THE COMPLETE
LAROUSSE
GASTRONOMIQUE

THE WORLD'S GREATEST COOKERY ENCYCLOPEDIA

hamlyn

First published in Great Britain in 1998
by Hamlyn, a division of Octopus Publishing Group Ltd
2–4 Heron Quays, London E14 4JP

Revised edition published in 2003

Robert J. Courtine compiled and directed the
1984 French language edition of Larousse Gastronomique
Abridgement: Lewis Esson Publishing

ISBN 0 600 60863 8

A CIP catalogue record for this book is available from the British Library

Printed and bound in Finland

10 9 8 7 6 5 4 3 2 1

Preface

Fifty years ago, in his preface to the first edition of *Larousse Gastronomique* Auguste Escoffier wrote: 'To undertake the task of writing the history of a country's food, to set out the changes which, through the centuries, have been made in the way in which it has been presented and served, to describe and comment upon the improvements in its cooking, is equivalent to painting a portrait evoking a country's whole civilization'. This was an elegantly phrased acknowledgement of the monumental work by Prosper Montagné, assisted by Dr Gottschalk in the compilation of the historical, scientific and medical sections.

Prosper Montagné related this history of cookery in the context of all the improvements made to the culinary art and to the refinements of the table from prehistoric times to our own days. He presented an anthology of haute cuisine and recipes for home cooking, but also made his readers aware of the great classic dishes of other countries. This is still the aim of the present edition of *Larousse Gastronomique*.

But time passes and monuments sometimes need restoration. Although the history of food, indissolubly linked to that of the countries that produced it, remains the same as do traditional recipes and basic methods, cookery itself has moved on. The pace of modern life has profoundly altered the eating habits of our contemporaries. Good food undoubtedly remains a major pleasure, but the time and the means devoted to its preparation no longer enjoy former scope and abundance, and nutritional concerns have had their influence upon taste. On the other hand, tourism, which has crossed provincial boundaries and now operates on a world-wide scale has enabled French people to experience a culinary change of scenery. They have been delighted to discover, first at the restaurant and then on their own table exotic dishes or dishes which are simply different from their usual fare. In its turn the taste for novelty has encouraged a renewal of curiosity about somewhat neglected regional dishes. The appearance of new utensils and new materials has also brought changes in methods of preparation and cooking. Finally, the lessons we have learnt from established wisdom combined with modern research have led to a growing interest in dietetics, a new science which has discovered the basic principles underlying the commonsense approach of our ancestors, much disregarded at the beginning of this century.

All this is sufficient justification for a new edition. Cooking is very much a child of its time. It constantly adapts itself to new requirements, to the tastes and desires of society, since its ties with civilization have always been very close. A notable new feature is recipes by leading contemporary chefs which add lustre to the book. They are in fact outstanding especially when compared to the classical preparations of Montagné or Philéas Gilbert, not to mention those of Carême, whose presence in this work, while occasionally anachronistic, is indispensable from the historical and documentary viewpoint.

Economic and social changes, improvements in household equipment, the growth of the tourist industry and dietary concerns have transformed not only behaviour but also tastes. We can well imagine the surprise of Madame de

Sévigné who noted, at Versailles, 'the passion for new garden peas', confronted with a salad of soya bean sprouts or a couscous garni, or the astonishment of Grimod de la Reynière (who witnessed the opening of the first restaurants), at a fast-food counter, or the amazement of a roast meat vendor, faced with a microwave oven!

Since the end of the last century this cultural and technical revolution has assumed such vast dimensions that a simple updating of Prosper Montagné's work was insufficient to ensure the *Larousse Gastronomique* continued to play its part as an informative and practical encyclopedia. While preserving the magnificent heritage bequeathed to us by this master of his craft – with his recipes, technical skills, knowledge and anecdotes – we believed it necessary to offer the reader a new *Larousse Gastronomique*, which would incorporate the contributions of modern research and answer contemporary needs.

The Concise Larousse Gastronomique is intended to be a synthesis of the science of nutrition and the art of cooking, but an attractive synthesis, as pleasing to the gourmet, cook and the aesthete as it is to the historian and the sociologist, contradicting Diderot, whose article *Cookery* claims: 'Cookery, a simple matter in the early stages of the world is now a most difficult study or science'.

Men and women today do not spend whole days at the dining table and ten-course menus have disappeared. But, more than ever before, food, through the choice of dishes and their preparation, forms an integral part of life and remains the natural expression of conviviality.

Robert J. Courtine

CONSULTANTS TO THE ENGLISH EDITION

Cookery consultants
Tricia Davis
Joan Hood
Carolyn Humphries
Bridget Jones
Frances Naldrett
Stella Vayne
Lorna Walker

Wine consultant
Pamela Vandyke Price

Spirits consultants
John Doxat
Jeffrey Wormstone

Paperback Editor
Lewis Esson

Translators of the French text
Lesley Bernstein Translation Services
Danielle de Froidmont
Margaret Hartley
Pat Hills
Jean Kirby

Edited by
Market House Books, Aylesbury, Bucks.

Editors
Susan Cope
Eve Daintith
Rosalind Fergusson
Janet Hammond
Robert Hine
Amanda Isaacs
Elizabeth Martin
Kate Smith
Stella Stiegeler

abaisse

A term used in French cookery for a sheet of rolled-out pastry. Hence, *abaisser* means to roll out thin, as for a pastry base. The term *abaisse* is also used for a biscuit (cookie) or a slice of sponge cake on which a filling such as jam or cream is to be spread.

abat-faim

An obsolete term (meaning literally 'hunger-killer') for the first of the main dishes (but not the first course of a meal) served to appease the guests' hunger. Nowadays hors d'oeuvres and appetizers fulfil this function.

abattoir

An establishment where livestock are slaughtered for their edible products (meat and offal) and their by-products (leather, bristles, horsehair, horns).

Until 1950, slaughtering was often carried out in France by butchers themselves on their own premises. But since 1972, for reasons of hygiene, it has had to be done in a public abattoir; improved abattoirs have been set up in animal production areas, since it is easier to transport carcasses and quarters than living animals. From the gas-tronomic point of view it is rather less desirable: less than a century ago, beef cattle from Normandy, Limousin, or the Nevers region would make their way slowly on foot for a distance of 200 to 400 km (125 to 250 miles) before being slaughtered in the big towns, and this made their meat firmer and more tasty.

Health and hygiene inspections take place at three stages – on the living animal, on the viscera (internal organs), and on the carcass; at the two latter stages this may lead to confiscation of all or part of the product. If all the inspections are satisfactory the carcass is branded as conforming to legal requirements, either national or for the EEC regulations governing exchanges between EEC countries.

Present-day abattoirs are becoming increasingly better equipped, incorporating cutting and sometimes packing departments, deep-freeze units, or workshops for processing and cooking the meat, particularly pork. Scientific research is constantly leading to improvements in this field, notably in matters of hygiene and preservation by rapid refrigeration. A recent technique, not yet used in France, consists of electrically stimulating carcasses after slaughter to prevent the muscle contraction caused by cold, which brings about an earlier start to the process of maturation.

☐ **Slaughtering in former times** The advanced technology now used in meat preparation makes it interesting to recall the relationships which existed in former times between people and their livestock. 'The meat of Greek animals is god-given. . . . For the Greeks, matters relating to butchery, religion, and cooking were all mixed up in what they called *thusia* and what we call sacrifice. . . . The moment when the sacrifice begins, after the procession, the moment when the blood spurts out, belongs to the gods. . . . The altar and the earth receive it all, then with a special implement and vessel it is collected and spread over the altar. . . . The principal ritual act is the extraction of the noble viscera, essentially the liver; then comes the cutting up of the animal, horizontally, according to a strict procedure. According to the nature of the parts, they are grilled (particularly the viscera, whose perfume is offered to the gods), cooked on a spit, or boiled (the manner of cooking preferred by the Greeks, particularly as fresh meat, already naturally tough and more so when cut in this way, is difficult to eat when roasted). The portions of meat are placed on the table as an offering to the gods, and afterwards they are at the priest's disposal. . . . The priest also receives that part which, at the start, contained the whole animal: the skin. . . . In taking their fill of the edible parts men recognized, at the same time as they replenished their energy, the inferiority of their mortal state. . . . In the language of Homer, to express the idea of the slaughter of livestock, there are no verbs other than those relating to offering up sacrifices to the gods.' (*La Cuisine du sacrifice en pays grec*, by M. Détienne & J.-P. Vernant, published by Gallimard.)

Even today, in some Greek villages, the public killing of livestock is practised as part of popular Orthodox rites, followed by the distribution and consumption of the meat, boiled in large cauldrons with vegetables and herbs. This is called *kourbani*.

abignades or abegnades

A term used in the department of the Landes for the intestines of a goose cooked in its blood. Abignades are found almost solely in the Chalosse region, where they are eaten on bread fried in goose fat, with slices of lemon.

ablutions at the table
ABLUTIONS DE TABLE

The custom of rinsing the fingers in the course of a meal. The origin of the word (from Church Latin *ablutio*) is a reminder that ablution was originally a ritual practice; the person offering up a sacrifice had to purify his hands before officiating at the ceremony. Table ablutions were customary in ancient Greece and Rome, when food was taken by hand directly from the plate, as is still the practice today in the East. In Europe, since the introduction of forks, the ewer – a basin used formerly for washing the hands – is no longer needed, and finger bowls appear on the table only with such foods as asparagus, artichokes, and sea food. Linked to the practice of ablutions is that of the mouth rinse, still current at the beginning of the 19th century. In the Far East it is customary to offer to each guest, on changing from one course to another, a damp perfumed towel.

aboukir

A dessert made of a sponge cake cooked in a charlotte mould, then cut horizontally in slices which are sandwiched with chestnut cream. The cake is iced with coffee fondant icing and decorated with chopped pistachio nuts.

Aboukir almonds are glazed petits fours made with green or pink almond paste, into each of which a blanched almond is pressed. They are glazed by holding them on a skewer and dipping them into caramel or briskly boiled sugar.

abricot-pays

A fruit from the West Indies, the size of a small melon. Its only resemblance to the apricot is the colour of its flesh, which is, however, firmer than apricot flesh. After removing the thick skin and the harder white parts, the pulp is used to make jams, sorbets, and fruit juices.

absinthe

Absinthe, or wormwood, is an aromatic plant containing an alkaloid known since ancient times for its properties as a tonic and febrifuge. The plant was used to make medicinal drinks in the Middle Ages. The liqueur absinthe was first made commercially by H. L. Pernod in 1797. Absinthe is sometimes served by pouring it over a lump of sugar placed on a small flat spoon with holes in, resting on the edge of the glass. The 'green Muse', as poets called it, became very popular at the end of the last century, but it was in fact a powerful drug, which had serious effects on the nervous system, and its manufacture and sale were prohibited by law on 16 March 1915. Pernod and the various forms of pastis are now flavoured with aniseed.

In his *Grand Dictionnaire de cuisine*, Alexandre Dumas relates the following anecdote:

'De Musset's fatal passion for absinthe, which incidentally perhaps gave his poetry its bitter flavour, caused the Académie to make a modest pun. De Musset was, in fact, missing many of the sittings of this august body, aware that he was in no state to attend.

'One day one of the distinguished forty members said to another: "Really, do you not think that Alfred de Musset absents himself rather too often?"

"You mean that he absinthes himself rather too often."'

accolade (en)

En accolade describes the presentation on the same plate of two similar kinds of food, leaning against each other. It is usually poultry and game birds which are displayed *en accolade*, but in former times meat and fish might also have been served in this manner.

accommoder

A French term meaning to prepare a dish, including the operations preceding the cooking as well as the seasoning and the cooking itself.

acetabulum   ACÉTABULE

In Roman times, a vessel for storing vinegar (*acetum* in Latin). The word also indicated a measure equivalent to 270 ml (9 fl oz). The Romans used wine vinegar, plain or strongly seasoned with pepper, but in non-vine-growing regions they made vinegar from fruit (figs, pears, or peaches).

acetomel   ACÉTOMEL

A syrupy mixture of honey and vinegar used in sweet-and-sour preserved fruits (grapes or quartered pears or quinces). The name comes from two Latin words, *acetum* (vinegar) and *mel* (honey).

achar   ACHARD

A strongly spiced pickle (usually saffron-coloured) relished throughout the Indian subcontinent, in Réunion Island, Indonesia, and the West Indies and brought to Europe by the English in the 18th century. It is made from a mixture of fruit and vegetables which are chopped and steeped in a spicy sauce. Exotic achars may be made from palm hearts, limes, dates, rose petals, ginger, and bamboo sprouts, but onions, pumpkins, cauliflower, and capers can be used in the same way. Some achars are very sharp-flavoured and piquant; others are milder and even sweet.

RECIPE

Vegetable achar with lemon   ACHARD DE LÉGUMES AU CITRON   Cut thin-rinded lemons into quarters and remove the seeds. Cut some carrots, peppers, and deseeded cucumbers into strips about 4 cm (1½ in) long, and cut some thin green beans and cabbage leaves into small pieces. Separate a cauliflower into tiny florets. Steep the lemons and the vegetables separately in coarse salt. After 12 hours, wash the lemons and soak them in cold water for 24 hours, changing the water several times, then boil them in water until the quarters have become soft. Drain and dry them. When the vegetables have been steeping for 36 hours, drain and dry them too. Finely mince or grate some onion and fresh root ginger (ginger root) (or use a blender). Add cayenne, vinegar, and powdered saffron, then some best-quality olive oil. Place the lemon quarters and vegetables in a jar and cover with the aromatized oil. Seal and store in a cool place.

Achard (Franz Karl)

German chemist (born Berlin, 1753; died Kunern, Silesia, 1821), whose French forebears had emigrated after the revocation of the Edict of Nantes. Carrying out research into a product designed to replace cane sugar, he succeeded in 1796 in perfecting the first industrial process for the extraction of beet sugar. This invention was disregarded by the Institut de France as of no value, but received the support of the Prussian King Frederick William III, who provided Achard with funds in 1802 for the establishment of a sugar factory in Silesia. This ended in failure as the sugar was too costly to produce, and Achard died in poverty.

acid   ACIDE

The term denotes a taste sensation (it is one of the four fundamental flavours – see *taste, flavour*) as well as a chemical function. Any substance is acid which, in a water solution, can give off hydrogen ions. The degree of acidity is defined by the hydrogen potential (pH), the scale of which varies from 0 (very acid) to 14 (very alkaline), 7 being the pH value of pure water, which is neutral.

Mineral acids, which are generally 'strong' (such as sulphuric acid), may be distinguished from the 'weak' organic acids, such as citric and malic acid in fruit, phosphoric acid in cheese, meat, and fish, and tartaric acid in wine. In addition to organic acids, foods contain other assimilable acids: ascorbic acid, amino acids, and fatty acids.

□ **Culinary applications** Acid foods and those to which acid (such as acetic acid or vinegar) is added are more easily preserved, for many microorganisms do not develop when the pH value is low. Also the vitamin C content is better preserved in an acid environment.

A weak acid, such as lemon juice, prevents artichoke hearts, avocados, sliced apples, bananas, chicory (endives), and peeled potatoes from going black through oxidation.

Acids help proteins to coagulate, which is why vinegar or lemon juice is used in a court bouillon and the cooking liquor of a blanquette or of poached eggs.

Acidification is a sign of deterioration. When the lactose in milk becomes lactic acid, the milk is said to have gone sour. Sour cream, however, is sometimes used in cooking; it can be made by adding a few drops of lemon juice to fresh cream.

acidulate   ACIDULER

To turn a liquid or a dish slightly acid, tart, or piquant by adding a little lemon juice, vinegar, or the juice of unripe fruit. Acidulate also means to make sour cream by adding a few drops of lemon juice to fresh cream.

acra or akra

A savoury fritter made by mixing a spiced purée of vegetables or fish with fritter batter. Acras, which are popular in the Caribbean, are served very hot as a starter, or with punch as cocktail snacks. Acras are also known as *marinades*, *bonbons à l'huile*, as well as 'stamp and go' in Jamaica and *surullitos* in Puerto Rico. They are most often made with salt cod, but alevin, mackerel, and crayfish are also used, as well as breadfruit, aubergines (eggplants), palm hearts, Caribbean cabbage, pumpkin, etc.

| RECIPE

Salt-cod acras   ACRAS DE MORUE
Place about 500 g (1 lb) salt cod in cold water for 24 hours to remove the salt, changing the water several times. Make a fritter batter with 200 g (7 oz, 1½ cups) flour, a pinch of salt, and enough water to obtain a thick batter, and leave it to stand for 1 hour. Place the desalted cod with a little cold water and a bay leaf in a saucepan; cook gently for 10 minutes. Drain and flake the fish then mix it with 4 teaspoons olive oil, salt, and cayenne. Finely chop 2 shallots and 4 or 5 chives, add these to the cod, and mix evenly with the batter. Stiffly whisk 2 or 3 egg whites and fold gently into the mixture. Slowly drop spoonfuls of the mixture into hot oil and fry until crisp and golden, turning once. Drain and serve hot.

acroama

A spectacle which livened up a banquet in Roman times: acrobats, flute players and dancers, mimes and parodies, even combats between men or animals. Of Greek origin, the name meant 'that to which one listens'. The acroama tradition continued in different forms, through the medieval story-tellers, jugglers, and mountebanks, to become a musical entertainment or accompaniment.

advocaat

A liqueur made with beaten egg yolks, sugar, and spirit, served both before and after meals. The best-known brands are made in the Netherlands. It is sometimes used in mixes, especially the snowball (when it is combined with fizzy lemonade).

affriander

A French term meaning to dress up and present a dish to give it an appetizing appearance.

affrioler

A French term meaning to entice to the table by offering tasty tit-bits.

affriter

A French term meaning to season or prove a pan or dish by rubbing coarse salt over the base with a piece of crumpled paper, or by heating a little oil in the pan, which is then dried with a cloth.

AFNOR

Association *française* de *nor*malisation: the French standards association. Created as a private organization in 1926 and recognized as a public utility in 1943, it centralizes and coordinates the laying down of standards in France. Some 950 standards, new or revised, are published each year. In 1981, there were about 11,000 standards, dealing with definitions, names, dimensions, characteristics, symbols, methods of testing, standard contracts, etc.

The official stamp N.F. (*normes françaises*) signifies that AFNOR certifies a product's conformity with the standards laid down by the association. This official stamp covers 64 fields of application and 1700 product types; it is used particularly in connection with domestic appliances and electrical household goods. AFNOR is also involved in the terminology relating to

commercially produced food products (fruit, fish, etc.) but these are governed by specific standards stipulating freshness, presentation, mention of origin, additives, etc. (see *labelling*).

The European Committee on Standardization (CEN) and the European Committee for Electro-technical Standardization (CENELEC) now exist to define standards in Europe generally.

Africa

See *Black Africa, North Africa, South Africa*.

africaine (à l')

The term *à l'africaine* is used to describe an accompaniment of olive-shaped potato pieces, which are browned in butter, and two other vegetables (cucumber, aubergine (eggplant), or courgette (zucchini)), which are sliced and either sautéed in oil or steamed. This accompaniment is served with large joints of roast mutton, which may be flavoured with powdered rosebuds (as in Tunisia) or with a combination of herbs and spices, including thyme, bay, cumin, cloves, or coriander. The sauce for dishes served *à l'africaine* is a rich demi-glace flavoured with tomato.

agape

A meal that the early Christians took together. The word comes from the Greek *agape*, meaning love, and was originally used to describe a frugal meal. After the Mass the faithful would come together to share a light meal of bread and wine, the aim of which was to recall the ideals of sharing and charity preached by the Christians. In the 4th century the agape celebrated the birthdays of martyrs, but primitive frugality had given way to a veritable banquet, the excesses of which were criticized by Saint Augustine. The Council of Laodicea (377) had forbidden the celebration of the agape in the churches themselves, but feasting went on to the same extent away from the holy places. In France, total prohibition under pain of excommunication dates from the Council of Orléans (541). The custom of distributing consecrated bread after the Mass is all that remains of this ancient ceremony.

In modern French parlance, the word

agapes (in the plural) indicates, often ironically, a meal among family or friends characterized by abundant food and a jolly atmosphere.

agar-agar

A viscous substance, also known as Bengal isinglass and Japanese or Ceylon moss, agar-agar is an extract of seaweed from the Indian and Pacific Oceans. It comes either in the form of small transparent crumpled strips of various colours, or in loaves or powdered form. When dissolved in water over a low heat, its gum blends with the water; on cooling, it sets to a jelly. The Japanese add it to soups, but it is principally used in the food industry, in desserts, ice creams, sauces, and canned soup.

agaric PSALLIOTE

Any of a genus of field and woodland mushrooms with a white cap, pink then brownish gills, and a stalk bearing a single or a double ring. According to the species, the flesh may be tinted with pink, reddish-brown, brown, or yellow. The group includes many edible mushrooms with a delicate flavour and smell, often of aniseed. They are prepared like cultivated mushrooms.

agave

A large plant with enormous fleshy leaves, originating from Mexico. The fermented sap is used in several Latin American countries to make fermented drinks, such as pulque, mescal, and tequila.

ageing of meat

MATURATION

The slow change that takes place in meat when it is left for a period of time and reaches a state in which it is suitable for consumption or further processing. After the animal is killed, the flesh is still warm and it passes through a stage known in France as *pantelante* (twitching). Then rigor mortis sets in. In the next stage, *rassise*, the flesh becomes more tender and flavoursome as the sinews are less taut and the muscles relax. The speed and intensity with which meat ages is influenced both by the quality of the meat (which is affected by the animal's diet) and the ambient temperature. See *hanging*.

Agnès Sorel

A garnish consisting of cooked button mushrooms, breast of chicken, and pickled ox (beef) tongue, cut according to the dish being garnished (omelette, fried or braised veal, or suprême of chicken). In Agnès Sorel soup the garnish is cut into thin strips and added to the thickened soup.

Mistress of the French King Charles VII, Agnès Sorel was a celebrated cook who gave her name to several dishes. 'To attract and keep the attentions of Charles VII, she engaged the best chefs of the time. She had no hesitation in making personal appearances in the kitchens. Two of her creations will go down to posterity: woodcock salmis and her little timbales.' (Christian Guy, *Une Histoire de la cuisine française*, published by Les Productions de Paris.)

RECIPES

Agnès Sorel tartlets TARTELETTES AGNÈS SOREL Fill tartlet cases with a layer of creamed chicken purée, containing chopped truffles if desired. Surround with a border of small rounds of cold cooked chicken breast and pickled ox (beef) tongue. On each tartlet place a mushroom cap which has been cooked in a white court-bouillon. Cook in a moderate oven 160 C (325 F, gas 3) for 10 minutes to heat through. Pour cream sauce over the mushrooms before serving.

agnolotti

A variety of ravioli in which the pasta is cut into small round pieces. These are filled with a stuffing, usually of chopped meat and vegetables, and the agnolotti are folded in half like small turnovers. They are particularly popular in Piedmont, where they are either poached in stock and served with melted butter and grated cheese or browned with cheese and breadcrumbs.

agraz

A sorbet made from almonds, verjuice, and sugar, popular in North Africa and Spain (its name means verjuice in Spanish). Agraz, which has an acid flavour, is served in large sorbet glasses and may be sprinkled with Kirsch.

aguardiente

An alcoholic spirit from Spanish-speaking countries. Made from must or marc in regions where the vine is cultivated, (Argentina, Chile), aguardiente may also be made from distilled sugarcane molasses (Central America). It is sometimes flavoured with aniseed.

Aïda

A way of serving flatfish fillets (brill or turbot). It is distinguished from preparations *à la florentine* by the addition of paprika to the Mornay sauce and the spinach.

aïgo boulido

Provençal name for a soup made from boiled water (hence its name, which may also be spelled *bouïdo* or *bullido*) and garlic. It is one of the oldest culinary traditions of this region, where they have the saying *l'aïgo boulido suavo lo vito* (garlic soup saves one's life).

RECIPE

Aïgo boulido Bring 1 litre (1¾ pints, 4 cups) water to the boil. Season with ½ teaspoon salt and 6 crushed cloves of garlic. Boil for about 10 minutes, then add a small sprig of sage, preferably fresh, one quarter of a bay leaf, and a small sprig of thyme. Remove at once from the heat and leave to infuse for several minutes; remove the herbs. Blend 1 egg yolk with a little of the cooled soup, then stir it back into the soup to thicken it. Pour the soup over slices of bread which have been sprinkled with olive oil.

aïgo sau d'iou

A Provençal fish soup, which is distinguished from bouillabaisse by the addition of potatoes. Using quantities as for bouillabaisse, the fish are cut into chunks and cooked in a large amount of water with the sliced onion, garlic, tomatoes, a bouquet garni, and eight potatoes cut into quarters. The soup is then strained and the liquor poured into a soup tureen onto slices of bread sprinkled with olive oil, while the fish is served separately with the potatoes.

This dish is accompanied by aïoli or rouille.

Aiguebelle

A monastery near Montélimar, founded by the Cistercians in 1137 and occupied by Trappist monks since 1815. The liqueur Aiguebelle is made from plants by the monks there, as well as syrups and jellied fruits.

aiguillette

The French name for a long narrow slice of flesh taken from either side of the breastbone of poultry (mainly duck) and game birds. However, an aiguillette can also be a thin strip of any meat.

In France the tip of a rump of beef is called *aiguillette baronne*.

RECIPE

Jellied beef aiguillettes AIGUILLET-TES DE BOEUF EN GELÉE Put 1 calf's foot and some veal bones in a saucepan, cover with cold water, and bring to the boil. Drain, then cool them and wipe dry. Peel and slice 750 g (1¾ lb) new carrots and 1 large onion, quarter 2 tomatoes, and peel 2 small cloves of garlic. Preheat the oven to about 180 c (350 f, gas 4).

Heat 2 tablespoons oil in a flameproof casserole and brown 1.25 kg (2¾ lb) slivers of beef aiguillettes which, if possible, have been larded by the butcher. Add the sliced carrot and onion, the calf's foot, and the veal bones; continue to cook until the onions are coloured. Remove any excess oil with a small ladle, then add the tomato quarters, a bouquet garni, a small piece of orange peel, a pinch of salt, pepper (a few turns of the pepper mill), a dash of cayenne, 2.5 dl (8 fl oz, 1 cup) dry white wine, and ½ litre (17 fl oz, 2 cups) water. Cover and slowly bring to the boil, then place the casserole in the preheated oven and cook for about 2½ hours or until the meat is tender, stirring the meat from time to time.

In a large uncovered pan, simmer 30 small peeled button onions with 20 g (1 oz, 2 tablespoons) butter, 2 teaspoons caster (superfine) sugar, a pinch of salt, and just enough water to cover them. Cook until the onions are tender and the liquid has evaporated. Toss the onions in the caramel which has formed. Drain the aiguillettes (keeping the cooking liquid) and arrange them in a deep dish or terrine with the sliced carrots and the small onions. Leave aside until cold, then refrigerate.

Remove the bones from the calf's foot and cut the flesh into cubes. Strain the cooking liquid back into a saucepan, add the calf's foot cubes, and boil for about 10 minutes, then strain. Dissolve 15 g (½ oz) powdered gelatine in the minimum of water add the strained cooking liquid and 100 ml (6 table-spoons, scant ½ cup) Madeira; check seasoning then leave to cool until syrupy. Coat the aiguillettes with the setting liquid then refrigerate until set and ready to serve.

aiguillon

A spicy sausage or slice of salted meat which creates a thirst. The name was originated by Rabelais.

aillade

A feature of the cuisine of southern France, which varies according to the region where it is made. In Provence, it is either a vinaigrette sauce with garlic or a slice of bread rubbed with garlic, soaked in olive oil, and grilled (broiled) (*pain à l'aillade*). In Languedoc, the aillade from the Toulouse area is a variation on aïoli mayonnaise made with blanched and ground walnuts, while in the region of Albi aillade is another name for aïoli

| RECIPE

Aillade sauce SAUCE AILLADE Skin 4 garlic cloves, crush or finely chop them, and place in a basin with salt and pepper. Gradually blend in 2 tables-poons corn or olive oil, stirring well. Mix in 2–3 teaspoons vinegar, a few sprigs of chopped parsley, and, if de-sired, 2 teaspoons chopped shallots and chives.

aillée

A condiment of the consistency of mus-tard, made with breadcrumbs, ground almonds, and garlic, mixed with stock. The origin of aillée is uncertain, but it is likely that it originated in Paris, where

in the 13th century no fewer than nine merchants are known to have dealt in it.

aïoli or ailloli

A kind of Provençal mayonnaise sauce; the name is formed from *ail* (garlic) and *oli* (Provençal dialect for oil). Léon Daudet maintained that the use of garlic in the food of Mediterranean peoples went back to the beginnings of cooking, and he considered the culinary use of garlic had achieved its peak of perfec-tion in aïoli. Frédéric Mistral, who in 1891 founded a journal entitled *L'Aïoli*, wrote: 'Aïoli epitomizes the heat, the power, and the joy of the Provençal sun, but it has another virtue – it drives away flies.'

Aïoli is served with cold poached fish, *bourride* (fish soup), hard-boiled (hard-cooked) eggs, salad, snails, or cold meats. But when a Provençal talks of a *grand aïoli*, which is eaten only two or three times a year, he means a sump-tuous dish which, as well as the sauce, includes poached salt cod, boiled beef and mutton, stewed vegetables (carrots, celery, green beans, beetroot (red beet), cauliflower, chickpeas, etc.) and, as a garnish, snails and hard-boiled (hard-cooked) eggs

| RECIPE

Aïoli sauce SAUCE AÏOLI Skin 4 large cloves of garlic (split them in two, and remove the germ if necessary). Pound the garlic with 1 egg yolk in a mortar or blender. Add salt and pepper and, while pounding or blending, very gradually add 2.5 dl (8 fl oz, 1 cup) oil, as for a mayonnaise. The sauce is ready when it has reached a homogeneous consistency. The bulk of the sauce is sometimes increased by adding 2 tea-spoons soft-boiled potato.

albacore GERMON

A small tuna fish of the Atlantic and tropical seas, which can measure up to 1½ m (5 ft) but is usually less than 1 m (3 ft) long. Also called 'white tuna' be-cause of its rather pale flesh, to disting-uish it from the large bluefin tuna, it is seldom marketed fresh (since it is rela-tively tasteless, it is braised in white wine with anchovies, tomatoes, onions, and garlic and served with capers).

However, it is the finest and most expensive of preserved tuna fish. Raw, it is highly prized in sushi and sashimi.

alberge

A variety of peach particularly esteemed in Touraine. Balzac considered jam made from alberges to be unrivalled. The fruit has a wrinkled skin and its juicy flesh, which has a tart flavour, clings to the stone. It was traditionally used in Anjou in certain ragouts. Lesser known today, its principal role is in jam making.

Albert

A sauce used in English cooking, dedicated to Prince Albert of Saxe-Coburg-Gotha, husband and consort of Queen Victoria. It is made from a white consommé seasoned with grated horseradish, thickened with breadcrumbs and enriched with fresh cream and egg yolks. Mustard thinned with vinegar or lemon juice is added to give a final piquant touch. This hot sauce accompanies joints of braised beef.

The name Albert is also given to a method of serving sole, dedicated to Albert Blazer, maître d'hôtel at Maxim's between the World Wars.

albigeoise (à l')

A garnish *à l'albigeoise* consists of stuffed tomatoes and potato croquettes; it accompanies joints of meat.

The term is also applied to methods of preparing dishes using specific products from southwestern France.

| RECIPE

Shoulder of lamb à l'albigeoise
ÉPAULE D'AGNEAU À L'ALBIGEOISE
Bone the shoulder and fill the bone cavity with a stuffing of half sausage-meat and half chopped pig's liver, seasoned with garlic, chopped parsley, salt, and pepper. Roll the shoulder as for a ballottine and tie to secure. Weigh the stuffed joint. Brown the rolled shoulder in very hot fat then place it in a roasting dish; surround with quartered potatoes (or whole small new potatoes) and 12 blanched cloves of garlic, season with salt and pepper, and sprinkle with a little melted fat. Cook the lamb in the oven at about 200 c

(400 F, gas 6), allowing 20 minutes per 500 g (1 lb) plus 20 minutes more. Sprinkle with chopped parsley to serve.

This dish is traditionally cooked and served in an ovenproof earthenware dish.

Albufera (à la d')

The name *à la d'Albufera* is given to several *haute cuisine* dishes (notably chicken and duck) dedicated by Carême to Marshal Suchet, Duc d'Albufera (the name of the lake at Valencia near which he won a victory over the English).

| RECIPE

Albufera sauce   SAUCE ALBUFERA
Prepare a suprême sauce using 500 ml (18 fl oz, 2 cups) thick rich chicken velouté sauce, 4 dl (14 fl oz, 1¾ cups) white chicken stock, 4 dl (14 fl oz, 1¼ cups) fresh cream, and 50 g (2 oz, 4 tablespoons) butter. While the sauce is cooking, sweat 150 g (5 oz) sliced peppers in 50 g (2 oz, 4 tablespoons butter.) Allow to cool, then liquidize the peppers in a blender. Add 150 g (5 oz, ¾ cup) butter and put through a sieve. Add to the suprême sauce (500 ml (18 fl oz, 2¼ cups) after reducing) 3 tablespoons veal stock and 2 teaspoons of the pepper butter. Rub through a fine sieve.

alcarraza   ALCARAZAS

A porous earthenware vessel used for cooling drinks. The name is Spanish and derives from the Arabic *al karaz* (pitcher). It was introduced into France in the 18th century. The alcarraza is suspended, preferably in the shade, in a draughty place. Liquid oozes out through the porous surface of the vessel and evaporates, thus lowering the temperature and cooling the contents of the pitcher.

alcazar

A gâteau made with a base of enriched shortcrust pastry covered with a layer of apricot marmelade and topped with a Kirsch-flavoured almond meringue mixture. The gâteau is decorated with apricot marmelade and a lattice of almond paste. It keeps well for two or three days.

RECIPE

Alcazar gâteau GÂTEAU ALCAZAR
Line a flan tin with 250 g (8 oz) *pâte sucrée* (see *doughs and batters*). Prick the base and spread with 2 tablespoons apricot marmelade or jam. Whisk 4 egg whites and 125 g (4½ oz, ⅔ cup) caster (superfine) sugar over heat to a stiff meringue, then fold in 60 g (2 oz, ½ cup) ground almonds, 60 g (2 oz, 1½ cups) flour, and 25 g (1 oz, 2 tablespoons) melted butter mixed with 1 tablespoon Kirsch. Pour this mixture into the prepared flan case and cook in a preheated oven (200 c, 400 f, gas 6) until the top has browned. Turn the gâteau out of the tin and cool it on a wire tray.

Using a forcing bag with a fluted nozzle, pipe softened almond paste into a lozenge-shaped lattice over the top of the gâteau and then as a border around the edge. Replace it in the oven to brown the almond paste. Over a low heat reduce 200 g (7 oz, ¾ cup) apricot marmelade or jam and fill each of the lozenge shapes with it, then place half a pistachio nut in the centre of each. If desired the border may also be glazed with apricot marmelade or jam and coated with chopped roasted pistachio nuts.

alcohol ALCOOL

Liquid resulting from the fermentation of sugar substances, which is isolated by distillation. The word was used first by the alchemists, who derived it from the Arabic *al kohl*, which originally meant pulverized antimony and then came to mean any product crushed to a powder. In the Middle Ages alcohol was considered an elixir of life (*aqua vitae*, from which it acquired the name *eau-de-vie*) and was mostly reserved for therapeutic use. It came to be used as a drink towards the end of the 15th century, when all kinds of herbs and plants were introduced into it. Finally, the invention of the rectification process and the continuous still transformed it into a product for a mass market. Distillation was nonetheless often a domestic art until recent times, hence the survival of recipes for homemade liqueurs and various digestives, and also for fruits preserved in alcohol.

The only alcohol suitable for consumption and therefore of interest to the chef and the gourmet is ethyl alcohol. It is obtained by the fermentation of a variety of different substances. Fruits (grapes, pears, apples, stone fruits, berries, etc.) can produce wine, cider, and perry, as well as a whole range of marcs, eaux-de-vie, and *alcools blancs* (Armagnac, Calvados, Kirsch, Mirabelle, Framboise, etc.). Cereals and grains (rice, barley, wheat, rye, maize, etc.) are also widely used (for beer, gin, whisky, vodka, etc.), as well as roots (mainly potato and beetroot) and various exotic plants (palm, millet, sugar cane, agave) which produce rum, tequila, and various alcoholic liquors produced and consumed locally.

Alcohol is the essential (though not the only) component of wine, 'noble' alcohols, and spirits. The alcoholic content of a drink is measured in various ways. In spite of international conventions tending to standardize systems of measurement, units of alcoholic concentration still vary from one country to another. Over most of Europe the Gay-Lussac scale is used (degrees GL), which corresponds to the percentage of alcohol by volume at a given temperature contained in the liquid.

Alcohol has antiseptic properties and nutritional value in the form of assimilable sugars, but it becomes toxic when there is more than a certain amount in the blood.

In cookery alcohol is used in pâtés, stuffings, ices, sorbets, soufflés, and many other recipes, as well as in various culinary operations, including deglazing, flaming, and marinating.

al dente

An Italian expression (meaning literally 'to the tooth') indicating the correct degree of cooking for pasta, which must be removed from the heat and drained while it is still firm enough to bite into. The expression may also be applied to certain vegetables, such as green beans, which are served while still retaining their crunchiness

alembic ALAMBIC

Apparatus used in distillation. The name derives from the Arabic *al'inbiq* (distilling vessel).

The traditional alembic, made of copper, comprises a boiler (called a cucurbit) in which the mixture to be distilled is heated, a cap where the vapours collect, and a bent pipe that carries the vapours to the serpentine, a spiral coil passing through a cold bath, where they condense. This type of alembic, known as *charentais, discontinu*, or *à repasse* (because the alcohol passes through it twice), is used for distilling most of the great eaux-de-vie or alcoholic spirits, but alembics of the continuous distillation type are also used – for Armagnac, for example – and double-towered alembics, in which the alcohol does not have to pass through twice, are used in industry.

Alexandra

The name given to several dishes (chicken consommé, Parmentier soup with vegetables, fillets of sole, sautéed chicken, pot-roast quail, noisette cutlets, and tournedos steak), served with a sauce and garnished with a thin slice of truffle and with asparagus tips (if the sauce is white) or quartered artichoke hearts (if it is brown).

Alexandra is also the name of a cocktail based on *crème de cacao* (chocolate liqueur).

RECIPE

Sautéd chicken Alexandra POULET SAUTÉ ALEXANDRA Joint a chicken and sauté the joints in butter until cooked. Remove and keep them hot. Add 100 ml (6 tablespoons, scant ½ cup) white stock to the sauté pan and cook briskly to reduce it, then add 1½ tablespoons Soubise purée, moisten with 100 ml (6 tablespoons, scant ½ cup) white stock, and reduce again. Finally stir in 2 tablespoons cream and 40 g (1½ oz, 2 tablespoons) butter, then strain the sauce. Arrange the chicken in a dish, coat with the sauce, and garnish with buttered asparagus tips.

algae ALGUES

Simple plants which constitute the flora of the seas, lakes, and coasts. According to their pigmentation, algae are classified as green (e.g. ulva or sea lettuce, chlorella, chondrus), brown (including fucus and laminaria), red (e.g. porphyra), or blue-green (primitive organisms resembling bacteria). Some of them are edible.

Ancient Britons, the Irish, the river-dwellers in Chad, and the Mexican Indians all appear to have been very early collectors of algae, with which they made bread and a type of pancake. In the Far East algae have always had particular gastronomic value. Apart from their present-day role in the food industry on account of their gum content (see *agar-agar, emulsifier, gelling agent*), there has been a revival of interest in algae as a source of protein, iodine, vitamins, and mineral salts. In France they still play only a minor alimentary role, being used, for example, in steaming fish, as a condiment, and as a vegetable. In the United States chondrus is used in making puddings.

Algae are quite widely used in Scottish and Japanese cookery. In Scotland the most commonly used are porphyra, rhodymenia, and chondrus, which are sold in different forms in health food shops. They are used to make traditional soups and sauces and they are served steamed with potatoes. Well washed, cooked for a long time in water, and served plain with butter or lemon or orange juice, they make a pleasant dish with a slight anchovy flavour. When mixed with porridge oats they may be used to make biscuits or small oatcakes, or a very nourishing bread called sloke. In Japan six kinds of algae are commonly eaten, constituting 10% of total food production. These algae are either taken from the sea or cultivated along the coasts. *Nori*, compressed into violet-coloured leaves, is used for wrapping balls of rice or fish; it is also used in powdered form as an iodized condiment. *Konbu* is used to season stocks, rice, and vegetables; it is also cut into strips and made into little baskets which are fried and served with vegetables. *Wakame* and *hijiki* are used to make soups and to colour various dishes.

Algerian wines

VINS D'ALGÉRIE

Algerian vineyards were planted by the French colonists in the 19th century, at a time when the French vines were ravaged by phylloxera; they reached their peak before World War II. Since independence Algeria has been in an ambiguous position, being a Moslem country (and therefore not officially consuming alcohol) whose economy rests largerly on wine production. It is therefore obliged to export almost its entire production. France used to take most of it for blending, but has modified its policy for the wine industry and no longer imports any Algerian wine. In attempts to find new markets, Algeria has turned to the production of quality wines. In spite of this its vine-growing area has been reduced by half, and wine production has fallen, being exported principally to the USSR.

algérienne (à l')

The garnish *à l'algérienne* consists of sweet potato, either as croquettes or sautéed, and chopped tomatoes seasoned with garlic. It is served with large or small pieces of meat (paupiettes) as well as sautéed chicken. Sweet potato purée is used for the soup *crème algérienne*.

alhagi

A small Mediterranean shrub with edible seeds, which in intense heat exudes a sugary substance; this may be the manna (from the Hebrew *mânhu*, 'what is it?') mentioned in the Bible.

Ali-Bab

One of the dishes named in honour of Henri Babinsky (born Paris, 1855; died Paris, 1931), whose pseudonym it was. A professional engineer from the École des Mines, he published *Gastronomie pratique* under this name in 1907. During his travels throughout the world prospecting for gold and diamonds, he collected many recipes and cooked for his travelling companions. His book was republished several times with various additions, including an interesting study on treatment for obesity among gourmands (1923). This well-documented and humorous work is still of great interest historically and gastronomically, though now of limited practical use.

RECIPE

Ali-Bab salad SALADE ALI-BAB
Turn some peeled shrimps in mayon-

naise, arrange them in a mound in the centre of a serving dish or salad bowl, and sprinkle with chopped fresh herbs. Surround with the following: courgette (zucchini) match-sticks, blanched in salted water; sweet potato, cut into small balls and boiled; hard-boiled (hard-cooked) egg cut into quarters; small tomatoes, peeled, deseeded, and quartered. Sprinkle the salad with vinaigrette and serve garnished with nasturtium flowers.

alica

Semolina made by the ancient Romans from a variety of semihard wheat known as *zea*, which was crushed in a wooden mortar. After sifting it was divided into three categories according to its fineness, and whitened by the addition of crushed chalk, which was extracted mainly from a hill in Campania called Leucogaeum ('white land'). It is said that the Emperor Augustus paid 20,000 sesterces to the Neapolitans for exclusive proprietorial rights over this land. Alica was used to prepare gruels, cakes, and a special bread known as Picenum bread, which was made by soaking the alica for nine days, kneading it on the tenth day with raisins, and baking in the oven in pots which were broken when the bread was cooked.

alicot or alicuit

A ragout of poultry giblets made in the Béarn and Languedoc regions of France. The name of this traditional rustic dish comes from *aile et cou* (wing and neck), in patois *ale y cot*, as it comprises mainly the pinions and necks of young turkeys (preferably) or geese. Each of the two provinces claims to have created this dish, and each prepares it in a different way: in Béarn, alicot is braised with garlic, carrots, and potatoes; in Languedoc the gizzard, liver, and feet are normally added.

aligot

A dish from the Auvergne region of France, made from potatoes, garlic, and Cantal cheese. The cheese used must not be fully ripe; fresh Tomme cheese may be used instead, the best being Tomme de Planèze. The most difficult part of the preparation is mixing the cheese with the cooked potatoes, either as a purée or simply mashed with a fork.

A sweet aligot may be made by pouring a generous helping of rum over the aligot in a gratin dish, and setting light to it.

RECIPE

Aligot (from Marinette's recipe) Smoothly mash 1 kg (2 lb) soft fondant potatoes (cooked very slowly in butter in a covered pan), add 1–2 crushed garlic cloves, 1 tablespoon bacon fat, and sufficient milk to make a purée. Turn the purée into a bain-marie, add 600 g (1¼ lb) thinly sliced fresh Laguiole cheese, and stir vigorously with a wooden spoon until the cheese is evenly blended into the potato. The aligot is cooked when a smooth flowing elastic purée is formed.

Aligoté

A white Burgundy wine produced from the Aligoté grape. Dry and assertive, it is the traditional base for the apéritif Kir or *vin blanc cassis*.

alize pâquaude or alise pâcaude

A traditional Easter girdle cake from the Vendée region of France, also called *gache vendéenne*. It is made with bread dough enriched with butter and eggs, sweetened, and flavoured with orange-flower water, and can weigh up to 2 kg (4½ lb). The cake is supposed to be made on Easter Saturday, and the dough is left to rise for only two hours. The name comes from Old French *alis* ('level' or, in this context, 'compact' or 'badly risen').

alléluia

A speciality of the French town of Castelnaudary, which the town's pastrycooks make especially for Easter. This citron sweetmeat has been known since the beginning of the last century. It is said that an old soldier gave the recipe to the pastrycook with whom he had been lodging by way of thanks, having picked it up in the course of his campaigns; legend has it that the pastrycook used the recipe on the occasion of a visit by Pope Pius VII to the town at Easter, and that he baptized the cakes *alléluias*.

allemande

A white sauce, described as 'German' to differentiate it from the brown espagnole sauce, although both these basic sauces are of French origin. Made with veal or poultry stock, allemande sauce accompanies offal, poached chicken, vegetables, and eggs; made with a fish or mushroom fumet, it is served with fish.

RECIPE

Allemande sauce SAUCE ALLEMANDE (from Carême's recipe) Prepare some velouté; pour half of it into a saucepan with an equal quantity of good chicken consommé containing some mushroom skins and stalks but no salt. Place the pan on a high heat and stir with a wooden spoon until it boils. Then cover the pan and simmer gently for about an hour to reduce the sauce; skim off the fat and return it to a high heat, stirring with the wooden spoon so that it does not stick to the pan. When the sauce is thoroughly reduced and well thickened, it should leave a fairly thick covering on the surface of the spoon. When poured, it should make a coating similar to that of redcurrant jelly at its final stage of cooking.

Remove the saucepan from the heat and make a liaison of 4 egg yolks mixed with 2 tablespoons cream. Put this through a sieve and add a knob of unsalted butter, the size of a small egg, cut up into small pieces. Pour this a little at a time into the velouté, taking care to stir with the wooden spoon to thicken as the liaison blends in. When completely thickened, place the allemande on a moderate heat, stirring all the time, and as soon as it has begun to bubble slightly remove from the heat and add a dash of grated nutmeg. When well blended, put it through a sieve.

allemande (à l')

The description *à l'allemande* is applied to a dish served with an allemande sauce, or alternatively to a method of preparing marinated game inspired by German cuisine: haunch or saddle of venison, saddle of hare, or rabbit roasted with the vegetables from the marinade. A sauce to serve with it is prepared by deglazing with the marinade.

RECIPE

Calves' brains à l'allemande CERVELLE DE VEAU A L'ALLEMANDE Poach the brains in a court-bouillon, drain them, and cut each into 4 slices. Coat these with flour and cook gently in butter. Arrange them on croutons fried in butter and coat with allemande sauce.

allonger

The French term for extending a sauce, i.e. adding a liquid (water, stock, wine, bouillon, etc.) to a sauce that is too thick or reduced too much. The sauce is thus made thinner but its flavour is less concentrated.

allspice

PIMENT DE LA JAMAÏQUE

A spice, also known as Jamaican pepper and (in France) as *poivre giroflée*, that is ground from the unripe berries of *Pimenta officinalis*, a tree which grows in the Caribbean, Honduras, and Mexico. Allspice has a strong odour of nutmeg, cinnamon, and cloves, which is why it is sometimes mistaken for a mixture of different spices. It is used to season sausages, salt beef and pork, pickles, sauces, soused herrings, stuffings, and even Christmas cake.

allumette

A small pastry strip cut from a long rectangle of puff pastry, topped with a savoury spread, garnished, and baked in the oven. If this savoury is to be served hot, the spread, whether made from one item (cheese, anchovies, shrimps, etc.) or a mixture, is sometimes sandwiched between two layers of pastry. Iced allumettes are small individual pastries which, according to Lacam, were created by a pastrycook called Planta, who came from Dinard but was of Swiss origin, when using up some leftover icing (frosting).

Allumette potatoes are very thin match-stick-shaped fried potatoes.

RECIPE

Savoury allumettes ALLUMETTES SALÉES Roll out some puff pastry to about 5 mm (0.2 in) thickness, and divide it into strips 8 cm (3 in) wide. Spread these with the chosen well-chilled filling, and top, if desired, with a pastry strip or a selected garnish. Cut the bands into rectangles 2–3 cm (0.8 –1.2 in) wide, and place them on a baking tray (sheet). Bake in a hot oven (about 200 c 400 F, gas 6) for 12–15 minutes. Serve very hot. Allumettes can be prepared with the following fillings:

■ *with anchovies:* anchovy butter filling, garnish with anchovy fillets (may also be served cold);

■ *à l'andalouse:* chicken filling with paprika and a salpicon of lean ham and onions cooked slowly in butter;

■ *à la chalonnaise:* chicken filling with cock's combs and kidneys and diced mushrooms;

■ *à la chavette:* fish filling with crayfish butter, garnished with crayfish tails and truffles;

■ *à l'écarlate:* veal filling with a salpicon of pickled tongue;

■ *à l'écossaise:* smoked haddock purée bound with béchamel sauce;

■ *à la florentine:* spinach gently cooked in butter, mixed with béchamel sauce and grated Gruyère; dust allumettes with Parmesan cheese before putting in the oven;

■ *à la toscane:* when giving the last 3 folds to puff pastry, sprinkle with very finely grated cheese. Dust allumettes with Parmesan cheese before putting in the oven.

almond   AMANDE

The fruit of the almond tree (in France the term is more loosely used for the seeds contained within the stones of such fruits as the apricot and peach) The outer layer of the almond is oval, green, and velvety to the touch; it encloses a thick-shelled nut containing one or two seeds. Originating in Asia and known by the Romans as 'Greek nuts', almonds were widely used in the Middle Ages to make soups, as well as sweet desserts (see *blancmange*).

There are two varieties of almond, both rich in sugar, albumen, and oil: the edible sweet almond, and the bitter almond, which has a very strong taste and is poisonous in large amounts, containing hydrocyanic acid. In France almonds are grown in Provence and Corsica, and imported from Sicily. The first fresh almonds appear in May; they are opened with a nutcracker and eaten for dessert. But almonds are mainly used dried, when they are also richer in proteins, sugar, fats, and vitamins (640 Cal per 100 g). They are served salted with apéritifs.

Dried bitter almonds are used in small quantities to flavour cakes, pastries, and confectionery. Dried sweet almonds – whole, flaked (slivered), ground, or made into paste or cream – are used in making cakes, biscuits (cookies), sweets, and various sweetmeats. In cooking, almonds may also accompany certain fish, such as trout, or meat, such as chicken or pigeon, and they are used as ingredients in such preparations as couscous, stuffings, and compound butters.

| RECIPE

Salted almonds   AMANDES SALÉES Heat some sweet blanched almonds in the oven until they turn slightly yellow, turning them once. Then fry them until golden in butter in a sauté pan, with a pinch of saffron, cayenne, and ginger. Drain on a cloth. When cold, coat with a clear solution of gum arabic and dust with fine salt.

almond milk
LAIT D'AMANDE

A liquid preparation based on ground almonds. In the Middle Ages almond milk was a soup made with crushed almonds, blanched onions, wine, and spices, heated with water until it thickened. The soup was served hot either as a main dish or as a course between savoury dishes. Later on, almond milk became almost synonymous with blancmange, a cold dessert made from ground almonds and sugar, which are stirred into hot milk and then strained, setting to a jelly when cooled. This dish, which is not as popular as it once was, is now set with gelatine and is used as a base for cold desserts or sundaes, finished off with fruit and ice cream.

The French term *lait d'amande* is also used in classic pâtisserie for a round cake made from a paste of almonds, sugar, and eggs. When cooked, it is coated with an apricot glaze, topped with a thin layer of almond paste, glazed again, iced (frosted), and then decorated with chopped roasted almonds.

| RECIPE

Almond milk jelly   LAIT D'AMANDE POUR COUPES GLACÉES   Soak 20 g (¾ oz, 3 envelopes) gelatine in cold water. Blanch 250 g (9 oz, scant 2 cups) sweet almonds and 15 g (½ oz, ⅛ cup) bitter almonds in ½ litre (17 fl oz, 2 cups) water for 2 minutes. Drain and skin the almonds and pound them thoroughly in a mortar, adding a few drops of iced water to prevent the nuts turning into oil. When the paste is completely smooth, strain the gelatine liquid into the almond paste (reserving the leaves) and stir. Stretch some muslin (cheesecloth) over a bowl and pour the mixture onto the cloth. Twist and squeeze the muslin to obtain ½ litre (17 fl oz, 2 cups) almond milk. Pour the milk into a saucepan. Crush the leaves of gelatine and add to the almond milk together with 200 g (7 oz, 1 cup) sugar. Bring slowly to the boil, stirring continuously. Then strain through a hair sieve. Spoon into individual dishes or into a ring mould. Put in the refrigerator to set.

almond paste
PÂTE D'AMANDES

A confectionery preparation consisting of ground sweet almonds mixed with their own weight of icing (confectioners') sugar and a little glucose syrup. Almond paste was traditionally prepared by adding the ground almonds to a sugar syrup, then crushing the mixture.

Coloured and flavoured, almond paste is sold in slabs or as individual sweets in the form of vegetables, fruits, animals, etc. (see *marzipan*). It is also used to fill sweets, chocolates, and dried fruits (such as dates and prunes) served as petits fours.

Almond paste is used extensively in pâtisserie, particularly for decorating or covering cakes. Granulated almond paste, in which half the icing sugar is replaced with caster (superfine) sugar, and egg yolk often replaces the glucose syrup, is used for coating cakes and petits fours.

RECIPE

Almond paste PÂTE D'AMANDES
Grind 250 g (9 oz, 2 cups) blanched sweet almonds in a blender, in small quantities, as they turn oily if too many are worked together. Cook 500 g (18 oz, 2¼ cups) caster (superfine) sugar, 50 g (2 oz) glucose, and 1.5 dl (¼ pint, ⅔ cup) water to the 'small ball' stage (see *sugar*). Remove the saucepan from the heat, add the ground almonds, and stir briskly with a wooden spoon until the mixture becomes granular. Leave to cool completely, then knead the paste by hand in small quantities until it is soft and easy to work.

Aloxe-Corton

A commune of the Côte de Beaune in eastern France, which produces some of the greatest Burgundy wines: both red and white are equally good, which is rare. The vineyards slightly overlap into two neighbouring communes, Ladoix-Serrigny and Pernand-Vergelesses.

Only the best red wines carry the name Corton, sometimes followed by that of the vineyard producing the grapes from which they are made (Corton Clos-du-Roi, Corton-Bressandes, Corton-Renardes). They are an exceptionally good class of Burgundy wines, balanced, potent, and having an incomparable bouquet. Of all the red wines of the Côte de Beaune, these are probably the ones that mature best. The *appellation*, which covers 78 hectares (193 acres) of vines, accounts for one-third of the total production of the commune.

The white wines, which are golden and full of aromatic savour, are considered by some enthusiasts to be perhaps the best in the world. Called Corton-Charlemagne or, more rarely, Charlemagne, they are produced by 25 hectares (62 acres) of vines.

The communal *appellation* Aloxe-Corton is given to red and white wines that are of very good quality, but are not in as high a class as the ones mentioned

above. They may mature more quickly, but keep for a shorter time.

Alsace

The abundance and variety of the natural resources of this region have made it an area of great gastronomic importance for several centuries. Its fish and game are plentiful and well flavoured. The breeding of livestock, particularly pigs, and poultry provides meats which are deservedly famous, as are the products of the vineyards, orchards, and kitchen gardens. The gastronomic reputation of Alsace also owes much to the talent of its chefs, who have harmoniously blended the culinary traditions of eastern France, and its taste for pork products and pastries, with German influence (beer, flour, and cherry soups) and Jewish influence too, particularly in the use of spices and the preparation of fish. Goose fat, lard, and the bouquet of the local wines give Alsatian cuisine its own characteristic flavour. Strasbourg and Colmar are the two poles of this gastronomic tradition, but it remains a major concern even in the smallest village, where the room (*Stube*) in which the dishes are prepared and eaten symbolizes family intimacy and the warmth of the home.

To give credit where it is due, it was the Benedictine monks of past centuries who encouraged the breeding of pigs, whose quality now makes Alsatian charcuterie worthy of repute. Pork products are largely responsible for the renown of sauerkraut, which, cooked with Riesling and seasoned with a glass of Kirsch, is the Alsatian dish *par excellence*. Also well known are *Schifela* (shoulder of smoked pork), boudin, saveloy, Strasbourg sausages, *Kälerei* (pork cheese), ham (salted, smoked, in pâté), and stuffed piglet *à la peau de goret*.

Another star attraction is the goose – a dish for special occasions either served in salmis or braised with potatoes – and the celebrated terrines and pâtés de foie gras with truffles rival those of southwestern France for their fine quality. Other poultry dishes enhance Alsatian cuisine: turkey with chestnuts, chicken with Riesling, chicken with morel mushrooms, and fricassee of chicken with cream. Red meat forms the basis of pies, stews, and ragouts, as typified by baekenofe.

Game provides some classic dishes, notably haunch of venison with pears and jugged hare with noodles. Among fresh-water fish dishes are carp *à la juive* and fish stew of the River Ill region, and there are numerous local ways of serving trout, pike-perch, pike, and eel. Crayfish, which are becoming increasingly rare, are traditionally cooked *cardinalisées* in a flan, or with Alsace wine. Frogs are used in stews, soups, and sauces.

The main vegetable is, of course, the cabbage, which is the basis of sauerkraut and is also served in salads. Equally good are red cabbage with chestnuts and kohlrabi with cream. The cabbage's place of honour can be challenged only by the onion, which is eaten in tarts (zewelewai) or in bread dough (flammenkuche). Hop shoots with cream should also be mentioned and, of course, the potato, which is one of the principal ingredients of everyday cooking and is also used to make knepfles, noques, and pflutters. Fresh noodles, such as spätzle, are often served as a garnish.

Alsatian fruit, which is full of flavour, is used to make white eaux-de-vie which are justly famous (Kirsch, Quetsche, Mirabelle, and Framboise). Fruits are used in tarts and provide colourful decoration on Alsatian pâtisserie, flavoured with aniseed, cinnamon, lemon, and almonds. In this field, the best-known speciality is kugelhopf. Not to be forgotten are such sweetmeats as cherries in Kirsch, crystallized (candied) mirabelle plums, macaroons, and gingerbread.

Alsace wines

VINS D'ALSACE

Vines seem to have been introduced into Alsace by the Romans and wine-making has continued, in spite of appalling vicissitudes of fortune within the region, ever since. During the Middle Ages, wine was made by three types of producer: the peasant growers, with their own plots; the nobility, owning vineyards and often dominating the small-scale growers within property they owned overall; and the great religious establishments of the Roman Catholic church, some of these being offshoots of many dominating the known world, such as sister houses to Cluny. Although the region was devastated on many occasions by invasions, notably in the Thirty Years' War, the wine trade was able to continue to a limited extent, especially as exports of Alsace wines to many countries via the River Rhine had been of importance since very early times. In the French Revolution the holdings of the church and the nobility were broken up, and in 1870 this part of France was annexed by Germany – Alsace wines had always been popular there, whereas the barrier of the Vosges Mountains and the independent spirit of the people of Alsace had limited the spread of Alsace wines within France. At the end of the 19th century phylloxera devasted the vineyards; soon after this came World War I, with another German occupation, and although much rehabilitation was undertaken after 1919, World War II brought an even more repressive occupation and, later, fighting in the wine villages when the Germans pulled out. After the war an overall programme of improvement in all aspects of wine-making was undertaken. In 1962 the wines of Alsace got their own *appellation d'origine contrôlée* and in 1972 a law was passed making it obligatory for all Alsace wines to be bottled in the region of production.

Despite being the northernmost vine-growing area of France, Alsace benefits from special climatic conditions. The Alsace plain was formed by a series of subsidences, revealing different layers of rock where faults occurred. It is in this area that the vines are situated, and this explains the great diversity of the rocks and resultant soils: yellow granite, pink sandstone, chalky clay soil, loess, sand, gravel, and marl. Planted on the lower foothills of the Vosges mountains and on the plain, facing the Rhine but sheltered from the cold northeast winds, the vineyards extend over 100 km (60 miles) from Thann, west of Mulhouse, to Marlenheim, west of Strasbourg, in a narrow strip 1–5 km (½–3½ miles) wide. They are protected from the Atlantic winds by the natural barrier of the Vosges and benefit from a semicontinental climate, sunny and dry.

Spring frosts, hail, and dull summers do some damage, although many of the vineyards, planted at an altitude varying from 200 to 450 m (650 to 1475 ft), face south, southeast, and east and enjoy microclimates that are quite exceptional in the Rhine valley. This great variety of microclimates and the unusual character of the soil types explain why generalizations about the wines are difficult to make.

The grapes used for Alsace wines are: Riesling, Gewurztraminer, Muscat, Tokay d'Alsace (or Pinot Gris), Pinot Blanc, and Sylvaner (the noble varieties) plus Chasselas, Knipperlé, and Goldriesling (for more ordinary types of wine). Edelzwicker is a blend of the noble varieties. Otherwise, the wines are labelled with the grape varieties that make them – 100%. It should be stressed, however, that each of the great firms will make a range of wines of different qualities, even from the same variety. In addition, there are now 22 *lieux-dits* (wines from specific sites), which may be shared between several owners, the names of which may be on the labels. Also, there are certain outstanding wines occasionally made in vintages when the grapes can be ripened beyond what might have been expected, and consequently the juice is concentrated. These very special wines, never in abundant supply, are labelled *vendange tardive* (late-picked) or *sélection de grains nobles* (from specially selected individual grapes).

Some red or pinkish-red wines are made in Alsace from the Pinot Noir, also an increasing quantity of sparkling wines. Some of these are made by the Charmat method but the better ones, known as Crémants d'Alsace, follow the Champagne procedure – although, makers are proud to point out, controls are even stricter for them!

Alsace wines are bottled in tall green bottles known as *flûtes*. Although the majority of the white wines are best enjoyed while fairly young, some of the finer examples are capable of lasting for some years. The marked fragrance of most Alsace wines is enhanced by not overchilling them.

alsacienne (à l')

The description *à l'alsacienne* is given to dishes garnished with sauerkraut, ham, salted bacon, Strasbourg sausages, etc. This garnish goes with roast or braised pork, fried pheasant, braised duck, and goose. *A l'alsacienne* is also used to describe timbales (pies and terrines containing foie gras), as well as fruit tarts covered with an egg mixture.

RECIPE

Pheasant à l'alsacienne   FAISAN À L'ALSACIENNE   Truss the pheasant and cook it (unbarded) in butter in a flameproof casserole until it is lightly brown; about 25 minutes are needed for a tender bird. Braise some sauerkraut and bacon in goose fat and put the sauerkraut in the casserole, placing the pheasant on top of it; cover and cook in a hot oven for about another 25 minutes or until the pheasant is tender. Cut up the pheasant. Slice some saveloys and cut up the bacon which has been braised with the sauerkraut. Make a bed of sauerkraut on a hot serving dish, and garnish with the pieces of pheasant, bacon, and saveloy.

aluminite

Fireproof porcelain, the alumina content of which makes it particularly resistant to heat. It is unaffected by acids, but is very sensitive to shock. Aluminite is used to make cooking utensils, either white or decorated. They are completely heat-resistant (suitable for ovens, charcoals, electric hobs, well spread-out gas jets) and may also be used for serving food (gratin dishes, soufflé dishes, egg dishes, scallop shells, ramekins, etc.). If the utensil has a metal mounting, particularly a saucepan, this should have sufficient clearance to allow the porcelain to expand under the effect of heat.

aluminium

A light and malleable white metal that is widely used for kitchen equipment and for food canning, particularly sauce tubes and beer cans.

A good conductor and diffuser of heat, and light in weight, aluminium is used for large cooking utensils (bain-maries, fish kettles, couscous dishes, etc.). In aluminium sauté pans, stew pans, and saucepans, food has a tendency to stick if it is not sufficiently liquid or fatty. This defect may be remedied by hardening the interior of the pan (anodized aluminium) and especially by coating with a nonstick surface (see *PTFE*). Pure aluminium, whether smooth or hammered, blackens in contact with alkalis, as in potatoes or artichokes, and lightens again in contact with acids, as in fruits or tomatoes. It can become pitted under the action of kitchen salt or mildew. It must be sufficiently thick not to become distorted. Utensils to be used on electric stoves, in particular, must have a perfectly flat base 5 or 6 mm (0.2 or 0.25 in) thick.

Aluminium foil is used for packing and freezing. Opaque, waterproof, and greaseproof, aluminium foil withstands high temperatures very well, e.g. for cooking *en papillotes*, and does not impede freezing. Laminated aluminium is also used to make disposable oven containers, with or without lids, which can go straight from the freezer to the oven.

amandine

An almond-based fancy pastry, of which there are several kinds. It may be a tart or individual tartlets made with enriched shortcrust pastry, filled with a mixture of whole eggs, sugar, ground almonds, flour, and melted butter, flavoured with rum, and sprinkled with flaked almonds. After cooking, the top is glazed with apricot jam and decorated with crystallized (candied) whiteheart cherries.

A classic variation is to make a sponge cake with sugar, egg yolks, vanilla, ground almonds, flour, stiffly whisked (beaten) egg whites, and butter. The mixture is poured into a savarin mould and, after cooking, is iced with white fondant.

The flavour of an amandine cake may be enhanced with lemon peel or bitter-almond essence.

Tartelettes amandines are small almond cakes, attributed to the pastry-cook-poet Ragueneau, whose recipe Edmond Rostand gives in verse in *Cyrano de Bergerac*.

Amanita   AMANITE

A genus of mushrooms including some edible as well as many poisonous, in-deed deadly, species; the latter include *A. phalloides* (death cap), *A. verna*, and *A. virosa* (destroying angel). The most sought-after edible species is *A. caesarea*, the *oronge*, or Caesar's mushroom, with an orange cap and yellow gills and stalk; a species of southern France, it grows in summer and early autumn in hot dry locations. It is excellent raw, in an entrée salad or a fruit salad with oranges, or grilled (broiled) and served with a sauce seasoned with parsley, and a trickle of oil or vinegar. It is also eaten stuffed, in fritters, and as a garnish for poultry or meat.

Two other species are regarded as delicacies, both eaten cooked: *Amanita rubescens* (blusher), with a reddish-brown cap (the flesh of which turns purplish-red in contact with the air), and *Amanita vaginata* (common grisette), which is ribbed around the edges of the cap.

amaranth   AMARANTE

An ornamental plant with purple flowers, whose name has been given to a synthetic product used as a red colouring agent (E123). About ten years ago amaranth was widely used to colour confectionery, pork products, cheese rind, and fruits in syrup. Suspected of being a carcinogen, it was prohibited in the USSR, then in the United States and Sweden, and finally, in 1977, in the EEC (except when used for caviar).

Amaretto di Saranno

An Italian liqueur flavoured with almonds, apricots, and aromatic extracts. It may be used to flavour fruit salads and whipped cream.

amaugette or amauguète

A dish characteristic of the Landes department of southwest France, consisting of sheep's offal. It is made from the paunch, intestines, and feet, boiled in a pot with herbs. The name comes from *amaugè*, which was 'the leather churn of the shepherds of old' (Simin Palay).

ambassadeur or ambassadrice

A dish involving very elaborate preparation, typical of classic cuisine on a grand scale. For large joints, ambassadeur or ambassadrice garnish includes artichoke hearts stuffed with duxelles, and duchess potatoes piped into rosettes and browned in the oven. The dish is accompanied by grated horseradish served separately. Ambassadeur soup is made with fresh peas.

RECIPE

Chicken ambassadrice POULARDE AMBASSADRICE Use a velouté sauce to bind a mixture of chopped lamb's sweetbreads, truffles, and mushrooms; stuff a good-sized chicken with this mixture. Cook the chicken until tender in a flameproof casserole with a purée of vegetables cooked in meat stock. Arrange the fowl on a round dish and surround it with tartlets filled- with sautéed chicken livers (formerly cocks' combs and kidneys would have been added). Place a thin slice of truffle on each tartlet. Deglaze the casserole with Madeira and veal stock, and coat the fowl with this sauce.

ambergris AMBRE GRIS

A waxy substance of greyish colour, giving off a strong musky scent, which is secreted in the intestine of the sperm whale and collected from the surface of tropical seas, where it floats. The Chinese were the first to use it as a spice. Throughout the Middle Ages it was used in ragouts, pies, custards, and jams. Richelieu was particularly fond of ambergris pastilles, and hot ambergris chocolate was a very popular drink in the 18th century, supposedly having aphrodisiac and restorative qualities. Today ambergris is used only in perfumery.

ambigu

'A mixed collation, where meat and fruit were served together', according to the *Dictionnaire de Trévoux*. Very fashionable in the 17th century, the ambigu was a kind of cold buffet served at the end of the evening, after a fête or entertainment. Pâtés and cold meats were served with desserts and pyramids of fruit, elaborately decorated, according to a strict etiquette.

ambrosia AMBROISIE

In Greek mythology, ambrosia was the food of the gods and gave them immor-

tality. Ancient authors are rather vague as to the nature of ambrosia, implying only that it was solid (while nectar, on the other hand, was liquid). The taste of this mysterious substance is described by the poet Ibicus as 'nine times sweeter than honey'.

The name ambrosia was also given to an apéritif liqueur with a sweet taste, for which *Larousse ménager* gives the following recipe:

'Macerate for one month in 10 litres (18 pints, 22 pints) old eau-de-vie 80 g (3 oz) coriander, 20 g (¾ oz) cloves, and 20 g (¾ oz) aniseed. Decant and filter it, then add 5 litres (9 pints, 11 pints) white wine, and finally a syrup made with 5 kg (11 lb) sugar in 6 litres (10½ pints, 13½ pints) water.'

américaine (à l')

The description *à l'américaine* is given to a classic dish of shellfish, particularly lobster, created by Pierre Fraisse, a French chef known as Peters who settled in Paris about 1860 after having worked in America.

The term is also applied to fish garnishes containing thin slices of lobster tail and américaine sauce, as well as to dishes consisting of egg and grilled (broiled) poultry or meat – chicken, steak, kidneys – garnished with tomatoes and bacon.

□ À l'américaine or à l'armoricaine? The description *à l'américaine* applied to lobster has given rise to much controversy, and continues to do so, many claiming that *à l'armoricaine* is the only valid name. Curnonsky received the following letter from a Monsieur Garrique, a restaurateur, on this subject:

'I think I can tell you the exact name given to this dish by its inventor.

As you quite rightly say, lobster *à l'américaine* was created in France and, of course, by a Frenchman, Peters, born in Sète and whose real name was Fraisse.

I knew Peters about 1900, when at about 78 or 80 years of age he was living quietly with his wife in the Rue Germain-Pilon. One evening when he felt in a confiding mood, he talked to me about this famous lobster. On returning to Paris from America where he had been a chef in Chicago, he founded the Peters restaurant; if I remember correctly, this was a little before 1860.

Now one evening when dinner was long over, eight or ten customers turned up almost at closing time and insisted that Peters serve them dinner, on the pretext that they had only one hour to spare.

Peters, who was kindness itself, agreed to return to his kitchens, not without wondering anxiously what he was going to be able to serve to them. 'While they are eating the soup and the hors-d'oeuvre,' he said to himself, 'I've got time to prepare a fish dish!' But there was no fish. There were only some live lobsters, reserved for the following morning . . . but there was not enough time to cook them in a court-bouillon.

It was then that Peters, in a flash of inspiration, threw into a pan some butter, tomatoes, crushed garlic, shallot . . . then some white wine, a little oil, and finally a good helping of brandy. . . . When it was all boiling, Peters said to himself: 'There is only one way to cook the lobster quickly – that is to cut it into pieces and throw them into the sauce!'

This he did, and the result was marvellous. His enthusiastic customers asked the great restaurateur what this exquisite dish was and what he called it. And Peters, still under the influence of his recent stay in America, said without thinking, 'Lobster *à l'américaine*!'

Peters himself gave me the recipe and it is the one I always use.

As far as the history of the creation of this famous dish is concerned, I believe it to be completely authentic, as Peters was the soul of frankness, honesty, and goodness.'

| RECIPE

Boiled (*or poached*) **eggs à l'amér-icaine** OEUFS MOLLETS (OU POCHÉS) À L'AMÉRICAINE Fry some croutons and top them with boiled or poached eggs and slices of lobster *à l'américaine*. Cover with the sauce (américaine sauce) in which the lobster was cooked (not all the sauce produced will be required for this dish).

amino acids
ACIDS AMINÉS
The basic constituents of proteins. Some

20 different amino acids occur in proteins. The human body is capable of synthesizing, according to its needs, most of these; there are, however, eight amino acids that the body cannot synthesize and that therefore must be provided through food. Known as the essential amino acids, they are isoleucine, leucine, lysine, methionine, phenylalanine, threonine, tryptophan, and valine. The lack of any one of these prevents the body from making its own proteins.

The biological value of proteins depends on their having a good balance of amino acids; animal proteins have a greater biological value than vegetable proteins. In eggs the amino acid distribution is almost ideal, while certain flours, for example, need enrichment with lysine. Certain essential amino acids, such as methionine, are industrially produced.

amiral (à l')
The term used to describe a particular garnish for such fish dishes as poached sole, fillets of sole, stuffed turbot, or braised salmon. It contains some of the following ingredients: fried oysters and mussels, crayfish tails or whole crayfish, mushroom caps, and truffle slices. The dish is coated with Nantua sauce.

The term also describes a type of consommé.

| RECIPE

Consommé à l'amiral Lightly thicken a fish consommé with arrowroot and garnish with small pike quenelles in crayfish butter, poached oyster halves, julienne of truffles cooked in Madeira, and sprigs of chervil.

amourette
The delicately flavoured spinal marrow of beef, mutton, or veal. Amourettes may be prepared and dressed like calves' brains; they can be cut into small pieces and used in fillings for croûtes, timbales, tarts, and vols-au-vent or used as an ingredient for salads.

| RECIPE

Preparation of amourettes PRÉPARA-TION DES AMOURETTES Clean the amourettes in cold water, remove the membranes, poach for a few minutes in a court-bouillon, and allow them to cool.

Amourettes au gratin Butter a gratin dish and cover the base with mushroom duxelles. Arrange the cold cooked amourettes on the mushroom layer and sprinkle with a little lemon juice. Cover with duxelles sauce and scatter with golden breadcrumbs. Pour melted butter over the top and brown in the oven or under the grill (broiler).

Amphicles AMPHICLÈS

A probably fictional chef of ancient Greece, noted for his opposition to very complicated dishes and the excessive use of spices. For him, a hare had to be served rare, roasted on a spit, and barely seasoned with fennel. He would cook red mullet in a fig leaf and lark in a vine leaf, among cinders. A defender of natural foods and opposed to the disguising of natural flavours, Amphicles can still serve as an example. He is probably an invention of the Abbé Barthélemy (author, in 1788, of *Voyage du jeune Anacharsis en Grèce au IVᵉ siècle de l'ère vulgaire*), included and embellished by Prosper Montagné in his dictionary.

amphitryon

A person who entertains guests at his table. According to mythology, Zeus, wishing to seduce the mortal Alcmene, took on the appearance of her husband, Amphitryon, and gave her a son, Heracles. In Molière's comedy inspired by this fable, the servant Sosie, embarrassed at having to serve two masters and deciding finally for the one who guarantees him board and lodging, says, 'The real Amphitryon is the host who provides dinner.'

But to provide dinner is not sufficient; one has to know the art of how to do it. Grimod de La Reynière was one of the first to indicate in his *Manuel des amphitryons* (1808) the rules of correct behaviour at the table. According to him, tact is necessary, as well as generosity, organization, a good chef, and the appreciation of good food. More recently, Auguste Michel, in the *Manuel des amphitryons au début du XXᵉ*

siècle, and Maurice des Ombiaux, in *L'Amphitryon d'aujourd'hui* (1936), have brought these rules into accord with modern tastes. Although the term is hardly used nowadays, one rule, decreed by Brillat-Savarin, remains unchanged: 'To invite someone to be our guest is to undertake responsibility for his happiness all the time that he is under our roof.'

amphora AMPHORE

A Greek or Roman two-handled jar (the Greek word means 'carried from both sides') that was used to store oil and wine. Some amphorae (*psykters*) had double walls between which iced water was poured to keep the contents of the jar cool. The *stamnos*, sometimes compared to a cooking pot, was also used for storing wine. It had a fairly narrow mouth with small horizontal handles, and was very popular in the 5th century B C.

Amphorae used for transporting wine were closed with clay corks and sealed with pitch or plaster. A label indicating the vineyard, the year, the capacity of the jar, and sometimes its maker's name, was either tied to the jar or engraved on it.

Amphoux (Madame)

19th-century French distiller. She owned a distillery in Martinique and the liqueurs des Îles (made from vanilla, tea, cocoa, coffee, etc.) were named after her. These liqueurs were very fashionable at the time of the Consulate and the Empire. Balzac refers to them several times, notably in *La Vieille Fille:* 'Finally, Mademoiselle sacrificed three bottles of the celebrated liqueurs of Madame Amphoux, the most illustrious of overseas distillers, a name dear to lovers of liqueurs'; and, further on: 'Bless my soul, there is nothing but liqueurs of Madame Amphoux, which are only brought out on high days and holidays.'

Amunategui (Francis)

French author of gastronomic articles and books (born Santiago, Chile, 1898; died Paris, 1972) who abandoned his career as an engineer in 1947 in order to write. He was responsible for one of the earliest series of articles dedicated to restaurants, which came into their own again after the Occupation. These appeared in the periodical *Aux écoutes*. He published *L'Art des mets* (1959), *Le Plaisir des mets* (1964), and *Gastronomiquement vôtre* (1971). He was a member of the 'Academy of the Psychologists of Taste' and founded the A.A.A.A.A., which extols the virtues of andouillettes. His style blends humour and historical and literary references, with an acute observation for everything connected with regional cuisine.

amygdalin

A French term derived from the Greek *amygdale* (almond), which was formerly used to describe pastries, cakes, and confectionery containing almonds.

anagnost ANAGNOSTE

In ancient Roman times, the slave whose task it was to read aloud during meals.

analect ANALECTE

In ancient Greek and Roman times, the slave whose task it was to gather up the remains of a meal.

anchovy ANCHOIS

A small sea fish, maximum length 20 cm (8 in), with a greenish-blue back and silvery sides. The anchovy is very abundant in the Mediterranean, the Black Sea, and the Atlantic and Pacific Oceans. It lives in tightly packed shoals and is fished for the canning industry. When sold fresh – which is rare – it may be fried or marinated like sardines.

Anchovies are sold salted, in jars, as whole fish in oil, or as fillets in cans (flat or rolled up, in oil, or in piquant sauce). As they will not keep long once opened, they must be stored in the refrigerator, as must anchovy pastes, creams, and butters.

In ancient times, anchovies were used to make a condiment (garum). There has always been a trade in anchovies, which were transported in special small casks called *barrots*. Today they are used mainly in the cuisine of southern France in such dishes as *anchoyade*, *tapenade*, *poutine*, *pissalat*, *pissaladière*, *pan-bagnat*, and pizza, but are also used in such traditional seasonings as ready-cooked anchovy butter and

English anchovy sauce. 'The temptation of Jansson', an extremely popular Swedish dish, is a gratin of anchovies and potatoes. See also *kilka*, *sprat*

RECIPE

Anchovy fillets à la silésienne FILETS D'ANCHOIS À LA SILÉSIENNE Poach some fresh soft herring roe in stock and then either rub through a fine sieve or purée in a blender. For 300 g (11 oz, 1 cup, firmly packed) roe, add 2–3 chopped shallots and a few sprigs of parsley (chopped). Place the mixture in an hors d'oeuvres dish and arrange a lattice of pickled anchovy fillets over the top. Make a salad with diced potatoes, dessert apples, and beetroot (red beet) moistened with a well-seasoned vinaigrette and arrange it around the purée. Sprinkle with chopped parsley.

anchoyade

A Provençal dish consisting of a purée of anchovies mixed with crushed garlic and olive oil, and sometimes a few drops of vinegar. It is usually served with raw vegetables and may also be spread on slices of bread and heated in the oven. At Draguignan, anchoyade (or *anchoïade*) *à la dracenoise* is an anchovy purée mixed with onions and chopped hard-boiled (hard-cooked) eggs. It is spread in a thick layer on slices of home-baked bread, moistened generously with olive oil, and browned in a hot oven.

ancienne (à l')

The description *à l'ancienne* is given to certain fricassees (chicken or lamb) or white stews (turkey, veal, or lamb) in which the garnish includes small sliced onions and button mushrooms (see *bonne femme*). This term, widely used in bourgeois cookery, may also be applied to braised dishes (sweetbreads, beef, or fowl) and to pastry cases (pie shells) baked blind and filled with ragouts of cocks' combs and kidneys or quenelles of truffles and mushrooms. See *béatilles*, *feuilleton*, *talmouse*, *tourte*.

RECIPE

Soft-boiled (*or poached*) **eggs à l'ancienne** OEUFS MOLLETS (OU POCHÉS) À

L'ANCIENNE Arrange the eggs on a bed of rice that has been cooked in meat stock. Coat them with velouté sauce and place between each egg 1 tablespoon julienne of truffles bound with a highly reduced Madeira sauce.

ancient Greece
GRÈCE ANTIQUE

The Homeric heroes apparently feasted on shoulder of mutton or roasted chine of pork, flavoured with oregano and cumin, and on olives, figs, walnuts, goats'-milk cheese, and cakes made with flour and honey. Vegetables, which were difficult to grow in the dry soil, are rarely mentioned. Nevertheless, they formed the basic diet of the common people, mainly in the form of cabbage and lentil purées. The ancient Greeks, in a country surrounded by sea teeming with fish, were very fond of seafood and fish. Salted tuna, eels, red mullet, sole, turbot, octopus, sea bream, porgy, torpedo fish, and conger eels are often mentioned in the texts. Game was also abundant: apart from pheasants, partridges, and wood pigeons, the ancient Greeks also hunted jackdaws, owls, flamingos, and even seagulls. Ground game included roebucks, wild boars, hares, foxes, white-breasted martens, moles, and even cats! The ancient Greeks originally drank hydromel, but from 2000 BC onwards this was superseded by heavy strong wines, always drunk with water (sometimes even sea water).

□ **The earliest cooks** In Homer's time cooks as such did not exist. Female slaves ground the corn and prepared the food. According to the *Iliad* and the *Odyssey*, the host himself, however exalted, prepared and cooked the meals with the help of friends when he received distinguished guests. Later, the baker (*mageiros*) cooked as well as baked for his masters. In time he became *archimageiros* (chef de cuisine) and was given assistants. Great houses had a hierarchy of slaves, under a steward, the *eleatros*. Each slave had definite duties. The *opsonomos* or *agorastes* (from *agora* or market place) bought the food, while the *opsartytes* looked after the fires, did rough jobs, and prepared food for the household slaves. A woman, the

demiourga, made sweetmeats and other delicacies. Women had free access to the kitchen. Other slaves prepared meals or served at table. The *trapezopoios* laid the table and washed the dishes, the *oinophoros* had charge of the wine, the *oinochoikos*, a young slave, filled the wine cups of the guests.

In the 4th century BC, Athenian cooks were often slaves. They played an important role in the life of the city and ruled as masters over all the other slaves in the household. A special law permitted the cook who invented a new dish the privilege of making it and selling it to the public.

Many Greek cooks left famous names behind. Cadmos was cook to the king of Sidon in Phoenicia, and, according to legend, introduced writing into Greece. As a result of the burning of the library in Alexandria, only a few fragments and the authors' names remain from the Greek literature of gastronomy.

□ **Hippocrates and dietetics** Even though there were few refined gourmets, the ancient Greeks, especially the Spartans and the Athenians, were discriminating in their eating habits, unlike the Boeotians, the Thessalians, and the Macedonians. Epicurus recommended 'simple dishes that satisfy us as much as sumptuous feasts'. In *The Republic*, Plato defines, through Socrates, the diet of the model citizen: bread, olives, cheese, vegetables, and fruit. Both Hippocrates (5th century BC) and later Galen (2nd century AD) studied the effects of food both on the sick and those in good health.

In *De la gastronomie française*, R. Dumay acknowledges that the ancient Greeks made four major contributions to cookery. First, they established the market (*agora*), where the master of the house himself often went to choose the food for his household. Secondly, they knew how to appreciate both their cooks and culinary art in general – in the town of Sybaris, in Magna Graecia, famous for its refined way of life, chefs were awarded patents to protect their recipes. Thirdly, they cultivated a simplicity in their cooking, using few basic ingredients, preferring roasts and grills to dishes with sauces, and including herbs to bring out the authentic flavour of the food. Finally, they left us a legacy of various recipes that have been handed down through the generations – black pudding (blood sausage), fried scampi, turbot with herbs, thrushes with honey, grilled (broiled) frogs' legs, etc.

ancient Rome

ROME ANTIQUE

The ancient Romans were pioneers of gastronomy, adding to their own culinary habits those of the Greeks and the peoples of Asia Minor and eagerly adopting new methods and ingredients. The traditional picture of orgies where great quantities of rare foods were served, drowned in spiced sauces and cooked in the most lavish fashion, is false. If the works of Petronius, Juvenal, and Martial are full of detailed accounts of sumptuous banquets, it is because these were the exception: flamingos' tongues, camels' heels, dormice stuffed with chestnuts, wild boar stuffed with thrushes, and other extravagant fancies were far from being everyday fare.

True, Maecenas was the first to taste mule flesh, which epicureans considered less tasty than wild ass, and Elagabalus feasted on elephant trunk and roast camel. To amuse the Emperor Aurelian, the actor Faron is said to have swallowed a ewe, a sucking pig, and a wild boar, with a hundred small loaves and as many bottles of wine. Petronius, in the *Satyricon*, paints an evocative portrait of Trimalcion. Nevertheless, true Latin cooking had its origins in a humble and frugal tradition. Stockrearing and agriculture were carried out in the Tiber valley, but it was due to the trade in salt, a commodity produced by evaporation at the river mouth, that commercial links were established with the Greek and Etruscan colonies.

From the earliest times, the staple food of the Romans was *pulmentum*, a porridge of millet, barley, or chickpea flour, sometimes diluted with milk. As the art of bread-making developed, the first bakers appeared in Rome. Other basic foods were: ewes'-milk cheese, boiled mutton, cabbage, cardoons, and broad (fava) beans. Fruit was important in the Roman diet: apples were no longer a scarce commodity as they had been in ancient Greece, but imported apricots from Armenia and peaches from Persia were very expensive. Lucullus is credited with introducing the cherry tree; figs grew in abundance and dates were imported from Africa. Melon growing developed in the region round Cantalupo (which gave its name to the cantaloupe melon).

It was after the defeat of Antiochus (III) the Great (189 BC) that the Romans, advancing into Asia Minor, gradually discovered the refinement of the Greek courts in the Hellenized East. The best-known fact about the General Lucullus is that he adopted their life style. According to Livy: 'The army returning from Asia brought foreign luxury to Rome. It became a lengthy and costly business to prepare a meal. Cooks, who used to be regarded as slaves, began to demand high wages. That which had been toil became art.'

In order to meet the tastes and needs of her citizens, Rome began to develop a more complex system of food production and distribution, operating chiefly through large warehouses and markets. The most famous of these was that of Trajan, where Romans could buy corn from Egypt, olive oil from Spain, spices from Asia, hams from Gaul, numerous varieties of fish, which were often farmed (Moray eels, sea bass, monkfish, plaice, and turbot), and various types of shellfish, including whelks, sea urchins, and especially oysters, which Sergius Orata believed were the first to be reared in oyster beds. It was the Romans who invented the process of force-feeding geese with figs, to enlarge their livers.

Wealthy Romans ate large quantities of meat, preferring pork to mutton. They enjoyed, for example, pork stuffed with oysters and small birds, roasted on one side, then spread with a paste of oats, wine, and oil and poached in boiling water on the other side. Apicius, author of many recipes, mentioned, among other things, fresh ham painted with honey and cooked in a pastry case with figs and bay leaves. Poultry was much esteemed: capons, Numidian fowl (guinea fowl), domestic pigeons, wild duck (of which only the brain and breast were eaten), roast goose, etc. In Marguerite Yourcenar's book *Memoirs of Hadrian*, the emperor reflects: 'It was

in Rome, during the long official re-
pasts, that I began to think of the relatively recent origins of our riches and of
this nation of thrifty farmers and frugal
soldiers, who formerly ate garlic and
barley, now suddenly enabled by our
conquests to revel in the cooking of
Asia, devouring this complicated food
with the greed of starving peasants.'

Several modern italian recipes go
back to the days of ancient Rome, such
as gnocchi and Ricotta cheese tart;
another very common cake made with
cheese was *libum* (or *savillum*),
flavoured with honey and poppy seeds.

Roman cooking was characterized by
the use of quite highly spiced sauces,
including *garum* based on fermented
fish. Particularly popular was a sweet-
and-sour condiment for which Apicius
gave the recipe: pepper, mint, pine nuts,
raisins, grated carrot, honey, vinegar,
oil, wine, and musk. As sugar was not
available, the Romans sweetened their
food with either honey or grape syrup.
They made a variety of different
cheeses, most of them from ewes' milk.
Great wine lovers, they preferred to
drink their wines young and diluted
with water. Several types of wine were
produced, which were sold quite
cheaply: straw wine (*passim*), honeyed
wine (*mulsum*), vinegar diluted with
water (*posca*), which was a thirst-
quenching drink favoured by soldiers
on campaign, imitation wines
(flavoured with wormwood, roses,
violets, etc.), and fruit wines.

The most highly prized wines, however, were the *grand crus* from the
Campania region: Capua, Pompeii,
Naples, Vesuvius, and Cumae. The
most famous of these, the red and white
Falernian wines, were aged over a long
period. These high-quality wines were
stored in amphorae and were usually
filtered at table before serving, to improve their clarity.

Wine was a common offering to the
gods and its use in religious ceremonies
gave rise to great wine festivals. A law of
Romulus forbade women to drink wine,
though apparently this prohibition applied only to fermented wines.

andalouse (à l')

The description *à l'andalouse* is given to
a garnish that includes peppers (stuffed
or sautéed), tomatoes (cooked halves,
chopped, or in a sauce), rice (pilaf, or
risotto with peppers), fried aubergine
(egg-plant) slices, and sometimes chipolata sausages or chorizo. It is served
with large joints of meat, particularly
red meat (leg, loin, and saddle (both
loins) of mutton; rib and fillet (sirloin)
of beef), but may also be served either in
a consommé or with sole fillets.

RECIPE

Andalouse sauce SAUCE ANDA-
LOUSE Reduce 3 dl (½ pint, 1¼ cups)
velouté sauce by one-third and add 2
tablespoons (3 tablespoons) tomato
purée (paste). Mix and reduce further.
Add a crushed clove of garlic and salt
and pepper. Wash and chop a small
bunch of parsley. Blanch a green pepper
and half a red pepper in boiling water,
peel and cool, remove the seeds, and
dice the flesh (2 tablespoons (3 tablespoons) altogether). Add the diced
peppers to the reduced velouté and the
chopped parsley.

andouille

A type of sausage made from the stomach and intestines of the pig to which
may be added other parts of the animal
(neck, breast, head, or heart), the whole
enclosed in a black skin. Rabelais, in
Pantagruel, names andouille as one of
the favourite dishes of his contemporaries: it features in 'the war of the
Andoyles against *Quaresmeprenant*'.
Various sausages, bearing the name of
the region where their recipes originated, are now called andouilles, but
there are only two authentic varieties –
those of Vire and those of Guémené.
Andouille is cut into thin slices and
eaten cold in hors d'oeuvres.

Guémené andouille, which is protected by a trademark, has the appearance of concentric circles when sliced, as
the intestines are placed one inside
another according to their size during
preparation. The andouille is then tied
up, dried, smoked, and, lastly, either
cooked in a bouillon or steamed.

The 'genuine Vire andouille' (with
guaranteed method and area of production) includes both intestines and stomach, cleaned, washed, cut up and
salted, and enclosed in a skin. The

andouille is smoked over beech wood for two months, which allows the natural black colour of the coating to develop. It is then tied and cooked either in water or in an aromatized court-bouillon. It measures 25–30 cm (10–12 in) in length and 4–6 cm (1½–2½ in) in diameter.

The 'Vire andouille' (without guarantee) is made all over France, by similar methods, using the same ingredients as for the genuine Vire andouille with the addition of the neck and the breast, which make it more fatty. The locally made 'andouilles de pays' also contain pig's heart and pig's head without the skin removed. The andouille of Val-d'Ajol and that of Aire-sur-la-Lys should also be mentioned. The andouille of Jargeau, made from shoulder and breast without any intestines, is not sold ready-cooked. Andouilles made from pork rind are a speciality of south-western France.

andouillette

A type of sausage made from pork intestines (*chaudins*), often with the addition of pork stomach and calf's mesentery, precooked in stock or milk and packed into a skin. Andouillettes, which are sold in 10–15-cm (4–6-in) lengths and are sometimes coated with breadcrumbs, aspic jelly, or lard, are eaten either grilled (broiled) or fried. Several regions are known for their production of andouillettes. The Troyes andouillette, made solely from pork, has a greasy consistency and is prepared from the intestines and belly of pork, cut into fairly wide strips. The andouillette from Cambrai is usually made from veal only. The Lyonnais andouillette is made from calf's mesentery with, sometimes, a bit of pork belly, while the Provençal andouillette consists of a mixture of thin slices of pork intestines and neck plus the rind. The drier andouillette from Rouen is made from pig's bowels without the belly and calf's mesentery. The andouillette is traditionally served with mustard and garnished with fried potatoes, red beans, lentils, and a purée of celery, apples, or red cabbage. In Strasbourg it is served on a bed of sauerkraut.

The association Amicale des Amateurs d'Authentiques Andouillettes (A.A.A.A.A.), a gastronomic society founded by F. Amunategui for those who appreciate authentic andouillettes, upholds the tradition, and Charles Monselet dedicated a sonnet to the andouillette.

RECIPE

Andouillettes à la tourangelle (from Charles Barrier's recipe) Lightly slit 6 andouillettes, pour some Armagnac over them, and let them steep for 24 hours. Slice 500 g (18 oz, 4–5 cups) button mushrooms and sprinkle them with lemon juice. Butter a cooking dish, place the mushrooms on it, add salt and pepper, and arrange the andouillettes on top. Pour a glass of dry Vouvray wine over the food and cook in a hot oven for 40 minutes, turning the andouillettes several times and basting them. Add a little more wine or boiling water if needed.

angelica ANGÉLIQUE

An aromatic umbelliferous plant from the Scandinavian countries, which was introduced into France by the Vikings and cultivated by the monks. Its green stalks are candied in sugar and used in cakes, gingerbreads, puddings, and soufflés. It is a speciality of the town of Niort, and Austin de Croze has described lyrically what he considers to be the best way to enjoy it: 'Have a dozen choice brioches, kept hot, a fruit dish filled with sticks of candied angelica, a bottle of angelica liqueur, a carafe of iced water, and a box of Egyptian cigarettes. Light a cigarette, take a draught of iced water, crunch a piece of Niort angelica with a mouthful of very hot brioche, inhale, draw in and distil a few drops of angelica liqueur in the mouth, then start again. Then you only need the room to be sprayed with a light fresh perfume, such as verbena or citronella, to know what blissful enjoyment a discreet sybaritism can give.'

Liqueur manufacturers also use the crushed stems and roots of angelica in the production of Melissa cordial, Chartreuse, Vespétro, and gin.

RECIPE

Candied angelica ANGÉLIQUE CON-FITE Cut some angelica stems into

15–20-cm (6–8-in) lengths. Soak them for 3–4 hours in cold water, then plunge into boiling water until the pulp softens Drain, cool, and peel carefully to remove all the stringy parts. Macerate the stems for 24 hours in a syrup of 1 cup sugar to 1 cup water. Drain. Boil the syrup to 102 c (215 f) and pour it over the pieces of angelica. Repeat this operation once a day for three days. On the fourth day cook the syrup until it reaches the 'pearl' stage, i.e. 105 c (221 f). Add the angelica and boil for a few moments. Remove the pan from the heat, cool, and drain the angelica in a sieve. When the angelica pieces are dry, lay them out on a slab, dust with caster (superfine) sugar, and dry in a slow oven. Store in hermetically sealed containers.

angel shark

ANGE DE MER

A fish of the shark family that resembles a skate with its wing-shaped pectoral fins. It is cooked in the same way as skate. There are several species, which are widespread in temperate European coastal regions and in tropical seas. The average size of the angel shark varies from 90 cm to 1.2 m (3–4 ft), but some individuals may reach 2 m (6½ ft) and weigh more than 60 kg (135 lb). Its skin is wrinkled, its back greenish-brown flecked with grey, and its underside a creamy-white colour. The flesh is quite tasty, but is not considered to be as palatable as that of the skate.

anglaise (à l')

The description *à l'anglaise* is given to vegetables, meat, and fish prepared in a variety of ways.

• Vegetables *à l'anglaise* are cooked in water and served plain with chopped parsley, knobs of butter, melted butter, a herb sauce, etc.: see *bean (French beans), Brussels sprout, cabbage, carrot, cauliflower, leek, pea, potato.*

• Meat and poultry *à l'anglaise* are poached, boiled, or cooked in a white stock. According to the dish, vegetables are cooked at the same time or separately, either boiled or steamed: see *beef, brain, breast, chicken, giblets, goose, head, heart, loin, rabbit, shoulder, turkey.*

• Fish or pieces of meat which are coated in breadcrumbs before being sautéed or fried are also described as *à l'anglaise*: see *brain, escalope, frog, kidneys, liver, suprême.*

• Fish grilled *à l'anglaise* (cut into steaks if they are large or slit if they are small) are brushed with oil or melted butter (and coated with flour if they have a delicate flesh); they must be cooked over a low heat. They are served with melted butter or maître d'hotel butter and, if desired, with steamed or boiled potatoes or with other boiled vegetables, such as spinach, the white part of leeks, etc.: see *cod, eel, herring, mackerel, monkfish, sardine, smelt, soft roe, sole, whiting.*

• Various dishes from the British gastronomic repertory are named *à l'anglaise*, including sauces, desserts, pies, and egg dishes.

• *Crème anglaise* is a basic preparation of classic cuisine: see *creams and custards.*

| RECIPE

Sauce à l'anglaise (from Carême's recipe) Chop 4 hard-boiled (hard-cooked) egg yolks very finely and mix them in a saucepan with some fairly thick velouté of the kind used as a sauce for an entrée. Then add a dash of pepper, some grated nutmeg, the juice of a lemon, and a little anchovy butter.

Angola pea

POIS D'ANGOLA

A pulse vegetable consisting of pale-green to dark-red seeds enclosed in long pods; the shrub itself is native to Asia but is also cultivated in Africa and the West Indies. Also known as *pois d'ambrevade, pois cajou, gandules,* or pigeon peas, the peas are used either fresh (in salads, soups, garnishes, etc.) or dried (when they are much more nourishing), in purées or as a base for sauces. A type of flour made from the peas is used to prepare fritters and cakes.

Angostura bitters

A brownish-red bitters made with various herbs (its exact formula is a secret). It has tonic and fever-reducing properties and was created at

Angostura (now Ciudad Bolívar, Venezuela) by a surgeon of Bolívar's army to combat the effects of the tropical climate. Angostura is now made in Trinidad and is used mainly for flavouring cocktails and 'pink gins'.

animelles

Animal testicles used for meat, especially those of the ram, the lamb, and the bull. Animelles were formerly very popular in the East, in Mediterranean countries, and in France under Louis XV. They are still popular in Italy and Spain (in the form of fried bull *criadillas*). They are either prepared in the same way as kidneys or served with a vinaigrette.

RECIPE

Preparation of animelles PRÉP- ARATION DES ANIMELLES Plunge the animelles into boiling water for about 2 minutes, cool under cold water, and immediately skin them. Soak them in cold water for about 10 hours to remove impurities, then drain and press between 2 plates.

Fried animelles ANIMELLES FRITES (from Plumerey's recipe) Skin 3 fresh animelles and cut each into 8 similar pieces. Put them into a terrine dish with salt, pepper, 2 tablespoons tarragon vinegar, 2 tablespoons olive oil, a little thyme, half a bay leaf, a sliced onion, and a few sprigs of parsley. Cover the dish. Drain them after an hour and replace in the terrine with all the ingredients and the juice of half a lemon. Just before serving, drain the animelles on a cloth and press lightly. Coat them with flour and fry them until lightly browned. Arrange in a pyramid on a napkin and garnish with friend parsley.

anise ANIS

An aromatic umbelliferous plant originating in the East (India and Egypt). It was also known to the Romans, and was regarded by the Chinese as a sacred plant. The seeds (aniseed) were used in early European cookery in pretzels, girdle cakes, and knackebrot and are now used to flavour soufflés, biscuits (cookies), and cakes, especially gingerbread. Aniseed is also used in con-fectionery (Flavigny dragés) and in distilling (pastis and anisette). The chopped leaves may be used to season pickled vegetables, salads, and fish soups in the south of France. See also *dill, star anise.*

RECIPE

Aniseed biscuits (cookies) PAINS À L'ANIS Mix 500 g (18 oz, 2¼ cups) caster (superfine) sugar and 12 eggs in a copper basin. Beat the mixture with a whisk as for an ordinary sponge cake.

When the mixture is well whisked, add 500 g (18 oz, 4½ cups) sieved flour, 200 g (7 oz, scant 2 cups) cornflour (cornstarch), and 50 g (2 oz, ⅓ cup) aniseed (in grains). Mix well.

Drop tablespoons of the mixture onto a wetted baking tray (sheet). Place in a warm place to dry. When the biscuits (cookies) begin to rise slightly, bake in a cool oven.

anisette

The flavour of the many liqueurs known as anisette or anise varies according to which seeds are used – aniseed or star anise. These liqueurs are very popular as digestives. Well known in France are the anisettes of Bordeaux (especially that of Marie Brizard), but most liqueur houses make a version of anisette. The aniseed-flavoured Mediterranean drinks – pastis, ouzo, etc. – are drunk either diluted with water or with water as an accompaniment.

Anjou

The cuisine of this region of the Loire Valley, which is well balanced and subtly blended, includes recipes dating from the Middle Ages and the Renaissance, particularly for river fish and sweet dishes.

The art of charcuterie is especially well developed with such dishes as rillettes, rillons, and rillauds, as well as white puddings and gogues. Sausages and andouillettes are also renowned.

The Loire fish are prepared in traditional ways, such as pike in white butter sauce (a recipe also claimed by Nantes), stuffed shad with sorrel, grilled salmon, perch with prunes, bouilleture and other fish stews, braised fish, and eel pie.

The meat of the region is excellent, particularly Le Mans beef, and tasty specialities are made from veal, such as rump of veal *à l'angevine* served with onion purée, matelote of veal with red wine, and stuffed breast of veal. Lamb's pluck is cooked in white wine. The tender plump poultry is used to make excellent fricassees, such as Taillevent's *cominée de gélines*.

The region is also noted for its vegetables: green cabbages (*piochons*) and cauliflowers are used to make fricassees. *Chouées* (boiled cabbage sprinkled with melted butter), stuffed artichokes, and *nouzillards* (chestnuts cooked in milk) are popular vegetable dishes.

Cheeses are often served with salad and walnut oil; specialities include the small local goats'-milk cheeses, as well as *chouze* from Saumur and *entrammes* (a forerunner of Port-Salut). Crémets make a delicate dessert.

The orchards of the region provide excellent fruit: Belle-Angevine pears, often cooked in red wine; dessert and cider apples; plums and mirabelles, used in pies; and strawberries, served with cream.

Sweet specialities include bottereaux, *bijane* (cold bread and wine soup) or soup *à la pie, millière* (maize and rice porridge), and *fouée* (a pancake made from dough covered with fresh butter), all of which date back to much earlier times, as do the fouaces appreciated by Rabelais and *guillaret* (a sweet pastry). Biscuits (cookies) are very varied and include sablés, croquets, the aniseed biscuits of Angers, almond and hazelnut balls, and macaroons.

Anjou wines

VINS D'ANJOU

Wines have been made in the region of Angers, capital of Anjou, for centuries, and as Henry II of England was the Count of Anjou, they certainly would have been familiar to the English court in medieval times. They are mentioned in an edict of King John, and, among the French kings, Philip Augustus, Louis XI, and François I are known to have enjoyed them. The River Loire provided a means of exporting them, as well as transporting them to other regions within France. The Anjou climate is influenced by the proximity of the Atlantic; it is usually mild in winter, with hot summers and long warm autumns – almost ideal for wine-making, although there can be dangers from spring frosts and sudden hailstorms. Soils are very varied, including shale, sandstone, clay, chalk, sand, and gravel. The vines tend to be planted on the slopes alongside the river and its tributaries, the vineyards ideally sited so that they face south and southwest.

A huge range of wines are made throughout the region: dry to medium-sweet and very sweet still whites, reds, rosés, and sparkling wines. They are numerous AOCs for the various areas within the region. The main grape for the white wines is the Chenin Blanc (here often called Pineau de la Loire or Blanc d'Anjou), which makes all the quality whites. The red wines come from the Cabernet Franc and some of the rosés are also made from this, although there are other red varieties planted, including the Gamay and Groslot. Most export markets feature the rosés, which vary from dry to sweetish, and the straightforward white wines. The red wines are unfortunately not very popular outside France – in their home region they are pleasant when served at cellar temperature – and the more luscious examples of wines affected by *Botrytis cinerea* are well worth discovering. The sparkling wines, many of them made around Saumur, are made as white and sometimes rosé wines following the Champagne process.

Anna

The name of a potato dish created by Adolphe Dugléré to accompany roast meat and poultry. It was dedicated to Anna Deslions, a woman of fashion at the time of the Second Empire. The dish is cooked in a special round two-handled casserole with an interlocking lid. The potatoes are sliced and covered during cooking. When the potatoes are cut into strips rather than rounds, the dish is called Annette potatoes.

RECIPE

Anna potatoes POMMES ANNA Peel 1 kg (2¼ lb) potatoes and cut into thin even round slices. Wash, wipe, and season with salt and pepper. Slightly brown 75 g (3 oz) butter in a special casserole (or in a sauté pan) and arrange the potatoes in circular layers, making sure that they are evenly coated with butter, then compress them into a cake with a wooden spatula. Cover and cook in a hot oven for 25 minutes. Quickly turn the whole cake over onto a flat dish and slide it back into the casserole to brown the other side.

annatto ROCOU

A food colouring extracted from the red wax coating around the seeds of the annatto tree of Central America. It is used to give an orange, yellow, or red colour to items of charcuterie, various cheeses (Edam, Mimolette, Cheshire, Cheddar), dried, salted, and smoked fish (notably haddock), and also to pastries, sweets, and butter.

antelope ANTILOPE

A ruminant mammal belonging to the cattle family, found chiefly in Africa and Asia. There are more than a hundred species of antelope, varying in size from that of a lamb to that of a horse. Their habits are similar to those of the European deer, but their meat is firmer and sometimes has a very strong flavour. According to the culinary traditions of the aboriginal populations who eat antelope, the meat may be roasted, braised, or boiled, although it is sometimes necessary to marinate it, or ripen it in the sun. The highly regarded meat of the gazelle (a small antelope) is prepared in the same way as venison.

antiboise (à l')

The description *à l'antiboise* is given to various dishes of Provençal cuisine that are specialities of Antibes. Such dishes include eggs cooked in the oven with browned *nonnats* (tiny Mediterranean fish), crushed garlic, and chopped parsley; a gratin of scrambled eggs in layers alternating with sautéed courgettes (zucchini) and a fondue of tomatoes in oil; oven-grilled tomatoes garnished with anchovy fillets, pieces of tuna, and breadcrumbs crushed with garlic; and cold stuffed tomatoes.

antillaise (à l')

The description *à l'antillaise* is applied to numerous ways of preparing fish, shellfish, and poultry, generally served accompanied either with rice coated with a thick sauce of small vegetables and tomato or with pineapple or banana. Desserts *à l'antillaise* are made by combining exotic fruits with rum or vanilla. All dishes *à la créole* are very similar.

Antilles cucumber

CONCOMBRE DES ANTILLES

A variety of cucumber that is common in the West Indies, which is oval in shape and prickly like a horse chestnut. Also known as *anguries* in French, they are eaten in salads or pickled in vinegar, like gherkins.

antioxidant

ANTIOXYGÈNE

An additive used to retard the oxidation of food, which can cause deterioration. Of the 37 authorized antioxidants, the most common is ascorbic acid, or vitamin C (E300), used in condensed milk, beer, syrups, lemonade, and salt provisions. Tocopherol or vitamin E (E306–E309) is used in dietetic products, oils, and fats, and BHT (butylhydroxytoluene, E321) in instant potatoes. Certain antioxidants may also have other functions: sulphurous anhydride (E220), used in beers, wines, and fruit juices, is also a preservative; lactic acid (E270), incorporated into yogurts and sodas, is also a thinning agent; and citric acid (E330) is also used as an acidifier. Finally, certain substances supplement the antioxidant action of other products; for example, tartrates are added to processed cheese and preserves.

antipasto

An Italian term for cold hors d'oeuvres. The name is derived from the Italian word *pasto* (meal), with the Latin prefix *ante* (before). An antipasto might consist of Parma ham with fresh figs, or a Piedmontese cheese fondue (raw vegetables accompanied by condiments and a melted cheese sauce), but is more usually a colourful assortment of starters served either as cocktail snacks with the apéritif or at the beginning of a meal instead of pasta. Typical antipasti, which are served with *grissini* (bread sticks), include marinated vegetables and fish, seafood with lemon, olives, cooked pork products, mushroom salad, artichoke hearts, etc., arranged in hors d'oeuvres dishes.

anversoise (à l')

The description *à l'anversoise* is given to a garnish composed essentially of young hop shoots cooked slowly in butter or cream. Primarily a garnish for eggs (soft-boiled, poached, or *sur le plat*), it may sometimes be used with potatoes (boiled or browned) or with roast contre-filet, veal paupiettes, etc. Hop shoots may also be served in tartlets or on artichoke hearts.

RECIPE

Lamb cutlets à l'anversoise CÔTE-LETTES D'AGNEAU À L'ANVERSOISE Sauté some lamb cutlets in butter. Arrange them in a ring on a round dish, alternating with triangular croutons which have been fried in butter. Garnish the centre of the dish with hop shoots in a cream sauce. Deglaze the cooking juices in the sauté pan with a little dry white wine and pour it over the cutlets.

AOC

See *appellation d'origine.*

apéritif

Since time immemorial, certain plants have been known to have the property of restoring, or 'opening' (from Latin *aperire* 'to open'), the appetite. Aperitive drinks were made from such plants, but these were more therapeutic than gastronomic, and were not drunk before meals. The Romans had a liking for wine with honey, and in the Middle Ages people believed in the benefits of wines mixed with herbs or spices. Then hippocras (an old English spiced wine), vermouths, bitters, and sweet wines came into being. The word apéritif has been in use as a noun only since 1888, and it was not until the 20th century that the habit of taking an apéritif before a meal became a generally accepted custom. Apéritifs include drinks based on wine (e.g. vermouth) or alcohol (e.g.

anise, bitters) and certain spirits and liqueurs.

The custom of having an apéritif follows fashions, and indeed rituals, which vary according to the country, the surroundings, and the circumstances. It is preferable to avoid very strong alcoholic drinks that may spoil the palate. *Larousse ménager* (1926) recommended: 'A bowl of bouillon with the fat skimmed off taken half an hour before a meal is an excellent apéritif. It stimulates the salivary and stomach secretions and promotes the production of pepsin in the gastric juice.' Some people would prefer a glass of champagne.

aphrodisiac
APHRODISIAQUE

Are there some dishes or types of cuisine that have the effect of arousing sexual desire? It is doubtful. In a sphere in which fantasy plays a large part, the décor, atmosphere, lighting, and music can have as much effect as the nature of the food. However, it is traditional to regard certain foods as stimulating: game, some offal (sweetbreads, animelles, amourettes, brains, and kidneys), oysters, lobster and crayfish, caviare and soft roe, truffles and morel mushrooms, and particularly condiments (pepper, pimiento, cinnamon, nutmeg, cloves, saffron, vanilla, and ginger) and certain ancient or exotic products (shark's fins, ambergris, and musk).

Recipes reputedly propitious to love games were particularly in vogue in the 18th century. They were, in fact, luxury dishes, offered as a token of love and considered as the prelude to an avowal. Champagne, too, has such a reputation. Furthermore, certain foods are popularly believed to have aphrodisiac effects – asparagus, celery, and bulbed chervil because of their shape, and pheasant and pigeon because of their courtship behaviour. However, it may be true that a diet based on food and drinks that expand the blood vessels predisposes to amorous behaviour. The following is an example of an 'aphrodisiac' menu extracted from a collection made last century: 'Turtle soup with ambergris, sole *à la normande*, reindeer fillet in cream sauce, salmis of teal, roasted young pigeon, watercress salad, asparagus in hollandaise sauce, bone-marrow pudding, port; Bordeaux, coffee, coca.'

Apicius

The name of three Romans famous for their taste for good living. The first, a contemporary of Sulla (2nd–1st century BC), is known only for his gluttony. The third Apicius, who lived in the 2nd century AD, deserves mention for having discovered a way of keeping oysters fresh, even at the end of a long journey. The most famous is Marcus Gavius Apicius, born about 25 AD, who is reputed to have compiled a recipe book, *De re conquinaria libri decem* ('Cuisine in Ten Books'), which was used as a reference work for several centuries. Regarded by some as a refined connoisseur, by others as a libertine, he was known for his extravagance and expensive tastes. He is credited with inventing a process for force-feeding sows with dried figs in order to fatten their livers, as well as devising recipes for flamingo or nightingale tongues, camels' heels, sow's udder, and a large number of cakes and sauces. Athenaeus relates that Apicius chartered a ship to go and check if the Libyan squillas (scampi (jumbo shrimp)) were as large as they were reputed to be. Disappointed, he did not even set foot on land. He spent all his fortune on sumptuous banquets until the day when, calculating how much money he had left, he decided to poison himself rather than turn to a more modest way of living.

aplatir

The French term for beating and thus flattening a small piece of meat (entre-côte, escalope) or fish with the flat part of a meat mallet. As this process breaks down muscle fibres, the flesh becomes more tender and easier to cook.

apotheka

A storeroom in which the ancient Greeks kept wine. (The Roman equivalent is a *fumarium*.) The wine was placed near the chimney shafts and developed a very good flavour. As the effects of the heat made it more concentrated until it acquired the consistency of honey, it had to be diluted before serving.

appareil

The French term for the mixture of different ingredients necessary to prepare a dish for cooking. The word *masse* is also used. Appareils are particularly common in cake- and pastry-making.

appellation d'origine

This, according to French law, is the 'name of a country, region, or locality used to designate a product which originates there, the quality and characteristics of which are due to the geographical situation, including natural and human factors'. Its use, which is strictly regulated, at present concerns wines, spirits, certain cheeses, and such local products as Le Puy lentils, Bresse poultry, Grenoble walnuts, and Charentes-Poitou butter.

Present legislation in France concerning *appellations d'origine* has been inherited from past laws in action up to the French Revolution (1792). At the beginning of the 20th century the quality of French wines had deteriorated as the vineyards, decimated by phylloxera in the previous century, had been replanted with inferior varieties. Series of laws passed in 1905 and 1909 were designed to protect the consumer. In 1919, under pressure from the vine-growers' lobby, further legislation ensured the protection of both the producer, who agreed to abide by precise regulations, and the consumer. The relevant law dates from 6 May 1919 and was modified by that of 6 July 1966.

To maintain the quality of French wines, an Order in Council of 1935 created an organization that united the wine professionals with the representatives of other interested bodies: this was the Institut National des Appellations d'Origine (INAO). It controls the production of wine at all stages. Although the organization is private, it has legal powers and has codified the denomination of quality wines in such a way as to determine their precise origin.

Four categories of *appellation d'origine* exist at present.

• AOC (*Appellation d'Origine Contrôlée*), which is reserved for the greatest wines, lays down strict rules concerning not only the place of production, but also the varieties of vines, the yield per hectare, and the cultivation and vinification methods. Today there are more than 250 AOCs, constituting the aristocracy of French viticulture.

● *VDQS* (*vins délimités de qualité supérieure*) describes excellent regional wines.

● *Vins de Pays*, the characteristics of which were specified in a decree of 1973, are good regional table wines. For a long time popular only in their area of origin, they are now beginning to reach a wider market.

● *Vins de Table* are a slightly humbler but still controlled category.

Appenzell

A Swiss cheese with a golden-brown rind made from cow's milk (45% fat). This compressed cooked cheese has holes and is very firm without being hard or brittle. It must be full-flavoured but never pungent. Originating from the canton of Appenzell, the cheese is manufactured in the form of a round weighing 6–12 kg (13–26 lb). It is of good quality from summer to winter. Appenzell is eaten at the end of a meal and can be used to replace Gruyère cheese in cooking. It is used in the preparation of the Swiss speciality *chäshappen* – spirals of pastry (made with melted cheese, milk, flour, yeast, and eggs) piped through a piping (pastry) bag into a pan and fried. They are drained and served very hot with a salad.

Appert (Nicolas)

French inventor (born Châlons-sur-Marne, 1749; died Massy, 1841). He learned the art of cooking from his father, who was an hotelier. He worked at first in the service of the Duke of Deux-Ponts and was *officier de bouche* to the Princess of Forbach. In 1780 he established himself in business as a confectioner in the Rue des Lombards in Paris. The Directory government offered a prize of 12,000 francs for the discovery of a process to preserve the food destined for the Army. Appert perfected a sterilization method which was named after him – *appertisation*. In 1804 he built a factory at Massy (on land where

peas and beans had been cultivated) and started up the production of bottled preserved foods. In 1810 the government officially recognized his discovery and awarded him the prize. In the same year, Appert published *L'Art de conserver pendant plusieurs années toutes les substances animales et végétales*, which generously made his process available to all. Moreover, his work was republished in 1811 and 1813 under the title *Livre de tous les ménages*. The fall of the Empire ruined him but in 1822, by which time others had become rich on his discovery, the state recognized his achievement in conceiving the process by granting him a small income. In the premises which were then allowed him, he pursued his experiments on the clarification of wines, the purification of bone gelatine, preservation in cans, etc., but he subsequently died in poverty.

appetite   APPÉTIT

Psychologists define under the term natural appetite the tendencies which instinctively cause us to satisfy the needs of the body.

In physiology appetite is defined as something rather different from hunger. Hunger in reality is nothing more than the need to eat, whereas appetite is the lure of pleasure which one experiences whilst eating.

The sensation of hunger, which usually develops at regular mealtimes, sometimes disappears if it is not satisfied at the usual hour. The appetite is stimulated by the sight and smell of food; bitter substances frequently awaken lost appetite by releasing digestive secretions.

In certain psychiatric conditions, appetite can degenerate into a craving for offensive and nonedible substances.

The opposite of appetite is *anorexia*, which means distaste for food.

In France spring onions (scallions), chives, and the small onions used for seasoning are known generally as *appétits*, as they all stimulate the appetite.

apple   POMME

The fruit of the apple tree, the most widely cultivated fruit tree in the world, which originated in Asia Minor and was growing wild in Europe by prehistoric times. Known throughout the ancient world, the apple began to be cultivated and was soon available in many varieties, being a popular dessert fruit and featuring in many ancient recipes. In his *Traité du sidre* (1588) Julien Le Paulmier lists several dozen varieties. Oliver de Serres refers to the *pomme appie* (today known as *pomme d'api*: small, red, and sweet), named after Claudius Appius, who brought it to Rome from the Peloponnese; he also mentions the Court-Pendu, the Reinette, the Rambure (the present Rambour, from the village of Rambures in the Somme region), the Grillot, the Rougelet, and the Curetin.

The apple is the most popular fruit in France, the United States, Britain, and Germany. In France, the eating apple (as opposed to the cider apple) is mainly produced in the southwest, southeast, and centre from July to November. Among varieties available in France are those of American and Australian origin (Golden Delicious, Melrose, Granny Smith, etc.) and the traditional varieties, such as Reine des Reinettes, Cox's Orange Pippin (an English variety developed by Richard Cox in the last century), the Reinette du Canada, the Grise du Mans, the Belle de Boskoop, and the now rare varieties Calville (named after a Norman village and dating back to the 15th century) and Grand-Alexandre. Unfortunately the choice of apples is getting smaller – in the United States, of the 7000 or so varieties known, only about 50 are marketed. In the United Kingdom the number of varieties available is far smaller though there is a campaign to increase crops of home-grown varieties.

Apples are available practically all the year round, but they are best as dessert fruit from October to April. They should be firm, without blemishes or wrinkles, and red- and yellow-skinned varieties should not be too green. The apple provides 52 Cal per 100 g; it has a high fruit-sugar content and is a good source of iron, potassium, and vitamins. Picked when ripe, apples can be stored in a ventilated room (stalk down, away from damp, heat, and draughts) or in cold store. They can also be sliced into thin rings and dried in a very cool oven, with the door open, for 30 minutes, then left overnight with the oven switched off

and the door closed, repeating the operation twice and raising the temperature slightly each time. Nowadays, however, with the use of domestic freezers, drying is an uneconomical time-consuming operation.

Apples can also be preserved in the form of jams, jellies, preserves in syrup, apple paste, and apple sugar, and also as the English specialities apple butter, apple cheese, and apple chutney.

In addition to its uses in distilling (for Calvados) and in cider and apple juice production, the apple is used in a wide variety of desserts, including fritters, turnovers, charlottes, flans, tarts, puddings, fruit salads, compotes, mousses, and two classic dishes: Austrian strudel and English apple pie. Stewed apple can be flavoured with cinnamon, vanilla, cloves, or lemon juice, and is excellent with fresh cream or a red fruit sauce. Apples are sometimes referred to in France as *pommes en l'air* (apples in the air) as opposed to *pommes de terre* (potatoes; literally earth apples), especially in savoury recipes, so as to avoid any ambiguity.

In savoury dishes, the apple is traditionally associated with black pudding (blood sausage), grilled (broiled) chitterlings, and roast pork (especially as apple sauce), but is also used with poultry (roast chicken, goose, duck, and turkey) and with grilled herring or mackerel instead of gooseberries (as an unsweetened compote or in quarters fried in butter) and with red cabbage or braised chestnuts. Apple goes well with dishes cooked in cider. It is also used for salads, especially with celery, lamb's lettuce, walnuts, raisins, beetroot (red beet), etc., together with a mustard vinaigrette or a rémoulade sauce.

The juice obtained by crushing fresh apples is very useful for making jellies from watery fruits, because it does not alter their flavour. The remainder of the pulp can be used to make confectionery fruit paste, a flan, or a soufflé.

RECIPES

Apple charlotte with brown sugar CHARLOTTE AUX POMMES À LA CASSONADE BRUNE (from Sylvie Beauvalot's recipe) Peel, core, and quarter 4

Belle de Boskoop or Granny Smith apples. Remove the crusts from 10 slices of white bread and fry in 60 g (2 oz, ¼ cup) butter. Drain and use to line the bottom and the sides of a charlotte mould. Melt about 75 g (3 oz, scant ½ cup) butter in a frying pan (skillet), add 200 g (7 oz, scant cup) soft brown sugar, then the apple quarters, and cook for 10 minutes, stirring from time to time. Flame with ½ liqueur glass warmed Calvados. Heap this mixture in the lined mould and bake for 30 minutes in the oven at 200 C (400 F, gas 6). Cool under a press, then turn out and serve with custard cream.

Apple conserve MARMELADE DE POMMES Peel and core some apples, cut into quarters, and weigh. For 500 g (18 oz) apples, allow 300 g (11 oz, scant 1½ cups) granulated sugar. Place the apples and sugar in a preserving pan and add 2 tablespoons (3 tablespoons) water. Cook gently until the apples crush under a spoon. Rub them through a strainer over a bowl. Put the purée back into the pan, bring to the boil stirring continuously, and cook until the purée reaches a temperature of 106 C (223 F). Pot in the usual way (see *jam, jellies, and marmalades*).

Apples bonne femme POMMES BONNE FEMME Make a light circular incision round the middle of some firm cooking apples. Core them and then place them in a large buttered ovenproof dish. Fill the hollow in each apple with butter mixed with caster (superfine) sugar. Pour a few tablespoons of water into the dish. Cook in the oven at 220 C (425 F, gas 7) until the apples are just tender. Serve the apples in the dish in which they were cooked.

Apple soufflé POMMES SOUFFLÉS Cut 8 large apples in half, core them, and then scoop out half the pulp without piercing the skin. Cook the pulp for 5 minutes with 2 tablespoons (3 tablespoons) water, without stirring, in a covered saucepan. Then add 300 g (11 oz, 1⅓ cups) caster (superfine) sugar and continue cooking, stirring to obtain a very smooth purée. Sprinkle the inside of the fruit halves with 1 dl (6 tablespoons, scant ½ cup) brandy, and add 1 dl (6 tablespoons, scant ½ cup) brandy to the apple purée. Stiffy whisk 5 egg whites and fold them into the apple purée using a wooden spoon. Arrange the apple halves in a wellbuttered ovenproof dish, fill them with apple purée, and sprinkle with 50 g (2 oz, scant ½ cup) icing (confectioners') sugar. Cook in a hot oven at 230 C (450 F, gas 8) for 10–12 minutes until browned. Serve immediately.

Le jeu de pommes (from a recipe by Jean and Pierre Troisgros) Make a fine pastry by mixing in the blender 200 g (7 oz, generous 1½ cups) flour, 140 g (5 oz, ⅔ cup) rather firm butter, a pinch of salt, 8 g (¼ oz, 1 teaspoon) sugar, and a little olive oil. Incorporate 1 dl (6 tablespoons, scant ½ cup) water and rotate a few times in the blender (the particles of butter should still be visible). Remove the dough and roll it out finely; cut out 16 circles approximately 12 cm (5 in) in diameter using a pastry (cookie) cutter. Place them on non-stick baking sheets, cover them with very thin slices of apple, brush with 50 g (2 oz, ¼ cup) melted butter, and sprinkle lightly with caster (superfine) sugar. Bake in a hot oven at 220 C (425 F, gas 7) for 15 minutes.

Turn each tartlet over on the baking sheet using a spatula and dust the reverse side with icing (confectioners') sugar. Put the tartlets under the grill (broiler). As it caramelizes, the sugar forms a glossy crackly film. Leave to cool for 15 minutes. Take 4 dessert plates and place 4 tartlets on top of each other on each plate (apples upwards). Just before serving, cover each *jeu de pommes* with 1 tablespoon warmed acacia honey and sprinkle with a little Calvados and a few drops of lemon juice. This dessert may be accompanied by a lemon sorbet.

apple-corer VIDE-POMME

A small kitchen gadget consisting of a tubular metal gouge attached to a handle, used for taking the cores out of apples. The corer can be made of steel or stainless steel. Apples are cored in this way before being baked in the oven or sliced into rings to be made into fritters. In France an apple-corer was formerly known as a *colonne*.

Main varieties of apples

variety and origin	size and shape	skin	flesh	comments
Belle de Boskoop (France) November to February	large; irregular and asymmetrical	rough and matt, yellowish-green	firm and sharp	good for tarts and charlottes
Calville (France) November and December	large	lemon yellow and shiny	very fine, tender, sweet, juicy, slightly acid	
Cox's Orange Pippin (England) (September to May	small and round	yellowish-green tinged with red	crisp, juicy, aromatic, sweet, some acidity	very popular dessert apple
Egremont Russet (England) October to December	medium	matt, reddish-brown	tender, very sweet, slightly acid	
Golden Delicious (America)	medium	pale green or yellow, depending on degree of ripeness	yellowish-white, sweet, juicy and soft, little flavour	intensively marketed, undistinguished
Granny Smith (Australia, USA)	medium	bright green and waxy	firm and very juicy, acid, crisp	good for raw vegetable salads, jellies, jams, and chutneys
Laxton's Superb (England) November to April	medium	green tinged with red	firm, crisp, sweet, juicy, some acidity	
Reine des Reinettes (France) August	medium to large	golden yellow, streaked with red	yellow, firm and fine, crisp, juicy and sweet	good for pâtisserie and savoury dishes
Starking Delicious (South Africa)	medium to large; elongated and thick-skinned	red-brown	yellowish, extremely mellow, fine and juicy	
Worcester Pearmain (England) September to November	medium	clear red	white and crisp, sweet and juicy	

apple sugar
SUCRE DE POMME
A confectionery speciality of the city of Rouen, where it was created towards the middle of the 16th century.

Apple sugar was formerly prepared by mixing one part of concentrated juice of cooked dessert apples to three parts of sugar syrup cooked to the hard crack stage; this mixture was used to form little sticks, tablets, or pastilles, which were coated with a layer of sugar. However, this apple sugar quickly became sticky, clouded, and soft. The present method consists of cooking sugar to the hard crack stage with a little glucose, then adding some natural apple essence and a little lemon juice; in this way a perfectly transparent apple sugar is obtained, which keeps well.

It is sold in traditional 10-cm (4-in) sticks in a grey, gold, and white wrapper decorated with the famous clock tower of Rouen; this design was created in 1865.

apprêt
The French word to describe all the culinary processes involved in the preparation of a dish.

apricot   ABRICOT
A round yellow-orange fruit with velvety skin, having tender, sweet, and fragrant flesh and very little juice. The smooth stone (pit), which comes away easily, contains an edible kernel which is used to flavour apricot jam.

The apricot tree grew wild in China several thousand years ago. It was later grown in India, then in Persia and Armenia, from where it gets its Latin name, *Prunus armeniaca*. It was probably introduced into Europe after the conquest by Alexander the Great. The ancient Greeks called the apricot 'golden egg of the Sun', but in the Middle Ages it was thought to cause fever. It was little known in France at the time of the Renaissance, but began to be cultivated in the south in the 17th century.

The name is derived from the Latin *praecoquus*, meaning precocious, or early-ripening.

□ Uses The apricot is particularly rich in carotene (provitamin A) and mineral salts (magnesium, calcium, phosphorus, iron, sodium, and fluorine); it also contains fructose, a sugar which is easily assimilated but has little calorific value. The fruit should be bought properly ripe, since once picked it stops ripening and might either be hard and bitter or become soft and floury.

Apricots usually do not travel well and are therefore frequently used canned (plain or in syrup, whole or in halves, and diced in fruit salad). They are also made into fruit juices and alcoholic spirit (*barack*).

The apricot is delicious eaten fresh. Its skin may be removed, if required, by dipping it in boiling water. The apricot is one of the fruits most widely used in sweet dishes (hot and cold desserts, cakes and pastries, fruit salads, ices) and in preserves (candied fruits, jams, and conserves).

□ Dried apricots In Europe, all dried apricots are imported. Those from Iran, California, and Australia are fairly large, pale, and a little dull-looking, while those from Turkey, which are the best, are dark orange with a muscatel flavour. Dried apricots have a much higher calorific value than the fresh fruit and usually must be rehydrated by immersing them in tepid water for two hours. They are used in much the same way as fresh apricots in desserts, particularly stewed in winter. Dried apricots are also good as an accompaniment to some meat ragouts.

Apricots can be dried at home, by splitting them to remove the stones, cutting in half if they are large, and either placing them in a very cool oven or leaving them in the sun on a wooden rack until they become dark red. After drying the apricots should be flattened with the fingers to give them a regular shape.

RECIPES

Apricot marmelade MARMELADE D'ABRICOTS Slowly cook 1 kg (2¼ lb) stoned (pitted) apricots in 1 dl (6 tablespoons, scant ½ cup) water for 15–20 minutes until soft, stirring frequently to prevent sticking. Liquidize the fruit in an electric blender then press it through a sieve to make a smooth thick purée. Return the purée to the pan, add 750 g (1¾ lb, 3½ cups) sugar (lump or granulated) and cook slowly, stirring until the sugar has dissolved, then increase the heat and continue cooking. To determine whether the marmelade is cooked drop a little onto a plate. If this remains in a blob without spreading out the marmelade is cooked. Jar as for jam.

Apricots Condé   ABRICOTS CONDÉ Poach apricot halves in a sugar syrup and arrange around a thick ring of cold rice pudding. Decorate with glacé cherries and angelica. Insert split blanched almonds between the apricots. Heat the apricot ring in a moderate oven (160 c, 325 f, gas 3) and serve wtih a Kirschflavoured apricot sauce.

Apricots preserved au naturel   ABRICOTS STERILISÉS AU NATUREL   Wipe the apricots and cut in half to remove the stones, then replace the halves together and pack tightly into preserving jars, without adding water or sugar. Screw on the lids (loosen bands a quarter turn) then immerse the jars in a large saucepan of lukewarm water. Bring the water up to 90 c (194 f) and maintain at this temperature for 15–20 minutes. Remove the jars, seal, dry, and store when cold.

Apricots preserved in syrup   ABRICOTS AU SIROP   Choose slightly under-ripe fruit. Prick them and put in a basin. Cover with a very heavy syrup.

Soak in the syrup for 3 hours. While the fruit is soaking prepare a 26° syrup (see *sugar*) with lump sugar. Clarify the syrup with white of egg – one white for 2 litres (3½ pints, 4½ pints) syrup. Strain the syrup through a straining bag or cloth. Leave to cool. Drain the apricots. Put them into wide-mouthed jars and cover with the boiling clarified syrup so that it reaches at least 3 cm (1 in) above the level of the fruit. Fix on the tops and screw bands tightly, then give the bands one half-turn to loosen them. Place a wire rack in the bottom of a large preserving pan and arrange the bottles on it so they do not touch. Fill the pan with cold water, making sure it covers the jars. Boil rapidly for a full 10 minutes. Remove the bottles, wipe and seal them. Keep in a cool place, away from the light.

Halved apricots can also be used for this recipe. Put in a basin and soak in a very heavy syrup. Crack half the number of stones, peel the kernels, and put into the preserving jars with the apricots.

apricoting   ABRICOTER

The process of spreading a thin layer of sieved apricot jam over the surface of a sweet or a cake, in order to give it a glossy appearance. If a cake is to be covered with fondant icing (frosting), this is made easier by apricoting the cake beforehand.

Characteristics of different varieties of apricot

variety	fruiting season	appearance	quality and uses
Rouge du Roussillon	end June	medium-sized and firm, golden red speckled with black	excellent eaten fresh or preserved
Polanais or Orangé de Provence	mid-July	large and firm, light pinkish-orange	rather tart, best in syrup or jams
Canino	mid-June	large and fairly soft	medium quality
Bergeron	mid-July to early August	large, firm, and elongated	fragrant, good for preserving
Luizet	early July	large and elongated	fragrant but fragile
Early Colomer	early June	small	travels well
Rouge de Sernhac	early June	medium-sized, highly coloured	fragrant

April fool

POISSON D'AVRIL

A practical joke that is played on an unsuspecting victim on 1 April, April Fools' Day or All Fools' Day. In France, it is traditional to eat chocolate, marzipan, or sugar fish, and in Alsace, cakes are moulded into the shape of fish.

Apparently, the origin of April fool goes back to the 16th century, at which time the new year started on 1 April in France. In 1564, Charles IX issued a decree that fixed the beginning of the year at 1 January instead of 1 April. This innovation was not very popular, and on 1 April 1565, both as a protest and as a joke, people started sending one another worthless presents as mock New Year's gifts. As the sun happened to be in the constellation of Pisces on this date, the gifts became sweetmeats in the shape of fish (*poisson d'avril*).

apron

A small river fish of the perch family, common in the Rhône and Saône basins. It is about 15 cm (6 in) long and weighs about 80 g (3 oz). It is only eaten fried.

aquavit or akvavit

A grain-based spirit flavoured with cumin, aniseed, or fennel that has been manufactured in Scandinavia since the 15th century. Its name comes from the Latin *aqua vitae* (water of life). It has a high alcoholic content and should be served really cold: ideally the bottle should be chilled in the freezer. Aquavit may also be distilled from potatoes.

araignée

The name given in French to the muscle in an ox that lines the socket of its hock bone. The membrane that covers it is streaked with veins like a spider's web (hence the name, which means 'spider').

As a highly prized piece of meat that is rarely for sale, the araignée is best eaten grilled (broiled) because of its succulence.

araignée à friture

See *skimmer*.

arak

A strong alcoholic spirit, usually flavoured with aniseed and popular in Eastern countries. Its name comes from the Arabic *araq* (juice, sap). Arak is distilled from dates in Egypt and the Middle East, grapes and seeds in Greece, palm sap in India, and sugarcane juice in Java.

Arbellot de Vacqueur (Simon)

French journalist, novelist, and historian (born Limoges, 1897; died St Sulpice-d'Excideuil, 1965). A member of the academy of gastronomes, he was one of the last witnesses of the Belle Époque. As well as *J'ai vu mourir le Boulevard* and *Un gastronome se penche sur son passé*, he wrote *Tel plat, tel vin* (1963) on the selection of the correct wines for the correct dishes, and in 1965 published the biography of his master and friend Curnonsky.

He wrote a large number of articles, particularly in *Cuisine et Vins de France*, in which he described the Parisian appreciation of good food in all walks of life. For example, of the modest Laveur guesthouse he wrote: 'A good smell of vegetable soup, the memory of tripe, the scent of a jam omelette comes back at once to my nostrils and keeps running through my mind, evoking the good eating experiences of our studious youth which, in some aspects, are well worthy of those of today.' On the other hand, at a sumptuous dinner at Larue, 'we heard one evening, under the eye of the imperturbable Paul, a foreign lady ask for a milk chocolate drink to accompany a fillet of sole Cubat, the chef's speciality. Sacrilege! Just as well that Marcel Proust and Boni de Castellane were not here to see that.'

Arbois

An AOC wine from Franche-Comté, in the Jura. Two famous men have contributed to the fame of the wines of this district – the gourmet Brillat-Savarin and the great scientist Louis Pasteur. The latter did much of his work in the region and it was because of the curious nature of certain of the Jura wines – those that form a 'veil' on the surface while they are in cask – that he worked out his theories about the action of bacteria.

The three main districts are Arbois,

Château-Chalon, and l'Étoile; although until very recently the wines were seldom seen outside their locality, even within France, some of them are beginning to feature on export lists. As well as red, white, and rosé wines, sparkling wines are produced, undergoing their second fermentation in bottle; these are sold as *vin fou* – (crazy or mad wine) – because of their ebullience. The grapes used for white wines are Savagnin, Melon d'Arbois (Chardonnay), and Pinot Blanc; for the reds the varieties are Poulsard, Trousseau, and Gros Noirien (Pinot Noir). Two very curious wines of the Côtes du Jura are the *vin de paille* (straw wine) and the *vin jaune* (yellow wine). The former is made by slightly drying the grapes before they are pressed (the name comes from the straw (*paille*) mats on which they were laid, but today they are usually hung on racks). Vin jaune is made solely from the Savagnin grape. When the wine is in its cask, this is then sealed and left for several years – not less than six and it may be as long as ten. During this time a film (the veil) forms on the surface of the wine, slightly changing its character but not spoiling it. Vin jaune is a table wine, but rather a powerful one, and it is such a rarity that it can never be cheap or in plentiful supply. The other red, white, and rosé wines of the area can be pleasant drinks, well worth sampling

arbolade or arboulastre

In the cuisine of former times, either a sweetened cream custard made with eggs, or a sweet or savoury omelette. The arboulastre mentioned in the *Ménagier de Paris* (1393) is a thick omelette made with a mixture of chopped herbs (such as wild celery, tansy, sage, beet, spinach, lettuce, and mint) and sprinkled with grated cheese. La Varenne's recipe for arbolade (1651) is a sweet dessert.

| RECIPE

Arbolade (from La Varenne's recipe) Melt a little butter and add some cream, egg yolks, pear juice, sugar, and a pinch of salt. Cook this mixture lightly, sweeten with flower water, and serve.

arbutus berry ARBOUSE

The fruit of a shrub that grows in the forests of North America and southern Europe and is cultivated in the south of France. The arbutus, or strawberry tree, produces rather tart berries that are red and pulpy but do not have the flavour of strawberries. They are used to make a fruit wine, spirits, and a liqueur, as well as jellies and jams. The city of Madrid was formerly surrounded by forests and has a strawberry tree and a bear on its coat of arms.

Archestratus

ARCHESTRATE

Greek poet and gastronome of the 4th century BC, who came from Gela, in Sicily. He wrote a long poem entitled *Gastronomy* (also known under the names of *Gastrology*, *Deipnology*, or *Hedypathy*). Only a few fragments, quoted by Athenaeus, remain: they are presented as a body of advice for the aesthete, the gourmet, and the gastronome. A great traveller, the author shares his discoveries with the reader, presenting such dishes as dog's or sow's abdomen cooked in oil and sprinkled with cumin and dispensing his advice on where to obtain the best products, such as wild boar from Lucania or sturgeon from Rhodes. Above all, he reveals his tastes, particularly with regard to fish; his recipes include conger eel boiled in brine and wrapped in herbs and eels cooked in beet leaves.

archiduc

The name given to dishes inspired by Austro-Hungarian cuisine at the time of the Belle Époque. Eggs, sole, and poultry are cooked with onion and paprika and coated with hongroise sauce. The pan juices are deglazed with either a fumet of fish or a demi-glace sauce, whichever is appropriate, and flavoured with brandy, whisky, Madèira, or port.

| RECIPE

Sauté of chicken archiduc POULET SAUTÉ ARCHIDUC Joint a chicken and sauté the pieces in butter. When half-cooked, add 2 tablespoons chopped onions softened in butter and ¼ teaspoon paprika. Drain the chicken pieces and keep hot. Deglaze the juices in the pan with 1 dl (5 tablespoons, 6 tablespoons) dry white wine, and heat to reduce. Add 1.5 dl (¼ pint, ⅔ cup) cream and reduce further. Finally, add a trickle of lemon juice and 50 g (2 oz) butter. Strain the sauce (if desired) and use it to coat the chicken pieces. Sliced cucumber, steamed in butter, may be served at the same time.

ardennaise (à l')

The name *à l'ardennaise* is given to several dishes of game, either birds (e.g. thrush) or animals (e.g. pickled hare or boar), in which juniper is used (in the form of spirits or berries).

RECIPE

Thrushes en croûte à l'ardennaise GRIVES EN CROÛTE À L'ARDEN NAISE Soak and dry pig's caul. Slit the backs of the thrushes to remove the backbone, ribs, and breastbone, and season the inside of the carcasses with salt, pepper, and a pinch of cayenne. Fill each bird with a little fine stuffing made from diced foie gras and truffle mixed with crushed juniper berries and sea soned with salt and pepper. Pull the birds back into shape and wrap each one in a piece of caul. Pack the thrushes close together in a buttered casserole and sprinkle with melted butter. Cook in the oven for 15–20 minutes until tender. Meanwhile, carefully remove the crumb from a round loaf, keeping the crust intact. Butter the inside of the crust, brown it in the oven, and line it with an *à gratin* forcemeat. Replace in the oven to keep hot. Drain and unwrap the thrushes and arrange them inside the loaf. Keep hot. Deglaze the casserole with 2 dl (¼ pint, ⅔ cup) sherry and 3.5 dl (12 fl oz, 1½ cups) demi-glace sauce, and reduce. Toss a few slices of truffle in butter and add them to the sauce. Serve the thrushes coated with the sauce.

Argenteuil

The name given to dishes with a sauce or garnish containing either asparagus tips or asparagus purée. The Argenteuil area of the Val-d'Oise has been famous for the cultivation of asparagus since the

17th century – there is even a society, the Compagnons de l'asperge d'Argen teuil. The description may also be ap plied generally to 'white' dishes, such as poached or soft-boiled eggs, sole or fillets of sole, and poached fowl.

RECIPE

Argenteuil salad SALADE ARGEN TEUIL Cook some potatoes in their skins, dice them, and dress with tarra gon mayonnaise. Pile into a salad bowl, and garnish with white asparagus tips seasoned with oil and lemon. Make a border with shredded lettuce and quar tered hard-boiled (hard-cooked) eggs.

Argentinian wines

VINS D'ARGENTINE

Argentina is fourth among major world producers of wine. However, at present its production seems to be oriented more towards quantity than quality. Its rather scanty wine legislation classifies wines into two categories: *comunes* or *ordinaires*, which represent about 90% of the harvest, and *reservados*. The first of these is designed essentially for the very large local market, but is also ex ported in bulk to several countries. Usually red, they are full-bodied table wines, normally sold in large con tainers. The second category of wines is bottled; when matured, they are popu lar with the Argentinians, but there are as yet few established controls. Spark ling wines and fortified wines of great variety are also made.

ariégeoise (à l')

The description *à l'ariégeoise* is given to typical dishes of the cuisine of south western France, particularly chicken and boned breast of mutton, which are served with stuffed cabbage and po tatoes. The chicken is poached in a broth (which is served first, as a soup) and then served with stuffed green cab bage leaves, pickled pork, and potatoes.

RECIPE

Stuffed breast of mutton à l'ariégeoise POITRINE DE MOUTON FARCIE À L'ARIÉGEOISE Make a cavity in a breast of mutton, season with salt and pepper, and fill with a fairly firm stuffing made with breadcrumbs soaked in stock and squeezed, fat and lean unsmoked bacon, chopped parsley, and garlic, bound together with eggs and well seasoned. Sew up the opening in the breast. Put the meat in a buttered braising pan, lined with fresh pork rinds and sliced onions and carrots. Add a bouquet garni, cover, and cook gently for 15 minutes. Moisten with 1.5 dl (¼ pint, ⅔ cup) dry white wine, and reduce. Add 3 teaspoons tomato purée and 3 dl (½ pint, 1¼ cups) thickened brown gravy. Keep covered and cook in the oven for a further 45–60 minutes. Drain the mutton breast and arrange it on a long dish. Surround with a garnish consisting of balls of stuffed cabbage and potatoes cooked in stock and butter. Strain the cooking juices, skim off the fat, reduce, and pour over the meat.

arlequin

In popular 19th-century French parlance, an assortment of leftover food from restaurants or large houses that was made to look palatable and resold at low prices either in certain markets or in cheap restaurants. Today in France they would be called *rogatons* (leftovers). In *Paris à table* (1846) Eugène Briffault recalls: 'all the remains that are thrown out which take on the lively name of *arlequin*, this *olla podrida* (pot pourri) of the Paris Bohemians.' The sellers were called 'jewellers', because of the care they took with the presentation of these disparate remnants, as colourful as Harlequin's coat.

arlésienne (à l')

The description *à l'arlésienne* is given to dishes with a garnish of aubergines (eggplants) fried in oil, sautéed tomatoes, and onion rings dredged in flour and fried. The garnish accompanies sole, tournedos steaks (filet mignons), or noisettes of lamb.

RECIPE

Snails à l'arlésienne ESCARGOTS À L'ARLÉSIENNE (from A. Hélie's recipe) Take some medium-sized snails, stand them in tepid water to remove the impurities, and then blanch with a handful of salt. Remove them from their shells and drain. Put a little diced bacon into a saucepan, sprinkle with flour, moisten with dry white wine and add the snails together with some garlic and plenty of herbs. Bring to the boil and cook gently for about 10 minutes. When the snails are cooked, drain and replace in their shells. Make a sauce with a glass of Madeira, a pinch of cayenne, and the juice of a lemon. Pour the sauce over the snails and sprinkle with chopped parsley.

Armagnac

Brandy made from wine from a region in Gascony almost entirely in the department of Gers. It has an *appellation d'origine contrôlée*.

The main production zone is Bas-Armagnac (in the west, around Gabarret, La Bastide-d'Armagnac, Cazaubon, Eauze, and Nogaro, up to Villeneuve-de-Marsan and Aire-sur-l'Adour), which produces very fine Armagnac with a particular bouquet. The Ténarèze region completes the Bas-Armagnac region to the east (around Nérac, Condom, Vic-Fezensac, and Aignan) and produces strongly scented and supple brandies. Haut-Armagnac, which extends to the east and south, around Mirande, Auch, and Lectoure, produces less of the total production.

Armagnac's name (and presumably the spirit itself) has been recorded as early as 1411, but since 1909 certain controls have defined its area and how it should be made and labelled. The main grapes used are: Piquepoul, St Émilion, Colombard, Jurançon, Blanquette, Mauzac, and Clairette Meslier. A special type of still is used to handle the white wines and this is now done by a continuous process, although the Armagnac still is quite different from the continuous still (Coffey or patent still) used in making other spirits. Some of the stills were, until very recently, travelling stills, going around the country making the brandy for the wine growers. Although some travelling stills are used today, the big firms mostly carry out their own distilling in their headquarters or buy from growers who do their distilling. Armagnac is matured in oak and the age of the spirit, when bottled, can be: three star or XXX (three years old); VO (from five to ten years); or VSOP (up to 15 years). 'Hors d'Age' means that the brandy is at least 25 years old, although, like Cognac, it will not improve indefinitely in wood. Sometimes bottled in a flagon-shaped bottle known as a *basquaise*, Armagnac may also be put into tall bottles. It should be served in a small tulip or flattish goblet-type glass, able to be cupped in the hand when it is drunk neat as a liqueur, although the more ordinary Armagnacs are useful in mixed drinks. Armagnac is different from Cognac but – a common delusion – it is not weaker in any way, nor is it, quality for quality, cheaper.

Armenonville

A garnish that bears the name of a Parisian restaurant in the Bois de Boulogne. The basic ingredients are either Anna or casseroled potatoes, together with morel mushrooms in cream sauce. It is served with noisettes of lamb, tournedos steaks (filet mignons), sautéed or casseroled chicken, and soft-boiled or poached eggs. These are coated with demi-glace sauce flavoured with either Cognac or Madeira.

The name is also given to a dish of sole or sole fillets.

> | RECIPE
>
> **Sole Armenonville** SOLES ARME-NONVILLE Prepare a pancake of Anna potatoes. Skin and prepare two good sole and poach them in a very shallow dish in fish stock. Make a white wine sauce and stir in the cooking juices from the sole. Cut some cep mushrooms into thin strips, cook them gently in butter in a covered pan, and add them to the sauce. Arrange the Anna potatoes on the serving dish, place the sole on top, coat with sauce, and serve immediately.
>
> In the traditional recipe, the sole are surrounded by a border of duchesse potatoes enriched with truffles.

armoricaine (à l')

The description *à l'armoricaine* is given to dishes with a sauce of prawns, shrimps, etc., which are cooked *à l'américaine*. *Armoricaine* is a corruption of *américaine*, but in fact the description applies to a Parisian dish. Moreover, the incorporation of garlic, tomatoes, and oil in its preparation and the fact that it was created by a chef of southern French origins, proves that the recipe has nothing to do with Brittany (Armorica is the ancient name for Brittany).

armottes

A speciality of Gascony, made from cornmeal paste mixed with crisp pieces of goose or pork. Served hot or cold, armottes are either grilled or fried in goose fat and may be used instead of bread. This paste may also be made into a sweet dish.

aroma   ARÔME

The distinctive smell of a food that is produced by a complex mixture of volatile compounds. A product is aromatized by introducing into it an aroma, natural or otherwise, that gives it a flavour or reinforces one that it has already.

Natural aromas or flavours are extracted from plants: mint, vanilla, the zest of citrus fruits, etc. Certain processes, such as smoking or maceration in alcohol, also give a natural flavour.

To keep costs down, and to maintain the quality and keeping properties of its products, the food industry is increasingly using artificial and synthetic flavourings. Artificial flavourings have chemical formulae identical to those of natural flavours, such as vanillin or menthol, while synthetic flavourings have chemical formulae that do not exist in nature. For example, amyl acetate, which smells of bananas, is used in liqueurs and processed cheeses; diacetyl is used in margarine; and the valerianates are widely used in preserves because of their fruity smell.

In France flavourings are not re garded as additives and their use is not governed by the same set of regulations. On the other hand, it is obligatory to include the word 'fantaisie' (imitation) on labels for aromatized alcohols and syrups, and the words 'natural flavour', 'reinforced natural flavour', or 'artificial flavour' on other food labels, depending on the circumstances. However, the actual nature of the flavouring remains a secret of the manufacturer.

The name *arômes* is given to Lyonnais cheeses, such as Rigotte and Pélardon, which are refined in grape marc or white wine to give them a piquant flavour.

aromatic AROMATE

Any fragrant plant that is used as a condiment or for flavouring. Various parts of the plant may be used: the leaves (basil, marjoram, mint, chervil, and tarragon), the flowers (caper and nasturtium), the seeds (dill, aniseed, caraway, coriander, and mustard), the fruits (juniper and pimiento), the roots (horseradish), the stems (angelica, savory, and wild thyme) or the bulbs (garlic and onion). Certain vegetables, such as carrots, celery, parsnips, and leeks, are also used in cooking as aromatics.

Although they have no nutritional value, aromatics constitute an indispensable item in cooking. They may be added directly to the preparation during cooking, to achieve a suitable blending of flavours and aromas (particularly for dishes that are boiled or braised for a long time) or are used indirectly in vinegars and oils, mustards, condiments, stuffings, court-bouillons, marinades, fumets, and macerations. They are also widely used to make alcoholic and nonalcoholic drinks and in the preserving industries.

Aromatics may be used fresh or they may be preserved by refrigeration, freezing, or drying; dried aromatics, whole or crushed, should be stored in opaque well-sealed pots.

Aromatics are distinguished from spices in that the latter are of exotic origin; for example, pepper, nutmeg, saffron, vanilla, and betel. A spice is necessarily aromatic but it may also be very pungent, while the aromatic is used essentially for its fragrance. To spice means 'to give taste to', while to aromatize means 'to perfume'. In ancient times, substances such as benzoin, myrrh, and rosewater were frequently used in cooking. In the Middle Ages, simples and herbs, both medicinal and culinary, played an essential role. Later, oriental spices competed with them, but different regions continued the local practice of aromatic cooking using indigenous plants, such as garlic, anise, basil, oregano, and thyme in the Mediterranean countries, dill and fennel in Scandinavia, and artemisia, juniper, and cumin in the East. In France, the situation is summarized by Raymond Dumay: 'We have only one condiment, in three shapes: garlic in Marseilles, shallots in Bordeaux, and onions in Dunkirk; these are the three pillars of our national cuisine.'

RECIPE

Aromatic sauce SAUCE AUX AROMATES Cover and infuse for 20 minutes a mixture consisting of 2.5 dl (8 fl oz, 1 cup) boiling consommé, a pinch each of chopped chives, savory, marjoram, sage, and basil, a chopped shallot, 4 pepper-corns, and a little grated nutmeg. Strain the infusion and then add it to a white roux made with 25 g (1 oz) butter and an equal amount of flour. Cook for 10 minutes. Add a trickle of lemon juice and a teaspoon each of chopped chervil and chopped tarragon. This sauce can be served with poached fish.

arquebuse

A herby liqueur that was originally supposed to possess therapeutic qualities in cases of gunshot wounds. The recipe for *eau d'arquebuse* or *d'arquebusade* was recorded in the 19th century by a Marist monk from the Hermitage Abbey (Loire) and includes agrimony and gentian. Today it is used as a digestive and 'pick-me-up' – it is said to be the French answer to Fernet Branca!

arracacia root
POMME DE TERRE-CÉLERI

The starchy rhizome of the arracacia, also known as the celery potato, native to Colombia. It can be ground to produce flour or cooked like the yam or the sweet potato.

arrêter

The French term used for stopping the cooking of an ingredient or a dish when it has reached the correct stage. Cooking may be stopped either by taking the food out of the oven (roasts, desserts, or soufflés) or out of the pan (fried or sautéed food) or by draining it (fried or poached food). In the latter case, cooking may also be stopped by adding cold water.

arrowroot

The starch extracted from the rhizomes (underground stems) of several tropical plants. It is so called because of the therapeutic qualities attributed to it by American Indians in the treatment of arrow wounds. A fine white powder, easily digestible, it is used to thicken sauces and soups and to prepare gruels and desserts.

RECIPE

Arrowroot liaison LIAISON À L'ARROW-ROOT Mix 2 tablespoons (3 tablespoons) arrowroot with a little cold veal or poultry gravy, or a little water. Pour into 1 litre (1¾ pints, 4¼ cups) boiling gravy, mix, and bring to the boil, stirring continuously.

Artagnan (à la d')

The name *à la d'Artagnan* is given to a garnish consisting of cep mushrooms *à la béarnaise*, small stuffed tomatoes, and croquette potatoes. It is served with poultry and meat joints.

Artemisia ARMOISE

A genus of aromatic plants with a scent of camphor. The species wormwood formerly provided the flavouring for absinthe. Another species is used in distillery to flavour the liqueur *génépi*. The leaves of some varieties are used as a fresh condiment to flavour fatty meats and fish, such as pork and eel, and may also be an ingredient in certain marinades. Artemisia is mainly used in Germany, the Balkans, and Italy.

artichoke ARTICHAUT

A perennial vegetable, also called globe artichoke, whose edible immature flower head is formed of a fleshy base, or heart (*fond*), surrounded by scaly leaves. The heart is eaten after the inedible hairy central core (choke) has been removed. The bases of the leaves are also edible. Originating from Sicily and still very widely used in Italian cooking, the artichoke was first regarded in France mainly as a remedy for various ailments. At the beginning of the 18th century, Louis Lemery said in his *Treatise on Food:* 'Artichokes suit elderly people at all times, and those of a phlegmatic and melancholy disposition.' It was also reputed to be an aphrodisiac, and women were often forbidden to eat it. Catherine de' Medici, who was fond of artichokes, encouraged their cultivation in France. They are grown today in the west (Brittany), the southeast, and around Paris. The artichoke, which has diuretic properties and is rich in iron and potassium, has a low energy value of 63 Cal per 100 g.

Available all year round, it is best in the summer. When selecting an artichoke, choose one that is firm and heavy, with stiff tightly packed leaves (these may be brilliant green, bluegreen, or violet-coloured, according to the variety). Because the artichoke is a flower bud, open leaves indicate that it is overripe, and will therefore be hard and have too large a choke. When it has been kept for a long time after picking, the tops of the scales go black.

Uncooked artichokes may be kept fresh for some days if their stalks are put into water, like a bunch of flowers. After cooking, they will keep for 24 hours in the refrigerator. When young and tender, artichokes can be served *au gratin*, as a filling for omelettes, and as fritters. The hearts are usually served stuffed, *à la barigoule*, in salad, or as a garnish for hot or cold dishes. Large artichokes, cooked in water or steamed, are served whole, either hot or cold, with a sauce. Only the small violet ones can be eaten raw with salt. The principal French varieties are:

- the Camus of Brittany, large, round, and heavy, with a large heart (April to December);
- the large green artichoke of Laon, with more pointed scales;
- the violet artichoke of Provence (autumn and spring), which may be eaten raw when young and small ('poivrade'; the choke is scarcely developed), and also cooked.

Canned artichoke hearts are formed from the heart and surrounding leaves of young artichokes. They are used as a garnish or in salads.

The whole artichoke or the heart only may be preserved in brine. A mixture of water, olive oil, lemon, thyme, bay leaf, coriander, etc., is often used for small artichokes. Artichokes may also be frozen and will keep their green colour if a little powdered vitamin C or lemon juice is added to the blanching water.

RECIPES

Artichoke hearts: preparation FONDS D'ARTICHAUT: PRÉPARATION Break off the stalk of the artichoke by bending it until it comes away from the base; the stringy parts will come away with the stalk. Using a very sharp knife, cut the base flat and then remove the leaves. Neatly trim the outside of the heart, then remove the choke. Rub with lemon to prevent it going black, even if it is to be used immediately.

Artichoke hearts à la cévenole FONDS D'ARTICHAUT À LA CÉVENOLE Blanch the artichoke hearts and gently cook them in butter. Garnish with chestnut purée flavoured with Soubise purée. Sprinkle with grated Parmesan cheese and melted butter and brown in the oven or under the grill.

Artichoke hearts à la niçoise FONDS D'ARTICHAUT À LA NIÇOISE Blanch the artichoke hearts and sauté in olive oil. Garnish with thick tomato fondue, sprinkle with white breadcrumbs and olive oil, and brown in the oven or under the grill.

Artichoke hearts cooked in butter *or* à la crème FONDS D'ARTICHAUT ÉTUVÉS AU BEURRE OU À LA CRÈME Prepare and trim the hearts. Rub with lemon and blanch for 10 minutes in boiling salted water with a few drops of lemon juice. Drain, arrange in a well-buttered sauté pan, and season with salt and pepper. Sprinkle with melted butter and cook, covered, for 18 to 25 minutes, according to size. The hearts may then be served *à la crème* by covering them with boiling fresh cream that has been reduced by half. They may be cut into slices if they are too large.

Stuffed artichoke hearts as garnish for cold dishes FONDS D'ARTICHAUT GARNIS POUR PLATS FROIDS Cook the hearts in white stock, drain, wipe, and allow them to cool completely. The usual fillings are: various compound butters, hard-boiled (hard-cooked) eggs, various vegetables (with or without mayonnaise), purées of shellfish, fish, meat, or poultry, or cold salpicons.

Stuffed artichoke hearts as garnish for hot dishes FONDS D'ARTICHAUT GARNIS POUR PLATS CHAUDS Half-cook the hearts in white stock, then gently cook them in butter and drain. The usual fillings are: anversoise, Argenteuil, bretonne, Conti, écossaise, macédoine of buttered vegetables, princesse, Saint-Germain, and Vichy. The hearts may also be stuffed with different salpicons.

Young artichoke hearts COEURS D'ARTICHAUT These may be braised without stuffing, devilled, cooked *à la lyonnaise* or *à la mirepoix*, or used in any of the recipes for artichoke hearts.

Artichokes à la lyonnaise ARTICHAUTS À LA LYONNAISE (from Paul Bocuse's recipe) Choose medium-sized artichokes with long spread-out leaves, either the green or the violet variety. Break off the stalks, cut the artichokes into four, cut the leaves down to two-thirds their length, and remove the choke. Plunge them into a saucepan of boiling water, half-cook them, and then drain. Heat a mixture of equal parts of oil and butter in a flameproof pan and soften a chopped onion in it. Add the artichokes, season with salt and pepper, and cook over a moderate heat until the vegetables begin to brown. Add 1 tablespoon flour and about 3 dl (½ pint, 1¼ cups) stock. When the artichokes are cooked, arrange them on a dish and keep them hot. Add a little more stock to the pan, and reduce. Add some chopped parsley and then stir in a good-sized piece of fresh butter and the juice of half a lemon. Pour the sauce over the artichokes and serve.

Boiled artichokes ARTICHAUTS BOUILLIS Using scissors or a very sharp knife, trim off the top third of the outer leaves of the artichokes and wash the heads in plenty of water. Break off the stalk (do not cut it) level with the leaves; the stringy parts will come away with the stalk. Tie up each artichoke with string so that the head retains its shape during cooking and plunge the vegetables into acidulated boiling salted water. Keep the water boiling vigorously. The cooking time (average 30 minutes) depends on the size and freshness of the artichokes. Allow 10–12 minutes after the steam begins to escape when using a pressure cooker. The artichokes are cooked if the outside leaves come away when pulled upwards. Drain the artichokes by placing them upside down in a colander, remove the string, and serve immediately. If they are to be eaten cold, put them under the cold tap as soon as they are cooked and then drain them; do not untie them until the last moment. To serve, take out the centre leaves which hide the choke and remove the choke with a small spoon.

Artichokes may be eaten hot with melted butter, a white sauce (prepared with the cooking water enriched with fresh cream), a cream sauce (or simply cream flavoured with lemon and heated), a hollandaise sauce, or a mousseline sauce. Cold artichokes may be served with mayonnaise, mustard sauce, soy sauce, tartare sauce, or vinaigrette, and flavoured if desired with chopped parsley or chervil.

Artois and Picardy

ARTOIS ET PICARDIE

These regions are particularly rich in food resources. The most interesting is seafood from the English Channel, an immense breeding ground for many species of fish and shellfish. Boulogne, the most important French fishing port, is a centre for herring and mackerel. In addition to the recipe for mackerel *à la boulonnaise*, the following are also noteworthy: jellied eel, *caudière de Berck* (a northern version of bouillabaisse), *craquelots* or *bouffis* (lightly smoked barely salted herrings), smoked herrings (*gendarmes*), kippers, herrings marinated in white wine, and red herring fillets marinated in oil. There are also good recipes for angler fish, turbot, grey mullet, smelt, hake, bass, sole, red mullet, and skate. Of the many kinds of fresh-water fish, salmon from the estuaries of coastal rivers, such as the Somme, and trout from the Canche are particularly noteworthy. Picardy has only a small stretch of coast, but good seafood is still abundant, in particular cockles (called *hénons*), which are found in great quantities in the bay of the Somme.

The animals of the region provide excellent meat, the salt meadow sheep being a well-known delicacy. In Picardy, the pigs are used to make good charcuterie, including andouilles, andouillettes, boudin, sausages, and smoked ham. Poultry is of medium quality, but water game is particularly abundant in Picardy and includes wild duck and geese, teal, sandpipers and snipe, lapwings, and water fowl.

The kitchen gardens of Artois produce good quality vegetables, especially those of the Saint-Omer region, but pride of place belongs to the *hortillonages*, intensively cultivated market gardens near Amiens that are drained by canals. The delicious vegetables grown there are well known even as far away as England. The climate is damp and changeable and does not favour fruit growing. Very little is grown except for cider apples; after beer, cider is the principal drink of these regions.

The characteristic local specialities include soups made with beer, tripe, pumpkins, frogs, and leeks, flamichre, fish pâté, woodcock or ducks from Amiens and Abbeville, hotchpotch, rabbit with prunes or grapes, goose *à la flammande*, and potato tarts and pies. Confectionery products and pastries include the spice-bread hearts and caramels of Arras, bêtises from Cambrai, chiques from Berck, apple pie, apple talibur, Peronne sablés, and macaroons and biscuits (cookies) from Amiens, Abbeville, and Ham.

Artois (d')

In classic cuisine, the name of the future Charles X of France (reigned 1824–30) is given to a haricot (navy) bean soup and a garnish for roast baron of lamb made with small potato croustades filled with young garden peas and accompanied by Madeira sauce.

RECIPE

d'Artois soup   POTAGE D'ARTOIS
To 1.5 litres (2¾ pints, 3½ pints) haricot (navy) bean soup, add 4 tablespoons

finely shredded vegetables softened in butter. Sprinkle the soup with 1 tablespoon chopped chervil.

asafoetida ASSA-FOETIDA

A resin extracted from an oriental umbelliferous plant. It is dried and crushed and sold as powder in Iran, India, and Afghanistan, where it is commonly used as a condiment. Its very bitter flavour and pronounced garlic smell make it distasteful to European (the Germans call it *Teufelsdreck*, or devil's dung). It was popular with the Romans (see *silphium*), but was later used mainly as a medicine to treat flatulence, etc.

asbestos AMIANTE

A natural fibrous silicate of calcium and magnesium, used as a heat insulator or filter constituent. In food and drink preparation, asbestos is used both indirectly, as insulated ovens, protective gloves, toasters, drinking-water pipes, and tanks, and directly, for filtering wine, beer, cider, and fruit juices. Since asbestos fibres cause lung disease, the use of asbestos is restricted in wine production. If an everyday object made from asbestos gets torn or is otherwise defective, it should be thrown away, even if it still appears to be useable.

ash FRÊNE

A tree of the genus *Fraxinus*, which grows in temperate climates. The leaves of the European ash (*F. excelsior*) are used for a fermented drink called *frénette*, or to make a type of tea. The very young green keys can be preserved in vinegar and used instead of capers.

RECIPE

Frénette cordial BOISSON FRÉNETTE Boil 50 g (2 oz) ash leaves with the thinly sliced peel of 10 oranges in 2 litres (3½ pints, 4½ pints) water for 30 minutes. Strain through a fine cloth. Dissolve 3 kg (6½ lb, 13 cups, firmly packed) granulated sugar in the strained infusion and add 50 g (2 oz) citric acid. Pour into a barrel with a capacity of about 50 litres (11 gallons, 14 gallons). Dissolve 30 g (1 oz) fresh yeast (1 cake compressed yeast) in 2 tablespoons (3 tablespoons) cold caramel and pour the mixture into the barrel. Fill with water, leave to ferment for 8 days, bottle, and cork.

Asiago

An Italian cow's-milk cheese (containing 30% fat) with a smooth rind. This compressed cheese has a granular appearance, a rubbery texture, but no smell. It is not crumbly and has a slightly piquant flavour. It was first manufactured from ewe's milk in the village of Asiago in the province of Vicenza. The cheese comes in rounds weighing 7–10 kg (16–22 lb). According to its maturing time (one, two, or six months), it is eaten fresh, medium, or mature, respectively (mature cheese may be grated). Its quality is good throughout the year.

asparagus ASPERGE

A perennial plant with an underground stem (crown) that produces edible shoots, which are regarded as a delicacy. Asparagus was known to the Egyptians and the Romans, but was not cultivated in France until the time of Louis XIV: the Sun King had a great liking for this vegetable, and received supplies from La Quintinie from December onwards. In about 1875, the Orleans district became the favourite area for growing asparagus – thanks to Charles Depezay, a cavalryman who took grafts from plants near Argenteuil during the siege of Paris, and afterwards dedicated himself to growing asparagus.

Three varieties of asparagus may be found in France from the beginning of March to the end of June. The white variety, harvested as soon as it appears above the ground, is grown in Alsace and Belgium and is also imported from north Africa. It is large and tender with little flavour. Purple asparagus, which is allowed to grow several centimetres high, comes from Aquitaine, the Charentes, the Loire, and also Italy. It has a full-flavoured delicious taste. Green asparagus from the Rhône (Lauris) is harvested when the stalks are about 15 cm (6 in) long; it is considered to be a luxury vegetable with the best flavour of all. Wild asparagus, with slender green shoots, has a slightly bitter taste, but is also good to eat.

For each variety in France, three grades may be identified (Extra, I, and II) according to the appearance of the shoot and the bud. The quality depends on how straight the shoots grow, whether they are starting to become woody or are showing any signs of mildew, and whether the buds are tightly closed.

Fresh asparagus stems should be firm and uniformly coloured. The cut ends of the shoots should be white. They may be kept for a maximum of three days if wrapped in a damp cloth.

Asparagus has a low energy value (25 Cal per 100 g), and is rich in vitamins A and C. 300 g (12 oz) per person should be allowed when serving the vegetable as a starter. However it is served – plain with a hot or cold sauce, in a salad, in a tart, *au gratin*, as a purée, in velouté sauce, as omelette filling, with scrambled eggs, etc. – asparagus should always be first cooked in water or steamed.

Canned asparagus is also available, either whole, sliced, in pieces, (sometimes called 'picnic'), or as asparagus tips.

A variety of equipment is available for cooking and serving asparagus. This includes a special steamer, a dish with a detachable draining rack, a plate with hollows for sauces, and various scoops and tongs. The tips may be eaten with a fork and the rest of the stem with the fingers, or the whole vegetable may be eaten with the fingers. A finger bowl is usually provided.

RECIPES

Preparation of asparagus PRÉPARA-TION DES ASPERGES   Lay the asparagus stalks flat on a chopping board and cut them all to the same length. Peel them, working from the tip to the base, and clean the tips with a pointed knife if necessary. Wash the asparagus in plenty of water but do not soak. Drain and tie into bunches or small bundles.

Cooking in water CUISSON À L'EAU   Plunge the bundles of asparagus into boiling salted water (1½ teaspoons salt to 1 litre (1¾ pints, 4¼ cups) water). When using fresh asparagus, allow 20–30 minutes of fast boiling, depending on the thickness of the stems. Remove the asparagus from the water as soon as it is tender, and drain either on a plate covered with a napkin or on the draining rack of an asparagus dish. There are special cylindrical saucepans for cooking asparagus. The stalks are placed upright in the saucepan and enough water is added to cover the stems but not the tips. The lid is replaced during cooking. The tips are more tender if they are cooked in the steam.

At the end of the season, asparagus becomes a little bitter. It needs to be blanched for 5 minutes and drained. The cooking is then completed in a fresh quantity of boiling salted water.

Asparagus served hot ASPERGES SER-VIES CHAUDES   The accompanying sauce may be clarified melted butter (flavoured with lemon if desired), noisette butter, or any of the following sauces: Chantilly, cream, hollandaise, maltaise, or mousseline.

Asparagus served warm ASPERGES SERVIES TIÈDES   The accompanying sauce may be mayonnaise, mustard sauce, tartare sauce, or a plain or seasoned vinaigrette. It is not advisable to serve asparagus cold.

Asparagus au gratin ASPERGES AU GRATIN   Cook the asparagus in salted water, drain, and arrange on an oven-proof dish, staggering the layers in order to expose the tips and hide the stalks. Coat the tips with Mornay sauce. Place a strip of greaseproof (waxed) paper over the uncoated parts. Sprinkle with grated Parmesan cheese, drizzle over melted butter, and brown in the oven or under the grill. Remove the greaseproof paper just before serving.

Asparagus tart TARTE AUX ASPERGES   Cover a pastry case (pie shell), baked blind, with a layer of creamed chicken purée. Garnish with asparagus tips that have been gently cooked in butter. Coat with cream sauce or suprême sauce. Sprinkle with fried breadcrumbs and brown in the oven.

Asparagus tips: cooking POINTES D'ASPERGE: CUISSON   Break or cut off the tips of a suitable variety of green asparagus, discarding the stalks where they start to become hard. Tie up these tips, about 10 cm (4 in) long, in bundles of 10 or 12. Peel the lower parts of the asparagus stems and cut into small pieces. Cook them in boiling salted water for 4 minutes, then add the bundles of asparagus tips. Cook them uncovered for 7–8 minutes, then drain the bundles and the pieces. Dip the bundles of tips in cold water. The asparagus pieces, together with the cooking water, may be used for soup or a garnish. White asparagus should be cut into tips 5–6 cm (2–2½ in) long.

Asparagus tips for cold garnishes POINTES D'ASPERGE POUR GARNI-TURES FROIDES Asparagus tips used for garnishes or cold salads should be dipped in cold water as soon as they have finished cooking, and then well drained. Depending on the dish being garnished, they may either be dressed with vinaigrette or mayonnaise, or glazed with meat aspic jelly.

aspic

A way of presenting cold cooked food (meat, poultry, foie gras, fish, shellfish, vegetables, or even fruit), by setting it in a moulded and decorated aspic jelly. Many authors believe that this name comes from the asp, a serpent whose icy coldness recalls that of the jelly, but it is more probably derived from the Greek word *aspis*, which means buckler or shield. It was, in fact, in this form that the first moulds were made; others were made in the shape of a coiled snake, doubtless to justify the name aspic. Today, aspics are made in plain moulds, charlotte moulds, savarin moulds, or in individual ramekins or darioles; aspic moulds may also be fluted or decorated. The type of aspic used (made from meat, poultry, or fish, or pectin-based for fruits) varies according to the nature of the principal ingredient (poultry slices, sole fillets, medallions of foie gras, sliced fresh vegetables, fruit segments, etc.). It is flavoured with port, Madeira, Marsala, or sherry.

RECIPES

Preparation of aspic moulds and dishes PRÉPARATION DE L'ASPIC Place the selected mould in the refrigerator until it is very cold. Prepare some

aspic jelly. Pour into the mould some jelly (which has cooled but not set), turning it so that it coats the base and sides. Replace the mould in the refrigerator so that the aspic just sets but is not too firm, and then place the items used for garnishing on the base and around the sides. The garnish (which should be chosen according to the principal item to go in the aspic), should be cut up into small pieces; for example, slices of truffle, rounds of hard-boiled (hard-cooked) egg, slices of lean ham or tongue, tarragon leaves, or smoked salmon may be used. When adding these items, the appearance of the jelly when it is turned out of the mould should be considered. Replace the mould in the refrigerator to allow the garnish to set firmly. Then carefully fill the mould with the prepared filling and press it down into the jelly. The preparation may be placed in layers alternating with layers of jelly, in which case, the jelly should be allowed to set before the subsequent layer of prepared food is laid on top. Alternatively, the mould can be filled with the prepared food and covered with a single layer of jelly. Replace the filled mould in the refrigerator until the moment of serving. Unmould the firmly set aspic by plunging the mould for a few seconds into boiling water. Turn it upside down on to a cold plate and replace in the refrigerator for a few moments before serving.

aspic of ham and veal (*or chicken*) ASPIC DE JAMBON ET DE VEAU (OU DE VOLAILLE) Prepare an aspic jelly flavoured with herbs, and coat the mould with it. Garnish the mould with some diced cooked ham and some casseroled veal (or chicken) cut into even-sized slices. Fill the centre with a layer of ham mousse, then a layer of Russian salad, finishing with a layer of aspic jelly. Place in the refrigerator to set. Unmould before serving.

foie gras aspic ASPIC DE FOIE GRAS Prepare an aspic jelly flavoured with herbs, and use it to coat the mould. Arrange slices of foie gras and thick slices of truffle in the mould. Fill the mould with half-set aspic and allow to set completely in the coldest part of the refrigerator. Unmould just before serving.

Smoked salmon aspic   ASPIC DE
SAUMON FUMÉ   Prepare an aspic jelly
flavoured with herbs, and use it to coat
the mould. Place some Russian salad on
slices of smoked salmon and roll them
up. Arrange in the mould, alternating a
layer of salmon rolls with a layer of
salmon mousse, and finishing with the
aspic jelly. Place in the refrigerator to
set. Unmould before serving.

aspic jelly

GELÉE DE CUISINE

A translucent savoury preparation
which solidifies on cooling because of
the gelatinous substances it contains.
Aspic jellies are prepared from basic
white or brown stocks (meat, poultry,
game, or fish). They are produced naturally when the stock is prepared with
items rich in gelatine (veal knuckle,
calf's foot, fresh bacon rind, poultry,
fish trimmings). In the absence of these
gelatinous items, some leaves of gelatine
(or powdered gelatine), softened in cold
water, must be added to the stock before
it is clarified. Clarification ensures that
an aspic is transparent. Nowadays,
aspic jelly can be made from a powder
which is simply dissolved in water, heated, and left to cool.

Aspic jellies are used in particular for
preparing such cold dishes as aspics and
terrines; as a garnish for cold dishes
(chopped or cut into triangles); and to
glaze cold preparations (suprêmes of
chicken, quails, steaks, or fillets of fish).
Meat, poultry, and game aspic stocks
are reserved for the aspics, terrines, etc.,
of which the dominant element is the
same as that of the jelly. For aspics of
fish or shellfish gelatine in powdered or
leaf form is dissolved in strained and
clarified fish fumet. Depending on their
use, aspic jellies can be coloured (with
caramel or edible carmine to obtain an
amber tint) and flavoured with a wine or
spirit (port, Madeira, sherry, brandy).

| RECIPES

Fish aspic   GELÉE DE POISSON   Prepare a strong fumet by putting in a
stockpot 1 kg (2¼ lb) white fish trimmings (bones and heads of brill, hake,
whiting, sole, or turbot), 2 onions, 150 g
(5 oz) mushroom parings, 2 shredded
carrots, a large bouquet garni, salt, pepper, 1 dl (6 tablespoons, scant ½ cup)
dry white wine (or red wine when cooking salmon, salmon trout, or carp), and
2 litres (3½ pints, 4½ pints) cold water.
Bring to the boil and then simmer for 30
minutes. Dissolve in water 45–75 g
(1½–3 oz) gelatine, depending on
the degree of firmness required for the
aspic. Chop up 2 whiting fillets. Mix the
dissolved gelatine with the whiting flesh
and 2 or 3 egg whites. Strain the fish
fumet, pressing the liquid out of the
ingredients, and pour it into a large
saucepan. Add the whiting mixture and
bring to the boil, stirring continuously.
When it boils, stop stirring and simmer
for 30 minutes. Gently strain through a
fine cloth and flavour the aspic with
champagne or sherry.

Meat aspic   GELÉE DE VIANDE
Brown in the oven 1 kg (2¼ lb) leg of
beef and 500 g (18 oz) knuckle of veal
cut into pieces, 1 calf's foot, 500 g (18
oz) veal bones, and 250 g (9 oz) defatted
bacon rind. Peel and shred 2 onions, 4
carrots, and 1 leek. Place all these ingredients in a stockpot together with a
large bouquet garni and 15 g (½ oz) salt
and pepper. Add 3 litres (5¼ pints, 6½
pints) water and bring to the boil. Skim,
then add a ladleful of very cold water,
and simmer for 5 hours. Carefully strain
the liquid through a strainer lined with
muslin (cheesecloth), let it cool completely, and put it in the refrigerator so
that the fat which solidifies on the surface can be removed easily. Clarify the
stock with 200 g (7 oz, scant cup) lean
beef, 2 egg whites and a small bouquet
of chervil and tarragon.

The aspic can be flavoured with
Madeira, port, sherry, or with any other
liquor. If this is done, the flavouring is
added just before straining the aspic.
White aspic is obtained in a similar
fashion but the meat and bones are not
browned. Game aspic is obtained by
adding to meat aspic 1¼ kg (2¾ lb)
game carcasses and trimmings, which
have been previously browned in the
oven, and several juniper berries.

Chicken aspic is obtained by adding
to meat aspic either a whole chicken or
1½ kg (3¼ lb) chicken carcasses and
giblets, both browned in the oven.

assation

The French term for cooking food in its own juice without adding any liquid.

assiette anglaise

An assortment of cold meats arranged on a plate or dish. It may consist of cooked ham, roast beef, tongue, galantine, etc., garnished with gherkins (sweet dill pickles) and jelly and served with mustard and condiments. The term *assiette froide* (cold plate) is also used.

assommoir

A French public house of the lowest category. The word is now practically obsolete, only surviving in a novel by Émile Zola (*L'Assommoir*, 1877), in which the author describes the downfall of the working classes of Paris, prisoners of the slums, work, and alcohol: 'The *assommoir* of Père Colombe was situated on the corner of the Rue des Poissonniers and the Boulevard Rochechouart.'

Asti

A town in Piedmont, Italy, south of Turin, centre of an important wine region. The best-known wines are the sparkling whites made from the Moscato Bianco, which produces Asti Spumante, made by a process, unique to the area, that combines the Charmat (*cuve close*) method with certain local variations. A sweeter sparkling wine is made from the Moscato d'Asti. The 'grapey' flavour and marked fragrance have made the sparkling wines of Asti popular all over the world.

Athenaeus ATHÉNÉE

Greek writer and grammarian, born at Naucratis, Lower Egypt, in the 3rd century AD. His compilation *Deipnosophistai* ('Authorities on Banquets') is a mine of information about the daily and cultural life of ancient Greece. There are numerous references to chefs and their recipes, discoveries, cooking utensils, and special dishes.

athénienne (à l')

The description *à l'athénienne* is given to various dishes (such as poultry, lamb, or kebabs) that are cooked with olive oil and lightly fried onion and usually garnished with aubergines (eggplants) (fried, sautéed, or stuffed), peppers (sautéed or stuffed) and rice pilaf *à la grecque*.

attelet

A small ornamental skewer with a decorative head in the shape of a hare, boar, fish, etc. The word comes from the Latin *hasta* (a rod or staff), and these skewers were used for decorating hot or cold dishes served in the grand style, sometimes being threaded with kidneys, sweetbreads, and other small items of food. *Le Nouveau Cuisinier royal et bourgeois* (1714) recommends a *plat du milieu* (a dish served between the main courses and the dessert) consisting of 'a piece of beef garnished with small pâtés and hâtelettes of sweet-breads.'

Attelets were never used during cooking as the soldiering on the decorative motifs would melt.

Today this form of decoration is hardly ever seen, as modern cooks tend to avoid any decoration that is not actually edible.

attendu

The French description for a dish or item of food that should be left for a period before being eaten or used, in order to improve its quality. For example, game is hung for a period of time before being cooked.

attereau

A hot hors d'oeuvre consisting of various raw or cooked ingredients that are threaded onto a skewer, dipped in a reduced sauce, coated with breadcrumbs, and fried. It is distinguished from brochettes, which are made up of raw ingredients and grilled. The skewer used to cook this dish is also called an attereau and is made of wood or metal. It may be replaced by an ordinary skewer for serving. The etymology of the two words is the same: both come from the Latin *hasta* (spear).

The principal ingredient of an attereau is usually offal, either cut in pieces or sliced, but it can also be made with seafood or vegetables. The supplementary ingredients, such as mushrooms, tongue, or ham, may be varied, as well as the sauce for coating. An attereau may also be a hot dessert, in which case it is made with fruit and pastry, dipped in a fried custard mixture (see *creams and custards*), and coated with breadcrumbs.

The name *attereau* is also given to a Burgundian speciality consisting of minced (ground) liver and neck of pork, wrapped in a caul. Shaped like large balls, they are placed side by side on an earthenware dish and cooked in the oven. They are eaten cold.

RECIPES

Savoury Attereaux

Attereaux of chicken livers à la mirepoix ATTEREAUX DE FOIES DE VOLAILLE À LA MIREPOIX Sauté some chicken livers in butter, drain, and allow to cool. Dice some cooked ham and clean some small button mushrooms. Assemble the attereaux with these 3 ingredients, threading the mushrooms on lengthways. Roll them in a mirepoix and coat them with breadcrumbs. Plunge them into very hot fat, drain, and season with salt and pepper. Serve with fried parsley.

Attereaux of oysters ATTEREAUX D'HUITRES Poach and drain several large oysters. Cut some mushrooms into thick slices and sauté them in butter. Assemble the attereaux by alternating the oysters with the mushrooms. Dip them in Villeroi sauce made with a fish fumet, coat them with breadcrumbs, and plunge them into very hot fat. Serve with fried parsley and lemon halves.

Sweet Attereaux

attereaux of pineapple ATTEREAUX D'ANANAS Peel a fresh pineapple and cut into cubes. Thread the cubes onto skewers, dip them into a *crème frite* mixture (see *creams and custards*), coat with breadcrumbs, and plunge them into the frying fat.

attignole

A speciality from Normandy, consisting of a ball of minced (ground) meat and pork fat mixed with bread soaked in a mixture of milk, beaten eggs, and flour, and seasoned with pepper, onion, and shallot. Attignoles are cooked in the oven and are served cold as an entrée, coated with their jellied cooking juices.

attriau

A type of sausage in the form of a flattened ball, made with a mixture of minced (ground) pork liver, veal, onion, and herbs and cooked in a frying pan (skillet). This rustic dish is found in several French provinces.

aubergine (eggplant)

An elongated or rounded fruit with a smooth shiny purple skin covering a light firm flesh. A white variety also exists. The largest and oldest fruits contain more seeds.

Originating in India, the aubergine was cultivated in Italy by the 15th century. It spread to the south of France in the 17th century and was grown north of the Loire by the time of the Revolution. Today it is grown in southeastern

variety	characteristics
Barbentane (named after a village near Avignon)	long and cylindrical, dark purple, flesh slightly green; choose when young and slender
Violette de Toulouse	elongated, lighter shade of purple, white flesh; suitable for stuffing
Ronde de Chine and Ronde de Valence	rounded, almost black shiny skin; very firm flesh
Baluroi	short and cylindrical, bright purple shiny skin; firm flesh, sometimes a little bitter
Bonica	plump oval shape, dark purple, delicate flesh, few seeds
Dourga	white skin; very delicate taste, with a mushroom flavour

and southwestern France from May to October. From October onwards it is imported from the West Indies, Israel, Senegal, and the Ivory Coast. It has a low energy value (30 Cal per 100 g, 4 oz) and is rich in potassium and calcium.

The aubergine has a pronounced flavour and is used as a vegetable in numerous Eastern and Mediterranean dishes together with tomatoes, courgettes (zucchini), garlic, and olives (see *imam bayildi, moussaka, ratatouille, tian*). It is delicious as an accompaniment to mutton and white meats. It may be eaten hot, either as a main dish (stuffed or in a soufflé) or as a garnish (sautéed, in fritters, or puréed), or cold (in the form of a purée, or as a salad ingredient).

RECIPES

Preparation of aubergines PRÉPARA-TION DE L'AUBERGINE Formerly, it was the custom to peel aubergines, but this is no longer done except for so-called 'white' dishes. The slightly bitter taste of the vegetable is minimized by sprinkling the flesh with salt and leaving it for 30 minutes. It should then be wiped thoroughly with absorbent kitchen paper before using.

Aubergines may be stuffed in two ways depending on their size and shape. They may be cut in half lengthways and the flesh scooped out of each half. Alternatively, the top may be removed and the aubergine hollowed out inside. Use a sharp knife to remove the flesh, leaving a thickness of 5 or 6 mm (¼ in) around the edge, and scoop out the remainder of the flesh from the base with a grapefruit knife. Sprinkle the empty case and the flesh with lemon juice to prevent discoloration.

Aubergine caviar CAVIAR D'AUBER-GINE Cook 3 good-quality whole aubergines in the oven at about 200 C (400 F, gas 6) for 15–20 minutes until tender. Hard-boil (hard-cook) 4 eggs, cool under a cold tap, and shell them. Skin and deseed 2 tomatoes and chop the flesh. Peel and finely chop an onion. Cut the aubergines in half, remove the flesh, and chop it up with a knife. Mix the tomatoes, aubergine flesh, and on-ion in a salad bowl. Season with salt and pepper and slowly work in 1 small glass olive oil, stirring as for mayonnaise, or mix in a blender. Place in the refrigerator until ready to serve. Garnish with quarters of hard-boiled (hard-cooked) eggs and tomato slices.

Aubergines au gratin à la toulousaine (*or à la languedocienne*) AUBER-GINES AU GRATIN À LA TOULOUSAINE (OU À LA LANGUEDOCIENNE) Cut the aubergines into thick slices and steep in salt for 30 minutes. Wipe dry, and sauté in olive oil in a frying pan (skillet). Fry some tomato halves in oil in a separate pan. Arrange the tomatoes and aubergines in alternate layers in a gratin dish and sprinkle generously with breadcrumbs mixed with chopped garlic and parsley. Pour on a little oil and brown in the oven or under the grill.

Sautéed aubergines AUBERGINES SAUTÉES Cut the aubergines into 2 cm (1 in) cubes. Sprinkle with salt and leave for 30 minutes, wipe, and coat with flour. Sauté the slices in olive oil in a frying pan (skillet). Arrange in a vegetable dish and sprinkle with chopped parsley.

Stuffed aubergines AUBERGINES FARCIES (from Roger Vergé's recipe) Prepare 6 small aubergines for stuffing as described above. Sprinkle each hollow shell with salt and a tablespoon olive oil and arrange in an ovenproof dish. Cook them in a hot oven (220 C, 425 F, gas 7) for 15 minutes. Place all the diced flesh in another dish, cover, and cook it in the oven at the same time. Meanwhile, stone (pit) and finely chop 100 g (4 oz) large black (ripe) olives and put them in a large bowl. Heat 1 tablespoon olive oil in a frying pan (skillet), add 6 anchovy fillets, and mash them to obtain an oily purée. Pour this purée into the bowl of olives and add the cooked crushed aubergine flesh together with a crushed garlic clove and some thyme. Season with salt and pepper and mix well. Fill the aubergine shells with the mixture and flatten with a fork. Heat thoroughly in a hot oven.

Aumale (à la d')

The description *à la d'aumale* is given to a dish of fattened pullet that is stuffed and braised. It was created by the head chef of Henri d'Orléans, the fourth son of Louis-Philippe. The particularly elaborate garnish consists of croustades garnished with trimmed cucumber pieces cooked in butter and scooped-out onion halves, filled with a salpicon of tongue and foie gras bound with a Madeira sauce.

Scrambled eggs *à la d'Aumale* include crushed tomatoes and diced sautéed kidneys in Madeira sauce.

aumonière (en)

The description *en aumonière* is given to an original apricot dessert: the apricots, whose stones are replaced with lumps of sugar, are encased in triangles of short-crust pastry (basic pie dough) sealed at the edges. These tarts are cooked in the oven, decorated with chopped grilled (broiled) almonds, and served with a hot apricot sauce.

aurore

The name given to a velouté sauce flavoured with tomato purée and also to some dishes containing tomato purée. The name is also applied to dishes of egg and chicken coated with the sauce.

RECIPE

Sauce aurore The traditional sauce is made by adding ½ litre (17 fl oz, 2 cups) very thick puréed tomato sauce to 2 dl (7 fl oz, ¾ cup) velouté sauce. Finish with 50 g (2 oz) butter and put the sauce through a sieve.

Today, however, sauce aurore is a light béchamel sauce flavoured with tomato purée and butter.

Ausonius   AUSONE

Roman poet (born Burdigala (Bordeaux), *c.* 310; died *c.* 395), who was tutor to Gratian, a son of Emperor Valentinian I. Ausonius was made a consul in 379 and retired in 383 to the region around present-day Saint-Émilion. He wrote: 'Happy are the inhabitants of Bordeaux, for whom living and drinking are one and the same!' His name survives in the red Bordeaux wine, Château-Ausone. He left a work concerning the breeding of oysters.

Australia and New Zealand
AUSTRALIE ET
NOUVELLE-ZÉLANDE

British and Dutch colonists took with them both the food products and the customs that have shaped the present-day cuisine of these two countries. Aboriginal culinary traditions include the cooking of such animals as cockchafer grubs, bats, and lizards. Kangaroo-tail soup is considered to be a delicacy, but the kangaroo is now a protected species.

Having developed breeds of exceptionally high-quality livestock, particularly sheep and cattle, Australians and New Zealanders consume large quantities of meat – beef and mutton are traditionally eaten grilled (broiled) on a barbecue. Rabbits are also abundant. Specialities include young spring chickens from Sydney, which are marinated in pineapple and wine and then roasted, and also leg of mutton in brine flavoured with cloves and juniper. Fish and shellfish, often giant-sized are very popular but are not cooked with any gastronomic refinement; seafood and beer are served in lobster and oyster bars. Tropical fruits and vegetables are produced in abundance, particularly passionfruit and custard apple in Australia and kiwi-fruit in New Zealand. Danish pastries are very popular in New Zealand. Local beers, tea, and fruit juices are the most usual drinks, although Australian vineyards have produced quality wines since the mid-19th century.

Australian wines
VINS D'AUSTRALIE

Australian viticulture is, by European standards, fairly recently established: the first vines are recorded as having been planted near Sydney on 26 January, 1788. Today, Australian vineyards range from enormous properties to quite small plots and great strides have been made in exporting the wines, which are now becoming popular all over the wine-drinking world, including France. The concept of Australian wines as being clumsy assertive drinks is thoroughly outdated. Indeed, many major wine companies from overseas, including a number of the Champagne establishments, are currently either buying into certain of the big Australian wine companies or actually setting up in production there.

The main regions of production are in New South Wales, Victoria, South Australia, Western Australia, and Tasmania. Some of the vineyards have been in operation for many years, including the family concerns, which often started by being cultivated as a part-time occupation by British settlers. Every type of wine is made – still, sparkling, dry, sweet, and also various fortified wines – and a wide range of classic grape varieties are grown, including the Cabernet Sauvignon, Shiraz (Syrah), Chardonnay, Sauvignon Blanc, Chenin Blanc, Gernache, Sémillon, Rheinriesling, several types of Muscat, and many others. The enormous size of the continent means that soils and climate vary tremendously and the oenological colleges of Australia achieve very high standards, both in terms of wine and other technicalities: only a few years ago, for example, it was Australia that pioneered the now familiar 'bag in box' method of presenting inexpensive wine.

Although the Australians themselves consume large quantities of their own wines, they also import many of the fine classic wines, including the best known reds and whites of France and also champagne. As the country is much influenced by the United States, fashions in drinking often follow those of that country; for example in the great vogue in recent years for light dry white wines, which caused a great increase in the plantings of white wine grapes.

Austria UTRICHE

Austrian cuisine is essentially a combination of the culinary traditions of the different nationalities who have left their mark on the country's history – the Germans, the Italians, and the Hungarians. This is why it includes not only cabbage, ragouts, and charcuterie, but also cream cheeses with poppy seeds, and a taste for onion and paprika (goulash is an Austrian dish as well as being a Hungarian speciality). Gastronomy holds a place of honour in Vienna, where the splendours of the Empire survive in such bastions of tradition as the Hotel Sacher, the Demel pâtisserie, and the old cafés (Hewelka, Landtmann), as well as the Naschmarkt, the oldest of the Viennese markets.

The river resources have inspired some classic fish dishes, such as trout *au bleu*, stuffed pike, and fried carp, which is traditionally eaten at Christmas, and also crayfish with fennel.

Tafelspitz (very well-hung boiled meat) is the pride of Austrian cooks. There are several variations and it is served with salads and compotes. However, the dish that is best known abroad is the Wiener Schnitzel (escalope of veal), which can also be made with beef or pork. Poultry has always featured in Austrian cuisine, particularly chicken. It may be roasted, coated with breadcrumbs and fried in lard, or prepared with soured (dairy sour) cream, paprika, or cabbage.

Small traditional restaurants (*Gasthof* or *Heuriger*) serve the best wines with regional dishes such as roast hare, goose with red cabbage, pork quenelles, stuffed crêpes (*Palatschinken*), Carinthian ravioli (*Nudln*), beef with onions and cumin (*Zwiebelfleisch*), and Styrian spiced ragouts, followed by salads dressed with pumpkin-seed oil. Soups and ragouts are popular everywhere. The classic ones are made with potatoes and mushrooms and served with bread or liver knödel. The Tyrol is famous for its charcuterie, and sauerkraut, bacon quenelles, and calves' liver with onions are also popular. *Nockerln* is the Austrian version of Italian gnocchi, and the same word is also used for a sweet soufflé from Salzburg. Above all, Austria is a country renowned for its pâtisserie, which is served, like coffee, with lashings of whipped cream (*Schlagobers*). As well as the three great classics – sachertorte, strudel, and linzertorte – other specialities are dried fruit and poppy-seed cream puffs, meringues, crystallized (candied) fruit, cream cheese or cherry tarts, *Kaiserschmarrn* (a thick very sweet pancake), krapfen (fritters), *Zwetschenknödel* (stoned (pitted) prunes coated in pastry and fried), and *Tascherln and Buchteln* (Swiss rolls or cakes filled with jam).

autoclave

A hermetically sealed vessel designed for sterilizing food products. The food is immersed in water that is heated under pressure so that the temperature rises to 120–180 c (250–350 f). No bacteria can survive in temperatures of 120 c (250 f) or above. The apparatus is provided with an adjustable safety valve.

The principle of the autoclave, derived directly from the Papin marmite (invented by Denis Papin), enabled Nicolas Appert to perfect his food-preservation method. The preserving industry still uses autoclaves. See *pressure cooker*.

autrichienne (à l')

The description *à l'autrichienne* is given to various dishes seasoned with paprika. Sometimes lightly fried onion, fennel, or soured (dairy sour) cream may be included.

auvergnate (à l')

The description *à l'auvergnate* is given to numerous dishes made with products of the Auvergne: pickled pork, bacon, and ham (used in stews, stuffed cabbage, and lentil and potato dishes), and also cheeses, such as blue cheese (for soup) and Cantal (for aligot and truffade).

Auvergne

The Auvergne, including the picturesque Velay region, is farming country with a good simple cuisine, described by Curnonsky as *droite en goût* (with unadulterated flavours). The copious food of the region, generally considered to be fortifying rather than refined, is not however limited to the traditional potée, a cabbage soup common to many provinces. Delicate dishes of the Auvergne include mourtayrol, cousinat, Cantal soup, and *soupe au farci* (a stew containing a cabbage stuffed with sausagemeat). The fresh-water fish are excellent: carp, pike, tench, eel, and perch are prepared in tasty matelotes (fish stews), while trout may be eaten *à la meunière*, *au bleu*, or *au lard* (with bacon). Salmon is found upstream as far as Brioude, where it is made into a delicious pie.

The pork of the Auvergne is renowned, and the charcuterie consists of dried and smoked hams, dried sausages, large country sausages, black puddings (blood sausages), fritons (crisp pork pieces), fricandeaux, etc. Stock breeding results in the production of excellent meats, notably beef from Salers, veal, used to make falette, and the sheep of Vassivières and Chaudes-Aigues, to which the famous gigot brayaude owes its reputation. Even though the poultry of the region does not have a national reputation, turkey with chestnuts is a delectable dish, as is the coq au vin cooked with Chanturgues, a local red wine. The high-quality game is used in such dishes as braised partridge with lentils and hare *à l'auvergnate*.

☐ **The regional produce** The land of the Auvergne is fertile. The vegetables are magnificent, and the orchards of the Limagne provide very good fresh fruit – apricots, peaches, apples, pears, and cherries – a large proportion of which is made into crystallized (candied) fruit by the local industries. Auvergne walnuts and chestnuts, appropriately used in cooking, are particularly tasty.

Varied and abundant mushrooms are found in the meadows, forests, and undergrowth. They feature in some classic dishes of the gastronomy of the Auvergne – *cul de veau aux mousserons* (rump of veal with St George's mushrooms), *crépinette de foie aux cèpes, aux bolets*, or *aux oronges* (a special flat sausage of liver with ceps, boletus, or Caesar's mushrooms), and *omelette aux girolles* (chanterelle omelette). In addition, many kinds of meat and poultry are served with morels, either in gravy or cream sauce.

Some other well-known specialities include omelette brayaude, aligot, friand de Saint-Flour, meat pie, truffade, pounti, and potatoes with bacon. The famous local cheeses – Cantal, Saint-Nectaire, Savaron, Bleu, Gaperon, Murol, and Fourme d'Ambert – are best eaten with the local wines. The excellent pâtisserie includes fouace du Cantal, the crisp petits fours of Mauriac, Murat pastry horns, and picoussel of Mur-de-Barrez.

Auxey-Duresses

Red and white Burgundies from the Côte de Beaune, not far from

Meursault. Some of them are allowed to add the suffix 'Côte de Beaune' to the parish name.

Avice (Jean)

French pastrycook at the beginning of the 19th century. A chef in the best pâtisserie of the time – Bailly, in the Rue Vivienne, Paris, he was also appointed purveyor to Talleyrand. He trained the young Carême, who, when he became famous, paid tribute to 'the illustrious Avice, master of choux pastry'. Avice is considered by some to be the creator of the madeleine.

avocado   AVOCAT

A pear-shaped or round fruit from a tropical tree originating in South America and cultivated today in Mexico, the West Indies, Florida, Africa, Israel, Spain, and France. Its skin, which may be grained or smooth and shiny, is dark green or purplish-brown in colour. It has pale-green flesh surrounding a large hard round stone, which comes away easily with the point of a knife. The flesh has a buttery consistency and a slight flavour of hazelnuts. The avocado is ripe when it gives under the pressure of the finger. It can then be stored in the refrigerator. An unripe avocado will ripen within a few days either wrapped in newspaper or at room temperature.

The Spanish discovered the avocado tree and sent saplings to several tropical countries. In France, the avocado is a more recent introduction, and it was not until the 1950s that it appeared in the recipe books. Rich in fats, vitamin A, and potassium (240 Cal per 100 g), the avocado is cut in half and served as an hors d'oeuvre with a sauce or garnish. It may also be used in salads, iced mousses, and soufflés. Avocados are prepared only at the last moment as they become discoloured on exposure to the air.

The largest number of dishes that include the avocado are found in Israel. The fruit is also popular in Mexico in such dishes as *guacamole* (crushed avocado with pimientos and spices), which may be served with tortillas and bread rolls. In Martinique, it is the basis of *féroce* (avocado mixed with chopped salt cod). It is used throughout South America for garnishing hot or iced soups and ragouts. In Africa, avocado leaves are used to make the sparkling and slightly alcoholic drink known as *babine.*

RECIPE

Avacado salad Archestrate   SALADE D'AVOCAT ARCHESTRATE   (from Alain Senderens' recipe) Cut the heart of a head of celery into thin strips. Dice 3 artichoke hearts (poached in white stock and cooled) and the flesh of 3 tomatoes. Halve 4 avocados and carefully remove the flesh, keeping each half intact. Slice the flesh and sprinkle with lemon juice. Season the avocado and vegetables with vinaigrette, arrange in a salad bowl, and sprinkle with chopped herbs.

Avocado sauce   SAUCE À L'AVOCAT Blend together avocado flesh with lemon juice in the following proportions: 2 tablespoons (3 tablespoons) juice to a medium-sized avocado. Add an equal volume of whipped cream and mix together. Pour into a sauceboat and serve very cold with hot or cold meat or poultry, together with quarters of lemon.

Avocados stuffed with crab   AVOCATS FARCIS AU CRABE   Prepare a mayonnaise and season it with mustard and cayenne. Crumble some crab meat (fresh, canned, or frozen). Halve the avocados and either scoop out the flesh with a ball-shaped spoon or cut it into even-sized cubes. Sprinkle the flesh and the insides of the shells with lemon juice and season with salt and pepper. Mix the mayonnaise with the crab meat and carefully add the avocado flesh. Pile the filling into the shells and garnish with mayonnaise coloured with tomato. (Use a piping (pastry) bag with a star (fluted) nozzle.) Dust with paprika.

Cornmeal pancakes with avocados CREPES DE MAÏS AUX AVOCATS (from Raymond Oliver's recipe) Make a pancake batter with 250 g (8¾ oz) cornmeal, 3 whole eggs, salt, pepper, 2 or 3 tablespoons oil or melted butter, and ½ litre (17 fl oz, 2 cups) warm milk, or a mixture of milk and water. Beat the ingredients together and set the batter aside. Remove the flesh from 3 avocados, adding cayenne, salt, pepper, and 3 tablespoons olive oil, and reduce to a purée in a blender. Put in a cool place and add some chopped tarragon. Make the pancakes and allow them to cool. Spread them with avocado purée, roll up, and hold them together with a cocktail stick (toothpick). Serve cold.

baba

A cake made from leavened dough that contains raisins and is steeped, after baking, in rum or Kirsch syrup. It is served either as individual small cakes baked in dariole moulds or as a large cake, often decorated with angelica and glacé (candied) cherries.

The origin of this cake is attributed to the greediness of the Polish king Stanislas Leszcsynski, who was exiled in Lorraine. He found the traditional *kouglof* too dry and improved it by adding rum. As a dedicated reader of *The Thousand and One Nights*, he is said to have named this creation after his favourite hero, Ali Baba. This recipe was a great success at the court of Nancy, where it was usually served with a sauce of sweetened Málaga. Carême writes, however: 'It was well known that the true Polish baba should be made with rye flour and Hungarian wine.'

Sthorer, a pastrycook who attended the court of the Polish king, perfected the recipe using a brioche steeped in alcohol; he made it the speciality of his house in the Rue Montorgueil in Paris and called it 'baba'. Around 1850, several renowned pastrycooks, taking their inspiration from the baba, created the *fribourg* in Bordeaux, the *brillat-savarin* (later known as the savarin) in Paris, and the *gorenflot*.

RECIPE

Rum babas BABAS AU RHUM Soak 100 g (4 oz, ¾ cup) raisins in 3 dl (½ pint, 1¼ cups) rum and soften 100 g (4 oz, ½ cup) butter at room temperature. Mix 25 g (1 oz) fresh yeast or 10 g (2 teaspoons) dried yeast with 2 tablespoons (3 tablespoons) warm water. Make a well in 250 g (8¾ oz, 2 cups) sifted flour and add 25 g (1 oz, 2 tablespoons) sugar, a generous pinch of salt, 2 whole eggs, and the yeast mixture. Mix with a wooden spatula until the dough is elastic, then add another egg. Work this in, and then add a further egg and work that in. Finally add the softened butter and the drained raisins.

Melt 50 g (2 oz, 4 tablespoons) butter over a low heat and brush the insides of 16 dariole moulds with the melted butter. Divide the dough into 16 small pieces and put a piece into each mould. Leave in a warm place until the dough has risen to fill the moulds. Preheat the oven to about 200 C (400 F, gas 6) and then bake for 15–20 minutes. Turn the babas out immediately onto a rack and allow to cool completely.

Prepare a syrup using 1 litre (1¾ pints, 5 cups) water and 500 g (18 oz, 2½ cups) sugar. Dip each baba in the boiling syrup and leave submerged until no more air bubbles are released. Drain and place on a cake rack resting over a dish. When they have cooled slightly, soak them in rum. As the rum syrup collects in this dish repeatedly spoon it back over the babas to keep them very moist.

Bacchus

In Roman mythology, the god of vines and wine, the counterpart of the Greek god Dionysus. His functions were many: he represented Nature (symbolized by the rod he carried, which was wrapped in ivy and vine leaves, with a pine cone at one end); he was the father of viticulture, since he had taught man to cultivate the vine and make wine; and he was the incarnation of fertility and became the god of procreation, often symbolized by a goat or a bull. Bacchus is usually accompanied by a cortege of satyrs, syleni, and bacchantes. Dionysus, in whose honour mysteries were celebrated, inspired the birth of Greek dramatic poetry, where as Bacchus has essentially remained part of the sensual and carnal world of drunkenness and the pleasure of drinking (hence 'bacchic').

bacon

Lean cured sides of pork, generally sold as thin slices which are eaten fried or grilled, usually with eggs (see *breakfast*). In France the name *bacon* also refers to cured loin which has been dried, steamed, and smoked. The word derives from the old French *bakko*, meaning ham. In French this became *bacon*, meaning a piece of salt pork or even the whole pig (a *repas baconique* was a festive meal where only pork dishes were served). It was then adopted by the English and returned to France with its present meaning.

| RECIPE

Calf's liver with bacon FOIE DE VEAU AU BACON Season slices of calf's liver with salt and pepper and then coat in flour, shaking them to remove any excess. Fry and then drain two thin slices of rindless bacon for each slice of liver. Cook the liver for approximately 10 minutes in the same frying pan, arrange on a plate, and garnish with the bacon and slices of lemon. Keep warm. Make a sauce in the frying pan using the meat juices and lemon juice or vinegar. Pour over the liver and sprinkle with chopped parsley.

Sausage and bacon brochettes SAUCISSES AU BACON EN BROCHETTES Place small frankfurter or cocktail sausages in a pan of cold water and heat through without boiling. Drain and wrap each sausage in half a slice of rindless bacon. Thread onto skewers and grill gently.

badoise (à la)

This is a term applied to preparations inspired by German cuisine from the Baden region, where game is plentiful. Small cuts of game (fillet and cutlets of venison and saddle and fillet of hare and rabbit) are sautéed and garnished with stoned (pitted) cherries. These are served with a sauce made from the meat juices, cream, and cherry juice and a pepper sauce. Large cuts (haunch and saddle (loins) of venison) are served with a garnish of braised red cabbage, lean bacon, and creamed potatoes.

baekenofe or backenoff

An Alsatian dish comprising a stew of various meats. The origin of this speciality is linked to the traditional way of life in the country. On their way to the fields in the morning, the peasants would leave earthenware pots prepared by their wives (containing meat marinated overnight, onions, potatoes, and seasoning added that morning) with the village baker, who would bake (*baeken*) them in his oven (*Ofen*) after the batch of bread. The baekenofe was usually prepared on Mondays (washing day) when the housewife was too busy to cook. The baker himself sealed the pots with bread dough.

The baekenofe, which is still prepared in Alsace, requires long slow cooking in the oven to bring out the full flavour. It is often served with a green salad.

Baekenofe Cut 500 g (1 lb) shoulder of mutton, 500 g (1 lb) shoulder of pork, and 500 g (1 lb) beef into large cubes and marinate overnight in a bowl containing ½ litre (16 fl oz, 2 cups) Alsace wine, 1 large finely chopped onion, 1 onion stuck with 2 or 3 cloves, 2 crushed garlic cloves, a bouqet garni, and salt and pepper. The next day, peel and slice 2 kg (4½ lb) potatoes and 250 g (½ lb) onions. Grease a large casserole with lard, then fill with layers of the ingredients, as follows: a layer of potatoes, a layer of meat, and a layer of onions. Repeat until all the ingredients have been used, ending with a layer of potatoes. Remove the bouquet garni and the onion stuck with cloves from the marinade and pour liquid into the casserole. The liquid should just reach the top layer. If necessary, top up with water. Cover and cook in a slow oven (about 160 c, 325 F, gas 3) for 4 hours.

Bagnes

A Swiss cheese made from cows' milk (45% fat content); it is a cooked pressed cheese with a slightly rough brushed crust. Firm but springy to the touch, it has a fruity flavour which makes it suitable for the table, but it is most widely known as a cheese for making raclettes. A product of Valais (particularly the Bagnes valley), it is a flat round cheese, 35–40 cm (14–16 in) in diameter, 7–8 cm (3–4 in) thick, and weighing approximately 7 kg (16 lb). Some gourmets prefer it slightly more mature (up to six months old instead of the usual three), which makes it quite a strong cheese.

Bagration

The name given to various dishes inspired by recipes dedicated by Carême to Princess Bagration, whose service he entered on his return from Russia in August, 1819. These recipes often include macaroni (to accompany meat soups, salad, and stuffed eggs), Russian salad (to accompany crayfish and fillet of sole), creamed chicken, or salpicon of truffles and pickled ox (beef) tongue, but the garnishes have changed and are now more simple than in the original recipes.

Bagration meat soup POTAGE BAGRATION AU GRAS Sauté 500 g (1 lb) diced lean veal in butter to seal in the meat juices. Add to 1 litre (1¾ pints, 4½ cups) velouté soup and simmer for 1 hour. Strain the veal, chop it finely, and return to the velouté. Stir in 3 egg yolks mixed with 1 dl (4 fl oz, 5 tablespoons) cream to bind the soup. Adjust seasoning. Stir in approximately 50–60 g (2 oz, 4 tablespoons) butter and hot chopped macaroni. Serve with grated cheese.

Baguette de Thiérache

A cheese made from cows' milk (45% fat content), sold in blocks weighing approximately 500 g (1 lb). Soft and fragrant, with a very definite flavour and a smooth shiny reddish-brown crust, it compares with Maroille cheeses. Created after World War II, the Baguette de Thiérache, or Baguette laonnaise, although manufactured commercially, is at its best from the end of June to the end of March. A half Baguette, weighing 250 g (½ lb), is also produced.

bahut

A deep cylindrical container with two handles. Of variable size, it has no lid and is made of tin, stainless steel, or aluminium (enamelled plate is to be avoided).

This catering vessel is designed for storing cooked food, sauces, creams, or anything that needs keeping.

bain-marie

A utensil used for keeping sauces, soups, or mixtures warm so that they can be used later, for melting ingredients without burning them, or for cooling dishes very slowly.

Bain-marie was originally a term used in alchemy. It was then referred to as *bain de Marie* (Mary's bath) after Moses's sister, who was known to be an alchemist. It was also considered to refer to the Virgin Mary, the symbol of gentleness, since the term implies the gentleness of this method of cooking.

A soup bain-marie is used in catering for keeping sauces and creams warm. It is cylindrical in shape, with a handle and a lid, and is placed in a shallow rectangular bain-marie dish, large enough to hold about ten such containers. The sauce bain-marie is the same shape but smaller. A special double saucepan (double boiler) is used for cooking sauces in this way. This pan is in two parts which slot one inside the other (the lower part contains hot water). In domestic cookery, a gratin dish or baking pan containing water is often used as a bain-marie for cooking pâté, vegetable loaves, fish loaves, chicken-liver mousse, baked eggs, ramekins, flans, etc., either on top of the stove or in the oven. Whichever method is used, the water must not be allowed to boil in case water in the form of condensation gets into the preparation.

Many self-service cafeterias and large restaurants have heated vats arranged according to the bain-marie principle. Prepared dishes are kept hot in these containers ready for serving.

baiser (kiss)

A petit-four consisting of two small meringues, joined together with thick cream, butter cream, or ice cream.

bake blind (blind-bake)

CUIRE À BLANC

To cook an empty pastry flan case (pie shell) before filling it with a liquid or creamy mixture, which would otherwise soak the bottom, or with delicate fruit that does not need to be cooked.

RECIPE

Flan case (pie shell) baked blind CUISSON À BLANC D'UN FOND DE TARTE Prepare the pastry (dough), roll it into a ball, and leave it to rest for at least 2 hours in a cool place – it can be left to rest for up to 24 hours. Roll out the pastry and line a greased and floured flan tin or dish. (To flour, pour a little sieved flour into the buttered dish and turn it so that a very thin even film of flour sticks to the butter. Then shake the dish to remove the excess flour.) Press the pastry into the dish so it fits well, and prick the base in several places with a fork. Cover the bottom with a piece of cooking foil or greaseproof (waxed) paper and pour a layer of dried beans onto the paper. Bake for about 12 minutes in a moderately hot oven (200 c, 400 f, gas 6) until the pastry is partially cooked, but not coloured: it should look dry and have lost its shiny appearance. Remove the dried beans and the paper, then bake the pastry for a further 5 minutes or until cooked and golden brown. The case is now ready for filling.

baked Alaska

OMELETTE NORVÉGIENNE

The novelty of this dessert lies in the contrast between the ice cream inside and the very hot meringue surrounding it. The classic baked Alaska consists of a base of Genoese sponge soaked in liqueur on which is placed a block of fruit or vanilla ice cream, the whole thing being masked with plain or Italian meringue. This is cooked in a hot oven for a very short time so that the meringue is coloured but the ice cream is not melted. It is served immediately, sometimes flamed.

The original recipe is said to have been perfected, or rather brought back into fashion, at the Hôtel de Paris in Monte Carlo, by the chef Jean Giroix. An American doctor called Rumford is credited with the invention of this dessert, which is based on the principle that beaten egg white is a poor conductor of heat. However, according to Baron Brisse, in his cookery column in *La Liberté* (6 June 1866), a chef to a Chinese delegation visiting Paris introduced this dessert to the French:

'During the stay of the Chinese delegation in Paris, the chefs of the Celestial Empire exchanged courtesies and recipes with the chefs at the Grand Hotel. The French dessert chef was delighted at this opportunity: his Chinese colleague taught him the art of cooking vanilla and ginger ices in the oven. This is how the delicate operation is performed: very firm ice cream is enveloped in an extremely light pastry crust and baked in the oven. The crust insulates the interior and is cooked before the ice can melt. Gourmands can then enjoy the twofold pleasure of biting into a crisp crust and at the same time refreshing the palate with the flavoured ice cream.'

RECIPE

Baked Alaska OMELETTE NORVÉ-GIENNE Prepare some vanilla ice cream using the following method: make a custard from 7–8 egg yolks, 200 g (7 oz, scant cup) caster (superfine) sugar, ¾ litre (1¼ pints, 3 cups) fresh cream, and a vanilla pod (bean) or 1 teaspoon vanilla sugar. Freeze in an ice-cream churn. When the ice cream is fairly hard, pack it into a square cake tin and leave it in the freezer for 1 hour.

Meanwhile, make a sponge by beating 125 g (4 oz, ½ cup) caster sugar with 4 egg yolks until the mixture turns thick and white. Sprinkle on 150 g (5 oz, 1¼ cup) sifted flour, then add 40 g (1½ oz, 3 tablespoons) melted butter and 4 egg whites whisked to stiff peaks with a pinch of salt. Pour the batter into a buttered square cake tin and cook for 35 minutes at 200 c (400 F, gas 6). Turn the sponge out and leave it to cool.

Heat the oven to 250 c (475 F, gas 9). Make a meringue mixture using 4 egg whites, a pinch of salt, and 75 g (3 oz, 6 tablespoons) caster sugar and put the mixture into a large piping (pastry) bag. Split the sponge in two through the middle and arrange the pieces side by side in an ovenproof dish; trim them into a regular oval shape. Sprinkle with ⅓ glass syrup flavoured with Cointreau or Grand Marnier. Unmould the ice cream and mould over the sponge. Mask the sponge and ice cream entirely with half of the meringue, smoothing it with a metal spatula. Use the rest of the meringue to decorate the top with whorls (see illustration on p. 56). Dredge with icing (confectioners') sugar and place in the hot oven until the meringue is coloured. Serve immediately.

Baked Alaska can be flamed when it is taken out of the oven, using the same liqueur that was used to flavour the sponge.

bakery BOULANGERIE

The place where bread is manufactured and sold. In France, bread was baked at home until after World War I, and even today bread-making is still carried out largely in small-scale establishments.

☐ **Pistores and tameliers** Well-organized bakeries were depicted on the frescoes of ancient Egyptian tombs. These establishments produced mainly unleavened girdle cakes but also, for the upper classes, bread leavened with brewer's yeast. Herodotus reported that the Greeks learned the secret of leavened bread from the Egyptians.

In 168 BC, following the victorious campaign against Perseus, King of Macedonia, the bakers who travelled with the Greek army were taken as slaves by the Romans. They were known as *pistores* (grinders) because they ground the corn with a mortar. Even today many Italian bakers have Greek names. In 100 AD, the emperor Trajan created a bakers' guild that was granted many privileges. In this way, he completed the measures taken by his predecessors to ensure that Rome was supplied with food, thus avoiding insurrection. Bread was distributed free to the poorest citizens, numbering about 300,000 to 400,000 people. In the reign of Augustus, there were 326 bakers in Rome catering for a million inhabitants. This led eventually to the nationalization of the bakers, who were paid directly by the state and were not allowed to sell their businesses. The brick ovens that were found in the bakeries among the ruins of Pompeii had flat beds and vaulted roofs and were very similar to those in the French countryside today.

After the Roman conquest and under Roman law, the Gallic bakers were united into organizations, and in this way the oldest food profession was created. As early as the beginning of the Middle Ages, feudal lords raised taxes by making their serfs grind their corn in the baronial mill and bake the dough in the communal oven.

In the 12th century the guild of bakers was established in France: they were known as *tameliers* (sifters) because they had to sift the flour that was delivered to them. There were 62 of them at the time and Philip Augustus granted them the monopoly on the manufacture of bread within the boundaries of Paris. According to the *Livre des métiers* of Étienne Boileau (c. 1268), the *tamelier* bought his entitlement from the king (the Grand Baker). He served an apprenticeship of four years and had to complete various formalities. The master baker had a junior, or first boy, at his command. The guild also provided insurance against illness; every day, the baker delivered one or two loaves to a hospital, and in return was guaranteed free priority hospitalization. The baker who supplied free bread to the executioner placed the bread that was intended for him upside down so that the other customers could be sure that the executioner's hand would not touch any other loaves. This gave rise to the superstition that it is unlucky to place bread upside down. The word *boulanger*, which eventually replaced the word *tamelier*, comes from the Picardy word *boulenc*, meaning 'one who makes round bread'. The quality, weight and price of bread were precisely fixed by royal decree. Any loaf below the prescribed weight was confiscated and distributed to the poor. The *Grand Panetier* judged the misdemeanours.

□ **Royal decrees** Philip the Fair reformed the legislation concerning the bakers so that any fines meted out became proportional to the misdemeanour. He also reduced the bakers' privileges and authorized private individuals to buy grain. In 1366, Charles V introduced regulations concerning the places and times for the sale of bread, as well as the price, which varied according to the type of flour used. In the reign of Charles VI, the rigours of war, the scarcity of cereals, and the uncertainty of payment incited many bakers to destroy their ovens. They were ordered to rebuild them without delay, under the threat of banishment. Charles VII introduced further regulations and imposed limits on the places and times wheat and flour could be bought. In the meantime, it became more and more usual to make bread at home.

In 1569, a strange decree was issued concerning bakers' dress: except on Sundays and statutory nonworking days, journeyman bakers always had to wear a shirt, pants, and cap, but no breeches; thus attired, they could not go out into the street without being identified and were thus obliged to stay at the oven all day. They were also forbidden to 'form groups or monopolies, carry a sword, dagger, or any other offensive weapon'.

The 17th century saw many changes in the Parisian bakery trade. Bread manufacture was improved, flour (without bran) was delivered in larger quantities, the use of brewer's yeast was prohibited, and the number of markets increased. In 1635, Richelieu introduced the following measures: 'Bakers of bread rolls and pastrycooks will not buy grain before eleven o'clock in winter and noon in summer; bakers of large loaves will not buy grain before two o'clock. This will enable the people of the town to obtain their supply first. Bakers shall put a distinctive trademark on their loaves, and keep weights and scales in their shops, under penalty of having their licences removed.' Bakers were also obliged to sell their own bread, and although they could be assisted by their wives and children, they were not allowed to sell it through a third party.

Towards 1710, markets were established in Paris for the sale of bread and they were frequented by 500–600 bakers from Paris and the suburbs. A further thousand came from the surrounding area because the bread they produced was famous – from Gonesse, Corbeil, Chilly, and Saint-Germain-en-Laye. In 1724 there were 1524 bakers, most of whom sold their bread in the Great Hall in the Place Maubert, at the Marché Neuf de la Cité in the Rue Saint-Honoré, and at the market of Marais-du-Temple. Marie de Medici brought in Italian bakers who introduced new products. Gradually, the Parisians became more and more partial to light white bread made with pure wheat flour.

□ **From the Revolution to modern bakery** During the 18th century, methods of wheat cultivation and production made real progress, and the spectre of famine was gradually eradicated. But the far-sighted royal administration accumulated large quantities of grain. When a shortage of food occurred in 1773, the people accused the farmers and merchants of signing a 'pact of famine' in order to speculate on grain. In reality, these preventative purchases were to be resold at the normal price.

In 1774, Turgot decided that there should be free trade in grain throughout the kingdom. Unfortunately, this decision was premature and in the following year there was rioting and pillaging of grain stores. This was called the 'war of famine'.

The day after the storming of the Bastille, the continuing shortage of food exasperated the people: the bakers asked for sentries to protect them and prevent their shops from being sacked. Paris did not have enough bread and, to cries of 'Let's get the baker, the baker's wife, and the baker's assistant', the people, led by the market women, took the road to Versailles. On 2 March 1791, the Constitution did away with guild wardenships and masterships and bakery supposedly became 'free', but was still subject to the regulations of the public authorities. Bakery products continued to evolve: in 1840, Viennese products became popular and many Austrian bakers came to Paris.

Today there are more than 40,000 bakers in France, employing approximately 60,000 people and baking 3 million tons of bread every year. The bakery continues to be one of the essential parts of village life, and bakers still sometimes agree to bake certain slow-cooking dishes, or even roasts and pastries, in their ovens. The craze for the Parisian baguette has resulted in the disappearance of many regional breads and some regional bakeries have now become merely bread shops. Bread is also sold in grocers' shops and supermarkets. Commercial bakeries have been in operation in France since 1959, but these only account for 10% of the total production: most bread-making continues to be carried on in numerous small-scale bakeries.

□ **Bakery equipment** From antiquity to the beginning of the 20th century, the baker's equipment changed very slowly. Roman frescoes show a kneading machine driven by animals and it is known that the workers of this period wore hygienic masks. The mechanical kneader used in modern bakeries dates from 1920. Ovens, formerly heated by burning wood and then coal, are now heated by gas, electricity, or oil. Since the original Roman vault-shaped cooking chamber, the bread oven has seen the introduction of the rotating disc and stacking in layers. The most commonly used oven nowadays rotates internally and contains a vertical trolley which can be removed when the bread is cooked.

There have been many improvements. High-speed kneading machines oxygenate and whiten the bread. Refrigerated fermentation chambers (instead of incubators) mean that the baker can prepare the bread the previous evening because the fermentation process takes longer. However, the high proportion of yeast required does not improve the quality. The latest technological contribution is deep-freezing, which is very commonly practised in the United States.

In addition to various types of bread, local bakers also make pastries and sell confectionery.

baking powder
LEVURE CHIMIQUE

A raising (leavening) agent consisting of bicarbonate of soda and cream of tartar mixed with a flour or starch. Baking powder is commonly used in domestic baking, particularly for cakes.

baking sheet   TÔLE

A tray, with only a very slightly raised edge, on which all kinds of unmoulded pastries, biscuits (cookies), small cakes, tarts, etc., are placed to be baked in the oven. It can be lined with greaseproof (waxed) paper or buttered or floured directly.

baking tin (pan)   PLAQUE

A wide flat cooking utensil that comes in various sizes and depths. The roasting tin (pan), made of aluminium or tinned copper plate, is usually rectangular with two handles and shallow vertical sides; it may be fitted with a grid so that the meat or poultry does not rest in its own cooking juices.

baklava

A cake of Eastern origin consisting of several very thin layers of pastry (made from semolina flour, oil, and eggs) stuffed with chopped grilled almonds, pistachios, and walnuts mixed with sugar and then cut into triangles before baking. When they are taken out of the oven, a honey or sugar syrup flavoured with rose water and lemon juice is poured over the baklavas.

Balkan states

The countries of central Europe, bordered by Austria, Russia, Italy, Greece, and Turkey, have a characteristic national gastronomy, in which soups and stews, cooked meats, ewes'- and cows'-milk cheeses, and strong liqueurs predominate. (Hungary, where the cuisine has a character of its own, is an exception.)

● BULGARIA – The long domination by the Turks left in its wake a taste for mezze, halva, and raki. Yogurt, characteristic of this region, is widely used in such stews as *ghivetch* (meat and vegetables simmered with spices and topped with eggs and yogurt) and with raw vegetable salads such as *tarator* (cucumber with yogurt and chopped nuts). The staple dish is *tchorba*, a soup made with chicken, lamb offal, or tripe, but dried salted meat (*pastirma*), *kebabcha* (sausage kebabs), and flaky pastry filled with cheese or vegetables are also highly appreciated. *Sirene* is a famous ewes'-milk cheese. Good red or white wines, a well-known example of which is Euxinograd, and *slivovica* (plum brandy) are drunk in Bulgaria.

● RUMANIA – The Black Sea and the Danube delta provide a plentiful supply of fish (one of which is sturgeon – hence caviar). But the staple dish is a soup (*ciorba*) made from fish, chicken, or veal. Hors d'oeuvres are very important, particularly aubergine (eggplant) purée with olive oil and lemon, and *mititei* (small grilled sausages); hors d'oeuvres are often served with fermented grape juice. Carp, crayfish, and pike are prepared in the Austrian style, but stuffed braised cabbage leaves or vine leaves are cooked in the same way as they are in Greece. Rumania produces several ewes'-milk cheeses (e.g. *brandza* and *kaskaval*), some mild and matured with milk, others piquant and matured in pine bark; its cows'-milk cheeses are sometimes eaten with corn broth (*mamaliga*) and prepared in as many different ways as the Italian polenta. Turkish domination left behind it a taste for sweet pastries and rose-petal jam.

● CZECHOSLOVAKIA – Pilsen beer, cooked meats (black puddings and sausages), and Prague ham, together with foie gras, are the best-known ambassadors of Czech gastronomy. The influence of Russian and Polish cuisine is also apparent (calves' lights (lungs) soup, fillets of carp with mushrooms), but the national dish is *hovasy maso* – boiled beef served with very spicy sauces. Poultry (particularly goose) and game are served with *brambory* (potatoes) and sauerkraut. They are followed by pastries inspired by Austrian cookery. The Czechs are very fond of plum dumplings, sweet omelettes, and *livances* (pancakes with jam).

● YUGOSLAVIA – There are as many culinary traditions as there are races in this country of contrasts, but the common factor is once again a thick soup (*corba*) made with vegetables and meat or fish. Pig's trotters (feet) in aspic and Dalmatian smoked ham are traditional hors d'oeuvres, often served in the Italian way. In Croatia, where the Austrian influence is again strong, schintzels are eaten and also plenty of fish and shellfish. Paprika is produced close to the Hungarian border and is used to season sauces for stews and onion fondues served with meatballs and kebabs. In Bosnia and Montenegro, the Turkish and Greek influence is evident in pilaf, stuffed cabbage leaves, moussaka (prepared with chicken or veal), and oriental pastries. There are several famous cheeses, and the wines (Marastina and Ljutomer and red Blatina), plum or juniper brandies, and the famous Zara Maraschino are also worthy of note.

ballottine

A hot or cold dish based on meat, poultry, game birds, or fish in aspic. The flesh is boned, stuffed, rolled, and tied up with string, usually wrapped in muslin (cheesecloth) – sometimes in the skin – then braised or poached (see *galantine*).

RECIPES

Ballottine of chicken in aspic BALLOTTINE DE POULARDE À LA GELÉE
Bone a 2.5 kg (5½ lb) chicken as in the recipe for braised ballottine of chicken. Dice the flesh from the chicken together with 150 g (5 oz) cooked ham, 150 g (5 oz) pickled tongue, and 150 g (5 oz, 7

slices) bacon. Combine this meat with 250 g (8 oz) sausagemeat, 250 g (8 oz) lean minced veal, 2 eggs, 1 dl (6 tablespoons, scant ½ cup) Cognac, 150 g (5 oz) truffles or pistachios, a generous pinch of mixed spice, and salt and pepper. Knead the mixture well with wet hands. Shape the stuffing into an oblong, place on the boned chicken, and shape the ballottine by drawing the skin all round the stuffing. Rinse and squeeze out a piece of muslin (cheesecloth) and roll up the ballottine tightly in it. Tie with string at both ends, slightly compressing the ballottine, then tie in the middle and between middle and each end.

Prepare a jelly (aspic) stock using 2 calf's feet, 300 g (11 oz) pork rind, 750 g (1¾ lb) buckle of veal, 2 carrots, 1 onion, 2 leeks (white part only), a bouquet garni, about 3.5 litres (6 pints, 4 quarts) chicken stock (or water), and 4 dl (14 fl oz, 1¾ cups) Madeira, adding the chicken carcass and giblets (except the liver) and other giblets if desired. Simmer the ballottine gently in the prepared stock for 1¾ hours. Remove from the stock and allow to cool. Unwrap. Rinse the muslin (cheesecloth) in warm water, squeeze out thoroughly, and wrap up the ballottine again. Tie up and allow to cool for 12 hours under a weight. Clarify the stock, adding gelatine as necessary, and coat the cold ballottine with the half-set aspic, then chill and serve when completely cold.

Ballottine of lamb in aspic BALLOTTINE D'AGNEAU À LA GELÉE Make a galantine stuffing mixture consisting of a salpicon of pickled tongue, ham, and stoned (pitted) black olives. Spread this mixture on a boned flattened shoulder of lamb, roll it up, wrap it in muslin (cheesecloth), and tie with string. Cook the lamb in a casserole on a bed of vegetables with bacon and stock for about 1¾ hours, as in the recipe for braised ballottine of lamb. Drain and unwrap the ballottine (straining and reserving the liquor), squeeze out the muslin (cheesecloth), and use it to wrap up the ballottine again. Tie at both ends and in the middle and allow to cool for 12 hours under a weight. Unwrap and place in an earthenware dish; warm the liquor and pour it over the ballottine,

adding more warmed jellied stock, if necessary, to cover. Refrigerate for at least 24 hours until firmly set before serving.

Ballottine of pork BALLOTTINE DE PORC Prepare a boned shoulder of pork in the same way as for braised ballottine of lamb.

Ballottine of veal BALLOTTINE DE VEAU Prepare using boned shoulder or breast of veal, in the same way as ballottine of lamb.

Balthazar

This word is used to describe both a magnificent feast and, since 1800, a large bottle of champagne. In both cases it refers to an episode in the Old Testament in which Balthazar, the last king of Babylon, offers a sumptuous banquet to a thousand of his dignitaries. During the banquet he has the wine served in sacred vases which his father, Nebuchadnezzar, has stolen from the Temple in Jerusalem. That same night the sacrilege is punished by the hand of God.

The word Balthazar has an ironic meaning when applied to a banquet. However, it still remains the technical name for a bottle of champagne containing the equivalent of 16 ordinary bottles. The next size up, containing 20 bottles, is known as a Nebuchadnezzar.

Balzac (Honoré de)

French author (born Tours, 1799; died Paris, 1850). During his creative periods Balzac, the author of *La Comédie humaine*, shut himself away, drinking too much coffee and eating only eggs and fruit. When he re-emerged however, he displayed a gargantuan appetite. At the Véry restaurant, he was seen to devour 'a hundred Ostend oysters, twelve cutlets of salt-meadow mutton, a duck with turnips, two partridges and a Normandy sole', followed by desserts, fruit, coffee, and liqueurs.

Balzac has created a number of gourmets in his novels, such as Cousin Pons, who loved *escargots au gratin* and *boeuf miroton*, Père Rouget (from *La Rabouilleuse*), who considered that an omelette was more delicate when the whites and the yolks were beaten separately, and the Vidame de Pamiers (from

Le Cabinet des antiques), who decreed that for a dinner party to be successful no more than six guests must be present.

The author often used famous restaurants of the Paris of the 1830s as his setting and described their specialities in his books: turbot with oysters from the Rocher de Cancale, cutlets Soubise from the Café de Paris, cod in garlic from the Frères Provençaux, and grilled meats from the Café Anglais, where Rastignac gave a princely welcome to Delphine de Nucingen. However, provincial cooking was often more highly esteemed by Balzac because dishes were 'more studied and better thought out'. Angevin potted meat (*Le Lys dans la vallée*), cling peach jam (*Eugénie Grandet*), and Isoudun marzipan (*La Rabouilleuse*) were considered worthy of his praise.

Balzac also edited a collection of gastronomic texts (*Le Gastronome français ou l'Art de bien vivre*, 1828), for which he wrote an unsigned preface, and published the *Physiologie gastronomique* in 1830. He also published a study of contemporary stimulants (1838) and wrote a treatise on the same subject as an appendix to the new edition (1839) of the *Physiologie du goût* by Brillat-Savarin.

bamboche (en)

The term applied to a preparation of fried cod, sometimes served with fried eggs. The word is derived from the Italian *bamboccio*, meaning jumping jack, perhaps fancifully referring to the way the pieces of cod jump around in the hot fat.

RECIPE

Salt cod en bamboche MORUE EN BAMBOCHE Soak the fish to remove the salt and cut into thick slices the size of fillets of sole. Moisten with milk, dust with flour, and plunge into boiling fat. Drain, pat dry, and arrange on a bed of assorted vegetables mixed with butter or cream.

bamboo BAMBOU

A plant common throughout tropical Asia, whose young, tender, and slightly crunchy shoots are served as a vegetable. The Japanese also enjoy bamboo seeds, which have a slightly floury texture, and in Vietnam and China food is steamed in bamboo leaves. In Cambodia, the bamboo canes themselves are used for cooking minced meat in.

Bamboo shoots, ivory white in colour, are conical in shape, averaging 7 cm (2½ in) in diameter at the base and 10 cm (4 in) in length. When fresh, the fine needle-sharp hairs which cover them must be removed before use. In Europe, they are only found dried or preserved in brine or vinegar (under their Japanese name of *taknoko* or their Chinese name of *sun ki*). They contain a good deal of water and have a low calorific value, but they are quite rich in vitamin B and phosphorus.

Popular throughout China and the whole of tropical Asia, bamboo shoots cut into strips or sticks are an ingredient of many soups and hors d'oeuvres. Sliced and boiled, sautéed, or braised, they are served as an accompaniment to meat and fish. In China they are used as a seasoning: the shoots are salted, dried in the sun, and macerated in sweet wine, with star anise and rose petals. In Japan bamboo shoots are the basic springtime vegetable, indispensable for the preparation of *sukiyaki*. They are used in family stews and in the delicate dishes of the tea ceremony all year round.

Once opened, preserved bamboo shoots may be kept for several days in the refrigerator in a closed container filled with water.

RECIPE

Chicken with bamboo shoots POULET AUX POUSSES DE BAMBOU Place a chicken in a large pan and cover with water. Bring to the boil. Immediately remove the chicken and drain, keeping the stock. Cool by standing container of stock in cold water. Skim the stock, replace the chicken, and bring back to the boil. Add 5 or 6 black Chinese mushrooms, 1 or 2 scented Chinese mushrooms, 6 tablespoons (4 fl oz, ½ cup) soy sauce, 3 tablespoons sugar, salt, and pepper and continue cooking. After 1 hour, drain 225 g (8 oz) preserved bamboo shoots, rinse in a colander with cold water, then cut into thick sticks, add to the pan, and simmer gently for another hour. Drain the chicken, remove the skin, and cut all the meat into thin strips. Arrange the chicken on a serving dish and surround with the mushrooms and bamboo shoots. Just before serving, trim 3 or 4 spring onions (scallions) and fry quickly in oil. Add 2 tablespoons (3 tablespoons) soy sauce and use to garnish the dish. The stock, highly seasoned with pepper and containing Chinese vermicelli, can be served at the end of the meal.

banana BANANE

The fruit of the banana tree, a long-leaved plant originating in India and cultivated in tropical regions (West Indies, Africa, and South America). Each plant bears clusters of 50–200 fruits with sweet, white, floury, and fleshy pulp.

There are two major kinds of banana: fruit bananas, which are eaten cooked or raw, and plantain bananas, which are cooked as vegetables.

☐ **Fruit bananas** According to an Indian legend, where Paradise is on the island of Sri Lanka, the banana was the forbidden fruit and Adam and Eve, banished from the Garden of Eden, covered their bodies with banana leaves. Because Europeans first called bananas figs, this explains the ancient names of 'Adam's fig' and 'Paradise banana'. Still rare in the Renaissance, bananas, introduced to France by the Portuguese, became common from the 18th century onwards.

Indigenous varieties bear a short roundish fruit with a purplish red skin and highly scented flesh. Bananas cultivated for export (*poyo, gros Michel*, Cavendish, *grande naine*) are long with brown-stained yellow skin; they are harvested green, shipped in banana boats at a temperature of about 13 c (55 f), and stored in a humid environment where they ripen at a temperature between 16.5 c and 20 c (59–68 f).

Very nourishing, with a high energy value (99 Cal per 100 g) and in potassium, vitamins A, C, and K, and starch, raw bananas are an ideal food for growing children. Cooking them brings out their full flavour, and when combined with sugar, butter, or alcohol, they make a delicious, if heavy, dessert.

Bananas also contain pectins, which contribute to the smoothness of the flesh, and malic acid, which makes them refreshing when eaten raw. Well protected by their thick skin, they continue to ripen after purchase and can be kept for several days (they should not, however, be put in the refrigerator because they turn black at very low temperatures). Whatever the method of preparation, the skin is generally removed, as are the white threads which cling to the flesh. As well as the many sweet dishes (poached, sautéed, flambéed, fritters, fruit salads, sweet omelettes, ice cream, flans, purées, etc.), bananas can also be served as a cooked vegetable to accompany West Indian dishes.

In South America and the Far East, curled banana leaves are used to steam or wrap food (rice, minced meat, etc.). Dried bananas have an even higher energy value than fresh bananas (285 Cal per 100 g) and are therefore often eaten by sportsmen, but can also be used in dried fruit salads or stews.

☐ **Plantain bananas** With its green skin and fairly firm pink flesh, the plantain banana is usually flatter and longer than the fruit banana and contains more starch and less sugar. Cooking time varies according to the variety and state of maturity, but they are usually cooked in salted water for 15–45 minutes. Fried, mashed, or used in stews, plantain bananas are served as an accompaniment to many West Indian, South American, or African dishes.

RECIPE

SAVOURY BANANA RECIPE

Mixed salad with banana SALADE COMPOSÉE À LA BANANE Liquidize the flesh of 4 large tomatoes with 2 tablespoons (3 tablespoons) lemon juice, 150 ml (5 fl oz, ⅔ cup) natural yogurt, salt, pepper, and a pinch of cayenne. Add 1 tablespoon chopped fresh herbs (chives, chervil, and parsley, or parsley and mint). Finely chop a few sticks of celery. Cut 6 small round tomatoes into 6 and remove the seeds. Peel 2 large firm bananas, slice, and sprinkle with lemon juice. Arrange the celery, tomato, and banana pieces in concentric circles in a salad bowl and cover with the sauce. Sprinkle with chopped chives or mint.

SWEET BANANA RECIPES

Bananas à la créole au gratin BANANES À LA CRÉOLE GRATINÉES Select firm bananas and peel off a wide strip of skin from each. Remove the flesh in one piece, without crushing and sprinkle with lemon juice. Blanch the skins for 2 minutes in boiling water, cool by dipping in cold water, and pat dry. Slice the flesh and soak for 30 minutes in lemon juice, sugar, and rum. Put a layer of cooked rice pudding mixed with finely chopped crystallized (candied) fruit into each skin. Arrange the banana slices vertically on top and cover with finely crushed macaroons. Coat with melted butter and place under a hot grill.

They can be served with a rum-flavoured apricot sauce.

Bananas flambé BANANES FLAMBÉES Peel some firm bananas and remove the threads. Cook in butter or a vanilla-flavoured sugar syrup, without allowing them to become soft. Drain. Warm some rum, Calvados, Armagnac, or Cognac and pour over the bananas. Set alight immediately before serving.

banana split

An ice-cream dish created in the United States, the main ingredient of which is a banana split in two lengthwise. This is topped with three balls of ice cream (of the same or different flavours: vanilla, chocolate, and strawberry), coated with chocolate sauce and decorated with whipped cream and glacé (maschino) cherries. The melted chocolate may be replaced by strawberry sauce. An alternative decoration is sliced almonds or chopped walnuts, with a meringue shell on either side.

bandège

A large display unit made of lacquered wood, with two lipped trays, with or without feet. Bandèges, imported from the East and India, were used to show off gold or porcelain ornaments or to serve refreshments. They were fashion-

able in the reign of Louis XIV, who was presented with one by the King of Siam (Thailand).

Ban des Vendanges

In medieval times, the proclamation of the date when the picking of grapes for the wine harvest could begin. The date depended on the condition of the grapes and certain local traditions; for example, the 'Hundred days after the flowering of the lilies' in Burgundy or the flowering of the vine anywhere else. The Ban des Vendanges might be subject to the control of the overlord or vineyard owner – in feudal times there were equally strict dates when pruning, sowing, and so on might start – and prevented anyone from making wine from grapes not fully ripe. Today, some of the wine fraternities still proclaim the Ban des Vendanges, holding reunions and ceremonies, such as that of the Jurade de Saint-Émilion, second oldest of all the wine orders, when the vintage is announced from the top of the Tour du Roi. Elsewhere the occasion is similarly just a ceremony – except in Alsace, where even today no one can begin to pick until the Ban des Vendanges is officially announced.

Bandol

An AOC wine produced in the wine-growing region of Bandol, a small Provençal port between Toulon and La Ciotat. The vines are cultivated in terraces (Provençal: *restanques*) on arid sandy limestone soil. The varieties grown for red and rosé wines are mostly Mourvèdre (50% at least since 1980), Cinsault and Grenache. Other varieties cannot exceed 20% of the entire crop. The main varieties grown for white wine are: Clairette, Ugni Blanc, and Bourboulenc. A subsidiary variety is Sauvignon, which does not exceed 40% of the crop.

Red wines of this region are rare but it is to these that Bandol owes its reputation. Clean, solid, generous, and harmonious, they have a good dark-red colour. They are a little rough when young, but mellow during the compulsory 18-month (at least) aging period and become remarkably velvety thanks to the Mourvèdre grape. The white and rosé wines are fresh and versatile with a pleasant bouquet and are best drunk fairly young.

Banon

A cheese bearing the name of a village in Haute Provence. Made from cows', goats', or ewes' milk (45% fat content), it has a soft texture, a natural crust, and is a squat round shape (7–8 cm (3 in) in diameter and 3 cm (1½ in) thick). It is presented wrapped in chestnut leaves steeped in brandy and tied up with raffia. With its sweet or nutty flavour, Banon is very good from May to November. It is sometimes scented with springs of savory and is then known as 'Banon au pèbre d'aï', *pèbre d'aï* being the Provençal name for savory.

banquet

An ostentatious or formal meal for a large number of guests, either for a festival or to mark the occasion of a political or social event. In view of the large amount of food to be prepared and served, banquets are rarely of great gastronomic quality, but their purpose is rather to unite people than to feed them lavishly. The word, which dates from the 14th century, comes from the Italian *banchetto*, meaning a small bench on which the guests used to sit.

□ **Sacred right and civic function** Since the earliest times the idea of the communal meal has been associated with a magical rite. Every man had to gain the favour of the mysterious forces of nature to be lucky in the chase; by eating the animal he had killed with his companions, he regenerated his mental and physical strength. Greek sacrifices were followed by a banquet: the meat was roasted, distributed amongst the participants and eaten close to the altar. This was one of the rare occasions on which citizens ate meat (especially beef). In this way, the banquet was a very important act of communion, as it was for the early Christians in their love feasts. There were also banquets in ancient Greece where the main purpose was conversation, philosophical debate, games, and song. Plato describes one of these in *The Banquet*.

The Greeks also held civic banquets to commemorate the Elders. These ceremonial 'city meals' took place within the Prytaneum and were attended by chosen citizens dressed in white and wearing a crown of flowers. They even became obligatory in Sparta. This tradition was revived during the French Revolution with 'Lacedaemonian Tables' for the nation 'to hold its great banquet' in the hope of seeing rich and poor united in joyful public reunions 'drinking toasts to the sound of all the bells'. But these convivial meals were short-lived.

□ **Private and public celebrations** With the Romans, the banquet became an occasion for ostentatious luxury with great attention to the setting, regardless of whether the occasion was public or private. From the time of Charlemagne, custom required that vassals offered a banquet to their lords at least once a year. Pomp and circumstance were the order of the day. Table settings, ever richer, were part of the sumptuous ostentation. Banquets were organized whenever an occasion brought the people and their sovereign together. In February 1548, Swiss ambassadors visiting Fontainebleau for the baptism of Claude, seventh child of Henry II and Catherine de Medici, were invited to an 'historical' banquet. As this was during Lent, fish was served instead of meat and included lamprey, turtle, trout, char, anchovy, herring, snails, frog pâté, carp, and eels. In 1571, the City of Paris celebrated the arrival of Elizabeth of Austria in the capital with a sumptuous banquet which included whale on the menu.

□ **Power and politics** Banquets inevitably became more numerous when used as the tool of political ambition. When Louis XIV entertained hundreds of courtesans in the gardens of Versailles, he sought to demonstrate his power by the splendour of the reception and Talleyrand, who used culinary art in the service of diplomacy, said to Louis XVIII: 'Sire, I have greater need of cooking pots than of instructions.'

The banquet was also an instrument of internal politics. Under Louis-Philippe, minister Guizot removed the right to hold public meetings for political purposes, so voters met at banquets where they discussed politics under the guidance of famous men such as Lamartine and Ledru-Rollin. Guizot eventually prohibited these banquets, but he was too late. It is reported that the king delcared confidently that 'the Parisians will never trade a throne for a banquet'.

□ **The biggest banquet in the world** On 14 July 1889, Gambetta assembled all the mayors of France at the Palace of Industry in Paris to celebrate the centenary of the storming of the Bastille. Eleven years later, the idea was repeated by Émile Loubet for the famous 'mayors' banquet' on 22 September 1900. The menu included fillet of beef Bellevue, Rouen duck loaf, chicken from Bresse, and ballottine of pheasant. This menu was designed to revive the republican spirit in the city officials: 22,295 mayors were entertained in the Tuileries Gardens in tents specially erected for the occasion and served by waiters from Porel and Chabot, who covered the seven kilometres of tables on bicycles.

Nowadays banquets are less extravagant. Although still fashionable for heads of state, they hardly ever take place otherwise, except for associations, corporations, and fellowships in banqueting halls rented out by restaurants equipped to provide this kind of service. Social events now tend to be celebrated at luncheons, cocktail parties, and garden parties.

banquière

A rich garnish (hence the name, which means banker) composed of quenelles of chicken, mushrooms, and slivers of truffle, served as an accompaniment to poultry and calves' sweetbreads and used as a filling for pies and vols-au-vent with banquière sauce. The same garnish (without mushrooms) also accompanies tournedos (filet mignons) or sautéed noisettes of lamb arranged on croutons and coated with the pan juices mixed with Madeira and stock.

RECIPE

Banquière sauce SAUCE BANQUIÈRE Add ½ dl (2½ tablespoons, 3½ tablespoons) Madeira to 2 dl (7 fl oz, ¾ cup) suprême sauce. Sieve. Add 2 tablespoons (3 tablespoons) chopped truffle or truffle peelings.

Banyuls

A high-class French vin doux naturel that rivals port. Its name comes from one of the four communes of Roussillon where it is produced (Banyuls, Cerbère, Collioure, and Port-Vendres). The vineyards, where the grape traditionally grown is the Grenache noir, are situated on the dry hillsides where the work of the vine growers is particularly hard. Little arable soil is available and this is washed away each year by torrential rain and must be brought back to the tops of the slopes. This happens in spite of the terraces which have been built in an attempt to control the run-off effect and protect the vines from the icy blast of the north wind.

When Banyuls has been muted to alcohol (by stopping fermentation), it retains the aroma of the grape and some of the sugar. The sugar content varies according to when muting is carried out – the later it occurs, the sweeter the wine. The AOC 'Banyuls' requires that muting take place before the end of the year in which the grapes are harvested and that the wine remain in the cellars until 1 September of the following year. The 'Banyuls grand cru' (vintage Banyuls) must be aged in wooden barrels for at least 30 months before sale. It is classed as *sec* or *brut* (dry) when it contains less than 54 g (2 oz) natural sugar per litre (1¾ pints). The name 'rancio' is given to the vintage when particular aging conditions have given it a mature taste.

bar

A retail outlet for drinks, which are generally consumed standing up (or sitting on a bar stool) in front of a counter fitted with a copper or wooden bar as a foot rest (hence the name). The word appeared in the French language in 1837 and also applies to the counter itself (see also *barman*, *pub*).

The tradition of the American bar began in Paris in about 1910 and developed between the wars with the fashion for cocktails. Some bars frequented by celebrities became famous. This fashion has been in decline since the 1950s.

Some French restaurants, such as the Coupole or the Closerie des Lilas, and some hotels, such as the Crillon or the George V, have bars reserved for their own customers, and these are sometimes used as a background for political, society, or artistic events. Other establishments, opening in the evening and sometimes all night, often with musical entertainment, are simply bars where only alcoholic beverages are consumed. Among the famous bars of Paris are Fouquet's, a meeting place for the world of cinema, the Bar Romain, a favourite haunt of show-business artistes, and the Pont-Royal, a focal point of literary life.

But by far the majority of French bars are *café-bars* or *bars-cafés-tabacs*, which are open all day and serve snacks, as well as alcoholic and nonalcoholic drinks.

Barack Pálinka

An unsweetened apricot brandy produced in Hungary from a distillation of fresh apricots, the best of which come from the orchards of Kecskemet. Barack Pálinka from Austria and Hungary are often sold in long-necked bottles known as *fütyülös*.

baraquilles

Cooked *à l'ancienne*, these were triangular puff pastry cases filled with a salpicon of truffles, foie gras, fillets of game birds, calves' sweetbreads, and mushrooms, mixed together with a Madeira-flavoured allemande sauce and served as hot hors d'oeuvres. They were sometimes deep fried.

barbadine

A climbing plant originally from South America, introduced to the West Indies in the 19th century. Related to the passion-flower, its green ovoid fruits are 25 cm (10 in) long and are used as vegetables. As they ripen they become yellowish, and their whitish tart flesh is then used in the preparation of drinks, jams, and sorbets. The bark is used to make a jelly. When very ripe, the fruit can also be flavoured with Madeira and eaten with a spoon.

Barbaresco

A red Italian wine from Piedmont made from the Nebbiolo grape, but lighter than Betolo. It comes from the communes of Barbaresco and Neive and is characterized by its fine fruity flavour.

barbecue (outdoor grill)

An open-air cooking apparatus, usually charcoal burning, for grilling or spit-roasting meat or fish.

Charcoal cookery is the most ancient of cooking methods. The barbecue method is of American origin, being associated with the legendary conquest of the West. It was subsequently adopted in Europe. The word probably comes from the Haitian *barbacoa*, meaning grill, but some attribute its origin to the French *de la barbe à la queue* (from the beard to the tail), referring to the method of impaling the animal on the roasting spit. There may even be a connection with the French *barbaque*, which comes from the Romanian *berbec*, meaning roast mutton.

Another barbecue tradition, recently imported from Japan, is the *hibachi* or table barbecue. This small round cast-iron hearth is equipped with a grid on which each guest grills (broils) his own kebabs or other items, which have been cut up in advance.

☐ **Equipment** Types of barbecue vary according to whether one has a garden, verandah, or just a table. The most basic consist of a hearth containing charcoal and a grid (rack). The most complex are complete garden cookers with a spit (often electric), removable hood, oven, dripping pan, etc. Camping barbecues are made to fold away and are equipped with a wind break.

The hearth is made either of cast iron (they do not lose their shape but are heavy and breakable) or steel plate (this must be fairly thick), which sometimes tips to a vertical position. The rectangular or circular grid is made of steel and the height is adjustable.

The most commonly used fuel is wood charcoal; there is a special kind of wood charcoal consisting partly of carbon-purified sticks which greatly prolong the intense heat of the charcoal. However, some barbecues operate with lava stones heated by butane gas or even solar energy. There are various accessories which may come in handy: poker, tongs, bellows, oven gloves, long-handled spoon and fork, cutting board, fish slice, etc.

☐ **Cooking methods** Almost anything can be grilled or roasted on a barbecue, with the exception of veal and delicate fish. Aluminium foil also makes it possible to barbecue some vegetables (e.g. potatoes) and even fruit (such as bananas). Corn cobs, peppers, tomatoes, and large mushrooms can be cooked directly on the grid, brushed with oil or melted butter. Cooking begins when the charcoal has reached the glowing ember stage.

● SPIT-ROAST MEAT – Distribute the weight of the meat to be cooked evenly along the length of the spit. If chicken is being cooked, hold the limbs in place with small wooden skewers so that they do not become charred. Initially place the meat close to the embers so that the heat causes a cust to form, sealing in the juices, and then move it further away so that the meat will cook slowly right through.

● GRILLED (BROILED) FISH OR MEAT – Since they are either enclosed in a folding grill rack or cooked directly on the grid, each item must be brushed with oil all over so that it does not stick to the hot metal. Large fish should be gutted (cleaned) and washed, but not scaled (so that the flesh remains tender). Remove the scales and skin together before serving. If cooking a small chicken, split it in two, remove the giblets, flatten, and season. Scampi (jumbo shrimp) and oysters (in their shells) can be placed directly on the grid without further preparation.

● KEBABS – Oil each piece of food before putting the kebabs on the grill. Wrap fragile pieces (such as shellfish) in a thin slice of lean bacon.

Some meats have a better flavour if they have been marinated. Barbecued food can be served with any of the sauces which traditionally accompany grills and fondue bourguignonne (pepper, béarnaise, or tartare).

barbel BARBEAU

A freshwater fish with a brown back, yellowish sides, and white abdomen, characterized by the beardlike projections from its lower jaw: four in the common river barbel (about 50 cm (20 in) long and weighing up to 2 kg (4½ lb)), but only two in the smaller southern barbel. Its flesh is bland and full of bones. In the Loire and Burgundy regions it is served poached or braised and flavoured with red wine and herbs. Young barbel are either fried or grilled (broiled).

Barbera

An Italian grape which has given its name to a red wine produced in large quantities in Piedmont. Barbera is a full-bodied dark wine. It is drunk when young and can produce a second fermentation in the bottle that makes the wine slightly sparkling, which is unusual for a red wine.

barberry ÉPINE-VINETTE

A prickly European shrub that favours dry soil and sunny spots. In October it produces tart bright-red berries, rich in tartaric and malic acids, which are used to make jellies and syrups. Cooked and dried, they can be made into a fine powder, which was formerly used as a seasoning. The unripe green berries can be preserved in vinegar, like capers.

barbouille (en)

Regional name for a preparation of rabbit (Nivernais) or chicken (Berry) casseroled in red wine. The blood of the animal is poured into the dish just before serving, which gives a thick highly coloured sauce that smears (French *barbouille*, hence the name) the lips of the diners.

| RECIPE

Chicken en barbouille POULET EN BARBOUILLE Reserve the blood of a chicken and add a little vinegar to prevent it coagulating (if chicken blood is not available, ask the butcher for some pigs' blood). Cut the chicken into quarters. Brown the pieces in 4 tablespoons oil in a casserole or large saucepan then drain. In the same oil, fry some pieces of fat bacon and small round onions, then drain. Clean some mushrooms, cut into quarters, add to the casserole, and cook rapidly until they stop losing water. Add the bacon and onions, dust with flour, stir, and add 2 dl (7 fl oz, ¾ cup) red wine, salt, and pepper. Bring to the boil, then reduce heat and add a crushed clove of garlic, a bouquet garni, and the chicken pieces. Cover the casserole and simmer gently for 1 hour. Stir a little of the chicken sauce into the blood, pour back into the casserole, and stir to bind. Reheat the sauce, remove the bouquet garni, adjust the seasoning, and serve.

bard BARDE

Thin slices of pork or bacon fat which are placed around joints of meat, some game birds and poultry, and even some fish before roasting, to prevent them from drying out in the heat of the oven. Barding is not advised for some very tender meats as the strong flavour of the bard might overshadow the taste of the meat. Bards are also used as a lining for pâtés cooked in pastry or terrines.

In order to bard a roasting joint, the joint is covered with strips of bard held in place with string. To bard terrines and pâtés, the inside of the pie crust or mould is lined with bards.

The bards are usually removed before serving, but it is usual to serve partridge, other game, and pâtés still barded.

bardatte

A Breton speciality from the region of Nantes, which used to be prepared at harvest time and eaten cold by the peasants in the fields. It consists of a cabbage stuffed with rabbit or hare meat flavoured with herbs, which is wrapped in a thick wide slice of bacon (*barde*, hence its name), put in an earthenware dish, moistened with stock, and baked slowly in the oven. Bardatte was eaten with steamed chestnuts and roast quail.

barigoule (à la)

The term used to describe a particular method of preparing stuffed braised artichokes. *Barigoule* is the Provençal name for the mushroom (genus *Lactarius*) used in the recipe. Originally, the country recipe consisted of cooking the artichokes like mushrooms, i.e. cut off flat at the base, sprinkled with oil, and grilled (broiled). Provençal cooks subsequently developed a stuffing of ham and mushrooms for the artichokes.

RECIPE

Artichokes à la barigoule ARTI-CHAUTS À LA BARIGOULE Prepare the artichokes for stuffing. Clean and chop 80 g (3 oz, 1 cup) mushrooms for each artichoke. Mince 50 g (2 oz, 3 slices) fat bacon and the same quantity of ham. Mix these ingredients together with chopped parsley, salt, and pepper. Fill the artichokes with the mixture, bard, tie up with string, and braise in white wine to which a little olive oil has been added. Thicken the cooking liquor with a very small amount of softened butter.

barley ORGE

The earliest known cereal to be cultivated. Because it is low in gluten it is not usually used to make bread, although in former times barley was mixed with wheat to make a heavy and nourishing bred which kept well. Nowadays (as formerly) it is used mainly as a basic ingredient in malting and beer brewing (the best varieties for brewing are those with a double row of seeds).

Pearl barley is used in cooking; this is grain that has been hulled and milled until it resembles small pearls. It is used chiefly in soups, broths, and stews, such as oxtail soup and Scotch broth.

RECIPE

Consommé with pearl barley CON-SOMMÉ À L'ORGE PERLÉ Wash 100 g (4 oz, ½ cup) pearl barley in warm water and add it, with a stick (stalk) of celery, to 2.5 litres (4½ pints, 11 cups) clarified beef stock. Simmer for 2 hours, then remove the celery and serve the soup in cups.

barley beer CERVOISE

An alcoholic drink that the Gauls made from fermented barley, oats, rye, or sometimes wheat, flavoured with various spices. It was the forerunner of beer, which appeared with the introduction of hops in the 14th century. The French word possibly derives from the Gallic *cerevisia*, a combination of Cerès, Roman goddess of harvests, and the Latin *vis* (strength). Barley beer was originally matured in pottery jars and later in casks. Throughout the Middle Ages, because of privileges granted by Charlemagne, monks were the major producers. In 1268 the *Livre des métiers* laid down regulations for the *cervoisier* (barley-beer maker): 'No one may brew barley beer from anything except water and grain, either barley, wheat and rye mixture, or *dragie* (barley residue)'. The maker was forbidden to add to it 'berries, spiced honey-sweetened wine, or resin'. In present-day Iberian languages, *cerveza* and *cerveja* are words for beer.

barley sugar
SUCRE D'ORGE

An ancient sweet (candy) of cooked sugar, made originally from a mixture of hot sugar syrup and a decoction of barley to colour it.

Back in fashion under the Second Empire because Napoleon III enjoyed it, barley sugar became a speciality of the spa towns of France (Évian, Plombières, Cauterets, and Vichy, in particular). It has been made in the form of small cylindrical sticks (from a ribbon of drawn sugar rolled by hand, then wrapped in coloured cellophane), twisted sticks, and flat tablets, cut out on an oiled baking sheet. Today it is made of cooked sugar without barley, with various flavourings, shaped into a round stick or cut out by a pressing machine.

Two specialities are worth mentioning: Tours barley sugar, flavoured with apple or cherry; and Moret barley sugar, amber-coloured, in the shape of a heart marked with a cross. The latter was created in 1638 by the nuns of the convent of Moretsur-Loing (Seine-et-Marne) and its recipe remains a secret: lost under the Revolution, it was preserved by one of the nuns and later sold to a lay confectioner of the town.

The Nancy bergamot, the Vosges *granit*, and the honey-flavoured pastille of Saint-Benoît-sur-Loire (in the shape of a little monk) are also made of barley sugar.

RECIPE

Old-fashioned barley sugar SUCRE D'ORGE À L'ANCIENNE Gently cook 250 g (9 oz, 1¼ cups) hulled barley in 5 litres (4½ quarts, 5½ quarts) water for 5 hours. Strain this liquid (which resembles white jelly) and return it to the pan. Add 1 kg (2 lb, 4 cups) warmed sugar, stir until dissolved over a gentle heat, then boil the mixture just to the hard crack stage and pour it over an oiled marble slab. As soon as the barley sugar begins to cool, cut it into long strips and twist them.

barman
A specialist in the preparation of cocktails. Normally the barman does not serve drinks (that is the job of the barmaid). He is a professional who, in theory, stays behind the bar and, like the great chefs, gives his name to the new cocktails that he invents. Harry MacElhone, who took over Harry's Bar in Paris in 1913, created (among others) the Bloody Mary in 1921 and the Sidecar in 1931. His son Andy invented the Blue Lagoon in 1972. Famous barmen, who are traditionally known by their first names, have international careers that take them from Rome to London, from Monte Carlo to Biarritz and Paris.

The barman's paraphernalia includes a certain number of essential utensils: a mixing glass, a shaker, a small spoon for measuring spirits, a dropper (for adding a 'dash' of a particular ingredient), a special sieve, a long-handled mixing spoon, nutmeg grater, lemon squeezer, straws, and an ice crusher.

Barolo
An Italian red wine from the hills of Piedmont around the village of Barolo. It is a wine with a fairly high alcoholic content made from the Nebbiolo grape, which is improved by being aged in the barrel before bottling. Dark in colour and reminiscent of some Côtes-du-Rhone, Barolo is a powerful but smooth wine with a burnt aftertaste.

baron
The joint of mutton or lamb that includes the saddle (loins) and both legs. The term was applied originally to beef, but since a baron of beef is so big, it is hardly ever cooked as such. Baron of lamb is oven- or spit-roast, served with vegetables (braised chicory (endives), green beans, flageolets, and potatoes), and moistened with the meat juices; it is

one of the most spectacular joints of French cuisine.

The noble title given to this joint has an historical origin. Henry VIII of England was presented with a spit-roast double sirloin and was so impressed by this magnificent joint that he dubbed it Sir Loin, Baron of Beef. The corresponding joint of mutton was subsequently given the same name.

In 1953, the Académie Française attempted to impose the name *bas-rond*, but because of the protests from butchers and restaurateurs, it was decided that the French would keep to the original English name.

RECIPE

Baron of lamb à la périgourdine
BARON D'AGNEAU À LA PÉRIGOUR-DINE Cook and shell 1 kg (2½ lb) chestnuts. Cover the baron with a light even coat of butter, and season with salt and pepper. Roast in a moderately hot oven (200 c, 400 f, gas 6) for 18–20 minutes per 500 g (1 lb). While the meat is cooking, fry some small tomatoes (preferably in goose fat) and keep warm. Repeat the process with the chestnuts. Arrange the baron on a warm plate surrounded with alternating tomatoés and chestnuts. Deglaze the dripping with boiling water and reduce until richly flavoured. Serve the meat juice in a sauce boat. The baron can also be served with potatoes lightly fried and enriched with truffle peelings.

barquette

A small boat-shaped tart made of short-crust pastry (basic pie dough) or puff pastry, baked blind and then filled with various sweet or savoury ingredients. Sometimes the pastry boats are filled before they are baked. Savoury barquettes are served hot or cold as hors d'oeuvres or entrées. Sweet barquettes, filled with fruit or cream, are served cold.

RECIPE

SAVOURY BARQUETTES

Anchovy barquettes (*hot*) BARQUETTES AUX ANCHOIS (CHAUDES) Remove salt from the anchovy fillets, by soaking them in a little milk. Dice some mushrooms and onions, fry in butter, and bind with a little béchamel sauce. Dice the anchovy fillets and add to the béchamel mixture. Fill cooked barquette cases with this mixture, sprinkle with fried breadcrumbs, and bake for a few minutes in a hot oven (240 c, 475 f, gas 9).

Cheese barquettes (*hot*) BARQUETTES AU FROMAGE (CHAUDES) Finely chop some mushrooms and sauté them. Prepare a béchamel sauce and add some grated Gruyère cheese then the sautéed mushrooms. Fill the cooked barquettes with the mixture, sprinkle with white breadcrumbs and melted butter, then brown under the grill (broiler).

Mushroom barquettes (*hot*) BARQUETTES AUX CHAMPIGNONS (CHAUDES) Prepare some scrambled eggs and a mushroom duxelles. Spread a layer of scrambled eggs and a layer of mushrooms in each cooked barquette. Fry some breadcrumbs and sprinkle over the barquettes. Bake for a few minutes in a moderately hot oven (200 c, 400 f, gas 6) just to warm the barquettes through.

SWEET BARQUETTES

Apricot barquettes BARQUETTES AUX ABRICOTS For about 15 barquettes, prepare a dough using 250 g (8 oz, 2 cups) sieved flour, 5 g (1 teaspoon) salt, 10 g (½ oz, 1 tablespoon) sugar, 1 egg yolk, 125 g (4 oz, ½ cup) butter, and about 1 dl (6 tablespoons, ½ cup) water. Roll out the dough to a thickness of 3–4 mm (⅛ in). Cut with a fluted oval pastry cutter (cookie cutter). Line the moulds with the pastry (dough), prick the bottom of each one, and sprinkle with a little icing sugar (confectioners' sugar). Remove the stones from the apricots and cut each one into four. Lay the apricot quarters lengthwise in the pastry boats, skin-side down. Bake in a moderate oven (200 c, 400 f, gas 6 (for about 20 minutes. Turn out and allow to cool on a cooling tray. Coat each barquette with sieved apricot jam and decorate with 2 blanched almonds. Puff pastry can also be used. Alternatively the pastry boats may be baked blind, filled with crème au beurre (see *creams and custards*) and topped with apricots cooked in syrup.

Barsac

A white Bordeaux wine, very similar to Sauternes, although a little less sweet and slightly more fruity. Its name comes from the commune of Sauternes from which it originates and which also produces Sauternes. Both wines receive the same care and are of equivalent quality. Nine chateaux, officially classified in 1855, produce wine with the Barsac AOC: Clemens and Coutet (first growth) and Broustet, Caillou, Doisy-Daëne, Doisy-Védrines, Myrat, Nairac, and Suau (second growth).

basella   BASELLE

A tropical climbing plant, also known as vine spinach, capable of acclimatizing to sunny regions. The stem, which can grow as high as 2 m (7 ft), bears leaves which are harvested as the plant grows and are eaten like spinach. In the West Indies, basella is prepared like brèdes.

basil   BASILIC

An aromatic plant, originating in India, whose name is derived from Greek *basilikos*, meaning royal; only the sovereign (*basileus*) was allowed to cut it. Sweet basil is now widely grown as a pot herb. The leaves, which have a strong flavour of lemon and jasmine, are much used for flavouring in the cuisines of southern France and Italy. Some of the aroma is lost in drying, but the leaves can be successfully preserved in olive oil. Basil is particularly favoured with tomatoes but can also be used to flavour salads, stuffings, sauces, and omelettes as well as soups (see *pistou*) and pasta dishes.

basin   BASSIN

Originally, a basin was a wide deep circular container made of copper or tin, which was used to collect the water poured over the hands during table ablutions. These gradually became richly worked gold pieces used more as ornaments on sideboards and dressers. From the 17th century onwards pottery basins were used in France either for ablutions or, more commonly, for serving meat or fruit. Some reached such dimensions that it required two men to carry them. They disappeared as serving dishes in the 18th century and were replaced by smaller basins or dishes.

basket   PANIER

A container with a handle, used for carrying or storing provisions or for preparing various foods. Baskets made of wicker-work, willow, or woven rushes are intended for fruit and vegetables or shell-fish. The bottle basket is a rack with compartments, made of metal or plastic, used for carrying bottles upright. The wire frying basket is an accessory of the deep frying pan or of the electric deep-fryer. The cylindrical wire vegetable basket is used in restaurants for boiling vegetables and removing them from the water without damaging them. The wire nest basket is a double basket on a handle used for making fried potato nests. The salad basket, made of wire or plastic, is used for shaking a green salad after it has been washed (a centrifugal salad-dryer is now usually used for this).

basquaise (à la)

The term used to describe several recipes (particularly for omelettes and sautéed chicken) using tomatoes, sweet peppers, garlic, and often Bayonne ham. A basquaise garnish, for large cuts of meat, consists of Bayonne ham with cep mushrooms and Anna potatoes.

RECIPE

Stuffed potatoes à la basquaise POM-MES DE TERRE FARCIES À LA BAS-QUAISE   Prepare a tomato fondue with garlic. Dice some red and green peppers and fry in oil. Hollow out some large peeled potatoes, place in boiling water for 5 minutes, and wipe dry. Dice some Bayonne ham and mix it with the tomato fondue and peppers. Fill the potatoes with the mixture. Oil a dish, arrange the potatoes in it, and season them with salt and pepper. Sprinkle with oil or melted goose fat. Cover the dish and bake in a moderate oven (about 180 c, 350 f, gas 4)) for 30–40 minutes. When the potatoes are cooked, sprinkle with breadcrumbs and melted fat and brown under the grill (broiler).

bass BAR

A marine fish caught principally in the Mediterranean, also known as sea perch (because of its similarity to the perch) and – around the Provençal coast – as *loup* (wolf), because of its reputed ferocity. It is a voracious predator, 35–80 cm (14–32 in) in length; it is also relatively rare and, therefore, expensive. Valued since Roman times, it has fine, compact, and delicate flesh with few bones. It is served poached, grilled (broiled), braised, stuffed, or flambéed.

The speckled bass, which is smaller and has less flavour, is fished off the coasts of Morocco. The striped bass lives in southern seas.

RECIPE

Preparation of bass PRÉPARATION DU BAR Clean the fish through the gills and through a small incision at the base of the stomach in order to grasp the end of the gut. If the bass is to be braised, fried, or grilled (broiled), remove the scales, working from the tail to the head. Do not remove the scales if it is to be poached because the scales help to hold the fragile flesh intact. Wash and dry the fish. When grilling (broiling), make a few shallow incisions with a sharp knife in the fleshy part of the back.

Bass à la portugaise BAR À LA PORTUGAISE Scale and clean 2 bass each weighing 400 g (14 oz). Make incisions in the back and season with salt and pepper. Butter an ovenproof dish, arrange the bass in the dish, and moisten wth a mixture of equal proportions of dry white wine and fish stock. Bake in the oven for about 15 minutes at 230 C (450 F, gas 8), basting the fish two or three times during cooking. Drain the fish. Pour the liquor into a small pan, reduce, and add butter. Cover the bottom of the cooking dish with tomato fondue, arrange the bass on top, and cover with the sauce. Glaze in a very hot oven and sprinkle with chopped parsley.

Bass braised in red Graves LOUP BRAISÉ AU GRAVES ROUGE (from a recipe by Pierre Laporte) Fillet a 1.5-kg

(3-lb) sea bass. Season with salt and pepper and fry both sides quickly in butter. Drain. In the same butter, fry 100 g (4 oz, 1 cup) thinly sliced mushrooms and 100 g (4 oz, 1 cup) small white onions. Put the fillets back in the frying pan (skillet) on top of the mushrooms and onions. Add ½ bottle red Graves and a little fish stock. Cover with buttered greaseproof (waxed) paper and simmer for 5 minutes over a low heat. Drain the fillets on kitchen paper, remove the skin, and place them in an ovenproof dish. Drain the garnish and arrange it around the fish. Reduce the cooking juices and thicken with butter; just before serving, stir in a little hollandaise sauce, strain, and pour over the fillets. Brown the preparation under the grill (broiler) and garnish it with croutons fried in butter.

Braised bass BAR BRAISÉ Select a bass weighing 1.25 kg (2½ lb). Peel 2 or 3 carrots, 2 onions, and 1 shallot and chop finely. Heat 15 g (½ oz, 1 tablespoon) butter in a frying pan, add the chopped vegetables, and cook until they begin to change colour. Chop a small bunch of parsley and mix with 20 g (¾ oz, 1 tablespoon) butter, salt, and pepper. Stuff the fish with the parsley butter. Spread the partly cooked vegetables in a large buttered ovenproof dish and gently place the fish on top of the vegetables. Add a bouquet garni and 3 dl (½ pint, 1¼ cups) dry white wine. Preheat the oven to about 220 C (425 F, gas 7). Melt 20 g (¾ oz, 1 tablespoon) butter, pour over the bass, then cover the dish and bake for approximately 25 minutes in the hot oven. Drain the fish, arrange on a serving dish, and keep warm. Discard the bouquet garni, sieve the pan juices, and reduce. If desired, add butter to the sauce. Skin the bass and cover in sauce. The braised bass may be served on a bed of mushroom duxelles or sorrel fondue, or surrounded by slices of aubergine (egg-plant) lightly fried in oil.

Escalopes of bass with pepper and cream of ginger ESCALOPES DE LOUP AU POIVRE ET À LA CREME DE GINGEMBRE (from a recipe by Michel Poitou) Prepare the cream of ginger: soften 4 chopped shallots in butter, add

1 dl (6 tablespoons, scant ½ cup) dry white wine and 2 dl (7 fl oz, ¾ cup) fish fumet, and reduce. Add ⅓ litre (11 fl oz, 1⅓ cups) double (heavy) cream and a pinch of salt. Reduce by half, until you have the required consistency. Add 1 tablespoon grated fresh root ginger and allow to simmer for 2 minutes. Strain through muslin (cheesecloth) or a fine strainer. To thicken the sauce, add 80 g (3 oz, 6 tablespoons) butter cut up into small knobs and whisk.

Prepare 400 g (14 oz, 3 cups) well-washed spinach with the stalks removed and braise in butter. Take 4 escalopes (scallops) of sea bass, each weighing 180 g (6 oz), and season with ground white pepper and salt. Fry quickly in oil. Drain them on kitchen paper so as to remove all traces of cooking oil. Make a bed of spinach in the middle of the plates and arrange the sea bass escalopes (scallops) on top. Pour the cream of ginger over them and garnish with sprigs of chervil.

Grilled (broiled) bass   BAR GRILLÉ Scale and clean a bass weighing not more than 1 kg (2¼ lb). Make a few small incisions in the back and brush with seasoned olive oil. Cook gently, preferably using a folding double grill grid to enclose the bass so it can be turned during cooking without breaking. In the south of France, small bass are cooked on charcoal, on top of sprigs of dry fennel, which flavour the fish. Serve with anchovy or garlic butter or one of the special sauces for grilled fish, such as béarnaise or rémoulade.

Hot poached bass   BAR POCHÉ CHAUD   Clean and wash the bass without removing the scales and place in a court-bouillon consisting of cold salted water (10 g (⅓ oz) salt per litre (1¾ pints) water). As soon as the liquid starts to boil, reduce the heat and poach the fish in barely simmering water. Drain the bass, arrange on a dish covered with a napkin (or on a rack), and garnish with fresh parsley. In a separate dish serve melted butter, hollandaise sauce, or any other sauce suitable for poached fish. Serve with boiled or mashed potatoes, spinach, fennel, broccoli, etc.

Basselin (Olivier)

15th-century French poet from Vire, in Normandy. A fuller by trade, he found his inspiration in the bottle. His lively satirical poetry, known as *vaudevire* after his birthplace, is the origin of many table songs. Basselin's *vaudevires* were published at the end of the 17th century. *Vaudevire* gave its name to the type of musical entertainment known as vaudeville.

baste   ARROSER

To lightly moisten a dish cooking in the oven or rotisserie by spooning over melted fat or the cooking juices from the dish itself. This operation is repeated several times and stops the surface of the food from getting too dry. A dish cooked *au gratin* may be basted with melted butter to facilitate browning.

bastella

In Corsican cookery, a turnover stuffed with vegetables and meat. *Bastelle* are called *inarbittate* when they are made with Swiss chard or spinach; *inzuchatte* when made with marrow (squash) or pumpkin, and *incivulate* when they are made with onions. The ingredients are blanched and drained then finely chopped and mixed with pork or veal. *Bastelle* should properly be made with bread dough, but puff pastry is now more commonly used.

bastion

A method of presenting cold food in the shape of a tower (hence its name). Little used today, the bastion was common in the days of Carême, particularly for decorating display tables and sideboards. The most classical was the bastion of eels.

| RECIPE

Bastion of eels   BASTION D'ANGUILLES   Stuff some eels with a forcemeat of pike or whiting, with or without diced truffles. Wrap each one in muslin (cheesecloth) and tie up. Poach in a well-seasoned fish stock made with white wine. Drain, unwrap, and cool under a weight. Cut into 10 cm (4 in) lengths. Coat each section with a previously prepared chaud-froid sauce. Decorate with truffle and hard-boiled (hard-cooked) egg white and glaze with aspic jelly. Use a sharp knife to shape a stale loaf (crust removed) into the form of a cylinder 8–9 cm (3½ in) high. Arrange the sections of eel around the cylinder pressed tightly together. Garnish the edge of the dish with lozenges of aspic jelly. Place in the refrigerator until required for serving. This can be served with Montpellier butter or any other butter preparation.

ba-ta-clan

A cake made from fresh almonds, ground using a pestle and mortar, to which the following ingredients are added: eggs (one at a time), sugar, rum, and flour. The cake is cooked in a flat or fluted mould and coated with vanilla-flavoured fondant icing (confectioners' frosting). Its name derives from the Parisan café-concert famous at the end of the 19th century, but the recipe is attributed to Lacam, a 19th-century pastry chef who wrote treatises on pâtisserie.

bâtarde

A hot sauce, also known as butter sauce, served with vegetables and boiled fish.

RECIPE

Sauce bâtarde   Mix together 25 g (1 oz, 2 tablespoons) melted butter, 25 g (1 oz, 2 tablespoons) flour, and 2.5 dl (scant ½ pint, generous cup) boiling salted water. Beat in 1 egg mixed with 1 tablespoon very cold water and 1 tablespoon lemon juice and then, over a very low heat, add 100 g (4 oz, ½ cup) butter, cut into small pieces. Season with salt and pepper and sieve or strain if necessary

bâtelière (à la)

Describing a fish dish made with poached button mushrooms, small glazed onions, fried eggs, and prawns (shrimp). The name also applies to a preparation of fillets of sole arranged as small boats (hence the name) on a salpicon of prawns (shrimp) and mussels in a white wine and herb sauce. Mackerel *à la bâtelière* is simply grilled (broiled) and served with a separate green sauce.

bâton or bâtonnet

A petit four in the form of a small stick made of puff pastry or almond paste. They are served with desserts and buffets.

Vegetables may be cut *en bâtonnets* (i.e. into thin sticks) for cooking. See *allumette, jardinière, pont-neuf potatoes.*

RECIPE

Almond bâtonnets   BÂTONNETS AUX AMANDES   Pound 250 g (8 oz, 1⅔ cup) blanched almonds with 250 g (8 oz, 1 cup) sugar, or combine in a blender. Bind to a thick paste with 2–3 egg whites and then add 1 dl (6 tablespoons, ½ cup) white rum. Roll out thinly on a floured marble slab or work surface. Cut into strips 8 cm (3½ in) wide and cut these into sticks 2 cm (¾ in) wide. Lightly beat 2 egg whites. Dip the sticks in the egg whites then in granulated sugar. Arrange on a buttered and floured baking sheet, and bake in a moderate oven (approximately 170 C, 325 F, gas 3) until the sugar crisps.

batters

See *doughs and batters.*

Baudelaire (Charles)

French poet (born Paris, 1821; died Paris, 1867). Baudelaire, who loved to play chess at the Café de la Régence and the brasserie in the Rue des Martyrs with his artist and poet friends, sang 'the profound joys of wine' in verse and prose (*Wine and Hashish*, 1851; 'The Soul of Wine', a poem in *Flowers of Evil*, 1857). Although his usual restaurant was Dinochau, he dreamed of a more exotic cuisine rich in truffles and spices, 'pimiento, English powders, saffron, musk and incense' (*Fanfario*, 1847), which was supposed to combine 'the violence of prussic acid with the volatile lightness of ether'.

Baumé scale

DEGRÉ BAUMÉ

An old scale of measurement for the density or specific gravity of sugary liquids, evaluated using a saccharometer. It has been replaced in the measurement of cane and beet sugars by the Brix scale. However, the Baumé scale is still used in the corn-refining industry for measuring the density of sugar syrups derived from cornstarch.

Bavarian cream
BAVAROIS

A cold dessert made from an egg custard stiffened with gelatine, mixed with whipped cream and sometimes fruit purée or other flavours, then set in a mould, It is not known whether there is a connection between this dessert and Bavaria, where many French chefs used their talents at the court of the Wittelsbach princes. Carême gives various recipes under the name of *fromage bavarois* (Bavarian cheese). Many cookery books confuse Bavarian cream with a similar dish, the *moscovite*, which was perhaps invented by a French chef in the service of a great Russian family.

RECIPES

Bavarian cream BAVAROIS À LA CRÈME Chill 3.5 dl (12 fl oz, 1½ cups) double (heavy) cream and 75 ml (3 fl oz, ⅓ cup) milk in the refrigerator. Soak 15–20 g (½–¾ oz, 2–3 envelopes) gelatine in 3 tablespoons cold water. Boil 6 dl (1 pint, 2½ cups) milk and a vanilla pod (vanilla bean). Work 8 egg yolks, 125 g (4 oz, ½ cup) caster (superfine) sugar, and a pinch of salt together, and when the mixture is smooth, blend in the milk (from which the vanilla pod (vanilla bean) has been removed). Then add the gelatine and mix well. Stir continuously over a gentle heat until the mixture coats the back of a spoon. It is important not to allow the mixture to boil. Pour into a bowl and allow to cool, then refrigerate until custard is cold and just beginning to thicken.

Whip together the chilled cream and cold milk. As soon as it begins to thicken, add 50 g (2 oz, 4 tablespoons) caster (superfine) sugar, then add to the cooled mixture. Brush the inside of a Bavarian cream (or soufflé or savarin) mould with oil, preferably almond oil. Fill to the brim with the Bavarian cream mixture. Cover with buttered paper and refrigerate until firmly set. To loosen the cream, dip the bottom of the mould in

hot water, place a serving dish on top of the mould, and quickly turn them over together.

A Bavarian cream may alternatively be flavoured with coffee (add 2 tablespoons instant coffee to the milk instead of the vanilla pod), with chocolate (add 100 g (4 oz) melted cooking chocolate to the milk), with lemon or orange (add the juice of 2 lemons or oranges), with liqueur (add approximately 2 teaspoons), with praline, etc.

Bavarian fruit cream BAVAROIS AUX FRUITS Soak 30 g (1 oz, 4 envelopes) gelatine in 5 tablespoons cold water. Warm 5 dl (¾ pint, 2 cups) heavy sugar syrup (see *sugar*), add the gelatine, and stir to dissolve. Cool slightly, then add the juice of 3 lemons and 5 dl (¾ pint, 2 cups) thick fruit purée (apricot, pineapple, blackcurrant, strawberry, raspberry, etc.) and refrigerate until on the point of setting. Whip 4.25 dl (15 fl oz, 2 cups) double (heavy) cream with 50 g (2 oz, 4 tablespoons) caster (superfine) sugar until softly thick and gently fold into the half-set fruit jelly. Turn the mixture into an oiled mould and refrigerate until firmly set then turn out. It may be served with a fruit sauce (the same as the flavouring used in the cream).

bavaroise

A drink made basically from tea, milk, and alcohol. Popular in Bavaria, it was imported from France by the Bavarian princes at the beginning of the 18th century. In Paris, the famous Café Procope seems to have been the first to serve it.

In the 19th century, *bavaroise au choux* was a French slang name for a mixture of absinthe and orgeat.

RECIPE

Bavaroise Put 1 egg yolk and 1 tablespoon caster (superfine) sugar in a bowl. Whip until the mixture becomes frothy. Add 2 dl (7 fl oz, ¾ cup) very strong tea (or coffee or unsweetened cocoa), 5 teaspoons Kirsch, rum, Maraschino, or other liqueur, and as much boiled milk as required.

bay LAURIER

A Mediterranean evergreen shrub that is widely cultivated in temperate regions for ornament and for its glossy aromatic leaves, which have a slightly bitter smell. Bay leaves are among the most commonly used culinary herbs: a leaf is always incorporated in a bouquet garni. Bay leaves may be used fresh or dried and either whole or powdered, to season stocks, ragouts, stews, pâtés, and terrines.

The bay tree is in fact a species of laurel (*Laurus nobilis*), also known as bay laurel or true laurel. In ancient times it was used to make the laurel wreaths with which poets and victorious soldiers were crowned as a sign of honour. It should not be confused with any of the other trees and shrubs called laurels, such as the cherry laurel, which has white flowers and small red berries and whose leaves contain prussic acid.

bazine

A leavened semolina cooked in boiling water with oil. In Arab countries, this boiled springy dough constitutes the traditional morning meal during Ramadan, served before sunrise. Bazine is served with butter, honey, and lemon juice. This basic preparation is also part of everyday cooking, served in fish soup or with raisins and small pieces of fried meat. It can also be cooked unleavened in chicken stock and served with scrambled eggs or shaped into balls to be cooked in stock.

bean HARICOT

A vegetable of which there are many varieties. They can be divided into two main groups: those with edible pods (green beans) and those of which only the seeds are eaten. The former group includes the French bean (*haricot vert*), called string bean in the United States, and the runner bean. The latter group includes the various types of haricot (navy) bean (described below), the broad bean (fava bean), and the Lima bean.

☐ **French (string) beans** The colour varies in different varieties from pale green or yellow to dark green, sometimes spotted with purple. Grown at first for their seeds, it was not until the end of the 18th century, in Italy, that the whole pods began to be eaten. In France they were still rare and expensive throughout the 19th century: as they were not widely cultivated, they were imported from Spain and Algeria. There are two main varieties of French bean.

Dwarf French beans (*haricots filets* or *haricots aiguilles*) have long thin green pods which are picked while still young, before they become stringy and tough. From November to May, when they are imported into France from Senegal and Kenya, they are expensive and have little flavour. In late autumn and early spring, when they are imported from Spain and Italy, they are cheaper and have a better flavour. But the best flavour of all is found in French-grown varieties, which are in season from May to September. French varieties include the following:

● *Fin de Bagnols* (Roussillon and the Rhône Valley): very thin, straight, and fairly juicy; obtainable from May to late August.

● *Triomphe de Farcy* (Val de Loire and Morhiban): dark green with a delicate flavour; obtainable until September but best in summer.

● *Violet* (Val de Loire): straight, long, very thin, and a mixture of green and purple, with a very good flavour; obtainable until September.

Snap beans (*mange-touts*), which are either green or yellow (*haricots beurre*), are large and plump without being stringy. When harvested young, they are used in the same way as dwarf French beans. The yellow variety is generally juicier than the green; the most successful and popular varities are *Processor*, *Victoire*, *Contender*, and *Rocquencourt*.

French beans are quite digestible but have a low calorific value (39 Cal per 100 g). They contain 7% carbohydrates and are rich in vitamins. Choose beans with a regular shape that are a good green or golden yellow colour and have a sheen. They should be firm and crisp. Snap one in two to make sure there are no strings. If a drop of moisture forms on the break, this shows that they are fresh. French beans must be cooked as soon as possible after gathering or buying. To prepare the beans, top and tail (stem and head) them, remove any strings, and cut very long ones into two. Then wash and drain them. They are always plunged into boiling water and cooked until still slightly crisp before any further preparation is carried out.

Fresh French beans are easily preserved by freezing, drying, or salting. Three-quarters of the French crop is now canned or frozen.

☐ **Haricot beans** The seeds can be eaten fresh or dried, but are always cooked. The haricot bean was introduced into Europe from North America in the 14th century. It may have been Pope Clement VII who brought it to France, for he presented them to his niece, Catherine de' Medici, at her wedding to the future Henri II. Piero Valeriano described them as 'these multicoloured red and white seeds, resembling precious stones that might have been lodged in the earth'. They were first cultivated along the banks of the Loire and spread rapidly to other regions of France. Over the centuries, different varieties appeared. Flageolets, for example, were produced by chance in 1872 by Gabriel Chevrier who lived near Arpajon. (Flageolets are therefore also known as *chevriers* in France.) Modern varieties can be distinguished by their size and colour.

• *Flageolets:* small pale green beans with a low starch content. They are grown in the Arpajon region, in Brittany, and in central France and are harvested in August and September before they have matured. They are seldom sold fresh, usually being dried or canned.

• *Cocos:* large white beans grown in Brittany, in the Vendée, and in southeastern France and harvested from July to October. *Cocos* are often used in ragouts and cassoulets. They are known as *mogettes* in Poitou and the Vendée.

• *Lingots:* large white beans grown in northern France and in the Vendée. When dried, they will keep for a long period.

• *Red (kidney) beans:* traditionally cooked in red wine with bacon. They are not grown much in France but are very popular in the United States, Spain, and the West Indies.

Haricot beans are very nourishing (300 Cal per 100 g). They contain more protein than meat (though not so well balanced) and are also very rich in mineral salts and vitamins.

Haricots are sold either fresh when harvested, or after being dried in the pod for several months. They can be dried in the home provided they are protected against heat and damp. Dried beans are sold ready-shelled and must be soaked for several hours in cold water before use. Whether fresh or dried, the beans are cooked in boiling water with various flavourings. They can be mixed with butter or cream, puréed, cooked as a gratin, or even served cold as a salad with a well-flavoured vinaigrette. In France, however, they are used chiefly as an ingredient of dishes typical of the French countryside (*à la lyonnaise*, *à la bérichonne*, with charcuterie, in thick soups, cassoulets, casseroles, pot-au-feu). They also feature in foreign dishes prepared in Europe, such as chilli con carne and puchero. Flageolet beans are the classic accompaniment to leg of lamb and blade of pork.

RECIPES

FRENCH BEANS

Cooking French beans CUISSON DES HARICOTS VERTS Top and tail (stem and head) the beans, remove strings (if necessary), and wash them. Plunge them into unsalted boiling water and boil rapidly, without covering them. Add salt after cooking for 10 minutes and continue to boil until the beans are cooked. They should retain some crispness and not be too soft. Drain them and complete the preparation. If they are to be used cold, refresh them under running cold water after draining and then drain them again.

French bean salad SALADE DE HARICOTS VERTS Cook the beans just long enough for them to remain slightly crisp. Drain them and dry off any remaining water. Cut them in two and leave them to cool. Add a few chopped spring onions (scallions) and some well-flavoured vinaigrette. Mix and sprinkle with chopped parsley. Alternatively, the beans can be tossed in olive oil, sprinkled with pine kernels, and arranged in a lattice with long strips of marinated red peppers.

French beans sautéed à la provençale HARICOTS VERTS SAUTÉS À LA PROVENÇALE Cook the beans in the usual way and drain them thoroughly. Heat some olive oil in a large saucepan and brown the beans lightly. At the last moment add some chopped garlic and parsley (use 1 clove of garlic and a small bunch of parsley for every 750 g (1¾ lb) beans).

HARICOT BEANS

Cooking haricot beans (white, red or flageolet) CUISSON DES HARICOTS (BLANCS, ROUGES, OU FLAGEOLETS)

■ *Fresh beans:* cook in boiling salted water with a bouquet garni and vegetables to flavour (e.g. carrots, turnips, leeks, diced celery).

Alternatively, cook either 1 onion and 1 carrot (sliced thinly) or the white parts of leeks and some sticks (stalks) of celery (sliced) in butter until soft. Then add sufficient water to amply cover the beans when they are put in, together with a bouquet garni and a 300-g (11-oz) piece of lean green bacon (previously blanched). Cook for 30 minutes, add the beans, and simmer until they and the bacon are cooked (the time required will depend on the freshness and tenderness of the beans).

■ *Dried beans:* these must first be soaked in water for at least 2 hours, preferably overnight. Drain them, and discard the water in which they were soaked. Put them into a large saucepan, cover generously with cold water, bring slowly to the boil, and skim the pan. Add salt and pepper, a bouquet garni, an onion stuck with 2 cloves, a clove of garlic, and 1 scraped diced carrot. Cover the pan and simmer very gently for 1½–2½ hours, taking care that the pan does not boil over. In certain regional dishes, a small piece of fat pork or some bacon rinds, tied together, are added.

haricot bean salad SALADE DE HARICOTS Cook the beans, allow them to cool, and then drain. Add a chopped

mild onion to the beans, mix with a well-flavoured vinaigrette, and sprinkle with chopped herbs (parsley, chervil, chives).

Haricot beans à la lyonnaise HARICOTS À LA LYONNAISE Cook and drain the beans. Cook some sliced onions gently in butter (allow 200 g (7 oz, generous 1½ cups) onions for each kg (2¼ lb, 5 cups) cooked beans). Add the beans, cover the pan, simmer for 6 minutes, and sprinkle with chopped parsley.

Haricot beans in cream HARICOTS À LA CRÈME Cook the beans, drain them, and warm them gently in a saucepan until nearly all the moisture has evaporated. Cover with fresh cream, warm through again, add some chopped savory, and serve very hot.

An alternative method is to butter a gratin dish, pour in the cooked beans mixed with cream, sprinkle the dish with white breadcrumbs and melted butter, and put in a very hot oven until browned.

Red (kidney) beans à la bourguignonne HARICOTS ROUGES À LA BOURGUIGNONNE Cook the beans (fresh or dried) by the second method, using lean bacon, but replace the water with a mixture of half water and half red wine. When they are cooked, drain them, but not too thoroughly, and put them into a sauté pan. Cut the bacon into dice, fry it in butter, and add it to the beans. Finally, mix in a knob of kneaded butter (*beurre manié*) and combine it with the beans.

bear OURS

A large quadruped, once common in Europe but now very rare, even in mountainous areas. In Canada and Russia the bear is still hunted as a game animal. The Gauls enjoyed it stewed, and in North America the fat was valued for cooking. At the beginning of the 19th century, a few Parisian restaurateurs, encouraged by Alexandre Dumas, brought bear back into fashion. Chevet created the speciality of 'bear ham'. The best parts of this animal are its paws. Urbain Dubois suggested a recipe for bear paws marinated and braised with bacon, then grilled (broiled) and served with a highly seasoned sauce. In China bear's palm is listed among the 'eight treasures' of traditional cuisine.

Béarn and the Basque country

BÉARN ET PAYS BASQUE

These two Pyrenean regions occupy a special place in French gastronomy because the cuisine is affected by the proximity of the sea and the mountains and combines the contrasting influences of France and Spain. But from the Atlantic coast to the Pau valley, the same basic recipes recur: vegetable soups, confits, and millas. Oil, garlic, and pimiento often give a southern flavour to dishes from these two regions.

☐ **Henri IV's birthplace** Béarn, where Henri IV of France was born, is the country of poule au pot, which the king wanted to make the Sunday meal of the French. Even more popular than poule au pot, however, is garbure, the most characteristic dish of Béarn cuisine: this vegetable soup is served with *trebucs* (pieces of preserved locally raised goose or pork). There are many variations on these substantial Béarn soups which consist basically of vegetables simmered in goose fat or lard. For instance, cousinat and cousinette use aromatic herbs to enliven the flavour of Swiss chard or carrots, and *ouillat* (known in Bigorre as *toulia*) is a kind of onion soup popular with the Pyrenean shepherds. Game (woodcock, quail, wild duck, and ortolan) and fish (Adour salmon, trout, lamprey, and crayfish) also form an important part of the local cuisine in this mountainous country. Wood pigeon shooting is popular, and a characteristic dish of the southwestern region is pigeon salmis (pigeon in red wine sauce with small onions, mushrooms, and chopped ham).

In the foothills of the Pyrenees, cattle and sheep graze in meadows still full of wild herbs which give a particular flavour to the meat. Generations of gourmets in Béarn and the neighbouring provinces have appreciated leg of lamb and beef stew from animals raised in the Ossau valley or the region of Barèges. Pork and poultry farming in the Béarn also have a good reputation and Oloron confits, hams, sausages, and chitterlings (intestines) are a must, as well as the pâté de foie gras from Orthez. In these mountainous regions, desserts are substantial: after savouring a Pyrenean cheese made from cows' milk or ewes' milk, the meal can be rounded off with a broye, a millas, pastis, galettes stuffed with prunes, or Béarnaise puff pastries made with goose fat.

Béarn vines, planted on the billsides, produce generous and potent wines (see *Béarn wines*).

☐ **The ubiquitous capsicum** All the Basque dishes take their flavour and colour from red or green peppers (capsicums): chicken, cod, rice, and particularly the famous piperade, a mixture of tomatoes and peppers and eggs which goes well with Bayonne ham. The village of Espelette organizes colourful annual festivals when visitors can sample such dishes as elzekaria, *tripotcha* (small sausages seasoned with spicy sauce), hachua, or *merluza salsa verde* (fish covered with a green garnish of peas, asparagus, and parsley), all washed down with Irouléguy, the typical wine of the Basque region. This meal comes to a tasty conclusion with Basque cake, filled with confectioners' custard (pastry cream) or black cherry jam.

The local fish also feature in Basque cuisine. In nearly all the coastal ports, sardines are served, usually fried in oil; tuna, mullet, or cod are prepared *à la basquaise* or flavoured with garlic and peppers, giving a strong flavour reminiscent of nearby Spain. And, as in Spain, squid cooked in their own ink are a favourite. Finally, *ttoro*, the fish soup characteristic of the Basque coast, combines all the Atlantic fish with Dublin Bay prawns (shrimp) and mussels and is flavoured with tomato and peppers.

Special mention must be made of Bayonne, the gastronomic capital of the Basque country, famous throughout the world for its ham, which is used in several preparations *à la bayonnaise*. Bayonne specialities also include *tourons* (nut pastries) and light creamy chocolate, the recipes for which came from Spain in the 16th century.

béarnaise

A hot creamy sauce made from egg yolks and reduced vinegar, beaten together over a low heat and mixed with butter. It is usually served with grilled (broiled) meat or fish. Sauces derived from it (arlésienne, Choron, Foyot, paloise, tyrolienne, Valois) include additional ingredients. A béarnaise sauce which has curdled can be saved by gradually beating in a tablespoon of hot water (if the sauce is cold) or cold water (if the sauce is hot).

The association between the name of this sauce and the birthplace of Henri IV has probably arisen because it was first made by Collinet in the 1830s in a restaurant in Saint-Germain-en-Laye called the Pavillon Henri IV. But a similar recipe appears in *La Cuisine des villes et des campagnes* published in 1818.

Some recipes are called *à la béarnaise* even when they are not accompanied by this sauce. These are dishes directly inspired by the cuisine of Béarn, such as daube, poule au pot, and game confits with cep mushrooms.

RECIPE

Béarnaise sauce   SAUCE BÉARNAISE
Put 1 tablespoon chopped shallots, 2 tablespoons chopped chervil and tarragon, a sprig of thyme, a piece of bay leaf, ½ dl (2½ tablespoons, 3 tablespoons) vinegar, and a little salt and pepper in a pan and then reduce by two-thirds, allow to cool slightly. Cut 125 g (4½ oz, ½ cup) butter into small pieces. Mix 2 egg yolks with 1 tablespoon water, add to the pan, and whisk over a very low heat. As soon as the egg yolks have thickened, add the butter a little at a time, whisking continuously. Adjust the seasoning, adding a dash of cayenne if desired, and a little lemon juice. Add 1 tablespoon each of chopped chervil and tarragon and mix. The sauce can be kept in a warm bain-marie until required, but it must not be reheated once it has cooled.

Béarn wines

VINS DU BÉARN

The vineyards of the region situated in the eastern portion of the Pyrénees-Atlantiques department overflow into the departments of Hautes-Pyrénées (six communes) and Gers (three communes). Since 1975, the three traditional *appellations* (Jurançon and Pacherenc-du-Vic-Bihl representing white wines and Madiran representing red) have been joined by the Béarn AOC. This *appellation*, which previously applied to VDQS wines, now covers very pleasant dry white wines and particularly reds and rosés with a low alcoholic content, popular with both tourists and locals.

beat   BATTRE

To work a substance or mixture energetically to modify its consistency, appearance, or colour. The operation is performed in many ways according to the nature of the ingredients, the utensils used, and the purpose. A variety of mixtures are beaten with a wooden spoon to incorporate air. To give volume to a yeasted dough, it is beaten with the hands either in a bowl or on a worktop. For stiffly beaten egg whites, the whites are beaten in a bowl using a metal whisk, but when eggs are to be used as a binding agent, they are lightly beaten with a fork.

béatilles

An old French term for various small ingredients (such as cocks' combs and kidneys, lambs' sweetbreads, diced foie gras, and mushrooms) bound with cream sauce and used as a filling for vol-au-vent cases or savoury tarts. This dish, which dates from the Renaissance period, was imported from Italy by Catherine de' Medici. The name comes from the Latin *beatus* (blissful), *béatilles* originally being small objects of devotion prepared by nuns.

RECIPE

Ragout of béatilles   RAGOÛT DE BÉATILLES   (from an old recipe) Gently cook 250 g (8 oz, 1 cup) lambs' sweetbreads (previously soaked in cold water and blanched) in butter. Cook 125 g (4¼ oz, ½ cup) cocks' combs (scalded to remove the skin and well soaked in cold water) in white stock with 25 g (1 oz) cocks' kidneys (which have already been cooked in 1 dl (6 tablespoons, scant ½ cup) Madeira wine and 1 tablespoon butter). Quickly sauté in butter 250 g (8 oz, 1 cup) sliced trimmed chicken livers seasoned with salt and pepper. Then cook 250 g (8 oz, 2 cups) trimmed washed mushrooms in butter.

Put the sweetbreads, livers, combs, kidneys, and mushrooms in a pan and add 125 g (4 oz, 1 cup) thickly sliced truffles and 1.5 dl (¼ pint, ⅔ cup) Madeira. Prepare a white velouté sauce using a very strong chicken stock and add to it half its volume of fresh cream. Boil until reduced in volume by half. Flavour with a little Madeira, add butter, and sieve. Pour the sauce over the ragout. The ragout can be used to fill the centre of a ring of veal or chicken forcemeat.

Béatrix

The name given to a garnish of spring vegetables for large cuts of meat, which includes fresh steamed morel mushrooms, small glazed carrots, sautéed artichoke hearts (quartered), and fried or boiled new potatoes.

It is also the name of a mixed salad which is made from chicken breasts with potatoes and asparagus tips. The seasoning consists of a light mayonnaise flavoured with mustard with a slice of truffle as the final touch.

Beaucaire

The name given to various recipes, including a mixed salad, soup, and chitterlings (intestines), associated with Provençal cuisine.

The Beaucaire fairs were celebrated by the poet Mistral, who wrote of merchants who 'ate celery hearts in the open air'. Celery still figures in the traditional Christmas supper salad which inspired a mixed salad: thin strips of celery and celeriac (celery root) with chicory, ham, and sharp apples, with beetroot (red beet) and potatoes arranged around the edge. The ingredients of Beaucaire soup are cabbage, leek, and celery (sweated in butter and mixed with white chicken stock flavoured with basil and marjoram). It is garnished with pearl barley and diced chicken liver and served with grated cheese. Eel Beaucaire is boned, stuffed with a fish mixture, placed on a bed of shallots, onions, and mushrooms, and braised in a mixture of white wine and Cognac.

RECIPE

Beef à la mode de Beaucaire BOEUF À LA MODE DE BEAUCAIRE (from a recipe by H. Philippon, from *Cuisine de Provence*, Albin Michel) This is the traditional dish of the Beaucaire fair. It is delicious but takes a long time to prepare. Take thin slices of beef cut from the thigh or shoulder blade (1.2 kg, 2½ lb) allowing about 200 g (7 oz) per person. Bard the meat with fat which has been rolled in salt and pepper and moisten with brandy. Then marinate for 24 hours in 4 tablespoons vinegar to which a chopped onion, a bouquet garni, 4 tablespoons brandy, and 4–5 teaspoons olive oil have been added.

Cover the bottom of an earthenware cooking pot with 250 g (8 oz) bacon cut into slices 12 mm (½ in) thick. Chop 4 onions and 2 cloves of garlic and place on top of the bacon. Place the slices of beef on this bed, season with salt and pepper, and then pour the marinade over the meat. Cover and cook gently for 2 hours (120 C, 250 F, gas ½). Then slowly (so as not to overcool the contents) add 1 litre (1¾ pints, 4¼ cups) red wine, a bouquet garni, 1 tablespoon capers, and an onion stuck with 3 cloves. Cover and cook gently for a further 2 hours.

A quarter of an hour before serving, bind the sauce with a generous tablespoon of flour and add 3 ground anchovy fillets. When the dish is finally cooked, pour over 3 tablespoons (¼ cup) olive oil and serve.

Beaufort

A French cows' milk cheese (at least 48% fat content), cooked and then pressed until it is firm and ivory-coloured with a natural brushed crust. It is a round cheese without holes (but occasionally with a few 'threads' thin horizontal splits). It is a round cheese and it has a concave base (these characteristics differentiate it from other Gruyères). It can weigh up to 60 kg (135 lb) with a diameter of 60 cm (24 in) and a height of 20 cm (8 in), but some rounds are smaller. Made from the milk of cows from the mountain pastures of Maurienne, Beaufortin, and Tarentaise, it has a fine fruity flavour.

The 'Haute Montagne' label may only be given to Beaufort cheeses which are matured for about six months in cool damp cellars in communes of the Albertville, Saint-Jean-de-Maurienne, and Bonneville districts. The best season is the month of October. The dairy Beaufort produced in cooperative cheese dairies is not entitled to the *appellation contrôlée*. It is finer than Emmental and is used for gratins and fondues.

Beauharnais

A garnish usually served with small grilled (broiled) or fried cuts of meat, made of stuffed mushrooms and sautéed or steamed artichoke quarters. Beauharnais also describes a recipe for soft-boiled (soft-cooked) eggs on a bed of artichoke hearts. It is thought that these recipes were dedicated to Countess Fanny de Beauharnais, cousin by marriage of Empress Josephine, who had a reputation for being a gourmet. Sweet Beauharnais recipes (based on bananas and rum) reflect the Creole origins of Napoleon's first wife.

RECIPE

SAVOURY PREPARATIONS

Beauharnais sauce SAUCE BEAUHARNAIS Mix together 2 dl (7 fl oz, ¾ cup) béarnaise sauce and 2 tablespoons (3 tablespoons) tarragon-flavoured butter. This sauce is served with grilled (broiled) and fried meat and grilled (broiled) fish.

SWEET PREPARATIONS

Beauharnais bananas BANANES BEAUHARNAIS Remove the threads from 6 peeled bananas and arrange in a buttered ovenproof dish. Sprinkle with sugar and 4 tablespoons (⅓ cup) white rum. Bake in the oven for 5–8 minutes. Pour over some fresh double (heavy) cream, sprinkle with crushed macaroons and a little melted butter, then glaze in a very hot oven. Serve in the baking dish.

Beaujolais

One of the best-known and best-loved red wines in the world, made from the Gamay grape (full name Gamay Noir à Jus Blanc). Although the region may be said to be a continuation of the Burgundy vineyard, Beaujolais is, in fact, more correctly a Lyonnais wine, because the vineyards are in that department, with the exception of one section which is actually in Burgundy. These days. however, Beaujolais is usually considered separately from Burgundy. The writer Léon Daudet said that three rivers flow through Lyon: the Rhône, the Saône, and the Beaujolais! Until fairly recently, the locals were the main consumers of this lip-smacking wine, often served in 45-cl 'pots' in the bistros. However, during World War II many Parisian writers – including the author of *Clochemerle*, came to live in the Beaujolais, discovered the local tipple, and publicized it with gusto. Much additional publicity has been gained by the announcement of when the 'Nouveau', or first consignments of the young Beaujolais, are released. It is carried literally all over the world and has inspired many other wine countries to publicize their own 'Nouveaux' within weeks of its being vintaged.

There are nine 'growths' (*crus*) of Beaujolais and, within them, a few estate wines, although the majority are sold under their regional names plus the name of the shipper. These growths are: Brouilly, Côte de Brouilly, Chénas, Chrioubles, Fleurie, Juliénas, Saint-Armour, Morgon, and Moulin-à-Vent. Each has its own AOC. In addition to straight 'Beaujolais', there are Beaujolais-Villages' wines from a number of communes (parishes) entitled to this AOC. Most Beaujolais is at its delectable best when fairly young, although the wines of both Morgon and Moulin-à-Vent can age agreeably for a few years. Traditionally, young Beaujolais is served cool – at cellar temperature – although this is a matter of personal preference.

In addition to the region's red wine, some white, rosé, and sparkling (white) Beaujolais are also made now.

Beaune

This town, 'capital of Burgundy', is situated at the southern end of the Côte de Nuits; the Côte de Beaune encircles and extends to the south. Both red and white wines are produced; there are a number of AOCs, many of them world-famous names, and also many specific vineyards of repute. It is generally true to say that, although the red wines of the Côtes de Beaune can be very good indeed, the region is chiefly famous for its white wines, of which the Meursaults, Puligny, the various Montrachet wines, and the exceptional Corton Charlemagne can be magnificent. The wine of the southern sections below the Côte de Beaune are becoming extremely popular too, now that other fine Burgundies are so expensive.

Beaune itself is one of the most attractive of wine towns, preserving much of its medieval character and rich in great works of art. In the centre, the Hôtel Dieu is part of the Hospices de Beaune; established in the 15th century by the Chancellor of Burgundy, Nicolas Rolin, and his wife Guigone de Salins, this charitable organization is now an important owner of farms, woods, and vineyards with which the founders and subsequent benefactors endowed it. The organization runs the Hospice de la Charité, which is an old peoples' home, and a modern hospital. The Hôtel Dieu itself, in use until quite recently, is a treasure house of wonderful tapestries, antiques, and Rogier van der Weyden's glorious *Last Judgment* painting.

Since the middle of the 19th century, wines from the vineyards belonging to the Hospices de Beaune have been publicly auctioned every November, on the second Sunday of the month (in very poor years they are sold privately). Originally the auction took place in the Hôtel Dieu, but it is now so famous that it attracts buyers from every part of the world and the sale takes place in the covered market nearby. Buyers who bid for the wines include restaurateurs, wine merchants, private wine lovers, great retail chains, and hoteliers, and the bottles are usually labelled proudly with their provenance. For the occasion, many other tastings and ceremonies take place in or near Beaune, including the 'Trois Glorieuses' (the Saturday banquet at Clos de Vougeot, the post-sale dinner in the Bastion de Beaune, and (on the Monday) the 'Paulée' luncheon at Meursault); art exhibitions are also held, together with much private entertaining. The occasion provides the first indication of the character of the year's vintage and the prices certain wines may fetch.

beauvilliers

A rich nourishing cake made of crushed almonds and sugar mixed with butter, eggs, and a lot of flour (wheat flour and rice flour). After cooking it is wrapped in tin foil to ensure that it keeps well. It is the oldest form of 'travellers' cake. It was invented at the beginning of the 19th century by a M. Mounier, a pastrycook of the Rue Monsieur-le-Prince in Paris, who named it after the great cook to whom he had been apprenticed.

A similar travelling cake, the *bouvalet*, also bears the name of a famous pastrycook and restaurateur to whom it was dedicated.

Beauvilliers (Antoine)

French cook (born Paris, 1754; died Paris, 1817). In 1782 he founded the Grande Taverne de Londres in the Rue de Richelieu, which was the first real restaurant in Paris. His success was so great that, on the eve of the French Revolution, Beauvilliers opened another restaurant in his own name in the Galerie de Valois du Palais-Royal. Brillat-Savarin wrote that 'he was the first to have an elegant salon, well turned-out waiters, a carefully chosen cellar and superb cuisine'. Beauvilliers' renown, despite a brief eclipse in the Reign of Terror (1793), was maintained under the Empire and the Restoration and the doors of his establishment did not close until 1825.

Having been the chef of the Count of Provence, Beauvilliers received his clients wearing his sword, in the uniform of an *officier de bouche de réserve*. He had an excellent memory and was able to recognize his guests and assist them in their selections. His menu included such dishes as fricandeau with spinach, sauerkraut with sausages, duck with parsnips, carp-roe pie, hot woodcock pâté, and calves' sweetbreads *à la dauphine.* In 1814 he wrote *L'Art de cuisiner*, in which he treats cooking, food management, and service as an exact science. He collaborated with Carême in writing *La Cuisine ordinaire*.

The surname of this famous restaurateur is used, among other things, for garnish for large braised joints of meat made from salsify sautéed in butter, small deseeded tomatoes stuffed with a purée of brains and grilled (broiled) and spinach kromeskies. The accompanying sauce is made from the cooking juices.

RECIPE

Small Beauvilliers timbales PETITES TIMBALES BEAUVILLIERS Fill some buttered dariole moulds with unsweetened brioche dough. Bake, remove from the moulds, and allow to cool. Hollow out the brioches, leaving a shell 5 mm (¼ in) thick. Heat these shells gently in the oven, then fill with a salpicon of chicken breasts mixed with allemande sauce. Arrange a bouquet of asparagus tips sweated in butter on each timbale.

beaver CASTOR

An aquatic rodent formerly hunted in France for its fur as well as for its meat. The church classed its meat with that of water fowl, and permitted its consumption during Lent. The meat was made into pâté and preserves. Nowadays it is a protected species.

It should not be confused with the South American coypu, which was introduced into Europe in the 20th century for fur ranching. Several French producers have promoted its meat for quality pâtés.

Béchameil (Louis de)

French financier (born 1630; died 1703). Farmer-general and steward of the house of the Duke of Orleans, Louis de Béchameil, Marquis of Nointel, became major domo to Louis XIV. Saint-Simon reported that he was rich, a gourmet, an informed art lover, and a handsome man, but it is very unlikely that he created the sauce which bears his name, abbreviated to béchamel. This sauce is probably an improvement of an older recipe by one of the king's cooks

who dedicated his discovery to the king's major domo, which made the jealous old Duke of Escars say: 'That fellow Béchameil has all the luck! I was serving breast of chicken *à la crème* more than 20 years before he was born, but I have never had the chance of giving my name to even the most modest sauce.'

béchamel

A white sauce made by adding milk to a roux. (The original béchamel sauce, which owes its name to the Marquis of Béchameil, was prepared by adding large quantities of fresh cream to a thick velouté.) Béchamel is widely used for egg, vegetable, and gratin dishes and for filled scallop shells. It can be kept warm in a bain-marie and used as a basis for other sauces (such as Mornay and Soubise sauces) by adding different ingredients.

● *Hints for preparation* – Avoid using aluminium utensils. It is quicker and easier to pour boiling milk onto a cold roux: if the milk is poured on cold, the mixture must be stirred constantly until it boils and throughout the cooking.

RECIPE

Béchamel sauce SAUCE BÉCHAMEL (from Carême's recipe) Reduce the velouté until it is thick, then bind it with egg yolks and thick cream. Stir with a wooden spoon to make sure the sauce does not stick to the pan. Remove it from the heat, add a piece of butter the size of a walnut and a few tablespoons of double (heavy) cream. Add a pinch of grated nutmeg, sieve through muslin (cheesecloth), and keep hot in a bain-marie.

Béchamel sauce SAUCE BÉCHAMEL (modern recipe) Melt 40 g (1½ oz, 3 tablespoons) butter over a low heat in a heavy saucepan. Add 40 g (1½ oz, 6 tablespoons) flour and stir briskly until the mixture is smoothly blended, without allowing it to change colour. Add ½ litre (17 fl oz, 2 cups) milk and whisk well with a wire whisk to prevent any lumps forming: season with salt and pepper and, if desired (according to what the sauce is to be used for), a little grated nutmeg. Continue to cook the sauce slowly until it is the correct consistency stirring from time to time, so that a skin does not form on the surface.

becqueter

A French slang word meaning to peck at food.

beechnut FAINE

The small triangular brown nut of the beech tree. Beechnuts grow in twos or threes in a hairy brownish capsule and are gathered in October. They have a high oil content and a similar flavour to the hazelnut. They can be eaten raw but have a slightly bitter taste; it is best to grill (broil) or roast them. The oil extracted from them is considered to be second only to olive oil in quality. It keeps well and is excellent for frying and salad dressings.

beef BOEUF

The meat of all the large domestic cattle, including heifer, cow, bullock, and bull.

Our prehistoric ancestors hunted the wild ox for food and domestic cattle are descended from it. Cattle have been domesticated for more than 40 centuries. In the Middle Ages, 'noble' dishes were prepared using the better joints of beef, the best of which was sirloin. Tournedos (filet mignons), chateaubriand, fillet (tenderloin) *en croute*, and rib are the great classics. In 1756, the Duke of Richelieu chose the menu for a famous meal that was given for his illustrious prisoners during the Hanoverian War. The 12 dishes of the first course and the 10 dishes of the second course were all of beef.

The quality and the yield (the weight of edible meat in relation to the weight of the live animal) vary according to the breed of cattle. Beef cattle (the most popular in France being Charolais and Limousin) are specially bred for meat production. The proportion of muscle is high with relatively little fat. Young males may be castrated to accelerate the fattening process. Bullocks are slaughtered at 24–40 months (before this they are termed *bouvillons* in France).

Heifers that are not required for breeding are also slaughtered at this age, providing meat which is very tender and full of flavour. Recently, there has been a trend towards rearing uncastrated males. They grow more rapidly and can therefore be slaughtered at 16–24 months, but their meat is sometimes criticized for its lack of flavour.

Dairy breeds also used for their meat. Cows that have calved (especially Normandy cows after four to six calvings) form a large proportion of marketable meat. The quality of this meat varies considerably according to breed, age, and degree of fattening, but it is usually considered to be good, especially if the animal is fairly young – between five and eight years.

□ **Quality meat** 4.5 million beef cattle are slaughtered each year in France, providing 1.5 million tons of carcass. The hindquarter provides the so-called 'noble' cuts, which can be cooked quickly, while the forequarter gives mostly slow-cooking and boiling pieces. In order to meet home demand for 'noble' cuts, the French have to import hindquarters and export forequarters. The main exporting countries are South America, Australia, and New Zealand, the principal importers being the United States and Japan.

Good-quality beef is bright red and shiny in appearance and firm and springy to the touch with a sweet light scent. It has a network of white or slightly yellowish fat; when a lot of fat is present in the muscle, the meat is described as marbled. In order to be tender, beef must be matured after slaughtering, for a period varying from a few days to a week. Beef consists of water (53–65%), proteins (16–20%), and fat (16–31%), with traces of phosphorus and iron. It supplies 220–340 Cal per 100 g.

Edible offal includes heart, liver, tongue, kidneys, brains, and tripe, but only tongue (smoked or pickled) and tripe are highly regarded in gastronomic circles.

Minced (ground) beef, either prepared as required or deep frozen, should preferably be made from less tender cuts, such as silverside (bottom round) or stewing beef (hind shank or neck). The meat is either naturally lean or has had the fat removed. Mince may be eaten raw as steak tartare. Cooked mince is used to make hamburgers and *bitoks*. It is also made into spiced meatballs (see *fricadelle, kefta*).

□ **Roast Beef** Cuts of beef for roasting are generally taken from the hindquarter and include fillet, sirloin, rump, topside, and rib; of these the prime roasts are fillet, sirloin, and rolled rib.

In France the meat is usually barded and tied up in advance by the butcher, but it will taste fresher when it is cut and prepared on demand. In England it is served pink and very tender inside, browned and a little dry outside; the traditional accompaniments are horseradish sauce and Yorkshire pudding. In France it is cooked with the inside a little bloody, the rest of the meat pink, and the outside rather browner.

● *Advice on cooking* – Take the beef out of the refrigerator at least an hour before cooking it; it can be studded with two or three pieces of garlic. The meat will be more tender if it is cooked steadily in a moderately hot oven, rather than rapidly in a hot oven. Place the meat in a hot oven 230 c (450 f, gas 8) for about 15 minutes, then lower the temperature to 200 c (400 f, gas 6), allowing 15–20 minutes per 450 g (1 lb) for a medium roast (a little longer if the joint is thick). A very tender prime roast can be cooked rapidly in a hot oven, allowing 12–15 minutes per 450 g (1 lb).

Before slicing the beef, leave it to rest for a few minutes in a warm place so that the juices are distributed throughout the meat and do not run too much when the joint is cut.

● *Making the gravy* – Put the roasting tin on top of the stove over a low heat. Brown the juices lightly without burning them, pour off some of the fat, then deglaze the pan with a little light brown veal stock or water. Make double the volume of gravy finally required, then reduce by half. Adjust the seasoning; add a little gravy browning to enhance the colour, if necessary. Strain and keep hot.

To serve, pour a little of the gravy into the bottom of the dish in which the sliced meat will be arranged, and serve the rest separately. Garnish the dish with watercress.

● *Accompaniments* – Dauphine potatoes, artichoke hearts filled with mushrooms, braised lettuce, sautéed tomatoes, potato croquettes, stuffed mushrooms; garnishes: Du Barry, bouquetière, forestière, Richelieu, etc.

RECIPE

Beef à la mode BOEUF À LA MODE Cut about 250 g (9 oz) fat bacon into thick strips and marinate for 5–6 hours in a mixture of 1 dl (6 tablespoons, scant ½ cup) Cognac and spices. Use the strips to lard a piece of rump weighing about 2 kg (4½ lb). Season with salt and pepper and marinate for 5–6 hours (turning the meat several times) in the Cognac used to marinate the bacon mixed with at least 1 litre (1¾ pints, 4¼ cups) good red wine, 1 dl (5 tablespoons, scant ½ cup) olive oil, 250 g (8¾ oz, 2½ cups) chopped onions, 1 kg (2¼ lb, 9½ cups) sliced carrots, 2 or 3 cloves of garlic, a bouquet garni, and a few peppercorns.

Blanch a boned calf's foot and some bacon rind from which some of the fat has been removed. Drain the meat and dry it, and then drain the other ingredients of the marinade. Brown the meat on all sides in olive oil, then place in a large casserole. Add the drained ingredients of the marinade followed by the bacon rinds and the calf's foot. Moisten with the marinade and about ¾ litre (1¼ pints, 1½ pints) stock and season with salt.

Place the covered casserole in the oven (200 c, 400 f, gas 6) and cook for about 2½ hours, until tender. When the beef is cooked, slice it evenly and serve surrounded with the carrots and the diced meat of the calf's foot. Strain the braising stock over the meat. Small glazed onions may be added to garnish.

Beef bourguignon BOEUF BOURGUIGNON Cut 1 kg (2¼ lb) braising steak (rump) into cubes and coat with flour. Cut 150 g (5 oz) belly pork into thin strips and fry in a casserole or heavy saucepan. Add the steak, a chopped shallot, and 2 sliced onions and continue to fry. If desired, add a small glass of brandy and set alight. Add ½ litre (17 fl oz, 2 cups) red wine and a generous glass of stock. Season with salt and pepper and add a bouquet garni and a crushed clove of garlic. Cover and simmer gently for at least 2 hours. A dozen

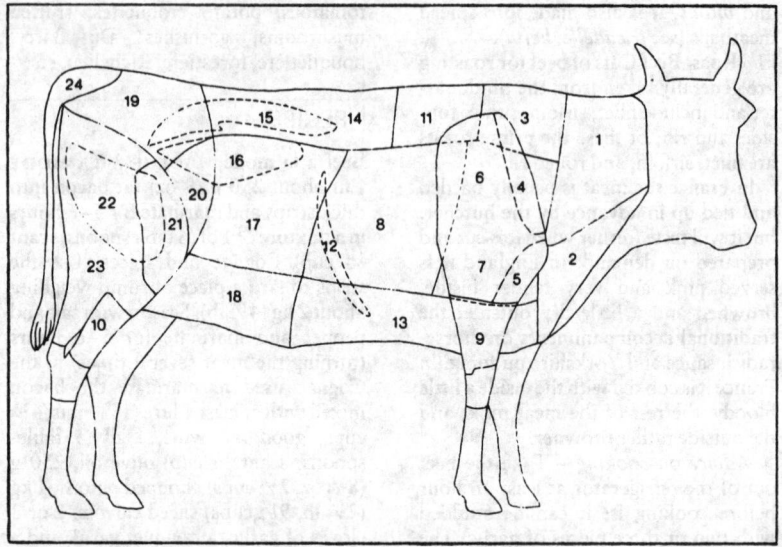

French cuts of beef.
1, 2. collier (neck); 3. basses-côtes; 4. jumeau for grilling or frying; 5. jumeau for stewing; 6. macreuse; 7. plat de côtes découvert (uncovered rib); 8. plat de côtes couvert (covered rib); 9. gîte de devant; 10. gîte de derrière; 11. entrecôte; 12. hampe; 13. poitrine; 14. faux-filet; 15. filet; 16. bavette for grilling or frying; 17. bavette for stewing; 18. flanchet; 19. romsteck (rump steak); 20. aiguillette baronne; 21. rond de tranche basse; 22. tranche; 23. gîte à la noix; 24. queue (tail).

small onions lightly fried in butter may be added 20 minutes before the end of cooking. Just before serving, bind the sauce with 1 tablespoon kneaded butter.

Boiled beef BOEUF GROS SEL OU BOEUF BOUILLI For 6 servings, place approximately 750 g (1¾ lb) beef or veal bones in a large saucepan with 2.5 litres (4¼ pints, 5½ pints) water, and bring to the boil. Skim the surface of the liquid and remove the foam deposited on the sides of the pan. Boil for about an hour then remove bones. Add 1.25–2 kg (2½–4½ lb) beef, depending on the cut and the proportion of bone to meat: silverside (bottom round), cheek, shoulder, chuck, flank, or oxtail may be used. Bring back to the boil and skim. Then add the following vegetables: 6 carrots, 3 medium turnips, 6 small leeks (tied together), 2 celery sticks (cut into short

lengths and tied together), a piece of parsnip, 2 onions (one stuck with 2 cloves), a good bouquet garni, and if desired, 1 or 2 cloves of garlic. Season with salt and pepper, cover to bring back to the boil, and simmer for about 3 hours. Drain the meat, cut into even-sized pieces, and serve surrounded with the drained vegetables. Serve with coarse salt, pickled onions, gherkins, and mustard.

If a marrow bone is available, wrap this in muslin (cheesecloth) and add it to the pan not more than 15 minutes before serving. The bone may be served with the dish (see illustration) or the marrow can be removed and spread on toasted croutons. To make the dish look more attractive, select vegetables of a similar size, cut the leeks and celery to the same length and form into neat bunches, and serve the onions slightly browned.

Pressed beef BOEUF PRESSÉ Take 3 kg (6½ lb) lightly larded brisket. Prick with a large larding needle and soak the meat in brine for 8–10 days, depending on the season (brine penetrates the meat more quickly in summer). The brine used is the same as that in the recipe for pickled ox tongue. The meat must be completely submerged and it is advisable to use a weighted board to achieve this. Just before cooking, wash the meat in cold water and cut into pieces the same size as the moulds that are to be used. Cook in water until tender with a carrot cut into pieces. Place the meat in square moulds, each covered with a small weighted board. When the meat is quite cold, turn it out of the moulds and coat with several layers of meat aspic, coloured reddish brown by adding caramel and red food colouring. This provides the meat with a strong protective coating that retards deterioration. To serve, cut into very thin slices and decorate with fresh parsley.

Salt beef BOEUF SALÉ This method is mostly used for preparing brisket, but may also be used for flank and chuck.

The meat is soaked in brine for 6–8 days in summer and 8–10 days in winter. It is then rinsed to desalt, and cooked in water for 30 minutes per kg (2¼ lb). Salt beef is served hot with vegetables that are traditionally associated with it, such as braised red or green cabbage and sauerkraut. It is also used for pot roasting.

Braised joint of beef PIÈCE DE BOEUF BRAISÉE Cut 200 g (7 oz, 1 cup) fat pork or bacon into larding strips. Season with spices, soak in Cognac, and use them to lard a piece of beef (cut from the rump) weighing 3 kg (6½ lb). Season the meat with salt, pepper, and spices and tie into a neat shape with string. Marinate for 5 hours in either red or white wine with thyme, bay, parsley, and 2 crushed garlic cloves. Blanch, cool, and tie 2 boned calf's feet. Peel and slice 2 large onions and 2 carrots and heat gently in butter. Crush into small pieces a mixture of 1.5 kg (3½ lb) beef bones and veal knuckle bones together with the bones from the calf's feet. Brown in the oven. Place the browned bones and the vegetables in a casserole

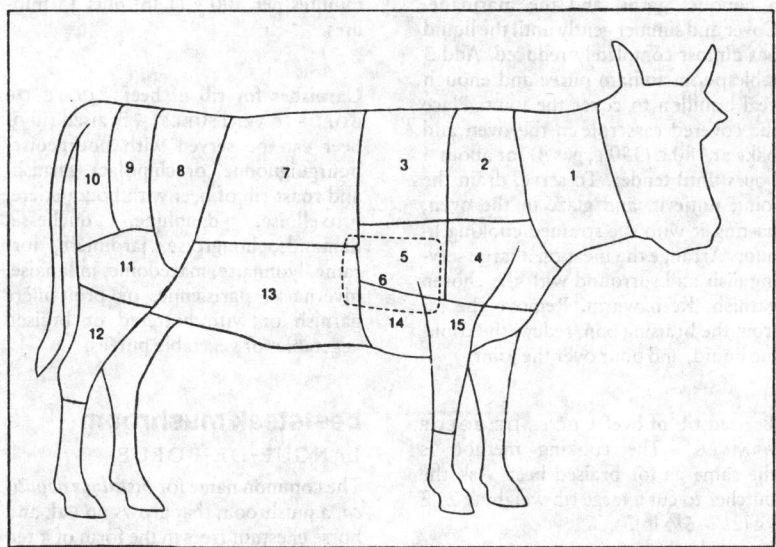

British cuts of beef.
1. neck and clod; 2. chuck and blade; 3. fore rib; 4. thick rib; 5. thin rib; 6. rolled ribs; 7. sirloin; 8. rump; 9. silverside; 10. topside; 11. thick flank; 12. leg; 13. flank; 14. brisket; 15. shin.

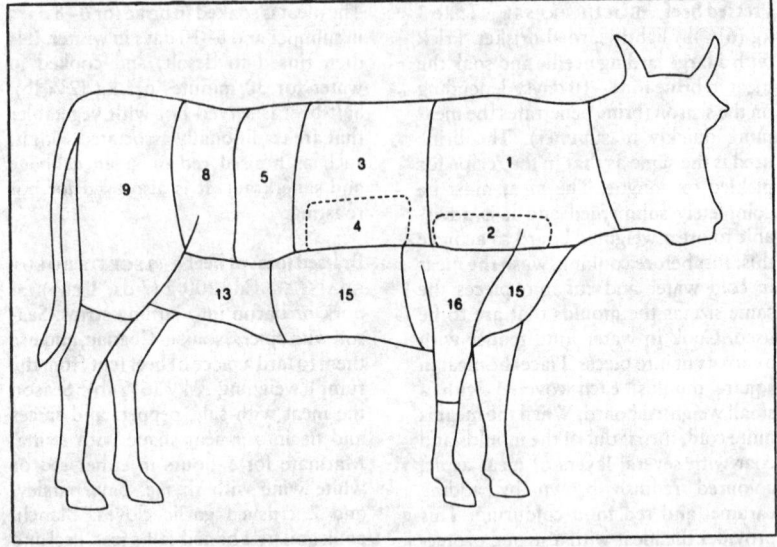

American cuts of beef.
1. chuck; 2. flanken-style ribs; 3. rib; 4. back ribs; 5. short loin; 6. Porterhouse steak; 7. tenderloin; 8. sirloin; 9. round; 10. boneless rump roast; 11. round steak; 12. hind shank; 13. flank; 14. flank steak rolls; 15. short plate; 16. brisket; 17. fore shank.

or a braising pan. Add the joint of beef, a bouquet garni, and the marinade. Cover and simmer gently until the liquid has almost completely reduced. Add 3 tablespoons tomato purée and enough veal bouillon to cover the joint. Place the covered casserole in the oven and bake at 180 C (350 F, gas 4) for about 4 hours until tender. To serve, drain the joint, untie it, and glaze in the oven, basting it with the strained cooking liquor. Arrange the meat on a large serving dish and surround with the chosen garnish. Keep warm. Remove the fat from the braising pan, reduce the cooking liquid, and pour over the joint.

Braised rib of beef CÔTE DE BOEUF BRAISÉE The cooking method is the same as for braised beef. Ask the butcher to cut a large rib weighing 2–3 kg (2¼–6½ lb).

Oven-roast rib of beef CÔTE DE BOEUF RÔTIE AU FOUR Place the rib in a roasting tin, brush with butter or dripping, and roast uncovered in a hot oven (240 C (475 F, gas 9) for 15–18 minutes per 500 g (1 lb) plus 15 minutes.

Garnishes for rib of beef CÔTE DE BOEUF (GARNITURES) Braised rib of beef can be served with bourgeoise, bourguignonne, or chipolata garnish, and roast rib of beef with bouquetière, bruxelloise, dauphine, duchesse, flamande, hongroise, jardinière, lorraine, lyonnaise, macédoine, milanaise, nivernaise, parisienne, or printanière garnish or with buttered or braised vegetables or vegetable purées.

beefsteak mushroom
LANGUE-DE-BOEUF
The common name for *Fistulina hepatica*, a mushroom that grows on oak and horse chestnut trees in the form of a red fleshy mass with a sticky surface. The thick flesh, which exudes an acidic reddish juice, can be sliced and fried like liver or eaten raw with a green salad. It is cut into thin strips, soaked in salted

water, then drained and dressed with chives and a vinaigrette.

beef tea

BOUILLON AMÉRICAIN

A highly nutritious concentrated meat juice used chiefly in the past as food for invalids. Lean beef is cut into small dice, placed in a hermetically sealed container without any water, and cooked in a bain-marie.

beer BIÈRE

An alcoholic beverage obtained by the fermentation of extracts of malted cereals, principally barley, and flavoured with hops. Most countries allow a percentage of maize and rice, but in Germany this practice is forbidden and beers are made solely from barley, malt, hops, yeast and water. British beer varies from 100% malt to 70% malt plus 30% unmalted cereals, together with sugar, hops, yeast, and water.

Beer is both the most widespread and the oldest alcoholic drink in the world. The first traces of 'liquid bread' based on fermented cereals were found in Mesopotamia. The Mesopotamians and the Egyptians were the greatest beer drinkers of the ancient world and drank their beer warm. It is made from barley bread crumbled in water and fermented in date juice flavoured with cumin, myrtle, ginger, and honey.

The Gauls, Celts, and Saxons produced beer which, like earlier fermented drinks, did not contain hops. Hops were introduced for making beer in the 13th century by Bavarian monks.

□ **Manufacture** The brewer's basic raw material is a cereal rich in starch; the latter does not ferment naturally in the presence of yeast (whereas the sugar contained in apples or grapes can be directly fermented to produce cider and wine). The cereal must therefore be 'processed' in order to obtain a fermentable extract (known to brewers as *wort*). For the cereal barley, this is usually done by first malting the raw grain and then extracting the soluble sugars with hot water using the natural enzymes of the malt.

● *Malting.* The grain is soaked, allowed to start germinating, then dried under controlled conditions in a kiln.

● *Brewing.* The malt is ground, then mixed with hot water. Malt enzymes release soluble sugars from the starch, the solution being run off from the insoluble husk. The resulting wort is heated to boiling point and hop flowers are added to give the beer its bitter flavour and hop bouquet. Yeast is added after cooling.

There are two major types of beer according to the type of yeast used. Traditionally, lager yeast is used at lower temperatures than ale yeast, therefore the fermentation period is longer.

● *Lager fermentation* – typically seven days at a temperature of 7–12 C (45–54 F), giving a lightly flavoured product whose character is mainly determined by the hops and the malt used. Lager beers dominate the world beer market.

● *Ale fermentation* – typically three days at a temperature of 18–25 C (64–77 F), giving more fruity beers in which the flavour is more directly influenced by the fermentation process. In continental Europe these are 'special' beers, Belgian Trappist beers, and brown beers, whereas in Great Britain they are the very popular ales. In very dark beers, such as stouts, the use of roasted cereals contributes significantly to the flavour as well as to the colour.

After fermentation the beer is placed in a cool cellar where it is allowed to mature. The maturation period can vary from a few days to several months, depending on the nature and strength of the beer. Finally it is clarified before being bottled, canned, or racked into barrels. Clarification is commonly done by a combination of settling and filtration; in Britain, however, settled beer is traditionally racked directly into casks, final clarification being achieved by addition of 'finings' directly into a cask followed by a period of 'stillage'.

□ **Colour and content** The colour is not related to the length of fermentation, degree of processing, or alcoholic strength, but to the degree to which the malt is heated during kilning. The heating produces caramel, which is extracted from the malt and eventually colours the beer brown. Highly kilned malt gives English stout, Belgian Chimay, and Munich basses their particular flavours. Pale beers (porter and ale, Czechoslovakian Pilsen, and German Dortmund) are distinguished by their bitter flavour.

Beer contains unfermentable sugar (except for 'light' low-calorie and diet beers), nitrogenous materials, mineral salts, and vitamins. 1 litre (1¾ pints) beer gives approximately 500 Calories.

□ **British and foreign beers** Among English beers, brown and pale Whitbread are typical, the latter being suitable as an apéritif. Pale ale is refreshing as well as being good for cooking. Scottish Gordon is prepared only at Christmas, whereas the dark and sweet Scotch ale is drunk all year round. Irish Guinness is a famous strong beer – very dark, dry, and bitter.

French beers have the reputation of being fairly uniform in flavour. Most are produced industrially for mass consumption with the emphasis on quenching thirst rather than on flavour. 'De luxe' beers, not generally drunk with meals, include Champigneulles, Kanterbräu, Mutzig, and Meuse, corresponding to the two main brewing regions of France: the north and Alsace. 'Special' French beers are finer (e.g. Kronenbourg and Ancre Old Lager).

German beer is usually rather bitter. Its produce is very widespread but the most famous German beers come from Bremen, Cologne, Dortmund, and Munich (Spaten, Kapuziner, and Löwenbräu). Also worthy of mention are Berliner Weisse, a 'white' beer from Berlin which is drunk with raspberry syrup or lemon, and 'smoked' Bamberg beer.

Belgian beers are noteworthy for their originality: Gueuze, which is strongly flavoured and similar to 'Mort Subite' (considered to be one of the best), Kriek (red beer with cherries), Roddenbach (amber-coloured, with a sharp flavour), and Chimay and Jumet brewed in abbeys (see *lambic*).

Danish and Dutch beers are light yet quite bitter (e.g. Carlsberg and Heineken).

Czechoslovakian Pilsen is an excellent beer which has given rise to the 'pils' or 'pilsener' type of beer imitated the world over.

In the United States beers are very light, delicately flavoured with just a hint of bitterness. They are drunk very cold.

□ **Consumption** Beer is served with meals and as a refreshment. It is also used in the preparation of cocktails and various cooked dishes (soups, fish (e.g. carp), stews, and carbonnades), to which it adds smoothness and a slight bitterness. It can also be served with some cheeses (e.g. Gouda and Maroilles) and is used instead of yeast in the preparation of pancakes and fritters.

There are three characteristic features of any beer: its bitterness (which should never reach acridity), produced by hops and tannin; its clarity, proving that it has been well produced and properly clarified; and finally its head, which must be well-formed and stable.

Lager should be served at 7–9 c (45–48 f); dark beer is consumed at room temperature. Bottles should be stored upright; once open, beer goes flat very quickly.

Balloon glasses and tumblers are suitable for normal beers. Very frothy beers are best served in tulip or tall beer glasses. In Germany stone tankards are used as they keep the beer cool. Pewter tankards are favoured by connoisseurs of English beer.

Beer is poured by directing the flow to the bottom of the glass to form a layer of froth, then along the side of the glass to prevent too much froth being formed, and finally righting the glass to produce the head. The great brewing nations of Europe are Germany (with its Munich Beer Festival in October and its custom of drinking beer all the year round and at every opportunity), Belgium (country of origin of the legendary Gambrinus, who is said to have invented brewing, and where cooking with beer is especially popular), and Great Britain (where beer is enjoyed at its best in the traditional British pubs).

RECIPES

Chicken cooked in beer COQ À LA BIÈRE Cut a 1.25-kg (2½-lb) chicken into pieces and brown in butter on all sides in a casserole dish. Add 2 chopped shallots and cook until brown. Pour 5 cl (3 tablespoons, ¼ cup) gin onto the chicken pieces and set alight. Then add 4 dl (14 fl oz, 1¾ cups) Alsatian beer, ½ dl (3 tablespoons, ¼ cup) fresh cream, a bouquet garni, salt, and a little cayenne. Cover and allow to simmer. Clean and chop 250 g (8 oz) mushrooms and add to the casserole. Cook for about 45 minutes, then drain the chicken pieces, arrange on the serving dish, and keep warm. Remove the bouquet garni from the casserole, add ½ dl (3 tablespoons, ¼ cup) fresh cream, and reduce by half. Mix an egg yolk with a little of the sauce, add to the casserole, and beat well. Pour the sauce over the chicken pieces, sprinkle with chopped parsley, and serve very hot with steamed new potatoes.

Home-brewed beer BIÈRE DE MÉN-AGE   To make 30 litres (6½ gallons, 8 gallons) beer, use 125 g (4½ oz) hops, 2 litres (3½ pints, 4½ pints) common barley, 1.125 kg (2½ lb, 5 cups) sugar, 50 g (2 oz) brewer's yeast, and 10 g (¼ oz) chicory (to colour). Add the barley to 20 litres (4¼ gallons, 5¼ gallons) water and cook for 2 hours. As soon as it is cooked, add the hops and the chicory and leave to infuse, then pour into a 30-litre (6½-gallon, 8-gallon) barrel. Mix and leave uncorked overnight. Then dissolve the yeast in a little water and add to the barrel. Stir with a stick and leave, again without corking, for 6 days, topping up with water to replace evaporation losses. Cork the barrel on the seventh day; on the eighth day, bottle the beer in strong bottles and cork tightly.

beet BETTERAVE

Any of several varieties of a plant with a fleshy root. Some are cultivated for the sugar industry and distilling (sugar beet), others for fodder (mangel wurzel). The beetroot (red beet), with its fine dark red flesh, is used as a vegetable and as a food colour. Beetroot was eaten in antiquity and was described in 1600 by Olivier de Serres, who was a self-appointed publicist of newly imported products in France, as 'a very red, rather fat root with leaves like Swiss chard, all of which is good to eat'. Nowadays, the leaves are rarely eaten, but then can nevertheless be prepared like spinach and are commonly used in soups in eastern Europe (see also *Swiss chard*).

Rich in sugar, vitamins, and calcium, beetroot can be eaten raw (grated), but is usually cooked and served cold (as an hors d'oeuvre, in salads, etc.). It is occasionally served hot as a garnish, particularly for game, or in soups. It is particularly characteristic of Flemish and Slav cuisine (see *borsch*, *botvinya*).

The long-rooted varieties (*rouge noir des vertus* or *rouge crapaudine*, which are both of good quality) have more flavour and are sweeter than the round varieties (red globe and dark red Egyptian), but the latter are more widely cultivated. They are harvested from the end of June to the first frosts; the roots are stored in silos or cellars and are mostly seen on the market in autumn and winter. They are usually sold cooked but can also be bought raw for cooking at home (baked in the oven or boiled in salted water). This takes at least two hours. Very small beetroots are also preserved in vinegar (especially in Germany where they are served with boiled meat) and are used for making pickles.

RECIPES

Beetroot à la lyonnaise BETTERAVES À LA LYONNAISE   Parboil some beetroot in salted water, peel, and slice. Cook until tender in butter with thinly sliced onions. Add a little thickened brown stock or bouillon to which a teaspoon of softened butter has been added. Heat through and serve.

Braised beetroot with cream BETTER-AVES ÉTUVÉES À LA CRÈME   Parboil some beetroot in salted water, peel, and slice. Cook in a little butter in a covered pan until tender. Remove the beetroot and keep hot. Boil some cream, add to the cooking liquor, and reduce to half its volume, seasoning with salt and pepper. Remove from the heat and stir in 1 tablespoon butter. Pour this sauce over the beetroot slices.

Cold beetroot soup POTAGE FROID DE BETTERAVES   Wash thoroughly 1 kg (2 lb) small raw beetroots, cook gently in salted water, then add the juice of 1 lemon and allow to cool. Set 3 or 4 egg whites in a small flat-bottomed dish in a bain-marie. Wash and chop a few spring onions (scallions), including the stems.

Peel the cold beetroot and slice into thin strips. Dice the cooked egg whites and 2 Russian gherkins. Add the diced egg whites, gherkins, beetroot, and the chopped onions to the liquid in which the beetroot was cooked, together with a generous pinch of sugar and 1.5–2 dl (¼–⅓ pint, ⅔–¾ cup) fresh double (heavy) cream. Stir well and place in the refrigerator. Just before serving, chop some parsley and sprinkle over the soup.

Scandinavian beetroot salad SALADE DE BETTERAVES À LA SCANDINAVE Peel some baked beetroot and cut into cubes. Peel and slice some onions and separate the rings. Hard-boil (hardcook) some eggs and cut into quarters. Chop some parsley. Cut some sweet smoked or unsmoked herring (a speciality of Scandinavia) into pieces. Sprinkle the beetroot with highly seasoned vinaigrette and place in a salad bowl. Garnish with the herrings, hard-boiled eggs, and onions, and sprinkle with the chopped parsley.

Belgium BELGIQUE

Well-known Belgian specialities include a portion of chips with mussels and a tankard of *gueuze* (a beer), bread and butter and coffee, and cold meats (pork) and a glass of gin, especially for the Liège Christmas table, which includes black and white puddings, pressed pig's head, and pigs' ears and trotters (feet). However, Belgian cuisine has many other things to offer. The following is an example of a typical Walloon festival menu: pea and smoked ham soup, followed by a casserole of St George's mushrooms in their own juice, saddle (both loins) of hare with mountain cranberries surrounded with crunchy *cwènes di gattes* (small Ardenne potatoes shaped like goat's horns), thrushes simmered with sage and juniper berries, a creamy runny Herve cheese, and finally a *rombosse* (apple cooked in a square of pastry) or a *doreye* (rice tart, sometimes filled with macaroons), served with coffee.

In addition to these regional, local, even family specialities, Belgian cruisine also has its own great classics, such as *hotch-potch*, *waterzooi*, and *vogel zonder kop* (literally birds without heads –

rolled beef 'olives'). Potatoes and chicory (*witloof*) dominate the vegetables, which also include asparagus, young hop shoots, and Brussels sprouts. Fish are particularly important, especially eel (*au vert* (in a sauce with nettle, mint, tarragon, chervil, etc.), also in pies and fish stews, and braised), whiting cooked in buttered paper or white wine, and herring in any shape or form.

☐ **Foreign influences** The vicissitudes of history have left their mark on Belgian cuisine; for example, both fish escabèche and goose *à l'instar de Visé* (casseroled, then cut into pieces coated with breadcrumbs and roasted, served with garlic and cream sauce) are recipes inspired by Spanish cookery dating back to the 16th century.

Moreover, trade has always been an essential activity in this country. In the 13th century, Norwegian butter, Portuguese grapes and honey, English cheese, and Moroccan cumin and sugar were imported into Damme. As early as the Roman Empire, the famous Ardenne ham was being sold in the markets of Lugdunum (Lyon), from where the Flemish brought back *couques*, said to be inspired from a Gallo-Roman recipe.

The other major ingredient of Belgian cuisine is beer (*chimay*, *gueuze*, *orval*, *trappistes*, *kriek*, etc.). This national drink (sometimes competing with French wine) is used in the preparation of several culinary specialities, including carbonade, rabbit with prunes, *choesels*, kebabs with *gueuze*, and Orval flan (with leeks and ham). Beer is often served with the fragrant cheeses: Herve, Boulettes de Charleroi, or Potkese (made of spiced curds).

Belgian cakes and pastries are rich and abundant, including Namur and Brussels waffles, Verviers brioches with sugar candy, cramiques with raisins, *spéculos*, Ghent *moques*, almond bread and gingerbread, and the famous flamiche from Dinant, oozing with melted butter.

See also *anversoise (à la)*, *brabançonne (à la)*, *bruxelloise (à la)*, *liègeoise (à la)*.

Belle-Hélène

In about 1865, several chefs from the restaurants of the Grands Boulevards of Paris started to use the title of this famous operetta by Offenbach to name several different recipes.

Grilled tournedos (broiled filet mignons) Belle-Hélène are garnished with crisp potato straws, sprigs of watercress, and artichoke hearts filled with béarnaise sauce. Sautéed chicken suprêmes Belle-Hélène are arranged on croquettes of asparagus tips crowned with a slice of truffle (deglaze the sauté pan for a sauce to pour over this dish). Large joints of meat Belle-Hélène are surrounded with chopped tomatoes, fresh green peas with butter, glazed carrots, and potato croquettes.

Belle-Hélène is also the name of a cold dessert consisting of fruit (usually pears) poached in syrup, cooled, drained, served on vanilla ice cream, and coated with hot chocolate sauce (the latter may be served separately in a sauceboat if desired).

Bellet

An AOC wine from Nice, which comes from the hillsides above the Var valley. The small vineyard produces delicate red wines, light rosés, and definite whites with a fresh bouquet. The reds and rosés are made from Folle and Braquet grapes and the whites are made principally from the Rolle, Roussanne, Clairette, and Chardonnay, but other varieties can be included in the wines.

bellevue (en)

The term applied to several cold preparations of shellfish, fish, or poultry glazed with aspic jelly. For lobster, the flesh is cut into medallions which are garnished, glazed, and arranged in the shell (see (*à la*) *parisienne*). For small birds (woodcock, quail, thrush, etc.), the animal is boned, stuffed, poached in game stock, cooled, coated in a brown chaud-froid sauce, garnished, and glazed with aspic. The name would appear to come from the Château de Belleville, owned by Madame de Pompadour, who used to prepare attractive dishes to stimulate the appetite of Louis XV.

⌐ RECIPE

Glazed salmon en bellevue SAUMON GLACÉ EN BELLEVUE Prepare and

poach the salmon whole in a concentrated fish stock. Allow to cool completely in the cooking liquor, then drain. Remove the skin from both sides and dry the fish gently with absorbent paper (paper towels). Clarify the stock to make an aspic jelly and glaze the salmon with several coats, allowing each coat to set in the refrigerator before applying the next. Coat the base of the serving dish with a thin layer of aspic and lay the glazed salmon on top. Garnish with diced or cut shapes of aspic and keep in a cool place until ready to serve. (Salmon steaks and fillets can be prepared in the same way.)

Bel Paese

An Italian cheese manufactured in Lombardy from cows' milk (45% fat content). Creamy and mild, it is an uncooked pressed cheese, creamy yellow in colour, with a washed crust; it is usually wrapped in aluminium foil in small rounds, 20 cm (8 in) in diameter. Bel Paese (Italian for beautiful country) is appreciated the world over. It can also be used for cheese tarts and croques-monsieur.

Benedictine
BÉNÉDICTINE

An amber-coloured herby French liqueur used primarily as a digestive. Dom Bernardo Vincelli, an Italian Benedictine monk from the old Abbey of Fécamp, is credited with first producing it. The old recipe was discovered in 1863 by a local merchant, Alexandre Le Grand, in some family archives. He perfected the formula and began selling the liqueur, which was immediately successful. As a homage to the monks, he called it Benedictine and printed D.O.M. (*Deo Optimo Maximo*, 'To God, most good, most great'), the motto of the Benedictines, on the bottle.

Benedictine is based on 27 different plants and spices, which are incorporated in what is still a secret formula at the distillery at Fécamp in Normandy. 'B and B' (Benedictine and Brandy) is a compounded version of the liqueur.

bénédictine (à la)

The term applied to several dishes using either a purée of salt cod and potato, or salt cod pounded with garlic, oil, and cream. Cod is traditionally eaten during Lent, hence the allusion to the Benedictine monks. Many of these dishes can be enriched with truffle.

| RECIPE

Bouchées à la bénédictine Add diced truffle to a purée of salt cod with oil and cream. Use to fill small cooked puff pastry bouchée cases. Garnish each bouchée with a slice of truffle. Heat through in a hot oven.

Berchoux (Joseph)

French solicitor (born Saint-Symphorien-de-Lay, 1768; died Marcigny, 1839). His name survives as the author of a long poem in four cantos entitled *Gastronomie ou l'Homme des champs à table*, published in 1801. This lively composition was very popular in the Directory period, following the Reign of Terror, during which the French rediscovered the joys of good food. In the first canto, 'Histoire de la cuisine des Anciens', Berchoux describes, in brisk Alexandrines, such subjects as the death of Vatel and Spartan gruel. In the following cantos, 'Le Premier Service', 'Le Second Service', and 'Le Dessert', he sings the praises of good simple cooking. His philosophy is summed up in the following lines: 'A poem was never worth as much as a dinner' and 'Nothing must disturb an honest man while he dines'. It was he who introduced the word *gastronomie* to the French language.

| RECIPE

Salmon trout Berchoux TRUITE SAUMONÉE BERCHOUX Stuff a 2 kg (5 lb) salmon trout with a creamy pike forcemeat with chopped truffles. Place the trout in a buttered ovenproof dish on a bed consisting of a chopped carrot, a medium-sized chopped onion (lightly fried in butter), a good handful of mushroom peelings, and a bouquet garni. Add fish stock with white wine until it comes halfway up the trout. Season with salt and pepper, cover, place in a preheated oven (175 C, 350 F, gas 4), and cook for approximately 40 minutes, basting frequently until fish is just cooked. Remove the central portion of skin and the dark parts of the flesh. Strain the cooking liquor, pour a few tablespoons of this liquor over the trout, and glaze slightly in the oven.

Prepare the garnish: 8 small pastry barquettes filled with soft carp roe and coated with normande sauce; 8 small croquettes made of diced lobster, mushrooms, and truffles bound with a thin velouté sauce; and 8 very small artichoke hearts, partly cooked in white stock, sweated in butter, filled with a salpicon of truffles bound with cream, sprinkled with Parmesan, and browned in the oven. Add 3 dl (½ pint, 1¼ cups) velouté fish sauce to the remaining cooking liquor and reduce over a high heat, gradually adding 3 dl (½ pint, 1¼ cups) fresh double (heavy) cream to the sauce. Add butter and then strain or sieve. Use to coat the bottom of the dish and serve the rest in a sauceboat.

This traditional recipe can be modified by simplifying the garnishes.

Bercy

A district of Paris, which for a long time had the largest wine market in Europe and has given its name to several cooked dishes based on a wine sauce. These dishes were originally prepared in small restaurants but from 1820 onwards spread into the surrounding area. These restaurants served fried fish, fish stews, and grills, very often prepared with wine and shallots or served with shallot butter (for instance, the famous entrecôte Bercy). Eggs Bercy are also typical of this suburban cuisine.

| RECIPES

Bercy butter or shallot butter BEURRE BERCY OU BEURRE D'ÉCHALOTE Poach 500 g (18 oz) diced beef marrow in salted water and drain. Add to the liquid 1 tablespoon chopped shallots to 2 dl (7 fl oz, ¾ cup) dry white wine. Cool till lukewarm. Soften 200 g (7 oz, 1 cup) butter and add to the liquid, together with the marrow, 1 tablespoon chopped parsley, the juice of half a lemon, 8 g (¼ oz) fine salt, and a generous pinch of milled pepper. This butter is poured on top of grilled (broiled) meat or fish and may also be served separately in a sauceboat.

Bercy sauce or shallot sauce SAUCE
BERCY OU SAUCE À L'ÉCHALOTE
Peel and chop 3 or 4 shallots (enough
for 1 tablespoon chopped shallots).
Cook gently in 1 tablespoon butter
without browning. Add 1 dl (6 tablespoons, scant ½ cup) white wine and 1 dl
(6 tablespoons, scant ½ cup) white wine
and 1 dl (6 tablespoons, scant ½ cup)
fish stock. Reduce to half the volume.
Add 2 dl (7 fl oz, ¾ cup) thin velouté
sauce and boil vigorously for a few moments. Chop a small bunch of parsley.
Remove the pan from the heat and add
50 g (2 oz, 4 tablespoons) softened butter; finally, add the chopped parsley,
salt, and pepper. This sauce is a suitable
accompaniment to poached fish.

Brill à la Bercy BARBUE À LA
BERCY Preparé a brill weighing
approximately 750 g (1¼ lb), making
an incision along the middle of the dark
side of the fish and gently lifting the
fillets. Season with salt and pepper inside and out. Butter an ovenproof dish,
sprinkle with chopped shallots and
parsley, and lay the brill on top. Add 1
dl (6 tablespoons, scant ½ cup) dry
white wine and the same quantity of fish
stock. Dot with 50 g (2 oz, 4 tablespoons) butter. Start cooking on top of
the stove then transfer to a moderate
oven (180 C, 350 F, gas 4) and bake for
15 minutes, basting frequently. Then
place the dish under the grill to glaze the
fish and reduce the volume of the cooking liquor. Finally sprinkle with a dash
of lemon juice and chopped parsley. The
fish stock may be replaced by dry white
wine diluted with the juice of half a
lemon and water.

Omelette à la Bercy OMELETTE À LA
BERCY Grill (broil) or fry some chipolata sausages. Make an omelette with
chopped mixed herbs added to the eggs;
fill with chipolatas and surround with a
ribbon of tomato sauce. The chipolatas
may be cut in two.

bergamot BERGAMOTE
A small yellow sour citrus fruit, similar
to the orange, the rind of which contains
an essential oil used in perfumery and
confectionery. The zest is used in pâtisserie. The bergamot is mostly cultivated
in Calabria.

Bergamot is also the name of a small
square honey-coloured barley sugar,
flavoured with natural bergamot
essence, which has been a speciality of
the town of Nancy since 1850.

Finally, there is a variety of pear
called bergamot: it is almost round with
a yellowish skin and very sweet fragrant
juicy flesh.

Bergerac
Wine from the Dordogne area of southwestern France. This wine-growing
region, situated in the district of Bergerac, has been famous since the Middle
Ages for the quality of its white wines; it
also produces reds and a few rosés,
appreciated locally.

Bergerac blanc, which may be a crisp
white wine or a full-bodied slightly
sweet one, is made from the Sauvignon,
Sémillon, and Muscadelle grapes, and
also sometimes from some Chenin
Blanc. The red wines are made from the
Bordeaux grapes Cabernet-Sauvignon,
Cabernet Franc, Malbec, and Merlot.
The reds from the left-bank vineyards of
the Dordogne are more full-bodied than
those on the right, where the wines are
more supple. All are subject to controls,
for the AOC 'Bergerac' and 'Côte de
Bergerac'.

berlingot
A pyramid-shaped boiled sweet, usually
flavoured with peppermint, with alternating clear and opaque stripes. Some
authorities say that it was created in the
Middle Ages, but its present formula
was perfected under Louis XVI by a
certain Madame Couet, who handed it
down to her descendants. In 1851, at
Carpentras, Gustave Esseyric revived
the recipe using peppermint cultivated
in Vaucluse. This peppermint gives a
particular flavour to the berlingots
which are produced in this town, using
sugar syrups left over from the preparation of crystallized (candied) fruit.
Nantes (since 1780), Saint-Quentin,
and Caen are also famous for their berlingots. Although most are flavoured
with peppermint, fruit-flavoured
mixtures are also used.

Berlingots are manufactured by
wrapping a sausage shape of boiled,
flavoured, and coloured sugar in bands
of transparent sugar alternating with

bands of beaten sugar. The sausage is then stretched and shaped in a *berlingotière* (a rotating machine with four blades) or a ring press.

The origin of the word is controversial. Some say that it is derived from the Italian *berlingozzo* (a very sweet cake), others from the Provençal *berlingan* (knuckle-bone). By extension, it is also used (in France) for a pyramid-shaped cardboard container for milk.

Bernis (Pierre de)

French diplomat (born Saint-Marcel-d'Ardèche, 1715; died Rome, 1794). A protégé of Madame de Pompadour, he was elected to the Académie Française at the age of 29 for his elegant verse; he then became a cardinal and ambassador, first to Venice, then to Rome at the Holy See. In all these posts, he proved himself to be a remarkable ambassador of French cuisine and his table was known as 'the best inn in France'. Chefs have given his name to various egg preparations using asparagus.

RECIPE

Soft-boiled or poached eggs Bernis OEUFS BERNIS MOLLETS OU POCHÉS Fill some puff pastry tarts with chicken mousse. Arrange the eggs in the tarts and coat with suprême sauce. Place the tarts in a ring on a serving dish and garnish in the centre with green asparagus tips coated with melted butter.

Berny

A method of preparing croquette potatoes, which are coated in chopped almonds then fried. A Berny garnish consists of small tarts filled with lentil purée and served with game.

berrichonne (à la)

A term applied to regional dishes from Berry. Large joints of meat garnished *à la berrichonne* are served with braised green cabbage (stuffed or plain), poached chestnuts, small glazed onions, and slices of lean bacon; the meat juice is slightly thickened. Chicken fricassee *à la berrichonne* is served with new carrots; potatoes *à la berrichonne* are cooked with onions and fat bacon.

RECIPE

Potatoes à la berrichonne POMMES DE TERRE À LA BERRICHONNE Peel 1 kg (2 lb) very small potatoes. Peel and chop 2 onions. Cut 100g (4 oz) streaky bacon into small strips. Brown the onions and bacon in a frying pan (skillet), then add the potatoes and brown slightly. Pour in just enough stock to cover, add a bouquet garni, salt, and pepper, then cover and cook gently for 20–25 minutes (depending on the cooking time for the potatoes: prick with a fork to test when they are cooked). Serve sprinkled with chopped parsley in a vegetable dish.

Berry

The gastronomy of this old French province is influenced by pig, poultry, and sheep farming, as can be seen from its most typical meat dishes: seven-hour braised leg of lamb, *saupiquet*, *sagourne*, Easter pâté (made from pork and hard-boiled (hard-cooked) eggs, *sanguette*, black roast turkey, and chicken *en barbouille*. Cuisine *à la berrichonne* is typified by the tasty, sometimes rustic, simplicity of its slow-cooked dishes. Soup and stew (with fritons known as *grignaudes*) play an important role, together with the accompanying vegetables, *tartoufes* (potatoes), and pumpkin (also used in a cake) Chestnuts and field mushrooms have inspired recipes for carp (steamed), lamprey, and salmon (braised).

One of the characteristics of this wine-growing region, which produces AOC wines (such as Reuilly, Chateaumeillant, Sancerre, Quincy, and Menetou-Salon) and rosé wines, is the use of wine in cooking: eggs in red wine and meat and fish stews cooked with wine. Cheeses are made mostly from goats' milk (Valençay, Pouligny, Chavignol, Levroux, Selles-sur-Cher). Fruit and nut trees are grown – cherry (for Kirsch), pear, walnut, and hazelnut – and fruit is used in sweet desserts (see *poirat*, *citrouillat*, *sanciau*) and fritters. *Lichouneries* (confectioners' shops) sell *forestines* from Bourges (with hazelnuts), marzipan, barley sugar, and *croquets*.

berry BAIE

Any small fleshy stoneless fruit containing one or more seeds. Berries occur singly, in bunches (e.g. grape and redcurrant), or in clusters (elderberry).

Wild berries, which may be eaten raw or cooked, are particularly rich in vitamins, particularly vitamin C, and were formerly widely used in pharmacopeias.

besugo

The Basque name for red mullet. The typical Christmas besugo dish (also called *arroséla*) is prepared by grilling (broiling) the fish, opening and boning it, and sprinkling with finely chopped red pepper and oil in which two or three cloves of garlic have been fried.

bêtise

A mint-flavoured boiled sweet manufactured in France since 1850. Although the Afchain company of Cambrai has long claimed to be sole inventor of bêtises, their exact origin is not known. Legend has it that a clumsy apprentice poured the ingredients (sugar, glucose, and mint) badly, but perhaps it was a flash of genius on the part of a confectioner who had the idea of blowing air into the sugar. The microscopic air bubbles incorporated into the hot boiled sugar make the sweet light and opaque. Bêtises remain a speciality of Cambrai but are imitated by the *sottises* made in Valenciennes.

bettelman

An Alsatian dessert (the name means literally beggar). It is made from small stale milk bread rolls. The crust is grated to make breadcrumbs and the crumb, soaked in vanilla-flavoured boiled milk, is crushed and mixed with sugar, egg yolks, finely diced candied orange peel, stoned (pitted) black (Bing) cherries, Kirsch, cinnamon, and stiffly beaten egg whites. The mixture is poured into a buttered china mould and the top is sprinkled with the breadcrumbs and dotted with butter. The bettelman is baked in a moderately hot oven (190 c, 375 f, gas 5) and served warm or cold.

beugnon

A type of fritter that is a traditional dish of central France. Similar to the bugne from Lyon, it is made of leavened dough shaped into a small ring, and is often fried in walnut oil.

beurre blanc

A sauce made with reduced vinegar and shallots to which butter is added; its English name is white butter sauce. It is the standard accompaniment to pike and shad. The Nantes region and Anjou both claim to be the birthplace of this famous sauce. It is said that a chef from Nantes called Clémence forgot to include the eggs when attempting to make a good béarnaise sauce for a pike for his master (the Marquis de Goulaine). It was nevertheless a success and Clémence subsequently opened a restaurant at La Chebuette near Nantes; this is where Mère Michel learned the secret of beurre blanc before opening her famous restaurant in the Rue Rennequin in Paris. Curnonsky praised the beurre blanc of La Poissonnière, a fish restaurant near Angers.

RECIPE

Beurre blanc Peel and chop 5 or 6 shallots. Place in a saucepan with ¼ litre (8 fl oz, 1 cup) wine vinegar, ⅓ litre (11 fl oz, 1⅓ cups) fish stock, and ground pepper; reduce by two-thirds. Cut 250 g (½ lb, 1 cup) very cold butter (preferably slightly salted) into small pieces. Remove the pan from the heat and add the butter all at once, beating briskly by hand until smooth. Season with salt and pepper. Pour the sauce into a warmed sauceboat and place in a lukewarm bain-marie until required for serving.

The emulsion can be stabilized by adding 1 tablespoon double (heavy) cream; this is Nantes butter (*beurre nantais*).

beurre manié

See *butter*.

biarrote (à la)

Describing a garnish for small cuts of meat, which are arranged on a base of potato galettes (prepared as for duchess potatoes) and surrounded by a ring of grilled (broiled) cep mushrooms. This name comes from the town of Biarritz, where several new restaurants were opened as a result of visits by the Emperor Napoleon III and the Empress Eugénie. It is also applied to a recipe for sautéed chicken in white wine, which may also be garnished with ceps.

RECIPE

Sautéed chicken à la biarrote POULET SAUTÉ À LA BIARROTTE Cut a 1.4-kg (3-lb) chicken into pieces and sauté until brown on all sides and cooked through. Deglaze with 1 dl (6 tablespoons, scant ½ cup) dry or medium white wine. After reducing, add 1 dl (6 tablespoons, scant ½ cup) tomato sauce and a dash of grated garlic. Using a separate pan, sauté 125 g (4 oz, 1 cup) ceps, 125 g (4 oz, ⅔ cup) diced potatoes, and 1 diced aubergine (eggplant) in olive oil. Fry a thinly sliced onion, separating the rings. Arrange the chicken in a heated serving dish, coat with sauce, and arrange the garnish in bouquets around it.

bib TACAUD

A coastal fish, similar to cod, commonly found in the English Channel and the Bay of Biscay. Shaped like an elongated triangle, with a copper-coloured back and silvery sides and belly, it measures 20–30 cm (8–12 in) and weighs about 200 g (7 oz). It has a short barbel on the lower jaw, long thin pelvic fins, and two abdominal fins connected by a membrane. The flesh, although lean, is rather tasteless and full of bones and deteriorates rapidly. Bib must therefore be prepared and eaten as soon as it is caught. It is cooked in the same way as fresh cod.

bicarbonate of soda

BICARBONATE DE SOUDE
An alkaline powder used in medicine as an antacid. In cookery, bicarbonate of soda is used to soften water for cooking vegetables and to preserve the colour of green vegetables.

Bicarbonate of soda is one of the main ingredients of raising (leavening) agents: it improves the action of baking powder in many commercial preparations (cake mixes, processed flour, etc.).

Bignon (Louis)

French restaurateur (born Hérisson, 1816; died Macau, 1906). He began his career in Paris as a waiter at the Café d'Orsay, then moved to the Café au Foy, which he acquired and passed on to his brother in 1847. He then took over the management of the Café Riche, redecorated it, and made it one of the best in Paris. His activities also extended into viticulture and agriculture. He was a founder member of the Société des Agriculteurs de France and during the World Fairs from 1862 to 1880 he won the highest prizes for various agricultural products, wines, and foods. He became a knight of the Order of the Legion of Honour in 1868 and officer in 1878, and was the first restaurant owner to wear the rosette of the Legion of Honour. Bignon was highly regarded by his colleagues and was elected president of the union of restaurateurs and dealers in soft drinks of the Seine department.

bigos

A Polish dish, also called 'hunter's stew', made of alternating layers of sauerkraut and cooked meat simmered for a long time in bouillon. Bigos is served with small grilled (broiled) sausages and traditionally precedes the soup course. It may be prepared with just one type of meat or with any mixture of duck, boiled beef, ham, mutton, pickled pork, or even venison.

RECIPE

Bigos Wash 4 kg (8½ lb) raw sauerkraut, changing the water several times. Place in a large saucepan and completely cover with cold water. Bring to the boil. Peel, core, and dice 4 apples, sprinkling the pieces with lemon juice. Drain the boiling sauerkraut in a colander and add the apples and 2 large chopped onions. Melt 4 tablespoons (⅓ cup) lard in a cooking pot and cover with a fairly thick layer of sauerkraut, then a layer of pieces of cooked meat. Continue filling the pot with alternate layers of meat and sauerkraut, finishing with sauerkraut and adding a little lard every now and then. Pour in enough stock to cover the sauerkraut. Cover the pot, and bake in the oven at 180 c (350 F, gas 4). After 1½ hours make a white roux and add some of the cooking liquor. Pour this sauce over the bigos and cook for a further 30 minutes.

bilberry MYRTILLE

A shrub native to northern regions of Europe and America and also cultivated; it is also known as whortleberry and huckleberry. Its small purplish-blue berries, which have an acid flavour, have a calorific value of 16 Cal per 100 g and are rich in vitamins B and C. Bilberries are usually used for making tarts, ices, and sorbets, as well as compotes, jams, jellies, syrups, and liqueurs. They freeze well.

RECIPE

Bilberry flan TARTE AUX MYRTILLES Make some shortcrust pastry (basic pie dough) with 200 g (7 oz, generous 1½ cups) flour, 100 g (4 oz, ½ cup) butter cut into pieces, a pinch of salt, 1 tablespoon caster (superfine) sugar, and 3 tablespoons (¼ cup) cold water. Form into a ball and leave it to stand for 2 hours.

Wash and dry 300 g (11 oz, 2¾ cups) fresh bilberries (or use frozen fruit). Prepare a syrup with 100 g (4 oz, ½ cup) sugar and ¼ litre (8 fl oz, 1 cup) water. Cook it for 5 minutes, then add the bilberries and leave to soak for 5 minutes. Return to a gentle heat and cook for 8 minutes, until all the syrup is absorbed.

Roll out the pastry and use it to line a buttered 22-cm (9-in) flan tin (pie pan). Cover the bottom with a piece of buttered greaseproof (waxed) paper and bake blind for 12 minutes in a moderate oven (200 c, 400 F, gas 6); remove the paper and continue cooking for a further 6–7 minutes until the flan base is golden. Leave until lukewarm before turning out.

When the pastry case is completely cold, fill it with the bilberries, smoothing the top. Dilute 2 tablespoons (3 tablespoons) apricot purée with 1 teaspoon water, warm over a gentle heat, sieve, and coat the bilberries with the glaze. Leave until completely cold.

Prepare a Chantilly cream by whipping 1 dl (6 tablespoons, scant ½ cup) double (heavy) cream with 1 tablespoon chilled milk, 1 teaspoon vanilla-flavoured sugar, and 1 tablespoon icing (confectioners') sugar. Using a forcing bag fitted with a fluted nozzle, pipe the cream on top of the tart and decorate with a few sugared violets.

Bilberry jam CONFITURE DE MYRTILLES Stalk and wash the berries (without letting them soak), then dry and weigh them. Put them into a preserving pan with water (½ glass (4 fl oz, ½ cup) water per kg (2¼ lb) berries). Bring to the boil, skim, and simmer for about 10 minutes. Then add a weight of sugar equal to the weight of the fruit. Bring back to the boil, skim again, then leave to cook for about 15 minutes, stirring regularly. Jar in the usual way (see *jams, jellies, and marmalades*).

billy by or bilibi

A mussel soup said to have been created by Barthe, the chef of Maxim's, for a regular customer called Billy, who adored mussels. Billy by is made of mussels cooked in white wine with onions, parsley, celery, and fish stock. The soup is served hot or ice-cold with fresh cream, the mussels and grated Parmesan cheese being served separately. Other sources claim that billy by was invented in Normandy, after the Normandy landings, when a farewell dinner was given to an American officer called Bill. So it was called 'Billy, bye bye', which degenerated to 'billy by'.

birds OISEAUX

Many varieties of wild and domesticated birds are used in cookery (see *game, poultry*). The consumption of small wild birds has declined as protection orders become more stringent. In France, all birds smaller than the thrush are protected, except for larks, ortolans, and sparrows in some regions. In times past, however, bird-catchers supplied the gourmand with many small birds: tits, warblers, curlews, jays, sandpipers, robins, wagtails, and sparrows (whose delicate meat was reserved for the sick and convalescent); as a general rule, the only birds to escape the slaughter were nightingales and wrens. The crow was much sought after for soup or, in England, for pies. In former times, the wild birds most esteemed were whole roast heron, scoter-duck and plover roasted with hot pepper, roast partridge and turtledoves served with cinnamon or ginger sauce, and turtledove pâté.

The rearing and consumption of domestic poultry, on the other hand, continues to expand. Quail-rearing has to some extent filled the gap left by the banning of other wild birds.

Birdseye (Clarence)

American businessman and inventor (born New York, 1886; died New York 1956). During a journey to Labrador in 1920, he observed that fish caught by the Eskimos and exposed to the air froze rapidly and thus remained edible for several months. On his return to the United States, Birdseye succeeded in perfecting a mechanical process for ultra-rapid freezing. In 1924 he formed a company to produce and distribute these frozen products, but the economic crisis forced him to sell his process and name to a food company. The name of this pioneer of cold storage, split into 'Bird's Eye', became an international tradename for deep-frozen food.

bird's-foot trefoil   LOTIER

A leguminous plant also known in France as *mélilot*, *trèfle de cheval*, *mirlirot*, etc., according to the species. When dried, the leaves, flowers, and stems give off a very pleasant smell and can be used to flavour marinades. In some areas it is used to flavour rabbit, which is stuffed with the leaves and flowers after it has been cleaned. In Switzerland *mélilot* is used to make herbal tea. Some cheeses (notably the German cows'-milk cheese Schabzieger and curd cheeses) are flavoured with the yellow flowers of bird's-foot trefoil.

birds' nests

NIDS D'HIRONDELLE

Nests built by the salangane, a type of Chinese swallow. Just before the breeding season, the birds feed on gelatinous seaweed, which makes their salivary glands secrete a thick whitish glutinous saliva with which they construct their nests. These nests are used in traditional Chinese cookery to make bird's-nest soup. After being soaked in water they become transparent and gelatinous, giving the soup its characteristic odour and sticky texture. The nests may also be used in stews and as an ingredient in certain garnishes. The first European travellers to discover them, at the beginning of the 17th century, believed that they consisted of a mixture of lime and sea foam, or else the sap of trees. It was the French naturalist Buffon who established their true composition, after hearing an eye-witness account of the nests from the explorer Poivre.

⎮ RECIPE

Bird's-nest consommé CONSOMMÉ AUX NIDS D'HIRONDELLE   Make some well-seasoned chicken consommé and clarify it. (In China it is traditional to use duck soup.) Soak some Chinese swallows' nests in cold water for 2 hours, allowing one nest per serving – each nest weighs about 12 g ($\frac{1}{2}$ oz). When the nests have become transparent, carefully remove any pieces of egg shell or other foreign matter, then blanch them for 5 minutes in boiling water. Drain the nests and place them in the boiling consommé. Poach gently, without boiling, for 30–45 minutes. Serve the soup boiling hot in small porcelain bowls.

bireweck

An Alsatian cake, also called *pain de fruits* ('fruit loaf'). It is made from leavened dough flavoured with Kirsch and mixed with fresh, dried, and crystallized (candied) fruit. Usually shaped into small balls, it can also be made in one large piece and sold in slices.

⎮ RECIPE

Bireweck   Cook 500 g (18 oz) pears, 250 g (9 oz) apples, 250 g (9 oz) peaches, 250 g (9 oz) dried figs, and 250 g (9 oz) prunes in a little water, but do not allow them to become pulpy. Mix 1 kg (2¼ lb, 9 cups) sifted flour and 30 g (1 oz) baker's yeast with enough cooking water from the fruit to form a soft dough. Leave to rise for 2 hours. Meanwhile, finely dice 100 g (3½ oz) candied citron and 50 g (2 oz) angelica. When the dough has risen, mix in the diced candied fruit, 250 g (9 oz, 1½ cups) sultanas, 125 g (4½ oz, ¾ cup) hazelnuts, 125 g (4½ oz, ¾ cup) almonds,

67797

125 g (4½ oz, 1 cup) walnuts, 50 g (2 oz) blanched strips of orange zest, 125 g (4½ oz, ¾ cup) stoned (pitted) dates, and the drained cooked fruit. Add 2 dl (7 fl oz, ¾ cup) Kirsch and mix well. Divide the dough into 200 g (7 oz) portions (about 28). Shape into rolls and smooth the surface with water. Bake at 160 c (325 F, gas 3) for about 1¾ hours.

biscotte parisienne

A light biscuit cooked once in the oven (unlike the true biscotte (see *rusk*), which is cooked twice). It is made from almonds, egg yolks, beaten egg whites, and cornflour (cornstarch), flavoured with Kirsch and piped onto a buttered baking sheet.

biscuit

A sweet or savoury dry flat cake with a high calorie content (420–510 Cal per 100 g).

As their name implies (it comes from the French *bis* = twice + *cuit* = cooked), biscuits should in theory be cooked twice. However, this is no longer practised, although the Reims biscuit was originally a flat cake that was put back in the oven after being removed from its tin. This made it drier and harder but improved its keeping qualities. This very hard, barely risen biscuit was for centuries the staple food of soldiers and sailors. Roman legions were familiar with it and Pliny claimed that 'Parthian bread' would keep for centuries. In his account of the Crusades, the Lord of Joinville talks of 'bread called "bequis" because it is cooked twice'. Soldiers' biscuits or army biscuits were known under Louis XIV as 'stone bread' (*pain de pierre*). In 1894, army biscuits were replaced by war bread made of starch, sugar, water, nitrogenous matter, ash, and cellulose, but the name 'army biscuit' stuck, even when the method of manufacture changed. It did not disappear until soldiers were supplied with proper bread, even on campaigns.

'Animalized' biscuits were also made. These were flat cakes containing meat juices and thought to be very nourishing. Vitamin biscuits appeared during World War II and these were distributed in schools in France. Nowadays, some special diet products are presented as vitamin-enriched biscuits with different flavours.

Biscuits were also a staple item in explorers' provisions. In his record of his adventures in the New World, Chateaubriand wrote: 'Reduced to a solitary existence, I dined on ship's biscuits, a little sugar and lemon.'

'Travellers' biscuits', in the 19th century, were hard pastries or cakes wrapped in tin foil, which kept well (see *beauvilliers*).

biscuit manufacture
BISCUITERIE

The industrial manufacture of biscuits (cookies and crackers) began in Britain. The Carr establishment, founded in Carlisle in 1815, was the first factory that specialized in the production of biscuits, and was soon followed by MacFarlane in Edinburgh and Huntley and Palmers in Reading. These manufacturers exported their specialities all over the world, often sponsored by famous names. For example, the Albert was a small savoury biscuit bearing the name of the Prince Consort. It was not until 1840 that Jean-Honoré Olibet, a baker's son from Bordeaux, founded the first French biscuit factory. Soon other industrialists followed suit. In 1882, the Lefèvre-Utile factory invented the petit beurre.

Biscuit-making has now become a very active branch of the food industry. The ingredients used include varying proportions of flour, vegetable fats (shortening) or butter, sugar (usually sucrose, but sometimes glucose or maltose), starch, milk, eggs, and baking powder. Permitted additives, such as antioxidants, colouring agents, emulsifiers, flavourings, etc., must be listed on the packaging. Flavours are extremely varied and include coffee, vanilla, chocolate, coconut, aniseed, cinnamon, and ginger. Liqueurs, jam, dried or crystallized (candied) fruit, nuts, etc. may also be incorporated. Production is completely automatic at all stages of manufacture, which include kneading, shaping, baking, cooling, sorting, and packing.

Sweet or savoury, biscuits are classified, in France, into three major categories depending on the consistency of the dough.

• *Hard or semi-hard dough* is used for petits beurres, tea biscuits (filled or plain), shortbread biscuits, girdle cakes, and various crackers and aperitif biscuits that may be seasoned with salt and other flavourings (cumin, cheese, paprika, etc.). These biscuits, which are the most widely consumed, contain approximately 70% flour and are made without eggs.

• *Soft dough* is used to make either dry biscuits (boudoir biscuits, cigarettes, tuiles, palets, langues de chat, and palmiers) or soft biscuits (sponge fingers, nonettes, madeleines, macaroons, rochers, petits fours, congolais and croquignoles). These biscuits are made with a high proportion of egg white.

• *Liquid dough* is used to make wafer biscuits (dry, iced, or filled). These biscuits have a high liquid content and may be made with water or milk and small amounts of fat and flour.

Biscuits are usually served with a drink, a dessert, or with ice cream: the choice of biscuit depends on what it is to be served with. Some biscuits are used in the preparation of desserts (charlottes, for example). Biscuit consumption is particularly high in Great Britain and northern Europe. Some regional specialities continue to be produced by small local manufacturers and include croquets, macaroons, almond biscuits, aniseed biscuits, schenkels and pretzels, etc.

Bishop BICHOF

An ancient mixed drink made with wine, citrus fruit, and spices, served either hot or iced. In his *Dictionnaire de cuisine*, Alexandre Dumas says that this drink was called Bishop (German *Bischof*) when made with red Bordeaux (because of its purple colour), Cardinal when made with red Rhine wine, and Pope when made with Tokay (white). Originating in the Rhineland, it came to France through Alsace, where hot spiced wines are popular. The classic English Bishop was made by heating claret with orange and lemon peel, cinnamon, and cloves. It is still a popular winter drink. There are many other traditional British recipes for mixed drinks of this sort, named after church officials: Prebendary, Beadle, Churchwarden, etc.

⎡ RECIPE

Rhine wine Bishop BICHOF AU VIN DU RHIN Dissolve 250 g (9 oz, 1 cup, firmly packed) granulated sugar in 3 dl (½ pint, 1¼ cups) water over a low heat with the peel of an orange and a lemon, 2 cloves, and a stick of cinnamon. Cook for 5 minutes. Add a bottle of Rhine wine and heat until a fine white froth begins to appear on the surface. Strain and serve in a jug or in a large punch bowl. This drink is sometimes flavoured with a little Madeira, sherry, or Marsala.

bison (buffalo)

A wild ox formerly widely distributed over the plains of North America. It was once a symbol of prosperity and plenty for the Indians, who used its meat, fat, hide, horns, etc. It was systematically hunted from the end of the 19th century onwards and now reconstituted herds live either on reserves or on ranches, where they are bred for the meat trade. Bison flesh is juicy with a pronounced flavour and is mostly eaten in the American West and Canada. (A cross between the bison and the cow has produced beefalo, whose meat is popular in some areas.) Bison is most commonly eaten either smoked (especially the tongue) or marinated. The hump is considered to be a delicacy. A typical Canadian dish is bison in brine, desalted, boiled for several hours, and then served with cabbage, carrots, potatoes, fresh cream, and seasoning. Bison meat may also be minced for making meat balls or smoked, powdered, mixed with fat, and used either to make soups or to spread on bread.

These methods of preparation are mostly inspired by ancient Indian recipes such as the Cheyenne recipe described by C. Lévi-Strauss in *The Origin of Table Manners*: 'They placed thin slices of hard meat carefully on a bed of charcoal, first on one side then the other. They beat them to break them into small pieces which they mixed with melted bison fat and marrow. Then they pressed it into leather bags, taking care that no air was left inside. When the bags were sewn up, the women flattened them by jumping on them to blend the ingredients. Then they put them to dry in the sun.'

bisque

A seasoned shellfish purée flavoured with white wine, Cognac, and fresh cream, used as the basis of a soup. The flesh of the main ingredient (crayfish, lobster, crab, etc.) is diced as for a salpicon and used as a garnish. The shells are also used to make the initial purée.

The word bisque has been in use for centuries and suggests a connection with the Spanish province of Biscay. It was originally used to describe a highly spiced dish of boiled meat or game. Subsequently, bisques were made using pigeons or quails and garnished with crayfish or cheese croûtes. It was not until the 17th century that crayfish became the principal ingredient of this dish, which soon after was also prepared with other types of shellfish.

RECIPES

Crayfish bisque BISQUE D'ÉCRE-VISSES Prepare 5–6 tablespoons mirepoix that has been cooked in 40 g (1½ oz, 3 tablespoons) butter until soft. Allow 1.25 litres (2¼ pints, 3 pints) consommé (or fish stock). Cook 75 g (3 oz, 6 tablespoons) short-grain rice in ½ litre (17 fl oz, 2 cups) of the consommé. Dress and wash 18 good-sized crayfish. Add the crayfish to the mirepoix together with salt, freshly ground pepper, and a bouquet garni, and sauté the crayfish until the shells turn red. Heat 3 tablespoons (¼ cup) Cognac in a small ladle, pour on to the crayfish, and set alight, stirring well.

Add 1 dl (6 tablespoons, scant ½ cup) dry white wine and reduce by two-thirds. Add 1.5 dl (¼ pint, ⅔ cup) consommé and cook gently for 10 minutes.

Shell the crayfish when cold. Finely dice the tail meat and reserve for the garnish. Pound the shells, the cooked rice, and the cooking liquor and rub through a fine sieve (or use a blender). Place the resulting purée in a saucepan with the remainder of the consommé and boil for 5–6 minutes. Just before serving, cool the bisque slightly then add a dash of cayenne and 1.5 dl (¼ pint, ⅔ cup) fresh cream, followed by 60 g (2¼ oz, 4¼ tablespoons) butter cut up into very small pieces. Add the diced tail meat and serve piping hot.

Lobster bisque BISQUE DE HO-MARDS Prepare in the same way as crayfish bisque, but replace the crayfish with an equal weight of small lobsters cut into pieces and sautéed in the mirepoix. If desired, it can be prepared using only the meat from the thorax, legs, and claws (the meat should be finely diced). The tails can then be used for medallions.

bistro BISTROT

A bar or small restaurant. The origin of this familiar word is obscure. It first appeared in the French language in 1884, but its etymology is often given as the Russian word *bistro* (quick), which the Cossacks used to get quick service at a bar during the Russian occupation of Paris in 1815. There also appears to be a relationship with the word *bistreau*, which in the dialects of western France describes a cowherd and, by extension, a jolly fellow – an apt description of the innkeeper. The most likely origin is doubtless an abbreviation of the word *bistrouille*. Modern French bistros are of modest appearance and frequently offer local dishes, cold meats, and cheese with their wine.

bistrouille or bistouille

In northern France, the term used for a mixture of coffee and brandy. It is derived from *bis* (twice) and *touiller* (to mix). It may also be used to describe a poor-quality brandy.

bitoke

A dish made with minced lean beef moulded into a flat, oval, or round shape. It was introduced into French cuisine by Russian émigrés in the 1920s. In Russian cookery, minced meat is often used for meatballs (*bitki*) and croquettes.

RECIPE

Bitoke To make a single bitoke, finely mince 125 g (4½ oz, ½ cup) lean beef and add 30 g (1 oz, 2 tablespoons) butter, salt, pepper, and a little grated nutmeg. Shape the mixture into a flattened ball, coat in flour, and sauté in clarified butter. Add 1 tablespoon fresh cream and 1 teaspoon lemon juice to the cooking liquor to make a sauce. Coat the bitoke with the sauce and garnish with fried onion. Serve with sauté potatoes. (The minced beef may also be coated with egg and breadcrumbs before cooking.)

bitter   AMER

Having a sharp or acid flavour. Certain bitter plants are used in cooking: they include chicory, bay, ginger, rhubarb, orange, and bitter almond. Others, whose bitterness is brought out by infusion or distillation, are used essentially in drinks: wormwood, camomile, centaury, gentian, hops, cinchona, etc. See *bitters*.

bitter orange

See *Seville orange*.

bitters   BITTER

An aromatic alcoholic or nonalcoholic drink with a bitter flavour. The very aromatic types are usually drunk alone or with soda; the others, such as peach or orange bitters, are used for flavouring mixed drinks. Many bitters come from Italy (for example, Campari and Fernet-Branca). They are usually wine-based and common flavourings are gentian and orange peel. Bitters may be served as apéritifs, digestives, or pick-me-ups and in various cocktails. French bitters include Amer Picòn, Selestat, Toni-Kola, Arquebuse, and Suze.

Black Africa   AFRIQUE NOIRE

The cuisine of the countries of Black Africa is little known in Europe, since it calls for ingredients which are difficult to obtain elsewhere. These include meats (buffalo, zebra, camel, snake, monkey and even elephant, hippopotamus, and lion, which are now protected species), fish (such as *tiof* – a near relative of the bass, *capitaine*, and the freshwater fish *manvi*), and plants (monkey bread, *n'dole* leaves, cassava, *fonio*, shea nuts, sorghum). African cooking is more varied in the west of the continent than in the east, except in Ethiopia (where it is very sophisticated: a characteristic dish is a rich and elaborately prepared meat sauce known as *went*). But it has generally retained a rustic character – in cooking over a wood fire and the use of a boiling pot in which everything cooks together. In Madagascar and Réunion Island there is a notable Indian influence (curry, rougails, achars).

□ **Unusual flavours** The most common African dishes are ragout and *canari* – a dish cooked without water in an earthenware vessel; both of these are seasoned with a vast assortment of condiments. As well as the traditional spices like pepper, ginger, garlic (*thoum*), pimiento (*pili pili*), and nutmeg, Africans use *atokiko* (mango stones), tamarind, *tô* (millet paste), *lalo* (powdered baobab leaves), and *soumbala* (dried and crushed fruit rind), as well as dried larvae and locusts. Peanuts, palm oil, and coconut also add their distinctive flavour to meat and fish dishes. Cassava is the basic starchy food, and sorghum the most extensively used cereal.

Salads and raw vegetables are unknown in African menus, but there is a great variety of soups: *nkui* (based on okra, husks, and maize dumplings) in Cameroon; *pepe supi* (in which meat is mixed with fish) in Guinea; 'churching' soup (made from hen and tripe) in Mali; and *caidou* (made from fish and rice) in Senegal. Many countries have a single traditional dish that is regarded as the national dish: *zegeni* from Eritrea (mutton with pimiento paste and vegetables, served with unleavened biscuits); *cosidou* from Benin (a kind of stew similar to Portuguese *cocido*); *dou louf* from Chad (shin (shank) and foot of beef with okra); *vary amin* from Madagascar (stew made of zebra, with chow-chow, tomatoes, and ginger); *yassa* from Senegal; *mafé* from West Africa (beef with peanuts and millet); *kourkouri* from Burkina Faso (pork stew); *bosaka* from the Ivory Coast (cockerel fried in palm oil); *massale* from Réunion Island (curried kid); etc.

Couscous is made throughout Africa, but based on millet rather than wheat, like *bassi salte* from Senegal; it is also made with maize in Cameroon, and with whole wheat in Chad. Vegetable accompaniments vary according to local resources: green cabbage and unroasted peanuts in Mali; dates, raisins, and artichoke hearts in Niger; pumpkin and aubergines (egg-plants) in Burkina Faso.

The basic dish which distinguishes African cooking relies on the association of two essential elements: (1) a starchy food (cassava, yam, sweet potato, taro, or plantain) or a cereal (rice, *fonio*, sorghum, or millet), reduced to a paste or gruel; and (2) a substantial ragout sauce, combining vegetables (spinach, palm seeds, tomatoes, okra), meat and/or fish, pistachios, peanuts, green mangoes, etc. According to its country of origin, this dish is called *foutou* (or *foufou*), *placali*, *gari*, or *aitiou* (based on maize).

Gourds and tuberous roots are the main African vegetables, with 'green leaves' (of pumpkin, aubergine (egg-plant) or beans) and all varieties of banana, which are eaten as paste, croquettes, sautéed (as in *dop* in Cameroon), or fried.

☐ **A wide variety of resources** While African cooking is closely related to local resources – ragout of viper in Cameroon, crocodile tail in Burkina Faso, monkey kebabs in Casamance (Senegal), camel with yams in Mali – it also includes dishes less unusual to European and North American palates. Chicken, in particular, is prepared in many ways – with coconut, ginger, unripe bananas, peanuts – while beef and pork are usually braised or cooked in a stew, and mutton is grilled (broiled).

On the coasts, the supply of fish provides variety in the menu, particularly in Benin (*ago glain* – ragout of crab with rice), Senegal (*tié bou diéné*), and in Guinea and Togo (sea perch with ginger, stuffed mullet). Giant oysters and crayfish are eaten fried. Tuna fish achar is a typical dish of Réunion Island, and cod, in salad or cooked in breadcrumbs, is a speciality of Guinea.

☐ **Desserts and drinks** Although goat milk curds are eaten, Africa produces practically no cheese, except henna cheese (in Mali, Niger, and Benin), which is crumbled into sauces. On the other hand, there is a great variety of fruits, many of which have high nut-ritional value – papaw, for instance. Avocado and custard apples are made into compotes and custards. Fruit also accompanies rice and semolina puddings, while bananas make delicious fritters and pancakes are made from sweet potato, which is also used with coconut to make cakes.

Drinks, too, are made from fruits – coconut or custard-apple milk, banana juice, and pineapple cider. A great quantity of alcoholic beverages is consumed: *mengrokom* (a spirit made with maize and cassava) in Gabon, millet beer in Togo, palm spirits and wine, and *babine*, a drink fermented from avocado leaves. Finally, there are many extracts which make refreshing drinks and at the same time have medicinal properties: infusion of *kinkeliba*, lemon-and-ginger water, and honey and lime drinks.

blackberry MÛRE

The fruit of a prickly European shrub, which is reddish-black, fairly firm, and ripens in September–October. It has a low calorific value (37 Cal per 100 g) but is rich in vitamins B and C. It is used to make jam, compote, jelly, tarts, pies, iced sweets, syrup, liqueur, and ratafia. It is also used in confectionery (fruit jellies, etc.).

RECIPES

Blackberry jam CONFITURE DE MÛRES Clean, stalk, and weigh the blackberries, place them in a deep bowl with 1 glass of water per kg (2¼ lb) cleaned fruit, and leave to soak for at least 12 hours. Pour the fruit and water into a preserving pan, add lemon juice (using 1 lemon per kg (2¼ lb) fruit), bring to the boil, and cook gently for 10 minutes. Then add 900 g (2 lb) sugar per kg (2¼ lb) fruit, bring back to the boil, skim, and cook for 15 minutes, stirring from time to time. Jar in the usual way (see *jams, jellies, and marmalades*).

Blackberry tartlets TARTELETTES AUX MÛRES Place 200 g (7 oz, 1¾ cups) flour, 60 g (2 oz, 4 tablespoons) sugar, and 1 egg in a mixing bowl and knead with the fingertips to obtain a coarse dough. Add 100 g (4 oz, ½ cup) softened butter cut into small pieces and continue to work the dough quickly until it is smooth. Form into a ball and leave it to stand for 2 hours. During this time, clean and stalk 800 g (1¾ lb) blackberries.

Roll out the dough and use to line 6 buttered tartlet tins (moulds). Prick the bottom with a fork, sprinkle with caster (superfine) sugar, and fill with blackberries, packing them closely together. Sprinkle with sugar again. Cook the tartlets in the oven at 200 c (400 f, gas 6) for about 30 minutes. Take them out and leave until lukewarm, then turn them out onto a wire rack. Serve warm or cold with plain fresh cream or decorated with piped Chantilly cream. A tart is prepared in the same manner.

blackbird MERLE

A bird of the thrush family. The female has a brown plumage and the male is black; both have yellow beaks. Its flesh has a fine texture and its taste varies depending on the diet of the bird, which itself depends on the region in which it lives and the season of the year. The flavour is usually slightly bitter but is at its most fragrant in the autumn. Blackbirds are cooked in the same way as thrushes, although they are less delicate. Corsican blackbirds are used to make a delicious pâté.

black bryony TAMIER

A perennial herb, common in Europe, also known in French as *herbe aux femmes battues* (battered wives' herb) and *vigne noire* (black vine). It has fairly large brown tubers with edible white pulp. However, the red shiny berries are poisonous.

blackcurrant CASSIS

A shrub naitve to northern Europe but now widely cultivated for its black juicy berries, which are sour and aromatic. The medicinal properties of both the fruit and leaves were known by the 14th century (the French *cassis* comes either from *casse*, the husk of the black-currant, or from *cassia* (senna), known for its purgative qualities). In France, its cultivation really began in the Côte d'Or following the perfection of blackcurrant liqueur (see *cassis*). The first stands were established in the park of the château at Montmuzard near Dijon in 1750.

Blackcurrants are grown especially in Burgundy but also in Orléanais and Haute Savoie, as well as in Germany, Belgium, and Holland. They are harvested at the end of June or the beginning of July. The variety Noir de Bourgogne, with dense clusters of small berries, is exceptionally tasty and aromatic. Varieties with large less dense fruit tend to be more watery. Black-currants are rich in vitamin C, citric acid, potassium, and calcium. They are used to make jellies, jams, fruit juice, syrups, and liqueur. Frozen or concentrated into a purée, the berries can also be used in the preparation of sorbets, Bavarian cream, charlottes, soufflés, and tarts. Dried blackcurrants are sometimes sold commercially; they can be used instead of sultanas in cake making.

RECIPES

Blackcurrant jelly I GELÉE DE CASSIS À CHAUD Wash, dry, and stalk some blackcurrants. Weigh them, place in a saucepan, and add 1.5 dl (¼ pint, ⅔ cup) water per kg (2¼ lb) fruit. Heat until the berries burst (if a perfectly clear jelly is required) then place the fruit in a cloth and wring to extract the juice. (If a thicker jelly is preferred, rub the contents of the saucepan through a sieve or mouli and weigh the liquid obtained.) Then, for every kg (2¼ lb) fruit juice, place 850 g (1 lb 14 oz, 3¾ cups) preserving sugar into a saucepan together with the juice of a lemon and 1 glass of water. Heat up to a temperature of 109 c (228 f) then add the blackcurrant juice. Stir thoroughly over a high heat until the jelly coats the back of the spoon. Skim and pour the boiling jelly into sterilized pots or jars. Allow to cool completely. Cover, label, and store in a cool place.

Blackcurrant jelly II GELÉE DE CAS-SIS À FROID Prepare a blackcurrant jelly as described in the previous recipe but using 1 kg (2¼ lb, 4½ cups) sugar per kg of fruit. Cook the sugar in the same way, then take the saucepan off the heat, add the juice, and stir thoroughly. Then pour the jelly into the sterilized jars, leave to cool, and proceed as in the previous recipe.

Blackcurrant sorbet SORBET AU CAS-
SIS Place 250 g (9 oz, generous cup)
sugar and 4 dl (14 fl oz, 1¾ cups) water
in a saucepan. Heat to dissolve the
sugar. The density should be 1.14. If it is
less than this, add a little more sugar.
Warm the syrup then add 3.5 dl (12 fl
oz, 1½ cups) blackcurrant juice and the
juice of half a lemon. Mix well and pour
the mixture into a sorbet machine.
'Real' sorbet is made by adding a quarter of the volume of Italian meringue to
the ingredients.

black pudding (blood sausage)

BOUDIN NOIR

A savoury sausage consisting largely of
seasoned pigs' blood and fat contained
in a length of intestine, which forms the
skin. They may be cut from a length or
sold in presealed pieces. Ox, calves', or
sheeps' blood can also be used, but this
results in a coarser pudding. The fat
consists partly of *chons*, which are
granular fragments (cracklings) recovered from melting down pig's fat.
One of the oldest known cooked meats,
black pudding is said to have been
invented by Aphtonite, a cook of
ancient Greece. Fried or grilled, it is
traditionally served with apples or
mashed potatoes.

In France there are as many types of
boudin noir as there are pork butchers.
Although the *boudin de Paris* traditionally contains equal portions of
blood, fat, and cooked onions, these can
vary widely; butchers may use a range
of different seasonings and add fruit or
vegetables, aromatic herbs, milk,
cream, semolina, crustless bread, etc. In
Lyon, they add raw onions, sometimes
marinated in brandy and herbs; in
Nancy, they add milk. The Auvergne
boudin contains milk together with a
pig's head cooked with its crackling.
Strasbourg smoked boudin contains
cooked pork rind and bread soaked in
milk. Poitou boudin is prepared without
fat but with cooked spinach, cream,
semolina, and eggs. Various regional
boudins contain fruit, including apples
(Normandy), prunes (Brittany), raisins
(Flanders), or chestnuts (Auvergne).
Alsace has two local specialities that are
similar to black pudding: *Zungenwurst*,
or tongue sausage, which in addition to
the basic ingredients includes pieces of
ox or pig's tongue, wrapped in bacon,
and arranged geometrically in ox intestine; and *Schwarzwurst*, or smoked
black sausage, which is made from a
paste of pig's blood, pork rind, ears,
boned head and trotters, fat trimmings,
and onions, with diced pork fat and
enclosed in ox intestine. See also *boutifar, galabart, gogues, tripotcha*.

RECIPES

Black pudding (blood sausage)
BOUDIN NOIR Add 1 tablespoon
wine vinegar to 1 litre (1¾ pints, 4¼
cups) pig's blood to prevent it coagulating. Chop 400 g (14 oz) onions and
gently cook them in 100 g (4 oz, ½ cup)
lard without browning. Dice 750 g–
1 kg (1¾–2¼ lb) fresh pork fat and
soften in a pan very gently without
frying, until it becomes translucent. Add
the onions and a bouquet garni and
cook for approximately 20 minutes. Remove from the heat and, stirring constantly, add the blood, 40 g (1¼ oz) salt,
1 glass (6 fl oz, ¾ cup) white wine, ½
teaspoon freshly ground pepper, and ½
teaspoon allspice. Sieve to remove remaining lumps of fat at this stage, if
desired, then add 2 dl (7 fl oz, ¾ cup)
fresh cream. Clean some pig's intestine
and make up the black puddings as in
the recipe for boudin antillais. Plunge in
boiling water and poach for approximately 20 minutes without boiling. As
the puddings rise to the surface, prick
them with a pin to release the air, which
would otherwise burst them. Drain
them and leave to cool under a cloth.

Black pudding (blood sausage) à la normande BOUDIN NOIR A LA NOR-
MANDE Peel some dessert apples
(about 750 g (1¾ lb) for a 1-kg (2¼-lb)
pudding). Chop, sprinkle with lemon
juice (if desired), and fry in butter. Cut
some previously poached black puddings into portions and fry in butter.
Combine the black pudding slices and
apple in a frying pan (skillet) and fry
together for a few seconds. Serve piping
hot.

bladder VESSIE

A membranous bag in animals in which

urine is stored; after slaughter it has various uses in cooking and charcuterie. Pig's bladder is used in cooking to poach poultry (chicken or duckling) in stock. It must be soaked in water with coarse salt and vinegar to remove impurities, then carefully rinsed and dried before use. The poultry poached in this way is served at table and is described in French as *en vessie* or *en chemise*. If the dish is to be served cold, it is left to cool in the intact bladder. This cooking method, in which the bird is effectively sealed, concentrates the flavours of the forcemeat and the aromatic cooking liquid inside the bladder.

In former times, dried pigs' bladders were used as containers for tallow and melted lard. Sometimes they were filled with air and used as shop signs for *charcutiers* (suppliers of cooked meat).

| RECIPE

Chicken en vessie Marius Vetard
POULARDE EN VESSIE MARIUS VET-
TARD (from Fernand Point's recipe) Singe and carefully clean a roasting chicken weighing 1.7–1.8 kg (3¾–4 lb). Leave it to soak in iced water for 4 hours to ensure that the flesh remains white. Meanwhile, soak a pig's bladder to remove any impurities.

Prepare a forcemeat with the chicken liver, 150 g (5 oz) fresh truffles, and 250 g (9 oz, generous cup) foie gras, using an egg to bind it. Season the forcemeat with salt and pepper and add about 150 ml (¼ pint, ⅓ cup) good-quality champagne. Stuff the chicken with the forcemeat and tie it.

Insert the chicken into the well-rinsed and dried bladder in such a way that the opening of the bladder is along the back of the chicken. Add 2 generous pinches of coarse salt, a pinch of pepper, and a glass each of Madeira and good-quality champagne. Sew up with fine string pulled tightly and prick it about 10 times all around to stop it from bursting. Then poach in a good consommé for 1½ hours. Serve the chicken in the bladder with shaped potatoes, carrots, turnips, and the white part of some leeks (or with rice pilaf). Open the bladder at the last moment, slitting it along the seam. A light Burgundy is a good accompaniment to this dish.

blaff

In Creole cuisine, a fish or shellfish dish in a sauce. The selected ingredients, usually sea-urchin eggs (*chadrons*) or firm-fleshed fish (even shark), are first marinated in lime juice with hot pepper and garlic. They are then simmered in stock flavoured with onion, thyme, parsley, and cloves. The name of this dish is onomatopoeic, derived from the noise the fish makes as it is plunged in boiling water. Blaff may also be cooked in white wine. The dish is served with rice and red kidney beans.

Blagny

An AOC wine from the Côte de Beaune. The vineyards of the hamlet of Blagny extend to the parishes of Meursault and Puligny-Montrachet. The elegant white wines are similar to Meursault and are sold as 'Meursault Premier Cru' or 'Meursault-Blagny'. Only the reds, made from the Pinot Noir grape and somewhat similar to the Volnay wines, carry the Blagny AOC.

blanc (à)

A term used to describe a stage of cooking when food is cooked or partially cooked but not coloured, for example by gently frying onions without allowing them to colour.

Cuire à blanc is also the French term for baking a pastry flan case (pie shell) blind.

blanc (au)

Describing a method of cooking food (especially poultry and veal) either in a blanc de cuisson or in a white stock.

| RECIPE

Chicken au blanc POULARDE AU BLANC Poach the chicken in white stock for 1¼–1¾ hours, depending on its size and tenderness. The legs and wings should come away in the hand without using a knife. Reduce a bowlful of the cooking liquor and add an equal volume of allemande sauce. Coat the chicken with the sauce and serve piping hot with rice and carrots cooked in stock.

blanc de blancs

White wine made solely from white grapes. Until recently, this term was used mainly in reference to champagne made from the Chardonnay and other permitted white grapes of the region. Today the term is often applied to other wines made only from white grapes and is used in many countires, both for still and sparkling wines.

blanc de cuisson

A specially prepared liquor used for cooking white offal and certain vegetables; it is used both to aid whitening and to prevent discoloration of the food. Blanc is prepared by blending a little flour with water then adding seasonings and lemon juice or white vinegar. See also *court-bouillon*.

RECIPES

Blanc for offal and meat   BLANC POUR ABATS ET VIANDES   This stock is used for cooking certain types of offal, such as sheep's tongue and trotters, calf's head, and cocks' combs and kidneys. Blend together 25 g (1 oz, ¼ cup) flour and 4 tablespoons water. Add a further litre (1¾ pints, 4¼ cups) water, mix, and strain. Season with 6 g (¼ oz, 1 teaspoon) salt. Add the juice of half a lemon, 2–3 tablespoons raw chopped calf's or ox kidney fat, a carrot (quartered), a bouquet garni, and an onion stuck with a clove. Place the ingredients to be cooked in the stock when it is boiling.

Blanc for vegtables   BLANC POUR LÉGUMES   This stock is used for cooking chard, artichokes, and salsify. It is prepared in the same way as the blanc for offal and meat, but the carrot, onion, clove, and bouquet garni are not essential as the vegetables are seasoned during their final preparation. Butter may be used instead of the fat from the offal: it forms an insulating layer to protect the vegetables from contact with the air.

blanc de noirs

White wine made from black grapes, the juice being run off before the skin pigments can tint it. The term is used in Champagne for wines made solely from the black Pinot Noir, and in other countries, including South Africa, for still white wines made from black grapes.

blanching

BLANCHIR, MONDER

This term is used for several different operations.

• Lightly cooking raw ingredients for varying amounts of time in boiling water with or without salt or vinegar. The ingredients are then refreshed in cold water and drained or simply drained and then cooked normally. Blanching may be carried out for several reasons: to make firmer, to purify, to remove excess salt, to remove bitterness, or to reduce the volume of certain vegetables. In some cases, the ingredients are placed in cold water and brought to the boil: potatoes (before frying), diced bacon (to be browned or sautéed), previously soaked white offal (prior to cooking), poultry, meat, and bones (when they are to be cooked in water), and rice (to remove starch and to facilitate cooking, especially in milk). In other cases, the ingredients are plunged directly into boiling water, for example, cabbage and lettuce (before braising). Blanching is equivalent to complete cooking with such vegetables as spinach, green beans, and fresh peas.

• The vigorous beating of a mixture of egg yolks and caster (superfine) sugar until the volume increases and it becomes light and fluffy. This method is used particularly for making custard cream, sponge cake mixture, etc.

• Preliminary frying of certain potato preparations (e.g. chips) so that they partially cook without changing colour. They become crisp and golden when fried for a second time at a higher temperature, just before serving.

• Covering fruit, vegetables, or nuts with boiling water for a few seconds to facilitate removal of the skin. Tomatoes, peaches, almonds, and pistachios are treated in this way; the skin can then be removed easily without damaging the pulp or kernel.

blancmange

BLANC-MANGER

A type of jellied almond cream. One of the oldest desserts, it was said by Grimod de La Reynière to have originated in Languedoc. In the Middle Ages, blanc-mange was a white meat jelly made of pounded capon or veal and a dessert made from honey and almonds. Although today there are many variations, often based on cornflour (cornstarch), traditional blancmange is made with sweet almonds and a few bitter almonds that are pounded, pressed, sweetened, and mixed with a flavouring and jelling agent. The latter was originally grated stag's horn, subsequently replaced by beef or mutton juice, isinglass, and finally gelatine. This dessert was often regarded as difficult to make because it had to be white and perfectly smooth.

RECIPES

Traditional almond blancmange (old recipe) Blanch 450 g (1 lb, generous 3 cups) sweet almonds and about 20 bitter almonds. Leave them to soak in a bowl of cold water, which renders them singularly white. Drain on a sieve and rub in a napking. Pound in a mortar, moistening them, little by little, with ½ tablespoon water at a time, to prevent them turning into oil. When they are pounded into a fine paste, put into a bowl and dilute with 5 glasses filtered water, added a little at a time. Spread a clean napkin over a dish, pour the blancmange into it and, with two people twisting the napkin, press out all the almond milk. Add to the milk 350 g (12 oz, 1½ cups) granulated sugar and rub through a fine sieve. Strain the liquid through a napkin once again and add 30 g (1 oz plus 4 grains) clarified isinglass a little warmer than tepid (or 25 g (1 oz, 2 envelopes) gelatine dissolved in warm water). Blend with the blancmange. Pour into a mould and place in a container with crushed ice.

To make rum blancmange, add ½ glass rum to the mixture described above. To make a Maraschino blancmange, add ½ glass Maraschino.

To serve this sweet in small pots, prepare two-thirds of the quantity given in the recipe; you will, however, need a little less isinglass, as the blancmange served in small pots has to be more delicate than when it is to be turned out.

Blancmanges can be flavoured with lemon, vanilla, coffee, chocolate, pis tachio nuts, hazelnuts, and strawberries. Whipped cream can also be incorporated.

Traditional almond blancmange (modern method) Blanch 450 g (1 lb, 3 cups) sweet almonds and 20 bitter almonds, then remove the skins. Liquidize the blanched almonds with 1 litre (1¾ pints, 4¼ cups) hot water; when the liquid is milky and the almonds are very fine, strain the mixture through a muslin. Stir 2 packets (25 g, scant 1 oz, 4 tablespoons) gelatine with 5 tablespoons almond milk. Leave aside to swell. Heat the remining almond milk with 125 g (4 oz, ½ cup) sugar, stirring frequently. When the sugar has dissolved and the liquid is almost boiling, stir into the gelatine, and continue stirring until the gelatine has melted. Pour the almond blancmange into a 1.1-litre (2-pint, 2½-cup) mould, leave aside until cold, then refrigerate until firmly set.

blanquette

A ragout of white meat (veal, lamb, or poultry) cooked in white stock or water with aromatic flavourings. Theoretically, the sauce is obtained by making a roux and adding cream and egg yolks. However, the roux is more often than not omitted. Blanquette had a very important place in historical cuisine and became a classic of bourgeois cookery. Blanquettes are also made with fish (monkfish) and vegetables (chard and celery).

RECIPES

Preparation of blanquette PRÉPARATION DE LA BLANQUETTE Cut the meat or fish into approximately 5 cm (2 in) cubes. Seal by frying the cubes in butter without browning. Cover with white stock or bouillon, season, quickly bring to the boil, and skim. Add 2 onions (one stuck with a clove), 2 medium-sized carrots cut into quarters, and a bouquet garni. Simmer gently (15 minutes for monkfish, 45 minutes for poultry, 1¼ hours for veal). Drain the pieces of meat or fish and place in a sauté pan with small onions and mushrooms that have been cooked *au blanc*, in a thin white sauce. Heat gently, and just before serving bind the sauce with cream and egg yolks and flavour with a little lemon juice. Place in a deep serving dish, sprinkle with chopped parsley, and garnish with heart-shaped croutons fried in butter.

Blanquette is usually served with rice *à la créole* but may also be served with celeriac (celery root), halved celery hearts, carrots, braised parsnips or leeks, cucumber (cut into chunks and blanched for 3 minutes in boiling salted water), braised lettuce, or lettuce hearts.

Blanquette of lamb à l'ancienne BLANQUETTE D'AGNEAU À L'ANCIENNE This is prepared with shoulder, breast, and best end (rib chops) of lamb. The stock for 1.8 kg (4 lb) lamb is made with 2 carrots cut into quarters, 2 medium onions (one stuck with a clove), and a vegetable bouquet garni consisting of 2 celery sticks and 2 small leeks (white part only). The garnish is made with 200 g (7 oz, 3¼ cups) baby onions, 200 g (7 oz, 2 cups) mushrooms (preferably wild), and 8 croutons fried in butter. To bind the sauce, use 50 g (2 oz, 4 tablespoons) butter and 50 g (2 oz, ¼ cup) flour for the roux, then 3 egg yolks, 1.5 dl (¼ pint, ⅔ cup) cream, the juice of half a lemon, and a pinch of grated nutmeg.

Blanquette of veal BLANQUETTE DE VEAU This may be prepared with shoulder, breast, or flank, either on or off the bone. For 1.5 kg (3 lb) meat use the same ingredients as for blanquette of lamb *à l'ancienne*. Seal the pieces of veal in butter without allowing them to brown and cook in bouillon.

Blanquette de Limoux

A sparkling white AOC wine produced in the department of Aude near the town of Limoux (near Carcassonne). It is made from the Mauzac grape, which used to be called Blanquette because the undersides of the leaves are covered in white down. After fermentation, the wine is bottled and the residual sugar undergoes a second fermentation – described as natural since no sugar is added – and produces a foam. The sediment resulting from this process must be removed for making champagne. Blanquette de Limoux is a light, golden, fruity, and very pleasant wine. The region also produces nonsparkling dry white wines with the AOC 'Limoux Nature'.

Blayais

A wine-growing region of Bordeaux situated on the right bank of the Gironde opposite Médoc. The communes of Blaye, Saint-Savin-de-Blaye, and Saint-Ciers-sur-Gironde produce smooth red wines with a rich bouquet and rather fruity dry white wines. The three AOC wines from this region are: 'Côte-de-Blaye' (usually red), 'Blaye', and 'Blayais' (red or white).

bleak ABLETTE

A small elongated fish, abundant in lakes and quiet waterways. Its scales, which are thin and silvery, come away easily. The flesh of the pond bleak is of poor quality, but that of the river variety is fairly good, although full of little bones. The bleak, which is about 15 cm (6 in) long, is invariably served fried.

blender MIXER

An electric device used to crush or mix foods. It is used in the preparation of sauces, soups, fruit and vegetable purées, fine forcemeats, mousses, and mousselines.

There are two kinds of blender: the hand-held type and the goblet type. The former consists of a motor unit with a handle and a column fitted with a blade which turns at approximately 10,000 r.p.m. It can be operated either in the receptacle used for cooking or preparing the food or in a tall narrow container useful for making mayonnaise. Sometimes it is equipped with a slower blade, which can be used to mash potatoes and purée chestnuts (otherwise the excessive rotary speed of the mixer would release the starch, making the purée sticky and viscous).

In the goblet type the motor unit serves as a base and the blade turns in the goblet. The goblet has a limited capacity, so only relatively small quantities can be processed at a time. It is particularly useful for puréeing soups and sauces, but when thicker mixtures are processed the machine may need to be stopped and the mixture scraped down from the sides of the goblet on to the blades.

blenny BLENNIE

A small river fish common in the south of France, where it is eaten in a fried dish known as *cagnette*. Up to 15 cm (6 in) long, it has a thick slimy fawn-coloured skin which lacks scales.

bleu (au)

The term applied to a method of cooking fish (trout, carp, or pike) by plunging it either alive or extremely fresh into a court-bouillon containing vinegar, salt, and herbs. A trout, for example, is skinned, cleaned, sprinkled with vinegar (which makes the slimy liquid covering its body turn blue), and immediately plunged into boiling court-bouillon.

blini

A small thick savoury pancake made with a leavened batter that contains both wheat flour and buckwheat flour. In Russian cuisine, blinis are served with soured (dairy sour) cream and melted butter as an accompaniment to hors d'oeuvres, caviar, or smoked fish. They are cooked in a special small frying pan, about 15 cm (6 in) in diameter, with a thick bottom and steep sides.

There are several types of blini: creamed rice (with a mixture of wheat flour and rice flour), egg (chopped hard-boiled (hard-cooked) eggs are added to the basic mixture), semolina and milk (instead of buckwheat and water), and carrot (puréed carrots are worked into the dough).

RECIPE

Blinis à la française Blend 20 g (¾ oz) fresh yeast (¾ cake compressed yeast) (or 1 tablespoon dried yeast) and 50 g (2 oz, ½ cup) sifted flour with 1 litre (17 fl oz, 2 cups) milk and leave to rise for 20 minutes in a warm place. Then mix in 250 g (8¾ oz, 2¼ cups) sifted flour, 4 egg yolks, 3 dl (½ pint, 1¼ cups) warm milk, and a generous pinch of salt. Mix the ingredients well, but do not let the mixture thicken. At the last moment, add 4 stiffly beaten egg whites and 1 dl (6 tablespoons, scant ½ cup) whipped cream. Leave the batter to rest for one hour and then make small thick pancakes by frying quantities of the batter in butter in a small frying pan (skillet).

blondir

A French culinary term meaning to lightly brown food by frying gently in fat. Onions and shallots may be cooked like this and also flour, which is lightly browned in melted butter to make a white roux.

blood SANG

The vital fluid of vertebrates. Pigs' blood, an ingredient of black pudding (blood sausage), is that most frequently used in cookery. Fresh blood, a symbol of vigour, has always been considered a fortifying food, especially in cold countries, hence the ancient Swedish *swartsoppa* (black soup), made with goose blood, and the Polish *czernina* (or *tchernina*), eaten with rice, noodles, or fried croutons, to which fresh poultry, game, or pigs' blood is added before it is thickened with a purée of chicken livers. There are also various French regional dishes using blood (see *sanguette*).

Thickening with blood is widely used in French cookery, mainly for ragouts, civets, and dishes *en barbouille*. When poultry or game blood is not available, fresh pigs' blood can be used instead.

Duck *au sang* is very popular in the cookery of Rouen.

The French expression *cuit à la goutte de sang* ('cooked to the drop of blood') is applied to young game or poultry which is just cooked; similarly, the term *saignant* (rare; literally, bleeding) corresponds to a specific degree of cooking for grilled (broiled) or roast meat.

blood sausage

See *black pudding*.

blue cheese BLEU

Many soft blue-veined cow's-milk cheeses are produced in France, mostly in the Auvergne, Savoy, and Jura. If the cheese is made from goat's or ewes' milk, the label must specify 'Bleu de Chèvre' (blue goat's milk cheese) or 'Bleu de Brebis' (blue ewes'-milk cheese).

In France, the name 'Bleu' also applies to white cheeses in which only the crust turns blue and is covered with a natural pale blue down, such as Olivet Bleu and Vendôme Bleu. The most important of the blue-veined cheeses are produced in Auvergne, Bresse, the Causses, Corsica (from ewes' milk), upper Jura, Lagneuille, Landes, Quercy, Saint-Foy, Sassenage, and Thiézac. They are all manufactured in the same way. The curds are cut into cubes, drained, and moulded. During coagulation, or, more frequently, during moulding, spores of the fungus *Penicillium glaucum* are added. This fungus gives the blue veining. The moulded curds are then salted and finely perforated to encourage the growth of the spores and finally matured for varying periods in damp cellars. The best seasons for blue cheese are summer and autumn.

A good blue cheese is ivory- or cream-coloured, firm and springy, and rather fatty, with evenly distributed light or dark green-blue veins. The naturally formed crust may be rough or smooth. Blue cheeses are sometimes wrapped in foil, eg. Bleu de Bresse, Bleu du Quercy, and Bleu d'Auvergne. Bleu d'Auvergne, Bleu des Causses (which also has a label of quality), and Bleu du Haut Jura are protected by *appellations d'origine*. Bleu du Quercy has a label of quality.

Outside France there are also numerous blue-veined cheeses, such as Gorgonzola from Italy, Danish Blue, Gamelost from Norway, Edelpilz from Germany, and Blue Stilton, Blue Cheshire, and Blue Wensleydale from Great Britain, not to mention certain American imitations of French and English blue cheeses, such as the renowned Maytag Blue Cheese from Iowa.

Blue cheeses are served at the end of a meal, preferably alone or as the last course, so that their often distinct flavour can be savoured with full-bodied aromatic red wines (for strong cheeses) or with more fruity red wines (for more mellow cheeses). They are often used for canapés (sometimes mixed with butter, chopped nuts, celery, etc.) and may also be used in the preparation of mixed salads, regional soups, and fondues. They are used to enliven such meat dishes as hamburgers, beef olives, and rabbit, and are often used in soufflés and pies.

● **Bleu d'Auvergne** (Cantal, Puy-de-Dôme, Haute-Loire) – Cylindrical, 10 or 20 cm (4 or 8 in) in diameter and 8–10 cm (3½–4 in) high, or a parallelepiped 29 cm (12 in) long, 11 cm (4½ in) high, and 8.5 cm (3½ in) wide, with a firm fatty paste (45% fat content), a strong smell, and a slightly piquant flavour.

● **Bleu de Bresse** (Ain) – Cylindrical, 6.8 or 10 cm (2½ or 4 in) in diameter and 4.5, 5, or 6 cm (1½, 2, or 2½ in) high, with a soft smooth paste (50% fat content), a fine smooth blue crust, and a medium to strong flavour.

● **Bleu des Causses** (Rouergue) – Cylindrical, 20 cm (8 in) in diameter and 8–10 cm (3½–4 in) high (formerly made with cows' milk mixed with ewes' milk), with a firm fatty paste (45% fat content), a strong smell, and a distinct bouquet.

● **Bleu de Corse** The name reserved for ewes'-milk cheeses that are not taken to Roquefort for maturing and are not, therefore, as fine as the famous cheese matured in the cellars of Aveyron. Cylindrical in shape, 20 cm (8 in) in diameter and 10 cm (4 in) high, it has a fine paste 45% fat content), a good piquant flavour, and a strong smell.

● **Bleu de Haut Jura** (Ain and Jura: Bleus de Gex and Septmoncel) – A flat wheel shape with a slightly convex base, 30 cm (12 in) in diameter and 8–9 cm (3½–4 in) high, springy to the touch with heavy veining, 45% fat content, slightly bitter and full of flavour.

● **Bleu de Laqueuille** (Auvergne) – Created in 1850 by a peasant, Antoine Roussel, who injected a white cheese with blue mould which was flourishing on rye bread. Cylindrical, 20–22cm (7 –8 in) in diameter and 8–10 cm (2–3 in) high, with a soft paste (45% fat), a pungent aroma, and a strong flavour.

● **Bleu de Loudes** (or **Bleu de Velay**) – Cylindrical, 12 cm (5 in) in diameter and 12–15 cm (5–6 in) high, with a firm paste (25–33% fat content), full of flavour, that hardens and becomes brittle.

● **Bleu du Quercy** (Aquitaine) – Cylindrical, 18–20 cm (7–8 in) in diameter and 9–10 cm (3½–4 in) high, with a firm full paste (45% fat content), a strong smell, and a definite taste.

● **Bleu de Sainte-Foy** (Savoy) – Cylindrical, 16–20 cm (5½–7 in) in diameter and 8–10 cm (2–3 in) high, with a firm fatty paste (40–45% fat content), and full of flavour. (Cows' milk is sometimes mixed with goats' milk.)

● **Bleu de Sassenage** (Dauphiné) – Quoted in 1600 by Oliver de Serres and described in Diderot's *Encyclopaedia*. Cylindrical, 30 cm (12 in) in diameter and 8–10 cm (3½–3¾ in) high, with a springy odourless paste (45% fat content), a fine light-coloured crust, and a pronounced, slightly bitter, flavour.

● **Bleu de Thiézac** (Cantal) – Cylindrical, 18–20 cm (7–8 in) in diameter and 9–10 cm (3¾–4 in) high, with a fatty smelly paste (45% fat content), and a strong flavour that is caused by it being salted when hot.

board PLANCHE

A slab, usually 4–6 cm (1½–2½ in) thick, made of solid wood (usually beech), rectangular, round, or oval in shape. It is used for slicing, chopping, or cutting up meat, fish, vegetables, and bread. Boards designed specially for cutting up roasted meat or poultry have a wide groove around the perimeter for catching the juice. Bread boards are sometimes made of horizontal laths fitted to a frame to prevent crumbs from scattering. Pastry boards, used for kneading and rolling out pastry dough, must be smooth and big enough to hold the rolled-out dough.

bochyn

A sparkling refreshing slightly alcoholic drink manufactured in the Soviet Union. It is obtained by fermenting raisins and yeast in whey containing sugar and hop extract.

bock

An earthenware or glass beer mug with a handle, about 12.5 cl (4 fl oz, 1 cup) in volume. The word may also be used to describe the contents. *Bockbier* originated in the town of Einbeck in Lower Saxony. It was exported to Bavaria, where it became traditional. The Bavarians pronounced Einbeck 'Oanbock', hence *bock*. In France and Belgium, *bière bock* is a light beer. Mr Binding, the owner of the Grand Balcon café on the Boulevard des Italiens in Paris, introduced the fashion for *bock* in about 1855. 'Dîners du Bon Bock' (Bock dinners) were instituted in 1873 in a café in Montmartre on the initiative of Manet and his friends when the artist sold one of his first paintings, entitled *Le Bon Bock*.

In Germany, however, bock beer is very strong, often brown, and the word is not used to refer to the container or glass. The strongest beer in the world is a Bavarian 'double bock'.

Bocuse (Paul)

French cook (born Collonges-au-Mont-d'Or, 1926). He comes from a line of restaurateurs and cooks established on the banks of the Saône since 1765. Michel Bocuse opened a café in an old Collonges mill which was taken over by his son Philibert. Philibert's son Nicolas bought the nearby Hôtel de l'Abbaye and ran it with his three sons, Jean-Noël, Nicolas, and Georges. Georges bought the Hôtel-restaurant du Pont, also in Collonges.

George's son, Paul, was first apprenticed to Fernand Point and then to Lucas-Carton and Lapérousse in Paris. He began working in 1942 in a restaurant in Lyon and in 1959 saved the small family restaurant in Collonges from ruin and made it into a gastronomic Mecca. Attached to the tradition and cuisine of Lyon, he renewed the great classics without entering into the excesses of *nouvelle cuisine*. His family nickname was 'primat des gueules' ('primate of the palate'). With his forceful personality, he became the ambassador of French gastronomy throughout the world, giving conferences and cookery classes, especially in Japan. He published *La Cuisine du marché* in 1980 and *Bocuse dans votre cuisine* in 1982. His creations include black truffle soup, lobster Meursault, and a chocolate gâteau that has become a speciality.

Boeuf à la mode

A restaurant founded in 1792 in Paris, close to the Palais-Royal, by two brothers from Marseille. Under the Directory, the ailing establishment was taken over by Tissot, who transformed it into an elegant restaurant noted for its southern cuisine; the new sign – an ox dressed in the fashion of the period – contributed to the restaurant's success. During the Restoration, Tissot changed the ox's dress to a shawl and bonnet, to conform with the current fashion (*à la mode du jour*), but this new decoration caused Tissot some problems, being considered by Louis XVIII's government to show too much of the Revolutionary colours – red, white, and blue.

The Boeuf à la mode closed down in 1936, having been run in its final years by Marcel Dorin. Its visitors' book contains the following praise by Berthe Bovy and Pierre Fresnay: 'J'aime ta cuisine, ô Boeuf, que cell d'en face; c'est moins vache . . .' – a play on words that can be roughly translated as: 'I prefer your cooking, Ox, to that of the Théâtre-Française; it's less of a cow . . .' (i.e. better).

Bofinger

One of the top bar-restaurants in Paris, established in 1864 in the Rue de la Bastille. It is famous for its Alsatian specialities, its lobster in mayonnaise, oysters, and its spirits cellar. It was owned by the same family for a long time. The new management has retained the authentic 1900 decor.

bohémienne (à la)

Various dishes have been named after Balfe's successful comic opera, *La Bohémienne* (1869). These include a soft-boiled egg dish, a salpicon, and also a sauce served with cold dishes, which uses a cold béchamel base to bind an emulsion of egg yolks and oil flavoured with tarragon vinegar.

The ingredients of sautéed chicken *à la bohémienne* – garlic, fennel, sweet peppers, and tomato – are similar to those of a Provençal dish called *boumanie*, which is a kind of ratatouille. The dish is served with plain rice. Rice with crushed tomato and fried onion rings are also ingredients in noisette of lamb *à la bohémienne*.

Salpicon à la bohémienne Dice some foie gras and truffles. Reduce some Madeira sauce, add some essence of truffle, and use the sauce to bind the salpicon of foie gras and truffles. Diced onions, cooked in butter and seasoned with paprika, may also be added. This salpicon may be used as a filling for vols-au-vent, small flans, poached eggs, tartlets, etc.

Sautéed chicken à la bohémienne POULET SAUTÉ À LA BOHÉMIENNE Season a medium-sized chicken with paprika and sauté in a casserole or large heavy saucepan until brown. Cover and continue cooking very slowly either on top of the stove or in a moderate oven. Cut 4 sweet peppers into thick strips. Peel 2 tomatoes and slice thickly. Peel and finely dice an onion and then blanch it. Prepare 1 tablespoon chopped fennel. Add all these ingredients, together with a pinch of grated garlic, to the pan when the chicken is half-cooked (after approximately 20 minutes). At the end of the cooking time, when the chicken is tender, deglaze the casserole dish with 1 dl (8 tablespoons, ½ cup) white wine. Add 50 ml (4 tablespoons, 5 tablespoons) thickened veal stock or well-reduced bouillon. Finally, add a dash of lemon juice. Pour the sauce over the chicken and serve with saffron rice.

Soft-boiled (*or poached*) eggs à la bohémienne OEUFS MOLLETS (OU POCHÉS) À LA BOHÉMIENNE Fill some puff pastry cases with liver purée. Place either a poached or a soft-boiled egg on top and coat with velouté sauce. Cook some thin strips of lean bacon in Madeira and use to garnish each egg. Coat thinly with a pale veal glaze.

boil BOUILLIR

To bring a liquid (water, stock, courtbouillon, etc.) to boiling point and maintain it at that temperature, thereby cooking ingredients that are placed in it. Boiling occurs at a fixed temperature, which for water is 100 c (212 F). If a recipe contains an instruction to 'boil rapidly', this does not mean that the cooking should be accelerated, but that the ingredients should be agitated to prevent them from sticking to each other or to the bottom of the pan. In most cases, it is sufficient for the liquid to simmer. Liquids are also boiled to reduce them.

Oil and other fats used for frying have boiling points of up to 200 c (400 F). The boiling point of sugar syrup varies according to the concentration, which increases as the water evaporates.

boiled beef

See *beef, bouilli*.

bolée

A small bowl with handles, traditionally used for serving cider in Normandy and Brittany. In Cotentin, it is known as a *moque*.

boletus BOLET

A wild mushroom that can be recognized by the spore-bearing tubes (rather than gills) on the undersurface of its cap. There are various edible species, one of the best known being the cep, *Boletus edulis*.

bollito misto

A type of stew originating in Piedmont. The name of the dish literally means 'boiled mixed' and its composition can vary according to region, availability of ingredients, and family traditions. As a general rule, it contains rump of beef, knuckle of veal, and chicken (stuffed or plain), often with a pork sausage or a *zampone* (stuffed pig's foot). Some recipes also include pigs' trotters, ox tongue, or rolled head of veal. The meat is cooked in stock with onions, carrots, and celery. The accompanying vegetables (carrots, turnips, celeriac (celery root), etc.) are then cooked in a little of the strained stock. It is customary to serve bollito misto with gherkins, capers, small pickled onions, green salad, and Cremona mustard – a sweet-and-sour fruit mustard similar to chutney.

bolognaise (à la)

The term applied to several dishes inspired by Italian cookery, especially that of Bologna, that are served with a thick sauce based on beef and vegetables. In Italy, bolognaise sauce is known as *ragu*, which is a corruption of the French word *ragoût*. It is richer than the French-style bolognaise sauce as it contains chopped ham, various vegetables, beef, lean pork, chicken livers, and white wine.

RECIPES

Bolognaise sauce SAUCE BOLOGNAISE Trim and chop 4 sticks (stalks) of celery. Peel and chop 5 large onions. Add 4 leaves of sage and 2 sprigs of rosemary to a traditional bouquet garni. Coarsely chop 500 g (18 oz) braising steak (chuck or blade beef or flank). Peel and crush about 10 large tomatoes and 4 or 5 garlic cloves. Heat 5 tablespoons olive oil in a heavy saucepan. Brown the meat and then the onion, celery, and garlic in the olive oil. Add the tomatoes and cook for about 10 minutes. Lastly, add the bouquet garni, 3.5 dl (12 fl oz, 1½ cups) beef stock, 2.25 dl (8 fl oz, 1 cup) wine, salt, and pepper. Cover and cook very gently for at least 2 hours, adding a little water from time to time. Adjust the seasoning.

Bolognaise sauce may be prepared in very large quantities. The length of the cooking time means that it can be kept for several days in the refrigerator, and several months in the freezer. It is served with spaghetti, macaroni, gratin dishes, and lasagne.

bombe glacée

A frozen dessert made from a bombe mixture, often enriched with various ingredients, and frozen in a mould. The dessert was named after the spherical mould in which it used to be made. Nowadays, cylindrical moulds with rounded tops are used.

Traditionally, bombe moulds are filled with two different mixtures. The bottom and sides of the mould are lined with a layer of plain ice cream, a fruit ice, or a sorbet; the inside is filled with the chosen bombe mixture. The mould is then hermetically sealed, clamped, and frozen. To serve, the bombe is turned out onto a folded napkin placed on the serving dish. The bombe may be decorated in a number of ways depending on its ingredients: crystallized (candied) fruit or violets, marrons glacés, jam, pistachios, fruit macerated in liqueur, whipped cream, etc.

RECIPES

Lining the mould with ice cream MÉTHODE POUR CHEMISER UN MOULE DE GLACE Chill the mould in the refrigerator for approximately 20 minutes. Place the ice cream or water ice chosen to line the mould in the refrigerator so that it softens. Spread it roughly on the bottom and sides of the mould with a plastic or stainless steel spatula. Place the mould in the freezer for about 15 minutes to harden and then smooth the ice with the spatula. Replace the mould in the freezer for a further hour before filling with the bombe mixture unless the mixture is a parfait, in which case pour it down the sides of the lined mould and place in the freezer for 5–6 hours.

Bombe mixture   APPAREIL À BOMBE   In traditional cuisine, the mixture is made with 32 egg yolks per litre (1¾ pints, 4¼ cups) syrup (specific gravity: 1.285). Pour the syrup and egg yolks into a saucepan and place the pan in a bain-marie over a moderate heat. Whisk vigorously until the mixture is thick and creamy, then press it through a very fine sieve. Whisk again, away from the heat, until completely cold: by this stage it should be light, fluffy, and white. Finally add an equal volume of whipped cream and the chosen flavouring.

Nowadays, bombes are made with much lighter mixtures. Gaston Lenôtre, for example, makes a 1-litre (1¾-pint, 4¼-cup) bombe Hawaii using ½ litre (17 fl oz, 2 cups) pineapple sorbet to line the mould and ½ litre (17 fl oz, 2 cups) Kirsch parfait made with 2 egg yolks, about 80 ml (4 tablespoons, ¼ cup) syrup (specific gravity 1.2407), and approximately 2.5 dl (8 fl oz, 1 cup) whipped cream mixed with ½ tablespoon Kirsch.

Bombe Aïda   Lining: tangerine ice cream. Filling: vanilla bombe mixture flavour with Kirsch.

Bombe Alhambra   Lining: vanilla ice cream. Filling: strawberry bombe mixture (a combination of strawberry purée, Italian meringue, and whipped cream). Turn out the bombe and surround with large strawberries macerated in Kirsch.

Bombe archiduc   Lining: strawberry ice cream. Filling: praline bombe mixture.

Bombe Chateaubriand   Lining: apricot ice cream. Filling: vanilla bombe mixture mixed with crystallized (candied) apricots macerated in Kirsch.

Bombe diplomate   Lining: vanilla ice cream. Filling: Maraschino bombe mixture mixed with diced crystallized (candied) fruit macerated in Maraschino.

Bombe Doria   Lining: pistachio ice cream. Filling: vanilla bombe mixture mixed with pieces of marrons glacés macerated in rum.

Bombe duchesse   Lining: pineapple ice cream. Filling: pear bombe mixture.

Bombe Grimaldi   Lining: vanilla ice cream. Filling: Kümmel-flavoured bombe mixture. Decoration: crystallized (candied) violets and halved pistachio nuts.

Bombe Monselet   Lining: tangerine ice cream. Filling: port-flavoured bombe mixture mixed with chopped crystallized (candied) orange peel that has been macerated in brandy.

bombine

A traditional Ardèche speciality made with roast salt pork, cooked in an earthenware pot with stock, onions, slices of potatoes, and garlic. The bombine may be sprinkled with breadcrumbs and browned in the oven. Just before serving, it is garnished with pieces of grilled black pudding (blood sausage) and slices of hot garlic sausage.

Bondard

The name of several Normandy cheeses made with cow's milk (60% fat content) also known as Bondart, Bonde, or Bondon. They are cylindrical, 8–9 cm (3½ in) in length, 6–7 cm (2½ in) wide, and weigh 200–300 g (7–11 oz). They originate in the Bray region and have a grey crust with a soft creamy paste and a distinctive flavour.

Bondon de Neuchâtel (*appellation contrôlée*) has a soft paste (45% fat content) and a downy crust. It is springy to the touch, has a fruity flavour, and weighs 100 g (4 oz).

bone   OS

The solid element in the carcass of a vertebrate animal. Bones are made of cartilage impregnated with calcium salts. When cooked in a boiling liquid they yield gelatine, essential for the smoothness and palatability of certain cooking stocks; veal bones are particularly valuable for this purpose. The crushed bones, which may be browned in the oven, are usually cooked with aromatic vegetables and herbs to make stock for sauces.

Some bones, particularly those from beef and veal, contain marrow. For those who are fond of marrow-bones the pot-au-feu can include thick slices of shin (shank) bone (fore or hind leg). Osso bucco, a traditional Italian dish, is prepared with slices of unboned veal knuckle.

Unboned rib of beef is a prime cut; it can be grilled (broiled) as it is or served *à l'américaine* (the famous T-bone steak of American barbecues). York ham cooked on the bone should also be mentioned – it is delicious.

Many cuts of meat are cooked on the bone, which may entail some extra preparation: for instance, loosening or shortening the bone. When serving, it can be decorated with a paper collar or frill.

bone marrow
MOELLE ANIMALE

A soft fatty substance in the cavities of long bones. In cooking, beef marrow is usually used. Slices of gently poached beef marrow are served with grilled (broiled) or roast beef. Marrow is also used as a filling for artichoke hearts, cardoons, omelettes, bouchées, and croûtes and it may be included in salpicons, garnishes, and soups. It is often used to prepare sauces for grilled meat or fish. A marrow bone is always included in a stockpot and often cooked with boiled rolled beef; the bone is then served with the meat and the marrow may be extracted with a teaspoon. Bone marrow may also be bought in jelly form.

RECIPES

Bone-marrow canapés CANAPÉS À LA MOELLE Wrap some fresh or frozen bone marrow in a small piece of muslin (cheesecloth), plunge it into boiling salted beef stock, and poach gently without boiling (approximately 5 minutes for fresh marrow and 7–8 minutes for frozen marrow). Lightly toast some small slices of bread. Unwrap the marrow, drain it carefully, and cut half of it into small dice and the other half into rounds. Garnish each canapé with diced marrow and place a round of marrow on top. Season with salt and pepper, sprinkle with finely chopped parsley, and serve immediately as marrow loses its creamy texture very quickly.

Bone-marrow sauce SAUCE À LA MOELLE Finely chop 3 good shallots. Moisten with 2 glasses white wine, season with salt and pepper, and reduce by half. Mix in 2 tablespoons (3 tablespoons) thickened veal stock or well-reduced meat sauce or 1 tablespoon meat extract. Poach 75 g (3 oz) bone marrow and cut into small dice. Remove the sauce from the heat and whisk in 100 g (4 oz, ½ cup) butter cut into tiny pieces, then add 1 tablespoon lemon juice and the diced bone marrow. Sprinkle with chopped parsley.

boning　DÉSOSSAGE

The removal of the bones from a joint of meat, poultry, fish, game, etc. Boning raw meat or poultry is carried out with a special boning knife and requires skill to avoid damaging the meat.

The same term is used for removing the backbone of a fish that is subsequently stuffed and reshaped before cooking.

bonito　BONITE

Any of several marine migratory fishes that are related to but smaller than the tuna and live in shoals in warm seas. The pelamid, a type of bonito with a striped back, lives in the Pacific Ocean, whereas the oceanic bonito (*listao*), with a striped belly, is fished in both the Atlantic and the Mediterranean. The bonito is an oily fish and is prepared in the same way as tuna.

bonne femme

The term applied to dishes that are prepared in a simple, family, or rustic manner, similar to dishes cooked *à la ménagère* and *à la paysanne*. Such dishes are often served in the container they are cooked in (a casserole dish, plate, pan, etc.).

RECIPES

Chicken bonne femme POULARDE À LA BONNE FEMME Trim a chicken weighing 1.8–2 kg (4–4½ lb), then season with salt and pepper and truss. Brown the chicken slowly on all sides in butter in a casserole or heavy saucepan. Blanch 100 g (4 oz, ½ cup) finely diced unsmoked streaky bacon. Add the diced bacon and 20 small onions to the casserole. Cover and cook gently for 15 minutes. Add 500 g (18 oz) potato balls or small new potatoes and continue cooking slowly, basting the chicken from time to time, until tender. Garnish with the cooked vegetables and serve.

Vegetable soup bonne femme POTAGE BONNE FEMME Cook 100 g (4 oz, 1 cup) finely sliced leeks (white part only in butter. Add 1.5 litres (2¾ pints, 3¾ pints) white consommé or chicken broth and 250 g (9 oz, 1½ cups) sliced potatoes. Season with salt and simmer until potatoes are soft. Just before serving add 50 g (2 oz, ½ cup) butter and some chervil. Serve with thin slices of French bread that have been dried in the oven.

Bonnefons (Nicolas de)

17th-century French writer who was a valet in the court of Louis XIV. He published a work in 1654 (which was reprinted several times until 1741), called *Les Délices de la campagne*. This book marks a turning point in the history of French culinary art, which, at that time, was still influenced by the precepts of the Middle Ages with its emphasis on decoration and overuse of spices, which detracted from the nature of the food.

The work was divided into three parts: *Drinks, bread, and wine* (this section was dedicated to the ladies of Paris); *Vegetables, fruit, eggs, and milk* (dedicated to the Capuchin monks famous for their skill as gardeners) and *Meat, poultry, and fish* (with a foreword for head waiters and, as a supplement, instructions for feasts). Bonnefons recommends cleanliness in the preparation of dishes, diversity of menus, and above all, simplicity: 'Let a cabbage soup be entirely cabbage . . . and may what I say about soup be a law applied to everything that is eaten'. He quotes recipes of the era, such as a dish using cod tripe, a special health soup (with four meats), and *poupelin* (a rich pastry cake). He advocated well-matched flavours, such as mackerel with green fennel.

Bonnes-Mares

A red Burgundy wine, one of the best Côtes-de-Nuits vintages, from an 11-hectare (27-acre) wine-growing region in the communes of Chambolle and Moray-Saint-Denis. Bonnes-Mares are rich-coloured wines, reminiscent of both Corton and Chambolle-Musigny wines. They age well, and after a few years attain a remarkable smoothness and fine bouquet.

Bonnezeaux

A smooth AOC white wine, produced in Anjou from the Chenin Blanc (or Pineau de la Loire) grape in a very small wine-growing region on a steep hillside on the right bank of the Layon (a tributary of the Loire). This aromatic Coteaux-du-Layon, which ages extremely well, rivals the best smooth wines of southwestern France.

Bontemps

A sauce made with cider and mustard that may be served with grilled meat and poultry.

RECIPE

Bontemps sauce SAUCE BONTEMPS Cook 1 tablespoon chopped onion in butter. Add salt, a pinch of paprika, and 2 dl (7 fl oz, ¾ cup) cider. Reduce by two-thirds. Add 2 dl (7 fl oz, ¾ cup) meat-based velouté and bring to the boil. Remove from the heat, add 40 g (1½ oz, 3 tablespoons) butter and 1 generous tablespoon white mustard, and sieve before serving.

boops BOGUE

A spindle-shaped fish abundant in the Mediterranean and the Bay of Biscay. It is 20–30 cm (8–12 in) long with spines along its back. It is mostly used in fish soups.

borage BOURRACHE

A herbaceous perennial plant with blue flowers that is used in cooking and in herbal remedies. The herb tea made from borage is used as a diaphoretic (it causes sweating), and its name derived from Arabic *abū 'āraq*, meaning literally 'father of sweat'. La Quintinie describes it as a soup vegetable. The young leaves can be used to flavour salads and the larger leaves to fill pies or pasta. They have a slight flavour of cucumber. The Germans use borage leaves in stews and stock and there are oriental recipes in which they are stuffed like vine leaves. The flowers are used locally to make fritters or they may be crystallized (candied), to decorate pastries.

bord-de-plat

A small kitchen utensil used to protect the border of a dish on which sauce is being served.

Bordeaux

Already known in the Gallo-Roman period and praised by Roman writers, Bordeaux wines became popular in England during the period 1154–1453, when the province of Aquitaine belonged to the English. Since then they have found new admirers and have been world-famous since the 19th century.

The vine-growing area lies on both sides of the Gironde in the department of the same name. It includes several wine regions, whose names are familiar to lovers of good wine: Médoc on the left bank of the Gironde; Graves and Sauternes on the left bank of the Garonne; Entre-Deux-Mers between the rivers Garonne and Dordogne; and St Émilion, Pomerol, Fronsac, Bourg, and Blaye on the right bank of the Dordogne and the Gironde. This vast wine-growing area extends mainly over stony undulations and the banks of rivulets that might seem ill-suited to vine-growing. But it produces a huge range of wines, distinguished by their overall regions, their specific areas, and their parishes. Each is subject to controls relating to area and quality.

☐ General appellations 'Bordeaux' and 'Bordeaux Supérieur' are good everyday red or white wines which do not have their individual *appellations* or those declassified wines whose owners did not consider a particular vintage good enough for marketing under the estate's name. There are also Bordeaux rosé wines, some sparkling Bordeaux (usually white, produced by the Champagne method), and 'Bordeaux clairet', which is not a rosé, but a light red wine fermented for a short period. It should be drunk young.

☐ Regional appellations These correspond to the main areas of production: Médoc and Haut-Médoc (red); Graves (red and white); the Entre-Deux-Mers (white), and so on. Each of these is governed by the regulations controlling the regional AOC.

☐ Commune or parish appellations These are the AOCs within the generic areas, also governed by the AOCs, but being somewhat stricter: thus, Sauternes, Barsac (white), and, in the Médoc, Pauillac, Margaux, St Estèphe, St Julien, also the subdivided categories of St Émilion and others.

☐ Classified growth The most famous classification is that of 1855, drawn up by the brokers of Bordeaux for the Paris Exhibition, although there had been earlier classifications of the better-known wines. The 1855 classification was based on the prices certain estates' wines were likely to fetch at the Paris Exhibition in that year; consequently, some estates that were undergoing a bad period, or that had been subdivided, were either not categorized or were placed in a lower category than would now be thought appropriate in terms of quality. The 1855 classification includes many of the famous growths of the Médoc and one red Graves (Haut Brion). Since then, the main regions of Bordeaux have been classified (with the exception of Pomerol), in some instances the outstanding estate wine being described as *grand cru*, above *premier cru*. The *crus bourgeois* have likewise been arranged in classified categories. Attempts to recategorize the Médoc estates have failed. While it is true to say that the term 'classified growth' in this context conveys the significance of a wine with a predigree and reputation, it is misleading to suppose that the five categories of the 1855 classification refer to quality: some wines in the fifth, fourth, third, and second growth sections might nowadays be rated higher, although the first growths (Lafite, Latour, Margaux,

Haut Brion and, since 1973, Mouton) are usually outstanding.

Bordelais and Guyenne

The old province of Guyenne extended from the Bordeaux region to the Query mountains. Guyenne today is usually regarded as corresponding only to the Gironde department in the west. Guyenne's capital, Bordeaux, dominates the gastronomy of the region, and rivals Lyon for cuisine and Burgundy for wine. Indeed, the region's cuisine employs wine to the full, both in the preparation of and as an accompaniment to its dishes. Moreover, Bordeaux offers a remarkable variety to lovers of fine food, probably a result of its position at the crossroads of shipping routes between northern and southern Europe and Africa and America.

Some dishes surprise visitors to Bordeaux by their unusual preparation. For instance, this is true of oysters, which are served with grilled *crépinettes* (flat sausages) or even country pâté; similarly grilled shad is served on a bed of walnut leaves, and lamprey *à la bordelaise* is cooked in its own blood mixed with red wine and flavoured with leeks. Shallots, like garlic in Provence, are used to flavour many dishes. They occur in almost all recipes for meat, fish, crayfish, and mussels and, of course, in the well-known entrecôte bordelaise, which is served with bordelaise sauce – made with shallots, beef marrow, and red wine.

Other typical dishes are tourin, in which a good measure of wine is traditionally mixed in the stock remaining at the bottom of the dish, *cagouilles* (small snails), which are eaten *à la Caudéran* during Lent, and ceps *à la bordelaise*, fried in olive oil and seasoned with garlic and parsley.

But, without doubt, it is the proximity of the sea that gives Bordeaux its most renouned specialities – fish and shellfish. Arcachon oysters, small soles (curiously named 'lawyers' tongues'), and mussels are particularly well known. Bordelais cooks also draw on the wealth of the surrounding countryside. Foie gras, conserves, wood pigeons, and buntings from Landes, meat from animals raised in the Pouillac region; dairy products from Charentes, brandy from Cognac and Armagnac, and fruit from the Dordogne all help to make Bordelais gastronomy one of the best in the world. The Bordeaux region may not produce cheese, but its pastries are famous. Macaroons from St Émilion, *fauchonettes*, *milliassons* with bitter almonds, and merveilles all provide a fitting end to a Bordelais meal.

bordelaise (à la)

The name given to a wide range of dishes (eggs, fish, shellfish, kidneys, steak, etc.) which use such ingredients as bone marrow, shallots, and – notably – wine (white for fish and white meat and red for red meat).

RECIPES

Bordelaise sauce I SAUCE BORDELAISE (from a recipe by Carême) Place in a saucepan 2 cloves of garlic, a pinch of tarragon, the deseeded flesh of a lemon, a small bay leaf, 2 cloves, a glass of Sauternes, and 2 teaspoons Provence olive oil. Simmer gently. Skim off all the fat from the mixture and mix in enough espagnole sauce to provide sauce for an entrée and 3–4 tablespoons light veal stock. Reduce the mixture by boiling down and add half a glass of Sauternes while still simmering. Strain the sauce when it is the right consistency. Just before serving add a little butter and the juice of half a lemon.

Bordelaise sauce II (for grilled meat) SAUCE BORDELAISE Boil down by two-thirds 2 dl (⅓ pint, scant cup) red wine with 1 tablespoon chopped shallot, a sprig of thyme, a piece of bay leaf and a pinch of salt. Pour in 2 dl (⅓ pint, scant cup) demi-glace sauce. Boil down by one-third, remove from heat, add 25 g (1 oz, 2 tablespoons) butter, and strain. Add 25 g (1 oz) beef marrow cut in dice, poached, and drained, and 1 teaspoon chopped parsley.

Grilled meats served with bordelaise sauce are usually garnished with slices of poached and drained beef marrow.

Fillets of sole à la bordelaise FILETS DE SOLE À LA BORDELAISE Prepare some button mushrooms and baby (pearl) onions and cook in butter. Butter a small fish kettle or casserole and sprinkle the bottom with finely chopped onions and carrots. Season the fillets of sole with salt and pepper and arrange in the fish kettle. Add a bouquet garni and 1–2 glasses white Bordeaux wine, according to the size of the dish. Poach the fillets for 6–7 minutes then drain, retaining the liquor. Arrange the fillets on the serving dish surrounded by the mushrooms and baby onions; cover and keep warm. Add 2 tablespoons (3 tablespoons) demi-glace or fish stock to the cooking liquor and reduce by half. Add a knob of butter, sieve, and pour over the fillets.

Sautéed calf's kidney à la bordelaise ROGNON DE VEAU SAUTÉ À LA BOR- DELAISE Poach 2 tablespoons diced beef marrow in salt water, drain, and keep warm. Trim the calf's kidney, slice thinly, season with salt and pepper, and fry briskly in very hot butter, turning the pieces over as they cook. Drain, retaining the juice, and keep the kidney warm. Deglaze the frying pan with 1 dl (6 tablespoons, ½ cup) white wine; add 1 level tablespoon finely chopped shallots and boil until dry. Then add 2.5 dl (8 fl oz, 1 cup) veal stock and the juice from the kidney, and reduce by half. Bind with arrowroot and adjust the seasoning. Replace the kidney in the sauce, add the beef marrow, and mix. Arrange in a mound and sprinkle with chopped parsley.

Sautéed chicken à la bordelaise POULET SAUTÉ À LA BORDELAISE Sauté the chicken in butter and oil as for chicken sautéed in white wine, but add some tomato sauce and a pinch of grated garlic. Garnish with 125 g (5 oz, ¾ cup) potato slices, fried raw in butter, blanched artichoke quarters cooked in butter, 2 onions, sliced and fried, and 25 g (1 oz, ¾ cup) parsley, fried. Spoon the sauce over the chicken before serving.

border or ring BORDURE

A mixture that is shaped, moulded, or cut to form a border around the edge of a dish, either for decorative effect or to hold other ingredients in the centre. The ingredients of the ring depend on whether the dish is hot or cold, sweet or savoury (see *crouton, dents-de-loup*).

● *For hot dishes:* rice, semolina, quenelle mixture, duchess potatoes.
● *For cold dishes:* hard-boiled (hard-cooked) eggs, aspic jelly (cut into triangles, crescents, cubes, etc.), sliced tomatoes, oranges, or lemons.
● *For desserts:* moulded creams, creamed rice, semolina.
Special round, plain, or ridged moulds or savarin moulds are usually used to shape the border.

RECIPES

SAVOURY RINGS

Egg ring à la princesse BORDURE D'OEUFS PRINCESSE Prepare in the same way as egg ring Brillat-Savarin, but flavour the eggs with diced truffle and asparagus tips. The latter may be replaced by crayfish tails, shelled prawns, shellfish, mushrooms, etc.

Egg ring Brillat-Savarin BORDURE D'OEUFS BRILLAT-SAVARIN Prepare a veal forcemeat ring as in the recipe for veal forcemeat ring with calves' marrow or brains; turn the hot ring out onto an ovenproof dish. Meanwhile, prepare some scrambled eggs and add either some Parmesan cheese or diced truffle (or truffle peelings). Now pour the scrambled eggs into the centre of the ring, sprinkle the eggs and the ring with grated Parmesan and melted butter, and brown rapidly in the oven.

Rice ring with various garnishes BOR- DURE DE RIZ GARNIE Butter a ring mould or savarin mould and fill with pilaf rice, risotto, or rice cooked in consommé and bound with egg. Cover the mould, bake in the oven (160 C, 325 F, gas 3) for approximately 10 minutes, then turn the ring out onto a serving dish. The filling can be a ragout of shellfish, poultry, or offal, medallions of lobster à l'américaine, crayfish à la bordelaise, curried fillets of fish, etc.

Ring of sole à la normande BORDURE DE SOLES a la normande Prepare a forcemeat of creamed fish. Generously butter a ring mould or savarin mould and fill with the forcemeat. Poach in a bain-marie in a warm oven then turn the ring out onto a serving dish. Fill the centre of the ring with a shellfish ragout mixed with normande sauce, then add some fried smelts. Poach some folded fillets of sole in white wine and arrange on top of the ring. Also poach some oysters and place one on each fillet. Garnish with sliced truffle. Garnish round the edges with shrimps cooked in court-bouillon.

SWEET RINGS

Rice ring à la créole BORDURE DE RIZ À LA CRÉOLE Butter a ring mould or savarin mould. Fill with thick rice pudding, press down, heat in the oven, then turn out onto a serving dish. Poach 16 half slices of pineapple in vanilla-flavoured syrup and fill the centre of the ring with them. Decorate with cherries and angelica. . Serve either slightly warmed or very cold, with apricot sauce flavoured with rum.

Semolina ring with fruit BORDURE DE SEMOULE AUX FRUITS Butter a ring mould or savarin mould and fill with a stiff cooked dessert semolina mixed with a salpicon of crystallized (candied) fruit. Place in the oven (160 c, 325 F, gas 3) for a few minutes, until set. Turn the ring out onto a serving dish. Fill the centre with whole, halved, or cubed fruit poached in vanilla-flavoured syrup. Heat again for a few minutes in the oven. Just before serving, sprinkle the ring with a very hot fruit sauce flavoured with rum or Kirsch.

börek BEURRECK

A type of Turkish cheese fritter served as an appetizer. Its preparation was described in the magazine *Le Pot au Feu* (1 January 1900): 'The true Turkish method consists of wrapping cigar-shaped pieces of *katschkawalj* cheese in thin sheets of noodle dough and frying them in oil.' This description remains valid, and böreks are in fact made with a very thick béchamel mixed with *katsch-kawalj* (a ewes' milk cheese common throughout the East); however, this cheese may be replaced by diced or grated Gruyère or Emmental. When cold the mixture is shaped into thin rolls, which are then wrapped in noodle dough (or puff pastry) rolled out to a thickness of 2 mm (⅛ in) and cut with a

pastry (cookie) cutter into oval shapes approximately 10 × 5 cm (4 × 2 in). The fritters are sealed with beaten egg and fried in deep fat for 8–10 minutes; when cooked, they rise to the surface. The dough can also be shaped into rectangles or circles and made into turnovers, which may be coated with breadcrumbs before frying.

borsch or bortsch
BORCHTCH

An eastern European soup that is popular in Poland and the Soviet Union. It was one of the first Russian dishes to become popular in France, with the arrival of Russian émigrés in the 1920s. There are many varieties of this very popular dish, some richer than others. The recipe given by Carême, who had the opportunity of preparing it for the court of St Petersburg, is one of the most elaborate, but the standard formula is based on stewing meat. The ingredient which gives borsch its basic characteristics and typical colour is beetroot (red beet), together with variable quantities of other vegetables.

Borsch is traditionally served with sour cream and diced meat as required, but it is customary to eat only the beetroot, mushrooms, and white kidney beans with the soup, reserving the meat cooked in the stock for another purpose. There is a fish borsch, also made with beetroot, and a green borsch made with sorrel, spinach, and either loin of pork or oxtail.

RECIPE

Borsch BORCHTCH (from a recipe by Carême) Place a spit-browned chicken in a soup cauldron with a round of veal, a marrow bone, 450 g (1 lb) very lean bacon, 2 carrots, a stick (stalk) of celery, 2 onions (one stuck with 6 cloves), a large bunch of parsley, and a little thyme, bay, basil, and mace. Add 25 g (1 oz) white peppercorns. Three-quarters fill the cauldron with beetroot (red beet) juice that has been prepared by boiling beetroots.

When you have skimmed it, boil for 1 hour, then add a duck, a half-roasted corn-fed chicken, and 6 large sausages. Remove and drain each of them when it is cooked. Take one of the beetroots used to make the beetroot juice and cut it into very thin strips; cut an equal amount of celery and onions in the same way. Fry these vegetables gently in clarified butter and add some of the soup liquid. Carefully remove the fat and allow to glaze. Mince 100 g (4 oz) beef fillet (sirloin) with 100 g (4 oz, ½ cup) fat. Add a little salt, pepper, grated nutmeg, and 2 egg yolks. Pound the mixture. Use half the mixture to make about 30 small pasties and simmer these for about 10 minutes or until just cooked in a little of the soup. Use the remainder of the minced beef mixture to make small quenelles about the size of hazelnuts. Roll on a table dusted with flour. Place in a sauté dish with a little clarified butter and brown just before serving. Hard boil (hard cook) 2 eggs and cut in half length-wise. Remove the yolks and pound with a raw egg yolk, a little salt, pepper, and grated nutmeg. Add a little grated horse-radish and chopped parsley. Garnish the egg whites with this mixture, then coat with beaten egg and breadcrumbs. Place the eggs in a small sauté pan containing clarified butter and brown slightly before serving.

When the soup has boiled for 5 hours, remove the fat, strain through a towel, and clarify in the normal manner. Then reduce in order to obtain a light clear soup with an excellent slightly sharp flavour. While it is reducing, trim a cooked oxtail and place in the soup tureen. Finely dice the bacon, fillet the chicken and duck, cut each sausage in four, and place all these in the soup tureen. Add the quenelles and the halved garnished eggs. Place the strips of vegetables and a sprig of parsley on top. Cover this garnish and keep warm. Grate a fresh raw beetroot, pound, and press through a sieve to obtain a red juice. Heat the juice and as soon as it begins to boil, pour it into the consommé to give it the colour of Bordeaux wine. Then pour the boiling soup into the soup tureen, adding a pinch of white peppercorns. Serve.

The marrow bone should be served on a very hot dish surrounded with heart-shaped croutons fried in butter.

Bossons macérés

Small soft cheeses made from goats' milk and containing about 45% fat.

Produced locally in Vivarais (Languedoc), the cheeses are steeped for three months in earthenware pots containing a mixture of olive oil, white wine, white brandy, and herbs, giving them a very strong flavour.

botermelk

A Belgian speciality, known in northern France as *lait battu* ('milk whip'). It consists of milk boiled very gently for 1½ hours with pearl barley (or rice, semolina, tapioca, or very fine vermicelli) and brown sugar. The mixture, which is sometimes bound with potato starch, is then mixed with molasses or honey; raisins or other dried fruits soaked in warm water are then added.

Botherel (Marie, Vicomte de)

French politician, financier, and originator of the modern restaurant car (born La Chapelle-du-Lou, 1790; died Dinan, 1859). In 1839 he had the idea of installing mobile kitchens on buses operating in the Parisian suburbs. In order to keep his bus-restaurants stocked with hot and cold food, he built vast and expensive kitchens, featuring such modern equipment as a steam machine that kept colossal pots permanently boiling. All Paris admired the venture, but the enterprise was doomed to failure and the Vicomte has passed into obscurity.

bottereaux

Geometrically shaped fritters (square, round, triangular, etc.) made from raised (leavened) dough that has been flavoured with brandy or liqueur. They are traditionally made during mid-Lent in the Charentes and Anjou regions and can be eaten hot or cold.

RECIPE

Bottereaux   Mix thoroughly together 400 g (14 oz, 3½ cups) flour, a pinch of salt, 3 tablespoons (scant ¼ cup) caster (superfine) sugar, and 2 tablespoons (3 tablespoons) rum. To this add 20 g (¾ oz) fresh yeast (¾ cake compressed yeast) mixed with 1 dl (4 fl oz, scant ½ cup) slightly warm milk to form a dough. Knead the dough thoroughly and roll out to a thickness of 5 mm (¼ in). Distribute 125 g (4½ oz, ½ cup) butter cut into small pieces evenly over the surface. Fold the dough in two and roll out evenly, then knead again to work the butter in. Roll into a ball, flatten, and roll into a ball again. Leave to rise for 3 hours. Roll out the dough very thinly (3 mm, ⅛ in) and cut out the shapes with a pastry (cookie) cutter. Fry them in very hot oil, then drain on kitchen paper before dusting with icing (confectioners') sugar.

bottle BOUTEILLE

A narrow-necked vessel for holding and storing liquids. Mineral water, fruit juice, wine, cider, beer, spirits, oils, and vinegar are marketed in bottles of various shapes, sizes, and materials.

☐ **Wine bottles and bottling** In ancient times, wine was stored and transported in amphorae; it could undergo an unpleasant change if exposed to air. The cask, supposedly invented by the Gauls, was a considerable improvement. Small quantities of wine were transported in goatskins, known as *boutiaux* or *boutilles* (from the Low Latin *butticula*, meaning a small cask) and this is probably the origin of the word bottle.

In the Middle Ages, wine was served at table either in tin vessels or pots – long-term storage in glass bottles did not become widespread until the 18th century. An etching, dated 1750 and showing wine bottles with driven-home corks (instead of mere bungs or stoppers), makes it possible to date their appearance. The first glassworks to specialize in making wine bottles was set up in Bordeaux in 1723, by an Irishman.

Bottling by hand is still done at certain wine estates, both large and small, according to the resources available. Automatic bottling is used for mass-produced wines, including those that are not intended for long-term keeping. On labels, the phrase 'Mise en bouteilles au château' or 'au domaine de la production' signifies that the wine has been bottled at the place where it has been made – this is now done for the major Bordeaux wines. Certain wines must be bottled in the region of production, such as those of Alsace. Inexpensive wines, shipped to export markets in bulk, will be bottled there.

☐ **Shape and size** Bottles were individually hand-blown until about the middle of the last century, so that their shape and size varied from one workshop to another. With the development of the wine trade, shapes varied according to the wine region. At first bottles were dumpy, like flagons, but they gradually became cylindrical and more refined. Before 1850, they had a more slender shape (the Burgundy type). Special basic shapes were created for certain wines, notably Bordeaux and champagne, but other shapes became associated with particular regions, such as Provence, parts of the Loire, the Jura, etc.

In 1866, the shape and size of Bordeaux, Burgundy, and Mâcon bottles was legally defined. Nevertheless, the creation of new types of bottles for commercial purposes continued – causing some confusion. The first bottles to be mechanically moulded were used at Cognac in 1894. The development of bottles made by machine, in moulds, enabled a greater standardization to be achieved, and today the 'standard' wine bottle is generally assumed to be one of 75 cl. This, however, can vary according to whether certain traditional shapes and sizes are used; in addition, the wine in the bottle does not always reach the level of the underside of the cork, so that a certain tolerance for ullage must be assumed as regards capacity. Certain very old wines, kept long in bottle, may be more ullaged than young inexpensive wines. Regulations vary according to the country of production and bottling, as with labelling.

In France, the 1-litre bottle of vin ordinaire bears six stars, 16 mm in height, at its base. Bottles of beer, cider, and lemonade also have a standard form, and plastic bottles, increasingly used for milk, mineral water, and oil, may be of virtually any size or shape, although the latter are usually of the 1-litre or 1.5-litre size. The principal types of bottle are shown in the table.

In spite of the fashion for 'special' bottles, each particular property or area claiming to have its own, it is the classical shapes that inspire the most confidence. One example is the bottle for rosé wine from Provence, which is conical with a bulge at the neck. Some foreign wines are also marketed in their characteristic bottles, a typical example being Chianti. Finally, it should be noted that Bordeaux classified growths have adopted a standard bottle shape made of darker refractive glass. This precaution ensures that the red wine keeps better. The colour of glass used for fine wines is subject to controls.

□ **Serving wine** Current practice is to serve wine from its original bottle, placed directly on the table or on a coaster. The practice of laying the bottle on its side in a basket is not advised except for very old wines, which may have a sediment and should be drawn from the wine bin in a recumbent position or, still lying down, be placed in a wine cradle, prior to decanting off the deposit. Such wines should be brought from the cellar well in advance of the meal. If they are not to be decanted, they should stand upright for some hours, to allow the deposit to slip to the bottom and remain in the punt at the base.

ALSACE

flûte d'Alsace		70 cl
bottle (for USA and Canada)		75 cl

ANJOU

fillette		37.5 cl
half-bottle		37.5 cl
bottle		75 cl

BEAUJOLAIS

half-bottle		37.5 cl
pot		50 cl
bottle		75 cl

BORDEAUX

fillette	½ bottle	37.5 cl
bottle		75 cl
magnum	2 bottles	1.5 l
demijohn	about 3 bottles	2.5 l
double magnum	4 bottles	3 l
jeroboam	6.67 bottles	5 l
impériale	8 bottles	6 l

BURGUNDY

half-bottle		37.5 cl
bottle		75 cl
magnum	2 bottles	1.5 l

CHAMPAGNE

quarter	¼ bottle	20 cl
half-bottle		40 cl
bottle		80 cl
magnum	2 bottles	1.6 l
jeroboam	4 bottles	3.2 l
rehoboam	6 bottles	4.8 l
methuselah	8 bottles	6.4 l
salmanazar	12 bottles	9.6 l
balthazar	16 bottles	12.8 l
nebuchad-nezzar	20 bottles	16 l

JURA

clavelin (yellow wine)	1 bottle	62 cl

MOSELLE

half-bottle	35 cl
bottle	72 cl

RHINE

half-bottle	35 cl
bottle	72 cl

SHERRY

bottle	75.75 cl or 70 cl depending on the bottling

UNITED STATES

tenth	½ bottle	37.86 cl
fifth	1 bottle	75.72 cl
magnum	2 bottles	1.51 l

bottling and canning food
CONSERVATION EN BOÎTE

A method of preserving food by hermetically sealing it in jars, bottles, or cans and then heating it to temperatures above 100 C (220 F), preferably 110–115 C (230–240 F), which destroys all the microorganisms and enzymes liable to cause spoilage. This form of sterilization is largely used at an industrial level, in preserving factories, but it can also be done at home, mainly for bottling fruit and vegetables.

Thorough sterilization necessitates heating the foodstuff for long enough to destroy the microorganisms but not so as to impair the nutritional qualities and taste of the product. To achieve this, new methods for industrial sterilization are being used, for example very high temperatures for a very short time. It is in the treatment of milk that methods have progressed most. The heating period for prepacked sterilized milk has dropped from 15 minutes at 125 c (257 F) to 4 minutes at 135 c (275 F). It is reduced even further for producing UHT (ultra-heat-treated) milk, which is heated to 140 c (284 F) for 1–3 seconds, normally by steam injection, and then cooled and further processed in sterile containers to eliminate the 'cooked' taste.

The original process was invented by Nicolas Appert and is still referred to as *appertisation* in France. When sterilizing on a domestic scale, fruit and vegetables are first of all peeled, trimmed, washed, and sometimes blanched, then placed in receptacles which can withstand high temperatures (hermetically sealed jars or metal cans which must be crimped); before being sealed, they are covered with a syrup or a salt solution to which lemon juice or ascorbic acid is sometimes added (this preserves the natural colour of the food and increases its acidity, a factor in good preserving). The sealed receptacles are placed in a sterilizer or an autoclave. Sterilization is carried out all at once or in several stages (see *tyndallization*).

bottom cuts

BAS MORCEAUX

Cuts of meat from the lower part of the animal (when it is in a standing position). The term is not derogatory but applies to second- and third-category meats (for braising and boiling) which are not considered as fine as fillet (sirloin) and other top cuts (for grilling (broiling) and roasting). The bottom cuts include shin, brisket, flank, skirt, and leg of beef; knuckle and shin, breast, and flank of veal; knuckle and breast of lamb and pork. Slow-cooking dishes (braised, stewed, navarin, etc.) are smoother and tastier when prepared with the bottom cuts, as these include a certain amount of fat and cartilage. The bottom cuts (i.e. the most economical) of a beef carcass represent 50% of the edible meat.

botvinya

A cold sweet-and-sour soup from Russia made from beetroot (red beet) leaves, spinach, and sorrel. It is garnished with either cucumber or small pieces of fish.

RECIPE

Botvinya Cut up 400 g (14 oz) spinach, 250 g (9 oz) beetroot (red beet) leaves, and 200 g (7 oz) sorrel. Cook gently in melted butter until soft then make into a purée by rubbing through a sieve or using a blender. When the purée is quite cold, mix it in a soup tureen with ¼ litre (8 fl oz, 1 cup) dry white wine, 1 litre (1¾ pints, 2 pints) stock, 12 g (½ tablespoon) salt, 10 g (½ tablespoon) sugar, 100 g (4 oz, 1 cup) diced cucumber, a chopped shallot, and 1 tablespoon each of chopped chervil and tarragon. Add about 10 ice cubes, allow them to melt, mix again, and serve very cold.

boucan

Originally, boucan was meat smoke-dried by the Caribbean Indians. Now, however, the word is used to describe a very different and more flavoursome dish from Caribbean cookery. This consists of a whole sheep, stuffed with the flesh of wild duck and geese, onions, and spices. Cooked outdoors, it is placed in a trench, heated with charcoal, then covered with hot sand and embers. Cooking takes about two hours.

bouche du roi

The service comprising all members of the royal kitchen staff at the French court before the Revolution (1789). The oldest order defining their duties dates from 1281, when there were ten people responsible for the bread pantry and for cupbearing, 32 for cooking and four for fruit (see *cupbearer*, *écuyer tranchant*, *serdeau*). A hundred years later, the number had more than tripled and under Louis XIV there were over 500. The bouche du roi became a very hierarchical structure managed by the highest officials and divided into eight offices, which were specified as 'bouche' if they served the king exclusively and 'commun' (common) if they worked for the rest of the court. The goblet office included the bouche pantry and the bouche cupbearers, and was closely allied to the office of bouche cuisine. These were followed by the three offices of common pantry, common cupbearing, and common cuisine. There were also the fruiterer's office and the

Home bottling and preserving of vegetables and fruit

product		additions (per litre, 1¾ pints, 4¼ cups water)	sterilization time	keeping time
vegetables	artichoke hearts	8 g (¼ oz) salt + 3 tablespoons (¼ cup) lemon juice	1¾ hours	10–12 months
	asparagus	20 g (¾ oz) slat + 3 tablespoons (¼ cup) lemon juice	1¾ hours	10–12 months
	new carrots	15 g (½ oz) salt	1¾ hours	12 months
	mushrooms	8 g (¼ oz) salt + 3 tablespoons (¼ cup) lemon juice	1½ hours	10–12 months
	Brussels sprouts	10 g (½ oz) salt + 3 tablespoons (¼ cup) lemon juice	1¾ hours	10–12 months
	chicory (endives)	20 g (¾ oz) salt + 3 tablespoons (¼ cup) lemon juice + 1 teaspoon sugar	1½ hours	12 months
	green beans	20 g (¾ oz) salt	2¼ hours	12 months
	shelled peas	10 g (½ oz) salt	1¾ hours	12 months
	peppers (peeled, seeded, browned for 5–10 mins in olive oil)		45 mins	10–12 months
	salsify (cooked for 30 mins in a blanc)	15 g (½ oz) salt	1¾ hours	12 months
	tomatoes (peeled and seeded)	20 g (¾ oz) salt	1¼ hours	8–12 months
	truffles	100 ml (4 fl oz, ½ cup) white wine, Madeira, or Cognac + a pinch of salt, without water (for 250 g (9 oz) truffles)	1¾ hours	12 months at least

fruit	au naturel	in syrup		
apricots (stoned, pitted)	1 tablespoon sugar without water	500 g (18 oz, 2 generous cups) sugar	30 mins	12 months
quinces (poached for 15 mins with the juice of 1 lemon per litre (1¾ pints, 4¼ cups) water)	1 tablespoon sugar, without water	750 g (1¾ lb, 3⅔ cups) sugar	30 mins	12 months
chestnuts (peeled)	20 g (¾ oz) salt + juice of 1 lemon	500 g (18 oz, 2 generous cups) sugar	1 hour	12 months
peaches (peeled)	1 tablespoon sugar	750 g (1¾ lb, 3⅔ cups) sugar	40 mins	12 months
pears (peeled)	1 tablespon sugar + juice of 1 lemon	500 g (18 oz, 2 generous cups) sugar	50 mins	12 months
plums (either stoned, or pricked to the stone in two or three places)	1 tablespoon sugar + juice of 1 lemon	500 g (18 oz, 2 generous cups) sugar + juice of 3 lemons	25 mins	12 months

quartermaster's office, which provided wood porters, carpenters, and others. The eighth office was that of tradesmen's kitchen. Each office was held by a high official, who was assisted by numerous officials of lower rank.

☐ **Bouche cuisine** The most important office was that of the king's kitchen, which had a team of four chefs, four roasters, four soup-makers, four pastry-cooks, three kitchen boys, ten equerries, keepers of the table service, who looked after the gold and silver table services, and washers, for washing-up and laundry. There were also chair carriers and table carriers. As the king moved around, he was accompanied by warners, who gave the cooks timely notice of when the king wished to eat. When the king went hunting, a wine runner followed, carrying a light snack with him on his horse. If a more substantial meal was required, it would be brought by carriage.

☐ **Expensive honours** All bouche du roi offices, which carried the right to wear a sword, were expensive to buy and gave little return. They were held by high noblemen; the grand master of the bouche du roi was the Prince of Condé. Towards the end of Louis XIV's reign, however, some of the rich bourgeoisie acquired these positions, which gave them the honour of *bouche à la cour*. The bouche was abolished by the Revolution but Napoleon re-established some offices, particularly that of *écuyer tranchant* (slicing equerry). Louis XVIII restored the system in its entirety but Louis-Philippe finally abolished it in 1830.

bouchée (savoury)
BOUCHÉE (SALÉE)

A small round puff pastry case with various fillings. Shortly before serving, bouchées are filled with a salpicon of one or more ingredients, with or without sauce. They are served hot. The first small bouchées (bouchées *à la reine*) were probably invented by Marie Leszczyńska, queen of Louis XV. It is safe to assume that the queen at least made them fashonable, as she did other dishes and delicacies – historians agree on the subject of her appetite!

RECIPE

Preparation of bouchées PRÉPARA-TION DES BOUCHÉES Flour the working surface and roll out some puff pastry to a thickness of about 5 mm (¼ in). Wipe a damp cloth over a pastry board. Using a round, crinkle-edged pastry (cookie) cutter, 8–10 cm 3–4 in) in diameter, cut out circles of pastry and place them on the damp board, turning them over as you do so. Glaze with beaten egg. Now, using a plain 6–8 cm (2½–3 in) pastry cutter, mark a circle in the pastry but do not cut right through. This will form the lid once the cases are cooked. Allow the cases to rest for approximately 30 minutes then place them on a baking sheet in a hot oven (around 220 C, 425 F, gas 7) for 12–15 minutes. Using the point of a knife, lift off the lids and if necessary remove any soft pastry inside the case. The bouchées are now ready to be filled.

Bouchées à la financière Fill the cases with a salpicon *à la financière*. Garnish with sliced truffle poached in Madeira.

Bouchées à l'américaine Prepare the bouchée cases as above and fill with a salpicon of lobster, crayfish, or monkfish *à l'américaine*.

Bouchées à la périgourdine Make some very small cases, approximately 4 cm (1½ in) in diameter. Prepare a salpicon of truffle and foie gra. .nd bind with Madeira sauce. Spoon into the cases.

Bouchées à la reine Prepare and bake some bouchée cases. Prepare a salpicon *à la reine* for the filling as follows. Dice some chicken breasts poached in stock; also, dice some truffle and poach this in white wine. Clean some button mushrooms, trim the stalks, and cut each mushroom into four; sprinkle with lemon juice and cook very gently in butter so they retain their original colour. Prepare a white sauce with the stock from the chicken, add some cream, and, if desired, some egg yolk. For ½ litre (17 fl oz, 2 cups) stock, use 40 g (1½ oz, 3 tablespoons) butter, 40 g (1½ oz, generous ¼ cup) flour, 1 dl (6 tablespoons, scant ½ cup) cream, and 1 egg yolk. Using this sauce, bind the chicken, truffles, and mushrooms together.

Heat the bouchée cases in a moderate oven (about 180 c, 350 f, gas 4) for 10 minutes. Fill them with the hot mixture and replace the lids. If the truffles are left out of the filling, equal quantities of chicken breast and mushrooms should be used. A salpicon of calves' sweetbreads, quenelles, and brains braised in white sauce may be added to the filling.

Bouchées with mushrooms
BOUCHÉES AUX CHAMPIGNONS
Make smaller cases using a 6 cm (2½ in) diameter pastry (cookie) cutter. Fill with morel mushrooms in cream or, if these are not available, with button mushrooms in a cream sauce.

Bouchées with prawns (shrimp)
BOUCHÉES AUX CREVETTES Fill the cases with a ragout of prawn (shrimp) tails in prawn sauce.

bouchée (petit four)
BOUCHÉE (SUCRÉE)
A petit four made from sponge-cake shapes which are hollowed out, filled with confectioners' custard (pastry cream) or jam, then sandwiched together and coated in coloured fondant icing (frosting). For instance, a filling of confectioners' custard flavoured with coffee or chocolate could be used with fondant icing of the same flavour; alternatively, a raspberry jam filling could be used with pink fondant icing. Other combinations include green confectioners' custard flavoured with Kirsch plus green fondant icing decorated with pistachios, and vanilla-flavoured confectioners' custard with white fondant icing.

RECIPE

Apricot bouchées Place 250 g (9 oz, 1 cup) caster (superfine) sugar and 8 eggs in a round-bottomed bowl and whisk together over a pan of hot water. When the mixture is thick and fluffy, fold in alternately 200 g (7 oz, 1¼ cups) sifted flour and 200 g (7 oz) melted butter to which a small glass of rum has been added. Three-quarters fill some small

round moulds with the mixture and bake for approximately 20 minutes in a moderate oven (180 c, 350 f, gas 4). Turn out onto a rack and allow to cool. Cut in two, spread the bottom half with apricot jam flavoured with rum, and sandwich the two halves together. Reduce some apricot jam, flavour with rum, and pour over the top and sides of the bouchées. Decorate with blanched toasted almonds and a glacé (candied) cherry.

bouchère (à la)
The name given to various dishes that feature a garnish of bone marrow. Examples are: chopped cabbage consommé, served with slices of poached bone marrow; soft-boiled or poached eggs *à la bouchère*; and omelette filled with diced poached bone marrow, surrounded with a ring of demiglace, and garnished on top with slices of bone marrow.

The name also applies to veal chops that are marinated in oil with salt, pepper, and chopped parsley, then grilled for approximately 15 minutes and served garnished with parsley and vegetables in season.

bouchon
A type of small bistro in Lyon where two of the gastronomic traditions of the city are maintained: the lavish mâchon and the *pot* – a 45-cl (¾-pint, 1-pint) bottle for tasting Beaujolais. The word comes from the Old French *bousche*, meaning a bottle stopper made of hay, straw, or leaves, and the insignia of taverns used to be a bunch of greenery or a bundle of straw, as recalled in an old marching song:
'My friend, we must take a break,
I can see the shadow of a *bouchon*.'

boudin
See *black pudding*.

boudin antillais
A Caribbean sausage, also called *boudin cochon*, that is grilled, fried in lard, or simply heated in very hot (not boiling) water. They are often eaten as an appetizer to accompany punch. The filling is fairly liquid and can be sucked out from one end of the skin.

RECIPE

Boudin antillais   For 6–8 sausages, add 2 tablespoons (3 tablespoons) vinegar to 1.5 litres (2¾ pints, 7 cups) fresh pigs' blood; this prevents the blood from coagulating. Moisten 250 g (9 oz, 2 generous cups) stale white breadcrumbs (without crusts) with 1.25 dl (4 fl oz, ¼ pint) milk. Turn some clean pig's intestines inside out, wash and dry them, rub with lemon juice, and turn right side out. Finely chop 250 g (9 oz) onions and brown gently for 7–8 minutes in 100 g (4 oz, ½ cup) lard. Make a purée of the breadcrumbs and blood in a blender and mix with the drained onions. Then add 5 large cloves of garlic, finely chopped, a small chilli pepper, about 20 chopped chives or the same quantity of spring onions (scallions), salt to season, and 1 tablespoon flour. Work together well by hand or with a spatula and adjust seasoning as required. The mixture must be highly flavoured.

Knot the end of one of the pieces of intestine and, using a funnel, fill the intestine with the mixture, pushing it with the hand towards the knotted end. When the sausage is about 10 cm (4 in) long, twist the intestine several times to seal it. Repeat for the other sausages. Place them together in boiling water seasoned with chives, bay leaves, peppers, and sandalwood and allow to barely simmer for about 15 minutes or until no more fat comes out when they are pricked. Drain the sausages and allow to cool completely.

boudin blanc

A kind of white-meat sausage sold in France mostly during the Christmas period. The filling is a fine white-meat paste (poultry, veal, pork, or rabbit) to which has been added pork or veal fat, and sometimes fish, cream, milk, eggs, flour (or crustless breadcrumbs), and spices. It is then put into intestine casings and poached, fried gently, baked in the oven, or cooked in buttered paper. White-meat sausages are made in many other countries: they are called white puddings (sausages) in Britain and the United States. Listed below are some of the many types of French boudin blanc, some of which contain truffles (see *bougnette, coudenou*).

● boudin *à la Richelieu* is based on chicken forcemeat and a salpicon *à la reine* and is cooked not in intestines but in small individual moulds.

● Le Havre boudin blanc is the only one sold all year round and contains no lean meat, only pork fat, milk, eggs, crustless bread, and rice flour.

● Avranches boudin blanc contains chicken breasts, calves' sweetbreads, fish fillets, and fresh cream.

● Le Mans boudin blanc combines hard back pork fat and lean pork (neck or leg) with eggs, onions, milk, and spices.

The traditional Christmas boudin blanc dates from the Middle Ages: after leaving Midnight Mass, the faithful would eat a milky gruel to warm themselves up. The pork butchers had the idea of binding it with eggs and adding minced (ground) meat.

RECIPES

Boudin blanc   Skin and bone a chicken and finely mince the flesh together with 250 g (9 oz) York ham. To 150 g (5 oz, 2½ cups) fresh breadcrumbs add just enough milk to moisten them. Work with a spoon over a gentle heat to thicken, then leave to cool. Prepare a duxelles using 400 g (14 oz, 4 cups) button mushrooms, the juice of half a lemon, and four finely chopped shallots. Thoroughly mix the bread mixture, the minced chicken and ham, and the duxelles with 2 egg yolks, 100 g (4 oz, 1 cup) ground almonds, 2 dl (7 fl oz, ¾ cup) fresh double (heavy) cream, a glass of Madeira or sherry, a large pinch of paprika, salt, pepper, a dash of cayenne, 2 tablespoons (3 tablespoons) chopped parsley, a generous pinch of powdered thyme, and (if desired) a few truffle peelings. Beat two egg whites until stiff and add to the mixture. Prepare and fill the intestines as for boudin antillais. Poach in the same way then allow to cool completely.

Boudin à la Richelieu   BOUDIN DE VOLAILLE À LA RICHELIEU   Butter some small ovenproof moulds, smooth-edged and oval in shape. Line the bottom and side of each with a finely ground chicken forcemeat. Now add a mixture similar to that used to fill bouchées *à la reine* but cut up more finely. Finally, cover with more forcemeat and smooth the surface using a knife blade dipped in cold water. Place the moulds in a bain-marie in a moderate oven (180 c, 350 f, gas 4) and cook for approximately 25 minutes. Turn the puddings out of the moulds and allow to cool. Arrange them in a circle on a serving plate with fried parsley in the centre. Serve with Périgueux sauce or suprême sauce to which has been added diced truffle or truffle peelings.

bougnette

A charcuterie speciality of southwestern France. The *bougnette de Castres* is a flat sausage made from chopped belly of pork combined with a mixture of bread and eggs, fried or baked in fat, and eaten cold. Bougnette from Albi is larger.

In the Cévennes, bougnette is a kind of fritter, while in Auvergne it is a type of coarse pancake.

bougras

A vegetable soup from Périgord, prepared with the water used for cooking black pudding (blood sausage). It was traditionally prepared at carnival time, when the pig was killed.

RECIPE

Bougras Cut the heart of a curly green cabbage into 4 pieces, blanch, then dip in cold water. Boil 2.5 litres (4½ pints, 5½ pints) water in which black puddings (blood sausages) have been poached. Add the cabbage, 6–8 carrots, 4 parsnips, and 3 onions (all quartered), 4 leeks and 4 sticks (stalks) of celery (tied in bunches), and a large bouquet garni containing plenty of thyme. Boil the ingredients for 45 minutes, then add 400 g (14 oz) thickly sliced potatoes and simmer for a further 25 minutes (approximately). Now remove a generous ladle of vegetables, drain, and fry in goose fat or lard, then add a ladle of stock: this is known as the *fricassée*. Pour the fricassée into the soup and cook for a further 15 minutes. Line a soup tureen with thin slices of stale farmhouse bread and pour in the boiling soup.

bouillabaisse

A dish comprising fish boiled with herbs, which is traditionally associated with the Provence region, especially Marseilles, although it has long been enjoyed further afield. The word is a contraction of two verbs, *bouillir* (to boil) and *abaisser* (to reduce), and in fact bouillabaisse is more a method of rapid cooking than an actual recipe; there are as many 'authentic' bouillabaisses as there are ways of combining fish.

Bouillabaisse was originally cooked on the beach by fishermen, who used a large cauldron over a wood fire to cook the fish that was least suitable for market, such as *rascasse* (scorpion fish or rockfish) – essential for an authentic bouillabaisse and hardly ever eaten otherwise. Shellfish are added, including squill fish, mussels, and small crabs (lobster is a city dweller's refinement). The dish is flavoured with olive, spices, including pepper and saffron, and dried orange peel.

In 1895, J.-B. Reboul listed in *La Cuisinière provençale* 40 types of fish suitable for bouillabaisse (including mackerel and sardines, which other experts reject as too oily). In fact, bouillabaisse should be prepared using rockfish, ideally caught with rod and line just before cooking. Species of the northen Mediterranean coast give even more authenticity to the dish and include sea bass, moray eel, rainbow wrasse, bonito, and wrasse.

The fish and its soup are served separately, with the soup traditionally poured onto slices of dried home-made bread (not fried or toasted); in Marseilles, a special bread called *marette* is used. But bouillabaisse can also be served with croutons rubbed with garlic and rouille sauce.

In 1980, the restaurateurs of Marseille signed a Bouillabaisse charter designed to protect and defend the authentic recipe, but this has since been contested by other 'specialists'.

Provençal cuisine offers several variations on the bouillabaisse soup. At Martigues, where it is usual to serve the soup with potatoes (cooked separately), there is also a black bouillabaisse, containing cuttlefish and their ink. Sardine and cod bouillabaisses are also characteristic of the region, as are bourride and revesset, (both Provençal fish soups). White wine is sometimes added to the liquid.

Other French coastal regions have their own local methods of preparing fish soups: *bouillinada* from Roussillon, cotriade from Brittany, chaudrée from Charentes (which gave rise to the American chowder), marmite from Dieppe, Flemish waterzooï, and ttoro, of the Basque region.

RECIPE

Bouillabaisse   For 8–10 servings, use about 3 kg (6½ lb) fish and shellfish. Place the following ingredients in a large deep flameproof casserole: 300 g (11 oz, scant 3 cups) chopped onions (or 100 g (4 oz) leeks, and 200 g (7 oz, scant 2 cups) onions), 3 large skinned and finely chopped tomatoes, 40 g (1½ oz) crushed garlic, a stick of fennel, a small bunch of parsley, a sprig of thyme, a bay leaf, and a piece of dried orange rind. Add the prepared shellfish, then the firm-fleshed fish cut into uniform pieces with heads, bones, and skin removed, as necessary. Moisten with 2 dl (7 fl oz, ¾ cup) olive oil and season with salt and freshly ground pepper. Add a generous pinch of powdered saffron and leave to marinate, covered and in a cool place, for a few hours.

Add sufficient water to cover the fish (or fish stock prepared with the heads and trimmings of the fish may be used). Cover and boil rapidly for 7–8 minutes. Then add the prepared soft-fleshed fish and continue to boil rapidly for a further 7 minutes. Now remove the fish and shellfish and place in a large round dish. Line a soup tureen with dry bread and strain the soup onto it. Sprinkle the soup and the fish with coarsely chopped parsley and serve both at the same time.

bouilleture or bouilliture

An eel stew thickened with kneaded butter and garnished with mushrooms, baby onions, and prunes; it is served with toast and sometimes quartered hard-boiled (hard-cooked) eggs. In Anjou, bouilleture is prepared with red wine; white wine is used in Poitou.

RECIPE

Angevin bouilleture   BOUILLETURE ANGEVINE   For 1 kg (2¼ lb) eel, allow ¾ litre (1¼ pints, 3 cups) red wine, 10 medium-sized shallots, 40 g (1½ oz, 3 tablespoons) butter, 1 glass brandy, 250 g (9 oz, 2 generous cups) button (or wild) mushrooms (sautéed), 150 g (5 oz) small glazed onions, 250 g (9 oz) prunes, 15 g (½ oz, 2 tablespoons) flour, a bouquet garni, salt, and pepper. Skin the eel and cut into thick slices. Peel and chop the shallots and soften in butter in a flame-proof casserole. Add the slices of eel, brown them, then flame with the brandy. Season with salt and pepper, add the red wine, the bouquet garni and the prunes. Cook for 20 minutes then remove and drain. Prepare some kneaded butter (see *butter*), add it to the casserole, and boil for 2 minutes, stirring constantly. Pour the sauce containing the prunes over the eel and garnish with the sautéed mushrooms and the glazed onions.

bouilleur de cru

In France, a landowner, vine grower, fruit producer, or owner of any other product that can be distilled (e.g. perry or cider) who is allowed to carry out the distillation for himself. The expression is much used in the Cognac region, where the large establishments may buy in brandy already distilled by a bouilleur de cru if they do not carry out the distillation process themselves. There are also some individual *bouilleurs ambulants*, who, as the term implies, travel around with some kind of portable still (alembic) and either operate this for anyone who hires them, or actually rent it out.

In the past such people were kept busy, but these days distilling carried out on a large scale is usually done at some centrally placed establishment and improved methods of transport enable the product intended for distillation to be brought to the distillery without loss of time. The more modest procedures of distillation can be – and sometimes are – carried out in a very small space, either in the distiller's actual house or some shed, so that an individual type of spirit may be produced. The systems of taxation and controls, however, have complicated what was at one time quite a common way of life, and though the person entitled to be a bouilleur de cru may still proudly continue to practice, the occupation is now both altered and not as numerous as in former times.

bouilli

The piece of beef cooked in the preparation of a pot-au-feu, bouillon, or consomé. It can be sliced and eaten cold with salad, or it can be grilled; it may also be diced and either fried or served in a spicy sauce. Minced, it is used for making meatballs, kromeskies, fritters, stuffed tomatoes, and hash.

RECIPES

Boiled beef à la hongroise BOUILLI DE BOEUF À LA HONGROISE Cut some boiled beef into large dice. Chop some onions, using 100 g (4 oz) for 500 g (18 oz) meat, and soften in butter. Add the diced meat and fry. Season with paprika. Coat with cream sauce and serve very hot.

boiled beef à la provençale BOUILLI DE BOEUF À LA PROVENÇALE Prepare in the same way as boiled beef *à la hongroise*, but instead of the cream sauce use the same quantity of tomato fondue flavoured with garlic. Sprinkle with chopped parsley before serving.

bouillinada

A fish soup from Roussillon, very similar to the Provençal bouillabaisse and likewise prepared with a variety of fish, most commonly wrasse and rock fish.

bouillon (restaurant)

A type of cheap restaurant that was opened in France at the end of the 19th century (see *Duval*), serving meals at a single price. Originally its main dish was boiled beef (*bouilli*) served with its stock but this ample and economical menu was later complemented by other dishes. In Paris, several chains of such restaurants were opened, including the Boulant and Chartier bouillons. One of these is still running, complete with its 1900 decor, sawdust on the floor, Thonet furniture, and a menu written with purple ink.

bouillon (stock)

The plain unclarified broth obtained from boiling meat or vegetables. It is used instead of water or white stock for cooking certain dishes and for making soups and sauces. 'Bouillon is the soul and quintessence of sauces' said F. Marin in 1739. The food industry has now developed solid or liquid extracts that can be mixed with water to obtain an instant meat or chicken stock.

In French cookery, the term 'bouillon' applies principally to the liquid part of a pot-au-feu.

RECIPES

Dietetic vegetable bouillon BOUILLON DE LÉGUMES DIÉTÉTIQUE This is easily prepared using a microwave oven. Take some vegetables normally used for a stock pot and cut into very thin strips or chop using a food processor. Place 2 tablespoons (3 tablespoons) of the chopped vegetables in a small bowl and add 4.25 dl (15 fl oz, 2 cups) water. Add a little salt if desired. Partially cover and cook at 100% (high) for 6 minutes in the microwave, stirring the mixture after 2 and 4 minutes. Add 1 teaspoon chopped parsley and a knob of butter (optional).

Giblet bouillon BOUILLON D'ABATTIS Place the giblets from 2 chickens in 2 litres (3½ pints, 4½ pints) cold water and bring to the boil. Peel and chop 4 medium-sized carrots, 2 turnips, 3 leeks (white part only), 2 sticks (stalks) of celery, and a small piece of parsnip. Skin the liquid, then add the vegetables together with an onion stuck with cloves, a bouquet garni, salt, and pepper. Boil gently until completely cooked (approximately 1½ hours). Just before serving, bone the giblets and return the meat to the bouillon, adding the juice of half a lemon and some chopped parsley. Adjust seasoning.

If desired, this can be prepared in the Greek way by cooking 2 handfuls of rice in the stock and thickening with a beaten egg yolk or, better still, a whole beaten egg.

Herb broth BOUILLON AUX HERBES (from a recipe in the 1884

Codex) Use 40 g (1½ oz) fresh sorrel leaves; 20 g (¾ oz) fresh lettuce leaves, 10 g (¼ oz) fresh chervil leaves, (½ teaspoon) sea salt 5 g (¼ oz) fresh butter, and 1 litre (1¾ pints, 4¼ cups) water. Wash the vegetables and cook them in the water. Then add the salt and butter. Strain.

Beet or spinach leaves may be added to the stock if desired, and, just before serving, parsley and lemon juice can be included.

Quick stocks BOUILLONS MÉNAGERS MODERNES Modern housewives no longer have stock pots bubbling away permanently on a corner of the stove. However, stock is still the basis of many recipes, so here are a few simple and quick recipes. The use of a microwave oven or pressure cooker considerably speeds up the cooking time of stock – see the manufacturer's recommended times. Stock can be kept for two or three days in the refrigerator (or longer if brought to the boil and refrigerated again).

▪ *Quick beef stock.* Coarsely chop 100 –150 g (4–5 oz) beef, a small carrot, a white leek, a small stick (stalk) of celery, a medium onion, and a clove. Place all the ingredients in 1.5 litres (2¾ pints, 7 cups) water and boil gently for 20 minutes. Strain.

▪ *Quick veal stock.* Use the same method as for quick beef stock but use lean veal (haunch or shoulder) instead of beef.

▪ *Quick chicken stock.* Use the same method as for quick beef stock but with 400–500 g (14–18 oz) chicken wings instead of the beef.

Depending on the purpose of these stocks, a little thyme or parsley and salt and pepper may be added.

Vegetable bouillon BOUILLON DE LÉGUMES Use vegetables that are generally included in a stock pot. Chop and drain them, cook gently in butter or fat, then pour boiling water over them to cover. A bouquet garni, salt, and pepper (optional) are added and the broth is simmered until the vegetables are cooked. Alternatively, simply add all the ingredients to boiling water and simmer until cooked, either conventionally or using a pressure cooker. In both cases, the broth must be strained before it can be served.

bouillon de noces

A stock pot for festive meals that features in the cuisine of the Périgord region of France. It is traditionally prepared using beef, knuckle of veal, stuffed chicken, and turkey portions, which are cooked in a stock along with the usual stock-pot vegetables plus Swiss chard stalks. When the meat is cooked, onion (which has been fried until golden in goose or bacon fat) and vermicelli are added and gently cooked in the bouillon.

boukha or boukhra

A Tunisian spirit made from figs and drunk as a digestive throughout north Africa. The figs most commonly used are Hordas figs from Turkey.

Boulanger

The owner of a Parisian café in the Rue des Poulies (now Rue du Louvre), who in 1765, became the first restaurateur of the capital. (Before this time, guests obtained their meals from inns, hostelries, and caterers.) Since he did not belong to the guild of caterers who sold sauces, cooked dishes, and stews, Boulanger was entitled to offer his clients only drinks and 'restorative broths'. One day in 1765, he served sheep's feet in white sauce and won his case against the caterers because Parliament had decreed that sheep's feet were not a stew. His success assured, Boulanger now added poultry *au gros sel* to his menu. Diderot said that at the Boulanger establishment 'one was well but expensively fed'. Grimod spoke of the 'first restaurateur of Paris, called Champ-d'Oiseau, established in the Rue des Poulies in 1770'; this may have been a nickname for Boulanger or an early competitor. A certain Roze de Chantoiseau set up in the same street, but his business foundered a few years later.

Boulanger is known only by this name (which means baker); some authorities claim that he was a baker whose real name has been lost.

boulangère (à la)

Describing certain dishes, usually of lamb but sometimes of fish (e.g. cod), that are baked in the oven (originally the baker's oven, hence the term), garnished with potatoes and chopped onions, and sometimes topped with butter.

RECIPES

Cod à la boulangère CABILLAUD À LA BOULANGÈRE Season a piece of cod with salt and pepper and place it in an ovenproof dish. Thinly slice some potatoes and onions and arrange these around the fish, seasoning with salt and pepper and adding a pinch of thyme and a pinch of powdered bay leaf. Sprinkle with melted butter. Place in a moderate oven (approximately 190 c, 375 F, gas 5) and bake for 40 minutes, covering the dish as soon as the fish turns golden to prevent it from drying out. Sprinkle with chopped parsley and serve, piping hot, in the cooking dish.

Roast leg of lamb à la boulangère GIGOT À LA BOULANGÈRE Season a 2.5 kg (5½ lb) leg of lamb with salt, pepper, and galic, rub with butter, and roast in a hot oven (220 c, 425 F, gas 7) for 40 minutes. Slice 600–750 g (1½– 1¾ lb) potatoes and 300 g (11 oz) onions. Arrange them round the joint and baste with the meat juices and about 50 g (2 oz) melted butter. Season with salt and pepper, reduce the oven temperature to 200 c (400 F, gas 6) and cook for a further 40–50minutes, basting four or five times. Finally, place a sheet of foil over the dish and leave it in the open oven for a good 15 minutes for the meat to relax.

boule-de-neige

A small cake in the shape of a ball, which is completely covered with whipped cream. It is made of layers of Genoese sponge spread with butter cream.

The same name is also used for a petit four, the size of a large marble. It consists of either two small meringues sandwiched together with a cream or small cakes made of a rum baba dough (without raisins) filled with Kirsch cream and decorated with white fondant icing.

Boule-de-neige is also the French name for a kind of ice-cream dessert (see *snowball*).

boulette

Minced, chopped, or puréed meat or fish shaped into a ball before cooking. They are usually coated with bread-crumbs and then deep-fried, but they may also be sautéed or poached. They are often made to use up leftover meat or fish and may be served with tomato sauce or brown sauce. See *fricadelle*, *kefta*, *knödel*.

Boulette d'Avesnes

A French cows'-milk cheese (containing 50% fat), made by mixing Maroilles cheese with parsley, tarragon, and spices. Its reddish crust is washed in beer. A speciality of Thiéraches, Boulette d'Avesnes is shaped by hand into a cone, 8 cm (3½ in) in diameter and approximately 10 cm (4 in) high. It has a very strong piquant flavour.

Boulette de Cambrai

A French cows'-milk cheese with a soft smooth paste (45% fat content) flavoured with parsley, tarragon, chives, and salt. It is shaped into a small ball, 6–8 cm (2½–3½ in) in diameter. It is not matured and has a milder flavour than the Boulette d'Avesnes. Caffut cheeses, also from the Cambrai region, have a stronger flavour and are made from either spoiled or old cheese mixed with herbs. They are not entitled to the 'Boulette' *appellation*. A similar type of aromatic, often strong-smelling, cheese is made in Belgium, especially in Charleroi and Romedenne. It is used to make cheese and leek flans. The Pierre-qui-Vire Abbey in Burgundy manufactures a Boulette with a soft drained paste flavoured with herbs and used for spreading.

bouquet

The aroma produced by the evaporation of the volatile products evident in wine. It is one of the main elements – together with colour, fruitiness, and vinosity – that may enable the origin of a wine and, for the experienced, also its area and vintage to be identified.

According to the age of a wine, there are three main types of bouquet: the first may be reminiscent of a flower or fruit, the second may evoke a woodland atmosphere, the third an animal smell (such as musk). Aeration, which consists of uncorking a bottle in advance, perhaps decanting it into a carafe, and gently turning the wine in the glass while warming the glass in the cupped hand, allows the bouquet to develop.

bouquet garni

A selection of aromatic plants used to flavour a sauce or stock. They are usually tied together in a small bundle to prevent them from dispersing in the liquid and are removed before serving. A bouquet garni generally consists of two or three sprigs of parsley, a sprig of thyme, and one or two dried bay leaves, but its composition may vary according to local resources. Celery, leek, savory, sage, etc., can be added. In Provence, rosemary is always included. In old French cookery, bouquets garnis contained cloves as well as herbs, and the whole bundle was wrapped in a thin slice of bacon. A bouquet garni may also be enclosed in a small muslin (cheesecloth) bag.

bouquetière (à la)

A garnish composed of vegetables that are arranged in bouquets of different colours around large roast joints of meat, fried chicken, or tournedos steaks. The term is also used for a macédoine of vegetables bound with béchamel sauce.

| RECIPES

Barquettes à la bouquetière bind a macédoine of vegetables with béchamel sauce and use the mixture to fill barquette pastry cases. Place a small bouquet of asparagus tips on top of each barquette, sprinkle with melted butter, and heat in the oven.

Roast rib of beef à la bouquetière CÔTE DE BOEUF RÔTIE À LA BOU-QUETIÈRE Prepare a bouquetière garnish by cooking some small carrots, pod-shaped pieces of turnip, small green beans, artichoke hearts, and small cauliflower florets in salt water. Drain the vegetables and warm them in clarified butter. Cook some peas and use them to stuff the artichoke hearts. Fry some small new potatoes in butter. Season a thick (two-bone) slice of rib of beef with salt and pepper, brush with melted butter, and roast at 250 c (500 f, gas 9) for approximately 18 minutes per kg (2¼ lb) or until cooked as required. Drain the fat and place the meat on a serving dish surrounded by the vegetables arranged in bouquets. Deglaze the dish in which the meat was cooked with a mixture of Madeira and stock. Reduce and pour the meat juices over the rib of beef.

Bourbon

An American whiskey named after Bourbon county in Kentucky. Bourbon is usually distilled from maize (corn), and malted rye and barley are added in varying quantities. It is aged for at least two years in charred wooden barrels. 'Straight' Bourbon has not been blended; 'blended straight' Bourbon is a mixture of several Bourbons, and 'blended' Bourbon is a mixture of straight Bourbon and neutral alcohol. The higher the proportion of maize (corn) the more full-bodied the Bourbon will be. Drunk mostly in the south and west of the United States, Bourbon varies in flavour according to the maker and has its own distinctive and individual taste. It may be drunk straight, with water, or in a mix.

Bourbonnais

The French province of Bourbonnais includes the department of Allier and part of Puy-de-Dome, Cher, and Creuse. Its rustic cuisine is similar in many ways to that of its neighbours – Auvergne, Berry, and Nivernais.

The natives of Bourbonnais are reputed to be hearty eaters and consume a wide variety of vegetable dishes. These include thick soups made with potatoes, celeriac (celery root), cabbages, and sometimes chestnuts; these become stews with the addition of smoked sausages and bacon. Other substantial dishes are enjoyed – truffiats, pompes *aux grattons*, meat pies, and sanciaux, also popular in other provinces of central France.

High-quality meat and poultry are produced here and the region has its own specialities, such as oyonnade and fricassin. The towns, especially Vichy, are famous for such vegetable dishes as Vichy carrots, vichyssoise soup, and carp *à la Vichy* (stuffed with mushrooms). In the area around Saintpourçain, wine is used in many recipes, such as *paupiettes bourbonnais* (beef olives), matelotes, and dishes *en meurette*. Many desserts are prepared with the choice fruit from the countryside: prune tarts, millias with black cherries, flaugnardes, *tartibas* (pancakes) with grapes, picanchâgnes with pears, and other fruit pies.

bourdaloue

A dessert created by a pastrycook of the Belle Époque whose establishment was in the Rue Bourdaloue in Paris. It consists of halved William pears that are poached and then immersed in vanillaflavoured frangipane cream. They are then covered with crushed macaroons and glazed in the oven. A tart bearing the same name is filled with this dessert.

Bourdaloue is also the name of a similar dessert made with semolina or pudding rice and other poached fruits (apricots, peaches, pineapple, etc.). Bombe bourdaloue is flavoured with anisette.

RECIPE

Apricots Bourdaloue ABRICOTS BOURDALOUE Poach 16 apricot halves in a light vanilla-flavoured syrup. Drain and wipe. Two-thirds fill a flameproof porcelain or glass dish with cooked dessert semolina. Place the apricot halves on top. Cover with a thin layer of semolina and top with 2 crushed macaroons and 1 tablespoon granulated sugar. Place in a very hot oven for a short time to glaze the top. Serve with apricot sauce. Pudding (short-grain) rice may be used instead of semolina and peaches or bananas instead of apricots.

bourdelot

A dessert from Normandy consisting of an apple or a pear baked in pastry. The core is removed (the fruit may also be peeled) and the centre of the fruit is filled with caster (superfine) sugar moistened with 1 teaspoon Calvados and topped with a knob of butter. The fruit is then placed on a square of shortcrust pastry (basic pie dough) or puff pastry that is large enough to wrap around it. The corners of the pastry square are folded and pressed together and glazed with egg yolk. Bourdelots are baked in the oven and may be eaten hot or cold. See *douillon, talibur.*

Bourgeais

A vine-growing region of Bordeaux, situated on the right bank of the Gironde opposite the Médoc, in a picturesque area nicknamed the 'Suisse girondine'. Under the 'Côtes-de-Bourg', 'Bourg', or 'Bourgeais' *appellations*, the region produces dry or medium-dry fairly full-bodied white wines and also well-balanced red wines with a good colour. They can age well and are good table wines.

bourgeoise (à la)

The term used for various dishes, particularly those made with braised meat (chuck, silverside (bottom round), fricandeau, knuckle of veal, calf's liver, or leg of mutton), that are typical family meals without a set recipe. Such dishes always include a garnish of carrots, small onions, and pieces of bacon, which are usually arranged in bouquets around the meat.

RECIPE

Calf's liver à la bourgeoise FOIE DE VEAU À LA BOURGEOISE Mix together a small glass of brandy and 2 tablespoons (3 tablespoons) oil, then add some chopped parsley, salt, pepper, and (optional) a small amount of cayenne. Marinate some pieces of bacon fat in this mixture for at least 30 minutes and then use to lard a piece of calf's liver. Tie the liver and braise it in a mixture of red wine and stock. Sauté some mushrooms in butter and glaze some small onions. When the liver is cooked, drain it, place it on the serving dish with the mushrooms and onions, and keep warm. Remove the fat from the cooking liquid, strain, and reduce to make a thick smooth sauce. Pour it over the liver and serve.

Bourgueil

Red or rosé wines from the Indre-et-Loire region of Touraine, made from the Cabernet Franc grape (known in the locality as 'Breton'). Rabelais celebrated them and put his legendary Abbey de Thélème in the region. The soils are partly sand, partly clay, producing light and fragrant wines; those from the flat sections make good drinking when young, while those from the slopes tend to be more full-bodied and benefit from moderate to long-term maturation. Crisp and delicate Bourgueil wines somewhat resemble those of their neighbour, Chinon, although Bourgueil tends to smell of raspberries, Chinon of violets.

bourguignonne (à la)

The name for several preparations cooked in red wine (poached eggs, meat, fish, sautéed chicken, etc.), the most famous of which is *boeuf bourguignon* (see *beef*). They are usually garnished with small onions, button mushrooms, and pieces of fat bacon. The term also applies to preparations inspired by the regional cuisine of Burgundy.

RECIPES

Bourguignonne sauce for fish   SAUCE BOURGUIGNONNE POUR POISSONS Prepare a fish stock using 1 litre (1¾ pints, 4¼ cups) red wine, the bones and trimmings of the fish to be used in the finished dish, a medium-sized chopped onion, a small bouquet garni, a handful of mushroom peelings, salt, and pepper. Strain, reduce to half its volume, and add some kneaded butter according to taste.

Bourguignonne sauce for meat and poultry   SAUCE BOURGUIGNONNE POUR VIANDES ET VOLAILLES Cut 75 g (3 oz, 4½ slices) bacon into small strips, blanch, drain, and cook in butter until golden brown. Finely chop some onions and mushrooms, mix together, and cook 4–5 tablespoons of the mixture in butter together with 2 generous tablespoons mirepoix. Stir in the diced bacon and place the mixture in the pan in which the chicken or meat has been cooked. Stir well and cook until golden brown. Add 2 tablespoons (3 tablespoons) flour and stir well. Then add 5 dl (17 fl oz, 2 cups) red wine, 2 dl (7 fl oz, ¾ cup) stock, a bouquet garni, salt and pepper. Reduce by two-thirds. When ready to use, sieve the sauce and thicken with 50 g (2 oz, 4 tablespoons) kneaded butter.

Chicken   à   la   bourguignonne   POULARDE À LA BOURGUIGNONNE For a chicken weighing about 2 kg (4½ lb), use 100 g (4 oz, 6 slices) fresh bacon, cut into larding strips and then blanched. Peel 20 small onions, and clean and slice 20 mushrooms. Place the cleaned and trussed chicken in a casserole dish and fry gently in 30 g (1¼ oz, 2¼ tablespoons) butter. Remove the chicken and fry the bacon, onions, and mushrooms in the same casserole dish. Remove and add 2 tablespoons (3 tablespoons) mirepoix, stirring well. Deglaze the casserole dish with 4 dl (14 fl oz, 1¾ cups) red wine and an equal quantity of chicken stock, boil down by half, and add a bouquet garni. Put the chicken back into the casserole dish, bring to the boil, then cover and cook gently for 20 minutes. Then add the prepared garnish of bacon, mushrooms, and onions, together with salt and pepper. Bring to the boil, cover, and cook gently for a further 45 minutes to 1 hour. Drain the chicken and its garnish and remove the bouquet garni. Add 1 tablespoon kneaded butter to the juices in the casserole dish, beat well for 2 minutes, adjust the seasoning, and then pour the sauce over the chicken.

bourguignotte (à la)

In *L'Art de la cuisine française au XIXe siècle*, Carême gives a recipe for a sauce for fresh-water fish that he calls *à la bourguignotte*:
'Prepare a medium-sized eel, cut it into pieces, and place the pieces in a saucepan together with 2 chopped onions, 225 g (½ lb, 2 cups) chopped mushrooms, 2 cloves of garlic, a pinch of ground pepper, 2 shallots, a bouquet garni, a pinch of all-spice, 4 washed anchovies, and ½ bottle Volnay wine. Simmer, allowing the sauce to reduce a little, then press it through a sieve. Return the sauce to the pan and add 275 ml

(½ pint, generous cup) reduced espagnole sauce and 225 g (½ lb, 2 cups) fried mushrooms together with their cooking liquor. Boil the mixture rapidly to reduce and add 1 glass of Volnay. When the sauce is sufficiently reduced, place it in a bain-marie to keep it warm. Just before serving, add some crayfish butter, about 30 crayfish tails, and the same number of white button mushrooms.'

bouribout

The name given by Alban of L'Alliance restaurant in Paris to a ragout of duck with grapes. The name is the result of a practical joke. In the 1950s, some travelling gastronomic historians grew tired of hearing one of their colleagues boasting that he had tasted everything. When passing through the town of Sens, they noticed the nameplate of the Rue des Bouribouts, and one of them turned to the boaster and said 'And what about bouribout? Have you eaten that?' 'Of course', the other replied immediately. When Alban heard this story, he decided to bring this imaginary dish to life.

bourriche

A long wicker basket used for transporting shellfish, especially oysters. The baskets were once used to transport game and fish. The word is also used to describe the contents of the basket.

bourride

A Provençal fish soup. After cooking, the liquid is strained and bound with aïoli (garlic mayonnaise). The authentic bourride from Sète is made with monkfish, but elsewhere whiting, sea perch, grey mullet, and red mullet are sometimes mixed together.

RECIPE

Bourride Cut 1 kg (2¼ lb) monkfish into pieces and boil rapidly for 20 minutes in a mixture of 1 litre (1¾ pints, 4¼ cups) water and an equal amount of white wine, together with the white part of a leek, 2 chopped onions, 2 chopped carrots, 2 chopped cloves of garlic, a little dried orange peel, salt, and pepper. When the fish is cooked, place each piece on a slice of stale bread, and sprinkle with a little saffron. Sieve the stock, reduce by half, remove from the heat, and blend in some very thick aïoli. Pour the sauce over the fish.

bourriol

A fairly thick pancake made from a leavened batter of potato purée, wheat flour, and buckwheat flour mixed with milk. It is a speciality of Auvergne.

boutargue or poutargue

A speciality of Provence, from Martigues, made with dried pressed grey mullet roe. The roe is taken from the fish in summer and salted and stored until November. This method of storing seems to have been invented either by the Phoenicians or the Jews. Boutargue, which is known as 'white caviar', is shaped into slightly flattened sausages. It is eaten as an hors d'oeuvre on thin slices of toast, sprinkled with vinaigrette or lemon juice. Boutargue is also made with tuna fish eggs and a 'false' boutargue is made with smoked cod's roe.

boutifar

A type of large black pudding (blood sausage) from Catalonia and North Africa, which is made with blood and pieces of fat and meat, it is about 8–10 cm (3½–4 in) in diameter and is eaten cold.

Bouton-de-Culotte

A French goats'-milk cheese that is classified as a soft paste cheese (40–45% fat content), but is eaten when it is very dry and brittle. Shaped like a truncated cone, with a greyish-brown crust, it has a strong piquant flavour. The cheese is made in the Mâcon area and is also called Chèvroton de Mâcon, Mâconnet, or Rougeret. It is often served at Beaujolais wine-tastings.

bouzourate

A refreshing drink consumed in Arab countries, made from dried melon seeds. The dried seeds are grilled, ground, soaked in water, and squeezed through fine cloth bags. The liquid thus obtained is sweetened and served very cold. It may also be used to make sorbets and water ices.

bowl BOL

A hemispherical container without a handle. Bowls are manufactured in different sizes and of different materials depending on the purpose to which they are to be put. In France breakfast bowls may be made of earthenware, porcelain, or toughened glass. They are used instead of cups as they hold more and are usually used for family breakfasts and by children.

Broth or onion soup is sometimes served in china bowls.

The plastic toughened glass or metal mixer bowl is an accessory of the food processor. It must be wide enough and deep enough to allow the beaters to operate efficiently.

Small crystal, porcelain, or metal bowls are also used as individual finger bowls.

A punch bowl is a very large container made of glass, crystal, or silver plate with a large ladle and matching cups and may be used for serving punch, sangria, hot wine, etc. In England, its use is a traditional part of Christmas festivities.

In the Far East, bowls are a fundamental part of the table setting. The sizes vary depending on their proposed use. There are sauce bowls, salad bowls, and bowls for eating from: the latter are often placed on a saucer. Plates are used only as serving dishes for putting scraps on during the meal. Each guest also has his own bowl of rice. Tea and soup may also be served in bowls. There are also bowls with lids and bowls that stack together for transporting food.

brabançonne (à la)

The name of a garnish made with typical produce from Brabant: Brussels sprouts, chicory (endives), and hops. It is served with large roast joints of lamb or mutton (such as baron, rack, or leg) and also with tournedos (filet mignon) and sautéed noisettes. The vegetables are arranged in barquettes, coated with Mornay sauce and glazed. They are served either with small round croquette potatoes that have been lightly browned in butter or with creamed potatoes.

Braganza BRAGANCE

A garnish named after the fourth and last Portuguese dynasty, made of croquette potatoes and small braised tomatoes filled with béarnaise sauce. It is used as a garnish for tournedos (filet mignon) or noisettes of lamb.

Braganza is also a dessert made with Genoese sponge cake. The cake is cut into two rounds and soaked in a syrup flavoured with orange liqueur. The rounds are sandwiched together with a layer of custard cream to which has been added orange liqueur, chopped candied orange peel, and butter, and the whole cake is completely covered with the same cream and decorated with candied orange peel.

brain CERVELLE

A white offal, rich in phosphorus, proteins, and vitamins. The best are lamb's brain, weighing about 100 g (4 oz), and sheep's brain, which weighs about 150 g (5 oz). Both are barely tinged with pink. Calf's brain, weighing 250–300 g (9–11 oz), has a similar flavour but is deeper in colour. Ox brain, weighing 500–700 g (18–20 oz) is firmer and is veined with red. Pig's brain is rarely used. Calf or ox brains, although less choice are also less expensive; they are used as a filling for pies and timbales and also in meat loves and gratins.

RECIPES

Preparation of brains PRÉPARATION DES CERVELLES Wash the brains in cold running water, then remove the membranes and blood vessels that surround them. Soak them in cold water for 1 hour and wash them again. The brains may then be blanched in salted water, cooked fairly gently in a court-bouillon, or cut into thin slices and cooked directly in butter or oil.

Brains in noisette butter CERVELLE AU BEURRE NOISETTE Cook the brains in a court-bouillon – about 10 minutes for lamb's or sheep's brain and about 15 minutes for calf's brain. Cut calf's brain into even slices; leave smaller brains whole or divide them into two. Melt some butter in a shallow frying pan (skillet) until it turns golden; then add some lemon juice or vinegar and some capers. Reheat the sliced or whole brains in this butter and serve with the butter, sprinkled with chopped parsley.

Calf's-brain fritots CERVELLE DE VEAU EN FRITOTS Cook a calf's brain in court-bouillon, cool under a press, and cut into even-sized cubes. Marinate as in the recipe for fried calf's brain *à l'anglaise*. Dip the pieces into a light batter, then plunge them into burning-hot oil. Remove, drain, wipe, and sprinkle with a little salt. Arrange the fritters on a dish in the shape of a pyramid, garnish with fried parsley, and serve with a well-reduced and well-seasoned tomato sauce.

Calves' brains en matelote CERVEL-LES DE VEAU EN MATELOTE Prepare 24 small glazed onions and 24 mushroom caps and sauté them in butter. Also prepare 8 dl (1¼ pints, 1½ pints) court-bouillon with red wine, and in it cook 2 calves' brains. Remove, drain, and cut into thin slices. Arrange these escalopes with the onion and mushrooms on a serving dish. Put the lid on and keep hot in the oven. Meanwhile, reduce the cooking liquid by half, then bind in with 1 tablespoon kneaded butter. Coat the brain and its garnishes with this sauce. Garnish with small triangular croutons fried in butter or oil.

Fried calf's brain à l'anglaise CER-VELLE DE VEAU FRITE À L'ANGLAISE Trim and cook a calf's brain in court-bouillon for about 10 minutes, then cool it in cold water, wipe it, and put it under a press. Cut into thin slices and marinate these for 30 minutes in 1 tablespoon cooking oil, lemon juice, chopped parsley, salt, and pepper. Coat the slices with breadcrumbs, fry them, and arrange on a serving dish with some fried parsley. A well-seasoned tomato fondue may be served at the same time.

braising BRAISAGE

A method of cooking food in a closed vessel with very little liquid at a low temperature and for a long time. Braising is used mostly for the tougher cuts of meat (see *daube*), certain vegetables (cabbage, chicory (endive), artichokes, and lettuce) and large poultry.

Braising is also a method of cooking certain firm-fleshed fish (monkfish, carp, and salmon): the fish is poached in the oven, in a small amount of liquid containing herbs, and basted during cooking.

When cooking was carried out directly on the hearth, braising meant cooking slowly in hot embers. The cooking container had a lid with a rim on which embers could be placed, so that heat came from both above and below.

☐ **Cooking hints** Braising joints are often ready barded or pricked and marinated beforehand. First of all the joint is fried in fat and sometimes allowed to brown. It is then cooked with a mirepoix. The initial frying concentrates the juices in the joint and the subsequent addition of liquid then allows them to draw out. Because the cooking takes place in a closed vessel and the action of the heat is long and continuous, a concentrated sauce is obtained that is full of flavour.

When the food to be braised contains a lot of water (particularly vegetables), it cooks in its own juice and no extra liquid is added.

The cooking liquid is chosen according to the type of food that is to be braised: it may be a strained marinade, white wine (for fish), red wine (for red meat), or meat or fish stock. Sometimes a few chopped tomatoes alone provide sufficient moisture for braising. However, the liquid added at the beginning is not sufficient to maintain the level of humidity required for long cooking (some joints of meat require a cooking time of five or six hours). In this case, liquid must be added during cooking: it must be at the same temperature and should be added gradually and in small quantities, so that the joint does not 'drown' (in which case it would begin to boil).

When the cooking is finished, the juice is strained, reduced if necessary, and the fat is removed. It is somtimes mixed with a suitable addition, such as a thickening agent, another sauce, or a garnish.

To make the dish darker, bacon rinds may be added (see *endaubage*). A braised dish may also be enriched by adding pieces of calf's foot because the gelatine makes the sauce smoother.

Braising is especially suitable for red

meat with a bourgeoise, *à la mode*, or bourguignonne garnish. White meat can also be braised, for example, fairly firm poultry and various cuts of veal, such as loin, shoulder, silverside, and breast. The cooking is carried out in very little liquid and is very similar to sautéing.

braising pan   BRAISIÈRE

An oval or rectangular two-handled cooking pan with a well-fitting lid, often made of aluminium or copper and lined with tin. Braising pans are used in catering for the long slow cooking (braising) of meat and vegetables. One type of braising pan has a hollow lid that is filled with water during braising. In the home, cast iron casserole dishes are suitable for braising. In French regional cookery, earthenware dishes (e.g. daube pans) are used as they can be placed directly into the embers of a fire. Embers are also placed on top of the lid to ensure simultaneous cooking above and below.

The word *braisière*, in restaurant terminology, is also used for a brown stock made with veal and beef bones, carrots, onions, and garlic, simmered for a long time in water with added herbs. The fat is removed and the stock is strained. This stock is used in the preparation of the classic brown sauces.

bran   SON

The husk of cereal grains, separated from the grain in the flour-making process. It takes the form of small scales and has a high vitamin B and phosphorus content. Since the discovery of the useful dietary properties of bran, bread made with bran, once considered to be of inferior quality, is now marketed as an alternative to highly refined white bread. The *boule de son* has become a bakers' speciality again in France.

Bran is now added to many proprietary breakfast cereals and can be bought separately to sprinkle on at home. It can also be added to soups, stews, pastry, and cakes during preparation.

Brancas

A garnish for small joints of red meat, white meat, and poultry, consisting of Anna potatoes and chiffonade of lettuce with cream. It was probably dedicated to Louis, a member of the Brancas family (originally from Italy). A friend of Voltaire, he also gave his name to a brill dish and to a consommé.

RECIPE

Escalopes à la Brancas   Soften a mirepoix or julienne of vegetables in butter. Cover some seasoned veal escalopes (scallops) with the vegetables and coat each one with breadcrumbs. Sauté in clarified butter. Place on top of a layer of Annette potatoes. Garnish each escalope with a fondue of lettuce and sorrel mixed with cream. Serve with buttered Madeira sauce.

brandade

A purée of salt cod, olive oil, and milk, which is a speciality of Languedoc and Provence. It does not include garlic, but in Marseille and Toulon crushed garlic is added to the dish, and even the croutons used as a garnish are rubbed with garlic. Some chefs have enriched the preparation further by adding truffles or even crayfish ragout *à la Nantua*. However, most recipes include a potato purée, even though this is not the true brandade.

The word is derived from the Provençal verb *brandar*, meaning to stir. Adolphe Thiers was known to be passionately fond of brandade and his historian friend Mignet sent him pots of it from Nîmes, which he ate alone in his library. Alphonse Daudet founded the Dîners de la Brandade in a café in the Place de l'Odéon in Paris: the meal cost 6 francs and included 'a brandade and two speeches'.

RECIPES

Brandade sauce à la provençale SAUCE BRANDADE À LA PROVENÇALE (from a recipe by Carême) This sauce is not made with salt cod but it is served with poached salt cod. Place 2 tablespoons (3 tablespoons) thin allemande sauce, 3 egg yolks, a pinch of grated nutmeg, a pinch of fine pepper, a pinch of crushed garlic, the juice of a large lemon, and a pinch of salt into a saucepan. Stir continuously over a low heat until the sauce is smooth and velvety. Remove the pan from the heat and add (a tablespoon at a time) a glass and a half of good Aix oil. Just before serving, add the juice of a lemon and 1 tablespoon chopped blanched chervil.

Nîmes brandade   BRANDADE DE MORUE NIMOISE   Desalt 1 kg (2¼ lb) salt cod, changing the water several times. Cut the fish into pieces and poach it very gently in water for 8 minutes. Drain, then remove the bones and skin. Heat 2 dl (7 fl oz, ¾ cup) olive oil in a thick flat-bottomed saucepan until it begins to smoke. Add the cod then crush and work the mixture with a wooden spoon, while heating gently. When it forms a fine paste, remove the pan from the heat. Continue to work the brandade then, while stirring continuously, gradually add 4–5 dl (14–17 fl oz, 1¾ –2 cups) olive oil, alternating with 2.5 dl (8 fl oz, 1 cup) boiled milk or fresh cream. Season with salt and white pepper. The result should be a smooth white paste with the consistency of potato purée. Pile the brandade into a dish and garnish with triangles of crustless bread fried in oil. It can also be put in the oven to brown, just before serving.

other recipes   See *benédictine (à la)*, *croque-monsieur*.

brandwine   BRANDEVIN

The old name for brandy. It means literally 'burnt wine' (i.e. distilled wine) and is derived from the Dutch word *brandewijn*. In Scandinavian countries, the word *branvin* refers to spirits such as aquavit, schnapps, and vodka.

brandy

A spirit distilled from wine, the best known being Cognac and Armagnac. (An English word, originally *brandwine*, it is derived from the Dutch *brandewijn* – 'burnt' or distilled wine.) The word is also used to denote a spirit distilled from certain fruits, such as Kirsch, Framboise, or Mirabelle, and it is used more loosely to signify a liqueur made from fruits, berries, etc., such as cherry brandy or apricot brandy. It is also a general term applied to distillates from the 'debris' of wine, such as marc

and the Italian grappa, and also to the spirit distilled from cider, such as applejack, the American version of Calvados.

braou-bouffat

Soup prepared from cabbage, rice, and thick vermicelli. The latter is cooked in the same stock used for poaching black puddings (blood sausages). The soup is a speciality of Credagne in Roussillon and is prepared in a similar way to bougras from the Périgord region.

brassadeau

A small cake that is traditionally eaten on Palm Sunday. It is a speciality of Languedoc and also Vivarais (especially at Privas), where it is known as *brassado*. In Velay it is known as *cordillon*, and in Dauphiné it is called *tortillon*. It consists of a small ring of sweet pastry that is sometimes coloured with saffron, which indicates how old the recipe is. The cake is poached in boiling water and then dried before being baked in the ove.

brasserie

Originally a brewery, a brasserie today is a café or restaurant where beer, cider, and other drinks are served. Dishes typically sold at brasseries include garnished sauerkraut and plates of oysters, but standard hot and cold dishes are also served. The distinction of all brasseries is that they serve a limited menu at any time of day and often fairly late at night.

In countries where a lot of beer is consumed, there was at first little to distinguish the brasseries from inns. They had the same wooden benches and wooden tables, like the traditional brasseries found in Bavaria – in Munich, one of the oldest (opened in 1589) is still in operation. In Paris, however, the refugees who came from Alsace-Lorraine, after the war of 1870 started a new fashion for brasseries. They became elegant places, and were as ornately decorated as the great cafés of the capital.

From 1870 to 1940, brasseries were frequented by writers, artists, journalists, and politicians: customers could argue, drink, play chess, write, and eat – all at the same table. Among the establishments that have now disappeared are the Brasserie Pousset, once the rendezvous of journalists and artists (a tradition continued by Lipp at Saint-Germain-des-Prés), the Brasserie Steinbach, which was situated in the Latin Quarter (and is now the Balzar), and the brasserie in the Rue des Martyrs, frequented by Nadar, Baudelaire, Courbet, and Manet. Today, Bofinger at the Bastille and Flo in the Passage des Petites-Ecuries are restaurants that have retained the turn-of-the-century decor and atmosphere. Over the past few years, renewed interest in beer has encouraged several brasseries to specialize in French and foreign beers. Some 'Belgian bars' or 'academies of beer' offer up to 300 different brands, mostly served with cold meats, cheese, or even mussels.

brawn (head cheese)
FROMAGE DE TÊTE

A charcuterie product consisting of rendered-down meat from a pig's head (excluding the brain) and aspic from the reduced cooking liquor, cooked with flavourings and herbs, then poured into a mould. When set firm the brawn is cut into slices and eaten as a first course. In French, it is also known as *pâté de tête* and *fromage de cochon.*

Hure is a type of brawn made with boar's or pig's head. Brawn made with boar's head is usually cooked in the kitchen (see *wild boar*). *Hure à la parisienne* consists of the tongue and the skin set in aspic in a mould. In Alsace there are three variations: *hure rouge* is a kind of brawn made from the head and packed into a large red skin from the animal's gut; *hure blanche* combines the head, cured forehock, and skin; and *hure de Francfort* is a smaller version.

brayaude

A term used in French cookery to indicate an association with Auvergne. Brayaude omelette, for example, is made with Auvergne ham, potatoes, cream, and cheese. The name is also used for a soup, but the most famous dish is *gigot brayaude*, in which a leg of lamb is pierced with cloves of garlic and braised slowly in white wine with potatoes. The potatoes may be replaced by cabbage, red beans, lentils, or lentil purée.

RECIPE

Brayaude omelette OMELETTE BRAYAUDE Dice some raw potatoes and some raw Auvergne ham. Fry the diced ham in butter, remove from the pan and drain. Brown the diced potatoes in the same pan and when cooked, replace the diced ham in the frying pan, add some beaten eggs, and season. Cook the omelette on one side, turn it over, and cook on the other side. Sprinkle the top of the omelette with very small cubes of fresh cheese and cover with fresh cream.

Brazil nut
NOIX DU BRÉSIL

A large nut with a very hard brown shell, cultivated in Brazil and Paraguay. The white kernel, very nutritious and with a high fat content, can be eaten as a dessert nut or used in cooking in the same way as coconut.

bread PAIN

Food made from a flour-and-water dough with yeast which is fermented, kneaded, and baked in the oven. The action of the raising agent gives bread its characteristic texture.

☐ **History** The invention of leavened bread is attributed to the Egyptians who cooked flat cakes made of millet and barley on heated stones and might have discovered fermentation by chance, with a piece of dough which had become sour. At the time of the Exodus, the Hebrews did not take with them any leaven, hence the tradition of unleavened bread to commemorate the crossing of the Red Sea. The Greeks cooked loaves made of rye or oats, or sometimes wheat, on a grid or in a kind of oven; the Romans cooked their bread in household ovens, made of brick and earth, and often flavoured it with the seeds of poppy, fennel, or cumin or with parsley. From Italy, the use of bread spread throughout the Roman empire. The Gauls kneaded barley beer into the dough and obtained a well-raised bread of good quality.

It was in the Middle Ages that the bakery trade began to develop; from this time, bread became very varied and many different kinds were produced.

These included hall bread, for distinguished guests; hulled bread (made from bran), intended for servants; wholemeal bread, with a well-cooked crust, kept for making breadcrumbs; and trencher bread, used as plates for cutting up meat. Soft or queen's bread was enriched with milk and egg yolk; German wheat bread had a very light-coloured crumb; chapter bread was flat and very hard; Gonesse and Melun loaves were supplied for a long time to the best bakeries of Paris; and variegated bread was made of alternate layers of brown and white bread.

In the 17th century a new method of fermentation was developed, using milk, salt, and beer barm, to manufacture finer loaves made in long moulds: Gentilly, Segovia, bread *à l'esprit*, bread *à la maréchale*, and horned bread. For a long time, the quality of bread depended on the flour used and therefore on its colour: white bread for the rich, black bread for the poor. In 1840, Viennese bread was introduced into France by a man called Zang, secretary of the Austrian embassy in Paris. He created the first bakery using Viennese methods; fine wheat flour was kneaded with milk and water to produce long loaves or rolls that became one of the classic French breads.

□ **Breads of the world** The consumption of bread has become almost universal. Made from wheat, rice, maize (corn), or rye, bread is usually baked in the oven, but certain breads of North Africa are cooked in oil, in an earthenware vessel, and some Chinese breads are steamed. In Scandinavia there is a great variety of bread, which is often made from rye. Germany produces many types of rolls, including pretzels, which are salted and flavoured with cumin or poppy seeds. German black breads are made from a mixture of rye and corn.

In Mediterranean countries, loaves are often made from a compact white dough, sometimes kneaded with oil; the oval Algerian breads with pointed ends and the flat round Tunisian breads are examples. In the United States and Great Britain bread is usually sold in the form of tin or sandwich loaves, which have a dense white crumb and a very thin crust; they are also available pre-sliced or prepacked. But wholewheat breads are becoming much more popular. The yellow corn bread, made from cornmeal, is an American speciality. In Russia, on the other hand, one finds round rye loaves with a compact brown crumb, typical of eastern countries.

In France the baguette is the most popular bread, but a wide variety of wholemeal and white breads are available as well as many regional variations.

□ **Gastronomy and dietetics** The only food which, like wine, is present on the table from start to finish of the meal, bread constitutes the traditional accompaniment to all dishes. It is also the basic ingredient of sandwiches, canapés, toast, croutons, and breadcrumbs. In addition to this, it is used widely in the preparation of other dishes, notably soups (particularly onion soup *au gratin*, gazpacho, and garlic soup), panadas, stuffings and forcemeats, timbales, charlottes, and puddings.

A good bread must have a crisp crust, an attractive golden colour, and a soft crumb. Growing stale too quickly is a sign of bad quality, as are tastelessness and insipidity. A good-quality bread can be kept for up to a fortnight in a box, preferably of wood (never in a plastic bag). If it is cut, it should be stored with the cut side against wood (or a slab of marble); bread freezes well if it is hermetically packed.

Most bread should be served fresh but not hot. Rye bread, however, should be slightly stale, and large farmhouse loaves are best left until the day after they have been baked. Loaves should not be cut until just before serving. The slices should not be too thin, in order to retain all the flavour of the bread; baguettes and other long loaves should be cut in small sections. Bread is best served in a wicker or cane basket.

A daily intake of 300 g (11 oz) bread provides 125 g (4½ oz) carbohydrate, 25 g (1 oz) protein, about 2 g fat, and mineral salts (calcium, phosphorus, magnesium, potassium); it gives 750 Cal (a third of the normal daily intake), but the input varies according to the nature of the flour. Nutritionists agree that a good bread constitutes an indispensable basic food.

□ **Making bread commercially** Bread

making comprises three main operations: kneading, fermentation, and baking.

• *Kneading* consists of combining the water, yeast or leaven, and flour, with a little salt to improve the final taste, into a homogeneous mixture. In the past, kneading (carried out by a workman called a *gindre*) was traditionally done with the arm, which was tiring and not very hygienic. Today, mechanical kneading is the norm. Kneading lasts for about ten minutes. It is in the course of kneading that the yeast or leaven is incorporated into the dough.

• *Fermentation* occurs at a favourable temperature when a raising agent is mixed into the flour-and-water dough. In endogenous fermentation, the leaven is taken from the previous day's batch of dough and added to the new; in exogenous fermentation, the raising agent is industrial yeast. The sole purpose of fermentation is to make the bread lighter; it also gives the bread its characteristic texture, appearance, and smell. Slow fermentation with leaven gives bread a slight acidity, which is a proof of quality. The ferments act on sugars in the damp hot dough to produce alcohol and carbon dioxide, which forms gaseous bubbles that raise (prove) the dough. The first stage of fermentation takes place in the kneading trough. The dough is then weighed and shaped into loaves and again left to rise until it has doubled its volume and is ready to be baked.

• *Baking* may be done in an oven heated by fuel oil, gas, or electricity, but traditional cooking over a wood fire is still preferred by some. The loaves are put in the oven as quickly as possible, with the aid of a wooden shovel with a very long handle. When cooked and a good colour, they are taken out of the oven and placed in the cooling-off room, ventilated but without draughts, where they gently cool to room temperature. Cooling-off is the last operation of bread making: the bread loses its humidity before being put on the shop shelves.

In present-day industrial baking, all the operations have been mechanized to a certain extent: a volumetric weighing machine measures the lumps of dough; other appliances shape the dough, put the loaves in the oven, and scarify their surfaces; the controlled-fermentation chambers control the fermenting action of the yeasts and the exact timing of the fermentation. For cooking, there is a tendency to use rotating ovens.

So-called 'fine' bread making is concerned with the manufacture of special bread products, such as bread sticks, French toasts, etc. Another sector of industrial baking includes dietetic breads and long-lasting breads.

Despite the wide variety of industrially produced bread that is available, many prefer to bake their own bread at home. Loaves of excellent quality can be produced as a whole range of flours is now available, but white bread and wholemeal bread are the most popular for home baking.

RECIPES

Bacon bread PAIN AUX LARDONS Grill (broil) 300 g (11 oz, 16 slices) smoked bacon, then cut it up into very small pieces. Knead 500 g (18 oz, 4½ cups) wholewheat flour with 300 m (½ pint, 1¼ cups) water and 15 g (½ oz) fresh yeast (½ cake compressed yeast) until soft. Add the bacon and leave to rise for 2 hours at 20–22 c (68–72 F). Shape the dough into an oblong mass and place it in a 1-kg (2¼-lb) earthenware dish. Leave to rise at the same temperature for another 2 hours. Bake in the oven at 200–220 c (400–425 F, gas 6–7). Turn out and leave to stand for 2 hours. This bread is served in particular with green salads (lamb's lettuce, endive (chicory), etc.).

Milk rolls PAINS AU LAIT Place 500 g (18 oz, 4½ cups) sifted flour on the worktop (work surface) and make a well in the centre. Add a generous pinch of salt, 20 g (¾ oz, 1½ tablespoons) caster (super-fine) sugar, and 125 g (4½ oz, generous ½ cup) softened butter. Mix the ingredients, then moisten with 2.5 dl (8 fl oz, 1 cup) tepid boiled milk. Knead, then add 200 g (7 oz) white bread dough. Knead together into a ball, cover it with a cloth, and leave it to rise, sheltered from draughts, for 12 hours. Then divide the dough into about 20 balls of approximately 50 g (2 oz). Make a cross-shaped cut on the top, glaze them with egg, and bake in a hot oven for about 25 minutes.

This type of Viennese bread is served at breakfast or tea.

Viennese currant buns PAINS AUX RAISINS Mix 15 g (½ oz) fresh yeast (½ cake compressed yeast) with 3 tablespoons (¼ cup) milk and 3 tablespoons (¼ cup) flour. Sprinkle with 3 tablespoons (¼ cup) flour and leave to rise in a warm place for about 30 minutes.

Put 300 g (11 oz, generous 2½ cups) flour in an earthenware dish, add the yeast mixture, then add 30 g (1 oz, 2 tablespoons) caster (superfine) sugar, 3 eggs, and 1 teaspoon fine salt. Knead for 5 minutes, slapping the dough flat on the table to make it elastic, then sprinkle it with 3 tablespoons (¼ cup) milk and mix well. Soften 150 g (5 oz, generous ½ cup) butter with a palette knife (spatula), blend it with the dough, then add 100 g (4 oz, ¾ cup) currants, previously swollen in tepid water and then drained. Knead for a further few minutes and leave to stand for 1 hour in a warm place.

Roll the dough into sausage shapes, coil each roll into a spiral, and leave to rise on a baking sheet for 30 minutes, sheltered from draughts. Glaze the buns with egg, sprinkle with granulated sugar, and cook in the oven at 220 c (425 F, gas 7) for about 20 minutes. Serve lukewarm or cold.

White bread PAIN BLANC Blend 15 g (½ oz) fresh yeast (½ cake compressed yeast) in 400 ml (¾ pint, 2¼ cups) warm water until dissolved, or dissolve 1 teaspoon sugar in the warm water, then sprinkle on 2 teaspoons dried yeast. Leave in a warm place for 10 minutes until dissolved and frothy.

Mix 675 g (1½ lb, 6 cups) white flour and 2 teaspoons salt together and rub in 15 g (½ oz, 1 tablespoon) butter. Add the yeast liquid to the dry ingredients and mix to form a firm dough, adding extra flour if it is too sticky to handle. Turn the dough onto a lightly floured surface and knead until smooth and elastic and no longer sticky. Shape the dough into a ball, place inside a large oiled polythene bag, and leave to rise until it has doubled in size. Remove

from the polythene bag, then knock back (punch down) and knead until the dough is firm. Shape into loaves or rolls; cover and prove (rise).

Bake in a hot oven for approximately 40 minutes for a large loaf, 30–35 minutes for small loaves, or 15–20 minutes for rolls.

Wholewheat bread PAIN COMPLET Blend 25 g (1 oz) fresh yeast (1 cake compressed yeast) in 400 ml (¾ pint, 2¼ cups) warm water until dissolved, or dissolve 1 teaspoon sugar in the warm water and sprinkle on 3 teaspoons dried yeast. Leave in a warm place for 10 minutes or until dissolved and frothy.

Mix together 675 g (1½ lb, 6 cups) wholewheat flour and 2 teaspoons salt. Rub in 15 g (½ oz, 1 tablespoon) butter. Add the yeast liquid and mix to form a firm dough, adding extra flour if it is too sticky to handle. Knead thoroughly until smooth and elastic. Shape the dough into a ball and place inside a large oiled polythene bag and leave to rise until doubled in size. Knock back (punch down) and knead until the dough is firm. Shape into loaves or rolls. Cover and prove (rise).

Bake in a hot oven for approximately 40 minutes for a large loaf, 30–35 minutes for small loaves, or 15–20 minutes for rolls.

breadcrumbs
CHAPELURE, PANURE
Dried and powdered breadcrumbs (*chapelure* in French) are used in cooking for coating items of food or as a topping for certain dishes. In France, these breadcrumbs used to be prepared from *chapelant* bread, made by removing the crust and then drying it in a warm oven. White breadcrumbs are made from stale bread that is rubbed through a sieve and then dried without being toasted. They are used to coat food before frying and only keep for two or three days. Golden breadcrumbs are prepared from bread that has been slowly baked in the oven or by crushing crusts of bread or rusks in a mortar. They will keep indefinitely in an airtight glass jar and are mainly used for sprinkling over preparations that are cooked

au gratin. Most of the dried bread-crumbs on sale today are manufactured industrially. They are either made from a very firm dehydrated paste or from breadcrumbs subjected to a specific type of heat treatment. The length and intensity of the heat treatment makes it possible to obtain a whole range of colourings from white to brown.

Fresh breadcrumbs (*panure* in French) are made by removing the crusts from a sandwich loaf and rubbing it through a sieve or grating it on a grater. They may also be made in a blender or food processor. They are used alone or mixed either with cheese (preparations *à la milanaise*), or with chopped garlic and parsley (*persillade*) for breaded preparations and for sprinkling on the top of gratins (in which case a few drops of melted or clarified butter helps the dishes to turn golden). They are also included in some forcements. Dishes coated with fresh breadcrumbs must be cooked slowly so that the crumbs do not brown before the foods are properly cooked.

There are three main breadcrumb preparations.
• *à l'anglaise* The food is dipped in flour, then in egg beaten with a little oil, water, salt, and pepper, and finally coated with breadcrumbs. This is suitable for fish fillets, escalopes, cutlets, croquette potatoes, etc.
• *à la milanaise* The breadcrumbs are mixed with one-third of their volume of grated cheese (preferably Parmesan, a dry cheese which mixes better with the breadcrumbs).
• *with butter* Meat to be grilled is covered liberally with clarified butter (or lard when grilling pigs' ears, trotters, or tails) and then covered with fresh breadcrumbs.

breadfruit   ARBRE À PAIN

A tree 15–20 m (50–65 ft) high that grows in the Sunda Islands, Polynesia, the West Indies, and India. Its egg-shaped fruits have a thick greenish warty skin, weigh from 300 g to 3 kg (11 oz–6½ lb), and form a staple part of the diet in the tropics. The white flesh has a texture like bread and its flavour is similar to that of the globe artichoke. It is very rich in starch, and its nutritive value is close to that of brown bread.

The breadfruit is peeled, the seeds are removed, and it is cooked in salted water like the potato. In Tahiti, these fruits are the subject of legend and religious rites: they may be roasted, cooked in water, or simmered in a stew (as in the West Indies, where they are also made into acras – savoury fritters). The large seeds are also edible and have an artichoke flavour.

bread sauce

An English sauce made with bread-crumbs and seasoned milk. It traditionally accompanies roast game and poultry.

RECIPES

Bread sauce   Place 275 ml (½ pint, 1¼ cups) milk, a bay leaf, and a small onion stuck with 2–3 cloves in a saucepan and bring to the boil. Set aside to infuse for 15 minutes. Remove the onion and bay leaf, add 5–6 tablespoons fresh white breadcrumbs, then stir over a low heat until boiling. Gradually beat in 25 g (1 oz, 2 tablespoons) butter, away from heat, and season to taste with salt and pepper before serving hot. The sauce may be thinned down with a little cream if desired.

Fried bread sauce   This sauce is served with small roast birds, such as quails. Chicken consommé, small cubes of lean ham, and finely chopped shallots are boiled together very gently for 10 minutes. Just before serving, add a few drops of lemon juice, some bread-crumbs fried in butter, and some chopped parsley.

bread sticks

See *grissini*.

breakfast

The first meal of the day, which literally breaks the fast of the night.

Before the end of the 18th century, breakfast was taken very early in the morning and consisted of cold meat, beer, pâté, and cheese. In Victorian England, it consisted of a fairly prolonged family meal of ham, galantine, omelette, ox tongue, kedgeree, or even roast partridge, followed by fruit, honey, and biscuits, and served with tea. Today the

English breakfast survives largely in hotels or at weekends in homes. Fruit juice or cereal, such as porridge or corn-flakes, is followed by eggs and bacon, grilled (broiled) tomatoes and sausages, or sometimes kippers (grilled or poached). The meal is rounded off with toast and marmalade and served with tea or coffee. Some regional traditions persist, such as lava bread and oat broth with buttermilk in Wales, and grilled black pudding (blood sausage) in Lancashire.

This traditional breakfast is usually more than the average British household can cope with on a daily basis, especially if all the members of a family have to go out to work. Much more common now is cereal followed by tea or coffee with toast and marmalade or alternatively the so-called continental breakfast, consumed in France, Switzerland, and elsewhere (see *petit déjeuner*).

bream BRÈME

A freshwater fish found in pools and slow rivers. 30–60 cm (12–24 in) long, it has a greenish-brown back and its sides and belly are grey with shiny gold spots. Bream was often used in medieval recipes. Although its flesh is soft, somewhat tasteless, and full of bones, it is used for matelotes (fish stews) and braised dishes, in the same way as carp. Only the large river bream are used: before being cooked they are soaked in fresh water to eliminate the taste of silt.

RECIPE

Bream à la vendangeuse BRÈME À LA VENDANGEUSE Gut (clean) a 1-kg (2-lb) bream and season the inside with salt and pepper. Butter an ovenproof dish and sprinkle the bottom with chopped shallots; add 2 sprigs of thyme and a bay leaf cut into four and lay the bream on top. Moisten with white wine (approximately 2.5 dl, 8 fl oz, 1 cup). Place in the oven at 230 C (450 F, gas 8) and bake for approximately 20 minutes, basting the fish 3 or 4 times. Meanwhile peel some large grapes, removing the seeds, and chop some parsley. When the bream is cooked, drain and keep warm. Strain the cooking liquor into a saucepan, add 1 dl (6 tablespoons, scant ½ cup) cream, and reduce by a quarter.

Adjust seasoning. Add 1 teaspoon kneaded butter (beurre manié) and 1 teaspoon lemon juice (optional). Heat the grapes in the sauce then pour the sauce over the bream. Sprinkle with chopped parsley.

breast POITRINE

A joint of meat consisting of the muscle of the chest. In beef this cut is known as brisket and is boiled, pot-roasted, salted, or used for minced (ground) meat.

Breast of mutton or lamb is slow-roasted whole, boned and stuffed. It can also be marinated or cooked in stock and then cut into pieces for frying, grilling (broiling), or baking in a barbecue sauce, or for stews or soups.

Breast of veal – a fairly lean cut – may be sautéed (for veal Marengo or blanquette) or braised (boned and stuffed).

Fresh breast of pork (known as belly) is used in ragouts or can be grilled or baked. When soaked in brine, it is known as salt or pickled pork (see *salt pork*). When cured (salted and sometimes smoked too) belly pork becomes streaky bacon (rashers (slices) and lardons).

Breast of chicken comprises the two pieces of white meat attached to the breastbone. When served with truffles, chaud-froid, or with a sauce, it is known as the suprême. Breast of chicken may be diced or chopped and used in the preparation of mixed salads or as a garnish for consommé.

RECIPES

grilled (broiled) and devilled breast of mutton POITRINE DE MOUTON GRILLÉE À LA DIABLE (from Carême's recipe) Take 2 fine fleshy breasts of mutton. With a single stroke of the knife, remove the part of the bone above the strip of gristle. Tie the breasts and put them into an oval casserole together with 2 carrots, 2 onions, and a bouquet garni. Completely cover with a good clear stock. Bring to the boil, skim, and cook for 2½ hours. Drain and cool under a press. When cold, trim the breasts and gently cut off the skin without removing the fat. Trim away the gristle. The bones at the lower edge of the breasts may be sawn off if they are too long. Coat the breasts in melted butter and grill under a gentle heat until they are well browned. Cut them into pieces along the bones, and arrange on a dish; serve with devilled sauce.

Alternatively, the cooled breasts may be cut into 5–6 pieces, dipped in egg and breadcrumbs, grilled, and served with a poivrade sauce.

Breast of lamb fritots POITRINE D'AGENEAU EN FRITOTS Braise a breast of lamb, then bone it and cool under a press. Cut the meat into long strips and marinate them in a mixture of oil, lemon juice, chopped garlic and parsley, salt, and pepper. Drain the meat, dip the pieces in batter, and deep-fry. Drain on absorbent kitchen paper and serve piping hot, garnished with fried parsley. Serve with a green salad and a tomato fondue seasoned with garlic.

Stuffed breasts of lamb POITRINE D'AGNEAU FARCIE Open 2 breasts of lamb (or mutton) and remove all the rib bones without piercing the meat. Rub the flesh with garlic, and season both the inside and outside with salt and pepper. Prepare a forcemeat by mixing 300 g (11 oz, 3 cups) stale breadcrumbs (soaked in milk and well strained) with 2 beaten eggs, 150 g (5 oz, generous ½ cup) finely diced ham, 150 g (5 oz, 1¼ cups) diced mushrooms, chopped parsley and garlic, and salt and pepper. Spread the stuffing on one piece of meat and cover with the second one, with the skin sides outwards. Sew up all round the edge.

Line a lightly buttered casserole with pork rind from which the fat has been removed, then add 2 sliced onions and 2 sliced carrots. Place the meat in the casserole, add a bouquet garni, cover, and cook gently on the hob for about 20 minutes. Add 2 dl (7 fl oz, ¾ cup) dry white wine and boil down to reduce. Then add 1 dl (6 tablespoons, scant ½ cup) tomato fondue seasoned with garlic and diluted with 2 dl (7 fl oz, ¾ cup) stock. Cover and cook in the oven at 220 C (425 F, gas 7) for approximately 45 minutes.

Meanwhile, prepare some small cabbage paupiettes and some sliced potatoes cooked in goose fat. When the meat is cooked, remove the thread, slice, and arrange on the serving dish. Surround with the cabbage paupiettes and the potatoes. Keep warm. Skim the fat from the cooking liquid, reduce if necessary to blend and thicken it, and pour over the meat. Serve piping hot.

brèdes

The name given in some of the old French colonies of the West Indies to a dish made from the leaves of various plants cooked with bacon and spices and served with rice *à la créole*. The most commonly used leaves are those of white or green cabbage, watercress, and lettuce, although spinach, manioc leaves, and pumpkin shoots are used as well. A variation of this dish, *bred*, is a mixture of pounded cassava leaves boiled with fish and coconut.

RECIPE

Watercress brèdes BRÈDES DE CRESSON Wash a bunch of watercress. Place some oil or lard in a cast-iron casserole dish and cook 150 g (5 oz, generous ½ cup) diced bacon and a chopped onion in the fat until brown. Crush 2 cloves of garlic with some salt and a peeled deseeded crushed tomato. Add them to the casserole. When the mixture is quite hot, add a large glass and a half of water. Slightly reduce the liquid and add the watercress. Cook for approximately 30 minutes. Serve with a separate dish of rice *à la créole*.

Use the same recipe to make lettuce brèdes, but soak the leaves in cold water beforehand. Blanch spinach leaves before making brèdes.

Bréhan

A garnish for large joints of meat, consisting of artichoke hearts filled with broad bean purée, cauliflower florets, hollandaise sauce, and potatoes with parsley.

bréjaude

A cabbage soup from the region of Limousin prepared with a joint of fresh bacon. The bacon is slit and then boiled for about an hour, so that the rind can be removed and the bacon can then be crushed (*bréjer* in Limousin dialect) with coarse salt. The rind is carefully scraped and then placed with the crushed bacon in a soup pan. Cabbage, leeks, beetroot, and potatoes are added and cooking is continued for a further hour. The bréjaude stock is served in soup dishes lined with slices of stale bread. It is topped with the vegetables and the scraped rind, which is called the *bréjou* and is traditionally reserved for the master's dish, which is served first.

brésolles

A meat dish prepared from an old French recipe, consisting of alternating layers of meat and forcemeat. The force-meat is made with lean ham, onions, chives, mushrooms, and a little garlic, seasoned with salt, pepper, and nutmeg and moistened with a dash of olive oil. A layer of forcemeat on the bottom of a buttered earthenware casserole dish is covered with thin slices of veal, beef, or mutton; alternating layers of forcemeat and meat are added until the dish is full. The dish is covered and baked in the oven, then turned out and served with Madeira sauce and braised chestnuts.

Controversy surrounds the origin of this recipe, which is traditionally attri-buted to the head cook of the Marquis de Brésolles: in 1742 Menon gave a variation under the name of *brézolles* (strips of veal with shallots), and Austin de Croze describes brésolles as a dish from Agen (round slices of veal with bordelaise sauce). The word could be derived from the verb *braiser* (to braise) or from the Italian *braciola* (a slice of meat).

bressane (à la)

A term applied to several dishes in which Bresse poultry is an important ingredient, including chicken stuffed with foie gras and mushrooms (some-times with slices of truffle slipped under the skin) and then braised or fried; flan or cake prepared with light-coloured Bresse chicken livers; and puff pastries and mixed salads.

| RECIPE

Bressane salad SALADE BRESSANE
Season some whole lettuce leaves with vinaigrette and use to line the bottom and sides of a salad bowl. Hard-boil (hardcook) some eggs, shell them, and cut into quarters. Cook and drain some asparagus tips (or drain a tin of aspar-agus). Finely chop the white meat of a chicken cooked in stock and season with vinaigrette. Cut some red and green peppers into very thin strips. Place all these ingredients on the lettuce leaves. Prepare a mayonnaise and col-our with a little sieved and well-reduced tomato sauce. Pipe a garnish of the tomato mayonnaise on the salad and sprinkle with chopped parsley. Serve the rest of the mayonnaise in a sauceboat (in the traditional recipe the top of the salad is garnished with slices of truffle).

Breese and Dombes

Covering an area between the valleys of the Saône and the Doubs and bounded to the south by the ancient principality of Dombes, Bresse has always been poultry country. Thanks to careful breeding and strict selection, free-range corn-fed Bresse chickens and capons reach perfection; they may be cooked with cream or truffles (chicken demi-deuil), seasoned with crayfish butter, or simply stewed (Bressane marmite). Eggs, cream, and the famous truffles of Valromey go perfectly with Bresse poul-try and contribute to the development of a sophisticated local cuisine, which has influenced that of the nearby city of Lyon.

Dombes, by contrast, is a clayey region covered in ponds, heathlands, and woods, which provide fish and game. These are skilfully prepared: pike in quenelles or with Nantua sauce, crayfish in puff pastry with cream, matelote with Beaujolais, and jugged hare. As in the entire Lyon region, car-doon is the vegetable speciality of Bresse: cooked in its juice, in cream, and with marrow (summer squash), it is part of the traditional end-of-year dishes. Sweet corn (corn), which has given the inhabitants of this region the nickname of 'yellow bellies', is still used for mak-ing rustic gaudes. Bressan cheese, made from goats' milk, competes with Bleu de Bresse, a blue cows'-milk cheese. Those with a sweet tooth will appreciate the chocolates from Bourg-en-Bresse and *corniottes* (cream cheese pas-tries or loaves) from Châtillon-sur-Chalaronne.

brestois

A cake with a firm consistency and which keeps well, once a speciality of the town of Brest. It is made from Genoese sponge to which are added blanched ground almonds, lemon essence, and orange liqueur. The mixture may be poured into small brioche moulds and baked gently until the cakes are golden brown. They are turned out of the moulds and allowed to cool on a cooling tray; wrapped in aluminium foil, they will then keep for several days. The mixture can also be cooked in a round cake mould. The cake is then split into two halves, filled with apricot jam, covered with apricot glaze, and garnished all over with sliced toasted or raw almonds.

breton

A table decoration, created in Paris around 1850 by the pastrycook Dubusc, made of almond biscuits of various sizes, glazed with fondant icing (frosting) of different colours, decorated, and arranged in a pyramid. It was mostly used to decorate large sideboards and side tables.

Breton is also the name of a large round fairly thick cake, rich in slightly salted butter and egg yolks. The surface is glazed with egg yolk and crisscrossed. The same mixture can also be used to make individual round or boat-shaped cakes.

bretonne (à la)

A dish having a garnish of whole or puréed haricot (navy) beans (of which Brittany is a famous producer), which go particularly well with mutton and lamb (leg or shoulder). However, Breton sauce, used to coat eggs (soft-boiled, poached, or fried) and fillets of fish *à la bretonne*, does not include haricot beans.

RECIPE

Breton sauce SAUCE BRETONNE (modern recipe) Cut the white part of a leek, a quarter of a celery heart, and an onion into thin strips. Soften gently in a covered pan with 1 tablespoon butter and a pinch of salt for approximately 15 minutes. Then add 2 tablespoons (3 tablespoons) thinly sliced mushrooms and 1 glass dry white wine. Reduce until dry. Add 1.5 dl (¼ pint, ⅔ cup) thin velouté sauce and boil vigorously for 1 minute. Adjust the seasoning and just before serving stir in 1 generous tablespoon double (heavy) cream and 50 g (2 oz, 4 tablespoons) fresh butter. If the sauce is to be served with braised fish, cook the sliced vegetables with the fish, adding 1 glass fish stock or white wine and finishing with cream and butter.

Brick

A cows'-milk cheese (45% fat content) which originated in the United States (the majority of American cheeses are imitations of European products). It has an elastic texture, full of holes, and its flavour is reminiscent of Cheddar but milder. Sold in blocks 25 cm (10 in) by 12.5 cm (5 in) by 7 cm (3 in), it is mostly used for sandwiches, canapés, cheeseburgers, etc.

Brie

A cows'-milk cheese (45% fat content), originating in the Île-de-France, which has a soft texture and a crust that is springy to the touch, covered in white down, and tinted with red. It is made in the shape of a disc of variable diameter, often placed on a straw mat; since it is drained on an inclined surface, the finished cheese is sometimes of uneven thickness. The thinnest part is the best matured. The body of the cheese is light yellow, flaxen, or golden in colour, with a delicate flavour and a bouquet of varying strength depending on whether the Brie is farmhouse (now rare) or dairy. Brie is retailed in portions like pieces of pie. It is served towards the end of a meal, but it is also suitable for vols-au-vent, croquettes, and canapés.

Brie appears to have been in existence in the tme of Charlemagne, who is said to have eaten it at the priory of Rueil-en-Brie. Philip Augustus offered it to the ladies of his court, and Charles of Orleans sang a madrigal about it. The poet Saint-Amant compares it to gold: 'Fromage, que tu vaux d'écus!' ('Cheese, you are worth your weight in gold!')

Condé the Great had it served to celebrate the victory of Rocroi, and bouchées *à la reine*, inspired by Marie Leszcynska, were originally made with Brie. In 1793, it was said that Brie, 'loved by rich and poor, preached equality before it was suspected to be possible'. Talleyrand, an informed diplomat and gastronome, had it proclaimed king of cheese during a dinner organized during the Congress of Vienna. He thus had his revenge on Metternich, who had had Sachertorte recognized as the king of cakes. Of the 52 different cheeses offered to the guests, it was a Brie from the farm of Estourville at Villeroy which was voted the best.

Brie was also once used to make a pie pastry (and brioches, according to Alexandre Dumas, who thus explained the etymology of the brioche, which was based on Brie). Eugène Sue quotes Brie in *The Seven Deadly Sins*.

Brie enjoys the same prestige today, even though it is usually dairy-manufactured. There are four types: Meaux and Melun (protected by *appellation contrôlée*), Montereau, and Coulommiers.

• *Brie de Meaux*: the most famous and the most widespread, 26 or 35 cm (10 or 14 in) in diameter and 2.5 or 3 cm (1 or 1¼ in) thick, it is matured for one month. The best come from the valleys of Grand Morin and Petit Morin; good from May to October, it goes well with Burgundy.

• *Brie de Melun*: moulded by hand with a ladle, like Meaux Brie; 27–28 cm (11 in) in diameter and 3 cm (1¼ in) thick, it is sold either matured for two months, or fresh and very white, with a very pronounced taste and smell of milk, or fresh and dusted with powdered wood charcoal (it is then described as blue). Matured, it is good from June to October and goes well with Bordeaux.

• *Brie de Montereau*: its fat content can be as little as 40%; 18 cm (7 in) in diameter and 2.5 cm (1 in) thick, the best is from Ville-Saint-Jacques. It is good from May to October.

• *Brie de Coulommiers*: 25 cm (10 in) in diameter and 3 cm (1¼ in) thick, matured for one month. The best is from Coulommiers itself; good from October to April, it goes well with Burgundy or Côte-du-Rhône.

brik

'A large triangle of very flaky pastry containing a soft-boiled egg surrounded by succulent minced (ground) meat; one can imagine nothing better.' This is how André Gide described this Tunisian speciality in his *Journal* in 1943. It is a very fine pancake garnished with lean mutton minced with onions and mint; a small hole is made in the meat and an egg is broken into the hole; the pastry is then folded and the brik fried in oil (it may also be prepared using only an egg). It is usually served with slices of lemon.

The success of this little appetizer lies entirely in the fineness of the pastry, which is called *malsouqa* (the equivalent of the Moroccan *pastilla*). A dough of elastic consistency is obtained by boiling semolina (semolina flour) in water; it is then cooked in olive oil in a frying pan (skillet) using a very delicate technique. The palm of the hand is dipped in cold water, then in the dough, which is spread out in the frying pan with circular movements; almost immediately, the malsouqa is lifted with a knife, (care must be taken not to make any holes in it), and laid on a dry cloth. It takes considerable dexterity and patience to make briks by hand, but commercially manufactured sheets of brik pastry can be obtained.

RECIPE

Brik with egg BRIK À L'OEUF Chop some parsley and coriander leaves. Spread out a sheet of brik pastry on the working surface and break an egg onto it; season with salt and pepper and add a pinch of each herb. Fold the pastry in two diagonally, then fold over both edges and finally the tip so that the egg is well sealed. Place straight into boiling oil. Fry till golden, basting with spoonfuls of oil so that it puffs up. Place the brik on kitchen paper and serve piping hot.

brill BARBUE

A marine flatfish similar to the turbot, with the same fine white nutritious flesh. Brill is less expensive than turbot, in spite of the considerable waste involved in its preparation. However, it is becoming scarcer in the sandy bed of the Atlantic from which it is fished. It is 30–75 cm

(12–30 in) long and weighs 1–2 kg (2¼–4½ lb), sometimes 3 kg (6½ lb). The top of the body is smooth, grey or beige in colour, with small pearly markings. The underside is creamy white.

Brill can be prepared in many ways, particularly with red or white wine, champagne, or cider. It can also be grilled (broiled) whole or baked. It can be served cold with various sauces. When poached, it can be garnished with prawns (shrimp), mussels, oysters, or crayfish. The famous chef Dugléré gave his name to a recipe for brill which he created at the Café Anglais in Paris.

RECIPES

Preparation of brill PRÉPARATION DE LA BARBUE Clean the fish by making a transverse incision underneath the head, on the dark side. Remove the scales. Trim all round the fish, slightly shortening the tail, and wash. If the brill is to be cooked whole, braised, or poached, make a longitudinal incision along the centre of the dark side. Slightly loosen the fillets and break the backbone in two or three places. If prepared in this way, the brill does not lose its shape during cooking.

In order to fillet the fish, lay the cleaned, scaled, and washed brill on the table, dark side underneath. Make an incision along the centre from top to tail, then slide the knife blade underneath the flesh and, keeping it flat against the bone, gently ease away the fillets and lift them, detaching them at the head (by cutting round the head) and the tail. Turn the fish over and repeat for the other side. Lay the fillets on the table, skin side down. Holding the fillet by the tail end, slide the blade of a filleting knife between the skin and the flesh with one quick movement.

Braised brill BARBUE BRAISÉE Season the brill and put it in a shallow pan on a foundation of sliced carrots and onions which have been lightly fried in butter. Add concentrated fish stock, thyme, parsley, and a bay leaf. Bring to the boil, and cook in a slow oven, basting frequently.

Drain the brill and remove the backbone. This is most easily done by placing the fish, dark side up, on a well-buttered long plate or dish, removing the fillets with a very sharp knife, taking out the bone, and replacing the fillets.

Garnish as indicated in the recipe you are using, and cover with a sauce to which has been added the braising liquor, boiled down and strained. Braised brill moistened with red wine fish stock reduced to the consistency of a fumet can be served with the following garnishes: bourguignonne, Chambertin, or mâconnaise. Brill braised in white wine can be served with one of the garnishes used for fish cooked in white wine, especially those recommended for sole.

Brill in Chambertin BARBUE AU CHAMBERTIN Prepare the brill whole. Surround with 24 small cleaned mushrooms and place on the rack in a fish kettle or large casserole; add equal quantities of fish stock and Chambertin. The liquid should only just touch the fish. Cook as for braised brill. Arrange the cooked brill on a serving dish with the white skin uppermost, surrounded by the mushrooms. Keep warm in the oven with the door open. Reduce the cooking liquor to half its volume. Whisk in a generous tablespoon of softened butter to bind then bring to the boil. Add a further 50 g (2 oz, 4 tablespoons) butter. Stir and strain. Remove the white skin from the brill and coat with sauce.

When prepared *à la bourguignonne*, the brill is garnished with small glazed onions.

Brill in champagne BARBUE AU CHAMPAGNE Prepare in the same way as brill in Chambertin but use dry champagne instead of Chambertin. This dish is traditionally garnished with small pieces of fillet of sole.

Brill stuffed with salmon BARBUE SAUMONÉE Clean a brill weighing about 2 kg (4½ lb) and slit it lengthwise down the middle on the dark side. Remove the central bone through this opening, taking care not to tear the white skin. Season the brill and stuff it with a cream forcemeat made of salmon and truffles. Lay the fish in a buttered ovenproof dish, season, moisten with 4 dl (¾ pint, scant 2 cups) white wine fish fumet, and poach gently in the oven with the lid on the dish. When the brill is cooked, drain, dry in a cloth, and arrange on a dish. Boil down the juices, add to normande sauce, and pour over the fish. The following garnishes are suitable: amiral, cancalaise, cardinal, champenoise, diplomate, Nantua, normande, Polignac, Victoria.

Brillat-Savarin

A cows'-milk cheese from Normandy. It has a soft triple-cream paste, a white downy crust, a mild flavour, and smells of cream. Brillat-Savarin is produced in discs measuring 13.5 cm (5½ in) in diameter and 3.5 cm (1½ in) thick. It is a more refined version of another cheese from Bray, called Excelsior.

Brillat-Savarin
(Jean-Anthelme)

French magistrate and gastronome (born Belley, 1755; died Saint-Denis, 1826). The eldest of eight children, Jean-Anthelme Brillat spent all his youth in Bugey, where he became interested in cooking: his mother, whose Christian name was Aurore, was an accomplished cordon bleu cook (see *oreiller de la Belle Aurore*). An aunt, called Savarin, left him her fortune on condition that he took her name.

After studying law at Dijon, followed by elementary chemistry and medicine, Brillat-Savarin joined the bar at Belley. In 1789 the young solicitor, elected deputy to the National Assembly, came to the notice of the Forum, in particular because of a speech against the abolition of the death penalty. Returning to his own region, he was elected president of the civil court at Ain, then mayor and commander of the National Guard. The fall of the Girondins forced him into exile because the Revolutionary tribunal accused him of moderatism and issued a summons against him. He himself said that the day before his departure for Switzerland, he had a memorable dinner at an inn in the Jura, where he enjoyed a 'fricasse of chicken liberally garnished with truffles', served with a 'sweet and generous' white wine.
□ **Exile and return** Brillat-Savarin went to Switzerland, then Holland, where he embarked for the United States. He stayed there for three years,

living on the proceeds of French lessons and as a violinist with the orchestra of the John Street Theater in New York. There he discovered roast turkey and Welsh rarebit, taught the art of scrambling eggs to a French chef in Boston (who subsequently sent him, by way of thanks, venison haunches from Canada), and enjoyed pot-roast goose, corned beef, and punch. In 1797 he obtained permission to return to France, but he had lost all his possessions, in particular a vineyard. After a few temporary jobs, he was appointed counsellor to the Supreme Court of Appeal and kept this post until his death.

He remained a bachelor and spent his leisure time drafting various treatises on economics and history and an essay on the duel. He was interested in archaeology, astronomy, chemistry, and, of course, gastronomy, appreciating good restaurants, especially Grand Véfour, Véry, Beauvilliers, and Tortoni. He entertained frequently at home in the Rue de Richelieu in Paris and cooked some specialities himself, including tuna omelette, stuffed pheasant garnished with oranges, and fillet of beef with truffles. Having survived all regimes, from the Empire to the Restoration, he died after catching cold at a mass celebrated in memory of Louis XVI in the basilica of Saint-Denis. On 8 December 1825, two months before his death, the book which was to make him famous had appeared in the bookshops: *Physiologie du goût ou Méditations de gastronomie transcendante, ouvrage théorique, historique et à l'ordre du jour, dédié aux gastronomes parisiens par un professeur, membre de plusieurs sociétés littéraires et savantes.*
□ **The professor of gastronomy** The work was immediately successful and aroused the enthusiasm of Balzac but the envy of others, such as Carême and the Marquis de Cussy, and even the contempt of Baudelaire. Grimod de La Reynière had led the way in gastronomic literature, but it was Brillat-Savarin's ambition to make the culinary art a true science, calling on chemistry, physics, medicine, and anatomy, which made the text somewhat pedantic. His didactic spirit led him to treat his subject as an exact science, tracing cause from

effect. But Brillat-Savarin was also a storyteller with numerous anecdotes, a defender of greed, and he had an elegant humorous style. His *Physiologie* remains a pleasant read, instructive in spite of certain omissions (such as the absence of a chapter on wine).

● **Storyteller and epicure** In spite of his sometimes excessive 'theorems' and some doubtful aphorisms, Brillat-Savarin's work has been constantly reissued. It came at the right time for the education of a well-informed and prosperous bourgeoisie, who respected the past and admired progress and who wanted to live well. As the author himself said, 'Greed is a passionate, reasoned, and habitual preference for those objects which flatter taste.'

The best pages of the *Physiologie* contain Brillat-Savarin's observations on certain foods and preparations: the pot-au-feu and broth, poultry and game (with his personal memories of hunting in the New World), truffles, sugar, coffee, and chocolate. His 'Théorie de la friture' combines anecdote with culinary accuracy. His 'Histoire philosophique de la cuisine' is both erudite and humorous and covers the period from the discovery of fire to the end of the age of Louis XVI; it ends with a description of the restaurants of Paris in the years 1810–1820. In his 'Variétés' there are still more tasty morsels to be found, such as the priest's omelette which was 'round, large-bellied, and cooked to a turn' and for which he gives the recipe. He expresses his indignation at the finger-bowl practice, finding it 'useless, indecent, and disgusting'; he imparts the secret of an improvised way of steaming turbot 'on a bed of pungent herbs'; he describes the Chevalier of Albignac demonstrating French salad before a British audience; and, after giving the recipe for Swiss fondue, he ends with a selection of gastronomic poems. As a postscript, the professor gives the reader the addresses of his favourite suppliers (the grocery shop of Madame Chevet at the Palais-Royal, the pastrycook Achard and his neighbour the baker). See *gastronomic tests, irror-ateur, magistère, osmazôme, savarin, Tendret.*

☐ **A ubiquitous surname** The name of the author of the *Physiologie du goût* has been given to a variety of preparations and to a garnish made of a salpicon of foie gras and truffles. This may be placed in small tarts or in shells of duchess potatoes to be served with game or noisettes of lamb, or it may be used as a filling for an omelette. Another Brillat-Savarin garnish is based on asparagus tips served with soft-boiled (soft-cooked) eggs.

RECIPES

Croûtes Brillat-Savarin Bake some small savoury pastry cases (pie shells) blind. Fill with a salpicon of calves' of lambs' sweetbreads and sautéed mushrooms and (optional) some cocks' combs and kidneys, all bound with a reduced demi-glace or Madeira sauce.

Eggs en cocotte Brillat-Savarin OEUFS EN COCOTTE BRILLAT-SAVARIN Butter some porcelain or fire-proof glass ramekin dishes and fill with noodles sautéed in butter. Break an egg into each ramekin dish and bake in a bain-marie. Heat some very short asparagus tips in butter and use as a garnish when the eggs are cooked. Add a ring of well-reduced Madeira sauce.

Flan Brillat-Savarin Make a flan case of fine savoury pastry and bake blind. When it comes out of the oven, fill with very creamy scrambled eggs with truffles. Clean some truffles, slice, heat in clarified butter, season with salt and pepper, and arrange on the eggs. Sprinkle with grated Parmesan cheese and melted butter. Brown well.

Timbale Brillat-Savarin Bake some brioche dough in a charlotte mould and scoop out the middle, leaving a thickness of 1 cm (½ in) lining the bottom and sides. Prepare a confectioner's custard (pastry cream) containing crushed macaroons, and cook some pear quarters in vanilla-flavoured syrup. Heat some apricot purée mixed with Kirsch and brush it round the inside of the timbale; heat in the oven. Fill the timbale with alternate layers of confectioner's custard and pears, finishing with a layer of pears. Decorate with crystallized (candied) fruit and warm in the oven. This timbale may be served with apricot sauce.

brilloli

A traditional dish of Corsican shepherds, made of a gruel of chestnut flour and goats' milk, which gives it a shiny surface (*brillare* is a Corsican word meaning 'to shine'). It can also be coated with cream.

Brimont

A name given in classic French cookery to certain decorative dishes, probably originally dedicated by a chef to his master.

> RECIPE

Brimont mixed salad SALADE PANACHÉE BRIMONT Cook some potatoes and artichoke hearts in water, peel, and wipe dry. Dice coarsely and mix with mayonnaise flavoured with sherry. Arrange in a dome in the centre of a serving dish and surround with clusters of stoned (pitted) black (ripe) olives, crayfish tails, and quartered hard-boiled (hard-cooked) eggs, all seasoned with olive oil and sherry vinegar. Garnish the salad with a few slices of truffle. The crayfish tails may be replaced by large peeled prawns.

brinde

A glass of wine drunk to someone's health. The word probably comes from the German *bringen*, meaning 'to raise a toast'. In the Middle Ages, it referred to a jug or vessel with handles, which was used for pouring wine into the guests' goblets. The Gascon verb *brindar* means 'to drink somebody's health'. Opera lovers will recall the 'Brindisi', or drinking song, in the first act of *La Traviata*.

brine SAUMURE

A salt solution used to preserve meat, fish, or vegetables. Brine sometimes also contains saltpetre, sugar, and flavourings. Small items can be pickled in brine on a domestic scale, but large items come within the sphere of industrial salting. Brine for industrial use contains about 18% salt (usually a mixture of sodium chloride and potassium nitrate (common salt and saltpetre)), 2–3% sucrose, and variable quantities of sodium polyphosphates.

The pink colour of ham is due to the saltpetre in the brine. In charcuterie brine is often injected into the meat before immersion. Cooked hams were traditionally treated either with old brine, brought to the required concentration by the addition of salt and nitrate, or with fresh brine mixed with the remains of the old brine, which provided some nitrate-reducing bacteria and some ready-made nitrite. Nowadays, however, fresh brines containing selected bacteria strains are usually used. Unfortunately this change has led to faster salting, which, with the addition of polyphosphates, does not improve the flavour of ham. Brines used for fish contain neither nitrates nor polyphosphates.

brinzen or bryndza

A Hungarian ewes'-milk cheese in the shape of a cylinder weighing 5, 10, 20, or 30 kg (11, 22, 44, or 66 lb). Left to ferment in brine and milk during the winter, it is eaten in spring and has a strong piquant flavour. Brinzen is similar to the Romanian *brandza* (which is milder, stored in salt water, and cut into cubes) and the Russian *brynza*.

brioche

A soft loaf or roll made from a yeast dough enriched with butter and eggs.

The word brioche first appeared in 1404, and for a long time its etymology was the subject of controversy. Some maintained that the pastry originated in Brie, and Alexandre Dumas claimed that the dough was originally kneaded with cheese from Brie. It is now considered that brioche is derived from the verb *brier*, an old Norman form of the verb *broyer* meaning 'to pound' (this is found in *pain brie*, a speciality of Normandy). This explanation is all the more likely since the brioches from Gournay and Gisors in Normandy have always been highly regarded.

The dough is a mixture of flour, yeast, water or milk, sugar (unless intended for a savoury dish), eggs, and butter. The substitution of baker's yeast (dating from the 18th century) for brewer's yeast made it lighter. Brioche dough can be moulded in many ways. The traditional *brioche à tête*, or Parisian brioche, is made of two balls placed one on top of the other: a small ball on top of a large one. Brioches are also moulded into hexagon shapes with marked-out sections: these are Nanterre brioches (or brioche loaves). The brioche mousseline is tall and cylindrical and is the most delicate. A traditional variation consists of adding raisins to the brioche dough.

The brioche, often in the shape of a ring, is one of the most widespread regional pastries, eaten by all sections of society. Worthy of mention are the *brioche coulante* (*fallue*) from Normandy, brioche with pralines from Saint-Genix, the Twelfth-Night cake (*tourtillon*) from Bordeaux, *gâtais de la mariée* from Vendée (which can measure up to 1.3 m (over 4 ft) in diameter), brioche stuffed with hazelnuts, raisins, and dried pears from the Vosges, brioche with cream cheese or Gruyère from Gannat, not forgetting fouaces, pompes, couques and cramiques, koeckbotteram from Dunkirk, campanili from Corsica, and pastis from Béarn, all of which are rustic brioches with various flavourings.

Brioche is served as a dessert or with tea, but it also has many culinary uses. Ordinary brioche dough is suitable for koulibiac and fillet of beef *en croûte*; brioche mousseline is served with foie gras, sausage, and cervelas (saveloy) from Lyons; rissoles are also made in brioche dough, but are deep-fried. Small individual brioches are used as cases for various sweet or savoury salpicons served as hot main dishes or as desserts.

RECIPES

Classic fine brioche dough PÂTE À BRIOCHE CLASSIQUE FINE Soften 225 g (8 oz, 1 cup) butter at room temperature. Crumble 8 g (¼ oz) baker's yeast and stir into 1 tablespoon warm water. In a separate container stir 15 g (½ oz, 1 tablespoon) granulated sugar and a pinch of salt into 2 tablespoons cold milk. Sieve 250 g (9 oz, 2 cups) flour, make a well in the centre, and place the yeast mixture and 1 whole egg in the well. After working in a little flour, add the sugar and salt mixture, and another egg. Continue to work the dough until it becomes smooth and elastic. It should stretch easily. Mix a third of the dough with the softened

butter, then add the second and finally the remaining third of the dough to the mixture. Place the dough in a 2-litre (4-pint) container, cover with a cloth, and leave to rise in a warm place (avoiding draughts) until it has doubled in volume (approximately 3 hours). Then separate the dough into 3 pieces, knead slightly, and leave to rise again (for 2 or 3 hours). Leave to rest for a few hours in a cool place: the dough is now ready to be shaped and baked.

Standard brioche dough PÂTE À BRIOCHE COMMUNE This is prepared in exactly the same way as the classic brioche dough, but the quantity of butter is reduced to 175 g (6 oz, ¾ cup).

Fruit brioche BRIOCHE AUX FRUITS Prepare some frangipane and some brioche dough. Coarsely dice some seasonal fruit (plums and apricots, or peaches and pears, or plums and pears), and macerate in fruit brandy, sugar, and lemon juice. Butter a shallow round mould, line with brioche dough, and cover the bottom with a layer of frangipane. Drain the fruit and arrange in the lined tin. Cover with brioche dough, seal the edges, and leave to rise for 1 hour. Bake in the oven until golden. Sprinkle with icing sugar (confectioner's sugar) and serve piping hot. The brioche may also be filled with a mixture of light confectioner's custard (pastry cream) and stoned (pitted) cherries.

Individual Parisian brioches BRIOCHES PARISIENNES INDIVIDUELLES These are made in the same way as the large brioches, using small brioche moulds. Allow only 15 minutes for cooking, but preheat the oven to approximately 225 C (425 F, gas 7).

Parisian brioche BRIOCHE PARISIENNE Having lightly floured the hands and the working surface, divide 280 g (10 oz) brioche dough into 2 balls, 240 g (8 oz) for the body of the brioche and the remaining 40 g (2 oz) for the head. Roll the large ball in the hands until it is perfectly round. Butter a ½-litre (17-fl oz, 1-pint) brioche mould and place the ball inside it. Roll the small ball of dough into a pear shape. Make a hole in the top of the large ball and insert the pointed end of the small ball; press down with the fingertips. Allow to double in volume at room temperature, for approximately 1½ hours. Heat the oven to medium (200 c, 400 f, gas 6). Make some small incisions in the large ball, from the edges towards the head, using wet scissors. Brush the brioche with beaten egg and bake for 30 minutes; turn out the mould while still warm.

FILLED SAVOURY BRIOCHES

Brioches with anchovies BRIOCHES AUX ANCHOIS Using standard brioche dough without sugar, prepare some very small Parisian brioches in fluted moulds. When cooked, allow to cool completely, wrap in aluminium foil, and place in the refrigerator for 1 hour. Then remove the heads of the brioches and carefully scoop out the insides of the brioche bases, using the bread taken out to make very fine breadcrumbs. Add these to the same volume of softened anchovy butter. Fill the brioches with this mixture and put the heads back on. Put in a cool place until required for serving. The mixture of breadcrumbs and anchovy butter can be lightened by adding a little whipped cream.

Brioches with cheese BRIOCHES AUX FROMAGE Prepare the brioches as for brioches with anchovies (but make them a little bigger). Fill with a thick Mornay sauce mixed with diced York or Bayonne ham. Reheat in the oven.

Brioches with mushrooms BRIOCHES AUX CHAMPIGNONS Prepare the brioches as for brioches with anchovies (they should however be bigger). Fill with duxelles of mushrooms mixed with a little béchamel sauce. Heat in the oven.

FILLED SWEET BRIOCHES

Brioche with raspberries BRIOCHE AUX FRAMBOISES Hollow out a large brioche mousseline in the same way as for Caribbean brioche. Add some Kirsch to melted butter and sprinkle this mixture over the inside of the brioche; fill with a mixture of raspberries and whipped cream. (Wild strawberries may be used instead of raspberries.)

The brioche may alternatively be filled with confectioner's custard (pastry cream) lightened with whipped cream and mixed with stoned (pitted) cherries, poached in syrup and drained.

Caribbean brioche BRIOCHE ANTILLAISE Make a large brioche mousseline and allow to cool completely. Slice off the top and scoop out the inside, leaving a thickness of approximately 1.5 cm (½ in) at the bottom and sides. Cut the bread removed from the inside into cubes and brown these in butter. Reduce the syrup from a tin of pineapple by three-quarters and flavour with rum. Cut the pineapple into large dice. Cut some firm ripe bananas into thin slices and heat these with the pineapple dice in butter; place the fruit in the reduced syrup. Add the cubes of brioche, mix together, and fill the brioche with the mixture. Replace the top and heat in the oven.

Briolet

A minor wine of mediocre quality which was formerly produced in Brie.

Brisse (Baron Léon)

French journalist (born Gémenos, 1813; died Fontenay-aux-Roses, 1876). Having begun his career in the Water and Forestry department, which he was obliged to leave after a scandal, he turned to journalism and specialized in gastronomic articles. It was his idea to print a different menu every day in the newspaper *La Liberté*. These recipes were put together in 1868 in a collection called *Les Trois Cent Soixante-Six Menus du baron Brisse*. He also published *Recettes à l'usage des ménages bourgeois et des petits ménages* (1868), *La Petite Cuisine du baron Brisse* (1870), and *La Cuisine en carême* (1873). He was often reproached for not being able to cook and his recipes are sometimes whimsical and even impossible, such as 'scoter duck with chocolate', a burlesque way of preparing a kind of duck with tough oily flesh. But he also gives a recipe for terrine of foie gras and *garbure* (cabbage and bacon soup). The 'paper gastrophile' as he was nicknamed by his colleagues, this enormous truculent character died at an inn in Fontenay-aux-Roses, where he had taken up lodgings. For several years his friends, including Monselet and Gouffé, observed the anniversary of his death by meeting at the inn, where the landlord, Gigout, symbolically laid Baron Brisse's place.

His name has been given to a garnish for large joints of meat, consisting of onions with chicken forcemeat and stuffed olive tartlets.

Bristol

A garnish served with large roast joints of meat (beef or lamb), noisettes of lamb, and tournedos. Consisting of small risotto croquettes, flageolet beans cooked in butter, and château potatoes, it probably takes its name from the Parisian hotel of the same name.

Brittany BRETAGNE

Breton cuisine benefits from being well supplied with the best products of land and sea; livestock rearing provides good meat, particularly 'salt-meadow' sheep. The most popular specialities are buckwheat and bacon soup, the substantial *potée bretonne* (shoulder of lamb boiled with duck, sausage, and vegetables), *pâte de Bécherel* (garlic pie), chitterling sausages (hot or cold), potted pork from Vallet, boudin blanc from Rennes, *courraye* or *pâté de courres* (galantine of offal), poached eggs *à la bretonne*, and a complete range of buckwheat savoury pancakes, garnished with eggs, cheese, various cold meats, fried sardines, etc., which constitute a complete meal in themselves.

The list of shellfish is impressive: razor fish, scallops, clams, oysters, etc.; sea urchins, prawns, and shrimps are used for specific regional dishes, but there are more varied recipes for crabs and lobsters – *à la vinaigrette*, *à la mayonnaise*, grilled (broiled), *au naturel*, *à l'armoricaine*, *à la morlaisienne*, etc. Scallops are prepared *à la nantaise*, *à la nage*, or cooked with cream; monkfish is cooked with cider; cod is prepared *à la bretonne*; tuna is fried; sardines are grilled (broiled); shad is stuffed; eel is cooked *à la ploërmelaise*

(marinated and grilled (broiled)); pike is cooked *au beurre blanc*; and lamprey is prepared *à la matelote*. Cotriade and conger eel soup are the delight of all fish lovers.

Meat specialities include côte au farci, casse, leg of lamb *à la bretonne*, potée bretonne, Nantes bacon (belly of pork braised with rind, offal, herbs, and white wine), and rabbit with nutmeg. Poultry dishes include duck with peas, bardatte, and grilled Janze chicken. These dishes are served with choice early vegetables and cooked vegetable dishes: cauliflower (stuffed, or served in its own cooking liquor or butter, or *à la crème*), artichokes, potato cakes, beans *à la bretonne*, etc., all washed down with excellent cider.

Among the desserts are the famous Breton crêpes made from wheat flour and eaten hot, spread with butter or jam, or with chocolate, lemon, or liqueur. Pastries include *crêpes dentelle* (very thin pancakes), *bigoudens*, Mam'Goz fritters, craquelins, Breton far, kouing aman (a rich yeast cake), Breton cake, and *maingaux* (a whipped cream dessert) from Rennes.

Brix scale

A scale of measurement for the density or specific gravity of sugary liquids made with cane or beet sugar, evaluated using a saccharometer. It replaced the Baumé scale in 1962.

broad bean (fava bean)

FÈVE

An annual leguminous plant cultivated throughout Europe for its flat seeds, used as food for man and animals. The broad bean was cultivated by ancient civilizations, particularly the Egyptians. It originated in Persia and Africa and has been used in the cuisine of the Mediterranean for centuries.

Dried beans are more nutritious than fresh ones: they are rich in amino acids and potassium salts and also contain large quantities of proteins and vitamins B and E. Broad beans contain a chemical substance that some people, particularly in the Mediterranean and Iran, are allergic to. The allergy, known as favism, is inherited and it leads to destruction of red blood cells resulting in severe anaemia.

The beans are shelled and the tough outer skin may be removed before cooking. They are cooked in boiling salted water. The classic preparation of broad beans is a purée, which is particularly good with pork. In Spanish cuisine they feature in *fabada*, a kind of cassoulet garnished with black pudding (blood sausage), chorizo, shoulder of pork, and white cabbage.

RECIPES

Fresh broad beans à la française FÈVES FRAÎCHES À LA FRANÇAISE Shell and skin the beans and cook, with a bunch of savory, as for peas *à la française*.

Fresh broad beans à l'anglaise FÈVES FRAÎCHES À L'ANGLAISE Shell the beans but do not remove the outer skin. Cook in boiling salted water with a bunch of savory. Drain and serve tossed in butter.

Broccio, Brocciu, or Brucciu

A cheese from Corsica made of ewes' milk, or sometimes goats' milk, with an oily texture (45% fat content). It is generally eaten fresh, from the end of autumn to the beginning of spring, but it can also be matured (demi-sec). It is used in the preparation of many local dishes and pastries (imbrucciata, fiadone, stuffed pancakes, omelettes, sardines, artichokes, and courgettes (zucchini)). Traditionally drained in small cane moulds, broccio (a corruption of *brousse*, meaning 'brush') is eaten within 48 hours. Otherwise it is salted and left to dry; when hard it is wrapped in dry asphodel leaves and stored in a cool place. When it is used to flavour a dish, it must be desalted for some time in cold water.

broccoli   BROCOLI

A brassica cultivated for its fleshy flower stalks which are approximately 15 cm (6 in) long. It is also known as sprouting broccoli and asparagus broccoli and is sold as green stalks ending in bunches of green or purple flower buds and surrounded with leaves. The stalks are sometimes eaten like asparagus and the flowers and leaves are prepared like cauliflower.

Originating in Italy (the name is derived from the Italina *broccolo*, meaning cabbage sprout), this vegetable was introduced to France by Catherine de' Medici. In Italy it remains one of the most popular spring vegetables, being cooked with olive oil, white wine, and garlic. The Chinese prepare it sweet and sour.

RECIPES

Broccoli à la vendéenne Completely desalt an approximately 500-g (1-lb) piece unsmoked streaky bacon by soaking in cold water, then place in a large saucepan with 2 litres (4 pints) cold water; simmer for approximately 1½ hours. Then add 1 kg (2 lb) cleaned broccoli, 2 crushed garlic cloves, and a little salt. Boil for 15 minutes; add quartered potatoes and finish cooking. Drain the broccoli, chop coarsely, and heat with 40 g (1½ oz, 3 tablespoons) butter. Cut the bacon into slices and brown in 30 g (1 oz, 2 tablespoons) butter. Drain the potatoes and slice. Arrange the broccoli, then the potatoes, and finally the slices of bacon in a heated dish. Sprinkle with the butter used for cooking. Add 25 g (1 oz, 2 tablespoons) butter to the water in which the bacon and vegetables were cooked; pour this stock into a soup tureen over thin slices of wholemeal bread dried in the oven. Sprinkle with chopped parsley just before serving.

Broccoli with cream BROCCOLI À LA CRÈME Carefully clean 1 kg (2 lb) broccoli, put into 2 litres (4 pints) boiling salted water, and boil for approximately 30 seconds, until just tender. Drain the broccoli and chop very coarsely. Lightly brown 50 g (2 oz, ¼ cup) butter in a frying pan (skillet) and add 1.5–2 dl (5–7 fl oz, ⅔–¾ cup) cream. When the cream is coloured, add the broccoli. Season with pepper and again with salt if necessary. Simmer for approximately 10 minutes. Serve the broccoli very hot with roast or sautéed meat, or with certain types of fish, such as bass, cod, hake, etc.

brochette

A large slightly flattened skewer, usually made of stainless steel, on which pieces of meat, vegetables, etc., are threaded for cooking under a grill or over charcoal. If the ingredients are to be fried, the skewer is made of wood. There are single brochettes, with a ring or handle, and double brochettes (with two needles). Electric rotating grills may be equipped with vertical brochettes, and some rôtisseries are fitted with brochette drums.

The preparation cooked in this way is also called a brochette. The principal ingredients are kidneys or pieces of calves' sweetbreads, scallops, large cubes of beef or mutton (sometimes marinated), small birds, etc., alternating with sliced mushrooms, lean bacon, quartered tomatoes, pieces of onion, pepper, etc. Most brochettes have more flavour–and are more tender – if their ingredients are marinated with oil, chopped herbs, sometimes garlic and brandy, salt, pepper, and various herbs and spices (since the ingredients of kebabs are small, 30 minutes' marinating is quite sufficient). The ingredients are then threaded onto the skewer and cooked. Brochettes are served as a hot hors d'oeuvre or as a main dish with a garnish of rice or ratatouille. (See *attelet, attereau, kebab, shashlyk*.)

RECIPES

BROCHETTES OF FISH AND SEAFOOD

Monkfish brochettes BROCHETTES DE LOTTE Cut the fish of a monkfish (taken from the tail, which is less expensive than the middle of the fish) into 2.5-cm (1-in) cubes and marinate with halved slices of aubergine (eggplant) for 30 minutes in the same mixture as for seafood brochettes. Thread the skewers, alternating monkfish and aubergine (egg-plant), and grill (broil) under a medium heat for 16–18 minutes.

Seafood brochettes BROCHETTES DE FRUITS DE MER Prepare a marinade using olive oil, plenty of lemon juice, finely chopped herbs and garlic, fresh crumbled thyme, and salt and pepper.

Marinate an assortment of seafood for 30 minutes: oysters poached for 1 minute in their liquor, mussels opened by heating in the oven, raw scallops, lobster tails, large prawns, scampi, etc. Thread onto skewers without draining, alternating with very fresh small mushrooms (pierced through the bottom of the cap) and fresh blanched pieces of bacon (optional). Grill (broil) under a high heat.

BROCHETTES OF MEAT AND POULTRY

Brochettes of marinated fillet of beef BROCHETTES DE FILET DE BOEUF MARINÉ Prepare a marinade using 1.5 dl (¼ pint, ⅔ cup) olive oil, salt, pepper, and chopped herbs. Cut up 500 g (18 oz) fillet of beef into 3-cm (1-in) cubes and cut 150–200g (5–7 oz) smoked belly pork into strips; marinate these for 30 minutes. Remove the seeds of a green pepper and cut the flesh into 3-cm (1-in) squares. Cut off the stalks of 8 large button mushrooms level with the cap, sprinkle the mushrooms with lemon juice, and sauté briskly in oil with the pieces of pepper; drain as soon as the pepper is slightly softened. Thread the following series twice onto each skewer: 1 new white onion, 1 very small tomato, 1 mushroom, 1 piece of pepper, 1 piece of bacon, 1 piece of fillet; finish with 1 onion. Grill (broil) under a very high heat for 7–8 minutes.

Lamb brochettes BROCHETTES D'AGNEAU Cut some well-trimmed fillet or leg of lamb into pieces 7–8 mm (¼ in) thick. Thread the pieces of meat onto skewers, alternating with blanched bacon strips and (optional) sliced wild mushrooms tossed in butter. Season with salt and pepper. Brush the brochettes with melted butter, roll in white breadcrumbs, sprinkle again with butter, and grill (broil) under a high heat.

Pork brochettes with prunes BROCHETTES DE PORC AUX PRUNEAUX Remove the stones (pits) from the prunes. Wrap each prune in half a slice of smoked streaky bacon and pin with a cocktail stick. Cut some pork loin (not as dry as fillet) into cubes.

Marinate all these ingredients for 30 minutes in a mixture of groundnut (peanut) oil, salt and pepper, and a little grated nutmeg and cayenne. Drain the pork and the prunes, thread onto skewers, and grill (broil) under a medium heat for about 10 minutes.

BROCHETTES OF OFFAL

Chicken liver brochettes BROCHET-TES DE FOIES DE VOLAILLE Remove the galls from the livers, cut them in two, and marinate. Add some small button mushrooms with lemon juice or, better still, wild mushrooms. Cut some fat bacon into fairly thick chunks, blanch for 2 or 3 minutes, then pat dry. Roll the livers in fresh breadcrumbs and thread the livers, mushrooms, and bacon onto the skewers. Grill (broil) under a high heat and serve with rice and sauce *à l'indienne*.

This recipe may also be made using duck livers.

Kidney brochettes BROCHETTES DE ROGNONS Skin some lambs' kidneys then cut in half and remove the white core. The kidneys may then be brushed with oil, seasoned with salt and pepper, and threaded onto skewers to be grilled (broiled) under a very high heat. Alternatively, the kidneys may be seasoned with salt and pepper, brushed with melted butter, rolled in white breadcrumbs, and threaded on the skewers, alternating with blanched strips of bacon; the whole is sprinkled with melted butter and grilled under a high heat. Serve the kidneys with maître d'hôtel butter.

Sliced calves' or lambs' sweetbreads, small pieces of beef or lamb, chicken livers, etc., can also be prepared in this way.

broiler
See *grill*.

broiling
See *grilling*.

Broodkaas
A Dutch cheese made from pasteurized cows' milk, with a firm compressed pale-yellow paste and a yellow or red wax covering. It is sold in the shape of loaves weighing 2–4 kg (4½–9 lb) and has all the characteristics of Edam except the shape. Broodkaas is imitated in France under the name of *galantine or édam français en pain* (French Edam loaf).

broth
See *bouillon*.

brou de noix
A liqueur made from green walnut husks. The soft shells are hollowed out, ground, flavoured with cinnamon and nutmeg, and macerated in alcohol. Sugar syrup is added and the mixture is then filtered. This traditional liqueur from Dauphiné, Quercy, and central France is served as a digestive.

brouet
Today in France 'brouet' is a pejorative term applied to any coarse and weak soup or stew. Originally it referred to the national dish of the Spartans, in particular under the tyranny of Lycurgus. 'Black brouet' was a sort of liquid stew made of fat, meat, blood, and vinegar. It was served at communal civic meals which all citizens aged between seven and sixty years were required to attend. It is said that Denys the Ancient brought a Spartan cook to Syracuse and ordered him to prepare a brouet according to the rules; when he indignantly rejected it, his cook pointed out to him that the essential seasoning was missing, i.e. hunger, fatigue, and thirst.

The word 'brouet' was commonly used in French cooking in the Middle Ages and had no pejorative meaning: it referred to a soup (brouet of oysters or fish), to a stew (brouet of pullets), or a sauce (white brouet with almonds, eggs, and ground meat). The *Ménagier de Paris* gives a recipe for brouet from Germany, a very popular soup at the time. From it was derived *brouet d'accouchée*, a broth made from eggs, milk, and sugar, which used to be given to women in labour and newly married women the day after their wedding.

broufado
A Provençal speciality made with marinated beef cooked in a casserole with herbs, gherkins (sweet dill pickles)

or capers, and fillets of anchovy. Mistral describes this dish as a 'fried meat with pepper sauce', but it is more of a stew or casserole, and is probably a very old seaman's recipe.

RECIPE

Broufado   Cut 800g (2 lb) stewing beef into 5-cm (2-in) cubes. Marinate in a cool place for 24 hours in a mixture of ½ glass red wine vinegar, 3 tablespoons (¼ cup) olive oil, a large bouquet garni, a large sliced onion, and some pepper. Desalt 6 anchovies. Drain the meat and heat in a casserole dish with 2 tablespoons (3 tablespoons) olive oil. Add a large chopped onion, then the marinade, and a glass of wine (red or white). Bring to the boil, then cover and cook in the oven at 200 c (400 F, gas 6) for 2 hours. Add a few small pickled onions and 3 or 4 sliced gherkins (sweet dill pickles). Cook for a further 15 minutes. Wash the desalted anchovies, remove the fillets and cut them into small pieces, mix with 2 teaspoons kneaded butter, and add to the casserole. Stir the broufado well for 2 minutes and serve piping hot with jacket potatoes.

Brouilly

A distinguished red wine from Beaujolais. The vineyards around the Montagne de Brouilly produce a very fruity wine, which must be drunk young. Côte-de-Brouilly, from the slopes of the mountain, owes its quite remarkable qualities to the soil and aspect. A little more full-bodied than Brouilly, it is not of the best Beaujolais wines and its bouquet is refined by a few years' maturation.

broulaï

A Caribbean fish stew cooked with sweet cassava roots or potatoes. The vegetables are browned in oil in a stewing pan, then removed and replaced by pieces of firm-fleshed fish, tomato purée, onion, and chilli pepper. Water is added and the mixture brought to the boil, then the vegetables are put back in the pan with a bay leaf. When the fish and vegetables are cooked, they are taken out of the pan and rice is cooked in the stock. Rice and stew are served together.

Brousse

A curd cheese (45% fat content) made in Provence from autumn to the beginning of spring; ewes' milk is used for Brousse du Rove (the most famous), and goats' or ewes' milk for Brousse de la Vésubie. White, mild, and creamy, unmatured and without crust, Brousse (from the Provençal *brousso*, meaning curds) is made from curds drained on muslin (cheesecloth), first into an earthenware dish with holes in to separate the buttermilk, then into cylindrical tin moulds with smaller holes. The paste must not be too dry.

Brousse is served with sugar and fresh cream, with fruit (fresh or stewed), or with vinaigrette, herbs, garlic, and chopped onions.

broutart

In France, a lamb or young calf which has grazed free in pasture until being slaughtered. Its meat is redder than that from milk animals, because the consumption of grass encourages the formation of the red blood pigment haemoglobin. The appearance of these animals on the market dates from World War II, when needs were too urgent to allow livestock to reach maturity.

broutes or broutons

In Béarn, leaves of old cabbages that are trimmed, washed, cooked in salted water, and served with vinaigrette. In some villages of the Pyrénées-Atlantiques, broutes are a mixture of cooked leeks and cabbage, drained, pressed, and cut into pieces.

brown   ROUSSIR

To cook meat or poultry in hot fat or oil until it takes on a golden-brown colour. The term is also applied to chopped or sliced onion which is first sweated then cooked until quite a dark colour.

broye and broyé

In Béarn, *broye* is a broth of maize flour (cornmeal). Simin Palay gives a recipe in *La Cuisine du pays* which differs by using white or browned flour.

In Poitou, *broyé* is a large biscuit made of a shortbread-type dough.

RECIPES

Broye béarnaise (from a recipe by S. Palay) Using white (i.e. raw) flour, broye is prepared like an ordinary gruel. Vegetable stock or plain salted water is boiled and flour is added little by little until the consistency is fairly firm. When the gruel is cooked, and it must be stirred constantly during cooking, it is served with a greased ladle so that the gruel does not stick to the utensil. If the flour is first baked to brown it, a well is made in the centre of the flour in an earthenware container, the stock or water is added and mixed well, and the mixture is cooked. The cold broye can be sliced and fried in very hot fat until well coloured.

Broyé poitevin Place 250 g (9 oz, 1 cup) caster (superfine) sugar and a pinch of salt in an earthenware dish; make a well and drop 1 whole egg and 250 g (9 oz, 1 cup) butter cut into pieces into the centre. Knead by hand to mix thoroughly. Add 500 g (18 oz), 4 cups) flour, a spoonful at a time, then 1 tablespoon rum or brandy and knead until the dough no longer sticks to the fingers (it should be fairly soft). Butter a pie dish 26 cm (10 in) in diameter and spread the dough in the dish, smoothing it with the palm of the hand. Brush the surface with 1 egg yolk mixed with 2 teaspoons black coffee. Draw a crisscross pattern or geometric designs with a fork. Bake for 30 minutes at 180 C (350 F, gas 4). Allow to cool before turning out of the mould as the cake is very crumbly.

brulé

A word, meaning literally 'burnt', used in various ways in French to describe ingredients, dishes, etc.

In France, dough is said to be *brûlée* when flour and fat have been mixed too slowly and the mixture has become oily (the same thing happens to brioche dough when the surrounding temperature is too high).

When egg yolks are left with caster (superfine) sugar without beating, small bright yellow particles appear and are difficult to mix into creams and doughs: the yolks are said to be *brûlés*.

brûlot

Alcohol that is flamed before being drunk (or poured into a drink) or before being added to food (as in an omelette flambée).

'Brûlot' in France is a familiar term for a sugar lump soaked in alcohol, held in a spoon over a cup of coffee, and flamed before being dropped into the coffee.

'Café-brûlot' is a typical drink of Louisiana. It is made by heating rum with sugar, cinnamon, an orange stuck with cloves, and lemon zest; when the sugar has dissolved, scalding coffee is poured onto the mixture and the resulting liquid is filtered and served in hot cups.

brunch

A meal originating in America, being a combination of breakfast and lunch. This type of meal is commonly eaten on Sundays, when parents, children, and sometimes friends gather round the table in a relaxed atmosphere between 10 a.m. and 2 p.m. The menu combines traditional English breakfast items with those of a cold meal: cereals, bacon, and fried or scrambled eggs, salads of fruit and green vegetables, pancakes with jam or maple syrup, fruit juice, tea, and coffee. Pies and cold meats may also be served. There is often a home-made fruit loaf (called a 'coffeecake'), corn bread, or French toast (slices of bread dipped in beaten egg, then fried and sugared). Brunch is still quite rare in France, but some hotel restaurants in Paris offer it to their customers on Sunday mornings.

brunoise

This term is applied both to a method of cutting vegetables into minute dice and to the resulting diced vegetables (either a single type or a mixture). Often braised in butter, brunoise is used as a garnish for soups, sauces, and stuffings and also serves as a flavouring (for preparing crayfish, osso bucco, etc.).

Brunoise is generally used as soon as it is ready, but it can be kept for a few minutes under a damp cloth.

| RECIPES |

Brunoise pannequets PANNEQUETS À LA BRUNOISE Stew a brunoise of vegetables in butter. Bind with a little light béchamel sauce. Make some pancakes (see *pannequet*) and fill with the mixture; roll up, cut into thick slices, coat in breadcrumbs, and fry.

Consommé à la brunoise For 4 servings, finely dice 200 g (7 oz) carrots 125 g (4 oz) new parsnips, 100 g (4 oz) leeks (white part only), 25 g (1 oz) onions, and 75 g (3 oz) well-trimmed celery. Braise gently in 25 g (1 oz, 2 tablespoons) butter, then add 8 dl (1¼ pints, 1½ pints) consommé and cook for 15 minutes. Just before serving, adjust seasoning and add 150 g (5 oz, 1 cup) green peas and the same amount of green beans cooked in water and cut into short lengths.

Brussels sprout

CHOU DE BRUXELLES

A vegetable that is widely cultivated for its green buds, which resemble tiny cabbages, 2–4 cm (¾–1½ in) in diameter, and grow in the leaf axils along a stem up to 1 m (3 ft) high. Although now cultivated mainly in northern Europe, the Belgians consider that Brussels sprouts were imported into their country from Italy by the Roman legions. In France, Brussels sprouts are available fresh from September to March; throughout the year they are available either canned (sterilized *au naturel* or precooked) or packed in foil sachets; they also freeze very well.

Brussels sprouts should be very green and compact, without yellow leaves; the best are usually found after the first frosts. They are prepared by removing the stump and one or two leaves around it, then washed in water to which vinegar has been added. Sprouts are rich in sulphur, potassium, and vitamins and contain 54 Cal per 100 g. Cooked in boiling water (preferably after blanching), they are generally served with meat (in butter, cream, or white sauce) but are also used for gratins and purées. They can also be braised and mixed with thin strips of bacon and chestnuts. They may be served cold in a salad.

Sprouts are essential for bruxelloise and brabançonne garnishes.

| RECIPES |

Brussels sprouts à l'anglaise CHOUX DE BRUXELLES À L'ANGLAISE Plunge the sprouts into boiling salted water and leave to cook briskly without a lid for about 30 minutes. Then drain and place them in a vegetable dish. Serve with fresh butter. If the sprouts are large, first blanch them in boiling water and cool them before proceeding as above.

Brussels sprouts au gratin CHOUX DE BRUXELLES GRANTINÉS Prepare some buttered Brussels sprouts. Butter a gratin dish, tip the sprouts into it, sprinkle with grated cheese and melted butter, and brown for about 10 minutes in a very hot oven.

Brussels sprout purée CHOUX DE BRUXELLES EN PURÉE Place some well-cooked buttered Brussels sprouts in a food processor to obtain a purée. Then pour it into a saucepan and heat, stirring so that it loses some moisture. Add a quarter of its volume of potato purée and fresh cream, using about 1 dl (6 tablespoons, scant ½ cup) cream for 1 litre (1¾ pints, 4¼ cups) purée. Season with salt and pepper and serve very hot, preferably with roasted or braised white meat.

Sautéed Brussels sprouts CHOUX DE BRUXELLES SAUTÉS Cook some sprouts in boiling water until tender, then drain thoroughly. Heat some butter in a frying pan (skillet) and toss the sprouts lightly in it. Transfer them to a vegetable dish and sprinkle with chopped parsley.

They may also be served with noisette butter (moistened first with lemon juice), *à l'indienne* (accompanied by a curry sauce and boiled rice), *à la milanaise* (sprinkled with grated Parmesan, then moistened with noisette butter), or *à la polonaise*, like cauliflower.

bruxelloise (à la)

A garnish consisting of stewed Brussels sprouts, braised chicory, and château potatoes, served with small joints of meat, either sautéed or roasted. Egg dishes *à la bruxelloise* are garnished with Brussels sprouts or chicory.

RECIPE

Eggs à la bruxelloise OEUFS À LA BRUXELLOISE Bake some small pastry cases (pie shells) blind. Gently cook some thinly sliced chicory (endive) in butter, bind with a little béchamel sauce, and put into the pie cases. Place a soft-boiled (soft-cooked) or poached egg in each case and coat with piping hot cream sauce.

bucket SEAU

A roughly cylindrical container with a handle. The champagne bucket, which is made of stainless steel or silver-plated metal, is used for keeping a bottle of champagne, dry white wine, rosé, Asti, or sparkling wine cool in iced water. The ice bucket, which is smaller, is used to serve ice cubes for drinks. It comes with a large pair of tongs or a spoon to pick up the ice cubes. Some ice buckets are insulated, with double walls and a lid, to prevent the ice cubes from melting.

buckwheat SARRASIN

A cereal plant originating in the Orient and cultivated in Europe since the end of the 14th century. The name is derived from the Middle Dutch *boecweite*, from *boeke* (beech) and *weite* (wheat), probably because the seeds resemble beechnuts. It is also known as Saracen corn, because of the dark colour of the grain, and (in French) as *blé noir*, *beaucuit*, or *bucail*.

Buckwheat flour is grey with black flecks; it is rich in minerals and B vitamins and has a lower calorific value than other cereals (290 Cal per 100 g). It is unsuitable for making bread, but is used in France for traditional buckwheat pancakes (*galettes*; see *crêpe*), porridge, and fars. When husked, crushed, and cooked, buckwheat forms the basis of the Russian dish kasha, and in Japan buckwheat flour is used for making noodles. Nowadays some pasta is made with buckwheat too.

Until the end of the 19th century, buckwheat was one of the staple foods of Brittany and Normandy, and also of north-eastern Europe, but its cultivation today has diminished considerably. In Basse-Normandie, buckwheat porridge was formerly a very common meal; the flour was soaked either in curdled skimmed milk or in plain water and then stirred in a pan over the heat. Then the pan was placed on a trivet and a hollow was made in the centre of the porridge and filled with melted butter. 'Everyone took a spoonful of the porridge, and then dipped it into the butter before eating it. When the meal was over, the leftover porridge was either put aside in a large dish, to be eaten with sweetened warm milk, or taken to the fields to be eaten later as a light meal. Thin slices of porridge, known as *soles de guéret*, were fricasseed and browned in sizzling butter.' (Jean Séguin, *Vieux Mangers, vieux parlers Bas-Normands*, Librairie Guénégaud.)

buffalo BUFFLE

A member of the ox family, which is wild in Africa and domesticated in India; it was first imported to Italy, Hungary, and the Balkans by the Romans. (The American buffalo, or bison, is a much larger animal.) The meat of the young animals, especially the females, is tender and tastes very similar to beef. Buffalo milk contains 40% fat (like cows' milk). In India, it is used to make *surati*, a cheese matured in earthenware vases which are also used to transport it. In Italy, *provolone* (a round cheese with a springy curd and mild paste) is produced from buffalo milk; it must be eaten a few days after manufacture. *Buriello* is an Italian cheese with a light paste and a ball of buffalo butter in the middle.

buffet

The word *buffet* means a large tiered table often set near the entrance of a restaurant, on which dishes of meats, poultry, fish, cold sweets, and pastries are arranged in a decorative manner. The buffet of a large restaurant is, in fact, a show of choice edibles.

Large tables with a display of foods set in or near a ballroom are also called buffets. The food is dispensed by a butler and the guests come to the table to be served with sandwiches, cold meats, pastries, and various drinks; or to have consommé served in cups. Buffets of this type are also arranged for wedding lunches.

In France, buffet restaurants (*buffets de gare*) were established in the principal railway (railroad) stations. The speed of transport has considerably reduced the importance of buffets, especially when there are restaurant cars or buffet cars providing food and refreshments during the journey. However, there are still some great buffets, such as those at Lille, Épernay, Avignon, Valenciennes, and Colmar. In Paris, the buffet at the Gare de Lyon (the Train bleu) is classed as an historic monument for its architecture and paintings; the quality of its cuisine attracts a clientele other than travellers.

Bugey

The region of Bugey, which lies in the eastern portion of the department of Ain, shares with Bresse and Dombes the reputation of being one of the centres of French gastronomy. Its capital, Belley, takes pride in being the birthplace of Brillat-Savarin, who gave many of the recipes of his country in his *Physiologie du goût*. Belley sausage and other items of charcuterie, crayfish, truffles, chicken, and game, all produced in this rich area, are well known by gourmets. Belley pâtés are noted for the complexity of their preparation; for example, the famous pâté *oreiller de la Belle Aurore*, created by Brillat-Savarin himself, contains more than six different types of meat and game.

Bugey rissoles, traditionally eaten at Christmas after Midnight Mass, are filled with roast turkey and tripe flavoured with currants. There is also chicken-liver cake, whose fine flavour is enhanced by a sauce made from crushed crayfish tails or, more modestly, from tomatoes. Like these specialities, other recipes from Bugey require elaborate preparation to enhance the flavour of poultry, freshwater fish, and crayfish, using cream and black or white truffles. Regional vegetables – cardoons, parsnips, or celeriac (celery root) – prepared in chicken stock or cream, complete these dishes, as well as the unusual *angurie* (watermelon) jam, which is served as an hors d'oeuvre in Belley.

The small Bugey vineyard produces fruity red and rosé wines, reminiscent of some Beaujolais wines, and light white wines (some sparkling), having similar characteristics to those of Savoy. These wines have been entitled to the VDQS label since 1963.

bugloss BUGLOSSE

A herbaceous plant common in Europe. Its name, derived from the Greek *buglossa* (meaning ox tongue), comes from its fleshy slightly rough leaves. Similar to borage, it has the same uses and its flowers are also used to prepare a refreshing drink.

bugne

A large fritter from the Lyonnais region, traditionally eaten on feast days, especially Shrove Tuesday. In the Middle Ages, fritter makers sold bugnes in the open air, from Arles to Dijon. They have become a speciality of Lyon, as common during the *vogues* (fairs) as waffles are in other regions. Bugne dough was originally made from flour, water, yeast, and orange flowers. When the eating of dairy products until Ash Wednesday became permitted, it was enriched with milk, butter, and eggs and bugnes have become true pastries. They are cut with a pastry wheel into ribbons which are then knotted. Bugnes are better hot than cold.

RECIPE

Bugnes Make a well in 250 g (9 oz, 2¼ cups) sifted flour. Add 50 g (2 oz, ¼ cup) softened butter, 30 g (1 oz, 2 tablespoons) caster (superfine) sugar, a large pinch of salt, 2 large beaten eggs, and a liqueur glass of rum, brandy, or orange-flower water. Mix well and knead thoroughly, then shape into a ball and allow to rest for 5 or 6 hours in a cool place. Roll the dough out to a thickness of 5 mm (¼ in). Cut the dough into strips approximately 10 cm (4 in) long and 4 cm (1½ in) wide; make a slit in the middle 5 cm (2 in) long. Thread one end of the dough through the slit; this makes a kind of knot. Fry the bugnes in hot oil, turning once; drain, place on kitchen paper, and sprinkle with icing sugar (confectioners' sugar).

buisson

A traditional method of arranging food in a pyramid, formerly widely used for vegetables (especially asparagus) and shellfish, and still used today for crayfish. The term is also used for fried smelts and goujonnettes of sole arranged in a dome with a garnish of fried parsley.

RECIPES

Buisson of asparagus in pastry BUIS-SON D'ASPERGES EN CROUSTADE (from a recipe by Carême) Boil some very thick white asparagus tips in salted water, keeping them slightly firm. Drain and wipe dry. One by one, coat them in a little mayonnaise stiffened with gelatine. Bake a thin pastry case (pie shell) blind and half-fill with a salad of green asparagus tips and very fine slices of truffle. Arrange the white asparagus tips on top in a pyramid.

Buisson of crayfish BUISSON D'ÉCREVISSES Boil the crayfish in plenty of water, then drain them. Roll a napkin into a cone shape, tucking in the bottom to make it flat and thus keep it stable, and place it on a round serving plate. Truss the crayfish by tucking the ends of the 2 claws over the top of the tail. Arrange the crayfish along the napkin, tails in the air, wedging them against each other. The top of the dish can be garnished with a sprig of parsley.

bulgur or burghul (cracked wheat)

BOULGHOUR, BULGHUR, PILPIL

A treated wholewheat grain, including the wheatgerm (it is therefore rich in protein, mineral salts, and carbohydrate). It is made by cooking the wheat, then drying and cracking it. It is then cooked in twice its volume of boiling water for approximately 10 minutes, until the liquid is absorbed. It is often used in vegetarian cooking – to make soups and gruels with pulses and flavourings, to stuff vegetables (in place of rice), or served as a salad garnished with raw vegetables in vinaigrette (like the Middle Eastern salad *tabbouleh*).

bullhead CHABOT

A fish, also called sea scorpion or sea devil, found in coastal waters of north-western Europe. It is distinguished by its large head and fan-shaped fins; the fins and the operculum (gill cover) are spiny. It can be eaten fried or in soup.

Bull's Blood

The best-known Hungarian red table wine, from vineyards around the town of Eger. It is made from the Kadarka, Merlot, and Pinot Noir grapes.

bun

A small round yeasted roll, flavoured with raisins, served for tea in Great Britain. Taken out of the oven when they have risen and turned golden brown, they may be sliced open, buttered inside, and served piping hot and dripping with melted butter: these are called Bath buns. Hot cross buns, traditionally eaten on Good Friday, are scored or patterned with a cross made from ribbons of dough arranged on the buns before baking. The dough is often flavoured with cinnamon.

RECIPE

Buns Crumble 25 g (1 oz) baker's yeast into a bowl, stir a cup of milk into it, and leave at room temperature. Soften 125 g (4½ oz, ½ cup) butter with a wooden spoon. Beat an egg with 1 teaspoon fine salt. Wash a lemon, grate the zest, and place this in a bowl with ½ litre (17 fl oz, 2 cups) milk, the softened butter, 100 g (4 oz, ½ cup) sugar, and 125 g (4½ oz, ¾ cup) raisins. Mix well, add the beaten egg, then the yeast mixture, and gradually mix in 650 g (1½ lb, 6 cups) flour. Knead these ingredients until the dough becomes elastic.

Cover with a cloth and leave until doubled in volume (approximately 5 hours), then divide the dough into balls about the size of a tangerine. Place the balls of dough in a large buttered metal tin, brush them with butter, place the lid on the tin, and allow to rise for a further 5 hours. The balls of dough may also be arranged on a baking sheet and placed in a draught-free cupboard. They will rise to 2½ times their original size. Heat the oven to approximately 200 C (400 F, gas 6). Place the buns in the oven and bake for 20 minutes. A few minutes before they are ready, mix 250 ml (8 fl oz, 1 cup) milk with 1 tablespoon sugar and brush the buns with the mixture.

burbot

LOTTE DE RIVIÈRE

A freshwater fish with a yellowish elongated cylindrical body, speckled with brown and covered in a slimy substance. The burbot can grow to a length of 1 m (3 ft), and in France is particularly abundant in the lakes of Savoy. Once caught, it is skinned and then prepared like eel or lamprey. Its oily and almost boneless flesh is very popular, but in France it is eaten primarily for its enormous liver. There is a French proverb: 'Pour un foie de lotte, femme vendrait sa cotte' (A woman would sell her soul for a burbot's liver). It is made into pâté or fried like calf's liver.

burdock   BARDANE

A large herbaceous plant common in uncultivated land. In cooking, the fleshy roots are prepared like salsify or asparagus; the young shoots and leaves, which have a refreshing and slightly bitter flavour, are used in soups or are eaten braised, especially in the south of France and Italy. The larger leaves are used in some areas for wrapping butter or soft cheeses. Burdock grows wild in Europe and is only eaten locally, but in Japan it is cultivated as a vegetable.

burghul

See *bulgur*.

Burgundy   BOURGOGNE

The former duchy of Burgundy covered a large area corresponding to Côte-d'Or, Saône-et-Loire, Yonne, and parts of Ain, Nievre, and Aube. Burgundy has a reputation not only for its wine but also for its prestigious cuisine, which is more aristocratic than provincial. Thanks to a carefully maintained tradition from the lavish period of the Dukes of Burgundy, this region considers itself to be the centre of French cuisine.

Dijon, the former capital of the duchy, could, on its own, sustain the reputation of the province on account of its famous products. Dijon mustard, which originated a very long time ago, is made from verjuice (from Burgundy grapes) mixed with mustard seeds, and no preparation *à la dijonnaise* would be complete without it. Another famous product, Dijon blackcurrant liqueur (cassis), is considered to be one of the best in the world, and its production continues to increase. Dijon gingerbread was introduced into the province by the Dukes of Burgundy, whose cooks imitated and perfected the recipes for cakes made in Flanders. Although mustard, cassis, and gingerbread are the best known specialities of Dijon, there are many other prestigious dishes – ham with parsley, salmon with Chablis, together with game, fish, and crayfish prepared in various ways. The excellence of Dijon cuisine has made the capital of the Dukes of Burgundy into the capital of the world of gastronomy conferences: these are held here every year in November.

Burgundy cuisine owes its liveliness to red or white wine, and spices, condiments, onions, garlic, and shallots add a certain piquancy to dishes which already have a strong flavour and colour. The quality of the country produce also contributes to this sophisticated cuisine, with the famous Charolais cattle, chicken from Bresse, fish from the Saône, ham and game from Morvan, crayfish and frogs from Dombes, and vegetables from the Auxonne area. All dishes *à la bourguignonne* or *à la meurette* include a sauce made with red wine and a garnish of mushrooms, small onions, and pieces of fat bacon. The sauce and the garnish may be used with meat, poultry, game, eggs, or fish. Famous recipes include boeuf bourguignon, coq au vin, chicken in Chambertin, hare in Pommard, ham fried in wine, pork chops sautéed in white wine, and chitterlings cooked in red wine. These few recipes prove, if proof were needed, that the bouquet of Burgundy wines is indispensible to the cuisine of the region.

The reputation of many other gastronomic specialities has travelled beyond the limits of the province. Although *potée bourguignonne* is similar to stews from other regions of France, snails simmered in garlic and butter or sometimes cooked *en meurette* remain a speciality of Burgundy. Pochouse, a very tasty soup made with freshwater fish, is another famous dish, said to have been invented by an innkeeper of Chalon-sur-Saône in the 16th century. Other specialities include gougère, with its strong smell of cheese, and ferchuse or pig's fry, which is traditionally eaten at meals to celebrate the wine harvest. Pork products, such as sausages, pâtés, and puddings, are specialities that each town and village prepares in its own way.

As well as being a great wine region, Burgundy also produces excellent cheeses: goats'-milk cheeses stored in grape marc, Saône-et-Loire cream cheeses, Saint-Florentin and Soumaintrain, and Époisses, with its orange crust washed in white wine. These strong cheeses, which have a powerful aroma and are often flavoured with marc, thyme, bay, or tarragon, are a perfect complement to the produce of the Burgundy vineyards.

The desserts of the region are comparable to those of the neighbouring provinces and include bugnes, flamusses, pumpkin pies, rigodons, and *corniottes* (triangular cream-cheese pastries). The towns of Burgundy also produce delicious confectionery, usually based on fruit.

Burgundy wines

VINS DE BOURGOGNE

Although wine was already being made in Burgundy in the Gallo-Roman era, it was the monks of the Middle Ages who were responsible for achieving its quality and renown. Beaune wines, which first introduced Burgundy vineyards to the world, did not begin to be appreciated outside the region until the 13th century, and the first large establishments of shippers who distributed and publicized the reputation of Burgundy throughout the world date only from the 18th century.

The Burgundy vineyard area extends over four departments – Yonne, Côte-d'Or, Saône-et-Loire, and Rhône – and is made up of six sub-regions: Chablis (near Auxerre), then, going north to south to the right of the River Saône, the Côte de Nuits, the Côte de Beaune, the Côte Chalonnaise, the Mâconnais, and the Beaujolais. All produce magnificent wines, mainly from two grapes: Pinot Noir for the reds, and Chardonnay for the quality whites; Gamay is used for red Beaujolais and Aligoté for some whites.

Compartmentalized in the extreme, the area produces a large number of wines, each of which has its own qualities and originality. There are 113 *appellations contrôlées* of various categories and thousands of single sites (*climats*) – more than 800 for the Côte de Beaune alone. Each *appellation d'origine contrôlée* (AOC) applied to Burgundy will stipulate, among other things, how much wine may be made in a delimited area (usually expressed in hectolitres per hectare) and also the minimum alcoholic content of the finished wine. The subdivisions that make up the AOCs within the larger AOCs are usually more detailed and stricter as regards yield and strength. The nomenclature is slightly complicated, but the suffix 'Supérieur' is what the word implies, and the suffix '-Villages', as in Côte de Beaune-Villages, Beaujolais-Villages, etc., means that the wines of certain villages within the area of the AOC are entitled to bear this *appellation*.

As each major property in the fine wine regions may belong to a number of different owners, the overall detailed designation of the wine is important. A particular village may carry the name of its famous vineyard after the village name – such as with Beaune les Grèves, Chambolle-Musigny les Charmes, and so on. It should be appreciated that, although an AOC establishes the origin, method of cultivation, and wine making, it cannot except by implication, guarantee quality, which is ultimately the responsibility of the grower, wine maker, *négociant* (shipper), and merchant.

Crémant de Bourgogne may be a white or a rosé sparkling wine.

Bourgogne Passe-Tout-Grains is a red wine produced by 'passing', or making the wine from the two Burgundy grapes (Pinot Noir and Gamay), of which at least one-third must be Pinot Noir.

Attempts have been made to categorize the Côte d'Or wines: those labelled 'Premier Cru' will give the name of the Specific vineyard. 'Deuxième Cru' wines tend to be sold with the village name only. The 'Grand Crus' may be labelled solely with the name of their respective great vineyards without that of their villages.

bustard OUTARDE

A migratory bird, now quite rare, which was formerly a highly prized game bird. The great bustard can still be found on the Belgian plains; the little bustard, or field duck, a much smaller bird, is fully protected. The bustard was roasted in the same way as a goose or a duck. In the Middle Ages it was considered to be more tender and less stringy than goose, while under the Ancien Régime it was described as 'a fine ceremonial roast dish'.

butcher's block BILLOT

A solid block of wood with a flat top used as a base for chopping meat with a cleaver. Butcher's blocks used to be set on three wooden feet. In some modern kitchens, a similar block made of a hardwood working surface set into a frame is installed with the other fitted units.

butcher's shop

BOUCHERIE

A shop for selling meat, especially lamb and beef. Horse and donkey flesh tends to be sold by specialist horse butchers, while pork, although sold in butchers' shops, is mostly retailed through delicatessens or specialist pork butchers.

☐ History In ancient Rome, the butcher's profession was regulated, carried privileges, and was specialized according to the various types of meat. The Roman legions were accompanied by butchers, who were responsible for buying the beasts required to feed both their own troops and the occupied countries. Inspired by the Roman master butchers, a tradition of hereditary butchers was well established throughout the ancient province of Gaul by the Middle Ages.

In 1096 the first butcher's shop in Paris began trading (on the present Place du Châtelet). Under King Phillip II Augustus, there were about 18 shops

and butchers obtained a permit from the king granting them the right to own their stalls in perpetuity. Thus was formed the rich and powerful butchers' guild, which, dominated for a long time by a few families, wielded considerable political power. Charles VI tried to limit the power of the butchers, who had taken the side of the Bourguignons against the Armagnacs and in 1416 the guild was dissolved, its privileges revoked and its shops destroyed. But it reformed a few years later. Philip the Bold had authorized the butchers to sell fish as well as meat, but they later lost this right and also had to abandon the pork trade to pork butchers. Statutes recorded in 1589 laid down the rights and obligations of butchers until 1789. These obliged them to own scales and sell meat by weight, not by guesswork as had previously been the practice.

Until abattoirs were set up under Napoleon I, the Grande-Boucherie quarter, around the Châtelet, remained a dreadful place: 'Blood flows in the streets and congeals under the feet' wrote Mercier in 1783. In his *Dictionnaire des rues de Paris*, Hillairet mentions the Rue de la Triperie ('Tripe Street'), previously known as Rue de l'Araigne ('Spider Street') after the four-pronged hook from which meat was hung in the open air; Rue Pierre-à-Poisson ('Fish Stone Street'), which alludes to the butchers' right to sell fish; Rue de la Tuerie ('Slaughterhouse Street'); Rue de l'Écorcherie ('Knacker's Yard Street'); and the Vallée de la Misère ('Vale of Tears'), the site of an open-air market that sold poultry, game, lamb, and goat as well as butter, eggs, and milk (in the former Paris meat market – Les Halles – the Vallée was the poultry and game section).

The traditions of the butchers' guild persisted until the Revolution. The feast day of their patron saint, St Nicholas, was celebrated on 6 December. Butchers were traditionally close to the religious authorities (until fairly recently, butchers' shops were closed on Fridays). Those aspiring to the title of master butcher had to give a candle and an egg cake to the head of the guild and four pieces of meat to his wife. Another important ceremony for Parisian butchers was the Fat Beef Procession, held at carnival time, just before Lent. A magnificent ox, decorated with ribbons and given a name that was often inspired by popular contemporary literature (for example, Monte Cristo or Wandering Jew), was paraded with great pomp through the streets of the capital. The tradition was maintained until the Second Empire.

Napoleon reorganized the profession by limiting the number of butchers' shops in Paris, but this measure was rescinded in 1863.

□ **The modern butcher's shop** Today, the butcher's profession remains one in which trade is combined with craftsmanship. Butchers can be wholesalers or retailers; some still buy animals on the hoof, slaughter them, cut them up, and sell the meat and offal. However, nowadays most retailers buy the meat they require directly from the abattoirs, either whole carcasses or special pieces ready to cut up for their customers.

The product that is bought by the consumer is the result of several operations, such as cutting, boning, cleaning, tying-up, larding, and stuffing. Many of these stages are carried out on the wooden butcher's block or table, cut across the grain of the wood to give more strength; however, more hygienic working surfaces made of strong plastic are increasingly being used. The butcher's tools have hardly changed since the very beginning: larding needles, cleavers, choppers, mallets, and knives and saws for boning, cleaning, and slicing; blades are nowadays made of durable tungsten steel. Serving tables, which are traditionally made of marble, are always white and often decorated with greenery to emphasize the red meat. The butcher does not have to wear a uniform but is usually dressed in white. In theory the wearing of a hat is compulsory. Legislation now ensures proper standards of sanitation in all areas of the trade, including cutting rooms, transportation vehicles, and cold stores, while refrigerated window displays help keep food fresh.

□ **Supermarket meat departments** Supermarkets and hypermarkets, which have developed over the last 20 years, now market 40% of retail meat. Although the methods of supply, cutting, and preparation are borrowed directly from the traditional trade, the method of selling is usually self-service and the meat is plastic-wrapped. The preparation and packaging are sometimes done in the sight of customers and, again, standards are strictly monitored by health officials.

butter BEURRE

A fatty substance obtained from churned cream, containing at least 80% fat, 2% milk solids, and not more than 16% water. It is washed and blended to make it smooth. Butter hardens at low temperatures and melts when heated. The colour varies from creamy white to golden yellow, according to the diet of the dairy cows (a pasture rich in carotene gives the yellow colour).

□ **The history of butter** Butter was known in ancient times and was introduced to the Greeks by the Scythians. Herodotus, quoted by Montesquieu, spoke of the Scythians who 'poked out the eyes of their slaves so that nothing would distract them from churning their milk'. The Greeks and Romans, however, used it mainly as a remedy (particularly for healing wounds) and relied almost entirely on oil for cooking purposes. Butter was produced by the Gauls, but it was the Normans, using knowledge acquired from the Danes, who firmly established the reputation of this product in their own country. By the Middle Ages, the small-scale local production of butter had become widespread. Large pats of butter, sometimes wrapped in leaves of sorrel or herbs, were sold at the markets and stored in earthenware pots covered in salt water. Colouring (with marigold flowers) was prohibited, as was selling butter on a fish stall. Butter was not supposed to be eaten during Lent, but a dispensation could be obtained by making a contribution to the 'butter chest'.

□ **Butter and dietetics** Butter is a very rich natural food with a high energy value (750 Cal per 100 g, which is less than oil or lard); it is a saturated fat containing vitamins A and D, calcium, and phosphorus (lighter butters are now on the market with 25% fat content). It decomposes at 120–130 c (250–260 f) releasing acrolein, an indigestible toxic substance which increases the cholesterol content. For a healthy diet, the recommended intake is 15–30 g (½–1¼ oz) per day.

☐ **Alternative butters** In Europe, butter is made exclusively from cows' milk, but in Africa and Asia the milk of the buffalo, camel, goat, ewe, mare, and donkey is used to manufacture butters with a very strong flavour.

The food industry has produced various butter substitutes. The best known of these is margarine, but various other 'spreading' products are available, many of which have a lower calorific value than butter and margarine.

☐ **Butter manufacture in France** The milk is skimmed, then the cream is pasteurized and placed in a maturation tank with selected yeasts (these give the butter its aroma). The cream is then churned so that globules of fat form and the buttermilk is eliminated. The butter is then washed and blended. Traditionally, the various stages of manufacture are performed in separate machines, but the whole process may be performed continuously in a butyrator. Various additives are permitted: antioxidant (ascorbic acid), deoxidizer (bicarbonate of soda), salt (sodium chloride), and colouring agents (roucou or carotene). At room temperature, good butter should not be brittle, lumpy, or sticky and should not sweat droplets of water; it should have a faintly fresh aromatic scent and a delicate nutty flavour.

Butter is usually packaged in 500-g, 250-g, or 125-g (1-lb, ½-lb, or ¼-lb) rolls or slabs and in individual portions of 7–30 g (¼–1¼ oz). It is wrapped in greaseproof or foil-lined paper or sealed in wax-coated cardboard pots or plastic boxes. Butter can also be sold in cans, mainly in tropical regions.

It is very easy to keep butter fresh in the refrigerator: the butter is placed in a special compartment or airtight butter dish because it readily absorbs odours. If a refrigerator is not available, a special earthenware butter container filled with salt water is necessary, especially in warmer climates. If left exposed to the light and air it will oxidize and become rancid. Salted butter keeps longer as the salt acts as a preservative.

☐ **Labels** There are two main types of butter to choose from: 'sweet cream' and 'lactic butter'. The sweet cream varieties, which are most common, are manufactured using pasteurized cream to which salt is added to give a longer shelf life. They have a mild and delicate flavour and keep well in the refrigerator for up to six weeks.

Lactic butter is made from cream that has been allowed to ripen under special conditions, giving the butter its distinctive full flavour and smooth texture. This type of butter is traditionally made in the Netherlands and Denmark and exported worldwide.

• *Farmhouse butter* – Manufactured on the farm with untreated (i.e. unpasteurized and naturally matured) cream. Prepared in the area of origin under strict conditions of hygiene, it is delicious but uncommon. It can be kept for a week in the refrigerator or it may be frozen, well wrapped, for up to three months.

• *Pasteurized butter* – Factory-produced and officially monitored, it has a fresh uniform taste (the milk is recultured with commercial fermenting agents); the labels 'fine' or 'superfine' have no legal value. Pasteurized butter will keep for up to one month in the refrigerator.

• *Dairy butter* – Pasteurized butter whose taste is not considered pure enough to deserve Ministry of Agriculture approval; called 'table butter' or 'cooking butter' (these names have no legal value), it does not keep as well as pasteurized butter.

• *Sweet butter* – Prepared using cream with low acidity; fragile and still uncommon on the open market, it is fine and delicate but does not keep well.

• *EEC butter* – Dairy butter purchased by the government during periods of over-production, deep-frozen for not more than one year, and placed on the market in periods of high demand at prices lower than that of the cheapest butter. It does not keep for more than one week.

• *Imported butter* – Imported from Denmark or the Netherlands, this butter is of uniform quality and often whiter than ordinary butter (the country of origin must be shown).

• *Restored butter* – Produced from poor-quality cream, reblended with bicarbonate of soda for deacidification; rare on the general market.

• *Salted butter* – Contains 1.5–2 g salt per 100 g butter. It enhances the taste and texture of foods when used for cooking and R. Oliver, talking about Échiré salted butter, considers that 'salt develops subtle and appreciable aromas in the whey of the butter'.

• *Regional butter* – Produced solely in its region using cream from the local dairy cows. Each region's butter has its own distinctive flavour, texture, and colour due to the quality of the pastures.

• *Concentrated* (or *cooking*) *butter* – Ordinary butter with the water, salt, and nonfat milk solids extracted from it; contains 96% butterfat. It has a firm texture and – due to the low moisture content – is excellent for shallow frying, braising, sautéing, as it does not decompose at high temperatures. It is used mainly for baking but recipes may have to be adapted by slightly increasing the liquid and salt content. Covered, it keeps well in the refrigerator for up to six months and freezes well for long periods.

□ **Butter in cooking** Butter is a good basic cooking ingredient, giving a delicious flavour to the preparations in which it is included. It is used for grilling (broiling), shallow frying, braising, and sautéing, but requires more care than oil or lard since it burns more easily. To help prevent this, a little oil may be added to the pan and the preparation is cooked over a low heat; alternatively, concentrated butter may be used, as it does not spit or burn at such low temperatures. Butter is essential for hot emulsified sauces (e.g. béarnaise and hollandaise), for roux and soups, and for binding sauces. It gives extra flavour to cakes and pastries (qualified as 'all butter' when butter is the only fat used), particularly brioches, croissants, sablés, sponge cakes, choux pastry, biscuits (cookies), and butter creams. Melted butter, applied with a brush to moulds, tins, etc., helps prevent food from sticking. Butter is also used extensively in confectionery.

Butter can be prepared in various ways, either plain or flavoured, for serving with grilled (broiled) meat or fish, boiled vegetables, rice, etc.

• **Flavoured butters** These are butters to which various herbs and other ingredients have been added, creating different colours and flavours. They are also known as compound butters or *beurres composés*. Flavoured butters are served cold with grilled meat and fish, boiled vegetables, etc., and are used in the preparation of allumettes, canapés, etc.; hot butters are used particularly for providing the finishing touch to certain sauces.

Butters that are prepared hot are flavoured with crushed crustacean shells (lobster for cardinal butter, crayfish for Nantua butter, etc.). Most flavoured butters are prepared cold, using raw or cooked ingredients. Raw ingredients (anchovy, garlic, shallot, tarragon, horseradish, etc.) are rubbed through a sieve, crushed, chopped, finely grated, or puréed. Cooked ingredients are always cooked in liquid until well reduced (for example, blanched shallots are reduced with white wine).

When accompanying grilled meat or fish, flavoured butter of a creamy consistency is served separately. Alternatively, it may be shaped into a small cylinder, wrapped in greaseproof (waxed) paper or aluminium foil, and hardened in the refrigerator. It is then unwrapped and cut into slices 1 cm (½ in) thick, which are placed on top of the meat or fish. These slices may also be kept in a container with water and ice cubes to retain their shape and appearance.

□ **Useful hints**

• Very cold grated butter is more easily incorporated in pastry (dough).

• Sweetened butter for pastries keeps even better than salted butter (mix with 20–25% caster (superfine) sugar).

• Sizzling butter will not spit if salt has previously been put in the frying pan (skillet) and a low heat is used.

• Clarify butter by melting it, then leaving it to stand in a bowl to cool. Skim off the pure fat for cooking, leaving the solids and water behind.

• To help prevent foaming and scum forming on jam (jelly) and skin forming on sweet sauces, add a piece of butter after cooking.

RECIPES

FLAVOURED BUTTERS

Preparation of flavoured butter PRÉPARATION DU BEURRE COMPOSÉ

Whatever the ingredients, the butter must first be creamed, using either a wooden spoon or (for large quantities) an electric mixer. The following recipes give ingredients for 250 g (½ lb, 1 cup) flavoured butter.

Almond butter BEURRE D'AMANDES Blanch 125 g (4 oz, 1 cup) sweet almonds and reduce to a paste using a mortar or mixer, adding 1 tablespoon cold water. Add to the softened butter and sieve. Very fresh ground almonds can also be used. This butter is used in the preparation of petits fours and cakes. Walnut butter is prepared in the same way.

Anchovy butter BEURRE D'AN-CHOIS Soak 125 g (4 oz) anchovies to remove the salt. Purée the fillets, either with a pestle and mortar or in an electric mixer. Season and, if desired, add a dash of lemon juice and mix with the softened butter. This butter is used for vols-au-vent, canapés, and hors d'oeuvres and to accompany grilled (broiled) meat and fish or cold white meat.

Crab or **prawn butter** BEURRE DE CRABE OU DE CREVETTES Finely pound in a mortar or blender 250 g (8 oz, 1½ cups) peeled prawns (shelled shrimp) or crabmeat (cooked in court-bouillon and with all cartilage removed). This butter is used to garnish canapés, cold fish, or hors d'oeuvres and to complete fish and shellfish sauces.

Garlic butter BEURRE D'AIL Peel 8 large cloves of garlic and plunge in boiling salted water. Boil for 7–8 minutes, dry, and purée. Add to the softened butter. Garlic butter is used to complete some sauces and adds the final touch to garnishes for cold hors d'oeuvres.

Green butter BEURRE VERT Wring 1 kg (2 lb) raw crushed spinach in a cloth until all the juice is extracted. Pour this juice into a dish and cook in a bain-marie until separated, then filter through another cloth. Scrape off the green deposit left on this cloth and add it to the softened butter; rub through a fine sieve. This butter is used to garnish hors d'oeuvres and cold dishes.

Hazelnut butter BEURRE DE NOI-SETTES Lightly grill (broil) some hazelnuts and continue as for almond butter. The uses are the same.

Horseradish butter BEURRE DE RAIFORT Grate 100 g (4 oz) horseradish and purée with a pestle and mortar or in a blender. Add to the softened butter and sieve. It is used in the same way as garlic butter.

Hôtelier butter BEURRE HÔTELIER Add to softened butter an equal quantity of chopped parsley, lemon juice, and mushroom duxelles. This butter is served with fish and grilled (broiled) meat.

Lemon butter BEURRE DE CITRON Blanch the zest of a lemon, chop as finely as possible, and add to the softened butter with a dash of lemon juice, salt, and pepper. This butter is used to garnish cold hors d'oeuvres.

Lobster butter BEURRE DE HOMARD This is prepared in the same way as prawn butter using the meat, shell, and eggs of the lobster cooked in court-bouillon. It is used for the same purposes.

Montpellier butter BEURRE DE MONTPELLIER Blanch 10 g (½ oz) parsley leaves, 10 g (½ oz) chervil leaves, 10 g (½ oz) cress leaves, 10 g (½ oz) spinach, and 20 g (¾ oz) shallots in salted water. Rinse in cold water and drain thoroughly. Blend with a gherkin, a small clove of garlic, and a hard-boiled (hard-cooked) egg. Add this mixture to the softened butter and season with salt and pepper. Montpellier butter is served with large cold fish. It is sometimes softened by adding a very fresh raw egg yolk and 80 ml (4 tablespoons, ⅓ cup) olive oil.

Mustard butter BEURRE DE MOUTARDE Add 2 tablespoons (3 tablespoons) tarragon mustard to the softened butter and season with salt and pepper. A hard-boiled (hard-cooked) egg yolk, some chopped herbs, and a dash of lemon juice may also be added. Uses are the same as for anchovy butter.

Pepper butter BEURRE DE PIMENT Remove the seeds from a large green or red pepper, dice, and cook very gently in butter until it is soft enough to be puréed. Add the puréed pepper to the softened butter, season with salt and pepper, add a pinch of cayenne, and sieve. Pepper butter is used to finish some sauces or garnish hors d'oeuvres.

Roquefort butter BEURRE DE ROQUEFORT Purée 150 g (5 oz) Roquefort cheese with 1 tablespoon Cognac or white brandy and 2 teaspoons white mustard (optional). Add to the softened butter. This butter is used to garnish canapés, vols-au-vent, and puff pastries or served with raw vegetables.

Sardine butter BEURRE DE SARDINES Prepare with trimmed sardines in the same way as anchovy butter. The uses are the same. Herring butter, smoked salmon butter, or tuna butter can also be prepared in this way.

Shallot butter BEURRE D'ÉCHALOTE Peel 150 g (5 oz) shallots and chop finely. Blanch for 2–3 minutes in boiling water, dry, and pound with a pestle and mortar or purée in a blender. Add to 150 g (5 oz, good ½ cup) softened butter. Season with salt and pepper. This butter is mainly served with grilled (broiled) fish and meat.

Soft-roe butter BEURRE DE LAITANCES Using a sieve or mixer, purée 150 g (5 oz) soft roe of pickled herring or poached carp (the roe should first be cooled and drained). Add to the softened butter and season with salt and pepper. This butter is added to some sauces for grilled (broiled) or poached fish.

Tarragon butter BEURRE D'ESTRAGON This is prepared in the same way as watercress butter and is used to finish sauces or garnish cold hors d'oeuvres.

Watercress butter BEURRE DE CRESSON Blanch 150 g (5 oz) watercress leaves, soak in cold water, and dry. Add the finely puréed leaves to the softened butter and season with salt and pepper. Watercress butter is used principally for canapés and sandwiches.

PLAIN BUTTERS AND BUTTER SAUCES

Black butter BEURRE NOIR This recipe for black butter is a very old one, dating from the 16th cnetury.

Cook some butter in a frying pan (skillet) until dark brown in colour. Add capers and chopped parsley, together with a little vinegar which is warmed through in the same pan.

Black butter was formerly an essential accompaniment to skate poached in stock.

Clarified butter BEURRE CLARIFIÉ Melt some butter gently in a thick-bottomed saucepan; do not stir. Remove the scum with a spoon then carefully pour the butter into another container so that the whitish sediment stays in the pan. Clarified butter is used particularly for emulsified sauces.

Creamed butter BEURRE MOUSSEUX Cream the butter in a warm earthenware container, carefully adding lemon juice and a little cold water. Serve with fish in court-bouillon and Vichy carrots.

Grilled butter BEURRE À LA BROCHE Beat 250 g (½ lb, 1 cup) butter until creamy in texture and add some chopped chervil, tarragon, and chives, and some lemon juice. Roll into the shape of a fat cigar, spear on a wooden stick, and allow to cool in the refrigerator; when the block of butter is quite set, coat with fresh breadcrumbs 3 times so that it is completely covered with a fairly thick layer. Cook under a hot grill, sprinkling with melted butter, for 8–10 minutes, turning regularly so that the crust is well coloured. Serve immediately. This unusual way of serving melted butter with poached or grilled (broiled) fish or boiled or steamed vegetables was formerly very popular but is now little used.

Kneaded butter BEURRE MANIÉ Mix together equal amounts of softened butter and flour (soften the butter with a fork to incorporate the flour). Kneaded butter is used to thicken stews and sauces. It is added in small knobs to the boiling liquid, which is then whisked until the butter melts and the sauce thickens.

Landais butter BEURRE LANDAIS
Roll small balls of butter in bread-crumbs until thickly and evenly coated, then cook under a hot grill to form a golden crust. Serve with grilled (broiled) meat and fish.

Melted butter BEURRE FONDU
Melt the butter very gently in a thick-bottomed saucepan with lemon juice, salt, and white pepper. This butter is used with poached fish or steamed or boiled vegetables.

Noisette butter BEURRE NOISETTE
Gently heat some butter in a frying pan (skillet) until it is golden and gives off a nutty smell. Serve scalding hot with lambs' or calves' sweetbreads, fish roe, vegetables (boiled and well drained), eggs, skate poached in stock, etc. Noisette butter is known as meunière butter when lemon juice is added.

butter dish BEURRIER

A container for keeping butter or serving it at the table. For storage it must have a lid since fresh butter is particularly delicate and readily absorbs smells. Butter dishes are usually made of plastic, glass, pottery, or stainless steel. Table butter dishes, which sometimes do not have lids, are usually individual containers (made of porcelain, silver plate, or stainless steel according to the style of the table setting) and are used for serving butter with certain cold hors d'oeuvre, shellfish, and cheese (flavoured butters are usually served in a sauceboat or a small dish).

Formerly, butter had to be stored either submerged in salted water or in a glass container placed in a double porous earthenware bell into which water was poured daily. Refrigerators removed these restrictions: they are usually fitted with a special compartment to prevent the butter becoming too hard and to protect it from smells.

buttermilk BABEURRE

A slightly sour whitish liquid obtained after churning cream. Rich in nitrogen and lactose but poor in lipids, buttermilk was once recommended for feeding children and was used for making soups. It is still a popular drink in Scandinavian countries. In France it is used commercially as an emulsifier (in bread, pastries, desserts, and ice creams). In some countries it is used in cheese making.

buvette

Under the Ancien Régime, a buvette was a small bar set up within the precincts of the courts of law where judges and lawyers could take light refreshments between sessions. The word has retained this meaning in the case of the Buvette de l'Assemblée nationale. Nowadays a buvette is a small bar in a station, theatre, or public garden. It can also serve ice creams, sandwiches, or sweets. In a spa, the buvette is the place where people drink the waters.

Cabardès

French red and rosé wines produced in the region of the Aude, to the north of Carcassonne, by a vineyard next to those of the Minervois. The varieties of vine from which these wines are made include Grenache Noir, Cinsault, Carignan, Cabernet Sauvignon, Merlot, etc. In 1973 they were granted the VDQS label. Fine wines with a good bouquet, Cabardès, Côtes-du-Cabardès, and Côtes-de-l'Orbiel are good to drink with grilled (broiled) dishes, roast pork, kidneys, and calf's liver.

cabaret (establishment)

The modern cabaret, a nightclub or restaurant with a floor show, has little in common with the original French cabaret, which until the end of the 19th century was a modest bar serving mainly wine.

Before the 17th century, there was a clear distinction in France between the taverne and the cabaret. Originally, the novelty of the cabaret consisted of selling wine à l'assiette, i.e. serving it on a table at which the customer could sit and possibly have something to eat. If the cabaret proprietor did not have permission to do this, the wine was sold au pot (by the jug).

King Henri IV reorganized the wine retailers as follows: (1) Wine merchants selling wine by the jug did so without having a taverne – an opening was made in the outer grille of the shop, through which the purchaser would pass his jug. (2) Tavern-keepers sold drinks in a place arranged for this purpose. (3) Proprietors of cabarets served not only drinks, but also food – they had permission to provide nappe et assiette (tablecloth and plate) service. Both tavern-keepers and proprietors of cabarets employed criers to go through the streets announcing the price of the wine.

In the 13th century, among the first cabarets were the Trois Mailletz, frequented by scholars from the Sorbonne who were extremely rowdy, according to the priests of Saint-Séverin, and the Pomme de Pin. In the course of the following centuries, the best-known cabarets were the Sabot (Saint-Marcel district), where Ronsard was a frequent customer, and the Écu d'Argent (near the Place Maubert), where Ménage was said to have set up in residence. The Épée de Bois and the Mouton Blanc (in the Rue de la Verrerie) were the meeting places of La Fontaine, Boileau, and Racine (who wrote Les Plaideurs there). Cabarets thus became fashionable in the

17th century and were frequented, in particular, by writers and artists, who later patronized the cafés, restaurants, and brasseries. In the 19th century, low-class cabarets again attracted the Romantics. Some of them were squalid hovels, like those described by Eugène Sue in *Les Mystères de Paris*. It was at the gate of one such cabaret – the Chat Blanc – that the body of Gérard de Nerval was found hanging.

The etymology of the word has given rise to various interpretations. Possible roots are the Hebrew word *cabar* (to meet), the Celtic words *cab* (head) and *aret* (ram – an animal sacrificed to Bacchus), the Latin *cabare* (to dig, to make a cellar), the Arabic *khamarat* (a place where drinks are sold), and, more recently, the Dutch *cabret*, itself derived from the old Picardy word *cambrette*, meaning 'little room'.

cabaret (furniture)

A pedestal table or a tray with legs from which tea, coffee, chocolate, or liqueurs may be served. The top may either be lacquered or made of marble. The word may also be used to describe a liqueur set used with such an item of furniture. The cabaret originated in the Far East, and appeared in France towards the end of the 17th century. Around 1900, it was used mainly as a tea trolley.

cabassol

A stew made from sheeps' heads simmered in white wine. It is a speciality of Albi in Languedoc (in this region *cabassol* means 'head'). At Réquista (Aveyron) there is a Cabassol Club, where it is customary to eat the stew on Shrove Tuesday. The tongue, brains, cheeks, and ears are considered to be delicacies. At Lodève near Hérault, cabassol is made with lambs' feet, heads, and mesentery (intestinal membranes), cooked with ham and knuckle of veal. It is served with vinaigrette and a purée of lambs' brains. Sometimes, it is eaten with stockpot vegetables and herbs. In Rouergue, cabassol is simply a lamb stock.

cabbage CHOU

A widely cultivated vegetable of the family Cruciferae. Wild cabbage, from which all the cultivated varieties are derived, is a perennial with broad thick curly leaves, growing in coastal regions of western Europe. Known for over 4000 years in Europe, it was at first valued for its medicinal properties but later was used as food, particularly as a basis for soups. Through cultivation and selection, white, green, and red varieties of cabbage were produced, as well as many other brassicas – Brussels sprouts, cauliflower, broccoli, etc.

The different varieties of full-hearted cabbage are distinguished by their colour (white, green, or red), their shape (rounded for winter cabbages, pointed for spring cabbages), and the texture of their leaves (crinkly (in Savoy cabbages) or smooth). Although low in calories, cabbage is rich in mineral salts and vitamins (especially when raw). Ideally, it should have crisp shiny leaves and a dense heart. It keeps badly. Cabbage is included in numerous garnishes (*à la flamande, à l'auvergnate, à la berrichonne, à la strasbourgeoise*, etc.) and can be prepared in many ways. It is used as a base for soups, stews, and stuffings. White and red cabbage predominate in cookery of eastern and northern Europe, while green cabbage is more popular in the west and south.

RECIPES

GREEN OR WHITE CABBAGE

Braised cabbage CHOU BRAISÉ Prepare a cabbage, blanch, drain, cool in cold water, and drain once again. Separate the leaves and discard the large ribs. Scrape and dice a carrot. Line a flameproof casserole with bacon rinds stripped of half their fat and add the diced carrot, then the cabbage, forming a heap. Add salt, pepper, a little grated nutmeg, an onion stuck with a clove, and a bouquet garni. Two thirds cover the cabbage with stock and put a very thin strip of bacon on top. Cover and bring to the boil over a ring. Then place the casserole in a moderate oven (180 C, 350 F, gas 4) and cook for about 1½ hours.

Cabbage à l'anglaise CHOU À L'ANGLAISE Remove any withered outer leaves, cut the cabbage into quarters, and remove the hard inner stalk. Blanch the quarters in plenty of boiling water for 5 minutes, drain, then plunge again into salted boiling water until cooked: the leaves should be very supple. Drain the cabbage, then press it hard between two plates; cut the resulting slab into even-sized pieces, lay the pieces on a dish, and serve with melted butter. The cabbage pieces may alternatively be arranged around meat and basted with the meat juices and with melted butter.

Green-cabbage salad SALADE DE CHOU VERT Remove any withered outer leaves, cut the cabbage into four, and blanch for about 12 minutes in boiling salted water. Drain, cool, and wipe. Cut the quarters into a julienne and season with a well-spiced vinaigrette. Sprinkle with chopped herbs or finely shredded spring onions (scallions).

Paupiettes of cabbage PAUPIETTES DE CHOU Blanch a whole cabbage for 7–8 minutes in boiling salted water, then drain and cool it. Pull off the large outer leaves, removing the tougher ribs. Chop the leaves from the central heart and to them add an equal volume of forcemeat. Make paupiettes by rolling this mixture in the large leaves, using 1 tablespoon per leaf; tie them up with kitchen thread. Braise as for stuffed cabbage, but reduce the cooking time to 1¼ hours. These paupiettes form a perfect garnish for braised meat.

Stuffed cabbage CHOU FARCI Blanch a whole cabbage in salted boiling water for 7–8 minutes, cool it in cold water, drain, and remove the stump (core). Moisten a piece of fine cloth or muslin (cheesecloth), wring it out, and lay it on the working surface. On top of the cloth lay four lengths of kitchen thread to form a star shape. Place the cabbage in the centre of the crossed threads and open out the larger leaves one by one. Remove the central heart, chop, and mix with an equal volume of fine well-seasoned pork forcemeat. Fill the centre of the cabbage with the mixture, then fold back the large leaves to recreate the original shape. On top place two very thin strips of fat bacon in a

cross and secure them by knotting the threads over them. Wrap the cabbage in the cloth and tie it up.

Line a flameproof casserole with bacon rinds stripped of half their fat, together with 100 g (4 oz) bacon, 150 g (5 oz) carrots, and 150 g (5 oz) finely diced onion. Put the cabbage on top and barely cover it with rich stock. Cover, bring to the boil over a ring, then cook in a moderately hot oven (about 200 c, 400 f, gas 6) for 1½ hours. Drain the cabbage, unwrap it, and remove the strips of fat bacon. (Alternatively, the cabbage may be prepared and cooked in a net without the strips of bacon.) Serve the cabbage in a deep dish, keeping it hot, and coat with the cooking juices, reduced by half.

RED CABBAGE

Pickled red cabbage CHOU ROUGE MARINÉ Prepare the cabbage, cut it into quarters, remove and discard the large ribs, then cut it into strips. Place in a large basin, sprinkle with a generous tablespoon of fine salt, and mix. Cover and leave for at least 48 hours in a cool place, turning over several times. Drain the cabbage and arrange it in layers in an earthenware jar, inserting between each layer 4–5 peppercorns, 3 small pieces of bay leaf, and half a clove of garlic, chopped. Boil enough red wine vinegar to cover the cabbage, leave to cool, then cover the cabbage with it. Seal the jar and leave to marinate for at least 36 hours. It can be served in various hors d'oeuvres or as a condiment with cold beef or pork.

Red cabbage à la flamande CHOU ROUGE À LA FLAMANDE Remove any withered leaves, slice off the stump (core) at the base of the leaves, ard cut the cabbage into four, then into thin strips. Wash and dry. Melt 40 g (1½ oz, 3 tablespoons) butter in a saucepan, add the cabbage, sprinkle with salt and pepper, moisten with 1 tablespoon vinegar, cover, and cook over a gentle heat. Meanwhile, peel 3 or 4 tart apples, cut them into quarters, remove the core, and slice them finely. Add them to the cabbage after 1 hour of cooking, sprinkle with 1 tablespoon brown sugar (coffee sugar), replace the lid, and cook

description	preparation	cooking	uses
White cabbage • June to February (northeast France and Holland): – round cabbage with very compact leaves. 'Yellow' cabbage is closely related.	Remove the stalk, cut into quarters, and prepare like green cabbage.	• Blanch for 10 minutes before cooking.	• Raw: finely chopped in salad (possibly using coarse salt to bring out the juice). • Poached in water: for purées, soups, or stews. • Braised (in European and oriental cookery). • Used for sauerkraut (*quintal d'Alsace*).
Green cabbage – October to March: – Savoy cabbage, with curly or crinkly leaves, dark green on the outside; Pontoise winter cabbage, excellent quality but takes longer to cook, except those picked after the first frosts. • May and June: – cabbage without much heart but pointed, called 'bullock's heart' (Nantes cabbage, *bacalan*); good quality. • July and August: – full-hearted pointed cabbage (Louviers); good quality. • July to October: – large round summer Savoy; full of flavour. • September and October: – autumn Savoy, pointed, very crinkly leaves, excellent quality (called 'Scotch kale').	– Discard the outer leaves, remove end of stalk, cut into quarters and remove the inside of the stalk without separating the leaves too much. – Wash in water to which vinegar has been added to remove any earth or insects. – Wash whole if the cabbage is to be stuffed, carefully separating the leaves and sprinkling them with vinegar.	• Blanch for 5–10 minutes in salted boiling water, drain, and rinse in cold water. • Second cooking: – boiled or steamed (20–30 minutes); – braised in an ovenproof dish (1½–2 hours); – stuffed or in a stew (2–2½ hours). Spring cabbage does not need to be blanched.	• Spring cabbage: poached (very occasionally braised). • Summer cabbage: mainly stuffed. • Autumn cabbage: braised (accompanies game). • Winter cabbage: braised, stuffed, or in stews.
Red cabbage • Practically all the year round, from northern Europe (Langedijk); – headed cabbage with a beautiful purple-tinted red colour.	As for green cabbage; chop finely, cutting the slices lengthways.	• Poach for 5–10 minutes before cooking. • Braising: 1½–2 hours (season with a little vinegar and sugar or add a dessert apple). • If the cabbage is eaten raw, use coarse salt to bring out the juice and rinse. Season and leave to marinate for an hour.	• Raw: finely chopped in salad (may be mixed with white cabbage and marinated in vinegar). • Cooked: – in stock or white or red wine; – braised in fat or lightly browned in lard, with chestnuts and apples; – accompanies fatty meats, game, and duck.

for a further 20 minutes. Serve to accompany boiled pork or boiled or braised beef.

Red-cabbage salad SALADE DE CHOU ROUGE Select a very fresh and tender red cabbage (break off a large leaf to test it), remove the large outer leaves, cut the cabbage into four, and remove the white centre. Slice the quarters into fine strips, about ½ cm (¼ in) wide, blanch them for 5 minutes in boiling water, then cool and wipe them. Place in a salad bowl, sprinkle with 2 dl (7 fl oz, ¾ cup) boiling red wine vinegar, mix, cover, and leave to marinate for 5–6 hours. Drain the cabbage and season it with salt, pepper, and oil. (Although unblanched red cabbage looks more attractive, it is more difficult to digest.)

Cabécou

A small soft French cheese (45% fat content) from Quercy and Rouergue, made from a mixture of goats' milk, ewes' milk, and cows' milk. (The literal meaning of the word is 'little goat'.) It is a fairly firm ivory-white cheese with a fine bluish crust and a nutty flavour. The main varieties of Cabécou are Cahors, Gramat, Entraygues, Livernon, Rocamadour, and Gourdon, all in season from April to November. Some of the cheeses are wrapped in vine leaves and stored in a jar with vinegar. They are eaten when they turn pink. In Quercy, the cheese is soaked in plum brandy.

Cabernet

One of the great black wine grapes of the world, grown both in France and many other countries. There are two main types.
• *Cabernet Franc* yields well in many regions. It has long bunches of small bluish grapes, which make a brilliant vibrant-toned wine, straightforward in flavour though sometimes a little lacking in bouquet. It is one of the basic grapes of the Bordeaux region, used in conjunction with the Cabernet Sauvignon, the Merlot, and the Malbec. In the Loire Valley it is used on its own and makes fine wines, such as Chinon, Bourgueil, and Saumur-Champigny.
• *Cabernet Sauvignon* is the principal grape of red Bordeaux. It flourishes on barren soil and has a dark blue fruit with a thick skin. The wine it makes is rich in tannin and with great depth, being hard in youth but softening with maturity. If made by itself, it is rather firm and austere in style, but it is the backbone and power behind the great clarets, being present up to 75% in the Mouton-Rothschild vineyard. It combines with other vines of breeding to compose the aristocrats of the cellar.

cabessal (en)

A method of preparing stuffed hare, which is tied up with string so that it forms a round and can be cooked in a circular dish. It is then said to be *en cabessal*. The method originated in the regions of Limousin and Périgord. A *cabessal* (or *chabessal*) is also a French dialect word for the twisted cloth that women wore on their heads to carry a pitcher of water.

RECIPE

Hare en cabessal LIÈVRE EN CABESSAL Skin and gut a hare, reserving the liver and blood. Pound the liver with a clove of garlic, then add the blood and 1 tablespoon vinegar. On the day before cooking, place the hare in a marinade of red wine, oil, carrots, thinly sliced onions and shallots, thyme, a bay leaf, a clove, salt, and pepper. Prepare a stuffing with 500 g (18 oz) fillet of veal, 250 g (9 oz) raw ham, 250 g (9 oz) fresh pork, 2 cloves of garlic, and 2 shallots. Chop the ingredients finely, season with salt and pepper, and bind with an egg. Remove the hare from the marinade, wipe, and stuff.

Sew up the opening in the belly. Bard the hare all over with larding bacon, then tie it with string so that it forms a round. Place it in a round dish with a little goose or pork grease, some pieces of larding bacon, and a few small onions. Add a small glass of brandy and a bottle of good-quality red or white wine, then a roux made with flour and goose grease. Cover the dish and cook in a slow oven and evenly for 4 or 5 hours. When three-quarters cooked, add the pounded liver and blood. Check the seasoning. When cooking is complete, the sauce should be substantially reduced.

When serving, remove the string, the larding bacon, and the bones (which should come away easily from the flesh). Serve with croutons of bread fried in goose grease, which may be rubbed with garlic if desired.

cabinet particulier

A private room placed at the disposal of customers by certain de luxe restaurants. They were very fashionable in Paris under the Second Empire and during the Belle Époque in such establishments as the Café Anglais, the Café de Prunier, and the Café de Lapérouse.

caboulot

A small French suburban or country café, or a small modest restaurant that permits dancing. The term appeared in 1852, being a Franche-Comté word meaning 'hut', 'small room'. It is described as a popular meeting place in a song by Francis Carco.

Cachat

A small white cylindrical Provençal cheese made from either ewes' or goats' milk (45% fat content), with a texture resembling cream cheese and no crust. It has a mild flavour that goes well with the local wines and is made mainly in the areas of Entrechaux and Malaucène. It is also used as the basis of the stronger Mont Ventoux cheese, which is mixed with flavourings and preserved in small pots.

Caciocavallo

An Italian cheese made from cows' milk (44% fat content) and often smoked. It is compact and straw-coloured with a pale fine oily crust. It is moulded into the shape of a narrow gourd with a smaller swelling on top and wieghs 3–4 kg (6½ –9 lb). Its name, a combination of the Italian words *cacio* (cheese) and *cavallo* (horse), could come from the fact that the ripening cheeses are tied together in pairs with wisps of straw, and hung on sticks (*à cheval*, i.e. mounted) to dry. Another possibility is that it was named after the seal of the kingdom of Naples, which depicted a galloping horse and was imprinted on the cheese in the 14th century. It is also possible that it was so named because Caciocavallo was originally made with mares' milk.

Today, the best Caciocavallo still comes from southern Italy. It is usually eaten at the end of a meal. If it is matured for a long period, it becomes very hard and is then grated before it is used.

cadenas

A box with a lock in which the royal cutlery, napkins, etc., were kept. It was used in the Middle Ages, and was also known as the *nef*. It was often boat-shaped and made of precious metal, enamelled and decorated with jewels. As well as holding the king's cutlery and table napkin (in a scented bag), it also contained salt, spices, and sometimes bread. Under Louis XIV, and until the end of the Ancien Régime, the cadenas became a tray on which the cutlery and napkin were presented to the monarch.

Cadillac

A rich white wine, which received its *appellation contrôlée* in 1973. The vineyard is in the Bordeaux region, across the Garonne River from the Sauternes vineyard. The wines are made from the Sémillon, Sauvignon blanc, and Muscadelle vines, the grapes being picked when ripe or overripe. Formerly Cadillac was included in the Premières Côtes de Bordeaux AOC but now it is produced in 21 parishes, including Langoiran and Gabarnac. Usually drunk as a dessert wine, it may also be enjoyed with foie gras or as an apéritif.

Caesar's mushroom

ORONGE

A large mushroom, *Amanita caesarea*, regarded since very early times as one of the best edible mushrooms – it is said that the Roman emperors valued it highly. Unfortunately it is now as rare as it is tasty.

Caesar's mushroom has an orange-yellow cap, distinguishing it from a closely related poisonous variety, which has a red cap sprinkled with white scales.

| RECIPE

Hazelnut and Caesar's mushroom soup POTAGE AUX ORANGES ET AUX NOISETTES (from a recipe of Dr Paul Ramain) Clean, peel, and finely dice 625 g (1⅓ lbk 5 cups) Caesar's mushrooms, then wash and shred 6 round lettuces. Season the lettuce with salt and pepper and ½ tablespoon caster (superfine) sugar. Heat 75 g (3 oz, 6 tablespoons) butter in a saucepan until it begins to turn brown, then put in the lettuce and the mushrooms; cook over a low heat, with the pan covered, for 30 minutes. Add a knuckle of veal, 1 litre (1¾ pints, 4¼ cups) milk, and 6 tablespoons rice which has been boiled for 1 minute. Salt lightly and mix in 1 tablespoon fairy-ring mushrooms (*Marasmius oreades*) or wood blewits (*Lepista nuda*) in dried and powdered form. Cook over a moderate heat for 2 hours.

Take out the knuckle and rub the soup through a fine sieve. Return it to a low heat. Pound a handful of shelled and skinned hazelnuts and mix them with 75 g (3 oz, 6 tablespoons) butter. Press this paste through a fine sieve into a hot soup tureen; add 3 egg yolks and 125 ml (5 fl oz, generous ½ cup) double (heavy) cream. Pour on the soup, beating vigorously.

café

A place selling drinks (particularly coffee, beer, wine, apéritifs, and fruit juices, and also snacks (sandwiches, salads, etc.). Originally, only coffee was served in these establishments.

The first café in the world was opened in Constantinople in 1550. In 1672, an Armenian called Pascal set up a little stall selling cups of coffee at the Saint-Germain fair in Paris. His success was only fleeting, and he left to try his luck in other European countries. For some time, the fashion of selling coffee to be drunk at home continued in Paris. The French had, however, discovered the social aspects of drinking coffee in a public place, combined with the delights of conversation. Until then, there had only been premises selling wine, such as the cabarets and tavernes. The cafés, or *maisons de café*, began to open: they sold brandy, sweetened wines, and liqueurs, as well as coffee. In 1696 the lemonade and brandy vendors' guild was formed.

☐ **Palais-Royal, Grands Boulevards, Left Bank, and bougnats** The first café (in the modern sense) was the Café Procope, opened in 1696 by an Italian.

Cafés soon became a new way of life: people read the news there, played chess or cards, exchanged ideas, talked politics, and smoked. The hero of Montesquieu's *Lettres persanes* said: 'If I were the king of this country, I would close the cafés, because the people who frequent those places become tediously overheated in the brain when they go there.' The 'club' cafés boasted a clientele of artists, officers, and writers. In the 17th century, and more especially the 18th century, the cafés became the meeting places of men of letters and literary critics: La Fontaine, Crébillon, Fontenelle, and the Encyclopedists were the habitués. The cafés of the Palais-Royal galleries – the 'porticoes of the Revolution' – included the Foy, Régence, Mille Colonnes, Aveugles, Caveau, etc.; they came to be highly fashionable meeting places for discussing politics and listening to the best orators.

After the revolutionary turmoil, rustic cafés, cafés with performers, and pleasure gardens, such as the Tivoli and Frascati, opened. However, the return of the Bourbons put the political cafés (for example, the Lemblin) back into fashion. Here, in front of the bourgeoisie, dandies vied for the limelight with journalists. The Romantics deserted the Palais-Royal, and literary life took refuge in the salons, where tea was the main drink.

Soon, when the Grands Boulevards became the focus of attention in the capital, it was the ice-cream seller and the restaurateur who drew the crowds with establishments such as the Café Riche, the Café de Paris, and the Tortoni, but nevertheless the café survived. It often took the form of a club or society. On the terraces of the fashionable cafés and in the first *cafés-concerts* (cafés with performers) – supervised by the 'garçon de café' clad in his black jacket and long white apron – artists and singers, writers, dandies, *grisettes* (French working girls), and young celebrities could be found. Such establishments included the Café des Variétés and the Divan Lepeletier. The cafés of the Left Bank also began to become important. These were the domain of writers, poets, and intellectuals, while the newly emerging brasseries constituted serious competition for the cafés-restaurants. In the 1900s, the Montmartre cafés served many artists. Later on, Montparnasse stole the limelight with the Closerie des Lilas, and the Parisian tradition of café life survived after the war in the Café de Flore and at the Deux Magots.

After the arrival of the *bougnats* (wine and coal merchants) in the last century, the corner cafés owned by the bougnats became firmly established; here the 'petit noir' (cup of black coffee), the 'ballon de rouge' (glass of red wine), and pastis are consumed at the bar and card games are played. (Note that in France, *café* or *vin de café* is a light red wine served in cafés at the bar.)

☐ **Cafés in Europe** In England, coffee was at first regarded as a panacea against alcoholism, and the coffee houses were all the more successful as the turmoil in the political parties at the end of the 17th century created a need for public meeting places. Also, English literature was then going through its 'French' period. Nowadays, an English café is a small establishment that sells coffee and tea by the cup, soft drinks, and sandwiches, cakes, etc. Coffee is automatically served with milk unless black coffee is specifically asked for.

In Germany, cafés were set up in Hamburg, Berlin, and especially Leipzig, a town of printers that was frequented by writers and wits (J. S. Bach even composed a Coffee Cantata). At the beginning of the 18th century, the right to sell coffee was restricted to four 'distillers', but the fashion for drinking coffee became so widespread that the law was flouted and coffee beans were illegally roasted. Boot-legging was organized, and ersatz versions of coffee appeared. In Berlin, cafés assumed the singing tradition of cabarets. However in Germany, most coffee was drunk at home, with plenty of cakes. It was, moreover, more of a woman's drink, as men usually preferred beer.

In Vienna, the café became firmly established in 1683, when the invading Turks abandoned 500 sacks of coffee. This was given to Kolschitzky, the hero of the victory over the invaders, and it was he who turned Turkish coffee into Viennese coffee. It was filtered, flavoured with honey, enriched with cream, and usually served with croissants. The Viennese had always considered the café to be a natural extension of their homes and offices. They spent many hours there – in the morning to read the news, in the afternoon to discuss business, and in the evening to talk, receive guests, and play billiards. It was in Vienna that the café-concert was born. The great Viennese cafés that perpetuate the tradition, with their hangings, soft lights, and wooden panelling, are the Landtmann, the Hewelka (with a literary and artistic tradition), and the Sacher, a veritable national institution. The same grand scale is seen in the *salon de thé* (tea room), an important meeting place for political and literary notables in Lisbon and Budapest.

Italian cafés existed before the first ones opened in France, especially in Venice, where the coffee shop (celebrated by Goldoni) was part of daily life. However, the most famous ones date from the 18th century: the Greco opened in Rome in 1760, and the Florian, which opened in Venice in 1720, held public concerts under the arcade of Saint Mark's Square; its elegant rooms were frequented by Mme de Staël, George Sand and Alfred de Musset, Marcel Proust, etc.

Café Anglais

An establishment set up in the Boulevard des Italiens in Paris in 1802. It was named in honour of the Peace of Amiens, which had just been signed and which, everybody hoped, would mark the start of a long period of peace with England. English breakfast was served there. At first, it was frequented by coachmen and servants, but in 1822 its new owner, Paul Chevreuil, made it into a fashionable restaurant, famous for its roast and grilled (broiled) dishes. According to Véron, this was 'the place in Paris where one dines best'. However, it was with the arrival of Adolphe Dugléré, that the Café Anglais acquired a great gastronomic reputation; it was here that this great chef created potage Germiny, poularde à la d'Albufera, sole Dugléré, and Anna potatoes. At that time, the clientele of the Café Anglais came from the world of finance and the smart Parisian set. The Grand Seize (one of its private rooms where the King of Prussia, Emperor Nicolas II, and Bismarck had supper) was immortalized in Offenbach's *La Vie parisienne*. The house was demolished in 1913, but its cellar, and the wood panelling of the Grand Seize, were purchased by André Terrail, the owner of the Tour d'Argent, who married the daughter of the last owner of the Café Anglais.

Before the Revolution, another Café Anglais existed in Paris, at the Quai Conti. Its habitués used to meet there to read the English newspapers.

café au lait

Coffee made with milk. It is usually drunk at breakfast in France. The fashion originated in Vienna and goes back to the end of the 17th century in France: café au lait was the favourite drink of Marie-Antoinette.

Opinions have always been divided about the benefits of this drink, which is said to be indigestible and rather unrefined. Madame de Sevigné, however, wrote in 1680: 'We have a fancy to skim the good milk and mix it with sugar and good coffee. It is marvellous, and will greatly console me for Lent. Du Bois, my doctor, approved it for the chest and for chills.' In those days it was called *lait cafeté*, or *café laité*, and was recommended for its nutritional properties. It rapidly became popular, and Sebastian Mercier remarked, in his *Tableaux de Paris*: 'Café au lait has become the eternal breakfast of workers on building sites. They say that in most cases, it keeps them going until evening.' However, Balzac, in his *Nouvelle Théorie du dejeuner*, was intransigent: 'To offer café au lait it is not a mistake, it is ludicrous. Only porters now drink such a vulgar mixture. The drink saddens the soul . . . and weakens the nervous systerm.' For many years in the countryside of northern and eastern France, the evening meal consisted of a bowl of café au lait with bread and cheese.

Café de Flore

A Parisian café in the Saint-Germain-des-Prés quarter, frequented by writers. It opened during the Second Empire and owes its name to a statue of the goddess Flora, which was erected nearby. In 1899 Charles Maurras made it his general headquarters, and later, Apollinaire and a crowd of admirers and followers, including André Salmon and André Billy, held the 'Soirées de Paris' there. During and after the Occupation, Simone de Beauvoir and Jean-Paul Sartre came there to write and made it one of the great centres of existentialism.

Café de Paris

An establishment that opened in Paris in 1822 in the Boulevard des Italiens. Regarded as the 'temple of elegance', it was frequented by dandies, fashionable ladies, and such celebrities at Musset, Balzac, Dumas, Gautier, and Véron. Successive managers brought with them a spectacular cuisine: Belle Alliance pheasant stuffed with truffles and rock partridges *sur piédestal*. The owner (the Marchioness of Hertford) specified in the lease that the café must always close its doors at 10 pm. It ran successfully for 20 years, but then declined and finally disappeared in 1856.

Another Café de Paris, just as splendid, smart, and expensive as the first one, was in business in the capital from 1878 to 1953, in the Avenue de l'Opéra. Opened by Auguste Joliveau, it was frequented by the Goncourts and their friends and the Prince of Wales, the future Edward VII. Léopold Mourier managed it from 1897 to 1923, engaging famous chefs (such as Tony Girod) whose creations marked a milestone in culinary history with such dishes as snipe *à la Diane*.

café liégeois

An iced dessert, made of coffee mixed with fresh cream. Alternatively, it may be made with coffee ice cream, served in a large glass, with a tablespoon of very strong coffee and topped with Chantilly cream. The origin of this dessert is actually Viennese. *Café viennoise* was popular all over Europe, but the Germanic sound of its name caused it to be changed during World War I.

Café Riche

A café founded in Paris on the Boulevard des Italiens in 1804. Initially a modest establishment, it was taken over by the elder Bignon and subsequently became famous. With its marble staircase and bronze banisters, its tapestries, velvets, and silver, it was patronized by theatre personalities and politicians, who were attracted by the sumptuous surroundings, the wines, and the cooking. Bignon created the fashion for red Bouzy, a still champagne. The great specialities of the restaurant (sole with shrimps and Riche sauce, woodcock on fried bread with Riche sauce) were enjoyed by Dumas, Véron, Flaubert, Sainte-Beuve, directors of the Opéra, actors, and composers. The Café Riche was badly affected by the war of 1870, though it survived until 1916.

cafeteria

A self-service restaurant. The ready-prepared hot and cold dishes are displayed on the counters or placed in automatic dispensers. In the latter, the choice is reduced to such food as sandwiches, pizzas, quiches, and cakes and pastries. The food may be eaten sitting down or standing. Hot and cold drinks may also be supplied, often in automatic vending machines. The word appeared in France in the 1950s, and came from Spain. In France, 'coffee-shops' are similar establishments that may be supplemented by table service.

caffeine CAFÉINE

An alkaloid present in coffee (1–2%), tea (1.5–3%), and cola nuts 2–3%), with stimulating, tonic, and diuretic properties. When taken in excessive amounts, caffeine can become toxic. The quantity of caffeine contained in a cup of coffee varies according to the origin of the beans. Robusta beans contain two and a half times more caffeine than arabica beans. Sri Lankan teas are normally richer in caffeine than China teas. Nowadays one can buy decaffeinated coffees and teas.

caghuse or caqhuse

A speciality from Picardy, made with a piece of pork knuckle, liberally covered with finely sliced onions and butter. It is cooked in the oven and served cold. The caghuse is traditionally made in an earthenware dish, greased with lard.

Cahors

A red wine from southwestern France. It was awarded the *appellation d'origine contrôlée* in 1976. After the fall of the Roman Empire, the Cahors region produced a red wine that was very famous in the Middle Ages. The Hundred Years' War and the protectionism practised by the citizens of Bordeaux curtailed the selling of Cahors wines, which had to be transported by boatmen down the Rivers Lot and Garonne to the Gironde region and the port of Bordeaux, from where they might be shipped to England and northern Europe.

The region of Cahors is situated to the east of Bordeaux and to the north of Toulouse, not far from the Bergerac vineyard. It is a limestone plateau (Les Causses) through which the River Lot flows. The vineyard extends over the reddish stony soil, along the banks of the Lot, between Cahors and Soturac. It is made up of small plots scattered over 50 km (31 mi) and is exposed to the south and southeast. The main vine variety is the Malbec (or Cot), which the Cahors vine-growers call Auxerrois. Other varieties are Merlot, Jurançon, Tannat, and Syrah. Cahors wine is so dark and tannic that it should traditionally be kept for three to five years in cask and five to ten years in bottle before being drunk. The young wine is inclined to be harsh and unrewarding but later it becomes fine, full of fragrance, well balanced, and dark red. It is an elegant accompaniments to many spices dishes, meats with sauce, and game.

caillebotte

In Poitou and Anjou, a dish made with curdled milk and served cold with fresh cream and sugar. The word comes from *cailler* (to curdle) and *botter* (to coagulate on a rush mat). In other regions, the name is given to a cream cheese made from cows' milk (in Aunis and Saintonge) or from goats' milk (in Saintonge and Poitou). When caillebotte is drained in a woven rush basket, it is called *jonchée*. The traditional preparation of Poitou caillebotte involves adding a pinch of cardoon flower to curdle the milk. Le Varenne's *Le Confiturier français* (1664) contained a recipe for this dish.

Poitou caillebottes CAILLEBOTTES
POITEVINES Infuse a pinch of cardoon flower in a very small amount of water for 5–6 hours. Pour the liquid into 1 litre (1¾ pints, 4¼ cups) fresh milk and leave until it coagulates. Using a knife, cut the resulting solid mass into squares and heat gently until it boils. The curds are cooked when the pieces separate and float in the whey. After chilling, remove the whey and replace it with fresh milk. Top with fresh cream and sweeten to taste.

caillette

A small flat sausage made of minced pork and green vegetables. It is cooked in the oven and may be eaten hot or cold. Caillettes are said to have originated in the Ardèche but they are prepared in the whole of southeastern France. The seasoning and secondary ingredients vary from region to region, and even from village to village: truffles are used in Pierrelatte, spinach in Soyans, greens in Chabeuil (where a caillette-tasting society, the Confrérie des Chevaliers du Taste-Caillette, was established in 1967), pig's liver and beet in Valence, and pig's liver *à la pugétoise* in Puget-Théniers. Caillettes are similar to a type of sausage made in Cornwall, which is served with mustard and mashed potato.

| RECIPE

Ardèche caillettes CAILLETTES
ARDÉCHOISES Blanch 250 g (9 oz), generous 3 cups) beet leaves, an equal quantity of spinach, and a large handful of dandelion leaves, nettles, and poppy leaves. Drain and chop finely. Also chop 250 g (9 oz, generous cup, firmly packed) pig's liver, an equal quanity of lights, and a little fat bacon and mix together. Brown a chopped onion in some lard and add the meat, vegetables, and a clove of garlic; season with salt and pepper. Cook for 5 minutes, stirring continuously. Remove from the heat, divide the mixture into 8 pieces, and roll each into a ball. Wrap each ball in pig's caul and pack them close together in an earthenware dish. Put a strip of fat

bacon on each caillette and cook in a hot oven (approximately 200 c, 400 F, gas 6) for 30–40 minutes. Cool the caillettes and store in earthenware pots, covered with lard. They may be served hot, browned in lard, or cold with a dandelion salad.

caillier

A wooden drinking vessel used in the Middle Ages and until the end of the 16th century. The largest of these vessels were used as containers for wine and the bowl-shaped lids were used as drinking cups.

caisses and caissettes

Cases used in cookery, pastry-making, and confectionery. Savoury preparations *en caisse* (in cases) or *en caissette* (in small cases) are served as hot hors d'oeuvres or small entrées. They are generally filled with salpicons, ragouts, or the various fillings used for barquettes, patties, pies, or tartlets. The cases are served in small round or oval receptacles made of oven-proof china, tempered glass, metal, plastic, or light aluminium (frequently used for caterers' preparations). Petits fours, certain sweetmeats (bouchées), and cakes (such as individual babas) are placed in caissettes made of pleated paper. 'Caisses de Wassy' are famous sweetmeats from Champagne made of meringue with almonds, apparently created because Mary Stuart stayed in the town.

The term *caisse* is also used in France to denote various tins and similar kitchen utensils.

cajasse

A sweet from Périgord, a speciality of the town of Sarlat. It is made from rum-flavoured crêpe batter mixed with fruit. It swells considerably during cooking and is eaten cold.

cakes and gâteaux

In France, the word 'gâteau' designates various pâtisserie items based on puff pastry, shortcrust pastry (basic pie dough), sweet pastry, pâte sablée, choux pastry, Genoese and whisked sponges, meringue, etc. To these may be added various additional ingredients, such as ground almonds, almond paste, chocolate, fruit (fresh, preserved, or dried), fondant or water icing (frosting), pastry and butter creams, liqueurs, fresh cream, etc.

The word 'cake' by itself is used in France for several types of rich fruit cake. In Great Britain and the United States the word is used more generally and can include various kinds of gâteaux (sponge cakes, iced cakes, chocolate cakes, Christmas cake, etc.).

The word 'gâteau' is derived from the Old French *waste* meaning 'food'. The first gâteaux were simply flat round cakes made with flour and water, but over the centuries these were enriched with honey, eggs, spices, butter, cream, and milk. From the very earliest times, a large number of French provinces have produced cakes for which they are noted. Thus Artois had *gâteaux razis*, and Bourbonnais the ancient *tartes de fromage broyé, de crème et de moyeux d'oeulz*. Hearth cakes are still made in Normandy. Picardy, Poitou, and in some provinces of the south of France. They are called variously *fouaces, fouaches, fouées* or *fouyasses*, according to the district.

Until the 17th century it was usual at Whitsuntide in Paris to throw down *nieules* and *oublies* (wafers), local Parisian confections, on the heads of the worshippers gathered under the vaulted roofs of the Cathedral of Notre-Dame. At the same time blazing wicks were showered on the congregation.

Among the many pastries which were in high favour from the 12th to the 15th centuries in Paris and other cities were: échaudés, of which two variants, the *flageols* and the *gobets*, were especially prized by the people of Paris; and darioles, small tartlets covered with narrow strips of pastry. Two kinds of darioles were made, one filled with cream cheese, the other with frangipane cream. *Talemouses*, which are known today as talmouses (cheese turnovers), were also much appreciated.

Casse-museau is a hard dry pastry still made today; *ratons, petits choux*, and *gâteaux feuilletés* are mentioned in a charter by Robert, Bishop of Amiens in 1311, which proves that puff pastry was known in France before the 17th

century, when, some writers claim, the process of making puff pastry was invented.

In the following centuries, pastrycooks, organized into guilds, produced not only the pastries listed above, but also brioches, spice cakes, waffles of various kinds, marzipan biscuits, tarts and flans garnished in various ways, *pâtes royales* (a kind of meringue), almond cakes, dough cakes, cracknels, and flamiches. Then came grand architectural creations (*pièces montées*), often more decorative than delectable. In the 18th and 19th centuries, cakes became masterpieces of refinement and ingenuity, especially where pastrycooks were in the service of a prince or a large house.

☐ **Traditional cakes** Many cakes have a ceremonial or symbolic significance, linked to a religious feast – Christmas, Easter, Epiphany (Twelfth-Night cake), Candlemas, etc. In addition, cakes have always featured prominently in family celebrations (for baptisms, birthdays, weddings, etc.). Formerly, tourteaux fromagés were served in Poitou at the wedding breakfast. In Brittany, the bride and groom were given the *gâteau de la demande*. In the country, cakes were provided for social evenings and gatherings, market days, threshing days, etc.

A number of foreign cakes are also well-known in France (strudel, fruit cake, baklava, vatrushki, linzertorte, panettone, etc.). On this subject, Jean-Paul Sartre gives a surprising example of culinary anthropomorphism: 'Cakes are human, they are like faces. Spanish cakes are ascetic with a swaggering appearance, they crumble into dust under the tooth. Greek cakes are greasy like little oil lamps: when you press them, the oil oozes out. German cakes are bulky and soft like shaving cream; they are made so that obese easily tempted men can eat them indulgently, without worrying what they taste like but simply to fill their mouths with sweetness. But those Italian cakes had a cruel perfection: really small and flawless, scarcely bigger than petits fours, they gleamed. Their harsh and gaudy colours took away any desire to eat them; instead, you felt like placing them on the sideboard like pieces of painted porcelain' (*Dépaysement*, published by Gallimard).

□ **Large and small cakes** In France distinction is usually made between individual cakes, or *gâteaux à la pièce* (éclairs, mirlitons, salammbôs, conversations, puits d'amour, etc.) and large cakes (Genoese sponge cakes, croquembouches, vacherins, etc.). Both sometimes bear the name of the person who created them (quillet, beauvilliers, etc.) or the person to whom they were dedicated (such as savarin), or the name indicates their place of origin (pithiviers, Paris-Brest, breton, etc.). However, cakes are usually given a fanciful name or a name which describes their method of preparation (manqué, quatre-quarts, mille-feuille, etc.).

The name *gâteaux secs* is given in France to plain petits fours, biscuits (cookies), etc., served with tea or ice cream.

Finally, the name *gâteau* is given to culinary preparations made with vegetable purée or various hashes moulded and cooked in a bain-marie and served as an entrée or a garnish (gâteau of chicken livers, carrots, cauliflower, etc.).

RECIPES

Black Forest gâteau GÂTEAU DE LA FORÊT-NOIRE Vigorously whisk 250 g (9 oz, 1 generous cup) caster (superfine) sugar with 6 whole eggs until very thick and frothy. Then gently fold in 100 g (4 oz, 1 cup) sifted flour, 50 g (2 oz, ½ cup) cocoa powder, and 150 g (5 oz, ⅝ cup) melted butter. Butter and flour 3 round 22-cm (9-in) cake tins and pour in the cake mixture. Bake in a moderate oven (180 C, 350 F, gas 4) for about 25 minutes. Turn the cakes out of the tins and allow to cool.

Make a syrup with 200 g (7 oz, 1 scant cup) caster sugar and 3.5 dl (12 fl oz, 1½ cups) water. Flavour with Kirsch. Grate 200–250 g (7–9 oz, 1½ cups) bitter chocolate into thick shavings and put in the refrigerator. Steep the cooled layers of cake in syrup.

Make some Chantilly cream by whipping together 8 dl (1⅓ pints, 3½ cups) chilled double (heavy) cream, 2 dl (⅓ pint) very cold milk, 80 g (3 oz, ⅔ cup) icing (confectioners') sugar, and 2 teaspoons vanilla sugar. Cover each layer of cake with a quarter of the cream and a dozen cherries in brandy. Cover the sides of the cake with the rest of the cream. Decorate the whole cake with chocolate shavings. Serve chilled.

Fruit cake CAKE Soften 125 g (4½ oz, generous ½ cup) butter at room temperature. Mix it with 125 g (4½ oz, ⅔ cup, firmly packed) caster (superfine) sugar and a pinch of salt. Add 3 eggs, one at a time. Mix 180 g (6 oz, 1½ cups) flour with 1 teaspoon baking powder. Wash and dry 250 g (9 oz, 1½ cups) currants or mixed dried fruit and add them to the flour, mix well with a wooden spoon, and blend with the mixture of butter, sugar, and eggs. Refrigerate the mixture for 30 minutes.

Preheat the oven to approximately 240 C (475 F, gas 9). Butter a loaf tin (pan) about 23 cm (9 in) long, line it with buttered greaseproof (waxed) paper, and fill with the cake mixture. Bake for about 12 minutes, then reduce the oven temperature to 180 C (350 F, gas 4) and bake for 45 minutes. Check that the cake is sufficiently cooked by piercing with the point of a knife, which should come out clean. Allow the cake to become lukewarm before removing from the tin. Cool on a rack.

Gâteau breton Cut 150 g (5 oz, ⅔ cup) crystallized (candied) fruit into very small cubes and soak in rum for 1 hour. Soften 190 g (6½ oz, ¾ cup) butter at room temperature. Separate the whites from the yolks of 5 eggs. On the work surface, make a well in 350 g (12 oz, 2¾ cups) sifted flour and put in a generous pinch of salt, 175 g (6 oz, ¾ cup) caster (superfine) sugar, ½ sachet dried yeast (1 oz fresh yeast, 1 cake compressed yeast), a liqueur glass of rum, and the 5 egg yolks. Mix well. Cut the softened butter into small pieces and blend them with the mixture, together with the crystallized fruit and rum. Butter a 23-cm (9-in) round flan tin (pie pan), put in the mixture, and smooth the top with a palette knife (spatula). Make a crisscross pattern with the point of a knife. Brush the cake with a beaten egg and bake in a moderately hot over (200 C, 400 F, gas 6) for 50 minutes until the cake is golden brown.

Gâteau le Parisien Remove the rind from a lemon, blanch it for 1 minute, cool, dry, and cut into short very fine julienne strips. Whisk 3 egg yolks with 110 g (4 oz, ½ cup) sugar until the mixture is almost white. Pour in 25 g (1 oz, ¼ cup) sifted flour, 35 g (1¼ oz, generous ¼ cup) cornflour (cornstarch), 1 teaspoon vanilla sugar, and the zest, then carefully fold in the 3 egg whites, whisked with a pinch of salt until very stiff. Pour this mixture into a buttered fairly deep 23-cm (9-in) sandwich tin (layer cake pan) or manqué mould and bake in a moderately hot oven (200 c, 400 F, gas 6) for 40 minutes.

During this time, make a frangipane cream with 3 egg yolks, 75 g (3 oz, 6 tablespoons) caster (superfine) sugar, 30 g (1 oz, ¼ cup) cornflour, 4 dl (14 fl oz, 1¼ cups) milk, 1 teaspoon vanilla sugar, and 125 g (4½ oz, 1 generous cup) ground almonds. Blend in 125 g (4½ oz, generous ½ cup) chopped crystallized (candied) fruits.

When the cake is cooked, leave it to cool. Make some Italian meringue with 3 egg whites, 2 tablespoons (3 tablespoons) icing (confectioners') sugar, and 185 g (6½ oz, ¾ cup) caster sugar. Cut the cooled cake into 3 equal rounds. Cover each layer with the frangipane cream and crystallized fruit mixture and re-form the cake. Spread some meringue on the top, then fill a fluted piping (pastry) bag with the rest of the meringue and decorate all round the cake with regular motifs. Sprinkle the meringue with icing sugar and put in a moderate oven (180 c, 350 F, gas 4). Take out the cake as soon as the meringue turns brown. Leave to cool completely.

Honey and cherry cake CAKE AU MIEL ET AUX CERISES CONFITES Soften 100 g (4 oz, ½ cup) butter at room temperature, divide into small pieces, and then cream with 100 g (4 oz, scant ⅔ cup, firmly packed) caster (superfine) sugar, a large pinch of salt, and 2 tablespoons liquid honey. Mix in 1 teaspoon baking powder, 200 g (7 oz, generous 1½ cups) sifted flour, and 3 eggs, added one at a time. Flavour with 2 tablespoons rum. Halve 125 g (4½ oz, ½ cup) glacé (candied) cherries and add them to the cake mixture. Pour im-

mediately into a buttered loaf tin (pan) and bake in the oven at 190 c (375 F, gas 5) for approximately 45 minutes. If the cake browns too quickly, cover it with aluminium foil. Turn the cooked cake out of the tin when lukewarm and leave to cool on a rack. Decorate with glacé cherries and pieces of angelica.

Marble cake GÂTEAU MARBRÉ Melt 175 g (6 oz, ¾ cup) butter very slowly, without letting it become hot. Whip it together with 200 g (7 oz, 1 scant cup) sugar, then add 3 egg yolks. Sift 175 g (6 oz, 1½ cups) flour and 1 teaspoon baking powder and blend with the egg mixture. Whisk 3 egg whites with a pinch of salt until very stiff and add them to the mixture. Divide the mixture into 2 equal parts. Blend 25 g (1 oz, ¼ cup) cocoa powder with one of them. Pour the two mixtures into a buttered 20-cm (8-in) cake tin (pan) in alternate thin layers. Bake in a moderately hot oven (200 c, 400 F, gas 6) for about 50 minutes.

calabash CALEBASSE

The fruit of various plants of the gourd family. The sweet calabash is a creeping shrub from America and Africa. Its soft delicate flesh may be eaten raw in a salad, baked in the oven, boiled, stewed with bacon and herbs (in Martinique), or curried with beef (in Sri Lanka). In Japan, the flesh of some calabashes is dried, cut into thin strips, and used as a garnish for soups. When dried, the fruit becomes hard and woody. These gourds are hollowed out and used as kitchen utensils, drinking vessels, and other articles.

In South America a liquid extracted from the pulp is used to make a syrup.

calamary

See *squid*.

calcium

A mineral that is essential for the development and functioning of the human body and is an important constituent of the bones and teeth. The daily calcium requirement for adults is 0.5 g, rising to 1 g during pregnancy and 2 g during breast-feeding. The principal sources of calcium are milk (0.15 g per litre), yogurt (0.15 g per litre), and cheese (0.15–1.25 g per 100 g). Calcium is also found in eggs and vegetables.

caldo verde

A Portuguese national dish consisting of a soup made with olive oil, potatoes, and dark green Portuguese curly cabbage. It is garnished with slices of garlic sausage and served with maize bread and red wine. The cabbage has a very strong flavour and is cut into very thin strips.

Californian wines

VINS DE CALIFORNIE

The United States produces 85% of the wine it consumes, over 80% of which comes from California. Although the Americans used to drink more spirits than wine, the proportion is changing, and the production of Californian wines, after a few setbacks due mainly to phylloxera and prohibition, is now expanding rapidly.

Vine-growing was introduced to Mexico by Cortés in the early 16th century, and slowly spread to the north via the Spanish missions. It was not until the second half of the 19th century, when California ceased to be Mexican and became one of the States of the Union, that modern vine-growing really began. The credit for this goes to a few pioneers, including the great Hungarian nobleman, Agoston Haraszthy, considered to be the 'father' of Californian vine-growing. They imported a large number of European vines to replace that of the Mission – a variety of grape formerly introduced by the Jesuits, which has a very high yield but produces only mediocre wines.

After a fairly erratic development, involving trial and error, the European vine finally became adapted to growth in the varied soils and climates of California. Two major vine-growing areas can be distinguished: the relatively cold north coast, which produces table wines, some of which are excellent, and the much warmer inland valleys, producing mainly sweet wines and dessert wines which are high in alcohol but in general of rather indifferent quality.

☐ **Table wines** The Californian wineries are outstandingly well equipped and planned. They make, in general, three main types of wine. The inexpensive red, white, and rosé 'jug wines' are often from table grapes (such as Thompson Seedless) and tend to be somewhat mediocre. Some of the better-quality wines bear European names, often those of classic grape varieties, but the use of classic regional names is declining and it must be said that such wines bear scant relation to their French counterparts. The 'varietal wines' bear the names of the grape or grapes from which they are made, although regulations do not yet insist on a 100% use of these varieties, which is something often stressed on labels by top producers. Such wines can equal in quality many European fine wines.

☐ **Sweet and sparkling wines** The apéritif and sweet wines are, in general, versions of European classics – sherry, port, Tokay, and so on, few of them attaining more than ordinary quality. The sparkling wines, however, made by the champagne process, can be really good, notably the dry versions.

calisson

A diamond-shaped sweetmeat from Provence produced on a small scale. Calissons are actually a centuries-old speciality of Aix-en-Provence. In the 17th century they were distributed among the congregation during religious ceremonies held in memory of the plague of 1630. Later, they were traditionally eaten at Easter. The Provençal word *calissoun* (or *canissoun*), which comes from the Latin *canna* (a reed), is used for the wire stand on which confectioners display crystallized (candied) fruit and calissons.

Calissons are made of 40% blanched almonds and 60% crystallized fruit (melon with a little orange) mixed with orange-flower water and syrup. The mixture is placed on a base of unleavened bread and coated with royal icing. Calissons should be bought when very fresh and soft and kept only for a short time. They must be protected from the air as they dry quickly.

calorie

A unit of heat equal to the amount of heat necessary to raise the temperature of 1 gram of water by 1 c at normal atmospheric pressure. A Calorie (or kilocalorie, or Cal) is equal to 1000 calories; this unit is used in dietetics to measure the energy value of foods and the energy needs of humans, although the international (SI) unit for expressing energy production is the joule (1 kilojoule = 1.24 Cal).

The amount of energy produced by food depends on its protein content (4.1 Cal per gram), its fat content (9.3 Cal per gram), and its carbohydrate content (4.1 Cal per gram). Mineral salts and vitamins do not produce Calories. Alcohol produces 7 Cal per gram (i.e. from 600 (wine) to 3000 (brandy) Cal per litre, depending on the drink).

Energy requirements are determined by age, sex, height, weight, climate and individual activity. An athletic adult man needs 3000 to 3500 Cal per day while a sedentary woman should use up from 1800 to 2200 Cal per day. Growth can increase the Calorie requirement by up to 50%. Nursing mothers need 700 additional Cal per day, while in pregnancy the requirement only increases in the last few weeks. Physical activity increases the requirements from 200 to 400 Cal per hour.

The source of the Calories is also very important. For a balanced diet, proteins should provide 12–15%, fats, 30–35%, and carbohydrates 50–55%. Many cases of obesity are due to excess intake of carbohydrates and fats. An excess of fat in the diet is one of the main causes of cardiovascular disease.

Calvados

Brandy made by distilling cider. Cider distillation is a very old tradition in Normandy – it was mentioned in 1553 in the diary of Gilles de Gouberville, a gentleman of the Cotentin. The best Calvados is made with cider that is over a year old.

Distilling may be carried out throughout the year, but it is usually from March to April and August to September. Traditional stills with a double distillation are used for the *appellation contrôlée* Calvados, which is made in the Auge region, comprising part of the department of Calvados and several communes of the Orne and Eure. The *appellation réglementée* Calvados are made by a single distillation process.

Calvados is a harsh rough brandy, 72°, which must mature for a time in oak casks. It may only be sold after a year's ageing. It is usually categorized as follows: 'Trois étoiles' or 'Trois Pommes' Calvados are aged for two years in wood; 'Vieux' or 'Réserve' are aged for three years; 'VO' (Very Old) or 'Vieille Réserve' for four years; 'VSOP' for five years; 'Extra', 'Napoléon', 'Hors d'Âge' or 'Âge Inconnu' for more than five years.

Since the middle of the 20th century, Calvados has been subject to strict controls and, in export markets, has become one of the most sought-after French spirits. (It is not, however, the same as the American spirit, applejack.) Old Calvados is to be enjoyed as a digestive, in a tulip glass. The Normans and Bretons have popularized the custom of *café-calva*: the brandy is either served in a small glass at the same time as the coffee, or else is poured into the empty coffee cup while this is still warm. (See *trou normand*.)

Like most spirits, Calvados may be used in cooking and pastry-making, particularly in dishes that are Normandy specialities, such as chicken or leg of mutton with cream and Calvados, apple desserts, omelettes, and crêpes flambées.

Camacho's wedding

NOCES DE GAMACHE

An episode in *Don Quixote* in which the hero and Sancho Panza attend the wedding feast of a wealthy farmer, Camacho. The enormous number of dishes served at this repast has become proverbial and the expression *noces de Gamache* is used to describe a particularly sumptuous feast costing an inordinate amount of money. 'The first thing that met Sancho's eyes was a whole ox spitted on the trunk of an elm and, in the hearth over which it was to roast, there was a fair mountain of wood burning. Six earthen pots were arranged around this blaze. . . . Whole sheep disappeared within them as if they were pigeons. Innumerable skinned hares and fully plucked chickens, hanging on the trees, were soon to be swallowed up in these pots. Birds and game too, of all kinds, were also hanging from the branches so that they were kept cool in the air. . . . There were piles of white loaves, like heaps of wheat in barns. Cheeses, built up like bricks, formed walls and two cauldrons of oil, bigger than dyer's vats, were used for frying pastries, which were lifted out with two sturdy shovels and then plunged into another cauldron of honey standing nearby.'

Cambacérès (Jean-Jacques Régis de)

French jurist, politician, and gastronome (born Montpellier, 1754; died Paris, 1824). During a particularly turbulent period in French history (from the French Revolution to the Restoration) Cambacérès adroitly advanced his career in the public sphere. He proved equally skilful in gastronomy. His table was reputed to be the most sumptuous and lavish in Paris, equalling that of Talleyrand, and the dinners that he gave at his house in Rue Saint-Dominique were celebrated. Cambacérès chose the dishes himself and knew all the gastronomic skills, so that he was regarded as a supreme arbiter of taste. But he was accused of stinginess and gluttony by the famous chef, Carême, probably in an effort to blacken the name of one who rivalled Carême's employer, Talleyrand, who also practised 'table politics'. During the Congress of Lunéville, when Bonaparte ordered that postal services should carry nothing but despatches and food parcels were banned, Cambacérès pleaded: 'How can one make friends without exquisite dishes! It is mainly through the table that one governs!' The First Consul decided in his favour.

More often than not, Cambacérès was accompanied by the Marquis d'Aigrefeuille, his faithful taster and table companion, to whom Grimod de La Reynière dedicated his first *Almanach des gourmands* ('Gourmets' Almanac'). Cambacérès also presided over Grimod's 'Jury of Tasters' from 1805 onwards. A hearty eater and generous host, who entertained distinguished guests on behalf of Napoleon, he died of apoplexy at the age of 70, after Louis XVIII granted him permission to return from exile.

Three very elaborate dishes were named after him: a cream soup of chicken, pigeon, and crayfish, garnished with quenelles made with the same meats; a timbale of macaroni and foie gras; and salmon trout with crayfish and truffles.

Cambridge sauce

An emulsified sauce in English cooking that is made from anchovies, egg yolks, and mustard. It is served as an accompaniment to cold meats.

RECIPE

Cambridge sauce SAUCE CAMBRIDGE Thoroughly desalt 6 anchovies, then remove the bones. Blend together 3 hard-boiled (hard-cooked) egg yolks, the anchovy flesh, 1 teaspoon capers, and a small bunch of tarragon and chervil. Add 1 teaspoon English mustard to the mixture and season with pepper. Thicken with groundnut (peanut) oil or sunflower oil, as for mayonnaise, then add 1 tablespoon vinegar. Adjust the seasoning. Add chopped chives and parsley.

camel CHAMEAU

A ruminant mammal of Asia and Africa, which possesses either one hump (dromedary) or two. Camel meat, mostly from young animals, whose tender flesh is similar to veal, is consumed in several countries of north Africa and the Middle East. The thigh joint of the dromedary is cooked chopped, as meatballs, or whole in a marinade. In Mongolia, the fat from the hump is used to make a widely used butter. The heart and other offal are also eaten. Considered unclean in the Bible, the camel was highly esteemed in Rome, where its grilled feet were a choice dish. In Paris, during the 1870 siege, it appeared on the Christmas Eve menu at the Voisin restaurant. Camel's milk is a nutritious and well-balanced food for humans.

cameline

A cold condiment for pâtés, roasts, and fish, used in medieval times. It was made of grilled bread soaked in wine, drained, squeezed, and ground with spices (cinnamon, ginger, pepper, cloves, and nutmeg), then diluted with vinegar. After sieving, the sauce was kept in a pot, ready for use. Taillevent criticized lazy people 'who, rather than make a pepper sauce to accompany stuffed young pig, are content to eat it with cameline.' A special version, served with fried fish, was called *aulx camelins* (bread, cinnamon, and garlic cloves ground with vinegar and fish liver).

Camembert

A soft cheese (45–50% fat content) made from cows' milk, pale yellow in colour with a white furry skin speckled with brown flecks. Each cheese measures about 11 cm (4½ in) in diameter and is 3–4 cm (about 1½ in) thick.

This cheese was invented at the time of the French Revolution in the Auge region of Normandy. A certain Marie Harel, who had hidden a recalcitrant priest from Brie, developed a new cheese by combining the method used in Normandy with that used in Brie. Marie Harel disclosed her secret to her daughter, who set herself up in the village of Camembert near Vimoutiers (Orne) to sell the cheeses. While passing through the region for the opening of the Paris-Granville line, Napoleon III tasted the cheese and found it delicious. On learning that it came from Camembert, the Emperor named it after the village. This name was never registered and a judgment of 1926 stipulated that Camembert could not have an *appellation d'origine*. This is why Camembert is now mass-produced throughout France and even in other countries.

Towards the end of the last century, a certain M. Ridel invented the cylindrical wooden box that enabled the cheese to be transported. The white mould with which Camembert is covered today was selected in 1910. (Originally, Camembert was covered with blue mould and wrapped in straw.)

□ **Manufacture** Real farmhouse Camembert cheeses are rare today, but dairy cheeses are manufactured on both a small and large scale. It takes 4 litres (7 pints) milk to make a Camembert. The best cheeses, made from raw milk curdled with rennet, are moulded with a ladle then drained, salted, turned over, removed from the mould, and left to mature for about a month in a dry cellar so that the skin forms naturally. The cheese should be wrapped in transparent parchment paper thereby showing the slightly bulging skin with its uneven coating of fur and orange streaks. The aroma should be delicate and full-flavoured.

Mass-produced Camemberts are made from pasteurized skimmed milk to which pasteurized cream is added. They are of uniform quality and keep longer than traditionally made cheeses but the taste is never as good. They are drained faster and moulded mechanically. *Demi-Camemberts* (half-Camemberts) and Camembert portions are also found. Since August 1983 the AOC Camembert de Normandie has been reserved for cheeses manufactured in the five departments of Normandy, which are sold in wooden boxes.

Camembert is one of the stalwarts of the cheeseboard and can be eaten on its own if it is in perfect condition.

Camerani
(Barthélemy-André)

Italian comedian and gastronome (born Ferrara, c. 1735; died Paris, 1816). Working mainly in France, he became administrator of the Favart and Feydeau theatres. But above all, Camerani was famous for his gourmandise, being a member of Grimod de La Reynière's 'Jury of Tasters' and giving his name to a soup which he invented and which was served around 1810 in the Café Anglais, when he was working at the Opéra-Comique.

In classic French cuisine, the name of Camerani is also applied to a garnish for poached chicken and calves' sweetbreads, consisting of small tartlets filled with a purée of foie gras (topped with slices of truffle and pickled ox tongue cut into the shape of cocks' combs) and macaroni *à l'italienne*, all bound together with suprême sauce.

RECIPE

Camerani soup POTAGE CAMBER-ANI (from old French cuisine) Slowly cook in butter 2 dl (7 fl oz, ¾ cup) finely shredded mixed vegetables, including a small turnip. Add 2 chicken livers, peeled and diced very finely, season with salt and pepper, and brown over a brisk heat. Meanwhile, cook 125 g (4½ oz) Naples macaroni in fast-boiling salted water. Drain, bind together with butter, and season. In a serving dish, buttered and sprinkled with grated Parmesan, arrange alternate layers of the macaroni and the chicken liver mixture, also sprinkled with Parmesan. Heat slowly for a few minutes before serving.

Canadian wines

VINS DU CANADA

Apart from a little production in British Columbia, sometimes using Californian must, all Canadian wines come from a narrow strip of land close to the border of the New York State, containing the famous Niagara Falls, which separates Lake Ontario from Lake Erie. The vineyards, dating back to the beginning of the 19th century, have been planted mainly with native American vines: Concord, Catawba, Niagara, and Agarvan. But recently several wineries have planted classic grape varieties and are making table wines of promising quality. Table wines made from native vinestocks have a characteristic 'foxy' taste due to the grapes from which they are made and are generally 'chaptalized', i.e. sugar is added to the must to compensate for low alcoholic strength resulting from insufficient warmth. The dessert wines, heavy and very sweet, are rather poor imitations of European ports, sherries, and vermouths. Sparkling wines are also made from the local white wines; drunk chilled, they are quite pleasant.

canapé

A slice of bread cut into various shapes and garnished. Cold canapés are served at buffets or lunches or with cocktails or apéritifs; hot canapés are served as entrées or used as foundations for various dishes. When served with game birds, canapés are generally fried in butter and spread with *à gratin* forcemeat, a purée made of the internal organs of the bird (cooked undrawn), or foie gras.

| RECIPES

Preparation of canapés PRÉPARATION DES CANAPÉS Unlike sandwiches, which consist of 2 slices of bread with a filling in the middle, canapés are made with a single slice of bread; they may be rectangular, round, or triangular in shape and the bread can also be lightly toasted. Cold canapés are usually made from white bread (slightly stale, so that it does not crumble, and with the crust removed) or rye bread; hot canapés are made from white or wholemeal bread. Cold canapés should be served as soon as possible after preparation so they do not dry out. They may be stored in a cool place covered with a cloth (a damp cloth if kept in a hot or dry place).

There is a wide variety of garnishes for canapés, including all the garnishes indicated for croûtes as well as various flavoured butters, spinach mixed with béchamel sauce and Parmesan (*á la florentine*), ham, scrambled eggs with cheese, sardines (fresh sardine fillets or purée of sardines in oil with hard-boiled (hard-cooked) egg and English mustard), etc.

COLD CANAPÉS

Canapés à la bayonnaise Spread some slices of bread with parsley butter and garnish with very thin slices of Bayonne ham cut to the exact size of the bread. Glaze with aspic.

Canapés with anchovies CANAPÉS AUX ANCHOIS Spread some Montpellier butter on lightly toasted rectangular slices of bread cut to the same length as the anchovies. Garnish each canapé with 2 anchovy fillets separated by cooked egg white and egg yolk (chopped separately) and chopped parsley.

Canapés with asparagus CANAPÉS AUX ASPERGES Spread some thickened mayonnaise on rectangular slices of bread. Arrange very small asparagus tips on each canapé and 'tie' each bunch with a thin strip of green or red sweet pepper.

Canapés with shrimps, lobster, or langouste CANAPÉS AUX CREVETTES (AU HOMARD, À LA LANGOUSTE) Spread shrimp (or lobster) butter on some round slices of bread. Garnish each canapé with a rosette of shrimp

tails (or a medallion of lobster or langouste tail) and a border of chopped
parsley or shrimp butter.

Canapés with smoked salmon CANA-
PÉS AU SAUMON FUMÉ Butter some
slices of bread and garnish with slices of
smoked salmon cut to the exact size of
the bread. Garnish each canapé with
half a slice of fluted lemon.

Canapés with watercress CANAPÉS
AU CRESSON Spread watercress butter on some round or rectangular slices
of bread. Garnish each canapé with a
centre of blanched watercress leaves
and a border of chopped hard-boiled
(hard-cooked) egg (yolk and white
together).

Danish canapés CANAPÉS À LA
DANOISE Spread horseradish butter
on some rectangular slices of black rye
bread. Garnish with strips of smoked
salmon or smoked herring, filling the
spaces with salmon roe or peeled rounds
of lemon cut in half and fluted.

Harlequin canapés CANAPÉS ARLE-
QUINS Spread some flavoured butter
or thickened mayonnaise on slices of
bread cut into various shapes. Garnish
with various chopped items: pickled ox
(beef) tongue, ham, truffles, yolks and
whites of hard-boiled (hard-cooked)
eggs, parsley, etc. Surround the canapés
with a thin border of butter.

HOT CANAPÉS

Canapés with cheese CANAPÉS AU
FROMAGE Butter some slices of
bread. Top with a thick layer of Gruyère
cheese (or Comté, Beaufort, Cheddar,
Appenzell, etc.) either grated or cut into
very thin strips. Brown in a hot oven.
The canapés may be served with seasoned tomato sauce. Alternatively,
grated Gruyère can be added to a well-
reduced béchamel sauce, seasoned with
cayenne, and spread over the slices of
bread, which are then sprinkled with
grated Gruyère or small cubes of
Gruyère and browned in a very hot
oven.

Canapés with crab CANAPÉS AU
CRABE Finely crumble the crab meat

(fresh or tinned), removing all the cartilage, and flavour with a little lemon
juice. Add an equal amount of béchamel
seasoned with nutmeg or saffron. Butter
some lightly toasted slices of white
bread and spread them with the crab
mixture. Sprinkle with fresh breadcrumbs and melted butter and brown in
a very hot oven. Garnish with half a
round of fluted lemon.

Canapés with mushrooms CANAPÉS
AUX CHAMPIGNONS Prepare a dry
well-browned duxelles of mushrooms
and add béchamel sauce (1 part to 3
parts duxelles). Spread this on lightly
toasted slices of bread and sprinkle with
fresh breadcrumbs and a little melted
butter. Brown in a very hot oven.

cancalaise (à la)

A term describing several fish dishes
using oysters from the Bay of Cancale,
in Brittany. Whiting, sole, or brill *à la
cancalaise* are stuffed with poached
oysters and prawn tails and coated with
Normandy sauce or white wine sauce.

Fish consommé *à la cancalaise* with
tapioca is garnished with poached oysters. Sometimes sole fillets cut into small
strips (*en julienne*) or small quenelles of
pike are added.

| RECIPE

Fillets of sole à la cancalaise FILETS
DE SOLE À LA CANCALAISE Fillet the
soles and poach some oysters, allowing
2 per fillet. Fold the fillets and poach
them in a full-bodied fish fumet to
which the poaching water from the oysters has been added. Drain the fillets,
retaining the juices, and arrange them
on a dish in the form of a turban. Garnish the centre of the dish with shelled
prawns and arrange 2 oysters on each
fillet. Coat with a white wine sauce to
which the reduced cooking juices have
been added.

cancoillotte

A speciality of the Franche-Comté
region based on *metton*, a skimmed
cows'-milk cheese. Metton takes the
form of hard hazelnut-sized grains with
a strong smell and has a long ripening
process. The cheese is mixed in a bain-
marie with salted water and fresh butter

to form a pale-yellow homogeneous paste, with a strong flavour. It is sweetened with white wine and eaten warm.

candied fruit

See *crystallized fruit*.

candies

See *sweets*.

candissoire

A flat rectangular cooking utensil with raised edges and a removable wire grid forming the base. The candissoire is used to hold such articles as crystallized (candied) fruits or fresh petits fours after glazing with melted sugar. It is also used for draining small pastries soaked with alcohol, especially individual babas.

Candlemas CHANDELEUR

The Christian festival held on 2 February to celebrate the Presentation of Christ at the Temple and the Purification of the Virgin Mary. The word comes from the Latin *festa candelarum* (feast of the candles) because many candles are lit in churches on that day. The origin of this festival is the ancient Roman festival of fertility, Lupercalia, dedicated to the god Pan. Pope Gelasius I abolished it in 492 and replaced it with processions holding lighted candles to symbolize the light of the divine Spirit. The festival also coincided with the resumption of work in the fields after the rigours of winter. This is probably why Candlemas is the occasion when flour-based dishes, such as pancakes and fritters, are made. Pancakes were considered to be a symbol of the sun because of their round shape and golden colour. To use the wheat from the previous harvest was also a means of attracting a blessing upon the future harvest.

The tradition of making pancakes is a very old one. It was mentioned in *Le Ménagier de Paris* (1393), and there are various superstitions attached to it. In Burgundy, you must toss one onto the top of the cupboard to avoid being short of money during the year! While pancakes are being made, shame on the clumsy one who drops it while turning it! At the Candlemas of 1812, prior to his departure for the Russian campaign, Napoleon made some crêpes *à la Malmaison*. It is said that four out of the five he made were successful, thus forecasting his victory in four battles. The fifth spoilt pancake worried him, and on the day of the Moscow fire, he might have said to Marshal Ney: 'It is the fifth pancake!'

candyfloss (cotton candy)

BARBE À PAPA

A confection made from coloured sugar syrup(usually white or pink), cooked and spun using a special machine into spidery threads which are rolled around a stick like wool on a distaff. The earliest machine, operated by a crank shaft, appeared in France at the Paris Exposition of 1900. Today, high-speed electric machines are used.

candy sugar

SUCRE CANDI

Refined crystallized sugar. The Arabic word *qandi* means 'cane sugar', but candy sugar can be made from sugar beet or sugar cane. It was used therapeutically from the 12th century onwards, and was often flavoured with rose, violet, lemon, or redcurrant.

Candy sugar takes the form of large crystals, which are obtained by slowly cooling a concentrated sugar syrup so that it crystallizes around threads stretched out in the tank. Brown candy sugar is obtained from a brown syrup.

Candy sugar dissolves very slowly and is preferred to ordinary sugar for preparing fruits in brandy and domestic liqueurs, since it allows time for the flavour of the fruits to emerge. It is also used in making champagne.

canelling CANNELER

The technique of making small V-shaped grooves over the surface of a vegetable or a fruit for decoration, using a canelle knife. The vegetable or fruit is often sliced after the canelle grooves have been cut, to make decorative borders to the slices.

canette

A traditional French beer bottle characterized by having a porcelain bung with a rubber washer, which is attached with a metal clamp. This bung has now been largely replaced with a seal. The word *canette* originated in Picardy and originally meant an elongated jug. It is also used to hold lemonade.

canna BALISIER

A vigorous tropical plant with a thick fleshy underground stem, which is eaten as a vegetable. Some varieties produce an edible starch used particularly in Australia, where it is known as 'Queensland arrowroot'.

cannelloni

A type of pasta dish originating in Italy. The word derives from *canna* (reed) and literally means 'big tubes'. Pasta squares are simmered in water and a knob of savoury filling is placed in the centre of each. They are then rolled up into cylinders to form the cannelloni, usually covered with tomato sauce, and cooked *au gratin*. Alternatively, cannelloni can be bought in the form of tubes, ready for filling.

RECIPES

Cannelloni pasta PÂTE À CANNELLONI Mix 200 g (7 oz, 1¾ cups) sifted flour and a large pinch of salt with 2 beaten eggs and enough cold water for the pasta to be flexible and smooth. Roll into a ball. Wrap in a damp cloth and keep cool for at least 1 hour. Cover the working surface with flour, and roll out the pasta to a thickness of about 3 mm (⅛ in). Using a pastry wheel, cut the pasta dough into rectangles measuring 6 × 8 cm (2½ × 3¼ in) and leave to dry for 1 hour. Bring a large saucepan of water to the boil, plunge in the pasta rectangles, and cook for about 10 minutes. Drain and fill.

Cannelloni à la béchamel Prepare some cannelloni pasta rectangles. Chop up 2 large onions and blanch them in 25 g (1 oz, 2 tablespoons) butter. Chop 3 slices of ham and about 250 g (9 oz) cooked chicken leftovers; add these to the onions and adjust the seasoning. Make a béchamel sauce with 50 g (2 oz, 4 tablespoons) butter, 50 g (2 oz, ½ cup) flour, 0.5 litre (17 fl oz, 2 cups) milk, salt, pepper, and grated nutmeg. Add 75 g (3 oz, ¾ cup) grated cheese and the chopped meat and onion. Fill the pasta

rectangles with this mixture, then roll them up. Butter an ovenproof gratin dish and arrange the cannelloni in it. Cover with the rest of the béchamel sauce. Sprinkle with 50 g (2 oz, ½ cup) grated cheese and a few knobs of butter. Brown in a very hot oven (240 c, 475 f, gas 9) or under a hot grill.

Cannelloni à la florentine Prepare some rectangles of cannelloni pasta. Hard-boil (hard-cook) 2 eggs and remove the shells. Boil some spinach and drain it. Make a very smooth béchamel sauce. Roughly chop the spinach and heat it gently in butter, allowing 30 g (1 oz, 2 tablespoons) butter to 1 kg (2 lb) spinach. Finely chop the hard-boiled eggs and add to the spinach. Also add 2 raw egg yolks mixed with 1 dl (5 tablespoons, scant ½ cup) fresh double (heavy) cream, 40 g (1½ oz, scant ½ cup) grated Parmesan cheese, salt, pepper, and grated nutmeg. Gently reheat the mixture without boiling, then leave to cool. Fill the pasta rectangles with this mixture and roll them up. Arrange in a buttered ovenproof dish, cover with the béchamel sauce, and sprinkle with grated Parmesan cheese and a few knobs of butter. Cook in a very hot oven (240 c, 475 f, gas 9) or under a hot grill until the surface is brown and crusty.

Meat cannelloni CANNELLONI À LA VIANDE Fill the pasta rectangles with a bolognaise sauce rich in chopped meat. Roll them up and arrange in a buttered ovenproof dish. Cover with tomato sauce, sprinkle with grated cheese, and place in a very hot oven (240 c, 475 f, gas 9) or under a hot grill until the surface is well browned.

Seafood cannelloni CANNELLONI AUX FRUITS DE MER Fill the pasta rectangles with a stuffing of crab meat or peeled prawns bound with a well-seasoned béchamel sauce. Roll up the cannelloni and arrange in a buttered ovenproof dish. Cover with normande sauce, sprinkle with a few knobs of butter, and cook in a very hot oven (240 c, 475 f, gas 9) or under a grill until the surface is well browned.

canole

A dry biscuit that is a speciality of Rochechouart (Haute-Vienne region). It originated in 1371, during the Hundred Years' War. The town, which had been under siege by the English, was relieved by du Guesclin. The inhabitants duly pillaged the enemy camp and found wheat and fresh eggs, with which they made these biscuits, mockingly named after the captain of the English troops, Sir Robert Canolles (or Knolles).

canotière (à la)

A name usually given to poached freshwater fish covered with bâtarde sauce. It is also given to a carp dish in which the carp is stuffed with a fish mousse, baked in a white wine stock, then arranged on a gratin dish with sliced shallots and mushrooms and lemon juice, and sprinkled with breadcrumbs. The sauce, which is made with the reduced cooking juices, is thickened with butter. The dish is garnished with crayfish cooked in court-bouillon, and with *fleurons* (crescents of puff pastry). The same stuffing and garnish are used for matelote *à la canotière*.

| RECIPE

matelote à la canotière Butter a frying pan (skillet) and make a bed of 150 g (5 oz) sliced onions and 4 crushed cloves of garlic. Add 1.5 kg (3¼ lb) freshwater fish (carp, eel, etc.) cut into equalized pieces, a large bouquet garni, and 1 litre (1¾ pints, 4¼ cups) dry white wine. Bring to the boil. Add 1 dl (3½ fl oz, scant ½ cup) brandy and flame. Cover and gently simmer for about 25 minutes. Drain the fish pieces, placing them in another frying pan, and retain the stock. To the fish add 125 g (4½ oz) cooked button mushrooms and 125 g (4½ oz) small glazed onions. Reduce the fish stock by two-thirds and bind with kneaded butter (for a litre of stock, bind with 50 g (2 oz, ½ cup) flour kneaded with 50 g (2 oz, 4 tablespoons) butter; finally, add a further 150 g (5 oz, ⅔ cup) butter. Pour the sauce over the fish and simmer gently. Serve the matelote in a deep round dish, garnished with gudgeons fried in breadcrumbs and crayfish cooked in a court-bouillon.

Cantal

A high-fat (45% fat) cows'-milk cheese from the Auvergne region of France. It is ivory in colour with a naturally darker crust, a flexible finely granulated texture, and a sweet nutty flavour; riper cheeses are a little firmer and more highly flavoured. It is also called Fourme du Cantal or Fourme de Salers, (where the cows produce a rich full-flavoured milk). An *appellation d'origine* label means that the production region is strictly defined as the department of Cantal and the arrondissements of Tulle, Ussel, Brioude, Clermont-Ferrand, and Issoire. Cantal is considered the ancestor of French cheeses: Pliny the Elder mentioned it, as did Grégoire de Tours. The similarity of its manufacture to that of British Cheddar suggests that Romans may have introduced the technique to the Bretons across the English Channel.

Cantal comes in the form of a cylinder, 35–40 cm (14–16 in) high and the same in diameter, weighing 35–45 kg (77–100 lb). Dairy Cantal is produced all the year round, whereas farm Cantal comes from the shepherds' huts of the Cantal. Connoisseurs prefer it when it has matured for three months: the thick crust sinks into the cheese, forming brown marks, and it has a fairly sharp taste. A smaller Cantal is also produced, called a *cantalet* or *cantalon*, weighing 4–10 kg (9–22 lb). An intermediate *petit cantal* weighs 20–22 kg (44–48 lb). Cantal is often served after a meal, with wine and fruit; it is also widely used in gratins, croûtes, soups, and soufflés, as well as in typically regional dishes (aligot, gâtis, patranque, truffade, etc.).

canteen CANTINE

Originally from the Italian *cantina* (a cellar), this word has several meanings. Firstly, it is a place where communal meals are eaten; for instance, on a worksite or in a barracks, school, or factory. A canteen is also a small shop where prisoners and soldiers can buy food to supplement their ordinary diets. From 1780 to 1914, regimental canteens were managed in France by a *cantinière* (originally *vivandière*) appointed by the administration. They would accompany the unit in the field, wearing a fancy military uniform.

A canteen is also a travelling box mainly used by the military and a metal container consisting of two superimposed boxes, one for transporting a ready-prepared dish and one for a water bath to reheat the dish.

Finally, the word is also used for a box containing a set of cutlery, and for the cutlery itself.

cantharus CANTHARE

A bell-shaped drinking vessel used by the Greeks and Romans. Made of ceramic, bronze, or silver, it stood on a single foot and had two vertical handles that rose above the rim.

cantonnaise (à la)

The French term for a garnished rice dish inspired by Cantonese cuisine, which is very popular not only in Canton but throughout China and in other countries. For Cantonese fried rice, the grains must be well separated from each other after cooking. The rice is cooked plain then left to rest for a few hours in the refrigerator; it should be fluffed up from time to time to aerate it. For the garnish, some lard is heated in a frying pan (skillet), together with salt, smoked bacon (or ham, or even lacquered pork) cut up into small pieces, chopped celery sticks (stalks), and prawns. After a few minutes the rice is added; when this is hot, some eggs are broken into the pan. The mixture is stirred until the eggs are just set.

The dish can also include crab meat, shellfish, bamboo shoots, or peas. The traditional Chinese seasoning is soy sauce and rice alcohol.

capacity and content
CAPACITÉ ET CONTENANCE

The volume of a vessel, which determines the quantity of a substance it can hold. In practice, the term capacity is used for bottles and cans of liquid and content for other receptacles. There is always a difference between the nominal content of a receptacle (the capacity) and the actual content (volume or net weight contained).

cape gooseberry
ALKÉKENGE

The fruit of a bush originating in Peru, which grows wild in hedgerows and thickets in warm countries, particularly in the south of France. Also called physalis, strawberry tomato, love-in-a-cage, and winter cherry, the cape gooseberry is yellow or red, the size of a cherry, and is enclosed in a brown papery bladder (calyx). It has a tart flavour and is used to make syrups and jams, as well as in fruit salads, sorbets, and ice creams.

RECIPE

Cape gooseberry compote COMPOTE D'ALKÉKENGES Dissolve 500 g (18 oz, 2 cups) sugar in 2 dl (7 fl oz, ¾ cup) water. Strip the fruits from their calyces and drop them into the boiling syrup. Cook for 5 minutes, then drain and put them into a compote dish. Add the rind of a lemon to the syrup, reduce this by a quarter, and pour it over the fruit. The rind should not be cooked with the fruit as it would affect its flavour.

caper CÂPRE

The flower bud of a shrub which is native to eastern Asia but widespread in hot regions. Capers are used as a condiment, either pickled in vinegar or preserved in brine. When pickled, they are sour but full of flavour. The Romans used them to season fish sauces. Capers are also used to flavour rice and meatballs (lamb and veal) and garnish pizzas; they go well with mustard and horseradish (see *gribiche*, *ravigote*). The flower buds of nasturtium, buttercup, marigold, and broom are sometimes used as substitutes for capers.

RECIPE

Caper sauces SAUCES AUX CÂPRES To accompany boiled fish, add 2 level tablespoons pickled capers, well drained, to 2.5 dl (8 fl oz, 1 cup) hollandaise sauce or butter sauce.

To accompany English-style boiled mutton, prepare melted butter sauce, adding the mutton cooking juices to the roux, followed by well-drained capers and a little anchovy essence or a purée of desalted anchovies.

capercaillie

COQ DE BRUYÈRE

The largest species of grouse. The adult male is the size of a turkey and can weigh up to 8 kg (18 lb). The hunting of female and young capercaillies is forbidden. The bird lives in coniferous hilly woodlands, feeding on conifer shoots, which gives its flesh a pronounced flavour of resin. It is rare in France, being found in the mountains of the Ardennes, Vosges, and Pyrenees. The black grouse is often preferred for cookery: its delicate flesh is whiter than that of the pheasant but is prepared in the same way.

capilotade

A ragout, originally from classic French cookery, made of cooked meat leftovers (poultry, beef, or veal) that are stewed until they disintegrate. The word comes from the Spanish *capirotada*, which was a brown sauce made with garlic, eggs, and herbs, used to cover the cut pieces of meat. The expression *en capilotade* (meaning in small pieces) is used in cookery, particularly for poultry dishes.

RECIPE

Chicken en capilotade POULET EN CAPILOTADE Take a chicken (boiled, braised, poached, or roasted) and remove the bones. Cut the meat into small pieces and place in a well-reduced cold sauce (for example, chasseur, Italian, Portuguese, or Provençal). Cover and leave to simmer gently until the meat forms a hash. Then pour into a deep dish.

Alternatively, the chicken and sauce can be poured into a gratin dish, sprinkled with breadcrumbs and knobs of butter, then cooked in a very hot oven (240 c, 475 F, gas 9) or under a hot grill until the surface is well browned. Serve with rice *à la créole*.

caplin CAPELAN

Either of two species of marine fish, up to 15 cm (6 in) long. One is a Mediterranean species; the other is common in the English Channel and the Bay of Biscay.

They have a fairly thickset body, brownish-yellow on the back, silver-grey on the sides, and white on the belly. The large head has large bulbous eyes and a barb under the chin. The two species are distinguished by the spacing of the caudal fins. The caplin, whose delicate flesh flakes easily, is used especially in fish soups.

capon CHAPON

A young cock that has been castrated and fattened. The meat is remarkably tender and this method of rearing poultry is a very ancient one. It was a speciality of the French city of Le Mans, but gradually disappeared because of the cost and the length of time involved. Recently, it has been taken up again in Bresse and Landes. Hormonal castration of cockerels has been banned since 1959. Capon is prepared in the same way as chicken.

The abundance and great delicacy of the flesh of a capon is due to the accumulation of fat, which is stored in successive layers in the muscles. A capon may weigh as much as 6 kg (13 lb).

Capons from Landes are fed on maize (corn) and are yellow, whereas those from Bresse are white. They are suitable for serving on festive occasions when there are plenty of guests.

caponata

A Sicilian speciality made of aubergines (eggplants), celery, and tomatoes, sliced and fried in olive oil and flavoured with capers, olives, and anchovy fillets. This dish is served as a cold hors d'oeuvre.

RECIPE

Caponata Peel 4 aubergines (eggplants), cut into large dice, and sprinkle with salt. When they have lost some of their water, wash and wipe them and fry in oil. Cut the following ingredients into very small pieces: 100 g (4 oz, scant 1 cup) olives, a head of celery scalded in salted water, 4 desalted anchovies, and 50 g (2 oz) capers. Slice an onion and brown in oil. Heat up 2 dl (7 fl oz, ¾ cup) tomato purée with 50 g (2 oz, 4 tablespoons) sugar until it is well reduced and darker in colour. Then add ½ glass vinegar and leave to simmer for a few minutes. Season with salt and pepper, add some chopped parsley, then mix the sauce with the aubergines and other ingredients. Allow to cool thoroughly. Arrange in the shape of a dome in a vegetable dish.

capsicum

POIVRON ET PIMENT

The fruit of several varieties of *Capsicum frutescens*, used as a vegetable. Capsicums may be mild, sweet, hot, or incredibly fiery, depending on the variety. Belonging to the same family as the tomato and aubergine (eggplant), they were discovered by Christopher Columbus in America and described by botanists at the beginning of the 16th century; they soon spread through Europe and the rest of the world. Capsicums are sold fresh, dried, or ground; there are two main types.

□ Sweet peppers (*poivrons*) These are large fleshy capsicums with a mild flavour. Green, yellow, orange, red, or black, they are now widely used in cooking with the increasing popularity of Mediterranean dishes. Sweet peppers have a low calorific value (22 Cal per 100 g) and are rich in vitamin C. Choose capsicums that are firm and glossy – avoid any with wrinkles or soft spots. Always remove the seeds and white fibrous membrane from inside before using. They may also be skinned by grilling (broiling) close to the heat until the skin blackens; it will then peel off. Alternatively, spear on a long fork or skewer and turn over and over in the gas flame until charred. The word 'capsicum' means box, and the hollow shape of these vegetables makes them perfect for stuffing. They are also used in salads, marinated condiments, and certain typical Mediterranean dishes, such as gazpacho, ratatouille, piperade, and caponata. They go well with chicken, rabbit, ham, tuna, mutton, eggs, and rice and they are a characteristic feature of many dishes, including those prepared *à la basquaise, à la portugaise, à la turque, à l'andalouse,* and *à la mexicaine.*

□ Chilli peppers (*piments*) Much smaller than sweet peppers, these, too, can be green, yellow, orange, red, or black. The seeds and flesh are extremely hot and should be used sparingly. By removing the seeds, the pepper is rendered less fiery. It is the volatile oil in the fruit, called capsicin, that accounts for its hot taste. Avoid contact with the eyes or any sensitive skin as the oil is an irritant. Chilli peppers soaked in cold salted water for a while will be less hot. They can also be charred like sweet peppers to give them a delicious smoky flavour. It is not, however, necessary to skin them before use.

There are many different varieties, the largest number being found in Mexico and the West Indies, where they are used liberally in local dishes.

● *West Indian pepper* (or *cherry pepper*): 2–3 cm (about 1 in) long, bright red, irregular in shape, and with a very strong hot flavour. It is sold fresh throughout the year.

● *Cayenne pepper*: 8 cm (3 in) long, thin, red, and with a strong and rather sharp flavour. Grown in South America and also in the south of France, it is sold fresh all the year round.

● *Bird pepper*: no more than 2 cm (1 in) long, copper-coloured, with a very strong hot flavour. It is sold fresh, dried, or ground (as cayenne) and is grown in Africa, Guyana, and Mexico.

● *Mild red chilli pepper*: 8 cm (3 in) long, pointed, with a strong flavour (but not as strong as most other varieties). It is grown in North Africa (where it is known as the *felfel*) and in the south of France. It can be bought fresh or dried.

● *Mild green chilli pepper*: quite strong, but milder than the mild red chilli, though similar in shape and size.

Besides these varieties there are a number of more exotic ones, including *ancho* (spicy, mild, and heart-shaped), *chipotle* (conical, brick-red, and very piquant), *pequin* (scarlet, minute, and very fiery; used dried), *malagueta* (very hot and stringy; most common in Bahia in Brazil), and *poblano* (dark red, quite large, and scented). Some West Indian varieties have colourful names, including the Zozio pepper (parrot's tongue), the Chinese lantern pepper, and the 'seven courts-bouillons pepper': all these have a fairly strong flavour.

The explorer Magellan introduced chilli peppers to Africa and Asia. In France they were confused with other spices for a long time, and even today they have only limited use in French cookery. In Mexico, on the other hand, chillies are used in nearly all ragouts and sauces (*moles*) to which they give their characteristic piquancy. Chilli pepper is also used to season black beans, avocados, fruit, and even cheese; it is also famous in the dish of beef and red beans, *chilli con carne*. In Britain and the United States, chilli peppers are used in pickles and mustard condiments. In Middle Eastern cuisine they are often served pickled whole. The North African harissa, which seasons couscous and other dishes, is made with red chilli peppers and garlic. Several kinds of chilli pepper are used in Indian curries, while the Chinese *öt* is a purée of red chilli pepper with salt and oil which is served with many dishes. Finally, chilli peppers are the principal ingredient of American Tabasco sauce. See also *paprika*.

RECIPES

CHILLI PEPPERS

Chilli-pepper oil   HUILE PIMENTÉE Boil 6 small Cayenne (or other chilli) peppers, crush them slightly, and place them in 1 litre (1¾ pints, 4¼ cups) olive oil. Cork the container, then shake. Leave to stand for 2 months away from the light before using.

Chilli purée   PURÉE DE PIMENT Cut open some strong chilli peppers lengthways and remove the seeds. Crush the flesh in a mortar or reduce it to a purée in a food processor. Add a little onion, ginger, and salt. Mix this purée thoroughly and place it in small tightly sealed bottles. Cover with oil. Leave to stand for 2 months before using. This purée will keep almost indefinitely provided it is always covered with oil. Since the oil may turn rancid, renew it at regular intervals.

SWEET PEPPERS

Grilled (broiled) pepper salad   POIVRONS GRILLÉS EN SALADE Cut some green peppers in half, removing the stalks and the seeds. Oil them very lightly and cook in a very hot oven under the grill (broiler), skin side up, until the skin blisters and blackens. Peel them and cut into strips. Make a vinaigrette with olive oil, very finely chopped garlic, chopped parsley, lemon juice, and a very small quantity of vinegar. Sprinkle over the pepper strips while they are still warm, leave to marinate at room temperature for at least 2 hours, then chill in the refrigerator. Serve as a cold hors d'oeuvre with toast spread with tapenade, shrimps, small octopuses in salad, etc.

Mille-feuille of scallops with sweet peppers   MILLE-FEUILLE DE SAINT-JACQUES AUX POIVRONS (from E. Tabourdiau's recipe) Prepare some puff pastry. Roll out thinly and divide into 16 equal rectangles, about 10 cm (4 in) by 7 cm (2½ in). Cook in a hot oven (220 C, 425 F, gas 7). Trim the edges and keep warm. Cook 6 peeled and crushed cloves of garlic in 2.5 dl (8 fl oz, 1 cup) whipping cream. Strain, season with salt and pepper, and add 25 g (1 oz, 2 tablespoons) butter. Keep in a warm place.

Clean, peel, and remove the seeds from 3 red peppers and 3 green peppers. Cut into strips and cook in 3 tablespoons (¼ cup) olive oil. Sauté 32 half-walnuts and 16 scallop corals in butter.

Construct 8 mille-feuilles by placing on top of each other a rectangle of puff pastry, a layer of red pepper, 4 half-walnuts and 2 scallop corals, a little garlic cream, a layer of green pepper, and finally a rectangle of puff pastry. Glaze the mille-feuilles with butter and arrange on a serving dish. Serve with scalloped mushrooms sautéed in butter, and beurre blanc.

Peppers à la piémontaise   POIVRONS À LA PIÉMONTAISE Grill (broil) some peppers or cook in a very hot oven until the skins blister and blacken. Peel them, remove the seeds, and cut into strips. Make a risotto *à la piémontaise*. Arrange alternate layers of peppers and risotto in a buttered gratin dish. Finish with a layer of peppers, sprinkle with grated Parmesan cheese and melted butter, and brown in a hot oven.

Peppers à l'orientale   POIVRONS À L'ORIENTALE Cut the stalk ends off 500 g (18 oz) green peppers and remove the seeds. Grill, peel, and cut into large dice. Gently fry 100 g (4 oz, 1 cup) chopped onions in a saucepan, without allowing them to brown, then add the peppers, a pinch of powdered garlic, 1.5 dl (¼ pint, ⅔ cup) clear stock, and pepper. Simmer for 30–35 minutes, then adjust the seasoning and serve very hot as a garnish for white meat or mutton.

Stuffed peppers   POIVRONS FARCIS
Cut the stalk ends off 12 very small green peppers. Remove the seeds and blanch for 5 minutes in boiling salted water. Prepare a stuffing by coarsely chopping 2 handfuls of very fresh sorrel leaves, 4 peeled deseeded tomatoes, 3 Spanish onions, 3 green peppers, and a small sprig of fennel. Place in a saucepan with 2 tablespoons (3 tablespoons) warm olive oil and cook gently, stirring, until soft but not brown. Strain to remove the liquid and mix with an equal volume of rice cooked in meat stock.

Stuff the peppers with this mixture. Pour a little oil in a deep frying pan and arrange the stuffed peppers in it, closely packed together. Half-fill the pan with thin tomato sauce to which lemon juice and 2 dl (7 fl oz, ¾ cup) olive oil have been added. Cook for approximately 25 minutes with the lid on. Arrange the peppers in a shallow dish together with the liquid in which they have been cooked. Leave to cool and then refrigerate for at least an hour. Serve as an hors d'oeuvre.

Capua delights
DÉLICES DE CAPOUE
A succession of gastronomic treats, enjoyed in a pleasant atmosphere, which make one lose one's sense of time and morals. After conquering the Italian town of Capua during the Second Punic War, Hannibal set up his winter quarters there to prepare for the siege of Rome. His soldiers nearly lost their fighting spirit there! The region of Campania is renowned for its cuisine, especially fried fish dishes, fruits, and light wines.

capucin
A small savoury tartlet, filled with Gruyère choux pastry and served as a hot entrée.

RECIPE

Capucins   Make some shortcrust pastry (basic pie dough) using 200 g (7 oz, 1¾ cups) flour, 100 g (3½ oz, ½ cup) well-softened butter, a large pinch of salt, and 2 or 3 tablespoons very cold water. Use this pastry to line 8 tartlet tins. Also make some choux pastry using 250 ml (8 fl oz, 1 cup) water, 50 g (2 oz, 4 tablespoons butter, a large pinch of salt, and 125 g (4½ oz, generous 1 cup) flour. Then, away from the heat and one at a time, add 3 whole eggs and 75 g (3 oz, ¾ cup) grated Gruyère cheese. Place a ball of the Gruyère choux pastry in each tartlet and bake in a moderately hot oven (about 190 c, 375 f, gas 5). Serve hot.

caquelon
An earthenware dish with a glazed interior, used in southern France to cook dishes that require simmering. Originally it was placed in hot ashes. When used on a cooker, a diffusing device must be placed between the caquelon and the gas flame or hotplate. It is customary to rub the inside with a clove of garlic the first time it is used, so it does not crack. In southwestern France, it is called a *toupin*.

carafe
A glass or crystal vessel with a wide base and narrow neck, which can sometimes be sealed with a glass stopper. It is used to serve water and wine at the table. Liqueurs and spirits may also be kept in carafes or stoppered *carafons* (small carafes). In the 19th century, a carafon was a metal bucket in which bottles were cooled.

Carafe wines are light, fresh, young, and inexpensive open wines, that restaurants serve in carafes, half or quarter carafes, or jugs. In the UK since 1976 the contents of a carafe used in a catering establishment must be stated.

carambola   CARAMBOLE
The fruit of a tree that is grown in the West Indies, Indonesia, and Brazil. Golden-yellow and elongated, with projecting ribs, the carambola is sliced and eaten fresh, either with cream and sugar for dessert, or with vinaigrette like avo-

cados. The fruit is star-shaped in cross section and the flesh is juicy and acidic.

caramel

Melted sugar that has been browned by heating. The word comes from the Latin *cannamella* (sugar cane). Heated above 150 C (300 F), sugar syrup changes colour, gradually losing its sweetness and giving off an increasingly strong 'burnt' odour. Eventually it becomes inedible. The end product is determined by temperature, depending on what the caramel is to be used for.

☐ **Preparing caramel**
— Use a small stainless-steel, thick aluminium, or untinned copper saucepan (no enamelled or tinned container should be used), to ensure good heat distribution.
— Select a very pure refined sugar.
— Add a little water to the sugar in the pan.
— Place the pan over a medium heat. The pan may be shaken to and fro to distribute the heat but the contents must not be stirred. Carefully watch the gradual colouring of the syrup.
● *Very pale caramel* – Almost white and used to glaze petits fours and sugar-coated fruits. Stop heating as soon as the syrup starts to turn yellow at the edges of the pan. A teaspoon of vinegar will help .. stay liquid for longer.
● *Pale caramel* – Used to caramelize choux pastry, coat citrus fruits, and bind meringues and other items. Make only small quantities at a time since, once hardened, it changes colour if reheated.
● *Medium caramel* – Mahogany in colour and used to coat moulds, make nougatine, and flavour puddings, creams, compotes, ice creams, etc. Never make the caramel directly in the cake mould.
● *Slaked caramel* – A small quantity of cold water is carefully added when the caramel has turned a mahogany colour, in order to stop the cooking process. Some of the syrup solidifies immediately. Used for flavouring, it is put back on a low heat and melted while stirring.
● *Brown caramel* – Amber-red and used to colour consommés, sauces, and stews.
● *Dry caramel* – Cooked without water but with a few drops of lemon juice. Used in a few recipes, including nougatine and caramel ice cream.
● *Liquid caramel* – Sold ready for use, in bottles or sachets, to flavour desserts, yogurts, and ice creams, or to caramelize moulds or cover desserts.

Caramel is also used commercially as a colouring agent (E150), particularly for liqueurs and alcohols, as well as for certain ready-made sauces.

RECIPES

Caramel sauce CARAMEL À SAUCE (from a recipe by Carême) Melt some caster (superfine) sugar without adding any water, and leave it to colour gradually over a gentle heat (this takes about 15 minutes). When it has turned amber-red, add a glass of water, turn up the heat to high, and boil for a few minutes. The result should be a beautiful amber-red caramel.

Coating caramel CARAMEL À NAPPER Place 200 g (7 oz, scant 1 cup) granulated sugar and 4 tablespoons water in a thick saucepan. Dissolve the sugar over a low heat. Add about 1 teaspoon lemon juice. When the liquid is boiling, stop stirring. When the mixture begins to change colour, shake the pan to obtain a uniformly coloured caramel; do not continue to stir as the caramel will stick to the spoon in a mass. When the caramel is a golden colour, add 1 tablespoon hot water and shake the pan to mix. Add the same quantity of water again, and stir. The mixture should still be very liquid. It will harden as it cools.

caramelize CARAMÉLISER

To turn sugar into caramel by gently heating it, an operation that requires care and precision. Alternatively, it can mean coating a mould with caramel, flavouring a pudding or similar preparation with caramel, glazing sugar-coated fruits, choux pastry, etc., with caramel, or colouring the top of a cake or biscuit by powdering it with sugar and putting it under the grill. Certain vegetables, such as small onions, carrots, or turnips, are 'glazed' – or lightly caramelized – by being heated with some sugar and a small quantity of water or butter in a saucepan.

RECIPE

Caramelizing a mould CARAMÉLISER
UN MOULE Place 100 g (4 oz, ½ cup)
sugar, 1 teaspoon lemon juice, and 1
tablespoon water into a small thick
saucepan. Heat until the mixture turns a
pale caramel colour (160 C, 320 F). Pour
the caramel into the mould and tilt the
mould in all directions to distribute the
caramel over the bottom and sides.
Continue to tilt until the caramel no
longer flows.

caramels

Sweets, often square-shaped, made
from a mixture of sugar, cooked glucose
syrup, and dairy products (milk, butter,
or cream), plus vegetable fats and
flavourings. There are various types –
hard and soft caramels, fudge, *hopje*,
and toffee – depending on the composition, degree of cooking, shape, and
flavour. The French town of Isigny,
famous for its milk, also makes famous
caramels.
• *Hard caramels* – These are made using glucose syrup, sugar, water, and
milk. Fats and flavourings are also
added. After homogenization, the mixture is heated until it reaches the required degree of hardness, then cooled,
cut up, and (if required) wrapped. Hard
caramel is also made into lollipops.
Although cocoa, coffee, or vanilla can
be used as flavouring, it is essentially
milk, more or less caramelized, that
gives it its flavour.
• *Soft caramels* – The glucose syrup is
dissolved in an emulsion of milk and
fats, then cooked and flavoured with
vanilla, cocoa, coffee, or hazelnuts.
Cutting is done after cooling.
    Making caramel at home requires
special equipment, particularly a
wooden frame in which the caramel
sets.

RECIPES

Hard coffee caramels CARAMELS
DURS AU CAFÉ Mix 250 g (9 oz)
granulated sugar with 100 g (4 fl oz, ½
cup) fresh cream, 2 cl (1 tablespoon)
coffee extract, and 12 drops of lemon
juice in a thick saucepan. Heat while
stirring with a wooden spoon, until the
temperature reaches 142 C (288 F). Oil a
marble or other heat-resistant surface
and a caramel frame, pour the caramel
into the middle of the frame, and leave
to harden, but do not allow to cool
completely. Remove the frame and pass
a flexible metal spatula under the sheet
of caramel to detach it from the surface.
Cut the caramel up into 2-cm (1-in)
squares.

soft butter caramels CARAMELS
MOUS AU BEURRE Place 250 g (9 oz)
granulated sugar, 1 dl (6 tablespoons,
scant ½ cup) milk, and 80 g (3 oz) honey
or glucose in a thick saucepan. Add a
vanilla pod split into two, and bring to
the boil while stirring continuously with
a wooden spoon. Add 150 g (5 oz, ⅔
cup) butter in small quantities, and
lower the heat. Continue to cook while
stirring, until the temperature reaches
120 C (248 F). Oil a marble or other
heat-resistant surface and 4 caramel
rules or an 18-cm (7-in) tart ring. Remove the vanilla pod from the saucepan
and pour the caramel into the ring or
between the rules, on top of the prepared surface. Leave to cool completely
for 2–3 hours before cutting up the
caramel with a large knife.

caraway CARVI

An aromatic plant, common in central
and northern Europe, that is grown
mainly for its brown oblong seeds.
When dried, these are used as a spice,
particularly in eastern Europe, to
flavour sauerkraut and stews and to
accompany certain cheeses (Gouda and
Munster). In Hungary and Germany,
where caraway is very popular, it is used
to flavour bread and cakes. In England,
it is added to cooked potatoes and
baked in cakes and biscuits
(Shakespeare's Shallow invites Falstaff
to partake of 'a last year's pippin of
mine own graffing, with a dish of car-
aways'). In France, it is used to flavour
Vosges dragées. Caraway is also widely
used in making liqueurs, such as Kümmel, Vespétro, schnapps, and aquavit.
There are various alternative names for
it in French, including 'meadow cumin',
'fool's aniseed', and 'mountain cumin'.
Caraway was used in prehistoric times
(the seeds have been found at ancient
sites) and was appreciated by the Romans, who ate the root like a vegetable.

carbohydrate GLUCIDE

One of a large group of chemical compounds, many of which are important sources of energy as foodstuffs. There are three major groups of carbohydrates in food: sugars (sucrose, fructose, glucose, etc.); starches; and cellulose, which occurs in fresh and dried vegetables, cereals, and fruit. Sugar and starches are easily digested and are an important energy source. Cellulose is not converted by digestive juices but provides dietary fibre.

carbonade

A Flemish speciality made of slices of beef that are browned and then cooked with onions and beer. The word comes from the Italian *carbonata* (charcoal-grilled). The name *carbonade* (or *cambonnade*) is also given to grilled (broiled) pork loin as well as to certain beef stews with red wine prepared in the south of France.

RECIPE

Carbonade à la flamande Slice 250 g (9 oz) onions. Take 750 g (1¾ lb) beef flank or chuck steak, cut into pieces or thin slices, and brown over a high heat in a frying pan (skillet) in 40 g (1½ oz, 3 tablespoons) lard. Drain. Fry the onions until golden in the same fat. Arrange the meat and onions in a small flameproof casserole in alternate layers, seasoning each layer with salt and pepper. Add a bouquet garni. Deglaze the frying pan with 6 dl (1 pint, 2½ cups) beer and half a glass of beef stock (fresh or made with concentrate). Make a brown roux with 25 g (1 oz, 2 tablespoons) butter and 25 g (1 oz, ¼ cup) flour, and add the beer mixture, then ½ teaspoon brown sugar (coffee sugar). Adjust the seasoning. Pour the mixture into the casserole, cover, and leave to cook very gently for 2½ hours. Serve in the casserole.

carcass CARCASSE

An animal after slaughter and processing at the abattoir. The ratio between the weight of the carcass and the weight of the live animal represents the killing out percentage and reflects the animal's meat yield. Large cattle, calves, and sheep are bled after slaughter, then skinned and eviscerated; the feet and head are cut off. Pigs, on the other hand, are not skinned, and the carcass includes the head and feet. For large cattle, the carcass is cut into four quarters: fast-cooking parts are at the back, slow-cooking parts at the front. The 'fifth quarter' comprises the offal and by-products. The carcasses are hung from large pegs, called *chevilles* in French, which is why butchers' wholesale suppliers are called *chevillards*.

cardamom or cardamon
CARDAMOME

An aromatic plant from the Malabar region of southwestern India, whose capsules contain seeds that are dried and used as a spice. Cardamom is used much more in the East than in Europe, except for Scandinavian countries, where it is used to spice mulled wines, stewed fruit, flans, and some charcuterie products. In France nowadays it is hardly used at all, except in gingerbread. Most common in India, cardamom is used to flavour rice, cakes, omelettes, meatballs, and noodles. In Arab countries its spicy flavour is appreciated with coffee.

cardinal

A fish dish that is garnished with lobster escalopes (or sometimes slices of truffle) or coated with a white sauce containing lobster stock. The name refers to the colour of the lobster after cooking, just as the French word *cardinaliser* is used to describe shellfish cooked in stock – their shells become red, like a cardinal's robes.

Cardinal is also the name of iced desserts containing red fruit (e.g. bombe cardinal) or fruit desserts. The fruit can either be cold (raw or poached), sometimes arranged on vanilla ice cream and coated with a strawberry or raspberry sauce, or hot (poached) and coated with the reduced cooking juice plus cassis (blackcurrant liqueur), as in pears cardinal, for instance.

RECIPES

Bombe cardinal Line a conical ice mould with strawberry or raspberry ice cream and fill the inside with vanilla mousse mixture flavoured with praline.

Brill cardinal BARBUE CARDINAL Prepare the fish, season with salt and pepper, then stuff with pike forcemeat to which lobster butter has been added. Poach the brill in white wine, drain, and arrange on the serving dish. Garnish with thin medallions of lobster, cover with cardinal sauce, and sprinkle with lobster coral.

Cardinal sauce SAUCE CARDINAL Heat 2 dl (7 fl oz, ¼ cup) cream sauce and 1 dl (6 tablespoons, scant ½ cup) fish stock and reduce by half. Add 1 dl (6 tablespoons, scant ½ cup) cream and bring to the boil. Remove from the heat and add 50 g (2 oz) lobster butter. Season with a little cayenne and sieve through a conical strainer. Garnish with a spoonful of chopped truffles, unless the recipe already contains them.

cardoon CARDON

A southern European plant, related to the artichoke, whose leafstalk is eaten as a vegetable. Cardoons are available at the end of autumn and in winter; in the south of France they were formerly traditionally eaten with Christmas dinner. In Tours, they are cooked *au gratin*.

When purchased, the stalks must be firm, creamy-white in colour, wide, and plump. They are sold with the leafy part and top of the root, which means they can be kept for a few days in cold salted water. The stalks are especially good fried or with bone marrow; they can also be served cold, with vinaigrette. They are usually used to garnish white or red meats (with the meat juice, butter, or béchamel sauce).

RECIPES

Cooking cardoons CUISSON DES CARDONS Clean the base of the cardoon, cutting off the hard stems. Remove the tender stalks, one by one, and cut into 8-cm (3-in) slices; sprinkle with lemon juice. Cut the heart into four, and plunge the stalks and heart into boiling water. Bring back to the boil, cover, and leave to simmer very gently until tender.

Buttered cardoons CARDONS AU BEURRE Braise some blanched cardoons in butter for 20 minutes. Arrange in a vegetable dish and sprinkle with roughly chopped mint or parsley.

Cardoon purée PURÉE DE CARDONS Prepare some buttered cardoons and reduce to a purée by forcing through a sieve or using a blender. If desired, a third of its volume of potato purée or a few tablespoons thick béchamel sauce may be added. Add butter to serve.

Cardoon salad SALADE DE CARDONS Cut some cooked cardoons into thick matchsticks. Add some well-seasoned vinaigrette and sprinkle with chervil and roughly chopped parsley.

Fried cardoons CARDONS FRITS Drain the cooked cardoons and marinate for 30 minutes in a mixture of olive oil, lemon juice, and chopped parsley. Then dip the cardoons in batter and deep-fry in hot oil. Drain and season with salt.

Carême (Marie-Antoine, known as Antonin)

French chef and pastrycook (born Paris, 1783; died Paris, 1833). Born into a large and very poor family, the young Carême was put out on the street at the age of ten, to be taken in by the owner of a low-class restaurant at the Maine gate, where he learned the rudiments of cookery. At 16, he became an apprentice to Bailly of the Rue Vivienne, one of the best pastrycooks in Paris. Amazed by Carême's abilities and willingness to learn, Bailly encouraged him, in particular by allowing him to study in the print-room of the National Library. Here Carême copied architectural drawings, on which he based his patisserie creations; these were greatly admired by Bailly's customers, including the First Consul himself. Carême met Jean Avice, an excellent practitioner of cuisine, who also advised and encouraged him. Then the young man's talents became noticed by Talleyrand, who was a customer at Bailly's, and he offered to take Carême into his service.

□ **Carême's genius** For 12 years Carême managed the Talleyrand kitchens. The culinary and artistic talents of his chef enabled Talleyrand to wield gastronomy effectively as a diplomatic tool. Carême also served the

Prince Regent of England, the future King George IV, and was then sent to the court of Tsar Alexander I; he was responsible for introducing some classic Russian dishes into French cuisine, including borsch and koulibiac. Carême numbered among his other employers the Viennese Court, the British Embassy, Princess Bagration, and Lord Steward. He spent his last years with Baron de Rothschild and died at 50, 'burnt out by the flame of his genius, and the charcoal of the roasting-spit' (Laurent Tailhade), but having realized his dream: 'To publish a complete book on the state of my profession in our times'.

The works written by Carême include *Le Pâtissier pittoresque* (1815), *Le Maître d'hôtel français* (1922), *Le Pâtissier royal parisien* (1825), and, above all, *L'Art de la cuisine au XIXe siècle* (1933). This last work was published in five volumes, the last two written by his follower, Plumerey. Written in majestic style, Carême's books invite the reader to the table of the emperors, kings, and princes for whom their author worked. Alexander I said to Talleyrand: 'What we did not know was that he taught us to eat.'

□ **Carême's contribution** A theoretician as well as a practitioner, a tireless worker as well as an artistic genius, Carême nonetheless had a keen sense of what was fashionable and entertaining. He understood that the new aristocracy, born under the Consulat, needed luxury and ceremony. So he prepared both spectacular and refined recipes, including chartreuses, desserts on pedestals, elaborate garnishes and embellishments, new decorative trimmings, and novel constructions.

A recognized founder of French *grande cuisine*, Carême placed it at the forefront of national prestige. His work as theoretician, sauce chef, pastrycook, designer, and creator of recipes raised him to the pinnacle of his profession. Some of his formulae are still famous, especially his sauces.

Carême was proud of his unique art: sensitive to decoration and struck on elegance, he always had a sense of posterity. He wanted to create a school of cookery that would gather together the most famous chefs, in order to 'set the standard for beauty in classical and modern cookery, and attest to the distant future that the French chefs of the 19th century were the most famous in the world.'

In parallel with his strictly culinary or literary activities, Carême was also concerned with details of equipment. He redesigned certain kitchen utensils, changed the shape of saucepans to pour sugar, designed moulds, and even concerned himself with details of clothing, such as the shape of the hat. The vol-au-vent and large meringues are attributed to him. Although an incomparable pastrycook, he was also famous for sauces and soups (there are 186 French ones and 103 foreign ones in *L'Art de la cuisine*). Yet on reading some of his recipes, one may wonder if he was concerned more with ceremony than gastronomy. In fact, Carême used money, political power, and social connections to enhance his reputation; indeed, he considered that only the great people in the world could appreciate him. Certainly, his name lives on in the recipes he created and the dishes named in his honour.

RECIPES

Eggs in moulds Carême OEUFS MOULÉS CARÉME Butter some dariole moulds; sprinkle the bottom and sides with truffles and pickled ox (beef) tongue cut up into small squares. Break an egg into each mould and cook in a bain-marie. Remove the eggs from the moulds and place on some artichoke hearts. Garnish with a ragout of lambs' sweetbreads, truffles, and mushrooms. Add some cream to a Madeira sauce and cover the eggs with the mixture. Place a round of pickled ox (beef) tongue, cut out in a saw-tooth pattern, on each one.

Soft-boiled (*or poached*) eggs Carême OEUFS MOLLETS (OU POCHÉS) CARÉME Braise some artichoke hearts in butter and arrange the eggs, either soft-boiled (soft-cooked) or poached, on them. Garnish as in the previous recipe.

cargolade

Snails grilled in the open air over the embers of a bonfire of vines, which are traditionally eaten on Easter Monday or

Whit (Pentecost) Monday in Roussillon and the county of Foix in southwest France. The snails are cleaned, then sprinkled with salt, pepper, and red pimiento, and arranged on special grills. When they start to sizzle, a few drops of bacon fat are dripped into each shell, using a 'torch' made with a piece of fat bacon wrapped in greased paper. The cargolade is eaten very hot, with garlic bread and roughly chopped parsley.

Caribbean cabbage
CHOU CARAÏBE

The edible root of an arum, which is cultivated in the West Indies as a vegetable. It is prepared like turnip, i.e. scraped, washed, cut into slices, and cooked in boiling water. The Caribbean cabbage and the closely related Asheen cabbage are ingredients in West Indian stews (the leaves are also used), and accompany colombos and curries. The grated root is used in the preparation of acras. The root is also a source of starch and even of a drink (*laodgi*, typical of Jamaica).

Caribbean cookery

See *Creole cookery, West Indies.*

Carignan (à la)

An *haute cuisine* dish made with lamb cutlets and fillet (sirloin) steak, sautéed, then arranged on Anna potatoes (shaped into little tarts) and served with a sauce made by deglazing the pan with port and tomato-flavoured veal stock. The garnish consists of buttered asparagus tips and eggs moulded in a duchesse mixture, breaded, fried, scooped out, and filled with foie gras purée.

The same name is used for a cold dessert in which a pear, peach, or apple is poached, hollowed out, filled with chocolate ice cream, then arranged on a Genoese sponge base and covered with vanilla fondant.

carmélite (à la)

A cold dish consisting of chicken suprêmes, covered with chaud-froid sauce, garnished with slices of truffle, and dressed with a mousseline of crayfish and crayfish tails.

The name, because of its association with the Carmelite nuns' white habit and black veil, is also used for an egg dish, in which soft-boiled (soft-cooked) or poached eggs are arranged in a flan crust, garnished with creamed mussels, and covered with white wine sauce.

Carmen

Any of various dishes, including consommé, eggs, or fillets of sole, that contain tomato or pimiento and, generally, a highly-seasoned garnish or flavouring *à l'espagnole.*

Carmen salad consists of boiled rice, diced white chicken, strips of red sweet pepper, and peas, all flavoured with a mustard and chopped tarragon vinaigrette.

RECIPE

Eggs sur le plat Carmen OEUFS SUR LE PLAT CARMEN Cook some eggs *sur le plat*, then cut round the whites with a circular pastry cutter (cookie cutter). Fry in oil some round slices of stale bread with the crusts removed. Cover each slice of bread with a slice of ham of the same size and place an egg on top. Cover with well-seasoned and reduced tomato sauce.

carmine CARMIN

A natural red food colouring, also called cochineal or carminic acid (E120). It is used especially in confectionery and patisserie – jams, jellies, filled biscuits, and preserved red fruits. Carmine is also used to colour delicatessen meats and cured meat products, preserved shrimps and dried fish, syrups, liqueurs and apéritifs, and flavoured cheeses and milks.

carnival CARNAVAL

A programme of popular festivities and masquerades that traditionally took place in the days preceding Shrove Tuesday and Ash Wednesday, the start of Lent. The word comes from the Italian *carnevale* (Shrove Tuesday), which derives from *carne levare* (leaving out meat), a reference to the Lenten fast immediately following the carnival period, during which the Church forbade the consumption of meat and cakes.

The carnival theoretically extended

from Twelfth Night to Ash Wednesday, but it used to reach a climax at the Shrove Tuesday meal, traditionally marked by an abundance of all types of meat (hence the custom of a procession with the fatted ox). In the Champagne region, this last rich meal had to include pigs' trotters (feet), and in Ardèche, pigs' ears. The cocks that had lost that day's fight were eaten in the Marne region, while in Touraine, the special dish was a leg of goat. Other traditional Shrove Tuesday dishes included a stuffed rabbit (in Limousin), a huge vol-au-vent containing chicken in salsify sauce (Quercy), and the famous aïoli (garlic mayonnaise) of Provence.

Carnival originated in the Roman feasts of the calends (first day) of March, which celebrated the awakening of nature. On this occasion, the rules were broken and disguises worn. Straw dolls were burned amidst shouting and chanting. (The word *carnaval* in folk tradition still means a grotesque mannequin that is solemnly burned or buried on Ash Wednesday.) Hence, in the country, magical rites are combined with feasting. In particular, the stock from the stockpot was sprinkled around the houses of the Morvan region to ward off snakes, around the hen houses to ward off foxes in Angoumois, or on the manure heap to make it bigger, in Limousin.

The large attendance at these festivities meant there was a need for fairly cheap cakes, quickly prepared using a blazing fire, hence the tradition of pancakes, and also waffles and fritters: *crespets des Landes*, *merveilles* and *bottereaux*, Sainte-Menehould *faverolles*, and Sologne *beugnons*. Also worthy of mention are Belfort *séchu* (dried apples or pears with slices of bacon) and the cheese soup in Isère. In Nivernais, the Shrove Tuesday meal consisted of: pasta bouillon, boiled beef with vegetables, *coq au sang* (or with white sauce), roast goose or turkey, garlic and nut-oil salad, white cheese with cream, and plum tart with flamed marc brandy.

carob CAROUBE

The bean from the carob tree, which grows in the Mediterranean region. Up to 30 cm (12 in) long, the carob bean has a nutritious refreshing pulp, as rich in

sugar as molasses. It contains hard reddish seeds, which in the Kabylia region of north Africa are crushed and used to make pancakes. In the food industry, carob meal (E410) is widely used as a gelling agent (for jams) and as a texturing agent.

caroline

A savoury miniature éclair, baked in the oven, then filled with a cheese or ham mixture, or with caviar, salmon mousse, or foie gras. Carolines, also known as Karoly éclairs, are served hot or cold as buffet snacks. They can also be made to the size of an ordinary éclair, and served as hors d'oeuvres or as a hot entrée.

RECIPES

Carolines à la hollandaise Prepare a sugarless choux pastry (see *chou*). Using a forcing (pastry:) bag, squeeze out some small éclairs, about 4 cm (1½ in) long, onto a baking sheet, brush with beaten egg, bake in the oven, and leave to cool. To make enough filling for 12 carolines, desalt 4 herring fillets, trim, and wipe them. Pound the fillets, or put them into a blender, together with 2 hard-boiled (hard-cooked) egg yolks and 80 g (3 oz, 6 tablespoons) butter. Add 1 teaspoon chives and 1 teaspoon chopped parsley. Gently split the éclairs along the side, and put the filling into this opening with a forcing bag. Brush the carolines with melted butter and immediately sprinkle with a little hard egg yolk and chopped parsley. Cool before serving.

Carolines Joinville Make some small éclairs as for carolines *à la hollandaise*. To fill 12 carolines, prepare a thick béchamel sauce using 30 g (1 oz, 2 tablespoons) butter, 30 g (1 oz, ¼ cup) flour, and 2 dl (7 fl oz, ¾ cup) milk. Heat 75–100 g (3–4 oz) peeled shrimps in some butter, flame them with marc brandy, and add to the béchamel sauce. Season with salt and pepper, and leave to cool. Finally, pipe the filling into the split éclairs and brush the éclairs with melted butter. Cool before serving.

carp CARPE

A freshwater fish, found in sluggish rivers and also reared commercially on fish farms. Up to 1 m (39 in) long, the carp's thick body is covered with thick scales and is brownish on the back, golden yellow on the sides, and whitish on the belly. Its small toothless mouth has four minute barbs. Improved yields have been obtained by crossbreeding, which has produced the leather carp, which has scales only in mid-body and at the base of the fins, and the mirror carp, which is the finest variety, with scales only at the base of the fins. When buying carp, choose a plump one that is carrying eggs, or milt. With spawning taking place between April and June, carp are 'empty' at this time. If a live carp is chosen, the fishmonger should kill and gut it, removing the gall bladder, which is at the base of the throat and is difficult to extract. It is advisable to soak the gutted and scaled fish in a bowl of vinegar and water (which should be replenished as necessary) in order to remove its 'muddy' taste.

The carp can be roasted, stuffed (especially *à la juive*), grilled (broiled), cooked in court-bouillon, or stewed in white wine or beer. Small fish can also be fried. Carp has been eaten since the Middle Ages, and used to be the dish of kings. They were usually cooked in wine with a lot of spices. The tongue was considered a delicacy. Carp is also the fish most prized by the Chinese; the lips are considered the finest part. Deep-frozen Asiatic carp are sold in France; their flesh is regarded as firmer and tastier than French carp.

RECIPES

Carp à la chinoise CARPE À LA CHI-NOISE Clean and gut a carp weighing about 1.5 kg (3 lb) and cut it into sections. Finely chop 2 large onions and fry in oil until slightly brown. Add 2 table-spoons (3 tablespoons) vinegar, 1 table-spoon sugar, 1 tablespoon freshly grated root ginger (or 1 teaspoon ground ginger), 1–2 tablespoons rice alcohol (or marc brandy), salt, pepper, and a glass of water. Stir, cover, and leave to cook for about 10 minutes. Fry the carp pieces in oil for 10 minutes, then add the sauce and leave to cook for another 4–5 minutes. Some strips of cucumber may be added to the carp along with the sauce, if desired.

Fried carp CARPE FRITE Select a small carp, weighing about 400 g (14 oz). Clean, gut, wash, and wipe the fish. Immerse it in milk, then in flour, and then deep-fry in hot oil. When cooked, remove, drain, and add salt. Garnish with fried parsley and lemon quarters.

Grilled (broiled) carp à la maître d'hôtel CARPE GRILLÉ À LA MAÎTRE D'HÔTEL Select a small carp, weighing 400–500 g (14–18 oz). Clean and gut the fish, slit open the back, season with salt, brush with oil, and grill gently. Garnish with fresh parsley and fluted lemon slices. Serve with maître d'hôtel butter.

Stuffed carp à l'ancienne CARPE FARCIE À L'ANCIENNE (from a recipe by Carême provided by Plumerey) Take a large carp that is carrying eggs (milt), remove the scales and bones, and lift off the flesh, taking care to leave the backbone intact, complete with head and tail. To the carp flesh, add the meat from a small eel as well as desalted anchovies and make a fairly firm quenelle forcemeat in the usual way but without adding any sauce. Scald the roes, cut into several pieces, sauté in butter with a little lemon juice, add some truffles and mushrooms, and bind with a few spoonfuls of thick allemande sauce.

Take a tin tray that is as long as the carp and butter it thickly. Spread a layer of stuffing on it, about 2.5 cm (1 in) thick, making it into the shape of the carp. On this place the carp backbone with head and tail still attached. Cover the backbone with a little stuffing, and cover this with the roe ragout; then add another layer of stuffing, 2.5 cm (1 in) thick, still in the shape of the carp. Smooth with a knife dipped in hot water.

Butter a baking sheet large enough to hold the carp, and sprinkle bread-crumbs on the butter. Carefully heat the tin tray so that the butter melts and slide the carp onto the baking sheet without damaging the shape. Brush with beaten egg, coat the top with breadcrumbs, press the breadcrumbs down firmly, and cover with clarified butter. Then, with the tip of a small spoon, press in a pattern of scales, starting at the head. Cook the carp in the oven for 45 minutes, basting frequently with clarified butter during cooking so that it turns a golden colour. When it is cooked, transfer it carefully from the baking sheet to the serving dish with a long fish slice. Work some fish essence into a financière sauce and serve in a sauceboat to accompany it.

carpaccio

An Italian first course consisting of very thin slices of raw beef served cold with a creamy vinaigrette sauce made with olive oil. This dish, named in honour of the Renaissance Venetian painter, originates from Harry's Bar in Venice (not connected with the famous American bar in Paris).

carpet shell (clam)

PALOURDE

A bivalve mollusc, 3–5 cm (1–2 in) long, that is more plentiful on the Atlantic coast and in the Channel than in the Mediterranean. Its thin shell, convex in the centre, is pale yellow to dark grey marked with brown spots and two series of very fine streaks, one radiating, the other concentric, forming a lattice. Carpet shells are eaten raw in a seafood platter or stuffed, like mussels.

Three very closely related species of false carpet shells (or clams) are distinguished by the colour of the inside of the valves (gold or pink instead of pale grey) and by the fineness of the radiating streaks, only visible with a magnifying glass. They are less delicate than the true carpet shells.

Carré de l'Est

A soft high-fat (45% fat) cheese made from pasteurized cows' milk and originating from Champagne and Lorraine, where it is now mass-produced. Sold in boxes 8–10 cm (3–4 in) square and 2.5–3 cm (1–1¼ in) deep, Carré de l'Est is a mild cheese with a white downy crust.

The term 'Carré' is also applied to Normandy cheeses, related to Bondart, from the Pays de Bray or the Pays d'Auge.

Carré (Ferdinand)

French engineer (born Moislains, Somme, 1824; died Pommeuse, Seine-et-Marne, 1900), who pioneered methods of refrigeration. One of Carré's machines was installed in 1859 at the Velten brewery in Marseille. In 1862 at the Universal London Exhibition, he exhibited an ice machine with an output of 200 kg (440 lb) per hour. In 1877, after setting up a business exporting machines to Germany, England, and the United States, he repeated Tellier's experiment: he equipped the ship *Paraguay* with refrigerated holds and loaded it with 80 tons of meat destined for Buenos Aires. On the return voyage, with Argentine meat on board, Carré's refrigerator ship ran aground on the coast of Senegal. In spite of a two-month delay, the meat arrived at Le Havre in perfect condition, and a great banquet was held to celebrate the event.

carrot CAROTTE

A vegetable grown widely for its orange-red edible root. It is one of the most popular vegetables in France, after the potato. The green tops can be used for soups.

Although the ancients recognized that carrot is good for the eyesight, they did not cultivate it as a vegetable. Until the Renaissance era, carrots had a yellowish tough root, very woody in the centre, and, like other root crops, never appeared among high-class foodstuffs. Little by little, the carrot was improved, and cultivated varieties were sold in the markets. Its orange colour dates from the middle of the 19th century.

☐ **Carrots throughout the year** April: the first new carrots appear – round or slightly elongated, grown in a hothouse, and sold in bunches with turnips. These are either Grelots – tender, sweet, and full of flavour – or the Bellot variety, which is slightly poorer in quality (do not scald them). They are suitable for cooking with cream or herbs, glazed, Vichy style, or in a jardinière.

May to June: Nantaise carrots are available – long, crisp, and grown in a frame. They can be cooked with butter, Vichy style, with cream, as a purée or soufflé, or grated.

June to October: long or semi-long carrots – grown in open soil, and very good if freshly dug. Use for garnishing stewed meats, served in their cooking juices, in a purée, or grated.

November to March: long, often

thick, carrots – average flavour, can be stored in a soil clamp or cold store. Use for soups, stock, or with lentils.

If the carrots are old, split them in half and hollow them, discarding the yellow core. Do not peel them like potatoes, as this removes the red part, which is the best bit.

Créances carrots, sold between the end of August and the end of May, are given a label guaranteeing the production area (seven communes in the south of the Manche department), crop quality (free of pesticides), and storage (in the soil under a layer of straw, heather, furze, or seaweed). Compare *Crécy*.

☐ **Nutrition and cooking** The carrot, which has a high water content, yields 42 Cal per 100 g. It is rich in sugar (9 g per 100 g), mineral salts, vitamins (mainly provitamin A), and pectin. It also contains a pigment called carotene. Theoretically, carrots should not be scraped or peeled, but brushed under running water, because the vitamins are concentrated in the skin. However, because of the risk of pesticide residues, it is advisable to scrape them (except the Créances variety), without soaking them.

Besides the culinary uses already mentioned, carrots are used in making soups, stews, and stocks (brunoise, court-bouillon). They can be cut into rounds, segments, sticks, dice, slices, or matchsticks, depending on use. When raw, they can be coarsely or finely grated. Carrots are widely used for canning and freezing, usually in the form of whole 'baby' carrots or in mixed vegetables, e.g., macédoines.

RECIPES

Boiled carrots CAROTTES À L'AN-GLAISE Scrape some new carrots and plunge into boiling salted water. Drain as soon as they are tender, arrange in a vegetable dish, and sprinkle with melted butter and roughly chopped parsley.

Carrot flan FLAN AUX CAROTTES Bake a pastry flan case blind and fill with a lightly sweetened carrot purée. Cover with slices of glazed carrot, pour over the cooking juices from the carrots, and place in a preheated very hot oven

(about 240 c, 475 f, gas 9) for a few minutes.

Carrot purée PURÉE DE CAROTTES Cook 500 g (18 oz) sliced new carrots in salted water to which 1 teaspoon granulated sugar and 1 tablespoon butter has been added. When the carrots are cooked, drain and make into a purée by forcing them through a fine sieve or using a blender. Heat the purée, adding a few spoonfuls of the carrots' cooking liquid if it is too thick. At the last moment, add 50 g (2 oz, 4 tablespoons) fresh butter. Mix well, and arrange on a vegetable dish. Carrot purée can also be made using the carrots from pot-au-feu.

Carrots with cream CAROTTES À LA CRÈME Cut some old carrots into segments and hollow out the centres. Cook in salted water, and before they become soft, drain, cover with boiling cream, and reduce by two-thirds. Arrange in a vegetable dish and serve very hot.

Carrots with raisins CAROTTES AUX RAISINS Cut some new carrots into slices and fry in melted butter. Lightly sprinkle with flour, then add just enough water to cover them and 1 tablespoon brandy. Cover. Halfway through cooking (after about 15 minutes), add a handful of raisins. Finish cooking with the lid on over a gentle heat.

Glazed carrots CAROTTES GLACÉES Clean some new, preferably fat, carrots, leaving medium-sized ones whole but cutting large ones into halves or quarters. Place in a frying pan (skillet) large enough to hold them all without overlapping. Cover with cold water. For every ½ litre (scant pint, 2 cups) water add 30 g (1 oz, 2 tablespoons) sugar, 60 g (2 oz, 4 tablespoons) butter, and 6 g (½ teaspoon) salt. (When old carrots are used, hollow out the centres, scald them, and drain before cooking with sugar and butter.) Bring to the boil over a high heat. When the water is briskly boiling, lower the heat, cover the pan, and leave to simmer until the liquid has almost completely evaporated. The carrots should now be cooked. Shake the pan so that the carrots are coated with the syrupy liquid.

Glazed carrots may be served with

béchamel sauce (add a few spoonfuls of the sauce at the last moment), butter, cream (cover with boiling cream and reduce by two-thirds), herbs (sprinkle with chopped parsley or chervil), or meat juices (add a few spoonfuls of roast veal or poultry cooking juices).

Grated carrots with anchovies
CAROTTES RÂPÉES AUX ANCHOIS
Flavour some mayonnaise with lemon juice and add some anchovy fillets in oil, cut into thin strips. Mix in some grated carrots and arrange in a mound on a salad dish. Garnish with stoned (pitted) green olives, black (ripe) olives, and fluted halfrounds of lemon.

Carthagène

A type of vin doux naturel made in the south of France, usually from the Grenache grape, which is high in sugar. After maturation in wood, spirit is added (formerly brandy, today more often marc). It tends to be a home-made product nowadays, produced mainly by bouilleurs de cru.

carving DÉCOUPAGE

The action of slicing or cutting up meat, poultry, game, or fish into sections, either for serving or for further preparation.

The art of carving was formerly held in great esteem and attended by a certain amount of ceremony (see *écuyer tranchant*). In ancient times, specialist carvers gave courses in cutting up and carving, using wooden 'chickens' with pieces that could be fitted together again. Noblemen in the Middle Ages liked to show off their skill, and Joinville recounts with pride that he carved one day at the King of Navarre's table. In the 17th century, young gentlemen were trained in the carving of meat and thus learned how to distinguish the best joints: 'the wing of birds who scratch at the earth with their feet; the leg of birds who live in the air; the white meat of large roast poultry; the skin and the ears of a suckling pig; the saddle and the legs of hares and rabbits'. Large fish, such as salmon or pike, were cut in two, and the front portion, considered the most delicate was placed at the head of the table, where the honoured guest sat.

Modern carvers, particularly in the catering trade, must combine culinary competence with knowledge of anatomy, manual dexterity, and a certain panache. Each joint of meat or species of poultry requires a particular carving technique. As a general rule, meat is carved perpendicularly to the direction of the muscle fibres; the slices should be as large as possible and of even thickness. The introduction of service *à la russe* (Russian style), in which meat is presented already cut up, has caused the disappearance from many tables of an operation that was formerly done with pride by the master of the house.

carving knife
TRANCHELARD

A knife with a very long (17–35 cm, 7–14 in) flexible blade and a sharp point. It is used for thinly slicing bacon and roast meat, hot or cold.

Casanova de Seingalt (Giovanni Giacomo)

Italian adventurer (born Venice, 1725; died Dux, Bohemia, 1798). Famous for his romantic and chivalrous exploits, Casanova was an attentive observer of contemporary gastronomic etiquette. This, and his own culinary tastes, occupy an important place in his *Mémoires*: he invented a special vinegar to season hard-boiled (hard-cooked) eggs and anchovies; he advocated Chambertin as an accompaniment to Roquefort cheese; and he claimed that forcemeat of béatilles and very frothy chocolate worked as an effective restorative. Between adventures, he would often make a detour to taste famous pâtés, the rare Hermitage Blanc of the Côtes du Rhône, Grenoble's liqueur, Genoese cep mushrooms, and Leipzig's skewered larks. Truffles, oysters, champagne, and Maraschino owe their reputation as aphrodisiacs largely to him. The Prince of Ligne once said of him: 'At 73, no longer a god in the garden or a satyr in the forest, he is a wolf at table.'

cashew apple
POMME DE CAJOU

A fleshy pear-shaped swelling that is part of the fruit of the cashew tree; the cashew nut hangs below this swelling. The cashew apple is picked when ripe and usually eaten with sugar because it is slightly tart. In Brazil, where it is widely used, it is made into jams, jellies, compotes, and beverages and fermented to produce a dessert wine and vinegar.

cashew nut

NOIX DE CAJOU

The fruit of the cashew tree, originally from South America but widely cultivated in India and other tropical countries since the 16th century. The nut contains a smooth creamy-white kidney-shaped kernel with a very high calorific content when roasted (621 Cal per 100 g); it is also rich in fat and phosphorus. In Europe it is usually eaten dried, roasted, and salted as an appetizer and in salads. In Indian cooking it is used in a variety of dishes, including lamb curry, beef stew, rice with prawns, vegetable dishes, stuffings for chicken, and cakes and biscuits (cookies).

cask TONNEAU

Wine casks come in a wide range of different sizes, some of which have special regional names, such as the Bordeaux *barrique*. The word *tonneau*, however, comes from *tonne*, a very large cask formerly used, especially in the port of Bordeaux, to store wine and then ship it, the mighty cask being rolled from the quayside into the hold of a ship in the wine fleet. According to how many *tonnes* the hold of a ship could take, the capacity of the vessel began to be given in terms of *tonnage*, a system still in use today. The *tonne* itself is no longer used, but the English word 'tun' perpetuates its association with a gigantic wooden container, such as are still used for cider, beer, and so on.

cassata CASSATE

An iced dessert of Italian origin, made of bombe paste set in a rectangular mould and lined with fruit ice cream. The name means 'little case', due to its brick shape, although triangular cassatas can be found. A cassata can also be an ice cream shaped like a brick, consisting of several ice creams of different flavours with a filling of Chantilly cream.

On the other hand, Sicilian cassata, also in the shape of a brick, is a cake. It is made with slices of Genoa cake steeped in Maraschino or Curaçao and covered with a mixture of Ricotta (white Italian cheese), flaked chocolate, crystallized (candied) fruits, and sugar syrup; the whole is finally coated with a thick layer of chocolate. This Christmas and Easter cake is also traditionally eaten at weddings.

RECIPE

Strawberry cassata CASSATE AUX FRAISES Prepare ½ litre (17 fl oz, 2 cups) strawberry ice cream (see *ices and ice creams*), the same quantity of vanilla ice cream, and 4 dl (14 fl oz, 1¾ cups) whipped cream mixed with crystallized fruits steeped in brandy or a liqueur. Spread the vanilla ice cream in a rectangular mould, cover with the whipped cream and fruits, and place in the freezer until the cream just hardens. Cover with the strawberry ice cream, press down firmly, smooth the surface, and leave to set.

cassava

See *manioc*.

casse

A French offal dish from the city of Rennes, made of pieces of boned (boneless) pig's head, pork rind, and calves' mesentery (intestinal membrane) and feet, all cooked with bacon fat, spices, and onions. The ingredients are first marinated with white wine in a hollow earthenware dish – the *casse* – and then cooked in the oven in the same dish with the marinade, plus braised onions and crushed garlic.

casse-museau

A very hard biscuit (cookie) that keeps well; it was formerly very common in France but is now only made in certain areas. The name, meaning 'jaw breaker', comes from its hardness and from the custom of tossing biscuits at one's face during certain popular festivals, such as the Rogation Procession held in Poitiers. In Corsica they are known as *sciappa denti* (tooth breaker). The casse-museau is usually made of a mixture of coarsely chopped almonds and curd cheese, which is rolled into a sausage shape, cooked, then cut into slices and returned to the oven; this double baking produces the very hard consistency.

casserole

A cooking utensil, made of metal or other ovenproof material, which is fitted with a lid and designed for long slow cooking in the oven. Many are decorative enough to use as serving dishes. The name is also given to the food cooked in a casserole.

In classic French cookery, a casserole is a dish generally made with cooked rice moulded into the shape of a casserole or timbale; it can also be made in a duchess potato mould. Rarely made nowadays, these dishes can have various fillings, including mousses, fat or lean minced meat, game purée, calves' or lambs' sweetbreads, escalopes of truffled foie gras, etc. Casseroles can also be garnished *à la Sagan, à la vénitienne, à la bouquetière, à la régence, à la Nantua*, etc. If the contents are cold they can be glazed with aspic jelly.

RECIPE

Rice casserole à l'ancienne CASSEROLE AU RIZ À L'ANCIENNE (from a recipe by Carême) Wash about 1kg (2 lb) long-grain rice in several changes of warm water then place it in a large saucepan. Cover with cold water and heat; after it has boiled for several seconds, drain, then moisten the rice with approximately two to three times its own volume of beef stock and thicken with fat skimmings from a chicken broth. Return the pan to the heat. As soon as the rice boils, take it off the heat and remove the scum from the surface. Now simmer gently, stirring after about 1 hour and again after a further 20–25 minutes. The rice should now be soft. (Further stock may be added during cooking in order to keep the rice moist.) Remove from the heat, stir for several minutes with a spatula, and allow to cool.

When the rice is only just warm, work it with a wooden spoon until the grains have all burst and the rice is a smooth paste, adding a little stock if necessary. Pile the rice into a baking tin, forming a casserole shape about 12 cm (4–5 in) high; smooth it well. Garnish with slices of carrot. Now coat the surface of the rice casserole with a little clarified butter and cook in the oven for about 1½ hours. During cooking, it will turn bright yellow. When cooked, carefully remove the garnished top crust and remove from the inside all the rice that does not adhere to the crust, even if this means that the crust is very thin. Mix a large spoonful of rice taken from the interior with a little sauce (béchamel, espagnole, or any other suitable sauce, depending on the filling to be used), and glaze the crust with this mixture after putting the filling in the case.

If good stock or fat are unavailable, the rice can be moistened with water, butter, and salt. This will make the rice much whiter.

Carême also gave a recipe for individual rice casseroles (*casserolettes*), approximately 6 cm (2½ in) tall and 5.5 cm (2¼ in) in diameter. They are placed on a baking sheet in a hot oven and cooked until evenly coloured.

Cassis

AOC wines from a vineyard close to the small Provençal part of Cassis, between Marseille and La Ciotat. This vineyard, famous since the 15th century, is known especially for its dry white wine. The vines, planted on the chalky cliffs overlooking the sea, include such varieties as Ugni Blanc, Colombard, Clairette, and Pascal. The sunny southerly aspect is sheltered by the hills, which shelter the vines from the Mistral. They are also protected from excessive heat by the proximity of the sea. Cassis also produces red and rosé wines from Grenache, Mourvèdre, Carignan, Cinsault, and other varieties of grape. But the white wines remain the most attractive and are enjoyed particularly for their fruitness, freshness, and delicacy. They are among the best white wines of Provence and are a delightful complement to bouillabaisse.

cassis

A liqueur of pronounced flavour made by macerating blackcurrants in spirit and sweetening the resulting liquid. There are several categories: 14° for most ordinary and culinary purposes; 15° for 'crème de cassis'; 20° for 'double crème' or 'super-cassis', and there are

even versions of 25°. Cassis is a speciality of Dijon and the Côte d'Or; it was
first made commercially in 1841 by one
Claude Joly. The popularity of Kir has
stimulated production. This drink, a
Burgundy apéritif consisting of a spoonful of cassis liqueur topped up with dry
white wine, has acquired the name of
the late Canon Kir, Mayor of Dijon and
Resistance hero. 'Kir royale' is made
with sparkling wine.

| RECIPE

Cassis LIQUEUR DE CASSIS For
every litre (1¼ pints, 4¼ cups) of eau de
vie, take 12 small washed leaves from
the tip of a blackcurrant branch and
place them in a bowl together with 1
clove and 1 g (a good pinch) stick
cinnamon. Wash and dry the blackcurrants and weigh them. Crush them
roughly and put them in the bowl,
allowing 1 kg (2¼ lb, 9 cups) blackcurrants per litre (1¾ pints, 4¼ cups) eau
de vie. Now add 750 g (1 lb 10 oz, 3¼
cups) sugar per kg (2¼ lb, 9 cups) of
blackcurrants and mix all the ingredients thoroughly. Pour into jars, seal,
and store, preferably in a warm sunny
place, for approximately 1 month. Then
pour the contents through a cloth secured over a large bowl and extract all
the liquid. Filter and bottle. If the liqueur is too strong, a little sugar dissolved in cold water can be added
(approximately 500 g (18 oz, 2¼ cups)
sugar per ½ litre (¾ pint, 2 cups) water).

cassolette

A small container with lugs or a short
handle, made of heatproof porcelain,
tempered glass, or metal, which is used
to prepare and serve hot entrées or certain hors d'oeuvres and cold puddings.
The word can also apply to a variety of
dishes that are served in cassolettes.
Savoury cassolettes may consist of salpicons and ragouts of all sorts, including
sweetbreads, chopped chicken, mushrooms, fish mousses, etc., bound with a
white or brown sauce; sweet cassolettes,
which are sometimes served in nougat
cups instead of the cassolette itself, can
include flavoured creams, custards, and
poached fruit.

cassonade

Raw crystallized sugar extracted directly from the juice of the sugar cane. The
small irregular crystals have a light-
brown colour and a slight taste of rum,
caused by the residues of gum and wax.
When further refined, cassonade gives
white cane sugar.

Cassonade is used to make chutneys
and features in certain recipes from
northern Europe, such as civet of hare,
Flemish red cabbage, and black pudding
(blood sausage), and in some southern
ones, for example, Pézenas mutton pie.
In cake making it gives a special flavour
to tarts and yeast cakes.

Until the 16th century cassonade was
called *casson* and took the form of an
irregular loaf of crumbly sugar.

| RECIPE

Belgian cassonade tart TARTE À LA
CASSONADE Make some pastry using
250 g (9 oz, 2¼ cups) flour, 125 g (4½
oz, generous ½ cup) butter, a pinch of
salt, and 8 cl (4 tablespoons, ⅓ cup)
cold water. Roll into a ball and leave to
rest for 3–4 hours. Then use it to line a
tart case and bake blind in a preheated
moderately hot oven (200 c, 400 f, gas
6). Grind 150–200 g (5–7 oz) almonds
in a blender and mix with 3 egg yolks, 2
dl (7 fl oz, ¾ cup) double (heavy) cream,
and 300 g (11 oz) cassonade (raw
brown sugar). Beat 3 egg whites until
they form stiff peaks and add to the
mixture. Pour into the tart case and
bake for about 40 minutes.

cassoulet

A dish, originally from Languedoc,
which consists of haricot (navy) beans
cooked in a stewpot with pork rinds and
seasonings. A garnish of meats, which
varies from region to region, and a
gratin topping are added in the final
stages. The word comes from *cassole*,
the name of the glazed earthenware
cooking pot traditionally used.

The haricot beans (known as *mounjetos*) are the essential ingredient, giving
cassoulet its creaminess and flavour.
(Originally, fresh broad (Lima) beans
were used; haricots come from Spain,
and were not used in France until the
19th century.) Cassoulet is divided into

three types according to the meats used. Prosper Montagné called them the 'Trinity', the 'Father' being the cassoulet from Castelnaudary, the 'Son' the cassoulet from Carcassone, and the 'Holy Ghost' that from Toulouse. The first, which is undoubtedly the oldest, contains pork (loin, ham, leg, sausages, and fresh rinds) with perhaps a piece of preserved goose. In Carcassone, leg of mutton and, during the shooting season, partridge are used. The same ingredients are used in Toulouse as in Castelnaudary but in smaller quantities, the difference being made up with fresh lard, Toulouse sausage, mutton, and duck or goose. Other variations exist, for example, Montauban (with Pamiers beans garnished with sausages and garlic sausage) and Comminges (with pork rinds and mutton). There is also a fish cassoulet, made with salt cod (which replaces the duck or goose).

Whatever the ingredients, the États Généraux de la Gastronomie française of 1966 decreed the following proportions for cassoulet: at least 30% pork (which can include sausage and Toulouse sausage), mutton, or preserved goose; 70% haricot beans and stock, fresh pork rinds, herbs, and flavourings. In France, canned cassoulet accounts for one-fifth of all precooked canned dishes.

The preparation of cassoulet requires that the beans and the meat are cooked at the same time (pork and mutton are cooked separately) while braising the rinds and cooking the sausages. A final coating of breadcrumbs is essential for a fine golden crust. Purists insist on certain refinements, such as rubbing the cooking pot with a clove of garlic and, above all, breaking the gratin crust several times (seven times in Castelnaudary and eight times in Toulouse).

Now far removed from the mutton and bean stew made by the Romans and Spaniards, cassoulet has become a classic dish. In 1909 at a journalists' lunch, President Fallières, a native of Lot-et-Garonne, had a cassoulet made to his own instructions, which he then ordered to be put on the menu at the Élysée Palace once a week. But this dish remains a subject of controversy, especially regarding the addition of mutton; this is considered by some a sac-

rilege (except in the Toulouse version, according to Clos-Jouve) and by others, such as Prosper Montagné and James de Coquet, as indispensable. Curnonsky, however, would only accept the inclusion of poached sausages, a small piece of shoulder of lamb, goose in tomato sauce, and garlic sausage.

The *Guide gourmand de la France* (Hachette) by Gault and Millau describes the preparation of the Toulouse cassoulet: 'We give this recipe for the cassoulet de Toulouse, as set out by the famous local cook and eminent gastronomic writer from the south-west, Louis Cazals. Soak the white haricot beans (known as *cocos*) for 12 hours. Boil them in salted water for a good hour, then drain. Return them to the cooker, this time into boiling water, and add the bacon rinds, which have first been blanched and rolled up, the carrots, cut into rounds, and some cloves of garlic. Add a sausage and leave the ingredients to cook together. Meanwhile, lightly brown a goose quarter with good-quality goose fat and two cloves of crushed garlic plus two peeled deseeded tomatoes. Add the goose to the haricot beans and leave to cook for a further two hours. Do not forget a bouquet garni. Put the sausage (cut into slices) and the haricot beans into a stewpot or earthenware casserole, add the fresh sausage, and cook in a slow oven. Allow a crust to form, which you then break eight times during the cooking. Serve in the cooking pot. To conclude, it is said that the Toulouse cassoulet is the most complete (or least simple) of all the regional cassoulets. It is of course subject to minor variations. The dish is generally accompanied by a Corbières wine (which is found more and more often on the wine lists of Toulouse) or, better still, by a hearty old Villaudric.'

The Syndicat d'Initiative (Regional Promotional Board) of Castelnaudary, who claims its city 'the world capital of cassoulet', provides the following recipe: 'Here we give the ingredients for the *true* dish as it is still prepared by local families in Castelnaudary. First of all is the choice of bean, preferably the *lingot*. Secondly the meat – hock of pork, pork ribs, pork rinds, local sausage, and preserved goose liver from

Lauragais. Place the beans in a pot (preferably earthenware), cover them with cold water, and blanch them by bringing to the boil for five to ten minutes. Drain off this water and cover the beans with fresh warm water. Garnish by adding a good helping of pork rinds cut into reasonably large pieces and add some hash made from a large piece of salted fat, a small piece of slightly rancid fat, and a generous quantity of garlic. Add some salt and leave to simmer for about two hours, preferably on the hearth. The beans should be well cooked but remain firm. In a large pan melt the fat off the preserved goose then remove the goose and fry the meat in the fat. (If preserved goose is not available, goose or pork fat can be used.) When these preparations have been completed place the ingredients in a *cassole* (never use any other type of utensil, for example, enamel or glass) as follows: first a layer of beans, rinds, and juice; then a layer of meat, which is then covered by the remaining beans. Pepper the surface generously. Separately cook a fresh sausage in a frying pan or in the oven until it is lightly browned. Then coil the sausage on the surface of the cassoulet, press down lightly, and sprinkle the whole surface with the boiling hot fat from the sausage. Put the *cassole* into the oven and leave to cook until a brown uniform crust forms on top. Break the crust and allow it to reform several times, as desired. Check the cassoulet from time to time and if it appears to be dry, sprinkle with warm water but be careful not to drown it. Allow to cook for three to four hours. Serve very hot in its cooking pot. Make it the day before to serve at lunchtime, or early in the morning for the evening meal.

• *Important note* – Never use smoked fat, smoked meat, Strasbourg sausages, or mutton.

RECIPES

Cassoulet (from a recipe by Prosper Montagné) For 8 people, soak 1 litre (1¾ pints, 4½ cups) white haricot (navy) beans in cold water for a few hours (but do not allow them to ferment). Drain, then add to them 300 g (11 oz) pork fat, 200 g (7 oz) fresh pork rind tied in a bundle, a carrot, an onion studded with cloves, and a bouquet garni containing 3 cloves of garlic. Season carefully, using very little salt as the fat contains salt. Add enough water to allow the beans to 'swim' well. Simmer gently so that the beans remain intact but are well cooked.

Place some dripping or goose fat in a separate pan and brown 750 g (1¾ lb) pork sparerib or bladebone and 500 g (1 lb) boned shoulder of mutton, well seasoned with salt and pepper. When the meats are well browned put them in a large frying pan (skillet) containing 200 g (7 oz, 1¾ cups) cooked chopped onion, a bouquet garni, and 2 crushed cloves of garlic. Cover and cook. Moisten from time to time with good meat juice or stock from the stockpot. If desired, add some spoonfuls of tomato purée or 3 peeled, seeded, and crushed tomatoes.

When the beans are almost cooked, remove the vegetables and bouquet garni and add the pork, mutton, and onions, together with some garlic sausage, a leg of preserved goose or duck, and, if desired, a piece of home-made sausage. Simmer gently for a further hour. Remove all the meat from the beans and drain. Cut the mutton, pork, and goose (or duck) into equal pieces and cut the rind into rectangles, the sausage into slices (removing the skin), and the fresh sausage into small rings.

Line a large earthenware dish with the rind, then make a layer of beans, a layer of the various meats (previously moistened with their sauce), and another layer of beans, seasoning each layer with freshly ground pepper. On top of the fina' layer place the pieces of fat, the remaining rind, and some sliced sausage. Sprinkle with white breadcrumbs and melted goose fat. Cook gently in the oven (preferably a baker's oven) for approximately 1½ hours. Serve in the cooking dish.

castagnacci

A dish from Corsica consisting of a thick batter or dough made with chestnut flour, which is used to make fritters or thick waffles or is baked as a flan.

In the high Cévennes, a country cake called *castanhet* was made by mixing butter and eggs with chestnut purée. It was cooked in a buttered mould in the oven. Traditionally it was served cold at the meal given to mark the end of the chestnut harvest.

Castiglione (à la)

A preparation in which small pieces of meat are fried, arranged on slices of aubergine (eggplant) fried in butter, topped with slices of poached bone marrow, and garnished with large mushroom caps stuffed with risotto and gratin mixtures. Sole or fish fillets (plaice, whiting, etc.) *à la Castiglione* are glazed with white wine and garnished with mushrooms, lobster pieces, and steamed potatoes.

castillane (à la)

A term used for tournedos (filet mignons) or noisettes of lamb, topped with crushed tomatoes thickened in olive oil (these are sometimes placed in tartlets and arranged beside the meat), and served with croquette potatoes and fried onion rings. The sauce is based on veal and tomato. This preparation is only used for lamb or mutton, which is a famous product of the Castile region of Spain.

cast iron FONTE

An alloy of iron and carbon, used to make various cooking utensils, especially casseroles, saucepans, frying pans (skillets), and griddles. Heavy and strong, cast iron retains heat for a long time and enables the quick sealing of meat, as well as long slow even cooking. Attractive enamelled cast-iron utensils, covered with two layers of enamel, are ideal for oven-to-table use. Unfortunately they chip easily, so enamelled cast iron should be handled carefully and not scratched. Cast aluminium, much lighter than cast iron, is being used increasingly for kitchen equipment.

catalane (à la)

A term used to describe garnishes inspired by Spanish cooking (Catalonia, in particular, was famous for its seafood and garlic). Chicken, lamb, or veal sautéed *à la catalane* is garnished with tomato quarters fried in butter, chestnuts poached in consommé, chipolatas, and stoned blanched olives. Large pieces of meat are garnished with diced

aubergines (eggplants) fried in oil and rice pilaf. Grilled tournedos and noisettes of lamb are arranged on a bed of artichoke hearts and surrounded by grilled tomatoes.

RECIPES

Fried eggs à la catalane OEUFS POÊLÉS À LA CATALANE Cook separately some deseeded tomato halves and aubergine (eggplant) rings in olive oil. Add salt, pepper, a little crushed garlic, and some chopped parsley. Cover a serving dish with the vegetables. Fry the eggs in the same pan and slide onto the vegetables.

Stuffed aubergines (eggplants) à la catalane AUBERGINES FARCIES À LA CATALANE Cut some good-sized aubergines (eggplants) in half lengthways to form boat shapes. Leaving a 1-cm (½-in) rim around the top, scoop out the flesh without damaging the skin. Chop the flesh together with a hardboiled (hard-cooked) egg, garlic (1 small clove per aubergine), and some parsley. In olive oil, lightly cook 1 large chopped onion per aubergine, add it to the egg and aubergine mixture, and fill the aubergine boats. Arrange in an oiled ovenproof dish, sprinkle with fresh breadcrumbs and oil, and cook in a preheated hot oven (225 C, 435 F, gas 7–8).

caterer TRAITEUR

One who prepares meals to order for private individuals or dishes to be taken away.

Under the Ancien Régime, traiteurs formed a corporation, specializing in weddings, feasts, and banquets. They also had the right to hire out cutlery, crockery, and table linen. The profession of traiteur was at that time considered more honourable than that of innkeeper or rôtisseur. The traiteur was the predecessor of the restaurateur, the difference being that customers were not able to eat on his premises. In addition, as Brillat-Savarin said at the end of the 18th century, traiteurs 'could only sell whole joints; and anyone wishing to entertain friends had to order in advance, so that those who had not the good fortune to be invited to some wealthy house left the great city without discovering the delights of Parisian cuisine.' Restaurants were not yet in existence, and respectable people did not frequent inns. However, following the success of restaurants towards the end of the 19th century, the term *traiteur* acquired a rather derogatory meaning and was applied to restaurants of the lowest class and wine merchants who provided meals.

The modern caterer specializes in banquets, cocktails, and lunches, served either in the clients' homes or in hired rooms. These services can be provided by pastrycooks, confectioners, restaurateurs, and delicatessen owners.

The kitchen of the pastrycook who provides a catering service is very different from that of the restaurateur, firstly because the transport and reheating of dishes require special methods, and secondly because he has to cater sometimes for several thousand and sometimes for a mere dozen. The dishes he provides typically include croustades, bouchées, timbales, vols-au-vent, pâtés, galantines and ballottines, chauds-froids, dishes in aspic, canapés, and, of course, set pieces for special occasions and a variety of desserts, ice creams, and petits fours. Restaurants providing a catering service often offer dishes from their menu which can be easily transported, such as cassoulet, sauerkraut, confit, civet, etc.

catfish   POISSON-CHAT

An American freshwater fish that inhabits calm waters and is found principally in the Mississippi basin. It is 30–35 cm (12–14 in) long with scaleless sticky blackish skin, a massive head with eight whisker-like barbels around the mouth, and a second fatty dorsal fin. Despite its ugly appearance, the flesh is excellent and practically boneless. It can be prepared in the same way as trout or perch.

The European catfish (*Silurus glanis*) is a very large freshwater fish of central European origin, which is found in the Danube, some Swiss lakes, and sometimes in the River Doubs in France. Growing up to 4 m (13 ft) long and weighing as much as 200 kg (450 lb), it has a massive six-barbed head, a small dorsal fin close to the head, and a very long anal fin which extends over more than half the abdomen. Its flesh, which is firm and white but rather fatty, resembles that of the eel.

catigot or catigau

A dish of mixed river fish, believed to have originated in Condrieu (Lyonnais); the ingredients of the dish change as one travels down the Rhône valley. Catigot is prepared with eels or carp (or both), either grilled in slices with onions and lard then simmered with sieved tomato sauce, or boiled briskly with slices of potato, leeks (whites), tomatoes, garlic, and bay leaf. Chilli pepper is added in the Arles region. The catigot was praised by Frédéric Mistral in the *Poème du Rhône*.

cauchoise (à la)

Describing dishes of the Caux region in France, especially saddle of hare or rabbit, marinated in white wine with herbs, cooked in the oven, then sprinkled with the reduced marinade and coated in a sauce made by binding the reduced juices with fresh thick cream and mustard. It is then garnished with Reinette apples fried in butter.

Sole *à la cauchoise* is braised in cider in the oven, then coated with a sauce made from the cooking juices and butter. It is garnished with shrimps (famous in the Caux region) cooked in courtbouillon to which fried mussels, poached oysters, and mushrooms have been added.

Cauchoise salad combines potato slices, slender sticks (stalks) of celery, and slivers of cooked ham. It is seasoned with a sauce made of fresh cream, cider vinegar, and chervil.

| RECIPE

Tart cauchoise   Prepare some shortcrust pastry (basic pie dough). Roll into a ball and leave to rest in a cool place for at least 1 hour. Line a flan case and bake blind. Soften 750 g (1 lb 10 oz, 6½ cups) finely chopped onion in butter. Beat 1 whole egg, mix in 2 dl (7 fl oz, ¾ cup) double (heavy) cream, then add salt, pepper, and a little grated nutmeg. Allow to thicken on a gentle heat, without boiling, then add the onions. Fill the flan case with chicken leftovers or finely chopped veal or ham, and cover them with the onion mixture. Dot with flecks of butter and cook for 15–20 minutes in a moderately hot oven (210 c, 410 f, gas 6–7).

caul (caul fat)
CRÉPINE, TOILETTE

A thin membrane veined with fat that encloses the stomach of animals, particularly that of the pig. In charcuterie the caul is soaked to soften it and make it easier to handle; it is used, for example, to wrap around the sausage-meat when making crépinettes. Numerous other culinary preparations use caul to hold together the ingredients during cooking: stuffed cabbage leaves, larded calf's liver, fricandeau, foie gras, pâtés, terrines, etc.

cauldron CHAUDRON

A large deep vessel made of cast iron or copper, with a detachable handle. It was formerly used for cooking thick soups and stews in the hearth, hanging from a chimney-hook. Varying in shape according to different regions (curved sides, with or without feet, etc.), it is used today mainly for decoration except for certain specific uses such as cooking cheese in the mountains or preparing preserves. In the Middle Ages, cauldrons often had diametrically opposed spouts; those produced in Beaucaire and Flanders (copperware districts) were famous.

cauliflower CHOU-FLEUR

Described by Arab botanists and known to the Romans, the cauliflower originally came from Cyprus and was introduced to France from Italy in the middle of the 16th century. Having been served to Louis XIV, the cauliflower was cultivated extensively, particularly in Brittany. The edible part is the flower head, popularly known as the 'heart' or 'head'; it is white, compact, and hard with many compressed flower buds. The heart is surrounded by crisp bluish-green leaves, whose condition is a good guide to the freshness of the heart. The leaf ribs and the stump (core) may be used to prepare soups or vegetable loaves.

□ **Calendar**

June to August: slightly yellow, the heart is neither compact nor very firm and the leaves afford it poor protection from the sun; weighs 1–1.5 kg (2¼–3¼ lb).

September to December: the hearts are white, compact, fleshy, and firm; numerous varieties are available, weighing 1.5–2.5 kg (3¼–5½ lb).

January to May: excellent quality but with slightly less body and a nutty taste.

Very small cauliflowers, weighing 400–700 g (¾–1¾ lb), can also be found. These are white and come either from Brittany or Italy; they do not have the flavour of the larger cauliflowers. The heart should be compact, white, firm, and undamaged, with no green shoots between the florets. The leaves should be very crisp; do not buy a cauliflower without leaves – it is probably old and has lost its vitamins. Cauliflowers are sold individually, not by weight, and only about half is usable. Allow about 200 g (½ lb) per person if served cooked and 100 g (4 oz) if served raw.

□ **Preparation** Containing only 30 Cal per 100 g and rich in sulphur, potassium, iron, and vitamins (C, B_1, and B_2 in particular), cauliflower is the most easily digested member of the cabbage family. It can be eaten raw (seasoned with salt), in a vegetable fondue, cooked in water (for soup, purée, or cold salad) in a soufflé, *au gratin, à la hollandaise, à la polonaise,* and also lightly braised, sautéed, or fried after blanching. It is included in pickles and is a feature of all Du Barry preparations.

Cauliflower can be cooked either whole (after soaking in water containing vinegar, then rinsing in clear water), or as small well-washed florets. It often gives off a strong smell during cooking. Ideally, it should be first blanched in fast-boiling unsalted water, then cooked in a white stock; a crust of stale bread can be added to absorb some of the smell. Lemon juice may be added after cooking to help it stay white and firm.

Cooked cauliflower does not keep long in the refrigerator, but, when blanched, it freezes well.

RECIPES

Cauliflower à l'anglaise CHOU FLEUR À L'ANGLAISE Cook the trimmed cauliflower, whole or divided into florets, either in salted boiling water (about 20 minutes) or by steaming (4 minutes in a pressure cooker, about 25 minutes in a saucepan). In England, it is usual to leave one or two rows of tender leaves around the head. Arrange the drained cauliflower in a vegetable dish, sprinkle it with chopped herbs or parsley, and serve with melted butter, flavoured with lemon if desired. It may also be served with a white sauce prepared using a little of the cooking liquid, a cream sauce, hollandaise sauce, or curry sauce.

Cauliflower au gratin CHOU-FLEUR AU GRATIN Divide the heart into florets and cook them in salted water or steam. Remove, drain, and toss them in butter. Transfer to a buttered gratin dish, coat with Mornay sauce, sprinkle with grated Gruyère cheese and melted butter, and brown for about 10 minutes in a very hot oven. The Gruyère may be replaced by Parmesan, which may be sprinkled in the dish before adding the cauliflower.

Cauliflower salad SALADE DE CHOU-FLEUR Divide the heart into florets and steam, keeping them slightly firm. Arrange them in a salad bowl, scatter chopped parsley or chervil on top, and sprinkle with a well-seasoned vinaigrette (the vinegar in the dressing may be replaced by lemon juice). Instead of vinaigrette, anchovy sauce, chantilly sauce, or mayonnaise may be used. If the cauliflower is very tender, the florets can be simply washed in water containing vinegar, thoroughly dried, and seasoned with vinaigrette as for a green salad.

Sautéed cauliflower CHOU-FLEUR SAUTÉ Divide the heart into florets and steam them until they are still slightly firm and do not disintegrate. Heat some butter in a frying pan (skillet) or sauté pan and lightly brown the florets. Arrange them in a vegetable dish and moisten with the cooking butter.

Cauliflower may also be sautéed in olive oil with chopped garlic.

other recipes See *Du Barry*.

caviar

Sturgeons' eggs that have been salted and allowed to mature. The word comes from the Italian *caviale*, itself derived from the Turkish *kâwyâr*. It appears as early as 1432 in Rabelais' *Pantagruel*, in which caviar is described as the choice hors d'oeuvre; Colbert organized the production of caviar in the Gironde using the sturgeons passing through the estuary. But the caviar we know today is Russian. It was introduced to France in the 1920s following the exile of Russian princes; during the Universal exhibition of 1925 the Petrossian Brothers learnt, through their Russian friends, that caviar was known to very few French people. Charles Ritz formally launched caviar by putting it permanently on the menu at his hotel.

The sturgeon lives in the sea but returns in winter to estuaries throughout temperate regions of Asia to lay its eggs. Today the Caspian Sea provides 98% of the world's caviar. The sturgeon was still common in the Gironde at the beginning of the century, but it has become so rare that fishing for it is now prohibited.

The Soviet Union was for a long time the sole producer of caviar. But since 1953, factories on Iran's Caspian coast have produced 180 tonnes annually; Russia produces 1800 tonnes every year.

The eggs constitute about 10% of the female's body weight. After they have been removed they are washed, sieved, put into brine, drained, and finally packed into tins. There are two sorts: caviar in grains and pressed caviar. The name 'red caviar' is sometimes used incorrectly for salmon eggs.

☐ **Types of caviar** Sold fresh or sometimes pasteurized, there are three types, differentiated by size, colour, and species of sturgeon.

• *Beluga* – The most expensive and produced by the largest species, which can weigh up to 800 kg (1750 lb). The eggs are more or less dark grey, firm, heavy, and well separated. These are the biggest but most fragile eggs, and if they burst the caviar becomes oily.

• *Ossetra* – Characterized by smaller more even grains, which are golden yellow to brown and quite oily; considered by many as the best.

• *Sevruga* – Produced by small sturgeons, which are the most prolific and give very small light- to dark-grey eggs. This is the cheapest type.

☐ **Pressed caviar** This is made from the ripest eggs, taken towards the end of the fishing season, which are then compressed. About 5 kg (11 lb) fresh caviar are needed to make 1 kg (2¼ lb) pressed caviar. It has a strong and rather oily taste and is sometimes considered too salty, although it is appreciated by Russian connoisseurs.

Caviar is a semi-conserve and perishable; it should be kept between −2 and +4 c (28–39 f). As an hors d'oeuvre allow 50 g (2 oz) per person. It should be served cold but not frozen, preferably on crushed ice; take the tin out of the fridge an hour before serving. Blinis and soured (dairy sour) cream or lightly buttered toast make an ideal accompaniment. Never use lemon, which affects the taste. Caviar has a calorific value of 140 Cal per 100 g; it is rich in phosphorus and contains (per 100 g, 4 oz), 20 g (¾ oz) lipids and 30 g (1 oz) protein.

RECIPE

Raw scallops with caviar COQUILLES SAINT-JACQUES CRUES AU CAVIAR (from a recipe by Michel Oliver) Open and trim the scallops. In an earthenware dish mix 2 tablespoons (3 tablespoons) pure olive oil and 3 tablespoons (¼ cup) groundnut (peanut) oil. Slice the raw white and coral meat into rings. Dip each ring in the oil mixture, wipe off the excess oil, and put them on a plate, allowing 2 scallops per serving. Season each plate with 3 pinches of salt and 3 turns of the pepper mill. With the tip of a coffeespoon handle, place 5–6 grains of caviar on each ring and surround the caviar grains with slices of coral meat. Serve with hot buttered toast.

Cavour

The name given to two garnishes inspired by Piedmontese cooking and named after the Italian statesman. One is used with veal escalopes (scallops) or veal sweetbreads, which are fried, drained, and arranged on polenta biscuits. They are then surrounded with grilled mushrooms and garnished with puréed chicken livers and slices of truffle.

The other Cavour garnish, for large pieces of meat, consists of croquettes of semolina and ravioli.

celeriac (celery root)
CÉLERI-RAVE

A variety of celery grown for its fleshy whitish root, which can weigh 800 g–1 kg (1¾–2¼ lb). In France it is cultivated in the north and the Paris region. It is sold without its leaves, looking like a heavy white ball, and should not be cracked. Celeriac is available from mid-September to the end of April, but is best in autumn.

Easily digested, it contains 44 Cal per 100 g and is rich in phosphorus and sodium chloride (common salt). It can be preserved, especially grated and seasoned with vinegar, in pickles, etc.

RECIPES

Preparation of celeriac PRÉPARATION DU CÉLERI-RAVE Peel like a potato, rinse, and sprinkle with lemon juice. To eat cooked, cut into pieces and blanch for 5 minutes in boiling salted water. To serve as a vegetable, it may be braised, cooked in its juices, or prepared as a julienne and braised. It can be prepared as a purée (like cardoons) and as a cream soup. Steamed in slices, it retains all its flavour.

Celeriac croquettes CROQUETTES DE CÉLERI Peel a celeriac root, cut it into pieces, and blanch. Then cook in salted water for approximately 30 minutes. Add the same weight of peeled potatoes and leave until cooked. Drain the vegetables and dry, either in the oven or in a saucepan. Pass them through a vegetable sieve and mix the resulting purée with egg yolks – 4 per kg (2¼ lb) of purée – and chopped parsley. Divide the paste obtained into little balls, flatten them out, and coat in batter. Plunge the croquettes into boiling oil or fat and leave to turn golden, then remove and drain on absorbent paper. Serve with roast beef, veal, pork, leg of lamb, or leg of venison.

Celeriac en rémoulade   CÉLERI EN RÉMOULADE   Peel a large celeriac root, grate it coarsely, and blanch for 2 minutes in boiling salted water. Drain and refresh with cold water. Dry thoroughly. Add rémoulade sauce and, if desired, sprinkle with chopped parsley.

Celeriac julienne   JULIENNE DE CÉLERI   Peel a celeriac root and cut into thick strips. Blanch for 3 minutes in boiling salted water, then refresh in cold water and drain. Put the strips into a pan with a knob of butter and a little sugar, to taste. Cover and sweat for approximately 15 minutes. Adjust the seasoning and sprinkle with finely chopped herbs. Use to garnish roast meats, fried meats, and braised fish, such as cod

celery   CÉLERI

A vegetable grown for its roots, stems, leaves, and seeds, all of which can be used. Wild celery, from which cultivated strains have been developed, was used both gastronomically, for soups and fish dishes, and therapeutically, as smelling salts. For a long time, both popular opinion and gastronomic writers considered celery to be an aphrodisiac.

Several varieties of cultivated celery are grown for their white fleshy stalks, which are easily broken when fresh. Canned celery hearts and slices, preserved in natural juice, are used as a garnish; celery is also very suitable for deep-freezing. It can be kept fresh for several days if the bottoms of the stems are stood in cold salted water; it becomes limp if simply put in the fridge. Yielding only 20 Cal per 100 g, and easily digested, celery is rich in sodium chloride (common salt). The stalks are eaten raw with salt, in mixed salads, or cooked.

The leaves, fresh or dried, can serve as a garnish for salads, soups, sauces, and stock and may be used in braised dishes. The seeds are used as a seasoning, having a taste similar to fennel.

Celeriac (celery root) is a variety of cultivated celery grown for its fleshy root. Celery salt, which is extracted from dried pulverized celeriac, is used as a condiment for tomato juice, vegetable moulds, and salad sauces. It is also used in salt-free diets.

RECIPES

Preparation of celery   PRÉPARATION DE CÉLERI BRANCHE   Remove the hard outer stems and the green leafy branches. Trim the base to a point and cut the stalks to a length of about 20 cm (8 in). For eating raw, detach the stalks from one another, wash them, and remove the stringy fibres. For cooking, wash the trimmed celery in cold water, splaying out the stems. Remove the stringy outer stalks, rinse the rest, then blanch in boiling salted water for 10 minutes. Drain, salt the insides, and tie the stalks in bunches. Braised celery hearts can accompany fatty meats, roasts, and chicken. Celery can also be cooked in béchamel sauce, au gratin, in meat juice or gravy, or with bone marrow. Celery purée is used in soups and in a sauce for boiled or braised poultry.

Braised celery (*au gras or au maigre*) CÉLERIS BRAISÉS (AU GRAS OU AU MAIGRE)   Spread some blanched celery stalks on a cloth, open them slightly, and season the insides with salt and pepper. Tie them in bunches of two or three, and place them in a buttered flameproof casserole lined with bacon rinds, chopped onions, and sliced carrots. Add sufficient stock to cover the vegetables. Bring to the boil over the heat, then cover and transfer to a moderate oven (180 C, 350 F, gas 4) to cook for 1½ hours.

Celery can be prepared *au maigre* by omitting the bacon rinds and replacing the stock with water.

Celery in butter   CÉLERIS AU BEURRE   Blanch and drain the stalks and place them in a well-buttered pan. Add salt and pepper. Moisten with several spoonfuls of white stock or water, cover, and cook for approximately 45 minutes.

Celery sauce   SAUCE AU CÉLERI Using only the tender stalks and hearts from two bunches of celery, remove the stringier fibres, slice widthways, wash, and dry. (Retain the hearts to eat with salt or anchovy sauce, if desired.) Put the slices in a saucepan with a bouquet garni and an onion studded with cloves. Add sufficient stock to just cover the contents, put the lid on, and bring to a gentle boil. When the celery is tender, put it into a blender with its cooking juices to make a purée. Put the purée into a saucepan, add 2 dl (7 fl oz, ¼ cup) cream sauce, and reduce until the desired texture is achieved. Adjust the seasoning and sprinkle with very finely chopped parsley. This sauce can accompany boiled or braised poultry.

Chicken with celery POULARDE AU CÉLERI Cook a chicken in butter in a flameproof casserole. While it is cooking, remove the stringier fibres from several sticks (stalks) of celery, slice them into matchstick strips, and blanch for 3 minutes in boiling water. Refresh and drain. When the bird has been cooking for 45 minutes add the celery strips and cook for a further 15 minutes. Arrange the bird in a serving dish and coat with its cooking juices; surround it with the celery strips and sprinkle with chopped parsley.

Célestine

A chicken dish named by the chef at the Cercle restaurant in Lyon in honour of the owner of the restaurant. A young chicken is fried with mushrooms and peeled tomatoes, flamed with Cognac, moistened with white wine, and served with powdered garlic and chopped parsley. This recipe was given by its creator to Lucien Tendret, who made it famous.

The name is also used for a chicken soup thickened with tapioca and garnished with strips of pancake seasoned with fines herbes, poached chicken breast, and a coating of chervil (a brunoise of truffles can replace the fines herbes in the pancakes). Certain ingredients of this soup are found in omelette *à la Célestine*.

| RECIPE

Omelette à la Celestine Prepare two small flat omelettes. Place one on a round plate, garnish with chicken

breast, and cover with a thick cream sauce containing chopped parsley. Place the second omelette on top and sprinkle with melted butter.

Cendré

One of various cows'-milk cheeses produced in Burgundy (Aisy Cendré, which contains 45% fat) or in Orléanais and Champagne (the Cendrés of Argonne, Riceys, and Rocroi, which contain 30% fat). Soft-centred and yellow in colour, Cendrés are fairly firm to the touch and disc-shaped. They are matured in wooden boxes or pots lined with the ashes, hence they are covered with a layer of wood ash.

cendre (sous la)

A rustic method of cooking, meaning literally 'under the ashes', which requires an open hearth or a wood fire. It is used mainly for cooking potatoes and truffles. One can also cook poultry or an animal with a protective coat, such as a hedgehog, in this way.
● *Potatoes sous la cendre* – Preferably choose some fine Fontenay potatoes; wash and dry them. Slide them under the hot coals (with the fire extinguished) and leave without disturbing for 35–40 minutes. Dust them off and serve with semisalted butter. They can be cooked wrapped in aluminium foil if the fire is still glowing and there are few ashes.
● *Truffles sous la cendre* – Brush the truffles carefully in cold water, wash, and wipe them. Dip them in Cognac or Armagnac, then wrap them singly in pieces of buttered foil or greaseproof (waxed) paper. If the embers are very hot, the truffles are placed in an earthenware pie dish with a lid, which is slipped under the embers. If the fire is almost out, the wrapped truffles may be placed directly under the cinders. Cooking takes 35–45 minutes.

centrepiece SURTOUT

An item of gold plate or porcelain which is placed in the centre of the table as a decoration for a large formal dinner. The centrepiece is usually in the form of a long tray lined with mirror, on which candelabra, baskets of fruit, or vases of flowers are displayed.

The use of centrepieces goes back to the Middle Ages, but it was in the 17th,

18th, and 19th centuries that this type
of table decoration had its heyday.

cep CÈPE

An edible boletus mushroom with a
large bulbous stalk that resembles a tree
trunk. There are over 20 edible varieties, which may be recognized by their
swollen stalks and the distinctive tubes
(the 'choke', or 'beard') that line the
inner surface of the cap.

Two varieties are highly valued in
gastronomy: the Bordeaux cep (whitish
to dark brown cap; swollen stalk; becomes cylindrical when the mushroom
is old) and the bronzed cep (very dark-
coloured; bulging stalk), which is particularly delicious and flavoursome in
mid-September. These varieties are
grown in southwestern France, Sologne,
and Alsace and are sold between July
and October. The pine cep (mahogany-
brown) and the reticulated cep (yellow-
ochre) are also very highly esteemed.

Ceps are always better when young;
then it is sufficient to wipe them gently
with a damp cloth. The bases of the
stalks are removed when they are too
ripe or maggoty. In wet weather, the
'choke' of certain ceps becomes slimy
and must be removed, as it would spoil
any dish.

The finest ceps may be eaten raw in
salad, cut into thin slices, but they are
especially delicious cooked, particularly
in an omelette, in a velouté, or as a
garnish (for confit, stew, or river fish).
They may be preserved by sterilization,
drying, or immersion in oil.

Many French regions have cep
specialities. In Auvergne, Châtaigneraie
ceps are eaten stuffed. In Aquitaine,
they are prepared *en cocotte*, stuffed, or
cooked in embers. In Poitou and southwestern France, they are grilled in walnut oil. Bordeaux ceps, always cooked
in oil (rather than butter), are dressed
with garlic or parsley. Auch is famous
for its ceps in white wine. In Gascony,
they are eaten *à la viande* (studded with
garlic and accompanied by raw ham),
grilled, in a stew, or with salmis. Brantôme is one of the most important
producing centres in France; several
hundred tonnes of ceps are sent to
Bordeaux and Paris each year.

The culinary value of ceps has only
been appreciated since the 18th century.

Their popularity can be traced to
the court of Stanislas Leszczyński in
Lorraine, hence the adjective *polonais*
(Polish) applied to the Bordeaux cep.

RECIPES

Ceps à la bordelaise Trim the ceps; cut
them into thin slices if they are very
large, halve them if of medium size, or
leave them whole if they are small. Put
them in a shallow frying pan (skillet)
with oil and lemon juice, leave to cook
slowly with the lid on for 5 minutes,
then drain. Heat some oil in another
frying pan, place the ceps in it, and
sprinkle with salt and pepper. Lightly
brown them then drain. Sprinkle with
chopped parsley and serve very hot.

In Paris, ceps *à la bordelaise* are
lightly fried and served with chopped
shallots, fried bread, and chopped
parsley.

Ceps à la mode béarnaise Trim and
wash some large ceps and put them in
the oven to release the excess juices.
Stud them with garlic, sprinkle with salt
and pepper, coat with oil, and grill
(broil) them. Chop and mix some breadcrumbs, garlic, and parsley and brown
this mixture in a frying pan (skillet) with
oil. Scatter the grilled ceps on top and
serve immediately.

Ceps au gratin Trim the ceps, separating the caps from the stalks; season with
salt and pepper, then coat with melted
butter or oil. Arrange the caps in a
buttered or oiled gratin dish with their
tops downwards. Chop the stalks and
add 1 chopped shallot for every 200 g
(7 oz) stalks, together with some parsley; brown in oil and season with salt
and pepper. Finally add 1 tablespoon
fresh breadcrumbs for every 200 g (7 oz)
stalks and mix all the ingredients
together. Fill the caps with this mixture,
sprinkle with some more fresh breadcrumbs, moisten with oil or melted
butter, and brown in a very hot oven
(240 c, 475 f, gas 9) or under a hot grill.

Ceps en terrine Trim and wash 750 g
(1¾ lb) ceps and separate the caps from
the stalks. Chop the stalks together with
3–4 cloves of garlic, 3–4 shallots, and a
small bunch of parsley and brown

everything in a shallow frying pan (skillet) with 3 tablespoons (¼ cup) olive oil. Add salt and pepper. Place the caps in a separate covered frying pan with 2 tablespoons (3 tablespoons) olive oil and some salt, and heat gently until they have discharged their juices. Drain them. Line the bottom and sides of an ovenproof earthenware dish with very thin rashers of smoked belly bacon. In it place a layer of the caps, then the chopped mixture, then a second layer of caps. Cover with more smoked rashers, put the lid on the dish, place in a moderately hot oven (about 200 c, 400 f, gas 6), and leave to cook for just under an hour.

Grilled (broiled) ceps CÈPES GRIL-LÉS Thoroughly clean and trim some fresh ceps. Lightly slit the caps and marinate the ceps for at least 30 minutes in a mixture of olive oil, lemon juice, chopped garlic, chopped parsley, a dash of cayenne, salt, and pepper. Drain the ceps and grill (broil) them. Sprinkle with chopped parsley and serve very hot. Alternatively, the ceps, moistened with melted butter or simply washed and wiped, may be sprinkled with salt and pepper, quickly grilled (broiled), and basted with oil or melted butter at the time of serving.

Marinated ceps CÈPES MARINÉS À CHAUD Trim and wash 750 g (1¾ lb) ceps and cut into thin slices. Plunge them into boiling oil for 2 minutes then cool them under cold water and wipe off excess. For the marinade, heat a mixture of 2 dl (7 fl oz, ¾ cup) olive oil, 3 tablespoons (¼ cup) wine vinegar, 1 tablespoon chopped fennel, 2 teaspoons lemon peel, a bay leaf cut into four, 2 small sprigs of thyme, salt, and freshly ground pepper. Bring this mixture to the boil and leave to boil for 5 minutes. Place the ceps in an earthenware dish and cover with the boiling marinade, poured through a sieve. Add 2 large cloves of garlic and 1 tablespoon chopped parsley. Stir, then leave in a cool place for at least 24 hours before serving.

cépage

The French word meaning variety of vine, or 'varietal'. The grape vine, *Vitis*

vinifera, has existed since before records were kept. There are thousands of varieties, but in France only about 50 types are in use. The Institut National des Appellations d'Origine specifies the cépages for each AOC wine and others subject to regional controls. Some wines, such as red Bordeaux (claret), are made from several grape varieties in conjunction; others are made from a single variety – red Burgundy and Beaujolais, Muscadet, Sancerre, and so on. In Alsace the wines are named after the single grape varieties that make them – Sylvaner, Riesling, Gewurztraminer, and others. It should be noted that in some regions a variety may have a local name or nickname; for example, the Chenin Blanc may be known as the Pineau de la Loire, and the Sauvignon is the Blanc Fumé of Puilly-sur-Loire.

cereal CÉRÉALE

Any of several grasses cultivated widely for their seeds (grain), which provide a staple food for humans and their livestock. Different cereals are grown in different regions of the globe: wheat and barley in temperate parts of Europe and Asia; rye and oats in northern and eastern Europe; rice in the wetter warm-temperate and subtropical parts of Asia; maize (corn) on the American continent: and millet and sorghum in Africa. Cereals remain the basic foodstuff in many countries, especially the poorest ones, although industrialized countries have tended to favour more elaborate processed foods. However, there is now a renewed interest in natural foods, including unprocessed cereals.

The nutritional value of cereals lies in their high carbohydrate content. They also provide proteins and certain B vitamins but are deficient in certain essential amino acids and are low in calcium. Consequently, for a balanced diet, cereals must be supplemented with dairy products, fresh vegetables, and fruit.

● *Whole cereals* (with only the husks removed; these are too hard for human consumption): highly nutritious; refined cereals have less flavour and provide less fibre and vitamins than whole cereals.

● *Flakes*: grains of wheat, oats, or maize (corn) that have been crushed,

cereals		food products
	soft	flour: bread, rusks, biscuits, and pastries; sprouted grains; cracked wheat.
wheat		
	hard	semolina: pasta, couscous
rice		grains (husked or not); rice crispies; rice flour; starch.
maize (corn)		corn on the cob; sweetcorn; cornflakes and popcorn; semolina and cornmeal.
rye		flour and bread; kasha.
barley		pearl barley; flour (gruel, galette).
oats		flour and flakes (porridge, oatmeal, muesli).
millet and sorghum		flour and semolina.

steam-cooked, crushed again, and grilled.

• *Puffed grains*: grains of maize (corn) or rice that have been subjected to a vacuum, thus causing them to swell up (and, incidentally, partly destroying their vitamin B_1; they are sometimes coated with sugar.

• *Pretreated grains*: grains that have been cooked slowly in their husks before refining; this operation concentrates the nutrients in the centre of the grain (blanched rice).

• *Precooked grains*: grains (whole or portions of grains) partially steam-cooked and then dried; this reduces the cooking time, for example, with rice.

cerisette

A fermented drink based on cherry juice. Not a liqueur, like cherry brandy or Maraschino, it is a refreshing slightly alcoholic drink.

The Morvan cerisette is a filled sweet, a speciality of Cosne-Cours-sur-Loire in Nièvre.

cervelas

See *saveloy*.

cervelle de canut

A speciality of Lyon, traditionally served in taverns as a mid-morning snack. It consists of fairly soft curd cheese known as *claqueret*, which is well beaten, seasoned with salt and pepper, and blended with shallot chopped with herbs, fresh cream, white wine, and a little oil.

cévenole (à la)

A term describing one of many sweet or savoury dishes that contain chestnuts, a speciality of the Ardèche region of France. Used in purées, stews, whole, poached, etc., chestnuts can accompany a range of roast and braised meats, including loin of pork, mutton, calves' sweetbreads, fillet of beef, and game. Marrons glacés are used in a variety of hot, cold, and iced sweets.

RECIPES

Savoury Dishes

Mutton cutlets (rib chops) à la cévenole CÔTELETTES DE MOUTON À LA CÉVENOLE Braise some trimmed mutton cutlets. Cook some chestnuts in meat stock; lightly fry some strips of smoked bacon. Add the chestnuts and bacon to the cutlets and cook for a further 5 minutes. Fry some chipolatas lightly in butter. Arrange the cutlets in a dish with the chestnuts and bacon and garnish with the chipolatas. Serve with braised red cabbage if desired.

Sweet Dishes

Bavarian cream à la cévenole BAVAROIS À LA CÉVENOLE Make a Bavarian cream mixture and add an equal volume of puréed marrons glacés flavoured with Kirsch. Brush a round mould with sweet almond oil and heap the mixture into it. Set in the refrigerator, then turn out onto the serving dish. Decorate with piped Chantilly cream and halved marrons glacés.

Crêpes à la cévenole Prepare some sweet pancakes (see *crêpe*). Spread them out on the worktop and cover each with a thin layer of marron-glacé purée flavoured with rum. Fold the pancakes over, arrange them in an ovenproof serving dish, dust with sugar, and glaze in the oven. Serve very hot.

ceviche or cebiche

A dish, characteristic of Peruvian cookery, that is based on raw fish marinated in lemon juice and is served with sweet limes, raw onion rings, tomatoes, and boiled sweetcorn.

Chabichou

A small goats'-milk cheese from Poitou, which contains 45% butterfat and has a soft centre and a natural crust. Usually in the shape of a truncated cone but sometimes cylindrical, it weighs about 100 g (4 oz) and is sold unwrapped when farm-produced, wrapped in paper from a dairy. It may be eaten fresh. When ripened, it is firm without being hard, with a fairly pronounced flavour and a strong goatlike smell. It is at its best in the summer.

Chablis

White Burgundy of worldwide repute. Situated between Tonnerre and Auxerre and crossed by the small unnavigable River Serein, the Chablis vineyard acquired fame because of the high quality of its white wines. Monks played a great part in the history of the vineyard. The first monks, in 867, were those of the abbey of Saint-Martin-de-Tours, the Cistercians of Pontigny not arriving until three centuries later. Since then, the sale of Chablis wines has been increasing all the time, in spite of the ravages of wars, vine phylloxera (in 1893), and, above all, frosts, which almost completely destroyed the vineyard in 1957 and did much damage in 1985. In the past considerable quantities of imitation 'Chablis' were sold, which proved very deceptive for foreign customers. Fortunately stricter controls are now in force.

Chablis, situated in the north of Burgundy, is nearer to certain vineyards of the Loire (Pouilly and Sancerre) than to Beaune. The vines are grown halfway up the hillsides in poor shallow chalky soil. The Chardonnay vine, which is called *beaunnois* (of Beaune) in the region, is today the only one authorized for the production of AOC Chablis. The work of the grower, already arduous on such a barren soil, is often ruined by May frosts, as the vineyard is particularly exposed.

Chablis is a very dry white wine that can keep well. Pale yellow in colour with glints of green, it is at the same time powerful and delicate. There are, in order of merit, four categories – Chablis Grand Cru, Chablis Premier Cru, Chablis, and Petit Chablis – originating from different soils and grown under conditions of varying exposure.

● Seven Chablis grands crus are officially recognized: Vaudésir, Les Clos, Grenouilles, Les Preuses, Bougros, Valmur, and Blanchots, to which is often added another, Moutonne.

● Chablis Premiers Crus, of which there are about 20, come from neighbouring parishes situated on the banks of the River Serein. Some well-known names are Montmain, Vaillons, Beugnon, Monte-de-Tonnerre, and Fourchaume.

● Chablis and Petit Chablis come from within the delimited AOC region.

chaboisseau

A small and very bony freshwater fish that is usually fried whole or used in a matelote.

chabrot or chabrol (faire)

To add red wine to a plate of soup or broth that has already been partly consumed. This rural tradition, associated with central and southwestern France, is customary with *bréjaude* soup.

chafing dish   RÉCHAUD

A small item of portable kitchen equipment consisting of a pan fitted over a source of heat, usually a spirit lamp but sometimes a butane gas burner or an electric element. Made of copper, stainless steel, or silver plate, it is used to cook dishes at table, such as fondues (when it forms part of the fondue set) or flambé dishes.

It can also serve as a hotplate, for keeping cooked dishes warm.

chai

This term, meaning 'wine store' is mostly used in the Bordeaux region, where underground cellars cannot be excavated, to designate the place where the wines mature, in vat or cask. The *maître de chai* decides when to draw off the wine and bottle it.

chakchouka

A traditional Arabian and north African dish comprising a ragout of potatoes and onions, cooked in oil and seasoned with chilli peppers, harissa, and tomato sauce, over which eggs are broken; when the eggs are cooked, the dish is sprinkled with dried mint. The potatoes may be replaced by green peas, beans, a mixture of sweet peppers and tomatoes, or courgettes (zucchini) and aubergines (eggplants). Chakchouka is often garnished with grilled merguez or slices of dried meat.

chaleuth

A sweet of Jewish cuisine, made from a mixture of breadcrumbs, finely sliced apples, eggs, and sugar, flavoured with rum, raisins, and cinnamon. The dish is baked in an oiled casserole and served warm. It is also prepared by cooking sliced apples with sugar and cinnamon, again in a casserole dish but between two pastry crusts, the top being sprinkled with small pieces of fat.

chalonnaise (à la)

A classic garnish, now rarely used, intended to accompany poultry and calves' sweetbreads. Named after the town of Chalon-sur-Saône in France, it consists of cocks' combs and kidneys, mushrooms, and then slices of truffle in a suprême sauce.

Chambertin

A famous red Burgundy vineyard in the Côte de Nuits which, together with Chambertin Clos de Bèze, make up a 28-hectare (70-acre) vineyard. The names derive from the plot (*clos*) at Gevrey, given in about 630 AD to the monks of the Abbey of Bèze. The owner of the adjacent field (*champ*), a man called Bertin, copied the monks' suc-

cessful methods. The Pinot Noir is grown on a chalky soil that also includes ferruginous marls. There are a number of other sites that may put their names before that of Chambertain – Charmes, Latricières, Mazy, Griottes, Reichottes, and Chapelle. They are all magnificent wines and should be served with respect and in the context of fine food.

RECIPES

Chambertin sauce SAUCE CHAMBERTIN Peel and dice 2 carrots and 2 onions. Soften them with 20 g (¾ oz, 1½ tablespoons) butter in a shallow frying pan (skillet). Add a bouquet garni, 100 g (4 oz, 1 cup) chopped mushrooms (including stalks and peelings), half a chopped clove of garlic, 250 g (9 oz) trimmings from white fish, salt, and pepper. Moisten with 5 dl (17 fl oz, 2 cups) Chambertin and cook for at least 20 minutes in a covered pan. Remove the lid and reduce by a third. Pass through a conical strainer and bind with 1 tablespoon kneaded butter.

Fillets of sole with Chambertin FILETS DE SOLE AU CHAMBERTIN Season some fillets of sole with salt and pepper and fold them in two. Butter an ovenproof casserole or dish and line the bottom with finely diced carrots, chopped onions, fresh and crumbled thyme, and a crushed bay leaf. Add some chopped mushroom stalks; the caps will serve for the garnish. Arrange the fillets in the dish, dab them with knobs of butter, and barely cover them with Chambertin. Put the lid on and bake in a preheated very hot oven (about 240 c, 475 f, gas 9). Remove and drain the fillets, then arrange them in the serving dish; keep hot. Reduce the cooking liquid by one-third, pass through a conical strainer, and bind the strained liquor with 1 tablespoon kneaded butter. Coat the fillets with this sauce and garnish with sautéed mushrooms caps and small glazed onions.

other recipes See *brill, duck, salmon (cold dishes).*

Chambolle-Musigny

A parish in the Côte de Nuits in Burgundy, famous for the Musigny and Bonnes Mares vineyards among others.

These cover about 24 hectares (59 acres). Other well-known wines originating here, and combining their names with that of the parish, include Les Amoureuses, Les Charmes, Les Combettes, and Les Grands Murs. A very small quantity of Chambolle-Musigny is made, and it is seldom found outside the region.

Chambord

A classic method of preparing large fish, such as carp, salmon, or sole, which are to be cooked whole. Requiring high-quality produce and meticulous preparation, the fish is stuffed and braised in red wine and garnished with a mixture of quenelles of fish forcemeat, fillets of sole, sautéed soft roes, mushrooms caps, truffles shaped like olives, and crayfish cooked in a court-bouillon.

| RECIPES

Carp Chambord CARPE CHAMBORD Select a carp weighing 2–3 kg (4½–6½ lb), trim it, stuff it with a cream fish forcemeat, and sew it up. Remove a thin strip of skin from the back on either side of the backbone and lard the bare area with small pieces of fat bacon. Butter a baking dish and line it generously with a brunoise of carrot, turnip, leek, celery, and onion mixed with mushroom peelings and softened in butter. Add a bouquet garni. Two-thirds cover the carp with a mixture of fish stock and red wine, and cook in a hot oven (about 225 C, 435 F, gas 7–8), basting from time to time. While the carp is cooking, slice some mushroom caps and cook them in a white court-bouillon. Remove the cooked carp, drain, and arrange on the serving dish, keeping it hot. Prepare a little brown roux, add it to the pan juices from the carp along with 2 tablespoons (3 tablespoons) tomato concentrate, and cook for at least 30 minutes. Pass through a conical strainer. Return the carp to the oven until it is glazed, then coat it with the sauce and surround it with a Chambord garnish, including the mushroom caps.

Chambord sauce SAUCE CHAMBORD Prepare a genevoise sauce with the braising stock of the fish that is being cooked; dilute it with red wine and coat the fish with it.

chambrer

A French term meaning to bring a wine to the temperature of the room where it will be drunk. White, rosé, and sparkling wines are most enjoyable served at 5–10 C (41–50 F), but reds should be served at 15–18 C (59–64 F). The bottle should take a room temperature gradually, and never be plunged into hot water or put near a fire. Not only will this shock the wine but currents will be created within it and churn up any sediment.

chamois

A wild mammal, resembling a deer, that is considered one of the finest venisons. The flesh is tender and has a distinctive flavour without being too strong, especially in animals under three years old. It is hunted in the mountainous regions where it lives, such as the southern Alps and the Pyrenees, where it is called izard (wild goat). It is prepared in the same way as venison; old animals must be marinated.

champagne

A sparkling wine produced in the delimited Champagne region of France. The champagne vines are reputed to be among the oldest in the world; there is, however, no proof that they were cultivated before the Roman occupation. The wine of the Champagne region was formerly a still wine, though always with a certain vivacity. It was in the 17th century that a Benedictine monk, Dom Pierre Pérignon, perfected the means of sealing the sparkle in the bottle, thanks to the rediscovery of the use of cork as a stopper. The gas in champagne is the result of secondary fermentation.

All wines tend to 'work' in the spring, and there is a secondary fermentation producing carbon dioxide gas, which, in the ordinary way, is given off when the wine is in the cask or vat. If the wine is in a bottle, however, the gas remains in it, and the bottle and the stopper must resist the pressure in the wine.

Situated northeast of Paris, the champagne wine-growing region is the most northerly in France, extending over the departments of Marne, Aube, and

Aisne. The main production areas are the Montagne de Reims, the Marne Valley, and the Côte des Blancs. There are several permitted vines but the main ones are the black Pinot Noir and the white Chardonnay. If the black grape skins are not left long enough in the must to tint it, a wholly white wine will result. First, the wine is made as usual and ferments. Then, in the spring, it is bottled before the secondary fermentation starts, a little sugar assisting the process. The *prise de mousse* (development of the sparkle) takes about three months. The bottles remain in the cellar and are rotated and shaken, so that the deposit slides down onto the cork. Then, when required, they are 'disgorged' – the first cork and the deposit are removed and, before the second cork goes in, any sweetening is added. The vogue for very dry champagnes is a recent one, being drunk as apéritifs and with certain first courses. The sweeter champagnes are agreeable at the end of a meal.

Champagnes should be served chilled but not iced. Great care should be taken when opening, as the force behind the cork is great – never point a bottle at anyone and never let go of the cork once the muzzle of wire is removed! Tulip glasses or goblets are correct – coupes tend to flatten the wine. Vintage champagne is usually considered to be at its best 5–10 years from its vintage. (Most champagne, however, is non-vintage). It is stored like any fine wine. If it becomes very old, it loses its freshness and sparkle and turns a deeper golden. Highly esteemed by Madame de Pompadour 'whom it left full of beauty after drinking it', champagne has, since the 18th century, been the supreme wine for celebrations, in France and throughout the world.

In addition to the various types of sparkling wine, the Champagne region also produces still wines, now with the AOC Coteaux Champenois. They can be red (that of Bouzy is famous), still white, and also rosé (the Rosé de Riceys is well known).

RECIPES

Salmon with champagne   SAUMON AU CHAMPAGNE   Cut some fairly thick salmon steaks. Butter a baking dish and line the bottom with chopped shallots and a few diced vegetables. Arrange the salmon steaks in it and half-cover them with a mixture of equal parts of fish stock and champagne. Cook in a hot oven (about 225 c, 435 f, gas 7–8), then remove the salmon steaks, drain, and keep hot. Strain the pan juice and add some cream, using 1 dl (6 tablespoons, scant ½ cup) per 2.5 dl (8 fl oz, 1 cup) juice, and reduce by half. Adjust the seasoning. Add a generous lump of butter cut into small pieces and beat energetically. Coat the steaks with this sauce.

Fillets of sole may be prepared in the same way.

Truffles with champagne   TRUFFES AU CHAMPAGNE   (from a recipe by Plumerey) Take 1.4 kg (3 lb) large well-rounded truffles, ideally ones that are of a good black colour. Brush them in two or three lots of water. When they are well drained, place them in a saucepan lined with slices of bacon and cover with more bacon.

Coarsely dice 450 g (1 lb) desalted ham, and also the same quantity of fillets of veal and fresh pork. Cook in butter in a saucepan, adding finely sliced carrots and onions, sprigs of parsley, a few pieces of thyme, bay leaf, basil, half a clove of garlic, and 2 cloves; season with a little salt, white pepper, grated nutmeg, and a dash of spices. When these ingredients begin to colour slightly, pour on two bottles of champagne (Ay is best); bring to the boil; skim, and leave to simmer on a low heat without reducing. Then press through a strainer and pour it over the truffles.

Start cooking the truffles 1 hour before serving. Leave to boil gently for 45 minutes then remove from the heat and keep very hot, without boiling. Just before serving, drain them and arrange them on a napkin folded on a silver dish; cover to keep them piping hot.

Champagne and Ardennes

Famous throughout the world for its wines, the French region of Champagne is not, however, noted for outstanding gastronomy. This paradox can be partly explained by the numerous political and social upheavals experienced by the province in the course of time. But the underlying causes are of a sociological nature: as one of the economic and military crossroads of western Europe, Champagne has been exposed to numerous influences. These conditions, unfavourable for the development of any great local traditions, could explain the modesty of the region's cuisine.

The adjective *champenois* as used in gastronomy must not be confused with the region; it is customarily used to describe any dish from any region that is cooked in champagne or in a still wine from the Champagne region.

The true culinary specialities of Champagne are staunchly rustic: stew (formerly pickled pork and cabbage; today bacon, smoked ham, sausages, cabbage, and other vegetables); dandelion salad with bacon; fish stew (young pike, bream, eels, and small carp with a still white wine); pike (in a blanquette, with white sauce, stuffed with ham, or in fillets); vine snails (stuffed with garlic); meat loaves, pâtés, and terrines of chicken, hare, goose, or pigeon; hams (in pastry or smoked); boudin blanc (with fresh ham); black pudding (blood sausage) or quenelles of rabbit; poultry, stuffed or stewed; small sausages made of chitterlings; and gougères and cheese fritters.

In fact the originality of Champagne depends on a method of preparation called *à la Sainte-Menehold*, which is applied to pigs' trotters and a great variety of other offal dishes. The traditional accompaniment is pease pudding.

In Ardennes, game reigns supreme: roebuck and wild boar (in roasts, pies, tarts, and terrines); hare (jugged, in pies, and terrines); and thrushes (roasted in sage leaves or stuffed with sage, or *en terrine* with juniper). Rabbit is often stuffed (with cooked ham). Fresh ham is served moulded or in paupiettes, rolled around chicory (endive). Fish is plentiful: trout and pike (dotted with pieces of diced bacon, carrots, gherkins (sweet dill pickles), in sauce, baked, etc.); eels (stewed); and small mixed fried fish. Red cabbage is cooked with apples; potatoes are cooked in the frying pan.

Apart from *gâteau champenois* (made with crushed pink Reims biscuits, raisins, crystallized (candied)

fruit, and champagne marc) and the soft Ardennes gâteau, desserts are fairly conventional. There is, on the other hand, a wide variety of biscuits and confectionery: Reims biscuits, croquettes, small meringue cases, galettes, madeleines, nonnettes, gingerbread, etc. Jam made from small black plums (*norbertes*) is a speciality of the Ardennes.

The best-known cheeses come from the Île-de-France: Bries, Coulommiers, Chaource, and Cendré.

Champeaux

A Parisian restaurant founded in 1800 in the Place de la Bourse by a man called Champeaux. It was a favourite haunt of stockbrokers and businessmen, who appreciated its substantial food and speedy service. It also possessed a winter garden. In 1903, the first Goncourt Prize was awarded at Champeaux's restaurant: the members of the Académie sometimes met there after leaving the Grand Hotel and before going to Drouant's house. The restaurant closed in about 1908.

champigny

A rectangular tart consisting of a puff pastry case filled with apricot jam.

| RECIPE

Champigny gâteau GÂTEAU CHAMPIGNY Stone (pit) 1 kg (2¼ lb) apricots and cook with 250 g (8¾ oz, 1 generous cup, firmly packed) granulated sugar and ½ glass of water until tender. Let the syrup reduce completely then add 1 small glass of fruit liqueur (apricot brandy or Kirsch) and a few kernels extracted from the apricot stones. Leave to cool thoroughly.

Roll out 500 g (18 oz) puff pastry into a long rectangle, about 3 mm (⅛ in) thick. Cut out two equal rectangles from the pastry and also strips 1.5 cm (½ in) wide that are long enough to fit around one of the rectangles. Coat the surface of one of the rectangles with some beaten egg. Press the strips of pastry around the rim of the rectangle so that they form a vertical edge.

Pour the stewed apricots into the centre and spread evenly over the pastry (the strips will prevent the apricots from running over during cooking). Brush the top of the pastry strips with beaten egg, put the second pastry rectangle over the top and press down very lightly with the fingers to make it stick. Add 2 tablespoons (3 tablespoons) milk to the remainder of the beaten egg and coat the top of the champigny. Score a latticework in the pastry with the point of a knife. Place in the oven at about 230 c (450 f, gas 8) and cook for 25–30 minutes. Serve when slightly warm.

The fresh apricots may be replaced by apricot jam flavoured with a fruit liqueur.

champoreau

A word derived from the Spanish *chapurrar*, meaning to mix two liqueurs. It was introduced into the slsng of the French troops in north Africa at the end of the 19th century and originally applied to an alcoholic drink made from a mixture of various kinds of spirits or liqueurs; it was then used to denote a mixture of milky coffee and rum. Today, it describes black coffee mixed with a small amount of spirit, such as Cognac, Calvados, or marc. The word is also used informally for a 'nip' or 'dram' poured into a cup still warm from the coffee it has contained.

Champvallon

A dish of mutton cutlets baked between a layer of onions and a layer of potatoes. This classic preparation dates from the reign of Louis XIV; it was invented by one of his mistresses, who supplanted the Marquise de Maintenon for a time by indulging the gluttony of the king. (The Marquise de Maintenon herself invented lamb chops *en papillotes*.)

| RECIPE

Mutton cutlets (rib chops) Champvallon CÔTELLETTES DE MOUTON CHAMPVALLON Take 6 trimmed mutton cutlets (rib chops). Peel 750 g (1¾ lb) potatoes and cut them into round slices. Peel and chop 125 g (4½ oz, 1 generous cup) onions and 1 clove of garlic. Brown the cutlets in 20 g (¾ oz, 1½ tablespoons) butter, drain them, and then soften the onions in the same butter with the lid on the pan. Place the onions in a buttered dish and arrange the chops on top. Sprinkle a little thyme,

salt, and pepper over the chops. Cover with 1 dl (6 tablespoons, scant ½ cup) stock and a further 20 g (¾ oz, 1½ tablespoons) melted butter. Place in the oven at about 240 c (475 f, gas 9) and cook for 20–25 minutes. Then arrange the potatoes over the chops, season with salt and pepper, and add the same amount of stock and melted butter as before. Return to the oven and cook for about 25 minutes.

chanfaina

A West Indian dish made with slices of fried lamb's liver arranged in an earthenware dish and covered with quarters of tomato fried in oil, crushed garlic, and thinly sliced sweet peppers.

In Spain, *chanfaina* (or *xanfaina*) is a typical Catalonian sauce made with onions, peppers, small pieces of various fresh vegetables cooked in very hot oil, fresh mint, parsley, cumin, and pepper. The sauce is served with poultry, white meat, or lobster escalopes.

chanoinesse (à la)

Describes various dishes that evoke the important role occupied by cookery in certain religious orders of canonesses during the Ancien Régime. Chicken *à la chanoinesse* is poached chicken served with tartlets filled with crayfish tails in a suprême sauce made with crayfish stock. A cream soup or velouté *à la chanoinesse* also contains crayfish stock. The name is also given to calves' sweetbreads and soft-boiled or poached eggs garnished with truffles and small carrots cooked in cream and coated with a sauce made from sherry-flavoured veal stock.

| RECIPE

Brain soufflé à la chanoinesse SOUFFLÉ DE CERVELLE À LA CHANOINESSE Cook some calves' brains in a court-bouillon, drain, and reduce to a purée. Mix 2 dl (7 fl oz, ¾ cup) béchamel sauce with, 250 g (9 oz, generous cup) brain purée, then add a little grated nutmeg, 60 g (2½ oz, ½ cup) grated Parmesan cheese, 1 tablespoon truffle peelings, and 4 egg yolks. Adjust the seasoning, then fold in 4 stiffly whisked egg whites. Pour the mixture into a buttered soufflé dish and bake in the oven for 30 minutes at 200 c (400 f, gas 6).

chanterelle

An edible mushroom with a funnel-shaped cap and thick swollen gills extending over the stalk. All chanterelles have a pleasant flavour, but they need to be cooked slowly as they become hard if they are sautéed too quickly. They are mainly used to garnish meat or fill omelettes. For recipes, see *girolle*.

Chantilly

Chantilly cream is fresh cream beaten to the consistency of a mousse, sweetened, and flavoured with vanilla or other flavours. It is used as an ingredient of, or an accompaniment to, various deserts, including meringues, sundaes, Bavarian creams, charlottes, custard creams, etc. Preparations *à la chantilly*, for example chicken *à la chantilly*, are made using whipped cream.

The name is also given to cold emulsified sauces (such as mayonnaise) and hot sauces (such as hollandaise) to which whipped cream is added; these sauces are also called mousselines.

Although the name is derived from the château of Chantilly, whose cuisine enjoyed a fine reputation under the supervision of Vatel in the mid-17th century, none of the preparations named after it was created there; they in fact date only from the last century.

RECIPES

Chantilly cream CRÈME CHANT-ILLY Chill some double (heavy) cream and some milk in the refrigerator. Mix the well-chilled cream with a third of its volume of very cold milk and whisk until frothy. Add some caster (superfine) sugar (60–75 g (2½–3 oz, 6–6 tablespoons, firmly packed) to each 5 dl (17 fl oz, 2 cups) cream), flavour with vanilla essence or vanilla-flavoured sugar, and continue to whip until the cream remains in the coils of the whisk. Return to the refrigerator immediately until ready to use.

Chantilly sauce SAUCE CHANTILLY Dilute 2 dl (7 fl oz, ¼ cup) very thick suprême sauce with 1 dl (6 tablespoons,

scant ½ cup) whipped cream. Use hot to coat a chicken or poached white offal.

Chicken à la chantilly POULARDE À LA CHANTILLY Make a stuffing with some boiled rice, truffle peelings, and diced foie gras. Stuff the chicken, sew up the aperture, and brown the bird in a stewpan with some butter. Take care not to overcook. Season with pepper, cover the pan, and cook for about 1 hour. Cook some truffles slowly in port and sauté some slices of foie gras in butter. When the chicken is cooked, drain it and arrange on a serving dish, surrounded by the truffles and foie gras. Keep it hot. Add some chicken velouté to the pan juice; reduce by half, and add several tablespoons of whipped cream. Coat the chicken with the sauce.

Chaource

A French cheese made in the Champagne region from cows' milk (50% butterfat). It is a very white soft creamy cheese with a whitened crust and a milky fruity flavour. It is named after the chief town of the canton of Aube and enjoys an *appellation d'origine*. It is cylindrical in shape, 11 cm (4½ in) in diameter and 7 cm (3 in) high, and weighs approximately 500 g (18 oz). The 'petit Chaource', weighing 280 g (10 oz), measures 9 cm (3½ in) by 5.5 cm (2 in). The cheese is in season in summer and autumn and is sold wrapped in a band of paper. It used to be wrapped in lettuce leaves to protect it during transport.

chapati

A small pancake served like bread in Indian cookery. It is fried in butter made from buffaloes' milk and when cooked is slightly swollen and crisp. Chapatis may be filled with chopped spinach flavoured with ginger and cumin, in which case they are not as crisp.

chapon

A crust of bread rubbed with garlic. Chapons are cut from a long thin French loaf (a *ficelle*) and left to harden for 24 hours. They are rubbed with a clove of garlic (which is itself sometimes called a *chapon*), and sprinkled with a little olive oil and vinegar. They are usually prepared half an hour in advance so that they have enough time to become well-impregnated. In the south of France, and especially in Languedoc, bread treated in this way is used to garnish a green salad, especially one made with endive (chicory).

The word *chapon* (meaning literally a capon) came to be used in this sense to describe the large piece of bread served with a thin soup when one could not afford to serve a real capon.

In Normandy, a crust of bread dipped in boiled milk is called a *chapon*.

chaptalization
CHAPTALISATION

The process of adding sugar to the must to enable the wine yeasts to do their work and raise the alcoholic content in the finished wine. It is subject to strict controls, but, correctly performed, is helpful to wines in some northerly vineyards, such as Burgundy. If carried to excess it unbalances the wine.

char   OMBLE CHEVALIER

A fish related to the salmon, found in the cold lakes of the Alps, the Pyrenees, Scotland, and Ireland: it is becoming increasingly rare. The char is a large deep-bodied fish with a very wide mouth, a grey-green back dotted with round pale spots, and an orange belly. It can weigh up to 8 kg (18 lb) and is one of the best-flavoured freshwater fish. It is cooked in the same way as salmon trout.

The lake trout, imported from Canada to Europe at the end of the 19th century, is related to, but smaller than, the char. Grey-green all over with lighter stripes on its back and sides, it has a very delicate flavour and is now widely farmed.

charbonnée

A term used to describe food cooked over a charcoal grill. In Berry, the term also describes pork civet thickened with blood. In the Île-de-France, it is used for a slow-cooking beef stew made with red wine, onions, carrots, and spices. This is also thickened with pig's blood towards the end of the cooking period.

charcuterie

Products based on pork meat or offal The word also designates the shop where this type of product is sold and also the group of tradesmen who sell it. Charcuterie, or pork butchery, is particularly well developed in regions and countries where rearing pigs has been a longstanding tradition, such as the Auvergne, Alsace, Italy, Germany, etc.

The Roman *porcella* law fixed the manner of rearing, feeding, slaughtering, and preparing pork, and the Romans were probably the instigators of pork butchery as a trade. It was not until 1475 that, in France, an edict of the provostship of Paris granted to 'maîtres chayrcutiers-saucissiers-boudiniers' the right to sell cooked and prepared pork flesh (and also fish during Lent). In 1476, these tradesmen formed a special category, distinct from the roasters (or *oyers*, with whom they had been confused until then), but they still formed part of the corporation of butchers. It was not until 1513 that the *chaircuitiers* (from *chair*, 'flesh' and *cuit*, 'cooked') had the right to lay in a supply of pork meat directly, without being obliged to go to the butchers.

The numerous preparations of charcuterie include cured meats, fresh and smoked sausages, pâtés, andouilles, andouillettes, black puddings, boudins blancs, sausagemeat, hams, galantines, pâtés en croûte, ready-cooked dishes, and forcemeats. For a long time these have remained regional specialities, dominated by the processes of salting and smoking. At the end of the 19th century, charcuterie began to appear on gala menus, partly thanks to a pork butcher named Louis-François Drone. He was born in 1825 in Sarthe and became established in Paris under the Second Empire, which imposed new methods in this field. Nicknamed 'the Carême of charcuterie', he published a monumental *Traité de la charcuterie ancienne et moderne*. On 9 December 1893, a menu entirely of charcuterie was published in *Le Figaro*, signed by Gustave Carlin, the great Parisian chef and author of *La Cuisine moderne* (1887). It consisted of cold hors d'oeuvres: mortadella, large sausages from Arles and Lyons, foie gras; hot hors d'oeuvres: Clamecy andouillettes, Richelieu croquettes stuffed with meat, and Tonnerre black pudding; entrées: pork pies, loin of pork in pepper sauce, pigs' trotters *à la Périgueux*, and ham in aspic with pistachios; roasts: sucking pig stuffed *à l'anglaise,* jellied brawn and lettuce in a green salad with grilled strips of larding bacon; entremets: spinach with roast-pork gravy, stuffed artichokes *à la barigoule,* and soufflé fritters.

In 1963 L'Association des Chevaliers de Sainte-Antoine was founded to study and promote the gastronomy of pork and charcuterie.

charcutière (à la)

Describing charcuterie preparations, such as *côte charcutière* (sautéed pork chop), roast loin of pork, crépinettes, and kromeskies, which are served with a charcutière sauce. This sauce is a Robert sauce containing thin strips of gherkins. Eggs *à la charcutière* are prepared with poached or soft-boiled eggs arranged on sautéed crépinettes and coated with reduced charcutière sauce.

| RECIPES

Charcutière sauce SAUCE CHARCUTIERE Soften 3 tablespoons (¼ cup) peeled chopped onions by frying gently in a covered pan, in 1 tablespoon lard. Sprinkle with 1 tablespoon white dried breadcrumbs until lightly coloured. Add ½ glass white wine and 1 small glass stock and boil for 3–4 minutes. Stir in 2 tablespoons (3 tablespoons) finely diced gherkins and then 1 tablespoon mustard. Adjust the seasoning before serving.

Fried eggs à la charcutière OEUFS FRITS À LA CHARCUTIÈRE Grill some crépinettes. Fry several eggs in lard and arrange them in a circle on a plate. Place the crépinettes in the centre and garnish with fried parsley. Serve with a charcutière sauce.

chard CARDE

The succulent leaves and stalks of a variety of beet, *Beta vulgaris cicla.* The name is also given to the edible inner leaves of the cardoon. Chards are used as a vegetable, especially in Provence and the Rhône Valley. Cooked in water or in a thin white sauce, they are served with the cooking juices or a well-seasoned white sauce, to enhance their rather neutral taste.

Compare *Swiss chard.*

Charente

The ancient provinces of Angoumois, Aunis, and Saintonge, which today form the Charente, pride themselves on their simple and straightforward cooking – described as 'peasant' by Curnonsky. Its charm is due mainly to the high quality of the products in the region. The sea provides shellfish, crustaceans, and fish, which are prepared in various ways: oysters (often eaten with grilled sausages) from Marennes, La Tremblade, and Châteaud'Oléron; mussels served in soup, *en éclade,* or *en mouclade;* scallops *aux fines herbes;* razor clams stuffed with breadcrumbs, garlic, and parsley (like snails); clams from Oléron and La Rochelle; cockles (*sourdons*); stewed *lavgnons* (cockle-like molluscs); fried cuttlefish (*casserons*), and *raiteaux* (small rays); prawns (*chevrettes*) or shrimps (*boucs*); hake in soup; sole and sardines from Royan, grey mullet and bass, roast eel, and fried elvers. All kinds of freshwater fish are also cooked, although the River Touvre, which flows through Angoulême, is no longer, as it was in the time of Clément Marot, 'paved with trout, and bordered by eels and crayfish'.

High-quality cattle and salt-meadow sheep are bred in the region. Typical dishes include Charente casserole, boned and rolled leg of veal, calf's head *saintongeaise,* Angoulême tripe, and gigorit. Charcuterie includes choice products such as rillettes, large and small sausages, saveloys and brawn, white and black puddings, terrines and pâtés (foie gras garnished with truffles at Barbezieux or Angoulême, partridges at Ruffec, larks at Excideuil). Game is plentiful and dishes such as jugged hare with redcurrant jelly and *salmis d'oiseaux de mer* (a stew made with sea birds) are specialities. Chicken recipes are varied and include chicken pie with salsify, sanguette, and chicken *à l'anglaise.*

The vegetables of the region are excellent. Peas from Aunis have a reputation for being tender and sweet – they are canned at Bordeaux and La Rochesur-Yon. Broad beans have as fine a flavour as haricot beans and red beans (*mojhettes*). Cabbages are often cooked *en farée.* Mushrooms, both cultivated and wild, are considered to be excellent, as are nectarines from Saintonge, apples from Saint-Porchain, and white grapes from the various vineyards.

The region also produces a butter, which is comparable to the best Normandy types, and is used to cook much of this produce, especially when cooking in a casserole. It goes well with radishes (*rifauts*), raw beans dipped in salt, and braised garlic. Cheeses are important products and include Oléron made with goats' milk, Ruffec made with cows' milk, Jonchée (a soft white cheese made in a rush basket), and also caillebotte (curds).

Among the sweets worth mentioning are merveilles, cruchade with jam, cheesecake, chocolate tartlets flavoured with Cognac, *gâteau d'assemblé*, Taillebourg brioches, *raisiné* (a jam), Pons sponge fingers (ladyfingers), frangipane tart, crystallized (candied) fruits, and angelica liqueur.

The red wines of the region are fairly ordinary but the whites are used for producing Cognac, for which the region is so well known.

charlotte

Two kinds of dessert, one hot and the other cold or iced, are known by this name.

The original charlotte (which appeared at the end of the 18th century, perhaps in honour of Queen Charlotte, the wife of George III of England) is inspired by English desserts. It is made from a thick fruit purée flavoured with lemon and cinnamon, poured into a round mould with a slightly flared rim, lined with slices of buttered bread. The dish is baked in the oven, then turned out of the mould and served warm with a cold custard cream. The classic example is apple charlotte, but other fruits may be used.

Carême invented charlotte russe. This is a chilled uncooked dish consisting of vanilla Bavarian cream (or chocolate mousse, coffee mousse, a bombe mixture, or Chantilly cream) poured into a charlotte mould lined with sponge fingers (ladyfingers). The latter can be soaked in liqueur or coffee beforehand. The preparation is allowed to cool and then turned out of the mould. Carême

named his creation *charlotte à la parisienne*, but this name was changed during the Second Empire, when Russian dishes became very fashionable.

Savoury charlottes may also be made, using vegetables or fish; they are cooked in an unlined charlotte mould.

RECIPES

COLD CHARLOTTES

Basic method for preparing cold charlottes METHODE DE BASE DES CHARLOTTES FROIDES For 20–22 sponge fingers (ladyfingers), prepare a syrup with 200 g (7 oz, scant 1 cup, firmly packed) sugar and 1 glass of water. Flavour the syrup (by adding 1 liqueur glass of rum, for example). Line the bottom of a charlotte mould with sponge fingers that have been cut into a point and then steeped in the syrup. Line the sides of the mould with sponge fingers that have been cut to the height of the mould and soaked in syrup. Place them tightly together (cut side down). Place the chosen filling in the mould and cover with the remainder of the sponge fingers, also dipped in the syrup. Smooth the mixture down well and place in the refrigerator until ready to serve (or in the freezer if it is an iced charlotte). Turn out the charlotte and decorate it just before serving.

Strips of bread (cut in the same way) may be used instead of sponge fingers.

Basic filling for cold charlottes APPAREIL À CHARLOTTE FROIDE Dissolve 15 g (½ oz) gelatine in 2 tablespoons (3 tablespoons) hot water over a pan of simmering water. Prepare ½ litre (17 fl oz, 2 cups) custard cream (see *creams and custards*), mix in the dissolved gelatine, and stir continuously with a wooden spoon until the mixture is almost completely cool. Prepare a Chantilly cream by whipping 2.5 dl (8 fl oz, 1 cup) double (heavy) cream diluted with slightly less than 1 dl (6 tablespoons, scant ½ cup) milk and 5 drops of vanilla essence (extract) or 1 teaspoon vanilla-flavoured sugar. Blend the Chantilly cream with the custard cream. Add the other ingredients to this preparation according to the recipe.

Chocolate charlotte CHARLOTTE AU CHOCOLAT (from a recipe by Pierre Mauduit) Break 250 g (9 oz) bitter chocolate into pieces and melt them very gently in a bain-marie to obtain a smooth paste. Remove from the heat, add 4 egg yolks one by one, mixing well. Then add 2 tablespoons (3 tablespoons) double (heavy) cream. Beat 6 egg whites into very stiff peaks and add 150 g (5 oz, ⅔ cup, firmly packed) caster (superfine) sugar. Blend the chocolate carefully into this mixture. Line a charlotte mould with sponge fingers (ladyfingers) (300 g (11 oz) are required). Fill with the chocolate mixture. Place in the refrigerator for at least 4 hours. Turn out the charlotte and serve it with a custard cream (see *creams and custards*). ˉ

Pear charlotte CHARLOTTE AUX POIRES (from a recipe by Pierre Mauduit) Dissolve 8 sheets (2½ tablespoons) gelatine in cold water. Prepare a custard cream (see *creams and custards*) with ½ litre (17 fl oz, 2 cups) milk, 250 g (8¾ oz, generous 1 cup, firmly packed) caster (superfine) sugar, 8 egg yolks, and 1 vanilla pod (bean). Remove from heat and add the gelatine. When the custard is completely cold, blend in ⅛ litre (generous 6 tablespoons, generous ½ cup) juice extracted from William pears and then ¾ litre (1¼ pints, 3 cups) Chantilly cream. Peel 1 kg (2¼ lb) William pears and poach them in a syrup prepared with ½ litre (8 fl oz, 1 cup) water and 500 g (18 oz, 2 cups, firmly packed) sugar. Cut them into medium-sized slices.

Line a charlotte mould with sponge fingers (ladyfingers) and then fill it with alternate layers of cream and slices of poached pears. Place in the refrigerator for 4 hours. Prepare a raspberry sauce with 300 g (11 oz, 1 cup) fruit pulp, 125 g (4½ oz, 1 cup) icing (confectioner's) sugar, and the juice of a lemon. Turn out the charlotte and serve it with the sauce.

Raspberry charlotte CHARLOTTE AUX FRAMBOISES (from a recipe of the Bistrot du Pont Notre-Dame) Make a syrup with 300 g (11 oz, scant 1 cup, firmly packed) sugar and ¼ litre (8 fl oz, 1 cup) water. Add 500 g (18 oz, 3½ cups) raspberries and cook for 30 minutes. Dissolve 15 g (½ oz) gelatine in 2 tablespoons (3 tablespoons) hot water over a pan of simmering water and mix with the raspberries. Allow to cool. Soak some sponge fingers (ladyfingers) in Kirsch and use them to line a charlotte mould. Whip ¼ litre (8 fl oz, 1 cup) double (heavy) cream and mix it with the raspberries. Fill the lined mould with the mixture and leave to set in the refrigerator for at least 3 hours. Serve with custard cream (see *creams and custards*).

HOT CHARLOTTES

Apple charlotte I CHARLOTTE AUX POMMES Peel and core 3 kg (6½ lb) apples and cut into quarters. Slice them thinly and place in a shallow frying pan (skillet) with 750 g (1¾ lb, 3½ cups, firmly packed) caster (superfine) sugar and 150 g (5 oz, generous ½ cup) butter. Place the pan over a brisk heat, stir the ingredients quickly with a wooden spatula, add a vanilla pod (bean), and reduce to a thick purée.

Butter a cold charlotte mould and dust it lightly with caster (superfine) sugar. Slice a loaf of bread. Remove the crusts and cut the slices into 8 heart-shaped pieces and 16 very thin strips, 4 cm (1½ in) wide and the exact height of the mould. Dip the pieces in 100 g (4 oz, ½ cup) melted butter. Place the 8 hearts in a rosette in the bottom of the mould and arrange the 16 strips around the sides of the mould, so that they overlap. To make it easier to unmould, brush the strips lining the inside with beaten egg: this coating will stiffen the lining during cooking.

Mix the well-reduced apple purée with 2 dl (7 fl oz, ¾ cup) thick sweetened apricot purée and pour into the mould. Cook in a hot oven (220 C, 425 F, gas 7) for 25–30 minutes. Leave to stand for short time before turning out; serve hot.

Apple charlotte II CHARLOTTE AUX POMMES Line the mould with sponge fingers (ladyfingers) as for a cold charlotte. Peel and slice about 12 apples. Melt 1 tablespoon butter in a shallow frying pan, add the apples, 250 g (9 oz, generous 1 cup, firmly packed) caster (superfine) sugar, 1 vanilla pod (bean), and a little grated lemon rind. Cover and leave to cook for 5 minutes. Remove the lid from the pan and cook for a further 10 minutes, stirring from time to time. Then add 4 tablespoons (⅓ cup) apricot purée. Remove the vanilla pod and pour the purée into the lined mould. Cover with pieces of sponge finger. Place in an oven heated to about 230 c (450 F, gas 8) and bake for 30–40 minutes. Take the charlotte out of the oven, leave it to stand for about 15 minutes, and then turn it out of the mould. Coat it with a hot apricot sauce.

ICED CHARLOTTES

Iced charlotte with chestnuts CHARLOTTE GLACÉE AUX MARRONS Line a charlotte mould with sponge fingers (ladyfingers). Prepare a syrup with 175 g (6 oz, ¾ cup, firmly packed) sugar, 1 tablespoon lemon juice, and ½ glass of water. Cook for 3–4 minutes. Gradually add the syrup to 500 g (18 oz, 2 cups) chestnut purée (fresh or canned). Prepare 1 litre (1¾ pints, 4½ cups) custard cream, using 9 or 10 egg yolks (see *creams and custards*). Put half on one side. Flavour the other half with rum and add it to the chestnut purée. Pour a little of this mixture into the mould, cover with a layer of sponge fingers soaked in the syrup, then fill the mould with the remainder. Cover with more sponge fingers. Place in the freezer for 30 minutes. Turn out and serve with the rest of the custard cream.

Vanilla ice cream charlotte CHARLOTTE GLACÉE À LA VANILLE Line a charlotte mould with sponge fingers (ladyfingers). When ready to serve, fill the inside of the mould with vanilla ice cream or vanilla-flavoured bombe mixture.

SAVOURY CHARLOTTES

Red mullet charlotte CHARLOTTE AUX ROUGETS (from a recipe of L'Ambroisie restaurant) Wash 1 kg (2¼ lb) aubergines (eggplants), dry them, and cut each in half. Make cuts on the flesh, sprinkle with salt, and leave for 1 hour so that the juice seeps out. During this time, skin and gut (clean) 6 150-g (5-oz) red mullet. Retain the livers and remove the fillets. Drain the aubergines

and wipe them. Brush them with olive oil and bake them in a hot oven (225 c, 437 F, gas 7). When the pulp is completely soft, remove it with a spoon and reduce it to purée. Add the juice of a lemon, and then stir it over a very gentle heat, adding 150 g (5 oz, generous ½ cup) butter, salt, pepper, and a clove of garlic. Chop the mullet livers and add them in their turn. Season the mullet fillets and fry them in olive oil. Drain them and use to line a buttered charlotte mould. Pour the filling into the mould and press down lightly with a plate. Place in the refrigerator for 2 hours. Serve with a tomato sauce.

Vegetable charlotte CHARLOTTE DE LÉGUMES (from a recipe by Alain Chapel) Trim 1 kg (2¼ lb) very fine green asparagus. Cook it in a generous quantity of salted water and then drain. Set aside 6 asparagus tips and pass the remainder through a fine sieve or a blender. Pour the resulting purée into a small saucepan and dry it out over a very gentle heat.

Plunge 12 small tomatoes into boiling water, peel them, and remove the seeds. Soften them over a gentle heat and add salt and pepper. Peel 12 small onions, brown them in butter, add some stock, and cook them until they are very tender. Make a zabaglione with 1 egg yolk.

Beat 2 eggs in a bowl with some salt and pepper. Add the tomatoes, asparagus purée, onions, and half the zabaglione. Stir gently with a wooden spoon until thoroughly mixed. Warm 1 dl (6 tablespoons, scant ½ cup) fresh double (heavy) cream in the oven, whisk it slightly, and add it to the vegetable mixture.

Pour the preparation into a buttered charlotte mould. Place it in the oven heated to about 170 c (335 F, gas 3–4) and cook for just under an hour. Heat the 6 asparagus tips in a bain-marie. Turn out the cooked charlotte onto a serving dish and surround with a rosette of asparagus tips. Coat with the rest of the zabaglione.

charmoula

In Arab cooking, a thick sweet-and-sour sauce prepared with a highly spiced hot ragout of onions (containing *rās al-*

hānout, bay leaf, and dried rose buds), vinegar, honey, and raisins, and sometimes carrots, celery, and shredded shallots. It may be served cold or hot with grilled meat, especially camel and game. It is also used to coat fish preparations, such as bonito, tuna, and sea bream. The fish are marinated, drained, coated with flour, and fried. They keep for several days in this sauce.

Charolais

One of the best French breeds of beef cattle. The name is often used in restaurant menus as a synonym for beef. An example is *pavé de charolais*.

charolaise

A piece of very bony beef from the region of the elbow that is used for making pot-au-feu.

Chartres (à la)

A method of cooking various egg and meat dishes in tarragon. Lamb chops are braised with tarragon and coated with tarragon-flavoured gravy. Fillet steak (sirloin) and noisettes are coated with a tarragon-based sauce and then sautéed. They are served with blanched tarragon leaves. The garnishes may vary and could consist of château potatoes, potato fondantes, stuffed mushrooms, braised lettuce, and pea purée.

Eggs *à la Chartres* are either hard-boiled (hard-cooked), coated with a tarragon-flavoured chaud-froid sauce, and covered with tarragon leaves and aspic, or soft-boiled (or cooked in a mould) and served on slices of toast with a tarragon-flavoured sauce and tarragon leaves.

Chartreuse

A herb liqueur made according to a very ancient recipe by the Carthusian monks at Voiron, near Grenoble.

The original recipe was probably created by Carthusians established at Vauvert (near Paris), who are thought to have sent it to the monastery of Grande-Chartreuse, near Grenoble, in 1735. Here the apothecary, Jérôme Maubec, could have used it to make a medicinal herb elixir. In 1789, the monks were dispersed and the formula for the elixir seemed doomed to disappear. However, by chance, in the time of the First Empire, a copy of the formula reached the Ministry for the Interior. It was intended for the archives, but as no-one understood the document, it was sent back to the now reconstituted monastery at Grande Chartreuse. In 1835, the monks resumed the production of both the elixir and a green liqueur. In 1838 officers visiting the monastery discovered the liqueur and decided to encourage its distribution. Today, the Carthusians prepare a 71° elixir, a 55° green Chartreuse, and a 40° sweeter yellow Chartreuse (created in 1840). During their second exile in Spain (1903–29), they continued to manufacture their liqueur at Tarragona and sold it under this name.

The composition of Chartreuse is a secret, but it is known that it is prepared from various plants and herbs, including balm, hyssop, angelica leaves, cinnamon bark, mace, and saffron.

chartreuse

A preparation of vegetables (particularly braised cabbage) and meat or game, moulded into a dome and formed of layers of alternating colours. It is cooked in a bain-marie, turned out, and served hot. Careme considered the chartreuse to be the 'queen of entrées'.

In former times chartreuse consisted solely of vegetables, and its name evoked the vegetarian diet of the Carthusian monks. Today, it is usually a dish of partridge with cabbage, called chartreuse of partridge.

Chartreuses may also be made with fish (such as tuna); lettuce is used instead of cabbage and it is seasoned with sorrel, which provides a slightly acid taste. Braised cabbage (with other vegetables) is still used to make chartreuse of eggs.

RECIPES

Chartreuse of eggs in a mould OEUFS MOULÉS EN CHARTREUSE Prepare and braise some cabbage. Dice some carrots and turnips, and cut some French beans into small even slices. Cook the vegetables in salted water: they must be just firm. Also cook some peas. Drain the vegetables and toss them in melted butter. Use them to line some buttered dariole moulds. Break an egg into each mould, season, and place the moulds in a bain-marie. Cook until the eggs set. Cover the serving dish with the braised cabbage and unmould the eggs on the top.

Chartreuse of partridge CHAR-TREUSE DE PERDREAU (from a recipe of Chef Denis) Braise some cabbage in goose dripping, together with an old partridge (the latter provides more flavour). Cut some turnips and carrots into very thin 1.5-cm (½-in) squares. Prepare a veal quenelle forcemeat and use it to line a small round casserole. Then cover the bottom and sides with the carrot and turnip squares to form a decorative chequered pattern. Place enough of the well-drained cabbage in the pan so that it comes a third of the way up the side. Put a piece of slightly salted bacon (which has been poached for at least 2 hours), on top of the cabbage. Roast one or two partridges to seal them. Cut them into pieces and arrange them on top of the bacon. Cover with the remaining cabbage. Cover the pan and cook in a bain-marie in a moderate oven (180 C, 350 F, gas 4) for 30–40 minutes. Remove from the oven. Cool for a short time and turn out onto the serving dish.

Chassagne-Montrachet

Red and white wines of the Côte de Beaune, in Burgundy. In the 18th century, the commune of Chassagne (which is present-day Chassagne-Montrachet) was noted for its red wines. Today, it is famous for its whites, which – like all fine white Burgundy – are made from Chardonnay grapes. They are dry elegant subtle wines, with a rich bouquet and lingering taste. They acquire full maturity after several years, but do not always improve after five or six years and may lose their bouquet and oxidize. The *appellation* covers three *grands crus* (a part of Montrachet, a part of Bâtard-Montrachet, and Criots-Bâtard-Montrachet), plus 18 *premiers crus*, the most famous of which are the Clos-de-la-Boudriotte, Clos-Saint-Jean, Grande Ruchotte, Caillerets, and Abbaye-de-Morgeot. The red wines, made from the Pinot Noir grape, are more full-bodied and robust than the other Côtes-de-

Nuits. They stand maturation (five years or more) quite well.

chasse-marée

A fish cart. In the 18th century, the carts were used to bring fish and especially oysters to Paris as quickly as possible from the coasts of Normandy and Picardy. The fish carts were given priority at the coaching inns and no-one was permitted either to stop them on the way, or to seize their horses. A special fund was provided to replace exhausted horses or to repay the cost of any fish that might be spoiled despite the speed of the journey. The oysters brought by these carts were known as *huîtres de chasse*, whereas those conveyed by boats coming up the Seine, and sold at a lower price, were called *huîtres de rivière*.

chasseur

Any of various sautéed dishes (such as chicken, kidneys, medallions, escalopes, and veal chops) that are served with a sauce made from mushrooms, shallots, tomatoes, and white wine.

This sauce, with the addition of sautéed chicken livers, is also suitable for poached or shirred eggs, and may also be used as an omelette filling.

In classic French cookery, *chasseur* describes various preparations which include game purée (including soup, bouchées, and eggs *en cocotte*).

RECIPES

Chasseur sauce SAUCE CHASSEUR Sauté 150 g (5 oz, 1 generous cup) finely chopped mushrooms (mousserons if possible) and 2 chopped shallots in butter. Add 1 dl (6 tablespoons, scant ½ cup) white wine and reduce by half. Then add 1.5 dl (¼ pint, ⅔ cup) stock and 2 tablespoons (3 tablespoons) reduced tomato sauce and reduce by a further third. Add 1 teaspoon kneaded butter (or arrowroot) and boil for 2 minutes. Finally add 30 g (1¼ oz, 2½ tablespoons) butter and 1 tablespoon chopped herbs (tarragon, chervil, and parsley).

Omelette chasseur Fill an omelette with sautéed chicken livers and mushrooms. Sprinkle with chopped parsley and surround with a ribbon of chasseur sauce.

Sautéed chicken chasseur POULET SAUTÉ CHASSEUR Sauté a chicken in a mixture of oil and butter. Season, cover, and cook for about 35 minutes. Add 150 g (5 oz, 1 generous cup) thinly sliced raw mushrooms and cook for about 10 minutes more. Drain the chicken and keep it hot. Brown 1 or 2 chopped shallots in the pan juices and add 1 dl (6 tablespoons, scant ½ cup) white wine and 1 tablespoon well-reduced tomato sauce. Reduce by a half and then add a small liqueur glass of marc and 1 tablespoon chopped tarragon. Bring to the boil and coat the chicken with the sauce. Sprinkle with parsley and serve very hot.

chasseur or saucisson du chasseur

A small sausage, weighing less than 250 g (½ lb) consisting of equal amounts of lean belly of pork and a fine paste of beef and pork. The chasseur is quickly dried and cold-smoked. It is golden in colour and is suitable for snacks and cold meals.

château

An estate or plantation, especially in the Bordeaux region, that produces wine. There are in some cases grand country houses (châteaux) attached to the estates, but in others there are not. A château wine is one that is produced from such an estate in the Bordeaux region; its label bears the name of its château, such as Château Ausone or Château Cheval-Blanc. This form of appellation is also used in other regions of France quite properly, although in Burgundy it is used only rarely as vineyards tend to belong to several proprietors.

Château Ausone

A red Bordeaux, one of the 12 classified *grands crus* of Saint-Émilion. Tradition has it that the vineyard occupies the site of the villa where the poet Ausonius lived in the 4th century. This generous and elegant wine matures in cellars hollowed out centuries ago in the soft stone below Saint-Émilion. The exceptional

quality of the great vintages justifies the prices fetched by this wine, which is classified – with Château Cheval-Blanc – with the best of the Saint-Émilions.

chateaubriand

A slice of very tender fillet steak about 3 cm (1¼ in) thick. Chateaubriand is grilled (broiled) or fried and served with a sauce (traditionally béarnaise). Restaurants sometimes serve a similar dish under the name of *château*, accompanied, like chateaubriand, by château potatoes.

This French version of English beef-steak was probably dedicated to the Vicomte de Chateaubriand (1768–1848) by his chef, Montmireil: at that time, the steak was cut from the sirloin and served with a reduced sauce made from white wine and shallots moistened with demiglace and mixed with butter, tarragon, and lemon juice. An alternative spelling is *chateaubriant*, and some maintain that the term refers to the quality of the cattle bred around the town of Chateaubriand in the Loire-Atlantique. Pellaprat, probably wrongly, specifies: 'The dish was created at the Champeaux restaurant; it was shortly after publication of Chateaubriand's book *L'Itinéraire de Paris à Jérusalem* (1811) that this grilled steak, comprising a thick slice from the heart of a beef fillet, made its first appearance; its cooking is a delicate process on account of the thickness, for if it is sealed too much, a hard shell is formed on either side and the centre remains uncooked; it must be cooked more slowly than a piece of ordinary thickness.'

RECIPES

Grilled (broiled) chateaubriand CHATEAUBRIAND GRILLÉ Brush the chateaubriand with oil, sprinkle with pepper, and grill (broil) under a brisk heat. Sprinkle with salt and serve very hot. A vertical grill is perfect for cooking chateaubriand to a turn: sealed on the outside, underdone inside.

Sautéed chateaubriand CHATEAUBRIAND SAUTÉ Sauté the chateaubriand briskly in butter: the outside must be sealed, the inside underdone. It may then be served like tournedos chasseur, or else drained, kept hot, and surrounded with the boiled vegetables mixed with the butter in which the meat was cooked. Alternatively the cooking butter may be removed and the chateaubriand served with a pat of maître d'hôtel or marchand de vin butter.

Château-Chalon

The best known of the yellow Jura wines, named after a small town in the region where it is produced, it is sold in a special 62-cl bottle called a *clavelin*. Golden amber in colour, Château-Chalon is produced from the Savagnin grape, and is aged in cask for six to ten years before being bottled. It then may keep remarkably well for decades.

Château Cheval-Blanc

A red Bordeaux, one of the 12 *grands crus* of Saint-Émilion. The vineyard is situated at the edge of the region of Saint-Émilion, next to the Pomerol vineyard. The 35 hectares (86 acres) of the estate consist of various types of soil. Curiously, this exceptional growth seems to combine the qualities of the land and the vines of the three great regions of the Bordeaux vineyard: Graves, Médoc, and Saint-Émilion. Its proximity to Pomerol makes it a finer vintage than most Saint-Émilions. Badly affected by the frosts of 1956, production was greatly reduced for many years. Today, however, Château Cheval-Blanc is on a par with the finest growth of Médoc. It combines delicacy and power and is one of the most celebrated wines of the world.

Château d'Yquem

A white Bordeaux, from the region of Sauternes, by many considered to be the best sweet white wine in the world. At the time of the classification of 1855, it was the only one of all the Bordeaux wines, red or white, entitled to the designation 'Grand Premier Cru'. The grapes are mainly Sémillon and Sauvignon Blanc and they are gathered, often individually, when the fungus *Botrytis cinerea* – the noble rot – has worked on the grapes. The yield is so small that each vine will produce only one glass of wine each vintage. This wine has to be perfect: in less than perfect years it is declassified and may be sold as just Sauternes. Golden and of incomparably smooth delicacy, it may benefit from ageing in wood, when it can retain all its qualities for more than a century.

Château Grillet

A white wine of the Rhône valley. The vineyard surrounds a 13th-century château and is the second smallest (2.5 hectares, 6¼ acres) to have its own AOC. It is planted with the Viognier Doré, a vine that does not begin to yield adequately for seven or eight years. Delicate, somewhat resembling both Hermitage Blanc and Condrieu, Château Grillet is a wine with an outstanding bouquet, dry yet at the same time mellow, well-balanced, and fragrant. Because of the minute size of the vineyard only small quantities are made.

Château Haut-Brion

Haut-Brion is the only Graves that was designated 'Premier Cru' in the 1855 classification of Bordeaux. The estate at Pessac, in the suburbs of Bordeaux, is one of the oldest estates of Bordeaux (the records go back to the beginning of the 16th century). The vineyard is planted with Cabernet Sauvignon, Cabernet Franc, Merlot, and Malbec vines. Its aspect, its soil, and its position encourage early ripening of the grapes. Tannic and succulent, like many Graves the wine can acquire a full-bodied character with age plus a bouquet of a rare delicacy, lingering flavour, and velvety power. A small quantity of white wine, fine and dry, is also made from the Sauvignon and Sémillon vines.

Château Lafite

One of the four first growths of the Médoc in the 1855 classification of Bordeaux. The vineyard is situated on a small hill, not far from Pauillac. It is planted with Cabernet Sauvignon, Cabernet Franc, Merlot, and Petit Verdot vines. The large proportion of Merlot is one of the reasons for the special character. Impeccably made, Château Lafite is the traditional claret. An aristocratic wine, it has a delicate bouquet and possesses smoothness, charm, and power.

Château Latour

One of the first four classified first growths of Médoc according to the 1855 classification of Bordeaux. It was already highly esteemed in the time of Montaigne, who speaks of it in his *Essais*. This great wine, with its incomparable bouquet, is named after a medieval fortress of which only a tower remains, restored under Louis XIII. The estate is situated on the upper region of Pauillac, which is particulary arid and stony, and is planted mainly with Cabernet Sauvignon, plus Merlot, Cabernet Franc, and Petit Verdot. The vines are allowed to produce up to an advanced age, which adds to the quality although to the detriment of the yield. The production of the wine is slow, both as regards fermentation and maturation. Considered by many wine-lovers as possibly the best balanced Bordeaux, Château Latour will keep for a long time, in a good vintage. It should not be confused with the very many 'Latour' or 'La Tour' estate wines of the Bordeaux region. There are nearly 80 of these! But there is only one Château Latour with the AOC 'Pauillac', which is the due for the great first growth.

Château Margaux

The first growth of the 1855 classification of Bordeaux. Château Margaux was already famous in the 15th century, when it was called 'Margou' or 'Margouse'. Today, its fame is justified. The 60 hectares (148 acres) of vines are planted on gravelly soil, which gives the wine delicacy and finesse. They produce red wine and sometimes a very small quantity of dry white, marketed as Pavillon Blanc du Château Margaux. The vineyard is planted with Cabernet Sauvignon, Cabernet Franc, and Merlot. A change in ownership in recent years has resulted in many changes at the estate and marked improvement in the wine. Wines bearing the generic parish name 'Margaux' should not be confused with the important wine of Château Margaux.

Château Mouton-Rothschild

A great Pauillac wine, which, after many years of campaigning by its owner, Baron Philippe de Rothschild, was rated as a first growth in 1973. (The price had, for a long while, been equal to that of other first growths). It is an important assertive wine, based very much on the Cabernet Sauvignon. Each year Baron Philippe commissions a well-known artist to design a label and these are now themselves the subject of exhibitions.

Châteauneuf-du-Pape

A famous vineyard at the bottom of the Rhône Valley. There are a number of quite well-known estates, some of them making a white wine as well as the better-known red. The vineyard, on the left bank of the river, owes its name to the residence of the popes, when they lived in Avignon in the 14th century during the period when the papacy abandoned Rome. Burned down during the later Wars of Religion, the château has been no more than a ruin since 1552, but it was not until the 19th century that it gave its name to the wine, called until then 'wine of Avignon'. Planted with a dozen or so different permitted varieties of vine, the region often suffers from drought. The hot sun is reflected from the huge orange stones which cover part of the ground, holding the heat, resulting in a powerful wine with a pronounced bouquet. Strict production controls make it one of the best Côtes-du-Rhône wines, having a minimum alcohol content of 12.5° but often higher.

Château Pétrus

An outstanding red wine of Pomerol, in the Bordeaux region, which often equals the prices at auction of the first growths of the Médoc. Made from Merlot, Malbec, and Cabernet grapes, it has a complex truffle-scented bouquet, full-bodied, generous, yet with great delicacy. Pétrus can, according to its vintage, have a long life.

château potatoes
POMMES CHÂTEAU

A dish consisting of potatoes cut into olives (or left whole if they are quite small and new), blanched, and sautéed in butter, with little strips of streaky bacon if desired, until they are well browned. They form the traditional garnish of grilled chateaubriand steak with béarnaise sauce and they are found in numerous garnishes (maraîchère, Orloff, Richelieu, etc.).

RECIPE

Château potatoes POMMES DE TERRE CHÂTEAU Brush some fairly small new potatoes, wash, and wipe. Heat some butter in a shallow frying pan (skillet), add the potatoes, and cook gently with the lid on. Add salt and pepper and serve with roast meat or with braised meat or fish.

châtelaine (à la)

A method of garnishing simple dishes to add refinement. For egg dishes, the châtelaine garnish includes chestnuts; for meat, artichoke hearts. For large joints of meat, these artichoke hearts are filled with Soubise chestnut purée, cooked au gratin, and accompanied by braised lettuces and noisette potatoes. Small pieces of meat are sautéed, a sauce is made from the pan juice and a court-bouillon, and the meat is simply drained and served with noisette potatoes.

The artichoke hearts may alternatively be cut into quarters, sautéed in butter, and accompanied by small skinned tomatoes, braised celery hearts, and château potatoes.

RECIPE

Soft-boiled (*or poached*) **eggs à la châtelaine** OEUFS MOLLETS OU POCHÉS À LA CHÂTELAINE Bake some tartlets blind using lining pastry (see *doughs and batters*). Prepare some chestnut purée and add a quarter of its volume of Soubise purée. Season well. Fill the bottom of the tartlets with this mixture, place 1 soft-boiled or poached egg in each of them, and coat with a chicken velouté sauce. Serve very hot.

Châtillon-en-Diois

Red and white wines made in the Drôme and having their own AOC since 1975. The reds are made from the Gamay grape and are pleasant to drink when young. The whites, made from the Aligoté and Chardonnay, are crisp and agreeable.

Chatouillard

A method of preparing potatoes by cutting them into long strips with a special utensil and frying them like soufflé potatoes. Rarely served in restaurants, the dish owes its name, according to Prosper Montagné, to the nickname given to an old chef skilled in roasting and frying.

RECIPE

Chatouillard potatoes POMMES CHATOUILLARD Cut some potatoes in a spiral to obtain strips 3 mm (⅛ in) thick; wash, wipe, and plunge into frying oil heated to only 160 C (325 F). Gradually increase the temperature until the strips rise to the surface (at about 170 C, 340 F). Drain them and leave them to cool slightly. Just before serving, plunge them into the frying oil heated to 180 C (350 F); they must swell up. Drain on absorbent paper before serving.

Chauchat

A preparation of fish (sole, brill, or whiting), either whole or in fillets, which are poached and coated with a béchamel sauce made from the cooking liquid bound with egg yolks and thickened with butter; the garnish is a simple border of rounds of boiled potatoes.

chaud-froid

A dish that is prepared as a hot dish but served cold. Chauds-froids are pieces of meat, poultry, fish, or game, coated with brown or white sauce, then glazed with aspic. Typically, they form part of a cold buffet, but are also served as an entrée.

Since the time of Carême, the presentation of chauds-froids has been simplified by eliminating the decorated stands or pyramid arrangements, but they remain very decorative dishes. The pieces of poultry or game, coated with chaud-froid sauce, are garnished with fine slices of truffle, rounds of hard-boiled (hard-cooked) egg whites, tongue coated with brown aspic, etc., before being glazed with a very clear jelly, containing little gelatine and therefore purer.

Philéas Gilbert asserts that chaud-froid was created in 1759 at the Château de Montmorency and was named by the marshal of Luxembourg (which casts doubts upon the existence of a certain Chaufroix, vegetable cook of the royal kitchens under Louis XV, to whom some people attribute the dish). 'One evening, the marshal of Luxembourg had invited a large number of illustrious guests to his château. Occupying a place of honour on the menu was a fricassee of chicken in white sauce. When it was time to sit down at table, a messenger arrived: the marshal was summoned without delay to the king's Council. The marshal gave orders that his absence should not delay the serving of the food, and he left. Returning late, and desiring only one dish, he was served with the cold chicken fricassee, congealed in the ivory-coloured sauce. He found this food succulent, and a few days later expressed a wish to have it served again. Presented under the name of *refroidi* (cooled), this term displeased the marshal, who insisted on the name of chaud-froid.'

RECIPES

Brown chaud-froid sauce for fish and game SAUCE CHAUD-FROID BRUNE POUR POISSONS ET GIBIERS (from a recipe by Chef Denis) Mix ½ litre (17 fl oz, 2 cups) demi-glace and ½ litre (17 fl oz, 2 cups) greatly reduced and clarified fish or game fumet (it must have the consistency of wobbly jelly). Gradually pour the hot mixture over 16 egg yolks and add 200 g (7 oz, ¾ cup) butter, whisking all the time.

Brown chaud-froid sauce for various meats SAUCE CHAUD-FROID BRUNE ORDINAIRE POUR VIANDES DIVERSES To make 5 dl (17 fl oz, 2 cups) sauce, put 3.5 dl (12 fl oz, 1½ cups) demi-glace glaze and 2 dl (7 fl oz, ¾ cup) light brown gelatinous stock into a thick-bottomed sauté pan. Reduce by a good third over a high heat, stirring with a spatula and gradually adding 4 dl (14 fl oz, 1¾ cups) aspic. Test the consistency by pouring a little sauce onto a chilled surface: if it is not thick enough, add several tablespoons of aspic and reduce again. Remove from the heat, add 2 tablespoons Madeira or any other

dessert wine; strain through muslin. Stir the sauce until completely cooled.

The following variations may be used:

■ *with game extract*: prepare a game fumet with the carcasses and trimmings of the game used; replace the light brown stock with 1 dl (6 tablespoons, scant ½ cup) game fumet and flavour the sauce with Madeira or any other dessert wine.

■ *à la niçoise*: add 3–4 anchovy fillets, completely desalted, reduced to a purée, and sieved, then strain the sauce and add 1 tablespoon coarsely shredded tarragon leaves.

■ *à l'orange* (for ducks and ducklings): prepare a duck fumet with the carcasses and giblets of the poultry and use it in place of the light brown stock; reduce the chaud-froid sauce more than usual so that adding orange juice does not make it too weak; blend the juice of 1 orange with the sauce, strain through muslin, add 2 tablespoons orange zest cut into fine strips, blanched, cooled, and drained.

Chaud-froid of chicken with tarragon CHAUD-FROID DE POULET À L'ESTRAGON (from a recipe by François Chatel) Take a chicken of about 2.5 kg (5½ lb) with its own giblets. Clean these giblets and two extra ones and place in a saucepan, cover with cold water, and bring to the boil; drain and rinse in cold water. Peel 3 onions, 2 carrots, a turnip, and the white part of a leek; stick 3 cloves into one of the onions. Put all the vegetables, a large bouquet garni, and the giblets into a saucepan; cover with plenty of water (about 3.5 litres, 6 pints, 15 cups), add salt and pepper, and cook quite gently (without a lid in order to reduce the stock) until the flesh of the giblets comes apart. Clean the chicken and season the inside with salt, pepper, and 3 or 4 sprigs of tarragon. Truss the bird, place it in the stock; cover the pan and leave to cook very gently for about 1½ hours. When the chicken is cooked, drain and leave it to cool on a rack.

To prepare the chaud-froid sauce, skim the fat from 1 litre (2 pints, 2½ pints) chicken stock and bring it to the boil. Mix enough powdered aspic with water to obtain 1 litre (2 pints, 2½ pints) liquid. Make a very pale roux with 125 g (4½ oz, ½ cup) butter and 100 g (4 oz, 1 cup) flour, leave it to cool, then gradually add the boiling broth, stir briskly over the heat; leave to boil gently for 10 minutes, then add a small glass of brandy and the same of port, 4 dl (14 fl oz, 1¾ cups) fresh cream, spoonful by spoonful, and finally the mixed aspic; leave this chaud-froid sauce to cook for about 5 minutes.

Having removed the skin, cut the chicken into pieces and put them into the refrigerator. When chilled, coat the pieces of chicken with several coats of chaudfroid sauce, putting them in the refrigerator between each application of sauce. In order to work more easily, arrange the pieces on a rack and collect the sauce which drains away; for the last two applications, dilute the sauce with a little cold broth. Garnish the pieces of chicken with blanched tarragon leaves, then coat with a very light layer of aspic to fix them.

Chaud-froid of salmon CHAUD-FROID DE SAUMON Poach some slices or steaks of salmon, simmering very gently in a plentiful and well-seasoned fish stock: this is later used for making the chaud-froid sauce.

When the slices are cooked (they must still be slightly firm), leave them to cool in the stock, then drain them on a rack. Prepare the chaud-froid sauce with the strained stock, keeping it fluid, and coat the slices of salmon with it in three successive applications. After the last, garnish with round slices of truffle (or black (ripe) olives) and small decorative shapes cut from a green pepper. Glaze with very light aspic.

Tomato chaud-froid sauce SAUCE CHAUD-FROID À LA TOMATE Add 3.5 dl (12 fl oz, 1½ cups) aspic to 5 dl (17 fl oz, 2 cups) blended tomato pulp; reduce by a third. Strain through muslin and stir until completely cooled.

White chaud-froid sauce for white offal, eggs, and poultry SAUCE CHAUD-FROID ·BLANCHE POUR ABATS BLANCS, OEUFS, ET VOLAILLES To make 5 dl (17 fl oz, 2 cups) sauce, place 3.5 dl (12 fl oz, 1½ cups) velouté and 1 dl (6 tablespoons, scant ½ cup)

mushroom fumet in a thick-bottomed sauté dish. Reduce over a full heat, stirring continuously with a spatula, and gradually add 4 dl (14 fl oz, 1¾ cups) aspic and 1.5 dl (¼ pint, ⅔ cup) cream. Reduce until the white sauce coats the spatula well. Ensure a good consistency by cooling a small quantity of sauce on ice: if it is not sufficiently firm, add a few spoonfuls of aspic to it and reduce again. Strain through a sieve or muslin and stir until completely cooled.

According to the dish being prepared, the sauce is used as it is or with various garnishes added.

■ *à l'andalouse*: flavour with sherry and with 2 tablespoons orange peel cut into fine strips, blanched, cooled, and drained.

■ *à l'aurore*: add 3 tablespoons thick tomato purée.

■ *à la banquière*: add 3 tablespoons Madeira and finely chopped truffles.

■ *Beauharnais*: colour with 2 tablespoons purée made from tarragon and chervil, which have been blanched, cooled, drained, and passed through a fine sieve or a blender.

■ *à l'écossaise* flavour with Madeira and add 2 tablespoons very finely diced carrot, the white parts of a leek and a stick (stalk) of celery cooked in white stock, 1 tablespoon tongue coated with brown aspic, and 2 tablespoons finely sliced truffle.

■ *à la Nantua* (for fish and shellfish): add 2 tablespoons crayfish purée and, after straining, 1 tablespoon finely diced truffle.

■ *à la royale*: add 2 tablespoons truffle purée diluted with 1 tablespoon sherry.

chaudin

The large intestine of a pig, used as a skin in charcuterie, particularly for chitterlings.

chaudrée

A fish soup of the Vendée and Saintonge coast, which is made with small skates, soles, small cuttlefish (*casserons*), and sometimes sections of eel, gurnets, etc. The fish are cooked in Muscadet with butter, thyme, bay leaf, and a little garlic, the hard varieties (such as conger eels) being placed in the saucepan first. Some recipes include potatoes. *Fouras chaudrée*, in which the stock is poured over bread and the fish served separately, is a famous bouillabaisse of the Atlantic coast. *Caudière* and *caudrée* are similar soups from the northern coastal regions of France.

chaudumer, chaudumé, or chaudumel

A medieval recipe similar to fish stew. Chaudumer (the name is probably derived from *chaudron*, a cauldron) consists of sections of eel and pike, first grilled (broiled), then cooked in a wine and verjuice sauce flavoured with ginger and saffron, and finally thickened with pike livers.

chayote

See *custard marrow*.

Cheddar

An English cows'-milk cheese (containing 45% butterfat), cylindrical in shape, with a compressed paste and a natural oily rind, wrapped in cloth. Firm to the touch, with a nutty flavour, and white or creamy yellow in colour, it originates from the town of Cheddar in Somerset. It is mass-produced in all English-speaking countries (often coloured with red): when it appeared towards the end of the 16th century it spread to the British colonies (in the United States, it is sold under the names of Daisy Longhorn, Flat or Twin; in Canada, it is called Store of Bulk). When it is well matured (up to two years in a dry cellar), dark marbling appears in its centre, and it is then called blue Cheddar.

The production of Cheddar involves the mechanical treatment of the curds (obtained according to the same method as for Cantal) while increasing the lactic acid; the particles of curds treated in this way are then slightly cooked at about 38 c (100 f), which then brings Cheddar close to cooked cheeses of the Gruyère type.

A giant 500 kg (1100 lb) Cheddar was offered to Queen Victoria on the occasion of her marriage, but this cheese normally weighs 27–35 kg (60–80 lb) and has a diameter and height of 35–40 cm (14–16 in). Commercially, it is sold in the form of 6.25 kg (14 lb) blocks. Its fairly strong flavour makes it a good cheese for cooking in English-speaking countries. At the end of a meal, it is eaten with Bordeaux or even port. It is often included in the manufacture of salted biscuits and used to prepare croûtes with cheese, mixed salads, canapés, hamburgers, etc.

cheek JOUE

Either side of the lower jaw of an animal, including the muscles. Sold as part of the whole head, the cheeks are regarded as offal; when sold separately, however, this cut (particularly in the case of beef) is very good boiled or braised.

The cheek of certain fish, especially the monkfish, is regarded as a delicacy.

RECIPE

Braised ox cheek JOUES DE BOEUF EN DAUBE   The day before they are required, clean 2–4 ox cheeks, removing all the gristle, fat, etc. Cut the meat into large pieces and put them into an earthenware bowl; leave overnight in a marinade consisting of salt and pepper, 3 tablespoons (¼ cup) olive oil, 1 glass (¾ cup) white wine, thyme, and bay leaves. Cut 4 carrots into small cubes. Cut 300 g (¾ lb) salted belly pork (salt pork) into strips, blanch for 3 minutes, then refresh them. Blanch 300 g (10 oz, 2 cups) stoned (pitted) green olives for 3 minutes in boiling water. Melt 500 g (2 oz, ¼ cup) butter in a flameproof pot and brown the drained meat, the strips of pork, the carrots, and the olives. Pour in the warm marinade, then add a bottle of white wine, 4 crushed garlic cloves, and 6 onions, peeled and quartered. Bring to the boil and cook for about 15 minutes, then cover the pot and cook for a further 3 hours over a very low heat or in the oven.

cheese FROMAGE

A dairy product made from coagulated milk, cream, skimmed milk, or a mixture of any of these, drained in a mould (or *forma* in Latin, hence its French name, *fromage*). A distinction is made between soft fresh cheeses (including cream and curd cheeses), fermented cheeses (which are more numerous and varied), and processed cheese.

◻ **The history of cheese** Cheese-making goes back to the earliest live-stock farmers: letting the milk curdle, then beating it with branches, pressing it on stones, drying it in the sun, and sprinkling it with salt, was an excellent way of converting surplus milk into a form that could be stored.

In ancient Greece, a number of pastries were based on goats'- or ewes'-milk cheese; when dried, this served as a long-lasting food for soldiers and sailors. The Romans were masters of the art of cheese manufacture; they preferred it fairly dry and, very often, smoked, according to a treatise on agronomy written by Columellus. This dates from the 1st century AD, when cheese presses were first used for press-ing the curd. Roman cookery used *moretum*, a condiment made from cheese, garlic, and herbs; it also featured a 'cheese stew' based on cheese, salted fish, brains, chicken livers, hard-boiled (hard-cooked) eggs, and herbs, a recipe which later reappeared in the works of Taillevent as 'cheese and egg gruel'. It was not until the time of Charlemagne and the chronicles of Eginhard (770 –840) that cheese was again mentioned in writing. The famous emperor disco-vered blue cheeses – the ancestors of Roquefort – while on a journey into the heart of his territory, and a stop at the priory of Rueil-en-Brie enabled him to sample the delights of Brie, which was given to him as a tithe.

Over the centuries, the development of various manufacturing techniques has led to a great diversity of cheeses and the emergence of the major regional characteristics of French cheeses: soft curd in the west and north, goats'-milk cheeses around Tours and Poitou, blue cheese from the central region, cooked cheeses in the Alps, etc. The monastic orders in particular played an important role in perfecting manufacturing pro-cesses, as the names of the cheeses indi-cate – Munster, Trappistes, Saint-Paulin, Saint-Nectaire, Tête-de-Moine, etc.

Cheese is a highly nutritious food enjoyed at all levels of society. Always a basic foodstuff of the peasants, it was 'ennobled' by Charles D'Orléans, who started the custom of offering it as a New Year's gift to the ladies of his court. It was also used in cookery, and some recipes from the Middle Ages have survived, such as arboulastre, tal-mouses, darioles, ramekins, and a num-ber of regional specialities, including tourteau, aligot, truffade, cheese flans, and various soups. At the end of the 15th century, Charles VIII returned from his campaigns in Italy with moulds for cooked curd cheeses, thus introduc-ing a new manufacturing method. From the Renaissance onwards there are many written accounts on the art of cheese-making. The most popular varieties of the time were the cream cheeses of Blois. Clamart, and Mon-treuil, the *angelots* of Normandy, Auvergne cheeses, and Brie. Dutch and Swiss products were also sold in French markets.

In the 17th century, cheese was used a great deal in cookery, particularly in sauces and pastry-making. During the Revolution, difficulties of supply dimi-nished the popularity of cheese, but it recovered from the time of the Empire onwards, and Cheshire, Maroilles from Hainaut, Normandy Neufchâtel (before the 'invention' of Camembert under Napoleon III), Swiss Gruyère, Roque-fort, and Italian Parmesan were all popular; Brie was hailed as the 'king of cheeses' during a dinner at the Congress of Vienna (1814–15). In the 20th cen-tury, pasteurization and industrializ-ation have tended to replace traditional manufacturing methods: some new pro-ducts, mostly very rich, creamy, and generally very mild in taste, have made their appearance, while genuine farm-produced cheeses have become in-creasingly rare.

◻ **Manufacture** The hundreds of varieties of cheese can be distinguished firstly by the type of milk used: cows', goats', or ewes' (sometimes mixed), or even mares' and buffaloes'; also, the milk can be whole, skimmed, or en-riched. In addition, the characteristics of the manufacturing methods give rise to several classes of cheeses. There are four stages in the basic process:

● *Acidification of the milk* – this is sometimes performed by lactic yeasts.

● *Coagulation* (or *curdling*) – the case-in (milk protein) coagulates following the addition of rennet or, more rarely, by natural lactic fermentation of the microorganisms in the milk. The milk then separates into the solid curds and liquid whey.

• *Cutting and draining the curds* – after being separated from the whey, the curds can either be made into fresh cheese or processed further, in which case the curds are stirred, kneaded, or cut; in some cases they are cooked. They are then put into moulds (sometimes a bacteria culture is added) and left to drain, an operation which is promoted by salting (either on the surface or by immersion in brine).

• *Ripening* – this allows the cheese to develop its characteristic texture, colour, and flavour. The cheese is left for varying lengths of time in a damp or dry atmosphere, often in special places (cellars, caves, or drying rooms).

□ **The classification of cheeses**

• Fresh cows'-milk cheeses: unripened, coagulated by the action of microorganisms in the milk without the addition of rennet, drained slowly, usually having a high water content, sometimes salted (Demi-Sel) or beaten with cream (Petit-Suisse).

• Soft cows'-milk cheeses with a downy rind: obtained by mixed curdling (i.e. rennet and natural fermentation), not kneaded, drained spontaneously, shaped, coated with a bacteria culture, then ripened. Examples: Camembert, Brie, Chaource, Neufchâtel, and Saint-Marcellin.

• Soft cows'-milk cheeses with a washed rind: made by mixed curdling and cut to accelerate draining; the surface is washed in salted water during ripening. Examples: Livarot, Munster, Feta, Caboc (Scottish), Époisses, Langres, and Pont-l'Évêque.

• Veined cows'-milk cheeses: cut after curdling, sometimes stirred, then cultured with bacteria at the time of shaping to give green or blue veins. Examples: blue cheeses, Fourmes, Stilton, Blue Cheshire, and Gorgonzola.

• Pressed cows'-milk cheeses: curdled by rennet and draining accelerated by cutting, stirring, and pressing. Examples: Cantal, Reblochon, Saint-Nectaire, Tommes, and Cheddar. Some, particularly Dutch cheeses like Edam, have a nonedible wax rind.

• Pressed and cooked cows'-milk cheeses: manufactured as above, but heated for more than one hour during the cutting and stirring stages. Examples: Comté, Beaufort, Gruyère, and Emmental.

• Goats'-milk cheeses: these are soft and have a downy rind (sometimes coated in ashes), except in fresh cheeses and some veined cheeses, such as Bleu des Aravis.

• Ewes'-milk cheeses: these can be fresh cheeses (Larzac and Broccio), soft cheeses (Venaco), veined cheeses (Roquefort), or pressed cheeses (Basco-Béarnais and Italian Pecorino).

• Mixed-milk cheeses (goats' and cows' milk, or ewes' and cows' milk): fresh or soft; includes some veined cheeses and Chevrotons.

• Shaped-curd cheeses: mainly Italian (Mozzarella, Provolone (only the immature ones), Caciocavallo); after cutting, the curds are mixed with whey, heated, kneaded to obtain an elastic slightly rubbery consistency, then shaped (hence the technical term 'plastic-curd' cheese); they are eaten fresh, dried, or smoked.

• Processed cheese: obtained by cooking several cheeses; often flavoured.

□ **Dietary value and regulations**
Cheese has a high energy (fat) and protein content and is less easily digested than milk; 100 g (4 oz) Gruyère, for instance, contains more protein than 250 g (9 oz) meat. Hard cheeses contain more lipids (fat) than most soft ones. The fat content is usually expressed as a percentage of the dry matter. Cheese is rich in calcium and phosphorus, cooked cheeses more so than soft ones. Vitamin A is present in cheese, but during processing a large part of the lactose and most B vitamins are destroyed with the whey as it drains away. Only minor changes in vitamin content occur during ripening and storage. Cheese only has a trace of carbohydrate and no vitamin C. Cheeses can be grouped according to their fat content: low-fat (less than 20% fat), medium-fat (20–40%), high-fat (40–45%), extra high-fat (more than 45%), double-cream (at least 60%), and triple-cream (at least 75%).

In France, some cheeses (such as Comté, Livarot, and Munster) are entitled to an *appellation d'origine*, which gives a guarantee of their origin, method of manufacture, and quality; others, for instance Tomme de Savoie and Camembert de Normandie, have a regional label.

□ **Choosing cheese** Farmhouse cheeses, made by craftsmen according to traditional methods, are always preferable to dairy cheeses, which are mass-produced in factories. Among the latter, cheeses manufactured from untreated milk are better than those made from pasteurized milk. One must also consider seasonal variations in quality and availability, besides, of course, compatibility with the meal.

Ideally, cheeses should be stored in a cool room, larder, or cellar; they may be kept in the bottom of the refrigerator in an airtight wrapping to prevent them from drying out. Cheeses should be taken out about one hour before they are to be eaten. Soft cheeses that are not ripe through to the 'heart' will improve if left for a few days in a cool place. Blue cheeses should be slightly damp, and there is an old tradition that Gruyère should be kept in an airtight box with a lump of sugar.

Formerly, cheese was frequently served instead of dessert. In the 19th century, it was considered 'masculine' taste and was served in the smoking room along with the liqueurs and brandy. Nowadays, besides its role in cookery, cheese is regarded as an extension of the meal. In France it is served after the salad and before the dessert, while in Britain and the United States it is usually eaten after the dessert. The cheeses may be served with butter, a controversial subject in France, as is the question of whether the rind should be eaten or not: experts are divided on both these points. In general, at least three types of cheese should be offered: a cooked cheese, a veined cheese, and a soft cheese with either a downy or a washed rind. Enthusiasts, however, like to have a choice of five or six cheeses: one goats'-milk cheese, one with a pressed curd, one hard cheese, one veined, one soft cheese with a downy rind, and one soft cheese with a washed rind. Sometimes a single cheese that has been carefully chosen and ripened is

Food value of cheeses *(all values given per 100 g, 4 oz)*

cheese	dry matter (g)	calorific value (Cal)	protein (g)	fat (g)	calcium (mg)	phosphorus (g)
blue cheese	60	410	24	34	490	280
Brie	43	271	17	21	184	188
Camembert	45	312	20	24	154	139
Cantal	63	387	23	30	776	462
goats' cheese	40–60	280–380	16–33	15–25	190	190
Comté	66	391	30	30	900	600
Coulommiers	45	279	15	22	205	147
Crème de Gruyère	51	280	18	22	750	620
Emmental	67	415	28	33	1080	810
Dutch cheese	61	331	29	25	777	332
Livarot	54	357	31	22	714	299
Munster	54	322	21	24	335	186
Parmesan	68	393	40	25	1350	990
Roquefort	60	405	23	35	700	360
Saint-Paulin	58	373	24	29	650	360

served; for example, a farmhouse Camembert, Vacherin, Brie, or Munster. Cutting the cheese is governed by certain rules of etiquette: they demand a special knife with a two-pronged blade for both cutting and picking up the desired piece, since cheese should never be touched with a fork.

Wine remains the best accompaniment to cheese. As a general rule, light red wines are mostly served with soft cheeses that have downy rinds and with goats'-milk cheese and pressed cheeses; more robust wines are best with soft cheeses that have washed rinds and with veined cheeses. Goats'-milk cheeses can also be served with dry fruity white wines, while cooked and processed cheeses go well with a rosé, blue cheeses and Roquefort with a smooth white, and Comté is delicious with a yellow Jura wine. Beer and cider are particularly suitable for drinking with some cheeses. Finally, in order to get the best out of a cheese, it is wise to have a choice of bread or biscuits; for example, farmhouse and rye bread, and even some crackers and crispbread.

□ **Cheese in cookery** Many cheeses can be used in cookery, as a basic ingredient or to add flavour. They can either be used raw (in mixed salads, canapés, pastry, and on bread) or, more often, cooked (for soufflés, omelettes, sauces, pancakes, puff pastries, pizzas, and soups). There is a large variety of dishes based on cheese: flamiche, fondue, keshy yena, Welsh rarebit, raclette, gougère, croque-monsieur, croûtes, patranque, goyère, truffade, imbrucciata, aligot, etc. Fresh soft cheese is used more in pâtisserie.

□ **Fresh soft cheeses** These are unripened cheeses that are made solely by natural lactic fermentation; they are drained slowly and have a water content of 60–82%. They are called *fromage frais* or *fromage blanc* in France, and varieties made with cows' milk, sold in pots marked with a 'sell by' date, are marketed under these names and as 'soft cheese' in Britain. Many are low-fat cheeses (less than 20% fat), but some contain up to 70% fat; they can either be smooth, with added cream (cream cheese), or have the appearance of curdled milk (curd and cottage cheeses). Variously flavoured, they can be eaten as a dessert – alone, with fruit, or with a compote. They can also top baked potatoes and various cooked vegetables.

Cheeses throughout the year

good all year round

Bel Paese, industrially made blue cheeses, Brillat-Savarin, Broodkas, Caciocavallo, Camembert, Cantal, Carré de l'Est, Chabichou, Cheddar, Cheshire, Comté, Coulommiers, Crème de Gruyère, Derby, Edam, Edelpilz, Emmental, Excelsior, Feta, Fontainebleau, Fourme, Gammelost, Gérardmer, Gjetöst, Gloucester, Gorgonzola, Gouda, Lancashire, Leyde, Limburger, Liptauer, Manchego, Mimolette, Mozzarella, Munster, Murol, Mysöst, Nantais, Neufchâtel, Parmesan, Pecorino, Port-Salut, Provolone, Reblochon, Ricotta, Saint-Nectaire, Saint-Paulin, Sbrinz, Scamorze, Schabzieger, Sovietski, Stracchino, Tilsitt, Tomme.

best between mid-April and mid-November

Bagnes, Banon (goats' milk), blue farmhouse cheeses, Bondard, Bossons macérés, Boulette, Broccio, Cabécou, Cachat, Cendré, Chevrotin, Coeur-de-Bray, Crottin de Chavignol, Dauphin, Époisses, Fontina, Herve, Labouille, Laguiole, Livarot, Maroilles, Mont-d'Or, Niolo, Pavé d'Auge, Pélardon, veined cheeses, Picodon, Poivre-d'Âne, Pouligny-Saint-Pierre, Pourly, Rigotte, Roquefort, Sainte-Maure, Saint-Marcellin, Selles-sur-Cher.

best between mid-November and mid-April

Appenzell, Asiago, Baguette de Thiérache, Banon (ewes' milk), Beaufort, Bouton-de-Culotte, Brie, Brousse, Feuille de Dreux, Frilbourg, Gaperon, Géromé, Gris de Lille, Gruyère, Katschkawalj, Olivet, Pithiviers, Pont-l'Évêque, Rollot, Saint-Florentin, Soumaintrain, Stilton, Vacherin, Vendôme.

Slightly salted cheeses (Demi-Sel) can also be bought, as well as such specialities as Petit-Suisse and Coeur à la Crème. Regional French cheeses, with a fat content of 40–75% or over, are sometimes eaten with sugar or various flavourings; they include Boursin, Caillebotte, Cerville de Canut, Crémet, Fontainebleau, Gournay Frais, and Jonchée. In northern France and Alsace, fresh soft cheese is mixed with horseradish, herbs, and other flavourings; this speciality is also found in Hungary, where Liptó (a cheese made from ewes' and cows' milk) may be flavoured with mustard, spices, herbs, capers, etc. These flavoured cheeses are often served with boiled potatoes.

Ewes' milk can also be used to make fresh soft cheeses, such as Broccio from Corsica, Brousse from Provence, Cachat, and Tomme Fraîche. Goats' milk is used for Claquebitou from the Burgundy region, Lusignan, and Sableau from Poitou. The Mediterranean and Balkan countries have several fresh soft cheeses made from ewes' and goats' milk, including Greek Feta, Rumanian Braidza, and Italian Ricotta, which are used mainly in cookery.

Russian pâtisserie uses soft cheese in such dishes as paskha (Easter cakes), vatroushki (patties made with cottage cheese), and cyrniki (cheese fritters). It is also found in some oriental preparations, such as böreks and stuffed aubergines (eggplants). In traditional French cookery, fresh soft cheese can sometimes partly replace cream to make a dish less rich; it is also used in salad dressings and stuffings for vegetables and fish. But, above all, it makes variously flavoured desserts and is used in pâtisserie for pies, galettes, soufflés, ice creams, etc.

□ **Processed cheese** This typically contains a variety of ingredients, combined together and melted by heat. A processed cheese spread, which may be based, for example, on Gruyère, Emmental, Cheddar, or Cheshire, contains – in addition – milk, cream, butter, casein, and various flavourings (ham, paprika, pepper, walnuts, raisins, etc.). A processed cheese contains at least 50% dry matter and at least 40% fat. A cheese spread contains less dry matter. In France, when the cheese makes up at least 25% of the product, it can be called 'Crème de . . .' followed by the name of the cheese.

Processed cheeses are sold in portions wrapped in foil (triangles or cubes) or in very thin slices; they are used on bread and for canapés, appetizers, croques-monsieur, and for gratins.

□ **Vegetarian cheese** This is usually a Cheddar-type cheese that has the same ingredients as normal Cheedar but uses microbial enzymes to clot the milk, instead of animal-derived rennet. It has the same qualities as Cheddar.

□ **Strong cheese** (*fromage fort*) This is made from one or more types of cheese (usually dry and matured) which are ground or coarsely grated and steeped in a mixture of oil, wine, spirits, stock, and flavourings in a sealed earthenware pot. After a few weeks or months this gives it a very strong flavour. Strong cheeses are mostly home-made and are a speciality of Beaujolais and the Lyon area, but they can also be found in Provence and northern France. They are eaten with bread and on toast. Special mention should be made of the strong cheeses from Mont Ventoux (based on Cachat, with salt and pepper and garnished with onion), from Beaujolais (Bouton-de-Culotte, dry Gruyère, oil, butter, and marc brandy), and from the Lyon area (dry goats'-milk Tomme, Saint-Marcellin, brandy, stock, thyme, and tarragon). Similar to strong cheeses are Pétafine from Dauphiné and Fremgeye from Lorraine (salted and peppered fresh cheese, left to ferment in a sealed pot), which is identical to the Belgian Pottekees.

RECIPES

Soft-cheese sauce SAUCE AU FROMAGE BLANC Mix 2 small 'pots' or 2 tablespoons (3 tablespoons) Petit-Suisse cheese with 5 tablespoons (6 tablespoons) fromage frais, 50 g (2 oz) finely crushed Roquefort, 1 tablespoon brandy, salt, pepper, a pinch of cayenne, and ½ teaspoon vinegar. Mix all the ingredients together in a blender.

As an alternative, mix 2 Petits-Suisses with 6 tablespoons (½ cup) fromage frais, 3 tablespoons (¼ cup) tomato ketchup, 1 teaspoon (or more) Worcestershire sauce, 2 drops of Tabasco sauce, salt, and pepper. Both sauces can be served with baked potatoes and cooked vegetables.

Soft fresh cheese with herbs FROMAGE BLANC AUX HERBES Chop some parsley, chervil, tarragon, and chives. Mix these into some full-fat or low-fat soft fresh cheese. Add salt, pepper, and a pinch of cayenne and mix well. Place in the refrigerator until required. Serve with farmhouse bread or rye bread and use to top potatoes baked in their jackets.

cheeseboard

PLATEAU DE FROMAGES
An assortment of cheeses offered on a tray of marble, olive wood, or wicker (sometimes decorated with vine leaves), with a matching knife. The board or tray may have a cover.

cheesecloth

See *muslin*.

cheese straw PAILLETTE

A small stick of puff pastry, generally spiced or flavoured with Parmesan cheese, served with apéritifs, consommés, fish, or cheese.

chef CUISINIER

A person who prepares food as an occupation in a restaurant, private house, hotel, etc. Chefs have occupied an important role in society from the 5th century BC onwards and in the Middle Ages, with the creation of guilds, they constituted a hierarchical community. In France, in the reign of Henri IV, the guilds split up into several separate branches: *rôtisseurs* were responsible for *la grosse viande* (the main cuts of meat), *pâtissiers* dealt with poultry, pies, and tarts, and *vinaigriers* made the sauces. The *traiteurs* (caterers) included the master chefs, the cooks, and the *porte-chapes* (the *chape* was a convex cover to keep dishes hot), and they had the privilege of organizing weddings and feasts, collations, and various meals at home. These *chefs cuisiniers* (head cooks), as they were now called, served a period of apprenticeship, at the end of which they had to create a masterpiece of meat or fish, and give £6 to each member of the association.

High-ranking chefs were revered, and some of them, like Taillevent, were raised to the nobility. The most famous of all was undoubtedly Carême. Under the Ancient Régime, a distinction was made between the *officier de cuisine*, who was the actual cook, and the *officier de bouche*, who was in fact the butler (Vatel held this office). From the 18th century onwards, chefs wore a large white hat to distinguish them from their assistants (hence their nickname of *gros bonnet*, 'big hat'). It seems that the hat first made its appearance in the 1820s. At the time when massive joints were served in England, the cook who supervised their preparation on the spit wore a black cap to facilitate carrying the roast to the table on a silver platter on his head. This form of headgear is retained at the Mansion House, official residence of the Lord Mayor of London, at Simpson's restaurant in the Strand, and at a single coaching inn in Devon. In these three establishments alone the chief cook holds the title 'Master Cook', not chef.

The patron saints of male and female cooks are Fortunat (bishop of Poitiers and a famous 7th-century poet), and Radegonde (who founded a monastery of which Fortunat became the chaplain). Radegonde was an excellent cook, as testified by this letter from Fortunat, thanking her for a meal that she had prepared for him: 'Next a superb piece of meat was brought, arranged in the shape of a mountain and flanked by high hills, the spaces between which were filled with a garden of various stews that included the most delicious products of earth and water. . . . A black earthenware jar provided me with milk of the utmost whiteness: it was quite sure to please me.'

□ **Modern chefs** 'Taste, ideas, skill, sincerity': this slogan of the great chefs of today might also have been that of Taillevent or Carême. What has really changed over the centuries is the mythology of cookery. The 'ninth art' formerly reserved for the privileged few, such as guests at large hotels, or guests in a few rich households possessing their own cook, is now popularized by the media and is gradually becoming accessible to everyone. Like any art, it has its idiosyncrasies, its masterpieces, its imitations, and its piracies and its very success has transformed the conditions in which it is practised.

Most of the great chefs and well-known cooks of today are restaurant-owners who have set up on their own and run their establishments with the help of their family. Often, they have learnt their trade from their parents: the third generation of the same family run Les Troisgros at Roanne. Raymond Thuillier, at Les Beaux-de-Provence, is the grandson of a Savoyard innkeeper; André Pic, at Valence, traced his family tree to the beginning of the 19th century, when one of his ancestors ran a small inn near Saint-Péray. Sometimes they began their apprenticeship or perfected their experience with a famous professional, although there are a few instinctive cooks who have made their way alone to the top of the professions.

A tour of gastronomic France would reveal the diversity and imagination of the great chefs of today. For it is no longer true to say that you can only eat well in Paris! Tourism, the motor car, and business have led to the discovery of the provinces by amateur gastronomes, talented cooks who have been able to adapt ancient recipes by using local produce.

Today's great chefs often acquire stardom through the media but they must also become business executives, concerned about public relations, promotion, and administration. Eloquent and scholarly, Raymond Oliver was the first to make use of television by introducing cookery programmes, in which, with a combination of knowledge and charm, he demonstrated his masterly skills.

Above all, cooks are writers: they publish their recipes. Not only do they tell you how to cook a dish, but they also tell you how to cook it successfully. One of the novelties of our time is that almost as much time is spent in digesting books about cooking as is spent in digesting food!

If there has been a development in the professionals of cookery, the world of gourmets has also changed. Even if everyone does not yet know how to make a vegetable charlotte or a Chiboust cream, at least everyone knows that light cooking preserves the flavour of a food better.

Cheilly-les-Maranges

A red or white AOC Burgundy, from the south of the Côte d'Or. It is often sold as 'Côte de Beaune' or, if made together with the wines of other parishes, 'Côte de Beaune Villages'.

chemise (en)

Denoting a dish in which the main ingredient is wrapped or retains its natural covering. Pigeons *en chemise* are wrapped in a slice of ham and cooked in a casserole (with spices and stock, diluted halfway through cooking with a little wine vinegar). Duckling *en chemise* is stuffed, wrapped in a napkin, and poached in a brown stock; it is served with orange quarters and a rouennaise sauce. Cloves of garlic *en chemise* are added whole, unpeeled, to a stew or a roast (they are removed before serving, but the pulp may be squeezed into the cooking juice). Potatoes *en chemise* are boiled in their skins. Truffles *en chemise* are baked in the oven, wrapped in buttered greaseproof (waxed) paper.

RECIPE

Quails en chemise CAILLES EN CHEMISE (from an old recipe) Clean some pork intestine. Stuff the quails with *à gratin* forcemeat, then truss, sprinkle with salt and pepper, and wrap each one separately in a small piece of intestine. Tie up each end. Plunge the quails into boiling clear stock and poach for about 20 minutes. Drain, reduce the stock, and coat the quails with it. Instead of stock, a well-seasoned and well-reduced clarified chicken consommé may be used.

chemiser

A French culinary term meaning to coat or line the sides or bottom of a mould either with something to prevent the food from adhering to the container and enable it to be turned out easily, or with different ingredients which form an integral part of the dish. In the case of an aspic, a thin film of jelly is spread on the bottom and against the inner sides of the mould. For caramelized desserts caramel is used. For bombe ices, the inside of the mould is first coated with cream or ice cream. The bottom and sides of a charlotte mould are coated with sponge fingers, rolled-out Genoese sponge, or slices of bread with the crusts removed. Some moulds are lined with buttered greaseproof (waxed) paper.

Chénas

One of the nine Beaujolais *crus* (growths). Most of the vineyard is in the Moulin-à-Vent region and therefore many of its wines are sold under this more famous name. Those made in the north of the parish, lighter in weight than Moulin-à-Vent, are sold as Chénas.

chère

In modern French, this word designates the food served during a meal: *bonne chère* is a savoury and plentiful food. Formerly, however, the word was used mainly in the expressions *faire bonne chère à* (someone) and *faire chère lie*, meaning to welcome someone in a friendly manner; *faire chère lie* now means to offer someone a good meal.

cherry   CERISE

A small round stone fruit with a skin varying from pale yellow to dark red and a pulp that can be sweet or sour, according to the variety. In Europe cherry trees cultivated for their fruits are mostly derived from two species: these originated from Asia Minor and were first cultivated in the Middle Ages.

• The wild sweet cherry tree was known by the Egyptians, Greeks, and Romans; its fruit is rather acid (though full of flavour) and is used mainly to make jams, syrups, and liqueurs. It has given rise to both the hard crisp bigarreaus and the soft sweet cherries known as *guignes* in France and geans in England. These are popular dessert fruit and are also used in tarts and for preserves (jams, liqueurs, and syrups).

• The bitter cherry was apparently brought to Rome by Lucullus after the campaigns against Mithridates; modern varieties, which are derived from it, produce the amarelle and morello cherries which are used for preserves in syrup or brandy, crystallized (candied) fruits, and jams. The sourish 'English' cherries are used mainly as fruits in brandy.

In France, the main cherry-producing regions are in the southeast – Vaucluse, Ardèche, Gard, Bouches-du-Rhône, Drôme, and the Rhône valley. Cherries are sold from mid-May until the beginning of July. The calorie content varies: 77 Cal per 100 g for bigarreaus; 56 Cal per 100 g for English cherries. They have a high content of sugar, mineral salts (especially potassium), and vitamins A and B. Cherry stalks and the dried flowers of the cherry tree are used for infusions.

Cherries are frequently used in pâtisserie and in other types of cooking. Fresh and thoroughly washed, they are used in compotes, fruit salads and ice-cream sundaes, as well as tarts, flans, soufflés, and Black Forest gâteau. Glacé (candied) cherries are popular in cakes and puddings and for decoration. In confectionary, cherry liqueur (particularly that made from morello cherries) is used to fill chocolates. Cherries are used to make soup in Alsace, in Germany they are employed in the preparation of sweet-and-sour dishes and pickles. They are also used as a condiment and as an accompaniment, particularly for game and duck (see *Montmorency*).

Of the cherry-based liqueurs and alcoholic drinks, the most noteworthy are the English cherry brandy, Guignolet from Anjou, Maraschino from Italy, and Kirsch from Alsace; a 'cherry wine' is made with fermented cherry juice, and the Belgian *kriek lambick* is flavoured with cherry.

Cherries can be frozen freshly picked with their stalks removed.

RECIPES

SAVOURY DISHES

Cherry soup   SOUPE AUX CERISES
Butter some slices of bread, dust them with flour, and fry in butter on both sides until golden. Heat some stoned cherries (preserved *au naturel*) in a mixture of equal parts of red wine and water. Season with a little salt, pepper, and sugar and pour the soup over the slices of bread arranged in each bowl.

In Alsace, this soup is traditionally made on Christmas Eve.

Hare with cherries LIÈVRE AUX CERISES Choose a hare weighing between 1.5–2 kg (3½–4½ lb) and cut into pieces. Place the pieces in a flameproof casserole containing very hot olive oil and cook until they are golden, then remove. In the same oil, brown a large onion and a shallot, both chopped, and a finely diced carrot; then replace the pieces of hare. Reheat, sprinkle in 1 tablespoon flour, and stir until it turns golden brown. Moisten with ½ bottle of red Burgundy and add a bouquet garni, a crushed clove of garlic, a clove, salt, and pepper. Cover and leave to cook gently for 1 hour.

Remove the stalks and stones from 1 kg (2¼ lb) cherries, cook them with 250 g (9 oz, 1 generous cup) sugar and a little water, then remove and drain. Caramelize the syrup slightly, then add 1 dl (6 tablespoons, scant ½ cup) wine vinegar, bring to the boil, and reduce to obtain a syrupy mixture. Roll the cherries in this syrup. Arrange the pieces of hare in the serving dish, coat with the strained cooking stock, and distribute the cherries around the dish.

SWEET DISHES

Cherries flambéed à la bourguignonne CERISES FLAMBÉES À LA BOURGUIGNONNE Remove the stalks and stones from some cherries and cook them with sugar and water, using 350 g (12 oz, 1½ cups firmly packed) sugar and ⅓ glass water per kg (2¼ lb) cherries. Cook gently for 8–10 minutes then add 2–3 tablespoons redcurrant jelly and reduce for about 5 minutes. Pour into a flambé pan, sprinkle with Burgundy marc, heated in a small saucepan or a ladle, and flame the cherries just before serving.

variety	characteristics	time of harvest
bigarreaus		
Early Burlat	large, dark red, and shiny; firm, full of flavour, and sweet.	late May
black	large, purple, and shiny; crisp, juicy, and fragrant.	late May
Napoleon	fairly large, pale yellow, tinged with light red; firm, fragrant, and slightly sour.	mid-June
Reverchon	large and round, glossy dark purple; firm and sweet.	early June
Hedelfingen Giant	large, black, and shiny; crisp and moderately fragrant; withstands transport and keeps well in a cool place.	mid-June to mid-July
William	large and pointed, bright purple; quite firm, fairly juicy, sweet, and fragrant.	late May
pigeon's heart	fairly large, bright red striped with dark red; firm, little flavour.	early June
geans		
Early Basle (or Ceret)	fairly small, blackish-purple; soft, juicy, sour, travels badly.	mid-May
Early Rivers	medium-sized, dark purple; sweet fragrant, and juicy; very small stone.	mid-May
English cherry	small, bright orange-red; soft translucent flesh.	late May
Montmorency	medium-sized, very sour.	early June
morello	small, dark red; fairly firm sharp flesh.	late June to early July

Cherries in brandy CERISES À L'EAU-DE-VIE Scald some storage jars in readiness. Dissolve some candy sugar in brandy, allowing 350 g (12 oz) sugar to 1 litre (1¾ pints, 4¼ cups) brandy. Choose sound morello or Montmorency cherries, cut off half of each stalk, and pierce each cherry opposite the stalk with a needle. Arrange the cherries in jars, cover them completely with the sweetened brandy, seal well, and store in a cool place away from the light. Wait 3 months before serving.

Cherries preserved au naturel CONSERVES DE CERISES AU NATUREL Remove the stalks from the cherries, wash, and wipe them. Pack them into jars, hermetically seal, and sterilize for about 20 minutes at 90 C (194 F).

Cherry-filled soufflé fritters BEIGNETS SOUFFLÉS FOURRÉS AUX CERISES Remove the stalks and stones from some cherries and cook them in syrup. Remove and drain the cherries and reduce the syrup until it coats a wooden spatula. Flavour it with Kirsch. Return the cherries to the syrup and coat them thoroughly. Prepare some fritter batter; dip the cherries in the batter and fry. Arrange the fritters in a bowl or compote dish and dust them with icing (confectioners') sugar.

Cherry jam CONFITURE DE CERISES Remove the stones from the cherries and weigh them. Use 1 kg (2¼ lb) sugar and 1 dl (6 tablespoons, scant ½ cup) water per kg (2¼ lb) fruit. Boil the water and sugar for 10 minutes, add the cherries, and cook until the fruit is transparent. Pour into jars.

Danish cherry flan FLAN DE CERISES À LA DANOISE Remove the stones from some bigarreau cherries and macerate the fruit with sugar and a dash of cinnamon. Line a flan dish with shortcrust pastry (basic pie dough) and fill with the stoned (pitted) cherries. Mix 125 g (4¼ oz, generous ½ cup) butter, 125 g (4½ oz, scant ⅔ cup) sugar, 125 g (4½ oz, generous cup) ground almonds, 2 whole beaten eggs, and the juice from the cherries. Cover the cherries with this mixture and bake in a hot oven (about 220 C, 425 F, gas 7) for 35–40 minutes.

Leave to cool, then cover with redcurrant jelly and a white rum-flavoured icing (frosting).

Jubilee cherries CERISES JUBILÉ They are prepared in the same way as flambéed cherries, but the syrup is thickened with a little arrowroot and the fruit is arranged in small individual ramekins and coated with syrup. Just before serving, pour 1 tablespoon Kirsch into each ramekin and flame.

cherry brandy

A liqueur obtained by macerating a purée of cherries and their crushed kernels in brandy. This liqueur, which may have first been made in England, is usually sweet, slightly syrupy, and ruby red in colour. (Most liqueur establishments now make a cherry brandy.) Its inventor in England was Thomas Grant, a distiller in Kent, a county famous for morello cherries. Depending on the whereabouts of the establishment, different varieties of cherry are used.

chervil CERFEUIL

An aromatic umbelliferous plant, originating from central Asia but now common throughout Europe, that is used as a condiment, particularly its freshly picked leaves. These are used to garnish soups or omelettes, and as a complement to sauces (béarnaise, gribiche, vinaigrette) and dishes of river fish cooked *au vert*. Its aroma is very volatile and care must be taken to avoid heating it excessively or mixing it with too much oil. Chervil keeps well when frozen.

In addition to common chervil and curly chervil (which is especially decorative), there is the delicate but rare bulbous chervil: its tuberous roots, aromatic and with a high starch content, are eaten like artichokes.

| RECIPE |

Chervil soup POTAGE AU CERFEUIL Wash and chop a large bunch of chervil. Soften it in a covered shallow frying pan (skillet) with 30 g (1 oz, 2 tablespoons) butter for 5–6 minutes, then add 1 litre (1¾ pints, 4¼ cups) thin white sauce made with chicken stock. Leave to cook gently for about 10 minutes, then pass through a blender.

Add 2 dl (7 fl oz, ¾ cup) fresh cream and reduce by boiling briskly for 5 minutes. Pour into a soup tureen and sprinkle with chervil leaves ready for serving.

chervis

A plant originating from China, widely cultivated in the past for its floury sweet roots. Olivier de Serres praised this vegetable, which was prepared like salsify; however, because of its low yield it was abandoned in favour of salsify.

Cheshire

An English cows'-milk cheese (containing 45% butterfat), with a compressed uncooked centre and a natural oily rind. Cylindrical in shape and 35–40 cm (14–16 in) high, it weighs 22–40 kg (50–90 lb). Granular in appearance, it is firm and oily to the touch, with a mild flavour which is more pronounced when it has been matured for a long time (up to two years); its particular taste is due to the deposits of salt in the pastures where the cows graze. It originates from Cheshire, where it appeared in the reign of Elizabeth I. There are three varieties: red (the best known), white, and blue (fairly rare).

Chester

The name given in France and Belgium to Cheshire and Cheddar cheeses, and also to similar French cheeses that are mass-produced by the Cheddar-making process (introduced in Castres after World War II). These cows'-milk cheeses (containing 45% butterfat) are used mostly for croûtes, canapés, etc.

chestnut

CHÂTAIGNE, MARRON

The fruit of the sweet chestnut tree, which is edible when cooked. The spiky husk generally contains three separate chestnuts, but improved cultivated varieties (called *marrons* in France) contain a single large nut.

Chestnuts were very popular in the days of the Roman empire and today are a basic food in Sardinia, Corsica, the Massif Central, and in parts of northern Italy. The main production areas in France are the Ardèche, the Dordogne, Lozère, and Corsica; chestnuts are also imported from Spain and Italy.

Chestnuts are energy-rich and highly nutritious, yielding 199–307 Cal per 100 g (depending on the variety). They contain a high proportion of starch, together with potassium and vitamins B and C. Fresh chestnuts, available in the winter months, should be heavy, hard, and shiny brown.

Whole chestnuts can be roasted in their shells, then peeled and eaten as they are. Alternatively they may be peeled and preserved, frozen, or puréed, with or without sugar added (see *chestnut cream*). Whole marrons are cooked and preserved in sugar and eaten as a sweetmeat (see *marrons glacés*). Chestnuts are also used to manufacture chestnut flour. Peeled chestnuts can be boiled, grilled (broiled), braised, or cooked in butter or milk for use as a garnish or vegetable. They make a good accompaniment to Brussels sprouts and are served with many winter dishes, particularly poultry and game. Puréed chestnuts are also used as a garnish, and are an ingredient of various stuffings. Chestnuts are also used for making sweet desserts and play an important role in the pâtisserie and confectionery industries.

In France, chestnuts are used in various regional recipes, such as chestnut estouffade, Ardèches salad, and Corsican *brilloli* (a chestnut polenta) and *castagnacci* (a chestnut cake). In the Cévennes and southwestern France they are used for making soups, gruels, and jams. In Valais, *brisolée* is a dish of chestnuts roasted with cheese.

RECIPES

Peeling fresh chestnuts ÉPLUCHAGE DES MARRONS FRAIS Slit the shells of the chestnuts on the domed face with a sharp knife. Put them in a baking tin (pan) with a little water and roast in a very hot oven for about 8 minutes. Peel them while they are still hot.

After slitting the shells, the chestnuts may alternatively be deep-fried for 2–3 minutes in very hot fat, cooked for 5 minutes in boiling water, or placed beneath very hot embers.

Some authorities recommend that chestnuts should be shelled when they are raw, and then boiled in slightly salted water for about 20 minutes. The inner skin can then be easily removed and the chestnuts are ready to eat or otherwise use.

CHESTNUT DESSERTS

Chestnut cream CRÈME DE MARRONS Make some chestnut preserve and put into sundae dishes. Decorate with Chantilly cream piped through a fluted nozzle and top each with a crystallized (candied) violet. The amount of sugar in the preserve may be reduced by a quarter if desired.

Chestnut preserve CONFITURE DE MARRONS Peel 2 kg (4½ lb) chestnuts, cover them with cold water in a saucepan, bring to the boil, and cook for 40 minutes. Drain and rub them through a sieve. Weigh the resulting purée and add an equal quantity of sugar. Put the sweetened purée in a preserving pan with 1 dl (6 tablespoons, scant ½ cup) water per kg (2¼ lb) sweetened chestnut purée and 2 vanilla pods (beans). Heat the mixture fairly gently, stirring continuously. The preserve is ready when it comes away from the bottom of the pan when stirred. Remove from the heat, take out the vanilla pods, and put into jars.

Chestnut soufflé Mont-Bry SOUFFLÉ MONT-BRY AUX MARRONS Boil 1 dl (6 tablespoons, scant ½ cup) milk with 40 g (1½ oz, 3 tablespoons, firmly packed) sugar and a pinch of salt. Blend 25 g (1 oz, ¼ cup) sifted flour with a small quantity of cold milk in a pan. Add the sweetened milk and cook for 2–3 minutes, stirring constantly. Remove from the heat and blend in 4 egg yolks and 10 g (½ oz, 1 tablespoon) butter, followed by 4 tablespoons (5 tablespoons) sweetened vanilla-flavoured chestnut purée, and a few pieces of marron glacé. Whisk 5 egg whites until very stiff and fold carefully into the mixture. Put the mixture into a buttered soufflé dish and bake in the oven at 200 c (400 F, gas 6) for 35 minutes.

SAVOURY CHESTNUT DISHES

Boiled chestnuts MARRONS BOUILLIS Place some peeled chestnuts in a saucepan and cover with cold water. Season with salt and pepper and add some chopped celery. Bring to the boil and simmer gently for 35–45 minutes. Drain the chestnuts well and serve with butter.

Braised chestnuts MARRONS BRAISÉS Peel the chestnuts and spread them over the base of a large greased ovenproof casserole. Place a bouquet garni and a stick (stalk) of celery in the centre, season with salt and pepper, and add enough stock to just cover them. Cover the casserole and cook in a hot oven (220 c, 425 F, gas 7) for about 45 minutes (do not stir the chestnuts during cooking in case they break). Serve with braised or roast meat.

Chestnut purée PURÉE DE MARRONS Boil some peeled chestnuts, drain them, rub them through a sieve, and place the purée in a saucepan. Add 1.5 dl (¼ pint, ⅔ cup) cream per 1 kg (2¼ lb) chestnuts and reheat, stirring constantly. Then add 50 g (2 oz, ¼ cup) butter and adjust the seasoning. If the purée is too thick, add a little of the strained cooking liquid.

Chestnut purée can be used to make soup or a savoury soufflé.

Roast chestnuts MARRONS GRILLÉS Using a sharp pointed knife, cut a circular incision around the chestnuts through the husk and the inner skin. Roast in a pan over hot embers, shaking them often.

They can also be roasted in a very hot oven. In this case, add a little water to the pan.

chestnut cream
CRÈME DE MARRONS

A sweetened chestnut purée with an oily consistency, used in confectionery and pâtisserie. It is a processed product, with good keeping qualities, that has become a speciality of the Ardèche region of France: since 1882, a Privas firm has manufactured a chestnut cream made from a purée of sweet chestnuts, fragments of marrons glacés, sugar, and glucose; it is often flavoured with vanilla. Chestnut cream is used for making iced desserts (Bavarian cream, ices, vacherins), sometimes finished off with marrons glacés; it also serves as a filling for pastries and sweets (gâteau roulé, barquettes, meringues, and pancakes). It may be served chilled with Chantilly cream and plain biscuits (cookies). It must not be confused with unsweetened chestnut purée, which accompanies game and is used in forcemeats.

cheval (à)

Describing small pieces of grilled beef (steak, hamburger, or entrecôte) with one or two fried eggs on top. Angels on horseback (*anges à cheval*) are grilled (broiled) oysters placed on a rasher of bacon on toast.

RECIPE

Steak à cheval   BIFTECK À CHEVAL Season a steak with salt and pepper and sauté in butter. Arrange it on a plate, place a fried egg on top, and sprinkle with the cooking butter.

chevaler

A French culinary term meaning to arrange the components of a dish (slices, cutlets, etc.) so that they partly overlap. On a long dish, the items are set out in a line or in a staggered arrangement; on a round dish, they are placed so as to form a crown.

chevalière (à la)

Describes two elaborately decorated preparations, one of sole and the other of eggs. The fillets of sole are poached, arranged on a fish forcemeat with crayfish trunks, surrounded by oysters, poached mushrooms, and crayfish tails bound with américaine sauce, and garnished with thin slices of truffle. The eggs are served with the garnish in a flan case.

RECIPE

Eggs à la chevalière   OEUFS À LA CHEVALIÈRE Bake a flan case blind. Arrange some soft-boiled or poached eggs around the edge and fill the centre with a ragout of mushrooms, cocks' combs, and kidneys bound with velouté sauce. Coat the eggs with suprême sauce. Dip some cocks' combs in egg and breadcrumbs and fry them. Place a

fried cock's comb between each egg and a thin slice of truffle on top of each egg.

Cheverny

A wine from the Loire valley. The *appellation* covers 23 communes of Loir-et-Cher, situated south of Blois and Chambord, not far from the famous 17th-century château, to the border of Sologne. The siliceous soil yields a relatively small quantity of dry white wines, fruity reds, and fresh rosés, which are particularly appreciated in the region. Sparkling Cheverny, produced according to the champagne process, is made from Chenin Blanc, Arbois, and Romorantin grapes.

Chevreton

One of several cheeses from the Auvergne made from goats' milk (or a mixture of goats' and cows' milk). Solely farm-produced, they contain 40–45% butterfat and have a soft centre and a natural crust. Blue-grey in appearance, yielding to the touch, and with a nutty flavour, the Ambert and Viverols Chevretons and the Brique du Forez are produced in the form of rectangular loaves 12–15 cm (5–6 in) long, 4–6 cm (1½–2½ in) wide, and 2–3 (1 in) high.

chevreuil (en)

Denoting meat prepared and served like venison: tournedos and noisettes of lamb are placed in a marinade, then drained, sautéed in butter, and served with a poivrade sauce and a chestnut purée, as for roebuck. Also prepared *en chevreuil* are filets mignons of beef (larded, marinated, and sautéed), and horse joints or legs of mutton (trimmed, larded, marinated, and roasted, served with a sauce for game).

RECIPES

Filets mignons of beef en chevreuil FILETS MIGNONS DE BOEUF EN CHEVREUIL Cut the filets mignons into triangles, flatten them slightly, and lard with fat bacon. Marinate them for between 36 hours (in summer) and 3 days (in winter), turning them frequently in the marinade. Drain, wipe, and sauté briskly in oil or clarified butter. They may be served with a purée (of celeriac (celery root), lentils, chestnuts, or onions) and a sauce (for example chasseur, hongroise, poivrade, or romaine).

Marinade for meats en chevreuil MARINADE POUR VIANDES EN CHEVREUIL Coarsely chop 75 g (3 oz) onions, 75 g (3 oz) carrots, 2 fine shallots, 3–4 sticks (stalks) of celery (stripped of their strings), and 1 clove of garlic. Brown these vegetables slightly in oil, adding ½ teaspoon chopped parsley, a little crumbled thyme, 1 clove, a piece of bay leaf, and some ground pepper. Moisten with ¾ litre (1¼ pints, 3 cups) white wine and a glass of white vinegar, and cook gently for 30 minutes. Leave to cool completely before pouring over the meat, which has been seasoned with salt and pepper.

additional recipe See *horse*.

Chevreuse

The name given to various preparations in classic French cookery. The Chevreuse garnish for noisettes of lamb or tournedos of beef consists of noisette potatoes and artichoke hearts garnished with a duxelles of mushrooms topped with a thin slice of truffle glazed with butter. The pieces of meat are coated with a sauce made with the pan juice flavoured with Madeira and a demiglace. Velouté Chevreuse is a thick cream of chicken soup flavoured with chervil leaves. Omelette Chevreuse is filled with a mixture of chopped chervil softened in butter and blanched chervil. Eggs Chevreuse are baked in the oven (*au miroir*), sprinkled with grated cheese, and bordered with a fairly firm purée of French beans. The presence of market-garden produce in the recipes explains the name, as the Chevreuse valley has been famous for its vegetables since the 18th century.

Chevrotin des Aravis

A Savoyard cheese made with goats' milk or a mixture of goats' milk and cows' milk. It has an uncooked pressed centre (45% butterfat) and a natural fine grey crust with a rough surface. Firm, mild, and slightly fruity, the cheese is disc-shaped, measuring 13 cm (5 in) in diameter and 4 cm (1½ in) high.

Chevrotin du Bourbonnais

The generic name given to various goats-milk cheeses (45% butterfat) with a soft centre and a natural crust. They include Chevrotin de Moulins, Chevrotin de Cosne-d'Allier, and Chevrotin de Souvigny, among others. They are shaped like truncated cones measuring 6–8 cm (2½–3 in) at the base and 5–6 cm (2–2½ in) high. Chevrotins are smooth and creamy when fresh and are eaten with spices or even sugar. When more mature, they become drier and have a nuttier flavour.

Chianti

An Italian red wine from Tuscany, served in carafes in restaurants. Young wine is sold in straw-sheathed flasks; the better wines are sold in dated bottles. The latter constitute 'classic' Chianti, originating from a very small region between Florence and Siena. They have a seal depicting a black cock on a gold background. The other Chiantis are described as *tolérés* and are produced in much greater quantities in six demarcated regions. The production varies between good-quality wine and very ordinary wine.

Chiboust

A 19th-century pastrycook, who in 1846 created the Saint-Honoré, a cake named in honour of the Paris district in which he worked, and also in honour of Saint Honoré, the patron saint of bakers and pastrycooks.

Chiboust cream, which traditionally accompanies the Saint-Honoré, is a confectioners' custard (pastry cream), usually flavoured with vanilla, and blended when still warm with stiffly beaten egg whites. Pastrycooks often use Chantilly cream instead as it is quicker to make.

| RECIPE

Chiboust cream CRÈME CHIBOUST Soak 4 sheets of gelatine in cold water then dissolve over hot water. Boil ½ litre (17 fl oz, 2 cups) milk with half a vanilla pod (bean). Beat 4 egg yolks with 130 g (4½ oz, ⅔ cup, firmly packed) sugar until the mixture lightens in colour Add 80 g (3 oz, ¾ cup) flour and mix well. Gradually pour in the boiling milk, whisking continuously. Pour the mixture into a saucepan, add the dissolved gelatine, and heat gently, stirring continuously. Remove from the heat as soon as it begins to boil. Add a pinch of salt to the 4 egg whites and beat the latter into stiff peaks. Reheat the cream until it starts to simmer and pour it immediately over the egg whites. Mix with a spatula, lifting the whole mixture, but taking care not to beat it, so that a smooth cream is obtained.

chicha

A Latin American highly alcoholic drink obtained from the fermentation of maize flour (cornmeal). In Peru, it is prepared on a small scale with grains of maize (corn) that the women chew, spit out, and then ferment with pieces of meat. The name derives from the expression *de chicha y nabo* (of little value), and the spirit is consumed by the rural and working classes. It is also mass-produced from maize that is fermented with molasses and then distilled.

chichifregi

A type of fritter from the region of Marseille and Aix-en-Provence. It used to be sold in the streets. Chichifregi are made of raised dough in the shape of little fluted puddings. They are fried and then rolled in sugar.

chicken

POULET, POULARDE

A domestic fowl reared (raised) for both its meat and its eggs. It is one of the most popular types of meat, being used in recipes the whole world over, from paella to chop suey, from jambalaya to *Brathendl*, from chicken pie to *waterzootje*, from curry to pilaf.

In France chickens are classified according to their age at slaughter, weight, diet, and methods of rearing (free-range or battery). The following types are found:

● *poussin* (spring chicken): a very young chicken with delicately flavoured flesh, killed when it weighs 250–300 g (9–11 oz); it is sometimes sold as *poussin de Hambourg*. It can be prepared in the same way as pigeon (devilled, fried, roast with peas, *à la piémontaise*, etc.).

Coquelets, which are a little older and larger but just as tender, are cooked in similar ways.

● *poulet quatre quarts*: a battery chicken killed at about 45 days old, weighing 1 kg (2¼ lb).

● *poulet de grain* (or *poulet de marque*): a battery chicken slaughtered at 50–70 days old, weighing 1.2–1.8 kg (2½–4 lb).

● *poulet d'appellation*: reared in large pens (not in batteries) and killed at 110–120 days old, weighing up to 2 kg (4½ lb). It has firm and well-flavoured flesh.

● *poulet de Bresse* (Bresse chicken): a top-quality bird which must be of the local breed, with a well-developed red comb (in the male), white plumage, and blue feet. There are strict regulations placed on rearing: at 35 days old it is set free onto pasture, with at least 10 square metres to itself; it stays there for 9 weeks, and then is put in a cage indoors for 8–15 days, so that its flesh will whiten; it is slaughtered at 16 weeks. It is the feeding which gives it its quality: cereal flour, maize (corn), and dairy products, together with the worms, snails, slugs, and insects which it finds in the ground.

● *poularde*: a young but large caponized hen reared in a cage in semi-darkness, which prevents the bird from reaching sexual maturity and produces a tender white flesh with a mild and very delicate flavour and a thick covering of fat. True poulardes have now almost completely disappeared, although some are still produced by Bresse breeders using traditional methods. The name is now often given (legally) by French poulterers to a male or female chicken weighing more than 1.8 kg (4 lb).

The poularde is normally roasted, braised (without too much liquid), fried, or poached (in a white or herb-flavoured stock), since sautéing or grilling (broiling) would cause all the fat to melt. Traditional recipes for poularde are often elaborate (using truffle and foie gras) and can be either hot or cold. The liver is sometimes prepared separately; the gizzard, neck, head, and feet are used for making stock.

The feed of a *poulet d'appellation* is made up of 60–70% cereals, 25% proteins (soya, alfalfa flour), and mineral supplements; an industrially raised chicken receives the same foodstuffs, but in different proportions. Yellow Landes chickens, however, are fattened on corn to give them their distinctive colour.

Chickens may still be bought at the butcher or poulterer, who will draw, clean, and truss them, but they are now usually bought ready-dressed, with the giblets in a bag inside the carcass. In France chickens are bought *effilés* (with the intestines removed, but still retaining the liver, gizzard, heart, and lungs) or *éviscérés* (ready-to-cook; completely drawn, with the neck cut off and the legs severed at the first joint). The latter is the form in which most chickens are bought in Britain.

Chicken flesh is very digestible, as it contains little fat; it is rich in iron and provides 120 Cal per 100 g.

☐ **Choosing a chicken for a particular dish** The main cooking methods suitable for chicken are roasting, sautéing, grilling (broiling), deep-frying (coated with breadcrumbs), poaching, and frying.

If the chicken is to be roasted, it is best if it is slightly fatty; the fat melts with the heat and prevents the flesh from drying out. If it is oven-roasted, it may be stuffed or sprinkled with a little thyme or tarragon. The bird is cooked when the juices run out colourless. If it is to be served cold, it should be wrapped while still hot in aluminium foil to preserve its softness and flavour.

A chicken for casseroling should be plump and really firm, but if it is too fatty the melted fat will accumulate in the bottom of the casserole. The accompanying ingredients of a chicken casserole can be fairly strongly flavoured (mushrooms, tomatoes, garlic, sweet peppers, etc.). Chicken also goes well with bananas, quinces, pineapple, lemons, and mangoes.

For a fricassee or a sauté, two fairly small chickens can be used, so that more of the best pieces are available.

When poaching a chicken, it is best to choose a really plump older bird that is not too fatty.

There is the greatest variety in the recipes for sautéed chicken, which range from the very simple to the very elaborate, but chicken can also be prepared in

a chaud-froid, a ballottine, a hash, *à la bonne femme*, *à la diable*, or in a civet. Its flesh can be made into crépinette sausages, shaped cutlets, fritters, kromeskies, pâtés, and mousses. Chicken giblets can be made into a consommé or stock; kebabs, terrines, or pilaf garnishes can be made from chicken livers.

● **Drawing a chicken** Cut through the skin down the length of the neck and remove the trachea (windpipe) and the oesophagus (gullet), pulling out the crop at the same time; leave the neck as it is or sever it at the base, without cutting through the skin. Make an incision at the tail end and pull out the intestines, gizzard, liver, heart, and lungs. Remove the gall bladder from the liver immediately. Split the gizzard on the rounded side and remove the grain sac. Singe the chicken to remove all the remaining down, etc. Clean the giblets and replace in the cavity if not to be used straight away. Cut off the pinions (wing tips), bend back the rest of the bottom joint, and tuck the ends underneath the bird to form a neat shape. Cut off the feet at the joint with the drumstick. Fold back the neck (if it is still on) under one wing, or else fold back the skin of the neck over the breast. Truss the chicken.

☐ **Jointing a raw chicken** Place the chicken on its back, pull out one leg, and cut the skin which joins it to the body. Lift up the leg and cut right through the joint and the flesh of the leg; repeat the process with the other leg. Lift up the wing and free most of the flesh with a knife. Cut right down through the white flesh to the wing joint and cut it free; repeat the process with the other wing. Separate the thighs from the drumsticks, cutting through the joints. Cut the remaining carcass in two, down the length of the back (or remove the backbone first and cut the breast in two). This gives eight pieces.

RECIPES

Chicken à la polonaise POULET À LA POLONAISE Sauté chicken pieces in butter in a flameproof casserole for about 20 minutes. When cooked, pour over the juice of a lemon and cover with about 30 g (1 oz, ½ cup) fresh breadcrumbs mixed with 125 g (4½ oz, ½ cup) noisette butter. Serve very hot with red cabbage, braised chestnuts, or braised celeriac (celery root).

Chicken casserole POULARDE EN CASSEROLE OU EN COCOTTE Clean a chicken weighing 1.8 kg (4 lb) and truss it. Heat 50 g (2 oz, 4 tablespoons) butter in a flameproof casserole and brown the chicken on all sides (if a poularde is not used, cover the chicken breast with strips of fat bacon to keep it moist). Sprinkle with salt and pepper and cover the casserole; place in a hot oven (230 c, 450 F, gas 8) and cook for about 1 hour. Serve the chicken with its own gravy, accompanied by glazed small (pearl) onions or carrots.

Chicken in a salt crust POULET EN CROÛTE DE SEL (from a recipe of Roger Vergé) In a bowl mix together 1 kg (2¼ lb, 9 cups) flour, the same weight of coarse sea salt, and 1 dl (6 tablespoons, scant ½ cup) cold water. Knead this dough and roll it out on a pastry board. Sprinkle the inside of a chicken with salt and pepper and insert a sprig of rosemary, a bay leaf, its own liver, and the livers of 2 other chickens. Place the chicken on the pastry, wrap it up and seal it, place on a baking sheet, and cook in the oven at 160 c (325 F, gas 3) for 1½ hours. Break off the hard salty crust and discard, remove the chicken, and carve. Serve with a salad dressed with walnut oil.

Chicken Maryland POULET FRIT MARYLAND Cut the raw chicken into joints and dip the pieces into cold milk. Drain them, coat with flour, and fry in butter until golden. Continue cooking over a very low heat, turning once, until cooked through. Meanwhile place the carcass and giblets in a saucepan with garlic, onion, a little stock, and some milk. Bring to the boil and simmer for a few minutes, then strain the liquid and pour over the fried chicken pieces. Garnish with fried bacon rashers (slices) and serve with grilled (broiled) corn-on-the cob or corn fritters and fried peeled bananas, cut in halves.

Chicken with rice and suprême sauce POULARDE AU RIZ SAUCE SUPRÊME Truss a large chicken as for roasting and

cook it in white stock, like chicken with tarragon, but for only 40 minutes. Blanch 250 g (9 oz, 1¼ cups) rice for 5 minutes, drain it, rinse it, and drain once more. Drain the half-cooked chicken, strain the stock, then return the chicken to the casserole; add the drained rice and the stock (it should come to about 3 cm (1 in) above the rice). Add 25 g (1 oz, 2 tablespoons) butter and continue cooking gently for 20 minutes. With the rest of the stock, make a suprême sauce. Place the chicken on a warm dish, pour over a little of the sauce, and surround with rice. Serve the rest of the sauce separately in a sauceboat.

Chicken with tarragon POULARDE À L'ESTRAGON Clean a large roasting chicken and put a bunch of tender tarragon sprigs inside it. Truss as for roasting, rub lightly with half a lemon, and bard the breast and back with thin slices of rindless bacon. Place in a flameproof casserole and just cover with white stock, adding a small bunch of tarragon. Cover, bring quickly to the boil, then cook gently for about 1 hour (when pricked, the juice which comes out of the chicken should be clear). Drain the chicken, untie it, and remove the barding fat and the tarragon from inside. Garnish with blanched tarragon leaves and put it in a warm place on a serving dish.

Thicken the cooking liquid with a little arrowroot or kneaded butter; strain it and add 2 tablespoons chopped fresh tarragon. Pour a little of this sauce over the chicken and serve the rest in a sauceboat.

Alternatively the casserole can be deglazed with a glass of white wine and a little thickened and strained veal stock to which a handful of chopped tarragon leaves has been added.

Chicken with tarragon in aspic POULARDE À L'ESTRAGON DANS SA GELÉE Cook a large roasting chicken in white stock as in the recipe for chicken with tarragon. Drain it, untruss it, and pat dry; leave it to cool, then place it in the refrigerator.

Skim the fat off the cooking liquid and strain it, then heat it, adding 20 g (¾ oz, 3 envelopes) powdered gelatine completely dissolved in cold water. In a saucepan, whisk together 100 g (4 oz, ½ cup) lean minced (ground) beef, the white of 1 egg, and a handful of tarragon leaves, roughly chopped. Add the cooking liquid, whisking all the time, and bring to the boil. Simmer gently for 30 minutes, then strain the liquid, add 1 dl (6 tablespoons, scant ½ cup) Madeira, and leave to cool.

When the aspic is nearly set, coat the chicken with several layers, placing it in the refrigerator after each application. Garnish the chicken with blanched tarragon leaves, arranged in a decorative pattern, before the last application of aspic. Finally place the chicken on a serving dish surrounded with any remaining set aspic cut into cubes.

Poached chicken à l'anglaise POULARDE POCHÉE À L'ANGLAISE Poach a large roasting chicken in white stock, as in the recipe for chicken with tarragon. Serve it surrounded with 8 small slices of pickled tongue alternating with small mounds of boiled celery, carrots, turnips, and peas. Pour over the chicken some béchamel sauce mixed with a little of the reduced cooking liquid.

Roast chicken POULET RÔTI Clean a chicken, weigh it, and calculate the cooking time, allowing 15 minutes per 500 g (1 lb) plus 15 minutes. Sprinkle with salt and pepper inside and outside, truss it, then brush lightly with clarified butter. Place it on its breast in a roasting dish and cook in a moderately hot oven (200 C, 400 F, gas 6) for half the cooking time. Then turn it onto its back to finish cooking. Baste it from time to time with its own juice. Transfer the chicken to a platter, deglaze the roasting dish with a little boiling water, and serve the chicken and its gravy separately.

Sautéed chicken à blanc POULET SAUTÉ À BLANC Joint a raw chicken: cut into four if it is small; separate the wings, legs, and breast if it is larger (the thigh bones can be removed if desired). Sprinkle the pieces with salt and pepper. Heat 40 g (1½ oz, 3 tablespoons) butter in a sauté pan or flameproof casserole and cook the pieces gently until firm but not coloured (first the thighs, which take longer to cook, then the wings and

breast, which are more tender). Then cover and cook gently for about 40 minutes. Remove the pieces in the same order that they went in. Pour off the cooking fat; deglaze the pan with white stock, wine, cream, mushroom stock, or any other liquid specified in the recipe.

Sautéed chicken à brun POULET SAUTÉ À BRUN Follow the recipe for sautéed chicken *à blanc* but fry the chicken pieces over a brisk heat until brown all over. Cover and finish cooking, removing the wings and breast first as these cook more quickly. Pour off the cooking fat, then add the sauce or garnish specified in the recipe and return the pieces of chicken to the pan. Reheat but do not allow to boil.

Sautéed chicken à la minute POULET SAUTÉ À LA MINUTE Sauté a chicken *à brun* and arrange it in a serving dish. Pour over a little lemon juice and the butter it was cooked in, very hot. Sprinkle generously with chopped parsley.

Sautéed chicken à la niçoise POULET SAUTÉ À LA NIÇOISE Sauté a chicken *à brun* in oil alone; drain it and keep warm. Deglaze the pan with 1 dl (6 tablespoons, scant ½ cup) white wine and 1.5 dl (¼ pint, ⅔ cup) tomato fondue. Add 1 crushed clove of garlic and reduce. Put the chicken back in the sauce and reheat without boiling, then arrange it in a serving dish, surrounded with artichoke quarters cooked in butter, braised courgettes (zucchini), and stoned black (pitted ripe) olives. Pour the sauce over and sprinkle with chopped herbs.

Sautéed chicken Annette POULET SAUTÉ ANNETTE Sauté a chicken *à brun* and prepare a base of Annette potatoes (see *Anna*). Arrange the drained chicken pieces on top of this and keep warm. Deglaze the cooking pan with 1 dl (6 tablespoons, scant ½ cup) white wine; add 1 chopped shallot, reduce, moisten with 1.5 dl (¼ pint, ⅔ cup) chicken stock, reduce a little more, then thicken with 1 tablespoon kneaded butter. Add a squeeze of lemon juice and some chopped parsley, chervil, and tarragon. Pour this sauce over the chicken.

Sautéed chicken with basil POULET SAUTÉ AU BASILIC Sauté the chicken *à brun*. Drain it and arrange on a warm dish. Deglaze the cooking pan with 2 dl (7 fl oz, ¾ cup) dry white wine. Add 1 tablespoon chopped fresh basil and whisk in 50 g (2 oz, 4 tablespoons) butter. Pour this sauce over the chicken.

Sautéed chicken with cep mushrooms POULET SAUTÉ AUX CÈPES Sauté a chicken *à brun* in a mixture of butter and oil in equal quantities. Three-quarters of the way through the cooking time, add 300 g (11 oz, 4 cups) ceps or other mushrooms, sliced and sautéed in oil, then 2 chopped shallots. Finish cooking. Arrange the drained chicken and mushrooms in a serving dish. Deglaze the casserole with 1 dl (6 tablespoons, scant ½ cup) white wine; reduce, then pour it over the chicken and mushrooms. Sprinkle with chopped parsley. A small crushed clove of garlic can be added to the sauce.

Sautéed chicken with cream POULET SAUTÉ À LA CRÈME Sauté a chicken *à blanc*; drain it, arrange on a serving dish, and keep warm. Pour off the cooking fat from the pan, add 1 wine glass of dry cider, and reduce until all the liquid has evaporated. Then mix in 2 dl (7 fl oz, ¾ cup) double (heavy) cream and reduce just enough to make the sauce very smooth; adjust the seasoning. Pour the sauce over the chicken and sprinkle with chopped parsley. The chicken can be flamed in Calvados, or the cider can be replaced with white wine.

Sautéed chicken with oysters POULET SAUTÉ AUX HUÎTRES Sauté a chicken *à blanc*. Poach 12 oysters in their own liquid. Drain the cooked chicken and keep warm in a serving dish. Deglaze the cooking pan with 1 dl (6 tablespoons, scant ½ cup) white wine and the liquid from the oysters; reduce by half and add 1 dl (6 tablespoons, scant ½ cup) chicken velouté sauce. Add a squeeze of lemon juice, then 40 g (1½ oz, 3 tablespoons) butter, whisking all the time. Arrange the oysters around the chicken and pour the sauce over.

Sautéed chicken with tarragon POULET SAUTÉ À L'ESTRAGON Sauté a chicken *à brun*, then drain it and keep warm in a serving dish. Deglaze the cooking pan with 1.5 dl (¼ pint, ⅔ cup) white wine; add 1 chopped shallot, reduce, then add 1.5 dl (¼ pint, ⅔ cup) thickened veal gravy (or chicken or veal stock thickened with a little arrowroot). Finally, add 1 tablespoon lemon juice and 2 tablespoons tarragon leaves, blanched and chopped. Pour this sauce over the chicken.

This dish can also be prepared in the same way as sautéed chicken with cream, replacing the parsley with tarragon. Another variation is to replace the tarragon with a mixture of parsley and chervil (unblanched) and blanched tarragon, all chopped.

Sautéed chicken with vinegar POULET SAUTÉ AU VINAIGRE Peel and dice 2 carrots, 1 turnip, the cleaned white parts of 2 leeks, and 1 stalk (stick) of celery; stud 1 large onion with 2 cloves. Brown the giblets of the chicken, plus those of 2 others, in a little butter. Place all these giblets into a stewpan with 1 litre (1¾ pints, 4¼ cups) cold water and bring to the boil; then add all the vegetables, a bouquet garni, 4 shallots, 2 peeled crushed cloves of garlic, 1 glass of dry white wine, some salt, pepper, and a small pinch of cayenne. Simmer gently for 45 minutes to 1 hour.

Heat 40 g (1½ oz, 3 tablespoons) butter in a flameproof casserole and cook the chicken, cut into 6 pieces, for about 10 minutes until golden brown; cover and simmer for another 35 minutes.

Reduce the liquid in which the giblets were cooked by half, then strain it and add 1 glass of vinegar; reduce again by one-third. Purée the chicken liver. When the chicken is cooked, pour the vinegar sauce into the casserole, stir well, and cook together for 5 minutes; thicken with 1 tablespoon kneaded butter. Dilute the liver purée with 1 tablespoon vinegar and blend into the sauce, away from the heat. Serve very hot.

Stuffed chicken à la mode de Sorges POULET FARCI À LA MODE DE SORGES Fill the inside of a chicken with a forcemeat made up of its liver chopped and mixed with stale breadcrumbs, chopped bacon, parsley, chives, shallots, garlic, salt, pepper, and mustard, and the bird's blood (if available), all bound together with an egg yolk. Truss it as for roasting.

Brown all over in goose fat then place it in a stewpan and cover with boiling water; season with salt and pepper. Bring to the boil, skim, then add 3 carrots and 2 turnips (peeled), the white part of 3 leeks tied together in a bundle, 1 celery heart, 1 onion stuck with a clove, and a few leaves of Swiss chard tied in a bundle. Simmer very gently for about 1¼ hours. Drain the chicken, untruss it, and place it on a dish, surrounded with the vegetables, cutting the carrots and turnips into pieces.

Prepare some Sorges sauce to be served separately: make a highly seasoned vinaigrette, add chopped parsley, chives, and shallots, then bind with the yolks of 2 eggs boiled for 3 minutes. Continue cooking the egg whites for 2 minutes in the chicken stock, dice them, and add to the sauce. As they do in Périgord, serve the strained chicken cooking stock first as a soup, either poured over slices of toast or garnished with large boiled vermicelli.

Spring Chicken

Devilled spring chicken POUSSIN GRILLÉ À LA DIABLE Prepare the spring chicken *en crapaudine*. Sprinkle with salt and pepper, brush lightly with clarified butter on both sides, and half-roast it in a very hot oven. Mix 2 tablespoons mustard with a little cayenne and brush this over the chicken. Coat generously with fresh breadcrumbs and sprinkle with a little clarified butter. Finish cooking under the grill (broiler), on both sides. Serve with gherkins, lemon halves, and a devilled sauce.

Spring chickens à la sicilienne POUSSINS À LA SICILIENNE (from a recipe by Prosper Salles) Boil some pasta shapes in salted water. Drain, reheat for a few minutes in very hot butter, then mix with a purée of pistachio nuts. Sprinkle with salt and pepper and leave to cool. Stuff the chickens with this mixture and truss them, then spit-roast, basting frequently. Three-quarters of the way through cooking, sprinkle with fresh breadcrumbs and allow to colour. Serve the cooking juices as a gravy separately.

chickpea POIS CHICHE

A bushy leguminous plant cultivated in southern Europe for its rounded edible pealike seeds, which are enclosed in pods. The English name is derived from the French *chiche*, from the Latin *cicer*: Cicero is said to have been so nicknamed because of the pea-shaped wart on the end of his nose. The plant originated in the Mediterranean basin and the seeds may be sold dried or precooked in cans.

Dried chickpeas should always be soaked before cooking. They have a very high energy content (361 Cal per 100 g) and are rich in carbohydrates, proteins, phosphorus, calcium, and iron. Used in garnishes, purées, soups, and stews, they feature in numerous dishes in the south of France and also in Spain and the Middle East: olla podrida, puchero, hummus, cocido, etc. They are the traditional garnish for couscous and are used in various preparations with dried beans and even in salads. They can be used as a substitute for lentils, in gratins covered wth Mornay sauce, and they can be ground into flour.

RECIPE

Ragout of mutton with chickpeas RAGOÛT DE MOUTON AUX POIS CHICHES Soak some chickpeas in cold water for at least 12 hours, changing the water several times. Place the peas in a large pan with cold water (2 litres (3½ pints, 4½ pints) per 500 g (18 oz, 2½ cups) peas). Bring to the boil, skim, add some salt, and simmer gently for approximately 2½ hours. Drain.

Prepare a mutton ragout *à la bonne femme* (see *mutton*), but add the chickpeas (instead of potatoes) at the same time as the bacon. Cook for a further 30 minutes.

chicory (endive) ENDIVE

A winter vegetable with tightly bunched white leaves that form a firm elongated heart. In about 1850, a peasant from the Brussels suburbs observed that wild chicory roots cultivated in warmth and shade grew elongated shoots with yellowish edible leaves. Later, a Belgian botanist called Brézier improved the technique of etiolation to produce the modern chicory. It first appeared at Les Halles in Paris in October 1879.

The nomenclature of this vegetable is rather confusing: it is called chicory in England and endive or Belgian endive in the United States (in England, endive is a curly-leaved salad plant called chicory in America). For the sake of clarity, the English nomenclature is used in this article.

Chicory is grown in northern France, Belgium (where it is called *chicon* or *witloof*), and the Netherlands, and is available from October to May. Carefully cleaned and packed, and kept in the dark to prevent it from turning green, the chicory should be firm, shiny, swollen, and unblemished. With a fairly high water content, it contains only 20 Cal per 100 g; it is also a source of potassium and vitamins.

☐ **Chicory for coffee** Certain varieties of chicory in the north of France and in Belgium have been selected for their large smooth roots, which can be used for the manufacture of chicory coffee. These roots are dried, cut, roasted, and then ground to make an infusion. Chicory is produced commercially in the form of grounds, a soluble powder, or as a liquid extract. It gives a bitter and very dark-coloured drink, which is often blended with breakfast coffee. Chicory has been used as a substitute for coffee since 1769, first in Italy, and then in Germany. It does not have the aroma or stimulating properties of coffee.

☐ **Trimming and preparation** Remove any damaged leaves, rinse the chicory quickly in water, dry, and wipe. Avoid soaking it in water, because this makes it bitter. Hollow out a small cone about 2.5 cm (1 in) high from the base using a knife. This is where the bitterness is concentrated. Never scald chicory.

Chicory can be served raw in salads – with vinaigrette and often with hard-boiled (hard-cooked) eggs and any of the various ingredients used in winter salads, such as beetroot (red beets), apples, nuts, cheese, and orange or grapefruit quarters. For cooked dishes,

chicory heads are braised and drained; then they can be coated with béchamel sauce, sprinkled with noisette butter, served with gravy or with plain butter and herbs, topped with grated cheese and then browned, or made into a purée. They can be served as an accompaniment to roasts and poultry. They can also be braised, made into a chiffonade, or prepared as fritters (especially when served with fish). As a main dish, chicory is braised, rolled in slices of ham, and coated with a port and raisin sauce, or stuffed (with a fatty or lean stuffing) and browned on top.

RECIPES

Braised chicory ENDIVES À L'ÉTU-VÉE Trim and wash 1 kg (2¼ lb) chicory and place in a flameproof casserole with 30 g (1 oz, 2 tablespoons) butter, a pinch of salt, the juice of a quarter of a lemon, and ½ dl (2½ tablespoons, 3½ tablespoons) water. Bring quickly to the boil without a lid, then leave to boil over a medium heat for 35 minutes.

The chicory can also be braised by cooking very gently in 50 g (2 oz, 4 tablespoons) butter, with a pinch of salt and a few drops of lemon juice but without water, for 45 minutes.

Chicory au gratin ENDIVES AU GRATIN Braise some chicory heads and drain them thoroughly. Arrange them in a gratin dish that has been buttered and sprinkled with grated cheese (Comté, Gruyère, Parmesan, or even dried Edam), sprinkle the chicory with more grated cheese and melted butter, then brown in a very hot oven.

Chicory fritots ENDIVES EN FRI-TOTS Braise some chicory heads, keeping them fairly firm, then drain thoroughly and leave to cool. Cut them into quarters and steep for 1 hour in olive oil containing some lemon juice and pepper. Drain, dip in batter, and deep-fry in very hot oil (180 c, 350 f). When the fritters have turned golden, remove, sprinkle with fine salt, and serve with fried parsley.

Chicory salad à la flamande SALADE D'ENDIVES À LA FLAMANDE Wash and wipe some fresh chicory. Separate the leaves and divide them in half, trimming if necessary. Wipe thoroughly. Sprinkle lightly with lemon juice to prevent discoloration. Add some diced cooked beetroot (red beet) and garnish with peeled orange quarters. Season with a mustard vinaigrette and sprinkle with chopped hard-boiled (hardcooked) egg yolk and chopped chives.

Chicory with ham ENDIVES AU JAMBON Braise some chicory heads. Prepare some very thick white sauce, (enough for 2–4 tablespoons (3–5 tablespoons) per head) and add 60 g (2 oz) Gruyère cheese per ½ litre (8 fl oz, 1 cup) sauce. Drain the chicory heads, wrap each in a slice of Paris ham, and arrange side by side in a buttered gratin dish. Cover with the hot white sauce, sprinkle with grated Gruyère cheese, and dot with butter. Brown in a very hot oven.

Scallop and chicory cassolettes CASSOLETTES DE SAINT-JACQUES AUX ENDIVES (from Fredy Girardet's recipe) Cut 1 kg (2¼ lb) chicory into 1-cm (½-in) segments, wash, drain, and sprinkle with lemon juice. Season with salt and sugar, add 2 tablespoons groundnut (peanut) oil, and fry for 7–8 minutes in butter without covering the pan. Shell and trim some scallops, put them in a frying pan (skillet), season with salt, pepper, and a little cayenne, and brown (3–4 minutes), keeping them fairly soft. Arrange them in cassolettes on top of the endives. Reduce ½ dl (2½ tablespoons, 3½ tablespoons) port by two-thirds, add the juice of a lemon and 50 g (2 oz) butter cut into pieces, then whisk into an emulsion. Add a little lemon zest, pour over the scallops, and serve.

chiffonnade

A preparation of sorrel, chicory (endive), or lettuce leaves, cut into strips of varying thickness. Cutting *en chiffonnade* consists of shredding green salad leaves on a chopping board to form a julienne. A chiffonnade may be softened in butter, moistened with stock, milk, or cream, and used as a garnish for soup. Lettuce chiffonnade may be used to garnish cold hors d'oeuvres.

RECIPE

Chiffonnade of raw lettuce CHIEFFONNADE DE LAITUE CRUE Wash and dry some lettuce leaves, discarding the coarser leaves. Roll up several leaves and cut each roll into very thin strips. Toss in vinaigrette if it is to be used as a garnish for meat, fish, or cold shellfish. It may also be mixed with green walnuts, a julienne of ham, meat, or cold chicken, and Emmental cheese, and then sprinkled with vinaigrette and chopped herbs.

chill FRAPPER

To cool an item of food, a drink, or a dish quickly. Ice cream (or a similar iced mixture) is chilled by surrounding it with crushed ice or by placing it in the freezer so that it sets. Jellies, cold mousses, terrines, etc., are chilled in the coldest part of the refrigerator prior to serving. When preparing some foods, such as certain forcemeats, the ingredients should be chilled when mixed by placing them in a bowl over crushed ice.

Champagne is chilled by placing the bottle in a bucket of crushed ice and water (never in the refrigerator). A cocktail is chilled by shaking it with ice in a cocktail shaker or pouring a liqueur over crushed ice.

chilli con carne

A Mexican speciality that has become popular in Britain and throughout the United States: it was a typical dish in the cookery of the pioneers of Texas. The name means literally 'chilli peppers with meat', and the authentic dish is a ragout of minced or cubed beef cooked with thinly sliced onions and seasoned with chilli peppers, powdered cumin, and other spices. Red kidney beans are sometimes added during the cooking, although purists object to them.

chilli pepper

See *capsicum*.

Chimay (à la)

The name of various preparations dedicated to the Princess of Chimay (formerly Madame Tallien), who was a regular guest at the sumptuous dinners given by the Vicomte de Barras under the Directory. Chicken *à la Chimay* is a dish of lightly braised chicken stuffed with buttered noodles and forcemeat, coated with gravy, and served with noodles and bunches of asparagus tips. Hard-boiled (hard-cooked) or soft-boiled eggs *à la Chimay* are prepared with mushrooms and cooked *au gratin*.

RECIPE

Hard-boiled (hard-cooked) eggs à la Chimay OEUFS DURS À LA CHIMAY Cut some hard-boiled eggs in half lengthwise and remove the yolks. Pound the yolks in a mortar with an equal amount of very dry mushrooms duxelles. Fill the whites with the mixture and arrange them in a buttered ovenproof dish. Coat with Mornay sauce and sprinkle with grated Gruyère cheese. Moisten with melted butter and bake for a few minutes in a very hot oven.

chimney CHEMINÉE

A small opening made in the pastry lid of a pie before it is placed in the oven, in order to allow steam to escape. The chimney generally has a small tube placed vertically, through which liquid jelly or fresh cream may be poured after cooking; this is removed before serving.

China CHINE

In China, nutrition and cookery have been subjects for discussion and reflection by philosophers, writers, and emperors throughout the centuries. There is no dividing line between philosophy, religion, and food, and everyone is obliged to know about and conform to the rituals associated with meals. Chinese meals have always been full of symbolism. Braised turtle signifies long life, and a ragout of stag with mushrooms means a favourable result and success in an undertaking.

Another fundamental feature of Chinese cookery is the quest for harmony, which is achieved through contrasts. A crisp dish is followed by a creamy preparation and a spicy course is served with a sweet garnish. The originality and subtlety of this cuisine is expressed by the mixture of four basic flavours (sour, salt, bitter, and sweet) in the same dish. For example, thinly sliced pork with scrambled eggs and lily flowers is served with black mushrooms, a plum sauce, and small salted pancakes.

☐ **Extravagance and mystery** Because of its paramount importance for centuries, Chinese cuisine has inevitably become more complicated in its struggle for perfection, and has become, to Western eyes, a somewhat terrifying mystery. Lao Tseu compared the art of governing the Chinese Empire to that of frying a small fish. Furthermore, in China, the preoccupation with diet has always played an equal part in the quest for flavour, with frequent developments in the direction of aphrodisiac recipes, such as sharks' fins, swallows' nests, tigers' bones, and hundred-year-old eggs. Finally, the traditional repertoire of Chinese recipes, which originates from the great mandarin tradition, includes dishes prepared from bears' palms, carps' lips, rhinoceroses' armpits, or frogs' stomachs, which combine flavour, aroma, and colour. The medicinal properties of these dishes were thought to be enhanced by magical properties.

☐ **The basic principles** Cooking methods were conditioned by the acute lack of fuel in China. Cooks invented dishes that were cooked on embers in 10–15 minutes, hence the basic feature in Chinese cookery of cutting all items of food into small pieces. This also enables the food to be easily impregnated by the seasonings. Ingredients may be cut into cubes, thin strips, dice, small sticks, round slices, or 'grains of rice', depending on the type of food being cooked. Cutting is also decorative – spring onion (scallion) 'feathers', tomato petals, and turnips or carrots shaped into stars. Cooks spend more time perfecting the mixtures than cooking them, and the art of obtaining the correct proportions is also fundamentally important. The most frequently used method of cooking is stir-frying, which retains all the natural juice and flavour of the foods – crisp vegetables and underdone beef, in particular. There are many soups, which are always cooked over a brisk heat and their garnishes are never allowed to become sticky. Stocks, which often form part of sauces, are always very clear. Finally, the artistic presentation of the dish is important, for the dish must appeal to the guest through his senses of sight and smell, and sometimes through touch and hearing. For example, a soup made with shrimps, ham, mushrooms and bamboo shoots is garnished with rice croûtes that may distinctly be heard to crackle!

☐ **Everyday cookery and regional recipes** The courses of a traditional Chinese meal are presented in a different order from those of a European meal: first cold dishes, then hot dishes, then a light soup, and finally, perhaps, a dessert. For a ceremonial meal, a thick soup is served, and a large festive dish, such as Peking duck, is also provided. This is followed by a light broth and then sweetmeats.

Rice is not necessarily the main accompaniment. North China produces and consumes little rice, steam-cooked bread rolls being eaten instead, and in central China pancakes are the usual accompaniment. Rice is placed on the table from the start of the meal in individual bowls. Good manners require that the rice is renewed at the end of the meal, but through politeness, no one touches it. (To do so would mean that people were still hungry.) Tea is not drunk at table, and meals are served with either a rice or sorghum wine, or even beer.

In the north, the delicate highly seasoned food is simmered, but may also be stir-fried (in the wok). The famous specialities of Peking are the most ancient dishes and include sweet and sour pork, beef sautéed with ginger, and eight-treasure rice pudding (a colourfully decorated dessert). In the east, soy sauce is the main ingredient for flavouring dishes and the method is known as 'red cooking'. Many seafood dishes are prepared and also soups, fritters, and pancakes (swallow's-nest soup originates from here). In western and central China, dried fish is popular, and mushrooms are an important ingredient in various dishes. Desserts often consist of crystallized (candied) fruits, such as kumquats. In the south, cookery is dominated by preparations of seafood such as stuffed perch, crab fritters, abalones in oyster sauce, shrimps with rice noodles, and shark's-fin soup.

☐ **Culinary resources** Several basic foods are eaten throughout China, particularly eggs. Fresh eggs may be fried, steamed, salted (like the famous 'hundred-years-old' duck eggs), or braised (hard-boiled and then simmered with onions and consommé). There is a great variety of noodles and vermicelli made from rice, soya, or wheat. Vegetables are always selected according to their texture and their taste. They are often steamed – a method of cooking used almost as much as stir-frying. This also applies to freshwater fish and shellfish, which are never eaten raw. There is a sufficient variety of fresh fruits to make desserts. They include lychees, longans, mangoes, and papayas, possibly served with almond sablés or sesame fritters, and always with tea!

The majority of Chinese recipes may be made with the same basic foods used in the West, including fresh cod, beff, cauliflower, and onion. Nevertheless, there are certain exotic products that are specifically Chinese. The vegetables include: black mushrooms and scented or 'straw' mushrooms; lily flowers (a dried yellow slightly sweet vegetable); soya beans, used in various ways (as seeds, bean sprouts, as an oil, or as soy sauce); lotus seeds, leaves, and roots; red dates; seaweed; water chestnuts; Chinese cabbage; bamboo shoots; and banana leaves. Seafood includes abalones, jellyfish (dried into small flat cakes that are finely sliced for salads), smoked eel, and fish bladders (a greatly prized ingredient of soups and stir-fried dishes). Among river fish, pike and carp are particularly enjoyed.

There are several varieties of rice, including gluey rice and scented rice. Spices, seasonings, and condiments are indispensable in Chinese cookery, especially 'five spices', star anise, ginger, Si-chouan black pepper, lemon balm, coriander, tangerine peel, monosodium glutamate, oyster sauce, and sesame sauce. Milk and its products are rare in Chinese cuisine.

Drinks naturally include tea; soya milk and syrup of sesame or ginseng seeds are also widely consumed. Rice wine, commonly known as yellow wine, is today used as a condiment in cookery and is served warm. The best known liqueur is *mei kuei lu* (rose dew), distilled from sorghum blended with rose petals. It is drunk during meals, between courses.

☐ **Table manners and customs** The simple place setting comprises a bowl and a plate, chopsticks, and a spoon. For a festive occasion, a wineglass, a tea cup, and a second bowl are added. In a Chinese restaurant it is customary to pass round hot scented table napkins after a fatty dish or one which has to be eaten with the fingers. At a family meal all the dishes are placed on the table simultaneously. It is easy to choose and mix, nothing is wasted, and a guest may be invited without notice. At the same time, the meal retains its intimate character. The festive meal has a succession of courses – usually between 12 and 20 – which include hot and cold dishes. The place of honour, which is allotted to the oldest guest, faces south and is opposite the entrance door of the dining room. Traditionally, women sat on one side of the table and men on the other.

Chinese cuisine was one of the first foreign cuisines to be introduced into Europe, and innumerable Chinese restaurants were firmly established in capital cities throughout the world. It has always been highly esteemed and has stimulated considerable interest.

Chinese artichoke
CROSNE

A plant cultivated for its edible tubers. Originating in Japan, this delicate vegetable was brought to France by the agronomist Pailleux and first cultivated in 1882 at Crosne (Essonne). Chinese artichokes have a slightly sweet taste, similar to that of the Jerusalem artichoke; once cleaned and blanched, they may be fried, cooked slowly in butter, or prepared like Jerusalem artichokes (see also (à la) japonaise). The Chinese artichoke was a very popular exotic vegetable between 1890 and 1920 but since then its popularity has declined, despite its delicate flavour, because it dries out quickly and takes a long time to peel.

| RECIPE

Preparation of Chinese artichokes
PRÉPARATION DES CROSNES Place the Chinese artichokes in a strong linen cloth with a handful of sea salt and shake them vigorously. Wash them and remove all the remaining skin. Blanch slightly in salted water, then cook them slowly in butter in a pan with the lid on, without letting them colour. Prepared in this way, Chinese artichokes may be served as a vegetable or as a garnish for roasts. They may also be dressed with cream, herbs, or gravy.

Chinese cabbage or Chinese leaves
CHOU CHINOIS

Of the numerous varieties of Chinese cabbage, two are generally available in European markets in the autumn: pe-tsai and pak-choi (bok choy). They are also available salted, in vinegar, or sweetened.

• *Pe-tsai* resembles a large cos (romaine) lettuce; the heart reaches 40 –45 cm (15–19 in) and its irregularly serrated leaves extend to the base of their stalks. It is eaten raw and finely shredded in salads or is poached in gravy or sweet-and-sour sauce.

• *Pak-choi* does not form a heart; its white and fleshy leaf stalks somewhat resemble celery stalks and it is served in the same way as celery. The elongated leaves have smooth edges and are 20 –50 cm (8–9 in) long.

In Chinese cookery, sautéed or braised cabbage, cut into thin strips, accompanies pork, fish, and shellfish, rather as a condiment than a true vegetable.

| RECIPE

Szechwan-style Chinese cabbage
CHOU CHINOIS À LA SSEU-TCH'OUANNAISE Clean a Chinese cabbage and cut it into pieces about 3 cm (1¼ in) long. Wash, blanch, cool, and drain. Heat 3 tablespoons oil in a frying pan (skillet). Chop a large clove of garlic and lightly brown it in the oil. Add the cabbage, a little Szechwan pepper, and some salt; stir well and leave to cook for 1 minute. Then add 1 teaspoon marc brandy and 1 teaspoon caster (superfine) sugar and stir well for 1 minute. Adjust the seasoning and serve very hot.

chinois

A conical strainer with a handle. There are various models: the chinois with a metallic mesh is used for straining broths, sauces, fine creams, syrups, and jellies, which need to be very smooth; the perforated tinplate chinois is used to strain thick sauces, which are pressed through with a pestle to remove the lumps.

chinois confit

The French name for a small bitter Chinese orange, macerated in several syrups of increasing concentration, then drained and crystallized (candied). The tree that produces this fruit is native to China but grows wild in Sicily. The chinois is usually green as it is picked before it is ripe, when it is considered to be at its best for crystallization.

Chinon

A red, rosé, or white AOC wine of the Loire. The area extends over the left bank and to the banks of the Vienne, its tributary, around the ruins of the castle where Joan of Arc came to find the Dauphin (Charles VII) and encouraged him to 'kick the English out of France'. Later, Rabelais, whose family had a vineyard at the foot of the citadel, sang the praises of the wine of Chinon. He called it 'this good Breton wine that does not grow in Brittany', because Chinon is made from the Cabernet Franc grape, known locally as the 'Breton'. White Chinon loses by comparison with Vouvray and Chinon rosé is at a disadvantage alongside the rosés of Anjou, but red Chinon, delicate, smooth and light, can improve with age and develops a charming bouquet, evocative of violets. Sparkling and *pétillant* (semi-sparkling) white wines are also made here.

chinonaise (à la)

In classic French cookery, a garnish for large joints of meat comprising potatoes sprinkled with chopped parsley and small balls of green cabbage stuffed with sausagemeat and braised.

In the region of Chinon, hare and lamprey, lightly browned in walnut oil, are also described as *à la chinonaise*.

chipolata

A small fresh sausage, about 2 cm (⅔ in) in diameter, made with medium or coarsely chopped sausagemeat enclosed in a natural casing (sheep's intestine) or a synthetic one. Chipolatas are eaten fried or grilled. The name comes from the Italian word *cipolla* (onion), and was originally applied to stew made with onions and small sausages.

RECIPE

Chipolatas with risotto CHIPOLATAS AU RISOTTO Prepare some risotto, place it in a buttered savarin mould, turn it out onto the serving dish, and keep hot. Lightly prick some chipolatas and quickly brown them in butter in a sauté pan. Add some white wine (1 glass for 6 sausages) and finish cooking with the lid half on. Arrange the chipolatas on the crown of risotto and keep hot. Add ½ glass well-reduced consommé to the pan juices, reduce by a half, and pour over the sausages.

chipolata (à la)

A garnish for game, braised poultry, meat, or eggs consisting of braised chestnuts, small glazed onions, glazed carrots, sautéed mushrooms, blanched and lightly fried strips of bacon, and fried chipolatas. The garnish may be bound with reduced Madeira sauce.

In classic French cookery, the term describes a pudding based on pig's kidney, forcemeat, and small sausages.

RECIPE

Pudding à la chipolata Stone (pit) 12 Agen prunes and steep for 1 hour in red wine. Brown a thinly sliced pig's kidney and a chopped shallot in some butter in a pan. Drain and flame with rum. Make a forcemeat with 200 g (7 oz) lean pork and an equal quanity of finely chopped veal. Flavour with mixed spice and salt. Cook *al dente* 4 tablespoons (⅓ cup) large macaroni. Grease and flour a fine cloth. Mix the kidney, macaroni, forcemeat, and prunes with 16 chipolatas and tie the mixture very tightly in the cloth. Poach for 1 hour in either a chicken broth or a very concentrated stock. Untie the pudding and serve hot with a charcutière sauce.

chips (French fries)

See *pont-neuf potatoes.*

chique

A large bonbon made of cooked sugar filled with almonds and flavoured with mint, aniseed, or lemon. Chiques from Montluçon and Allauch (Bouches-du-Rhône) are famous.

chiqueter

A French culinary term meaning to indent the margins of vol-au-vent cases, pies, cheese straws, etc., with a small knife. This helps them to swell during cooking and is decorative.

Chiroubles

One of the Beajoulais regional wines, smooth, light, and fruity, and possibly the one that, of them all, is the most enjoyable when drunk young and cool.

chives CIBOULETTE

An alliaceous plant, related to the spring onion (scallion), that produces small elongated bulbs and clumps of tubular green leaves. The leaves are chopped and used for seasoning salads, omelettes, etc.

Chivry

A flavoured butter containing herbs that may be used with cold hors d'oeuvres. It is also used to flavour Chivry sauces. The Chivry sauce served with fish is made with a fish stock, while the sauce served with poached chicken or soft-boiled or poached eggs is prepared with a chicken velouté.

RECIPES

Chivry butter BEURRE CHIVRY To prepare about 250 g (9 oz, generous cup) butter, use 150 g (5 oz) parsley, tarragon, chervil, chives, and, if possible, burnet, and 20 g (¾ oz, scant ¼ cup) chopped shallot. Blanch the mixture for 3 minutes in boiling water, drain, cool immediately in cold water, and wipe dry. Chop very finely (or pound in a mortar), add (7 oz, generous ¼ cup) butter, season with salt and pepper, and rub through a fine sieve.

Chivry sauce for eggs and poultry SAUCE CHIVRY POUR OEUFS ET VOLAILLES Put 1 dl (6 tablespoons, scant ½ cup) dry white wine, 1 teaspoon finely chopped shallot, and 1 tablespoon chopped chervil and tarragon in a small saucepan. Reduce by half. Add 3 dl (¼ pint, ⅓ cup) chicken velouté and reduce by a third. Finally add 2 generous tablespoons (3 generous tablespoons) Chivry butter and rub through a fine sieve.

chlodnik

An iced soup of Polish origin, common to several Slavonic countries. The word literally means refreshment. The soup is made with sorrel, beetroot (red beet) leaves, and cucumber purée. It is sometimes thickened with wheat semolina, flavoured with fennel and tarragon, and garnished with various ingredients, such as slices of hard-boiled (hard-cooked) eggs, crayfish, and fresh diced cucumber.

chocart or choquart

A large puff pastry turnover filled with a thick apple purée flavoured with cinnamon and lemon zest. Chocarts are eaten hot and are a speciality of Yffiniac (Côtes-du-Nord). They are prepared in large quantities for the *fête des Chocarts* in November.

chocolate CHOCOLAT

A food product consisting essentially of a mixture of cocoa and sugar, to which milk, honey, dried fruits, etc., may be added.

The first French chocolate factory was situated in Bayonne, where a guild of chocolate-makers had existed since 1761. The city exported chocolate to Spain and Paris, and its trade calendar of 1822 quotes more than 20 prestigious firms. (Cocoa also provided a nutritious food for the fishermen of Saint-Pierre-et-Miquelon.)

In 1778 the first hydraulic machine for crushing and mixing the chocolate paste appeared in France, and in 1819 Pelletier built the first factory to use steam. It was at about this time that the famous family businesses were set up in Europe: Van Houten in the Netherlands (1815) – C. J. Van Houten discovered a method of solubilization in 1828 (now known as 'dutched' in English); Menier in France (1824); Cadbury and Rowntree in England; and Suchard, Nestlé, Lindt, and Kohler in Switzerland. Docteur Peter, a Swiss, was responsible for the invention of milk chocolate in 1818. After 1850, the chocolate industry was developed throughout the world.

Chocolate is not only used in confectionary but is also an essential ingredient of numerous cakes, pastries, desserts, etc.

☐ **Chocolate and dietetics** Soon after its introduction into France, the medical profession considered chocolate to be a panacea for fevers and chest or stomach illnesses. Cocoa was registered in the Codex in 1758, and the confectioners of the 18th and 19th centuries gladly became apothecaries: chocolate was believed to have medicinal properties and various types of medicinal chocolates were sold by Debauve (a former pharmacist of Louis XVI) and others of his profession. These included purgatives, cough mixtures, aids to digestion, aids to put on weight, antispasmodics (with orange blossom), anti-inflammatories (with milk of almonds), tonics, carminatives, etc. The expression health chocolate, for the mixture containing only sugar and cocoa, remained common until the beginning of the 20th century.

Chocolate is a concentrated food with a high energy value: 100 g (4 oz) chocolate produces about 500 Cal (the equivalent of nine eggs or three slices of ham).

According to whether or not it contains milk, chocolate contains 55–62% glucose, 30% lipids, and 2–9% proteins, as well as potassium, calcium, magnesium, iron, and vitamin D. Contrary to popular belief, it does not by itself have any harmful effect upon the liver.

☐ **The various products of the chocolate industry**

• Cocoa powder is normally unsweetened and may include an alkalizing agent to render it more soluble and milder-tasting.

• Powdered or drinking chocolate is a mixture of sugar and cocoa consisting of at least 32% cocoa. If the mixture contains other ingredients, in particular certain types of flour, it is not a true chocolate product.

• Chocolate covering (coating), called *couverture* in French, is made of chocolate containing a higher proportion of cocoa butter or other fat, which lowers its melting point. It is sold either in a solid or a liquid form and is intended mainly for moulding, for coating different types of confectionery, for covering biscuits (cookies), or for decorating cakes.

• The different categories of chocolate (e.g. cooking chocolate, milk chocolate, milk cooking chocolate) may contain up to 40% milk, almonds, hazelnuts, puffed rice, or other products. They are manufactured as filled or plain blocks, sticks, or bars.

☐ **The quality of chocolate** The quality of chocolate depends both on the quality of the raw materials and on the care taken at the different stages of manufacture: roasting and crushing the cocoa beans and mixing the cocoa paste or 'mass' with sugar and possibly milk.

A good chocolate is shiny brown, breaks cleanly, and is free of lumps, tiny burst bubbles, and white specks. It melts on the tongue like butter, has a true aroma of chocolate rather than of cocoa powder, and is neither greasy nor sticky.

The more cocoa butter it contains, the softer and creamier is the chocolate. The less it contains, the harder and more brittle it is. The more bitter the chocolate, the more flavour it has.

Chocolate without milk in it may be kept for many months (or even years) if it is protected from damp and stored at a temperature of about 18 C, (64.4 F).

For cakes and desserts, it is best to choose a chocolate with a high cocoa content; the aroma may be intensified by adding unsweetened cocoa. For coating, decoration, icing, or making fondants, special *couverture* chocolate is used. The basis of chocolate cakes is often a sponge cake mixture, a Genoese cake mixture, or a meringue. *Sachertorte*, *Doboschtorte* (made with caramel and chocolate), and Black Forest gâteau bear witness to the quality of chocolate patisserie in Germany and Austria. Italy is renowned for the *pan pepato* of Ferrara (a brioche flavoured with cocoa, sweetened with honey, enriched with almonds and lemon zest, coated with chocolate, and decorated with sweets), the traditional New Year's

Eve cake and Sicilian cassata. In France, the great classics are the Queen of Sheba (a sponge cake filled and coated with chocolate), the tête de nègre, the Yule log, the dacquoise, marble cake, pavés, and the various desserts that are decorated with chocolate vermicelli or grated chocolate. Chocolate can also be added to confectioners' custards (pastry creams) and it may be mixed with butter (see *ganache*) and used as a filling, for example in éclairs and choux. It may also be used in the sauce that coats profiteroles, nègre en chemise, Belle-Hélène fruits, puddings, brioches, or iced desserts.

Chocolate is a basic flavouring for ices, ice-cream desserts, and cooked custard creams. It is also used in various charlottes, soufflés, and mousses.

In biscuit (cookie) making, it may be used as a filling or a coating, and in Viennese baking it is used to make small chocolate loaves.

Chocolate is used extensively in confectionery for making a great variety of bouchées, truffles, chocolates, Easter eggs, etc. Demel, the celebrated Viennese pâtisserie, is the sole producer of a rare delicacy – whole cocoa beans coated with fine chocolate. In France, there is small-scale production of very famous chocolate confectionery, such as those of Bayonne, Lourdes, Bordeaux, Grenoble, Chambéry, and Lyons. But some industrial firms have also acquired a reputation for producing certain types of high-quality chocolate that are consumed in much greater quantities.

The use of chocolate in savoury cookery is less well-known. Chocolate was commonly used by the Aztecs, and one of the great dishes of Mexican cookery is still *mole poblano de guajolote* (a turkey stew with unsweetened chocolate, flavoured with chilli peppers and sesame). In 1869, Baron Brisse suggested cooking scoter (a type of sea duck) with chocolate. In Spain, two dishes use bitter chocolate in a sauce: calf's tongue and langouste, specialities of Aragon. Finally, in Sicily, there is a popular recipe for jugged hare with chocolate.

RECIPES

Chocolate cake GÂTEAU AU CHOCOLAT Preheat the oven to about 190 C (375 F, gas 5). Sieve 125 g (4½ oz, generous cup) flour. Break 3 eggs, separating the white from the yolks. Add 125 g (4½ oz, scant ⅔ cup, firmly packed) sugar to the yolks and beat with a wooden spoon until the mixture has increased in volume and has become foamy.

Break 150 g (5 oz) unsweetened cooking chocolate into small pieces in a saucepan. Heat it gently with 3 tablespoons (2 fl oz, ¼ cup) milk in a bain-marie with the lid on. Whip the egg whites into very stiff peaks with a pinch of salt.

Blend 125 g (4½ oz, generous ½ cup) softened butter with the chocolate, stir until it has melted and become smooth (possibly adding 1 tablespoon instant coffee) and then pour the chocolate mixture into a warm mixing bowl. Immediately add the mixture of egg yolks and sugar and stir briskly. Then add the sifted flour and quickly blend in the stiff egg whites.

Pour the mixture into a buttered manqué mould and bake in the oven for about 45 minutes. During this time, prepare a caramel with 2 tablespoons (3 tablespoons) sugar, 1 tablespoon water, and 1 tablespoon vinegar. Roll 10 walnuts in the caramel, and set aside on an oiled plate.

When the cake is cooked, leave it to cool in its mould, and prepare a chocolate icing (frosting) according to the recipe below. Turn out the cold cake onto a rack above a dish. Pour the icing over the cake and spread it over the top and sides with a palette knife. Decorate with the walnuts and keep in a cool place until ready to serve.

Chocolate ice cream GLACE AU CHOCOLAT Place 8 egg yolks and 200 g (7 oz, scant cup, firmly packed) sugar in a bowl and beat the mixture with a wooden spoon until it forms a ribbon. Melt 250 g (9 oz, 1½ cups) grated cooking (unsweetened) chocolate in a covered pan with 2 dl (7 fl oz, ¾ cup) water. Add 1 litre (1¾ pints, 4¼ cups) boiling milk to the chocolate and stir well until the mixture is completely smooth. Pour the boiling chocolate mixture over the mixture of sugar and egg yolks and cook over a very gentle heat until the cream coats the spoon. Then dip the saucepan in cold water to prevent further cooking and continue to beat until the cream is luke warm. Stir it occasionally until it is completely cold. Complete the ice cream in the usual way.

For a richer ice cream, 2 dl (7 fl oz, ¾ cup) of the milk may be replaced by the same volume of fresh cream, and 10 egg yolks may be used instead of 8.

Chocolate icing (frosting) GLAÇAGE AU CHOCOLAT Sift 100 g (4 oz, 1 cup) icing (confectioners') sugar. Melt 125 g (4½ oz) cooking (unsweetened) chocolate in a bain-marie, working it with a wooden spoon. Add the sifted icing sugar, then 60 g (2½ oz, 5 tablespoons) softened butter (in small pieces). Continue to stir until the mixture is completely melted and remove from the heat. Then dilute gradually with 6 tablespoons (scant ½ cup) cold water. Use the icing (frosting) when slightly warm.

Chocolate sauce SAUCE AU CHOCOLAT Melt 100 g (4 oz) cooking (unsweetened) chocolate in a bain-marie with 1 dl (6 tablespoons, scant ½ cup) milk and 20 g (¾ oz, 1½ tablespoons) butter. When the mixture is completely smooth, add 30 g (1½ oz, 2½ tablespoons) sugar and 1 generous tablespoon fresh cream. Bring to the boil, stirring continuously, then remove at once from the heat.

chocolate (beverage)
CHOCOLAT
A cold or hot drink made by mixing chocolate or cocoa in water or milk.

It was in the form of a drink that chocolate was discovered in Mexico and then introduced into Europe by the Spanish. The Aztecs prepared a highly spiced beverage (*xocoatl*) with cocoa beans that were roasted, pounded in a mortar, and mixed and flavoured with pepper, chillis, vanilla, annatto (to dye it red), and sometimes honey and dried flowers. The emperor Montezuma had *xocoatl* of different colours served in gold cups at the end of the meals. The

people also consumed large quantities of chocolate in the form of a thick paste, often thickened with cornflour.

The Jesuits were the first to improve this exotic product in order to make a profit from it. Chocolate, at this time, was always prepared with water, but it was very sweet and flavoured with vanilla, strengthened with ambergris and musk. Soon, chocolate became fashionable among the high society of Spain.

In 1615, Ann of Austria introduced this novelty to the French court, and her maids of honour circulated the recipes. Even under Louis XIV, who had little sympathy for his queen's liking for this drink, chocolate was still regarded as a curiosity. It was in England that it became customary to prepare it with milk, and even to add Madeira and beaten eggs. The Church did not consider that chocolate broke the fast (although doctors thought it more nourishing than beef and mutton), and the days of Lent became agreeably sweetened! Society ladies had the drink served in church during the sermons. The Marquise de Sévigné wrote: 'The day before yesterday, I took some chocolate to digest my dinner in order to sup well, and I took some yesterday evening so as to nourish myself well and be able to fast until the evening: that is why I find it pleasant, because it acts according to the purpose.'

☐ **A rapid rise in popularity** In about 1670, Paris had only one chocolate merchant, but in 1705 an edict allowed café owners to sell it by the cup, like coffee. It was not until the time of the Regency, under Louis XV, that chocolate became fashionable in high society. To be admitted to the 'Regent's chocolate' was a special honour. The Marquise de Sévigné then retracted her previous statements and wrote: 'All those who spoke well of it to me now speak badly. It is cursed, accused of all the ills that one has, it is the cause of vapours and palpitations.' Nevertheless, chocolate had become part of the way of life. It was served at collations (light meals), drunk at breakfast, and served with the afternoon snack.

It was in Austria, Spain, and France, the countries where most chocolate was drunk, that chocolate powder began to be retailed during the 19th century. Balzac did not think highly of it: 'Who knows whether the abuse of chocolate has not had something to do with the debasement of the Spanish nation, which, at the time of the discovery of chocolate, was about to recreate the Roman Empire.' But Brillat-Savarin rose to its defence: 'Chocolate is one of the most powerful restoratives. Let any man who has spent working a considerable portion of the time that should be spent sleeping, let any man of wit who feels himself temporarily become stupid, let any man who finds the air damp, the time long, and the atmosphere difficult to tolerate, let any man who is tormented by an obsession that prevents him from thinking clearly, let all those men dose themselves with a good half-litre of amber-coloured chocolate . . and they will see a miracle.'

Today, thanks to instant products, chocolate may be quickly prepared. However, true hot chocolate needs to be prepared the previous day in order to be full of flavour and frothy. As Brillat-Savarin had already recommended, on the advice of a mother superior: 'When you wish to take some good chocolate, make it the evening before in an earthenware coffee-pot, and leave it. The night rest concentrates it and gives it a smoothness that improves it.'

| RECIPES

Foamy chocolate CHOCOLAT MOUSSEUX For 1 litre (1¾ pints, 4¼ cups) milk, allow 200–250 g (7–9 oz) chocolate and 1 tablespoon vanilla-flavoured sugar (or a pinch of powdered cinnamon). Break the chocolate into small pieces in a saucepan and heat gently. When the chocolate begins to soften, add the chosen flavouring together with a small cup of boiling milk. Beat the chocolate thoroughly with a whisk. Then gradually pour in the rest of the hot milk. Warm over a gentle heat, whisking all the time to make the chocolate foamy. 1 dl (6 tablespoons, scant ½ cup) thin cream may also be added to it, or the vanilla (or cinnamon) may be replaced by 1 tablespoon instant coffee.

Iced chocolate CHOCOLATE FRAPPÉ Prepare a foamy chocolate as in the recipe above but reduce the quantity of chocolate to 125–150 g (4½–5 oz) and add 2–3 tablespoons (3–4 tablespoons) caster (superfine) sugar. Allow the chocolate to cool completely and then put it in a blender, adding crushed ice. Serve immediately.

Viennese chocolate CHOCOLAT VIENNOIS Melt 200 g (7 oz) chocolate in a bain-marie with a cup of milk. Stir, while letting it come to the boil, for about 10 minutes. Heat ¾ litre (1¼ pints, 1½ pints) milk with 1 tablespoon sugar. Pour it into a saucepan and whisk for 5 minutes. Make a Chantilly cream by whisking 5 tablespoons (6 tablespoons) double (heavy) cream with 15 g (1½ oz, 2 tablespoons) icing (confectioners') sugar and flavour with vanilla. Pour the chocolate into cups and top each with a dome of Chantilly cream.

chocolate pot
CHOCOLATIÈRE
A tall vessel for serving hot chocolate. It is often shaped like a truncated cone or like a jug, with a spout and a horizontal wooden handle. The chocolate pot has a lid pierced with a hole for a beater to pass through. This is intended to make the chocolate foam when it is poured into the cups. The pot may be made of silver-plated metal, solid silver, porcelain, or earthenware. The first models, which came from Spain with Maria-Theresa of Austria, appeared in France under Louis XIV.

chocolates
BOUCHÉES AU CHOCOLAT
Confectionery made from chocolate or covered in chocolate.

There are many different types of filled chocolate; the filling may consist of coloured and flavoured fondant cream, praline, almond paste, soft caramel, nougat, liqueur, liqueur soaked fruit, etc. The chocolate coating is very liquid when hot and rich in cocoa butter. In the case of liqueurs, these are first poured into starch moulds to crystallize; the liqueur sweets are then removed from the starch and carefully brushed before being coated. Fruit, such as cherries in brandy, are first dipped in fondant and then coated in chocolate; after about two weeks, the moisture from the cherry causes the fondant layer to liquefy, producing a cherry liqueur.

The coating for moulded chocolates is poured into moulds, which are immediately turned over, thereby emptying most of the chocolate and leaving only a thin film, which forms the outside of the chocolate. The filling is then poured into the mould and allowed to set. Finally the chocolates are sealed with chocolate coating, which becomes the base.

French regional specialities include *bouchons de champagne*, *cabaches de Châlons* (chocolate praline sweets iced (frosted) with pistachio-flavoured sugar), *chardons des Alpes* (white chocolate balls filled with liqueur), *granits de Sémur-en-Auxois* (toasted almond clusters dipped in orange-flavoured white chocolate), *guignes de Bordeaux* (cherries in brandy, coated in chocolate, with the stalk sticking out), *joyaux de Bourgogne* (white chocolate shells tinted green or pink and filled with almond paste), *mojettes de Poitou* (small bean-shaped chocolates), *quernoux d'Angers* (nougatine dipped in white chocolate that has been tinted blue and shaped like small roofing slates), *muscadins nantais* (truffles stuffed with grapes), etc.

chocolate truffle

TRUFFE EN CHOCOLAT

Confectionery made of chocolate, melted with butter or cream, sugar, and sometimes eggs, then flavoured (with brandy, rum, whisky, vanilla, cinnamon, coffee, etc.) and shaped into balls, which are coated with chocolate or rolled in cocoa powder.

Chocolate truffles, which keep only for a short time, are traditionally given at Christmas in France. They are a good accompaniment to coffee. *Muscadines* are long truffles, immersed in chocolate then sprinkled with icing (confectioners') sugar. Chambéry truffles, or *truffettes*, a speciality of the town, are made of praline mixed with chocolate, fondant icing, and butter, then coated with cocoa powder and sugar or rolled in grated chocolate.

RECIPES

Chocolate truffles with butter TRUFFES EN CHOCOLAT AU BEURRE To make 20 truffles, melt in a bain-marie 250 g (9 oz) plain (semisweet) chocolate with 1 tablespoon milk. When the mixture is very smooth, add 100 g (4 oz, ½ cup) butter in small pieces and mix well. Blend in 2 egg yolks, then 50 ml (3 tablespoons, ¼ cup) fresh cream and 125 g (4½ oz, 1 cup) icing (confectioners') sugar. Leave in the refrigerator for 24 hours. Shape the truffles rapidly, spooning out the paste with a teaspoon and rolling it into walnut-sized balls on a marble surface with the palm of the hand. Drop them one by one into a bowl containing 50 g (2 oz, ½ cup) unsweetened cocoa powder, twisting the bowl to coat the truffles with cocoa. Store in a cool place.

Chocolate truffles with cream TRUFFES EN CHOCOLAT À LA CRÈME (from Dominique Nahmais's recipe) Melt 300 g (11 oz) dark bitter chocolate and 75 g (3 oz, ¾ cup) pure cocoa with ½ cup strong coffee in a bain-marie. Mix well. Heat 250 ml (10 fl oz, 1¼ cups) double (heavy) cream and, as soon as it starts to boil, mix with the chocolate paste. Remove from the heat and leave for a few hours in a cool place. Pipe into small balls on aluminium foil, leave in a cool place for 1½ hours, then roll in pure cocoa powder.

Truffles in paprika TRUFFES AU PAPRIKA (from André Daguin's recipe) Melt 150 g (5 oz) cooking chocolate (unsweetened chocolate). Add 1 glass boiling whipping cream and mix well. Leave to cool. Finely chop 40 g (1½ oz) prunes in Armagnac and incorporate into the paste. Shape into small balls and roll in a mixture of half bitter cocoa, half mild paprika. Store in a cold place.

choesels

A speciality of Belgian cookery consisting of a ragout made with various kinds of meat and offal, especially beef pancreas, simmered with onions and beer.

RECIPE

Choesels à la bruxelloise (from a recipe by Paul Bouillard) Clean and

blanch a choice calf's sweetbread, cool
it under a press, and cut it into thin
slices. Cut an oxtail into pieces. Clean a
heifer's kidney and cut it into pieces.
Peel and finely slice 100 g (4 oz, 1 cup)
onions. Heat 100 g (4 oz, ½ cup) clarified beef dripping in a frying pan (skillet), add the pieces of oxtail and sweetbread, and brown gently for 45 minutes.
Then add 1 kg (2¼ lb) breast of veal cut
into even-sized pieces, together with the
thinly sliced onions. Brown again, still
stirring, for 30 minutes. Add the pieces
of kidney. When they have stiffened,
add 3 dl (½ pint, 3¼ cups) lambic
(Belgian beer), a bouquet garni, salt,
and a dash of cayenne. Cook very gently
for 30 minutes. Finally, add a bottle of
lambic and 5 dl (17 fl oz, 2 cups)
mushroom stock to the choesels.

Choiseul

A preparation of poached sole or fillets
of sole coated with a white wine sauce
containing a julienne of blanched
truffles.

Choisy

Any of various preparations containing
lettuce. The Choisy garnish for meat
(tournedos steak, veal chops, or rib of
veal) combines château potatoes with
braised lettuce. Choisy omelette is filled
with a creamed lettuce chiffonnade and
surrounded by a thin border of cream
sauce. Sole Choisy is poached, coated
with white wine sauce, and garnished
with a julienne of lettuce and
mushrooms. Potage Choisy is a cream
of lettuce soup.

chope

A large cylindrical goblet with a handle,
used for drinking beer. (The word
comes from the German *schoppen*.) It
appeared in France in about 1845, at the
time when the great Paris brasseries
were set up. The chope is made of stoneware, pottery, thick glass, or sometimes
pewter and may be fitted with a hinged
lid. Its capacity is generally 33 cl (11 fl
oz, 1⅓ cups), but there are also chopes
holding 50 cl (17 fl oz, 2 cups), 1 litre
(1¾ pints, 4¼ cups), and even 2 litres
(3½ pints, 4½ pints). 20 cl (7 fl oz, ¾
cup) whisky glasses are also called
chopes.

chop or cutlet

CÔTE OU CÔTELETTE

A small cut of meat comprising a rib
bone and the meat attached to it. The
animals whose meat is sold by butchers
normally have 13 pairs of ribs, commonly called 'ribs' for beef, 'chops' or
'cutlets' in veal and lamb, 'chops' in
pork, and 'cutlets' or 'noisettes' in stag
or venison.

□ **Beef** The rib with the bone in is a
prime cut, for roasting in the oven or
grilling (broiling). It is marbled and full
of flavour and can be of various thicknesses. The back ribs, which are cut into
slices entrecôte style, are somewhat
firmer in texture; when boned, they can
be roasted in the same way as boned
middle rib, whose flavour is very fine.

□ **Veal** Prime and best end of neck
cutlets (ribs) are lean and tender in the
centre, more fatty at the edge, and can
be fried or grilled. Middle neck cutlets
(shoulder chops), which are firmer and
more sinewy, are better fried. Loin
chops are fairly wide; they are often
stuffed, and sometimes coated in breadcrumbs. The 'Parisian' chop is a slice
from the breast.

□ **Pork** Loin chops from the hind loin
have lean and fairly dry meat. When cut
from the foreloin they are more fleshy,
wider, and more tender. When taken
from the spare rib (shoulder), they are
more fatty. Chinese spare ribs come
from the belly and are often barbecued.
In wild boar, both mature and young,
the cutlets can be eaten marinated and
fried (escalopes can also be cut from
them).

□ **Mutton and lamb** Best end of neck
cutlets (rib chops), cut from the loin
with a long bone (which is often decorated with a paper frill when serving),
have lean flesh which forms a central
'nut' surrounded by fat. The middle
neck cutlets are more fatty, with meat
which extends along the bone. Loin
chops (both loins) do not have the long
bone and the 'nut' is joined to a band of
meat with strips of fat in it, rolled up on
itself.

What the French call 'mutton chops'
are very thick cutlets cut from mutton
fillet; a skewer is stuck through them
before grilling, to keep the round part in
place.

What the French call 'lamb chops' are lamb cutlets cut across the best end (ribs) and comprising two cutlets joined together at the bone, but cut less thick than a single one. They are also known as 'lunettes d'agneau' ('lambs' spectacles'), or, in England, as butterfly chops, and are eaten grilled.

chopping   HACHAGE

The division of an item of food into very small pieces, using either a knife or a mincer (see *mincers and choppers*). The resulting texture varies from very coarse to very fine, depending on the requirements of the recipe. The French term *hachage* can also describe the food that has been chopped, although the more common French word is *hachis* (see *hash*).

chopsticks   BAGUETTES

Chopsticks are used in the Far East to transfer food from the individual plate or dish to the mouth, sometimes after dipping the food in a sauce. (Spoons may not be used, even with soup; solid pieces are eaten with chopsticks and the liquid is drunk from the bowl.) The strongest chopsticks are made of bamboo, but they can also be made from lacquered wood, plastic, or ebony and often bear designs or ideograms.

Chopsticks must not be sucked (since they are considered to be an extension of the fingers), and the tips should be at the same level; the ends, however, must never be stood on the table in order to bring them together. According to Chinese etiquette, they must be held in the middle. If they are held too high, it is considered a sign of arrogance; too low means lack of elegance. In Japan, however, the higher they are held, the better.

There are also bigger longer chopsticks which are used in the preparation of the meal, for example for stirring the ingredients during cooking.

chop suey

A popular Chinese-style dish invented at the end of the 19th century in the United States by immigrant Chinese cooks for their American customers. It consists of a mixture of chopped simmered vegetables, sometimes accompanied by strips of meat (such as chicken or pork).

RECIPE

Chop suey   LÉGUMES CHOP SUEY Prepare a julienne of young vegetables in season (carrot, turnip, leek, onion, peppers, courgette (zucchini), etc.). Place them in a shallow frying pan (skillet) with some oil (2 tablespoons (3 tablespoons) for 500 g (18 oz, 4½ cups) vegetables). Stir well, cover the pan, and stew gently for 4–5 minutes. During the cooking time, cut some spring onions (scallions) into small sticks. Scald some bean sprouts, cool, and drain. Chop finely 1 small clove of garlic and dice some skinned and deseeded tomatoes. Add the bean sprouts to the pan, mix well, and leave to heat for 1 minute. Finally add the tomato, onion, garlic, pepper, soy sauce (1½ tablespoons (2 tablespoons) to 500 g (18 oz, 4½ cups) vegetables), and a little salt if necessary. Mix and serve hot. This mixture may also be seasoned with 1 teaspoon sesame oil.

chorizo

A long dry Spanish sausage, flavoured with red peppers (either sweet or spicy) and garlic. The meat content is very varied: pure pork, pork and beef, or even horse, donkey, or mule may be used. It may be eaten raw or fried and is used in making the Spanish stew cocido and in paella. The best known chorizo is from Jabugo in Andalusia.

Choron

A French cook from Caen who became chef de cuisine of the famous Voisin restaurant. He invented a hot emulsified sauce to serve with grilled fish, tournedos steaks, and soft-boiled or poached eggs and also a garnish for sautéed meat consisting of noisette potatoes with artichoke hearts filled with either green peas or asparagus tips in butter. During the siege of 1870, Choron served several dishes at Voisin's based on elephant – elephant's trunk in chasseur sauce, elephant bourguignon, etc.

RECIPE

Choron sauce   SAUCE CHORON Dilute 2 dl (7 fl oz, ¾ cup) béarnaise sauce with 2 tablespoons (3 tablespoons) tepid tomato purée which has been well reduced and sieved. It is essential to use a very concentrated purée.

chou

A small sweet or savoury bun, made from double-cooked choux pastry, which is eaten cold, often filled with a cream or garnish. In pâtisserie, choux are often used to make croquembouches or are filled or iced to make éclairs, profiteroles, etc. Savoury choux, filled with savoury mixtures, such as shellfish, vegetables, cream cheese, foie gras etc., are served as hors d'oeuvres.

RECIPES

Choux pastry PÂTE À CHOUX To make about 12 choux, measure out ¼ litre (8 fl oz, 1 cup) water or milk and water (in equal proportions) into a thick saucepan. Add a large pinch of salt, 2 teaspoons caster (superfine) sugar (for sweet choux), and 65 g (2½ oz, 5 table-spoons) butter cut into small pieces. Bring to the boil over a gentle heat. Heat the oven to about 180 C (350 F, gas 4). As soon as the mixture begins to boil, take the pan off the heat, add 125 g (4½ oz, 1 generous cup) flour all at once, and mix quickly. Return the saucepan to the heat and thicken the paste, stirring all the time with a wooden spatula: it takes about 1 minute for the pastry to leave the sides of the saucepan. When this happens, remove from the heat and quickly blend in 2 eggs, stirring briskly, then 2 more eggs, one after the other, continuing to stir until a really smooth paste is obtained.

Transfer the pastry to a piping bag (pastry bag) fitted with a plain nozzle, 1 cm (½ in) in diameter, and pipe small pastry balls, 4–5 cm (1½–2 in) in diameter, onto a lightly oiled baking sheet, spacing them out so they do not stick to each other as they swell during cooking. Place in the oven and cook for about 15 minutes or until the buns have turned golden. Leave them to cool with the oven switched off and the door open.

SAVOURY CHOUX

For six people, allow 200 g (7 oz) choux pastry and 400–450 g (14–16 oz) filling. Split each chou along one side and insert the filling with a piping bag (pastry bag) fitted with a plain nozzle, 1 cm (½ in) in diameter.

Cheese puffs CHOUX AU FROMAGE Prepare a béchamel sauce using 30 g (1 oz, 2 tablespoons) butter, 30 g (1 oz, ¼ cup) flour, and 3 dl (½ pint, 1¼ cups) milk and add to it 75 g (3 oz) grated Gruyère or Cheddar cheese, or 50 g (2 oz, ½ cup) Parmesan, a little grated nutmeg, salt, and pepper. Leave to cool until lukewarm. Fill the split choux with this mixture. Cover with aluminium foil and reheat gently in a moderate oven (about 160 C, 325 F, gas 3). As an alternative, the quantity of cheese may be reduced by half and 75 g (3 oz) finely diced ham added.

Choux à la Nantua Fill some small cooled choux with cold crayfish mousse. Keep them cool. They can be served with a hot Nantua sauce if desired.

Choux with foie gras mousse CHOUX À LA MOUSSE DE FOIE GRAS To some foie gras mousse add an equal volume of unsweetened whipped cream. Fill the cooled choux with the mixture and keep them cool until time to serve. If desired, a small cube of truffle steeped in Madeira may be placed inside each bun.

SWEET CHOUX

Almond chous fritters PETITS CHOUS AMANDINES EN BEIGNETS To make about 20 fritters, use 500 g (18 oz) choux pastry and 100 g (4 oz) shredded almonds. Scatter the almonds over a baking sheet and bake in a hot oven until golden. Mix these almonds with the choux pastry. In a deep pan, heat some oil to 175 C (345 F). Drop tea-spoonfuls of pastry into the oil to make the fritters, which turn over by them-selves in the oil when they are cooked (about 6 minutes). Cook them in batches of 10. Drain the fritters on ab-sorbent paper and serve them hot, sprinkled with plenty of icing (confec-tioners') sugar. They may be accompa-nied with a fruit sauce, such as apricot, cherry, or raspberry.

Chantilly cream puffs CHOUX À LA CRÈME CHANTILLY These are made to resemble swans. Heat the oven to about 180 C (350 F, gas 4). Prepare some choux pastry, using the quantities in the basic recipe, and place it in a piping bag (pastry bag) fitted with a plain 1.5 cm (⅔ in) diameter nozzle. Onto a lightly oiled baking sheet pipe 10 oval-shaped buns, each about the size of a soupspoon. Now replace the nozzle with one 4–5 mm (about ¼ in) in diameter and pipe onto the sheet 10 S shapes, 5–6 cm (2–2½ in) long. Cook the S shapes, which will be the swans' necks, for 15 minutes and the buns for 18–20 minutes.

During this time, prepare the Chantilly cream, using 4 dl (14 fl oz) very cold fresh cream, 1 dl (6 tablespoons, scant ½ cup) very cold milk, 40 g (1½ oz, 3 tablespoons, firmly packed) caster (superfine) sugar, and 1 tablespoon vanilla sugar. Place the cream, milk, and vanilla sugar in a chilled bowl and begin to whip. When the cream starts to thicken, add the caster sugar while continuing to whip. Place the cream in cool place.

Leave the choux to cool in the switched-off oven, with the door open. Then cut the top off each bun and cut the tops in half lengthways; they will form the swans' wings. Fit the piping bag with a large-diameter fluted nozzle, fill the bag with the Chantilly cream, and fill the chou buns with it, forming a dome on each. Place a 'neck' at one end of each bun and stick the 'wings' into the cream on either side. Dust generously with icing sugar (confectioners' sugar).

Chocolate cream puffs CHOUX AU CHOCOLAT Prepare some confectioner's custard (see *creams and custards*) and flavour it with melted chocolate. Separately prepare some chocolate fondant icing (frosting) using 200 g (7 oz) fondant icing and 50 g (2 oz, ½ cup) cocoa blended with 2 tablespoons water. Fill and decorate the choux as in the recipe for coffee choux.

Choux à la normande Fill some choux with a well-blended mixture of thick apple purée and a third of its weight of confectioners' custard (see *creams and custards*) flavoured with Calvados. Dust the choux generously with icing sugar (confectioners' sugar).

Coffee cream puffs CHOUX AU CAFÉ Fill some cooked choux with confectioners' custard (see *creams and custards*) flavoured with coffee essence (strong black coffee). Prepare 200 g (7 oz) fondant icing (frosting), flavour it with coffee essence (or instant coffee made up with 2 tablespoons of water), and heat until it is runny. Ice the tops of the puffs with the fondant and leave to cool completely.

choulend TCHOULEND
A kind of Jewish ragout made with braised beef. Since the rules of the Sabbath forbid fires being lit from sunset on Friday until sunset on Saturday, dishes are placed in the oven on Friday evening and allowed to simmer until midday on Saturday. The prolonged slow cooking gives these dishes a remarkable flavour.

choum
An alcoholic beverage consumed in China and southeast Asia and obtained by distilling fermented rice. It is sometimes flavoured with flower or fruit essences. It should not be confused with rice wine (including Japanese saké).

chouquette
A small unfilled chou bun sprinkled with a little granulated sugar. Made from ordinary choux pastry, chouquettes are sold at bakers' and confectioners' shops.

choux pastry
See *chou*.

Christmas NOËL
The feast of the Nativity of Christ, some of whose customs and celebrations are taken from the pagan festival of the same date, which it officially replaced in 336 AD.

Prominent among the festivities is the giving of gifts, a custom often associated with one of the great figures of popular myth – St Martin in Belgium, Germany, and the Netherlands; St Nicholas in the north and east of France; and Father Christmas. An ancient custom in many regions of France is for godparents to give their godchildren a cake in the shape of a human figure – a puppet, a swaddled infant, or perhaps just a spindle. In Ardèche, this cake is known as *Père Janvier*. In northern France it is called *cougnou* (*cugnot* or *cougnat*; *kerstborden* in Flemish) and consists of a brioche cake decorated with raisins and sprinkled with icing sugar (confectioners' sugar). In Berry the cake is called *naulet*.

The custom of the village children going from house to house on Christmas Eve is a very ancient one. Good wishes and Christmas carols brought their reward, traditionally food – bacon, eggs, flour, sweets (candies), dried fruit, cakes, etc. In Burgundy the *cornette*, a cornet-shaped wafer made from cornmeal, has given its name to the annual round of visits. In Touraine, children are given the *guillauneu*, a long cake split at both ends, specially made for the event.

☐ **The Christmas meal** The main celebration of Christmas centres on a special meal, although what is eaten varies from country to country. In France, the traditional Christmas meal was the *réveillon*, a supper eaten on Christmas morning, immediately on returning from Midnight Mass. The word comes from *re-veiller*, meaning, to begin a new watch (*veillée*) after Midnight Mass. The length of the three low masses and the time taken to walk to church and back used to justify a substantial meal eaten in the early hours of Christmas morning.

Virtually throughout France, roast turkey with chestnuts has become the classic Christmas dish. In former times different regions of France had their own specialities: a daube (beef in red wine) in Armagnac, sauerkraut and goose liver in Alsace, aligot in Auvergne, black pudding (blood sausage) in Nivernais, and goose in southwestern France. In the southeast, a large supper was eaten before Mass, consisting of cauliflower and salt cod with raïto, or perhaps snails, grey mullet with olives, or omelette with artichokes and fresh pasta. It always ended with the so-called 'thirteen Christmas desserts', recalling the 13 participants at the Last Supper: a fruit pastry known as *pompe à l'huile*, raisins, quince paste, marzipan sweets, nougat, *fougasse* (a rich cake), crystallized (candied) citrons, walnuts and hazelnuts, winter pears, Brignoles plums, dried figs, almonds, and dates.

All over the Christian world, the traditional dishes of Christmas are handed down from generation to generation. E. de Pomiane mentions that 'the Russians eat *koutia*, wheat grain cooked with dried fruit. The Poles break a Host and eat foods containing poppy seeds. The French gorge themselves on onion soup, grilled black pudding (blood sausage), and truffled turkey. Every year the English eat Christmas pudding.' In Italy, *pan pepato*, originally from Ferrara, appears mainly on New Year's Eve, although it is also a traditional dessert during the week preceding Christmas. In Rome, the festivities begin during the night of Christmas Eve with a grand procession: here the main item of food is eels, together with a stuffed roast capon. In Bologna, home of fresh pasta, Christmas begins with tortellini stuffed with minced (ground) pork, turkey, sausage, cheese, and nutmeg. For sweetmeats there may be *nocciata*, made with walnuts and honey and cut into triangles, cassata flavoured with Ricotta cheese and chocolate, and *torrone*, made with almonds.

In Germany, carp is the traditional Christmas dish, and in some regions carp are still fattened for Christmas from August onwards. However, the main dish today is more likely to be goose, turkey, venison, wild boar, a roast, or even Schnitzel. Some traditional foods are always eaten, particularly apples, walnuts, and almonds (the first being the symbol of the Tree of Knowledge, and the nuts, with their shells, representing life's difficulties).

In Sweden, a centuries-old tradition at Christmas was marinated ling (a fish related to cod), served in a white sauce with butter, potatoes, mustard, and black pepper. Nowadays, the favourite dish, as in Denmark, is roast goose stuffed with apples and prunes and garnished with red cabbage, caramelized potatoes, and cranberry sauce; dessert may be rice porridge or rice with almonds covered with cherry compote. In Norway, large roast pork chops are served with sauerkraut flavoured with cumin, while the Finns cook a ham in a rye-flour pastry case. All Scandinavian countries celebrate Christmas with a sumptuous smorgasbord.

In most European countries a special cake is eaten at Christmas: in England it is the Christmas cake, in Germany the stollen (containing crystallized (candied) fruit), and in France the Yule log. In Alsace the seasonal cakes are bireweck (containing nuts and dried and crystallized (candied) fruit), served with compotes, and *lebkuchen* (gingerbread), traditionally eaten before Midnight Mass; in Brittany the traditional cake is a star-shaped fouace.

☐ **Christmas in Paris** In his *Almanach des gourmands*, Grimod de La Reynière gives us a picture of a Parisian Christmas which in spirit is not unlike those of today: '. . . *révillon*, this word says it all; it is just as well that it comes only once a year, on 25 December, between two and three o'clock in the morning. This meal . . . is designed to restore the faithful, who are exhausted after a session of four hours in church, and to refresh throats hoarse from singing praises to the Lord. . . . A poularde or a capon with rice is the obligatory dish for this nocturnal meal, taking the place of soup, which is never served. Four hors d'oeuvres, consisting of piping hot sausages, fat well-stuffed andouilles, boudins blancs *au crème*, and properly defatted black puddings, are its attendants. This is followed by ox (beef) tongue, either pickled or (more likely) dressed as it would be at this time of the year, accompanied by a symmetrical arrangement of a dozen pigs' trotters (feet) stuffed with truffles and pistachio nuts, and a dish of fresh pork cutlets. At each corner of the table are two plates of petits fours, including tarts or tartlets, and two sweet desserts, which may be a cream and an Engllish apple pie. Nine more desserts round off the meal, and the faithful – thus fortified – retire to their devotions at the early morning Mass, preceded by Prime and followed by Tierce.'

The first *grand réveillon* at Maxim's, on New Year's Eve, 1906, offered for 50 francs the following menu served with champagne, which was already *de rigueur*: hot hors d'oeuvres, bone-marrow croustades, Parmesan cheese tartlets, consommé, *délices de barbue*

au chablis (brill), stuffed chicken *à l'américaine*, ragout of mushrooms Villeroy, foie gras with port, salad, and New Year's ice cream.

Here is a Christmas menu suggested by Edmond Richardin in his book *Art du bien manger* (1913):

Langoustine bisque
Sole Mornay
or
Chicken turbot
Pheasant soufflé
or
Curried chicken
or
Poularde *à la Montmorency*
Grated cardoons
Orange fritters
Pineapples Fontanges

Christmas cake

A cake traditionally eaten in Great Britain over the Christmas period. English Christmas cake (there are similar Irish and Scottish versions) is a large round flat-topped fruit cake, rich in dried fruits, almonds, spices, and sometimes alcohol. After baking, the top and sides are spread with apricot jam, covered with a thin layer of almond paste, then coated with royal icing (frosting), which is often decoratively piped or sculpted. Glacé (candied) cherries and sprigs of holly can provide a seasonal finishing touch.

Christmas pudding

A pudding traditionally served at Christmas in Britain. Containing beef suet, breadcrumbs, flour, and dried fruit, it is boiled for several hours and often served flambéed with rum or Cognac. It improves with keeping and can be stored for up to a year beforehand. The pudding was formerly shaped like a large ball and cooked in a cloth; nowadays a cloth-wrapped pudding basin is used.

Charles Dickens, in *A Christmas Carol*, alluded to this distinctive pudding, to which the English remain greatly attached: 'Oh! All that steam! The pudding had just been taken out of the cauldron. Oh! That smell! The same as the one which prevailed on washing day! It is that of the cloth which wraps the pudding. Now, one would imagine oneself in a restaurant and in a confectioner's at the same time, with a laundry next door. Thirty seconds later, Mrs Cratchit entered, her face crimson, but smiling proudly, with the pudding resembling a cannon ball, all speckled, very firm, sprinkled with brandy in flames, and decorated with a sprig of holly stuck in the centre. Oh! The marvellous pudding!'

RECIPE

Christmas pudding (simplified recipe) Finely chop 500 g (18 oz) beef suet. Wash and dry 500 g (18 oz, 3 cups) seedless raisins, the same amount of sultanas (seedless white raisins), and 250 g (9 oz, 1½ cups) currants. Finely chop 250 g (9 oz) candied peel (or 125 g (4½ oz, ½ cup) glacé (candied) cherries), 125 g (4½ oz) orange peel and 125 g (4½ oz) blanched almonds, and the zest of 2 lemons. Mix all the ingredients together with 500 g (18 oz, 9 cups) fresh breadcrumbs, 125 g (4½ oz, 1 generous cup) flour, 25 g (1 oz, ¼ cup) mixed spice, the same amount of cinnamon, half a nutmeg (grated), and a pinch of salt. Add 3 dl (½ pint, 1¼ cups) milk and, one by one, 7 or 8 beaten eggs. Next add 2 glasses of rum (or brandy) and the juice of 2 lemons. Mix everything together thoroughly to obtain a smooth paste.

Wrap the mixture in a floured cloth, shaping it into a ball, or fill a greased pudding basin (heatproof mould). Cook in boiling water for about 4 hours (a little longer if the basin is cooking in a bain-marie, a little less if the pudding is wrapped in a cloth and in direct contact with the water; in any case cooking may be prolonged by at least 1 hour without harm).

Keep the pudding in its cloth or basin for at least 3 weeks, in a cool place. Before serving, heat the pudding in a bain-marie for 2 hours, then turn it out, sprinkle it with rum or brandy, and serve it flambéed, decorated with a sprig of holly.

Christmas yule log

BÛCHE DE NOËL

A log-shaped cake, traditionally prepared for the Christmas festivities. It is usually made of rectangular slices of Genoese sponge, spread with butter cream and placed one on top of the other, and then shaped into a log; it is coated with chocolate butter cream, applied with a forcing (piping) bag to simulate bark. The cake is decorated with holly leaves made from almond paste, meringue mushrooms, and small figures. A Swiss roll may be used instead of sliced Genoese cake. There are also ice cream logs, some made entirely of different flavoured ice creams and some with the inside made of parfait or a bombe mixture.

This cake is a fairly recent creation (after 1870) of the Parisian pastrycooks, inspired by the real logs which used to be burned in the hearth throughout Christmas Eve. Before then, the cakes of the season were generally brioches or fruit loaves.

RECIPES

Chestnut log BÛCHE AUX MARRONS Heat the oven to approximately 180 C (350 F, gas 4). Take 2 shallow square cake tins measuring approximately 22–24 cm (9 in) square; cut 2 squares of greaseproof (waxed) paper and line the tins. Prepare a Genoese cake mixture using 125 g (4½ oz, 1 cup) flour, 4 eggs, and 125 g (4½ oz, ⅔ cup) sugar. Spread the mixture in the buttered lined tins with a moistened metal spatula, leaving a gap of 2 cm (1 in) between the mixture and the top of the tin. Put straight into the oven and bake for 25–30 minutes. Take the tins out of the oven, turn over onto a cloth, and immediately remove the paper from the bottom of the cakes. Cover with another cloth and allow to cool.

Prepare 2 dl (7 fl oz, ¾ cup) sugar syrup by boiling 100 g (4 oz, ½ cup) sugar with 1 dl (4 fl oz, ½ cup) water and flavour it with rum or vanilla. To prepare the chestnut mixture, soften 225 g (8 oz, 1 cup) butter with a spatula and add 450 g (1 lb) chestnut cream and, if desired, 2 tablespoons rum. Whisk (beat) the mixture for 6–8 minutes until light and fluffy, then separate into 2 portions. Soak the 2 slabs of cake with the cooled sugar syrup and spread each with half the chestnut mixture. Place the 2 pieces of cake facing each other and roll the first one up tightly, then wrap the second one on top of the first. Cut both ends off diagonally and stick these to the top of the log to represent knots in the wood. Place the cake in the refrigerator for 1 hour. Soften the remaining cream again and cover the entire log with it. Mark with the prongs of a fork to imitate the bark. Decorate with 8 marrows glacés, put back in the refrigerator, and dust with icing sugar (confectioners' sugar) just before serving.

Chocolate log BÛCHE DE NOËL AU CHOCOLAT Prepare Genoese cakes as for the chestnut log. To prepare the syrup, boil 1 dl (8 tablespoons) water and 100 g (4 oz, ½ cup) sugar in a small saucepan, allow to cool, then add 2 tablespoons rum. Finally, prepare a chocolate-flavoured butter cream (see *creams and custards*) using 400 g (14 oz, 1¾ cups) butter. Using a pastry brush, cover the 2 cakes with rum syrup; coat with three-quarters of the cream and roll up as for the chestnut log. Completely cover the log with the remaining cream and make uneven furrows along it with a fork. Decorate with small sugar or meringue figures and store in a cool place until required for serving (the butter cream may also be flavoured with coffee or vanilla).

chrysanthemum

CHRYSANTHÈME

An ornamental plant whose petals are used in Japan, China, and Vietnam for preparing salads. Their taste is similar to that of cress.

chtchi, tschy, or stschy

A thick Russian soup, based on braised sauerkraut cooked in a thickened stock, to which are added pieces of blanched brisket of beef, poached duck or chicken, salted bacon, and smoked sausages. Chtchi is served in a soup tureen with soured (dairy sour) cream (*smitane*) and fennel or chopped parsley. Chtchi is also prepared with green vegetables (spinach, sorrel, nettle).

chub

CHEVAINE, CHEVESNE

A fairly widespread freshwater fish, 30–50 cm (12–20 in) long, with a greenish-brown back and silvery belly. Several species are known: the common chub has a big round head, others have angular heads. All have quite soft flesh but are full of bones; they are therefore kept for fish stews (except for the smallest ones, which are sometimes eaten fried).

chuck MACREUSE

A lean boneless cut of beef from the shoulder, also known as blade. This traditional cut for casseroles and stews is gelatinous and best braised slowly in dishes such as carbonade, daube, or beef *à la mode*. The name *macreuse* is used for a type of wild duck whose flesh could formerly be eaten during Lent.

chump end (loin) SELLE

A joint of lamb, mutton, or venison lying between the leg (gigot) and loin. It may be tied up, boned, and stuffed before roasting or cut into succulent chops for grilling (broiling).

The French equivalent, *selle*, means 'saddle', but it should not be confused with the English saddle of meat, which consists of the two joined loins. The two legs, chump end and saddle together, make an elegant banqueting dish called a baron.

The chump end is a prime piece of meat, which inspired Monselet to write:

'Sors du mouton qui te recèle,
Selle,
Et sur un coulis béarnais
Nais!'

This is a witty little command to the chump end to emerge from the animal, to be eaten with béarnaise sauce!

RECIPE

Chump end of lamb Callas SELLE D'AGNEAU CALLAS (from Alex Humbert's recipe) Bone a chump end of lamb weighing about 2.75 kg (6 lb), trim the excess fat, and season with salt and pepper. Prepare a mushroom julienne, cook it in butter, and leave it to cool. Also prepare a julienne of fresh truffles. Put the truffle julienne down the centre of the meat with the mushroom julienne on each side. Roll and tie up the joint. Roast in a hot oven (220 c, 425 F, gas 7), allowing 12 minutes per lb. Deglaze the roasting pan with a little veal stock and sherry. Serve with buttered asparagus tips.

chunk TRONÇON

A regular-shaped piece obtained by cutting up an elongated foodstuff or preparation, such as a celery stick (stalk) or a croquette mixture. The French word *tronçon* also refers to a short wide piece cut from the middle of a large flatfish (turbot, brill, etc.).

churn BARATTE

The apparatus used for agitating cream to make butter. The traditional churn is a teak barrel which rotates about a horizontal axis. The plungers fixed to the walls assist the churning process. Modern commercial churns are made of stainless steel and the churning process is continuous. They are equipped with beaters and mixers which give the butter the required consistency and are maintained at a constant temperature of 10–13 c (50–55 f). The speed of rotation varies from 25 to 50 rpm.

Small plastic household churns (3 litres, 5¼ pints, 6½ pints) with stainless steel beaters are also available. They should only be half filled to allow the mechanical action to take place, as the weight of the cream falls from one end to the other.

chutney

A sweet-and-sour condiment, made of fruits or vegetables (or of a mixture of the two) cooked in vinegar with sugar and spices until it has the consistency of jam. Considered as typically Indian, chutney – from the Hindustani *chatni* (strong spices) – is in fact a British speciality dating from the colonial era (like pickles). Chutneys, sold in jars under various trade names, may contain exotic fruits (mango, coconut, pineapple, tamarind pulp), as well as temperate ones (aubergine (eggplant), tomato, onion, melon, grapes, cherries, apple, etc.). Some chutneys are reduced to a purée; others retain recognizable pieces of their ingredients; all are characterized by a syrupy and sometimes highly spiced juice which coats the ingredients. Cooked for about two hours, chutneys are put in glass jars and keep like jams. They enliven slightly insipid dishes, mainly cold ones (chicken, fish, ham, leftovers).

RECIPES

Apple and mango chutney CHUTNEY AUX POMMES ET AUX MANGUES Peel and finely slice 1.5 kg (3¼ lb) cooking apples. Bring 1 litre (1¾ pints, 4¼ cups) white vinegar to the boil, put the apples in it, and cook for 5 minutes. Add 500 g (18 oz) brown sugar (coffee sugar), 30 g (1 oz) finely sliced chillies (chili peppers), 200 g (7 oz, 1¼ cups) stoned raisins, 200 g (7 oz, 1¼ cups) sultanas (seedless white raisins), 100 g (4 oz, ¾ cup) sorted and washed currants, 500 g (18 oz) candied citron cut into large dice, and 2 crushed cloves of garlic. Season with 30 g (1 oz) salt, 125 g (4½ oz) mustard seeds, and 15 g (½ oz, 2 tablespoons) ginger. Finally add 500 g (18 oz) well-drained canned mangoes. Cook for about 25 minutes. Scald some jars and pour the hot chutney into them; cover and seal.

Spanish-onion chutney CHUTNEY AUX OIGNONS D'ESPAGNE Peel and slice 2 kg (4½ lb) onions. Tip them into a large saucepan along with 700 g (1½ lb) brown sugar (coffee sugar), 400 g (14 oz, 2½ cups) raisins or sultanas (seedless white raisins), 4 dl (14 fl oz, 1¾ cups) dry white wine, 4 dl (14 fl oz, 1¾ cups) white wine vinegar, 2 cloves of garlic, 300 g (11 oz) crystallized ginger cut into pieces, a pinch of curry powder, and 5 cloves. Boil for 1¾–2 hours, leave to cool completely, then put in jars.

cider CIDRE

A drink produced by the natural fermentation of apple juice (pears are sometimes mixed with the apples). The word comes from the Greek *sikera* (intoxicating drink), and the production of cider certainly dates from antiquity. In France regulations were introduced under Charlemagne, and in the 12th century cider-making became established in Normandy and Brittany, where the climate is very favourable for growing apples. Here, cider completely supplanted barley beer.

Calvados, Manche, Orne, Ille-et-Vilaine, and Mayenne remain the most important areas of production. The ciders of Dinan and Fouesnant are equally famous. Great Britain also produces and consumes a great range of ciders, generally pale in colour with a higher alcohol content than in France, where processes such as sweetening and reconstitution with apple concentrate are prohibited.

Several hundred varieties of apple are used for the manufacture of cider (including Bedan, Duret, Bisquet, Fréquin, Saint-Martin, etc.); some are sweet, but most are rather bitter or even sour. The cider-maker's skill lies in blending different varieties to obtain an agreeable and well-balanced cider. The apples are gathered when ripe, then left in a heap for several days before being crushed and pressed. Fermentation, which occurs naturally without the addition of yeasts or sugar, takes about a month. According to its style and quality and the intended market, it may then be filtered to clarify it, and pasteurized to make it keep longer. Both still and sparkling ciders are produced. With its thirst-quenching and fruity flavour, cider makes a refreshing drink.

The use of cider in cooking is a characteristic of Brittany and Normandy, particularly in recipes for fish (matelote, sole, brill), rabbit, and tripe. In Brittany, 'one sits by the fire in the evenings eating chestnuts and drinking sweet cider', as Théodore Botrel sang in *La Paludicie*. The 'bowl' or cup of cider traditional in Brittany is an excellent accompaniment to the region's pancakes.

RECIPES

Chicken with cider COQ AU CIDRE Peel, quarter, and core 500 g (18 oz) sour apples; cut half of them into thin slices. Season the inside of a large chicken with salt and pepper, stuff it with the apple slices, and sew up the opening. Baste the chicken with melted butter and brown in a casserole for about 20 minutes. Meanwhile, chop up 3 shallots and brown them lightly in butter. When the chicken is golden brown, surround it with the remaining apples and add a little crumbled thyme, 2 crushed cloves, salt, freshly ground pepper, the shallots, and ½ bottle of cider, already heated. Bring to the boil,

partly cover, and cook for about 40 minutes. Remove the chicken and keep it hot. Add 2 dl (7 fl oz, ¾ cup) thick cream to the casserole and reduce by a third. Cut the chicken into portions and serve coated with the sauce.

Cider fruit cup COUPE DE FRUITS DU CIDRE Peel some fresh fruit, sprinkling with lemon juice those that tend to turn brown. One can use apples, pears, oranges, pineapples, and bananas; or cherries, strawberries, apricots, melon, and pears; or melon, peaches, plums, and grapes. Leave the smaller fruit whole, and cut the others into thin slices. Add a liqueur glass of Calvados for every litre (1¾ pints, 4¼ cups) of sweet cider, add sugar, and mix. Sprinkle the fruit generously with the cider and place in the refrigerator for at least 1 hour before serving.

Fillets of fish in cider FILETS DE POISSON AU CIDRE Prepare a fish stock but replace the white wine and half the water with rough cider. Poach the fish fillets in this stock, then drain and arrange on the serving dish, keeping them hot. Pass the cooking liquid through a strainer and reduce by half. To it add the same volume of fresh cream and reduce a little more. Coat the fillets with the sauce and glaze in a very hot oven.

Wild rabbit with farm cider LAPEREAU DE CAMPAGNE AU CIDRE FERMIER (from a recipe by Patrick Jeffroy) Remove the bones from a baron (saddle and legs) of young rabbit weighing about 1.5 kg (3¼ lb). Prepare a brunoise of carrots, celeriac (celery root), sticks (stalks) of celery, and leeks (green parts). Blanch the vegetables separately, then cool and bind together using 3 egg yolks. Sprinkle with salt and pepper. Prepare 2 dl (7 fl oz, ¾ cup) rabbit stock using the bones, 1 carrot, 1 onion, a bouquet garni, 2.5 dl (8 fl oz, 1 cup) farm cider, 2.5 dl (8 fl oz, 1 cup) water, salt, and peper. Spread the baron of rabbit out on its back, season with salt and pepper, and stuff it with the brunoise. Pull the sides of the legs and belly together over the brunoise and tie up with string. Lay the rabbit in an ovenproof earthenware dish or casserole containing a bed of diced vegetables (2 carrots, 2 red onions, and 2 shallots) mixed with diced dessert apple. Roast it with butter in a very hot oven (about 240 c, 475 f, gas 9) for 15–20 minutes so that it remains pink. Keep it hot, covered with a sheet of aluminium foil.

Boil 1 litre (1¾ pints, 4¼ cups) milk and allow to cool. Peel and slice 1 kg (2¼ lb) potatoes. Shred half a green cabbage, blanch, and cool. Butter an ovenproof, preferably earthenware, dish and arrange in it a layer of the potatoes, sprinkled with salt and pepper, then a layer of the cabbage, a layer of Emmental cheese, and so on, finishing with a layer of potatoes and Emmental. To the cooled milk add 4 well-beaten eggs and a few knobs of butter and pour over the potatoes. Cook in a moderately hot oven (about 210 c, 415 f, gas 6–7) for 45 minutes. Keep hot.

For the sauce to accompany the rabbit, add ½ litre (17 fl oz, 2 cups) farm cider to the pan juices and reduce by two-thirds; add a small glass of demiglace, the rabbit stock, and 2.5 dl (8 fl oz, 1 cup) fresh cream. Cook over a gentle heat for 5 minutes. Chop some chives and chervil and sprinkle over the sauce.

Surround the rabbit with cress and serve it with the sauce and the potato cake.

cigarette

A cylindrical biscuit (cookie), also called *cigarette russe*, prepared with langues-de-chat mixture. After baking, the discs are rolled into a cylinder shape around a wooden stick while they are still lukewarm and malleable.

RECIPE

Cigarettes russes Butter a baking sheet and heat the oven to 180 c (350 f, gas 4). Melt 100 g (4 oz, ½ cup) butter in a bain-marie. Whisk 4 egg whites into very stiff peaks, adding a pinch of salt. In a mixing bowl, blend 90 g (3½ oz) flour, 160 g (5½ oz) caster (superfine) sugar, 1 tablespoon vanilla-flavoured sugar, and the melted butter. Carefully add the egg whites. Spread this mixture on the baking sheet, making very thin discs about 8 cm (3 in) in diameter. Bake only 3 or 4 at a time. Place them in the oven and cook for 10 minutes or until the biscuit turns golden. Loosen them and roll each around the handle of a wooden spoon while still hot. Leave them to cool completely and store in a tin.

cinchona   QUINQUINA

A tree originating in Peru and cultivated chiefly in Indonesia for its bark, which is rich in quinine. Cinchona bark is also used in the manufacture of apéritifs and alcoholic drinks (see *quinquina*).

cinghalaise (à la)

Describes preparations of cold fish or white meats accompanied by cinghalaise sauce, a kind of vinaigrette to which a salpicon of vegetables in oil and herbs is added, and in which only the presence of curry is evocative of Sri Lanka.

RECIPE

Cinghalaise sauce SAUCE CINGHA-LAISE   Peel a courgette (zucchini) and cook it in water until it is just slightly firm. Finely dice equal quantities of green and red peppers, tomato pulp, cucumber, and the cooked courgette. To this salpicon add some sieved hardboiled (hard-cooked) egg yolk, curry powder, salt, pepper, lemon juice, oil, and chopped parsley and chives.

cinnamon   CANNELLE

A spice obtained from the bark of several tropical trees (cinnamon trees). The bark is removed, dried, and rolled up to make a tube (*cannella* in Italian), light fawn or dark grey in colour, depending on the species. The most popular varieties of cinnamon are from Sri Lanka and China. Cinamon gives off a sweet penetrating aroma and has a hot spicy flavour. It can also be found in the form of a powder and an extract. It is one of the oldest spices, mentioned in Sanskrit texts and the Bible and used by the ancients to flavour wine. In the Middle Ages it was widely used in stews, soups, custards, and poultry fricassees. In France it is mainly used in compotes and desserts, and to flavour mulled wine. In eastern Europe and Asia its uses are much more numerous, in patisserie, soups, and meats.

RECIPE

Mulled wine with cinnamon and cloves VIN CHAUD À LA CANNELLE ET AU GIROFLE Wash a small orange and stick 2 cloves into it. Leave to macerate for 24 hours in 1 litre (1¾ pints, 4¼ cups) red wine. Remove the orange, pour the wine into a pan, sweeten to taste, and add 1 cinnamon stick. Bring to the boil, then remove from the heat and allow the cinnamon to infuse according to taste. Remove the cinnamon and reheat the wine.

cioppino

A dish from San Francisco (California) consisting of a stew of white fish, large shrimps, clams, and mussels, with a garlic, tomato, and white-wine base.

citron CÉDRAT

A citrus fruit originally from China (not Persia, as was formerly believed) and similar to the lemon. It has been used since the 16th century or before. In France the citron tree is cultivated particularly in Corsica and on the Côte d'Azur. The fruit is larger than the lemon and slightly pear-shaped, with a thick glossy skin. It is rarely eaten raw and gives little juice, which can be used like lemon juice. Although employed in jams and marmalades, the citron is used mainly for its peel, which is candied as

an ingredient for cake-making and for biscuits and puddings, etc. In Corsica it is also used to make a liqueur, Cédratine, and to fill sweets.

citronner

A French culinary term meaning to flavour or sprinkle a dish with lemon juice (see *acidulate*). The term also means to rub the surface of certain vegetables (artichoke hearts, celeriac (celery root), mushrooms) with a cut lemon, or to sprinkle them with lemon juice, to prevent discoloration.

citrouillat

A savoury or sweet pumpkin pie from the south of the Berry region of central France. Served lukewarm, it is made with shortcrust pastry (basic pie dough) rolled out into a rectangle and spread with scalded diced pumpkin (together with sugar and fresh cream for the dessert version); the pastry is folded in four and stuck together with milk before being placed in the oven.

citrus fruits ARGUMES

Fruits of the genus *Citrus*, including the orange, Seville (bitter) orange, bergamot, grapefruit, pomelo (shaddock), tangerine, clementine, lemon, lime, citron, and sweet lime, as well as hybrids of this genus (citrange) and related genera (kumquat). Originally from Asia, the citrus fruits – whose French name comes from the Latin *acrumen* (bitter flavour) – gradually spread throughout the world, particularly to

Composition of citrus fruits and their juice
(per 100 g (4 oz) edible matter)

		calorific value (Cal)	potassium (mg)	vitamin A (international units)	vitamin C (mg)
grapefruit	pulp	41	135	80	38
	juice	39	162	80	38
lemon	whole fruit	20	145	30	77
	juice	25	141	20	46
orange	whole fruit	40	196	250	71
	juice	45	200	200	50
tangerine	whole fruit	46	126	420	31
	juice	43	178	420	31

Mediterranean countries (Israel, Spain, Italy) and to the United States (Florida, California).

These fruits, which are rich in vitamin C and potassium, have an acid flavour to varying degrees. They are widely consumed either as fresh fruit or in cakes, pastries, and preserves (crystallized (candied) fruit – particularly citron and bergamot – jams, and sweets). They are also used in distilling (Curaçao) and in some recipes are combined with meat and poultry (pork, duck). The most important role of citrus fruits, however, is in the fruit juice industry (natural or concentrated). Several by-products play an important part in the food industry: aromatic essential oils, extracted from the skin; pectin, which comes from the white part of the rind; and oils made from some pips. (*Agrume*, in the singular, is the French name for the Ente plum, from which Agen prunes are made.)

civet

A game stew typically made from wild rabbit, hare, venison, or young wild boar, prepared with red wine, and thickened with the animal's blood or pig's blood; this gives it its oily texture and distinctive colouring. Small onions and pieces of larding bacon are generally included. The name is derived from *cive* (spring onion or scallion), which was formerly used to flavour all stews, particularly hare.

Certain seafood and fish dishes served in sauce are also called civet; at Dinard, abalones *en civet* are cooked in red wine with onions and strips of larding bacon. In French provincial areas civets are also prepared from goose giblets or squirrel; in southwestern France, squirrel is cooked in a roux moistened with red wine, with onions and orange peel.

RECIPES

Civet of hare or **jugged hare (basic preparation)** CIVET DE LIÈVRE Skin and gut the hare. Carefully collect the blood and put to one side along with the liver, having removed the gallbladder; add 1 tablespoon vinegar. Detach the thighs and forelegs and chop each thigh in half, splintering the bones as little as possible; cut the saddle into 4

pieces. Place all the pieces in a deep dish and season with salt, pepper, thyme, and powdered bay leaf. Add a large finely sliced onion, 3–4 tablespoons oil, and at least 1 tablespoon Cognac. After marinating for 24 hours, the hare is ready to be cooked *en civet à la flamanade, à la française*, or *à la lyonnaise*.

Civet of hare CIVET DE LIÈVRE (from a recipe by Paul Haeberlin) Skin and gut a choice hare, keeping the blood and the liver. Cut the hare into pieces and marinate overnight in red wine containing 3 onions (halved), a sliced carrot, and a sprig of thyme.

The following morning, drain the hare in a colander. Heat a cup of oil and 40 g (1½ oz, 3 tablespoons) butter in a frying pan (skillet) and lightly brown the pieces of hare on each side, as well as the onions and carrots from the marinade. Then place the pieces in a saucepan and sprinkle with flour. Moisten with the wine from the marinade, a trickle of Cognac, and 1 tablespoon tomato purée; add 2 cloves of garlic crushed in their skins, a bouquet garni, a quarter of a bay leaf (crushed), salt, and pepper. Mix well and leave to simmer for 2 hours.

Separately, cook 20 small onions in a little water to which 1 teaspoon caster (superfine) sugar has been added. Cut 250 g (9 oz) small mushrooms into quarters and brown them in some butter. Dice 150 g (5 oz) smoked or salted bacon, blanch it, then cook it gently in a frying pan.

When the hare is cooked, arrange the pieces in a dish and keep hot. Chop up the hare's liver and mix it with the blood. Add it to the cooking liquor and bring to the boil. Pass through a fine strainer to form a sauce. Add the garnish of onions, mushrooms, and pieces of bacon. Adjust the seasoning, pour the sauce over the hare, and serve accompanied by fresh noodles.

Civet of lobster CIVET DE HOMARD (from a recipe by Roger Vergé) Cut a lobster into 6 pieces and remove the shell from the claws. Collect the coral and creamy parts (the liver), not forgetting to discard the pouch of grit in the head. Season the flesh with salt and pepper and brown it in 2 tablespoons very hot oil. Remove the lobster, drain, and keep hot.

Return the saucepan to the heat and add 25 g (1 oz, 2 tablespoons) butter, 2–3 chopped shallots, and half a carrot, diced. Stir. Add the lobster pieces and 4 tablespoons Cognac, then flame. Moisten with three-quarters of a bottle of red Burgundy and add a bouquet garni. Season with salt and pepper, cover, and leave to simmer gently for 15 minutes.

Peel about 20 small onions and place them in a saucepan with some salt, a knob of butter, and a pinch of caster (superfine) sugar. Barely cover with water and reduce completely so that the onions brown slightly. In a frying pan (skillet), sauté some small very fresh mushrooms in butter, then drain them. Using a fork, mush 50 g (2 oz, 4 tablespoons) butter with a spoonful of flour and the lobster coral in a bowl. When the lobster pieces are cooked, remove the shell and arrange them in soup plates adding the onions and mushrooms. Keep hot.

Reduce the cooking liquid by half, beat into it the coral mixture, adjust the seasoning, and rub through a fine sieve. Coat the lobster with it and serve hot.

clafoutis

A dessert from the Limousin region of France, consisting of black cherries arranged in a buttered dish and covered with fairly thick pancake batter. It is served lukewarm, dusted with sugar. As a rule, the cherries are not stoned (pitted) but simply washed and stalked (stemmed), since the kernels add their flavour to the batter during cooking. The Académie française, who had defined clafoutis as a 'sort of fruit flan', were faced with protests from the inhabitants of Limoges, and changed their definition to 'cake with black cherries'. Nevertheless, there are numerous variations using red cherries or other fruits. The word comes from the provincial dialect word *clafir* (to fill).

RECIPE

Clafoutis Remove the stalks (stems) from 500 g (18 oz) washed black cherries, dust them with 50 g (2 oz, 4 tablespoons firmly packed) sugar, and leave for at least 30 minutes. Butter a baking tin and fill it with the cherries. Sieve 125 g (4½ oz, 1 generous cup) flour into a mixing bowl and add a pinch of salt, 50 g (2 oz, 4 tablespoons) caster (superfine) sugar, and 3 well-beaten eggs; mix, add 3 dl (½ pint, 1¼ cups) milk, and mix thoroughly again. Pour the mixture over the cherries and bake in a moderate oven (about 180 c, 350 F, gas 4) for 35–40 minutes. Wait until it is lukewarm before dusting with icing sugar (confectioners' sugar).

clairet

A light-coloured French wine, deeper in tone than pink but not a vibrant red. It can be made in various regions (subject to local controls) and is usually nonvintage or a wine to be drunk young. In the past, it might have been made by mixing red and white wine – illegal for pink wines today (with the exception of champagne).

The word derives from the colour of the wines of Bordeaux, which in the Middle Ages, when the English Crown owned the entire region of the Gironde, were lighter in tone (*plus clair*) than the wines of the hinterland that were shipped through the port of Bordeaux. This is why the English term for red Bordeaux is still claret – in spite of attempts within the EEC to impose the use of 'red Bordeaux', it had to be agreed that centuries of use of the word claret entitled the UK to retain the expression.

Clairette

A white wine grape, grown mainly in the Midi. Because of its 'grapey' flavour it has often been used with the Muscat. It is found in many wines of the south of France, including some with AOC. Clairette de Die, made in the Drôme, is a sparkling wine that may be produced either according to the champagne process, with the second fermentation taking place in the bottle, or according to the traditional method of Die, fermentation taking place immediately, without any addition of *dosage* (sweetening). Wines produced by the first method are made wholly or mostly (75%) from the Clairette grape; for the second method, there is at least 50% of Muscat in the wine.

The Clairettes of Bellegarde and of Languedoc are full-bodied dry white wines, of a definite yellow colour. The former are at least 11.5°, the latter about 13°.

clam

A bivalve mollusc, 5–10 cm (2–4 in) across, whose large smooth shell is marked with fine circular striations. Clams, introduced to France by the Americans in 1917, are gathered from sandy and muddy estuaries, particularly on the east coast of the United States, but also in the French region of Charente. They are eaten raw or cooked like oysters or *à la commodore*.

The American hard clam, measuring 3–6 cm (1¼–2½ in), has a thick yellowish-grey domed shell marked with deep concentric grooves and covered with warty lumps. It is rarely found in the Mediterranean, but is abundant on the Atlantic and English Channel coasts, living in the sand on seashores. Also known in France as *rigadelle* or *coque rayée*, it can be eaten raw (preferably without lemon juice, so as not to hide its subtle flavour) or cooked (stuffed like mussels, or in soup).

Clam chowder is a soup made from vegetables, onions, and clams garnished with strips of larding bacon; it originated in New England. A clambake is a picnic, originally along the east coast of the United States, at which clams and other shellfish are cooked on heated stones under a layer of seaweed.

RECIPE

Clam soup SOUPE AUX CLAMS Dice 100 g (4 oz) salted bacon, 1 medium-sized onion, 2 sticks (stalks) of celery, 1 red pepper, and 1 green pepper. Blanch the bacon for 3 minutes in boiling water, then cool it, wipe it, and soften it in a pan containing some butter, without colouring it. Then add the vegetables, sprinkle on 1 tablespoon flour, and cook for 2 minutes, stirring all the time. Sprinkle with 1.5 litres (2¾ pints, 7 cups) stock and bring to the boil.

Open 36 clams near a heated oven, retaining the liquid. Prepare the clams; chop up the trimmings and put them in a saucepan with the clam liquor plus 2 dl (7 fl oz, ¾ cup) water. Cook for 15 minutes, strain, and add this stock to the soup. Return the soup to the boil, add the clams, bring to the boil again, cover, then turn off the heat. Boil 3 dl (½ pint, 1¼ cups) thick cream and add it to the soup along with 1 tablespoon chopped parsley and 100 g (4 oz, ½ cup) butter. Heat and serve with crushed or whole crackers.

Clamart

Any of various dishes that include green peas, either whole or in a purée. It is named after a district of the Hauts-de-Seine that used to be famous for its pea crops. Clamart soup is a purée of fresh green peas in consommé, served with fried croutons; poached eggs Clamart are served on canapés spread with purée; scrambled eggs Clamart is served with the peas left whole. The name is also given to puff-pastry patties filled with creamed purée, to chicken *en cocotte*, to a sauté, and to sweetbreads served with fresh green peas or a Clamart garnish.

The true Clamart garnish, for small items of sautéed red meat, comprises tartlets or artichoke bottoms filled with green peas in butter; for larger pieces, château potatoes are added.

RECIPES

Artichokes Clamart ARTICHAUTS CLAMART Clean a lettuce and cut it into long thin shreds. Wash 12 small young artichokes; break off the stalks and cut away the large leaves. Butter a casserole and arrange the artichokes in it. Add ½ litre (17 fl oz, 2 cups) shelled fresh green peas, the lettuce, some salt, 1 teaspoon caster (superfine) sugar, and 3 tablespoons water. Cover and cook very gently. Serve in the cooking dish, adding 1 tablespoon fresh butter at the last minute.

Chicken Clamart POULARDE CLAMART Truss a chicken and half-cook it in butter in a casserole. Also half-cook 1 litre (1¾ pints, 4¼ cups) green peas *à la française*. Pour them around the chicken, cover, and finish cooking in a hot oven (about 225 C, 440 F, gas 7–8).

clarequet

In old French cookery, a transparent jelly prepared with verjuice and apples or gooseberries. The fruits were reduced to a purée, mixed with their weight in sugar, then put in glass moulds, called clarequet moulds; these were placed in a drying oven to set the jelly, so ensuring that it would keep.

claret

See *clairet*.

clarification

The process of rendering a turbid or cloudy substance clear. Clarification is applied mainly to liquids, especially stocks and drinks, but the term is also used for sugar, butter, and eggs (clarified egg white contains no trace of yolk).

● *Clarification of stock* – In domestic cookery, poultry or other stock can be served like soup, garnished in different ways, without having been clarified – this is white consommé, which can also be used in sauces, stews, or braised dishes. In the catering (food service) industry, clarified consommé is used. Clarification involves using chopped lean beef, egg white, and an aromatic vegetable brunoise. When the broth boils, the egg whites coagulate, trapping the particles that were making the liquid cloudy. The consequent loss in flavour is restored by the lean beef and the vegetables.

Clarification is essential when stock from the pan is used to make a jelly by adding gelatine. For charcuterie items with a jelly base, the egg whites are often replaced by blood.

● *Clarification of wine* – This is achieved by various processes, including filtration and fining – the addition of a suitable agent (egg white, blood, albumen, bentonite) to the wine in cask or vat. The fining agent will attract any particles in suspension in the young wine. Filtration usually takes place prior to bottling.

● *Clarification of beer and cider* – Before it is put in barrels or bottles, beer is filtered (under pressure so that the carbon dioxide gas does not escape).

Cider is cleared by coagulating the pectin with enzymes as soon as it comes out of the press; it is then siphoned off and drawn into casks.

● *Clarification of syrups, liqueurs, and household drinks* – Syrups and fruit and vegetable juices are filtered through paper or a piece of muslin.

Fermented fruit drinks are clarified with egg white whisked to a fluffy consistency, then filtered.

Liqueurs and creams are filtered through cotton in a funnel; fining with egg white is sometimes necessary.

RECIPE

Clarification of stock CLARIFICATION DU BOUILLON In a deep thick-bottomed saucepan, put 750 g (1 lb 10 oz) finely chopped lean meat and 100 g (4 oz) very finely diced vegetables. Add the white from a very fresh egg and mix well. Gradually add 2½ litres (4¼ pints, 5½ pints) tepid stock. Whisk while heating until it boils. Reduce the heat and simmer very gently for 1½ hours. Strain the consommé through a napkin.

clavaria CLAVAIRE

Any mushroom of a genus containing many species. Usually found in woodland, they are generally whitish or yellow and shaped like a club, lacking a distinct cap, hence their name, from the Latin *clava* (a club). Nearly all are edible but they are not great delicacies. After removing the tip of the stalks, they may be cooked *au gratin*, sautéed with garlic, or preserved in vinegar.

clean VIDER

To remove the viscera from fish, poultry, or game before cooking.

Sea fish, usually sold partly cleaned, must be trimmed and scaled and the grey skin should be removed. Large round fish, such as hake, are cleaned through an incision made in the belly. Smaller fish, such as whiting or trout, are cleaned by removing the viscera through the gill covers, thus avoiding opening the belly (unless they are to be stuffed). Large flatfish such as turbot are cleaned on the dark side, while smaller flatfish, like sole, are cleaned by removing the grey skin and then making an incision on the right side. In most cases, the gills are removed. After cleaning, the fish are carefully washed.

Poultry is often sold with the intestines already removed. Drawing, which takes place after singeing and trimming, is carried out by first loosening the skin around the neck to remove the digestive and respiratory tracts, fat, glands, and crop. Then the index finger should be inserted through the neck to loosen the lungs. Finally, the anal orifice should be enlarged slightly and the gizzard, liver, heart, and lungs pulled through together, taking care not to damage the gall bladder. If the intestines have not previously been removed from the birds they are taken out at this point. The bird is then ready to be trussed or jointed.

clementine CLÉMENTINE

A hybrid of the tangerine and Seville (bitter) orange, produced in 1902 in Algeria by Père Clément. It is grown mainly in Mediterranean countries. Small, orange-coloured, and spherical, the clementine has a firm skin, which adheres to the juicy pulp. On sale from the end of October until February, it is consumed mainly as a table fruit.

Clementines, which are more acid and less aromatic than tangerines, come mainly from Spain, Morocco, Italy, or Algeria. Three varieties are recognized:
• the *Corsican clementine*, the best, is protected by an official regional mark; its skin is orange-red, it is highly scented, and it contains no seeds. It is usually sold with its leaves (two per fruit) from the beginning of November until the beginning of February;
• the *Spanish clementine* comes in several varieties: the choice smaller fruit and the larger Nules and Oroval varieties (2–10 seeds);
• the *Monréal clementine*, fairly rare, appears from mid-October, from Spain or Algeria (10–12 seeds).

Juicy, sweet, and rich in vitamin C, the clementine keeps well in a cool place. It may also be crystallized (candied) or preserved in brandy. The juice is used for sorbets and drinks. It is used in patisserie and confectionery in the same way as the orange. A liqueur is made from it and in England it is used with vinegar and spices to make pickles.

Clermont

Any of several dishes containing chestnuts or cabbage, characteristic products of the Auvergne, of which Clermont-Ferrand is the capital.

Clermont garnish for large pieces of red meat combines paupiettes of green cabbage with lightly fried potatoes; a sauce is made from the pan juices of the meat plus the liquid in which the paupiettes of cabbage were cooked; with braised meat, the braising base or a demi-glace sauce is used.

Clermont garnish for small sautéed pieces of meat comprises fried artichoke quarters and onions stuffed with chestnut purée and braised; the whole is coated with a Madeira déglaçage. Bavarian cream *à la Clermont* is a cold sweet made from rum and chestnut purée.

climat

In Burgundy, each of the different parcels of land that comprise a *vignoble* – a wine-growing region. The Burgundian *climat* is equivalent to the *cru* of Bordeaux.

clitocybe

Any mushroom belonging to a genus containing numerous species, some of which are edible. Clitocybes are characterized by having gills that extend along the stalk and a drooping cap with a depression in the centre; the name comes from the Greek *klitos* (sloping) + *kubê* (head). The best for eating are the funnel-shaped clitocybe (pale-buff or yellow-ochre cap), the nebulous or *petit-gris* clitocybe (grey-brown), the geotropic or *tête-de-moine* clitocybe (yellow-ochre), and the sweet-smelling clitocybe (green). All must be picked when young and consumed fresh, with the stalks discarded. Their aniseed, bitter almond, or mint flavour is sometimes fairly strong, so they are used in small quantities to flavour a dish of more insipid mushrooms. They must be cooked thoroughly.

RECIPE

Omelette with green clitocybes
OMELETTE AUX CLITOCYBES VERTS
(from a recipe by Dr P. Ramain) Choose 18 caps of aniseed-flavoured green clitocybes and clean them thoroughly. Brown the 6 choicest ones whole in butter with ½ tablespoon chopped onions. Cook in a covered pan for 10 minutes over a gentle heat. Season with salt and pepper and keep warm. Cut the

remaining 12 caps into thin strips and cook in butter for 5 minutes over a moderate heat. Remove and drain on a fine sieve.

Beat 8 fresh eggs lightly as for an omelette, add salt and a little curry powder, and blend in 8 knobs of butter, then the drained julienne of mushrooms. Cook the omelette in very hot olive oil, constantly moving the frying pan (skillet) over a brisk heat, and lifting up the edges. Serve garnished with the 6 whole caps and accompanied with a green salad dressed in walnut oil containing ½ teaspoon anisette.

clitopile petite-prune

A greyish-white edible mushroom, also called *meunier* or *mousseron*. Its tender flesh has a delicate smell of fresh flour and cooks rapidly. It is used to flavour blander mushrooms and, when dehydrated, serves as a condiment.

cloche

A convex dish-cover made of stainless steel or silver-plated metal with a knob or a handle. The cloche is used mainly in restaurants to keep food hot. Some restaurants, which provide 'plate service', use individual cloches for their dishes. It was formerly widely used in Great Britain, where hot breakfast or dinner dishes were traditionally placed on the sideboard.

The cheese cloche, hemispherical and made of glass or wire gauze, protects cheeses from the air and from flies; it generally rests on a round wooden or marble tray. It has become rarer since the advent of refrigeration.

clod   JUMEAU

Butcher's term for a neck muscle of beef. The clod is soft and gelatinous and can be braised, cooked *à la mode*, in a carbonade, and in a pot-au-feu.

Clos-de-Vougeot

A classified *grand cru* of the Côte de Nuits and one of the most famous wine-growing regions of Burgundy. The vineyard, created by Cistercian monks in the 12th century, is a true *clos* (i.e. it is enclosed by walls). But it is subdivided between over 60 owners, each with his own methods of viticulture, winemaking, and marketing. The soil of the 50-hectare (124-acre) site is not uniform: the ground is drier at the top of the slope than at the bottom. The Clos-de-Vougeot (or Clos-Vougeot) wines cannot therefore be all the same. They are, however, usually magnificent reds of substance, but delicate, well-balanced, and with a lingering taste and a strong aroma. In the centre of the vineyard stands the original establishment constructed by the monks in the 16th century to house the press. This has been altered and enlarged many times since then and today is owned by the Confrérie des Chevaliers du Tastevin, who hold their 'chapters' or ceremonies there.

Close (Jean-Joseph)

French cook (born Dieuze, Moselle, 1757; died Strasbourg, 1828). He did not invent foie gras, as the legend claims, neither was he responsible for its truffle garnish, but he did have the idea of wrapping goose livers in a thin veal forcemeat and covering them with a pastry crust. This pie was named *à la Contades* because in about 1782 Close was in the service of the Maréchal de Contades, governor of Alsace. It was sent as a gift to the king from the Maréchal, who was rewarded with an estate in Picardy. It is said the cook received a gratuity of 20 pistoles. When his master left Strasbourg in 1788, Close married the widow of a pastry-cook of the city and opened a shop in order to sell his *pâtés à la Contades*, thus creating the first production centre of Alsatian foies gras.

clove   CLOU DE GIROFLE

The sun-dried flower bud of the clove tree, used since ancient times as a spice. Brown and hard, cloves are about 12 mm (½ in) long, with a head 4 mm (⅙ in) in diameter.

Introduced into Europe in about the 4th century, cloves were for a long time in as much demand as pepper. The Chinese used them well before the Christian era for their medicinal and culinary properties. They originated in the Moluccas, where the Dutch for a long time held the monopoly of their cultivation, but they were introduced into Réunion in the 17th century and then into the West Indies. In the Middle

Ages, great use was made of cloves for their medicinal properties: oranges studded with cloves were supposed to guard against the plague, and in Naples clove pastilles were made as aphrodisiacs.

Cloves act as a preservative of meat and meat products. The great cooks of the 18th century continued to use recipes inherited from the Renaissance, but in Europe nowadays cloves are limited to a few specific uses: onions studded with a few cloves in braised and boiled meat dishes; matelots in red wine; marinades in vinegar; gherkins and pickles; pastries with honey and dried fruits; fruits in brandy. In mulled wine, cloves are often combined with cinnamon. In India and China they are included in several mixtures of spices.

club

The 'gentlemen's club', where men dine and spend their moments of leisure away from any feminine presence, is a British tradition.

The word was introduced to France in 1702. In *Paris à table* (1846), E. Briffault writes: 'The clubs in which we have introduced British customs are slow to gain popularity in France. The Jockey Club is almost the only one which has become successfully established. There the diner is treated as if he is at a very great house. The conversation at table and after dinner, the lounges, billiard room, and on the balcony, sums up in an original fashion society gossip concerning the life of pleasures and amusements. . . . What is known as a club in London, in Paris bears the name of *circle*.' The author quotes the circle of the Deux-Mondes, concerned with utmost luxury, and those of the Rue de Gramont 'where dinner sometimes assumes extraordinary proportions: whole roebucks have been served, and piles of still life as in the great Flemish paintings'. Today, this type of establishment has practically disappeared, although there are still gastronomic clubs (Club des Cent, Chaîne des Rôtisseurs). See also *confréries, orders, and brotherhoods.*

coat ENROBER

To cover an item with a batter, sauce, or other preparation in order to protect it during cooking or improve its appearance or taste, etc. Food with a relatively high water content is dipped in batter to protect it during deep-frying (in particular vegetable and offal fritters). Confits should always be completely coated with fat for better preservation.

In pâtisserie, petits fours, cakes, sweets, and chocolates can be coated with chocolate, icing (frosting), or glazed sugar. Individual ice creams can be coated with chocolate or praline.

In the food industry, many foodstuffs are coated with a neutral substance to improve presentation and extend shelf-life (especially delicatessen sausages). 'Coated' coffee has been treated to make the beans black and shiny.

cochon au Père Douillet

A dish of suckling pig popular in an earlier age. Pierre de Lune, the official in charge of the catering in the household of the Prince of Rohan, gave the recipe in *Le Cuisinier* (1654): 'Cut the pig into pieces. Blanch the pieces and interlard with pork fat cut partly from the outer layer and partly from the belly. Put them in a cloth and season with salt, pepper, whole cloves, nutmeg, bay leaves, limes, and spring onions. Cook in a pot with stock and a little white wine. Make sure that the finished dish is highly seasoned. Leave to stand until lukewarm. Serve with slices of lemon.'

Menon, in *La Cuisinière bourgeoise* (1742), gives a more elaborate version of *cochon par quartiers au Père Douillet*: the animal is cooked in bouillon, allowed to get cold in its jelly, and served reshaped on a large dish, garnished with crayfish. There is also a recipe using sweetbreads, in a sauce flavoured with pomegranate seeds and verjuice.

The name of the dish is attributed to Madame de Maintenon, who named it after her confessor. Although Pierre de Lune does not explicitly call his recipe *au Père Douillet*, this name appears in *L'Art de bien traiter* (1674) in the recipe for *cochon de lait au perdouillet.*

cochonnaille

A synonym for charcuterie, sometimes used jokingly or ironically, suggesting the idea of abundance. The traditional French country buffets and village feasts featured vast assortments of sausages, galantines, hams, pâtés, and other charcuterie.

cocido

A Spanish pot-au-feu (from the verb *cocer*, to cook). The ordinary cocido originated in Castile, but numerous regional varieties exist. The cocido of Madrid consists of three dishes served in turn from a pot that has simmered for a long time: firstly the stock, strained, enriched with vermicelli, and traditionally served with white wine; next a dish of chickpeas and boiled vegetables, i.e. potatoes, carrots, and cabbage, which are added to the cocido in the final stages of cooking and become impregnated with the juices from the meats; and finally a dish of meats comprising pieces of beef, chorizo, pickled pork, loin of pork, chicken, and little meat balls (sometimes also marrow bones, black pudding (blood sausage), and fresh bacon). The vegetables and meats are served with red wine and accompanied by sauces (tomato, cumin, and mint), and each dish is eaten with crusty bread.

In Castile, the three dishes are called *sota*, *caballo*, and *rey* (the knave, queen, and king of playing cards) – cocido is 'ennobled' as it progresses!

Lavish or simple (it may be only a dish of chickpeas with a piece of bacon), easy to make, and nourishing (the only precaution is to soak the chickpeas overnight beforehand), cocido is a staple dish throughout Spain and Portugal. The three major variants are Catalan cocido (dried beans and sometimes rice, local sausages, boutifar, oxtail), in which the three dishes are served together; Andalusian cocido (lighter and fragrant, with chilli peppers, mint, saffron, and green beans); and Galician cocido (which always contains pork, turnips with their tops, bacon, and several varieties of dried beans).

Cockaigne

PAYS DE COCAGNE

A mythical land of plenty, where men live happily without working and there is an abundance of everything. The myth, which is found in Germany and in Italy, is particularly deeply rooted in Flemish tradition and dates back to a time when the spectre of famine often became reality. In the legend, the lucky man arrives at the land of plenty by travelling through a tunnel cut into a mountain of buckwheat flour; there he discovers a roasted pig walking about with a carving knife in its belly, a table covered with pies and tarts, hedges made of sausages, etc., and roast pigeons drop into his mouth. All these images appear in a famous painting of 1567 by Brueghel, which depicts representatives of the three states, replete and satisfied.

By extension, *cocagne* used to refer to a table generously provided and richly loaded. In 17th-century Naples, the *cocagne* (or *cuccagna*) was a traditional feast, when a heap of victuals was arranged as a sign of rejoicing and reconciliation.

cock-a-leekie

A Scottish speciality, whose name means literally 'cock and leek'. It is a substantial soup, based on chicken and leeks, thickened with barley, and traditionally served with stewed prunes. A more refined version is based on chicken consommé, leek, and chicken.

RECIPE

cock-a-leekie   Prepare a chicken consommé. Cut the white parts of some leeks into fine strips; 200 g (7 oz) are required for 1 litre (1¾ pints, 4¼ cups) consommé. Cook this julienne slowly in 20 g (¾ oz, 1½ tablespoons) butter for 15 minutes. Cut into strips the white chicken flesh that was used to prepare the consommé and add the leek and chicken juliennes to the consommé.

cockle   COQUE

A bivalve mollusc, 3–4 cm (1–1½ in) long, which is found near or on the seabed. The two equal shells have 26 clearly marked ribs and enclose a knob of flesh and a tiny coral. Sold by volume, cockles may be eaten raw but are generally cooked, like mussels. Since they retain sand inside the shell they should be left to clear in salt water for 12 hours or so before they are consumed. The cockles of Picardy, called *hénons*, are highly regarded.

cock's comb

CRÊTE DE COQ

A fleshy red outgrowth on the top of the head of a cock. For use in cookery it needs to be fairly large, but nowadays most breeds of domestic fowl have small combs and in any case are usually slaughtered when young. Today cocks' combs are used in recipes as a garnish for barquettes and croustades. They were frequently used in traditional French cookery (often with cocks' kidneys) in numerous garnishes, including ambassadeur, chalonnaise, financière, gauloise, Godard, Régence, etc.

Pickled ox (beef) tongue and fine slices of truffle are sometimes cut into the shape of cocks' combs for decoration.

RECIPE

Preparation of cocks' combs PRÉPARATION DES CRÊTES DE COQ Prick the combs lightly with a needle and put them under the cold tap, pressing them with the fingers to dispel the blood. Cover with cold water and cook until the water reaches a temperature of 40–45 c (110 f), when the skin of the combs begins to detach itself. Drain the combs and rub them one by one in a cloth sprinkled with fine salt.

Remove the outer skin; put the combs in cold water, and when they are white plunge them into a boiling white courtbouillon (see *blanc de cuisson*). Cook for 35 minutes.

Cocks' combs en attereaux à la Villeroi CRÊTES DE COQ EN ATTEREAUX À LA VILLEROI Cook the cocks' combs as described above, drain and dry them, and cover with Villeroi sauce. Leave to cool on a grid. Cover the combs with egg, sprinkle with breadcrumbs, and fry in clarified butter.

cocktail

A mixed drink made according to a variety of recipes and containing liqueurs, spirits, syrup, spices, and so on, the end product being pleasant to both eye and palate. The origin of the word is somewhat obscure: it may refer to the shades of colour in a cock's tail, but it is more likely to derive from American racecourse slang, dating from the early part of the 19th century.

Drinking cocktails became particularly fashionable between the two World Wars, a time when famous bars were opened in all the capitals of Europe. Barmen, expert in the art of making cocktails, christened their creations with names that have become classics – Manhattan, gin fizz, Bloody Mary, and so on. A competent barman should have a wide repertoire of cocktails, ranging from the world's most famous – the dry martini – to the more complicated sours, smashes, fizzes, crustas, sangarees, flips, shrubs, and drinks that may be created for topical events. Cocktails that are based on spirits without much dilution are usually served in a smallish glass, as shorts. Longer drinks, such as juleps, Pimm's, and recipes incorporating soda or sparkling wine, may be in tall glasses, large goblets, or tumblers.

There is a fine distinction between those cocktails that are stirred and those that are shaken – subsequently to be poured though crushed ice; the garnish also varies: lemon zest, olive, cherry, and so on. Touches such as frosting the edges of glasses (by damping them and then turning them in sugar) or serving any 'frappé' with straws are all part of the barman's expertise.

Recently, nonalcoholic cocktails using fruit or vegetable juices or even flavoured milk have become popular.

The word cocktail is also used in cookery to describe various cold hors d'oeuvres, such as prawn cocktail, lobster cocktail, etc. A macédoine of fruit may also be called fruit cocktail.

RECIPE

CLASSIC COCKTAILS

Alexandra: 1 part fresh cream, 1 part crème de cacao, 1 part Cognac.

Americano: 1 part Campari, 2 parts sweet Italian vermouth, a splash of soda, lemon zest.

Bacardi: 3 parts white Bacardi rum, 1 part grenadine, 1 part lime juice.

black velvet: 1 part Guinness, 1 part nonvintage champagne.

Bloody Mary: 1 small can of tomato juice, 1 dash of lemon juice, 2 dashes of Worcestershire sauce, 3 dashes of vodka, salt, and cayenne.

Bronx: 3 parts gin, 1 part orange juice, 1 part sweet red Italian vermouth, 1 part dry Italian vermouth.

Canasta: 1 part sweet white Italian vermouth, 1 part gin, 1 part Maraschino.

Champagne cocktail: 2 drops angostura bitters on a lump of sugar, 1 teaspoon brandy or Cognac, topped up with nonvintage champagne and garnished with a slice of orange.

Cherry blossom: 1 part Cognac, 1 part cherry brandy, 1 dash of Curaçao, 1 dash of grenadine, 1 dash of lemon juice.

Curnonsky: 2 parts Cognac, 3 parts Cointreau, 1 tablespoon orange juice.

Daiquiri: 3 parts white rum, 2 parts lemon juice, 1 part sugar syrup.

Dubonnet fizz: 1 glass of Dubonnet, the juice of half an orange, topped up with champagne.

Evening delight: 1 glass of rye whisky, 1 dash of Curaçao, 1 dash of apricot brandy.

Gin fizz: 1 glass of gin, the juice of 1 lemon, 1 tablespoon sugar, soda water.

Half and half: 1 part pale ale, 1 part stout.

Manhattan: 2 parts rye whisky, 1 part sweet vermouth, 2 dashes of angostura bitters, 1 cherry.

Manhattan dry: as Manhattan, but substitute dry for sweet vermouth and a twist of lemon for cherry.

Negroni: 1 part gin, 1 part Campari, 1 part vermouth (sweet or dry), lemon slice.

Planter's: 4 parts white rum, 1 part lemon or lime juice, 1 part orange juice.

Sherry cobbler: 1 glass of sherry, 2 dashes of Curaçao, 3 dashes of orange juice, 1 slice of orange, 1 slice of lemon.

Sidecar: 1 part lemon juice, 1 part Cognac, 1 part white Curaçao.

Tom Collins: 1 measure of gin, 1 teaspoon sugar, 1 tablespoon lemon juice, soda water.

Cocktails Based on Fruit Juice

Cocabana: 1 glass of pineapple juice, 1 tablespoon milk, 1 tablespoon honey, 1 mashed banana.

Cocabricot: 1 large glass of apricot juice, ¼ cup skimmed milk, 1 tablespoon honey.

Cocktomate: 1 glass of tomato juice, 1 tablespoon lemon juice, 1 tablespoon chopped parsley.

Complete cocktail: 1 glass of pineapple juice, 1 tablespoon crushed walnuts, 1 teaspoon yeast, 1 tablespoon honey, 10 wild strawberries.

(These cocktails were specially devised by the dietician Gayelord Hauser)

Caribbean cocktail: ½ glass of orange juice, ½ glass of pineapple juice, 1 teaspoon mint syrup, 1 teaspoon lemon juice, topped with fresh mint leaves.

Spiced tomato juice: 1 glass of tomato juice, 1 tablespoon lemon juice, 1 dash of Worcestershire sauce, a pinch of celery salt, a pinch of grated nutmeg, a pinch of caster (superfine) sugar.

Milk-based Cocktails

Apricot cocktail (*make in the blender*): 1 litre (1¾ pints, 4¼ cups) semi-skimmed milk, 500 g (18 oz, 3 cups) stoned (pitted) apricots, the juice of 1 orange, 3 tablespoons sugar, 6 tablespoons crushed ice.

Banana cocktail (*make in the blender*): 1 sliced banana, 1 teaspoon lemon juice, 1 tablespoon sugar, 1 glass of milk.

Brazilian cocktail: ⅓ glass of evaporated milk, 2 teaspoons instant coffee dissolved in 2 tablespoons boiling water, ¼ teaspoon powdered cinnamon, sugar to taste, ice cubes.

Cherry cocktail *(make in the blender)*: 1 litre (1¾ pints, 4¼ cups) semi-skimmed milk, 1 egg yolk, 500 g (18 oz, 3 cups) stoned (pitted) cherries, juice of half a lemon, 2–3 tablespoons caster (superfine) sugar.

Five-fruit cocktail *(make in the blender)*: ½ glass of skimmed milk, 125 g (4½ oz, scant 1 cup) strawberries, 125 g (4½ oz, scant 1 cup) raspberries, the juice of 125 g (4½ oz, ¾ cup) redcurrants, the juice of 125 g (4½ oz, generous 1 cup) blackcurrants, the juice of 1 orange, caster (superfine) sugar to taste (the gooseberry and blackcurrant juices are very acid.

Mint cocktail: 1 glass of semi-skimmed milk, 1 liqueur glass of mint syrup, 1 tablespoon crushed ice. Serve with a few leaves of fresh mint.

Négrillonne: 1 glass of diluted evaporated milk, 1 tablespoon chocolate powder, ¼ teaspoon vanilla, sugar to taste, ice cubes.

Tea-based Cocktails

Casbah This Algerian drink is extremely thirst-quenching. Drunk hot, or even very hot, during the hottest season, it is delightfully refreshing. Use 1 tablespoon green tea, 1 tablespoon chopped mint leaves, 100–150 g (4–5 oz, approximately ⅔ cup) loaf (or granulated) sugar, ¾ litre (1¼ pints, 1½ pints) boiling water. Mix the green tea and mint together and leave to infuse in the water for some time. Crush the sugar and add small quantities gradually to the tea until it dissolves. The infusion must be very strong and very sweet, rather like a syrup in consistency. Serve very hot with a fresh mint leaf in each glass.

This drink may be made entirely with mint leaves, in which case the sugar is replaced by honey.

Tea punch Use 3 teaspoons tea, the zest of half a lemon, 3 tablespoons caster (superfine) sugar, 1 dl (6 tablespoons, scant ½ cup) rum, water, and ice cubes. Make the tea with ¼ litre (8 fl oz, 1 cup) boiling water. Allow to stand and then strain. Add the lemon and then 3 dl (½ pint, 1¼ cups) boiling water. Add the sugar. Allow to cool and then place in the refrigerator. To serve, put an ice cube in each glass, pour in the rum, and lastly, the cold tea. This cocktail is often drunk through a straw inserted through a slice of lemon.

Hors-d'oeuvre Cocktails

Crab cocktail Cook fresh crabs in a court-bouillon, or use canned or frozen crabmeat (about 400 g (14 oz) crabmeat is required). Prepare the sauce as follows. Cook 3 finely chopped shallots in a glass of white wine, and reduce completely. Add the shallots to a well-seasoned mayonnaise prepared with 1 egg yolk, ¼ litre (8 fl oz, 1 cup) oil, 1 tablespoon strong mustard, and 1 tablespoon vinegar. Blend in 1 tablespoon tomato purée and 1 tablespoon chopped tarragon. Season to taste with salt, pepper, and cayenne. Flavour, if desired, with 1 liqueur glass of Cognac. Mix the sauce with the flaked crabmeat. Place some shredded lettuce seasoned with vinaigrette in 4 sundae glasses. Divide the crab cocktail among the glasses and place in the refrigerator until ready to serve. (Do not prepare the lettuce if the serving time is delayed.) At the time of serving, sprinkle with finely chopped tarragon leaves.

Prawn cocktail Prepare in the same way as crab cocktail, but garnish with quarters of tomato and slices of hard-boiled (hard-cooked) egg.

Vegetable-based Cocktails

The chosen vegetables must be young and very fresh. They are washed, peeled if necessary, and chopped as finely as possible, then put in a food processor or blender. Water, soda water, or lemon juice, together with the specified spices, can then be added.

Cucumber and tomato cocktail Mix equal amounts of chopped cucumber and tomato in a blender. Add some lemon juice (the juice of half a lemon for each cucumber used), 1 glass of water, salt, pepper, and a dash of cayenne.

Six-vegetable cocktail Chop together 4–5 fresh carrots, 3 large tomatoes, 5 onions, 3 sticks (stalks) of cleaned celery, 1 fresh turnip, half a desceeded green pepper, and the juice of 1 lemon. Place all the ingredients in a blender together with some salt, pepper, and enough water for the drink to have the desired consistency. Place in the regrigerator until ready to serve. Pour into the glasses and decorate with 2–3 basil leaves.

cocktail party

A social gathering in which the guests usually remain standing and cocktails, other alcoholic drinks, fruit juices, and canapés are served. A cocktail party generally takes place at the end of the afternoon in a hotel or private house.

cocktail snack

AMUSE-GUEULE

A small bite-sized savoury item that is served with apéritifs. Depending on the occasion, cocktail snacks may comprise an extensive or limited range of hot or cold hors d'oeuvres. Examples include plain or stuffed olives, salted nuts, savoury biscuits (crackers) flavoured with cheese, paprika, ham, etc., potato crisps (chips), small hot cocktail sausages, cubes of hard cheese on small sticks, canapés, miniature pizzas or quiches, savoury allumettes, and shredded raw vegetables.

cocoa CACAO

A powder made from cocoa (cacao) beans, which are the seeds of the cacao, a tropical tree 4–12 m (13–39 ft) high. Each fruit (pod) contains 25–40 beans, rounded or flattened in shape and grey, purplish, or bluish in colour depending on the variety. The beans are extracted from the ripe pods and heaped up into mounds so that they ferment. This process destroys the germ and helps to develop their flavour. They are then sorted, washed, dried, and roasted.

The word cocoa is derived from the Aztec word *cacahuatl*. According to legend, the cacao tree was the most beautiful tree in the paradise of the Aztecs, and they attributed many virtues to it. It was thought to appease hunger and thirst, give universal knowledge, and cure sickness. In 1502, Christopher Columbus was offered, as a sign of welcome, weapons, fabrics, and sacks of brown cocoa beans, the latter, in Aztec society, serving as currency as well as food. In 1519 Cortés discovered the New World civilization, and the first cargo of cocoa reached Spain in 1524. It was not until the 17th century that cocoa, or chocolate, became a fashionable drink, and it was not until the 19th century that chocolate bars were first manufactured.

There are several varieties of cocoa. The best variety comes from Venezuela. The finest and most aromatic, it is known as Caracas cacao. Brazilian cocoa, known as Maranhão cacao, has a pleasant bitter taste, like the cocoas of Ecuador and the West Indies. The latter two varieties are used to flavour weaker cocoas, with which they are mixed. The African cocoas, which give a high yield but are poor in quality, are used mainly for commercial products. Cocoa beans are also produced in Sri Lanka and Java.

The raw material of all cocoa- or chocolate-based products is cocoa paste (chocolate liquor). This bitter oily substance is made by crushing the cocoa beans after they have been fermented, roasted, and shelled. The fat content of cocoa paste amounts to 45–60%, according to the quality of the beans. Crushing is very important, as it determines the fineness and smoothness of the paste.

Cocoa butter is the natural fatty material in cocoa beans. It is a relatively firm product, yellowish-white in colour, and is pressed from the paste in variable proportions when manufacturing cocoa powder. Extra cocoa butter is sometimes added in the manufacture of block chocolate, in order to enrich and improve the consistency.

Cocoa powder is obtained by grinding cocoa cake, which is cocoa paste with most of the fat removed. Cocoa powder contains between 8 and 20% fat, depending on how much cocoa butter has been extracted from the cocoa cake.

coconut NOIX DE COCO

The fruit of the coconut palm, a tall tree probably originating in Melanesia but now widely cultivated throughout the tropics. The coconut has a very hard woody shell and is enclosed in a thick fibrous husk. The shell is lined with a firm white pulp and the hollow centre contains a sweet milky-white liquid which makes a refreshing drink. The pulp is rich in fat and has a high calorific value – 370 Cal per 100 g fresh; 630 Cal per 100 g dried. It also contains phosphorus, potassium, and carbohydrates.

Used as food in southeast Asia and Polynesia from the earliest times, the coconut was 'discovered' by Marco Polo, who described 'the Pharaoh's nut' as a fruit full of flavour, sweet as sugar, and white as milk, providing at the same time both food and drink. A Portuguese doctor who made a detailed study of the coconut in the 16th century wrote: 'This fruit is called *coquo* because it has three pores on its surface, giving it the appearance of a human head.' The first specimen to arrive in Paris was presented to the Académie Française by Charles Perrault in 1674.

In western countries coconut is most commonly used in desiccated (shredded) form, for biscuits (cookies), cakes, and confectionery, as well as for jam and ices. However in Indian, Indonesian, African, and South American cooking the pulp is used fresh (grated and sieved) or dried (grated and mixed with water) in condiments, to season raw vegetables and fish, and as an ingredient in chicken, beef, or shellfish stews. Coconut milk, much used in Indian cooking, gives a distinctive taste and smoothness to curries, sauces, and rice. In Polynesia it is used in soups, jams, and fish marinades. In Brazil and Venezuela coconut cream is poured over desserts and pastries, while in Vietnam and the Philippines, pork, beef, and poultry are marinated in it.

A coconut can be opened either by cracking the shell with a hammer, or by first piercing the two ends so that the liquid runs out and then heating it in the oven until it cracks; the pulp can then be extracted quite easily. The dried pulp (copra) is refined and deodorized to produce coconut butter, used as a cooking fat.

RECIPES

Coconut cake GÂTEAU À LA NOIX DE COCO Prepare a syrup using 200 g (7 oz, scant 1 cup) caster (superfine) sugar and 2 dl (7 fl oz, ¾ cup) water. Whisk 4 egg yolks in a bowl over hot (but not boiling) water, then slowly pour in the sugar syrup, whisking constantly. When the yolks have almost doubled in volume, remove the bowl from the hot water and continue to whisk until the mixture is cold. Make ½ litre (8 fl oz, 1 cup) fresh Chantilly cream, adding 1 teaspoon vanilla sugar and a glass of rum. Blend well then add the egg-yolk mixture and 300 g (11 oz, 4 cups) fresh or desiccated (shredded) grated coconut. Pour into a deep sandwich tin (layer cake pan) and put in the freezer until the mixture is firm to the touch. Then remove the cake from the mould, cover with grated coconut, and keep in the refrigerator until required.

Coconut preserve CONFITURE DE NOIX DE COCO Open some coconuts, extract the pulp, and grate it. Prepare a syrup using 1 kg (2¼ lb) sugar to 1 litre (1¾ pints, 4¼ cups) water and flavour it with either vanilla essence (extract) or 1 teaspoon vanilla sugar. Mix together equal quantities of the grated pulp and the syrup and cook very gently until the jam becomes transparent. Pot as for jam.

coco or icaco plum

ICAQUE

The plumlike fruit of a tropical tree cultivated in the West Indies and Central America. The skin is yellow, white, red, or purplish, depending on the variety. The white flesh is soft with a rather sour taste and the kernel is edible. The fruit is also known as the handle plum or the cotton plum and may be eaten raw or used as a preserve.

cocotte

A round or oval cooking pan with two handles and a well-fitting lid, used for slow-cooking dishes such as daubes, braised dishes, and casseroled meat. The pan is also used for various preparations described as *en cocotte* or *à la bonne femme*.

The origin of the cocotte goes back to the beginning of the 19th century. At first it was made of black cast iron, which is a good conductor of heat but tends to break and rust. Nowadays, the cocotte (or coquelle) is usually made of enamel, aluminium (which is lighter), stainless steel (which is unbreakable but not such a good conductor of heat), copper (for small pans), tempered glass (ovenproof, but not able to withstand direct heat), or glazed ceramic (a good conductor of heat, easy to clean, and without the drawbacks of tempered glass).

Dishes *en cocotte* or *en casserole* almost always need to be fried lightly over a brisk heat before they are put on to simmer. It is therefore necessary that the material from which the cocotte is made will be able to withstand differences in temperature and it is also important that the food does not stick. In order to ensure a more gentle heat, the bases of some cocottes are grooved, but these cannot be used on the hotplates of an electric cooker, when a flat-bottomed pan must be used. Some cocottes have a lid designed to hold cold water. This is poured onto it during the cooking period and causes internal condensation, thus preventing the food from drying out.

cod CABILLAUD

A large fish, up to 1.8 m (6 ft) long, with an elongated powerful body, very pronounced fins, and a large head. It has a heavy whisker-like barbel on its lower jaw. Its colour varies from greyish-green to brown and it has dark spots on the back and sides and a whitish belly. Cod is abundant in the cold seas of the North Atlantic (0–10 c, 32–50 f). The female is very fertile, and can lay up to 5 million eggs. The eggs, known as roe, can be sold freshly boiled or smoked.

Fresh cod has a white flaky delicate flesh that can be prepared in many different ways. Small and medium-sized fish, weighing from 1 to 3 kg (2¼–6½ lb), are sold whole, although there is a large amount of waste. They can be roasted in the oven (which concentrates the flavour), braised in white wine like brill, or poached in a flavoured court-bouillon. They are served hot or cold with a sauce. Large cod, which are more generally used, are cut into fillets, slices, or pieces. The skinned fillets are good value, and can be prepared in many different ways. Slices have little waste (only the backbone, skin, and part of the fin); they are prepared *à l'anglaise* or *à la meunière*. The cod's delicate flesh requires careful cooking because of the whitish liquid that seeps from it. Prolonged cooking harms both the flavour and the presentation. Cod pieces are especially suited to cooking in the oven or in a court-bouillon, usually in white wine. Cod is rarely grilled (broiled), because of the flaky texture of its flesh. The tail yields a nicely presented piece of flesh for roasting or braising, whereas the part near the head, which has a very fine flavour, has a less elegant appearance and needs to be tied up with string before cooking.

Cod is also used to make croquettes, fish cakes, gratins, coquille dishes (served in scallop shells), and mousses. Cod may be frozen whole, in fillets, or in the form of croquettes or fingers, covered with breadcrumbs and ready for frying. Cod is rich in mineral salts and is not a fatty fish (68 Cal per 100 g, 1% lipids); it is available practically all the year round.

In France, cod that has been salted and dried is sold under the name of *morue*. Recipes for cod preserved in this way are given under the article *salt cod*.

RECIPES

Braised cod à la flamande CABILLAUD BRAISÉ À LA FLAMANDE Season slices of cod with salt and pepper. Butter an ovenproof dish and sprinkle with chopped shallots and parsley. Arrange the cod in the dish and just cover with dry white wine. Place a slice of peeled lemon on each piece of cod. Bring to the boil, then cook in the oven at 220 c (425 f, gas 7) for about 15 minutes. Remove the fish and drain. Arrange the slices on the serving dish and keep warm. Reduce the juices by boiling, then add some pieces of butter, stir, and pour the sauce over the cod. Sprinkle with roughly chopped parsley.

Cod à l'anglaise   CABILLAUD À L'ANGLAISE   Cut the cod into slices 3 cm (1¼ in) thick, taken from the middle of the fish for preference. Season with salt and pepper and dredge in flour. Dip in beaten egg mixed with oil, cover with white breadcrumbs, and fry in clarified butter until both sides are golden. Arrange the cod on a hot serving dish and coat with half-melted maître d'hôtel butter.

Cold poached cod   CABILLAUD POCHÉ FROID   Poach the fish as in the recipe for hot poached cod until nearly cooked. Leave to finish cooking as it cools in the salt water. Drain the cooled fish, wipe, and arrange on a napkin. Garnish with either fresh parsley or lettuce hearts and quarters of hard-boiled (hard-cooked) eggs. Serve with a suitable cold sauce, such as gribiche, mayonnaise, ravigote, rémoulade, tartare, sauce vert, vinaigrette, or Vincent.

Fried cod   CABILLAUD FRIT   Cut the fish into thin slices, dip them in cold boiled milk, and coat them with flour. Deep-fry in oil over a high heat. Drain the fish, and wipe with absorbent paper (paper towels) to soak up the excess oil. Garnish with fried parsley and lemon quarters. The fish may alternatively be dipped in egg and breadcrumbs before frying.

Grilled (broiled) cod   CABILLAUD GRILLÉ   Season some cod steaks with salt and pepper. Coat lightly with flour or oil and sprinkle with melted butter. Alternatively, the cod steaks can be soaked in a mixture of olive oil, garlic, chopped parsley, and lemon juice for 30 minutes. Cook under a moderate grill. Garnish the cod with slices of peeled lemon and fresh parsley. Serve with maître d'hôtel butter or one of the sauces recommended for grilled fish.

Hot poached cod   CABILLAUD POCHÉ CHAUD   Place a piece of cod, either whole or cut up into chunks, in a pan of salt water (allow 10 g (generous ¼ oz, 1 tablespoon) salt per litre of water). Bring to the boil, then lower the heat and poach gently with the lid on, taking care not to boil, until flesh flakes easily. Drain the fish, arrange on a napkin, and garnish with fresh parsley. Serve with a sauce suitable for poached fish, such as anchovy, butter, caper, prawn, herb, hollandaise, lobster, or ravigote.

Roast cod   CABILLAUD RÔTI   Trim a cod weighing 1.5–1.75 kg (3–4 lb). Season with salt and pepper, sprinkle with oil and lemon juice, and leave to steep for 30 minutes. Drain the cod, place it on a spit, and brush with melted butter. Then roast before a brisk fire, basting frequently with melted butter or oil, for 30–40 minutes. Arrange on a serving dish and keep hot. Deglaze the pan with dry white wine, reduce, and spoon the juice over the fish. The fish may also be roasted in the oven, provided that is placed on a wire rack so that it does not lie in the cooking juices.

Coeur de Bray

A Normandy cheese made from cows' milk (45% fat content), with a soft smooth paste and a downy white rind, flecked with red. It has a fruity flavour and is excellent in summer when freshly made.

coffee   CAFÉ

The coffee tree, native to the Sudan and Ethiopia but now widely cultivated, bears small red berries that contain the seeds (coffee beans). The word coffee comes from the Italian *caffè*, derived from the Turkish *kahve* and the Arabic *qahwah*. The Arabic word originally designated any stimulating drink.

□   **From Turkey to the tropics** The invention of the drink itself and the discovery of its properties is the subject of many stories and legends. One version attributes its discovery to a goatherd, who noticed that his goats became agitated when they chewed the leaves of certain bushes. Another story is that a dervish, mullah, or hermit used coffee to stay awake at night in order to pray. Some people attribute its discovery to the famous Arabic doctor, Avicenna. Whichever story is true, coffee was being drunk in Aden as early as 1420. The custom passed on to Syria, and then in 1550 to Constantinople. Italian ambassadors in Turkey called it 'black water extracted from seeds called *cavee*'. The first Westerners to import coffee were the Venetians in 1615. It was introduced to France in 1644 by a French traveller called La Royne, but in fact it was Soliman Aga, the ambassador of the Turkish government to Louis XIV, who, in 1669, made it popular. Initially, it was considered to be an exotic and rather therapeutic product. The 'new flavour', as it was called, became a fashionable drink at court and among the nobility. The invention of the coffee mill in 1687 greatly contributed to the widespread use of coffee and coincided with the publication of *Le Bon Usage du thé, du caffé, et du chocolat pour la préservation et pour la guérison des maladies.*

In 1690, a coffee plantation was established at the Jardin des Plantes, but the coffee tree remains an essentially tropical plant. Its cultivation spread throughout Africa, South America, and the West Indies. The price fluctuations of this colonial commodity together with such political vicissitudes as the Continental System caused various substitutes for coffee to appear, such as acorns, barley, maize, rye, butcher's broom, dried beans, dried peas, but especially chicory.

Nowadays, two species of coffee tree provide 95% of world production. They are *Coffea arabica* and *Coffea robusta*. Arabica coffees, having beans that are elongated, oval, and flat, are mild and aromatic and generally considered to be the best. They come mainly from Brazil but also from Arabia, Ethiopia, and India (Mocha). They are also grown in Mexico and Costa Rica, but although this coffee is full of flavour, the quality is not as good. However, the arabica coffee from Colombia has a good slightly acid flavour and is highly rated by connoisseurs. Robusta coffee beans are smaller and have an irregular convex shape. The beans contain two and a half times more caffeine than arabica coffee beans and yield a more full-bodied and bitter drink. They are grown in the Ivory Coast, Angola, and Zaïre. More full-bodied arabica coffees can be obtained by mixing them with other varieties, such as canephora, liberica, and excelsa.

☐ **From harvesting to grinding** The fruits of the coffee tree are treated to remove the pulp, and the yellowish-grey beans are hulled, graded, and bagged. In this form the beans are known as green coffee, which keeps for a long time provided that it is protected from damp. It may then be sold and exported.

Roasting the coffee beans releases various complex volatile constituents, which are responsible for the characteristic flavour and aroma of coffee. The beans are continuously stirred during the roasting process. At 200 c (392 F), they are light brown and have doubled in volume. At 250 c (482 F), they are noticeably darker. Well-roasted coffee should be fairly dark reddish-brown, but never black or shiny. Insufficient roasting produces a harsh colourless tasteless infusion, whereas excessive roasting yields a very black, bitter, and astringent brew. Until the end of the 19th century, green coffee was still roasted at home in special coffee burners. (Alexandre Dumas tells how Napoleon, coming upon a priest in the middle of roasting his coffee during the Continental System, heard him reply: 'I am doing the same as Your Majesty, I am burning colonial produce!'. Nowadays, the food industry makes more or less standardized flavours according to prevailing tastes: very lightly roasted coffee for North Americans; slightly more heavily roasted coffee for the French and the Italians; fairly dark coffee for the Dutch; and 'burnt' coffee for countries in the Middle East. After roasting, coffee does not retain its aroma for long, and becomes stale in the open air: it should therefore be stored in a sealed jar and kept in a cool place.

The final operation is grinding. The fineness of the grounds depends on which method is used to brew the coffee. It is always preferable to grind only enough coffee for one's immediate needs, as ground coffee loses its aroma very quickly. Ideally, grinding should be done just before the coffee is made.

The stimulating effect that coffee has on the body is due to the alkaloid called caffeine. In his *Treatise on Modern Stimulants*, Balzac remarked: 'Coffee sets the blood in motion, so that the driving force springs from it. This stimulation speeds up digestion, takes away the desire for sleep, and enables one to exercise one's mental faculties for a little longer.'

The 19th-century *Larousse* states that coffee 'is particularly indicated for men of letters, soldiers, sailors, and all workers who have to stay in hot surroundings, lastly, to all inhabitants of a country where cretinism is rife'.

☐ **Different types of coffee** Coffee sold and labelled as an arabica variety must contain only that particular variety: Mocha, Manilla, or Bourbon (for a choice aromatic coffee), Colombia or Menado (for a very mild coffee), or Haiti (for a full-bodied coffee). If sold without such a label, it will be either a robusta (if cheap) or a mixture of arabica and robusta (if more expensive). Coffee lovers of the 19th century recommended the following as best: 'a Mocha coffee, mixed with Bourbon coffee and Martinique coffee'. Nowadays, so-called superior coffee is sold with a guarantee that there are no more than 10% of faults in the beans. It must also be labelled with the date of roasting. Coated coffee (for industrialized packaging) is very black and shiny because of the addition of glucose, gum arabic, or vegetable oil after roasting. It keeps longer, and has a full-bodied flavour, but is slightly syrupy.

After roasting, coffee is sold either in the form of coffee beans or as ground coffee. It should preferably be ground in a coffee mill, which preserves the flavour as much as possible. Ground coffee is often vacuum-packed, but must be consumed quickly once the packet has been opened. Since the 1930s, decaffeinated coffee has been produced. Instant coffee is a great commercial success. Either spray-dried or freeze-dried (which denatures it less), with or without caffeine, it is instantly soluble in hot water.

Lastly, there is liquid coffee essence (extract), which is widely used as a flavouring in desserts, cakes, and confectionery.

☐ **The history of coffee-drinking** At the end of the 17th century, it was the custom in French high society to serve coffee after a meal. By about 1860, coffee-drinking in France was firmly established at all social levels. Also at this time, coffee became an integral part of military rations. The French slang term *jus* was widely used for black coffee by the end of the 19th century, and

indicates how popular it had become. It is served in a variety of ways, depending on the country or region. In Greece, Turkey, and the Arab countries, it is highly concentrated, often sweetened, and served with a glass of cold water. In Switzerland, Germany, and Holland it is served with a chocolate, while in Belgium and the UK it may be served with biscuits. In northern France it is very often served with a small jug of cream. Coffee after a meal is traditionally served with liqueurs and cigars. Finally, there are many regions of France (especially Normandy and Lorraine) where coffee is served with a 'dash' of alcohol. (*See brûlot, champoreau, gloria.*)

The United States is the prime consumer of coffee (12 kg (26 lb) per person per annum, double the amount consumed in France), followed by the EEC and Brazil.

☐ **French or Turkish coffee** There are two basic methods of brewing coffee:

● The Turkish method consists of pouring coffee (which has been reduced to an extremely fine powder) into boiling water, together with an almost equal quantity of sugar. The mixture is then heated until it is on the point of boiling. This operation is repeated three times. A special small conical pan with a wide base is used for the process. Before serving, a few drops of cold water are poured into the saucepan to settle the grounds. The piping hot coffee is served either in cups or in small glasses.

● The French method is to pour boiling water onto ground coffee (which is less finely ground than that used to make Turkish coffee), held between two perforated discs that act as a filter. This procedure is known technically as *lixiviation*. (See *percolator*.)

Turkish coffee is commonly drunk in the Mediterranean countries and the Middle East. In Arab countries, two Madagascan cardamon seeds are often added. In Greece, coffee may be very strong and sweet, moderately strong with only a little added sugar, or tepid and sugarless; sweetened coffee may be reboiled several times.

French coffee, on the other hand, must never be boiled, and certainly not reheated. (In the 19th century, however, the taste of boiled coffee was highly appreciated in the French provinces.) Purists recommend the use of bottled still water rather than tap water, as the chlorine in tap water ruins the flavour. One tablespoon of coffee per person (10–12 g (approximately ⅓ oz) per cup) is generally advised. A porcelain or earthenware coffee pot is preferable to one made of metal, as the latter spoils the flavour. The water must be just below boiling point when it is poured over the coffee. Cups should be filled three-quarters full.

□ **Variations** Espresso coffee is a black Italian-style coffee. It is also very popular in Austria, where it is usually known as *moka*, even if it is not made from Mocha coffee beans. It is made in a special pressurized apparatus by forcing steam from boiling water through the ground coffee.

The Italians have also produced cappuccino coffee, so called because of its pale brown colour, reminiscent of the robes of the Capuchin monks. This consists of strong coffee to which frothy cream or milk is added. It is sometimes served with a pinch of powdered chocolate on the top. This type of coffee is the same as the Austrian *Kapuziner*. White coffee (coffee with milk) was in fact introduced by the Viennese. True Austrian white coffee is made by putting a spoonful of either whipped cream or fresh double (heavy) cream onto the surface of the coffee, without stirring. In France, white coffee is mixed with hot milk before serving (see *café au lait*).

In South America, where coffee-growing was introduced in 1720, the best varieties are exported, but large quantities of *tinto* (strong black very sweet coffee) are consumed there. In Argentina and Mexico, people also drink a type of coffee that has been roasted with sugar and has a pronounced caramel flavour. In the West Indies, coffee is flavoured with vanilla, cinnamon, ginger, etc.

RECIPES

Arabic coffee CAFÉ ARABE (from *La Cuisine arabe*, R. Khawam, Albin Michel) Put 50 g (2 oz, ½ cup) very finely

ground arabica coffee and 100 g (4 oz, 8 tablespoons, firmly packed) granulated sugar into a coffee pot that has a wide bottom and a narrow neck. Boil 500 ml (17 fl oz, 2 cups) water in a small saucepan and pour it into the coffee pot all at once. Heat the coffee pot until the coffee boils, stirring continuously. Remove the pot from the heat, and then replace it. Repeat this procedure twice more. When the coffee boils for the third time, tap the bottom of the coffee pot sharply on a flat surface. The coffee grounds will then begin to sink towards the bottom. Pour the coffee into cups, adding 1 teaspoon hot water to each cup. The grounds will then settle completely.

Coffee ice cream GLACE AU CAFÉ Blend together 6 eggs, 200 g (7 oz, scant cup, firmly packed) sugar, and 3 tablespoons instant coffee to make a custard cream. Whip 2 dl (7 fl oz, ¾ cup) cold thick cream with a quarter of its volume of very cold milk and 1 tablespoon vanilla sugar. Fold the whipped cream gently into the cold custard and leave it to freeze in an ice-cream maker. The ice cream can be decorated with sugar coffee beans or coffee sugar crystals.

Coffee syrup SIROP DE CAFÉ Finely grind 500 g (17½ oz, 4¼ cups) coffee, and pour 1.5 litres (2¾ pints, 3½ pints) boiling water very slowly over it. Add the hot coffee to 2.5 kg (5½ lb, 11 cups, firmly packed) sugar in a pan, and dissolve over a very low heat to prevent it from boiling. Remove the syrup from the heat just before it reaches boiling point.

Iced coffee CAFÉ GLACÉ Use 300 g (11 oz, 3⅔ cups) freshly ground coffee and ¾ litre (1⅓ pints, 1¾ pints) boiling water. Pour into a bowl with 575 g (1¼ lb, 2½ cups) granulated sugar. Dissolve the sugar and chill the infusion. Add to the coffee 1 litre (1¾ pints, generous quart) vanilla-flavoured cold boiled milk and ½ litre (scant pint, 2¼ cups) fresh cream. Serve chilled.

coffee maker CAFETIÈRE

A utensil for making or serving coffee. The word *cafetière* appeared in 1685, when coffee-drinking began in France, and the use of the *cafetière* became widespread in the reign of Louis XV; it was later provided with a heating plate and a spirit lamp. Flaubert recalls this antique device in *Madame Bovary*: 'Madame Homais reappeared, bearing one of those unsteady machines that have to be heated with spirit of wine, for Homais liked to make his coffee at the table, having, besides, roasted it himself, ground it himself, and compounded it himself.'

For a long time only two models of coffee maker were known in France: the infuser, in which the coffee was held in a filter, and the Dubelloy *cafetière*, in which the coffee was filtered. The latter, which appeared after 1850 and is known as *cafetière de grandmère*, was a wide pot, made of fire clay. Another method of making coffee became widespread in the period between the World Wars – the Cona. It consists of two interconnecting toughened glass vessels placed one on top of the other and heated either with a spirit lamp or with an electric or gas heater. The water in the lower glass container is forced up, by vacuum, into the top glass container which contains the ground coffee. The coffee drains down into the lower container and then rises again two or three times.

During the 1950s Italian coffee makers began to be widely used in many coffee bars and restaurants. These aluminium or stainless steel coffee makers are placed directly over heat. Water is heated up in the base until it boils, then it is forced up under pressure, through a metal filter basket filled with ground coffee. As soon as the water starts to rise into the top section of the coffee maker it must be removed from the heat source. The hot coffee is then ready to be poured out from the top jug.

At about this time coffee makers using filters (either filter paper or filter pistons) began to be used for very finely ground coffee. The coffee is quickly made using this method.

Electric coffee makers use the filter method; they work by heating water in a container and passing it through a filter full of coffee into a jug. The glass jug stands on a thermostatically controlled hotplate keeping the coffee hot for a limited period of time. Espresso coffee makers make stronger coffee using finely ground coffee; they work under pressure using the same principle as that of the Italian coffee makers. Both electric and espresso coffee makers have the advantage of making only the required number of cups.

The traditional coffee pot, which is often part of a coffee service, may be made of porcelain, earthenware, silver, silver plate, or stainless steel. It is used for making coffee using the 'jug method', the simplest and quickest way of making coffee. Allow 1 level tablespoon medium-ground coffee per person, and scald the pot before adding the coffee. Although this method is still quite widely used, electric coffee makers are gaining in popularity (see *percolator*).

Cognac

A world-famous brandy distilled from wine, made in the delimited region around Cognac in the Charente region of France. Distillation of the local wine began in the 17th century, when the market for both wine and salt, especially to the Dutch and Hanseatic League export markets, suffered a decline and was also at a disadvantage because of the popularity of Bordeaux wines. Distillation not only disposes of the surplus crop, but brandy as such was easier to transport. History attributes the invention of Cognac to a certain Chevalier de la Croix-Marrons, who is said to have been the first to have had the idea of heating wine to 'capture its soul'. He then put the distilled wine through the still once more. This distillation, at first considered to be a last resort in times of glut, came into general use. The brandy from the Cognac region soon gained an exceptional reputation for quality. The name 'Cognac' was not applied to the brandy itself until 1783.

Today, Cognac is made exclusively by the distillation of white wine from selected grapes, including Colombard and Saint-Émilion des Charentes. The wine is made and distilled within the delimited area, which spreads over two departments. Brandies distilled elsewhere have neither the same taste nor the same quality.

Six main areas within the region have

been defined. The Grande Champagne region (around Cognac and Segonzac) produces the finest, most delicate, and most fragrant brandies. Petite Champagne, which surrounds the Grand Champagne region from the southwest to the east, produces less subtle brandies that mature more rapidly. The brandies of the Borderies (a series of hills to the north of Grande Champagne) are rounder and softer. Encircling these three areas are the Fins Bois, the Bons Bois, and the Bois Ordinaires, which produce brandies of a more straightforward type. They are used mainly for blending with other brandies and are rarely sold commercially under their regional names. 'Fine Champagne' Cognac is a blend of the first two types, which must have at least 50% Grand Champagne in it.

☐ **Manufacture** Cognac results from a double distillation in what is known as the Charentais alembic. The wine is heated for the first time to give a *brouillis*, of about 30°. This is distilled a second time giving *la bonne chauffe*. The 'heads' and 'tails' of the process are removed from what is known as the 'heart' or 'flower of the vine', to be redistilled; it is a matter of great skill to 'cut' these out, once the still is running and the brandy coming across. It takes 9 litres of white wine to make 1 litre of the resulting clear spirit, which has a distinctive smell but is rough and not agreeable in flavour. It is now 70° and must mature. The maturing is carried out in casks made of oak from the forests of Limousin and Tronçais, seasoned out of doors. Cognac acquires much of its character from the cask. Up to five years old, it is pale yellow with a sight vanilla taste; aged between five and ten years, the colour deepens and the flavour becomes pronounced; up to 30 years, there is a slight drop in the alcohol content. It takes around 50 years for the alcohol content to begin to decline to around 40°, when the brandy may be used as a drink, but brandies of different ages and styles go into the great commercial blends. Their content can be reduced by breaking them down with distilled water. Maturing Cognac is expensive – the quantity of spirit evaporated (known traditionally as the 'angels' share') is equivalent to more than 20 million bottles each year from the whole region.

Each season's brandy is given the number 0 on the 31 March following the vintage and it cannot be sold commercially until it has been numbered 2 (two years later). This is often known as 'Three Star'. There are other categories, such as 'VO', 'VSOP', and 'Réserve', corresponding to five years' maturing, and 'Napoléon', 'Extra', and 'Vieille Réserve', which are seven years old or more. In fact, the different qualities sold are the result of blending spirits both of different ages and from different areas – old brandies (10, 20, 30 years old or more) can be blended with younger ones, the age given to the overall blend always being categorized as that of the youngest Cognac in the blend.

☐ **Drinking Cognac** When Cognac is drunk by itself, as an after-dinner liqueur, it should be served in a small balloon or tulip glass, which can be held in the hand, the only means of slightly warming the spirit and releasing the bouquet. (The heating of the glass is anathema to anyone who appreciates fine brandy of any kind!) Some people, however, prefer to drink Cognac quite cool.

Depending on the quality of the Cognac, it may be served alone, diluted with water or soda, or sometimes in mixes. Cognac (or brandy) and ginger ale is enjoyed in Britain; in the United States Cognac is an ingredient in many cocktails; in Canada iced Vichy water is often added; and in the Far East Cognac may be drunk straight, throughout an entire meal. It should be noted that the stars system as used on the labels of Cognac can be applied to other brandies, but does not indicate equivalent quality (in Greece, for example, a 'three star' brandy is a very rough spirit: for a brandy and water, one should ask for 'five star').

The incomparable bouquet of cognac is also utilized in cookery. It is used in various sauces, flamed preparations, and marinades and in such dishes as rabbit casserole, fricassee of chicken, pancakes, and zabaglione, not to mention fruit preserves and chocolates.

cola or kola nut

NOIX DE COLA OU KOLA

The seeds of the cola tree of Africa and South America. Rich in caffeine, they are chewed for their stimulating effects. The caffeine content is similar to that of coffee, but its tonic effect is less harsh and more prolonged.

In the United States and Europe, cola nuts are used to make biscuits (cookies) and, more importantly, in the manufacture of nonalcoholic fizzy cola drinks. These drinks are made with natural fruit extracts and also contain caffeine and preservatives. They are drunk chilled and are sometimes flavoured with lemon. Colas are an ingredient in certain cocktails, particularly those containing whisky or rum. The oldest and best-known is Coca-Cola, which was created in Atlanta in the United States in 1886.

Colbert

The name given to a method of preparing fish, especially sole, in which the fish is filleted and dipped in egg and breadcrumbs before frying. It is served with a flavoured butter, such as maître d'hôtel butter or Colbert butter. Colbert butter is also served with grilled (broiled) meat, other grilled fish, fried oysters, and soft-boiled eggs. Colbert sauce is used as an accompaniment to vegetables as well as grilled meat and fish. Finally, the name Colbert is also given to a chicken consommé (containing diced vegetables and garnished with very small poached eggs), to an egg dish, and to a dessert made with apricots.

All these preparations are probably dedicated to Jean-Baptiste Colbert, a minister of Louis XIV, who employed Audiger as the head of his household.

RECIPES

Colbert butter   BEURRE COLBERT
Add 1 tablespoon chopped tarragon and 1 tablespoon meat glaze to 200 g (7 oz, scant 1 cup) maître d'hôtel butter.

Colbert sauce   SAUCE COLBERT
Blend 2 tablespoons (3 tablespoons) meat glaze with 1 tablespoon water in a saucepan and bring to the boil. Remove from the heat and incorporate 125 g

(4½ oz, generous ½ cup) softened butter. Season, and add a generous pinch each of grated nutmeg and cayenne. Stir continuously while adding the juice of half a lemon, 1 tablespoon chopped parsley, and 1 tablespoon Madeira.

Sole Colbert   Remove the dark skin from the sole and slit the flesh on either side of the backbone. Raise the fillets and break the backbone in 2 or 3 places so that it may be easily removed after cooking. Dip in milk and coat in egg and breadcrumbs. Fry the sole, drain it, and remove the backbone. Fill the cavity left with Colbert butter. Serve on a long dish and garnish with fried parsley.

colcannon

A very popular Irish dish made from mashed potatoes and green cabbage, mixed with butter or milk and strongly flavoured with chopped chives, parsley, and pepper.

colère (en)

A method of preparing whole fried whiting in which the fish is served with its tail between its teeth. It is garnished with fried parsley and quarters of lemon. A tomato sauce is served separately.

Colette (Sidonie Gabrielle)

French novelist (born Saint-Sauveur-en-Puisay, 1873; died Paris, 1954). She spent her childhood on the borders of Burgundy and Nivernais, and retained a lasting love of the countryside and of nature in general. She excelled in describing the pleasures of the table, and wrote that drinking wine and sucking sugar 'loosened the tongue and revived the spirit'. In her novels and narratives, she describes how she would go hunting for truffles in the Lot, keeping a small sow with her on a leash, and intersperses her pages with genuine recipes, such as her famous one for chicken à la cendre (in ashes). She wrote about the sensual pleasures of eating good food, exemplified by the following description of beef à l'ancienne: 'which, besides its dark velvety flavour and its almost melting consistency, shone with a lustrous caramel-like sauce edged with light golden-coloured fat'. An orange wine, served as an apéritif in the south of France, is sometimes called *vin de Colette* (she often used to stay in Saint Tropez).

This is what Colette thought of a particular trend in the art of French cooking: 'an ignorant and pretentious bunch try to improve on what is already the finest. . . . The improviser sets himself up at the stove just as he does anywhere else. With his eyes turned to heaven instead of on his saucepans, he drops in a pinch of curry powder here, a spoonful of brandy there, and somewhere else, something even worse – a few drops of custard! He uses any old stuffing, he dribbles in some frightful additive. . . . Old words, classic terms, and traditions are all flouted by these priests of improvisation – it seems that we are a long way removed from the discreet combinations of flavours, thought out at length, that were once the basis of French gourmandise. . . .' (*Prisons et paradis*, Hachette, 1933).

colifichet

A term borrowed from women's fashion (where it referred to a small fancy ornament fixed onto a headdress) that describes small ornamental items in pâtisserie. They were used to decorate the table and buffets and were called *colifichets* to distinguish them from the main dishes. Colifichets are rarely seen nowadays, except at culinary exhibitions, wedding receptions, and christenings. Carême said, 'I compare a pastrycook who makes good colifichets to a distinguished fashion designer, endowed with perfect taste, who can make charming things with very little material. In the same way, out of almost insignificant scraps of pastry, we have to create pleasing and graceful things that also tempt the appetite.'

colin

The name given to hake in Paris markets. The name *colin* is also commercially to denote other white-fleshed sea fish, such as cod and haddock.

collage

The French term for 'fining' – separating particles in suspension in young wine. This is done by adding a fining agent; according to the region and the wine, this may be egg white, blood, albumen, gelatine, or bentonite. The fining agent is mixed with the wine in cask or vat and attracts the particles to itself, so that the wine may then be racked off. See also *clarification.*

collation

Originally, a light meal eaten by Roman Catholics on fasting days. The word comes from the Latin word *collatio*, meaning 'coming together'. It marked a devotional meeting of monks that was followed by a light repast. Nowadays, a collation means a quick meal usually eaten outside normal mealtimes.

colle

The French term for gelatine that has been softened in water ready to dissolve in certain savoury or sweet preparations that require thickening. The word is also applied to melted aspic added to some cold sauces.

RECIPE

Clarified fish colle for desserts COLLE DE POISSON CLARIFIÉE POUR ENTREMETS (from a recipe by Carême) Take about 46 g (2 oz) leaf gelatine. Cut it into small pieces, wash it, and place it in a medium-sized casserole with 8 glasses of filtered water and 60 g (2½ oz, 5 tablespoons) sugar. Boil rapidly, removing any froth as soon as it appears. When it is reduced sufficiently to give 1 good glass of gelatine, it should be strained through a napkin over a thoroughly clean bowl. The fine clarifying of sugar and gelatine is considered the secret of success in making attractive fruit and liqueur jellies.

coller

The French word for adding dissolved gelatine to give body to a preparation. Gelatine is added to consommés, to aspic jellies to clarify them, to fruit jellies, to Bavarian creams, and to mayonnaise.

The word can also be used when slices of truffle, hard-boiled egg white, leek, or carrot are stuck together with a small amount of jelly and used to decorate certain cold dishes.

Collioure

A red wine from the Roussillon. The *appellation contrôlée* refers only to the table wine, the vin doux naturel (produced in the same region) being known as Banyuls. They are named after the towns of Collioure and Banyuls-sur-Mer, both nearby on the Mediterranean coast, near the Spanish border. Collioure table wine, made mainly from the Grenache Noir grape, is dry, robust, and full-bodied, about 12°–15°. It matures in wood and cannot be bottled and sold until the July after its vintage.

colombine

A croquette consisting of a moulded outer layer of semolina mixed with Parmesan cheese, filled with a salpicon, a purée, or any filling used for vols-au-vent or barquettes. Coated with breadcrumbs and fried, colombines are served as a hot hors d'oeuvre.

colombo

A mixture of spices that are often used in the French West Indies. It was imported by Ceylonese coolies who had come to work in the Caribbean and was named after Colombo, the capital city of Sri Lanka. Colombo powder is a mild variation on curry powder and contains garlic, coriander, 'Indian wood' (Jamaican chilli), saffron, curcuma, dried mango pulp, and cinnamon.

The term colombo is also used for any West Indian dish that is seasoned with colombo powder. Locally, turtle, agouti, and even iguana flesh is used, but the most common colombos are based on chicken, crab, pork, or firm-fleshed fish. They are served with rice *à la créole* and red kidney beans. Yams, breadfruit, aubergines (egg-plants), and pieces of custard marrow (chayote) are sometimes added to the stew.

Colombo is also the name of an African climbing plant whose root is used to make tonic and apéritif drinks.

colouring agents

COLORANTS

Additives used in confectionery, cake-making, dairy products, and drinks. Their function is essentially a psychological one – to give the products a more appetizing appearance, and this can often mislead the consumer about the composition of the products.

Some colouring agents are natural or manufactured according to a natural formula; others are synthetic.

The use of colouring agents in food is not new. In the Middle Ages, butter was coloured with marigold flowers, and even at this time their use was subject to certain regulations. Saffron, spinach, and caramel have been used as colouring agents for many centuries.

□ **Natural colouring agents** These are almost all of vegetable origin, except for cochineal and carmine (E120), obtained from insects. They include yellow lactoflavin (E101), obtained from milk, wheat, liver, or eggs, caramel (E150), and vegetable carbon (E153). Others include:

• *yellow* – curcumine (E100), an extract from turmeric root: used in curry powders, margarine, and processed cheese.

• *yellow/red* – carotenoids (E160, carotene (alpha, beta, and gamma), bixin, annatto, norbixin, capsanthin, lycopene), extracts from carrot, tomato, and paprika: used for butter, cheese, margarine, cakes, and confectionery.

— xanthophylls (E161), extracts of various plants; used for butter, cheese, jams, drinks, soups and sweets.

• *red* – beetroot red (E162), made from boiled beetroots (red beets): used in soups.

• *violet* – anthocyanins (E163), extracts of aubergines (eggplants), blackcurrants, and red cabbage: used for ice creams and confectionery.

• *green* – chlorophyll and its derivatives (E140): used for fats, preserved vegetables, and oils.

□ **Synthetic colouring agents** The red azo dyes form the most important group: carmoisine (E122), amaranth (E123), ponceau (E124), and pigment rubine (E180, for cheese rind only). The same group also includes brilliant black (E151) and tartrazine (E102), a yellow dye used especially for fizzy drinks – now used less and less. Patent blue (E131), brilliant green (E142), erythrosine red (E127), and indigotine (E132) are all synthetic coal-tar dyes.

Surface colourings for sweets, etc., include calcium carbonate (E170), titanium dioxide (E171), and the oxides of aluminium, silver, and gold (E173, 174, and 175).

Food colourings are sometimes used in association with each other. For example, E151, E122, and E102 are used for black lumpfish caviar. Their use is limited to carefully calculated maximum doses, and regulations stipulate that they should be mentioned on the packaging.

☐ **Colouring food during cooking** The colour of a dish may be intensified or changed during cooking by adding vegetable colouring matter, such as spinach juice, beetroot juice, caramel, tomato purée, crustacean shells, etc. Meat is coloured by sealing it in very hot fat, which has the effect of browning the surface. The same effect is achieved by placing it under a hot grill before cooking.

coltsfoot TUSSILAGE

A plant with yellow flowers, the dried leaves of which are smoked, like eucalyptus, to soothe coughs. They are also used to make tisanes and, in Canada, as an aromatic, especially with fish.

cominée

In ancient times, a culinary term for dishes that contained cumin. This spice was widely used in the Middle Ages for seasoning soups, poultry dishes, and fish dishes. Taillevent's *Viandier* gives recipes for *cominée d'amandes* (a sort of poultry soup made with verjuice and flavoured with shelled almonds, ginger, and cumin), *cominée de gélines* (i.e. of chickens), and *cominée d'esturgeon* (sturgeon cut into pieces and boiled with cumin and almonds).

RECIPE

Cominée de gélines (from an ancient recipe) Boil some chickens in wine and water. Skim off the fat and remove the chickens. Beat some egg yolks, mix them with the cooking liquid from the chickens, and add cumin. Replace the chickens.

commodore

A term used to describe a very elaborate garnish for poached fish, in which fish quenelles, crayfish tail croquettes, and mussels *à la Villeroi* are mixed together in a crayfish bisque.

Consommé commodore is made with a fish stock thickened with arrowroot and garnished with pieces of poached clam and diced tomatoes cooked in the stock.

compote

A preparation of fresh or dried fruit, cooked either whole or in pieces in a sugar syrup. It does not keep for as long as jam.

Fresh fruit should be cooked by poaching it in syrup over a gentle heat, or else by fast boiling. A compote can be made with several different kinds of fruit. The fruit should be arranged in a fruit bowl or dish and served as a dessert. It may be served either slightly warm or chilled, accompanied by whipped cream or sprinkled with cinnamon, vanilla sugar, or biscuit (cookie) crumbs. Fresh fruit compotes may be used to prepare rather more elaborate desserts, such as sundaes and mousses. This kind of fruit purée can also be used as an ingredient in turnovers, tarts, and charlottes.

Before cooking, dried fruit should be soaked for varying lengths of time in cold or warm water, to which some kind of alcohol (such as Kirsch, rum, or Frontignan) or tea may be added.

Whether the fruit is fresh or dried, the cooking syrup (or the compote itself) can be flavoured with various ingredients, such as vanilla, lemon or orange peel, cinnamon powder (or cinnamon sticks in the case of syrup), cloves, ground almonds, grated coconut, crystallized (candied) fruit, or raisins.

The term compote is also used for certain dishes containing game, such as pigeons, partridges, or rabbit, that have been cooked in a roux for a fairly long time over a gentle heat. The game is usually cooked with small onions and bacon; at the end of the cooking time, the flesh has disintegrated completely. Onions and peppers may also be reduced to a compote.

RECIPES

Apple compote COMPOTE DE POMMES Prepare a syrup as for apricot compote. Peel the apples, cut them into quarters, remove the pips (seeds), and cover them with lemon juice. Boil the syrup, add the apples, and remove as soon as they are tender. Serve either warm or cold.

Apricot compote COMPOTE D'ABRI-COTS Halve the apricots, remove the stones, and extract and blanch the kernels. Cook the fruit for about 20 minutes in syrup: use 350 g, (12 oz, 1½ cups) sugar to 6 dl (1 pint, 2½ cups) water. Arrange the apricot halves in a fruit bowl with half a kernel on each; pour the syrup over.

Cherry compote COMPOTE DE CE-RISES For each 1 kg (2¼ lb) stoned (pitted) cherries use 300 g (11 oz, 1½ cups, firmly packed) caster (superfine) sugar and ½ glass of water to make a sugar syrup. Cook until it has reached the 'large ball' stage. Add the cherries and cook with the lid on for 8 minutes over a low heat. Drain the cherries and place in a bowl. Mix 1 liqueur glass of Kirsch with the syrup and pour over the cherries. Cool before serving.

Chestnut compote COMPOTE DE MARRONS Slit the shells of the chestnuts, plunge them into boiling water for 5 minutes, and peel them while they are still hot. Cook them gently in a vanilla-flavoured syrup (using proportions of sugar and water as for apricot compote) for about 45 minutes. Pour the chestnuts and syrup into a bowl, cool, and refrigerate before serving.

Fig compote (*dried figs*) COMPOTE DE FIGUES SÈCHES Soak the figs in cold water until they swell. Prepare a syrup with half red wine and half water, using 350 g (12 oz, 1½ cups) sugar to 6 dl (1 pint, 2½ cups) liquid; flavour it with finely grated lemon peel. Bring the syrup to the boil, add the figs, and cook very gently for 20–30 minutes.

Fig compote (*fresh figs*) COMPOTE DE FIGUES FRAÎCHES Peel some white or black figs. Put them in boiling vanilla-flavoured syrup, made with 350 g (12 oz, 1½ cups) sugar to 6 dl (1 pint, 2½ cups) water and poach for a few minutes only. Drain, reduce the syrup, and pour it over the figs.

Four-fruit compote COMPOTE DE QUATRE FRUITS Use equal quantities of apples, quinces, and oranges, together with a few large grapes. Prepare a syrup as for apricot compote. Peel the apples and quinces, remove the pips (seeds), slice thickly, and sprinkle with lemon juice. Plunge the slices of quince in the boiling syrup; 15 minutes later, add the apples. Meanwhile, peel and slice the oranges and add them to the other fruit 20 minutes after the beginning of the cooking time. Continue to cook for another 10 minutes. Peel and, if possible, remove the seeds from the grapes. Add them to the syrup as soon as the pan has been removed from the heat. Allow to cool, and chill in the refrigerator.

Peach compote COMPOTE DE PÊCHES Prepare a vanilla-flavoured syrup using proportions of sugar and water as for apricot compote. Plunge the peaches for about 30 seconds in boiling water and cool them under cold running water. It should then be easy to peel them. Either leave them whole or cut them in half and remove the stones (pits). Poach them in boiling syrup for 13 minutes if cut in half, or 18 minutes if they are whole.

Pear and apple caramel compote COMPOTE POIRES-POMMES CARA-MÉLISÉE Cook the apples and pears separately, as described in the individual recipes. Drain them and arrange them in layers in a fruit bowl. Place the bowl in the refrigerator. Mix the two lots of syrup together and reduce until it begins to turn pale gold in colour. Pour this boiling syrup over the cold fruit and set aside to cool. Do not refrigerate.

Pear compote COMPOTE DE POIRES Peel the pears, cut them into quarters, and remove the seeds. (If the pears are small, leave them whole.) Cook them in boiling vanilla-flavoured syrup (prepared as for apricot compote) until they become translucent. Remove and place in a bowl. Reduce the syrup and pour it over the pears. Cool before serving. Some pear brandy may be added to the cold syrup if desired.

Pineapple compote COMPOTE D'ANANAS Remove the skin and core of a pineapple. Slice the fruit and cook in some vanilla-flavoured syrup for about 15–20 minutes. Arrange the pineapple slices in a dish, reduce the syrup, and pour it over the pineapple. Cool completely, and store in the refrigerator until ready to serve.

Plum compote COMPOTE DE PRUNES Stone (pit) the plums carefully without splitting them in two. Poach them in boiling syrup (prepared as for apricot compote) for 10–12 minutes. Serve well chilled, with or without cream.

This recipe can also be prepared using mirabelle plums.

Preserved fruit compote COMPOTE DE FRUITS EN CONSERVE This preparation is the same whether apricots, cherries, peaches, or plums are used. Choose fruits that are ripe but not overripe. Prick them with the point of a knife and place them in an earthenware dish. Cover with a cold syrup (made with 350 g (12 oz, 1½ cups) sugar to 6 dl (1 pint, 2½ cups) water) for 3 hours. Scald the preserving jars and their rubber seals.

Make a syrup with a density of 1.2197, using sugar cubes. Clarify the syrup with egg white (use 1 egg white to 2 litres (3½ pints, 4½ pints) syrup), and then filter it through a cloth. Leave to cool completely. Drain the fruit, put it into the jars, and pour the boiling clarified syrup over it so that it reaches a level in the jar that is 3 cm (1¼ in) higher than the top of the fruit. Seal the jars.

Line the bottom of a preserving pan with a cloth. Wrap each jar individually in a cloth so that they do not touch one another and place them in the pan. Fill the pan with enough cold water to cover the jars and bring to the boil. Fast-boil for 10 minutes and then remove the preserving pan from the heat. Allow the water to cool completely before removing the jars. Wipe them, and store them in a cool place.

Rhubarb compote COMPOTE DE RHUBARBE Only use fresh sticks and carefully remove the strings. Cut the sticks into pieces 6–8 cm (2½–3 in) long. Blanch them in boiling water for 3 minutes, drain, and cool. Place them in a preserving pan and cover with a syrup

made as for apricot compote. Cover, and cook without stirring. Serve either warm or cold. This compote can be used as a filling for tarts.

Strawberry compote COMPOTE DE FRAISES Wash, hull, dry, but not cook the strawberries. Arrange them in a dish and pour boiling syrup (prepared as for apricot compote) over them. The syrup may be flavoured with orange or other flavourings.

compoter

A French term meaning to cook a dish very gently so that the ingredients are reduced to a sort of compote or purée (see *capilotade*). Onions and rabbit pieces may be cooked in this way.

compotier

A large dish (made of porcelain, crystal, glass, or earthenware) on a raised base. It is used for serving compotes, cream desserts, or other sweet dishes. Earthenware or glass compotiers may also be used for arrangements of fresh fruit.

Comté

A cheese made with cows' milk (minimum 45% fat content), which is cooked and pressed. It is ivory-coloured or pale yellow and has a natural brushed rind, varying from golden yellow to brown. It is matured for three to six months. The cheese comes from the Franche-Comté region of France and is also known as Comté Gruyère. Traditionally, it should have small 'eyes' or holes, not much smell, a fruity flavour, and a strong (but never pungent) bouquet.

Its manufacture is governed by an *appellation d'origine*. The name is followed by a clear indication of the department or district in which it has been made. The departments include the Doubs, the Jura, and the Haute-Saône, together, with the area around Belfort, and the districts of Belley, Bourg-en-Bresse, Gex, Nantua, Beaune, Dijon, Langres, Chalon-sur-Saône, Louhans, Épinal, and Neufchâteau. The origin and also the month of its manufacture is marked on a piece of green casein attached to the cheese.

The cheese has a straight or slightly convex rind and measures 40–70 cm (16–28 in) in diameter and 9–13 cm

(3½–5 in) in height. Comté is a very ancient cheese, and the first dairy to make it is recorded as far back as the 13th century. It is served at the end of a meal and is widely used in cooking. It may be grated or sliced and used for topping, soufflés, mixed salads, canapés, fondues, fritters, etc.

Comus

The ancient Roman god of drinking and revelry. He was invoked during nocturnal feasts that were accompanied by music and dancing. Comus was represented as a young man crowned with flowers, holding a flaming torch in his right hand. See also *Marin*.

concasser

The French term for chopping or pounding a substance, either coarsely or finely. When skinned deseeded tomato pulp is finely chopped, it is known as tomato *concassée*. The term may also be applied to parsley, chervil, or tarragon that has been chopped on a flat board with a few rapid strokes of a knife. Meat, poultry, game, and fish bones can be 'concasséed' with a cleaver or chopper when preparing a stock or flavouring. The term may also be used for the crushed ice used to line a serving dish for chilled melon, caviar, etc.

concentrate   CONCENTRÉ

A substance in which the water content has been reduced by evaporation or some other process. In cookery, the method is used for meat, poultry, or fish glazes. These are stocks that have been cooked slowly over a long period. The juices are concentrated and form a syrupy substance used to enhance the flavour of certain sauces.

Tomato purée, a concentrate that can be home-made or bought, is made by reducing the liquid extracted from tomatoes and filtering it to remove the skins and seeds. It is widely used in the preparation of sauces and stews. Fruit juices are industrially processed to obtain concentrates, which, when diluted with water, give reconstituted drinks.

Evaporated and condensed milks are prepared in a vacuum and are sold in cans. Condensed milk is sweetened,

evaporated milk is not, but both keep for a long period. They are particularly useful in the preparation of iced desserts and are much used in the industrial preparation of confectionery, cakes, and pastries.

concorde

A garnish for large joints of meat, consisting of creamed potatoes, trimmed and glazed new carrots, and peas in butter.

Condé and à la Condé

Names given to various methods of preparing food which were dedicated to the French general Condé the Great (1621–86) and his descendants by family chefs.

Savoury dishes are characterized by the presence of a purée of red kidney beans.

Condés, or Condé cakes, are small cakes made of puff pastry covered with a layer of royal icing with almonds (Condé icing).

The terms are also applied to cold desserts based on rice and poached fruit; classically, the fruit should be apricots in syrup, arranged in a crown around a 'cake' of rice coated with an apricot and Kirsch sauce and decorated with cherries and crystallized (candied) fruit. This basic recipe has many variations, using slices of pineapple, peaches, strawberries, etc., but always including rice cooked in milk and a fruit sauce.

RECIPES

SAVOURY PREPARATIONS

Condé soup POTAGE CONDÉ Cook some red kidney beans with a very little salt until they can be reduced to a fine purée. Add sufficient chicken stock to obtain a liquid soup. Thicken with fresh butter and serve very hot, with or without small croutons fried in butter or oil.

Shirred eggs Condé OEUFS SUR LE PLAT CONDÉ Grease an individual egg dish; pipe a border of puréed red kidney beans round the edge. Gently fry 2 slices of bacon in butter and lay them on the dish. Break 2 eggs on top and cook in the oven.

SWEET PREPARATIONS

Cherries Condé CERISES CONDÉ
Stone (pit) the cherries and poach them
in syrup. Fill an ovenproof dish with rice
cooked in milk, smooth over the top,
and decorate with some of the drained
cherries, candied angelica cut into diamond shapes, and shelled almonds.
Purée the rest of the cherries and add
enough of the syrup to obtain a very
liquid sauce; reduce this sauce until it
becomes syrupy. Reheat the garnished
rice in the oven. Serve with the cherry
sauce.

Condé icing APPAREIL À CONDÉS
Chop 250 g (8 oz, 1½ cups) shelled
almonds finely in a blender, without
reducing them to a paste. Mix 350 g (12
oz, 3 cups) icing sugar (confectioners'
sugar), 1 tablespoon vanilla sugar, and
the chopped almonds in an earthenware
dish. Beat 2 whites of egg and a small
pinch of salt with a fork until fluffy but
not stiff, and add them little by little to
the sugar – the mixture should be liquid
enough to spread easily over the cakes,
without overflowing while cooking.

Strawberries Condé FRAISES CON-
DÉ Bind some rice cooked in milk,
flavoured with sugar and vanilla, with
egg yolk, and fill a ring mould. Cook in a
bain-marie for 30 minutes in an oven
heated to about 200 c (400 F, gas 6),
then leave to cool and turn out of the
mould onto a serving dish. Wash some
large strawberries, drain, hull, and divide into 2 equal quantities. Sprinkle
half with sugar and brandy and leave in
a cool place to macerate for at least 1
hour. Sieve the other half of the strawberries, together with some raspberries
(a quarter of the weight of strawberries); add some lemon juice (1 tablespoon per 500 g (18 oz) strawberries)
and just enough caster (superfine) sugar
for the purée not to taste sour. Drain the
whole strawberries and arrange in the
middle of the rice, serving the fruit purée
at the same time.

condiments

Food substances used to heighten the
natural flavour of foods, to stimulate
the appetite, to aid digestion, or else to
preserve certain products (the word
comes from the Latin *condire*, to preserve). The term condiment is used today to include spices, seasonings,
sauces, fruit, and various cooked or uncooked preparations. Strictly speaking,
however, a seasoning is a substance
added to food while it is being prepared,
whereas a condiment, chosen to harmonize with the taste of the food, can be
either an accompaniment (e.g. mustard,
pickled fruit, ketchup, gherkins), or an
ingredient (truffles, dried fruit, alcohol,
herbs, or spices), or a preserving agent
(vinegar, salt, oil, or sugar).

The custom of adding condiments to
food is as ancient as cookery itself.
Originally, it was a means of preserving
(in very spicy sauces such as the Roman
garum, or in the saltpetre and verjuice of
the Middle Ages). Most condiments are
of vegetable origin (herbs, spices, dried
or crystallized (candied) fruit, and
aromatic vegetables); some, such as the
Vietnamese *nuoc-mâm*, are based on
dried and pounded fish or shellfish.

Condiments are used either raw and
untreated (e.g. onion, fresh herbs, cress,
etc.), or else after some form of preparation (sweet-and-sour sauces, purées,
mustards, capers, chutneys, etc.). Customary use varies from one country to
another: in Britain and the United States
large quantities of bottled sauces and
condiments are used to accompany
salads, cold meat, charcuterie, etc.,
whereas in oriental and northern countries sweet-and-sour sauce is a basic
ingredient of many condiments. Mention should also be made of products
such as cocoa, sometimes used as a condiment in Mexico. Finally, the term can
also include natural colourings
(caramel, beetroot juice, spinach green,
etc.), as well as essences and extracts
(anchovy, aniseed, almond, etc.), wines
and spirits, some flowers, and even
cheese (Parmesan, Gruyère, Mozzarella, and blue cheeses).

Condrieu

An AOC white wine from the Rhône
Valley which is produced in such small
quantities that until recently it was practically unknown outside the region.
Only one type of vine (the Viognier) is
used. Condrieu, which is capable of
ageing (though it is usually drunk while

young) is an unusual wine, firm in style with a distinctive bouquet.

confectioners' custard

See *creams and custards*.

confectionery

CONFISERIE

Food products based on sugar. The French term can be applied not only to sweets and candies, but also to the confectioner's shop and to the techniques of the craftsman or the whole industry. Several broad categories of confectionery products can be listed:
- boiled sweets (acid drops, barley sugar, lollipops, mint humbugs, soft-centred sweets, etc.);
- caramels and toffees;
- chews;
- chewing gum;
- liquorice, etc.;
- marzipan (almond paste);
- nougat;
- fruit jellies, crystallized (candied) fruit, and marrons glacés;
- fondant creams (various different fillings);
- jellied products (made of starch, jelly, or pectin, such as marshmallows);
- sugared almonds and other sugar-coated products;
- pastilles and tablets;
- oriental confectionery (Turkish delight and halva);
- pralines.

Numerous raw materials are used in the manufacture of confectionery products – sugar, glucose syrup and invert sugar, honey, milk (whole or skimmed, fresh, concentrated, or powdered), animal and vegetable fats, fruit (fresh, preserved, frozen, or in pulp), cocoa, dried fruit, gum arabic, pectin, starches, gelatine, liquorice juice, certain acids, natural or synthetic aromatic products, and permitted colourings.

In France, the average consumption of confectionery has been estimated at 3 kg (6½ lb) per year per person (among European countries, only Italy's consumption is lower). The large majority of confectionery products are bought on impulse, particularly by children, and purchases are spread out over the year. Some kinds are eaten mostly on special occasions (christenings, Easter, and Christmas) in France: this is particularly true of sugared almonds, marrons glacés, bonbons, and crystallized fruit, which are sold in fancy wrappings and are most often given as presents. Packaging has always been particularly important for confectionery.

☐ **Development of confectionery** The confectioner's art is very old. Its evolution has followed the ingredients available; before sugar became available, honey was used to coat grains and fruits and to make the type of sweets (candies) still eaten in the Middle East. The introduction of cane sugar into Europe by the Crusaders allowed confectionery to develop. Like the chemists, the confectioners of Paris were members of the grocers' guild, whose charters date from 1311. Until the end of the 17th century, the chemists and confectioners, quarrelled over the right to make and sell sugar products, but the confectioners with their growing specialization obtained the definitive right to produce sweets for everyday consumption, so that they were no longer available only for the rich. The first important producer was the house of Oudard in the Rue des Lombards, Paris, who was praised by Grimod de La Reynière. The extraction of sugar from sugar beet gave the profession a boost; mechanization was also coming in.

At the end of the 19th century confectionery comprised biscuits (cookies) and iced biscuits, chocolate, cooked sugar sweets, shaped fruit jellies, sugar-coated nuts, and ices. In France today there are about 300 small family firms where the cooking is done on an open fire; there are also large industrial firms which are entirely mechanized. As a general rule these manufacturers do not make the same type of product: boiled sweets, toffees, sugar-coated sweets, and chewing gums are produced by the large firms, while fruit jellies, marzipan, and marrons glacés are made by small firms or craftsmen. Certain regional specialities are still made, such as the sugar-coated almonds of Verdun, nougat from Montélimar, and fruit jellies from the Auvergne.

confire

A French culinary term for preparing certain foods in particular ways in order to preserve them, either by cooking them slowly in their own fat (confits of pork, goose, and duck), by coating them with sugar syrup (confectionery and crystallized (candied) fruit), or by bottling them in alcohol (cherries and prunes in brandy), in vinegar (capers, gherkins, and pickles), or in a sweet-and-sour preparation (chutneys).

confit

A piece of pork, goose, duck, or turkey cooked in its own fat and stored in a pot, covered in the same fat to preserve it. The confit is one of the oldest forms of preserving food and is a speciality of south-western France. Simin Palay, in *Cuisine du pays*, described this speciality from the Basque and Béarn regions: lean pork or a quarter of fowl is rubbed with salt, soaked in brine, then drained and dried and cooked slowly in fat with flavourings and seasonings; finally, it is put into a pot and stored in a cool dry place. Confit of goose or duck, fattened on maize (corn), is often prepared with a mixture of pork and poultry fats. If the pot is made of tin plate the confit must always be well covered by fat.

The long life of confit, the fact that it can be eaten hot or cold, and its delicate flavour have won it a high place in the gastronomy of the Gers, Périgord, and Landes regions. It is used in the preparation of garbure and cassoulet, but it is above all eaten as a meat dish, accompanied by a variety of vegetables: cep mushrooms (*à la basquaise*), fried potatoes (*à la béarnaise* or *à la sarladaise*), fresh peas and Bayonne ham (*à la landaise*), a sorrel fondue (*à la périgourdine*), or white beans, cabbage, or lentils. When eaten cold, with the fat removed, it is often accompanied by a dandelion, endive (chicory), or white cabbage salad.

Neighbouring regions have their own confit specialities, such as confit of mallard served with new potatoes in Saintonge, confit of duck or truffled turkey in Brantôme and confit of young turkey in Bordeaux.

The leg (thigh) is considered the most succulent part of preserved poultry and the wing the tenderest. The weight of meat, without the fat, must represent at least 55% of the total weight of a pot of preserved poultry.

Goose is most commonly used for making confit as its meat is often too tough to roast. A special container known as a *grésale* (stoneware pot) is used to marinate the meat in brine with a clove, thyme, pepper, a bay leaf, and garlic. Traditionally, it is cooked the day after a pig is slaughtered, when pâtés, terrines, and pork dishes are prepared; a deep copper cauldron is the most suitable utensil for this. To check that the legs and wings (which are surrounded by fat) are cooked, a knitting needle is inserted: if it comes out without a trace of blood the meat is cooked. The confit is stored in stoneware pots (called *toupins*), which are preferable to glass jars as they allow no light to get in. Either goose fat or dripping is used to make a hermetic final seal.

Other meats can be prepared as confits, especially chicken, guinea fowl, rabbit, woodcock (in the Gers region), and veal.

RECIPES

Confit of goose CONFIT D'OIE (from a recipe by R. Lamazère) Clean the inside of a fat goose thoroughly and remove the bones, keeping the carcass whole. Cut into quarters. Place in a container and season with coarse salt (12 g per kg, ¼ oz per lb), then leave in a cold place for 26 hours to allow the salt to penetrate thoroughly into the flesh. Cook in a large copper cauldron with 2 kg (4½ lb) goose fat for 2 hours. Make sure the fat simmers while cooking but do not allow it to boil. While the fat is still hot, strain it into a stoneware pot and place the pieces of goose in the fat so they are completely covered. Leave to cool, and then cover the pot. To obtain an authentic confit, store in a cellar for 5–6 months. For confit of duck follow the same method.

Confit of goose à la béarnaise CONFIT D'OIE À LA BÉARNAISE Heat a quarter of preserved goose in its own fat and keep hot in a serving dish. Peel and slice some potatoes and fry them in the confit fat. Chop some parsley and garlic together, add to the potatoes, and reheat. Surround the confit with the potatoes and serve very hot.

Confit of goose à la landaise CONFIT D'OIE À LA LANDAISE Peel 6 small onions and dice 75 g (3 oz) Bayonne ham. Heat 1 tablespoon goose fat in an earthenware casserole and cook the onions and ham for 5 minutes, then add 1 litre (2 pints, 4 cups) freshly shelled peas. Sprinkle with 1 tablespoon flour and stir for a few moments with a wooden spoon. Moisten with 1.5 dl (¼ pint, ⅔ cup) water; add pepper and ½ teaspoon sugar (salt is not needed because the ham is already salty). Add a bouquet garni with chervil, cover, and leave to cook for about 30 minutes. Then add a quarter of preserved goose and leave until cooked, the total cooking time depending on the tenderness of the peas.

confréries, orders, and brotherhoods

In the Middle Ages in France, many of those involved with wine formed associations devoted to preserving local traditions and upholding the quality of their particular wines, in addition to acting as benevolent societies to assist members and their families in need. They exercised considerable control over the production and marketing of wines and spirits, but at the time of the French Revolution many ceased their operations, both because of the civic disturbance and because, in many regions, the great estates and vineyards changed hands. But records and certain traditions were not quite lost. In Alsace, for example, where the Confrérie Saint-Étienne was founded in the 14th century, in former times the *ban* (proclamation of the vintage) announced to growers that they could start picking their grapes. To this day, no one can begin the harvest in Alsace before the official date – an old survival of an ancient practice.

Since the 1930s, however, many confréries have been revived and those that had managed to keep going have progressively engaged in many activities, most of them now of a promotional rather than restrictive type. In some regions in France, where wine growing has become more organized and the wines are enormously improved, there are a number of recently formed similar organizations. All of them usually have a set of rules and an annual list of fixtures, such as chapters at which new members are admitted by the organizing council, banquets, and festivals, especially at the times of the flowering of the vine in the spring, the vintage, and on the feast day of any of the numerous saints associated with wine. In many instances, would-be members have to submit themselves to a preliminary test and the insignia they wear denotes their rank within the fraternity – apprentice, fellow, master, or some similar honorary title.

Although the best-known confréries are those concerned with wine, there are many others associated with other commodities, such as those of the cheese makers, that are similar to the medieval guilds and livery companies of the City of London.

☐ **Wine orders** Often originating many centuries ago, possibly as dining clubs, wine orders evolved as corporations administering the business of the wines of their particular locality. Few regions of France today are without some organization of this sort, from the Ordre des Coteaux in Champagne, founded as an aristocratic 'Bacchic society' (really a version of a drinking club) in the 17th century, to the humbler groupings of regions such as those of the Auvergne or Jura. Both the highly reputed Sacavins d'Anjou (1905) and the Chevaliers du Tastevin are examples that are widely known. The latter was re-established in 1934 at a gala dinner at Nuits Saint Georges and subsequently acquired the great building of Clos de Vougeot. Here their ceremonies, 'oiled' by wine and song and followed by lengthy banquets, have done much to promote Burgundy throughout the world, including Britain and the United States (where there are now branches of the Tastevins).

● BORDEAUX – In order to combat the economic problems of 1949, the wine trade of the Médoc decided to found both an Academy of Bordeaux wines and a wine order, following the example of the successful Chevaliers du Tastevin; this was approved and supported by the leading wine personalities of the area. The wine order, the Commanderie du Bontemps de Médoc et des Graves, takes its name from the little wooden bowl (*bontemps*) used for whisking the egg whites for fining the wines. The 'baptism' of the order was inaugurated by well-known personalities from the worlds of art and literature as well as businessmen, civic dignitaries, and the heads of the university, wearing the claret-coloured velvet robes and medieval toque headdresses topped by a piece of pleated white silk – to represent the egg whites. (Those officers belonging to the Graves wear golden velvet robes.) There are annual reunions and celebrations, notably at the flowering of the vine in June and the Ban des Vendanges at vintage time in September. The Bontemps have been followed by other regions within the Gironde, such as the Commandeurs du Bontemps de Sainte-Croix-du-Mont (1963) and the Commandeurs du Bontemps de Sauternes et de Barsac (1959). Many of these orders have chosen a name historically associated with the region: for example, the Jurade de Saint-Émilion (1948) took their name from the charter given to the local council by King John of England in 1199; the *jurade* was equivalent to the town council – there was one in Bordeaux. The Compagnons de Loupiac (1971) like to associate themselves with the Roman poet Ausonius, who is said to have had a villa in the region. The Hospitaliers de Pomerol (1968) have taken as their emblem the Maltese Cross, in honour of the Knights Hospitallers of St John of Jerusalem (the St John's Ambulance Brigade is their descendant in Britain), some of whom were landowners and wine makers in the region. The Gentilshommes de Fronsac associate themselves with the famous – one might almost say notorious – Duc de Richelieu, marshal of France and governor of the old province of Guyenne. These and other confréries are represented at the Grand Conseil de Bordeaux, which coordinates their activities.

● BURGUNDY – The part played by the wine orders in the economic and social life of the various regions is both recognized and approved. In Burgundy, the Chevaliers du Tastevin organize many functions throughout the year, notably the great banquet at Clos de Vougeot on the Saturday before the annual sale of the Hospices de Beaune wines in November. They also arrange processions throughout the region to celebrate the Feast of St Vincent, patron of wine growers, on 22 January. The Confrérie Saint-Vincent de Mâcon, representing the wines both of Mâcon and Pouilly Fuissé, have chosen the same saint who, local legend says, was able to offer the very first *vin nouveau* to the Father Almighty! The Piliers Chablisiens (1952), so called because Chablis is the 'golden gate' to Burgundy, hold their jollifications in a real cellar; at the end of November they celebrate 'Saint Cochon', a survival of the medieval period when pigs were killed and preserved in various ways for winter. The Master of the Piliers is known as the 'Grand Architrave' – typical Burgundian humour. The Confrères des Trois-Ceps (1965), an offshoot of the Piliers, celebrate the 'Sauvignon Festival' on 11 November – indicating that Chardonnay is not the only white grape of the area!

● LOIRE – It is not surprising that there are plenty of Bacchic brotherhoods in the Loire, especially around Chinon, birthplace of François Rabelais. Although many of the wines he wrote about have disappeared, there are plenty more. Since 1937 the Chevaliers de la Chantepleure de Vouvray have gathered every mid-June and mid-September in various places, in and out of doors, sometimes in cellars hollowed from the limestone cliffs of the Loire banks, to sample Vouvray. There are many orders associating themselves with Rabelais: the Entonneurs Rabelaisiens (1962) who meet at Chinon (the word *entonnoir* means a funnel, signifying the copious draughts of wine under consideration); the Compagnons de Grandgousier at Onzain (1958); and the Fins Gouziers d'Anjou, who wear black velvet hats in the style of Henri III. The Confrérie des Tire-Douzils (1953) in Marigny-Brizay in Poitou and the Fripe-Douzils (1952) of Ingrandes-de-Touraine in the Bourgeuil region have chosen as their emblem the little wooden peg inserted into a barrel to draw out the wine for tasting. The Chevaliers de Sancerre (1964), on the Berri side of the Loire, and the Baillis de Pouilly (1949) aim to promote the wines of Sancerre and Pouilly-sur-Loire; the Chevaliers Bretvins at Nantes vow to drink Muscadet and Gros Plant, while at Angers the Sacavins d'Anjou quaff the wines of their region. The majority of the Loire wine orders have fine robes for their officers: the Commandeurs des Grands Vins d'Amboise (1967) wear plumed hats and red robes with sleeves slashed open to reveal yellow under-sleeves (the colours representing both red and white wine). The Compagnons d'Honneur des Sorciers et Birettes (1951), concerned with Bué and the Sancerre area, have a reunion on the first Sunday in August, when they wear white capes with red and green facings and wizards' masks.

• THE SOUTHWEST AND THE MEDITERRANEAN – There are plenty of wine orders maintaining the names and traditions of the past in other parts of France. Some of the better known include the Viguiers Royaux du Juran-çon (1953), who wear a Béarn beret and a ruffled collar in the style of Henri IV, the Chevaliers du Tursan (1963), the Confrères du Vin de Cahors (1966), and the Consuls de la Vinée de Bergerac (1954). There are also the fraternities of the spirit producers: the Mousquetaires d'Armagnac (1952), the Principauté de Franc-Pineau (1950), and the Confrérie des Alambics Charentais (1946), who wear green coats and toque-style headgear. All organize festivities in France and abroad to promote Cognac, Armagnac, and Pineau des Charentes.

As the wines of the Mediterranean coast and hinterland are possibly the most ancient of France, the Latin name is retained in the names of some of the wine orders: the Consuls de Septimanie (1970) are associated with this classical poet; they celebrate the Narbonne vineyards in August. The name of the Échansons du Vidauban (1970), who wear an apron and a red scarf, comes from the Latin *vitis albanus* (white vine). The Ordre Illustre des Chevaliers de Méduse (1951) of Arcs-sur-Argens, holding its annual chapter in Septem-ber, wear azure blue capes lined with purple. The Échansons des Papes (1967) of Châteauneuf-du-Pape chose a bronze key (the sign of St Peter) as their emblem; the Commandeurs de Tavel wear a red cape with a black velvet collar when they celebrate the rosé wine of the Gard. In south-eastern France and near the Spanish frontier, in the Roussillon and Corbières border re-gions, there are the Senhores de la Vinhas (1971) in Lézignan-Corbières, sumptuously attired in purple coats with gold facings, and the Seigneurs de Commande Majeure de Roussillon (1964), wearing a caped Catalan cos-tume in honour of King Peter of Aragon.

□ **Gastronomic confréries** These societies, whose aim is to publicize the quality and fame of French cooking, are as varied and numerous as the wine lodges. They are often created to pro-mote a regional product – cheese, char-cuterie, and other specialities, and the members may be professional cooks, food-producers, or simply gourmets.

The confréries today no longer spend 18 hours enjoying three successive meals lasting from Saturday evening to Sunday lunchtime, as did the famous Club des Grands Estomacs during the Second Empire. Today's gourmets often meet friends or members of the same profession to enjoy a good meal. The famous Club des Cent, which was founded in 1912 at the time of the birth of the motorcar, was the inspiration of the journalist Louis Forest and had a gastronomic and sporting aim. The rules only allowed the admission of 'gourmets who have travelled forty thousand kilometres for a fine meal'. The great Académie des Gastronomes was founded in 1928 by Curnonsky, along with Édouard de Pomaine, Maeterlinck, Paul Reboux, and the Marquis de Polignac, and was directly inspired by the Académie Française: each of its 40 members had to write an eulogy to an ancestor. Also founded in 1928, the Compagnie des Gentils-hommes de Gueule organize a monthly dinner for their president, who is a well-read scholar. The Académie des Psycho-logues du Goût, established in 1922, are a sort of gastronomic Jockey Club whose members include ambassadors and other well-known personalities. The Académie du Malt Whisky, founded in 1970, awards two prizes each year.

• DIPLOMAS AND MEDALS – Some of these associations are more directly in-volved in cookery and award diplomas and medals. Among the first was Joseph Favre's Académie de Cuisine (1883), which was the first school of cookery. It served as a model for the Académie Granet at Bourg-en-Bresse, the Académie des Chroniqueurs de Table, the Maîtres Cuisiniers de France (1949), the Poulardiers de Bresse, and the Club Prosper-Montagné (1948): all share the same aims and work to promote the quality of cookery throughout France. The Chaîne des Rôtisseurs, founded in 1950 and allied with the Ordre Mondial des Gourmets, favour the use of the spit which 'by its neat and straitforward operation is the symbol of true French cookery'.

The old French tradition of charcuterie has given rise to many confréries in every province. Remembering Rabelais' famous battle of the andouilles, two or three confréries dispute the science of making andouilles; the learned and distinguished gourmands of the Confrérie des Taste-Andouilles du Val d'Ajol (1965) have founded an interesting andouille museum. The Confrérie du Goûte-Andouille de Jargeau (1970) is a more recent group, while the Association Amicale des Amateurs d'Authentiques Andouillettes is one of the most exclusive clubs as it has only five members, who have awarded diplomas to charcutiers and restaurateurs since 1960. In charcuterie western France is represented by the Confrérie du Goûte-Boudin de Mortagne-au-Perche (1963), the Confrérie des Chevaliers des Rillettes Sarthoises (1968), and the Confrérie de Gastronomie Normande la Tripière d'Or (1952); in Paris the Chevaliers de Saint Antoine (1963), wearing a white jacket and blue cape lined with black silk, hold all the secrets of charcuterie. The Confrérie du Jambon de Bayonne was founded in 1962 in the Basque country.

There is also a great variety of societies concerned with cheese: the Chevaliers de Taste-Fromage wear a green costume braided with gold (1954), and the Chevaliers de Faste-Fromage have violet costumes. In Carvagna (Italy) the Guilde des Maîtres Fromagers et Compagnons de Saint Uguzon holds chapter on 12 July, in robes bordered with fur, in memory of the saint, a Lombard shepherd who was persecuted to death – pilgrimages to his birthplace are organized.

The numerous culinary specialities of France have given birth to almost as many associations: the Confrérie du Cassoulet de Castelnaudary (1970), the Ordre du Collier de l'Escargot de Bourgogne (1956), the Ordre du Taste-Quiche (1969), the Confrérie des Chevaliers de la Pochouse (1949), the Confrérie des Taste-Cancoillotte de Franche-Comté (1970), the Ordre des Fines Goules du Poitou (1972), and the Compagnie de la Madeleine de Commercy (1963). Oysters are adored by the Galants de Verts-Marennes (1957), and vegetables by the Tastos Mounjetos du Comminges, the Mangeux d'Esparges de Sologne, and the Compagnons de l'Asperge d'Argenteuil. Whether great public bodies or simply gatherings of friends, these confréries continue to develop and there appears to be no lack of progress in conviviality.

conger eel   CONGRE

A common fish in the English Channel and the Atlantic. It is called *sili mor* in Brittany, *orratza* in Gascony; it is also found in the Mediterranean, where it is known as *fiela* or *fela*. Its body is long and smooth and its skin is of a brownish-grey colour without visible scales. It is a carnivore and has large jaws and strong teeth. Normally it measures 0.5–1.5 m (1½–5 ft) and weighs 5–15 kg (11–33 lb) but it can reach 3 m (10 ft) and 50 kg (110 lb). The conger can be found on the market all the year round, either whole (gutted (cleaned) and without the head), in pieces, or sliced. The flesh, which is firm but rather tasteless, is particularly suitable for soups and matelotes (e.g. chaudrée, cotriade). Slices cut between the middle of the body and the head (having less bones than the tail) can be roasted.

congolais

A small biscuit or sweet made of Italian meringue with grated coconut, cooked in a slow oven. It is also known as 'coconut rock'.

consommé

Meat, poultry, or fish stock served hot

or cold, generally at dinner, at the beginning of the meal. Simple consommé, taken from the stockpot, is sometimes served in home cookery as a clear soup, garnished if required with thinly sliced meat, vermicelli, tapioca, mixed vegetables, bone marrow, poached eggs, grated cheese, croutons, little quenelles, ravioli, etc. True consommé is clarified, thereby enriching it with nutritive and aromatic substances. This 'double' consommé may be garnished in many different ways depending on the base from which it is made. Beef and chicken are the most common bases; fish and game are rarely used nowadays. Consommés may be thickened with egg yolks, fresh cream, or with arrowroot. Cold consommés are normally placed in the refrigerator one or two hours before serving. Their sometimes gelatinous appearance (which may be heightened by adding gelatine) is due to the concentration of nutritive elements.

RECIPES

Basic Consommés

Clarified white consommé (1) CONSOMMÉ BLANC CLARIFIÉ For 3 litres (5 pints, 6 pints) stock, use 750 g (1½ lb) lean beef, chopped and trimmed, 100 g (4 oz) carrots, 100 g (4 oz) leeks, and the whites of 2 eggs. Clean the vegetables and cut into small dice. Put them into a pan with the chopped beef and the egg whites. Add the stock cold, or at most, tepid. Bring to the boil stirring constantly, then reduce the heat and simmer slowly for 1½ hours. Remove surplus fat and strain the consommé through a damp cloth.

Simple game consommé (2) CONSOMMÉ SIMPLE DE GIBIER For 5 litres (9 pints, 11 pints) consommé, use the following: 2 kg (4½ lb) shoulder or neck of venison, 1 kg (2¼ lb) forequarter of hare or the equivalent of rabbit, an old pheasant and an old partridge (these proportions may be modified according to availability), 300 g (11 oz) carrots, 300 g (11 oz) leeks, 300 g (11 oz) onions, 150 g (5 oz) celery, 50 g (2 oz) parsley sprigs, 2 cloves of garlic, 2 sprigs of thyme, a bay leaf, 50 g (2 oz) juniper berries, 3 cloves, and 40 g (1½ oz) salt.

Clean the game, then brown it in a lightly greased pan in an oven set at about 250 C (475 F, gas 9). Put the game (including the meat juices) into the stock-pot, add 6 litres (10 pints, 13 pints) cold water, and bring to the boil. Meanwhile prepare and chop the vegetables, and brown them in the pan. Tie the juniper berries and the cloves in a muslin (cheesecloth) bag. When the stock has come to the boil, add the vegetables and herbs and return to the boil. Simmer gently for 3½ hours. Remove surplus fat and strain the stock. It is now ready to serve as a soup or to be clarified in the same way as beef stock.

The game used in this consommé can be boned, made into a purée or salpicon, and used for various garnishes.

Simple fish consommé (3) CONSOMMÉ SIMPLE DE POISSON For 5 litres (9 pints, 11 pints) consommé use 1.5 kg (3 lb) pike, 600 g (1¼ lb) white fish bones, 1 kg (2¼ lb) turbot heads, 300 g (11 oz) onions, 200 g (7 oz) leeks, 80 g (3 oz) parsley sprigs, 30 g (1 oz) celery, a sprig of thyme, a bay leaf, 40 g (1½ oz) salt, and 6 dl (1 pint, 2½ cups) white wine.

Proceed as for simple white consommé, but chop the onions and leeks finely and boil slowly for 45 minutes only. Strain the stock through a sieve. To clarify the consommé use 1.5 kg (3 lb) whiting or chopped pike, 150 g (5 oz) leeks, 50 g (2 oz) sprigs of parsley, and 4 egg whites. Proceed as for clarified white consommé but cook very slowly and only for about 30 minutes; finally strain the consommé.

Simple chicken consommé (4) CONSOMMÉ SIMPLE DE VOLAILLE Proceed as for simple white consommé but replace the lean beef by a small chicken and 3 or 4 giblets browned in the oven, and the shin of beef (beef shank) by 750 g (1¾ lb) veal knuckle. For clarification, proceed as for clarified white consommé, using 4 or 5 chopped chicken giblets instead of the chopped beef. The chicken may then be used for croquettes, patties, etc.

Simple white consommé CONSOMMÉ BLANC SIMPLE Cut up 2 kg (4½ lb) lean beef and 1.5 kg (3¼ lb) shin of beef

(beef shank) (with bone) and put them into a big stockpot. (To extract the maximum amount of flavour from the bones, ask the butcher to break them into chunks.) Add 7 litres (12 pints, 15 pints) cold water. Bring to the boil and carefully remove the scum that forms on the surface. Season with coarse salt (it is better to adjust seasoning at the end than to add too much at the beginning). Add 3 or 4 large carrots, 400 g (14 oz) turnips, 100 g (4 oz) parsnips, 350 g (12 oz) leeks tied in a bundle, 2 sticks (stalks) of celery, sliced, a medium-sized onion with 2 cloves stuck in it, a clove of garlic, a sprig of thyme, and half a bay leaf. Simmer very slowly so that boiling is hardly perceptible, for 4 hours. Remove the meat and very carefully strain the stock. Remove surplus fat carefully.

COLD CONSOMMÉS

The number indicates the type of basic consommé to be used. These recipes will make about 1.5 litres (3 pints, 3½ pints) consommé.

Consommé flavoured with game fumet CONSOMMÉ AU FUMET DE GIBIER   (2) Add to the consommé 1 tablespoon Madeira per guest.

Consommé with wine CONSOMMÉ AU VIN   (1) Strain the consommé and when nearly cold add 1.5 dl (¼ pint, ⅔ cup) Madeira, Marsala, port, or sherry.

Tarragon-flavoured consommé CONSOMMÉ À L'ESSENCE D'ESTRAGON (4) Add 20 g (¾ oz) fresh tarragon leaves to the consommé after it has been clarified and before straining, and leave to infuse.

Truffle-flavoured consommé CONSOMMÉ À L'ESSENCE DE TRUFFE   (1 or 4) Add 40 g (1½ oz) fresh truffle peelings to the consommé 5 minutes before it has finished clarifying, and pour 1 tablespoon port or sherry into each soup dish.

HOT CONSOMMÉS WITH GARNISHES

Consommé à la parisienne   (4) Garnish the consommé with shredded vegetables lightly cooked in butter, rounds of plain royales, and chervil leaves.

Consommé Brillat-Savarin   (4) Thicken the consommé with tapioca and garnish with 1½ tablespoons finely shredded breast of poached chicken, 1½ tablespoons savoury pancakes cut up into very small diamond shapes, and 1½ tablespoons of a mixed lettuce and sorrel chiffonnade. Sprinkle with chervil leaves.

Consommé chasseur   (2) Cook 2 tablespoons finely shredded mushrooms in 5 cl (3 tablespoons, ¼ cup) Madeira. Thicken the consommé slightly with tapioca. Add the mushrooms and sprinkle with chervil leaves. Small profiteroles filled with game purée may be served at the same time.

Consommé Colbert   (4) Garnish the consommé with 3 tablespoons finely shredded vegetables cooked in butter and poach in the consommé 1 egg for each guest. Sprinkle with chervil leaves.

Consommé croûte au pot   (1) Dry some hollowed-out bread crusts in the oven. Sprinkle each one with a little stockpot fat and brown lightly or garnish with chopped stockpot vegetables. Serve with the consommé.

Consommé Dalayrac   (4) Thicken the consommé with tapioca. Garnish with shredded breast of chicken, mushrooms cooked in a court-bouillon, and truffles.

Consommé Florette   (1) Cook 150 g (5 oz) shredded leek lightly in butter, moisten with consommé, and reduce. Cook 1½ tablespoons rice in consommé and add the leek. Serve with fresh double (heavy) cream and grated Parmesan cheese.

Consommé Léopold   (1) Lightly cook 2 tablespoons (3 tablespoons) shredded sorrel in butter. Cook 4 teaspoons semolina (semolina flour) in the consommé, then add the sorrel and some chervil leaves.

Consommé Monte-Carlo   (1) Cut some very thin slices of bread into circles; butter, sprinkle with Parmesan, and toast lightly. Serve with the consommé.

Consommé Princess Alice (1) Separately cook shredded artichoke hearts (enough for 2 tablespoons) and finely shredded lettuce (enough for 1 good tablespoon) in butter. Cook 2 tablespoons (3 tablespoons) fine vermicelli in the consommé, add the artichoke and lettuce garnishes, and finally some chervil leaves.

Consommé princesse (4) Cook 15 green asparagus tips in butter. Prepare 15 small chicken forcemeat quenelles and poach them in stock. Add them to the consommé with the asparagus tips and some chervil leaves.

Consommé with profiteroles CON-SOMMÉ AUX PROFITEROLES (1, 2, or 4) Prepare 20 small profiteroles filled with a purée of meat, game, vegetables, or chicken. Thicken the consommé with tapioca and sprinkle with chervil leaves. Place the profiteroles in an hors d'oeuvre dish and serve with the consommé.

Consommé with rice or semolina CONSOMMÉ AU RIZ OU À LA SEMOULE (1, 3 or 4) Cook 60–80 g (2½–3 oz, scant ½ cup) rice in simple white consommé. Add it to the consommé chosen for a base and cook for about 20 minutes. Serve wth grated cheese.

Constantia

A wine from one of the oldest wine estates in South Africa, planted towards the end of the 17th century in the vicinity of Cape Town. It became very popular in Britain in the 19th century and also in France, where it was known as 'Vin de Constance' – a full-bodied sweet dessert wine, based on the Muscadelle grape. Today, however, fine table wines are made on the property, which has recently been rehabilitated by the government.

consumer associations

ASSOCIATIONS DE CONSOMMATEURS

The earliest associations to defend the interests of consumers appeared in the United States after World War II under the impetus of the solicitor Ralph Nader, who started by concerning himself with motor car safety. The farming and food industries soon followed this example. Consumer associations are essentially concerned with maintaining the health standards of products, publicizing precise information on their composition, and ensuring they are offered at a fair price.

Conti

The name given, in classic French cookery, to dressings made from lentils. For meat which is roasted, fried, or braised, the garnish consists of a lentil purée cooked with streaky bacon cut into strips. Another Conti garnish consists of croquettes of lentil purée accompanied by potato rissoles. For eggs *sur le plat à la Conti*, the lentil purée should be piped along the edge of the dish. For Conti soup, the purée is diluted with stock and fresh butter and croutons are added.

It is possible that these dressings were originally dedicated to the Prince of Conti, who employed in his kitchen two of the three famous 'Provençal brothers', Barthélemy and Simon.

contiser

A term for the process of encrusting chicken fillets, or those of game or fish (chiefly sole), with truffles or other ingredients cut in the shape of little cocks' combs. These are soaked in egg white in order to make them adhere properly and set at regular intervals into cuts made in the fillets.

contre-filet

See *faux-filet*.

conversation

A small pastry with an almond filling. According to the *Dictionnaire de l'Académie des gastronomes*, they were created at the end of the 18th century, taking their name from the title of a popular work, *Les Conversations d'Émilie*, by Mme d'Épinay (1774). They consist of covered puff pastry tartlets filled with a rum-flavoured frangipane or with almond cream and topped by a layer of royal icing. The tartlets are decorated with thin bands of pastry crisscrossed over the top.

RECIPE

Conversations Break 3 eggs, separating the yolks from the wites. Work 150 g (5 oz, ⅔ cup) butter into a paste with a wooden spatula, adding 150 g (5 oz, ⅔ cup) caster (superfine) sugar, then the 3 yolks one by one. Mix well, then add 175 g (6 oz, 1½ cups) ground almonds, 50 g (2 oz, ½ cup) cornflour (cornstarch), and 1 teaspoon vanilla-flavoured sugar. Beat thoroughly to obtain a well blended mixture.

Cut 400 g (14 oz) puff pastry into 3 portions, 2 of them equal, the third smaller. Roll out the 2 equal portions into sheets and use one of them to line 8 greased tartlet moulds. Fill each tartlet with the almond cream and moisten the edges of the pastry with water. Then place the moulds close together and cover them with the second sheet of pastry. Pass the rolling pin over this, cutting the pastry off on the rims of the moulds.

Whisk 2 of the egg whites until stiff, adding 200 g (7 oz, 1½ cups) icing sugar (confectioners' sugar). Spread this icing (frosting) over the tartlets. Roll out the rest of the pastry, cut it into thin strips, and intertwine these in diamond shapes on the icing. Leave for 15 minutes before cooking in a moderate oven (190 C, 375 F, gas 5) for 30 minutes. Allow them to cool before serving.

conviviality
CONVIVIALITÉ

The satisfaction felt by people enjoying a meal together. In *L'Amphitryon d'aujourd'hui* (1936), Maurice des Ombiaux wrote 'The spirit of sociability, of cordiality, of conviviality, lies at the heart of all gastronomy.'

Among all traditions the communal partaking of nourishment has been of socially fundamental importance. Hence the symbols of welcome, especially in Russian civilization and in the civilizations of the Middle East: a stranger is welcomed by the sharing of bread and salt, or by the offer of a drink of tea. A meal shared creates mutual rights and obligations: the host protects his guest, but the guest respects the rules of whoever receives him and should not betray the confidence of his host.

In feudal society, the knight about to be honoured had the right to carve the peacock or the pheasant; it was the custom for one partaker of the feast to have a morsel of his choosing carried to another by a page. In all societies, every circumstance in life from birth to death, every event of a social or religious nature, is celebrated by a meal, the distribution of cakes or confectionery, or by some sort of special food. Meals taken together for some special occasion even today proceed in accordance with protocol and good manners.

cooker (range)
CUISINIÈRE

A cooking appliance operating by gas, electricity, oil, or solid fuel. Gas and electric cookers are the most popular today, and have largely replaced the more traditional cooking range that was fired by coal or wood. Most cookers consist of a cooking top (hob) with several burners and an oven. There is usually a separate compartment for grilling (broiling) food situated either at eye level or just above the oven. Split-level cookers are becoming increasingly popular in modern kitchens – the oven is housed in a specially constructed cupboard and is usually situated at eye level, whereas the hob is situated separately, usually flush with a kitchen worktop. (See *oven, microwave oven*.)

In Britain the words 'cooker' and 'range' remained synonymous for a considerable period of time. Édouard de Pomiane called the gas cooker a range in 1934 when he wrote an article describing its merits: 'The gas range has a much greater heating surface than your enormous coal-burning cooker. On the front, you have two burners, but both burners provide equal amounts of heat, while on an average coal-burning cooker, there is one very good source of heat and another on which it is impossible to boil a saucepan of water! The gas range is one of the most important discoveries made by the inventive genius of man.' Shortly afterwards, electricity began to be used, first for special boiling rings, and then for complete cookers. Gas and electricity from then on were the two greatest sources of power for cookers, but certain models, especially those used in the country, are still designed to operate with wood, coal, or other domestic fuel. These appliances also ensure a supply of hot water as well as heating a room. In general, chefs prefer to cook on a visible flame, which can be regulated more quickly, but an electric cooker heats the kitchen less and presents fewer risks.

☐ **The hob (range top)** This has between three and five sources of heat, either gas burners, or electric hotplates, or a combination of both.

The fast or ultra-fast gas burner is simple or sequential and is extinguished and relit automatically, allowing a very flexible reduction of heat for simmering, or heating milk, for example. Visual control of the power of the flame is immediate, and the adjustment instantaneous.

The electric hotplate has a built-in thermostat that cuts off the current when the desired temperature is reached. Heat reduction is both easy and controlled, but the maximum power is only obtained after several minutes, and it also takes some time to cool (which may be useful for slow cooking). There are no flames and no fumes but the saucepans need to be thick-bottomed and strong and are therefore more expensive.

The independent ceramic hob is quite flat. It consists of a large sheet of opaque glass, beneath which are the heating elements. These transmit the heat by radiation towards points marked on the glass surface. Finally, the electric induction plate, covered by ceramic, transmits the electricity through an inductor, which transforms it into a magnetic field. The ceramic remains cold, as the power from the magnetic field is collected solely by the metal pans.

☐ **The choice of cooker (range)** Nowadays, there are several useful improvements in the design of cookers, including the electric rotisserie and the lighting system inside the oven. Electronic or electric lighting in gas cookers is becoming widespread, as is the autotimer, which automatically controls the switching on and switching off of the oven at preset times and temperatures.

The position of a cooker is important. It is best to place it next to a worktop, away from the refrigerator or freezer, and within easy reach of an exit for cooking fumes; a gas cooker should be sheltered from draughts.

cookery books
LIVRES DE CUISINE

The oldest cookery book in the world was undoubtedly that of Archestratus (4th century BC), but unfortunately it has not survived. A few centuries later, however, Apicius and Athenaeus produced works that were for many centuries considered to be the main authorities on culinary matters. The first medieval cookery book was written in French (rather than Latin) and dates from the early 14th century. Two of its most striking aspects are that the recipes require large quantities of spices and that it contains a wealth of recipes for fish and game. But the first real cookery books, giving details of the different ways of preparing food, cooking techniques, and recipes, were Taillevent's *Viandier* (c. 1380) and the anonymous *Ménagier de Paris* (1392–94). These two books, which were the authoritative works until virtually the 17th century, are full of recipes for spicy sauces, stews, soups, tarts, pâtés, roast meat, and flans. A treatise by the Italian humanist Platina in 1474 brought the art of good cooking back into fashion.

The first important changes came with the Italian cooks who arrived in France with Catherine de Medici. Their influence was seen in the introduction of new sweet dishes, jams, candied fruit, etc. *Le Bastiment de recettes*, published in Venice and translated in Lyon in the same year (1541), was a manual for making fruit preserves. It inspired the Frenchman Jehan Bonfons to write *La Manière de faire toutes confitures* (1550), and Nostradamus to produce his *Opuscule à tous nécessaire qui désirent avoir connaissance de plusieurs exquises receptes* (1555). During the Renaissance and the period up to the beginning of the 17th century, the royal physicians contributed to culinary literature. Jacques Pons' *Le Traité des melons* (1583) and Joseph du Chesne's *Le Pourtraict de santé* (1606) recommended certain fruit remedies, preferred game to domestic animals, and laid down set times for meals, and *Le Trésor de santé* (J. A. Huguetan, 1607) contained a wealth of vegetable and herb recipes. Books on agriculture also had an influence on the cuisine of that period, especially *Le Théâtre d'agriculture* (1600) by Olivier de Serres and *La Maison rustique*, published at the end of the 17th century.

An important turning point came in the 17th century with the publication of La Varenne's *Cuisinier français*, which was a proper recipe book, concentrating on soups, egg dishes, vegetables, and meat. La Varenne also wrote one of the first books about pâtisserie. Another great cook, Pierre de Lune, produced a treatise on cookery (*Le Cuisinier*, 1656), while servants' duties at table and in the house were set down in *L'École des officiers de bouche* (1662). New food products brought new books, including *Traités nouveaux et curieux du café, du thé, et du chocolat* (1685), by Philippe Sylvestre Dufour. French cookery became more sophisticated and simpler, as seen in *L'Art de bien traiter* (1674), signed 'L.S.R.', one of the most remarkable collections of recipes of its time. Two important contributions to culinary literature date from the end of the 17th century: Massialot's *Le Cuisinier royal et bourgeois* (he had already published *Nouvelles Instructions pour les confitures*) and Audiger's *La Maison réglée* (1692).

The 18th century brought with it a boom in the publication of cookery books, most notable of which were: *L'Abstinence de la viande rendue aisée* (1700), by Doctor B. Linand, which claimed that Lenten fasts did no harm to the body and also provided many vegetarian recipes: *Le Traité des aliments* (1702) by Louis Lemery, a great advocate of vegetarian food, famous for the lessons in chemistry and natural science that he gave in the Jardin du Roi; *Le Cuisinier moderne* (1735: first published in English as *The Modern Cook* in 1733) by La Chapelle, the creator of a sophisticated and methodical way of cooking and the only man acknowledged by Carême to be his superior; *Le Festin joyeux* (1738) by J. Lebai, in which cookery is perceived as a challenge of orchestration; *Les Dons de Comus ou les Délices de la table* (1739) by Marin, who came down on the side of 'modern' cookery in this, the first

complete manual on the theory of the culinary arts; *Le Cuisinier gascon* (1740), published anonymously by the Prince des Dombes, which brought together some rather strange-sounding dishes (chicken in bat, wooden-leg soup, veal in donkey's dung), which are nevertheless delicious. Menon's works mark the return of the great classic tome: *La Cuisinière bourgeoise* (1746) and *Les Soupers de la Cour* (1755), among others, are massive volumes (400 pages on poultry in the latter, and countless recipes using truffles, sweetbreads, foie gras, as well as some amazing pâtisserie recipes). Sweets and desserts were also in their heyday, as shown by *Le Cannaméliste français* (Gilliers, 1751) and *L'Art de bien faire les glaces d'office* (Emery, 1768).

The democratic wind of the Revolution even extended to the kitchens. A Parisian bookseller, Madame Mérigot, wrote and published *La Cuisinière républicaine* (1794), a collection of basic and inexpensive recipes (potato was a popular ingredient). The following year saw the appearance of *Le Petit Cuisinier économe* by Jannet, another bookseller, who published his *Le Manuel de la friandise ou les Talents de ma cuisinière Isabeau mis en lumière*, inspired by the works of Menon, in 1796.

The great renaissance in French cuisine did not come until the first decades of the 19th century, with such chefs as Viard, with his *Cuisinier impérial* (1810), and, of course, Carême, whose writings on all kinds of cookery were seminal – *Le Pâtissier royal parisien* (1815), *Le Cuisinier parisien* (1828), and *L'Art de la cuisine française au XIXe siècle* (finished by Plumerey, 1843–44). The 19th century also saw restaurateurs putting pen to paper, including Beauvilliers with his *L'Art du cuisinier* (1814), and their more discerning customers were not to be left out: Grimod de la Reynière (*Almanach des gourmands*, 1803–12), Brillat-Savarin (*La Physiologie du goût*, 1825), the Marquis de Cussy (*L'Art culinaire*, 1835), Colnet (*L'Art de dîner en ville*, 1810), Cadet de Gassicourt (*Les Dîners de Manant-Ville*, 1809), and Berchoux (*La Gastronomie*, 1801). Gastronomy and the art of cooking had become a literary genre, with Alexandre Dumas *père* as its foremost exponent (*Le Grand Dictionnaire de cuisine*, 1873); it was even the province of journalists, with Monselet's *Almanach des gourmands* (1863–70) and *La Cuisinière poétique* and Baron Brisse's 366 menus which appeared in *La Liberté*.

But the great chefs continued to publish theoretical and practical books which are accurate guides to the way that cooking in that era was practised and taught. Among these are Urbain Dubois' *La Cuisine classique* (1856), Jules Gouffé's *Livre de cuisine* (1867), and works by Garlin.

With the dawn of the 20th century, cookery books began to become very diversified. The great French chefs of those days, almost without exception, put down their spoons and picked up their pens at some stage in their career, from Montagné, Nignon, Escoffier, Guillot, Denis, and Oliver to Paul Bocuse and Chapel. As new media emerged, cooks used them to explain their techniques: books were still the most popular vehicle, but now had the advantage of colour illustrations; there were also specialist magazines, the radio, and, later, television.

Alongside recipe books written by famous chefs, another kind of book appeared that proved to be just as popular with the public: the works of gourmets and food critics, whose careers as authors were made possible by the trailblazing Curnonsky. The book-buying public seemed to be fascinated by works dealing with the history of food, regional and exotic recipes, and culinary arts in general, and this led to a rich and varied assortment of publications, from collections of 'card' recipes to reprints of old works and 'health food' books.

The contents of a cookery book depend on the market at which it is aimed: books of family-meal recipes (after the style of Mrs Beeton) go side by side with specialist volumes on wine, other drinks, cheese, cakes, preserves, freezer cookery, etc. Cookery books are, in fact, becoming increasingly specialized, and are often designed for use with a particular item of kitchen equipment, such as the microwave oven, mixer, deep-fryer, blender, etc.

cookery correspondent (food writer)

CHRONIQUEUR GASTRONOMIQUE

A newspaper or magazine journalist or a broadcaster who specializes in cookery, nutrition, and gastronomy. The cookery correspondent deals with culinary products and materials, reviews books or events, and appraises restaurants, an activity on which there can be too much emphasis. One of the first specialized cookery magazines in France was *Cuisine et Vins de France*. Some writers have tried their hand at cookery journalism, including Colette.

'French literature includes ... the gastronomic column, in which the cookery of restaurants is analysed as if it were a book, stage play, painting, or opera. Cookery is an art too. It is therefore quite natural that the *feuilleté de homard* of such and such a chef calls for the same vocabulary as *Le Chevalier à la rose* conducted by Karajan. ... Gastronomic critics are as controversial as evangelists, because they are committed narrators. They do not tell us how one lunches at a certain place, but how they themselves lunched there.' (James de Coquet, *Lettre au gourmets, aux gourmands, aux gastronomes et aux goinfres sur leur comportement à table et dans l'intimité*, Simoën, 1977).

Cookery correspondents share their task with the writers of food guides, which are normally published annually and offer a list of selected hotels and restaurants. Their origin can be traced to the itineraries that were mapped out for the use of medieval pilgrims, particularly in the fifth book of the *Liber Sancti Jacobi* (the pilgrims' guide to St James of Compostella), drawn up by Aymery Picard in 1150, which comments on the amenities of monasteries along the pilgrimage route. But a more recent predecessor was the list published over eight years from 1803, by Grimod de la Reynière.

The increasing popularity of restaurants boosted sales of the guides, one of which was de Blanc's *Guide des dîneurs* (1814). But it was the development of the motor car and tourism which brought about the proliferation of works designed especially for *gastronomades* (gastronomic tours), according to Curnonsky. The *Michelin* guide (started in 1900), published by a tyre firm, covers the whole of France. More recent ones are the *Guide de l'Auto-Journal*, the *Guide Gault et Millau* (Paris, London, and Austria) and the *Bottin gourmand*.

The ratings given by the guides (stars, cocks, chef's hats) are awaited each year with a certain anxiety by restaurant owners; they are sometimes downgraded. The *Michelin's* star rating serves as a model. The 1951 edition awarded three stars to seven restaurants, of which three were in Paris and four in the provinces. By the 1980s there were 19, 13 of which were in the provinces – an indication of the part played by the guide in encouraging high-grade restaurants outside the capital.

cookie

See *biscuit*.

cooking CUISSON

The culinary operation of subjecting food to the action of heat, which either renders it fit to eat or improves its flavour. Most fruits and many vegetables may sometimes be eaten raw, but most other foods are cooked. There are seven basic cooking techniques: frying, grilling (broiling), roasting, sautéing, cooking in water (or steam), braising, and pot-roasting.

☐ **Changes brought about by cooking**
● Chemical changes: through softening, coagulation, swelling, or dissolving, foods become either edible (rice, flour) or easier to digest (the collagen in meat is destroyed, which makes it more tender; the cellulose fibres of vegetables are also softened; the pectin of fruits is released; starch increases in volume).
● Changes to the external appearance: these render cooked preparations more appetizing and include the browning of grills and roasts, the glazing of vegetables, the caramelization of sugar, etc.
● Development of aroma and flavour: the taste of the basic ingredients is improved by incorporating extra flavours, condiments, herbs, wine, etc., especially in ragouts,soups, and daubes. Reducing liquids by cooking gives a more pronounced flavour, and marinating foods adds flavour before cooking.
● Elimination of the harmful elements which are destroyed by heat, particularly through boiling.

See also *French cooking*.

cooking ball
BOULE DE CUISSON

A metal utensil of variable size consisting of two halves that open either to enclose food that needs to be cooked in boiling water, or to immerse dried plants for infusion.

● The *tea egg* is a round or oval utensil, the size of an egg, made of aluminium or stainless steel and perforated with small holes. It is filled with tea or any other plant for infusion and plunged into boiling water in a teapot. It prevents the dispersion of the tea leaves and makes it easier to clean the teapot. A spoon version also exists for making tea directly in the cup.

● The *rice ball* is an aluminium spherical utensil with a diameter of approximately 14 cm (6 in) and with slightly larger holes than the tea egg. It should never be more than half filled as rice swells during cooking. It is primarily used for cooking rice in the stock remaining after a chicken has been cooked. It is then used as a garnish. Rice balls are also used to enclose aromatic ingredients used to flavour a dish, at the same time prevening their dispersal through the liquid.

● The *vegetable ball* is an oval wire basket in two halves joined by a hook. It enables the vegetables to be removed from the liquid in which they were cooked without having to decant the liquid.

cooler
RAFRAÎCHISSOIR,
RAFRAÎCHISSEUR

A deep cylindrical or oval receptacle made of glass, china, or metal. Bottles are plunged into the iced or salted water in the container to keep cool. The cooler can also be set on the table to serve certain foods which must be eaten very cold, such as caviar; it sometimes has a double bottom, which contains crushed ice.

Coolers have been in use since the

Middle Ages; in the 17th and 18th centuries they formed part of the table setting. Glasses, particularly champagne glasses, could be cooled in china receptacles with sloping deeply channelled sides in which the glasses were placed upside down.

coppa

Italian or Corsican charcuterie made by deboning and trimming loin of pork, seasoning it with salt, and marinating it with garlic and red wine. It is then rolled out and tied in a sectin of gut. The coppa is first braised, then dried, and eaten before it hardens. Rather fatty but with a fine flavour, it is cut in thin slices and is eaten plain, or as a garnish for pizza. It can also be used as bacon. The word means 'nape of the neck' in Italian and in fact it is the part of the loin near the neck that is used.

copper CUIVRE

A reddish metal used in the manufacture of many cooking utensils. It is an excellent conductor of heat, and copper cooking pans distribute heat evenly. Copper heats up and cools down rapidly and therefore enables greater control to be exercised in certain cooking methods (such as simmering). The major disadvantage of copper is the formation of verdigris on its surface in humid conditions. This coating is unsightly and toxic and the utensils need to be polished frequently. Copper utensils are also very costly to buy and tend to be used more in restaurants than in the home. Copper also destroys vitamin C.

To avoid all direct contact with food, copper pans are coated inside, the older or cheaper ones with layer of tin. This is carried out by electrolysis, and the lining should be renewed regularly. Good-quality solid copper pans are usually lined with a coating of stainless steel. Tin is not used for bowls in which egg whites are whisked or beaten as the metal whisks would scrape the tin and cause oxidation of the eggs. Tin is not used to line preserving pans or pans for heating sugar as the high temperature is likely to melt the tin.

Decorative copper utensils (pastry moulds, sets of saucepans, etc.) are coated with a colourless varnish that must be removed if they are to be used for cooking. In certain food industries, such as brewing or jam-making, the fermentation vats and cauldrons are made of copper.

Copper is present in the human body and in certain foods in minute but measurable doses.

copra COPRAH

The dried kernel of the coconut, from which an oil is extracted. This oil, called coconut oil or copra oil, is then refined and used in the manufacture of margarine.

coq

The French word for a cock, and now used as a synonym for chicken in certain dishes. In traditional stock farming, cocks which were good breeders were kept as long as they could fulfil their function. They would be several years old before they were killed and therefore needed long and slow braising in a casserole (coq au vin). Nowadays, coq au vin is usually made with a chicken or hen.

The combs and the kidneys of the cock serve as a garnish or decoration, rare now but frequently used in the elaborate cuisine of former days.

RECIPES

Coq au vin (from an old recipe) Cut up a young chicken of about 1.75 kg (4 lb) into 6 pieces. Gently fry 90 g (3½ oz, ½ cup) lean bacon cut into small cubes and about 20 small onions in 45 g (1½ oz, 3 tablespoons) butter in an earthenware or cast-iron pot. When these are lightly browned, add the chicken pieces, a garlic clove chopped finely, a bouquet garni, and about 20 morels or other mushrooms. Sauté with the lid on over a brisk heat until golden. Remove the lid and skim off the fat. Pour a little good brandy over the chicken, set light to it, then pour on ½ litre (17 fl oz, 2 cups) old Auvergne wine (a Chambertin or a Mâcon). After cooking over a brisk heat for about 1¼ hours, take out the chicken, thicken the sauce with kneaded butter, and pour it over the chicken.

Mme Maigret's coq au vin COQ AU VIN DE MME MAIGRET (from a recipe by Georges Simenon) Prepare and finely slice a carrot, a leek, and an onion. Cut up a chicken of about 2 kg (4½ lb) into pieces. Put the vegetables, a bouquet of parsley, and the chicken legs into a pot. Pour over 3 dl (½ pint, 1¼ cups) water and cook gently for 30 minutes to obtain a chicken stock.

Meanwhile cut 2 carrots in round slices, and chop 4 shallots and 2 cloves of garlic. In another pot brown the rest of the chicken pieces in 2 tablespoons lard over a brisk heat. Take these out and put in the carrot slices and the chopped shallots and garlic. Reduce the heat and lightly brown for 10 minutes. Put the chicken pieces back into the pot. Sprinkle with 1 tablespoon flour and stir.

Pour over the chicken stock (there should be about 1 dl, 6 tablespoons, ½ cup, after reduction) with the same quantity of Riesling. Season with salt and pepper, a little grated nutmeg, and dried thyme. Cook for about 1½ hours (depending on the age of the chicken). Take out the chicken pieces and place them on a warm dish. Thicken the sauce away from the heat with an egg yolk thinned with 1 dl (6 tablespoons, ½ cup) fresh cream. Finally, add the juice of a lemon and 2 tablespoons sloe brandy. Pour the sauce over the dish and serve.

coque

A cake made in the south of France for the Easter celebrations. Shaped like a crown, it is made with brioche dough and crystallized (candied) fruit. The Limoux coque is flavoured with citron; in the Aveyron it is flavoured with citron, orange-flower water, or rum. Very large coques were formerly made for the Feast of the Boatmen of the Tarn at Whitsun (the seventh Sunday after Easter), when the priest would bless the waters of the river (this tradition disappeared during the 1960s).

coque (à la)

The French term for describing the familiar method of cooking a soft-boiled egg, i.e. by immersing the whole egg for three to four minutes in boiling water and eating it from the shell. This expression is also applied to any food which is poached without peeling (peaches, for instance) or indeed to any

which is eaten directly from its skin, such as avocados or artichokes. Some authors prefer the spelling *à la coq*, an allusion to the name given to the ship's cook.

RECIPE

Avocado à la coque AVOCAT À LA COQUE Cut an avocado in half just before serving and remove the stone (pit). Pour into the centre a vinaigrette flavoured whith chopped shallots, or a mayonnaise to which a little lemon juice and tomato ketchup have been added, or a tomato sauce with a dash of Worcestershire sauce.

coquelet

A young cock weighing 500–600 g (1–1½ lb). Its meat, which has scarcely had time to mature, is rather tasteless. It may be roasted, grilled (broiled), or fried in breadcrumbs, and requires a sauce with a strong flavour (lemon, green pepper). Young cocks should not be cut into pieces; they are generally cut in two, lengthwise.

RECIPE

Coquelets en crapaudine à l'américaine Prepare 2 young cocks as spatchcocks (see *(en) crapaudine*). Chop 2–3 cloves of garlic and some parsley. Add salt, 3 tablespoons oil, a good quantity of pepper, 2 teaspoons powdered ginger, and a dash of cayenne. Cover the cocks inside and outside with this mixture, marinating them in this way for 1 hour, then grill (broil) briskly and serve them with a green salad or mixed salad.

coques à petits fours

Shell shapes made with ground almonds and a meringue mixture, joined together in pairs with a stiff fruit *marmelade* or other filling and glazed with fondant icing. These petit fours can alternatively be filled with flavoured French butter cream or chestnut cream.

coquille à rôtir

An old cooking utensil resembling a round box, made of cast iron or thick terracotta. This was filled with charcoal and used to roast meat and chicken on the spit, making it the ancestor of the modern spit-roaster (see *rotisserie*). It was still in use in many households at the end of the 19th century.

Corazza

A café and ice-cream parlour which opened in Paris in 1787 under the arcades of the Montpensier galleries at the Palais-Royal. The Corazza belonged to the same proprietor as the Café de Foy, M. Le Noir, and was managed by his wife, 'one of the most beautiful limonadières in Paris', according to Grimod de La Reynière in *Itinéraire gourmand*. The café was known for its Maraschino sorbets and ice-cream concoctions. The French revolutionaries made it their headquarters, and Barras, Talma, and Napoleon all frequented it. The Café Corazza was brought back by a former major domo of Charles X, who turned it into a restaurant. This survived until 1915.

Corbières

A Languedoc vineyard, extending from Narbonne nearly to Carcassonne and as far as the northern regions of Roussillon. Its wines are categorized as VDQS and account for 40% of French production in this sector. The main grape varieties are Carignan and Grenache and the bulk of the production is red, although a little rosé and an even smaller quantity of white wine is also made. The hot hillsides are conducive to full-bodied fruity wines, sometimes able to develop a pronounced bouquet with some bottle age, which are required to be 11°. A characteristic of red Corbières wines is that they are agreeable to drink when lightly chilled.

Corcellet

A famous Parisian seller of gourmet foods who moved into the Beaujolais galleries, at the Palais-Royal, during the Empire. In his *Itinéraire gourmand*, Grimod de la Reynière enthusiastically praised his shop: 'One should be happy to know that it is hither that Strasbourg goose pâté de foie, Toulouse duck liver, Pithiviers larks, chickens and plovers from Chartres, Périgueux partridges, etc., are inclined to make their way when they arrive in Paris. Here they find themselves in familiar country with Nérac terrines, mortadellas from Lyons, sausages from Arles, little tongues from Troyes, the galantines of M. Prévost, and other succulent compatriots.'

M. Corcellet left the Palais-Royal for the Avenue de l'Opéra at the end of the 19th century. His shop is still in business today, after several changes of management, on the Avenue Victor Hugo.

Paul Corcellet, a distant descendant of the original caterer from the Palais-Royal, has opened a shop in Paris which sells hippopotamus stew, smoked boa, elephant trunk, alligator tail, sautéed reindeer, and other exotic products, which have been cooked and frozen. Apart from this amusing side it is a first-class grocery shop which specializes in vinegar, chutneys, mustard, and especially in green peppercorns, which Paul Corcellet has made popular in France.

cordée

A pastry is described as *cordée* when too much water has been used in the mixing, making it hard and tough. A purée is said to be *cordée* when the potatoes are crushed through a sieve with a rotary movement, which makes them sticky. (The potatoes should be crushed by pressing them through the sieve vertically.)

cordial

A beverage, often sweet, which is generally alcoholic and aromatic. It is supposed to have a tonic effect, as the etymology of cordial suggests (from the Latin *cor*, heart). In France, the word has fallen into disuse, being used only for the names of certain so-called 'household' preparations (various squashes, creams, and liqueurs), but in English-speaking countries it is occasionally used as a synonym for liqueur or brandy, to designate spirits with particular strength as well as a distinctive flavour.

cordon bleu

This was originally a wide blue ribbon worn by members of the highest order of knighthood, L'Ordre des Chevaliers du Saint-Esprit, instituted by Henri III of France in 1578. By extension, the term has since been applied to food prepared to a very high standard and to outstanding cooks. The analogy no doubt arose from the similarity between the sash worn by the knights and the ribbons (generally blue) of a cook's apron. In *Paris à table* (1846), the words of Eugène Briffault have lost none of their force: 'Those who underestimate the feminine sex where culinary matters are concerned forget their high level of achievement which has earned them the accolade of cordon-bleu. It is impossible to bring more skill and delicacy, more taste and intelligence to the choice and preparation of dishes than women have brought.'

coriander CORIANDRE

An aromatic umbelliferous plant used mainly for its dried seeds, either whole or ground. The Hebrews flavoured their cakes with coriander and the Romans made use of it for preserving meat. Charlemagne encouraged its cultivation. In the 18th century, the seeds, covered with sugar, were chewed. However, coriander has played only a modest role in France (except in making such liqueurs as Izarra and Chartreuse) compared with the place it occupies in Mediterranean cookery (in soups, with vegetables, in marinades and pastries). In Germany, coriander is used for seasoning cabbage and in marinades for game. Its most classic uses are for the preparation of vegetables *à la grecque* and of pickles in vinegar.

Coriander leaves, commonly known as Arab parsley or Chinese parsley in France and as Greek parsley in Britain, can be used like parsley: the leaves feature especially in the cuisine of China, Southeast Asia, South America, and Mexico.

cork LIÈGE

The thick outer part of the bark of the cork oak, which grows in Portugal, Morocco, the Landes region of France, and generally throughout the western Mediterranean. Cork has a very low density, is a good insulating material, does not rot, is flame-resistant, and is almost impermeable to water and air. It is also remarkably elastic, so that it can be compressed without expanding sideways. As it will stick to smooth surfaces, even when they are wet, it is an ideal material for bottle stoppers. Because of its insulating property, it is also used to manufacture place mats, drip mats, etc.

corkscrew
TIRE-BOUCHON

An implement used to open a bottle sealed by a cork. The standard corkscrew has a spiral thread, which can be flat or rounded, and is usually nickel-plated. The rounded stem is preferable because there is less risk of causing the cork to crumble. The spiral must be 60–80 mm (2½–3¼ in) long so that the cork, which is quite long in a good bottle, is pierced all the way through. Its tip must be sharp and designed in such a way that it is not centred in the spiral.

There are numerous models of corkscrew, some fitted with a casing to protect the neck of the bottle, others with a lever or even with a gearing-down system to limit the strain but also to avoid moving the bottle too much. Some corkscrews are also fitted with a bottle opener and a blade for cutting the seal.

Another system operates with two blades of unequal length, which are inserted between the neck and the cork, and this obviates the need to pierce the cork. There is also a device which pierces the cork and injects gas underneath. This has the effect of effortlessly forcing out the cork. It is only recommended for a crumbly cork which is in danger of breaking.

corn

See *maize*.

Cornas

A Côtes du Rhône AOC red wine, from the Vivarais side of the river valley. The Syrah is the basic grape. The Romans probably laid down the original vineyard when they came up the Rhône from the south and began to settle around here and in the foothills of the Massif Central. Emperor Charlemagne is said to have esteemed the full robust wine and, with some bottle age, it can develop very pleasantly.

corned beef

Cured beef, of American origin, which can be sold in cans. Pieces of beef are cooked, preserved with salt or brine, and then canned with beef fat and jelly. From the end of the last century military slang gave the name 'bully beef' to the preserved beef distributed by the army. During World War I, the corned beef salvaged from American stocks was known as bully beef. It can be eaten cold with salad, or heated up and served with an onion sauce; in the United States it is mostly eaten in sandwiches.

cornelian cherry

CORNOUILLE

The edible fruit of a species of cornel, a shrub which grows in undergrowth and hedges in central and southern Europe. Cornelian cherries are picked in September, when they are red, fleshy, oval, about the same size as olives, and taste sharp and slightly oily. They can be eaten when very ripe on their own, made into jelly, or preserved in sugar or honey; if they are picked when barely ripe, they can be preserved in brine.

cornet

A cone-shaped pastry. The cornets used as ice-cream cones are made from wafer pastry. Filled cornets (often known as cream horns) are usually made from puff pastry, cooked while rolled around cornet moulds, and then filled with confectioners' custard (pastry cream), Chiboust cream, or Chantilly cream and decorated with chopped crystallized (candied) fruit. Murat cornets (a speciality of the Auvergne) are made from the mixture used for langues de chats, filled with sweetened whipped cream, and sometimes decorated with candied violets.

The name *cornet* is also given to a slice of ham or salmon rolled up, filled with a cold preparation, and served as an hors d'oeuvre.

RECIPES

Ham cornets with foie gras mousse
CORNETS DE JAMBON À LA MOUSSE
DE FOIE GRAS Roll up some small but fairly thick slices of ham into cornets. Fill them with foie gras mousse (using a piping (pastry) bag). Arrange on a bed of lettuce or on a dish garnished with cubes of port-flavoured aspic jelly.

Smoked salmon cornets with fish roe
CORNETS DE SAUMON FUMÉ AUX
OEUFS DE POISSON Roll up some small slices of smoked salmon into cornets. Fill them with fish roe (caviar, salmon, or lumpfish). Arrange them on a bed of shredded lettuce dressed with vinaigrette. Garnish with fluted lemon halves. The base of the cornet can be filled with a little cream mixed with a few drops of lemon juice and grated horseradish, or else this cream can be served in a sauceboat at the same time as the cornets, with hot blinis.

Cornish pasty

A turnover of short or puff pastry with a filling of meat, onions, and potatoes. Originally from the county of Cornwall in England, it is served as a hot snack, sometimes garnished with parsley.

corn salad

See *lamb's lettuce*.

correct CORRIGER

To modify a flavour which is too pronounced by adding to the preparation another substance with a contrasting effect. Salt and pepper are usually used to correct the seasoning of a dish; they are added when cooking is completed, before the food is served. A little sugar in tomato purée corrects excessive acidity. A few slices of raw potato or a sugar lump are used for correcting a preparation which is too salty.

corsé

The French term used to describe strong black coffee. It is also used to describe a wine with a high alcoholic strength, of definite character, whose taste fills the mouth: the English equivalent is 'full-bodied' or 'robust'.

Corsica CORSE

A Mediterranean island, which is a French department. Corsican cookery is not well known internationally. The diversity of the natural resources of the island, which often do not travel well, give considerable individuality and refinement to Corsican cuisine. As well as typically Mediterranean products, such as olives, citrus fruits, tomatoes, aubergines (eggplants), etc., it uses chestnuts (in brilloli, fritters, pancakes, and cakes) and also fairly rare berries, such as those of the arbutus. Corsican dishes are not highly spiced; they make use of the herbs of the maquis (rosemary and thyme) and those of the garden (basil and mint), which are almost absent from Provençal and Italian cookery.

This originality can also be found in the traditional technique of the *fucone*: the fire lit on a clay slab heats the family room, while its smoke, filtering through the laths of the ceiling to the loft, adds its flavour to the various products made from the pig killed in the autumn. The fame of Corsican charcuterie rests on the quality of its smoked specialities, such as figatelli, coppa, and lonzo. Pickled pork (*petit salé*) is also used in some wonderful ragouts with broad beans and red kidney beans. However, other meats are also worthy of the attention of the gastronome: roast kid, blackbirds fed on myrtle and arbutus, woodcock in salmis, and mutton stew (stufatu). There is an even wider range of fish specialities in an island well provided with rivers and streams. They include the bouillabaisse (ziminu) from Corte, dried cod, eel in red wine (*tiano*), and fried trout. As in Provence, anchovies appear in many dishes, including anchoyade. The shellfish have a reputation for freshness.

The Corsicans know how to enhance the flavour of their quality products with spiced tomato purée (sometimes using mushrooms, which are very numerous and diverse in the countryside) but above all with Broccio. Thanks to this cheese, which is made from the whey of ewes' milk, some Italian specialities (such as lasagne and cannelloni) have a special flavour; the same is true of vegetables, which are either stuffed or used in fritters, such as courgettes (zucchini), aubergines (eggplants), artichokes, onions, and leeks. Polenta, another dish that appears in Italy, is generally made from chestnut flour, whose bitter smoky taste is very different from that of wheat flour. On the other hand, recipes such as *sciacce* have no equivalent on the mainland, neither do the local tarts made with vegetables, herbs, and Broccio.

Corsican housewives are skilled at making desserts, in which Broccio is a prime ingredient – without it, neither the fritters (fritelles) nor the custard creams (fiadone) would have their delicacy. Honey, pine kernels, bitter almonds, and aniseed are also included in various specialities. Mention should also be made of Corsican crystallized (candied) citrus fruit, tomato, fig, and wild fruit conserves, ratafias made from cherry, fig, and sorb apple, and myrtle liqueur.

Corsican wines
VINS DE CORSE

The vin de pays name for certain wines of Corsica is 'Île de Beauté' and, although the terrain is well suited to vine cultivation, for many years the wines were neither well known nor well reputed outside their homeland. More recently, however, the vineyards have been expanding and the wines are mostly being made by producers well acquainted with modern technology, so that the overall standard of Corsican wines is much improved and certain of them have an AOC, notably those of Patrimonio. The fine wine region is the Cap Corse peninsula, homeland of the island's world-famous apéritif of the same name, but other wine areas include Bastia, Ajaccio, Calvi Caro, Sartène, Bonifacio, and Santa Lucia di Tallano. The Corsican grapes tend to be of Italian rather than of French origin: Sciaccarello, Nielluccio, Barbarosso (for the reds); Vermentino, Riminese, Rossola Bianca (for the whites); but in recent times some of the classic varieties, including Carignan, Cinsault, and Syrah, have been successfully introduced.

Napoleon is said always to have had a bottle of Patrimonio on his table, and generations of tourists have appreciated the red, white, and rosé wines. As might be expected from this sunny island, these are full-bodied and aromatic (Corsica is often referred to as 'the scented isle'), the rosé in particular being very charming and distinctive.

cortinarius CORTINAIRE

A genus of mushrooms of which there are very many species, most of them inedible. Most celebrated is the oddly named remarkable (or Berkeley) cortinarius, which has a brown cap marked with white and violet. This mushroom is fleshy, has a pleasant fragrance, and is well suited to stuffed preparations. The mountain cortinarius, a species which is fairly rare in France, is deadly.

Corton-Charlemagne

An AOC white wine, from the parish of Aloxe-Corton in the Côte de Beaune. It is a very great white Burgundy, but the vineyard, which is smallish anyway, suffers from being on fairly steep slopes, so that there is a risk of the topsoil being brought down in heavy rain. Corton-Charlemagne is a noble and powerful fine wine, comparable in breeding to Meursault, although somewhat less soft.

A section of the vineyard, thought to have been the personal property of Emperor Charlemagne, has the right to the AOC 'Charlemagne', although this is seldom used, as the vine growers prefer to use the name 'Corton', which has a high reputation for red wines as well as a little white.

Costières-du-Gard

Red, rosé, and white wines produced on the right bank of the Rhône, to the south of Nîmes. They come from 24 parishes in the Gard and the Hérault, and are the product of such grape varieties as are suited to its stony soil and the heat. In style the wines are similar to those of the Côtes-du-Rhône and they are in the VDQS category.

Coteaux

The word *coteau* means hillock and is often used to indicate the small undulations in the ground, as differentiated from the more definite slopes or foothills (*côtes*). The name was applied sarcastically in the 17th century to those who today would be dubbed wine snobs – gourmets who boasted that they could not only pick out (blind) the finest wines, but could actually distinguish the particular slope or the very vineyard from which a wine came. These self-styled connoisseurs came to be known as members of the 'Ordre des Coteaux'.

The original joke is said to have been made by the then Bishop of Le Mans, who had invited the Marquis de Saint-Évremond to dinner. (It was this gentleman who, exiled to England, introduced Charles II and his court to the pleasures of champagne, which he used to order to be sent to London from his friends' vineyards, including those owned by the Comte d'Olonne and the Marquis de Bois-Dauphin.) 'These gentlemen,' commented the Bishop 'carry everything to extremes in an attempt at refinement. They disdain to drink unless the wine comes from one of the vineyards (*coteaux*) of Ai (Ay), Hautvillier (Hautvillers), or Avenay.' Saint-Évremond passed on this remark and soon the three friends became known as 'Les Trois Coteaux'. There is today an Ordre des Coteaux, for celebrating and promoting the wines of Champagne.

Coteaux-Champenois

Still wines, with their own AOC. They may be red, white, or rosé and are produced within the delimited Champagne area. Formerly they were referred to as 'Champagne nature'.

Coteaux-d'Aix-en-Provence

Red, white, and rosé wines from 28 parishes around Aix-en-Provence. Those labelled 'Coteaux-d'Aix or Coteaux-des-Baux' come from six other parishes in the region. All these wines are VDQS.

Coteaux-d'Ancenis

VDQS wines from the north bank of the lower Loire. The Cabernet Franc and Gamay grapes are used for the red and rosés, Chenin Blanc or Pinot Gris for the whites. They are lightweight, but pleasant and fragrant.

Coteaux-de-l'Aubance

An Anjou white wine, with its own AOC, from the banks of the Aubance, a small tributary of the Loire. The Chenin Blanc is used: if the 'noble rot' (*Botrytis cinerea*) develops on the overripe grapes, sweetish wines can be made; otherwise they are medium dry to dry. Some rosé is also made, from the Cabernet Franc, with the AOC 'Cabernet d'Anjou'.

Coteaux-de-Pierrevert

VDQS red, white, and rosé wines from Provence, coming from about 40 parishes near the confluence of the Rivers Verdon and Durance. These light-bodied fairly fruity wines are usually most enjoyable when drunk young.

Coteaux-du-Giennois

VDQS wines produced around Gien, in the upper Loire region. Gamay is used for the reds, Sauvignon Blanc or Chenin Blanc for the whites. As production is small, the majority are drunk in the locality.

Coteaux-du-Languedoc

Red and rosé VDQS wines from the Hérault department (the biggest region of wine production in France) plus those of two parishes in the Gard and five in the Aude. These days some good wines are made here, meriting consideration in their own right; in former times many went for blending into the branded wines, for vermouth, and even for distillation. A variety of grapes are used, including the Carignan Noir, and there are a number of different regional names beginning to be widely known, including Saint Chinian, La Clape, Cabrières, and Montpeyroux.

Coteaux-du-Layon

White wines from Anjou, with their own AOC. They are made from the Chenin Blanc grape, locally known as the Pineau de la Loire. They are usually sweetish and those produced from grapes affected by the 'noble rot' (*Botrytis cinerea*) can be extremely luscious and may have an alcohol content of up to 15° in certain years. Among the famous wines of the region are those of Quarts-de-Chaume and Bonnezeaux.

Coteaux-du-Loir

An *appellation contrôlée* covering red, rosé, and white wines of Touraine, which should not be confused with the Coteaux-de-la-Loire, which are white wines from Anjou. The red and rosé Coteaux-du-Loir are made mainly from the Cabernet Franc, which is rapidly superseding the old Pineau d'Aunis. The whites, which are more popular, are made from the Chenin Blanc, known locally as Pineau de la Loire. They are fine and fruity, varying in dryness according to the vintage, and also include sparkling wines.

Coteaux-du-Tricastin

AOC red, rosé, and white wines from the Rhône Valley. The vineyard area is in the Drôme and near to the region covered by the AOC 'Côtes-du-Rhône'. The same grape varieties are used and the wines are somewhat similar, notably the well-constituted reds, in which some drinkers detect an aroma and flavour of truffles.

Coteaux-du-Vendômois

VDQS wines from the small area alongside the River Loir, west of Vendôme. The rosé, made from the Pineau d'Aunis grape, is dry and fruity, with an unusual fragrance. The red, made from the Gamay Noir and the Pineau d'Aunis, is a 'cosy' type of wine, slightly akin to those of the Coteaux-du-Loir. The dry white, made from the Chenin Blanc and Chardonnay, is liked locally.

cotechino

A fresh Italian sausage, rather like a saveloy but not smoked or dried. It is used in stews.

Côte-de-Beaune

Red and white Burgundies, coming from 19 parishes in the south of the Côte-d'Or, around Beaune itself and running from Ladoix in the north to Santenay in the south. The predominant vines are Pinot noir (for the reds) and Chardonnay (for the whites). The red wines may not often be as outstanding in quality and style as those of the neighbouring Côte-de-Nuits, but they are generally very good. It is the dry whites that are superb – the best of Burgundy. The AOC 'Côte-de-Beaune-Villages' is used for the wines from two or more of the parishes along the slopes, as specified.

Côte-de-Nuits

The Burgundy region stretching from Nuits-Saint-Georges up to the outskirts of Dijon in the Côte-d'Or. Here, nearly all the wines are red, made from the Pinot Noir, and many of them are world-famous. Each one, from the different specific sites, will possess an individual character, due to the portions into which the vineyards are divided, so that the owner of even a small plot can endow the wine he makes with its own special style. The majority are certainly wines for keeping, possessing a most beautiful character and outstanding bouquet. The AOC 'Côte-de-Nuits-Villages' applies to wines (mostly red) coming from the parishes at the north and south extremes of the region; they are usually not quite as good as those bearing specific parish names, but are higher in overall quality than the wines that are merely categorized by the AOC 'Bourgogne'.

Côte-Roannaise

VDQS red and rosé wines from vineyards on the banks of the upper Loire, near Roanne. The grape is Gamay-Saint-Romain à Jus Blanc. The wines are light and fresh in style and are drunk young.

Côte-Rôtie

Red wines from the right bank of the Rhône, opposite Vienne. The steep slopes have been terraced and are, as the name suggests, very sunny. Côte-Rôtie (AOC) is, together with Châteauneuf-du-Pape, the best-known of the Côtes-du-Rhône wines. Many grape varieties are used, including Syrah and Viognier, Côte-Rôtie wines are full-bodied easy drinks, with a bouquet that, for some, is evocative of raspberries.

Côtes-Canon-Fronsac

AOC red wines from Fronsac, east of Bordeaux and near Libourne. The vineyards overlook the Dordogne. The area comprises two regions but Côtes-Canon-Fronsac should not be confused with Saint-Émilion's Château-Canon. The wines are full-bodied, well-balanced, and deep in tone; they usually benefit by three to five years' bottle age.

Côtes-d'Auvergne

Red, rosé, and white VDQS wines from 53 parishes of the Puy-de-Dôme region. The vineyard, which is large and extensive, produces light pleasant wines with a definite fragrance and character. They are drunk young and are liked locally. The white wines are made from the Chardonnay grape and the reds and rosés from the Pinot Noir and the Gamay Noir à Jus Blanc.

Côtes-de-Blaye

White and red AOC wines from Blaye, on the right bank of the Gironde, facing the Médoc. The best may have the AOC 'Premières Côtes de Blaye', about 85% of which is red.

Côtes-de-Buzet

Red and white AOC wines from a small wine-growing area situated east of Agen, in southwestern France. The white, from the Sémillon, Sauvignon, and Muscadelle grapes, are dry and clean-tasting, with a pronounced bouquet. The reds are from Bordeaux grapes – Cabernet Sauvignon, Cabernet Franc, Merlot, and Malbec. They are usually matured in wood, thanks to the efforts of the Buzet-sur-Baise cooperative. Up to the end of the last century the region was large, but the vineyard was completely destroyed by phylloxera and has only recently been rehabilitated. The whites are best enjoyed when young and fresh. The reds can benefit by some bottle age.

Côtes-de-Duras

AOC red and white wines from the Lot-et-Garonne region in southwestern France, between the Bordeaux and Bergerac areas. The reds are made from the grape varieties used for Bordeaux – Cabernet Sauvignon, Cabernet Franc, Merlot, and Malbec. The whites are also made from grapes grown in Bordeaux – Sémillon, Sauvignon Blanc, Muscadelle, and some Mauzac. Both red and white are agreeable, the whites often slightly sweet.

Côtes-de-la-Malepère

VDQS red and rosé Languedoc wines, from vineyards near Carcassonne. They are beginning to show marked quality.

Côtes-de-Provence

Red, white, and especially rosé wines, harvested between Nice and Marseilles. In 1977 they were given an *appellation d'origine contrôlée*. The three main wine-growing regions are the coast between La Ciotat and Saint-Tropez, the north of the Maures massif, and the valley of the Argens, near Fréjus. The wines produced include full reds, dry assertive whites, and fruity rosés with a pronounced bouquet. They are considered to be the perfect accompaniment to the cuisine of the south. The rosés come mainly from the Grenache, Cinsault, Mourvèdre, and Mourvaison grapes. They are drunk chilled and usually while young.

Côtes-de-Toul

A VDQS wine from Lorraine, now made in fairly small quantities from vineyards around Toul. The French description is *vin gris* ('grey wine'), as the wine is a pale pinkish colour, evocative of a lilac-blue.

Côtes-du-Forez

VDQS red and rosé wines from the top of the Loire, the vineyards being on the foothills of the Forez Mountains.

Côtes-du-Frontonnais

Red and rosé AOC wines from southwestern France, produced in the Tarn-et-Garonne and the Haute-Garonne, to the south of Montauban. The main grape is the Négrette and the *appellation* may be followed by the suffixes 'Fronton' or 'Villaudric'.

Côtes-du-Jura

An AOC used for various wines from the rocky spurs of the Jura, covering a dozen districts in the Apremont region. The AOC covers dry whites, made from the Savagnin grape, yellow wines (see *vin jaune*), and straw wines (see *vin de paille*). There are also some fruity rosés, made from both black and white grapes; good full-bodied reds; and fully sparkling wines. Formerly mostly drunk locally, many are now exported.

Côtes-du-Luberon

VDQS red, white, and rosé wines from Haute-Provence. Pleasantly fruity, they are beginning to be widely known, thanks to improvements in vine growing and wine making.

Côtes-du-Marmandais

VDQS red and white wines from southwestern France, the vineyards extending along both banks of the Garonne and really being a continuation of the Entre-Deux-Mers.

Côtes-du-Rhône

Red, rosé, and white AOC wines, from the section of the Rhône valley between Lyon and Avignon. In the north, the river banks are steep, and the granite slopes, exposed to the strong sun of the Midi, are admirably suited to vines. About 20 different permitted grape varieties produce varied wines. The most famous are sold under their own *appellations*: Côte-Rôtie, Château-Grillet, Hermitage, Crozes-Hermitage, Clairette-de-Die, Châteauneuf-du-Pape, Tavel, and many more. Wines bearing the AOC 'Côtes-du-Rhône' are appealing, on account of their immediate attractiveness, redolent and evocative of their warm homeland. The best have the name of their parish added: Côtes-du-Rhône-Cairanne, Côtes-du-Rhône-Chusclan, etc. However, the Côtes-du-Rhône-Villages come from a number of delimited specified districts.

Côtes-du-Roussillon

Red, rosé, and white AOC wines from the Pyrénées-Orientales department, covering the same regions as Rivesaltes. The *appellation* covers the robust dark reds, produced mainly from the Carignan and the Grenache noir, also the fruity rosés and the crisp whites. The AOC 'Côtes-du-Roussillon-Villages' applies to reds of superior quality from 25 parishes specified in the *appellation*.

Côtes-du-Ventoux

AOC wines from the Rhône Valley and the sunny slopes of Mont Ventoux. They are mainly red wines with a beautiful ruby-red colour, and in smaller quantities, elegant fruity rosés. White wines are produced in very small quantities.

Côtes-du-Vivarais

VDQS wines from the Ardèche region, on the right bank of the Rhône. They can be very pleasant and appeal in style and value to today's drinkers.

cotignac

A pink sweetmeat, popular in France, made from a sweetened quince paste. It is sold in small round boxes made of thin wood, and its pink colour is due to the natural oxidation of the fruit while it is drying out. It can be home-made, although the most famous cotignac is the one made industrially at Orléans. It is said that cotignac was made in France in the time of Joan of Arc, and her effigy is used to decorate the boxes, but there is no evidence of its existence before the time of Louis XI.

Quince paste has its origins in antiquity, and ancient recipes indicate that it was formerly made with honey. Greek legend recounts how the nymphs offered it to Jupiter when he was a child. This has given rise to the popular 19th-century tradition that to eat cotignac from Orléans benefited the minds of unborn children – a good pretext for satisfying the craving of pregnant women for sweet things!

RECIPE

Cotignac Wash and peel some quinces; remove the seeds and tie them in a small piece of muslin (cheescloth). Cut the quinces into quarters and place them in a pan with a small amount of water (½ glass per kg (2¼ lb) fruit), together with the seeds in a muslin (cheesecloth) bag. Cook over a very low heat until the quinces are soft and squeeze the bag of seeds to obtain the maximum flavour. Remove the seeds and reduce the pulp to a purée.

Weigh the purée and pour it into a basin with 400 g (14 oz, 1¾ cups, firmly packed) sugar to each 500 g (18 oz, generous 2 cups) purée. Reduce the purée, stirring continuously with a wooden spoon, until a small ball of the mixture is able to retain its shape. Spread the paste evenly on an oiled baking tray (sheet) and leave to dry out, preferably in a very cool oven. Cut the paste into squares and coat with sugar. Pack into boxes, separating the layers with greaseproof (waxed) paper, and store in a dry place.

Cotignac can also be made with the leftover pulp when the fruit is used to prepare a jelly.

côtoyer

The French term for turning a joint while it is roasting so that the entire surface is exposed to the heat source.

cotriade

A fish soup from the coast of Brittany, prepared with butter or lard, onions, and potatoes. The word is said to have been derived from *cotret*, one of the pieces of wood on which the cauldron rested when the fish was cooked over a wood fire. Another possibility is that it is derived from the French word *coterie*, a former name for the ship's crew, who were given certain fish as food. Thus, a cotriade would have been made with the more common types of fish, the more rare or expensive ones, such as turbot or sole, being reserved for sale.

RECIPE

Cotriade The fish should be selected from the following: sardines, mackerel, sea beam (porgy), angler, hake, conger eel, gurnard, and horse mackerel (saurel). (For a more delicate dish, do not allow the proportion of oily fish, such as sardines and mackerel, to exceed a quarter of the total weight.) 1 or 2 large fish heads may also be included.

Cut 3 good-sized onions into quarters and cook in a large pan with 25 g (1 oz, 2 tablespoons) butter or lard until they are pale golden. Add 3 litres (5 pints, 6½ pints) water and 6 peeled sliced potatoes. Flavour with thyme, bay leaf, and other herbs. Bring to the boil and cook for about 15 minutes, then add 1½ kg (3 lb) cleaned pieces of fish. Cook for a further 10 minutes. Pour the stock from the resulting soup onto some slices of bread and serve the fish and potatoes separately, with a sauceboat of vinaigrette.

coucoulelli

Small diamond-shaped cakes from Corsica and the area around Nice, made with flour, olive oil, and white wine, blended together.

coudenou

A boudin blanc (white pudding or sausage) made with equal quantities of pork rind and a paste made with egg and breadcrumbs. The mixture is stuffed into ox (beef) intestines and poached in water. The dish is a speciality of Mazamet.

coulemelle

See *parasol mushroom*.

couler

The French term for pouring an aspic jelly into a cold cooked meat pie through a hole in the top of the pastry. A piece of card rolled into a tube can be used to make the operation easier. The warm jelly fills the spaces beneath the crust that form when the pie is cooked. When the jelly sets, it improves the consistency of the filling, and makes it easier to cut the pie into slices.

coulis

A liquid purée of cooked seasoned vegetables or shellfish (see *bisque*). It may be used to enhance the flavour of a sauce, it may itself be used as a sauce, or it may be used as an ingredient in soup. Fruit coulis are sauces made with raw or cooked fruit. Red fruit (redcurrants, strawberries, or raspberries), yellow fruit (apricots or mirabelle plums), berries (blackberries or bilberries), or exotic fruit (kiwi fruit) may be used; the sauces are served as an accompaniment to hot or cold desserts, ice creams, etc.

In the past, sauces of any kind were called coulis and were prepared in advance using type of funnel known as a *couloir* (hence the name).

RECIPES

Fresh fruit coulis COULIS DE FRUITS FRAIS Prepare 1 kg (2¼ lb) fresh fruit (apricots, strawberries, peaches, redcurrants, or any other suitable fruit in season). Chop into pieces where necessary, and purée in a blender with some caster (superfine) sugar (use 600–750 g (1¼–1¾ lb, 2½–3½ cups, firmly packed) depending on the acidity of the fruit). Add the sugar a little at a time while blending.

Raspberry coulis COULIS DE FRAMBOISE Sort, clean, and wipe 1 kg (2¼ lb) raspberries. Reduce to a purée in a blender together with about 500 g (18 oz, 2¼ cups, firmly packed) caster (superfine) sugar.

Tomato coulis (*condiment*) COULIS DE TOMATE (CONDIMENT) Choose firm ripe tomatoes. Cover them with boiling water for 20 seconds and then put them in cold water (this makes them easier to peel). Halve them and remove the seeds. Sprinkle the cut surface of each tomato with salt and turn them over so that the juice drains away. Then put the pulp into a blender with a little lemon juice and 1 teaspoon caster (superfine) sugar for each kg (2¼ lb) tomatoes used. After blending, reduce the resulting purée further by boiling it for a few minutes (this is not always necessary). Pass through a sieve, season with salt and pepper, and cool.

Tomato coulis (*sauce*) COULIS DE TOMATE (SAUCE) Peel 1½ kg (3 lb) ripe tomatoes and cut them into quarters. Brown a mixture of 50 g (2 oz, ⅔ cup) chopped carrots and 50 g (2 oz, ½ cup) chopped onions in a pan. Add the tomatoes, salt, pepper, 1 teaspoon caster (superfine) sugar, and a small bouquet garni. Stir, bring to the boil rapidly, cover, and cook either in the oven or on the hob until the mixture has reduced to a purée. Pass through a sieve, and reheat to reduce to the desired consistency.

Coulommiers

A French cows'-milk cheese (50% fat content) with a soft paste and whitish rind. It is similar to Coulommiers Brie, but smaller (13 cm (5 in) in diameter) and often contains more fat. When it is wrapped in fern leaves it is called *fougeru*.

country wines

VINS DE FRUITS

Beverages, usually of fairly low alcoholic strength, made from fruits, flowers, or even roots or vegetables. They are not widely produced commercially, but they are made extensively at home. The ingredients are crushed and allowed to ferment naturally in their own juice, which often has water and sugar added to it to facilitate fermentation and storage. Home wine-making is an excellent way of using up a glut of garden produce and is becoming an increasingly popular hobby.

Of course these 'wines' are no substitute for commercial wines made from grapes according to officially defined procedures, although such beverages make very enjoyable drinks.

RECIPES

Blackcurrant wine   VIN DE CASSIS
Select ripe sound blackcurrants, crush them by hand, and allow to stand for 24 hours. Rub through a sieve or coarse cloth; measure and reserve the juice. Add to the fruit residue a volume of water equal to that of the measured juice and macerate for 12 hours. Press through the sieve again, then mix the two lots of juice. Measure the volume of the mixture, and add to it 50 g (2 oz, ¼ cup) granulated sugar per litre (1¾ pints, 4¼ cups) juice. Pour into a small cask and leave to ferment.

At the end of about 4 weeks, cork up the cask, leaving a very small opening. A week later, uncork the cask to allow any carbon dioxide to escape; repeat this operation from time to time until no more gas remains in the cask. (Alternatively, pour into a demijohn fitted with an airlock and leave in a warm place until fermentation ceases.) Bung the cask (or demijohn) and draw off at the end of 6 months.

Cherry wine is made in the same way.

Orange wine   VIN D'ORANGES   Peel some good-quality sweet oranges and press them in a fruit press to extract the maximum amount of juice (or use a juice extractor). Add 1 kg (2¼ lb, 4½ cups) granulated sugar per 4 litres (7 pints, 9 pints) juice, mix in, and put into bottles. Cork, wire as for bottles of cider, and leave to ferment for 6 months before drinking.

coup

A French term for three customs at table during the Ancien Régime. The *coup d'avant* was a glass of vermouth, generally served in the drawing room while the guests were waiting to go to the table. The *coup d'après* was a glass of wine drunk after the soup, and the *coup du milieu* was a small glass of spirit that was drunk after the roast meat (see also *trou normand*). Between 1850 and 1900, this was often replaced by either a rum sorbet or a glass of sherry.

These are extracts from *L'Almanach des gourmands*, by Grimod de La Reynière:

'A few years ago, the *coup du milieu* was introduced to Paris, having been popular for a considerable time in Bordeaux and other maritime towns.

'It is drunk immediately after the roast meat and consists of a small glass of a bitter liqueur or spirit, often both, which aids digestion. Normally an extract of Swiss absinth is served, or failing that, Jamaican rum, or else simply very old Cognac.

'There are two ways of serving the *coup du milieu*: either the host pours it into small crystal glasses especially designed for this purpose and passes them to each guest, starting on his right; or else a young blonde girl, aged between 15 and 19, wearing no ornament on her head and with her arms bare to above the elbow, serves each guest. She holds a glass tray in her right hand and the bottle in her left and goes around the table serving each guest in succession. They must not take any liberties with this new kind of Hebe, who should be a virgin if possible (though 19-year-old virgins are extremely rare in Paris).

'However the *coup du milieu* is served, no pretext can be used to dispense with drinking it.

'Whether all the guests have arrived or not, five minutes before the meal is due to start the host will appear in the drawing room (unless there's nobody there). After greeting the guests collectively or individually, the *coup d'avant* will be served (if this is a custom of the house). It consists, as is well known, of a glass of vermouth. The host will then invite his guests to follow him into the dining room.'

coupage

In wine and spirit making, the process of blending the components in order to achieve a balanced and harmonious product. The skill of the maker is required to ensure that all the components – grapes, vineyards, vintages, etc. – contribute satisfactorily to the whole.

In Champagne and Bordeaux the similar process of *assemblage* involves the blending of the contents of various vattings or casks made at vintage time, which, the following spring, are blended together according to the judgment of the maker in order to attain the required uniformity and consistency of the wine.

coup de feu

The French term describing the browning, charring, or other changes that result from the sudden exposure of a piece of meat to too high a temperature during roasting. It also describes a cake mixture that has been overbaked in too intense a heat. This can be prevented by covering the cooking dish with buttered greaseproof (waxed) paper.

In catering (food service), the expression is used colloquially to describe the hurried last-minute preparations that have to be carried out in a restaurant to serve the food to perfection.

coupe

A rounded receptacle of varying size. Individual coupes are cups or goblets of glass, stainless steel, or silver plate, often on a stem, in which ice cream, fruit salads, or similar desserts are served. These desserts themselves are also known as coupes. They may be simple or elaborate, coated with syrup or chocolate sauce, and decorated with whipped cream, crystallized (candied) fruit, biscuits or wafers, etc. Coupes made with ice cream (*coupes glacées*) are known as sundaes in Britain and the United States.

The champagne coupe is a stemmed glass goblet that us wider than it is high. Large glasses, with or without a stem, are used for arranging fresh fruit, fruit salads, desserts, etc.

RECIPES

Coupes à la cévenole Prepare ½ litre (17 fl oz, 2 cups) vanilla ice cream, as described in the recipe below. Macerate 300 g (11 oz, 1⅓ cups) split marrons glacés in 2 dl (7 fl oz, ¾ cup) rum for 1 hour. Chill 6 sundae dishes in the refrigerator. 15 minutes before serving, divide the marrons glacés among the sundae dishes and cover with vanilla ice cream.` Decorate the dishes with whipped cream piped through a forcing (pastry) bag. Each dish can be topped with crystallized (candied) violets.

Coupes Malmaison Prepare ½ litre (17 fl oz, 2 cups) vanilla ice cream, as described in the recipe below. Remove the seeds from 400 g (14 oz) Muscat grapes, plunge them into a saucepan of boiling water and then immediately into cold water, then drain and peel them. Boil together 5 cl (2½ tablespoons, 3½ tablespoons) water with 150 g (5 oz, ⅔ cup, firmly packed) caster (superfine) sugar until the sugar just caramelizes. Divide the ice cream among 4 sundae dishes, cover with the grapes, and top with the caramel.

Hawaiian cream coupes COUPES DE CRÈME HAWAI Prepare ½ litre (17 fl oz, ½ cup) almond milk and keep it in a cool place. Wash, pat dry, and hull 300 g (11 oz, generous 2 cups) strawberries, cutting large ones in half. Peel and dice the flesh of a fresh pineapple. Line some sundae dishes with the strawberries and diced pineapple and completely cover with the almond milk. Top with a layer of raspberry coulis (approximately 100 g, 4 oz, ½ cup). Decorate each dish with piped rosettes of whipped cream.

Pear and caramel-cream coupes COUPES AUX POIRES À LA CRÈME AU CARAMEL Prepare 250 g (9 oz, ⅔ cup) caramel cream (see *creams and custards*) and keep in a cool place. Divide ½ litre (17 fl oz, 2 cups) almond milk among 8 sundae dishes and place in the refrigerator. Divide 16 diced canned pear halves amongst the dishes, cover with caramel cream, and put into a cool place. A few moments before serving, decorate with piped rosettes of whipped cream.

Vanilla ice cream for coupes glacées GLACE À LA VANILLE POUR COUPES GLACÉES For about ½ litre (17 fl oz, 2 cups) ice cream, use 4 egg yolks, ¼ litre (8 fl oz, 1 cup) milk, 1 vanilla pod (bean), 130 g (4½ oz, ⅔ cup) caster (superfine) sugar, and 2 tablespoons double (heavy) cream. Split the vanilla pod in two, add it to the milk, and bring to the boil. Work the egg yolks into the sugar with a wooden spoon. When the mixture lightens in colour, add the boiling milk, little by little, whisking constantly. (Remove the vanilla pod from the milk beforehand.) Heat the mixture, add the cream, and continue to heat until the mixture is thick enough to coat the wooden spoon. Strain the mixture into a bowl and allow to cool, stirring continuously. Pour into an ice-cream churn and operate this until the ice cream is frozen.

Coupole

A restaurant, bar, and brasserie situated on the Boulevard du Montparnasse in Paris. It opened in 1927, and was frequented by such customers as the painters of 'La Ruche', the musicians of the group 'Les Six', political exiles such as Lenin and Trotsky, and various foreign poets and artists who were at that time unknown in France (Foujita, Hemingway, Picasso, Eisenstein, etc.). These faithful habitués, nicknamed the 'Montparnos', also met at Le Dôme and Le Sélect (which opened in 1923). People also came to La Coupole to listen to jazz in the bar, and Louis Armstrong composed several pieces there. The ceiling of the restaurant is decorated with frescoes by Othon Friesz. In the 1930s, La Coupole was considered to be a mecca for artistic, talented, and creative people, and it continues to be patronized by the world of show business, the arts, and literature.

couque, couke, or koucke

A Flemish cake that is served at breakfast or with tea. It is eaten warm, split in half, and buttered. Couques are made from a brioche mixture with currants, or a gingerbread mixture (a speciality of Verviers), or from puff pastry (topped with icing). The couques from Dinant in Belgium are famous. The name is derived from the Dutch word *koek* (cake).

courbine

A fish with a slight resemblance to bass, commonly found in the Mediterranean and the Bay of Biscay. It is usually about 1 m (3 ft) long, but may measure up to 2 m (6½ ft). The courbine can be cooked like bass, but its flesh does not have such a delicate taste.

courgette (zucchini)

A variety of marrow (summer squash) usually eaten when young and immature. It has a shiny outer skin and the firm watery flesh has a delicate taste and has a low calorific value (30 Cal per 100 g). For a long time it was used primarily in Mediterranean cookery, but in recent years its popularity has become more widespread. It is sold throughout the year in the south of France, and is also grown in the north of France and in England. It is also imported from Spain, Italy, and Morocco. Of the varieties that are available practically all year round in France, the best is Diamant, which is seedless, small, and mid-green, with a delicate flavour. Other varieties have varying numbers of seeds and can be distinguished by the colour of their skin – grey in Grisette de Provence, mid-green in Aurore, and dark green in Reine des Noires.

If the courgettes are tender, it is not necessary to peel them. In general, 250 g (9 oz) per person is allowed (150 g (5 oz) for a ratatouille or a caponata). From the nutritional point of view, it is best to eat them either steamed or cooked in their own juice. When fried, deep-fried, or cooked as fritters, they are a good accompaniment to Mediterranean fish, mutton, and veal. They tend to be rather insipid when boiled, and it is best to enhance their flavour by serving them with a béchamel flavoured sauce with nutmeg, or with a curry sauce. They are equally delicious stuffed or cooked *au gratin*. They can be used as a salad vegetable, served sliced and chilled with olives and hard-boiled (hard-cooked) eggs. They can also be pickled. Courgettes freeze well, sliced and blanched beforehand.

RECIPES

Preparation of courgettes (zucchini) PRÉPARATION DE LA COURGETTE Remove the stalks from the courgettes and wipe them. Depending on the recipe, courgettes may or may not be peeled (it is essential to peel them for purées, but optional for fritters). Strips of peel may be removed from the courgettes to make them look decorative – in a ratatouille, for example.

Courgette purée PURÉE DE COURGETTES Peel and slice the courgettes, place them in a saucepan, and just cover them with water. Add some salt and 3–4 cloves of garlic, and cook them with the lid on for about 15 minutes. If the resulting purée is very watery, dry it carefully on the heat without allowing it to stick to the bottom of the pan. Add some butter. Pour the purée into a vegetable dish and sprinkle with chopped herbs, or spread it in a greased gratin dish, top with grated Gruyère cheese and butter, and brown in the oven.

Courgette salad SALADE DE COURGETTES Peel the courgettes, cut the flesh into small strips, and blanch them for 5 minutes in salted boiling water. Cool them under running water, and pat dry. Pour over some well seasoned vinaigrette and sprinkle with a mixture of chopped chervil and tarragon.

Courgettes à la niçoise Partially peel the courgettes, slice them thinly, and sauté them in oil with an equal quantity of peeled tomatoes. Add some parsley and garlic, and season with salt and pepper.

Courgettes à la provençale Do not peel the courgettes. Cut them into long thick slices, sprinkle them with salt, and leave for 15 minutes. Then pat them dry, coat them with flour, and sauté them in oil in a frying pan (skillet). Brush a gratin dish with oil, cover the bottom with rice cooked in meat stock, then add some of the courgette slices. Sauté some slices of tomato and onion in oil and add chopped parsley and garlic. Place the onion and tomato slices in the gratin dish on the courgettes, and cover with the rest of the courgettes. Sprinkle with grated cheese, and brown in a very hot oven.

Courgettes à l'indienne Peel the courgettes, cut them into olive-shaped pieces, and braise them in butter with salt and curry powder.

Glazed courgettes COURGETTES GLACÉES Cut the courgettes into small uniform olive-shaped pieces. Blanch them lightly in salted water and drain them. Place them in a sauté pan with 2 tablespoons butter, a pinch of salt, and a small amount of sugar. Cover with cold water, bring to the boil, and cook with the lid on over a low heat until the liquid has almost completely evaporated. Sauté the courgettes in this reduced sauce.

Glazed courgettes may be used as a garnish for poached fish or roast, fried, or sautéed white meats.

Sautéed courgettes COURGETTES SAUTÉES Do not peel the courgettes. Cut them into thick slices, sprinkle with salt, and then coat with flour. Fry them in oil or butter.

Stuffed courgettes COURGETTES FARCIES Cut the courgettes in half lengthwise, hollow them out, blanch them in salted water, and drain.

Prepare the following stuffing: cook some rice, drain it, rinse it under running water, and drain again. Add some fairly fatty minced (ground) mutton, chopped onion softened in butter, chopped fennel, a little garlic, and some salt and pepper to the rice.

Fill the courgette halves with the stuffing and place them close together in a sauté pan. Add some tomato sauce. Cook them on the top of the cooker for a while, then cover the pan and cook at 185 c (350 f, gas 4) until tender. Baste frequently during cooking.

courquinoise

A soup from the northern coast of France, particularly Calais, made with conger eel, crabs, gurnard, mussels, and sliced leeks. It is browned in the oven at the end of the cooking time.

court-bouillon

A spiced aromatic liquor or stock used mainly for cooking fish and shellfish but also for preparing white offal and certain white meats (such as chicken and veal). Wine and vinegar may sometimes be added to the court-bouillon, which is usually prepared in advance and allowed to cool. Food cooked in the liquid absorbs the flavour of the ingredients. Freeze-dried court-bouillon is available in France; it is easy to use and time-saving, as it is simply diluted with water.

☐ Cooking in court-bouillon Depending on the size of the item to be cooked, either a fish kettle or a large saucepan can be used. Large fish should be wrapped in a cloth (and tied to the grid if a fish kettle is used). The cooled court-bouillon is poured into the receptacle first. (If the court-bouillon is boiling hot, the liquid makes the flesh shrink and delays the cooking time.) The liquid is brought to the boil, and the heat is then reduced so that the fish simmers. (Cook for 25 minutes for fish 5 cm (2 in) thick and 1 hour for fish 12 cm (4 in) thick). When cooked, the flesh should be firm but supple.

If there is not enough court-bouillon, the fish should be covered with either a cloth or some celery leaves, to prevent the surface from drying out. Cold water should never be added.

When cooked, fish that are to be served hot are drained, arranged on a dish, and served with sauce (separately) and, traditionally, steamed potatoes, although other vegetables can be served. When served cold, the fish should be allowed to cool in the cooking liquid. The skin may then be removed. However, the court-bouillon should not be discarded as it can be strained and used in a soup or white sauce. It can be kept in a sterilized jar and used over again for a number of cooking sessions. In this way, its flavour is progressively enriched.

RECIPES

Court-bouillon eau de sel COURT-BOUILLON EAU-DE-SEL This is the easiest kind of court-bouillon to prepare as it consists only of salted boiling water (use 15 g (⅓ oz) coarse sea salt per litre (1¾ pints, 4¼ cups) water). It is not usually flavoured, but a little thyme and a bay leaf may be added if desired.

Court-bouillon with milk COURT-BOUILLON AU LAIT Add 1 finely shredded onion, a sprig of thyme, salt, and pepper to equal quantities of milk and water (the court-bouillon should cover the food that is to be cooked). It is used principally for cooking flatfish, such as brill or turbot, or smoked or salted fish, such as smoked haddock or salt cod (in the latter case, do not add salt).

Court-bouillon with wine COURT-BOUILLON AU VIN For every 2.5 litres (4½ pints, 5½ pints) water, add 50 cl (17 fl oz, 2 cups) dry white wine, 50

g (2 oz, ½ cup) grated carrot, 50 g (2 oz, ½ cup) grated onion, a sprig of thyme, a piece of bay leaf, 30 g (1 teaspoon) coarse salt, and possibly a small stick (stalk) of celery (chopped) and a sprig of parsley (although these have a strong flavour). Add 10 g (¼ oz) peppercorns 10 minutes before the end of the cooking time.

The wine should be chosen for its fruity flavour. The amount of wine can be increased if the amount of water is reduced by the same quantity. Red wine may also be used, especially if the court-bouillon is to be used to make an aspic jelly, which will then have a pale pink colour. Court-bouillons with white wine are used for cooking shellfish and fish of all types. Court-bouillons with red wine are used for cooking lean white-fleshed fish such as bass, which are served cold.

Lemon or vinegar court-bouillon COURT-BOUILLON AU CITRON OU AU VINAIGRE For every 3 litres (5 pints, 6½ pints) water, allow 250 g (9 oz) sliced carrots, 150 g (5 oz) onions (quartered, and, if desired, studded with a clove), a sprig of thyme, a bay leaf, 1–2 sprigs of parsley, 30 g (1 oz) coarse sea salt, either the juice of 2 lemons or 20 cl (7 fl oz, ¾ cup) vinegar, and finally 10 g (¼ oz) peppercorns (added 10 minutes before the end of the cooking period).

This court-bouillon can be used when the natural colour of the fish is to be preserved, for example, when cooking salmon or salmon trout, and also when cooking shellfish, as it makes the shell turn red.

COUSCOUS

A traditional north African dish made with hard wheat semolina and sometimes with barley or, in Tunisia, with green wheat. It was discovered by the French during the reign of Charles X during the conquest of Algeria. There is still some doubt about the original meaning of the word, which is derived from the Arabic *kouskous*. Some experts believe that the word was originally used for the food in a bird's beak used to feed its young. Léon Isnard, who considers that it is the Gallic form of *rac keskes* ('to pound until small'), maintains that it is derived phonetically from the words *koskos*, *keuscass*, *koskosou*, and *kouskous*, used in different parts of north Africa for a cooking pot in which semolina is steamed. Made of earthenware or alpha glass, the pot, which is pierced with holes, sits on top of another similar pot containing water or stock. Other experts believe that the sound of the word describes the noise made by the steam as it passes through the holes in the pot.

Couscous (in Arabic: *t'âam*) is the national dish of Algeria, Morocco, and Tunisia. It is served in Algeria after the *méchoui* (the barbecued food), and in Morocco after the tajines. The grain is shaped into small balls with the fingers and quickly put in the mouth. Even though the basic components are the same in all three countries – semolina and stock (or *marga*) – the ingredients vary. In Algeria, couscous is served with chickpeas, broad (fava) beans, a wide variety of other vegetables, including artichokes, courgettes (zucchini), potatoes, aubergines (eggplants), chard, fennel, and peas, and sometimes meat. *Mesfouf*, a couscous made with fresh broad beans and raisins, is served at dawn during the month of Ramadan. It is eaten while drinking whey (*leben*) or curdled milk (*raib*). Saharan couscous is served without vegetables or stock. In Tunisia, couscous can be made with rabbit, partridge, or mutton, but chickpeas are an essential ingredient. The most original recipe is for couscous made with fish (such as sea bream or groupers), but there is also a type of couscous in which the meat, fish, and vegetables are replaced by raisins, almonds, pistachios, dates, and walnuts, which are mixed with fresh milk and sprinkled with sugar. In Morocco couscous is served with chicken and (usually) two stocks – one to moisten the semolina, the other (seasoned with red pepper) to spice it. The numerous ingredients (turnips, courgettes, raisins, chickpeas, onions, etc.) are cooked for a very long time until they are reduced to a sort of mash. Another Moroccan recipe is for sweet couscous flavoured with cinnamon.

Whatever the variations in each country, there are two rules that must be observed in the preparation of an authentic couscous. First, the grain must be of the right quality and consistency, which depends on the art of rolling the grain by hand and cooking the semolina correctly. Secondly, the vegetables and spices used to prepare the stock must be carefully chosen to give the meat its unique flavour.

RECIPES

Preparing the grain for couscous PRÉPARATION DE LA GRAINE DU COUSCOUS In country villages, where couscous is simply a dish of semolina flavoured with rancid butter (*smeun*) and served with whey, the women prepare the grain in the traditional way by skilfully rolling it by hand. Hard-wheat semolina and flour are placed in a wooden dish (a *kesra*) or in an earthenware dish, together with a small amount of cold salted water. By rolling the semolina, the flour progressively binds itself around each grain. The grain is then sieved, which enables the particles to be sorted according to their size.

As this method of preparation requires skill and practice, it is preferable to use ready-made grain, which is now available in the shops (choose medium-sized grain). Put the grain in a dish with a little salted water, and work it with the hands until it has absorbed all the water. Coat the hands with oil and roll the grain between the palms to break up the lumps. The grain is then ready for cooking.

Cooking the grain CUISSON DE LA GRAINE The grain is steamed in a couscous pan. Fill the pot two-thirds with water or stock and bring it quickly to the boil. Then fit the *keskès* (steamer) containing the semolina onto the pot. Tie a damp cloth around the part where the *keskès* and the pot meet so that no steam escapes. After about 30 minutes, remove the semolina from the couscous pan, put it in a large round dish with a raised edge, coat the grains with oil, and break up the lumps with the hands. Put the couscous back in the *keskès* to steam it, and repeat the operation twice more, without forgetting to work the grain between each steaming. After the third steaming, arrange small knobs of butter on the semolina and serve.

During the second and third steaming, vegetables or meat are added to the pot, and raisins are mixed with the grain.

Couscous with fish COUSCOUS AU POISSON (Tunisian recipe) Steam some whiting fillets in the *keskès* (for 10 minutes). Flake them, and mix them with a purée of onions, some finely chopped garlic, paprika, harissa, chopped parsley, salt and pepper, 1 egg, and some stale bread that has been soaked in cold water. Form the mixture into balls and brown them in a frying pan (skillet).

Steam 1.5 kg (3 lb, 8 cups) semolina. Scale, trim, and gut 4 sea breams or 1 grouper weighing in total about 1.5 kg (3 lb). Marinate the fish in a mixture of 3 tablespoons (¼ cup) olive oil, 2 teaspoons each of fennel seeds and ground caraway, a generous pinch of cayenne, and 1 teaspoon paprika for 30 minutes.

Meanwhile, brown 3 grated onions, 3 chopped courgettes (zucchini), 4 chopped carrots, and 2 artichoke hearts (cut into quarters) in olive oil. Then cover with 1.5 litres (2¾ pints, 3½ pints) water and add 225 g (8 g, 1 cup) soaked chickpeas, fresh broad beans, a pinch of cayenne, 3 peeled and roughly chopped tomatoes, 2 cloves, 1 small cinnamon stick, 1 teaspoon caraway seeds, and, if desired, some harissa mixed with water. Bring the vegetables to the boil and then reduce the heat. Grill the fish 15 minutes before serving. Pile the semolina onto a dish and garnish it with the grilled fish and the fish balls. Serve the vegetables and stock separately.

Some people prefer to cook the fish in the stock with the vegetables. In this case a cabbage, 6 medium-sized potatoes, and 4 sweet peppers (cut in half) are also added.

Couscous with meat COUSCOUS À LA VIANDE Steam 1.5 kg (3 lb, 8 cups) semolina once only. Pour away the water in the pot. Use the meat from a 1.8-kg (4-lb) chicken and a small shoulder of mutton. Cut the meat into pieces and place it in the couscous pot with 8 pieces of neck of mutton and 5 tablespoons (6 tablespoons) olive oil. Brown the meat in the oil and add 4 onions, cut in half. Make sure that the onions brown without burning. Add 8 carrots (split in two), 4 chopped leeks, 1 chopped fennel bulb, 6 roughly chopped tomatoes, tomato purée thinned with water, 4 crushed cloves of garlic, a bouquet garni, and a small pinch of coarse salt. Cover the ingredients with cold water and then add 225 g (8 oz, 1 cup) chickpeas (previously soaked for 24 hours). Put the lid on the pot and bring to the boil. Cook for 20–25 minutes.

Add 4 turnips (cut into quarters), 4 large chopped courgettes (zucchini), and 4 small quartered artichokes (with the chokes and large leaves removed). Place the *keskès* containing the semolina on top of the pot and continue cooking for about 30 minutes.

Meanwhile, prepare some meatballs by mixing 450 g (1 lb) minced (ground) mutton with a small bunch of parsley, 2 chopped cloves of garlic, 2 chopped onions, 4 slices of bread (crumbled, moistened with milk, and squeezed out), 1 teaspoon harissa, salt, and pepper. Work the mixture well and divide it into 8 small balls. Roll each ball in flour and brown them in a frying pan (skillet) with olive oil over a brisk heat.

When the grain is cooked, turn it into a large dish, add butter, and garnish with the pieces of meat, merguez fried in oil, and the meatballs. Serve with the vegetables and the stock.

Couscous with vegetables COUSCOUS AUX LÉGUMES The preparation is almost the same as for couscous with meat. All the vegetables are placed in the pot when the grain is being cooked. Use chickpeas (soaked for 24 hours), broad beans (preferably fresh), grated onions, chopped turnips, chopped carrots, and sliced tomatoes, all seasoned with salt. Just before serving, enhance the flavour by seasoning with black pepper or mixed spices, (*qâlat daqqāa* or *rās al-hānout*) according to taste. Add small knobs of butter (rancid, if preferred). A wider range of vegetables can be used, such as cabbage, artichokes, potatoes, beet, chard, courgettes (zucchini), peas, etc.

Sauce for couscous SAUCE FORTE Mix 2 tablespoons harissa with ½ litre

(17 fl oz, 2 cups) stock, adding a little 'four spices' if desired. This sauce is served with all types of couscous dishes to enhance their taste. However, it should not be too strongly spiced.

couscous pan
COUSCOUSSIER

An aluminium or stainless steel utensil consisting of two parts, one fitting on top of the other. The lower part consists of a curved pot with handles for the vegetable or meat stock or plain water. The upper receptacle is a type of basin called the *keskès*, in which the semolina or other ingredients are steamed. Its base is pierced with small holes. The couscous pan has a lid that is also perforated to allow the steam to escape.

Formerly in north Africa, a couscous pan was either a simple earthenware utensil pierced with holes, or it was made of interlaced grasses. The semolina was placed inside and the receptacle was then placed on top of an ordinary cooking pot filled with water or stock.

cousinat

In the Auvergne, a soup made with chestnuts, celeriac (celery root), onions, and the white parts of leeks. It is traditionally finished with fresh cream and Salers butter.

On the Basque coast, cousinat is a ragout consisting of Bayonne ham cooked in lard, with beans, poivrade artichokes, carrots, and pieces of pumpkin.

cousinette

A soup from Béarn made with spinach, sorrel, lettuce and other finely chopped green vegetables. When served, it is poured into dishes containing thin slices of bread.

RECIPE

Cousinette Wash 150 g (5 oz) spinach leaves, 150 g (5 oz) Swiss chard leaves, 150 g (5 oz) lettuce leaves, 50 g (2 oz) sorrel leaves, and a small handful of wild mallow leaves. Shred all the leaves into a very fine chiffonnade and brown them gently in 50 g (2 oz, 4 tablespoons) butter or goose fat. Cover and braise gently for 10 minutes. Add 1.5 litres

(2¾ pints, 3½ pints) water or preferably chicken stock and, if desired, 250 g (9 oz, 1½ cups) finely sliced potatoes. Continue cooking for about 30 minutes. Just before serving, adjust the seasoning and add a knob of fresh butter. Pour the soup onto thin slices of bread that have been dried in the oven.

couve

A cake from the Dauphiné region in southeastern France. Made in Crest, originally for the Palm Sunday feast but nowadays all the year round, it is a sort of galette (French Twelfth-Night cake) flavoured with vanilla and lemon and cut in the shape of a broody hen. The cake is glazed with egg, pricked so that it does not swell, and baked in the oven. It is generally served with Clairette de Die, a sparkling white wine.

cover   COUVERT

The set of table implements (plate, glass, cutlery, etc.) that mark a place at table. In a more restricted sense, it can mean simply the knife, fork, and spoon, or even just the spoon and fork.

Until the 15th century, it was customary to serve 'under cover' (*à couvert*), that is, to cover the courses and dishes with a large white napkin to show the guests that all precautions had been taken to avoid poisoning. Hence the expression *mettre le couvert* (to lay the table – literally 'to put on the cover'). Since the word also meant the diner's place at the table, it began to be applied to the meal itself: *avoir son couvert mis chez quelqu'un* (to have one's place set at someone's house) means to have breakfast or dinner there regularly.

Under the Ancien Régime, a distinction was made between *le grand couvert*, the large setting or banquet reserved for the king alone or the royal family; *le petit couvert*, the small setting or ordinary meal, which the king ate with his initmate friends; and *le très petit couvert*, the very small setting which, although a very intimate meal, nevertheless consisted of three courses. Modern table conventions, with their tendency towards simplification, were introduced during the 18th and 19th centuries.

Table setting is classically based on precise rules governing such aspects as the folding of napkins, the number of glasses (up to five glasses of various capacities were used in the 19th century), and the position of the fork (on the left, prongs against the tablecloth), the knife (on the right, blade facing inwards), and the soupspoon if required (on the outer right, convex side upwards). Knife rests, which imply that the setting is not changed between courses, are disappearing with the introduction of modern facilities for laundering table linen, and the rules for table settings are becoming much less formal.

Since silver-plated metal came into general use, tableware designs have often merely reproduced previous styles. The early 20th century saw the beginning of a modern style, influenced by such people as Jean Puiforcat who, after World War I, created a style in which shape took precedence over decoration. German, and later Scandinavian, silversmiths have led the development of European designs, emphasizing the functional aspects and the beauty of the materials, which include wood, steel, and Plexiglas. However, Louis XIV shells, Louis XV festoons, Louis XVI pearls, and 18th-century fillets still adorn many items of household tableware, whether silver-plated or stainless steel. The standard setting is often supplemented with special implements, depending on the dish being served, such as snail tongs, a leg-of-mutton sleeve, fish knife and fork, grapefruit spoon, etc.

covering food COUVRIR

Food often needs to be cooked covered, particularly when the heat is lowered or when liquid is added after preliminary cooking over a brisker heat. For certain vegetables (e.g. cauliflower), the lid can be replaced by a cloth. Covering food with greaseproof (waxed) paper (buttered or unbuttered) prevents the formation of a skin during cooling (in the case of confectioner's custard (pastry cream), for example) and prevents food from drying out.

Some dishes (daubes, pâtés, terrines) should be cooked in a hermetically sealed utensil and the lid is further sealed by a strip of paste (*see lute*).

Other foods, cooked by rapid boiling (pasta, green vegetables) or simmering (eggs, poached fish), are cooked uncovered.

COW VACHE

The female of the domestic cattle from the time of its first calving (before this it is called a heifer). The cow is generally bred for producing milk and calves, but in France a good proportion of 'beef' comes from milch cows which are no longer needed for milk. Such cows are fattened up for the butcher at about five years old (much earlier than they used to be), giving meat which is often more tender and has more flavour than that from a bullock.

crab CRABE

One of a large group of decapod crustaceans characterized by a wide flat body protected by a hard carapace (shell); the small abdomen is tucked underneath. The five pairs of legs vary in size according to the species but the first pair (pincers) are generally much larger and equipped with strong claws.

Crabmeat is fine and delicate, although removing the meat, especially from the legs, is a painstaking and time-consuming operation. The dark meat from the body cavity is particularly good spread on buttered rye bread.

The four main species eaten in France are the spiny spider crab, with a spiny forward-pointing shell; the *tourteau* (common edible crab), which is larger, has a well-developed pair of pincers, and can weigh up to 5 kg (11 lb); the shore (or green shore) crab, which measures only 8–10 cm (3–4 in) across; and the velvet (or swimming) crab, which has an almost square shell and webbed legs.

Crabs live on sheltered coasts where vegetation grows, although the *tourteau* prefers more rocky or shingly sea beds. They should be purchased live and should be heavy and plump; a sign of plumpness is when the abdomen ('tail'), tucked under the shell, is slightly lifted.

Some fishmongers sell crabs already cooked, and only the common edible crab can be stuffed. It can also be cooked in a court-bouillon and eaten cold with mayonnaise; in Saint-Malo it is served shelled, with mayonnaise and quartered hard-boiled (hard-cooked) eggs. Crabs are served with special tongs and eaten using thin forks with two prongs; finger bowls should be provided. Small crabs are used for soups, bisques, and coulis. One can also buy canned crabmeat (shredded or in pieces), the best of which is imported from the Soviet Union.

RECIPES

Crab à la bretonne CRABE À LA BRETONNE Plunge a live crab into boiling lemon or vinegar court-bouillon. Cook for 8–10 minutes, then drain and cool. Remove the legs and claws and take out the contents of the shell. Clean the shell thoroughly. Cut the meat from the shell in two, put it back in the clean shell, and arrange the legs and claws around. Garnish with parsley or lettuce leaves and serve with a mayonnaise.

Crab salad SALADE DE CRABE Clean and cook 2 large crabs. Wash, scald, and cool 500 g (18 oz) bean sprouts and dry them. Mix 4 tablespoons mayonnaise, 1 tablespoon ketchup or very concentrated sieved tomato purée, and at least 1 tablespoon brandy. Mix the crabmeat, the bean sprouts, and the sauce and serve on a bed of lettuce leaves. Sprinkle with chopped herbs.

Stuffed crabs à la martiniquaise CRABES FARCIS À LA MARTINIQUAISE Clean 4 medium-sized *tourteau* crabs and cook them in court-bouillon. Add 1 cup of milk to a bowl of stale breadcrumbs. Trim and finely chop 3 good slices of ham and, separately, 5–6 shallots. Brown the shallots in oil or butter. Chop together a small bunch of parsley and 3–4 cloves of garlic, add them to the shallots, and stir. Crumble the crabmeat and add it to the pan together with a good pinch of cayenne, the breadcrumbs, (softened but well squeezed), and the chopped ham. Thoroughly stir the whole and reheat.

Adjust the seasoning so that the forcemeat is highly spiced. Mix 2 egg yolks with 2 tablespoons white rum, bind the forcemeat with this mixture, then fill the shells with the forcemeat. Sprinkle with white breadcrumbs, pour

on some melted butter, and bake gently in the oven.

Stuffed crabs au gratin CRABES FARCIS AU GRATIN Wash and brush some crabs. Plunge them in court-bouillon with lemon. Bring back to the boil, cook for about 10 minutes, then drain and leave to cool. Detach the claws and legs and remove their meat. Take out all the meat and creamy parts from the shells, discarding any gristle. Crumble or dice the meat finely. Wash and dry the shells.

Mix the creamy parts with a few spoonfuls of Mornay sauce (the quantity depends on the size of the crabs) and spread this mixture over the bottom of each shell. Then fill with diced or crumbled crabmeat and top with Mornay sauce. Finally, sprinkle with grated cheese, pour on some melted butter, and bake in a very hot oven until the surface is brown.

cracked wheat

See *bulgur*.

cracker

A light crisp savoury biscuit of British origin. The manufacturing method gives it a flaky crumbly texture. In Anglo-Saxon countries, crackers are served mainly with cheese. In France, they are usually flavoured and accompany apéritifs.

cracklings BEURSAUDES

The remains of salted and cooled cooked pork fat, which are used to flavour omelettes, spinach, purées, and soups. Cracklings are also used for making black pudding (blood sausage) and are eaten as a snack, either cold or crispy and hot (especially sweet and sour, with bread and redcurrant jam).

cramique

In Belgium and northern France, brioche bread with currants or raisins in it. It is served warm with butter.

RECIPE

Cramique (Belgian recipe) Warm ½ glass milk and mix it with 40–50 g (1½–1¾ oz) fresh (compressed) yeast. Gradually add enough flour to obtain a soft paste. Place it on the working surface and cover it with 1 kg (2¼ lb) flour. Soak 150–200 g (5–7 oz, 1 cup) small currants in warm weak tea. When cracks have formed in the flour, add a generous pinch of salt, 2 tablespoons sugar, 3 eggs (beaten), and, gradually, 3–4 dl (10–14 fl oz, 1¼–1¾ cups) warm milk. Work the dough until it is soft and elastic. When it no longer sticks to the hands, add 150–200 g (5–7 oz, ¾ cup) butter cut into small pieces and softened to room temperature, then add the drained currants.

Brush a baking sheet with melted butter. Lightly stretch the dough into an oval, put it on the baking sheet, and glaze the top with egg. Leave it to rise at room temperature away from draughts, until the dough has doubled in volume. Bake in a very hot oven (approximately 240 C, 475 F, gas 9) for 10–15 minutes, then reduce the temperature to 210 C (410 F, gas 6–7) and finish baking (about 50 minutes in all). Cool on a rack.

cranberry AIRELLE

The red berry of any of several related shrubs of the genus *Vaccinium*. Cranberry sauce is a traditional accompaniment to roast turkey.

The mountain cranberry is found in heath and woodland in cold mountainous regions. Also known as lingonberry and cowberry, it is eaten mainly in Scandinavia and Germany. The mountain cranberry has a very tart flavour and is rich in vitamin C and pectin. It is used to make compotes and sweet jellies, as well as sauces and condiments to accompany savoury dishes. The traditional roast goose of the Danish Christmas dinner is served with red cabbage and stewed lingonberries. Plain lingonberries may also accompany game and boiled meat and are used to make iced mousse (*kissel*) and puddings.

| RECIPES

Cranberry jam CONFITURE D'AIRELLES Clean and stalk 2 kg (4½ lb) berries. Heat 1.5 kg (3¼ lb) lump or granulated sugar in a preserving pan with 500 ml (17 fl oz, 2¼ cups) water until the sugar dissolves. Then add the berries and cook briskly, stirring frequently with a spatula until the gelling stage is reached. Remove the pan from the heat and jar the jam.

Cranberry jelly GELÉE D'AIRELLE Clean and stalk 2 kg (4½ lb) cranberries and 1 kg (2¼ lb) redcurrants. Press the berries to extract their juice (a vegetable mill may be used). Pour the juice into a pan with 3 kg (6¾ lb) sugar and mix. Bring to the boil, skim, then leave to cook for about 5 minutes. When the syrup has reached setting point remove from the heat and jar.

Cranberry sauce SAUCE AUX AIRELLES Cook 250 g (9 oz, 2 cups) cranberries with 500 ml (17 fl oz, 2 cups) water over a high heat until the fruit splits. Strain immediately and press through a fine sieve. Add a few spoonfuls of the cooking liquid and a little sugar to this purée. Heat through well until the sauce is fairly thick.

crane GRUE

A large migratory long-legged wading bird, formerly a prized game bird but no longer used for food as it is a protected species. The Romans prized this bird and fattened it specially to give it a richer flavour. From the Middle Ages until the 18th century cranes were highly regarded as food, although the flesh is tough: they were served reconstituted and decorated with their feathers.

Lémery, in his *Traité des aliments* (1702), sets great store by them: 'The younger they are, the more tender, delicate, easy to digest, and tastier they are.' But Liger, in *La Nouvelle Maison rustique* (1749), comments: 'They have a tough skin that needs to be hung.'

crapaudine (en)

A method of preparing a small chicken or pigeon as a spatchcock, i.e. the bird is split and flattened so that it looks like a toad (hence the name, from *crapaud*, a toad), coated with breadcrumbs, and grilled (broiled). The flavour is retained, since the juices are concentrated and the flesh does not dry out. It is frequently garnished with two rounds of egg white topped with a small round of truffle to represent the eyes, and is served with lemon slices, bunches of cress, and maître d'hôtel butter, devilled sauce, or sauce Robert.

RECIPES

Preparation of pigeon (*or chicken*) en crapaudine PRÉPARATION DU PIGEON (OU DU POULET) EN CRAPAUDINE Draw and singe the bird. Cut off the feet at the first joint as well as the pinions. Place the bird on its breastbone and split it open down one side of the backbone from the neck to the rump. Part the two sides and make the bird lie flat by cutting the small bone situated near the neck. Remove the backbone and detach the ribs with the point of a knife. Make a small slit in the skin at the base of each leg and pound the end to distend the skin or crush the small bones.

Grilled pigeon (*or chicken*) en crapaudine PIGEON OU POULET GRILLÉ EN CRAPAUDINE Prepare the bird as described above. Coat it with a mixture of olive oil, garlic, finely chopped herbs, salt, and pepper. Leave for 30 minutes, then grill gently over charcoal or in a vertical grill for 25–30 minutes.

crapiau or grapiau

A large savoury pancake from the Morvan region of France, which is cooked in melted bacon fat. Crapiau batter is sometimes made more substantial with grated potato. In Nevers, sweet crapiaux are made from batter containing finely sliced apples steeped in brandy.

Crapiaux with apples CRAPIAUX AUX POMMES Prepare a pancake batter using 250 g (9 oz, 2¼ cups) flour, 3 eggs, ½ litre (17 fl oz, 2 cups) milk, a generous pinch of salt, and 50 g (2 oz, 4 tablespoons) sugar. Peel and core 5 firm dessert apples, slice thinly, and sprinkle with sugar and a small glass of rum. Steep for at least 1 hour, then add both the apples and rum to the batter. Grease a pan with butter and make the pancake. Sprinkle with sugar and serve hot.

craquelin

A small light crunchy cake or biscuit (cookie). It can be a dry petit four (a speciality of Saint-Malo, Binic, Vendée, and Beaume-les-Dames), a sort of échaudé (in Cotentin), or a cake of unrisen unsweetened dough made into various shapes, Craquelins formerly resembled three-cornered hats or eggs. The word, known as early as 1265, derives from the Dutch *crakeline*.

RECIPE

Craquelins as petits fours CRAQUELINS EN FORME DE PETITS FOURS Knead 250 g (9 oz, 2¼ cups) sifted flour with 125 g (4½ oz, generous ½ cup) butter, 2 egg yolks, 3 tablespoons cold milk, 30 g (1 oz, 2 tablespoons) sugar, and a generous pinch of salt. Leave the dough to rest for 2 hours then roll it out to a thickness of 1.5 cm (½ in). Cut it into 5-cm (2-in) squares, arrange the squares on a baking sheet, glaze them with egg, and bake in a very hot oven (approximately 240 c, 475 f, gas 9) until golden brown. Sprinkle with vanilla-flavoured sugar when cooked.

craquelot

A young herring, lightly smoked (traditionally in walnut leaves), eaten in northern France from October to December, usually two or three days following its preparation. In Dunkirk it is served grilled (broiled) with fresh butter after being soaked in milk.

crater CRATÈRE

A large vessel in which the Greeks mixed water with wine during meals (wine was rarely drunk undiluted as it was very thick). Craters were made of pottery or bronze and varied in size and shape. Big-bellied craters with *colonnettes* had small vertical double handles; *volute* craters, such as the famous example found at Vix in the Côte d'Or, had a more slender shape with vertical handles ending in scrolls; the chalice crater is so called because of the shape of the belly, at the base of which are the two handles. A pitcher with a trefoil-shaped mouth, the *oenochoé*, or an elongated version, the *olpé*, were used to draw wine from the crater in order to fill a cup (*kylix, cantharus*) or a goblet (*skyphos*). Each guest could also serve himself with a *cotyle*, a drinking and drawing vessel, or with a *kyathos*, which had a long handle and was also used as a measure for determining the proportions of the mixture.

crayfish ÉCREVISSE

A freshwater crustacean resembling a small lobster, 15–20 cm (6–8 in) long. Formerly plentiful, crayfish have now become very rare in France. The four species now fished in France are as follows: the red-clawed crayfish, which is found particularly in the Auvergne and is the best and most sought-after variety; the white-clawed variety, which is smaller and usually restricted to mountainous regions; the mountain-stream crayfish, which lives in the rushing torrents of Alsace and Morvan; and the American crayfish, which is of poorer quality and was introduced into French rivers at the end of World War I.

The rarity of crayfish is due not only to water pollution but also to the fact that they are caught faster than they reproduce (they take five to seven years to reach the adult stage). This is why the commonest variety on the market is the slender-clawed crayfish, also known as the Turkish crayfish, which reaches adulthood in two to three years and is imported frozen or alive from central Europe. This variety of crayfish has a rough greenish shell with orange joints.

Most of the flesh of a crayfish is in its tail (approximately one-fifth of its total weight), although the claws, when crushed in a nutcracker, also yield a little meat. The shell is pounded to make bisques (thick soups and savoury butters. Before the preparation of any crayfish dish, the bitter-tasting gut must be removed. The 17th-century writer Nicolas de Bonnefons described the task: 'They have to be cleaned by removing the gut, which is attached to the media lamina at the end of the tail. After giving it half a turn, pull it, and the gut comes out at the end.' This task is not necessary if the crayfish are kept without food for two days and hung up in a net in a cool place.

Crayfish have been eaten in France since the Middle Ages. They took their place in haute cuisine in the 17th and 18th centuries, in recipes such as pigeon with crayfish, crayfish *cardinalisées* (plunged in boiling court-bouillon), or crayfish pudding. However, it was in the 19th century that they became really fashionable. In the days of the Second Empire and the Belle Époque they became more and more rare and expensive. Crayfish bisque and a *buisson* of crayfish were then the great classics (a *buisson*, which literally means a bush, was a special tiered dish on which cooked crayfish were mounted).

Crayfish remain the major ingredient in some of the most famous recipes of the gastronomic provinces: Jura, Alsace, Bordelais, and Lyonnais, in particular, offer gratins, soufflés, turnovers, rissoles, pies, mousses, moulds, veloutés and dishes *à la nage*. When they are served whole, cooked in stock, crayfish may be picked up in the fingers in order to shell them easily. When served as an accompaniment to other dishes, they are trussed (the ends of the claws are tucked into the base of the abdomen before cooking).

RECIPES

Crayfish à la bordelaise ÉCREVISSES À LA BORDELAISE Prepare a finely diced mirepoix of vegetables. Toss 24 crayfish in butter and season with salt, pepper, and a little cayenne. Pour brandy over the crayfish and set alight, then just cover with dry white wine. Add the vegetable mirepoix and cook together for a maximum of 10 minutes. Drain the crayfish and arrange them in a deep dish. Keep hot. Bind the cooking stock with 2 egg yolks, then beat in 40 g (1½ oz, 3 tablespoons) butter. Adjust the seasoning to give the sauce a good strong flavour. Cover the crayfish with this sauce and serve at once, piping hot.

Crayfish sauce SAUCE AUX ÉCREVISSES (from Carême's recipe) Wash 50 medium-sized crayfish. Cook them with half a bottle of champagne, a sliced onion, a bouquet garni, a pinch of coarsely ground pepper, and a little salt. When the crayfish have cooled, drain them and strain the cooking liquor through a silk strainer. Boil down by half, then add 2 tablespoons (3 tablespoons) white sauce. Reduce again to the desired consistency and add half a glass of champagne. After reducing again, strain the sauce through a sieve. Just before serving, add a little glaze and best butter, then the shelled crayfish tails. Add to the sauce crayfish butter made with the pounded crayfish shells.

Crayfish tails au gratin GRATIN DE QUEUES D'ÉCREVISSE Prepare some ragout of crayfish tails *à la Nantua*. Put it in a buttered gratin dish, sprinkle with grated Parmesan cheese, and pour on melted butter. Brown slowly in the oven.

The ragout can alternatively be placed in a flan case (pie shell) which has been baked blind.

Crayfish tails au gratin à la façon de Maître La Planche GRATIN DE QUEUES D'ÉCREVISSE À LA FAÇON DE MAÎTRE LA PLANCHE Make a ragout of crayfish tails thickened with highly seasoned crayfish purée, using crayfish cooked in a mirepoix, as for crayfish *à la bordelaise* (see above). Put this ragout in a buttered gratin dish, alternating with layers of fresh truffles which have been cut in thick slices, seasoned, and quickly tossed in butter. Sprinkle with finely grated cheese and brown in a moderate oven, standing the dish in a tray of warm water to prevent the sauce from curdling.

Grilled crayfish with garlic butter ÉCREVISSES GRILLÉES AU BEURRE D'AIL (from a recipe by Georges Blanc) Prepare some garlic butter by mixing 100 g (4 oz, ½ cup) softened butter with 1 crushed clove of garlic, 1 finely chopped shallot, and 2 teaspoons chopped herbs (tarragon, chives, and parsley). Gut the crayfish and fry them on their fronts in a little olive oil for a few minutes only (until they turn red). Turn them over, grease with a little garlic butter, and finish cooking in a moderate oven for 3 or 4 minutes.

cream

A dairy product consisting of the part of milk, rich in fact, which has been separated by skimming or otherwise. Often an increase in the thickness of cream denotes an increase in fat content, but this is not always true as the viscosity of cream can now be controlled by manufacturing processes, giving a variation in the thickness of creams of the same fat content.

Originally the cream was separated from the milk by gravity. When milk is left to stand in a vessel, fat globules cluster or aggregate and, being lighter than the rest of the milk, rise to the surface to form a layer of cream. This can be skimmed off by hand.

Nowadays commercial cream manufacturers use centrifugal force to separate the cream. In the UK the cream regulations of 1970 control the composition and descriptions of cream on the basis of milk-fat content. The label should bear a description, and the fat content of the cream should comply with the requirement for that description.

The following are the most common types of cream available in the UK with the legal minimum milk fat content by weight.
• *Clotted cream* (55%) is produced by scalding, cooking, and skimming milk or cream. The traditional farmhouse method of making clotted cream is to pour milk into shallow pans and leave undisturbed for 12–24 hours for the cream to rise. The pans are then heated or scalded to about 82 C (180 F) and held at this temperature for about an hour. The surface cream develops a rich yellow wrinkled crust. The pans are then cooled slowly and the cream crust skimmed off. The heating of the cream improves its keeping qualities by destroying bacteria which may cause souring.

Clotted cream is produced commercially, mainly in Devon, Cornwall, and Somerset, by heating pans of 55% cream in water jackets. Commercial clotted cream tends to be smoother than farmhouse cream but has the same distinctive scalded flavour. Clotted cream is traditionally served with scones, fruit, and fruit pies.
• *Double cream* (48%) is produced commercially by centrifugal separation and sometimes slightly homogenized; it may be pasteurized. It can be used as a rich pouring cream, whipped or floated on coffee or soup.
• *Whipping cream* (35%) is commercially produced by centrifugal separation. It is not usually homogenized but may be pasteurized. Whipping cream will double its volume when whipped and is less likely to curdle through overwhipping. It is ideal in its whipped form for piped decorations on desserts and gâteaux.
• *Whipped cream* (35%) is sold

pasteurized and mainly in frozen form, although some is sold chilled. Commercially whipped cream may have a fairly high sugar content. It is served on fruit or desserts.

- *Single cream* (18%) is normally homogenized to prevent separation during storage. It may be pasteurized. Single cream is used as a pouring cream in coffee, on fruit and cereals, and to enrich soups and sweet and savoury dishes.
- *Half cream* (12%) is homogenised to prevent separation; it may also be pasteurized. It is sometimes known as 'coffee cream' or 'top of the milk'.
- *Soured (dairy sour) cream* (18%) is pasteurized homogenized single cream soured by the addition of a culture of harmless bacteria which grow in the cream and convert the natural sugar, lactose, into lactic acid. The piquant refreshing flavour enhances many sweet and savoury dishes. It is used as a jacket-potato topping and in cooking for cheesecakes.
- *UHT cream* is subjected to ultra-heat treatment, which destroys any viable microorganisms and their spores that may be present in the cream without significantly affecting its nutritional value. There is a slight change in the flavour. The heat treatment is carried out either by heating cream to at least 140 c (284 f) for not less than 2 seconds or by heating cream to any other time/temperature combination which renders it free from viable microorganisms and their spores. The treated cream is homogenized, poured into sterile containers, and sealed under antiseptic conditions. Double, whipping, and single cream can all be preserved by UHT.
- *Frozen cream* (single, whipping, or double) is pasteurized, cooked, and commercially frozen either by blast freezing for about 45 minutes or by passing the cream, sandwiched between two belts, through a zone where it is frozen to −18 c (0 f) in 2–4 minutes. It is usually sold in chips (pats) or stick form to make it easy to select the amount needed.
- *Aerosol cream* is a recent development in which the cream is ultra-heat treated and filled into aerosol containers. Nitrus oxide is used as a propellant to release the whipped cream and

aid aeration. There is a volume increase of 400%. It provides easy, convenient, and instant use, but the whipped cream starts to collapse soon after it has been applied to desserts, etc.

See also *crème fraîche*.

creams and custards
CRÈMES D'ENTREMETS ET DE PÂTISSERIE

Sweet preparations with the consistency and appearance of cream. Made with milk, eggs, and sugar (and sometimes flour and butter) and variously flavoured, creams and custards are generally cooked and can be eaten either cold or warm. They can be used as desserts, as the basis for desserts, or as fillings, toppings, or accompaniments for pastries, cakes, etc. (See also *ices and ice creams*.)

□ **Dessert creams** Quickly prepared, variously flavoured, and served cold (either set or liquid), dessert creams form the basis of a large number of desserts in family cooking; they are also a basic ingredient in Bavarian creams, charlottes, and many puddings. The food industry has developed a variety of powder mixtures which are made up simply by adding milk: these 'instant' custards and desserts, which are usually flavoured with vanilla, chocolate, caramel, or fruit, usually contain gelling agents or starch, rather than eggs.

- *Set (moulded) creams*: the basic type is egg or caramel custard (*crème renversée*), which is set in a mould and turned out. Other set creams include blancmanges and moulded custards. Velouté creams contain starch or flour instead of eggs. If egg yolks are used instead of whole eggs, the cream is thicker and has a finer texture but it cannot be turned out. A set cream must be thoroughly cooled before turning it out. When moulded in a ring mould, fruit or whipped cream make an excellent decoration. (See *diplomat pudding, île flottante, malakoff, pudding*.)
- *Custards*: the basic recipe is that for custard cream (*crème anglaise*), which has many uses in pâtisserie. In France and Britain it can be bought in the form of custard powder. Zabaglione also belongs to this category.

The smoothness of custard cream

depends on whether the egg yolks co-agulate well in the milk: this binds the preparation and should be done carefully. The consistency depends on the proportion of eggs and milk: more egg yolks make it thicker and richer (up to 18 yolks per litre of milk can be used). The texture is improved by adding fresh cream when cool: use 200 g (7 oz) cream for 1 litre (1¾ pints, 4¼ cups) custard. Adding egg white makes it lighter; in this case the mixture is cooked in ramekins in a bain-marie. Custard cream is a classic accompaniment for eggs *à la neige*, or 'floating islands' (made using the egg whites left over from the custard), and it is also served with sponges, Genoese cakes, brioches, charlottes, puddings, etc.

FLAVOURS – Although there are few basic recipes for dessert creams, many flavours, sometimes in combination, can be added:

• Citrus fruits: finely grated zests of lemon, orange, tangerine, grapefruit, or citron are infused in hot milk.

• Spirits and liqueurs: two liqueur glasses of rum, Curaçao, Kirsch, Maraschino, etc. per litre of milk are added when the cream or custard has cooled.

• Almonds, hazelnuts, pistachios, coconut: ground or finely grated, they are infused like the zest.

• Coffee: coffee beans are heated, crushed, and infused in boiling milk; instant coffee is mixed with water or coffee essence.

• Cinnamon: ground or in sticks, is infused in milk.

• Caramel: heated until it caramelizes then dissolved in a little water to form liquid caramel and added to the cream.

• Chocolate: melted solid chocolate or dissolved chocolate powder. Since chocolate is sweet, the proportions of sugar in the cream are reduced. Reduce the quantity by half if cocoa is used.

• Fruit: purée of fresh or tinned fruit; finely chopped dried or crystallized (candied) fruit.

• Praline: crushed pralines or praline mixture.

• Vanilla: pod (bean) is split and infused in boiling milk; vanilla-flavoured sugar or vanilla essence in powder or liquid form are also used.

• Other flavours: in the past, desserts, especially nulle, jellies, creams, and blancmanges, were flavoured with flowers (such as violet, rose, orange blossom, and marjoram) and with amber and musk. Orange-flower water is still used. In some countries poppy or lotus seeds are used.

□ **Pastry creams** A number of creams are not served alone as desserts but are used as ingredients, fillings, or decoration for pastries, cakes, and desserts. They can be divided into four groups: Chantilly cream and its derivatives (e.g. Chiboust and Saint-Honoré creams); confectioners' custard (French pastry cream) and frangipane; butter creams (mocha, nougatine, ganache, praline, etc.); and almond cream.

• *Chantilly or whipped cream*: whipped fresh cream sweetened with sugar and flavoured with vanilla. It accompanies fruit desserts, fresh fruit, waffles, etc. It is used as a filling (for cream puffs, Saint-Honoré cake, savarins, charlottes, meringues, etc.) and often for decoration, especially for iced desserts (vacherins, etc.). Finally, it is an ingredient of parfaits, iced soufflés, and iced Bavarian creams and charlottes. It can also be flavoured with coffee, chocolate, or liqueurs. Aerosol cans of whipped cream can be bought and kept in the refrigerator.

• *Confectioners' custard (French pastry cream)*: made with eggs, sugar, milk, and flour, it can keep for 24 hours in the refrigerator. The proportions vary according to its use: with egg yolks only it has a finer texture; egg whites added make it lighter (for Saint-Honoré cake). It can be flavoured in different ways (in particular with almond flavouring for frangipane cream), and it can be enriched with butter. It is used for filling (éclairs, cream horns, cream puffs, mille-feuilles, croissants, etc.), as a garnish (for tarts and flans), and for some hot desserts (soufflés, charlottes) and cold desserts (diplomats).

• *French butter creams (crèmes au beurre)*: made with butter, sugar, eggs, and flavouring, they can be prepared in various ways but always using high-quality butter and very fresh eggs. Butter cream *au sirop cuit* (made with cooked syrup) is the most common and provides a fine, light, and smooth preparation. Butter cream *à l'anglaise* is made by beating small pieces of butter into lukewarm custard cream.

Butter creams (flavoured with coffee, chocolate, praline mixture, or vanilla) keep well in the refrigerator. They are used to fill and decorate Genoese and sponge cakes, Paris-Brest, sponge rolls, yule logs, etc.

• *Almond cream*: a mixture of sugar, butter, ground almonds, and eggs, sometimes flavoured with rum. It is an essential ingredient of many brioches and pastries, including pithiviers gâteau, galette des Rois (Twelfth-Night cake), *conversations*, *jalousies*, filled brioches, and almond tartlets.

RECIPES

ALMOND CREAM

Almond cream CRÈME D'AMANDES Beat 2–3 whole eggs as for an omelette and put them aside. Blend in a mixer 150 g (5 oz) blanched or ground almonds and the same weight of sugar and of butter (creamed). When the mixture is thoroughly blended, beat in the eggs one by one.

CARAMEL CREAM

Caramel cream for garnishing desserts CRÈME AU CARAMEL POUR GARNIR DES ENTREMETS Cook 200 g (7 oz, scant cup) caster (superfine) sugar in 1 dl (6 tablespoons, scant ½ cup) water to obtain a golden caramel. Pour ¼ litre (8 fl oz, 1 cup) fresh cream into a large deep basin, sprinkle it with the caramel, and whisk. Then transfer the mixture to a saucepan and cook over a gentle heat. Meanwhile work 230 g (8 oz, 1 cup) butter with a spatula in the deep basin until soft. Test a drop of the caramel cream in a bowl of cold water: if it forms a firm ball, the cream is cooked. Then pour it over the butter, whipping briskly. Put in a cool place until time to use.

CHOCOLATE CREAMS

Chocolate cream CRÈME AU CHOCO-LAT Place 125 g (4½ oz) grated bitter chocolate in a saucepan and moisten it with 2 dl (7 fl oz, ¾ cup) tepid water.

Work it over a gentle heat until it boils. Cook for 15 minutes then add 3 tablespoons fresh cream and 1 tablespoon butter. This cream can be served either hot, as a sauce, or cold, as a dessert.

Individual chocolate creams CRÈME EN RAMEQUINS Melt 90–100 g (3 –3½ oz) cooking chocolate in a bain-marie with 1 tablespoon milk; make the quantity of milk up to ½ litre (17 fl oz, 2 cups) and bring to the boil. Beat 6 egg yolks with 100 g (4 oz, ½ cup) caster (superfine) sugar; when the mixture has turned white, slowly add the chocolate-flavoured milk, beating it in quickly. Strain this cream and divide it between 6 ramekins. Place the ramekins in a bain-marie, bring the water to simmering point on top of the stove, then place the bain-marie in a moderately hot over (190 C, 375 F, gas 5) and cook for about 25 minutes. Remove the ramekins from the bain-marie and leave to cool before putting them in the refrigerator to set.

CONFECTIONERS' CUSTARD (PASTRY CREAM)

Confectioners' custard (pastry cream) I CRÈME PÂTISSIÈRE In a thick-bottomed saucepan, place 60 g (2 oz, ½ cup) flour, 175 g (6 oz, ¾ cup) sugar, a pinch of salt, 15 g (½ oz, 1 tablespoon) choice butter, and 4 whole eggs. Work this mixture with a whisk. Infuse a vanilla pod (vanilla bean) in ½ litre (17 fl oz, 2 cups) milk, bring to the boil, and add it to the mixture. Stir well, place the saucepan over the heat, and boil for a few minutes, stirring all the time to prevent the cream from sticking to the bottom. Remove the vanilla pod, pour the cream into an earthenware dish, and allow to cool, stirring from time to time.

Confectioners' custard (pastry cream) II CRÈME PÂTISSIÈRE Split a vanilla pod (vanilla bean), boil it in ½ litre (17 fl oz, 2 cups) milk, then take it out. Beat 3 egg yolks with 80 g (3 oz, 6 tablespoons) caster (superfine) sugar; when the mixture has turned white, add 40 g (1½ oz) cornflour (cornstarch). Then gradually add the boiling vanilla flavoured milk, whisking all the time. Put the mixture in a saucepan over a gentle heat and boil for 1 minute, whisking vigorously. Pour the cream into a deep bowl and leave to cool.

Chocolate-flavoured confectioners' custard (pastry cream) CRÈME PÂTISSIÈRE AU CHOCOLAT Use 80–100 g (3–4 oz) cooking chocolate for 500 g (18 oz) confectioners' custard. Cut the chocolate into small pieces, add them to the hot custard, and stir with a wooden spoon until they have melted completely.

Coffee-flavoured confectioners' custard (pastry cream) CRÈME PÂTISSIÈRE AU CAFÉ Stir 1 teaspoon coffee essence or 1 tablespoon instant coffeee into every 500 g (18 oz) hot confectioners' custard.

CUSTARD CREAMS

custard cream CRÈME ANGLAISE Blend 250 g (9 oz, generous cup) caster (superfine) sugar, a pinch of salt, and 8 egg yolks in a pan using a whisk. Boil ½ litre (17 fl oz, 2 cups) milk flavoured with vanilla or the zest of either a lemon or an orange. When the sugar-egg yolk mixture forms ribbons, gradually add the warm (not boiling) milk. Mix well, keeping the pan on the heat and stirring continuously until the first signs of boiling. At this point the yolks are sufficiently cooked and the custard should cling to the spoon. Pass the hot custard through a fine sieve or a silk strainer. Keep it hot in a bain-marie if it is to accompany a hot dessert; otherwise pout it into a basin, stir until it is completely cool, and keep it in a cool place.

A simpler and lighter version of this can be made by reducing the number of egg yolks to 5–6 and adding 1 small teaspoon arrowroot, starch, or cornflour (cornstarch) when mixing the eggs and sugar. This gives a firmer consistency to the custard and prevents it from curdling if allowed to overheat.

Caramel-flavoured custard CRÈME AU CARAMEL Add caramel to the boiling milk used for preparing the custard.

custard cream with gelatine CRÈME ANGLAISE COLLÉE Prepare the custard as described above. When it is cooked, add 10–15 g (¼–½ oz, 1–2 envelopes) gelatine (4–5 sheets) softened in cold water and drained. Strain into the custard and stir until completely cool. This custard is used in the preparation of Bavarian cream and charlotte russe.

Custard cream with liqueur CRÈME ANGLAISE À LA LIQUEUR When the custard is completely cold add 1 tablespoon liqueur (Curaçao, Kirsch, Maraschino, or rum, for example).

Custard flavoured with coffee or tea CRÈME AU CAFÉ OU AU THÉ Add coffee essence (strong black coffee) or instant coffee to the milk used for preparing the custard. Alternatively, tea can be infused in the milk, which is then strained.

Lemon custard CRÈME AU CITRON For the quantities given in the basic recipe, add the finely grated zest of a lemon to the milk and allow to infuse for 1 hour before making the custard.

EGG CUSTARDS

Egg or caramel custard CRÈME RENVERSÉE Boil ½ litre (17 fl oz, 2 cups) milk with a vanilla pod (bean) split in two. In a mixing bowl, blend 2 whole eggs, 4 egg yolks, and 125 g (4½ oz, generous ½ cup) caster (superfine) sugar; gradually add the boiling milk (having removed the vanilla), whisking it quickly. Pour the resulting custard into a buttered or caramel-coated mould, place the mould in a bain-marie, and heat the latter on top of the stove. When the water begins to simmer, place the bain-marie in a moderately hot oven (about 200 C, 400 F, gas 6) and cook for about 35 minutes. Then take the mould out of the bain-marie and allow it to cool completely. Turn out onto a dish and cool before serving.

Chocolate egg custard CRÈME RENVERSÉE AU CHOCOLAT Melt 100 g (4 oz) cooking (unsweetened) chocolate in a bain-marie with 1 tablespoon milk; when the mixture is quite smooth, add ¾ litre (1¼ pints, 3 cups) milk, bring to the boil, then remove from the heat. Beat 6 eggs with 150 g (5 oz, ⅔ cup, firmly packed) caster (superfine) sugar; when the mixture has turned white, gradually add the chocolate-flavoured milk, whisking it all the time. Strain the custard, pour it into ramekins or buttered dariole moulds, and cook in a bain-marie in a moderately hot oven (200 c, 400 f, gas 6) for 30—35 minutes. Take the moulds out of the bain-marie, leave to cool, and turn out.

French Butter Creams

French butter cream made with syrup CRÈME AU BEURRE AU SIROP Boil 130 g (4½ oz, scant ⅔ cup) caster (superfine) sugar in ½ litre (17 fl oz, 2 cups) water for 10 minutes to a temperature of 120 c (250 f). Meanwhile, beat 4 egg yolks in a small bowl. Gradually pour on boiling syrup, whisking for 3 minutes. Continue to whisk until the mixture is lukewarm. Then whisk in 130 g (4½ oz, generous ½ cup) butter cut into small pieces and whisk for a further 5 minutes.

French butter cream à l'anglaise CRÈME AU BEURRE NATURE À L'ANGLAIS Prepare the recipe for custard cream. Bring 225 g (8 oz, 1 cup) butter to room temperature then cut it into small pieces. Blend the butter with the custard cream, working with a whisk, and flavour as desired (with coffee, chocolate, liqueur, praline, lemon zest, or orange zest).

French butter cream made with sugar CRÈME AU BEURRE NATURE AU SUCRE Beat together 250 g (9 oz, generous cup) caster (superfine) sugar and 6 egg yolks. Then blend in a few drops of vanilla essence (extract) and 1 dl (6 tablespoons, scant ½ cup) fresh cream until the mixture is quite smooth. In a separate bowl, work 225 g (8 oz, 1 cup) butter into a soft paste using a wooden spatula. Place the first basin in a bain-marie and whisk the mixture until it becomes white and foamy. Remove it from the bain-marie and continue to whip until completely cool. Then gradually blend this mixture with the creamed butter.

French chocolate butter cream CRÈME AU BEURRE AU CHOCOLAT Follow the recipe for butter cream à l'anglaise, but dissolve plain (unsweetened) chocolate in the milk, using 100 g (4 oz) chocolate to ½ litre (17 fl oz, 2 cups) milk. For butter cream made with sugar syrup, dissolve the chocolate in a bain-marie and incorporate in the finished butter cream.

French coffee butter cream CRÈME AU BEURRE AU CAFÉ To flavour butter cream à l'anglaise, add coffee essence (strong black coffee) or instant coffee to the milk used in the custard. To flavour butter cream made with syrup, blend the coffee essence or instant coffee with the fresh cream, using 1 teaspoon coffee essence to 300 g (11 oz) cream; the mixture should become homogeneous when heated.

Praline butter cream CRÈME AU BEURRE PRALINÉE Blend some powdered praline with one of the French butter creams (made with syrup or à l'anglaise), using 60 g (2 oz) praline for 300 g (11 oz) butter cream.

Fried Custard

Fried custard fritters CRÈME FRITE EN BEIGNETS Boil ½ litre (17 fl oz, 2 cups) milk with 1 tablespoon vanilla-flavoured sugar. In a mixing bowl, beat 5 egg yolks with 10 g (4½ oz, scant ⅔ cup) caster (superfine) sugar until the mixture is white. Beat in 80 g (3 oz, ¾ cup) flour, and gradually add the boiling milk, whisking it well. Pour the mixture into a saucepan, boil on a gentle heat for 3 minutes, stirring all the time, then remove from the heat and leave to cool until lukewarm. Spread the custard evenly over a buttered baking sheet to a thickness of 1.5 cm (½ in) and leave it to cool completely. Cut it into rectangles, diamonds, or circles, dip these in batter and plunge them into hot oil at a temperature of 170—180 c (340—350 f). Drain and dust with sugar.

Lemon Cream

Lemon cream CRÈME AU CITRON For 8 people, use 2 lemons, 5 eggs, 130 g (4½ oz, generous ½ cup) butter, and 200 g (7 oz, 1¾ cups) icing sugar (confectioners' sugar). Grate the rind from one of the lemons. Then squeeze both lemons and strain the juice. Beat the eggs with a fork. Melt the butter over a very gentle heat, add the sugar and lemon juice, and bring to the boil. Sprinkle the beaten eggs with this mixture, whisking quickly to obtain a very smooth cream. Return to the saucepan, add the grated lemon rind, and bring to the boil over a gentle heat, whisking all the time. Pour the lemon cream into a bowl and leave to cool before placing it in the refrigerator.

WHIPPED CREAM

Whipped cream CRÈME FOUETTÉE To some chilled double (heavy) cream, add one-third of its volume of chilled milk and whisk carefully until the cream has doubled in volume.

Cream soup CRÈME

A soup made with a white base (formerly milk and a white roux) or a béchamel sauce, thickened with flour, rice flour, or cornflour (cornstarch) and finished by adding fresh cream or possibly egg yolks, which gives it the characteristic creamy consistency. The basic ingredients can be vegetables, rice, barley, shellfish, or poultry. It is often garnished with chervil leaves, croutons, etc.

RECIPES

Basic method of preparing cream soups CRÈME-POTAGE (MÉTHODE DE BASE) Shred and blanch the chosen vegetable then cook it in butter in a covered pan, using 40–50 g (1½–2 oz, 3–4 tablespoons) butter per 500 g (18 oz) vegetables. Prepare 8 dl (1⅓ pints, 1¾ pints) béchamel sauce by adding 8.5 dl (1½ pints, 2 pints) milk to a white roux consisting of 30 g (1 oz, 2 tablespoons) butter and 40 g.(1½ oz, 6 tablespoons) flour. Mix this béchamel with the cooked vegetable and simmer gently for 12–18 minutes depending on the vegetable used. Purée in a food processor or blender, then sieve if necessary. Dilute with a few tablespoons of white consommé (or milk if the soup is to be meatless). Heat and adjust the seasoning. Add 2 dl (7 fl oz, ¾ cup) fresh cream and stir while heating.

Cream of asparagus soup CRÈME D'ASPERGES Clean and blanch 400 g (14 oz) white or green asparagus tips and cook them in butter in a covered pan. Add 8 dl (1⅓ pints, 1¾ pints) béchamel and purée in a food processor or blender. Do not cook the asparagus and béchamel together. Finish as described in the basic method.

Cream of chicken soup CRÈME DE VOLAILLE Put a small tender chicken into a saucepan containing 1 litre (1¾ pints, 4¼ cups) white consommé, bring to the boil, and skim. Add a bouquet garni supplemented with the white parts of 2 leeks and 1 stick (stalk) of celery. Simmer very gently with the lid on until the meat comes away from the bones. Drain the chicken, retaining the stock, and remove the skin and bones. Keep the breast fillets and reduce the rest of the meat to a purée using a food processor. Rub through a sieve. Shred the breast fillets finely and keep them hot in a little consommé. Add 8 dl (1⅓ pints, 1¾ pints) béchamel to the chicken purée and bring to the boil. Add a few spoonfuls of the chicken stock and whisk. Adjust the seasoning and sieve again. Add 1 dl (6 tablespoons, scant ½ cup) fresh cream and whisk while heating. Add the finely shredded breast fillets just before serving.

Cream of mushroom soup CRÈME DE CHAMPIGNONS Clean 600 g (1½ lb) mushrooms, putting 100 g (4 oz) aside. Cook the remaining mushrooms) in butter in a covered pan, and proceed as in basic method. Meanwhile, finely shred the reserved mushrooms and sprinkle them with lemon juice. Add them to the soup just before serving.

Crécy

Any of various dishes that contain carrots. Purée Crécy is a carrot purée used as a base for a soup and as a garnish for various dishes, including poached eggs, omelette, and fillets of sole. In consommé Crécy, the carrots are shredded into a brunoise, while for tournedos Crécy they are turned and glazed.

It is not known whether the name derives from the produce of Crécy-la-

Chapelle (Seine-et-Marne) or Crécy-en-Ponthieu in Somme.

RECIPES

Crécy soup POTAGE CRÉCY Scrape 500 g (18 oz) very tender carrots, slice thinly, and cook them with 50 g (2 oz, 4 tablespoons) butter in a covered pan. Add 1 tablespoon shredded onion, a pinch of salt, and ½ teaspoon sugar. When the vegetables are soft, add 1 litre (1¾ pints, 4¼ cups) beef or chicken consommé, bring to the boil, and add 100 g (4 oz, ½ cup) rice. Cook slowly with the lid on for about 20 minutes, then put it through the blender and strain. Add a few more spoonfuls of consommé, heat, and add 30 g (1 oz, 2 tablespoons) butter. Adjust the seasoning. Serve with small croutons fried in butter.

Fillets of sole Crécy FILETS DE SOLE CRÉCY Wash, clean, and fold up the fillets of sole. Poach them in a fish fumet for 5 minutes, drain them, and arrange on a long dish. Strain the stock, reduce, and add 2 tablespoons béchamel sauce and the same amount of carrot purée. Mix well and heat. Coat the fillets with this sauce and garnish them with very small glazed new carrots.

Crémant

A sparkling wine most often associated with the Champagne region, where it has slightly less sparkle than the fully sparkling wines – about 4 atmospheres of pressure behind the cork as compared with 5.6. The Crémant of the Cramant area is well known. Other regions make Crémant wines, including the Loire and Burgundy, but it should be noted that the Crémants d'Alsace are fully sparkling. All these wines are subject to strict controls.

crème

A sweet liqueur with a syrupy consistency. Crèmes are obtained by soaking various substances in brandy or spirit containing sugar syrup: fruits (pineapple, bananas, blackcurrants, strawberries, tangerines, sloes, raspberries), various plant parts (vanilla, mint, cocoa, tea, coffee), or flowers (violet, rose). These liqueurs were very fashionable in the 19th century and often had exotic names, such as *crème de Barbade* and *crème créole*. Crèmes are usually drunk as a digestant in small glasses. They are included in cocktails and are sometimes served as an apéritif with ice and water.

The French word crème is also used for cream soups, for dairy cream (see *crème fraîche*) and for a wide variety of sweet preparations (see *creams and custards*).

crème fraîche

A French dairy product obtained from pasteurized cows' milk. It is cream to which a lactic bacteria culture has been added, which thickens the cream and gives it a distincive sharp flavour without souring the cream.

Crème frîche is used extensively in French cooking. In Normandy, where it is sometimes combined with Calvados, it is used extensively in dishes made with sole, leg of mutton, chicken, and mussels. Crème fraîche is also used in cooking north of the Loire (fricassee of rabbit or poultry in Anjou), in Lorraine and Alsace (soups, vegetable flans), in the traditional stockpot of Dieppe, for hare *à la crème* in the Bourbonnais, for chicken with morels in Franche-Comté, etc. More generally, crème fraîche enlivens vegetables (green beans, mushrooms, cauliflower, etc.), is sometimes used as a salad dressing (for lettuce hearts, cucumber), adds a finishing touch to soups and blanquettes, and, above all, is an essential ingredient in numerous sauces (bonne femme, Breton, normande, poulette, princesse, rémoulade, suprême, etc.). Finally, crème fraîche is used in pâtisserie, as an ingredient, filling, or decoration, and in confectionery, for caramels. It is also added to certain drinks (coffee, cocktails).

● *Crème fleurette* (12–15% fat) is light and semi-liquid and must be consumed within 48 hours (unless it is UHT). It is used for preparing Chantilly cream and for accompany fromage frais, pastries, fruits, or coffee.

crémer

A French culinary term meaning to add fresh cream to a preparation (such as a soup or sauce) in order to bind it and obtain a smooth consistency and a softer taste. Eggs *en cocotte* are covered with fresh cream before cooking.

crémet

A dessert made with cows'-milk fromage frais, stiffly beaten egg whites, and whipped cream. Crémets are a speciality of Angers and Saumur. When the mixture is quite firm, it is placed in small perforated moulds, each lined with a piece of muslin (cheesecloth), and left to drain in a cool place. This delicate and light dessert is served with fresh cream and sugar.

créole (à la)

The name given to numerous sweet and savoury preparations inspired by West Indian cookery. In particular, the term refers to a method of preparing rice by cooking it in plenty of water, draining it and then drying it in the oven in a buttered dish. It is finished with tomatoes, sweet peppers, onions, etc., and served with various meats, poultry, fish, and shellfish. Sweet dishes *à la créole* contain rum, pineapple, vanilla, or banana.

RECIPES

Savoury Preparations

Calves' liver à la créole FOIE DE VEAU À LA CRÉOLE Cut some fat bacon into very small strips and marinate them in a mixture of oil, lime juice, salt, and pepper. Use them to lard some slices of calves' liver and then marinate the liver for 20 minutes in the same mixture. Drain them, coat them with flour, and cook them in a frying pan (skillet) in some lard. Remove the slices of liver from the pan and keep them warm in a buttered dish. For every 6 slices of liver, flavour the juice in the frying pan with 2 tablespoons (3 tablespoons) chopped onion and 1 tablespoon chopped parsley. Brown the onion and parsley and then add 1 tablespoon white breadcrumbs, salt, pepper and 1 tablespoon tomato purée diluted with 3–4 tablespoons white wine. Heat the sauce, stirring continuously, and adjust the seasoning. Coat the liver with the sauce.

Chicken à la créole POULET À LA CRÉOLE Cut a chicken of about 1.5 kg (3 lb) into 8 pieces and season with salt and pepper. Heat 3 tablespoons (¼ cup) oil in a sauté pan and brown the chicken pieces. Cover, and cook gently for 20 –30 minutes. Then add a small glass of rum, flame the chicken pieces, and keep them hot on a serving dish. Skim the fat off the cooking juices and add 4 slices of canned pineapple (cut into pieces) to the sauté pan, together with 3–4 tablespoons of the pineapple syrup. Then add 2 tablespoons (3 tablespoons) lime juice and a dash of cayenne. Reduce the sauce and adjust the seasoning. Coat the chicken pieces with sauce and garnish them with pineapple.

Sweet Preparations

Fritters à la créole BEIGNETS À LA CRÉOLE Slit and stone (pit) some large dates and stuff them with sweetened rice mixed with finely chopped orange zest and flavoured with Curaçao. Wrap each date in a very thin layer of Viennese fritter dough. Allow the dough to rise in a warm place for about 30 minutes. Drop the fritters into very hot deep fat and cook until they are golden brown. Drain, and dust with fine sugar. Serve hot.

Iced pineapple à la créole ANANAS GLACÉ À LA CRÉOLE Slice the top off a pineapple and keep it in a cool place, wrapping the leaves so that they do not wilt. Carefully scoop out the flesh of the pineapple and discard the core. Make a pineapple water ice with the pulp. Soak some finely chopped crystallized (candied) fruit in little rum. When the pineapple ice is frozen, fill the pineapple by placing the crystallized fruits between two layers of pineapple ice. Replace the top of the pineapple and keep it in the freezer until ready to serve. Serve on a bed of crushed ice.

Creole cookery
CUISINE CRÉOLE

'A mixture of Caribbean, African, and Hindu recipes, in which there is a blend of subtlety and violence, embellished by the scent of herbs, spices, and peppers'

(Albert Veille). There are, in fact, as many types of Creole cookery as there are African culinary traditions. They have been introduced gradually into the cuisine of various tropical countries, such as Brazil and former French, British, Spanish, and Dutch colonies.

According to Jim Plauché, the five essential elements of good Creole cookery are a well-used iron stockpot, a brown roux, some meat or fish stock, herbs and spices, and finally alcohol. It is a type of cuisine with jealously guarded secrets.

Creole cooking is characterized by the use of specific local ingredients, including herbs, shellfish, and various tropical fruits and vegetables. There is usually a very wide variety of ingredients combined in the same dish; these are often cooked in a stew, although fried food and fritters are also popular. The basic ingredients are salt cod, chicken, pork, a variety of fish, rice, red beans, and manioc. Rum, pineapple, and banana are frequently used to flavour both sweet and savoury dishes. See *Black Africa*, *West Indies*.

crêpe

A pancake: a sweet or savoury dish made with a batter that is poured sparingly into a frying pan (skillet) and fried on both sides. The word comes from the Latin *crispus*, meaning curly or wavy (in France the dish used to be called a *galette crêpe*).

Crêpe batter is prepared in advance so that it may settle before use. Wheat or buckweat flour may be used and either milk or water to mix. If beer is used to mix the batter, it rises slightly. The number of eggs used depends on the individual recipe, but the batter must always have a pouring consistency. Some recipes require the addition of sugar. The crêpes may be fried in oil or butter.

Pancakes are traditionally served on Candlemas and Shrove Tuesday, to celebrate renewal, family life, and hopes for good fortune and happiness in the future. It is customary in France to touch the handle of the frying pan, and make a wish while the pancake is turned, holding a coin in the hand. In French rural society, crêpes were also considered to be a symbol of allegiance: farmers offered them to their landowner. Pancakes are popular not only throughout France but also in other countries, including Germany, the United States, and Austria. In the United States they are soaked in butter, coated with maple syrup, or filled with blueberries, cranberries, apple purée (apple sauce), etc. Some regional French crêpes are the *tantimolles* of Champagne, the *landimolles* of Picardy, the *chialades* of Argonne, the *sanciaux* of Limousin and Berry, the *crespets* of Béarn, etc.

In western France, particularly in Brittany, crêpes are prepared throughout the year and served with salted butter. *Crêpes dentelles* (lace pancakes), a speciality of Quimper, are crisp biscuits made of small thin tongue shapes of batter, baked, and then rolled up. In central France, the Auvergne, Lorraine, and the Lyonnais district, the batter is often enriched (or even replaced) by finely sliced or purée potatoes in such dishes as bourriols, criques, and matafans.

Crêpes, a speciality of Agen (particularly on the occasion of the Fête des Félibres), were extolled by Anatole France in *Le Temps*. He wrote, 'sprinkled with sugar and eaten hot, they form an exquisite dish. They have a golden hue and are tempting to eat. Thin and transparent like muslin, their edges are trimmed to resemble fine lace. They are so light that after a good dinner, a man from Agen is still willing to sample three or four dozen of them! Crêpes form an integral part of every family celebration. Served with white wine, they take pride of place on all joyful occasions.'

In traditional cookery, crêpes are served as a hot hors d'oeuvre, filled with a fairly thick mixture based on a béchamel or velouté sauce with mushrooms, ham, Gruyère cheese, seafood, etc. They may also be cut into fine strips and used to garnish soup. Most often, however, crêpes are prepared as sweet dishes. They may be served plain and dusted with sugar, or filled with jam, cream (sometimes mixed with salpicon of fruits), honey, melted chocolate, chestnut cream, etc. They may be served warm, or flamed, or even layered on top of one another to form a cake.

RECIPES

SAVOURY CRÊPES

Savoury crêpe batter PÂTE À CRÊPES SALÉE Mix 500 g (18 oz, 4½ cups) sifted flour with 5–6 beaten eggs and a large pinch of salt. Then gradually add 1 litre (1¾ pints, 4¼ cups) milk or, for lighter pancakes, ½ litre (17 fl oz, 1 pint) milk and ½ litre (17 fl oz, 1 pint) water. The batter may also be made with equal quantities of beer and milk, or the milk may be replaced by white consommé. Finally, add 3 tablespoons oil, either one with little taste (such as groundnut (peanut) oil or sunflower oil) or, if the recipe requires it, use olive oil. 25 g (1 oz, 2 tablespoons) melted butter may also be added. Leave the batter to stand for 2 hours. Just before making the crêpes, dilute the batter with a little water (1–2 dl, 4–8 fl oz, ⅓–¾ cup).

Buckwheat crêpes (*or galettes*) CRÊPES (OU GALETTES) DE SARRA-SIN Mix 250 g (9 oz, generous 2 cups) sifted buckwheat flour and 250 g (9 oz, generous 2 cups) sifted wheat flour (or use all buckwheat flour) in a bowl with 5 or 6 beaten eggs and a large pinch of salt. Add, a little at a time, ½ litre (17 fl oz, 1 pint) milk and 7 dl (scant 1¼ pints, 1½ pints) water (or ½ litre (17 fl oz, 1 pint) water), and then 3–4 tablespoons oil. Leave the batter to stand for 2 hours at room temperature. Just before making the crêpes, thin the batter with 1 dl (6 tablespoons, ½ cup) water.

Egg and cheese crêpes CRÊPES À L'OEUF ET AU FROMAGE Prepare some buckwheat crêpes as described above. After turning each crêpe over in the pan to cook the other side, break an egg on top. As soon as the white is set, season lightly, sprinkle with grated cheese, and fold each crêpe into a square. Serve immediately, very hot.

Ham crêpes CRÊPES AU JAMBON Prepare 12 savoury crêpes. Prepare separately a béchamel sauce with 40 g (1½ oz, 3 tablespoons) butter, 40 g (1½ oz, 5 tablespoons) flour, ½ litre (17 fl oz, 1 pint) milk, nutmeg, salt, and pepper. Add 150 g (5 oz, generous ½ cup) diced Paris or York ham and 50 g (2 oz, ½ cup) grated cheese to the sauce. Cool

and fill each crêpe with one-twelfth of this mixture. Roll up the crêpes and arrange them in a buttered dish. Sprinkle with 50 g (2 oz, ½ cup) grated cheese and 25 g (1 oz, 2 tablespoons) melted butter, and brown in a very hot oven.

Mushroom crêpes CRÊPES AUX CHAMPIGNONS Prepare some savoury crêpe batter as above, and leave it to stand. Meanwhile, prepare a duxelles with 500 g (18 oz, generous 4 cups) mushrooms, 1 or 2 shallots, a small clove of garlic, 20 g (¾ oz, 1½ tablespoons) butter, salt and pepper, and 3 dl (½ pint, 1¼ cups) béchamel sauce.

Make 12 crêpes, cooking each one as follows: melt a knob of butter in a frying pan (skillet) and pour a small quantity of batter into the pan, tilting it in all directions to spread a thin film of batter. Cook over a moderate heat until the crêpe slides when the pan is shaken. Then turn the crêpe over, and cook the other side for about 2 minutes. Place a tablespoon of the mixed béchamel sauce and duxelles on each crêpe and roll it up. Arrange the crêpes close together on a lightly buttered dish and sprinkle them with 60 g (2½ oz, generous ½ cup) grated cheese. Top with 25 g (1 oz, 2 tablespoons) melted butter and either brown them under the grill or reheat them in a very hot oven. Serve very hot.

The béchamel sauce may be replaced by 6 tablespoons (½ cup) double (heavy) cream.

Roquefort-cheese crêpes CRÊPES AU ROQUEFORT Make 12 savoury crêpes. Mix approximately 12 table-spoons béchamel sauce with 4 tablespoons (5 tablespoons) Roquefort cheese that has been pounded into a paste. Season with pepper and a little nutmeg. Fill each crêpe with a heaped tablespoon of the mixture, roll them up, and place in a lightly buttered oven-proof dish. Sprinkle with grated cheese and brown them in a very hot oven.

Brie, blue cheese, or Gruyère cheese may be used instead of Roquefort cheese.

Spinach crêpes au gratin CRÊPES GRATINÉES AUX ÉPINARDS Prepare

12 savoury crêpes and approximately 12 tablespoons creamed spinach. Put 1 tablespoon spinach on each crêpe and roll it up. Finish as for mushroom crêpes.

SWEET CRÊPES

Sweet crêpe batter PÂTE À CRÊPES SUCRÉE Mix 500 g (18 oz, 4½ cups) sifted wheat flour with 1 tablespoon vanilla-flavoured sugar (or a few drops of vanilla essence (extract)), 5–6 beaten eggs, and a small pinch of salt. Gradually stir in ¾ litre (1¼ pints, 1½ pints) milk and ¼ litre (8 fl oz, 1 cup) water. Flavour with a small glass of rum, Cognac, Calvados, or Grand Marnier, depending on the recipe. Finally, add 40 g (1½ oz, 3 tablespoons) melted butter, or a mixture of 25 g (1 oz, 2 tablespoons) melted butter and 2 tablespoons oil. Leave the batter to stand for 2 hours. Just before making the crêpes, dilute the batter with a little water or milk (1–2 dl, 4–8 fl oz, ⅓–¾ cup).

It was formerly the custom to add 2–3 tablespoons caster (superfine) sugar to the batter, in addition to the vanilla-flavoured sugar. Today, the crêpes are usually sprinkled with sugar when cooked, according to individual tastes.

Chartreuse crêpes CRÊPES DES CHARTREUX Prepare a crêpe batter in the usual way. 15 minutes before making the crêpes, prepare the filling. Beat 50 g (2 oz, 4 tablespoons) butter to a soft paste and add 50 g (2 oz, 4 tablespoons, firmly packed) caster (superfine) sugar, 3 crushed meringues, and 5 cl (2 tablespoons, 3 tablespoons) green Chartreuse. Add 6 crushed macaroons, the grated zest of an orange, and 5 cl (2 tablespoons, 3 tablespoons) Cognac to the batter and mix well. Thin the batter with 1 dl (6 tablespoons, ½ cup) water and cook the crêpes. Spread each one with the filling and fold in four. Dust with icing (confectioners') sugar and serve very hot.

Cherry crêpes CRÊPES AUX CE-RISES Prepare a crêpe batter with 250 g (9 oz, generous 2 cups) sifted flour, 75 g (3 oz, 6 tablespoons) caster (superfine) sugar, a pinch of salt, 3 beaten eggs, and 1 egg yolk, gradually adding ½ litre (17 fl oz, 2 cups) milk. Leave to stand for 2 hours at room temperature. Remove the stalks and stones (stems and pits) from 400 g (14 oz) fresh cherries (or use 300 g (11 oz) cherries preserved in syrup). Cut them in two, mix them with the batter, and allow to stand for 2 hours.

Cook the crêpes and keep them hot on a plate over a saucepan of boiling water. Coat each crêpe with a thin layer of orange marmalade (about 200 g (7 oz, generous ½ cup) is required). Roll up the crêpes and arrange them on an ovenproof dish. Sprinkle with caster (superfine) sugar and glaze in the oven.

Crêpes à la cévenole Prepare some sweet crêpes and coat each one with a thin layer of rum-flavoured chestnut cream. Roll up the crêpes and arrange them in a buttered dish. Dust generously with caster (superfine) sugar and grill to caramelize the sugar. Serve with Chantilly cream if desired.

Crêpes normandes Prepare a crêpe batter with 250 g (9 oz, generous 2 cups) flour, 3 eggs, 3 dl (½ pint, 1¼ cups) milk, 2 dl (7 fl oz, ¾ cup) water, a pinch of salt, 1 tablespoon thin (light) cream, 2 tablespoons (3 tablespoons) Calvados and 1 tablespoon melted butter. Leave to stand for 2 hours at room temperature. Peel and slice 2 dessert apples and toss them in 40 g (1½ oz, 3 tablespoons) butter in a frying pan (skillet) until they brown lightly. (The apples may be soaked in a little Calvados before they are cooked.) Cool and add them to the crêpe batter. Make the crêpes and pile them up on a serving dish. Sprinkle with fine sugar and serve very hot with fresh cream.

Gâteau de crêpes Make a dozen sweet crêpes. Prepare a Chantilly cream with 2 dl (7 fl oz, ¾ cup) double (heavy) cream, 5 dl (17 fl oz, 2 cups) milk, 1 tablespoon vanilla-flavoured sugar (or a few drops of vanilla essence (extract)), and 30 g (1 oz, 2 tablespoons, firmly packed) caster (superfine) sugar. Lay a crêpe on the serving dish and spread with strawberry jam. Cover with a second crêpe and spread with Chantilly cream. Continue in this way, alternating the layers of jam and cream. Finish with a crêpe. Sprinkle with icing sugar (confectioners' sugar) and trace a pattern of diamond shapes for decoration. Serve immediately.

Jam crêpes CRÊPES À LA CONFITURE Make some sweet crêpes and keep them hot. Sieve some apricot, plum, or peach jam and heat it, possibly adding some rum or a fruit liqueur. Spread the crêpes with jam, roll them up, sprinkle them with fine sugar, and serve immediately. The crêpes may also be placed for a few moments under the grill to caramelize the sugar.

Lemon crêpes CRÊPES AU CITRON Add the grated zest of a lemon to ½ litre (17 fl oz, 2 cups) milk. Bring to the boil, and leave to cool. Make a crêpe batter with the lemon-flavoured milk, 250 g (9 oz, generous 2 cups) flour, 3 eggs, and a pinch of salt. Strain and let it stand for at least 1 hour at room temperature. Add 25 g (1 oz, 2 tablespoons) butter to the batter and thin with 1 dl (6 tablespoons, ½ cup) water. Make the crêpes and keep them hot on a plate over a saucepan of boiling water. Fold the crêpes in four, arrange them on a buttered serving dish, and dust generously with caster (superfine) sugar.

crêpe pan CRÊPIÈRE

A shallow flat-bottomed frying pan (skillet) for cooking crêpes. Cast-iron pans, used mainly for buckwheat crêpes (or galettes), are also called *tuiles, galettières,* or *galetoires.* There are also electric nonstick pans for use at table, with either a flat or a convex hotplate. When using the flat pan, the batter is poured onto it and then spread out with a scraper. The pan with a convex base usually has a handle and is turned upside down so that the surface is immersed in the batter. The pan is then turned over with the batter covering the surface. When the crêpe is cooked on one side, it is loosened with a spatula and cooked on the other side.

crêperie

A restaurant or shop specializing in serving various sweet and savoury crêpes. Crêperies were originally established in Brittany, but are now found throughout France. Cider is the traditional Breton drink to serve with crêpes and sometimes there are other Breton specialities on the menu, such as grilled sardines.

crépinette

A small flat sausage, generally made of sausagemeat mixed with chopped parsley and wrapped in caul (*crépine*). Crépinettes may also be made with lamb, veal, or poultry, prepared with a salpicon of meat and mushrooms, sometimes garnished with truffles, and bound with white or brown stock. This mixture is enclosed in fine forcemeat and the whole is wrapped in caul. Crépinettes are brushed with melted butter (and sometimes coated with white breadcrumbs) and may be grilled (broiled), sautéed, or cooked in the oven. They are served with a potato purée, lentils, or boulangère potatoes. They can be served with a strongly seasoned sauce or, if they are truffled, with a Périgueux sauce.

Cinderella pork crépinettes (*pieds de Cendrillon*) are made of fine truffled pork forcemeat. A salpicon of pigs' feet is mixed with diced truffles and mushrooms, bound with concentrated veal stock, and placed in the middle of each crépinette. Traditionally cooked in wood-ash, wrapped in pieces of buttered paper, today they are wrapped in caul or in paper-thin pieces of pastry before being cooked in the oven.

Crépinettes may be used to stuff game and poultry with rather dry flesh, such as rabbit, guinea fowl, etc. In the Gironde, crépinettes are fried and served with oysters from the Arcachon basin and white wine.

RECIPES

Chicken crépinettes CRÉPINETTES DE VOLAILLE Prepare a forcemeat of 3 parts minced chicken and 1 part fat bacon. Shape into small sausages, wrap them in caul, and cook them as for pork crépinettes.

Pork crépinettes CRÉPINETTES DE PORC Prepare some small flat sausages using either fine pork forcemeat or sausagemeat flavoured with chopped herbs and Cognac (a few diced truffles may also be added to the mixture). Divide the forcemeat into portions of about 100 g (4 oz, ½ cup) and wrap each one in a rectangular piece of previously soaked and dried pig's caul. Coat each crépinette in egg and breadcrumbs, brush with melted butter, and grill (broil) under a moderate heat. (The crépinettes may be grilled or fried without a coating of breadcrumbs.) The classic garnish is a purée of potatoes or of haricot beans (navy beans), but they may also be served with buttered green vegetables.

Crépy

A white wine from Haute Savoie, coming from slopes alongside Lake Geneva and made from the Chasselas grape. The wines are light-bodied and some are slightly sparkling (*pétillant*).

cress CRESSON

Any of various plants of the mustard family which are cultivated for their sharp-tasting leaves, which can be eaten raw or cooked.
● *Alénois cress* – A type of cress that grows abundantly in the region of Orléans (*alénois* is a corrupt form of *orléanais*). The young plants are sold in bunches throughout the year and are easily recognized by their small leaves arranged in a rosette. The leaves have a piquant flavour and are used as a condiment in salads and sauces, as a garnish for canapés and sandwiches, and sometimes for garnishing grilled (broiled) dishes.
● *Garden cress* – This is available from July to March. It has shiny leaves and a strong flavour and is used raw in salads or cooked in soups and purées.
● *Watercress* – This is the most popular type of cress and is available all the year, but at its best from April to October. It grows in running water and is widely cultivated. It has a distinctive peppery taste and is delicious eaten raw, but it can also be cooked in soups and forcemeats.
● *Meadow cress* – This plant grows wild in damp places, and its leaves resemble those of watercress except that they are firmer.

Cress is believed to be native to the Middle East but is now naturalized and widely cultivated in Europe. In the 14th century, it was used mainly for medicinal purposes but gradually began to be used in soups. It was not until about 1810 in France that methods of cultivating the cress in cress beds were introduced from Germany. The district of Senlis specialized in growing cress and it soon found a niche in gastronomy – in about 1850, the Café Riche included cress purée on its menu.

Today, cress is produced in France mainly in Oise, Essonne, and Seine-Maritime. When cress is to be eaten raw, it should be picked over carefully, the thicker stems and yellowing leaves removed, and the rest washed and drained carefully. It should not be left to soak in water. Wild cress should not be eaten as it can transmit parasites. It has a low calorific value (21 Cal per 100 g), but is rich in vitamin C and also in iron.

RECIPE

Cooked watercress CRESSON ÉTUVÉ Blanch some watercress in boiling salted water, drain, dry, and simmer in butter in the same way as spinach.

Watercress purée PURÉE DE CRESSON Simmer some watercress in butter and sieve. Add one-third of its volume of either potato purée or a purée of split peas. Add some fresh butter or cream and finish with a little finely chopped raw cress.

Watercress salad SALADE DE CRESSON Trim, wash, drain, and dry some watercress. Season with an appropriate salad dressing and garnish with walnut halves, small cubes of Gruyère cheese, small cubes of apple sprinkled with lemon juice, or quarters of hard-boiled (hard-cooked) eggs.

cressonnière (à la)

A name given to preparations that contain watercress. Potage *à la cressonnière* is a cream of watercress and potato soup thickened with egg yolks and cream and garnished with blanched watercress leaves. Salad *à la cressonnière* is a mixture of potatoes and watercress topped with chopped hard-boiled (hard-cooked) eggs and chopped parsley.

RECIPES

Baked eggs à la cressonnière OEUFS SUR LE PLAT À LA CRESSONNIÈRE Edge a buttered dish with a border of very thick watercress purée (see *cress*). Break 2 eggs in the centre, pour a little fresh cream around the yolks, and bake in the oven until the eggs have set.

Poached eggs à la cressonnière OEUFS POCHÉS À LA CRESSONNIÈRE Coat a buttered dish with a layer of watercress purée. Arrange some soft-boiled or poached eggs on the purée, and coat with cream sauce.

Watercress sauce SAUCE CRESSONNIÈRE Remove the leaves from some watercress. Wash, drain, and dry them, chop finely, and blend them with a mixture of chopped hard-boiled (hard-cooked) eggs, salt, pepper, oil, and vinegar.

cretonnée of peas

CRETONNÉE DE POIS

A very old recipe in which a purée of stewed green peas, which has been browned in lard, is mixed with breadcrumbs soaked in milk containing saffron and ginger and some cooked chicken. To finish, the mixture is bound with egg yolks and served garnished with thinly sliced breast of chicken.

crever (faire)

A French culinary term meaning to remove part of the starch from rice by boiling the grains in salted water for several minutes. This operation reduces the cooking time for rice pudding. (The literal meaning of the word (to burst) has sometimes given people the mistaken idea that the rice has to be cooked to the point of bursting.)

crible

A large-meshed sieve made of metal or nylon used mainly for sieving fruit in the preparation of jam and marmalade. The crible used in the food industry is a machine that consists of a succession of sieves with meshes of different sizes used to sort vegetables, dried fruit, and sweets.

crique

A small pancake from the Viverais made with grated raw potato and eggs. In the Auvergne, criquettes are potato cakes.

crispbread

A small thin crisp rectangular biscuit made from wholemeal (whole-grain) rye flour (or, less frequently, from wheat flour). It is sometimes flavoured with sesame seed, linseed, or cumin. It was originally made by Swedish peasants and was intended to be stored for long periods. Today it is manufactured on a large scale, especially in Scandinavia, Germany (where it is called *Knäckebrot*), and Great Britain. Exported all over the world, it is buttered and eaten with cheese, smoked fish, etc., and is also recommended for low-calorie diets.

crisps (potato chips)

CHIPS

Thin round slices of fried salted potato that are mass-produced and sold in bags. Crisps are served in France and Britain with apéritifs or with grills and roasts. This method of preparing fried potatoes is a very old one: it used to be called *pommes en liards* (the *liard* being a former small coin of various European countries).

RECIPE

Potato crisps (chips) POMMES CHIPS Wash and peel some large firm potatoes. Cut them into very thin round slices (preferably with a mandolin cutter or in a food processor), and immediately place them in cold water. Leave them to soak for 10 minutes and then dry them thoroughly. Plunge the slices once only into very hot frying oil (185 C, 365 F). Drain on absorbent paper and sprinkle with salt.

crockery VAISSELLE

All the items and accessories made of earthenware or china needed for service at the table or use in the kitchen: plates, cups, saucers, bowls, dishes, egg cups. etc.

crocodile

A reptile with strong-smelling flesh, highly appreciated in Africa and South

America and by lovers of unusual dishes. The legs and the tail of young crocodiles are used: the firm white meat is seasoned and either stewed in palm oil or roasted. Crocodile tripe is considered to be a delicacy in Ethiopia, and apparently the eggs make excellent omelettes. Only the yolks are used, as the whites do not contain any albumin and therefore do not coagulate.

croissant

A crescent-shaped roll generally made with puff pastry or with a leavened dough for which the recipe is given below.

This delicious pastry originated in Budapest in 1686, when the Turks were besieging the city. To reach the centre of the town, they dug underground passages. Bakers, working during the night, heard the noise made by the Turks and gave the alarm. The assailants were repulsed and the bakers who had saved the city were granted the privilege of making a special pastry which had to take the form of a crescent in memory of the emblem on the Ottoman flag.

Bakers usually sell two sorts of croissants: those made with butter and 'the others', which no law obliges him to declare are 'made with margarine'. Croissants may be served at breakfast or tea, or as hot hors d'oeuvres filled with ham or cheese or with a salpicon of mushrooms or chicken.

The term 'croissant' is also used for a semicircular petit four made with almond paste and garnished either with pine seeds or flaked almonds.

RECIPES

Parisian crossants CROISSANTS PARISIENS Blend 30 g (1 oz) fresh yeast (2 cakes compressed yeast) or 15 g (½ oz) dried yeast (2 packets active dry yeast) with ¼ litre (8 fl oz, 1 cup) lukewarm milk. Put 500 g (18 oz, 4½ cups) sifted flour into a mixing bowl and add 60 g (2½ oz, ⅓ cup) sugar and 10 g (¼ oz, 1½ teaspoons) salt. Make a well in the flour mixture and pour the mixture of milk and yeast into the centre. Mix quickly with the fingertips, and as soon as the liquid is completely absorbed by the flour, cover the dough with a cloth and leave it to stand for 30 minutes to 1 hour, depending on the room temperature.

Roll out the dough into an oblong and dot with butter. Fold into three and repeat rolling, dotting with butter, and folding twice more using 250 g (9 oz, generous 1 cup) softened butter. Allow the dough to stand for 30 minutes.

Then roll it out to an oblong about 45 cm (18 in) by 15 cm (6 in) and cut it into triangles. Roll up the triangles, starting at the base and working towards the top. Place the croissants on a baking sheet, bending them into crescents. Allow them to rise further in a draught-free place for 15–45 minutes, depending on the room temperature. Brush with beaten egg yolk and bake in the oven at 220 C (425 F, gas 7) for about 10 minutes.

Viennese croissants CROISSANTS VIENNOIS Blend 12–15 g (½ oz) fresh yeast (1 cake compressed yeast) or 7 g (¼ oz) dried yeast (1 packet active dry yeast) with 1 tablespoon tepid water. Dissolve 30 g (1 oz, 2 tablespoons, firmly packed) caster (superfine) sugar and a pinch of salt in 1 tablespoon milk. Place 25 g (1 oz, 2 tablespoons) butter in a saucepan and heat with a mixture of 5 tablespoons water and 5 tablespoons milk. Put 260 g (9 oz, scant 2½ cups) flour into a large bowl, make a well, and add the sugar/salt/milk mixture followed by the mixture of butter, water, and milk. Finally add the diluted yeast. Mix all these ingredients together thoroughly to obtain a smooth paste. Leave the dough in a warm place for 1 hour so that it doubles in volume.

Spread out the dough on a floured dish and cool in the refrigerator for 30 minutes. Then roll out the dough into a thin rectangle on a floured surface. Cut 70 g (3 oz, 6 tablespoons) butter into small pieces and distribute them over two-thirds of the rectangle. Fold it into three, starting with the unbuttered third. Roll the dough out a second time, cover, and replace in the refrigerator for 1 hour. Repeat the operations again using a further 70 g (3 oz, 6 tablespoons) butter and finish by rolling out the dough into a square of about 20 cm (8 in). Cover and refrigerate again for a further 30 minutes.

Then roll it out into a very thin rectangle measuring 30 cm (12 in) wide and 60 cm (24 in) long. Cut the rectangle into two lengthwise, and cut each half into 6 triangles. Roll up each triangle from base to top. Arrange the croissants on a buttered baking tray (sheet), allowing plenty of space between them. Leave them to stand for 1 hour. Brush the croissants with beaten egg and cook for 3 minutes in a very hot oven. Lower the heat to 200 C (400 F, gas 6) and bake for a further 12 minutes. Watch them carefully during the last few minutes so they do not overcook.

SAVOURY CROISSANTS

Cheese croissants CROISSANTS AU FROMAGE Split some baked croissants on one side. Butter the inside and fill with thin slices of Gruyère or Emmental cheese. Sprinkle with pepper and heat in a very hot oven. Serve immediately. The butter and cheese may be replaced by a well-reduced béchamel sauce containing cheese.

Shrimp croissants CROISSANTS AUX CREVETTES Use 6 croissants baked without sugar. Make 2 dl (7 fl oz, ¾ cup) well-reduced prawn sauce (see *shrimps and prawns*). Split the croissants on one side and fill them generously with the sauce. Heat in the oven and serve very hot.

SWEET CROISSANTS

Small almond croissants PETITS CROISSANTS AUX AMANDES Pound together in a mortar 300 g (11 oz, 2 cups) whole shelled almonds and 150 g (5 oz, ⅔ cup, firmly packed) vanilla-flavoured sugar, gradually moistening with sufficient egg white to obtain a paste that can be rolled in the hand. Add 2 tablespoons (3 tablespoons) flour to the paste, and divide it into pieces about the size of a walnut. Roll each piece with the hands into the shape of a cigar with slightly pointed ends (flour your palms if necessary). Dip each 'cigar' in beaten egg, roll in some flaked almonds, and shape into small croissants. Arrange them on sheets of greaseproof (waxed) paper on baking trays (sheets). Glaze with egg yolk and cook for approximately 12 minutes in a moderate oven

(about 200 C, 400 F, gas 6) until they are golden brown. As soon as they are cooked, brush them with sweetened milk.

Viennese jam croissants CROISSANTS VIENNOIS À LA CONFITURE Prepare 500 g (18 oz) dough as for Viennese croissants. Roll it out into a rectangle 30 cm (12 in) wide and 60 cm (24 in) long. Cut it lengthwise into 2 strips, and cut each strip into 6 triangles using a fluted pastry cutter. Place 1 tablespoon sieved strawberry, raspberry, or apricot jam at the base of each triangle, and shape the croissants by rolling them up from the base to the top. Place the croissants on a buttered baking tray (sheet), leaving plenty of space between them, and brush with beaten egg. Cook for 18–20 minutes. When cooked, dust them with icing sugar (confectioners' sugar).

croquante

A large item of pâtisserie formerly used as a table decoration. It was made of interlaced strips of cooked almond paste, placed on a pastry base, and iced with green or pink sugar; the whole preparation was decorated with hollowed-out rounds of puff pastry, garnished with glacé cherries. Croquantes were also made of iced brandy snaps, built up like a croquembouche.

A croquante (or croquant) is also a small dry crunchy petit four. Saint-Geniez croquants are made of a mixture of almonds and hazelnuts. Parisian croquants are sweets made of worked sugar.

croque au sel (à la)

Describing vegetables served raw with salt as the only seasoning, but sometimes accompanied by fresh butter. New young artichokes, radishes, and beans can be served in this way, providing that they are very fresh. Roger Lamazur and other gourmets maintain that this is the best way of eating fresh truffles.

croquembouche

A decorative cone-shaped preparation built up of small items of pâtisserie or confectionery and glazed with a caramel syrup to make it crisp. The croquembouche is usually placed on a base of nougat. It is built around a conical mould, also called a croquembouche, which is removed through the base when the small pieces are securely fixed to each other by the solidified caramel. It is traditionally served at buffets, weddings, and first-communion meals.

The traditional croquembouche is made of little chou buns, sometimes filled with some kind of cream and dipped in sugar cooked to the crack stage. Croquembouches are also made with crystallized (candied) or sugar-coated fruits, brandy snaps, marzipan sweets (almond paste candies), meringue, or nougat. They can be decorated with sugar-coated almonds, sugar flowers, or spun caramel.

RECIPE

Chestnut croquembouche   CRO-QUEMBOUCHE DE MARRONS   (from Carême's recipe) Take 60 choice roasted chestnuts, peel them carefully, and remove any traces of burning. Glaze by dipping them in sugar cooked to the crack stage (see *sugar*), one by one, and place them on a smooth round mould, 18 cm (7 in) in diameter and 12.5 cm (5 in) deep. This croquembouche must be piled up at the last minute before serving, because the moisture in the chestnuts tends to soften the sugar and make it lose both its consistency and its brilliance.

croque-monsieur

A hot sandwich, made of two slices of buttered bread with the crusts removed, filled with thin slices of Gruyère cheese and a slice of lean ham. The croque-monsieur is lightly browned on both sides, either in butter in a frying pan (skillet) or under the grill (broiler). The top may be coated with a Gruyère béchamel sauce and cooked *au gratin*. There are several possible variations on the basic recipe: the ham can be replaced by white chicken meat, the Gruyère cheese by Gouda, and a slice of tomato, or even pineapple, can be added. If the croque-monsieur is served with a baked egg on top, it is then called a *croque-madame*.

The first croque-monsieur was served in 1910 in a Parisian café on the Boulevard des Capucines. It is still a popular dish in cafés and snack bars, and is also served as an entrée or a hot hors d'oeuvre.

RECIPE

Croque-monsieur à la brandade
Lightly coat with oil 2 slices of bread from which the crusts have been removed. Spread brandade of salt cod on one of the slices, cover with slices of tomato, then place the second slice of bread on top. Brown on a grid in a very hot oven or under a grill.

croquet

A dry petit four in the shape of a small stick, generally made of almonds, sugar, and egg white. Croquets are very often regional specialities. The best-known are the croquets of Berry, Sologne, and Périgord, the golden croquets of Sens, the lacelike croquets of Nivernais, the croquets of Bar-sur-Aube and Bordeaux (made with unskinned almonds), and the croquets of Vinsobres and Valence (made with whole almonds).

RECIPE

Almond croquets   CROQUETS AUX AMANDES   Soften 50 g (2 oz, 4 tablespoons) butter with a palette knife; coarsely chop 70 g (3 oz, ¾ cup) unskinned almonds. In a basin, mix 200 g (7 oz, 1¾ cups) flour with 5 g (½ teaspoon) baking powder, 70 g (3 oz, ⅓ cup) caster (superfine) sugar, 1 egg, and the butter; add the chopped almonds and knead the paste to make it smooth. Heat the oven to about 200 C (400 F, gas 6). Shape the paste into a sausage 20 cm (8 in) long and flatten it with the hand into a rectangle 10 cm (4 in) wide. Place on a buttered baking tray (sheet) and leave to stand for 15 minutes.

Prepare a caramel with 1 tablespoon sugar and the same amount of water, leave until lukewarm, then add 1 egg and beat all together with a fork. Brush the rectangle with this mixture and use a fork to score the surface. Cook for 10 minutes, remove from the oven, and immediately cut into rectangles about 2 cm (¾ in) wide and 5 cm (2 in) long.

croquette

A small savoury or sweet preparation.

Savoury croquettes, made with a salpicon of fish, meat, poultry, ham, mushroom, calves' sweetbreads, etc., are served hot as an hors d'oeuvre or as a garnish (especially potato croquettes); sweet croquettes are made with rice, chestnuts, semolina, etc.

The basic mixture is bound with a fairly thick sauce (white, suprême, velouté, curry, tomato, or cheese béchamel for savoury croquettes; confectioners' custard (pastry cream) for sweet croquettes). Croquettes are shaped into corks, sticks, balls, or rectangles. They are usually coated with breadcrumbs, plunged into very hot oil, and fried until they are crisp and golden. They are arranged in the shape of a pyramid, turban, or crown on a dish lined with a doily or napkin, and savoury croquettes are sprinkled with fried parsley. Croquettes are always served with a sauce related to the main ingredient of the mixture (salt cod croquettes with tomato sauce, chicken croquettes with Périgueux or Villeroi sauce, game croquettes with chasseur sauce, etc.; custard cream or fruit coulis for sweet croquettes). The most common are fish croquettes (made with salt cod, for example, and all the preparations frozen in 'sticks') and croquette potatoes, served with sautéed or grilled meat.

Sweet croquettes may also be made with very thick confectioners' custard, cut into diamond shapes or rectangles, which are coated with breadcrumbs and fried (fried custard; see *creams and custards*).

RECIPES

Savoury Croquettes

Preparation of croquette mixture PRÉPARATION DE L'APPAREIL À CROQUETTES Mix 500 g (18 oz) of the main ingredient of the croquettes (cooked poultry, game, veal, lamb, offal), minced (ground) or cut into very small dice, with 250 g (9 oz) cooked diced mushrooms (and possibly 75 g (3 oz) diced truffles). Moisten with 1 dl (6 tablespoons, scant ½ cup) Madeira, place in a covered pan, and heat gently. Then add 4 dl (¾ pint, 1¾ cups) well reduced velouté sauce, thickened with 3 egg yolks. Stir the mixture well, on the heat, then spread evenly on a buttered baking tray (sheet) and dab the surface with butter to prevent it from forming a crust. Leave to cool completely before making the croquettes.

When the croquette mixture is made with various meats, poultry, or game, a salpicon of cooked lean ham or tongue is often added to it. When it is made with fish or shellfish, the only additional items it contains are truffles and mushrooms. Croquette mixtures may also be made by replacing the velouté sauce with reduced demi-glace sauce.

Shaping Divide the cold mixture into portions of 60–70 g (2–3 oz. Roll these out on a floured flat surface and shape them into corks, balls, eggs, rectangles, etc. Dip them in a mixture of egg and oil beaten together and then cover them completely with fine breadcrumbs.

Cooking Place the croquettes in a frying basket, plunge into very hot oil (175–180 c, 340–350 f), and cook until they are crisp and golden. Drain on absorbent paper, sprinkle lightly with salt, and arrange on a napkin in a pyramid or turban shape. Garnish with parsley and serve with an appropriate sauce.

Garnish When the croquettes are served as a small entrée, they are often accompanied by a garnish of fresh vegetables coated in butter or a purée of vegetables. The croquettes themselves, if they are made very small, may be used as a garnish for large roasts, joints, poultry, game, or fish.

Beef croquettes CROQUETTES DE BOEUF Cut some boiled beef and some lean ham into very small dice. Make a well-reduced béchamel sauce with 50 g (2 oz, 4 tablespoons) butter, 50 g (2 oz, ½ cup) flour, ½ litre (17 fl oz, 2 cups) milk, grated nutmeg, and salt and pepper; beat in 1 egg yolk. Bind the salpicon with the béchamel and leave to cool. Finish according to the basic preparation and serve with a well-seasoned tomato sauce.

The béchamel may be replaced by rice, using two-thirds salpicon to one-third rice cooked in meat stock.

Cheese croquettes I CROQUETTES DE FROMAGE Make a béchamel sauce with 50 g (2 oz, 4 tablespoons) butter, 50 g (2 oz, ½ cup) flour, 4 dl (14 fl oz, 1¾ cups) milk, a little grated nutmeg, salt, and pepper. Add to the boiling béchamel 1 dl (6 tablespoons, scant ½ cup) cream and 125 g (4½ oz, 1 cup) grated cheese (Gruyère, Emmental, or Edam). Stir until the cheese is melted, and adjust the seasoning. Leave to cool. Finish the preparation as in the basic recipe.

Cheese croquettes II CROQUETTES DE FROMAGE Beat together 3 whole eggs and 2 yolks. Boil ½ litre (17 fl oz, 2 cups) milk. Pour into a saucepan 50 g (2 oz, ½ cup) sifted flour and 50 g (2 oz, ⅓ cup) rice flour. Add the beaten eggs and mix well. Dilute with the boiled milk and season with salt and pepper, grated nutmeg, and a dash of cayenne. Bring to the boil and cook for 5 minutes, stirring all the time. Add 125 g (4½ oz, 1 cup) grated cheese (Gruyère, Emmental, or Edam) and stir until melted. Leave to cool and finish the preparation as in the basic recipe.

Macaroni croquettes CROQUETTES DE MACARONI Cook some macaroni in salted water, keeping it slightly firm. Drain it. Add some grated cheese to a thick béchamel sauce (60 g (2½ oz, ½ cup) cheese to 3 dl (½ pint, 1¼ cups) béchamel). Bind the macaroni with béchamel mixture (use the same amounts of béchamel and macaroni). Spread the mixture on a greased baking tray (sheet), smooth the surface and brush it with melted butter, and leave to cool completely. Then cut the mixture into small rectangles. Flour them, coat with egg and breadcrumbs, and deep-fry in hot oil (175–180 c, 340–350 F) until golden. Drain on absorbent paper and dust lightly with salt. Serve the croquettes with a well-seasoned tomato sauce.

Potato croquettes CROQUETTES DE POMMES DE TERRE Peel and quarter 1.5 kg (3½ lb) floury potatoes and cook in salted boiling water until they are quite tender (at least 20 minutes). Drain the potatoes and dry them out over a low heat. Sieve or blend them to a purée,

add about 50 g (2 oz, 4 tablespoons) butter, and gradually work in 4 beaten egg yolks with a fork. Spread the purée in a butteed dish and leave to cool completely.

Work the purée into a ball, using floured hands, and roll the ball into a long narrow cylinder; cut it into sections about 6 cm (2½ in) long. Round these sections slightly. Roll them in flour, coat with a mixture of 2 eggs lightly beaten with 1 tablespoon oil, and cover with breadcrumbs. Deep-fry the croquettes in oil (at 180 c, 350 F) for about 3 minutes, until they turn golden. Drain on absorbent paper and serve very hot with roast or grilled meat.

Rice croquettes CROQUETTES DE RIZ Mix together 500 g (1 lb, 3½ cups) rice cooked *au gras* with 125 g (4½ oz, 1 cup) grated Parmesan cheese. Bind with a beaten egg and check the seasoning. Mould into cork shapes and finish according to the basic preparation. Serve with a well-seasoned tomato sauce.

Rice croquettes à l'indienne CROQUETTES DE RIZ À L'INDIENNE Mix some boiled rice with a quarter of its volume of a salpicon of onions softened in butter or oil and some beaten egg. Bind with a little curry sauce (see *(à l')indienne*). Finish the croquettes according to the basic method, moulding them into disc shapes. Serve with curry sauce.

Salt-cod croquettes CROQUETTES DE MORUE Soak some salt cod in water to desalt it. Poach in water, then crumble it very finely. Add one-third of its volume of duchess potatoes and just enough béchamel sauce to bind the mixture well. Finish the croquettes according to the basic method, moulding them into ball shapes. Serve with a well-seasoned or garlic-flavoured tomato sauce.

SWEET CROQUETTES

Chestnut croquettes CROQUETTES DE MARRONS Dip some chestnuts in boiling water and peel them. Cook them in a light syrup (500 g (1 lb, 2 cups) sugar per litre (1¾ pints, 4¼ cups) water) flavoured with vanilla. Sieve the chestnuts to obtain a purée and thicken it with egg yolks and butter (5 egg yolks and 50 g (2 oz, 4 tablespoons) butter per 500 g (1 lb, 2¼ cups) purée). Spread the mixture on a buttered baking tray (sheet) and leave to cool completely. Cut into rectangles of about 60 g (2 oz), cover with egg and breadcrumbs, and deep-fry in oil heated to 180 C (350 F). Serve the croquettes very hot with a fruit sauce flavoured with Cognac or Armagnac.

500 g (1 lb, 4½ cups) sieved marrons glacés may be used instead of chestnuts, blended with 4 dl (¾ pint, scant 2 cups) confectioners' custard (see *creams and custards*) flavoured with rum, Cognac, or Armagnac.

Rice croquettes CROQUETTES DE RIZ Prepare some rice in milk using 125 g (4½ oz, 2 cups) rice; after cooking, add 5–6 egg yolks (or 3 whole eggs beaten as for an omelette). Leave to cool completely, then divide into portions of about 60 g (2 oz). Mould them into cork shapes, coat with egg and breadcrumbs, and deep-fry in oil (180 c, 350 F) until golden. Drain on absorbent paper. Serve with a hot fruit sauce flavoured with Grand Marnier.

croquignole

A very small light crisp cake, served with tea, creams, or ices. It is made from a mixture of sugar (or royal icing), flour, and egg white and the top is covered with vanilla-flavoured icing (frosting or a light syrup. The best-known croquignoles, made since the 16th century, are those of Paris and Navarrenx (in the Pyrenees).

The word seems to come from *croquer* (to crunch) and from *nieule* (a kind of wafer). It also means a flick of the finger, which presumably derives from the ancient custom of people throwing small cakes at each other at certain festivals.

RECIPE

Parisian croquignoles CROQUIGNOLES PARISIENNES Heat the oven to a low temperature (about 160 C, 325 F, gas 3) for 15 minutes. Whisk 6 egg whites, add 450 g (1 lb, 3½ cups) icing (confectioners') sugar, and 3 tablespoons vanilla-flavoured sugar, and continue whisking until the mixture forms stiff peaks. Gradually blend in 300 g (11 oz, 2¾ cups) sifted flour, mixing quickly in order to obtain a smooth paste. Using a piping (pastry) bag with a small smooth nozzle, pipe some croquignoles, in various shapes, on a buttered baking tray (sheet). Place the latter in the oven (which has been switched off) and leave to dry slowly for 1½ hours. Then reheat the oven to 200 C (400 F, gas 6) and cook the croquignoles for a further 15 minutes. Take the baking tray out of the oven and brush the croquignoles with sugar syrup. Let them cool completely before storing in a jar or an airtight tin.

Crottin de Chavignol

A French goats'-milk cheese made in Sancerre. Containing at least 45% butterfat, it has a soft centre and a natural crust, mottled with white, blue, or brown mould. Crottin can be eaten when it has ripened for three months until dry, when it is crumbly, with a piquant flavour, and gives off a fairly strong smell; it is also eaten fresh, when it is milder and white. Originally, only very mature cheeses, with a strong smell and almost black colour, were entitled to be called Crottin. Crottin comes in the form of a small flattened ball, weighing about 60 g (2oz). A distinction is made between farm Crottin, which is enjoyed with a full-bodied wine, and dairy Crottin, slightly more insipid and rarely matured, which may be used for soufflés, salads, etc. In Berry, Crottin was traditionally prepared by placing it under the grill for a few minutes, sometimes coated with breadcrumbs, and then serving it hot accompanied by a green salad of endives or dandelions.

croupion

The rear end of the body of birds, consisting of the last two dorsal vertebrae and bearing the tail feathers. Called the parson's nose in Britain, it is a very tasty part, particularly from chickens and turkeys.

In the duck and the goose, the sebaceous glands situated on either side of it must be removed before cooking as they can give the meat an unpleasant taste.

croustade

A preparation consisting of a case of lining pastry, puff pastry, hollowed-out bread, duchess potato mixture, semolina, or rice, which is fried or heated in the oven and filled with a salpicon, ragout, vegetables, or a purée, bound with a suitable reduced sauce. Croustades, which were originally made in the south of France, are eaten as hot hors d'oeuvres, but they are also used in certain garnishes for large-scale cookery (filled with kidneys, vegetables, crayfish tails, etc.).

RECIPES

Preparation

Bread croustades CROUSTADES DE PAIN DE MIE Cut some thick stale bread into slices 5–6 cm (2–2½ in) thick, remove the crusts, and trim to the desired shape. On the top, make a circular incision with the tip of a knife to a depth of 4–5 cm (1½–2 in) to mark the lid. Deep-fry the croustades in hot oil (175–180 C, 350 F) until they are golden. Drain. Take off the lid and remove all the crumb from the inside. Line the croustades with a thin layer of forcemeat (according to the filling). Leave for 5–6 minutes at the front of a hot oven with the door open. Fill with the chosen mixture. All the fillings recommended for timbales and vols-au-vent are suitable for bread croustades. These croustades may also be made using round bread rolls.

Duchess potato croustades CROUSTADES DE POMMES DE TERRE DUCHESSE Spread the duchess potato mixture in a thick layer (4–5 cm, 1½–2 in) on an oiled baking tray (sheet) and leave to cool completely. Use a smooth round cutter to cut into shapes 7 cm (2¾ in) in diameter. Coat these croustades with egg and breadcrumbs. To mark the lid, make a circular incision in the top 1 cm (½ in) from the edge and 3–4 cm (1–1½ in) deep. Deep-fry in very hot oil (180 C, 350 F) until golden. Drain and dry on absorbent paper. Re-

move the lid and hollow out the inside, leaving only a base and a wall, about 1 cm (½ in) thick. Fill the croustades according to the instructions given in the recipe.

Puff pastry croustades CROUSTADES DE PÂTE FEUILLETÉE Sprinkle the worktop with flour and roll out the pastry to a thickness of about 1–2 cm (½–¾ in). Using a pastry (cookie) cutter, cut rounds 7–10 cm (3–4 in) in diameter. With a smaller cutter, make a circle centred on the first, with a diameter 2 cm (¾ in) smaller, taking care not to cut right through the pastry: this smaller circle will form the lid of the croustades. Glaze with egg yolk and place in a hot oven (230 C, 450 F, gas 8). As soon as the crust has risen well and turned golden, take the croustades out of the oven. Leave until lukewarm, then take off the lid and, with a spoon, remove the soft white paste which is inside. Leave the croustades to cool completely.

Alternatively, roll the pastry to a thickness of only 6 mm (¼ in) and cut half of it into circles 7–10 cm (3–4 in) in diameter, and the rest into rings of the same external diameter and 1 cm (½ in) wide. Brush the base of the rings with beaten egg and place them on the circles; glaze the whole with beaten egg and cook.

Rice *or* **semolina croustades** CROUSTADES DE RIZ OU DE SEMOULE Cook some rice or semolina *au gras.* Bind with egg yolks (5 yolks per 500 g (1 lb, 3 cups) rice or semolina). Spread out in a layer 4–5 cm (1½–2 in) thick and leave to cool completely. Finish as for duchess potato croustades.

Fillings

Croustades à la grecque Fill some rice croustades with a fondue of tomatoes *à la grecque.* Garnish each croustade with 3 round slices of onion, coated in butter and deep-fried.

Croustades à la marinière Prepare some mussels *à la marinière.* Strain the juice and mix with fresh cream to make a thick velouté sauce. Fill croustades made of puff pastry with the mussels. Coat with the sauce and serve very hot.

croûte

A pastry case or slice of bread used to hold a savoury or sweet preparation. Pastry croûtes (puff or shortcrust) are cooked blind and then filled; they include timbales, vols-au-vent, and bouchées.

Croûtes served as hot hors d'oeuvres are round or square slices of bread from which the crusts have been removed, fried in butter until they are a golden colour and topped with various preparations (ham, mushrooms, anchovies, seafood, etc.); they are sometimes coated with a little thick sauce and cooked *au gratin* (see *Welsh rarebit*).

Croûtes served as hot desserts are stale slices of savarin, brioche, or milk bread, dried in the oven and spread with poached or crystallized (candied) fruits, moistened with syrup, sprinkled with shredded almonds, coated with jam, etc., and often arranged in a border or crown shape.

RECIPES

Savoury Croûtes

Preparation Cut some round pieces of bread, 4–5 cm (1½–2 in) in diameter and 2 cm (¾ in) thick, from a stale loaf. Take a round cutter with a diameter smaller than that of the croûtes, and lightly press it on each croûte to mark the lid. Fry the croûtes in butter, oil, or margarine. When they are golden, drain and hollow out. Fill according to the instructions of the recipe. Instead of frying the croûtes in butter, they can be brushed with butter and browned in the oven.

Croûtes à la diable Fill some croûtes with a salpicon of York ham and mushrooms which have been cooked slowly in butter, bound with well-reduced demiglace and seasoned with a dash of cayenne. Sprinkle the top of the croûtes with breadcrumbs fried in butter, and brown in a very hot oven.

Mushroom croûtes CROÛTES AUX CHAMPIGNONS Prepare some croûtes

and fill them with mushrooms (preferably field mushrooms) *à la crème*. Sprinkle with breadcrumbs and brown in a very hot oven or under the grill. Serve hot.

Seafood croûtes CROÛTES AUX FRUITS DE MER Cut some slices of bread and remove the crusts. Lightly fry them in butter and then coat them with a cheese béchamel sauce. Place on these slices various types of shellfish (oysters, mussels, clams, etc.), cooked in white wine as for a marinière, and coat them with a sauce prepared with their cooking stock. Sprinkle with fresh breadcrumbs, moisten with melted butter, and brown quickly in a very hot oven. (Peeled prawns (shelled shrimp) may be added to the shellfish.)

Sweet Croûtes

Crown of croûtes à la Montmorency CROÛTES EN COURONNE À LA MONTMORENCY Cut stale brioches into slices 1.5 cm (½ in) thick. Arrange these slices on a baking tray (sheet), dust them with sugar, and glaze them in the oven. Cover each slice with a thin layer of frangipane cream flavoured with cherry brandy, then arrange them in a crown on a round dish, placing them very close to one another. Fill the centre of this crown with a dome of stoned (pitted) cherries, cooked in a vanilla-flavoured syrup and drained well. Decorate the border of the crown with more cherries. If liked, coat with redcurrant sauce laced with cherry brandy and serve more of this sauce separately.

Fruit croûtes CROÛTES AUX FRUITS Cut a stale savarin into slices 1.5 cm (½ in) thick. Place these slices on a baking tray (sheet), dust them with fine sugar, and glaze them in the oven. Reassemble the savarin on a large round dish, alternating the croûtes with slices of canned pineapple. Place around this crown, alternately, quarters of pears and apples, cooked in vanilla-flavoured syrup and well drained. Fill the inside of the crown with a salpicon of various fruits cooked in syrup and drained. Decorate the top with glacé (candied) cherries, angelica lozenges, quarters of crystallized (candied) apricots, small golden and green preserved oranges, and halved almonds. Warm the crown in a cool oven (150 c, 300 f, gas 2).

When ready to serve, coat it with apricot sauce flavoured with rum or Kirsch, and serve more of this sauce separately. Croûtes containing other types of fruit cooked in syrup (apricot, peach, pear, plum, nectarine, etc.) are prepared in the same way.

croûtes for soup
CROÛTES À POTAGE

Thick slices of French bread (*flûte*) which have been partly hollowed out or cut in two lengthwise and dried in the oven. Croûtes are served with all kinds of soups, usually separately, either plain, garnished, or filled.

Croûtes *à l'ancienne* are stuffed with stockpot vegetables (chopped or sieved) and cooked *au gratin*. Croûtes *au pot* are moistened with the stockpot fat and browned in the oven. The name *consommé croûte au pot* is sometimes given to the stockpot broth garnished with vegetables cut into small pieces, grated Gruyère cheese, and round slices of *flûte*, hollowed out and grilled (broiled) in the oven. (Served separately, these are also called *croûtes en dentelle*.) Diablotins are croûtes covered with reduced béchamel sauce, sprinkled with grated cheese and a pinch of cayenne, then cooked *au gratin*. Plain croûtes lightly browned and sometimes rubbed with garlic) are usually called croutons.

In the Middle Ages, the thin slices of bread soaked in stock, wine, or milk, which were served with gruels or liquid stews, were called *soupes*. Later, the name croûtes was given to lightly browned slices of bread served after the soup: these were coated with purée, garnished with crayfish or asparagus tips, and moistened with partridge gravy or cooked *au gratin* using Parmesan cheese.

RECIPE

Croûtes for consommé croûte au pot
Divide a French loaf (*flûte* or *ficelle*) into slices 5 cm (2 in) long. Cut each slice in half lengthwise and remove the soft part. Dry out the croûtes in the oven and arrange them in a dish. Alternatively, the slices can be sprinkled with stock-

pot fat and baked in the oven until golden. Serve separately with the broth from the pot-au-feu or a consommé.

crouton CROÛTON

A small piece of bread which is toasted, lightly browned in butter, fried in oil, or simply dried in the oven. Diced croutons are used to garnish certain preparations (soups, green salads, scrambled eggs, omelettes, buttered spinach) and are included in composite garnishes (such as *grenobloise*). Cut into hearts, diamonds, crescents, triangles, circles, or stars, they are used as a complementary garnish for dishes in sauce (salmis, blanquettes, matelotes, sautés) or purées and to decorate the border of the serving dish. Croutons spread with *à gratin* forcemeat are used as a base for some types of game and poultry (see *canapé*). Large crouton supports are used to raise large hot or cold items so that garnishes can be arranged without masking the food. They are used for buffets and are not intended to be eaten.

The name crouton is also given to small decorative aspic shapes used to garnish cold dishes.

RECIPES

Aspic croutons CROÛTONS DE GELÉE The aspic must be well set and very clear. In order to cut out a large number of croutons, set it in a shallow rectangular tray. When set, place the strips of aspic flat on a damp napkin and cut out with a knife or a cutter into geometric shapes.

Crouton omelette OMELETTE AUX CROÛTONS Beat some eggs for an omelette, add some small diced croutons which have been fried in butter (1 cup for 6 eggs), and cook the omelette. Serve the omelette with a ribbon of well-reduced spiced tomato fondue poured around it and sprinkle with chopped herbs.

croûtonner

A French culinary term meaning to arrange croutons of aspic cut into cubes, triangles, crescents, etc., as decoration around cold items served as hors d'oeuvres or entrées.

crown COURONNE

A method of arranging certain sweet or savoury dishes in the form of a ring (using a ring mould), or a border (e.g. rice), or a crown (e.g. lamb cutlets arranged back to back). The centre of the arrangement is usually decorated or garnished. The terms 'turban' or 'border' are also used.

Brioches and bread *en couronne* are shaped in the form of a crown or ring.

Crozes-Hermitage

Red and white AOC wines of the Rhône Valley from vineyards adjacent to those producing Hermitage.

crozets or crousets

Quenelles made from a mixture of flour (wheat or buckwheat), potato purée, eggs, water, and walnut oil: a speciality of the Dauphiné. Crozets are poached, drained, then arranged in layers in a gratin dish, with crumbled blue cheese and grated Gruyère cheese between layers, sprinkled with melted lard, and cooked in the oven until golden. Crozets are often the traditional dish served on Christmas Eve.

cru

The French word meaning 'a growth', which is widely used in wine growing. In the Bordeaux area, a *cru classé* is a wine from a specific estate that has been officially classified, usually according to the famous classification of 1855. Wines classified by this system were appraised according to the prices they were likely to fetch at the Paris Exhibition, rather than exclusively on their quality. Categories include the *premiers crus* (first growths), *grands crus* (great growths), and *crus exceptionnels* (exceptional growths). Subsequent categorization has been attempted in certain areas, but it should be remembered that each region's labelling laws are likely to be individual.

cruchade

A gruel made from cornflour (cornstarch) with milk or water, traditional in south-western France. In the Béarn, the gruel is cooled, then cut into evensized pieces which are then fried. The Saintonge cruchade is a thin round cake made from maize (corn), fried and served with jam. Cruchades in the Landes region are small savoury or sweet biscuits which can be fried.

crudités

Raw vegetables or fruits served as an hors d'oeuvre, generally thinly sliced, grated, or cut into little sticks and accompanied by cold sauces. Crudités include carrots, celeriac (celery root), cucumber, sweet peppers, red cabbage, celery, fennel, fresh broad beans, cauliflower (in very small florets), tomatoes, mushrooms, radishes, small artichokes, quarters of grapefruit, orange, and apple, round slices of banana sprinkled with lemon, slices of avocado, and, although it is cooked, beetroot (red beet). The various items are often presented as an assortment, with several sauces (fondue of vegetables). A plate of crudités may also include a hard-boiled (hard-cooked) egg in mayonnaise.

RECIPE

Basket of crudités PANIER DE CRUDITÉS Choose some very fresh raw vegetables: little carrots, sticks (stalks) of celery, radish, cucumber, sweet peppers, very small artichokes known as *poivrades*, cauliflower, mushrooms, fennel.

Scrape the carrots and radishes, leaving the small green leaves on the radishes. Thoroughly remove the strings from the sticks of celery, cut them into sections of about 10 cm (4 in), and split the heart into four. Skin the pepper (optional), cut open, take out the white partitions and seeds, and cut the flesh into thin strips. Peel the cucumber and cut into sticks. Pull the cauliflower apart into small florets. Wipe and slice the mushrooms. Clean the fennel bulb and cut it into thick slices. Just before serving, break the stalks of the artichokes, cut them in four, remove the chokes, and sprinkle the cut part with lemon juice.

Line a wickerwork basket with a napkin and arrange the vegetables in it, in bunches. If it is not to be served immediately, cover it with a cloth and put in a cool place. Serve accompanied by a mayonnaise with herbs, a tarragon vinaigrette, an anchovy sauce, and a cream cheese sauce.

cruet stand
HUILIER, MÉNAGÈRE

A table set consisting of a base holding containers for oil and vinegar, a salt-cellar, a pepper pot, and a mustard pot. It may be made of glass, porcelain, or metal.

crumb tray
RAMASSE-MIETTES

A small dustpan equipped with a soft-bristled brush, used for brushing the crumbs off the tablecloth, usually before the dessert is brought in (the bread basket and the saltcellar should be removed at this point), and sometimes between other courses. There is an automatic model, consisting of a case containing a brush, which picks up the crumbs as it is rolled over the table.

crumpet

A small spongy yeast cake with holes on the top surface, cooked on a griddle in a special ring about 7 cm (3 in) in diameter. In England, crumpets are usually served at tea-time, toasted and spread with plenty of butter.

RECIPE

Crumpets In a bowl, mix 2 table-spoons tepid water, 25 g (1 oz, 1 cake) fresh yeast, and ½ teaspoon sugar until completely dissolved. Leave the bowl in a warm place until the mixture has doubled in volume. Put 145 g (5 oz, 1¼ cups) sifted flour and a pinch of salt in a large mixing bowl. Make a well and pour 1 dl (6 tablespoons, scant ½ cup) milk into the middle. Add 1 whole egg. Stir the batter with a spoon, add 1 tablespoon butter and the yeast, and continue to mix until a really smooth batter is obtained. Cover the bowl with a napkin and put it in a warm place, sheltered from draughts, for 1 hour until the batter has doubled in volume.

Clarify 4 tablespoons (5 tablespoons) butter and use to grease the bottom of a large heavy griddle or skillet and also the insides of some 7-cm (3-in) rings. Place 3 or 4 rings on the griddle over a moderate heat. Drop 1 tablespoon batter into each ring: it spreads immediately and fills the ring. When the crumpets begin to bubble, turn them over with a palette knife (spatula), then lightly brown the other side for 1–2 minutes. Place the crumpets on a dish and cover them with foil. Butter the rings and the griddle again and continue making crumpets until the batter is used up. Toast before serving.

crustaceans CRUSTACÉS

See *shellfish*.

crystallized (candied) fruit FRUITS CONFITS

Whole fruit or pieces of fruit preserved in sugar syrup. By putting the fruit into increasingly concentrated syrup solutions, the syrup gradually replaces the water in the fruit. The concentration of the syrup depends on the type, size, and origin of the fruit. It is heated to precise temperatures, so that it neither crystallizes nor caramelizes. The impregnation must be progressive so that the fruit flesh does not break or shrivel up.

The method is described by Olivier de Serres in his *Théâtre d'agriculture* (1600). But the reputation of the crystallized fruits of Apt was established as long ago as the 14th century, their manufacture having begun at the start of the Avignon papacy (1309). In the Middle Ages, crystallized fruits, then known as *épices de chambre*, were very popular, especially plums, apricots, pistachios, pine kernels, and filberts.

In theory, any fruit can be crystallized, but the process works better for some than others in practice. Besides whole fruit or fruit slices, it is also possible to use angelica stems, the peel of citrus fruits (citron, orange, lemon), and even certain flowers (particularly violets).

The fruit is picked before it is fully ripe so that it has plenty of flavour but will not disintegrate. Then it is blanched (except strawberries and apricots), cooled, and drained. The sugaring process starts with a light syrup, which is then made more and more concentrated; the syrup is heated in a copper pan. Between each step, the fruit rests in its syrup in an earthenware terrine. The duration of the process varies from a few soakings for bigarreau cherries to a dozen or so for large fruit, which takes a month or two. This traditional method is always used for apricots, strawberries, plums, pears, figs, pineapples, and small green oranges; less fragile fruit (such as melon and bigarreau cherries), citrus peel, and angelica are crystallized continuously in batteries of vats, taking, on average, six days to complete.

Crystallized fruit may be sold plain or glazed with sugar, either loose or in packaged assortments. Glazing improves the appearance of the fruit, makes it less sticky and better to handle, and prolongs its shelf life (up to six months away from heat). The glazing process involves coating the fruit with a concentrated syrup just when it has started to crystallize; it is then cooled and drained. Some fruit is reconstituted; for example, large crystallized strawberries can be hollowed out and filled with smaller crystallized strawberries, and stoned (pitted) apricots are filled with crystallized apricot pulp.

In the 19th century, the Auvergne was the leading area for crystallizing fruit; nowadays it has been overshadowed by the south of France. Apt, a traditional Mecca for lovers of these delicacies, exports to the whole world. Dauphiné and Provence are also noted for crystallized fruit, while Clermont-Ferrand remains the specialist town for the glazed varieties. Privas is the capital for marrons glacés.

Although widely known as confectionery items, crystallized fruits are also used in baking, for certain cakes (fruit cakes, brioches), and also for ice creams. When diced, they are used to decorate desserts and puddings (cherries, angelica, and citron in particular). In Great Britain, candied peel is an ingredient of mincemeat, for mince pies.

cucumber CONCOMBRE

The fruit of an annual climbing plant of the gourd family, which may be eaten raw or cooked.

Originating in the foothills of the Himalayas, where it once grew wild, the cucumber has been cultivated in India for more than 3000 years. It was introduced into Egypt and carefully cultivated by the Hebrews in Galilee. Pliny recounts that the Romans and Greeks were very fond of cucumber. In France, cucumber was eaten during the reign of Charlemagne, but it was La Quintinie who organized its cultivation under cover, so that it could be served at Louis XIV's table as early as April. It is long and cylindrical in shape, with firm watery pale green flesh, which is crisp, cool, and slightly bitter to the taste; its fine green skin is shiny and usually smooth.

□ **Varieties** There are several varieties of cucumber, classified in two types – those grown exclusively in greenhouses, known as Dutch, and those cultivated either in the open or under cover, known as ridge; they differ more in size, shape, and shade of green than in taste.

The cucumber is very watery (96% water) and has a low calorific value (12 Cal per 100 g), but it contains minerals and vitamins A and C. It should be bought very fresh and firm, never wrinkled. It is often peeled, since its skin can be quite bitter. When served raw, it is sometimes salted and drained to make it more digestible and get rid of any bitterness; on the other hand, the flesh becomes soft and less aromatic; careful draining prevents the water it produces from affecting the flavour of the seasoning (tarragon dressing, cream, or yogurt, for example).

Cucumber can also be eaten cooked, either baked in the oven, sautéed in butter, or else cooked *au gratin*. Served in its own juice or in a sauce, it can accompany meat or fish. It can also be stuffed, either raw or cooked. Cucumber is just as popular in northern and eastern European cookery (sweet-and-sour cucumber, cold Russian soups) as in Mediterranean countries (minted cucumber, gazpacho, cucumber *à la grecque*, mixed salads).

RECIPES

Preparation of cucumbers PRÉPARATION DES CONCOMBRES *For hot dishes*: peel the cucumbers, split in half lengthwise, and remove the seeds; cut the flesh into regular-sized chunks, and then again into segments; plunge into boiling water for 2 minutes to blanch them, then drain.

For cold dishes: peel the cucumbers,

split in half lengthwise, and remove the seeds; they can then either be kept intact for stuffing, cut into segments, or else simply cut into semicircular slices or quarters; the flesh can also be cut into circular slices without splitting lengthwise.

COLD DISHES

Cold cucumber soup POTAGE FROID AU CONCOMBRE Peel a large cucumber, remove the seeds, and cut into small pieces. Peel 12 small new onions and cut into quarters. Chop these vegetables with a food processor and put them into a blender with the same quantity of low-fat cottage cheese and some salt and pepper: the purée obtained should be well seasoned. Place in the refrigerator until ready to serve. Then dilute the purée with iced water to obtain the consistency of a fairly thick soup and sprinkle with chopped chives or parsley.

Cucumber salad SALADE DE CONCOMBRE Cut the cucumbers into semicircular slices. Add a well-seasoned vinaigrette generously flavoured with herbs (parsley, chervil, chives) or roughly chopped fresh mint leaves. This salad can be served as an hors d'oeuvre, or to accompany cold white meat or fish.

Cucumber stuffed with crab CONCOMBRES FARCIS AU CRABE Split in two and hollow out 3 medium-sized cucumbers of regular shape. Sprinkle with fine salt and leave to sweat for about 1 hour. Mash 250 g (½ lb, 1 cup) crabmeat (fresh or tinned) and dice some fennel finely (enough for 3 tablespoons, ¼ cup). Also dice very finely 150 g (5 oz) cooked ham heel (rind). Make some mayonnaise with 1 egg yolk, 2 teaspoons mustard, and ¼ litre (8 fl oz, 1 cup) oil; add salt, pepper, and 1 tablespoon each of vinegar and tomato ketchup. Mix together the mayonnaise, crabmeat, fennel, and ham. Adjust the seasoning. Drain the cucumber halves well and fill with the stuffing. Keep in a cool place; when ready to serve, sprinkle the cucumbers with chopped herbs and arrange on lettuce leaves.

Instead of mayonnaise, double (heavy) cream flavoured with tomato ketchup, lemon juice, and cayenne can be used, and shelled prawns (shrimps) can be substituted for the crabmeat.

HOT DISHES

Buttered cucumber CONCOMBRES ÉTUVÉS AU BEURRE Place blanched segments of cucumber into a sauté pan with some butter (50 g per kg (1 oz, 2 tablespoons per lb) cucumber), salt, pepper, and 2 tablespoons (3 tablespoons) water. Begin by boiling fast, then cover and simmer very gently for about 30 minutes. Just before serving, add a fresh piece of butter, stir, pour into a vegetable dish, and sprinkle with chopped herbs. Buttered cucumber can be served with poultry and white fish.

Cucumbers with cream CONCOMBRES À LA CRÈME Cut the cucumber flesh into segments and blanch. Grease a sauté pan, add the pieces of cucumber with some salt and pepper, cover, and cook very gently for about 10 minutes; then add some heated cream (2 dl per kg (6 tablespoons, scant ½ cup per lb) cucumber flesh) and continue cooking uncovered. The cucumber can also, after salting and draining, be cooked *au gratin* or served with Mornay sauce.

Stuffed cucumber CONCOMBRES FARCIS Peel 2 medium regular-shaped cucumbers, split them in half lengthwise, and remove the seeds and a little of the flesh. Prepare an *à gratin* forcemeat. Grease a gratin dish or, better still, line it with pieces of pork rind with the fat removed. Cover with a layer of finely chopped carrots and onions and sprinkle with a little chopped parsley. Fill the cucumber halves with the stuffing and arrange them in the dish. Add beef or chicken stock until it comes two-thirds of the way up the cucumber boats.

Bring to boiling point on the top of the cooker, then transfer to the oven and cook at about 225 C (425 F, gas 7) for 35 minutes. Cover with aluminium foil as soon as the top of the stuffing starts to dry out. Arrange the cucumbers on a serving dish and keep warm. Reduce the cooking liquid to 2 dl (7 fl oz, ¾ cup), thicken with *beurre manié* (kneaded butter), pour over the cucumber, and serve very hot.

Cuisinier Gascon

An anonymous cookery book, published in 1740. It is thought that the author was the very person to whom the book is dedicated, namely, the Prince de Dombes (1700–55). He was the grandson of Louis XIV and Madame de Montespan, who had the opportunity of exercising his talents as a cook for Louis XV on many occasions. He was credited with introducing Gascon cuisine into the sphere of gastronomic literature. The recipes included in the book given an indication of the author's taste for Italian cuisine, and a large proportion are devoted to such regional dishes as *soupe à la jambe de bois* ('wooden-leg soup'). More elaborate recipes with picturesque names are also included: *hachis d'oeufs sans malice* ('chopped eggs without malice'), *poulet en chauve-souris* ('bat-like chicken'), and *veau en crottes d'âne roulées à la Neuteau* ('veal as rolled-up donkey droppings à la Nantua').

cul-de-poule

A hemispherical basin with a rolled rim. It lacks a handle but is fitted with small ring to hang it up when not in use. It is used mainly for whisking egg whites or for holding mixtures which are cooked over a pan of hot water. Traditionally, the cul-de-poule was made of untinned copper, but it is now usually made of stainless steel.

culinary exhibitions and shows

SALONS ET EXPOSITIONS CULINAIRES

Until 1914, there were two rival exhibitions in Paris, dating back to the beginning of the century: the Salon Culinaire and the Exposition Internationale d'Alimentation et d'Hygiène. Consisting mainly of demonstrations of very elaborate and decorative dishes, this type of exhibition is rarely found today. However, the food industry still organizes shows to demonstrate new materials, products, and services.

cultivateur

A clear soup made with vegetables and salted belly of pork (salt pork). It is the 'restaurant' version of the classic vegetable and bacon soup. It is served with diced lean bacon, which may be placed on thin slices of bread.

RECIPE

Potage cultivateur Cut 2–3 small carrots and a small turnip into large dice; prepare 6 tablespoons (½ cup) diced leeks (white part only) and 2 tablespoons (3 tablespoons) diced onions. Season with salt and a pinch of sugar. Cook in 50 g (2 oz, ¼ cup) butter in a covered pan. Moisten with 1.5 litres (2¾ pints, 3¼ pints) white consommé and cook for 1¼ hours. About 25 minutes before serving, add 150 g (5 oz, ¾ cup) sliced potatoes and 75 g (3 oz) well-blanched diced bacon.

The potatoes can be replaced by rice.

Cumberland sauce

A traditional English sweet-and-sour sauce that is usually served cold with venison, braised ham, mutton, or roast or braised duckling. It is made with port, orange and lemon juice and zest, and redcurrant jelly.

RECIPE

Cumberland sauce Remove the zest from an orange and a lemon and cut into fine strips; cook 1 generous tablespoon of the zest very gently in 2 dl (7 fl oz, ¾ cup) port for about 20 minutes. Remove the zest and add to the port 2 tablespoons (3 tablespoons) redcurrant jelly, then a pinch of cinnamon and a pinch of cayenne. Mix, bring to the boil, add the juice of the orange and lemon, then strain. Mix in the cooked strips of zest.

cumin

An aromatic plant with long spindle-shaped seeds that are used as a condiment and a flavouring. They have a hot, piquant, and slightly bitter taste. Cumin is cultivated today in Mediterranean countries, and also in Germany, the Soviet Union, and even as far north as Norway. There are biblical references to its use in soup and bread, and the Romans used it to flavour sauces and grilled (broiled) fish and to preserve meat. It was often included in the recipes of the Middle Ages (see *cominée*). Today, it is a classic condiment for bread (especially in eastern Europe) and is also used in certain preparations of cold meat and cheeses, such as Munster cheese.

RECIPES

Aubergines (eggplants) with cumin AUBERGINES AU CUMIN Prepare a court-bouillon with ½ litre (17 fl oz, 2 cups) water, the juice of a large lemon, 1 dl (6 tablespoons, scant ½ cup) olive oil, 1 teaspoon coriander seeds, 1 tablespoon cumin seeds, 12 peppercorns, a large bouquet garni, and a generous pinch of salt. Peel 4 large aubergines, cut the flesh into small even-sized cubes, and sprinkle with lemon juice. Boil them in the court-bouillon for about 10 minutes, remove, and drain. Remove the bouquet garni from the court-bouillon, strain the liquid, and reduce by half. (2 tablespoons (3 tablespoons) tomato purée may be added to the court-bouillon). Pour it over the aubergines and refrigerate before serving.

Cumin allumettes ALLUMETTES AU CUMIN Roll out a strip of puff pastry to a thickness of about 5 mm (¼ in) and about 7–8 cm (3 in) wide. Cut this strip into 1-cm (½-in) strips and arrange them on a baking tray (sheet). Glaze with egg yolk, sprinkle with cumin seeds, and bake in a very hot oven until golden.

cup TASSE

A drinking receptacle manufactured in various shapes, sizes, and materials and provided with a handle.

Cups are made of porcelain, faïence, earthenware, glass, plastic, or even metal. In former times, cups were made without a handle, or with two handles, or even with a lid and they were not always accompanied by a saucer. In the 15th century, cups were used for both hot and cold drinks. Peasants drank from plain or engraved wooden cups. Before the French Revolution, the wine provided in cabarets was served in cups made of heavy faïence. Decorative cups, usually made of hard stone mounted in gold or silver, were embellished with precious stones. From the 18th century onwards, faïence and porcelain services became very widespread, but individual cups were also made, such as the *trembleuse* (the base of which is placed on a saucer with a slightly larger centre) and the *tasse à moustaches*, with an inner lip that enabled men to drink from it without wetting their moustaches.

There are four traditional sizes of cup: breakfast cups, tea cups, coffee cups, and mocha cups. There are also cups for drinking chocolate, broth, and tisanes. The consommé cup is shallow and wide and has two handles. It is generally placed on a small matching plate.

cup (drink)

A mixed drink usually with one ingredient used as a base and often prepared for several servings. Cups may be made by macerating fruit (such as peeled citrus fruits, cherries, pears, peaches, or bananas) in liqueurs, spirits, wine, or sometimes cider, beer, champagne, or sparkling wines. Cups were enormously popular in the 19th century and, more recently, for parties given for young people, because ideally a cup is a thirst quencher and not usually high in alcohol. Pimms is perhaps the best-known commercial cup. See also *Bishop, mulled wine, sangria*.

RECIPES

Cider cup (makes about 15 glasses) Mix together 1 glass of Calvados, 1 glass of Maraschino, 1 glass of Curaçao, and 1 litre (1¾ pints, 4¼ cups) sweet cider. Add some ice cubes, slices of peeled orange, and soda water. Stir gently and decorate with thin slices of fruit.

Saint James's cup (makes about 15 glasses) Dissolve 200 g (7 oz, 1 cup) sugar in ¼ litre (8 fl oz, 1 cup) water. Add ½ litre (17 fl oz, 2 cups) Cognac, an equal quantity of rum, 1 glass of Curaçao, 1 litre (1¾ pints, 4¼ cups) very strong cold tea, and some crushed ice. Mix with 1 bottle of dry sparkling cider just before serving.

Sauternes cup (makes about 10 glasses) Mix together 1 glass of Curaçao, 1 glass of Cognac, about 12 cherries in brandy, 1 bottle of Sauternes, and a little soda water. Add a few slices of lemon, cucumber peel, and ice cubes.

cupbearer ÉCHANSON

An officer in charge of serving drinks to kings and princes under the Ancien Régime. The position of cupbearer, which was instituted in France during Carolingian times, can be traced back to the Byzantine court. This was one of the most prestigious and lucrative posts concerned with serving the royal food and drink, but in practice the cupbearer himself only fulfilled this function at coronations.

The *grand échanson* ('grand cupbearer') was a high-ranking officer of the court, who had the privilege of adding two silver-gilt flagons stamped with the king's arms to his own heraldic arms. The *échansonnerie de l'hostel du roi* was the staff of cupbearers, which varied in numbers depending on the epoch. In 1285, besides the grand cupbearer, there were four ordinary cupbearers, two butlers (to receive the wine), two cellar-men (in charge of the cellars and barrels), two bottle-men (to prepare the drinks), a potter, and a clerk (for the accounts). Under the reign of Louis XIV, there were 12 *chefs par quartier* (head officers), four assistants, four butlers (for receiving the wine and looking after the cellars and the plate), one cellar master, four wine runners, and two leaders of the horse, who went with the king on his hunting expeditions (loaded with all his requirements), as well as a number of underlings.

Curaçao

A liqueur based on sweet or bitter oranges (originally it was made from the dried peel of the bitter oranges from the island of Curaçao, off the west coast of Venezuela). It is now made by many liqueur houses and often sold as 'triple sec'; it may be colourless, yellow, or orange (or even blue). Curaçao is used in various cocktails and also for culinary purposes, notably for flavouring cakes, pastries, soufflés, and above all, for making crêpes Suzette. The best-known form of this popular liqueur is the one evolved by Cointreau, one of the top-selling liqueurs of the world.

| RECIPE

Curaçao (household recipe) Macerate 250 g (9 oz, 1½ cups) dried orange peel and the grated rind of 2 Seville (bitter) oranges in 3 litres (5 pints, 6½ pints) alcohol in a large hermetically sealed jar for 1 month. Make a syrup with 1.25 litres (2¼ pints, 5¾ cups) water and 2.5 kg (5½ lb, 11 cups) sugar. Strain the maceration, mix with the syrup, bottle, and leave to mature. If liked, the liqueur may be coloured with a little caramel.

curd CAILLÉ

Milk coagulated either by the action of rennet or by natural fermentation. Curdling is the first stage in the manufacture of cheese. In the French countryside, naturally, curdled milk has always been a standard dessert, sometimes forming an essential part of the dinner. It may be eaten sweetened or mixed with fruit, or savoury and seasoned with herbs. The savoury dish is usually accompanied by boiled potatoes, particularly in Brittany (where it is called *lait cuit* (cooked milk) or *marri*) and in Lorraine (where it is called *matton* or *brocq*). In Corsica, it is the custom to give a young bride on the threshold of her new home a bowl of goats' milk curdled with the stomach (*caillette*) of a suckling kid.

Curnonsky (born *Maurice Edmond Sailland*)

French writer, journalist, and gastronome (born Angers, 1872; died Paris, 1956). After secondary-school education, he went on to study literature at the Sorbonne. The attractions of journalism speedily enticed him away from a university career, and in 1892 he began to frequent newspaper offices and literary circles. He made friends wherever he went.

On the advice of one of these friends, Alphonse Allais, the young Sailland decided to choose a pseudonym. It was the period of Franco-Russian entente. 'Why not Sky?' someone suggested. He replied, translating this suggestion into

Latin, 'Cur non Sky?' The pseudonym had been found.

Simon Arbellot, his biographer, gives the following description of the life and career of this unrivalled prince-elect of gastronomes.

'Tracing Curnonsky's life through the early part of the century means reliving all the gay ostentation of the boulevard and breathing again the perfumed air of what is called *la belle époque*. He was to be found wherever imagination triumphed over conformity. P. J. Toulet and Jean de Tinan were friends of his; Willy invited him into his circle and Curnonsky was later to become one of his favourite collaborators. Everyone knew that the old master humorist, author of so many licentious novels, had the knack of surrounding himself with young intellectuals who had fun ghosting for him. *Un petit vieux bien propre* is attributed to Curnonsky; Toulet is supposed to have written a part of *Maugis en ménage*; and the two together wrote a great many now-forgotten works signed "Willy", the titles of which have a strong *fin de siècle* savour: *Le Bréviaire des courtisanes*, *Le Métier d'amant*, *Jeu de prince*, etc.

'Curnonsky was to be found wherever there was a meeting of minds. Léon Daudet, in his *Souvenirs*, gives us a picture of him as a regular visitor to Weber's, joining in the debates of Forain, Maxime Dethomas, Adrien Hébrard, Maurice de Fleury, while the slight and vaguely disturbing shadow of Marcel Proust hovered in the background. He was also to be found at Maxim's conversing with Feydeau and Maurice Bertrand. He used to join Paul Fort occasionally in the evenings at the Closerie des Lilas, but secretly he preferred the poetry of George Fourest and Raoul Ponchon to symbolism.

'One day he yielded to the temptations of travel and distant horizons. On his return he wrote the account of the African expeditions of the duc de Montpensier. He was to become a skilful 'biographer' of this hunting prince. He moved on to China where the cuisine of the country left an indelible imprint on his mind; he proclaimed it to be the best of the world.

'This somewhat bohemian way of life was, nonetheless, marked by a consider-able literary output. Novels, short stories, an anthology, and collections of anecdotes made the name of Curnonsky a familiar one in the press and in the publishing world. For Dranem he wrote *Une Riche Nature*, for Charles Barret, *Un Homme qui a bien tourné*.

'Writing was his passion. And his masters? First and foremost was La Bruyère, whose advice he loved to repeat to his young friends: 'If you wish to say it is raining, then *say* it is raining.' The Anatole France (the Anatole France of *Jacques Tournebroche* rather than of *M. Bergeret*), for the clarity of his old-fashioned methodical style. I have heard Curnonsky cry out in indignation at the sight of a solecism. Language was no mere form of words to him.

'Then came the gastronomic period, together with princedom and public acclaim. Fifty or so academies and clubs fought for his presidency and solicited his presence at their feasts. 'Cur' had always loved his food. The Anjou wine and the rillauds of his childhood had trained his appetite, and while the Rue Jacob period – so discreetly touched on by Madame Colette – seems to have been somewhat disappointing in this respect, the Maxim and Weber era followed closely on its heels. Later, with the collaboration of an epicure and great amphitryon, Marcel Rouff, Curnonsky undertook what amounted to a tourist crusade. It was to this cause that he began to devote all his time. *La France gastronomique* (32 volumes, interrupted at the 28th by the death of his collaborator) is a monument of erudition, and a tribute to the richness of our soil. There are also dozens of cookery books, each one no less a literary than a gastronomic delight.

'A public referendum in May 1927 crowned him Prince of Gastronomes, and there was no respite for him after that. He went from *disnées* to light snacks, inaugurations and enthronements, *tastevins* and barbecues without a break. Wherever he went there was a table laid ready for him, the finest wines placed at his disposal.

'On 23 March 1928 he founded the Academy of Gastronomes, modelled on the Académie française, with 40 seats and with symbolic titles ranging from Epicure to Talleyrand. His friends joined him – Maeterlinck in Vergilius Maro's seat, Marcel Rouff in that of Honoré de Balzac. For himself he chose the seat of Brillat-Savarin, in whose honour he gave an address.

'Curnonsky enjoyed a sprightly old age. Honoured and fêted wherever he went, he had the satisfaction of seeing his young disciples carrying on his good work and realizing the idea that was so close to his heart, that of linking the route to the good restaurant to the interests of tourism. He died as the result of an accident in 1956.'

currants

See *dried vine fruits.*

curry CARI

A dish flavoured and coloured with a mixture of spices (curry powder) of Indian origin.

In India the ingredients of curry powder vary according to the individual cook, the region, caste, and customs. In Europe the mixtures were prepared to fixed formulas during the era of the East India Company and sold by the Dutch and British; the first were published at the beginning of the 18th century. Beauvilliers proposed one in 1814. In 1889, at the Universal Paris Exhibition, the composition of curry powder was set by decree: 34 g (1.2 oz) tamarind; 44 g (1.5 oz) onion; 20 g (0.7 oz) coriander; 5 g (0.17 oz) chilli pepper; 3 g (0.1 oz) turmeric; 2 g (0.08 oz) cumin; 3 g (0.1 oz) fenugreek; 2 g (0.08 oz) pepper; 2 g (0.08 oz) mustard.

Nowadays, curries are categorized as mild, hot, and very hot. A standard curry powder would include, for example, turmeric, coriander, cumin, pepper (essential), cloves, cardamom, ginger, nutmeg, tamarind, and chilli pepper. It may be further seasoned with fennel, caraway, ajowan, ginseng, dried basil, mustard seeds, and cinnamon. The spices are finely powdered and stored in fragrant wooden boxes. In Sri Lanka, coconut milk or yogurt is added. In Thailand, dried shrimp paste is added. In India, curries are oily, liquid, dry, or powdery, and their colour ranges from white to golden-brown, or from red to green. In the East, curry may be one of many vegetarian dishes (based on chickpea flour, lentils, and rice), as well as meat or fish dishes. In the West, curries are mainly prepared with pork, chicken, or lamb, but the Indian curry sauce has many other uses. There are three methods for preparing a curry.

● *Indian style* – Meat, cut into pieces, is browned in a pan with sliced onions and shallots, then removed and replaced with a stew of tomatoes, curry powder (sometimes with coconut milk), and spices which are simmered before replacing the meat plus a little stock and simmering again.

● *Chinese style* – Meat, cut up into very small pieces, is marinated with curry mixture and soy sauce, then placed in a pan containing lard and browned with the spices.

● *English style* – This is a standard stew of meat (cut in pieces and sprinkled with flour then curry powder) with stock added.

Curry mixture can also be used to season seafood pilafs, bisques, tomato soup, lentil stew, vegetable dishes (salsify, sweet potatoes), mayonnaise for fish, and flavoured butters.

RECIPES

Chicken curry CARI DE POULET (from Mont-Bry's recipe) Draw, singe, and clean a medium-sized chicken, then cut it into quarters and divide each quarter into 3 or 4 pieces (make sure the chicken bones are cut cleanly, without splintering). In a flameproof casserole containing lard or butter, cook 2 medium onions, 100 g (4 oz, ½ cup) ham, and 2 peeled dessert apples, all chopped and seasoned with crushed garlic, thyme, bay leaf, cinnamon, cardamom, and powdered mace. Then add the chicken pieces and cook until they are firm, stirring them in the mixture without letting them get too coloured.

Now sprinkle in 2 teaspoons curry powder. Add 2 tomatoes, peeled, crushed, and deseeded, and mix well. Moisten with 2.5 dl (8 fl oz, 1 cup) coconut milk (or almond milk). Simmer with the lid on for about 35 minutes. 10 minutes before serving, add 1.5 dl (¼ pint, ⅔ cup) fresh double (heavy) cream and the juice of a lemon. Continue to reduce the sauce until the desired consistency is achieved.

Arrange the chicken pieces in a dish

and serve with rice prepared as follows: boil 250 g (9 oz, 1¼ cups) rice for 15 minutes in salted water, stirring often; drain, and wash several times in cold water. Empty onto a metal plate, wrap in a towel, and dry in a very cool oven (110 c, 225 F, gas ¼) for 15 minutes.

Chicken curry can also be made using the recipe for lamb curry.

Lamb curry CARI D'AGNEAU Mix 1 tablespoon freshly grated root ginger (or 1 teaspoon ground ginger), a pinch of saffron, 3 tablespoons oil, a large pinch of cayenne, salt, and pepper. In this mixture, roll 1.5 kg (3 lb) neck or shoulder of lamb cut up into pieces, and leave to marinate for 1 hour. Peel and crush 3 large tomatoes. Brown the pieces of meat in a large saucepan containing 25 g (1 oz, 2 tablespoons) lard, then remove from the pan.

In the same fat, fry 4 large sliced onions until golden, then add the crushed tomatoes, 2 teaspoons curry powder, 3 finely chopped cloves of garlic, and a bouquet garni. Leave to brown for 5 minutes. Peel and grate an acid apple, add to the pan, and stir for 2–3 minutes. Replace the meat in the pan, stir, add a small cup of coconut milk or semi-skimmed milk, cover, and leave to finish cooking gently for about 40 minutes. Adjust the seasoning.

Serve this curry very hot with boiled rice, cashew nuts, raisins, and pineapple and banana dice flavoured with lemon juice, all in separate dishes.

Monkfish curry à la créole CARI DE LOTTE À LA CRÉOLE Cut about 1 kg (2¼ lb) monkfish into pieces, fry in oil until golden, then drain. In the same oil, fry 100 g (4 oz, 1 cup) finely chopped onion until golden then add 2 or 3 peeled crushed tomatoes, a pinch of saffron, 1 tablespoon freshly grated root ginger (or 1 teaspoon ground ginger), 2 finely chopped cloves of garlic, a bouquet garni, a piece of orange peel, and 1 teaspoon curry powder. Stir over a medium heat for 5–6 minutes, then add 250 ml (8 fl oz, 1 cup) hot water, cayenne, salt, and pepper. Cover and leave to cook very gently for 30 minutes. Remove the bouquet garni and orange peel, and serve with rice *à la créole*.

Cussy (Louis, Marquis de)

One of the wittiest gastronomes of the early 19th century (born Coutances, 1766; died Paris, 1837). He held the post of prefect of the palace under Napoleon I. If his great friend Grimond de La Reynière is to be believed, Cussy invented 366 different ways of preparing chicken – a different dish for each day, even in a leap year.

In 1843 he published *Les Classiques de la table*, in which he devoted many pages to the history of gastronomy. He also wrote several articles. As principal steward of the emperor's household, he looked after the wardrobe, the furniture, and the provisions of the court. When Louis XVIII succeeded Napoleon, it is said that at first he refused to have anything to do with Cussy, but that later, learning that he was the creator of strawberries *à la Cussy*, he gave him a post of responsibility.

Chefs have dedicated several recipes to him, including a garnish for meat or poultry consisting of artichoke hearts filled with mushroom purée, cooked *au gratin*, topped with cocks' kidneys and fine slices of truffle, and coated with a port or Madeira sauce.

RECIPE

Potatoes à la Cussy POMMES DE TERRE CUSSY (from Plumerey's recipe) Take big yellow potatoes, cut off the 2 ends, and cut them with a special cutter (called a *colonne*) into cork-shaped chunks, about 2½ cm (1 in) in diameter. Cut them into slices 5 mm (¼ in) thick. Dry on a cloth to absorb all water. Put them into a big pan with 225 g (8 oz, 1 cup) hot clarified butter and cook gently so that they colour without sticking to the pan or drying up. In the meantime, slice 6–8 truffles, toss them in butter with 1 tablespoon Madeira and a piece of chicken aspic the size of a walnut. When the potatoes are cooked and acquire a fine golden colour, remove them from the heat and add the truffles and the juice of half a lemon and serve piping hot.

custard

See *creams and custards*.

custard apple ANONE

The fruit of a tree that originated in Peru and is now cultivated in many tropical countries. Similar fruits produced by related species include the soursop (or bullock's heart) and the cinnamon apple. The custard apple is imported from the Near East, Central America, or the south of Spain, and is sold in French shops from October to February. It is the size of an orange, with a rough green skin, which turns blackish-brown when the fruit is properly ripe. The flesh is white and juicy and has a sweet-sour flavour with a rose-like scent. The chilled fruit is cut in half, the black seeds are removed, and it is usually eaten with a small spoon. It can also be used in sorbets and fruit salads.

custard marrow

CHAYOTE

A species of climbing gourd which is eaten as a vegetable; it is called *christophine* or *brionne* in the West Indies and *chouchoute* in Madagascar and Polynesia. Originating from Mexico, where its young shoots are eaten like asparagus, the custard marrow is cultivated in tropical countries and in north Africa. It resembles a green or white pear, with a fairly rough skin and several spines, and is as big as two fists, with deep longitudinal ribs. Its firm homogenous white flesh does not have a very pronounced flavour, but it is sweet and has a high water content; it has a low calorific value (12 Cal per 100 g).

The custard marrow keeps for a long time. Before completely ripe, it may be consumed raw in salads, peeled, cored, and finely sliced. It is especially common in Caribbean cookery. Not fully ripe until it starts to germinate, the gourd is boiled and puréed for making acras and very fine gratins. It is an essential ingredient in *mange-mêle* (ratatouille with streaky bacon and coconut milk), and accompanies spiced dishes such as kid colombo or pork curry (it is then diced for sautéing or braising). It may also be made into a soufflé.

RECIPES

Custard marrows à la martiniquaise
CHAYOTES À LA MARTINIQUAISE

Press some boiled custard marrows in a cloth to extract the maximum amount of water and mix this pulp with bread soaked in milk. Brown some peeled and finely sliced green onions in butter, then blend with the mixture of bread and custard marrow. Season and spread out in a gratin dish, smoothing the top. Moisten with olive oil, sprinkle with fresh breadcrumbs, and reheat in the oven.

Custard marrows braised in gravy
CHAYOTES BRAISÉES AU JUS Divide the custard marrows into quarters and cut into lozenge shapes; blanch for 5 minutes in salted water and drain. Cover a shallow frying pan (skillet) with bacon rinds, carrots, and onions peeled and cut into rings, and arrange the custard marrows on top. Season with salt and pepper and cover with stock made from clarified bouillon. Cook quite gently, first with the lid on, then without. When the liquid is three-quarters reduced, add some meat juice and leave to simmer for a few minutes. Drain the custard marrows and keep them hot in the serving dish. Strain the pan juice, add butter, and pour it over the custard marrows. Sprinkle with chopped parsley.

cutlet CÔTELETTE

See *chop or cutlet*.

A shaped cutlet (*côtelette composée*) consists of boned minced meat, poultry, or fish that is bound with a sauce and shaped into a cutlet. It may then be dipped in egg and breadcrumbs, and fried in butter. Egg cutlets are made in a similar way. Hard-boiled (hardcooked) eggs are chopped, bound with a reduced béchamel sauce containing raw egg yolks, coated with breadcrumbs, and fried. Mushrooms, ham, or pickled tongue can be added. Shaped cutlets are served as a hot starter.

RECIPE

Shaped cutlets CÔTELETTES COMPOSÉES Chop cooked poultry, game, or meat into small dice or reduce to a very dry paste. Slowly and gradually add a thick béchamel sauce (with or without tomato purée), or a thick Mornay sauce, or an allemande sauce.

The resulting mixture must have an even consistency. Add some chopped herbs (parsley, tarragon, mint, etc.). Roll out the mixture evenly on a greased surface and allow it to cool completely. Divide the mixture into portions weighing about 75 g (3 oz). Shape each portion into a cutlet, dip in beaten egg with a little added oil, and coat with fresh breadcrumbs. Cook them in clarified butter. To imitate the shape of a cutlet, stick a piece of macaroni decorated with a frill into the narrow end. Serve garnished with vegetables and quarters of lemon.

cuttlefish   SEICHE

A mollusc related to the squid, which is about 30 cm (12 in) long and lives on weedy coastal sea beds. Its body resembles a greyish oval bag with a mauve sheen and it has a fairly large head with ten irregular tentacles, two of which are very long. The 'bag' is almost completely surrounded with fins and encloses a hard part – the cuttlebone. The cuttlefish has several French nicknames (*margate*, *sépia*, *supion*, etc.), which are used in certain regional dishes. Like the squid, the cuttlefish has an ink sac, which means that it can be cooked in its ink as it is in Spain (*ens u tinta*). Cuttlefish, which are sold whole or cleaned, are cooked like squid, but the flesh is quite tough and has to be beaten vigorously. The Romans were very fond of it and it is still eaten in Italy, Spain, and southwestern France, especially stuffed or *à l'américaine*.

cuvée

The contents of a wine vat (*cuve*), and hence a blending of various vats or casks into a harmonious whole. The term is used particularly in Champagne, where the ingredients of the cuvée come from different wines of different vineyard plots, different grapes, and, from the nonvintage wines, of different years.

Terms associated with this word include *tête de cuvée* and *première cuvée*, but the legality of their use depends on the region's laws.

Cyprus wines

VINS DE CHYPRE

Since ancient times, the island of Cyprus, situated in the eastern Mediterranean off the Turkish and Syrian coasts, has been known for its vineyards. Egyptians, Greeks, and Romans in turn enjoyed its wines, and the Crusaders spread their fame throughout the West. The most famous of Cyprus wines, Commandaria, is a deep brown dessert wine. It was named after the *commanderies* into which the vineyards were divided. That of the Knights Templars was outstanding. How many wines can boast of bearing the same name for eight centuries?

Today, the Cyprus vineyards are on the foothills of the mountains and the wines are a major product of the island. The red table wines, which account for much of the production, are based on the Mavron vine. Robust, strongly coloured, and with a high tannin content, they are enjoyed by both the people of Cyprus and holidaymakers. Cyprus also produces a wide range of other wines for export as well as home consumption. The dry fresh rosés may be made from the Mavron, and are often referred to as Kokkineli; they are drunk chilled. The white wines are dry with a flinty taste; they are produced in small quantities, some from the Xynisteri vine, and the best-known makes are Aphrodite and Arsinoé. Commandaria is traditionally made in huge stone jars, from a basic 'mother' or culture, but nowadays most is produced in the modern wineries of Limassol and Paphos. Cyprus Muscat wines are also made: in export markets, the sherry-style fortified wines are well known and many attain true quality.

cyrniki or cierniki

Dumplings made with cottage cheese, served as a hot hors d'oeuvre with soured (dairy sour) cream. They may alternatively be poached and served with melted butter, or cooked in timbales with grated cheese and butter. Cyrniki are of Polish origin but also form part of the repertoire of Russian cuisine. The cheese is mixed with eggs and flour (seasoned with salt and pepper) until it forms a soft dough. Small triangles or dics, about 2 cm (¾ in) thick, are cut out of this dough, floured, and then lightly browned in butter in a frying pan (skillet).

dab LIMANDE

Any of several related flatfish found in the North Sea, the English Channel, and the Atlantic, although not further south than the Bay of Biscay. There are several varieties of dab. The true (or European) dab is lozenge-shaped; its upper surface is brownish with orange-yellow spots. The false dab (or red dab) is a rather elongated oval in shape, brownish-grey on the upper surface and light sandy grey underneath. The lemon dab (or lemon sole) is rounder and has a superior flavour; it is reddish-brown with darker spots, and the gills are bordered with an orange line. The American dab is similar to the European species. Dabs are 20–35 cm (8–14 in) long and weigh 180–250 g (6–9 oz). However, 40% of their body weight is lost during cleaning and filleting. They are sold either whole or filleted (also deep-frozen), and are cooked in a similar way to brill.

dacquoise

A traditional gâteau of southwestern France, also called *palois* (the Dacquois are the inhabitants of Dax, the Palois those of Pau). It consists of two or three layers of meringue mixed with almonds (or with almonds and hazelnuts). The layers are sandwiched together with fresh whipped cream or French butter cream, variously flavoured. The base, a variant of *succès*, is light and crisp and should be stored as for meringue. Fresh fruit may be added to the filling, particularly strawberries *à la chantilly*. The top is usually dusted with icing sugar (confectioners' sugar).

RECIPE

Coffee dacquoise DACQUOISE AU CAFÉ Whisk 8 egg whites with a pinch of salt until they form stiff peaks. Then gradually add 200 g (7 oz, scant cup) caster (superfine) sugar and 2 teaspoons vanilla sugar, and continue whisking until the whites are firm and shiny. Gently fold in 150 g (5 oz, 1¼ cups) ground almonds and 80 g (3 oz) blanched chopped hazelnuts. Butter 3 22-cm (8-in) flan rings (pie rings), place them on a buttered baking sheet, and divide the mixture between them. Cook in a moderate oven (160–180 C, 325–350 F, gas 3–4) for about 20 minutes.

Meanwhile prepare a French coffee butter cream (see *creams and custards*) using 250 g (9 oz, generous cup) sugar cooked to the thread stage (see *sugar*) in 1 dl (6 tablespoons, ½ cup) water, 8 egg yolks, 250 g (9 oz, generous cup) butter, and 1 tablespoon coffee essence. When the meringue rounds are cooked, turn them out and allow to cool. Grill (broil) 100 g (4 oz, 1 cup) flaked almonds. Place the coffee cream in a piping bag (pastry bag) fitted with a fluted nozzle and cover 2 of the meringue rounds with a thick layer. Place one above the other and put the third disc on top. Sprinkle the top with the grilled flaked almonds and dust with icing sugar (confectioners' sugar).

daikon or dai-co

A kind of radish, widely cultivated as a vegetable in the Far East, also called Japanese radish or Satsuma radish. Its large fleshy root can grow up to 1 m (3 ft) in length and weigh several kilograms. In Japan it is eaten raw, either cut into slices or strips to garnish salads or grated, particularly to accompany fish. When cooked, daikon has the same uses as turnip; for example, it may be finely sliced in soups. It is also pickled in salt.

daiquiri

A rum cocktail, named after a small village on the Cuban coast near Santiago, where, in the 19th century, the Americans supposedly landed after defeating the Spanish. Generally served in a frosted glass, it may be diluted with mineral water.

RECIPE

Daiquiri Frost a wine glass. Into a cocktail shaker put 1 measure of cane sugar syrup, 2 of lemon juice, 3 of white rum, and 1 tablespoon crushed ice. Shake for several seconds, then pour into the frosted glass.

dal

A Hindi word meaning 'leguminous' and applied to various kinds of peas and beans. Owing to the importance of vegetarian dishes in Indian, Pakistani, and Sinhalese cooking, dal vegetables are major ingredients; they are also good sources of protein.

The three most common are: *mung dal*, green, brown, or red lentils that are eaten fresh, raw in salads, sautéd in *ghee* or butter, mixed with rice, cooked fish, or meat in a ragout, or used as a purée to thicken sauces and seasonings; *urid dal*, which has black beans that are dried, reduced to a powder, and used to make pancakes and purées; and *maisur dal*, small pink lentils that are cooked and ground and used mainly for fritters. Dal, of whichever kind, is prepared by cooking it in water spiced with turmeric, ginger, and chilli (or with cumin and coriander); it is served with onion purée seasoned with mustard seeds. Rice or potatoes and flaked almonds are often added.

dame blanche

Any of various desserts in which white or pale colours predominate. The name applies particularly to vanilla ice cream used as a bombe filling or served with whipped cream and a chocolate sauce to provide contrast; fruit in syrup or alcohol may also be added. Other kinds of dame blanche include a sponge cake filled with cream and crystallized (candied) fruits and completely covered with Italian meringue, a lemon île flottante, and an almond ice cream.

RECIPE

Peaches dame blanche PÊCHES DAME BLANCHE Macerate 4 slices of pineapple in a bowl containing 1 tablespoon Kirsch and an equal quantity of Maraschino. To a saucepan containing ¼ litre (8 fl oz, 1 cup) water, add 250 g (9 oz, generous cup) caster (superfine) sugar and half a vanilla pod (bean) split in two; boil until the mixture becomes syrupy. Peel 2 large peaches and poach gently in the syrup for about 10 minutes, turning them frequently, then remove from the heat.

Prepare some Chantilly cream by whipping 1.5 dl (¼ pint, ⅔ cup) fresh double (heavy) cream with 1 tablespoon milk, 1 tablespoon caster (superfine) sugar, and a little vanilla sugar or essence to taste; chill in the refrigerator Drain the peaches, halve them, and remove the stones (pits). Divide ½ litre (17 fl oz, 2 cups) vanilla ice cream between 4 sundae glasses, add a slice of pineapple and peach half to each, and decorate with a 'turban' of Chantilly cream using a piping bag (pastry bag) fitted with a fluted nozzle. Serve immediately.

dame-jeanne

The French name for a large glass or earthenware vessel holding up to 50 litres (11 gallons, 13 gallons) liquid. Usually encased in basketwork, it was traditionally used to transport wines and spirits. In the Bordeaux region its capacity is about 2.5 litres (4½ pints, 5½ pints) – between a magnum and a double magnum. The close link between this region and England explains how *dame-Jeanne* was corrupted to 'demi-john' in English.

damier

A gâteau made of rum-flavoured Genoese sponge filled with butter cream and covered with praline. The sides are coated with flaked almonds and the top is decorated in a chequerboard pattern.

RECIPE

Damier Make a Genoese sponge cake using 40 g (1½ oz, 3 tablespoons) butter, 3 egg yolks, 90 g (3¼ oz, generous ⅓ cup) caster (superfine) sugar, 90 g (3¼ oz, generous ¾ cup) flour, and a pinch of salt; allow it to rest in its tin for 24 hours. Prepare a syrup by boiling 300 g (11 oz, scant 1½ cups) caster sugar in 3 dl (½ pint, 1¼ cups) water, allow to cool, then add 5 cl (2½ tablespoons, scant ¼ cup) rum.

Prepare a butter cream (see *creams and custards*) using 3 egg yolks, 150 g (5 oz, generous ½ cup) butter, 125 g (4½ oz, scant ⅔ cup) caster sugar, 2 tablespoons water, and 50 g (2 oz) ground praline. Gently melt 250 g (9 oz) chocolate in a bain-marie. Prepare some royal icing (frosting) using 1 egg white and 80 g (3 oz, ¾ cup) icing sugar (confectioners' sugar). Brown some flaked almonds in the oven and roughly chop them.

Cut the sponge into two equal rounds and sprinkle the rum syrup over them. Spread half the butter cream over one of the rounds with a palette knife (spatula). Cover with the second round and decorate this with the rest of the butter cream. Sprinkle the sides of the gâteau with flaked almonds. Using a piping bag (pastry bag), pipe the royal icing over the butter cream to form a chequerboard pattern of 3-cm (1-in) squares. Fill alternate squares with royal icing and the rest with the melted chocolate.

dampfnudeln

A sweet dessert, made in Germany and Alsace, consisting of rounds of leavened dough baked in the oven and served either with compote, fruits in syrup, jam, or vanilla cream; dusted with sugar and cinnamon. It may alternatively be filled with a compote of apricots in rum and folded like a small turnover.

Originally dampfnudeln was a savoury dish (the name means 'steamed noodles'), usually accompanied by green salad.

RECIPE

Dampfnudeln Prepare a leavening dough using 125 g (4½ oz, generous cup) flour, 15 g (½ oz) fresh yeast (or 8 g (1½ teaspoons) active dried yeast) and 2 dl (7 fl oz, ¾ cup) warm milk. Squeeze the fresh yeast in the milk until dissolved (sprinkle the dried yeast over the milk and stir until dissolved) and leave in a warm place until frothy. Then mix into the flour. Leave the dough in a warm place until it has doubled in volume.

Now gradually work into the dough 100 g (4 oz, ½ cup) melted butter, a pinch of salt, the zest of a lemon, 5 egg yolks, 100 g (4 oz, ½ cup) caster (superfine) sugar, and 375 g (13 oz, 3¼ cups) flour. Roll out with a rolling pin and leave to rest for 5 minutes. Cut the dough into rounds and leave to rise in a warm place for 1 hour. Brush with melted butter, dust with icing sugar (confectioners' sugar), and bake in a moderate oven (about 180 c, 350 f, gas 4) for about 15 minutes until lightly browned.

dandelion PISSENLIT

A perennial flowering plant that grows wild in Europe. The name is derived from the alternative French name *dent-de-lion* (literally 'lion's tooth', referring to its serrated leaves); *pissenlit* is a reference to its supposed diuretic properties! Dandelion leaves are low in calories but rich in iron and vitamins A, B_1, B_2, and C. They are usually eaten raw in salads, but may be cooked like spinach. Wild dandelion leaves should be picked before the plant has flowered

(January–March), when they are small and sweet. In France cultivated varieties of dandelion are available from October to March; they have longer more tender leaves but sometimes lack flavour. In salads, dandelions are traditionally accompanied by pieces of bacon and garlic-flavoured croutons (as in *salade du groin d'âne*, literally 'donkey's snout salad', typical of Lyons), hard-boiled (hard-cooked) eggs, or walnuts.

| RECIPE

Dandelion and bacon sald SALADE DE PISSENLIT AU LARD Thoroughly wash 250 g (9 oz) dandelion leaves, then dry. Dice 150 g (5 oz) green or smoked streaky (slab) bacon and brown gently in a frying pan (skillet). In a salad bowl prepare some vinaigrette using 1 tablespoon white wine, 2 tablespoons (3 tablespoons) oil, salt, and pepper. Add the dandelion leaves and toss thoroughly. Pour 1 tablespoon vinegar over the diced bacon and stir with a wooden spoon, scraping the bottom of the frying pan. Pour the contents of the frying pan into the salad bowl. Quartered hard-boiled (hard-cooked) eggs may be added to the bowl before adding the bacon if wished.

danicheff

A mixed salad comprising a julienne of artichoke hearts cooked in white stock, raw mushrooms, blanched celeriac (celery root), asparagus tips, and thin slices of potato. The salad is dressed with mayonnaise and garnished with hardboiled (hard-cooked) eggs, truffles, (either sliced or in a julienne), and crayfish tails.

The name danicheff is also given to a gâteau and a praline parfait ice with coffee and rum. The origin of the name is unknown, but it seems to date from the beginning of this century.

| RECIPE

Danicheff gâteau Prepare a Genoese sponge cake using 4 egg yolks, 50 g (2 oz, 4 tablespoons) butter, 125 g (4½ oz, scant ⅔ cup) sugar, and 125 g (4½ oz, generous cup) flour; leave the cake to rest for 24 hours. Boil 300 g (10 oz, 1¼ cups) caster (superfine) sugar with 3 dl (½ pint, 1¼ cups) water in a saucepan, then allow to cool and add 2½ tablespoons (scant ¼ cup) Kirsch. Prepare some confectioners' custard (pastry cream; see *creams and custards*) using ¼ litre 8 fl oz, 1 cup) milk, 2 egg yolks, 50 g (2 oz, ¼ cup, firmly packed) caster (superfine) sugar, and 15–20 g (½–¾ oz) cornflour (cornstarch). Also make an Italian meringue using 4 egg whites, 200 g (7 oz, scant cup) caster sugar, and 5 cl (2½ tablespoons, scant ¼ cup) water.

Cut the sponge cake into two equal rounds and spoon the syrup over them. Place one of the rounds on a baking sheet and thickly spread with the confectioners' custard. Dice a large tin of pineapple rings, sprinkle with Kirsch, place them on top of the confectioners' custard, and cover with about 100 g (4 oz) apricot jam. Place the other round of sponge cake on top and completely coat the surface of the gâteau, including the sides, with the Italian meringue paste, spreading it with a palette knife (spatula). Sprinkle with about 200 g (7 oz, 2 cups) flaked almonds and dust with icing sugar (confectioners' sugar). Brown for about 5 minutes in a moderately hot oven (about 200 c, 400 F, gas 6). Allow to cool before transferring to a serving dish.

Danish Blue   DANABLU

A Danish cows'-milk cheese, blue with a whitish rind, containing about 45% fat. It has a strong and slightly piquant flavour and is sold, wrapped in aluminium foil, in rounds 20 cm (8 in) in diameter, 10–12 cm (4–5 in) thick, and weighing 2.5–3 kg (5½–6½ lb).

Danzig Goldwasser

EAU DE DANTZIG

A liqueur made from spirits in which citrus fruit zest, aromatic balm, and mace have been steeped. It is filtered and sweetened, and then tiny particles of gold or silver leaf are added. Of Polish origin, it was especially popular in the 19th century and it is the classic flavouring for soufflé Rothschild.

Darblay

A Parmentier (potato) soup mixed with a julienne of vegetables, thickened with egg yolks and cream, and garnished with chervil.

RECIPE

Potage julienne Darblay Prepare 1 litre (1¾ pints, 2 pints) puréed potatoes and dilute with about ½ litre (18 fl oz, 1 pint) consommé. Add 4 tablespoons (⅓ cup) julienne of vegetables which have been gently cooked in butter. Mix 3 egg yolks with 1 dl (6 tablespoons, ½ cup) fresh cream and use this liaison to thicken the soup. Before serving, blend in about 50 g (2 oz, 4 tablespoons) butter and garnish the soup with chervil.

dariole

A small steep-sided cylindrical mould, or the preparation cooked in such a mould. Dariole moulds are used to make small pastries, cheese flans, small cakes, rice puddings, and vegetable pasties.

The original dariole, mentioned by Rabelais, was a small puff pastry filled with frangipane; its name is derived from an old Provençal word *daurar* (to brown, turn golden), referring to its crust. It is still traditional fare in Reims, on the feast of St Rémy, and also in Beauvais, where the frangipane is flavoured with Kirsch and dusted with sugar.

RECIPES

Almond darioles DARIOLES AUX AMANDES Lightly butter 6 dariole moulds and line them with puff pastry. Prepare some frangipane cream using 80 g (3 oz, 6 tablespoons, firmly packed) caster (superfine) sugar, 80 g (3 oz, ¾ cup) flour, 1 whole egg, 3 egg yolks, ½ litre (17 fl oz, 2 cups) milk, 6 crushed macaroons, 1 tablespoon ground almonds, and 30 g (1 oz, 2 tablespoons) butter. Allow to cool completely, then fill the pastry-lined moulds with this mixture and bake in a hot oven (220 C, 425 F, gas 7) for about 30 minutes. Remove the pastries from the moulds and dust with sugar. Alternatively, the moulds may be simply filled with frangipane cream, without the puff pastry.

Cheese darioles DARIOLES AU FROMAGE Butter 6 dariole moulds. Boil ½ litre (17 fl oz, 2 cups) milk. In a mixing bowl, beat 2 whole eggs and 4 egg yolks; add 70 g (2 ½ oz, generous ½

cup) grated cheese, salt, and pepper. Use a whisk to blend in the boiled milk. Fill the buttered moulds with this mixture, place them in a bain-marie, and bring the water to the boil; then transfer to a hot oven (220 C, 425 F, gas 7) and cook for about 20 minutes. Remove the firm custards from the moulds onto a serving dish, coat with a very hot fondue of tomatoes to which mushroom duxelles or a light béchamel sauce has been added, and serve immediately.

darne

A thick transverse slice of a large raw fish, such as hake, salmon, or tuna. The word comes from the Breton *darn* (meaning 'piece'). A *dalle*, on the other hand, is a thin slice or escalope of fish. Both darnes and dalles may be poached, braised, or grilled (broiled); dalles may also be sautéed.

Darphin

A flat potato cake made of grated or julienne potato, cooked first in a frying pan (skillet), then in the oven, until it is brown on both sides but soft in the centre. Named after the chef who created the recipe, this dish is served with Madeira or Périgueux sauce to accompany fillet of beef and fried tournedos steaks (filet mignons). It may also be called *paillasson de pommes de terre* ('potato doormat').

RECIPES

Darphin potatoes POMMES DE TERRE DARPHIN Peel 1 kg (2¼ lb) potatoes, rinse, soak in cold water for 1 hour, then grate or cut into thin straws and remove excess moisture with a cloth. Pour ¼ litre (8 fl oz, 1 cup) oil into a flan tin or dish and heat in a very hot oven (240 C, 475 F, gas 9). Melt 50 g (2 oz, 4 tablespoons) butter in a frying pan (skillet), add half the potatoes, and sauté them for 5 minutes. Then transfer them to the flan tin and press down. Repeat with the rest of the potatoes. Sprinkle with a little extra oil and cook in the oven for about 20 minutes. Turn out the potato cake and serve very hot.

dartois

A hot pastry or hors d'oeuvre comprising two strips of puff pastry enclosing a savoury or sweet filling. It is said to have been named after the vaudeville artist François-Victor Dartois, who was very well known in the 19th century.

The fillings for savoury dartois (also called *sausselis*) are the same as for allumettes: anchovies, sardines, crayfish, chicken, and truffled foie gras are most often used. Sweet dartois are filled with confectioner's custard (pastry cream), sometimes flavoured with crystallized (candied) fruits, frangipane, jam, or fruit purées. Frangipane dartois is also called *gâteau à la Manon*, in honour of the composer Massenet, who was very fond of it.

RECIPES

Savoury Dartois

Anchovy dartois DARTOIS AUX ANCHOIS Prepare some puff pastry and a fish forcemeat. Roll and cut the pastry into two rectangular strips of equal size and thickness. Add some anchovy butter to the forcemeat and spread one of the strips with it, leaving 1 cm (½ in) of pastry all around. Arrange some drained anchovy fillets in oil on top. Cover with more fish forcemeat, then place the second pastry strip on top and seal the edges down. Cook in a hot oven (220 C, 425 F, gas 7) for 20–25 minutes.

Seafood dartois DARTOIS AUX FRUITS DE MER Prepare 400 g (14 oz) puff pastry. Poach 8 scampi in a court-bouillon for 5 minutes. Prepare 8 scallops and poach in a small casserole for 6–7 minutes with 1 dl (6 tablespoons, ½ cup) white wine, 1.5 dl (¼ pint, ⅔ cup) cream, 1 good-sized shallot (chopped), salt, and pepper. Drain the scampi, shell the tails, and cut into sections. Drain the scallops and dice. Add 50 g (2 oz) shelled shrimps and gently heat all the seafood ingredients together in butter. Add some Calvados or marc brandy and set it alight. Pour the cooking juices of the scallops over the mixture and thicken with 1 tablespoon *beurre manié* (kneaded butter). Adjust the seasoning, allow to cool completely, and proceed as for anchovy dartois, but using the seafood filling instead.

Sweet Dartois

Apricot jam dartois DARTOIS À LA CONFITURE D'ABRICOTS Prepare 500 g (18 oz) puff pastry and chill for 1 hour in the refrigerator. Then divide the pastry in half and roll each half into a rectangle 15 cm (6 in) wide, 25 cm (10 in) long, and about 3 mm (⅛ in) thick.

Place one of the rectangles on a baking sheet and cover with about 400 g (14 oz) apricot jam. Cover with the second rectangle of pastry and bake in a hot oven (220 c, 425 f, gas 7) for about 15 minutes. Dust with icing sugar (confectioners' sugar) and return to oven to caramelize for 5 minutes. Preferably serve warm.

Frangipane dartois DARTOIS À LA FRANGIPANE Prepare 500 g (18 oz) puff pastry and chill for 1 hour in the refrigerator. To make the frangipane, soften 100 g (4 oz, ½ cup) butter with a wooden spatula. Blend 2 egg yolks in a mixing bowl with 125 g (4½ oz, generous cup) ground almonds, 125 g (4½ oz, scant ⅔ cup) caster (superfine) sugar, a little vanilla sugar, and the softened butter. Cut the pastry into two rectangles 25 cm (10 in) long and 15 cm (6 in) wide. Complete as for apricot jam dartois.

Dartois or à la d'Artois

The name of various preparations, all dedicated to the Comte d'Artois, future Charles X of France. The Dartois garnish for large pieces of meat consists of glazed carrots and turnips, braised celery hearts, and lightly fried potatoes (*pommes de terre rissolées*) arranged in bouquets around the meat. Dartois soup is a purée of white beans with the addition of a light julienne of vegetables. In baron of lamb Dartois, the joint is surrounded by potato cases (shells) filled with petits pois and served with Madeira sauce.

dashi

A bouillon stock used in Japanese cookery, made from crushed *konbu* (algae) and dried bonito fish, variously spiced, and used for soups, basting or cooking meat, rice or fish, and the preparation of hot and cold sauces. It may be sweetened for sweet-and-sour dishes, seasoned with sake or soya paste, or garnished with finely sliced vegetables. Like instant bouillon cubes in Europe, it can be bought in small packets of soluble paste and in powder form.

date   DATTE

The fruit of the date palm. Brown and fleshy, about 4 cm (1½ in) long, and growing in clusters, the date is rich in sugar and also contains calcium, potassium, phosphorus, magnesium, and vitamins B_1 and B_2. The Greeks, who called it *daktulos* (finger) because of its shape, used it in sauces for meat or fish and made it into cakes and pastries.

Originating in the Persian Gulf, the date palm was the 'tree of life' for the Chaldeans, who ate both the fruit and buds, drank the sap, used its fibres for weaving, and its nuts as fuel. Today it is cultivated throughout north Africa and Arabia. Only a few of the many varieties are exported to Europe, notably the nutmeg date from Tunisia, which has a smooth skin. Others include the *halawi*, which is very sweet, and the *khaleseh*, which has orange-brown skin and is very fragrant. Dates are sold in their clusters or in boxes.

In France, dates are mainly eaten as sweetmeats, often stuffed or iced. North African cuisine makes varied use of them, notably in tajines (ragouts), sweet couscous, and curry-flavoured dishes, and even for stuffing fish (shad). Dates are also used for fritters, nougats, and jam, and are crystallized (candied). The sap of the date palm produces a 'wine', greyish and sweet, which ferments rapidly to become sparkling. This refreshing drink is also consumed in India, where dates are used to make spiced sauces, confectionery, and cakes. In Iraq, date juice serves as a condiment for soups and salads.

｜ RECIPES

Date fritters   BEIGNETS DE DATTES
Remove the stones (pits) from some dates and fill each one with very thick confectioner's custard (pastry cream) flavoured with Kirsch or rum (see *creams and custards*). Coat the dates in batter and deep-fry them, then drain and dust with fine sugar.

Date nougat   NOUGAT DE DATTE
Remove the stones from 1 kg (2¼ lb) dates. Brown 250 g (9 oz, generous 2 cups) blanched almonds in a frying pan (skillet), without fat. Prepare a syrup by boiling 250 g (9 oz, generous cup, firmly packed) sugar with half a glass of water until the temperature reaches 110 c (230 f). Remove from the heat, stir in 250 g (9 oz) honey, then quickly mix in the dates, almonds, 2 pinches of white pepper, 1 teaspoon ginger, and the same quantity of sesame. Form the mixture into a sausage shape and slice into rounds. Store in an airtight container.

Stuffed dates   DATTES FOURRÉES
Prepare some almond paste as follows: heat 150 g (5 oz, ⅔ cup, firmly packed) caster (superfine) sugar in a heavy saucepan with 5 dl (17 fl oz, 2 cups) water and 15 g (½ oz) glucose. When the temperature reaches soft ball, i.e. 115 c (240 f), remove from the heat and add 75 g (3 oz, ¾ cup) ground almonds. Stir with a wooden spatula to obtain a granular texture. Allow to cool.

Remove the stones (pits) from about 30 dates, without separating the two halves. When the paste is cold, knead it in small quantities until supple and then form it into a large ball. Hollow this out, and pour into the hollow a good tablespoon of Kirsch and 3 drops of green food-colouring. Knead the paste again to spread the colour evenly. With the palm of the hand, roll the paste into a large sausage, slice it, and roll each slice into an olive shape; use one to fill each date. Serve the stuffed dates in individual paper cases. They may also be sprinkled with crystallized sugar.

daube

A method of braising meat (beef, mutton, turkey, goose, pheasant, rabbit, pork, chicken), certain vegetables (boletus mushrooms, palm cabbage), and some fish (tuna). Meat cooked *en daube* is braised in red-wine stock well seasoned with herbs, the name is thought to come from the Spanish *dobar* (to braise). The word *daube* alone generally means a joint of beef braised in wine, a popular dish in several southern provinces of France, where it is served hot or cold.

Daube of beef à la provençale DAUBE
DE BOEUF À LA PROVENÇALE Cut 1½
kg (3¼ lb) lean chuck or silverside (bottom round) into 6-cm (2½-in) cubes.
Lard each cube crosswise with a piece of
fat bacon rolled in chopped parsley and
garlic. Put the meat into an earthenware
dish or casserole with a calf's foot and
cover with white wine containing 2
tablespoons olive oil, 1 tablespoon
brandy, salt, and pepper. Marinate for
24 hours. Mix together 150 g (5 oz)
mushrooms, 75 g (3 oz) chopped raw
onion, 2 crushed tomatoes, 150 g (5 oz)
thick streaky bacon, diced and blanched, and 100 g (4 oz) black (ripe)
olives.

Remove the fat from some bacon
rinds, blanch, wipe, and use the rinds to
line the base of an earthenware casserole
just large enough to contain the meat
and its garnishes. Add 2 sliced carrots,
then add alternating layers of meat
cubes and the vegetable and bacon mixture. In the centre of the meat place a
large bouquet garni composed of parsley stalks, thyme, a bay leaf, and a small
piece of dried orange peel. Add the
white wine of the marinade plus an
equal volume of beef stock so that it just
covers the meat.

Cover the casserole, seal the lid with a
flour-and-water paste, and cook in a
cool oven (about 120 c, 250 F, gas ½)
for 6 hours. Remove the bouquet garni,
allow to cool, then skim off the fat.
Serve the daube cold in slices, like a
terrine, or hot (reheated in the oven).

daubière

A braising pot of stoneware, earthenware, or galvanized copper, used for
making daubes and other braised dishes
which require a long slow cooking time.
Like the *braisière* (stewpan), it was
originally designed for cooking over
charcoal; the daubière has a lid with a
raised edge for holding burning
charcoal or boiling water.

Daudet (Léon)

French writer and journalist (born
Paris, 1867; died Saint-Rémy-de-
Provence, 1942). Founder, with Charles
Maurras, of *L'Action française*, Daudet
was an unashamed polemicist and one
of the greatest gastronomes of his time.

In *Paris vécu*, he evokes Parisian life
through its restaurants and its chefs,
from the best known to the humblest. At
the pension Laveur, he invented *kaul-
back* (which he said was dedicated to a
Bulgarian general), comprising white
haricot beans, sautéed potatoes, and
eggs *sur le plat*. He was a regular customer at La Grille, a bistro where journalists from *L'Humanité* and *L'Action
française* rubbed shoulders over the beef
hash and pickled pork. But he also
patronized the Tour d'Argent, where,
with his friend Babinsky, he discussed
such topics as the merits of an endive
(chicory) salad, 'lightly crushed in
absinthe', to accompany foie gras; his
description of Frédéric cutting up
canard au sang (duck cooked in its
blood) is famous. At Weber's house, he
described Marcel Proust, 'a doe-eyed
young gentleman muffled up in an
enormous overcoat', being served with
grapes or pears.

A founder member of the Académie
Goncourt, he organized the lunch at
which the first Prix Goncourt was
awarded. For this first lunch at the
Grand Hotel and for subsequent ones at
Champeaux, the Café de Paris, and
Drouant, Daudet compiled the menus
until his death. He sang the praises of
Provençal and Lyonnaise cooking, as
well as that of Beaujolais, the 'third river
of Lyon'.

His famous judgments on his contemporaries reflect the acerbity of a committed journalist and his love of the
good life: the eloquence of Jaurès was
'full like a Gruyère of which each hole is
a metaphor'; Renan was 'gracious with
lust and sauce'; Briand started to 'wrig-
gle like shellfish sprinkled with lemon';
as for Clemenceau, he was 'as appetizing as a cabbage soup in which the
spoon of eloquence would stand up'.

Persuaded that 'the best therapy for
all ills is good food', he waxed lyrical
when he met a chef who fully satisfied
him, such as Madame Génot, his
favourite restaurateur of the Rue de la
Banque, who was 'to gastronomy what
Beethoven is to music, Baudelaire to
poetry, and Rembrandt to painting'.

Daudet's second wife was Marthe
Allard, his cousin, who was responsible,
under the pseudonym of Pampille, for
the gastronomic column in *L'Action*

française and who edited *Les Bons Plats de France* (1924).

Daumont (à la)

Designating an opulent garnish dating from the time of the Restoration (and no doubt dedicated to the Duc d'Aumont), designed principally for large braised fish, such as shad, salmon, or turbot. It comprises fish quenelles, slices of truffle, crayfish tails *à la Nantua* (in shells or barquettes), button mushrooms, and soft roe, all coated with breadcrumbs and sautéed in butter. The dish is served with a normande sauce finished with crayfish butter.

Today, the name is given to simpler fish dishes, as well as to a dish of soft-boiled (soft-cooked) or poached eggs with crayfish and mushrooms.

| RECIPE

Poached eggs à la Daumont OEUFS POCHÉS À LA DAUMONT Cook some large mushroom caps in butter, drain, and top each one with a spoonful of a salpicon of crayfish tails *à la Nantua*. Arrange a poached egg on each mushroom cap, coat with Nantua sauce, and garnish with a slice of truffle.

Dauphin

A soft cows'-milk cheese from French Hainaut, with a brown rind and containing at least 50% fat. Excellent from September to May, Dauphin cheese is made from the same type of curds as Maroilles cheese but is flavoured with parsley, tarragon, pepper, and cloves, and has a highly seasoned taste. It can be shaped like a croissant, heart, shield, or rod. Created in the reign of Louis XIV, it owes its name to a royal edict that exempted carters from Maroilles from the penny tithe payable to the Dauphin, which was levied at Cambrai on each waggon coming from Belgian Hainaut.

Dauphiné

A region of France that extends from Savoy to Provence. Its geographical diversity gives rise to a wide range of produce, including cattle and sheep, chestnuts, walnuts, almonds, olives, peaches, plums, grapes, mushrooms (boletus, morels, and truffles), fish (trout and crayfish), and game (hares, songbirds, quail). The abundance and quality of the Dauphiné's milk have made cream a feature of the region's cuisine; it is used in Dauphinoise soup, Vercors salmon trout, and the famous gratins: gratin dauphinois, based on potatoes, is the best-known, but gratins may also be made of macaroni, minced meat, pumpkin, beets, cardoons, ceps, and crayfish tails.

Beef and veal daubes – particularly those of Vienne – are also very popular. Thrushes are cooked *à la dauphinoise*, with juniper berries, in pâtés, and in salmis. The young guinea fowl and chickens of Drôme are well known.

The region's cheeses include Sassenage blue, Sérac, and fresh or dried Tomme from Saint-Marcellin. The local pastry speciality is a tart called *pogne*, which has a thick-edged crust and is filled with fruit – plums, peaches, or pumpkin – according to the season. In the Drôme area, the *pogne* is a large brioche; those from Romans are renowned. Grenoble is famous for its walnut gâteau. Noted among its sweetmeats are the *pruneaux fleuris* (a type of prune) of Sahune, the honey *touron* from Gap, and Montélimar's nougat. Of the local wines, white or red Hermitage and Clairette de Die are well known. Finally, the liqueurs of Grenoble and Voiron, and above all the green or yellow Chartreuse, are world-famous.

dauphine (à la)

A method of preparing vegetables, such as celeriac (celery root) or aubergines (eggplants), in the same way as dauphine potatoes. If the purée obtained is too watery – as can happen with courgettes (zucchini) – it is dried off in the oven.

The name is also given to joints of meat or game garnished with dauphine potatoes.

dauphine potatoes
POMMES DAUPHINE

Potatoes reduced to a purée, added to choux pastry, shaped into balls, and fried in very hot fat. They are used to accompany grilled or roast meat or game. The mixture may be enriched with grated cheese or Bayonne ham, especially for croquettes (see *Lorette*).

RECIPE

Dauphine potatoes POMMES DAUPHINE Peel 1 kg (2¼ lb) floury potatoes, cut into quarters, and cook in salted water until very soft. Drain thoroughly and mash to a purée. Prepare some choux pastry (see *chou*) using ½ litre (17 fl oz, 2 cups) water, 130 g (4½ oz, generous ½ cup) butter, 250 g (9 oz, 2¼ cups) sieved flour, 7 eggs, a pinch of grated nutmeg, salt, and pepper. Mix the dough with an equal volume of the potato purée. Heat some cooking oil to about 175 c (345 F) and drop the mixture into it a spoonful at a time. When the potato balls are puffed up and golden, drain on absorbent paper, dust with fine salt, and serve very hot.

dauphinoise (à la)

A method of preparing potatoes that is a speciality of the 'country of the four mountains' (Lans-en-Vercor, Villard-de-Lans, Autrans, and Sassenage). The potatoes are cut into *taillons* (round slices) and placed with fresh cream in a gratin dish which has been rubbed with garlic and buttered. However, *gratin dauphinois* is often made by pouring a mixture of eggs, milk, and cream over the potato slices and sprinkling the dish with grated cheese. *Gratin savoyard*, from the neighbouring region, is made without milk, cream, or eggs, consisting of alternating layers of potato and grated Beaufort cheese with knobs of butter, all covered with bouillon.

débarrasser

A French word meaning literally 'to clear away', used in cuisine to describe the transfer of food from the cooking vessel to a place, such as a cupboard or a marble slab, where it can cooled or be kept for later use.

In catering, *débarrasser une mise en place* is to remove from the vicinity of the cooker or work station the utensils that were employed in preparing a dish or meal.

decant DÉCANTER

To transfer a liquid from one vessel to another after allowing suspended impurities to settle. In French, *décanter* is used in a variety of contexts: melted butter is decanted after skimming, as is deep-frying fat and stock after use. The same word is even used for extracting meat from the stock or sauce in which it has been cooked; the cooking liquid is then strained, thickened if necessary, and used to make a sauce in which the meat is given a final simmer.

Wine is decanted by transferring it carefully into a carafe so that any deposit that has formed in the bottle during maturation is left behind. Decanting wine also permits oxygenation, which is often beneficial. In practice, only old red wines are habitually decanted; the bitter tannin and solid pigments they contain must remain in the bottle.

decoction DÉCOCTION

The extraction of the constituents of a food by boiling it in water for varying lengths of time. In this way meat or vegetable bouillons, court-bouillons, and aromatic extracts are made. This procedure should not be confused with infusion, in which boiling water is poured over the substance but the boiling is not continued.

decoration DÉCORATION

Any operation designed to enhance the appearance of a dish. Decoration is used throughout cuisine and may depend on the method of preparation, especially for cold dishes (aspics, chaud-froid, fish *à la parisienne*, etc.), or on the addition of trimmings and garnishes, particularly with meats, poultry, salads, pâtisserie, and desserts.

There is much less emphasis on decoration in French regional cooking, in which dishes are often served straight from the pot; typical decorated dishes are Taillevent's reconstituted birds and symbolic colours and Carême's architectural *pièces montées*. 20th-century decoration concentrates on using ingredients of different colours and shapes for contrast or harmony.

The chef's palette is well provided with colours – the green of spinach and watercress, the red of beetroot (beets) and radish, red or black lumpfish roe, yellow and white of eggs, etc. Shape and size can be varied – dice, cubes, balls, tracery on meringue, chequerboard design on grilled (broiled) meat, etc. – as can texture (solid, powdery, granular, soft, gelatinous). Japanese and Chinese cooks pay much greater attention to decoration and have raised, in particular, the cutting up of vegetables and fish to the level of art.

The principal items of culinary decoration are as follows:
• lemons and oranges, grooved or embellished, for fish *à la meunière*, Viennese escalopes, and duck with orange;
• bunches of watercress for grills and roasts;
• puff pastry fleurons (crescents) dents de loup, and other croutons for meats in sauce, fish bonne femme, and spinach;
• hard-boiled (hard-cooked) eggs (chopped or in rounds) for salads and hors d'oeuvres;
• fresh parsley for poached or grilled fish and hors d'oeuvres;
• duchesse potatoes, potato nests, potato straw potatoes and chips;
• tomatoes in slices, fan shapes, or 'roses', tarragon, lemon rind, red apple peel, radish, truffle, mayonnaise, etc. Non-edible items are also used:
• plate papers and fluted paper cases of various shapes for hot hors d'oeuvres, pies, etc.
• frills and ruffles, for loin of lamb, veal chops, leg of lamb, haunch of venison, etc.
• folded napkins, in boat shapes for fish, in squares for toast and iced bombes;
• stands and tiers for fish, suprêmes, medallions of foie gras, etc.

In patisserie and for sweetmeats, decoration plays a particularly important role, and all sorts of decorative designs can be created in sugar (extruded, cut, twisted, etc.). Sundaes, desserts, large gâteaux, etc., are commonly decorated with such materials as caramel, chocolate (shavings, beads, vermicelli), piped butter cream, almonds (flaked, grilled, or chopped), sauces, royal icing (frosting), icing sugar (confectioners' sugar), fondant icing, almond paste, coffee beans, crystallized violets, crystallized (candied) fruits, Chantilly cream, and marrons glacés.

découpoir

A small slightly conical cutter, of stainless steel or galvanized iron, that cuts decorative slices in the form of a star, trefoil, heart, diamond, spade, leaf, etc. from truffles, tomatoes, jelly, etc. It should not be confused with a pastry (cookie) cutter, used in pâtisserie.

décuire

A French term meaning to lower the cooking temperature of sugar syrup or jam by adding to it, gradually while stirring, sufficient cold water to give it the correct consistency.

deep-fat frying   FRITURE

The process of cooking food by immersing it in a large deep pan of very hot fat or oil. (The French term, *friture*, can also be applied to the fat itself.) When done carefully at the right temperature, deep-frying should give food a crisp dry golden coating without making it too greasy.

☐ **What can be fried?** Foods for deep-frying should be dried well to remove any excess moisture, because water evaporates at 100 c (212 f) and bubbles through the oil, causing the fat to spit and splash. Foods that naturally contain albumin (which coagulates) or starch can be plunged directly into the oil. Others should be sealed in a coating, especially if they contain a lot of water.

WITHOUT COATING – The following foods can be deep-fried directly, without first being coated:
• potatoes: peel, wash, wipe, and cut into straws, chips (sticks), or slices; their starch content makes any other preparation unnecessary;
• eggs (the white coagulates immediately);
• small fish (for example, whitebait, smelts, sand-eels);
• brioche, puff, or choux pastry (for example, dauphine potatoes, rissoles, soufflé fritters).

WITH COATING – There are three basic methods of sealing food for frying:
• Whole fish and fish fillets are sometimes soaked in cold milk, then seasoned and dipped in flour, the excess being shaken off gently.
• Meat, offal, poultry, and croquettes, which all contain a fair amount of water, are sealed by a triple coating of flour, beaten egg, and fresh or dried breadcrumbs (known in French as *panure anglaise*).

• Fruit and vegetables, which have a very high water content, must be coated in batter; a range of fritters can be made in this way. A savoury or sweet mixture (such as minced meat or fish, sliced mushrooms, or spinach, bound with white sauce, cream, etc.) can also be fried if it is sealed in an airtight short-crust pastry (basic pie dough) case.

Pieces of food to be fried should be fairly small, since the heat must reach the centre rapidly without burning the outside of the food; this is why potatoes are cut into chips (sticks) or thin slices, fruit and vegetables are sliced into rounds or divided, and dough preparations are cut into individual portions.

☐ **What fat should be used?** The fat or oil should be pure, clean, fairly heat-resistant, and relatively neutral-tasting. Butter, margarine, and low-fat spreads should not be used, since they decompose at around 100 C (212 F), giving a burnt taste to food. Temperatures in deep-frying reach 140–180 C (275–360 F) – above that, many fats start to turn brown and give off acrid smoke. The range of fats that can be used includes:
• vegetable oils (olive, groundnut (peanut), palm, sunflower, soya, grape-seed, and corn oils) are suitable for all uses; they keep well and can be heated to over 200 C (400 F);
• the fat from ox kidneys, veal, and horsemeat, and also pork fat (mutton fat smells of wool grease) can be heated satisfactorily, as can clarified goose fat. Animal fats tend to be used less often and are less desirable from a dietary point of view, since they have a high content of saturated fatty acids.

After use, allow the fat or oil to cool, decant it, and then strain to remove remaining food debris and impurities. Never add fresh fat or oil; it is better to use a batch until it starts to discolour and smell stale, then get rid of it. Store in an airtight container away from the light. Discard after using six or seven times.

☐ **How can deep-frying be done successfully?**
• Only one-third fill the pan or deep-fryer, thereby avoiding splashes or spillages. Allow one part (by volume) of food to three of fat or oil. So, when cooking for four to six people, use 2.5–3 litres (4½–5¼ pints) oil so that the temperature does not drop quickly when adding the food: the temperature should remain constant once it has been brought up to the required level.
• Heat the fat on its own to the required temperature; this will prevent it from foaming and avoid the risk of it bubbling over; it also prevents the fat from being absorbed too much into the food.
• Cook with the fat at the optimum temperature: test by dropping a small piece of the food into the pan – if it returns to the surface, bubbling, after about 20 seconds, the fat is ready.
• Never allow fat or oil to brown or smoke: above the so-called 'critical' temperature – generally 210–220 C (410–425 F) – it becomes unpleasant and starts to taint the food.

☐ **The three degrees of frying** Three different temperature levels for deep-drying can be distinguished:
• *Medium frying*, at 140–160 C (275–325 F), is suitable for the first frying of certain potato preparations which require cooking through before browning and for cutlets or thick fillets of fish.
• *Hot frying*, at 160–175 C (325–350 F), is required for all coated foods, fritters, cutlets, etc., and for precooked preparations that simply require colouring (croquettes).
• *Very hot frying*, at around 180 C (355 F) or before the fat begins to smell, is reserved for small fish (such as whitebait) and for the second frying of potato chips (French fries) and crisps (chips).

Whatever the frying temperature, the food should float to the surface when cooked (ensure that fritters, etc., are turned to cook both sides). The food should then be removed immediately, drained first in its frying basket and then on absorbent kitchen paper (paper towels), and served, sprinkled with salt or sugar, on paper or a napkin.

deep-freezing
SURGELATION

A method of commercially preserving food in which it is subjected to rapid and intense freezing (as low as −50 C, −58 F) so that the temperature at the centre of the food is lower than −18 C (0 F) but the degree of crystallization is not such as to cause moisture loss at the time of defrosting. This is why deep-freezing (invented at the beginning of this century by Clarence Birdseye and practised only on an industrial scale) is used on products of limited thickness (maximum 10 cm, 4 in) which must already be at a very low temperature (it is always preceded by chilling). Because of its speed, deep-freezing is suitable for fragile products, which are not destroyed by the process.

• *Deep-freezing by contact*, applied to thin products of regular shape (such as fillets of fish or packets of spinach), is performed between metallic elements in which fluid circulates at −35 C (−31 F).
• *Deep-freezing by pumped air* is carried out either in a static tunnel, where very cold air (up to −50 C, −58 F at a speed of 5−6 metres per second) is circulated, or in a deep-freezer with a conveyor belt, on which foods move along while icy-cold air is blown upwards and downwards, or in a continuous deep-freezer with a fluidized bed inserted in the appliance, through which pass very small foods (bilberries, raspberries, diced vegetables, shrimps), carried along by a violent air current at −40 C (−40 F) by which they are each coated in frozen water.
• *Deep-freezing by immersion*, in a liquid at very low temperature, is used for products of medium size and irregular shape (such as chickens wrapped in plastic film, or whole fish or shellfish).

Packaging precedes or immediately follows deep-freezing. After this the temperature must be kept consistently low until the product is used (−18 C, 0 F).

Deep-frozen products must, according to legislation, meet the following conditions:
• be, at the time of deep-freezing, in a state of prime freshness (i.e. freezing should be carried out as quickly as possible after fishing, slaughtering, picking, or preparation), and be completely free from disease-producing organisms;
• be subject to a very rapid fall in temperature (−18 C, 0 F), as quickly as possible (whereas the time allowed for ordinary freezing, is, on average, 24 hours);

• be kept, between deep-freezing and sale, at a temperature below or equal to −18 C (0 F);
• be packed in an absolutely airtight container or wrapping suitable for use with foodstuffs;
• bear a label clearly indicating the name of the producer, the origin, the date of deep-freezing, the recommended date of use, the net weight, and the method of defrosting.

It is possible to deep-freeze most food products and culinary preparations: vegetables, soups, fish (whole, in fillets, or in fingers), shellfish, frogs' legs, the flesh and corals of scallops, stuffed snails, beefburgers, fruit juices, meatballs, cakes and bakery products, and many ready-cooked dishes. Fruit and vegetables for deep-freezing should be carefully selected for suitability and the right degree of ripeness, with thorough bacteriological control for all preparations.

It is very important to maintain the low temperature of deep-frozen products, so the following precautions

Keeping time for products frozen at −18 C (0 F)

	months
fruits, fruit juices, and vegetables	30
meat (in quarters or in portions)	18
minced meat	9
poultry	18
brains	24
other offal	18
fish (whole, in slices, or filleted)	18−24
breaded fish	24
pastry dough (rolled or in slabs)	24
bakery products	12
cooked pastries	18
potatoes prepared for frying or sautéing	24
ready-cooked dishes	18−24

should be taken before buying them: check the temperature of the freezer compartments (which should always be provided with a thermometer); ensure the packaging is not torn or damaged in any way; the products may be covered by a very thin layer of frost (caused by the freezing of the surrounding air), but not by trails of ice; chopped vegetables and individually frozen small products must sound like pebbles rattling in the packet. It is also necessary to check that the display cabinets are not filled higher than 10 cm (4 in) from the top, since products which are above this level are no longer at the necessary temperature.

The foods should be taken home in insulated bags as quickly as possible, and stored preferably in a freezer or in the 4-star compartment of a fridge-freezer; if these are not available, they may be stored for 24 hours only in a refrigerator or for three days in the ice-making compartment.

There is one absolute rule which applies to the use of deep-frozen foods: never refreeze a defrosted product. A number of frozen products may go directly from the freezer into the oven or the microwave oven. It is essential, however, to defrost certain products: fruits, fruit juices, shrimps, pastries, poultry, joints of meat, and meatballs. The operation should be carried out in the least cold part of the refrigerator, in a specially designed fan oven, or in a microwave oven set to the defrosting position (or, if time is short, by placing the packet under running cold water). Defrosting should never be carried out by applying heat (in the oven of a cooker, on a radiator, or in hot water) and preferably not at room temperature.

Small cuts of meat, vegetables, croquettes, and fillets of fish can be cooked in the frozen state (baked, grilled (broiled), fried, or stewed in court-bouillon); the cooking time for grilling or frying is longer than for a fresh product, but when cooking in water or court-bouillon, once the preparation has been brought to the boil, it is actually shorter. Ready-cooked dishes can be reheated in the oven or in a bain-marie in a fairly short time. All recipes for fresh products may generally be applied to frozen foods, which makes

them of great value in household cookery, but their principal use is for large organizations and restaurants.

Natural products are not necessarily superior to frozen ones: fresh spinach, for example, possesses only 35% of its vitamins after 36 hours, whereas frozen spinach after being kept for a year still possesses 85%. Deep-freezing is not a form of sterilization: the cold scarcely inhibits the multiplication of microbes, and at −10 c (14 f) certain kinds still develop. It is therefore essential that before freezing the product is perfectly fresh.

deer CERF

A ruminant of temperate regions. The flesh of the fawns (up to six months old) and young stags (up to one year old) is tender, dark red, and makes good eating (see *roebuck*). The flesh of older beasts is firmer and can be tough. The hind, especially when young, is always more tender. In the Middle Ages, deer were the most highly prized game animals, reserved exclusively for the nobility. They inspired some highly decorative culinary displays, in which the beast was virtually reconstructed lying on gigantic dishes. Deer meat was also used to lard poultry. Both stag and hind were eaten roasted, stewed, or jugged; deer-knuckle soup was a famous dish. In the 16th century, stag's antlers, cut into sections and fried, were considered fit for a king, as were the *menus droits* (comprising the tongue, muzzle, and ears). Stag's horn was commonly sold by grocers: when ground, it was used to prepare jellies and sweets.

deffarde or défarde

A speciality of the Dauphiné region of southeastern France, especially of Die and Crest, comprising lambs' feet and intestines cooked in a court-bouillon with carrots, onions, leeks, bay leaf, and cloves, then simmered in the oven with white wine and tomato sauce; it is sometimes seasoned with capers and a trickle of vinegar. Deffarde is served with chopped garlic and parsley.

de fructu

In former times, the minor expenses (fruit, service, etc.) incurred by a person who lent his table for a meal at which all the participants paid a share. The term comes from the Latin legal expression *curare de fructu* (to look after the provision of fruit). Another explanation of the word is associated with the custom, maintained until the 17th century among the gentry, of receiving the clergy in their homes the night before Christmas: the meal, eaten after Vespers, is supposed to have been blessed with the first words of the antiphon chanted by the canons in the afternoon: *de fructu ventris tui* (from the fruit of thy womb).

deglaze DÉGLACER

To heat wine, stock, or other liquid together with the cooking juices and sediment left in the pan after roasting or sautéing in order to make a sauce or gravy. It may be necessary to caramelize the sediment by heating it or to skim off excess fat before adding the wine or stock. Deglazing is done by pouring a small quantity of liquid into the pan over the heat, dissolving all the pan juices in it, leaving it to cook and take on colour, then reducing it until the right consistency is achieved. In the course of this operation, wines lose their acidity. Deglazing is sometimes preceded by flaming the contents of the pan after sprinkling with spirits. When the deglazing liquid is well reduced, it is moistened with stock (clear or thickened), bouillon, fumet, etc., in order to make gravy or sauce. Finally, the seasoning is adjusted and the sauce may be sieved before being served.

dégorger

A French term meaning to soak meat, poultry, fish, or offal in cold water (with or without vinegar) to eliminate impurities and blood, particularly for 'white' dishes, or to dispel the 'muddy' taste of river fish. The term is also used for the process of sprinkling certain vegetables, particularly cucumber and cabbage, with salt to eliminate water. It also applies to the preparation of snails.

dégraisser

A French culinary term meaning to remove excess fat from an ingredient, dish, or cooking vessel. Fat is removed from raw or cooked meat using a small butcher's knife; for hot bouillons, gravies, or sauces, a small ladle or spoon is used to skim off the fat; and for cold liquids, where the fat has solidified, a skimming ladle should be used, or the liquid may be sieved. Fat can be completely removed from hot clarified consommé by putting absorbent paper on the surface. It is necessary to remove excess fat from a cooking vessel before deglazing the vessel. For white wine which has become oily and insipid, the method is to add tannin, then to clarify and preserve the wine.

dégraissis

The fat removed from a bouillon, stock, sauce, or dish. Formerly, the fat was filtered and stored in stone jars for cooking vegetables. Today day this 'economy fat' is no longer desirable on dietetic grounds.

dehydrated foods
PRODUITS DÉSHYDRATÉS

Foods from which some or most of the natural water has been extracted. Dehydration is carried out in the food industry for several reasons: to preserve the product for a considerable period of time; to reduce the weight and usually the volume of the product, thus making it easier to transport and store; and to reduce the preparation time (as with instant coffee and dried soups).

The concentration of a product involves partial dehydration by evaporation, filtration, or centrifugation. Certain products (such as milk, soups, meat extracts, vegetable concentrates, and fruit juices) retain between a third and half of their natural water content and always remain in a liquid form. Concentration alone does not ensure preservation of the product; it must then be bottled, canned, or frozen.

Desiccation, or dehydration in the true sense of the word, is achieved by different processes.

• *Drying on trays:* solid foods are cut into small pieces and constantly moved forward in an oven or tunnel through which a current of hot dry air is directed in the opposite direction. The moisture is gradually absorbed.

• *Drying on drums:* soft foods (purées, baby foods, soups, etc.) are spread in a

Principal dehydrated foods and their uses

products	method of use	remarks
CONCENTRATED PRODUCTS		
unsweetened condensed milk	Mix with an equal volume of cold water. Use undiluted to replace fresh cream (in soups, ice cream, etc.).	Used alone, it has a rather 'cooked' taste; this disappears when mixed with other items. By reducing the proportion of water a special smoothness is obtained (in creams, soups, desserts, etc.).
canned soups	Mix with an equal volume of warm water and heat.	
fruit juice	Mix with three times its volume of cold water and allow to thicken.	Tastes of fresh juice.
tomato concentrate	Many uses, either as it is or diluted as required.	
DRIED PRODUCTS		
packet soups	Mix with the volume of cold water indicated on the packet and allow to thicken.	Flavour varies greatly from one brand to another; often too salty.
powdered milk (or in granules)	Mix with hot or cold water or milk: 1 tablespoon to 1 dl (4 fl oz, ½ cup) liquid.	Used alone, it is more inspid than fresh milk, particularly the skimmed variety. Powdered skimmed milk added to liquid skimmed milk doubles the latter's nutritive value and gives it a better taste.
instant mashed potatoes	Pour into the quantity of hot water (or hot water and milk) indicated on the packet. Wait a few moments before stirring to allow the flakes or granules to swell.	
coffee powder	Pour 1 cup of hot (but not boiling) water onto 1 teaspoon (or 1 sachet) powder.	Often bitter, due more to the composition of the blend than to the dehydration process.
FREEZE-DRIED PRODUCTS		
instant soups	Mix with the volume of hot water indicated on the packet.	
freeze-dried coffee	Pour 1 cup of hot (but not boiling) water onto 1 teaspoon (or 1 sachet) powder.	Good results if the quantity is not increased. Some blends leave an aftertaste of caramel. Very useful for flavouring creams, custards, and pâtisserie.

thin layer on the outside wall of a rotating drum that is heated from the inside. Special knives scrape off the dry film, which is subsequently reduced to a powder or to flakes.

● *Atomization:* liquids (such as milk or coffee) are atomized to form a fine spray. The tiny particles in the vapour are dehydrated with a current of hot air and collected in powder form.

Products subjected to desiccation contain no more than, on average, 6% of their original water content, and will keep for very long periods in hermetically sealed containers.

See also *freeze-drying.*

déjeuner

The French word for lunch. Nowadays the déjeuner is the midday meal, as opposed to *petit déjeuner* (breakfast) and *dîner* (dinner). But according to its etymology (from the Latin *disjejunare*, later *disjunare*, to break one's fast), the word originally meant the first meal of the day, ·comprising essentially bread, soup, and even wine (before coffee, tea, and chocolate appeared on the scene).

The introduction of the midday déjeuner dates from the French Revolution. Until that time, the midday meal was called *dîner*. But because the sessions of the constituent Assembly began at midday and finished about 6 p.m. dinner had to be eaten at the end of the afternoon. The deputies, being unable to go without food from breakfast until dinner, acquired the habit of eating at about 11.00 a.m., a second breakfast that was more substantial than the first. A certain Madame Hardy, who in 1804 ran a café on the Boulevards near the Théâtre des Italiens, invented the *déjeuner à la fourchette* (fork lunch), offering her customers cutlets, kidneys, sausages, and other grills served on a sideboard. The development of cabarets and cafés, then the birth of restaurants, turned the déjeuner into an important social occasion.

Nowadays in France, lunch is eaten generally at about 12.30 p.m. to 1.00 p.m. It is often a quick and light meal, although in the professional sphere, it has become more substantial as the 'business lunch'. Certain events, such as the awarding of literary prizes, often take place at a special lunch (see *Drouant*). But even today, the Sunday lunch remains a symbol of family life, not so far removed from the type of lunch served in the 1850s, mentioned by Marguerite Yourcenar: 'Every Sunday, Reine presides over a meal to which all the family are invited. The tablecloth laid for this ceremony, hardly less sacred than High Mass, is resplendent with silverware and the soft gleam of old porcelain. Poultry quenelles are served at midday; the dessert and sweetmeats at about five o'clock. Between the sorbet and the saddle of lamb, it is understood that the guests have the right to take a turn about the garden or even, with a slight apology for taking pleasure in such a rustic amusement, a game of bowls.' (*Archives du Nord*, Gallimard).

Delessert (Benjamin)

French industrialist and financier (born Lyon, 1773; died Paris, 1847). Having founded a sugar refinery in 1801 in the district of Passy in Paris, in 1812 he perfected the process of sugar extraction from sugar beet (see *Marggraf, Achard*). Napoleon visited the factory and saw the potential of this discovery, which could make it unnecessary to import cane sugar from the West Indies. He granted large funds to Delessert, earmarked a great deal of land in the north for sugar beet cultivation and, on Delessert's advice, opened one of the first 'sugar schools' at Douai. Meanwhile, Delessert plunged into political life and became one of the founders of savings banks in France.

delicatessen

DELIKATESSEN

A shop selling high-quality groceries and luxury food products such as German sausages, preserved meats, fine wines and spirits, sweetmeats, exotic fruits, foreign cheeses, sweet-and-sour preserves, and spiced loaves. The word, meaning delicacies, originated in Germany in the 18th century.

délice and délicieux

Fancy names given by pastrycooks to various desserts, gâteaux, and sweetmeats.

RECIPES

Apple délicieux DÉLICIEUX AUX POMMES Prepare and bake 650 g (1½ lb) apples on a baking sheet in a moderately hot oven (190 C, 375 G, gas 5). Reduce the pulp to a purée and allow to cool. Whisk 5 egg yolks with 100 g (4 oz, ½ cup) caster (superfine) sugar until the mixture becomes light and foamy. Whisk the 5 whites stiffly and fold a little at a time into the egg–sugar mixture alternately with the apple purée and 70 g (2½ oz) dried white breadcrumbs. Empty the mixture into a buttered and floured soufflé dish and cook in the moderately hot oven for 40–45 minutes. Dust with granulated sugar and serve very hot.

Délicieux surprise Gently melt 130 g (4½ oz) chocolate in a bowl over hot water. Add 1 tablespoon fresh cream, 20 g (¾ oz, 1½ tablespoons) butter, 1 tablespoon milk, and the grated rind of an orange. Keep the sauce hot over the hot water. Cut a large brioche mousseline into 6 thick slices, put them in a dish, and sprinkle with 1 dl (6 tablespoons, ½ cup) rum. Peel 3 pears, remove the seeds, slice, and place on the brioche slices. Whip 1.5 dl (¼ pint, ⅔ cup) fresh double (heavy) cream with 1 tablespoon very cold milk and slowly add 60 g (2 oz, ¼ cup, firmly packed) caster (superfine) sugar. Cover the brioche and pears with a dome of the whipped cream and cover with the hot chocolate sauce. Serve immediately.

Lemon délice DÉLICE AU CITRON Melt 100 g (4 oz, ½ cup) butter in a bain-marie. Measure 250 g (9 oz, 2¼ cups) self-raising flour into a mixing bowl, then add the melted butter, 4 eggs, 200 g (7 oz, scant cup) caster (superfine) sugar, the grated zest and juice of a lemon, and 100 g (4 oz) crystallized (candied) fruits cut into very small dice. Mix until evenly blended, then turn the mixture into a 25-cm (9-in) round loose-bottomed cake tin and cook for 40 minutes in a moderately hot oven (about 190 C, 375 F, gas 5).
Meanwhile, prepare a French butter cream (see *creams and custards*) using 125 g (4½ oz, scant ⅔ cup) caster sugar cooked to the thread stage (see *sugar*) in ½ dl (2½ tablespoons, 4½ tablespoons) water, 4 egg yolks, 125 g (4½ oz, generous ½ cup) butter, and the grated zest and juice of a lemon.
When the cake is cooked, turn out onto a wire tray, allow to cool, and cut into three rounds. Cover two of the rounds with a thick layer of the lemon butter cream. Place one on top of the other and put the last round on top. Dust generously with icing sugar (confectioners' sugar) and keep in a cool place (not the refrigerator) until ready to serve. (The layers may be sprinkled with lemon sugar syrup if desired.)

Nut délices DÉLICES AUX NOIX Blend 125 g (4½ oz, generous cup) flour with 60 g (2 oz, ¼ cup) softened butter, 1 egg yolk, 1 tablespoon water, 40 g (1½ oz, 3 tablespoons, firmly packed) caster (superfine) sugar, and a pinch of salt. When the dough is smooth, roll it into a ball and place in the refrigerator.
Cream 70 g (2½ oz, 5 tablespoons) butter; add 70 g (2½ oz, ⅓ cup, firmly packed) caster sugar and 1 egg, then 70 g (2½ oz, generous ½ cup) ground almonds, and finally 30 g (1 oz) fecula (potato flour); mix well. Roll out the chilled pastry to a thickness of 2 mm (⅛ in). Cut out 8 discs and line tartlet moulds with them. Prick the bases and cover with the almond cream. Cook in a moderately hot oven (190 C, 375 F, gas 5) for 15 minutes.
Meanwhile, prepare a French butter cream (see *creams and custards*) using 125 g (4½ oz, scant ⅔ cup) sugar cooked to the thread stage (see *sugar*) in ½ dl (2½ tablespoons, 3½ tablespoons) water, 4 egg yolks, 125 g (4½ oz, generous ½ cup) butter, and 1 teaspoon coffee essence. Chop 100 g (4 oz) fresh walnuts and mix with the cream. Allow the tartlets to cool, then turn out and top each with a dome of the walnut cream. Put in a cold place for 30 minutes.
Warm 250 g (9 oz) fondant icing to about 32 C (90 F), flavour it with a few drops of coffee essence, and add just sufficient water to make it spread easily. Dip the top of each tartlet into the fondant, smoothing it evenly over the cream with a palette knife. Place a fresh walnut on each délice and store in a cool place.

Strawberry délices DÉLICES AUX FRAISES Work together in a mixing bowl 125 g (4½ oz, generous 1 cup) flour with 1 egg, 50 g (2 oz, ¼ cup, firmly packed) caster (superfine) sugar, a pinch of salt, 1 tablespoon water, and 50 g (2 oz, 4 tablespoons) butter cut into small pieces, When the mixture is a smooth dough, place it in the refrigerator to cool. Meanwhile, wash and hull 175 g (6 oz, generous cup) strawberries and macerate in 60 g (2 oz, ¼ cup, firmly packed) sugar for 1 hour. Roll out the dough to a thickness of 3 mm (⅛ in), cut out 6 rounds, and use them to line 6 buttered tartlet moulds; prick the bases with a fork and bake blind for about 10 minutes in a moderately hot oven (190 c, 375 f, gas 5).

Meanwhile sieve the macerated strawberries and blend with 130 g (4½ oz, generous ½ cup) butter. Fill the tartlet cases with this mixture and decorate with 175 g (6 oz, generous cup) washed fresh strawberries.

demi-deuil

Meaning literally 'half-mourning', this term describes dishes containing both black and white ingredients. In classic cuisine, the 'white' foods (poached poultry and eggs, sweetbreads in white stock, potato salad, shellfish) are *contisés* (encrusted) with slices or strips of truffles and coated with suprême sauce.

Chicken demi-deuil is one of the most renowned dishes of Lyonnais cuisine, particularly the version given by Mère Fillioux: the chicken is stuffed with truffle, poached, garnished with slices of truffle between skin and flesh, served with the vegetable ingredients of the cooking stock, and coated with the strained cooking juices.

RECIPE

Chicken demi-deuil POULARDE DEMI-DEUIL Poach a chicken in white stock, place on the serving dish, and keep hot. Prepare 8 tartlets or croustades and fill them with a salpicon of calves' or lambs' sweetbreads braised in white stock and mushrooms gently cooked in butter – all mixed with suprême sauce. Garnish each tartlet with a slice of truffle heated in Madeira.

Arrange the tartlets around the chicken and coat it with suprême sauce.

Demidof

A chicken dish dedicated to Prince Anatole Demidof, the husband of Napoleon's niece, Princess Mathilde. Demidof was one of the celebrated bons viveurs of the Second Empire and an habitué of the Maison Dorée, where this recipe was created.

The name is also given to a dish of sautéed chicken.

RECIPES

Chicken Demidof POULARDE DEMIDOF Stuff a large chicken with a mixture comprising one-third quenelle stuffing and two-thirds *à gratin* forcemeat. Prepare a very thick matignon vegetable fondue using 125 g (4½ oz) carrots, 50 g (2 oz) celery, 25 g (1 oz) sliced onion, half a bay leaf, a sprig of thyme, a pinch of salt, and a pinch of sugar. Soften the vegetables in butter, moisten with 1 dl (6 tablespoons, scant ½ cup) Madeira, and reduce until dry.

Brown the chicken in the oven. Cover it with the vegetables, then wrap it in a pig's caul, tie it up, and braise it. Arrange on a serving dish and surround with artichoke hearts cooked in butter and topped with the vegetable fondue. Garnish each artichoke heart with an onion ring (covered in batter and fried) and a slice of truffle. Deglaze the cooking vessel used for the chicken with Madeira and pour over the chicken.

Sautéed chicken Demidof POULET SAUTÉ DEMIDOF Remove the giblets from a chicken and cut off the breast, wings, and legs. Brown the remaining carcass and giblets in oil, dust with flour, brown again, moisten with 1.5 dl (½ pint, ⅔ cup) dry white wine and bouillon, and cook gently for 30 minutes. Strain and reserve this cooking liquid. Cut 2 carrots, 1 turnip, 2 celery sticks (stalks), and 1 onion into thin julienne strips. Flour the chicken portions and brown them in a saucepan. Add the vegetable julienne and the strained cooking liquid, cover, and cook gently for 30 minutes. Add a slice of smoked ham and a diced truffle. Cook for a further 15 minutes, then deglaze with Madeira and demi-glace sauce.

demi-glace

A rich brown sauce made by boiling and skimming espagnole sauce and adding white stock or estouffade. It usually has the addition of Madeira, sherry, or a similar wine.

RECIPE

Demi-glace Boil down to reduce by two-thirds a mixture of 5 dl (17 fl oz, 2 cups) espagnole sauce and 8 dl (generous 1¼ pints, generous 3 cups) clear brown stock. Remove from the heat, add 5 cl (3 tablespoons, scant ¼ cup) Madeira, and strain. A handful of sliced mushroom stalks may be added during cooking.

Demi-Sel

A soft French cheese made from pasteurized cows' milk. It has a mild flavour and contains 40–45% fat and less than 2% added salt. It is sold in small squares wrapped in aluminium foil and is used as a cheese spread. It may be flavoured with herbs, paprika, or pepper. Demi-Sel was first made at the end of the last century and is a speciality of Normandy.

dénerver

A French culinary term meaning to remove tendons, membranes, etc., from raw meat, poultry, or game. It facilitates the cooking and improves presentation.

Denis (*born* Lahana Denis)

French chef and restaurateur (born Bordeaux, 1909; died Paris, 1981). He opened the restaurant Chez Denis in Paris and devoted himself to perfecting inventive and luxurious dishes. A cultured man, motivated by his love of cooking, he replied to certain chefs who criticized him for not having worked his way up through the profession: 'I have eaten my way through six inheritances in the great restaurants, so I know what good cuisine is all about.' He persuaded himself that the gourmets of today were, like him, capable of spending fortunes on such dishes as suprêmes of Bresse chicken, chaud-froids of ortolan *au chambertin*, and fresh truffles *à la ser-*

viette and on bottles of Château-Latour 1945. Consequently, he was ruined and forced to close his restaurant.

He published *La Cuisine de Denis* (Laffont, 1975), in which fundamental techniques, various tricks of the trade, and basic recipes are presented with simplicity, precision, and good sense. His recipe for scallops, is as follows: 'Sauté the scallops quickly in clarified butter, without browning. Moisten with a fumet (use about 1 tablespoon for 6 scallops). Add a few drops of absinthe or, failing this, of Pernod, some pieces of very cold butter (10 g (generous ¼ oz, ½ tablespoon) per scallop), herbs, salt, and pepper. Keep moving the sauté pan back and forth over a high heat. When the cooking liquor boils, pour the entire contents of the pan onto the serving dish.'

density

The mass of a substance per unit of volume; in practice, the weight of something divided by its volume. Density has units of grams per cc, etc.

The term density is sometimes used loosely (especially in cookery) to mean *relative density*, which is the mass of a given volume of substance divided by the mass of an equal volume of water (strictly, the water should be at 4 c (39.2 f) but this is unimportant in cookery). Relative density is also called *specific gravity*. It is used in wine-making, brewing, cider-making, the fats industry (oil, margarine), and the dairy industry (fat content of milk). Sugar concentration – important in making sweets, jams and other preserves – is now also expressed by relative density (rather than by degrees Baumé). Relative density can be measured by a hydrometer – an instrument which floats in the liquid, the relative density being read directly from its graduated stem.

dentex   DENTÉ, DENTI

A Mediterranean fish with long sharp sometimes hooked teeth and powerful jaws. The young fish are silvery grey and the adults are reddish-brown. Related to but much larger than the sea bream (up to 90 cm (36 in) long), it has firm, rather tasty, flesh and is cooked in the same way as sea bream.

dents-de-loup

Triangular croutons used for decoration or garnish, arranged as a border around the edge of a dish with the points to the outside (hence the name, which means wolves' teeth). The dents-de-loup to garnish hot dishes are triangles either cut from sandwich bread and fried in oil or butter or made from puff pastry and baked in the oven. Cold dishes are garnished with dents-de-loup cut out of strips of aspic.

The name is also used for certain kinds of crisp biscuit. One variety, a speciality of Alsace, is a long pointed biscuit flavoured with lemon and brandy. Another kind is crescent-shaped and flavoured with cumin or aniseed.

Derby

An English cheese made with cows' milk, containing approximately 45% fat. It is a firm pressed milk cheese which resembles Cheddar, but is slightly flakier and moister. The cheese is traditionally wheel-shaped, 38 cm (15 in) in diameter, 12 cm (5 in) high, and weighing approximately 14 kg (31½ lbs). The usual ripening period is two months, but mature Derby, with a richer slightly piquant flavour, ripens for ten months. Sage Derby is marbled with green and is made by adding chopped sage leaves to the curd for additional colouring and flavouring. It was traditional to make this speciality at Christmas and at harvest time.

Derby (à la)

A method of preparing chicken, created in the 1900s by Giroix when he was chef at the Hôtel de Paris at Monte Carlo. It was dedicated to a member of a distinguished British family with a predilection for French cuisine. Chicken *à la Derby* is stuffed with truffled rice and foie gras; truffles cooked in port and slices of foie gras sautéed in butter provide the garnish, and the chicken is coated with the cooking juices deglazed with port.

Derby soup is a cream of onion and curried rice soup, garnished with poached rice, quenelles of foie gras, and chopped truffle.

dérober

A French culinary term meaning to remove the skins of shelled broad (fava) beans. It also means to remove the skins of blanched tomatoes or almonds and unpeeled boiled potatoes.

Derval

A garnish for beef tournedos and noisettes of lamb, made with artichoke quarters sautéed in butter.

desalting   DESSALAGE

The removal of salt from certain foods that have been preserved in brine. Desalting is carried out by soaking the food in cold still or running water so that the salt dissolves gradually and forms a deposit on the base of the vessel. Salt cod needs to be soaked the day before it is required, changing the water several times. Salted ham must be soaked for several hours before cooking. Lardons (cut from streaky bacon) are desalted by blanching. The salt used for preservation should not be used for seasoning – it is better to desalt too much and reseason again later.

Désaugiers (Marc Antoine)

French songwriter and poet (born Fréjus, 1772; died Paris, 1827). The author of numerous table songs, he was secretary of Caveau Moderne, a gastronomic and somewhat bacchanalian literary society. His philosophy may be summed up in this verse which he wrote in the form of an epitaph:

'Je veux que la mort me frappe
Au milieu d'un grand repas,
Qu'on m'enterre sous la nappe
Entre quatre large plats,
Et que sur ma tombe on mette
Cette courte inscription:
"Ci-gît le premier poète
Mort d'une indigestion".'
(I pray that death may strike me
In the middle of a large meal.
I wish to be buried under the tablecloth
Between four large dishes.
And I desire that this short inscription
Should be engraved on my tombstone:
'Here lies the first poet
Ever to die of indigestion'.)

Descar

A garnish for large joints of meat consisting of potato croquettes and artichoke hearts cooked gently in butter and stuffed with diced breast of chicken. The garnish was created in honour of the Duc des Cars, the head of the royal household in the reign of Louis XVIII of France. He was a celebrated gourmet who unfortunately died of indigestion!

dessert

The last course of a meal. Nowadays in France, dessert comprises cheese, sweet dishes, and fresh fruit. In an ordinary menu, cheese alone sometimes replaces the dessert, especially at lunchtime.

The word comes from *desservir* (to remove that which has been served) and consequently means everything offered to guests after the previous dishes and corresponding serving utensils have been cleared away. However, its meaning has gradually changed, especially as far as sweet dishes are concerned. In former times at great banquets, dessert, which was the fifth course of the meal, was often presented in magnificent style. Large set pieces fashioned in pastry, described often and in great detail by Carême, whose accounts are accompanied by splendid illustrations, were placed on the table at the beginning of the meal. These owed more to architecture than to the art of cooking, and had a purely decorative function. Just before the sweet course, a multitude of sweets were elegantly arranged on the table with the set pieces, for every ceremonial table was laid in accordance with a detailed plan. The dishes had to harmonize with gold plate, crystal, magnificent baskets of fruit, and the tall candelabra: a magnificent spectacle. It was not until about 1850 that the word 'dessert' took on its present meaning.

In ancient times, meals generally ended with fresh or dried fruit, milk or cheese dishes, or honey. In France in the Middle Ages, the main sweet dishes, often served between meat courses, consisted of jellies, flans, blancmanges, tarts, compotes, *nieules* (flat round cakes), *fouaces* (fancy pastry), *échaudés* (poached pastry), waffles, and various other small cakes. The dessert proper consisted of the *issue*, a glass of hippocras served with *oublies* (wafers), followed by *boutehors* (dragées with spice and crystallized (candied) fruit). In the 17th century, desserts had become more elaborate and were decorated with flowers. They included marzipan, nougat, pyramids of fruit, dry and liquid preserves, biscuits, creams, sugar sweets, sweet almonds in sugar and orange-flower water, green walnuts, pistachios, and marrons glacés. At the end of the century, ice creams made their appearance, and at the same time pâtisserie became extremely diversified, with different basic mixtures, such as puff pastry, sponge, choux pastry, and meringue.

In the 20th century, instant desserts have been provided by the food industry in the form of various powders, etc., which can be mixed with milk to produce flavoured desserts.

□ **Regional and foreign specialities** Apart from the creations of the Parisian master pastrycooks, the desserts of the provinces provide a good example of the diversity of French cuisine: kouing-aman from Brittany, poirat from Berry, bourdelot from Normandy, eierkückas from Alsace, crémets from Angers, pogne from Romans, pithiviers and flaugnarde from the Auvergne, clafoutis from Limousin, etc., in addition to brioches, waffles, pancakes, and various fritters, not forgetting the 'thirteen desserts' from Provence, traditionally served at Christmas.

In Great Britain, Germany, Austria, and Belgium, where good-quality butter, cream, milk, eggs, and chocolate are also abundant, there is also a wide selection of desserts and pâtisserie. In the Mediterranean countries, the Far East, and South America, sweetmeats and fruits clearly predominate. In eastern Europe, cooked fruits, brioches, and spiced biscuits are served at the end of the meal, while in China and Japan, dessert does not exist! Ice creams, pies, and filled biscuits are particularly popular in the United States, together with fruit and pancakes.

□ **The choice of a suitable dessert** When choosing a dessert, the nature and quantities of food served in the previous courses must be taken into account. At the same time, the need for a well-balanced menu must be satisfied. The wide range of hot and cold desserts now available simplifies the task of choosing an appropriate dessert. The choice depends on the content of the main course,

whether or not a cheese course is provided, and also on the season of the
year. Moreover, the inclusion of a
regional or exotic dish in the menu may
be complemented by an appropriate
dessert that harmonizes with it. Nowadays, many restaurants offer a *grand
dessert* display or a sweet trolley, bearing a whole range of desserts from
which the diner may choose. This
attractive eye-catching display of
desserts originated in Italy, where it was
introduced to encourage the young
women and girls to stay at table during
family gatherings.

The opinions of writers are divided
on the subject of desserts. Maurice des
Ombiaux writes in his *Traité de la table:*
'The wisest choice of dessert is one that
is confined to ripe cheese, preserves, and
wines that are dry, old, and warm, like
sherry. La Chapelle, major-domo of
Louis XIII, was of the opinion that any
man who sets store by a dessert after a
good dinner is a madman who allows
his judgment to be affected by his
stomach! . . . The best desserts consist
of well-flavoured good foods that do
not take long to eat. What could be
more suitable than cheese? . . . Take
care not to introduce a new course with
gâteaux and sweetmeats, which would
be bad for digestion, only out of sheer
gluttony! However, we are not dogma-
tic, and we offer the ladies (after the
ices) petits fours, morello cherries, and
other delicacies.' Chef Denis disagrees:
'There is no good formal dinner without
a dessert of pâtisserie and preserves. The
idea of a dinner finishing with the cheese
course would be, for me, so incon-
gruous that it would never even cross
my mind!' Eugène Briffault admires the
visual splendour of a good dessert,
while at the same time agreeing with
Maurice des Ombiaux: 'The dessert
crowns the dinner. To create a fine dessert, one has to combine the skills of a
confectioner, a decorator, a painter, an
architect, an ice-cream manufacturer, a
sculptor, and a florist. The splendour of
such creations appeals above all to the
eye – the real gourmand admires them
without touching them! The magnificence of the dessert should not allow
one to forget the cheese. Cheese comple-
ments a good dinner and supplements a
bad one.'

desserte

The French term for the food that is left
over after a meal. In some instances, it
may be used as a basis for another meal.
The simplest type of desserte consists of
slices of various cold meats with gherkins or pickles. Desserte may be used to
prepare certain cold dishes, such as
mixed or meat salads, canapés,
mousses, etc., or hot dishes, such as
shepherd's pie, various stuffings, croquettes, bouchées, pilaf, risotto, etc.
Under the Ancien Régime, the members
of the royal household in charge of food
did a brisk trade in desserte with outside
caterers and restaurateurs. In certain
French restaurants, such food (apart
from a few items) belongs to the waiters.

A desserte is also a small sideboard on
which the dishes are stacked after their
removal from the table.

détailler

A French term meaning to cut up
various items of food into dice, rounds,
slices, cubes, etc. Vegetables cut up in
this way can be used for preparing a
julienne, brunoise, mirepoix, or macédoine. The *détail* of meat includes all the
joints cut up by the butcher, especially
the pieces cut into a special shape or
thickness – escalopes, medallions,
noisettes, grenadins, etc.

détendre

A French culinary term meaning to
soften a paste or a mixture by adding an
appropriate substance, such as beaten
eggs, milk, or stock.

détrempe

The French culinary term for a paste
made with flour and water in the first
stage of pastry-making, before the addition of butter, eggs, milk, etc. It is best
to let the détrempe rest in a cool place
for about ten minutes before adding the
remaining ingredients. (A détrempe is
rarely used on its own, except as a luting
paste.)

Détremper a paste or dough is to
allow the flour to absorb all the necessary water, kneading it with the tips of
the fingers without working it too
much.

Deux Magots

A Parisian café frequented by the literary fraternity of Saint-Germain-des-Prés. It adjoined the rival Café de Flore and took its name from a draper's shop which previously occupied the site. Today the café has become a rendezvous for Left Bank intellectuals: at first patronized by the journalists of the *Mercure de France*, it was later frequented by Giraudoux, André Breton, Sartre, Simone de Beauvoir, and other literary figures.

devilled À LA DIABLE

The name given to dishes of meat, poultry, fish, shellfish, offal, etc., that are seasoned, usually coated with mustard, dipped in egg and coated with breadcrumbs, grilled (broiled), and served with a piquant devilled sauce. These dishes are very popular in English cookery. Devilled chicken or pigeon, for example, is prepared by slitting the bird open along its back, spreading it out flat, seasoning it, and then grilling it. It is then dipped in egg and coated with coarse or fine breadcrumbs and browned. It is served with a devilled sauce.

| RECIPES

Devilled herrings HARENGS À LA DIABLE Scale, wash, and dry the herrings, then slit them along the back and sides. Season and coat with mustard, sprinkle with white breadcrumbs and oil, and cook slowly under the grill (broiler). Serve with mustard sauce, ravigote sauce, or devilled sauce.

Devilled meat dishes METS ENDIABLÉS (from A. Suzanne's recipe) In England, this is a way of using pieces of leftover poultry or game or the remains of a joint to make a tasty meal. Mix together the following: 1 tablespoon English mustard, 1 tablespoon mustard with herbs, 2 tablespoons (3 tablespoons) olive oil, 2 egg yolks, 1 teaspoon each of Worcestershire sauce, salt, and anchovy paste, and a pinch of cayenne. (Curry, tomato purée, or a concentrated onion purée may be added if desired.) Coat the meat with this mixture and grill (broil) under a medium heat until brown. Serve piping hot with a good gravy.

Devilled oyster HUÎTRES À LA DIABLE Poach, drain, and remove the beards of the oysters. Thread them on small kebab skewers, coat with melted butter seasoned with a little cayenne, and dip them in white breadcrumbs. Grill (broil) under a low flame and serve with devilled sauce.

Devilled sauce SAUCE À LA DIABLE (English recipe) Add 1 tablespoon chopped shallots to 1.5 dl (¼ pint, ⅔ cup) vinegar, and reduce by half. Then add 2.5 dl (8 fl oz, 1 cup) espagnole sauce and 2 tablespoons (3 tablespoons) tomato purée. Cook for 5 minutes. Just before serving, add 1 tablespoon Worcestershire sauce, 1 tablespoon Harvey sauce or spiced vinegar, and a dash of cayenne. Strain the sauce. This sauce is generally served with grilled (broiled) meat.

diable

A cooking pot consisting of two porous earthenware pans, one of which fits over the other as a lid. It is designed for cooking certain vegetables without adding water, e.g. potatoes, beetroot, chestnuts, and onions. Each pan has a flat base; half-way through cooking, the diable is turned upside down. The diable from Charentes resembles a small round casserole dish, with a handle and a tightly fitting lid.

The diable is never washed, because the dryer it is, the more tender are the vegetables. Sometimes the inner surfaces are rubbed with a clove of garlic. It was originally meant to be used when cooking on hot charcoal, but may also be used in an ordinary oven. If placed directly onto an electric hotplate or a gas ring, it is advisable to start off the cooking very slowly over a gentle heat; otherwise, a heat diffuser should be placed beneath the base.

diable (à la)

See *devilled*.

diablotin

A very thin small round slice of bread (sometimes first coated with reduced béchamel sauce) sprinkled with grated cheese and browned in the oven. Diablotins are usually served with soup, particularly consommé. If Roquefort cheese is used, they can be served as cocktail snacks.

Formerly the name *diablotin* was used for a small fritter made of a deep-fried thick sauce. It is also the name of a small spoon used to measure spices for cocktails.

RECIPES

Cheese diablotins DIABLOTINS AU FROMAGE Cut a *ficelle* (long thin French loaf) into slices 5–6 mm (¼ in) thick. Butter them, and coat with grated cheese (Comté, Emmental, or Beaufort, which melt, or Parmesan, which doesn't melt). A thin slice of Gruyère or Edam may be used instead. Brown the slices quickly and serve with soup.

Diablotins with walnuts and Roquefort cheese DIABLOTINS AUX NOIX ET AU ROQUEFORT Cut a long French loaf into slices about 5 or 6 mm (¼ in) thick. Mix some butter with an equal quantity of Roquefort cheese and add some roughly chopped green walnuts (1 tablespoon walnuts per 75 g (3 oz) of the mixture). Spread the mixture on the slices of bread and quickly heat in a very hot oven.

diabolo

A refreshing nonalcoholic drink made with lemonade and fruit syrup. The most common diabolos are those made with mint and grenadine.

Diane (à la)

The description *à la Diane* is given to certain game dishes that are dedicated to the goddess Diana (the huntress). Joints of venison *à la Diane* are sautéed and coated with sauce Diane (a highly peppered sauce with cream and truffles). They are served with chestnut purée and croutons spread with game forcemeat. The name may also be given to a game purée, used to garnish either soft-boiled eggs on croûtes (with a salmis sauce) or mushroom barquettes with sauce chasseur. This purée can also form the basis of a cream soup, flavoured with port. Quails *à la Diane* are simmered in stock and tomato-

flavoured demi-glace, then garnished with small quenelles and braised lettuce.

dieppoise (à la)

A method of preparing fish named after the port of Dieppe, which is famous for the excellence of the sole fished in its waters. Sole, whiting, or brill *à la dieppoise* are cooked in white wine, garnished with mussels, shrimps, and often mushrooms, and masked with a white wine sauce made with the cooking stock of the fish and mussels. This method is also suitable for cooking pike and even artichokes. Dieppoise garnish consists of mussels, prawns (shrimp), and mushrooms cooked in white wine and is used for bouchées, barquettes, salads, and a velouté sauce.

Mackerel and herrings marinated in white wine are considered to be a speciality of Dieppe; they are also called *à la dieppoise*. See also *Marmite dieppoise*.

RECIPES

Brill à la dieppoise BARBUE À LA DIEPPOISE Prepare ½ litre (17 fl oz, 2 cups) fish fumet. Clean 1 kg (2¼ lb) mussels and cook them *à la marinière*. Make a white roux with 25 g (1 oz, 2 tablespoons) butter and 25 g (1 oz, ¼ cup) flour and gradually add the fish fumet together with 1 dl (6 tablespoons, scant ½ cup) strained cooking stock of the mussels. Add 1 tablespoon roughly chopped mushrooms and a bouquet garni. Check the seasoning and boil gently for 20–25 minutes to reduce. Shell the mussels and keep them hot in the remainder of their cooking stock, taking care not to boil them.

Season a brill weighing about 750 g (1¾ lb) with salt and place in a buttered flameproof dish. Pour over 1.5 dl (¼ pint, ⅔ cup) white wine. Bring to the boil, uncovered, then cook in the oven for 15–18 minutes at about 220 c (425 F, gas 7), basting the fish frequently. Mix 2 egg yolks with a little of the partially cooled mushroom sauce. Add 60 g (2¼ oz) peeled prawns (shelled shrimp) and the cooking liquor from the fish to the rest of the mushroom sauce. Mix well, heat, add the hot drained mussels, then the egg-yolk mixture, and coat the brill with this sauce. This recipe may also be used for fresh cod.

Scallops au gratin à la dieppoise CO-QUILLES SAINT-JACQUES GRATINÉES À LA DIEPPOISE Poach the white flesh of 16 good scallops very gently for 4 minutes in ½ litre (17 fl oz, 2 cups) fish fumet mixed with 2 dl (7 fl oz, ¾ cup) dry white wine. Cook 1 kg (2¼ lb) small mussels *à la marinière*. Prepare a sauce from a roux, the mussel cooking liquor, and the fish fumet as described in the previous recipe. Add 1 tablespoon chopped mushroom stalks and a bouquet garni to the sauce; check the seasoning and cook gently for 20–25 minutes.

Keep the scallops hot in a covered lightly buttered gratin dish over a saucepan of hot water. Shell the mussels and keep hot in the rest of their cooking liquor, without boiling. Add 75 g (3 oz) peeled prawns (shelled shrimp). When the sauce is cooked, strain it through a sieve and add the strained mussels and prawns. Dilute an egg yolk with a little of the sauce and whisk it in. Coat the scallops with the sauce, scatter with very fine fresh breadcrumbs, sprinkle with melted butter, and brown quickly in the oven or under the grill (broiler).

dietetic products
PRODUITS DIÉTÉTIQUES

Food preparations that are manufactured for the specific needs of certain categories of consumer such as babies, pregnant women, sportsmen, etc., or for people suffering from a specific illness, such as diabetes, various cardiovascular conditions, obesity, etc. Dietetic and dietary products in France are regulated by a decree (23 January 1975) and subsequent enactments that control the composition, the conditions of manufacture and sale, the labelling, and the advertising of such products. The principal categories of dietetic products are those concerned with salt-free diets, low-sugar diets, low-calorie diets, and those requiring a very precise composition and/or calorific value. Some food preparations have a guaranteed content of certain vitamins, amino acids, mineral salts, etc., and there are also specific products to aid and promote growth, and/or to provide extra energy.

dietetics DIÉTÉTIQUE

The study of everything concerned with diet and all that relates to the therapeutic use of food. Dietetics can be defined as the art of nourishing oneself naturally. The importance of a sensible balanced diet has been amply proved where health is concerned.

The science of dietetics is still mainly applied to invalid diets, diets for chronic diseases, such as diabetes, heart disease, etc., and slimming diets. But it is just as important for dietetics to be used in the service of the healthy. To feed oneself badly means depriving the body of nutrients that it requires, or providing these in overgenerous or insufficient amounts, practices which often lead to disease and disorders.

It is important, therefore, to know the body's quantitative and qualitative requirements, and to discover what percentage of vital elements are present in the various foods. With this knowledge it is possible to compile diets suited to various needs.

dietician DIÉTÉTICIEN

A specialist in the study and regulation of food intake and food preparation (dietetics), who has had scientific and paramedical training. The profession is a relatively new one in France and is usually practised by women. Dieticians may work in hospitals, supervising and dealing with all aspects of the patient's diet; in various educational establishments or with health authorities, etc., advising on and supervising the formulation of menus and various dietary aspects of health; and also in the food industry. A dietician is also called upon to carry out investigations, to give private consultations, and to prepare information for the mass media.

digestive DIGESTIF

A liqueur or spirit that may be taken after a meal, more for the pleasure of drinking it than for any digestive action. Digestives are served plain or with ice.

dijonnaise (à la)

The description *à la dijonnaise* is given to various dishes prepared with a speciality of Dijon, particularly mustard (for savoury dishes) or blackcurrants (for sweet dishes). Dijonnaise sauce is a mustard-flavoured mayonnaise-type sauce served with cold meats.

RECIPES

Dijonnaise sauce Pound together 4 hard-boiled (hard-cooked) egg yolks and 4 tablespoons (5 tablespoons) Dijon mustard. Season with salt and pepper. Work in some oil (up to ½ litre, ¾ pint, 2 cups) and lemon juice, like a mayonnaise.

Sweet omelette à la dijonnaise OMELETTE SUCRÉE À LA DIJONNAISE Beat 8 eggs together, then add 5–6 finely crushed macaroons, 2 tablespoons (3 tablespoons) fresh cream, and 1 tablespoon caster (superfine) sugar. Make 2 flat omelettes. Mix about 3 dl (½ pint, 1¼ cups) thick confectioners' custard (see *creams and custards*) with 1 tablespoon ground almonds and 2 tablespoons (3 tablespoons) blackcurrant jelly. Cover one of the omelettes with the mixture and place the second omelette on top. Cover completely with a meringue made with 3 or 4 egg whites. Dust with 1 tablespoon icing (confectioners') sugar and glaze in a very hot oven. Serve surrounded with a border of blackcurrant jelly.

dill ANETH

An aromatic umbelliferous plant originating in the East and introduced into Europe in ancient times. It is commonly called false anise or bastard fennel. The French name comes from the Greek *anethon* (fennel), and in Roman times it was the symbol of vitality.

Dill leaves are used as a culinary herb and the seeds are used in cooking in north Africa (in the preparation of meat), the Soviet Union, and particularly in Scandinavia, where they are used in the preparation of salmon and crayfish. Dill is also used to make an aromatic vinegar and as a flavouring for various pickles, including gherkins.

dinner DÎNER

Today, dinner is normally the evening meal, but in France before the Revolution, dinner was eaten in the morning or at midday. It is generally thought that the French word *dîner* is derived from the Latin *disjunare* (to break the fast), as is *déjeuner*, the French word for lunch. This is because the word was originally used for the morning meal that was eaten after mass, first at 7 a.m. and later at 9 or 10 a.m. It consisted of bacon, eggs, and fish and was one of the two main meals of the day, the other being supper (taken at about 5 p.m.). However, other theories concerning its origin have also been put forward: *dîner* might have been derived from *decim hora* (the tenth hour, i.e. ten o'clock), or from the words of the blessing *dignare dominum*, or even from the Greek word *deipnon* (the meal eaten after sunset).

The hour for eating dinner became progressively later when the daily rite of Mass was observed less strictly, and in time, the habit of serving a light meal on rising developed. This meal, the *déjeuner* later became the *petit déjeuner* (breakfast). Dinner was at midday in the reigns of Louis XIII and Louis XIV, and Furetière describes the meal thus: 'Midday is the normal time for dinner. When one wants to go and see people, it is advisable to do so between eleven o'clock and midday, certainly not later, for then one would be preventing them from taking their meal.'

In the 18th century, dinner was moved on to 2 p.m., but supper often remained the principal meal of the day. Finally, at the time of the Revolution, dinner was eaten at the end of the afternoon, lunch was taken at midday, and supper was served (in the towns) when there was a soirée. In the country, there was less change and supper continued to be the main meal for a considerable period of time.

Today, dinner usually takes place at about 7 p.m., earlier in Scandinavian countries, later in Mediterranean countries. It may be a formal occasion for receiving guests. Alexandre Dumas defined dinner as the 'principal act of the day that can only be carried out in a worthy manner by people of wit and humour; for it is not sufficient just to eat at dinner. One has to talk with a calm and discreet gaiety. The conversation must sparkle like the rubies in the entremets wines, it must be delightfully suave with the sweetmeats of the dessert, and become very profound with the coffee.' According to the chef Denis, the composition of a formal dinner must be varied and abundant, and hot dishes must alternate with cold ones. For a big occasion, he recommends: consommé, followed by a cold entrée, a large hot entrée, a sorbet, a hot roast, a cold roast, vegetables, sweet dessert, pâtisserie, and fruit. This prescription is now simplified to: consommé, fish served in a sauce, roast meat and garnish, and pâtisserie. Some gastronomes advise against serving cheese at dinner.

diot

A small vegetable and pork sausage made in Savoy. Diots may be dried like saucissons; fresh diots are browned in lard with sliced onions then gently simmered in a little white wine.

diplomate (à la)

The description *à la diplomate* is given to dishes that include truffles and lobster, thus evoking the idea of luxury and refinement. Diplomat sauce, also called riche sauce, is made with lobster butter, truffles, and lobster flesh and accompanies delicate fish, such as John Dory, sole, and turbot.

RECIPES

Diplomat sauce SAUCE DIPLO-MATE Add 2 tablespoons (3 tablespoons) truffle parings or chopped mushroom stalks to 2 dl (7 fl oz, ¾ cup) fish fumet and reduce by half. Make 80 g (3 oz) white roux and add 8 dl (generous 1¼ pints, generous 3 cups) fish stock (use the cooking liquid of the fish specified in the recipe). Strain the reduced fumet and add it, together with 2 dl (7 fl oz, ¾ cup) cream, to the sauce. Reduce again by half. Add 50 g (2 oz, 4 tablespoons) lobster butter, 4 tablespoons (⅓ cup) cream, 1 tablespoon brandy, and a pinch of cayenne. Strain through a sieve. If the sauce is served separately, add to it 1 tablespoon diced lobster flesh (cooked in a court-bouillon) and 1 tablespoon diced truffles.

Sole diplomate Remove the skin from a good-sized sole, slit its flesh along the backbone, and free the top fillets, working outwards from the centre. Cut the backbone at the head and tail and re-move it completely. Prepare 125 g (4½ oz) whiting forcemeat *à la crème*, adding 1 tablespoon diced truffles. Insert the forcemeat underneath the top fillets. Gently poach the sole in a fish fumet but do not cover. Drain, remove the small lateral bones, arrange on the serving dish, and surround with diced lobster flesh. Keep hot. Use the cooking liquid to make some diplomat sauce as described above and coat the fish with it.

diplomat pudding
DIPLOMATE

A cold dessert prepared in a mould by two different methods. The more common version consists of sponge fingers (lady-fingers) soaked in a rum- or Kirsch-flavoured syrup, layered with crystallized (candied) fruits, apricot jam, and an egg custard or a Bavarian cream. After refrigeration, the pudding is unmoulded and coated with fruit sauce or custard cream. in the second version, the sponge fingers are replaced by layers of stale brioche soaked in milk and the pudding is cooked in a bain-marie. It is then chilled and unmoulded, and served with custard or chocolate sauce.

Individual diplomats are barquettes filled with a cream containing crystallized fruits, glazed with apricot jam, covered with fondant icing (frosting), and garnished with a crystallized cherry.

Bombe diplomate is made with ice cream and crystallized fruits (see *bombe glacée*).

RECIPES

Diplomat pudding DIPLOMATE AU BAVAROIS Make a syrup with 1 dl (6 tablespoons, scant ½ cup) water and 100 g (4 oz, 8 tablespoons, firmly packed) caster (superfine) sugar. Bring to the boil and add 50 g (2 oz, ⅓ cup) sultanas. Leave for a few minutes, drain, and reserve the syrup. Dice 50 g (2 oz, ¼ cup) crystallized (candied) fruits and soak in 5 cl (2½ tablespoons, 3 tablespoons) rum.

Soak 15 g (½ oz, 1 tablespoon) powdered gelatine in 3 tablespoons cold water. Boil ½ litre (17 fl oz, 2 cups) milk with half a vanilla pod (bean). Beat 4 large egg yolks with 125 g (4½ oz, scant ⅔ cup) caster sugar until the mixture is light and creamy, then add the boiling milk a little at a time, stirring with a wooden spatula. Pour the mixture into a saucepan and cook over a low heat, stirring continuously, until the custard cream is just thick enough to coat the spoon. Stir the gelatine into the custard cream, then pass through a sieve. Leave to cool. Whip 2 dl (7 fl oz, ¾ cup) double (heavy) cream until stiff with 1 tablespoon very cold milk and fold into the cold custard.

Strain the rum from the crystallized fruit and add it to the reserved syrup Use the rum-flavoured syrup to soak 200 g (7 oz) sponge fingers (ladyfingers). Put some of the crystallized fruit in the bottom of a greased mould, cover with a layer of the Bavarian cream, and then with a layer of sponge fingers sprinkled with sultanas and crystallized fruit. Coat with a little apricot jam. Continue to fill the mould with layers of Bavarian cream, sponge fingers, sultanas, crystallized fruits, and apricot jam. Refrigerate for at least 2 hours.

Heat some apricot jam until liquid and add to it 5 cl (2½ tablespoons, 3 tablespoons) rum. Unmould the diplomat pudding onto a dish and coat it with the apricot sauce or, if preferred, with a little thin custard.

Individual diplomats with crystallized fruit PETITS DIPLOMATES AUX FRUITS CONFITS Make a pastry with 130 g (5½ oz, generous 1 cup) flour, a pinch of salt, 35 g (1½ oz, 3 tablespoons, firmly packed) sugar, 1 egg yolk, and 70 g (3 oz, 6 tablespoons) softened butter. Roll the dough into a ball; wrap and chill.

Mix in a bowl 70 g (3 oz, 6 tablespoons) softened butter with 70 g (3 oz, 6 tablespoons, firmly packed) caster (superfine) sugar, 1 egg, and 70 g (3 oz, ¾ cup) ground almonds. Roll 50 g (2 oz, ⅓ cup) sultanas and 50 g (2 oz, ¼ cup) diced crystallized (candied) fruits in 20 g (¾ oz, 3 tablespoons) flour. Stir the fruit into the almond mixture, then add 5 cl (2½ tablespoons, 3 tablespoons) rum and mix well. Heat the oven to about 200 c (400 F, gas 6).

Roll out the pastry until it is about 2 mm (¼ in) thick, then cut out about 10 oval shapes with a pastry cutter (cookie cutter). Butter some barquette moulds and line them with the pastry shapes, leaving an excess of about 2 mm (¼ in) around the edges. Fill with the fruit-cream mixture and bake in the oven for 30 minutes. Remove the moulds from the oven, and cool. Turn the barquettes out of the moulds and glaze with apricot jam that has been liquefied over a low heat.

Heat 100 g (4 oz) fondant icing (frosting) very gently so that it liquefies, and use to coat the diplomats. Decorate each diplomat with a glacé cherry and keep in a cool place until ready to serve.

dipping pin
BROCHE À TREMPER
A small confectionery utensil consisting of a stainless steel rod with a wooden handle and a spiral, a ring, or a two- or three-pronged fork at the end. The pin (or ring) is used for plunging a sweet in sugar fondant or melted chocolate to coat it, or for dipping a petit four or a sugar-coated fruit in boiling sugar to glaze it.

distillation
The process of boiling a liquid and cooling and collecting the vapour, so as to separate components of the liquid mixture. It is the basic process in making strong alcoholic spirits, either from wine or from other fermented material (e.g. grain or potatoes). It depends on the fact that different substances boil at different temperatures; alcohol, in particular, boils more easily than water, so the vapour from boiling wine (say) will contain more alcohol than the original wine. Distillation, then, is a method of increasing the alcohol content – over and above that possible by normal fermentation. The distilled liquor also contains other substances from the original mixture, giving it its flavour. In many distillation processes, a second distillation (or rectification) is used. This is sometimes followed by the addition of aromatic substances (e.g. Cognac is matured in oak barrels; gin is flavoured with juniper berries). Usually, the process is carried out in an alembic – a large copper vessel with a long neck in which the vapour condenses and from which

the distillate drips (The word 'distillation' comes from the Latin *distillare* – to fall drop by drop).

Divan-Le Peletier

A brasserie situated in the Rue Le Peletier in Paris, founded in 1837 and called the Café du Divan. At that time, the Opéra was situated nearby in the same street and so the café was frequented by writers and actors. Balzac and Gavarni rubbed shoulders with Alfred de Musset (who went there to drink beer laced with absinthe), Meissonier, Daumier, and Henri Monnier. Besides the beer, the clientele enjoyed the brasserie's sweet liqueurs, which were sold under such picturesque names as 'Parfait Amour', 'Crinoline', 'Alma', 'Sebastopol', 'Lique Impériale', and 'Le Retour de Banni'. The establishment closed in 1859.

dodine

A dish of boned, stuffed, and braised poultry (particularly duck) or meat, similar to a ballottine.

In medieval cookery the term dodine was used for a classic sauce for which Taillevent gives three recipes: white dodine (milk boiled with ginger, egg yolks, and sugar), red dodine (toast soaked in red wine, rubbed through a sieve, and boiled with fried onions, bacon, cinnamon, nutmeg, cloves, sugar, and salt), and verjuice dodine (egg yolks, verjuice, crushed chicken livers, ginger, parsley, and bouillon). These sauces were placed under roasting poultry, so that the fat and meat juices ran into the sauce and were thus blended in. Dodines were used to accompany duck, teal, plover, and capons. The dish was served with roast potatoes.

Nowadays, the names 'duck *à la dodine*' or 'guinea fowl *en dodine*' are still given to certain haute cuisine dishes in which the bird is roasted and carved, the legs and sliced breast meat are set aside, and the carcass is browned with carrots, and onions (or mushrooms), wine, spices, and the cooking juices. The sauce is then sieved and the uncooked chopped liver of the bird is added, together with fresh cream. The sauce is poured over the joints before serving. Dodine of duck is a wel. known speciality in Aquitaine, Burgundy (served with Chambertin wine), the Morvan, and Touraine.

RECIPE

Dodine of duck DODINE DE CANARD Bone a duck without damaging the skin, keeping the breast meat intact as far as possible. Remove all the flesh from the skin. Cut the breast meat into aiguillettes (thin slices) and marinate them for 24 hours in 2 tablespoons (3 tablespoons) brandy, a pinch of fennel, salt, and pepper. Chop the remaining flesh and mix it with 250 g (9 oz, 13 slices) chopped fat bacon, 250 g (9 oz) chopped lean pork, 250 g (9 oz) chopped veal, 250 g (9 oz, generous 2 cups) button mushrooms, 50 g (2 oz, generous 2 cups) ground almonds, and a small bunch of parsley. Work 2 tablespoons (3 tablespoons) truffle parings (or diced truffles), 1 egg, salt, and pepper into the mixture. Toss a knob of the mixture in a sauté pan, and after a few minutes taste it and adjust the seasoning if necessary.

Spread out the skin of the duck and cover it with half of the stuffing. Arrange the slices of breast on top and cover with the remaining stuffing. Fold the skin towards the centre at the neck and the tail, roll, and tie up the dodine. Either wipe a soaked pig's caul and tie it around the dodine or tie the dodine in shape with string. Braise the dodine in a little white wine in the oven at 180 C (350 F, gas 4), basting it several times. Cook from 1½ to 1¾ hours, until the juices that run out when it is pricked are clear.

If the dodine is to be served hot, cut the thread and remove any parts of the caul that have not melted. Skim the fat off the cooking juices and add 2 tablespoons (3 tablespoons) port and a few tablespoons of stock. Reduce by half. Cut the dodine into slices, garnish with watercress, and serve with the sauce.

If the dodine is to be served cold, allow it to cool completely before cutting the thread. Serve with a green or mixed salad.

dogfish ROUSSETTE

A small shark, two species of which are sold as food, under the name of rock

salmon. The smaller dogfish is 40–60
cm (16–24 in) long and has a grey skin
marked with numerous brown spots.
The larger species is less common; up to
1.2 m (47 in) long, it is redder in colour
and has larger and fewer spots. Dogfish
have small round fins and flat heads;
their skeletons are made of cartilage,
which is easy to take out. The thick
rough skin is usually removed before
sale. The dogfish is cheap to buy, with
little waste, and can be cooked in
numerous ways (recipes for monkfish
and skate are suitable). The high season
is in January and February.

dolichos

DOLIC, DOLIQUE

A genus of pulses of which several
varieties are cultivated in warm and
tropical regions. The most common is
the mongette dolicho, which is widely
cultivated in China and Louisiana
(United States) and is also grown in the
south of France (where it is known as
bannette) and in Italy. It is similar to a
haricot bean (navy bean), but the seeds
are smaller. The young pods may be
cooked and eaten like French beans.
The asparagus bean has very long pods
– up to 1 metre (3 feet) – and its beans
vary in colour. The lablab dolicho (or
bonavist bean) is cultivated in Africa
and the West Indies.

dolma

A Turkish and Greek dish, the main
form of which comprises a vine leaf
stuffed with cooked rice and minced
lamb, rolled into a cylinder, and braised
in a little stock with olive oil and lemon
juice added. Dolmas (or dolmades) are
usually served cold as hors d'oeuvres.
They may also be made with cabbage or
fig leaves, or even with the leaves of
the hazel tree. In Turkey, they are
traditionally cooked in sheep-tail fat.

RECIPE

Yalanci dolmas Choose large sound
vine leaves. Blanch for a maximum of 2
minutes, cool under running water, and
wipe dry. For about 50 dolmas, half-
cook 125 g (4½ oz, scant ½ cup) rice in
meat stock. Peel and roughly chop 400 g
(14 oz) onions and cook gently in olive

oil until soft but not brown. Mince 250
g (½ lb) mutton or lamb and gently
brown it. Finally chop 1 tablespoon
fresh mint. Mix all these ingredients
together. Place a small ball of stuffing on
each vine leaf, fold up the tip and base of
the leaf, roll into a cylinder, and tie with
kitchen thread.

Oil a sauté pan and place the dolmas
in it, packing them closely together.
Sprinkle with 4 tablespoons olive oil,
the juice of 2 lemons, and about 1 glass
stock flavoured with 1 tablespoon
coriander seed. Cover and simmer
gently for about 30 minutes. Drain the
dolmas and let them get completely cold
before removing the thread.

domyoji age

A Japanese dish consisting of fried
shrimps coated with dried rice, accompanied by sliced peppers and aubergines
(eggplants) and slices of lemon. It is a
classic example of the type of dish that
combines contrasting textures, colours,
and flavours, much favoured in
Japanese cookery.

donkey   ÂNE

A mammal used essentially as a draught
or pack animal; its meat is only a subsidiary edible product. In some oriental
countries young donkey meat is very
popular, as it was in France at the time
of the Renaissance. Nowadays, the
meat of large donkeys (the Poitou
breed) is put into the same class as
horsemeat. In the south of France,
where donkeys are smaller, their meat,
which is firmer and has a stronger
flavour, is used mainly in such products
as the Arles sausage. Ass's milk, which
has a composition similar to human
milk, has been used for a long time to
feed nursing babies; it was also considered to have restorative properties. In
the Balkans it is made into cream cheese.

This is what Alexandre Dumas says
of the donkey in his *Grand Dictionnaire
de cuisine*: 'Tastes change. We have
recently seen the horse on the verge of
replacing the ox, which would be quite
just, since the ox had replaced the
donkey. Maecenas was the first in
Roman times to make use of the flesh of
the domestic donkey.... Monsieur
Isouard of Malta reports that, as a result
of the blockade of the island of Malta by

the English and the Neapolitans, the inhabitants were reduced to eating all the horses, dogs, cats, donkeys, and rats: 'This circumstance,' he says, 'led to the discovery that donkey meat was very good; so much so, in fact, that gourmands in the city of Valetta preferred it to the best beef and even veal. . . . Particularly boiled, roast, or braised, its flavour is exquisite. The meat is blackish and the fat verging on yellow. However, the donkey must only be three or four years old and must be fat."'

Doria

The name of various classic dishes, probably dedicated to a member of the famous Genoese Doria family who was an habitué of the Café Anglais in Paris in the 19th century. These dishes evoke the image of Italy, either by combining the colours of the Italian flag (green, white, and red) or by including Piedmontese white truffles.

RECIPES

Bombe Doria Coat a bombe mould with pistachio ice cream. Macerate some pieces of marron glacé in Curaçao, then add them to a vanilla-flavoured bombe mixture. Fill the mould with this mixture and set in the refrigerator.

Chicken Doria POULARDE DORIA Wrap a chicken in a pig's caul and poach in white stock. Drain, remove the caul, and untruss the bird. Slit at the breastbone, remove the suprêmes (breast and wings), then take out all the small bones inside the carcass. Mix together 100 g (4 oz, 1 cup) very small peeled and trimmed mushrooms, 100 g (4 oz) cooked cocks' combs and kidneys, and 100 g (4 oz) white truffles trimmed to the shape of olives and bind the mixture with 3 dl (½ pint, 1¼ cups) thick chicken velouté sauce.

Use this stuffing to reshape the chicken. Cut up the suprêmes into thin slices and arrange them on the reshaped carcass. Coat with very thick allemande sauce, dust with grated Parmesan, and brown lightly in a hot oven. Arrange the chicken on a dish and surround with 8 large chicken quenelles studded with pieces of truffle, 8 fried cocks' combs, and 8 large trimmed mushrooms cooked in butter. Garnish with cucumbers cut into small pieces and cooked in butter.

Doria salad SALADE DORIA Place a heap of shredded celeriac (celery root), dressed with rémoulade sauce, in a deep salad bowl and cover with thin slices of white truffle. Surround with a border of cooked green asparagus tips and thin strips of cooked beetroot (red beet) that has been seasoned with vinaigrette. Sprinkle with sieved hard-boiled (hard-cooked) egg yolk and chopped parsley.

dorine

A tartlet filled with chestnut purée and confectioners' custard (pastry cream), sprinkled with flaked almonds, and glazed with apricot jam.

RECIPE

Dorines Mix 150 g (5 oz, 1¼ cups) flour with 80 g (3 oz, 6 tablespoons) butter (cut into pieces), 45 g (1½ oz, 3 tablespoons, firmly packed) sugar, a pinch of salt, 1 egg yolk, and a little water. Knead the ingredients together quickly to obtain a smooth dough. Roll the pastry into a ball, wrap, and place in the refrigerator. Prepare some confectioners' custard (pastry cream) with ¼ litre (8 fl oz, 1 cup) milk, 3 egg yolks, 75 g (3 oz, 6 tablespoons, firmly packed) caster (superfine) sugar, and 20 g (¾ oz, scant ¼ cup) cornflour (cornstarch).

Roll out the pastry to a thickness of about 2 mm (¼ in) and cut out 8 rounds with a pastry cutter (cookie cutter). Line 8 buttered tartlet moulds with the pastry. Mix the contents of 1 can of sweetened chestnut purée with 5 cl (3 tablespoons, ¼ cup) rum and half-fill the tartlets with this mixture. Top with the confectioners' custard and sprinkle with flaked almonds. Cook on a baking sheet in a moderately hot oven (about 190 c, 375 f, gas 5) for 20–25 minutes. Glaze the cooked dorines with 100 g (4 oz, scant ¼ cup) apricot jam that has been gently heated. Turn them out of the moulds when completely cold.

dormouse　LOIR

A small rodent that nests in the branches of trees and feeds on nuts, berries, and seeds. In ancient times it was considered to be a delicacy, but is no longer eaten. The Romans were so fond of dormice that they bred them in special containers made of mud with holes through which the animals were fed with chestnuts, acorns, and nuts. When the dormice had been fattened up, they were either stewed or roasted and then coated with a sauce made from honey and poppyseeds. As late as the 17th century, it was still possible to find dormouse pie in France.

doughnut

A small cake made from enriched bread dough or a baking-powder dough. Doughnuts may be round or ring-shaped; the former are often filled with jam. After being fried in hot fat, they are dusted with sugar and eaten hot or cold.

| RECIPE

Doughnuts　Mix 15 g (½ oz) baker's yeast (1 cake compressed yeast) with 5 fl oz (⅔ cup) warm milk. Alternatively, use 1½ teaspoons dried yeast. Put 500 g (18 oz, generous 4¼ cups) sifted flour, 100–125 g (4–4½ oz, 8–9 tablespoons, firmly packed) caster (superfine) sugar, a generous pinch of salt, and ½ teaspoon grated nutmeg in a large bowl. Make a well in the centre and mix a beaten egg with the dry ingredients as thoroughly as possible. Add 2 more eggs, one at a time. Work 60 g (2¼ oz, 4½ tablespoons) melted butter into the mixture, then add the warm yeast mixture. Knead the dough until it becomes elastic. Leave to rise until the volume doubles.

Roll out the dough on a floured surface to a thickness of about 1 cm (⅓ in) and cut it into rounds with a pastry cutter (cookie cutter) 6–7 cm (2½ in) in diameter. Fry the doughnuts in hot fat (at least 185 c, 360 f), until they swell up and become golden brown. Drain on absorbent paper, dust with icing (confectioners') sugar, and serve very hot with maple syrup or a cranberry compote.

doughs and batters

PÂTES DE CUISINE ET DE PÂTISSERIE

The basis of all doughs and batters is a mixture of flour and water. At this stage, when a little salt is added, unleavened bread and pasta can be made. The addition of raising (leavening) agents is required for bread dough and its variants. All pastry doughs are enriched with fat (butter, oil, or margarine), and some of them have in addition eggs, milk (instead of water), sugar, and various other ingredients, such as ground almonds, vanilla, dried fruit, etc.

All doughs and batters, even sweet ones, are seasoned with a little salt to bring out the flavour. Wheat flour, which is the basis of most doughs and batters, contains gluten and starch, which ensure the cohesion of the finished product. The water (or milk) disperses the starch, dissolves the salt (and sugar when present), and enables the raising agent to work. (An effect similar to that of a raising agent is sometimes obtained by adding beer, especially when making pancakes and brioches.) The fat gives the pastry its final texture (flaky or crumbly, for example). It must be firm in consistency, yet malleable enough to be mixed into the flour or incorporated into the dough. When beaten with sugar, the fat becomes lighter.

Eggs facilitate the emulsification of the fat and also increase the richness of the dough after baking. Adding whisked egg whites makes the dough lighter, while the yolks colour it golden brown.

Baking powder and flour are sieved together so that they are thoroughly mixed. Dried yeast must be dissolved in water.

According to the type of handling to which the dough is to be subjected (kneading, knocking back, folding and rolling, beating, drying, pressing, proving (rising) resting, etc.), leavened, dry, soft, or runny doughs can be made.

Although some people consider pastry-making to be an art, most people can achieve success by following the directions carefully and weighing the ingredients precisely.

Doughs and batters and their uses

type	cooking method	savouries	pâtisserie and desserts
baba dough	baking		baba, savarin
bread dough	baking	white or wholewheat loaves and rolls	
brioche dough	baking	koulibiaca, sausage, foie gras or fillet steak in brioche, piroshki	brioche, milk bread, fruit loaf, fouace, pogne, couque, kugelhopf, cramique
	deep-frying		Viennese fritters, krapfen
choux pastry	over the heat, then in the oven	gougère, ramekins, talmouse, profiteroles, carolines	éclairs, religieuse, pont-neuf, Paris-Brest, Saint-Honoré, salammbô, Mecca bread, bâton de Jacob, profiteroles, duchesse, polka
	boiling	quenelles, gnocchi à la parisienne	
	deep-frying	dauphine potatoes, lorette, fritters, soufflés	soufflé fritters
crêpe batter	shallow-frying	savoury crêpes (filled and rolled), pannequets, ficelle picarde, kromeskies	sweet crêpes (filled, soufflé, and flamed), pannequets
croissant dough	baking	croissants filled with ham or cheese	sweet croissants, croissants with almonds, filled croissants
fritter batter	deep-frying	savoury fritters	sweet fritters
frying batter	deep-frying	fritters, fritots, fritto misto, attereaux	sweet fritters, fruit and cream fritters
Genoese mixture	bain-marie then baking		Genoese sponge, mocha cake, mascotte, little fancy cakes, swiss rolls.

meringue mixture	baking	basic meringues, vacherins, succès, progrès, petits fours, baked Alaska, decorations
pâté pastry	baking	pâtés en croûte, pies, tarts, timbales
puff pastry	baking	chaussons, allumettes, mirlitons de Rouen, dartois cakes, friands, paillettes, allumettes, vols-au-vent, fleurons, talmouse, bouchées, dartois, croustades	pithiviers, tarts, mille-feuilles, palmiers, sacristains, cream horns, condé, champigny, conversations, petits fours, jalousies, puits d'amour
	deep-frying	rissoles
raised sweet batter	baking	madeleine, gingerbread, Madeira cake, Genoa cake, marble cake, bugnes
rich sweetened shortcrust pastry	baking	pastry bases, marcellins, amandines, tarts, barquettes, tartlets, biscuits, sablés, petits fours, milanais
savarin mixture	baking	marignan, savarin, gorenflot
shortcrust or lining pastry	baking	barquettes, croustades, quiches, tarts, pâtés en croûte, timbales, pies
	deep-frying	rissoles
sponge cake batter	baking	Savoy sponge, sponge fingers, sponge rolls, Genoese sponge, langues de chat, manqué
waffle batter	in waffle iron	sweet waffles, filled waffles, wafers
yeast dough		See baba dough, brioche dough, croissant dough, bread dough

The cooking process is of prime importance. The oven must be preheated so that it is at the correct temperature when the dough or pastry is put in.

• *Raised doughs and batters*: bread, brioche, baba, savarin, and kouglof doughs are made with either yeast or baking powder. The dough rises when carbon dioxide is released by the action of heat and moisture on the raising agent. Sponge, Genoese, and meringue mixtures rise solely by the action of heat on the air trapped either in the egg yolks that have been whisked with sugar, or in the stiffly whisked egg whites. Other raised doughs include creamed cake mixtures, which rely on air trapped during beating and on a raising agent, and choux pastry (see *chou*), which swells in the oven, in hot oil, or when poached. Frying and fritter batters contain either a raising agent or whisked egg whites, which are responsible for the puffy appearance of the finished product.

• *Pastry*: this is made with flour, fat, salt, and a binding agent. The French have the following varieties: *pâte brisée* (shortcrust pastry, basic pie dough), *pâte sablée* and *pâste sucrée* (rich sweetened shortcrust pastries), and *pâte feuilletée* (see *puff pastry*). French shortcrust pastry is dry and light. Made quickly and set aside to rest before use, it is the classic base for tarts, pâtés *en croûte*, pies, etc. Pâte sablée, which is reserved for fine pâtisserie, is very crumbly and is used to make biscuits (cookies) or pastry bases that are to be kept for some time and filled or decorated at the last moment. Puff pastry, which is richer in fat than the other types, takes longer to make but can be prepared in advance. It uses are very varied, both in baking and pâtisserie.

• *Frying batters*: these are more fluid than dough but are based on the same ingredients (though in different proportions). Waffle and crêpe batters are included in this category.

In all cases, it is the effect of heat which gives the cake or pastry its final texture: dry for pie crusts, soft for sponge cakes, crisp for puff pastry, elastic for crêpes, aerated for choux pastry or brioche dough, etc.

Most doughs and batters are prepared cold by mixing the ingredients fairly quickly, but some types, notably choux pastry, are mixed together over heat before being baked. Depending on the recipe, the same dough may be cooked in different ways. Choux pastry, for example, is poached in water for gnocchis, baked for éclairs, or deep-fried for dauphine potatoes or soufflé fritters (beignets); puff pastry may be baked in the oven (for tarts, etc.) or deep-fried (for rissoles).

It is now easy to buy frozen pastry, especially puff and shortcrust pastry.

RECIPES

Frying batter PÂTE À FRIRE Sieve 200 g (7 oz, 1¾ cups) flour into a bowl. Add ¼ sachet (2 teaspoons) baking powder, 2 tablespoons (3 tablespoons) groundnut oil (peanut oil), a pinch of salt, and 2.5 dl (8 fl oz, 1 cup) warm water. Mix the ingredients thoroughly and leave the batter to rest in a cool place for at least 1 hour. Just before using, add 2 stiffly whisked egg whites and a pinch of salt.

Lining pastry PÂTE À FONCER Sieve 250 g (9 oz, generous cup) flour onto a board. Make a well in the centre and add 5 g (½ teaspoon) salt and 125 g (4½ oz, generous ½ cup) butter (softened at room temperature and cut into pieces). Start to mix the ingredients and then add 2 tablespoons (3 tablespoons) water (the quantity of water required may vary depending on the type of flour used). Knead the dough gently, using the heel of the hand, shape it into a ball, wrap it in aluminium foil, and set aside in a cool place for at least 2 hours if possible until ready to use.

A richer pastry can be made by increasing the quantity of butter to 150 g (5 oz, scant ¾ cup) and by adding 1 small egg and 25 g (1 oz, 2 tablespoons, firmly packed) sugar.

Rich sweetened shortcrust pastry I PÂTE SABLÉE Sieve 250 g (9 oz, generous cup) flour. Cream 125 g (4½ oz, generous ½ cup) butter. Quickly mix the flour and butter by hand, draw the mixture together, and make a well in the centre. Add 1 whole egg, 125 g (4½ oz, 9 tablespoons, firmly packed) caster (superfine) sugar, and a few drops of vanilla essence (extract). Quickly blend the ingredients together, roll the pastry into a ball, and leave in a cool place for 1 hour.

Alternatively, the pastry can be made by first mixing the egg and sugar, then rubbing in the flour, and finally kneading in the butter.

Rich sweetened shortcrust pastry II PÂTE SUCRÉE (DITE 'SÈCHE') Heap together 250 g (9 oz, generous cup) sieved flour, a pinch of salt, and 75 g (3 oz, 6 tablespoons, firmly packed) caster (superfine) sugar and make a well in the centre. Add 1 large egg (or 2 small ones), 100 g (4 oz, ½ cup) softened butter, and ½ tablespoon orange-flower water and work all the ingredients together, drawing the flour into the centre. Knead the dough quickly and gently with the heel of the hand, form it into a ball, cover, and keep cool.

Shortcrust pastry PÂTE BRISÉE This can be made by hand or in a food processor and may be prepared with or without eggs.

■ *By hand*: Sieve 250 g (9 oz, generous cup) flour into a bowl or onto a board. Add a pinch of salt and 20 g (¾ oz, 1½ tablespoons, firmly packed) sugar (to taste). Spread the mixture into a circle and make a well in the centre. Add 125 g (4½ oz, generous ½ cup) butter and a beaten egg, and knead the ingredients together as quickly as possible with 2 tablespoons (3 tablespoons) very cold water. Form the dough into a ball, even if there are still some whole pieces of butter visible. Wrap it in aluminium foil and leave it to rest for at least 1 hour in the refrigerator. Knead the dough, pushing it down gently with the heel of the hand, and roll it out on a lightly floured worktop to the required thickness.

■ *In a food processor*: Put 250 g (9 oz, generous cup) flour (no need to sieve), a pinch of salt, 20 g (¾ oz, 1½ tablespoons, firmly packed) sugar (optional), and 130 g (4½ oz, 1½ tablespoons, firmly packed) sugar (optional), and 130 g (4½ oz, generous ½ cup) softened butter (cut into thick pieces) into the bowl. Switch on and mix the ingredients until they are evenly distributed. Then add 1½ tablespoons (2 tablespoons)

very cold water all at once. Switch off the machine as soon as the dough binds and comes away from the sides of the bowl. Roll it into a ball and proceed as above. It will be smoother and easier to roll out than pastry made by hand.

Yeast dough for tarts PÂTE LEVÉE POUR TARTES Prepare like brioche dough, but use 250 g (9 oz, generous cup) sieved flour, 7 g (¼ oz) fresh baker's yeast, 5 g (½ teaspoon) salt, 10 g (generous ¼ oz, generous ½ tablespoon) caster (superfine) sugar, 2 eggs, 100 g (4 oz, ½ cup) butter, and 6 tablespoons (½ cup) milk.

dough trough HUCHE

A large wooden trough used in the past for kneading dough or for keeping bread. A regional name for this trough is *la maie*.

douillon

A speciality of Normandy, consisting of an apple or pear wrapped in a pastry case and baked in the oven. See also *bourdelot*.

| RECIPE

Douillons Mix 500 g (18 oz, scant 4¼ cups) flour, 350 g (12 oz, 1½ cups) softened butter, 2 eggs, 3 tablespoons (¼ cup) milk, 20 g (¾ oz, 1½ tablespoons, firmly packed) caster (superfine) sugar, and 1 teaspoon salt to make a smooth dough. Roll it into a ball and place in the refrigerator.

Heat the oven to about 190 C (375 F, gas 5). Peel 8 small pears, remove the cores, and place a knob of butter in the centre of each. Cook in the oven for 10 minutes. Remove, and allow them to get completely cold. (Do not turn the oven off.)

Roll out the pastry to a thickness of about 2 mm (¼ in) and cut it into 8 squares of equal size. Place a well-drained pear in the centre of each square and fold the corners upwards, stretching the pastry a little. Seal the sides and the top by pinching with damp fingers. Draw lines on the pastry with the point of a knife. Glaze the douillons with an egg yolk beaten in 2 tablespoons (3 tablespoons) milk and bake in the oven for 25–30 minutes. Serve hot, warm, or cold, with fresh cream.

doum palm

An African palm tree with edible fruits. Palm wine is made from the sap of this tree. Alexandre Dumas writes in his *Grand Dictionnaire de cuisine*: 'The doum palm produces a refreshing fruit, in which I was able to detect the taste of gingerbread. A lady in Cairo . . . once offered me a cool sorbet of doum fruit.'

dove   TOURTERELLE

A bird similar and related to the pigeon, but smaller. There are several varieties, including the rock dove and ring dove (see *pigeon*), the turtledove, the collared dove, the palm dove, and the rufous turtledove. The latter four species are hunted in France, though they are of minor gastronomic interest. Plump young doves were formerly considered to make a delicious meal. In the 16th century, doves, together with curlews, wood pigeons, squabs, and egrets, were more highly prized by some than beef, veal, and pork. In Arabic cookery, doves cooked in a cocotte with artichoke hearts, nutmeg, and raisins are a choice dish.

dragée

An item of confectionery consisting of an almond with a hard coating of sugar. The sugar coating may be white or coloured, and hazelnuts, pistachio nuts, nougat, almond paste, chocolate, or liqueur may also be used as centres for these sweets.

Honey-coated almonds were popular sweetmeats with the ancient Greeks and Romans, and the name 'dragée' is derived from the Greek word for these sweets (*tragemata*). The dragée was mentioned for the first time in 1220, in the archives of the town of Verdun. At that time, the apothecaries (with whom confectioners were still confused) coated certain spices (aniseed, coriander, and fennel) with honey. These *épices de chambre* were considered to be medicinal spices, eaten to sweeten the breath or as an aid to digestion. When cane sugar was introduced into Europe, dragées as we now know them appeared – sugar-coated almonds, pumpkin seeds, or cucumber seeds. In 1660, Colbert noted that Verdun was the centre of trade in dragées, and it remains famous for their production to the present day. Dragées are traditionally given at christenings, first communions, and weddings. The *obus de Verdun* is a chocolate novelty fitted with a fuse which, when lighted, explodes to release dragées and small party novelties.

Before 1850, dragées were handmade by craftsmen. The almonds were suspended in rotating vats of sugar syrup so that they would be evenly coated. In that year, however, the first mechanical turbine was invented, and the process is now carried out mechanically by spraying sugar syrup onto the kernels under pressure, and drying them in warm air.

☐ **The range of dragées** The sugar-coating process is the same for every type of filling. The most popular varieties of almonds are the flat Italian *avolas* and the slightly rounded Spanish *planetas*. The almonds are put into the turbine, dipped three times in a mixture of gum arabic and sugar, dried, and then coated with a concentrated sugar syrup. They are then blanched in a sugar syrup with added starch, smoothed, and coloured if required.

Chocolate, nougat, fondant icing, almond paste, or liqueur fillings are moulded before being coated with sugar. Specialities include *olives de Provence*, different types of *cailloux* and *galets*, and *anis de Flavigny*.

Perles d'argent are made by coating a sugar centre with a gelatine-based solution, and then with pure silver.

Soft dragées (also called *dragées à froid* or *dragées Julienne*) are shaped like beans or peas and their centres consist of clear or opaque boiled sugar coated with a dilute glucose solution and then with icing (confectioners') sugar.

drain   ÉGOUTTER

To drain the water from raw foodstuffs which have been washed or from foods which have been cooked or blanched in water. Various utensils are used for this purpose. Most green vegetables are drained in a colander or over a grid, while cauliflower should be lifted with a straining spoon and placed in a colander, sometimes lined with a cloth. Rice and pasta are poured, together with their cooking liquids, into a colander or sieve. Poached eggs are drained on a folded cloth. Spinach can be squeezed with the hands, and bread soaked in milk (used to make a stuffing) is treated in the same way.

Foods which have been deep-fried are also drained to remove the excess oil or fat. French-fried potatoes, fritters, small fried fish, etc. are lifted from the oil with a wire spoon or in a frying basket, and then placed on kitchen paper.

Draining is also important in cheese-making, to separate the whey from the curds (see *faiselle*).

drainer ÉGOUTTOIR

A grid or trellis support made of wood or plastic, for draining washed dishes, etc. A bottle drainer is a tin-plate column studded with rods which hold inverted bottles by the neck after they have been washed.

Drambuie

A Scotch whisky-based liqueur, which can be drunk at any time. Its formula is the property of the Mackinnon family, who keep it a secret. The origin of the name apparently comes from the Gaelic expression *an dram buidheach* ('the liqueur that satisfies'). Drambuie, little known in continental Europe, is very popular in the United States.

dresser (presentation of food)

A French culinary term with several different meanings. In cooking, it means to arrange attractively on the serving dish all the items that comprise a particular preparation, including the principal ingredient, the garnish, the sauce, and any decorations. In pâtisserie, *dresser* means to roll out pastry for lining a mould, flan tin (pie pan), etc., or to force dough through a piping (pastry) bag.

In restaurants, *dressage* takes place as soon as the dishes are *à point* (ready to be served). Garnishes must always be kept in perfect condition for use. For example, sprigs of parsley and bunches of watercress are kept in fresh water; maître d'hôtel butter is kept cold in water with ice cubes; mushrooms are sprinkled with lemon juice; and flavoured butters are shaped into rolls, wrapped in aluminium foil, and stored in the refrigerator.

The items used in dressage include serving dishes, radish dishes, hors-d'oeuvre dishes (divided into sections), sundae glasses, timbale dishes, copper platters for serving game, vegetable dishes, sauceboats, salad dishes, soup tureens, terrine dishes, fruit dishes, toast racks, etc. *Fonds de plat* and *bords de plat* were used at one time. The former were either round or oval pieces of wood that were placed on the bottom of a plate to form a raised base for cold dishes. They were usually covered with silver paper. *Bords de plat* were wide-rimmed decorative dishes made of solid silver or silver plate on which the garnishes were arranged around the principal item.

Certain dishes require a particular item of dressage; for example, oysters and other seafood are served on a large plate covered with crushed ice, mounted on a support. Other dishes need to be on a plate-warmer. Certain items call for specific utensils: special plates and tongs for snails, asparagus cradles, etc.

☐ **Methods of dressage** The items of food may be presented in various ways. Game and poultry are often served on slices of fried bread. Potatoes are often used in various ways for dressage – borders, duchess potatoes, nests of potato straws, little piles of noisette potatoes, etc. Artichoke hearts, tomatoes, and mushrooms are also used in this way.

The plates and dishes for dressage must be kept at the correct temperature for the food they are to hold (for example, sundae glasses must be ice-cold).

The present tendency in French restaurants is for *service à l'assiette*, in which the individual portion is placed directly on the plate, coated with sauce and garnished with vegetables.

dresser (furniture)
VAISSELIER

A sideboard surmounted by shelves on which dishes are displayed. It is a traditional piece of kitchen furniture still used today: the normal items for setting the table are kept in it, ready to hand – plates standing up, cups hanging on hooks under the shelves, and cutlery placed in open compartments or arranged on racks. Nowadays dressers may be used simply to display collections of decorative plates or pottery.

dressing fish, poultry, and game HABILLAGE

The preparation of fish, poultry, and game birds for cooking.

• *Dressing fish*. The fish must be successively trimmed, scaled, gutted (cleaned), and washed (some of this may be carried out by the fishmonger). The dressing will vary depending on the type of fish (flat, round, small, or large) and on the way it is to be served. For example, if a whole sole is to be served only the black skin is removed, whereas a sole fillet is not trimmed, but the skin is removed completely.

• *Dressing poultry and game birds.* The bird must first be plucked, carefully picked over, and singed. Poultry is then drawn, usually trussed, and often larded, but the preparation will vary according to the type of bird. Feathered game is not always completely gutted; trussing or tying, and sometimes larding, complete the dressing. All the above operations apply to birds that are to be cooked whole. When they are to be cut into portions, the giblets, white meat, breasts, etc., are removed, and it is therefore only necessary to pluck, singe, and draw the bird.

dried vine fruits

RAISINS SECS

Currants, sultanas, and raisins, which are all produced by exposing ripe grapes to hot dry air so that the moisture is drawn out to leave the flesh and skin so concentrated that the activities of enzymes and the growth of moulds and bacteria are inhibited.

It takes 1.8 kg (4 lb) grapes to produce 450 g (1 lb) currants, sultanas, or raisins. None of the nutrients are affected by drying (with the exception of some vitamin C); therefore dried grapes contain all the goodness of fresh fruit in a concentrated form.

Dried vine fruits contain 60–70% natural fruit sugar. Minerals (particularly calcium, iron, and copper) are present in substantial amounts, as are vitamins (particularly vitamins in the A and B groups) and a high fibre content. They contain virtually no fat, no cholesterol, and a low sodium content, although having lost 90% of their water they have a high calorific value – 324 Cal per 100 g.

For all types of dried vine fruits the grapes are dried naturally in the sun or artificially by hot air. The dried fruit is sorted and graded, the seeds and stalks are removed, and the fruit is then usually spin-washed, dried, and a light coating of preservative applied before it is finally packed.

• *Currants* are produced mainly in Greece. The quality varies with the type of grape used and the soil conditions. Traditionally, the finest are Vostizza but excellent fruit is produced in the Zante Gulf and Patras regions. The grapes are gathered in August and September and generally are sun-dried. Currants are also grown in Australia, California, and South Africa, but the limited production is usually required for domestic consumption.

• *Sultanas* come from grapes that are green when fresh but darken in colour when dried. Light-coloured fruit is generally obtained by drying in the shade and darker fruit by sun-drying. In both cases drying is natural, using the hot dry harvest weather. Many countries in the northern hemisphere produce sultanas – Greece, France, Turkey, Iran, Afghanistan, China, the United States, and Mexico. In the southern hemisphere the producers are Australia, South Africa, and Chile.

• *Seedless raisins* are produced in the United States, Mexico, and South Africa. They are obtained from the Thompson sultana grape and are green when harvested. They are sun-dried, the action of the sun caramelizing the sugars and causing the fruit to darken to a purplish-brown colour. A red raisin grape is produced in Afghanistan; after drying, it is essentially of the same appearance as the other.

• *Stoned raisins* come from large red grapes that are usually used as wine and table grapes, although some are sun-dried. To extract the seeds the fruit is steamed to soften it, then put through special machinery that squeezes the seeds out. The skin is then sealed by a light coating to prevent the fruit from sugaring. Australia, South Africa, and Spain are the main producers.

Dried vine fruits are used to flavour cooked dishes, especially poultry stuffings, black pudding (blood sausage), some types of meat loaf, patties, pies, etc.; they are also added to couscous, tajines, pilafs, and some West Indian dishes. In Sicily, they are used to stuff sardines *en papillotes*: they are also an ingredient of stuffed vine leaves and of the port sauce which accompanies braised ham.

They have many uses in cake- and pastry-making, often being soaked first in warm water, wine, or rum. They may form part of the filling for fruit cakes, buns, brioches, kugelhopf, savarin, and other cakes made with yeast dough. They also form an essential ingredient in a number of desserts.

RECIPE

Raisin tart TARTE AUX RAISINS SECS (from Pierre Romeyer's recipe) Soak 500 g (18 oz, 3 cups) raisins in brandy. Beat 8 whole eggs lightly, then whip them together with 1 litre (1¾ pints, 4¼ cups) double (heavy) cream, 300 g (12 oz, 1½ cups) caster (superfine) sugar, and 2 teaspoons vanilla sugar (or a few drops of vanilla essence). Line a tin at least 28 cm (11 in) in diameter with 450 g (1 lb) puff pastry. Pour the cream into the pastry case, add the raisins, and bake in the oven at 210 C (415 F, gas 6–7) for at least 30 minutes.

additional recipe See *carrot*.

drink BOISSON

The simplest and most natural drink, and the only one essential for the survival of all living organisms, is water. The average consumption of liquid in a temperate climate is 1 litre (1¾ pints, 2 pints) per day, but needs vary according to the climate and the diet. For example, meat and salted, spiced, or sweetened dishes all increase the thirst. Man has used his intelligence to vary the flavour of drinks, which may be sweet, aromatic, fermented, or spirit-based.

Water-based drinks, which may be still or sparkling, hot or cold, include lemonades, sodas and syrups, broths, infusions, tea, coffee, chocolate, and chicory. Drinks of vegetable origin may or may not be alcoholic, for example, fruit and vegetable juices, wine, cider, beer, perry, etc. Such drinks can be transformed by distillation into brandy, liqueurs, and spirits. These different liquids have given rise to countless variations – cocktails, liqueur wines, apéritifs, punches, grogs, etc. Milk from animals is really a liquid food, but may also be used to prepare drinks, such as milk shakes, kefir, etc.

Drinking habits vary considerably depending on the customs of a country and the latitude. As a general rule, Orientals and Russians do not drink with their meals, but take tea at the end of a meal. Tea is the most widely consumed drink in the world after water.

In France, water, beer, and wine are the drinks that traditionally accompany meals. Family and social life also offer numerous other occasions to consume drinks for pleasure.

☐ **Drinking establishments** Drinking establishments considerably predate restaurants; they include pubs and taverns, bars, milk bars, tea rooms, etc. Such establishments may even vary from region to region in the same country; in France, for example, there are the *bouchons* of Lyon, the *estaminets* of the north, and the *guinguettes* (pleasure gardens) and bistros of Paris.

The code of drinking establishments classifies drinks into five groups: non-alcoholic drinks (water, fruit juice, lemonade, etc.); fermented nondistilled drinks (wine, beer, cider, etc.); wine-based apéritifs and red fruit liqueurs; rums and spirits obtained by distillation; and all other alcoholic drinks.

In former times, most drinks were either produced in the home or by local makers – home-made beers and liqueurs, orgeat, mulled wine, etc. Today, drinks are produced commercially and the market has grown considerably, particularly for the sale of fruit juices. Drinks are sold in various packagings (bottles, cans, etc.) and in a variety of forms (concentrated, powdered, frozen, etc.).

dripping pan LÈCHEFRITE

A shallow rectangular metal pan placed in the oven, or under the grill (broiler) or spit, to catch juices or melted fat from a roasting joint or any liquid that boils over the edge of a pudding dish. It is usually too shallow to be used for roasting. The French word, *lèchefrite*, has been used since the end of the 12th century; before this the pan was called a *belle-bouche*. In former times these receptacles were made of wrought iron and were fitted with a long handle, so that they could be slipped under the joints which were being roasted in huge fireplaces. They were also made of silver.

droit de banvin

The monopoly on the sale of new wine reserved by the landlords on their own land during a set period (generally 40 days before the opening of the selling season). In some areas this feudal right, dating back to the time of Charlemagne, began at Easter and ended at Whitsun, seven weeks later.

Drouant

A restaurant opened in Paris in 1880 by an Alsatian, Charles Drouant, on the corner of Place Gaillon and Rue Saint-Augustin. Specializing in seafood, it attracted a clientele of writers and journalists, such as Jean Ajalbert, Léon Daudet, Octave Mirbeau, and the Rosny brothers. Drouant enlarged his business and his fame spread, thanks to his cellar (particularly white vintages). In October 1914 the restaurant really found a place in literary history, when the Académie Goncourt decided to hold its lunches there. There were numerous gourmets among the Goncourt academicians, particularly Léon Daudet, who introduced the serving of blanc de blancs. Edmond de Goncourt's will stipulated that the meal must cost 20 francs per person, and the academicians still pay that sum. Here are a few menus for Goncourt lunches, which are traditionally served in the Louis XVI salon on the second floor, at a round table with a damask tablecloth.

● 1933 (prizewinner: André Malraux for *La Condition humaine*): oysters, pike boulangère, roast turkey with thinly sliced roast potatoes, cep mushrooms à la bordelaise, cheeses, praline ice, and fruit.

● 1954 (prizewinner: Simone de Beauvoir for *Les Mandarins*): oysters, grilled turbot, Bresse chicken with champagne, cheeses, liqueur soufflé, and fruit.

● 1981 (prizewinner: Lucien Bodard for *Anne-Marie*): beluga caviar, foie gras in port aspic, lobster Drouant, haunch of venison Saint-Hubert, chestnut cream, cheeses, iced hazelnut soufflé with *mignardises* (Small biscuits or cakes).

drumstick   PILON

The lower leg of a fowl or game bird, consisting of the bone, meat, and a thin layer of fat, giving it the shape of a pestle (hence the French name, which means pestle). It is fleshier and juicier than the white meat, but inferior to the thigh.

drying   SÉCHAGE

One of the oldest methods of preserving food. Drying slows down the proliferation and activity of the bacteria that cause spoilage and decay, but it considerably alters the appearance of food, due to the loss of its water. Since prehistoric times, cereals, nuts, and fruit have been dried in the sun before being stored. The American Indians used to dry buffalo meat in the same way to make pemmican. Pastirma and various salted meats are dried quite heavily, and may subsequently be smoked. The process of drying in the open air and wind is applied to fish (generally salted fish) in Scandinavia, Senegal, and India. The drying of fruit and vegetables has been widely practised since time immemorial – in Greece (for grapes), in Turkey (for apricots), in Iran and Spain (for tomatoes), in Hungary (for peppers), and in most other countries for pears, sliced apples, plums, whole cherries, and grapes. Vegetables are usually dried flat on hurdles in the sun, the drying often being completed in the oven.

In industry, the selection of the drying process depends mainly on the texture and size of the foodstuff, but factors such as ease of transport and convenience in use must also be considered. For modern industrial methods of drying, which eliminate a very large proportion of water, the term dehydration is used (see *dehydrated foods*). Drying is done:

● in the open air, in a ventilated room

(dried vegetables, salt cod), or in a drier, either on a conveyor belt or suspended in a current of air (dried vegetables);

• in an oven at a controlled temperature (dried fruit);

• in a drier with a controlled atmosphere, in which the temperature and humidity are progressively reduced (dried sausage);

• in an enclosed area using microwaves on a conveyor belt (crisps (chips)).

Drying is often supplemented (or preceded) by smoking, salting, fumigation (dried vegetables), or spraying with sulphur dioxide (dried fruit).

RECIPES

Drying apples and pears SÉCHAGE DES POMMES ET DES POIRES Peel and core some cooking apples. Cut them into slices 1 cm (½ in) thick and put into water containing lemon juice (or 10 g (¼ oz) citric acid per litre (1¾ points, 4¼ cups) water). Drain and place flat, without overlapping, on a wooden hurdle in the sun. Leave the fruit (bringing it in at night) for 2–3 days; if necessary finish off the drying in the oven on its coolest setting. The apple rings should be flexible but must contain no more water.

Pears (sound ones only) may be dried whole and unpeeled in the sun. Finish off in the oven as for apples. When cooled, dried pears may be flattened between boards.

In countries where the weather is not so clement, the fruit may be dried completely in the oven or suspended from the ceiling, threaded on string.

Drying herbs SÉCHAGE DES FINES HERBES Gather the herbs just before they flower (avoid picking them after it has been raining). Wash, then shake off the water. Roll up small-leaved herbs (thyme, rosemary, and savory) in muslin (cheesecloth) loosely, without squashing them together, then hang them up in a warm place. Herbs with large leaves (bay, mint, sage, parsley, and basil) can be dried in bunches, tied together by the stalks and hung upside down. Alternatively, the leaves may be removed and wrapped in muslin. When the herbs are dried, leave them whole or crush them with a rolling pin. Keep

them in sealed jars in a dark dry place. Drying in a microwave oven gives perfect results.

Drying vegetables SÉCHAGE DES LÉGUMES Using a needle, thread some young sound French (green) beans onto thick thread. Ensure that they are not too tightly packed together, tying a knot occasionally to separate them. Dip in boiling salted water (use 10 g (¼ oz) salt per litre (1¾ pints, 4¼ cups) water), drain them, and hang them in a fairly shady place for 3–4 days, bringing them inside at night (or suspend from the ceiling).

Mushrooms can be dried in the same way, once the earthy part of the stalk has been cut off. Small green chilli peppers, which become dark red when dried, can be threaded through the stalk, as can baby onions, garlic bulbs, and shallots. Store green beans, peppers, and mushrooms out of the light in sealed jars. Rehydrate before use by soaking for 12 hours in tepid water.

drying off DESSÉCHER

The elimination of excess water from cooked food by heating it over a low heat. It is necessary to dry off mashed potatoes in this way before adding milk and butter. The excess moisture absorbed by vegetables during cooking may be evaporated by tossing them rapidly in a sauté pan before coating with butter.

In France, the term *dessécher* is used particularly for the initial cooking of choux pastry. The mixture of water, butter, and flour is worked vigorously over a high heat with a wooden spatula until the paste detaches itself from the walls of the pan and forms a ball. Thus, excess water evaporates before the eggs are added and before the choux is baked.

Drying off is not synonymous with reducing, which refers only to the process of boiling down certain liquids so that they are reduced in volume.

Du Barry

The name given to several dishes that contain cauliflower. A Du Barry garnish for joints of meat consists of château potatoes and small florets of blanched cauliflower coated with Mornay sauce, sprinkled with grated cheese, browned under the grill, and arranged *à la serviette*. These dishes were dedicated to the Comtesse du Barry, the favourite of Louis XV.

RECIPES

Du Barry salad   SALADE DU BARRY Steam some very small white cauliflower florets for about 4 minutes in a pressure cooker or about 12 minutes in an ordinary saucepan. Drain and cool completely, and heap them in a salad bowl. Garnish with radishes and small sprigs of watercress. Pour some well-seasoned vinaigrette with added lemon over the salad, and sprinkle with chopped herbs. Toss the salad just before serving.

Potage à la Du Barry   Cook a cauliflower in salted water, then rub it through a sieve (or purée in a blender). Mix with it a quarter of its weight of potato purée, then add enough consommé or milk to obtain a creamy consistency. Finally, add some fresh cream (1–2 dl (4–7 fl oz, ¼–⅔ cup) for 5 portions). Adjust the seasoning, and sprinkle with chopped parsley. Butter may also be added.

other recipes See *lamb, omelette (flat omelettes)*.

Dubley

A garnish for large joints of meat, consisting of grilled (broiled) mushrooms and duchess potato croustades surrounded by a border of mushroom purée.

duchesse

A sweet or savoury preparation of choux pastry that may be served as an entrée, a garnish, or a dessert (like profiteroles). Savoury duchesses are filled with a mousse or a salpicon. Duchesses for dessert are filled with vanilla-flavoured confectioners' custard (pastry cream) or whipped cream, dusted with icing sugar (confectioners' sugar), and scattered with chopped pistachio nuts, flaked almonds, or dusted with chocolate (cocoa) powder.

Duchesses are also petits fours consisting of meringue shells or circles of langue-de-chat biscuit mixture, stuck together in pairs with flavoured butter cream.

Duchesse is also the name of an excellent variety of winter pear, and of certain desserts that include pears.

RECIPE

Duchesses (petits fours)   Grease 3 baking sheets and dust with flour. Mix together 100 g (4 oz, 1 cup) ground almonds, 100 g (4 oz, 8 tablespoons, firmly packed) caster (superfine) sugar, and 40 g (1½ oz, 6 tablespoons) flour. Whisk 6 egg whites until very stiff, and fold into the mixture with a metal spoon. Melt 40 g (1½ oz, 3 tablespoons) butter and add to the mixture. Put the mixture into a piping bag (pastry bag) and pipe small rounds onto the baking trays. Cook in the oven at 190 C (375 F, gas 5) for 7–8 minutes, remove from the oven, and carefully lift off the rounds of meringue with a palette knife. Mix 200 g (7 oz, ⅔ cup) ground praline with 225 g (8 oz) French butter cream (see *creams and custards*) and use to sandwich the duchesses together. Store in a cool place.

duchesse (à la)

The description *à la duchesse* is given in French cuisine to various dishes garnished, surrounded, or served with duchess potatoes. In pâtisserie, the name applies to certain preparations containing almonds.

RECIPES

Peaches à la duchesse   PÊCHES À LA DUCHESSE   Heat the oven to about 200 C (400 F, gas 6). Make a dough with 150 g (5 oz, 1¼ cups) flour, a pinch of salt, 40 g (1½ oz, 3 tablespoons) caster (superfine) sugar, 80 g (3 oz, 6 tablespoons) softened butter, 1 tablespoon water, and 1 egg yolk. Roll into a ball and place in the refrigerator. Dice 8 slices of canned pineapple and macerate them in Kirsch. Put 50 g (2 oz, ½ cup) flaked almonds onto a baking sheet, moisten with water, dust with sugar, and bake in the oven until golden brown, turning often.

Roll out the chilled dough to a thickness of about 2 mm (¼ in) and cut out 8 circles with a pastry cutter (cookie cutter). Use to line 8 tartlet moulds, prick with a fork, place a piece of greaseproof (waxed) paper in each, and fill with lentils. Cook for 5 minutes in the oven, remove the paper and lentils, and cook for a further 7 minutes. Cool and turn out of the moulds.

Prepare a zabaglione by whisking 100 g (4 oz, 8 tablespoons, firmly packed) caster sugar and 3 egg yolks in a bain-marie until the mixture is warm and frothy. Add 5 cl (3 tablespoons, ¼ cup) Kirsch and an equal quantity of Maraschino, whisking until the mixture has thickened. Soften ½ litre (17 fl oz, 2 cups) vanilla ice cream by crushing it with a wooden spatula. Add the diced pineapple. Place some of the icecream mixture in the bottom of each tartlet, put a canned peach half on each, and coat with the zabaglione. Sprinkle with flaked almonds and put in the refrigerator for a short time.

The peaches may be replaced by pears.

Poached eggs à la duchesse OEUFS POCHÉS À LA DUCHESSE Spread some cold duchess potato mixture on a buttered dish and cut out circles about 7 cm (2¾ in) in diameter. Bake in the oven until golden brown and arrange a poached egg on each. Coat with béchamel sauce, Mornay sauce, tomato fondue, cream sauce, or any other suitable sauce.

duchess potatoes

POMMES DUCHESSE
Potatoes puréed with butter and egg yolk, piped into decorative shapes, and baked in the oven. Duchess potatoes are served with joints of meat or they may be used as a garnish. They are also used to make croquettes, Berny potatoes (mixed with chopped truffles, coated with flaked almonds, shaped into rounds, and fried) and Saint-Florentin potatoes (mixed with chopped ham, coated with fine uncooked vermicelli, shaped into small corks, and fried).

RECIPES

Duchess potato mixture APPAREIL À POMMES DUCHESSE Cut 500 g (18

oz) peeled potatoes into thick slices or quarters. Boil them briskly in salted water. Drain, put in the oven for a few moments to evaporate excess moisture, and rub through a sieve. Put the purée into a saucepan and dry off for a few moments, turning with a wooden spoon. Add 50 g (2 oz, ¼ cup) butter, season with salt, pepper, and a little grated nutmeg, bind with 1 whole egg and 2 yolks, and mix. Spread the purée on a buttered baking sheet, leave until cold, and shape as indicated in the recipe.

When this mixture is intended for borders to be piped through a forcing bag, it is used while still hot. It is then not so thick as when it is intended for croquettes, or to be served as duchess potatoes proper.

Duchess potatoes for garnish POMMES DUCHESSE POUR GARNITURES Heat some frying oil to about 175 C (347 F). Place some cooled duchess potato mixture into a piping bag with a plain nozzle (about 2 cm (¾ in) in diameter), and pipe the mixture into the hot oil, cutting it off into about 4 cm (1½ in) sections. Cook until golden brown, drain on absorbent paper, and serve very hot.

The duchess potato mixture may also be spread out on a buttered baking sheet, cooled, and divided into even-sized rectangles that can be rolled into cylinders and then deep-fried.

duck CANARD

A web-footed bird that was domesticated in China over 2000 years ago. In France, the most common breeds are the Nantes duck and the Barbary duck. The mulard duck, produced by crossing these two breeds, is mainly reared in southwestern France for the production of foie gras. The excellent Rouen duck, in particular the Duclair (named after a village in Normandy), is mainly sold locally. Finally, there is a wild cross-breed (mallard male × domestic female) that has been in existence for about 12 years and is highly esteemed by gourmets. Whatever the breed, duck should be consumed within three days of killing.

• Rouen duck: very fine flesh, tinged with red, with a special flavour due to the fact that the bird is smothered, not bled, so that the blood remains in the muscles.

- Nantes duck (or Challans duck – after the name of the marshland where it is raised in a semi-wild state): smaller but fatter, with fine delicately flavoured flesh.
- Barbary duck: raised in the wild; firmer and leaner flesh with a slightly musky flavour.
- Pekin duck: now rare since it is too small for commercial purposes; very fine and delicate flesh.

In French cookery, the term *canard* applies to birds two to four months old. *Caneton* (duckling) is used for younger birds and in grande cuisine. The female duck (*cane*) is smaller but plumper than the drake; it is preferred for roasts because its meat is finer and tastier. A female duckling is called a *canette*.

Ducks' eggs, which have a greenish-white shell and weigh 80–120 g (3–4½ oz), are very popular in the Far East. Because they often carry germs, ducks' eggs should only be eaten cooked.

☐ **Cooking method**
Very tender: roast on a spit
Tender: roast in the oven
 (for both these the cooked meat should be pale pink)
Less tender: braise or roast (stuffed), and garnish with onions, turnips, olives, and acid fruits.
Very large birds: use for pâtés and ballottines and also for cassoulets.

Choose for preference a fairly young bird with a flexible beak; the pinion flesh as well as the skin should be supple and the breast plump. When a duckling is killed too young, the breastbone is still soft and the flesh is not developed sufficiently. The current tendency in restaurants is to use ducklings, although some preparations can only be successfully made with more mature birds. The cold dishes using duck are the same as those made with roasting chicken. (See *confit, foie gras, gizzard, magret*.)

☐ **Pressed duck** Created at the beginning of the 19th century by a restaurateur from Rouen called Méchenet, the recipe for pressed duck owed much of its immediate success to the Duke of Chartres, who commended it highly in Paris. When the famous cook Frédéric took over the restaurant La Tour d'Argent, he began numbering all the pressed ducks that he served, intending to make the dish the speciality of his restaurant. Today the number has exceeded 600,000. Number 328 was served to Edward VII, then Prince of Wales, in 1890; No. 33,642 was provided for Theodore Roosevelt and No. 253,652 for Charlie Chaplin.

Léon Daudet, in *Paris vécu*, describes the cook at work: 'You ought to have seen Frédéric with his monocle, his greying whiskers, his calm demeanour, carving his plump quack-quack, trussed and already flamed, throwing it into the pan, preparing the sauce, salting and peppering like Claude Monet's paintings, with the seriousness of a judge and the precision of a mathematician, and opening up, with a sure hand, in advance, every perspective of taste.'

Pressed duck is prepared in front of the customer. The aiguillettes (thin slices of breast) are cut from the bird and placed in a dish of well-reduced red wine standing on a hotplate. The rest of the duck (except the legs, which are served grilled (broiled)) is pressed in a special screw press. The juice obtained is flavoured with Cognac, thickened with butter, and poured over the aiguillettes, which finish cooking in the sauce.

☐ **Wild duck** The most common species in France is the mallard (*colvert*). It is also the largest and has exquisite flesh. The male has green and grey plumage with a touch of brown and white. The female is brown. Practically sedentary from October to March, the mallard migrates south only in very cold weather.

Other wild ducks that are well known in gastronomy include the shoveler duck (*souchet*), which has a spatulate beak, the gadwall (*chipeau*), which is grey and white with a brown border on the wings (in eastern France), the baldpate (*siffleur*), which is a smaller, coastal species, and the pintail (*pilet*), which is less highly regarded. The sheldrake (*tadorne*) and the merganser (*harle*) are now protected species.

Generally speaking, only the legs and fillets of wild ducks are eaten (this is why one bird is required for every two servings). These game birds are not hung, but used fresh: young tender birds are roasted on a spit or in the oven;

older birds are prepared as a salmis or fricassee. Dishes made using domestic duck are also applicable to wild duck.

RECIPES

Amiens duck pâté   PÂTÉ DE CANARD D'AMIENS   (from a recipe by M. Dumont-Lespine)

■ *Preparing the pastry* – Ingredients: 500 g (18 oz) sifted flour; 125 g (4½ oz, ½ cup) lard; 1 tablespoon olive oil; 10 g (1 teaspoon) table salt; and about 1½ tablespoons cold water. Spread the flour on a board or working surface, make a well in the centre, and put the salt in the well. Break an egg into the well, mix with the salt, then add the olive oil. Soften the lard by kneading if necessary, then mix it with the liquid part in the middle of the flour. Now blend the flour and lard, without moistening at all. When the pastry is well blended, spread it out and sprinkle with cold water. Roll the pastry together into one lump and leave to rest in a cool place for at least 2 hours before use. (This pastry has the advantage of rising very little during cooking.)

■ *Preparing the duck* – To make these pâtés, use only young ducklings, which can be cooked very quickly. Pluck, draw, and singe the bird, carefully removing any innards which may remain. Cut off the wing tips just below the first joint from the shoulder. Cut off the feet at the joint. Season the inside and outside with spiced salt. Cut up a scalded breast of streaky bacon and fry over a low heat in a little cooking fat. Remove it and brown the duck in the fat over a low heat, turning so that it browns all over. Drain the duck on a dish and leave to cool before making the pâté.

■ *Preparing the forcemeat* – À gratin forcemeat is always used for this pâté. The ingredients may vary, depending on what is available, and may include veal or poultry liver, in addition to the liver from the duck. Ingredients: 500 g (18 oz) veal or poultry liver; 150 g (5 oz, scant ¾ cup) finely chopped fat; 1 medium-sized onion, chopped; 15 g (½ oz) spiced salt; chopped thyme and bay leaves; and 2 chopped shallots. Melt the fat over a low heat and use it to brown the liver, which has been suitably trimmed and coarsely diced. When the liver is well browned, add the chopped onion and shallots, and season with the spiced salt, thyme, and bay leaves. Cover and leave for a few minutes on a low heat. Remove and allow to cool, then pound the mixture in a mortar and pass through a fine sieve.

■ *Making the pâté* – Divide the pastry into two equal portions and roll one half into an oval about 1 cm (½ in) thick so it is a little longer and wider than the duck. Place this pastry in the centre of a metal baking sheet or ovenproof pie dish that has been lightly moistened with a little cold water. Next, spread a quarter of the forcemeat in the middle of the pastry and lay the duck, on its back, on top; season the duck with more spiced salt and a little cayenne. Completely cover the duck with the rest of the forcemeat. Roll out the remaining pastry in an oval shape and place over the duck, sealing it well at the edges. Crimp up the sides, decorate the top with some pieces of pastry cut into fancy shapes, and make an opening in the centre for the steam to escape. Finally, glaze the pastry with beaten egg. Bake the pâté in a hot oven (220 C, 425 F, gas 7) for 1¼–1½ hours, depending on the size.

Braised duck   CANARD BRAISÉ Singe and truss a duck weighing approximately 2 kg (4½ lb). Put it into an oven-proof braising pan lined with fresh bacon rind and containing a carrot and a medium-sized onion cut into rounds and tossed in butter. Add a bouquet garni, season, and cook with the lid on for 15 minutes, browning the duck on all sides. Now moisten with 1 dl (6 tablespoons, scant ½ cup) white wine, reduce, and add 3 dl (½ pint, 1¼ cups) chicken stock. Bring to the boil then transfer to a hot oven and cook with the lid on for about 1 hour. Drain the duck, untruss it, arrange on a serving dish, and surround with fresh garden peas. Sprinkle with a few spoonfuls of the braising juices, reduced and strained, and serve the rest in a sauceboat.

The same method is used to prepare duck à l'alsacienne, which is surrounded with braised sauerkraut and a garnish of streaky bacon and Strasbourg sausages, duck *à la chipolata*, which is garnished with braised chestnuts, small glazed onions, lean rashers of blanched bacon, and chipolata sausages cooked in butter, and duck with olives, which uses green olives, stoned (pitted) and blanched.

Cold duck pâté   PÂTÉ DE CANARD FROID   This is made using a boned duck, stuffed with *à gratin* forcemeat to which foie gras and truffles have been added, either *en pantin* (see *pâté pantin*), like cold lark pâté, or a mould, like cold timbale of woodcock.

Duck à l'agenaise   CANARD À L'AGENAISE   Singe a duck weighing approximately 2 kg (4½ lb). Season the inside with salt and pepper, stuff with a dozen or so stoned (pitted) prunes soaked in Armagnac, and sew up. Brown the duck in a pan containing 25 g (1 oz, 2 tablespoons) butter, sprinkle with a glass of Armagnac, and set alight. Cover the pan and cook for about 40 minutes. Meanwhile, poach the grated rind of half an orange for 5 minutes in half a bottle of Bordeaux wine together with 2 cloves, a little grated nutmeg, 5 or 6 crushed peppercorns, a sprig of thyme, and a bay leaf. In a saucepan, brown 100 g (4 oz) very small lardons of smoked bacon, 2 tablespoons diced carrot, 1 tablespoon diced celery, and a large chopped onion, adding a knob of butter if required. Sprinkle with 1 tablespoon flour, then add the orange-flavoured wine, having strained it. Season with salt and pepper, stir well, and cook slowly for 20 minutes. Drain the duck and keep it hot. Pour the wine sauce into the juices from the duck, add a small glass of Armagnac and about 20 stoned (pitted) prunes. Reheat the sauce. Garnish the duck with prunes and cover with the sauce.

Duck à l'orange Lasserre   CANARD À L'ORANGE LASSERRE   (from a recipe of the Lasserre restaurant) Prepare a Nantes duck weighing approximately 2 kg (4½ lb), fry it in butter, then cook gently for 45 minutes. Sprinkle with 1 dl (6 tablespoons, scant ½ cup) Grand Marnier and leave to cook for a further 5 minutes. Remove the duck from the pan and keep hot. Strain the liquor and pour it into a saucepan, adding 1 tablespoon vinegar, the same amount of caster (superfine) sugar, the juice of 3 oranges, and 1 dl (6 tablespoons, scant ½ cup) each of Mandarin and apricot liqueur to make the sauce. Peel 6 oranges down to the flesh, cut them into slices, removing all fibres and seeds, and place them in a frying pan (skillet) with a few spoonfuls of the sauce. Heat without boiling. Now carve the duck, arrange it on a hot dish, and surround with slices of orange. Cover with some of the sauce and serve the rest in a sauceboat.

Mallard with green peppercorns   COLVERT AU POIVRE VERT   (from a recipe of the Restaurant Lapérouse) Select a mallard duck weighing about 1.4 kg (3 lb). Season the inside and outside with salt and pepper and place in a roasting dish. Sprinkle with 2 tablespoons oil and cook for 30 minutes in a moderately hot oven (about 200 C, 400 F, gas 6). Then cover the dish with aluminium foil to keep the duck hot. Peel 2 good-sized Granny Smith apples, cut them into halves, and remove the seeds and cores. Cook in a moderate oven (180 C, 350 F, gas 4) for about 10 minutes. For the sauce, pour 8 cl (4 tablespoons, ⅓ cup) white wine and 2 cl (1 tablespoon) Armagnac into a saucepan, and reduce by about two-thirds. Add the juice of a tin of green peppercorns and 6 cl (3 tablespoons, ¼ cup) stock (duck or other poultry). Reduce again for 2–3 minutes. Add 20 cl (7 fl oz, ¾ cup) fresh cream, lightly season with salt, and cook until the sauce achieves a uniform consistency. Check the seasoning, and at the last moment add 2 cl (1 tablespoon) port and 15 g (½ oz) green peppercorns. Cut off the breast fillets of the duck and arrange on a serving dish. Cover with the sauce and garnish with the apple, cut into quarters.

Roast duck   CANARD RÔTI   Season the duck with salt and pepper both inside and out, truss, and roast in the oven or on a spit. A duckling weighting approximately 1.3 kg (2¾ lb) should be cooked in a hot oven (220 C, 425 F, gas 7) for 35 minutes or for 40–45 minutes on a spit.

Roast duck with peaches CANARD RÔTI AUX PÊCHES Roast the duck. Meanwhile, peel some medium-sized peaches and poach them whole in a light syrup. When the duck is roasted, drain it and keep it hot. Dilute the pan juices with a little peach syrup and reduce to the consistency of a sauce. Add the peaches to the sauce to flavour them, heat them through, and arrange them around the duck. Serve the sauce in a sauceboat.

wild duck à la tyrolienne CANARD SAUVAGE À LA TYROLIENNE (from Plumerey's recipe) Stew some cooking apples, adding a little cinnamon and mace, to form a hot apple purée (applesauce). Stuff a wild duck with this purée, tie securely, and place the duck on a spit for roasting. Boil one-third of a glass of vinegar together with a small knob of butter (about the size of a walnut), ½ teaspoon caster (superfine) sugar, and a few grains of coarsely ground pepper. Baste the duck continually with this preparation while it is cooking on the spit, placing a small pan beneath to catch the juices. Cooking should take about 30–35 minutes. When finished, take the duck off the spit, untruss, and arrange on a dish. Strain the collected juices into a saucepan and heat, adding ½ tablespoon redcurrant jelly. Finally pour this sauce over the duck.

Wild duck à la Walter Scott CANARD SAUVAGE À LA WALTER SCOTT (from a recipe by L. Dépée) Draw, singe, and truss a wild duck. Cook in a hot oven (about 220 C, 425 F, gas 7). Meanwhile fry the duck's liver in butter, mash it, and mix it with 20 g (¾ oz) foie gras. Fry 2 croutons in clarified butter and spread them with the liver paste. Core 2 apples, stud each with 4 cloves, and cook as for apples bonne femme. Dilute some Dundee marmalade with 2 tablespoons whisky and heat gently. When the duck is cooked, arrange it on a serving dish. Remove the cloves from the apples and place the latter on the croutons, then pour the marmalade into the holes in the apples. Arrange the croutons around the duck. Serve the juice in a sauceboat, without skimming off the fat.

Wild duck au chambertin CANARD SAUVAGE AU CHAMBERTIN Roast the duck for 18–20 minutes in a very hot oven (about 240 C, 475 F, gas 9) or fry over a brisk heat, so that the flesh stays slightly pink. Arrange on a serving dish and cover with Chambertin sauce to which the pan juices have been added. Garnish with mushrooms and, if desired, with strips of truffle.

Dugléré (Adolphe)

French chef (born Bordeaux, 1805; died Paris, 1884). A pupil of Carême, he became head of the kitchens of the Rothschild family and later managed the restaurant Les Frères Provençaux. In 1866 he became head chef at the Café Anglais, with which his name is always associated. He is described as 'a taciturn artist who revelled in contemplative isolation', and his culinary creations made the Café Anglais one of the most famous restaurants in Paris during the Second Empire. His creations included potage Germiny, Anna potatoes, sole and sea bream *à la Dugléré*, and soufflé *à l'anglaise*. It was Dugléré who drew up the menu for the historic dinner of the 'Three Emperors'. Among the illustrious guests who attended were Alexander II (the Russian emperor), his son (the future Alexander III), Wilhelm I of Prussia (the German emperor), and Bismarck. The dinner, it is said, cost 400 francs a head!

7 June 1867
Menu for the dinner
arranged by Adolphe Dugléré,
The 'Mozart of cuisine'
SOUPS
Impératrice and Fontanges
HORS D'OEUVRES
Soufflés à la reine
REMOVES
Fillets of sole à la vénitienne
Escalopes of turbot au gratin
Saddle of mutton with Breton purée
ENTRÉES
Chicken à la portugaise
Hot quail pâté
Lobster à la parisienne
Champagne sorbets
ROASTS
Duckling à la rouennaise
Canapés of ortolan

ENTREMETS
Aubergines à l'espagnole
Asparagus spears
Cassolettes princesse
DESSERTS
Bombes glacées
WINES
Retour de l'Inde Madeira, sherry,
Château-d'Yquem 1847,
Château-Margaux 1847, Château-
Lafite 1847,
Château-Latour 1848,
Chambertin 1846, Champagne
Roederer

Dumaine (Alexandre)

French chef (born Digoin, 1895; died Digoin, 1974). At the age of 12 he became an apprentice at a hotel in Paray-le-Monial, and gradually worked his way up in the profession, eventually becoming *grande toque* (head chef) in such famous establishments as the Carlton (in Vichy then in Cannes), the Café de Paris and the Hotel Louvois in Paris, and the Oasis Hotel at Biskra. In 1932 he opened a restaurant at Saulieu, which, with the help of his wife Jeanne, became a gastronomic shrine. The Hôtel de la Côte-d'Or was, with Point at Vienne and Pic at Valence, one of the three outstanding centres of provincial cuisine in France from 1930 to 1950. After retiring in 1964, Dumaine collaborated with Henry Clos-Jouve in producing *Ma cuisine*, a book of recipes interspersed with various reminiscences.

Dumas (Alexandre)

French author (born Villers-Cotterêts, 1802; died Dieppe, 1870). In 1869 Dumas, best known as the author of *The Three Musketeers* and other historical romances, accepted an assignment from a young publisher, Alphonse Lemerre, to write a *Grand Dictionnaire de cuisine*. To find the peace and quiet necessary to compile such a monumental work (1152 pages). Dumas retired to Roscoff (Finisterre) with his cook Marie. The work was completed in March 1870, a few weeks before his death, and was published in 1872. It is not considered to be a very reliable work from a strictly culinary point of view, in spite of the friendly collaboration of Joseph Vuillemot, a pupil of Carême who published a revised and abridged version in 1882. But in spite of its errors, its gaps, and its trenchant opinions, the work is written in an alert and amusing style and is full of anecdotes.

Dumas was a great habitué of Parisian restaurants: he had his own private room at the Maison Dorée, and attended the 'Bixio dinners' at Brébant-Vachette, the Rocher de Cancale, the Jockey Club where his protégé Jules Gouffé presided, and the Restaurant de France in the Place de la Madeleine. Here his friend Vuillemot gave a famous dinner in his honour with 'lobster *à la Porthos*', 'fillet of beef Monte-Cristo', 'salad *à la Dumas*', *gorenflot* (rum-soaked sponge cake), etc.

Dumas made it a point of honour to dress the salad himself: 'I place in a salad bowl one hard-boiled egg yolk for every two persons. I pound it in oil to make a paste. I then add chervil, crushed thyme, crushed anchovies, chopped gherkins, and chopped whites of the hard-boiled eggs, salt, and pepper. I mix it all with a good vinegar, then I put the salad into the salad bowl. Then I call a servant and ask him to toss the salad. When he has finished, I scatter a pinch of paprika over it. It remains only to be served'. Another famous Dumas salad was made with truffles 'peeled with a silver knife' and seasoned, according to the mood of the host, with champagne, a liqueur, or almond milk.

dumpling

A savoury or sweet ball of dough that is poached and served as an accompaniment to meat or as a desert. Dumplings are popular in Britain and the United States.

In England dumplings made with either a suet or bread dough were traditionally served with boiled beef and carrots and pease pudding. Today they are served with boiled meat or stews or in soups; they are made with a mixture of flour and shredded beef suet and are simmered gently in a meat stock. The English apple dumpling (an apple encased in pastry) is made with suet crust and boiled or with pastry and baked.

In the United States, dumplings can accompany roast and boiled meat dishes. Made with flour, baking powder, egg, and milk, they are shaped into walnut-sized balls and simmered very gently in vegetable soups, stews, and beef and poultry consommées. They may also contain cornmeal, potato purée, grated cheese, or breadcrumbs. Sweet-pastry dumplings sometimes made with a yeasted dough are poached in fruit juice and served with compotes, fruit purées, melted butter, or cream. They are sometimes stuffed with fruit.

Dunand, Dunan, or Dunant

The surname of two Swiss cooks, father and son. The father was in charge of the kitchens of the Prince of Condé. His son inherited the post and, in 1793, followed the prince into exile. He returned to France 12 years later and entered the service of Napoleon I. Chicken Marengo is attributed to him even though the French victory over the Austrians took place in 1800, and Dunand remained in the service of the Prince of Condé until 1805! On the other hand, it is known that Napoleon greatly enjoyed his crêpinettes. On the fall of the Empire, Dunand went into the service of the Duc de Berry, but resumed his post with the emperor during the Hundred Days.

Durand

A Parisian restaurant that was situated in the Place de la Madeleine. In the 1860s, according to A. Luchet, it was considered to be 'the third wonder in the art of good living' (after the Café Riche and the Café Hardy). It was frequented by writers and politicians, notably Boulanger, Anatole France, and Émile Zola (who wrote *J'accuse* there). The chef Voiron created Mornay sauce in this restaurant.

Durand (Charles)

French chef (born Alès, 1766; died Nîmes, 1854). Called 'the Carême of Provençal cooking', he was chef to the bishops of Alès, Nîmes, and Montpellier before opening restaurants in Alès (1790) and Nîmes (1800). Above all, he was responsible for popularizing French regional cuisine at a time when it was practically unknown elsewhere. *Le Cuisinier Durand* (1803) is a collection of authentic Provençal recipes that enabled brandade (a dish of salt cod) and other specialities of the south to be enjoyed in Paris.

durian

A tree that is widely cultivated in Southeast Asia, especially in Vietnam and the Philippines, for its fruit. Durian fruits are oval, up to 20 cm (8 in) in diameter and weighing up to 5 kg (11 lb), with a hard greenish rind covered with large thorns. The flesh is whitish or coffee-coloured with a creamy texture and a distinctive putrefying smell that becomes nauseating when the fruit is over-ripe. It is ready to eat when the skin begins to crack, and is usually eaten raw either as an hors d'oeuvre or as a dessert. It may also be eaten as a compote with sugar and fresh cream, and in Java it is made into a fruit jelly with coconut milk. The large shiny seeds are also edible and are prepared in the same way as chestnuts. The fruit appeared in European markets in about 1975.

Duroc

A dish dedicated to General Duroc, a soldier at the time of the Empire. It consists of small joints of meat or sautéed poultry garnished with new potatoes browned in butter, covered with crushed tomatoes, and coated with chasseur sauce.

Duse

A garnish named in honour of the great Italian actress, Eleonora Duse. It consists of fresh green beans cooked in butter, with deseeded steamed tomatoes and Parmentier potatoes. It accompanies large joints of meat. The name is also given to poached stuffed fillets of sole arranged in a ring with rice, coated with Mornay sauce, and glazed. The centre is filled with a salpicon of shrimps bound with a white wine sauce and sprinkled with finely chopped truffles.

Dutch cheeses
FROMAGES DE HOLLANDE

The best-known Dutch cheeses are Edam and Gouda. Cheeses made in the Netherlands always carry a government control stamp which gives the name of the cheese, the fat content in the dry matter, the country of origin – expressed as Holland – the number indicating where, on what date, and from which curd batch the cheese was made, and the code of the relevant government control station.

Duval (Pierre-Louis)

French butcher (born Montlhéry, 1811; died Paris, 1870). He supplied the Tuileries kitchens and owned several retail butcher's shops in Paris. In 1860 he had the idea of creating a number of small restaurants serving a single dish – boiled beef and consommé – at a fixed price. The first 'bouillon', in the Rue de Montesquieu, was soon followed by a dozen others.

His son Alexandre successfully developed the chain of restaurants and made an immense fortune. A well-known figure of Parisian life, nicknamed 'Godefroi de Bouillon' by humorists of the time, he composed a *Marche des petites bonnes* in honour of his waitresses, who all wore a coif of white tulle and, for the first time, replaced the traditional garçons in restaurants.

duxelles

A basic preparation of chopped mushrooms, onions, and shallots sautéed in butter. Duxelles is used as a stuffing or garnish, as a complementary ingredient of a sauce, and in the preparation of various dishes called *à la duxelles*. The derivation of the word is disputed: some claim that duxelles was created at Uzel, a small town in the Côtes-du-Nord, while others attribute it to La Varenne, chef of the Marquis d'Uxelles.

RECIPES

Duxelles sauce SAUCE À LA DUXELLES Prepare 4 tablespoons (⅓ cup) mushroom duxelles. Add 1 dl (6 tablespoons, scant ½ cup) white wine and reduce until almost completely dry. Add 1.5 dl (¼ pint, ⅔ cup) demi-glace sauce and 1 dl (6 tablespoons, scant ½ cup) sieved tomato fondue. Boil for 2–3 minutes, pour into a sauceboat, and sprinkle with chopped parsley.

Alternatively, the duxelles may be moistened with 1.5 dl (¼ pint, ⅔ cup) consommé and 1 dl (6 tablespoons, scant ½ cup) sieved tomato fondue and thickened with 1 tablespoon kneaded butter.

Mushroom duxelles DUXELLES DE CHAMPIGNONS Clean and trim 250 g (9 oz, 2 cups) button mushrooms and chop them finely, together with 1 onion and 1 large shallot. Melt a large knob of butter in a frying pan (skillet), add the chopped vegetables, salt and pepper, and a little grated nutmeg (unless the duxelles is to accompany fish). Cook over a brisk heat until the vegetables are brown and the water from the mushrooms has evaporated. If the duxelles is for use as a garnish, add 1 tablespoon fresh cream.

Omelette à la duxelles OMELETTE FOURRÉE À LA DUXELLES Prepare 4 tablespoons (⅓ cup) mushroom duxelles with cream added. Make an omelette with 8 eggs and fill it with the duxelles. Stud the omelette with small fried croutons and serve with duxelles sauce.

Poached eggs à la duxelles OEUFS POCHÉS À LA DUXELLES Prepare 4 croûtes. Cut 4 slices of ham to the size of the croûtes and fry quickly in butter. Poach 4 eggs. On each croûte place a slice of ham and a poached egg. Coat with duxelles sauce and sprinkle with chopped parsley.

Sautéed veal chops à la duxelles CÔTES DE VEAU SAUTÉES À LA DUXELLES Prepare 4 tablespoons (⅓ cup) mushroom duxelles. Sauté 4 veal chops in butter. When the chops are almost cooked, add the duxelles to the pan and complete the cooking over a low heat. Drain the chops and arrange on a serving dish; keep hot. Add to the duxelles in the pan 1 dl (6 tablespoons, scant ½ cup) fresh cream and half a glass of white wine (or 2 tablespoons (3 tablespoons) Madeira) and reduce until the cream thickens. Coat the chops with this sauce and serve very hot.

ear OREILLE

A piece of offal, usually from pigs or calves, used in cooking or in the preparation of brawn and various other forms of charcuterie. It can be boiled, fried, sautéed, braised, stuffed, made into a gratin, or grilled (broiled) and is an ingredient of great number of tasty recipes.

RECIPES

CALVES' EARS

Grilled (broiled) and devilled calves' ears OREILLES DE VEAU GRILLÉS À LA DIABLE Braise the calves' ears in a mirepoix. Drain them, cut them in half lengthwise, and leave to get cold under a weight. Spread them liberally with mustard and sprinkle with melted butter; roll them in fresh breadcrumbs and grill (broil) them gently. Serve with a devilled sauce.

Stuffed calves' ears du Bugey OREIL-LES DE VEAU FARCIES DU BUGEY (from Alain Chapel's recipe) Blanch, refresh, then carefully clean 1 calf's ear per guest. Rub the ears with lemon and sew each one into the form of a cornet. Put them into a pan with 1.5 litres (2¾

pints, 7 cups) well-flavoured beef stock, 1 litre (1¾ pints, 4¼ cups) dry white wine, herbs, and some pot vegetables. Add plenty of salt and pepper and cook gently for about 2½ hours. Drain the ears and put them aside, covered with a damp cloth.

Dice 1 calf's sweetbread which has been braised in white wine, 1 chicken wing, and 1 fresh truffle. Fry 100 g (4 oz, 1 cup) coarsely chopped wild mushrooms in butter; add salt and pepper. When they are half-cooked, add the truffle, the sweetbread, and the chicken meat; continue to cook over a low heat. Add 2 dl (7 fl oz, ¾ cup) slightly soured cream, then take the pan off the heat and add 2 egg yolks. Blend everything well and leave to get cold.

Spoon the cold mixture into the ear cornets. Dip the ears in flour, then beaten egg, then breadcrumbs, and fry in butter, without allowing it to get brown. Drain, arrange on a serving dish, and sprinkle with fried parsley.

PIGS' EARS

Boiled pigs' ears OREILLES DE PORC BOUILLIES Singe 4 pigs' ears and clean the insides thoroughly; cook them in boiling salted water (1 teaspoon salt

per litre, 1¾ pints, 4¼ cups water) with
2 carrots, 1 onion studded with 2 cloves,
and a bouquet garni. Simmer for about
50 minutes, then drain.

Boiled pigs' ears can be used in several
ways. They can be chopped, dipped in
batter, and deep-fried; or spread with
butter, dipped in fresh breadcrumbs,
and grilled (broiled), to be served with
mustard or horseradish sauce and
mashed potatoes or purée of celeriac
(celery root). Pigs' ears *à la lyonnaise* are
cut into large strips and sautéed in butter with sliced onion. They can also be
served cold with vinaigrette, or
browned in the oven with a white or
Mornay sauce.

Braised pigs' ears   OREILLES DE
PORC BRAISÉES   Singe 4 pigs' ears and
clean the insides thoroughly. Blanch
them for 5 minutes in boiling water,
drain them, and cut them in half lengthwise. Grease a casserole, cover the bottom with pieces of pork rind, put in 1
sliced onion and 1 sliced carrot, and
arrange the pieces of ear on top in a flat
layer; put a bouquet garni in the middle.

Begin cooking on the hob with the
casserole covered, then pour in 2 dl (7 fl
oz, ¾ cup) white wine and reduce completely. Add 4 dl (14 fl oz, 1¾ cups)
thickened veal juices or stock and cook
in the oven, covered, for 50 minutes.
Drain the ears and arrange them on a
serving dish. Garnish with braised celery hearts or steamed cauliflower. Pour
over the strained and reduced braising
liquid.

Stuffed and fried pigs' ears   OREILLES
DE PORC FARCIES ET FRITES   Braise
the ears whole. Meanwhile, make a
chicken forcemeat and some Villeroi
sauce. Let the ears get cold, slit them,
and stuff them with the chicken forcemeat. Dip them into the Villeroi sauce
and leave them for 30 minutes. Roll the
ears in egg and breadcrumbs and fry
them in very hot oil. Drain, arrange on
the serving dish, and serve with tomato
sauce.

earthenware
POTERIE À FEU

A ceramic made of clay paste and sand
with chalk and *chamotte* (fired and
crushed earth), which is moulded, dried,

and baked at a high temperature. This
pottery is naturally porous, but it can be
glazed with a clear or coloured glaze.
Unglazed containers need to be sealed
before they are used for the first time:
this is done by filling them with water
and simmering them over a low heat for
an hour. Glazed earthenware is perfect
for simmering food for a long period
over a low heat (the dish should rest on
an insulating plate if it is to be cooked
over a naked flame). Sudden changes of
temperature must be avoided or the
containers will crack.

The main earthenware vessels are
oven dishes (glazed), diables (porous),
pots, casseroles, gratin dishes, and
covered braising dishes (glazed; formerly placed in the embers but now in the
oven). Earthenware dishes are typically
found in regional French kitchens; examples are the green varnished *daubière*
of Provence and the *guichon* from
Normandy (a small soup tureen).

Easter   PÂQUES
The major festival of the Christian
calendar, which celebrates the resurrec-
tion of Jesus Christ. It was associated in
the early days of Christianity with the
Jewish feast of the Passover, commemorating the Exodus from Egypt
(the French word for Easter is derived
from the Greek *Paskha* and the Hebrew
Pesah, meaning 'passage'). The Passover is celebrated for a week at the
beginning of spring (from the 14 to the
21 of the month of Nisan), during which
no alcohol or leavened food must be
consumed; the feast begins with a formal meal of a roasted lamb, sacrificed
according to the kosher method.

Easter Day, fixed at the Council of
Nicaea in 325 AD to fall on the first
Sunday after the first full moon following the spring equinox, can occur on any
Sunday between 22 March and 22
April. It corresponds to the height of the
period of the renewal of life after winter
and, as Easter also follows the abstinence of Lent, numerous culinary
traditions mark this festival.

In all countries, eggs are the symbol of
Easter. In France, the custom of offering
painted or decorated hard-boiled (hard-
cooked) eggs goes back to the 15th century, when it was particularly common

in Alsace. The paschal omelette, sometimes made with eggs laid on Good Friday, is usually enriched with bacon or sausage to emphasize the end of the period of abstinence.

The omelette is traditionally followed by a dish of meat, generally roebuck or lamb but also pork (grilled sucking pig at Metz, ham sprinkled with chopped parsley in the Côte-d'Or). In Charente, Poitou, Touraine, Berry, and Bresse the Easter Sunday menu includes a pie filled with a mixture of chopped meats and hard-boiled eggs. Little noodles in vinaigrette (*totelots*) are typical in Lorraine, fritters in Roussillon, and large thick pancakes (*pachades*) in Auvergne. A variety of special cakes and pastries are prepared for Easter: *pognes* and *pompes* in Provence, Savoy, and the area around Lyon; *alise pacaude* in the Vendée; *cavagnats* in Menton (shaped like baskets and containing eggs dyed red); *cacavelli* (crowns topped with eggs) in Corsica; *alléluias* in Castelnaudary; *pagnottes* in Forez; gingerbreads in the shape of horses in Touraine; darioles in Reims; *flônes* in the Aveyron region; and *soupe dorée* in Savoy (called *soupe rousse* in the Creuse), which is a kind of French toast (*pain perdu*).

Russian cookery includes several traditional cakes for Easter Day, such as kulich and pashka. In Germany the Easter cake is the *Ostertorte*, a type of sponge cake filled with a mocha-flavoured butter cream and decorated with chocolate eggs.

The British simnel cake is now traditional at Easter although originally it was a cake made to celebrate Mothering Sunday.

eau-de-vie

A French term meaning 'water of life', from the Latin *aqua vitae*. It is nowadays generally applied to brandy (not necessarily Cognac or Armagnac) and also to the *alcools blancs* (white alcohols) – spirits distilled from fruits or herbs and kept in glass (not wood) without any sweetening. The various marcs are known as *eaux-de-vie-de-vin*, as they are distilled from wine. Distillates from other basics, such as Scotch, vodka, gin, schnapps, and so on, are not strictly speaking eaux-de-vie, although the Gaelic for Scotch whisky – *usque béatha* – means 'water of life'.

écailler

A French culinary term meaning to open shellfish. An *écailler* is the person employed to open the oysters in a restaurant having its own oyster bed. Écailler are also traders specializing in the sale of shellfish and seafoods.

The verb *écailler* also means to scale fish.

écarlate (à l')

The French term describing pickled pork or beef, especially ox (beef) tongue. (The pickling process colours the meat bright red, hence the name, meaning 'scarlet'.) Pickled tongue is served hot with vegetables or cold as an hors d'oeuvre. It is also an ingredient of dishes described as *à l'écarlate*, which are served with some kind of red sauce (e.g. tomato), and it is often used as a decoration (cut into cocks' combs). Beef can also be pickled, cooked, pressed, and used in the same way.

Fromage à l'écarlate, a speciality of classical cookery, is a type of butter made with crayfish (and therefore reddish in colour): a recipe is given by the chef Menon in *La Science du maître d'hôtel cuisinier* (1749).

RECIPES

Pickled ox (beef) tongue LANGUE DE BOEUF À L'ÉCARLATE Soak a trimmed ox (beef) tongue in cold water for 24 hours, drain and wipe it, and then prick it lightly all over, rubbing the surface with salt mixed with saltpetre. Put the tongue in a stoneware container. Prepare a liquid brine by adding 2.25 kg (5 lb, 6¼ cups) coarse salt, 150 g (5 oz) saltpetre, 300 g (11 oz, 1½ cups) brown sugar, a sprig of thyme, a bay leaf, 12 juniper berries, and 12 peppercorns to 5 litres (9 pints, 11 pints) water. Boil for a few minutes, then leave it to cool completely. Cover the tongue with this brine, place over it a wooden board with a weight on top, and leave it to steep in a cool place for 6 days in summer, or 8 days in winter.

Drain the tongue, soak it for a few hours in fresh water to draw out the salt, then cook in water without any seasonings or condiments for 2½–3 hours, depending on its size. Drain the tongue, then strip the skin off completely while still hot. Cover it with buttered paper to prevent blackening, and leave it to cool. Wrap the tongue in very thin pieces of fat bacon, tie it up, and wrap the whole thing in muslin (cheesecloth), tying it at each end. Poach the tongue in a large quantity of simmering water for about 10 minutes. Drain immediately, remove the muslin, and brush the tongue with liquid carmine. Hang it up and leave to cool. Prepared in this way, the tongue will keep for several weeks in a cool dry place.

Canapés à l'éscarlate   Cut some thin slices of bread into rounds or rectangles, and spread them with a little butter which has previously been softened and then mixed with paprika, cayenne, and a little Worcestershire sauce. Place a slice of pickled tongue on each round and garnish with a thin line of the same butter.

échaudé

A small light crisp biscuit, very popular in France up to the last century. It was made of a mixture of water and flour (to which an egg and some butter was added), poached in boiling water (hence its name, which means 'scalded'), and then drained and dried in the oven. Formerly, during Lent, the egg was omitted and the butter replaced with oil.

Échaudés are mentioned for the first time in a charter dated 1202, under the name of *panes qui discuntur eschaudati* ('bread known as scalded'). In the 13th century they were scalloped; later they were round, triangular, or heart-shaped. They used to be sold in the street, like wafers. In his *Grand Dictionnaire de cuisine*, Alexandre Dumas describes them as 'a sort of unsweetened cake which is made for the birds and for children rather than for adults'. The Parisian pastrycook Favart, who brought them back into fashion at the beginning of the 18th century, in the Rue de la Verrerie, was thought for a long time to have invented them.

The échaudé remains a traditional biscuit in several provinces, particularly in Aveyron (aniseed-flavoured) and in the west of France (along with the craquelins). It can also be made with a raising (leavening) agent.

Echézeaux

A region in the Côte de Nuits, Burgundy, where 11 vineyards entitled to the AOC make fine red wine, labelled according to their specifications: one of them is a *grand cru*, the highest rating in Burgundy. Very few of the wines are sold just as 'Échézeaux', as many Vosne-Romanée people have difficulty pronouncing the name!

éclade or églade

A traditional dish prepared from mussels, which is typical of Saintonge on the Atlantic coast of France, particularly of La Tremblade. The mussels are scraped and cleaned and then arranged on the *fumée*, a thick plank of hard olive wood, which is sometimes covered with a layer of clay so that the mussels will stay in place. The plank and mussels are then covered with a layer of dry pine needles, which are set alight. When the needles have been reduced to ashes, the mussels are ready. They are eaten very hot and plain, with country bread and butter.

éclair

A small log-shaped bun of choux pastry, filled with cream and coated with fondant icing (frosting). The dough is piped from a forcing bag onto a baking sheet and cooked until crisp and hollow.

After baking, the éclair is split lengthwise and traditionally filled with cream or confectioners' custard (pastry cream), usually coffee- or chocolate-flavoured, but rum or fruit flavours are also used. The top is iced with fondant icing of the same flavour as the filling; if whipped cream is used as a filling, chocolate or coffee fondant is used. Éclairs can also be filled with chestnut purée or a filling made of fruits in syrup.

RECIPES

Chocolate éclairs   ÉCLAIRS AU CHOCOLAT   Prepare some choux pastry (see *chou*) with 125 g (4½ oz, generous cup) flour, 65 g (2½ oz, 5 tablespoons) butter, a large pinch of salt, ¼ litre (8 fl oz, 1 cup) water, and 4 medium-sized eggs. Using a piping bag with a smooth nozzle, 2 cm (¾ in) in diameter, pipe some thick lengths of dough, 6–7 cm (2½–3 in) long, onto a baking sheet, well spaced apart so that they will be able to swell without sticking together. Beat an egg yolk with a little milk, and glaze the eclairs with it. Heat the oven to about 190 c (375 f, gas 5) and bake the éclairs until pale golden in colour. This will take 20 minutes at the most. The inside must still be soft. Leave the éclairs to cool completely, then split them down one side.

Make a confectioners' custard (see *creams and custards*) wth 50 g (2 oz, 8 tablespoons) flour, 1 whole egg, 2 egg yolks, and 50 g (2 oz, 4 tablespoons) caster (superfine) sugar. Add 1 tablespoon cocoa powder (unsweetened cocoa) to the cream mixture. Leave to cool completely. Fill a piping bag with this mixture and fill the éclairs with it. Heat up 200 g (7 oz, 1 cup) fondant icing (frosting) over a low heat, add 50 g (2 oz, ⅓ cup) melted chocolate, and mix well. Coat the top of the éclairs and leave in a cool place.

Coffee éclairs ÉCLAIRS AU CAFÉ Use the same process as for chocolate éclairs, but flavour the cream filling with 2 teaspoons instant coffee dissolved in ¼ litre (8 fl oz, 1 cup) milk brought to the boil with 40 g (1½ oz, 3 tablespoons) butter. Add coffee essence (strong black coffee), drop by drop to taste, to the icing (frosting).

éclanche

A French word formerly used in classic cookery to mean a shoulder of mutton. The word comes from the Old French *esclenc* ('left side', then 'arm' or 'shoulder', and finally 'shoulder of mutton'). The word was still being used in Balzac's time, but has now disappeared.

École de Salerne

A collection of the health precepts of an Italian school of medicine which was highly regarded in the Middle Ages. Translated from Latin into French in about 1500, and edited and enlarged several times, these precepts were rewritten in the form of little verses, easy to remember; for example:
  Fennel seeds when soaked in wine
  Revitalize a heart that love makes pine,

  And reawaken the old man's flame;
  The salutary usage of the seed, you
        know,
  From liver and lung doth banish pain,
  And quells the wind that in the gut
        doth blow.
For a long time it served as a dietetic and therapeutic recipe manual.

écossaise (à l')

A French term primarily used to describe a soup inspired by Scottish cookery (Scotch broth). This is a clear mutton soup made with diced boiled mutton, pearl barley, and a vegetable mixture. This mixture is also used to make écossaise sauce, served with white offal, eggs, or poached fish and poultry. The name is also used for various dishes, particularly egg dishes, containing salmon.

RECIPES

Écossaise sauce SAUCE ÉCOSSAISE Gently braise in butter 4 tablespoons vegetable brunoise and some green beans cut up into very small dice. Prepare 2 dl (7 fl oz, ¾ cup) cream sauce and put through a strainer. Add the vegetable mixture.

Soft-boiled (*or poached*) **eggs à l'écossaise** OEUFS MOLLETS (OU POCHÉS) À L'ÉCOSSAISE Prepare 4 tablespoons salmon purée by mixing some finely crumbled poached salmon with the same quantity of thick white sauce. Heat up this purée and use it to fill 4 puff pastry croustades previously warmed in the oven. Arrange 1 soft-boiled or poached egg in each case, and cover with shrimp sauce. Each egg may be garnished with a slice of truffle.

écot

A French term meaning each diner's share in a meal paid for communally. The word, which comes from the Old French *skot* ('contribution'), is now hardly used at all except in the expression *payer son écot* (to pay one's share).

écuelle

A small round rimless bowl for individual portions of food. Wooden, earthenware, or tin écuelles are among the most ancient of table utensils. In the Middle Ages, one bowl was sometimes used by two people. Nowadays écuelles are usually made of earthenware or pottery, and are generally only used to serve thick vegetable soups or rustic dishes.

écuyer tranchant

An officer in charge of cutting the meats and serving at the king's table under the Ancien Régime. The post was sometimes shared, the *écuyer tranchant* doing the cutting and the *grand écuyer tranchant* the serving (known as the *premier tranchant* when he officiated for the queen). The écuyer tranchant was a nobleman, who had the right to display representations of a knife and fork with fleur-de-lis on the· handles under his heraldic arms. The post itself gradually became honorary, but remained highly lucrative owing to the privileges attached to it.

In the 15th century, Olivier de La Marche· reported that the écuyer tranchant had to 'keep his knives clean' at his own expense. These knives were luxury utensils bearing his lord's emblem or coat of arms, and at this time there were three of them. The largest one, which had a wide blade with two cutting edges, served not only for cutting, but also for presenting morsels to the diners; the second knife was for carving roasts and poultry; and the third one, which was smaller and known as the *parepain*, was for cutting the slices of bread used as trenchers for the meat.

Edam ÉDAM

A Dutch cows'-milk cheese, containing 30–40% fat, in the shape of a large ball with a yellow or red waxed coating. The semihard pressed cheese is firm but elastic, free of holes, and light yellow to yellow ochre in colour, depending on its degree of maturity. Edam is described as 'young' after two or three months in a dry cellar, when it has a sweet nutty flavour; after six months it is 'semimatured', with a stronger flavour; at the end of a year's maturing it is described as 'matured' and has a slight bite. Edam is also known on the continent as *tête de mort* or *tête de Maure* (dead man's head or Moor's head), *Manbollen*, and *Kat-*

zenkopf, due to its characteristic head-like shape. Measuring about 13 cm (5 in) in diameter, it weighs between 1.5 and 1.7 kg (3–4 lb). A 'baby' Edam is also available, weighing 1 kg (2¼ lb), and a triple Edam, weighing 6.5 kg (14½ lb).

Edam is made everywhere in the Netherlands, and even in France and Belgium, but authentic Edam, from the small port in the northern Netherlands, is protected by a label of origin. It is usually served after a meal, often with pale ale, but it is also used a good deal in cookery. Young or semimatured cheese is suitable for sandwiches, pastries, canapés, croque-monsieurs, and mixed salads; matured cheese is used in gratins, soufflés, and tarts. In Bordeaux it is sometimes cut up into small cubes and served at wine tastings in the vineyards. Lastly, it is used in a traditional dish called *keshy yena* from Curaçao, the main island in the Dutch East Indies.

RECIPE

Keshy yena Using a young Edam, cut a round slice from the top and hollow out the inside of the cheese with a knife, leaving the walls 1.5 cm (½ in) thick. Cut the hollowed-out cheese into small cubes, mix with a cooked ragout made of diced or chopped pork or beef, then add some stoned (pitted) olives, tomatoes cut into small segments, and sliced onion. Fill the Edam ball with this mixture; replace the round slice at the top and hold it in place with sticks. Bake in a cool oven for 1 hour.

Edelpilz

A German cows'-milk cheese containing 55% fat. A blue-veined pale-yellow cheese with a natural crust, it has a sweet flavour with a slight tang. Made in the Bavarian Alps, Edelpilz is sold in a round, a loaf, or individual portions, wrapped in silver paper. Its name means literally 'noble mushroom'.

Edelzwicker

A white Alsace wine made from a blend of certain permitted 'noble' grapes. A pleasant drink, it goes well with various Alsatian recipes.

Edward VII
ÉDOUARD VII
While still the Prince of Wales, the future king of England was a notable personality in fashionable Paris at the end of the 19th century. He was an habitué of the great restaurants (Voisin, Café Hardy, Paillard) and sumptuous dishes were dedicated to him. For example, *turbot prince de Galles* was a dish of poached turbot garnished with oysters and fried mussels and coated with a champagne sauce seasoned with curry spices and enriched with crayfish butter.

When he became king, he continued to receive the honours of haute cuisine. *Barbue Édouard VII* is brill poached in white wine, garnished with duchess potato rosettes, and served with an oyster mousseline sauce. *Poularde Édouard VII* is chicken stuffed with foie gras, rice, and truffles, coated with a curry sauce containing diced red pepper, and served with cucumbers in cream. In *oeufs Édouard VII*, soft-boiled (soft-cooked) or poached eggs are arranged, with slices of pickled tongue, on a risotto mixed with diced truffles, and garnished with slices of truffle. *Édouard VII* itself is a small boat-shaped cake filled with rhubarb and topped with green icing (frosting).

eel ANGUILLE
A snakelike fish with a smooth slippery skin. Eels mature in fresh water where they are fished, and migrate to the Sargasso Sea to breed. The larvae (leptocephali) are carried by the ocean currents over a period of two or three years to the coasts of Europe. When they enter the estuaries, they are transparent and have grown to a length of 6–9 cm (2½–3½ in). These are the glass-eels or elvers, which make a popular fried dish in Nantes, La Rochelle, Bordeaux, and the Basque country. Those larvae which survive grow larger and the skin becomes pigmented. The 'yellow' eel has a brown back, becoming greenish, with a yellowish underbelly that later becomes silvery white. It is at this time, when it starts to travel back to the Sargasso Sea, that the eel, now described as 'silvered' or 'descending', is most prized. It measures from 50 cm (20 in) (male) to 1 m (40 in) (female) and is sold alive. It is killed and skinned at the last moment as the flesh deteriorates rapidly, and the raw blood is poisonous if it enters a cut, e.g. on one's finger. Eel is a very fatty fish, but tasty, nourishing, and rich in nitrogen.

The eel was popular with the Romans and widely eaten during the Middle Ages. Taillevent's *Viandier* gives a whole range of recipes for preparing eel dishes: in broth, in galantine, in tarts or pâtés (English eel pie is similar), as Lent flan, with garlic or mustard, roasted, salted, 'dusted with spices', or as a roulade. Today, it appears in numerous regional recipes (catigot, matelote, bouilleture, *au vert, à la flamande*). However, classic haute cuisine dishes (ballottine, pâté), or even more simple ones (*à la tartare, à la poulette*), are less often prepared than they used to be.

Smoked eel is a popular dish in Scandinava and in northern Germany. The skin should be shiny and almost black, and it is served as an hors d'oeuvre, with rye bread and lemon.

Paul Forgerit, a chef from the Charente, has compiled a comprehensive collection of recipes for this fish.

RECIPES

Preparation of eel PRÉPARATION DE L'ANGUILLE To kill an eel, seize it with a cloth and bang its head violently against a hard surface. To skin it, put a noose around the base of the head and hang it up. Slit the skin in a circle just beneath the noose. Pull away a small portion of the skin, turn it back, take hold of it with a cloth, and pull it down hard. Clean the eel by making a small incision in its belly. Cut off and discard the head and the end of the tail. Wash and wipe dry. Alternatively, when the eel has been killed, it can be cut into sections and grilled (broiled) for a short time. The skin will puff up and can then be removed. This method has the advantage of removing excess fat from the eel, particularly if it is large.

Devilled eel ANGUILLE À LA DIABLE Cook an eel of about 750 g (1¾ lb) in a court-bouillon of white wine and let it cool in the liquor. Drain and wipe the eel, then smear it with mustard, brush with melted butter, and grill (broil) slowly. Arrange the eel on a round dish and garnish with gherkins if desired. Serve with a devilled sauce.

Eel à la bonne femme ANGUILLE LA BONNE FEMME Soften 4 large tablespoons chopped onion in butter and place in a sauté pan. Put slices of a medium-sized eel (about 750 g (1¾ lb)) on top of the onion layer. Add salt and pepper, a bouquet garni, and 3 dl (½ pint, 1¼ cups) white wine. Cover and poach slowly for 25 minutes. Drain the slices of eel and arrange them on croutons of sandwich bread fried in butter. Garnish with large diced potatoes sautéed in butter. Coat the eel with the liquor from the pan, after reducing it by half and thickening it with 1 tablespoon *beurre manié* (see *butter*). Sprinkle with chopped parsley.

Eel à la provençale ANGUILLE À LA PROVENÇALE Cook 2 tablespoons (3 tablespoons) chopped onion gently in a large pan with a little oil. Cut a medium-sized eel into even-sized slices, add to the pan, and cook until they have stiffened. Season with salt and pepper and add 4 peeled deseeded chopped tomatoes, a bouquet garni, and a crushed clove of garlic. Moisten with 1 dl (6 tablespoons, scant ½ cup) dry white wine, cover the pan, and cook slowly for 25 to 30 minutes. 10 minutes before serving, add 12 black (ripe) olives. Arrange on a dish and sprinkle with chopped parsley.

Eel brochettes à l'anglaise ANGUILLE À L'ANGLAISE EN BROCHETTES Cut a boned eel into even-sized pieces and marinate them for an hour in a mixture of oil, lemon juice, pepper, salt, and chopped parsley. Drain the eel pieces, roll in flour, and coat with breadcrumbs. Thread the eel onto skewers, separating the pieces with slices of rather fat bacon. Grill (broil) on a low heat until the flesh separates easily from the bone. Arrange on a long dish, garnished with fresh parsley and surrounded with half-slices of lemon. Serve with tartare sauce.

Eel pie PÂTÉ D'ANGUILLE Bone an eel, cut the fillets into slices of 5–6 cm (2–2½ in) and blanch them in salted water. Drain and cool the eel slices. Hard-boil (hard-cook) and slice some eggs. Season the fish and eggs with salt, pepper, and grated nutmeg and sprinkle them with chopped parsley. Layer the eel and egg slices in a deep, preferably oval, dish. Add sufficient white wine to just cover the fish and dot with small knobs of butter. Cover with a layer of puff pastry, leaving a hole for the steam to escape. Coat the pastry with beaten egg and score the top for decoration. Bake in a moderate oven (180–200 c, 350–400 F, gas 4–6) for 1½ hours. Just before serving, pour a few tablespoons demi-glace sauce (made with fish stock) into the hole at the top of the pie. The pie may also be eaten cold.

Eel pie aux fines herbes (*called à la ménagère*) PÂTE D'ANGUILLE AUX FINES HERBES (DIT À LA MÉNAGÈRE) Bone an eel and cut the fillets into slices. Flatten each slice and season with salt, pepper, and spices to taste. Arrange in a deep dish and moisten with a few tablespoons dry white wine, a little Cognac, and a few drops of oil. Leave to marinate for 2 hours in a cool place. Drain and wipe the slices, and keep the marinade. Cook the fish briskly until stiff in butter in a sauté pan, then sprinkle generously with chopped parsley and shallots. Take the pan off the heat and pour the marinade over the fish. Leave to get completely cold.

Line a shallow oval pie dish with short-crust pastry (basic pie dough) and spread the base and sides with a layer of pike forcemeat containing chopped parsley. Fill the pie with alternating layers of the flattened eel slices and the pike forcemeat. Moisten each layer with a little of the marinade. Finish with a 2-cm (¾-in) layer of forcemeat and sprinkle with melted butter. Cover with a layer of pastry (dough) and trim the top with leaves cut out of the pastry trimmings. Make a hole in the top for the steam to escape and coat the pastry (dough) with beaten egg. Bake in the oven at 180 c (350 F, gas 4) for 1¾–2 hours.

Remove the pie from the dish and place it on a long serving dish. Pour a few tablespoons demi-glace sauce, made with fish stock, through the hole into the top of the pie. Anchovy fillets may also be included with the eel slices, or some anchovy butter or dry duxelles may be added to the pike forcemeat. If the pie is served cold, pour enough fish jelly into the hole in the top of the pie to fill the gaps left by the cooking process. Leave for 12 hours to get completely cold.

effiler

A French culinary term meaning to prepare green beans for cooking by breaking off the ends with the fingers, as close as possible to the tip, and removing the strings, if any.

When applied to almonds and pistachio nuts, *effiler* means to cut into thin slices lengthwise, either with a knife or with a special instrument. The word is also used for slicing chicken or duck breasts.

Some chefs use the term *effilocher*, particularly for cutting leeks into fine shred.

egg   OEUF

The round or oval reproductive body laid by the female of many animals, containing the developing embryo and its food reserves and protected by a shell or skin. Although the eggs of many birds, fish, and even reptiles can be used as food, the word 'egg' unqualified applies exclusively to hens' eggs. All other types of egg offered for sale must be labelled appropriately – quails' eggs, duck eggs, plovers' eggs, etc. There are also exotic rarities such as crocodile or ostrich eggs.

The average weight of a hen's egg is 60 g (2 oz). The shell weighs about 12% of the total weight of the egg and is made of a calcareous porous substance which is pervious to air, water, and smells. It is lined with a delicate pellucid membrane which separates itself from the shell at the larger end of the egg to form the air chamber. The size of this chamber is in inverse proportion to the freshness of the egg – the fresher the egg the smaller the chamber.

The albumen, or white of the egg, is a thick viscous transparent liquid containing half the 14% protein content of the egg; it also has a high percentage of water and some mineral substances. Albumen is soluble in cold water, congeals at 70 C (158 F), and remains from then on insoluble. It forms about 58% of the total weight of the egg.

The yolk of the egg (30% of the total weight) is an opaque soft substance which congeals in heat. The yolk is composed of albumins, fats containing vitamins, lecithins, nucleins, chlorestins, and mineral substances including a ferruginous pigment called *haematogen*, which gives it its colour. It contains the germ (visible in a fertilized egg – this does not mean the egg is inedible), the remaining proteins, and all the fats (especially lecithin), together with iron, sulphur, and vitamins A, B, D, and E.

Eggs are a nourishing and perfectly balanced food, fairly low in calories (76 Cal per 100 g); they supply all the amino acids essential for human nutrition and are easy to digest provided they are not made up into rich dishes. However, those on a low-animal-fat diet should restrict their consumption of egg yolks.

Soft-boiled eggs, poached eggs, and eggs *en cocotte* are easily digested, unless served with a heavy garnish such as foie gras, truffles, mushrooms, etc. The same applies to omelettes and scrambled eggs, although these, even without a garnish, are not as easily digested as those mentioned above. Fried eggs are fairly digestible if they are not over browned in the butter or fat in which they are cooked. Hard-boiled (hard-cooked) eggs take longer to digest than any of the others. A hard-boiled egg cut into very small fragments is more easily digested. The average diet should not contain more than two or three eggs weekly (in whatever form they are served) and these should preferably be eaten at the midday meal.

□ **Varieties and qualities** Contrary to popular opinion, a brown egg is neither better nor more 'natural' than a white one; it is, in fact, usually smaller and less well-filled. However, it is easier to examine for freshness against a bright light because the shell is thinner and less opaque. The colour of the yolk (deep or pale yellow) has no bearing on the quality of the egg, and any blood spots that may be found in the white or the yolk have no significance.

Fresh eggs should be used within a month and stored unwashed, with the pointed end down, in the least cold part of the refrigerator. Washing an egg makes the shell permeable to smells. A hard-boiled egg will keep for four days unshelled, two days if shelled. Hard-boiled eggs pickled in flavoured vinegar and sterilized will keep for months. A raw egg yolk will keep for 24 hours and a raw egg white from 6 to 12 hours. A dessert containing raw eggs, such as a mousse, should be eaten within 24 hours. Fresh eggs can be frozen if they are broken into a bowl, beaten, and poured into suitable containers.

☐ **Freshness of eggs** A fresh egg is heavy and should feel well-filled. An egg loses a tiny fraction of its weight every day by evaporation of water through the porous shell. It is easy to test the freshness of an egg by plunging it into salted water (125 g (4¼ oz, ½ cup) salt per litre (1¾ pints, 4¼ cups) water). An egg up to three days old will fall at once to the bottom; an egg three to six days old will float halfway up the water; if it is bad, it floats horizontally on top of the water. Another method is to break an egg onto a plate. If the yolk is compact and positioned in the centre, the egg is fresh. If the egg is one week old, the yolk is not in the centre, and in an egg that is two to three weeks old, the yolk has a tendency to spread. The freshness of an egg can also be tested by holding it up to the light – a very small air chamber indicates a very fresh egg. There are three categories of quality of eggs, A, B, and C, although in practice, only the first is available in retail shops.

In Europe eggs are graded, according to weight, from size 7 (less than 45 g, 1¾ oz) to size 1 (70 g (2¾ oz) and over). The commonest grades are 4 (55–60 g, 2¼ oz) and 3 (60–65 g, 2½ oz); these are the sizes on which most recipes are based.

☐ **Uses** Eggs are nutritious, inexpensive, and probably the most versatile ingredient in cooking. They are of prime importance in many branches of the food industry, especially those concerned with making pasta, ices, biscuits, and cakes. In the kitchen they have innumerable uses (liaisons, egg and breadcrumb coatings, glazing pastry, preparing emulsified sauces and forcemeats, etc. They are an ingredient in many basic doughs and batters and are used to make certain drinks, such as eggnog.

But an egg is also a food in itself, which can be cooked in a great variety of ways and served with all sorts of garnishes. According to James de Coquet, 'There is not a celebrity, a marshal, a composer, or an opera singer who has not given his name to a method of preparing eggs.'

The nutritive value and versatility of eggs ensured that they became part of the human diet all over the world from the earliest times; they were frequently associated with rites and traditions. Enormous numbers of eggs were eaten in the Middle Ages and, as in ancient Rome, the diner crushed the shell in his plate to prevent evil spirits from hiding there. Eggs were forbidden during Lent because of their 'richness', and it was traditional in France to search for and collect eggs on Maundy Thursday and Good Friday and have them blessed on Easter Saturday ready for their prolific consumption over Eastertide. The French word for the yolk at that time was *moyeu*, meaning centre or hub, and some people believe that the word 'mayonnaise' is derived from it. The French word for the white was *aubun* (now *blanc*).

☐ **Basic egg dishes**

● *Eggs en cocotte* – Eggs cooked in individual dishes in a bain-marie, in the oven.

● *Eggs à la coque* (*boiled eggs*) – Eggs cooked in their shells in boiling water, so that the yolk remains liquid and the white is just coagulated, and eaten straight from the shell.

● *Eggs sur le plat* (or *shirred eggs*) – Eggs cooked in a pan or in individual dishes in a cool oven.

● *Fried eggs* – Eggs fried in oil, butter, goose fat, or lard or in a deep-fryer.

● *Hard-boiled eggs* – Eggs cooked in their shells in boiling water for 10–12 minutes until both white and yolk are firm.

● *Omelettes* – See separate entry under *omelette*.

● *Poached eggs* – Eggs removed from their shells and cooked in boiling liquid (usually water with vinegar added).

● *Scrambled eggs* – Eggs that have been mixed (rather than beaten) and cooked with butter over a low heat.

● *Soft-boiled eggs* – Eggs cooked in their shells in boiling water like eggs *à la coque*, but shelled before being eaten.

RECIPES

Eggs à la Coque

Preparation PRÉPARATION There are three methods of preparing these: (1) plunge the eggs into boiling water and leave them for 3 minutes; (2) plunge them into boiling water, boil for 1 minute, remove the pan from the stove, and leave them to stand for 3 minutes before taking them out of the hot water; (3) put the eggs into a saucepan with cold water, heat, and remove the eggs as soon as the water boils. Whichever method is chosen, ensure that the eggs are at room temperature before cooking them.

When several eggs are to be boiled at once, they can be cooked together in a special egg-holder.

Eggs En Cocotte

Preparation PRÉPARATION Break the eggs into small buttered cocottes or ramekins and cook in a bain-marie in a hot oven for 6–8 minutes.

Eggs en cocotte à la tartare OEUFS EN COCOTTE À LA TARTARE Mix some minced (ground) raw beef with chopped chives, salt, and pepper. Put a layer of the mixture into some buttered ramekins and break the eggs on top. Pour a ribbon of fresh cream around the yolks. Cook in the oven in a bain-marie in the usual way.

Eggs en cocotte with cream OEUFS EN COCOTTE À LA CREME Pour 1 tablespoon boiling cream into each ramekin. Break 1 egg on top and place a knob of butter on the yolk. Cook in a bain-marie in the oven. When cooked add salt and pepper. The eggs may also be sprinkled with a little grated Parmesan and moistened with melted butter before cooking.

Eggs en cocotte with tarragon OEUFS EN COCOTTE A L'ESTRAGON Cook the eggs *en cocotte* and pour some reduced tarragon-flavoured veal gravy around each yolk. Garnish with blanched drained tarragon leaves arranged in the form of a star. If wished, chopped tarragon can be sprinkled in the bottom of the buttered ramekins and the veal gravy can be replaced with reduced tarragon-flavoured cream.

Eggs in a Mould

Preparation PRÉPARATION This dish from the *grande cuisine* is rarely made nowadays but is very simple to prepare. Break the eggs into buttered dariole moulds and sprinkle with some type of chopped flavouring (parsley, ham, truffle, etc.). Cook in a bain-marie and turn out onto a croustade, fried bread, or an artichoke heart. Coat with sauce.

Eggs in a mould Bizet OEUFS MOULÉS BIZET Butter the dariole moulds and line them with a mixture of minced (ground) pickled tongue and diced truffle. Break the eggs into the moulds and cook them in a bain-marie. Unmould them onto braised artichoke hearts. Cover with Périgueux sauce and garnish with a slice of truffle.

Eggs Sur Le Plat (Shirred Eggs) and Au Miroir

Preparation PRÉPARATION Eggs *sur le plat* are cooked in individual dishes in a cool oven. The size of the cooking dish is important as the yolks do not cook as well when the whites have too much room to spread out. Some cooks recommend separating the whites from the yolks, cooking the whites first until they begin to set, and then placing a yolk in the centre of each white. It is advisable to put salt on the white only as it will show up as white specks on the yolk.

Eggs *au miroir* are also baked in the oven but at a higher temperature, so that the yolks when cooked are shiny.

Eggs au miroir OEUFS AU MIROIR Put a knob of butter into a small flameproof egg dish and melt it on top of the stove. When it begins to sizzle, break 2 eggs onto a plate and slide them into the dish. Sprinkle with a pinch of salt and top with soft butter. Cook in the oven at 240 C (475 F, gas 9) until the white has set. Serve very hot while the yolks are still shining. Alternatively, the eggs can be cooked on top of the cooker, basting them constantly with the hot butter in the cooking dish.

Eggs sur le plat à la Chaville OEUFS SUR LE PLAT À LA CHAVILLE Cook a salpicon of mushrooms in butter and put a tablespoon into individual egg dishes. Break the eggs on top and cook them. Garnish with 1 tablespoon tomato fondue flavoured with chopped tarragon.

Eggs sur le plat à l'agenaise OEUFS SUR LE PLAT À L'AGENAISE Line some individual egg dishes with 1 tablespoon chopped onion that has been sautéed in goose fat. Break an egg into each dish and bake in a cool oven. When they are cooked, add a little chopped garlic and parsley. Garnish with coarsely chopped sautéed aubergines (eggplants). Alternatively, the eggs can be cooked in a single large dish.

Eggs sur le plat à l'antiboise OEUFS SUR LE PLAT À L'ANTIBOISE Roll 4 tablespoons (5 tablespoons) nonnats in flour and sauté them in olive oil. When they are brown, add 1 tablespoon finely diced Gruyère cheese and a little crushed garlic to the pan. Break 4 eggs into the same pan and cook them in the oven. Serve on a hot plate and sprinkle with chopped parsley.

Eggs sur le plat à l'orientale OEUFS SUR LE PLAT À L'ORIENTALE Soften some chopped onions in butter and spread 1 tablespoon on the bottom of individual egg dishes. Break the eggs into the dishes and bake in the oven.

To serve, garnish with a ragout of sweet peppers *à l'orientale* and saffron-flavoured rice *au gras*. Pour tomato sauce round the eggs.

Eggs sur le plat Montrouge OEUFS SUR LE PLAT MONTROUGE Butter individual egg dishes and pipe a border of mushroom duxelles in each. Break the eggs into the dishes, surround the yolks with a ribbon of fresh cream, and bake in the oven.

Eggs sur le plat with bacon OEUFS SUR LE PLAT AU BACON Heat a little butter in a frying pan (skillet) and lightly fry some thin rashers (slices) of bacon.

Break the eggs onto the bacon and cook, basting them with the fat that runs from the bacon. Alternatively, line small individual dishes with thin strips of lightly browned bacon. Break an egg into each dish, pour bacon fat over them, and bake in the oven.

FRIED EGGS

Preparation PRÉPARATION Break each egg into a cup, season with salt, and pour into a frying pan (skillet) containing hot oil, butter, goose fat, or lard. (Alternatively, use a deep-fryer.) Immediately draw the white around the yolk with a wooden spoon to seal it. Shake the pan occasionally to shape the egg. As soon as it is lightly browned, remove and drain. The white should be crisp and the yolk soft.

Fried eggs à la bayonnaise OEUFS FRITS À LA BAYONNAISE Deep-fry some small round slices of bread and on each place a slice of fried Bayonne ham cut to the same shape. Fry the eggs in oil and place one on each slice of bread. Garnish with sautéed mushrooms (preferably ceps).

HARD-BOILED EGGS

Preparation PRÉPARATION Cook the eggs in their shells in boiling water for 10–12 minutes, then plunge them into cold water for 7–8 minutes to cool them before shelling. The white and the yolk should be completely set. The eggs must not be allowed to boil for longer because the white becomes rubbery and the yolk crumbles.

Gargantuan hard-boiled egg OEUF DUR GARGANTUA (from a recipe by Danielle Spieghel) Thoroughly clean 2 pigs' bladders, one larger than the other. Separate the yolks and the whites of a dozen fresh eggs. Pour the lightly beaten yolks into the smaller bladder, tie the ends to form a ball, and plunge it into boiling water. Cook it for 8 minutes, then cool and untie it. Pour the whites into the larger bladder, then add the enormous yolk; because of its weight, it will automatically settle in the centre. Tie the bladder and shape it into an oval with both hands. Plunge it into boiling water and cook until it is set. Leave it to cool. Remove the 'egg' from the bladder and cut into large slices. It can be eaten cold sprinkled with vinaigrette or browned in the oven with béchamel sauce.

Hard-boiled-egg cutlets OEUFS DURS EN CÔTELETTES Dice the whites and yolks of 4 hard-boiled (hard-cooked) eggs and blend them with 4 tablespoons (5 tablespoons) thick béchamel sauce to which 2 raw egg yolks have been added. Chill. Divide the mixture into 60 g (2 oz) portions and shape them into cutlets. Dip in egg and breadcrumbs and deep-fry at 175 c (347 F) or shallow-fry in clarified butter. Arrange them in a circle on a dish, and put a paper frill on the narrow end of each cutlet. Sprinkle with fried parsley. Serve with tomato sauce and a garnish of green vegetables blended with butter or cream, or with a vegetable macédoine, tomato fondue, or risotto.

The recipe may be varied by adding diced mushrooms, truffle, lean ham, or tongue to the egg mixture.

Hard-boiled eggs in breadcrumbs OEUFS DURS PANÉS (from a recipe by Hubert) Hard-boil 8 eggs, cool under running cold water, and shell them. Wash half a bunch of watercress, dry it, and arrange it on a dish. Grate 150 g (5 oz, 1¼ cups) dry Tomme cheese. Mix half of it with 50 g (2 oz, ½ cup) stale breadcrumbs. Beat 2 eggs lightly and season with salt and pepper. Cut 8 very thin slices from a sandwich loaf and fry them in oil until golden brown. Sprinkle the remaining cheese onto the pieces of fried bread and put them in a medium oven for 5 minutes. Roll the eggs in the breadcrumbs, dip them in the beaten egg, then once more in the breadcrumbs. Fry them quickly, turning them in the oil. Arrange the pieces of fried bread on the watercress and put an egg on each.

Hard-boiled eggs with sorrel OEUFS DURS À L'OSEILLE (from a recipe by Paul Bocuse) Take a good handful of young sorrel, remove the stalks, wash and dry the leaves, and shred them finely. Cook slowly in a saucepan with 40 g (1½ oz, 3 tablespoons) butter until

all the moisture has evaporated. Add 1 tablespoon flour, cook for 5 minutes over a gentle heat, and allow it to cool. Gradually add 4 dl (14 fl oz, 1¾ cups) boiling milk, stirring constantly with a wooden spoon. Add salt and pepper and simmer for 15 minutes. Rub the mixture through a fine sieve. Replace in the pan and bring to the boil. Remove from the heat and add 2 tablespoons (3 tablespoons) cream. Adjust the seasoning. Hard-boil 4 eggs, arrange them in a hot dish, and pour the sauce over them.

POACHED EGGS

Preparation PRÉPARATION Break the egg into a cup and then slip it quickly into boiling water with vinegar added (1 tablespoon per litre, 2 pints, 4½ cups). Cook for 3–5 minutes with the water barely simmering, depending on how firmly set the yolk needs to be. If the egg is very fresh, it will not spread out in the water and the white will coagulate instantly. When cooked, remove with a slotted spoon, refresh in cold water, drain on a cloth, and trim. The eggs should be poached one by one so that they do not merge together in the water. They can be kept warm in water at 70 c (158 F).

Poached eggs Almaviva OEUFS POCHÉS MASQUÉS ALMAVIVA (from a recipe from La Tour d'Argent) Cook 4 artichoke hearts in salted water, drain them, and braise them in butter. Spread a knob of foie gras over each and top with a poached egg. Coat them with Mornay sauce and glaze in the oven. When the eggs are browned, sprinkle with finely chopped fresh truffles and serve immediately.

Poached eggs in aspic OEUFS POCHÉS EN GELÉE (from Fouquet's recipe) First make a good aspic jelly: prepare a stock with a knuckle of veal, 2 calf's feet, and the usual vegetables. Strain the stock, bring it to the boil, and add some gelatine leaves previously soaked in cold water. Boil for 5 minutes and then proceed to clarify: whisk 3 egg whites until stiff and add a diced tomato and some chopped chervil and tarragon. Pour the stock onto this mixture and bring it slowly to the boil so that the egg whites mass together on the top of the liquid. After boiling gently for 20 minutes, strain through a sieve lined with muslin (cheesecloth) and containing a few tarragon leaves – these will flavour the jelly.

Poach 2 eggs per person for 3 minutes in barely simmering unsalted water containing a glass of wine vinegar. Then chill the eggs in iced water. Arrange some strips of ham, previously dipped in the jelly, and 2 tarragon leaves in the bottom of each ramekin and pour a thin layer of the cold jelly over the top. Drain and trim the poached eggs and place one in each ramekin. Surround each egg with a julienne of cooked ham and fill the dishes with jelly. Leave to set in the refrigerator. Unmould when ready to serve.

Alternatively, place the drained and trimmed eggs in ramekins and surround with a julienne of ham. Coat with aspic. Decorate with chervil, ham, and tarragon and cover with aspic. Leave to set.

Poached eggs with caviar OEUFS POCHÉS AU CAVIAR (from a recipe by Marc Pralong) Boil 3 dl (12 fl oz, 1½ cups) fresh cream until it is reduced by half. Make a sabayon sauce (see *zabaglione*) with 3 egg yolks, and mix it with the reduced warm cream. Season with salt and add some lime juice. Keep warm. Poach 8 eggs, drain and trim them, and either arrange them in a hot dish or place them in small individual shortcrust pastry cases. Put 1 tablespoon caviar on each egg and add 60 g (2 oz) caviar to the sauce. Pour the sauce over the eggs.

SCRAMBLED EGGS

Preparation PRÉPARATION Melt 50 g (2 oz, ¼ cup) butter in a small heavy-bottomed saucepan but do not let it boil. Beat 8 eggs together lightly and season with salt and pepper. Pour into the pan and cook over a low heat (a double saucepan can be used), stirring constantly with a wooden spoon. As the eggs begin to set at the edge of the pan, draw them into the centre and ensure that they do not stick to the bottom. Remove from the heat and add 40 g (1½ oz, 3 tablespoons) fresh butter cut into small pieces (or add 2 tablespoons (3

tablespoons) double (heavy) cream. Mix well and keep hot in a double saucepan or a bain-marie until ready to serve.

Gratin of scrambled eggs à l'antiboise GRATIN D'OEUFS BROUILLÉS À L'ANTIBOISE Sauté some sliced courgettes (zucchini) in olive oil and prepare a concentrated tomato fondue. Make some scrambled eggs and arrange them in a deep ovenproof dish with alternate layers of the courgettes and tomato fondue. Finish with a layer of eggs. Sprinkle with grated Parmesan cheese and melted butter and brown quickly in a hot oven.

Scrambled eggs with cep mushrooms OEUFS BROUILLÉS AUX CÈPES Slice some cep mushrooms, season with salt and pepper, and sauté them in butter or oil with a little garlic. Make the scrambled eggs and add the ceps. Place in a serving dish with a generous tablespoon of fried ceps in the centre. Sprinkle with fried croutons.

Other varieties of mushroom may be used: chanterelles, blewits, horn of plenty, or cultivated button mushrooms.

Scrambled eggs with chicken livers OEUFS BROUILLÉS AUX FOIES DE VOLAILLE Make the scrambled eggs and pile them into a heated dish. Garnish with sliced chicken livers, sautéed in butter and blended with demi-glace sauce. Sprinkle with chopped parsley.

Scrambled eggs with shrimps OEUFS BROUILLÉS AUX CREVETTES Add some peeled (shelled) shrimps or prawns heated in butter to the scrambled eggs. Arrange them in a heated dish and garnish with peeled shrimps that have either been tossed in butter or blended with shrimp sauce. Surround with croutons fried in butter and a ribbon of shrimp sauce.

This recipe can be varied by using crayfish tails and Nantua sauce.

Scrambled eggs with smoked salmon OEUFS BROUILLÉS AU SAUMON FUMÉ Cut some smoked salmon into thin strips (allow 25 g (1 oz) salmon per 2 eggs). Pile the scrambled eggs into a hot dish or into a warm puff-pastry case. Garnish with the smoked salmon and croutons fried in butter.

Scrambled eggs with truffles BROUIL-LADE DE TRUFFES Prepare some scrambled eggs. Cut fresh truffles into dice or fine strips and toss them in butter, add them to the eggs, and pile the mixture into a dish. Garnish with slices of truffle and croutons fried in butter.

SOFT-BOILED EGGS

Preparation PRÉPARATION Plunge the eggs into boiling water and cook for about 6 minutes from the time the water comes back to the boil. The shelling of these eggs is quite a delicate operation because they are so fragile. Crack the shells by rolling them on a flat surface, then refresh them under the tap (the cold water penetrates through the cracks in the shell, which can then be removed more easily).

All the recipes given for soft-boiled eggs can also be used for poached eggs.

Soft-boiled eggs Aladdin OEUFS MOLLETS ALADIN Prepare some saffron-flavoured rice *au gras*. Peel and dice some sweet peppers and fry them in oil together with some chopped onion. Spread the rice over the bottom of a hot dish and arrange the peppers in the centre. Place the cooked eggs in a circle round the peppers. Cover with tomato sauce seasoned with a pinch of cayenne.

Soft-boiled eggs Béranger OEUFS MOLLETS BÉRANGER Make a flan case and bake it blind. Line it with a fairly thick onion purée (see *Soubise*). Arrange the cooked eggs on top and coat them with Mornay sauce. Sprinkle with grated cheese and melted butter and brown quickly in the oven.

Soft-boiled eggs Chénier OEUFS MOLLETS CHÉNIER Make some saffron-flavoured pilaf rice and shape it into small round cakes in individual ramekins. Place a cooked egg on top of each and surround with slices of fried aubergine (eggplant). Coat with tomato sauce.

egg cup COQUETIER

A small wooden, metal, or china cup designed as a holder for boiled eggs and placed on a saucer or plate. Sets of two, four, or six egg cups are often presented together on a tray.

Called *oviers* in France in the Middle Ages, *coquetiers* (or *coquetières*) in the 16th century were little tables with a cover and several cavities where the eggs were placed. These egg stands often incorporated a salt cellar. Today in France a coquetière is an egg-holder used for boiling several eggs at the same time.

egg custard

OEUFS AU LAIT

A dessert made by pouring sweetened boiling milk onto lightly beaten eggs. The milk can be flavoured with vanilla, orange or lemon zest, coffee, etc. It is cooked in the oven in a bain-marie, either in a shallow ovenproof dish or in individual moulds. Care must be taken to ensure that the water in the bain-marie never boils. The custard is served cold in the cooking dish.

RECIPE

Egg custard OEUFS AU LAIT Boil 1 litre (1¾ pints, 4¼ cups) milk with 125 g (4½ oz, generous ½ cup, firmly packed) sugar and a vanilla pod (bean). Beat 4 eggs lightly in a deep bowl. Gradually pour the boiling milk over the eggs, stirring constantly. Strain into an ovenproof dish or into ramekins and cook in a bain-marie in the oven at 170 C (325 F, gas 3) for about 40 minutes. Serve cold.

eggnog LAIT DE POULE

A nourishing drink served either hot or cold. To make it, beat an egg yolk with one tablespoon sugar. Add a glass of hot milk, and lace with rum or brandy.

Prosper Montagné gave a recipe for beer eggnog (*lait de poule à la bière*), a German speciality that they call *Biersuppe*. It is actually more like a substantial soup.

RECIPE

Eggnog with beer LAIT DE POULE À LA BIÈRE Boil 2 litres (3½ pints, 4½ pints) pale ale with 500 g (18 oz, 2¼ cups) sugar, a pinch of salt, a little grated lemon peel, and a pinch of cinnamon. Add 8 egg yolks beaten with 1 tablespoon cold milk, strain, and chill in the refrigerator. Soak 120 g (4½ oz, scant 1 cup) each of raisins and currants in ½ litre (¾ pint, 2 cups) warm water until plump. Drain well and add to the eggnog, together with a bowl of fried wholemeal (wholewheat) croutons, just before serving.

eggplant

See *aubergine*.

egg sauce

A hot English sauce made of diced hard-boiled (hard-cooked) eggs and butter, served particularly with poached fish.

Scotch egg sauce is a béchamel sauce containing sieved hard-boiled egg yolks and whites cut into small strips. It is used for the same dishes.

RECIPE

Egg sauce Boil 2 eggs for 10 minutes, then remove their shells and dice them. While still hot, add the diced egg to 125 g (4½ oz, 9 tablespoons) melted butter, season with salt and pepper, and flavour with lemon juice. Sprinkle with chopped parsley.

egg threads OEUFS FILÉS

Eggs poached in such a way that they form long threads, used to garnish consommé or soup. The raw eggs are lightly beaten and poured through a fine strainer into the boiling consommé. The fine threads of egg dropping through the strainer set instantly in the boiling liquid. They can be cooked in boiling water, drained, and added to thicker soups, such as vegetable soup, cream of watercress soup, or cream of sorrel soup.

egg timer SABLIER

A small gadget consisting of two transparent bulbs linked by a very narrow opening. The upper bulb contains sand or some other powdery material, which runs into the lower bulb in a given length of time. Many egg timers are designed so that the time taken for the sand to run through is three minutes, the average cooking time for a soft-boiled egg. Some are graded from three to five minutes to suit varying tastes.

égrugeoir

A small wooden mortar (usually of boxwood) used for crushing coarse salt and peppercorns. The word *égrugeoir* is also used for a small salt or pepper mill. Salt crushed in an égrugeoir keeps the flavour of coarse salt, and freshly crushed pepper also has a better flavour.

Egypt ÉGYPTE

Cookery at the time of the Pharaohs had certain refinements. Some game dishes were prepared, and asparagus, several types of onions and leeks, and many spices (including turmeric) and fruit were used. Contemporary Egyptian gastronomy, however, is relatively frugal, and can hardly be distinguished from that of other Middle Eastern and Mediterranean countries.

The staple food is bread made from maize (corn). Brown beans called *foul medames* are used in large quantities; green vegetables include okra and bamia. *Molokheya* (or *mouloureija*) soup is regarded by Egyptians as their national dish. It is a thick sweetish soup seasoned with herbs, to which chicken or rabbit, spices, and tomato sauce are added. The commonest meat is mutton, which is grilled (broiled), minced (ground), or stewed with eggs and vegetables. Beef is not usually eaten, since it is tough. A type of very large prawn is prepared in a risotto containing peppers and tomatoes, and mullet roe is also popular. Dried vegetables are used a great deal.

Egyptian pâtisserie is typical of the Middle East, with loukoums and baklavas predominating. Dates are widely consumed in many forms. They are used in pâtisserie, especially to make *menenas*, a dough ball flavoured with almonds and orange flower, filled with stoned (pitted) dates, almonds, pistachio nuts, and cinnamon, and baked in the oven. Other fruits include plums, pomegranates, mangoes, bananas, limes, and watermelons.

The Egyptians mainly drink water flavoured with orange-flower water or rose water, unfermented sugar cane juice, and a typical red brew called *kar kade*, tasting of redcurrants, made with redcurrant blossom from Guinea. They have also tried to revive the famous wines the Pharaohs used to have buried in jars in their tombs. Some interesting wines are produced for export, the best known of which are whites: Cru-des-Ptolémées and Queen Cleopatra. Omar Khayyam is a mellow red wine smelling of dates.

égyptienne (à l')

Describing various dishes using rice, aubergines (eggplants), or tomatoes, together or separately. Aubergines *à l'égyptienne* are stuffed with a mixture of chopped aubergine pulp and onions and served with fried tomatoes. A garnish *à l'égyptienne* is made of fried aubergine rounds, rice pilaf, and tomato fondue. The term also describes a mixed salad of rice with chicken livers, ham, mushrooms, artichoke hearts, peas, pulped tomatoes, and red peppers. Fried eggs *à l'égyptienne* are served with tomato halves filled with saffron rice, and potage *à l'égyptienne* is a cream of rice soup made with leeks and onions softened in butter, sieved, and then finished with milk.

RECIPE

Chicken medallions à l'égyptienne MÉDAILLONS DE VOLAILLE À L'ÉGYPTIENNE Cut the breasts off a raw chicken and trim and flatten them into round or oval medallions. Cut some large aubergines (eggplants) into rounds about 1.5 cm (½ in) thick and sprinkle them with lemon juice. Prepare some rice pilaf. Fry the chicken medallions and aubergine rounds separately in olive oil, then arrange them alternately round a serving dish. Fill the centre of the dish with rice pilaf. Deglaze the pan in which the chicken was cooked with white wine, add this juice to a thick and well-seasoned tomato fondue, and serve separately in a sauceboat.

eierkückas

A pancake made of batter enriched with fresh cream (the word means 'egg cake'). It is a speciality of Alsace.

RECIPE

Eierkückas Make a sweet pancake batter (see *crêpe*), substituting 1 dl (6 tablespoons, scant ½ cup) single cream for the same quanity of milk. Leave this batter to rest for 2 hours. Grease a frying pan (skillet) with butter and make the pancakes. As soon as they are cooked, fill with redcurrant jelly or raspberry jam and fold twice. Sprinkle generously with icing sugar (confectioners' sugar). Either draw crisscross patterns on them with a red-hot skewer or glaze in the oven.

elder SUREAU

A common European tree or shrub whose aromatic flowers are prepared as fritters (like mimosa fritters) and used to flavour jams, vinegars, and various fermented drinks. The young shoots contain an edible and delicate core, which is prepared like asparagus. Elderberries are used to make jam, jelly, and wine.

RECIPES

Elder-flower wine with lime blossom VIN DE SUREAU AU TILLEUL Pour 7 litres (6 quarts, 7½ quarts) water over a handful of elder flowers and a handful of lime blossom. Add 250 g (9 oz, 1 cup) sugar, 2 lemons cut into slices, and 1 glass white-wine vinegar; leave to macerate for 3 days. Stir each day. Strain off the liquid and bottle it; tie up the corks with string. Leave to stand for 5 days before consuming.

Elder shoots MOELLE DE SUREAU Peel some elder shoots, stripping the woody parts away from the core. Cut the core into sticks about 8 cm (3¼ in) long; tie the sticks into bundles like asparagus and cook them in boiling salted water for 10–15 minutes. Drain them thoroughly and serve them hot, with cream, gravy, or melted butter containing chopped hard-boiled (hardcooked) egg yolk, or cold, with a vinaigrette dressing.

electrical appliances
ÉLECTROMÉNAGER

Electrical appliances have undergone spectacular development in the kitchen during the 20th century. At the beginning of the 1920s most household appliances were mechanical, but soon the first electrical ones began to appear. The ancestor of the dishwasher was introduced by 1930 together with waffle irons and electric boiling rings. Ten years later toasters, kettles, and refrigerators were readily available.

It was after 1948 that electrical appliances really started to take off in Europe: electric mixers were followed by mincers, peelers, and automatic toasters. During the 1960s the first electric carving knives, the first fully automatic dishwashers, and the first electric deep-fryers appeared.

□ A variety of appliances Small electrical appliances include mixers, kettles, coffee-makers, cream separators, electric knives, pancake griddles, slicing machines, peeling machines, fryers, waffle irons, toasters, meat grills, mincers, blenders, coffee grinders and mills, can-openers, fruit presses, slicers, sorbet-makers, yogurt-makers, and food processors. Some appliances have now reached a high degree of sophistication, as in the multifunction electronic robot with programmable cooking; others are subject to the fluctuations of fashion (such as the raclette oven, a type of grill for cheese). Small household electrical appliances save time and energy, but to be worthwhile they must be used often and regularly.

Besides dishwashers, most large electrical appliances for the kitchen comprise cooking and refrigerating equipment, i.e. cookers, hotplates, spit-roasters, built-in ovens, refrigerators, and freezers. A family's requirements depend on the number of people living in the home, their ages, and their eating habits.

electric deep-fat fryer

FRITEUSE

An electrical appliance that, to a certain extent, has replaced the traditional chip (deep-fry) pan. It usually has a capacity of 1.5–3.5 litres (2¾–6 pints, 3½–7½ pints), depending on the model. A cool zone, which may or may not be built in, ensures that it is cooler at the bottom of the fryer, so that food residues do not burn. The appliance also has a graduated thermostat, so that frying can be

carried out at optimum temperatures. The lid sometimes has a filter to absorb the cooking smells. There is also a draining basket and an on/off indicator light. The fryer should be used without a lid on unless it has a filter. As the items are fried at exactly the right temperature, the surface is sealed and they do not become sodden with fat or oil. This also stops the flavour of the food from contaminating the fat or oil, which can thus be reused to fry different foods, sweet and savoury.

Some domestic fryers can be used to braise, stew, roast, steam, and boil, as well as to fry food. Their thermostatic control enables perfect jams and jellies to be made in them.

elephant ÉLÉPHANT

A large mammal of which there are two species: the Indian elephant, trained as a beast of burden, and the African elephant, formerly widely hunted as game and a source of ivory. Strict protective measures are now in force to preserve the species. Reports by travellers and hunters from the 17th century onwards indicate that elephant meat is tough but tasty, provided that it is cooked for more than 15 hours or has been hung for a long time in the open air. The feet and the trunk are of greatest culinary interest: their flesh, which is muscular and gelatinous, resembles ox (beef) tongue.

During the 1870 siege of Paris, the flesh of elephants from the Jardin des Plantes appeared in butchers' shops and restaurants. The menu of the Café Anglais offered braised elephant's feet with ham, garlic, spices, and Madeira, and one butcher was selling elephant blood pudding.

elf-cup fungus PEZIZE

A cup-shaped fungus of the genus *Peziza*, usually brown or orange in colour. Elf-cups grow wild on the surface of the ground or on dead branches of trees. They are prepared in the same way as morel mushrooms, but are not as good. However, Doctor Ramain, in his *Mycogastronomie*, believes that they are underestimated and recommends the veined hare's (or ass's) ear variety, which loses its smell of chlorine when cooked and has delicate tasty flesh. He also recommends the orange variety, which can be eaten raw with sugar and Kirsch.

elixir ÉLIXIR

A solution of aromatic substances in alcohol. In the Middle Ages elixirs were used as potions to which magical properties were sometimes attributed. The word comes from the Arabic *al-iksir* (essence), from the Greek *ksêron* (dry medicine). Some elixir formulae, most of which are prepared by monks, have lasted for centuries and are still being made up today (notably the Grande-Chartreuse plant elixir). Many plant liqueurs bear the name 'elixir' and are sweet and scented to the taste, such as the golden-coloured Anvers elixir, made of plants steeped in wine brandy, and elixir of Garus, made of vanilla and saffron steeped in alcohol, to which is added syrup flavoured with maidenhair fern and orange-flower water.

The elixir of Père Gaucher, mentioned by Alphonse Daudet in *Les Lettres de mon moulin*, requires 'Provençal herbs, sound, grey, serrated, and burnt with sun and fragrances'.

elk ÉLAN

A large deer living wild in Scandinavia and Siberia (where attempts are being made to tame them); it also occurs in North America, where it is known as a moose. Its meat is prepared in the same way as venison, which it resembles. In the Rocky Mountains, minced (ground) moose meat is used to make hamburgers and also pies (with apples and grapes).

elzekaria

A rustic soup from the Basque country in southwestern France, made of sliced onions, white cabbage cut into strips, dried white beans, and bacon (sometimes also some crushed cloves of garlic). It is served with a dash of vinegar.

emballer

A French culinary term meaning to wrap up an article which is to be poached or stewed in stock (a large fish, stuffed cabbage, a ballottine, any dish cooked in a caul, etc.). The food is wrapped in a pig's caul or a piece of muslin (cheesecloth) or linen, to hold it together while cooking. In French charcuterie, *emballer* means to fill the moulds with a mixture to be cooked (pâté de foie, galantine etc.).

émincer

A French culinary term meaning to cut vegetables, fruit, or meat into thin slices or rounds. This is usually done with a slicing knife on a chopping board (for cucumbers, leeks, mushrooms, pears, and apples), but a mandolin can be used (for carrots, turnips, and potatoes), and a food processor with a slicing disc for potatoes. There is a special instrument for slicing tomatoes thinly without spoiling them and for cutting them into a 'fan', with the slices still joined at the base.

émincés

A dish consisting of thin slices of leftover meat (roast, braised, or boiled) placed in an ovenproof dish, covered with a sauce, and gently heated in the oven. (An *émincé* is a thin slice of meat.) Émincés are most often made with beef, lamb, or mutton, sometimes with game (venison), and less frequently with pork, poultry, or veal, as white meats are always drier when reheated.

Beef émincés are prepared with Madeira sauce and mushrooms, bordelaise sauce and slices of bone marrow, or with chasseur, lyonnaise, piquante, Robert, tomato (well-reduced and highly seasoned), or Italian sauce; they are accompanied by sautéed potatoes, green vegetables tossed in butter or cream, braised vegetables, purées, pasta, or a risotto. Venison émincés are covered with poivrade, grand veneur, or chasseur sauce and served with chestnut purée and redcurrant jelly. The sauces for mutton émincés are mushroom, tomato, paprika, or Indian sauce; the accompanying vegetables are rice and courgettes (zucchini). Pork émincés are made with piquante, Robert, or charcutière sauce and served with a potato or split pea purée. Veal or poultry émincés are covered with tomato, royal, or suprême sauce; the accompanying vegetables are the same as for beef émincés.

By extension, the word *émincé* is also used for various other dishes made of items sliced thinly before cooking. In veal émincé, for example, thin slices of veal cut from the noix (the fleshy uppper part of the leg) are quickly fried and then covered with stock, gravy, or sometimes fresh cream; the dish is served with fried mushrooms.

| RECIPE

Beef émincés with mushrooms ÉMIN-CÉS DE BOEUF AUX CHAMPIGNONS Arrange some thin slices of boiled beef in a long ovenproof dish. Prepare some Madeira sauce. Trim and slice some mushrooms and heat them in butter. Place the mushrooms on the meat and cover generously with hot Madeira sauce; heat through gently in the oven.

Veal or chicken émincés à blanc ÉMINCÉS DE VEAU OU DE VOLAILLE À BLANC Lightly butter an ovenproof dish. Cut some poached or boiled veal or chicken into thin slices. These slices can then be treated as for beef émincés with mushrooms, or they can be coated with tomato, Breton, royal, or suprême sauce.

Emmental

A Swiss cows'-milk cheese containing 45% fat, named after the Emme valley in the canton of Bern, where it was first made. It is a hard ivory-coloured cheese with a good many holes and a golden-yellow to brown rind. Emmental is matured for 6–12 months in a cool cellar and marketed in a wheel shape with convex edges, 80–85 cm (31–34 in) in diameter, 22 cm (8¾ in) thick, and weighing 80–100 kg (176–220 lb). The edge of the cheese bears the word 'Switzerland' stamped in red.

The cheese was introduced into Haute-Savoie in the middle of the 19th century by German Swiss immigrants, and a Savoy Emmental, made in the cheese dairies of Savoy, is very similar in appearance and flavour to the Swiss cheese. Savoy Emmental is marketed in wheels weighing 60–130 kg (132–286 lb), 70–100 cm (27½–39 in) in diameter and 13–25 cm (5–10 in) thick. Swiss and Savoy Emmentals are used for the table.

Another type of French Emmental (also spelt Emmenthal) is produced in the flatter regions of France, such as Franche-Comté and Burgundy. It is matured for two months in a warm cellar and resembles Gruyère, with large holes. It is used for cooking (especially grating).

| RECIPE

Croque-Emmental Take 4 slices of ham. Place on each a slice of Emmental or Gruyère (cut to half the size of the ham slice), fold over, and secure with a cocktail stick (toothpick). Coat with flour, then batter, and fry in hot oil. Put 1 fried egg on each croque-Emmental and serve very hot.

empanada

A pie or pasty filled with meat or fish, popular all over Spain and in parts of South America. The classic empanada comes from Galicia and is made with chicken, onions, and peppers. It can also be made with seafood, sardines, eel, or lamprey. Formerly made with bread dough, empanada is now usually made with flaky pastry and often eaten cold. It is also prepared in the form of small individual pies.

In Chile and Argentina, empanadas are small pasties with scalloped edges. They are filled with a mixture of minced (ground) meat, raisins, olives, and onions, spiced with pepper, paprika, and cumin. They are served as a hot hors d'oeuvre or snack, often with wine.

emulsifier ÉMULSIFIANT

A food additive used to preserve the texture of emulsions. Among natural emulsifiers are lecithins (E322), extracted from almonds or other seeds (especially soya beans in chocolate-making) or from egg yolk (in powdered milk). Mono- and diglycerides of fatty acids (oleic, palmitic, ec.) are used in making margarine and mayonnaise. Gums (gum arabic and gum tragacanth) are also often used to stabilize emulsions.

emulsion ÉMULSION

A preparation obtained by dispersing one kind of liquid (in the form of tiny droplets) in another liquid, with which it does not mix. An emulsion consisting of a fatty substance, such as oil or butter, dispersed in vinegar, water, or lemon juice will only remain smooth and stable if it is bound with an emulsifier, usually egg yolk. This preparation is the basis of emulsified sauces, such as hollandaise, mousseline, and their derivatives. Milk is a natural emulsion consisting of globules of cream suspended in a watery solution containing protein (which acts as an emulsifier).

en-cas

The French word for a light meal, usually cold, eaten between main meals (the word literally means 'in case', i.e. of hunger). In the old châteaux, an *en-cas de nuit*, consisting of cheese, fruit, and cold meats, was arranged on a pedestal table for the refreshment of travellers returning home late at night. At Versailles, the king's *en cas de nuit* consisted of three loaves, two bottles of wine, and a carafe of water. Wishing to publicize his support for Molière, Louis XIV invited him to share his snack, in order to teach a lesson to the courtiers who refused to allow the famous dramatist to sit at their table.

enchaud

A speciality from Périgord consisting of a piece of boned pork fillet (tenderloin) rolled up, tied with string, and cooked in the oven in a casserole. It can also be stuffed. Cold enchaud is particularly delicious.

| RECIPE

Enchaud Bone a piece of pork fillet (tenderloin) weighing about 1.5 kg (3½ lb), and keep the bone. Spread out the fillet on the work surface. Season with salt and pepper, sprinkle lightly with crushed thyme, and insert small pieces of garlic. Roll up the meat tightly, tie it up with string, and keep it cool.

The next day, heat 2 tablespoons lard in a flameproof casserole and brown the enchaud on all sides. Add 1 small glass of warm water, a sprig of thyme, and the pork bone. Season with salt and pepper. Cover, and seal the lid with a flour and water mixture. Cook in the oven for about 2 hours at 180 c (350 f, gas 4). When the enchaud is cooked, drain it and keep it hot on the serving dish. Remove the bone and the thyme from the casserole and skim as much fat as possible from the cooking juices; add 1

small glass of stock and reduce. Serve the enchaud with this sauce, accompanied by potatoes sautéed with garlic.

The garlic can be replaced by small sticks of truffle. In this case, the pork is stuffed with about 400 g (14 oz, 1¾ cups) well-seasoned fine forcemeat, to which 1 teaspoon brandy and some truffle peel have been added. Roll up and cook the enchaud as in the previous method and serve cold, with salad dressed with walnut oil.

endaubage

A mixture of ingredients used for braising; it can include bacon, sliced carrots, onions, shallots, a bouquet garni, wine, spirits, oil, vinegar, garlic, peppercorns, salt, various flavourings, etc. Endaubage formerly described a conserve of stewed meat with lard, which was stored in barrels and used, in particular, by the navy.

endive (chicory)

CHICORÉE

A plant whose leaves may be eaten raw in salads or cooked as a vegetable. Most varieties have bitter leaves. The variety commonly used is the curly endive. The stumps, known as *gourilos*, may also be eaten.

There is confusion about the names endive and chicory. In England, endive usually means the curly-leaved salad plant, generally called chicory in the United States. Chicory in England is what the French and Americans call endive or Belgian endive. For the sake of clarity, preference is given in this article to the English usage.

• *Wild endive* – When young and tender, it is eaten in salads in the spring. It may be found growing on the roadsides. It is usually cut into fine strips (a chiffonnade) and has a very bitter flavour. It is an ingredient of mesclun niçois. If planted out in a shady place, winter 'improved' varieties of endive are produced, including 'Capucin's beard'. This is tender, white, and slightly bitter and is tossed in vinaigrette or cut into small sticks for pickling in vinegar.

• *Curly endive* – There are several summer and winter varieties of curly endive. In France it is cultivated in the Paris area and in the west and is eaten mainly in salad. The heart is white or yellow, and the leaves, which are very thin and serrated, are yellow in the centre and greener towards the outside. Curly endive is seasoned with vinaigrette flavoured with shallot, mustard, or garlic. It is often served with chapons or strips of larding bacon. In the west of France, the vegetable is served with haricot (navy) beans in butter with a walnut-oil dressing.

RECIPES

Braised endive CHICORÉE BRAISÉE Prepare the endive as for endive *au gratin*. Make a white roux, using 40 g (1½ oz, 3 tablespoons) butter and 40 g (1½ oz, 6 tablespoons) flour for every 500 g (18 oz) endive); season with salt, pepper, a little sugar, some grated nutmeg, and add 6 dl (1 pint, 2½ cups) stock. Add the chopped endive and cook on top of the stove for a short time. Then place a lid on the pan and cook in the oven (1½ hours cooking time in all). Veal gravy may be added to enhance the flavour.

Endive au gratin CHICORÉE AU GRATIN Remove the hard or dark green leaves from the heads of curly endive. Cut the remaining leaves at the beginning of the stump, and rinse well in water. Drain and blanch for 10 minutes in plenty of boiling salted water. Cool, drain, chop finely, and then mix with béchamel sauce (4–5 tablespoons per 500 g (18 oz) endive). Arrange the endive on a buttered gratin dish and sprinkle with 75 g (3 oz, ½ cup) grated Gruyère cheese and 2 tablespoons (3 tablespoons) melted butter. Brown in a very hot oven

Endive salad with bacon SALADE DE CHICORÉE AUX LARDONS Cut some smoked bacon (250 g (9 oz) for each head of curly endive) into very fine strips and brown them in butter in a frying pan (skillet). Clean the endive, rinse it, and dry it as thoroughly as possible Season with a well-flavoured vinaigrette and then pour the sizzling-hot bacon strips over the top. Tiny fried garlic-flavoured croutons are usually added. Serve immediately.

Gourilos fritters BEIGNETS DE

GOURILOS Trim and blanch 12 *gourilos* (stumps of curly endive). Marinate them for 45 minutes in 2 tablespoons (3 tablespoons) oil, 1 tablespoon lemon juice, and salt and pepper. Then dip them in thin batter and deep-fry them in very hot oil. Drain on absorbent paper, sprinkle with salt, and serve.

entoloma ENTOLOME

A genus of mushrooms, one of which is edible. The edible species is the buckler entoloma, *Entoloma prunuloides*, a fleshy mushroom with a grey-brown cap and pink gills. The majority of mushrooms in this genus are poisonous, so great care should be taken to select only the edible variety.

Entraygues-et-du-Fel

A VDQS wine from the Aveyron and Cantal. Red, white, and rosé are made, but are seldom seen outside the region.

entrecôte (rib steak)

A piece of prime-quality beef, which should be cut from 'between two ribs' (*côtes*) – hence the name. However, it is usually cut from the boned set of ribs. Marbled and tender, entrecôte steak should be grilled (broiled) or fried. Steaks cut from the lower ribs are prepared in the same way but tend to be firmer. Ideally, the steak should be about 1.5 cm (¾ in) thick, flat, and well-trimmed, with just a thin margin of fat, which is cut at intervals to prevent it curling up during cooking.

RECIPES

Fried entrecôte (rib steak) ENTRECÔTE POÊLÉE Season the steak with salt and pepper. Heat some butter in a frying pan (skillet). When it bubbles, add the steak and brown both sides over a high heat. Then drain, arrange on the serving dish, and garnish with a knob of butter (plain butter, maître d'hôtel butter, or marchand de vin butter). Alternatively, serve with a red wine sauce or sprinkle with the cooking butter plus a few drops of lemon juice and some chopped parsley.

Fried entrecôte (rib steak) à la bourguignonne ENTRECÔTE POÊLÉE À LA BOURGUIGNONNE Fry a 400–500-g

(14–18-oz) steak in butter, drain, and keep hot on the serving dish. Pour 1 dl (6 tablespoons, scant ½ cup) each of red wine and demi-glace into the frying pan (skillet), reduce, and coat the steak with this sauce.

The demi-glace can be replaced by the same amount of well-reduced consommé bound with 1 teaspoon kneaded butter.

> *Letter to gourmets, gourmands, gastronomes, and gluttons ...*
> (James de Coquet, Simoën, 1977)
>
> 'Grilled? Fired? It doesn't matter. The only essential thing is that it should be properly sealed. Season well and brown until it is slightly charred outside but bright red inside. In passing, let us make a recommendation to the profane: do not scorn the end of the entrecôte steak, the crusty part. It is delicious. The entrecôte steak has a penchant for shallots, which is where the famous *entrecôte maître de chai* comes from. This dish is grilled, needless to say, on an open grill or barbecue. But not just any old fuel will do; it must be vine shoots, and not just any old vine shoots! You have to use Cabernet Sauvignon vine shoots, which were put away to dry for this very purpose at least a year ago. Once the first side is done, turn the steak over and slice the shallot over it. Add some melted butter. When the second side of the steak is duly sealed, turn it over quickly and put it in a very hot dish in which a knob of butter is gently melting. Sprinkle with shallot, add a second knob of butter, and place another very hot dish over the top, thus making an oven in which your steak can poach for two or three minutes. Next, take a large knife and ...'

Fried entrecôte (rib steak) with mushrooms ENTRECÔTE POÊLÉE AUX CHAMPIGNONS Fry a 400–500-g (14–18-oz) steak in butter. When three-quarters cooked, add 8–10 mushroom caps to the frying pan

(skillet). Place the steak in a serving dish and keep hot. Finish cooking the mushrooms, then arrange them around the steak. Deglaze the frying pan with 1 dl (6 tablespoons, scant ½ cup) each of white wine and demi-glace, and reduce. Sieve, add 1 tablespoon fresh butter, stir, and pour the sauce over the steak.

Instead of demi-glace, the same quantity of well-reduced consommé bound with 1 teaspoon kneaded butter can be used.

Grilled entrecôte (broiled rib steak) ENTRECÔTE GRILLÉE Lightly brush the steak with oil or melted butter, season with salt and pepper, and barbecue over very hot wood charcoal or grill (broil) in a vertical grill, under the grill (broiler) of the cooker, or over an iron grill. The surface of the steak must be sealed so that the juices will not escape. (Some cooks advise against seasoning with salt before cooking because this draws out the blood.) Serve with château potatoes, bunches of cress, and béarnaise sauce (separately, if desired.

Entre-Deux-Mers

An AOC white wine from the Bordeaux region. There is, in fact, some red wine made there, but this is only entitled to the AOC 'Bordeaux'. The production area is between two rivers, the Garonne and Dordogne, hence its name (which means 'between two seas'). In the past, the wines tended to be made soft and were not very highly rated in the UK, because of their somewhat nondescript character. Today, however, the white wines are much improved, being crisp, dryish or definitely dry, and sometimes capable of pleasant improvement in bottle. They provide a good accompaniment to most fish and shellfish, including the oysters that are a speciality of the Gironde region.

entrée

Today, the entrée is usually the main course of a meal, but in a full French menu it is the third course, following the hors d'oeuvre (or soup) and the fish course and preceding the roast. At a grand dinner, the entrée is either a hot dish in a sauce or a cold dish. Mixed entrées are composite dishes, such as croustades, timbales, and small pâtés. When more than one entrée is served, they must be clearly differentiated: distinctions were formerly made between *entrées volantes de boucherie* (meat entrées), *entrées d'abats* (offal entrées), and *entrées diverses* (various entrées).

With the trend towards simplification and reduction in the number of courses, today's menu usually centres on a main dish, preceded by an hors d'oeuvre or soup and followed by a salad, cheese, and dessert. In the Middle Ages, entrées included such items as crystallized (candied) melon peel, oyster tarts, andouillettes, forcemeats, cheese ramekins, etc. Today (when present) they include fish, shellfish, caviar, foie gras, fish terrine, pasta dishes (such as gnocchi, macaroni, spaghetti, and ravioli), quenelles, savoury pastries (such as quiches, patties, timbales, tarts, and vols-au-vent), egg dishes (including soufflés), and even vegetable dishes (artichokes and asparagus). In theory, cold charcuterie, fish in marinades or oil, raw vegetables, mixed salads, melon, radishes, etc., are considered to be hors d'oeuvres.

entremets

The sweet course, which in France is served after the cheese (the word is also used to mean a specific dessert). Formerly, all the dishes served after the roast, including vegetables and sweets, were entremets. In the royal households of the Middle Ages, the entremets were a real showpiece, being accompanied by music, juggling, and dancing. In restaurants, the word still embraces the vegetable dishes (which in large establishments are the responsibility of the *entremettier*), as well as the *entremets de cuisine* (soufflés, savoury pancakes and fritters, pastries, croquettes, and omelettes) and the sweets. The latter are subdivided into three categories:
● hot entremets (fritters, pancakes, flamed fruits, sweet omelettes, soufflés);
● cold entremets (Bavarian cream, blancmanges, charlottes, compotes, pastries, creams, fruits with rice or semolina, chilled fruits, meringues, puddings, rice or semolina desserts, moulds);
● iced entremets (fruit ice creams, sorbets, iced cups, frosted fruits, ice-cream

cakes, bombes, mousses, parfaits, soufflés, vacherins).

□ **From the Middle Ages to the 19th century** Taillevent proposed the following as entremets: frumenty, broth, oyster stew, rice pudding, fish jelly, stuffed poultry, almond milk with figs, etc. All these dishes were served throughout the meal, alternating with the roasts and fish dishes, and mixing sweet and savoury (the word entremets means literally 'between dishes'). Certain spectacular entremets, such as 'swan in its skin and all its feathers', were purely decorative showpieces, presented with great pomp and musical accompaniment. At the marriage of Charles VII's daughter to the king of Bohemia, an entremets was served consisting of a huge château built on a high strong rock, with damsels at the windows, waving Hungarian banners, and groups of singing children. One of the most theatrical on record must be the 'pheasant's vow', presented in 1454 at the court of Philip the Good: a gigantic pâté was followed by a circus show with trumpet players and an elephant, and a procession of knights and ladies preceded a long gold dish, which held a live pheasant decorated with precious stones.

In 1655, Nicolas de Bonnefons gave as entremets: 'dishes cooked with butter and fat, all types of egg dishes, lamb cooked in its juices in the oven; also sweet dishes, both hot and cold, jellies of all colours and blancmanges, with artichokes, cardoons, and celery with pepper in the middle.'

During the reign of Louis XIV and until the 19th century, the entremets continued to be a combination of sweet and vegetable dishes. After the entrée, a sweet was sometimes served as an entremets (croquembouche or nougat, for instance) or a ham or a small fowl. After the roast a second entremets would be served: fruit and green vegetables, jellies, and fritters.

Towards the 1850s, the menu of the famous Véry restaurant offered the following under 'entremets': a range of hot vegetable dishes, mushroom pastries, herb omelette, poached eggs with verjuice, and Italian macaroni. The 'sweet entremets' comprised small pots of rum jelly, cream meringues, jam omelettes, apricot fritters, cherry tart, apricot charlotte, and soufflé omelette with rice.

éperons bachiques

Literally meaning 'drinking spurs', this expression was coined by Rabelais to describe spicy salty dishes, such as andouilles and other sausages, which act on the thrist like spurs on a horse. The expression (in the singular) is now little used, except perhaps at reunion dinners of Bacchic societies by guests who wish to evoke the atmosphere of the past.

The expression (in the singular) is also used for a cheese, called 'the drunkard's biscuit' by Grimod de La Reynière and 'Bacchus' cotignac' by Saint-Amand.

épigramme

A dish consisting of two cuts of lamb, both cooked dry. These two pieces are a slice of breast and a cutlet or chop, dipped in egg and breadcrumbs and grilled (broiled) or fried.

Philéas Gilbert explains the origins of the term *épigramme* as follows: 'It was towards the middle of the 18th century. One day a young marquise overheard one of her guests at table remark that when he was dining the previous evening with the Comte de Vaudreuil, he was charmingly received and, furthermore, had had a feast of excellent epigrams. The marquise, though pretty and elegant, was somewhat ignorant of the meaning of words. She later summoned Michelet, her chef "Michelet," she said to him, "tomorrow, I shall require a dish of épigrammes!"

The chef withdrew, pondering the problem. He looked up old recipes, but found no reference to anything of the kind. None of his colleagues had ever heard of the dish. But no French master chef is ever at a loss. Since he could discover nothing about the dish he set about inventing one. Next day, inspiration came and he created a most delicate dish.

At dinner, the guests fell into ecstasies over the dish put before them and, after complimenting the lady of the house, desired to know its name. The chef was called. With perfect composure he replied, "Epigrammes of lamb *à la Michelet.*"

Everyone laughed. The marquise was triumphant, though she could not understand the amusement of her guests. From that moment, the culinary repertoire of France was enriched by a name still used to this day.

But whereas this name was originally used for slices of breast of lamb dipped in breadcrumbs, fried in butter, and arranged in a circle round a blanquette of lamb, by the end of the 18th century it had been completely transformed into what it is today, cutlets and slices of breast, dipped in egg and breadcrumbs and fried in butter or grilled.'

RECIPE

Épigrammes Braise a breast of lamb, or poach it in a small quantity of light stock. Drain and bone the meat, and cool it in a press. Cut it into equal portions and coat with egg and breadcrumbs. Take the same number of lamb cutlets and coat with egg and breadcrumbs. The cutlets and breast portions should then be grilled (broiled) or fried in butter and oil, and arranged in a round dish. Garnish the cutlet bones with paper frills, then put a few spoonfuls of reduced and sieved braising stock around the épigrammes. Garnish with glazed vegetables (carrots, turnips, and baby onions), mushrooms, tomatoes fried in oil, or aubergine (eggplant) fritters, arranged in the centre of the dish.

Epoisses

A soft French cows'-milk cheese named after a village on the Côte d'Or and made in almost every part of Burgundy. Containing 45% fat, it has an orange washed crust (first with sage, then with Burgundy marc brandy) and a soft creamy inside that is light- to brownish-yellow (depending on the degree of maturity), with a very strong flavour. Brillat-Savarin considered it the 'king of cheeses', and it was highly appreciated by Napoleon I. Each cheese is flat and round, 10 cm (4 in) in diameter and 3–6 cm (1–2½ in) thick, with a slight depression in the middle. It is sometimes sold surrounded with vine leaves, or boxed. It may be flavoured with cloves, fennel, and black pepper. Époisses is given the collective regional brand mark 'Bourgogne'. It is eaten fresh in the summer; mature cheeses are very good from June to the end of March, but are best in winter.

Esau ÉSAÜ

The name of this biblical character, who sold his birthright to his brother Jacob for a mess of pottage, is given to a thickened soup made from lentil purée and white stock or consommé. This also serves as a basis for other soups, such as Conti. Soft-boiled (soft-cooked) or poached eggs Esau are arranged on lentil purée, garnished with heart-shaped croutons, and coated with concentrated veal stock with butter added. Alternatively, the eggs are arranged in a croustade of crustless bread, fried, hollowed out, and filled with lentil purée; the whole is covered with concentrated veal stock with butter added.

escabèche

A spicy cold marinade intended for preserving cooked foods and originating in Spain. It is used chiefly for small cooked fish (sardines, mackerel, smelt, whiting, red mullet, etc.). The fish are beheaded (hence the name, from *cabeza*, 'head'), then fried or lightly browned; they are then marinated for 24 hours in a cooked and spiced marinade. The fish then keep for up to a week in the refrigerator.

The preparation has spread throughout the Mediterranean region: it is called *scabetche* in North Africa, *escabecio* or *scavece* in Italy, and *escavèche* in Belgium. In Berry a similar preparation of fried gudgeon is called *à la cascamèche*. Escabèche is also used for poultry and game birds. In Spain, partridge is fried quickly in oil with garlic, then drained and marinated in its cooking juices with spices, and served cold. In Chile, chicken in escabèche is prepared in the same way and served cold with lemon and onions.

RECIPE

Fish in escabèche POISSONS EN ESCABÈCHE Cut some small fish (smelt, sand eels, weevers, etc.) and remove the heads; clean, wash, and wipe the fish. Dip in flour and fry in olive oil until golden. Drain and arrange in an earthenware dish. Peel an onion and a carrot and slice thinly. Heat the oil used for cooking the fish until it begins to smoke, then fry the onion and carrot and 5–6 unpeeled cloves of garlic for a few moments. Remove from the heat and add 1.5 dl (¼ pint, ⅔ cup) vinegar and 1.5 dl (¼ pint, ⅔ cup) water. Add a bouquet garni containing plenty of thyme and season with salt, pepper, a dash of cayenne, and a few coriander seeds. Cook for about 15 minutes then pour the boiling marinade over the fish and leave to marinate for at least 24 hours. Serve as an hors d'oeuvre.

escalope

A thin slice of white meat. The word comes from the Old French *eschalope* (nut-shell), probably because the slice tends to curl up during cooking (it is sometimes cut on one side to prevent the flesh from shrinking). If taken from the fillet, veal escalopes (veal scallops) are usually tender and lean; escalopes from further down the leg are firmer and more sinewy. Italian *scaloppine* (small escalopes), prepared as saltimbocca or piccata, are cut from the fillet. Turkey escalopes, cut from the breast or wing, may be prepared in the same ways as veal.

Veal escalopes, usually oval in shape, are flattened before being lightly fried or sautéed. Because they tend to be slightly dry and can lack flavour, they are often cooked in sauce, with cream, or with mushrooms. The classic method of preparing escalopes is to coat them with breadcrumbs (*à la milanaise* or *à la viennoise*). Paupiettes are prepared from escalopes.

An escalope can also be a slice cut from a fillet of a large fish (particularly salmon) or from lobster flesh.

RECIPES

Escalopes à la Mandelieu Flatten some escalopes, sprinkle them with salt and pepper, and sauté in clarified butter until golden. Then flame in Cognac, using 1 tablespoon Cognac for 4 escalopes. Cover each with a thin slice of Gruyère or Comté cheese and sprinkle with a few golden breadcrumbs. Moisten with melted butter and brown in a very hot oven. Prepare 250 g (½ lb, 2 cups) mushrooms and sauté them in the butter in which the escalopes were cooked. Add 2 tablespoons (3 tablespoons) tomato purée and 250 ml (8 fl oz, 1 cup) reduced consommé; cook for about 5 minutes. Adjust the seasoning and serve this sauce with the escalopes.

Escalopes à l'anversoise Cut some round slices of bread, 1.5 cm (½ in) thick, and fry them in butter. Lightly fry in butter some very small new potatoes, and prepare some hop shoots in cream. Flatten some round escalopes, sprinkle with salt and pepper, and sauté them in a frying pan (skillet) containing clarified butter. Drain and arrange while hot on the fried bread slices. Add to the frying pan a little white wine or beer and some very concentrated consommé. Reduce to a sauce and pour over the escalopes. Serve piping hot with the potatoes and the hop shoots.

escaloper

A French culinary term meaning to carve thin slices (escalopes) of meat (e.g. veal or poultry), large fish fillets, lobster, or certain vegetables (e.g. mushroom caps or artichoke hearts).

escarole SCAROLE

A vegetable, also called batavia, similar to curly endive (chicory), but with broader leaves (which are fairly curly and very crisp). It usually has a heart of white leaves edged with yellow.

Escarole is generally eaten raw, in a green salad (often with seasoning flavoured with mustard or shallots), possibly with tomatoes or scalded French (green) beans, or in a winter salad with nuts and raisins. It can also be cooked like spinach.

escauton

A Gascon meat stock prepared with local ham and various vegetables and spices.

Escoffier (Auguste)

French chef (born Villeneuve-Loubet, 1846; died Monte-Carlo, 1935). He began his career at the age of 13 with his uncle, who ran a famous restaurant in Nice, then worked in Paris, Nice, Lucerne, and Monte-Carlo. In 1890, in association with Ritz and Echenard, two masters of the hotel business, he opened the Savoy Hotel in London and remained in this illustrious establishment until 1898, when, for personal reasons, he gave up the direction of the Savoy kitchens to take charge of those of the Carlton Hotel, then one of the most famous in Europe.

Escoffier's culinary career was brilliant. He was regarded as the emperor of the world's kitchens, a title conferred upon him by the Emperor William II, who spent some time on the steamer *Imperator* of the Hamburg-America Line, which Escoffier had joined to take charge of the imperial kitchens. In the course of a conversation with Escoffier, the Emperor, congratulating him, said: 'I am the Emperor of Germany, but you are the Emperor of chefs.'

As a reward for all he had done to enhance the prestige of French cooking throughout the world, Escoffier was made a Chevalier of the Legion of Honour in 1920, and Officer of the Legion in 1928. Escoffier retired in 1921. He was then 74 years of age and had practised his art for 62 years. In all the history of cookery, there is no other example of such a long professional career. He died in February 1935, nearly 89 years old.

The culinary writings of Escoffier are works of authority. The best-known are *Le Guide culinaire* (1903) and *Le Livre des menus* (1912), both written in collaboration with Philéas Gilbert and Émile Fétu, and *Ma cuisine* (1934). Other works include *Le Riz* (1927), *La Morue* (1929), the magazine *Le Carnet d'Épicure* (1911), and *Les Fleurs en cire* (1910, a new edition of *Le Traité sur l'art de travailler les fleurs en cire*, 1886). Escoffier created numerous recipes, most notably peach Melba, in honour of the Australian singer Nellie Melba. His other recipes include chaud-froid Jeannette (in memory of a ship trapped in polar ice), *cuisses de nymphe aurore* (a dish of frogs' legs) for the Prince of Wales, and Réjane salad and Rachel mignonettes of quail, in homage to two great actresses.

The house where he was born was transformed into a museum of culinary art in 1966, at the suggestion of one of his former cooks, Joseph Donon.

escuedella

A Catalan pot-au-feu traditionally made in the Perpignan region. The ingredients include beef and vegetables with eggs, a mixture of chopped meat and pasta, and sometimes stuffed turkey. Its full name is *escuedella de Nadal* (literally 'Christmas bowl'), but it is also cooked on many other festive occasions.

espagnole (à l')

The name of several preparations inspired by Spanish cuisine. The main ingredients are tomatoes, sweet peppers, onions, and garlic, and they are usually fried in oil. The garnish *à l'espagnole*, used for small sautéed or lightly braised items, consists of tomatoes stuffed with tomato-flavoured rice, braised sweet peppers, small braised onions, and Madeira sauce. Mayonnaise *à l'espagnole* contains chopped ham, mustard, a dash of garlic, and red pepper.

There are a considerable number of ways to cook eggs *à l'espagnole*. Soft-boiled (soft-cooked) or poached eggs are arranged on cooked tomatoes (stuffed with a salpicon of sweet peppers), coated with tomato sauce, and garnished with fried onion rings. Baked eggs are arranged on a bed of finely sliced onions and garnished with tomato fondue, fried diced peppers, halves of tomato, and fried onion rings. They are served with a tomato sauce to which a salpicon of sweet peppers has been added. Scrambled eggs are garnished with diced tomatoes and peppers and always served with fried onion rings.

RECIPES

Calf's liver à l'espagnole FOIE DE VEAU À L'ESPAGNOLE Season slices of calf's liver with salt and pepper. Coat with flour and sauté them in oil. Arrange the liver slices on tomatoes that have been softened in olive oil and seasoned with garlic. Garnish with fried onion rings and fried parsley.

Ragout of sweet peppers à l'espagnole POIVRONS EN RAGOÛT À L'ESPAG-

NOLE Deseed and peel 6 sweet peppers, and cut them into large strips. Fry 100 g (4 oz, 1 cup) finely sliced onions in some olive oil in a shallow frying pan (skillet). Add the strips of pepper, some salt, pink pepper, and a large clove of garlic, crushed. Stir in 1 tablespoon flour and add 3 dl (½ pint, 1¼ cups) beef stock and 2 tablespoons (3 tablespoons) tomato purée. Cook very gently with the lid on for 35 minutes. Adjust the seasoning. Serve in a vegetable dish sprinkled with chopped parsley.

Spanish omelette OMELETTE FARCIE À L'ESPAGNOLE Dice some sweet peppers and cook them slowly in olive oil. Cut some tomato pulp into cubes, add a little garlic and some chopped parsley, and fry briskly in butter. Beat some eggs and add some of the sweet peppers and tomato pulp (1 large tablespoon of each vegetable for 6 eggs). Season with salt and pepper. Make an omelette, roll it up, and serve with a highly seasoned tomato sauce.

espagnole sauce

A basic brown sauce, which is used as a basis for a large number of derivative brown sauces (Robert, genevoise, bordelaise, Bercy, Madeira, Périgueux, etc.). It is made with a brown stock to which a brown roux and a mirepoix are added, followed by a tomato purée. Cooking takes several hours and the sauce needs to be skimmed, stirred, and strained when a particular stage in the cooking is reached. The meat stock may be replaced by a fish stock, depending on the requirements of the particular recipe. Carême's recipe is considered to be the classic method of preparing an espagnole sauce. Nowadays, a shoulder of veal is used instead of a noix, and partridge is not used in the stock.

RECIPES

Espagnole sauce SAUCE ESPAGNOLE (from Carême's recipe) Take a deep saucepan. Put in 2 slices of Bayonne ham. Place on top a noix of veal and 2 partridges. Add enough stock to cover the veal only. Boil down the liquid rapidly. Move the pan to a cooler part of the stove to extract all the juice from the contents. When the stock is reduced to a coating on the bottom of the pan, remove it from the stove. Prick the noix of veal with the point of a knife so that its juice mingles with the essence. Put the saucepan back on the stove on a low heat and leave for about 20 minutes. Watch the essence as it gradually turns darker.

To simplify this operation, scrape off a little of the essence with the point of a knife. Roll it between the fingers. If it rolls into a ball, the essence is perfectly reduced. If it is not, it will stick the fingers together.

Remove the saucepan from the stove and put it aside for 15 minutes for the essence to cool. It will then dissolve more readily. Fill the saucepan with clear soup or stock and heat very slowly. As soon as it comes to the boil, skim it, and pour 2 ladles into a roux.

For the preparation of this roux, melt 100 g (4 oz, ½ cup) butter and add to it enough sieved flour to make a rather liquid roux. Put it on a low heat, stirring from time to time so that little by little the whole of the mixture turns a golden colour. When adding the liquid, do not forget that the roux must not be on the stove while you are mixing in the first spoonfuls of stock; but it should be put on afterwards, so that it may be added boiling hot to the rest of the stock.

When the 2 ladles of stock are poured into the roux, stir so as to make the mixture perfectly smooth. Now pour it into the saucepan with the veal noix. Add parsley and spring onions (scallions), seasoned with half a bay leaf, a little thyme, 2 chives, and mushroom trimmings. Leave to simmer, stirring frequently. After a full hour skim off the fat. 30 minutes later skim off the fat again.

Strain through a cloth into a bowl, stirring from time to time with a wooden spoon so that no skin forms on the surface, as easily happens when the sauce is exposed to the air.

Espagnole sauce SAUCE ESPAGNOLE (from the modern recipe of Chef Denis) Make a brown roux with 30 g (1 oz, 2 tablespoons) butter and 30 g (1 oz, ¼ cup) flour. Add 1 tablespoon mirepoix, 50 g (2 oz, ½ cup) chopped mushrooms, and 1 kg (2¼ lb) crushed tomatoes. Stir in 2.25 litres (4 pints, 5 pints) brown stock and simmer gently for 3–4 hours, carefully skimming the sauce from time to time. Pass through a very fine sieve, or (better still) strain through muslin (cheesecloth), preferably when cold.

essai

The ceremony of tasting of the king's food and drink at the French royal courts. The cups which were used for tasting wines, etc., were also called *essais*.

The fear of poison in the Middle Ages gave rise to a complicated ceremonial attending the sovereign's meals. In France, this was minutely regulated by court etiquette, which continued with slight modifications up to the Revolution, to be revived under the Empire.

The knife, fork, spoon, salt cellar, spices, and napkin were locked in the cadenas or nef. The maître d'hôtel rubbed all the cutlery and the dishes with balls of breadcrumbs which he made sure were eaten by the squires of the pantry, who, previously, had subjected the servants who had handed them the dishes to the same ordeal.

For drinks, the ceremonial was equally complicated. When the king called for a drink, the cupbearer made a sign to the wine butler and his assistant. The first of these brought the wine in a flagon, and the king's glass, covered; the second brought a silver jug full of water. The cupbearer took the glass and uncovered it; the wine butler poured in the wine, then the water. The cupbearer poured some of this watered wine into two little silver-gilt cups. He drank from one; the wine butler drank from the other. Only then did the cupbearer proffer the cup, now covered once more, across the table to the king. He did not uncover it until the very moment that the king was about to drink.

The same ceremonial took place for the queen. By special favour, Louis XIV bestowed the same prerogative upon the dauphine (the wife of the heir to the throne).

essence or extract

A concentrated aromatic liquid used either to enhance the flavour of certain culinary preparations or to flavour certain foods that have little or no flavour of their own. They are plant extracts obtained by distillation or infusion and include lemon oil, rose oil, and essence of oranges, cinnamon, vanilla, etc. Natural essences are obtained by three methods: by extracting the essential oil of a fruit or a spice (lemon, bitter almond, orange, rose, cinnamon, etc.); by reducing an infusion or a cooking liquid (mushroom, tarragon, chervil, tomato, game carcass, fish trimmings, etc.); or by infusing or marinating items in either wine or vinegar (truffles, onions, garlic, anchovy, etc.).

Essences sold commercially sometimes contain artificial flavourings and colourings.

RECIPES

Chervil essence ESSENCE DE CER-FEUIL Infuse some fresh chervil in either white wine or vinegar, strain, and reduce by boiling.

Coffee essence ESSENCE DE CAFÉ Pour some boiling water over ground coffee placed in a filter (500 g (1 lb, scant 6 cups) coffee per litre (1¾ pints, 4¼ cups) water). Collect the coffee and pour it through the filter 3 more times. The colour may be intensified by adding a little caramel.

Garlic essence ESSENCE D'AIL Pour boiling vinegar or white wine onto crushed cloves of garlic, leave for 5 or 6 hours, strain, and boil down. (1 glass of wine or half a glass of vinegar are needed for 12 cloves of garlic.)

Mushroom essence ESSENCE DE CHAMPIGNON Strain some liquid in which mushrooms have been cooked and reduce it considerably. It is used to flavour sauces or stuffings.

Tarragon essence ESSENCE D'ESTRA-GON Infuse some very fresh tarragon in either white wine or vinegar, strain, and reduce.

Tomato essence ESSENCE DE TO-MATE Rub 500 g (generous 1 lb) very ripe raw tomatoes through a fine sieve. Boil the pulp until it is reduced to half its volume. Pass through a sieve, pressing hard with a spoon. Boil this pulp until it

thickens to a syrupy consistency. Rub through muslin (cheesecloth).

Truffle essence ESSENCE DE TRUF-FE Infuse some truffle peelings in Madeira or any other heavy wine for at least 24 hours. Strain before using.

essential oil
HUILE ESSENTIELLE

An oily substance which has a strong flavour and is extracted from the flowers, fruit, leaves, seeds, resin, or roots of certain plants. Essential oils are used principally in the perfume industry but they are also used to flavour food. Examples are citrus oils, almond oil, and peppermint oil.

estaminet

Until the 18th century in France, an estaminet was a café where people could drink beer and wine, and were permitted to smoke. Today, the term is rare and often pejorative, being used in northern France and Belgium to designate a bistro or, more specifically, the room in a café reserved for smokers. It derives from a word of Germanic origin, meaning 'column' (the ceilings of tavern rooms were supported by wooden columns).

estofinado

A local name in Provence for salt cod *à la provençale* (it is also called *stoficado*, *estoficado*, and *stocaficado*). The word is a Provençal transcription of 'stockfish' (Norwegian dried salt cod). In Marseille and Saint-Tropez, the dish is a well-seasoned ragout of salt cod cooked with tomatoes, onions, garlic, olive oil, and various spices. (In Nice, it is also prepared with hake.)

Under the name *stoficado*, it is also a speciality of Aveyron, especially at Villefranche-de-Rouergue and Deca-zeville: the cod is poached and mixed with potatoes. The mixture is then mashed with very hot walnut oil, butter, garlic, parsley, beaten raw eggs, and fresh cream.

There have been a number of theories to explain why salt cod has been so popular for such a long time in Provençal cookery. One suggestion is that recipes were brought back from

Holland and Scandinavia by southern French soldiers. Another seemingly more probable theory is that salt cod was introduced by northern European merchants travelling to the Italian cities. Its presence in the Rouergue could also be associated with the fact that it was introduced into the area when there was a constant trade in iron ore between the mines of Auvergne and the fishing port of Bordeaux.

estouffade

A dish whose ingredients are slowly stewed. The word comes from the Italian *stufato* (a daube), and is applied most often to beef in wine sauce, with carrots and small onions.

In traditional cookery, *estouffade* is also a clear brown stock used to dilute brown sauces and moisten ragouts and braised dishes.

RECIPE

Estouffade of beef ESTOUFFADE DE BOEUF   Dice and blanch 300 g (11 oz, 15 slices) lean bacon. Brown the bacon in butter in a sauté pan, drain, and set aside. Cut 1.5 kg (3¼ lb) beef into cubes of about 100 g (4 oz), half chuck steak, half rib, and brown in the same pan. Cut 3 medium-sized onions into quarters, add them to the beef, and brown. Season with salt, pepper, thyme, a bay leaf, and a crushed garlic clove. Then add 2 tablespoons (3 tablespoons) flour, stir in well, and add 1 litre (1¾ pints, 4¼ cups) red wine and an equal quantity of stock. Add a bouquet garni and bring to the boil. Cover and cook in the oven (heated to about 180 c, 350 f, gas 4) for 2½–3 hours.

Drain the ragout on a sieve placed over an earthenware dish. Place the pieces of beef and the strips of bacon in a pan and add 300 g (11 oz, scant 3 cups) sautéed sliced mushrooms. Skim the fat from the cooking liquid, strain, and boil down. Pour it over the meat and mushrooms and simmer gently with the lid on the pan for about 25 minutes. Serve in a deep dish.

estouffat

A Languedoc dialect word for a dish that is stewed very slowly. In that region it is used mainly for a stew of pork and haricot (navy) beans, flavoured with garlic, onions, and tomatoes.

In southwestern France the word is also used for various braised dishes (made with game, tripe, etc.).

RECIPE

Estouffat of haricot (navy) beans à l'occitane ESTOUFFAT DE HARICOTS A L'OCCITANE   Brown a diced carrot and a sliced onion in either goose fat or lard in a pan. Add 1.5 litres (2¾ pints, 3½ pints) water and a bouquet garni, bring to the boil, and simmer for about 20 minutes. Add 1.5 litres (2¾ pints, 3½ pints) fresh white haricot beans (navy beans) and three-parts cook. Drain them. Cut 250 g (9 oz) slightly salted belly bacon into cubes, blanch, and brown in goose fat or lard. Add to the pan 150 g (5 oz, 1¼ cups) peeled chopped onions, 2 large tomatoes (peeled and crushed), and 1 crushed clove of garlic, and cook for a further 10 minutes. Then add the drained beans, cover the pan, and gently simmer until cooking is completed.

200 g (7 oz) rind from preserved pork may be added to the bean cooking liquid. When cooked, the rind is cut into squares and added to the beans in the serving dish.

étuvé

The French term used to describe Dutch cheeses, such as Edam or Gouda, that are matured for a long time. This is sometimes carried out in an *étuve*, a heated humidified cellar that has the effect of reducing the maturing time of these cheeses. A *demi-étuvé* cheese spends four to six months in a dry cellar or two to five months in an *étuve*. An *étuvé* cheese is matured for five to nine months in an *étuve*.

ewe   BREBIS

A female sheep. The ewes of breeds reared for meat are allowed to breed for four to six years and are then fattened up for slaughter. (In the past, ewes were allowed to breed for longer before being slaughtered, but consumers today prefer meat with a milder flavour.) Ewes' meat provides most of the joints sold as mutton.

Ewes' milk contains more fat, nitrogen, and minerals than cows' milk (8.5%, 6.2%, and 0.85% as opposed to 4%, 3.2%, and 0.7% respectively), but the proportion of lactose is lower (4.2% as opposed to 5%). It is used for making cheese that is traditionally manufactured in dry mountainous areas. The most famous is Roquefort, but other regions produce notable cheeses: Broccio and Niolo from Corsica, Oloron and Laruns from Béarn, and Esbareich and Arnéguy from the Basque region. Cachat and Rocamadour also deserve a mention.

In Spain and Portugal, the best cheeses are made from ewes' milk, for example, Hecho, Villalon, and Serra, and in Italy, Pecorino and Fiore Sardo are good ewes'-milk cheeses. Liptai is the Hungarian national cheese. In Greece, the Balkans, and the Caucasus, Feta and various types of Katschkawalj and Brandza are the most common cheeses. Fresh ewes'-milk cheese is served with sugar or fresh cream. It may also be used for making tarts or as a filling for puff pastry turnovers.

ewer AIGUIÈRE

A tall vessel formerly used for serving water at table – for washing the hands at the start and finish of a meal rather than for drinking. It had a base, spout, and handle and a tray or bowl beneath it to catch the water poured over the hands. Ewers were made of gold or silver until the 18th century; materials used later included pewter, glazed earthenware, and marble.

Excelsior

A cows'-milk cheese from Normandy with 72% fat content. The skin is white with brown markings and the ivory-coloured paste is soft, fine, and dense in texture, with a mellow, slightly nutty, flavour.

Created in 1890, Excelsior is the oldest of the double- or triple-cream cheeses (along with Fin-de-Siècle, Explorateur, Lucullus, and Brillat-Savarin).

excelsior

A garnish for lamb tournedos and noisettes that consists of braised lettuce and *pommes fondantes* (potatoes cut into small pieces and cooked, covered, in butter). The term also refers to a method of preparing sole, which is rolled into paupiettes, poached, and arranged in a crown around diced lobster *à la Newburg*. The fish is then coated in normande sauce and garnished with slices of truffle and prawn tails.

extra

An adjective printed on French labels to denote special characteristics of certain products when they are marketed. In France, 'extra' eggs have a special label with white letters on a red background and this indicates to the customer that they are fresh and have been packed within three days of being laid. They retain this label for seven days. 'Extra' fruit and vegetables have a red label and are of superior quality and perfect. An 'extra gras' cheese has a fat content of between 45% and 60% (and is also labelled as 'crème'). An 'extra sec' champagne is fairly dry (really dry champagne is labelled 'brut').

extract EXTRAIT

See *essence*.

faggot FAGOT

A ball of coarsely minced pork and liver mixed with breadcrumbs, onion, and herbs and wrapped in caul fat. Faggots are eaten fried or baked.

faïence

A type of white or patterned pottery used a lot for tableware. The earthenware is covered with tin glaze (lead glaze made opaque by the addition of tin ashes) so that the colour of the earthenware is completely masked. This pottery takes its name from the Italian town of Faenza.

Very little is known about the origins of faïence pottery, but from the very earliest times a brilliant vitreous lead glaze, coloured by means of metalic oxides, was known to potters. It is to be seen in the hypogeum of ancient Egypt, on its vases, funeral images, and also in the glazed bricks which decorated the walls of Nineveh and Babylon. The ancient mosques of Asia Minor have preserved for us the magnificent craftsmanship of the Persians, who passed on their skill to the Arabs.

From the 13th century there were important centres for the manufacture of faïence in Spain, at Malaga and Majorca, which gave its name to the Italian *majolica*. Up to the 17th century the most famous factories were in Valencia. But it was mainly through the discovery of tin glaze by Luca della Robbia towards the middle of the 15th century, that the ceramic industry was able to develop, first at Faenza and then in various other Italian towns, notably Urbino, Gubbio, Druta, Durante, Venice, Milan, and Turin.

In France, in the 16th century, faïence pottery called Henry II faïence was made, the most important being the very individual pieces made by Bernard Palissy. During the same period Italian potters tried to introduce the faïence industry into France. The Conradi, coming from Savona, settled at Nevers. Early abortive attempts to produce faïence in Rouen were made in the 16th century, but it was not until the 17th century that this city began to produce the beautiful specimens which remain one of the glories of the French faïence industry. These were very fashionable in the 18th century and were copied everywhere, both in France and other countries. Moustiers, from the end of the 17th century, made famous faïence pieces in the style of Tempesta, or copied from Bérain and Bernard Toro. At Strasbourg, in the 18th century, the Hannong family created a style which was quickly adopted by the factories of Lunéville and Niederwiller. In Paris, Saint-Cloud, Meudon, Lille, and Marseille, there were also a large number of less important factories.

Outside France, some of the finest work was produced at Delft in Holland, which was, for a long time, the most active centre of the faïence industry in Europe.

Fine pottery, called clay pottery, made its appearance towards the middle of the 18th century, and this industry was most fully developed in England, at Leeds and at Burslem in Staffordshire, where Josiah Wedgwood opened the first of his factories. In France, this type of pottery was made especially at Pont-aux-Choux, Paris, Lunéville, and Orléans.

With the advent of porcelain, faïence became less sought-after and less highly prized. But modern manufacturers have given it a new lease of life.

fairy-ring mushroom
MARASME D'ORÉADE

A small mushroom with a pleasant smell that is fairly common in meadows. Its Latin name is *Marasmius oreades* and in France it is also known as *faux mousseron* The stalk is tough and should be discarded, but the cap can be dried. The dried caps can be crushed and used as a condiment, or rehydrated by soaking in water and then added to meat dishes, sauces, omelettes, and soups.

faiselle   FAISSELLE

A type of basket with perforated sides used for draining cheese. The material from which it is made varies, depending on the type of cheese and the region where it is manufactured. Faiselles may be square, cylindrical, or heart-shaped and can be made of wood, earthenware, pottery, wicker, or plastic. *Faisselle* is also the French name for a table on which the apple residue is drained after the brewing of cider.

Falerno   FALERNE

An Italian wine harvested on the sunny slopes of the Massico mountains, in Campania, to the north of Naples. This moderately vigorous wine is sometimes red but more usually white: the latter is a beautiful golden colour.

The Falerno of today is nothing like the highly prized Falernian wine of the ancient Romans, which rivalled the prestigious Greek wines. The poet Horace praised it in verse but deplored its high price – too expensive for him to drink it in the quantities that he would have liked! Pliny the Elder described three types: a light dry white, a fairly sweet yellow, and a dark red – all very highly regarded. He also divulged that Falernian was the only wine that ignited on contact with a flame. The wine was also reputed to keep indefinitely; the Greek physician Galen was of the opinion that it was not good until it had matured for ten years and that it was at its best between 15 and 20 years old. Although it is not known which grape the ancient Falernian was made from, it is supposed to have resembled the present-day Lacrima Christi.

falette

A dish made with breast of mutton browned with carrots and onions and cooked slowly in the oven for a long time. It is sliced and served with haricot (navy) beans. It is a speciality of the Auvergne, particularly Espalion.

RECIPE

Falettes   (from a recipe from L'Ambassade d'Auvergne) Bone and season 2 breasts of mutton. Make a stuffing with 300 g (11 oz, 4 cups) chopped Swiss chard leaves, 200 g (7 oz, scant 3 cups) spinach, 50 g (2 oz, 1½ cups) fresh parsley, 2 cloves of garlic, and 1 large onion. Mix the ingredients carefully together with 100 g (4 oz, 4 slices) bread (without crusts and soaked in milk) and 100 g (4 oz, ½ cup) sausagemeat. Season with salt and pepper.

Flatten out the boned breasts on top of some bacon rashers. Spread the stuffing along the length of each breast, roll up, including bacon, and tie. Brown the 2 falettes in a flameproof casserole with 200 g (7 oz, 1¾ cups) sliced onions and 100 g (4 oz, generous 1 cup) sliced carrots. Deglaze the casserole with some white wine and add a generous quantity of liquid, preferably mutton stock. Add half a clove of garlic and a bouquet garni, and cook with the lid on in a medium oven for 2½ hours.

Meanwhile, blanch 500 g (generous 1 lb) haricot (navy) beans that have previously been soaked for 2 hours in cold water. Cool them quickly under the cold tap. Sauté 100 g (4 oz, 1 cup) sliced onions, 100 g (4 oz, ½ cup) chopped Auvergne ham, and 100 g (4 oz) chopped tomatoes until soft in a second casserole dish. Add the beans, a bouquet garni, and a generous quantity of mutton stock and simmer gently for about 1½ hours.

Remove the falettes from the casserole, cool for a short time, untie them, remove the bacon, and cut them into slices. Strain and reduce the cooking liquid and pour it over the sliced falettes. Serve the beans separately.

fallow deer   DAIM

A small deer of temperate regions. The strong-tasting flesh of adult stags should be marinated in a tannin-rich wine; methods of preparation are as for roebuck. Females and fawns have a less pronounced flavour and may be roasted.

fallue

A type of brioche that was traditionally made in Normandy for the feast of Epiphany. Long and narrow, with transverse markings, it is made with a mixture of flour, softened butter, cream, egg yolks, lightly whisked egg whites, sugar syrup, and a small quantity of baking powder. It is also known as *brioche coulante* or *gâche améliorée*.

fanchonnette or fanchette

A little tart made with puff pastry filled with confectioners' custard (pastry cream), coated with meringue, and decorated with tiny meringue balls. The larger version is known as *gâteau fanchette*.

Fanchonnette and *fanchette* are also the names of certain petit fours. One type consists of a boat-shaped piece of nougat filled with a hazelnut-flavoured confectioners' custard and covered with coffee-flavoured fondant icing. Another consists of a macaroon base with strawberry-flavoured butter cream and covered with pink fondant icing.

far breton

A flan with prunes that may be eaten warm or cold. The French word *far* was originally used for a porridge made with durum wheat, ordinary wheat, or buckwheat flour, with added salt or sugar and dried fruit. It was a popular dish throughout Brittany. Traditionally, it was cooked in a linen bag, pocket, or sleeve, hence its various dialect names: *far sach*, *far poch*, and *far mach*. Slices of the flan are usually served as a dessert or as an accompaniment to meat or vegetables.

RECIPE

Far breton   Soak 125 g (4½ oz, scant cup) currants and 400 g (14 oz, 2⅓ cups) stoned (pitted) prunes in some warm weak tea. Drain them. Make a well in the centre of 250 g (9 oz, generous 2 cups) flour and mix in a large pinch of salt, 2 tablespoons (3 tablespoons) granulated sugar, and 4 well-beaten eggs to make a batter. Thin the batter with 4 dl (14 fl oz, 1¾ cups) milk, mix in the currants and prunes, pour into a buttered tin, and bake in the oven at 200 c (400 F, gas 6) for about 1 hour, until the top is brown. Sprinkle with icing sugar (confectioners' sugar).

farcement

A cake made with grated raw potato mixed with prunes, dried pears, sultanas, eggs, flour, salt, and pepper. The mixture is poured into a special covered tin resembling a charlotte mould, which is greased and lined with rashers of smoked bacon, and then cooked in a bain-marie. The cake is turned out of its mould and served with cooked meats or on its own as a dessert. It is a speciality of Savoy and is traditionally made on festive occasions. (See *farçon*.)

farci

A speciality of Périgord consisting of forcemeat wrapped in cabbage leaves. It is traditionally cooked inside a boiling bowl in meat or vegetable stock. However, it is more usually cooked by wrapping the stuffed cabbage leaves in muslin (cheesecloth) or securing with string and cooking directly in stock.

RECIPE

Farci   Crumble 350 g (12 oz) stale bread (without the crusts) and soak in fatty stock or in milk. Mix together 350 g (12 oz) fresh chopped ham or bacon, 2 chopped cloves of garlic, 2 chopped shallots (or 1 chopped onion), and a bunch of chopped parsley, tarragon, or other herbs. If liked, add some chopped chicken liver. Squeeze out the bread and mix it with the chopped ingredients. Season with salt, pepper, and a generous pinch of spice and bind with 2 or 3 egg yolks. Mix well until smooth, and keep in a cool place.

Blanch some large cabbage leaves in boiling water for 5 minutes. Cool quickly under the cold tap, pat them dry, and arrange them like flower petals on a flat surface. Shape the forcemeat into a ball, place it on the cabbage leaves, and fold them over to wrap it up. Secure with string to keep the shape, or wrap the leaves in muslin (cheesecloth), and cook in vegetable or meat stock for about 1¾ hours. Remove the muslin or string. Cut the farci into slices and serve very hot with the stock or with a chicken, depending on the recipe. (Farci can also be served cold.)

farcidure

A speciality of Limousin, consisting of poached balls of forcemeat or chopped ingredients. In Guéret, where farcidure (or *farce dure* – literally 'hard stuffing') is particularly famous, the balls are made with buckwheat flour and a mixture of chopped green vegetables, as sorrel, Swiss chard, cabbage, etc. When made with wheat flour, they are known as *poule sans os* ('boneless chicken'), contain chopped bacon and sorrel, and are deep-fried. If garnished with salt pork, they are boiled in cabbage soup. Farcidure with potatoes is made with a mixture of puréed potatoes, herbs, garlic, onions, and rashers of bacon, to which beaten eggs are sometimes added. The balls are poached and then fried in lard or goose fat.

farçon

A speciality of Savoy, made with puréed potatoes mixed with eggs, herbs, milk, sugar, and spices The mixture is then browned in a hot oven or under the grill (broiler).

In the Dauphiné, *farçon* is a large saveloy in the shape of a melon.

far du Poitou

A speciality of Poitou, also known as *farci au pot*, prepared *au gras* or *au maigre*. The most common *far (au gras)* is made with chopped green vegetables (Swiss chard, green cabbage, lettuce, sorrel, etc.), mixed with chopped fat bacon, bound with cream and eggs, and seasoned with chives and various herbs. This forcemeat is wrapped in green cabbage leaves and lettuce leaves and then enclosed in a net or muslin and cooked in a hotpot containing fresh and salt pork flavoured with vegetables. *Far au maigre* is prepared similarly but without the bacon, and is cooked in vegetable stock. This *far* can also be cooked *au gratin* and served either on its own or with meat.

farée

A speciality of Charentes, consisting of cabbage stuffed with bacon or sorrel and served with bacon and crustless bread. It is cooked in the stock from a pot-au-feu or a soup.

farinaceous   FARINEUX

Containing flour, or a high content of starch. The term is applied particularly to cereals and pulses (peas, beans, lentils, broad beans, etc.). In France, the consumption of farinaceous foods has diminished considerably during the last 50 years, as it has in all industrialized countries, where there has been an increase in the consumption of meat. It is still high in the Mediterranean area (for example, chickpeas and broad (fava) beans are widely consumed in Spain and north Africa) and in South America (where red and black beans are very widely used).

farinade

A Corsican gruel made from chestnut flour mixed with olive oil. When cooked, it is poured onto a floured cloth so that it forms a ball. It is then sliced and either served on its own, while still hot, or with fresh Broccio or goats' milk. The slices may also be fried in oil.

farinage

The French term for any dish or dessert based on flour. Generally, it is used to describe pasta dishes served as a main course, as well as quenelles, knödel, knepfles, *floutes* (quenelles made with mashed potatoes), gnocchi, etc., which are popular dishes in Italian, Austrian, German, and Alsatian cookery. Farinages also include dishes made with cornmeal (such as polenta, gaudes, and miques), and potato flour (such as gruels and panadas), and also semolina puddings. Pastries and crêpes are not included.

farinette

A sweet or savoury pancake made with beaten eggs and flour. There are several variations to be found in the different parts of the Auvergne, where they are also known as *omelette enfarinée* ('floured omelette'), *pachade* (in Aveyron), and *farinade*.

fast   FAIRE MAIGRE

To eat neither meat nor fat as instructed by the Roman Catholic Church during Lent and on fast days.

Originally only vegetables were allowed to be eaten on fast days. Meats and all animal products (butter, fats, milk, and eggs) were proscribed. Over the years the rules were relaxed, and gradually eggs, then fish and shellfish, were allowed to be eaten on fast days. However, the eating of butter necessitated the payment of extra offerings. When fish was permitted, wild duck and other waterfowl were also included. Brillat-Savarin tells the amusing story of a fasting cleric who enjoyed an omelette with tuna tongues and carp's roe. The last restrictions were removed for Catholics in 1966 with the lifting of Friday fasting, but the tradition of serving fish on that day remains.

In cookery, dishes (sauces, stuffings, salpicons) prepared *au maigre*, as opposed to those prepared *au gras*, do not include lard, bacon, sausagemeat, or any other meat-based ingredients, especially pork. Butter, however, can be used.

fat
CORPS GRAS, GRAISSE, MATIÈRE GRAS

Lipid substances containing glycerol and fatty acids. Fats are solid at low temperatures; oils, however, are liquid at room temperature, due to their higher content of unsaturated fatty acids, and will solidify in the refrigerator. Fats and oils do not dissolve in water, but they may be emulsified with water (for example in margarine and butter making).

Foods containing fats usually have a small amount of fat-soluble substances, including vitamins A (retinal), D (containing varying amounts of cholesterol), and E, as well as flavour components.

There are basically two types of fats: saturated fats (or saturates) and unsaturated fats (these include polyunsaturated fats, or polyunsaturates). Saturated fats are found in dairy products (butter, milk, cheese), animal fats (lard, pork fat, suet, etc.), cakes, biscuits and 'hardened' margarine. They are also found in vegetable fats like coconut oil and palm oil. On food labels they may be listed in the ingredients as 'hydrogenated vegetable fat/oil'. Unsaturated fats are found in vegetable oils (such as sunflower, corn, or soya oils), spreads and margarines (which are high in polyunsaturates), nuts, and in oily fish, such as herring and mackerel. Fats are widely used for cooking and preparing food: frying, baking, roasting, and pastry-making, as well as preparing liaisons and emulsions.

Of the animal fats, lard, obtained from pork fat, is most widely used for cooking in Europe. However, beef suet is also used, particularly in England. Sheep suet or sheep-tail fat is used especially in oriental cookery. In France, goose fat, which is highly esteemed by gastronomes, is specific to Gascony, Béarn, and Languedoc, being used especially for confits. It is also used in Scandinavian and Jewish cookery. Calf fat is used in certain forcemeats. The use of some fats is limited to particular culinary traditions: smeun in north Africa and ghee in India, for example.

In French cooking, recipes or dishes are described as *au gras* (literally, 'fat') when they contain meat products, and *au maigre* when they do not contain meat, being based on fish or vegetables. The introduction of vegetable oils and fats has led to a significant reduction in the role played by animal fats in cooking.

Most vegetable fats are extracted from copra, shea, or palm cabbage. Vegetable fats are traditionally used as cooking fats in many African and eastern countries; when manufactured for cooking, vegetable fats usually take the form of white waxy rectangular blocks. Their melting point is lower than that of animal fats but, like oils, they have high boiling points, which enables them to be used for frying food. (The culinary uses of oils are discussed in the article on *oil*.)

The trend today in western countries, following medical advice, is to reduce consumption of fats, both to avoid weight problems and to prevent the build-up of cholesterol, which may lead to cardiovascular disease.

fatty acids ACIDES GRAS

The basic elements of lipids, which are mainly triglycerides composed of one molecule of glycerol and three fatty acids. There are about 20 common fatty acids, distinguishable by the degree to which they will bond with each other. They may be saturated (when no bonding is possible) or unsaturated (allowing a double bonding for the monounsaturates, and several double bondings for the polyunsaturates). Of the polyunsaturated fatty acids some, such as linoleic acid, are essential as they cannot be synthesized by the body. They play an important part in growth, cellular structures, and the maintenance of a good skin. The body can make the best use of dietary lipids if they represent a sensible combination of the three types of fatty acids. Saturated fatty acids are to be found mainly in meat and pork products, cheese, butter, and animal fats; monounsaturates in olive and peanut oil; polyunsaturates in oil made from corn, sunflower seeds, and grape pips, as well as soya (soy) beans and rapeseed.

Faubonne

A thick soup made with a purée of white haricot (navy) beans, split peas, or peas, mixed with a white stock or a consommé containing finely shredded vegetables (carrots, turnips, leeks, celery) and seasoned with parsley and chervil. Formerly, Faubonne soup was garnished with thin strips of roast or braised pheasant.

Fauchon (Auguste Félix)

A famous French grocer (born 1856; died Paris, 1939). He arrived in Paris from Normandy in 1886 and opened a food store in the Place de la Madeleine that dealt exclusively in the best French products, including groceries, poultry, charcuterie, cheese, biscuits, confectionery, wines, and liqueurs. Auguste Fauchon did not stock exotic products, and sent customers requiring such items to his friend Hédiard. Between the two wars, he opened a *salon de thé-pâtisserie* and also started a catering service. After the death of its founder, the store began to stock specialities from all over the world, at the same time maintaining a selection of luxury French products.

faux-filet or contre-filet (tenderloin)

Part of the beef sirloin located on either side of the backbone above the loins. It is fattier and less tender than the fillet but has more flavour; when boned and trimmed, it can be roasted or braised. Unlike fillet, it is not essential to bard the meat, unless it is to be braised. Slices of faux-filet can be grilled (broiled) or fried.

RECIPE

Roast faux-filet FAUX-FILET RÔTI Bone and trim the meat. Bard it on top and underneath, shape into a square, and tie. Cook in a very hot oven so that the outside is sealed but the inside remains pink or rare (10 minutes per 500 g, 1 lb). 5 minutes before the end of the cooking time the meat can be untied and debarded to brown the outside thoroughly. Season with salt and pepper.

fava bean

See *broad bean*.

Favart

A sumptuous garnish for poultry or calves' sweetbreads, dedicated to

Charles Simon Favart, an 18th-century
playwright and director of the Opéra-
Comique. It is made of poultry quenelles with tarragon, and small tarts filled
with a salpicon of cep mushrooms and
cream. The accompanying sauce is a
chicken velouté flavoured with crayfish
butter.

The name is also given to a preparation of soft-boiled (soft-cooked) or
poached eggs, served in little tarts garnished with a salpicon of lamb sweetbreads, truffles, and mushrooms, bound
with a velouté sauce.

favorite (à la)

Describing various preparations created
during the last century in honour of a
popular Donizetti opera, *La Favorita*
(1840). Soup *à la favorite* is a cream
soup of asparagus and lettuce garnished
with asparagus tips. Asparagus tips also
feature in a garnish for small sautée
joints of meat (together with slices of
foie gras topped with slivers of truffle,
coated with the meat juices deglazed
with Madeira and demiglace) and in a
mixed salad. There is also a garnish of
the same name for large roasting joints,
consisting of sautéed quarters of prepared artichoke hearts, celery hearts, and
château potatoes.

RECIPE

Salad à la favorite   SALADE À LA
FAVORITE   Arrange in a salad dish, in
separate heaps, asparagus tips, shelled
crayfish, and sliced white truffles. Season with oil, lemon juice, salt, and pepper. Sprinkle with chopped celery and
herbs.

Favre (Joseph)

Swiss-born chef (born Vex, 1849; died
Paris, 1903). After his apprenticeship in
Switzerland, he finished his studies in
Paris, with Chevet, then worked in Germany, England, and again in Paris, with
Bignon. He is best known as a theoretician: his *Dictionnaire universel de
cuisine et d'hygiène alimentaire* (1st edition 1889–1891, 2nd edition 1902)
contains not only a large number of
recipes but also a very interesting history of cookery. In 1877 he founded the
journal *La Science culinaire* in Geneva,

and in 1893 he founded the first
Academy of Cookery.

Fédora

A garnish for large roasting joints, consisting of barquettes filled with asparagus tips, pieces of glazed carrot and
turnip, quarters of orange, and braised
shelled chestnuts.

feet and trotters   PIEDS

The feet and trotters of slaughtered
animals are classified as white offal.
Sheep's or lambs' trotters, which can be
obtained from the butcher already
blanched, must be boned, singed, and
the little tufts of hair between the cleav-
age in the hoof removed. They are first
cooked in a court-bouillon, and can
then be braised, grilled (broiled), fried,
prepared *à la poulette*, or used for a
fricassee or a salad. They are also included in the Provençal speciality pieds
et paquets, particularly popular around
Marseille.

Pigs' trotters are also sold blanched
and cleaned. A particularly savoury way
of cooking them is *à la Sainte-
Menehould*: they are parboiled, dipped
in egg and breadcrumbs, then grilled
and served with mustard or Sainte-
Menehould sauce. They may also be
boned and mixed with forcemeat, often
with truffles. Pigs' trotters may also be
cooked in a flavoured stock, grilled,
cooked *en daube*, braised, etc.

Calves' feet are used primarily as a
source of gelatine in stock, but they may
also be prepared separately after being
boned, cleaned, blanched, and then
cooked in white stock. They can then be
fried, curried, prepared *à la poulette*, or
dipped in egg and breadcrumbs, grilled,
and served with devilled or tartare
sauce. All the recipes for calf's head can
be used for calves' feet.

RECIPES

CALVES' FEET

Cooking calves' feet   CUISSON DES
PIEDS DE VEAU   Calves' feet can be
bought already blanched and partially
boned (the long foot bones only). They
are usually cooked in a white court-
bouillon for approximately 2 hours, like

a calf's head. They can be served, for example, with a curry sauce and curried rice.

Alternatively, they can be left to cool under a press, brushed with melted butter and coated in breadcrumbs, grilled (broiled), and served with a tartare sauce.

Calves' feet with tartare sauce PIEDS DE VEAU À LA TARTARE Cook the calves' feet in a white court-bouillon until really tender. Bone them completely while they are still warm and cut the flesh into pieces. Drain them on a cloth and dip each piece in flour, then coat with beaten egg and fresh breadcrumbs. Brown them lightly in hot deep oil at 180 C (350 F), drain on absorbent paper, and serve very hot with tartare sauce.

PIGS' TROTTERS (FEET)

Cooking pigs' trotters CUISSON DES PIEDS DE PORC Buy blanched trimmed pigs' trotters. Tie them in pairs and place them in a pan of cold water. Bring to the boil, skim, and add carrots, turnips, leeks, celery, an onion studded with cloves, and a bouquet garni. Simmer gently for 4 hours. Drain and cool. If they are to be grilled (broiled), place them between 2 thin boards tied with string, while still hot, to press them as they cool.

Daube of pigs' trotters DAUBE DE PIEDS DE PORC (from a recipe by Michel Oliver) Cut 3 pigs' trotters in half and place the 6 halves in a stewpan, together with a slightly salted knuckle of veal and 2 slightly salted pigs' tails. Cover with cold water and leave to soak for 3 hours. Drain and rinse the meat, then place in a flameproof casserole. Cover with cold water. Bring to the boil, skim, and cook gently for 10 minutes with the lid off. Drain the meat.

Rinse and wipe the pan, add 3 tablespoons (4 tablespoons) groundnut (peanut) oil, and return to the heat. When the oil is hot, add 4 diced carrots, 3 diced onions, and 2 chopped sticks (stalks) of celery. Cook for approximately 6 minutes until the onions are transparent, stirring occasionally. Then add 3 or 4 crushed cloves of garlic, a few

chopped sage leaves, 1 tablespoon (2 tablespoons) flour, 1 tablespoon tomato purée, and 4 peeled diced tomatoes. Cook for 2 minutes. Add 4 dl (2 tablespoons, 3 tablespoons) dry white wine, 2 pinches of caster (superfine) sugar, and 3 pinches of salt. Bring to the boil. Add a bouquet garni and a pinch of cumin seeds tied in a muslin (cheesecloth) bag. Add the meat, remove from the heat, cover the casserole with a lid, and cook in the oven at 140 C (275 F, gas 1) for at least 3 hours.

Arrange the meat on a heated serving dish, cover it with the sauce and vegetables, and sprinkle with chopped parsley.

Grilled (boiled) pigs' trotters PIEDS DE PORC GRILLÉS Cook the trotters in stock until really tender. Drain and cool. When cold, cut them in half lengthwise. Brush them with melted butter or lard and coat with fresh breadcrumbs. Cook gently under the grill. Serve with mustard and mashed potatoes or celery, or with potato straws (the traditional accompaniment).

SHEEP'S TROTTERS (FEET)

Sheep's trotters à la poulette PIEDS DE MOUTON À LA POULETTE Cook 250 g (9 oz, 3 cups) sliced mushrooms. Bone 12 trotters, split in half, and cook in white court-bouillon. Put into a shallow pan with the cooked mushrooms. Add 4 tablespoons (⅓ cup) white stock and the same amount of the mushroom cooking liquor. Boil to reduce almost entirely. Add 3 dl (½ pint, 1¼ cups) velouté sauce and 3 tablespoons (scant ¼ cup) cream. Simmer for 5–6 minutes.

Bind the sauce with a liaison of 3 or 4 egg yolks mixed with 3–4 tablespoons (scant ¼–⅓ cup) cream. Simmer the trotters but do not boil. Add 3 tablespoons (scant ¼ cup) butter, a dash of lemon juice, and 1 tablespoon chopped parsley. Mix well.

Sheep's trotters à la vinaigrette PIEDS DE MOUTON À LA VINAIGRETTE Cook the trotters in a white cour. bouillon until really tender. Drain and bone them completely. Cut them into even slices and season while hot with oil, vinegar, salt, pepper, and finely chopped herbs. Serve as an hors d'oeuvre flavoured with chopped spring onions (scallions).

feijoa

A fruit tree native to South America, now grown mainly in New Zealand. Sometimes called pineapple guava, the fruit, which is 2–8 cm (¾–3 in) long, has a thin green skin and coarse white flesh, which combines the flavours of strawberries and pineapple. It is rich in iodine and can be eaten raw when very ripe. It can also be used to make sorbets, jams, and jellies, and when poached can be included in exotic fruit salads.

feijoada

A Brazilian speciality whose basic ingredient is the black bean (*frijol negro*). It is a complete dish served on special occasions, not dissimilar to cassoulet. A large pot is used to cook slightly salted pork meat, such as shoulder, trotters (feet), rib, and tail, that has been previously soaked, and black beans. Flavourings include chopped onions, celery, garlic, pepper, and bay leaf, and other meat may be added, such as smoked streaky bacon, dried beef, and cooked sausage.

Feijoada is served as follows: a mixture of meat and beans is poured into the centre of the plate and surrounded by rice *au gras*, green cabbage (thinly sliced and fried in oil), and a few slices of orange (with the peel and pith removed). Grilled (broiled) cassava flour is sprinkled over the whole plate, together with small pieces of bacon (*farofa*). The dish is served with a very spicy sauce, *molho carioca*, which is made with cayenne, vinegar, the cooking liquid from the beans, and chopped tomatoes and onions.

Fendant

A Swiss white wine, produced mainly in the Valais on the right bank of the Rhône. It is made from the Fendant, a local name for the Chasselas, and is a dry, elegant, and refreshing wine. Fendant is sometimes slightly sparkling (*pétillant*), which accentuates its freshness. It is generally sold under the name of the commune in which it is harvested, or, more rarely, under the name of a particular vineyard.

fennel FENOUIL

An aromatic umbelliferous plant of Mediterranean origin, which is now widely cultivated. It is a hardy perennial which grows to 1.2–1.5 m (4–5 ft) high. The feathery leaves and seeds have a slight aniseed flavour and both are used in a variety of recipes. The leaves are also used as a garnish.

Florence fennel resembles ordinary fennel but it is a short plant – about 30 cm (1 ft) in height – with a swollen leaf base. This is similar in texture to celery. The feathery leaves, which grow to about 60 cm (2 ft), are used as a herb or as a garnish. The fennel bulb can be used raw in salads or it can be cooked.

RECIPES

Fennel braised in meat stock FENOUIL BRAISÉ AU GRAS   Trim the fennel stems. Parboil for 5 minutes in boiling salted water. Cool under running water. Drain, and dry in a cloth. Quarter them or, if they are small, leave whole. Put them in an ovenproof dish lined with bacon rinds, sliced onions, and carrots. Moisten with a few tablespoons of rather fat stock. Bring to the boil. Cover the pan and cook slowly in the oven.

Raw fennel salad FENOUIL CRU EN SALADE   Hard-boil (hard-cook) 2 eggs and shell them. Boil 100 g (4 oz, generous ½ cup) rice. Leave to cool. Peel 12 small pickling onions. Clean 1 large bulb of fennel and slice it finely. Cut 4 small tomatoes into quarters. Add a little well-seasoned vinaigrette to the rice and put into a salad bowl. Place all the other ingredients on top of the rice, together with some black (ripe) olives. Sprinkle with chopped herbs and serve with anchovy sauce.

fennel flower

See *nigella*.

fenugreek FENUGREC

An aromatic Mediterranean plant originating in the Middle East. It is a leguminous plant belonging to the pea family. It produces long slender curved pods containing oblong flattened brownish seeds. The seeds, which have a slightly bitter taste, are roasted and ground, then used as a flavouring in curries. They are very hard and can only be ground with a heavy pestle and mortar or in a special grinder.

The leaves have a very strong smell and in Turkey, various Arab countries, and India, they are used either fresh or dried, as a vegetable or herb. In north Africa, the seeds were traditionally used to fatten women, who regularly consumed a mixture of fenugreek flour, olive oil, and caster (superfine) sugar. Fenugreek is used in the West only as one of the main ingredients in curry powder or to flavour spiced vinegar.

féra

A rare fish of the salmon family that is now found only in Lake Geneva, and is becoming scarce even there. The féra, which is highly prized, is about 50 cm (20 in) long and has white, delicate, but very fragile flesh. It has very few bones, which is rare in a freshwater fish.

It may be prepared *à l'anglaise*, *à la meunière*, *au bleu*, with red wine (Bercy), or poached.

ferchuse

A culinary speciality of Burgundy, made from pigs' offal, which was traditionally prepared on the day when the pig was killed. (*Ferchuse* is a corruption of the French word *fressure*, offal.) The heart, lungs, and liver are cut into pieces, browned in lard with shallots and garlic, then floured and moistened with two parts red wine and one part stock. The dish is simmered for an hour. A bouquet garni, some thinly sliced onions, and slices of sautéed potato are then added and the dish is cooked for a further 45 minutes.

fermentation

The biochemical change brought about by the action of certain yeasts or bacteria on certain food substances, particularly carbohydrates. These microorganisms are either naturally present in the food or are added because of the requirements of a particular process. The type of fermentation varies depending on the type of food, the nature of the fermenting agent, and the length of time the process takes, resulting in the formation of acids or alcohols. For example, alcohol is produced by the fermentation of natural sweet juices such as grapes, sugar cane, etc. Vinegar is a dilute solution of acetic acid produced by the fermentation of various dilute alcoholic liquids, such as wine or beer. Lactic acid is produced in the souring of milk by bacteria.

The main foods that are fermented include dough, milk products (curds, yogurt, and cheese), meat (raw sausage), and alcoholic drinks, such as beer, wine, cider, etc. Certain cereal preparations are also fermented, especially in India and Africa. Fermented vegetables include sauerkraut, cucumber, and beetroot (in eastern Europe) and mixed thinly sliced vegetables (in China).

The greatest variety of fermented foods can be found in the Far East. They are based on soya, rice, leguminous plants, and even fish (*nuoc-mâm*). In the Middle East, cereals and milk are fermented, and in eastern and northern Europe, vegetables, alcohol, bread, and cheese. Fermentation is an excellent method of preservation and also improves the nutritive value of foods.

fermière (à la)

A special method of preparing braised or pot-roasted meat, poultry, or fish, using a garnish of vegetables that have been cooked slowly in butter until tender and are sometimes added to the main ingredient while it is being cooked. Vegetables prepared in this way can also be used to garnish omelettes and soups.

RECIPES

Potage fermière   Finely shred 2 or 3 small carrots, 1 small turnip, 6 tablespoons (½ cup) leeks (white part only), 4 tablespoons (⅓ cup) onions, and 75 g (3 oz, 1¼ cups) cabbage heart. Season, and simmer slowly in 50 g (2 oz, ¼ cup) butter in a covered pan. Moisten with 8 dl (1⅓ pints, 1¾ pints) water in which white beans have been cooked, and 6 dl (1 pint, 2½ cups) white consommé. Cook for 1¼ hours. Add 1 dl (6 tablespoons, scant ½ cp) cream, 4 tablespoons (⅓ cup) cooked white beans, and some chervil leaves.

Sautéed chicken à la fermière POULET SAUTÉ À LA FERMIÈRE Sauté a chicken in some butter until brown. Prepare 2 dl (12 tablespoons, ¾ cup) of the vegetable mixture used for brill *à la fermière* (see recipe above), ensuring that the vegetables remain fairly firm. Add the vegetables 15 minutes before the chicken is cooked. Place all the ingredients in an ovenproof casserole, add 2 tablespoons (3 tablespoons) diced ham, and simmer, covered, in a preheated oven at about 220 c (425 F, gas 7) for about 10 minutes. The cooking liquid can be deglazed at the last moment with 1 dl (6 tablespoons, scant ½ cup) thick gravy or thick veal stock.

Ferval

A garnish for main courses consisting of braised artichoke hearts and potato croquettes filled with finely diced ham.

festive cookery

CUISINE CALENDAIRE

In France a number of dishes and pastries are traditionally prepared especially for festive occasions, such as religious holidays or important events in country life (the wine harvest, crop harvest, etc.).

Folklorists, such as A. Van Gennep in the *Manuel de folklore contemporain* and G. Bidault de l'Isle in the *Vieux Dictons de nos campagnes*, have written well-documented works on ceremonial dishes, which made up a long and varied list, differing from region to region and sometimes from village to village. These dishes had two points in common: they are exceptionally nutritious, in contrast to the dull and frugal daily fare, and, most important, they had a magical or a symbolic significance.

festonner

A French culinary term meaning to arrange decorative items in festoons around the edge of a serving dish. This is a garnish which is added on the dish, rather than on the food. Croutons, slices of aspic, half slices of fluted lemon, etc., can be used for this.

Feta

The best-known Greek cheese, made from ewes' milk or sometimes from goats' milk and containing 45% butterfat. It is made by traditional methods, even though it is now manufactured on an industrial scale. The curdled milk is separated and allowed to drain in a special mould or a cloth bag. It is cut into large slices that are salted and then packed in barrels filled with whey or brine. Feta is used mostly in cooking, for gratins and feuilletés. It is often crumbled over the top of mixed salads and may be cut into cubes and served as a snack with olives and farmhouse bread.

Feuille de Dreux

A French cheese made in the Île-de-France from partially skimmed cows' milk. It contains between 28 and 40% butterfat and has a soft golden yellow centre and a bluish-grey powdery crust that is spotted with mould. It is a round flat cheese, 16–20 cm (6½–8 in) in diameter and 2–3 cm (¾–1) thick. It is yielding to the touch and has a fruity taste. The *feuille* (leaf) of its name comes from the fact that it is wrapped in chestnut leaves.

feuilleté

A piece of puff pastry cut into the shape of a finger or triangle and filled or garnished with cheese, ham, seafood, etc. Feuilletés are served hot as an entrée.

The name is also given to small sticks of flaky pastry brushed with a little egg yolk and sprinkled with cumin seeds, cheese, or paprika. They are served hot or cold as cocktail snacks.

RECIPES

Crab feuilletés FEUILLETÉS AU CRABE Prepare 500 g (18 oz) puff pastry. Wash and scrub 2 crabs; plunge them into boiling water for 2 minutes and then drain them. Pull off the claws and the legs, crack the shells, and cut the round bodies in two. Remove the 'dead man's fingers' and discard. Chop a carrot, an onion, a shallot, half the white part of a leek, and a stick (stalk) of celery into small dice.

Heat 40 g (1½ oz, 3 tablespoons) butter in a shallow frying pan (skillet), add the pieces of crab, then the chopped vegetables, and cook, stirring frequently until the crab shell turns red. Add 5 dl (2½ tablespoons, 3 tablespoons) heated

Cognac, and flame. Then add 1 bottle of dry white wine, 1 generous tablespoon tomato purée, a piece of dried orange peel, salt, pepper, a dash of cayenne, a crushed clove of garlic, and a small bunch of parsley. Cover the pan and cook for 10 minutes. Remove the crab and cook the sauce for a further 10 minutes. Shell the pieces of crab to remove the meat. Strain the sauce and mix half of it with the crab meat. Allow to cool completely.

Roll out the pastry to a thickness of 6 mm (¼ in). Cut it into rectangles measuring about 13 cm by 8 cm (5 in by 3 in), and make crisscross patterns with the tip of a knife. Glaze them with beaten egg and cook them for about 20 minutes in the oven at 230c (450 F, gas 8). When the feuilletés are cooked, split them and insert the crab filling. Reheat the remaining sauce and serve it with the feuilletés.

Roquefort feuilletés FEUILLETÉS AU ROQUEFORT Prepare some puff pastry. Mix together 200 g (7 oz) Roquefort cheese, 200 g (7 oz) soft cream cheese, 2 dl (7 fl oz, ¾ cup) double (heavy) cream, some chopped herbs, and some pepper. Then add 4 eggs, one by one, beating the mixture continuously. Adjust the seasoning. Roll out the dough into 2 rounds about 3 mm (⅛ in) thick. Line a tart plate with one of the rounds, and prick with a fork. Spread it with the cheese filling and cover with the second round. Seal the edges carefully. Bake in the oven at 230 c (450 F, gas 8) for about 35 minutes, protecting the top with a sheet of foil if it is browning too quickly. Cut into triangles before serving.

feuilleton

Thin slices of veal or pork beaten flat, spread with layers of forcemeat, and laid one on top of the other. The layers are then wrapped in strips of bacon or caul and tied with string. It may also be made with a single piece of meat that is cut into parallel slices but not completely through. Forcemeat is then spread between each adjoining slice and the meat is tied up with string. The feuilleton is stewed or braised and served with a bourgeoise garnish or with braised vegetables (celery, chicory (endive), lettuce, etc.).

| RECIPE

Feuilleton of veal l'Échelle FEUILLETON DE VEAU L'ÉCHELLE (from a recipe of Prosper Montagné) Season a boned fillet of veal and brown it quickly in very hot butter to seal. Leave it to cool. Cut it into slices lengthwise, but do not cut completely through the joint. Prepare a forcemeat with a mixture of dry mushroom duxelle, chopped lean ham, diced truffles, and a vegetable mirepoix, bound with a beaten egg. Spread each of the slices with the forcemeat and reshape the fillet.

Cover the feuilleton wih mirepoix and wrap it in pig's caul. Braise the feuilleton for 2–3 hours in butter, very slowly, then place it in a long dish. Garnish it with lettuce and potatoes that have been braised in butter. Pour over a little of the pan juices and replace it in the oven to glaze. Make a sauce with the remainder of the juices in the pan by adding some Madeira and some veal stock.

This feuilleton may be served cold in aspic. In this case, a boned calf's foot is added to the cooking stock.

fiadone

A Corsican cake prepared with a mixture of eggs, sugar, fresh Broccio cheese, and lemon peel. Several recipes exist, one of which consists of blending the stiffly whisked eggwhites with a mixture of the egg yolks, the mashed cheese, and the lemon peel. The cake is sometimes flavoured with a little brandy.

fiasque

The French word for a type of Chianti bottle. It is derived from the Italian *fiasco*, meaning flask or straw-covered bottle. The bottle has a long narrow neck and is uually wrapped in woven straw.

ficelle

A long thin loaf of French bread (the word literally means 'string').

ficelles picardes

Savoury pancakes filled with a slice of ham and chopped creamed mushrooms with cheese. They are rolled up,

fig **509**

arranged in an ovenproof dish, covered with cream and grated Gruyère cheese, and then brownd in the oven. They are a speciality of northern France and are served as a hot entrée.

fig FIGUE

The fruit of the fig tree, which is pear-shaped or globular and is eaten fresh or dried. Probably originating in Asia Minor and now widespread throughout the Mediterranean region, the fig is mentioned in the Old Testament and was highly prized by the Ancients.

☐ **Fresh figs** There are three types of fig: the white fig (including green figs), the purple fig, and the red fig. These three types are subdivided into a large number of varieties. French figs are grown in the Midi, mostly in Var. The best-known varieties are *buissone*, *bellone*, *bourjasotte*, *célestine*, *col de dame*, and *dauphine violette*. These figs are exported fresh between June and November. The fig is also grown throughout the Mediterranean basin. Algeria is the principal supplier of dried figs.

Besides being the sweetest of all fruits, the fig contains appreciable quantities of vitamins A, B, and C. It has laxative and digestive properties (although if eaten when underripe it may cause an irritation of the mouth and lips). Figs are more nourishing when dried and, like prunes, are improved by soaking for 24 hours before use.

Fresh or canned figs are usually eaten in their natural state. They can be served as an hors-d'oeuvre with raw ham (Parma ham) in the same way as melon. Figs can also be cooked in various ways. All recipes for apricots are suitable for figs.

A fermented drink is made from figs and also a spirit which is highly prized by the Arabs. In central Europe roast figs are used to flavour coffee, as chicory is in France.

☐ **Dried figs** These have a high calorific value (275 Cal per 100 g) and are rich in sugar and vitamins. Very ripe autumn fruit is used. The figs, spread out on hurdles, are exposed to the sun. They have to be turned over several times during the drying and, before they are completely dried, they are slightly flattened. Treated in this way, figs will keep for a very long time. The best dried figs are sold tied up with a piece of raffia and selected for their size and ripeness. They may be eaten plain or stuffed with almonds or walnuts. Dried figs are also sold in blocks. They are eaten in compotes, cooked in wine, accompanied by milky rice pudding, vanilla cream, etc. They are also served with pork or rabbit, like prunes, and are particularly delicious with braised pheasant and guinea fowl (soaked in port until swollen, then added to the pan a the end of cooking). A drink is also made from them (see *figuette*).

RECIPES

Corsican anchoyade with figs ANCHOYADE CORSE AUX FIGUES Soak 5 anchovy fillets in cold water to remove the salt, then wipe them dry. Pound them with 500 g (1 lb) fresh figs and 1 small clove of garlic. Spread the resulting paste on slices of bread moistened with olive oil. Sprinkle with chopped onions and serve as an hors-d'oeuvre.

Fig jam CONFITURE DE FIGUES Peel and quarter some large white figs that are just ripe but firm. Prepare a syrup, using 200 g (7 oz, scant cup) sugar and half a glass of water per kg (2¼ l) fruit. Boil it, then add the figs and cook until the jelling stage is reached. Pot and cover in the usual way.

Figs with raspberry mousse FIGUES À LA MOUSSE DE FRAMBOISE Peel some ripe fresh figs and cut them into quarters. Make a raspberry mousse with 2 dl (7 fl oz, ¾ cup) Chantilly cream for each 250 g (8¾ oz, 1½ cups) sieved sweetened raspberries. Arrange the fig quarters in a shallow bowl, cover with the raspberry mousse, and refrigerate for 30 minutes before serving.

Fig tart TARTE AUX FIGUES Prepare 350 g (12 oz) shortcrust pastry (basic pie dough) or shortbread pastry and use it to line a 23-cm (9 in) flan. Prick and bake blind. Allow it to cool. Peel and halve some fresh figs, and leave for 3 minutes. Mix a little rum with some apricot jam, sieve the mixture, and spread it over the base of the flan.

Arrange the drained fig halves on top, coat them with apricot jam, and decorate with Chantilly cream.

Fresh figs with Parma ham FIGUES FRAÎCHES AU JAMBON CRU Choose some very fresh green or purple figs that are ripe but still slightly firm. Split them into four without completely separating the quarters (these should be held together by the stalk). Gently loosen the skin near the stalk. Roll some very thin slices of Parma or Bayonne ham into cornets, arrange the figs and ham in a dish, and serve cold.

Lamb cutlets with figs and honey CÔTELETTES D'AGNEAU AUX FIGUES ET AU MIEL (from a recipe by Christiane Massia) Wash and wipe 1 kg (2¼ lb) fresh figs, but do not peel. Place them, stalks upwards, in a generously buttered ovenproof dish. Cover with a glass of water, add some pepper and a little cinnamon and nutmeg, and cook in a moderate oven (200 c, 400 f, gas 6) for 30–35 minutes. 10 minutes before the end of the cooking time, melt 40 g (1½ oz, 3 tablespoons) butter in a frying pan (skillet) and fry 4–8 lamb cutlets (depending on their size) for 3 or 4 minutes per side. Season with salt and pepper and arrange the cutlets in a warmed serving dish. Keep hot. Melt 2 tablespoons (3 tablespoons) honey in a little hot water and add the pan juice from the cutlets to make a sauce. Adjust the seasoning. Arrange the figs around the meat. Coat the cutlets and the figs with honey sauce. Serve immediately.

figatelli

A Corsican charcuterie product in the form of long thin sausages, smoked and very spicy, made with liver (*fegato*), lean and fat pork, and sometimes heart and kidney. They are flavoured with garlic, bay leaf, and white wine and are eaten raw or grilled (broiled).

figuette

A drink made from dried figs and juniper berries soaked in water for a week (5 juniper berries per 500 g (1 lb) figs in 5 litres (1 gallon) water). The liquid is then strained, bottled, and left for four or five days before drinking.

fillet FILET

The undercut of the sirloin of beef and – in France – the same cut in pork, veal, and lamb. In Britain the word can also refer to the fleshy part of the buttocks of other animals. Either cut is prime meat, tender and with a delicate flavour.

If it is to be served whole, fillet of beef must be trimmed, larded or barded, and secured with string. It may be roasted in the oven or on a spit, fried, or braised, according to the recipe. The fillet may alternatively be cut into steaks and grilled (broiled) – chateaubriands are cut from the middle of the fillet and tournedos from the end. The end of the fillet also provides pieces of meat suitable for kebabs.

In France, fillet of veal is used for grenadins and for fillet chops (*côtes-filet*), which are broader than ordinary chops, and fillet of lamb provides fillet cutlets (without knuckle) and mutton chops. Pork fillet (tenderloin) provides particularly tender cuts of meat, especially from the middle or end of the fillet. The boned end of pork fillet provides a slightly dry roast joint, which it is advisable to bard with rashers (slices) of bacon. *Filet de Saxe* (Saxony fillet) is a fillet of smoked salted pork wrapped in a caul. It resembles bacon but is smoother.

● The filet mignon of beef and veal is a small choice cut of meat from the end of the fillet. Pork filet mignon is cut from the boned fillet and is particularly tender. It may be lightly braised in a single piece, sliced into two lengthways and stuffed, or cut into pieces for kebabs.

● In poultry and game birds, the fillet is the underside of the breast, or the entire breast, cut off before cooking and prepared in various ways. However, the breasts of poultry and game are more often known as suprêmes. (The fillet of a duck reared for its foie gras is called a *magret*.)

● In fish, the fillets are cut lengthwise off the backbone. There are four in a flatfish, and two in a round fish. They may be removed before cooking and poached, fried, marinated, or rolled into paupiettes. When a fish is cooked whole, the fillets are removed at the time of serving.

RECIPES

Cold fillet of beef à la niçoise FILET DE BOEUF FROID À LA NIÇOISE Garnish the cold roasted fillet with small tomatoes that have been marinated in olive oil and stuffed with a salpicon of truffles, small artichoke hearts filled with a salad of green asparagus tips, large olives, anchovies, and pieces of aspic jelly.

Cold fillet of beef in aspic FILET DE BOEUF FROID EN GELÉE Cold roasted fillet either whole, or cut into thin slices, may be covered with aspic jelly. If the piece is big enough to be served whole, place it on a grid and coat with several layers of aspic jelly, which may be flavoured with Madeira, port, or sherry. (It must be placed in the refrigerator between each coating.) Then arrange it on a serving dish and decorate with chopped jelly or with croutons and watercress. Slices of fillet are either covered with jelly separately or placed in a row on the serving dish and coated with aspic. They are decorated in the same way.

Serve with a cold sauce, such as mayonnaise or tartare sauce, and barquettes of cold vegetables, artichoke hearts garnished with vegetables, or a salad.

Fillet of beef à la périgourdine FILET DE BOEUF À LA PÉRIGOURDINE Trim the fillet of beef, stud it with truffle, cover it with bacon rashers (slices), tie it with string, and braise in a Madeira-flavoured stock. Drain, remove the bacon, glaze in the oven, and arrange it on the serving dish. Surround it with small slices of foie gras that have been studded with truffles and sautéed in clarified butter. Reduce the braising stock by half, strain it, and pour it over the fillet.

Fried fillet steaks TRANCHES DE FILET DE BOEUF A LA POÊLE Cut the trimmed fillet into thick 125–150-g (4–5-oz) steaks. Slightly flatten, then seal the steaks in very hot butter. Season with salt and pepper. Remove the steaks and keep them hot. Make a sauce with the pan juices mixed with a little Madeira. Reduce and coat the steaks with the sauce.

Grilled (broiled) beef fillet steaks TRANCHES DE FILET DE BOEUF GRILLÉES Cut the trimmed fillet into thick steaks each weighing 125–150 g (4–5 oz). Slightly flatten each steak, sprinkle with pepper, brush with oil, season with herbes de Provence (or mixed dried herbs), and cook under a hot grill (broiler) or over glowing embers, so that the outside is sealed while the inside remains pink or rare. Top each steak with a pat of maître d'hôtel butter.

Grilled (broiled) filets mignons FILETS MIGNONS GRILLÉS Slightly flatten some filets mignons of beef, each weighing about 125 g (4–5 oz). Season with salt and pepper, dip in melted butter, and coat with fresh breadcrumbs. Moisten them with clarified butter and cook under a low grill (broiler). Serve with maître d'hôtel butter, Choron sauce, lemon butter, or tarragon-flavoured tomato fondue mixed with white wine.

Roast fillet of beef FILET DE BOEUF RÔTI AU FOUR Trim the fillet, bard it top and bottom (or brush with melted butter), and tie with string. Cook it in a very hot oven (240 c, 475 f, gas 9), allowing 10–12 minutes per 500 g (1 lb), basting it several times with the meat juices, to which a very small amount of water has been added. Drain the meat, remove the barding strips, and keep it hot on the serving dish. Make a sauce with the pan juices mixed with stock or reduced veal gravy. Reduce and serve with the fillet.

Sautéed filet mignons FILETS MIGNONS POÊLÉS Slightly flatten some filets mignons of beef, season with salt and pepper, and sauté them quickly in very hot clarified butter. Garnish as for tournedos.

Spit-roasted fillet of beef FILET DE BOEUF RÔTI À LA BROCHE Trim the fillet, put it on the spit, season with salt and pepper, and coat with melted butter. Roast, allowing about 10–12 minutes per 500 g (1 lb). Remove from the spit and allow the meat to stand for a few minutes. Cut it into even slices and serve with the reserved meat juices.

filleting fish   FILETER

The process of removing the fillets from a whole fish that has been cleaned. Filleting is often carried out on a board reserved for this purpose, using a filleting knife known in France as a *couteau à filets de sole.*

filter   FILTRE

A utensil or a material that is porous or perforated, enabling the separation of solid matter from a liquid by retaining the solid material and allowing the liquid to pass through. In cookery, liquids can be filtered through a clean cloth strainer or a piece of muslin (cheesecloth), a colander, or a sieve.

A coffee filter holds ground coffee and near boiling water is poured over it. It can be made of perforated metal, earthenware, porcelain, or cloth (*la chaussette*), or a cone of filter paper that is placed in a special cone-shaped holder. *Café-filtre* (or *filtre*) is coffee made this way filtered directly into the cup.

financier

A cake made from a sponge mixture made with ground almonds and whisked egg whites. Small financiers are oval or rectangular in shape; they may be used as a base for iced petits fours.

Large cakes made with the same mixture are decorated with shredded almonds and crystallized (candied) fruits. These large financiers may be cooked in cake tins of decreasing size and then built up in layers to form a large gâteau.

RECIPE

Almond financiers   FINANCIERS AUX AMANDES   Heat the oven to about 200 C (400 F, gas 6). Butter 16 cake tins 10 cm (4 in) long by 5 cm (2 in) wide. Sift 100 g (4 oz, 1 cup) flour and pour it into a mixing bowl. Add 100 g (4 oz, 1 cup) ground almonds, 300 g (11 oz, generous 1⅓ cups) caster (superfine) sugar, 2 or 3 tablespoons vanilla-flavoured sugar, and a pinch of salt. Mix everything thoroughly. Add a pinch of salt to 8 egg whites and whisk them into very stiff peaks. Fold them carefully into the cake mixture. Quickly pour in 150 g (5 oz, generous ½ cup) melted butter and fold into the mixture. Divide the mixture between the cake tins and bake in the oven for 15–20 minutes until the financiers are golden brown. Turn them out of the moulds. Cool on a wire rack. They may be coated with Kirsch- or chocolate-flavoured fondant icing (frosting).

financière (à la)

A very rich classic garnish for joints of meat, calves' sweetbreads, or braised poultry. It may also be used as a filling for croûtes, timbales, bouchées, or vols-au-vent. It consists of a ragout of cocks' combs, chicken quenelles, finely sliced mushrooms, and shredded truffles flavoured with Madeira, all bound with a sauce containing Madeira and truffle essence. The same ingredients are used to make attereaux *à la financière*, the quenelles being optional. There is also a financière sauce flavoured with Madeira and truffles.

RECIPES

Financière garnish   GARNITURE FINANCIÈRE   Prepare some poached chicken quenelles and some cocks' combs. Slowly cook some finely sliced mushrooms and shredded truffles in butter. Add a little Madeira. Bind all these ingredients with financière sauce (see recipe below).

Financière sauce   SAUCE FINANCIÈRE   (from Carême's recipe) Put some shredded lean ham, a pinch of mignonnette (coarsely ground white pepper), a little thyme and bay leaf, some shredded mushrooms and truffles, and 2 glasses of dry Madeira into a saucepan. Simmer and reduce over a gentle heat. Add 2 tablespoons (3 tablespoons) chicken consommé and 2 tablespoons (3 tablespoons) well-beaten espagnole sauce. Reduce by half, pass through a fine sieve, strain, then heat again, stirring in half a glass of Madeira. Reduce to the desired consistency and serve the sauce in a sauceboat.

When this sauce is intended for a game entrée, the chicken consommé is replaced by an appropriate game fumet. Add a little butter just before serving.

Suprêmes of chicken à la financière SUPRÊMES DE VOLAILLE À LA FINAN-CIÈRE   Sauté some suprêmes of chicken in clarified butter. Arrange them on fried croutons or flaky pastry croustades. Coat with financière sauce and surround with a financière garnish.

fine

The French word for a brandy distilled from wine (as opposed to another alcoholic liquid). It should be distinguished from marc, which is distilled from the mass of grape debris left after pressing.

fine champagne

A category of Cognac coming from the delimited regions of Grande and Petite Champagne and containing not less than 50% Grande Champagne Cognac in the blend (it has nothing to do with the delimited area producing champagne).

RECIPE

Woodcock à la fine champagne BÉCASSES À LA FINE CHAMPAGNE Remove the meat from the woodcocks and cut it into pieces, reserving the carcasses and trimmings. Cook the meat in a sauté pan with a little butter. Cover and simmer for 8–10 minutes. Drain the meat and keep hot on a serving dish. Press the carcasses and pound them. Finely chop the trimmings (intestines, livers, hearts, etc.). Make a sauce by adding some fine champagne brandy, the juice from the pounded and sieved carcasses, and the chopped trimmings to the pan juices in which the meat was cooked. Add a dash of lemon juice and a pinch of cayenne and pour the sauce over the woodcocks. Serve piping hot.

fines herbes

A mixture of chopped aromatic herbs, such as parsley, chervil, tarragon, and chives, in various proportions. The mixture is used to flavour sauces, cream cheeses, meat, sautéed vegetables, and omelettes. In the past, chopped mushrooms were added, and today some chefs include sticks (stalks) of celery, fennel, basil, rosemary, thyme, and bay leaf.

RECIPES

Omelette garnished with fines herbes OMELETTE GARNIE AUX FINES HERBES   Add enough coarsely chopped parsley, chervil, tarragon, and chives to the beaten eggs to colour the omelette green (allow 3 tablespoons (4 tablespoons) chopped fines herbes for 8 eggs).

Sauce with fines herbes SAUCE AUX FINES HERBES   Make ¼ litre (8 fl oz, 1 cup) demi-glace sauce or brown stock and add 2 tablespoons (3 tablespoons) chopped parsley, chervil, and tarragon. Reduce, rub through a very fine sieve, add a few drops of lemon juice, and adjust the seasoning. This sauce is served with poached poultry.

Veal chops aux fines herbes CÔTES DE VEAU AUX FINES HERBES   Sauté some veal chops in butter in a frying pan (skillet), drain them, and arrange on a hot serving dish. Add some chopped shallots and some white wine to the butter and cook for a few minutes to reduce. Then add some chopped parsley, chervil, and tarragon, adjust the seasoning, mix, and pour the sauce over the chops. Formerly, demi-glace sauce was added to the white wine to make a richer, smoother, and creamier sauce.

finger bowl
RINCE-DOIGTS

A small individual metal, glass, or china bowl that is filled with warm water, usually perfumed with lemon, and used for rinsing the fingers at the table. It is an essential component of the table setting when serving shrimps, prawns, etc., which need to be shelled with the fingers, or asparagus or artichokes, which are eaten with the fingers. The finger bowl is placed to the left of the dinner plate towards the end of the course and is removed as soon as the course is finished and the guest has rinsed his or her fingertips, an operation which should be carried out rapidly and with the minimum of fuss.

finish FINIR

To complete the preparation of a dish, for example by adjusting the seasoning or the consistency, adding decorations or garnishes, etc. Certain soups are finished by adding chervil leaves, fresh butter, or cream. A civet (rich game stew) is generally finished by thickening it with the blood of the animal used in the recipe. A dish coated with Mornay sauce is finished by browning under the grill (broiler). A sweet dish, such as an iced sundae, a fruit salad, or a fruit cocktail, is finished by decorating it before serving with whipped cream, extra fruit, sugar, etc.

fish POISSON

Aquatic vertebrates with fins (for swimming) and gills (for breathing), which represent an important source of food. At present, more than 30,000 species are known (as many as all other vertebrates put together). Most fish live in the seas and oceans, at varying depths. Freshwater fish are much less numerous. Some fish, such as eels and salmon, are migratory, spending part of their life in the sea and part in fresh water.

Fish are classified into two broad groups, according to their skeletons: cartilaginous fish (sharks, rays, dogfish, skate) and bony fish (the vast majority). Several basic body shapes can be distinguished:
● tapering, adapted to swimming in the open water (herring, cod, salmon, mackerel, carp, pike, etc.) – these are the most numerous;
● flatfish compressed vertically, with the eyes on the darker dorsal (upper) surface (e.g. skates and rays) – the ventral (lower) surface is white;
● flatfish compressed laterally, with both eyes either on the right side of the head (e.g. plaice, flounder, dab, sole) or on the left (e.g. turbot, brill), the blind side usually being without pigment;
● elongated and snakelike (e.g. eels).

Fish can also be differentiated by colour, the number and shape of the fins, the width of the mouth, the presence or absence of teeth, the thickness of the skin, and the presence of spines, spurs, barbels, etc.

□ **Buying fish** There are three main factors to consider when buying fish: its availability (depending on the season), its freshness, and the percentage of waste. The season is less important now than it used to be, because fish caught off the African or northern coasts are sold almost all the year round. However, it is always better to eat fish in season: it tastes better and is cheaper.

Freshness is the most important quality of fish. Fish is subject to speedy decay by bacterial action and often causes food poisoning if it is not absolutely fresh. It is at its best when first caught, but the speed of modern transport and the excellent methods of preservation mean that fish can be enjoyed far from the fishing grounds without loss of flavour. In France before a fish auction, the fish are sorted under the supervision of a veterinary surgeon and are classified into batches marked A and B and labelled with different colours. Identical controls, using tests for the presence of additives, radioactivity, mercury, etc., are carried out on imported fish. Fish is refrigerated for transport and sold in melting ice, care being taken that the melting water drains off properly. This practice is sometimes considered to detract from the flavour, but it still remains the only method of transporting fresh fish for long distances from the fishing grounds. Most methods of preserving fish date back to ancient times: freezing (practised by the Romans), drying (especially for herring and cod), smoking (salmon, haddock, eel, etc.), and salting in casks or barrels. Preservation by canning has considerably increased the consumption of tuna, sardines, pilchards, and salmon in particular, and deep-freezing has enabled many more types of fish to be made available all the year round.

Fish is an excellent source of protein. It is also rich in phosphorus, magnesium, copper, iron, iodine, and the B vitamins, and oily fish have significant amounts of vitamins A and D. Fish have a low or average fat content, which decreases even further after spawning. The eel, which is considered to have the highest fat content (25% fats), contains no more fat than mutton or pork.

For culinary purposes, fish can be divided into the following categories: 'lean' or white fish (0.5–4% fats), the most numerous, which include all the

What to look for when buying fish

	odour	fresh and pleasant: sea fish should smell of seaweed; freshwater fish of waterweeds
whole fish	*body*	glossy, with metallic and iridescent colours; firm elastic flesh; shiny close-fitting scales that feel damp to the touch and are covered with a light transparent mucus
	head	bulging eyes, damp bright-red gills
	guts	belly should not be torn, sagging, swollen, or taut; when the fish is opened, the guts should be smooth and clean
gutted fish		belly wall quite pale, never dark red or brown; backbone adhering well to the flesh
steaks		section of backbone embedded in the flesh; firm flesh, not dark in colour around the backbone
fish fillets		firm pale flesh

(*from Gousset, Tixerand, Roblot*)

cod family (haddock, whiting, etc.), the white flatfish (plaice, sole, etc.), and the perch family (including bass, red mullet, and skate); 'semi-oily' fish (4 –10% fats, i.e. less than lean meat), which include sardines, mackerel, herring, and trout; and oily fish, which are not very numerous and include (as well as eel) tuna (13%), salmon (8–12%), moray, and lamprey (13–17%).

☐ Cooking fish This always requires a lot of care, to avoid undercooking (the flesh is pink and sticky) on the one hand and overcooking (when it is flaky and dry) on the other. Fish may be cooked dry (grilled (broiled) or baked), poached in water or stock, cooked in fat, steamed, or wrapped in buttered paper, foil, etc., before cooking in the oven. Raw fish is considered to be a delicacy by some, but it needs to be absolutely fresh and carefully prepared. Such dishes include *ceviche* from Mexico, *gravad lax* from Scandinavia and sashimi from Japan.

Hot or cold fish dishes can be accompanied by a wide variety of sauces, flavoured butters, vegetables, and even fruit. Fish can also be cooked in soups (e.g. chaudrée, bouillabaisse, cotriade), in pies (e.g. koulibiaca), in mousses, quenelles, aspics, salads, or scallop shells, in gratin dishes, on skewers, curried, as a matelote, and in many other ways.

In France, the Association des Gastronomes Amateurs de Poisson is working to increase the consumption of fish, which in that country does not occupy such an important place as in some others (Japan and Scandinavia, for example). In the Middle Ages, river fish were much more common than they are today, but even then coastal fish from the English Channel, especially mackerel and herring, were being sold in Paris. However, the eels of Maine, the barbels of Saint-Florentin, the pike of Chalon, the lampreys of Nantes and Bordeaux, the loach of Bar-sur-Seine, the dace of Aisne, and the carp of the lakes of Bondy continued to be highly regarded. During the Renaissance period, haddock, anchovies, turbot, skate, and whiting were eaten more frequently, but the river continued to supply most of the fish markets. The following is an extract from *Blasons domestiques* (by G. Corrozet, 1539): 'There you can see the eel and the lamprey ... the fresh salmon, the stubnosed carp, the large pike, the frisky sole, the fat porpoise, the savoury shad, then the sturgeon and the amorous trout, some boiled, the others roasted to sharpen human appetites.'

In the 15th century, salt cod was considered to be worthy of the best tables, while the so-called 'royal fish' (basically dolphin, sturgeon, and salmon) were

Proportion of waste

	fish	proportion of waste	made up of
whole	sea bream, hake, cod, coley, John Dory	50–60%	large head, large backbone, skin, fins, guts
	plaice, sole, herring, mackerel, sardine, dab	30–40%	average or small head, backbone, skin, fins, guts
headless	monkfish, dogfish (rock salmon), hake, cod, coley	15–25%	backbone, skin, fins
steaks		about 10%	section of backbone, possibly pieces of fin, skin
fillets		nil	

reserved for the king's table. Today in France certain fish, especially river species, are becoming rare (pike, char, shad, dace), while others are less frequently cooked (eel, sturgeon). On the other hand, some are in greater demand than in the past (red mullet, sea bass, and sea bream). Among the most popular fish today are sardine, hake, cod (fresh and salt), mackerel, and herring. Exotic fish from American and African coasts are now appearing on the market.

fish kettle POISSONNIÈRE

A long deep cooking receptacle with two handles, a grid, and a lid. The fish kettle may be made of aluminium, stainless steel, tin-plated iron, or tin-plated copper on the inside; it is used to cook whole fish (hake, salmon, pike, etc.) in a court-bouillon. The removable grid enables the fish to be taken out without breaking it. The turbot kettle is specially designed for cooking large flatfish.

fish slice TRUELLE

A table utensil, in the form of a silver-plated or stainless steel spatula, for serving fish. It is used to open, turn over, or take hold of boiled or poached fish, whether whole or in pieces or fillets. It is usually perforated, since fish cooked in a court-bouillon, even if it has been drained, is often rather watery. The

blade is rounded, pointed, or has its corners cut off. The French word *truelle* may also be applied to the cake slice.

Fitou

A red AOC wine from Languedoc, produced around Corbières, south of Narbonne, on the arid hillsides. The main grapes are Carignan and Grenache. The wine is assertive, deep in tone, and full in flavour. It must have a minimum of nine months in wood. It can benefit by some bottle age, and when mature is among the most popular wines from the south of France.

five spices CINQ-ÉPICES

A mixture of five Chinese spices: star anise, clove, fennel, cinnamon, and pepper. It is widely used in Chinese cookery.

Fixin

A fine red Burgundy (AOC), from the most northerly of the Côte de Nuïts vineyards. It includes the wines of six first growths labelled with the vineyard names. The other wines are sold as 'Vin Fin de la Côte de Nuits'. Fixin wines are particularly fragrant, capable of long lives, and are appreciated for their finesse and breeding.

flamande (à la)

The name given to various preparations derived from the regional cookery of

.northern France. The flamande garnish consists of stuffed braised balls of green cabbage, shaped pieces of glazed carrot and turnip, potatoes *à l'anglaise*, and, sometimes, diced belly of pork (salt pork) and slices of sausage that are cooked with the cabbage. It is also the name of a garnish and a hotpot which is used especially for large cuts of meat (such as rump of beef) or for braised goose. The entire dish is coated with demi-glace, veal stock, or a sauce made with the pan juices from the meat.

Among other preparations described as *à la flamande* are Brussels sprouts (puréed, mixed with an equal quantity of potatoes, or used to garnish a consommé) and chicory (endive) (either raw in a mixed salad, or cooked in a chiffonnade for garnishing an omelette served with cream sauce). *À la flamande* is also a method of preparing asparagus with sieved hard-boiled egg yolks.

RECIPES

Asparagus à la flamande ASPERGES À LA FLAMANDE Cook some asparagus in salted boiling water. Serve hot with melted butter to which sieved yolks of hard-boiled (hard-cooked) eggs and chopped parsley have been added.

Flemish salad SALADE FLAMANDE Cook some peeled potatoes in salted water and blanch some large peeled onions. Cut the potatoes into slices and chop the onions coarsely. Clean some chicory (endive) and cut the leaves lengthwise and across. Place all the ingredients in a salad bowl and mix with a fairly well-seasoned vinaigrette. Arrange in a dome and garnish with fillets of salt herring cut into strips. Sprinkle with chopped parsley and chervil.

flamber

A French culinary term meaning to pour spirits over food, then ignite it. The aim is to enhance the flavour and for culinary showmanship.

When flaming a savoury dish the spirit must be warmed, and then ignited, preferably with a long taper. As it catches fire, it is poured over the dish. Brandy, rum, or whisky are the spirits most commonly used, and the procedure is usually carried out when making a sauce from the pan juices.

In some restaurants, sweet dishes, such as crêpes or sweet omelettes, are flamed with rum, Grand Marnier, etc., at the serving table on special hotplates.

flambé trolley
TABLE À FLAMBER
A small table on castors, fitted with one or two burners (spirit, butane, etc.) and used in restaurants for flaming dishes at table. The flambé trolley often has a bottle rack and a cabinet for cutlery.

flamiche or flamique

A type of sweet or savoury tart made in northern France and Flanders (*flamiche* is the Flemish word for cake). Formerly, it was a cake made of bread dough and eaten freshly baked, spread with butter. Nowadays, a flamiche contains vegetables or cheese. The vegetables are cooked slowly in butter, then mixed with egg yolks and seasoned. The best-known flamiche is made with leeks; in Picardy, where it is known as *flamique à porions*, it is also prepared with pumpkin or onions.

Cheese flamiches are usually made with a Maroilles or a similar full-flavoured cheese. Flamiche *à l'ancienne* is made with a three-turn puff pastry mixed with semi-matured Maroilles cheese and butter. It is cooked in a very hot oven and is eaten as a hot entrée with beer. Another way of making a flamiche is to line a tart plate (pie tin) with bread dough and fill it with slices of Maroilles cheese, alternating with cream seasoned with black pepper and butter. Yet another variation is prepared in Hainaut, where cheese flamiche is made as a pie (with a pastry lid). In Dinant the tart plate is lined with shortcrust pastry (basic pie dough) but the covering is a mixture of strong cheese, butter, and eggs.

RECIPE

Leek flamiche FLAMICHE AUX POIREAUX Make 500 g (18 oz) shortcrust pastry (basic pie dough). Roll out two-thirds of the dough to line a 28-cm (11-in) pie plate. Cut and thinly slice 1 kg (2¼ lb) leeks (the white parts only) and slowly cook them in butter. Add 3 egg yolks and adjust the seasoning. Spread the mixture over the pastry on the tart plate. Roll out the remaining dough large enough to cover the top of the dish. Dampen and pinch the edges together to seal and mark a crisscross pattern on the top with the tip of a knife. Glaze with some beaten egg. Make a slit in the centre and bake in the oven at about 230 c (450 f, gas 8) until the pastry is golden brown. Serve very hot.

flammenküche

An Alsatian speciality, whose name means literally 'flame cake'. Traditionally prepared by the baker, it consists of a large rectangle of very thin bread dough with a raised edge; it is filled with finely sliced lightly fried onions mixed with fresh cream and topped with small strips of fried smoked bacon. Flammenküche may also be filled with a mixture of cream cheese, cream, and egg yolks and topped with onions and strips of bacon. It must be cooked very quickly in a very hot oven.

flamri or flamery

A baked semolina pudding prepared with white wine instead of milk and served cold. It is coated with a purée of sweetened red fruit.

RECIPE

Flamri Place ½ litre (17 fl oz, 2 cups) sweet white wine and ½ litre (17 fl oz, 2 cups) water in a saucepan and bring to the boil. Gradually stir in 250 g (9 oz, 1½ cups) fine semolina and simmer gently for 25 minutes. Remove from the heat and add 250 g (9 oz, 1 generous cup) caster (superfine) sugar, 2 beaten eggs, and a generous pinch of salt. Then stir in 6 stiffly whisked egg whites. Pour the mixture into a buttered charlotte mould in a bain-marie. Cook in the oven at 200 c (400 f, gas 6). Cool, then turn out onto the serving dish and coat with a sauce made from a purée of uncooked red fruit that has been sweetened with sugar.

flamusse

An apple pudding made in the same way as clafoutis. It is a speciality of Burgundy and Nivernais.

RECIPE

Apple flamusse FLAMUSSE AUX POMMES Place 60 g (generous 2 oz, generous ½ cup) flour in a mixing bowl. Make a well in the centre and add 75 g (3 oz, 6 tablespoons, firmly packed) caster (superfine) sugar, a generous pinch of salt, and 3 beaten eggs. Mix with a wooden spoon to obtain a smooth mixture. Gradually add ½ litre (17 fl oz, 2 cups) milk and mix well. Peel 3 or 4 dessert apples and cut them into thin slices. Arrange them on a buttered tart plate so that they overlap. Pour the mixture over the top and cook for 45 minutes in a very cool oven (about 150 c, 300 f, gas 2). When cooked, turn the flamusse over to serve, and sprinkle the apples generously with caster sugar.

flan

An open tart filled with fruit, a cream, or a savoury mixture. A flan may be served as a hot entrée or as a dessert. The word comes from the Old French *flaon*, from the Latin *flado* (a flat cake).

Flans have been in existence for centuries. They are mentioned in the works of the Latin poet Fortunatus (530–609 AD), and featured in medieval cookery – Taillevent gave numerous recipes for flans.

The word *flan* in France and Spain is also used for an egg custard, often caramel-flavoured, that is made in a mould and then turned out and served cold.

RECIPES

Flan case baked blind CROÛTE À FLAN CUITE À BLANC Prepare 350 g (12 oz) pastry dough (shortcrust, sweet, fine lining, or puff) and roll out to a thickness of 3 mm (⅛ in). Grease and flour a 28-cm (11-in) tart plate (pie tin) or flan ring and line it with the pastry, pressing firmly around the edges to ensure that it stays in place, taking care not to stretch the pastry. Leave a thicker edge of pastry at the top so that it does not shrink while it is being baked. Trim off the excess pastry by rolling the rolling pin around the rim of the plate or by trimming with a sharp knife. Prick the bottom with a fork and completely cover the pastry with lightly buttered greaseproof (waxed) paper or aluminium foil, greased side down. To keep the base of the flan flat sprinkle the surface of the paper with baking beans or dried peas or beans. Bake in the oven at 200 c (400 f, gas 6) for about 10 minutes. Remove the paper or foil and baking beans, glaze the crust with beaten egg, and return to the oven for 3–4 minutes or until the pastry is cooked and dried out. The pastry case may ten be filled.

Savoury Flans

Cheese flan FLAN AU FROMAGE Bake a flan case blind. Heat ½ litre (17 fl oz, 2 cups) double (heavy) cream with 50 g (2 oz, 4 tablespoons) butter. Season with salt, pepper, and grated nutmeg and add 100 g (4 oz, 1 cup) sifted flour. Whisk over a gentle heat to obtain a fairly smooth cream. Remove from the heat and add 4 egg yolks and 150 g (5 oz, 1¼ cups) grated cheese. Whisk 4 egg whites into very stiff peaks and fold them into the cream mixture. Fill the flan and bake in a moderate oven (200 c, 400 f, gas 6) for about 30 minutes or until set.

Chicken-liver flan Chavette FLAN DE VOLAILLE CHAVETTE Bake a flan case blind. Thickly slice 50 g (18 oz) trimmed chicken livers. Season and sauté quickly in hot butter. Drain and keep warm. Sauté 200 g (7 oz, scant 2 cups) sliced mushrooms in the same butter. Season, drain, and keep warm with the chicken livers.

Make a sauce by adding 2 dl (7 fl oz, ¾ cup) Madeira to the juices in the pan in which the chicken livers and mushrooms were cooked. Reduce a little. Add 3.5 dl (12 fl oz, 1½ cups) thin béchamel sauce and 2 dl (7 fl oz, ¾ cup) single (light) cream and reduce the sauce until it has a creamy consistency. Strain it, then add the chicken livers and mushrooms. Simmer gently without allowing the sauce to boil.

Prepare some very soft scrambled eggs (using 8–10 eggs) and then add 2 tablespoons (3 tablespoons) grated Parmesan cheese and 2 tablespoons (3 tablespoons) butter.

Arrange the chicken livers and mushrooms in the bottom of the flan case. Top with the scrambled egg mixture and sprinkle with grated cheese. Pour some melted butter over the top and brown very quickly in the oven so that the scrambled eggs are not overcooked.

Flan à la florentine Bake a flan case blind. Fill the flan with a layer of spinach that has been cooked in a little butter (squeeze it well, coarsely chop, and drain well). Cover with Mornay sauce and sprinkle with grated cheese. Pour some melted butter over the top and brown in a hot oven or under the grill.

Seafood flan FLAN AUX FRUITS DE MER Bake a flan case blind. Prepare a ragout of shellfish (such as oysters, mussels, cockles, etc.). Blend the shellfish with a fairly thick normande sauce and fill the flan case with the mixture. Sprinkle with toasted breadcrumbs and a little melted butter and brown in a very hot oven.

Sweet Flans

Cherry flan FLAN AUX CERISES Line a flan ring with sweetened pastry and bake blind. Remove the stalks and stones (stems and pits) from 400 g (14 oz, scant 3 cups) black cherries (Bing cherries). Boil 3 dl (½ pint, 1¼ cups) milk with a vanilla pod (bean) split in two and then stir in 50 ml (2 fl oz, generous ¼ cup) double (heavy) cream. Beat 3 eggs with 100 g (4 oz, ⅔ cup) caster (superfine) sugar in a bowl, add the vanilla-flavoured milk, and whisk until the mixture has cooled completely. Place the cherries in the flan case and carefully pour the mixture over. Cook in the oven at 190 c (375 f, gas 5) for 35–40 minutes. Serve either lukewarm or cold, sprinkled with granulated sugar if desired.

Milk flan FLAN AU LAIT Prepare a flan case, but do not bake it. Mix together 100 g (4 oz, 1¼ cups) flour, 250 g (9 oz, generous 1 cup) caster (superfine) sugar, 6 eggs, 20 g (¾ oz, 1½ tablespoons) melted butter, a pinch of salt, and 1 tablespoon vanilla-flavoured sugar. Mix well and blend with 1 litre (1¾ pints, 4¼ cups) milk. Fill the flan case with the mixture and bake in a moderate oven (190 C, 375 F, gas 5) for about 20 minutes or until set.

Flanders FLANDRE

The cuisine of this northern province has much in common with that of the neighbouring provinces of Artois and Picardy. The North Sea provides maritime Flanders with an abundance of fish, particularly mackerel and herrings. Crops and vegetables of the interior include wheat, potatoes, endive (chicory), hops, and sugar beet. High-quality livestock is also important and includes pigs and sheep, and also dairy and beef cattle, whose meat is highly regarded. With all these resources, the cuisine of Flanders is a rich one – dishes are usually cooked slowly in a covered pan.

The most typical Flemish soups are beer soup, *soupe verte* (green soup), and beetroot (red beet) soup. Fish specialities include Dunkerque bloaters, *wam* (dried fish), mackerel stuffed with shallots, spring onions (scallions), parsley, and butter, cod *à la flamande* (sautéed with shallots and cooked in white wine), red herring salad (with potatoes and beetroot), and eels in beer.

Typical meat dishes include smoked tongues of Valenciennes, baby chitterlings (andouillettes) of Cambrai and Armentières, the traditional Flemish hotchpotch, carbonades, potjevfleisch, rabbit *à la flamande* (with prunes and raisins), *coq à la bière* (in beer), and *poule au blanc* (chicken in white stock).

Vegetables are used to make flamiches and also to make such specialities as red cabbage *à la lilloise* (cabbage, apples, and onions, simmered for three hours, reduced to a purée, and cooked briefly in the oven in a soufflé mould). The best-known cheeses, which all have a strong flavour, are Bergues, Mont-des-Cats, Coeur d'Arras, Boulette d'Avesnes, Dauphin, Vieux-Lille, and Maroilles. Omelettes and flamiches are made with Maroilles cheese, as is the goyère (Maroilles cheese tart) of Valenciennes.

The production of sugar from sugar beet has given rise to a variety of regional pastries and confectionery. The best known are the apple pies of Avesnes, plum tarts, craquelins of Roubaix, *carrés* of Lannoy, *galopins* (little oblongs of bread dipped in milk, mixed with eggs, and fried), couques, and the bêtises (mint humbugs) of Cambrai.

The local drink is beer, and good-quality spirits are distilled from beetroot or cereals, often flavoured with juniper berries.

flank BAVETTE

The abdominal muscles of beef, which form a second-category joint. Thick flank steaks cut perpendicularly from the internal muscles are lean, tasty, coarse-grained, and slightly tough (they must therefore be hung); they are eaten grilled (broiled) or sautéed. Thin flank is similar but slightly tougher. Cuts taken from the two external muscles give fibrous, rather tough, meat suitable for broths and stews.

RECIPES

Flank with shallots BAVETTE À L'ÉCHALOTTE Chop some shallots, allowing 1 level tablespoon chopped shallots for each steak. Fry the steaks quickly in butter, add the chopped shallots to the frying pan (skillet), and brown. Season with salt and pepper. Remove the steaks and deglaze the meat juices with vinegar (1 tablespoon per steak) and a little stock, then reduce. Pour the shallots and juice over the steaks.

Grilled (broiled) flank BAVETTE GRILLÉE Brush some steaks with oil, sprinkle with chopped herbs (fresh thyme and parsley), and grill (broil) quickly for 7–8 minutes. Season with salt and pepper at the end of cooking.

flan ring

See *tart or flan ring*.

flaquer

The French word meaning to slit a fish along its back in order to remove the backbone. It is usually used for round fish such as trout.

flaugnarde, flangnarde, flognarde, or flougnarde

A flan made in the Auvergne, Limousin, and Périgord regions of France. The name is derived from the Old French *fleugne*, meaning soft or downy. The flan resembles clafoutis and is made with apples, pears, or prunes, flavoured with cinnamon, vanilla, rum, brandy, orange-flower water, lemon rind, etc. It resembles a large pancake and is served either lukewarm or cold (Curnonsky recommended the latter), generously sprinkled with icing (confectioners') sugar, and sometimes spread with jam.

| RECIPE

Flaugnarde Beat 4 whole eggs with 100 g (4 oz, 8 tablespoons, firmly packed) sugar in a bowl until the mixture is light and frothy. Gradually add 100 g (4 oz, 1 cup) flour and a pinch of salt. Slowly beat in 1.5 litres (2¾ pints, 7 cups) milk. Mix well, then flavour with 1 dl (6 tablespoons, scant ½ cup) rum or orange-flower water. Peel and core 3 pears, cut them into thin slices, and add them to the mixture. Butter an ovenproof dish, pour in the mixture, and dot the surface with small pieces of butter. Bake in a hot oven (220 c, 425 f, gas 7) for 30 minutes. Serve hot or cold.

flavour SAVEUR

The sensation produced when food comes into contact with the taste buds on the tongue. There are four basic tastes – sweet, salty, sour, and bitter – which are detected by taste buds on different parts of the tongue. The particular flavour of a dish comes from the combination of several of these basic tastes: when one predominates, the dish is described as sweet, salty, sour, or bitter.

Extreme temperatures (very hot or very cold) temporarily numb the sense of taste. When flavours are mixed, they can mask each other or bring each other out. Salt masks the sweetening power of sugar, but a pinch of salt in a sweet dish (especially in pastries and doughs) makes it seem sweeter. A little sugar added to some savoury foods (peas, tomatoes, sauces, etc.) enhances their flavour. A contrasting taste will modify the flavour of a food-stuff; for example, fruit tastes sour after a sweet dish and sweet after cheese or a spiced dish. The skilful cook combines contrasting or similar flavours to produce a harmonious whole, the flavours being enhanced by the texture, consistency, colour, and temperature of the dish.

flavouring PARFUM

A substance added to a preparation to improve its flavour. Before the 18th century, it was customary to use exotic flavourings which are today usually reserved for perfumery, such as essence of rose and other flowers, benzoin, amber, musk, etc. Today, the herbs and spices commonly used for flavouring include thyme, bay, savory, coriander, cinnamon, cumin, aniseed, pepper, and ginger. Orange-flower water, almond essence, vanilla, and zest of citrus fruits are used for flavouring cakes, pastries, and confectionery.

Wines, fortified wines (Madeira, Frontignan, port, sherry, etc.), spirits, and brandies are used extensively for flavouring sauces and gravies and for enhancing the taste of game stews, salmis, shellfish *à la bordelaise* or *à l'américaine*, and flamed meat and poultry dishes. A variety of extracts, essences, and fumets are also used. Other methods of flavouring include steam-cooking with aromatic plants, smoking with specially scented wood, and macerating with spices.

fleur de lys

The French name for a vegetable used in Chinese cooking. The plant's Chinese name can be translated as 'golden needle', and its appearance is reminiscent of the fleur de lys motif in heraldry (hence its French name). It is a kind of bulb which is cooked in sugar. Its long filaments, often sold dried, are used in the preparation of many sweet and savoury dishes (soups, omelettes, sweet soups, ragouts, and salads).

Fleurie

One of the nine Beaujolais regions distinguished by an AOC. Charming and fruity, the wines are sometimes associated with the 'floweriness' of the place name. They are usually at their best when drunk young.

fleuriste (à la)

Describing a preparation of small cuts of sautéed meat garnished with château potatoes and tomatoes. The latter are hollowed out, slowly baked, and filled with a jardinière of vegetables mixed with butter.

fleuron

A small puff-pastry shape used to garnish pie crusts or served with dishes of fish cooked in sauce. Fleurons are cut into crescents or other shapes from the leftover pastry trimmings, rolled out very thinly. They are then brushed with beaten egg and baked or fried.

flip

Formerly, a flip was a hot alcoholic drink made with beer, rum, and beaten eggs. Today it is usually a cold cocktail made with wine or spirits mixed with beaten eggs, sugar, nutmeg, and various flavourings. The best-known is the port flip.

floating islands
OEUFS À LA NEIGE

A cold dessert consisting of a light egg custard topped with egg whites that have been stiffly whisked with sugar, shaped with a tablespoon, and poached either in boiling water or in the milk used to make the custard. In the latter case, the dish is more difficult to make successfully and the whites are not as meltingly soft. Floating islands are served sprinkled with pale caramel or crushed praline.

RECIPE

Floating islands OEUFS À LA NEIGE Boil 8 dl (generous 1¼ pints, 1½ pints) milk with a vanilla pod (bean) or 1 teaspoon vanilla sugar. Whisk 8 egg whites to stiff peaks with a pinch of salt, then fold in 40 g (1½ oz, 3 tablespoons, firmly packed) sugar. Using a tablespoon, drop portions of the whisked egg whites into the boiling milk. Turn the whites so that they are cooked all over. Remove after 2 minutes and drain on a cloth. Make an egg custard with the same milk, the 8 egg yolks, and 250 g (9 oz, generous 1 cup, firmly packed) sugar. When completely cold, pour the custard into a deep dish, place the cooked egg whites on top, and chill until ready to serve.

flône

A tartlet from Rouergue filled with a cream made from eggs and ewes'-milk whey flavoured with orange-flower water. At Lodève in Languedoc, they are known as *flaunes* or *flauzonnes* and are prepared from flour, eggs, grated ewes'-milk cheese, and orange-flower water. Spoonfuls of this paste are dropped onto a greased baking sheet and baked in the oven until light golden brown.

florentine (à la)

A method of preparation used mainly for fish, white meat, or eggs in which spinach (and usually Mornay sauce) are included. The connection between the city of Florence and spinach is not known and seems strange, as the vegetable is consumed throughout Italy.

In Italy the term *alla fiorentina* is used for dishes that are typically Florentine, such as tripe cooked in chicken stock, garnished with green vegetables, and served with Parmesan cheese, or saddle of pork simmered with spices, or omelette with artichoke hearts, or *bistecca alla fiorentina*, a beefsteak that is marinated before being grilled.

RECIPES

Fritters à la florentine BEIGNETS À LA FLORENTINE Prepare 250 g (9 oz) spinach purée and dry it out gently over the heat, turning it with a wooden spoon. Mix the purée with 2 dl (7 fl oz, ¾ cup) well-reduced béchamel sauce and blend in 50 g (2 oz, ½ cup) grated Gruyère cheese. Cool the mixture completely and divide it into about 15 portions. Roll each portion in flour, dip into a prepared batter, and deep-fry in oil, heated to 180 C (350 F), until golden brown. Drain on absorbent paper, sprinkle with salt, and serve very hot.

Soft-boiled (*or poached*) **eggs à la florentine** OEUFS MOLLETS (OU POCHÉS) À LA FLORENTINE Slowly cook some spinach in butter and drain well. Butter some small ramekin or soufflé dishes and place some spinach in each, making hollows to hold 2 soft-boiled (soft-cooked) or poached eggs. Coat the eggs with Mornay sauce, sprinkle with grated cheese, and brown under a hot grill (broiler).

Suprêmes of chicken à la florentine
SUPRÊMES DE VOLAILLE À LA FLORENTINE Season some suprêmes of chicken or young turkey with salt and pepper and brush with melted butter. Melt some butter in a pan, add the suprêmes, and flavour with a little lemon juice. Cover the pan and place it in the oven at 220 c (425 f, gas 7). Cook for 12–15 minutes. Cook some spinach slowly in butter and spread it over a dish. Arrange the suprêmes on top, coat with Mornay sauce, sprinkle with grated cheese and melted butter, and brown in a very hot oven.

Florian

A garnish for large joints of meat made with braised lettuce, small glazed onions, shaped glazed carrots, and potato fondantes (small croquettes).

flounder FLET

A flatfish that is often found in estuaries, although it is actually a sea fish. The European species, *Platichthys flesus*, has a greenish or brownish mottled skin covered with tiny scales and can be up to 50 cm (20 in) long.

In France, the flounder is sometimes known as *flandre* (or *flondre*) *de rivière* or *de picard*. In former times, it was incorrectly called *fléton*, which means halibut.

In northern Europe, especially in Norway, flounders are preserved by drying and smoking. Recipes for turbot, brill, dab, and plaice are suitable for flounders. In American cuisine, the word flounder is used for a larger variety of flatfish than in Europe.

flour FARINE

Finely ground cereal, such as wheat, barley, oats, rye, rice, and maize (corn). In Britain, the word 'flour' usually refers to flour produced from wheat. The milling of grain dates back to prehistoric times, and over thousands of years this has developed into an important and highly automated industry. There is evidence that wheat or corn was crushed and used as food at least 6000 years ago. The pounding stones used for this purpose have been discovered in archaeological digs throughout Europe.

The Romans were the first to apply rotary motion to milling. This involved grinding the grain between circular stones, one rotating and the other stationary. The domestic quern mills were turned by hand; the larger mills by slaves or donkeys. The milled flour was sifted through a boulting bag of linen or rushes, which separated the white flour from the bran and wheatgerm.

The water wheel came to Britain from Rome. The earliest were laid horizontally in the water; later they were vertically set. Windmills first appeared about 1200 and were widely used until the Industrial Revolution. After this, steel roller mills were introduced from Hungary. These produced finer flours as we know them today and roller milling is still the system used in all large commercial mills.

The wheat grain is composed of three parts: endosperm, germ or embryo, and bran. The object of milling is to separate the endosperm from the bran and germ, because white flour is derived from the endosperm, which generally comprises 85% of the grain (compared with 2% germ and 14% bran). Today wheat is cleaned before milling, foreign matter being removed on the basis of shape, size, and density. After this the wheat is moistened and allowed to 'temper', a process which toughens the bran and makes separation more complete.

Wheat grains are initially ground on break (or fluted) rolls that are designed to shear open the grains and release the endosperm. The ground material is then sieved; the bran flakes with endosperm still attached to them are reground by finer break rolls, and large endosperm pieces are sent to purifiers which remove small bran particles using air currents. The purified endosperm pieces (semolina) are then ground on mat-surface rolls (reduction rolls) to produce flour. A number of reduction passages are required to convert the semolina into flour. Flour is removed from the sifters at various stages throughout the milling process. These various machine flours are blended to produce a range of flours to meet bakery specifications. Wheatgerm is removed during the milling of wheat into white flour and is sold separately.

Hard milling wheats mill easily to give high yields of granular free-flowing flour, whereas soft milling wheats produce fine flours of poor sieving and packing qualities.

In Britain, white flours are fortified by the addition of vitamins and minerals and may be bleached to remove yellow endosperm colour.

Flours of different properties are required for different commercial baked products. Bread flour is of high protein content with good gluten strength and high water-holding capacity. Biscuit flours are mainly produced from soft wheats with low protein content and weak glutens.

Wholemeal flour is made from the whole wheat; it is becoming increasingly popular with trends towards high-fibre diets.

flouring

FARINER, FLEURER

The process of lightly covering an item of food with flour, or sprinkling a mould, cake tin, etc., or a work surface with flour. Items of food are often floured before frying or sautéing; the excess flour can be removed by shaking or tapping. Flouring should not be done too far in advance as the flour should be dry. Foods may also be floured before being coated with egg and breadcrumbs. Finally, items of sautéed meat or poultry may be floured after being browned as a method of thickening a ragout or casserole (the French word for this process is *singer*).

A work surface or a pastry board is floured before the dough is rolled out to prevent it from sticking. Some baking tins and sheets need to be floured lightly before mixtures are poured in or before being lined with pastry. The tin, tray, etc., is usually greased beforehand. This makes it easier to turn out the item after cooking or to prevent a mixture from spreading out too much on a baking tray when cooking begins.

In bakery, *bannetons* (wicker moulds lined with cloth) are dusted with a special rye flour: this process is known as *fleurage*.

floutes

See *pflutters*.

flower FLEUR

Throughout history, flowers have always been used in cookery. The Romans used them to flavour certain dishes – the recipes of Apicius include brains with rose petals, sweet marjoram flowers in various hashes, and a sauce with safflower petals – and Roman wines were flavoured with roses or violets. Today flowers are used mostly in oriental cookery – dried rose buds are used as a condiment, jam is made from rose petals, salads incorporate chrysanthemum, nasturtium, or marigold petals, jasmine and hibiscus flowers flavour poultry and fish dishes, and yellow lilies provide seasoning for sauces and stocks.

In Europe, flowers are mostly used in aromatic drinks but also in wines and spirits (elderflower wine, hyssop syrup, and pink ratafia). Some well-known spices and flavourings are made from flowers and buds, notably cloves, capers, nasturtium flowers in vinegar, and orange-flower water.

Several chefs have invented recipes that include flowers, either as an ingredient or as decoration. Jules Maincave, a great French chef at the beginning of this century, declared that seasonings were 'pitifully limited, whereas the progress of modern chemistry would enable us to use rose, lilac, and lily-of-the-valley'. Alexandre Dumas suggested a recipe for herb soup *à la dauphine* containing marigold flowers. Usually flowers are added to soups at the end of cooking. In salads they obviously play a more decorative role, particularly nasturtium but also red poppy, borage, violet, and honeysuckle. They can be arranged in a crown or in bunches, and the colours are used to match or complement the colours of the other ingredients. Vinegar changes the colour of flowers, and if they are to be used in a salad with a vinaigrette dressing they must be added at the last moment and the salad must not be tossed until it is time to serve. Certain flowers are especially suitable for fritters, especially those of the mimosa, gourd, elder, and jasmine. Pumpkin flowers can be eaten stuffed and are also used to garnish omelettes. Flavoured butters are seasoned with the petals of jasmine, orange, lemon, or garlic flowers. Flowering mint is suitable for fish, together with lime and jasmine flowers. The latter may also be used in various forcemeats. Aromatic infusions are also made from flowers and may be drunk or used in certain steamed dishes. Wild violets complement the taste of beef, savory flowers complement veal, sage is used with pork, and mint and thyme with mutton.

Flowers have always been used in confectionery, for example in rosewater jellies, rose jam, crystallized (candied) violets, mimosa, forget-me-not, and primula, and praline-flavoured orange blossom. These sweet delicacies and decorations were very popular in France at the time of the Second Empire.

flûte

A long thin French roll, weighing about 100 g (4 oz), midway between a baguette and a ficelle in size. Flûtes are usually split in half and grilled (broiled) for croûtes, served with soups and broths.

flute glass FLÛTE

A glass with a stem and a narrow body, for serving champagne and other sparkling wines. The narrow body (as opposed to a wide one) enables the wine to keep its sparkle, as the gas bubbles are not released so quickly.

In France, a flûte is also a tall thin bottle used traditionally for white Alsace wines.

fluting CANNELER

The technique of making V-shaped grooves over the surface of a purée, cream, or mousse, using a spatula. Pieces of pastry are described as fluted when they have been cut out with a serrated pastry (cookie) cutter. A toothed piping nozzle is also described as fluted.

flying fish EXOCET

A small fish, 18–25 cm (7–10 in) long, common in warm and tropical seas. It has a blue back and a silvery belly and its pectoral fins are winglike, enabling it to glide above the surface of the water. It

is often fished in the Caribbean islands; its tasty flesh is prepared like mackerel.

foie gras

Goose or duck liver which is grossly enlarged by methodically fattening the bird. The cramming (force-feeding) of geese was done as early as Roman times (the Romans used figs for this). As soon as the bird was slaughtered, the liver was plunged into a bath of milk and honey, which made it swell as well as flavouring it. Nowadays the birds are fattened with maize (corn); each liver weighs 700–900 g (1½–2 lb) for geese (the record is 2 kg, 4½ lb), 300–400 g (11–14 oz) for ducks.

Foie gras from Toulouse geese is ivory-white and creamy; that from Strasbourg geese pinker and firmer. It is a highly prized delicacy, yet opinions vary as to its suitability for culinary preparation in comparison with duck foie gras, which is also delicate (but slightly darker in colour than goose liver) but melts and breaks down more during cooking and has a slightly more pronounced flavour. André Daguin, a leading chef of Auch, many of whose recipes are given below, prefers duck foie gras. France also imports foies gras from Austria, Czechoslovakia, Hungary, Israel, and Luxembourg, as demand exceeds French production.

Charles Gérard, in *L'Ancienne Alsace à table*, wrote: 'The goose is nothing, but man has made of it an instrument for the output of a marvellous product, a kind of living hothouse in which there grows the supreme fruit of gastronomy.' Foie gras is available in four forms in France.

• Raw foie gras (*foie gras cru*), increasingly in demand, is sold during the holiday season at the end of the year. It must be well-lobed, smooth, and round, not too large (so that not all its fat is rendered down in the cooking process), and putty-coloured (if yellowish, it has a tendency to be grainy). Its preparation and cooking must be meticulous, and are only worthwhile for fine-quality livers.

• Fresh foie gras (*foie gras frais*) can be purchased cooked from a delicatessen, usually in pots. It will keep at the most for a week covered in the refrigerator.

• Semi-cooked pasteurized foie gras

(*foie gras mi-cuit pasteurisé*) in cans will keep for three months in the refrigerator once opened. It retains the taste of fresh foie gras quite well, and its manufacture is governed by very strict regulations. The best quality must have a perfect consistency, aroma, and flavour, and must not exude fat. The labels 'foie gras d'oie entier' (whole goose foie gras), 'foie gras d'oie entier truffé' (whole goose foie gras prepared with truffles), 'foie gras de canard entier' (whole duck foie gras), and 'foie gras de canard entier truffé' (whole duck foie gras prepared with truffles) apply to pure whole livers (formerly labelled 'foie gras au naturel'). Goose or duck 'parfait de foie gras', with or without truffles, is a liver reconstituted from small pieces (formerly labelled 'bloc de foie gras'). 'Pâté de foie d'oie truffé' (goose-liver pâté with truffles) is a whole goose liver coated with forcemeat (formerly called 'parfait de foie d'oie truffé'). The labels 'délice', 'lingot', 'suprême', 'timbale', 'roulade', and 'tombeau' designate products coated with forcemeat, or barding, or both (with a minimum of 20% foie gras). When the foie gras is referred to as 'truffé', with no other indication, it contains at least 3% truffles.

• Preserved foie gras (*foie gras de conserve*) in jars is the most traditional preparation. Sterilized and preserved in its own fat, it will keep for years in a cool dark dry place and improves like wine.

In addition to the labels for semicooked foie gras, there is also the label 'purée de foie d'oie' (goose-liver purée). This contains 50–75% finely pounded goose liver, and the term replaces the former 'mousse'. Foie gras yields 700 Cal per 100 g.

□ **Tradition and innovation** Whether from the goose or the duck, foie gras has always been considered a rare delicacy, but the way in which it is served has changed according to culinary fashion. At one time it was served at the end of the meal. The traditional truffle and aspic accompaniments are now thought to be superfluous by some, who prefer to serve it with farmhouse bread (leavened and slightly acid) which has been lightly toasted, rather than with plain slices of toast. Nouvelle cuisine sets as much store by foie gras as classic

cuisine, and sometimes gives it novel accompaniments, such as green leeks, pumpkin, or even scallops. However, the classic recipes, both hot and cold, still retain their prestige.

Most dishes described as *à la périgourdine* or *Rossini* are prepared with foie gras.

RECIPES

Preparation of raw foie gras PRÉPARATION DU FOIE GRAS CRU (from a recipe of Roger Lamazère) Carefully remove all the tubes and skin from the liver, using the point of a thin-bladed knife. First make an incision in each lobe starting from the larger end, where the main vein is located. Separate it. Still using the knife, pull on the vein. It will come away by itself, showing the rest of the network, which can then be easily removed. Once the lobes are open, season them with fine salt (6 g (½ teaspoon) per lb) and freshly ground pepper (2 g (⅓ teaspoon) per lb). Close up each lobe, wrapping it tightly in muslin (cheesecloth), and refrigerate overnight.

The next day, place the liver in a terrine, cover it with goose fat, and poach it (allow 4 minutes per 100 g (4 oz) foie gras when the fat starts to simmer). When it is cooked, cool and drain the liver on a wire cooling tray, then refrigerate for at least 24 hours. Remove the muslin before serving the foie gras cold, possibly with a hot truffle cooked *en papillote*.

The taste of the liver can be enhanced by marinating it for 48 hours in port mixed with 10% Armagnac.

DUCK FOIE GRAS

Cold duck (*or goose*) foie gras escalopes with grapes and truffles ESCALOPES FROIDES DE FOIE GRAS DE CANARD (OU D'OIE) AU RAISIN ET AUX TRUFFES Prepare the raw liver and cook as described in the basic preparation above. Cut the liver into equal-sized slices. On each of these escalopes place 1 large slice of truffle dipped in aspic jelly, leave to set, then glaze the whole escalope with aspic. Arrange the escalopes in a crown shape in a shallow glass bowl. In the middle of the crown, heap a dome of fresh peeled seeded grapes which have been steeped in a little liqueur brandy. Coat everything lightly with clear port-flavoured aspic. Cover and then chill in the refrigerator well before serving.

duck foie gras with banana purée and truffles FOIE GRAS DE CANARD À LA PURÉE DE BANANES TRUFFÉE (from a recipe by Jean Laustrait) Prepare a foie gras weighing about 400 g (14 oz) in the usual way, then leave to swell in very cold milk for 24 hours. Cut the liver into slices 1 cm (½ in) thick. Rub 6 peeled bananas through a sieve (or blend in a food processor) and gently reduce the resulting purée over a low heat, carefully stirring all the time. Make a light hollandaise sauce with 3 egg yolks and 300 g (11 oz, 1½ cups) clarified butter, then add the banana purée and a few chopped truffles to the sauce. Fry the liver slices in very hot butter for 1 minute on each side. Arrange the slices on the serving dish and surround with the banana purée.

Duck foie gras with oysters and crayfish FOIE GRAS DE CANARD AUX HUÎTRES ET AUX ÉCREVISSES (from a recipe by Gérard Vié) Put the following through a blender: 150 g (5 oz) raw duck foie gras, ¼ litre (8 fl oz, 1 cup) milk, 4 whole eggs, salt and pepper, and 50 g (2 oz) hot beef marrow poached in stock. Put this mixture into some ramekins and bake in a very slow oven (140 c, 275 F, gas 1) for about 25 minutes. Leave for 5 minutes, then turn out. Place 2 poached shelled oysters and 2 boiled crayfish on each plate. Coat with white butter sauce flavoured with Monbazillac (a sweet white wine).

Duck foie gras with white pepper and green leeks FOIE GRAS DE CANARD AU POIVRE BLANC ET AU VERT DE POIREAU (from André Daguin's recipe). Prepare a foie gras weighing 300–400 g (11–14 oz) in the usual way. Boil some young green leeks in salted water and purée them with a little cream. Put this purée in a small greased cake tin. Season the foie gras with salt and ground pepper (not too fine) and arrange it on the leek purée. Cover the tin with aluminium foil and bake in the

oven at about 140 c (275 F, gas 1) for 35 minutes. Leave to cool for 45 minutes (the last 15 minutes in the refrigerator).

Duck (*or goose*) foie gras mousse MOUSSE DE FOIE GRAS DE CANARD OU D'OIE Rub a cooked foie gras through a fine sieve, and place the purée in a bowl. For each litre (1¾ pints, generous quart) purée, add 2.5 dl (8 fl oz, 1 cup) melted aspic jelly and 4 dl (14 fl oz, 1¾ cups) chicken velouté sauce. Beat the mixture lightly over ice. Season, then add 4 dl (14 fl oz, 1¾ cups) partly whipped double (heavy) cream. Line a round mould with aspic jelly and garnish with slices of truffle, the thinly sliced whites of hard-boiled (hard-cooked) eggs, and tarragon leaves. Then fill with the mousse up to 1.5 cm (¾ in) from the top. Cover the mousse with a layer of aspic jelly, allow to cool, and chill in the refrigerator.

Turn out the mousse onto a serving dish, or a buttered crouton, and surround it with chopped aspic jelly. The foie gras mousse can also be served in a silver dish or a crystal bowl at the bottom of which a layer of aspic jelly has been left to set. Smooth the top of the mousse, which should be slightly dome-shaped. Garnish with slices of truffle and glaze lightly with any remaining aspic jelly.

Foie gras fritters à l'ancienne BEIGNETS DE FOIE GRAS À L'ANCIENNE Coat some thin savoury pancakes (see *crêpe*) with duck foie gras purée mixed with some diced truffles and some good-quality champagne for flavouring. Roll them up, folding in the ends, and divide into 2 or 3 pieces. Dip them in light batter and fry them in a good-quality hot oil (about 180 c, 350 F).

This recipe can also be prepared using goose foie gras which is not good enough to be prepared *au naturel*.

Glazed duck foie gras FOIE GRAS DE CANARD GLACÉ (from a recipe by Claude Peyrot) Season a fine duck foie gras with salt and pepper, then marinate it in port for at least 24 hours. Draw a 2.5-kg (5½-lb) duck through the neck, remove the breastbone, and open out the tail end. Put the liver into the duck, and truss it up. Oil the duck and cook in a covered casserole in the oven at 200 c (400 f, gas 6) for 1 hour 20 minutes. While the duck is cooking, prick the skin frequently with a fork so that it does not burst. Remove from the casserole and leave to cool. Add to the pan juices the port marinade and some aspic jelly made with the duck's giblets. Clarify. Glaze the duck with this clarified aspic and refrigerate.

Poach some prunes in water, some cherries in a red-wine jelly, and some apple quarters in butter. Flavour all these fruits with ginger and glaze with the remaining duck aspic. Stuff some stoned (pitted) green olives with foie gras or ham mousse. Peel the segments of a large orange. Arrange the duck in the serving dish with all the fruits, making the orange segments into a rosette.

Hot duck (*or goose*) foie gras escalopes with grapes ESCALOPES CHAUDES DE FOIE GRAS DE CANARD (OU D'OIE) AU RAISIN Trim the raw liver and remove the tubes. Slice it into escalopes (slices). Fry these in very hot butter, drain them, arrange each one on an oval piece of bread fried in butter, and garnish with large peeled and seeded grapes. Deglaze the frying pan with Frontignan or another heavy wine, and reduce. Add a few spoonfuls of thickened veal stock, and reduce again. Coat the escalopes with this sauce.

Preserved potted duck (*or goose*) foie gras in goose fat CONSERVE DE FOIE GRAS DE CANARD (OU D'OIE) AU NATUREL EN TERRINE Trim the liver, season with spiced salt, and steep in brandy for about 6 hours. Wipe dry and poach very gently in clarified goose fat (5 minutes per 100 g, 4 oz liver). Drain the liver, place it in a terrine just large enough to hold it, cover with the strained fat used in the cooking process, and leave it to cool completely. Pour a thin layer of melted lard over the goose fat. Cool again completely. Adjust the lid of the terrine and stick some masking tape along the join or melt down some special wax or cooking lard between the lid and the terrine to make it airtight. Place the terrine in a cool dry place. The foie gras will keep for several weeks if prepared in this way.

Steamed duck foie gras with Sauternes FOIE GRAS DE CANARD À LA VAPEUR AU FUMET DE SAUTERNES (from a recipe of Gérard Vié) Prepare some stock with duck bones, 1 bottle of Sauternes, and 2 carrots, 1 turnip, 2 sticks (stalks) of celery, 2 shallots, and the white part of a leek (all sliced). Season with salt and pepper. Trim the foie gras and remove the tubes, season with salt and pepper, and refrigerate (with the strained stock) for 24 hours. Pour the stock into a steamer, place the foie gras in the steamer basket, and cook for about 15 minutes. Cut the foie gras into slices, pour over a little of the stock, and serve hot or cold.

GOOSE FOIE GRAS

Baked foie gras FOIE GRAS AU FOUR (from Raymond Oliver's recipe) Prepare a foie gras weighing about 600 g (1¼ lb), season it with coarse salt, and keep in a cool place for 24 hours. Wash the liver, wipe it, and marinate for 48 hours with ground paprika, spices, and Armagnac brandy. Drain the liver, place it in an ovenproof dish, and half-fill the dish with melted goose fat. Bake in the oven at 190 c (375 f, gas 5), turning it over while cooking, for about 15 minutes per lb. To see if it is done, pierce with a skewer: the drop of juice which appears should be only just pink.

baked potatoes with raw goose foie gras POMMES DE TERRE AU FOUR AU FOIE D'OIE CRU (from a recipe by Gérard Vié) Bake 2 large potatoes in their skins in the oven. Cut them in half while they are still hot. On top of each one, place a thin slice of raw foie gras (trimmed and with the tubes removed). Season with a little salt and some pepper.

Foie gras en brioche (*hot*) FOIE GRAS EN BRIOCHE (CHAUD) Soak a pig's caul in cold water, then prepare some unsweetened brioche dough. Take a firm foie gras weighing 700–900 g (1½ –2 lb) and stud it with truffles, which have been seasoned and moistened with brandy. Then season the foie gras itself with spiced salt, moisten it with brandy, and leave to marinate for a few hours. Drain the pig's caul, wipe it dry, and wrap the foie gras in it. Gently cook in a moderately hot oven (190 C, 375 F, gas 5) for 18–20 minutes, then leave to cool.

Line the bottom of a plain greased timbale mould with a fairly thick layer of brioche dough, then add the liver and cover it with another, thinner, layer of dough. Cover the mould with a piece of buttered greaseproof (waxed) paper, and tie with string to prevent the dough from spilling out when cooking. Leave the dough to rise for 2 hours in a warm place, then bake in a moderately hot oven (200 C, 400 F, gas 6) for 50–60 minutes. To see if the brioche is done, pierce with a needle, which should come out clean. Turn out the brioche and serve.

Goose foie gras with sultanas FOIE GRAS D'OIE AUX RAISINS (from a recipe of Raymond Oliver) Prepare a foie gras weighing about 600 g (1¼ lb) in the usual way. Cook in a saucepan over a gentle heat for 5–6 minutes, drain, and remove the fat. Chop 1 peeled onion, fry in goose fat, sprinkle with a little flour, then add the liver cooking juices, a little white wine, 1 chopped tomato, a bouquet garni, and some stock. Cook for 30 minutes, then strain. Put the liver in a heavy-bottomed casserole with this sauce, add some sultanas which have been soaked in warm Madeira until swollen, and leave to simmer for 20 minutes. Serve with croutons fried in goose fat and drain well.

Potted foie gras with truffles TERRINE DE FOIE GRAS AUX TRUFFES Remove the tubes from a goose foie gras, and divide it in half. Trim the lobes, and reserve the trimmings. Stud the liver with pieces of truffle. Season with spiced salt, pour over some brandy, and leave to marinate for 5–6 hours. Prepare a forcemeat made of 375 g (13 oz, 1½ cups) lean pork meat, 475 g (17 oz, 2 cups) fresh pork fat, the foie gras trimmings, 150 g (5 oz, 1 cup) diced truffles, ½ dl (3 tablespoons, scant ¼ cup) Madeira, and 25 g (1 oz) spiced salt.

Line the bottom and sides of an oval terrine or ovenproof dish with thin slices of pork fat, then cover the inside with a thin layer of the forcemeat. Place half the foie gras on top of the forcemeat

and press down. Cover with another layer of forcemeat, then place the other half of the foie gras on top. Finish with the rest of the forcemeat. Cover with a thin slice of pork fat. Press well to flatten the ingredients and place half a bay leaf and a sprig of thyme on top. Cover the terrine, seal the lid with a flour-and-water (lute) paste, and place in a bain-marie. Bring to the boil, then place in a moderate oven (about 180 C, 350 F, gas 4) and bake for 1¼–1½ hours, depending on the size of the terrine.

Cool, uncover, then leave under a light weight until the next day. Turn out the potted foie gras by putting the dish in hot water for a few seconds. Remove the pork fat and dry the top of the foie gras with a cloth, pressing down a little to firm it. Pour a thin layer of lard mixed with goose fat (rendered during cooking) over the bottom of the terrine and leave it to set. Replace the foie gras in the terrine and pour some more lard and goose fat mixture (just warm) over the top. Refrigerate for at least 12 hours and serve in the terrine.

Truffled pâté de foie gras PÂTÉ DE FOIE GRAS TRUFFÉ Prepare 1 kg (2¼ lb) pâté pastry dough (made with butter or lard) and leave to rest for 12 hours. Prepare 2 firm foies gras in the usual way. Stud the lobes with peeled truffles cut into sticks, seasoned with spiced salt, and moistened with brandy. Season the livers well. Soak them in brandy and Madeira for 2 hours. Prepare 1 kg (2¼ lb) pork and foie gras forcemeat.

Line a hinged pâté mould (round or oval) with some of the dough, then spread a layer of forcemeat over the bottom and sides of the mould. Put the foie gras into the mould, pressing it well. Cover with a domed layer of forcemeat. On top of this lay a slice of pork fat, half a bay leaf, and a small sprig of thyme. Cover the pâté with a layer of dough and seal the edges. Garnish the top with decorative pastry motifs shaped with pastry (cookie) cutters (lozenges, leaves, crescents, etc.) or strips of plaited dough. In the middle put 3 or 4 round pieces of dough shaped with a fluted pastry cutter. Make a hole in the middle of these for the escape of steam during baking. Brush with egg. Bake in a fairly hot oven (190–200 C, 375–400 F, gas 5

–6) until the dough is cooked thoroughly and golden brown.

Cool. When it is lukewarm pour into it either half-melted lard (if it is to be kept for some time) or Madeira-flavoured aspic (if it is to be used at once).

Pâté de foie gras must be made at least 12 hours before using. The mould can be lined with a forcemeat made entirely of foie gras instead of with pork and foie gras forcemeat.

fond

See *stock*.

fondant

Sugar syrup containing glucose, cooked to the 'soft ball' stage, then worked with a spatula until it becomes a thick opaque paste. This is then kneaded by hand until smooth, soft, and white. It can also be bought ready made. Fondant keeps well in an airtight sealed container.

Coloured and flavoured fondant is used in confectionery, to fill chocolates and sweets. When heated in a bain-marie with a little water, light syrup, or alcohol, it can be used to coat marzipan, fresh or dried fruits, and brandied cherries. Diluted in this way and flavoured with chocolate, coffee, lemon, etc., it can also be used to ice cakes and pastries.

RECIPE

Fondant icing GLACE AU FONDANT Put the following ingredients in a thick-bottomed saucepan: 2 kg (4¼ lb) lump sugar, 80 g (3 oz, 6 tablespoons) glucose, and 1.2 dl (6 tablespoons, ½ cup) water. Cook over a high heat, skimming regularly. Take the pan off the heat when the sugar reaches the 'soft ball' stage, at about 118 c, 245 f (see *sugar*). Oil a marble slab, pour the sugar mixture over it, and allow to cool until just warm. Working with a metal spatula, alternately spread out and scrape up the fondant until the mixture is uniformly smooth and white. Place in a bowl, cover, and keep cool. When it is needed, heat the fondant gently in a small saucepan and add a little syrup cooked to the 'short thread' stage (101.5 c, 215 f) and the selected flavouring (coffee liqueur,

essence, or extract or melted chocolate). Alternatively, add a few drops of edible food colouring.

fond de pâtisserie

A French term meaning a sweet base or shell used for a gâteau or dessert. It may be made of shortcrust pastry (basic pie dough), flan pastry, puff pastry, Genoese sponge, meringue, or various biscuit (cookie) mixtures. In the catering trade, the *fonds* are prepared in advance and filled, decorated, mounted into set pieces, or iced (frosted) when required.

RECIPES

Pearl fond FOND PERLÉ Whisk 350 g (12 oz) egg whites (10–12 whites, depending on the size) into very stiff peaks with a pinch of salt. Mix together 250 g (9 oz, 2 generous cups) ground almonds and 250 g (9 oz, 1 generous cup) caster (superfine) sugar, and carefully fold in the whisked egg whites. Place a hot flan ring on a greased and floured baking sheet and fill with the mixture. Spread evenly with a spoon and dust with icing sugar (confectioners' sugar). Remove the flan ring and bake the base in the oven at about 180 c (350 f, gas 4) until just dried out, crisp, and light golden brown.

Walnut or **hazelnut fond** FOND NOIX OU NOISETTES Crush 250 g (9 oz, 2 cups) walnuts or unblanched hazelnuts, add 250 g (9 oz, 1 generous cup) caster (superfine) sugar, and mix together. Work into this mixture 450 g (1 lb) egg yolks (12–13 yolks, depending on the size) and 100 g (4 oz, 8 tablespoons) butter softened with a wooden spatula. Mix in 125 g (4½ oz, 1 cup) potato starch or cornflour (cornstarch) and then carefully fold in 350 g (12 oz) egg whites (10–12 whites), which have been whisked into stiff peaks with a pinch of salt. Spread the mixture on lightly greased and floured baking sheets (it can be used for large gâteaux or small individual cakes) and bake in the oven at 180 c (350 f, gas 4) until light golden brown.

fondre

A French culinary term meaning to cook certain vegetables in a covered pan in a little fat but no other liquid apart from their natural moisture. The contents of the pan should be stirred regularly to prevent them from sticking. This method is also used to prepare potato fondantes.

fondu creusois

A Limousin speciality made of cows'-milk cheese melted over a low heat in a saucepan with water and milk. Fresh butter and egg yolks are added, plus salt and pepper. This fondu (which must be smooth and even-textured) is served with French fried potatoes, which are dipped one by one into the pan. Alternatively it can be poured over potato purée and browned under a hot grill (broiler).

fondue

A Swiss speciality consisting of one or more cheeses melted in a special pottery fondue dish with white wine and flavouring. When the mixture becomes creamy, the dish is placed over a spirit lamp on the table to keep it hot. The diners spear pieces of bread on a long two-pronged fork, dip them in the fondue, and eat them piping hot.

The fondue recipe which Brillat-Savarin gives in his *Physiologie du goût* is in fact a dish of scrambled eggs with cheese. However, there are several Savoy and Swiss recipes that may be considered authentic. Androuet, in *La Cuisine au fromage*, mentions several. *Fondue comtoise* is made with mature full-flavoured Comté cheese, semi-matured Comté cheese, dry white wine, Kirsch, and garlic. *Fondue des Mosses* from Vaud is made with Gruyère, Appenzell, and Bagnes or Tilsitt, dried boletus mushrooms, dry white wine, garlic, and plum brandy. *Swiss Jura fondue* is made with full-flavoured salty Jura Gruyère, dry white wine, Kirsch, garlic, and nutmeg. *Fondue savoyarde* uses mature salty Beaufort and full-flavoured Beaufort, dry white wine, and Kirsch. A classic variant is *fondue normande*, made of Camembert, Pont l'Évêque, and Livarot (with the crusts removed), cream, milk, Calvados, and shallots. *Fondue piémontaise* is made with Fontina from the Aosta Valley, butter, milk, and egg yolks, to which chopped white truffles are added. This fondue is not served in a fondue dish, but poured into dishes garnished with croutons. Swiss raclette (melted cheese served with boiled potatoes and pickles) is a rustic variant of fondue.

There are several other dishes derived from, or inspired by, cheese fondue. *Fondue bourguignonne*, like cheese fondue, is prepared on the table in a metal fondue dish placed over a heating device and filled with hot oil. A long-handled fork is used to skewer cubes of beef (fillet steak, sirloin, or rump steak) and dip them in the very hot oil until they are cooked. They are then dipped in one of an assortment of flavoured sauces (béarnaise, barbecue, aïoli, mayonnaise, horseradish, tomato, etc.) and eaten. Condiments such as gherkins, pickles, chutneys, or pickled onions can also be served at the same time, as well as potato crisps (chips).

Chinese fondue is prepared using the same principle as *fondue bourguignonne*. Strips of beef and pork, thin slices of chicken breast, little pieces of fish, etc., are cooked in a chicken stock kept simmering in a fondue pot over a special charcoal burner incorporated into it. This traditional Chinese dish was introduced to the Far East by the Mongols in the 14th century, and was originally made with mutton. It is accompanied by sliced fresh vegetables arranged in bowls (Chinese cabbage, spinach, and onions), a purée of haricot beans (navy beans), and rice vermicelli. This fondue is also served with soy, ginger, and sesame oil based sauces. In Vietnam, where this fondue is served on festive occasions, it is made with beef, prawns, and fish, cooked in coconut milk and served with a prawn sauce and sweet and sour condiments. Scallops and strips of prepared squid are sometimes also included.

Chocolate fondue consists of chocolate melted in a bain-marie and kept liquid over a spirit lamp on the table. It is used for dipping pieces of cake, biscuits, pastries, fruit, etc.

Finally, the name *fondue* is given to a preparation of vegetables cut into thin pieces and cooked slowly in butter over a very low heat until they are reduced to a pulp. Vegetable fondues made with chicory (endive), fennel, onions, sorrel, carrots, leeks, celery, or celeriac (celery root) can be used as an ingredient in another dish (as a braising sauce for ragouts, baked fish, etc.) or as an accompaniment. Tomato fondue is most often used in egg dishes, sauces, and Mediterranean garnishes (*à la madrilène*, *à la provençale*, and *à la portugaise*). It can also be added to certain forcemeats, and when cold can be used to give piquancy to hors d'oeuvres or fish (as can onion fondue). When seasoned with coriander, it is used for preparations *à la grecque*.

RECIPES

Cheese fondue FONDUE (from Brillat-Savarin's recipe) Weigh the number of eggs you wish to use, according to the number of diners. Grate a piece of good Gruyère cheese weighing one-third of this, and take a piece of butter weighing one-sixth. Break the eggs into a heavy-based saucepan and beat them well, then add the butter and cheese. Put the pan over a moderate heat and stir with a spatula until the mixture is thickened and smooth. Season with a little salt and a generous amount of pepper, which is one of the distinguishing characteristics of this ancient dish. Serve in a warmed dish.

Fondue du Valais Rub the bottom of an earthenware fondue dish with garlic. Cut into very thin slices 150–200 g (5–7 oz, 1 cup) good-quality Gruyère cheese per person. (Alternatively, use a mixture of Beaufort, Emmental, and Comté.) Put the cheese into the fondue dish and just cover it with dry white wine (in Switzerland Fendant is normally used). Stir over the heat until the cheese has melted, then add a little freshly ground pepper and 1 liqueur glass of Kirsch. In Switzerland this fondue is served with Grisons (air-cured) meat or raw ham cut into very thin slices.

Tomato fondue FONDUE DE TOMATE Peel and chop 100 g (4 oz, 1 cup) onions. Peel, deseed, and finely chop 750 g (1¾ lb) tomatoes. Peel and crush 1 clove of garlic. Prepare a bouquet garni rich in thyme. Soften the onions in a thick-bottomed saucepan with 25 g (1 oz, 2 tablespoons) butter (or 15 g, ½ oz, 1 tablespoon butter and 2 tablespoons olive oil, or 3 tablespoons olive oil). Then add the tomatoes, salt and pepper, the garlic, and the bouquet garni. Cover the pan and cook very gently until the tomatoes are reduced to a pulp. Remove the lid, stir with a wooden spatula, and continue cooking (with the lid off) until the fondue forms a light paste. Adjust the seasoning, strain through a sieve, and add 1 tablespoon chopped parsley or herbs.

Fontainebleau

A soft fresh cows'-milk cheese containing 60–75% fat, originating in Île-de-France. It is not matured or salted, but wrapped in cheesecloth and sold in a small waxed cardboard container. It is prepared from a foamy mixture of whipped cream and slowly coagulating curds, which is drained for 30 hours and then smoothed. It is served with sugar, and often with strawberries or jam. Enthusiasts often add fresh cream.

Fontainebleau is also the name of a classic garnish consisting of a macédoine of vegetables cut up into very small pieces, cooked with butter, and arranged in barquettes made of duchess potato mixture browned in the oven.

Fontanges

A soup probably dedicated to Mlle de Fontanges, who was a favourite of Louis XIV for a short time. It is made of a purée of fresh peas, topped up with beef or chicken consommé, and contains shredded sorrel cooked slowly in butter. Just before serving it is enriched with an egg yolk mixed with double (heavy) cream and sprinkled with chervil.

Fontenelle (à la)

Describing a preparation of asparagus served with melted butter and soft-boiled eggs. The asparagus is dipped first in the melted butter, then in the egg yolk. The name commemorates the greediness of Bernard Le Bovier de Fontenelle (1657–1757), a philosopher and permanent secretary of the French Academy of Sciences. Once when he invited his friend, the Abbé Terrasson, to dinner, Fontenelle had arranged to have half the asparagus served with butter (which he preferred) and half with vinaigrette (favoured by the Abbé). Approaching the table, the Abbé suddenly dropped dead of apoplexy, and it is said that Fontenelle immediately shouted to his chef, 'Serve them all with butter! All with butter!'

Fontina

An Italian cows'-milk cheese (containing 45% fat and about 384 Cal per 100 g), with a pressed cooked centre and a brushed, sometimes oiled, crust. Elastic to the touch, and with a few small holes, the cheese tastes delicately nutty. It originated in the Aosta Valley in the Alps, where it has been made since the 12th century, and it comes in rounds 40–45 cm (16–18 in) in diameter and 7–10 cm (3–4 in) high. It is made almost all over northern Italy, and even in France (under the name of Fontal and made mainly from pasteurized milk). The name Fontina is reserved for the cheese which comes from the Aosta Valley. Young Fontina is served at the end of a meal or on canapés, and it is also used in cookery, particularly in fondue piémontaise. When matured, it is grated and used like Parmesan.

food ALIMENT

A substance eaten to sustain life; as part of a well-balanced diet, it promotes growth and maintains health. No one food is nutritionally perfect as it does not supply all the nutrients in the right proportions to support health. So, to satisfy nutritional needs and individual tastes, we need to eat, in moderation, a variety of different foods. There are many combinations of foods that supply the right balance of nutrients and energy. A good diet in Mexico, for example, is based on very different foods from an equally nutritious diet in France, Japan, or Italy, since the daily diet of a country still reflects its social, religious, and family traditions, as well as its agricultural practices. In addition, the diet will vary according to the habits and way of life of the individual. There is no need to try to achieve the correct balance of nutrients for every meal and snack, as long as the diet as a whole is well-balanced. Most foods – sweets, cakes, chips (French fries), etc. – have a place in a healthy diet, provided that no one food forms an unduly large part of the total food intake.

food additive

ADDITIF ALIMENTAIRE

A substance added to prepacked or processed food to help improve its keeping qualities, taste, or colour; additives do not necessarily improve the nutritional value of the food.

Under European and American law, since January 1986 each food item must show clearly each food additive on the label or packet under its own E number rather than just quoting 'preservatives' or 'colourings' in the list of ingredients. Water that has been added to foods (such as ham or bacon) must also be listed clearly on the label. Labelling regulations state that ingredients must be clearly listed in descending order by weight, as a guide to the quantity of additives included.

The use of additives in foods is by no means a recent practice; indeed, without them many foods we consume would quickly become unsafe to eat and have a very short storage life. Salt, sugar, spices, vinegar, and such products as caramel or spinach-green have been used for years. The growth of the food industry, however, has considerably enlarged the number of additives and changed their nature and conditions of use. Many food additives are essential and harmless, but there are indications that some are nonessential and may cause allergies and other reactions; for example, the yellow colouring tartrazine (E102), found in puddings and sweets, is believed to cause hyperactivity in children, and sulphur dioxide, used as a preservative, destroys vitamin B_1. The type of additive varies according to whether it is introduced at the manufacturing stage or in processing, packaging, transport, or storing of the food product, and several additives can be included in the same product. Each additive is tested by law to make sure it is safe to use in food products. The 300 or so existing additives include permitted colouring agents, preservatives, permitted antioxidants, flavourings, mineral hydrocarbons, emulsifiers, and stabilizers.

□ **Current regulations** In France, no additive may be used without prior authorization from the quality control department of the Ministry of Agriculture, following advice from the Council for Public Hygiene and from the Academy of Medicine on its nontoxicity. In England and Wales, legislation on food additives is made by the Minister of Agriculture and the Secretary of State for Social Services on advice from the Food Advisory Committee. The authorization is given for specific products and often lays down maximum quantities which may be used. According to this principle, everything which is not authorized is prohibited. This system certainly provides the maximum guarantees – certain additives have been struck off the list and others, although in use for a very long time, are only provisionally permitted.

France permits certain additives prohibited in other countries, such as amaranth (E123), which is prohibited in the Soviet Union, Britain, Sweden, and the United States. In European countries and the United States, the label on a packaged food product must state the nature of the additive with its identification number – E for Europe, followed by a figure: E100 to E199 for colouring agents, E200 to E299 (in the UK E296 and E297 are under consideration) for preservatives, E300 to E399 for antioxidants, and E400 to E499 for texturing agents.

Dietetic products, which have been regulated since 1975, incorporate some common additives and other substances (proteins, amino acids, vitamins, mineral salts, dietary fibre) for enrichment purposes.

food processing machines
ROBOTS MÉNAGERS

Electrically powered items of kitchen equipment designed to carry out various operations in the preparation of food. They can, in fact, do nearly all the time-consuming tasks involved in food preparation. The actual time saved is significant: a processor requires only 3 seconds for grating, 5 for slicing, 10 for chopping meat, 20 for making pastry, etc.

● *Food processors* consist of a motor with a medium-power drive, and a bowl in which the accessories operate under a protective lid. The chosen accessory (a double-bladed curved knife for chopping, beating, and mixing; a slicing disc; a coarse or fine grating disc; a chip (French fry) cutter; a whisk, etc.) revolves at the desired speed to chop vegetables, purée soups, chop meat or fish, emulsify sauces, mix forcemeats and doughs, and whisk egg whites. The appliance generally has sufficient power to grate or grind food (cooking chocolate, Parmesan cheese, nuts, etc.); it may even be able to cruch ice. Some models also have a juice extractor or a centrifuge.

● *Food mixers* are often supplied with a very powerful motor that drives specialized appliances: dough kneaders, mincers (grinders), vegetable cutters, a centrifuge, peelers, can openers, etc. A mixer of this type is really a collection of different appliances (rather than accessories), driven by a single motor. Each appliance is designed to perform one particular function: a mixer with mixing blades, hooks, etc., for making different kinds of dough; vegetable cutters with discs for various slicing operations; etc. The mincer may either be the screw type with interchangeable cutters, or the knife type (which may also be used for vegetables, fruit, and fish). A mixer may also have attachments for coffee grinding, pasta making, and sausage making.

food safe
GARDE-MANGER

A type of cage with a wooden frame and wire mesh for storing foodstuffs away from flies and other insects. The food safe was often equipped with a handle and hung in the cellar or in a cool place. Sometimes food was stored in an outside larder with shutters or ventilation grilles, installed in big old houses under the kitchen window square with the wall. Nowadays both types have been replaced by the refrigerator, but they are still sometimes used for cheeses, which are spoiled if they are kept at too low a temperature.

In France in the Middle Ages and up to the end of the 18th century, the word *garde-manger* was applied to the cool well-aired place where provisions were stored.

food substitute

SUCCÉDANÉ

A food product used as a substitute for another, usually because the latter is very rare or expensive but sometimes because of health reasons (artificial sweeteners instead of sugar, for example). It is often during wars or during times of shortage that substitutes are devised, such as Guinea pepper (seeds from a plant related to the cardamom) for real pepper, and safflower for saffron.

In a book of recipes published in 1941, Prosper Montagné suggested malt extract and concentrated grape juice as acceptable substitutes for sugar in pastries, cakes, and confectionery. Some substitutes are for emergency use only, until the genuine article becomes available, like roasted acorns for making coffee; others, such as chicory (for coffee), margarine, and beet sugar, have however acquired universal acceptance. Certain substitutes have remained acceptable in everyday use, though acknowledged as inferior products; for example, slices of gherkins as substitutes for pistachios in mortadella, and lumpfish roe for caviar.

Some novel substitutes appeared at the end of the 19th century: at the time of the Paris Exhibition of 1878, machines were introduced for cutting out mares' udders into the shape of tripe, for twisting ox lights into the shape of *petit-gris* (edible brown snails), for graining cheeses with verdigris using copper needles to sell them as Roquefort, and for making bread with starch or with couch-grass powder.

The most famous substitute preparations were cooked by Chavette, chef of the Brébant Restaurant, in order to mystify Monselet, a well-known gastronome. Monselet praised the swallows'-nest soup, brill, chamois cutlets, and capercaillie, served with hocks and Tokay wines, which proved to be a purée of noodles and small kidney beans, fresh cod cooked on a fine comb (to simulate the brill's backbone), lamb cutlets marinated in bitters, and a young turkey sprinkled with absinthe; the 'Tokay' was Mâcon wine mixed with punch, and the 'Johannisberg' an ordinary Chablis flavoured with thyme essence!

fool

A chilled dessert of English origin, made of fruit purée strained through a fine sieve, sweetened, and chilled (but not frozen). Just before serving, the purée is mixed with twice its volume of whipped cream.

forced fruit and vegetables

PRIMEURS

Horticultural products which appear on the market before their normal season. Often expensive and sometimes lacking the flavour of fruit and vegetables in season, these forced products are the result of cultivation under glass or shelter of produce normally sensitive to weather conditions (peas, asparagus, etc.). Improved transport facilities have made forcing less important in regions with a poor climate.

forcemeat or stuffing

FARCE

A seasoned mixture of raw or cooked ingredients, chopped or minced (ground), used to stuff eggs, fish, poultry, game, meat, vegetables, or pasta (ravioli, cannelloni, etc.). Forcemeats are also the basis for several pâtés, meat pies, terrines, galantines, and ballottines, not to mention all the different kinds of sausages. They are also used to make forcemeat balls, quenelles, and some borders, and to fill barquettes, vols-au-vent and tartlets. A *gratin* forcemeats are used to garnish croûtes, croutons, and hot canapés.

There are three major categories of forcemeat: those made with vegetables; those made with meat, game, or poultry; and those made with fish. In addition, there is a fourth more minor category of forcemeat based on egg yolk.

The composition of a forcemeat depends in principle on the food that it is intended to stuff or fill. The basis for a forcemeat is usually minced meat or fish; the additional ingredients, for example, gherkins (sweet dill pickles), herbs, onion, ham, foie gras, crustless bread soaked in milk, or egg whites, give it its character and consistency. Seasoning is also extremely important. A panada may be added to give it some substance, and most forcemeats made of meat, poultry, or game are bound with eggs. The stuffing for a food that is to be boiled needs to be more strongly seasoned than one for food to be roasted. However, in the latter case, the stuffing must contain sufficient fat to prevent the food from drying out, especially in the case of poultry.

RECIPES

Preparation of forcemeats PRÉPARATION DES FARCES The ingredients for some forcemeats need to be very finely minced or even ground in a mortar or food processor and then forced through a sieve. Fine forcemeats need to be minced twice. Sometimes only some of the ingredients need to be minced. Add seasoning to taste and about 6 tablespoons brandy per kg (2¼ lb) forcemeat. Allow 1 large egg to bind 500 g (1 lb) forcemeat.

FORCEMEATS MADE WITH EGG YOLKS

Cold egg yolk stuffing FARCE DE JAUNES D'OEUF À FROID Sieve 10 hard-boiled (hard-cooked) egg yolks and place them in a terrine together with 100 g (4 oz, ½ cup) softened butter. Season with salt and white pepper and mix all the ingredients together. This is used as a spread for cold canapés and as a filling for halved hard-boiled egg whites, artichoke hearts, etc.

Hot egg yolk stuffing FARCE DE JAUNES D'OEUF À CHAUD Add some sieved hard-boiled (hard-cooked) egg yolks to half their weight of hot thick béchamel sauce. Rub through a very fine sieve and season with salt and pepper. A teaspoon of dry duxelles and some chopped parsley are usually added as well. This mixture is used to fill halved hardboiled eggs, vols-au-vent, or barquettes or to stuff vegetables prepared *au gratin*.

FORCEMEATS MADE WITH FISH AND SHELLFISH

Cream forcemeat FARCE À LA CRÈME This is a mousseline forcemeat made by replacing the meat with either boned and skinned whiting or pike.

Mousseline forcemeat for fish mousses and mousselines FARCE MOUSSELINE POUR MOUSSES ET MOUSSELINES DE POISSON Skin and bone 1 kg (2¼ lb) fish (pike, whiting, salmon, sole, or turbot) and season with 20 g (¾ oz, 3 tablespoons) salt, a generous pinch of pepper, and ground nutmeg. Pound the fish in a mortar, add 4 lightly beaten egg whites (one by one), put into a blender, and then through a fine sieve. Place the resulting purée in a terrine, smooth out with a wooden spatula, and chill in the refrigerator for at least 2 hours. Then place the terrine in a bowl of crushed ice or ice cubes and incorporate 1.25 litres (2¼ pints, 5¾ cups) cream, working it in gently with a spatula. Keep in the refrigerator until needed. This forcemeat can also be used for quenelles and to garnish large braised fish or fillets of sole or turbot.

Prawn (shrimp) forcemeat FARCE DE CREVETTES Cook 125 g (4½ oz, ¾ cup) prawns or shrimps in some salted water. Pound them in a mortar with 100 g (4 oz, ½ cup) butter and then rub the mixture through a fine sieve. Add to this mixture half its weight of finely sieved hard-boiled (hard-cooked) egg yolks. Mix together well.

Shellfish forcemeat FARCE DE CRUSTACÉ This is a mousseline forcemeat made with crayfish, lobster, or crab meat. Allow 4 egg whites, 1.5 litres (2¾ pints, 3½ pints) cream, 25 g (1 oz) salt, and a generous pinch of white pepper for each kg (2¼ lb) shellfish meat.

Smoked herring or sardine forcemeat FARCE DE HARENGS SAURS OU DE SARDINES Make a white roux with 1 tablespoon butter and 2 tablespoons (3 tablespoons) flour. Add 1 dl (6 tablespoons, scant ½ cup) warm milk and cook for about 10 minutes, stirring continuously with a wooden spoon. Remove from the heat when very thick.

Add 1 whole egg and 2 egg yolks. Place either 1 large smoked herring fillet (soaked in a little milk to remove some of the salt if necessary) or 4 medium sardines in a blender, and reduce to a purée. Incorporate this into the roux and cook for 3–4 minutes. Rub through a sieve. This forcemeat is used as a filling for croustades, dartois, and small pastry cases.

FORCEMEATS MADE WITH MEAT, GAME AND POULTRY

À gratin forcemeat FARCE À GRA-TIN Fry 150 g (5 oz) finely chopped unsmoked bacon in a sauté pan until soft. Add 300 g (11 oz) chicken livers, 2 thinly sliced shallots, 50 g (2 oz) finely chopped mushrooms, a sprig of thyme, and half a bay leaf. Season with a generous pinch of salt, some pepper, and a little spice. Sauté quickly over a high heat. Allow to cool completely, then pound in a mortar (or purée in a blender) and rub through a fine sieve. Cover with buttered or oiled greaseproof (waxed) paper and place in the refrigerator until needed.

This forcemeat is spread on croutons of fried bread that are used as a base for small roast game birds or served with salmis or civets.

Foie gras forcemeat FARCE AU FOIE GRAS Finely pound in a mortar (or purée in a blender) 375 g (13 oz) lean pork meat, 450 g (1 lb) unsmoked streaky bacon, and 250 g (9 oz) thinly sliced foie gras. Add 15 g (½ oz) spiced salt and 1 dl (6 tablespoons, scant ½ cup) brandy, and rub through a sieve. This forcemeat is used for making pâtés and terrines.

Forcemeat for poultry FARCE POUR VOLAILLES This consists of fine sausagemeat mixed with one-fifth of its weight each of breadcrumbs and finely chopped onion cooked in a little butter until soft, together with chopped parsley. Refrigerate until required.

Game forcemeat FARCE DE GIBIER Prepare with the appropriate game meat in the same way as poultry forcemeat. To make it richer, add thin slices of fresh

foie gras or game liver forcemeat. This forcemeat is used for making pâtés and terrines.

Liver forcemeat FARCE DE FOIE Brown 250 g (generous ½ lb, 12 slices) diced unsmoked streaky bacon in 30 g (1 oz, 2 tablespoons) butter in a sauté pan. Remove and drain. In the same fat, sauté 300 g (11 oz) liver cut into cubes (pig's (pork) liver, calf's liver, game liver, or chicken liver may be used). Mix 40 g (1½ oz, generous ½ cup) finely chopped shallots and 75 g (3 oz, 1 cup) finely chopped cultivated mushrooms together. Replace the bacon in the sauté pan, add the mushrooms and shallots, and season with salt, ground white pepper, and allspice; then add a sprig of thyme and half a bay leaf. Mix together and sauté for 2 minutes.

Remove the cubes of liver. Deglaze the pan with 1.5 dl (¼ pint, ⅔ cup) dry white wine, pour the sauce over the cubes of liver, and purée all the ingredients in an electric blender or food processor, together with 70 g (2½ oz, 5 tablespoons) butter and 3 egg yolks, until very smooth. Pass the forcemeat through a sieve and store, covered, in the refrigerator.

This forcemeat is used for making pâtés, terrines, or meat loaves. Minced cleaned truffle peelings can be added to it if desired. (If game liver is used, add an equal amount of rabbit meat and replace the white wine with 1 dl (6 tablespoons, scant ½ cup) Madeira.)

Mousseline forcemeat FARCE MOUS-SELINE Pound 1 kg (2¼ lb) boned veal, poultry, or game in a mortar (or reduce to a purée in a blender). Then rub through a fine sieve. Whisk 4 egg whites with a fork and add them to the meat purée a little at a time. Season with 20 g (¾ oz) salt and a generous pinch of ground white pepper. Rub through the sieve a second time, place in a terrine, and then store in the refrigerator for 2 hours. Chill well. Remove the terrine from the refrigerator and place in a bowl of crushed ice. Then work in 1.5 litres (2¾ pints, 3½ pints) double (heavy) cream using a wooden spoon. (It is essential to keep the cream and the pâté as cold as possible to prevent curdling.)

This forcemeat is used for fine quenelles, mousses, and mousselines.

Panada forcemeat with butter FARCE À LA PANADE ET AU BEURRE Purée 1 kg (2¼ lb) boned veal or poultry in a blender with salt, ground white pepper, and grated nutmeg. Also blend 500 g (generous 1 lb) panada with an equal quantity of butter. Add the puréed meat and beat the mixture vigorously. Then add 8 egg yolks, one at a time. Rub the forcemeat through a fine sieve, place in a terrine, and work with a spatula until smooth. Store in the refrigerator, covered, until required.

This forcemeat is used for quenelles, borders, and meat loaves and to stuff poultry, joints of meat, etc.

Panada forcemeat with cream FARCE À LA PANADE ET À LA CRÈME Pound 1 kg (2¼ lb) boned minced (ground) veal or poultry in a mortar (or reduce to a purée in a blender). Season with 10 g (generous ¼ oz) salt, a generous pinch of white pepper, and some grated nutmeg. Add 4 lightly beaten egg whites one at a time, followed by 400 g (14 oz) bread panada. Beat vigorously until the mixture is very smooth. Rub through a fine sieve over a terrine and refrigerate for 1 hour, together with 1.5 litres (2¾ pints, 3½ pints) double (heavy) cream and 2 tablespoons (3 tablespoons) milk. Then place the terrine in a basin of crushed ice or ice cubes. Add one-third of the cream to the forcemeat, working it in vigorously with a spatula. Lightly beat the remaining cream with the milk and then fold it into the forcemeat. Refrigerate until needed.

This forcemeat is used for quenelles.

Poultry forcemeat FARCE DE VO- LAILLE Dice 600 g (generous 1¼ lb) chicken or other poultry meat, 200 g (7 oz) lean veal, and 900 g (2 lb) bacon; work together in a blender until smooth. Add 3 eggs, 15 g (generous ½ oz) salt, and 2dl (7 fl oz, ¾ cup) brandy. Mix well, rub through a sieve, and re- frigerate until required. This forcemeat is used for pâtés and terrines.

Veal forcemeat FARCE DE VEAU Pound 1 kg (2¼ lb) lean minced (ground) veal in a mortar (or reduce to a

purée in a blender). Season with 15 g (½ oz) salt, some white pepper, and some grated nutmeg. Purée 300 g (11 oz) flour panada; when really soft, add the veal, together with 60 g (2¼ oz, 4½ table- spoons) butter, and beat the mixture well. Finally add, beating continuously, 5 whole eggs and 8 yolks, one by one. Then add 1.2 litres (scant 2¼ pints, 5½ cups) thick béchamel sauce. Rub through a fine sieve and work with a spatula to make the forcemeat smooth. Refrigerate until required.

This forcemeat is used for borders and large quenelles.

FORCEMEATS MADE WITH VEGETABLES

Forcemeat for fish FARCE POUR POISSONS Crumble 250 g (9 oz) bread (with the crusts removed) and soak it in milk. Sauté 75 g (3 oz, ¾ cup) chopped onions and 150 g (5 oz, gener- ous cup) chopped button mushrooms in 30 g (generous 1 oz, generous 2 table- spoons) butter. Add a small handful of chopped parsley and cook for a few minutes. Meanwhile, add half a glass of white wine to 3 chopped shallots in a separate pan and reduce. Add the shal- lots to the other vegetables and mix. Squeeze out the bread and place in a terrine. Add the vegetable mixture and work together well. Then bind with 2 egg yolks and season with salt and pep- per and, if liked, a generous pinch of nutmeg and half a clove of garlic, chopped.

Mushroom forcemeat FARCE AUX CHAMPIGNONS Sauté 2 peeled and finely chopped shallots and 175 g (6 oz, 2 cups) wiped button mushrooms, also finely chopped, over a high heat in a frying pan (skillet), with 40 g (1½ oz, 3 tablespoons) butter and a generous pinch of ground nutmeg. When cooked, allow to cool. Make 100 g (4 oz) bread panada and purée it in a blender, adding the mushrooms and shallots. Finally, add 3 egg yolks and mix thoroughly (it is not necessary to sieve this forcemeat). It is used to stuff vegetables, poultry, game, and fish.

forestière (à la)

A method of preparing small cuts of

meat or chicken (or even eggs or vegetables), which are garnished with mushrooms (usually chanterelles, morels, or ceps) cooked in butter, usually accompanied by potato noisettes or rissoles and blanched browned bacon pieces. It is served with gravy, thickened veal stock, or the deglazed pan juices.

RECIPES

Carrots à la forestière CAROTTES À LA FORESTIÈRE Braise some carrots in butter, then add half their volume of mushrooms, also braised in butter. Adjust the seasoning and sprinkle with fresh parsley.

Soft-boiled (*or poached*) **eggs à la forestière** OEUFS MOLLETS (OU POCHÉS) À LA FORESTIÈRE Clean some mushrooms and fry them in butter. Cut some lean bacon into small dice, scald them, and brown them in butter. Mix the mushrooms and bacon together and spread the mixture over bread croustades. Place a soft-boiled or poached egg on top of each. Add a few drops of lemon juice, pepper, a little cayenne, and some chopped parsley to some melted butter and pour it over the eggs.

fork FOURCHETTE

An implement usually made of metal with two, three, or four prongs on the end of a handle, used at the table either for lifting food to the mouth or for serving food. Forks are also used in the kitchen for turning food in cooking, etc.

The fork has a very ancient origin and is mentioned in the Old Testament. It was first used as a ritual instrument to grip pieces of meat destined for sacrifices; later it was used in the kitchen. According to the 11th-century Italian scholar Damiani, forks were introduced into Venice by a Byzantine princess and then spread throughout Italy. But it was Henri III of France who first introduced to the French the custom of using a two-pronged fork at the table. Before this time, it had been regarded as a decorative item fashioned in gold or silver; forks were mentioned in 1379 in an inventory of the French king, Charles V. After visiting the court at Venice in 1574, Henri III noted that a two-pronged table fork was being used and he launched this fashion amongst the nobility. It seemed a very useful implement for putting food into the mouth above the high collars and ruffs that were worn at that time! In 14th-century England, it is recorded that Piers Gaveston, a favourite of Edward II, ate a pear with a fork, but it was not until the 18th century that it became widely used. Louis XIV ate with his fingers, and in the reign of Louis XVI, it was common to eat food from the tip of the knife.

Forks then came to have three prongs, and later four, and their use spread from Italy and Spain into France and England. Nowadays, only the carving fork has two prongs. These may be straight or slightly curved. Table forks are more diversified and are made in many sizes and many metals. They may even be made of wood or plastic. Salad servers consist of a fork and spoon, and carving sets consist of a knife, a fork, and often a steel for sharpening the knife. There are table forks, fish forks, fruit forks, etc., diminishing in size down to the small pastry fork. Certain forks are modified for a particular use; for example, snail forks, oyster forks, shellfish forks, and fondue forks.

Etiquette varies as to the proper way of holding and using a fork, and in which hand. E. Briffault ends his *Paris à table* (1846) with this assessment: 'The two-pronged fork is used in northern Europe. The English are armed with steel tridents with ivory handles – three-pronged forks – but in France, we have the four-pronged fork, the height of civilization.'

fortified wine VIN VINÉ

Wine to which a certain quality of spirit is added in the course of production. Increasing the alcoholic strength has the effect of interrupting the work of the yeasts in the fermentation of the must, so that the grape sugar cannot be converted into alcohol. The resulting wine may retain a considerable proportion of its natural sugar. Fortified wines include port, sherry, and Madeira.

fouace, fouasse, or fougasse

One of the oldest of French pastries. It was originally a pancake made of fine wheat, unleavened, and cooked under the cinders in the hearth (in Latin *focus*, hence the name *focacia pasta*, which became *fouace*, *fouasse*, or *fougasse*). Rabelais gave the recipe for it in his *Gargantua*: 'Best-quality flour mixed with best egg yolks and butter, best saffron and spices, and water.' The fouaces from the regions of Chinon and Touraine have had a fine reputation for centuries.

Fouaces are still produced in many areas of France. Nowadays they are usually rustic dough cakes baked in the oven, sometimes salted and flavoured, and usually made for Christmas or Twelfth Night. They used to be very widespread in western and central France (Caen, Vannes, La Flèche, and Tours), but are now most common in the south. At Najac, in Rouergue, a 'fouace festival' is held every year. In Languedoc, a *fouace aux grattons* is eaten with Frontignan wine. In Auvergne, the fouace is made with crystallized (candied) fruits. In Provence, where it is called the *fougasse*, sometimes a little orange-flower water is poured onto the pastries and brushed over the top and sides. This is one of the desserts traditionally eaten at Christmas. The *fougassette*, which is made of brioche dough, is a speciality of the Nice area. This small fougasse is shaped like a plaited loaf and flavoured with orange-flower water and saffron. It sometimes contains candied citron.

RECIPE

Fouace or fougasse Dissolve 15 g (½ oz) baker's yeast (½ cake compressed yeast) in a few tablespoons of warm milk or water. Add 125 g (4½ oz, 1 generous cup) sieved flour, and then enough milk or water to make a slightly soft dough. Cover the dough with a damp cloth or greased polythene and leave to rise until it has doubled in volume.

Heap 375 g (13 oz, 3 cups) sieved flour on a worktop, make a well in the centre, and add a large pinch of salt, 100 g (4 oz, 8 tablespoons) softened butter, 1 liqueur glass of rum, brandy, or orange-flower water, 50 g (2 oz, 4 tablespoons) sugar (optional), and 4 beaten eggs. Knead this mixture together,

adding a little milk or water to obtain a smooth dough. Then add the risen dough and (if desired) a filling of crystallized (candied) fruits (150–200 g, 5–7 oz, 1 cup). Work the dough again until it is elastic, knead it into a ball, cut a cross in the top, and leave it to rise, loosely covered (it should double in volume).

Place the fouace on a lightly buttered baking sheet, in a ball, loaf, or crown shape, glaze with beaten egg, and bake in the oven at 230 c (450 f, gas 8) for about 40 minutes or until golden brown (the base should sound hollow when tapped).

fougasse
See *fouace*.

Fouquet's

A restaurant and café in the Champs-Élysées in Paris. Originally (in 1901) it was a small public house for cabmen, which bore the name of its owner, Louis Fouquet. In 1910 Léopold Mourier, well-known in the Parisian restaurant trade and the tutor of the founder's children, purchased it, anglicized its name to 'Fouquet's' (like Maxim's), redecorated it in the Belle Époque style (which survived until 1961), and set up an English bar and a grill room, where 'the Longchamp racegoers were accustomed to meeting before or after the races, with their grey top hats over their ears, and their binoculars in deerskin cases over their shoulders' (R. Héron de Villefosse). A restaurant was also opened on the first floor. Since World War II, most of Fouquet's regular customers have been actors.

four fruits
QUATRE-FRUITS

The phrase used in French to designate four red summer fruits – strawberries, cherries, redcurrants, and raspberries – which are cooked together to make jams, syrups, or comptes. The phrase 'four yellow fruits' (*quatre-fruits jaunes*) is sometimes used to refer to oranges, lemons, Seville (bitter) oranges, and citrons. In practice, 'four fruit' jams and compotes may be made from a combination of any four fruits, fresh or dried.

RECIPE

Four-fruits compote COMPOTE DE QUATRE-FRUITS Wash and deseed 2 bunches of Muscat grapes. Peel 4 bananas and cut them into thick rounds and peel and finely dice 4 apples and 4 pears. Put all the fruit into a saucepan with the juice of a lemon, a pinch of cinnamon, 300 g (11 oz, scant 1½ cups) caster (superfine) sugar, the juice of 2 oranges, and ½ glass (4 fl oz, ½ cup) water. Bring to the boil, cook very gently for 30 minutes, and then pour into a glass fruit bowl. When the compote is cold, chill until ready to serve. If desired, liquid caramel can be poured over it just before serving.

Fourme

Any of various cows'-milk cheeses from central France that usually contain parsley and are used in the same way as blue cheese. The French word *fourme* is derived from the Latin *forma* (a mould); it then became *formage* and later *fromage*.

• Fourme d'Ambert (45% fat content), which has a special label of origin (an AOC), comes from the Loire, Puy-de-Dôme, and the district of Saint-Flour. It has a firm paste flavoured with parsley and a dry dark-grey crust mottled with yellow and red. It has a strong flavour and is shaped into tall cylinders, 13 cm (5 in) in diameter and 19 cm (8 in) high. It is usually served cut horizontally. Fourme de Pierre-sur-Haute, Fourme du Forez (named after Monts du Forez), and Fourme de Montbrison are similar cheeses.

• Fourme du Mézene (30–40% fat content) is also known as Bleu du Velay, Bleu de Loudes, or Bleu de Costaros. It is flavoured with parsley and has a natural crust. Like Fourme d'Ambert, it is cylindrical and has a pronounced flavour.

The name 'Fourme' is also used, albeit incorrectly, for Cantal, Salers, and Laguiole.

fourrer

The French term meaning to insert a raw or cooked filling into a sweet or savoury item. For example, omelettes and pancakes may be filled with various mixtures before being folded. Chou pastries, éclairs, and sponge cakes can be filled with butter cream, almond cream, confectioners' custard (pastry cream), or a fruit filling. Bread rolls, served as hors d'oeuvres, can be filled with various savoury mixtures.

four spices
QUATRE-ÉPICES

A mixture of spices, usually consisting of ground pepper, grated nutmeg, powdered cloves, and ground cinnamon. It is used in stews, civets, terrines, and game dishes. (It should not be confused with five spices (*cinq-épices*) or allspice (*toute-épice*).)

Nigella (or black cumin) is also known in France as *quatre-épices* or *toute-épice* on account of its spicy taste and smell. It was in great demand up to the 16th century and is still used in certain spice mixtures. In Egypt it is mixed with flour to flavour bread and cakes.

foutou

A traditional African dish based on cassava (manioc root) together with plantains (green bananas) or yams. The cassava and bananas (or yams) are boiled in water, drained, and then pounded into a smooth paste that is shaped into several small rounds or a single large one. Foutou is always served with very rich and highly spiced sauces, which are based on meat and vegetables or on fish. These sauces are actually more like ragouts, and their composition is very varied. Foutou is very common in Africa, particularly in Benin and the Ivory Coast.

Foyot

A Parisian restaurant which was situated on the corner of the Rue de Tournon and the Rue de Vaugirard. It was originally a hotel, and the emperor Joseph II, brother of Marie Antoinette, once stayed there. In 1768 it was converted into a restaurant, known as the Café Vachette, and in 1848 it was bought by Foyot, the former chef of Louis-Philippe, and renamed.

The proximity of the Palais du Luxembourg meant that the clientele included many senators. The specialities served by Foyot at that time included the famous veal chops Foyot, sheep's trotters (feet) *à la poulette*, pigeons Foyot, and Ernestine potatoes. No-one is certain that these dishes were actually invented by Foyot himself, but they certainly made the restaurant very famous. It was while breakfasting at Foyot in 1894 that the poet Laurent Tailhade was seriously injured by an anarchist's bomb.

The restaurant was finally closed in 1938 and the building was demolished.

RECIPES

Foyot sauce SAUCE FOYOT Make 2 dl (7 fl oz, ¾ cup) béarnaise sauce and strain it. Add 2 tablespoons (3 tablespoons) meat glaze or stock, stirring well. If the sauce is not to be served immediately, keep it warm in a bain-marie. (The meat glaze is made by boiling down a concentrated meat stock until it becomes thick and syrupy.)

Veal chop Foyot CÔTE DE VEAU FOYOT Make a thick cheese paste with 20 g (¾ oz, scant ¼ cup) dried breadcrumbs, 30 g (generous 1 oz, generous ¼ cup) grated Gruyère cheese, and 20 g (¾ oz, 1½ tablespoons) butter. Season and flour a large veal chop (about 250 g, 9 oz) and roast it in a cool oven (150 c, 300 F, gas 2) with 20 g (¾ oz, 1½ tablespoons) butter for 20–30 minutes. When half-cooked, turn it over and cover with the cheese paste. Stuff a small tomato with a mixture of breadcrumbs, parsley, and butter and place it in the roasting pan. Finish cooking the chop and baste regularly with the butter. Drain the meat and the tomato and arrange them on a serving dish. Add a peeled and chopped shallot to the cooking juices and deglaze with half a glass of dry white wine and an equal quantity of veal stock. Boil and reduce by half. Add 10 g (generous ¼ oz, generous ½ tablespoon) butter and pour the sauce over the veal.

fraisier

A gâteau consisting of two squares of Genoese sponge moistened with Kirsch syrup and sandwiched altogether with a layer of Kirsch-flavoured butter cream and strawberries. The top of the gâteau is covered with a layer of butter cream coloured red with cochineal and decorated with strawberries. When the gâteau is cut, the strawberries can be seen, cut in half.

There are several variations of this gâteau, which is also called *fragaria* or *fraisalia*. The sponge may be made with ground almonds and covered with several layers of Kirsch-flavoured strawberry jam. It is then brushed with apricot glaze, covered with pink fondant icing (frosting), and edged with sugar and chopped blanched almonds. The top is decorated with a large strawberry made with red marzipan (almond paste) and leaves made with boiled sugar. Another method is to fill the sponge with a layer of strawberry cream and ice it with a pink fondant icing containing crushed strawberries. Fresh strawberries are then used for the decoration. Finally, it may be filled with strawberry jam, covered with a thin layer of pink almond paste, dusted with icing sugar (confectioners' sugar), and edged with chopped roasted almonds.

framboise

A spirit made from raspberries, especially in the Alsace region.

française (à la)

Describing a preparation of joints of meat served with asparagus tips, braised lettuce, cauliflower florets coated with hollandaise sauce, and small duchess-potato nests filled with diced mixed vegetables. The sauce served with dishes *à la française* is a thin demi-glace – or a clear veal gravy.

Peas *à la française* are prepared with lettuce and onions (see *pea*).

Franche-Comté

This province comprises the Jura, Doubs, and Haute-Saône districts and contains mountainous regions, high plateaux, and valleys.

A variety of excellent foods is produced in this province. The cattle of Franche-Comté and the Jura are famous for their well-flavoured meat and high-quality milk, from which cheese and other dairy products are made. In the orchards of Franche-Comté, excellent fruit, particularly stone fruit, is grown. This part of France has an abundant variety of game. In the rivers, streams, and ponds numerous kinds of fish are found in great quantities. The inhabitants cook them in delicious ways, notably in succulent stews. Known for their delicacy are Saulon carp, red mullet, pike from Ognon, Doubs and Dessoubs trout, and Breuchin salmon trout, the flesh of which is very well flavoured. In the Breuchin there are also good crayfish.

Cheeses from Franche-Comté include Septmoncel, which some people consider a rival to Roquefort, and Comté cheese, a kind of Gruyère.

Foremost among the culinary specialities are maize (corn) porridge, *potée franc-comtoise*, which is prepared like potée from other regions but has Morteau sausage added to it; frog's-leg soup; panada, a dish like a soup with bread and butter boiled to a pulp; cherry soup; and a whole range of soups made with fresh vegetables.

The charcuterie of Franche-Comté is excellent and can be bought in Paris and many other large towns. It includes smoked ham, mainly from Luxeuil; different kinds of sausages, including caraway sausage from Montbozon; and stuffed tongue from Besançon.

The most famous dishes to be found in Franche-Comté are fish stews made from freshwater fish with white or red wine, onions, and herbs; meat braised in wine, cooked very slowly in a covered casserole to preserve all the meat juices; pike quenelles of Vesoul; jugged hare *à la franc-comtoise*; cheese fondue; *pain d'écrevisses* (crayfish loaf); marrow *au gratin*; cheese potatoes; morels on toast; onion tourte; matefaim; ramekins; fritters; *flamusse* (a cheese tart specially made in Burgundy); *sèche* (flat bread made with eggs and sugar); craquelins of Baume-les-Dames; almond pastry and biscuits (cookies) of Montbozon; *viques* (bread rolls made with milk) of Montbéliard; *malakoff* (almond pastry) of Dole; quiche comtoise; *galette de goumeau* of Saint-Amour; *gaufres* (waffles) *de chanoinesses* of Baume-les-Dames; chestnut cakes; gingerbread of Vercel and Dole; quince paste from Baume-les-Dames; and bilberry and whortleberry jam from Melisey.

Franche-Comté (particularly the department of Jura) produces white, red, and rosé wines of different qualities as well as vin jaune and vin de paille (straw wine), which are specialities of the region. The vin jaune is made from the Savagnin white grape. It demands strictly controlled and highly specialized methods of vinification, fermentation, and conservation. The best-known vin jaune is that of Château-Chalon. Vin de paille is so-called because the grapes are sun-dried on straw mats before being pressed.

Francillon

A mixed salad consisting of potatoes marinated in a white wine vinaigrette, mussels cooked *à la marinière*, and chopped celery, garnished with sliced truffles. The original recipe was given by Dumas *fils* in his play *Francillon*, first performed at the Comèdie-Française on 9 January 1887. The Paris restaurateurs took advantage of the event by putting the new salad on their menus. The restaurant Brébant-Vachette substituted Japanese artichokes for the potatoes, and Francillon salad was renamed 'Japanese salad' (it is often called Japanese salad even when it is made with potatoes).

Below is a passage from the play, in which Annette, a cordon-bleu cook, gives the recipe to Henri, the leading man, who intends to make the salad as a special treat for his mother, a great gourmand. In the modern recipe, the truffles are omitted and the vinaigrette is flavoured with Chablis.

A bombe glacé coated with coffee ice cream and filled with a champagne-flavoured bombe mixture is known as *bombe Francillon*.

frangipane

A pastry cream used in the preparation of various desserts, sweets, cakes, and pancakes. It is made with milk, sugar, flour, eggs, and butter, mixed with either crushed macaroons (to give a lighter cream) or with ground almonds. A few drops of bitter almond essence may be added to intensify the flavour. The name is derived from that of a 16th-century Italian nobleman, the Marquis Muzio Frangipani, living in Paris. He invented a perfume for scenting gloves that was based on bitter almonds. This inspired the pastrycooks

ANNETTE
Boil some potatoes in stock, cut them into pieces as for an ordinary salad, and while they are still warm, season them with salt, pepper, very good-quality fruity olive oil, and vinegar. . .

HENRI
Tarragon vinegar?

ANNETTE
Orléans vinegar is better, but that's not important. What is important is to add half a glass of white wine, Château-Yquem if possible, and plenty of herbs, chopped very very small. At the same time cook some very large mussels in stock with a stick of celery, drain them thoroughly, and add them to the seasoned potatoes. Mix everything together gently.

THÉRÈSE
Less mussels than potatoes?

ANNETTE
One-third less. One has to become gradually aware of the mussels. They must be neither anticipated nor imposed.

STANISLAS
Very well put!

ANNETTE
Thank you sir. When the salad is finished and stirred . . .

HENRI
Gently . . .

ANNETTE
Cover it with rounds of truffle. That puts a finishing touch to it.

HENRI
Cooked in champagne.

ANNETTE
That goes without saying. Do all this two hours before dinner so that this salad will be cold when served.

HENRI
We could surround the salad bowl with ice.

ANNETTE
No! It mustn't be rushed. It is very delicate, and all the flavours have to combine together slowly.

of the time to make an almond-flavoured cream which they named frangipane. La Varenne mentions *tourtes de franchipanne* (frangipane tarts) several times in his treatise on pâtisserie.

In classic cookery, frangipane is also the name of a kind of panada made with flour, egg yolks, butter, and milk and cooked like a choux pastry. It is used in poultry and fish forcemeat.

RECIPES

Frangipane cream CRÈME FRANGI-PANE Boil 7.5 dl (1¼ pints, 1½ pints) milk with a vanilla pod (bean) or 1 teaspoon vanilla sugar. Place 100 g (4 oz, 1 cup) sieved flour, 200 g (7 oz, 1 cup) sugar, 4 beaten eggs, and a pinch of salt in a thick-bottomed saucepan and mix together thoroughly. Gradually add the hot milk and cook slowly for about 3 minutes, stirring all the time, until the cream thickens. Pour the cream into a bowl and stir in 75 g (3 oz, ¾ cup) crushed macaroons and 50 g (2 oz, 4 tablespoons) softened butter. Mix well.

Crêpes à la frangipane Make some crêpes and prepare some frangipane cream, using ½ litre (17 fl oz, 2 cups) milk for the cream and an equal quantity for the crêpe batter. Coat the crêpes with the cream and fold into four. Arrange in a buttered ovenproof dish, dust with icing sugar (confectioners' sugar), and lightly caramelize in a very hot oven or under the grill. Serve very hot.

Frangy
VDQS white wine from Savoy, entitled to the prefix 'Roussette de Savoie' and made from the Roussette grape. Pleasantly fragrant, it can have a slightly honeyed flavour although it is essentially a dry wine.

Frascati
A gaming house-cum-restaurant situated on the corner of the Rue de Richelieu and the Boulevard des Italiens in Paris. It was founded in 1796 by the Neapolitan ice-cream merchant Garchi, who named it after one of the most famous holiday resorts for well-to-do Romans. Its gardens were illuminated at

night and during the Directory and the Empire it had the reputation of being the most famous gaming house in Paris. In addition, the clientele could dine, eat ice cream, and watch the firework displays. It was also frequented by women of easy virtue.

The restaurant was eventually closed after 50 years with the suppression of gaming houses and was subsequently succeeded by the Pâtisserie Frascati.

The name Frascati is used for a garnish for meat dishes and for various desserts. It is also the name of a famous Italian dry white wine.

| RECIPE

Fillet of beef à la Frascati FILET DE BOEUF À LA FRASCATI Prepare a demi-glace sauce flavoured with port. Sauté some very large mushrooms in butter, or bake them in the oven. Cook some very short green asparagus tips in butter, and quickly sauté some small slices of foie gras (preferably duck) in butter. Keep all these ingredients hot. Roast a fillet of beef and place it on a serving dish. Fill two-thirds of the mushroom caps with the asparagus tips and the remainder with a salpicon of truffles braised in Madeira. Arrange the mushrooms and the slices of foie gras around the meat. Pour the demi-glace over the top.

fraudulent misrepresentation of food
FRAUDE ALIMENTAIRE

Deception in the manufacture and sale of food products. In the EEC, fraud occurs when the type and origin of the food product does not correspond to the name under which it is sold (for example, pâté de foie gras containing other than goose or duck liver, or Bresse chicken that does not in fact come from Bresse) or when the quantity of goods is not specified.

In the manufacture of many products certain practices are forbidden, such as adding water to milk and beer, adding margarine to butter, artificially ageing alcoholic drinks, etc. Some frauds can be more directly harmful; for example, the use of antibiotics or oestrogens in chicken or livestock feed, the sale of

shellfish without a health label (in France), the sale of milk from cows suffering from foot-and-mouth disease, and breaches of hygiene regulations (meat coming from nonapproved slaughterhouses, etc.).

All perishable foods sold should have a 'sell by' date on them.

fréchure

A ragout of pig's (pork) lights (lungs), also called *levadou*, which is made in Languedoc, especially at Sainte-Eulalie, a famous pig-rearing district.

freeze-drying
LYOPHILISATION

A method of preserving food, known also as cryodesiccation and lyophilization, in which the product is frozen and then dehydrated. The food is treated in three stages: first the product is deep-frozen; next it is subjected to a vacuum, which sublimates the ice trapped in it; and finally the water vapour is removed, leaving the product dry and stable. A solid food which has been processed in this way becomes extremely light because it contains only 1–2% of its original water content; but it retains its volume, cellular structure, and shape, allowing rapid and even rehydration. The nutritional qualities remain more or less the same as those of fresh food. As it is a costly process it is only used for quality products. The best results are obtained with liquids and small pieces of food. Coffee is still the principal freeze-dried product, but mushrooms, onions, and prawns are also preserved successfully in this way.

freezer CONGÉLATEUR

A domestic appliance, either in chest or cupboard form, run on electricity and used to preserve food for up to 12 months at a temperature of −18 c (0 F) after it has been frozen at −24 c (−11 F) minimum. The volume of freezers varies between 40 and 600 litres (1½ and 22 cu ft); the useful average capacity per person is 80–100 litres (3–4 cu ft) in the country and 40–50 litres (1½–2 cu ft) in town.

There are four types of freezers:
• The two-door model is a combined fridge-freezer with the freezer usually on top.

- The upright model is like a cupboard with storage drawers and occupies a minimum of floor space.
- The chest is horizontal and offers a greater usable volume for the same capacity.
- The combination model consists of an upright freezer placed beside a refrigerator.

The icebox in a three-star refrigerator is intended for the preservation of deep-frozen or frozen foods but is unsuitable for deep-freezing.

☐ **Structure** The interior chamber of a freezer is refrigerated by a circuit of metal tubes containing Freon gas. Food is frozen between −24 c and −40 c (−11 f and −40 f) in a special compartment or packed against the sides of the walls. The apparatus then sets itself on the storage program, its power and freezing ability being measured by the maximum quantity of lean beef that can be frozen in 24 hours per 100 litres (4 cu ft) of usable capacity. An external indicator shows when the freezer is in storage mode, a second indicator signals the freezing mode, and finally a light appears to show if a door is not properly closed, or if the temperature is rising abnormally. A thermometer that can be read from the outside means that the door does not have to be opened. Various accessories can be useful: a temperature register (which indicates changes in temperature during a period of absence), a special knife-saw (for frozen products), a thermo-wrapper, and a vacuum pump to eliminate air when packing the food.

☐ **Choice of position** The freezer should be placed in a room where the average temperature varies little (between 16 and 22 c, 60 and 70 f), not in a cold place which is unheated in winter, nor near a heater or a cooking appliance. The room should be well ventilated and the air should circulate freely around the freezer.

freezing CONGÉLATION

Submitting a perishable foodstuff to the action of cold to preserve it. The temperature at the centre of the food must be brought to between −10 and −18 c (14 and 0 f) as quickly as possible. It is the speed with which the water contained in the food crystallizes which prevents all microbial development and preserves the palatability and nutritional qualities of the food until it is defrosted. Freezing is distinguished from deep-freezing by the length of the operation and the level of temperature attained; a product deep-frozen at −40 c (−40 f) becomes merely a frozen product if it is kept and transported at −10 to −15 c (14 to 5 f). Deep-freezing is the usual industrial method of preservation, freezing usually being restricted to domestic use. The whole process can be completed on the spot: the products are stored in the apparatus in which they were frozen, after being packed and carefully labelled, so that there is no break in the freezing process.

☐ **What to freeze** Almost all foods can be frozen, although some require preliminary preparation: eggs, for example, cannot be frozen in their shells but can be stored when lightly beaten. The only rule is that one should not freeze anything that is not completely fresh. In the country the possibilities are enormous (game, freshly harvested foods, etc.); in towns and cities the products are not sufficiently fresh. Cooked dishes and pastry (dough) constitute a large part of family freezer products.

☐ **How to freeze large quantities of food** Set the apparatus to 'maximum freeze' six hours before starting.

- Never overload.
- Work quickly and package in small quantities: this avoids defrosting larger quantities than required. Base quantities on the number of people usually eating together.
- Make the best use of the space available. Food should be packed flat against the walls of the freezer during freezing and then piled up to store, without taking too much space. Small items are piled on trays and quickly frozen, then packaged quickly to finish the operation as swiftly as possible.
- Do not forget to label the food, noting the contents, date of freezing, number of portions, and optimum date of storage.
- Once the freezing is finished, arrange the products as closely together as possible as this preserves the cold.
- Set the apparatus at 'store'.

☐ **Preparing food for freezing**
- Vegetables: blanch quickly in boiling

Rules for freezing

food	choice	preparation	packaging	defrosting	cooking	storage time
meat	• Meat from the butcher	• Prepared by a butcher	• In plastic film	• Thin cuts for grilling (broiling): not necessary	Very hot, then moderate	8–10 months
	• Freshly slaughtered meat	• Remove fat, cut up as for immediate cooking		• Roasts: 12–24 hours in the fridge	As usual	
	• After 3–5 days ageing in a cold room			• Other preparations: not necessary	A little longer	

NOTE: Never freeze minced meat

food	choice	preparation	packaging	defrosting	cooking	storage time
poultry, rabbits, game	• Poultry and rabbits: plucked and singed (or skinned), gutted straight after killing, and kept 24 hours in the fridge	• For roasting: stuff body cavity with crushed kitchen foil, tie, and treat as for fresh meat	• In plastic film	• Whole: 24 hours in the fridge	As usual, or a little longer	8–10 months
	• Game: bled as much as possible, stored for 2–3 days, then plucked and gutted as for poultry and rabbits	• Other preparations: cut into pieces	• In sealed freezer bags	• Pieces: 12–15 hours in or out of the fridge		
	• Venison: as for meat		• In plastic film			
	• Water fowl: raw or cooked		• In aluminium foil containers			

food	choice	preparation	packaging	defrosting	cooking	storage time
fish and shellfish	• Fresh fish (caught less than 4 hours beforehand)	• Whole: gut, scale, or skin, then wash, dry with absorbent paper, and stuff body cavity with crushed foil. Wrap in foil or plastic film and freeze on a tray, turning over	• In sealed freezer bags	• For grilling, poaching, or cooking in the oven: not necessary	A little longer	Fish 4–6 months
		• Slices: freeze raw, on a tray		• For frying: several hours in the fridge		Shellfish 2–3 months
		• Small fish: gut, dry, and freeze raw on a tray				
		• Shellfish: cook as usual				
vegetables	• Fresh vegetables (gathered less than 12 hours beforehand)	• Peel, clean, wash, and if necessary cut into dice or slices	• In sealed freezer bags: artichokes, carrots, cabbage, turnips, peas	• For boiling: not necessary	In boiling salted water Medium heat	6–9 months
	• Most suitable varieties	• Blanch in unsalted boiling water (1 litre (2 pints, 4¼ cups) water for 50–100 g (2–4 oz) vegetables) for 3–10 minutes according to texture and thickness	• In aluminium or plastic containers: asparagus, spinach, sorrel, leeks, salad vegetables	• For braising: not necessary	As usual	
		• Drain, then plunge into very cold water	• In double wrapping: onions (smell)	• For frying: not necessary, unless to be coated (fritters; 12 hours in the fridge)		
		• Drain again and dry in warm air		• For gratins: 12 hours in the fridge		
		• Variation: sweat for 5 minutes, then chill.				

EXCEPTIONS – Do not peel aubergines (eggplants) or courgettes (zucchini)
– For artichokes, salsify, and mushrooms, add lemon juice to blanching water
– Tomatoes: hollow out if they are to be stuffed, otherwise freeze in quarters or crushed
NOTE: For fruit and vegetables the amount of time required for blanching, and the final result, varies according to the variety and – within the same variety – from one year to another, and even from one part of the season to another. Be guided by experience

		Preparation	Packaging	Defrosting	Storage time
fruit	Fresh fruit (gathered less than 12 hours beforehand)	• Clean, wash, and (if necessary) stone (pit) and chop • Dry in warm air • Freeze on a tray before packing, either as they are or dusted with sugar (for small fruit) • Or, put into containers and sprinkle with a light syrup	• In plastic containers	• For cooking: not necessary • For salads, garnishes, or pâtisserie: 2–3 hours in the fridge	8–12 months
cooked dishes	Roast meats, casseroles, etc.	• Usual preparation, but stop about 10 minutes before the end of cooking time	• In aluminium containers • In waxed cartons (soup, fruit juice)		1–3 months
pastry	Raw dough	• Usual preparation • Divide into required amounts • Roll out and line mould or tin	• In plastic film • In thin aluminium foil and freezer bag	• 3–6 hours in the fridge • 1–2 hours in the fridge or not at all	Cook longer / About 3 months

unsalted water (except for tomatoes and mushrooms), then drain, wipe, plunge into iced water, drain again, and dry thoroughly.

● Fruit: peel and remove the stones (pits), wipe thoroughly without washing.

● Meat: remove as much fat as possible and cut into joints or serving-sized pieces (the larger the pieces the less damage to the meat from freezing).

● Poultry: pluck, draw, singe, remove fat, stuff with crumpled kitchen foil, and truss (or cut into pieces).

● Fish: gut (clean), scale, dry, stuff with kitchen foil if whole (or cut into slices), trim, and dry.

● Soft-fat (soft-ripened) cheeses: choose when just ripe and wrap.

● Cooked dishes: reduce cooking time by 10–20 minutes.

● Pastry (dough): wrap portions of pastry or roll out and shape onto aluminium trays.

☐ **Packaging** The package must be impermeable to smells; it should be light and not bulky. This excludes glass, tin, and round dishes and favours kitchen foil and plastic freezer bags, which must be hermetically sealed by thermowrapper (freezer paper). Square and rectangular foil or plastic boxes are also used (for liquids).

☐ **Defrosting of frozen products** Preliminary defrosting is not necessary for small cuts of meat, fish, or vegetables. They should be heated immediately to maximum temperature in boiling water or in a preheated oven or under a grill so that they are defrosted, sealed, and cooked in one. In general, frozen vegetables cook more quickly than the same fresh vegetables (since the former have been blanched before freezing), while frozen meats require longer cooking than fresh meats. Precooked dishes which are placed directly in a saucepan or in the oven in their container always heat very quickly. Defrosting is, however, essential for large meat items (whole birds, roasts), shellfish, pastry, pastry dishes, and cheeses. This should preferably take place in the refrigerator (2–20 hours according to the type and size of the product) or in a microwave oven set on the defrost position. No food should ever be refrozen.

French cooking
HISTOIRE DE LA CUISINE FRANÇAISE

Throughout history, bread has always been an important part of the French diet. In ancient Gaul, which was essentially an agricultural region, the peasants used to prepare flat cakes of millet, oats, barley, and wheat. They were good hunters and ate game, poultry, and also pork, the fat of which was used in various culinary preparations. Because of the abundance of herds of wild pigs in the forests, the Gauls perfected the art of preserving meat by salting and smoking and the pork butchers (*lardarii*) of the time had such a high reputation that they even exported their pork to Rome. Meals were washed down with *cervoise* (barley beer), and in the Marseilles region, wine was drunk as well. Centuries earlier, the Greeks had introduced vines into the region and Marseilles also imported wine from Italy.

☐ **From the Romans to the barbarians** The Romans, with their refined habits and their tradition of great cookery, exerted a profound influence on the Gauls from the 1st century onwards, above all on the wealthy classes: the recipes of Apicius were handed down until the Middle Ages. Whereas their ancestors took their meals seated around the table, the Gallo-Roman noblemen dined on reclining couches and enjoyed, as did the Romans, beans, chickpeas, grilled snails, oysters, dormouse stuffed with walnuts, and jam made from violets and honey. Cooking food in olive oil gained ground, and orchards were developed. It is even recorded that fig trees used to grow in little Lutetia (ancient Paris). However, the most important and influential factor of all was the widespread establishment of wine-growing areas: Italian vine plants were introduced into the Bordeaux region, the Rhône valley, Burgundy, and Moselle. Soon, the wine merchants of Gaul invaded the markets of the Empire to the detriment of Roman wines, all the more successfully since the Gauls had discovered that wine could be kept longer if it was stored in casks. Competition became so lively that in 92 AD the emperor

Domitian ordered half the vineyards of Gaul to be destroyed.

After the Germanic invasions, Gaul went through a tragic period of food shortage and famines marked the beginning of the Middle Ages. The Merovingian and, later, the Carolingian nobles imitated the luxurious example set by the Romanized Gauls and feasted on a wide variety of highly spiced game (boar, wild ox, reindeer, and even camel), while the masses contented themselves with oatmeal gruels, and the basic dish was a hearty soup made with root vegetables enriched with bacon. Meat was eaten only on special occasions. Agricultural techniques regressed, the economy became autarkic, and until the 8th century, there was a massive slump in trade.

☐ **The influence of the church** What remained of the ancient culture had found a refuge in the monasteries. The great religious orders extolled manual labour, and vast areas of land were cleared for cultivation. Kilns, workshops, and hostelries for pilgrims were also established near the abbeys. The monks undertook the essential responsibility for selecting vine plants, and also supervised the manufacture and maturing of cheeses. Above all, however, the Church altered the diet of the population by forcing people to abstain on certain days in the year from eating any kind of animal fat or meat, which 'kindle lust and passion'; as a result, this encouraged both fishing and the breeding of pike, eels, and carp in the fish ponds. Whale blubber, a greatly prized food, was permitted during Lent; furthermore, the increased consumption of fish brought about improved methods of salting and smoking.

Consequently, the attics and cellars of the great Carolingian cities and those of the abbeys were always well stocked, and the banquets were sumptuous. The emperor Charlemagne personally supervised the good management of the imperial estates. Above all, he enjoyed hunting, and the word *gibier* (game) dates from this time. But abundance was still preferred to culinary elegance, and serious food shortages continued. The study of monastic meals reveals impressive rations of leguminous plants rich in proteins: 200 g (7 oz) dried vegetables, 2 kg (4½ lb) bread, 100 g (4 oz) cheese, together with honey, salt, and wine (about 6000 Cal per meal for each person). Such a keen appetite can be explained by the struggle against the cold, by fear of food shortages, and by the lack of protein and other fortifying foods with a small volume. The population, which had dropped to perhaps 8 million inhabitants, lived mainly as its ancestors had done, but in a world where insecurity and the lack of communications often caused shortages, or even famine. The absence of methods of food preservation meant that food frequently went bad: for example, flour infected with ergot caused ergot poisoning.

☐ **The opening up of the Mediterranean** The setting up of the feudal society in the 8th and 9th centuries contributed to the restoration of relative security. The resumption of trade caused new cities to be built and a new class to develop – the middle class or *bourgeois*, a group dominating the poorer citizens, such as journeymen, labourers, and unskilled workers. The cities needed regular provisions, which brought about the establishment of fairs and markets.

The taste for fish and poultry predominated, but products became more varied with the gradual expansion of trade in the Mediterranean and also because of the pilgrimages and the Crusades. Plums from Damascus (damsons), figs from Malta, dates, pomegranates, pistachio nuts, rice and buckwheat, and above all spices (cinnamon, ginger, aniseed, cloves, and nutmeg) appeared on the tables of the rich together with various seasoned dishes whose freshness sometimes left much to be desired! Soon, condiments became indispensable aids to cooking, and the citizens of Dijon added their contribution in the 12th century by discovering mustard, an adaptation from an old Roman recipe. Also, by the 10th century, the sugar trade was established in the Mediterranean, centred on Venice.

City dwellers are traditionally eaters of bread and meat and guilds of butchers and bakers were powerful organizations in the cities, where people's fortunes were assessed by the quantities of bread that they bought. Pork was the main type of meat, but joints of mutton and beef formed part of the menus of the rich, and at the same time, *rotisseurs* (sellers of roast meat) and pie makers multiplied. Cheeses were made in all parts of France and, gradually, wine ousted beer in popularity, except in Flanders and Picardy. Cider, which had been made for several centuries, gained ground in Brittany from the 14th century onwards.

☐ **Prestigious meals** Because of his rank, the nobleman was obliged to keep open house in his château: he was responsible for feeding his *maisnie*, which included not only his family but also his equerries and vassals. The menservants set up the table with trestles and planks of oak in the communal rooms. There was no tablecloth and the plates and dishes were very basic, made of baked clay, wood, or tin. The cutlery consisted of spoons and knives, and in the 12th century a type of two-pronged fork came into use. As the kitchen was separated from the keep through fear of fires, the servant brought the dish to the table covered with a cloth to keep it warm. The meal consisted of either game or roast pork, poultry of some kind, eggs prepared in various ways, either cheese or curdled milk, and cooked fruits.

These meals were sometimes veritable feasts. The elaborate arrangement of the dishes on the table, following the recipes of Apicius, demonstrated the power, generosity, taste, and prestige of the nobleman. The famous 14th-century chef Guillaume Tirel, known as Taillevent, was head cook to Charles V. He was the author of *Le Viandier*, a collection of his recipes and a complete record of the cuisine of that period. The edible game at that time included almost all species of feathered or furred animals, including the cormorant, swan, and whale. The royal menus consisted of five dishes, with roasted peacocks and herons, partridges with sugar, young rabbits in spiced sauce, stuffed capons, and kids, together with pies, cress, creams, pears, walnuts, honeyed wines, *nulles* (dessert creams), etc.

The discovery of the Americas at the end of the 15th century resulted in the introduction of a new variety of foods, including sweetcorn, guinea fowls, turkeys, tomatoes, and potatoes. At the same time, table manners became more refined, individual plates were used, and the tables were beautifully decorated with various items of silver.

☐ **The splendour of the Renaissance** The Renaissance heralded a new way of life. The marriage of Catherine de' Medici and the future Henri II marked the beginning of the Italian influence on French cuisine, destined to play an important role. It had only very slightly impinged in the reign of François I, a great lover of veal and poultry who, according to Rabelais, had revived the days of feasting and drinking. The middle classes had also acquired an interest in cooking. Whale meat and even donkey were still popular and garlic was widely used as a flavouring, but new foods had also become part of the diet: pasta (such as macaroni and vermicelli), Italian sausages, vegetables (such as artichokes and asparagus), and aromatic herbs (such as basil, sweet marjoram, and sage), which had gradually become more popular than the traditional herbs inherited from the Romans, such as cardamom and cumin.

Catherine de' Medici was also responsible for introducing the Florentine art of decorating the table, considered to be the most advanced in Europe. The fine tablecloths, earthenware, glassware, and silverware, together with the introduction of the fork (which was welcomed with uncertainty) contributed to the pleasure of meals. At the end of the 16th century, Italian cooks and pastrycooks came to France under the influence of Catherine and Marie de' Medici. At this time, the Italian *maîtres queux* (head chefs) were considered to be the best in the world. They taught the French many recipes that have remained in the French culinary repertoire. Cooks of this era were already aware of their role and social importance.

Banquets were magnificent, and a meal served to Henri II himself included a profusion of lampreys in hippocras sauce, hotpots, ducklings *à la Malvoisie*, slices of muraena (an eel-like fish) served with a sauce of egg yolks and herbs, ducks *à la didone*, sturgeon fillets *à la lombarde*, quarters of roebuck, partridges *à la tonelette*, and a whole series of puddings, such as darioles and échaudes.

☐ **French cooking in the 17th century**
The reign of Henri IV is symbolized by the famous *poule au pot*, which the king promised that his subjects would enjoy once a week, as a symbol of modest comfort and an improvement in the condition of the serfs. In fact, the beginning of the 17th century was marked by the contribution of the agronomist Olivier de Serres, who introduced all garden vegetables into cookery, for example, cauliflowers and asparagus. However, the king had a preference for sweet things and so sugared almonds, marzipan (almond paste), and tarts with musk and ambergris became fashionable, together with all kinds of jam. As early as 1555 the Italian café owners had taught the French how to make sorbets, and ice creams followed a century later. Heavily spiced food declined in popularity and a number of cookery books were written, the best-known of which is *Cuisinier français*, by François de la Varenne, which appeared in 1651. It was the first book to fix rules and principles and thus to establish some order in cooking. It included recipes for cakes and also for the first mille-feuilles. In 1691, the *Cuisinier royal et bourgeois* by Massaliot was published. Its instructions were precise and it showed that the cuisine was becoming more varied.

In the reign of Louis XIV, cooking was spectacular rather than fine or delicate, and the festivities of the Prince of Condé at Chantilly, for example, were particularly sumptuous. The famous Vatel was maître d'hôtel of Condé the Great, a very important position! A great number of dishes were served at each meal, and there are many descriptions of the meals served at the table of Louis XIV, who ate too heavily for a true gourmet.

The Palatine Princess wrote: 'I have very often seen the king eat four plates of different soups, an entire pheasant, a partridge, a large plateful of salad, mutton cut up in its juice with garlic, two good pieces of ham, a plateful of cakes, and fruits and jams.'

However, Louis XIV established the habit of having dishes served separately. Before this time, everything was piled up together in a large pyramid. In his reign, the culinary utensils of the Middle Ages were replaced by a *batterie de cuisine*, which included many new pots and pans in tinplate and wrought iron and, later, the introduction of silver utensils.

Louis had a passion for vegetables, which led La Quintinie to develop gardening: green peas were produced in March and strawberries in April. Oysters and lamb were particularly highly prized, and elaborate dishes were concocted. One sauce became famous: béchamel, named after the financier Louis de Béchameil, who drafted recipes and precepts in verse.

Coffee, tea, and chocolate were favoured by the aristocracy, and doctors debated about their advantages and drawbacks. Establishments were set up specializing in these exotic drinks. For example, in 1680 the Café Procope opened in Paris. Here, fruit juices, ices and sorbets, exotic wines, hippocras, orgeat pastes, crystallized (candied) fruits, fruits preserved in brandy, etc., were sold. In addition to the coffee houses, taverns, inns, and cafés had multiplied in the city and were visited frequently by princes and their courtiers.

☐ **French cooking from the Regency to Louis XVI** The Regency and the reign of Louis XV are regarded as the golden age of French cookery. At the same time, the produce of rural France slowly improved both in quality and quantity and there was no further famine. The Age of Enlightenment united the pleasures of the table with those of the mind, and gastronomy, a new word, was the main topic of conversation: the *petits soupers* (little suppers) of the Regent and the choice meals prepared for the king and his great noblemen did more to perfect the culinary art than the showy banquets in the reign of Louis XIV. Great chefs rivalled each other in imaginative cookery. They discovered how to make stocks from meat juices and began to use them to add flavour to sauces. Mahonnaise sauce appeared at the table of the Marshal de Richelieu, the conqueror of Port-Mahon; pâté de foie gras garnished with truffles might have been the idea of Nicolas-François Doyen, chef of the first president of the Parliament of Bordeaux; La Chapelle, the chef of Marie Leszczynska, prepared *bouchées à la reine* (chicken vols-au-vent), and Marin, the butler of the Marshal de Soubise, was the first to glaze meat and deglaze (i.e. make a sauce from) the juices. It was in the mansions of rich financiers that the culinary art expanded. Food shops, pastrycooks, and confectioners achieved perfection and people also learnt how to recognize foreign specialities, such as caviar, beefsteak, curry, and Madeira. At the same time, the concern for maintaining regular food supplies encouraged methods of cultivating and storing grain.

During the first years of the reign of Louis XVI, culinary methods continued to become more refined, more order and logic was established, menus for festive occasions became more elegant, and there were further improvements in all branches of catering. The first restaurant was established during this period and menus of the restaurants at that time provide valuable information about the cuisine of the era. The menus included 12 soups, 24 hors d'oeuvres, 15–20 entrées of beef, 20 entrées of mutton, 30 entrées of fowl or game, 12–20 entrées of veal, 12 dishes of pâtisserie, 24 dishes of fish, 15 roasts, 50 entremets, and 50 desserts.

Louis XVI is also famous for encouraging Parmentier, the economist and agronomist, in his written works on food. These included several reports on ways of using potatoes, and he finally succeeded in popularizing this once-scorned vegetable.

☐ **From the Revolution to the Second Empire** The Revolution caused a distinct slowing-down in the development of French cuisine, but Carême, a young pastrycook already famous for his *pièces montées*, saved it from sinking into obscurity. Furthermore, science contributed to its revival with the discoveries of Appert (food-preserving techniques) and Delessert (sugar extraction from sugar beet). Already the chef Laguipière and the gastronome Cussy showed a taste for the display of the Empire; two tables were particularly famous, that of Cambacérès and that of Talleyrand. At the same time, the fashion for restaurants made accessible to a greater number what had until then been the privilege of an elite. Gastronomic literature, invented by Grimod de La Reynière and illustrated by Brillat-

Savarin, played an important part. Louis XVIII himself created recipes. Under Charles X, the French discovered couscous, and trout farming was developed. The kneading machine improved the quality of bread, and after 1840 railways ensured that provisions were fresher. Stock rearing made considerable progress, and the quality of the meat produced superb results. In about 1860, horse meat, less expensive than beef, was widely available for sale; horse butchers multiplied. The invention of the gas cooker was another great milestone, and many more cafés and restaurants were established, particularly on the country side of toll-gates near Paris. Meals during the Second Empire reached a peak of excellence. This period was marked by an obsession with good living, particularly among the great writers: Flaubert, the Goncourt brothers, and Sainte-Beuve.

After the Palais Royal, the 'boulevard' became the centre of famous restaurants. Joseph Favre pursued his career at the Café de la Paix, then at the Café Riche; Dugléré composed succulent menus for the Café Anglais, where he received the king of Prussia (1867) and Czar Alexander II, who had come to hear Offenbach's *La Grande-Duchesse de Gérolstein*.

The meals included in turn soups, entrées, roasts, and desserts. It is not so much the quantity of dishes which is surprising but the position of the courses: there was no hesitation in serving a pâté as an entremets and sweet dishes as an entrée.

☐ **The 20th century** At the beginning of the 20th century, French cooking gained supremacy throughout the world. Its chefs reigned supreme in the kitchens of Buckingham Palace, the Winter Palace of St Petersburg, and in the great international hotels. Paris became the Mecca of gastronomy. The Edwardian era was the age when great books were written about cooking by such authors as Urbain Dubois, Auguste Bernard, Escoffier, and Bignon. The Académie Goncourt organized its first dinner in 1903, and Prosper Montagné, the most famous chef of the last 50 years, opened the most luxurious restaurant of this frivolous era. There was also a fashion for local bistros, run by natives of the Auvergne and Périgord, and also by gastronomic associations. Now, as the 20th century draws to a close, the influence of Curnonsky still prevails and the great classic dishes of the cuisine of provincial France continue to uphold the reputation of French cookery with such dishes as pot-au-feu, blanquette, tripe, bouillabaisse, cassoulet, bourguignon, and Tatin tart. French cookery has also been introduced to, and influenced by, other culinary traditions, with the result that exotic and foreign restaurants flourish. The great classics of European cuisine were incorporated early on, but the Frenchman is now discovering Chinese, Indian, and Scandinavian cookery. See also *nouvelle cuisine*.

French dressing

See *vinaigrette*.

French fairs and markets

FOIRES ET MARCHÉS

The oldest market in Paris, in the heart of the city, was established at the beginning of the 12th century for selling wheat. Not long afterwards Louis le Gros established another market in the place where Les Halles operated right up to 1969, when it moved out to Rungis. Nowadays the art of selecting the right ingredients and looking for top-quality food is still practised. All over France, markets take place on fixed days, once or twice a week, in the open air or in market buildings. No matter how small the purchase, the customer is keen to obtain the best goods that are available. Careful inspection of the foods which the traders have on offer is still part of the shopping process.

The great annual fairs used to be held in the church square on the parish saint's day. In Paris, the ham fair, which began on the last Tuesday of Lent, was held in the church square of Notre-Dame before being moved to the Boulevard Richard-Lenoir and then to Pantin. The Lendit fair, established by King Dagobert, was held on the Plaine Saint-Denis for a fortnight in June. The products of this fair came from all over France and even from abroad, especially Flanders. The Saint-Germain fair, established by Louis XI in 1482 near the church of Saint-Germain-des-Prés, started on 3 February and lasted until Holy Week: it flourished until 1785 and sold all types of goods in small wooden booths. Plays were also performed and coffee was served for the first time in France by an Armenian called Pascal. The Saint-Laurent fair, the Saint-Ovide fair, and the Temple fair were the forerunners of the great annual exhibitions now known as the Salon de l'agriculture (Agricultural Show) and the Foire de Paris (Paris Show). Several other towns in France specializing in certain types of products also hold fairs, including Arpajon (beans) and Excideuil (foies gras).

French toast   PAIN PERDU

A dessert consisting of slices of stale bread (or brioche or milk bread) soaked in milk, dipped in eggs beaten with sugar, then lightly fried in butter. French toast is served hot and crisp. It was formerly called *pain crotté, pain à la romaine,* or *croûtes dorées.* In the south of France, it was traditionally eaten on feast days, particularly at Easter. Originally intended to use up crusts and leftover pieces of bread, French toast today is usually made with milk bread. It may be accompanied by custard cream, jam, or compote.

> RECIPE

French toast   PAIN PERDU   Boil ½ litre (17 fl oz, 2 cups) milk with half a vanilla pod (bean) and 100 g (4 oz, ½ cup) sugar, then leave it to cool. Cut 250 g (9 oz) stale brioche into fairly thick slices. Soak them in the cooled milk, without letting them fall apart, then dip them in 2 eggs beaten as for an omelette with a little caster (superfine) sugar. Heat 100 g (4 oz, ½ cup) butter in a pan and fry the slices. When golden on one side, turn them over to cook the other side. Arrange them on a round dish and dust them with caster sugar.

Freneuse

A soup made with turnips and potatoes in light stock or consommé, thickened with fresh cream. It can be garnished with small turnip balls.

Frères Provençaux

A Paris restaurant run by three brothers-in-law from Provence – Maneille, Simon, and Barthélemy (its full name was Les Trois Frères Provençaux). In 1786 they opened a cheap restaurant in the Rue Helvétius (now the Rue Sainte-Anne). It quickly became successful because of the novelty of the dishes that were served – brandade, bouillabaisse, tomatoes and salt cod with garlic, and mutton chops *à la provençale*. Maneille continued to run the establishment, while his brothers-in-law went to work for the Prince of Condé and remained with him until he emigrated. When reunited once again, they transferred the restaurant to the arcades of the Palais-Royal, at 38 Galerie de Beaujolais. The restaurant was now a luxury establishment and very fashionable. It was in vogue throughout the early 19th century, still serving specialities of Provence and Marseille. 'The cooking, the cellar, and the host are all equally delightful,' said Grimod de La Reynière. In 1836 the restaurant was sold and lost both its reputation and its customers. It became successful once more under the second Empire, under the supervision of Godin, Dugléré, Hurel, and lastly Goyard. It was finally closed in 1869.

friand

A small puff-pastry case filled with sausagemeat, minced (ground) meat, ham, or cheese, baked in the oven, and served as a hot hors d'oeuvre.

A *friand* is also a small sweet pastry – a barquette often made with an almond paste filling and elaborately decorated.

RECIPE

Sausage rolls FRIANDS À LA VIANDE Mince together 2 peeled shallots, 100 g (4 oz) mushrooms, 200 g (7 oz) veal, 200 g (7 oz) smoked pork, and a bunch of parsley (a food processor may be used). Add 1 tablespoon cream and season with salt and pepper. Mix together well. Dust the worktop with flour and roll out 500 g (18 oz) puff pastry to a thickness of about 3 mm (¼ in); cut it into 6 rectangles of equal size. Divide the filling into 6 portions and roll into sausage shapes the same length as the width of the pastry rectangles. Put a 'sausage' at one end of each rectangle and roll it up. Score the top with the point of a knife and glaze with beaten egg. Bake in the oven at 220 C (425 F, gas 7) for about 30 minutes.

The filling can also be made with fine sausagemeat mixed with chopped onion, parsley, salt, and pepper.

friandise

The French word for a delicacy when referring to pâtisserie or sweetmeats. The word is often used for petits fours or sweets eaten between meals. It used to mean a treat in the general sense, and the term *friandises de confiseur* (confectioner's treats) was used for chocolates, crystallized (candied) fruits, nougats, fruit jellies, etc., which were also referred to as *mignardises*. Friandises may be served with coffee or tea, or at the end of a meal following the dessert, in which case an assortment of such delicacies may be served.

Fribourg

The name sometimes used in France for Swiss Gruyère cheese, because the Gruyère Valley, where the best Gruyère cheese is manufactured, is in the district of Fribourg.

fricadelle

A meatball or burger made of minced (ground) meat or forcemeat. Fricadelles may be deep- or shallow-fried or cooked in a ragout. They are Belgian or German specialities and are sometimes cooked in beer. They are served with a sauce (tomato, paprika, or curry), together with fresh pasta, rice, or a vegetable purée.

fricandeau

A dish made of noix of veal larded with bacon and braised, roasted, or fried. It is usually served with spinach, a sorrel fondue, peas, or a jardinière of vegetables. It can also be served cold, having been left to cool in the cooking juices.

The name is also applied to slices or fillets of fish, mainly those of sturgeon, tuna, or even salmon steak, braised in a fish stock.

Fricandeau is also a special item of

charcuterie from southwestern France. It consists of minced pork neck, liver, and kidneys flavoured with herbs, shaped into balls, wrapped in caul, and cooked in the oven. They are served cold, coated with aspic jelly and lard.

RECIPE

Veal fricandeau with sorrel FRICAN-DEAU DE VEAU À L'OSEILLE Lard a slice of noix of veal, about 3–4 cm (1 in) thick, with some thin strips of fat bacon that have been marinated for 30 minutes in a mixture of oil, chopped parsley, salt, and pepper. Then brush the veal with melted butter or with oil containing crushed veal bones. Sauté 2 diced carrots and 2 sliced onions in butter until golden brown and put them in a braising pan. Place the veal on the vegetables with the crushed bones, a bouquet garni, and half a calf's foot that has been boned and blanched. Add enough white or red wine to half-cover the meat; season with salt and pepper. Cover the pan and bring to the boil. Place the pan in the oven preheated to 220 c (425 f, gas 7) and cook uncovered for 1 hour. Remove the pan and replace on the top of the cooker. Mix 1 tablespoon tomato purée with ½ litre (17 fl oz, 2 cups) stock and add it to the pan so that the veal is now covered. Bring back to the boil, return to the oven, and cook for a further 1½ hours. Drain the meat and arrange it on an ovenproof dish. Strain the liquid in the pan, pour some of it over the meat, and glaze it in the oven. Serve the fricandeau with a sorrel fondue and the remainder of the sauce in a sauceboat.

fricassee FRICASSÉE

A preparation of chicken in a white sauce (veal and lamb may also be prepared in this way). Formerly in France, the term denoted various kinds of ragout of chicken meat, fish, or vegetables in white or brown stock. The meat is cut into pieces, an aromatic garnish is added, and it is then sautéed over a low heat, without browning. The meat is then coated with flour, some white stock is added, and the meat is cooked in the thickened liquid. A fricassee is usually cooked with cream and garnished with small glazed onions and lightly cooked mushrooms. Fricassees are also made with fried fish which is subsequently cooked in a sauce.

In the 17th century, when La Varenne referred to fricassees of calves' liver, calves' feet, chicken, young pigeon, potato, and asparagus, this method of cooking was very common and not highly regarded. Subsequently, the word became distorted to *fricot*, which, in popular parlance, designates any simple but popular tasty dish.

RECIPES

Fricassee of chicken à la berrichonne FRICASSÉE DE POULET À LA BER-RICHONNE Cut a chicken into medium-sized pieces. Brown 350 g (12 oz, 3 cups) new carrots in 50 g (2 oz, 4 tablespoons) butter in a pan (leave them whole if small; quarter if large). Drain them, and then brown the chicken pieces in the same butter. Add 2.5 dl (8 fl oz, 1 cup) chicken stock, the carrots, a bouquet garni, and some salt and pepper. Cover the pan and cook gently for 30 minutes. Remove the chicken pieces and keep them warm. Mix 2 egg yolks and a pinch of fine sugar with 2 dl (7 fl oz, ¾ cup) double (heavy) cream, 1 tablespoon wine vinegar, and a few drops of the chicken stock. Pour the mixture into the pan and mix thoroughly with the pan juices. Heat without boiling so that the sauce thickens a little. Serve the chicken coated with the sauce and sprinkled with chopped parsley.

Fricassee of sea fish with Bellet zabaglione FRICASSÉE DE MER AU SABAYON DE BELLET (from a recipe by Pierre Estival) For 6 persons, you will need 800 g (1¾ lb) young turbot, 1.5 kg (3½ lb) John Dory, 4 slices of monkfish, 2 red mullet, 4 scampi, and ½ litre (17 fl oz, 2 cups) white Bellet wine or a good Provençal wine. Fillet the turbot and the John Dory. Wash the fillets and season with salt and pepper. Heat 3 tablespoons (¼ cup) olive oil and 40 g (1½ oz, 3 tablespoons) butter in a large frying pan (skillet). When the mixture foams, add all the fish and the scampi. Add a large chopped shallot and cook for a few seconds. Add about 1 dl (6 tablespoons, scant ½ cup) Bellet. Remove the red mullet, fillet them, and replace in the pan. Add 5 cl (3 tablespoons, ¼ cup) fish stock reduced by half and finish cooking. Arrange the fish on a dish and keep hot.

Make a zabaglione with 8 egg yolks and 4 dl (14 fl oz, 1¾ cups) Bellet. Season with salt and pepper and add ½ litre (17 fl oz, 2 cups) hot fresh cream. The zabaglione should be hot and foamy, but must not boil. Adjust the seasoning. Coat the fricassee with the zabaglione. Sprinkle with fresh chervil, and serve with lightly cooked (*al dente*) French beans, with a knob of butter on top.

Lamb fricassee   FRICASSÉE D'AG-NEAU   Wash and wipe some pieces of lamb (fillet, lean leg, or shoulder), fry in butter without browning, and season with salt and pepper. Sprinkle with 2 tablespoons (3 tablespoons) flour and stir over the heat. Add some white stock or consommé and a bouquet garni, and bring to the boil. Simmer with the lid on for 45–60 minutes. Fry some mushrooms in butter and glaze some button onions. Remove the pieces of lamb from the pan, replace with the onions and mushrooms, and stir them into the pan juices. Take off the heat and add an egg yolk to thicken. Pour the sauce into a large heated dish, add the lamb, and sprinkle with chopped parsley. Serve hot.

Minute fricassee of chicken   FRICAS-SÉE DE POULET À LA MINUTE   (from Plumerey's recipe) Joint 2 chickens in the usual way and place them in a saucepan with 175 g (6 oz, ¾ cup) good-quality melted butter. Fry the chicken without browning, add 2 tablespoons (3 tablespoons) flour, season with salt, pepper, and grated nutmeg, and add sufficient water to make a lightly thickened sauce. Add 6 blanched button onions and a bouquet garni and cook over a brisk heat, ensuring that the chicken pieces do not burn and the sauce is gradually reduced. After 25 minutes, test one of the thighs to see that it is cooked. Add 250 g (9 oz, 2 generous cups) button mushrooms and skim the fat off the sauce. Blend in 4 egg yolks to thicken the sauce and add a dash of fresh lemon juice.

fricassée périgourdine

The name given in Périgord to the vegetables of a pot-au-feu. Before this is quite cooked, the vegetables are removed, drained, sliced, browned in butter or oil, sprinkled with flour, moistened with a little stock, and put back in the pot-au-feu to finish cooking.

The same name is given to a mixture of aromatic vegetables cooked in butter or oil with garlic and ham. It is used in various soups and stews.

fricassin

A speciality of Bourbonnais (especially of Gannat) made from the *fraise* (mesentery) of a young goat. The membrane is washed, then boiled with onions, bay leaf, thyme, and parsley. When cooled and drained, it is cut into pieces and fried in butter. Fresh cream is added towards the end of the cooking time, and the dish is served with chopped parsley.

fricasson

A speciality of Bourbonnais (especially of Montluçon) made from the offal of a young goat. Clotted blood is cooked and cut into small cubes. It is then mixed with pieces of head, tongue, brain, and mesentery (also cooked) and fried in butter. Cream is added towards the end of the cooking time, and the dish is served with a dash of vinegar.

frichti

A colloquial French name for a light meal or snack cooked at home. The word was probably introduced into the French language in the 1860s by Alsatian soldiers and is derived from the German *Frühstück* (breakfast).

fritelle

A Corsican fritter made with leavened dough containing egg yolks and oil. It contains a mixture of chopped beet, mint, and marjoram leaves, or a slice of Corsican sausage, or a square of Broccio (a fresh cream cheese). Fritelles can also be made with chestnut flour and flavoured with fennel seeds. They are then sweetened with plenty of sugar.

friton

A charcuterie speciality from southwestern France. Resembling a rillette, it is made with the residue of melted pork fat and fatty pork pieces, such as belly, which is mixed with pieces of offal (tongue, heart, kidneys, or even head) and cooked in lard.

The word *fritons* is also used for the crisp residues of goose fat and cubes of pork fat, although the more usual word is *grattons* or *gratterons*.

fritot or friteau

A kind of savoury fritter made from small pieces of cooked marinated food that are dipped in a light batter and deep-fried. Fritots are usually made with frogs' legs, shellfish, leftovers of fish, poultry, or meat, various types of offal, or vegetables. They are usually arranged on a paper napkin, garnished with fried parsley and slices of lemon, and served as a hot hors d'oeuvre, accompanied by a spicy tomato sauce.

| RECIPES

frogs'-leg fritots FRITOTS DE GRE-NOUILLES Trim the frogs' legs and marinate them for 30 minutes in a mixture of oil, chopped garlic, chopped parsley, lemon juice, salt, and pepper. Then dip them in a light batter and deep-fry until they are golden brown. Drain on absorbent paper and serve with fried parsley, quarters of lemon, and either curry sauce (see *(á l')indienne*) or gribiche sauce. The frogs' legs can also be threaded onto small skewers before being dipped in the batter and fried.

Fritots of meat or poultry FRITOTS DE VIANDE OU DE VOLAILLE Bone some poached or braised meat or poultry (or use leftovers), cut into even-sized pieces, and marinate in a mixture of oil, brandy, chopped parsley, salt, and pepper. Finish as for frogs'-leg fritots.

Mussel fritots FRITOTS DE MOULES Prepare the mussels *à la marinière*, remove from their shells, drain, and dry. Finish as for oyster fritots.

Oyster fritots FRITOTS D'HUÎTRES Remove the oysters from their shells and poach gently in their own liquor.

Drain and dry, then marinate as for frogs'-leg fritots, but add a pinch of cayenne to the marinade. Finish as for frogs'-leg fritots and serve with Italian sauce (see *(à l')italienne*).

Salmon fritots FRITOTS DE SAUMON Cut some raw salmon into thin slices or large dice and marinate in a mixture of oil, lemon juice, chopped parsley, salt, and pepper. Finish as for frogs'-leg fritots and serve with tomato or hollandaise sauce or sauce verte.

Sole fritots FRITOTS DE SOLE Cut some sole fillets in two (or four if large fillets) and prepare as for frogs'-leg fritots. Serve with a flavoured mayonnaise sauce.

fritter BEIGNET

A preparation consisting of a piece of cooked or raw food coated in batter and fried in deep fat or oil. Other types of fritter can be made using choux pastry, yeast dough, or waffle batter. Some believe that fritters were of Saracen origin and were brought back by the Crusaders. They are served, according to their ingredients, as an hors d'oeuvre, a main course, or a dessert, almost always hot and dusted with fine salt or sugar.

When cooking fritters, plenty of oil must always be used because the fritters drop to the bottom of the pan when they are placed in the oil and then rise to the surface as the heat cooks the batter. Fritters should be turned halfway through cooking. The temperature of the oil is usually moderate but can vary considerably according to the type of batter used, whether the food coated in the batter is raw or cooked, and whether the fritter is sweet or savoury.

The principle of the fritter is simple, but the dishes vary enormously in shape and taste and range from regional specialities to classical dishes.
● **Fritters made with batter** – Some foods containing a large amount of water must be coated with batter for making fritters. Raw ingredients are cut small so they cook quickly; ready-cooked ingredients may or may not be marinated. Savoury fritters (made with vegetables, fish, cheese, etc.) are served as an hors d'oeuvre, a main course

(sometimes with a sauce) or as a cocktail snack (e.g. prawn (shrimp) fritters).

Sweet fritters are made with fruit or flowers. The best known of the former are apple fritters, but they can also be made with bananas, apricots, etc. Flower fritters were very popular in the Middle Ages, using violets, elderflowers, lilies, etc.; but today mimosa flowers, elderflowers, and marrow (squash) flowers are practically the only ones still used. Sweet fritters can also be prepared with a cold cream sauce, cold rice pudding, or semolina cut into squares or rectangles and coated in batter.

• **Fritters made with choux pastry –** Fritters made using sweet or savoury choux pastry are known as soufflé fritters; they are served as hors d'oeuvres or desserts. In savoury recipes, the pastry can be flavoured with grated cheese, diced ham, almonds, etc. Sweet choux pastry gives a basic sweet fritter.

• **Fritters made with yeast dough –** These fritters are made of sweet dough rounds, sometimes filled with jam, plunged into boiling oil. When puffed and golden they are removed from the oil and dusted with sugar.

• **Fritters made with waffle batter –** Fritters made of waffle batter are moulded in long-handled waffle irons of various shapes (stars, boats, hearts, roses, etc.). In France they are mostly used for decoration, but in the USA they are served for breakfast or as a dessert, often with maple syrup.

Fritters are among the most ancient and widespread of regional dishes. Made of special flavoured dough, they are often associated with traditional celebrations: for instance, *bugnes* from Lyon, *merveilles* and *oreillettes* from Montpellier, *beugnons* from Berry, *bignes* from Auvergne, *roussettes* from Strasbourg, *tourtisseaux* from Anjou, and *bottereaux* from Nantes.

RECIPES

Fritter batter I PÂTE À BEIGNETS (OU PÂTE À FRIRE) Sieve 250 g (9 oz, 2¼ cups) flour into a bowl. Heat 2 dl (7 fl oz, ¾ cup) water until just lukewarm. Make a well in the flour and put 1.5 dl (¼ pint, ⅔ cup) beer, the warm water, and a generous pinch of salt in the middle of it. Mix, drawing the flour from the sides to the centre of the well. Add 2 tablespoons (3 tablespoons) groundnut (peanut) oil and mix. Leave to rest for 1 hour if possible. When required for use, stiffly beat 2 or 3 egg whites and fold into the batter. Do not stir or beat. For sweet fritters, flavour the batter with Calvados, Cognac, rum, etc. The batter may also be sweetened with ½ tablespoon granulated sugar and the oil replaced with the same amount of melted butter.

Fritter batter II PÂTE À BEIGNETS (OU PÂTE À FRIRE) Place 250 g (9 oz, ¾ cup) sifted flour in a mixing bowl. Make a well in the centre and add 5 g (1 teaspoon) salt, 2 whole eggs, and 3 dl (½ pint, 1¼ cups) groundnut (peanut) oil. Whisk the eggs and oil together, incorporating a little of the flour. Add 2.5 dl (8 fl oz, 1 cup) beer and, stirring well, gradually incorporate the rest of the flour. Allow to stand for approximately 1 hour. A few minutes before using the batter, stiffly beat 3 egg whites and fold into the batter using a wooden spoon or rubber spatula.

DESSERT FRITTERS

Apple fritters BEIGNETS DE POMMES Core the apples with an apple corer, peel, and cut into rounds about 4 mm (⅛ in) thick. Sprinkle with lemon juice and macerate for 30 minutes in Cognac or Calvados. Drain, dip in batter, and continue as for apricot fritters.

Apricot fritters BEIGNETS D'ABRICOTS Stone (pit) some ripe apricots and macerate for 30 minutes in sugar and rum (or Kirsch, Cognac, etc.). Drain thoroughly, dip in sweetened or unsweetened batter, and deep-fry in hot oil. Remove the fritters, and drain. Dust with caster (superfine) sugar and arrange on a napkin. Fritters may also be served on a plate, dusted with icing (confectioners') sugar and glazed in a hot oven or under a grill (broiler).

Banana fritters BEIGNETS DE BANANES Peel some bananas and cut in half lenghtwise. Macerate for 1 hour in white or dark rum with sugar. Dip in batter and deep-fry in hot oil. Drain and continue as for apricot fritters.

Fig fritters BEIGNETS DE FIGUES
Peel and quarter figs and macerate for
30 minutes in brandy (or liqueur) and
sugar. Dip in batter and continue as for
apricot fritters.

Pineapple fritters BEIGNETS D'ANA-
NAS Slice a peeled fresh pineapple (or
use canned pineapple). Sprinkle the
slices with caster (superfine) sugar and
Kirsch or rum and allow to macerate for
30 minutes. Complete as for apricot
fritters.

Rice fritters BEIGNETS DE RIZ Prepare a thick rice pudding. Spread in a
layer 1.5 cm (½–¾ in) thick and allow
to cool completely. Cut into small
squares, rectangles, or lozenges. Dip in
batter and continue as for apricot fritters.

SAVOURY FRITTERS

Anchovy fritters BEIGNETS D'AN-
CHOIS Soak anchovy fillets in milk to
remove all the salt. Mix together with a
fork (or in a blender) some hard-boiled
(hard-cooked) egg yolk, a little butter,
and some chopped parsley. Spread the
mixture on the anchovy fillets and roll
up. Dip in batter, deep-fry in hot oil, and
serve on a napkin with fried parsley.

Aubergine (eggplant) fritters BEIG-
NETS D'AUBERGINES Peel some
aubergines (eggplants), slice them, and
marinate for 1 hour in oil, lemon juice,
chopped parsley, and salt and pepper.
Continue as for anchovy fritters. The
same method may be used for broccoli,
cardoons, celery, celeriac (celery root),
courgettes (zucchini), cauliflower, marrow (squash) flowers, salsifies, tomatoes, Jerusalem artichokes, and vine
leaves.

Cheese fritters I BEIGNETS DE FROM-
AGE Cut some Gruyère or Comté
cheese into 5 cm (2 in) squares about 4
cm (1½ in) thick. Dip in batter and
continue as for anchovy fritters. Serve
with highly seasoned tomato fondue.

Cheese fritters II BEIGNETS DE
FROMAGE Add grated cheese
(Gruyère or Parmesan), chopped pars-
ley, and pepper to a thick béchamel

sauce. Allow to cool completely. Continue as for chicken liver fritters II.

Chicken liver fritters I BEIGNETS DE
FOIES DE VOLAILLE Remove the gall
from the chicken livers (if present) and
marinate for 30 minutes in oil seasoned
with salt, pepper, and chopped herbs to
taste. Then dry and dip in batter. Continue as for anchovy fritters.

Chicken liver fritters II BEIGNETS DE
FOIES DE VOLAILLE Make a salpicon
of diced chicken livers and mushrooms.
Sauté in butter and bind with some thick
béchamel sauce. Season with salt and
pepper and allow to cool. Divide into 25
g (1 oz) portions and roll into balls. Dip
in batter and continue as for anchovy
fritters.

Mushroom fritters BEIGNETS DE
CHAMPIGNONS Wash some small
fresh tightly closed button mushrooms.
Pat dry and coat with flour. Dip in
batter and continue as for anchovy
fritters. They can be served with a highly
seasoned tomato fondue.

Scampi fritters BEIGNETS DE LAN-
GOUSTINES Cook fresh or frozen
scampi in court-bouillon. Shell the tails
(discarding the heads) and marinate for
30 minutes in oil, lemon juice, and
cayenne. Dip in batter and continue as
for anchovy fritters.

Soft roe fritters BEIGNETS DE
LAITANCES Poach some soft roes (of
herring, carp, or mackerel, for example)
in fish stock, drain, and marinate for 30
minutes in oil, lemon juice, and
cayenne. Dip in batter and continue as
for anchovy fritters.

Soufflé fritters BEIGNETS SOUF-
FLÉS Prepare 250 g (9 oz) unsweetened choux pastry (see *chou*). Using a spoon, divide the pastry into small
balls the size of a walnut. Plunge into
hot oil until the fritters are puffed and
golden. Drain on a cloth and arrange in
a heap on a napkin. The following are
some alternative recipes for soufflé
fritters:

■ *with anchovies* – add 2 tablespoons

finely chopped anchovy fillets (previously soaked in milk) to the choux pastry;

■ *à la hongroise* – add 3 tablespoons onions lightly fried in butter and seasoned with paprika to the pastry;

■ *with cheese* – add 50 g (2 oz, ½ cup) grated cheese (preferably Parmesan) seasoned with a little nutmeg to the pastry;

■ *à la toscane* – add a little cooked lean ham and a little chopped white truffle to the pastry.

fritto misto

An Italian speciality (meaning literally 'fried mixture'), made from an assortment of savoury fritters: sliced chicken, calves' brains or sweetbreads, chicken livers, cauliflower, asparagus tips, artichoke hearts, rice or macaroni croquettes, etc. The ingredients are sometimes marinated, then dipped in a light batter and plunged into very hot deep fat. They are served hot, with lemon quarters, and sometimes accompanied by very small marinated veal escalopes (scallops), coated in breadcrumbs and sautéed in butter.

frog GRENOUILLE

A web-footed amphibian found in damp marshland or alongside ponds and streams. Certain species are edible, but only the leg meat. Frogs' legs were regarded as a tasty dish in the Middle Ages, particularly during Lent. In France two main species are found – the green or common frog, and the rusty or mute frog (so called because the male has no larynx). The green frog has three dark bands on its back and is considered to be more tasty. The draining of marshlands has considerably reduced its numbers, but it can still be found in the Dombes (hence its fame in Lyonnais gastronomy), in Auvergne, Sologne, Brittany, and Alsace. The rusty or mute frog is darker and only approaches the water to mate. It generally inhabits cool places, not necessarily near water. Its flesh is rather less delicate than that of the common frog.

Most of the frogs eaten in France are imported from central Europe and Yugoslavia. They tend to be larger and have more meat than the local species.

Frozen frogs' legs, from bullfrogs, are also imported from Cuba or the United States. These are nearly as big as the legs of guinea fowl but they have very little flavour.

The delicate flavour of the meat is enhanced by seasoning, and frogs' legs are often prepared with herbs, garlic, and chopped parsley. They are also made into blanquettes, soups, omelettes, and mousselines and can be fried or sautéed. The most highly regarded recipes come from Lyon, Alsace, and Poitou. The *Ménagier de Paris* contained recipes for cooking them in soups and in pies.

Frogs' legs are also eaten in Germany and Italy, but they have usually filled the British with disgust. When Escoffier was chef of the Carlton Hotel in London, he managed to have them accepted at the table of the Prince of Wales by calling them *cuisses de nymphes aurore* (legs of the dawn nymphs).

RECIPES

Preparation of frogs' legs PRÉPARA-TION DES GRENOUILLES Skin the frogs by slitting the skin at the neck and pulling it back. Cut the backbone so that the legs are still joined to it and can be cooked in pairs. Cut off the feet. Skewer the legs and soak them in very cold water. Change the water 3 or 4 times over a period of 12 hours, so that the flesh whitens and swells. Dry the legs and cook them according to the recipe. Usually 3 pairs per serving are allowed.

Brochettes of frogs' legs CUISSES DE GRENOUILLE EN BROCHETTES Marinate the frogs' legs for at least 2 hours in a mixture of olive oil, lemon juice, grated garlic, finely chopped parsley, and a pinch each of cayenne. powdered bay leaf, salt, and pepper. Drain, dry, and thread them on skewers. Fry for 7–10 minutes in the oil in which they were marinated, or grill (broil) them gently for 15–20 minutes. Test with a fork to see if they are cooked. Sprinkle with chopped parsley and serve very hot, garnished with slices of lemon.

Fried frogs' legs CUISSES DE GRE-NOUILLE AUX FINES HERBES Season the prepared frogs' legs with salt and pepper and dip them in flour (or in egg and breadcrumbs). Sauté them in butter or olive oil in a shallow frying pan (skillet) for 7–10 minutes over a brisk heat. Drain, and arrange in a heated serving dish. Sprinkle with chopped parsley and lemon juice. If they were cooked in butter, pour it over them; otherwise use maître d'hôtel butter. Serve with boiled potatoes.

fromage glacé

A cone-shaped ice cream of the 18th and early 19th centuries. They originally consisted simply of ice cream in various flavours, but later became what we now call bombes. At that time, the name *fromage* (cheese) was used not only for fermented milk products but for all preparations based on milk, cream, and sugar, provided they were shaped in a mould: thus, a Bavarian cream was known as a *fromage bavarois*. Grimod de La Reynière stated that it was 'in error that this name is given to all sorts of ice creams made in large quantities in moulds. . . . Whatever one calls them, however, these fluted iced cheeses are the most beautiful ornamental desserts. They have the advantage over ice creams served in sundae dishes that they keep longer without melting, and they are better than slabs of ice cream because they are softer.'

Among the fromages glacés popular during the Second Empire were *fromage à l'italienne* (flavoured with lemon marmalade and orange blossom), *fromage de parmesan* (with cinnamon and cloves, poured into a mould and sprinkled with grated Parmesan), and *fromage à la chantilly* (with whipped cream and citron peel).

fromagère

A serving utensil, made of silver plate or stainless steel, containing a small glass dish and a folding lid, which is used for serving grated cheese at the table.

The term is also used for an electric domestic cheese-maker that makes a variety of soft curd cheese using rennet and milk at a thermostatically controlled temperature.

froment

A French term for various types of wheat – soft, hard, and spelt. In cookery, the word *froment* is used in preference to *blé* to avoid any confusion with buckwheat, commonly known as *blé noir* (black wheat). *Fine fleur de froment* (fine wheaten flour) traditionally denotes a superior quality flour used for baking.

Frontignan

A vin doux naturel made from the Muscat Doré grape around the town of Frontignan in the Hérault. Very popular with our ancestors (as 'Frontignac' or 'Frontiniac'), it is less well-known outside France today, because its alcoholic strength (15°) makes it liable to higher duty in export markets.

frost GIVRER

To shake some ice cubes in an empty glass so that an opaque mist forms on the sides of the glass before a cocktail or a fruit-based spirit is poured in. Alternatively, a glass is frosted by moistening the rim with lemon juice or egg white, then dipping it upside down in caster (superfine) sugar (which may be coloured), chocolate powder, or vanilla sugar.

Frosted fruit is whole pieces or clusters of fruit brushed with egg white or lemon juice then dusted with caster sugar.

frosting

See *icing*.

fruit

Botanically speaking, the fruit is the part of the plant that develops from the ovary of the flower and contains the seeds. This definition covers not only the sweet fleshy fruits but also certain vegetables (courgettes (zucchini), aubergines (eggplants), cucumbers, etc. and nuts. Fruits can be divided into three main groups:
- Fleshy fruits with a high water content (up to 90%) – include citrus fruits, pears, pineapples, apples, peaches, mangoes, and strawberries; some are rich in vitamin C (especially citrus fruits) and minerals; their calorific value depends on their sugar content.
- Fleshy fruits with a high sugar content – include dates and dried fruits; they are a good energy source, containing 200–300 Cal per 100 g.

• Dry fruits with a high fat content and low water content – include the nuts (walnuts, hazelnuts, almonds, etc.); these are rich in calcium and B vitamins, contain around 650 Cal per 100 g, and are usually considered in a separate category (see below).

☐ **Desserts and pastries** Raw fruit for dessert should always be sound and just ripe. Fresh fruit can also be served chilled (pineapple, strawberries), poached in wine (peaches, pears), flamed (bananas), with rice, semolina, or soft cheese, in fritters or kebabs, or baked (apples bonne-femme, apricot meringue). Fruit is also used for a wide range of mousses, creams, ice creams, sorbets, charlottes, soufflés, jellies, pies, and tarts. Finally, diced fruit can be used in omelettes, pancakes, and puddings and as a sauce or purée to accompany ice creams and desserts.

☐ **Fruit in cookery** Fruit can be used for making jam, marmalade, compotes, and jellies, as well as for drinks, either alcoholic (liqueurs, brandies, spirits, wines, and cider) or nonalcoholic (fruit juices, syrups). Natural fruit extracts are used in confectionery, baking, dairy products, and drinks.

Although fruit is mostly used in sweet preparations, it also goes well with meat, fish, poultry, or vegetables. Apart from lemon, the following fruits can be used in cooking: pineapples and bananas (with pork and chicken), cranberries and redcurrants (game and turkey), figs (cured ham, partridge), grapefruit (crab and fish), cherries (duck and game), quince (tajines), mango (beef), orange (duck, calf's liver), grapes (quail and fish), prunes (rabbit and pork), and apple (black pudding (blood sausage) and red cabbage).

☐ **Preserving fruit** Various preservation methods are used for fleshy fruit, depending on the type. Many fruits can be sterilized and then preserved (with or without syrup) in bottles or jars. This method does not alter the vitamin content very much but the mineral content may be affected. Fruits preserved in this way may be used for fruit salads, sundaes, compotes, etc., and in cooked dishes; they are not suitable for jams or ice creams or (except as decoration) for pastries.

Freezing is particularly successful for raspberries, cherries, bilberries (blueberries), and redcurrants, as well as for fruit purées.

Fruits can also be preserved in sugar (see *crystallized (candied) fruit*).

• *Fruit in alcohol* Fruit can be preserved in brandy or other alcohol. Examples are morello cherries in marc brandy, bigarreau cherries in Maraschino, prunes and plums in Armagnac, pears in Calvados, grapes in brandy, and tangerines in orange liqueur. They can be used in fruit salads, sundaes, and confectionery (sugar-coated and marzipan fruit) and are served after coffee.

• *Pickled fruit* Small fruits can be bottled in vinegar (spiced with cinnamon, cloves, pepper, etc.) and sugar. The fruits most commonly used are cherries (morello cherries or very firm bigarreau cherries), oranges, peaches, grapes, small green melons, and green walnuts. Pickled fruits are used to accompany cold and boiled meats, fish, and cheese; they are also ingredients of mixed pickles and chutneys.

• *Dried fruit* Fruit can be dried in the sun or in a very slow oven. Fruits suitable for drying include apples, pears, peaches, dates, apricots, figs, and bananas; plums are dried to produce prunes, and grapes to produce raisins, sultanas, and currants (see *dried vine fruits*). Dried fruits retain many of the qualities of fresh fruit, but their energy content is concentrated. They can be eaten on their own as a sweetmeat (see *mendiants*) and are often included in breakfast cereals and health bars. If soaked for a few hours in tea, warm water, fruit juice, or alcohol, they can replace fresh fruit in compotes and some desserts; they are also used in baking (fruit cakes, puddings, etc.) or flamed (raisins in rum). They can also be used in preparing other dishes (mutton stew with apricots, partridge with figs, various stuffings, rabbit with prunes, etc.).

☐ **Nuts** These are dry fruits with an edible kernel enclosed in a hard woody shell. Examples are almonds, walnuts, hazelnuts, pistachios, pine kernels, pecans, cashew nuts, and peanuts; they are very rich in fats, have a low water content, and are a good energy source. When roasted and salted, they are eaten as appetizers with apéritifs. They are also used in desserts and confectionery (almond paste, nougat, pralines, flavourings for cream desserts and ice creams, etc.), in charcuterie (pistachios), in forcemeats, and in preparing other dishes (e.g. almonds with trout, walnuts or pine kernels in mixed salads and sauces).

☐ **Sugar-coated and marzipan fruit** Sugar-coated fruits are small fruits (strawberries, blackcurrants, cherries, plums, etc.), either fresh or preserved in brandy, which are coated with fondant icing (frosting) or caramel. Marzipan fruits are made from very thick fruit purée or a few drops of edible food colouring mixed with almond paste, moulded into the shape of the fruit.

• *Caramel-coated fruit* – The sugar used for the caramel should contain a generous amount of glucose to stop it crystallizing and should be heated to caramel setting (extra-hard crack; 154 c, 310 F); the pieces of fruit should be lightly dried with kitchen paper to remove any excess moisture, placed on a fork or dipping skewer, dipped in the caramel, then placed on an oiled marble slab until cool and set.

• *Fondant-coated fruit* – Any small fruits preserved in brandy and some fresh fruit (strawberries, slices of tangerine, pineapple segments, cape gooseberry, etc.) can be dipped in fondant. Greengages and mirabelle plums are normally blanched and soaked in syrup before being coated. The fondant is flavoured and sometimes coloured: small whole apricots preserved in brandy (the stone is replaced by a ball of almond paste) are coated with pink or white fondant; large blackcurrants are coated with violet fondant flavoured with brandy; cherries in brandy, fresh raspberries, and fresh strawberries are all coated with pink fondant. Small green oranges or kumquats are coated with yellow or white fondant, small pears (soaked in brandy flavoured with Kirsch and raisins) with orange fondant, and greengages with green fondant flavoured with vanilla or Kirsch.

RECIPES

Fondant-coated or marquise cherries
CERISES DÉGUISÉES DITES 'MARQUISES' Thoroughly drain about 50 cherries (complete with their stalks) pre-

served in brandy or eau-de-vie. Pat dry, removing any excess liquid. Put 375 g (13 oz) fondant into a small heavy-based saucepan and heat rapidly, adding half a glass of Kirsch; mix well with a wooden spatula. When the fondant is liquid, remove from the heat and incorporate 3–4 drops of red food colouring, mixing briskly. Hold each cherry by the stalk and dip it in the fondant; let any excess drip back into the saucepan. Then lay the cherries on a worktop or marble slab sprinkled lightly with icing sugar (confectioners' sugar) to prevent the fruit from sticking. Transfer each cherry to a small paper case.

Alternatively, add colouring to only half the fondant, to give 25 pink and 25 white cherries. (The same method can be used for large blackcurrants preserved in brandy; use pink fondant.)

Fruit brochettes en papillotes
BROCHETTES DE FRUITS EN PAPILLOTES Peel some oranges, remove the pith and seeds, and cut the segments into pieces; peel some pears, apples, and bananas, cut into cubes or slices, and sprinkle with lemon juice; cut some fresh or canned pineapple into cubes. Macerate all these ingredients for 30 minutes with some granulated sugar to taste and a liqueur or spirit (Curaçao, brandy, rum, or Grand Marnier), then thread the pieces onto small skewers, mixing the various fruits. Lay each skewer on a piece of lightly buttered aluminium foil or greaseproof (waxed) paper and dot the fruit with small pieces of butter. Wrap the brochettes in the foil or paper, lay them on the shelf (rack) in a very hot oven, and cook for about 15 minutes. Serve the brochettes in their wrapping. (If you have a microwave oven, use buttered greaseproof paper and cook the brochettes for about 3 minutes on full power.)

Glacé (candied) cherries filled with almond paste CERISES CONFITES FOURRÉES À LA PÂTE D'AMANDE Prepare some almond paste with 125 g (4½ oz, 1 generous cup) ground almonds, 250 g (9 oz, 1 generous cup) granulated sugar, 25 g (1 oz) glucose powder, 8 cl (4 tablespoons, ⅓ cup) water, and some Kirsch. Split 50 glacé (candied) cherries in half, but without separating the halves completely. Shape the almond paste into small balls and insert one into each cherry. Serve on a tray sprinkled with icing sugar (confectioners' sugar).

fruit givré

An iced dessert consisting of a hollowed-out fruit skin filled with ice cream, sorbet, or iced soufflé made with the flesh of the fruit. This method is particularly suitable for citrus fruit (such as oranges, lemons, or tangerines), pineapple, melon, and persimmon.

fruitier

During the Ancien Régime, the member of the royal household charged with supervising the supply of fruit, as well as tapers and candles.

fruit juice and essence
JUS ET SUC DE FRUITS

The liquid extract from a fruit by pressure or by centrifugal force.

Fruit juice is a refreshing drink, rich in vitamins, which can be drunk plain or diluted with water or soda water. Concentrated fruit juices have been developed, either in liquid form or in crystals, which can be diluted to taste. The calorific value of a juice depends on the fruit from which it was extracted, and also on the proportion of added sugar. The fruit juices most widely consumed are apple, grape, orange, grapefruit, pineapple, and tomato. For fruits that are more fleshy (apricots, mangoes, pears) or more acid (gooseberry, blackcurrant, raspberry) the juices have a larger proportion of added water and sugar.

Fruit juices are used mainly as drinks, but they are also used to make ices and sorbets as well as in more general cooking (especially citrus fruits and pineapple). Lemon juice has its special uses. In many diets, natural fruit juices are complemented by vegetable juices, served as non-alcoholic apéritifs (for example carrot juice, red cabbage juice, and spinach juice, often mixed together).

Fruit essences are highly concentrated fruit juices, used mainly in confectionery.

| RECIPES |

Fermented cherry juice SUC DE CERISE Remove the stones (pits) from 1 kg (2¼ lb) red cherries and 100 g (4 oz) black cherries. Press the fruit into a sieve placed over a mixing bowl, crushing them hard; place the crushed pulp in a fruit press to extract all the juice, then add this to the juice in the bowl and leave to ferment at a temperature of 12–15 c (54–59 F), until the juice is no longer cloudy (about 24 hours). Strain through a jelly bag, then add 450 g (1 lb, 2 cups, firmly packed) sugar to every 600 ml (1 pint, 2½ cups) juice. Stir until dissolved, strain through muslin (cheesecloth), bottle, and seal.

Raspberry, gooseberry, or blackberry fermented juice is prepared in the same way.

fruit paste
PÂTE DE FRUITS

A confectionery item made with fruit pulp, sugar, and pectin. It is prepared in a similar way to jam, but is a much drier mixture. The fruit pulp represents 50% of the finished product (40% for quinces and citrus fruits). In industrially manufactured fruit paste, this pulp usually consists of one-third apricot pulp, one-third apple pulp, and one-third pulp of the fruit which gives its name to the paste, usually with a flavouring and sometimes a colouring. The pulp is cooked with sugar, glucose syrup, and pectin, then flavoured, coloured, and poured into moulds of starch (or onto trays to be cut into shapes later). After 12–24 hours the fruit pastes are turned out, brushed (if they have been moulded in starch), dried, then rolled in caster (superfine) sugar or icing (confectioners') sugar. They are stored at a moderate temperature in a slightly humid atmosphere.

Certain French regional specialities have a basis of fruit paste: Vosges 'apricots' (with a filling of Kirsch liqueur), Dijon *cassissines* (blackcurrant paste filled with blackcurrant liqueur), Auvergne *guignolettes* (cherry paste filled with a Kirsch-soaked cherry), and Dauphiné 'mulberries' (mulberry paste in the shape of a mulberry).

RECIPES

Apple paste   PÂTE DE POMMES
(from the recipe in *Le Confiseur moderne*) Peel and core some good desert
apples. Put them in a pan with water
(about 7 dl (1¼ pints, 1½ pints) per kg
(2¼ lb) apples) and cook, turning them
over occasionally with a wooden spoon,
until they are soft. Remove the apples
and put them in a sieve over a bowl.
When they are cold, rub them through
the sieve and reduce the pulp by half
over the heat. Pour the thick pulp into a
glazed earthenware dish or a terrine.
Make a syrup with the same quantity of
sugar, cook it to the 'soft ball' stage,
take the pan off the heat, and pour in the
apple pulp. Stir well over a low heat,
with the mixture gently bubbling, until
the bottom of the pan can be seen. Pour
into a mould (as for apricot paste).

Apricot paste   PÂTE D'ABRICOTS
Choose some very ripe apricots, stone
(pit) them, put them in a pan, just cover
them with water, and bring to the boil.
Drain and peel the fruits, then pass them
through a vegetable mill. Weigh the
pulp obtained. For 1 kg (2¼ lb) pulp,
weigh 1.1–1.2 kg (2¼–2½ lb) caster
(superfine) sugar. Mix 100 g (4 oz, ½
cup) of this sugar with 60 g (2 oz, 2
tablespoons) powdered gelatine. Pour
the pulp into a thick-bottomed saucepan and bring to the boil. Add the sugar
–gelatine mixture and bring back to the
boil, stirring with a wooden spatula.
Pour in half of the remaining sugar,
bring back to the boil, then add the rest
of the sugar, still stirring. Keep it boiling
fast for 6–7 minutes.
  Place a sheet of very lightly oiled
greaseproof (waxed) paper on a marble
slab and place on top a rectangular
wooden frame, specially for making
fruit paste. Pour the paste inside the
frame, smooth the surface, and leave to
cool completely (about 2 hours). Then
cut the paste out into squares or rectangles, roll them in caster sugar, and
store them in an airtight tin, separating
the layers with greaseproof paper.

Cherry paste   PÂTE DE CERISES
Stalk and stone (pit) the cherries and put
them through a vegetable mill. Prepare
as for apricot paste but use equal

weights of sugar and cherry pulp and 70
g (2½ oz, 2½ tablespoons) gelatine per
kg (2¼ lb) pulp.

Plum paste   PÂTE DE PRUNES   Use
ripe greengages and the same procedure
as for apricot paste.

Strawberry paste   PÂTE DE FRAISES
Wash and hull the strawberries and put
them through a vegetable mill. Use
equal weights of sugar and strawberry
pulp and 70 g (2½ oz, 2½ tablespoons)
gelatine per kg (2¼ lb) pulp. Prepare as
for apricot paste but note that the brisk
boiling stage should last only 5 minutes.

fruit salad
FRUITS RAFRAÎCHIS, SALADE DE FRUITS

A dessert consisting of pieces of sliced or
chopped fruit or whole small fruit (such
as grapes), peeled, stoned (pitted), and
skinned if necessary, macerated in sugar
and often in alcohol (sweet wine or
liqueur), and served in a fruit dish,
usually with the flavoured fruit juice
poured over. The dish is placed on
crushed ice or chilled in the refrigerator
and the fruit salad may be served
with small cakes or biscuits or with ice
cream. As a variation, the bottom of the
bowl can be filled with a layer of ice
cream.
  The fruit used varies according to the
season; sometimes exotic fruits are
used, such as lychees, kiwi fruit, mangoes, or passion fruit. The fruit can be
raw, poached and cooled, or dried,
soaked, and poached. Canned fruit can
also be used (in this case the fruit juice or
syrup is used instead of sugar) and crystallized (candied) or dried fruit can be
used as decoration.

RECIPES

Exotic fruit salad with lime   SALADE
EXOTIQUE AU CITRON VERT   Peel a
very ripe pineapple and dice the flesh.
Peel and stone (pit) 3 mangoes; cut the
flesh into strips. Peel 3 bananas, slice
them, and roll (but do not soak) the
slices in the juice of a lime. Put all these
ingredients in a bowl, sprinkle with 3–4
tablespoons granulated sugar, and chill
for at least 3 hours before serving.

Fruit salad à la maltaise   FRUITS RAF-
RAÎCHAIS À LA MALTAISE   Macerate
an assortment of sliced bananas, stoned
(pitted) cherries, and cubes of fresh
pineapple in a mixture of Curaçao and
granulated sugar. Chill in the refrigerator. Put a layer of orange-flavoured ice
cream in the bottom of a glass fruit
bowl; place the drained fruit on top.
Decorate with whipped cream and
peeled orange segments. Alternatively,
the ice cream can be omitted and orange
juice mixed with Curaçao poured over.

Fruit salad à la normande   FRUITS
RAFRAÎCHIS À LA NORMANDE   Peel
and core a pineapple and cut the flesh
into cubes. Peel and slice some bananas.
Peel and core some apples, cut them into
cubes, and sprinkle with lemon juice.
Macerate all the fruit in some Calvados
mixed with granulated sugar. Chill in
the refrigerator. Arrange the fruit in a
glass bowl and pour the fruit liquid over
it. Cover with single (light) or Chantilly
cream.

fruit salad à l'occitanienne   FRUITS
RAFRAÎCHIS À L'OCCITANIENNE
Peel and core some pears, slice thickly,
and sprinkle with lemon juice. Peel and
slice some figs. Peel some large black
and white grapes. Arrange the ingredients in layers in a glass bowl, sprinkle
with granulated sugar, and pour over
some Blanquette de Limoux (a sparkling white wine) and a little brandy.
Refrigerate for 1 hour at least. Cover
with Chantilly cream and decorate with
peeled grapes.

Fruit salad with gin   SALADE DE
FRUITS AU GIN   Chill 4 shallow glass
sundae dishes in the refrigerator. Peel 2
pink grapefruit; detach the segments
and skin them completely. Peel 2
papaws, remove the seeds, and cut the
flesh into thin slices. Peel 4 kiwi fruit
and slice the flesh. Shell about 20
lychees (and remove the stones (pits) if
wished) or carefully drain 20 canned
lychees.

Remove the dishes from the refrigerator; arrange the grapefruit segments
alternately with the slices of papaw,
insert slices of kiwi fruit here and there,
and arrange the lychees in the centre of
each dish. The decoration can be completed with a large raspberry in the middle. Put the filled dishes in the least cool
part of the refrigerator.

Squeeze 2 oranges, dissolve 2 tablespoons granulated sugar in the juice,
and add 4 tablespoons gin. Just before
serving, divide the juice between the
dishes. Serve with vanilla-flavoured
meringues.

**Fruit salad with Kirsch and Maras-
chino**   FRUITS RAFRAÎCHIS AU
KIRSCH ET AU MARASQUIN   Peel 6
peaches, 3 pears, and 2 apples and slice
thinly; slice 4 bananas and cut 6 apricots into chunks. Mix all the fruit in a
bowl; then add 25 g (1 oz) hulled strawberries, 75 g (3 oz) raspberries, and 125
g (4½ oz) white deseeded grapes.
Sprinkle with 5–6 tablespoons (½ cup)
caster (superfine) sugar; pour over 3 dl
(½ pint, 1¼ cups) Kirsch and 3 dl (½
pint, 1¼ cups) Maraschino. Gently mix
the ingredients together. Surround the
bowl with crushed ice and leave to
macerate for 1 hour. Then pour the
contents into a glass fruit bowl, also
surround by crushed ice. Decorate with
about 50 g (2 oz) strawberries, some
grapes, and 25 blanched and halved
almonds.

Fruit stoner (pitter)
DÉNOYAUTEUR,
ÉNOYAUTEUR
A special utensil designed to remove the
stones (pits) from certain fruits, particularly cherries and olives, without spoiling the flesh. It is a type of pincers with a
cup-shaped depression at the end of one
arm in which the fruit is held and a short
rod at the end of the other arm that acts
as a pusher and buries itself in the fruit.
When the pincers are squeezed together,
the stone is pushed out. The stones are
removed from olives before stuffing
them. A type of cherry stoner with a
receptacle for catching the stones is
quicker and more efficient to use.

fruit store   FRUITIER
A room used for storing fresh fruit, such
as apples, pears, quinces, etc., after harvesting. The room must be cool and
well-ventilated with moderate humidity. It is fitted with shelves and grids
covered with straw or bracken on which
the fruit is laid, ensuring that individual

items do not touch. The fruit should be protected from direct sunlight.

frumenty   FROMENTÉE

A very old country dish, consisting of a porridge or gruel made from wheat boiled with milk, then sweetened and spiced. Originating in Touraine, it is mentioned as a dessert in *Le Ménagier de Paris* (1383), being made with milk in which almonds have been boiled to give flavour and served either warm and semi-liquid or cold and set.

In the Berry region, frumenty was made with water and served with butter or fresh cream.

frying pan (skillet)   POÊLE

A round or oval shallow pan with a long handle, used for frying or sautéing food. The French word comes from the Latin *patella*, meaning a small dish. Meat, fish, vegetables, eggs, and various mixtures (croquettes, omelettes, pancakes etc.) may be sautéed or fried. The classic frying pan, made of steel with a matt black finish, is thick and heavy so that it does not buckle and food does not burn. To prevent it from rusting, it must be dried thoroughly after cleaning and lightly oiled using a cloth pad or absorbent kitchen paper.

Many people prefer lighter pans because they are easier to work with and maintain: pans of glazed aluminium with a ceramic interior are light and good conductors of heat. Stainless steel pans are bad conductors of heat, and must have a copper or aluminium base lining; they also tend to make the food stick. Enamelled cast iron is heavy but can easily be damaged, and only gives moderate results. Aluminium frying pans with a nonstick coating (PTFE) are good conductors of heat, easy to clean, and require a minimum of cooking fat, but the nonstick surface is easily scratched and spoilt. The base of such a pan must be strengthened so that it does not buckle.

The classic frying pan is round, with a slightly raised rim, and is a very versatile utensil, being used for potatoes, omelettes, meat, etc. There are also frying pans which have been designed for a specific use. The trout pan is oval and suitable for cooking fish *à la meunière*. The crêpe pan is round and very shallow so that the pancakes can be turned over easily. The omelette pan is often lined with copper plate and is deeper, enabling the eggs to be cooked evenly throughout. The blini pan is similar to the omelette pan but smaller. Chestnuts can be grilled in a special round perforated pan with a very long handle designed for use over hot coals. The chafing dish is an elegant copper pan used especially for flaming food at the table. Finally there is an electric frying pan with a lid fitted with a safety valve. This can be used for roasting meat or poultry as well as for frying or even for baking.

fudge

A very soft caramel that melts in the mouth and is not sticky. It originated in the 19th century from an error made during the manufacture of normal toffee, when the sugar recrystallized. It can be flavoured with fruit, nuts, chocolate, coffee, etc., and is cut into squares when cold.

Fulbert-Dumonteil (Jean Camille)

French journalist and writer (born Vergt, 1831; died Neuilly-sur-Seine, 1912). He was the author of numerous articles and about 30 books, starting his career with the *Mousquetaire* newspaper (owned by Dumas *père*) and later moving to *Le Figaro*. In 1906 he published a collection of articles on gastronomy entitled *La France gourmande*, which reflects his Belle Époque spirit and love of food. He chose as his coat of arms 'truffles and smiles on a field of roses'. Besides gastronomy, he was passionately interested in zoology and travel, which inspired some flights of lyricism on exotic cookery: 'If I had magic powers, I should like to wave my golden fork over the confined cookery of Europe and enlarge it to infinity; I would like to . . . offer French nationality to the many hardly known but delicious foreign dishes; . . . I would like to put the whole of natural history on the spit, in stews, in fricassees, in court-bouillon, in grills . . .'

fumet

A liquid, obtained by reducing a stock or cooking liquid, that is added to a sauce or cooking stock to enhance its flavour or give it extra body. Literally meaning 'aroma', the word *fumet* is used for concentrated mushroom and fish stocks; for meat, poultry, and game stocks, the word *fond* is used.

• *Mushroom fumet* – The concentrated cooking liquid obtained by boiling cultivated mushrooms in salted lemon-flavoured water with butter; it is used to improve the flavour of some sauces and can be kept, in a well-sealed bottle, in the refrigerator or freezer. Truffle fumet can be made by cooking truffle peelings with Madeira and reducing the liquid.

• *Fish fumet* – Made with fish trimmings and bones, onions, shallots, mushrooms, and other flavourings boiled in water and wine (white or red, according to the intended use). It is used for braising or poaching fish and for making sauces to accompany a dish (normande, suprême, white wine).

RECIPES

Fish fumet FUMET DE POISSON
Crush 2.5 kg (5½ lb) bones and trimmings of white fish (sole, lemon sole, whiting, brill, turbot, etc.). Peel and thinly slice 125 g (4½ oz) onions and shallots; clean and thinly slice 150 g (5 oz) mushrooms or mushroom stalks and trimmings; squeeze the juice from half a lemon; tie 25 g (1 oz) parsley sprigs into a bundle. Put all the ingredients in a stewpot, add a small sprig of thyme, a bay leaf, 1 tablespoon lemon juice, and 10 g (⅓ oz) coarse sea salt. Moisten with 2½ litres (4½ pints, 5½ pints) water and ½ litre (17 fl oz, 2 cups) dry white wine (or red for some recipes). Bring to the boil, skim, then boil very gently for 30 minutes. Strain through muslin (cheesecloth) and leave to cool.

Mushroom fumet FUMET DE CHAMPIGNON Boil ½ litre (17 fl oz, 2 cups) water, 40 g (1½ oz, 3 tablespoons) butter, the juice of half a lemon, and 6 g (¼ oz) salt in a saucepan; add 500 g (18 oz) cleaned mushrooms to this mixture and leave to boil for about 10 minutes. Remove the mushrooms (which can be used as a garnish) and reduce the cooking liquid by half. This fumet will keep in the refrigerator, covered, until required.

funnel ENTONNOIR

A utensil for filling bottles or other containers. Generally conical (oval for brandy), with a long narrow stem, funnels are made of glass, stainless steel, tin plate, enamelled metal, or plastic. There is sometimes a tap for controlling the flow. An icing funnel has a wooden stick to control the aperture and is used to pour certain types of confectionery into moulds.

In charcuterie, a type of funnel called an *embossoir*, equipped with a wooden rammer, is used to fill sausage skins, etc.

gâche

In Normandy, a small soft flat cake made of a yeasted dough and baked in a very hot oven. In Brittany, sugar and butter (or lard), and even slices of apple, are included. Gâche from the Vendée is a kind of half-risen, sometimes twisted, brioche.

Gaillac

Wine from southwestern France, produced on both banks of the Tarn by one of the oldest vineyards in France. Of the four AOCs made there, the best known is the sparkling Gaillac, which is sometimes rosé but more often white; the white wine comes mainly from the Mauzac (the grape used for Blanquette de Limoux).

The appellation Gaillac applies to the white, red, and rosé wines produced by 73 communes around Gaillac. The most unusual wines are those described as *perlé*, which are slightly *pétillant*. A sweet version of white Gaillac is made in addition to the dry version. Gaillac is best drunk young.

galabart

A large black pudding (blood sausage) from southwestern France, made with pig's head (including the skin and the tongue), lungs, heart, and blood mixed with bread. It measures 9–10 cm (3½–4 in) in diameter and is usually eaten cold, in thick slices.

galangal GALANGA

A spice which comes from the Far East, obtained from a rhizome with orange or whitish pulp and a reddish skin. Its colour and flavour are slightly reminiscent of saffron. Galangal was mentioned by Marco Polo and was widely used in the Middle Ages under the name of 'garingal' or 'galingale'. It is still a commonly used spice in Indonesia and Thailand.

galantine

A dish made from lean pieces of poultry, game, pork, veal, or rabbit, mixed with a forcemeat containing eggs, spices, and various other ingredients and pressed into a symmetrical shape. Galantines are cooked in an aspic stock and served cold as an entrée, glazed with aspic (the name comes from the Old French *galatine*, meaning 'jelly').

Galantines are sometimes cooked wrapped in a cloth, which gives them a cylindrical shape; they should then, strictly speaking, be called ballottines. Galantines can also be made with fish; a *soupresse* of fish, which was cooled under a board with a weight on top, was a form of galantine.

RECIPE

Galantine of chicken GALANTINE DE VOLAILLE Singe and draw a 2-kg (4½-lb) chicken. Cut off the feet and pinions. Slit the bird along the back and, with a small sharp-pointed knife, bone it completely without tearing the flesh. (This operation, which at first sight seems awkward, is actually fairly simple. It is necessary only to follow the joints of the chicken and to work inwards towards the carcass, shaving off the flesh as close to the bone as possible. This first boning operation separates the carcass from the body of the chicken, leaving them both whole). Now remove the bones from the legs and wings, still being careful not to tear the skin. Spread the bird out on the table and cut away the breast and the fleshy part of the thighs and wings, then cut these pieces into squares.

Now prepare the forcemeat: finely mince 250 g (9 oz, 1 cup) boned loin of pork and 250 g (9 oz, 1 cup) shoulder of veal. Dice 150 g (5 oz, ⅔ cup) fat bacon, 150 g (5 oz, ⅔ cup) ham, and 150 g (5 oz, ⅔ cup) pickled tongue into 1½-cm (½-in) cubes; mix with the chicken squares, 150 g (5 oz, 1¼ cups) blanched pistachios, the minced meat, 2 beaten eggs, 1 dl (6 tablespoons, scant ½ cup) brandy, salt, pepper, and ½ teaspoon allspice. Wet your hands in order to work this mixture and blend it together. Shape it into a ball, then into a rectangular block.

To prepare the galantine, place the block of forcemeat over the central third of chicken and enclose it by folding over the parts of the chicken skin which project at the sides and ends, stretching it without tearing. Soak a coarse linen cloth in water and wring it out, then spread it flat on the table. Place it so that a flap about 25 cm (10 in) wide hangs over the edge of the table. Place the galantine lengthwise on this cloth, about 10 cm (4 in) from the edge of the table, breast upwards. Wrap the galantine in the cloth as tightly as possible. Tie both ends of the cloth securely. Tie tne galantine with string in 3 places to keep it in shape.

Prepare an aspic stock with 2 partly boned calf's feet, 500 g (1 lb) fresh pork skin, 2 kg (4½ lb) knuckle of veal, 2 large sliced carrots, a large onion studded with cloves, 2 shredded leeks, a bouquet garni enriched with celery, 5 litres (8¾ pints, 11¼ pints) white stock, 4 dl (¾ pint, 1¾ cups) Madeira (optional), salt, and pepper. Cook the stock for 1½ hours, then add the galantine, bring rapidly to the boil, and simmer for 2¾–3 hours. Remove the galantine. Let it stand for 15 minutes before unwrapping it. Remove the cloth, rinse in lukewarm water, and wring thoroughly. Spread it on the table and carefully wrap the galantine in it as before, taking care to keep the slit part of the chicken underneath. Tie up the galantine. Press it on a slab, covering it with a wooden board with a weight on top. Allow to cool for at least 12 hours; it can be kept for several days if it is stored in a cool place.

The galantine is served garnished with its own clarified aspic jelly.

galette

A flat round cake of variable size. The galette probably dates back to the Neolithic era, when thick cereal pastes were cooked by spreading them out on hot stones. In ancient times, people made galettes from oats, wheat, rye, and even barley, sweetened with honey. Then came the hearth cakes of the Middle Ages and all the regional varieties: the galette of Corrèze (made with walnuts or chestnuts), the galette of Roussillon (made with crystallized (candied) fruits), the marzipan galette of the Nivernais, the curd-cheese galette of the Jura, the puff-pastry galette of Normandy, filled with jam and fresh cream, the famous galette of Perugia (a delicate yeasted pastry, like brioche, flavoured with lemon zest and topped with butter and sugar), and, of course, the traditional puff-pastry Twelfth-Night cake (*galette des Rois* or *gâteau des Rois*).

Galettes are not always sweet. In the French countryside, it is traditional to make galettes with potatoes (finely sliced or puréed) or with cereals (maize, millet, oats). In Brittany, Basse-

Normandie, and the Vendée, galettes are buckwheat crêpes garnished with cheese, an egg, a sausage, grilled (broiled) sardines, etc.

The word 'galette' also applies to a small shortbread biscuit (cookie) made with butter, which is a great Breton speciality, and to dry round crunchy cakes, sometimes with crimped edges, which are variously flavoured, filled, or iced (especially with coffee or chocolate).

RECIPES

Galette de plomb Make a well in 300 g (11 oz, 1⅓ cups) sifted flour and add 10 g (1 teaspoon) caster (superfine) sugar, 1 scant tablespoon fine salt dissolved in 1 tablespoon single (light) cream, and 200 g (7 oz, scant cup) softened butter cut up into small pieces (dot these pieces all over the flour). Mix all the ingredients together with the tips of the fingers. Beat together 1 .whole egg and 1 yolk. Add them to the dough and knead towards the centre. If necessary, add a second tablespoon cream. Work the dough into a ball, cover with a cloth, and leave to stand for 30 minutes.

Flour the work surface, spread out the dough with the flat of the hand into a rectangle, fold it 3 times upon itself, roll it into a ball again, and flatten it into a round shape, 2–3 cm (¾–1¼ in) thick. Place it on a buttered tart dish, trace rosettes on the top with the point of a knife, brush it with beaten egg, and bake in a hot oven (220 c, 425 f, gas 7) for about 30 minutes. Serve lukewarm or cold.

Potato galette GALETTE DE POMME DE TERRE Bake 6 large floury (baking) potatoes in the oven for 35–40 minutes until soft. Cut them open and remove the flesh, then mix 400 g (14 oz, 3¾ cups) of this with 4 egg yolks, added one by one, and 1 teaspoon salt. Soften 150 g (5 oz, generous ½ cup) butter with a spatula and mix it in. Roll the potato dough into a ball and flatten it with the palm of the hand. Shape it into a ball again and repeat the operation twice more. Butter a baking tray (sheet) and flatten the dough to form a galette 4 cm (1½ in) thick. Trace a pattern on the top with the point of a knife, brush with

egg, and bake in a hot oven (220 c, 425 f, gas 7) until golden brown. (If the galette is to be served as a dessert, add to the dough 125 g (4½ oz, ⅔ cup) sugar, orange-flower water, and chopped blanched orange and lemon zest.)

Small orange galettes PETITES GALETTES ORANGINES Make a well in 250 g (9 oz, 2¼ cups) sifted flour. In the centre place 120 g (4½ oz, ⅔ cup) sugar, 150 g (5 oz, ⅔ cup) butter, a pinch of salt, the zest of 2 oranges rubbed on lumps of sugar, and 6 egg yolks. Mix these ingredients together and gradually blend the flour into the mixture. Knead the dough into a ball and allow it to stand for a few hours in a cool place. Roll out the dough to a thickness of about ½ cm (¼ in). Cut it into rounds with a fluted cutter 5–6 cm (2–2½ in) in diameter. Place the galettes on a buttered baking tray (sheet), brush with egg beaten with a pinch of sugar, and bake in a hot oven (240 c, 475 f, gas 9) for about 6 minutes until lightly golden.

Twelfth-Night cake GALETTE DES ROIS Make about 250 g (9 oz) puff pastry and roll it out into a round shape 1½–2 cm (½–¾ in) thick. Place the dough on a baking tray (sheet). Push a bean into the dough (during baking, the dough closes up and conceals the bean). Trace a pattern on the top of the dough with the point of a knife and brush it with egg. Bake in a very hot oven (240 c, 475 f, gas 9) until the top is golden brown. The pastry can also be rolled into 2 rounds and sandwiched together with frangipane cream before baking.

This cake is traditionally served on Twelfth Night. Whoever finds the 'lucky bean', symbolizing the baby Jesus, becomes king or queen of the evening.

galicien

A type of sponge cake filled with pistachio-flavoured cream, iced green, and decorated with finely chopped pistachio nuts. It was apparently created at the old Pâtisserie Frascati in Paris.

RECIPE

Galicien Prepare a round Genoese sponge cake using 45 g (1½ oz, 3 table·

spoons) butter, 3 eggs, 95 g (3½ oz, ½ cup) caster (superfine) sugar, 95 g (3½ oz, scant cup) plain flour, and a pinch of salt. Slice the cake across. Spread on each half a layer of confectioners' custard (see *creams and custards*) flavoured with finely chopped pistachio nuts. Sandwich the 2 halves together. Spread the cake with apricot jam. Make some icing with 3 egg whites, the juice of a lemon, 300 g (11 oz, 2⅓ cups) icing (confectioners') sugar, and 3 drops of green colouring. Cover the cake with the icing, decorate with chopped pistachios, and keep cool until ready to serve.

galingale SOUCHET

A perennial Mediterranean plant producing scaly brown tubers the size of hazelnuts, the sweet white farinaceous pulp of which earned them the French name *amandes de terre* (earth almonds). They may be eaten dry, raw, or roasted like chestnuts.

In North Africa, the tubers are generally ground and used in forcemeats for poultry, meatballs, and spice mixtures.

In Spain, the galingale is called *chufa*; grown in the Valencia region, it is used for making a popular drink, *horchata*, which is similar to orgeat. It also yields an oil, which has a lower freezing point than water and does not turn rancid, and a flour used in confectionery.

gall bladder

POCHE DU FIEL

The organ that stores bile – a greenish very bitter substance secreted by the liver. When poultry or game birds are drawn, care must be taken not to pierce or break the gall bladder attached to the liver as the bile is so bitter that it would taint the flesh.

gallimaufry GALIMAFRÉE

In the Middle Ages, a dish of finely sliced cooked meat (usually chicken or mutton), fried in lard or goose fat, mixed with finely chopped onions, and then moistened with wine and verjuice sauce spiced with ginger. At that time, gallimaufry was the feast dish of the people (its name comes from *galer*, to enjoy oneself, and *mafrer*, to eat ravenously). It was only in the 17th century that the word took on the pejorative

meaning that it has today: a badly prepared and unappetizing dish.

game GIBIER

All wild animals and birds that are hunted. The French word comes from the Old French *gibecer* (to hunt), which derives from the Latin *gibbosus* (hunchback). Hunters carried home the game they killed in a bag that they usually carried on their backs. Thus, the hunter's bag was called a *gibecière*, from which it was an obvious step to *gibier* (the contents of the bag).

In former centuries hunting was an important means of providing meat for the table. Today, in industrialized countries, game is only a minor and occasional foodstuff, but hunting continues to be enjoyed as a sport. In France there is one hunter per 15 square miles and this has caused a serious reduction in the amount of small game (partridges, pheasants, hares), whereas large game (deer and wild boar) are more abundant, being well protected by hunting regulations.

In Europe, game only appears on the market during the open season, when hunting is permitted, unless the animals or birds have been specially bred (quails, pheasants, etc.). In Britain, several birds are protected all the year round, including blackbird, bustard, cygnet, heron, lapwing, lark, rail, swan, and swift. Other birds and animals are no longer hunted at all, tastes having changed (e.g. crow, beaver, dormouse).
□ **Ground and winged game** Game can be divided into two broad categories: ground and winged. Ground game is subdivided into large game (deer, roebuck, and wild boar) and small game (hare and wild rabbit). The French term *bête fauve* applies specifically to the large herbivorous game (deer of both sexes) as distinct from the *bête noir* (wild boar) and *bête rousse* (fox, badger). Winged game in France includes woodcock, pheasant, hazel grouse, grouse, partridge, partridge poult, rail, wood pigeon, capercaillie, and black grouse. Small game birds include lark, garden warbler, thrush, blackbird, ortolan, and plover, while water game includes godwit, wild duck, curlew, wild goose, moorhen, teal, and lapwing. Other birds and animals are

hunted in other regions or have been hunted in the past (bear, reindeer, heron, turtle, hedgehog, yak, zebu, etc.).

☐ **Digestibility of game** The way of life and the feeding habits of game are reflected in the texture and flavour of its flesh, which has a strong fragrant aroma becoming stronger with age. The flesh is more compact and almost leathery in old animals, with a strong colour and less fat than other meat, but richer in albumin. It is considered difficult to digest and must be consumed in moderation.

Before cooking, game meat is generally hung for a certain length of time to allow it to mature, which makes it tender and gives it a stronger flavour (see *hanging*). Care must be taken, however, not to overhang game as it can become toxic. When this is not carried out, the game is drawn as soon as possible, then hung in a cool dark place, by the hind legs in the case of ground game, or by the head in the case of winged game. It is not skinned or plucked until just before use. Some birds, like the thrush and woodcock, are not drawn. In this case, the digestive tract is made into a strongly flavoured paste which is spread on toast or fried bread to accompany the roast bird.

The length of time for which the game is left to mature varies according to its age and type: four days for a woodcock or a pheasant, three for a thrush or a duck, two for a hare, six to eight days for large game. This is best done in the refrigerator. During the maturing process the carbohydrates are converted into lactic acid, which improves the flavour and tenderness of the game.

Game sold commercially is already matured. When purchasing, it is advisable to choose a young animal or bird that is not 'high'.

☐ **Cooking game** The cuts of meat and the culinary methods are the same for large game as for other meat, except that game is often marinated: haunches, saddles, and loins are roasted; breasts, shoulders, and necks are eaten in ragouts and civets; noisettes and cutlets are sautéed or grilled (broiled). Winged game is prepared like poultry. A sweet accompaniment (whortleberries, red fruits, apples, grapes, chestnuts) is sometimes chosen in order to bring out the strong taste of the dark meat, which is often served with highly seasoned sauces (grand-veneur, poivrade, Périgueux, Cumberland). Full-bodied wines with a distinct bouquet are usually served with game.

Terrines and pâtés can be made from game, which can now be used in different ways since the advent of cold storage and deep-freezing. Ready-cooked dishes and preserves of varying quality are sold on the market.

Gammelöst

A Norwegian semisoft yellowish-brown cheese made from cows' or goats' milk. Its rind is brown and becomes darker as it ages. Maturing can take up to six months, but Gammelöst, which has a strong aromatic flavour, can also be eaten after one month. It is made in 15-cm (6-in) blocks, either rectangular or cylindrical in shape, depending on whether it is made of goats' or cows' milk.

ganache

A flavoured cream made with chocolate, butter, and fresh cream, used to decorate desserts, fill cakes or sweets, and make petits fours. It was created in Paris in about 1850 at the Pâtisserie Siraudin.

RECIPE

Ganache cream   CRÈME GANACHE Melt 250 g (9 oz, 1½ cups) sweetened chocolate over a low heat and add 60–75 g (2½–3 oz, 5–6 tablespoons) butter. Cool, then fold in whipped cream, either 2.5 dl (8 fl oz, 1 cup) whipping cream or 2 dl (7 fl oz, ¾ cup) double (heavy) cream whipped with at least ½ dl (3 tablespoons, ¼ cup) milk.

Gaperon or Gapron

A cheese from the Auvergne region of France made of skimmed cows' milk or buttermilk (*gape* in the local dialect), shaped like a ball flattened at one end, 9 cm (3½ in) in diameter. The cheese is compressed, uncooked, and flavoured with garlic and pepper, which gives it a pronounced flavour, but a strong smell is a sign that it is overripe. The best season for Gaperon is between October and March.

Cooking times for game

	roasted in a hot oven (200 c, 400 f gas 6–7)	casseroled	fried
wild duck	25–30 mins		
pheasant (per lb)	20–25 mins	30–35 mins	
young partridge	20–30 mins	40 mins	
partridge	20–30 mins	2–2½ hrs	
small birds	10–15 mins	15–20 mins	
roebuck (per lb)	15–20 mins	1½ hrs	noisettes: 2–3 mins each side
young wild boar (per lb)	12–15 mins	1½–2 hrs	cutlets: 3–4 mins each side
hare saddle (per lb) civet (jugged hare)	15–20 mins	2 hrs	
rabbit		45 mins	

garbure

In the Béarn region of France, a kind of stew based on vegetable stock, cabbage, and *confit d'oie* (preserved goose). However, there are several variants of varying richness, including *briscat* (maize garbure). According to some authors, the word comes from the Spanish *garbías* (ragout or stew). This etymology is disputed by Simin Palay: 'The root is undoubtedly *garbe* (a sheaf or bunch). And indeed it is a bunch of vegetables which is the very basis of the garbure.'

RECIPE

Garbure (from Simin Palay's recipe) Boil some water in an earthenware pot glazed on the inside (cast-iron or iron pots spoil the delicacy of the flavour). When it is boiling, throw in some potatoes, peeled and cut into thick slices. Add other fresh vegetables in season: haricot (navy) or broad beans, peas, or French beans. Season with salt and pepper. Red peppers may be used in place of white pepper. Flavour with garlic, a sprig of thyme, parsley, or fresh marjoram. Leave the stock to cook, making sure that the water is constantly on the boil.

Shred tender green cabbage as finely as possible into strips, cutting across the width of the leaves, having removed any tough portions. When the rest of the ingredients are thoroughly cooked, throw the cabbage into the boiling stock. Cover the pot to keep the cabbage leaves green and, 30 minutes before serving, put in a piece of pickled meat, preferably goose (*lou trébuc*); the fat on this will be sufficient. If pickled pork *trébuc* is used, the addition of a little goose fat will enhance the flavour of the stew. Cut stale wholemeal (wholewheat) bread into thin slices and add to the stock and vegetables. The mixture must be thick enough for the ladle to stand up in it when set in the centre of the tureen.

It is possible to make a good garbure without *trébuc*, but in that case it is necessary to put a piece of ham bone, or a sausage, or, at the very least, lean bacon (thin flank) in the cold water. White cabbage may be used instead of green cabbage. For an everyday garbure, it is usual to make do with a piece of bacon or ham, or bacon chopped with crushed garlic. According to the time of year, a few slices of swede or roast chestnuts are added.

If dried beans are used, these have to be cooked in advance and drained after cooking, as their water would destroy the characteristic flavour of the garbure. To thicken the broth, the cooked beans are sometimes crushed and rubbed through a sieve. The meat is served separately from the broth, either by itself or with the vegetables, like the boiled beef of a hotpot. Some cooks brown the *trébuc* in a pan before putting it in the stock. In this case some fat must be added but the fat in which the *trébuc* was browned should not be used.

Simin Palay concludes: 'A good *goudale* is an indispensable complement to every garbure.' (A *goudale* is the broth remaining when the vegetables have been eaten, which is enriched with red or white wine.)

garde-manger

In a classic French kitchen, the member of the staff in charge of cold items, hors d'oeuvres, some desserts, and all decorative work.

garfish   ORPHIE

An elongated sea fish with a long spear-like snout which has earned it the nickname of sea-snipe. The garfish has a bluish-green back, a whitish belly, and can reach a length of 80 cm (31 in) and a weight of 1.5 kg (3 lb). The flesh has a delicate flavour and is prepared in the same way as conger eel; it can also be fried. Unfortunately its strong smell and the fact that its bones, green in their natural state, become mauve when cooked are disconcerting to some people.

gargote

Originally, a gargote was an inn where one could eat inexpensively. Since the 19th century, the word has come to mean any small cheap dirty restaurant serving poor-quality food, its proprietor being called a *gargotier*. The word appears to come from the Old French *gargate* (throat). R. Dumay, in *Du silex au barbecue*, gives a more amusing etymology: according to him, the word is derived from *cargator*, the cook on board the boats carrying pilgrims to Jerusalem, packed together uncomfortably.

gargouillau

A dessert from the Limousin and the Bourbonnais regions of France, made with a thick pancake batter to which peeled, cored, and finely sliced pears are added; it is cooked in a flan tin. Like clafoutis, gargouillau is eaten lukewarm or cold. In Auvergne, *gargouillou*, a near homonym, is a country ragout of vegetables.

gargoulette

A porous earthen vessel in which water is cooled by evaporation. The gargoulette usually has a handle and a spout which makes it possible to drink from it without the vessel touching the lips.

garlic   AIL

A bulbous plant, probably originating in central Asia, known since ancient times for its curative properties. The Greeks and Romans held garlic in high esteem; Hippocrates classified it as a sudorific medicine, stating that garlic was 'hot, laxative, and diuretic'. (It is noteworthy that the Latin word for garlic, *allium*, derives from a Celtic word meaning 'hot'.) The Crusades helped to make it known in Europe, where it soon took on the role of a panacea, even against the plague and possession by devils. One of the most widely used medieval sauces was *sauce d'aulx*, in which crushed garlic was mixed either with parsley and sorrel to accompany fish dishes, or with vinegar and breadcrumbs to go with grills. Rabelais concurred with Ambroise Paré and the Salerno school in praising the merits of garlic. However, space does not permit an exhaustive list of the therapeutic properties attributed over the centuries to the 'poor man's antidote' (an allusion to an opiated medicine created, according to tradition, by Mithradates).

☐   Varieties Garlic is used today mainly as a condiment in most parts of the world except northern and eastern Europe, where the onion reigns supreme. The bulb or 'head' of garlic is formed of 12–16 bulblets, commonly called 'cloves', each protected by a parchment-like skin. The most widely used garlic has a white or grey skin and is grown in Provence and southwest France. The smaller and less popular variety of garlic, cultivated in the Auvergne, has a violet or rose-coloured skin (Billom pink garlic); garlic from the Douai region has a red-brown skin. Garlic from the Charentes is considered to be less pungent, while Spanish garlic, or rocambole, is similar to a shallot.

☐ **Use in cooking** The bulbs must be thoroughly dry. They can be stored in a cold place (from −0.5 c to +1 c, 31−34 f) or at a moderate temperature (18 c, 64 f), either laid out flat or hanging in bunches to improve aeration. If spots appear on them or the cloves become soft, the garlic is no longer usable. Generally speaking, white garlic keeps for about six months, pink garlic for nearly a year.

● skinned whole raw cloves: may be rubbed on bread (*frottée à l'ail*, *aillade*, fried *chapons*) or around the sides of a salad bowl or pan;

● chopped or crushed raw garlic: seasoning raw vegetables; *aioli* (garlic mayonnaise); pesto sauce; garlic butter; garlic purée;

● pressed raw garlic: aromatized oils;

● whole cooked cloves (sometimes with the skin *en chemise*): ragouts and braised dishes (cassoulet); roasts (remove the cloves before serving); soups;

● larded garlic: leg of mutton;

● peeled cloves, sliced or chopped: sautéed dishes – fish, meat, frogs, snails, tomatoes, potatoes, salsify, mushrooms. Add the garlic at the end of the cooking time, as it introduces a bitter flavour if fried for too long.

RECIPES

Garlic oil HUILE D'AIL Blanch and crush cloves of garlic, add olive oil, and pass through a sieve. Alternatively grated garlic may be added to olive oil and pressed through a muslin cloth. Garlic oil is used to season salads or raw vegetables.

Garlic purée PURÉE D'AIL Blanch some garlic cloves then gently sweat them in butter. Add a few spoonfuls of thick béchamel sauce and either press through a sieve or liquidize in a blender. Garlic purée is used in certain sauces and stuffings.

Garlic stuffing FARCE D'AIL Crush the yolks of hard-boiled (hard-cooked) eggs in a mortar with an equal quantity of blanched garlic cloves. Add fresh butter (half the volume obtained in the mortar), season with salt and pepper, and put through a sieve or crush in a blender. Chopped herbs may also be added. This stuffing is used to garnish cold hors d'oeuvres, to spread on canapés, and for various other dressings.

garnish GARNITURE

A single item or combination of various items accompanying a dish. The garnish can be placed around meat, chicken, fish, game, etc., or served separately.

Whether simple or composite, the garnish always blends with the flavour of the basic dish and the sauce (if there is one). The range of garnishes in French cookery is very diverse, although the blending of flavours necessitates the use of certain traditional garnishes (leg of mutton with small kidney beans, poached fish with boiled or steamed potatoes, venison with chestnut purée, etc.).

● *Simple garnishes* – These consist of a single element, usually a vegetable (braised, sautéed, bound with butter, or cooked in cream), rice, or pasta.

● *Composite garnishes* – These are made from several ingredients whose flavours blend with each other and with the main dish. They consist of ordinary items (such as pieces of bacon, small onions, fresh vegetables, mushrooms prepared in a variety of ways) or more elaborate ingredients (cocks' combs, crayfish tails, truffles, filled croustades, quenelles, croutons, etc.) depending on the nature of the dish. Examples of such garnishes are bonne femme, ménagère, paysanne, bourgeoise, forestière, financière, duchesse, ambassadeur, châtelaine, maréchale, royale, etc. The garnish may also be a kind of ragout, made of a composite salpicon (chicken, calves' sweetbreads, quenelles, mushrooms), blended with brown or white sauce, and arranged in barquettes, patties, etc.

In all cases, the garnish should be placed around a dish so as to achieve an overall harmony of shapes and colours which is pleasing to the eye.

Some garnishes were invented by chefs of old (Voisin, Choron, Foyot, Laguipière); some are dedicated to historical figures (Cavour, Condé, Du Barry, Meyerbeer, Rossini, Talleyrand); some bear the name of the town or region where their main ingredient originates (anversoise, Argenteuil, Nantua, Clamart, Périgueux, bordelaise); while others evoke either the preparation of which they are part (grand veneur, batelière, commodore) or their own arrangement (bouquetière, jardinière).

garum

A condiment widely used by the ancient Greeks and Romans, obtained by soaking intestines and pieces of fish in brine with aromatic herbs. (Pissalat from Nice and the Vietnamese nuoc-mâm both have a similar formula.) According to contemporary writers, the best garum was made in Carthage using mackerel, but it was also made with fry, salmon, sardines, and shad, and there were many variants: with wine, with vinegar, with water, or strongly seasoned with pepper. Garum had a very strong smell and flavour and formed part of most recipes; it was also used as a condiment added at the table.

Gascony GASCOGNE

This French province, which extends from the Landes on the coast to Haute-Garonne and from Gers to Hautes-Pyrénées, enjoys a reputation for good and abundant food, which was recognized by the ancient Romans in their nickname for it: 'the granary of the Gauls'. A wide variety of fruits (including the grape) and vegetables (the garlic of Beaumont-de-Lomagne is famous for its quality) are grown in Gascony. The cep mushrooms of its woods (*cèpes des Landes*) are much sought-after. Its cattle, pigs, and sheep (Landes lambs) produce tasty meat. The poultry, fed on corn and maize – especially the geese and ducks – are one of the glories of the region. Its game, in addition to the famous wood pigeons and ortolans of the Landes, includes ducks, larks, thrushes, and woodcocks, as well as wild boar in the woods of the Adour and wild goats in the Hautes-Pyrénées. There is a wide range of fish: trout with delicate flesh from the mountain

torrents and the Adour, salmon, shad, lamprey, pike, carp, elver (young eels), sardines, mullet, gilthead bream, bonito, and other sea fish on the Landes coast, not forgetting the oysters and pullet shells of Arachon and Cap Breton.

Gascon cookery, based on goose fat, pork fat, or oil rather than butter, is flavoured with garlic, shallots, and spices. Highly flavoured, though not to excess, the cookery of this vast region offers a wide variety of dishes. In the Gers, garbure and tourin are prepared; in the Landes, *chaudeau* (hot broth) and bouillon of goose giblets; in Hossegor, fish soup.

The raw hams of the Landes, Dax, and Saint-Sever and the sausages of Masseube are well known. The goose and duck foies gras are among the gems of the region, prepared with grapes or made into pâtés and terrines. The flesh of these birds, like pork, is used for making confits (preserves), and their giblets are used in the preparation of alicot. Goose intestines, cooked with onions, garlic, blood, and wine, make abignades (Landes). Pork stewed with haricot beans makes estouffat. Other specialities include daubes of beef or goose from Auch and Condom, tripe *à la landaise*, civet of hare in Armagnac, stuffed fowl, leg of lamb *à la gasconnade*, roast lamb from the Landes, wood pigeons, larks, or woodcocks cooked in a salmis or roasted, stuffed ortolans (buntings) in Armagnac from Chalosse, matelotes of lampreys and eels, fried elvers, and aillade. There is also a wide variety of sweets: cruchade, Gascon pastis, *feuillantines* (prune or apple pastries) from the Gers, madeleines from Dax, chocolate from Lourdes, and prunes and fruit in Armagnac.

The local wines are of high quality, the most highly esteemed being Madiran. The liqueurs include *eau de noix* (made with walnuts), *eau de coings* (made with quinces), and cassis, but the glory of the province is Armagnac.

Gascony butter
BEURRE DE GASCOGNE

A mixture of fine melted and seasoned veal fat and puréed blanched garlic cloves. This condiment is badly named since it does not contain butter. It is served with grills, breadcrumbed preparations, and boiled vegetables.

gastrique

A reduced mixture of vinegar and sugar used in the preparation of hot sauces accompanying dishes made with fruit (such as duck with orange). Gastrique is prepared by heating the ingredients together (seasoning as necessary) until the liquid has almost entirely evaporated.

gastronome (à la)

A term used to describe a dish of pot-roasted stuffed chicken or calves' sweetbreads with small poached truffles, chestnuts, and morels in butter, garnished with cocks' combs and kidneys. The cooking pot is deglazed with champagne and demi-glace, seasoned with truffle essence and used as a sauce.

The name is also given to a dish of sautéed potatoes accompanied by truffles, attributed to the Marquis of Cussy.

gastronomic tests

ÉPROUVETTES
GASTRONOMIQUES

'Some dishes are of such indisputable excellence that their appearance alone is capable of arousing a level-headed man's degustatory powers. All those who, when presented with such a dish, show neither the rush of desire, nor the radiance of ecstasy, may justly be deemed unworthy of the honours of the sitting, and its related delights.'

This test, described by Brillat-Savarin in Meditation XIII of the *Physiologie du goût*, was intended to identify the true gourmet. However, the test would have to be adapted according to the gourmet's income and social status. Brillat-Savarin therefore suggested three series of tests, according to the gourmet's prescribed income (mediocre, comfortable, or large). The first was fillet of veal larded with fat bacon and cooked in its own juices, or a dish of garnished sauerkraut, followed by *oeufs à la neige* (floating islands); the second was leg of salt-meadow lamb *à la provençale* and petits pois, or haunch of venison with chopped gherkin sauce; and the third

was a pheasant *à la Sainte-Alliance*, or a seven-pound fowl stuffed with Périgord truffles until quite round.

gastronomy

GASTRONOMIE

The art of good eating, which Monselet defines as 'the joy of all situations and of all ages'. Derived from the Greek *gastros* (stomach) and *nomos* (law), the word came into general use in France in 1801, the year that *La Gastronomie ou l'Homme des champs à table* by J. Berchoux was published. Two years later, *Le Gastronome à Paris* by Croze Magnan appeared.

In 1835, the Académie Française made the word *gastronomie* official by including it in its dictionary: it therefore rapidly gained currency despite being rather pedantic and unwieldy. It was Rabelais who introduced the Greek stem word into his play *Pantagruel* through the character of the god Gaster, honoured by gluttons. Various neologisms have been coined from the same model, such as *gastrolâtrie* and *gastromanie*, which designate various degrees of excessive love of eating, and *gastrotechnie*, invented by E. de Pomiane, meaning the science of cooking. But the best verbal invention is attributed to Curnonsky, the founder of the Académie des Gastronomes, who coined the term *gastronomades* to designate tourists who are lovers of regional specialities.

The true gastronome, while appreciating the most refined products of the culinary art, enjoys them in moderation; for his normal fare, he seeks out the simplest dishes, which are, however, the most difficult to prepare to perfection. Although he is not himself a practitioner of the culinary art, he knows enough of its methods to be able to pass judgment on a dish and to recognize the ingredients of which it is composed. In addition, he is familiar with the history of cooking and food and interested in foreign and exotic dishes.

On the other hand, as J.-F. Revel says in *Un festin en paroles*: 'The gastronome is at the same time inquisitive and timid; he explores faint-heartedly. He spends half his time remembering past satisfactions and the other half sceptically calculating future possibilities.'

Often, however, gastronomy is reduced to following fashion and reflects contemporary social attitudes. In 1925 a well-known journalist, Clément Vautel, wrote a report on 'snobbish gastronomy': 'The curious thing is that snobbish gastronomes look for a traditional classic – even rough and rustic – simplicity. They leave the bourgeois eating swallows' nests in pseudo-Chinese restaurants and go to inns with a Norman décor to enjoy blanquette de veau served unpretentiously by skilled cooks.'

gâteau

See *cakes and gâteaux*.

gâteau à la broche

A speciality that is claimed to come from both the Aveyron and the Ariège regions. It is made with a thick oily paste flavoured with rum or orange-flower water, which is gradually poured over a special rotating spit. The spit rod is a long cone of wood which is wrapped in oiled paper; the mixture is ladled onto this as it turns slowly in front of a very hot fire. The cake then cooks in a series of layers, which are wound in a long jagged band. When the cake mixture is used up, the cone is carefully withdrawn and the cake is left to cool. It keeps perfectly well for several days.

gâte-sauce

Now synonymous with 'scullion', this term originally designated the *gars de sauce*, the kitchen assistant or cook's boy whose job was to prepare the sauces under the instructions of the sauce chef or head chef.

gâtis

A speciality of the Rouergue region of France, made of a yeasted dough. It was created in about 1900 in Saint-Affrique by Léonie Cazes. Today the gâtis is made of a ball of brioche dough in the centre of which a mixture of Laguiole and Roquefort or Roquefort and Cantal cheese is inserted; the whole is covered with a slice of Laguiole or Cantal. The brioche is then left to rise, brushed with egg, and baked in the oven.

gaudebillaux

An old French dish akin to tripe, which Rabelais describes in *Pantagruel*: 'Gaudebillaux is fatty tripe from coiraux. Coiraux are oxen fattened at the manger and in guimaux meadows. Guimaux meadows are those which have two crops of grass a year.' Rabelais states that this tripe, prepared immediately the ox was slaughtered, did not keep for very long, 'from which it was concluded that people should stuff themselves with it, so as not to waste anything.'

gaudes

A cornmeal porridge which used to be the traditional evening meal in Burgundy, Franche-Comté, and Bresse. The word is derived from *gaude*, a type of plant yielding a yellow dye, which was grown in France in the 19th century. However, some inhabitants of Franche-Comté claim that it comes from the Latin *gaudeamus* (let's enjoy ourselves).

Gaudes is served hot in a soup plate or a bowl topped up with milk, cream, or even wine. Sometimes pieces of larding bacon are added. The thick porridge may also be poured into a large dish, spread out, and left to cool. It can then be cut up into pieces, browned in the frying pan (skillet) in butter, and served as a dessert with caster (superfine) sugar, jam, or honey.

gauloise (à la)

The term applied to a number of quite elaborate dishes incorporating cocks' combs and kidneys. These include a chicken consommé blended with tapioca and garnished with poached cocks' combs and kidneys; soft-boiled (soft-cooked) eggs on croutons with a salpicon of ham in tomato sauce, garnished with browned kidneys and cocks' combs; and a garnish for bouchées or tartlets, made of cocks' combs and kidneys with a salpicon of truffles and mushrooms added, thickened with suprême sauce flavoured with Madeira.

However, cocks' combs and kidneys are not included in the garnish *à la gauloise* for large braised or poached fish. This consists of barquettes filled with a salpicon of truffles and mushrooms in cream, thickened with matelote sauce, and garnished with trussed crayfish cooked in court-bouillon.

gayette

A small flat sausage from Provence. It is made of pig's liver and fresh raw pork fat, garlic, and parsley, sometimes with kidney and lung added. Gayettes are cooked in the oven, soaked in olive oil, and served piping hot or (more often) cold, as an hors d'oeuvre.

gazelle's horn

CORNE DE GAZELLE

An oriental crescent-shaped pastry made from two types of paste. One is a mixture of ground almonds, sugar, butter, and orange-flower water, which is rolled into small sausage shapes about the size of a finger. The other is a very smooth and elastic dough, which is rolled out to a thickness of 2–3 cm (about 1 in). This dough is cut into 10–12 cm (4–5 in) squares, on each of which is placed an almond-paste sausage, diagonally across. Each square is then rolled up into a crescent shape. Gazelles' horns are cooked in a warm oven and sprinkled with icing sugar (confectioners' sugar).

Gazetin du Comestible

A periodical which appeared between January and December 1767, the object of which was to tell its readers how to obtain all the necessary foodstuffs to eat well. Although this forerunner of modern culinary guides only ran for 12 issues, it provides valuable information on the provisioning of Paris in the 18th century and the prices charged.

gazpacho GASPACHO

A Spanish soup made with cucumber, tomato, onion, red pepper, and bread-crumbs, seasoned with olive oil and garlic, and served ice-cold. It is sometimes served with croutons rubbed with garlic. Its name, of Arabic origin, means 'soaked bread'. Traditionally prepared in a large clay bowl which gives it a characteristic taste, gazpacho originally came from Seville but there are numerous variants. In Jerez it is garnished with raw onion rings; in Malaga it is made with veal bouillon and sometimes garnished with grapes and almonds; in Cadiz it is served hot in winter; in Cordoba it is thickened with cream and maize (corn) flour; in Segovia it is flavoured with cumin and basil and prepared with a mayonnaise base.

Alice Toklas, in her *Cookery Book*, states that a Chilean writer of Catalonian origin, Marta Brunet, describes gazpacho as the meal of the Spanish muleteers, who 'take with them on their travels an earthen dish, garlic, olive oil, tomatoes, and cucumbers, as well as some dry bread which they crumble up. By the side of the road, they crush the garlic between two stones with a little salt, then add some oil. They coat the inside of the dish with this mixture. Then they cut up the cucumbers and tomatoes and place them in the dish in alternate layers with breadcrumbs, finishing with a layer of breadcrumbs and oil. Having done this, they take a wet cloth, wrap the dish in it, and leave it in the sun. The contents are cooked by evaporation and when the cloth is dry, the meal is cooked.'

RECIPE

Seville gazpacho GASPACHO DE SÉVILLE (from Alice Toklas' recipe, published by Éditions de Minuit) Put 4 crushed cloves of garlic, 1 teaspoon salt, ½ teaspoon ground cayenne, and the pulp of 2 crushed medium-sized tomatoes in a bowl. Thoroughly mix these ingredients and add 4 tablespoons olive oil, drop by drop. Then add a Spanish onion cut into slices as thin as tissue paper, a green or red pepper (cored and diced), a cucumber (peeled, deseeded, and diced), and 4 tablespoons croutons. Add ¾ litre (1¼ pints, 3 cups) water and mix well. Serve chilled.

gelatine GÉLATINE

A colourless odourless substance extracted from the bones and cartilage of animals and also from certain algae (agar-agar, alginates). Gelatine can either be in the form of powder or translucent leaves. It is soaked in cold water until it swells and is then dissolved either over or with a little boiling water and blended with the mixture for which it is intended. Gelatine is used for making jellies, numerous cold or iced desserts, and also for the fining of wines and fruit juices. It is also used in industrial confectionery.

gelling agent GÉLIFIANT

A food additive used to give a preparation a jelly-like consistency. The main gelling agents are pectins, alginic acid and its derivatives (E400–405), agar-agar, carrageen, starch, and carob bean meal, which is used in flans, ice creams, jams, and porridge.

gendarme

A popular French name for pickled herring, referring to the stiffness of the fish when it is dried and smoked.

The name is also given to a small flat sausage of Swiss origin (called *Landjäger*) but also common in Germany and Austria. Rectangular in shape, it is made of lean beef and pork fat, dried and smoked, and eaten raw or cooked.

génépi

An alpine species of wormwood, well known for its tonic properties. It is used in the preparation of herb teas and is the main ingredient in a number of plant liqueurs, including the famous *génépi des Alpes*.

genevoise (à la)

A term used to describe fish dishes served with genevoise sauce, made of fish fumet, mirepoix, and red wine, thickened with butter. Genevoise sauce was originally called *génoise* (Carême's recipe is made with consommé and espagnole sauce), the name being changed to avoid confusion with Genoese sponge. Nevertheless, some cookery books still include a 'génoise sauce', made in the same way as genevoise sauce but with white wine. A variant of genevoise sauce, called *gourmet sauce*, includes lobster butter, crayfish tails, quenelles, and truffles and is used to coat slices of eel cooked in court-bouillon.

RECIPES

Genevoise sauce SAUCE GENEVOISE Crush 500 g (18 oz) salmon trimmings. Peel and dice a large carrot and a large onion. Cut 10 parsley sprigs into small pieces. Sauté all these in 15 g

(½ oz, 1 tablespoon) butter for 5 minutes over a low heat. Add a sprig of thyme, half a bay leaf, pepper, and the fish trimmings. Cook very slowly in a covered pan for 15 minutes. Add a bottle of red wine (Chambertin or Côtes-du-Rhône) and a little salt to the pan juice. Boil down slowly for 30–40 minutes. Strain the sauce, then thicken it with 1 teaspoon kneaded butter (1 tablespoon anchovy butter may also be stirred in). Adjust the seasoning.

Génoise sauce SAUCE 'GÉNOISE' (from Carême's recipe) Pour into a saucepan 2 glasses (8 fl oz, 1 cup) red Bordeaux wine. Add 2 tablespoons (3 tablespoons) fines herbes (consisting of mushrooms, truffles, parsley, and 2 shallots, all blanched and chopped), a small pinch of *quatre-épices* ('four spices'), and a pinch of finely ground pepper. Boil down almost completely, add 2 tablespoons (3 tablespoons) consommé, 2 ladles (8 fl oz, 1 cup) espagnole sauce, and 1 glass (4 fl oz, ½ cup) Bordeaux wine. Boil down to the desired consistency and transfer the sauce to a bain-marie. Blend in a little Isigny butter just before serving.

Genoa cake
PAIN DE GÊNES

A type of rich sponge cake made with ground almonds, not to be confused with Genoese sponge cake. Of varying degrees of lightness depending on whether or not the beaten egg whites are incorporated separately, Genoa cake is traditionally cooked in a round mould with a fluted edge. It is served plain or with various decorations and fillings.

RECIPE

Genoa cake PAIN DE GÊNES Work 125 g (4½ oz, generous ½ cup) butter into a soft paste with 150 g (5 oz, ⅔ cup) caster (superfine) sugar, then beat with a whisk until the mixture becomes white. Blend in 100 g (4 oz, 1 cup) ground almonds, then add 3 eggs, one by one, 40 g (1½ oz, ⅓ cup) starch or cornflour (cornstarch), and a pinch of salt. Work everything well together. Flavour the mixture with 1 tablespoon liqueur (such as Curaçao). Butter a round cake tin (pan), line the bottom with a circle of buttered greaseproof (waxed) paper, and pour in the mixture. Cook for 40 minutes in the oven at 180 c (350 f, gas 4). Turn out immediately onto a wire rack and remove the paper.

Genoese sponge
GÉNOISE

A light sponge cake which takes its name from the city of Genoa. Genoese sponge is made of eggs and sugar whisked over heat until thick, then flour and melted butter are added to the cooled mixture. It can be enriched with ground almonds or crystallized (candied) fruits and flavoured with liqueur, the zest of citrus fruits, vanilla, etc. Genoese cake (which should not be confused with Genoa cake) differs from ordinary sponge cake in that the eggs are beaten whole, whereas in the latter the yolks and whites are usually beaten separately. Genoese cake is the basis of many filled cakes. Cut into two or more layers, which are covered with jam, cream, fruit purées, etc., it is coated, iced, and decorated as required.

RECIPES

Genoese sponge PÂTE À GÉNOISE Melt 125 g (4½ oz, ½ cup) butter gently without allowing it to become hot. Put 275 g (10 oz, 1⅓ cups) caster (superfine) sugar, 8 beaten eggs, 2 large pinches of salt, and 1 teaspoon vanilla sugar into a basin and place it in a tepid bain-marie; whisk the mixture until it becomes thick, pale, and foamy. Remove from heat and continue to whisk until it cools down completely. Carefully fold in 250 g (9 oz, 2¼ cups) sifted flour and then trickle in the tepid melted butter at the side of the bowl. Mix in gently until it is evenly blended. Pour this mixture into a large buttered sandwich tin (layer cake pan) and bake for 10–15 minutes in the oven at 200 c (400 f, gas 6).

Apricot Genoese sponge GÉNOISE À L'ABRICOT Bake a Genoese sponge cake. When completely cold, slice it horizontally into 3 layers of equal thickness. Cover each with apricot jam rubbed through a fine sieve, flavoured with a little rum, and warmed over a gentle heat. Reform the cake. Ice with fondant icing and decorate with browned almonds and crystallized (candied) fruits.

gentian   GENTIANE

A plant from the mountains of Europe, picked especially in the Jura and the Alps. The root is used as a substitute for cinchona. Before the latter was introduced into the Old World (1639), the large yellow gentian (*Gentiana lutea*), the panacea of the mountain dwellers, was prescribed as an infusion or a syrup as a tonic, stimulant, and febrifuge. Nowadays, it is mainly used for its apéritif and digestive properties. Gentian essence, amber yellow in colour, is an excellent bitter tonic with a strong pungent flavour; it is an ingredient of many apéritifs.

Georgette

A name given to various dishes at the end of the 19th century. It was the title of a play by Victorien Sardou, which had a successful run at the Vaudeville in 1885. Pommes Georgette, which were served for the first time at the Paillard restaurant near the theatre, are potatoes cooked whole, hollowed out, then stuffed while still hot with a ragout of crayfish tails *à la Nantua*. Poached or scrambled eggs Georgette are served in potatoes with the same garnish. There is also a Georgette soup – cream of tomato and cream of carrot mixed and blended with *perles du Japon* (tapioca). Finally, crêpes Georgette are sweet pancakes filled with a salpicon of pineapple in rum thickened with apricot jam, sprinkled with sugar, and glazed in the oven.

Gérardmer

A soft cows'-milk cheese (containing 45–50% fat) with a washed rind, generally eaten fresh. Commonly called 'Lorraine' or 'Gros Lorraine', it is cylindrical in shape, weighs 5–6 kg (11–13¼ lb), and gives off a pungent lactic smell.

Gerbaudes

A traditional festival held at the end of the harvest in the central provinces of France, also called 'Revolle' in Dauphiné and Lyonnais and 'Chien de Moisson' 'Tue-Chien', or 'Chien' in

Franche-Comté, Lorraine, Côte-d'Or, and Champagne. Elsewhere, there were different festivals to mark the end of other great agricultural events, such as walnut gathering. The common feature of all these festivals was a gargantuan communal meal, accompanied by singing and dancing. Ceremonial dishes were served on these occasions: roast cockerel in Sologne, rabbit *au sang* in Cher and Indre, and tripe in Creuse, served with galettes, fritters, and matefaims (thick pancakes). In Burgundy the meal consisted of charcuterie meats followed by stuffed mutton with parsley, braised shoulder of veal, hot pies, *corniottes au fromage* (triangular creamcheese pastries), and, varying from village to village, flamusse (sweet fruit omelette), prune galette, or brioche. The table was decorated with a sheaf of ears of corn tied up with ribbons. The festival expressed people's satisfaction at having laid in a sufficient store of food to guard against scarcity in winter.

German wines

VINS D'ALLEMAGNE

Because of the northern latitude of German vineyards vintages in Germany vary a great deal, but in spite of the cold, modern technology makes it possible to produce some pleasant wines in most years and some remarkable ones every two or three years. The German Wine Law of 1973 has established a somewhat complicated system of controls, which make the interpretation of wine labels difficult. The finer wines are grouped into the following categories: *Kabinett*, *Spätlese*, *Auslese*, *Beerenauslese*, and *Trockenbeerenauslese*. The differences between the wines of individual growers can be considerable, so that one producer's *Spätlese* may be the equivalent, in apparent sweetness, to another producer's *Auslese*. Knowledge of who makes what is of great importance where wines of superior quality are concerned. The more everyday wines come from the following 11 wine regions: Ahr, Baden, Franconia, Hessiche Bergstrasse, Mittelrhein, Mosel-Saar-Ruwer, Nahe, Rheingau, Rheinhessen, Rheinpfalz (Palatinate), or Württemberg.

The bulk of German wine is white,

although some reds are made, notably in the Ahr Valley. They tend to be lightweights. An enormous quanity of white sparkling wine is produced, often referred to as *Sekt*; some of it is made by the Champagne process but most is produced by a version of the Charmat method. Recently, German producers have been attempting to make dry or dryish wines to suit the current preference for drinking wines with a meal, but the very finest German wines are usually appraised on their own, unaccompanied by food. Among the inexpensive wines offered for drinking with food are those made by blending in wines of suitable type from other EEC countries: as the overall production of wine in Germany is comparatively small, producers who can make the quality wines prefer to concentrate on these. In Württemberg a type of pale rosé is made, called Schillerwein because of its 'shimmering' colour. In Baden one of the local specialities is Weissherbst, a white wine which is made from black grapes, but vinified as white – like a blanc de noir.

The great German grape is the Riesling, but because of its susceptibility to the climatic conditions in some years, increasing numbers of plantations are producing sturdier varieties. In most regions, however, it is the Riesling that makes the finest wines; an exception is Franconia, where the Silvaner can yield outstandingly in some years. Other substantial plantings are of the Gewurztraminer, Müller-Thurgau, Weisser Burgunder (Pinot Blanc), and Ruländer (Pinot Gris) varieties, and recently some successful crossings have been achieved, such as the Kerner, Morio-Muskat, and Scheurebe. The red wines are often made from the Trollinger and also from the Pinot Noir and Portugieser. Rosés are made with the Rotberger.

Bottles for the finer German wines vary somewhat according to the region, but in general brown glass is used for Rhine wines and green glass for the Mosels. The flagon-shaped bottles used for certain of the finer Franconian wines are somewhat similar to the *basquaise* in which some Armagnac establishments bottle their brandy.

Huge quantities of brandy are made in Germany, together with other spirits usually generally referred to as schnapps.

As so much German wine is consumed where it is made, it should be noted that the wines of some regions tend to be scarce on export markets – this applies particularly to Baden and Württemberg, the latter having the highest per capita consumption of wine in West Germany.

Germany ALLEMAGNE

German cooking is famous for being substantial and served in copious portions, it is less well known for the variety it offers. In cold damp north Germany, where Dutch, Scandinavian, and Polish influences mingle, thick soups are popular, as well as smoked meat and fish. Central Germany is known for the famous 'beer–rye bread–ham' trilogy, but ragouts, fresh vegetables, and Slav pastries are equally appreciated. In the south, the cuisine is lighter, particularly in the province of Baden and in the Rhineland, the wine country, where game is predominant. In Bavaria the accent is mainly on meats and pâtisserie.

German cooking has an ancient tradition: stuffed roast goose with potatoes and peppered hare are dishes which go back to Charlemagne. The princely courts in each state cultivated a taste for haute cuisine, often securing the services of French chefs. Nevertheless, there are also time-honoured rustic dishes, such as the popular *Himmel und Erde* ('Heaven and Earth'), which is a purée made of potatoes and tart apples, topped with a grilled sausage.

One of the characteristics of German cuisine is its marked emphasis on sweet–savoury combinations, which is evident both in Hamburg's cherry soup and eel soup (with carrots, peas, asparagus, prunes, and dried apricots) and also in Black Forest saddle of venison, served with apples stuffed with whortleberries.

□ **The land of charcuterie** It is above all the products of the pork butcher which have made the gastronomic reputation of the region beyond the Rhine, particularly in Swabia, Westphalia, and Bavaria, where the hams are renowned, as they are in Holstein and Saxony. There is an astonishing range of sausages, both hot and cold: sausages for sandwich spreads, made of liver, paprika, or smoked pork; sausages for grilling, smoked or stuffed with herbs, particularly in Nuremberg; and sausages for poaching, lightly or heavily spiced, including the delicious white weisswurst made from veal, beef, and parsley, the large bockwurst, crunchy and juicy, and, of course, the frankfurter, which is always eaten with a round roll and mustard. There are also the saveloys, brawns, and black puddings (blood sausages). All this charcuterie, often served cold, forms the main part of the family dinner.

Other basic foods, such as bread and milk products, are equally varied: *Quark*, a soft creamy white cheese eaten in great quantities, is mixed with onion, paprika, or herbs; hard cheeses contain ham or are smoked; and blue cheeses are eaten with beer. Bread comes in different forms with varying degrees of colour: wholewheat, wheaten, or rye bread, flavoured with linseed, sesame, or cumin (knackebrot, pumpernickel).

□ **Meat and fish** Meat platters are encountered everywhere, served with the two major condiments of German cuisine – horseradish and onion. Stews and ragouts are generally well spiced and sometimes cooked with soured (dairy sour) cream; for example, boiled pork knuckle from Berlin, the four-meat ragout (beef, lamb, pork, and veal) of the traditional *Pichelsteiner Fleisch*, and the chine of smoked pork as cooked in Kassel, on a bed of sauerkraut. Also popular are beef paupiettes stuffed with gherkins in a piquant sauce, meatballs with capers, *Labskaus*, and minced (ground) meat as prepared in Berlin or Hamburg (which became the hamburger in the United States).

Poultry, particularly chicken, has a prominent place. It is spit-roasted by the thousand during the Munich Beer Festival, and in Berlin it is cooked in a fricassee with asparagus and mushrooms – a French-inspired dish, imported by the Huguenots. Certain places are particularly renowned for their products: Hamburg for its fowls, which are cooked in a ragout with white wine, mushrooms, and oysters or mussels; and its *poussins* ('chicks'), which are actually tender and tasty spring chickens. Equally famous is the Pomeranian goose, the breasts of which are set aside to be smoked.

Game provides dishes of a high quality, such as the stuffed pheasant of the Rhine and venison cutlets with mushrooms. Sea fish is predominant in the north, particularly herring, which is prepared in innumerable ways (served in a sauce, smoked, marinated, fried, with horseradish, with mustard, with beer, or as rollmops), and turbot; shellfish and oysters are also popular, as are eels, Rhine salmon, pike from the Mosel, and trout from the Black Forest, which are cooked *en papillotes*.

□ **Vegetables, fruit, and desserts** Among vegetables, cabbage reigns supreme: white, red, or green, it may be marinated or served raw, in salads or as sauerkraut. The potato is equally popular, being prepared with unparalleled ingenuity: as purée, croquettes, pancakes, but above all as dumplings, klösse and knödel, served in a sauce or as a garnish to soup. Some regions are well known for their fresh vegetables: small turnips from Teltow (Berlin), green beans and kidney beans from Westphalia, the Leipzig macédoine (young peas, carrots, and asparagus), and asparagus from Brunswick.

The fruit from German orchards, known for their apples and cherries, is often dried or made into a sweet-and-sour conserve. Jellies made from wild berries and the clear eaux-de-vie are excellent.

German pastries, though less distinguished than the Viennese variety, are very popular with the Germans, who eat them at all hours of the day in the *Konditoreien* (tea-rooms), which are as numerous as the *Bierstuben* (beer bars). There is a vast range of tarts and filled biscuits, not to mention Nuremberg gingerbread and marzipan cakes from Lübeck, traditionally eaten at Christmas, as well as the great classic confections: stollen from Dresden, Black Forest gâteau, and *Baumkuchen* from Berlin (gigantic Christmas cakes in the shape of trees). Cinnamon, dried fruit, lemon, almonds, and poppyseeds are popular in homemade pastries.

Germiny

A soup made with sorrel, which Francis Amunategui called 'a soup fit for the governor of the Bank of France'. Indeed, the soup is attributed to the cook of Charles Gabriel Le Bègue, Count of Germiny and governor of the Bank of France. According to another version, it was created in his honour by the chef of the Café Anglais.

RECIPE

Germiny soup POTAGE GERMINY Wash 300 g (11 oz) sorrel, shred into a chiffonnade, and soften in butter. Add 1.5 litres (2¾ pints, 3½ pints) beef or chicken consommé. Mix 4–6 egg yolks with 3–5 dl (½–1 pint, 1¼–2 cups) fresh cream. Use this to thicken the soup until the consommé coats the spatula. Do not allow to boil. Add 1 tablespoon chervil leaves and serve with slices of French bread, dried in the oven.

Géromé

A cows'-milk cheese (containing 45–50% fat) made in the Vosges. Its name is that of the town of Gérardmer in local dialect. A soft cheese with a washed reddish rind, it is always ripened (unlike Gérardmer). Pliable to the touch, it has a strong smell and a highly seasoned taste; it may be flavoured with caraway seeds. It is marketed in round blocks, 11–20 cm (4½–8 in) in diameter and 2½–3½ cm (1–1½ in) thick.

Gevrey-Chambertin

Red Burgundy AOC from the Côtes de Nuits. This parish owes its reputation to two top wines – Chambertin and Clos de Bèze – the latter bearing the vineyard name of 'Chambertin' before its own. The other great wines in the parish, also of the highest quality, are only entitled to put this place name after their own: Latricières-Chambertin, Mazoyères-Chambertin, Charmes-Chambertin, Mazis-Chambertin, Ruchottes-Chambertin, Griotte-Chambertin, and Chapelle-Chambertin. Gevrey-Chambertin and Gevrey-Chambertin-Premier-Cru are also of high quality; they are mainly produced in Gevrey-Chambertin but can also come from the vineyards of the adjacent parish of Brochon.

Gewurztraminer

White Alsace wine made from the spicy (*Gewurz*) Traminer grape and having a very pronounced bouquet. It can make outstanding wines in the special categories of the late pickings in certain years. The Gewurztraminer grape is grown in Germany, Italy, Austria, and in California and some other New World vineyards.

ghee

Clarified fat, commonly used in Indian cooking. An ancient food, it is mentioned in the *Purāna*, a collection of legends, religious precepts, and rules for practical living, in which the human body is represented in the form of circles associated with primordial foods: palm sugar, wine, ghee, milk, yogurt, and water. The best ghee is made of butter from buffaloes' milk (twice as rich in fat as cows' milk). It is used as an ingredient in pâtisserie, as a cooking fat, to season dry vegetable purées, rice, etc. Among poorer people ghee is made of sesame oil or mustard. In Nepal it is made of yaks' milk.

gherkin CORNICHON

A variety of cucumber whose small fruits are picked while still unripe, then pickled in vinegar and used as a condiment (the French word *cornichon* means 'little horn'). The tradition of preserving small cucumbers in vinegar is an old one in several countries.

In France the plants are grown in open fields, especially in southwestern and central areas, and harvested from June to September. They consist of the following varieties:

• *Paris small green*: prickly and straight, light green, fine, and crunchy; picked when 5 cm (2 in) long.

• *Meaux fine*: less prickly, longer, darker in colour, and more watery; most used industrially.

• *Massy green*: fairly prickly, long, and deep green; particularly suitable for gherkins *à la russe* or sweet-and-sour gherkins.

The fruits are washed, brushed, left to sweat, and then plunged into a bath of brine (or placed into wooden vats and sprinkled with salt, or rubbed with salt and then immersed in brine). They are then rinsed to get rid of the salt, washed, blanched, and covered with spirit vinegar. Finally they are drained and placed in glass or earthenware jars, where they are steeped in vinegar flavoured according to each manufacturer's particular recipe (with tarragon, pepper, thyme, bay leaves, nasturtium buds, or small onions). The best gherkins are pickled in white wine vinegar. Pasteurization has become more common, and this normally produces gherkins which are more crunchy, less salty, less acid, and which keep for longer, but with a slight loss in flavour and aroma. Gherkins can be preserved equally well on a domestic scale.

In some countries they are eaten as a vegetable rather than as a condiment. Gherkins *à la russe*, *à la polonaise*, or *à l'allemande* are made according to Russian, Polish, or German recipes, respectively. These use large smooth-skinned gherkins, in a sweet-and-sour preparation, only mildly acid, and usually not very crunchy. Before being plunged into vinegar, to which sugar is added, they are steeped in brine with herbs, dill, and some leaves of oak, blackcurrant, or wild cherry.

In France and elsewhere gherkins are used principally as an accompaniment for cold meat and boiled dishes (salt beef, brisket, pastrami, and poule au pot), pâtés, terrines and other charcuterie, and dishes using aspic. They are an ingredient of some sauces (piquante, charcutière, hachée, ravigote, gribiche, reform, etc.) and can be used in mixed salads.

RECIPES

Gherkins à la russe CORNICHONS À LA RUSSE Boil some salted water with caster (superfine) sugar, using 15 g (1 tablespoon) salt and 1 teaspoon sugar per litre (1¾ pints, 4¼ cups) water. Allow to cool completely. Wash some large fresh gherkins in warm water, then cool them in cold water. Drain and pat dry. Lay them in a jar in layers, separating each layer with a few fragments of fennel sprigs and, if available, a few fresh blackcurrant leaves (taken from the ends of the twigs). Press down well. Fill the jars with salted water (it should completely cover the gherkins) and leave to marinate in a cool place for at least 24 hours before serving.

When preserving these gherkins, they

can be sterilized in the ordinary way, but they become softer in the process.

Gherkins pickled in vinegar (*prepared cold*) CORNICHONS AU VINAIGRE, À FROID Prepare and marinate the gherkins with salt as in the previous recipe. Then wash them in vinegared water, wipe them dry one by one, and place them in jars. Add some peeled white pickling onions, some fragments of bay leaf, sprigs of thyme and tarragon (which have been scalded, cooled, and dried), 2–3 cloves, 1 or 2 small cloves of garlic, 1 small chilli, a few black peppercorns, and a few coriander seeds. Cover with white vinegar, seal the jars hermetically, and store in a cool place. These gherkins can be eaten after 5 or 6 weeks, but they will improve with time (up to a year).

Gherkins pickled in vinegar (*prepared hot*) CORNICHONS AU VINAIGRE, À CHAUD Rub the gherkins with a rough cloth, then place them in a terrine. Add some coarse salt, stir, and leave for 24 hours. Remove the gherkins and dry them one by one. Place them in a terrine and cover with boiled white wine vinegar. Marinate for about 12 hours. Strain off the vinegar and add ½ litre (17 fl oz, 2 cups) fresh vinegar to each 3 litres (5 pints, 13 cups) boiled vinegar, bring to the boil, and while still boiling pour over the gherkins. Repeat the process the next day, then leave to cool completely. Scald some jars with boiling water and let them dry. Lay the gherkins in them in layers, adding seasoning every 2 layers (fragments of bay leaf, sprigs of thyme and tarragon, which have been scalded, cooled, and dried, cloves, and 1 or 2 chillies per jar). Cover with vinegar, seal the jars with cork stoppers, and store in a cool place.

gibassier or gibassié

A traditional cake made in Provence, especially at Christmas and Epiphany. It is a large brioche in the shape of a crown, flavoured with aniseed, lemon or orange zest, or orange-flower water. Of very ancient origin, the gibassier owes its name (derived from the Provençal *gibo*, meaning lump) to its lumpy surface. It is also known by the name of *pompe à l'huile*. See also *Twelfth-Night cake*.

gibelotte

A savoury stew of rabbit in white or red wine. The word derives from the Old French *gibelet* (platter of birds), which was prepared in this way. Pieces of rabbit are browned in the fat of some blanched and sautéed bacon. They are then floured, put in a cocotte with the bacon, some small onions, and a bouquet garni, and moistened with bouillon and wine. Mushrooms are added during cooking and pounded liver when the rabbit is cooked.

giblets ABATTIS

The edible inner parts of poultry, including the gizzard, heart, liver, and kidneys, plus the external giblets – the head, neck, pinions (wingtips), feet, etc.

The external giblets of large poultry (chickens, turkeys, geese) can be bought separately in France and are used to make ragouts (see *alicot*, *oyonnade*), fricassées, or pot-au-feu. Giblets are a common ingredient in French home cooking, the internal giblets being used in stuffings, garnishes, terrines, pies, and even kebabs or fritters.

☐ **Duck or goose giblets** Only the neck, gizzard, liver, and heart are used. The feet are not cooked, and the pinions are not separated from the body. *Heart*: simply take it out. *Neck*: cut it off close to the head and the body, then remove the skin. *Liver*: separate it from the entrails, then remove the gall, taking care to cut generously around this in order not to burst the bladder as the bitter bile would make this particularly tasty liver inedible. *Gizzard*: remove the thick skin with the tip of a sharp knife and only use the two fleshy parts.

☐ **Chickens and turkey giblets** These are prepared in the same way but, while the head and feet of the chicken are eaten, only the turkey's pinions, heart, liver, gizzard, and neck are used. *Pinions*: separate them from the bird at the first joint and cut them off at the second. *Neck*: slice it off close to the head and body, then remove the skin. *Heart and liver*: prepare these as for duck. *Gizzard*: slit it on the fleshy side without piercing the gravel-sac, which should be thrown away. *Chickens' feet*: cut off the claw-joint, then singe and skin the rest. *Head*: singe the head of a chicken (do not use a turkey's head).

RECIPES

Fricassee of giblets ABATTIS EN FRICASSÉE Place 450 g (1 lb) prepared turkey and duck giblets into a saucepan with a knob of butter, a bouquet garni, a chopped spring onion (scallion), chopped basil, a clove of garlic, 2 cloves, and 250 g (8 oz) mushrooms. Fry lightly then sprinkle with 25 g (2 tablespoons) flour and add about 600 ml (1 pint, 2½ cups) water or stock to cover; season with salt and freshly ground pepper. Cover the pan and cook gently for about 20 minutes then remove the lid, increase the heat, and cook briskly to allow the sauce to reduce. Just before serving, remove the bouquet garni, blend an egg yolk with 2 tablespoons cream and 4 tablespoons of the hot liquid, and stir into the giblets. Add a dash of vinegar and gently reheat without allowing to boil until sauce has thickened.

Giblet ragout ABATTIS EN RAGOÛT Cut the necks, pinions, and gizzards of the poultry of choice into similar-sized pieces, including the feet if desired, to make 700 g (1½ lb) prepared giblets. Heat 15 g (½ oz, 1 tablespoon) butter in a sauté pan, add the giblets, and stir until slightly brown, adding a little chopped garlic if desired. Dust with 1 tablespoon flour, and cook until lightly coloured. Moisten with 1 tablespoon wine and 600 ml (1 pint, 2½ cups) stock or water, add a bouquet garni, and bring to the boil. Season, cover the pan, and simmer for 30 to 35 minutes. Strain the giblets (keeping the liquid), trim them and remove any spinters of bone (the meat will have separated from the bones during cooking). Clean the sauté pan and replace the giblets, adding 225 g (8 oz, 2 cups) prepared diced vegetables of your choice. Strain the cooking liquid and skim off the fat, mix in 2 teaspoons tomato purée, and pour over the giblets. Bring to the boil, then transfer the ragout into a casserole, cover, and complete cooking in a moderate oven (160 c, 325 F, gas 3) for about 45 minutes until the vegetables are tender. Add the liver 10 minutes before the end.

Giblets à l'anglaise ABATTIS À L'ANGLAISE Scald or singe the heads, necks, pinions, and feet of chickens and carefully remove any remaining feathers. Prepare the gizzard and remove the gall from the liver. For about 750 g (1¾ lb) prepared chicken giblets, peel and slice 500 g (18 oz) potatoes and 250 g (8 oz) onions and finely chop a small bunch of parsley. Place half the onions, potatoes, and parsley in a shallow saucepan and add the giblets (except the liver) and a bouquet garni. Cover with the remaining onions, potatoes, and chopped parsley. Season, cover with water, and bring to the boil quickly. When boiling vigorously, cover the pan, reduce to a medium heat, and cook for 35 minutes. Add the liver and cook for a further 10 minutes. Turn the cooked giblets into a shallow dish, sprinkle with chopped chervil or parsley, and serve very hot.

Giblets Babylas ABATTIS BABYLAS Clean and singe 1 kg (2¼ lb) giblets of choice; peel and chop 3 medium onions. Brown the giblets in a sauté pan with 40 g (1½ oz, 2 tablespoons) butter, add the chopped onions, stir, and cook until the onions are golden. Add 850 ml (1½ pints, 3½ cups) poultry stock and a bouquet garni. Bring to the boil, cover, and leave to simmer for 25 to 30 minutes. Meanwhile, clean and slice 250 g (8 oz, 2 cups) button mushrooms and sprinkle them with lemon juice. Add the mushrooms to the pan with 1 dl (6 tablespoons, scant ½ cup) fresh cream. Stir and continue slowly cooking, uncovered, for a further 10 minutes. Then mix 4 teaspoons mustard in a little of the cooking liquid, return to the pan, and stir. To serve, sprinkle with chopped parsley.

Turkey giblets with turnips ABATTIS DE DINDE AUX NAVETS (from a recipe by Robert, in *La Grande Cuisine simplifiée*) Fry 225 g (8 oz, 1 cup) coarsely chopped unsalted streaky bacon with 25 g (1 oz, 2 tablespoons) butter in a large pan until lightly browned. Add 1 kg (2¼ lb) prepared turkey giblets and fry until they are slightly coloured. Dust with 25 g (1 oz, 2 tablespoons) flour then mix in 700 ml (1¼ pints, 3 cups) stock or water. Add an onion stuck with 4 cloves, salt, pepper, and a bouquet garni. Cut 225 g (8 oz) turnips to the size of large olives and place in a frying pan (skillet) with 25 g (1 oz, 2 tablespoons) butter and 2 teaspoons sugar, fry until brown, then moisten with 150 ml (¼ pint, ⅔ cup) liquid from the giblets. Transfer turnips and liquid to the giblet pan and continue to cook gently until the turnips are tender and the sauce has thickened. Skim off the fat. Check the seasoning and adjust if necessary. Remove the bouquet and the onion stuck with cloves. Serve hot.

Giblets can be prepared in the same way with mushrooms, celeriac (celery root), artichoke hearts, cucumber, etc.

Gigondas

Red or rosé AOC Rhône wine from vineyards in the foothills of Mont Ventoux, in an outcrop of the Dintelles de Montmirail. Full and amiably assertive the red from certain producers is capable of development in the bottle; the rosé, however, should usually be drunk young because, after a while, it tends to 'madeirise' (i.e. become like Madeira).

gigorit

A speciality of Charente and Poitou consisting of pork offal cooked in a ragout with red wine. There are several variations. Curnonsky mentions the gigorit of Aunis and Saintonge ('galantine of pig's fry and blood in wine'), while Paul Berthelet describes Charente gigorit (or *gigourit*) as follows: 'Pig's head fondue mixed with fatty pork rind which scrapes the throat a little on the way down.' Gigorit to which poultry, pork rind, onion, and spices can be added, is also called *tantouillet* (or *tantouillée*) in Poitou.

gigot

A French cut of meat corresponding to a leg of mutton or lamb. The name derives from the word for an ancient musical instrument (*gigue*), which had the same shape. The whole gigot (haunch or long leg) comprises the actual leg itself (or *gigot raccourci*, short leg) and the muscles extending from it, which form the French cut *quasi* or *selle de gigot* (chump end – not to be confused with the English saddle). The two pieces can be cut and cooked separately: the chump end, tied up with string, can be a very fine roast, whereas the short leg may be roasted, boiled *à l'anglaise*, pot roasted, braised, or even sliced and grilled (broiled). By steeping a short leg of mutton in a marinade before cooking in the oven, it is transformed into gigot chasseur, tasting of venison. The flavour of lamb combines well with garlic and roast gigot of lamb studded with garlic and garnished with kidney beans is the French traditional dish for family celebrations and special meals. The leg can also be cooked with white wine, bacon, and onions (see *brayaude*); with juniper berries, garnished with red cabbage; or with caper sauce, garnished with steamed potatoes and turnips. Other recipes include brochettes *à la turque* (lamb on skewers) and daubes or braised dishes, such as famous *gigot de sept heures* or *à la cuiller*, which is cooked for a long time over a very gentle heat, so it can be cut with a spoon, and is served with the braising liquor, strained and boiled down. Gigot of lamb can also be served cold with aïoli or in aspic with a green salad.

Leg of lamb is carved either parallel to the bone (the slices are all equally cooked) or perpendicular to the bone, slightly on the slant (the meat is more tender, but cooking is graduated). (Note: lamb cooked in the French style is generally pink in the centre, hence the cooking graduation.)

Manche de gigot ('handle' of leg of lamb) is the name given to the knuckle bone, which is traditionally decorated with a paper frill for presentation purposes and to which can be attached the *manche à gigot* (meat-carving tongs), a utensil for keeping the piece of meat steady while carving.

By analogy, the word *gigot* is also used for the drumstick and leg of a turkey or a chicken, tied together (and possibly stuffed) for roasting or braising. The term is also applied to monkfish (braised with tomato and white wine).

RECIPES

Braised leg of lamb with baby onions
GIGOT BRAISÉ AUX PETITS OIGNONS NOUVEAUX (from Alain Chapel's

recipe) Cook a leg of lamb in a casserole with butter in the oven for 25 minutes, then drain. Brown 1 kg (2¼ lb) baby onions sprinkled with sugar in butter. Place the lamb on the onions and return to the oven. When the onions are tender, add 2 peeled tomatoes cut into eight and 2 glasses of white wine. Complete the cooking, turning the lamb over to glaze it properly and moistening it as and when required with reduced beef stock. Drain and carve the lamb; cover the slices with the onions, bound with butter.

Léa's roast leg of lamb GIGOT RÔTI DE LÉA (from Léa Bidaut's recipe) Crush 4 anchovy fillets in 4 tablespoons (5 tablespoons) olive oil mixed with 2 level tablespoons mustard, sage, basil, rosemary, and crushed garlic. Rub the joint with this mixture and marinate for 2 hours, turning from time to time. Drain and roast in a hot oven.

While the meat is cooking, boil down the marinade with some butter, gradually adding ½ bottle champagne. Strain and thicken with softened butter.

Leg of lamb boiled à l'anglaise GIGOT BOUILLI À L'ANGLAISE Season a trimmed leg of lamb, wrap in a buttered and lightly floured muslin (cheesecloth), and tie up with string. Put it into a pan of boiling salted water, together with 2 carrots cut into quarters, 2 medium-sized onions (one studded with a clove), a bouquet garni, and a clove of garlic. Simmer steadily, allowing 30 minutes per kg (15 minutes per lb). Drain, unwrap, and place on a long serving dish, with the vegetables around it. Serve with an English butter sauce, made with the cooking stock of the mutton and 2 tablespoons (3 tablespoons) capers. This dish may be accompanied by a purée of turnips or celeriac (cooked with the leg of mutton), steamed potatoes, or white haricot (navy) beans.

In Provence, leg of lamb is boiled in a reduced full-bodied stock. The meat remains pink and is served with the pot vegetables and aïoli. In Normandy, near Yvetot, leg of lamb is cooked in a vegetable stock flavoured with a tablespoon of Calvados; it is served surrounded by pot vegetables and accompanied by a white sauce with capers.

Roast leg of lamb GIGOT RÔTI Stud the joint near the projecting bones with 2 or 3 cloves of garlic. Cook it on a spit or in the oven, allowing 20–22 minutes per kg (9–10 minutes per lb). Place it on a long serving dish and serve with a sauce made from the cooking juices, kept quite fatty, with slices of lemon and chopped watercress. Roast leg of lamb is accompanied by French beans in butter, white haricot beans (navy beans) in juice, or vegetables prepared *à la jardinière* or as a purée.

Note: this is the French method for roasting lamb, and the flesh will be pink. For fully cooked meat allow 45 minutes per kg (20 minutes per lb) and add 20 minutes to the total time.

Roast leg of lamb en chevreuil GIGOT RÔTI EN CHEVREUIL Completely skin a very fresh leg of lamb and lard with best lardons, as for a haunch of roebuck, then put it in a special marinade – see *chevreuil (en)*. Leave it to steep for some time, depending on the tenderness of the meat and the temperature (2 days in summer, 3 or 4 days in winter). Dry the leg with a cloth, then roast. Serve a roebuck sauce or a poivrade sauce separately.

Roast leg of lamb with forty cloves of garlic GIGOT RÔTI AUX QUARANTE GOUSSES D'AIL Desalt some anchovy fillets. Trim a leg of lamb as necessary. Stud it with slivers of garlic (2 or 3 cloves) and the anchovy fillets cut into fragments. Brush with a mixture of oil, thyme, powdered rosemary, and freshly ground pepper. Roast on a spit or in the oven (for cooking times, see recipe for roast leg of lamb), basting occasionally with a little of the aromatized oil. As the meat starts to cook, put 250 g (9 oz) unpeeled cloves of garlic into boiling water. After boiling for 5 minutes, drain the garlic and put into a saucepan with 2 dl (7 fl oz, ¾ cup) stock. Simmer for 20 minutes. Add a small cup of this liquor to the meat juices and pour over the joint. While completing the cooking, select some watercress, wash thoroughly in running water, and chop coarsely. Arrange the leg on a serving dish, surrounded by the cloves of garlic and chopped watercress. Serve the juice in a sauceboat.

Roast leg of lamb with pineapple

GIGOT RÔTI AUX ANANAS Marinate a leg of lamb for 48 hours in red wine, brandy, and aromatics. Dry it, inject some of the marinade with a syringe, and cook it in the oven (for cooking times, see the recipe for roast leg of lamb).

Serve with a sauce made from the marinade and a compote of crushed pineapples, browned in butter.

Spit-roast leg of lamb with parsley

GIGOT À LA BROCHE PERSILLÉ Spit-roast a leg of lamb (salt-meadow or milk-fed). Before cooking is completed, cover it evenly with a layer of fresh breadcrumbs mixed with chopped parsley and possibly some chopped garlic. Finish cooking the lamb until the surface turns golden brown. Put it on a long serving dish and garnish with chopped watercress and halved lemons. Serve the juice separately in a sauceboat.

gigue

Haunch of roebuck or deer, also called *cuissot* in French. Once the sinews are drawn, a haunch is usually studded with lardoons, marinated if necessary, then roasted in the oven (15–18 minutes per lb). Celery or chestnut purée, mushroom fricasse, and red- or white-currant jelly are the conventional garnishes.

Gilbert (Philéas)

French cook (born La Chapelle-sur-Dreuse, 1857; died Couilly-Pont-aux-Dames, 1942). After an apprenticeship as cook/pastrycook in Sens he travelled around France, working with Escoffier, Émile Bernard, Ozanne, and Montagné. He became a great practitioner, theoretician, and scholar. The author of numerous books, including *La Cuisine rétrospective*, *La Cuisine de tous les mois*, and *L'Alimentation et la Technique culinaire à travers les âges*, he collaborated in the writing of Escoffier's *Guide culinaire*. He also wrote numerous articles in professional magazines and cookery journals, becoming known for raging controversies with his colleagues.

Gilliers

The official chef of King Stanislas Lesz-czyński. In 1751 he published *Le Cannaméliste français* (this word comes from *cannamelle* or *canne à miel* an old French word for sugar cane). This is a valuable document both for its history of *friandises* (sweet delicacies) and for its illustrations by Dupuis, engraved by Lotha, which depicted the masterpieces of 18th-century glassware and goldsmiths' work.

gimblette

A small ring biscuit (cookie) in the shape of a crown, a speciality of Albi. The word seems to come from the Italian *ciambella* (a ring-shaped cake similar to an échaudé). The dough (flour, ground almonds, sugar, egg yolks, yeast, zest of citron, orange, and lemon) is not the same as that for échaudés, but the cooking principle is the same: the biscuits are first immersed in boiling water, then drained, dried, and browned in the oven. Fernand Molinier, pastrycook in Albi and author of *Recherches historiques sur les spécialités gourmandes du Tarn*, thinks that gimblettes were invented by the monks of Nanterre, who entrusted the recipe to the canons of Albi in the 15th century.

RECIPE

Orange gimblettes GIMBLETTES À L'ORANGE (from Carême's recipe) Grate the rind of half an orange on a lump of sugar; crush the sugar to a fine powder and mix it with more (superfine) sugar so that the whole amount measures 175g (6 oz, ¾ cup). Pound thoroughly 100 g (4 oz, scant cup) fresh almonds. Place 225 g (8 oz, 2 cups) sifted cake flour in a circle round this mixture, and in the centre put 15 g (½ oz) fresh yeast dissolved in a quarter of a tumbler (2½ fl oz, generous ¼ cup) milk. Add 50 g (2 oz, 4 tablespoons) butter, 2 egg yolks, a pinch of salt, the almonds, and the orange-flavoured sugar. Knead all these ingredients in the usual way and leave the dough in a warm place for 5–6 hours to allow the yeast to ferment.

Now break the dough and divide it into 5–6 strips, each the width of a little finger. Cut the strips diagonally into pieces 13 cm (5 in) in length. Make these into little rings so that the joins are invisible. Drop the rings into a large saucepan of boiling water. Stir gently with a spatula for a few minutes to prevent the rings from sticking and to bring them to the surface. Drain them and drop them into cool water. When cold, drain in a large sieve, then toss to dry them.

Dip each ring in a little beaten egg (2 eggs should be used in all) 2 or 3 times. Leave them to drain for a few minutes. Arrange them carefully on 3 lightly greased baking sheets and bake them in a slow oven until they are a good colour.

Little plaited biscuits (cookies) or little rolls about as long as a thumb can also be made this way. These gimblettes may also be flavoured with the rind of lemon, citron, or Seville (bitter) orange, or with aniseed, vanilla, or orange-flower water.

gin

Pure alcohol, distilled usually from grain, into which are infused aromatic plant products, particularly oil of juniper. The two basic types are Dutch and British. Dutch gin (genever), directly stemming from medicinal compounds evolved in the Netherlands in 16th century, is heavily aromatic; it is usually drunk chilled and neat. Dry gin, the universal style, originated in London in the 1870s. Much lighter and more popular than older genever, it is essentially a versatile mixing spirit – with tonic water, juices, and in numerous cocktails. Dry gin is made in many countries, premier brands carrying English names. Flavoured gins have declined, but sloe gin is still popular in Britain and the United States. Gin's culinary uses are confined mainly to offal and game dishes.

ginger   GINGEMBRE

A plant of southeast Asian origin that is cultivated in hot countries for its spicy aromatic rhizomes (underground stems), which are used fresh, preserved in sugar, or powdered. Widely appreciated in the Middle Ages, ginger was used as a flavouring and as a sweetmeat. Since the 18th century it has fallen out of use in Europe, except in pâtisserie and confectionery (sweets, biscuits (cookies), cakes, and jams, particularly in England, Alsace, and the Nether-lands) and for flavouring drinks. However, it continues to be an important seasoning in eastern cookery – fresh or dried, grated, or preserved in sugar, syrup, or vinegar. In India and Pakistan it is used to flavour meat, fish in sauce, rice, and vegetable purées, to season curries, and to flavour tea. In China and especially in Japan, it is widely used fresh, shredded in courts-bouillons, marinades, and soups. It is an essential seasoning for fish and whale fillets. It is even eaten pickled between courses. In southeast Asia crystallized (candied) ginger is the most widespread sweetmeat.

RECIPE

Ginger cake   CAKE AU GINGEMBRE Cut 100 g (4 oz, ½ cup) preserved ginger into very small cubes. Soften 100 g (4 oz, ½ cup) butter with a wooden spatula. Vigorously whisk together 3 large eggs, 1 tablespoon rum, and 2 tablespoons (3 tablespoons) hot water: when the mixture is thick and foamy, gradually add 175 g (6 oz, ¾ cup) caster (superfine) sugar, continuing to whisk. Sift together 250 g (9 oz, 2 cups) flour and 2 teaspoons baking powder, make a well in the middle, and blend in the beaten eggs, the softened butter, and the ginger. Mix well and pour into a buttered manqué mould or deep sandwich tin (layer cake pan) 22 cm (8¾ in) in diameter. Bake in oven at 220 C (425 F, gas 7) for about 40 minutes.

ginger beer

A frothy slightly alcoholic drink, widely consumed in Britain, obtained by fermenting a mixture of sugar, ginger, and cream of tartar in water. Its bitter spicy taste is popular in Britain, where ginger is also used in ginger ale (aerated water to which colouring and ginger essence is added, often used to make gin or whisky into a long drink) and ginger wine (water, ginger, yeast, sugar, lemon, raisins, pepper, and sometimes alcohol), which is mixed with whisky to make Whisky Mac.

gingerbread

PAIN D'ÉPICE

British gingerbread is a cake flavoured with ginger and treacle. The French equivalent (*pain d'épice*), whose name means literally 'spice bread', is a cake with a basis of flour, honey, and spices (it need not contain ginger). The use of honey as the only sweetening product for breads or cakes goes back to ancient times. Aristophanes mentions *melitunta*, which was made with sesame flour, eggs, and fresh cheese and coated generously with honey after cooking. The Romans prepared *panis mellitus* with German wheat flour, honey, pepper, and dried fruit. The Chinese *mikong* (honey bread) is mentioned as part of the rations of the horsemen of Genghis Khan. It is generally believed that gingerbread was introduced to Europe during the time of the Crusades. At Pithiviers, however, it is held that gingerbread was introduced into the city by St Gregory, an Armenian bishop who took refuge there in the 11th century. Whatever the case, it was from that time that the manufacture of gingerbread spread into Holland, England, Germany, Belgium, France, and Italy.

The guild of *pain d'épiciers*, founded at Reims, was officially recognized by Henri IV in 1596. According to A. Sloïmovici in *Ethnocuisine de la Bourgogne* (1973), *pain d'épice* 'was the monopoly of the city of Reims, and at first manufactured exclusively with rye flour. In Burgundy, however, the *boichet* or *boichée*, made with wheat flour, honey, and leaven, had been known since the 14th century, and *gaulderye* bread, made of honey and millet flour, was known in the 15th century.' Reims retained the monopoly until the Revolution, then Dijon, where the local production gave rise to a flourishing trade, finally took it over.

Gingerbread was formerly regarded primarily as a fairground delicacy. In Paris, the Gingerbread Fair, which became the Throne Fair in the 19th century, had been held since the 11th century on the site of the present Saint-Antoine Hospital, where there was then an abbey. The monks sold their own gingerbread cakes there, in the shape of little pigs. Gingerbread was sold in many different shapes (animals, little men, flowers, etc.) as well as the large traditional *pavé* or the ball. Belgian *spéculos*, which are made of gingerbread, depict all kinds of popular characters (Harlequin, Columbine, Saint Nicholas, etc.).

Today, two types of gingerbread are made in France: that of Dijon, made with wheat flour and egg yolks; and *couque*, made with rye flour. The *demi-couque*, or *couque bâtarde*, made with a mixture of flours, is used mainly for the large gingerbread *pavé* loaves. In industrially manufactured products, the honey is totally or partially replaced by other sweetening materials (invert sugar, glucose, grape must) and the spices are often artificial essences. However, it is always prepared according to the traditional method: the flour and sweetening materials are mixed together and matured in a cool dry place for about a month (formerly for several months). It is then mixed with baking powder and spices, shaped, glazed with milk and eggs, and baked in the oven. Ordinary gingerbread is baked in *pavé* loaves, while fancy gingerbread is cut out into hearts and various other shapes.

Although it is mainly eaten at teatime or at festivals (particularly in Belgium and Germany), gingerbread also has some uses in cookery, for thickening sauces, ragouts, and carbonades, especially when beer is used in the recipe.

Gingerbread (French or English varieties) can easily be made at home. The best results for *pain d'épice* are achieved with a strong-flavoured honey, such as buckwheat or heather honey. What flour is generally used (sometimes mixed with rye flour); flavourings can include orange-flower water, ginger, orange or lemon zest, star anise or cinnamon, or a mixture of spices. For both kinds, orange or apricot marmalade may also be added to the mixture. After baking, the top of the cake may be decorated with pieces of angelica, green walnuts, or candied orange peel.

RECIPES

gingerbread Warm together 100 g (4 oz, ½ cup) margarine or lard and 200 g (8 oz, ¾ cup) black treacle or molasses. Add 125 ml (¼ pint, ⅔ cup) milk and allow to cool. Sieve 200 g (8 oz, 2 cups) plain flour, 1 teaspoon mixed spice, 2 teaspoons ground ginger, and 1 teaspoon bicarbonate of soda into a bowl.

Add the treacle mixture, 50 g (2 oz, ¼ cup) brown sugar, and 2 eggs. Beat well. Pour into a 18-cm (7-in) square tin lined with greaseproof (waxed) paper. Bake in a slow oven (150 c, 300 F, gas 2) for 1¼–1½ hours, until firm to the touch.

Pain d'épice Heat 500 g (18 oz, 1½ cups) honey to boiling point, then skim it. Place in an earthenware bowl 500 g (18 oz, 4½ cups) sifted flour, make a well in the centre, pour the honey into it, and mix with a wooden spoon. (Certain flours absorb more liquid than others: it may be necessary to add more liquid in order to obtain a firm paste.) Gather the paste into a ball, wrap it in a cloth, and let it stand for 1 hour. Then add 12 g (2½ teaspoons) baking powder and knead the paste thoroughly. Mix in 2 teaspoons aniseed, a generous pinch of cinnamon, the same amount of powdered cloves, and ½ teaspoon grated lemon or orange peel.

Alternatively, mix the sifted flour directly with the same amount of liquid honey. Let the paste stand, then knead it hard with 100 g (4 oz, ½ cup) caster (super-fine) sugar, 12 g (2 teaspoons) cream of tartar, 5 g (1 teaspoon) bicarbonate of soda, 50 g (2 oz, ½ cup) skinned and chopped almonds, and 60 g (2½ oz, ½ cup) mixed and chopped candied orange and lemon peel.

Pour the mixture into a 23-cm (9-in) square cake tin or a buttered manqué mould. Cook in the oven at 190 c (375 F, gas 5) for about 30 minutes. As soon as the cake is cooked, quickly brush the top with some milk sweetened to a thick syrup or with sugar cooked to the 'fine thread' stage and glaze for a few seconds in a cool oven.

ginkgo nut NOIX DE GINKGO

The oval pale-green fruit of the Asian ginkgo tree. The olive-sized kernel is much used in Japanese cooking, either roasted or grilled (broiled), as a garnish for fish or poultry, or, in the autumn, simply as a dessert nut. A typical dish comprises large prawns mixed with ginkgo nuts, pieces of chicken, and mushrooms cooked on hot cooking salt in an earthenware casserole.

ginseng

The root of a plant growing in mountainous regions of Korea and Manchuria. It is considered to be the 'root of life' by the Chinese, who have attributed all kinds of therapeutic, magical, and even aphrodisiac properties to it. Used mainly in a tonic drink, ginseng is also used to make sweets, pastilles, dyes, and ointments. It can also be preserved whole in alcohol or dried and used as seasoning, in the same way as ginger. Its taste is similar to that of fennel.

giraumon

A type of gourd cultivated mainly in the West Indies and in certain tropical countries. There are two varieties: one with a large fruit (3–4 kg, 6½–9 lb), the other with smaller fruit (about 1 kg, 2 lb), the latter being preferred since giraumons do not keep once they are opened. Its firm flesh is sweet and slightly musky. Also called *bonnet turc* (Turkish bonnet) and *citrouille iroquoise* (Iroquois pumpkin), it is rich in water and has a low caloric value (31 Cal per 100 g). Giraumon can be eaten raw like cucumber, but is usually cooked like the pumpkin, especially in West Indian cookery (in a ratatouille called *giraumonade* and in ragouts). When green, it is used to make jam, like the tomato. Its leaves are sometimes used like sorrel.

girella GIRELLE

A small brightly coloured Mediterranean rock fish, with spiky rays on its dorsal fin. Its flesh is delicate and tasty but full of bones. Girella is sometimes served fried, but it is used mainly in bouillabaisse.

girolle

The French name for the chanterelle – a funnel-shaped mushroom picked between June and October in hardwood and coniferous forests. Several varieties are used, but there are two particularly good ones: the fragile girolle is very delicate and tasty, orange-yellow in colour, with a delicate stalk; the cockscomb girolle, slightly less flavoured, has a thicker and shorter stalk. Sautéed, they are used as a filling for omelettes and scrambled eggs, or to accompany rabbit or veal. They can also be eaten raw, after being marinated in a herb-flavoured vinaigrette. It is important to clean them carefully – young girolles, which are usually quite clean, are simply brushed; others are washed quickly under the tap, then drained on absorbent paper.

| RECIPE

Salad of girolles with endive (chicory) SALADE DE GIROLLES À LA CHICORÉE (from Daniel Metery's recipe) Wash and drain a large endive and 250 g (9 oz) girolles. Season the mushrooms with salt and pepper and sauté in butter for 3 minutes, adding during the final minute 2 chopped shallots and 4 tablespoons (5 tablespoons) chopped parsley (not curly leaved). Make a vinaigrette with 2 tablespoons (3 tablespoons) old wine vinegar, 6 tablespoons (½ cup) olive oil, 2 tablespoons (3 tablespoons) groundnut (peanut) oil, 1 tablespoon walnut oil, salt, and pepper. Separately season the endive and warm girolles with the vinaigrette. Arrange the endive on plates and on top place the girolles. Sprinkle with chopped chives, parsley, and chervil.

gîte à la noix

A French cut of beef from the top of the leg. With the round of beef which extends from it, it was formerly classified as braising meat, but the growing demand for beefsteak has promoted it to grilling (broiling) or roasting meat of the second category. The round of beef is lean, tender, and tasty. Gîte à la noix is also used to make steak tartare and beef on skewers. For roasting, it is larded and tied with string.

gîte-gîte

The French term for the fleshy part of the fore or hind shin of a ox. Its name comes from the verb *gésir* (to be lying down), for these muscles can touch the ground when the animal is in this position.

Gîte-gîte is a gelatinous cut of meat used in ragouts, for braising, and for stewed beef (boned). The bone provides good marrow bone for pot-au-feu.

Givry

Red and white AOC wines from the Côtes Chalonnaire vineyard in southern Burgundy. The reds are made from the Pinot Noir, the whites from the Chardonnay. The Côtes Chalonnaire has a proud history and is said to have been under vines since Roman times.

gizzard GÉSIER

A digestive pouch in birds, consisting of a thick muscle. If the gizzard is not cooked with the bird, or if it is not minced (ground) in the stuffing, it can be fried or roasted separately (particularly duck or goose gizzard) or prepared in a ragout of giblets. It is also often preserved. When a chicken is drawn, the gizzard is slit in two to remove the small stones and the thick envelope which surrounds them.

| RECIPE

Ragout of pasta with preserved ducks' gizzards and necks RAGOUT DE PÂTES AUX GÉSIERS ET AUX COUS DE CANARDS CONFITS (from *Les Menus de fête*, by Marie Abadie and Colette Olive, published by Grasset) Brown some preserved duck giblets (gizzards, necks, pinions) in a fairly large saucepan until the fat in which they are encased softens. Add 2 or 3 shredded onions, a bowlful of sliced carrots, and a slice of ham cut into coarse strips. Season with salt and pepper. Add 1 or 2 cloves of garlic and just enough water to cover. Bring to the boil and cook gently for 30 minutes. After removing the fat, add a large handful of macaroni or fresh noodles. Add more water if necessary for the pasta, and cook until it is swollen and soft. Serve very hot.

Gjetöst

A dark brown strongly flavoured Norwegian cheese made of skimmed cows' and goats' milk, or just goats' milk (*gjei* in Norwegian). It is moulded in brick shapes weighing between 200 g (7 oz) and 4 kg (9 lb).

glacé

Describing fruits (crystallized (candied) or in liqueur) and petits fours that are coated with a syrup cooked to the 'crack stage' so that they have a hard shiny layer. The word is also used for fruits and chestnuts (marrons glacés) preserved in syrup.

In France, the term is also applied to many iced desserts and drinks, and also to cakes and pastries covered with icing (frosting).

glass and glassware

VERRE ET VERRERIE

Common soda glass is a transparent or translucent material made from the fusion of silica (sand), sodium carbonate (soda), and calcium carbonate (lime). Crystal glassware is made from flint glass, a very clear glass containing lead oxide, silica, potassium carbonate, and potassium nitrate; good-quality crystal glass makes a clear ringing sound when struck. Common and crystal glassware may be engraved, coloured, or gilded. In spite of its fragility and poor resistance to sudden changes in temperature, glass is widely used for table- and kitchenware, not to mention bottles, because of its transparency and resistance to chemicals.

☐ **The history of glass** Egyptian paintings show that the art of glass-blowing was known as far back as the 4th century BC, and glass objects have been in existence for more than 5000 years. Until the Middle Ages, however, pottery utensils were more common in ordinary households, glassware being rather rare and reserved for luxury use. The glass industry in France dates from the Gallo-Roman era. In the 6th century, the glassware of Clotaire I consisted of cone-shaped stemless goblets, their borders decorated with a fine strip of coloured glass. There were also bottles and white enamelled dessert cups. But the use of glass in tableware as we know it today did not come until the 14th century. The 16th-century Venetian glass-blowers were the first to obtain a colourless glass, which they named *cristallo*. Shortly afterwards, the glass makers of Bohemia discovered that clear glass could also be made by adding limestone to the glass paste. However, it was an Englishman, George Ravenscroft, who in 1675 discovered lead crystal. In France, the Cristalleries de Baccarat dates, in its present form, from 1816.

The industrial and technical progress made during the 19th and 20th centuries has produced a wide range of drinking glasses, in a style either based on past models or reflecting modern taste. Venetian glasses ornamented with filigree work, heavily patterned Bohemian crystal, coloured engraved tall wine glasses from the Rhine, and wide-mouthed flute glasses from Dutch glassworks have become collectors' items. Coloured glass is not often used for present-day wine-glasses, so that the natural colour of the wine may be appreciated. The wineglass should never be completely filled, and it must be wide enough for the aroma of the wine to be appreciated, since part of the pleasure of drinking wine is to sample its bouquet.

☐ **Glassware** For a carefully prepared meal, three matching glasses are required, in decreasing size: for water, for red wine, and for white wine; the Madeira glass is tending to be less fashionable. The set is sometimes completed by a champagne glass, if the meal is to end with champagne. However, it is inadvisable to set out too many glasses as they can get in the way of the cutlery; therefore the setting is often reduced to two glasses, one for water and the other for wine. For an informal meal, the latter may be used for several different wines or be changed in the course of the meal.

Glasses come in a wide range of shapes and sizes. Most wine-producing regions have designed thin-walled glasses of a particular shape to allow the best possible tasting of their wine (for Alsace wine, Chambertin, etc.). Thin-walled balloon glasses are used for Cognac, Armagnac, marc brandy, etc.; liqueur glasses are usually short and narrow, made of thicker glass, and often without a stem. A tumbler is used for long drinks, and beer is usually served in a tankard. 'Short' cocktails are served in a fluted cocktail glass of 8–12 cl (2½–4 fl oz) capacity while long drinks are served in a tall 30-cl (10-fl oz) Collins glass (tumbler). Large glass goblets may be used for mineral waters and cups, medium goblets for wines and for apéritifs with water or a mixer, and small goblets for dry apéritifs, port, and short drinks such as sherry. There are also various specially designed glasses, such as champagne tulips and brandy goblets. A mixing glass may be used instead of a cocktail shaker to prepare cocktails based on alcohols; it has a capacity of 60–70 cl (20 fl oz).

Innumerable poets have sung the praises of wine and yet others have waxed lyrical about the glasses. For example, Remi Belleau, a member of the Pléiade, a group of seven French poets led by Pierre de Ronsard, was inspired by the work of medieval lapidaries to write:

'Crystal hanté mignardement
Sur un pied qui fait justement
La base d'une colonette
Où règne pour le chapiteau
À feuillage un triple rouleau.
Le seul appuy de la cuvette,
Jamais ne se puisse casser,
Esclatter, feller ou froisser
De ce crystal la glace belle,
Mais toujours pris de mon soulas
Comble de vin ou d'hypocras
Demeure compagne fidèle.'

('Crystal delicately poised
On a stem which in fact is like
The base of a little column
Where a triple coil provides
The carved capital,
The only support for the cup.
May this beautiful glass
Never be broken,
Burst, cracked, or crushed,
But always be filled with my solace
Overflowing with wine or hippocras
And remain a faithful companion.')

glasswort SALICORNE

A small fleshy plant with salty sap, also called marsh samphire, which grows in European salt marshes as far north as Norway and also in the Camargue (Mistral calls it *sans-souiro*). It is similar to rock samphire. The plant is harvested in summer for its tender green tips, which can be eaten in a salad, cooked like French (green) beans, or pickled and used as a condiment, like gherkins.

glaze or stock glaze
GLACE DE CUISINE

A syrupy substance obtained by boiling down an unthickened stock of meat, poultry, more rarely game, or even fish.

Stock glazes are used as an essence to be added to certain sauces, in order to enhance their flavour, or to baste dishes to be browned in the oven. They are also used as the base for a sauce when adding other ingredients.

Stock glazes may be used to speed up the preparation of soups, coulis, aspics, etc. Ready-made meat glazes, marketed as 'extracts' or 'essences', are available: they are mostly made of beef and vegetable matter. They offer a more limited range of flavours than cooked glazes, but the latter no longer play as important a role in cooking as they used to because they take a long time to prepare, as is demonstrated in this impressive recipe taken from *Secrets de la nature et de l'art concernant les aliments* (1769):

'Take a quarter of a large ox, a whole calf (or a part only, depending on its size), two sheep, two dozen old hens and two old cocks, or a dozen old turkeys, plucked and drawn. After defatting all this meat and scalding and cleaning the calf's and sheep's feet separately, put it all in a large boiler. Add the hot liquor from 12–14 litres of stag's horn gratings, boiled separately and put through the press. Then pour four buckets of spring water over it all. Put the lid on the boiler, sealing the edge with a flour-and-water paste. Apply a weight of 50–60 pounds. Boil the meat over a low even flame, without skimming it, for six hours or more if necessary, until it is sufficiently cooked, when the bones can be easily detached. Remove the largest bones, leaving the boiler over the heat to keep the meat very hot. Take the meat out as quickly as possible, chop it up immediately, and then put it in a large press with hot iron plates to extract all the juices. As soon as this operation is completed, add the extracted juices to the hot stock left in the boiler and strain immediately through a large horsehair strainer.'

The word 'glaze' is also used for any substance used to give food a glossy surface (see *glazing*).

RECIPE

Meat glaze GLACE DE VIANDE Remove all the fat from a brown stock. When it is as clear as possible, boil it down by half. Strain through a muslin cloth (cheesecloth), then boil it down again and strain. Continue this process until it will coat the back of a spoon, each time reducing the temperature a little more as the glaze becomes more concentrated. Pour the meat glaze into small containers and keep it in the refrigerator.

A similar method is used with a poultry or game stock to obtain a poultry or game glaze.

By boiling down a fish fumet to a syrupy consistency, then decanting it and straining it through muslin, a light-coloured fish stock is obtained, which is used to enhance the flavour of a fish sauce or to pour over fish before putting it in the oven.

Similarly, white poultry stock is boiled down to obtain a light-coloured poultry glaze, used to supplement certain sauces or for glazing.

glazing GLAÇAGE

The process of creating a glossy surface on food. This may be achieved by several different methods according to the effect required.

Cold food is brushed with such glazes as arrowroot, aspic jelly, stock glazes, sugar syrup, etc.

Desserts such as fruit tarts and flans, babas, savarins, etc., are coated with a fruit glaze – a liquid jelly made from finely sieved apricot jam or redcurrant jelly, usually with gelatine added. As well as being decorative, this prevents the fruit from drying out or oxidizing.

Food that is to be baked, particularly pastry, is coated with whole beaten egg, egg yolk only, milk, milk and sugar, etc.

Hot cooked food, particularly vegetables, can be glazed either by cooking with butter, sugar, and very little liquid or by brushing with melted butter when cooked.

Food coated with sauces that are rich in egg yolk, cream, or butter is grilled (broiled) or baked under a very high heat to form a shiny brown surface.

In France, the term *glaçage* is also used for glazing cakes with icing (frosting) and for the preparation of many cold or frozen desserts and chilled drinks.

gloria

Black coffee with brandy or rum added. First used in 1817, the term is now obsolete.

Balzac mentions the Flicoteaux restaurant, where 'friendships were sometimes sealed in the warmth of half a cup of coffee, blessed by a gloria of some kind.'

Gloucester

A traditional English cows'-milk cheese, with a firm close texture. Double Gloucester is twice the size of Single Gloucester, which is seldom made now. Gloucester is compact and smooth, with a delicate and creamy flavour. It is used for making sandwiches, canapés, etc., but it is also sometimes served as a dessert, with a salad or a fruit compote.

glucose

The simplest of the carbohydrates and the preferred energy source of cells, especially those of the brain. It is glucose into which the digestive juices reduce the sugars and starches in foods in order to assimilate them. It is found naturally in ripe fruit and honey and also forms part of the formula of many carbohydrates.

Glucose is made industrially by heating starch with various acids. This produces first dextrins and then an impure form of glucose itself. Two forms of glucose are used commercially, viscous and semisolid. Glucose has many industrial uses, notably to increase the sugar content of wine and beer. It is also used in the manufacture of syrup and jam. French law lays down that when glucose is used in this way the fact must be indicated on the label.

gnocchi

Small dumplings made of flour, semolina (semolina flour), potato, or choux pastry. They are usually poached, then cooked *au gratin* in the oven and served as a hot entrée. This dish is Italian in origin (the word means 'lumps'), but it is also found in Austro-Hungarian and Alsatian cookery in the form of knödel, noques, knepfle, or even quenelles, which are all quite similar.

Gnocchi *à la romaine* are made with semolina, egg yolks, and cheese; gnocchi *à la parisienne* are prepared from choux pastry with milk and cheese; and gnocchi *à la piémontaise* or *à l'alsacienne* are made with potato purée, eggs, and flour. The basic ingredients can be varied by incorporating various cooked vegetables (pumpkin, spinach, green vegetables, beetroot), which colour the gnocchi; by varying the cheese (Emmental, Parmesan, Ricotta) or the flour (maize, wheat); and by including chicken liver or brains, herbs, and condiments (nutmeg, fines herbes, paprika (paprika pepper), oregano, parsley).

RECIPES

Gnocchi à l'alsacienne   Cook 3 medium-sized potatoes in boiling salted water for about 20 minutes. Meanwhile grate 6 or 7 medium-sized peeled potatoes and squeeze them in a cloth to extract as much water as possible. Peel and mash the cooked potatoes, then mix them with the grated raw potatoes. Add 100–125 g (4–4½ oz, 1 cup) flour, a little grated nutmeg, salt, pepper, then 2 whole eggs, one after the other. Mix thoroughly. Boil some salted water and use 2 spoons to shape the paste into small round portions. Drop them into the water, and leave to simmer for 6–8 minutes. Drain the gnocchi and place them on a cloth. Butter a gratin dish and arrange them in it, coated with 2 dl (⅓ pint, ¾ cup) fresh cream and sprinkled with grated cheese. Brown in a very hot oven.

Gnocchi à la parisienne   Make some choux pastry using milk instead of water, and flavour with grated nutmeg. Add some grated Parmesan – 75 g (3 oz, ¾ cup) per 500 g (1 lb) dough. Boil some salted water, using 8 g (¼ oz) salt per litre (1¾ pints). Push the dough through a forcing bag fitted with a large plain nozzle so that it drops into the water in pieces measuring about 3 cm (1¼ in). Poach for a few minutes, then drain and arrange on a cloth. Line a gratin dish with some Mornay sauce, place the gnocchi in it, cover them with more sauce, sprinkle with grated Gruyère, and pour over melted butter. Brown quickly in a preheated oven (250 c, 480 f, gas 9)

Gnocchi à la romaine   Pour 125 g (4½ oz, ¾ cup) semolina into ½ litre (scant pint, 2 cups) boiling milk and stir to obtain a very thick smooth porridge. Add salt, pepper, and grated nutmeg, then 100 g (4 oz, 1 cup) grated cheese and 25 g (1 oz, 2 tablespoons) butter. Allow to cool and then add 1 lightly beaten egg and 1 yolk. Brown small balls of this paste in boiling oil (about 175 c, 350 f), drain on absorbent paper, and serve immediately with tomato sauce if liked.

Alternatively, spread the paste evenly on a moistened slab, leave to cool completely, then cut with a pastry cutter (cookie cutter) into rounds about 5 cm (2 in) in diameter. Arrange the rounds in a buttered gratin dish and sprinkle with grated Gruyère or Parmesan cheese. Pour over melted butter and brown slowly in the oven. (The paste can also be made without butter or grated cheese.)

goat   CHÈVRE

A domestic animal bred mostly for its milk. In France, where goat cheeses are increasingly in demand, the main rearing areas are Poitou, Berry, Dauphiné, and Touraine.

Goats' meat is fairly firm, with a pleasant flavour but a strong smell. It is consumed principally in the regions where the goats are bred; when the animal is young, it is eaten roasted or marinated, sometimes even smoked and dried (in the mountains). The male (*bouc*) is today eaten only when a kid, but for centuries, in spite of its leathery flesh and pungent smell, it was a basic meat of the poor (the word *boucherie* (butcher's shop) is derived from *bouc*).

goats'-milk cheeses

CHÈVRES

In France, cheeses prepared exclusively from goats' milk contain at least 45% butterfat. *Mi-chèvre* cheeses are made from a mixture of cows' milk and goats' milk (at least 25%). Among the best-known French goats'-milk cheeses are Sainte-Maure,   Pouligny-Saint-Pierre, Valençay, Cabécou, Chabichou, Chevreton, Crottin, and Selles-sur-Cher.

goblet GOBELET

A wide-mouthed drinking vessel. Antique goblets were made of gold and silver, often exquisitely engraved and embellished with precious stones.

gobo

A root of a variety of burdock. It is long, thin, and brown and is commonly used in Japan as a condiment, finely chopped and usually blanched. Gobo has a flavour similar to that of cardoon and is used in cooking stocks and vegetable mixtures.

goby GOBIE

A small sea fish, known in France as *goujon de mer*, of which there are numerous types. Its flesh has a delicate taste, but because it is so small it is usually served fried.

Godard

A classic garnish for large cuts of meat, poultry, and calves' sweetbreads. According to the *Dictionnaire de l'Académie des gastronomes*, it was dedicated to the farmer-general and man of letters Godard d'Aucour (1716–95), but other authorities say that it is named after the chef de cuisine of the Élysée Palace at the time of Sadi-Carnot. The garnish consists of quenelles, lambs' sweetbreads (braised and glazed), cocks' combs and kidneys, small truffles, and fluted mushroom caps. These are covered by a sauce made of white wine or champagne with a ham mirepoix.

RECIPE

Godard sauce SAUCE GODARD Cook 2 tablespoons (3 tablespoons) ham mirepoix in butter, add 2 dl (⅓ pint, ¾ cup) champagne, and boil down by half. Moisten with 2 dl (⅓ pint, ¾ cup) demi-glace sauce and 1 dl (6 tablespoons, scant ½ cup) mushroom essence and boil down again by one-third. Strain.

godiveau

The delicate forcemeat, consisting of veal and fat, used to make quenelles, which are served as a hot entrée or used to fill vols-au-vent or to accompany meat dishes. The word seems to be a corruption of *gogues de veau* (gogues of veal). Godiveau can also be made from fish (pike in particular) or poultry. The mixture must be very smooth, springy, and yet firm, which requires quite a long preparation time as the raw meat and fat is pounded with cream or panada, eggs, and seasoning.

RECIPES

Godiveau lyonnais or pike forcemeat à la lyonnaise GODIVEAU LYONNAIS OU FARCE DE BROCHET À LA LYONNAISE Pound together in a mortar 500 g (18 oz) trimmed diced beef suet, 500 g (18 oz) frangipane panada, and 4 egg whites (these ingredients may first be put through a blender). Add 500 g (18 oz) pike flesh and season with salt and pepper. Work vigorously with a spatula, then a pestle. Rub through a fine sieve, place in an earthenware dish, and work with a spatula until smooth.

The forcemeat is shaped into quenelles and poached in salted water when served as a garnish for pike.

Godiveau with cream GODIVEAU À LA CRÈME Chop up 1 kg (2¼ lb) noix of veal and pound it. Also chop up and pound 1 kg (2¼ lb) beef suet. Mix these ingredients together and add 1 tablespoon salt, 5 g (¼ teaspoon) pepper, a pinch of grated nutmeg, 4 whole eggs, and 3 egg yolks, grinding vigorously with a pestle the whole time. Rub the forcemeat through a fine sieve and spread it out on a board. Leave on ice or in the refrigerator until the next day. Put the forcemeat back in the mortar and pound it again, gradually adding 7 dl (1¼ pints, 3 cups) fresh cream.

To test the consistency of the godiveau, poach a small ball and rectify if necessary, adding a little iced water if it is too firm or a little egg white if it is too light. Shape into quenelles and poach.

gogues

Savoury puddings (blood sausages) that are a speciality of Anjou. Made of vegetables, bacon, fresh cream, and blood, they are poached in boiling water, then cut into slices and fried.

RECIPE

Gogues Chop 250 g (9 oz) onions, 250 g (9 oz) spinach beet leaves, 250 g (9 oz) spinach leaves, and 250 g (9 oz) lettuce leaves. Season with salt and pepper, leave to stand for 12 hours, then braise over a very gentle heat with 40 g (1½ oz, 3 tablespoons) lard in a casserole. Dice 250 g (9 oz) fat bacon and cook without browning. Add to the chopped vegetables and season with a pinch of cinnamon and mixed spice. Take off the heat and add 1 dl (6 tablespoons, scant ½ cup) double (heavy) cream and 2½ dl (scant ½ pint, 1 cup) pigs' blood. Adjust the seasoning. Fill a pig's intestine with this mixture, twisting it every 10–15 cm (4–6 in) after filling. Poach the gogues in salted water, just below boiling point, for about 30 minutes. When they rise to the surface, prick them with a pin to prevent them bursting. Drain and leave to cool. When they are cold, cut the gogues into thick slices and brown them in butter or lard in a frying pan (skillet).

gold OR

A precious metal used for decorative tableware or as a veneer, in the form of silver gilt. Gold also has some culinary uses: in the Middle Ages, pâtés and roast birds were wrapped in thin gold leaf. Even today, chocolates (*palets d'or*) are decorated with a tiny piece of gold leaf, and minute pieces of gold are suspended in the liqueur Danziger Goldwasser, which is used to flavour soufflé Rothschild. It is also an authorized food additive (E175), a colouring agent for charcuterie, confectionery, and cake decorations.

gomphide

A fleshy viscous mushroom which grows under conifers. It is edible if peeled carefully, although its flesh turns black when cooked. It is usually sautéed in oil and served with noisette butter and a little fresh cream.

gondole

A decoration consisting of a white stiffened table napkin, reinforced by a sheet of greaseproof (waxed) paper or kitchen foil, and folded using a particular technique into the shape of a curved horn. In catering, gondoles are used to decorate the two ends of a long dish when serving fish.

goose OIE

A migratory bird originally prized as a game bird and later domesticated. The Romans practised the force-feeding of geese; the preparation of foie gras therefore has a long history.

All breeds of domesticated goose are probably descended from the greylag goose. In France, geese providing foie gras may weigh up to 12 kg (26½ lb) after fattening; they are found mainly around Toulouse, Landes, Strasbourg, etc. White geese, from Bourbon or Poitou, are descended from the snow goose; they weigh less (5–6 kg, 11–13 lb). Laying birds may be kept until they are five or six years old; as their meat is by then very tough and dry it is usually stewed or preserved (see *confit*). Table geese are killed at three months, by which time the breast is well developed and the meat has a delicate flavour. In areas where geese are bred primarily for foie gras, the remainder of the bird (the meat and carcass, called the *paletot*) is sold as it is, or cut up and preserved, or made into rillettes. The gizzard, heart, tongue, neck, and giblets are all used in various savoury dishes. Today, in spite of competition from the turkey, roast goose is still the typical dish cooked at Christmas and New Year in Scandinavia and Germany. Formerly in Britain roast goose with sage and onion stuffing was served at Christmas and Michaelmas. Two famous recipes for cooking goose come from northern Europe: goose *à l'instar de Visé* from Belgium and smoked goose from Pomerania. Many of the recipes given for cooking turkey and chicken can be used for goose.

RECIPES

Ballottine of goose with Savigny-lès-Beaune BALLOTTINES D'OIE AU SAVIGNY-LÈS-BEAUNE (from a recipe by Marc Pralong) Take a young goose weighing about 3.5 kg (8 lb) and cut off the wings and legs. Bone the legs and remove the meat from the wings to make the forcemeat. Remove the suprêmes from the carcass and refrigerate until required.

Stuffed goose legs en ballottines
Mince (grind) the reserved wing meat
and the liver very finely. Place in a bowl
over a dish of ice and work the mixture
until smooth. Then blend in an egg
white followed by 3 dl (10 fl oz, 1¼
cups) double (heavy) cream. Add salt,
pepper, and cayenne and 50 g (2 oz, ½
cup) boiled diced chestnuts. Stuff the
boned legs with this mixture, shape
them into ballottines, and tie them.
Spread some sliced onion over the base
of an ovenproof dish and lay the carcass
of the goose on top. Then place the
ballottines on top of the carcass and
braise them for 45 minutes to 1 hour,
basting frequently so that they remain
moist. (The remainder of the stuffing
can be used to make godiveau).

Chestnut custards Mix 3 dl (10 fl oz,
1¼ cups) single (light) cream, 3 whole
eggs, 150 g (5 oz, ½ cup) chestnut
purée, and 100 g (4 oz, 1 cup) boiled
diced chestnuts. Butter 8 small dariole
moulds and divide the mixture between
them. Cook in a bain-marie in the oven
at 170 c (325 f, gas 3). Leave for a few
minutes before unmoulding.

Onions stuffed with garlic purée
Blanch 8 medium-sized Spanish onions
in fast-boiling salted water, refresh
them, and drain them carefully. Peel
500 g (18 oz) garlic cloves, cook them in
milk, drain them, and rub them through
a fine sieve. Reheat them with a little
cream. Stuff the onions with the garlic
purée, filling them to the top.

Accompanying sauce Remove the fat
from the liquor in which the ballottines
were braised and deglaze the pan with a
bottle of Savigny-lès-Beaune. Reduce by
one-third, strain, and thicken the sauce
with 200 g (7 oz, scant 1 cup) butter.
Adjust the seasoning.

Fried sûpremes Fry the suprêmes in
the goose fat until the outside is golden
brown but the inside is still pink.
 On each plate, place a thin slice of
suprême, a slice of ballottine, a stuffed
onion, and a chestnut custard. Pour the
sauce around the items without covering the sliced meat. Serve the rest of the
sauce separately.

Goose à la bourguignonne OIE À LA
BOURGUIGNONNE Dice 100 g (4 oz)
blanched lean bacon and fry it in 25 g (1
oz, 2 tablespoons) butter. Using the
same pan, fry 20 small onions and then
20 sliced mushrooms. Remove them
and brown the goose all over in the same
butter. Remove the goose, deglaze the
pan with 5 dl (17 fl oz, 2 cups) red wine,
boil down to reduce it by half, and then
add 4 dl (14 fl oz, 1¾ pints) demi-glace
sauce (or reduced stock). Boil for 5 minutes, and add a bouquet garni. Put the
goose back into the pan. Start the cooking over a high heat, then reduce the
heat, cover the pan, and cook gently for
30 minutes. Add the bacon, onions, and
mushrooms and continue to cook over a
moderate heat, with the pan still covered, for 45 minutes to 1 hour. Remove
the bouquet garni, and either serve the
goose and its accompaniments in the
cooking dish or arrange it on a large
serving dish and pour the sauce over it.

Goose à l'anglaise OIE À L'ANG-
LAISE Roast 1 kg (2¼ lb) large unpeeled onions in the oven. Let them get
cold, then peel and chop them. Soak an
equal weight of crustless bread in milk,
then press out as much milk as possible.
Mix the bread with the chopped onion
and season with 10 g (1½ teaspoons)
salt, a pinch of pepper, a little grated
nutmeg, and 50 g (3 tablespoons, scant
¼ cup) chopped fresh sage.
 Stuff the goose with this mixture and
sew up the vent. Roast the bird in the
oven, preferably on a spit, for about
1½–2 hours. Place it on a long serving
dish, pour over the deglazed cooking
juices, and serve with unsweetened or
very slightly sweetened apple sauce.

Goose in the pot OIE AU POT (from
a recipe by Simone Lemaire) The day
before it is required, stuff a young goose
weighing about 3½ kg (8 lb) with the
following mixture: the chopped liver
and heart, 2–3 diced apples, and 3–4
desalted anchovy fillets pounded to a
paste. Leave the goose in a cool place for
24 hours. The following day, make a
stock with 20 unpeeled garlic cloves, a
bouquet garni, and an onion studded
with 2 cloves. Stud the goose all over
with garlic and poach it in the stock for

1½ hours, skimming the pan when it comes to the boil.

Stew some dessert apples, and add to them 2 desalted pounded anchovies and 1 cup of the strained cooking stock. Prepare some small gougères: for every 2 eggs used for the dough, add 100 g (4 oz) Gruyère cheese and 1 puréed anchovy fillet.

Serve the goose very hot, accompanied by the apple and garnished with the gougères.

Roast goose with fruit OIE RÔTIE AUX FRUITS Stuff a goose and roast it as for goose *à l'anglaise*. While it is cooking, poach some quartered pears in boiling syrup until transparent. Peel and core some small apples and sprinkle them with lemon juice. Fill the centres with redcurrant jelly. Half an hour before the goose is cooked, place the apples around it and baste with the goose fat that has collected in the pan. Complete.the cooking. Place the goose on a long serving dish and arrange the apples and the drained pear quarters around it. Keep hot at the front of the oven. Deglaze the cooking pan with a little of the pear syrup, reduce the liquid by half, and pour it into a sauceboat.

goose barnacle OPERNE

A type of barnacle which is permanently attached to a rock by a long stalklike foot. In Biarritz it is called *operne*; in Brittany it is called *poche-pez*; while in Saint-Jean-de-Luz it is known as *lamperna*. It is found in large numbers on rocky reefs battered by the sea but is so difficult and dangerous to harvest that it rarely appears on the dining table. However, the natives of Biarritz insist that it is delicious when cooked for 20 minutes in a court-bouillon (only the foot is edible). It is the emblem of a gastronomic society, Les Chevaliers de l'Operne, which is dedicated to increasing the consumption of seafood.

gooseberry

GROSEILLE À MAQUEREAU

The fruit of the gooseberry bush, a large berry with a slightly hairy skin, usually green or amber-green in colour. In France gooseberries are mainly grown in Normandy, on a small scale. The French name derives from the use of the fruit to prepare a sauce traditionally served with mackerel. Gooseberries are produced on a larger scale in the Netherlands and in Great Britain.

Gooseberries have a low calorific value (30 Cal per 100 g) as they contain little sugar, but they are rich in potassium, vitamin C, and certain trace elements. They may be eaten raw with sugar or used to make tarts, sorbets, fools, jellies, and syrups. They are an ingredient in puddings, chutneys, and fruit salads, and are used to garnish fish and duck. They freeze well.

RECIPES

Gooseberry jelly GELÉE DE GROSEILLE À MAQUEREAU Remove the stalks from 3 kg (6½ lb) gooseberries and put them in a pan. Cover and heat them, shaking them from time to time until the skins burst. Purée the fruit in a blender, then strain. Pour the juice obtained back into the pan. Add 2½ kg (5½ lb, 11 cups) granulated sugar and the juice and grated rind of 2 lemons. Cook over a high heat for 5 minutes then lower the heat and cook for 15 minutes. Skim and put into jars.

Gooseberry sauce SAUCE AUX GROSEILLES À MAQUEREAU Cook 500 g (18 oz) gooseberries in a saucepan with ½ litre (17 fl oz, 2 cups) water and 75 g (3 oz, 6 tablespoons, firmly packed sugar. When the pulp becomes very soft, strain and serve piping hot. If the gooseberries are very ripe, add a few drops of lemon juice.

Gorenflot

The name of one of Alexandre Dumas' heroes, a larger-than-life monk who appears in *La Dame de Monsoreau* and *Les Quarante-Cinq*. In the middle of the 19th century, this name was given to a large hexagonal baba created by the Parisian pastrycook Bourbonneux, and also to a garnish for pieces of braised meat, consisting of a julienne of red cabbage, slices of saveloy sausage, and stuffed potatoes.

Gorgonzola

An Italian cows'-milk cheese (48% fat), white or light yellow in colour and streaked with blue. Gorgonzola should be delicate and creamy with a natural grey rind, pitted with red. It has a distinct smell and can have a mellow, strong, or sharp flavour, depending on its degree of maturity (it is ripened dry, in a cold damp cellar). Cylindrical in shape, 25–30 cm (10–12 in) in diameter and 16–20 cm (6¼–8 in) high, it is wrapped in silver paper bearing its trademark. It is good to eat all the year round, its qualities being due to its special manufacturing technique: the hot curds from the morning milking are used to line the moulds, while the cold curds from the evening milking are placed in the middle. Contrary to the normal manufacturing technique for blue cheeses, the mould *Penicillium glaucum* is not included.

The history of Gorgonzola is connected with the migration of cattle from the Alps to the south of the plains of the Po. Tired from their journey (*stracche* in the Lombard dialect), the cattle were rested in-the small town of Gorgonzola in the region of Bergamo. Their milk was used to make a soft cheese, Stracchino di Gorgonzola. Apparently, it was not until the beginning of the 11th century that this cheese became blue-veined, although the exact circumstances of this innovation are not known. In Lombardy they still make a cheese similar to Gorgonzola, but not a blue cheese – Panerone.

Gorgonzola is served in small cubes with apéritifs, included in mixed salads, spread on canapés, or presented on a cheese board. It can also be used to season sauces or forcemeats and to flavour gratins, soufflés, and flaky pastries. In Lombardy hot polenta may be served with a piece of melted Gorgonzola in the middle. In the Trieste area, a mixture of Gorgonzola, Mascarpone (a fresh creamy cheese), fresh cream, anchovy paste, cumin, chives, and sweet mustard is served as a dessert.

Gottschalk (Alfred)

Swiss doctor and scholar (born Geneva, 1873; died Paris, 1954). Founder of the medical gastronomy review *Grand-gousier* (1934–48), he also published *Histoire de l'alimentation et de la gastronomie* (1948) in two volumes. This is a lively and well-documented study, which describes the way in which people have eaten and cooked from prehistory up to the 20th century. He collaborated with Prosper Montagné in the first edition of the *Larousse Gastronomique*, published in 1938.

Gouda

A Dutch cows'-milk cheese (30–40% fat) with a compressed paste. Firm to the touch, it is light yellow to yellow ochre in colour, depending on whether it has matured for two or three months (waxed rind, tinged with yellow or colourless), has been semi-oven-dried (golden rind) or oven-dried (yellow rind). Its flavour can be mellow or pronounced. Gouda owes its name to a small Dutch port near Rotterdam, from which it was originally exported; it is made in flat rounds with a curved edge, 25–30 cm (10–12 in) in diameter and 7 cm (2¾ in) high, weighing 3–5 kg (6½–11 lb). In France and Belgium it is usually made in a rectangular block (*galantine*) weighing 2–3 kg (4½–6½ lb). 'Genuine' Gouda, originating in the south of Holland, is protected by a label. Imitated all over the world, it is very similar to Edam both in taste and in the way it is used.

gouéron, gouerre, or gouère

A country cake made in various areas of central France. In Berry the word means an apple pie. In Nivernais *gouerre au cirage* is a prune cake. In Touraine gouéron is made of flour, eggs, and fresh goats'-milk cheese.

Gouffé (Jules)

French cook (born Paris, 1807; died Neuilly, 1877). Having been an apprentice pastrycook to his father in Paris, at the age of 17 Jules Gouffé became the disciple of Carême, who took him on when he saw his skill in producing *pièces montées* (decorative set pieces). Between 1840 and 1855 Gouffé ran a famous restaurant in the Faubourg Saint-Honoré. Later, although he was semiretired, Emperor Napoleon III always called upon Gouffé to prepare banquets for him, and Alexandre Dumas and Baron Brisse managed to persuade him to become the head chef at the Jockey Club. It was at this time that he published various culinary works.

His most important work, *Livre de cuisine* (1867), was republished several times and eventually revised and enlarged by Prosper Montagné. *Le Livre des conserves* (1869), *Le Livre de pâtisserie* (1873), and *Le Livre des soupes et des potages* (1875) should also be mentioned.

His name has been given to a dish consisting of small pieces of sautéed meat, coated with a Madeira-flavoured demi-glace sauce and garnished with potato nests filled with morels in cream and buttered asparagus tips.

gougère

Savoury choux, usually in round or ring shapes, flavoured with cheese (Gruyère, Comté, or Emmental). In Burgundy cold gougères traditionally accompany wine-tasting in cellars. Individual or large gougères are also served warm as an entrée.

RECIPE

Gougères   Make 500 g (18 oz) salted choux pastry (see *chou*). After adding the eggs, blend in 100 g (4 oz, ½ cup) grated Gruyère cheese and a pinch of white pepper. Butter a baking sheet and shape the dough into small balls (using a spoon) or into a ring (using a forcing bag). Brush with beaten egg, sprinkle with flakes of Gruyère, and cook in the oven at 200 c (400 f, gas 6) for about 20 minutes until golden brown. Leave to cool in the oven with the heat switched off and the door half-open.

goulash   GOULACHE

A Hungarian beef soup named after the keepers of Magyar oxen (*gulyas*). The origin of this dish, which is now made with onions and paprika and garnished with potatoes, dates back to the 9th century, before the foundation of the Hungarian state, when nomadic tribes prepared a meal that was in keeping with their way of life. At that time, it consisted of chunks of meat stewed slowly until the cooking liquid completely boiled away. The meat was then dried in the sun and could be used later to prepare a stew or a soup, by boiling it up in water.

Traditionally, goulash is made in a special cauldron (*bogracs*). There are a number of regional variants according to the cut of beef and the cooking fat used (pork fat or lard), but purists agree that goulash should not include flour or wine, nor should soured (dairy sour) cream be added just before serving. Hungarians regard Viennese *Goulasch* as a flour-thickened version of genuine goulash soup; in Hungary the latter is sometimes served with potatoes and *csipetke* (small quenelles of egg pasta, poached in stock).

RECIPE

Hungarian goulash   GOULACHE Peel 250 g (½ lb) onions and slice them into rings. Cut 1½ kg (3¼ lb) braising steak (chuck beef) into pieces of about 80 g (3 oz). Melt 100 g (4 oz) lard in a casserole. When it is hot, put in the meat and onions and brown them. Add 500 g (1 lb) tomatoes, peeled, deseeded, and cut into quarters, then a crushed clove of garlic, a bouquet garni, salt, pepper, and finally 1 tablespoon mild Hungarian paprika. Add enough stock to cover the meat, bring to the boil, then reduce the heat, cover, and cook very gently for 2 hours. Add 6 dl (1 pint, 2½ cups) boiling water and 750 g (1¾ lb) potatoes, peeled and cut into quarters. Again bring to the boil and continue boiling until the potatoes are cooked. Adjust the seasoning. Serve very hot.

goumi

A wild berry that originated in the Far East, but is now grown in the United States. The goumi has a fleshy red or orange skin covered with silvery dots. When raw, its flesh is rather sour; it is therefore usually cooked and used in compotes or as a filling for tarts.

gourd (squash)   COURGE

The fruit of several plants of the family *Cucurbitaceae*. Originating in tropical Asia and Africa, they have a thick skin and watery flesh and are used as vegetables. They include the summer and autumn pumpkins (yellow gourd), vegetable marrows, courgettes (zucchini), and various squashes. Pumpkins are large round fruits with yellow or red skin and flesh. They are eaten in winter in soups, gratin dishes, purées, soufflés, and pies. The courgette is a summer vegetable, but can now be obtained all year round. Squash melons have firm flesh and a flavour rather like an artichoke. The very small varieties can be pickled in vinegar. Custard marrows are eaten mostly in the West Indies. Winter and muscat squashes (the latter do not keep so well) are longer, wider, and tend to be more insipid and watery than courgettes, but they can be cooked in the same way. Their seeds must always be removed.

Calabashes and colocynths are grown as ornamentals because of their attractive colours, shapes, and patterned skins.

RECIPES

Marrow (summer squash) au gratin COURGE AU GRATIN   Peel a large marrow and cut it into several medium-sized pieces. Blanch them in salted water for 4–5 minutes, drain, and pat them dry. Place them in a greased gratin dish on a layer of grated cheese. Pour some melted butter over the top and brown them in a medium oven.

Marrow *au gratin* may also be prepared with alternating layers of pieces of marrow and sliced onions (softened in butter), or with rice cooked in meat stock.

Marrow (summer squash) flower fritters FLEURS DE COURGE EN BEIGNETS   Pick very fresh marrow flowers, and only wash them if really necessary. Pat them dry, dip them in a light batter, and then fry them in very hot deep fat (175–180 C, 350 F) until golden brown. Drain the fritters, sprinkle with salt, and serve very hot as an hors d'oeuvre.

gourd-melon   BENINCASE

An oriental plant, the fruit of which looks like a marrow (squash), tastes something like a cucumber, and is eaten as a vegetable in Southeast Asia and China. It is cooked in water and preserved in vinegar.

gourmands and gourmets

Synonymous until the 18th century, these two words later became clearly differentiated: a gourmand merely enjoys good food, whereas a gourmet knows how to choose and appreciate it. In *Caractères*, La Bruyère describes the gourmand as follows: 'Above all, he has a discerning palate which is never deceived, and so he never experiences the ghastly problem of eating a bad stew or drinking a mediocre wine. . . .' In fact, there is a hierarchy which starts at the bottom with the *goinfre* (greedyguts), progresses to the *goulu* (glutton), then the *gourmand*, the *friand* (epicure), and the *gourmet*, and finally the *gastronome*. Every era has had its famous gourmands and gourmets. A greater knowledge of dietetics, a totally different way of life, and the standardization of foodstuffs have caused the breed of large eaters to disappear, although gourmandism and gastronomy have nevertheless remained.

goûter

A light meal eaten in France between lunch and dinner. Until the 18th century, goûter was eaten at about 5.00 p.m. and constituted a proper meal, generally cold, with cakes, cheese, fruit, and wine. With the change in mealtimes following the Revolution, goûter was increasingly omitted, as noted by Grimod de La Reynière: 'Now that people dine at six o'clock, they hardly ever have a goûter, except children.' Indeed, nowadays the goûter or quatre-heures is only eaten by children (fruit juice, bread, chocolate, biscuits (cookies), milk).

Even when it was a full meal, the goûter was always considered common and unstylish. It was replaced by the English meal of afternoon tea, with tea and cakes. But in the countryside, *goûter dinatoire* (high tea) was traditionally served at the end of the afternoon, after working in the fields. It was so substantial that it took the place of dinner, a simple snack of soup or milk and bread being served at night. In Spain, where mealtimes are later, 6.00 p.m. marks the middle of the afternoon and is the time for the *merienda*, which usually consists of a cup of coffee or chocolate and cakes (dinner is eaten at about 10.00 p.m.).

goyère

A speciality of the north of France,

particularly Valenciennes. Its origin dates back to the Middle Ages. It was originally a cheesecake made with cream cheese, eggs, and cassonade (or honey), flavoured with orange-flower water. Today it is a Maroilles cheese flan (a mixture of matured and white Maroilles, or of Maroilles and drained cream or curd cheese) which is eaten very hot, as an entrée, with fairly strong beer or red wine. Some think that goyère owes its name to a pastrycook called Gohier (hence the old spelling *gohière*). Others maintain that the name is derived from the Old French *goguer*, meaning to enjoy oneself.

RECIPE

Goyère Make some pastry with 250 g (9 oz, 2 cups) flour, 1 egg, 125 g (4½ oz, ½ cup) butter, and a generous pinch of salt. Roll it out to a thickness of 3 mm (1¼ in), line a pie dish with it, and bake blind for 10–12 minutes. Leave to cool.

Remove the rind from half a Maroilles cheese, cut the cheese into cubes, and rub through a sieve with 200 g (7 oz, scant cup) well-drained curd cheese. Add to this mixture 3 beaten eggs, 2 tablespoons (3 tablespoons) fresh cream, and a pinch of salt. Season generously with pepper and mix well. Pour the filling into the flan case (pie shell), level the surface, and bake in a preheated oven at 220 c (425 f, gas 7) for 20 minutes. Take the goyère out of the oven and trace a diamond pattern on the top with the tip of a knife. Dot with cubes of butter and put back in the oven for about 15 minutes. Serve piping hot.

gradin

A tiered plinth, usually cut from sandwich bread, used for the presentation of cold dishes (such as chauds-froids), particularly for buffets. In former times gradins were widely used for the presentation of set pieces of confectionery: they were carved wooden stands, decorated with sugarwork (*pastillage*), almond paste, sugar motifs, nougat, etc. Carême describes this decoration:

'Let us suppose, for example, that you wish to decorate a gradin with laurel leaves. You first cut out a laurel wreath in paper. Next you give the base of the gradin a light coating of icing (frosting)

and stick the paper wreath to it. Now you cover the rest of the gradin with a medium grade of coarse sugar. When this is done, you remove the paper, after which you sprinkle the imprint of the leaves with green pistachio sugar. Now, you have a laurel crown surrounding the base of the gradin.

For a large set piece with three gradins, each one can be individually decorated. This creates a graceful and elegant effect.

I have also sometimes embellished my gradins with laurel crowns made from biscuit pastry shaped like laurel leaves and coloured green, or with garlands of spun sugar. This last decoration has both brilliance and elegance.

I have also created gradins out of almond paste, moulded in basket moulds.'

But although he favoured the presentation of set pieces on gradins, Carême maintained that young practitioners should not forget 'that gradins of German or Italian waffles, of nougat, of glazed duchesse cakes, of puff pastry, . . . of Genoese cake, or of croquembouche are immensely effective and truly belong in the realm of the great pastry-making establishments.'

And, in fact, Carême is right: all the types of gradin that he mentions above are edible, whereas the other types, regardless of how decorative they might be, were merely pieces of wood.

Graham (Sylvester)

American nutritionist (born West Suffield, Connecticut, 1794; died Northampton, Massachusetts, 1851). He became the leader of a crusade against the bad eating habits of his compatriots, denouncing excessively spicy condiments and overindulgence in meat. For him, the cure-all was bran and it was essential to make bread exclusively from wholemeal flour. Bread and biscuits (cookies) sold under his trademark have to be made with flour containing all the original bran. Graham bread, marketed in the United States and in Europe since the mid-19th century, was the first internationally consumed bread. It is a wholemeal (wholewheat) bread with a very dense texture and it keeps extremely well. Graham crackers, still one of the most popular American crackers, are made with wholemeal flour and named after Sylvester Graham.

grainer

The French word *grainer* applies to cooked sugar tending to crystallize and turn cloudy or to a fondant mixture which has been overheated. The word also describes whisked egg whites lacking cohesion and the property of holding air. Instead of becoming thick and foamy the egg whites form a multitude of small particles when beating stops. This defect is often due to greasy equipment. It may be possible to correct this by adding two or three drops of vinegar just as the egg whites are beginning to form small bubbles before rising.

graisse normande

A cooking fat that is peculiar to Norman cookery, used especially in the Cotentin. Also called *graisse de Cherbourg*, it was traditionally prepared twice a year by gradually melting together, over a period of 20 hours, a mixture of beef suet, pork fat, and mutton fat with vegetables and herbs (carrots, onions, cloves, leeks, parsley, celery, chervil). Strained and stored in stoneware pots, the fat constituted a food supply which kept very well. It could then be used to extend vegetable soups and also to grease pans used for dishes that require a long cooking period (tripe and daubes).

gramolate or gramolata

A type of sorbet made from a granita mixture. It is served between main courses or as a refreshment during an evening party. It should not be confused with *gremolata*, a condiment in Italian cookery, which is made of a mixture of orange and lemon zest, chopped parsley, and garlic and used in ragouts and, most often, in osso bucco.

grand-duc

The name given to various dishes created in the Parisian restaurants frequented by the Russian aristocracy during the Second Empire and at the turn of the century. These dishes all contain asparagus tips and truffles: poached fillets of sole covered with Mornay sauce, arranged in a ring around asparagus tips and crayfish tails, and garnished with thin slices of truffle; soft-boiled (soft-cooked) or poached eggs covered with Mornay sauce, browned, garnished with a slice of truffle, placed on a bed of fried croutons or puff-pastry croustades, and surrounded by asparagus tips in butter; sautéed meat served with the cooking liquid mixed with Madeira and périgourdine sauce, topped with thin slices of truffle, and surrounded with bundles of asparagus tips. Stuffed turkey grandduc is a very elaborate recipe created in 1906 by M. Valmy-Joyeuse, while he was in charge of the kitchens of the Marquise de Mazenda.

RECIPE

Stuffed turkey grand-duc DINDE ÉTOFFÉE GRAND-DUC (from M. Valmy-Joyeuse's recipe) Slit open a turkey along the back and stuff with the following mixture: 500 g (1 lb) chicken rubbed through a fine sieve, ½ litre (scant pint, 2 cups) double (heavy) cream, 250 g (½ lb) foie gras poached in port wine and rubbed through a sieve. Mix all these ingredients thoroughly and season. Add 12 truffles, peeled and cooked for 10 minutes in a little liqueur brandy, and 24 chicken hearts with the blood vessels removed, which have been soaked in water, steeped in white Malaga wine, drained, dried in a cloth, stuffed with a purée of York ham, and poached for 15 minutes in truffle essence.

Carefully reshape the stuffed turkey. Cover with slices of raw ham or bacon, and enclose in a large layer of lining pastry, taking care to keep the shape of the bird as far as possible. Bake in a slow oven for 2½ hours. During cooking, cover the turkey with greaseproof (waxed) paper folded into four, so that it will cook all through without browning the pastry too soon. Serve the turkey as soon as it comes out of the oven, with a sauceboat of demi-glace sauce flavoured with truffle essence.

Grand Marnier

A liqueur evolved by the Marnier-Lapostolle family firm in 1880. It is based on oranges and there are two types. *Cordon rouge* includes Cognac; *cordon jaune* is slightly lower in strength. Grand Marnier is often used in sweet dishes, such as soufflés, or with crêpes, or in whipped cream.

grand-mère

Describing dishes similar to those called *bonne femme* or *en cocotte*. The term is applied particularly to a chicken casserole served with pieces of fried bacon, small brown-glazed onions, sautéed mushrooms, and fried new potatoes. The same garnish can accompany fried entrecôte (sirloin) or rump steak.

| RECIPE

Entrecôte grand-mère Prepare 12 small glazed onions, 12 blanched mushroom caps, and 50 g (2 oz) diced blanched salt pork or bacon. Sauté the steak in butter, browning both sides, then add the vegetables and bacon to the pan and cook all together. Meanwhile, prepare and fry some small new potatoes until browned. Arrange the steak on the serving dish surrounded by the garnishes and keep hot. Dilute the pan juices with a little stock, bring to the boil, and pour over the steak. Sprinkle with chopped parsley and serve with the potatoes.

Grand-Roussillon

An AOC of the Perpignan area, applying to vins doux naturels coming mainly from the Muscat, Grenache, and Macabeo grapes. Riveslates, Maury, and Banyuls, which are located in the area of the 'Grand-Roussillon' *appellation*, are entitled to a special *appellation* of their own. Seldom seen outside France, these sweetish wines make pleasant apéritifs or occasional drinks.

Grand Véfour

A Parisian restaurant situated in the Galerie de Beaujolais in the Palais-Royal. Founded by Aubertot in 1784 and initially called the Café de Chartres, it was first taken over by Charrier, who served English breakfasts and whose scallops with mushrooms were famous, and then (in 1820) by Jean Véfour. Bonaparte, Brillat-Savarin, Murat, Grimod de La Reynière, Lamartine, Thiers, and Sainte-Beuve all frequented

this well-known restaurant and enjoyed chicken Marengo and poultry mayonnaise. Other proprietors succeeded Jean Véfour but the restaurant kept his name. When, under the Second Empire, one of Véfour's brothers opened his own restaurant in the Palais-Royal, a distinction was made between the Grand Véfour and the Petit Véfour (which closed in 1920). At the end of the 19th century the Grand Véfour ran into difficulties, but after World War II, Louis Vaudable (whose restaurant, Maxim's, closed) took it over and in 1948 went into partnership with a young chef, Raymond Oliver, who became the maître of the restaurant two years later. Jean Cocteau and Colette, to whom several recipes are dedicated, frequented the restaurant and helped to establish its excellent reputation; its 18th-century décor has remained intact.

grand veneur

A term used to describe dishes of ground game, roasted or sautéed, covered with grand veneur sauce (also called 'venison sauce'). This is a poivrade sauce (sometimes made with the blood of the animal) with redcurrant jelly and fresh cream added. Grand veneur dishes are usually accompanied by chestnut purée.

| RECIPES

Grand veneur sauce SAUCE GRAND VENEUR Prepare a poivrade sauce using the trimmings of a piece of cooked venison, and boil it down to obtain at least 2 dl (⅓ pint, ¾ cup). Strain, then blend it with 1 tablespoon redcurrant jelly and 2 tablespoons (3 tablespoons) cream. Whisk. If the sauce is to accompany hare, mix 1 tablespoon hare's blood with 2 tablespoons (3 tablespoons) strained marinade and add this mixture to the reduced and strained sauce.

Saddle of roebuck grand veneur SELLE DE CHEVREUIL GRAND VENEUR Trim the saddle, then lard it with strips of bacon which have been marinated in Cognac with chopped parsley, salt, pepper, and a little oil. Roast it and arrange on a serving dish surrounded by braised chestnuts or chestnut purée and dauphine potatoes. Serve with a grand veneur sauce.

granita GRANITÉ

A type of Italian sorbet popularized by Tortoni in Paris in the 19th century. It is a half-frozen preparation with a granular texture (hence its name), made of a lightly sweetened syrup or of a syrup flavoured with coffee or liqueur. Unlike sorbet, granita does not contain any Italian meringue.

It is served in sundae dishes or a glass bowl, either between courses or as a refreshment.

| RECIPE

Granita GRANITÉ Make a light syrup with fruit juice (such as lemon, orange, tangerine, passion fruit, or mango) or very strong coffee. Cool the syrup, then pour it into an ice tray and freeze for 3–4 hours without stirring. The granita will then have a granular texture.

grape RAISIN

The fruit of the vine, which grows in bunches on a stalk. The skin may be green, yellow, or purple and encloses a sweet pulp with one to four seeds. Both white and black varieties are used to make wine. There are also varieties cultivated as dessert grapes, which are served as fresh fruit or used in cooking, and other varieties are dried to produce raisins, sultanas, and currants.

It is known that in the Stone Age wild vines were already established in the Caucasus, where they originated, as well as in the Mediterranean region. Very early on, man discovered how to make a fermented drink from grapes. The cults of Osiris and Dionysus, as well as the biblical story of Noah, are evidence of the antiquity of the cultivation of vines and the manufacture of wine. After the Greeks and Romans, who learnt the technique of drying grapes, came the Gauls, inventors of the cask. The Gauls made great progress in the cultivation of vines, while later still the monks became progressively more adept in the art of wine making. Throughout this period, fresh and dried grapes were always available.

Grape juice, valued for its invigorat-

ing and purifying properties, gave rise to the cult of the 'grape cure' in France. A grape cure centre (called the 'Uvarium') was opened in Moissac in 1927; in 1930, a grape centre was set up at the Saint-Lazare station in Paris, which sold the juice of five tonnes of grapes daily. The development of bottled fruit juices led to the disappearance of these public outlets, but in Avignon, Béziers, and Narbonne freshly pressed grape juice is still sold during the grape harvest.

France is the second largest European supplier of dessert grapes, after Italy; the three main French producing regions are Provence, Languedoc-Rousillon, and the southwest. Both black and white varieties are grown, and the harvest lasts from the end of July to mid-November. Grapes are also imported from Spain, Italy, and, in winter, South Africa. Nourishing and thirst-quenching, grapes have a high calorific value (81 Cal per 100 g) and a high content of water and sugar (18 g per 100 g). They are also rich in potassium, iron, vitamins, and trace elements.

When buying dessert grapes, choose fruit that is clean, ripe, firm, and not too closely packed on the stalk, which should be firm and crisp. The grapes should be of equal size, uniformly coloured, and with the bloom still on. Ripe grapes do not keep well; they can, however, be stored for a few days in the centre of a refrigerator, wrapped in a perforated paper bag. They should be taken out an hour before they are required.

Before they are eaten, grapes should be carefully washed in water which has been slightly acidulated with lemon juice or vinegar. If served as a dessert, they can be arranged in a basket or dish, alone or with other seasonal fruits, together with a special pair of scissors designed for cutting off small bunches from the main stalk. Grapes are also used in pâtisserie and other forms of cookery; fresh grapes are served with veal and duck livers, roast quails and thrushes, and *boudin blanc*. They are used in fruit salads, tarts and flans, jams (including raisiné), and rice dishes. Grape-seed oil, a table oil very rich in fatty acids (but said not to increase blood cholesterol), is extracted from the seeds. See also *verjuice*.

	size and shape	skin	flavour	country of origin
white grapes				
Perlette (seedless)	small	thin	bitter sweet to sweet	Israel, Cyprus
Sultana (seedless)	medium, elongated	thin	very sweet and juicy	South Africa, Cyprus
Thompson (seedless)	medium, elongated	thin	very sweet and juicy	South Africa, Australia, Israel, Chile, USA
Italia	very large, elongated	fairly thin, greenish-yellow	juicy, plump, with musky flavour	Italy
Almeria	medium	fairly thin	dry-sweet	Argentina, Chile, Spain
black grapes				
Barlinka	large	crisp	sweet, very juicy	South Africa, Chile
Alphonse Lavalle	large, spherical, in a compact bunch	thick and dark	firm, crisp, juiciness varies	South Africa, France, Spain
Napoleon	small	fairly thin	sweet	Spain
Ribier	large	thick	very sweet	USA
Dan Ben Hannah	large	thick	very sweet	South Africa
Flame (seedless)	medium	fairly thin	very sweet and juicy	Chile

RECIPES

Duck foie gras with grapes FOIE GRAS DE CANARD AU RAISIN Skin and deseed 8 large white Muscat grapes for each slice of foie gras. Slice the foie gras fairly thickly, season the slices with salt and pepper, and sauté them rapidly in butter. Drain and keep hot. Deglaze the pan with a small glass of Sauternes, Monbazillac, or a liqueur wine (or use half wine and half thickened veal stock), then add the grapes and shake them about in the pan. Adjust the seasoning. Pour the sauce and the grapes onto the foie gras and serve very hot.

Fresh grape tart TARTE AU RAISIN FRAIS Make some tart pastry with 250 g (9 oz, generous 2 cups) flour, a generous pinch of salt, 100 g (4 oz, ½ cup) caster (superfine) sugar, 1 egg yolk, ½ glass water, and 125 g (4 oz, ½ cup) softened butter. Roll the dough into a ball and chill it for an hour. Wash and deseed 500 g (18 oz) white grapes.

In a bowl, mix 3 eggs with 100 g (4 oz, ½ cup) caster (superfine) sugar and 2.5 dl (8 fl oz, 1 cup) fresh cream; beat the mixture with a whisk and while whisking gradually add 2.5 dl (8 fl oz, 1 cup) milk, then 1 dl (6 tablespoons, scant ½ cup) Kirsch.

Roll out the dough and use it to line a 24-cm (9½-in) tart tin. Prick the bottom with a fork, spread the grapes over the tin, and bake in the oven at 200 C (400 F, gas 6) for 10 minutes. Pour the cream into the tart and continue to cook for 25–30 minutes (cover the tin with foil if the cream browns too fast). Leave the tart to get cold, then unmould it onto a serving dish and sprinkle with icing (confectioners') sugar.

Grape jam CONFITURE DE RAISIN Pick the grapes off the stalk, removing any bad ones, and deseed them if the grapes are large. Weigh the fruit. Weigh out 500 g (18 oz, 2¼ cups) granulated sugar for every 1 kg (2¼ lb) grapes. Put the sugar into a pan with ½ glass water per kg (2¼ lb) grapes and dissolve it over a low heat. Bring to the boil and boil for 4 minutes, then add the grapes and a split vanilla pod (bean). Bring back to the boil and skim the pan. Cook for 10 minutes over a medium heat, then

15 minutes over a low heat. Take out the grapes with a slotted spoon and put them to one side. Boil the syrup to the pearl stage (107 C, 225 F; see *sugar*), then replace the grapes and bring the pan back to the boil. Take off the stove and pot in the usual way (see *jams, jellies, and marmalades*).

Muscat grape tartlets PETITES TARTES AU MUSCAT (from Lucien Vanel's recipe) Make some *pâte sablée* (see *doughs and batters*), roll it out very thinly, cut out 4 circles 18 cm (7 in) in diameter, and use to line 4 tartlet tins. Prick the bottom of each lined tin, leave to rest, then bake blind for 15 minutes.

Mix together 2.5 dl (8 fl oz, 1 cup) black Muscat grape juice, 1.5 dl (5 fl oz, ⅔ cup) fresh cream, 100 g (4 oz, ½ cup) melted butter, 2 egg yolks, 2 whole eggs, and 25 g (1 oz, 2 tablespoons) sugar. Fill the tarts with this mixture and bake in the oven at 180 C (350 F, gas 4) for 20 minutes.

Other recipes See *foie gras, quail, raisiné, thrush.*

grapefruit
PAMPLEMOUSSE

A large round citrus fruit, 11–17 cm (4½–7 in) in diameter, the most common varieties of which have a yellow skin and a refreshing slightly acid-tasting pulp. There are also pink varieties which have a pinkish-red tinge to the skin and pink flesh which is much sweeter. The grapefruit tree probably originated in the West Indies but a large percentage of the world's crop is now grown in the southern United States.

The grapefruit has a low calorific value (43 Cal per 100 g) as it contains less sugar than the orange, but is rich in vitamins A, B, and C as well as potassium. It is usually served as an hors d'oeuvre, cut in two, each segment being detached from the skin with a special saw-knife with a curved point. It is eaten either plain and fresh or quickly grilled (broiled) after being brushed with melted butter. Grapefruit is also an ingredient in garnished cocktails and salads (the fruit is then peeled and the seeds removed from the segments) and – like pineapple – can accompany chicken and pork dishes.

As a dessert, the grapefruit is divided in half, dusted with sugar, and decorated with a glacé cherry or caramelized under the grill. It can also be used in the preparation of ices, fruit salads, cakes, and various sweet courses, in the same way as the orange.

The fruit is also used to make marmalade and the juice is widely consumed as a fruit drink.

RECIPES

Grapefruit ices PAMPLEMOUSSES GLACÉS Cut the tops off some grapefruit, hollow them out with a special grapefruit knife without piercing the rind, and separate the segments. Press the segments (or put them through a blender then strain) to obtain the juice and use this to prepare a grapefruit ice in the same way as an orange ice. Put the grapefruit skins in the freezer. When the ice has just started to freeze, fill the grapefruit skins with it. Place the caps on the fruits and return to the freezer until the ice has frozen. Transfer to the refrigerator 40 minutes before serving.

Grapefruit salad SALADE DE PAMPLEMOUSSE Mix some cubes of grapefruit pulp with some slices of apple sprinkled with lemon juice, some chopped celery, and a few lettuce leaves. Season with fresh cream, rum, and lemon juice.

Grapefruit with prawns (*shrimp*) PAMPLEMOUSSES AUX CREVETTES Prepare a vinaigrette with 1 tablespoon vinegar, 3 tablespoons (¼ cup) oil (groundnut (peanut) or sunflower seed), pepper, ½ teaspoon sugar, 1 tablespoon soy sauce, 1 teaspoon powdered ginger, 1 tablespoon tomato ketchup, and 1 tablespoon honey. Mix everything well together. Peel (shell) 150 g (5 oz, scant cup) prawns (shrimp). Peel a small cucumber, remove the seeds, and cut the pulp into thin slices. Peel 2 grapefruit and cut out the segments. Mix the dressing well with the prawns and the cucumber and adjust the seasoning. Finally add the grapefruit segments. Stir very gently, arrange in individual dishes, and put in a cool place until time to serve.

The prawns may be replaced by crabmeat, langoustines, or crayfish tails poached in court-bouillon and shelled.

grappa

A marc brandy made in Italy, from the residue of grapes left after pressing. It should ideally be matured so that the harsh initial taste is refined. Grappa is made in various regions and may be used for certain dishes, such as the Piedmontese speciality braised kid.

grater RÂPE

A flat or convex utensil with a rough surface perforated with small holes of different sizes and shapes, some of them toothed. By rubbing a solid substance repeatedly over the holes it is reduced to coarse or fine threads (cheese, carrots, celery, etc.) or to powder or very fine fragments (coconut, nutmeg, zest of citrus fruits, Parmesan cheese, etc.). A nutmeg grater is the smallest (3 cm (1¼ in) long), while a cheese or vegetable grater may be 20 cm (8 in) long. Some graters are in the form of mechanical mills in which the interchangeable drums provide the grating surface. For large quantities, some food processors are equipped with grating accessories.

gratin

The golden crust which forms on the surface of a dish when it is browned in the oven or put under the grill (broiler). Usually the top of the dish has been coated with grated cheese, breadcrumbs, or egg and breadcrumbs. Formerly, 'gratin' was the crust adhering to the cooking receptacle, which was scraped off (*gratté* in French) and eaten as a titbit.

The term has been extended to denote a method of cooking fish, meat, vegetables, pasta dishes, and even sweets. The preparation is cooked or reheated in the oven so that a protective layer forms on the surface, preventing the food from drying up and improving its taste. This layer consists of strongly flavoured grated cheese (such as Gruyère or Parmesan) or breadcrumbs, sprinkled with melted butter. The length of cooking time depends on whether the dish is to be cooked from scratch or merely reheated or browned. In all cases a number of rules apply: use dishes that are flameproof and can be transferred directly to the table; butter them generously so that the preparation does not stick; if the dish is to be browned under the grill, it must already be very hot; for a gratin that is to be fully cooked, the dish must be set on a metal tray separating it from the oven shelf or placed in a bain-marie.

Gratins are served straight from the dish they are cooked in. They are frequently made using minced (ground) leftover meat, pasta, and poultry, but the method can also be applied to more elaborate preparations (lobster thermidor, scallops *à la parisienne*, sole or calves' sweetbreads *au gratin*, crayfish, etc.).

RECIPE

Gratin dauphinois Peel and thinly slice 1 kg (2¼ lb) potatoes and arrange them evenly in a generously buttered dish. Mix 2 whole eggs with a little milk, add 1 teaspoon salt, then whisk together with 6 dl (1 pint, 2½ cups) warmed milk or fresh cream. Pour this mixture over the potatoes and dot with knobs of butter. Cook in the oven at 220 c (425 F, gas 7) for about 50 minutes, if necessary protecting the top of the dish with aluminium foil towards the end of the cooking period.

The bottom of the dish can be rubbed with garlic and a little grated nutmeg may be added at the same time as the salt. Some grated Gruyère may also be added: one layer on the bottom of the dish and another on the top.

gratinée

Onion soup poured into a tureen or individual casseroles made of ovenproof porcelain, topped with dried bread and grated cheese, and cooked *au gratin* in a very hot oven. Gratinée is a Parisian speciality, traditionally served for late supper in the bistros of Montmartre and the district around the Halles.

In general, the cheese used is Gruyère, Comté, or Emmental, but gratinée can also be made with Cantal or Bleu d'Auvergne.

RECIPE

Gratinée Peel and finely slice 4 large onions. Heat 40 g (1½ oz, 3 tablespoons) butter and 4 tablespoons (5 tablespoons) oil in a shallow frying pan (skillet). Add the onions and stir with a wooden spatula until they are golden brown. Sprinkle with 30 g (1 oz, ¼ cup) flour and stir until brown. Add 2 dl (⅓ pint, ¾ cup) dry white wine, reduce for a few minutes over a gentle heat, then pour in 1 litre (1¾ pints, 4¼ cups) water or stock. Season with salt and pepper, add 2 small crushed cloves of garlic and a bouquet garni, then bring to the boil and cook very gently for 1 hour.

Meanwhile, dry some slices of bread cut from a long thin French loaf in the oven. Mix 3 egg yolks with 1 dl (6 tablespoons, scant ½ cup) Madeira or port. Preheat the oven to 220 c (425 F, gas 7) and put a bain-marie into it. When the onion soup is cooked, remove the bouquet garni, gradually add the mixture of egg yolks and Madeira, then divide the soup between 4 individual ovenproof soup bowls. Generously sprinkle the dried slices of bread with Gruyère and arrange on the surface of the soup. Place the soup bowls in the bain-marie in the oven and cook until the top of the bread is well browned. Serve immediately.

grattons or gratterons

The name given in certain regions of France to the residue of melted pork or goose fat, containing small pieces of meat, which are eaten cold as an hors d'oeuvre (See also *friton*.) Grattons from Auvergne are strips of pork neck and fatty meat cooked together, then pounded or minced (ground) and pressed in a mould. Lyonnais grattons are formed into rissoles and not moulded. Bordeaux grattons combine melted pork fat and lean pork. In *Odeurs de forêt et Fumets de table*, Charles Forot gives the recipe for Vivarais grattons: 'The pork fat, cut into small pieces, is melted for 5–6 hours over a very low heat. When it has completely melted, it is put into jars. Salt, pepper, spices, chopped parsley, and a pinch of grated garlic is added to the remains of meat left on the bottom of the pan. This mixture is stirred for a long time so as to mix together the ingredients and flavours, then it is put in a stone jar.'

Goose grattons are obtained during the preparation of confit, by draining the residue of goose fat and the tiny fragments of flesh while they are still hot. They are then pressed, sprinkled with fine salt, and eaten cold.

Grattons can also be pieces of fatty pork cooked until crisp (cracklings).

gravenche

A small fish of the salmon family, found in the calm water of alpine lakes. It resembles the féra and is prepared in the same way. Its flesh is firm and fairly delicate but it has become very rare.

Graves

Red and white AOC Bordeaux wines from the gravelly vineyards mostly to the south of the city of Bordeaux, along the left bank of the River Garonne and down into the Landes. The area is often considered as two regions: the northern part, particularly famous for its red wines, and the southern region, abutting and enclosing the Sauternais. However, as some parts of each region (and some of the famous estates) make both red and white wines, generalizations are risky. The Graves region, named after the type of ground (gravel and sand), is possibly the oldest part of the Bordeaux vineyard to have been planted.

The red wines are made from the same grapes as other red wines of the Bordeaux area: Cabernet Sauvignon, Cabernet Franc, and Merlot in the main, and they are somewhat similar, although sometimes slightly more spicy and warmer in character. The best-known is the world-famous Château Haut-Brion, categorized as a 'first growth' in the 1855 classification, but the estates of Pape Clément, La Mission Haut-Brion, Haut-Bailly, and others are now equally renowned.

The white wines of the Graves, more numerous than the reds, are made from the same grapes as the Sauternes – Sémillon, Sauvignon Blanc, and Muscadelle – and they are basically of two types: the truly dry wines and those that are somewhat softer in taste. The dry whites are excellent accompaniments to fish.

Graves de Vayres, AOC wines from the left bank of the Dordogne, in the Entre-Deux-Mers region, are red and white wines, the whites being slightly soft in style, the reds agreeable. They should not be confused with the wines coming from the Graves region itself.

gravy

See *jus*, *sauce*.

grayling   OMBRE

A freshwater fish similar and related to the trout; it is distinguished by its small mouth and its dorsal fin. Weighing about 1.2 kg (2½ lb) and 40–50 cm (16–20 in) long, it has a good flavour and is cooked in the same way as trout. It will not travel or keep, however, and must be cooked and eaten without delay.

greasing   GRAISSER

The process of coating a baking sheet, cake tin, mould, etc., with cooking fat to prevent the preparation from sticking to the container during cooking and to enable it to be removed easily.

Great Britain

GRANDE-BRETAGNE

It is perhaps surprising to realize that English and continental cookery draw on a common tradition. The first English cookery book, *Form of Cury*, ('Cooking Methods'), attributed to the cooks of Richard II, is from the same period as *Viandier* by Taillevent. The French words *boudin*, *pudding*, *bacon*, *rosbif*, and *bifteck* all have English origins.

British cookery is basically medieval, as shown by the predominance of cereals in foodstuffs, the sweet-and-sour contrasts (such as roast pork with apple sauce, roast lamb with redcurrant jelly or mint sauce), and the traditions of a large breakfast and of cheese served as a dessert.

Even those most distrustful about the value of British cookery acknowledge the high quality of Scottish smoked salmon, York ham, Dover sole, Finnan haddock, Dundee marmalade, and Stilton, not forgetting pure malt whisky, British ales and stouts, and Earl Grey tea.

Carême, and later Escoffier, who both worked in London, introduced French people to a number of great British specialities: turtle soup, oxtail soup, oyster soup, fried whitebait from the Thames estuary, John Dory with lobster sauce, curry and its numerous variants, eel pie, Irish stew, and, of course, eggs and bacon, fruit cake, and a wide range of puddings.

☐ **Regional specialities** British cookery is full of highly characteristic regional specialities, which sometimes have surprising names: hindle wakes from Lancashire (chicken stuffed with prunes, served cold with a lemon sauce), toad-in-the-hole (sausage in batter), angels on horseback (fried oysters on croutons), petticoat tails (a kind of shortbread), maids of honour (almond tartlets), etc.

Traditional country cookery, which is usually of a fortifying nature, based on oats, potatoes, and meat also makes great use of fish and fruit. Porridge oats are included in several dishes: black pudding (blood sausage), parkins, Scottish sweet bannocks (hearth scones), not to mention porridge itself. Bread also has numerous traditional variants, particularly in Ireland, Scotland, and Wales: for example, soda bread (made with bicarbonate of soda) and potato bread in Ireland, and bara brith (made with currants) in Wales.

Potatoes are widely used throughout Great Britain but particularly in Ireland, in colcannon (potato purée with cabbage and sometimes spring onions) and boxty bread and pancakes. Cornwall's specialities include pasties (individual pies with a vegetable and meat filling) and stargazey pie (made with pilchards or herrings). Yorkshire is famous for Yorkshire pudding, the classic accompaniment to roast beef.

☐ **Meat, vegetables, and fish** The British are great meat eaters: John Bull, the typical Englishman, was based on a fictional 18th-century landowner whose diet consisted of beef and beer. Roast meat is the traditional Sunday lunch, and fresh or cooked meat is used in innumerable pies (chicken and ham, steak and kidney, ham and veal, etc.) and meat puddings. Cooked vegetables, such as cabbage and Brussels sprouts, are usually served with the main dish; leeks are traditionally associated with Wales and turnips with Scotland. Vegetables are also enjoyed pickled (particularly pickled onions), being used in various chutneys and mixed pickles. The main dish is nearly always served with potatoes, whether or not there are other accompanying vegetables: they may be mashed, boiled, roasted, baked in their skins in the oven, or fried as chips – the latter are such a popular accompaniment to fried fish that, there are special fish and chip shops where they are sold. Potatoes are also used in soups, cakes, bread, pies, pancakes and hotpots.

As so many dishes are served with boiled vegetables (which have a rather bland flavour), they are often enlivened with a variety of sauces and condiments, often quite spicy: chutneys, curry, Worcestershire and Cumberland sauces, anchovy sauce, butter sauce, etc. This habit dates back to the Indian influence in the period of the British Empire.

Fish, too, constitutes an important food item, both sea and freshwater fish as well as shellfish and seafood. Fresh cod, plaice, and haddock are often served fried with tartare sauce, sole is grilled, and crab is prepared mainly in salads. Mackerel is traditionally accompanied by gooseberry sauce. Halibut, herring, and whiting are also popular. Fish is also enjoyed simply poached and served with a complimentary sauce, such as shrimp, oyster, fennel, parsley, horseradish, cucumber (especially with salmon), or mustard.

As in France, game and venison have featured in festive cookery and have been eaten by the well-to-do since the Middle Ages. However, the practice of poaching led to more humble traditional dishes – rook pie (in the absence of pigeons and pheasants) and hare pie (with its numerous variants). Winged game is enjoyed roasted with bread sauce and cranberry or redcurrant sauce. Grouse, a Scottish speciality, is served with bread sauce and redcurrant or rowan jelly; duck is served with orange sauce and hare is jugged.

Poultry (turkey, goose, and chicken in particular) are used in traditional recipes, including chicken pie, boiled chicken with oysters or parsley sauce, mulligatawny (a chicken curry soup of Indian origin), and the traditional roast turkey at Christmas, stuffed with chestnut stuffing and sausage meat, accompanied by bacon and small chipolata sausages.

☐ **Fruit and desserts** In that 'large garden cultivated by a nation of gardeners' which is Great Britain, fruit has always played an important part in cookery, particularly apples (including the famous Bramley and Cox), strawberries, and raspberries. Fruit tarts, jams, pies, jellies, fools, and trifles (made with sponge cake, jam, fruit, custard, and cream) are very popular. But the hot puddings, with their infinite variety reign supreme among desserts. All the recipes have been carefully catalogued, particularly by Mrs Beeton in her famous cookbook; some of them have royal names (Coburg or Prince Albert); others are more traditional such as bread and butter pudding, apple dumplings, Cabinet pudding, plum pudding, and the milk puddings (rice, semolina, and tapioca).

There is a British cheese to satisfy every taste: Cheshire, Cheddar (mild or mature, excellent grilled), Stilton (eaten with port), Welsh Caerphilly (mild and white), Derby, Red Leicester (delicious on canapés), Double Gloucester (very mellow), and Scottish Crowdie (eaten with oatcakes). Cheese is used to flavour a number of savoury biscuits and is also cooked (Brillat-Savarin was very fond of Welsh rarebit). Cheese goes well with beer, the British traditional drink, which takes a variety of forms: brown or pale ale, the popular amber-coloured bitter, or the famous draught stout, black and creamy, all of which are sold in pubs at their special opening hours. The British also continue to develop their taste for wine.

☐ **Traditional dishes** Great Britain is a country of traditions, and traditional foods are eaten on festive occasions.

Scottish haggis is served on New Year's Eve (Hogmanay) or on the anniversary of the death of the famous Scottish poet Robert Burns, who dedicated an ode to it. There are a number of culinary traditions going back to ancient times, such as hot cross buns, marked with a cross and served on Good Friday, or Shrewsbury Easter biscuits or the Easter cake, decorated with 12 balls of almond paste, the origin of which, some say, dates back to the ancient Greeks. The strongest of all traditions remains that of Christmas. Hot punch, roast turkey or goose, Christmas pudding, flambéed and

accompanied by brandy butter or sauce, mince pies, and then port served with the cheese: all these make up the traditional menu of the British Christmas dinner. At the time of Elizabeth I, the Christmas menu consisted of a boar's head, spicy beer in which baked apples were steeped, stuffed pike and mead, syllabub, and dried fruit.

British cookery today is simple and unpretentious, but with the high quality of indigenous ingredients that need no more than simple cooking, the cuisine is in a class of its own.

grecque (à la)

Describing dishes of Greek origin, but more loosely used for dishes inspired by Mediterranean cuisine. Vegetables *à la grecque* are cooked in a marinade flavoured with olive oil and lemon and served cold, either as an hors d'oeuvre or an entrée. Pilaf *à la grecque* consists of rice mixed with sausage, peas, and cubes of red pepper. Fish *à la grecque* is coated with a white wine sauce flavoured with celery, fennel, and coriander seeds.

RECIPES

Marinated fish à la grecque POISSONS MARINÉS À LA GRECQUE Gently cook 100 g (4 oz, 1 cup) finely chopped onions in 1.5 dl (¼ pint, ¾ cup) olive oil without browning them. Add 1.5 dl (¼ pint, ⅔ cup) white wine, 1.5 dl (¼ pint, ⅔ cup) water, and the strained juice of a lemon. Add 2 finely shredded peppers, a crushed clove of garlic, and a bouquet garni consisting of parsley, a sprig of thyme, a bay leaf, and a sprig of fresh fennel. Season with salt and pepper and boil for 15 minutes. Pour piping hot over the selected fish, allow to cool, and keep in the refrigerator. This quantity of sauce is sufficient for 500 g (generous 1 lb) fish. Suitable fish include sardines and red mullet.

Sauce à la grecque for fish SAUCE À LA GRECQUE POUR POISSONS Heat a finely sliced quarter of a celery heart and 3 finely sliced onions in 3 tablespoons (4 tablespoons) olive oil. Add a bouquet garni (including a sprig of fennel), 1 dl (6 tablespoons, scant ½ cup) white wine, and 12 coriander seeds. Boil down by two-thirds and add 1 dl (6 table-spoons, scant ½ cup) thin velouté sauce and the same quantity of cream. Boil down by one-third. Blend in 50 g (2 oz, 4 tablespoons) butter and strain before serving.

The velouté sauce may be replaced by an equal volume of strained fish fumet and 1 tablespoon kneaded butter, added in small knobs to the boiling liquid, which is whisked for 1–2 minutes.

Vegetables à la grecque LÉGUMES À LA GRECQUE Choose very fresh tender vegetables, such as aubergines (eggplants), cardoons, mushrooms, cauliflower, courgettes (zucchini), fennel, artichoke hearts, or small onions. Small onions may be left whole, but the other vegetables should be washed thoroughly and cut into fairly small pieces so that they can be cooked properly. They should be sprinkled with lemon juice if there is a risk of discoloration. Make a court-bouillon by boiling 1 dl (6 tablespoons, scant ½ cup) olive oil, 7 dl (1¼ pints, 1½ pints) water, and the strained juice of 2 lemons with a bouquet garni (consisting of parsley, celery, fennel, thyme, and bay leaf), 12–15 coriander seeds, and 12–15 peppercorns for 20 minutes. Lightly brown the vegetables in a little olive oil, then pour over the very hot court-bouillon and finish cooking. 2 tablespoons (3 tablespoons) concentrated tomato purée may be added to the court-bouillon if desired.

Greece GRÈCE

Contemporary Greek cuisine is dominated by fish, mutton, and various Mediterranean vegetables, flavoured with aromatic herbs, olive oil, and lemon. The Eastern influence is apparent in the custom of eating mezze (small appetizers) with ouzo, the habit of drinking very strong sweet black coffee served with cold water, and in the sweet greasy pâtisserie.

Mutton is relatively abundant in the north; it is cooked in stews (often with leeks and herbs), in a sauce blended with eggs and lemon juice (*avgolemono*), on skewers, or in spicy meatballs (see *kefta*). In the south, where meat is more scarce, offal is used in such dishes as *souvlakia* (kidney on skewers with tomatoes and peppers), grilled (broiled) lamb's intestine on skewers, and sausages made with lamb's liver, spleen, and lungs (*kokoretsi*). Fish, abundant everywhere, is usually. either brushed with olive oil, grilled, and garnished with lemon, or cooked in the oven with aromatic herbs (fennel, aniseed, or coriander). Fish roe is used in the preparation of taramasalata, an hors-d'oeuvre that is also widely enjoyed outside Greece. Mussels are cooked in piquant sauce and another popular dish is dried meat with garlic (see *pastirma*). Lemon is used extensively in Greek cuisine, in *avgolemono* soup (a consommé with rice, flavoured with egg and lemon), garnishes for ragouts, marinated vegetables, sweet desserts, cakes, etc.

It is in the preparation of vegetables that the originality of Greek cookery can be seen. Aubergines (eggplants) are used in a variety of ways: they are an essential ingredient in moussaka; they can also be stuffed, prepared *au gratin*, and puréed to make *tarato*, a thick cold soup including peppers and yogurt, seasoned with vinaigrette (French dressing).

Other specialities include courgettes (zucchini) stuffed with minced (ground) mutton flavoured with saffron and marjoram, stuffed artichokes à l'athénienne, and stuffed vine leaves or cabbage leaves (dolmas). Marinated vegetables à la grecque have been popular in France for many years. Yogurt is used with cucumber and garlic to make tzatziki, a refreshing hors d'oeuvre.

As in other Balkan countries, dairy products play an important part in Greek cuisine. Greek cheeses, made of ewes' or goats' milk, are highly thought of and quite varied. The hard cheeses include Agrafaou, Kefalotyri (highly salted), Kasseri, and Skyros. Feta, the best-known soft cheese, is a crumbly goats'-milk cheese which is eaten fresh. There is also a blue cheese, Kopanisti. Cheese is often used in stuffings, gratins, sauces, or to fill *bourekakia* (small pastries served as an entrée, filled with minced vegetables, meat, or fish mixed with Feta cheese and herbs). Curd cheeses are flavoured with herbs, onion, and soured (dairy sour) cream, and tomato and cucumber salads are mixed with black (ripe) olives and cubes of fresh salted cheese.

Greek wines

VINS DE GRÈCE

Although the Greeks were not the first to make a drink fermented from the fruit of the vine, they were nevertheless the creators of viticulture and their wines were highly esteemed throughout the ancient world. Unfortunately this is not so in our times. Greece continues to grow grapes and make wine on its arid soil and hilly terrain. Although much of this grape crop is exported as table grapes, raisins, and currants, wine and olives represent the principal agricultural wealth of the country. About 5 million hectolitres (132 million gallons) of wine is produced annually, of which approximately one-fifth is exported to northern Europe and the United States. The remainder is sold to the domestic market and consists of cheaper wines and the distinctive resinated wine retsina.

Since 1976, legislation has brought wine-growing in Greece in line with other Common Market countries. The vineyards are divided into two categories: those producing quality wines, which have an *appellation d'origine*, and those making table wines that are sold without any indication of their place of origin.

There are various dessert wines, including the famous Muscat of Samos, available in both dry and sweet versions, and the Mavrodaphne of Patras. Monemvasia, the vine that is known elsewhere as Malvoisie or Malmsey, is grown in many regions to make a sweet wine. It is true to say that though wine is so widely produced in Greece and the Greek islands, it is rare for it to be of more than pleasant quality, although the big wineries all produce a wide range.

See also *ancient Greece*.

greengage

REINE-CLAUDE

A variety of plum with a green skin, sometimes tinged with yellow, red, or purple, and greenish-yellow flesh with good flavour; there are many different strains. Greengages are delicious eaten fresh and make good jam. They can also be bought canned in syrup.

The French name is an abbreviation of *prune de la reine Claude* (Queen Claude's plum), because the fruit was dedicated to Claude of France, wife of Francis I.

grenadin

A small slice of fillet of veal, about 2 cm (¾ in) thick and 6–7 cm (2½–3 in) long, cut from the loin, the noix (fillet), or the noix pâtissière (chump end of the loin). Grenadins are usually interlarded with best larding bacon and then grilled (broiled), fried, or even braised. A small unbarded grenadin of veal fried in butter is called a *noisette*. Grenadins may also be cut from white turkey meat.

RECIPE

Braised veal grenadins GRENADINS DE VEAU BRAISÉS   Trim some 100-g (4-oz) grenadins and interlard with bacon fat. Butter a casserole dish and line it with unsmoked bacon rinds or pork skin with the fat removed. Peel and finely slice a large carrot and a medium-sized onion and brown them in butter, together with any trimmings of meat from the grenadins. Put the vegetables on top of the bacon rinds, arrange the grenadins on top, cover, and cook gently for 15 minutes. Add 2 dl (7 fl oz, ¾ cup) white wine and boil down almost completely. Then add a little stock, bring to the boil, cover the casserole dish, and cook in the oven preheated to 220 C (425 F, gas 7) for about 40 minutes, basting the meat several times. Arrange the grenadins on an ovenproof serving dish, coat them with a little of the strained cooking juice, and glaze in the oven. Dilute the cooking juices in the casserole with some consommé, strain, and remove the fat. Boil down further if necessary and pour the sauce over the grenadins. Serve with buttered spinach.

grenadine

A refreshing drink made of water and grenadine syrup. The latter was originally made from pomegranates only, but today it contains vegetable matter, citric acid, and certain red fruits.

Grenadine syrup is used as a colouring agent for certain cocktails, diabolos, and apéritifs.

grenobloise (à la)

Describes preparations of fish *à la meunière* garnished with capers and finely diced lemon flesh. Croutons may also be added.

gribiche

A cold sauce based on mayonnaise in which the raw egg yolk is replaced by hard-boiled (hard-cooked) egg yolk. Capers, fines herbes, and the chopped white of a hard-boiled egg are added. Gribiche sauce is served with calf's head (*tête de veau*) or cold fish.

RECIPE

Gribiche sauce   SAUCE GRIBICHE
Thoroughly pound or mash the yolk of a hard-boiled (hard-cooked) egg and gradually add 2.5 dl (8 fl oz, 1 cup) oil, beating constantly and keeping the mixture smooth as for a mayonnaise. As it thickens, add 2 tablespoons (3 tablespoons) vinegar, salt, pepper, 1 tablespoon each of capers, chopped parsley, chervil, and tarragon, and the white of the hard-boiled egg cut into a julienne.

griffe

A French cut of beef consisting of the muscle between the shoulder and the neck. When the fat is removed, it can be used with other more fatty or more tasty cuts to make soups and stews.

grill (broiler)   GRIL

An item of kitchen equipment for grilling (broiling) meat and fish; that is, equipment used for cooking food by radiant heat. The heat source may be gas, electricity, charcoal, or coke. The best form of grill is heated from below, as in charcoal grilling. When the heat comes from above the grill is often referred to as a salamander. One of the oldest grill models consisted of a wrought-iron grid with four legs and a handle. Food was placed on the grid, which was then rested on top of the glowing embers of a fire, the legs preventing the food from actually touching the embers. It was oiled before use and was suitable for cooking large pieces of meat, such as rib of beef or entrecôte. Another old model that is still used today consists of two grids hinged together, the food being placed between them. This type was especially useful for sardines, sausages, or small cutlets, which are often difficult to turn over on an ordinary grill. Some grills consist of a cast-iron or sheet steel plate that is placed in direct contact with the hotplate or burner of the stove.

One of the heating elements of electric or gas cookers is a grill, consisting of burners or infrared elements. They may be situated above the oven or in the roof of the oven itself. This grill is only effective if the heat radiation is intense. When situated inside an oven it operates exposed to the air, with the door open, as a salamander.

In France, the most up-to-date models are independent electric grills. There are two main types. One type operates by radiation, the other by contact. In the first type, the food is cooked either on a horizontal grill or between two vertical grills, and the juices are collected in a trough. The grills that operate by contact consist either of a single hotplate or of two hinged hotplates, which may be smooth or grooved and usually have a nonstick surface. The single hotplate is suitable for mixed grills, fish, or even mushrooms and peppers. The advantage of the model with the hinged hotplates is that a piece of meat can be rapidly sealed on both sides at the same time.

grill or grill-room

A restaurant or room where, in theory, only grills are served. It is usually used to describe a restaurant in a large hotel, where the service is faster and the meals are less elaborate than those served in the large dining room. The name was first used in England in the 1890s.

grillade

The French name for food that has been grilled (broiled), particularly meat.

A prime French cut of pork taken from along the blade bone or loins and usually grilled is also known as a grillade. These cuts are scarce, since there are only two per pig. Weighing about 400–500 g (14–18 oz), a grillade is slightly fatty, tender, and tasty and is characterized by long fibres, which are cut crosswise before cooking. Grillades are fried or grilled over à medium heat. They may also be coated with egg and breadcrumbs, stuffed, or rolled into large paupiettes.

grilling (broiling)

GRILLADE

A method of cooking by intense heat, the nourishing juices being sealed into the meat by the crust formed on the surface. The fuel traditionally used for grilling in France is small charcoal (known as *braise*). The charcoal, when thoroughly alight, is spread out to form a bed in a grill pan with a well-regulated draught. This bed of charcoal varies in depth according to the size and kind of meat to be grilled. Nowadays there are also gas and electric grills, both of which are very good and extremely practical.

The grill must be scrupulously clean, and heated before the meat is laid upon it or under it. The food to be grilled must be basted with clarified butter, oil, or fat, and seasoned. Meat should be gently flattened and trimmed before cooking.

Fish should be scored with a knife, well coated with butter and oil, and seasoned. Fish which is rather dry has a tendency to stick to the bars of the grill, and should therefore be floured before being coated with butter or oil. This will form a covering which will enable the fish to cook without becoming too dry. Turn grilling meat or fish over once or twice during cooking, and baste frequently with the butter or oil, using a brush.

Grilled food is ready when it resists pressure if lightly touched with the fingertip. Tiny pinkish droplets appearing on the browned surface are another indication that it is fully cooked. Grilled white meat should be less browned than red meat and a less intense heat should be used. Grill fish at moderate heat, and baste frequently.

Grill poultry first if it is to be cooked in breadcrumbs. When three-parts cooked, cover with butter or oil and roll in the breadcrumbs.

Grimod de La Reynière
(Alexandre Balthasar Laurent)

French writer and gastronome (born Paris, 1758; died Villiers-sur-Orge, 1837. His father, who was a farmer-general, was himself the son of a pork butcher. Born disabled, with one hand shaped like a claw and the other like a goose's foot, the boy was rejected by his aristocratic mother and eventually rebelled against his entire family. While pursuing his law studies, his extravagant behaviour made him quite notorious.

☐ **Taste for scandal** Shortly after becoming a qualified barrister, the young Alexandre, who had already published *Réflexions philosophiques sur le plaisir par un célibataire*, organized a memorable dinner at the end of January 1783. He sent the following invitation card to his guests: 'You are invited to attend the funeral procession and burial of a feast that shall be given by Master Alexandre Balthasar Laurent Grimod de La Reynière, Esquire, barrister to the high court, drama correspondent of the *Journal de Neuchâtel*, at his residence in the Champs-Élysées. You are invited to attend at nine o'clock in the evening and the meal will be served at ten.' Bachaumont, in his *Mémoires secrets*, relates the details of this curious dinner: 'In the middle of the table . . . there was a catafalque. . . . We took our seats at the table. The meal was magnificent, consisting of nine courses, one of which was entirely of pork. At the end of this course, Monsieur de La Reynière asked his guests whether they had enjoyed it; after everyone had replied in chorus "excellent", he said: "Gentlemen, those cooked meats were from Mr So-and-so, the pork butcher, living at such-and-such a place *who is the cousin of my father*." After another course where everything was prepared with oil, the host again asked his guests if they were pleased with the oil, then said: "It was supplied by Mr So-and-so, the grocer, living at such-and-such a place, *who is the cousin of my father*. I recommend him as highly as I do the pork butcher."' By proclaiming the plebeian origin of his paternal forebears, Alexandre, who was indeed the grandson of a pork butcher, simply aimed to upset his mother, but at the same time he managed to gain a reputation as a madman, which he carefully fostered.

In the private residence of his father, he held gatherings twice a week. Besotted with literature, he invited not only Beaumarchais, Chénier, and Restif de La Bretonne, but also would-be poets and public letter-writers. The sole qualification for admission was the ability to drink 17 cups of coffee, one after the other. The food served was simply bread and butter with anchovies and, on Saturday, sirloin. At this stage in his life, Grimod was passionately fond of the theatre: he became one of the best drama critics of his time.

☐ **From retreat to the grocery business** Following a particularly shocking scandal, the young barrister's family obtained an order against him under the king's private seal. In April 1786 Alexandre was sent to a Bernardine monastery near Nancy, where he spent three years. It was at the table of the abbot that Grimod discovered the art of good eating, and his knowledge of this improved in Lyon and Béziers, where he next took refuge.

In order to make a living, he decided to set up in business. In the Rue Mercière, Lyon, he started a business selling groceries, hardware, and perfumery. Then he travelled through the fairs in the south of France. But the death of his father in 1792 brought him back to Paris. He renewed his ties with his mother, whom he saved from the gallows, and endeavoured to pick up a few fragments of his father's estate, including the mansion in the Champs-Élysées, where he again organized extravagant dinner parties. At the same time he resumed his drama criticism. But Talma, whom he had often attacked, managed to have his review *Le Censeur dramatique* suppressed.

☐ **A vocation for gastronomy** Banned from drama criticism, Grimod turned to writing about restaurants. This gave rise to the series *Almanach des gourmands* (1804–12), an anecdotal and practical guide to Paris, including a food guide that proved to be very successful. In 1808 Grimod published his *Manuel des amphitryons*, to instruct the new rich in the conventions and proprieties that

they must observe. In his *Variétés nutritives*, he wrote the following: 'Soup must be eaten boiling hot and coffee drunk piping hot – happy are those with a delicate palate and a cast-iron throat. The local wine, a dinner at your friends' house, and music performed by amateurs are three things to be equally dreaded – cheese is the biscuit of drunkards.' Grimod de La Reynière established his authority on gastronomic matters by setting up a 'jury of tasters', who awarded a kind of academic certificate called *légitimtatmion* to various dishes or foods that were presented to them. The jury of tasters met at intervals at Grimod's home in the Champs-Élysées. There, in solemn fashion, they tasted the choice dishes sent by tradesmen who sought publicity by making known to their customers the judgment, always favourable, pronounced by this gastronomic Areopagus. Among the most influential members of this jury were Cambacérès, the Marquis of Cussy, and Gastaldy, doctor and gastronome, who died at table when he was almost a hundred years old! Gastaldy conceived an original way of classifying Burgundy wines: the king – Chambertin; the queen – Romanée-Conti; the regent – Clos-de-Vougeot; the princes of the blood – Romanée, Romanée-Saint-Vivant, Clos-de-Tart, Musigny, La Tâche, Nuits-Échezaux, Bonnes-Mares; the first cousin of Chambertin – Richebourg; etc. However, the jury of tasters soon had to give up its sittings because some of its judgments aroused protest. Grimod was even accused of partiality!

Threatened with lawsuits, Grimod had to suspend publication of the *Almanach*. His mother had died, and he inherited the remains of a vast fortune. He married the actress with whom he had been living for 20 years and retired to the country, to live among his lifelong friends the Marquis of Cussy and Doctor Roques. He died on Christmas Eve, during the midnight feast, and left, among other extravagances, the following recipe for an 'unparalleled roast', punctuated with references to the actresses of his time: 'Stuff an olive with capers and anchovies and put it in a garden warbler. Put the garden warbler in an ortolan, the ortolan in a lark, the lark in a thrush, the thrush in a quail, the quail in a larded lapwing, the lapwing in a plover, the plover in a red-legged partridge, the partridge in a woodcock – as tender as Mlle Volnais, the woodcock in a teal, the teal in a guinea fowl, the guinea fowl in a duck, the duck in a fattened pullet – as white as Mlle Belmont, as fleshy as Mlle Vienne, and as fat as Mlle Contat, the pullet in a pheasant, the pheasant in a duck, the duck in a turkey – white and fat like Mlle Arsène, and finally, the turkey in a bustard.'

Gris de Lille

A soft cows-milk cheese from Flanders (45% fat), also called Puant Macéré and Vieux Lille. It has a pale pinkish-grey washed rind and is matured by soaking in brine and washing with beer. It is sold in slabs 12–13 cm (5 in) square and 5–6 cm (2–2½ in) thick. It is a very strong-smelling cheese with a highly seasoned salty taste.

grissini   GRESSIN

Italian bread sticks. Long, thin, and crunchy, they are made from a dough containing butter or oil and sometimes eggs or malt. They were first made in Turin and are either eaten as appetizers or served with soup or pasta dishes.

grocery   ÉPICERIE

Originally, the grocers' guild was an important and highly esteemed trade guild, to which grocers, confectioners, candle-makers, and apothecaries belonged. They also had a monopoly over the control of weights and measures. Grocers therefore sold not only groceries but also other goods, such as apéritif wines, rose water, medicinal preparations, and wax. From 1742 onwards, the *épiciers-droguistes* (general grocers) formed their own guild separate from the apothecaries and confectioners. After grocers obtained the vote under the July Monarchy, they became the subjects of caricature and abuse by writers and artists and a symbol of the conformist petit bourgeoisie. A satirical drawing of the time depicts a grocer wearing an otter-skin cap, a large apron, and oversleeves, with the cap-

tion: 'He is found in large numbers in towns and eats candles, string, and treacle.'

Nowadays, groceries cover a wide range of foodstuffs: basic commodities, such as sugar, flour, coffee, tea, salt, rice, pasta, biscuits (cookies), crackers, and chocolate, as well as fresh or preserved fruits, drinks, dairy products, and even exotic and special dietary foods. The appearance of prepackaged products (particularly bread) and the diversification of preservation methods (freezing, drying, freeze-drying) has transformed the modern grocery business.

In the old days, the grocer himself packaged loose products, such as dried vegetables, confectionery, sugar loaves, and coffee roasted to order. Personal attention could be given to each customer. Problems of storage and preservation meant that housewives made daily shopping expeditions. Nowadays, the traditional grocery store is being increasingly replaced by self-service stores and by specialized delicatessens.

grog

A traditional winter drink, made with a mixture of boiling water, rum, sugar (or honey), and lemon. The rum may be replaced by Cognac, Kirsch, or whisky.

Originally, grog was simply a glass of rum topped up with water. Its name comes from 'Old Grog', a nickname borne by Edward Vernon, a British admiral, because of the grogram cloak he used to wear. In 1776, he ordered his crew to put water in their ration of rum.

The name may also be used informally (especially in Australia) for any alcoholic drink.

Gros-Plant

An AOC white wine from the lower reaches of the River Loire, made from the grape of the same name (also called Folle Blanche). Pale in colour, it is light in character and very dry, a pleasant wine to drink with seafood and shellfish as its acidity enables it to stand up to mayonnaise and similar sauces.

groundnut

See *peanut*.

grouper MÉROU

A large marine fish that can grow to a length of more than 1.5 m (5 ft) and weigh about 50 kg (110 lb). It is a member of the sea perch family. There are two closely related species: one is found in the Mediterranean; the other, also called stone bass or wreckbass (*cernier* in French), is more widespread, also occurring in the Atlantic. It is brown, speckled with yellow, and has an enormous head (representing one-third of its weight), a wide mouth with a protruding bottom lip, and numerous teeth. A peaceful fish that prefers the warm seas of the Caribbean and Mediterranean, it is a favourite catch of underwater fishermen. It is rarely sold by fishmongers, although its flesh is excellent. It is cooked like tuna, but is particularly tasty when grilled over charcoal.

RECIPE

Grouper with Corcellet sauce MÉROU SAUCE CORCELLET (from a recipe of the restaurant Chez Max) Trim, gut, and clean a small grouper, poach it in very concentrated court-bouillon, and allow it to cool in the stock. Take out the fish, remove the skin, and garnish with blanched tarragon leaves and thin slices of tomato.

Finely chop 6 large very ripe peeled deseeded tomatoes and rub them through a sieve. Store the resulting fresh tomato purée in the refrigerator. Just before serving, add 2 generous tablespoons (3 generous tablespoons) aniseed-flavoured Corcellet mustard to the tomato purée. Serve well chilled.

grouse TÉTRAS

Any of several game birds belonging to the same family. They resemble fowl and are mostly ground-living. British species include the red grouse, black grouse, and the capercaillie. The common French species is the hazel grouse (*gelinotte*), and the pin-tailed grouse (*ganga*) is found in the south of France (this species has very delicate flesh and is usually spit-roasted). In North America there are many species, including the ruffed grouse, blue grouse, and sage grouse.

Grouse may be roasted, braised, or made into pâtés or terrines.

RECIPE

Roast grouse TÉTRAS RÔTI Mash 50 g (2 oz, ¼ cup) butter with 2 tablespoons lemon juice, salt, and pepper. Wipe 2 plump or 4 small prepared grouse and place some of the butter inside each bird. Cover the breasts of the birds with bacon and tie in place, then wrap each bird in foil. Place the birds, breast side down, on a rack resting in a baking tin (pan) and roast at 200 C (400 F, gas 6) for about 25 minutes for small birds and 35 minutes for the larger ones. While the birds are roasting, fry the grouse livers in butter, then mash together to make a paste. Fry 2–4 slices of bread, crusts removed, in a mixture of butter and oil until crisp and golden. Spread these croutons with the liver paste. Unwrap the birds, baste each one well with hot fat, then dust the breasts with flour, baste again, and return to the oven for about 5 minutes until well browned. Serve the grouse resting on the croutons, garnished with watercress. Serve hot game chips and rowan or redcurrant jelly separately. The birds should be moist enough to serve without gravy.

gruel BOUILLIE

A liquid food made by boiling a cereal flour in milk, water, or vegetable broth. Gruel is one of the oldest forms of nourishment. The Egyptians made gruel from millet, barley, and wheat; the Greeks added olives, and the daily diet of the Roman legionaries was usually gruel made from wheat and the related cereal, spelt, together with onions, salted fish, and cheese. The Germans and Franks ate mostly gruel made from oats (see *porridge*). In the French provinces, the evening meal traditionally consisted of sweet corn or buckwheat gruel (see *gaudes*, *kasha*, *polenta*, *rimotte*).

Nowadays gruel is used mainly as food for babies and young children.

grumeau

A French word meaning a small lump, also used to describe a clot of blood, a coagulum formed in milk, or the lumps found in the lumpy sauce or batter.

Gruyère

A Swiss or French cows'-milk cheese (45% fat content) with a firm but pliable texture and a brushed and washed rind. It takes about six months to mature in a damp cellar, and has a nutty flavour. It is ivory yellow or golden brown in colour.

Gruyère is made in Switzerland in the cantons of Fribourg, Neuchâtel, and Vaud; in France, it is manufactured in Savoy, Franche-Comté, and Burgundy. By analogy, the word is often incorrectly used in France for all cooked compressed cheeses sold in large rounds, including Emmental, Beaufort, and Comté.

According to the Swiss, Gruyère cheese is named after the Counts of Gruyère, whose coat of arms was embellished with a crane (*grue*) and who settled in the Gruyère valley in the canton of Fribourg at the beginning of the 9th century (in France, Swiss Gruyère is called 'Fribourg'). The French believe that the word comes from *agent gruyer*, an officer of the waterways and forestry authorities who, in the Middle Ages, used to collect certain taxes in the form of timber and cheese.

Gruyère cheese is made in rounds weighing 30–45 kg (66–100 lb), 50–65 cm (20–26 in) in diameter and about 11 cm (4 in) thick. It should not be confused with Emmental cheese, which has larger holes.

The cheeses that are exported are less salty than those made for local consumption, and to enhance the pungent flavour of this excellent cheese the Swiss preserve it in a cloth soaked either in salt water or in white wine. The cheese is made in cheese factories in the mountains, close to the pastures. It keeps for a very long time if uncut. Some connoisseurs demand a very mature cheese; others prefer it to be fairly fresh. It is eaten at the end of meals or in sandwiches and is used to prepare many dishes, such as fondues, gratins, soufflés, croûtes, croque-monsieur, and mixed salads; it also serves as a condiment for pasta and rice, etc.

Gruyère is used to make processed cheese called Crème de Gruyère. This is also made from Comté cheese and is sold in small triangles wrapped in silver paper. Gruyère de Comté is one of a number of Gruyère-type cheeses made in the United States and all over Europe. For a long time, a type of Gruyère cheese was manufactured in the Jura, but Gruyère de Comté manufacturers themselves now insist that the *appellation* Gruyère de Comté be replaced simply by Comté.

guava GOYAVE

A fruit originating in Central America and the West Indies but now grown in many tropical countries. There are several varieties: some are pear-shaped, some apple-shaped, and some are shaped like walnuts. The thin yellow skin of the guava is dotted with black spots when ripe and sometimes mottled with green; it covers an orange-pink, white, or yellow pulp. Highly flavoured and refreshing, yet rather sour, it contains a large number of hard seeds. The variety called 'pear of the Indies', which is the size of a hen's egg, is the most popular. Imported from Brazil and the West Indies (December to January) or from India and the Ivory Coast (November to February), it is a fairly good source of energy (52 Cal per 100 g) and, above all, very rich in vitamins C, A, and PP and in phosphorus. When it is ripe it is eaten on its own, after being peeled and deseeded (it may be flavoured with sugar or a little rum). It is also used to make drinks, ice creams, and jellies. In Brazil, the pulp collected when making jelly is often used to make a firm jellied fruit paste or cheese, which is sliced and served as a dessert with fresh goats'-milk cheese. Guava is also preserved in syrup and is included in exotic fruit salads. In China there is a variety called the strawberry guava, which is the size of a walnut, with a white, black, yellow, or red skin and a strong flavour.

gudgeon GOUJON

A small freshwater fish with a large head, thick lips, and very delicate flesh. Formerly abundant, gudgeon were a speciality of the small eating houses on the banks of the Seine and Marne which served fried food; at the turn of the century, customers could enjoy 'that small fish – a crunchy tasty mouthful', as described by Fulbert Dumonteil, who also states: 'In a good lunch, there is no second course more delicate than a splendid plateful of fried gudgeon, skilfully browned.'

Gudgeon must be gutted (cleaned), wiped (but not washed), dipped in milk or beer, then drained, seasoned with salt and pepper, rolled in flour, and fried in boiling oil. As soon as they are crisp and golden, they are drained, sprinkled with fine salt, and served with lemon as an hors d'oeuvre. (If the fish are fairly large they are fried twice, first in oil that is at the correct temperature to cook them, then in very hot oil to brown them.)

By extension, *goujonnettes* is the name given to fillets of sole and other fish cut diagonally into strips, fried, and served like gudgeon or used as a garnish.

guignolet

A cherry liqueur made from a specific variety of cherry, from around the River Loire. It is one of the liqueurs of Anjou and, in the region, is sometimes combined with Kirsch. It is quite different from the cherry brandies of other areas and not to be confused with Kirsch, which is a distillate of the fruit and an alcool blanc.

Guillot (André)

French chef (born Faremoutiers, 1908). Apprenticed at the age of 16 in the kitchens of the Italian Embassy, he later pursued his career in various private houses; his employers included Raymond Roussel, an extremely rich epicurean who had his early fruit and vegetables brought from the Côte d'Azur in a Rolls Royce, and the Duke of Auerstaedt. From 1952 he worked at the Auberge du Vieux-Marly, which he turned into a restaurant of great renown. After retiring, he wrote about his experiences and recorded his expertise in *La Grande Cuisine bourgeoise* (1976) and in *La Vraie Cuisine légère* (1981).

He is outspoken and does not hesitate to attack well-established traditions: 'I am certain to annoy many restaurateurs when I say that all these flambé dishes set alight under the customers' noses are no more than play-acting. The flambé process must be carried out at the start of cooking, in the privacy of the kitchen.'

guinea fowl   PINTADE

A gallinaceous bird, all domesticated varieties of which are descended from an African species that was known and appreciated by the Romans, who called it Numidian hen or Carthage hen. Before the introduction of modern rearing methods, young guinea fowl (*pintadeaux*) – a speciality of the Drôme region – were sold at Whitsun (the seventh weekend after Easter) at about 11 weeks old, while adults, weighing over 1 kg (2¼ lb), were killed in the autumn.

Intensification and artificial insemination have now enabled guinea fowl to be bred all the year round. In France they are sold with a red label guaranteeing their origin, feeding, and rearing. The term *fermier* (free-range) is reserved for birds reared with access to runs, as opposed to those which are battery-reared. The most tender and succulent birds are the young *pintadeaux*. They can be roasted and prepared in any way suitable for a young pheasant, partridge, or chicken. The flesh of the adult guinea fowl is firmer and is usually fricasseed or prepared in any other way suitable for chicken, being well basted, barded, and larded or casseroled to keep the flesh moist.

RECIPES

Breast of guinea fowl with potatoes Alex Humbert BLANCS DE PINTADE AUX POMMES DE TERRE ALEX-HUMBERT (from a recipe by Jean and Pierre Troisgros) Prepare 750 g (1¾ lb) potatoes by the Alex Humbert method: slice thinly and soak in cold water for about 10 hours, then cook for approximately 20 minutes in 150 g (5 oz) clarified butter seasoned with salt and pepper. Drain off the excess butter and brown the potatoes in the oven.

Remove the breast meat from 2 guinea fowl each weighing about 1.5 kg (3¼ lb), slicing along the breastbone. Season with salt and pepper. Heat 100 g (3½ oz, scant ½ cup) butter in a large flameproof casserole and brown the guinea-fowl breasts on both sides (8 minutes in all), then remove. Add 4 chopped shallots to the casserole. Cook them for a few seconds and then mix in 50 g (2 oz, 1 cup) fresh breadcrumbs to absorb all the cooking butter. Brown slightly, and stir in 4 cl (2 tablespoons, 3 tablespoons) wine vinegar, then add 6 chopped basil leaves. Put to one side and keep warm.

Onto each of 4 warmed plates, pour 2 tablespoons previously made brown gravy, place some of the potatoes in the centre, and cover with a guinea-fowl breast cut into 5 or 6 slices. Give one twist of the pepper mill and add a little salt. Finally, sprinkle with the breadcrumb mixture and serve immediately.

Guinea fowl salad with fruit SALADE DE PINTADEAU AUX FRUITS (from a recipe by Nicole Cruaud) Roast half a guinea fowl weighing about 1 kg (2¼ lb) for approximately 30 minutes. Leave to cool completely. Wash and dry some radiccio lettuce, and cover the serving dish with it. Peel and finely slice 1 Granny Smith apple and 2 peaches. Sprinkle with lemon juice. Arrange these items on the bed of lettuce, together with the finely sliced meat of the guinea fowl and 25 g (1 oz, ¼ cup) blackcurrants. Blend 1 carton (150 ml, ¼ pint, ⅔ cup) natural yogurt with 1 tablespoon cider vinegar, seasoned with salt and pepper. Cover the guinea fowl with this dressing.

Guinea fowl with chestnuts PINTADEAUX AUX MARRONS (from a recipe by René Lasserre) Cut 2 small guinea fowl in half lengthways. Brown them in hot butter in a flameproof caserole, together with 150 g (5 oz) diced belly of pork and 3 chopped shallots. Cook gently for approximately 40 minutes, turning occasionally, then dilute the meat juices with 1 glass red Burgundy. Add a bouquet garni and 300 g (11 oz) cooked chestnuts. Cook gently for a further 10 minutes. Remove the bouquet garni, bind the sauce with 80 g (3 oz, 6 tablespoons) butter, adjust the seasoning, and serve hot straight from the casserole.

Guinea pepper
POIVRE DE GUINÉE

A condiment prepared from the berries of an African tree related to the carda-

mom (genus *Xylopia*). Its flavour is less subtle than real pepper.

guinguette

A type of French suburban tavern, usually situated in pleasant surroundings, where people go to eat, drink, and dance on public holidays. Some etymologists believe that the name is derived from *guinguet*, a rather sour wine cultivated in the Paris suburbs; others that it might be derived from the Old French *guinguer* (to jump), which has given rise to the French word *guincher* (to dance). In the 18th century guinguettes were spread out along the Seine, in the district of the Tuileries. Their name is especially linked to the Romantic period, when they were found outside the gates of Paris and on the hilltops of Belleville.

gum GOMME

A viscous translucent substance which exudes from certain plants.

• *Gum arabic* is secreted from acacia trees in Sudan and Egypt. The basic ingredient of chewing gum, marshmallow, and liquorice, it is also used to glaze certain items of confectionery and as a clarity stabilizer in the chemical treatment of wines.

• *Gum tragacanth* is the most mucilaginous kind of gum and is extracted from shrubs of the genus *Astragalus*. It is used in the manufacture of stabilizers, emulsifiers, and thickeners for the food industry. It prevents crystallization in ice cream and jam. Guar gum, produced by a leguminous plant, can be used for the same purposes as gum tragacanth.

Gums extracted from certain algae are also used in cooking, as well as synthetic gums.

Gumpoldskirchner

An Austrian white wine of quality, made in the Wienerwald-Steinfeld area, on the foothills of the Vienna woods. Very pale in tone, it is fruity, light, and elegant, attaining a marked sweetness in years when it is possible to make it from late-picked grapes. Gumpoldskirchner is often labelled with the grape variety used to make it, such as Riesling, Gewürztraminer, Grüner Veltliner, and so on.

gurnard or gurnet

GROUDIN

Any of several European fish of the family *Triglidae*. The French name, meaning 'grunter', derives from the grunting sound it is said to make when it comes out of the water. In England, it is also called sea robin. All gurnards have a cylindrical body, a spindle-shaped tail, a large head protected by bony plates, an elongated muzzle, and a wide mouth. Their pectoral fins are finger-shaped and are used to explore the muddy sea bed. They are 20–60 cm (8–24 in) long and their weight varies between 100 g (4 oz) and 1.2 kg (2¾ lb). There are several types of gurnard, mainly distinguished by their colour: the cuckoo gurnard is red mottled with green, the grey gurnard is brownish-grey, the red gurnard and the trigle lyre are pink or red, with lighter-coloured bellies.

The fish should always be carefully trimmed with the fins removed. The flesh is lean, white, firm, and sometimes rather tasteless, but it is rich in protein, iodine, and phosphorus. It is usually poached or used in soups and bouilla-baisse. It can also be cooked in the oven or even grilled (broiled), but in this case the fish must be protected as the fragile skin is damaged by excessive heat.

Gurnard is often sold in France as 'red mullet', but although it has a delicate flavour it cannot really be compared with this fish. However, all recipes for red mullet are suitable for gurnard.

RECIPE

Baked gurnard GRONDINS AU FOUR Choose 2 good-quality gurnards, each weighing about 400 g (14 oz). Draw, clean, and dry them. Score oblique cuts on the back of each fish from the backbone outwards and pour in a few drops of lemon juice. Butter a gratin dish and spread in it a mixture of 2 large onions, 2 shallots, and a small clove of garlic, all very finely chopped. Sprinkle with chopped parsley. Place the fish in the dish and add 2 dl (7 fl oz, ¾ cup) white wine and 50 g (2 oz, 4 tablespoons) melted butter. Season with salt and pepper and sprinkle with a little thyme. Arrange slices of lemon along the backs of the fish and sprinkle with chopped fresh bay leaf. Bake in the oven for about 20 minutes at 240 C (475 F, gas 9), basting the fish several times during cooking.

Just before serving, flame the gurnards with 4 tablespoons (⅓ cup) heated pastis.

Gyrocephalus rufus

GYROCÉPHALE ROUSSÂTRE

A funnel-shaped mushroom, split at the side and orange-pink to reddish-brown in colour. It grows in damp meadows and under conifers. Fleshy and tender, it is eaten raw in salads when unripe; otherwise it can be eaten only after thorough cooking.

hachée sauce

SAUCE HACHÉE

A sauce of ancient origin, so called because all the ingredients are chopped and therefore appear as separate pieces in the finished sauce. Carême gives this recipe:

'Put 2 tablespoons (3 tablespoons) vinegar into a saucepan. Add 1 level tablespoon chopped mushrooms, half this quantity of parsley, 2 chopped shallots, a little garlic, a fragment of thyme and bay leaf, 2 cloves, a generous pinch of white pepper, and a little grated nutmeg. Cook this seasoning over a low heat. Remove the thyme, bay leaf, and cloves and add 2 tablespoons (3 tablespoons) consommé and 2 tablespoons (3 tablespoons) espagnole sauce. Boil down to reduce and transfer to a bainmarie. Just before serving, stir in a small piece of anchovy butter, 2 small gherkins chopped very finely, and some capers.'

This sauce can accompany roast red meat or venison.

hachua

A Basque dish made from sirloin of beef and fat ham, braised for several hours in white wine with carrots, onions, and a bouquet garni (according to Simin Palay). *Hachua* is also the name of a ragout of veal or beef braised with diced Bayonne ham, peppers, and onions.

haddock ÉGLEFIN

A fish belonging to the cod family but generally smaller than cod – up to 1 m (3 ft) long and weighing 2–3 kg (4–6½ lb). When sold whole and gutted (cleaned), fresh haddock can be recognized by its brownish-grey colour, with a dark lateral line and a black mark under its first dorsal fin. The flesh is white and delicate, containing only 1% fatty acids. Haddock is also sold in fillets.

Fresh naddock is prepared and cooked in the same way as cod, both fish lending themselves to a great number of culinary treatments.

Smoked haddock is very popular in Britain and the United States. As soon as it is caught, the fish is split lengthwise, lightly rubbed with salt, hung by the tail, and left to smoke for 24 hours. Smoked haddock is usually poached in milk and served either with boiled potatoes and leaf spinach or with a poached egg and covered with a white cream sauce. In Britain, smoked haddock is a traditional breakfast dish, and in Scotland, home of the famous Finnan haddock, it may be served for high tea. Other members of the cod family, especially cod itself, may be lightly smoked in the same way as haddock, but they have neither the texture nor the subtle flavour.

The following recipes are methods of preparing smoked haddock.

RECIPES

Curried haddock HADDOCK A L'IN-DIENNE Soak the smoked haddock in cold milk for 2–3 hours. Prepare a curry sauce (see (*à l'*)*indienne*). Dry the haddock thoroughly, then bone, skin, and dice the flesh. Cook thinly sliced large onions in butter (allow 2 onions per 500 g (1 lb) fish). Cool. Add the haddock to the onions, moisten with the curry sauce, then cover and simmer for about 10 minutes. Serve with boiled rice.

Grilled (broiled) haddock HADDOCK GRILLÉ Place the smoked haddock in a dish, cover it with cold milk, and leave for 2–3 hours. Dry the fish thoroughly, brush with melted butter or oil, and grill (broil) gently. Serve with melted butter seasoned with pepper and lemon juice (but no salt), accompanied by boiled potatoes or buttered spinach.

Haddock gâteau GÂTEAU DE HAD-DOCK (from a recipe of Christian Schuliar) Boil 1 kg (2¼ lb) potatoes in their skins. Clean and slice the white part of 5 leeks and braise them in a little water and 40 g (1½ oz, 3 tablespoons) butter for 8 minutes. Thinly slice 2 smoked haddock fillets weighing about 350 g (12 oz) each. Clean 150 g (5 oz, generous 1 cup) mushrooms and slice them thinly. Peel the potatoes and cut them into thick slices. Spread two-thirds of the haddock in the bottom of a buttered ovenproof mould and cover with the mushrooms, potatoes, leeks, and the remaining haddock. Top with 10 cl (6 tablespoons, ½ cup) fresh cream. Sprinkle with pepper, but not salt. Cover the mould with kitchen foil and cook in a bain-marie in a very hot oven for 30 minutes. Unmould the gâteau, and retain the juices that will have

formed. Cook 1 chopped shallot in 10 g (¼ oz, ½ tablespoon) butter, add the juices, and boil down until reduced by one-third. Add 1 dl (6 tablespoons, scant ½ cup) single (light) cream. Pour this sauce over the gâteau.

Haddock rillettes RILLETTES DE HADDOCK (from a recipe of Daniel Metery) Poach 900 g (2 lb) smoked haddock for 3 minutes in a mixture of unsalted water and milk. Simmer very gently, but do not boil. Remove the fish and drain well. Using a food processor, mix together 5 hard-boiled (hard-cooked) eggs, 2 large tablespoons (3 tablespoons) butter, 3 tablespoons (4 tablespoons) parsley, and 2 tablespoons (3 tablespoons) chopped chives. Then add the haddock, the juice of half a lemon, and 1 dl (6 tablespoons, scant ½ cup) olive oil, and mix together very rapidly. Place the mixture in a bowl. Skin and deseed 2 large tomatoes and place in a food processor or blender. Add the juice of half a lemon, 3 finely chopped shallots, 1 dl (6 tablespoons, scant ½ cup) olive oil, salt, and pepper. Blend together to obtain a smooth sauce. Cover the bottom of each plate with 2 tablespoons (3 tablespoons) of this sauce. Arrange 3 ovals of the haddock mixture (formed with a spoon) in a star pattern on the sauce. Serve with toast.

Poached haddock HADDOCK POCHÉ Soak the smoked haddock in cold milk for 2–3 hours, then remove it. Bring the milk to the boil, add the haddock, and poach without boiling (otherwise it will become stringy) for 6–10 minutes, depending on the thickness of the fish. Serve with melted butter strongly flavoured with lemon juice and chopped parsley, accompanied by boiled potatoes.

haggis

A national Scottish dish, consisting of a sheep's stomach stuffed with a spicy mixture of the animal's heart, liver, and lungs, onions, oatmeal, and mutton fat. The haggis is boiled for 2 hours in stock. It is served either with a purée of turnips or with the vegetables that have been boiled with it in the stock. The traditional accompaniments are pure malt whisky or strong beer. It is served on high days and holidays, such as the anniversary of the birth of the Scottish poet Robert Burns (25 January), who wrote an 'Ode to Haggis', or at Hogmanay. The name probably comes from the verb *haggen* (to hack), although some authorities suggest that it is derived from the words *au gui l'an neuf* (mistletoe for the New Year), the cry of the mistletoe sellers in the Middle Ages, possibly inspired by a vague memory of ancient druidic ceremonies.

hake MERLU

A sea fish that has a long cylindrical body with two dorsal fins, one anal fin, and no barbs. It belongs to the genus *Merluccius* and there are about ten species. In France the fish is called *colin* in many recipes and even in fishmongers. Small hake are called *merluchons*.

The hake can measure up to 1 m (39 in) and weigh up to about 4 kg (9 lb). The head and back are dark grey (hence the French name *colin*, which comes from the Dutch *koolvisch*, meaning 'coal fish'); the undersurface is silvery-white. It is a lean fish (containing 1% fat), and although it has little flavour, it is very much in demand, probably because it has few bones and these are easy to remove. Although it is intensively fished, it is always expensive. Before the opening up of North Atlantic fishing, colin was salted and used instead of salt cod in European markets. Medium-sized fish are sold whole (in which case there is 40% waste). Larger fish are sold in sections or steaks. The piece of hake just behind the head tastes the best, but its appearance is less pleasing. The head itself, which is cartilaginous, imparts a smooth texture to fish soups.

Hake should always be cooked for a short time, particularly when poached, and care should be taken to ensure that the flesh does not disintegrate. There are numerous ways of preparing hake, both hot (with delicate sauces, mousseline, normande, or caper sauce, and often with Morney sauce, *au gratin*) and cold (with mayonnaise or sauce verte). All recipes for cod are suitable for hake.

RECIPES

Hake à la boulangère COLIN À LA BOULANGÈRE Season a piece of hake weighing 1 kg (2¼ lb), taken from the middle of the fish. Put it into a greased gratin dish and coat with melted butter. Arrange 750 g (1¾ lb) thinly sliced potatoes and 200 g (7 oz, 1¾ cups) sliced onions around the fish. Sprinkle with salt and pepper, thyme, and powdered bay leaf. Pour 30 g (1 oz, 2 tablespoons) melted butter over the top. Place the dish in the oven preheated to about 210 C (410 F, gas 6) and cook for 30–35 minutes. Sprinkle the fish with a little water several times during the cooking period. Serve in the gratin dish garnished with chopped parsley.

Steaks of hake à la duxelles TRANCHES DE COLIN À LA DUXELLES Clean and chop 500 g (18 oz, 4½ cups) button mushrooms and 2 shallots and mix together with 1 tablespoon lemon juice. Fry the mixture in 20 g (¾ oz, 1½ tablespoons) butter over a high heat for 5 minutes. Line a greased gratin dish with the mushroom duxelles and arrange 4 steaks of hake on top. Add 1 glass of white wine and 1 glass of fish stock (or 2 glasses of fish fumet). Top with small pieces of butter, season, and add a bouquet garni. Place in a very hot oven and cook for 25 minutes. Moisten with small quantities of water during the cooking period. Drain the fish and keep warm. Reduce the cooking liquid, replace the fish in the dish, pour over some cream, and replace in the oven for 5–6 minutes.

Halévy

The name given to two dishes, one of poached or soft-boiled (soft-cooked) eggs, the other of poached fish (cod, turbot, or halibut), both dedicated to the French lyric composer Jacques Halévy and his nephew Ludovic, who wrote the libretti for various comic operas (particularly by Offenbach). These dishes, now seldom prepared, are unusual in using two different sauces for the same dish. Eggs Halévy are served in pairs, sometimes in tartlet cases filled with a savoury filling of chicken in a velouté sauce. One egg is coated with either allemande sauce or suprême sauce and garnished with chopped truffles; the other is coated with tomato sauce and garnished with chopped egg yolk. Cod Halévy is surrounded by a border of duchess potatoes and served with the same sauces as for the eggs, each sauce covering one half of the dish. Turbot Halévy is also bordered with duchess potatoes, but one half is covered with a white wine sauce and chopped truffles and the other half with a Nantua sauce and chopped egg white.

halibut FLÉTAN

A large flatfish (genus *Hippoglossus*) found in northern waters of Britain and extending northwards to the whole of the North Atlantic and the Barents Sea. It may grow to a length of 2 m (6½ ft) and weighs 150–200 kg (330–440 lb). Its firm white flesh is greatly valued as food, and all recipes for brill can be used for this fish.

halicot

A mutton stew, whose name is derived from the Old French verb *halicoter* (to cut into small pieces). The dish is also known as *haricot de mouton*, even though it did not originally contain beans: it is mentioned in the recipes of Taillevent and La Varenne before the haricot (navy) bean was introduced into France. Today, the stew is made with chopped meat, turnips, onions, potatoes, and sometimes haricot beans.

RECIPE

Halicot of mutton HALICOT DE MOUTON Cut about 800 g (1¾ lb) neck or breast of mutton into pieces. Season, and put into a casserole with 3 tablespoons (¼ cup) oil. Add a large sliced onion, 1 teaspoon granulated sugar, and 2 level tablespoons (3 level tablespoons) flour. Stir thoroughly. Then add 2 tablespoons (3 tablespoons) tomato purée diluted with a little stock. Completely cover the meat with more stock, stir well, add a small crushed clove of garlic and a bouquet garni, and cook for 45 minutes. Skim the fat from the sauce and add 500 g (18 oz) potatoes (cut into quarters or neat oval shapes), 400 g (14 oz) small turnips, and 200 g (7 oz) small peeled onions. Add sufficient stock to cover the vegetables and continue to cook for about 40 minutes.

Halles (Les)

One of the main market places in central Paris, dating back to the reign of Philip Augustus in 1183. The other important markets were the corn and flour market (established in 1765) and the fresh fish and oyster market (in the Rue Montorgueil). Until 1969 all the wholesale food markets of central Paris were grouped together under metal pavilions that were constructed by the architect Victor Baltard in the reign of Napoleon III (1852–70). These pavilions, known as 'umbrellas', replaced the stalls and booths that had stood on this site, which was called Les Champeaux, since the time of Louis le Gros. In the 15th century the market halls of Les Champeaux were reserved exclusively for food trading. In 1958 an enquiry was opened into the possibility of moving Les Halles from their central position to a site on the outskirts of Paris, and since 1973 the wholesale markets for meat and poultry have been operating from Rungis.

halva or halvah

An Eastern sweetmeat based on roasted sesame seeds, which are ground into a smooth paste (*tahin*) and then mixed with boiled sugar. It has a high fat content and, although very sweet, a slightly bitter taste. Other types of halva can be aerated and whipped and cream or crystallized (candied) fruit may be added.

ham JAMBON

A leg of pork, cured in various ways. The ham may be sold whole or sliced, cooked (for example, Paris ham or York ham) or raw, i.e. pickled in brine, dried, and sometimes smoked (for example, the hams of Bayonne, Auvergne, Westphalia, Parma, Prague, etc.). A good ham should be plump with an ample, though not too thick, layer of fat under the rind. Pork shoulder is cured in the same way, but it is not entitled to be called 'ham'; the flavour is not so good, but it can be used in cooked ham dishes.

Ham is cut from the leg and brined separately. Gammon is also from the leg but is cut from the carcass after brining. It may be smoked separately or left unsmoked. In French cookery the term *jambon* not only means ham but also applies to a leg of fresh pork. This cut can be cooked in a great many ways, either whole or divided into smaller cuts. It is also used as an ingredient for stuffing, and in various manufactured pork products.

The salting and smoking of pork to produce ham is of French origin. It was the Gauls, great devotees of pork and efficient pig breeders, who first became renowned for the salting, smoking, and curing of the various cuts of pork. After salting, the Gauls subjected them for two days to the smoke of certain selected woods. They then rubbed them with oil and vinegar and hung them up, to dry and preserve them. The Gauls ate ham either at the beginning of a meal to sharpen their appetites, or at the end to induce thirst.

Today, the curing of ham involves two main operations, salting and smoking. The hams are either salted in brine or dry salt, or rubbed over with dry salt, saltpetre, and sugar and left for three days well covered with this mixture. Alternatively, the brine is injected into the veins before the joints are boned. The salted joints are then put into brine, washed, brushed, and dried, and finally smoked in special chambers, starting with a light smoke which grows denser as the operation proceeds. This treatment varies according to the type of ham, and whether it is to be eaten cooked or raw.

Fresh ham is an excellent dish when it is cooked whole, accompanied by rice, mushrooms, or pineapple (unless it is cooked *en croûte*, i.e. in a pastry case). The type of ham known in France as *jambon blanc* (cooking ham, unsmoked or slightly smoked, often sold boned and cooked) is an ingredient of many different dishes (stuffings, mousses and pâtés, pancakes, omelettes and egg dishes, soufflés, aspics, gratins, croque-monsieur, mixed salads, ham cornets, quiches, sandwiches, and cocktail snacks); raw (or dried) ham is eaten cold as an hors d'oeuvre but is also an ingredient of cooked dishes (*à la bayonnaise, à la basquaise, à l'alsacienne, à la limousine*, etc.).

Formerly, the characteristic flavours of both raw and cooked hams varied with the type of salt, the curing process, and the breed, diet, and age of the pig: hence their regional names. In many cases these names still designate a local product, but others merely describe a method of curing and are applied to hams from any breed of pig or place of origin. This is the case with York ham, Prague ham, and even Bayonne ham.

□ **Cooked ham** The traditional method is to steep the ham in brine for some weeks; this is still done in some country places on a small scale. It results in a good quality cooking ham (sometimes described as *cuit au torchon*, or cooked in a cloth). The best hams are salted by injecting brine into the veins before the joint is boned; it is then put into brine for four days and subsequently cooked in stock, wrapped in a cloth. Prime-quality ham is prepared industrially with no additives; it is boned, injected with brine, put into brine, then pressed into a mould and steamed. The result is block-shaped (Paris ham), oblong ('mandoline'), or cylindrical.

'Ordinary' ham is prepared industrially with brine containing polyphosphates, which tend to give it a moist appearance; it is sometimes sold sliced, in packets. Even when described as 'best quality', it is often a rather second-rate product.

□ **Ham cooked on the bone** York ham is the best-known variety. After salting, it is sometimes lightly smoked. It is cooked on the bone either in stock or steamed. It can be served hot or cold, often accompanied by a Madeira or port sauce and spinach.

Prague ham is soaked in sweetened brine and may also be smoked. It is sold ready-cooked, or ready for cooking (either poaching or in a pastry case).

□ **Raw hams** This includes all the dried hams, whether smoked or not. The various trade names are not usually protected. Traditionally the ham is treated by repeatedly rubbing salt into the meat, but not by injecting brine (though this may be done to certain 'mountain' or 'country' hams); the most important aspect of the curing process is the maturing period.

Bayonne ham is manufactured all over France, although the original product was made in that region and is still made at Orthez and Peyrehorade. The red seal guarantees that the ham comes from good-quality carcasses, has been rubbed with a mixture of salt from Salies-de-Béarn, saltpetre, sugar, pepper, and aromatic herbs, and has been dried for 130–180 days.

Hams from the Alps, the Morvan, the Causses, Savoy, and the Ardennes are all smoked to some extent; they may be excellent but can also be indifferent quality. The injection of brine and polyphosphates along the length of the bone hastens the curing and the ham can be sold two months after processing, but its keeping quality is poor and the flavour insipid. If, however, it has been produced by local tradesmen supplied direct from the farms, then it is full of flavour. It is eaten in thin slices, either raw or fried with eggs, or it may form part of one of the regional dishes.

Parma ham (*prosciutto di Parma*) is particularly tasty, being matured for 8–10 months. Connoisseurs are very fond of the ham from San Daniele. It is eaten very thinly sliced, with melon or fresh figs.

Westphalian ham is protected by trademark. It is dry-salted, brined, desalted, and cold-smoked over strongly resinous wood, then dried. Mainz ham is brined, desalted, soaked in brandy or wine lees, and smoked for a long period. Both these German products are excellent.

Nutritionally, the calorific value of lean cooked ham is 170 Cal per 100 g; the food value of raw ham, whether smoked or salted, is higher.

A leg of wild boar is also called a ham; it is soaked in a sweet-and-sour marinade then braised in the same liquid, often with fruit such as prunes, raisins, or candied orange peel.

Other specialities include Reims ham (prepared with pieces of cooked shoulder and ham, covered with aspic and pressed in a mould), which is traditionally sold coated with breadcrumbs; *jambon persillé* from Burgundy or the Morvan, also made with cooked shoulder and ham, with jelly and a large proportion of parsley added before moulding. According to Austin de Croze, the very best of all hams is from Artigues-de-Lussac, cooked but not smoked, fried with garlic and vinegar, left in the vinegar for 24 hours, and served very cold.

RECIPES

Braised ham JAMBON BRAISÉ A few hours before cooking a fresh ham (or a corner or middle gammon), rub it with salt mixed with powdered thyme and bay leaf. When ready to cook, wipe the ham dry, then brown it lightly in 50 g (4 oz, ½ cup) butter. Prepare a meatless matignon with 250 g (½ lb) finely diced peeled and cored carrots, 100 g (4 oz) celery sticks (stalks) with the strings removed, and 50 g (2 oz) peeled and roughly chopped onions. Cook these vegetables gently in 50 g (2 oz, ¼ cup) butter in a covered pan with a bay leaf, a sprig of thyme, salt, pepper, and a pinch of sugar for about 30 minutes. Then add 2 dl (7 fl oz, ¾ cup) Madeira or 2 dl (7 fl oz, ¾ cup) Meursault or Riesling and let it reduce with the lid off until the vegetables are soft and all the liquid has been used up.

Put the ham in a roasting tin (pan), coat it with the matignon and sprinkle it with melted butter, then cover with buttered greaseproof (waxed) paper. Cook in the oven at 200 C (400 F, gas 6), allowing 20–25 minutes per 450 g (1 lb), basting frequently with the cooking butter (if this seems to be getting too brown, add a few tablespoons of stock). When the ham is cooked, remove the greaseproof paper and the matignon and place the ham on a hot serving dish. Deglaze the roasting tin with a mixture of one-third Madeira and two-thirds stock, and reduce by half. Put the matignon and the cooking juices through a blender and pour this sauce over the ham.

Braised ham with pineapple JAMBON BRAISÉ À L'ANANAS (from Raymond Oliver's recipe) Put a fresh ham weighing about 5 kg (11 lb) into cold water, bring to the boil, and simmer very gently for 2 hours. Drain the ham and leave until cold, then remove the rind, leaving a 1-cm (½-in) layer of fat on the joint. Stud the ham with cloves and sprinkle with 125 g (4½ oz, ½ cup) caster (superfine) sugar. Cook in a roasting tin (pan) for 1½ hours in a hot oven (220 C, 425 F, gas 7).

Heat a dozen or so canned pineapple slices in their syrup. Put ¼ litre (8 fl oz, 1 cup) wine vinegar and 20 peppercorns into a saucepan, bring to the boil, and then add ½ litre (17 fl oz, 1 pint) stock. Prepare a pale caramel with 125 g (4½ oz, ½ cup) caster sugar and strain the flavoured stock onto the caramel. Add 2 glasses of sherry and reduce until syrupy; pour into a sauceboat. Put the ham on a hot dish and surround it with the drained slices of pineapple; serve the sauce separately.

Cold ham mousse MOUSSE FROIDE DE JAMBON Mince (grind) 500 g (18 oz) cooked lean ham, adding 2 dl (7 fl oz, ¾ cup) cold thick velouté sauce. Purée in a blender then put it into a bowl and stand it on ice; season and stir with a spatula for a few minutes, adding 1.5 dl (¼ pint, ⅔ cup) melted aspic a little at a time. Finally, gently fold in 4 dl (¾ pint, 1¾ cups) cream whisked until fairly stiff. Pour into a mould lined with aspic, and refrigerate. Turn out onto the serving dish and garnish with chopped aspic.

Glazed ham with caramel JAMBON GLACÉ AU CARAMEL Soak a medium-sized ham (York, Bayonne, or West-phalian) in cold water for at least 6 hours, then scrub it and bone it at the loin end. Put it in a large saucepan with plenty of cold water but no seasoning. As soon as the water boils, reduce the heat and let it simmer very gently, allowing no more than 20 minutes per 450 g (1 lb). After draining and skinning the ham, put it in a roasting tin (pan), sprinkle with icing sugar (confectioners' sugar), and glaze in the oven. As it caramelizes, the sugar turns into a sort of golden lacquer, enhancing the appearance and flavour of the ham. It is usually served with spinach and a Madeira sauce.

Poached ham in pastry à l'ancienne JAMBON POCHÉ EN PÂTE À L'ANCIEN-NE Poach a York ham in water until it is two-thirds cooked, then drain. Remove the skin and glaze on one side with caramel, then let it get cold. Prepare 600 g (1¼ lb) lining pastry, about 250 g (½ lb) vegetable mirepoix, and 3 table-spoons (¼ cup) mushroom duxelles. Mix the mirepoix and the duxelles together, adding 1 chopped truffle.

Roll out the pastry to a thickness of about 4 mm (¼ in) and spread the vegetable mixture over an area in the centre about the same size as the ham. Place the ham on the vegetables, glazed side down, wrap it in the pastry, and seal the edges. Put it in a buttered roasting tin (pan), sealed side down. Brush the top of the pastry with beaten egg yolk and decorate with shapes cut from the pastry trimmings. Make a hole in the top for the steam to escape, and cook in the oven at 180–200 c (350–400 f, gas 4–6) for about 1 hour. Place the ham on a serving dish. If liked, a few spoonfuls of Périgueux sauce can be poured in through the opening.

hamburger

Minced (ground) beef shaped into a flat round cake and grilled (broiled) or fried. It is one of the main items of a tradit-ional American barbecue. The name is an abbreviation of Hamburger steak, i.e. beef grilled in the Hamburg style, and the hamburger was introduced into the United States by German immig-rants. Widely available in snack bars and takeaways, it is sandwiched in a round bread roll. Accompaniments are tomato ketchup, mayonnaise, lettuce, and slices of tomato, and it may be topped with cheese (a cheeseburger).

RECIPES

Hamburgers Cook 50 g (2 oz, ½ cup) chopped onion in butter. Mince 400 g (14 oz) best-quality beef, and mix with the softened onion, 2 beaten eggs, a pinch of grated nutmeg, salt, and pepper (1 tablespoon chopped parsley may also be added). Shape the mixture into 4 thick flat round cakes, dredge them with flour, and fry in very hot clarified butter. They are cooked when droplets of blood appear on the surface. Fry 100 g (4 oz, 1 cup) chopped onion in the same butter to garnish the hamburgers. Serve very hot in a round bun.

Fish hamburgers HAMBURGERS DE POISSON (from a recipe by Michel Oliver) Crumble a thick slice of bread (without crusts) into a bowl and mix with a beaten egg. Carefully remove the flesh from a piece of hake weighing about 250 g (9 oz), mince, mix with half an onion (chopped), and add the mixture to the ingredients in the bowl, together with salt and pepper. Beat with a fork to obtain a thick smooth mixture. Shape the mixture into 2 round flat cakes and coat them with flour. Heat some butter and oil in a frying pan (skillet) until foamy and fry the hamburgers gently for 6 minutes. Turn them over and cook for a further 6 minutes. Fry 2 eggs in a separate pan. Serve each hamburger topped with a fried egg.

hanap

A large drinking goblet with no handle. Used in France in the Middle Ages, it was made of wood, pewter, silver, or even hard polished stone. In his glossary, Jean de Garlande mentions the hanap repairers whose street cry was: 'Have your hanaps mended with gold or silver wire.'

hanging FAISANDAGE

The operation of leaving red meat, especially game, in a cool place for a varying length of time to make the flesh more tender and improve the flavour.

The French word is derived from *faisan* (pheasant). When it is fresh, pheasant is tough and without much flavour. It grows tender and its aroma develops after it has been hung, the length of time depending upon the temperature. Nowadays, pheasant is no longer hung, as advocated by Montaigne, 'until it develops a marked smell'. In Brillat-Savarin's time, pheasant was not considered fit for the gastronome's table except in a state of complete putrefaction. This authority recommends, in effect, that it should be kept, unplucked, until its breast turns green, so that for roasting on the spit it has to be held together by a slice of bread tied on with ribbon. The habit of hanging meat until it is high is properly reprehended by those concerned with hygiene, and also by the true gastronome.

Game which is wounded in the belly or damaged by lead shot should never be hung, as it will rot very quickly. Woodcock and certain other game birds are not drawn, but large game should be drawn as quickly as possible. Game birds are wrapped in muslin or a cloth, and suspended by the legs in a cool, dry, and preferably well-ventilated place. Woodcock needs to be left for the longest time, followed by wild duck, pheasant, and partridge. Small birds are generally not hung. Game animals are hung for two to four days. Both winged game and ground game when hung acquire a similar flavour to that of pheasant.

Meat should be hung in a cool airy place. In theory, beef requires to be hung for three to four weeks at −1.5 c (29 F), 15 days at 0 c (32 F), two days at 20 c (68 F), or one day at 43 c (109 F). In practice, however, it is hung in a cold room at 2 c (35 F) for five or six days.

hare LIÈVRE

A game animal belonging to the same family as the rabbit, but larger and having dark flesh. The male is called a 'buck', the female a 'doe'. Hunting has cut down the hare population drastically, and new stock has been imported into France from Hungary. The best French wild hares are found in Beauce, Champagne, Brie, Normandy, Poitou, Gascony, and Périgord (the last being the region where the most famous French hare dish, *à la royale*, originated). The meat is highly flavoured and excellent to eat, the mountain variety having a more delicate flavour than that of the plains.

Hare meat has 132 Cal per 100 g and is cooked in different ways according to its age. A leveret (between 2 and 4 months) weighs about 1.5 kg (3 lb) and is usually roasted. A one-year-old hare (called a *trois-quarts* in France) weighs 2.5–3 kg (5½–6½ lb) and yields excellent saddles for roasting and meat for sautéing. Hares more than a year old (known in France as *capucins*), weighing 4–6 kg (9–13 lb), are mostly made into civets (jugged hare). A year-old hare is best for the table. If it is much older, it should be made into a terrine or cooked *en daube*.

Hares are not hung, since they deteriorate after about 48 hours. A marinade based on a rough red wine is used for civets. Hare fillets and legs are sometimes used for specific recipes. Hare with cherries is a German speciality.

RECIPES

Fillets of hare (*preparation*) FILETS DE LIÈVRE (PRÉPARATION) Separate the saddle from the forequarters of a hare as far behind the ribs as possible, and place the saddle on its back. With a pointed knife, cut away the meat on both sides of the backbone. Ease off the flesh to halfway up the backbone, then place the blade of a very heavy knife against the backbone and by tapping on the blade complete the separation of the fillets. Do the same on the other side. Separate the fillets from each other, then lard them with fat bacon. Season with salt, pepper, and a pinch of cayenne; pour over a dash of brandy and leave to marinate until time for cooking.

Roast fillets of hare FILETS DE LIÈVRE RÔTIS Prepare the fillets and place them in a buttered roasting dish. Pour over melted butter and cook them in a preheated oven at 240 C (475 F, gas 9), covering them with aluminium foil once they are browned. Serve on slices of bread fried in butter and coat with financière or Périgueux sauce, or a fruit sauce (cranberry or redcurrant).

Hare cutlets with mushrooms CÔTELETTES DE LIÈVRE AUX CHAMPIGNONS Finely chop a boned hare. Add one-third of its weight of bread soaked in cream and an equal quantity of chopped mushrooms, parsley, and shallots. Season with salt and pepper, add a pinch of 'four spices', and blend all the ingredients together into a firm paste. Divide the mixture into portions of 50–60 g (2–2½ oz), roll into balls, then flatten into cutlets. Coat with flour and fry in clarified butter. Serve with a game sauce, such as poivrade.

Hare pâté PÂTÉ DE LIÈVRE Bone a hare and set aside the fillets (including the filets mignons) and the thigh meat. Remove the sinews from these cuts, lard them, and season with salt and pepper and a little mixed spice. Then marinate them in brandy together with an equal weight of thin slices of lean unsmoked ham, fat bacon, and quartered truffles. Prepare a game forcemeat with the rest of the meat; rub it through a sieve and then thicken it with the hare's blood.

Butter an oval hinged mould and line with lining pastry. Cover the pastry with very thin slices of fat bacon, and spread a layer of forcemeat over the bottom and up the sides. Arrange a layer of marinated hare fillets in the mould and cover with a layer of forcemeat. Continue to fill the mould with alternate layers of hare and forcemeat, finishing with a layer of forcemeat. Cover with slices of fat bacon, then with a layer of pastry. Seal well around the edges. Shape the crust with a pastry crimper and decorate the top with pastry shapes. Insert a chimney in the centre of the pie to allow the steam to escape during cooking. Brush with beaten egg and cook in a moderately hot oven (190 C, 375 F, gas 5), allowing 35 minutes per kg (15 minutes per lb).

Let the pâté cool in the mould. When it is cold, pour a few spoonfuls of Madeira-flavoured aspic through the central hole (or, if the pâté is to be kept for any length of time, a mixture of melted butter or lard). The pâté should be prepared at least 24 hours before serving.

Hare with chocolate LIÈVRE AU CHOCOLAT (from Alain Dutournier's recipe) Skin a hare, detach the saddle and thighs, season these with salt and pepper, and marinate for 3 days in oil. Break up the rib cage, the forelimbs, and the offal, and marinate these for 3 days in a marinade made with 2 bottles of red wine, 2 onions, a head (bulb) of garlic broken into cloves, 2 carrots and a leek (roughly chopped), thyme, bay leaves, grated nutmeg, pepper, the juice of a lemon, chopped root ginger, cinnamon, and cloves.

After 3 days, strain the marinade and sauté the pieces of carcass in olive oil until brown. Remove the fat. Add a little of the marinade and a calf's foot. Cook very gently for 4 hours, then remove the fat. Strain the sauce obtained and thicken it with 50 g (2 oz) bitter chocolate and 100 g (4 oz, ½ cup butter. Heat together the juice of a lemon with 5 cl (2½ tablespoons, 3 tablespoons) poultry blood without boiling, and add to the sauce. Cook the saddle and thighs in butter in a casserole (the meat should remain pink). Cut into portions. Pour over the sauce and serve with spiced pears sautéed in butter.

Roast hare en saugrenée LIÈVRE RÔTI EN SAUGRENÉE (from Alain Chapel's recipe) Let the hare hang, unskinned, in a cool place for 24 hours, then joint it and reserve the blood and liver. Place the joints in a dish containing 1 glass of cider, 3 tablespoons (¼ cup) olive oil, an onion and a carrot (finely chopped), 6 juniper berries, 12 shallots, and a pinch of spice. Leave to marinate for 12 hours.

Blanch the shallots from the marinade and put them in a roasting dish with a slice of fat bacon. Place the hare on top and roast for 30–40 minutes. Prepare the hearts of 2 heads of celery, wash them, blanch them in salted water, and drain. Braise the celery for 40 minutes in a buttered dish, moistened with stock.

Place the cooked hare in a warm dish. Deglaze the roasting dish with 1 small ladle of stock and 1 tablespoon brandy. Remove from the heat and thicken carefully with the puréed liver of the hare and the reserved blood. Pour this sauce over the hare. Serve the celery separately.

Roast legs of hare CUISSES DE LIÈVRE RÔTIES Remove the sinews from a hare's legs. Stud with lardons to form rosettes. Pour over melted butter and roast in a very hot oven. Serve with a poivrade sauce and chestnut purée.

haricot beans

See *bean*.

harissa

A condiment from north Africa and the Middle East. It is a purée (*tabal*) made from small peppers, cayenne, oil, garlic, and coriander, pounded with cumin and either dried mint or verbena leaves. The harissa must be left for 12 hours before using. Covered with olive oil, it keeps well in a sealed container. It is diluted with a little stock and served with couscous, soups, and dried meat.

hash HACHIS

A preparation of finely chopped raw or cooked meat, poultry, fish, or vegetables. Hashes are nearly always pre-

pared from leftovers and usually either piled in the centre of a ring of duchess potatoes and browned in the oven, or accompanied by a pilaf of rice or a risotto. The classic example of this dish is *hachis Parmentier*, in which finely chopped beef is topped with mashed potato, then with breadcrumbs and butter, and browned in the oven. (The meat is chopped very small rather than minced (ground) as it will taste better and look more appetizing.)

A purée of vegetables (e.g. aubergines (eggplants), tomatoes, courgettes (zucchini), pumpkin, dried vegetables) can be substituted for the potato. Diced beef, mutton, rabbit, or pork is sometimes enriched with mushrooms, and diced veal or poultry is often mixed with cream, béchamel sauce, or Mornay sauce (see *moussaka*). Finely chopped or minced meat is also used for meatballs, croquettes, and fricadelles. Pork is used for certain regional dishes, such as caillettes and attignoles.

Fish for hashes should be firm-fleshed (such as tuna or cod) and it is best to use only one variety of fish.

RECIPES

BEEF HASHES

Beef hash à l'italienne HACHIS DE BOEUF À L'ITALIENNE Sauté 2 tablespoons (3 tablespoons) chopped onion in 2 tablespoons (3 tablespoons) olive oil until slightly brown, sprinkle with 1 tablespoon flour, and mix well. Then add 2 dl (7 fl oz, ¾ cup) water or stock, 2 tablespoons (3 tablespoons) tomato concentrate diluted with 1 dl (6 tablespoons, scant ½ cup) stock, a bouquet garni, and a crushed garlic clove. Cook gently for about 30 minutes. Remove the bouquet garni, and allow to cool. Add some of this sauce to some finely chopped braised or boiled beef and reheat gently. Serve with tagliatelle and the remainder of the sauce.

Boiled beef hash HACHIS DE BOEUF BOUILLI Chop very finely (by hand or in a food processor) 500 g (18 oz boiled beef. Cook 2 large finely chopped onions in 1 tablespoon butter until tender. Sprinkle with 1 tablespoon flour and cook until golden brown. Add 2 dl (7 fl oz, ¾ cup) stock, season with salt and pepper, and bring to the boil, stirring constantly. Simmer for 15 minutes. Allow to cool, add the boiled beef, and cook in a covered dish in the oven for 25 minutes.

Curried beef hash HACHIS DE BOEUF À L'INDIENNE Prepare a border of cooked rice. Dice some braised beef and mince it in a food processor or mincer. Mix it with some curry sauce (see *(à l')indienne*). Pour the hash into the centre of the rice border and serve the remaining curry sauce separately.

An alternative method is to sauté 2 tablespoons (3 tablespoons) chopped onion in 1 tablespoon oil or butter without browning. Sprinkle with 1 teaspoon curry powder and 1 tablespoon flour. Stir well. Then add 2 dl (7 fl oz, ¾ cup) stock, mix well, and cook gently for 15–20 minutes. Add the minced braised beef, heat through, and pour it into the centre of the rice border.

CHICKEN HASH

Small hot entrées with chicken hash PETITES ENTRÉES CHAUDES AU HACHIS DE VOLAILLE Make one of the following sauces: allemande, béchamel, cream, or velouté. Dice poached, braised, or roast chicken meat very finely and mix it with the tepid sauce. Heat the mixture thoroughly in a saucepan. Chicken hash can be used to stuff mushroom caps, artichoke hearts, or hard-boiled (hard-cooked) eggs (mix the crushed yolks into the hash): sprinkle with grated Gruyère cheese, cover with melted butter, and brown in the oven. The hash can also be used to fill warmed croûtes, croustades, or vol-au-vent cases.

MUTTON OR LAMB HASH

All the recipes for beef hash can also be used for mutton or lamb hash.

PORK HASH

The recipes for beef hash can be used for leftovers of pork if the meat has been braised. If it has been boiled or roasted, the recipes for veal hash should be used.

VEAL HASH

Veal hash à la Mornay HACHIS DE VEAU MORNAY Finely dice some leftover roast or sautéed veal. Prepare some well-seasoned béchamel sauce and add a little fresh cream. Divide the sauce into 2 equal portions. Add some chopped fines herbes to one portion, and some grated Gruyère cheese to the other. Mix the sauce containing the herbs with the diced veal, and pour into a buttered gratin dish. Smooth the surface and cover with the cheese sauce. Sprinkle with some more grated Gruyère, pour some melted butter over the top, and brown in a very hot oven. Sliced mushrooms, braised in butter with a little lemon juice, can be added if desired.

Hauser (Gayelord, *born* Helmut Eugene Benjamin Gellert Hauser)

American nutritionist (born Tübingen, Baden-Württemberg, 1895; died Los Angeles, 1984). He suffered from tuberculosis of the hip but was cured by following the advice of a Swiss doctor, who convinced him of the power of natural foods: wholewheat flour, brewer's yeast, yogurt, dried pulses, cereals, soya, etc. Having written *Message of Health* and a *Dictionary of Foods*, he achieved worldwide recognition with *Live Young, Live Longer* (1950). In this book he propounds several basic theories concerning a balanced diet, discusses the importance of fruit diets and aromatic herbs, and suggests cooking methods that preserve vitamins and mineral salts. Various dietetic products have been marketed under his name.

Haut-Médoc

An AOC applied to certain red wines of the northern section of the Médoc. Within this region – the birthplace of such world-famous clarets as Châteaux Lafite-Rothschild, Latour, Mouton-Rothschild, and Margaux – there are various parishes, each having its own AOC. For example, the first three of the estates mentioned above are AOC Pauillac. Other parishes with their own AOC here are Margaux, St Julien, and St Estèphe.

Haut Poitou wines
VINS DU HAUT POITOU

VDQS wines, red, white, and rosé, produced in the Vienne and Deux-Sèvres. Thanks to the high quality of those from the local cooperative, they are very popular now in export markets. The whites, made from either the Sauvignon or the Chardonnay grape, and the reds, from a blend of classic black grapes, are small-scale but first-rate and good value.

havir
A French culinary term that originally meant to cook the outside of a dish at a very high temperature, i.e. to sear. Nowadays, it is more likely that anything described as *havi* will be burnt on the outside and raw on the inside.

hawthorn AUBÉPINE
A thorny shrub frequently found in woodlands and hedgerows throughout Europe. Its leaves and flowers are used for tisanes, as it is traditionally thought to have a calming action on the heart. A Mediterranean species of hawthorn, known as the Mediterranean or Neapolitan medlar, is very widespread in the south of France; its red fleshy fruits have a tart flavour and are used to make jellies and jams.

hazel grouse GELINOTTE
A game bird of the grouse family. It is also called hazel hen or wood grouse and is about the size of a partridge. Now very rare in France, the hazel grouse only survives in the Vosges and in certain regions of the Alps. It is imported frozen from Scandinavia and the Soviet Union. The hazel grouse has succulent flesh and is cooked like partridge; it can be hung briefly, but not until high. When the hazel grouse has fed on fir cones, its flesh tastes of resin. This flavour can be made less strong by soaking the bird in milk.

hazelnut NOISETTE
A hard-shelled nut with an oval or round kernel that is produced by one of several species of hazel tree. Harvested in August and September, the nuts can be eaten fresh but are usually dried.

French hazelnuts come from Corsica, Pyrénées-Orientales, and the southwest; they are also imported from Turkey, Italy, and Spain.

Hazelnuts have a high calorific content (656 Cal per 100 g) and comprise about 60% fat. They also contain sulphur, phosphorus, calcium, potassium, and nicotinic acid. An oil is extracted in small quantities for use as a flavouring; it should not be heated. Fresh hazelnuts are always sold in their green husks (involucres). The whole dried nuts should have shiny shells, not too thick and free from blemishes, holes, and cracks; they can only be broken with a nutcracker. Once shelled, the kernels should be kept in an airtight container or they will go rancid. They can be served on their own, salted or perhaps toasted, as an appetizer; they are also used whole, grated, or ground in many dishes (for example, stuffings, terrines, with chicken and in fish meunière, in the same way as almonds). They make a good flavouring for butter as well. Their chief role, however, is in pâtisserie and confectionery: the *noisetier* (a cake from Pontarlier), hazelnut cake, and *noisettine* (a puff pastry with hazelnut-flavoured butter cream) are some examples.

The filbert (*aveline* in French) is a variety of large cultivated hazelnut, although the name is sometimes used loosely to describe dishes containing ordinary hazelnuts, for example *truite aux avelines*.

RECIPES

Chicken with hazelnuts POULET AUX NOISETTES Cut an uncooked chicken into 4 pieces. Sprinkle the joints with salt and freshly ground pepper, dip them in flour, then brown them in butter. Moisten with stock made from the giblets and cook with the lid on for 30 minutes. Keep hot. Lightly toast 150 g (5 oz, 1 cup) shelled hazelnuts in the oven, then grind them and blend with 150 g (5 oz, ⅔ cup) butter. Reduce the cooking liquid from the chicken, then add the nut butter and 3 tablespoons (¼ cup) crème fraîche; cook for 5–6 minutes over a low heat. Pour this sauce, to which some whole nuts can be added, over the chicken.

Hazelnut cake GÂTEAU AUX NOISETTES Spread 50 g (2 oz) ground hazelnuts on a baking sheet and brown them lightly in a cool oven. Whisk 5 egg yolks with 150 g (5 oz, ⅔ cup, firmly packed) caster (superfine) sugar for 5 minutes, then beat in 150 g (5 oz, 1¼ cups) sifted flour and the ground hazelnuts. Melt 90 g (3¼ oz, 6½ tablespoons) butter over a very low heat, blend in the nut mixture, then carefully fold in 5 egg whites whisked to stiff peaks. Pour this mixture into a 20-cm (8-in) buttered deep round sandwich tin (layer cake pan) and cook in a moderate oven (180 C, 350 F, gas 4) for 30–35 minutes. Turn the cake out onto a wire rack and leave to cool.

Meanwhile make some butter cream using 4 egg yolks, 150 g (5 oz, ⅔ cup, firmly packed) caster sugar, 175 g (6 oz, ¾ cup) butter, and 50 g (2 oz) ground hazelnuts. Then prepare the decoration: soften 50 g (2 oz, 4 tablespoons) butter and blend in 50 g (2 oz, 4 tablespoons, firmly packed) caster sugar, 1 teaspoon vanilla sugar, and 1 egg; using a whisk, beat in 50 g (2 oz, ½ cup) flour. Roll this dough out, cut it into small rounds with a biscuit cutter (cookie cutter), and place the rounds well apart on a lightly buttered baking sheet. Bake for 3–4 minutes in a very hot oven. Remove the rounds when cooked and leave to cool.

Cut the cake into 3 equal layers, spread butter cream over each layer, then put the cake together again. Coat the sides with the remaining butter cream and decorate with the baked rounds. The spaces between the rounds can be filled with toasted hazelnuts. Store in a cool place.

Jerusalem artichoke and hazelnut salad SALADE DE TOPIN-AMBOURS AUX NOISETTES Peel the Jerusalem artichokes and cook them for 10 minutes or so in salted white wine. Drain and slice. Put the slices into a salad bowl and season with oil, mustard, and lemon juice. Crush the hazelnuts and scatter them over the artichokes.

head TÊTE

A gelatinous variety of white offal. Cer tain parts of the head are particularly appreciated and prepared separately: brain, tongue, ears, and cheeks, for example. Only calf's head is used as a whole in classic cuisine, although lamb's or sheep's head is prepared whole in certain regional dishes from Auvergne and southwestern France.

Ox head (head of beef) is always sliced or prepared as a terrine (*museau de boeuf*, made of salted ox muzzle and chin and served with vinaigrette).

Pig's head is quite widely used in charcuterie for *pâté de tête* (made with cooked boned head and cooked salted pork with the rind), *museau de porc* (boned pieces of head and tail that are cooked, pressed, and moulded), *hure à la parisienne* (head and loin of pork), and *tête de porc roulée* (boned pig's head and tongue cut into cubes, then cooked, set in aspic, moulded, and garnished with pressed pigs' ears; it is sliced when cold and served with vinaigrette). It is similar to the British brawn but in the latter the head is cooked and then the meat removed.

Calf's head is always cooked in a white court-bouillon. It is sold at the tripe butcher's already boned, wrapped, and blanched (the flesh must be bright pink and there must be a marked contrast in colour between the flesh and the white gelatinous part). Calf's head has always been of major importance in French cookery and can be prepared in a wide variety of ways, either hot or cold, and served with such sauces as herb, Madeira, caper, ravigote, tomato, gribiche, piquante, etc. It is also cooked stuffed, *au gratin*, or fried in batter. Traditionally, it was prepared *en tortue*, a prestigious dish with a rich garnish of tuffled quenelles, cocks' combs and kidneys, calves' sweetbreads, and mushrooms.

RECIPES

Preparation and cooking of calf's head PRÉPARATION ET CUISSON DE TÊTE DE VEAU Clean the head thoroughly, soak it in cold water, then blanch it. Prepare a white court-bouillon: mix 2 generous tablespoons (3 generous tablespoons) flour with 3 litres (5 pints, 6½ pints) water in a saucepan. Season with salt and pepper, then add the juice of half a lemon, an onion studded with 2 cloves, and a bouquet garni. Bring to the boil and immerse the head wrapped in muslin (cheesecloth) in this court-bouillon. Simmer very gently for about 2 hours.

Serve with the chosen garnish.

Calf's head à l'anglaise TÊTE DE VEAU À L'ANGLAISE Thoroughly clean half a calf's head (with half the tongue and brain) in cold water. Sprinkle the tongue and head with lemon juice, then roll it up to enclose the tongue and brain. Tie and leave to stand for 2 hours. Cook as in the basic preparation. Untie the head and serve with a bâtarde sauce mixed with lemon juice and chopped parsley.

Calf's head bonne femme TÊTE DE VEAU BONNE FEMME Boil the calf's head in a white court-bouillon as in the basic preparation, but double the quantity of liquid. When cooked, drain and cut into uniform pieces. Simmer these gently for 10 minutes in a demi-glace sauce with pieces of bacon lightly browned in butter, glazed mushrooms, and small onions. Serve piping hot.

Hot calf's head with cold sauce TÊTE DE VEAU CHAUDE EN SAUCE FROIDE Arrange the cooked head on a dish with slices of tongue and brain. Garnish with fresh parsley. Serve with any of the following cold sauces: aïoli, anchovy, gribiche, mayonnaise, ravigote, rémoulade, tartare, Vincent, or vinaigrette.

Hot calf's head with hot sauce TÊTE DE VEAU CHAUDE EN SAUCE CHAUDE Cut a calf's head into pieces and cook them in a white court-bouillon. While still hot, drain and arrange the pieces on a napkin together with slices of tongue and brain. Garnish with fried parsley and serve with any of the following: a white sauce (caper, fines herbes, hongroise, ravigote), a brown sauce (charcutière, diable, piquante, Robert), tomato sauce, or mint sauce. The calf's head may also be cut into small cubes, heaped on a serving dish in a pyramid, and garnished with a sauce of one's own choice.

Ragout of calf's head TÊTE DE VEAU EN RAGOÛT (from Joël Robuchon's recipe) Choose a very white whole calf's head and soak for 24 hours in cold water. Blanch for about 15 minutes in salted water with the juice of a lemon. Cool, trim, and singe, then scrape out the inside of the muzzle and sprinkle all over with lemon juice. Mix 75 g (3 oz, ¾ cup) flour with 10 litres (8¾ quarts, 11¼ quarts) water. Add the juice of a lemon and 5 cl (3 tablespoons, ¼ cup) white vinegar. Bring to the boil, skim well, then add 2 medium-sized onions (each studded with 2 cloves), 4 carrots, 1 head of garlic, a large bouquet garni, 1 dl (6 tablespoons, scant ½ cup) oil (to prevent the head from coming into contact with the air and turning black), 60 g (2 oz, ½ cup) salt, and 1 tablespoon peppercorns. Add the head and cook gently for about 2 hours.

To prepare the sauce, pour 1 dl (6 tablespoons, scant ½ cup) very dry white wine into a saucepan and boil down to reduce by half. Then add 3 dl (½ pint, 1¼ cups) boiling veal stock, 1 dl (6 tablespoons, scant ½ cup) boiling white chicken stock, 6 g (¼ oz) sage, a pinch each of marjoram, rosemary, basil, thyme, and powdered bay leaves, and 8 crushed peppercorns. Cover and allow to infuse for 20 minutes on the corner of the stove, without boiling. Strain the infusion and add 2 cl (1½ tablespoons, 2 tablespoons) Madeira and 1 teaspoon ginger, cut into thin strips.

Prepare a garnish with 500 g (18 oz) glazed carrots, 250 g (9 oz) glazed spring onions (scallions), 750 g (1¾ lb) chanterelles tossed in 100 g (4 oz, ½ cup) butter, 2 chopped shallots, salt, and pepper. Carefully mix all the vegetables together.

Cut the calf's head, brain, and tongue into pieces. Place them in a dish and cover with the vegetables. When the sauce is very hot, pour it over the top. Simmer the whole dish for 5 minutes, sprinkle with chervil, and serve immediately.

head cheese
See *brawn.*

heart COEUR
A type of red offal from various animals, which must be bright red and firm when bought. Remove the hard fibres and any clots of blood, if necessary by

soaking it in cold water. Heart is devoid of fat and inexpensive. It is considered to be an excellent dish despite its lack of gastronomic repute. Ox (beef) heart is eaten roasted or braised and may be stuffed. It may also be cut into cubes and grilled (broiled) on skewers (like *anticucho*, a popular Peruvian dish). Heifer's heart is more tender and is considered to be better than ox heart. However, calf's heart has the most flavour and may be either roasted whole or cut into slices and fried. Pig or sheep hearts are used to make a ragout or a civet. Poultry hearts are either grilled on skewers, used in terrines, incorporated in mixed salads, or merely seized in butter.

RECIPES

Calf's heart à l'anglaise COEUR DE VEAU À L'ANGLAISE Clean a calf's heart and cut it into slices about 1.5 cm (½ in) thick. Season with salt and pepper, brush with melted butter, coat with egg and breadcrumbs, and grill (broil) lightly. Also grill some rashers of bacon. Arrange the slices of heart and the bacon rashers alternately on a round dish. Coat the slices of heart with half-melted maître d'hôtel butter. Serve with boiled potatoes.

Casserole of calf's heart COEUR DE VEAU EN CASSEROLE Clean the heart and season it with salt and pepper. Melt 2 tablespoons (3 tablespoons) butter in a casserole, add the heart, and cook until lightly brown. Then cook in the oven (heated to about 230 C, 450 F, gas 8) for 30–35 minutes, basting the heart several times. Serve immediately. (In traditional cookery, the heart was covered with a thickened veal gravy before serving.)

Grilled calf's heart on skewers COEUR DE VEAU GRILLÉ EN BROCHETTES Clean the heart and cut it into large cubes. Clean some small mushrooms and marinate the heart and mushrooms in a mixture of olive oil, lemon juice, chopped garlic, chopped parsley, salt, and pepper. Thread the cubes of heart and the mushrooms alternately on some skewers, finishing each skewer with a small tomato. Cook under a hot grill.

Lambs' hearts à l'anglaise COEURS D'AGNEAU À L'ANGLAISE Clean the hearts and cut them into thick slices. Sprinkle the slices with salt, pepper, and flour and cook them briskly in butter in a frying pan (skillet). Arrange them in a warm serving dish. Make a sauce with the juices from the pan, a little Madeira, and Harvey sauce. Pour the sauce over the hearts and sprinkle with chopped parsley.

In England, this method is used to prepare all pluck, including liver, heart, spleen, and lungs. The latter two need to be blanched beforehand.

Roast calf's heart COEUR DE VEAU RÔTI Clean the heart, season with salt and pepper, cover with oil and 1 tablespoon lemon juice, and marinate for 1 hour. Drain and remove the heart, cut it into large slices, and wrap each slice in a piece of pig's caul. Put the slices on a spit or skewers and roast for 30–35 minutes. Make a sauce from the juices in the grill pan mixed with a little white wine. Reduce, and pour over the pieces of heart.

Sautéed calf's heart COEUR DE VEAU SAUTÉ Clean the heart and cut it into thin slices. Season with salt and pepper. Sauté the slices quickly in butter in a frying pan (skillet). Remove, drain, and keep warm. Brown some sliced mushrooms in the same butter and mix them with the slices of heart. Deglaze the frying pan with some Madeira. Reduce, add 1 tablespoon butter, and pour the sauce over the heart and mushrooms.

Sautéed lambs' hearts COEURS D'AGNEAU SAUTÉS Clean the hearts, cut them into slices, and sauté them briskly in butter or olive oil in a frying pan (skillet). Add parsley sauce and 1 tablespoon wine vinegar for each heart.

Stuffed calf's heart COEUR DE VEAU FARCI Clean the heart, season with salt and pepper, and stuff with forcemeat (fine or mushroom). Wrap it in a piece of pig's caul and tie with string. Follow the same procedure as for casserole of calf's heart but cook for an additional 30 minutes. Keep the heart hot on the serving dish and make a sauce with the pan juices and some white wine. Reduce, then thicken with 1 tablespoon kneaded butter. Pour the sauce over the heart and serve with vegetables such as carrots, turnips and glazed onions, or a printanière of vegetables.

heat diffuser DIFFUSEUR

A specially designed mat that is placed between a pan or other cooking utensil and the source of heat, either to slow down the heating process or because the material from which the vessel is made is not resistant to intense heat. It may be round or square, generally with a handle, and is made of asbestos, wire gauze, or a double thickness of perforated sheet metal.

heat-resistant glass
VERRE À FEU

A material that is resistant to sudden changes of temperature and mechanical shocks. It is used to make various cooking and serving utensils, being a better conductor of heat than common glass and having a low coefficient of expansion. Made from silica, soda, and oxides of boron and aluminium, this type of glass is usually fairly thick; a common type has the brand name Pyrex, which was first marketed in 1937 and is widely used for oven-to-table ware (gratin dishes, soufflé dishes, ramekins, etc.), as well as plates, glasses, bowls, cups, and teapots. Pyrex dishes are especially recommended for long slow cooking. Duralex is a similar toughened glass, used mainly for the manufacture of preserving jars, as it withstands temperatures of up to 150 C (300 F) and can be cooled without risk of cracking when it is removed from the sterilizer. Corelle is an almost unbreakable material consisting of a thin core of transparent heat-resistant glass that has been welded with a coating of opaque glass. It can be used in the oven or the freezer, but should not be used over a source of direct heat, nor is it advisable to subject it to extreme changes of temperature. Arcopal is a toughened heat-resistant glass that is used to make dishes and cooking utensils for use in the oven or over a flame (provided it is used with a heat diffuser).

hedgehog HÉRISSON

An insect-eating mammal, two varieties of which can be found in France: the dog hedgehog and the edible pig hedgehog. Boiled hedgehog was a common dish in Paris in the early 16th century, but nowadays it is only eaten by gipsies, who either roast it or stew it. The meat has a stronger flavour than wild rabbit. It is roasted by wrapping it in wet clay and cooking it in a pit full of hot embers. When the clay has hardened, it is broken open and the quills remain embedded in the clay. The hedgehog can also be skinned (starting from the belly), or scalded and then marinated to make a civet. The gipsy *niglo* is eaten with a purée of potatoes cooked in red wine with diced bacon.

heifer GÉNISSE

A young cow aged between 8 and 20 months. Its meat and liver are of good quality and heifer meat has become much more common since the 1970s. This is due to improvements in dairy cattle and overcapacity in dairy farming, resulting in an increase in the numbers of heifers being killed for beef rather than being kept for milk.

Helder

A dish of small pieces of sautéed meat garnished with noisette potatoes and a thick tomato sauce. Helder was the Dutch port that General Brune, commander-in-chief of the Dutch army, captured from the English in 1799. A Parisian café was named after the port; it became very popular with army officers and the students at Saint-Cyr, and it was in the Café du Helder that the dish was created. The name is also used for a dish of shaped chicken cutlets with tomato sauce but a different vegetable garnish.

RECIPES

Shaped chicken cutlets Helder
CÔTELLETTES DE VOLAILLE HELDER Make a velouté from some chicken carcasses (the white meat that has been removed is shaped into cutlets). Add some tomato concentrate to the velouté and reduce over a gentle heat. Incorporate some butter and then

strain the sauce. Season the cutlets with salt and pepper, brush with melted butter, and place them in a buttered casserole. Sprinkle with a little lemon juice, cover, and cook in a very hot oven for 6–10 minutes. Braise some diced carrots in butter and boil some diced artichoke hearts and mushrooms in water. Arrange the cutlets on a warmed serving dish and garnish with the vegetables. Coat with the tomato sauce.

Tournedos Helder Prepare a béarnaise sauce and a very thick tomato fondue. Also prepare some noisette potatoes. Brown the steaks in butter, drain them, and keep them warm. Deglaze the pan with white wine and consommé, and boil down to reduce to a thick syrupy consistency. Put a ribbon of béarnaise sauce on each steak with a little tomato fondue in the centre. Garnish with the noisette potatoes. Pour the reduced pan juices over the steaks.

Heliogabalus
HÉLIOGABALE
Roman emperor (born 204; died 222), who was notorious for his many excesses, particularly his culinary extravagances. It is said that his kitchens were equipped with silver utensils. A different-coloured dinner service appeared at every feast he gave, and he served meals composed entirely of pheasant, chicken, or pork. He also devised an itinerant feast moving around the city of Rome, eating the hors d'oeuvre at one house, the main course at another, and the dessert at a third. These lengthy meals could take up an entire day! He also organized mock naval battles fought out on wine-filled canals, and for a single feast he ordered 600 ostrich brains to be prepared.

hen POULE
The female of various gallinaceous birds, particularly the domestic fowl but also the pheasant (hen pheasant). The word 'hen' normally denotes a chicken kept for laying.

Hens are slaughtered between 18 months and 2 years of age, weighing 2–3 kg (4½–6½ lb). Known as boiling fowl in Britain, they have firm flesh which is always a little fatty. They are usually cooked by gentle simmering, to make them tender.

Henri IV
The name given to a dish consisting of small pieces of grilled (broiled) or sautéed meat or offal (kidneys), garnished with potatoes pont-neuf and béarnaise sauce. The presentation of sautéed tournedos Henri IV is precisely defined: watercress in the centre of the dish, the steaks separated by potatoes pont-neuf arranged in pairs crisscross fashion, each pair resting across the one beneath, and the sauce in a ribbon across the steaks. Artichoke hearts stuffed with noisette potatoes sometimes replace the potatoes pont-neuf.

herbs HERBES
Various aromatic plants that are used in cookery. Among the most common herbs used for seasoning are chervil, thyme, rosemary, dill, tarragon, chives, and parsley (see *aromatic, fines herbes*). Pot herbs traditionally include six vegetables: orache, spinach, lettuce, sorrel, chard, and purslane. They are used not only to flavour soups and stews but also as vegetables, salad ingredients, and as a garnish. *Herbes à soupe*, which were traditionally used to flavour soups and stews consisted of various green vegetables (carrot and celery tops, radish leaves, parsley stalks, etc.). *Herbes de Provence* consist of a mixture of aromatic plants (thyme, rosemary, bay, basil, savory), which are sometimes dried and are used especially to flavour grills. *Herbes vénitiennes* are a mixture of aromatic herbs (tarragon, parsley, chervil, and sorrel), which are finely chopped and incorporated into kneaded butter.

In former times, the term 'herbs', when used in cookery, included all edible plants and vegetables which grow above ground; those growing below ground were called 'roots'.

Hermitage
AOC red and white wines from the left bank of the Rhône, the vineyards being on the steepish slopes above Tain-l'Hermitage. The young red wine can be somewhat assertive, even rough-textured, but with time it mellows admirably and is justifiably esteemed as

one of the great Côtes-du-Rhône wines. Although a variety of grapes may be used, the finest examples of Hermitage are predominantly Syrah, which endows the wine with a wonderful bouquet, a full but fine-textured flavour, and great length. The white wine, mainly made from the Marsanne grape, is full-bodied and aromatic; it is dry, with slight mineral overtones of taste (some describe its taste as that of a gun-flint). Hermitage – which appears in some reference books as 'Ermitage' – should not be confused with the nearby Crozes-Hermitage vineyards, which also make first-rate red and white wines (although these wines lack the breeding of Hermitage).

herring HARENG

Any of various sea fish of the family Clupeidae. The common herring (*Clupea harengus*) is seldom more than 30 cm (12 in) long; it has a tapering body, silvery bluish-green with a silver belly. The large scales are easily removed. Herring are found mainly in the cold waters of the Atlantic and the North Sea.

Despite its prodigious fertility, intensive fishing and pollution have resulted in a scarcity of herring, but its swarming shoals have provided an essential part of our diet since the Middle Ages, especially in northern Europe, where its economic importance rivalled that of spice. It was because of the herring that the first maritime fishing rights were established, and the herring trade was one of the reasons for the foundation of the Hanseatic League. It served many purposes – food, barter, ransom, and gift.

There are many varieties of herring, each one confined to its own sea area (the North Sea and the Baltic where the largest fish are caught; the Atlantic off the coast of Norway, and the Irish Sea), and each variety has its own spawning season (which influences the taste and nutritional value of the fish). A prespawning herring, caught from October to January while still carrying its eggs (hard roe) or milt (soft roe), has the most flavour, but also contains the most fat (6% lipids). When caught after spawning (January to March) the herring is said to be 'spent', i.e. it is only half the weight and the flesh is drier.

Fresh herring can be cooked in foil, grilled (broiled), fried, baked, stuffed, etc. It can also be preserved in various ways.
• *Sa herring*: found in two forms – the small herring from Dieppe or Boulogne, which is salted at sea after the head is removed; and the large herring from the Baltic, cut into thick fillets and preserved in brine.
• *Smoked (or dried) herring*: salted for two to six days, then lightly cold-smoked. Smoked herring fillets are sold in packets.
• *Bloater*: very lightly salted (for one day at most), then smoked until it becomes straw-coloured. It will keep for ten days in a refrigerator.
• *Buckling*: salted for a few hours, then smoked at a high temperature, thus being partly cooked.
• *Kipper*: slit open and flattened, salted for an hour or two, then lightly smoked on both sides over a wood fire. It is a traditional breakfast dish in Great Britain, where it is sold fresh, frozen, canned, or in ready-to-cook bags. It will keep for 24–48 hours in the refrigerator.
• *'Gendarme' (pickled herring)*: salted for nine days and then smoked for 10–18 hours.
• *Rollmops and Baltic herring* (formerly *Bismarck herring*): slit open like a kipper, marinated in vinegar and spices, rolled up, and secured with a sliver of wood. Baltic herring are sold as flat fillets.

There are many forms of canned herring in various sauces: lemon, tomato, horseradish, mushroom, etc.

All north European countries have a great many recipes for serving herring: it is an ingredient of zakouski in Russia and of smörgasbord in Scandinavia; in Berlin fresh herring is fried and eaten either hot or cold; in Norway it is prepared in a sweet-and-sour dressing of vinegar, mustard, sugar, and ginger; and in Flanders smoked herring and warm potato salad is a classic dish, eagerly adopted by the French.

It was J.-K. Huysmans who praised the herring most highly: 'Your raiment, O herring, displays the rainbow colours of the setting sun, the patina on old copper, the golden-brown of Cordoba leather, the autumnal tints of sandalwood and saffron. Your head, O herring, flames like a golden helmet, and your eyes are like black studs in circlets of copper.'

RECIPES

Preparation of herring PRÉPARATION DES HARENGS If fresh, scale the fish but do not slit them in half. Gut (clean) them through the gills, leaving the hard or soft roes inside. Wash and dry them. If they are to be cooked whole, score the skin lightly on both sides. The fish is filleted by running a very sharp knife between the backbone and the fillets, starting from the tail end. The fillets can then be eased off the bone, trimmed, washed, and dried.

If the herring is smoked, take out the fillets, then skin and trim them. Before cooking, soak them for a while in milk to remove some of the salt.

If the fish is salted, wash the fillets and soak them in milk, or a mixture of milk and water, to remove the salt. Drain, trim, and dry them.

FRESH HERRING

Fried herring HARENGS FRITS Choose small herrings weighing about 130 g (4½ oz). Clean, trim, and score them and soak them in milk for about 30 minutes. Drain. Coat with flour and deep-fry in oil at 175 C (347 F) for 3–4 minutes. Drain well on absorbent kitchen paper. Sprinkle with salt and serve them with quarters of lemon.

Fried herring fillets à l'anglaise FILETS DE HARENGS FRITS À L'ANGLAISE Remove and clean the herring fillets. Dip them first in beaten egg, then in breadcrumbs, and deep-fry them in oil at 175 C (347 F) for 3–4 minutes. Drain well on absorbent kitchen paper. Serve with maître d'hôtel butter. If the fish still contains its soft roe, poach this in a court-bouillon for 4 minutes and then drain. The roe can then be either mashed and added to the maître d'hôtel butter, or dipped in egg and breadcrumbs and fried with the fillets.

Grilled (broiled) herring HARENGS GRILLÉS Clean and trim some medium-sized herrings. Brush them with oil or melted butter, season with pepper, and cook under a moderate grill (broiler). Sprinkle with salt and serve with maître d'hôtel butter or a mustard sauce.

Marinated herrings HARENGS MARINÉS Clean and trim 12 small herrings, sprinkle them with fine salt, and leave for 6 hours. Chop 3 large onions and 3 carrots. Choose a dish just big enough to hold the herrings and half-fill it with the chopped vegetables. Add a pinch of chopped parsley, a pinch of pepper, 2 cloves, a bay leaf cut into small pieces, and a little thyme. Arrange the fish in the dish and pour in enough of a mixture of half white wine and half vinegar to just cover the fish. Top with the remaining vegetables, cover the dish with foil, and bring to the boil on the top of the cooker. Then cook in the oven at 225 C (437 F, gas 7) for about 20 minutes. Leave the herring to cool in the cooking liquid and refrigerate until ready to serve.

Sautéed herring à la lyonnaise HARENGS SAUTÉS À LA LYONNAISE Clean and trim 6 herrings. Chop 2 medium-sized onions. Season the fish with salt and pepper, coat with flour, and fry in butter until golden brown on both sides. Fry the onions until golden brown in a separate pan. Turn the herrings over, add the onions, and continue cooking for about 10 minutes. Arrange the fish on a serving dish, cover with the onions, and sprinkle with chopped parsley. Deglaze the frying pan (skillet) in which the fish was cooked with a generous tablespoon of vinegar and pour the sauce over the fish.

Swedish herring balls BOULETTES DE HARENGS À LA SUÉDOISE Fillet 3 fresh herrings. Boil 3 large floury potatoes in salted water, peel, and mash. Cook 3 finely chopped onions slowly in a covered pan for about 10 minutes. Chop the herring fillets finely, add the potato, onions, salt, pepper, and, if desired, a little grated nutmeg. Mix everything together thoroughly and form into small balls. Fry them in butter or oil and serve with hot cranberry sauce.

SMOKED HERRING

Herring fillets à la livonienne FILETS
DE HARENGS À LA LIVONIENNE Re-
move the fillets from some large smoked
herrings, trim them, and cut into dice.
Boil some potatoes in salted water, peel
them, and slice them into rounds. Peel
and halve some sweet crisp apples, core
them, cut into slices, and dip in lemon
juice. Arrange the herring, potato
rounds, and apple slices in concentric
circles. Sprinkle with vinaigrette and
chopped parsley, chervil, and fennel.
Refrigerate until required.

Herring fillets marinated in oil FILETS
DE HARENGS MARINÉS À L'HUILE
Put some lightly smoked herring fillets
into an earthenware dish. Soak them in
milk and leave in a cool place for 24
hours. Drain the fillets and wipe them
dry. Wash the dish. Slice 2 onions (for
every 450 g (16 oz) fillets) and spread
half over the bottom of the dish.
Arrange the fillets on top and cover with
the rest of the onion, some sliced carrot,
some coriander seeds, and half a bay
leaf cut into pieces. Sprinkle a little
thyme over the top, pour on some
groundnut (peanut) oil, cover the dish,
and leave to macerate for several days at
the bottom of the refrigerator.

Herve

A Belgian cows'-milk cheese with a fat
content of 45%. It is soft, close-
textured, pliable, and cream-coloured,
with a smooth pinkish-yellow washed
rind. The cheese has been made since the
16th century on the plain of Herve, in
the province of Liège. It tastes mild and
creamy after six weeks of ripening, but
after eight weeks the taste becomes
more pronounced. Cube-shaped, each
side measuring 5–10 cm (2–4 in), it is in
season in summer and autumn. The
strong-flavoured cheese is best eaten
with brown ale; red wine or even very
sweet black coffee are good accompaniments to the mild cheese.

hippocras HYPOCRAS

A spicy drink based on red or white
wine, popular during the Middle Ages
and up to the 17th century. It was made
by macerating various fruits and spices
in wine: angelica and nutmeg; raspberries and brandy; juniper berries, fruit
stones, vanilla, wormwood, citrus
fruits, and violets; cinnamon, nutmeg,
mace, cloves, ambergris, and so on.
Hippocras was sweetened, then filtered,
and could be served cool or iced as an
apéritif or at the end of a meal. It was
also used in cooking, particularly by
Taillevent for his *partridge trimolette* (a
sweet-and-sour salmis) and for poached
pears. The word probably comes from a
Greek verb meaning 'to mix', though an
analogy has been suggested with the
name Hippocrates (the Father of Medicine) (the tammy cloth through which
the wine was passed was called 'Hippocrates' sleeve'). Today hippocras is a
home-made drink.

RECIPES

Hippocras with angelica HYPOCRAS
À L'ANGÉLIQUE Infuse 8 g (¼ oz)
fresh angelica and a pinch of grated
nutmeg in 1 litre (1¾ pints, 4¼ cups)
red or white wine for 2 days. Sweeten to
taste and add a glass of brandy. Strain.

Hippocras with juniper berries THY-
POCRAS AU GENIÈVRE Infuse 30 g (1
oz, ¼ cup) crushed juniper berries in 1
litre (1¾ pints, 4¼ cups) red or white
wine for 24 hours. Add a little
powdered vanilla or vanilla essence and
75 g (3 oz, ½ cup) caster (superfine)
sugar. Mix and strain.

hob (cooking surface)

TABLE DE CUISSON
A cooking appliance, made of
enamelled cast-iron, stainless steel, or
ceramic glass with a stainless-steel rim,
designed to be built into the work surface of a kitchen. Hobs are fitted with
two, three, or four gas rings or electric
plates, or both. The ceramic hob
(burner) has a completely smooth
surface made of a special glass panel,
which is highly shock-resistant and can
withstand large variations in temperature; the heating elements are situated
beneath this panel, which transmits heat
by radiation to saucepans, etc., the positions for which are marked on the top of
the unit. It is advisable only to use pans
with thick flat bottoms that are dry and
clean, and to ensure that containers are

properly positioned on the cooking surface.

Another type is the induction hob, sometimes known as the cold-heat hob; the active element is a coil that creates a powerful magnetic field when an alternating (inducing) current is passed through it. This magnetic field heats the pan intensely, rapidly, and evenly. The hob itself consists of one or more heating areas with a corresponding number of inductors and has a perfectly flat surface, made of a material that does not conduct heat (ceramic, for example). The efficiency of an induction hob far exceeds that of any gas or electric versions.

hollandaise (à la)

The name given to a dish of poached eggs, boiled vegetables (artichokes, asparagus, chard, cauliflower), or poached fish, with hollandaise sauce either poured over or served separately. It also describes dishes of Dutch cuisine, such as eggs in cups *à la hollandaise*.

RECIPE

Eggs in cups à la hollandaise OEUFS EN TASSE À LA HOLLANDAISE Butter the insides of 3 cups and coat them with grated cheese. Put a layer of diced bacon in the bottom of each cup, pour in a beaten egg, cover with another layer of diced bacon, and then with a thick layer of grated cheese. Cook for 10 minutes in a bain-maire. Serve with a well-flavoured tomato sauce.

hollandaise sauce

A hot emulsified sauce based on egg yolks and clarified butter. It is the foundation of several other sauces, including chantilly (or mousseline), maltaise, mikado, and mustard sauce, depending on the ingredients added (fresh cream, zest and juice of an orange or tangerine, white mustard). It is served with fish cooked in a court-bouillon, or with boiled or steamed vegetables. The sauce should be made in a well-tinned copper or stainless steel sauté pan; an aluminium pan will turn it a greenish colour. As it must not get too hot, hollandaise sauce should be kept warm in a bain-marie. If it does curdle, it can be re-emulsified by adding a spoonful of water, drop by drop; use hot water if the sauce is cold, and cold water if the sauce is hot.

RECIPES

Hollandaise sauce SAUCE HOLLANDAISE Pour 5 cl (3 tablespoons, ¼ cup) water into a pan with a pinch of salt and a pinch of ground pepper. Place the base of the pan in a tepid bain-marie. In another saucepan, melt 500 g (18 oz, 2¼ cups) butter without letting it get too hot. Beat 5 egg yolks with 1 tablespoon water and pour into the pan containing the warmed water. With the pan still in the bain-marie, whisk the sauce until the yolks thicken to the consistency of thick cream; add the melted butter slowly, whisking all the time, and then add 2 tablespoons water, drop by drop. Adjust the seasoning and add 1 tablespoon lemon juice. The sauce can be strained through a sieve.

Hollandaise sauce au suprême (from Carême's recipe) Put 6 egg yolks in a saucepan; add about 50 g (2 oz) best-quality butter, a pinch of salt and pepper, a pinch of grated nutmeg, 1 tablespoon allemande sauce, and 1 tablespoon chicken stock. Stir this sauce over a very low heat and, as it begins to thicken, gradually add a further 100 g (4 oz) butter, taking care to stir constantly.

Just before serving, pour in a little good plain vinegar and add a generous knob of butter.

honey MIEL

A sweet substance manufactured by bees from nectar and stored in the cells of the hive as food. Its flavour varies depending on the season, the species of flower from which it is derived, and when it is collected from the hive. Honey contains 17–20% water, 76–80% sugar (primarily glucose and fructose), small amounts of pollen and wax, and mineral salts (especially calcium, potassium, magnesium, and phosphorus), but practically no vitamins. It is a valuable source of natural unrefined sugars in a form easily assimilated by the body.

Commercial honey is extracted centrifugally from the combs of the hive, and then filtered and purified: this is 'cast' honey. 'Pressed' honey, which is rarer nowadays and does not keep so well, is obtained by crushing the honeycombs. Honey is specified as coming from a certain type of flower (e.g. heather honey, lavender honey) or from a certain region or country. Some foreign honeys are also imported into France, particularly from Canada (white clover), Hungary (acacia), and Romania (lime blossom, mint, acacia, and sunflower). Honey from Spain is particularly full-flavoured (rosemary, orange-blossom, or eucalyptus honey).

A distinction is made between blended honey, which is derived from honeys from different parts of the world, and honey from a single variety of flower or from one country. Honey can be liquid or thick, but the liquid forms usually crystallize with age. The colour varies according to the flowers from which the honey nectar came: alfalfa, rape, and clover honeys are white, heather honey is reddish-brown, lavender honey is amber, and acacia and sainfoin honey are straw-coloured.

Naturally, the flavour also depends on the flower source: honey from leguminous plants is relatively neutral, while honey from conifers, buckwheat, and heather has a stronger flavour; aromatic plants such as thyme and lime blossom impart a distinctive flavour to the honey.

In ancient times, honey was regarded as the food of the gods, a symbol of wealth and happiness used both as a food and as an offering. In the Bible, the Promised Land is described as 'the land of milk and honey'. In the Middle Ages honey continued to be regarded as a precious commodity and was used medicinally. As in Greek and Roman times, it was used for confectionery and as a condiment for savoury or sweet dishes, including pork with honey, dormouse *en sauce*, mead and honeyed wine, and gingerbread. Nowadays, honey plays a major role in pâtisserie, being used in gingerbread, *nonnettes* (small round cakes of iced gingerbread), *croquets* (crisp almond biscuits (cookies)), oriental cakes, and various types of confectionery. Grog, egg nog, and certain liqueurs also contain honey and it is used instead of saltpetre in pickling brine for fine delicatessen meats. But it also has a role in cooking meat dishes, particularly in North Africa (couscous, stuffed pigeons, roast lamb, chicken tajines with prunes, mutton tajine, etc.), in the United States (e.g. Virginia ham), and in China (duck).

RECIPES

Aiguillettes of duckling with honey vinegar AIGUILLETTES DE CANARD AU VINAIGRE DE MIEL (from a recipe by Christiane Massia) Cut 2–3 aiguillettes per serving (there are 2 per duckling). Season with salt and pepper. Cook a chopped shallot in butter over a gentle heat. When it begins to brown, add 1 tablespoon liquid honey (preferably acacia honey); boil for about 2 minutes until it thickens. Grill (broil) the aiguillettes separately and arrange them on a warm dish. Pour the sauce over the top and serve immediately.

Serve with potato straws (*pommes paille*), rice, or a mixture of sautéed carrots and turnips.

Caramel cream with honey CRÈME CARAMEL AU MIEL (from a recipe by Simone Nouyrrigat) Make a caramel with 50 g (2 oz, 3 tablespoons) honey and 50 g (2 oz, 4 tablespoons, firmly packed) sugar and use to line the bottom and sides of a charlotte mould. Mix together 8 whole eggs and 350 g (12 oz, 1 cup) honey with a spatula. Pour 1 litre (1¾ pints, 4¼ cups) boiling milk onto the egg and honey mixture, mix well, and pour it into the mould. Cook in a bain-marie for 1 hour in a preheated oven at 180 C (350 F, gas 4).

Honey pastry for tarts PÂTE À TARTE AU MIEL (from a recipe by Christiane Massia) Mix 2 tablespoons (3 tablespoons) liquid honey with 100 g (4 oz, ½ cup) creamed butter using a fork. Quickly blend in 1 tablespoon fresh cream, followed by 200 g (7 oz, generous 1½ cups) flour. Set the dough aside to rest. Knead the dough again with a little flour, then roll it out on a well-floured working surface. Line a tart plate and bake blind. Fill the tart case with raw fruit. If the fruit is not sufficiently sweet, add a little honey. If it is too dry, add a little purée or jam made from the same fruit.

Characteristics of the principal types of pure honey

plant	region/country	appearance and use
acacia	Provence, Gironde, Rhone valley, Auvergne, Paris basin, Canada, Hungary, Romania	Liquid, very pale, and very fine. Used mainly for serving at the table and also for sweetening drinks.
alfalfa	Many regions	Very crystalline, thick, and yellow. Suitable for cooking.
buckwheat	Sologne, Britanny, Canada, California	Dark reddish-brown, coarsely crystalline, with a strong taste. Should be used for gingerbread.
clover	All regions of France, Canada, California, Britain	Very pale, fairly oily, and full of flavour. Used as a table honey.
heather	Landes, Sologne, Auvergne, Britain	Reddish-brown and fairly thick, rich in mineral salts. Used mainly in baking (cakes, biscuits, gingerbread, etc.).
lavender, lavandin	Alpes, Provence, Cévennes	Amber-coloured, aromatic, and full of flavour, rich in iron. Used mainly for serving at the table.
lime blossom	All regions of France, Far East, Poland, Romania	Greenish-yellow and thick with a very pronounced flavour and aroma; crystallizes rapidly. Suitable for the table and for cooking.
orange blossom	Algeria, Spain, South Africa	Very pale golden yellow, oily and smooth, and full of flavour. Suitable for serving at the table.
pine	Vosges, Alsace	Greenish (sometimes almost black), slightly aromatic, with a malted flavour. Almost exclusively for table use.
rosemary	Provence, Lower Alps, Narbonne, Spain	White or golden, fairly soft, and with a fine delicate flavour when pure and a more pronounced flavour when mixed with thyme honey. Suitable for serving at the table.
sainfoin	Gâtinais, Beauce, Champagne	Pure sainfoin honey, which is very rare, is pale golden, finely crystalline, and full of flavour. It should be reserved for the table.
thyme	Provence, Larzac	Dark golden yellow, oily and aromatic, with a distinctive taste. Excellent for spreading.

NOTE: Other honeys worth mentioning are: colza honey (all regions except mountainous ones; pale and smooth, rich in sucrose, produced in large quantities for the table and for cooking); ling honey (Landes; full-flavoured, slightly bitter, with a strong floral scent); black alder honey (Auvergne; greenish-brown and aromatic); eucalyptus honey (North Africa, Spain, Australia, and tropical regions; rare but very aromatic, dark brown); hymettus (an aromatic Greek honey which combines the flavours of thyme, savory, and marjoram, dark brown in colour).

Landes ham with honey JAMBON LANDAIS AU MIEL (from a recipe by Christiane Massia) Cook 2 cups rice in salted water and drain. Coat 4 slices of slightly salted raw ham on both sides with a little liquid honey (such as chestnut honey). Butter an ovenproof dish, line it with the rice, top with the slices of ham, and sprinkle with cinnamon. Grill (broil) for 10 minutes. Sprinkle with pepper and serve piping hot.

Onion and honey tart TARTE AUX OIGNONS ET AU MIEL (from a recipe by Christiane Massia) Peel and thinly slice 1 kg (2½ lb) new onions. Cook in boiling water for 3 minutes and drain. Melt 30 g (1 oz, 2 tablespoons) butter in a thick-based saucepan, add the well-drained onions, and cook without allowing them to brown. Add 2 generous tablespoons (3 generous tablespoons) mixed-flower honey, salt, 1 teaspoon ground cinnamon, and a little pepper. Stir thoroughly and remove from the heat.

Line a flan tin (pie pan) with 300 g (11 oz) thinly rolled out shortcrust pastry (basic pie dough). Fill with the onions and bake in the oven at 230 C (450 F, gas 8). When the tart is half-cooked, cover it with aluminium foil. Serve the tart warm either as an entrée or as a dessert.

honey fungus

ARMILLAIRE COULEUR DE MIEL

A mushroom (*Armillaria mellea*) that grows on old tree stumps from summer to early winter. The yellow cap has brownish scales, and is edible only if young and cooked: it should be plunged in very hot oil and then cooked in butter on a low heat. The fibrous stalk should be thrown away.

hongroise (à la)

Describing dishes which contain paprika. Hongroise (Hungarian) sauce is based on onion, paprika, and white wine, with velouté or tomato concentrate added. Depending on what it is to be served with it is finished with Mornay sauce (for eggs), a reduced fumet thickened with butter (for fish), demi-glace (for meat), or velouté or suprême sauce (for poultry).

Meat dishes *à la hongroise* are garnished with cauliflower florets coated with paprika-flavoured Mornay sauce, which are arranged in duchess potato cases or browned in the oven and served with potato fondantes.

RECIPES

Gratin of potatoes à la hongroise GRATIN DE POMMES DE TERRE À LA HONGROISE Bake the potatoes in their skins in the oven or in hot embers. Cut them in half and scrape out the insides; rub this through a sieve. Peel and chop some onions (use half the weight of the sieved potato) and soften them in butter in a covered pan. Season with salt, pepper, and a sprinkling of paprika, then mix with the sieved potato. Stuff the potato jackets with this mixture, and put the stuffed potatoes into a buttered ovenproof dish. Cover with breadcrumbs, moisten with melted butter, and brown in a very hot oven.

Hungarian omelette OMELETTE À LA HONGROISE Fry 150 g (5 oz, generous ½ cup) diced lean ham in butter over a very low heat. Peel and dice 150 g (5 oz, 1¼ cups) onions, and fry in butter. Season with salt, pepper, and paprika. Lightly beat 8 eggs, season with salt and pepper, then pour over the onions. Add the diced ham. Cook as for a flat omelette, without folding. Serve with Hungarian sauce (see recipe below).

Hungarian sauce SAUCE HONGROISE Peel and chop some onions and fry them in butter, without browning them. Season with salt and pepper and sprinkle with paprika. For 5 tablespoons (6 tablespoons) cooked onion add 2.5 dl (8 fl oz, 1 cup) white wine and a small bouquet garni. Reduce the liquid by two-thirds. Pour in 5 dl (17 fl oz, 2 cups) velouté sauce (with or without butter enrichment). Boil rapidly for 5 minutes, strain through a muslin-lined (cheese-cloth-lined) strainer, and finish with 50 g (2 oz, ¼ cup) butter.

hop HOUBLON

A vigorous climbing plant which grows in temperate regions. The female flowers are used mainly in the brewing industry to give the bitter taste to beer.

The flowers of the male plant, known in France as *jets de houblon* (hop shoots), are edible and are used particularly in Belgian cooking; dishes including hop shoots are termed *à l'anversoise*. The shoots are prepared in the same way as asparagus: they are first boiled in salted water with lemon juice added, then they can either be cooked in a covered pan in butter or simmered in cream, veal juices, etc. Hop shoots in cream are the classic accompaniment to poached eggs (plain or on fried croûtons, possibly with hollandaise sauce) and poached sole.

| RECIPE

Hop shoots in cream JETS DE HOUBLON À LA CRÈME Put 350 g (12 oz) fresh hop shoots into salted boiling water; take them out while they are still firm. Drain them, braise in butter in a covered pan, then add 2 dl (7 fl oz, ¾ cup) fresh cream. Season with salt and pepper and simmer until cooked.

Horace
(Quintus Horatius Flaccus)

Roman poet (born 65 BC; died 8 BC). A friend of Virgil and Maecenas and one of the favourites of Augustus, he preferred the simple family pleasures of rural life to the tumult of Rome. When the fashion in cookery was for pretentious and complicated dishes, he advocated simple straightforward meals: farm-reared chicken, roast milk-fed kid, a salad from the garden, and fruit from the orchard.

horn of plenty
CRATERELLE

A common woodland mushroom, also called trumpet of death (in France its common names are *corne d'abondance* and *trompette-de-la-mort*). Resembling a smoke-grey or black funnel, it is not very fleshy and is slightly tough but is nevertheless highly edible. It is chopped and added to sauces (poivrade with red wine), mixed with blander mushrooms to enhance their flavour, or prepared in the same ways as the chanterelle. It can be dried easily and is ground for a con-

diment. This mushroom is being increasingly cultivated.

hors d'oeuvre

The first dish to be served at a meal, particularly luncheon (dinner usually starts with soup). As the hors d'oeuvre is, by definition, additional to the menu, it should be light and delicate, stimulating the appetite for the heavier dishes to follow. Some restaurants have an hors-d'oeuvre trolley from which each diner chooses his or her own assortment. The presentation of an hors d'oeuvre is very important: it should always look decorative.

There are two main types of hors d'oeuvre: cold and hot. Cold hors d'oeuvres include the following: fish or seafood which can be either marinated, smoked, in oil, or in vinegar; vegetables *à la grecque*; various types of charcuterie; fish roes; various raw vegetables; stuffed or jellied eggs; mixed salads; stuffed grapefruit; prawn cocktail; etc. They are arranged in hors-d'oeuvre dishes, on plates, or in glass dishes. Hors-d'oeuvre dishes are small and usually oblong or rectangular; at least two are used together, so that different foods can be displayed without mixing them. These dishes can be arranged in fours or sixes in a ring or some other pattern, to present the hors d'oeuvres as attractively as possible.

Hot hors d'oeuvres include vols-au-vent, croquettes, rissoles, kromeskies, fritters, fritots, etc. These are, in fact, more likely to be served at dinner after the soup, but they may also appear at luncheon.

France has adopted and modified the Russian custom of serving an assortment of hors d'oeuvres as a small meal preceding the main one. Under the name of *hors d'oeuvre à la russe*, these snacks are arranged on trays and served to the guests at table.

horse CHEVAL

A domestic animal used for centuries for transport and agricultural work, but not sold in France as meat for human consumption until the last century. When it was first sold, draught animals were slaughtered and the cheap meat was sold in special horse butchers' shops in order to avoid any attempt to sell it as beef. Today Ardennes and Postier Breton horses are specially bred for meat. Colts are preferred as their flesh is tender and full of flavour, although slightly sickly; it provides markedly fewer calories than beef (94 Cal per 100 g as compared with 156 Cal per 100 g for lean beef), with a high content of glycogen, and is reputed to be strengthening and easily digestible. Ass and mule meat may also be sold as horsemeat.

Horsemeat lends itself to all beef dishes, but is particularly suitable for raw dishes (such as the authentic steak tartare), as the animal is unaffected by tuberculosis and tapeworm. Nevertheless, it does not keep as well as other meats and its degree of freshness is difficult to assess. Some charcuterie products (e.g. Arles sausage) are based on horsemeat.

The consumption of horse flesh has been controversial for a long time, and was strictly prohibited until 1811, when it was decreed legal. Its fervent supporters included the naturalist Geoffroy Saint-Hilaire, Parmentier, Cadet de Gassicourt (Napoleon's pharmacist), and Larrey (a surgeon during the Empire, who testified that horse flesh had saved a number of human lives during the Napoleonic campaigns). On 6 February 1856, a horse butchers' banquet was organized to prove that horse flesh was perfectly healthy and, furthermore, good to eat. The feast took place at the Grand Hôtel, under the supervision of a chef named Balzac. Among the guests were Dr Véron, Roqueplan, Flaubert, and Dumas. The menu consisted of the following: horse-broth vermicelli, horse sausage, and charcuterie, then boiled horse and horse *à la mode*, followed by horse stew and fillet of horse with mushrooms, potatoes sautéed in horse fat, salad in horse oil, and finally rum gâteau with horse bone marrow. The wine was Château Cheval-Blanc. At the time of this banquet, Edmond de Goncourt did not conceal his hostility towards this 'watery and blackish-red' meat.

Another ten years passed before statutory regulations controlled the butchery of horses in France; it was already strictly controlled in England, Germany, and Scandinavia.

horse mackerel (saurel)
CHINCHARD

A sea fish resembling mackerel, with a body 40–50 cm (16–20 in) long, a bluish-grey back, and silvery sides. The lateral line on each side is studded with bony scales that become more pointed nearer the tail. It is widespread in temperate seas and plentiful in summer and autumn. It is prepared like mackerel and is very suitable for fish soups. It is also used for canning, plain or in a tomato sauce.

In the United States, horse mackerel is the name given to an Atlantic species of tuna. The Atlantic bluefish is also sometimes called horse mackerel.

horseradish   RAIFORT

A perennial plant originating in eastern Europe, where it grows wild; it is cultivated for its root, used as a condiment.

Horseradish is a traditional condiment in Scandinavia, Alsace, Russia, and Germany. The root has a grey or yellowish skin and white flesh, which has a sharp hot taste and a strong smell. After being washed, peeled, and grated, it can be used either as it is or with the flavour softened by cream or by breadcrumbs soaked in milk. It is sometimes grated and dried, and then has to be reconstituted before use. It can also be thinly sliced. It accompanies a wide range of dishes: beef and pork (boiled, braised, or cold), fish (herrings and smoked trout), poached sausages, potato salad, etc. Horseradish is also an ingredient of sauces (hot or cold), relishes, vinaigrettes, mustards, and flavoured butters, which are served with the dishes mentioned.

RECIPES

Cold horseradish sauce   SAUCE AU RAIFORT FROIDE   Soak some breadcrumbs in milk, then squeeze them dry. Add grated horseradish, salt, sugar, some double (heavy) cream, and vinegar (adjust the quantities of these ingredients to give the desired taste).

This sauce can be served with smoked fish, potatoes, or beetroot (red beet) salad.

Hot horseradish sauce (*or* **Albert sauce**) SAUCE AU RAIFORT CHAUDE, ALBERT SAUCE Cook 4 tablespoons (⅓ cup) grated horseradish in 2 dl (7 fl oz, ¾ cup) white stock. Add 2.5 dl (8 fl oz, 1 cup) English butter sauce. Boil to reduce, then strain. Mix 2 tablespoons (3 tablespoons) English mustard with 2 tablespoons (3 tablespoons) wine vinegar. Bind the sauce with 2 egg yolks, then add the mustard.

This sauce is served with boiled or braised beef.

hotchpotch HOCHEPOT

A Flemish stew that can be made with pig's ears and tails, breast of beef, oxtail, shoulder of mutton, salt bacon, and all the usual pot vegetables (cabbage, carrots, onions, leeks, and potatoes). However, it is more usually made with oxtail only. The vegetables are served whole or mashed into a purée. Formerly, hotchpotch was made with chopped meat, turnips, and chestnuts cooked in an earthenware pot with stock, as described in *L'Agronome, ou le Dictionnaire portatif du cultivateur* (1760). The word *hochepot* is derived from the Old French *hottison* (to shake) and its origin is obscure, especially as the term can also be applied to a chicken cooked in a pot with cheap cuts of beef and vegetables.

RECIPE

Oxtail hotchpotch QUEUE DE BOEUF EN HOCHEPOT Cut an oxtail into uniform pieces and put them into a casserole with 2 raw quartered pig's trotters (feet) and a raw pig's ear. Cover the meat with water and bring to the boil. Skim, and simmer for 2 hours. Then add a firm round cabbage (cut into quarters and blanched), 3 diced carrots, 2 diced turnips, and 10 small onions. Simmer for a further 2 hours. Drain the pieces of oxtail and trotters and arrange them in a large round deep dish with the vegetables in the centre. Surround with grilled (broiled) chipolata sausages and the pig's ear cut into strips.

Serve boiled potatoes separately.

hot dog

A long roll split and filled with a frankfurter sausage spread with mustard. Hot dogs originated in the United States in the 1930s; the name was taken from a humorous drawing of a dachshund in the form of a sausage.

hôtelière (à l')

The name given to grilled or sautéed meat and fish dishes which are served with hôtelier butter (creamed butter to which lemon juice, chopped parsley, and a dry duxelles are added.

hotplate RÉCHAUD

An electric heating device consisting of one or two heating rings sunk into an enamelled metal framework. It is used for keeping serving dishes and their contents warm at the table.

Hotplates were used in Roman times; made of bronze, they were filled with embers and were used to cook or reheat certain dishes at the table. In the 13th century, they were made from wrought iron and mounted on wheels. In the 18th century they were even made of silver and filled with boiling water.

Chafing dishes can also be used as hot-plates.

hummus HOUMMOS

An Arabic and Greek dish made from cooked chickpeas crushed with sesame oil, sometimes with the addition of soy sauce. It usually accompanies hors d'oeuvres or crudités.

hundred-year-old eggs
OEUFS DE CENT ANS

A Chinese speciality consisting of duck eggs that are enclosed in a coating made of lime, mud, saltpetre, fragrant herbs, and rice straw, which preserves them for a very long time. They can be eaten after the third month, but their smell grows stronger with age. When they are broken out of their covering, the eggs are black and shiny. They are eaten cold as they are or with slices of ginger, cucumber, or pieces of preserved chicken gizzard.

Hungarian wines
VINS DE HONGRIE

Hungary is a huge producer of wine of many categories, including the world-famous Tokay; because of the latter, it has retained its reputation and acceptance as a source of quality wines in general. Significantly, although the present régime controls wine production overall, individual makers are still able to run their own vineyards and wineries. Although the phylloxera plague, followed by peronospora, attacked the Hungarian vineyards at the turn of the century, some of them, especially those planted in the sandy soil of the Great Plain, escaped phylloxera, because the aphis cannot live in sand and therefore the vines did not have to be uprooted and replaced with vines grafted onto resistant American rootstocks, as had to be done throughout most of Europe.

The wine regions are subdivided into 15 different areas, each vineyard being registered and classified – approximately 200,000 hectares are now under vines. A number of native grapes are grown, notably Furmint and Hárslevelü (important in making Tokay), as well as Kéknyelü, Szürkebárat, Ezerjó, and others. Much use is also made of other varieties that are planted throughout Europe: Olaszrizling, Rheinriesling, Sylvaner, Traminer, Pinot Blanc, and Sauvignon Blanc are among the white grapes; the black grapes include Kadarka (much planted in the eastern European countries) Médoc Noir (Merlot), Kekfrankos (Gamay), Cabernet Sauvignon, and Cabernet Franc. It should be remembered, when looking at labels, that the Hungarian versions of the names of some grapes and wines may look strange although in fact they are really familiar, due to use of the suffix -i – 'Tokaji', for example, for Tokay, and 'Burgundi' for Burgundy.

It is not often realized that Tokay is available as a dry wine, in addition to the various degrees of sweetness, expressed in terms of *puttonyos*, for which it is best known. There is an enormous range of Hungarian white table wines from many regions, varying from light, crisp, and fresh in style to fuller and rather aromatic ones. Among the reds, Egri Bikavér (Bull's Blood of Eger) is very well known, but there are many others, notably the Villányi-Burgundi. Hungary does a great deal of business exporting wine, especially to the Eastern bloc countries (as might be expected) but also to West Germany and to Britain, where the low price and agreeable quality make Hungarian wines popular.

Hungary   HONGRIE

Hungarian cuisine is rooted in the ancient traditions of the Magyar nomad people who used preserved foods, which could be prepared rapidly as soon as a halt was made on the journey. In the 16th century *tarhonya*, a granulated dried pasta made from flour and eggs, was boiled and eaten with dried meat; today it is used to garnish dishes made with a sauce.

The principal ingredients in the modern cuisine are lard and bacon, onions, and soured (dairy sour) cream. But it is undoubtedly paprika that characterizes modern Hungarian dishes, although it was not introduced until the 18th century. It is an essential ingredient in four typically Hungarian dishes: goulash, pörkölt, tokány, and paprikache; these recipes can be adapted for cooking red and white meat, poultry, and fish.

Other Hungarian dishes include a thick soup sometimes flavoured with caraway, garlic, and paprika; *tarhonya* fried in lard; *galuska* (small dumplings made with flour); noodles with a sweet or savoury flavouring; ravioli filled with damson preserve; and *lecso*, a sort of ratatouille made from peppers, tomatoes, and onions with pieces of bacon or sliced sausage. Freshwater fish are highly regarded, in soup, in aspic, filleted and cooked in a court-bouillon, in a ragout, or baked. They are often combined with green peppers and bacon, mushrooms, cream, and dill. The *fogas*, from Lake Balaton, is worth special mention: unknown elsewhere but closely related to the pike-perch and with very delicate flesh, it is grilled (broiled) or poached in white wine and served whole. Crayfish are often cooked in a ragout, with paprika or cream, and used as a garnish for pancakes or flaky pastries. Foie gras is one of the most characteristic of all Hungarian ingredients.

☐   **Famous names** Many classic dishes in Hungarian cuisine are named after famous people or historical events; examples are *Ujházi*, a chicken casserole named after a famous actor, and

Munkácsy, jellied eggs on a macédoine in rémoulade with dill, named after a great 19th-century painter. Poached eggs on a pörkölt of carp's roes is called *à la Kapisztrán*, in memory of a Franciscan monk, Capistrano, hero of the defence against the Turks, and the cake *Rigó Jancsi* (a famous gipsy violinist) is a delicious pavé layered with chocolate mousse and covered with chocolate icing.

Meat is usually prepared according to one of the four main paprika recipes. Other noteworthy meat dishes include sauerkraut served with pork, bacon, and smoked sausages and flavoured with dill, and grills (*fatányeros*), which combine on one large wooden platter a fillet of beef, a veal escalope, a pork chop, and smoked bacon, the whole garnished with crudités. Another dish that is typical of Hungarian cookery without paprika is entrecôte steak braised with marjoram, tomatoes, and cumin and garnished with peppers and semolina dumplings (*rostélyos*). However, paprika is often used in the cooking of pork chops, for which there is a great variety of recipes, many of them including lard and tomatoes. Nowadays, these rich and filling dishes are accompanied by various salads (such as salted cucumber, beetroot (red beet) with cumin and horseradish, lettuce with vinaigrette dressing, fresh or marinated green peppers). Vegetables are sometimes seasoned with paprika; for example, gratin of asparagus with cream, stewed mushrooms (frequently served with fried eggs), and potatoes, which are served with everything. Soured cream is nearly always used in the cooking of French (string) beans, cabbage, or marrow (squash) with dill.

The national pâtisserie speciality is *rétès*, strudel pastry which may be filled with apples, cherries, poppy seeds, morello cherries, or nuts; it is sometimes filled with savoury mixtures. One of the many classics of the Hungarian pastrycook is *dobos torta*, made from seven layers of Savoy sponge filled with mocha cream and covered with a crisp caramel coating. Other specialities include rissoles, stuffed pancakes (especially stuffed with cream cheese, jam, and crushed nuts), soufflé fritters, tarts,

and quenelles made with curd cheese and sprinkled with melted butter.

hunting CHASSE

Once the means of providing an essential part of man's diet, hunting became – and continues to be – a popular sport for the well-to-do. In France, until the abolition of such privileges, it was reserved strictly for the nobility. All the grounds around Paris devoted to the royal hunts were called the king's pleasures. The game shot during hunting by the king, princes, or noblemen was sold in the market known as La Vallée at the Quai des Grand-Augustins, and thus competed with other suppliers of meat. Official inspectors were commissioned to draw up a written return of all the items put up for sale, but that did not prevent poaching from flourishing.

By analogy, the term *chasse* was also given to a meat course consisting solely of roast game arranged on an enormous dish.

hure

The French word for a type of brawn (head cheese) made with boar's or pig's head.

The word is also used for the head of a pike or a salmon.

husk GRUAU

The tough outer casing of the seedlike fruits of cereal plants, such as wheat, barley, rye, oats, etc. The French expression *farine de gruau* is used for wholewheat flour.

hussarde (à la)

The name usually given to a dish of braised beef garnished with potatoes and stuffed aubergines (eggplants). It is masked with a sauce made from the pan juices deglazed with demi-glace and served with grated horseradish.

Hussarde is also the name of a sauce and a garnish. The former is an espagnole sauce with tomatoes, shallots, sliced onions, diced ham, grated horseradish, and chopped parsley. A hussarde garnish, which is served with sautéed meat, consists of halved tomatoes stuffed with a purée of onions and mushrooms stuffed with spinach purée, all moistened with a tomato-flavoured demi-glace.

hydnum HYDNE

A mushroom characterized by soft spines or pegs under the cap. The various species grow in deciduous woods in autumn. The best are the *pied de mouton* and the pink hydnum, which is more delicate. They are prepared in the same way as chanterelles and should be cooked slowly for a long time. They go particularly well with stuffed tomatoes and ragouts.

hydria HYDRIE

A Greek jar or pitcher made of ceramic or bronze, originally used by women to fetch water from the well. It has three handles: one vertical, on the neck of the vessel, the other two lateral, on the rounded portion. The hydria had various domestic uses, including that of wine container.

hydromel

A drink made from honey and water. It was very popular with the Greeks, who regarded bees as a symbol of immortality, and was consumed in large quantities by the Romans. The Celts, Saxons, Gauls and Scandinavians drank as much hydromel as beer, calling it *met*. It was drunk throughout the Middle Ages and up to the 18th century.

hygrophorus
HYGROPHORE

A mushroom of which there are many varieties, some of them edible. Some species grow in November or in March, when few other mushrooms grow. Of the edible varieties, the very delicate snow-white hygrophorus (*blanc de neige*) is recommended. These mushrooms should be peeled and cooked like agaric (true) mushrooms. Species which are not very fleshy or have a bitter smell are mixed with other mushrooms or used as a seasoning.

hypholoma HYPHOLOME

A mushroom often found growing in clumps on old tree stumps. The edible variety is identifiable by the complete absence of green or yellow in the gills. It goes without saying that it is vital to use an infallible visual aid when picking mushrooms for eating.

hyssop HYSOPE

An aromatic plant from the Mediterranean region, with a pungent taste and a strong rather acrid smell. In ancient times and during the Middle Ages it was very popular as a flavouring for soups and stuffings. Nowadays, its main use is in the distillation of liqueurs, such as Chartreuse, but the young leaves can be used as a seasoning for oily fish or to flavour stuffings, some charcuterie products, fruit salads, and compotes.

ice box GLACIÈRE

A hermetically sealed insulated chest containing blocks of ice, maintaining a sufficiently low temperature to cool drinks and preserve foodstuffs for a relatively short time. This type of ice box has now been superseded by the refrigerator.

However, portable versions are still in use, in which refrigeration is provided by blocks containing water or other substances which are frozen in the freezing compartment of a refrigerator and maintain their refrigerating power over a period of several hours.

ice cream

See *ices and ice creams*

ice-cream cake

BISCUIT GLACÉ

A dessert made of alternate layers of different flavoured ice creams and a bombe mixture (a very light-textured ice cream), frozen in a brick-shaped mould (see *Neapolitan slice*). After removing from the mould the ice cream is cut into even slices, which are then arranged in small paper cases and kept in a cold place until serving.

The same name is used to describe a round or oblong cake having a sponge cake or meringue base with ice cream (or sorbet, parfait, or a bombe mixture) on top. It is decorated with whipped cream, crystallized (candied) fruit or fruit in syrup, and chocolate vermicelli (chocolate sprinkles).

Comtesse-Marie cake is made in a special square mould lined with strawberry ice cream; the inside is filled with vanilla-flavoured whipped cream.

RECIPE

Blackcurrant ice-cream cake BISCUIT GLACÉ AU CASSIS Trim some sponge fingers to the height of a rectangular cake tin. Prepare a sugar syrup flavoured with blackcurrant liqueur and allow to cool. Soak some whole sponge fingers in the syrup and use to line the bottom of the tin. Repeat the process for the cut sponge fingers and use these to line the sides.

To make about 700 g (1½ lb) filling, beat 6 egg yolks and 200 g (7 oz, ¾ cup) sugar until white and fluffy. Add 5 cl (2 fl oz, ¼ cup) blackcurrant liqueur and, if available, some blackcurrants macerated in sugar. Add 1 dl (6 tablespoons, scant ½ cup) milk to 4 dl (14 fl oz, 1¾ cups) very thick double (heavy) cream (both cream and milk having first been chilled in the refrigerator) and whisk until the cream will stand in peaks. Mix the whipped cream with the blackcurrant mixture and pour into mould.

Place in the freezer until slightly set, then soak some more sponge fingers in the syrup and cover the mixture with them. Leave in the freezer until completely set. Just before serving, turn out of the mould and pipe with whipped cream. This dish may be served with a hot or cold blackcurrant sauce.

ice-cream maker

SORBETIÈRE

An electric appliance consisting of a container with a mixer or paddle blades driven by a motor. It can be used to make ice creams and sorbets. The old type of manual machine, which used crushed ice and salt as a freezing agent, is rarely round today. The modern electric ice-cream maker is round or rectangular and is placed directly in the freezer. Rectangular models tend to be shallower (about 10 cm (4 in) high); round ones can be up to 20 cm (8 in) tall. They all hold around 1 litre (1¾ pints, 5 cups). During its running time (from 45 minutes to 2 hours) the motor drives the blades, which churn the preparation. When the required consistency is obtained the blades are raised and the motor stops automatically. Ice-cream makers have one or two compartments (to prepare two flavours at the same time).

ices and ice creams

GLACES ET CRÈMES GLACÉES

Cold desserts made by freezing a flavoured mixture. Freezing is carried out commercially in an ice-cream maker or a churn freezer, mainly consisting of a refrigerated tank in which a number of electrically driven blades stir the mixture throughout the operation to incorporate air and make it smooth. The tank can act as a mould, but the ices are usually spooned into individual tubs or put into moulds after they are taken out of the ice-cream freezer. There are moulds of all shapes, made of metal or plastic, enabling various combinations to be made by mixing up the flavours. The mould is filled, then frozen. To

remove the ice cream from it, the mould is rapidly immersed in warm water. The ice cream can be decorated with fresh or crystallized (candied) fruit, Chantilly cream, coffee beans in liqueur, grated chocolate, etc.

☐ History The history of ice cream is linked with that of gastronomy and refrigeration. The Chinese knew the art of making iced drinks and desserts long before the Christian era. They taught this art to the Arabs, who began making syrups chilled with snow, called *sharbets* (hence the words 'sherbet' and 'sorbet').

At the court of Alexander the Great, and later under Nero, fruit salads and purées were served, mixed with honey and snow. It was not until the 13th century, however, that Marco Polo brought back from the East the secret of cooling without ice, by running a mixture of water and saltpetre over containers filled with the substance to be cooled. Thus the great fashion for water ices began in Italy.

When Catherine de' Medici arrived in France to marry the future Henri II, she introduced iced desserts to the court, among other culinary novelties, but the Parisian public only discovered them a century later, when Francesco Procopio opened a café. People went there to read news-sheets, discuss politics and literature, and above all to sample drinks and delicacies, among which there were ices and sorbets (sherbets) that soon became all the rage. Procope (as he was now called) was soon imitated by his colleagues: in the 18th century, 250 *limonadiers* were selling ices in Paris, but only in summer. In about 1750 Procope's successor, Buisson, had the idea of selling ices all the year round. The fashion at the time was to walk under the arcade of the Palais-Royal where the fashionable cafés sold their iced specialities, but these were still of poor quality.

Around 1775, ices became more delicate in flavour, richer, and with more body, so that they could be moulded into different shapes. Ices made with milk, cream, and eggs appeared. In fact, they had been discovered in 1650 by a French cook of Charles I of England, who paid him to keep his method secret. The end of the 18th century saw the great fashion for *fromages glacés*. The manufacture of ices continued to develop. The ice bombe appeared and it became customary to serve it during any meal of any significance. Two Italians, Pratti and Tortoni, were especially famous for their fine ices; in particular, Tortoni launched the iced sponge cake in 1798. Under the Second Empire the surprise omelette was invented, then the first coupes, mousses, and parfaits. Ices were served at the end of meals, and also became common during balls and receptions. Very refined blends of flavours were invented (apricot and wild cherries, Mignonne peaches, Malmsey wine from Alicante, angelica liqueur, the yolks of finch eggs, sugary melon, hazelnuts and mint liqueur, green tea and citron juice, pistachios and peach juice, etc., according to the recipes in the *Préceptoral des menus royaux* of 1822). By the beginning of the 20th century, itinerant ice-cream vendors were already selling in the streets. The United States have been particularly inventive as regards the ice-cream industry.

Ancient recipes were gradually modified and adapted to the needs of industrial manufacture. Nowadays stabilizers are included, such as edible gelatine, egg white, agar-agar, and carob.

RECIPES

ICE CREAMS

Caramel ice cream GLACE AU CARAMEL Whisk together 9 egg yolks and 300 g (11 oz, 1⅓ cups) caster (superfine) sugar until the mixture becomes white and foamy. Boil 1 litre (1¾ pints, 4¼ cups) milk. Make some caramel without water: warm 100 g (4 oz, ½ cup) sugar in a thick-bottomed saucepan over a gentle heat, stirring with a wooden spoon. As soon as the sugar has melted and turned into a smooth mass, add a further 100 g (4 oz, ½ cup) sugar, melt, then blend in another 100 g (4 oz, ½ cup). Continue to stir until the caramel has turned brown. Add 1 teaspoon lemon juice or vinegar straight away, and remove from heat.

Mix the boiling milk with the hot caramel over a gentle heat, stirring with a wooden spoon. Pour this boiling mixture over the sugar/egg yolk mixture,

whisking vigorously, then stir this cream in the saucepan, over a low heat. When the cream begins to coat the spoon, remove the saucepan from the heat and immerse the bottom in cold water. Continue to stir until the cream is completely cool. Freeze in an ice-cream maker.

Coffee and brandy ice cream GLACE AU CAFÉ ET À LA FINE CHAMPAGNE Chill a 1-litre (1¾-pint) bombe mould in the freezer. Make some custard cream (see *creams and custards*) with ½ litre (scant pint, 2 cups) milk, 6 egg yolks, and 125 g (4½ oz, ½ cup) caster (superfine) sugar, then add 1 tablespoon instant coffee. Work this cooled cream in an ice-cream maker, then remove the beaters and leave to freeze for about 30 minutes.

Make a bombe mixture: bring to the boil a syrup made with 2 dl (⅓ pint, ¾ cup) water and 250 g (9 oz, generous cup) caster sugar. While still boiling, pour the syrup over 8 egg yolks and beat with an electric mixer until cool. Whip 1 dl (6 tablespoons, ½ cup) milk with 2½ dl (scant ½ pint, 1 cup) very cold double (heavy) cream until very stiff. Blend this cream with the cooled sugar/egg yolk mixture, flavour it with 5 cl (3 tablespoons, scant ¼ cup) liqueur brandy, and put in the refrigerator.

Cover the bottom and walls of the mould with coffee ice cream in an even layer about 2 cm (¾ in) thick. Fill with the brandy-flavoured cream. Pack down well, then freeze for about 4 hours. Remove from the mould and decorate with coffee beans soaked in liqueur.

other recipes See *bombe glacée, chocolate, coffee, mousse, parfait, plombières, vanilla.*

WATER ICES

Grand Marnier ice GLACE AU GRAND MARNIER Make 1 litre (1¾ pints, 4½ cups) syrup with density of 1.2407. Whisk in the juice of half a lemon and 1 dl (6 tablespoons, ½ cup) Grand Marnier. Freeze in an ice-cream maker.

Liqueur ice GLACE À LA LIQUEUR Mix cold sugar syrup (density 1.1407) with the chosen liqueur (generally 1 dl

(6 tablespoons, ½ cup) liqueur to 1 litre (1¾ pints, 4¼ cups) syrup), adding a little lemon juice. The density of the mixture must be between 1.1425 and 1.1799.

Mango ice GLACE À LA MANGUE Choose mangoes that are very ripe and in perfect condition. Cut them in two, remove the stone, and put the pulp into a blender, adding the juice of half a lemon (or lime). For about 5dl (scant pint, 2 cups) pulp reduced to a purée, prepare 4 dl (⅔ pint, 1¾ cups) syrup with a density of 1.2407. Whisk the syrup and mango pulp together. Freeze the mixture in an ice-cream freezer.

icing (frosting)
GLACE DE SUCRE

A preparation of icing sugar (confectioners' sugar) used to coat pastries, cakes, and confectionery of all kinds. Uncooked water icing is a simple solution of icing sugar mixed with water (200 g, 7 oz, 1½ cups sugar to half a glass of water) with a spatula until a thick consistency is obtained. It can be flavoured with a fruit juice, a liqueur, or coffee essence. It is mainly used to cover cakes before they cool, forming a glittering smooth coating which hardens. Royal icing, made with egg whites and icing sugar, is also mixed cold.

RECIPE

Royal icing GLACE ROYALE Gradually add some icing sugar (confectioners' sugar) to lightly beaten egg whites, stirring continuously and gently until it forms a mixture that is thick enough to spread without running. Stop stirring when the mixture is smooth. A few drops of filtered lemon juice may be added (10 drops for 2 egg whites). Keep the icing cool, covered with damp paper. To cover a Genoese cake 20 cm (8 in) in diameter, use 1 egg white, 175 g (6 oz, 1⅓ cups) icing sugar, and 1 teaspoon lemon juice. If a piped decoration is to be used, the icing must be firmer (300 g, 10½ oz, 2⅓ cups sugar per egg white).

Île-de-France and Paris

Some people say that Paris, the symbol and home of the whole gastronomic tradition of the Île-de-France, does not possess culinary specialities which are particularly her own. Such people take no account of the magnificent work carried out by the master chefs of Parisian restaurants, from Carême to Escoffier. There were also Gouffé, Urbain Dubois, Philéas Gilbert, Marguery, Paillard, Mourier, Nignon, and a host of others.

In this vast city there are the best cooks and most skilful cordons bleus of all France. Paris abounds with foodstuffs imported from abroad and brought in from every corner of France, not to mention the produce of the fertile soil of the Île-de-France, and the livestock reared in all the departments around Paris, which provide it with savoury fish, delicate poultry, every kind of game, and a host of other delicious things.

The finest vegetables are grown in the Île-de-France, and the most delicately flavoured fruit is picked in the orchards of Paris. Here is a list of a few of the gastronomic delights to be found in the Île-de-France, and in the Paris region in paticular: Argenteuil asparagus, which with that of Lauris has the reputation of being the best in France; Clamart green peas; the French beans of Bagnolet; the cauliflower of Arpajon; the carrots of Crécy-sur-Morin; Laon artichokes and asparagus; the white beans of Soissons, or more accurately of Noyon; the lettuces of Versailles; the fragrant morels of the woods of Verrières, Viarmes, and Rambouillet; the cultivated mushrooms of the Paris region, called *champignons de Paris*; the pot-vegetables grown at Bagneux, Châtillon, Saint Denis, and other places in the area; onions, small and large, leeks, cabbages, carrots, turnips, cucumbers, shallots, various salads, spinach, sorrel, chervil, parsley, parsnips, horseradish, beetroot.

The fruits of the Paris orchards have a great reputation: the peaches of Montreuil; the strawberries of the Bièvre valley; the Héricart strawberry which the barrow-men call 'Ricart'; and many other sweet-smelling fruits which melt in the mouth, such as pears, apples, plums, figs, apricots, and nectarines.

Excellent meat is sold in Paris. What is more, the Parisian butchers are true artists and their cuts are flawless. Pontoise veal, called river veal, is as tender and as delicate as any to be found. In the woods and forests around Paris, in the regions of Versailles, Marly, and Saint-Germain-au-Laye, there is an abundance of excellent game. The poultry of Houdan is held in high esteem for its delicate flavour. The freshwater fish caught in the Seine, the Marne, the Oise, and the Aisne are especially delicious.

Very good cheeses are made round about Paris, among which are Coulommiers, Brie, Brie de Melun, and the fresh cream cheese known as the Crémet of Fontainebleau, which rivals the famous fresh cream cheese of Saumur and Angers.

On the hillsides of the Marne, which are an extension of the neighbouring Champagne vineyards, the grapes gathered produce table wines that are fresh and pleasant to taste. Excellent cider is brewed in the Aisne and Oise districts, and among the liqueurs distilled in the Paris region there is one, the Noyau de Poissy, which enjoys a great and long-established reputation.

☐ **Culinary specialities** The following soups were invented in Paris, in Parisian restaurants by Parisian chefs, and may be classed among the culinary specialities of Paris and the Paris region; Crécy, Saint-Germain, Parisien, bonne-femme, cressonnière, santé, Bonvalet, Compiègne, Cormeilles, Briard, Soissonnais, Argenteuil, Ambassadeurs, Balvet, Faubonne, Germiny (invented by Dugléré at the Café Anglais), Darblay, Longchamp, and Saint-Cloud.

Among the pork specialities of the Paris region are: andouillettes, black and white puddings, petit-salé, veau piqué (misnamed since it is not made from veal but from pork), friands parisiens, pig's liver pâté, *fromage de tête de porc* (pork brawn), *hure de porc à la parisienne* (boar's head brawn), roulade of pig's head, *pâté de porc de Paris*, rillons and rillettes, saveloys, *jambon glacé de Paris* (glazed Paris ham), ribs of pork *à la charcutière*, and pig's trotters *à la parisienne*.

Among the dishes made from other meat are: beef miroton, shoulder of mutton *à la boulangère*, entrecôte Bercy and entrecôte marchand de vin, the celebrated navarin of mutton, the old halicot (now called haricot) of mutton,

fillet of beef *à la béarnaise*, rib of veal *à la bonne femme*, calves' tendons *à la paysanne*, calf's head du Puits Certin, sauté of veal chasseur, mutton chops Champvallon, sheep's trotters *à la poulette*, and épigrammes of mutton or lamb.

Among the special poultry and game dishes of Paris are: sautéed chicken Bercy, Boivin-Champeaux, chasseur, Durand, Lathuile, and Parmentier; spring chicken *en cocotte, à la Clamart, à la bonne-femme*, and *à la diable*; squab *à la crapaudine, en compote*, and *en papillotes*; Rouen duckling *à la presse*; timbale of duckling Voisin; gibelotte of young rabbit; pheasant *à la Sainte-Alliance*, a majestic creation from the hands of Brillat-Savarin; snipe *à la fine champagne* and *à la Riche*; and pressed wild duck.

Vols-au-vent, flans, and tarts filled in many different ways have for a very long time been regarded as culinary specialities of Paris.

Special Parisian fish (sea and freshwater) and shellfish dishes are: lobster *à l'américaine*; the various stews of eels and freshwater fish, for example *matelote du Moulin de la Râpée* and *matelote à la canotière*; eel *à la tartare*; carp *à la canotière*; bouillabaisse *à la parisienne* (doubtless disapproved of by natives of Marseilles, but excellent all the same, and invented by a Parisian master chef); whiting Bercy, Colbert, and *au gratin*; brill Dugléré; young turbot *au plat*; sole *à la normande* and Marguery; turbot *à la parisienne*; spring lobster *à la parisienne*; coquilles Saint-Jacques (scallops) *à la parisienne*; and frogs' legs *à la poulette*.

The sauces in the Paris repertoire are numerous. Among the brown sauces may be mentioned charcutière, chasseur, Colbert, diable, hachée, moelle, and Robert. Among the white sauces the following are the best known: béarnaise, Bercy, Bonnefoy, Chantilly, Choron, Fayot, Laguipière, mousseline, mustard, poulette, ravigote, Riche, and Véron.

Here is a random selection of some other Parisian specialities: green peas *à la française* and *à la parisienne*; matelote de Beauvais; the partridge pâtés of Laon; the poultry pâtés of Houdan; the lark pâtés of Étampes; échaudés; puits d'amour; oublies; the Paris brioche; the aniseed bread of Fère-en-Tardenois; the stuffed pears of Provins; the cakes of Compiègne and Étampes; the green walnuts of Faucaucoure; the barley sugar of Moret; and the sugared almonds of Melun.

île flottante

A very light dessert made from egg whites and sugar cooked in a bain-marie then unmoulded onto a custard cream and usually coated with caramel. Known in English as floating island, it can be decorated with toasted slivered almonds, chopped praline, or very fine strips of lemon zest (the latter dessert is also called *dame-blanche*).

Formerly, île flottante was made with slices of stale Savoy sponge or brioche that were moistened with liqueur and sandwiched together with apricot jam containing chopped almonds and raisins. It was served cold with custard cream or a purée of strawberries, raspberries, or redcurrants.

RECIPE

Île flottante with caramel ÎLE FLOTTANTE AU CARAMEL Prepare a custard cream (see *creams and custards*) with 1 litre (1¾ pints, 4¼ cups) boiled milk, 10–12 egg yolks, and 150 g (5 oz, ⅔ cup, firmly packed) sugar. When it has cooled completely, pour it into the serving dish. Whisk 10 egg whites with a generous pinch of salt and 1 teaspoon vanilla sugar until very stiff. Grease a deep cake tin and carefully fill with the egg-white mixture. Put the tin a bain-marie and cook in the oven at 150 c (300 F, gas 2) until the top just begins to brown 30–50 minutes). Cool completely, and unmould it onto the cold custard.

Put 6 tablespoons (½ cup) caster (superfine) sugar in a small saucepan with just enough water to dissolve it. Boil until the mixture becomes a pale caramel. Trickle the boiling caramel over the unmoulded dessert to form a lattice. Store in the refrigerator until ready to serve, but for not more than 4 hours.

imam bayildi

A Turkish dish of stuffed aubergines (egg-plants) whose name means 'the imam fainted'. According to legend, when aubergines prepared in this way were offered to a certain *imam* (priest), he was so moved by the fragrant odour of the dish that he fainted from sheer gastronomical joy! The stuffing is made with a mixture of the aubergine pulp, onions, and tomato. Cooked rice is sometimes added, together with various other ingredients (especially raisins), spices, and aromatic herbs, but not meat. The dish may be served hot or cold. Aubergines (stuffed or plain) are used a great deal in Turkish cooking as a garnish for roast lamb or mutton. In classic cuisine, the garnish *à l'imam bayildi* consists of slices of fried aubergine, sautéed halved tomatoes, and pilaf rice; it is served with tournedos steaks or noisettes of lamb.

RECIPE

Aubergines (eggplants) imam bayildi Soak 200 g (7 oz, generous 1 cup) currants in a little tepid water. Wipe 4 long aubergines and, without peeling them, slice them in half lengthwise. Carefully remove the pulp without piercing the skin, cut it into small dice, and sprinkle with lemon juice. Peel and chop 4 large onions, skin, deseed, and squeeze 8 large tomatoes, and chop a small bunch of parsley. Heat 4 tablespoons (5 tablespoons) olive oil and brown the diced aubergine, the tomato pulp, the chopped onion, and the parsley. Add salt, pepper, a sprig of thyme, and a bay leaf. Cover the pan and cook gently over a low heat for about 20 minutes. Then add 2 crushed garlic cloves and the drained currants. Mix everything together thoroughly and cook for a further 5 minutes. Grease an ovenproof dish, remove the thyme and the bay leaf, arrange the aubergine halves in the dish, and fill them with the mixture. Pour some olive oil around the aubergines, and add a little fresh thyme and some crumbled bay leaf. Cook slowly in the oven at 160 c (325 F, gas 3) for 2 hours.

imbrucciata

Any of various Corsican pastries containing Broccio, a white cheese made from ewes' and goats' milk. The name is applied particularly to a savoury tart and sweet fritters.

RECIPE

Fritters à l'imbrucciata BEIGNETS À L'IMBRUCCIATA Sieve 500 g (18 oz, 4½ cups) flour into a bowl, add 3 eggs, a pinch of salt, 2 teaspoons baking powder, and 2 tablespoons (3 tablespoons) olive oil, and mix together. Add 8 fl oz (1 cup) water and mix to obtain a smooth batter. Cover the bowl with a cloth and leave the batter to stand for 3 hours at room temperature. Cut some fresh Broccio cheese into slices, dip them in a little of the batter, and deep-fry them in very hot oil until golden brown. Drain and sprinkle with sugar.

Impératrice (à l')

The name given to various sweet or savoury classic dishes characterized by the richness of their ingredients. Consommé *à l'impératrice*, made from chicken stock, is garnished with cocks' combs and kidneys, chervil, and asparagus tips. Chicken and sole *à l'impératrice* are finished with suprême sauce. However, the name is most commonly applied to a dessert made with rice, crystallized (candied) fruits, and a Bavarian cream mixture. All fruit deserts *à l'impératrice* are based on this preparation.

RECIPE

Rice à l'impératrice RIZ À L'IMPÉRATRICE Soak 15 g (½ oz, 2 envelopes) gelatine in 2 tablespoons (3 tablespoons) warm water. Dice 125 g (4½ oz) crystallized (candied) fruit and soak in 2 tablespoons (3 tablespoons) rum. Add 250 g (9 oz, 1⅓ cups) short-grain rice to 1 litre (1¾ pints, 4¼ cups) boiling water and boil for 2 minutes. Drain, and then add the rice to 1 litre (1¾ pints, 4¼ cups) boiling milk containing a vanilla pod (bean), a pinch of salt, and 1 tablespoon butter. Cook gently for about 20 minutes until the rice is just beginning to soften. Now add 200 g (7 oz, scant 1 cup, firmly packed) caster (superfine) sugar and cook for a further 5 minutes. Remove from the heat and add the crystallized fruit.

While the rice is cooking, prepare a custard cream (see *creams and custards*) with ¼ litre (8 fl oz, 1 cup) milk, half a vanilla pod (bean), 4 eggs, 60 g (2½ oz, 5 tablespoons, firmly packed) caster sugar, and a tiny pinch of salt. While the custard is still hot, add the soaked gelatine and stir until dissolved. Then rub the custard through a fine sieve and flavour with 1 tablespoon rum if desired. Leave the rice and the custard to cool.

Whip 2.5 dl (8 fl oz, 1 cup) fresh cream with 3–4 tablespoons very cold milk until thick, then add 1 teaspoon vanilla sugar and 2 tablespoons (3 tablespoons) caster sugar. Mix the custard into the chilled rice, then very carefully fold in the cream. Pour into a savarin mould or a deep sandwich tin (layer cake pan) and keep in the refrigerator until required. Unmould onto a serving dish and decorate with crystallized fruit or fruit in syrup.

impériale (à l')

The name given to various dishes of grande cuisine, for example: a consommé garnished with small quenelles, cocks' combs, and kidneys; fish dishes (such as sole or trout) garnished with crayfish tails, poached soft roes, and finely sliced truffle; and chicken dishes garnished with foie gras and truffles.

incise INCISER

To make shallow incisions in meat or fish using a sharp knife. For example, small incisions are made in a leg of lamb to insert cloves of garlic, and shallow incisions are made in thick pieces of fish before they are grilled (broiled) or fried to reduce the cooking time.

incorporate INCORPORER

To add an ingredient during the preparation of a dish or to a basic mixture, and to blend it in thoroughly. When making choux pastry, the eggs are incorporated one by one. Whisked egg whites are always incorporated into a mixture gently, being folded in rather than stirred in.

India and Pakistan

INDE ET PĀKISTĀN

Indian and Pakistani cookery is based to a large extent on rice, spices, pulses, and fruit and is influenced by the various religious practices of the subcontinent, including vegetarianism. However, each area can still offer its own specialites: Kashmir is famous for its meat and chickpeas, Delhi for its tandoori food, Bombay for its pork in vinegar, Bengal for its intensely sweet desserts and its fish, and Madras for its vegetarian dishes, made with tamarind, semolina, and coconut. Extensive British influence was responsible for the spread of dishes and seasonings derived from Indian cuisine, particularly curries and chutneys, but they are not really representative of authentic Indian cooking.

☐ **Basic ingredients** Indian cookery is based on rice, dried pulses (see *dal*), and chapatis (Indian bread). Methods of preparing fruit and vegetables sometimes differ from those practised in Western countries. Pineapple is used in dishes that need to be cooked for a long time; peanuts may be eaten fresh, salted, or grilled (broiled); arrowroot is an ingredient of cakes and sweets; the pith of the banana tree is eaten as a vegetable in Bengal, while the bitter seeds of cucumber are popular as an hors d'oeuvre, and water chestnuts are crunched as a sweetmeat. Dates are cooked to a thick sugary paste, indispensable in confectionery making; figs are used mainly as a vegetable; leaves of the margosa, or bead tree, are served fresh or fried as a first course with rice, or they are dried and used as a condiment; mango and papaya are also cooked as vegetables. Ready-made curry powder is never used in India: each cook prepares his or her own spices as required at each stage in the cooking of a particular dish. There are two other ingredients that are essential to Indian cuisine: ghee (a clarified butter) and a form of condensed milk called *khir*, in liquid or solid form, depending on how concentrated it is.

☐ **Snacks and rice dishes** Indians are very fond of snacks, which are served as appetizers or at teatime and may be savoury or sweet. Some examples are *chanachur*, which is made from split peas, peanuts, lemon, peppers, and lentil flour, all the ingredients being fried separately; little meat pies; spiced fish balls; fritters of fish roe or aubergine (eggplant) served with chutney; lentil fritters with yogurt sauce; grilled

cashew nuts; and little fried cakes spiced with fennel flower and covered with syrup. Indian bread is usually in the form of thin flat cakes made from wheat flour, lentil flour, or potato pulp; they are sometimes stuffed with different mixtures of spices, mutton, or spinach, and cooked in ghee until golden brown in the *kodai*, a basic kitchen utensil shaped like a frying pan (skillet) but without a handle.

Rice is served with all savoury dishes. It is never eaten plain but is either mixed with a sauce or mashed vegetables, or cooked with browned onions and spices. For special occasions, a delicately flavoured long-grain rice called *basmati* is used, especially to make the dish *pulao* (basmati rice cooked with raisins, flaked almonds, small peas, cardamom, cinnamon, and cloves, served with crayfish or meat) or *murghi biriani* (basmati rice with chicken marinaded in spices and yogurt, flavoured with nutmeg flowers, and served with vegetables).

☐ **Fish and meat** Fish is prepared in many different ways. Small slices of fried fish are coated in turmeric and served with dal; bass fritters are eaten with onion salad; gilthead is cooked with spices and yogurt; curried carp is served with rice cooked with vegetables; shad is cooked in aubergine sauce; boiled giant prawns are served with ginger, coconut, or mint; spiced ragout of mullet with mustard oil, garnished with aubergines, tomatoes, and potatoes, is served with rice and freshly fried croûtons made with lentil flour. The latter is a typical Bengali dish.

The most commonly eaten meats are chicken, mutton, and pork, either stewed with spices or marinated and then grilled. Examples are chicken pieces in a sauce made with yogurt, garlic, and pepper, and chicken with coconut or vinegar, garnished with hard-boiled (hard-cooked) eggs. *Murghi tandoori* is a famous speciality: pieces of chicken are marinated in chillies and spices, coated with saffron, grilled, and served with a salad of raw vegetables. Mutton is cooked with spices and yogurt in a stew, but may also be chopped finely and formed into balls; pork is often served in a sweet-and-sour sauce. There are innumerable lamb and chicken curries; other curried dishes are made with offal (lamb's liver and sheep's kidneys) and vegetables (green cabbage, green papaya, spinach, and aubergines).

□ **Vegetables and desserts** Vegetables are eaten with rice or chapatis, contrasting flavours being combined in one dish. Examples are sour gherkins with potatoes and peppers; courgettes (zucchini) stuffed with prawns, ginger, and turmeric; potatoes with poppy seeds; and *chachadi* – a sweet-and-sour ratatouille with either mustard or coconut. True vegetarian dishes often contain cream cheese and lemons as well as various dals. To offset so many highly spiced dishes there is an equally wide range of crudités (raw vegetables): onions, cauliflower, cucumber, tomatoes, etc., served with yogurt, coriander, and tamarind sauces.

Yogurt is also used to make desserts, as are dried fruit, spices, rice, and semolina. *Halva* is a cake made from semolina cooked in milk and decorated with raisins, almonds and cardamom seeds; vermicelli cooked in milk is flavoured wth cinnamon and cashew nuts. Other popular desserts are curd cheese with pistachios, raisins, or rose petals, green mangoes cooked in milk, and very sweet cakes made with banana, almonds, or rice. *Sandesh*, made from casein (milk solids), sugar, and milk, is flavoured with coconut and cooked like a fritter.

indienne (à l')

The name given to many dishes of curried fish, eggs, meat, or poultry. They are usually served with boiled rice.

| RECIPES

Cod à l'indienne CABILLAUD À L'IN-DIENNE Season 4 steaks (or 2 fillets) of fresh cod with salt and pepper. Peel and chop 3 large onions. Peel, deseed, and chop 4 tomatoes. Chop together 2 cloves of garlic and a small bunch of parsley. Heat 4 tablespoons (5 tablespoons) oil in a sauté pan and brown the onions and tomatoes. Cover the pan and cook gently for about 20 minutes. Add salt, pepper, and the chopped garlic and parsley, and continue to cook for a further 10 minutes. Pour the contents of the pan into a casserole and arrange the cod on top. Sprinkle with 1 generous tablespoon curry powder and add 2 tablespoons (3 tablespoons) oil and 1.5 dl (¼ pint, ⅔ cup) dry white wine. Bring to the boil on top of the stove and then transfer to the oven, heated to 220 c (425 F, gas 7). Cook for about 20 minutes, basting the fish 3 or 4 times. Serve with boiled rice.

Curry or Indian sauce SAUCE À L'IN-DIENNE Cook 4 large sliced onions slowly in 4 tablespoons (5 tablespoons) oil. Add 1 tablespoon each of chopped parsley and chopped celery, a small sprig of thyme, half a bay leaf, a pinch of mace, salt, and pepper. Sprinkle with 25 g (1 oz, ¼ cup) flour and 1 generous tablespoon curry powder and stir. Then add ½ litre (17 fl oz, 2 cups) chicken stock, stir, and cook slowly for about 30 minutes. (The sauce is even better if a quarter of the chicken stock is replaced by coconut milk.) Rub the sauce through a sieve, add 1 teaspoon lemon juice and 4 tablespoons (5 tablespoons) fresh cream, and reduce a little. Adjust the seasonong.

This sauce is served with eggs, mutton, and poultry. With fish and shellfish, a fish fumet is used instead of the chicken stock.

A cold Indian or curry sauce is made with mayonnaise flavoured with curry powder and chives.

Rice à l'indienne or à l'orientale RIZ À L'INDIENNE OU À L'ORIENTALE Pour the required amount of long-grain rice into boiling salted water, using 1 teaspoon salt for each litre (1¾ pints, 4¼ cups) water. Cook for about 15 minutes, stirring the rice 2 or 3 times. Drain, and rinse with plenty of cold running water. Line a strainer with a table napkin and pour the rice into the strainer. Fold over the ends of the napkin to enclose the rice completely, and put it in a very cool oven (about 100 c, 212 F, gas ¼) for 15 minutes to dry out.

indigo carmine or indigotine INDIGOTINE

A blue food colouring (E132) originally extracted from plants but now synthesized from aniline. It is used mainly in cooked meats, pastries, ices, cheese, jams, and confectionery, and also to colour green teas. The colouring is either incorporated into the foodstuff or applied externally.

Indonesia INDONÉSIE

The staple food in the Indonesian archipelago is rice, which is accompanied by various garnishes (some very rich, others less so) and a whole range of spices and sauces. Two famous rice dishes are *rijsttafel*, a classic of Dutch cuisine, and *nasi goreng*, a dish of rice garnished with chicken, lobster, peppers, and tomatoes. Other dominant elements in this cuisine are chicken and pork, yams and palm hearts, and also seafood.

Indonesian cuisine is characterized by its variety of spices and seasonings. These include not only those that are familiar in Europe (onions, shallots, garlic, bay leaves, nutmeg, saffron, cloves, etc.), but also sambal (for seasoning rice, vegetables, and meat), dried powdered roots, fruit such as *djerek purut* (a small aromatic lemon) and tamarind, red peppers, and cooked seasonings such as *trasi* (a paste of fermented prawns). The influence of Indian cuisine is evident in the use of curry powder, and the Chinese influence is seen in the use of rice vermicelli and soy sauce.

There are, of course, many exotic fruits. These are eaten raw and in salads, especially in *rudjak* (pineapple, cucumber, green mango, and *bengkuang* (a type of large juicy turnip) flavoured with sugar, tamarind, vinegar, and trasi). But the great Indonesian speciality is *satay* (or *satai*): small pieces of meat threaded onto bamboo skewers, grilled (broiled), and dipped in a spicy sauce. Satay can be made with chicken, mutton, or pork. In Jakarta, mutton satay is eaten with a thick sauce made with peanuts and various seasonings; Chinese pork satay is accompanied by a tomato sauce; and the chicken satay from Madura is served off the skewers with a thick purée of chopped meat. The garnish, of course, is rice.

Indonesians normally drink tea, coconut milk, and fruit juices, but there are also locally made alcoholic drinks, such as arak, made from fermented vegetable fibres, and *bromi*, based on rice alcohol.

industrial oven ÉTUVE

A sealed oven operating at a constant temperature of about 150 c (300 f) and used for the industrial dehydration of fruit, vegetables, rice, and other products.

infusion

The process of steeping an aromatic substance in a boiling liquid until the liquid has absorbed the flavour. The resulting flavoured liquid is also called an infusion; examples are tea and tisanes (herbal teas). White wine is infused with truffle peelings for flavouring sauces; red wine can be infused with cinnamon and cloves; and vanilla-flavoured milk is obtained by infusing a vanilla pod (bean) in boiling milk.

inn AUBERGE

An establishment where travellers can obtain food and lodging. The provision of lodging on a commercial basis started at the beginning of the 16th century (before this it was undertaken free of charge by the monasteries). Modern inns are small, often modest, country hotels run on a family basis. Restaurants of rustic appearance, tastefully decorated and offering good food and overnight accommodation, are also called inns.

insect larvae VER

Certain species of insect larvae are eaten as food in several tropical countries. In Cameroon, about 20 different species of larvae are sold in the markets. They are usually grilled (broiled) or they may be prepared in a sauce with peanuts or gourd seeds, cooked over charcoal, wrapped in banana leaves, or cooked on skewers. The Pygmies, who are very partial to them, crush them in palm oil and use them as a condiment. The Japanese eat grilled mantis, wasp, and dragonfly larvae, whereas in Latin America, agave grubs and bamboo caterpillars are popular.

The French anthropologist Lévi-Strauss, writing in his book *Tristes Tropiques*, takes great delight in describing a larva known as *koro*: 'A stroke of the axe opens up thousands of channels deep down in the wood. In each one, there is a large cream-coloured animal, rather similar to the silkworm . . . From its body comes a whitish fatty substance . . . it has the consistency and fineness of butter and the flavour of coconut milk.' In the West Indies, palm grubs are a choice delicacy. They are grilled on skewers and served sprinkled with breadcrumbs and lemon juice.

The French missionary Père Favaud recounts the following experience in China at the beginning of the century: 'For centuries, our farmers in the Midi have devoted themselves to the rearing of silk-worms, but never, to my knowledge, have they dreamed of using them as food. It is different in China. During my long stay, I have often seen people eat silk-worm chrysalids, and indeed, I have eaten them myself. I can affirm that they make an excellent stomach medicine, both fortifying and refreshing, and often a successful remedy for those in poor health.

'After the cocoons have been spun, a certain number of chrysalids are taken and grilled in a frying pan (skillet), so that the watery fluid runs out. The outer coverings come away easily, leaving behind a quantity of small yellow objects that resemble a mass of carp roe.

'These are fried in butter, fat, or oil, and sprinkled with stock . . . After boiling them for 5 minutes, they are crushed with a wooden spoon and the whole mass is carefully stirred so that nothing remains at the bottom of the pan. Some egg yolks are beaten, in the proportion of 3 to every 100 chrysalids, and poured over them. In this way, a beautiful golden yellow cream with an exquisite flavour is obtained.

'This is the way the dish was prepared for the mandarins and the wealthy. On the other hand, the poor people, after grilling the chrysalids and removing their outer coverings, fry them in butter or fat and season them with a little salt, pepper, or vinegar, or even eat them just as they a₁ . with rice.'

interlarding PIQUAGE

The process of inserting thin strips (lardons) of pork fat into lean cuts of meat using a larding needle. Interlarding is similar to larding, but the lardons are left protruding from the surface of the meat (in larding, they are pushed right into the flesh). Interlarding is usually done on the top side of the joint only; its purpose is to keep the joint basted and therefore moist, throughout the cooking time, as the lardons will melt in the heat of the oven.

Joints that are interlarded include fillet of beef, leg of veal, saddle of mutton, haunch of venison, and baron of hare. Small cuts, poultry, and game birds can also be interlarded, using very small lardons.

intestine BOYAU

The intestines of slaughtered animals are used mainly as casings for various types of sausages. Pig's intestine is most commonly used. For large sausages, the large intestine and caecum are used; the small intestine is used for chitterlings and small sausages. The small intestine of sheep is used for some sausages, and ox intestines are used to make black pudding (blood sausage). Artificial intestines made from viscose are also used.

iodine

An essential element in food. The intake per person per day should be 200–500 micrograms, perhaps more in those regions where the water is completely iodine-free. In the latter case, iodine can be added to table or cooking salt to supplement the diet. The chief sources of iodine, which is essential for the synthesis of the thyroid hormones, are seafood, milk, bread, and vegetables grown in soil containing iodide. Iodine deficiency leads to goitre, a swelling of the neck due to the enlargement of the thyroid gland.

Irish coffee

An alcoholic drink made from black coffee, sugar, and Irish whiskey, topped with fresh cream. To prepare Irish coffee, warm a tall glass and pour in 1 good measure of Irish whiskey. Add about 2 teaspoons sugar, then fill the glass to within 3 cm (1 in) of the top with very strong hot coffee. Mix to dissolve the sugar, then carefully pour double (heavy) cream over the back of a teaspoon which is just touching the surface of the coffee, so that the cream floats on the surface of the coffee. Once the cream is added, do not stir.

Irish stew

A stew of mutton and potatoes which, according to Courtine, 'is witness, if not of the art of living, at least of the art of staying alive in difficult times, and has thus become a legendary dish'. The potato was introduced into Ireland in the 16th century and, together with mutton, became the staple food. Pieces of neck end of mutton are arranged in alternate layers with sliced potatoes and onions. Water is added, and the pot is left to simmer over a very low heat. The traditional accompaniment is pickled red cabbage.

iron FER

An essential element contained in haemoglobin, the pigment of the red blood cells. The recommended daily intake is estimated to be 10–12 mg per day (iron requirements are higher for pregnant women and children than for adult men.) The principal food sources are liver and red meats, and also egg yolk, dried vegetables, certain green vegetables (such as spinach), and bread.

Irouléguy

A red, rosé, or white wine from the Basque country, awarded an AOC in 1970. The red wine is made from the Cabernet Sauvignon or Cabernet Franc and the Tannat grapes. Production is limited and the wine tends only to be available in the locality.

irradiation

A method of preserving food by irradiating it with gamma rays. The treatment destroys microorganisms and inactivates enzymes, thus sterilizing the food. At present irradiation is mainly used to inhibit the sprouting of potatoes, garlic, shallots, and onions. Any produce that has been irradiated to prevent sprouting must be labelled accordingly when sold.

irrorateur

A type of spray gun, invented by Brillat-Savarin, which was used to perfume rooms, especially the dining room.

Brillat-Savarin writes in the preface to *La Physiologie du goût*: 'I submitted to the council of the Society for the Encouragement of National Industries my *irrorateur*, a piece of apparatus invented by me, which is none other than a compressor spray which can fill a room with perfume. I had brought the spray with me, in my pocket. It was well-filled. I turned on the tap and, with a hissing sound, out came a sweet-smelling vapour which rose right up to the ceiling and then fell in tiny drops on the people present and on their papers. It was then that I witnessed, with indescribable pleasure, the heads of the wisest men in the capital bending under my *irroration*. I was enraptured to note that the wettest among them were also the happiest.'

The pedantic name of this device comes from the Latin verb *irrorare*, meaning to sprinkle or to bedew.

issues

A term used in the French butchery trade to describe the inedible parts of animal carcasses, such as the skin, hair, horns, etc. In some regions, the word *issues* can also mean both edible offal and also the parts of the animal that are forbidden by law to be sold for human consumption.

When the term is used in the flour industry, it refers to the by-products of milling, such as bran.

Italian wines
VINS D'ITALIE

Italy is the largest producer of wine in the world in most years (with France and Spain not far behind) and a major exporter, although huge quantities of Italian wines are consumed per capita on the home market annually. Virtually every province makes not only a wide range of table wines, but also wines that come into the dessert or sweetish category, sparkling wines (made mainly in the north), and an enormous quantity of vermouth and numerous liqueurs, both sweetish and digestive. In fact the country (including Sicily and its islands) is one long vineyard, and as the climate, soils, and grape varieties also vary so much, it is no wonder that, until recently, Italian wines were somewhat happy-go-lucky, enjoyed where they were made but not always able to maintain a continuity of quality sufficient to satisfy export markets.

As Italy has been a wine producer since very early times, many local traditions have become established; in recent times, therefore, attempts have been made by the Ministry of Agriculture in Rome to set up various controls. The problem has been that wines made according to traditional methods have had to be appraised alongside those made for purely commercial considerations. Here the great vermouth firms have achieved much, because in many instances the wines they used to buy from other regions (such as those in the south) for their vermouths are now made by them and considered as wines in their own right, albeit of modest quality. Owners of some of the great estates have also been able to progress in the making of their wines, sound capital backing the development of the wines in both instances. The main controls are, as elsewhere, referred to mainly by their initials: in ascending order, they are Denominazione di Origine Semplice (DOS), Denominazione de Origine Controllata (DOC), and Denominazione di Origine Controllata e Garantita (DOCG), the latter wines being in the highest category. It should be noted that the wines must be tested and tasted in order to attain such categories, and this may take time; in addition, the *consorzi* (wine associations) in the various regions do not always include all the producers – some of the most reputable and famous may choose not to belong to these associations.

Certain Italian native grapes, such as the black grapes Sangiovese (the foundation of Chianti) and Nebbiolo, are augmented by many classic varieties, including Cabernet Sauvignon and Cabernet Franc, Pinot Blanc, Pinot Noir, Merlot, Riesling, Sylvaner, Traminer, Pinot Gris, and many others. Wines labelled 'Riesling' are made from the Riesling Italico (or Wälschriesling), rather than the Rheinriesling. The white Trebbiano is in fact the Ugni Blanc.

A wine made in the north – Tuscany and Piedmont are two of the main areas of quality wine production – will be quite different from a wine made in the south or in Sicily, even if made from similar or identical grapes. In very general terms, the north makes the finest red and white wines, also the quality sparkling wines, such as those of Asti. Emilia Romagna is famous for Lambrusco, both red and white; the northern Alto Adige region is becoming famous for very fine white wines of many different styles; and the wines of Frascati, both dry and sweet, come from the region around Rome.

The Sicilian wines have recently made a considerable name for themselves, but this island is best known for the rich wines of Marsala, which can be dry as well as sweet, and also the table wines from the volcanic slopes of Mount Etna.

In addition to the many great wine estates in the Italian provinces there are also huge firms, who put out as table wines many that in former times would probably have gone to the vermouth houses for blending, as well as the small growers, who usually sell their wines locally to catering trade outlets. Some special wines are made by allowing grapes to dry on mats or racks, in a way similar to the *vins de paille* (straw wines) of the Jura in France. One interesting thing about many of the more important Italian wines is that years which are not wholly successful in France (such as 1968) may be triumphs in Italy, so that generalizations should not be made about them.

The huge range of apéritifs includes many types of vermouth – dry white and red, sweetish red, rosé, and others, each possessing the house style of the maker. There are possibly thousands of liqueurs of different types, of which the herby Strega and the cherry-based Maraschino are widely known; *grappa*, the spirit made from the distillation of the debris of the pressed grapes, should also be mentioned.

italienne (à l')

In French classic cuisine this name is given to dishes of meat, fish, vegetables, or eggs which are either dressed with Italian sauce (based on a duxelles of mushrooms, ham, and chopped herbs) or garnished with artichoke hearts or macaroni. It is also applied to pasta cooked *al dente* and to many other dishes typical of Italian cookery.

RECIPES

Fried eggs à l'italienne OEUFS FRITS
À L'ITALIENNE Prepare some Italian
sauce (see recipe below), allowing 1
tablespoon for each egg. Cook some
very small slices of ham in butter over a
very low heat, taking care that they do
not become tough. Fry the eggs in oil
and arrange them in a circle, alternating
them with the slices of ham. Pour the
Italian sauce over the top.

Italian sauce SAUCE ITALIENNE
Clean and chop 250 g (9 oz, 2 generous
cups) button mushrooms, 1 onion, and
1 shallot. Heat 4 tablespoons (5 tablespoons) olive oil in a saucepan, add the
chopped vegetables, and cook over a
high heat (the juices from the mushrooms must be completely evaporated).
Add 1.5 dl (¼ pint, ⅔ cup) stock, 1 dl (6
tablespoons, scant ½ cup) tomato
purée, salt, pepper, and a bouquet garni
and cook gently for 30 minutes. Just
before serving, add 1 tablespoon diced
lean ham and 1 tablespoon chopped
parsley.

Lettuce à l'italienne LAITUES À
L'ITALIENNE Braise some lettuce
hearts, then drain them well and
arrange them in a buttered gratin dish.
Moisten with Italian sauce (see recipe
above), using 1 tablespoon per lettuce.
Cover the pan and simmer over a gentle
heat for about 20 minutes. Place the
lettuces in a ring and arrange some
sautéed veal around the outside. If desired, the lettuces can be sprinkled with
a little lemon juice.

Sliced meat à l'italienne
ÉMINCÉS À L'ITALIENNE Prepare
some Italian sauce (see recipe above)
and keep it very hot. Cut thin slices of
beef, mutton, or veal that has been
boiled or braised. Pour some of the
sauce into a greased flameproof dish
and arrange the slices of meat on top.
Cover with the remaining sauce and
sprinkle with grated Parmesan cheese.
Reheat on top of the stove without
allowing it to boil.

Italy ITALIE

Italian cuisine is one of the best-known
outside its country of origin. Pasta,
risotto, fritto misto, and pizza are enjoyed practically worldwide, together
with excellent charcuterie (including
mortadella, salami, Parma ham, and
zampone) and cheeses, notably Gorgonzola and Parmesan, which goes so well
with all pasta dishes. The fine quality of
Italian ice cream and water ices is also
widely acknowledged.

Italian cuisine in one of the oldest in
Europe. It is derived from Greek gourmet traditions, these being derived in
their turn from oriental cuisine.
Throughout the centuries these culinary
traditions became firmly established in
Italy. They gradually attained perfection in the country that had adopted
them. Choose any ordinary Italian dish
and it is the replica of one that was once
enjoyed by gourmands in ancient Rome.
Italian polenta, for example, is the same
as the *puls* that the Romans prepared en
route when they set out to conquer the
world. They toasted grains of wheat,
crushed them, and made a gruel from
the result. The only difference is that
polenta is now made from coarse maize
(corn) flour, not wheat flour.

☐ **Regional cooking** The great attraction of modern Italian cooking lies in
the quality and variety of its ingredients
and it is for this reason that the true
Italian specialities are regional – even
local.

Not so very long ago, a 'culinary
frontier' separated northern Italy, with
its butter, cows'-milk cheese, rice, and
Barolo or Valpolicella wines, from the
south, the land of olive oil, pasta, Marsala, and mares' milk. It was the Tuscans who forged the first link with the
regions of the south, with the opening of
restaurants where Lucca oil, entrecôte
steak *à la florentine*, white haricot
(navy) beans, and Chianti could be enjoyed. Other regions followed suit: pizzas became known in the north, while
risotto and polenta were eaten in the
south. However, regional cookery continues to dominate. Lombardy is still the
home of dishes prepared *à la milanaise*,
which are rich in butter, and of vegetable soups and osso bucco. Venice has
its fish and seafood specialities and
shows the influence of Austrian cuisine.
Liguria specializes in highly seasoned
stuffed food, and the province of
Emilia-Romagna is dominated by

Bologna, a city that is to Italy what Lyon is to France. It is especially noted for its charcuterie and its endless range of *pasta asciutte* (pasta with butter). Tuscany is the orchard and vegetable garden of Italy and is famous for its red meat. Other regions must not be forgotten: the Marches, with their game (wood pigeon with lentils) and olives; Latium, offering fried fish and stewed tripe; Campania, home of macaroni in tomato sauce; Apulia, where the figs and melons come from; Calabria, producing both aubergines (eggplants) and tuna; Sicily, land of citrus fruits and fish cooked *en papillote* with aromatic herbs; and Sardinia, renowned for its honey, wild boar ham, and its thrushes.

□ **Rice and pasta** Those who enjoy rice and pasta will find that the Italians have developed the preparation of dishes based on these simple foods to a fine art. Herbs are used extensively, especially basil, thyme, sage, oregano, rosemary, and parsley. These herbs flavour the hearty minestrone soup from Lombardy, as well as delicate chicken consommés with vermicelli. Rice will absorb any flavour. It may be cooked in a savoury stock, flavoured with saffron, prepared *à la milanaise* or *à la piémontaise* (with chicken and white truffles), used as a stuffing for tomatoes or peppers, flavoured with garlic and basil, used as a garnish for fish and seafood, and mixed with sautéed mushrooms or garden peas, as in the famous *risi e pisi* of Venice. Italian pasta has a worldwide reputation. In Italy it is served as a first course, sometimes mixed with butter and Parmesan cheese or covered with a thick tomato sauce, a meat sauce (*à la bolognaise*), a *carbonara* sauce (made with ham, eggs, fresh cream, pepper, and grated cheese), or any of a variety of other sauces. Pasta can be the basis of some delicately flavoured dishes, such as the Neapolitan spaghetti *alle vongole*, which is cooked in a fish fumet with clams, tomatoes, and garlic. *Pesto* is a Genoese sauce made with basil, parsley, and marjoram pounded with oil, Parmesan cheese, and garlic; it is eaten with spaghetti or tagliatelle. Everyone is familiar with cannelloni, ravioli, and tortellini, but there are also *capelletti* from Emilia (cone-shaped pasta stuffed with minced chicken, cheese, and eggs), *pansotti* from Rapallo (filled with spinach and served with a walnut sauce), macaroni *à la sicilienne* (braised with meat balls, Mozzarella cheese, and fried aubergines), and finally, pasta *con le sarde*, a gratin of macaroni in sardine sauce with fennel and raisins, topped with fresh sardines.

□ **Meat and fish** Italian cookery does justice to its meat. As with pasta, there are many regional variations and they do not begin and end with osso bucco. The Lombards, who are hearty eaters, and very fond of *bollito misto* (mixed boiled meats seasoned with sweet-and-sour sauce and vinegar) and *busecca* (a thick soup made from veal tripe, haricot beans, and green vegetables). The Tuscans and Italians from Campania prefer roast baby lamb or a stew of kid, while Florentines remain faithful to *bistecca* (grilled entrecôte steak). Dishes described as *alla pizzaiola* are found all over Italy. They consist of beef or veal sautéed in very hot oil and then simmered with tomatoes, garlic, and herbs. There is an amazing variety of recipes for veal: saltimbocca from Rome, *involtini* (thin slices of stuffed rolled veal with ham) from Milan, *picatta* (thin slices of meat with a lemon or Marsala sauce), loin of veal cooked *en papillote* with small artichokes, the celebrated *vitello tonnato* from Naples (veal in a tuna and anchovy sauce garnished with capers), veal with olives from Leghorn, and from Sicily *messicani* (very thin stuffed escalopes, threaded on skewers, sautéed in butter, and deglazed with white wine and Marsala) and *farsumagru* (a terrine of veal with sausages and hard-boiled (hard-cooked) eggs, simmered with Mozzarella and tomatoes). There are fewer recipes for cooking poultry, but two worth mentioning are chicken breasts *à la Valdostana* (covered with white truffles and Mozzarella cheese, sautéed, and deglazed with white wine) and fried chicken *à la toscane* (small birds threaded on skewers and served on a bed of polenta).

Fish is prepared in a variety of ways. Examples of dishes made with fresh water fish are salmon trout from the lakes, cooked in a court-bouillon and served with a very fruity olive oil and lemon sauce, and lampreys braised with bacon and covered with a tomato and garlic sauce. However, sea fish predominate. They are cooked quite simply as they are, *en papillote*, *à la sicilienne* (stuffed with almonds and raisins), grilled, or fried. The fish soups are less highly flavoured than those found in Provence.

□ **Vegetables and desserts** There is an abundance of vegetables and they are used in a wide variety of ways: chopped spinach with vinaigrette, marinated courgettes (zucchini), stuffed peppers, and artichokes. Some less well-known recipes are worthy of note: cardoons *à la piémontaise* (mixed with a hot sauce made with oil, butter, and garlic); *fagioli* (white haricot beans) with herbs, served warm in vinaigrette; asparagus served with fried eggs; and broad beans mixed with bacon, onion, and bay leaf and simmered with a chiffonade of lettuce. *Capon magro* consists of slices of bread rubbed with garlic and covered with layers of cooked vegetables, the whole being covered with boiled fish and a thick mayonnaise containing a mixture of chopped herbs. It is served with olives, prawns, hard-boiled eggs, and anchovy fillets.

An Italian meal will often end either with cheese (Gorgonzola, Provolone, Bel Paese, or perhaps Mozzarella with herbs) or fruit followed by very strong espresso coffee. However, there are also many kinds of desserts and cakes including the Milanese panettone, Venetian *bacioli* (delicately flavoured lemon biscuits), Genoese marzipan, Florentine zabaglione, Sicilian *amaretti* (almond macaroons), cassata, *torta di ricotta*, and *zuppa inglese* (trifle), not to mention all the magnificent fresh fruit.

ivoire

A variety of suprême sauce enriched with white meat glaze or reduced veal stock, used especially for poached chicken. It is used thick for a chaud-froid sauce.

RECIPES

Chicken à l'ivoire POULARDE À L'IVOIRE Poach a chicken in white stock; prepare ½ litre (17fl oz, 2 cups) ivoire sauce (see recipe below). Make 24 small chicken quenelles. Clean and trim 24 button mushrooms, sprinkle with lemon juice, and place in a sauté pan with a little butter. Just cover with chicken consommé and cook for about 10 minutes.

Drain the chicken and arrange on a serving dish, surrounded by the mushrooms and quenelles. Coat with ivoire sauce; serve the remaining sauce in a sauceboat.

Ivoire sauce Add 2 tablespoons (3 tablespoons) reduced veal stock or meat glaze to 2 dl (7 fl oz, ¾ cup) suprême sauce.

izard ISARD

A variety of the chamois found in the Pyrenees. Tender and full of flavour, the meat (particularly the haunch and the fillets) is much sought-after, being either roasted or stewed. As the animal is in danger of becoming extinct it is now a protected species. Therefore mutton, from sheep slaughtered the day after they return from pasture, is marinated to produce a similar taste.

jackfruit JAQUE

The fruit of a tropical tree which originated in India. Oval in shape and studded with small protuberances, a jackfruit can weigh up to 30 kg (67 lb). The skin is bluish, pale green, yellow, or brown; the flesh is white or yellowish, full of large seeds. Blanched and then peeled, it is eaten in stews or baked in the oven as a vegetable. The seeds are cooked in the same way as chestnuts, either roasted or in a purée.

Jacob's bâton

BÂTON DE JACOB

A small stick-shaped éclair filled with confectioners' custard (pastry cream) and iced (frosted) with fondant icing.

jailles

A stew from the Alps, consisting of pieces of pork chine cooked with aromatic herbs and seasonings; halfway through cooking, quartered dessert apples and breadcrumbs are added, and when the stew is cooked, a trickle of vinegar is poured over the dish.

jalousie

A small rectangular pastry consisting of a strip of puff pastry spread with vanilla-flavoured marzipan (almond paste) and topped with a slatted pastry lid resembling a Venetian blind (*jalousie* in French). Apple compote, apricot jam, or a fruit preserve can be used instead of the marzipan. The jalousie can also be made in the form of one large pastry.

RECIPE

Jalousies with apricot jam JAL-OUSIES À L'ABRICOT Roll out 500 g (18 oz) puff pastry into a rectangle about 3 mm (⅛ in) thick and cut it into 2 equal strips about 10 cm (4 in) wide. Brush all round the edges of one of the strips with beaten egg and spread 500 g (18 oz, 1½ cups) apricot jam in the centre. Fold the second piece of pastry in half lengthwise, and with a knife make slanting cuts from the folded side to within 1 cm (½ in) of the other edge. Unfold the strip and place it over the first one. Press the edges firmly together to seal them, trimming if necessary to a neat rectangle, then make decorative indentations with the point of a knife. Brush the top with beaten egg, put in a preheated oven at 200 c (400 f, gas 6), and cook for 25–30 minutes. When it is cooked, brush the top lightly with apricot jam which has been mixed with double its volume of water and boiled to reduce it slightly; finally, sprinkle the top with caster (superfine) sugar.

Cut the strip into 4 cm (2 in) slices and serve warm or cold.

jambalaya

A speciality of New Orleans, inspired by Spanish paella and made of highly spiced rice, chicken, and ham. Various ingredients can be added; for example, sausage, peppers, tomatoes, prawns, or oysters.

RECIPE

Chicken jambalaya JAMBALAYA DE POULET Poach a chicken in stock, then drain. When it is quite cold, remove the skin and bones, weigh the meat, and dice it finely. Sauté half this weight of raw diced ham in 50 g (2 oz, 4 tablespoons) butter over a low heat, with the pan covered. While it is cooking, prepare some rice *à la grecque* using 300–400 g (12–14 oz, 2 cups) uncooked rice and the stock from the chicken. When the ham is cooked, add the diced chicken together with some cayenne, salt, and pepper so that the mixture is highly seasoned. Finally, add the rice, mix everything together thoroughly, and serve very hot.

jambe de bois

The French term for shin or knuckle of beef (beef shank) left on the bone, when used as an ingredient of a pot-au-feu. In former times, the preparation of *potage à la jambe de bois* was a major undertaking; according to a receipe from 1855 it required a chicken, a brace of partridges, 2 lb boned fillet of veal, and a variety of vegetables. The dish came originally from Lyon.

jambonneau

The French name for the knuckle end of a ham or pork leg. It is eaten fresh, semi-salted, or smoked. Braised or poached like ham, but for a longer time, it is served with sauerkraut and used in thick soups. It can be bought ready cooked and skinned.

The name *jambonneau* is also given to a preparation of stuffed leg of chicken, because of its similar shape.

RECIPE

Chicken jambonneaux JAMBONNEAUX DE VOLAILLE Bone some plump uncooked chicken thighs, making only one cut so as to keep them as intact as possible. Spread 1 tablespoon forcemeat onto the cut surface of each thigh (use the chicken forcemeat for pâtés and terrines, or for poached, braised, or roast chicken, or a mushroom forcemeat). Reshape the thighs round the stuffing so that they look like small ham knuckles and tie them in this shape. Braise as in the recipe for braised ham *à la crème*.

jambonnette

Cooked charcuterie made from pork shoulder (50–60%) and bacon (40–50%), chopped, seasoned, and enclosed in rind to make a pear shape. A jambonnette can be decorated and glazed in the same way as a galantine.

jambonnière

A deep-sided cooking utensil with a handle at each end and a lid, having the same shape as a ham. Used for cooking a whole leg or shoulder of pork, this pan was formerly made of beaten copper but modern ones are of aluminium.

jam pot CONFITURIER

A small container made of glass, porcelain, or stainless steel, the lid of which has a small opening for a spoon and is sometimes made of wood. It is used to serve jam or marmalade at breakfast or tea time.

The French word *confiturier* is also used for a small cupboard with a single door used to store jars of jam.

jams, jellies, and marmalades CONFITURE

Preparations of fruit cooked in a sugar syrup.

The art of jam making began in the Middle East. It was introduced into Europe by the Crusaders, who had discovered cane sugar and certain previously unknown fruits.

□ **The choice of fruits** Certain regions and towns in France have made a speciality of a particular jam; for example, redcurrant jam from Bar-le-Duc, bilberry (blueberry) jam from Alsace, and green tomato jam from Provence. In Britain many types of fruit are grown for jam in the Vale of Evesham, Kent, and Essex. Speciality jams, such as mulberry, quince, and medlar, are grown and made in the Tiptree area.

To make good jam, the fruit should be sound and not overripe. Pears, peaches, apricots, strawberries, and raspberries should be slightly underripe, while plums and cherries should be just ripe but still full-flavoured. The flavour of jams can be enhanced by spices (vanilla and cinnamon), a little alcohol (rum, Kirsch), caramel (for apples), or another fruit of more robust flavour (peaches, respberries, cherries, redcurrants, mixed citrus fruits, rhubarb, and strawberries). The colour may be deepened by adding blackberries or raspberries to peaches and melon. Some less common fruits, such as watermelon, tomatoes, or fresh walnuts, as well as exotic fruits, like mango, guava, and coconut, can also be used. Small wild fruits, such as haws, elderberries, blackberries, bilberries, rosehips, etc., can also be used successfully. At one time flowers (such as violets, roses, and pumpkin flowers) and many spices (especially ginger) were used. Lastly, there is milk jam, which does not contain fruit. Widely eaten in South America, where it is known as *dulce de leche* ('milk sweet'), it is made by slowly reducing sweetened vanilla- or cinnamon-flavoured milk.

□ **Utensils**
• stoner (pitter), rustproof peeling knife, nutcracker.
• stoneware pot for storing fruit.
• scales.
• preserving pan made of copper (not tin-plated because of the risk of oxidation and the tin linings would melt at the temperature of boiling jam) or of thick stainless steel, brass, or aluminium, or, failing these, a pressure cooker without its lid or a large thick-bottomed saucepan. Whichever is used, the vessel should be thick enough to prevent the jam from burning and its volume should be twice that of the fruit to be cooked in it when boiling rapidly (to prevent overflowing and to facilitate evaporation). It should be thoroughly cleaned before use.

• skimming ladle of copper, aluminium, or stainless steel.
• hydrometer or sugar thermometer.
• spatula or long-handled wooden spoon.
• ladle with an insulated handle.
• jam jars (not too large as the contents can deteriorate before they have been used up).
• waxed paper, paraffin, or cellophane, labels, and elastic bands.

□ **Jam-making seasons**
• December to March: oranges, grapefruit.
• May: rhubarb.
• June: strawberries.
• July: strawberries, raspberries, cherries, redcurrants.
• August: redcurrants, blackcurrants, apricots.
• September: peaches, blackberries, tomatoes, black and gold plums, bilberries, raspberries, etc.
• October: pears, figs, apples, grapes.
• November: quince, oranges, apples, chestnuts, pumpkins.

□ **The sugar** This is the essential element in jam making. As a rule, use equal weights of refined sugar (preserving sugar and lump sugar (cubes) are more expensive than granulated sugar) and fruit (when washed, dried, peeled, and stoned (pitted). The weight of sugar may be increased slightly for more watery fruit and decreased slightly for pectin-rich fruit (a setting agent always tends to thicken the jam). If the proportion of sugar is insufficient or the jam is not sufficiently cooked, the jam may ferment and will not keep. If there is too much sugar, the jam is too concentrated and tends to crystallize. Part of the sugar can be replaced by honey, especially in redcurrant and raspberry jam. Also available is a white coarse sugar with added pectin, specially prepared for making jams and preserves.

□ **Cooking** Below a certain temperature, which varies according to the fruit (strawberries and raspberries, for example, are 'seized' by the syrup rather than actually cooked), the jam will remain too liquid. Above this temperature it may burn. It is therefore necessary to keep to the temperature indicated in the recipe. There are two stages of cooking:
• *first stage:* the evaporation of the

water contained in the fruit. Thick steam will escape from the jam pan. At the end of this stage the jam should be skimmed to ensure its clarity. The fruit should be covered when the sugar has boiled and the jam is skimmed.

● *second stage:* cooking the fruit. The steam lessens and the bubbles merge together. A sugar thermometer or a hydrometer may be used instead of the traditional test of putting a small amount of jam on a cold saucer to test its consistency.

Most jams are cooked when they coat the back of a wooden spoon. When the skimmer is put into and taken out of the jam, the jam runs together and sets (density 1.2964 and temperature 103 c (217 f); for certain fruits a density of about 1.25 (102 c, 213 f) is sufficient. The fruits will retain their flavour if they are cooked quickly over a high heat (to accelerate evaporation) but should be stirred from time to time, especially if the jam is thick; use a heat diffuser if there is a danger of overheating.

□ **To remedy failures in jam making**
● *Mouldy jam:* remove and discard every trace of mould from the jam, together with the underlying jam to a depth of 1 cm (½ in); use the remaining jam straight away. Remember to store the jam in a cool dry place and check occasionally.
● *Fermented jam:* jam ferments if insufficiently cooked, or if too little sugar has been added, or if poor-quality fruit has been used.
● *Crystallized jam:* reheat and add lemon juice or a little citric acid and water. Pay special attention to the temperature and density.
● *Unset jam:* this is due either to underboiling, to a lack of pectin, or to the use of too much sugar.

□ **Bottling**
● Carefully wash and boil the jars. Stand them upside down on a clean tea towel and leave to drain without wiping them. Pour the jam into the hot sterilized jars.
● Allow jams like strawberry and cherry to cool slightly before filling the jar to prevent the fruit from rising to the top. Ladle the jam into the jars in small quantities while still boiling, leaving as little space as possible between the top of the jar and the jam. If the jam should

spill over, clean the rim of the jar carefully.
● Some jam makers prefer to cover the jam before it cools so that a hard skin cannot form (if this happens, stir the contents with a small boiled wooden spoon). Others prefer to let the jam cool completely, allowing the steam to escape rather than condensing and encouraging the formation of mildew. Jellies must always be allowed to set before covering, but with jams and marmalades experience is the best guide.
● There are three methods of covering the jars:
— for hot or cold jam: cover the jar with a piece of moistened cellophane pulled tightly across the opening and held in place by an elastic band.
— for cold jam: pour over the surface of the jam a very thin layer of paraffin wax that has been melted in a bain-marie. Turn the jar so the wax covers the complete surface and sides giving an airtight seal. This is the commonest and most successful method.
— Place a circle of paper soaked in alcohol (brandy or rum can be used) or waxed paper on top of the jam. A second paper is placed over the top of the jar or, better still, it can be left without the second paper in a cool dry well-ventilated place protected from the light (the second paper may trap some moisture, risking mildew formation). This is the oldest method.
● When labelling the jars it is important to indicate the type of fruit or fruit mixture and the date the jam was made.

□ **Jellies** Only fruits rich in pectin are suitable for making jellies (redcurrants, whitecurrants, mulberries, quinces, bilberries, apples, etc.). Alternatively, one of these fruits can be combined with a strong-flavoured fruit that is low in pectin (such as raspberries or blackcurrants). The acidity of the fruit and the sugar concentration are also important. To extract the juice, first the berries are burst by cooking them with a little water until the skins break. In the case of citrus fruits, apples, and quinces, the prepared fruit is presoaked with the cores and seeds collected in a knotted piece of muslin (cheesecloth) and then cooked in little water. The resultant liquid is then put through a very fine strainer Sugar, equal to the weight of the juice obtained, is added to the juice. The boiling time varies according to the fruit (3–4 minutes for red- or whitecurrants to 20–30 minutes for apples and quinces). To test whether or not the jelly has begun to set, a few drops are poured onto a cold plate. If it solidifies in a few minutes, the jelly is ready for potting.

□ **Uses** Jams, jellies, and marmalades are eaten with bread or toast (or brioches) for breakfast and tea. They are also used to accompany desserts (rice pudding, bread pudding, poached fruits, iced desserts, pancakes, waffles, etc.) and to fill or cover cakes, to flavour yogurt and soft cream cheese (e.g. fromage frais), and to make sauces for desserts. Jams also accompany meat: red fruits with game, orange with duck or pork, for example.

RECIPES

Apple jelly GELÉE DE POMME Take 3 kg (6½ lb) slightly acid apples (e.g. Granny Smiths). Wash and quarter them without peeling or coring. Place the quarters in a saucepan containing 3 litres (5¼ pints, 6½ pints) water. Boil gently for about 50 minutes. Then pour the contents of the pan into a strainer and let the juice run through without pressing the fruit. Pour the juice back into the pan and add 3 kg (6½ lb, 13 cups) granulated sugar. Add the juice of 6 lemons, bring to the boil, and cook for about 1¾ hours until the syrup coats the spoon. Jar.

Apricot jam CONFITURE D'ABRI-COTS For 1 kg (2¼ lb) ripe stoned (pitted) apricots, use 1 kg (2¼ lb) sugar (granulated or lump) and 1 dl (6 tablespoons, scant ½ cup) water. Dissolve the sugar in the water in a pan, bring to the boil for 5 minutes, and then skim. Add the apricots and cook until the setting stage is reached (approximately 30 minutes). A few half-kernels from the apricot stones may be added to the jam when it has finished cooking. Pour into sterilized jars.

Greengage (plum) jam CONFITURE DE REINES-CLAUDES For 1 kg (2¼ lb) ripe stoned (pitted) greengages, allow 750 g (1½ lb, 3 cups) granulated sugar and 1 dl (6 tablespoons, scant ½ cup) water. Dissolve the sugar in the water in a pan, bring to the boil for 5 minutes, and then skim. Add the greengages and cook until the setting stage is reached (about 104 C, 220 F). Pour into sterilized jars.

Japan JAPON

To Western palates, Japanese cooking seems frugal but refined. Although there are few basic ingredients, they are set out with great delicacy and elegance.

□ **Heritage of the past** The pantheistic worship of nature and her bounty – especially seafood, rice, soya, and vegetables – is reflected in Japanese cookery by the term *sappari* (i.e. clarity, lightness, simplicity, and order). Japanese gastronomy relies as much on the intrinsic flavour of ingredients, often subtly combined, as on the presentation of the food and the tablesetting. However, some important Western influences have filtered through, notably the technique of frying (*tempura*), introduced by Portuguese Jesuits in the 17th century, and the marked increase in meat consumption (especially chicken and pork), which was formerly condemned by Buddhist precepts. Sukiyaki, now the Japanese national dish, was formerly prepared in secret by the peasants.

□ **Food and the seasons** One of the basic principles of Japanese cookery is that every product should be served at the right season.

Spring is celebrated with the 'nightingale cake', made from pounded sticky rice stuffed with a paste of sweetened haricot (navy) beans. April is the time for raw squid; in May the Japanese drink *shincha*, the new season's tea (traditionally green but mellow and perfumed), and eat *ayu*, a small freshwater fish with delicate flesh, grilled (broiled) with salt and garnished with green vegetables. Also during spring the Japanese hold a 'children's feast', formerly for boys only; the dishes offered are intended to symbolize virility and courage: scampi presented with their claws erect to look like a samurai warrior's helmet, and rice cakes wrapped in leaves from the oak tree, symbol of vigorous growth.

Summer is the time for eel, grilled over charcoal and served with soy sauce; for soya (soy) bean paste, garnished with dried bonito, spring onions (scallions), and ginger; and for glazed buckwheat noodles. August is the hot season, when the food is particularly light and refreshing: fried chicken, cucumbers stuffed with prune paste, trout cooked in stock, and sea urchins.

Autumn is the season for mushrooms, especially the *matsutake*, which has a delicious flavour of grilled meat: these mushrooms are marinated in soy sauce and *sake*, then roasted or steamed with chicken, fish, and nuts from the ginkgo (or maidenhair) tree. This is also the season of the *kaki* (or Japanese persimmon) and chestnuts, excellent with sweetened rice. September is the month of the moon, and the food is often symbolic: slices of abalone cooked with steamed cucumbers, boiled bamboo shoots, and rolled eel with hard-boiled (hard-cooked) eggs.

In winter the food is more substantial, with such dishes as terrine of octopus with *daikon* (a large white radish) or dried mushroom soup. November heralds some particularly savoury dishes made with rice, the cornerstone of Japanese cookery and the symbol of good fortune. Its Japanese name is *gohan*, which means cooked rice (usually steamed) and, by extension, a meal. Winter is also the season for white fish, served raw, grilled, or fried, in stews and in soups. Noodle soups containing meat and vegetables are eaten all the year round, but are particularly fortifying against the rigours of winter. The mandarin orange (tangerine), a delicious symbol of the sun, is offered as a traditional New Year's Day gift.

☐ **Basic ingredients of Japanese cooking** The basic ingredients are combined in a great variety of ways. At the head of the list are the soya bean (used in miso, tofu, and sauces) and rice, which can be either savoury or sweet. The other most commonly used ingredients are rice wine, either weak and sweetened for use in cooking (*mirin*) or strong (*sake*); rice vinegar; sesame oil; green horseradish (*wasabi*); daikon, which is either cut up or grated; dried marrow (squash), burdock; *shirataki* (noodles made from the dried tubers of devil's tongue plant, a subspecies of the sweet potato); bamboo shoots; and lotus roots. The

Japanese are fond of the taste of marinades, and there is a whole range of pickles (including prune, radish, ginger, and sea urchin). A great variety of noodles and vermicelli of all sizes are made from wheat, buckwheat, or rice flour. Finally there is seafood, which includes the dried, powdered, and compressed seaweeds added to sauces, soups, and garnishes (such as *nori*, *konbu*, and *wakame*). Dried bonito fish (*katsuobushi*) is used in a variety of ways. Ginger, pepper, pimientos, mustard, glutamate, and all the spices and fresh herbs (including parsley and chives) are indispensable.

The preparation of food follows a characteristic pattern. Fish can be salted and grilled, or boiled in a strongly flavoured sauce, but it is often finely sliced and eaten raw (see *sashimi*). Chicken is grilled with salt or left in a sweet-and-sour marinade, then fried and sprinkled with the marinade. Cooking times are always very precise, particularly for eggs. Beef is usually finely sliced, grilled, then rapidly immersed in a vegetable soup. Two typically Japanese culinary processes can be applied to many dishes; *nabemono* (food cooked at table, on a grill (broiler) or in a fondue pan) and *nimono* (food cooked in aromatic stock). Steaming is another common method, the food then being accompanied by sauces and various seasonings. Beef, pork, and seafood may be cooked in coarse salt in a casserole. Fried marinated chicken, pork (either sliced and coated with breadcrumbs or threaded on skewers), and oysters coated with breadcrumbs are all highly esteemed. Frying is in fact the pride of Japanese cooking. More than one oil may be used, in carefully measured proportions, especially for prawn fritters, fish, scallops, peppers, mushrooms, aubergines (eggplants), etc., which are served separately with a galaxy of sauces. Finally, the Japanese excel in the art of presenting food decoratively, cut into rounds, squares, petals, filaments, small tongues, roses, and other complicated shapes; this is skilled work, requiring special tools and great dexterity on the part of the cook.

☐ **Riches from the sea** Japan is one of the world's greatest consumers of seafood. Japanese coastal waters support a great variety of fish, many edible sea-weeds, cetaceans (e.g. whales), and shellfish (including abalone, oysters, clams, crabs, lobsters, and prawns). All these are present in huge numbers and are of exceptionally high quality. Tuna, bonito, gilthead bream, and cuttlefish are the current favourites, the most popular dishes being bite-sized slices of raw fish (*sashimi*) served with soy sauce sharpened with mustard and horse-radish; *nigiri zushi*, small balls of *sushi* (rice flavoured with vinegar) topped with a small slice of seafood; and *maki zushi*, raw seafood rolled up in vinegar-flavoured rice and crisp seaweed. A famous speciality is blowfish, *fugu* (or *diodon*), a fish whose organs contain a highly poisonous substance but whose flesh is much prized; it is served only in selected restaurants where the chef has a special licence guaranteeing the safety of the diners. Fried fish is eaten a great deal and, like other fried dishes, is accompanied by soy sauce with grated daikon and a pinch of ginger, or simply with salt and lemon.

□ **Eating at home** The Japanese breakfast normally consists of a bowl of rice and dried seaweed, a miso-based soup, or eggs. Lunch, which is relatively light and is always eaten in a great hurry, may be rice with eggs and meat (pork chops or minced (ground) steak) or noodles, either cold or in a soup. Dinner, on the other hand, is a more extensive and sophisticated meal. Tra-ditionally it consists of at least four different dishes combining liquid, crisp, and simmered foods, some spicy and others bland: the alternation of consist-encies and tastes is one of the golden rules of Japanese cuisine. Colour, tex-ture, and shape are as important as the taste. Tea and beer are the most com-mon accompaniments to the meal.

The Western sweet dessert has re-cently become popular in Japan; tra-ditionally, however, sweets and cakes are reserved for feast days or enjoyed between meals, as is fresh fruit. Sym-bolic dishes are served on feast days and important occasions, such as clam soup at a Shinto marriage ceremony (the two halves of the shell symbolizing union); red rice (sticky rice cooked with *azuki*, small dried red beans, also known as aduki beans) is a symbol of happiness.

The most typical food for the New Year feast is *mochi*: pounded sticky rice, formed into pancakes and simmered with vegetables (for savoury dishes) or with red beans and sugar (for dessert). In addition, there may be fish loaf, oranges, chrysanthemum leaves, chest-nuts, carp, and good-luck ferns. The culinary art and Japanese tradition reach their apogee in the tea ceremony and attendant *kaiseki*, a formal meal consisting of several courses, served in a symbolic tea house, representing a time-honoured ritual symbolizing great har-mony.

Japanese quince
COING DU JAPON

The fruit of an ornamental Japanese tree or shrub with clusters of red flowers. The Japanese quince is a juicy greenish oval fruit, which tastes rather like a lemon. The fruit is very hard and ripens in the autumn. It is not sold commer-cially and is only edible when cooked. Japanese quinces are usually mixed with apples to make a jelly, using three parts by weight of quinces to one part of apples.

japonaise (à la)

In classic French cuisine, this name is given to various dishes containing Chinese artichokes (called Japanese artichokes in French). It applies particu-larly to large cuts of roast meat gar-nished with Chinese artichokes (braised in butter or cooked with the meat juices and demi-glace), or to a filled omelette. Francillon salad is known as Japanese salad when Chinese artichokes replace the potatoes, but there is another Japanese salad, served as an hors d'oeuvre, which combines diced tom-ato, pineapple, and orange on lettuce leaves, covered with fresh cream to which lemon juice has been added, and sprinkled with sugar. Finally, there is a bombe glacée called *japonaise*, consist-ing of peach ice cream filled with tea mousse.

RECIPE

Filled omelette à la japonaise OMELETTE FOURRÉE À LA JAPO-NAISE Clean 300 g (11 oz) Chinese artichokes and blanch for 3 minutes in boiling water; drain, rinse, and wipe dry. Braise over a low heat in a covered pan without browning; add salt, pepper, and a little cream sauce. Make an omelette with 8 eggs and fill it with the artichoke mixture. Fold the omelette and slide it onto the serving dish; sprinkle with chopped parsley. The rest of the cream sauce is served separately in a sauceboat.

jar JARRE

Any of various wide-mouthed containers, usually lacking handles. Glass jars are widely used for storing jams, preserves, etc. Large stoneware jars are used chiefly for storing oil or for salting meat or fish by traditional methods. The word is derived from the Arab word *djarra*, meaning 'earthenware vessel'.

jardinière

A mixture of vegetables, essentially carrots, turnips, and French beans, served as a garnish for roast or sautéed meat, casseroled poultry, braised calves' sweetbreads, etc. Carrots and turnips are cut into chunks 3–4 cm (1½ in) long, trimmed to a regular shape, cut into slices 3–4 mm (¼ in) thick, then cut again into matchsticks 3–4 mm (¼ in) wide; the French beans are cut into chunks, sometimes diamond-shaped, 3–4 cm (1½ in) long. The vegetables are cooked separately, then mixed with garden peas and bound together with butter. The jardinière often also includes flageolet beans and small sprigs of cauliflower. Meat juices or some clear veal stock can be added. A jardinière can also consist of a simple macédoine of vegetables.

RECIPE

Flat omelette à la jardinière OMELETTE PLATE À LA JARDINIÈRE Prepare a standard jardinière, cooking the ingredients in water or in consommé and making sure that they retain their crispness. Add some cooked garden peas and tiny sprigs of cauliflower cooked in the same way. Brown gently in melted butter in a large pan, adding salt and pepper. Beat some eggs as for an omelette, adding a pinch of salt and pepper, and pour over the vegetables;

cook like a thick pancake. Garnish with steamed asparagus tips and coat with cream sauce.

jasmine JASMIN

A sweetly scented flower used mostly in the perfume industry. In the Far East, sambac jasmine is used to perfume tea, while Chinese jasmine is used in pastry-making and cooking.

RECIPE

Red mullet with jasmine ROUGETS AU JASMIN (from a recipe by René Lasserre) Gut, trim, and clean the mullet. Remove the backbone. Stuff the fish with a mousse made of whiting flesh bound with cream and flavoured with essence (extract) of jasmine. Wrap each fish in buttered paper and cook in a moderate oven for 25 minutes. Take the fish out of their wrappings and arrange them on a hot dish. Cover with a tomato-flavoured white wine sauce.

Jasnières

An AOC dry white wine from the Coteaux de Loir in Touraine. It is made from the Chenin Blanc grape.

jelly (dessert)
GELÉE D'ENTREMETS

A cold dessert made of fruit juice, wine, or liqueur to which sugar and gelatine are added (see *kissel, rodgrod*). Jellies from fresh and dried vegetables or cereals, formerly highly prized as savouries, are now only used as food for invalids.

Dessert jellies are made with a clarified base of gelatine or with calf's-foot jelly. These jelly bases are flavoured with a liqueur, a dessert wine, or a fruit juice.
• For *liqueur jellies*, the liqueur is added to the clarified base in the proportion of one part liqueur to nine parts jelly base.
• For *wine jellies* (champagne, Frontignan, Madeira, Marsala, port, sherry, etc.), the wine is added in the proportion of three parts to seven parts jelly base.
• For *red fruit jellies* (cherries, strawberries, raspberries, redcurrants, etc., the fruit, which must be very ripe, is rubbed through a fine sieve. Between 1 dl (6 tablespoons, scant ½ cup) and 3 dl

(½ pint, 1¼ cups) water is added to its juice for every ½ litre (17 fl oz, 2 cups) fruit juice, according to the pectin content of the fruit. The juice is filtered, then added in two stages to the previously prepared and highly clarified jelly base, in order to obtain the right consistency.

• For *jellies made from juicy fruits* (lemons, oranges, tangerines, pineapples, grapes, etc.), the filtered fruit juice is added to the jelly base.

• *Stone fruits* (apricots, nectarines, peaches, plums, etc.) are used mainly for making jelly preserves (see *jams, jellies, and marmalades*). However, jelly bases can be made with these fruits as follows: dip the fruits in boiling water and skin them. Cook slowly in syrup and leave in this syrup until cold. Make the jelly from the syrup and clarify it.

Fruit jelly bases are often flavoured with Kirsch, Maraschino, or some other liqueur.

jelly (preserve)
GELÉE DE FRUIT
See *jams, jellies, and marmalades*.

Jerusalem artichoke
TOPINAMBOUR
A perennial plant cultivated for its edible tubers, which are cooked and eaten as a vegetable or used in distilling. The French name is the name of a small tribe in Brazil, but in fact the vegetable originated in North America and was introduced into France by Champlain. Called *pommes de terre* by Nicholas de Bonnefons and *poires de terre* by Lemery, 'because they are born in the earth, attached to the branches of the root which bears them', the tubers are knobbly and quite difficult to peel.

Fairly firm in consistency, they have a taste similar to that of real artichokes. On sale in winter and spring, very nourishing and rich in phosphorus and potassium, they are boiled, steamed, or braised with butter and can be served with cream or béchamel sauce, sprinkled with parsley, or used in salads, fried in batter, puréed, or souffléed.

| RECIPES

Jerusalem artichokes à l'anglaise
TOPINAMBOURS À L'ANGLAISE Peel

some Jerusalem artichokes, cut into quarters, and trim to egg shapes if they are large. Blanch for 5 minutes in boiling water, then dry them. Cook gently in butter in a covered pan for about 30 minutes. Stir in a few tablespoons light béchamel sauce or double (heavy) cream and simmer for about 10 minutes. Serve as a garnish for veal, for example, sprinkled with chopped chervil and tarragon.

Salad of Jerusalem artichokes
SALADE DE TOPINAMBOURS Prepare like a potato salad, using small new Jerusalem artichokes, cooked in water for 20 minutes, peeled, and cut into uniform pieces. Dress with a sunfloweroil vinaigrette seasoned with shallot and sprinkle with plenty of parsley.

Jessica
A garnish for poultry suprêmes, veal escalopes or grenadins (small slices of fillet of veal interlarded with best larding bacon), and soft-boiled (softcooked) or poached eggs. It consists of small artichokes braised in butter and filled with a salpicon of bone marrow with shallots, and morels sautéed in butter, both arranged on tartlets made from Anna potatoes; these are accompanied by an allemande sauce enriched with thickened veal stock and flavoured with truffle essence (extract). An omelette Jessica is filled with sliced morels and asparagus tips bound with cream, then folded and surrounded with a ribbon of chateaubriand sauce.

jésuite
A small triangular puff pastry filled with marzipan (almond paste) and covered with royal icing (frosting). Formerly, these pastries were covered with a darkcoloured praline or chocolate icing shaped like the hat with a rolled brim worn by the Jesuits.

jésus
A large sausage made in Franche-Comté (especially at Morteau) and in Switzerland, consisting of coarsely chopped pork (or sometimes pork and beef) encased in the widest part of the gut. It has a small wooden hook inserted in the end so that it can be hung up to be lightly smoked. A *morteau* (or *saucisson de*

Morteau) is one that is made in the same way in Alsace and the Jura. Both these sausages can be poached and used to garnish thick soups, but they are also used in particular regional recipes.

RECIPE

Jésus à la vigneronne (from a recipe by André Jeunet) Make a court-bouillon with 2 litres (3½ pints, 4½ pints) Arbois wine, 2 litres (3½ pints, 4½ pints) water, 2 peeled onions each studded with 2 cloves, a bouquet garni, salt, and pepper. Simmer for 1 hour. Place a handful of vine shoots in the pan. Prick 1 or 2 jésus with a fork and rest them on the vine shoots so they are just above the surface of the liquid; leave them to cook in the steam from the court-bouillon. Serve with fresh butter and baked potatoes.

Red wine can be used instead of the Arbois, and red or white haricot beans (navy beans), according to the colour of the wine, can be substituted for the potatoes.

Jewish cookery
CUISINE JUIVE

Jewish cookery is closely linked to religious feast days and the Sabbath, but it incorporates culinary specialities from all the countries of the Diaspora. It is a family-based art, with a unity derived from ancient traditions. The rules imposed by the *kashruth* do not in any way limit the variety of dishes; they merely ensure that food is completely fresh: meat (only beef and mutton) is carefully washed, then salted and seared to remove any blood (see *kosher*). Tradition plays a great part: for example, the fish prepared on Friday for Saturday's meal is eaten fried by eastern Jews and stuffed by European Jews; eggs, symbols of totality and death, are part of many feast-day dishes; honey is a reminder of the Promised Land. Plaited bread (*hallah*) is a reminder of the sacrificial bread. Even the shape of some foods can relate to a biblical character, like the 'ears of Haman', a cake served at the feast of Purim. Fasts (at least three of 24 hours' duration during the year) are the excuse for some splendid feasts before

and after: although Jewish religious precepts forbid greed and drunkenness, they do not condemn good eating.

The cooking of the Sephardic Jews (from Mediterranean countries) and of the Ashkenazi Jews (from central Europe) is derived from a common source. For example, the *tchoulend* of the latter and the *tfina* of the former (meat and vegetable stews) are both cooked in the baker's oven so as to ensure a hot meal on Saturday, when the religious laws forbid the lighting of a fire. However, tastes have been strongly influenced by the foods that are available in the region and the local recipes. North African Jews enjoy couscous; Iranian Jews like to eat *gipa* (ox stomach stuffed with rice) and pilaf; Ashkenazi Jews cook potatoes, puddings (*kugel*), and pasta (such as *lockshen*, noodles made with water, and *kreplech*, pasta filled with meat), as well as Austrian and Russian dishes (borsch, strudel, and torten). On the whole, Jewish cookery relies a great deal on frying, for example in stuffed carp, onions with sugar and meat (a dish served at Sephardic wedding feasts), and the Moroccan *pastelas*, pastry rissoles stuffed with meat, honey, and vegetables.

Since Israel became an independent nation it has developed its own native cuisine. Each wave of immigrants tends to retain its ethnic cookery, but in everyday life Israelis eat simply; their meals are based mainly on raw vegetables (particularly cucumbers and avocado pears), dairy produce, and citrus fruits. Like their Middle Eastern neighbours, they are fond of vegetable purées, spiced meatballs, etc. Israeli farmers rear large numbers of turkeys and ducks, of which they have developed a new breed. They also export foie gras.

Jews's-ear fungus
AURICULAIRE
OREILLE-DE-JUDAS

A blackish mushroom shaped like an ear lobe that grows in clusters on old tree trunks. Its body is partly hard and partly jelly-like. It was originally eaten raw in salad, but is now mainly served in Chinese restaurants in France under the name of *champignon noir* ('black mushroom').

Johannisberg

A world-famous white wine from the Rheingau, the best-known vineyard being that of Schloss Johannisberg where the great estate of the Prince Metternichs uses different coloured seals to demarcate the quality of the wines. There is also a Swiss Johannisberg, made from the Sylvaner grape, whereas the great Rheingaus are all Rheinriesling. The term often used in California for the Rheinriesling is Johannisberger Riesling.

John Dory   SAINT-PIERRE

An oval deep-sided fish found along rocky coasts. 30–50 cm (12–20 in) long, it has a large head with an enormous mouth and a prominent lower jaw, and the dorsal fin is extended into filaments (the other fins are spiky). On each side of the body, which is bronze-coloured with silvery glints, is a large black spot, which according to tradition is the thumbprint of St Peter, who seized the fish to throw it back into the water because it was moaning (which in fact it does when removed from the water). Tradition also has it that the apostle took a coin from the fish's mouth, on Jesus' instructions. (It should be pointed out, however, that the Sea of Galilee, which is a freshwater lake, does not harbour this fish.)

The John Dory rarely provides more than four servings, since the enormous head, the fins, and the bones account for nearly 60% of its weight. But it is one of the best sea fish: its firm white flesh comes off the bone easily and can be used for many different dishes. It can be cooked like turbot or brill, is used in bouillabaisse and fish soups, and many chefs have created original recipes for it.

The English name is a corruption of one of its French nicknames, *jean-doré*.

RECIPES

John Dory fillets in a soufflé   FILETS DE SAINT-PIERRE SOUFFLÉS (from J.-Cl. Ferrero's recipe) Steam 4 John Dory fillets, each weighing 150 g (5 oz), for 4 minutes. Sprinkle with salt and pepper. Whisk 8 egg whites until stiff and fold in 3 tablespoons (¼ cup) mustard. Arrange the fillets in an ovenproof dish, pile up the egg whites on top, and cook in a hot oven (230 C, 450 F, gas 8) for about 4 minutes.

John Dory fillets with lemon   FILETS DE SAINT-PIERRE AU CITRON (from Aldo Funaro's recipe) Fillet a John Dory weighing about 1.25 kg (2½ lb); this should provide 600 g (generous 1¼ lb) flesh. Remove the skin and cut the flesh into 1-cm (½-in) dice. Finely shred the zest of 2 lemons, blanch and refresh it, then cook it in a little water and ½ dl (2½ tablespoons, scant ¼ cup) olive oil. Remove the white pith from the lemons, break up the lemon segments, and dice them. Cut 350 g (12 oz) courgettes (zucchini) into small pieces, trim them to the shape of olives, and blanch them.

Lightly grease 4 pieces of aluminium foil large enough to wrap round a piece of fish and some vegetables. On each one place a quarter of the fish, courgettes, lemon dice, and rind, 20 g (¾ oz, 1½ tablespoons) butter, and some salt and pepper. Seal the foil envelopes and bake in a hot oven (230 C, 450 F, gas 8) for about 8 minutes. Open the envelopes and sprinkle with chopped chives.

John Dory fillets with melon   FILETS DE SAINT-PIERRE AU MELON (from J.-Cl. Ferrero's recipe) Fillet a John Dory weighing about 1.5 kg (3¼ lb) and quickly sauté the fillets in a nonstick frying pan (skillet) without fat, allowing 2 minutes for each side. Keep the fillets warm. Blanch a julienne of 2 carrots and 1 leek for 1 minute in boiling water. Pat them dry and sauté briskly in 20 g (¾ oz, 1½ tablespoons) butter for 2 minutes. Sprinkle with salt and pepper and keep warm.

In another pan, fry slices of a 400-g (14-oz) melon in 30 g (1 oz, 2 tablespoons) butter, sprinkle with salt and pepper, and allow to caramelize slightly. Arrange a quarter of the melon slices and a John Dory fillet in a ring on each plate, place a spoonful of the vegetables in the centre, and sprinkle with fresh chopped mint.

John Dory fillets with red peppers FILETS DE SAINT-PIERRE AU POIVRON ROUGE (from Pierre Estival's recipe) Fillet a John Dory. Braise the fillets in fish fumet: they should be just cooked. Arrange them on a dish and keep warm. Reduce the braising liquid, add 2 dl (7 fl oz, ¾ cup) double (heavy) cream, and reduce once again. Remove from the heat, add 2 tablespoons (3 tablespoons) hollandaise sauce, and adjust the seasoning. Bake 4 whole sweet red peppers in a very hot oven or put under the grill until the skin blackens and blisters. Peel and deseed them and purée the flesh in a blender. Season with salt and pepper and heat the purée. Coat the fish with the sauce and with 4 tablespoons (⅓ cup) pepper purée. Garnish with sprigs of chervil. Serve with French (green) beans.

John Dory steaks in whisky velouté sauce with vegetable julienne BLANCS DE SAINT-PIERRE AU VELOUTÉ DE WHISKY ET SA JULIENNE DE LÉGUMES (from Gilbert Picard's recipe) Fillet 2 John Dorys, each weighing 1.25 kg (2½ lb). Grease an ovenproof dish and sprinkle it with 2 finely chopped shallots. Season the fillets with salt and pepper and lay them in the dish. Moisten with 1 dl (6 tablespoons, scant ½ cup) dry white wine and 1 dl (6 tablespoons, scant ½ cup) whisky. Cover with buttered paper and bake in a medium oven for 10–12 minutes.

Drain the fillets and reduce the cooking liquid by one-third. Remove from the heat, whisk in 50 g (2 oz, ¼ cup) butter in small pieces, then add ½ litre (17 fl oz, 2 cups) whipped double (heavy) cream. Mix well, still off the heat. Put the fish back in the oven (or under the grill) for 2 minutes, then coat with the sauce.

Serve the fish with steamed potatoes and a vegetable julienne made with 2 carrots, 1 celery heart, the white parts of 2 leeks, a bulb of fresh fennel, and 4 large mushroom caps.

John Dory with rhubarb SAINT-PIERRE À LA RHUBARBE (from Louis Outhier's recipe) Fillet a John Dory weighing 1.5 kg (3¼ lb) and cook the fillets in a little butter over a gentle heat, allowing 1 minute for each side. Keep warm. Add to the butter in which the fish was cooked 150 g (5 oz) rhubarb, peeled and thinly sliced, and cook for 30 seconds. Add 2 dl (7 fl oz, ¾ cup) cream

and reduce by half. Season with salt and pepper and add a pinch of sugar and a pinch of chopped basil. Mix well and pour the sauce over the fish.

jointing DÉPEÇAGE

The action of cutting up meat, poultry, etc. into large pieces at the joints, using a very sharp knife.

jointoyer

A French culinary term meaning to fill in any surface unevenness and to smooth the joined edges of cakes and pastries that are made up of several layers. Using a cream as the filling agent, the object is to ensure a smooth and uniform surface on the top and sides of the cake; this is essential if the cake is to look its best or if it is to be iced (frosted).

Joinville

The name of a dish of sole fillets arranged in a circle, which was dedicated to the third son of Louis-Philippe, the Duc de Joinville. The garnish for fillets of sole Joinville usually consists of prawns, poached mushrooms, and truffles, while the sauce is made from a sole velouté bound with cream and egg yolks with oyster liquor, mushroom essence (extract), and a purée of prawns and crayfish added to it. There are a number of simpler variations.

The name is also applied to a normande sauce with prawn butter, and to a prawn sauce with crayfish butter and a julienne of truffles when it is to accompany braised fish. Joinville garnish is also used to fill barquettes, tartlets, bouchées, etc., and an omelette (which is then surrounded with a prawn sauce). Finally, there is a gâteau Joinville, made from two squares of flaky pastry filled with raspberry jam.

RECIPE

Fillets of sole Joinville FILETS DE SOLE JOINVILLE Clean 250 g (½ lb) mushrooms; dice them, sprinkle with lemon juice, and cook slowly in butter over a low heat. Fillet 2 sole. Make a fumet from the sole trimmings and poach the fillets in this for 6 minutes. Drain. Cook 8 giant prawns in boiling salted water for 4 minutes. Prepare 3 dl (½ pint, 1¼ cups) normande sauce using the fish fumet and the mushroom cooking juices; add 1 tablespoon prawn butter to the sauce. Mix 100 g (4 oz, ⅔ cup) peeled prawns (shelled shrimp) with a finely diced truffle and the mushrooms; bind with a little sauce. Arrange the sole fillets in a circle on a round dish; stick a prawn into each fillet. Put the garnish in the centre of the dish and cover with the sauce.

Formerly, the fillets were arranged on a border of fish forcemeat and truffle slices, with the garnish in the middle.

Jonchée

A fresh soft French cheese (fat content 45%) drained in moulds of different sizes (formerly made of rush) and sold unwrapped on rush or straw mats. The cheese is made from cows' milk, which is sometimes flavoured with bay leaves (in Brittany and Saintonge); from goats' milk (in Aunis and Poitou); or from ewes' milk (in Béarn and the Basque country). Very white, soft to the touch, and with a slightly acid smell, it has a mild and creamy flavour.

joule

Since 1980 this has been the official international unit of measurement for energy. The kilojoule is the metric replacement for the Calorie or kilocalorie (1 kJ = 0.24 Cal or kcal). Calories continue to appear without the metric equivalent on some information labels. When kilojoules are given, the calorific equivalent also appears, generally expressed *kJ/kcal*.

Judic

A garnish for small or large cuts of meat, sautéed chicken, braised calves' sweetbreads, etc., usually consisting of braised lettuce, small stuffed tomatoes, and château potatoes. The accompanying sauce is made by deglazing the pan with Madeira and demi-glace sauce, or with a tomato-flavoured demi-glace. According to the *Dictionnaire de l'Académie des gastronomes*, tournedos Judic was supposed to have been named after the comedienne Anna Damiens, known as Dame Judic: the steaks are garnished with braised lettuce and a ragout of sliced truffle and cocks's combs and kidneys, covered with a Madeira demi-glace. The name is also

given to poached fillets of sole garnished with lettuce and fish quenelles, the whole dish being coated with Mornay sauce and browned.

judru

A short thick dry sausage made from pure pork, a speciality of Chagny in Burgundy. The meat is steeped in marc brandy and cut into small pieces (rather than minced (ground) or chopped).

juice

See *fruit juice and essence, jus*.

juice extractor
CENTRIFUGEUSE

An electrical appliance used to extract juice from vegetables and fruit by means of rapid rotation (citrus fruits, which are pressed are an exception). A sieve retains the pulp, seeds, and skin. Some models have a system for ejecting the waste and can operate continuously, producing large quantities of juice; others require frequent cleaning of the filter. The juices obtained are used in drinks, ices, sorbets, and jellies.

juive (à la)

Describing a dish of carp, generally served cold. In the authentic Jewish recipe, the carp is cleaned with salt, quickly browned in hot oil, then braised in a white roux with the roe, garlic, and parsley. This recipe is adapted in classic French cookery, the fish being sautéed in onion then braised in white wine with herbs. This dish has many variations; for example, chopped almonds and saffron, or fresh parsley, raisins, sugar, and vinegar, can be added to the cooking juices.

A dish of artichokes stuffed with breadcrumbs, chopped fresh mint, and garlic, cooked in oil, is also described as *à la juive*.

RECIPE

Carp à la juive   CARPE À LA JUIVE (Jewish recipe) Scale and gut (clean) a carp weighing about 1 kg (2 lb), taking care to reserve the roe. Cut it into slices and rub it with coarse salt. Leave for 20–30 minutes, then drain the pieces, dry them with a cloth, and add the roe. Mix 2–3 chopped garlic cloves with some parsley in a small bowl. Heat 3–4 tablespoons oil in a saucepan and seal the fish and the roe. Add enough water to almost cover the fish, then salt and pepper and the parsley and garlic, and simmer for about 20 minutes. Take out the pieces of fish and the roe and arrange them in a deep dish.

Make a smooth paste with 2 table-spoons (3 tablespoons) cornflour (corn-starch) and a little water, then mix in two-thirds of the liquid from the sauce-pan. Simmer the sauce until it has re-duced by one-third. Pour it over the fish and leave in the refrigerator to set.

jujube

An oval olive-sized fruit with a smooth tough red skin, soft sweet yellowish or green flesh, and a hard stone. The jujube tree, which originated in China, was known to Homer, and the fruit (usually dried) was used medicinally for hun-dreds of years. It is much more calorific dried than fresh (314 Cal per 100 g, as against 135 Cal, per 100 g). The jujube is grown in the south of France; the Far East exports large jujubes, either fresh or dried, known as 'red dates'. The ju-jube can be eaten as it is, either fresh or dried, and is also used in pastry-making (cakes, fritters, etc.) and in savoury dishes (such as meat stuffings and soups).

Jules-Verne

A garnish for large cuts of meat consist-ing of stuffed braised potatoes and tur-nips, arranged alternately with sautéed mushrooms. It was dedicated to the famous novelist by a 19th-century chef.

Juliénas

One of the nine classified growths of the Beaujolais, which in good years may have good keeping qualities, although its somewhat fleshy character makes it pleasant when drunk young. It is sup-posed to be the most popular wine of the Lyonnais.

julienne

Foodstuffs, especially vegetables, which are cut into thin sticks. They are cut with a knife or a mandoline into even slices 1–2 mm (¼ in) thick and then into strips 3 cm (1 in) long. The julienne is cooked in butter in a covered pan until quite soft and then used for various garnishes, particularly for soups and consommés.

Raw vegetables to be served as an hors d'oeuvre can also be cut as a juli-enne: for example, carrots in vin-aigrette, celeriac in spicy mayonnaise, or pickled red cabbage. Many other foods can be cut in this way: gherkins, truffles, peppers, mushrooms, ham, ton-gue, chicken breasts, citrus-fruit peel, etc.

The origin of the word is obscure, but it appears in the 1722 edition of *Le Cuisinier royal*.

RECIPES

Bouchées à la julienne Cut the follow-ing vegetables into fine strips: carrots (discarding any hard core), turnips, the white stem of leeks, some celery sticks (stalks) with the strings removed, and some mushrooms sprinkled with lemon juice (use twice as much carrot as each of the other vegetables). Cook the julienne in melted butter in a covered sauté pan over a low heat, so that the vegetables retain a little bite. Add 1 dl (6 tablespoons, scant ½ cup) fresh cream for every 500 g (1 lb) vegetables, and reduce until the mixture is thick. Add some Bayonne ham, also cut into strips (1 part ham to 5 parts mixture), and heat through without boiling. If liked, a little very fine julienne of truffle can be added. Adjust the seasoning.

Heat some small puff-pastry cases and divide the mixture between them. Serve immediately before the pastry goes soggy.

Consommé julienne Make a julienne of 100 g (4 oz) carrot (discarding any hard core), 75 g (3 oz) turnip, and 40 g (1½ oz) each of white of leek, onion, and celery. Sprinkle with a pinch of salt and a pinch of sugar. Soften the veget-ables in 50 g (2 oz, ¼ cup) melted butter over a low heat, with the pan covered, for 10 minutes. Cut 50 g (2 oz) white cabbage into julienne strips and blanch for 10 minutes in boiling water, then refresh and drain; do the same with the heart of a medium-sized lettuce; add these to the other vegetables.

Cook them all together, covered, for

15 minutes. Pour in 3 dl (½ pint, 1¼ cups) consommé and simmer for 5 minutes; and 25 g (1 oz) sorrel cut into fine ribbons and 1 tablespoon fresh garden peas, and cook for a further 25 minutes. Add another 1.25 litres (2¼ pints, 6 cups) consommé and boil for a few seconds; skim the pan, and at the last moment add some chervil leaves.

The consommé can be garnished with pearl barley, rice, semolina, tapioca, or vermicelli, or with quenelles, profiteroles, or royales.

juniper berries GENIÈVRE

The darkish berries of the juniper tree, which are used in cooking and the manufacture of wines and spirits because of their pungent and slightly resinous flavour. Used either whole or ground, juniper berries are particularly appreciated in Scandinavian cookery. They are the indispensable seasoning for marinades and courts-bouillons, dishes of game animals (wild boar) and birds (thrush, blackbird, woodcock), pork dishes (knuckle, pâtés), and sauerkraut. They are generally used in dishes *à la liégeoise* or *à l'ardennaise*.

A highly aromatic brandy, mostly drunk in northern Europe, is flavoured with juniper berries: it is known as *genièvre* in France, *genever* and *schiedam* in the Netherlands, and *péquet* in Belgium. English gin, as well as a number of schnapps and brandies, are also flavoured with juniper berries. In addition, they are used to flavour Scandinavian beers.

Jurançon

One of the best-known wines from south-western France, produced in limited quantities in the foothills of the Pyrenees from vineyards which are difficult to work because of their steepness. The white wine has been famous since the day it was used to moisten the lips of the newborn future Henri IV. It is made from local grape varieties (Petit-Manseng, Gros-Manseng, and Courbu), which may in ideal conditions be picked late and affected by 'noble rot'. There are two *appellations contrôlées*: Jurançon, a softish slightly sweet wine, and Jurançon Sec, which is traditionally drunk young. The other Jurançon grapes are Camaralet and Lauzet.

jus

This French word is roughly equivalent to 'juice', but has more specific meanings in French cookery than the English word.

It is used primarily for the gravy of a roast, made by diluting the pan juices with water, clear stock, or any other suitable liquid and then boiling it until all the goodness in the pan has been absorbed into the stock. Dishes described as *au jus* are prepared or served with this gravy.

It is also used for a thickened or clear brown stock, especially veal stock (*jus de veau*).

Finally, it is used for the juice squeezed from raw vegetables or fruit (see *fruit juice*).

Jussière

A garnish for small cuts of meat, consisting of stuffed onions, braised lettuce, and château potatoes, sometimes with carrots cut into neat shapes and glazed.

kaltschale

A Russian dessert consisting of a fresh
fruit salad that has been macerated in
wine and is covered with a purée of red
fruit (strawberries, raspberries, redcurrants, etc.). It is served in a large bowl
that traditionally should rest on a dish
of crushed ice. (The word *kaltschale* is
actually German, and its literal meaning
is 'cold cup'.)

RECIPE

Kaltschale   Rub 1 kg (2¼ lb, 7 cups)
strawberries and 250 g (8 oz, 2 cups)
very ripe redcurrants through a sieve.
Boil 1 litre (1¾ pints, 4¼ cups) light
sugar syrup with ½ bottle of champagne, and allow to cool. Add the syrup
mixture to the fruit purée. Peel and
remove the seeds or stones from several
different fruits (such as melon or watermelon, apricots, peaches, pears, or fresh
pineapple). Cut them into thin slices and
sprinkle with lemon juice. Place all the
fruit into a large bowl and pour the
liquid purée over them. Refrigerate until
ready to serve. Add some raspberries at
the last moment.

kasha or kacha

An eastern European dish made from
crushed or powdered buckwheat. There
are several ways of preparing it. In
Russia it is baked in the oven, mixed
with butter, rolled out, and shaped into
small pancakes. These are served with
soups or stews, possibly flavoured with
cheese, eggs, or mushrooms or cooked
au gratin. In Poland, kasha is a type of
sweet pudding made either from hulled
barley (cooked in milk and served with
cream) or from semolina (served with
melted butter).

RECIPES

Polish kasha with barley   KACHA
POLONAISE À L'ORGE   Pick over 350
g (12 oz, scant 1½ cups) hulled barley
and blanch in boiling water for 2 minutes. Bring 3 litres (5¼ pints, 6½ pints)
milk and 60 g (2½ oz, 5 tablespoons)
butter to the boil, add the barley, and
stir frequently until it is cooked. Take
the pan off the heat and add 200 g (7 oz,
scant 1 cup) butter, 6 lightly beaten
eggs, and 1 dl (6 tablespoons, scant ½
cup) soured (dairy sour) cream. Pour the
mixture into a buttered charlotte mould
and cook in a preheated oven at 200 c
(400 F, gas 6). Serve it in the mould with
double (heavy) cream served separately.

Russian kasha KACHA RUSSE Crush 500 g (18 oz, generous 3½ cups) fresh buckwheat and soak in sufficient warm water to make a thick paste. Season with salt and put it in a deep cake tin or charlotte mould (traditionally an earthenware pot is used). Bake in a preheated oven at 180 C (350 F, gas 4) for 2 hours. Remove the thick crust formed on the surface, and pour the remaining soft paste into a dish. Add 60 g (2½ oz, 5 tablespoons) butter and mix well with a spatula. Spread the paste out on a greased surface, cover it with a board, and press it until it is about 1 cm (½ in) thick. Cut into shapes with a pastry cutter (cookie cutter) and fry in clarified butter until golden brown. Serve with soup.

Russian kasha with Parmesan cheese KACHA RUSSE AU PARMESAN Prepare a kasha of buckwheat as described in the recipe above. Spread a thin layer of the soft paste over the bottom of a buttered gratin dish. Sprinkle with grated Parmesan cheese and a little melted butter, alternating the layers until all the ingredients are used up. Smooth the final layer of kasha carefully, sprinkle with Parmesan cheese, top with melted butter, and brown in the oven. Serve melted butter separately.

Katshkawalj

A Bulgarian cheese made from ewes' milk, which is similar to the Italian Cacio-cavallo. It is found in various central European countries: in Yugoslavia it is known as *Kackavalj*, and in Hungary as *Kaskaval Sajt*. It has a fat content of about 45% and its paste has a springy texture. Katshkawalj is served fresh at the end of a meal, or as an hors d'oeuvre with raw vegetables. When it is dry it can be grated and used in the same way as Parmesan cheese.

kebab

A dish consisting basically of small pieces of meat threaded on skewers and grilled or roasted, which originated in Turkey and eventually spread to the Balkans and the Middle East. The name is a shortened form of the Turkish *şiş kebab*, *şiş* meaning skewer and *kebab* meaning roast meat. Şiş (or shish) kebab consists of cubes of marinated mutton threaded onto wooden or metal skewers, traditionally alternating with cubes of mutton fat, but the latter is often replaced by large pieces of belly of pork (fat pork). The skewered meat is grilled over hot embers and usually served with quarters of lemon, yogurt, or soured (dairy sour) cream. There are many variations of this dish: it may be made with or without vegetables (tomatoes, peppers, onions), or with veal, lamb, or even buffalo or meatballs. Sometimes the kebabs are slipped off the skewers and served on a bed of rice with chickpeas, raw onions, and a salad of chopped raw vegetables.

| RECIPE

Shish kebab CHICHE-KEBAB Cut some shoulder or leg of mutton into cubes. Marinate the meat for 30 minutes in a mixture of olive oil and lemon juice seasoned with pepper and salt, thyme, powdered bay leaf, and a little finely chopped garlic. Cut an equal quantity of belly of pork (fat pork) into cubes and blanch them. Thread the mutton and pork alternately onto skewers and grill them under a very high heat, or, preferably, over charcoal. Serve with quarters of lemon and either a green salad or saffron rice.

kedgeree

An English dish that came originally from India. The word comes from the Hindi word *khicari*, from Sanskrit *khiccā*, the origin of which is obscure. It consists of a mixture of rice, cooked flaked fish, and hard-boiled (hard-cooked) eggs. (The fish is usually smoked haddock, but it may be salmon or even turbot.) Peas may be added, or it can be bound with a curry-flavoured béchamel sauce seasoned with cayenne and nutmeg.

The original Indian dish, known as *kadgeri*, consists of rice garnished with onions, lentils, and eggs. Fish was added by the British.

kefir KÉPHIR

Fermented milk drunk in the Middle East and in southern Russia. Strictly it should be made from camels' milk, but in practice cows' milk, skimmed or not, is usually used. Kefir is frothy or creamy (like yogurt) and its alcohol content varies according to the period of fermention. It is sometimes flavoured with aromatic herbs or eaten with cream. Kefir is a refreshing drink and resembles *kumiss*, another traditional central Asian drink, prepared from fermented mares' milk. As kefir is easily digestible, it is often recommended for invalids.

kefta KEFTEDES

A central European dish made from chopped meat with bacon and spices, sometimes bound with egg, and made into flat rounds that are coated with flour and then sautéed. The word itself is Hungarian, but kefta is also a German, Austrian, and Greek dish. In Greece it is flavoured with chopped onion. The meat can be beef, veal, poultry, or game.

Kellogg (William Keith)

American industrialist (born Battle Creek, Michigan, 1860; died Battle Creek, 1951). He worked as an assistant to his brother, who was a well-known nutritionist and the director of a hospital specializing in nutritional disorders. In 1894 he discovered a process for making flakes out of grains of maize (corn). These could be eaten as part of the vegetarian diet recommended by the Seventh Day Adventists, to which sect both brothers belonged, and in 1898 the process was industrialized. In 1906 a company was formed to market cornflakes, and ever since then they have been regarded as an integral part of both the English and American breakfast.

ketchup

A sweet-and-sour condiment with one flavour predominating, usually based on tomatoes but sometimes on mushrooms or walnuts. Tomato ketchup is very popular in Britain and North America and is the variety usually sold in France; it is used to flavour meat sauces or served with fish, hamburgers, eggs, rice, and pasta. It is made from tomato purée, vinegar, sugar, and spices.

kettle BOUILLOIRE

A container with a spout, handle, and lid, used for boiling water. Kettles are made of aluminium, stainless steel, chrome-plated copper, enamel, Pyrex, plastic, etc. They may have steam whistles, which blow when the kettle boils.

Ancient kettles, known in French as *coquemars*, were often very large and made of earthenware or, more usually, copper. These are now used as ornaments.

A milk kettle or boiler is a cylindrical pot used for boiling milk. It has a perforated lid designed to stop the milk boiling over. See also *fish kettle*.

kholodetz

A Russian dish of jellied meats. The meats (generally beef, veal, and chicken, or perhaps pig's trotters (feet) and knuckle of veal) are cooked in stock, placed in a dish garnished with slices of carrot, tarragon, and dill, then covered with aspic. When the aspic has set, the kholodetz is unmoulded and served with gherkins, plums, or pears macerated in vinegar.

kid CHEVREAU

A young goat. Only the very young males (six weeks to four months old) are slaughtered for meat, as the females are reserved for milk production. They are available from mid-March until the beginning of May. Kids' meat is insipid and rather soft, similar to that of milk lamb. It is generally eaten roasted and, in most recipes (particularly in Corsica and Spain), well seasoned and spiced.

kidneys ROGNONS

A type of red offal. Ox and calves' kidneys are multilobed, while pigs' and sheep's kidneys are shaped rather like a haricot (navy) bean. The kidneys of young animals, such as calves, heifers, and lambs, have the most delicate flavour; pigs' kidneys are rather strongly flavoured, while those of the ox and sheep tend to be tough as well as strongly flavoured (it is best to boil the latter for a few minutes and drain them before preparing them for cooking).

In all cases, the transparent membrane that surrounds the kidneys must be removed so that they do not shrink when cooked. Any blood vessels, together with the central core of fat, must also be removed. When grilled (broiled) or sautéed, they should be served when still pink, otherwise they may become tough. They can also be braised in a medium oven. Calves' kidneys are particularly good when fried (whole or sliced) without trimming the surrounding fat, which gradually melts; they are ready when golden brown.

Cocks' kidneys, which are now becoming rare, feature with cocks' combs in several classic garnishes.

RECIPES

CALVES' KIDNEYS

Calf's kidney à la bonne femme ROG-NON DE VEAU À LA BONNE FEMME Fry 50 g (2 oz) coarsely diced streaky bacon and 4 small onions in butter in a small casserole. Remove these from the casserole, and in the same butter toss a whole calf's kidney with most of the outer fat removed, just to stiffen it. Fry 12 small new potatoes in butter until they are three-quarters cooked, then add the diced bacon, the onions, and the kidney and season with salt and pepper. Continue the cooking in the oven at 240 C (475 F, gas 9) for about 15 minutes. Just before serving, sprinkle with 3 tablespoons (¼ cup) veal stock. Serve the kidney in the casserole. It may be garnished with mushrooms tossed in butter if desired.

Calves' kidneys with chicken livers ROGNONS DE VEAU AUX FOIES DE VOLAILLE (from a recipe by Raymond Thuillier) Skin 4 calves' kidneys and remove the fat. Halve them and chop into small pieces. Slice 12 chicken livers. Using a tinned copper saucepan (or a stainless steel saucepan with a copper base), fry the kidneys and the chicken livers in a knob of butter for about 5 minutes, taking care not to let them brown. While they are still pink, flame them with ½ glass (3 fl oz, scant ½ cup) Armagnac and set aside, keeping them hot. Pour 1 glass (6 fl oz, ¾ cup) port and ½ litre (17 fl oz, 2 cups) red Gigondas wine into the cooking liquor. Boil down to reduce, and thicken with 15 g (½ oz, 1 tablespoon) kneaded butter. When the sauce is ready (about 15 minutes), strain it. Arrange the kidneys

and chicken livers in the serving dish, coat with the sauce, adjust the seasoning, and sprinkle with chopped parsley.

Grilled (broiled) calf's kidney ROG-NON DE VEAU GRILLÉ Remove some of the fat from a calf's kidney, slit it lengthways without cutting it through completely, and keep it open and flat by threading it on 2 small metal skewers. Season with salt and pepper, brush lightly with oil, and cook rapidly under a hot grill. Serve with Bercy butter, maître d'hôtel butter, or anchovy butter.

Sautéed calf's kidney with three mustards ROGNON DE VEAU SAUTÉ AUX TROIS MOUTARDES (from a recipe by Raymond Oliver) Remove some of the fat from a calf's kidney, season with salt and pepper, and cook for 10–15 minutes in a small pan with a little oil and butter (this is known as cooking *à la coque*). Drain all the fat away and flame the kidney with a generous liqueur glass of young good-quality Armagnac. Drain the kidney and slice it thinly on a plate; keep hot.

Pour 1 Bordeaux glass (4 fl oz, ½ cup) sherry or Madeira into the pan and boil to reduce the liquid by half. Pour any kidney juices on the plate into the sauce, boil rapidly for a few minutes, add the kidney, and place the pan at the side of the stove. Do not let it boil again.

Blend 50 g (2 oz, 4 tablespoons) butter with a mixture of Dijon, Champagne, and Bordeaux mustards. Add this mixture, a little at a time, to the pan, stirring constantly, so that the sauce becomes smooth and creamy. This is the most critical process in the whole preparation, and should be carried out away from the heat. Serve the kidney with sautéed potatoes.

COCKS' KIDNEYS

Cocks' kidneys for garnishing ROG-NONS DE COQ POUR GARNITURES Wash 125 g (4½ oz) firm white cocks' kidneys in several changes of water. Put them into a small saucepan with 1 dl (6 tablespoons, scant ½ cup) water, a pinch of salt, 25 g (1 oz, 2 tablespoons) butter, and a few drops of lemon juice. Start to cook over a high heat; as soon as the liquid begins to simmer, reduce the heat, cover the pan, and poach the kidneys very gently for 10–12 minutes, taking care not to let the liquid boil. Drain and use according to the recipe.

OX OR HEIFERS' KIDNEYS

Ox kidney with lardons ROGNON DE BOEUF AUX LARDONS Slit an ox kidney (or preferably a heifer's kidney) in half and take out the central core. Cut the kidney into thin slices. Sprinkle 250 g (9 oz, 3 cups) washed sliced mushrooms with a little lemon juice. Cut 200 g (7 oz) rindless streaky bacon into thin strips; peel and chop 2 shallots. Melt 25 g (1 oz, 2 tablespoons) butter in a sauté pan, add the sliced kidney, and brown quickly over a high heat. Then add the mushrooms, the lardons, and the shallots and cook until all the ingredients are lightly browned. Season with salt and pepper, lower the heat, cover the pan, and cook for about 20 minutes. Then add a small glass of Madeira and 1.5 dl (¼ pint, ⅔ cup) fresh cream and reduce the sauce over a high heat. Pour the preparation into a serving dish and sprinkle with chopped parsley.

PIGS' KIDNEYS

Preparation of pigs' kidneys PRÉ-PARATION DE ROGNONS DE PORC To reduce the rather strong taste of these kidneys, skin them, cut them open without separating the halves, take out the white central core, wash them under running water, cover them with milk, and leave them in a cool place for 3–4 hours. They can then be grilled (broiled) or sautéed (with lardons or mushrooms) in the same way as calves' kidneys.

SHEEP'S AND LAMBS' KIDNEYS

Lambs' kidneys à l'anglaise ROG-NONS D'AGNEAU À L'ANGLAISE Remove the skin of the kidneys and cut them in half without separating the halves completely. Remove the white central core and tubes. Thread the kidneys on skewers, pushing the skewer through each half of the kidney to keep them open. Season with salt and pepper, brush with melted butter, and (if desired) roll them in fresh breadcrumbs.

Grill (broil) the kidneys under a high heat for about 3 minutes on each side, then arrange in a long dish with grilled rashers (slices) of bacon, small boiled new potatoes, and fresh watercress. Put a pat of maître d'hôtel butter on each half kidney.

Lambs' kidneys sautéed with mushrooms ROGNONS D'AGNEAU SAUTÉS AUX CHAMPIGNONS Clean and slice 8 large button mushrooms and sprinkle with lemon juice. Clean 8 kidneys, cut them in half, season with salt and pepper, and sauté them quickly in very hot butter. (Do not overcook; ensure that they remain pink.) Drain and keep hot in a serving dish.

Sauté the sliced mushrooms in the same butter, drain them, and arrange around the kidneys. Keep hot. Pour 2.5 dl (8 fl oz, 1 cup) stock into the pan and boil down to reduce by one-third; add 1 dl (6 tablespoons, scant ½ cup) Madeira, port, champagne, or Riesling and again reduce by one-third. Thicken with 1 teaspoon arrowroot, then add 40 g (1½ oz, 3 tablespoons) butter. Pour the sauce over the kidneys and sprinkle with chopped parsley.

kilka

A Russian fish similar to the sprat, three species of which are fished intensively in the Caspian Sea. It is sometimes eaten fresh but is usually frozen at sea and then canned in oil, salted, or marinated. It is served as a cold hors d'oeuvre with slices of lemon.

Kir

Originally, a Burgundy mixture of dry white Aligoté wine and cassis (the blackcurrant liqueur for which Burgundy is famous). Referred to as *vin blanc cassis*, it became associated with the late Canon Félix Kir, a hero of the French Resistance who, as Mayor of Dijon, insisted on its being the only drink offered at official receptions. Kir Royale was originally made with champagne, but like ordinary Kir is now based on any dry and sparkling wine. Kir Communard is red wine plus cassis; in the Beaujolais region this mix is known as a *rince cochon*.

Kirsch

A white spirit (*alcool blanc*), a true fruit brandy distilled from cherries; it should not be confused with the sweetened cherry brandies made by most of the great liqueur establishments. The type of cherry used depended originally on where the distillate was made, but nowadays firms reputed for their Kirsch, such as those in Alsace, Franche-Comté, and the Black Forest in Germany, may have to buy in fruit to supplement the local cherries. The kernels of the cherries are included in the 'mash'. As with many spirits that are widely used for culinary purposes, there are less expensive types of Kirsch, which are used for flaming pancakes, incorporating with whipped cream and fillings for pastries and cakes, and in confectionery. The top-quality liqueurs are particularly appreciated as a digestive after a meal.

RECIPE

Apples with cream and Kirsch POMMES À LA CRÈME AU KIRSCH Peel and core some crisp sweet dessert apples, sprinkle them with lemon juice, and cook them in boiling vanilla-flavoured syrup until transparent. Drain and leave to cool. Mix some very cold fresh double (heavy) or whipping cream with a quarter of its volume of very cold Kirsch, and whip until the whisk leaves a trail. Pour this over the apples.

kiss

See *baiser*.

kissel

A Russian dessert made from sweetened red fruit purée thickened with arrowroot or flour and sometimes flavoured with white wine. Kissel can be served warm or cold with fresh cream.

RECIPE

Kissel with cranberries KISSEL AUX AIRELLES Put 1 kg (2¼ lb, 9 cups) cranberries through a vegetable mill. Mix with 2–2.5 litres (3½–4½ pints, 9–11 cups) water, pour the mixture into a bowl through a cloth, and wring out the cloth to extract the maximum quantity of juice. Alternatively, purée the fruit and water in a blender. Mix 6 tablespoons (1½ cup) potato flour, cornflour (cornstarch), or tapioca into the juice and pour into a saucepan. Add 200 g (7 oz, 1 cup) caster (superfine) sugar and bring to the boil on top of the cooker. Stir constantly until the mixture thickens and becomes transparent. Pour into a fruit bowl and serve warm or cold.

kissing crust BAISURE

In baking, the kissing crust is the pale, slightly underdone, portion of a loaf that was in contact with the loaf next to it during baking.

kitchen CUISINE

A room set aside for the preparation of food. The kitchen as a separate room in a house first appeared in about the 5th century BC, but in ancient times it was also associated with religious practices: the hearth where meat and vegetables were cooked was also the altar of the cult of the household gods. Roman kitchens in great residences were particularly well-equipped, with a water tank, sink, cavities provided in worktops for pounding spices, bronze tripods, etc.

In medieval chateaux, the kitchen was one of the most important rooms and the scene of constant activity. Very spacious and endowed with one or several gigantic chimneys, particularly in abbeys (Fontevrault) and palaces (Avignon, Dijon), it extended into numerous annexes (bread store, fruit store, cupbearer's room, etc.). In middle-class houses and farms, on the other hand, it was usually the communal room where guests were received, cooking was done, and meals were eaten.

During the Renaissance, fittings and decoration were improved. Under the reign of Louis XV, when the culinary art underwent a true renewal, the kitchen of a noble house could even be luxurious, as the Abbé Coyer proves (in *Bagatelles morales*, 1755, quoted by Franklin): 'I am dragged into kitchens and made to admire the taste of the master; it is the only room in the house which is pointed out to the curious.

Elegance, solidity, cleanliness, conveniences of all kinds, nothing is missing from this vast workshop of Comus, a modern masterpiece where architecture has enjoyed displaying its resources.'

In the 19th century, technical progress (improved kitchen utensils, and above all the range, then the cooker) transformed the kitchen into a veritable *laboratoire* (as great chefs called it). A room distinctly separated from the rest of the house, possessing a service entrance, it was sometimes situated in the basement (particularly in Victorian England) or at the end of a long corridor. Its equipment abounded in various utensils: scales and weights, a canteen of cutlery, a draining board, spice boxes, a set of saucepans, etc. It was the domain of the housewife, as epitomized by the German *hausfrau* in the cliché of the 'three Ks' (*Kinder, Kirche,* and *Küche,* children, church, kitchen).

The 20th century has seen progress in lighting and heating, improvements in interior decoration, and the introduction of refrigerating and preserving appliances. In many households the reduction of available space has necessitated the introduction of a composite room with a kitchen recess and a dining area. Nevertheless, the traditional kitchen, with its large table and sink and its dresser with rows of crockery, jars of preserves, and pots of jam, still represents, in all classes of society, the symbol of the home and of domestic economy. As declared in *La Parfaite Cuisinière bourgeoise et économique* (1853): 'Order and cleanliness must reign in the kitchen; everything must be in its place, well polished, well cleaned.'

kitchen equipment

BATTERIE DE CUISINE

All utensils and accessories used to prepare and cook food. Of widely varying shapes and materials, such utensils range from skewers, which are as old as the invention of fire, to the latest applications of modern technology.

□ **Origins** We know very little about the first kitchen utensils. The Egyptians, the Assyrians, and the Persians principally used earthenware and bronze vessels, big-bellied in shape, with and without handles. They also used the spit and,

for cooking cakes and biscuits, they had baking dishes rather like those we use nowadays.

The Jews did not generally use earthenware vessels for cooking purposes; most of their pots and pans were made of metal. To extract the meat from the big pots in which food destined to be offered to God was prepared, they used a big two-pronged fork, the forerunner of our table fork, which did not make its appearance until the 17th century.

The Greeks, for their culinary preparations, used greatly improved bronze, iron, or silver vessels. They also had some in earthenware. Almost all these vessels were conical in shape and therefore not very deep. They were provided with lids, and either handles or detachable rings.

Among the principal kitchen utensils used by the Greeks was the *chytra*, a kind of earthenware pan used for cooking meats and stews. It was apparently in these utensils that the famous Spartan broths were prepared. Or perhaps this historical dish was made in the *kakkabi*, a fairly large three-legged pot. The Greeks also had another pot, which can be considered as the prototype of the earthenware casserole which we use nowadays for the pot-au-feu. This, filled with cooked fruit (probably cooked in wine and sweetened with honey), was carried to the altar of the god, Bacchus, on the third day of the feast of Anthesteria, the famous festival in honour of Dionysus.

The Greeks also had bronze casseroles which resembled those now in use. For cooking meat and fish cut in pieces they had a pan similar to the type which in France today is called *coupe lyonnaise*, and which the Greeks called *teganon*. In order to place all these metal or earthenware receptacles on the fire, the Greeks used a triangular support, the tripod, that is still in use in country kitchens.

Kitchen utensils used by the Romans were similar to those of the Greeks. It is also a known fact that Greek cooks brought the art of cooking to Rome. The Romans, who were sensual voluptuous people, with a great love of luxury in all things, made kitchen utensils not only of bronze but also of silver. Among the treasures of Bosco-Reale, which are kept in the Louvre, various kitchen utensils of this type can be seen. Kitchen utensils used by the Romans included the *clibanus*, an earthenware utensil with holes pierced in it, used for cooking various dishes, mainly pastry, in hot ashes; *craticula*, a grill for cooking meat and fish on the glowing embers; and the *apala*, a dish with cavities of varying sizes hollowed out, which was used for cooking eggs.

The Gauls and the Gallo-Romans had earthenware and metal kitchen utensils somewhat similar to those of the Greeks and Romans. The Celts knew nothing of the refinements of the sumptuous cookery of Imperial Rome and their pots and pans were rudimentary. With the coming of the Merovingian era, kitchen utensils began again to improve. Some specimens of these have survived, and we can see in museums the magnificent bronze vessels in which the food was prepared.

From reading Charlemagne's *Capitularies*, it seems evident that in succeeding centuries French kitchen utensils were improved still further. After the Crusades a great number of richly worked metal utensils – ewers, salvers, cauldrons – were brought to Europe and served as models for the artisans of the West in the manufacture of magnificent utensils.

In French museums and private collections can be seen, for example, cooking pots in engraved bronze or artistically beaten copper; wrought-iron pot-hangers, which are veritable works of art; kitchen forks, which in those days were called *roables*; turning gridirons; big-bellied pots and kettles; the *acoste-pot* (old version of the *accote-pot*, 'tilt-pot'), and other kitchen implements which are all excellent examples of ironmongery.

Among the many utensils used was the horsehair sieve or tammy, which, it is said, was invented by the Gauls. The following utensils were also in use: the *couloir*, a large strainer with a handle which was used for draining foods; the *rastels* or *rastelrier*, iron hooks on which food was hung; pots and kettles of all sizes; *tartières* (baking tins); skillets, saucepans, frying pans, etc.; the *féral* – a large metal vessel used as a water container; the *becdansne*, a pot

with a handle and a long curved spout; funnels, mostly in copper; the *esmieure*, a grater used for grating nutmeg and cheese.

In the kitchens of those times they also used gridirons, mortars, spice-grinders, various ladles which were called *potlouches* and *poches*, *minchoirs*, which were long-bladed knives used for slicing pork fat into rashers, mincers, and various other utensils which are still in use in the present day.

□ **Modern times** Most of the basic utensils we know today already existed during the Renaissance, but technical improvements and the emergence of new materials (not to mention the imagination of manufacturers) have led to great variety in modern kitchen equipment, providing utensils for preparing food, large cooking apparatus, cooking dishes, smaller items of equipment, cutlery, and electrical devices (an essential and growing addition to the kitchen since the 1950s). There are in addition many small accessories which soon go out of fashion. More than a century ago, Brillat-Savarin, who followed the latest developments of his era very closely, already owned 'an economical cooking pot, a roasting shell, a pendulum spit roaster and a steamer'. Nowadays, basic kitchen equipment can include the following items:

EQUIPMENT FOR PREPARING FOOD
● chopping boards, sharp cooks' knives and other kitchen cutlery, knife sharpener, larding and trussing needles (optional extras), scissors;
● vegetable peeler, grater, colander, sieve, whisks, salad basket, hand rotary beater, vegetable mill;
● spatulas and wooden spoons, ladle, skimmer (optional), funnels, can opener, corkscrew, bottle opener;
● lemon squeezer, mixing bowls and pudding basins, rolling pin, forcing bag (pastry bag), pastry cutters (cookie cutters);
● storage containers, greaseproof (waxed) paper, aluminium foil, self-adhesive film (plastic wrap);
● weighing scales:
● measuring jug (cup);
● oven gloves.

EQUIPMENT FOR COOKING
● large cooking pot (for cooking large quantities of soup, large joints of meat,

etc.), if necessary, two of different sizes:
- heavy stew pan, assorted casseroles, large oval cocotte (for cooking poultry);
- pressure cooker (optional extra);
- roasting pan;
- omelette and crêpe pans and two frying pans (skillets), one large and one small;
- deep frying pan (deep frier) and fitted basket;
- set of five saucepans (12–20 cm (5–8 in) in diameter) with lids;
- gratin and ovenproof dishes of various sizes;
- pâté dishes (optional extras);
- pie plates, flan dishes, assorted cake tins, baking sheets, dessert moulds, soufflé dishes;
- preserving pan with skimmer;
- steamer.

ELECTRICAL EQUIPMENT
- blender with accessories (or a food processor);
- mincer (grinder);
- coffee grinder;
- electric mixer with accessories;
- ice-cream maker (optional).

NEW EQUIPMENT

The popularization of certain foreign dishes has introduced new utensils to current kitchen equipment, such as the Moroccan tajine, the Chinese wok, and the Japanese hibachi (table barbecue), not forgetting other less exotic items, such as the paella dish and the pasta-making machine.

kitchen scales BALANCE

An instrument used for measuring weight, essential for keeping to the correct proportions (especially in pastry making) and for weighing ingredients. In home cooking apart from the traditional balance with two pans and a series of weights, automatic scales which indicate the weight by means of a moving needle are widely used. These compact scales, with a range of 2–5 kg (4–11 lb), include a removable washable bowl or tray, so that they can also be used for weighing liquids.

kitchen staff

BRIGADE DE CUISINE

In a large catering establishment, the staff consists of a brigade (team) of cooks and others providing kitchen ser-

vices. The team is directed by a head chef, who divides the staff into parties (sections) each contributing to the total food production. He is assisted by an underchef who manages the section leaders, each of whom is responsible for a particular section of work with the aid of an assistant and sometimes an apprentice. The kitchen staff varies according to the requirements of each establishment, tasks being shared or distributed between the workers.

The kitchen staff and their functions are as follows:
- *Chef de brigade* (head chef, assisted by underchef) – Drawing up of menus; purchasing; coordination of kitchen work; hiring personnel.
- *Saucier* (sauce chef) – Preparation of stocks and sauces, braised, fried, sautéed, and sometimes poached meat and poultry, and game (except roast or grilled dishes).
- *Garde-manger* (larder chef, sometimes assisted by a cold chef) – Preparation of all cold articles (hors d'oeuvres, terrines, pâtés, galantines, etc.) and cold sauces; cutting up and distribution of meat and fish; stock control as required.
- *Rôtisseur* (roast chef: may also act as staff cook) – Preparation of food cooked in the oven or spit roasted and grilled (broiled) and fried food; cutting up potatoes for frying (formerly assisted by a fryer, a griller, and a spit roaster).
- *Entremettier* (vegetable chef, sometimes assisted by a soup-maker) – Preparation of vegetables, egg dishes (except grilled (broiled) and fried), and soups; cooked side dishes prepared by small teams.
- *Poissonnier* (fish chef) – Preparation of all fish (except grilled (broiled) and fried); hollandaise and béarnaise sauce; boiled potatoes.
- *Pâtissier* (pastry chef, sometimes assisted by an ice-cream maker and a confectioner) – Preparation of cooked desserts, pastries, ice creams, savoury cooked pastries, pasta (formerly assisted by an oven boy and an outworker).
- *Communard* (staff cook, sometimes assisted by a keeper) – Preparation of food for the kitchen staff.
- *Tournant* (relief chef) – Replacement for an absent section leader.

Associated services, including

washing-up, are provided by the pot washer (who is also responsible for cleaning fish), the silver plater, the washer-up, the kitchen boy, and the vegetable boy (responsible for peeling).

Since the end of the last century, some chefs of famous restaurants have become well known: Léopold Mourier, first with Marie then at the Café de Paris and at Fouquet's; Marc Soustelle, with Lucas-Carton; Alex Humbert at Maxim's, etc.

kiwi fruit

A fruit about the size of a large egg, with a greenish-brown hairy skin. The plant is a climber and belongs to the genus *Actinidia*. It originated in China but is now cultivated chiefly in New Zealand (hence the name) and also in California, western France, and Israel. The flesh is pale green, highly perfumed, and juicy, with a slightly acidic taste. It contains 53 Cal per 100 g and is rich in vitamin C. The fruit is ripe when soft to the touch. It is used in various ways – it may be halved and eaten from the skin as a dessert, or peeled and cut into cubes or slices for fruit salads, tarts, etc., or as a garnish for roast quail, baked mackerel, or fried pork chops. It is also an ingredient in a sweet-and-sour sauce served with cold meat or fish.

RECIPES

Fruit salad with kiwi fruit SALADE DE FRUITS AUX KIWIS Choose the fruit according to the season. Divide oranges and grapefruits into segments, peel, and remove the pith. Peel, core, and slice apples and pears and sprinkle with lemon juice. Peel peaches and melon and cut into cubes; sprinkle the peaches with lemon juice. Hull strawberries and raspberries. Peel and slice the kiwi fruit (they should represent a quarter of the total volume of fruit).

Place all the fruit (except for the raspberries) into a large salad bowl, sprinkle with sugar, and moisten with Kirsch or some other fruit-based liqueur. Leave in a cool place until ready to serve. Add the raspberries at the last moment.

The whole strawberries can be replaced by strawberry purée: put the fruit through a blender, sieve the purée, sweeten with sugar, and pour it over the other fruit just before serving.

Kiwi fruit sauce SAUCE AUX KIWIS (from a recipe by Paul Corcellet) Peel 2 kiwi fruit and mash them with a fork. Add 1 tablespoon single (light) cream, a pinch of 'five spices', a few drops of Worcesterhsire sauce, and a pinch of salt. Serve the sauce with cold roast veal or cold hake that has been cooked in a court-bouillon.

Pork chops with kiwi fruit CÔTES DE PORC AUX KIWIS Fry 4 pork chops in butter. While they are cooking, peel 8 kiwi fruit, cut them into thick slices or quarters, and sprinkle with a little lemon juice. Drain the chops and keep them hot in the serving dish. Add the fruit to the frying pan (skillet), cover the pan, and heat in the pan juices. Arrange the fruit around the chops. Deglaze the pan with ½ glass (¾ cup) pineapple juice and an equal quantity of stock. Boil down to reduce the sauce to a thick syrup. Add a generous pinch of pepper and pour over the chops.

klösse

A German and Austrian dish consisting of spiced dumplings made from a mixture of flour, breadcrumbs (or potato purée) eggs, milk, and sometimes chopped ham. The dumplings are poached in boiling water and served on their own with melted butter and fried breadcrumbs or used as a garnish for soups or dishes in a sauce. A similar Polish dish, *klouskis*, consists of dumplings made from a mixture of flour, eggs, sugar, and yeast, which are poached, coated with noisette butter, and served as a dessert.

RECIPE

Klösse à la viennoise Remove the crust from 550 g (19 oz) brown bread, cut the crumb into small dice, and soak the diced bread in boiling milk. Cook 175 g (6 oz, 1½ cups) chopped onions in 15 g (½ oz, 1 tablespoon) butter in a covered pan until soft. Add the onions to the bread, together with 1 tablespoon chopped chervil, 1 tablespoon chopped tarragon, and 250 g (9 oz, generous 1 cup) chopped ham. Bind with 1 tablespoon flour and 3 lightly beaten eggs, and season with salt, pepper, and nutmeg. Divide the mixture into 50-g (2-oz) pieces and roll them into balls. Coat with flour and poach for about 12 minutes in a large pan of salted water. Fry some fine breadcrumbs in butter. Drain the dumplings and sprinkle them with the fried breadcrumbs.

knackwurst

A type of fresh German sausage similar to a frankfurter, but shorter and thicker. It is made with 50% lean pork, 30% beef, and 20% fat pork, finely minced (ground) and flavoured with cumin and parsley. Saltpetre is added to give it a pinkish colour, and the sausage is eaten poached or grilled. The name is derived from the German *knacken* (to make a cracking sound), referring to the sound made when the sausage is bitten into.

kneading   MALAXAGE

The process by which a mixture or dough is made smoother and softer or more elastic and by which air or additional ingredients are evenly incorporated at the same time. Doughs are usually kneaded on a board by applying a gentle pressing and stretching action with the hand. Butters or stuffings can be worked in a bowl.

kneading trough   PÉTRIN

The large wooden trough in which bread dough was kneaded. In the 19th century it was replaced in the bakery trade by the mechanical kneader. The latter is made of stainless steel and the dough is continuously stirred by rotating metal arms. Domestic electric food mixers and certain food processors have special attachments for kneading dough. Some electric hand mixers are fitted with attachments suitable for kneading light and semi-liquid dough or batter, but their motors are not powerful enough for thick doughs.

knife   COUTEAU

A cutting instrument with a handle and a blade. The blade has a pointed end (tang) that fits into the handle and is encircled with a bolster. Between the tang and the blade there is a projection, the rocker, which prevents the blade from touching the table surface when the knife is lying flat. When a knife has no bolster, the blade is held in place by two plates that form the handle. Before stainless steel came into general use, the blades were made of carbon steel except for fruit knives and fish knives, which were made of silver. However, carbon steel is best for kitchen knives as the blade stays sharp longer than blades made with stainless steel. Table knives match the style of the forks and spoons.

The ancestor of the knife was a sharpened piece of flint, and the first blades were made of bronze and later of iron. In Greek and Roman times, knives were luxury articles, but were already fairly similar to modern knives. Until the end of the 16th century, knives were used both for cutting and for spearing food (particularly meat) and also to cut bread. A knife was a personal object that the host would not necessarily make available to his guests. It was therefore worn on the belt. The colour of the handle could vary according to the time of year (ivory for Easter, ebony for Lent). The first round-ended knives appeared around 1630 as the social conventions of the time demanded that the knife should no longer be used as a toothpick. Handles were made of wood, hard stone, horn, shell, or metal and were often decorated with grotesque figures or fantastic animals. Later, they were made of gold and silver plate, and sometimes even of porcelain or china, especially in the 18th century. In the 17th century, table knives began to differ according to their use.

Nowadays, a standard set includes knives for cutting meat, for serving fish, for serving cheese (curved with a double-pointed end), and for serving cakes. Each person at the table has a large knife (or table knife), sometimes a steak knife (with a serrated or special cutting edge), and small knives of various types according to the type of dish being served (grapefruit, fish, cheese, fruit, or dessert). Butter knives are specially designed for spreading and have blunt edges and a rounded end. Bread knives have teeth along one edge like a saw. There are also electric knives with sawlike edges that are used for cutting meat, etc.

□ **Kitchen knives** A chef's knives are as personal to him as an instrument is to a musician; their weight, balance, and shape are all important features. A standard French set comprises the following main items:

a *boning knife* (used mostly by butchers but also by cooks): small, with a short blade that is wide near the handle and sharply pointed at the end;

a *carving knife* large, with a long wide sharply pointed blade;

a *chopping knife*, with a heavy strong thick blade for breaking up and crushing bones and chopping meat;

a *filleting knife*, with a long flexible sharply pointed blade for filleting fish;

a *ham knife*, with a long flexible blade rounded at the end, that may be smooth, pitted, or fluted, for carving ham and cold or hot meat;

a *chef's kitchen knife*, with a very wide stiff sharply pointed blade, for carving, slicing, shredding, and chopping;

an *all-purpose knife*, the smallest and most frequently used kitchen knife, with a narrow pointed blade, used for peeling vegetables and fruit and many other tasks;

a *slicing knife*, specially designed for vegetables.

A housewife's set generally includes a saw-edged knife, a chopping knife, two all-purpose knives, a carving knife, and possibly a ham knife and a knife for filleting fish.

Various small tools complete the set: a potato peeler (or parer) for peeling vegetables and fruit; a tomato knife, with a very fine saw edge; an oyster knife, with a short thick pointed blade protected by a guard; a knife for scraping lemon zest; and a cannelle knife for fluting. Knives used in pâtisserie include a long round-ended spreading knife; a palette knife (spatula), pliable with no cutting edge, for lifting tarts and pancakes; and a saw-edged knife for cutting biscuits (cookies), cakes, and brioches.

□ **Professional tools** Many knives are designed specifically for use in commercial cookery and butchery:

a *chopper*, with a very thick rectangular blade for breaking up bones;

a *cleaver*, with an almost rectangular blade, fine and rounded, used particularly for cutting up saddles and loins of mutton and pork;

a knife for cutting fat into bards and lardons, which is fitted with milled screws for adjusting the thickness of the slices;

a *meat knife*, in the form of a spatulate chopper, for separating minced meat and sausagemeat;

a *chevalier*, for drawing the sinews from meat;

a *chip knife*, which has small perpendicular blades spaced at regular intervals and is used for cutting potato slices into chips (French fries) (if the blades are closer together, it is a julienne knife);

an *onion knife*, which may have a transparent plastic hood over the blade to prevent tears;

a *fish knife*, which has a serrated edge for cutting large pieces;

a *smoked-salmon knife*, with a long flexible serrated blade;

a *salami knife*, with a saw-edged blade at an angle to the handle, used for thinly slicing all firm-textured charcuterie;

a knife for frozen foods, which has a thick serrated blade, irregularly indented on one or both sides, for sawing through frozen foods.

knife sharpener

AIGUISOIR, AIGUISEUR

A tool made of two steel discs joined side by side and mounted onto a wooden handle. A knife blade is passed between the discs to give it a new cutting edge. This is an effective tool but quickly wears out the knife blade, as does the electric grindstone sharpener, which grinds knives with straight or serrated blades.

knock back (punch down)

ROMPRE

To stop temporarily the fermentation (or rise) of yeast dough by folding it over onto itself several times. This process is carried out twice during the preparation of the dough and improves the final result.

knödel or knödl

A type of sweet or savoury dumpling found all over eastern Europe from Alsace to Czechoslovakia, including southern Germany and Austria. In Alsace and Germany, knödel are small dumplings made from pasta dough and served with cream or melted butter. The dough may be enriched with bone marrow to produce *markknödel* or with puréed liver to form *leberknödel*. They are served as a hot entrée or as a garnish. In Czechoslovakia, knödel may be made from breadcrumbs soaked in milk, from potato purée, or from yeast dough, mixed with chopped onions and meat.

The size and shape varies: some knödel are formed into sausages, which are poached and then sliced. The Austrian *zwetschenknödel* are large plum fritters eaten as a dessert. Another type of dessert knödel consists of squares of dough filled with stewed cherries or apricots, formed into dumplings, and poached in boiling water. These are served with melted butter and sugar, and may be sprinkled with poppy seeds or chopped almonds.

Knorr (Carl Heinrich)

German industrialist (born Meedorf, 1800; died Heilbronn, 1875). He was the son of a teacher and his second marriage to a wealthy lady farmer enabled him to set up, in 1838, a small industrial plant for roasting coffee and chicory. After his death, his two sons expanded the business and began to manufacture pea, lentil, haricot (navy) bean, and sago flours, which were marketed in packets. These were the precursors of today's packet soups.

knuckle or shin JARRET

That part of the leg of an animal carcass lying below the thigh or the shoulder. In France, shin of beef is called the gîte-gite, and shin of mutton corresponds to the manche de gigot (see *gigot*). In veal, the fore or hind knuckle is gelatinous and lean; the bone is rich in marrow. Boned and cubed, it is added to sautéed and braised dishes and blanquettes; whole, it can be cooked in stock with vegetables or form part of a thick meat and vegetable soup. Osso bucco is made from slices of veal knuckle. Pork knuckle or jambonneau can be roasted, braised, or boiled like a ham, but it is less tender. The fore knuckle can be braised, boiled, or cut up and stewed; a semisalted pork knuckle is an excellent addition to sauerkraut, meat and vegetable soups, and dishes which require a slightly salty flavour.

┌──────────────────────────
│ RECIPE

Knuckle of veal à la provençale JARRET DE VEAU À LA PROVENÇALE Cut about 800 g (1¾ lb) veal knuckle (shank) into slices 4 cm (1½ in) thick and season with salt and pepper. Brown in a sauté pan in 3 tablespoons (scant ¼ cup) very hot olive oil. Peel 150 g (5 oz) onions, chop finely, and fry until golden in the sauté pan; add 600 g (1¼ lb) peeled, deseeded, and roughly chopped tomatoes – or 500 g (1 lb) tomatoes and 1 tablespoon tomato purée – together with 1.5 dl (¼ pint, ⅔ cup) dry white wine and a bouquet garni. Stir well, then add 1 dl (6 tablespoons, scant ½ cup) stock or consommé and 2 crushed garlic cloves. Cover the pan and cook gently for about 1 hour 20 minutes, then remove the lid and reduce the liquid for 10 minutes. Adjust the seasoning.

knusper

A large cinnamon-flavoured shortcake covered with chopped almonds and crushed lump sugar. An Austrian speciality, it is cut into squares or rectangles and eaten with tea or coffee. (The name is derived from the German *knusprig*, meaning crunchy.)

koeckbotteram

A cake made with milk, butter, and raisins which is a speciality of Dunkirk. It is similar in texture to the Flemish *couques* (small sweet brioches) but is formed into a small loaf or a large brioche. The literal meaning of the name is 'butter cake'.

kohlrabi CHOU-RAVE

A vegetable of the cabbage family whose fleshy stalk swells like a turnip. Tender when young, kohlrabi is available in autumn and is prepared like turnip or celeriac (the water should be changed after several minutes of cooking).

konbu

An edible seaweed frequently used in Japanese cookery. The large black leaves are dried; when rehydrated they are used as a garnish and stock base for soups or fish (see *dashi*) or as a seasoning for the garnishes.

kosher or kasher

Describing food that is permitted to be eaten according to Jewish dietary laws (the word is a Hebrew one meaning 'permitted', 'ritually correct'). Fruit and vegetables can be eaten without further preparation, but there are strict rules governing the eating of meat. The Old Testament distinguishes between *tahor* (authorized meat) and *tame* (prohibited meat). Rabbinical proscriptions forbid the eating of pork, game, horsemeat, shellfish, fish without scales (eels), snakes, not to mention camel, hippopotamus, and bear. Fermented drinks are also forbidden except for wine, which is subject to certain rules. If a kosher food comes into contact with one that is forbidden, it becomes itself forbidden. Strictly Orthodox Jews therefore only buy foods such as sugar, milk, flour, etc., that are certified kosher. In addition, the *kashruth* (the Jewish dietary laws) lays down two basic principles: no blood must be eaten, and 'the calf shall not be cooked in the milk of its mother'. Therefore meat can only be eaten if it comes from an animal that has been ritually slaughtered: its throat is cut and the meat is then salted and washed. Milking is also carefully supervised. Milk or dairy products must not be used to prepare meat dishes, or even appear at the same meal. Orthodox Jews usually have two sets of kitchen equipment so that accidental contamination can be avoided.

kouing-aman

A Breton cake from the Douarnenez region, whose name means 'bread and butter'. This large flat cake is made from bread dough enriched with butter (unsalted or slightly salted) or double (heavy) cream, cooked in a hot oven, and caramelized with sugar. It is best eaten warm.

⌐ RECIPE

Kouing-aman Dissolve 12 g (½ oz) fresh yeast (1 cake compressed yeast) in 2 tablespoons (3 tablespoons) warm water and mix with 50 g (2 oz, ½ cup) flour. Cover with a cloth and leave to rise in a warm place. When its volume has doubled, sift 200 g (7 oz, 1¾ cups) flour and a pinch of salt into a bowl and add the yeast, kneading it in with the tips of the fingers and adding just enough water to obtain a pliable dough. Knead it well, then leave it to rise again in a warm place.

When its volume has doubled place it on a floured working surface and roll it into a large circle. Dot the surface with 125 g (4½ oz, generous ½ cup) softened butter cut into pieces and sprinkle with 60 g (2 oz, 4 tablespoons, firmly packed) caster (superfine) sugar. Fold the dough into three, roll it out, and fold it again into three. Leave it for 15 minutes. Roll it out into a circle again, fold it in three, and leave it to rest. Repeat the operation once more.

Shape the dough into a circle about 22 cm (9 in) in diameter and put it into a buttered and floured flan tin (pie pan). Score the top of the dough with diamond shapes and brush with egg. Bake at 250 C (475 F, gas 9) for about 20 minutes, basting the top with the butter that will run out of the dough. Sprinkle with icing (confectioners') sugar and continue to bake until the cake is cooked (it should still be fairly moist inside). Unmould straightaway and serve warm.

koulibiaca or coulibiaca
KOULIBIAC

A Russian pie filled with fish, vegetables, rice, and hard-boiled (hard-cooked) eggs. This speciality has been known in France since the 19th century. The filling is topped with *vésiga* (dried spinal marrow of the sturgeon), an essential element of an authentic koulibiaca. European cooks have adapted and varied the recipe in many ways. It can be made with brioche dough or puff pastry, and it may be filled with rice, chicken, and mushrooms or with salmon (or even turbot), onions, parsley, shallots, etc. Hard-boiled eggs are an essential ingredient, but *vésiga* is now very rarely used. Koulibiaca is often cooked without being enclosed in a dish, but traditionally it is baked in an earthenware dish shaped like a fish.

⌐ RECIPE

Salmon koulibiaca KOULIBIAC DE SAUMON Make some puff pastry with

350 g (12 oz, 3 cups) flour, 275 g (10 oz, 1¼ cups) butter, 2 dl (7 fl oz, ¾ cup) water, and 7 g (¼ oz) salt. While the dough is resting, prepare the filling. Hard-boil (hard-cook) 3 eggs, shell them, and cut into quarters. Cook 100 g (4 oz, 8 tablespoons) rice in boiling salted water, then drain. Skin about 400 g (14 oz) boned fresh salmon and poach it in salted water, adding 1 glass (¾ cup) white wine, a bouquet garni, and 10 g (¼ oz) paprika.

Cook for about 12 minutes, remove from the cooker, and allow the salmon to cool in its own cooking liquid. Chop 3 shallots and 350 g (12 oz, 3 cups) mushrooms, season with salt and pepper, and cook briskly in 15 g (½ oz, 1 tablespoon) butter. Finally, cook 3 tablespoons (4 tablespoons) semolina in boiling salted water.

Roll out two-thirds of the dough into a rectangle 3 mm (¼ in) thick. Leaving a narrow border free, spread over a layer of rice, then a layer of flaked salmon, then the mushrooms, then the semolina, and top with the hard-boiled eggs. Roll out the rest of the dough and cover the pie. Pinch the edges to seal them, decorate with strips of pastry, and brush with beaten egg. Cook in the oven at 230 c (450 f, gas 8) for about 30 minutes. Serve the koulibiacà very hot, with melted butter.

kounafa

A cake made in eastern countries, comprising alternating layers of pastry (cut into strips and browned in butter or sesame oil) and sweetened chopped almonds or hazelnuts (pistachios or pine kernels, or a mixture of these nuts, can be used instead). When cooked, the cake is moistened with a thick syrup flavoured with lemon and rosewater. There are many variations:
• *Lakhana:* the nuts are replaced with drained cream cheese, and the strips of pastry are rolled instead of forming flat layers.
• *Basma:* very long pastry strips are arranged in a lattice pattern and the nuts are chopped more coarsely.
• *Gouch:* the pastry strips are very wide, moistened with syrup, and covered either with whole toasted nuts or halves.

The Arab kounafa is similar to the Turkish *kadaif,* which consists of long vermicelli-like strands of pastry and finely chopped nuts, saturated with a heavy syrup.

krapfen

A doughnut made with yeast dough, usually filled with apricot jam, raspberry jam, or almond paste and served hot with a light custard cream or apricot sauce. Also known in France as a *boules de Berlin* or *berlines,* they originated in Germany and Austria.

kromesky CROMESQUI

A hot hors d'oeuvre originating in Poland. It is made by binding a salpicon with a thick sauce and then, when cold, cutting it into rectangles, which are dipped in flour. These are then wrapped in a thin savoury pancake or enclosed in a pig's caul before being dipped in batter and fried. Kromeskies may also be made with a sweet salpicon and served as a sweet.

RECIPES

Preparation of kromeskies PRÉPARATION DES CROMESQUIS

■ *à l'ancienne:* prepare a rich or plain croquette mixture, allow it to cool, and divide it into portions weighing about 60–70 g (2½ oz). Enclose each portion in a thin layer of duchess potato purée and then in a very thin savoury crêpe.

■ *à la française:* the portions of croquette mixture are floured and shaped into pavés or cork shapes.

■ *à la polonaise:* each portion of croquette mixture is wrapped in a very thin savoury crêpe.

■ *à la russe:* the portions of salpicon are wrapped in pieces of pig's caul.

Each kromesky is dipped in melted butter and fried in very hot oil until golden brown. They are drained on absorbent paper, sprinkled with salt, and served garnished with fried parsley. A sauce, corresponding to the basic ingredient of the kromesky mixture, is also served.

Kromeskies à la bonne femme Boil

500 g (18 oz) beef and retain the cooking stock. Soften 2 tablespoons (3 tablespoons) chopped onion in 1 tablespoon butter or lard and add 1 tablespoon flour. Brown lightly and then add 2 dl (7 fl oz, ¾ cup) very reduced beef stock. Stir well, and cook over a very gentle heat for about 15 minutes. Dice the beef very finely and mix it with the sauce. Reheat, and then cool completely. Divide the mixture into portions weighing about 60–70 g (2½ oz), shaping them into cork shapes. Roll them in flour, dip them in batter, and fry in very hot fat.

The beef may be replaced by pieces of cooked chicken or game.

Kromeskies à la florentine Cook some spinach slowly in butter and mix with a well-reduced béchamel sauce and some grated Parmesan cheese. Enclose the mixture in some very thin savoury crêpes, dip them in batter, and fry them in very hot fat.

kugelhopf

A yeast cake from Alsace, of Austrian origin, containing raisins or currants and cooked in a special high crownlike mould. The word is spelt in various ways (*kougelhof*, *gougelhopf*, or *kouglof*) and is derived from the German *Kugel* (a ball). It is said that Marie Antoinette's fondness for this type of dough made such cakes very fashionable. However, some authorities consider that it was Carême who popularized the cake in Paris, when he was pastry chef at the Avice. It is said that he was given the recipe by Eugène, head chef to Prince Schwarzenberg, the Austrian ambassador to Napoleon. Others claim that the first pastrycook to make true kugelhopfs in Paris was a man named Georges, who was established in the Rue de Coq in 1840.

In Alsace, kugelhopf is eaten at Sunday breakfasts, and traditionally prepared the night before, as it is always better when slightly stale. It goes well with Alsace wines.

| RECIPE

Kugelhopf Soak 40 g (1½ oz, ¼ cup) currants in a little warm tea, and soften 175 g (6 oz, ¾ cup) butter at room temperature. Mix 25 g (1oz) fresh yeast (2 cakes compressed yeast) with 3 tablespoons (4 tablespoons) warm milk, add 90 g (3½ oz, scant 1 cup) flour, and mix well. Add just enough warm milk to obtain a soft dough. Shape the dough into a ball, put it in a basin, mark a cross on the top with a knife, cover it with a cloth, and leave it to rise in a warm place, away from draughts.

Sift 250 g (9 oz, scant 2½ cups) flour into a heap on the working surface, make a well in the centre, and into this put 2 eggs and 1 tablespoon warm water. Mix these ingredients and knead the dough well. Dissolve 40 g (1½ oz, 3 tablespoons, firmly packed) caster (superfine) sugar and 1 teaspoon salt in a little water and add this to the mixture, together with the softened butter. Finally add 2 more whole eggs, one at a time, continuing to knead the dough. Roll this out on the board, put the yeast mixture on top, then mix it all together by gathering the dough up, kneading it out on the board, and then repeating the procedure. Finally, add the currants. Put the dough into a bowl, cover it with a cloth, and leave it to rise in a warm place until it has doubled in volume.

Butter a kugelhopf mould and sprinkle the inside with 100 g (4 oz, 1 cup) shredded almonds. When the dough is ready, shape it into a long sausage and put it into the mould, turning the mould as the dough is fed in (it should half-fill the mould). Leave it to rise again in a warm place until the dough reaches the top of the completely cold, sprinkle it lightly with icing (confectioners') sugar.

kulich KOULITCH

A traditional Russian Easter cake, shaped like a tower. It is made from yeast dough and contains raisins, crystallized (candied) fruit, saffron, cardamom, mace, and vanilla. The cake is sprinkled with icing (confectioners') sugar, cut into slices crosswise, and traditionally eaten with hard-boiled (hard-cooked) eggs.

Kümmel

A liqueur flavoured with caraway seeds, probably first made in Holland in the 16th century. (It should not be confused with cumin, another semimedicinal plant, which is not an ingredient of

Kümmel.) Caraway is an ingredient of gripe water, the old remedy for treating wind in babies, and it was recommended for flatulence as long ago as ancient Egyptian times. Production of Kümmel was fairly widespread in the Baltic countries in the 19th century, some being made in Danzig, where the gold-flecked Danziger Goldwasser may be flavoured with both aniseed and caraway.

Today Kümmel is a speciality of the northern European countries: some versions are rather sweet and are therefore served 'on the rocks' to make the drink more refreshing. Because of the pronounced flavour, its culinary uses are somewhat limited, although in English-speaking countries the old-fashioned seed cake, made with caraway seeds, can incorporate Kümmel as an addition.

kumquat

A citrus fruit originating in central China and now cultivated in the Far East, Australia, and America. It resembles a small orange, the size of a quail's egg, and has a sweet rind and a sour flesh. It contains 65 Cal per 100 g and is rich in vitamin A, potassium, and calcium.

It may be eaten fresh (unpeeled) or preserved and is also used to make conserves and jams. It is an ingredient in various cakes, and is particularly good in stuffings for poultry.

kun pod

A Breton speciality from Belle-Île-en-Mer, consisting of dumplings made with salted dough and raisins, served as a garnish for mutton ragouts and chicken blanquettes.

kvass   KWAS

A Russian beer, made locally from rye and barley must or from soaked and fermented black bread, flavoured with mint or juniper berries. It is brown in colour with a low alcohol content and a bitter-sweet taste. It is sold in the streets of Moscow in summer from the backs of small tankers. Kvass can be drunk either as it is, or mixed with spirits or tea; it is also used in cooking, particularly for making soups.

labelling ÉTIQUETAGE

☐ **Food labelling** The information given on the labels of food products must conform to EEC regulations in the country where the product is sold. As well as telling consumers what they are buying, labels on most foods give the weight or volume, a full list of ingredients and additives, the country of origin, and the name and address of the manufacturers. They also often give additional information, such as calorific values, serving suggestions, and the date after which the product must not be sold or used.

☐ **Wine labelling** Everything on the label of a French wine and on the labels of most good and fine wines throughout the world is subject to control, but these vary considerably and the situation is complicated by the difference in labelling laws within the EEC overall and those prevailing in France itself. The information on the capsule, the cork, and the strip label is also controlled, although most back labels can provide general information. The size of the type on a label is usually also controlled, and a code number will enable the bottling establishment to be identified if its name and address is not given. In France, words such as 'Château', 'Domaine', 'Clos', and so on may not be used as a name on a label unless the wine in the bottle actually comes from such a specific area. The use of the terms 'AOC', 'VDQS' (to be phased out in the fairly near future), 'Vin de Pays', and 'Vin de Table' are likewise controlled; the only French wine that is AOC and not obliged to put this on the label is champagne, but champagne labels are equally strictly controlled and bear a code number enabling them to be identified by the CIVC (the local body in charge of the regulations).

Generally speaking, the more detail given on a label, the finer the wine. The bodies governing the controls must comply with the labelling requirements of markets to which they export. For example, it is quite legal to describe a sparkling wine as 'champagne' in the New World countries in which it is made, but this would be prohibited both in France and in the EEC. Nor can such classic wine names as 'Sauternes', 'Claret', 'sherry', and 'port' be put on labels regardless: there is a regulation, for example, that requires a wine similar to sherry to bear the name of its country of origin in the same sized lettering and type on its label if the word 'sherry' is used.

☐ **The French 'label'** In France the word 'label' is used to denote the qualities and specific characteristics of particular items of food. Any product described as *sous label* must meet any standards set down for that product and must have the specific qualities associated with its place of origin, its production methods, and its manufacture.

In 1965 the *label rouge* (red label) was introduced. This is a seal with a ribbon that is awarded to certain food products that have been approved by the Ministry of Agriculture (although such awards do not constitute government guarantees of quality).

La Bouille

A soft double-cream Normandy cheese with a fat content of 60%, made from enriched cows' milk. It is produced in the village of La Bouille and has a fruity flavour and a strong bouquet. Firm to the touch and with a decorated rind, it is cylindrical in shape, measuring 8 cm (3 in) in diameter and 5.5 cm (2 in) deep. La Bouille is best from July to March or April and should be served with a strong country cider or a full-bodied red wine.

The local Normandy milk churns are also called *bouilles*.

Labskaus

A dish from northern Germany, made with marinated minced (ground) beef, onions, and either herrings or anchovies, which are browned in lard and then added to a potato purée seasoned with pepper and nutmeg. It is garnished with a poached egg, marinated beetroot (red beet), and gherkins.

Labskaus is a variation on the old Norwegian dish *lapskaus* – salt cod with potatoes – which acquired its name from the nickname 'lobscouse', given to it by British seamen.

Lacam (Pierre)

French pastrycook and culinary historian (born Saint-Amand-de-Belvès, 1836; died Paris, 1902). Lacam created many petits fours and desserts, notably puddings topped with Italian meringue. He is best known for his masséna, which he dedicated to the Duc de Rivoli: an oval of sweet shortcrust pastry (basic pie dough) and an oval-shaped base of sponge cake are sandwiched together with chestnut purée, covered with Italian meringue, and iced (frosted) half with chocolate, and half with coffee icing (frosting). Lacam is also credited with the invention of the pastry crimper. Among his literary works are *Le Nouveau Pâtissier-Glacier français et étranger* (1865), the massive *Mémorial historique et géographique de la pâtisserie* (1890), and *Le Glacier classique et artistique en France et en Italie* (1893). He also edited a professional magazine, *La Cuisine française et étrangère*.

La Chapelle (Vincent)

French chef, born in 1703, who began his career in England in the service of Lord Chesterfield. His work *The Modern Cook* was published in 1733 in three volumes; it was subsequently reprinted several times. He returned to France to work for the Prince of Orange-Nassau, then for Madame de Pompadour, and finally, for Louis XV. His book was first published in French (as *Le Cuisinier moderne*) in 1735 in four volumes. It was enlarged to five volumes in its final edition in 1742. *Le Cuisinier moderne* was praised by Carême and, as recently as 1930, it was considered by Nignon to be perfectly up to date. La Chapelle's recipes were intentionally simple, and are therefore eminently suitable for the cooks of the 1980s. Among his dishes are stuffed sole (with anchovies, parsley, shallots, and spring onions (scallions), cooked in white wine, and sprinkled with orange juice), mackerel with fennel and gooseberries, and lamb *ratons* (paupiettes of leg of lamb stuffed with chicken and roasted on skewers).

La Clape

Red, rosé, or white wine (VDQS) from Languedoc, produced in a village on a spur of the Corbières hills. The wines are typical of this part of the south of France – dryish, aromatic, lightweight whites and fullish reds, most enjoyable while young, although a few can improve with some bottle age.

lacquered duck

CANARD LAQUÉ

A traditional Chinese dish in which a duck is coated with a sweet-and-sour 'lacquer sauce', roasted, and served, hot or cold, cut into small pieces. Pork is prepared in the same way. The sauce is a mixture of soy sauce, *cinq-épices* (five spices), liquid honey, oil, garlic, vinegar, flour, ginger, red colouring, rice alcohol, chilli oil, and baking powder.

The duck should be drawn, pierced in several places with a needle, left to marinate overnight in the sauce, and then hung. It is then brushed with sauce several times and allowed to dry between each coat. It is this process which will make the skin golden and crispy. The duck is then roasted on a spit and basted several times with a juice and lacquer sauce while cooking. Success depends on the degree to which the duck absorbs the sauce. If the duck is roasted in the oven and not on a spit, it must not lie in the dripping pan, otherwise the skin will be dry and shrivelled. Finally, the duck should be cut (across the grain of the meat) into small pieces. These are served with fresh lettuce leaves and heads of sweet-and-sour leeks or gherkins.

Lacrima Christi

An Italian white wine produced on the volcanic slopes of Mount Vesuvius. Pale gold in colour, it is either dry or sweetish. It gets its name ('tear of Christ') from an old legend: when Lucifer was banished from Heaven, he fell to earth in what is now Campania, and the impact created the Bay of Naples. Sad to see such a beautiful country falling prey to the devil, Christ shed a tear, which landed on Vesuvius. Where the tear fell, a vine sprang up. The vineyard is today planted with Greco and Fiano vines. Lacrima Christi is unusual in that it is a white wine traditionally served at room temperature, not chilled.

Lacroix (Eugène)

German chef (born Altdorf, 1886; died Frankfurt, 1964). He was the son of restaurant owners in Heidelberg, and became apprenticed to one of the chefs of Napoleon III. He established himself and made his name in Strasbourg, but left the city in 1918. He moved to Frankfurt, where he created a foie gras *en croûte* and a clear turtle soup.

lactary LACTAIRE

Any mushroom of the genus *Lactarius*, which exudes a white or coloured milky juice when cut. Lactaries are bitter, with an unpleasant smell, and are frequently inedible. They should therefore be tasted when picked, and only those with a sweet-tasting juice should be retained. None of them is poisonous, but few are worth eating. The best is *Lactarius sanguifluus*, which has dark red juice and is common in the Midi; it should either be grilled (broiled) or cooked slowly with meat, particularly in a gibelotte of rabbit. The orange-coloured lactary, which smells of either crayfish or herrings, may be seasoned and eaten raw. The curry milk cap (*Lactarius camphoratus*). smells like celery and can be dried and used as a condiment. It can also be used to flavour omelettes. Lastly, the saffron milk cap (*Lactarius deliciosus*) has an orange-coloured juice that changes to green, and is usually pickled when it is small, or used to make a piquant sauce.

RECIPE

grilled (broiled) saffron milk caps à la Lucifer LACTAIRES GRILLÉS À LA LUCIFER Take the caps from 600 g (1¼ lb) young saffron milk caps, blanch them for 3 minutes, drain, and blot dry.

Prepare 2 dl (7 fl oz, ¾ cup) devilled sauce, boil down to reduce, and add 1 teaspoon paprika, 300 ml (½ pint, 1½ cups) brown sauce, and 2 tablespoons (3 tablespoons) tomato purée. Stir, cook over a moderate heat, and season with salt. Add 1 tablespoon Worcestershire sauce and a generous pinch of cayenne. Strain through a sieve, return to the saucepan, and keep hot in a bain-marie.

Chop a small bunch of parsley and a little fennel. Brush the mushroom caps with olive oil and grill (broil) for 4 minutes. Then rub them with garlic and arrange them on a dish. Sprinkle them generously with the chopped parsley and fennel, together with about 100 g (4 oz, 1 cup) grated Parmesan cheese and some salt. Whisk the hot sauce and pour it over the mushrooms.

ladle LOUCHE, POCHON

A large bowl-shaped spoon with a long handle, used for serving soups and

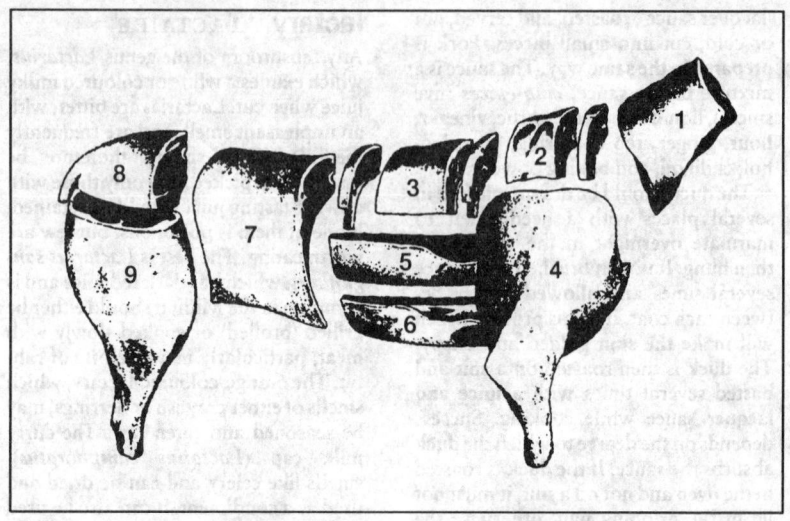

French cuts of lamb. *1. collet (small animals) or collier (large animals); 2. carré de côtes découvertes; 3. carré de côtes premières: côtes premières and côtes secondes; 4. gigot; 5. haut de côtelettes; 6. poitrine; 7. filet; 8. selle de gigot, 9. gigot entier (with selle) or raccourci.*

stews. A smaller ladle with a lip is used in cooking for basting and for spooning out cooking juices and sauces; it is made of aluminium or tin. There is another kind of ladle for punch or mulled wine, which is also lipped and sometimes made of glass. The ladle used in cheese-making for pouring the curds into the moulds is known in France as a *poche*.

Ladoix-Serrigny

AOC red and white Burgundy from the northern end of the Côte de Beaune. The name rarely appears on labels because the growers of the two villages under-standably prefer to use the names of wines that may be classified as Grand and Premier Cru Aloxe-Corton, and also may declassify Ladoix-Serrigny as Côte-de-Beaune-Villages.

Laguiole-Aubrac

A cows'-milk cheese from Rouergue, containing 45% fat. It is a pressed un-cooked cheese with a natural brushed rind that is either light or dark grey, depending on its storage time (from three to six months in a damp cellar). Made in Aubrac and protected by an *appellation contrôlée*, Laguiole-Aubrac, or Fourme de Laguiole, is shaped into a cylinder 40 cm (16 in) in diameter and 35–40 cm (14–16 in) high. A straw-coloured strong-flavoured cheese that is springy to the touch, it is very similar to Cantal. It is best in March or April. Laguiole-Aubrac is served at the end of a meal or as a snack and is also used in cabbage and bread soup. It is manufactured on a small scale in the mountain pastures.

Laguipière

French chef (born mid-18th century; died Vilnius, 1812). He learned his trade in the household of Condé and followed the family into exile. On his return to France, he went to work for Napoleon and Carême was one of his pupils. Laguipière then moved into the service of Marshal Murat, travelling to Naples with his employer and then accompanying him on the Russian cam-paign. He died during the retreat of the French army from Moscow, and his body was brought back to France on the back of his master's carriage. Carême paid his respects to Laguipière in his introduction to *Le Cuisinier parisien*: 'You were a man of outstanding gifts which brought you the hatred of those who should have admired your efforts to improve our existence. You should have died in Paris, respected by all for your great work.'

This great chef left no literary legacy, but his name lives on in several recipes, some of which may have been merely dedicated to him by other chefs: sauces; fillets of sole, turbot, or brill (poached, then coated in a white wine or normande sauce, and sprinkled with a julienne of truffles marinated in Madeira); and a salmis of pheasant (part-roasted, jointed, then casseroled in a stock made from the bones, onions, bacon, red wine, Madeira, and a little bouillon).

RECIPES

Dartois Laguipière Prepare some strips of puff pastry. Sandwich them together with a salpicon of braised calves' sweetbreads and truffles mixed with finely diced vegetables and bound together with a thick velouté sauce. Bake in a hot oven, cut into rectangles, and serve.

Laguipière sauce SAUCE LAGUIPIÈRE (from Carême's recipe) Put into a saucepan 1 large tablespoon butter sauce, 1 tablespoon good consommé or a little chicken glaze, a pinch of salt, some nutmeg, and either plain vinegar or lemon juice. Boil for a few seconds, then stir in a generous knob of fine butter. The sauce may also be made with fish glaze instead of chicken glaze.

Laguipière sauce is often known as *sauce au beurre à la Laguipière*

Laguipière sauce for fish SAUCE LAGUIPIÈRE POUR POISSONS Prepare some normande sauce. Infuse 2 tablespoons (3 tablespoons) chopped truffles in 1 tablespoon Madeira. Mix the 2 preparations together thoroughly.

lamb AGNEAU

The male or female young of the sheep. Lambs killed for the market in France fall into three categories. The milk lamb, known in France as *agnelet*, is killed before being weaned, at the age of 30 to 40 days, and weighs from 8 to 10 kg (18 to 22½ lb). The meat of the milk lamb is very tender and delicate, if a little lacking in flavour. Milk collection areas for Roquefort cheese specialize in this type of lamb production, as the ewes must be freed as soon as possible after lambing for milking.

The second category is the *agneau blanc* or *laiton*, which is mainly available from Christmas to June and provides 70% of the lamb that comes into the French market. Slaughtered at an age of 70 to 150 days, it weighs from 20 to 25 kg (45 to 56 lb). It has had a rich milk-based diet and its dark pink meat, firm at the time of purchase, becomes very tender on cooking; its fat is white.

Lastly, the grazing lamb, known as *broutart* as it has fed on pasture, is killed at between 6 and 9 months and weighs from 30 to 40 kg (67 to 90 lb). Its diet causes its fat to lose its whiteness, giving rise to its French name of *agneau gris* ('grey lamb'). Its flesh is fully developed, firmer, and of a stronger flavour, and many gourmets prefer it to the *agneau blanc*. It is sold at the butcher's mainly from September to December and is increasingly replacing mutton, which – having a stronger flavour – is now hardly ever in demand. (See *salt-meadow sheep*.)

Lamb is cut up in the same way as mutton and is usually eaten roasted, although lamb cutlets and chops may be grilled. There is an old French tradition of serving lamb on Easter Sunday.

The lamb often appears in the coats of arms of butchers' guilds, particularly in Paris.

RECIPES

Breaded lamb cutlets (rib lamb chops) CÔTELETTES D'AGNEAU PANÉES Season the cutlets (chops) with salt and pepper and coat them with a beaten egg, then with breadcrumbs. Sauté on both sides in clarified butter, then arrange in a crown in a serving dish and sprinkle with noisette butter.

Grilled lamb cutlets (broiled rib lamb chops) CÔTELETTES D'AGNEAU GRILLÉES Season the cutlets (chops) with salt and pepper, brush them with melted butter or groundnut oil, and

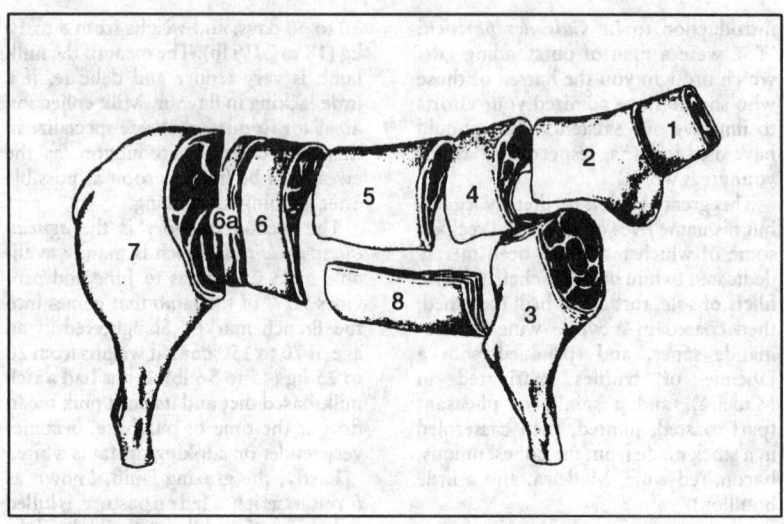

British cuts of lamb. *1. scrag end of neck; 2. middle neck; 3. shoulder; 4. best end of neck; 5. loin; 6. chump; 6a. chump chops; 7. leg; 8. breast.*

cook either over a barbecue or under the grill. Arrange on a serving dish: the protruding 'handle' bone may be covered with a white frill. Garnish with watercress or with a green vegetable, which may be steamed (and tossed in butter or cream if desired), braised, puréed, or sautéed. Serve with noisette potatoes.

Sautéed lamb cutlets (rib lamb chops)
CÔTELETTES D'AGNEAU SAUTÉES
Season the cutlets with salt and pepper then sauté on both sides in clarified butter, goose fat, or olive oil. The sautéed cutlets (chops) may be served with any of the following garnishes: *à la financière, à la française, à la portugaise, à la romaine.*

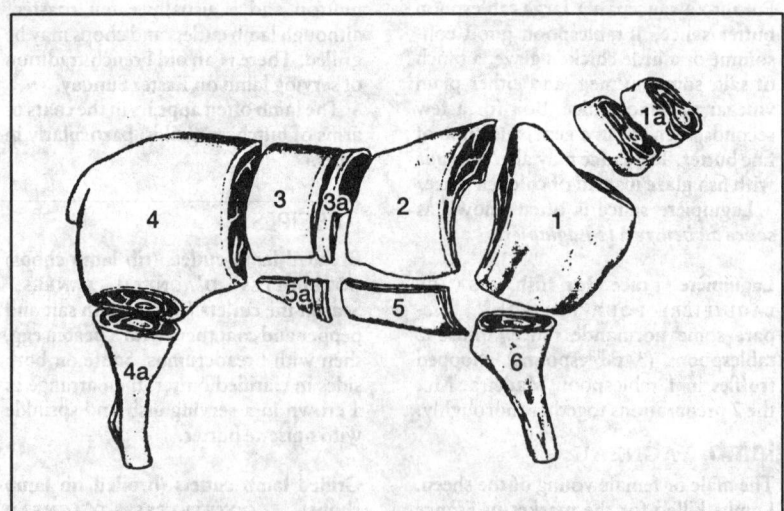

American cuts of lamb. *1. shoulder; 1a. neck slice; 2. rib; 3. loin; 3a. loin chop; 4. leg; 4a. hind shank; 5. breast; 5a. riblets; 6. fore shank.*

Grilled (broiled) loin of lamb CARRÉ D'AGNEAU GRILLÉ Shorten and trim the bones of a loin of lamb and lightly score its skin in a criss-cross pattern. Season the joint with salt and pepper and brush with melted butter. Cook very slowly on both sides either under the grill or over a barbecue well away from the source of heat until the meat is cooked through. Garnish with watercress or young vegetables and serve with maître d'hôtel butter.

Loin of lamb à la bonne femme CARRÉ D'AGNEAU À LA BONNE FEMME Lightly brown a dozen button onions in melted butter and set aside. Cut 250 g (9 oz) potatoes into large olive-shaped pieces. Coarsely chop 50 g (2 oz) unsalted streaky bacon. Blanch the bacon for 1 minute in boiling water, then drain, pat dry, and lightly fry in butter with the potatoes. Shorten and trim the bones of a 1 kg (2¼ lb) loin of lamb joint. Brown the joint on all sides in butter over a fairly high heat, then place it in a large casserole, season with salt and pepper, and add the onions, bacon pieces, and potatoes. Spoon 1–2 tablespoons melted butter over the joint, cover the casserole, and cook in a moderate oven (180 C, 350 F, gas 4) for about one hour until the lamb is cooked. Serve the lamb in slices with the casserole vegetables and juices spooned round.

Loin of lamb à la bordelaise CARRÉ D'AGNEAU À LA BORDELAISE Cut 250 g (9 oz) potatoes into large olive-shaped pieces. Slice 225 g (8 oz) mushrooms (preferably cep mushrooms) and fry them quickly in a little oil. Shorten and trim the bones of a 1 kg (2¼ lb) loin of lamb, then brown on all sides in equal quantities of melted butter and oil. Place the joint in a large casserole with the mushrooms and potatoes, and season. Cover and cook the joint in a moderate oven (180 C, 350 F, gas 4) for about 1 hour, then add a small clove of crushed garlic mixed with several tablespoons stock and a little tomato purée. Continue to cook until the lamb is tender.

Roast loin of lamb CARRÉ D'AGNEAU RÔTI Shorten and trim the bones of a loin of lamb. Brown it on all sides in butter, then place in a roasting tin, season with salt and pepper, and, adding a little more melted butter, roast in the oven at 220 C (425 F, gas 7) allowing 25 minutes per kg (11 minutes per lb). When cooked place the lamb on a serving dish and keep hot. Add 150 ml (5 fl oz, ¾ cup) white wine to the meat juices and boil vigorously to reduce; add 2 or 3 tablespoons jellied stock to make a gravy. Sprinkle the joint with chopped parsley to serve.

Note: loin may also be spit-roasted allowing the same time. Cooked by either method, the meat will be rare.

Stuffed milk lamb AGNEAU DE LAIT FARCI Ask the butcher to dress a whole baby lamb ready for stuffing and spit-roasting. Finely slice the liver, heart, sweetbreads, and kidneys and fry quickly in butter, seasoning with salt and pepper. Add these to half-cooked rice pilaff and loosely stuff the lamb cavity with the mixture. Sew up the openings and truss the animal by tying the legs and shoulders close to the body to give it a regular shape. Pierce the lamb evenly with the spit, season with salt and pepper, and cook over a high heat (20 minutes per kg, 15 minutes per lb). Place a pan under the lamb to catch the juices; blend sufficient stock into the pan juices to make a gravy and keep it hot. Remove the lamb from the spit, untruss it, and place it on a long serving dish. Garnish with watercress and lemon quarters and serve the gravy separately.

Reheated sliced lamb in sauce ÉMINCÉS D'AGNEAU Cut cold cooked shoulder or leg of lamb into very thin slices and arrange on a lightly buttered dish. Coat with one of the following boiling hot sauces: bordelaise, bourguignonne, charcutière, chasseur, duxelles, Italian, lyonnaise, Madeira, or poivrade. Cover the dish and reheat gently on the top of the stove or in a bainmarie.

Lamballe

The name given to various dishes in honour of the Princess de Lamballe, a friend of Marie-Antoinette. These include a soup made from a purée of garden or split peas mixed with tapioca cooked in consommé and also a dish of stuffed quails in paper cases.

RECIPES

Lamballe soup POTAGE LAMBALLE Prepare 8 dl (1¼ pints, 1½ pints) purée of fresh peas (see *Saint-Germain*). Add 7 dl (scant 1¼ pints, 1½ pints) consommé with tapioca cooked in it and mix well. Garnish with chervil leaves.

Stuffed quails in cases à la Lamballe CAILLES FARCIES EN CAISSES À LA LAMBALLE Prepare the stuffed quails in cases (see *quail*), lining the base of each greaseproof (waxed) paper case with a julienne of mushrooms and truffles blended with cream. Add some port to the pan juices in which the quails were cooked, blend in some fresh cream, and pour the resulting sauce over the quails.

lambic

The highly intoxicating slightly bitter Belgian beer made with malt and uncooked wheat. Lambic is produced by spontaneous fermentation and may either be sold from the keg and pumped under pressure into the glass or it may be bottled. In the latter case, some new beer is added just before bottling. This induces a secondary fermentation, and the resulting beer is known as *gueuze*.

Cherry flavouring is added to make *Kriek-Lambic*.

lamb's lettuce MÂCHE

A plant with rounded leaves in a rosette form which is usually eaten raw in a salad, mainly in France and Italy. It is also known as corn salad and, in France, as *doucette*, *valérianelle potagère*, *raiponce*, and *oreille-de-lièvre*. It grows wild in fields, usually in the autumn, but is cultivated in France from September to March and gives a good flavour to a winter salad. It yields only 36 Cal per 100 g but is rich in cellulose and vitamins. There are several varieties: Northern Green, with large leaves, is inferior to the round variety, which has smaller leaves and is juicy and tender; Italian corn salad has lighter leaves, slightly velvety and indented, and is less tasty. The lettuce must be carefully washed and dried, leaf by leaf, before it is eaten. It is used in mixed salads with potatoes, walnuts, beetroot (red beet), etc., and enriches poultry stuffings. It can also be cooked like spinach.

RECIPES

Lamb's lettuce mixed salad SALADE DE MÂCHE PANACHÉE Peel and chop 200 g (7 oz, 6¼ cups) cooked beetroot (red beet). Trim, wash, and cut into rings 200 g (7 oz) chicory (endive). Wash 250 g (9 oz) lamb's lettuce. Peel, core, and thinly slice an apple, and sprinkle with lemon juice. Place all these ingredients in a salad bowl. Prepare a vinaigrette with 1 teaspoon mustard, pour onto the salad, and mix well. A small handful of walnut kernels can be added to the salad or a little Roquefort cheese can be mixed into the vinaigrette.

Lamb's lettuce salad with bacon SALADE DE MÂCHE AUX PETITS LARDONS Cut 150 g (5 oz) half-salted belly of pork into pieces and blanch for 3 minutes in boiling water. Trim, peel, and wash 400 g (14 oz) lamb's lettuce. Arrange in a salad bowl. Brown the bacon pieces in a little butter and add to the salad. Sprinkle with vinaigrette.

lamprey LAMPROIE

An eel-like fish, up to 1 m (3 ft) long, with small fins and no scales. Using its sucker-like mouth, it attaches itself to other fish and feeds on their blood. The European species are marine but they migrate upriver to spawn in fresh water. In France they are caught in the lower reaches of the Gironde, Loire, Rhône, and other large rivers. Lampreys have been a delicacy since ancient times. Roman patricians ate them, and Saint Louis had them brought from Nantes in barrels of water. Gloucester (in England) was famous for its lamprey pies, and in France, braised lamprey *à l'angevine* and lamprey *à la bordelaise* are still popular dishes. The fish is bled, washed, and then scalded so that the skin can be easily removed. Then the head and the dorsal nerve that runs down the body from it are removed. The lamprey can then be sliced and cooked in a similar way to eel. It is fatty like eel, but is considered to be superior.

RECIPE

Lamprey à la bordelaise LAMPROIE À LA BORDELAISE Bleed a medium lamprey, reserving the blood to flavour the sauce. Scald the fish and scrape off the skin. Remove the dorsal nerve (cut off the lamprey's tail, make an incision around the neck just below the gills, then take hold of the nerve through this opening and pull it out). Cut the fish into slices 6 cm (2½ in) thick and put them into a buttered pan lined with sliced onions and carrots. Add a bouquet garni and a crushed garlic clove, season with salt and pepper, and add enough red wine to cover the fish. Boil briskly for about 10 minutes, then drain the lamprey slices.

Clean 4 leeks, cut each into 3 slices, and cook in a little butter with 4 tablespoons (5 tablespoons) finely diced ham. Add the lamprey. Make a roux with 2 tablespoons (3 tablespoons) butter and an equal quantity of flour. Add the cooking stock of the lamprey and cook for 15 minutes. Strain the sauce and pour it over the lamprey in the pan with the vegetables. Simmer very gently until the fish is cooked.

Arrange the lamprey slices on a round dish, stir the reserved blood into the sauce, and pour over the fish. Garnish with slices of bread fried in butter.

Lancashire cheese

An English cows'-milk cheese containing 45% fat. It is a pressed uncooked soft-bodied cheese, with a natural tendency to crumble. Although it is delicious eaten on its own, it is equally good grilled on toast and its crumbly texture makes it suitable as a condiment in cooking. Lancashire cheese is increasingly mass-produced, but the farmhouse version can still be found and has a much stronger flavour. This is because a second quantity of fresh curds is added to a batch that has been prepared the previous evening. Sage Lancashire is flavoured and veined with sage.

landaise (à la)

Describing dishes inspired by cooking techniques of the Landes region of France. The most common ingredients are Bayonne ham, goose fat, and mushrooms. The name can be applied both to basic dishes (such as potatoes) and to more elaborate preparations (such as garden warblers, or goose or duck livers), as well as to such regional culinary classics as *confit d'oie* (preserved goose).

RECIPE

Potatoes à la landaise POMMES DE TERRE À LA LANDAISE Fry 100 g (4 oz, 1 cup) chopped onions and 150 g (5 oz, generous ½ cup) diced Bayonne ham in goose fat or lard. When both are browned, add 500 g (18 oz) potatoes cut into large dice. Season with salt and pepper, cover, and cook, stirring from time to time. Just before serving add 1 tablespoon chopped garlic and parsley.

other recipes See *confit*, *warbler*.

langouste

A crustacean also known as spiny lobster, thorny lobster, rock lobster, and crawfish (it differs from the true lobster in having no claws). In addition, it is also sometimes known as crayfish, a cause of confusion with the freshwater crayfish (which resembles a diminutive lobster). To cap the confused nomenclature, in the United States the freshwater crayfish is also known as crawfish. To avoid confusion, the French name is used in this article and elsewhere in the book.

It takes five years for a langouste to grow to the regulation size (in France) for the table – 23 cm (9 in) long – during which time it sheds its shell more than 20 times. When it reaches its maximum size, it can weigh up to 4 kg (9 lb). Despite the fact that it produces up to 100,000 eggs at a time, the langouste is becoming scarcer. Attempts have been made to breed them near Roscoff, in northwestern France.

Langoustes inhabit rocky seabeds at a depth of between 20 and 150 m (65 and 490 ft) and are found in the Atlantic, the Mediterranean, and around the coasts of the West Indies and South America. There are several different kinds:

• The *red*, *Breton*, or *common langouste*, also known as thorny lobster, is considered to be the best, being fished in the English Channel, the Atlantic Ocean, and the western Mediterranean.

Its shell is reddish-brown or purplish-red and is covered with sharp spines. It has two light spots on each segment.

• The *pink* or *Portuguese langouste* is found in the seas off southwestern Ireland and as far south as Senegal. It is the same length as the common variety but its body is narrower and its shell is covered with light blotches.

• The *green* or *painted langouste* has the longest antennae, plus an additional elongated pair. Its carapace is bluish-green and there are a light-coloured stripe and two pale blotches on each segment.

• The *brown* or *Cape langouste* has a reddish-brown scaly shell and is usually sold frozen, sometimes as lobster tails.

• The *Florida langouste* is also brown and has large pale spots on its second and sixth segments. It is also usually marketed frozen and often sold as lobster tails.

Fresh langoustes should be bought live and undamaged, with all their legs intact and no holes in their shells. Inevitably, the antennae are sometimes broken, but this is unimportant. Females are considered to be superior, and they can be recognized by the egg sacs beneath the thorax. Like all shellfish, langouste should be cooked alive. The pale delicate firm flesh has a milder flavour than that of the true lobster, but the same recipes can be used for both. However, the langouste is more suitable for highly seasoned recipes. The most visually appealing methods of preparing langouste are *en bellevue* and *à la parisienne*.

There are also two other delicious recipes worthy of mention, one from Spain and one from China. The Spanish recipe is for Catalonian langouste with unsweetened chocolate, cooked with a tomato-based sauce seasoned with chopped almonds and hazelnuts, red pepper, and cinnamon chocolate. The Chinese speciality is langouste with ginger, in which the shellfish is sautéed in sesame oil with onions, chives, and fresh ginger.

RECIPES

Grilled (broiled) langouste with basil butter LANGOUSTE GRILLÉE AU BEURRE DE BASILIC (from Roger Vergé's recipe) Cut a langouste in two. Place the halves in a roasting dish (carapace side down). Season the cut surface with salt and pepper and moisten with olive oil. Grill for 10 minutes, turning once. Turn once more, so that the flesh faces upwards, and baste with a mixture of melted butter and roughly chopped fresh basil. Continue to baste at regular intervals until the langouste is cooked (about 20 minutes). Serve piping hot.

Langouste croustades CROUSTADES À LA LANGOUSTE Line some tartlet tins with pastry and bake them blind. Fill them with a macédoine of vegetables blended with mayonnaise and top with a slice of langouste. Brush with aspic. Using a star (fluted) nozzle, pipe a ring of thick mayonnaise around the edge.

Langouste des chroniqueurs (from Fernand Point's recipe) Brown 2 chopped carrots and 3 chopped onions in butter in a saucepan. Add the diced flesh of a langouste together with salt, a generous pinch of cayenne, a glass of slightly stale Château Grillet, 2–3 tablespoons brandy, and 4–5 tablespoons fresh tomato juice. Cook for 15 minutes. Remove the langouste pieces and keep hot. Reduce the sauce, add a knob of butter, remove from the heat, and add 2 egg yolks. Pour the sauce over the langouste and sprinkle with chopped parsley.

Langouste du grincheux (from Alex Humbert's recipe) Cut the langouste into thick slices. Heat equal quantities of butter and oil in a deep frying pan and brown the slices with salt, pepper, and cayenne. Add 1½ glasses of port and 2 glasses of fish stock. Cover and cook gently for 15 minutes. Remove the langouste slices and discard the shells. Keep the flesh hot and moisten with a little port. Reduce the liquid in the pan. Beat together 3 egg yolks and 1 glass of port. Remove the pan from the heat, add the egg yolks and port to the pan juices, and stir well. Return the langouste flesh to the pan and heat through. Do not allow to boil.

Langouste salad SALADE DE LAN-

GOUSTE Poach a langouste in court-bouillon, drain, and leave to cool completely. Cook 500 g (1 lb) small French (string) beans in an uncovered pan for 15–20 minutes, but do not let them go soft. Allow to cool completely. Separate the thorax of the langouste from the tail. Remove the tail flesh and cut into even slices. Finely dice the remaining flesh. Also remove the creamy part of the flesh. Using a melon baller, make small balls from the flesh of an avocado and sprinkle with lemon juice. Peel and dice a cucumber.

Make a vinaigrette from 9 tablespoons (generous ⅔ cup) oil, 3 tablespoons (¼ cup) tarragon vinegar (or sherry), 2 tablespoons (3 tablespoons) lemon juice, salt, pepper, and chopped herbs. Incorporate the creamy flesh of the langouste in this dressing. Mix the drained French beans, the diced langouste and cucumber, and the vinaigrette in a salad bowl. Garnish with the avocado balls, and arrange the langouste slices in a circle on the salad. Sprinkle with chopped basil. Serve the remaining vinaigrette separately.

langoustine

A marine crustacean resembling a crayfish, which is widely available in western Europe; scampi are a type of langoustine. Similar to the Dublin Bay prawn, the langoustine is 15–25 cm (6–10 in) long with a yellowish-pink shell. Its pincers are characteristically ridged and, like the legs, are white-tipped. Langoustines cannot live for long out of water and they are therefore usually sold cooked, displayed on a bed of ice. When buying langoustines look for bright black eyes and shiny pink shells (they do not change colour when cooked). They can be poached and served whole, but many dishes require only the shelled tails. They are one of the ingredients of paella, and are often used instead of king prawns in European versions of Chinese and Vietnamese cookery.

⎸RECIPES

Brochettes of langoustine tails BROCHETTES DE QUEUES DE LANGOUSTINE Choose some medium langoustines. Shell the tails and marinate them for at least 30 minutes in the same preparation as that for the langoustine fritters. Then thread them on skewers and cook gently, either over glowing embers or under a grill (broiler). Serve with a piping hot ratatouille or with rice with green peas and mushrooms.

Langoustine fritters BEIGNETS DE LANGOUSTINES Choose 12 medium langoustines and shell the tails. Marinate for 30 minutes in a mixture of olive oil (3 tablespoons, ¼ cup), lemon juice (1½ tablespoons, 2 tablespoons), chopped parsley (1 generous tablespoon), chopped garlic (1 small clove), Provençal herbs (1 small teaspoon), salt, pepper, and a dash of cayenne. Prepare some fritter batter. Drain the langoustine tails, dip them in the batter, and deep-fry until golden. Drain on absorbent paper and serve with lemon halves and tartare sauce.

Poached langoustines LANGOUSTINES POCHÉES Add the langoustines to a cold court-bouillon, bring to the boil, and simmer gently for 6 minutes (or until cooked). Drain and leave to cool.

The dressings are the same as for lobster or crayfish.

Langres

A cows'-milk cheese (45% fat content) from Bassigny (Haute-Marne department) in the Champagne area of France. Langres is a soft cheese with a reddish-brown rind and is produced in rounds 10 cm (4 in) in diameter and 5 cm (2 in) deep), which are slightly hollowed out in the middle. It is springy to the touch, with a creamy yellow paste. It has a strong aroma and flavour, and is best served with a full-bodied wine or with beer.

langue-de-chat

A small dry finger-shaped biscuit whose name (meaning cat's tongue) is probably derived from its shape. Langues-de-chat are thin and fragile, but they keep well and are usually served with iced desserts, creams, fruit salad, champagne, and dessert wines.

RECIPES

Langues-de-chat I   Cut 125 g (4½ oz, generous ½ cup) butter into pieces and cream with a wooden spatula until smooth. Add 1 tablespoon vanilla sugar and 75–100 g (3–4 oz, ½ cup) caster (superfine) sugar; work for about 5 minutes with a whisk or a wooden spatula. Blend in 2 eggs, one at a time. Finally, add 125 g (4½ oz, generous cup) sifted flour a little at a time, mixing it in with a whisk. Lightly grease a baking tray (sheet). Using a forcing (piping) bag with a round nozzle, pipe the mixture into strips 5 cm (2 in) long, leaving a space of about 2.5 cm (1 in) between them. Bake in a hot oven for about 8 minutes: remove as soon as the languesde-chat have begun to turn golden.

Langues-de-chat II   Work together in a mixing bowl 250 g (9 oz, generous cup) caster (superfine) sugar, 200 g (7 oz, 1¾ cup) flour, and 1 tablespoon vanilla sugar. Gently fold in 3 egg whites beaten into stiff peaks. Pipe the mixture and bake as described in the previous recipe. When the langues-de-chat are cooked, turn off the heat and leave them to cool in the oven.

Languedoc

This area of southwestern France, which stretches from the Garonne to the Rhône and from the Lozère to the Mediterranean, is rich in arable land, natural resources, and culinary traditions. The fertile countryside around Toulouse yields garlic, asparagus, onions, tomatoes, and plums, while the cereal crops support excellent poultry (geese, ducks, and chickens). Some of the finest French lamb is produced on the limestone Causses, and the Gard is the site of many fruit orchards (cherries, peaches, apricots, figs, etc). Freshwater fish include pike, perch, tench, lampreys, and eels, and the Mediterranean provides tuna, mackerel, anchovies, and red mullet, as well as the delicious Bouzigues blue-ribbed oysters. The marshy coastal areas are visited by quail, woodcook, and waterfowl, while hares, rabbits, thrushes, and red-legged partridge are plentiful in the Cévennes.

From the Lozère to the Haute-Garonne, the woodlands provide such mushrooms as ceps, morels, and orange-milk agarics; truffles can be found in the Uzès region, and the whole Languedoc area is ideal for viniculture.

The principal cooking media for this wealth of food resources are lard, goose fat, and olive or walnut oil (rather than butter), and garlic is almost invariably used as a seasoning.

Languedoc has many regional specialities: pot-au-feu, made with stuffed chicken (in Toulouse) or with stuffed goose necks (in Albi) and garlic soups give way to fish soup, cockle soup, bourride, and bouillabaisse on the coast. There are many varieties of pâté: goose or duck foie gras (Toulouse, Gaillac, Bédarieux, Quillan), thrush and hare (Lozère), lamb (Nîmes), and the sweet meat pâtés of Pézenas and Béziers.

Two of the most famous fish dishes of the region are brandade of salt cod from Nîmes and tuna tripe from Palavas. Snails are prepared in many different ways: *à la sommiroise*, *à la gayouparde*, *à la narbonnaise*, *à la lodévoise*, etc. The same holds true for the famous cassoulet, which differs depending on whether it is prepared in Toulouse, Castelnaudary, or Carcassonne. Other specialities worthy of note are the goose and duck confits (Toulouse), duck *à l'agenaise*, civet, tripe, gigot of lamb with juniper berries, and salted pig's liver (Albi), as well as thrushes *à la cévenole*, herb sausages from Mont Lozère, carbonade of veal, potatoes *à la persillade*, and tomato and aubergine (eggplant) gratin.

Pastries and confectionery are represented by crystallized violets from Toulouse, *caladons* and *croquants* (bonbons and cakes) from Nîmes, *minerves* from Nîmes and Uzès, Florac madeleines, *biscotins* from Bédarieux and Montpellier, Limoux tourons (petits fours), Castelnaudary alléluias, Uzès liquorice, almond navettes, gimblettes and *petits janots* from Albi, together with marrons glacés from Montpellier and Carcassonne.

As well as table wines, the Languedoc region produces some superior vintages, such as Tavel rosé, Gaillac white, Limoux sparkling white, and many others.

languedocienne (à la)

The name for various dishes that include tomatoes, aubergines (eggplants), and cep mushrooms, either individually or together. Fried eggs *à la languedocienne* are served on a bed of aubergine rings and accompanied by a tomato and garlic sauce. The languedocienne garnish for joints of meat and poultry consists of cep mushrooms fried in butter or oil, sliced or diced aubergines fried in oil, and château potatoes (or fried sliced ceps and aubergines with chopped tomatoes). The accompanying sauce is a demi-glace with tomatoes, often seasoned with garlic. The term *à la languedocienne* is also used to describe certain dishes that are typical of Languedoc cookery, in which the principal ingredients are garlic, ceps, and olive oil or goose fat.

| RECIPES

Best end of neck (rack) of lamb à la languedocienne CARRÉ D'AGNEAU À LA LANGUEDOCIENNE Lightly brown in goose fat a piece of best end of neck (rack) of lamb which has been trimmed and shortened. Add 12 small onions tossed in butter with 12 small pieces of raw smoked ham, 6 blanched cloves of garlic, and 200 g (7 oz) ceps or small mushrooms sautéed in oil. Sprinkle with salt and pepper. Arrange the meat and its garnish in a flameproof earthenware dish and cook in a slow oven, basting frequently. If necessary, cover with kitchen foil towards the end of the cooking time. Sprinkle with chopped parsley and serve in the cooking dish.

Pheasant à la languedocienne FAISAN À LA LANGUEDOCIENNE Cut a pheasant into 4–6 pieces; season with salt and pepper. Prepare 4 tablespoons mirepoix; cook slowly in butter with a little thyme, powdered bay leaf, salt, and pepper. Add the pieces of pheasant and lightly fry, then sprinkle with 1 tablespoon flour; cook until the flour turns golden. Moisten with 3 dl (½ pint, 1¼ cups) red wine and mix well. Add a few tablespoons of stock and a bouquet garni, cover, and cook for 20 minutes. Drain the pheasant and arrange it in a flameproof earthenware dish with 12 cep or button mushrooms and a truffle cut into fine strips; moisten with 2 tablespoons (3 tablespoons) Cognac or marc brandy. Strain the pan juice, add some butter, whisk, and pour over the pheasant. Put the lid on the dish, seal it with flour-and-water paste, and cook in a bain-marie in the oven preheated to 190 C (375 F, gas 5) for 40 minutes. Serve in the cooking dish.

Salt cod à la languedocienne MORUE À LA LANGUEDOCIENNE Completely desalt 1 kg (2¼ lb) salt cod, cut it into square pieces, and poach in water, without boiling. Cut some potatoes into even-sized pieces, brown them in oil, sprinkle them with a spoonful of flour, and fry for a few seconds, shaking the pan, until the flour has turned brown. Add a crushed clove of garlic, the fish, a few spoonfuls of the fish cooking stock, a bouquet garni, some pepper, and very little salt, as the water in which the cod was cooked is already salty. Cook gently in a covered pan for 25 minutes. Take out the bouquet garni and pour the contents of the pan into a deep ovenproof dish, placing the cod in the centre. Sprinkle with chopped parsley, moisten with a little olive oil, and finish cooking in a hot oven (about 5 minutes).

Lapérouse

A Parisian restaurant on the Quai des Grands-Augustins, which was opened in the 19th century by a certain Monsieur Lauvergniat. It started off as a humble tavern frequented by carters and traders from the nearby game and poultry market, who were attracted by the establishment's oysters and steak. In 1850, encouraged by his booming trade, Lauvergniat's nephew, Jules Lapérouse, opened a room on the first floor to accommodate his clientele. The old servants' bedrooms were later turned into private dining rooms and the restaurant acquired an excellent reputation for its food. Among Lapérouse's greatest creations were duck Colette, named by the famous author herself, and chicken Docteur, named in honour of Dr Paul, a famous medical expert at the beginning of the century (the chickens is three-quarters cooked, soaked in port, simmered in veal gravy, and served with tarragon and strips of veal).

lapwing VANNEAU

A bird with black, bright green, and white plumage and a black crest. Through Brillat-Savarin it acquired a great gastronomic reputation, and the Catholic Church did not regard it as a meat (therefore being suitable for days of abstinence). As large as a pigeon, with fairly delicate flesh, the lapwing is usually roasted undrawn (except for the gizzard) for about 18 minutes, sometimes stuffed with stoned (pitted) olives.

Lapwings' eggs came into fashion in Paris in the 1930s, imported at that time from the Netherlands, where the first egg from the nest is traditionally offered to the sovereign. They are prepared as hard-boiled (hard-cooked) eggs and are used in aspics or in mixed salads.

RECIPE

Lapwings' eggs princesse OEUFS DE VANNEAU PRINCESSE Hard-boil (hard-cook) some lapwings' eggs for 6 minutes; cool and shell them. Place each egg in a barquette shell baked blind, containing small asparagus tips seasoned with vinaigrette. Coat with white chaud-froid sauce flavoured with sherry, decorate with a slice of truffle, and glaze with aspic jelly. Surround each egg with chopped aspic.

La Quintinie (Jean de)

French horticulturalist (born Chabanais, 1626; died Versailles, 1688). La Quintinie began his working life as a barrister in Poitiers, but left the bar to devote himself to the culture of fruit trees. By a process of trial and error, he perfected techniques of pruning and transplanting. He introduced the espalier method of training trees to grow against a wall by means of a trellis. He also created many famous kitchen gardens, including those at Versailles, Chantilly, Vaux, and Rambouillet. The king's kitchen garden near the château of Versailles benefited from a remarkable irrigation and drainage system, in addition to cold frames and greenhouses introduced by La Quintinie. This garden supplied the royal table with asparagus in December, cauliflowers in March, strawberries in April, and melons in June. His work *Instructions pour les jardins fruitiers* was published by his son in 1690.

lard SAINDOUX

A cooking fat obtained by melting down pork fat. Lard is a fine white fat, which is not used as much these days as formerly because of its high animal-fat content. It is used particularly for slow cooking, but also for deep-frying (it has a high smoking point) and for making pastry. It has a fairly pronounced flavour which is associated traditionally with dishes from the north and east of France. It is used in the cookery of Alsace, Brittany, Britain, Scandinavia, and Hungary, for ragouts and dishes featuring cabbage, onion, and pork, and also in specialities of the Auvergne region. Lard is also used a great deal in China.

larding LARDER

The process of adding fat to cuts of meat or certain types of fish to make them more moist or tender. Larding consists of threading thin strips (lardons) of pork fat into a large cut of meat with a larding needle. The lardons can be seasoned with salt and pepper, sprinkled with chopped parsely, and marinated in brandy for an hour in a cool place before use. Strips of ham or pickled tongue may also be used, but it is essential that the lardon is very firm (taken straight from the refrigerator) so that it can be threaded through the meat easily. Larding a joint with various ingredients improves both its flavour and its appearance (when it is carved).

larding needle LARDOIRE

An implement used for larding cuts of meat, poultry, and game. It consists of a hollow stainless steel skewer, pointed at one end and with the other slotted into a wooden or metal handle. A lardon is threaded into the needle, which is then pushed into the meat. When the needle is extracted, the lardon is left behind in the meat.

lardons or lardoons

Strips of larding fat, of varying lengths and thicknesses, which are cut from the belly fat (*lard maigre*) of pork (see *pork fat*). Lardons about 1 cm (¼ in) wide are used to lard lean meat and roasting joints (see *larding*). Lardons cut at right angles are used in the cooking of ragouts, fried dishes, stews, and fricassees, and as a garnish for certain vegetables and salads (dandelion leaves, endives, etc.). These lardons can also be cooked with potatoes, used in omelettes, and threaded on skewers as an ingredient of kebabs.

lark   ALOUETTE

A small passerine bird with delicate flesh. There are several species, but it is mainly the crested lark and skylark that are shot: EEC legislation is shortly to protect all lark species. In French cooking larks are called *mauviettes*. From two to four per person are needed if the larks are served roasted or *en caisse* (wrapped in greaseproof (waxed) paper and casseroled), but according to Grimod de La Reynière in his *Almanach des gourmands*, they are hardly more than 'a little bundle of toothpicks, more suitable for cleaning the mouth than filling it'. They are mainly used for making pies, but can also be prepared *à la bonne femme*, *en caisse*, *à la Lucullus*, and *minute*. Pies from Pithiviers, particularly pâté pantin, have been well known for centuries. According to tradition, when Charles IX was held to ransom in the forest of Orléans and then set free, he promised to spare the lives of his captors if they told him the provenance of the delicious lark pie they had shared with him. This brought fame to a pastrycook from Pithiviers, called Margeolet and known as Provenchère.

RECIPE

Cold lark pie   PÂTÉ FROID D'ALOUETTES   Slit sufficient larks along the back to fill the pie mould and bone them. Line the inside of a deep oval hinged pie mould or dish with very thin overlapping slices of bacon. Cover the bottom with a thick layer of stuffing consisting of a mixture of equal quantities of *fine* (cream and bread) and *à gratin* forcemeats. Arrange the boned larks on top of the stuffing, inserting thin slices of truffle and foie gras between them. Cover with more stuffing and top with a bay leaf and 2 sprigs of thyme. Fold the ends of the bacon slices over the top of the filling then cover the pie with a layer of pastry, pinching the edges to seal. Make a chimney, using a small smooth-edged piping nozzle, to allow the steam to escape, then decorate the top of the pie with pastry shapes. Brush the pie with beaten egg and cook in the oven at 200 c (400 f, gas 6) for 1¼ hours for a medium-sized pie and 1¾ hours for a large one. If necessary cover the top of the pie with aluminium foil to prevent it from browning too much. Leave it to cool in the mould. Pour in some liquid jellied stock through the chimney then leave the pie in a cool place for 24 hours or until really firm before serving.

lasagne

Italian pasta cut into wide flat ribbons. Green lasagne is flavoured with spinach, pink lasagne is flavoured with tomato, and the pasta can also be made with wholewheat. The dish called lasagne is usually prepared with alternate layers of minced meat and pasta coated with tomato sauce and topped with grated Parmesan cheese, then baked in the oven until browned.

Lavallière

The name given to several great culinary dishes, although it is not known whether they were dedicated to Louise de la Vallière, mistress of Louis XIV, or to a famous actress in the Belle Époque. The dishes include: poultry or calves' sweetbreads garnished with trussed crayfish and truffles *à la serviette*; a cream soup of chicken and celery, garnished with a salpicon of celery and royale, served with profiteroles filled with chicken mousse; poached sole fillets garnished with poached oysters, fish quenelles, and mushrooms, the whole dish being coated with a normande sauce; and grilled lamb cutlets garnished with artichoke hearts stuffed with a purée of asparagus tips and served with a bordelaise sauce with beef marrow.

La Varenne (François Pierre)

French chef (born Dijon, 1618; died Dijon, 1678). He was in charge of the kitchens of the Marquis d'Uxelles, the governor of Chalon-sur-Saône, after whom mushroom duxelles was probably named, since this dish was perfected by La Varenne. This master chef is also remembered as the author of the first systematically planned books on cookery and confectionery, which revealed his attention to detail and showed how French cuisine, having been influenced by Italian cookery during the previous 150 years, had now developed a style all of its own. *Le Cuisinier français* was published in 1651, followed by *Le Pâtissier français* (1653), *Le Confiturier français* (1664), and *L'École des ragoûts* (1668). These books – especially the first – were reprinted several times before the end of the 18th century and marked a new direction in French cookery, a move away from the overelaborate dishes of the past. His books are now rare, but they have been consulted for centuries and contain recipes that can still be used today.

La Varenne is particularly remembered for his *potage à la reine*, invented in honour of Marguerite de Navarre, the recipe for which is still usable, as well as his *soupresse* (terrine) of fish, his stuffed breast of veal, and his *tourte admirable* (a marzipan (almond paste) base covered with a lime cream and preserved cherries, then topped with meringue). His name is still linked with various dishes that include mushrooms, either as a salpicon or as duxelles.

RECIPES

La Varenne sauce SAUCE LA VARENNE To ¼ litre (8 fl oz, 1 cup) mayonnaise add 2–3 tablespoons duxelles cooked in oil and cooled, then some chopped parsley and chervil (1 tablespoon of each).

Loin of lamb La Varenne CARRÉ D'AGNEAU LA VARENNE Trim and completely bone a loin of sucking (baby) lamb. Flatten it slightly and season with salt and pepper. Dip it in beaten egg and cover with finely crumbled fresh breadcrumbs (press the breadcrumbs well in to make them stick). Cook the loin in clarified butter, allowing it to turn golden on both sides. Prepare a salpicon of mushrooms

bound lightly with cream and coat the serving dish with it; place the loin on top. Moisten with noisette butter and serve piping hot.

lavaret

A fish closely related to the trout. In France it is found almost exclusively in the Lac du Bourget. Its pinkish delicate flesh has a subtle flavour. It is cooked in the same way as trout, especially *à la meunière*.

lavignon

A bivalve mollusc sometimes called the 'false calm'. It is about 5 cm (2 in) long, and lives in the mud of French bays and estuaries. Like the clam, it can be eaten either raw or stuffed. It has a slightly peppery flavour.

leaven   LEVAIN

Loosely, any substance that can produce fermentation in dough or batter. In a bakery, this is a dough used to make bread rise. It is prepared by taking a piece of dough from a previous batch and 'refreshing' it by kneading it with flour and water until it has matured sufficiently to act as a raising (leavening) agent for the next batch of bread. As this is a long, finicky, and laborious operation, many modern bakers have changed to much simpler processes, using yeast, for example.

Lebanon   LIBAN

Having its roots in European, Arabian, and oriental cuisines, Lebanese cookery is characterized by a very cosmopolitan range of dishes in which rice and Mediterranean vegetables predominate. However, the widespread use of sesame oil, together with cracked wheat (see *bulgur*), makes Lebanese cookery quite distinctive. Chicken is a popular ingredient and is almost always served with rice. It may be stuffed with meat hash, pine kernels, or almonds, or else chopped, marinated, and grilled (broiled) on skewers; another common method is to grill the chicken whole, flavoured with garlic. Mutton is also widely used, as it is throughout the Middle East: roast, on skewers, and in meatballs. The national dish of Lebanon is *kibbeh*: balls or patties of minced (ground) mutton mixed with bulgur, onion, parsley, pine kernels, or almonds, and either baked in the oven or grilled, often on skewers. This dish is found in many Islamic countries, although the spelling varies – *kobba* in Syria and Jordan, *koubba* in Iraq. Other typical dishes include *moghrabié*, a chicken couscous, prepared without vegetables, using quite large grains and seasoned with saffron; and *chawurma*, lamb grilled on a vertical spit, sliced thinly, and served with a rice salad.

There are also some very sophisticated dishes in the Lebanese repertoire, served for special occasions. One such dish is the classic pheasant *à la libanaise*: boned, stuffed with grated bacon fat, pine kernels, cloves, and cinnamon, wrapped in a cloth, boiled in stock, and finished off on the spit. It is sliced and served with rice and a pepper sauce.

One of the most outstanding features of Lebanese cookery is the large selection of hors d'oeuvres, which can make a meal in themselves. These include lambs' tongues, brains, chicken livers, chopped kidneys, spinal marrow, etc., dressed with vinaigrette; puff-pastry cases filled with spinach or minced meat; *foul* (broad beans in a hot salad); *falafel* (broad beans puréed with sesame oil, garnished with salad; a purée of aubergines (eggplants) (*baba gannoj*) or chickpeas (see *hummus*), both prepared with sesame oil; cucumber with mint and yogurt; stuffed vine leaves; small marinated fish; courgette (zucchini) balls with cheese, coated in breadcrumbs and fried; and many others. The dish that is most characteristic of Lebanese cookery is tabbouleh, in which bulgur, mint, spices, and tomatoes are marinated in oil and lemon.

The Lebanese are extremely fond of very sweet pastries with an oriental flavour: crystallized (candied) dates, baklava, Turkish delight, halva, and preserves made from whole figs or sliced quinces. They also enjoy some very subtle ice creams, made from milk and grape juice and flavoured with orange-flower water.

lèche

A French word meaning a thin slice, usually of bread or meat. It is now rarely used except in its diminutive forms, *léchette* and *lichette*. Taillevent, in *Le*

Viandier, spelled it *lesche*, and also used the verb *lescher*, meaning to cut meat into thin escalopes. Another derivative still used today is the verb *licher* – to drink or eat greedily.

leckerli or lecrelet

A spiced biscuit (cookie) with a very distinctive flavour, sometimes coated with icing (frosting). It is a Swiss speciality, originating in Basle. The name is an abbreviation of *leckerli kuchen*, meaning 'tempting cake'.

RECIPE

Leckerli Sift 500 g (18 oz, 4½ cups) flour into a bowl, add 350 g (12 oz, 1 cup) liquid honey, and beat with a spoon. Add 75 g (3 oz, scant ½ cup) candied orange peel, 40 g (1½ oz, ⅓ cup) flaked almonds, 20 g (¾ oz, scant ¼ cup) spices (half mixed spice, half ground ginger), and 1 teaspoon bicarbonate of soda. (The candied peel and almonds can be replaced with chopped hazelnuts and cinnamon.) Mix well until blended. Butter some square biscuit tins and spread the mixture in them to a depth of 2.5–3 cm (1 in). Bake in a moderate oven; when cooked, brush with milk and cut into even rectangles.

Le Doyen

A restaurant that opened in the gardens of the Champs-Élysées towards the end of the 18th century. The establishment was originally a fairly humble drinking house called Le Dauphin, near the Place de la Concorde. In 1791 it was rented by a certain Antoine Nicolas Doyen, who numbered among his customers members of the National Convention, including Robespierre. In his *Mémoires*, Barras mentions dining there, and Grimod de La Reynière, who was also a patron, wrote about Doyen's brother, who had a restaurant of his own in the courtyard of the Tuileries orangery. In about 1848, Le Doyen moved to a new location near the Rond-Point, taking over a house that is said to have belonged to Marie de Medici. The restaurant became very fashionable during the Second Empire. A tradition grew up of dining at Le Doyen's on the first day of the Paris Salon, when the customers could enjoy *sauce verte Le Doyen*, a herb mayonnaise. This sauce was created for Napoleon III by his chef Balvay, in 1855, before he took over the ownership of the restaurant.

leek POIREAU

A vegetable believed to have originated from a Near Eastern variety of garlic. Leeks are usually eaten cooked, either hot or cold, though they can be finely shredded in a salad. The plant consists of a bulb and stem completely ensheated by leaves, to form a cylindrical shaft. It is set deep in the soil so that most of the plant is blanched; this white and tender part is considered to be the best. Most of the green leaves are usually cut off and used in stews and for purées.

The leek was cultivated by the Egyptians and the Hebrews. The Romans believed that leeks had the property of imparting and maintaining the sonority of the voice. The emperor Nero had leek soup served to him every day, to develop a clear and sonorous voice for delivering his orations, and was nicknamed 'the Porrophage' (*porrum* meaning leek in Latin).

The Romans introduced the leek to Great Britain, where it has become the national emblem of Wales. In France it has been used for centuries to make soups, and the names *porreau* and *pourreau* eventually became *poireau* at the beginning of the 19th century.

The leek has a low calorific value but is rich in vitamin A, sulphur, and other mineral salts and is a good source of dietary fibre.

In France leeks are cultivated mainly in the Loire-Atlantique region, the north, the Yvelines, and the Bouches-du-Rhône and they are available throughout the year. The most common varieties from November to April are those with large white stems, 10–20 cm (4–8 in) long, and dark-green leaves, and the Créance leeks, which are very delicate, with a slight hazelnut flavour. The new leeks appear from May to July, notably the tender Nantes leeks, barely 1 cm (½ in) in diameter, and the 'baguettes', which are not as tender and have a slightly bulbous base. From mid-July onwards the winter varieties are planted out. They have more flavour but are less tender. The very large leeks, including the Malabar of the southwest,

5 cm (2 in) in diameter, are marketed in the autumn and are also considered to be very good.

Leeks must be bought when very fresh. They should be smooth with a good fresh colour and erect foliage. To prepare, the roots and base are removed, then the green part is cut off and set aside. The white part must be washed several times and is then usually blanched in boiling salted water before further preparation. They may be served cold with vinaigrette or mayonnaise or hot with béchamel sauce, white sauce, melted butter, or cream, au gratin, or braised. They are also used in soups, tarts (see *flamiche*), fritters, *à la grecque*, or even stuffed. They go equally well with beef, chicken, lamb, and fish. The white part of the leek can also be cut or shredded for a brunoise or julienne and the green part used to flavour a court-bouillon or stock.

RECIPES

Boiled leeks POIREAUX À L'ANGLAISE Trim and clean some young leeks, keeping only the white parts. Cut these all to the same length, split them, wash well, and tie together in bunches. Cook for about 20 minutes in plenty of boiling salted water until just tender (they must not fall to pieces). Untie them, drain thoroughly on a cloth or absorbent kitchen paper, and arrange them in a warm dish. Garnish with chopped parsley and serve fresh butter separately.

Alternatively, coat with melted butter (seasoned and flavoured with lemon juice) or with reduced and seasoned cream.

Braised leeks POIREAUX BRAISÉS Trim and wash 12 leeks, keeping only the white parts. Cut into slices and place in a casserole with 3 tablespoons (4 tablespoons) butter, salt and pepper, and 5 tablespoons (scant ½ cup) water or meat stock. Braise for approximately 40 minutes. Arrange the leeks in a vegetable dish and pour the braising liquid (enriched with an extra tablespoon of butter) over them.

Leek flan with cheese FLAN DE POIREAUX AU FROMAGE Butter a 26-

cm (10-in) flan ring and line it with 350
g (12 oz) unsweetened lining pastry (see
doughs and batters). Prick the base and
bake blind for 12 minutes in the oven at
200 c (400 F, gas 6). Allow to cool.
Clean, trim, and slice 750 g (1¾ lb)
leeks (the white part only) and braise
them gently for about 14 minutes in 40 g
(1½ oz, 3 tablespoons) butter. Strain.
Make 4 dl (14 fl oz, 1¾ cups) Mornay
sauce and allow to cool. Completely
cover the base of the flan with half the
sauce. Spread the leeks on top and cover
with the remainder of the sauce. Sprinkle with 40 g (1½ oz, ¾ cup) grated
Parmesan cheese and 30 g (1 oz, 2 tablespoons) knobs of butter and brown in a
very hot oven.

Leeks à la crème POIREAUX À LA
CRÈME Put the well-washed white
parts of leeks into a buttered casserole.
Add salt and pepper, cover, and braise
in butter for 15 minutes. Completely
cover with fresh cream, then continue to
simmer, with the lid on, for 30 minutes.
Arrange the leeks in a vegetable dish,
add a few tablespoons of fresh cream to
the pan juices, and pour over the leeks.

Leeks à la vinaigrette POIREAUX À LA
VINAIGRETTE Use the white part of
the leeks only, wash well, and cook in
boiling salted water. Drain on a cloth to
remove any surplus liquid and arrange
in an hors-d'oeuvres dish. Season with
vinaigrette containing mustard if liked.
Sprinkle with chopped parsley and chervil or sieved hard-boiled (hard-cooked)
egg yolk.

Leeks au gratin POIREAUX AU GRA-
TIN Trim the leeks and use only the
white parts. Wash them well, blanch for
5 minutes in plenty of boiling salted
water, drain them, then cook slowly in
butter. Arrange the cooked leeks in an
ovenproof dish, sprinkle with grated
cheese (preferably Parmesan) and
melted butter, and brown in a very hot
oven.

Rump of beef with leeks and beer
CULOTTE DE BOEUF AUX POIREAUX À
LA BIÈRE (from a recipe by Loïc Martin) Trim and wash the white parts of 1
kg (2¼ lb) leeks and slice them into
large rings. Cut 1 kg (2¼ lb) rump of

beef or chuck steak into cubes. Put the
meat and leeks into a casserole and
season with salt and pepper. Add 1 litre
(1¾ pints, 4¼ cups) light ale together
with 40 g (1½ oz, 3 tablespoons) butter,
cut into small pieces. Bring slowly to the
boil, then cover and cook for 3 hours in
the oven at 160 c (325 F, gas 3).

Soles with leek fondue SOLES DE
LIGNE À LA FONDUE DE POIREAU
(from a recipe by Alain Chapel) Braise
some well-washed trimmed young leeks
with 10 g (¼ oz, ½ tablespoon) butter,
a little water, and a pinch of salt. Remove the leeks with a draining spoon
and keep warm. Reduce the cooking
liquid, stirring frequently. Add a generous amount of cream and reduce until
the sauce is thick. Cook some lemon or
Dover soles on a bed of seaweed in the
oven, arrange the leeks in bunches
around them, and spoon the sauce over.

lees LIE DE VIN

The deposits that settle in a cask or vat,
consisting mainly of tartrates and
yeasts. A wine bottled directly 'off the
lees' (*sur lie*) may be slightly 'working'
or lively, and this is appreciated by some
drinkers, notably those buying Muscadet. Normally, wine is pumped off its
lees prior to bottling.

Legrand d'Aussy (Pierre Jean Baptiste)

French historian (born Amiens, 1737;
died Paris, 1800). He planned to write a
massive work called *Histoire de la vie
privée des Français, depuis l'origine de
la nation jusqu'à nos jours,* dealing with
the housing, dress, leisure activities, and
food of the French. However, only three
volumes, all on the subject of food, were
published (1782). They gave a detailed
account of the diet, menus (especially at
Versailles), table customs, and regional
traditions of former times. Legrand
d'Aussy also included information
about the guilds of the butchers, cooks,
and pastrycooks, together with a collection of proverbs illustrating the most
popular customs of the times. After his
appointment as chief librarian of the
National Library, Legrand d'Aussy devoted his time to other topics of research.

Leiden

A Dutch cows'-milk cheese (containing 40% fat) named after the city where it was originally made; it is also called Leidse Kaas and Leyde. The cheese is flavoured with cumin seeds or cloves and has a brushed washed waxy rind. It is shaped into a flattened globe weighing between 5 and 10 kg (11 and 22 lb, and its mild flavour is dominated by the flavour of the spices. Leiden is used in sandwiches and for canapés and croûtes as well as being served at the end of a meal.

lemon CITRON

A citrus fruit with an acid juicy pulp surrounded by an aromatic yellow rind of varying thickness (see *zest*).

Originally from India or Malaysia, the lemon was introduced into Assyria, and from there passed to Greece and Rome, where it was used as a condiment and a medicament. The Crusaders brought the lemon and other citrus fruits back from Palestine, and its cultivation became widespread in Spain, north Africa, and Italy. Until the 18th century, it was traditional for French schoolboys to give lemons to their masters at the end of the school year. The lemon was also used as a beauty product – it was thought to make the lips red and the complexion pale. Above all, it was a vital remedy against scurvy, being a good source of vitamin C, and was used especially by sailors.

Today, lemons are available throughout the year; although they are cultivated on the Côte d'Azur, they are mainly imported by France from Spain and the United States. The different varieties are distinguished by shape, size, ranging from 5 to 8 cm (2–3 in long, thickness of the skin, and the number of seeds; the quality of flavour is fairly consistent. A good lemon should be heavy, fragrant, and have a close-grained peel. As the lemon becomes very ripe, it gets less sour and more juicy. There are numerous uses for the lemon in cookery, especially in pâtisserie, confectionery, and drinks.

☐ **The juice** Obtained simply by hand-squeezing or with a lemon-squeezer, lemon juice serves firstly as a natural antioxidant, with which certain fruit and vegetables can be coated to prevent discoloration due to oxidation. It is also an ingredient in numerous dishes, including blanquettes and ragouts; it appears in marinades and courts-bouillons, and replaces vinegar in dressings for raw vegetables and salads; it seasons mayonnaises and certain sauces (butter or white); large quantities are used in the preparation of ice creams, sorbets, and various refreshing drinks. Finally, marinating raw fish in lemon juice is a method of 'cooking' widely practised in South America and the Pacific islands. See *fruit juice, cocktail, lemonade.*

☐ **The zest and the rind** As citrus fruits are often treated with diphenyl (this should be marked on the label but usually isn't), it is preferable, if the rind is to be used, to choose untreated lemons, or failing this to wash and dry them carefully. The zest may be obtained by grating, peeling it with a special utensil, or by rubbing it with a sugar lump (cube), depending on the intended use. It serves as a flavouring, usually in pâtisserie for creams, soufflés, mousses, tarts, and flans; candied lemon peel is used for flavouring biscuits and cakes.

☐ **The fruit** Lemon slices are an essential accompaniment for a seafood platter, most fried food and savoury fritters, and many dishes coated in breadcrumbs. They are also a necessary ingredient of lemon tea. Lemon quarters may serve as a condiment for certain ragouts and sautés (of veal or chicken) and also for tajines. Preserved lemons are widely used for flavouring fish and meat in north African cookery. Lemon is included in jams, compotes, lemon curd, and chutneys. Finally, whole lemons are prepared frosted or iced.

☐ **The extract** Lemon extract or flavouring is used in confectionery and in wines and spirits. It also flavours certain aromatic teas.

RECIPES

SAVOURY DISHES

Chicken with lemon POULET AU CITRON Cut a chicken into portions. Squeeze 2 lemons and to the juice add salt, pepper, and a dash of cayenne. Marinate the chicken portions in this juice for at least 1 hour, then drain them, retaining the marinade. Wipe the portions then brown them in butter in a casserole. Reduce the heat, sprinkle the chicken with crumbled thyme, cover, and leave to cook gently for 30 minutes. Drain the chicken portions and keep them hot. Now add the marinade to the casserole along with 1 dl (6 tablespoons, scant ½ cup) thick fresh cream. Stir well and heat, stirring constantly as the sauce thickens. Adjust the seasoning. Coat the chicken portions with this sauce.

Duckling with lavender-honey and lemon CANETON AU MIEL DE LAVANDE ET AU CITRON (from a recipe by Pierre and Jany Gleize) For 4 people, allow 2 ducklings, each weighing about 1.5 kg (3¼ lb), and their giblets. Soften 2 tablespoons mirepoix in a shallow frying pan (skillet). Add the giblets and turn them over in the mirepoix. Barely cover with a mixture of half white wine and half water. Season with salt and pepper. Cover and leave to cook gently for about 30 minutes. Strain. Season the ducklings with salt and pepper. Fry them lightly in butter for 20 minutes, taking them out while they are still pale pink.

Discard the cooking butter and deglaze the pan with the juice of 2 lemons; then add 1 small teaspoon lavender honey to make a sauce. Leave to reduce almost completely. Then add 2 tablespoons strained duck giblet juices, and finally stir in a knob of butter. Adjust the seasoning.

Cut the breast of the ducklings into long thin slices; grill (broil) the legs briefly on both sides. Coat with the seasoned sauce.

Preserved lemons CITRONS CONFITS Wash 1 kg (2¼ lb) untreated lemons, wipe, and cut into thick round slices. (Small lemons can simply be quartered lengthways.) Dust with 3 tablespoons fine salt and leave them to discharge their juices for about 12 hours. Drain them, place in a large jar, and cover completely with olive oil. Leave in a cool place for a month before use. Close the jar firmly after opening and keep in a cool place away from light.

Sea bream with preserved lemon DAURADE AU CITRON CONFIT Scale and gut (clean) a large sea bream and make a shallow incision in the back. Oil a gratin dish and in it place 6–8 slices of lemon preserved in oil. Arrange the bream on top and sprinkle with salt and pepper. Add a small handful of coriander seeds and garnish the bream with 6 more slices of preserved lemon. Sprinkle with 2 tablespoons lemon juice and several tablespoons olive oil, and cook in a hot oven (about 230 C, 450 F, gas 8) for about 30 minutes, basting the fish several times during cooking.

Stuffed lemons CITRONS FARCIS Remove the stones (pits) from about 30 black (ripe) olives; put 6 of them aside and chop the rest together with a bunch of parsley. Cut the stalk ends off 6 large thick-skinned lemons; using a small spoon with a cutting edge, scoop out all the flesh, leaving the rind intact. Separate the pulp from the fibrous partitions and seeds. Crumble a medium-sized tin of tuna or salmon and remove the skin and bones. Mix the lemon pulp and juice (or half the juice if the lemons are very sour) with the crumbled fish and the chopped olives and parsley, plus 4 hard-boiled (hard-cooked) egg yolks and a small bowl of aïoli. Adjust the seasoning. Fill the lemon shells with this stuffing, garnish each lemon with a black (ripe) olive, and place in the refrigerator until time to serve.

The tuna (or salmon) and aïoli mixture may be replaced by a mixture of sardines in oil-and-butter.

SWEET PREPARATIONS

Frosted lemons CITRONS GIVRÉS Cut the stalk ends off some large thick-skinned lemons and, using a spoon with a cutting edge, remove all the pulp without piercing the rind. Then chill the rinds in the refrigerator. Press the pulp, strain the juice, and use it to prepare a lemon sorbet. When the sorbet is set, fill the chilled rinds with it, and cover with the section that was removed. Freeze until time to serve. Decorate with leaves of almond paste.

Lemon jam CONFITURE DE CIT-RON Allow 1.1 kg (2½ lb) sugar per kg (2¼ lb) lemons. Wash the lemons (ideally untreated ones) and carefully peel the outer rind from one-third of them. Blanch these rinds for 2 minutes in boiling water, then cool in cold water, and cut into fine strips. Squeeze these peeled lemons to extract the juice and cut the remaining ones into thick slices.

Put the juice and slices of lemon in a preserving pan, bring to the boil, and boil for 5 minutes, stirring all the time. Add three-quarters of the strips of lemon peel, the sugar, and 1 dl (6 tablespoons, scant ½ cup) water per kg (2¼ lb) sugar. Stir and cook for 20 minutes over a gentle heat. When the jam is cooked add the rest of the peel, either mixing it in over the heat for 3 minutes, or adding it after passing the jam through a strainer and reheating it (the jam is then clear like a jelly). Pour into scalded jars.

Lemon meringue pie TARTE MER-INGUÉE AU CITRON Butter a baking tin 24–26 cm (9–10 in) in diameter and line it with 350 g (12 oz) shortcrust pastry (basic pie dough). Cook the tart case (pie shell) blind in a moderately hot oven (200 C, 400 F, gas 6) for 10 minutes.

Boil 3.5 dl (12 fl oz, 1½ cups) water in a saucepan. In another saucepan put 65 g (2½ oz, generous ½ cup) flour, 65 g (2½ oz) cornflour (cornstarch), and 250 g (9 oz, 1 generous cup) caster (superfine) sugar and gradually add the boiling water, stirring all the time. Bring to the boil, still stirring, then remove from the heat and leave to cool slightly.

Wash and wipe 2 or 3 lemons, grate the outer zest, and squeeze the juice. Add the grated zest, the juice, 4 egg yolks, and 30 g (1 oz, 2 tablespoons) butter to the cooled mixture and cook in a bain-marie for 15 minutes, whisking from time to time. Pour the mixture into the flan case, cook for 10 minutes, still in a moderate oven, then leave to cool.

Add a pinch of salt to 4 egg whites, whisk into stiff peaks, then gradually fold in 125 g (4½ oz, scant 1 cup) caster (superfine) sugar and 20 g (¾ oz) icing sugar (confectioners' sugar). Spread this meringue over the tart using a metal spatula, and return to the oven for 10 minutes, browning lightly. Serve lukewarm or cold.

Lemon sorbet SORBET AU CITRON Cut away the zest from 3 lemons, chop it, and add it to ½ litre (17 fl oz, 2 cups cold syrup with a density of 1.2850. Leave to infuse for 2 hours. Add the juice of 4 lemons, then strain. The density should be between 1.1699 and 1.1799. Complete by the usual method (see *sorbet*).

Lemon tart TARTE AU CITRON Prepare a pastry using 200 g (7 oz, 1¾ cups) flour, 100 g (3½ oz, ½ cup) butter, 60 g (2 oz, 4 tablespoons firmly packed) caster (superfine) sugar, 1 egg, and a pinch of salt. Use it to line a baking tin that has been well-greased with butter. Heat the oven to about 190 C (375 F, gas 5).

Break 2 eggs into a mixing bowl containing 50 g (2 oz, 4 tablespoons firmly packed) sugar and beat the mixture until it turns white. Remove the outer peel from a lemon and chop it finely; squeeze the juice from the pulp. To the eggs and sugar add 100 g (4 oz, 1 cup) ground almonds, the lemon peel, and the juice. Mix well. Fill the flan case with this cream and cook in the oven for at least 30 minutes.

Meanwhile, wash 2 lemons and slice them very thinly. Measure into a saucepan 200 g (7 oz, scant 1 cup) sugar, ¼ litre (8 fl oz, 1 cup) water, and 1 tablespoon vanilla-flavoured sugar. Cook for 10 minutes then add the lemon slices and cook for a further 10 minutes. Leave them to cool completely before using them and some glacé (candied) cherries to decorate the tart, which should also be cool.

Preserved lemon peel ÉCORCES DE CITRON CONFITES Peel some fresh lemons and, using a spoon with a serrated edge, remove the pith, keeping only the zest. Blanch this zest for 5 minutes in boiling water, drain, place in a very concentrated sugar syrup, and leave overnight. The next day, remove the peel and cook the syrup until it reaches a density of 1.2095; then return the peel and leave to macerate for 24 hours. Repeat this operation until the syrup reaches a density of 1.3319.

lemonade

CITRONNADE, LIMONADE

A refreshing drink made from lemon juice (3 tablespoons per glass), sugar, and still or aerated (sparkling) water. The liquid is often left to infuse with the peel of the fruits before being passed through a cloth strainer (cheesecloth). *Citron pressé* (pressed lemon) is made in a glass just before serving.

lemon balm

CITRONNELLE, MÉLISSE

A lemon-scented herbaceous plant native to Europe. The leaves are used in salads, drinks, soups, stuffings, and sauces and to flavour white meat and fish; fresh or dried leaves are also used in tisanes. The sweet-scented flowers are distilled to make melissa cordial, especially that known as *eau de Carmes*.

lemon curd

An English speciality, made from a mixture of sugar, butter, eggs, and lemon juice, used to fill tartlets or to spread on bread and butter. It should be kept in an airtight jar in the refrigerator.

| RECIPE

Lemon curd Finely grate the peel of 2 large lemons. Squeeze them, and reserve the juice. Melt 100 g (4 oz, ½ cup) butter in a double saucepan over a very gentle heat. Gradually add 225 g (8 oz, 1 cup, firmly packed) caster (superfine) sugar, 3 beaten eggs, the grated lemon peel, and the lemon juice. Stir until thickened. Put into jars while still hot.

Lent CARÊME

In the Roman Catholic calendar, 46 days of abstinence before Easter, intended as a time of penitence. The original strictures of Lent forbade one to eat meat, fat, and eggs, so the diet comprised mainly vegetables, usually dried since fresh ones were not in season, and fish, especially dried fish, such as herring and salt cod. However, the rules of abstinence were circumvented by various means: special alms enabled one to eat butter and eggs in measured quantities (the proceeds of these particular alms financed the construction of Rouen cathedral's 'Butter Tower'). Moreover, certain waterfowl were permitted, particularly teal and plover, because of a tenuous association with fish, as well as the beaver, because of its 'fish-like' scaly tail. In the kitchen, pâtés and pies were brushed with mashed pike's eggs, and egg thickenings, very common at the time, were made with carp meat. Even the pastrycook got round the difficulty: croquants, craquelins, échaudés, and cakes of flour and honey boiled with almonds demonstrate this.

The rule of abstinence, which has become more and more lenient in modern times until it has almost disappeared, in fact did much to develop the cook's imagination: salt cod, served at many tables for 40 days on end, has probably more recipes than any other fish eaten in France. Fresh fish were also served, with a great variety of sauces.

lentil LENTILLE

A small annual leguminous plant with small round dry flat seeds that are borne in pairs in a flat pod. They are always eaten shelled and cooked. Lentils have been cultivated since ancient times, originating in central Asia and forming the staple diet of the poor for many centuries. Ancient Rome imported whole shiploads from Egypt.

Several varieties are now grown in France. The *green Puy lentil* flourishes in the volcanic soil of the Velay. The seeds are dark green with blue marbling and have an excellent flavour. The *green lentil* comes from the Haute-Loire, Indre, etc., and is small, with a thin skin. The *Champagne brown lentil* is almost entirely restricted to that area and is reddish. The *blonde lentil* is oval and flat and is grown in the Cantal.

Lentils from other countries are usually fatter than the French varieties.

Nourishing, and with a high energy value (336 Cal per 100 g), lentils are rich in protein (24%), carbohydrates (56%), phosphorus, and iron, as well as the B vitamins. They are prepared and cooked in the same way as white haricot (navy) beans, but some people prefer not to soak them as they cook quickly without soaking. Once cooked, lentils are used as an accompanying vegetable (puréed, in gravy, creamed, with parsley, etc.), as well as for soup. They are the traditional accompaniment for pickled pork, and can also be used in salads.

Lentils are particularly good for children, anaemics, and nursing and expectant mothers, provided that there is no history of digestive problems. They are best puréed or mixed with potato to counteract the effect of the indigestible lentil husks.

RECIPES

Hot lentil salad SALADE DE LENTILLES CHAUDE Cook the lentils as for lentil purée (see recipe below), but keep them slightly firm. Cut belly of pork (salt pork) into strips; blanch, drain, and brown the strips in a little butter (for 1 kg (2¼ lb) cooked lentils, use 250 g (½ lb) pork). Prepare a vinaigrette and add to it 1 tablespoon red wine. Drain the lentils and place them in a warm dish. Add the pork, dress with the vinaigrette, and sprinkle with chopped parsley. Mix the salad and serve hot.

Lentil purée PURÉE DE LENTILLES Pick over the lentils and, if desired, soak them for 1–2 hours in cold water. Place them in a large saucepan, cover with plenty of cold water, bring to the boil, and skim. Add salt, pepper, a bouquet garni, a large onion stuck with 2 cloves, and a small diced carrot. Cover and simmer gently (the cooking time will depend on the freshness of the lentils). Remove the bouquet garni and the onion. Reduce to a purée in a blender while still hot, then heat the purée through gently, beating in a knob of butter. If desired, add a little stock, water, boiled milk, or cream before beating in the butter.

L'Étoile

An AOC wine from the Jura. The parish of L'Étoile and the neighbouring communes of Plainoiseau and Saint-Didier produce a small quantity of good dry white wines, plus a little *vin jaune* and *vin de paille*. The white wines tend to be naturally 'lively' (*pétillant*).

lettuce LAITUE

A plant that grows wild all over the northern hemisphere and is cultivated in many varieties for its large edible leaves. It has been cultivated in Egypt and Asia for thousands of years, and was popular with the ancient Greeks and Romans because of the milky juice it exudes when cut (its Latin name, *lactuca*, is derived from *lac*, meaning milk).

Lettuce was introduced into France in the Middle Ages, some think by Rabelais, who is said to have brought some seeds back from Italy, although others believe that the popes in exile at Avignon were responsible. Until the time of Louis XVI, lettuce was eaten as a hot dish. Raw lettuce with a vinaigrette proved a great success in London when it was introduced by the Chevalier d'Albignac, a French nobleman who had emigrated to England. He made his fortune by visiting various private hotels and fashionable restaurants to dress the salads. Brillat-Savarin described him as a fashionable salad maker going from one dining room to another complete with his mahogany tools and his ingredients, which included flavoured oils, caviar, soy sauce, anchovies, truffles, meat juices, flavoured vinegars, etc.

Nowadays, several varieties of lettuce are available commercially. The most common is the *cabbage* or *round* (*butter*) lettuce, which has a rounded head with a yellow heart and smooth or curled floppy leaves. *Webb* (*Bibb*) or *iceberg* lettuces are crisp and round, with very large firm hearts. The *cos* (*romaine*) lettuce has long dark-green leaves with thick veins and a relatively open crisp heart.

All lettuces have a very high water content and few calories (18 Cal per 100 g). They also contain a variety of mineral salts and vitamins. Although lettuce is available all the year round the cabbage lettuce is at its best in spring and the other varieties are best in summer. Those grown in the open have a better flavour than those grown in hothouses, and also contain more mineral salts.

Great care must be taken to clean lettuces thoroughly in plenty of water so that all the soil is removed. It is important to dry the leaves gently. The way lettuce is prepared depends on the size of the leaves (see *chiffonnade*). Lettuce can be seasoned and served raw in green or mixed salads, and the leaves are often used as a garnish. In addition it can be braised, stuffed, cooked with cream, and used to prepare peas *à la française* and mange-tout (snap) beans.

| RECIPES

Braised lettuce au gratin LAITUES BRAISÉES AU GRATIN Braise the lettuces in meat stock or water and arrange in an ovenproof dish. Cover with Mornay sauce, sprinkle with grated cheese, top with melted butter, and brown in a hot oven.

Braised lettuce in meat stock LAITUES BRAISÉES AU GRAS Trim the lettuces by discarding the tough outer leaves. Blanch for 5 minutes in boiling salted water, cool under the tap, then squeeze to extract as much water as possible. Tie the lettuces together in twos or threes. Butter an ovenproof dish and line it with bacon rinds, sliced carrots, and onions. Lay the lettuces in the dish and cover with slightly fatty stock. Bring to the boil, cover, and cook in a preheated moderate oven for about 50 minutes. Drain the lettuces and remove the string. Halve each lettuce lengthwise. Trim the leaves at both ends and fold each half in two. Place the lettuces in a buttered pie dish. Pour over a few tablespoons of strained reduced veal stock (or broth), some meat gravy, or a few tablespoons of noisette butter.

Lettuce à la crème LAITUES À LA CRÈME Braise the lettuces in stock or water. Divide each lettuce in two, folding each half, and place in a buttered pan. Moisten with cream and simmer until the cream has reduced by half. Transfer to a serving dish and garnish with fried croutons.

Lettuce purée PURÉE DE LAITUES Braise the lettuces in water then purée them in a blender, together with the cooking stock. Heat the purée and add one-third of its volume of béchamel sauce to give it body. Add butter, and season to taste just before serving.

Lettuce salad SALADE DE LAITUE Prepare a lettuce chiffonnade, incorporating a julienne of unsmoked ham, breast of chicken, and either Gruyère or Emmental cheese. Dress with a vinaigrette made with walnut oil and sprinkle with chopped herbs.

Stuffed lettuce LAITUES FARCIES Trim the lettuces, blanch for 5 minutes, cool under running water, and blot dry. Halve each lettuce without cutting through the base. Season them inside. Fill each lettuce with a generous tablespoon of fine forcemeat mixed with mushroom duxelles. Tie each lettuce back together and braise in meat stock or water. Stuffed lettuce can be served on its own with fried croutons, or it may be used as a garnish for roast or sautéed meat.

Vegetarian braised lettuce LAITUES BRAISÉES AU MAIGRE Follow the recipe for braised lettuce in meat stock, omitting the bacon rinds and using water instead of stock.

Levroux

A French goats'-milk cheese (45% fat content) from the province of Berry. Shaped like a truncated pyramid, it is made in the countryside around Levroux, in the Indre department. It is similar to Valençay, and some say that the latter is derived from Levroux; they share the same characteristics.

liaison

Any mixture used for thickening or binding sauces, soups, stews, etc. Commonly used liaisons are kneaded butter (*beurre manié*), egg yolks, arrowroot, cornflour (cornstarch), a roux, and cream. See *thickening*.

libation

An ancient religious ritual in which wine, milk, oil, or blood were sprinkled on the ground or on an altar to honour the gods. A libation was made standing with cup in hand, looking up towards the heavens. A few drops of liquid were sprinkled and this was followed by a short prayer uttered with the arms extended towards the sky; finally, the offering was drunk from the cup. In ancient times, no one would dream of eating a meal without first performing a libation (see *symposium*). As well as being a display of deference to a deity, a libation was also intended to enlist help in times of need, especially before a battle or a journey. It was also used to seal a truce or a peace treaty.

In modern parlance, the word libation is used, often facetiously, to describe the act of taking an alcoholic drink.

lid COUVERCLE

A flat cover with a handle or knob, placed over cooking pots, casseroles, stewpans, etc., to prevent splashing and to stop the evaporation of water and juices. Some serving utensils, such as vegetable dishes and soup tureens, also have lids. Lids may be convex (for sauté pans) or concave (for holding water on certain types of casserole). For utensils without a purpose-made lid, so-called 'universal' lids are used. These have three concentric notches so they can fit on pans of different diameters. Other lids have special uses: a filter lid, made of double aluminium mesh, lets steam through but prevents fat from splashing and reduces cooking smells; an anti-vapour and anti-splash lid, with a row of small holes around the circumference, slows down evaporation and prevents fat from splashing; a strainer lid makes it possible to drain the cooking water while retaining the solid contents of the pan.

Liebig (Justus, Baron von)

German chemist (born Darmstadt, 1803; died Munich, 1873). Professor of chemistry at Giessen, Heidelberg, and then Munich, he was particulary interested in the agricultural and industrial applications of organic chemistry; his most important work on this subject was published in 1823. Realizing that the transport of enormous quantities of meat imported from South America and Australia was proving expensive, he had the idea of extracting the nutritional part of the meat. In 1850 he produced the first meat extract; this was followed by concentrated stock powder.

In 1862 the Fray Bentos Giebert company was formed in Belgium, the forerunner of what was eventually to be a giant industrial concern. In 1865 Liebig was involved in founding Liebig's Extract of Meat Company in England – the name survives today in an industrial brand of meat concentrates and soups.

liégeoise (à la)

Describing certain dishes that include alcohol and juniper berries. Kidneys *à la liégeoise* are casseroled, garnished with crushed juniper berries, potatoes, and bacon, and served in a sauce made from the meat juices, gin, and white wine. Small birds cooked *à la liégeoise* are flamed with gin and casseroled with juniper berries and Ardennes ham.

RECIPE

Thrushes à la liégeoise GRIVES À LA LIÉGEOISE Pluck the thrushes, flame them with gin, and discard the eyes. Do not draw the birds, but simply remove the gizzards. Truss the thrushes by folding and crossing the feet, or tie them with kitchen thread. Brown the birds all over in melted butter in a casserole. Cover the pan and cook gently for 20–25 minutes. Add some crushed juniper berries, stir, and add 1 tablespoon chopped Ardennes ham per bird. Fry some half-slices of bread (with the crusts removed) in butter, lay the birds on top, and keep warm. Add a little stock to the casserole juices and boil down to reduce. Pour the sauce over the thrushes and serve.

lights MOU

The lungs of certain animals, used as food. Calves' lights are usually used. After being beaten to expel the air, they can be cooked in a civet (with wine, mushrooms, strips of bacon, and onions), *à la poulette*, or *à la persillade* (cut into thin slices and sautéed in butter, with garlic and parsley).

ligurienne (à la)

Describing large cuts of meat garnished with small stuffed tomatoes alternating with a saffron risotto shaped in dariole moulds, and piped duchess potatoes brushed with egg yolk and browned in the oven.

Lima bean
HARICOT DE LIMA

A bean plant grown in tropical countries and the United States, also known as Cape bean or pea, Siéva bean, sword bean, jack bean, and Chad bean. The seeds are normally pale green and the same size as broad beans; they are prepared in the same way as fresh white haricot beans. Butter beans are a variety of Lima bean, grown in the southern United States.

Limburg

A Belgian cows'-milk cheese (containing 40% fat) with a soft smooth yellow paste, the crust varying in colour from reddish-yellow to brick red. It weighs 500–600 g (1–1¼ lb) and has a strong aroma and a full-bodied flavour. Many people enjoy it with a glass of beer. Originally from the Belgian province of Limburg, it has been copied in Germany, the United States, and the Netherlands.

lime   CITRON VERT

A citrus fruit closely related to the lemon. Rounded, with bright-green peel and very sour pulp, it is smaller, more fragrant, and juicier than the lemon. The lime is cultivated in tropical countries, including the Ivory Coast, Brazil, and the West Indies, and is often used in Caribbean and Brazilian dishes, particularly fish or meat stews, marinated chicken, jams, sorbets, punches, and cocktails. The zest is used like lemon zest and will keep for a long time steeped in caster (superfine) sugar or rum. Sugar rubbed with the zest is kept in an airtight jar for flavouring tea, creams, or milk. See also *sweet lime*.

RECIPE

Roast pork with lime sorbet and mint
RÔTI DE PORC AU SORBET DE CITRON
VERT ET À LA MENTHE   Roast a 1-kg
(2¼-lb) fillet of pork (pork tenderloin) for 1 hour 10 minutes in a hot oven (225 c, 437 f, gas 7–8) and leave to cool completely. To make the sorbet, dissolve 600 g (1 lb 6 oz) sugar in 2 dl (7 fl oz, ¾ cup) water, heat just sufficiently to dissolve the sugar completely, and leave to cool. Squeeze enough limes to collect 5 dl (17 fl oz, 2 cups) strained juice. Add it to the syrup. Pour into ice trays and place in the freezer. After about 1 hour, stir and leave to set completely for at least a further hour.

Slice the roast thinly and arrange on the serving dish; garnish with sprigs of fresh mint. Prepare a lettuce salad and

sprinkle it with chopped mint. Serve the sorbet in small sundae glasses alongside the cold roast meat and the salad.

lime blossom   TILLEUL

The highly fragrant flowers of the lime tree, or linden, which are dried and used to prepare soothing infusions, sometimes to flavour creams, ices, and desserts, and more rarely as an aromatic in cooking. Édouard Nignon made a powder of dried, crushed, and sifted lime blossom to season sauces and stocks, and R. Lasserre created a recipe for chicken with lime blossom. Veal chops can also be flavoured with lime blossom, as can cream sauces and dishes cooked in white wine or cider. The most aromatic lime blossom comes from the Drôme in France, where a lime-blossom ratafia was formerly made. Lime-blossom honey has a. pronounced aroma and flavour.

limoner

A French word meaning to remove the skin, blood, and impurities from certain foods (brains, fillets of fish, pieces of meat) by dousing them in water or holding them under running water. Certain freshwater fish are washed in this way to remove any slimy covering. The word is also a synonym for *écailler*, meaning to remove the scales of a fish or to open osyters.

Limousin and Marche

These two provinces, corresponding to the departments of Haute-Vienne, Corrèze, and Creuse, have the same specialities and products, despite the differences in their climate and soil. The plateaux with their grasslands and forests provide game (hares and partridges) and mushrooms (ceps and chanterelles); they also provide pasture for rearing some very fine livestock (sheep and pigs, but mostly cattle). Where the fields are cultivated, these plateaux also yield excellent vegetables and many kinds of fruit and nuts (especially plums, cherries, and chestnuts). The rivers and swamps sustain a variety of fish, including trout, carp, pike, gudgeon, and sometimes crayfish.

The culinary specialities of the region include bréjaude, miques, and other hearty soups made with cabbage, pickled pork, and beans; all these are traditionally finished off with red wine (see *chabrot*). The Limousin pigs are used for making pickled pork, confits, and black pudding (blood sausage) with chestnuts, not to mention ham, sausages, and various pâtés. Among the excellent farcidures are stuffed cabbage and stuffed mushrooms. The great Limousin speciality is hare *en cabessal*, but some excellent braised veal dishes are also cooked. Among the desserts, apart from the famous clafoutis, should be mentioned the Limousin fruit tarts, plum pies, marzipan, and *cornues* (two-horned brioches made at Easter time), the rustic *tartes sèches* (cooked in water, covered with aniseed, and finished in the oven), madeleines from Saint-Yrieix, croquants from Bort-les-Orgues, and macaroons from Dorat. Special mention should be made of the Limousin chestnuts, which have formed a staple part of the diet of the rural population and are still enjoyed boiled (*boursadas*), roasted, or blanched (shelled and braised).

The vineyards on the slopes of Corrèze and in the Vienne valley produce a modest amount of table wine, but the Limousin peasants also make cider and some very good fruit brandies, based on cherries, plums, and prunes, as well as various home-made liqueurs, including walnut cordial.

limousine (à la)

Describing a method of preparing red cabbage. It is sliced very finely and cooked in lard with a little stock, a dash of vinegar, and a pinch of sugar. When the cabbage is almost cooked, grated or finely diced potato and crushed raw chestnuts are added. This garnish is served with roast pork and other roasted joints. Chicken *à la limousine* is stuffed with sausagemeat and fried mushrooms, cooked in a casserole, coated with the pan juices mixed with veal gravy, and garnished with bacon and poached chestnuts. An omelette *à la limousine* is filled with fried diced ham and potato.

limpet   PATELLE

A marine gastropod mollusc with a conical shell, 3–7 cm (1½–2 in) in diameter, dull grey on the outside and orange-yellow on the inside. Limpets are common on the rocky shores of the Atlantic coast. The Mediterranean limpet is similar, but the inside of the shell is iridescent blue. Limpets may be eaten raw, flavoured with lemon juice or vinaigrette, or they may be grilled (broiled) with a little butter in each shell. They can also be shelled and used as a forcemeat, in which case the flesh is reduced to a purée in a blender or food processor.

line   FONCER

To cover the bottom and sides of a casserole, mould, or terrine with a thin layer of bacon, pork fat, flavouring ingredients, or pastry. A braising pan can be lined by covering the bottom with such ingredients as sliced onions and carrots, thyme, bay leaf, parsley, and garlic, which enhance the flavour, or with fatty or nutritious ingredients, such as bacon rind, bones, meat trimmings, etc. A pâté terrine is lined with strips of pork fat or fatty bacon.

Lining pastry should be cut to match the size and shape of the container, either by using a pastry (cookie) cutter before lining, or by passing a rolling pin over the edges of the container after lining to cut off the excess. In general, pastry linings are placed on lightly greased surfaces. Lining a tart plate or flan ring often involves making a ridge around the top, which is pinched with a special tool or with the fingers to improve the final appearance.

ling   LINGUE

A fish of the cod family, also called sea burbot or long cod. The common ling, found in the North Sea, can reach a length of 1.5 m (5 ft); a smaller variety, fished in the Mediterranean, is rarely more than 90 cm (3 ft) long. The ling is a slender olive-grey fish with a silver stripe along its length and a small barbel on its lower jaw. It is sold in fillets and is prepared in the same way as cod.

In the United States the name ling is sometimes given to the freshwater burbot.

linzertorte

An Austrian pastry that takes its name from the town of Linz. It is made from a sweet shortbread dough flavoured with lemon and cinnamon, topped with raspberry jam, and decorated with a lattice of pastry.

RECIPE

Linzertorte Leave 70 g (3 oz, 6 tablespoons) butter to reach room temperature. Remove the zest from a lemon and shred two-thirds of it into fine julienne strips. Blanch, drain, and chop these strips. Sift 175 g (6 oz, 1½ cups) flour onto the work surface and add 75 g (3 oz, ⅔ cup) ground almonds, 75 g (3 oz, 6 tablespoons, firmly packed) caster (superfine) sugar, 1 egg, 2 teaspoons powdered cinnamon, the softened butter, the lemon zest, and a pinch of salt. Knead the ingredients thoroughly and refrigerate the dough for 2 hours.

Butter a 22-cm (9-in) round flan tin (pie pan). Roll the dough out to a thickness of about 3–4 mm (¼ in) and line the flan tin carefully, trimming off the excess around the top. Prick with a fork and fill with 125 g (4½ oz, ½ cup) raspberry jam. Gather the pastry trimmings together and roll them out into a rectangle about 2 mm (⅛ in) thick. Cut it into strips a little under 1 cm (½ in) wide and make a lattice pattern on top of the flan, pressing the ends into the top of the pastry case. Bake at 200 c (400 f, gas 6) for about 30 minutes.

Remove the flan from the tin, place on a serving dish, and allow to cool completely. The tart may be lightly brushed with an apricot glaze.

lipids LIPIDES

The scientific term for a group of substances that include the natural fats and oils (simple lipids), as well as the sterols, phospholipids, and glycolipids (compound lipids). Lipids are the principal source of energy provided by food, yielding 9.3 Cal per gram. They are also important as one of the forms in which the body can store energy, but excessive fat reserves lead to weight problems. Lipids are also essential for the absorption of fat-soluble vitamins A, D, E, and K and they contain essential fatty acids that cannot be synthesized naturally in the body. The lipids in our bodies, like those in food, are made up basically of triglycerides (a triglyceride consists of one glycerol molecule combined with three fatty acids). Food containing a high proportion of lipids include cooking oils and fats, dairy products, and nuts. An excessively high consumption of these foods (both in quantity and in proportion to other food constituents) should be avoided.

Lipp

A brasserie that was opened in 1871 on the Boulevard Saint-Germain in Paris by Léonard Lipp. It was known at that time as the Brasserie des Bords du Rhin. His successors (Hébrard, then Cazes) enlarged it, renamed it Lipp, and succeeded in attracting customers from the literary and political clientele of the Café Flore and the Deux Magots.

Léon-Paul Fargue, whose father was responsible for the ceramic-tiled interior design, used to remark that it was the only place in Paris where 'for the price of a beer you can have a full and frank summary of the day's political and literary happenings'. The same could still be said today. Saint-Exupéry, Léon Daudet, and Galtier-Boissière, together with members of the French parliament, presidents of the Council, actors, and men of letters, all flocked to the doors of Lipp's, more to be seen there than to enjoy the culinary fare, which was always the same traditional selection (Baltic herrings, savelog with rémoulade sauce, sauerkraut, stuffed pig's trotters, skate with black butter, and entrecôte steak). Bordeaux and champagne are now more the order of the day than beer!

Liptauer

The German name for a Hungarian cheese spread; the base is a fresh cheese originally made in the province of Liptó and also called Liptai or Juhturó. This cheese is made with ewes' milk, sometimes mixed with cows' milk, and sold in small wooden cases. It has a creamy colour, a buttery consistency, and a slightly spicy flavour. The spread is usually made by mixing the fresh cheese with cream, paprika, chopped capers, onions, and anchovies; it is spread on wholemeal (wholewheat) bread as a snack. It is also used as a stuffing for sweet peppers for an hors d'oeuvre: this dish is very popular in Czechoslovakia, where it is called *liptovsky sir* and is usually accompanied by a glass of lager.

liqueur

An alcoholic drink of more than table-wine strength, usually incorporating some form of spirit. Liqueurs may be sweet or sweetish, herby (this type is often used as a digestive after meals), distillates of fruit (the *alcools blancs*), and flavoured spirits (such as fruit brandies). They are served at different times and in different ways – some as apéritifs, especially when poured 'on the rocks', some after a meal, some as between-times drinks, often as an ingredient of cocktails and mixes. Liqueurs are widely used in recipes for desserts, confectionery, cakes and pastries, and fruit dishes. A large number are made in France, and many formerly independent producers have now become part of a few huge organizations.

From very early times compounded mixtures of herbs, spices, and other ingredients were used for medicinal purposes. After the evolution of distilling, the monastic orders made many drinks with spirits and other ingredients to serve as remedies, preventives, and ultimately as enjoyable drinks. In France, so rich in many of the ingredients required, the influence of immigrant Italians during and after the 15th century encouraged the practice of making liqueurs in many religious houses and subsequently by lay organizations, as a commercial concern. In regions where the basic materials for liqueur-making were cheap or free, the French often made such drinks in their own homes and many old recipes are still followed, especially when there is a glut of fruit or some other ingredient and when the necessary spirit is fairly cheap. It should be noted, however, that the process of distilling by the general public is illegal and those who wish to make liqueurs in their homes may only do so by macerating and/or infusing the ingredients in different forms of alcohol. There are many liqueur recipes, but the formulae for many of the most famous, such as Chartreuse, Bénédictine, and Izarra, are closely guarded secrets, unlikely to be fathomed by the amateur and impossible to reproduce in the domestic kitchen.

The use of the word 'liqueur' as applied to certain spirits (liqueur brandy, for example) implies that it is a superior version of the product, usually intended for drinking without dilution.

RECIPES

Apricot liqueur   LIQUEUR D'ABRICOT   Stone (pit) 30 apricots and put them in a preserving pan with 4 litres (3½ quarts, 4½ quarts) white wine; bring to the boil. When boiling, add 1 kg (2¼ lb, 4½ cups) sugar, 10 g (1½ tablespoons, 2 tablespoons) cinnamon, and 1 litre (1¾ pints, generous quart) 33° eau-de-vie. Take the pan off the heat, cover, and leave to infuse for 4 days. Strain, filter, and bottle. Cork the bottles tightly and store in a dry place.

Cherry liqueur   LIQUEUR DE CERISE   Crush 4 kg (8¾ lb) Montmorency cherries with their stones. Place in an earthenware dish and leave to macerate for 4 days. Dissolve 1 kg (2¼ lb, 4½ cups) sugar in 4 litres (3½ quarts, 4½ quarts) 22° alcohol and add it to the macerated cherries. Decant the mixture into a large jar, cork it, and leave to infuse for 1 month. Then squeeze the mixture through muslin (cheesecloth) to extract the liquid. Filter and bottle. Cork tightly and store in a cool place.

Orange liqueur   LIQUEUR D'ORANGE   Wash 6 oranges, pare off the rind very thinly, and chop it. Squeeze the oranges and pour the juice into a jar. Add 500 g (18 oz, 2¼ cups) sugar and stir until it dissolves. Add the rind, a pinch of cinnamon, and a pinch of ground coriander. Pour in 1 litre (1¾ pints, generous quart) Cognac or white eau-de-vie, mix, and leave to macerate for 2 months. Filter, bottle, cork, and store in a cool place.

The same recipe may be used for lemons or tangerines.

Strawberry liqueur   LIQUEUR DE FRAISE   Hull 1.25 kg (2½ lb, 8 cups) very ripe strawberries, place in a large jar, and cover with 4 litres (3½ quarts, 4½ quarts) eau-de-vie. Cork and leave to infuse for 2 months, placing the jar in the sun whenever possible. Add 500 g (18 oz, 2¼ cups) caster (superfine) sugar and shake well. When the sugar has completely dissolved, shake again and filter. Bottle, cork tightly, and store in a cool place.

Raspberry liqueur can be made using the same recipe with 1 kg (2¼ lb, 8 cups) ripe raspberries.

liqueur cabinet

CAVE À LIQUEURS

In the past, an ornate wooden cabinet in which spirits were stored. Today this is outmoded, but any bottle of spirit should be kept upright, otherwise the spirit may rot the cork or stopper.

liquorice   RÉGLISSE

A shrub cultivated in temperate regions for its root, from which liquorice sticks for chewing are cut and liquorice juice is extracted. This juice, purified and concentrated, is used principally to make various types of confectionery; it is also used for flavouring medicines and apéritifs and in brewing. The plant grows wild in Syria, Iran, and Turkey; in France, it is cultivated mainly around Uzès in the Gard region. It was grown extensively around Pontefract during the 16th century and was used to manufacture Pontefract cakes, lozenges of liquorice sold as sweetmeats.

Depending on its origin, liquorice juice contains 5–10% glycyrrhizine, the ingredient responsible for its sweet taste and its reputed therapeutic properties, known since very early times. Assyrian tablets and Chinese and Indian papyruses give evidence of its early medicinal use. During the 19th century, liquorice began to be made into sweets, presented in elegantly decorated little boxes or given as a treat to children. There are two basic types.

● *Hard liquorice* (in the form of sticks, pastilles, etc.) is made from a mixture of liquorice juice, sweeteners, gum arabic, and perhaps a flavouring (mint, aniseed, violet); liquorice sweets contain at least 6% glycyrrhizine.

● *Pliable liquorice* (ribbons, laces, twists, etc.) is made from a paste of liquorice juice plus sweeteners, hard-wheat flour, starch, and icing (confectioners') sugar; this is cooked, then flavoured and extruded in a thread. Gums, pastilles, and chewing gum made

from liquorice are flavoured with at least 4% pure liquorice juice.

RECIPE

Orange-flavoured liquorice water
EAU DE RÉGLISSE À L'ORANGE   Cut 100 g (4 oz) liquorice root sticks into small slices and wash them; place in a saucepan with 10 g (¼ oz) grated orange peel and 4 litres (7 pints, 8 pints) water. Boil for 5 minutes then strain and leave to cool. Serve very cold.

liquorice water   COCO

A refreshing drink made from liquorice sticks soaked or infused in water with added lemon juice. The French name comes from the fact that the drink resembles coconut milk in appearance. it was popular in the 18th and 19th centuries, when it was sold in the streets and public gardens by the *marchand de coco*, who carried a small cask on his back from which he served it in goblets very cheaply.

Lirac

A wine from the Côtes du Rhône with its own *appellation contrôlée*, produced in the Gard around Roquemaure. The most famous is Lirac rosé, which is similar to its neighbour, Tavel. It is made principally from the Grenache and Cinsault vines. The red wines, which are robust and full-bodied, and the whites, which are aromatic and lightweight, are made in only limited quantities.

Listrac

AOC wine from the delimited area in the Haut-Médoc region within the Bordeaux vineyard. The wines are red and can be extremely pleasant – drinkers should not be confused by the slightly pejorative categorization of 'bourgeois'. There are a number of well-maintained properties whose wines are of fine quality.

Livarot

A cows'-milk cheese (containing 40–45% fat) from the Calvados region of Normandy. It has a soft smooth paste and a washed brownish-red rind, traditionally tinted with annatto (an orange dye from the fruit of a tropical American flowering tree). It is left to mature for three or four months in a damp cellar. Livarot is one of the earliest traditional Normandy cheeses. Thomas Corneille, in his *Dictionnaire universel géographique et historique* of 1708, mentioned its excellent qualities. Its region of origin is the Auge, and it is still only made in the villages of the Livarot area. It is a cylindrical cheese, 11–12 cm (5 in) in diameter and 4–5 cm (2 in) deep, and is sold boxed or unboxed, encircled by five thin strips of ribbon (the stripes left by this binding gained it the nickname 'colonel'), which were originally intended to maintain its shape. Livarot is at its best from November to June and has a fine firm elastic texture, with no holes. It has a distinctive but not overwhelming aroma, and a full-bodied flavour that is neither bitter nor spicy. It is protected by an *appellation d'origine* and is still made on farms by the traditional method using fresh milk, although there is some mass production and smaller versions of the cheese, known as *petits lisieux*, are made.

liver FOIE

Red offal from carcasses of animals, poultry, and game.

Apart from chicken liver, the most tender and savoury variety is calf's liver, which is pale pink and firm and cooked whole (larded with bacon and roasted) or in slices (grilled (broiled) or fried and served with a saue). Next, in decreasing order of quality, is lamb's liver, which is often fried or grilled on skewers. Ox (beef), liver, which has a strong flavour and is usually tougher, is less expensive, and sheep's liver, which is mediocre, can also be fried or grilled. Pig's (pork) liver can be casseroled, but it is used mainly in the charcuterie and delicatessen trade, for patés, terrines, cooked sausages, etc., because it has a slightly stronger flavour.

Chicken livers are widely used in cookery, particularly for cooking on skewers and risottos, pilafs, pâtés, forcemeats, and various garnishes. In France, Bresse chicken livers (*foies blonds*) are regarded as a delicacy and used in chicken-liver terrines. Duck's liver, even when the duck has not been fattened, is of very high quality, excellent when cooked with Armagnac brandy and grapes.

The liver of certain fish is also edible. Skate's liver (in fritters) and monkfish liver (poached) are especially used. Cod liver is smoked and preserved in oil, and then used to make cold canapés.

RECIPES

Calf's Liver

Calf's liver à la bourguignonne FOIE DE VEAU À LA BOURGUIGNONNE Fry some slices of calf's liver in very hot butter over a high heat. Keep hot on a serving dish. Deglaze the pan with red wine and stock (in equal proportions), and reduce. Pour this sauce over the slices of liver and surround with bourguignonne garnish.

Calf's liver à l'anglaise FOIE DE VEAU À L'ANGLAISE Cut some calf's liver into thin slices; fry in hot butter on both sides quickly over a high heat (allow 25 g (1 oz, 2 tablespoons) butter to 4 slices), drain, and keep hot on the serving dish. Fry some thin rashers (slices) of bacon in the same pan, and use to garnish the liver. Sprinkle with chopped parsley, a squeeze of lemon juice, and the cooking juices. Serve with small steamed potatoes.

Fried calf's liver à florentine FOIE DE VEAU SAUTE À LA FLORENTINE Braise some spinach in butter. Peel some large onions, cut into thick slices, and separate into rings. Dip the onion rings in batter and fry in very hot oil until golden brown. Drain and keep hot. Lightly grease a serving dish, cover it with drained spinach, and keep it hot. Quickly fry some very thin slices of calf's liver in very hot butter and arrange on the spinach. Deglaze the liver pan with white wine, reduce, and pour the juice over the slices. Garnish the liver with the fried onion rings and (if liked) with lemon wedges.

Roast calf's liver FOIE DE VEAU RÔTI Cover the liver with thick rashers (slices) of bacon, season with salt, pepper, a pinch of fennel, and some chopped parsley, then moisten with brandy. Wrap in a pig's caul (which should first be soaked in cold water, wiped dry, and stretched) and tie up with string. Cook on a spit or in a moderately hot oven (200 c, 400 f, gas 6) allowing a cooking time of 12–15 minutes per 500 g (1 lb). Dilute the pan juices with white wine or veal stock and pour over the liver. Serve with glazed carrots.

CHICKEN LIVER

Bresse chicken-liver terrine GÂTEAU DE FOIES BLONDS DE VOLAILLE (from a recipe by Paul blanc) Select 8 Bresse chicken livers (preferably white ones; ordinary chicken livers can be used instead but will give a darker result); rub through a sieve together with 150 g (5 oz, ¾ cup) beef marrow. Add 50 g (2 oz, ½ cup) flour. Mix thoroughly, then add 6 whole eggs and 4 yolks (one by one), 2 tablespoons double (heavy) cream, and ¾ litre (1¼ pints, 3 cups) milk. Season with salt, pepper, and ground nutmeg. Add a generous pinch of chopped parsley and half a peeled crushed clove of garlic. Place the mixture in a greased mould and cook slowly in a bain-marie for about 45 minutes or until set. Turn out of the mould just before serving.

Prepare a sauce by reducing some cream, port, and fresh tomato purée, enriched with a little butter. Pour the sauce over the dish and garnish with a few slices of truffle. Serve warm or cold.

Chicken-liver brochettes à l'italienne BROCHETTES DE FOIES DE VOLAILLE À L'ITALIENNE Clean some chicken livers and cut each in half. Roll up each piece of liver in a thin slice of smoked bacon, then thread them onto skewers, with pieces of onion and sage leaves in between each piece. Moisten lightly with oil and season with salt, pepper, and a little dried thyme. Leave to stand for 30 minutes. Grill (broil) the brochettes under a fierce heat for about 10 minutes, brushing them with oil when necessary. Serve with lemon halves and a green salad.

Chicken-liver croustades CROUS-TADES DE FOIES DE VOLAILLE Make some small pastry cases (see *croustade*). Clean the chicken livers (turkey or duck livers can be used instead), separate the pieces, season with salt and pepper, and fry quickly in very hot butter. Drain. Fry some sliced mushrooms and chopped shallots in butter, then season with salt and pepper. Warm the empty croustades in the oven.

Add enough Madeira sauce to the mushroom pan to make a filling for the croustades, then add the livers. (Alternatively, deglaze the liver and mushroom cooking juices with Madeira, then thicken with a small amount of kneaded butter.) Heat up this mixture and use to fill the pastry cases. Serve very hot. The croustades can be garnished with slices of truffle poached in Madeira.

Chicken-liver timbale TIMBALE DE FOIES DE VOLAILLE Prepare some chicken livers and mushrooms as in the recipe for chicken-liver croustades. Cook some shell-shaped pasta (or macaroni) *al dente*. Drain well. Add the chicken livers to the pasta, together with the mushrooms and some Madeira sauce (or a Madeira sauce thickened with blended arrowroot or kneaded butter) and cream. Adjust the seasoning and serve very hot in a timbale mould or large dish.

LAMB'S LIVER

Lamb's liver with garlic FOIE D'AG-NEAU À L'AIL Peel and chop very finely as many cloves of garlic as there are slices of liver. Heat some butter in a frying pan (skillet) and sauté the liver over a high heat, on both sides. Season with salt and pepper, drain, and keep hot. Put the garlic in the frying pan, stirring well so that it does not turn brown. Immediately deglaze the pan with as many tablespoons of wine vinegar as there are slices of liver, and allow to reduce by half. Coat the liver with this sauce, sprinkle with chopped parsley, and serve immediately.

PIG'S LIVER

Pig's (pork) liver with mustard FOIE DE PORC À LA MOUTARDE (from a recipe of Simone Nouyrigat) **Lard** a pig's liver with strips of bacon and brush generously with strong mustard. Sprinkle with chopped parsley, crushed garlic, and a little butter and cook in a covered casserole for about 45 minutes in a low oven. Cut and arrange the liver in slices on a hot dish. Deglaze the casserole with 1 tablespoon mustard and 2 tablespoons wine vinegar; coat the liver with this sauce.

loach LOCHE

A freshwater fish with an elongated slimy body, greenish-grey or orange-yellow with black spots and covered with very delicate scales. Three species are found in Europe. The *pond loach* can grow up to 35 cm (14 in) long and has ten barbels around the mouth. The *river loach* is the smallest species (8–10 cm, 3–4 in), with six barbels and a spine beneath each eye. The *common loach*, 10–12 cm (4–5 in) long and the most popular, has six barbels and no spines. All these fish live in the mud, which sometimes gives them a somewhat earthy taste. They should be soaked for a few hours in vinegar and water before being cooked, either *à la meunière* or *en matelot*. They are considered to be at their best between October and March.

loaf PAIN DE CUISINE

A preparation made from a moulded forcemeat, generally cooked in the oven in a bain-marie. The basic ingredient of the forcemeat is fish (pike, carp, salmon, whiting, etc.) or shellfish (lobster, crab, crayfish, etc.), poultry, white meat, game, or even foie gras.

Vegetable loaves are usually prepared with green vegetables (endive (chicory), spinach, lettuce, etc.), braised and mixed with beaten eggs, but artichoke hearts, aubergines (eggplants), cauliflower, and carrots can also be used. Cooked in a mould and often coated with a cream sauce, vegetable loaves are served as an entrée or accompany meat, fried or braised chicken, a whole fish, or poached or soft-boiled eggs.

Some loaves (fish, shellfish, or chicken) can be set in a mould lined with aspic and served chilled.

RECIPES

carrot loaves PAINS DE CAROTTE Scrape 750 g (1¾ lb) carrots and cook them in salted water. Drain them, reduce them to a purée, and dry out over the heat without letting it burn. Prepare a béchamel sauce with 50 g (2 oz, ¼ cup) butter, 50 g (2 oz, ½ cup) flour, and 4 dl (14 fl oz, 1¾ cups) milk. Mix the purée and the béchamel sauce, season with salt and pepper, and add 4 beaten whole eggs. Generously butter 10 small dariole moulds, fill them with the mixture, and cook in the oven at 200 c (400 F, gas 6) for 15–20 minutes. Turn out onto warmed plates.

Turnip loaves are prepared in the same way. The mixture may also be poured into a buttered crown mould, cooked for about 30 minutes, and turned out onto a hot dish.

Fish loaf PAIN DE POISSON Dice 500 g (18 oz) pike, carp, salmon, or turbot flesh (net weight after trimming). Dust with salt, a pinch of white pepper, and a little grated nutmeg. Pound finely in a mortar or put through a blender. Pound 250 g (9 oz) flour panada, add 250 g (9 oz, generous cup) butter, and mix with the fish purée. Work everything in a mortar or blender to obtain a homogeneous mixture. Still working the preparation, add 1 whole egg and 4 yolks, one by one. Rub the mixture through a fine sieve, place it in an earthenware dish, and beat it with a mixer until very smooth. Pour this preparation into a round smooth buttered mould, then cook in a bain-marie in the oven at 200 c (400 F, gas 6), for 45–50 minutes. Turn out onto the serving dish and serve with white butter sauce or any sauce for hot poached fish.

Meat, game, or **poultry loaf** PAIN DE VIANDE, DE GIBIER, OU DE VOLAILLE Prepare a mousseline forcemeat with veal, poultry, or game (woodcock, pheasant, young partridge, or roebuck). Fill a well-buttered savarin mould with this forcemeat up to 1 cm (½ in) from the rim. Cook in a bain-marie in the oven at 200 c (400 F, gas 6) for 45–60 minutes. When the loaf is cooked, leave it to stand for a few minutes before turning it out onto warmed round dish. Coat with cream sauce.

Shellfish loaf PAIN DE CRUSTACÉ Prepare a cream forcemeat with 500 g (18 oz) crab, lobster, or crayfish flesh, 7.5 dl (1¼ pints, 3 cups) double (heavy) cream, 2 egg whites, 9 g (2 teaspoons) salt, and a pinch of white pepper. Butter a savarin (ring) mould and fill it with this forcemeat. Cook in a bain-marie in the oven at 200 c (400 f, gas 6), for 45 minutes. Turn out onto a warmed round dish and coat with américaine, normande, or cardinal sauce.

lobster HOMARD

A marine crustacean related to the crayfish, crawfish, and crab and found in cold seas. It is the largest and most sought-after shellfish. It has a thick shell and its small pointed head bears long red antennae. The abdomen is in seven sections and terminates in a fan-shaped tail. The first pair of claws, which are full of meat, end in large powerful pincers. The thorax contains a creamy substance (the liver), and hen lobsters often have a coral, often used in the sauces served with lobster. The abdomen, or tail, is filled with dense-textured white meat that can be cut into escalopes or medalions.

There are two main types. The European lobster, found in British and Norwegian waters, is a violet-blue or greenish colour and has a very delicate flavour. The Northern lobster, fished off the east coasts of Canada and the United States, is said to have less flavour. When cooked, the lobster turns red, which is why it is sometimes called 'the cardinal of the seas' (Monselet); it is therefore difficult to distinguish the origins of a lobster when it is bought cooked from a fishmonger. Although a prolific breeder, the lobster has had to be protected: since 1850 experiments in lobster farming have been carried out on both sides of the Atlantic, but it is still regarded as a rather special delicacy.

A live lobster, which can be identified by the reflex actions of the eyes, antennae, and claws, should not show any signs of damage from fighting or have any pieces missing when it is bought, especially if it is to be boiled. A female is generally heavier and better value than a male of the same size and in the opinion of gourmets has a better flavour. An average lobster is about 30 cm (12 in) long and weighs 300–500 g (¾–1 lb). Lobsters can reach a length of 75 cm (2½ ft) and a weight of several kilos, but such specimens are very rarely sold on the open market.

The British Universities Federation for Animal Welfare has discovered that lobsters can be humanely killed by putting them in a plastic bag in the freezer (at a temperature at least as low as −10 c) for two hours. The lobster will gradually lose consciousness and die. It can then be plunged into boiling water. If a freezer is unavailable, make sure that at least 4.5 litres (1 gallon) water per lobster is boiling fast over a very hot flame before plunging the lobster in head first, ensuring it is totally immersed. Hold it under the water with wooden spoons for at least 2 minutes. The lobster should die within 15 seconds. If the recipe calls for uncooked lobster, remove it after 2 minutes.

Lobster meat is low in fat (90 Cal per 100 g) and rich in proteins and mineral salts, but it can be rather indigestible. There are numerous methods of preparing lobster; these are some of the best-known: *à l'américaine*, *à la parisienne*, Thermidor, Newburg, grilled (broiled), or spit-roasted. Other dishes include lobster in scallop shells (hot or cold), soufflés, and mousses. As a garnish for rice pilaf, canned lobster is preferable to fresh.

RECIPES

Grilled (broiled) lobster HOMARDS GRILLÉS Plunge 2 lobsters, each weighing about 500 g (1 lb), head first into boiling salted water for about 3 minutes. Drain them, split in half lengthwise, and crack the claws. Season the meat with salt and pepper, sprinkle with melted butter or oil, and grill (broil) under a medium heat for about 25 minutes. Arrange each half lobster on a napkin. Serve with melted butter flavoured with lemon, maître d'hôtel butter, or hollandaise sauce.

Lobster à l'américaine HOMARD À L'AMÉRICAINE Cut a lobster weighing about 1 kg (2 lb) into even-sized pieces; split the body in two lengthwise; crack the shell of the claws; reserve the liver and the coral, which will be used to thicken the sauce. Season all the pieces of lobster with salt and pepper. Heat 4 tablespoons (¼ cup) olive oil in a pan. Put in the lobster pieces, brown quickly on both sides, and remove from the pan. Finely chop a large onion and cook it gently in the oil; when it is nearly done add 2 finely chopped medium-sized shallots and stir well, Peel, deseed, and chop 2 medium-sized tomatoes and put them in the pan; add 1 tablespoon tomato purée, a piece of dried orange peel, a small clove of garlic, and 1 tablespoon chopped parsley and tarragon. Arrange the pieces of lobster on this mixture. Pour over 1 dl (6 tablespoons, scant ½ cup) white wine, 1 dl (6 tablespoons, scant ½ cup) fish fumet, and 2 tablespoons (3 tablespoons) brandy. Season with cayenne. Bring to the boil, then cover and cook gently on top of the stove for a maximum of 10 minutes. Drain the lobster pieces and remove the flesh from the claws; arrange all the pieces in the split body halves in a long serving dish. Keep warm.

To prepare the sauce, reduce the cooking liquid by half. Chop the coral and liver and work them into 40 g (1½ oz, 3 tablespoons) butter, then add this mixture to the cooking liquid. Take the pan off the heat and blend the mixture well, then whisk in 60 g (2 oz, 4 tablespoons) butter cut into small pieces. Season the sauce with a pinch of cayenne and a few drops of lemon juice. Pour the boiling sauce over the lobster and sprinkle with chopped parsley.

The chopped onion and tarragon can be replaced by 3–4 tablespoons (¼–⅓ cup) finely chopped mirepoix, added to the lobster while it is cooking.

Lobster en chemise HOMARD EN CHEMISE Plunge a lobster head first into boiling water to kill it and drain immediately. Season with salt and pepper and brush with oil or melted butter. Wrap it in a double thickness of oiled greaseproof (waxed) paper, tie it securely, and put it on a baking tray (sheet). Cook at 230 C (450 F, gas 8) for 40–45 minutes (for a medium-sized lobster).

Remove the string and serve the lobster in the paper in which it has been cooked.

It can be accompanied either by half-melted maître d'hôtel butter or by an américaine, béarnaise, Bercy, bordelaise, hongroise, or curry sauce.

Lobster escalopes à la parisienne ESCALOPES DE HOMARD À LA PARISIENNE Cook a medium-sized lobster in court-bouillon and leave to cool. Remove the shell and cut the meat into thick slices. Coat each slice separately with gelatine-thickened mayonnaise and garnish with a slice of truffle dipped in the half-set mayonnaise jelly; brush over with more jelly to give a glaze. Finely dice the rest of the lobster flesh and mix it with a salad; finely diced truffles can also be added. Bind with thickened mayonnaise and pack this salad into a dome-shaped mould. Turn the mould out into the centre of a round serving dish and arrange the lobster slices all around it in a border. Garnish with chopped jelly.

Lobster in court-bouillon HOMARD AU COURT-BOUILLON Prepare a really well-flavoured court-bouillon: to 2 litres (3½ pints, 4½ pints) water add the following ingredients: 2 medium carrots, 1 turnip, the white of a leek, and a stick of celery (all finely diced), a large bouquet garni, an onion stuck with 2 cloves, a small clove of garlic, ½ litre (17 fl oz, 2 cups) dry white wine, ½ glass vinegar, salt, pepper, and a pinch of cayenne. Bring to the boil and simmer for 30 minutes. Plunge the lobster head first into the boiling court-bouillon and let it simmer gently, allowing 10–15 minutes per 450 g (1 lb). Drain. If it is to be served cold, tie it onto a small board so that it keeps its shape and leave it to get completely cold.

A lobster weighing 400–500 g (1 lb) should be split lengthwise and served in 2 halves. If the lobster is large, take off the tail, remove the meat and cut it into medallions. Split the body in half lengthwise, and remove and crack the claws. Arrange the medallions on the tail shell and place the 2 halves of the body together to resemble a whole lobster again. Garnish with the claws. Serve with mayonnaise.

Lobster sauce SAUCE HOMARD
Prepare 3 dl (½ pint, 1¼ cups) fish
fumet made with white wine. Reduce it
by two-thirds, let it cool, and add 4 egg
yolks; whisk over a low heat until thick
and light. Melt 250 g (8 oz, 1 cup) butter
and blend it into the sauce, whisking
constantly. Add 2 tablespoons (3 tablespoons) lobster butter. Still whisking,
season with salt and pepper and add the
juice of half a lemon. At the last moment
a little diced lobster meat can be added.

Lobster sautéed à l'orange HOMARD
SAUTÉ À L'ORANGE (from Jean Minchelli's recipe) Split a lobster in half
length wise, reserving the coral and the
liver. Cut off the claws and crack them.
Season the meat with salt. Crush and
pound the small claws, which should be
cut off close to the body. Brown them in
a little oil with crushed cloves of garlic
and a pinch of cayenne. Add enough oil
to just cover the contents of the pan and
cook on the lowest possible heat so that
the oil does not smoke.

Rub the mixture through a sieve and
adjust the seasoning. Put 4 tablespoons
(⅓ cup) of this oil into a sauté pan, slice
4 shallots and 1 onion, and brown them
in the oil, together with half an orange
cut into large dice and some tarragon
leaves. Push this mixture to the sides of
the pan to leave the centre tree and put
in the lobster, flesh side down. Boil for 3
minutes to reduce the liquid.

Pour the juice of half an orange into
the pan. Turn the lobster halves over
onto the shell sides and add the claws.
Purée the coral and the intestines with 2
tablespoons (3 tablespoons) single
(light) cream in a blender. Add a little
brandy, a pinch of cayenne, and some
chopped tarragon. Garnish the lobster
halves with this mixture. Put under a
grill (broiler) for 3 minutes and serve at
once.

Lobster surprise HOMARD SUR-
PRISE (from Fernand Point's recipe)
Prepare the lobster as for lobster *à
l'américaine* and arrange the shelled
meat with some cooked sliced
mushrooms on a very large pancake.
Roll up the pancake. Cover with the
sauce, sprinkle with grated parmesan,
and brown rapidly in a hot oven or
under the grill (broiler).

locust SAUTERELLE
A herbivorous insect living in desert
areas, particularly in Africa, which is an
important item of food in these regions.
There are two edible species: the smaller
one has green wings and a silver belly;
the larger, species has a red head and
legs. Locusts are eaten grilled (broiled),
roasted, or boiled; dried and ground to
a powder or a paste, they are also used
as a condiment.

loganberry
See *raspberry*.

loin CARRÉ, LONGE
A joint of veal, lamb, pork, or mutton
that includes some of the ribs. It is usually roasted or braised.

Boned (boneless) veal loin is cooked
with the bones placed alongside the
roast to add their flavour to the meat.
When cooking loin of mutton (or lamb,
which is more delicate), the fat is lightly
trimmed, the tops of the cutlet bones are
scraped, and the joint chined in order to
make carving easier. (See *saddle*.)

Although boned pork loin, tied up
and lightly barded, makes an excellent
roast, the meat is tastier when cooked
on the bone. The butcher should be
asked to split the vertebrae and separate
the top of each rib. Then tie all the ribs
together to form a crown before roasting. Boned loin can also be cut into
cubes and cooked on skewers.

RECIPE

Loin of veal LONGE DE VEAU Have
the loin boned without removing the
kidney and leaving the top part long
enough to be wrapped around the fillet
Remove some of the fat from the kid
ney, so that it is no more than 1 cm (½
in) thick. Season the side which will be
on the inside with salt and pepper, then
roll the loin up and tie it together. Season again with salt and pepper. Melt
some butter in a large casserole and fry
the loin until golden brown all over,
turning all the time. Put the lid on the
casserole and place it in the oven at 200
C (400 F, gas 6). Peel some small onions
and fry them in butter until golden
brown. Five minutes before the meat is
ready, add the onions and complete the

cooking. Remove the joint from the pan, allow it to drain, and keep it warm on a dish. Deglaze the casserole with 1 glass of stock and 1 glass of white wine and reduce the liquid by half. Serve it in a sauceboat with the onions.

Loire wines

VINS DE LA LOIRE

For a little more than half its length, between Pouilly-sur-Loire and Nantes, the longest river in France is bordered by gently sloping hills where vines have been cultivated since Roman times. Different varieties of vines are grown on the different kinds of soil, the main ones being Cabernet Franc (and some Gamay) for red and rosé wines and Chenin Blanc (or Pineau de la Loire) and Sauvignon Blanc for whites. These produce a wide range of wines, ranging from sweet to dry, still to sparkling. Much rosé wine is produced. All the wines are inclined to be elegant and refreshing, and some of the whites can attain a very high quality; most should be drunk while relatively young, although this depends on both the vintage and the maker.

From east to west, the Loire Valley is divided into nine main wine-producing areas of varying sizes. Upriver, Pouilly-sur-Loire uses Sauvignon grapes to produce its fine Pouilly Blanc Fumé, the more ordinary Pouilly wines being made from the Chasselas. Sancerre, next to it, produces many respected dry whites, made only from the Sauvignon Blanc, a very good rosé, and some red wines made from the Pinot Noir. The small regions of Quincy and Reuilly make dry whites from the Sauvignon Blanc. The extensive vineyards of Touraine produce all kinds of wine: red, white, and rosé, still and sparkling. The reds include Chinon, Bourgueil and St Nicolas de Bourgueil, and Champigny. The whites, which include Montlouis and Vouvray, range from still to fully sparkling, from dry to sweet and luscious. Slightly to the north, in the Sarthe, Jasnières makes dry and sweetish whites. The Coteaux du Loir area is known mainly for its rosés. Anjou, like Touraine, produces a huge range of wines, notably rosés and pleasant whites; the finest wines are the reds of Saumur-Champigny and the sparkling

white and rosé Saumur wines. Further down the river, the sweeter wines of the Coteaux du Layon, including Quarts de Chaume and Bonnezeaux, are famous and Savennières makes distinguished dryish whites. Nearer the sea, the dry whites Muscadet and Gros Plant, named after the grapes from which they are made, are now widely known.

lollipop SUCETTE

A sweetmeat made of boiled sugar mounted on a little stick, which is held in the hand for sucking. Lollipops, which appeared at the end of the 19th century, are flavoured with fruit, caramel, or mint; some types are trimmed with strips of opaque sugar or combined contrasting colours.

longan LONGANE

A fruit originating in India and China, which is oval and about the same size as a plum or a greengage. Its red, pink, or yellow skin covers firm white translucent flesh which is quite sweet and surrounds a large black stone with a white eye-shaped marking (hence the Chinese name for the fruit – *lung-yen*, meaning 'dragon's eye'). The longan is somewhat similar to lychee, but has a fainter aroma. It is rich in vitamin C and yields 65 Cal per 100 g. In France it can be bought canned in syrup, or sometimes crystallized (candied). It is used in fruit salads and can be liquidized to make a refreshing drink.

longaniza

A half-dried half-smoked Spanish sausage rather like a fat chorizo sausage. Made from fatty sausagemeat, which is highly coloured and seasoned with hot peppers and aniseed, it is eaten fried, particularly with egg dishes, or uncooked.

Longchamp

The main racecourse of Paris, whose name was given to a thick soup, based on a pea purée.

RECIPE

Longchamp soup POTAGE LONGCHAMP Cut some sorrel into fine strips and soften it in butter in a covered saucepan. When well braised, add 3 tablespoon (¼ cup) sorrel to 1 litre (1¾ pints, 4¼ cups) puréed fresh peas. Add ½ litre (17 fl oz, 2 cups) stock with vermicelli and stir well. Heat up the soup and sprinkle with parsley.

longeole

A sausage from Switzerland or Savoy, made with vegetables (spinach beet, cabbage, leeks) which are cooked, drained, and pounded, then mixed with pork fat and pluck (heart, lungs, and spleen). Longeoles are braised and can be preserved in oil.

longuet

A long cylindrical dry bread roll cooked in a gutter-shaped tin. The fact that it is made with a little fat and sugar, and is cooked in a slow oven, gives it its characteristic crumbly texture and enables it to be stored for a long time.

lonzo

An item of Corsican charcuterie prepared in the same way as coppa, but using the fillet instead of the faux-filet. The fillet is boned, rubbed with salt, and coated with saltpetre, then washed with garlic-flavoured red wine, dried, and dusted with paprika. It is then pressed into a pig's intestine and tied up with string. Lonzo is eaten in thin slices as an hors d'oeuvre.

loquat NÈFLE DU JAPON

The pear-shaped fruit of an ornamental evergreen tree that is native to China and Japan and is widely cultivated in the Mediterranean basin. The loquat, which is the size of a crab apple, is also called Japanese medlar or Japanese plum; it has a slightly downy skin and white, yellow, or orange flesh that may be firm or soft, depending on the variety. The fruit may contain one or more seeds. A few trees, imported from Madagascar, are grown in Provence, and the fruit is available in France from April to the end of June. It has a low calorific value (38 Cal per 100 g) and is rich in calcium and vitamin A. The loquat is eaten raw as a dessert fruit when very ripe, having a slightly acid refreshing flavour. It can also be made into jam, jelly, syrup, or a liqueur.

Lorette

A garnish for large joints of roast beef and smaller sautéed ones. It consists of chicken croquettes and small bunches of asparagus tips garnished with sliced truffles. A demi-glace sauce is used for large roasts; for the sautéed steaks, the pan is deglazed with Madeira and demi-glace.

Lorette potatoes are deep-fried cheese-flavoured dauphine potatoes. Lorette salad consists of corn salad, with a julienne of celeriac (celery root) and cooked beetroot (red beet).

RECIPE

Lorette potatoes POMMES DE TERRE LORETTE Prepare a dauphine potato mixture and add grated Gruyère cheese (100 g (4 oz) for 700 g (1½ lb) potato mixture). Divide the mixture into portions weighing approximately 40 g (1½ oz, 3 tablespoons) and mould into crescent shapes, or use a piping bag to make stick shapes or knobs. Allow to dry for 30 minutes in the refrigerator, then deep-fry until golden brown in very hot oil (at least 175 C, 345 F). Drain on absorbent kitchen paper.

Lorraine

This province comprises widely differing regions. The Vosges mountains are rich in forests and pastures. The rugged countryside of the Vôsge – with its narrow steep valleys, numerous thermal springs (Vittel, Contrexéville, Plombières) and beautiful oak and beech forests – is famous for wild boar, mushrooms, and bilberries and for the rearing of horned cattle, whose milk is used for making some well-known cheeses (often strong or flavoured). The Lorraine plateau, with its fertile soil, is increasingly used for growing maize (corn) and animal feed (for horned cattle – both beef and dairy breeds – and also for sheep and pigs). The slopes of the Meuse region, with its varied agricultural activities, are covered in vineyards (*vin gris de Toul*), orchards (mirabelle plums, quetsche plums, and cherries) and pastures. The rivers – the Meuse, Moselle, and Ornain – are rich in carp, pike, and trout.

The Lorraine cuisine is based principally on pork, which is an important ingredient in *potée* (smoked ham soup), in the famous quiche, and in *tourte de porc et de veau* (marinated meats baked in a piecrust with egg custard), not to mention the andouillettes of Épinal, the black puddings (blood sausages) of Nancy, the sauerkraut of Saint-Dié, fresh pork liver, sucking pig in aspic, and the wide range of charcuterie from Jametz, Dannevoux, and Vaucouleurs. Goose is often prepared *en daube*, and the pâtés de foie gras of Lorraine rival those of Alsace.

The local fish is used for delicious fish stews, while frogs and crayfish are served *en gratin*.

Lorraine pâtisserie has been famous ever since Stanislas Leszczyński ruled in Nancy, but even before then the province was renowned for its traditional specialities: the quetsche, mirabelle, bilberry, and grape tarts, the biscuits (cookies) of Stenay, *chemitrés* (a kind of waffle), cream puffs from Pont-à-Mousson, macaroons from Nancy, madeleines from Commercy, and ginger cakes and gingerbread from Remiremont. Its confectionery is equally famous: bergamots, sugared almonds, barley sugar, Kirsch chocolates from Charmes, redcurrant jam from Bar-le-Duc, and bilberry jam from Remiremont.

Lorraine beer no longer enjoys the fame it once did, but mirabelle, raspberry, quetsche, and cherry brandies are still, rightly, highly appreciated.

lorraine (à la)

Describes a preparation of large cuts of meat, usually braised, which are garnished with red cabbage cooked in red wine, and apples. The braising juices are served as an accompanying sauce after the fat has been skimmed from them.

The term is also used to define other specialities from Lorraine such as *potée* (smoked ham soup) and quiche, as well as various egg-based dishes, all of which include smoked bacon and Gruyère cheese.

| RECIPE

Flat omelette à la lorraine OMELETTE PLATE À LA LORRAINE For a 6-egg omelette, dice 150 g (5 oz, 6 slices) smoked bacon and sauté in butter. Shred 60 g (2½ oz, ½ cup) Gruyère cheese. Prepare 1 tablespoon finely chopped chives. Beat the eggs and add the rest of the ingredients, then season with pepper. Melt 15 g (½ oz, 1 tablespoon) butter in a frying pan (skillet); pour in the mixture. Cook on one side, then turn and cook the other side.

lotus

An Asian plant related to the water lily. Its large seeds are eaten raw, boiled, or grilled (broiled), while the roots are prepared like celery.

Sometimes the leaves are eaten like spinach. In Vietnam lotus seeds, which taste of almonds, are used in a very popular sweet soup. In Java lotus leaves are stuffed with prawns and rice; while in China they are stuffed with chopped meat and onion, and the seeds are either pickled in vinegar or candied in syrup. In Europe, it is possible to buy canned lotus roots, sliced and pierced with holes. They are used as a garnish for meat or poultry.

Louisiane

A chicken dish in which the bird is stuffed with a mixture of creamed sweetcorn and diced red and green peppers, browned on top of the stove, then baked in the oven in a covered casserole, with a few herbs. It is basted frequently. When it is nearly cooked, some chicken stock and Madeira are added. The chicken is served with a garnish of sweetcorn in cream (sometimes in tartlets), rice moulded in darioles and thick fried slices of banana (possibly arranged on fried slices of sweet potato). The accompanying sauce consists of the cooking liquid strained and skimmed.

Loupiac

A sweetish AOC white wine, from the right bank of the River Garonne, opposite Barsac, within the Premières Côtes de Bordeaux. Full-bodied and with a pronounced bouquet, Loupiac is somewhat similar to Sauternes, though on a smaller scale than many of these. It is even more closely akin to its neighbour, Sainte-Croix-du-Mont.

louquenka

A small raw sausage from the Basque

area, flavoured with pimiento and garlic. It is traditionally eaten grilled (broiled), with oysters.

lovage LIVÈCHE

An aromatic herb which originally came from Persia but is now naturalized in many parts of Europe. The leaves taste rather like celery, and the plant is quite popular in England and Germany, where its leaves and seeds are used to flavour salads, soups, and meat dishes. The leafstalks are blanched and eaten in salads, but they can also be candied, rather like angelica. The roots, too, are used as a salad vegetable (raw or cooked) and can be dried and ground for use as a condiment.

loving cup VIDRECOME

A large drinking vessel, usually with two handles, originating in Germany and used in the Middle Ages at banquets, when it was passed from one guest to another. The French name, which comes from the German *wieder* (again) and *kommen* (come), means literally 'to start drinking again'.

Lucullus (Lucius Licinius)

Roman general (106–56 BC), now remembered chiefly for the splendour and luxury of his feasts. After winning a brilliant victory over Mithridates, Lucullus retired to his country villa, where he lived on a grand scale. Each of his various dining halls was used according to the amount of money spent on the meals served there. Thus, surprised one day by the unexpected arrival of Caesar and Cicero, who wanted to share his meal but would not allow him to change anything on their account, he served them in the Apollo room, where the cost of meals had been fixed at 100,000 sesterces. One night, when he was on his own, he reprimanded his cook for preparing a less elaborate meal than when there were guests, and shouted at him: 'Today Lucullus is dining at Lucullus's!'

It was Lucullus who introduced the pheasant, the peach tree, and the cherry tree to his native country.

The name Lucullus has been given to numerous classic dishes characterized by the richness of their ingredients. Pheasants, ortolans, or quails Lucullus

are stuffed with foie gras and truffles, cooked in a casserole, deglazed with Madeira and demi-glace, then garnished, with truffles poached in Madeira, cocks' combs, and cocks' kidneys. In tournedos Lucullus, the steak is sautéed, placed on a crouton, decorated with a thin slice of truffle and a poached mushroom cap, then coated with a sauce prepared by deglazing the pan with Périgueux sauce; the garnish consists of cocks' combs and cocks' kidneys with asparagus tips. There are even poached eggs Lucullus, which are served on artichoke hearts stuffed with a salpicon of lambs' sweetbreads, cocks' combs, and truffle.

| RECIPES

Macaroni Lucullus MACARONIS LUCULLUS Boil some macaroni until cooked *al dente*. Prepare a very concentrated Madeira sauce, then add it to a salpicon of truffle and foie gras. Arrange alternate layers of macaroni and salpicon in a dish. Garnish with strips of truffle.

Stuffed quails Lucullus CAILLES FARCIES LUCULLUS Bone some quails and reshape them. Cut some foie gras into 25–30-g (1-oz) portions, season with salt and pepper, and insert a small piece of peeled truffle into each one. Garnish the quails with these and cook as for stuffed quails in cases. When cooked, unwrap them and keep warm. Deglaze the cooking juices with Madeira and brown veal stock. Reduce by half and add some chopped truffle. Arrange each quail in small pastry case (pie shell) and coat with the sauce.

lumpfish LUMP

A fish found in cold seas and therefore very abundant in the North Sea and the Baltic. About 50 cm (20 in) long, it leads a sedentary life, attaching itself to the rocks by means of a sucker on its belly. It is fished mainly for its eggs. These are laid in large quantities in March and are yellow in their natural state. They are artificially dyed black or red and sold as caviar substitute, but they do not have anything like the delicious flavour of sturgeon's eggs.

lunch

The midday meal in many English-speaking countries. It is lighter than its continental counterpart because of the British tradition of eating a filling breakfast. Lunch typically includes cold meats, pies, sausage rolls, eggs, a variety of salads, and sandwiches.

The word was introduced into France in the first half of the 19th century, and is used for a cold buffet served at a reception where a large number of guests have to be catered for, often standing up. In addition to canapés, a lunch of this type consists of cheeses, fruit, petits fours, chilled puddings, and a few larger dishes, such as chaud-froid of chicken, fish in aspic, and cold hams. See also *déjeuner*.

luncheon meat

A cooked meat eaten in Britain and the United States. Related to the sausage used widely in Germany for putting on bread, luncheon meat is made of a fine pork paste, often with the addition of chunks of lean meat, thickened with flour, and seasoned with salt, saltpetre, and spices. The product is available canned or put inside a skin, which has been smoked and rubbed with olive oil. In the United States, the name 'luncheon meat' is also used for various kinds of cold sliced meats used for sandwiches.

Lunel

A vin doux naturel made in Languedoc, from the Muscat Doré, as in Frontignan, but Lunel is a little less sweet. It can be quite elegant and has the obvious 'grapey' bouquet typical of wines made from any variety of Muscat.

lute   LUT

A mixture of flour and water, also known in France as *repère*, used to seal the lid onto an earthenware cooking pot. The lute hardens as it dries in the heat. This means that the food is cooked in a hermetically sealed container, avoiding evaporation; therefore all the flavour is retained.

lychee or litchi

A fruit that originated in China, and which is now grown in the Far East and the West Indies. It is about the size of a small plum and has a thin hard knobbly shell that can be removed easily. The shell is green when unripe, but turns either pink or red. The white, juicy, and translucent flesh surrounds a large dark-brown stone; the fruit has a sweet rather musky flavour. Lychees contain 68 Cal per 100 g and are rich in vitamin C and glucose (16%). In Chinese cookery they are often served with meat or fish. In Europe, lychees can be purchased fresh from November to January, and enhance a winter fruit salad. However, they are most often sold canned, preserved in sugar syrup. If the fruit is allowed to dry in its shell, it eventually turns black like a prune. These 'litchi nuts' are very sweet with a slightly acid flavour.

Lyonnais

Lyon is a gastronomic centre of high repute, famous for its mâchons served with jugs of Beaujolais. It owes its place in French cuisine to its own local resources (notably, onions, fruit and vegetable produce, and a wide range of local charcuterie) as well as to imports from bordering provinces: beef from Charolais, fruit and vegetables from the Rhône valley, poultry from Bresse, and freshwater fish and game from Dombes.

As an important communication point between Gaul and Cisalpine, Lyon (then called Lugdunum) enjoyed a reputation as a gourmet town even in times of antiquity. Its local fairs attracted craftsmen, tradesmen, moneylenders, and later manufacturers and industrialists, who met together around sumptuously laden tables. Rabelais joined Erasmus in singing the praises of Lyon and its cuisine. The prosperous bourgeoisie of the town ensured that the tradition of good food was perpetuated. The fame of their rôtisseurs and caterers spread as far as Paris, even before the first restaurants were established. Then there was the period of the Mères Lyonnaises (mothers of Lyon), before the great chefs of modern times turned Lyon, Roanne, and other large towns of Lyonnais into the centres of the district's cuisine.

As well as being the home of great chefs, Lyonnais is also the cradle of a traditional hearty cuisine which is as delicious as the more elegant and refined cuisine that extended its reputation beyond its own borders. This dual tradition is upheld by a number of typically Lyonnais gastronomic societies, such as the Club Brillat-Savarin, which held its meetings at Morateur's; the Société des Amis de Guignol, which preserves the popular recipes of the Lyonnais; and the Académie Rabelais and the Francs-Mâchons, also enthusiasts for the traditional local cuisine.

☐ **Lyonnais specialities** Lyonnais cuisine is undoubtedly dominated by the onion, indispensable for the preparation of omelettes and other egg dishes, miroton, sautéed vegetables, and many other dishes. However, it is an extremely varied cuisine, with a particularly wide range of charcuterie. These include the rosette, the sabodet and the saucisson de Lyon (a 'product with a gnarled uneven surface, held in tightly by its string casing, this giving it a swollen appearance'). Then there are the andouille and andouillettes of Charlieu, *cervelas truffé* (truffled saveloy), *grasdouble* (tripe), tablier de sapeur, roulade of pig's head, grattons, *paquet de couennes*, *jambonneau* (knuckle of ham), and the pigs' ears and tails that featured in the Rabelaisian snacks in the taverns of the town.

Typical Lyonnais soups are bone-marrow consommé, onion soup, pumpkin soup with cream, and egg yolk soup (thickened in a bain-marie, like a baked custard). Lyonnais pike quenelles are famous, and local freshwater fish and crustaceans form the basis of both sumptuous and simple dishes: *matelote* (fish stew) with red wine, fried Rhône gudgeons, gratin and mousse of crayfish tails, trout and pike *au bleu*, braised carp with onion, and frogs with cream or garlic.

The peaks of culinary art have been reached with Lyonnais meat and poultry dishes: *grillades de boeuf à la moelle* (grilled beef with marrow), *farci de veau en vessie* (veal sausage), *poulet Célestine* and *poularde demi-deuil*, seven-hour braised gigot, *rouelle de veau roulé*, and *potage à la jambe de bois* are just a modest selection from the range of Lyonnais cuisine. Vegetable specialities include cardoons *au gratin*, with bone marrow, or with chicken, artichoke hearts with foie gras, galette lyonnais (made with potatoes and onions), dandelion salad with diced bacon, and sautéed green beans. Cheeses from neighbouring areas that are eaten in Lyon include Bleu de Bresse, Pélardon du Vivarais, Reblochon, Rigotte, and Brique du Forez. But Mont-d'Or (once made exclusively from goats' milk) and cervelle de canut are typically Lyonnais.

The desserts, cakes, and confectionery of the region show the same sort of range as the other products. For example, there is vacherin with whipped cream and strawberries, Bernachon chocolates, the sablés of Noirétable, as well as the more homely bugnes du carnaval (a sort of fritter), matefaims (a type of pancake), almond and Kirsch tart *à la lyonnaise*, *radisses* (large elongated brioches), pumpkin cakes, marrons glacés, and mimosa blossom fritters.

lyonnaise (à la)

Describing various preparations, usually sautéed, characterized by the use of chopped onions, which are glazed in butter until golden and often finished off with the pan juices deglazed with vinegar and sprinkled with chopped parsley. Preparations of leftover meats, cardoons, calf's head, etc., are also described as *à la lyonnaise* if they are served with a lyonnaise sauce, which has an onion base.

RECIPES

Lyonnaise potatoes POMMES DE TERRE À LA LYONNAISE Parboil some potatoes and slice them. Heat some butter in a frying pan (skillet) and add the potatoes. When they start to go golden brown, add some peeled and finely chopped onions that have been softened in butter (allow 4 tablespoons onion per 750 g (1½ lb) potatoes). Sauté the mixture well. Arrange in a vegetable dish and sprinkle with chopped parsley.

Lyonnaise sauce SAUCE LYONNAISE Cook 3 tablespoons finely chopped onions in 1 tablespoon butter. When the onions are well softened, add ½ litre (17 fl oz, 2 cups) vinegar and ½ litre (17 fl oz, 2 cups) white wine. Reduce until almost evaporated, then add 2 dl (7 fl oz, ¾ cup) demi-glace. Boil for

3–4 minutes, then strain the sauce or serve it unstrained. 1 tablespoon tomato purée may be added to this sauce.

Alternatively, sprinkle the cooked onions with 1 tablespoon flour and cook until golden, deglaze with 1 glass of vinegar and 1 glass of white wine, then add some meat stock or pan juices. Boil for a few minutes and serve as above.

Omelette à la lyonnaise Peel some onions and chop finely. Brown them in butter and add some chopped parsley. Season with salt and pepper. Break the eggs into a bowl, add the onions, and beat together (allow 1 level tablespoon fried onion per egg). Cook the omelette and roll it onto a serving dish. Pour over it a few spoonfuls of vinegar heated up in the same frying pan (skillet) and a little noisette butter.

Salt cod à la lyonnaise MOURUE À LA LYONNAISE (from Carême's recipe) Prepare and cook some salt cod. Drain, separate the individual flakes, and put them in a saucepan. Cover the saucepan and place over a low heat to dry out any water the cod might still contain. Dice 3 large white onions and cook them gently over a low heat in 225 g (½ lb, 1 cup) melted butter. As soon as they are golden brown, add the cod and sauté. Season with pepper, grated nutmeg, and the juice of a lemon before serving.

macadamia nut

NOIX DE MACADAM
The fruit of an Australian tree. Also known as Queensland nut, it has a thin green fleshy husk; a very hard light-brown shell encloses the edible white kernel, which has a flavour reminiscent of coconut. In Asia the nut is used in curries and stews; in the United States it is a flavouring for ices and cakes, and is also eaten as a sweetmeat, dipped in honey or chocolate.

Macaire

A flat potato cake used as a garnish for roast or sautéed meats. The dish is named after Robert Macaire, brigand hero of the 19th-century melodrama *L'Auberge des Adrets*, who was popularized by Frédérick Lemaître and the Daumier lithographs.

RECIPE

Macaire potatoes POMMES DE TERRE MACAIRE Cook 4 large floury unpeeled potatoes in the oven. Cut in half and remove the pulp. Mash the potato pulp with butter until smooth, allowing 100 g (4 oz, ½ cup) butter per kg (2¼ lb) potato. Season with salt and pepper. Heat some butter in a frying pan (skillet) and add the potato, spreading it out into a flat round cake. Cook until golden, then, with the aid of a plate, turn the potato cake over and cook the other side.

macaroni MACARONIS

Tubes of pasta, 5–6 mm (about ¼ in) in diameter, which originated in Naples. Macaroni is cooked in boiling water and may be served with grated cheese, tomato sauce, butter, or cream, or *au gratin*. It may also be put in a timbale mould or ring mould and served with seafood, vegetables, mushrooms, etc. The word comes from the Italian *maccherone*, meaning 'fine paste'. In Rome the popular method of serving macaroni is *alla ciociara*, with sliced fried vegetables, smoked ham, and slices of sausage. In Naples it is served *all'arrabbiata* (with a spicy sauce with pimientos) or with Mozzarella cheese, mushrooms, peas, and giblets. Macaroni has been known in France since the 17th century. In the 19th century it was also served as a dessert.

RECIPES

Cooking macaroni CUISSON DE MACARONIS Put 2.5 litres (4½ pints,

5½ pints) water in a pan large enough to allow the macaroni to swell. Add salt in the ratio of 1 teaspoon per litre (scant quart, generous quart). Bring it to the boil and put in 250 g (9 oz) macaroni, broken into pieces if necessary. Boil very fast for 16–20 minutes, according to the thickness of the macaroni. Like all pasta products, macaroni must not be overcooked and should be tender but firm. Take the pan off the heat and add a little cold tap water to halt the cooking process. Drain the macaroni well through a colander.

Proceed according to the recipe used.

Macaroni à l'anglaise MACARONIS À L'ANGLAISE Cook 250 g (9 oz) macaroni as described above and place in a serving dish. Serve hot, with fresh butter (added according to taste).

Macaroni à l'italienne MACARONIS À L'ITALIENNE Cook 250 g (9 oz) macaroni and drain thoroughly. Mix in 75 g (3 oz, ¾ cup) grated cheese (a mixture of Gruyère and Parmesan) and 75 g (3 oz, 6 tablespoons) butter cut into small pieces. Season with salt, pepper, and a pinch of grated nutmeg. Mix well together, pour into a serving dish, and serve very hot. The cheese can be replaced by cooked chopped chicken livers bound with a velouté sauce or by fine slices of white truffles, which can be bound with a tomato fondue.

Macaroni croquettes MACARONIS EN CROQUETTES Cook the macaroni in salted water, drain thoroughly, then, if necessary, cut into pieces 1 cm (½ in) long. Bind with an equal volume of thick béchamel sauce and add grated Gruyère cheese. Mix well and leave to cool completely. Divide the mixture into small portions and form into sausage shapes, coat them with beaten egg and breadcrumbs, and deep-fry. When the croquettes are golden, drain them on absorbent paper. Serve very hot with tomato fondue.

Macaroni in stock MACARONIS AU JUS Boil the macaroni until three-parts cooked. Drain thoroughly and place in a frying pan (skillet) with 2 dl (7 fl oz, ¾ cup) concentrated brown veal or beef stock. Cover and leave to simmer for 10 minutes. Serve very hot.

Macaroni with seafood MACARONIS AUX FRUITS DE MER Prepare a seafood ragout. Cook the macaroni in salted water and drain thoroughly. Place half the macaroni in a serving dish, cover with the ragout, and pile the remaining macaroni on top. Serve very hot.

macaroon MACARON

A small round cake, crunchy outside and soft inside, made with ground almonds, sugar, and egg whites. Macaroons are sometimes flavoured with coffee, chocolate, nuts, fruit, etc., and then joined together in pairs.

The origin of this cake goes back a long way. The recipe originally came from Italy, particularly Venice, during the Renaissance: the name is derived from the Italian *maccherone* and the Venetian *macarone* (meaning fine paste), from which *macaroni* is also derived. Some authorities claim that the recipe for the macaroons of Cormery is the oldest. Macaroons have been made in the monastery there since 791 and legend has it that they used to be made in the shape of monks' navels. The macaroons of many French towns are famous, including those of Montmorillon (shaped like coronets and sold on their cooking paper), Niort (made with angelica), Reims, Pau, Amiens, and Melun. The Nancy macaroons are probably the best-known. During the 17th century they were manufactured by the Carmelites, who followed Theresa of Avila's principle to the letter: 'almonds are good for girls who do not eat meat'. During the Revolution two nuns, in hiding with an inhabitant of the town, specialized in making and selling macaroons. They became famous as the 'Macaroon Sisters' and in 1952 the street in which they had operated was named after them; macaroons are still made there today.

| RECIPES

Classic macaroons MACARONS CLASSIQUES Line a baking tray (sheet) with rice paper or buttered greaseproof (waxed) paper. Mix 350 g (12 oz, 1½ cups) caster (superfine) sugar with 250 g (9 oz, 3 cups) ground almonds. Lightly whisk 4 egg whites with a pinch of salt and mix thoroughly with the sugar and almond mixture. If liked, a little finely chopped candied orange peel or cocoa powder can be added to the mixture before cooking. Pipe or spoon small heaps of this mixture onto the baking tray, spacing them so that they do not run into one another during cooking.

Cook in the oven at 200 c (400 F, gas 6) for about 12 minutes. Lift the macaroons off the baking tray with a spatula, transfer to a wire rack, and leave to cool completely. Macaroons can be stored in an airtight container for several days in the refrigerator, or for several months in the freezer.

Hazelnut macaroons MACARONS AUX NOISETTES Use the recipe for soft macaroons (see below) but replace the ground almonds with crushed hazelnuts.

In accordance with a regulation regarding the naming of foodstuffs, these biscuits (cookies) may no longer commercially be called macaroons in France.

Soft macaroons MACARONS MOELLEUX Mix together 250 g (9 oz, 3 cups) ground almonds, 450–500 g (16 –18 oz, 3½–4 cups) icing (confectioners') sugar, and 1 teaspoon vanilla sugar (or a few drops of vanilla essence (extract)) in a bowl with 4 lightly beaten egg whites. Whisk 4 additional egg whites into stiff peaks with a pinch of salt and fold very gently into the mixture. Place the mixture in a piping (pastry) bag with a smooth nozzle 5 mm (¼ in) in diameter. Pipe small amounts of the mixture onto a baking tray (sheet) lined with rice paper or greaseproof (waxed) paper, spacing them so that they do not stick together during cooking. Cook in the oven at 180 c (350 F, gas 4) for about 12 minutes. Finish as for classic macaroons (see recipe above). A little finely chopped angelica can be added to the almond mixture if liked.

mace MACIS
A condiment derived from the fibrous outer coating of the nutmeg seed which is pressed, dried, and used as it is or reduced to powder. It is golden brown when dried, with a combined flavour of cinnamon and pepper. Mace is often used in pork dishes and spice mixtures. It can also be used to improve the flavour of sauces for meats and can replace nutmeg in omelettes, béchamel sauce, and potato purée.

macédoine
A mixture of vegetables or fruit cut into small dice.

A vegetable macédoine is usually composed of carrots and turnips, which are peeled and cut into slices 3–4 mm (⅛ in) thick, then into sticks, and finally into 3–4 mm (⅛-in) cubes. French (green) beans are cut into small pieces. The vegetables are cooked separately and then mixed together with some well-drained peas and possibly other vegetables. The macédoine is bound with butter and is served hot as a garnish for meat and poultry. Roast meat juices are often added, particularly veal, as are chopped herbs and fresh cream. It can also be served cold, either in an aspic mould or bound with mayonnaise and used to stuff tomatoes or to accompany hard-boiled (hard-cooked) eggs or ham cornets.

A fruit macédoine consists of diced fruit soaked in fruit syrup which is served cold, often sprinkled with Kirsch or rum. It can be used to garnish grapefruit and many other dishes.

The name 'macédoine' is derived from Macedonia, the ancient royal kingdom formed from the various Balkan states united by Philip II, father of Alexander the Great.

RECIPE

Vegetable macédoine with butter or cream MACÉDOINE DE LEGUMES AU BEURRE OU À LA CRÈME Peel and dice 250 g (9 oz) each of new carrots, turnips, French (green) beans, and potatoes. Prepare 500 g (18 oz, 3¼ cups) shelled peas. Add the carrots and turnips to a pan of boiling salted water. Bring back to the boil and add the beans, then the peas, and finally the potatoes. Keep on the boil but do not cover. When the vegetables are cooked, drain and pour into a serving dish and add fresh butter or cream (keep the cooking water for a soup base). Sprinkle with chopped herbs.

macerate MACÉRER

To soak raw, dried, or preserved foods in liquid (usually alcohol, liqueur, wine, brandy, or sugar syrup) so that they absorb the flavour of the liquid. Maceration is usually applied to fruit; it imparts flavour to the fruit, softens it, and draws out the fruit juices. Dried fruits for winter compotes and other dishes are often treated in this way as maceration gives them a better flavour.

To prepare jams, fruit is often macerated with the sugar in which it will later be cooked.

maceron

A herbaceous plant formerly grown in the south of France for its young shoots, which were eaten like celery. Also known as 'black parsley' and 'giant Macedonian parsley', it has a strong rather bitter smell and tastes like celery, which has replaced it as a vegetable and flavouring.

mâchon

A traditional snack in the region around Lyon in France, which is served in a bouchon, at 9 a.m. or at 5 p.m., with several jugs of Beaujolais. The word comes from the verb *mâcher*, meaning 'to chew'. Certain bistros in Lyon have made it a speciality. The snack usually consists of pork products (garlic sausage, brawn (head cheese), etc.) served with a salad of potatoes, lentils, or dandelion leaves and bacon. Certain other dishes are also typical, such as *salade de clapotons* (lamb's trotters in vinaigrette with sheep's testicles), *lapin huppé* (thin slices of saveloy in vinaigrette), *tablier de sapeur* (sliced ox tripe coated with egg and breadcrumbs, grilled (broiled) and served with garlic butter, tartare sauce, or a spiced mayonnaise), *cervelle de canut*, (a mixture of fermented curds, white wine, and oil and vinegar seasoned with garlic), *ragoût de béatilles* (a fricassee of gizzards, hearts, livers, and combs of

poultry), *boudin de crépieu aux pommes* (a frothy sorrel omelette on a bed of tripe with potatoes), and *barboton* (slices of potato cooked with tomatoes and spices in a stock thickened with flour). The most ardent supporters of the mâchon have formed an association called the Francs-Mâchons to perpetuate the enjoyment of these traditional dishes.

mackerel MAQUEREAU

An important food fish found throughout the North Atlantic, in the North Sea, and in the Mediterranean. It can be fished throughout the year, in surface waters during the summer months and in deep waters during the winter. The main season is from November to March, when it comes close to the shores. Mackerel migrate in large shoals to specific breeding grounds each year. The small mackerel, known as *lisettes* in France, are caught in the Channel, especially off the coast of Dieppe, and are widely consumed. Mackerel caught by line fishing are always fresher and tastier than those caught by trawler.

The mackerel has a streamlined body, greenish-blue with black and green bands on the back and a silvery underside. When freshly caught, the flesh is firm and crisp and the eyes are very bright. Mackerel is a somewhat oily fish (6–8% fats; a little more before spawning). It can be prepared in many ways – grilled (broiled), classically served with gooseberry sauce; stuffed; prepared *à la provençale* or with white wine; made into a soup (cotriade); or poached and served with mustard sauce, tomato sauce, or cream sauce. In about 1885 mackerel fillets (marinated in white wine and herbs) were marketed in Boulogne. Brittany soon followed suit. Mackerel fillets can also be smoked, preserved in oil or tomato sauce, or served with mustard sauce, cream sauce, with mushrooms, horseradish, etc.

RECIPES

MACKEREL FILLETS

Fillets of mackerel à la dijonnaise FILETS DE MAQUEREAUX À LA DIJONNAISE Fillet 4 large mackerel. Season the fillets with salt and pepper and coat with white seed mustard.

Soften 2 chopped onions in 2 tablespoons (3 tablespoons) oil in a saucepan. Add 1 tablespoon flour and mix well. Pour a glass of stock or fish fumet into the saucepan, together with a glass of dry white wine. Stir well, add a bouquet garni, and cook for 8–10 minutes.

Arrange the fillets in a buttered ovenproof dish, and add the sauce. Place the dish in a moderately hot oven (200 c, 400 f, gas 6) and cook for about 15 minutes. Drain the fish and arrange on a serving dish. Remove the bouquet garni from the sauce, add a little mustard, check the seasoning, and pour the sauce over the fillets. Garnish with slices of lemon and sprigs of parsley.

Mackerel in cider Pierre Traiteur MA-QUEREAUX AU CIDRE PIERRE TRAITEUR (from a recipe by Guy Nouyrrigat) Trim and wash the mackerel and season them thoroughly. Place them on a base of onions and chopped apples in a pan. Cover with cider, add 5 cl (3 tablespoons, ¼ cup) cider vinegar, and bring to the boil. Simmer for 5 minutes. Allow the fish to cool in the pan. Remove the fillets and arrange them on a serving dish surrounded by pieces of apple that have been fried in butter. Boil down the cooking liquid in the pan and pour over the mackerel while still hot. Sprinkle with pepper and chopped chives.

WHOLE OR SLICED MACKEREL

Mackerel with noisette butter MA-QUEREAUX AU BEAURRE NOISETTE Clean 6 medium-sized mackerel and cut them into thick slices of a similar size. Poach for about 12 minutes in a court-bouillon made with vinegar. Drain, place on a serving dish, and keep warm. Sprinkle with a little vinegar. Prepare 100 g (4 oz, ½ cup) noisette butter and add 1 tablespoon capers and chopped parsley. Pour the butter over the mackerel and serve very hot.

Mackerel with sorrel MAQUEREAUX À L'OSEILLE (from a recipe by Fernand Point) Trim 6 mackerel, slit them along the back, and dry them. Melt a large knob of butter in a frying pan (skillet), place the fish in the hot butter, and cook on one side for 5 minutes. Turn, and cook the other side. Remove the fish from the pan, season, and keep warm.

Pick over 500 g (18 oz) sorrel, wash it thoroughly, and add it to the juices in the frying pan. Heat the mixture, stirring constantly, until the sorrel is reduced to a purée (do not allow it to dry out). Check the seasoning, then bind the mixture with fresh butter and 1–2 eggs. Serve the mackerel on a long dish, garnished with the sorrel purée.

Mackerel with two-mustard sauce MAQUEREAUX AUX DEUX MOUTARDES (from a recipe by Dominique Nahmias) Wash and gut (clean) 8 small mackerel (*lisettes*). Place them in an ovenproof dish, season with salt and pepper, moisten with a glass of dry white wine, and cook in a very hot oven (240 c, 475 f, gas 9) for 8 minutes. Mix 1 tablespoon strong mustard with 1 tablespoon mild mustard in a saucepan. When the mackerel are cooked, add their cooking juices to the mustard mixture. Add 2 tablespoons (3 tablespoons) butter, bring to the boil, and cook for 2 minutes. Coat the fish with the sauce and serve with rice *à la créole*.

Mâcon

The region between the southern end of the Côte de Beaune and the Beaujolais. It produces red, white, and rosé AOC wines, of which the white Pouilly-Fuissé and St Véran are well known. Although Mâconnais wines do not usually attain the character and quality of Côte d'Or Burgundies, they can be both agreeable and varied. Since Pouilly-Fuissé became popular in the United States, it is no longer reasonably priced.

mâconnaise (à la)

Describing dishes cooked with Mâcon wine or slices of fish cooked in red Mâcon wine with herbs, garnished with small brown glazed onions, fried mushrooms, croutons, and shrimps.

Macquée

A fresh soft cheese made from skimmed cows' milk, which is sold in small blocks or muslin (cheesecloth) bags. It is used to make a tart which is very popular in northern France and Belgium. The cheese is thoroughly drained, mixed with egg yolks (and sometimes with herbs and pepper – although the original recipe does not include these items), then spread out on a raised dough base. When the tart is cooked, the top is pricked and spread with butter, which melts and soaks into the tart. It should be served warm as an entrée.

macrobiotic
MACROBIOTIQUE
Denoting a system of diets inspired by the Zen sect of Japanese Buddhism, based on balancing the opposing principles of Yin (feminine) and Yang (masculine). It was founded by Sakurazawa Nyoiti, known as Oshawa (1893–1966), and appeared in France in the 1950s. It comprises a dozen diets, adapted to the individual's physical and spiritual requirements, based on wholegrain cereals and dried vegetables. Some diets include some green vegetables and a little fish, but meats, fruits, and alcoholic drinks are forbidden. The only beverage permitted is tea and then only in small quantities. This method of nutrition is considered unbalanced and, in certain cases, a health hazard. Dieticians recognize thorough chewing as its only advantage.

Macvin
A regional speciality of the Jura, reputedly dating from the 9th century. Essentially it is spiced wine, sweetish and fairly high in strength due to the addition of marc.

Madeira MADÈRE
A fortified wine from the island of the same name, which belongs to Portugal. The vineyards are terraced and the vines trained vertically. The wine is produced by a process known as the *estufa*, in which the wine in the cask is very gradually heated and then allowed to cool down. Most Madeiras are named after the grapes that make them: Sercial is the driest, Verdelho is nutty and mellow, Bual (or Boal) and Malmsey are sweetish and full-bodied. The wine from each Madeira establishment has its own distinctive character and there are in addition a few blends sold under brand names, such as Rainwater. Madeira is

regaining its previous popularity. It can have a very long life in the bottle – there are 18th-century Madeiras still in existence, but these are exceptional vintage wines. Dry Madeiras are good drunk as apéritifs or with clear soup, while the sweeter wines may be drunk at any time, or with dessert, fruit, and nuts.

RECIPES

Braised ham with Madeira JAMBON BRAISÉ AU MADÈRE Braise the ham and cut it into slices. Remove the fat from the meat juices, reduce them, and add Madeira. Strain and then thicken with arrowroot or cornflour (cornstarch). Arrange the slices of ham in an ovenproof dish and cover with the Madeira-flavoured stock. Cover and heat through in the oven without boiling.

Madeira sauce SAUCE MADÈRE (old recipe) Add 3 tablespoons (¼ cup) Madeira to 2 dl (7 fl oz, ¾ cup) reduced meat juices and warm up.

madeleine
A small cake shaped like a rounded shell, made with sugar, flour, melted butter, and eggs, flavoured with lemon or orange-flower water. The mixture is cooked in ribbed oval moulds which give the cakes their shell-like appearance.

The origin of this 'seashell cake so strictly pleated outside and so sensual inside' (Marcel Proust) is the subject of much discussion. It has been attributed to Avice, Talleyrand's chef, who had the idea of baking a pound-cake mixture in aspic moulds. Other authorities, however, believe that the recipe is much older and originated in Commercy, a town in Lorraine, which was then a duchy under the rule of Stanislaw Leszczynski. It is said that during a visit to the castle in 1755 the duke was very taken with a cake made by a peasant girl named Madeleine. This started the fashion for 'madeleines' (as they were named by the duke), which were then launched in Versailles by his daughter Marie, who was married to Louis XV. The attribution of the cake to Madeleine Paumier, cordon-bleu cook to a rich burger of Commercy, seems doubtful.

RECIPES

Classic madeleines MADELEINES CLASSIQUES Melt 100 g (4 oz, ½ cup) butter without allowing it to become hot. Butter a tray of madeleine moulds with 20 g (¾ oz, 1½ tablespoons) butter. Put the juice of half a lemon in a bowl with a pinch of salt, 125 g (4½ oz, scant ⅔ cup) caster (superfine) sugar, 3 eggs, and an extra egg yolk. Mix well together with a wooden spatula and then sprinkle in 125 g (4½ oz, scant 1¼ cups) sifted flour and mix till the mixture is smooth; finally add the melted butter. Spoon the mixture into the moulds but do not fill more than two-thirds full. Bake in the oven at 180 C (350 F, gas 4) for about 25 minutes. Turn out the madeleines and leave to cool on a wire tray.

Commercy madeleines MADELEINES DE COMMERCY Cream 150 g (5 oz, generous ½ cup) butter with a wooden spoon. Add 200 g (7 oz, ¾ cup) caster (superfine) sugar and mix well. Add 6 whole eggs, one at a time, then 200 g (7 oz, 1¾ cups) flour sieved with 1 teaspoon baking powder, and finally stir in 1 tablespoon orange-flower water. Butter and lightly flour some madeleine moulds and spoon in the mixture. Bake in the oven at 220 C (425 F, gas 7) for about 10 minutes. Turn out the madeleines onto a rack to cool.

Madiran

AOC red wine from southwestern France. It has a pronounced character and may be a little acid when young but ages well and is sometimes compared to Burgundies. Madiran is produced on the same communes as the white wine Pacherenc-du-Vic-Bilh.

madrilène (à la)

The name given to a poultry consommé enriched with tomato pulp, sometimes served hot but usually served chilled or iced, as in the Spanish tradition for soups.

RECIPE

Consommé à la madrilène Prepare a chicken consommé for 5 people. When clarifying, add 3 dl (½ pint, 1¼ cups) chopped fresh tomato pulp. Strain the soup through a very fine strainer, add a pinch of cayenne, and leave to cool completely, then refrigerate. Serve cold in cups. The soup can be garnished with finely diced red pepper which has been cooked in stock.

magistère

A very nourishing concentrated consommé invented by Brillat-Savarin to combat the effects of 'muscular, intellectual, or sexual exhaustion'. There are two types: one for robust temperaments, based on a stock made with chicken (or partridge) and beef bones and meat; and one for weak temperaments, made from shin of veal (veal shank), pigeon, shrimps, and cress. These dishes were recommended by Ambroise Paré to nourish invalids without overexciting them.

magnesium MAGNÉSIUM

A mineral which is found mainly in cocoa, whole-grain cereals, soya (soy) beans, brewer's yeast, and nuts. Magnesium is required in minute amounts for all metabolic processes and is essential for the health of the nervous system.

magret

A portion of meat from the breast of a duck (mallard or Barbary, traditionally fattened for foie gras). Magrets are presented with the skin and underlying layer of fat still attached. For a long time they were used only for confits. A renewed interest came when the restauranteurs from the Landes region in France served magrets grilled in the traditional country way (skin side first so that the fat impregnates the flesh), so that the skin is crunchy but the meat remains bloody or very rare. The best magrets (the name means the lean portion of a fat duck) come from ducks boned the day after they are killed, and are served the day after that.

RECIPE

Magrets de canard (from André Daguin's recipe) Place 4 chopped shallots and 3 dl (½ pint, 1¼ cups) Madiran in a small saucepan and reduce over a high heat until the wine has been absorbed. Then add 125 ml (4 fl oz, ½ cup) fresh cream and reduce again until syrupy. Lower the heat. Remove from the heat and gradually whisk in one or two pieces cut from 350 g (12 oz, 1½ cups) semisalted butter, returning the casserole to the heat for a few moments and then removing it. Continue in this way until all the butter has been incorporated. Keep the sauce warm in a bain-marie.

Quickly brown 6 ducks' breasts (magrets) in a thick-bottomed saucepan, placing the fatty side down. Turn them over as soon as they are golden, cook the other side similarly, and reduce the heat. Leave to cook for about 15 minutes. Remove the breasts from the pan and keep warm in a serving dish. Skim off the cooking fat and deglaze the pan with 1 dl (6 tablespoons, scant ½ cup) Madiran. Reduce for a few minutes, then remove from the heat and thicken the sauce with 1 tablespoon of the butter sauce prepared earlier. Pour this sauce over the ducks' breasts and serve the remainder of the butter sauce separately.

maidenhair fern

CAPILLAIRE

A species of fern with aromatic and mucilaginous leaves that are used to make infusions and syrups to ease bronchial conditions. Maidenhair fern syrup was once used to sweeten hot drinks, particularly Bavarian cream. *Capilè*, a very popular drink in Portugal, especially in Lisbon, is made of maidenhair fern syrup, grated lemon zest, and cold water.

maid of honour

A small English tart with an almond, curd cheese, and lemon filling. Tradition has it that Anne Boleyn created the recipe while she was lady-in-waiting to Catherine of Aragon and that an enchanted Henry VIII named the cake maid of honour. Many English cities produce maids of honour as a speciality but it is in Richmond, a suburb of London, that the most delicious maids of honour are to be found.

Maille

An 18th-century French mustard and vinegar manufacturer. In 1769 he succeeded Leconte as vinegar distiller to the king but his reputation had already been established. He had invented the famous 'four thieves' vinegar in 1720, the antiseptic qualities of which protected the doctors and nuns treating plague victims in the great epidemic in Marseilles.

100 varieties of vinegar for health or beauty and 53 varieties of flavoured table vinegars (nasturtium, caper, game, ravigote, distilled, etc.) were produced in his laboratories in Paris as well as mustards (such as the tarragon and trois fruits rouges mustards praised by Grimod) and fruits preserved in vinegar. These products were exported to Hamburg and Moscow. Mme de Pompadour, a faithful client of M. Maille, especially liked his aniseed vinegar and the vinegar *à la dauphine*. The name Maille is still used on a range of mustards and vinegars, the recipes of which date back to the 18th century.

Maintenon

The name given to a savoury dish made with mushrooms, onions, and béchamel sauce, sometimes containing truffles, tongue, and chicken breasts. This style of preparation is usually applied to delicate meats (lamb chops, veal, sweetbreads, etc.), but stuffed omelettes, poached eggs, and stuffed potatoes can also be prepared in this way. Sweetbreads *à la Maintenon* are braised, arranged on croutons, decorated with a slice of truffle, garnished with onion purée, and surrounded by a ring of suprême sauce. Dishes *à la Maintenon* were probably created by a chef in the service of the Noailles family, who owned the Château de Maintenon, but Mme de Maintenon was also interested in cooking: she created lamb chops *en papillotes* for Louis XIV.

RECIPES

Lamb (*or mutton*) chops Maintenon
CÔTELETTES DE MOUTON MAINTENON Quickly brown the chops in butter on one side only. Coat the cooked side of each chop with 1 tablespoon Maintenon mixture (see recipe below),

shape into a dome, and coat with bread-crumbs. Lavishly butter a baking dish and arrange the chops on it. Sprinkle with melted butter and cook in the oven, preheated to 250 c (475 F, gas 9). Serve with Périgueux sauce.

Maintenon mixture APPAREIL À MAINTENON Clean and slice 150 g (5 oz, 1¼ cups) mushrooms and sweat in 10 g (½ oz, 1 tablespoon) butter. Prepare a Soubise purée with 500 g (18 oz, 4½ cups) sliced onions blanched and sweated in butter and 500 ml (17 fl oz, 2 cups) thick béchamel sauce, salt and pepper, and a little grated nutmeg. Add the mushrooms and bind with 2 egg yolks. Check the seasoning.

Stuffed potatoes à la Maintenon POMMES DE TERRE FARCIES À LA MAINTENON Bake some floury medium-sized unpeeled potatoes in the oven. Cut in half and remove the pulp without breaking the skin. Prepare a salpicon with chicken, pickled tongue, mushrooms, and truffles, bound with a light Soubise purée. Fill the potato skins with this mixture, forming a dome shape. Sprinkle the tops with grated cheese, breadcrumbs, and melted butter. Brown in the oven.

maison

This descriptive term, when used honestly, indicates that the dish concerned has been prepared according to an original recipe and is served only in the establishment which claims it. It is more commonly used today to refer to a speciality of the house, or to a dish that is home-made to the chef's own recipe. Nevertheless, the term does lack precision. It would be more satisfactory to say *de notre maison* or *à la manière de notre maison*, since *maison* as it stands is vague enough for unscrupulous restaurateurs to offer as a *tarte maison*, for instance, a pastry which comes from an establishment other than their own, from a wholesale confectioner, in fact! Maurice des Ombiaux points out in his *Traité de table* (1947): 'In many restaurants the menu offers *sole maison*, *filet maison*, *poulet maison*, *fine maison* (a liqueur brandy), etc. But which maison does this refer to? A chef tells us that it was after World War I that this strange and ungainly word first appeared. Previously the specialities created in a restaurant bore its name, which was simple and logical. Today the expression is used constantly, misleading the customer who sees on the menu of the same restaurant a *poulet maison à la sauce brune* one day, *poulet maison à la sauce blanche* the next, *poulet maison à la sauce au vin* the following day, *à la sauce tomate* after that . . .'.

Maison Dorée

A restaurant on the Boulevard des Italiens in Paris, which was founded in about 1840 on the site previously occupied by the Café Hardy. It was used as a setting by Balzac and Zola, who had a number of their characters dine there (they called it Maison d'Or). It became extremely fashionable; the late diners particularly enjoyed boudin Richelieu, grilled before them on silver grills. Champagne was the order of the day, although the cellars contained the greatest variety of wines in the Second Empire. The establishment was owned by the Verdier brothers, sons of a restaurateur from Les Halles. The master chef, Casimir Moisson, is said to have invented timbale Nantua. The restaurant's reputation declined after 1870. It had seen all the literary, political, and artistic celebrities of the era, including the famous *cocottes* who played a prominent role in Zola's *Nana*. The Maison Dorée was closed in 1902, but the façade – with its gilded balconies and friezes depicting hunting scenes – is classed as a historic monument.

maître d'hôtel

The man in charge of the dining room in a hotel or restaurant. He is assisted by a team of senior, junior, and assistant waiters.

Previously in royal, princely, and other noble households, the office of maître d'hôtel was always held by noblemen of the highest rank, sometimes princes of the blood royal. Although at that time the office was a sinecure, the maître d'hôtel was, at least nominally, in charge of all departments of the royal household, including the kitchens and cellars, and all the functionaries and servants. In *La Maison réglée* (1692), Audiger sets out the maître d'hôtel's duties in a private house: he should supervise the accounts, choose the cooks, buy the bread, wine, and meat, and 'regulate and arrange the table settings of all the different services the nobleman might require'.

The maître d'hôtel's function has almost ceased to exist in private houses as it is rare to require someone's services just to arrange tables and buy provisions. However, in the large restaurants it has lost none of its importance. The maître d'hôtel of a modern restaurant or a great private establishment must have a very extensive range of technical knowledge. He must have qualities of leadership which will enable him to command his staff with authority and courtesy. He must be a first-class administrator and a tactful diplomat.

He must be thoroughly familiar with details of the special work of the dining room, kitchens, and cellars. He must be able to talk to the clients – in several languages – politely but not obsequiously. He must be able to advise his clients, to guide them in their choice of dishes, the wines to go with them, and the fruit to follow.

These are the qualities which the modern maître d'hôtel must possess. If he is no longer a *grand seigneur*, as were the important personages who filled this office in the great royal households, he is usually a man of distinction, good education, and, particularly, a master of his art, for service at the table is as much an art as cooking.

maître d'hôtel butter

A savoury butter containing chopped parsley and lemon juice and served with grilled (broiled) or fried fish, grilled meat, or vegetables, either in liquid form in a sauceboat or solidified, in rounds or slices.

| RECIPES

Maître d'hôtel butter BEURRE MAÎTRE D'HÔTEL Work 200 g (7 oz, generous ¾ cup) butter to a smooth paste with a wooden spatula, add ½ teaspoon fine salt, a pinch of freshly ground pepper, a squeeze (about 1 tablespoon) of lemon juice, and 1 table-spoon chopped parsley. This butter can be kept in the refrigerator for 2 or 3 days.

maize (corn) MAÏS

A cereal with white, yellow, or rust-coloured grains, rich in starch, which are attached to a cob protected by layers of fibrous leaves with tasselled tops. Also known as corn (in the United States) and Indian corn, it originated in America, being discovered by Christopher Columbus and introduced into Europe by Cortés. For many years it was only grown in southwestern France, Spain, and Italy: it was usually ground to a powder, boiled, and eaten as porridge (polenta, millas, etc.). Maize plays a very important part in the nutrition of the American continent. Yielding 354 Cal per 100 g, it is also rich in lipids, proteins, and carbohydrates. It is, however, devoid of certain essential amino acids. There are several varieties.

● **Grain maize** is hard and bright yellow with a fairly small cob. It is usually used as an animal feedstuff but can also be ground into flour or semolina and used to make bread, pancakes, fritters, waffles, and many cakes. It is also served boiled. Cornflakes are also made with maize flour. Cornflour (cornstarch) is widely used as a thickening agent both in domestic cookery and in the food industry. This type of maize is also used to make Bourbon whiskey and certain types of beer, as well as corn oil.

● **Sweetcorn** is bought fresh on the cob from July to October. The grains are pale yellow and the cob is larger than that of grain maize. It is harvested while still unripe and must be eaten quickly as it deteriorates rapidly after picking. It should be chosen with milky grains and covered with pale green leaves. It is sold either fresh, canned, or frozen. The fresh cobs are cooked in boiling salted water with their inner leaves on or grilled (broiled) without their leaves. They are served with fresh or melted butter, lightly flavoured with lemon, fresh cream, or, especially in America, with redcurrant jelly or maple syrup. Small cobs are pickled in vinegar. Sweetcorn can be served hot, on or off the cob, as an accompaniment to meat dishes or roast poultry. The grains can also be used in mixed salads.

● **Popcorn** is prepared by heating the grains in oil until they puff up and burst, forming soft white light masses which can be caramelized. Popcorn is eaten as a snack or sweetmeat.

RECIPES

Cornbread PAIN DE MAÏS (American cookery) Mix 500 g (18 oz, 3½ cups) cornmeal, 250 g (9 oz, generous 2 cups) sieved wheat flour, 4 teaspoons sugar, 1½ tablespoons baking powder, 1½ teaspoons salt, and 100 g (4 oz, ½ cup) butter in a bowl. Blend in 4 egg yolks beaten with ½ litre (scant pint, 2¼ cups) milk and 1 dl (6 tablespoons, scant ½ cup) double (heavy) cream, stirring as little as possible. Fold in 4 egg whites, whisked stiffly, and pour into well-buttered patty tins (muffin pans), filling them three-quarters full. Bake in a hot oven for 25–30 minutes. This bread is served hot, straight from the oven, at breakfast.

Corn en soso with chicken giblets MAÏS EN SOSO AUX ABATTIS DE POULET (Creole cookery) Soso is a porridge made from cornmeal. It must not be too thick and should be simmered slowly for a long time.

Cut the giblets into equal pieces. Brown in fat and add a little water. Add 2 tablespoons (3 tablespoons) tomato purée and season. When completely cooked, drain off the stock and keep it to moisten the flour. Wash some cornmeal. Put it in the pan in which the giblets have been browned, together with chopped onion. Add the giblets, then the stock (gradually), and cook slowly until thick.

Fresh corn au naturel MAÏS FRAIS AU NATUREL Cook as for corn with béchamel sauce, then drain the cobs and remove the leaves. Serve the cobs with fresh butter or melted lightly lemon-flavoured butter, or remove the grains and serve with butter as a vegetable.

Fresh corn with béchamel sauce MAÏS FRAIS À LA BÉCHAMEL Choose very fresh cobs with tender grains. Leave only one layer of leaves on and cook in boiling salted water for about 15 minutes (be careful to keep the water on the boil). Drain the cobs and remove the leaves. Detach the grains from the cob and serve with a light béchamel sauce.

Grilled (broiled) fresh corn on the cob MAÏS FRAIS GRILLÉ Choose very fresh cobs with tender grains. Remove the leaves and fibres and either grill (broil) on all sides or cook the cobs in a hot oven until the grains are swollen and golden. Serve either on or off the cob, with melted butter and lemon, if desired.

Málaga

A Spanish wine produced around the town of the same name in Andalusia. It is made according to a type of solera system, in which the casks of maturing wine are repeatedly topped up with younger wines to perpetuate the quality and character of the original. Although Málaga is not fortified, it is higher in alcohol (about 16°) than table wines. Most Málaga is sweet, some is luscious, but a little dry wine is also made. Very popular a century or so ago, it is now seldom drunk in quantity in the UK, although it remains popular in other northern countries.

malakoff

The name given to various classic cakes, often containing nuts. The most common type is made of two thick round dacquoise (nut meringue) cakes, each of which is coated in coffee mousse; the top is sprinkled with icing (confectioners') sugar and the sides coated with chopped grilled (toasted) almonds. Another version of malakoff is composed of a choux pastry crown placed on a puff pastry or sponge cake base, the centre filled with ice cream containing crystallized (candied) fruits, Chantilly cream, or any other cold frothy filling.

malanga

A large firm root vegetable with a brown skin and white flesh, which is used grated in the West Indies for the preparation of acras.

mallow MAUVE

A common plant that grows in fields, hedgerows, and on roadsides. There are about 20 different species found all over the world. In France the best-known variety is the greater mallow, which can reach a height of about 1 m (3¼ ft). Its leaves contain a mucilage used as an emollient and in infusions. The leaves can also be eaten in salad or as a vegetable, like spinach. The flowers are soothing to chest troubles and sore throats.

Malmsey

See *Malvoisie*.

malsat or melsat

A boudin blanc made in southwestern France, with belly pork bound with an egg panada and usually flavoured with herbs.

Malsat from Albi is made from chopped spleen and eggs. It is served fried, cold, or heated up in a vegetable soup.

malt

Barley that is prepared for brewing or distilling by being steeped, germinated, roasted, and then crushed in a mill. The extent to which the malt is roasted determines the colour of the beer: the higher the caramelization, the darker the beer. The main constituent of malt is starch, which is converted to sugar by fermentation when the crushed malt is soaked and heated. This process, called saccharification, results in the production of wort, which is processed further to produce beer or distilled to produce whisky.

Malt extract – a concentrated infusion of germinated barley – is used as a sugar substitute, especially for young children.

maltais

A petit four made with crystallized (candied) orange and ground almonds and iced with fondant icing (frosting).

RECIPE

Maltais Mix 100 g (4 oz, 8 tablespoons) caster (superfine) sugar and 100 g (4 oz, 1 cup) ground almonds. Add a liqueur glass of rum and 60 g (2½ oz, ⅓ cup) finely chopped candied orange peel. If the paste is very thick add 2–3 tablespoons (3–5 tablespoons) strained orange juice. Roll out the paste on a cloth until it is about 5 mm (¼ in) thick

and cut into rounds with a 3-cm (1¼-in) pastry (cookie) cutter. Leave the rounds to dry out for about 12 hours, taking care not to break them as the paste is very fragile.

Heat 100 g (4 oz) fondant icing (frosting) to 35 c (85 f) and colour half of it pink. Ice half of the petits fours with pink icing and the other half with white icing. Cut candied angelica into lozenge (diamond) shapes and decorate each petit four with an angelica star. Store in a cool place until serving.

maltaise (à la)

The term used to describe sweet or savoury preparations which are based on oranges, particularly the Maltese blood orange. Maltaise sauce is a hollandaise sauce flavoured with blood-orange juice and shredded rind, served with poached fish or boiled vegetables (such as asparagus, Swiss chard, and cardoons). The bombe glacée *à la maltaise* is coated in orange ice and filled with tangerine-flavoured Chantilly cream.

RECIPES

Banana croûtes à la maltaise CROÛTES AUX BANANES À LA MALTAISE Cut a stale brioche mousseline into slices, and then cut the slices into rectangles a little longer and wider than the bananas. Arrange them on a baking sheet, sprinkle with sugar, and lightly glaze in the oven. Peel 6 bananas, cut them in half lengthwise, and sprinkle lightly with lemon juice. Place the bananas on a buttered baking sheet and cook in a hot oven for 5 minutes. Arrange the bananas, alternating with slices of brioche, in a circle in an ovenproof dish. Fill the centre with a confectioners' custard (pastry cream) favoured with orange zest (see *creams and custards*). Sprinkle the whole dish with finely crushed macaroons and melted butter and brown in the oven. Before serving, decorate with candied orange peel.

Maltaise sauce SAUCE MALTAISE Mix the juice of a blood orange with 2 dl (7 fl oz, ¾ cup) hollandaise sauce. Add 1 tablespoon grated and blanched orange peel.

Malvoisie

The French name for a grape and a wine originating in the Peloponnese, the Greek name being Monemvasia. In Italy it is called Malvasia, in Spain Malvasía, and in Britain Malmsey. The wine, which is sweet, was very popular in former times when sugar was expensive. The grape, which belongs to the great Pinot grape family, is grown in Madeira, Brazil, California, South Africa, and France.

It is no longer only used to make sweet wines, although Malmsey Madeira is rich and luscious.

mancelle (à la)

The name given to dishes which originated in the town of Le Mans and the surrounding area, notably poultry (roast capon, chicken fricassee), pork rillettes, wild rabbit, and an omelette in which the eggs are mixed with artichoke hearts and diced potatoes.

Manchego

A Spanish cheese made from ewes' milk (57% fat), which originated in La Mancha. It is cylindrical, 10 cm (4 in) deep and 25 cm (10 in) in diameter, and is sold either fresh or matured for 5, 20, or 60 days. The cheese is very fatty and firm to the touch, cream in colour, and sometimes pierced with small holes; it has a strong bitter taste if it is not very fresh. Manchego used to be stored in olive oil but today it usually has a waxed rind.

manchette

A paper frill used to decorate the projecting bones of a leg of lamb, a ham, chops, etc.

manchon

A small petit four made of almond paste and shaped into a small tube by rolling it around a wooden handle. It is filled with Chiboust cream or praline butter cream and the ends are dipped in coloured ground almonds or in chopped pistachio nuts.

mandoline

A vegetable slicer consisting of two adjustable stainless steel blades, one plain, one grooved, held in a wooden or metal frame. A folding support enables the mandoline to be tilted during slicing. It is used particularly to slice cabbage, carrots, turnips, and potatoes.

mange-tout

See *bean, snow pea.*

mango   MANGUE

A large tropical fruit of which there are many varieties. Mangoes are typically oblong and greenish, ripening to yellow, red, or violet (particularly on the side of the fruit which has been exposed to the sun). The skin should be slightly supple. The orange juicy flesh clings to a large flattish nut; it is soft and sugary with an acid aftertaste. Certain varieties are fibrous, with a flavour of lemon, banana, or mint.

The mango tree came originally from Malaysia and has been known in Asia for a long time; it was introduced into Africa and then South America in the 19th century. Mangoes are available nearly all the year round in France, being imported from Brazil from September to January and from Burkina Faso and the Ivory Coast from March to July.

Yielding 62 Cal per 100 g, the mango is a rich source of iron and vitamin A, and contains some of vitamins B and C. In Asia and the West Indies unripe mangoes, either raw or cooked, are used as an hors d'oeuvre or as an accompaniment to fish or meat. Mango chutneys are among the best-known chutneys. Ripe mangoes, which do not keep long, can be used as a garnish for chicken, as an ingredient in mixed salads, and to make sorbets, jams, marmalades, and jellies. Fresh mangoes can be cut in two like an avocado and eaten with a spoon; alternatively the flesh can be removed and diced.

RECIPES

Mango dessert with passion fruit and rum DESSERT DE MANGUES ET DE FRUITS DE LA PASSION AU RHUM VIEUX (from a recipe by Michel Poitoux) Remove the pulp from 500 g (18 oz) passion fruit and discard the seeds. Whisk the pulp together with an equal quantity of sugar syrup and freeze to make a sorbet.

Cut some Genoese sponge cake into 4 rounds, 10 cm (4 in) in diameter and 1 cm (½ in) thick, and scoop out a slight hollow in each. Cut the flesh of 4 well-ripened mangoes into slices. Fill the hollows in the sponge rounds with the passion fruit sorbet and arrange the slices of mango in the shape of a fan over the top. Place in the coldest part of the fridge.

Prepare a zabaglione with rum: whisk 4 egg yolks with 10 cl (6 tablespoons, scant ½ cup) rum in a bain-marie. When the mixture is light and fluffy, add 4 tablespoons (⅓ cup) fresh whipped cream. Coat the slices of mango with the zabaglione, glaze for a short time under the grill (broiler), and decorate with cape gooseberries.

Mango sorbet SORBET À LA MANGUE Choose ripe mangoes, peel them, and rub the flesh through a fine sieve. Add an equal volume of sugar syrup and some lemon juice (the juice of 2 lemons is needed per litre (1¾ pints, 4¼ cups sorbet). Add a little extra lemon juice if the syrup is too heavy, or some sugar if it is too light. Freeze and finish the preparation in the usual way (see *sorbet*).

Sautéed chicken with mangoes POULET SAUTÉ AUX MANGUES Cut a chicken into pieces and sauté in butter for about 20 minutes. Soften a chopped onion and a peeled crushed tomato in a mixture of 2 tablespoons (3 tablespoons) oil and 20 g (¾ oz, 1½ tablespoons) butter with a pinch of ground ginger. Add the crushed pulp of 2 or 3 mangoes, a squeeze of lemon juice, and the chicken pieces, together with a cup of water, salt, pepper, and a pinch of cayenne. Cover and cook for about 30 minutes over a medium heat.

mangosteen
MANGOUSTAN

A round ribbed fruit, the size of an orange, native to Malaysia. The thick tough dark red skin covers a delicate juicy white flesh divided into five or six segments. The mangosteen is eaten fresh, peeled and cut in half. It is also used in jams, sorbets, and exotic salads. In Indonesia it is made into a vinegar and a concentrated oil is extracted from the seeds to make *kokum* butter.

manioc

The edible root of a tropical plant, also called cassava, having a white starchy flesh beneath a brown rind; it is used as a vegetable or to make tapioca. Originally from Brazil, the plant is cultivated throughout South and Central America and has been introduced into Africa, where it is now a basic foodstuff (ground into semolina, salted or sugared in flat cakes, or boiled in *foutou*). It is also grown in Asia.

There are two varieties of manioc: sweet and bitter. Sweet manioc is rich in calories (262 Cal per 100 g) and carbohydrates but deficient in proteins, vitamins, and mineral salts. The root is peeled, washed, cut into pieces, cooked in salted water, and used like potatoes to accompany meat or fish. A flour is also extracted to make cakes, soups, stews, bread, and biscuits. The starchy leaves are prepared like spinach (West Indian *brèdes*). Bitter manioc is used in the food industry. It contains a poisonous juice which contains hydrocyanic acid, which is eliminated by washing; the fresh roots are then grated and left to ferment. The starch is extracted by centrifugation, cooked, crushed, dried, and made into tapioca. In Brazil manioc is used to make a spirit called Cavim.

maniveau

A small basket or reed tray in which certain foods (such as mushrooms) are sold.

manouls

A speciality of the Languedoc region in France, consisting of veal tripe stuffed with ham, garlic, parsley, and spices. In the Rouergue region, however, manouls is lamb's tripe cooked in portions with a rich spicy garnish.

manqué

A type of sponge cake that is a speciality of Paris. It is said to have been invented by a famous 19th-century Parisian pastrycook called Félix, while preparing a Savoy sponge cake. When the egg whites would not whisk up, in order not to waste the mixture he had the idea of adding melted butter and flaked (slivered) almonds, and covering the cake with praline when it was cooked.

The customer who bought it thought it was so good that she ordered another and wanted to know the name of the mystery cake. The baker said it was a *manqué* (failure), but it became such a success that a special mould was invented.

The *moule à manqué* is a round deep-sided mould which is also used for other cakes. The original manqué mixture has been considerably modified since Félix first made it. It is now often flavoured with flaked hazelnuts, raisins, crystallized (candied) fruit, aniseed, liqueur, alcohol, etc. It can be decorated with cream, jam, crystallized fruit, or coated with fondant icing (frosting).

RECIPES

Gâteau manqué   Melt 100 g (4 oz, ½ cup) butter without allowing it to brown. Separate 6 eggs. Put the yolks into a bowl with 200 g (7 oz, scant 1 cup, firmly packed) caster (superfine) sugar and 1 teaspoon vanilla sugar. Whisk until the mixture becomes light and frothy. Then fold in 150 g (5 oz, 1¼ cups) flour, the melted butter, and half a liqueur glass of rum, mixing until evenly blended. Whisk the egg whites together with a pinch of salt into firm peaks and gently fold them into the mixture.

Grease a deep sandwich tin (cake pan) or a manqué mould with butter, pour in the mixture, and bake in the oven at 200 c (400 f, gas 6) for 40–45 minutes. Leave for a few minutes in the tin, then turn out onto a wire rack to cool completely.

Lemon manqué   MANQUÉ AU CIT-RON   Remove the peel from a lemon and blanch it for 2 minutes in boiling water. Refresh it in cold water, dry it, and shred it very finely. Finely dice 100 g (4 oz, ½ cup) crystallized (candied) citron. Prepare a manqué mixture (see recipe above) and add the shredded lemon peel and citron before incorporating the egg whites. Bake the cake, remove from the tin while still warm, and cool completely.

Lightly whisk 2 egg whites and mix in 1 tablespoon lemon juice, then some icing (confectioners') sugar, until the mixture has a spreading consistency. Coat the cake with the icing (frosting)

and decorate with small pieces of crystallized citron.

Manzanilla

A type of sherry produced from around Sanlúcar de Barrameda, in Andalucia. It is very light and dry and may sometimes be unfortified, though seldom for export markets. It is very popular in the locality with the shellfish of the coasts around Cádiz and should be served chilled.

maple   ÉRABLE

One of about 200 species of tree or shrub which grow in temperate climates. The North American sugar maple has orange sap, which is collected from the trunk in the spring and yields a clear golden syrup. Rich in sugar, with an aromatic flavour, maple syrup is very popular in the United States and Canada. It is spread on roasts and ham, served with pancakes, and puddings, and used to glaze carrots and caramelize sweet potatoes. Maple-syrup tart is another favourite.

Centrifugation of maple syrup produces a 'butter'; an essence used as a flavouring in pâtisserie and confectionery is obtained by distillation. Concentrated maple syrup produces a type of candy sugar. Lastly, maple sap can be used to make a cider-like drink (especially in Louisiana) which, after fermentation, yields an aromatic vinegar.

RECIPE

Maple-syrup tart   TOURTE AU SIROP D'ÉRABLE   Boil 1 dl (6 tablespoons, scant ½ cup) maple syrup with a little water for 5 minutes. Blend in 3 tablespoons cornflour (cornstarch) mixed with cold water, then 50 g (2 oz, 4 tablespoons) butter. Line a tart plate (pie tin) with shortcrust pastry (basic pie dough) and spread the lukewarm syrup mixture over it. Decorate with chopped almonds. Cover with a fairly thin pastry lid, pinch round the edge, prick with a fork, and bake in a hot oven (220 c, 425 f, gas 7) for about 20 minutes.

maraîchère (à la)

Describing preparations that incorporate a selection of fresh vegetables. The term is applied particularly to large roast or braised cuts of meat that are garnished with glazed shaped carrots, small glazed onions, braised stuffed cucumber, and quarters of artichoke heart cooked gently in butter. Another maraîchère garnish consists of Brussels sprouts in butter, salsify, and château potatoes. The accompanying sauce consists of the deglazed and thickened meat juice or the strained skimmed braising liquid.

| RECIPE

Eggs sur le plat à la maraîchère OEUFS SUR LE PLAT À LA MARAÎCHÈRE Finely shred 250 g (9 oz) lettuce leaves and 100 g (4 oz) sorrel and cook in 30 g (1 oz, 2 tablespoons) butter with 1 tablespoon chopped chervil until soft. Arrange this chiffonnade in a ring around the edge of an ovenproof dish, break 4 eggs into the centre, sprinkle with salt and pepper, and bake in the oven. Lightly fry 4 small slices of smoked streaky bacon in butter. Add them to the baked eggs just before serving.

Maraschino MARASQUIN

A colourless liqueur made from the distillate of fermented Maraschino cherries. It originated in Dalmatia (now part of Yugoslavia) and is much used in flavouring sweet dishes.

marble MARBRE

Marble working surfaces are used by professional pastrycooks and confectioners when working with chocolate, sugar, and pastries that need to be kept fairly cool. For the preparation of delicate pastries (shortbread and puff pastry), the marble slabs are kept cool by convection. A marble surface always remains clean and cool as it does not absorb fat or atmospheric moisture. However, the surface should not be exposed to acid substances, which will cause pitting. When making toffee at home, a small marble slab brushed with oil can be used.

marbrade

A charcuterie speciality from southwestern France, similar to brawn (head cheese). It is made with pieces of pig's head loosely packed in aspic and served in a mould.

marc

A spirit distilled from the debris left after the final pressings of grapes for wine. In Italy it is known as *grappa*. It can be used as brandy in cookery, although marc that has not been matured can be a fiery spirit and should be actually cooked or set alight, and not used neat. The marcs of several French regions are famous, notably the marc de Bourgogne. In Alsace there is one made from Gewurztraminer grape pressings.

marcassin

The French name for a wild boar under the age of six months. Up to the age of three months, its coat is marked with black stripes; boars of this age are said to be *en livrée* ('in livery'), and it is forbidden to hunt them. The flesh of the young wild boar is tender and full of flavour, without the musky taste of the adult animal. It is unnecessary to marinate the meat which, when well oiled, keeps for three or four days in the refrigerator. The carcass yields cutlets and escalopes, and the fillet provides cuts for roasting (which should be barded). The meat can also be prepared as a fricassee or a civet cooked with wine.

| RECIPE

Cutlets of marcassin with quinces CÔTELETTES DE MARCASSIN AUX COINGS (from a recipe by Daniel Bouché) Peel and finely dice 100 g (4 oz) carrots, an equal quantity of onions, the white part of a leek, and a stick (stalk) of celery. Place in a saucepan with 500 g (1 lb) bones and trimmings of a marcassin, a clove of garlic, and a small bouquet garni and cook until well-browned. Then pour 1 bottle of a robust red wine into the pan and add 100 g (4 fl oz, ½ cup) cream. Add salt, stir, and cook very gently for 1½ hours. Skim off the fat, rub through a fine sieve, and boil down to reduce until about 30 cl (½ pint, 1¼ cups) liquid remains. Put this sauce on one side.

Prepare a stuffing: cook 400 g (14 oz) peeled diced salsify in boiling water with a little lemon juice. Cook 200 g (7 oz, generous 1½ cups) thinly sliced onions and 200 g (7 oz, scant 2 cups) diced pears in a covered pan with a knob of butter for 30 minutes. Add the cooked salsify and adjust the seasoning. Prepare 6 crêpes. Spread the stuffing over the crêpes, roll them up, place in a greased gratin dish, and bake in a preheated oven at 200 c (400 f, gas 6) for 15 minutes.

Peel 300 g (11 oz) quinces, cut into dice or segments, and boil in water with lemon juice until tender but slightly firm. Fry 12 marcassin cutlets like pork chops until they are just slightly pink. Cover them with the quinces and add a dash of rum. Bring the sauce to the boil and blend in 100 g (4 oz, ½ cup) butter, stirring over a low heat. When the sauce becomes glossy, pour it over the cutlets. Serve with the stuffed crêpes.

This recipe can also be used for cutlets and noisettes of venison or adult wild boar.

marcelin

A cake consisting of a pastry base covered with strawberry jam, coated with a mixture of eggs and ground almonds and sprinkled with icing (confectioners') sugar.

marchand de vin

The name for certain preparations that are made with red wine and shallots, especially a flavoured butter served with grilled (broiled) meat (usually entrecôte steak or kidneys). Whiting or sole *à la marchand de vin* are poached in red wine with chopped shallots, then coated with the cooking liquid, reduced and whisked with butter, and sometimes glazed in the oven.

RECIPES

Entrecôte marchand de vin Grill (broil) an entrecôte steak under a high heat. Season with salt and pepper and garnish with rounds of marchand de vin butter.

Marchand de vin butter BEURRE MARCHAND DE VIN Add 30 g (1 oz, ¼ cup) finely chopped shallots to 3 dl (½ pint, 1¼ cups) red wine and boil down to reduce by half. Add 3 dl (½ pint, 1¼ cups) beef consommé and reduce further until almost dry. Cream

150 g (5 oz, 10 tablespoons) butter and mix it with the reduced wine mixture. Add 1 tablespoon finely chopped parsley and a little lemon juice and season with salt and pepper. Chill until firm.

maréchale (à la)

In classic cuisine, describing small cuts of meat (such as lamb chops or noisettes, veal escalopes or cutlets, calves' sweetbreads, or poultry suprêmes) that are coated with breadcrumbs and sautéed. They are garnished with bundles of asparagus tips and a slice of truffle on each item and served in a ring of thickened chateaubriand sauce or veal gravy. They may also be served with maître d'hôtel butter. Fish *à la maréchale* are poached in white wine and fish fumet, with mushrooms and tomatoes. The sauce is made from the reduced cooking liquid mixed with meat glaze and butter.

RECIPE

Lamb cutlets (chops) à la maréchale CÔTELETTES D'AGNEAU À LA MARÉCHALE Braise some asparagus tips in butter. Cut a truffle into thin strips and braise in butter for 2 minutes. Prepare a liquid maître d'hôtel butter. Season the cutlets with salt and pepper, coat them with breadcrumbs, and sauté them in clarified butter. Arrange the cutlets in a crown, garnish each one with a strip of truffle, and place the asparagus tips between the cutlets. Serve with the maître d'hôtel butter in a sauceboat. Very finely chopped truffle parings may be added to the breadcrumb coating.

marée

A French collective name for all sea fish, shellfish, and seafood that are sold in a fish market. The Parisian fish markets had a regular supply of fresh fish as early as the Middle Ages. Louis IX (reigned 1226–70) had two extra buildings added on to Les Halles in Paris especially for the fish trade, whose wares arrived from the English Channel and the North Sea via a road that led right into the centre of the capital. There was a special service of carts to transport the fish (see *chasse-marée, Vatel*).

Marengo

A dish of chicken or veal sautéed with white wine, tomato, and garlic.

Chicken Marengo is named after the Battle of Marengo (14 June 1800), at which Napoleon Bonaparte defeated the Austrians; it was created on the battlefield itself by Dunand, Napoleon's chef.

Bonaparte, who on battle days ate nothing until the fight was over, had gone forward with his general staff and was a long way from his supply wagons. Seeing his enemies put to flight, he asked Dunand to prepare dinner for him. The master chef at once sent men of the quartermaster's staff and ordnance corps in search of provisions. All they could find were three eggs, four tomatoes, six crayfish, a small hen, a little garlic, some oil, and a saucepan. Using his bread ration, Dunand first made a panada with oil and water, and then, having drawn and jointed the chicken, browned it in oil and fried the eggs in the same oil with a few cloves of garlic and the tomatoes. He poured over this mixture some water laced with brandy borrowed from the general's flask and put the crayfish on top to cook in the steam.

The dish was served on a tin plate, the chicken surrounded by the fried eggs and crayfish, with the sauce poured over it. Bonaparte, having feasted upon it, said to Dunand: 'You must feed me like this after every battle.'

The originality of this improvised dish lay in the garnish, for chicken *à la provençale*, sautéed in oil with garlic and tomatoes, dates from well before the battle of Marengo. In the course of time the traditional garnish was replaced by mushrooms and small glazed onions and the preparation was also used for veal.

Some authorities believe that the dish was created in the town of Marengo (now Hadjout) in Algeria.

RECIPE

Sautéed veal Marengo SAUTÉ DE VEAU MARENGO Cut 1 kg (2¼ lb) shoulder of veal into large even-sized cubes and sauté in 30 g (1 oz, 2 tablespoons) butter and 2 tablespoons (3 tablespoons) oil in an ovenproof casserole until lightly brown. Add 2 chopped onions to the casserole and brown them, sprinkle with 1 tablespoon flour, and cook until golden brown. Add 1 glass of white wine, scraping the bottom of the casserole to incorporate all the residue, then 500 g (18 oz) deseeded chopped tomatoes, a bouquet garni, a crushed clove of garlic, and salt and pepper. Add enough hot water to just cover the ingredients, bring to the boil, cover, and simmer for 1 hour.

Meanwhile, glaze 24 small (pearl) onions in 1 tablespoon granulated sugar, 30 g (1 oz, 2 tablespoons) butter, salt, and pepper. Keep hot. Sauté 150 g (5 oz, generous 1 cup) finely sliced mushrooms in 20 g (¾ oz, 3 tablespoons) butter. Cut 2 slices of bread into croutons and fry them in 3 tablespoons (4 tablespoons) oil until golden brown. 5 minutes before the meat is cooked, add the mushrooms and complete the cooking.

Pour the sautéed veal into a deep preheated dish, sprinkle with chopped parsley, and garnish with the glazed onions and the croutons.

margarine

A fat invented in 1869 by the French chemist Henri Mège-Mouriès. It was based on beef fat and skimmed milk and was sold commercially from 1872. Various attempts were made to use other fats. A new process was discovered in Germany to raise the melting point of vegetable fats and also to prevent them from going rancid; this helped to make margarine more popular. Today margarine is any food substance that resembles butter and can be used in the same way. By law, margarine contains 80% fat and no more than 16% water, the same proportions as in butter.

Margarine may be made with a single oil, or a blend of a number of oils, including animal fats, such as soft beef fat, oil from fish such as herring, anchovy, and pilchard, and vegetable oils from sources like soya (soy) bean, sunflower, palm, rapeseed, safflower, and corn. A number of vegetable oils used in making margarine – sunflower, safflower, and soya, for example – are high in polyunsaturated fats and a margarine made entirely from one of these may be selected by people following a low-cholesterol diet. Flavouring, colouring, emulsifiers, and whey are added; vitamins A and D are added to table margarine. No preservatives are added to margarine in the UK, although a variable quantity of salt is added and this acts as a natural preservative.

A distinction is made between margarines used for baking and cooking, those used for spreading, and those specially made for the catering profession. Hard margarines, usually employed in cooking and baking, are sold in rectangular packets. They contain either mixed animal and fish, fish and vegetable oils, or vegetable oils only and can be used for all kinds of cooking except deep-frying. They are particularly suitable for baking, roasting, braising, frying, and making roux. Spreading margarines are soft and sold in tubs. They often consist of vegetable oils only and are manufactured to resemble butter as closely as possible as regards texture and taste. They may be eaten on bread, toast, etc., and used in home baking and can be used instead of butter in compound butters, on vegetables and grilled (broiled) meat, in purées, and with noodles and rice. The margarines used in catering differ both in their consistency and their melting point, depending on their subsequent use: making puff pastry, raised doughs, croissant pastry, cake mixes, or creams and fillings.

Margaux

A parish (commune) in the Médoc region of Bordeaux; it has its own AOC, Margaux, separate from that of the more general one of Haut-Médoc. Many fine wines are within the Margaux area, including a number of classed growths, such as Palmer, Issan, Lascombes, Rausan-Ségla, Rauzan-Gassies, and the great first growth, Château Margaux.

Marggraf (Andreas Sigismund)

German scientist (born Berlin, 1709; died Berlin, 1782). In 1747 he discovered that the root of sugar beet contained a white crystalline substance with a sweet taste. He envisaged that it could be used in the same way as cane sugar but was unable to find a practical application for his discovery. It fell to other researchers (Achard and Delessert) to perfect its manufacture. During the Napoleonic wars, beet sugar was used when France was prevented from importing its supplies of cane sugar by the Continental Blockade.

Marguery (Nicolas)

French chef (born Dijon, 1834; died Paris, 1910). He began his career as a dishwasher at the Restaurant Champeaux in Paris, during which period he married the owner's daughter. He then became an apprentice chef first at the Rocher de Cancale and later at the Frères Provençaux. Eventually, in 1887, he opened a restaurant of his own on the site of the former Maison Dauphin on the Boulevard Bonne-Nouvelle. The Marguery became an elegant opulent rendezvous for gourmands and was famous for its marvellous cellar and, especially, for its fillets of sole Marguery (cooked in white wine). Marguery invented a number of other dishes, particularly tournedos Marguery (served on artichoke hearts).

RECIPES

Fillets of sole Marguery FILETS DE SOLE MARGUERY Fillet 2 good sole. Using the bones and trimmings, make a white wine fumet, adding a little chopped onion, a sprig of thyme, a quarter of a bay leaf, and a sprig of parsley. Season with salt and pepper and boil for 15 minutes. Add to the fumet the cooking liquid from 1 litre (1 quart) mussels cooked in white wine. Season the sole fillets with salt and pepper and lay them in a greased dish. Pour over a few spoonfuls of the fumet and cover with a sheet of buttered greaseproof (waxed) paper. Poach gently, then drain the fillets and arrange them in an oval dish; surround with a double row of cooked shelled mussels and peeled prawns (shelled shrimp). Cover and keep warm while the sauce is being made.

Strain the fumet and the cooking liquid from the sole, reduce by two-thirds, remove from the heat, and, when slightly cooled, mix in 6 egg yolks. Whisk the sauce over a gentle heat, like a hollandaise sauce, incorporating 350 g (12 oz, 1½ cups) softened butter. Season the sauce with salt and pepper and strain it; pour over the fillets and their mussel and prawn garnish. Glaze quickly in a very hot oven and decorate with pastry motifs pointing outwards.

Tournedos Marguery Braise some artichoke hearts in butter and fill them with a salpicon of truffles *à la crème* and morels sautéed in butter. Cook some cocks' combs and kidneys in brown stock and prepare a sauce by deglazing the cooking juices with port, adding some cream, and boiling to reduce. Sauté the steaks in butter and place on top of the artichoke hearts. Garnish the dish with the mushrooms, cocks' combs, and kidneys. Serve with the sauce.

Marie-Louise

A garnish dedicated to the second wife of Napoleon I and served mainly with cuts of lamb or mutton. It consists of either noisette potatoes and artichoke hearts stuffed with a mushroom dux-elles and onion purée, the sauce being made by deglazing the pan with demi-glace; or small tarts filled with peas and tiny balls of carrot and turnip.

marignan

A savarin cake spread with sieved apricot jam and covered with Italian meringue; it is traditionally decorated with a ribbon of angelica fashioned like the handle of a basket.

| RECIPE

Marignan Soak 75 g (3 oz, ½ cup) raisins in warm water until plump. Weigh out 250 g (9 oz, 2¼ cups) flour. Dissolve 15 g (½ oz) fresh yeast (½ cake compressed yeast) in a very small amount of water, stir in a little of the flour, then cover the mixture with the rest of the flour and leave to rise. When cracks appear in the flour (after about 15 minutes), transfer the yeast and flour to a mixing bowl and add 25 g (1 oz, 2 tablespoons, firmly packed) caster (superfine) sugar, a pinch of salt, and 3 very lightly beaten eggs; knead the dough well until it becomes elastic. Gradually incorporate about 3 cl (1½ tablespoons, 2 tablespoons) water to

make a very soft smooth dough. Let it stand for 30 minutes.

Melt 80 g (3 oz, ⅓ cup) butter and add this to the dough, together with the drained and dried raisins. Turn the dough into a buttered and floured man-qué mould or deep-sided cake tin, 19 cm (7½ in) in diameter, and leave it to rise. When the dough has doubled in volume, bake in a moderately hot oven (190 c, 375 f, gas 5) for about 40 minutes.

Meanwhile, prepare a syrup with 125 g (4 oz, ½ cup) sugar, 2.5 dl (8 fl oz, 1 cup) water, and 1 dl (6 tablespoons, scant ½ cup) rum. Pour this over the warm cake. Spread the cake with warmed and sieved apricot jam (about half a jar is required). Prepare an Italian meringue mixture with 400 g (14 oz, 1¾ cups) sugar, 4 egg whites, and 1 liqueur glass of rum. Completely cover the sides and top of the cake with this mixture. Bend a long strip of angelica over the cake to resemble the handle of a basket, and fix it to the cake at each end.

Marigny

Any of a variety of dishes dedicated to the Marquise de Pompadour's brother. The Marigny garnish for small sautéed cuts of meat consists either of fondante potatoes, peas, and French beans cut into sticks (buttered and arranged in tartlet cases); or artichoke hearts stuffed with sweetcorn in cream and small noisette potatoes. The sauce is made by deglazing the pan with white wine (or Madeira) and thickened veal stock. Marigny soup has peas and French beans as its basis.

| RECIPES

Marigny soup POTAGE MARIGNY Mix 1.5 litres (2¾ pints, 3½ pints) Saint-Germain soup (thinned with a little consommé) with 2 tablespoons sorrel chiffonnade gently cooked in butter and 1 tablespoon each of boiled peas and diced French beans. Garnish with 1 tablespoon chopped chervil.

Tournedos Marigny Gently cook some artichoke hearts in butter. Prepare some buttered sweetcorn and some noisette potatoes. Sauté the steaks in butter and keep them warm. Deglaze the pan with a little white wine and reduce; complete the sauce by adding some thickened veal stock. Surround the steaks with the artichoke hearts stuffed with sweetcorn and noisette potatoes. Serve with the sauce.

marigold SOUCI

A garden plant with yellow flowers, the petals of which were once used to heighten the colour of butter. Traditionally they are used to enrich such dishes as Jersey conger soup (with cabbage, leeks, and peas), garnish green salads, and season vinegar. Alexandre Dumas proposed a herb soup *à la dauphine*, which included marigold flowers. Special care must be taken not to boil the slightly bitter petals.

marinade

A seasoned liquid, cooked or uncooked, in which meat, offal, game, fish, or vegetables are steeped for varying lengths of time. (See also *marinate*.) Its principal purpose is to flavour the food, but it also makes certain meats more tender by softening the fibres, and it enables fish and meat to be kept rather longer than would normally be possible.

The length of time that foodstuffs should be left in a marinade depends on the nature and size of the item and also on external conditions. In winter, large cuts of meat and venison can be left in the marinade for five or six days. In summer, however, they should not be marinated for longer than 48 hours, except in the case of large cuts of venison, which require a longer period. Small cuts of meat for grilling (broiling) or frying need be marinated only for an hour or two – 30 minutes is sometimes sufficient for meat for kebabs. When the marinade is used for its preserving effect, the food should be completely submerged and not removed until required.

An essential distinction is drawn between cooked, uncooked, and instant marinades. The two former marinades (based on carrots, shallots, onions, pepper, salt, bouquet garni, parsley, vinegar, garlic, and red or white wine) are used for meat and game. A cooked marinade must be cooled before use, whereas uncooked and instant marinades can be used immediately as they require no cooking. Instant marinades are used to impart flavour and not generally for tenderizing, as this requires a longer marinating time. They are used for fish (lemon, oil, thyme, and bay leaf), for the ingredients of fritters or fritots (lemon, oil, parsley, salt, and pepper), and for the ingredients of terrines, pâtés, galantines, etc. (brandy, Madeira or port, salt, pepper, and shallots).

In general, the food that is being marinated is turned over with a slotted spoon from time to time. Because of their high acid content uncooked marinades are made in glass, porcelain, or glazed earthenware dishes.

The food should be removed from its marinade just before cooking and drained well; in the case of fried or roasted items, the marinade may be later used for deglazing or to make the accompanying sauce. When the marinade is used in the cooking, the meat should be totally or partially immersed in it before braising.

RECIPES

COOKED MARINADES

Marinade for meat and venison MARINADE POUR VIANDES DE BOUCHERIE ET VENAISON Take the same vegetables and herbs as listed for the uncooked marinade for large cuts of meat and game and brown them lightly in oil. Moisten with a mixture of 7.5 dl (1¼ pints, 1½ pints) wine (red or white according to the recipe) and 1 dl (6 tablespoons, scant ½ cup) vinegar then simmer gently for 30 minutes. Season the meat with salt and pepper and put it in a bowl; when the marinade is completely cold pour it over the top. Stand it in a cool place for 2–6 days.

UNCOOKED MARINADES

Marinade for ingredients of pâtés and terrines MARINADE POUR ÉLÉMENTS DE PÂTÉS ET DE TERRINES Season the ingredients with salt, pepper, and mixed spice. Add a little crushed thyme and a finely chopped bay leaf. Moisten with brandy (about 1.5 dl (¼ pint, ⅔ cup) brandy for the ingredients of a duck terrine) and marinate for 24 hours in a cool place.

Marinade for large cuts of meat and game MARINADE POUR GROSSES VIANDES DE BOUCHERIE ET GIBIER Season the meat with salt, pepper, and mixed spice. Place in a dish just large enough to hold it. Add 1 large chopped onion and 2 chopped shallots, 1 chopped carrot, 2 crushed cloves of garlic, 2–3 sprigs of parsley, a sprig of thyme, half a bay leaf (coarsely chopped), and a clove. (For a daube add a piece of dried orange peel.) Cover completely with red or white wine (according to the recipe) fortified with 1 liqueur glass of brandy. Cover and marinate for 6 hours to 2 days in a cool place, turning the meat 2 or 3 times so it is thoroughly impregnated with the marinade. The marinade can be used in the cooking if the meat is to be braised.

Marinade for small cuts of meat, fish, and poultry MARINADE POUR PETITES PIÈCES DE BOUCHERIE, VOLAILLES ET POISSONS Season the meat or fish with salt and pepper and sprinkle with the following: 1 large chopped onion and 2 chopped shallots, 1 finely chopped carrot, a sprig of thyme, a finely chopped bay leaf, 1 tablespoon chopped parsley, a small crushed clove of garlic, a clove, and 12 black peppercorns. Moisten with the juice of a lemon and 3 dl (½ pint, 1¼ cups) oil (preferably olive oil) and marinate in a cool place for 2–12 hours.

marinate MARINER

To steep meat or game in a flavoured liquid (see *marinade*) for a certain length of time to tenderize and flavour the flesh. It is one of the oldest culinary procedures: wine, vinegar, salted water, herbs, and spices not only counteract the very strong taste of game, for example, but also increase the length of time that the meat can be preserved. The word is ultimately derived from the Latin *marinus* (marine), referring to the sea water or brine that was used for preserving foods in ancient times. Nowadays, foods are usually marinated to improve their flavour rather than to preserve them.

In Mediterranean countries, it is traditional to marinate vegetables and fish (sardines, tuna, achars, peppers, onions, mushrooms, etc.). In Sweden goose is salted and marinated; other items marinated in Scandinavia include pickled tongue, ham, damsons, and mackerel (in white wine). In India, many ingredients are marinated in spiced curdled milk; in Peru raw fish are marinated in lemon juice (see *ceviche*).

Meat such as pork or beef, or even horsemeat or mutton, is sometimes marinated to give it a gamey taste.

marinette

A small puff-pastry tartlet filled with vanilla-flavoured apple purée containing raisins and lemon peel and topped with rum-flavoured pink or green fondant icing (frosting).

Marin (François)

18th-century French chef. In 1739 he published *Les Dons de Comus ou les Délices de la table*, a work that ran to four editions and was added to regularly (the 1750 edition is in three volumes). Its preface, signed by two Jesuit priests, Father Brumoy and Father Bougeant, is an excellent summary of the history of French cooking up to the beginning of the 18th century and emphasizes the progress that had been made in culinary art: 'Modern cookery, although established on the foundations of the older cuisine, requires less fuss and less equipment, but is just as varied and is simpler, cleaner, and, perhaps, more scholarly. The science of the chef consists . . . of blending the flavours of different meats to achieve a harmonious result.' This is a fundamental principle, which makes cooking the art of creating new combinations of flavour rather than simply using spices to flavour a dish.

Among Marin's original recipes are *oeufs à l'infante* (poached eggs coated with a sauce made with champagne, orange, garlic, and shallots, blanquette of fillets of sole, fillets of lamb *à la Condé* (with gherkins and anchovies, covered with chopped mushrooms, herbs, and capers, enclosed in a caul and roasted), ox (beef) tongue with cucumbers, chicken with parsley (flavoured with parsley butter inserted beneath the skin, then roasted), and lettuces Dame Simone (stuffed with chicken and rice).

marinière (à la)

A method of preparing shellfish or other seafood, especially mussels, by cooking them in white wine, usually with onions or shallots. The term is also applied to certain fish dishes which are cooked in white wine and garnished with mussels. Marinière sauce is a kind of Bercy sauce made with mussel cooking juices, and the marinière garnish always includes mussels and sometimes also prawns (shrimp). Langoustines, crayfish, frogs, and various types of seafood used to garnish croûtes, timbales, vols-au-vent, etc., are also cooked in this way.

| RECIPES

Marinière sauce SAUCE MARINIÈRE
Prepare a Bercy sauce using the juices from moules marinière. Add 2 egg yolks per 1.5 dl (¼ pint, ⅔ cup) sauce and whisk continuously over a low heat until the sauce thickens.

Moules marinière Trim, scrape, and wash some mussels. Peel and chop 1 large shallot per kg (2¼ lb) mussels. Put the chopped shallots in a buttered pan with 2 tablespoons (3 tablespoons) chopped parsley, a small sprig of thyme, half a bay leaf, 2 dl (7 fl oz, ¾ cup) dry white wine, 1 tablespoon wine vinegar, and 2 tablespoons (3 tablespoons) butter (cut into small pieces). Add the mussels, cover the pan, and cook over a high heat, shaking the pan several times, until all the mussels have opened. Remove the pan from the heat and place the mussels in a large serving dish. Remove the thyme and bay leaf from the saucepan and add 2 tablespoons (3 tablespoons) butter to the cooking liquid. Whisk the sauce until it thickens and pour it over the mussels. Sprinkle with chopped parsley.

Marivaux

A garnish for large cuts of roast meat served with thickened veal stock. It consists of French (green) beans in butter together with oval nests of duchess potato, browned in the oven, filled with a mixture of finely chopped carrots, celery, artichoke hearts, and mushrooms which have all been softened in butter and blended with a béchamel sauce; the nests are sprinkled with grated Parmesan cheese and lightly browned in the oven.

marjoram MARJOLAINE

A herb of which there are various types, the most popular being sweet marjoram (*Origanum majorana*) and wild marjoram (*Origanum vulgare*), more commonly known as oregano. Sweet marjoram is one of the most popular herbs in European cookery; it has a strong aromatic scent but a fairly delicate flavour, which is good in salads and combines well with meat, game, poultry, pulses, and some vegetables, particularly carrots, salsify, and cucumber. To avoid losing its mild flavour with prolonged cooking it is best added towards the end of the cooking period.

Wild marjoram, or oregano, has a much more pungent flavour that is popular in Mediterranean dishes, such as pasta and pizza sauces and tomato dishes. In Greece it is used frequently with lamb.

When dried, both sweet and wild marjoram become much stronger in flavour and should be used sparingly.

marmalade
CONFITURE D'ORANGES

An orange jam invented by a manufacture from Dundee in Scotland in about 1790. In domestic cookery marmalades can, in principle, be made with any fruit, but in 1981 the EEC issued a directive that limited the term to those items prepared with citrus fruit (sweet or bitter oranges, lemons, and grapefruit). Originally marmalades were made with quinces: the word is derived from the Portuguese *marmelada*, quinces cooked with sugar or honey (see *melimelum*). See also *jams, jellies, and marmalades*.

marmelade

A thick sweet purée prepared from fruit that is stewed for a long time with sugar. The fruit, whole or cut into pieces, is first macerated in a sugar syrup (made with 500 g (1 lb) sugar per 500 g (1 lb) fruit) for about 24 hours. In a *marmelade*, unlike jam, the fruit is no longer identifiable.

marmite

A metal or earthenware covered pot with two handles, with or without feet, depending on whether it is used for cooking in a hearth or on the stove. Its large capacity (up to 50 litres, 11 gallons, 14 gallons) makes it suitable for boiling large quantities of food (soups, large cuts of beef, stews, pâtés, shellfish, various types of seafood, etc.). The kitchens of restaurants and residential institutions use even larger marmites, with such a large capacity (100–500 litres, 22–110 gallons, 28–140 gallons) that they are fitted with a tap at the bottom for emptying. Metal marmites can be made of cast iron, enamelled cast iron, aluminium, stainless steel, or copper lined with tin. The tallest kind in France are called *pot-au-feu*, and the smallest, *fait-tout*. The *huguenote* is an earthenware marmite with short legs.

The word 'marmite' is derived from an Old French word meaning 'hypocrite', which was applied to the vessel because its contents were concealed. In France it was formerly known as *oille*, *ouille*, or *oule* (see *olla podrida*). From the 14th century onwards, the marmite was made of cast iron with a lid, a handle, and three feet. It was suspended from the trammel of the chimney and used for boiling water and washing laundry, as well as for preparing the soup, hence the French expression *faire bouillir la marmite* meaning literally 'to get the marmite boiling' but actually 'to support one's family'. In the 17th century the marmite was reserved for making soups. Special silver marmites, decorated with coats of arms, medals, and inscriptions, were manufactured to serve the soup at table.

marmite dieppoise

A fish soup from the Normandy coast made of sole, turbot, and anglerfish cooked in white wine with vegetables (celery, leeks, onion, fennel), garnished with mussels, prawns (shrimp), and scallops, and blended with cream. The recipe was devised by Pierre Monquet, a gastronome from Dieppe.

marmite mongole

The French name for a cylindrical cooking utensil used in Asia for steaming food. It consists of a number of separate units that can be stacked one on top of the other. The bottom unit, usually made of aluminium, is filled with water. The remaining three or four components are made of metal, or sometimes bamboo, and are perforated. They are filled with different items of food and stacked up. The top unit is covered with a lid. The water in the base is brought to the boil and the food in the various compartments is steamed.

Thinly sliced or chopped meat, fish, vegetables, and small sweet or savoury noodles can be cooked simultaneously by this method.

marmite norvégienne

The French name for a double cooking pot in which food is cooked very slowly and economically over a low heat. The inner container is an ordinary aluminium or stainless steel casserole. When its contents have been brought to the boil, it is taken off the heat and immediately placed inside the second container, which has double walls filled with an insulating material such as cork or fibreglass.

The temperature of the food in the casserole falls very slowly (to 30 c, 86 f in six hours), thus the food can continue to cook without using any more fuel.

Marmite Perpétuelle

An establishment that was situated in the Rue des Grands-Augustins in Paris, near the old poultry market. It was very famous at the end of the 18th century, especially for capons and beef boiled in consommé, which could either be taken away or eaten on the premises. It is said that the fire under the marmite never went out, and that more than 300,000 chickens were cooked successively in the same stock, which the proprietor, Deharme, simply watered down every day.

marocaine (à la)

The name given to sautéed noisettes of mutton or lamb arranged on mounds of pilaf rice (lightly seasoned with saffron) and coated with a sauce made by deglazing the pan juices with tomato purée. They are served with sautéed diced courgettes (zucchini) and sometimes braised green peppers stuffed with chicken forcemeat.

Maroilles

A French cows'-milk cheese (containing 45–50% fat) with a soft yellow paste and a smooth shiny reddish-brown rind. Named after the Abbey of Maroilles (Thiérache), where it was first made around 960, it is a semi-hard full-flavoured cheese with a strong smell. Philippe Auguste, Louis XI, François I, and Fénelon, in particular, greatly appreciated Maroilles cheese, which today is protected by an *appellation d'origine contrôlée*. It is manufactured in the towns of Vervins, Avesnes-sur-Helpe, and Cambrai. Maroilles is excellent in summer, autumn, and winter and is matured for four months in a damp cellar. It is sold in 13-cm (5-in) squares, 6 cm (2½ in) deep and weighing 800 g (1¾ lb). Sorbais, Mignon, and Quart de Maroilles are related cheeses that benefit from the same *appellation d'origine*. All of them are good to eat at the end of a meal, especially with beer. They are also used in various regional recipes.

marquise

Any of various delicate desserts. Chocolate marquise is a glazed dessert halfway between a mousse and a parfait. It is based on chocolate, fine butter (which makes it remarkably smooth), eggs, and sugar, chilled in a mould, and served with vanilla-flavoured custard cream or Chantilly cream. Another type of marquise is a granita (usually flavoured with strawberry, pineapple, or Kirsch) to which very thick Chantilly cream is added just before serving.

The name is also used for chocolate dacquoise and for a Genoese sponge or almond cake filled with chocolate-flavoured confectioners' custard (pastry cream) and covered with chocolate fondant icing (frosting).

Formerly, marquise was a refreshing drink made with sweetened white wine or champagne mixed with Seltzer water. It was served very cold with paper-thin slices of lemon.

| RECIPES

Chocolate marquise MARQUISE AU CHOCOLAT Break 250 g (9 oz) plain chocolate into small pieces and melt it gently in a covered bain-marie. Separate the yolks and whites of 5 eggs. Add 100 g (4 oz, ½ cup, firmly packed) granulated sugar to the yolks, beating the mixture until it becomes light and fluffy. Then add the melted chocolate and 175 g (6 oz, ¾ cup) melted butter and mix well. Whisk the egg whites with a little salt until very stiff, and carefully fold them into the chocolate mixture. Cool a deep sandwich tin(or charlotte mould) under running water and pour the mixture into it, smoothing it down well.

Chill for 12 hours in the refrigerator before removing from the mould.

Marquise (*the drink*) BOISSON MARQUISE Dissolve 500 g (18 oz, 2¼ cups, firmly packed) sugar in a little water, then add a bottle of dry white wine and 1 litre (1¾ pints, 4¼ cups) sparkling mineral water. Cut 2 lemons into thin slices, remove the pips, and add them to the drink. Store in the refrigerator and serve with ice cubes.

marrons glacés

Chestnuts that have been poached in syrup and then glazed; they are packaged as luxury sweetmeats and are also used in pâtisserie. Marrons glacés were created during the reign of Louis XIV and are today manufactured chiefly at Privas, in the Ardèche. The chestnuts should be well-rounded and smooth, without deep grooves. They are shelled, washed, cooked, peeled, and then poached in vanilla-flavoured syrup for 48 hours. During this time they are basted constantly with the sugar syrup, which gets more and more concentrated as the heat is gradually increased. The marrons are then cooled and glazed (coated with liquid sugar), which gives them a shiny appearance. Marrons glacés were formerly sold in the syrup in which they were prepared.

marrow

See *bone marrow, gourd*.

Marsala

A Sicilian fortified wine, made around the town of the same name. It is produced in a type of solera system (see *sherry*) and the finer examples are matured for some while – the type described as *vergine* must be at least five years old. Marsala tends to be full in character and brownish, and – which will surprise many – it can be dry as well as sweet. There are also Marsalas that are flavoured with almonds, coffee, chocolate, tangerines, and other fruits. Marsala *all'uovo* is a rich sweet drink consisting of Marsala enriched with egg yolks. Marsala is used in various recipes, notably veal piccata and zabaglione.

marsh mallow   GUIMAUVE

A medicinal plant (*Althaea officinalis*) with sweet-tasting roots used to make cough lozenges and syrup. The mucilage from the roots was formerly used to make the spongy sweets known as marshmallows. Now, however, marshmallows are prepared with sugar, flavouring, colouring, then either starch and gelatine or gum arabic and egg white.

Marshmallows are commonly eaten as a sweet; in the United States they are also used as an ingredient in cooking to make cakes, icings (frostings), and sauces.

marsh marigold

POPULAGE

A vigorous colonizing meadow plant, also known in France as *souci d'eau*, the flower buds of which are pickled in vinegar and used like capers.

marzipan   MASSEPAIN

A thick paste made with ground almonds, sugar or sugar syrup, and egg whites, cooked together. It is used in making cakes and pastries, especially as a base for the icing (frosting) on a Christmas or wedding cake, and it can be coloured and flavoured and used in confectionery to make petits fours, usually coated with sugar or praline (these are known in France as *massepains*). Other marzipan sweetmeats are formed into the shapes of fruits, vegetables, etc.; these are a speciality of Aix-en-Provence, and are also made in Castille, Sicily, Belgium, and Germany.

Marzipan sweetmeats are said to have been perfected by the Ursuline order of nuns at Issoudun. Dispersed by the Revolution, the nuns subsequently opened a pastry shop in the town: the fame of the massepains of Issoudun reached as far as the Russian court, the Tuileries, and even the Vatican (both Napoleon III and Pope Pius IX were partial to them).

In 1844 a rumour spread around Paris that Balzac, who had just included a eulogy of massepains in his novel *La Rabouilleuse*, which is set in Issoudun, was turning confectioner. In fact an announcement appeared, stating that the novelist was opening a shop in the Rue Vivienne, and would be selling Issoudun massepains 'whose reputation in the province of Berry is more than a century old . . . , one of the greatest creations of French confectionery'. For a time the shop was very fashionable, although Balzac never showed his face there, but these sweetmeats soon fell into oblivion. Doctor Cabanès, who tells this story, points out that Balzac, while never actually being involved in their manufacture, had subsidized the sale of these sweets.

The words 'marzipan' and 'massepain' are derived from the Italian *marzapane*, originally meaning a sweet box, and later its contents.

RECIPES

Marzipan sweets I   MASSEPAINS
Blanch 250 g (9 oz, 1¾ cups) sweet almonds and 2 or 3 bitter almonds and pound them in a mortar (or use a food processor), moistening from time to time with a little cold water. When the almonds have been reduced to a fine and fairly firm paste, put them in a copper pan with 500 g (18 oz, 4 cups) caster (superfine) sugar, a pinch of powdered vanilla, and a few drops of orange-flower water. Dry out over a gentle heat, stirring with a wooden spoon.

Put the paste back into the mortar and grind it with the pestle, then work it with the hands on a marble slab until smooth, adding a small handful of fine sugar, sifted through a fine sieve. Roll the paste out to a thickness of 2 cm (¾ in), lay it out on a sheet of rice paper, and cut it up into various shapes with a cutter. Lay the pieces on a baking sheet lined with paper and dry out in a very cool oven.

Marzipan sweets II MASSEPAINS In a mortar, finely pound 500 g (18 oz, 3½ cups) blanched almonds with 450 g (1 lb, 2 cups) sugar and 50 g (2 oz, ¼ cup) vanilla sugar (or use a food processor). Add 4 egg whites, little by little. Leave the mixture to rest for a few minutes. Roll out this paste to a thickness of 5 mm (¼ in) and cut into various shapes with a pastry (cookie) cutter. Ice (frost) the pieces with some slightly liquid royal icing flavoured with a few drops of orange-flower water. Lay the sweets on a baking sheet lined with a sheet of greaseproof (waxed) paper and dry out in a cool oven.

Plain marzipan sweets (candies) MASSEPAINS COMMUNS (from a recipe in *Le Confiturier royal*) Take 1½ kg (3 lb, 9½ cups) sweet almonds and peel them under hot water; drain and wipe them. Pound them in a marble mortar, sprinkling them from time to time with egg white, so that they do not become too oily (or use a food processor). When they are pounded to a smooth paste, cook 700 g (1½ lb, 3 cups) sugar to the feather stage. Add the almonds to the sugar and mix together with a spatula, carefully scraping the bottom and sides to prevent sticking, which may occur even when the pan is removed from the heat. The paste is ready when it does not stick to the back of the hand when touched.

Take the paste from the pan and lay it on a board. Sprinkle with caster (superfine) sugar on both sides and leave it to cool. Roll out the paste to a moderate thickness and cut out different shapes with cutters (round, oval, fluted, heart-shaped, etc.), pressing them gently with the fingertips onto sheets of rice paper before baking. Cook on one side only, then ice (frost) the other side and bake in the same way.

Mascara

A wine-producing area in Algeria, near Oran, where white, rosé, and red wines are made. Before controls became strict, the red wines were much used in blending – even for wines of considerable fame. These days the reds are satisfying for some export markets and all the wines are quite pleasant.

mascotte

A Genoese sponge cake soaked in Kirsch or rum, filled and coated with praline butter cream or coffee-flavoured butter cream, and decorated with praline or with caramelized or grilled (toasted) shredded almonds.

RECIPE

Mascotte Make a Genoese mixture with 4 eggs, 125 g (4½ oz, scant ⅔ cup) granulated sugar, a pinch of salt, and 125 g (4½ oz, generous 1 cup) flour. Bake in a buttered round cake tin 22 cm (9 in) in diameter.

Prepare a syrup with 100 g (4 oz, ½ cup, firmly packed) granulated sugar and 1 dl (6 tablespoons, scant ½ cup) water. When it has cooled, blend in 1 dl (6 tablespoons, scant ½ cup) rum. Make a coffee-flavoured butter cream (see *creams and custards*) with 4 tablespoons (5 tablespoons) instant coffee powder, 250 g (9 oz, generous 1 cup, firmly packed) sugar, 6 egg yolks, 300 g (11 oz, scant 1½ cups) softened butter, and 5 cl (3 tablespoons, ¼ cup) rum. Divide the butter cream into 2 equal portions and add 2 tablespoons (3 tablespoons) grilled crushed almonds to one half.

Cut the cake horizontally into 2 halves and soak them in the rum-flavoured syrup. Sandwich together with the butter cream without almonds and coat the top and sides of the cake with the remainder of the butter cream. Store in a cool place.

mascotte (à la)

A garnish for small sautéed cuts of meat and poultry. It consists of olive-shaped pieces of potato and sliced artichoke hearts sautéed in butter, with a few slices of truffle and, sometimes, some small stewed whole tomatoes. The sauce is made by deglazing the meat juices in the sauté pan with white wine and thickened veal stock. Dishes *à la mascotte* were named after an operetta by Audran, 1880. They are usually served in an ovenproof casserole or an earthenware dish.

mask MASQUER, NAPPER

To coat food with a sweet or savoury substance, usually just before serving but sometimes during preparation (of a chaud-froid, aspic, etc.). The masking substance can be a sauce, a cream, a salpicon bound with a sauce, a purée, fondant icing (frosting), aspic, etc. The French word *masquer* also means to line a dish with some kind of preparation or with various ingredients that are spread out evenly.

massacanat

A large omelette with various fillings (diced veal sautéed in butter with onions and parsley, small pieces of sausage, slices of black pudding (blood sausage), etc.). It is a speciality of the south of France and the Pyrenees, and is the traditional dish for Easter morning in Haute Bigorre.

Masséna

A method of preparing sautéed tournedos steaks or lamb noisettes, in which the pan is deglazed with Périgueux sauce and the garnish is artichoke hearts and slices of poached beef bone marrow. Soft-boiled (soft-cooked) or poached eggs Masséna are served with artichoke hearts and béarnaise sauce and topped with slices of bone marrow.

RECIPE

Tournedos Masséna Gently cook some medium-sized artichoke hearts in butter and poach some slices of bone marrow (2–3 per steak) in a court-bouillon. Prepare a thin Périgueux sauce. Sauté the steaks in butter and arrange them on a dish with the artichoke hearts. Garnish each of the steaks with 2–3 slices of bone marrow and pour a little of the Périgueux sauce over the artichoke hearts. Serve the remaining sauce separately.

Massenet

A garnish for large and small cuts of meat dedicated to the French composer Jules Massenet. It consists of Anna potatoes baked in individual moulds, small artichoke hearts filled with a salpicon of bone marrow, and French (green) beans in butter. The sauce is made from the meat juices or from a demi-glace sauce flavoured with Madeira. Massenet also gave his name to various egg

dishes garnished with asparagus tips and artichoke hearts.

RECIPE

Scrambled eggs Massenet OEUFS BROUILLÉS MASSENET Cook some asparagus tips in butter. Boil or steam some artichoke hearts, dice them, and sauté them in butter. Prepare some scrambled eggs, mix them with the diced artichoke hearts, and garnish them with the asparagus tips. Add some thin slices of foie gras and slivers of truffle.

Massialot (François)

French chef (born 1660; died 1733). He was chef de cuisine (*officier de bouche*) to various illustrious personages, including the brother of Louis XIV, the dukes of Chartres, Orléans, and Aumont, Cardinal d'Estrées, and the Marquis de Louvois. In 1691 he published anonymously *Le Cuisinier royal et bourgeois*. His name did not appear on the title page until the work was republished in 1712. He also wrote an *Instruction nouvelle pour les confitures, les liqueurs et les fruits*, published in 1692. These two works were relatively unknown to the general public but were held in great esteem by the professional cooks of the 18th century and certainly had an influence on the development of French cuisine. When bookshops had sold out of *Le Cuisinier royal*, La Chapelle had it republished at his own expense in 1739. Massialot's recipes include chicken with green olives and herbs, ragout of salmon's head with white wine, verjuice, capers, and mushrooms, and also *benoiles* (soufflé fritters flavoured with orange-flower water and served very hot, sprinkled with sugar).

massillon

A petit four consisting of a barquette made of pâte sucrée filled with vanilla-flavoured almond paste and covered with almond glaze or with Kirsch-flavoured fondant icing (frosting). This sweetmeat was dedicated to the preacher Massillon and was created in the town of Hyères, where he was born.

RECIPE

Massillons Make some pâte sucrée (see *doughs and batters*) with 150 g (5 oz, 1¼ cups) flour, a pinch of salt, 35 g (1½ oz, 3 tablespoons) sugar, 60 g (2½ oz, 5 tablespoons) butter, and 1 egg. In a separate bowl, mix together 100 g (4 oz, 1 cup) ground almonds, a pinch of powdered vanilla (or 1 teaspoon vanilla sugar), and 150 g (5 oz, ⅔ cup, firmly packed) caster (superfine) sugar. Add 2 eggs, one at a time, and then a stiffly beaten egg white.

Roll out the pastry to a thickness of about 2 mm (¼ in) and use to line some small buttered and floured barquette moulds. Fill them with the almond mixture and bake for 15 minutes in the oven at 210 C (41p F, gas 6).

Prepare a glaze by mixing together 1 egg white, 130 g (4½ oz, 1 cup) icing (confectioners') sugar, and 40 g (1½ oz, ⅓ cup) ground almonds. When the tartlets are cooked, remove them from the oven, coat them with the glaze, and put back in the oven at 180 C (350 F, gas 4) to dry out the glaze (about 3 minutes). Remove from the oven and leave to cool.

masticatory

MASTICATOIRE

A substance of vegetable origin that is chewed simply for pleasure. These substances are popular in Asia, Africa, and America and often contain flavoured substances or stimulants.

Among the most widely used are betel (nuts of the betel palm wrapped in leaves of the betel pepper and sprinkled with lime) in south and southeast Asia; chicle (sapodilla gum) in Mexico, which was originally chewed by the Mayas and forms the basis of chewing gum; liquorice; and coca (the dried leaves of the coca tree), which contain cocaine and are chewed by the people of the Andes.

matafan or matefaim

A large thick nourishing pancake made in Burgundy, Bresse, Lyon, Franche-Comté, Savoy, and the Dauphiné. The dish was first named *matafan* in Franch-Comté when the province was occupied by the Spanish in the 15th century. The word is derived from the Spanish *mata*

hambre (kills hunger), which in French became *mate le faim*, hence the frequent spelling *matefaim*. In the environs of Lyon and in the mountains, matafans are savoury and contain spinach, potatoes, pieces of bacon, or even lean pork. In Burgundy and Bresse, they are served as sweet desserts, dried fruit replacing the savoury ingredients.

RECIPES

Besançon matafans MATAFANS BISONTINS Blend 5 tablespoons (6 tablespoons) flour, 1 whole egg, 2 egg yolks, a little caster (superfine) sugar, a pinch of salt, and 1 teaspoon oil with a little milk. Flavour the batter with Kirsch and let it stand at room temperature for 1 hour. Melt a little butter in a frying pan (skillet); when it starts to smoke, pour in some batter, tilting the pan so that the batter spreads out to cover all the surface. When the first side is cooked, turn the pancake over and brown the other side.

Savoy matefaim MATEFAIM SAVOYARD Make a batter with 125 g (4½ oz, generous 1 cup) flour, 2 dl (7 fl oz, ¾ cup) milk, 4 whole eggs, salt and pepper, and a little grated nutmeg. Then blend in 1 tablespoon melted butter. Melt 20 g (¾ oz, 1½ tablespoons) butter in a heavy-based frying pan (skillet) and pour in the batter, tilting the pan in all directions so that the batter spreads out to cover the base. Cook gently until the pancake is set. Turn it out onto a buttered ovenproof plate, sprinkle generously with grated Gruyère cheese, and cook under a grill or in a very hot oven for 5 minutes.

maté

A tealike beverage prepared from the leaves of a South American holly shrub. Both the shrub and the beverage are also known as yerba maté and Paraguay tea. The leaves – dried, roasted, and powdered – are infused to produce a tonic drink, rich in caffeine, which is popular in Argentina, Brazil, and other South American countries. It can be flavoured with lemon, milk, or brandy. Originally, the South American Indians chewed the fresh leaves without any previous preparation.

matelote

A French fish stew made with red or white wine and aromatic flavourings. The term is generally applied to stews made with freshwater fish: eel in particular, but also carp, small pike, trout, shad, and barbel. Matelote is a standard recipe in the regions of the Loire and the Rhône, in Languedoc, and as far as Hendaye (where a matelote of eel is made with mushrooms, Armagnac, and red wine); there are also several tasty regional variations (see *bouilleture*, *catigot*, *meurette*, *pochouse*). In Normandy a matelote is made with sea fish: turbot, gurnard, conger eel, brill, etc.; it is flamed with Calvados, cooked in cider, bound with butter, and enriched with shrimps and mussels or oysters. All matelotes are usually garnished with small onions, mushrooms, and rashers of bacon and sometimes with crayfish cooked in court-bouillon and fried croutons.

By extension, the term matelote (originally *plat de matelots*, 'sailors' dish') is also used for a similar preparation of brains, sautéed veal, or hard-boiled (hard-cooked) or poached eggs.

RECIPE

Eel matelote MATELOTE D'AN-GUILLE Skin 1 kg (2½ lb) eels and cut them into thick slices. Cook them in 60 g (2½ oz, 5 tablespoons) butter until firm, then flame them in 1 liqueur glass of marc or brandy. Add 2 onions, a stick (stalk) of celery, and a carrot, all thinly sliced. Cover with 1 litre (1¾ pints, 4¼ cups) red wine and add salt, a bouquet garni, a crushed clove of garlic, a clove, and 4–5 peppercorns. Bring to the boil and simmer for about 20 minutes.

Meanwhile, glaze 24 pickling (pearl) onions in butter and keep them warm, then sauté 250 g (9 oz, generous 2 cups) thinly sliced mushrooms. When the eel is cooked, drain and keep warm. Put the cooking liquid through a blender together with 1 tablespoon kneaded butter. Return the sauce to the pan, replace the eel, add the mushrooms, and simmer for 5 minutes.

Fry 12 small croutons. Pour the matelote into a deep dish, add the glazed onions, and garnish with the fried croutons. About 20 small fried pieces of sliced streaky bacon may be added just before serving.

matignon

A vegetable fondue that is prepared *au gras* (with bacon) or *au maigre* (without bacon). It is used as a complementary ingredient in various braised or fried dishes. Matignon is also the name of a garnish for various cuts of meat, consisting of artichoke hearts stuffed with vegetable fondue, sprinkled with breadcrumbs, and browned, accompanied by braised lettuce and sometimes Madeira or port sauce.

RECIPES

Matignon mixture APPAREIL À MATIGNON For the *au maigre* (meatless) version, cook 125 g (4½ oz, 1¼ cups) sliced carrots, 50 g (2 oz, ½ cup) chopped celery, and 25 g (1 oz, ¼ cup) sliced onions gently in butter. Add salt, a sprig of thyme, half a bay leaf, and a pinch of sugar. When the vegetables are very soft, add 1 dl (6 tablespoons, scant ½ cup) Madeira and boil to reduce until nearly all the liquid has evaporated.

For the *au gras* version (with meat), add 100 g (4 oz, ½ cup) lean diced bacon to the preparation above.

Chicken à la matignon POULARDE à LA MATIGNON Soak a pig's caul (caul fat) in cold water. Stuff a chicken with *à gratin* forcemeat mixed with veal forcemeat. Brown it in the oven at 220 C (425 F, gas 7), then remove it and leave to cool slightly. Coat it with a matignon mixture and wrap it in the drained caul. Tie it firmly, place it in an ovenproof casserole, and braise in the oven.

When it is cooked, untie it and remove the caul and the matignon. Skim the fat from the cooking liquid and add one-fifth of its volume of Madeira. Pour a few tablespoons of the cooking liquid (strained) over the chicken and glaze it in the oven. Serve the chicken surrounded by a matignon garnish and serve the remainder of the gravy separately.

mattyè

A dish from ancient Greece, of Thessalian or Macedonian origin, based on poultry, usually guinea fowl. The bird was bled to death the previous day, then cooked in a very spicy stock and served coated in a sauce made with green grapes and vinegar. Chickens, thrushes, and other birds were cooked in the same way. This recipe, similar to the French recipe for chicken in vinegar, had such a high reputation that the word *mattyè* was sometimes used as a synonym for a sumptuous and delectable dish.

maturing of cheese

AFFINAGE

The final stage in the manufacture of French cheese (except for fresh soft cheeses). In this stage the curds have set and been turned out of their moulds, the rind forms, and the cheese acquires its texture, aroma, and flavour. The maturing takes place in a cellar, vault, or similar place, at a particular temperature – 10–18 c (50–64 f) – and a specific degree of humidity, sometimes in the presence of bacterial flora. The lower the temperature and the larger the cheese, the longer is the maturing process (from four to eight weeks for a Brie; three to six months for a Cantal cheese).

During this process the cheese is subject to the action of microorganisms that are present in the atmosphere or deliberately introduced into the cheese. In the case of blue cheese, the action progresses from the interior towards the outside, but for most cheeses, ripening starts at the rind. Meanwhile certain treatments are necessary: brushing of the cheese, washing of the rind, steeping, regular turning, and coating with ash, grass, or hay. When the maturing is complete, the cheese is said in France to be *fait* or, in the case of a soft cheese, *à coeur*. If it has overripened, it loses its characteristic qualities.

Many continental sausages, being similarly fermented products, also go through the maturing process. They are subjected to a ripening and drying period which ensures their stability, taste, and aroma.

Maultaschen

A German speciality from Swabia, consisting of large ravioli stuffed with meat and spinach, flavoured with marjoram, nutmeg, and onion, and poached in meat stock. They are used to garnish a type of vegetable soup made with fried

chives and onion or a pot-au-feu. They may also be browned and covered with a layer of sautéed onions, or coated with breadcrumbs, fried, and served with tomato sauce, or used as filling for an omelette.

Maultaschen (meaning literally 'bags for the mouth') are thought to have been introduced into Swabia by immigrant Italian workers, whose Italian-style ravioli were considered to be too small. They are traditionally served on Fridays.

Maury

A sweetish fortified wine served mainly as an apéritif. After ageing and oxidation, it may develop a curious pleasant aroma, referred to as *rancio*.

Maxim's

A Parisian restaurant that opened in 1893 in the Rue Royale. Formerly the premises belonged to Imoda, an ice-cream maker, who had gone bankrupt three years earlier (Imoda had decorated his shop window on 14 July with the colours of the German flag: consequently the shop was wrecked and he lost his clientele). Maxime Gaillard, who worked in Reynolds Bar nearby, bought the premises with his friend Georges Everaert, with the financial backing of the president of the Distillers' Union, a butcher, and a champagne merchant. They converted the establishment into a café and ice-cream parlour with the name Maxim's et George's; the second part of the name disappeared fairly rapidly.

After the death of M. Gaillard in 1895, his chef Henri Chaveau and his maître d'hôtel Eugène Cornuché became partners and took over the management of the business. Cornuché, who had studied with Durand in the Place de la Madeleine, brought a new snobbish clientele to Maxim's. They were the friends of Max Lebaudy, an immensely rich sugar industrialist nicknamed 'the little sugar maker', and members of the exclusive Club de la Rue Royale, which had its premises on the first floor of the building. Maxim's premises were remodernized and became the meeting place for multimillionaires, princes, and opera singers. The most famous cocottes of the era took over a small room nicknamed the *saint des seins*, to which only a favoured few were admitted. Maxim's was bought in 1907 by an English company, and its success continued. After World War I, it was acquired by Oscar Vaudable and thereafter classified as an historic monument. Maxim's retained its reputation, the eccentricities of the twenties giving way to quiet dinners for the wealthy élite.

Several illustrious dishes have been created by the great chefs at Maxim's, including saddle of lamb Belle Otéro, soufflé Rothschild, and fillets of sole Albert. The latter was dedicated to Albert Blazer, who was maître d'hôtel at Maxim's for 50 years.

mayonnaise

A cold emulsified sauce consisting of egg yolks and oil blended together and flavoured with vinegar, salt, pepper, and mustard.

There are four possible etymologies of its name, whose spelling has also changed several times. Some sources attribute the name to the Duke of Richelieu, who captured Port Mahon on the island of Minorca on 28 June 1756. Either the duke himself or his chef created the sauce during this period and named it *mahonnaise*. Others believe that the sauce was originally a speciality of the town of Bayonne, known as *bayonnaise* sauce, which has since become modified to mayonnaise. However, Carême claimed that the word is derived from the French verb *manier* (to stir) and called it *magnonnaise* or *magnionnaise*; in his *Cuisinier parisien: Traité des entrées froides* he wrote: '. . . it is only by stirring the liquids together that one can achieve a velouté sauce that is very smooth, very appetizing, and unique of its kind, as it does not bear any resemblance to the sauces that are obtained only by boiling and reducing on the stove.' Finally, Prosper Montagné suggested that the word was 'a popular corruption of *moyeunaise*, derived from the Old French *moyeu*, meaning egg yolk. Now when all is said and done, the sauce is simply an emulsion of egg yolk and oil.'

The incorporation of complementary ingredients into plain mayonnaise allows a very wide range of derivative

sauces to be obtained: andalouse, italienne, tartare, verte, Cambridge, indienne, dijonnaise, gribiche, maltaise, rémoulade, russe, or Vincent, depending on whether herbs, curry powder, tomato purée, chopped watercress, caviar, anchovy essence, garlic, capers, gherkins, chervil, or chopped truffle, respectively, are added.

In order to make a successful mayonnaise, it is important that all the ingredients should be at the same temperature. Some recommend that the egg yolk should be left to stand with some mustard for a few minutes before adding the oil. If a mayonnaise has curdled, this can be rectified by adding the mixture, a little at a time, to another egg yolk plus a pinch of mustard and a few drops of vinegar or water. Mayonnaise should be stored in a cool place, but not in the refrigerator.

Mayonnaise is served as an accompaniment to cold dishes (hors d'oeuvres, eggs, fish, meat, etc.). It can also be used for decoration (piped through a forcing (pastry) bag) or as a seasoning (Russian salad, macédoines of fish, shellfish, poultry, or vegetables, etc.); such dishes are, by extension, known as mayonnaises. When mixed with aspic, mayonnaise is used for coating cold food or binding the ingredients of a salad.

RECIPES

Mayonnaise Sauces

Mayonnaise (from Carême's recipe) Place 2 fresh egg yolks, a little salt and white pepper, and a little tarragon vinegar in a medium-sized bowl. Stir quickly with a wooden spoon and as soon as the mixture is smooth use a tablespoon to blend in about 250 ml (½ pint, 1¼ cups) olive oil. Add the oil a little at a time, with a few drops of vinegar, taking care to beat the sauce against the sides of the bowl. The whiteness of the sauce depends on this continued beating. As it increases in volume, larger quantities of oil can be added at a time and also more vinegar and, at the beginning, a little aspic. It is essential to add the ingredients slowly and sparingly to avoid curdling.

This recipe requires 2 glasses (12 fl oz, 1½ cups) oil, ½ glass (3 fl oz, 4½ tablespoons) aspic jelly, and enough tarragon vinegar to give it an appetizing taste. To make it whiter, add lemon juice.

Classic mayonnaise MAYONNAISE CLASSIQUE Half an hour before making the mayonnaise, ensure that all the ingredients are at room temperature. Put an egg yolk into a bowl and add a pinch of salt and a pinch of white pepper. Mix these ingredients with a wire whisk, but do not beat too hard. Add the oil (olive, groundnut (peanut), corn, or sunflower) drop by drop, beating continuously with the whisk, stirring in the same direction and at the same speed. When the mayonnaise begins to thicken, increase the quantity of oil, adding it in a thin trickle. (1 large or 2 small egg yolks will emulsify 2.5 dl (8 fl oz, 1 cup) oil.) Then flavour with vinegar (tarragon if available) or lemon juice and adjust the seasoning. Before adding the oil, 1 teaspoon white mustard can be mixed with the egg yolk.

Anchovy mayonnaise MAYONNAISE AUX ANCHOIS Add 1 teaspoon anchovy essence (paste) or 3 desalted puréed anchovies to 2.5 dl (8 fl oz, 1 cup) mayonnaise. Mix well.

Aspic mayonnaise MAYONNAISE COLLÉE Prepare 1 dl (6 tablespoons, scant ½ cup) meat aspic (see *aspic jelly*). When cooled but before it sets, add 2.5 dl (8 fl oz, 1 cup) mayonnaise and whisk thoroughly. The sauce must be used promptly because it will set very rapidly. It can be flavoured in the same way as classic mayonnaise.

Caviar mayonnaise MAYONNAISE AU CAVIAR Pound 25 g (1 oz) caviar in a mortar and add 3 tablespoons (4 tablespoons) mayonnaise. Continue to pound. Rub the mixture through a fine sieve and blend with 2 dl (7 fl oz, ¾ cup) classic mayonnaise.

Russian mayonnaise MAYONNAISE À LA RUSSE Make 4 dl (14 fl oz, 1¾ cups) aspic (see *aspic jelly*) and leave to cool. Before it sets, add 3 dl (½ pint, 1¼ cups) mayonnaise and 1 tablespoon vinegar. Place the bowl in a larger one containing ice cubes and beat until the mixture becomes foamy.

Shrimp or prawn mayonnaise MAYONNAISE AUX CREVETTES Pound or mix 50 g (2 oz, ⅓ cup) prawns or shrimps with 3 tablespoons (4 tablespoons) mayonnaise in a mortar or blender. Sieve the mixture and blend with 2 dl (7 fl oz, ¾ cup) mayonnaise. The sauce can be coloured by adding a drop of cochineal (red food coloring) or a little tomato ketchup.

Watercress mayonnaise MAYONNAISE AU CRESSON Add 2 tablespoons (3 tablespoons) very finely chopped watercress to 2.5 dl (8 fl oz, 1 cup) very thick classic mayonnaise. Mix well.

MAYONNAISE DISHES

Lobster mayonnaise MAYONNAISE DE HOMARD Cook a lobster in court-bouillon. Drain, chill, shell the claws and the tail, and cut into uniform slices. Sprinkle with salt, pepper, oil, and vinegar (or lemon juice) and add some chopped parsley and chervil. Dice the remaining flesh and season in the same way. Arrange a thick layer of seasoned shredded lettuce in a salad bowl, add the diced flesh, and then the slices of lobster. Cover with mayonnaise. Garnish with a lettuce heart, quarters of hard-boiled (hard-cooked) egg, anchovy fillets, olives, and capers.

Langouste, langoustines, crab, prawns, shrimps, and various types of fish (particularly fresh poached salmon), either sliced, diced, or left whole, can be prepared in the same way.

Poultry mayonnaise MAYONNAISE DE VOLAILLE Prepare in the same way as lobster mayonnaise, using poached or braised chicken or turkey or braised duck. Garnish with lettuce and hard-boiled (hard-cooked) eggs. Strips of grilled (broiled) pepper seasoned with vinaigrette may be added if liked.

mazagran

An earthenware goblet in which coffee and certain iced desserts are served (the name is also given to the dessert itself).

Originally, iced coffee laced with brandy or rum was served in a mazagran and drunk through a straw. The name is derived from the town of Mazagran, in Algeria, where the French garrison withstood a memorable siege in February 1840. According to tradition, the Zouaves held their ground thanks to this drink! The goblet was created in their honour by a pottery manufacturer from Berry.

In classic cuisine, mazagran is the name of a case made with duchess potato mixture and filled with chopped or diced savoury ingredients; the filling is covered with duchess potatoes, piped on with a fluted nozzle. Mazagrans are baked in a hot oven and served hot with a suitable sauce. A single large mazagran can be prepared in a manqué mould or deep-sided sponge tin (cake pan).

mazarin

A two-layered cake made with dacquoise mixture and filled with praline mousse.

Formerly, a mazarin was a very large Genoese cake with a cone-shaped hollow in the centre. This was filled with crystallized (candied) fruit in syrup and topped with the cone-shaped piece of cake that had been removed, which was inverted, replaced, and iced (frosted) with fondant. The cake was decorated with crystallized fruit. A third type of cake named mazarin (by Jules Gouffé) was made with raised (leavened) dough and filled with a butter cream mixed with diced candied citron.

mazarine (à la)

Describing preparations of small cuts of meat which are garnished with rice, button mushrooms, and artichoke hearts stuffed with mixed diced vegetables cooked in butter.

meal   REPAS

A relatively fixed occasion at which food is consumed each day. The three principal meals of the day are breakfast (or brunch), lunch, and dinner; snacks may be eaten at other times of the day, such as tea, supper, etc. Religious feasts, such as Christmas, Easter, or Ramadan, are commemorated by meals consisting of traditional dishes.

measuring jug or glass
VERRE GRADUÉ

A vessel, usually made of hard plastic or toughened glass, sometimes with a handle and a pouring lip, which is used to measure the volume of liquids and is often graduated to measure certain dry provisions, such as flour, sugar, rice, tapioca, semolina, etc., as well. The capacity ranges from 25 cl to 1 litre (8–32 fl oz) and up to 4¼ cups.

meat   VIANDE

The flesh of animals and birds used as food. There are three main categories: red meat (mutton, lamb, and beef), white meat (veal, pork, rabbit, and poultry), and dark meat (game). In France the categories are often 'butcher's meat' (beef, mutton, veal, horsemeat, pork, and offal), poultry, and game.

The French word for meat, *viande*, comes from the Latin *vivenda*, meaning 'that which maintains life'. It was formerly used in the sense of foodstuffs in general, as in Taillevent's *Viandier* (1380), and in the 17th century the term was still used for all food, *viande creuse* ('hollow food') meaning a foodstuff that was not very substantial or nutritious. In the reign of Louis XIV, a meal was announced by the phrase '*La viande est servie*'.

There are numerous rites and customs concerning meat: the slaughtering of the animal, how it should be eaten, how it should be served, and how it should be preserved. Even today, in certain rural areas of France, the slaughter of a pig (*tuerie*) is an important occasion in the life of the community. Festive meals (at Christmas and Easter) are still associated with copious meat dishes, or meat cooked according to special recipes, and the 'Sunday roast' remains a firmly established family tradition to the present day.

Meat is composed of small fibres which are bound together in bundles to form the muscles of the animal. In an edible animal, about 200 of the muscles may be eaten, weighing from a few ounces to several pounds. Some of them are surrounded by thick sheaths of tendon or connective tissue (the fascia): the various cuts of meat are classified into categories according to the amount of this connective tissue present. Cuts for roasting or grilling (broiling) (the first-category expensive cuts) have almost none so are very tender and can be cooked quickly in dry heat. Cuts for slow-roasting, braising, and casseroling have a moderate amount (second-category medium-priced meats) and so need more gentle cooking with some moisture to break down this tissue and make the meat tender. If there is a high proportion of this tissue, or if the tissues are thick because the animal is old, then the cut needs long moist cooking to render it tender so is used for stewing or boiling (third-category cheaper cuts). The muscular tissue is enclosed in a layer of fat of variable thickness. If there is fat between the bundles of fibres making up the muscle, the meat is said to be marbled (*persillée*), a desirable quality particularly sought after in beef as it helps tenderize the flesh when cooked.

□ **Meat and dietetics** The proportion of protein in meat is constant (about 20%, including many essential amino acids) but the amount of fat is very variable, depending both on the animal and the cut. Carbohydrates are totally absent, as any stored in muscles in the form of glycogen are broken down into lactic acid when the animal is slaughtered. This chemical reaction is important in the maturing of the meat and in its tenderness. Meat also contains mineral salts (mainly iron, and also phosphorus) and group B vitamins, particularly B_{12}.

The water content of meat varies (60 –70%), depending on the age of the animal; it will be higher if the animal is young, and therefore lean. Generally speaking, the lean meats (*viandes maigres*), with 5–10% fat, are chicken, rabbit, game, horse, veal, and some of the offal of beef, mutton, and pork; semi-lean meats (*viandes demi-grasses*), with more than 20% fat, include pork, goose, many cuts of beef, and certain cuts of lamb and mutton. The way in which a joint has been trimmed and cooked is very important, as it affects its fat content: a leg of mutton with all its outer fat removed, cooked in the oven without any added fat, and eaten without the fat that has collected in the roasting pan during cooking becomes a lean meat, even though mutton is considered to be rather fatty (17–25% fats).

Like other products of animal origin, meat is a good source of protein, but it is also rich in saturated fatty acids; a daily ration of 200 g (7 oz) meat is considered sufficient, and many nutritionists now recommend that meat is not eaten every day. In contrast to other foods, meat retains its mineral salts and vitamins during cooking, especially when roasted or grilled. For those who enjoy eating meat, the smell and taste of cooked meat stimulate the digestive juices; meat is easy to digest and totally assimilated into the body. Being high in protein, meat gives a feeling of being well fed.

□ **The qualities of meat** Immediately after slaughter, the still warm meat is described as being *pantelante* (twitching) and is not edible; the muscles are soft, the water in the meat is strongly bonded to the proteins and the glycogen in the muscles is breaking down into lactic acid. After several hours, rigor mortis sets in and the muscles become stiff. However, at this stage the meat would be extremely tough after cooking; 24 hours after slaughter, the meat is hung to mature; once it is 'settled' it becomes suitable for eating.

There are five factors to consider when judging the quality of meat.

● *Colour*: this – the first sign that the consumer is aware of – depends on the level of myoglobin in the blood, the breed and age of the animal, and possibly its feed. Beef is a vivid shiny dark red, with a fine network of yellow fat; veal is slightly pink with white fat; lamb is bright pink with white fat, mutton a little darker; pork is pale pink.

● *Tenderness*: this depends on the following: the age and breed of the animal; its feed; the proportion of connective tissue around the muscle fibres; the treatment of the carcass (whether it was stored in a well-ventilated place and at the correct temperature); the period of maturing; and correct butchery (cutting up) of the carcass into joints and cuts of meat. In addition to all these factors, the cooking method is also very important: boiling and stewing increase the tenderness, even of very poor cuts of meat; indeed, expensive first-category meat from a young animal, which is considered to be very tender, becomes tough if roasted for too long.

• *Water retention*: this relies on the strength of the bond between water and proteins in the meat and is also an important factor, both when preserving meat and when eating it fresh.

• *Succulence*: this depends on the ability of the meat to give up its juices on being chewed. Prolonged chewing of meat that is not very succulent causes salivation and leaves a sensation of dryness in the mouth, which is often attributed to the meat not being tender, which may not be the case. Succulence, or juiciness, is linked to the presence of intramuscular fat (marbled meat); however, some young meat (veal raised on the udder, for example) which has a high water content may also seem to be succulent if the water remains in the meat after it has been cooked.

• *Flavour*: this comes essentially from the fat and is therefore linked with the succulence, which itself is determined by the feed of the animal. The flavour is more pronounced in an adult animal that has been well reared for the table, often with more highly coloured meat.

The quality of the animal and the category of meat should not be confused. A piece of stewing steak (a third-category cheaper cut) of high quality makes a delicious pot-au-feu, while a piece of rump steak (a first-category expensive cut) can be disappointing if it comes from an animal of mediocre quality.

The category of a cut of meat determines its culinary treatment: the first category comprises cuts for rapid cooking (grilling, frying, roasting), which mainly come from the back part of the animal; the second category includes the braising cuts, generally from around the legs at the front and (a few) at the back; the third category consists of what is left (neck, knuckle, shin, breast, tail, etc.), cuts that need to be boiled or stewed for a long time.

☐ **Cooking meat** In former times, the main rule to be observed when cooking meat was to poach it in boiling water before roasting or, alternatively, to start by sealing the meat over the heat if it was to be subsequently cooked in a sauce or stew. In fact, meat was tougher then than it is today, as cattle were not specifically selected and bred for butcher's meat. At the time of the Renaissance, when large quantities of salt beef were eaten, the best beef came from Normandy and the Auvergne; veal, choice meat for roasting, was from male animals, heifers being slaughtered at two or three years of age; the best sheep were those from Berry and Limousin; kids from Poitou were also well-known; but it was primarily the pig and its offal that provided meat for the table.

Methods of cooking meat are divided today into two basic procedures: rapid cooking and slow cooking.

There are three techniques for rapid cooking: frying tender slices of meat in cooking fat; grilling thin tender cuts over embers or under a grill (broiler), which reduces the proportion of fat; and roasting in the oven, either on a spit or in a roasting pan, with little or no fat but frequent basting (longer cooking is required in a cooler oven for a second-category roast).

There are three methods of slow cooking: braising (browning the meat, then cooking it covered in a small amount of well-flavoured stock); simmering in stock, wine, or even beer, cider, or milk, to tenderize the meat; and boiling in a greater quantity of liquid (water) with vegetables and herbs.

Meat is most often eaten cooked and hot, but it is also served cold and sometimes even raw and well-seasoned to alleviate the insipid flavour (e.g. steak tartare). Very rare meat, lightly cooked so that the blood runs out when it is cut, is perfectly easy to digest and retains all its nutrients, provided the meat juices are also eaten. Boiled meat undergoes much greater chemical changes, most of its nutrients enriching the stock in which it is cooked. The liquid should therefore always be served as part of the meal, either before or with the meat. Roast or grilled meat has a better smell and flavour than boiled meat and is considered by some people to be more appetizing. Fried and braised meats are intermediate between roast and boiled meat, but have more flavour than the latter (particularly ragouts). Small sautéed cuts of meat are frequently cooked with a sauce, which makes them less easily digestible. Frying, usually after coating with breadcrumbs, is only suitable for very small cuts of meat.

□ **Minced (ground) meat** If meat is not to be minced at home, the purchaser should ask the butcher to mince it on request. This applies particularly to beef. However, many people buy it ready-minced or deep-frozen, in which case they should check whether it is minced steak or simply minced beef from any part of the animal. Ready-minced pork, lamb, or veal can also come from any part of the animal.

The flavour of minced meat depends largely on the mincing: if the meat is minced fairly coarsely and has larger pieces in it, its juices are retained as well as its flavour; if meat is crushed to a fine pulp it becomes insipid. The description *à tartare* is reserved for freshly minced very lean beef with only 5% fat. As well as steak tartare, there are many uses for minced meat (beef, mutton, or veal): hamburgers, meat pies, fritters, different kinds of meatballs, hash, meat loaves, forcemeats, etc.

□ **Preserving meat** Cooking the meat may be regarded as a means of preserving it, but it will only keep for a limited time. This is also true when fresh meat is stored in the refrigerator. Man discovered, very early on, various ways of preserving meat, quite apart from charcuterie. One method is cooking in fat, to make confits of goose, duck, and pork. Coating cooked meats with aspic is another way of preserving them, but only for a limited time.

Salting, practised since ancient times, is a method of preserving raw meat: pickled pork, cured bacon, salt beef, pickled tongue, etc.

Smoking is applied to pork and charcuterie, as well as to poultry; some cuts of beef were also traditionally treated in this way, although this meat does not adapt itself so well to the changes in flavour brought about by smoking.

The drying of meat takes place in regions where the air is dry and pure (*brési* from Jura, Swiss *Bundenfleisch*, South American *charqui*, *pastirma* in the East, South African *biltong*, etc.); drying was the traditional method used by the American Indians to conserve the meat of the bison (pemmican).

Freeze-drying is a new method of preparing dried meat; arranged in thin layers, it is frozen and then dried by sublimation.

Appertization (sterilization by heating, see *Appert*) is currently used for preserving cooked meats: jellied beef, corned beef, but also beef bourguignon, blanquette, daube, etc.

Freezing is the most suitable method for preserving meat, either by commercial deep-freezing or, for smaller quantities, in the domestic freezer.

meat-carving tongs
MANCHE À GIGOT

Tongs with a turnkey and handle, fixed to the projecting bone of a leg of lamb (called the *manche*) or a ham and held in position by turning the key to facilitate carving. Made of stainless steel, silver plate, horn, or (die-cast) aluminium, it forms a set with the carving knife and fork.

Mecca cake
PAIN DE LA MECQUE

A small sweet chou bun, glazed with egg and sprinkled with granulated sugar or shredded almonds. Mecca cakes are served without fillings, usually with tea.

méchoui

A North African or Arab dish served on festive occasions, the cooking of which is traditionally supervised by men. It consists of a whole lamb or sheep that is roasted on a spit in the open air over the embers of a wood fire. Before cooking, the entrails are removed and the carcass is seasoned. Méchoui (*kharouf machwi* in Arabic) can also be prepared with a small camel, a gazelle, or a mouflon (wild sheep).

| RECIPE

Méchoui Choose a fat lamb, one year old at most. Trim it, leaving the head attached. Make a 30-cm (12-in) slit lengthwise along the belly near the kidneys. Remove the entrails through this opening, but leave the kidneys inside. Wash the interior and sprinkle with a handful of fine salt. Then insert 250 g (9 oz, generous 1 cup) butter, a little pepper, and either a few finely chopped onions or a large bunch of fresh mint, thyme, and rosemary. Close up the opening with a large wooden skewer stuck through obliquely (metal would give a nasty taste to the meat, and string would burn).

Brush the lamb with melted butter, sprinkle with salt and pepper, and impale it from head to tail on a pointed wooden spit that is long enough to protrude considerably at either end. Tie the front legs to the neck with a piece of the intestines and stretch the hind legs backwards and tie them to the spit with a piece of intestine.

The cooking area is prepared by digging a ditch about 1 m (39 in) square and about 50 cm (20 in) deep. Two X-shaped trestles are driven into the ground at opposite ends of the ditch so that the spit can be suspended over the fire. The fire is lit and there must be an adequate supply of wood to keep the fire burning throughout the entire cooking period. The spit with the lamb firmly secured is then suspended on the trestles in the correct position. In some areas, a second ditch is dug parallel to the first one. A fire is kept burning in the second ditch, and the embers are transferred when necessary to the ditch over which the lamb is roasting.

The lamb should be turned slowly so that it is completely and evenly exposed to the fire; it can be basted with butter, especially if one part seems to be on the point of burning. The lamb is cooked when the skin is crackly and the juice no longer pink when the meat is pricked with the point of a knife.

The kidneys are traditionally offered to the guest of honour. The guests should be given very hot plates so that the fat does not solidify. Since tradition demands that méchoui should be eaten with the fingers, finger bowls containing warm water perfumed with rose or lemon should be provided. Guests should also be provided with salt, powdered cumin, and chillies. Méchoui is normally served with couscous or bulghur and chickpeas.

medallion MÉDAILLON

An item of food cut into a round or oval shape. The word is synonymous with tournedos when applied to small cuts of beef. Medallions of various thicknesses can be prepared from meat, poultry, fish, shellfish, and even from slices of foie gras. Medallions of veal or poultry are sautéed or fried and can be served hot or cold.

Médaillons composés are medallions made with various croquette mixtures. The mixture is shaped into rounds weighing about 70 g (3 oz), coated in breadcrumbs, then sautéed in butter.

RECIPE

Chicken medallions Beauharnais
MÁDAILLONS DE VOLAILLE BEAU-
HARNAIS Remove the breasts from a large chicken and cut each into 2 or 3 slices of equal thickness; flatten them slightly and trim them into round or oval medallions. Season with salt and pepper and sauté in butter. Prepare an equal number of artichoke hearts and cook them in butter. Fry some round bread croutons, the same size as the medallions, in butter. Arrange an artichoke heart on each crouton, cover with Beauharnais sauce, and top with a chicken medallion. Serve any remaining sauce separately.

médianoche

A Spanish word meaning midnight and used to denote a meal that was eaten in the middle of the night as soon as the fast of the previous day had finished. The fashion for this was introduced to the French court by Anne of Austria and was carried on by her stepdaughter, Marie-Thérèse. By extension, the term was also used for an exquisite meal that was eaten very late, on such occasions as New Year's Eve.

Médicis

A method of preparing sautéed noisettes of lamb or tournedos, which are either coated with béarnaise sauce or surrounded by a ring of sauce made by deglazing the meat juices with Madeira and a thickened stock. The garnish consists of noisette potatoes and artichoke hearts cooked in butter, with peas and tiny balls of carrots and turnips arranged alternately. It is thought that it was named in honour of Marie de Médicis, who was renowned for her love of food.

medlar NÈFLE

A yellowish-brown pear-shaped fruit, 3–4 cm (about 1½ in) in diameter, with greyish flesh enclosing five seeds (certain varieties are seedless). It is native to central Asia and southeastern Europe and was known in ancient times. It sometimes grows wild in Britain and Europe. The medlar is edible only when overripe, after the first frosts if it is still on the tree, or after it has been left to ripen slowly on straw. Yielding 97 Cal per 100 g, it has a mildly acid and rather winelike flavour. The fruit is usually made into compotes or jellies.

Médoc

One of the most important regions of the Bordeaux vineyard. It runs from an area just north of the city of Bordeaux almost to the Pointe de Grave, the tip of a peninsula jutting into the Atlantic. The vineyard is divided into the Bas-Médoc in the north and the Haut-Médoc to the south, which includes some of the most famous of all the Bordeaux parishes (*communes*): Pauillac, St Julien, St Estèphe, Margaux, and certain others, such as Listrac and Moulis. Within these districts some of the greatest red wines of the world are made. Very little white is produced, and that mainly for local consumption.

The term *cru classé* (classified growth) refers to the 1855 classification of many of the Médoc wines (and one red Graves) into five categories established by brokers for the Paris Exhibition, according to the price each was expected to fetch (see *Bordeaux*). Each of the parishes has its own special character, each of the great estates among the *crus classés* possesses considerable individuality, and these days the *crus bourgeois* and *crus artisans* can be extremely good wines too. Wines from the different parishes, both vintage and nonvintage, may be offered simply as 'generics', merely bearing the name of the commune. People are sometimes puzzled that some good wines (such as Mouton Cadet) may now bear the nonspecific AOC 'Bordeaux' or 'Bordeaux Supérieur'. This is because the demand for these wines is so great that wines of regions outside the specific AOC de-

limitation are used, and therefore a different AOC must be given.

The great estates also produce 'second' and *sous marque* wines, which may not be quite up to the quality of their finest wines. It is up to the individual wine-makers to decide whether they will declassify their wine – for example, in a very poor year, the château label may not be put on a wine that does not attain its usual high standard, but which may be perfectly acceptable as a 'second wine' or *sous marque*.

The red Bordeaux wines (clarets) are made from a blend of several permitted grapes, notably Cabernet Sauvignon, Cabernet Franc, Merlot, and sometimes Petit Verdot, the proportions of each varying according to the estate.

Mège-Mouriès (Hippolyte)

French scientist (born Draguignan, 1817; died Neuilly-sur-Seine, 1880). Napoleon III commissioned him to perfect a cooking fat for the French navy that would be cheap and would keep well. In 1869 he obtained a fat from mutton suet which he named 'margarine' because of its pearly appearance (from the Greek *margaron*, 'pearl'). Later, margarine was manufactured from vegetable oils. As early as 1883, the chef Joseph Favre underlined the culinary advantages of Mège-Mouriès' invention: 'It is an excellent product for deep-frying, roasts, and soups, but will never replace butter for sauces or vegetables.'

Melba

The name of various dishes dedicated to Dame Nellie Melba, the famous 19th-century Australian opera singer. The best known is peach Melba, created in 1892 by Escoffier when he was chef at the Savoy, in London, at the time when Melba was starring in the opera *Lohengrin*. It was first served at a dinner given by the Duke of Orléans to celebrate her triumph: Escoffier conjured up a dish of a swan of ice bearing peaches resting on a bed of vanilla ice cream and topped with spun sugar. Escoffier first included peach Melba on a menu in 1900, for the opening of the Carlton, where he was in charge of the kitchens. In this version the peaches were coated with raspberry purée and the swan was omitted. Today peach Melba consists of poached stoned (pitted) peach halves placed on a bed of vanilla ice cream and coated with raspberry purée. The latter can be replaced by slightly melted redcurrant jelly flavoured with Kirsch, and pears, apricots, or strawberries can be substituted for the peaches.

Melba is also the name of a garnish for small cuts of meat consisting of small tomatoes stuffed with a salpicon of chicken, truffles, and mushrooms bound with velouté sauce.

RECIPES

Lamb noisettes Melba NOISETTES D'AGNEAU MELBA Stuff 8 very small tomatoes with a salpicon of chicken, truffles, and mushrooms bound with velouté sauce. Brown them in the oven or under the grill (broiler) and then keep warm. Fry 8 croutons cut the same size as the noisettes of lamb. Sauté the noisettes in butter and arrange them on the croutons on a serving dish. Keep warm.

Deglaze the sauté pan with 2 glasses (1½ cups) stock and boil down to reduce by three-quarters. Blend 1 tablespoon arrowroot with 1 glass (¾ cup) Madeira, pour the mixture into the sauté pan, and whisk until the sauce thickens. Add 20 g (¾ oz, 1½ tablespoons) butter, cut into small pieces, and continue whisking. Pour the sauce over the noisettes and arrange the stuffed tomatoes in a circle around them.

Peach Melba PÊCHES MELBA Prepare ½ litre (17 fl oz, 2 cups) vanilla ice cream and 3 dl (½ pint, 1¼ cups) raspberry purée. Plunge 8 peaches into boiling water for 30 seconds, then drain, cool, and peel them. Make a syrup with 1 litre (1¾ pints, 4¼ cups) water, 500 g (18 oz, 2¼ cups, firmly packed) sugar, and 1 vanilla pod (bean). Boil for 5 minutes, then add the peaches and poach them in the syrup for 7–8 minutes on each side. Drain and cool completely.

Cut each peach in half and remove the stones (pits). Either line a large fruit bowl with the vanilla ice cream, lay the peaches on top, and coat them with the raspberry purée or spoon the ice cream into individual glasses, top with the

peaches and Melba sauce, and serve scattered with flaked (slivered) almonds.

melimelum

In ancient Greece and Rome, a sort of jam made with honey and apples. The word comes from Latin *mel* (honey) and *malum* (apple) and is itself derived from the Greek *melimelon*, from *mel* (honey) and *mēlon* (apple). The word *melimelum* also denoted a variety of sweet apple, similar to quince. See *marmalade*.

melokhia MÉLOCHIE

A plant of the mallow family, with green slightly serrated leaves, several species of which are cultivated in Egypt and Israel as a green vegetable. The leaves may be eaten raw in a salad or cooked like spinach. *Molokhia*, a popular soup in Egypt, is made with fried onions and fried crushed garlic and coriander, cooked in very fatty beef stock with chopped melokhia leaves. It can be served with lemon juice and is often thickened with rice.

melon

The roundish fruit of several varieties of climbing plant belonging to the family Cucurbitaceae. Melons have a hard rind and a juicy sweet flesh that is usually eaten fresh at the beginning of a meal, as an hors d'oeuvre, or at the end, as a fruit. It can also be used to make jams and pickles.

The melon originated in Asia and was known in China at least 1000 years BC. It has been cultivated in southern Europe for centuries and was introduced into France from Italy by Charles VIII (reigned 1483–98), who brought it back from Cantalupo, a papal estate near Rome. Successive popes developed its cultivation near Avignon (during the period of the Avignon papacy). Later, La Quintinie perfected cultivated varieties in the kitchen garden at Versailles.

Melon production in France, which is concentrated essentially in the departments of Vaucluse, Bouches-du-Rhône, Tarn-et-Garonne, and Lot-et-Garonne, lasts from June to October. Three main groups of melon varieties can be distinguished: musk, cantaloupe, and winter melons. Musk melons are oval or round with a net-veined, sometimes, ribbed, rind and a green to pinkish or orange flesh. They are not cultivated much in France; the best-known French variety is the Sucrin, a sweet melon from Tours. The cantaloupes usually have a warty rind and yellowish scented flesh. However, the popular Charentais variety has a practically smooth pale green rind and represents 95% of melons cultivated in France. Winter melons, which are oblong, have a smooth or finely ribbed rind and a lightly scented yellow or greenish flesh. This type of melon keeps for the longest time and is therefore good for exporting. A common member of the group is the Honeydew.

The melon yields 30 Cal per 100 g and has a very high water content. It contains vitamins B and C. To prevent the flesh discolouring it should not be cut with a steel knife. A good-quality melon should feel heavy for its size and should have a thick unmarked rind that should 'give' slightly when pressed gently with the fingers at the stalk end. The 'female' melon is the most sought-after and can be distinguished when the end opposite the stalk has a large coloured circle that resembles the areola of a woman's breast. The cantaloupe melon can be kept for five or six days in a cool airy place (not in the refrigerator, as it tends to taint other foods with its smell). It freezes very well when peeled, sliced, sprinkled with lemon juice and sugar, and packed in a plastic box.

Among the great lovers of the melon were Henri IV of France and Alexandre Dumas. In his *Mémoires*, the Duc de Sully, chief minister to Henri IV, recalls the king refreshing himself with melons on returning from the hunt: 'They never do me any harm when they are very good, when I eat them while very hungry and before the meat, as the doctors order.' Dumas was even more extreme. He offered to the municipal council of Cavaillon all of his published works and future publications in exchange for 'a life annuity of twelve melons per year'.

As an hors d'oeuvre, melon can be seasoned with salt and freshly ground pepper or with ginger. As a dessert, it is usually sprinkled with caster (superfine) sugar. A number of connoisseurs consider that the only admissible seasoning is salt, possibly with pepper, unless it is preferred plain. Larger melons are usually cut into wedge-shaped slices for serving, but it is better to serve the smaller ones either whole with the top and the seeds removed or cut in half. Melon can also be served *à l'italienne*, with very thin slices of raw ham (Parma or San Daniele). It is considered wrong to serve melon with a fortified wine poured over it. However, a glass of port or Frontignan, served separately or drunk afterwards, is a pleasant accompaniment.

For pickling, melon is cut into pieces and prepared like gherkins. Pickled melon goes well with hot (boiled) or cold meats and cold poultry. The rinds of large melons can also be pickled. The outer layer of skin is removed and the remainder is cut into tiny pieces. Finally, when iced or filled with fruit salad, melon is a popular summer dessert.

The following is an extract from the article *Propos de table* by J. de Coquet in the 1982 June edition of *Figaro*: 'How should melon be eaten? Not with a spoon, as is usual in restaurants. . . . The back of the spoon anaesthetizes the taste buds! In this way, it loses half of its flavour. Melon should be eaten with a fork.'

RECIPES

Chilled melon ices MELON FRAPPÉ Take 6 small individual melons and 2 large melons. Prepare a granita with the flesh of the latter. Cut a generous slice from the end nearest the stalk of the small melons, remove the seeds, then gently scoop out the flesh taking care not to damage it or to pierce the rind. Cut the flesh into cubes, place them in a shallow bowl, and add a large glass of port. Store in the refrigerator, together with the empty rind and the slices from the tops. Leave to macerate for 2 hours. Just before serving, fill the shells with alternating layers of granita and melon cubes. Pour the port over, replace the tops, and serve in individual dishes, surrounded by crushed ice.

Melon en surprise à la parisienne Choose a good-quality ripe firm melon weighing about 2 kg (4½ lb). Remove a thick slice from the stalk end. Carefully remove the seeds and then scoop out the flesh without piercing the rind. Dice the flesh and place in the refrigerator. Select some fruit in season (apricots, peaches, pears, etc.) and cut it into cubes. Add some grapes, stoned (pitted) plums, strawberries, raspberries, and pineapple cubes. Mix this fruit with the melon cubes, sprinkle with a little caster (superfine) sugar, and pour over some Kirsch, Maraschino, or other liqueur.

Sprinkle the inside of the rind with a little sugar, pour in a liqueur glass of the same liqueur, fill with the fruit, replace the top of the melon, and store in the refrigerator. Serve the melon in a dish containing crushed ice.

Alternatively, ripe small melons can be used. Cut them in half and prepare each half as above to serve as individual portions.

Melon jam CONFITURE DE MELONS Dice 1 kg (2¼ lb) melon flesh (net weight after peeling). Put in a large dish in layers, sprinkled with 750 g (1¾ lb, 3½ cups) sugar. Leave to macerate in a cool place for 3–4 hours. Then cook in a preserving pan until the setting point is reached.

Pickled melon rind ÉCORCE DE MELON AU VINAIGRE (from a recipe by Jacques Pons, physician to Henri IV of France) Remove the rind of a large melon, keeping the green inside layer. Cut the rind into slices 2 cm (¾ in) wide and then peel off the thin outer skin. Put the peeled pieces of rind into a glazed earthenware pot, cover with white wine vinegar, and leave to marinate for 8 days. Drain. Place them in a saucepan and cover with water. Bring to the boil and drain again.

Cover the slices with very hot fresh water and boil until they are tender without being too soft. Drain a third time. Stud each slice with a clove and a small piece of crushed cinnamon bark. Return the slices to the earthenware pot and add a few sprigs of fennel. Just cover with white wine vinegar. When they are required, plunge the slices into warm water for 10 minutes, pat them dry, and season with salt, pepper, and oil.

melt FONDRE

To heat a product (such as sugar, chocolate, fat, etc.) until it liquefies. To prevent it from burning, a bain-marie or a heat diffuser is sometimes used, and the substance is stirred with a wooden spoon.

ménagère (à la)

The name given to various dishes in plain domestic cookery in which simple and relatively inexpensive ingredients are used, prepared according to recipes that are accessible to any good housewife.

RECIPES

Entrecôte à la ménagère Gently cook 250 g (9 oz) small carrots, 150 g (5 oz) small glazed onions, and 150 g (5 oz, generous 1 cup) mushrooms in butter. Season the steak with salt and pepper and brown it in butter in a frying pan (skillet) over a brisk heat. Add the vegetables and fry for a further 3–4 minutes. Arrange the entrecôte and the vegetables on a serving dish and keep hot. Make a sauce in the frying pan by adding ½ glass (4½ tablespoons) white wine and ⅓ glass (3 tablespoons, ⅓ cup) stock. Boil down to reduce and pour it over the entrecôte.

Omelette à la ménagère Cut some boiled beef into small dice and fry lightly in butter. Fry an equal quantity of diced onions in butter. Put the meat and onions in the same frying pan (skillet). Beat some eggs, add some chopped parsley, and season with salt and pepper. Pour the beaten eggs into the frying pan and cook.

Ménagier de Paris

An anonymous treatise on domestic ethics and economics written in about 1393 by a well-to-do Parisian for his young wife. The work was published for the first time in 1846 by Baron J. Pichon, a scholar who assumed that the author was either a *prévôt des marchands*, a barrister, or the treasurer of Charles VI (see *Taillevent*).

The *Ménagier* contains lessons on household economics, instructions on the management of servants, examples of menus for receptions, and numerous recipes, possibly taken from Taillevent, but sufficiently detailed for non-professional cooks. The work, which is interspersed with stories and poems, gives a vivid picture of Parisian life for the wealthy in the 14th century.

mendiants

A dish consisting of four types of dried fruit and nuts: almonds, figs, hazelnuts, and raisins, whose colours are those of the habits of the four Roman Catholic mendicant orders (Dominicans in white, Franciscans in grey, Carmelites in brown, and Augustinians in deep purple). Mendiants was traditionally served at Christmas.

In Alsace, *mendiant* is the name of a type of moist fried bread (*pain perdu*) made with apples, crystallized (candied) fruit, and cinnamon. This is also a very popular dessert in Germany, where it is known as *armer Ritter* (see *bettelman*).

Menetou-Salon

A wine from the Berry region, south-west of Sancerre. The Sauvignon grape makes pleasant dry white wines and there are also a few reds and rosés made from the Pinot Noir grape.

Menon

The author of several cookery books published in the 18th century. Highly regarded at the time, they were also appreciated by later generations of cooks. The most influential of these books was *La Cuisinière bourgeoise* (1746), which Franklin describes in *La Vie privée d'autrefois* as: 'A precious book which, rightly or wrongly, certainly had more editions than Pascal's *Les Provinciales*' (over 30, in fact, up to the middle of the 19th century). Menon's other publications include *Le Nouveau Traité de cuisine* (1739), *La Nouvelle Cuisine* (1742), *La Science du maître d'hôtel* (1750), and *Les Soupers de la cour* (1755).

Menon believed in simplicity but was not against invention and refinement, as shown, for example, by his *omelette au joli coeur* (filled with spinach, anchovies, and crayfish tails), his *raie au fromage* (skate with cheese), his marinade of pigeons with lemon, and his vine-leaf fritters filled with frangipane.

mentonnaise (à la)

The name for various dishes inspired by the cuisine of the south of France. For fish prepared *à la mentonnaise*, the main ingredients are tomatoes, black (ripe) olives, and garlic, while meat dishes are garnished with courgette (zucchini) halves stuffed with tomato-flavoured rice, small braised artichokes, and château potatoes. Courgettes *à la mentonnaise* are stuffed with spinach.

RECIPE

Courgettes (zucchini) à la mentonnaise Cut the courgettes (zucchini) in half lengthways. Make an incision around the pulp, 1 cm (⅓ in) from the edge, and several smaller incisions in the centre of the pulp. Season the courgettes with salt and put them upside down on absorbent paper to remove the excess moisture. Dry and sauté gently in olive oil until they are golden brown. Drain, remove the pulp from the centre without damaging the skin, and chop it.

Blanch some spinach in boiling water, then drain, cool, chop, and cook it in butter in a covered pan. Mix the courgette pulp with an equal amount of cooked spinach and fill the courgette halves with this mixture. Sprinkle with 1 tablespoon grated Parmesan cheese and add a little garlic and some chopped parsley. Sprinkle with breadcrumbs and olive oil and brown in the oven.

menu

A list, in specific order, of the dishes to be served at a given meal. In French restaurants, all the dishes that are available are listed on the *carte*; the *menu* lists the dishes for set meals, the composition of which is decided by the restaurant manager. The word menu dates back to 1718, but the custom of making such a list is much older. In former times, the *escriteau* (bill of fare) of ceremonial meals was displayed on the wall and enabled kitchen staff (*officiers de la bouche*), in particular, to follow the order in which dishes should be served.

Modern menus did not appear until the early 19th century in the Parisian restaurants of the Palais-Royal; customers were provided with small handy-sized reproductions of the menu displayed on the door. In 1894, Émile Goudeau, in *Paris qui consomme*, noted that: 'The development of menus in the smaller establishments and their simplification in the larger ones is a characteristic sign of the times. In the olden days there were dictionary-type menus, volumes with sections covering each type of dish: 100 soups, 100 *relevés* (courses following the soup), 300 entrées, 200 roast meat courses, 400 entremets, and 200–300 wines. In actual fact, nothing was available from this list except for a number of dishes of the day, which were basically always the same. Nowadays we have short cards usually consisting of a single sheet with an ornamental border, which ... only offer those dishes which can be served: 50–60 dishes, some always available and others varying according to the season or the day.'

Great illustrators and famous painters, including Toulouse-Lautrec, Manet, Picasso, and Chagall exercised their talents in this field.

The variety and number of dishes served at banquets in the time of Louis XIV would be unbelievable if one did not know that the guests tasted only a few of the dishes served *à la française*, that is arranged in order all together on the table, within one course. The five regulation courses of the gala meal offered to Louis XIV by Madame de La Chancellière in 1656, in her château at Pontchartrain, totalled 168 dishes or *assiettes garnies*, without counting the desserts. In the early 19th century, after the French Revolution which, according to Grimod de La Reynière, destroyed the basic concept of savoir-vivre, the *Manuel des amphitryons* (1808) still offered its readers, some 20 menus, each consisting of at least two soups, eight entrées, two relevés, two large cuts of meat, two roast dishes (*rôts*), and eight entremets. However, Carême advocated that the number of dishes should be reduced and that 'they should be served one after the other, so that they are hotter and better'.

Until the early part of the 20th century, menus were still very unbalanced from the dietary point of view. The almost total absence of vegetables and crudités, the small number of milk and cheese dishes, the preponderance of meat, game, fish, and pickled foods, and the high fat content would have made these menus highly detrimental to health had they been served regularly twice a day. But these were exceptional meals – banquets, state dinners, receptions, weddings, and so on; the everyday meals of most people were far more frugal.

Menus today reflect the current concern for a healthy balanced diet without neglecting the pleasures of gastronomy. Meals are less rich and cooking methods are aimed at preserving essential nutrients. Here are some examples of menus devised by today's leading chefs for different seasons of the year:

- Point's spring menu: liver mousse *en brioche*, braised turbot with vermouth, beef with bone marrow, gratin dauphinoise, cheese platter, sorbet, gâteau succès.
- Thuillier's summer menu: eggs *en surprise*, sea bass with fish mousseline, chicken with crayfish, leg of lamb *en croûte*, artichoke mousseline, strawberry gâteau.
- Guérard's autumn menu: freshwater crayfish soup, feuilleté of truffles with Graves wine sauce, braised scallops in their shells, navarin of pheasant with pigs' trotters, hot tart apple flan.
- Pic's winter menu: lobster salad with sherry, truffles wrapped in puff pastry, fillet of sea bass with caviar, Bresse chicken *en vessie*, iced orange soufflé.

Escoffier maintained that the menu was one of the most difficult aspects of the work of a restaurant proprietor. He has to find the right balance between the available products, the specialities on which the restaurant's reputation is built, and the specific requirements of the customer. There is one important basic rule: no dish should be included on the menu unless the chef is absolutely confident that it is worthy of being there. A chef often spends months or even years trying out a new creation before making such a decision.

menu-droit

A strip cut from a poultry fillet, 2 cm (1 in) wide and 2 cm (1 in) thick. Marinated in double (heavy) cream, menus-droits are grilled (broiled) for two minutes on each side and served with lemon juice and noisette butter. They can also be heated gently for a few minutes in a suitable sauce for poultry. Formerly, menus-droits denoted a ragout made with the tongue, muffle, and ears of a deer.

Mercédès

A garnish for large cuts of meat, consisting of tomatoes, large grilled (broiled) mushrooms, braised lettuces, and croquette potatoes. It is also the name of a chicken consommé with sherry, seasoned with cayenne, garnished with cocks' combs (split into two and cut into various shapes) and slices of cocks' kidneys, and sprinkled with chervil.

Mercier (Louis Sébastien)

French writer critic, and playwright (born Paris, 1740; died Paris, 1814). He is principally known for his *Tableau de Paris* in 12 volumes, published in 1781, to which six volumes (*Le Nouveau Paris*) were added in 1800. It is a series of short articles about everyday life in the French capital and contains valuable information on the history of food and catering, which was in its infancy at the time. The author also condemns certain culinary fashions, such as jellies, consommés, ragouts, and mousses, which were very much in vogue during the 18th century: 'What the nobility wants today are dishes that bear neither the name nor any resemblance to what one is actually eating. If the eye is not surprised in the first place, then the appetite is not sufficiently stimulated. Our cooks are busy changing the appearance of all the dishes that they prepare.'

Mercurey

A wine from the Côte Chalonnaise in southern Burgundy, a region most famous for its reds, made from the Pinot Noir grape. A small amount of white wine, made from the Chardonnay grape, is also produced. These wines are excellent value now that the Côte d'Or Burgundies have become so expensive.

Mères Lyonnaises

The nickname given to several cooks who set up in business in Lyon towards the end of the 19th century. Françoise Foujolle, known as Mère Filloux, was one of the first to achieve fame. After spending ten years in the service of an exacting gourmet, she married Louis Filloux, the proprietor of a wine bar. She added a number of her own specialities to the menu of cold meats served in her husband's tavern, including velouté soup with truffles, quenelles *au gratin* with crayfish butter, artichoke hearts with foie gras, and chicken demi-deuil. Between 1890 and 1925 her success inspired a large number of rivals: Mères Brigousse, Blanc, Niogret, Bigot, Brazier, Guy, Brijean, Pompon, Charles, etc. They were all cordon-bleu cooks, formerly employed in middle-class homes, who opened small restaurants (*bouchons*) that were frequented by a regular clientele.

The last of the authentic Mères Lyonnaises was Léa, born at the turn of the century, whose establishment finally closed in 1981.

These cooks frequently gave their customers a surly welcome. They did not offer a very extensive range of dishes, but those they offered were cooked to perfection and they made a considerable contribution to the fame of Lyonnais cuisine. They also prepared the way for the great cooks of this region, such as Fernand Point, Paul Bocuse, and Chapel.

merguez

A sausage made of beef and mutton and coloured red because it is seasoned with red pepper. It originated in North Africa and Spain, but has become popular in France since the 1950s. It is fairly thin (18–20 mm (¾ in) in diameter) and may be fried or grilled (broiled) and used to garnish couscous.

meringue

A very light item of pâtisserie made from stiffly whisked egg whites and sugar. Some historians of cookery believe that the meringue was invented by a Swiss pastrycook called Gasparini, who practised his art in the small town of Meiringen (now in East Germany). Others maintain that the word comes from the Polish word *marzynka* and that the preparation was invented by a chef in the service of King Stanislas I, Leszczyński, who later became Duke of Lorraine. The king passed on the recipe to his daughter Marie, who introduced it to the French. Queen Marie Antoinette had a great liking for meringues and court lore has it that she made them with her own hands at the Trainon, where she is also said to have made vacherins, which are prepared from a similar mixture. Until the early 19th century, meringues cooked in the oven were shaped with a spoon; it was Carême who first had the idea of using a piping (pastry) bag.

There are three types of meringue.

• *Meringue ordinaire* (and its professional variation, *meringue suisse*) is made with whisked egg whites and sugar. It can be used as it is for making *oeufs à la neige* (floating islands) or *norvégienne omelette* (baked Alaska) or as a topping for various desserts. When baked in the oven, it can be used for making meringue shells (which can be flavoured, coloured, and filled in various wàys) as well as vacherin cases. Ground almonds or hazelnuts can be added to produce *progrès*, *succès*, or *dacquoise* mixtures.

• *Meringue italienne* (Italian meringue) is made by pouring hot sugar syrup onto whisked egg whites. Rarely used on its own, this meringue mixture is used as a topping for tarts, flans, and desserts, for finishing *zuppa inglese* (meringue-topped trifle), for coating Polish brioche, and for folding into sorbets. It is used in the preparation of icings (frostings), butter creams, sorbets, iced soufflés, petits fours, etc.

• *Meringue cuite* or *sur le feu* is prepared by whisking the egg whites and sugar over a gentle heat (as for a Genoese sponge mixture) and then baking it in the oven. It is used principally for making meringue baskets and petits fours and to decorate desserts and cakes.

RECIPES

'Cooked' meringues MERINGUES CUITES Put 8 egg whites and 500 g (17 oz, 4 cups, firmly packed) icing (confectioners') sugar into a bowl resting on a pan of simmering water over a low heat and whisk the mixture until it is very stiff and holds its shape. Flavour with coffee essence, vanilla sugar, or a little rum. Pipe the mixture into small mounds on a baking sheet either oiled or lined with non-stick kitchen paper and bake in a very cool oven for about 2 hours.

Italian meringue MERINGUE À L'ITALIENNE Put 300 g (11 oz, scant 1½ cups, firmly packed) caster (superfine) sugar and 1 dl (6 tablespoons, scant ½ cup) water in a thick-based saucepan and boil to the 'large ball' stage (see *sugar*). Whisk 4 egg whites stiffly and add the boiling sugar syrup in a thin stream, whisking continuously until the meringue is cold. It can then be stored in the refrigerator until needed.

Meringue-topped fruit and rice FRUITS MERINGUÉS AU RIZ Spread a layer of rice pudding 2 cm (1 in) thick on a round ovenproof plate without going right to the edge. Poach 24 apricot halves in vanilla-flavoured sugar syrup, drain, and place them in an even layer over the rice. Whisk some egg whites until stiff then whisk in some sugar to make a meringue mixture. Cover the dessert with the meringue, smooth the surface, and decorate the top with piped meringue circles. Cook in a moderate oven until the meringue is firm, then increase the temperature or place under the grill (broiler) at the last minute to brown the surface. After removing from the oven, fill the hollows in the meringue decoration with apricot jam and redcurrant jelly, alternating the colours. This dessert is usually served hot but can also be served cold.

Pineapple, bananas, cherries, peaches, pears, and apples can be substituted for the apricots. The fruit may be used whole, halved, sliced, or diced and poached in vanilla syrup, except for apples and bananas, which are browned in butter.

Swiss meringues MERINGUES SUISSES Work 500 g (18 oz, 4 cups) icing (confectioners') sugar with 2 egg whites, 3 drops of white vinegar, 1 teaspoon vanilla sugar, and a pinch of salt. When the mixture is white and smooth, add 4 stiffly whisked egg whites. Mix well and pipe the mixture onto a buttered floured baking sheet. Bake in a very cool oven (less than 100 c, 212 F) for 12 hours. Decorate with crystallized (candied) fruit or sprinkle with sugar of different colours.

Vanilla meringues with Chantilly cream MERINGUES VANILLÉES À LA CHANTILLY To make approximately 800 g (1¾ lb) meringues, whisk 12 egg whites with a generous pinch of salt. When the mixture thickens but is not yet stiff, add 2 teaspoons vanilla sugar and then, gradually, 500 g (18 oz, 4 cups, firmly packed) caster (superfine) sugar, whisking continuously. The resulting mixture should be very stiff.

Put the mixture into a large piping (pastry) bag with a plain nozzle 1 cm (½ in) in diameter. Pipe some meringues onto a lined or buttered and floured baking sheet and bake in a very cool oven. When the meringues have cooled, sandwich together in pairs with Chantilly cream piped onto the flat side of one of the meringues using a piping bag with a star (fluted) nozzle. Small meringues can also be sandwiched together with butter cream, coffee cream, or chocolate cream (see *creams and custards*).

meringuer

A French verb meaning to top or decorate a dessert or item of pâtisserie with a meringue mixture. It is usually placed in the oven to brown the surface. In France, the part of the cake or dessert consisting of the cooked meringue mixture is called the *meringage*.

When applied to a sorbet mixture, *meringuer* means to add a certain amount of Italian meringue to make it more frothy.

merlan

A French cut of beef from the thigh near the topside (beef round). It is so called because its long flat shape resembles that of a whiting (the French name for whiting is *merlan*). This cut of meat is very good for steaks and constitutes, together with the *poire*, one of the *morceaux du boucher* (choice cuts of meat).

merveille

A traditional French pastry made from dough cut into different shapes and deep-fried. Merveilles are sometimes made with a raised (leavened) dough, and the mixture contains a large quantity of flour. The dough is rolled out and either cut into strips and formed into small plaits (braids), which are sometimes called *noeuds* or *bunyètes*, or cut with a pastry (cookie) cutter into rounds, diamonds, heart shapes, animal shapes, etc. Merveilles are sprinkled with sugar and served hot, warm, or cold; they keep for a fortnight in a sealed tin. Closely related to roussettes and oreillettes, merveilles are made in several regions of southern France. Traditionally, they were made at Shrovetide. In Provence they are fried in olive oil, while in the Landes they are made into biscuits (cookies) with goose fat and baked.

RECIPES

Merveilles Make a dough with 500 g (18 oz, 4½ cups) sifted flour, 4 lightly beaten eggs, 150 g (5 oz, ⅔ cup) softened butter, a generous pinch of salt, 30 g (1 oz, 2 tablespoons, firmly packed) sugar, and 1 liqueur glass of orange-flower water, rum, or Cognac. Roll the dough into a ball and leave it to stand for at least 2 hours, covered with a cloth. Roll it out to a thickness of about 5 mm (⅓ in) and cut it into various shapes with fluted pastry (cookie) cutters. Deep-fry in boiling fat (175 c, 347 F) until golden brown. Drain on absorbent paper, sprinkle with a mixture of icing (confectioners') sugar and vanilla-flavoured sugar, and pile up on the serving dish. Leave to stand for 2 hours in a cool place.

mescal

A Mexican spirit made from a distillate of the agave plant. In Mexico it is often drunk by itself, but for export markets the more complex spirit tequila, also made from the agave, is more familiar.

mesclun

A mixture of young shoots and leaves of wild plants used to make a salad. It originated in the south of France and the name is derived from the Niçois word *mesclumo* (a mixture). Mesclun generally consists of various types of wild and cultivated endive (chicory), lamb's lettuce, and dandelion, but traditionally it may also include rocket (arugula), groundsel, chervil, salsify, purslane, oak leaf lettuce (*latitue feuille de chêne*), etc.

It is seasoned with vinaigrette made with olive oil and flavoured with fines herbes, garlic, and even anchovies. This slightly bitter salad is sometimes served with croutons, small baked goats'-milk cheeses, small pieces of bacon, preserved gizzards, or chicken livers fried in butter.

A similar salad mixture is found in Rome and also in the Rouergue, where it is known as *mescladisse* and is served with walnuts.

mesentery FRAISE

A membrane covering the intestines of animals. In France calf's mesentery (*fraise de veau*) is usually used in cookery, although the mesentery of lambs and young goats can also be used. The mesentery is washed and poached in boiling water before being sold and must be white and firm to the touch. It may be cut into squares and eaten cold with a ravigote sauce or prepared as a hot dish in the same way as tripe *à la lyonnaise* or tripe *à la poulette*. It is also used as a filling for vols-au-vent. It is not used or sold in the United States.

RECIPES

Calf's mesentery à l'indienne FRAISE DE VEAU À L'INDIENNE Cut the poached mesentery into uniform slices, and simmer them gently in some curry sauce (see (*à l'*)*indienne*) for a few minutes. Serve with boiled rice.

Fried calf's mesentery FRAISE DE VEAU FRITE Cut the poached mesentery into squares, season, coat each square in egg and breadcrumbs, and deep-fry. Arrange the squares on a napkin and garnish with fried parsley and wedges of lemon. Serve with a spiced sauce, such as devilled sauce.

metal MÉTAL

Any one of a number of dense opaque chemical elements or alloys that are insoluble in water and in normal solvents. Many metals can be highly polished and easily worked by smelting or forging when hot, or by rolling, stamping, embossing, etc., when cold. Because of these qualities, metals have been used for making plates and dishes from the earliest times. As metals are also good conductors of heat and electricity, they are used for most cooking utensils.

Copper heats up and cools down most rapidly, which enables cooking times to be measured precisely. However, it is expensive and should be looked after carefully because it oxidizes easily and becomes discoloured. Copper pans are often lined with tin for this reason. Aluminium is cheaper, lighter, and easier to clean but it is easily dented and also reacts with certain foods. Cast iron heats up and cools down more slowly. Its disadvantages are that it is brittle, very heavy, and rusts unless it is enamelled, but enamel is fragile and reduces heat transfer even further. Stainless steel is strong and noncorrosive, but it is a poor conductor of heat and therefore the bottom of stainless-steel utensils is often lined with another metal, such as copper. Iron in sheet form is used, with or without an enamel coating, for making frying pans (skillets) and deep-fryers. Tin plate, made from sheet steel coated with tin, is used in the food industry for the manufacture of cans.

méteil

The French term for a mixed crop of wheat and rye, sown and harvested together. The flour made from this crop is used for making various regional breads. Méteil bread is common in central France, the Lot, and the Alps. At Douarnenez in Brittany a type of méteil bread is made with a mixture of wheat flour and buckwheat (or barley) flour.

mets

The French word for any dish prepared for the table. It can be hot or cold, savoury or sweet. The word is derived from the Latin *missum* (that which is served on the table).

méture

In the Basque and Béarn regions, a porridge made with maize (corn) and eggs, to which strips of raw ham are added. The word is derived from the Latin *mixtura* (mixture). In the Landes region, mêture is a very heavy yellow bread made with cornmeal and yeast. It is traditionally baked in a round high mould – often an old saucepan lined with cabbage leaves. The bread is eaten

Principal uses of metals in the kitchen

metal or alloy	use	type
steel	cooking utensils, dishes, cutlery	stainless steel
	frying pans (skillets)	sheet steel
	cooking utensils	enamelled sheet steel
	cooking utensils	'pearled', anodized, or lined with a nonstick (PTFE) coating
aluminium	cooking utensils	cast aluminium
	wrappings, containers for freezing, disposable cooking utensils	aluminium foil
silver	cutlery, dishes	silver and silver plate
	decoration for confectionery	silver leaf
copper	cooking utensils	lined with tin or stainless steel
	preserving pans and mixing bowls	untinned copper
iron	frying pans, deep-fryers	tin-plated iron
cast iron	cooking utensils	black cast iron and enamelled cast iron
gold	decoration for confectionery	gold leaf
silver gilt	cutlery, dishes, teapots, coffee pots	gilded silver

toasted, with goose rillettes, or dipped in soup.

In Normandy, *méture* is a synonym for méteil.

meunière (à la)

A method of cooking that can be used for all types of fish (whole, filleted, or steaks). The fish is always lightly floured (hence the name of the dish – *meunière* means miller's wife) and fried in butter. It is arranged on a long dish and sprinkled with lemon juice, then noisette butter, and finally chopped parsley. Frogs' legs, scallops, brains, and soft roes can also be prepared *à la meunière*.

| RECIPE

sea bream (*or bass*) à la meunière
DAURADE (OU BAR) À LA MEUNIÈRE
Scale and gut (clean) the fish (each

weighing less than 600 g, 1¼ lb) and make a few incisions along the back. Season with salt and pepper and coat with flour (shake the fish lightly to get rid of the excess flour). Heat some butter in a frying pan (skillet) and brown the fish on both sides. Drain them, arrange on a long dish, sprinkle with chopped parsley and lemon juice, and keep them hot. Add some butter to the frying pan and cook until golden (noisette butter), then pour the bubbling butter over the fish.

meurette

Any of certain dishes cooked in a red wine sauce, such as a matelote of river fish (eel, carp, tench, etc.) or a stew of veal or chicken. It is a speciality of Burgundy, the Dombes, and Bresse. The word *meurette* is derived from the Old French *muire* (pickling brine). Apart from red wine, it is traditional to add strips of bacon and often baby onions and mushrooms. Meurette is usually served with fried croutons. Eggs and brains *en meurette* are poached in this sauce.

RECIPE

Meurette of fish MEURETTE DE POIS-SON Clean 1.5 kg (3 lb) freshwater fish (small carp, barbels, young pike, small eels, tench, etc.) and cut them into pieces. Brown them in butter in an oven-proof casserole, then flame them with Burgundy marc (use at least 1 liqueur glass). Peel and shred a carrot, an onion, and a shallot and add them to the casserole. Stir thoroughly. Cover the contents of the casserole with red Burgundy wine, add a small crushed clove of garlic and a bouquet garni, and season with salt and pepper. Cover and simmer very gently for about 20 minutes. Rub some small croutons of bread with garlic and fry them in butter. Thicken the sauce with 1 tablespoon kneaded butter, adjust the seasoning, and serve in a hot deep dish. Garnish with the small fried croutons.

Méursault

One of the most famous vineyard areas of Burgundy's Côte de Beaune. It includes the parishes of Meursault, Puligny-Montrachet, and Blagny. Most of the wine is white, made from the Chardonnay grape, but there are some reds, made from the Pinot Noir. There is much variation in the styles of the white wines, many of them being outstanding in quality and capable of long lives in bottle.

mexicaine (à la)

Describing a preparation for braised or roast meat, which is garnished with grilled (broiled) mushrooms stuffed with chopped tomato, sweet peppers, aubergine (eggplant) halves, etc. The accompanying sauce is a tomato demi-glace to which finely shredded red peppers are added (hence the name of the dish).

Paupiettes of fish *à la mexicaine* are poached and garnished with the stuffed grilled mushrooms only. They are served with a white wine and tomato sauce containing finely diced red peppers.

Mexico and Central America

MEXIQUE ET AMÉRIQUE CENTRALE

Mexican cookery, which has strongly influenced the cuisine of other Central American countries, combines old Indian traditions with the influence of the Spanish colonists. The latter introduced pig rearing, the cultivation of rice, and a new method of cooking – frying. The cuisine of the indigenous population relied on steaming, cooking in a tightly covered pan with very little liquid (*à l'étouffée*), and braising, which explains the great diversity of ragouts and sauces, which are also served with boiled or roast dishes.

The main contribution of the Aztec civilization was the cultivation of maize (corn), which together with red beans and rice constitutes the staple food throughout the whole of Latin America: tortillas (pancakes made of cornmeal) are eaten in a number of ways. They may be served plain, fried, or baked, either flat or folded, and topped or filled with various stuffings. Crisply fried pieces of tortilla (*tostadifas*) are used as a garnish or for dipping into sauces; fried whole and piled high with a savoury assortment they are called *tostadas*. *Enchiladas* are folded stuffed tortillas, usually topped with a sauce and baked. *Tacos* are plain tortillas stuffed, rolled, and sometimes fried. The grain of maize, cooked in water, is used as a garnish for stews and fish dishes, while maize leaves are stuffed with minced (ground) meat and seasonings (see *tamal*). The leaves are also used for cooking chicken with red pepper *à l'étouffée*, and banana leaves are used for cooking kid. Haricot (navy) beans (white, red, and black) accompany pork and chicken. The fruits include avocado (used especially for *guacamole* sauce), bananas (of which there are over 20 varieties), pineapple, and papaw; they are served both as desserts and as vegetables.

But the most characteristic feature of Mexican and Central American cookery is the widespread use of chilli peppers. About 100 varieties exist, ranging from bright red to dark brown, most of which have a hot pungent taste. They are used in the famous dish chilli con carne, and one variety is ground to produce cayenne. Ground or crushed with tomato, they are used as an accompaniment to salt cod and chicken; larger varieties are often cooked stuffed with meat, walnuts, and almonds, mixed with soured (dairy sour) cream. Goats'-milk cheeses are also sprinkled with powdered chilli.

Meat is not very plentiful; apart from pork (especially in Guatemala, cooked with bananas), chicken is the main dish. *Mole poblano de guajolote*, a ragout of turkey with spices and cocoa, is the Mexican dish *par excellence*. The most popular drink is beer. Alcoholic drinks of various strengths are distilled from the yucca and the agave plants (see *mescal*, *pulque*, *tequila*). All Mexican cakes are very sweet.

The cookery of other Central American countries is very similar and includes tortillas, tamales and empanadas, omelettes, fried black beans, vegetable soups, and fish soups (particularly in Nicaragua).

Meyerbeer

A dish of eggs *sur le plat* dedicated to the German composer Giacomo Meyerbeer, whose operas were very successful in Paris during the Romantic era.

RECIPE

Eggs sur le plat Meyerbeer OEUFS SUR LE PLAT MEYERBEER Cut a lamb's kidney in half without separating the halves completely. Clean, season with pepper, and grill (broil). Sprinkle with salt. Cook 2 shirred eggs (*sur le plat*), garnish them with the kidney, and surround with a border of Périgueux sauce.

mezze or mezes MÉZÈS

An assortment of hors d'oeuvres consisting of (usually cold) spiced snacks, served in Greece and Turkey with ouzo or raki. Mezze almost take the place of a meal: in addition to taramasalata, stuffed vine leaves, and böreks, they include mussels in piquant sauce, green and black (ripe) olives, dried meat with gar-

lic (pastirma), marinated mushrooms, haricot (navy) beans in sauce, and a highly spiced dry sausage (*sucuk*), which is eaten with *cacik* (chopped cucumber with yogurt, seasoned with garlic, and served very cold).

miche

Pure wheat bread that was originally made for well-to-do citizens and then gradually became the daily bread of the rural areas. Originally a small loaf (the word comes from the Latin *micca*, meaning 'morsel' or 'crumb'), it became larger when used as the standard family loaf and is now a round loaf, weighing 1–3 kg (2½–6½ lb).

microwave oven
FOUR À MICRO-ONDES

An electric cooking apparatus whose source of energy consists of high-frequency ultra-short waves produced by a magnetron. These microwaves are fed into the oven compartment, through a wave guide, then distributed within the oven cavity by a stirrer, which bounces them off the metal walls and floor so that the food is bombarded from all angles, ensuring even cooking. The food is put into microwave-proof containers. Ovenproof glassware and china are suitable for microwave cooking but all dishes with metallic trims should be avoided. Specially manufactured plastics are ideal but some thin plastics melt in the microwave, so these materials must be carefully selected. Metallic material reflects the waves, so dishes made of these materials should not be used as the energy will not pass through them. The dish is placed on a turntable or on the base of the oven. The waves are absorbed by the food and produce heat by the agitation of the water molecules. Microwave cooking is a moist cooking method because of the steam created by heating the water molecules. It is this extremely rapid friction inside the food which creates the heat and cooks the food, and the cooking time is much shorter than in a conventional oven. However, the absence of radiated heat prevents food from browning or from developing a crisp outer crust.

The lack of browning, or crisp cooking, means that meat cannot be roasted as in a conventional oven and the speed of microwave cooking does not allow time for any tougher cuts of meat to tenderize.

However, fish, tender poultry, and vegetables all cook very successfully in the microwave oven. Sauces, soups, and fruit also cook well. Although it is not possible to achieve perfect results with bread and cakes, sponge puddings can be cooked quickly with good results.

The microwave oven can be used to defrost foods quickly and for reheating food speedily without any loss of flavour and without giving a 'reheated' flavour. Combination microwave ovens offer the facility for simultaneous use of conventional heat and microwaves.

mignon

A dish of chicken, calves' sweetbreads, or small cuts of meat, which are sautéed, coated with Madeira-flavoured demiglace sauce, and served with artichoke hearts filled with garden peas *à la française* and topped with slices of truffle.

mignonette

MIGNONNETTE

Coarsely ground pepper, particularly from the more flavoursome white peppercorns. (Formerly, a mignonette was a small muslin (cheesecloth) sachet filled with peppercorns and cloves, used to flavour soups and stews.)

The name is also used for elaborate preparations of noisettes of lamb, suprêmes of chicken, filet mignon, etc. Escoffier created mignonettes of chicken (suprêmes cut into rounds and studded with pickled tongue and truffle) and mignonettes of foie gras (small slices coated with chicken mousseline, dipped in egg and breadcrumbs, and sautéed). Potatoes cut into thick matchsticks are also called mignonettes.

RECIPE

Mignonettes of milk lamb MIGNONNETTES D'AGNEAU DE LAIT (from a recipe by André Guillot) Season 8 noisettes of lamb with salt and pepper, sprinkle them with a little thyme and rosemary, and marinate them for 24 hours in grape-seed oil. Drain them and coat lightly with strong mustard. Add 1 tablespoon chopped shallot to ½ glass (5 tablespoons) white wine vinegar mixed with ½ glass (5 tablespoons) white wine vinegar mixed with ½ glass (5 tablespoons) white wine and an equal quantity of beef stock. Boil down over a brisk heat until almost dry, add 6 dl (1 pint, 2½ cups) fresh cream, and season with salt and pepper. Drain the noisettes and grill (broil) them briskly for about 2 minutes on each side. Put them in the sauce and cook with the lid off while the sauce boils down.

Mignot

A celebrated Parisian restaurateur of the 17th century. He was immortalized by Boileau who, in his satire *Le Repas ridicule*, called him a poisoner.

A cook of some talent and a conscientious restaurateur, Mignot was much enraged by such criticism and took his complaint to court. His suit was rejected and he resolved to take vengeance himself. At that time he was making a kind of biscuit (cookie) much prized by Parisians. He conceived the idea of wrapping these biscuits in a sheet of paper upon which, at his own expense, he had printed a violent satire on Boileau written by the latter's enemy, the Abbé Cottin.

The success of these pastries, which were called *biscuits Mignot*, was enormous. All Paris wanted to taste them so as to be able to savour, at the same time, the verses in which Cottin reviled Boileau. Mignot's rage subsided somewhat when he discovered that, far from doing him any harm, the couplet had contributed to his greater prosperity.

migourée

A fish soup, similar to a matelote, that is a speciality of Aunis and Saintonge. Hake, anglerfish, skate, cuttlefish, mullet, conger eel (and sometimes gurnard, weever, and John Dory, depending on their availability) are cut into pieces, seared in butter and olive oil, and cooked in a court-bouillon made with white wine, water, onions, shallots, parsley, tarragon, a bouquet garni, and spices. Finally, the cooking liquid is thickened with kneaded butter.

Migourée de Matata has become a speciality of Meschers-sur-Gironde; the dish is named after the caves for which the area is famous.

mijoteuse

An electric cooking utensil containing a heating element on which a casserole rests. The casserole dish, which may be either movable or fixed, can be made of pottery, earthenware, metal with a non-stick finish, or fireproof glass. The element, which has a low power rating, is controlled by a thermostat. It enables food to be cooked very slowly for 4–10 hours, without any risk of burning or sticking, and is therefore ideal for ragouts, stews, cassoulets, sauerkraut, etc. If the casserole dish is removable and flameproof, meat can be browned in it over a brisk heat before being simmered; otherwise the meat must first be browned in a separate pan.

mikado

The name for various classic French dishes garnished or flavoured with ingredients that are reminiscent of Japanese cuisine. Escalopes of veal or chicken mikado is prepared by arranging the meat on croquettes of curried rice, coated with a curry sauce to which a little soy sauce has been added; the dish is served with tartlets filled with soya (soy) bean sprouts in cream. Tournedos or noisettes mikado are arranged on grilled (broiled) tomato halves, coated with a mixture of chopped tomatoes and a small quantity of tomato sauce, and garnished with Japanese artichokes cooked in butter in a covered pan. Mikado sauce is made by adding the juice and shredded blanched peel of tangerines to a hollandaise sauce.

RECIPE

Mikado salad SALADE MIKADO
Boil 750 g (1¾ lb) unpeeled potatoes in salted water. Allow them to cool, remove the skin, and dice them. Prepare 3 tablespoons (4 tablespoons) mayonnaise, replacing the salt with 1 tablespoon soy sauce. Remove the seeds from a green pepper and cut it into very fine strips. Peel, deseed, and dice the flesh of 3 firm tomatoes. Blanch 6–7 small chrysanthemum flowers for 2 minutes in boiling water, drain, dry, and season lightly with vinaigrette. Mix the diced potatoes with the mayonnaise and 150 g (5 oz, scant 1 cup) peeled prawns (shelled shrimp). Arrange the mixture in a dome in a salad bowl and garnish the top of the salad with chrysanthemum petals. Surround the salad with clusters of finely shredded green pepper and diced tomato.

milanais

Any of various cakes or biscuits (cookies).

The small biscuits known as milanais are made with lemon- or orange-flavoured almond paste cut into various shapes and decorated with almonds or crystallized (candied) fruit. They can also be shaped by hand into rounds, plaits, etc., and decorated with sliced almonds.

Milanais are also small cakes made of sponge or Genoese mixture flavoured with rum and raisins or with aniseed, covered with apricot glaze, and sometimes iced (frosted) with fondant.

Milanais sablés are small round biscuits sandwiched together in pairs with jam and sprinkled with icing (confectioners') sugar. They are more commonly known as *lunettes*, because the two small circles cut out of the top resemble spectacles.

RECIPE

Milanais sablés SABLÉS MILANAIS
Using the fingers, blend 250 g (9 oz, 2¼ cups) flour with 125 g (4½ oz, generous ½ cup) softened butter. Add 1 whole egg, 125 g (4½ oz, ⅔ cup) sugar, and either ½ teaspoon powdered vanilla or 1 teaspoon vanilla sugar. Knead the dough quickly, shape it into a ball, put it into a floured bowl, and cool in the refrigerator for 1 hour. Preheat the oven to 180 c (350 f, gas 4).

Roll out the dough to a thickness of 5 mm (¼ in) and cut it with a 5–6-cm (2½-in) oval pastry (cookie) cutter into an even number of sablés. Using a small round pastry cutter approximately 1.5 cm (½ in) in diameter, cut out 2 circles of dough from half of the sablés. Place the sablés on a buttered baking sheet and bake for approximately 12 minutes: they should be just golden. Allow them to cool completely.

Sprinkle the pieces in which holes have been cut out with icing (confectioners') sugar (these will form the tops) and spread the others with a layer of redcurrant jelly. Lightly press the tops and bottoms together.

milanaise (à la)

Food prepared *à la milanaise* is generally dipped in egg and breadcrumbs mixed with grated Parmesan cheese, then fried in clarified butter.

The name also describes a method of preparing macaroni (served in butter with grated cheese and tomato sauce), and a garnish for cuts of meat, made from macaroni with cheese, coarsely shredded ham, pickled tongue, mushrooms, and truffles, all blended in tomato sauce.

Dishes cooked *au gratin* with Parmesan cheese are also described as *à la milanaise.*

RECIPE

Celery à la milanaise CÉLERI-BRANCHE À LA MILANAISE Cut the sticks (stalks) from a head of celery into strips, chop them into small pieces, and cook them *au blanc* for 10 minutes. Drain thoroughly, and place half of them in a buttered ovenproof dish. Sprinkle with grated Parmesan cheese, top with the remaining celery, and sprinkle with more Parmesan cheese. Pour melted butter over the top and brown in a very hot oven. Just before serving, pour a few spoonfuls of noisette butter over the top.

milk LAIT

A white opaque slightly sweet nutritious liquid secreted by the mammary glands. Milking animals was originally a religious ritual among the early human societies that raised livestock. Milk has always been a symbol of fertility and wealth: in the Bible the Promised Land is described as 'flowing with milk and honey', and Moses proclaimed that the milk of cows and ewes were gifts from God. In Asia and India, zebus' and water-buffaloes' milk are sacred. Like the Greeks, the Romans were partial to goats' and ewes' milk, but they also drank mares', camels', and asses' milk.

The composition of milk varies according to the type and breed of animal, its state of health, and the diet on which it has been reared.

In most western countries the word 'milk' without specification means cows' milk, the most readily available kind. Cows' milk is a very nourishing food, yielding 65 Cal per 100 g, and 1 litre (1¾ pints, generous quart) contains, on average, 870 g water, 39 g emulsified fats (which give milk its white colour), 33 g proteins (including casein, which is coagulated by rennet as curds), 45 g lactose (milk sugar, which some people find difficult to digest and is the cause of some allergies), 7–10 g minerals (mainly calcium), and a variety of vitamins.

The composition of milk has a significant influence on the type of cheese that is made from it: very fresh milk with a low level of acidity is used for Gruyère cheese; Pont l'Évêque is made with milk that is virtually straight from the cow; while the milk can be slightly acid for Camembert cheese. The flavour of butter is also affected by the diet on which the animal has been reared.

Milk has a flourishing population of microbes. This is vital for the natural coagulation of milk, but it can be harmful. This is why various methods are used to pasteurize or sterilize milk, thus avoiding deterioration and prolonging the length of time it can be stored.

☐ **Different kinds of European milk**

● *Untreated milk* retains all its natural flavour. It must come from brucellosis accredited herds, be bottled on the farm where it was produced, and sold under licence. Untreated milk has to be labelled 'raw unpasteurized milk'. Some people advise boiling untreated milk for 5 minutes before drinking it. It is especially good in the spring and will keep for 24 hours in the refrigerator.

● *Pasteurized milk* undergoes mild heat treatment, which destroys any harmful bacteria and improves the milk's keeping qualities. A small amount of the vitamin content is lost in pasteurization; otherwise there is little significant change. It will keep for one to two days in a cool place, three to four in a refrigerator. Three types are available: *ordinary* (silver top) milk has a visible cream line; *homogenized* (red top) milk has no cream line because the fat is broken up into small particles; *Channel Islands* (gold top) milk has a marked cream line and is rich. Domestic boiling spoils the flavour of milk and also produces a skin in which some of the nutritious substances are often lost.

• *Sterilized milk* (blue top on plastic bottle or long-necked glass bottle) is homogenized milk heated to about 150 c (300 f) for several seconds. Sterilization destroys all germs and increases the shelf life of an unopened bottle, which can be kept at room temperature for several weeks. Date-stamped plastic bottles and cartons have a shelf life of several months. After opening, it should be stored in the refrigerator. Its flavour is caramel-like.

• *UHT (or long life)* milk is homogenized milk given ultra-heat treatment, then rapidly cooled. Nutritionally, it is similar to pasteurized milk, although some vitamin B$_{12}$ may be lost during storage. Unopened, it has a shelf life of six months, but once opened should be kept in the refrigerator. It tastes quite different from pasteurized milk.

• *Skimmed milk* is pasteurized milk from which nearly all the fat has been removed. The vitamin and mineral content is also reduced.

• *Semi-skimmed milk* is pasteurized milk from which some of the fat has been removed, with a consequent reduction in vitamin and mineral content.

• *Evaporated milk* is a concentrated homogenized milk, which is sterilized in the can and which, unopened, will keep almost indefinitely.

• *Condensed milk* is made from whole, semi-skimmed, or skimmed milk, to which sugar is added. Unopened, it will keep almost indefinitely.

• *Powdered or dried milk* is made from skimmed or semi-skimmed milk to which vegetable fat has been added. Water is evaporated from the milk by heat to produce solids. Powdered milk is packed in airtight containers and can be kept for a long time if stored at a moderate temperature. It dissolves readily in water, but once reconstituted should be treated as fresh milk.

☐ **Uses of milk** Milk is a very versatile food: it is the basic ingredient of fresh cream, butter, cheese, and yogurt, and it makes a delicious drink, either on its own or flavoured with fruit, vanilla, chocolate, etc. It is stirred into tea and coffee and forms the basis for many hot drinks, notably chocolate. Milk shakes are popular, and this versatile liquid can even be used in cocktails. Milk can also be thickened and flavoured to produce various desserts. Fermentation preserves milk and alters its flavour. Apart from spontaneous coagulation, due to the action of the lactic microbes in the milk producing curds and curdling by means of rennet, there are many other types of fermented milk. *Leben, kumiss,* and *kefir* from the Middle East, Indian *khir* and *gioddu sarde,* Icelandic *skyr,* etc., are examples. Curdled milk was formerly used as a basis for many French rural dishes: *lait ribot* is churned milk poured over mashed potato; *lait cuit* (cooked milk) is left to curdle naturally, then heated gently, and eaten with buckwheat pancakes; *lait marri* is boiled, mixed with *lait ribot,* and sweetened with sugar; etc.

Milk is an indispensable ingredient in modern cookery and is essential for many sauces, such as béchamel, Nantua, and soubise. It may also be added to soups, used in gratin dishes, court-bouillons for certain fish, and even in meat cookery (roast pork with milk). Desserts such as custard and cooked creams require large quantities of milk, as do ice creams and batters for pancakes, waffles, and fritters. Another, more unusual, use is in milk jam, where the milk is reduced to a heavily sweetened caramel and then flavoured with vanilla.

mill MOULIN

A mechanical or electric implement used to reduce a solid foodstuff to powder. The hand-worked coffee mill has largely been replaced by the electric coffee grinder.

The pepper mill and the coarse-salt mill are mechanical crushers, with a serrated roller or grinding wheel, operated by a handle or by a rotating movement of the lid. Freshly ground pepper gives a more pronounced aroma and flavour.

A vegetable mill with a handle and interchangeable plates is often preferable to an electric blender or processor, particularly for preparing purées of starchy vegetables, which can easily be overworked in the electric appliance.

Small spice mills formed part of kitchen equipment as early as the 14th century, but the mortar was more commonly used. From the 18th century the spice mill was used mainly for coffee, while the pepper mill became part of the table service.

millas, millasse, or millias

In the Languedoc, a kind of porridge made with either cornmeal or a mixture of wheaten flour and cornmeal. When cold, it is shaped into flat cakes and fried. The cakes are eaten like bread, either seasoned with salt or sweetened with sugar. The word is derived from the Old French *millet*, meaning fine-grained maize (corn).

In Anjou, *millière*, a porridge of sweet or savoury millet, can also be prepared with rice or maize.

RECIPES

Millas porridge MILLAS EN BOUIL-LIE Heat 1 litre (1¾ pints, 4¼ cups) water in a large saucepan. When it boils, flavour it with orange-flower water and a small piece of lemon peel, and gradually add 300–350 g (11–12 oz, 2¼–2½ cups) cornmeal. Cook over a gentle heat, stirring with a wooden spatula. When the porridge is thick, serve it on warm plates with caster (superfine) sugar. Alternatively, leave it to cool, cut into slices, and either fry in butter sprinkled with caster sugar or icing (confectioners') sugar, or fry in lard or goose fat and serve with stews, casseroles, etc.

Millas with fruit MILLAS AUX FRUITS Cook the millas, flavouring it with Kirsch or brandy. Put a layer of millas about 1.5 cm (½ in) thick in a buttered pie dish. Cover with drained cherries that have been cooked in a Kirsch- or brandy-flavoured syrup. Then put a layer of millas on top of the cherries, smooth the surface carefully, and decorate with a border of drained cherries. Sprinkle lightly with crushed macaroons, pour on some melted butter, and bake gently in a preheated oven at 220 C (425 F, gas 7).

The cherries can be replaced by apri-

cots, peaches, pears, apples, pineapple, plums, or even prunes, and rum can be used as a flavouring.

mille-feuille

A pastry consisting of thin layers of puff pastry separated by layers of cream (which may be flavoured), jam, or some other filling. The top is covered with icing (confectioners') sugar, fondant icing (frosting), or royal icing. Mille-feuilles are usually small rectangular pastries, but they can also be made as large gâteaux, which may be round. The origin of the millefeuille dates back to the late 19th century. Savoury dishes may be prepared in a similar way using puff pastry with a filling of fish or shellfish. They are served as hot entrées.

RECIPES

Mille-feuille gâteau MILLE-FEUILLE ROND Prepare some puff pastry with 300 g (11 oz, scant 3 cups) flour, a generous pinch of salt, 1 dl (6 tablespoons, scant ½ cup) water, and 225 g (8 oz, 1 cup) softened butter. Divide the dough into 3 equal portions and roll them out to a thickness of 2 cm (¾ in). Cut out 3 circles 20 cm (8 in) in diameter, place them on a baking sheet, and prick them with a fork. Sprinkle with 50 g (2 oz, ½ cup) icing (confectioners') sugar and bake for 15 minutes in a hot oven (225 C, 437 F, gas 7).

Meanwhile, prepare ¾ litre (1¼ pints, 1½ pints) rum-flavoured confectioners' custard (pastry cream; see *creams and custards*) and allow it to cool. Roughly chop 100 g (4 oz, 1 cup) blanched almonds and brown them gently in a frying pan (skillet). Leave the circles of pastry to cool completely. Use two-thirds of the cream to cover 2 circles of pastry, arrange them one on top of the other, and cover with the third circle. Cover the entire gâteau with the remaining cream, sprinkle with the browned almonds and some icing sugar, and store in a cool place.

Mille-feuille of fresh salmon au beurre rose MILLE-FEUILLE DE SAUMON FRAIS AU BEURRE ROSE (from a recipe by Élisabeth Cagnaire) Cut some thinly rolled puff pastry into 4 rectangles measuring 10 × 7 cm (4 × 2½ in) and bake them in the oven. Arrange some thin slices of fresh uncooked salmon on 3 of the pastry rectangles and place them on top of each other, spreading each layer with a mixture of fresh cream and lemon juice seasoned with chopped tarragon, salt, and pepper. Cover with the fourth rectangle of puff pastry, bake for 5–10 minutes in a very hot oven, then cool. Blend some butter with cream and mix with cranberry compote. Coat the cold mille-feuille with this butter.

millésime

The French word for the vintage year of a wine. Only certain wines are demarcated with a date (*millésimé*) when they are made; the bulk are nonvintage. A vintage date on a bottle of wine enables one to judge when it will be at its best (for a wine that is drunk young and fresh) or when it is approaching its prime (for a great wine, capable of long-term maturation and improvement).

millet

Any of several varieties of cereal grain. The main types of millet include the common millet (*Panicum miliaceum*) used for flour milling or as a poultry feed, pearl millet (*Penniseutum glaucum*), cultivated for food and for animal fodder in dry arid soils, Italian millet (*Setaria italica*), cultivated for grain and animal fodder, and Japanese millet.

Millet has been cultivated from the earliest times; in ancient Rome a kind of milk porridge was made from the grains after removing the husks. This method of preparation is still used by certain African tribes. Millet continues to be important in the diet of many African and Asiatic countries, but in Europe and North America it is cultivated mainly as a pasture grass and fodder crop. Millet is rich in magnesium, iron, manganese, and vitamins A and B and is sold in the form of grain, flakes, and flour. It is easy to prepare, being cooked for 20 minutes in twice its volume of boiling water or milk. According to the chef André Guillot in *Vraie Cuisine légère*: 'It can be buttered and seasoned and then moulded in a savarin mould and served in the same way as a rice mould.'

RECIPE

Millet tartlets TARTELETTES AU MILLET Put 200 g (7 oz, 1¼ cups) millet flour, 400 g (14 oz, 1¾ cups) caster (superfine) sugar, and 8 beaten eggs into a bowl. Work the mixture well and add a generous pinch of salt and the finely chopped zest of 2 lemons. Add 1.5 litres (2¾ pints, 3½ pints) boiling milk and mix well. Pour the mixture into small plain round buttered moulds and cook for 25–30 minutes in the oven at 220 C (425 F, gas 7).

Mimolette Français

A cows'-milk cheese (45% fat content), characterized by its orange colour and shaped like a flattened ball, 20 cm (8 in) in diameter. It is a compressed cheese with a dry hard grey or brown rind. Depending on its maturity (young, semi-matured, or matured up to 18 months), the cheese may be supple, dry, or hard and flaky; the nutty flavour of the young cheese gradually becomes more piquant. (The word *mimolette* comes from the French *mollet*, meaning fairly soft.) The cheese is eaten at the end of a meal, but may also be used in mixed salads and in the preparation of croûtes, canapés, cocktail snacks, etc. The cheese can be steeped in port or Madeira for one week before eating. The Mimolette manufactured in France is sometimes called Boule de Lille or Vieux Lille.

RECIPE

Panaché of chicken and mushrooms with Mimolette PANACHÉ DE VOLAILLE ET DE CHAMPIGNONS À LA MIMOLETTE (from a recipe by Édouard Carlier) Cook 4 suprêmes of chicken in a concentrated chicken stock and leave them to cool in the cooking liquid. Drain them and cut them into small cubes. Carefully wash 500 g (18 oz) *Craterellus* (horn of plenty) mushrooms in water mixed with vinegar. Drain them and cut in half. Cut 250 g (9 oz) semi-matured Mimolette into 1-cm (⅓-in) squares. Put all the ingredients into a salad bowl and season with a light vinaigrette made with white wine vinegar *à l'ancienne* and walnut oil.

mimosa ACACIA

An ornamental species of acacia whose yellow flowers can be made into fritters and used to garnish salads and prepare home-made liqueurs.

The name is also given to certain egg dishes using sieved hard-boiled (hard-cooked) egg yolk (which superficially resembles mimosa flowers), particularly a cold hors d'oeuvre consisting of stuffed hard-boiled eggs. The yolks are sieved, mixed with mayonnaise and parsley, and piped in flower shapes into the egg-white cases. Mimosa salads are mixed salads sprinkled with sieved hard-boiled egg yolk.

RECIPES

Mimosa flower fritters BEIGNETS DE FLEURS D'ACACIA Select very fresh flower clusters, and remove any fading flowers. Dust with caster (superfine) sugar, sprinkle with rum or brandy, and leave to macerate for 30 minutes. Coat the flower clusters with batter and plunge them into hot deep fat. Drain, place on a doiley or absorbent paper, and dust with sugar.

Mimosa ratafia RATAFIA D'ACA-CIA Strip very fresh mimosa flowers from their stalks. Weigh out 100 g (4 oz) and place them in a jar with 1 litre (1¾ pints, 4 cups) 50° white alcohol. Seal well and leave to infuse at room temperature for one month. Then add 125 g (4 oz, ⅔ cup) caster (superfine) sugar. Stir from time to time to allow it to dissolve (about 15 days). Filter and pour the liquor into bottles, corking them well. Store away from the light.

Mimosa salad SALADE MIMOSA Boil some unpeeled potatoes, then peel them, cut into cubes, and keep warm. Poach some artichoke hearts in salted water and cut them into quarters. Boil and chop some French (green) beans. Mix the ingredients and season them with a very spicy vinaigrette. Rub the yolks of some hard-boiled (hard-cooked) eggs through a coarse sieve and sprinkle over the salad. Serve immediately.

Mincemeat

A spicy preserve in English cookery, consisting of a mixture of dried fruit, apple, beef suet, candied fruit, and spices steeped in rum, brandy, or Madeira. It is the traditional filling for individual mince pies served warm at Christmas.

In the 17th century, a mince pie was a huge covered tart filled with ox (beef) tongue, chicken, eggs, sugar, raisins, lemon peel, and spices. Gradually, the small tartlets replaced the single large tart and the filling was reduced to a mixture of beef suet, spices, and dried fruit, steeped in brandy.

Mincemeat, which can be stored in jars like jam, can also be used in various hot desserts; for example, mincemeat fritters, served with apricot and rum sauce; mincemeat omelette, flavoured with brandy; and mincemeat rissoles.

RECIPES

American mincemeat MINCEMEAT AMÉRICAIN Put the following ingredients in a large bowl: 450 g (1 lb, 3 cups) minced beef suet, 450 g (1 lb, 3½ cups) cooked and finely diced beef, 450 g (1 lb, 3 cups) seedless raisins, 450 g (1 lb, 3 cups) washed currants and sultanas, 450 g (1 lb, 4 cups) peeled and chopped dessert apples, 150 g (5 oz, 1 cup) finely diced candied citron, 100 g (4 oz, ¼ cup) chopped candied orange peel, the chopped rind and juice of 1 orange, 450 g (1 lb, 2 cups) soft light brown sugar, 25 g (1 oz, ¼ cup) mixed spices, 2½ teaspoons salt, a half-bottle of brandy, 1 dl (6 tablespoons, scant ½ up) rum, and 1 dl (6 tablespoons, scant ½ cup) Madeira.

Mix all the ingredients thoroughly. Leave the mixture to steep for 1 month in a cool place. Stir every 8 days.

English mincemeat MINCEMEAT ANGLAIS Combine the following ingredients in a large mixing bowl: 450 g (1 lb, 3 cups) shredded suet, 450 g (1 lb, 3 cups) currants, 450 g (1 lb, 3 cups) seedless raisins, 450 g (1 lb, 4 cups) chopped apples, 450 g (1 lb, 2 cups) sugar, 450 g (1 lb, 3 cups) sultanas, 100 g (4 oz, ⅔ cup) chopped mixed candied fruit peel, 3 tablespoons (4 tablespoons) brandy or rum, the juice and rind of 1 lemon, and 1 teaspoon each of cinnamon, nutmeg, clove, and mace.

Pack closely in jars and cover tightly. This yields about 2 kg (4–5 lb) mincemeat.

Mince pies Line some tartlet tins with ordinary lining pastry and fill with mincemeat. Cover with a thin layer of puff pastry and seal the edges. Make a small hole in the centre of each pie to allow the steam to escape. Brush with egg and bake for 20 minutes (maximum) in a hot oven (220 c, 425 f, gas 7). Serve hot.

mincers and choppers
HACHOIRS

Hand- or electrically-operated utensils designed for minching or chopping meat, fish, vegetables or herbs. The traditional chopper (known in France as a *berceau*) consists of a wide curved blade with an upright handle at each end. It is held in both hands and operated on a chopping board with a rocking movement. It is used chiefly to chop spinach, sorrel, cooked salads, and herbs. The mechanical mincer is used only for meat and is fixed to the table by a screw-on attachment or suction. The meat is placed in a funnel and is drawn towards the knives by a screw operated by a cranking handle. Nowadays, mincers are usually powered by electricity.
• The *screw mincer*, similar in shape to the mechanical mincer, is supplied with interchangeable cutters, designed to produce coarser or finer grades of mince as required. It is often fitted with an attachment for grating or slicing.
• The *food processor* resembles a large vertical cylinder with a funnel for dropping in food. Blades revolve at the base. It is fitted with a lid, which incorporates a safety device. It not only chops meat and fish but can also deal with nuts (e.g. almonds, walnuts) and raw vegetables. It often comes with accessories (includ-.ng a grater and a slicer).

mineral salts
SELS MINÉRAUX

Mineral substances contained in most foods and needed for nutritional balance. The major elements are calcium phosphorus, iron, potassium, sodium, and chlorine; these, together with a number of trace elements, have various different functions. Calcium and phosphorus are the main constituents of bony tissue; iron and potassium are concerned with metabolism; calcium is necessary for blood coagulation; magnesium and calcium are required for nerve activity; and potassium and sodium regulate general hydration and the acid-base balance.

Minervois

Red, white, or rosé VDQS Languedoc wines. The area has been under vines since Roman times and, thanks to modern vinification methods, the wines (especially the reds) are now often seen in export markets.

minestrone

An Italian mixed vegetable soup containing pasta or rice. Italians often start a meal either with *minestra* (a vegetable soup), *minestrina* (a lighter soup), or minestrone, which – with its garnish of pasta – virtually constitutes a meal on its own. Sometimes several types of pasta are used, or it can be made with macaroni alone or with rice. The latter is usually used in minestrone in Milan.

Minestrone is characterized by the variety of vegetables it contains, which vary from region to region. In Tuscany it is always made with white haricot (navy) beans, together with garden peas, celery, courgettes (zucchini), leeks, onions, potatoes, tomatoes, and carrots. It is generally thought that minestrone originated in Genoa, where it is made with pumpkin, cabbage, broad (Fava) beans, courgettes, red (kidney) beans, celery, and tomatoes and garnished with three sorts of pasta – *cannolicchi* (small cubes filled with meat and herbs), small finger, shaped *ditalini*, and feather-like *penne*. It is mainly served with *pesto*, a thick oily sauce made with fresh basil, olive oil, garlic, and grated Parmesan cheese. Elsewhere, minestrone is classically flavoured with garlic; grated cheese is served separately.

RECIPE

Minestrone Soak 200 g (7 oz, 1 cup) dried white haricot (navy) beans in cold water for approximately 12 hours. Clean 200 g (7 oz) courgettes (zucchini) without peeling them; slice 250 g (9 oz) French (green) beans; shell 250 g (9 oz) garden peas; peel 250 g (9 oz) each of carrots, turnips, and potatoes; clean 150 g (5 oz) cabbage leaves. Cut the courgettes and potatoes into large cubes and dice the carrots and turnips; chop the French beans into small pieces.

Put the drained haricot beans into a pan, add 3 litres (5 pints, 6½ pints) cold water, and bring slowly to the boil. Add a large bouquet garni and 3 crushed cloves of garlic. Boil the beans until they are three-quarters cooked. Blanch the cabbage leaves for 5 minutes in boiling water, cool, and drain. Add the carrots to the haricot beans and, after 10 minutes, add salt and pepper, 2 tablespoons (3 tablespoons) olive oil, and the French beans, peas, turnips, potatoes, and cabbage leaves. Bring back to the oil, then add 250 g (9 oz) tomatoes (cut into quarters) and a handful of macaroni (broken into pieces). Cook for a further 10 minutes. Finally, add a large handful of chopped basil leaves. Serve piping hot.

mingaux or maingaux

A speciality of Rennes, consisting of whipped cream made from two different types of cream – one is kept in a cool place for 3–4 days after being skimmed from the milk; the other is fresh. As the cream is whipped (traditionally with a wooden whisk consisting of a small bundle of sticks), the froth that forms is removed and placed in a bowl until all the liquid cream has disappeared. Mingaux is served with strawberries, mulberries, or raspberries sprinkled with sugar. In former times, it was served wtih échaudés or galettes. In some versions of this cream, stiffly beaten egg whites are added.

minnow   VAIRON

A very small fish with a bluish back and pink belly, commonly found in streams and used mainly as a bait for trout. Although not much used in cookery, it may be eaten fried: the heads are removed and the fish soaked in cold milk until they swell up. If cooked in a courtbouillon, they may be used to fill an omelette.

mint   MENTHE

A very fragrant aromatic plant of the genus *Mentha*, used in infusions, to flavour liqueurs, sweets, and syrups, and as a culinary herb. There are about 25 species, widely distributed in temperate and subtropical regions. Garden mint, or spearmint (known in France as *menthe verte* or *menthe douce*), is the most common. Its leaves are used to flavour sauces (particularly mint sauce) and salads, in cooking vegetables (especially peas and potatoes), and to season roast lamb and other meat dishes. Mint tea is made by infusing the leaves. Dried mint will retain its flavour for two years.

Other species used in cookery are water mint (*menthe aquatique*) and horsemint (*menthe pouliot*), both water-loving mints. The leaves of peppermint (*menthe poivrée*) produce a very pungent oil used mainly in confectionery and to flavour spirits, liqueurs, jellies, etc. Bergamot or eau-de-Cologne mint (*menthe citronnée* or *menthe bergamote*) is a Mediterranean species, *Mentha citrata*, which produces a lemon-scented essential oil similar to essence of bergamot. It is rarer but in great demand because of its fruity flavour and is used to flavour drinks and marinades. Japanese mint (*menthe du Japon*) is the species from which menthol is extracted. *Menthe à l'eau* (peppermint cordial) is a refreshing drink made of mint syrup mixed with still or carbonated water.

RECIPES

Haunch of rabbit with mint BARONS DE LAPEREAU À LA MENTHE (from a recipe by Louis Albistur) This dish is prepared with 2 small boned haunches of young wild rabbit. Prepare a courtbouillon with the rabbit bones, a bouquet garni, the chopped white parts of 2 leeks, 1 chopped carrot, 1 onion stuck with cloves, 1 litre (1¾ pints, 4¼ cups) water, and an equal quantity of white wine. Cook gently for 2 hours. Steam the rabbit joints over this stock for about 1 hour.

Slice some tomatoes and courgettes (zucchini), allowing 4 slices of each per person. Stack the sliced vegetables alternately to form 4 small columns and bake them in a very hot oven. Carve the joints into fillets, garnish them with the columns of vegetables, and keep them hot. Prepare the sauce: thicken the strained stock with about 10 g (½ oz) cornflour (cornstarch) and 3 tablespoons (4 tablespoons) whipping cream. Pour the sauce over the fillets and sprinkle with 8–10 fresh finely chopped mint leaves.

Mint sauce SAUCE À LA MENTHE Pour 1.5 dl (¼ pint, ⅔ cup) vinegar over 50 g (2 oz) very finely chopped fresh mint leaves in a bowl. Add 25 g (1 oz, 2 tablespoons, firmly packed) brown sugar or caster (superfine) sugar dissolved in 4 tablespoons boiling water, a pinch of salt, and a little pepper and leave to marinate.

Mint sauce is the traditional accompaniment for roast leg of lamb in England.

Mint tea THÉ À LA MENTHE Pour boiling water onto a mixture of equal quantities of Chinese green tea and finely chopped mint leaves, allowing 2 dl (7 fl oz, ¾ cup) boiling water for each tablespoon of the mixture. Immediately sweeten with caster (superfine) sugar, according to taste (the tea is usually drunk very sweet). Infuse for 2–3 minutes, strain, and serve very hot.

Mint tea can also be made by the above method by adding 2 teaspoons finely chopped mint to the boiling water. Sweeten with sugar or honey and serve with a thin slice of lemon.

additional recipe See *pea*.

mint julep

A cocktail made by placing crushed ice, mint leaves, and sugar in a tall glass and pouring over Bourbon. Although the drink is American, 'julep' is an Old French word derived from the Arabic *julāb*, from the Persian *gulāb*, meaning rose water. Juleps are served decorated with fresh mint leaves and sprinkled with sugar.

mique

A kind of dumpling made in the countryside around Périgord since the Middle Ages. Originally made with flour and fat, miques today are prepared with a mixture of cornmeal and wheat flour, or wheat flour only, and either lard, goose fat, or butter. Yeast and milk are sometimes added, as well as eggs. The dough can be used to make one large ball, which is cut into slices after being cooked, or several small balls. They are poached in salted boiling water or in stock and accompany such dishes as pot-au-feu, pickled pork with cabbage, soup, or civet of hare or rabbit. They can be flattened before being poached and cooled and then fried and served as a dessert with jam or sugar. They can also be sliced, browned in goose fat, and served as an entrée with grilled (broiled) bacon.

Miques are also eaten in Béarn and in the Basque country, especially black miques (*pourrous negres*), made from maize (corn) and wheat, poached in the cooking water of black puddings (blood sausages), and then grilled.

RECIPE

Miques Mix 250 g (9 oz, 2¼ cups) cornmeal, 250 g (9 oz, 2¼ cups) wheat flour, 1 large tablespoon lard, a generous pinch of salt, and 1 glass (¾ cup) lukewarm water. When the dough is well kneaded, divide it into 100-g (4-oz) portions and shape them into balls by rolling them in floured hands. Drop the balls into a saucepan of salted boiling water and turn them twice so that they cook evenly. After boiling for about 25 minutes, strain, put them on a cloth, and keep them warm.

Mirabeau

A dish of grilled (broiled) meat (especially beef), fillets of sole, or shirred eggs garnished with anchovy fillets, stoned (pitted) olives, tarragon leaves, and anchovy butter.

RECIPE

Entrecôtes Mirabeau Stone (pit) about 15 green olives and blanch them in boiling water. Prepare 2 tablespoons anchovy butter. Blanch a few tarragon leaves. Grill (broil) 2 thin entrecôte (sirloin) steaks. Garnish with strips of anchovy fillets arranged in a crisscross pattern, the tarragon leaves and olives, and anchovy butter, which may be piped into shell shapes.

mirabelle

A small yellow plum with a firm sweet-tasting flesh; it is grown mainly in Alsace and Lorraine – the Metz mirabelle is regarded as one of the best varieties. Mirabelle plums are stewed, made into jam, preserved in syrup, and used to make a white brandy. They are also used in flans and tarts. In Lorraine, mirabelle brandy is protected by an *appellation*.

RECIPES

Mirabelle custard pudding FLAN AUX MIRABELLES Wash and stone (pit) 300 g (¾ lb) mirabelle plums. Mix 4 eggs with 80 g (3 oz, 6 tablespoons, firmly packed) caster (superfine) sugar, then add 4 dl (14 fl oz, 1¾ cups) milk and a generous pinch of salt. Gradually add 100 g (4 oz, 1 cup) flour and whisk well until smooth. Blend in 20 g (¾ oz, 1½ tablespoons) melted butter. Put the plums into a buttered ovenproof dish and cover them with the mixture, tilting the dish so that the mixture penetrates down between the fruit. Bake in the oven at 220 C (425 F, gas 7) for 35–40 minutes. Remove from the oven, sprinkle with caster sugar, and serve hot, warm, or cold.

Mirabelle jam CONFITURE DE MIRABELLES Stone (pit) the plums without separating the halves and weigh them. Place them in a bowl with an equal weight of caster (superfine) sugar. Mix well and leave to macerate for 24 hours, stirring several times during this period. Pour the plums and sugar into a preserving pan, bring to the boil, and cook for 20 minutes. Pot as for jam.

mirepoix

A culinary preparation created in the 18th century by the cook of the Duc de Lévis-Mirepoix, a French field marshal and ambassador of Louis XV. It consists of a mixture of diced vegetables (carrot, onion, celery); raw ham or lean bacon is added when the preparation is *au gras* (with meat).

A mirepoix is used to enhance the flavour of meat, game, and fish, in the preparation of sauces (notably espagnole sauce), and as a garnish for such dishes as frogs' legs, artichokes, macaroni, etc. When a mirepoix is used in braised or pot-roasted dishes, it should be simmered gently in a covered pan until all the vegetables are very tender and can impart their flavour to the dish. Mirepoix *au maigre* (meatless mirepoix) is mainly used in the preparation of shellfish or mussels *à la bordelaise* and may also be used for braised vegetable dishes in certain white sauces.

RECIPES

Mirepoix with meat MIREPOIX AU GRAS Peel and finely dice 150 g (5 oz) carrots and 100 g (4 oz) onions. Cut 50 g (2 oz) celery and 100 g (4 oz) raw ham (or blanched streaky bacon) into fine strips. Heat 25 g (1 oz, 2 tablespoons) butter in a saucepan and add the ham and vegetables, together with a sprig of thyme and half a bay leaf. Stir the ingredients into the butter, cover, and cook gently for approximately 20 minutes until the vegetables are very tender.

Vegetable mirepoix MIREPOIX AU MAIGRE This mirepoix is cooked in the same way as mirepoix with meat, but the ham or bacon is omitted and the vegetables are shredded into a brunoise.

mirliton

A puff-pastry tartlet filled with almond cream and decorated with three almond halves arranged in the form of a star.

Crisp petits fours flavoured with orange-flower water are also called *mirlitons*.

RECIPE

Mirlitons de Rouen Roll out 250 g (9 oz) puff pastry to a thickness of approximately 2 mm (⅛ in). Line 10 tartlet tins (moulds). Mix 2 beaten eggs, 4 large crushed macaroons, 60 g (generous 2 oz, generous 2 tablespoons, firmly packed) caster (superfine) sugar, 20 g (¾ oz, scant ¼ cup) ground almonds in a bowl. Three-quarters fill the tartlets with the mixture and leave to stand for 30 minutes in a cool place. Halve 15 blanched almonds and arrange 3 halves on each tartlet. Sprinkle with icing (confectioners') sugar and bake for 15 –20 minutes in the oven at 200 c (400 f, gas 6). Serve warm or cold.

miroton

A dish of sliced cooked meat (usually boiled beef or leftovers) cooked in a sauce with sliced onions. The origin of the word is unknown but it is known to have existed since 1690. In *Le Cousin Pons*, Balzac gave a very exact description of this dish without naming it: 'It consisted of boiled leftovers of beef purchased from a rôtisseur ... and fricasseed in butter with thinly sliced onions until the butter was absorbed by the meat and the onions, so that this dish looked like a fried meal.'

RECIPE

Beef miroton BOEUF MIROTON Cook about 10 tablespoons finely sliced onions in 125 g (4½ oz, generous ½ cup) butter in a covered pan. Sprinkle with 1 tablespoon flour. Brown slightly, stirring continuously, then add 2 tablespoons (3 tablespoons) vinegar and an equal amount of stock or white wine. Bring to the boil, then remove from the heat. Pour half the sauce into a long ovenproof dish. Cut 500 g (18 oz) cold boiled beef into thin slices and arrange them in the dish on top of the sauce. Pour the rest of the sauce over the top, sprinkle generously with breadcrumbs, and pour on some melted butter (or dripping). Brown in a hot oven without allowing the sauce to boil. Sprinkle with chopped parsley and serve piping hot.

mise en place

The French term for all the operations carried out in a restaurant prior to serving the meal. In the dining room, this constitutes laying the tables; in the kitchen it means setting out the ingredients and utensils required for the preparation of the dishes on the menu. The apprentice or assistant is generally in charge of preparing the vegetables, bouquets garnis, chopped onions, parsley, etc., while the initial preparation of stocks, fumets, sauces, and compound butters and the preparation of meat and game, consommés, soups, and desserts is the responsibility of the appropriate cook or section chef.

miso

A Japanese condiment consisting of a red or white paste of fermented soya, made from cooked soya (soy) beans mixed with rice, barley, or wheat grains and salt.

mistelle

Grape juice to which spirits have been added in order to prevent fermentation from taking place, so that the natural sweetness of the fruit is retained. Mistelle is used in the making of various apéritifs and vermouths.

mitonner

A French cooking term that originally meant to simmer stale bread for a long time in soup or stock so that it absorbs the liquid and thickens the soup. The verb is derived from *miton*, a dialect word in western France for the crumb of bread. *Mitonner* is now synonymous with *mijoter* (to simmer) and is also sometimes used to refer to the detailed preparation of a meal at home.

mixed grill

An assortment of various meats (steak, lamb cutlets (chops), sausages, kidneys, etc.) barbecued or grilled and usually served with a garnish of watercress, grilled tomatoes, and mushrooms. It is a popular dish in English-speaking countries.

mocha MOKA

A variety of Arabian coffee bean grown on the borders of the Red Sea, named after the Yemenite port from which they were traditionally exported. Mocha is a strong coffee with a distinctive aroma, but some people find it bitter, with a musky flavour. It is normally served very strong and sweet in small cups.

Mocha is used as a flavouring for cakes, biscuits (cookies), ice creams, and confectionery, and the word is used to describe various cakes with a coffee flavour, particularly a large Genoese sponge cake with layers of coffee or chocolate butter cream. This type of cake was probably created when coffee drinking was introduced into Paris.

RECIPE

Mocha cake GÂTEAU MOKA Melt 90 g (3½ oz, 7 tablespoons) butter, taking care not to let it get too hot. Whisk 5 egg yolks with 150 g (5 oz, ⅔ cup) sugar until the mixture has turned white and thick. Mix in 150 g (5 oz, 1¼ cups) sifted flour and 50 g (2 oz, ½ cup) ground hazelnuts, then incorporate the melted butter and fold in 5 stiffly whisked egg whites. Pour this mixture into a deep 22-cm (8-in) buttered cake tin (pan) and bake in the oven at 180 C (350 F, gas 4) for about 35 minutes. As soon as the cake is cooked, turn it out onto a rack and allow it to cool completely. Then cover and refrigerate for at least 1 hour.

Dissolve 150 g (5 oz, ⅔ cup) sugar with 2 tablespoons (3 tablespoons) water and very slowly bring it to the boil. Gently mix the boiling syrup with 4 egg yolks and beat briskly until it has cooled and is thick and mousse-like. Now whisk in 175 g (6 oz, ¾ cup) soft butter, cut into small pieces, and 1 teaspoon coffee essence (extract). Finely grind 150 g (5 oz, 1¼ cups) toasted hazelnuts. Cut the cake into 3 layers. Mix two-thirds of the ground nuts into half the cream and spread on 2 of these layers. Sandwich the cake together and cover it completely with half the remaining cream. Sprinkle the surface of the cake with the remaining ground hazelnuts, put the rest of the cream into a piping (pastry) bag with a fluted nozzle, and pipe a regular design of rosettes on the cake. Place a grain of coffee covered in bitter chocolate at the centre of every rosette. Refrigerate the cake in a sealed container for at least 2 hours; serve very cold.

Mocha cake can also be filled and coated with coffee cream, then decorated with toasted flaked (slivered) almonds and crystallized (candied) violets and mimosa. Mocha cake is best eaten the day after its preparation.

mode (à la)

Describing a preparation of braised beef, to which diced leg of veal, sliced carrots, and small onions are added when it is three-quarters cooked. Beef *à la mode* is eaten either hot or cold (in aspic).

The term is also used to describe dishes that are a speciality of a particular town or region, such as tripe *à la mode de Caen*.

moderne (à la)

Describing a preparation for large cuts of meat in which the garnish includes braised lettuce (stuffed or plain) and sometimes noisette potatoes and quenelles decorated with slices of truffle or pickled tongue. The sauce is made from thickened veal stock. Tournedos and lamb noisettes *à la moderne* are sautéed, served on a bed of grilled (broiled) mushroom caps, and coated with the pan juices deglazed with Madeira and demi-glace; the garnish consists of croquette potatoes, braised lettuce, and whole peeled and stewed tomatoes.

Moïna

A dish consisting of poached fillets of sole garnished with quartered artichokes braised in butter and morels *à la crème*.

moisten MOUILLER

To add a liquid to a culinary preparation, either in order to cook it (for stews, braised dishes, etc.) or to make the sauce or gravy. The liquid, which may be water, milk, broth, stock, or wine, usually just covers the items to be cooked, but in certain cases (for example, baked fish) the ingredients are only half-covered.

molasses MÉLASSE

The thick brownish uncrystallized residue obtained from cane or beet sugar during refining. This dense viscous syrup, which is separated out last during the process, consists of sugar (about 50%), water, mineral salts, and nitrogenous substances. Molasses can be used for various purposes. Only sugarcane molasses, known as 'black treacle', is sold for domestic consumption, for certain items of pâtisserie (such as treacle tart) and also for sweet-and-sour cooking. It is also used in confectionery and for the manufacture of rum. Sugarbeet molasses is used mainly for the production of industrial alcohol, baking powders, and animal feeds.

mole poblano

A festival dish in Mexican cookery (its full name is *mole poblano de Guajolote*), consisting of a turkey stew with a chocolate sauce. It is supposed to have been invented in the 16th century by nuns of the convent of Puebla. The story goes that the nuns were taken unawares by a visit from their bishop, so they cooked the local poulterer's only turkey in a sauce typical of Aztec cookery. Originally, the turkey was cooked in a casserole but it can also be roasted in the oven or fried in lard. The sauce (*mole*) is prepared as follows. Various red peppers (*ancho*, very aromatic; *mulato*, large and scented; and *pasilla*, very hot) are pounded in a little turkey stock. Onions, tomatoes, pieces of tortilla, garlic, and crushed almonds are added to this mixture, as well as aniseed, sesame seeds, cinnamon, cloves, and coriander. The mixture is then thoroughly pounded, strained, and simmered with turkey stock to which lard and plain chocolate are added. The turkey is cut into pieces, liberally covered with the sauce, and served sprinkled with sesame seeds, sweetcorn, or small tortillas.

mollusc MOLLUSQUE

A soft-bodied animal, usually with a shell. The bivalves (or lamellibranchs), which have a shell consisting of two valves hinged together, include the mussels, oysters, cockles, and scallops. The gastropods have a single spiral shell and include the periwinkles, whelks, snails, and limpets. Bivalves and gastropods are sold as shellfish. The third group of molluscs – the cephalopods – do not have shells; they include squid, octopuses, and cuttlefish.

Monaco

A dish consisting of poached fillets of sole covered in a sauce made with white wine, tomatoes, and mixed herbs and garnished with poached oysters and croutons in the shape of wolves' teeth. The name is also applied to a chicken consommé thickened with egg yolks and garnished with slices of bread powdered with sugar. The latter dish is similar to consommé Monte-Carlo (chicken consommé thickened with arrowroot, sprinkled with small pieces of Genoese cake made with cheese, and browned in the oven).

monasteries ABBAYES

In these privileged centres of religion, order, and culture, the monks combined the role of settlers, architects, stockbreeders, doctors, and hotel-keepers, and from the earliest times played an essential part in spreading knowledge of Christianity and its practices. In the field of food and gastronomy, three kinds of products owe much to the monastic orders: drink and alcohol, cheeses, and pastries. The monks were the first to plant vines, select suitable varieties, and perfect their cultivation, as evidenced in the Burgundian vineyards of Cistercian origin. As apothecaries, moreover, only the monks understood the uses of plants, from which they created many liqueurs (Chartreuse, Benedictine, Aiguebelle, etc.).

The monks also perfected techniques for ripening cheeses; among others, Saint-Paulin, Saint-Nectaire, Port-Salut, and Munster (from *monasterium* = monastery) may be mentioned.

The third category of product in which the religious orders specialized was pâtisserie – pastry- and cake-making. For example, gingerbread, *nonnettes* (small cakes of iced gingerbread), *oublies* (wafers), and *nieules* (small flat cakes from Flanders) go back to the Middle Ages; more recent products are *sacristains* (caramelized puff pastry twists), *religieuses* (a type of chocolate éclair), *jésuites* (small almond and praline pastries), and *pets-de-nonne* (soufflé fritters).

Finally, the monasteries patronized the fairs, one of the main objects of which was the sale of wine. As indicated by Raymond Dumay in his book *Du silex au barbecue*, published by Julliard: 'Living on their lands, producing their bread and wine, with the stimuli of travel and visits, and being observant, well-informed, and gluttonous, it was the monks who made the most genuine and constant contribution to the development of regional gastronomy.' The pilgrims were the first to know the good stopping places, and the

Guide de pèlerin à Saint-Jacques-de-Compostelle, written in 1150 by Aymery Picard, describes in great detail not only places to seek sanctuary, but also monasteries with a high standard of board and lodging.

Monbazillac

An AOC white wine from southwest France, produced on the left bank of the River Dordogne not far from Bergerac. It is made from the same grape and by the same methods as Sauternes. Monbazillac is a mellow dessert wine with a delicate bouquet.

monégasque (à la)

Describing a dish of cold stuffed tomatoes, served as an hors d'oeuvre. The tomatoes are hollowed out, seasoned with salt and pepper, dressed with oil and vinegar, then stuffed with a mixture of mayonnaise, pieces of tuna, chopped onions, mixed herbs, and (if desired) chopped hard-boiled (hard-cooked) eggs.

monkey SINGE

A mammal from tropical and subtropical regions, the arboreal, vegetarian, and fruit-eating varieties of which are edible. Monkeys form part of the staple diet of the Amazon forest tribes. In Casamance (Senegal), monkey meat is marinated in lime juice and cooked in a spicy stew like chicken. Ali-Bab thought macaque meat resembled squirrel, which is not a compliment, while Lévi-Strauss thought marmoset stew tasted like goose. The Baoulas of Central Africa eat roast monkey with a spicy groundnut (peanut) sauce. Finally, monkey brains are one of the 'eight treasures' of the Chinese cuisine of the mandarins. In Europe, however, the only gastronomic allusion to monkeys is in World War I slang, in which corned beef is called 'monkey meat'.

monkfish LOTTE DE MER

An ugly-looking sea fish, hence its French nicknames of *crapaud* (toad) or *diable de mer* (sea devil). It has an enormous head with a very large mouth and a scaleless brownish body. The head is unfamiliar to the consumer, because the fish is always sold as *queue de lotte* (monkfish tail), with the head removed.

Its flesh, which is lean, delicate, and firm, is prepared rather like meat (with a sauce, sautéed, grilled on skewers, or baked). There is very little waste, and the thick backbone is very easy to remove.

RECIPES

Escalopes of monkfish with creamed peppers ESCALOPES DE LOTTE À LA CRÈME DE POIVRON (from Pierre Poirier's recipe) Take 500 g (18 oz) thoroughly cleaned monkfish and cut into 8 small escalopes. Season with salt and pepper. Coat them with breadcrumbs, roll in 50 g (2 oz, ½ cup) grated Parmesan cheese, then brown in butter. Cut open 3 green peppers and remove the seeds. Blanch for about 10 minutes in boiling water, then cut into pieces and purée in a blender. Enrich the purée with about 60–75 g (2½–3 oz, 5–6 tablespoons) butter. Season with salt and pepper and add a dash of Worcestershire sauce. Place 2 escalopes of monkfish on each plate and surround them with a ribbon of the green pepper purée.

Fillets of monkfish à l'anglaise FILETS DE LOTTE À L'ANGLAISE Remove the backbone from the monkfish tail. Separate the 2 fillets; trim and flatten them lightly. Season with salt and pepper, then coat them with flour and dip in beaten egg and fresh breadcrumbs. Melt some butter in a frying pan (skillet) and fry the fillets until golden brown on both sides. Turn the heat down and cook for another 10 minutes. Arrange the fillets on a warm dish; serve with maître d'hôtel butter.

Fillets of monkfish braised in white wine FILETS DE LOTTE BRAISÉS AU VIN BLANC Remove the backbone from a monkfish tail (or from a piece cut from the middle of the fish) and separate the 2 fillets. Trim and flatten lightly. Season with salt and pepper. Arrange the fillets on a buttered roasting dish just big enough to hold them and half-cover them with reduced fish stock mixed with white wine. Bake them in an oven preheated to 220 c (425 f, gas 7) for 7–8 minutes. Turn the fillets over and bake for another 7–8 minutes, then cover with aluminium foil and bake for a further 5 minutes. Place them on a serving dish and keep warm. Add cream to the juices in the roasting dish and reduce until the sauce has thickened. Adjust the seasoning if necessary. Pour the sauce over the fish, sprinkle with chopped parsley, and serve very hot accompanied by braised spinach or puréed broccoli.

Fillets of monkfish with leeks and cream FILETS DE LOTTE À LA CRÈME ET AUX POIREAUX Clean 300 g (11 oz) leeks (the white part only), a stick (stalk) of celery, and 2 turnips. Peel 2 shallots. Shred all these vegetables finely. Melt 30 g (1 oz, 2 tablespoons) butter in a flameproof casserole, add the shredded vegetables, and cook until golden, stirring all the time; then cover and cook gently for about 5 minutes, until soft. Take some fillets of monkfish (about 1 kg, 2¼ lb) and place them on top of the vegetable mixture, then turn them over carefully in it. Add 2 more chopped shallots, a clove of garlic (also chopped), a small bouquet garni, 1 glass of dry white wine, 1 glass of water, and salt and pepper. Cover the casserole. When the mixture begins to boil, turn the heat down and simmer.

5 minutes before cooking is completed, add 250 g (9 oz, 2 cups) mushrooms which have been cleaned, chopped, sprinkled with lemon juice, and lightly fried in butter. Adjust the seasoning if necessary and cook until ready (the fish must remain slightly firm). Drain the fillets and keep them warm in a dish. Remove the bouquet garni from the casserole. Leave the juices on the heat and pour in 1.5 dl (¼ pint, ⅔ cup) cream. Reduce until the sauce is slightly thickened. Mix in another 30–50 g (1–2 oz, 2–4 tablespoons) butter, beating all the time. Pour this piping hot sauce over the fish.

Medallions of monkfish with a red-pepper sauce MÉDAILLONS DE LOTTE AU BEURRE DE POIVRON ROUGE (from Guy Savoy's recipe) Prepare a court-bouillon with water and white vinegar, 1 carrot and 1 onion (thinly sliced), a bouquet garni, and salt and pepper. Cook for 20 minutes. Cut a red pepper in half and remove the seeds.

Cook slowly in olive oil, in a covered saucepan, for 6 minutes, then press through a fine sieve.

Cut up 700 g (1½ lb) monkfish fillets into medallions 1 cm (½ in) thick. Soften 2 small chopped shallots in white wine and reduce until all the liquid is absorbed. Add 2 tablespoons double (heavy) cream and boil for 2 minutes, whisking all the time, then, over a low heat, incorporate 150 g (5 oz) butter, whisking all the time. Add the puréed pepper, season with salt and pepper, and add a squeeze of lemon juice.

Arrange the medallions well separated in a gratin dish. Season with pepper and salt. Pour the court-bouillon over the fish and simmer for 4 minutes over a low heat. Remove from the heat and drain. Arrange the medallions on a serving dish and coat with the sauce.

Monkfish pieces in cabbage leaves BOUCHÉES DE LOTTE AU CHOU NOUVEAU (from Nicole Cruaud's recipe) Prepare an aromatic court-bouillon flavoured with tarragon, fennel, thyme, rosemary, and a few fragments of bay leaf, plus the juice of 1 lemon. Remove the skin from 2 monkfish tails. Lift the fillets away and cut each one in two. Season with salt and pepper. Wash and drain 4 large inside leaves of a fresh young cabbage; roll each fillet up in a leaf. Bring the court-bouillon to the boil and steam the fillets for 10 minutes. Prepare a sauce with 300 g (11 oz) very ripe tomatoes (peeled, deseeded, and liquidized), a little lemon juice, salt, pepper, a pinch of sugar, and a few tarragon leaves. Serve the cabbage rolls on warm plates with the cold sauce.

Poached monkfish LOTTE POCHÉE Take a piece of monkfish cut from the middle of the fish and trim it thoroughly. Place in cold court-bouillon to which some white wine has been added. Bring this to the boil, skim, then turn the heat down, and leave to cook (the fish must remain slightly firm). Adjust the seasoning, then drain the fish, place it in a serving dish, and surround with quarters of lemon. Serve with melted butter well flavoured with lemon, or with a sauce for poached fish. It can also be served with a cream sauce mixed with a sorrel fondue.

Roast monkfish LOTTE RÔTIE Prepare a fondue of tomatoes. While this is cooking, fry some very small button mushrooms together with some chopped garlic in a little olive oil. Oil a roasting dish and place in it a piece of well-trimmed monkfish seasoned with salt and pepper. Bake in a hot oven (240 c, 475 f, gas 9) for 10 minutes, then reduce the heat to 200 c, 400 f, gas 6 and leave until cooked, basting from time to time. Serve the fish surrounded with mushrooms; the tomato fondue should be served separately.

monosodium glutamate

GLUTAMATE DE SODIUM

A seasoning used in Far Eastern and some Western cookery, developed in 1905 by a Japanese called Ikeda. Chemically extracted from the gluten of cereals, it is a common additive used to enhance the flavour of foodstuffs.

Monselet (Charles Pierre)

French journalist and author (born Nantes, 1825; died Paris, 1888). Of particular value among his numerous works is *La Cuisinière poétique* (1859), a work on which Dumas, Banville, and Gautier collaborated, among others. Every Sunday from 21 February to 1 August, 1858, Monselet published *Le Gourmet*, the gastronome's journal. This sheet was subsequently republished under the title of *Almanach des gourmands* (the title was borrowed from Grimod de La Reynière, whose work it endeavoured to continue). The *Almanach* appeared in 1861 and 1862 and then from 1866 to 1870. *Gastronomie* (1874), a collection of anecdotes and recipes, *Les Lettres gourmandes* (1877), and *Les Mois gastronomiques* (1880) complete his brilliant and witty gastronomical works. 'Gastronomy,' he once said, 'has been the joy of all peoples through the ages. It produces beauty and wit and goes hand in hand with goodness of heart and a consideration of others.'

A friend of numerous restaurateurs of his time, Monselet had many recipes containing artichokes and truffles dedicated to him, including poached oysters, steamed quarters of artichoke, and truffle slices on skewers, coated with Villeroi sauce and breadcrumbs, and fried; and an omelette filled with a salpicon of artichoke hearts and truffles simmered in cream, garnished with slices of truffles cooked in butter, and served with a well-reduced Madeira sauce. Various other rich dishes are also dedicated to him.

RECIPE

Partridge Monselet PERDREAU MONSELET Trim a partridge and stuff it with foie gras to which a truffle salpicon has been added. Truss it, season with salt and pepper, and brown in a small heavy casserole. Cover and cook in a low oven. After about 15 minutes, add 2 thin slices of artichoke hearts which have been tossed in lemon and butter. Allow to cook for about a further 15 minutes. Cut a truffle into small dice and add to the casserole. Add 2 tablespoons (3 tablespoons) warmed brandy and set alight. Serve in the casserole.

Montagné (Prosper)

French chef (born Carcassonne, 1864; died Sèvres, 1948). Son of a hotelier from Carcassonne, he was to have studied architecture but adopted his father's occupation when his parents opened a hotel in Toulouse. He worked his way up through the kitchens of the most famous establishments in Paris, Cauterets, San Remo, and Monte Carlo. He then returned to Paris, where he became chef first at the Pavillon d'Armenonville, then at Ledoyen, and finally at the Grand Hotel (where he had had his first job), finishing there as head chef. It was then that he published his first culinary work, with Prosper Salles, *La Grande Cuisine illustrée* (1900), to be followed by the *Grand Livre de la cuisine* (1929). With Dr Gottschalk, he published the *Larousse gastronomique*, the first edition of which dates from 1938. Among his other works are *La Cuisine fine* (1913), *Le Trésor de la cuisine du Bassin méditerranéan, le Festin occitan* (1929), and *Cuisine avec et sans ticket* (1941).

During World War I Montagné organized the kitchens of the Allied armies. After the war he visited the

United States, where he was adviser to the management of the Chicago abattoirs. He then returned to Paris and opened a restaurant in the Rue de l'Échelle, which was considered by some to provide the best fare in the whole of France and was frequented by celebrities during the 1920s. Here he created numerous dishes, but management difficulties forced him to close this establishment. In addition to this Prosper Montagné organized the first Concours de Cuisine and several gastronomic exhibitions. His name will live on, thanks largely to the Club Prosper Montagné, an association of gastronomes and professionals founded by René Morand in memory of the master. See also *Mont-Bry*.

Montagny

An AOC white Burgundy wine from the Côte Chalonnaise. The wines, made from the Chardonnay grape, can be very good, though not great, and the monks of Cluny are supposed to have enjoyed them. They usually represent excellent value, now that the white wines of the Côte de Beaune tend to be expensive.

Montbazon

A garnish for chicken, comprising lightly fried lambs' sweetbreads, quenelles, mushroom heads, and slices of truffle.

mont-blanc

A cold dessert made of vanilla-flavoured chestnut purée, topped with a dome of Chantilly cream and decorated. Alternatively, the cream may be surrounded by a border of sweetened chestnut purée and mounted on a base of sablé pastry or meringue.

RECIPES

Mont-blanc Shell 1 kg (2¼ lb) chestnuts and simmer them until soft in 1 litre (1¾ pints, 4¼ cups) milk with 150 g (5 oz, ⅔ cup) sugar, a pinch of salt, and a vanilla pod (bean) split in two. Press the chestnuts through a potato ricer and pack the vermicelli-like chestnut purée into a buttered ring mould. Refrigerate for at least 30 minutes. Whip 4 dl (14 fl oz, 1¾ cups) fresh cream together with 1 teaspoon vanilla sugar and 30 g (1 oz,

¼ cup) icing (confectioners') sugar to make Chantilly cream. Turn the chestnut ring out onto a dish and fill the centre with the Chantilly cream. Decorate with pieces of marrons glacés and crystallized (candied) violets. Refrigerate until served.

Mont-Bry

The pseudonym of Prosper Montagné, used to name various dishes which he created or which were dedicated to him. The Mont-Bry garnish for small cuts of meat consists of little cakes of spinach purée bound with Parmesan cheese and cep mushrooms cooked in cream; the meat pan juices are deglazed with white wine and thickened veal stock and used as a sauce.

RECIPES

Fritters Mont-Bry BEIGNETS MONT-BRY Prepare sweetened semolina as for a dessert, let it cool down, and spread it on a buttered metal sheet in a layer 1 cm (½ in) thick. When completely cold, cut it into small rectangles 4 × 5 cm (1½ × 2 in). Boil down some apricot jam mixed with rum until reduced by half, then add a fine salpicon of walnuts and figs. Coat half the semolina rectangles with this mixture and cover with the remaining rectangles. Dip into batter and deep-fry (at 175 c, 315 F). Drain on absorbent paper, dust with caster (super-fine) sugar, and serve very hot.

Soles meunière Mont-Bry (from Philéas Gilbert's recipe) Prepare in advance 200 g (7 oz) fresh finely cut noodles. Scald, peel, and deseed 6 tomatoes, then crush them to remove any liquid. Chop a medium-sized onion and brown in butter. Add the crushed tomatoes, a pinch of salt, a pinch of caster (superfine) sugar, and a small amount of crushed garlic; cover and cook slowly.

Then prepare 3 sole of about 300 g (11 oz) each. Remove the brown skin and carefully detach the fillets from the backbone. Season the fillets with salt and pepper, roll them in flour, and cook in clarified butter in a frying pan (skillet) until golden brown on both sides.

Using another frying pan, sauté the noodles in 5–6 tablespoons (½ cup)

clarified butter until they are lightly browned and slightly crisp. Place the sole fillets in a hot long serving dish, sprinkle with lemon juice and chopped parsley, and arrange the tomato mixture around them. Pile mounds of noodles at each end of the dish. Baste the fish copiously with noisette butter, which should be bubbling and frothy.

Mont-d'Or

A French cheese made from goats' milk, a mixture of cows' and goats' milk, or (now increasingly common) from cows' milk only. Containing 45% fat, it is a soft cheese with a crust which is slightly blue with a hint of red in it. The best Mont-d'Or is made in the region around Lyon and is becoming rare. Sold in the form of small discs, 8–9 cm (3–3½ in) in diameter and 1.5 cm (½ in) thick, it has a delicate flavour, like that of a mature Saint-Marcellin. It is at its best in winter, eaten with Beaujolais. (Mont-d'Or cheese should not be confused with the Mont-d'Or Vacherin.)

Mont-Dore

A method of preparing potatoes. The potatoes are puréed and mixed with egg yolks (and often cream) and grated cheese. The mixture is piled into a dome shape on a gratin dish, sprinkled again with grated cheese, and put in the oven to brown.

monter

A French culinary term meaning to give body to or to increase in volume. Egg whites, fresh cream, and meringues or other sweet mixtures are whisked to increase their volume (by incorporating air) and thickness.

In making hot emulsified sauces, egg yolks are whisked over a low heat until the mixture has become thick and mousse-like. Egg yolks are whisked with fat or oil when making cold or hot emulsions (e.g. béarnaise sauce or mayonnaise).

The term is also used for stirring small amounts of butter into a sauce to make it smoother or creamier.

Montglas

A salpicon dedicated to the Marquis of Montglas, an 18th-century French diplomat. It consists of shredded pickled tongue, poached mushrooms, foie gras, and truffles bound with thick Madeira sauce. (Less frequently, the tongue and mushrooms are replaced by poached lambs' sweetbreads and cocks' combs and kidneys and the mixture is bound with a Madeira-flavoured demi-glace sauce.) The salpicon is used to fill bouchées, which are then garnished with strips of foie gras and truffle.

Lamb chops Montglas are cooked on one side, covered with this salpicon and breadcrumbs, browned in the oven, and surrounded with a border of demi-glace sauce. Lambs' sweetbreads and chicken Montglas are braised and covered with their deglazed pan juices mixed with the salpicon.

Monthélie

AOC Burgundies from the Côte de Beaune. They are mostly red wines though some white is made and also some sparkling white wines. The still wines may be labelled Monthélie or Monthélie-Côte-de-Beaune-Villages. The Monthélie wines are akin to those of neighbouring Volnay but are usually cheaper.

Montilla

Wines from near Córdoba in southern Spain that slightly resemble sherry, although they have their own specific controls. They are traditionally made in huge earthenware jars and range in style from very dry and light to rich and luscious. They may be naturally as alcoholic as the most alcoholic table wines and so do not always require fortification.

Montlouis

AOC white Touraine wines, still or sparkling, from the south bank of the River Loire, opposite Vouvray. Like the wines of Vouvray, they are made from the Chenin Blanc grape.

Montmartre

A tiny vineyard surviving in the heart of Paris, where formerly much wine was produced. When the vintage (about 400 bottles annually) is sold, the proceeds go to charity. In 1961 vines from certain famous Bordeaux estates were planted here.

Montmorency

The name given to various savoury or sweet dishes that include the sour Montmorency cherries. Duck Montmorency, cooked with herbs in a frying pan (skillet), is garnished with stoned (pitted) cherries poached in a Bordeaux wine; the sauce is made by deglazing the pan with cherry brandy and adding strained veal stock. The classic gâteau called Montmorency is a Genoese sponge topped with cherries in syrup and covered with Italian Meringue; the top is decorated with glacé or crystallized (candied) cherries. The ice creams, bombes, iced mousses, croûtes, tarts, and tartlets called Montmorency all include cherries, which may be fresh, crystallized, or macerated in brandy.

There are, however, other dishes in classic cookery dedicated to the Montmorency family, which do not include cherries. For example, the Montmorency garnish for cuts of meat consists of artichoke hearts stuffed with balls of glazed carrot and balls of noisette potatoes.

RECIPES

Bombe glacée Montmorency
Coat a bombe mould with Kirsch ice (see *ices and ice creams*). Prepare a bombe mixture flavoured with cherry brandy and add cherries macerated in Kirsch. Fill the mould with this. Finish off the bombe in the usual way (see *bombe glacée*).

Gâteau Montmorency Separate the yolks from the whites of 3 eggs. Whisk the 3 yolks with 60 g (2 oz, ½ cup) ground almonds and 125 g (4½ oz, scant ⅔ cup) caster (superfine) sugar. Drain 400 g (14 oz) cherries in syrup, cut them in two, stone them, and roll them in flour. Incorporate 60 g (2 oz, ½ cup) flour and the cherries into the almond mixture, then carefully fold in the 3 egg whites stiffly whisked with a pinch of salt. Pour the mixture into a buttered cake tin and bake in the oven at 200 c (400 F, gas 6) for about 30 minutes. Turn the cake out onto a rack and allow to cool.

Melt 200 g (7 oz) fondant over a low heat, stirring all the time. Add a liqueur glass of Kirsch and 2–3 drops of cochineal (red food colouring). Spread the fondant over the cake with a spatula and decorate with 12 glacé (candied) cherries and a few pieces of angelica.

Alternatively, the cake may be cut into 2 layers, steeped in Kirsch, and sandwiched together with butter cream mixed with cherries in brandy.

Montpensier

The name given to various savoury or sweet dishes that may have been dedicated to the Duchesse de Montpensier (1627–93), but were more probably dedicated to the fifth son of Louis Philippe. Gâteau Montpensier is a Genoese sponge enriched with ground almonds, raisins, and crystallized (candied) fruit. By extension, cakes cooked in a tin lined with the ingredient which gives them their flavour are termed *à la Montpensier*.

The Montpensier garnish for small cuts of meat and poultry consists of artichoke hearts, asparagus, tips, sliced truffles, and Madeira sauce.

RECIPES

Gâteau Montpensier Steep 50 g (2 oz, ⅓ cup) crystallized (candied) fruit and 50 g (2 oz, ⅓ cup) sultanas (seedless white raisins) in 1 dl (6 tablespoons, scant ½ cup) rum. With the fingertips, work 125 g (4½ oz, generous cup) flour with 80 g (3 oz, 6 tablespoons) butter cut into small pieces. Beat 7 egg yolks with 125 g (4½ oz, scant ⅔ cup) caster (superfine) sugar until the mixture is white, then mix in 100 g (4 oz, 1 cup) ground almonds and finally 3 stiffly whisked egg whites. Drain the fruit and sultanas then add them to the mixture, together with the flour-and-butter mixture. Work briskly with a wooden spoon for a short time.

Butter a 2-cm (8½-in) cake tin (mould) and sprinkle it with 50 g (2 oz, ½ cup) sliced almonds. Pour the mixture into the tin and bake for 30 minutes in a preheated oven at 200 c (400 F, gas 6). Turn out the cake onto a rack and allow to cool. Melt 150 g (5 oz, ½ cup) apricot jam over a low heat, strain, and spread over the surface of the cake. Keep cold until serving.

Noisettes of lamb Montpensier
NOISETTES D'AGNEAU MONTPEN-
SIER Braise some asparagus tips in
butter and fry as many round slices of
bread as there are noisettes. Fry some
coarsely shredded truffles in butter.
Sauté the noisettes briskly in the same
butter, place them on the slices of fried
bread, sprinkle with the truffles, and
keep hot. Mix the pan juices with
Madeira, thicken with a little arrowroot
mixed with 1 tablespoon stock, and
pour over the noisettes. Garnish with
the asparagus tips and serve very hot.

Montrachet

One of the most famous of all white
Burgundies, produced by two parishes
in the Côte de Beaune, Puligny-
Montrachet and Chassagne-Montrachet. It is made from the Chardonnay
grape and usually achieves great
distinction. However, the specific vineyard (*climat*) is tiny and the wine is
therefore scarce and expensive.

Montravel

AOC white wines, some of which are
dryish and others slightly sweet, from
vineyards on the right bank of the River
Dordogne, about 80 miles east of Bordeaux. The red wines of the region are
AOC Bergerac.

Montreuil

A garnish for beefsteaks and other small
cuts of meat consisting of artichoke
hearts braised in butter and stuffed with
garden peas and tiny balls of glazed
carrot. Poached fish Montreuil are covered with white wine sauce and garnished with balls of boiled potato coated
with a shrimp velouté sauce.

Montrouge

The name given to various dishes which
include cultivated mushrooms. They are
so called because of the mushroom beds
which used to be at Montrouge, near the
gates of Paris.

RECIPE

Croquettes Montrouge Prepare a dry
mushroom duxelles and add half its
volume of chopped ham and a third of
its volume of bread soaked in milk and
then dried. Add some chopped parsley

and 2 egg yolks (for 250 g (9 oz) mixture), mix well, and season to taste.
Shape the preparation into balls the size
of tangerines. Flatten them slightly, coat
with egg and breadcrumbs, and fry in
very hot fat. Drain on absorbent paper
and sprinkle with fine salt.

moorhen POULE D'EAU

A black water bird, living by lakes and
ponds. It used to be considered suitable
for eating during Lent by the Catholic
Church, but its dark dry flesh has a
rather strong and somewhat muddy
flavour. Before cooking, it should be
skinned and singed to remove the sub-
cutaneous oil. Then it can be prepared
like chicken chasseur or casseroled with
strips of bacon.

moque

A kind of earthenware cup used as a
measure for liquids, particularly in
northern France. Cider is traditionally
served in a moque.

moques

A speciality of Belgian (Ghent) pâtisserie. A fat sausage of pastry made with
brown sugar and cloves is rolled in
granulated sugar, cut into thick slices,
and cooked in a slow oven.

moray MURÈNE

A large eel, up to 1.3 m (4 ft) long, found
in warm and tropical seas. It is dark
brown with yellow and black markings
and its wide mouth is armed with several rows of strong pointed teeth; its bite is
poisonous. The flesh of the moray is
fatty but fairly delicate and boneless.
The Romans bred morays in fishponds
and are said to have fed them on live
slaves; this fish continued to be regarded
as a delicacy until the Renaissance and
history relates that Henry I of England
died from indigestion caused by eating
moray. Today, moray is hardly ever
found except in certain markets in the
south of France. It is eaten cold with
garlic mayonnaise and included in
bouillabaisse, but it may also be prepared in all the same ways as eel.

Morbier

A French cows'-milk cheese (45% fat
content) from Franche-Comté. Maturing in two to three months, it is a firm

cheese with a natural light-grey or slightly orange crust and a firm creamy paste with a dark horizontal line running through the middle of it. It should have a fairly strong flavour. Morbier is disc-shaped, 35–40 cm (14–16 in) in diameter and 8 cm (3 in) thick. It is traditionally made by superimposing the curd obtained from the evening's milking on that obtained from the morning's milking, with a protective layer of fat between them. Morbier (named after a commune in the Jura) is particularly good in the spring, the result of the winter's production from the chalets of the foothills.

morel MORILLE

A very tasty but rare mushroom which is found in the spring. Its globular or conical cap is deeply furrowed in a honeycomb pattern, and therefore the morel must be very carefully cleaned to get rid of any earth, sand, or insects which may be inside. This can be done either by rinsing the mushroom several times in water and then draining it or by cleaning the cap with a fine brush so as not to destroy its delicate scent. Morels with dark caps (from dark brown to black) are the most highly prized ones. The paler (*blonde*) variety is less tasty, and mushrooms with a longer stalk and a conical cap are regarded as inferior.

All morels should be well cooked. A classic dish is morels braised in butter, the pan juices being thickened with fresh cream or deglazed with Madeira. They can also be cooked *au gratin*, used in a forestière garnish for omelettes, chicken, red meat, or calves' sweetbreads, or as a seasoning for soups and sauces. Morels may be preserved *au naturel*, in oil, or by drying.

RECIPES

Chicken oysters with morels SOT-L'Y-LAISSE AUX MORILLES (from Jean-Claude Ferrero's recipe) Carefully wash 4–5 morels and split them in two lengthwise. Dredge 6–8 chicken oysters with flour and fry briskly in 25 g (1 oz, 2 tablespoons) butter in a shallow pan together with 1 chopped shallot. When golden brown, season with salt and pepper and add the morels. Cover the pan and cook gently for 7–8 minutes, then add 1 dl (6 tablespoons, scant ½ cup) Sauvignon and finish the cooking with the lid off. (A little grated nutmeg will further improve the flavour.) Add 1 tablespoon double (heavy) cream and cook for another 10–12 minutes. Serve in a hot dish.

Morel creams GÂTEAUX DE MORILLES (from Daniel Metery's recipe) Wash 250 g (9 oz) morels 6 or 7 times in water and vinegar. Peel and dice 150 g (5 oz, 1¼ cups) courgettes (zucchini), season with salt and pepper, and brown them briskly in butter for 2 minutes. Then brown the morels (seasoned with salt and pepper) for 3 minutes in butter, and add 2 tablespoons (3 tablespoons) meat extract, half a shallot (finely chopped), 5 cl (2 fl oz, ¼ cup) white wine, and 4 cl (2 tablespoons, 3 tablespoons) brandy. Remove the morels from the pan and cut them into small pieces. Wash and finely chop 100 g (4 oz, 1 cup) leeks and season with salt and pepper. Cook slowly in butter in a covered pan for 10 minutes then allow to cool. Dice 2 preserved duck gizzards.

Mix the morels, courgettes, and leeks in a salad bowl. Add the diced gizzards, 3 beaten eggs, and 4 dl (14 fl oz, 1¾ cups) double (heavy) cream and season with salt and pepper. Butter 6 oval dariole moulds, fill them with the mixture, and cook in a moderate oven (180 C, 350 F, gas 4) in a bain-marie for 30 minutes.

For the sauce, add 2 small chopped shallots to 1.5 dl (¼ pint, ⅔ cup) white wine and boil down to reduce. Add 5 tablespoons (6 tablespoons) crushed tomatoes, then reduce a little more. Enrich the sauce with 30 g (1 oz, 2 tablespoons) butter and season with salt and pepper. Cover the bottom of a serving dish with sauce. Turn out the creams into the dish and sprinkle with fresh mint.

Morels à la crème MORILLES À LA CRÈME Clean 250 g (9 oz) morels. Wash them briskly in cold water and dry them thoroughly. Leave them whole if they are small, cut them up if they are large. Put the morels in a shallow frying pan (skillet) with 1 tablespoon butter, 1 teaspoon lemon juice, 1 teaspoon chopped shallots, salt, and pepper. Braise for

5 minutes, then cover with very hot cream and reduce until the sauce has thickened. Just before serving, add 1 tablespoon fresh cream and some chopped parsley.

Morels in herb sauce SAUCE AROMATIQUE AUX MORILLES (from Carême's recipe) Put into a saucepan a pinch of rosemary, sage, thyme, and basil, a quarter of a bay leaf, a clove, a little coarsely ground peper, and a little grated nutmeg. Add a shredded onion and a ladle of good consommé and simmer for a few minutes, then strain through coarse muslin (cheesecloth). Add about 30 cleaned morels to the strained liquid and bring it to the boil, pour in some thick allemande sauce, and reduce. Just before serving, add a little chicken stock, a little fine butter, some lemon juice, and 1 tablespoon chopped and blanched chervil.

Morey-Saint-Denis

A red Burgundy, or more rarely a white wine, from the Côte de Nuits. The *grands crus* of the parish are sold under their own names: Clos de la Roche, Clos Saint-Denis, Clos de Tart and Les Bonnes Mares (the greater part of the latter being in the parish of Chambolle-Musigny). Morey-Saint-Denis is between Gevrey-Chambertin in the north and Chambolle-Musigny in the south. Its wines sometimes possess the vigour of the former and the delicacy of the latter. The Clos de Tart is perhaps the most famous name.

Morgon

One of the *crus* of the Beaujolais region and possibly the only one that is capable of attaining some age in the bottle.

Mornay

A béchamel sauce enriched with egg yolks and flavoured with grated Gruyère cheese. It is used to coat dishes to be glazed under the grill (broiler) or browned in the oven, including poached eggs, fish, shellfish, vegetables, filled pancakes, etc. The invention of this sauce and its use is attributed to Joseph Voiron, chef of the restaurant Durand at the end of the 19th century, who is thought to have dedicated it to the cook Mornay, his eldest son.

RECIPES

Fillets of sole Moray FILETS DE SOLE MORNAY Season some fillets of sole with salt and pepper, place them in a buttered dish, spoon over a little fish stock, and poach gently in the oven for about 7–8 minutes, until cooked. Drain them and arrange in a buttered gratin dish, cover with Mornay sauce, sprinkle with grated Parmesan cheese and clarified butter, and brown in a very hot oven.

Mornay sauce SAUCE MORNAY Heat ½ litre (17 fl oz, 2 cups) béchamel sauce. Add 70 g (3 oz, ¾ cup) grated Gruyère cheese and stir until all the cheese has melted. Take the sauce from the heat and add 2 egg yolks beaten with 1 tablespoon milk. Bring slowly to the boil, whisking all the time. Remove from the heat and add 2 tablespoons (3 tablespoons) cream (the sauce must be thick and creamy). For browning at a high temperature or for a lighter sauce the egg yolks are omitted. If the sauce is to accompany fish, reduced fish cooking stock is added.

Soft-boiled (*or poached*) **eggs Mornay** OEUFS MOLLETS (OU POCHÉS) MORNAY Soft-boil or poach some eggs. Remove the crusts from some round slices of bread (one for each egg) and fry in butter. Prepare a Mornay sauce (see recipe above). Place each egg on a slice of fried bread in a buttered gratin dish. Coat generously with Mornay sauce, sprinkle with grated cheese and melted butter, and brown in a very hot oven.

Moroccan cookery

See *North Africa*.

Moroccan wines

VINS DE MAROC

Vines have been grown and wine made in Morocco since the time of the Roman Empire. In the 8th century, when the country was officially Islamic, the vineyards fell into disuse, except for those growing grapes for the table. Morocco has begun to produce wine again in the 20th century, but the better profit derived from other fruit crops has hampered much development. Red, white, and rosé wines are made, and also some that are referred to as *vins gris* on account of their pale pink tones. Those wines that are exported provide pleasant inexpensive drinking, but red wines used for blending form a more important part of the export trade.

mortadella

A lightly smoked Italian sausage served cold and very thinly sliced as an hors d'oeuvre. A speciality of Bologna, it has a basis of meat (pure pork, pork and beef, or veal and ham) or a mixture of meat and offal and is flavoured in various ways, particularly with parsley; originally it included myrtle (*mortella* in Italian), hence its name. (Another etymology suggests that the word is derived from *mortaio della carne*, a reference to the mortar used for pounding the meat.) It is also studded with pistachios or green olives. 15 cm (6 in) in diameter, it appears in cross section as a fine light-coloured paste, dotted with diced fat. The first recipe, dating from 1484, was given in *Du plaisir honnête et de la santé* by Platina. Later on a variety of recipes were devised, not only in Italy but also in Bavaria, Lyon, Paris, etc.

mortar MORTIER

A bowl made of wood, earthenware, marble, or stone in which foods are pounded or ground to a paste or powder using a pestle. Mortars have been used in cookery since ancient times. In the Middle Ages and earlier herbs and spices were pounded in mortars of hard stone, which were also used to crush garlic, buckwheat, beans, and pulses. In rural areas salt was still ground in granite mortars as recently as the 19th century, and in Provence mortars made of olive wood are still used for emulsifying *aïoli* (garlic mayonnaise) and pounding aromatic herbs with oil.

The mortar has gradually been replaced by food processors and vegetable mills or rendered superfluous by the increase in the number of products which are sold in powder form. But it remains very useful for certain preparations, such as forcemeats and flavoured butters, as well as for aïoli and *brandade* (pounded salt cod). It is still a basic kitchen utensil in India (for spices and lentil flour), Africa (for manioc and millet), and Central America (for cornmeal).

morvandelle (à la)

Describing various preparations which include raw Morvan ham, particularly potée, omelette, baked eggs, tripe, and veal cutlets.

RECIPE

Omelette à la morvandelle   Dice 125 g (4 oz, generous ½ cup) raw Morvan ham and fry it lightly in butter. Beat 8 eggs as for an omelette, season with pepper, and add the ham. Cook the omelette in the usual way. Garnish with small thin slices of Morvan ham heated gently in butter and rolled up into cornets.

mosaic   MOSAÏQUE

In charcuterie, a decoration on the top of a terrine or a galantine using ingredients of various colours cut into circles, squares, stars, etc.

In pâtisserie, a mosaic is a round Genoese sponge, filled with butter cream, glazed with apricot jam, and iced (frosted) with white fondant. The top is decorated with apricot and redcurrant jam piped in parallel lines and scored with crossing lines, using the tip of a knife.

moscovite

Any of various cold moulded desserts similar to Bavarian cream. Moscovites were originally iced desserts made in special sealed domed hexagonal moulds (*moules à moscovite*). Today the name is given to a Bavarian cream containing fruit, a plombières ice cream, or a chilled sponge cake soaked in Kirsch and topped with a dome of ice cream or fruits mixed with cream.

moscovite (à la)

Describing various preparations inspired by Russian cookery or perfected by French chefs who had worked in Russia in the 19th century. Salmon *à la moscovite* is poached whole, cooled, skinned, covered with jellied mayonnaise, garnished with slices of truffle, hard-boiled (hard-cooked) eggs, and blanched tarragon leaves, and finally glazed with aspic. The garnish includes artichoke hearts stuffed with Russian salad and halves of hard-boiled eggs filled with caviar. Sauce *à la moscovite*, served with game, is a poivrade sauce to which pine kernels, sultanas (seedless white raisins), and juniper berries have been added. Consommé *à la moscovite*, based on sturgeon and cucumber, is garnished with a julienne of Russian mushrooms (*gribouis*) and diced *vésiga* (sturgeon's spinal marrow). Eggs *á la moscovite* are poached and served either cold with Russian salad or hot with sauerkraut.

Moselle or Mosel

Wines from the River Moselle and its tributaries, the Saar and Ruwer. The vineyard extends from Germany into Lusembourg and also into the Lorraine region of France, where the River Moselle flows. The Luxembourg and Lorraine wines can be very pleasant, but are seldom outstanding. The German wines, notably those made from the Riesling grape, can be great and the vineyards are spectacular, very steep and presenting a remarkable panorama because of the winding of the river. The German Moselles are all white wines and can range from light and dry to very sweet. Some sparkling wines are also produced.

mouclade

In Aunis and Saintonge, a preparation of cultured mussels cooked in white wine with shallots and parsley and coated with their cooking liquid enriched with cream and butter and thickened with egg yolks or cornflour (cornstarch).

RECIPE

Mussel-farmers' mouclade MOUC-LADE DES BOUCHOLEURS (from Guy Épaillard's recipe) Clean and wash 2 kg (4½ lb) mussels. Toss them in a saucepan over a brisk heat until they open. Remove the empty shells and place the ones containing the mussels in a dish; keep hot over a saucepan of boiling water. Strain the juice from the mussels through a fine sieve. Finely chop a clove of garlic and a sprig of parsley and blend with 100 g (4 oz, ½ cup)

butter. Warm the mussel juice in a saucepan over a gentle heat. Add the flavoured butter, a pinch of curry (or saffron), a pinch of powdered celery seed, a dash of pepper, and the mussels. Stir well, then simmer for 5 minutes. Sprinkle with 1 teaspoon cornflour (cornstarch), stir well, and simmer for 2 minutes. Add 1.5 dl (¼ pint, ⅔ cup) fresh cream and serve.

mouflon

A wild sheep, ancestor of the domestic sheep, which is still found in Corsica and Sardinia (other species exist in Asia Minor and Canada). Its strongly flavoured flesh must be marinated for a long time before being roasted or cooked in a ragout or a civet.

mouillette

A small finger-shaped piece of fresh or toasted bread which is dipped into the yolk of a soft-boiled egg and then eaten (the white is then eaten with a small spoon). The fingers of bread can be buttered and dipped in finely chopped parsley, tarragon, or chervil, or small steamed asparagus tips can be used instead of bread.

moulds and tins MOULES

A mould is a hollow receptacle that holds a preparation in a certain shape while it sets or is baked so that it retains this shape when turned out. In France, tins for cooking cakes and pastries are also referred to as moulds. Moulds can be tall, shallow, shaped, plain, or with patterned indentations. Porcelain or glass moulds are used where heat or cold retention is an important factor, but most moulds are made of metal because of its quick reaction to heat change. The variety is enormous, so the following list covers only a selection of those most commonly used in pâtisserie, baking, desserts, and charcuterie.

☐ **General moulds and tins**

• Decorative moulds: made of copper lined with tin, aluminium, glass, porcelain, for jellies and mousses, both sweet and savoury; may be tall or shallow. They are often in the shape of fish or fruit to indicate the main ingredient of the dish.

• Pie moulds: made of tinned steel or aluminium. They may be oblong or oval with hinged sides or loose sides which clip together for easy unmoulding.

• Deep cake tins: made from tinned steel or aluminium with either a fixed or a loose base. Some Continental cake tins are adjustable rings of metal, which have to be placed on a baking sheet for use. The sides are 5–9 cm (2–3½ in) deep. Deep cake tins are available in a wide range of sizes and may be round, square, hexagonal, or heart-, number-, or letter-shaped. Deep cake tins should be lined with greaseproof (waxed) paper.

• Shallow cake tins: made from tinned steel or aluminium, sometimes with a nonstick coating. They are available in a large variety of shapes and sizes, round, square, oblong, and heart-shaped being the most common. The sides are 1–5 cm (½–2 in) deep. The base of shallow cake tins should be lined with greaseproof paper.

• Loaf tins and bread moulds: made from steel, tinned steel, ovenproof glass, or earthenware. They can be oblong or round.

• Small cake tins (patty tins): made from tinned steel or aluminium, in the form of trays containing six, nine, or twelve indentations with rounded or sloping sides. Some have special shapes for baking particular items, such as éclairs or madeleines.

• Flan dishes: made from tinned steel, aluminium, or porcelain. The metal ones often have loose bases. They are usually round but can be square, oblong, or oval. The sides slope and may be fluted. They come in several sizes ranging from 7.5 cm (3 in) to 38 cm (15 in).

• Ring moulds: made from aluminium, porcelain, and ovenproof glass. They can be deep or shallow, plain or decorated. They are used for cakes, sweet or savoury mousses, and jellied desserts.

□ **Moulds and tins for special purposes**

• Confectionery moulds: made of tin, plastic, or rubber, either individual or in 'mats'. They are small decorative moulds for making chocolates and fondants.

• Chocolate moulds: made of tinned steel in two halves for easy unmoulding and held together by clips. They are usually in the shape of animals, eggs, or figures for making festive hollow chocolate novelties.

• Ice-cream moulds: made of tinned steel or copper with a lid, for making iced bombes and layered iced desserts. They can be conical, square, or shaped like a bombe.

• Cheese moulds: made of plastic, aluminium, stainless steel, porcelain, or glazed earthenware, in various shapes and sizes. They have holes in the bottom and sometimes in the sides as well for releasing whey when moulding soft cheeses or cheese-based desserts, such as paskha.

• Charlotte mould: made from aluminium, tinned steel or copper, or ovenproof glass. The shape is deep and round with slightly sloping sides and two small handles. The sloping sides facilitate the lining of the sides of the mould with fingers of bread or sponge. These moulds can also be used for Bavarian creams.

• Butter moulds: made of wood, which should be dampened before use. They can be trough-shaped, to take a large slab of butter, or small and cylindrical in shape, with a decorative plunger, for individual butter pats.

• Shortbread mould: a wooden mould usually engraved with a thistle pattern in which the shortbread dough is rolled to shape it before being turned out onto a baking sheet for cooking.

• Savarin mould: made from tinned steel or aluminium. It is a shallow ring mould with a smooth rounded base in large or individual sizes for rum babas and savarins.

• Kugelhopf mould: made from tinned steel or aluminium. It is a deep ring mould with heavy patterning.

• Brioche tin: made from steel or tinned steel in large or individual sizes. It is deeply fluted.

• Barquette tins: tinned steel boat-shaped tins in various sizes from 3.5–13 cm (1.5–5 in) used for sweet and savoury pastries.

• Cream horn mould: tinned steel conical-shaped mould for forming individual pastry shapes for pâtisserie.

• Tartlet tins: tinned steel fluted individual tins in various shapes for petits fours and pâtisserie.

• Croquembouche tin: conical-shaped stainless steel tin which is filled with tiny caramel-dipped choux buns. When the caramel is set the tin is removed to leave an impressive cake, which is served at festive occasions in France.

• Manqué mould (*moule à manqué*): made from aluminium or tinned steel. It is the classic French cake tin, 18–23 cm (7–9 in) in diameter; the sides are about 5 cm (2 in) deep and slope slightly to give the turned-out cake an attractive shape.

• Dariole mould: made from tinned steel or aluminium. It is a small flowerpot-shaped mould used to make individual steam puddings, small cakes, timbales, and savoury or sweet mousses.

• Swiss (jelly) roll tin: made from aluminium or tinned steel. It is an oblong tin, 1.5 cm (¾ in) deep.

Moulin-à-Vent

One of the Beaujolais regions, where the wines can achieve considerable quality and, unlike most Beaujolais, can age for a longish period in certain vintages.

Moulis

A vineyard region in the Médoc area of Bordeaux, making wines capable of achieving subtlety and finesse.

mounjetado

A dish of haricot (navy) beans cooked *à la languedocienne*: a speciality of Saint-Gaudens and Montréjeau. Haricot beans are a typical product of the region. Traditionally, on Monday mornings, an earthenware pot filled with *mounjetos* (beans) was placed in the hearth; part of it was eaten in the evening and the remainder was reheated the following day – and sometimes the day after – with onions. The addition of pork rinds transformed this dish of beans into *mounjetado*, a kind of poor man's cassoulet. The order of the Tastos Mounjetos du Comminges was created to promote the quality of the bean and the gastronomy of Saint-Gaudens.

mourtayrol or mourtaïrol

In the Rouergue region of France, a saffron-flavoured soup with a chicken-stock base, also called *tusset*. In the Auvergne, mourtayrol is a hearty stew containing beef, ham, chicken, and all kinds of vegetables; the addition of saffron is its distinguishing feature. This dish is prepared in particular for Easter, when it is also called *mortier*. After the meat has been cooked, the stock from the mourtayrol is poured into a stewpan lined with slices of stale farmhouse bread, where it must simmer for half an hour before being served as soup; the meat and vegetables are served together to follow it.

moussaka

A dish common to Turkey, Greece, and the Balkans, made with slices of aubergine (eggplant) arranged in layers, alternating with chopped mutton, onions, and aubergine pulp, often with the addition of a thick béchamel sauce. Moussaka is cooked in a round dish or mould lined with aubergine skins and is served, either in the dish or turned out, with tomato fondue.

| RECIPE

Moussaka Cut 5 aubergines (eggplants) in half lengthwise. Lightly score the pulp with a knife, without piercing the skin, and arrange them in a gratin dish. Sprinkle each half with 1 tablespoon oil and cook for about 15 minutes in the oven at 200 c (400 f, gas 6). Then remove the pulp (reserving the skins) with a spoon and chop it with 2 large peeled onions, a bunch of parsley, and 2 cloves of garlic. Mix with 3 tablespoons (¼ cup) very thick tomato sauce, 750 g (1¾ lb) chopped navarin of mutton, 1 whole egg, salt and pepper, and (if desired) a pinch of cayenne. Work the mixture together thoroughly.

Cut 2 large raw aubergines into round slices and brown them lightly in olive oil. Oil a manqué mould and line it with the aubergine skins, glossy side downward, so that they radiate from the centre with the tops projecting above the mould. Fill the lined mould with alternate layers of the chopped mixture and rounds of aubergine, finishing with the former. Turn down the ends of the aubergine skins and press lightly into the mixture.

Place the mould in a bain-marie, bring to the boil on top of the stove, then cook in the oven at 180 c (350 f, gas 4) for 1 hour (cover with kitchen foil during the final stages of cooking if necessary). Turn off the oven and leave the moussaka inside, with the door ajar, for about 15 minutes before turning out and serving.

Moussaka may be accompanied by a reduced tomato fondue or a tomato sauce, made by putting large ripe tomatoes (peeled and deseeded) through a blender with fresh basil, a small clove of garlic, a pinch of sugar, the juice of a lemon quarter, and salt and pepper.

mousse

A light soft preparation, either sweet or savoury, in which the ingredients are whisked or blended and then folded together. Mousses are often set in a mould and usually served cold. Savoury mousses, served as an hors d'oeuvre or entrée, may be based on fish, shellfish, poultry, foie gras, ham, a vegetable, etc.; sweet mousses are usually based on fruit or a flavouring such as chocolate or coffee.

RECIPES

Chicken mousse MOUSSE DE VOLAILLE Prepare in the same way as fish mousse (see recipe below) but use poached chicken meat instead of fish and season the mixture well using curry powder or nutmeg.

Fish mousse MOUSSE DE POISSON Clean 500 g (18 oz) fillets or steaks of either pike, whiting, salmon, or sole and pound them in a mortar or put in a food processor. Sprinkle with fine salt and freshly ground pepper, then blend in 2–3 egg whites, one after the other. Rub this forcemeat through a sieve and refrigerate for 2 hours. Then place the bowl in crushed ice and gradually add 6 dl (1 pint, 2½ cups) thick fresh cream, stirring the mixture with a wooden spatula. Adjust the seasoning, pour the mousse into a lightly oiled plain mould, and poach gently in a bain-marie in the oven at 190 C (375 F, gas 5) for about 20 minutes. Wait about 10 minutes before turning out and serve the mousse lukewarm, coated with a sauce for fish.

Shrimp *or* lobster mousse MOUSSE DE CREVETTE OU DE HOMARD Cook the shellfish as for crayfish *à la bordelaise* and shell them. Reduce the cooking mirepoix, then rub through a sieve (or put through a blender) with the flesh of the shellfish. For every 250 g (9 oz, generous cup) purée obtained, add 75 g (3 oz, ½ cup) well-reduced fish velouté and 1 dl (6 tablespoons, scant ½ cup) fish aspic (see *aspic jelly*). Cool but do not allow to set. Line a small charlotte mould with fish aspic. Add 1.25 dl (7 tablespoons, scant ⅔ cup) half-whisked fresh cream to the shellfish purée, then pour the mixture into the mould. Pour over it a thin layer of aspic and refrigerate for at least 2 hours. Turn out onto a serving dish and garnish with prawns.

ICED MOUSSES

Iced cream mousse MOUSSE GLACÉE À LA CRÈME Prepare a custard cream (see *creams and custards*) with ½ litre (17 fl oz, 2 cups) milk, 350 g (12 oz, 1½ cups) sugar, and some egg yolks (8 for a liqueur mousse; up to 16 for a fruit mousse). Leave to cool completely. Then add the chosen flavouring (vanilla, orange or lemon zest, liqueur, or ½ litre (17 fl oz, 2 cups) fruit purée), 20 g (¾ oz) powdered gum tragacanth (optional), and ½ litre (17 fl oz, 2 cups) double (heavy) cream. Place the mixing bowl in a basin containing crushed ice and whisk the preparation well. Pour into a mould and put in the freezer for at least 4 hours to set.

Iced fruit mousse MOUSSE GLACÉE AUX FRUITS Prepare an Italian meringue with 300 g (11 oz, 1⅓ cups) sugar, 1 dl (6 tablespoons, scant ½ cup) water, and 4 egg whites and put it in the refrigerator. Prepare a fruit purée (with 375 g (13 oz, 2½ cups) strawberries, for example). Whisk ½ litre (17 fl oz, 2 cups) very cold double (heavy) cream with 1.5 dl (¼ pint, ⅔ cup) very cold milk until stiff. Mix the meringue and the fruit purée and then add the whisked cream. Pour into a mould and put in the freezer for at least 4 hours to set.

SWEET MOUSSES

Chocolate and strawberry mousse MOUSSE AU CHOCOLAT ET AUX FRAISES CONFITES (from Étienne Bigeard's recipe) Melt 500 g (18 oz) plain bitter chocolate with a little water.

Separate the whites from the yolks of 8 eggs. Add the yolks, one by one, to the cooled melted chocolate and then blend in 6 tablespoons (½ cup) fresh cream. Place in the refrigerator. Very lightly cook 200 g (7 oz, 1½ cups) strawberries in 1 dl (6 tablespoons, scant ½ cup) syrup. Drain and leave them to cool. Stiffly whisk the egg whites with a pinch of fine salt. Fold them carefully into the chocolate cream. Serve the mousse in individual moulds, topped with a few drained strawberries.

Chocolate mousse MOUSSE AU CHO-COLAT Melt 150 g (5 oz) plain (semi-sweet) chocolate in a bain-marie, remove from the heat, and add 80 g (3 oz, scant ½ cup) butter. When the mixture is very smooth, quickly blend in 2 large egg yolks. Whisk 3 egg whites with a pinch of salt until very stiff, then whisk in 25 g (1 oz, 2 tablespoons) caster (superfine) sugar and 1 teaspoon vanilla-flavoured sugar. Carefully mix the chocolate preparation with the beaten egg whites, using a wooden spatula. Pour into a glass dish and refrigerate for at least 12 hours.

Lemon mousse MOUSSE DE CIT-RON (from Alain Chapel's recipe) Beat together 2 egg yolks and 5 tablespoons (6 tablespoons) sugar. When the mixture is foamy, add 2 tablespoons (3 tablespoons) cornflour (cornstarch) and then the hot juice of 6 limes and 2 lemons. Bring the mixture to the boil, stirring all the time. Stiffly whisk 2 egg whites and fold into the mixture. Pour this mousse into ramekin dishes and serve chilled with a salad of blood oranges and pink grapefruit.

mousseline

Any of various mousse-like preparations, most of which have a large or small quantity of whipped cream added to them. This term is used particularly for moulds made of various pastes enriched with cream (poultry, game, fish, shellfish, foie gras, etc.).

Mousselines are served hot or cold. If cold, they are also known as small aspics.

Mousseline is used as an adjective to denote a sauce enriched with whipped cream mayonnaise mousseline, hollandaise mousseline). It is also used of the paste or forcemeat used to make fish balls and mousses.

The term *mousseline* is much used in confectionery to describe certain cakes and pastries made of delicate mixtures (e.g. brioche mousseline).

RECIPES

Mousseline of apples with walnuts MOUSSELINE DE REINETTES AUX NOIX (from Paul Bocuse's recipe) Peel and core 8 medium-sized dessert apples, cut into slices, and make a compote by stewing them until soft with 2 knobs of butter, 3 tablespoons (¼ cup) caster (superfine) sugar, 1 teaspoon vanilla-flavoured sugar, and a small piece of finely chopped lemon peel.

Peel and core 3 more apples and cut each into 8 pieces. Poach these pieces of apple slowly in a syrup prepared with 350 ml (12 fl oz, 1½ cups) water, 125 g (4½ oz, scant ⅔ cup sugar, and a vanilla pod (bean): the fruit should be just softened. Remove 15 pieces of apple and complete the cooking of the other 9. Drain the fruit and put the syrup on one side.

As soon as the compote is cooked, mash it with a fork and reduce it over a high heat, turning it over with a spatula until a sort of thick fruit paste is obtained. Remove from the heat and cool. Thicken with 125 ml (4 fl oz, ½ cup) whisked double (heavy) cream, 3 eggs beaten as for an omelette, and 3 yolks. Add 2 tablespoons (3 tablespoons) crushed fresh walnuts and the half-poached apple pieces.

Butter a charlotte mould well and pour this mixture into it. Pile it up slightly and cook in a bain-marie in the oven at 190 C (375 F, gas 5) for about 40 minutes. Remove from the oven and turn out 15 minutes later onto a hot dish.

Prepare a sauce by reducing the syrup in which the apples were cooked to 100 ml (4 fl oz, ½ cup), remove it from the heat, and add 50 g (2 oz, 4 tablespoons) fresh butter and then 225 ml (8 fl oz, 1 cup) whisked fresh cream. Flavour with Noyau liqueur. Coat the mousseline with this sauce and decorate with the 9 fully cooked pieces of apple. Serve some langues-de-chat biscuits separately.

Mousseline sauce SAUCE MOUSSELINE Prepare a hollandaise sauce. Just before serving, blend into it half its volume of stiffly whisked cream.

Zeeland oysters with mussel mousseline MOUSSELINE DE FUMET DE MOULES AUX HUÎTRES DE ZÉLANDE (from Michel Theurel's recipe) Prepare a hollandaise sauce with some mussel cooking juice. Reduce ¼ litre (8 fl oz, 1 cup) mussel cooking juice and thicken it slightly with the hollandaise sauce. Finish with 2 tablespoons (3 tablespoons) whipped cream. Pack some large Zeeland oysters into an ovenproof dish and heat gently. Coat with the mousseline sauce and place under the grill for a short time.

mousseron

The common French name for several species of small white or beige mushrooms with a delicate flavour, including St George's mushroom, the fairy-ring mushroom, and blewits. They are cleaned and prepared like chanterelles. Lémery, in his *Traité des aliments* (1702), described the mousseron as a 'white, tender, and fleshy mushroom with a strong smell. It grows in the woods in spring and is called *mouceron* because it is enveloped in moss'.

mouvette

The French term for a round flat wooden spoon of varying size, used principally for stirring (or 'moving') sauces and creams and for mixing various preparations.

Mozart

A garnish for small cuts of meat consisting of artichoke hearts, slowly cooked in butter and stuffed with celery purée, and potatoes, cut into strips (called 'shavings') and fried.

Mozzarella

An Italian cheese originating from Latium and Campania, still made with buffaloes' milk in these areas but with cows' milk (40–45% fat) in the rest of Italy. It is a fresh cheese, springy and white; the mild flavour has a slight bite. Mozzarella is kept in salted water or whey, shaped into balls or loaves of varying size (100 g to 1 kg (4 oz to 2½

lb)). The buffaloes'-milk cheese, which has a more delicate flavour, is eaten at the end of a meal; the cows'-milk cheese is used mainly for cooking, particularly for pizzas, but also (with the addition of Ricotta) for preparing a lasagne gratin or for stuffing fried rice croquettes. *Mozzarella in carrozza*, a popular Neapolitan snack, is a small sandwich filled with cheese, rolled in flour, dipped in beaten egg, fried in oil, and eaten very hot.

muesli

A mixture of cereals, dried fruit, and fresh fruit served with milk (and sometimes sugar). Perfected at the beginning of the century by a Swiss nutritionist called Bircher-Brenner, muesli (from the German *Muësli*, meaning mixture) was then popularized as a nutritious breakfast cereal in Switzerland, Germany, and Great Britain. Mixtures of cereals and dried fruit have been marketed under several trade names, but any variation is possible. A standard mixture is rolled oats, wheat germ, roasted almonds, raisins, and grated apple served with milk. Sliced banana, grated carrots, walnuts and hazelnuts, condensed milk or yogurt, orange juice or grapefruit juice, honey, and malt extract may also be used as desired.

muffin

In Great Britain, a muffin is a traditional light-textured roll, round and flat, which is made with yeast dough. Muffins are usually enjoyed in the winter – split, toasted, buttered, and served hot for tea, sometimes with jam. In the Victorian era muffins were bought in the street from sellers who carried trays of them on their heads, ringing a handbell to call their wares.

In North America muffins are entirely different. The raising (leavening) agent is baking powder and the muffins are cooked in deep patty (muffin) tins. Cornmeal and bran are sometimes substituted for some of the flour.

RECIPE

English muffins Prepare the yeast liquid: blend 15 g (½ oz) fresh yeast (½ cake compressed yeast) in 300 ml (½ pint, 1½ cups) warm water. (Alternatively, dissolve 1 teaspoon caster (superfine) sugar in the warm water and sprinkle in 1½ teaspoons dried yeast.) Allow to stand until frothy (about 10 minutes).

Mix 450 g (1 lb, 4 cups) strong white (unbleached) flour and 1 teaspoon salt together. Add the yeast liquid and mix to form a soft dough. Turn out onto a lightly floured surface and knead until smooth and elastic (about 10 minutes by hand). Shape into a ball and place inside an oiled polythene (plastic) bag; leave to rise until doubled in size. Remove from the polythene bag, knock back (punch down), and knead until the dough is firm (about 2 minutes). Cover the dough and rest it for 5 minutes. Roll out on a floured surface to a thickness of 1 cm (½ in). Cover again and rest for a further 5 minutes.

Cut into 9-cm (3½-in) rounds with a plain cutter. Place on a well-floured baking sheet and dust the tops with flour or fine semolina. Cover and prove in a warm place until doubled in size (about 15–30 minutes).

Heat a griddle, hotplate, or heavy frying pan (skillet) and grease lightly. Cook the muffins for about 3 minutes or until golden brown on each side, or bake towards the top of a hot oven (230 c, 450 f, gas 8) for about 10 minutes, turning over carefully with a palette knife after 5 minutes. Cool on a wire rack.

mulberry MÛRE

The fruit of the mulberry tree, which is somewhat similar to the blackberry but has a higher calorific calue (57 Cal per 100 g) and lower vitamin content. For uses, see *blackberry*.

mule MULET

An animal resulting from the crossing of an ass and a mare. The flesh of the mule is rather dry and its taste is often quite musky. This meat, highly prized in mule-breeding regions, is becoming increasingly rare. It is still used in some countries for preparing sausages.

mulled wine VIN CHAUD

An aromatic alcoholic drink made with red wine, sugar, and spices and served very hot, traditionally in winter; examples are grog, punch, and Bishop. Mulled wine is particularly popular in mountainous regions, in Germany and Scandinavia. It is traditionally prepared by slowly heating the contents of a bottle of Bordeaux, Burgundy, or a similar red wine for about ten minutes with lemon or orange peel, sugar or honey, and spices (cinnamon, cloves, mace), but this should never be brought to the boil; the liquid is sieved and served in glasses or cups with handles. In the country it may be served in a pottery jug. To strengthen the aroma of the spices, these are sometimes left to infuse for half an hour in a glass of wine brought up to the boil, before the rest of the heated wine is added. If spirits are added or the wine is sufficiently high in alcohol, its vapours may be flamed.

mullet

One of several unrelated fish which can be divided into two broad groups.

□ Grey mullets (*mulets* or *muges* in French) These are found in coastal waters and there are several species. The largest is the striped mullet (*mulet cabot*), up to 60 cm (2 ft) long, with a large head, silvery-grey back, and brown sides. The golden mullet (*mulet doré*) is the smallest (20–45 cm, 8–18 in); it has gold spots beside its eyes and a yellowish tint to the sides. The thick-lipped grey mullet (*mulet lippu*) has wide thick lips. The thin-lipped mullet (*mulet porc*) resembles the golden mullet but is larger and lacks spots. The first two are the most highly prized and the most common. They are prepared like bass – cooked in court-bouillon, baked, or grilled (broiled), after they have been carefully scaled. The flesh is lean, white, and slightly soft; it contains few bones but sometimes smells of mud.

□ Red mullets (*rouget-barbet* in French, goatfish in the United States) These fish are distinguished from the grey mullets by their smaller size (40 cm (16 in) maximum length), reddish coloration, and the pair of barbels beneath the chin. They are highly valued as food fish, especially in the Mediterranean region. The best variety is bright pink streaked with gold and has a black striped front dorsal fin and two scales under its eyes; in France it is fished chiefly in the Vendée and Cherbourg area. The sand mullet (fished round Arcachon, Provence, Corsica, and Tunisia) is inferior in quality. It is reddish-brown and has three scales under the eyes. Both fish can be bought in France from February to June. From October to May, red mullet from Senegal is available, imported from Dakar. This is a smaller fish (maximum length 20 cm, 8 in) and less colourful, with a spine on the gill cover. Its flesh is dry and more bony than the other varieties.

The colour of the red mullet is brighter if the fish is scaled as soon as it is caught. This is a difficult operation, however, as the skin is fragile. Mullet are therefore generally sold unscaled. The fish are extremely perishable and must be sold and consumed within a short time.

Very fresh small red mullet do not need to be gutted (cleaned); if they are, the liver should be reserved. They can be grilled, after being dried and lightly salted. Mullet with drier flesh can be fried or baked. Medium-sized fish are grilled or cooked *en papillote* (taking care always to reserve the liver, which is used in the sauce). Large mullet are cooked in the oven, *en papillote*, or on a bed of herbs, with butter or olive oil.

Red mullet is a lean fish, with a calorific value of 80 Cal per 100 g; it is rich in protein, iodine, iron, and phosphorus. An infallible guide to freshness is the colour: if this begins to fade, the fish is going off. The flesh should be quite firm, the body almost rigid, the skin tight, and the eyes prominent and clear.

RECIPES

Baked red mullet à la livournaise ROUGETS AU FOUR À LA LIVOURNAISE Gut (clean) 4 red mullet, make some light incisions on their backs, season them with salt and pepper, and lay them head to tail in a buttered or oiled gratin dish. Cover with a reduced tomato fondue, sprinkle with breadcrumbs and 2 tablespoons (3 tablespoons) oil or melted butter, and bake at 240 C (475 F, gas 9). When the top is brown (after about 15 minutes), add some chopped parsley and a few drops of lemon juice. Serve from the cooking dish.

Baked red mullet with fennel ROUGET AU FOUR AU FENOUIL Soften 25 g (1 oz, ¼ cup) chopped onion in oil, then add 1 tablespoon very finely chopped fresh fennel. Gut (clean) a mullet, make some light incisions on its back, and season with salt and pepper. Butter a small ovenproof dish, spread the base with the onion, and lay the fish on top. Sprinkle with breadcrumbs and a little olive oil and bake in the oven at 220 C (425 F, gas 7) for 25 minutes. Sprinkle with chopped parsley and a little lemon juice.

Fried red mullet ROUGETS FRITS Gut (clean) some small mullet, dry them, and make a few shallow incisions on their backs. Soak them for 30 minutes in salted boiled milk, then drain them, dip in flour, and fry at 175 C (347 F). Drain on kitchen paper and arrange them in a dish lined with a table napkin, garnished with sliced fluted lemon and fried parsley.

Grilled (broiled) red mullet ROUGETS GRILLÉS (from Raymond Oliver's recipe in *La Cuisine*, Bordas, 1981) Scale 800 g (1¾ lb) red mullet. Cook whole if they are small, but make some light incisions in the skin. Brush them with oil, applied with a small bunch of thyme or rosemary sprigs. Grill (broil) the fish under a moderate heat. Oil them lightly from time to time while cooking, using the herb brush. Turn them as few times as possible so as not to damage them. Sprinkle with salt and serve either as they are or accompanied by a béarnaise or Choron sauce or with melted butter. A traditional Provençal method is to grill them without any previous preparation, complete with scales and fins, and without salt. They should be eaten, unsalted, when still barely cooked.

Red mullet grilled (broiled) in cases ROUGETS GRILLÉS EN CAISSE Grill (broil) some red mullet. Cut pieces of greaseproof (waxed) paper large enough to enclose the fish and spread them with mushroom duxelles. Put a fish on each piece of paper and pour over some duxelles sauce; sprinkle with breadcrumbs and melted butter and brown in a very hot oven for a few minutes.

Red mullet poached à la nage with basil ROUGETS POCHÉS À LA NAGE AU BASILIC (from Raymond Thuillier's recipe) Prepare the sauce in advance: finely chop 20 fresh basil leaves, 5 tarragon leaves, and 5 sprigs of parsley. Peel and chop a tomato. Marinate these ingredients with a little garlic in ·250 ml (8 fl oz, 1 cup) first pressing virgin olive oil. Add a few drops of wine vinegar and season with salt and pepper.

On the day of the meal, prepare an aromatic poaching liquid (see *nage*) for the fish and cook it for 30 minutes. Meanwhile, scale 4 red mullet, each weighing 180–200 g (6–7 oz), but do not gut (clean) them. Place a slice of orange, a slice of lemon, and a bay leaf on each fish and wrap in kitchen foil. Cook the fish gently in the poaching liquid for about 10 minutes; they should still be firm and have retained their shape. Serve with the sauce.

mulligatawny

A soup of Indian origin, adopted by the British and particularly popular in Australia. It is a chicken consommé to which are added stewed vegetables (onions, leeks, celery, etc.) highly seasoned with curry and spices (bay leaf and cloves), garnished with chicken meat and rice *à la créole*. In the original Indian preparation the garnish also includes blanched almonds and coconut milk (possibly replaced by cream). The Australians generally add tomatoes and smoked bacon.

mung bean

HARICOT MUNGO

A bean plant, originating in the Far East, having small green, yellow, or brown seeds. It is widely cultivated for its shoots, commonly known as bean sprouts, which are eaten either raw or blanched. They can be served as a vegetable accompanying a main dish, in hors d'oeuvres, or in mixed salads with oriental overtones. Bean sprouts can be bought canned or fresh from shops selling Indian and Asian foods and in many supermarkets.

Munster

An Alsatian cheese made from cows' milk (45–50% fat); it has a soft yellow paste and a washed straw- to orange-coloured rind. After it has matured for two to three months and had regular washings it has a strong smell and a full-bodied flavour. It is eaten with Gewürztraminer in Alsace and with well-balanced red wines elsewhere. Created in the 7th century by monks – the name is derived from *monastère* (monastery) – it is protected by an AOC which applies to certain districts of the Haut- and Bas-Rhin, Meurthe-et-Moselle, the Haute-Saône, the Vosges, and the Territory of Belfort.

Munster is best eaten in summer and autumn. It is a flat round cheese, 13–20 cm (5–8 in) in diameter and 2.5–5 cm (1–2 in) thick, and is sold unwrapped or boxed (when it is small). Cumin seeds are sometimes added to the paste, but it is better to serve them separately. In Alsace Munster is often eaten young and is traditionally served with unpeeled boiled potatoes.

Murat

A method of preparing fillets of sole, which are cut into small strips, cooked *à la meunière*, and arranged in a timbale with potatoes (boiled in their skins and peeled) and poached artichoke hearts, cut into dice and sautéed. The whole preparation, which may be garnished with slices of tomato sautéed in oil, is sprinkled with coarsely chopped parsley, mixed with lemon juice, and moistened with noisette butter.

Murfatlar

A Rumanian dessert wine produced in the Dobroudja region, not far from the Black Sea. The use of overripe grapes gives a golden liqueur-like wine, with a bouquet reminiscent of orange blossom.

Murol

A cows'-milk cheese (45% fat) from the Auvergne, with a compressed centre and a pink or reddish washed crust. Its centre, which is yellow and yielding to the touch, has a mild flavour. Named after a village in Puy-de-Dôme, where it was created (according to Androuet) by a man called Jean Bérioux, Murol is best eaten in summer and autumn. It is shaped like a flat cylinder, 12 cm (5 in) in diameter and 3.5 cm (1½ in) thick, pierced in the centre by a hole 4 cm (1½ in) in diameter (made to speed up maturing). The central part is shaped into a truncated cone, coated with red wax, and sold under the name of Murolait.

Muscadel MOSCATEL

The Spanish and Portuguese name of the Muscat grape. Setúbal wine, from the area around Lisbon, is based on it.

Muscadet

White AOC wine made from the Muscadet grapes in the region south of Nantes, at the sea end of the Loire. There are three areas: Muscadet, Muscadet du Coteaux de la Loire, and Muscadet de Sèvre et Maine. The description *sur lie* means that the wine is bottled directly off the lees, without being first pumped off them. This can result in a slight pétillance. Muscadet was formerly mostly drunk locally or mainly in France, but nowadays this dry light-bodied wine is famous throughout the world.

Muscat or Muscatel

One of the great white grapes of the wine world, available in various forms. Muscat wines have a marked 'grapey' fragrance, but although some varieties of Muscat wines are sweet (such as the vins doux naturels) there are also plenty of dry ones. Muscat wines are made not only in Alsace and the south of France, but also in Italy (Asti Spumante is made from the Moscato) and in many other countries.

museau

The muzzle of an ox or pig, which is used chiefly in charcuterie. Ox muzzle, comprising the edible part of the muffle and chin, is treated by curing. In France it is usually sold ready prepared and it is used as a cold hors d'oeuvre, served in a herb-flavoured vinaigrette. Pig's muzzle (*museau de porc*) is also sold as a cooked meat speciality, similar to brawn (head cheese); it is prepared using the whole head (and sometimes the tongue and the tail), which is boned, cooked, pressed, and moulded.

RECIPE

Ox muzzle MUSEAU DE BOEUF
Soak some trimmed and cleaned ox muzzle for 2 hours in cold water, changing the water several times. Then simmer it very gently in salted water for about 6 hours (1½ hours in a pressure cooker). Leave it to cool, then cut it into thin slices, sprinkle with vinaigrette, and add a little chopped onion or shallot and some coarsely chopped herbs, according to taste. Serve chilled.

---

mushroom CHAMPIGNON

A type of fungus (a plant with neither chlorophyll nor flowers) generally found growing in cool damp places in woodland and meadows, where the soil is rich in humus. A mushroom consists of a stalk and an umbrella-shaped cap. Sometimes the whole mushroom may be eaten, in other cases just the cap. Although many mushrooms have a high water content, they have a greater food value than green vegetables, but are not as nutritious as root vegetables. The cultivated protein-rich parasol mushroom provides eight times as many calories as the chanterelle. Edible mushrooms include cultivated species of the genus *Agaricus* and numerous varieties of field mushrooms that are sold in season, such as boletus, chanterelle, and horn of plenty. The morel and truffle have enjoyed gastronomic fame for centuries. They are rare and expensive and are generally used for haute cuisine dressings. Some mushrooms are used in rustic or traditional recipes.

□ **Field mushrooms** Wild mushrooms, like berries, have been gathered for food throughout history. In France in the Middle Ages, the most highly prized mushroom was the field mushroom belonging to the genus *Agaricus*, which was easily identifiable. Ceps were not known to be edible until the 18th century.

In order to collect mushrooms, it is essential to be able to identify them properly. Some species are very poisonous, others are without gastronomic interest, but many are prized as food. There is no empirical means of distinguishing poisonous species from edible ones. Therefore, it is wise to use cultivated mushrooms if one has no knowledge and no experience of identifying mushrooms. Although this may present a rather terrifying picture in a work dedicated to gastronomy, there are frequent fatal accidents that occur every year from eating poisonous mushrooms, and it is very necessary to stress this point. Mushrooms must be bought when fresh and young, and must not be maggoty. It is advisable to cook them as quickly as possible. Chanterelles and ceps may be kept for two or three days, but others, like amanitas, lepiotas, and especially coprinus mushrooms, must be consumed immediately.

□ **Preparation** In order to retain the full flavour of mushrooms, it is best not to peel or wash them, but simply to wipe them with a damp cloth and then dry them. If the stalks are tough, stringy, or maggoty, they are removed. Otherwise, the base of the stalk is sliced off. Only the mushrooms that become sticky in damp weather (including certain boletus mushrooms) and those with a bitter outer skin (cortinae and pholiotae) are peeled. The fleshy tubes of boletus mushrooms are removed if they are too spongy, and the gills of certain other mushrooms are trimmed if they are too ripe. If absolutely necessary, the mushrooms may be washed very quickly, but never allowed to soak. Varieties such as morels, which have a cap that is pitted like a honeycomb, are cleaned with a small brush. The flavour of the delicate kinds is completely destroyed by blanching and only a few varieties with a bitter, peppery, resinous, or earthy flavour (such as certain milk caps and russulae) stand up to this treatment.

□ **Culinary uses** Mushrooms are considered to be a flavoursome delicate condiment rather than a true vegetable. Ceps, chanterelles, and cultivated mushrooms may be used as a garnish or as a separate dish. Dr Paul Ramain, author of an important *Mycogastronomie* (1954), was one of the first to treat field mushrooms from the culinary angle. A few species may be eaten raw (Caesar's mushroom (*Amanita caesarea*), coprinus, and cultivated mushrooms); the majority are edible only after they are cooked (preferably in an enamelled, earthenware, or glass

container). When cooked on a gentle heat in a covered pan, they give out a liquid in which they simmer. This is set aside for soup. They may be sautéed in olive oil, vegetable oil, or butter. If they are an ingredient of a sauce or a stew, they are added directly. The cooking time varies according to the species: coprinus and Caesar's mushrooms require a few minutes, but most other species require from 45 minutes to 1 hour. The respective cooking times must be taken into account if a mixture is used in a recipe. If overcooked, the mushrooms lose their flavour and become hard; salt is not added until the end of cooking. If required, mushrooms may be seasoned with garlic, shallots, or parsley, but in moderation, so that their often delicate flavour is not masked.

□ **Preserving** Drying is suitable for the species with dry flesh (chanterelle, craterellus, morel) and for ceps (the caps of which are cut into thin strips). Dried mushrooms may be reduced to a powder and used as a condiment. If they are preserved in liquid, they may be treated as fresh mushrooms. The fleshy types of mushrooms are bottled and sterilized, or frozen. Mushrooms may also be preserved in oil, vinegar, or brine. (They may be canned *au naturel*, or sometimes in brine, but their flavour is not as good.)

□ **Cultivated mushrooms** These belong to the genus *Agaricus*, with a fleshy cap and pale pink gills that become dark brown at maturity. The erect stalk has a membranous ring of tissue about halfway up. These mushrooms are extensively cultivated around Paris (hence the French name – *champignon de Paris*) in two varieties: *blanc* (white) and *blond* or *bistre* (golden), of which the latter has more flavour. Cultivated mushrooms are rich in phosphorus, nitrogenous substances, and vitamin B, but have a low calorific value. They are sold throughout the year and have a firm soft flesh. The widespread use of these mushrooms in many dishes is due to their abundance rather than their flavour.

In France the cultivation of the field mushroom began in the Middle Ages and was intensified by La Quintinie. It was renamed 'Paris mushroom' during the reign of Napoleon, when large quantities were produced in the abandoned racecourses of the XVth arrondissement of Paris. They were then cultivated in the north, in the Gironde, and in the Val de Loire, and these regions, together with districts near Paris, remain the major areas of production.

Cultivated mushrooms may be eaten raw when they are young and closed, or white and firm. Raw mushrooms are served with cream and *aux fines herbes*, with Roquefort sauce, with a vinaigrette sauce, with seafood, in mixed salads, *à la grecque*, and in assorted hors d'oeuvres.

Sautéed mushrooms are served with various meats, fish, and poultry and in omelettes. They are included in numerous classic preparations such as Belle-Hélène, *à la bourguignonne*, Chambord, *à la forestière*, *à la gauloise*, Richelieu, etc. They are widely used in sauces, either thinly sliced or cooked in a court-bouillon (chasseur, financière, Godard, italienne, matelote, Polignac, Régence, suprême, etc.). They are the main ingredient of duxelles. Finally, cultivated mushrooms are often cooked with cheese or ham, used in pies, patties, and flans, in gratins, on canapés, stuffed, etc.

☐ **Exotic mushrooms** A good many mushrooms are used in the cuisine of the Far East and are sold in Europe either in a dried form or in mixtures of marinated or ready-cooked vegetables. The Chinese black mushroom is an ingredient of salads, soups, hashes, garnishes, and sautéed vegetables; in Chinese restaurants in Paris it is often replaced by the auricularia (jew's-ear). The Chinese scented mushroom (*xiang xin*, 'perfumed heart') is cooked like the black mushroom in China and Japan.

RECIPE

Preparation of cultivated mushrooms PRÉPARATION DES CHAMPIGNONS DE PARIS Do not peel the mushrooms, but cut off the base of the stalk. Wash them quickly several times in cold water, dry, and sprinkle with lemon juice if they are not to be used immediately.

Freezing mushrooms CONSERVE DE CHAMPIGNONS PAR LE FROID Choose very firm mushrooms. Clean them in the usual way, arrange them on a flat dish, and freeze. When frozen, place them in freezer bags or boxes. The mushrooms may be cooked without defrosting.

Mushroom blanc BLANC DE CHAMPIGNONS Boil 1 dl (6 tablespoons, scant ½ cup) water with 40 g (1½ oz, 3 tablespoons) butter, the juice of half a lemon, and 6 g (scant ¼ oz, scant tablespoon) salt. Add 300 g (11 oz, 3 cups) mushrooms and boil for 6 minutes. Drain and retain the cooking stock to flavour a white sauce, a fish stock, or a marinade.

Mushroom croquettes CROQUETTES AUX CHAMPIGNONS Clean and dice some mushrooms, sprinkle with lemon juice, and sauté them briskly either in oil or in butter. Add some chopped shallot and parsley, a little thyme and powdered bay leaf, a chopped clove of garlic, salt, and pepper. Bind this salpicon with a thick béchamel sauce and leave to cool. Divide the mixture into equal portions and roll them into cylinders. Dip the cylinders in batter, plunge into very hot oil, and brown. Drain and dry on absorbent paper. Serve very hot (possibly with a tomatoe fondue), either as an entrée or as a vegetable.

Mushroom salad SALADE DE CHAMPIGNONS Clean some very fresh mushrooms. Slice them finely along their full length and sprinkle with lemon juice to prevent them from turning brown. They may be served with either a very highly seasoned vinaigrette dressing with added lemon juice and chopped herbs, or with a mixture of fresh cream, vinegar or lemon juice, salt, pepper, and chopped chives. Keep in a cool place until ready to serve.

Mushrooms à l'anglaise CHAMPIGNONS À L'ANGLAISE Choose good-quality cultivated mushrooms. Trim, wash, and remove the stalks. Season the caps with salt and pepper. Butter small round lightly toasted pieces of bread. Place a mushroom, hollow side up, on each slice, garnished with a little maître d'hôtel butter. Arrange the toast in a gratin dish, cover, and bake in a moderate oven for 12–15 minutes.

Mushrooms cooked in cream CHAMPIGNONS À LA CRÈME Sauté the mushrooms in butter, cover them with fresh boiling cream, and simmer until reduced (8–10 minutes). This preparation may be used as a filling for flans or vols-au-vent.

Mushrooms for garnishing CHAMPIGNONS EN GARNITURE Sauté the mushrooms in butter and drain. Make a Madeira sauce in the frying pan and reduce. Add stock or demi-glace, reduce by half, and strain. Add the mushrooms to the sauce. The garnish may then be included in a wide variety of dishes, (such as blanquettes, fricassees, escalopes, noisettes, calves' sweetbreads, fish, eggs, etc.) or used to fill small vol-au-vent cases, patties, flaky-pastry flans, etc.

Mushroom soufflés SOUFFLÉS AUX CHAMPIGNONS Add 4 egg yolks to 4 dl (14 fl oz, 1¾ cups) mushroom purée, followed by 4 stiffly beaten egg whites. Butter some small ramekins and divide the mixture between them. Place them in the oven at about 190 C (375 F, gas 5) and cook for about 20 minutes without opening the oven door. The soufflés are cooked when they have filled the mould and the top has browned. Serve immediately.

Mushroom stuffing FARCE DE CHAMPIGNONS Clean some mushrooms, remove the caps, and set them aside to use as garnishes. Chop the stalks and toss them in very hot butter (or olive oil) with chopped shallots, salt, pepper, and (optional) a dash of grated nutmeg. Then add some fresh breadcrumbs, chopped parsley, 1 egg (either whole or just the yolk), salt, and pepper.
    The stuffing may be used to fill mushroom caps or other vegetables (tomatoes, aubergines (eggplants), courgettes (zucchini), and cabbage) and also as a fish or meat stuffing.

Preserved mushrooms (au naturel) CONSERVE DE CHAMPIGNONS AU NATUREL Clean some small mushrooms and blanch them for 4 minutes in boiling water with added lemon juice. Drain and cool in cold water, drain again, wipe, and dry. Place them in jars,

seal, and sterilize at 100 C (212 F) for about 30 minutes.

Stuffed mushrooms CHAMPIGNONS FARCIS Choose large mushrooms of a similar size. Remove the stalks so that the cavities of the caps are fully exposed. Wash and wipe the caps, arrange them in a buttered or oiled dish, and season with salt and pepper. Coat them with oil or melted butter and place them in the oven for 5 minutes. Stuff each one with a heaped tablespoon of duxelles. Dust with fine breadcrumbs, sprinkle with olive oil, and brown.
    Like all stuffed vegetables, mushrooms may be filled with different mixtures, such as chopped vegetables, forcemeat, mirepoix, purée or salpicon, risotto, etc.

Musigny

Red and white Burgundies from the parish of Chambolle-Musigny in the Côte de Nuits. Mostly red, the great growths are world-famous, being extremely fine and delicate and very expensive.

musk MUSC

A strong-smelling substance extracted from the glands of the musk deer and Ethiopian civet or from various seeds (especially musk mallow, cultivated in Africa and in the West Indies). Now used chiefly in perfumery, musk was formerly used as a spice and is still included in certain African and oriental dishes.

muslin (cheesecloth)
ÉTAMINE

Loosely woven cloth used for straining thick liquids, such as sauces and purées. The liquid is either pressed through the cloth with a spatula or enclosed in the cloth, the two ends of which are twisted in opposite directions.
    Small muslin bags (*nouets*) are used to hold ingredients intended to flavour a dish. The flavouring ingredients are placed on a small square of muslin (or chiffon); the muslin is then drawn up and knotted to form a bag. In this way the flavouring material does not escape into the dish and can be removed when cooking is complete.

mussel MOULE

A bivalve mollusc of which there are many species. European mussels have thin oblong shells which are bluish and finely striped. The common mussel is fished or cultivated on the coasts of the Atlantic, the English Channel, and the North Sea, especially between the mouth of the Gironde and Denmark. It is small, convex, and tender. The Toulon mussel, which is larger, flatter, and less delicate, is found only in the Mediterranean, where it is seriously threatened by pollution. Natural mussels are usually smaller and more leathery than those which have been cultivated.

Mussel culture has been practised in France since the 13th century but mussel beds date back to Roman times. The story goes that an Irish traveller, Patrick Walton, was shipwrecked in the region of La Rochelle in 1290 and then settled in the district. One day he noticed that the posts hung with nets which he set up in the sea to catch birds were covered with mussels. This gave him the idea of increasing the number of posts, placing them closer together, and joining them with bundles of branches (*bousches*). This is the origin of *bouchot*, the modern French word for the wooden hurdles on which mussels are bred. Today the hurdles are stocked with young mussels taken from lines for catching seed oysters. Mussel culture in France is practised mainly on the west coast, from Cotentin to the mouth of the Charente, and produces mussels which are small but full of flavour and very fleshy.

Two other methods of rearing mussels are used: rearing *à plat*, which is similar to oyster farming and originated in Croisic, where the hurdles were not successful; and rearing *sur cordes*, which is a method peculiar to the Mediterranean. As French mussel breeding is not sufficient to meet the demand, mussels are also imported, mostly from the Netherlands and Portugal.

Mussels are sold by the litre (pint or quart) or by weight (1 litre = 700–800 g; 1 pint = 14 oz–1 lb). Mussels are also sold preserved in oil or sauce, used for garnishing rice timbales or mixed salads. Mussels bought live must be firmly closed and cooked within three days of being caught (mussels with half-opened shells which do not close when they are tapped must be thrown away). The mussels must be completely cleaned of any filaments and parasites which may be attached to them before they are used. This is done by brushing and scraping under running water. If the mussels are consumed raw, they must be eaten the same day that they are bought. Cooked mussels may be kept for 48 hours in the refrigerator.

Mussels have a calorific value of 80 Cal per 100 g and a high content of calcium, iron, and iodine. Nicknamed 'the poor man's oyster' because of its abundance and its reasonable price, it is a very popular shellfish, often cooked very simply: *à la marinière*, in cream, fried, sautéed, *au gratin*, or in an omelette. Some delicious French regional mussel dishes include stuffed mussels from Île de Ré, éclade, and mouclade. Mussels also feature in a number of recipes from other parts of the world, including paella, *zuppa di cozze* from Liguria (soup made from garlic, celery, and onion), English mussel broth (soup made from cider, milk, leeks, and parsley, bound with fresh cream), and in various Belgian dishes, made with white wine or cream and parsley.

RECIPES

Fried mussels MOULES FRITES Prepare some mussels *à la marinière*, remove the shells, and leave to cool. Marinate for 30 minutes in olive oil, lemon juice, chopped parsley, and pepper. Then dip in frying batter and cook in oil heated to 180 C (350 F). Drain them on absorbent paper and serve as an hors d'oeuvre (with lemon quarters) or with apértifs (on cocktail sticks).

Hors d'oeuvre of mussels à la ravigote HORS-D'OEUVRE DE MOULES À LA RAVIGOTE Cook some mussels *à la marinière*, remove their shells, and leave them to cool completely in a salad bowl. Prepare a well-seasoned vinaigrette and add to it some chopped hard-boiled (hard-cooked) eggs, parsley, chervil, tarragon, and gherkins. Pour over the mussels and stir. Put in a cool place until time to serve.

Iced mussel soup   SOUPE GLACÉE AUX MOULES   (from Alain Dutournier's recipe) Place a red pepper in a very hot oven for a few minutes, to loosen the skin, then peel it. Clean 2 litres (3½ pints, 4½ pints) mussels and cook over a brisk heat with half a glass of white wine for 2 minutes. Remove the shells and reserve the cooking liquid. Peel and deseed a cucumber, cut it into dice, then place in a colander and sprinkle with coarse salt; leave to drain. Cut half a bunch of radishes into round slices. Shell and skin 500 g (18 oz) broad (fava) beans. Wash and dice 5 mushroom caps (preferably wild) and sprinkle them with lemon juice.

Finely slice one half of the peeled red pepper and dice the other half. In a food processor, blend 6 peeled tomatoes, the slices of pepper, the mussel cooking juices, 2 tablespoons (3 tablespoons) olive oil, a little sauce *à l'anglaise*, and 10 drops of Tabasco sauce. Add the diced and sliced vegetables, the broad beans, and the mussels. Adjust the seasoning. Refrigerate for several hours before serving.

Mussel brochettes   BROCHETTES DE MOULES   (from Dominqiue Nahmias' recipe) Open some mussels over a brisk heat. Remove the shells and thread the mussels on skewers, alternatiing them with thin pieces of smoked bacon and tomato. Season with pepper. Cook under the grill (broiler) for 1 minute.

Mussel salad   SALADE DE MOULES   Prepare 1 kg (2¼ lb) mussels *à la marinière*, drain them, and remove the shells. Boil, without peeling, 750 g (1½ lb) potatoes; peel while still hot and cut into cubes. Shred 2–3 sticks (stalks) of celery. Peel and chop a shallot and a clove of garlic and mix with plenty of chopped parsley. Mix all the ingredients together in a salad bowl. Sprinkle with a vinaigrette made with 2 tablespoons (3 tablespoons) hot vinegar, 6 tablespoons (scant ½ cup) oil, 1 tablespoon white mustard, salt, and pepper. Serve immediately.

Mussel sauce   SAUCE AUX MOULES   Prepare 500 g (18 oz) small mussels *à la marinière* with 3 dl (½ pint, 1¼ cups) white wine; remove the shells and keep the mussels hot. Strain the cooking liquid and reduce it to ½ dl (2 tablespoons, 3 tablespoons). Let it cool until lukewarm, then beat in 2–3 egg yolks, followed by 100 g (4 oz, ½ cup) butter and a few drops of lemon juice. Add the mussels and adjust the seasoning. This sauce accompanies white fish or poached fillets of fish.

Mussels in cream   MOULES À LA CRÈME   Prepare 2 kg (4½ lb) mussels *à la marinière*, drain them, remove one of the shells from each mussel, and place them in a vegetable dish. Keep hot. Strain the cooking liquid through a fine cloth. Prepare 3 dl (½ pint, 1¼ cups) light béchamel sauce, add 2 dl (7 fl oz, ¾ cup) fresh cream and the cooking liquid from the mussels, and reduce by at least one-third. Season with salt and pepper and pour this hot sauce over the mussels.

The béchamel cream sauce may be flavoured with curry or 1 tablespoon chopped onion, softened in butter.

Stuffed mussels (or clams)   MOULES (OU PALOURDES) FARCIES   Prepare *à la marinière* 3 dozen Toulon mussels (or clams). Remove the shells, keeping half of them, and leave the shellfish to cool completely. Prepare 150 g (5 oz, generous ½ cup) snail butter. Put a little of this butter in each half-shell, place a mussel in each, then cover with butter. Sprinkle with breadcrumbs and brown in a hot oven until the butter bubbles.

must   MOÛT

Grape juice before it has been acted on by the yeasts that convert the natural sugar in it to alcohol. See *wine*.

mustard   MOUTARDE

A herbaceous plant, originating from the Mediterranean region, whose seeds are used to prepare the yellow condiment of the same name. There are three varieties: black mustard (spicy and piquant), brown mustard (less piquant), and white mustard (not very piquant but more bitter and more pungent).

French mustards are sold in the form

of a paste; the main centre for production is Dijon, followed by Meaux, Orléans, and Bordeaux. In France, the term 'mustard' is reserved for the product obtained only from black or brown mustard seeds (or both). These seeds contain two elements, myronate and myrosin: when crushed in the presence of water, they release a volatile and piquant essence which gives mustard its distinctive flavour. White mustard does not contain myronate and the product obtained from its seeds is known simply as 'condiment'. The only exception is Alsace mustard, which contains white mustard and is manufactured in the Upper Rhine, the Lower Rhine, and the Moselle. English mustard is sold either as a fine powder consisting of a mixture of black and white mustard with turmeric added, which is mixed with water before use, or ready-mixed in jars or tubes.

Mustard has been known and used since ancient times. Black mustard seed is mentioned in the Bible; the plant, cultivated in Palestine, was introduced into Egypt, where its crushed seeds were served as a condiment (as they still are in the East). The Greeks and Romans used the seeds in the form of flour or mixed in tuna-fish brine (*muria*), for spicing meat and fish. Black mustard then reached Gaul: an early 'recipe' appeared in the 4th century and spread to Burgundy. Pope John XXII, who was a great enthusiast, created a sinecure for his nephew, the post of *grand moutardier du pape* (great mustard-maker to the Pope). The medicinal properties of the plant were also highly valued in the Middle Ages.

In 1390 the manufacture of mustard was governed by regulations: it had to be made from 'good seed and suitable vinegar', without any other binder. The corporation of vinegar and mustard manufacturers was founded at the end of the 16th century at Orléans and in about 1630 at Dijon. In the 18th century, a Dijon manufacturer called Naigeon fixed the recipe for 'strong' or 'white' mustard, the production of which was synchronized with the wine harvest, as the black and brown seeds were mixed with verjuice. Today, Dijon mustard is prepared with verjuice and white wine, Orléans mustard with wine

vinegar, and Bordeaux mustard, which is milder and brown in colour, with grape must (the French word for mustard is derived from *moût ardent*, i.e. 'piquant must'). Meaux mustard, which owes its flavour and colour to coarsely crushed seeds of various colours, is prepared with vinegar, particularly at Lagny.

Mustard is a condiment that can be flavoured in many different ways: with tarragon, garlic, fines herbes, paprika, and (more recently) with orange or lime. Grimod de La Reynière speaks of the countless mustards of M. Bordin. Today Corcellet names about 20 kinds. Mustard is made at home in France by mixing crushed mustard seeds with white wine and a little oil or with vinegar flavoured with herbs or aromatic plants. Mustard is best kept in a stone or glass pot, preferably in the bottom of the refrigerator.

In addition to its uses as a condiment for meat and charcuterie, mustard is used in cookery for coating rabbit, pork, chicken, and oily fish before cooking. It may be added to the cooking stock of a ragout or a blanquette, and it is the basis of numerous sauces, both hot and cold (vinaigrette, mayonnaise, rémoulade, devilled sauce, dijonnaise, Sainte-Menehould, Cambridge, etc.). In English cookery, mustard sauce is often enriched with egg yolk or flavoured with anchovy essence, to accompany fish. Cremona mustard, from Italy, resembles chutney rather than mustard, as it is made from fruits macerated in a sweet-and-sour sauce containing mustard; it generally accompanies boiled meat.

RECIPES

Macaroni with mustard MACARONIS À LA MOUTARDE (from a recipe of the restaurant La Bourgogne) Cook 250 g (9 oz, 2 cups) macaroni in plenty of salted water, cool, then drain. Rub a gratin dish with garlic, butter it generously, and tip the macaroni into it. Warm ¼ litre (8 fl oz, 1 cup) double (heavy) cream in a saucepan and season with salt and pepper. Add 1 egg yolk, 2 tablespoons (3 tablespoons) strong mustard, and the same amount of grated cheese (preferably Parmesan).

Pour this sauce over the macaroni and brown in a hot oven.

Mustard sauce (English recipe) Melt 2 tablespoons (3 tablespoons) butter in a small saucepan, then blend in 2 tablespoons (3 tablespoons) flour and mix well. Next pour in ¼ litre (8 fl oz, 1 cup) milk, beat, and leave to cook over a brisk heat until the sauce thickens. Lower the heat and simmer for 3 minutes, then add 4 tablespoons (⅓ cup) fresh cream, 1 teaspoon white vinegar, 1 teaspoon English mustard powder, some salt, and a little pepper. Serve immediately with poached fish.

Mustard sauce (for cold fish) SAUCE MOUTARDE Heat some fresh cream to reduce it by one-third. Cool, then add to it a quarter of its volume of Dijon mustard and a squeeze of lemon juice. Whisk until light and foamy. Adjust the seasoning.

Mustard sauce (for grills) SAUCE MOUTARDE Peel and finely chop 50 g (2 oz, ½ cup) onions and soften them in butter. Add 1.5 dl (¼ pint, ⅔ cup) white wine, salt, and pepper and reduce until almost dry. Then add 2.5 dl (8 fl oz, 1 cup) demi-glace sauce and reduce by one-third. Blend in 1 tablespoon Dijon mustard, a squeeze of lemon juice, and 1 tablespoon butter. Adjust the seasoning.

mustard pot
MOUTARDIER

A small pot in which mustard is served at table; it sometimes forms part of a cruet. Its lid is notched to allow the mustard spoon to pass through. The oldest models, which are made of pewter and very large, date from the 14th century. In the 17th century mustard pots were made of silver, silver-gilt, and even gold. It was only after the 18th century that mustard pots were manufactured in porcelain, pottery, glass, or wood.

mutton MOUTON

The meat from a castrated and fattened male sheep over a year old. Rams and ewes can also be slaughtered for mutton, but the flesh of the ram does not have such a good flavour and has a stronger smell of wool grease, and the ewe is fatter and of inferior quality. With a calorific value of 250 Cal per 100 g, mutton is a fattier meat than beef and spoils more quickly. The criteria of quality are firm compact dark-red flesh and hard fat, pearly white in colour and plentiful around the kidneys. Mutton is at its best at the end of the winter and in the spring; in summer (shearing time) the smell of wool grease tends to impregnate the flesh.

In France, the best mutton traditionally comes from Pauillac, Sisteron, and Bellac. The flesh of animals reared in the open takes on the taste of the grass consumed (oily in Limousin, fine and fragrant in the southern Alps, salty from the salt meadows), whilst sheep kept under cover, in cereal-producing areas, have a fattier flesh.

Australia is the greatest worldwide exporter of mutton and lamb. Great Britain is also a large producer, exporter, and consumer of mutton, as witnessed by such traditional dishes as: Irish stew, mutton broth, haggis, and Lancashire hotpot. Mutton is an essential meat in North Africa, the Middle and Near East, and also in the Indian subcontinent. Able to subsist in a rugged environment, the sheep is a most useful animal, supplying milk, leather, meat, and wool. Mutton itself is eaten much less in western countries than formerly, as people now prefer lamb.

Highly prized in ancient times, mutton in Gaul was superseded by pork, then by poultry during the Middle Ages; it returned to favour under Louis XIV. Its flesh was then termed 'black', as opposed to beef and to white meats. For centuries the production of wool made it necessary to keep the animals for a long time before slaughter, and the oldest recipes are devised to tenderize the meat and eliminate the taste of wool grease: boiled leg of mutton in England, marinated and larded mutton in France, whole roast sheep in Mediterranean countries. Sautéed and braised ragouts, which make up the majority of recipes for mutton, are usually accompanied by starchy foods, to counteract the fattiness of the meat. For roasts and grills it is generally better to use lamb.

□ **Cooking mutton** The joints for roasting are cut from the leg (shank or fillet end), the saddle (double un-separated loin), the best end, and the shoulder (sometimes boned). As well as being roasted, the leg may also be boiled as in the traditional English fashion and served accompanied by caper sauce.

The pieces for grilling (broiling) are essentially chops (chump, loin, or neck).

Pieces of mutton for cooking on shewers are cut from the breast, shoulder, or neck.

Cuts for braising, sautéing, or stewing are supplied by the neck, the breast, and the shoulder.

Certain items of sheep's offal are in great demand in France: the brains, kidneys, tongue, and feet.

| RECIPES

Braised mutton cutlets CÔTELETTES DE MOUTON BRAISÉES Trim some thick cutlets and season with salt and pepper. Butter a shallow frying pan (skillet), line it with bacon rinds from which all the fat has been removed, and add some thinly sliced carrot and onion. Arrange the cutlets in the pan, cover, and cook gently for 10 minutes. Add enough white wine to just cover, then reduce with the lid removed. Moisten with a few spoonfuls of brown gravy or stock, add a bouquet garni, and cook with the lid on for about 45 minutes. Drain the cutlets and keep them hot on the serving dish. Surround with boiled Brussels sprouts (the garnish may also consist of chestnuts, sautéed potatoes, or a vegetable purée). Reduce the braising stock, strain it, and pour it over the cutlets.

Mutton broth POTAGE AU MOUTON Finely dice a carrot, a turnip, the white part of 2 leeks, a stick (stalk) of celery, and an onion. Soften this brunoise in butter, then add 2 litres (3½ pints, 4½ pints) white consommé. Add 300 g (11 oz) breast and collar of mutton and 100 g (4 oz, generous ½ cup) pearl barley blanched for 8 minutes in boiling water. Cover and cook gently for 1½ hours. Remove and dice the meat and put back in the soup. Sprinkle with chopped parsley just before serving.

Mutton cutlets à la fermière

CÔTELETTES DE MOUTON À LA FERMIÈRE Season 6 thick cutlets with salt and pepper. Fry them lightly in butter in a shallow flameproof serving dish. Add 3 dl (½ pint, 1¼ cups) vegetable fondue, 6 tablespoons (½ cup) very fresh green peas, and 1.5 dl (¼ pint, ⅔ cup) white wine. Reduce, then add a bouquet garni and 2 dl (7 fl oz, ¾ cup) brown stock and cook with the lid on for 20 minutes. Then add about 20 small potatoes and continue cooking with the lid on for a further 35 minutes. Serve in the cooking dish.

Mutton cutlets chasseur CÔTELETTES DE MOUTON CHASSEUR Sauté 6 cutlets in butter in a shallow frying pan (skillet), then drain and keep them hot. Place in the pan 1 tablespoon chopped shallots and 6 large thinly sliced mushrooms and stir for a few moments over a brisk heat. Sprinkle with 1.5 dl (¼ pint, ⅔ cup) white wine and reduce until almost dry. Pour in 2.5 dl (8 fl oz, 1 cup) thickened brown stock and 1 tablespoon tomato sauce, boil for a few moments, then add 1 tablespoon butter and ½ teaspoon chopped chervil and tarragon. Coat the cutlets with this sauce.

Mutton fillets in red wine FILETS MIGNONS AU VIN ROUGE Cut the fillets of mutton into small squares. Season with salt and pepper, then cook them quickly in very hot butter, keeping them slightly pink inside. Drain them and put on one side. In the same butter quickly cook (for 6 fillets) 125 g (4½ oz, 1 cup) thinly sliced mushrooms and add them to the meat. Make a sauce by adding 3 dl (½ pint, 1¼ cups) red wine to the pan juice, reduce, then add several spoonfuls of brown veal gravy. Reduce once again, add some butter, and strain. Mix the meat and the mushrooms with this sauce and serve very hot.

Ragout of mutton a la bonne femme RAGOÛT DE MOUTON À LA BONNE FEMME Cut 750 g (1¾ lb) mutton into cubes, season with salt and pepper, and fry quickly in oil with a chopped onion. Skim off some of the oil in which the meat was cooked, dust the meat with a pinch of caster (superfine) sugar and 2 tablespoons (3 tablespoons) flour.

and mix. Then add a small crushed clove of garlic and moisten with 1 litre (1¾ pints, 4¼ cups) water or stock. Add 3 tablespoons (4 tablespoons) tomato purée (or 100 g (4 oz, ½ cup) fresh tomatoes, peeled and crushed) and a bouquet garni. Cook, covered, in the oven at 220 c (425 f, gas 7) for 1 hour. Drain the meat and reserve the cooking stock (strained and skimmed).

Return the meat to the pan and add 400 g (14 oz, 2⅓ cups) potatoes cut into olive shapes, 24 glazed baby (pearl) onions, and 125 g (4½ oz, ½ cup) streaky bacon (diced, blanched, and lightly fried). Pour the cooking stock over the ragout. Boil, cover, and finish cooking in the oven for 1 hour. Arrange in a timbale or in a round dish.

This ragout may also be prepared with celeriac (celery root) (cut into small pieces and blanched), kohlrabi, haricot (navy) beans, or chickpeas. It may alternatively be served with a macédoine of vegetables, a ratatouille, boiled rice, etc.

Other recipes See *breast, cévenole (à la), Champvallon, chickpea, couscous, epigramme, feet and trotters, gigot,* *halicot, kidneys, lamb, Maintenon, moussaka, navarin, noisette, pieds et paquets, shoulder, tongue.*

muzzle

See *museau.*

myrtle MYRTE

A Mediterranean shrub whose aromatic evergreen leaves have a flavour like that of juniper and rosemary. Myrtle leaves are used particularly in Corsican and Sardinian cookery, to flavour roast thrushes, boar, charcuterie, and bouillabaisse. An essence extracted from the leaves is used to prepare a liqueur, *nerto.* The Romans used myrtle leaves and berries extensively for flavouring ragouts and certain wines.

Mysöst

A Scandinavian cheese made from cows'-milk whey (20% fat). Mysöst is a brown compressed cheese: the water from the whey is evaporated leaving only the whey albumen and lactose, which acquires the consistency of very hard butter and a slightly sweetish flavour. See also *Gjetöst.*

nage

An aromatic court-bouillon in which crayfish, langoustes, small lobsters, or scallops are cooked. They may be served either hot or cold in the cooking stock, which is either seasoned, or mixed with fresh cream. Dishes prepared in this way are described as *à la nage* (literally, 'swimming').

RECIPE

Scallops à la nage COQUILLES SAINT-JACQUES À LA NAGE Prepare the court-bouillon (*nage*) as follows: slice 100 g (4 oz) carrots into thin rounds and place them in a saucepan; add 100 g (4 oz, 1 cup) finely sliced small onions, 4 chopped shallots, a crushed clove of garlic, a sprig of thyme, half a bay leaf, and some sprigs of parsley. Season with salt and pepper and add 1 dl (6 tablespoons, scant ½ cup) white wine and 2 dl (7 fl oz, ¾ cup) water. Simmer gently for 20 minutes, and cool.

Wash and scrub 16 scallops and put them in a cool oven with the rounded sides downwards, until they open. Remove them, take out the flesh, the greyish beard, and the coral 'tongue', which is a great delicacy, and wash very thoroughly to remove any sand. Put the flesh, beards, and coral into the cold nage, bring it slowly to the boil, and poach very gently for 5 minutes. Drain the flesh and the coral and keep them hot. Simmer the beards in the liquid for a further 15 minutes, then remove.

If desired, fresh cream can now be added to the nage. Reduce the nage by one-third and pour it over the hot scallops and coral arranged on a serving dish and garnished with rounds of carrot.

Nanette

The name given to a classic dish of lamb cutlets, veal escalopes, or calves' sweetbreads garnished with small artichoke hearts and mushroom caps braised in butter. The former are stuffed with a chiffonnade of lettuce in cream, the latter with a salpicon of truffles blended with a reduced demi-glace. The dish is served with a sauce made from the pan juices deglazed with Marsala and blended with chicken velouté, cream, and concentrated chicken stock.

Nantais

A Breton cows'-milk cheese made with pressed curds (40% fat content). It has a smooth washed rind and the paste is springy to the touch and pale to deep yellow in colour. It has a pronounced flavour and is manufactured in 9-cm (3½-in) squares, 4 cm (1½ in) deep. Nantais is also known as 'Curé' or 'Fromage du Curé' because it was first made in the 19th century by a priest from the Vendée.

nantais

A cake made of pâte sablée (similar to shortbread dough) mixed with ground almonds or chopped crystallized (candied) fruit and flavoured with Kirsch or rum. It may be baked as a large flat cake or as small biscuits cut out with a round fluted pastry (cookie) cutter and decorated with chopped almonds, chopped crystallized fruit, or raisins.

RECIPE

Gâteau nantais Cream 150 g (5 oz, ⅔ cup) butter with a spatula. Mix 250 g (9 oz, 2¼ cups) plain flour, 150 g (5 oz, ⅔ cup, firmly packed) sugar, and a pinch of salt in a bowl. Add the butter, 3 egg yolks, 1 tablespoon rum, and 125 g (4½ oz, scant cup) diced candied angelica. Work these ingredients together to make a smooth paste, roll it into a ball, flatten it out with the palms of the hands, again roll into a ball, and leave in a cool place for 2 hours. Roll the paste out into a circle 2 cm (¾ in) thick and place it on an oiled baking sheet. Mix an egg yolk with 1 tablespoon water and brush it over the surface of the gâteau. Sprinkle with chopped almonds. Cook for 35 minutes in a moderately hot oven (200 c, 400 f, gas 6). Serve when cold.

nantaise (à la)

The name given to various dishes served with a white wine sauce enriched with butter. Scallops *à la nantaise* are poached, sliced, and then reheated in white wine together with poached oysters and mussels. They are then served in the scallop shells with the sauce poured over, and glazed under the grill (broiler). (Chopped mushrooms and peeled (shelled) shrimps coated with a mixture of velouté and hollandaise sauce can also be added.) Grilled (broiled) fish *à la nantaise* is served with a sauce made with white wine and shallots and thickened with butter. Roast or braised meat *à la nantaise* is garnished with glazed turnips, garden peas, and creamed potatoes.

RECIPE

Red mullet à la nantaise ROUGETS À LA NANTAISE Put 1.5 dl (¼ pint, ⅔ cup) white wine and 2 or 3 finely chopped shallots into a pan and boil down to reduce. Trim and gut (clean) 4 mullet but do not remove the livers. Wipe the fish, season with salt and pepper, brush with oil, and grill (broil). Then remove the livers from the fish, mash them, and beat them into the reduced sauce together with a few drops of lemon juice and about 50 g (2 oz, 4 tablespoons) butter. Pour the sauce into a long serving dish and arrange the grilled mullet on top. Garnish with half slices of lemon with fluted edges.

Nantes cake

PAIN DE NANTES

A small round cake flavoured with lemon or orange and cooked in a tin (mould) lined with shredded (slivered) almonds. The cooked cakes are glazed with apricot jam, iced (frosted) with fondant, and dusted with sugar.

RECIPE

Nantes cakes PAINS DE NANTES Cream in a mixing bowl 100 g (4 oz, ½ cup) butter, 100 g (4 oz, ½ cup) caster (superfine) sugar, a pinch of salt, ½ teaspoon bicarbonate of soda, and the zest of a lemon or an orange, rubbed on sugar or grated. Work these ingredients thoroughly until they are of the consistency of cream, then quickly beat in 2 whole eggs and 125 g (4½ oz, generous cup) sifted flour, beating the mixture well. Butter some tartlet moulds and sprinkle with shredded (slivered) almonds. Pour in the mixture and cook in the oven at 190 c (375 f, gas 5) for about 20 minutes. Turn the cakes out onto a wire rack. Coat them with warmed apricot jam, then ice (frost) them with fondant flavoured with Maraschino and dust with pink sugar grains.

Nantua (à la)

The name given to various dishes containing crayfish or crayfish tails, either whole or in the form of a savoury butter, a purée, a mousse, or a thick sauce. These dishes often contain truffles as well. Nantua is a small town in Bugey, with a centuries-old reputation for gastronomy.

RECIPES

Chicken à la Nantua POULARDE À LA NANTUA Poach a chicken in white stock. Bake some small barquette cases. Prepare a ragout of crayfish tails (see recipe below) and also some crayfish butter. Use the chicken stock to make a suprême sauce and flavour with the crayfish butter (add 1 tablespoon crayfish butter to 2.5 dl (8 fl oz, 1 cup) sauce). Fill the barquettes with the ragout of crayfish tails. Joint the chicken and place on the serving dish, arrange the filled barquettes around it, and coat with the sauce. The barquettes and chicken may be garnished with slices of truffle and with crayfish.

Fillets of sole Nantua FILETS DE SOLE NANTUA Poach some fillets of sole in a little court-bouillon made with white wine or concentrated fish stock. Arrange them in a circle on a serving dish and garnish the centre of the circle with a ragout of crayfish tails (see recipe below). Coat with Nantua sauce (see recipe below) and garnish with slices of truffle.

Nantua sauce SAUCE NANTUA Make 2 dl (7 fl oz, ¾ cup) béchamel sauce. Add an equal volume each of strained crayfish cooking liquor and single (light) cream. Boil to reduce by one-third. While the liquid is boiling, beat in 100 g (4 oz, ½ cup) crayfish butter, 1 teaspoon brandy, and a tiny pinch of cayenne. Rub through a very fine sieve and use in the appropriate recipe.

Ragout of crayfish tails à la Nantua RAGOÛT DE QUEUES D'ÉCREVISSE À LA NANTUA Cook 1.5 dl (¼ pint, ⅔ cup) vegetable mirepoix for about 10 minutes on top of the stove. Add 4 dozen crayfish, season with salt and pepper, and cook until the crayfish turn red. Moisten with 2 dl (7 fl oz, ¾ cup) dry white wine, cover, and cook for 8 minutes. Drain the crayfish and shell the tails.

Pound the mirepoix and the shells in a mortar, then add 2 dl (7 fl oz, ¾ cup) béchamel sauce to the resulting purée. Set the sauce aside.

Put the crayfish tails into a small sauté pan with 1 tablespoon butter. Heat through without allowing them to brown, add 1 tablespoon flour, and mix well. Stir in 2 tablespoons (3 tablespoons) brandy and 1 dl (6 tablespoons, scant ½ cup) double (heavy) cream and cook over a low heat for 7–8 minutes. Then add either all or part of the prepared sauce. Remove from the heat and incorporate 60 g (2½ oz, 5 tablespoons) fresh butter.

This ragout may be used to fill vols-au-vent, a timbale, or pastry barquettes. Add more crayfish if necessary, depending on the recipe. It is often finished with mushrooms, truffles, oysters, etc.

Napolitain

A former Parisian café, opened in 1875 on the corner of the Boulevard des Capucines and the Rue Louis-le-Grand and originally named Café de la Ville de Naples. Its name was soon shortened to 'Napo', and its reputation was founded not so much on the ices and absinthe that were sold there as on its customers. Two generations of journalists and writers sat at its tables: Jules Renard, Maupassant, Courteline, Alphonse Allais, Tristan Bernard, etc. During the Belle Époque, it cost 8 sous to buy a glass of beer there, despite the fact that other cafés in the Boulevard charged only 6 sous, probably because the high society of Paris at that time selected the Napolitain as its rendezvous. An old cab driver, who was nicknamed 'Marquis', knew all the pretty Parisian actresses and used to wait in front of the café to take them up as his fares. The Napolitain closed down in 1965.

napolitain

A large cylindrical or hexagonal cake with a hollow centre. It is made of layers of almond pastry, sandwiched together with apricot jam, redcurrant jelly, or other preserve and usually lavishly decorated with marzipan (almond paste) and crystallized (candied) fruits. It was formerly used as the set piece of elaborate buffets. The name of the cake suggests that it originated from Naples, but it was more probably created by Carême, who made a number of elaborate cakes for set pieces and named them himself.

Although the large cake is rarely seen today, small biscuits known as *fonds napolitains* are still made; they are decorated with butter cream or jam.

Napolitain (neapolitan) is the name given to very small tablets of fine, often bitter, chocolate served with coffee.

RECIPES

napolitain Pound 375 g (13 oz, 2½ cups) sweet almonds in a mortar, together with 5 g (¼ oz, 1 teaspoon) bitter almonds, if desired. Gradually incorporate an egg white to prevent the almonds from becoming oily. Then add 200 g (7 oz, 1 cup) caster (superfine) sugar, the very finely grated rind of a lemon, 250 g (9 oz, generous cup) softened butter, and 500 g (18 oz, 4½ cups) sifted plain flour. Work all the ingredients together in the mortar. Add 4 whole eggs, one by one, until the dough is very smooth but still firm.

Leave the dough in a cool place for 2 hours. Then roll it out to a thickness of 1 cm (½ in) on a lightly oiled surface and cut out circles 20–25 cm (8–10 in) in diameter. Leaving 2 rounds whole, cut out the centres of the remaining rounds with a pastry (cookie) cutter 6 cm (2½ in) in diameter. Place the rounds on a baking sheet and bake in a moderately hot oven (200 c, 400 f, gas 6) for 20–25 minutes.

When completely cold, cover one of the whole rounds with very reduced sieved apricot jam, then build up the cake by placing the rounds with the centres cut out one on top of the other, covering each of them with apricot jam. Place the remaining whole round on the top and cover it with apricot jam. Put the cake in a cool place. Finish by covering the cake with marzipan (almond paste) or royal icing (frosting) and decorate the top with crystallized (candied) apricot halves.

Napolitain biscuits (cookies) FONDS NAPOLITAINS Rub together 250 g (9 oz, generous cup) chilled butter with 250 g (9 oz, 2¼ cups) plain flour until the mixture resembles breadcrumbs. Then add 250 g (9 oz, generous cup, firmly packed) caster (superfine) sugar, 250 g (9 oz, 2¼ cups) ground almonds, and 2 or 3 egg yolks. Mix together as quickly as possible without kneading and roll out to a thickness of about 1 cm (½ in). Cut into rounds with a pastry (cookie) cutter and bake in a moderately hot oven (200 c, 400 f, gas 6). Decorate the biscuits (cookies) with butter cream or jam when cold.

napolitaine (à la)

A method of serving buttered macaroni or spaghetti either in a tomato sauce or with peeled, chopped, and deseeded tomatoes, sprinkled with grated cheese. It can be served either as a main dish or as an accompaniment to small cuts of meat. Napolitaine sauce, invented by Carême, is made with horseradish, ham, Madeira, espagnole sauce, redcurrant jelly, raisins, and (sometimes) candied citron.

This sauce has nothing in common with Neapolitan cooking, which is characterized by the famous *pizzaiola* sauce, consisting of peeled chopped deseeded tomatoes, garlic, basil or marjoram, and olive oil. It is served with pasta, grilled (broiled) dishes, and pizzas.

RECIPE

Napolitaine sauce SAUCE NAPOLITAINE (from Carême's recipe) Put 1 tablespoon grated horseradish, a little chopped lean ham, a seasoned bouquet garni, a little ground white pepper, some grated nutmeg, and 1 glass (4 fl oz, ½ cup) dry Madeira into a pan. Reduce over a very low heat. Remove the bouquet garni and add 2 tablespoons (3 tablespoons) consommé and 2 tablespoons (3 tablespoons) espagnole sauce. When the sauce has reduced, strain and reduce it again, gradually adding 1 glass (4 fl oz, ½ cup) Málaga and a quarter of a jar of redcurrant jelly. Just before serving, add a little butter and game glaze.

This sauce goes well with game and venison. If well-washed sultanas (seedless white raisins) are added, the sauce can be served with braised or roast fillet (sirloin) of beef á la napolitaine. A little candied citron rind, diced and blanched, may also be added.

nasi goreng

An Indonesian speciality with rice as its foundation. Finely chopped onion, garlic, and chilli are fried in oil, then boiled and cooled rice is added, together with diced cooked pork or chicken and peeled (shelled) cooked prawns (shrimp). Finally, a plain omelette is made and cut into strips which are laid in a lattice pattern on top of the rice mixture. The dish is served with cucumber and roasted peanuts.

The Dutch adopted this dish during their colonial period and adapted it to European tastes; it is known in the Netherlands as rijsttafel (literally, 'rice table').

nasturtium   CAPUCINE

An ornamental plant whose leaves and flowers are sometimes used as an ingredient or garnish for salads or as a condiment. The flower buds and seeds, picked when soft and pickled in tarragon vinegar, can be used as a substitute for capers. They are a little tougher, but more aromatic. Tuber nasturtiums, which come from Peru, yield tubers that can be pickled and used to garnish hors d'oeuvres and cold meats.

nature

A French term used to describe dishes which are served plainly cooked with no additions other than those necessary to make them edible.

The term is applied chiefly to boiled or steamed unseasoned vegetables, but also to meat or fish that has been grilled (broiled) *au naturel* (that is without butter or sauce), plain omelettes without garnish or filling, and fresh fruit served either as a dessert (such as strawberries or raspberries) or as a first course (e.g. melon).

navarin

A ragout of mutton with potatoes and/ or various other vegetables, particularly yo g spring vegetables (when it becom.s navarin printanier). The dish is popularly supposed to have been named after the Battle of Navarino, at which British, French, and Russian ships destroyed the Turkish and Egyptian fleets on 20 October 1827, during the Greek War of Independence. However, the dish existed well before 1827, and was more likely to have been named after the *navet* (turnip), originally the main accompanying vegetable. Some chefs therefore use the name navarin, quite justifiably, for other types of ragout (of shellfish, poultry, monkfish, etc.) garnished with turnips.

RECIPE

Navarin of mutton with spring vegetables   NAVARIN DE MOUTON PRINTANIER   Cut 1 kg (2¼ lb) mutton (middle or scrag and of neck, or shoulder) into pieces of about 75 g (3 oz). Brown the meat in 3 tablespoons (4 tablespoons) oil in a casserole dish and season with salt and pepper. Add a pinch of sugar to caramelize and colour the sauce. Mix with 2 tablespoons (3 tablespoons) flour and cook until lightly browned. Then add enough warm water to just cover the meat, bring to the boil, stirring continuously, and add 4 medium chopped tomatoes (or tomato purée), a crush clove of garlic, and a bouquet garni. Cover and cook gently (preferably in the oven) for 1 hour.

Remove the pieces of meat and strain the sauce. Rinse the casserole in hot water, then replace the meat and sauce. Bring to the boil again and add 12 small onions, 15 small carrots, 15 turnip quarters cut into olive shapes, and 20 small new potatoes. Continue to cook very gently for another hour.

About 25 minutes after adding the vegetables, add 100 g (4 oz, ¾ cup) freshly shelled peas and 100 g (4 oz) French (string) beans, cut into pieces. Just before serving, skim off the fat and transfer the ragout to a deep serving dish.

navette

A dry boat-shaped cake, made from butter, flour, and sugar syrup flavoured with orange-flower water. In Marseille, navettes are traditionally made at Candlemas and sold at the *four des navettes*, near the Abbaye Saint-Victor, made to the same recipe for over a century.

The cake is believed to have originated in ancient Egypt, and its shape is thought to represent the boat that carried Isis, the goddess of fertility and harvests (the name comes from the Latin *navis*, a boat). However, another theory suggests that the shape represents the boat that brought the Virgin of the Sea to the Camargue, together with Lazarus, whom Jesus raised from the dead.

Navettes can also be found at Albi, where they are sometimes made with crystallized (candied) fruit or almonds. In this region, the shape represents the weaver's shuttle, which was the secret emblem of the Cathars, a medieval heretical Christian sect.

Néac

A region north of the St Émilion vineyard in the Bordeaux region. It was officially joined to Lalande-de-Pomerol in 1954 and Néac wines are somewhat similar to the Pomerols in style.

Neapolitan slice

TRANCHE NAPOLITAINE

A slice of ice-cream cake made with mousse mixture and ordinary ice cream, presented in a small pleated paper case. Neapolitan ice cream consists of three layers, each of a different colour and flavour (chocolate, strawberry, and vanilla), moulded into a block and cut into slices. Neapolitan ice-cream makers were famous in Paris at the beginning of the 19th century, especially Tortoni, creator of numerous ice-cream cakes.

neck or scrag

COLLIER OU COLLET

Part of the neck of slaughtered animals that provides economical cuts of meat. The neck contains a lot of fat and gristle and must be cooked slowly. Neck of beef is used in stews and carbonades, and may be braised. Neck (or scrag) of veal or mutton is usually cut into fairly large cubes and used for braised dishes or stews such as blanquettes, marengos, navarins, and Irish stew.

Neck of pork is not used as a cut as such, but is used to make sausagemeat, etc.

In poultry, the neck forms part of the giblets. Goose necks may be eaten stuffed.

nectar

In Greek mythology, the drink of the gods, which conferred immortality on those who drank it. In the botanical sense, nectar is the sugary liquid produced by flowers and turned into honey by bees.

In the French soft-drinks industry, the term 'nectar of . . .' followed by the name of a fruit is only applied to sweetened fruit juices with added water, the juice being considered unpalatable in its pure state because it is too acid or too thick. The most common fruits from which nectars are made are apricots, peaches, pears, guavas, sour cherries, and blackcurrants. In the United States, in particular, undiluted fruit juice is known as nectar, as are certain mixtures of fruit juices.

nectarine

A variety of peach with a smooth skin, reddish tinged with yellow, and firm sweet juicy flesh. Nectarines are eaten plain and can be used instead of peaches in desserts.

nègre en chemise

A chilled chocolate dessert covered with Chantilly cream.

RECIPE

Nègre en chemise Melt 250 g (9 oz) chocolate in a double saucepan with 1 tablespoon milk. Soften 250 g (9 oz, generous cup) butter with a spatula. Mix the melted chocolate with the butter, beat thoroughly, and then add 75 g (3 oz, 6 tablespoons, firmly packed) sugar and 4 or 5 egg yolks. Whisk 5 egg whites until very stiff and fold them carefully into the mixture. Oil a bombe or charlotte mould, pour in the chocolate cream, and refrigerate for at least 12 hours.

Just before serving, make some Chantilly cream by whisking 2 dl (7 fl oz, ¾ cup) double (heavy) cream and 75 ml (4 tablespoons, ⅓ cup) very cold fresh milk, adding 40 g (1½ oz, generous ¼ cup) icing (confectioners') sugar and either 1 teaspoon vanilla sugar or a few drops of vanilla essence. Unmould the chocolate cream onto a serving dish then pipe the Chantilly cream over it, taking care that the chocolate shows through in places.

neige

The French term for egg whites whisked until they form stiff peaks. They are used to prepare many different desserts and pastries (meringues, soufflés, floating islands, etc.).

Neige is also a type of sorbet made with red fruit juice and sugar. *Neige de Florence* (Florentine snow) – featherlight flakes of pasta – is used in consommés and clear soup. It is served separately, and stirred into the soup by the person eating it.

nélusko

An iced petit four consisting of a stoned (pitted) cherry steeped in brandy, filled with Bar-le-Duc redcurrant jelly, and covered with fondant icing (frosting) flavoured with cherry brandy. *Nélusko* is also the name of a chocolate and praline bombe glacée flavoured with Curaçao.

According to the *Dictionnaire de l'Académie des gastronomes* the name, which was given to one of the heroes in Meyerbeer's opera *L'Orientale*, was originally applied to a sweet soup made from coconut, arrowroot, and almonds.

Nemours

A garnish for small entrées, consisting of duchess potatoes, buttered garden peas, and shaped and glazed carrots. It is also the name of a dish of poached fillets of sole coated with shrimp sauce, topped with a slice of truffle, and garnished with quenelles and small mushrooms in normande sauce. Nemours soup is made with potato purée moistened with consommé, thickened with cream and egg yolk, and garnished with tapioca.

neroli   NEROLI

A volatile oil extracted from orange blossom and used in perfumery. The name is derived from the family name of a 17th-century Italian princess, Anne-Marie de la Tremoille of Neroli, who is thought to have created the perfume. Neroli, which has a bland, though penetrating, scent, is also used in confectionery and in the manufacture of certain liqueurs.

Nesselrode

The name given to various cooked dishes and pastries, all containing chestnut purée, dedicated to Count Nesselrode, the 19th-century Russian diplomat who negotiated the Treaty of Paris after the Crimean War. Braised calves' sweetbreads or sautéed roebuck steaks in poivrade (pepper) sauce are served with salted chestnut purée. For consommé Nesselrode, the purée is used to fill profiteroles, which are served with a game consommé.

Among the desserts, one of the best-known is Nesselrode pudding, created by M. Mouy, head chef to Count Nesselrode. It consists of custard cream mixed with chestnut purée, crystallized (candied) fruit, currants and sultanas (seedless white raisins), and whipped cream. In bombe Nesselrode, the bombe mousse mixture contains Kirsch-flavoured chestnut purée and the mould is lined with vanilla ice cream.

RECIPES

Consommé Nesselrode   Prepare some game consommé and make some small savoury chou buns. Mix some chestnut purée with one-third of its weight of onion purée and use the mixture to fill half of the choux. Fill the remainder with a very dry mushroom duxelles. Garnish the consommé with the profiteroles.

Nesselrode pudding   PUDDING NES-SELRODE   Mix 1 litre (1¾ pints, 4½ cups) custard cream (see *creams and custards*) with 250 g (9 oz, generous cup) chestnut purée. Macerate 125 g (4½ oz, scant cup) candied orange peel and diced crystallized (candied) cherries in Málaga, and soak some sultanas (seedless white raisins) and currants in warm water. Add all the ingredients to the custard cream together with 1 litre (1¾ pints, 4¼ cups) whipped cream flavoured with Maraschino. Line the base and sides of a large charlotte mould with greaseproof (waxed) paper and add the mixture. Cover the mould with a double thickness of kitchen foil and secure it with an elastic band. Place the mould in the freezer. When the pudding is frozen, unmould it onto the serving dish, peel off the paper, and surround the base with marrons glacés.

nest NID

A small basket made with potato matchsticks and shaped like a bird's nest. Potato nests are used to hold small roast birds, such as thrushes or quails, the preparation being described as *au nid* (in a nest). The nests are built up and deep-fried in a special wire basket, called *panier à nids* (nest basket), which is made up of two parts, one fitting into the other. Potato nests are sometimes lined with pancakes, particularly when the birds are served with a garnish and a sauce. The nests may be decorated with poached cherries and small bunches of parsley or watercress.

Other preparations described as *au nid* include soft-boiled (soft-cooked) or poached eggs placed in hollowed-out tomatoes or in 'nests' made of piped Montpellier butter garnished with chopped aspic and watercress.

See also *birds' nests*.

RECIPE

Potato nests NIDS DE POMMES PAILLE OU GAUFRETTES Peel some firm potatoes and wipe them (do not wash). Using a mandoline, cut them into very fine strips (matchsticks). Line the larger nest basket with an even layer of potato matchsticks, overlapping them slightly. Press them against the sides and trim them. Place the smaller basket inside the larger one so that the matchsticks are held in position. Deep-fry in hot oil (180 C, 350 F) for 5–6 minutes. Open the basket and the nest should come out quite cleanly.

Netherlands PAYS-BAS

Dutch cookery is closely related to that of Belgium and north Germany. Being a country of rich pasturelands, there is an abundance of high-quality dairy produce, which goes into its famous cheeses. The best known of these are Gouda, a yellow cheese with yellow or black rind, shaped like a flattened cylinder, and sometimes flavoured with cumin; Edam, a large spherical yellow-orange cheese with a red or yellow rind; and Leyde cheese, which is round and flattened and flavoured with cumin or aniseed.

The Netherlands is a country of both fishermen and livestock farmers, so the Dutch table features a wide variety of salted and smoked meats and fish. Together with many different breads, these make up the famous *koffietafel*, a cold buffet which is served at lunchtime. The main meal is served in the evening.

There is a Dutch proverb which says: '*Haring in't land, dokter aan de kant*' ('As long as the herring is there, the doctor stays away'). Herring is a popular food of the Dutch people. So it is not surprising that the herring is the centrepiece of countless feasts. One of these is the 'New Hollanders' (first fishing of the year) celebrated in gaily decorated coastal villages. The first barrel of herring is offered to the queen.

Dutch cooking is quite filling. Favourite winter dishes include split pea soup, *hutspot* (a stew served with a plate of chops), *balkenbrij* (brawn (head cheese) served with an apple compote), *hazepepper* (jugged hare), and knuckle of veal with sauerkraut. Other typical dishes are *rolpens* (fried marinated meat served with potatoes and pineapple) and escalope of veal with a creamy cheese sauce, seasoned with nutmeg, and served with green vegetables.

Rice is imported in large quantities from the former Dutch colonies and is a frequent ingredient in both sweet and savoury dishes. *Rijsttafel* (literally 'rice table') is a direct result of the influence of Indonesian cookery. It consists of rice garnished with different types of highly spiced meat, fish, sauces, and vegetables, and is a typically Dutch dish.

In pâtisserie and confectionery, ginger, cinnamon, and nutmeg are used a great deal, for example in *spéculos* (tiny cakes) served at Christmas, spiced pancakes, *boterkoek* (butter cake), and the famous *hopjes* (coffee caramels).

From Indonesia comes excellent coffee, tea, and high-quality cocoa and chocolate. The Dutch love good coffee and drink it often, from small porcelain coffee cups. Apart from their own national beer, the Dutch drink French and Rhine wines. Two famous Dutch liqueurs are Curaçao and Advocaat.

nettle ORTIE

A plant whose leaves have stinging hairs which cause a rash on contact; because of this, people are generally unaware of its therapeutic qualities and its food value. The young leaves of the annual small nettle (known in France as *grièche*) can be chopped and used in salads. The leaves of the perennial large, or common, nettle can be used in green vegetable soups, on their own or combined with sorrel, leeks, watercress, or cabbage, thickened with broad beans or potatoes. Both types of nettle can be cooked like spinach. Nettles are even richer in iron than spinach and contain the same amount of vitamins A and C.

Neufchâtel

A cows'-milk cheese (45% fat content), with a white downy rind mottled with red and a soft smooth creamy golden-yellow paste. It has a mild flavour and is sold in various shapes – rectangular, square, cylindrical, or heart-shaped. It has been made in Neufchâtel, a small town in the Seine-Maritime region, since the Middle Ages and is now protected by an AOC, guaranteeing its source of manufacture. Several other cheeses are very similar to Neufchâtel, e.g., Coeur de Bray, Bondon, Gournay, etc.

Néva (à la)

The name given to a dish of stuffed chicken coated with a white chaud-froid sauce and glazed with aspic. The reference to the River Neva, which flows through Leningrad, is justified because it is served with Russian salad.

RECIPE

Chicken à la Néva POULARDE À LA NÉVA Prepare a chicken weighing about 3 kg (6½ lb) and remove the breastbone. Stuff it with a mixture of 750 g (1¾ lb, scant 3¼ cups) fine chicken forcemeat, small cubes of raw foie gras, and truffles. Truss the bird, poach it in white stock, and leave to cool in the liquid. When it is quite cold, wipe dry and coat with a white chaud-froid sauce prepared with some of the cooking liquor. Garnish with slices of truffle, glaze with aspic, and allow to set firmly. Place the chicken on a long serving dish.

Prepare some Russian salad (see (*à la*) *russe*) mixed with a thick mayonnaise, divide the mixture into two, and shape each half into a dome. Garnish each dome with slices of truffle and place them on the serving dish at each end of the chicken. Garnish the edges of the dish with chopped aspic.

Newburg

A method of cooking lobster created by a Mr Wenburg, a former head chef at Delmonico's, the famous New York restaurant. The first letters of Wenburg have been transposed to give Newburg. Lobster Newburg is basically lobster sautéed in cream, although there are many variations on both sides of the Atlantic.

Newburg sauce is made by preparing lobster *à l'américaine* and adding cream and fish stock. It can also be used to accompany fish, particularly sole or fillets of sole garnished with lobster medallions.

RECIPE

Lobster Newburg HOMARDS À LA NEWBURG Wash 2 lobsters weighing about 500 g (1 lb) each and joint them as for lobster *à l'américaine*. Remove the coral and liver and keep for use later. Season the lobsters with salt and paprika and brown them in 75 g (3 oz, 6 tablespoons) butter. Cover the pan and cook with the lid on for 12 minutes. Drain off the butter, add 3 dl (½ pint, 1¼ cups) sherry, and boil down over a high heat. Add 3 dl (½ pint, 1¼ cups) fish stock and an equal quantity of velouté sauce. Cover the pan and simmer gently for 15 minutes. Take out the pieces of lobster and arrange them in a deep dish. (The tail pieces may be shelled if wished).

Boil down the cooking liquid and add 4 dl (14 fl oz, 1¾ cups) cream. When the sauce is thick enough to coat the back of the spoon, add the coral and liver, rubbed through a fine sieve and blended with 100 g (4 oz, ½ cup) fresh butter. Beat the sauce vigorously and pour it over the lobster.

New Zealand spinach

TÉTRAGONE

A climbing plant, *Tetragonia tetrago-*

nioides, native to New Zealand and Australia, also called summer spinach. It is cultivated in many warm regions for its dark green fleshy leaves, which have a pleasant though slightly acid flavour and are eaten as a vegetable.

It was introduced into Europe from New Zealand by Sir Joseph Banks, who travelled with Captain Cook on his voyage round the world in 1771. Nowadays it is available in April and May and from July to October. It will grow well in a drier climate than spinach. It contains less iron and oxalic acid than spinach, but is prepared in the same way.

The following is an extract from *Le Livre de cuisine*, by Alice Toklas (published by Minuit, 1981): 'It is better to cook them as they are, without adding water, after they have been washed. Cook them for ten minutes in a covered saucepan, drain, rinse them under the cold-water tap, drain again, squeeze, and replace them in the saucepan. Half a teaspoon of salt and a pinch of ground nutmeg or ground ginger, or both, gives them the necessary flavour.'

Nice and its environs
NICE ET PAYS NIÇOIS

The city of Nice is situated on the French Riviera, in the southeastern corner of Provence, close to the Italian border. Although influenced by both Provençal and Italian cooking, the cuisine of the region still retains its own specific characteristics. The Mediterranean provides the region with a variety of seafood. Sardines are stuffed or sautéed in oil, as in sartagnano, and anchovies are used in a host of different dishes (see *anchoyade, niçoise (à la), panbagnat, pissaladière, pissalat*). Sea bass, scorpion fish, squid, and octopus are usually cooked with tomatoes and garlic. However, the truly original dishes of this cuisine are stockfish, or *stoficado* (see *estofinado*), omelette *à la poutine* (filled with sardines and anchovies), and *favouille* soup (made with little crabs).

Olive trees growing on the hills behind Nice provide both oil and the celebrated small black (ripe) Nice olives. Bellet wines are produced from the grapes of the region and are used locally to cook moray eels with tomatoes and

olives. Oranges, especially bitter oranges, are a speciality of Nice. Cultivated or wild flowers are a source of honey. Other fruits and vegetables of the region include aubergines (eggplants), tomatoes, courgettes (zucchini), and peppers, combined in the famous ratatouille or cooked separately (sautéed or stuffed); also to be mentioned are small purple artichokes, fresh broad (fava) beans, and medlars, figs, and strawberries.

Among other typical dishes of the region are *trucha* (an omelette of spinach or Swiss chard), *tourte aux feuilles de bettes* (a dessert using Swiss chard leaves), *socca* (flat cakes made of chickpea flour and fried in oil), and ravioles, which are served with daubes or with estouffade of beef *à la niçoise*, garnished with tomatoes and olives. Tripe, stewed kid, medallions of lamb, and veal paupiettes are also garnished with tomatoes and olives.

Among the cheeses, Cachat and Brousse de la Vésubie are highly esteemed. Most cakes and sweetmeats are based on preserved flowers and fruits, and there is also the famous local pastry known as *pompe à l'huile*.

nickel
A lustrous silvery-white metal that is resistant to oxidation and corrosion. It is used mainly for electroplating copper, and it forms a base for chrome-plating. Nickel is a constituent of numerous alloys, including stainless steel and nickel silver (nickel, copper, and zinc). The latter is used in the manufacture of cutlery and tableware that are subsequently silver-plated.

niçoise (à la)
The name given to various dishes typical of the cuisine of the region around Nice, in which the most common ingredients are garlic, olives, anchovies, tomatoes, and French (green) beans.

Fish grilled (broiled) *à la niçoise* (mullet, sole, or whiting) is served with coarsely chopped peeled deseeded tomatoes, anchovy fillets, olives, and sometimes anchovy butter.

The niçoise garnish for large cuts of meat and poultry consists of tomatoes stewed in oil and flavoured with garlic, buttered French beans (or stewed courgettes (zucchini) and small artichokes), and château potatoes. The sauce that coats the meat is made by deglazing the pan with veal stock thickened with tomato.

Finally, *salade niçoise* is a typically southern dish containing tomatoes, cucumber, locally grown fresh broad (fava) beans or small artichokes, green peppers, raw onion, hard-boiled (hard-cooked) eggs, anchovy fillets or tuna, black (ripe) Nice olives, olive oil, garlic, and basil. Neither potatoes nor cooked vegetables should be added to this salad.

RECIPES

Grilled (broiled) red mullet à la niçoise ROUGETS GRILLÉS À LA NIÇOISE Clean, wash, and dry the fish, season with salt and pepper, brush with olive oil, and marinate for 30 minutes. Make a well-flavoured tomato fondue and boil down until very thick. Grill (broil) the mullet gently for 15 minutes. Cover the bottom of the serving dish with the tomato fondue (capers may be added if desired) and place the grilled fish on top. Garnish with strips of anchovy fillets in oil, arranged in a lattice, and small black (ripe) Nice olive. Place a slice of lemon on the head of each fish.

Rack of lamb à la niçoise CARRÉ D'AGNEAU À LA NIÇOISE Trim a rack of lamb and brown it lightly in butter in a flameproof earthenware casserole. Add a coarsely diced peeled courgette (zucchini) fried quickly in olive oil, a large peeled deseeded chopped tomato fried in olive oil, and 20 or so small peeled new potatoes tossed in olive oil. Season with salt and pepper and cook in the oven at 230 c (450 F, gas 8). Serve in the casserole, sprinkled with chopped parsley.

nieule

A small round cake with fluted edges from Flanders, made with flour, milk, a little butter, eggs, and sugar. In *Moeurs populaires de la Flandre française* (1889), Desrousseaux describes nieules as 'pastries shaped like large Communion wafers, made in a waffle iron' and says that they were made on feast days all over Flanders. The town of Armentières claims to have originated nieules: in 1510, when Jacques, Duke of Luxembourg and lord of the town, was presiding at a banquet, he went out onto the balcony and threw the remains of a great cake to the children of the town. The event was such a success that it became an annual custom known as the 'Feast of Nieules'. The name is derived from the Spanish word *ñolas*, meaning crumbs – at that time, Flanders was ruled by Spain. The tradition survived until 1832, then fell into disuse. In 1938 Pierre Baudin, a pastrycook in the town, revived the custom for the carnival.

niflette

A cake that is traditionally made for All Saints' Day in Brie. It consists of puff pastry filled with frangipane cream.

nigella NIGELLE

Any of several chiefly Mediterranean plants of the genus *Nigella* (family *Ranunculaceae*), also known as fennel flower, whose aromatic or pungent seeds were formerly used as a seasoning. The seeds of the species N. *sativa*, also known as black cumin, allspice, and (in France) *poivrette* and *quatre-épices*, can be used as a substitute for pepper. Seeds of the species N. *damascena* (cultivated as the garden plant love-in-a-mist in temperate regions) are scattered over bread and cakes in Eastern countries.

Nignon (Édouard)

French chef (born Nantes, 1865; died c.1934), regarded as one of the greatest masters of French cuisine. His apprenticeship and his exceptionally successful career took him to the most famous restaurants in France – Potel et Chabot, the Maison Dorée, the Café Anglais, Bignon, Magny, Noël Peter's, Paillard, and Lapérouse – and also to Claridges in London and L'Ermitage in Moscow. He was head chef to the Tsar, the Emperor of Austria, and President Woodrow Wilson. In 1918 he took over the management of the restaurant Larue, exchanging his white chef's waistcoat for the black suit of a maître d'Hôtel, causing Sacha Guitry to comment: 'He spent two-thirds of his life dressed all in white or all in black.' He wrote three cookery books in which he recorded his experiences: *L'Hepta-méron des gourmets ou les Délices de la cuisine française* (1919); *Éloges de la cuisine française* (1933), with a preface by Sacha Guitry; and *Les Plaisirs de la table* (1926). Some of his recipes, such as *beuchelle tourangelle* (rice, calves' kidneys, and morels in a cream sauce), are still much appreciated by gourmets.

Nimrod NEMROD

A biblical character, described as 'a mighty hunter before the Lord', to whom various classic game dishes were dedicated during the last century. The Nimrod garnish for ground game consists of small pastry barquettes or vols-au-vent filled with stewed cranberries, croquette potatoes, and large grilled (broiled) field mushrooms, stuffed with chestnut purée. Consommé Nimrod is made with game consommé mixed with port, thickened with arrowroot, and garnished with small quenelles of game forcemeat enriched with chopped truffle. Finally, attereaux Nimrod consist of quenelles of game and ham forcemeat, mushrooms, and hard-boiled (hard-cooked) lapwings' eggs, threaded onto skewers and deep-fried.

Ninon

The name given to various classic French dishes dating from the last century. The Ninon garnish for small sautéed cuts of meat served with marrow sauce consists of small nests of duchess potato filled with a salpicon of cocks' combs and kidneys blended in a velouté sauce, together with asparagus tips in butter. This garnish is also used as a filling for Ninon canapés, which are cut from a round loaf and crisped in a very hot oven.

In a variation of the garnish, the meat is arranged on a base of Anna potatoes and covered with a sauce made with the pan juices deglazed with Madeira and concentrated veal stock. A small pastry case (shell) filled with asparagus tips cooked in butter and sprinkled with a finely shredded truffle is arranged on each piece of meat.

The Ninon mixed salad consists of lettuce leaves and orange segments, flavoured with lemon and orange juice, salt, and a few drops of oil.

Niolo

A Corsican cheese made either from ewes' milk or a mixture of goats' and ewes' milk (fat content at least 45%). Niolo has a soft texture and a natural greyish-white rind. After being soaked for three or four months in brine it is firm to the touch, with a sharp flavour and a strong smell. Niolo is a farmhouse cheese, made in 13-cm (5-in) squares, 4–6 cm (1½–2½ in) deep. It is best from May to December.

Nivernais and Morvan

The culinary repertoire of this ancient province does not pretend to be *grande cuisine*, but the dishes that it does offer are full of flavour, using local produce of excellent quality. The rich pastures of Nivernais and the meadows of Morvan are the home of a highly prized breed of beef cattle, the Charolais, yielding high-quality meat suitable for lavishly garnished roast or braised dishes. The rearing of sheep with delicately flavoured meat is also being developed, and the pork and poultry are of equally fine quality. The forests of Morvan are full of winged and ground game, while trout, pike, and perch are fished in the rivers. Particularly favoured dishes are gudgeon *à l'escabèche* (fried, marinated, and served cold), frogs' legs *au pouilly*, delicious matelotes cooked in wine, and trout *au bleu*.

Other culinary specialities include *potée morvandelle* (a substantial meat and vegetable soup); andouilles and andouillettes from Clamecy, *beursaudes* (pork rillons), saveloys and smoked ham from Morvan, and the game pâtés of Lormes and Prémery. Some of these dishes have a very ancient history, like the veal grenadins from Nevers, chicken or rabbit *en barbouille*, potatoes *en tourtière*, daube with carrots, tripe *à la morvandelle*, saupiquet, civet of hare, and veal stewed in red wine.

There is a wide variety of cheeses, including those of Lormes, Toucy, Tracy, and Dornecy.

Typical pastries from Nivernais are flamusse, crapiaux, fritters made with curds, and almond biscuits (cookies). The confectionery, which has been famous for centuries, includes nougatines from Nevers, marzipan from Decize, and barley sugar from Morvan.

nivernaise (à la)

Describing preparations of large roast or braised cuts of meat or braised duck garnished with glazed carrots cut into olive shapes, small glazed onions, and sometimes braised lettuce. This garnish may also be arranged in croustades and it is usual to pour the braising liquid over the entire dish.

noces

A type of gruel formerly made in the Ille-et-Vilaine region. A paste of unsifted oat flour and warm water was diluted with more water and then wrung out in a cloth; the resulting liquid was boiled over a wood fire. In Normandy, noces was an oat porridge mixed with fresh butter. It was diluted with cider and eaten cold.

Noël Peter's

A Parisian restaurant that opened in the Passage des Princes in 1854 and became very popular during the period of the Second Empire. At first it was known simply as 'Peter's', after the proprietor, Pierre Fraisse. Having lived in the United States, he served dishes that were then new to France, such as turtle soup, roast beef sliced at the table to the customer's requirements, and, above all, lobster à l'américaine, which he created. The restaurant was much patronized by journalists, including the writer Monselet, who was exempted from paying a cover charge. When the place was bought by Vaudable, father of the manager of Maxim's, it became known as Noël Peter's because of its association with a certain Noël. During the 1880s, the restaurant pioneered the concept of a *plat du jour*: each day of the week was allotted its particular dish.

When covered arcades fell out of fashion the restaurant declined and eventually closed.

noisette

A small round steak, usually of lamb or mutton, cut from the rib or loin. Surrounded by a thin band of fat, like a tournedos steak, noisettes are very tender and can be fried in butter and served with a variety of garnishes, including

Anna potatoes and fried onions, morels sautéed with herbs, artichoke hearts, sautéed aubergines (eggplants) or cucumber shells, buttered French (green) beans or garden peas, or asparagus tips. The accompanying sauce often consists of the pan juices deglazed and reduced with Madeira, tomato sauce, or wine.

The name 'noisette' is also given to: a small round slice of beef fillet, fried in butter and served with the same garnishes; a small grenadin of veal, which can be cooked like a veal escalope; or the 'eye' of a roebuck cutlet, grilled (broiled) or sautéed in butter.

RECIPES

Noisettes chasseur Sauté 8 lamb noisettes in a mixture of oil and butter then drain. Add 100 g (4 oz, 1 cup) finely sliced mushrooms and 1 tablespoon chopped shallots to the pan, deglaze with white wine, and moisten with veal stock to which a little tomato sauce has been added. Arrange the meat on a hot dish, garnish with the mushrooms, and pour the sauce over.

Noisettes des Tournelles (from a recipe of the Tour d'Argent) Sauté some lamb noisettes in clarified butter and arrange them on a hot dish. Deglaze the cooking pan with a mixture comprising equal quantities of vermouth, sherry, and veal stock. Thicken with butter. Put 1 teaspoon Soubise purée on each noisette and grill (broil) for a few seconds. Serve the sauce separately in a sauceboat.

noisette butter
BEURRE NOISETTE

Butter heated until it becomes nut brown; it is used to add a finishing touch to a variety of dishes, particularly fish.

Noisette sauce is a hollandaise sauce to which a few spoonfuls of noisette butter are added. It is served with salmon, trout, and turbot cooked in a covered pan on top of the stove.

noisette potatoes
POMMES NOISETTES

Small potato balls, cut out with a melon baller, lightly fried and browned in butter. They are used as a garnish, usually for small cuts of meat.

noix

The fleshy upper part of the fillet end of a leg of veal, cut lengthwise. Below this cut are two other fleshy cuts – the *sous-noix* and the *noix pâtissière*. The meat is lean and tender but tends to be rather dry. It can be sliced into escalopes (scallops) or grenadins or it can be roasted. Various garnishes may be used to accompany it, for example bouquetière, bourgeoise, Clamart, milanaise, or piémontaise; it can also be served with mushrooms, braised chicory (endives), buttered spinach, mixed vegetables, or a risotto. The noix can also be braised, a method which enhances its tenderness.

The lean plump 'eye' of a veal cutlet (chop) is also known as the noix.

RECIPES

Noix of veal Brillat-Savarin NOIX DE VEAU BRILLAT-SAVARIN (from a recipe by Alexandre Dumaine) Flatten a whole noix of veal, bone it, then sew the cut parts together to reform the noix. Chop 3 shallots. Cook 100 g (4 oz) black morels in cream. Spread a 1-cm (½-in) layer of *à gratin* forcemeat mixed with the shallots over the veal. Sprinkle on some of the cooked morels, then place a piece of duck foie gras, weighing about 200 g (7 oz), in the centre. Roll up the noix to form a roast and tie it securely. Stud with strips of fat pork, brown the veal in butter, then place in a braising pan on a bed of mirepoix. Moisten with equal quantities of dry white wine and beef stock. Add some peeled deseeded roughly chopped tomatoes and a bouquet garni. Cover the pan and cook slowly for 2 hours.

Take out the meat, then reduce and strain the cooking liquid. Serve the veal sliced, with a little of the sauce poured over, accompanied by leaf spinach and the remaining morels. Serve the rest of the sauce in a sauceboat.

Roast noix of veal NOIX DE VEAU RÔTI Heat some butter in a flameproof casserole on top of the stove. Stud a noix of veal with thin pieces of bacon and brown it on all sides in the butter. Sprinkle with salt and pepper, then cook in a moderately hot oven (200 C, 400 F, gas 6), allowing 35 minutes per kg (16 minutes per lb).

nonnat

The common name for several species of small white fish found off French coasts, particularly the sandsmelt from the Atlantic and the Mediterranean rockling. They are normally deep-fried.

nonnette

A small round iced gingerbread cake. The cakes were originally made by nuns in convents, but today they are commercially produced. The nonnettes of Reims and Dijon have a good reputation.

nonpareille

A small round caper pickled in vinegar. In France, the name is also used for 'hundreds and thousands', the multi-coloured sugar crystals used as a decoration on cakes and pastries.

noodles NOUILLES

Pasta made from flour, eggs, and water and cut into thin flat strips. The name comes from the German *Nudel*. The best noodles are made with egg yolks; whole eggs give a rather tougher pasta.

Noodles can be used fresh or dried. Famous Italian noodles are tagliatelle and the slightly broader fettuccine. Noodles are cooked in a large quantity of boiling salted water and can be served as a main dish (with butter, cheese, *au gratin*, with tomato or meat sauce, etc.) or as the classic accompaniment to rich game stews, coq au vin, and white meat. They are also used as a garnish for soups and consommés, often in the form of small short noodles.

Noodles are used extensively in Chinese and Vietnamese cookery. Yellow noodles are made from eggs and wheat flour, with monosodium glutamate or nuoc-mâm added, and accompany sautéed meat or garnish soups. Rice noodles include very fine vermicelli, which is steamed and served with lacquered pork, brochettes, or chop suey, as well as ordinary flat noodles.

RECIPES

Buttered noodles à l'alsacienne NOUILLES AU BEURRE À L'ALSAC-

IENNE Cook 300 g (11 oz) noodles *al dente* in plenty of boiling salted water. Drain thoroughly and pour them into a sauté pan; add 60 g (2 oz, 4 tablespoons) fresh butter cut into pieces (or the same amount of noisette butter) and sauté the noodles until the butter is incorporated. Season with salt and pepper and transfer to a hot serving dish. In a frying pan (skillet), lightly brown some raw noodles in butter (the noodles can be broken up or not) and sprinkle them over the boiled noodles. Serve very hot.

Fresh noodles NOUILLES FRAÎCHES Sift 500 g (18 oz, 4½ cups) flour and arrange it in a circle on the work surface. Dissolve 12 g (2 teaspoons) salt in 2 tablespoons (3 tablespoons) water, put it in the middle of the flour, then add 3 whole eggs and 6 egg yolks. Gradually work the flour into the liquid. Knead the dough thoroughly, working it with the heel of the palm until the dough is smooth and firm. Wrap it in a cloth and leave for 1 hour so it loses its elasticity. Then divide the dough into pieces about the size of an egg and roll these into balls. Roll out each piece into the shape of a very thin pancake. Spread these pancakes on baking sheets covered with sheets of paper and leave them to dry for 50 minutes. Lightly dust each pancake with flour, roll it up, cut into strips 2–3 mm (⅛ in) wide, then gradually unroll the strips on a flat surface.

To cook the noodles, plunge them into boiling salted water, using 2.5 litres (4½ pints, 5½ pints) water and 25 g (1 oz) salt for every 250 g (9 oz) fresh noodles. Boil fast for 10 minutes, drain, and transfer to a sauté pan over a low heat to dry off any excess moisture.

Noodles à la lyonnaise NOUILLES À LA LYONNAISE Prepare some buttered noodles (see recipe above), pour them into a deep dish, and garnish with finely chopped onion fried in butter, allowing 1 tablespoon per person. Just before serving, sprinkle some hot vinegar over the top.

Noodles au gratin NOUILLES AU GRATIN Prepare some buttered noodles (see recipe above), adding 60 g (2 oz, ½ cup) mixed grated Gruyère and Parmesan cheese and a little grated nutmeg. Pour into a buttered gratin dish, cover with more grated cheese, sprinkle with melted butter, and brown in a very hot oven.

noque

In Alsace, a small round quenelle (dumpling) made from flour, eggs, and butter. Also called *knepfles*, they are poached and served as a first course or in soup. Noques *à l'allemande* are quenelles of flour with pork liver added, or are made with choux pastry and lean veal; they are served with meat and gravy or used as a garnish in soup.

Noques *à la viennoise* are small light balls made of dough containing eggs, fresh cream, and butter; they are poached in vanilla-flavoured milk and served with custard.

RECIPES

Noques à l'alsacienne Bring 250 g (9 oz, generous 1 cup) butter to room temperature, then cut into pieces and place in a bowl. Sprinkle with salt, pepper, and a little grated nutmeg, then work to a paste using a wooden spatula. Blend in 2 whole eggs and 2 yolks, add 150 g (5 oz, 1¼ cups) sifted flour (all at once), and finally 1 stiffly whisked egg white. Scrape this mixture into a clean bowl and leave it in a cold place for 30 minutes. Shape the dough into walnut-sized balls. Poach them in simmering salted water, turning them so they puff up on both sides. Drain, turn into a deep serving bowl, sprinkle with Parmesan cheese and noisette butter, and serve as a first course or with soup.

Noques à la viennoise Cream 125 g (4½ oz, generous ½ cup) butter in a bowl and blend in a generous pinch of salt, 30 g (1 oz) semolina (semolina flour), 5 egg yolks (one by one), and ½ dl (2½ tablespoons, 3½ tablespoons) double (heavy) cream. Beat the mixture until smooth then add 100 g (4 oz, 1 cup) sifted flour all at once and beat this in; then fold in 1 stiffly whisked egg white and finally 3 unwhisked egg whites, one by one.

Add 60½ g (2 oz, 4 tablespoons, firmly packed) sugar and 1 teaspoon vanilla sugar to ½ litre (17 fl oz, 2 cups) milk and bring to the boil. Poach spoon-fuls of the dough in the simmering milk, turning them so they puff up on both sides. Drain them, arrange in a bowl, and allow to cool.

Prepare some custard by beating together ½ dl (2½ tablespoons, 3½ tablespoons) double (heavy) cream and 5–6 egg yolks. Blend with the poaching milk and heat gently until the custard thickens. Strain it onto the noques.

nori

An edible scented seaweed used for cen-turies in Japanese cookery. Several varieties are grown along the coasts us-ing traditional methods. Rich in vit-amins, nori is sold as a powder, in strands, or pressed and dried into papery sheets. Sometimes it is flavoured with saké or soy sauce, or even sweetened. It is used to wrap around small portions of rice and as a garnish for soups, pasta, or rice.

normande (à la)

Describing various dishes based on the cooking of Normandy, or made using typically Norman products, notably butter, fresh cream, seafood, apples, cider, and Calvados. The term can be applied to a host of fish, meat, poultry, and egg dishes as well as to desserts, such as pancakes, omelettes, puff-pastry galettes, Genoese sponge cake, and fruit salad.

Sole *à la normande* (a model for several dishes of fish braised in white wine) was in fact invented by a Parisian called Langlais, chef at the Rocher de Cancale at the beginning of the 19th century. The original dish was based on fish braised in cream and was prepared with cider, not white wine. However, it evolved to become an *haute cuisine* dish with an elaborate garnish comprising oysters, mussels, prawns (shrimp), mushrooms, truffles, fried gudgeon, and crayfish in court-bouillon that was no longer typically Norman.

Normande sauce, which accompa-nies many fish dishes, is a fish velouté with cream and mushroom fumet. Small cuts of meat and chicken *à la normande* are sautéed, deglazed with cider, mois-tened with cream, and sometimes flavoured with Calvados. Partridge *à la normande* is cooked in a covered pan with Reinette apples and cream. Apples also accompany black pudding (blood sausage) *à la normande* and are used as the filling for pastries, pancakes, and galettes *á la normande*. Cream is used as a dressing for French beans and for matelote normande (seafood flamed in Calvados and moistened with cider).

RECIPES

Apple puffs à la normande FEUIL-LETE AUX POMMES À LA NOR-MANDE Roll out 600 g (1 lb 5 oz) puff pastry to a thickness of 2 cm (¾ in), cut it into two 20-cm (8-in) squares, prick them with a fork, and place them side by side on a baking sheet. Blend 1 egg white with 80 g (3 oz, ¾ cup) icing (confec-tioners') sugar for 2 minutes using a wooden spoon. Spread this icing (frost-ing) over one of the squares, then bake both squares for 12–15 minutes in a moderately hot oven (200 C, 400 F, gas 6).

Peel and slice 750 g (1 lb 10 oz) apples and cook them in 50 g (2 oz) melted butter with 150 g (5 oz, ⅔ cup, firmly packed) caster (superfine) sugar for 15 minutes. Brown 30 g (1 oz) flaked (slivered) almonds in a frying pan (skil-let) over a low heat, stirring them with a wooden spoon. Spread the cooked apples over the plain square, cover with the iced square, and sprinkle with the toasted almonds. Serve warm.

Normande sauce SAUCE NOR-MANDE In a heavy-based saucepan heat 2 dl (7 fl oz, ¾ cup) fish velouté sauce and 1 dl (6 tablespoons, scant ½ cup) each of fish fumet and mushroom essence. Mix 2 egg yolks with 2 tables-poons (3 tablespoons) cream, add to the pan, and reduce by one-third. Just be-fore serving, add 50 g (2 oz, ¼ cup) butter (cut into small pieces) and 3 tab-lespoons (¼ cup) double (heavy) cream. If necessary, pass the sauce through a very fine strainer.

An alternative method is as follows: mix 2 tablespoons (3 tablespoons) mushroom peelings with 2 dl (7 fl oz, ¾ cup) fish velouté; add 1 dl (6 table-spoons, scant ½ cup) double cream and boil down by half. Then add 50 g (2 oz, ¼ cup) butter cut into pieces and 4 tablespoons (⅓ cup) cream. Strain through a very fine sieve.

Potatoes à la normande POMMES DE TERRE À LA NORMANDE Peel 800 g (1¾ lb) potatoes, slice them thinly, wash and dry them, and sprinkle with salt and pepper. Butter a flameproof casserole and put in half the potatoes. Clean and slice 3 large leeks and chop a small bunch of parsley. Spread the leeks and parsley over the potatoes in the casserole, then cover with the rest of the potatoes. Add sufficient meat or chicken stock to cover the potatoes and dot with 50–60 g (2 oz, 4 tablespoons) butter cut into small pieces. Cover the casserole, bring to the boil, then transfer to a hot oven (220 C, 425 F, gas 7 and cook for about 45 minutes, or until the potatoes are done.

Sole à la normande For a sole weighing about 400 g (14 oz), prepare a garnish of 4 debearded and poached oysters, 12 mussels cooked in white wine, 25 g (1 oz) peeled (shelled) shrimps, 4 fluted mushrooms cooked in white wine, 6 slices of truffle, 4 gudgeon (or smelt) coated with breadcrumbs and fried, 4 trussed crayfish cooked in court-bouillon, and 4 heart- and lozenge-shaped croutons of bread fried in butter (or puff-pastry crescents).

Trim the sole, split it, skin one side only, and carefully raise the fillets a little. Break the backbone in 2 or 3 places to facilitate its removal after cooking. Poach the fish in a little fish fumet made with white wine, to which the cooking liquids from the oysters, mushrooms, and mussels have been added. Drain the fish on absorbent paper and remove the backbone.

Arrange the fish on a long buttered serving dish, together with the various garnishes and cover with normande sauce made from the fish cooking stock. The fish can be garnished with a ribbon of light fish aspic or meat glaze.

Sweet omelette à la normande OMELETTE SUCRÉE À LA NOR-MANDE Peel, core, and slice 3 Reinette (dessert) apples. Cook them in 50 g (2 oz, 4 tablespoons) butter and some caster (superfine) sugar. Add 2 dl (7 fl oz, ¾

cup) double (heavy) cream and reduce to a creamy consistency, then flavour with 2–3 tablespoons (3–4 tablespoons) Calvados.

Beat 10 eggs with a pinch of salt, sugar, and 2 tablespoons (3 tablespoons) fresh cream. Cook the omelette and fill it with the apple mixture; glaze under a hot grill.

Normandy NORMANDIE

This maritime and agricultural region, described by the chronicler Froissart as 'a rich and flavoursome country in all its aspects', possesses many resources which are employed in a culinary tradition developed over many hundreds of years.

The coastal waters teem with fish and shellfish, shad, eel, and trout are fished in the rivers, the rich pastures of the interior support herds of dairy cattle, while delicious mutton is obtained from sheep reared on the salt meadows of Avranchin. There is also a thriving pig-rearing industry.

Normandy apples provide the raw material for cider and Calvados and are also used in cooking and pâtisserie; dessert varieties, such as Colville, are also grown. Market gardening, too, is important in the region.

The most famous dishes of Normandy cuisine are *canard au sang* (duck killed by smothering to retain the blood), tripe *à la mode de Caen*, chicken with cream and Calvados, and roast leg of mutton. Less well known is graisse normande, which is used as a cooking fat (particularly for roast sirloin of beef) and as the basic ingredient of a rich vegetable soup. Although omelette *à la crème de la Mère Poulard* is famous, those filled with cockles, mussles, or shrimps (and sometimes topped with poached oysters) are just as delicious. And while the *tripes de Caen* are universally acclaimed, those of Ferté-Macé and Coutances are close rivals.

Helped by the ritual of the trou normand (a glass of Calvados taken between courses), Normandy meals tend to be rich and plentiful. Poultry dishes include duckling *à la rouennaise*, sautéed chicken *yvetois*, flamed partridges with Reinette apples, and goose *en daube*. Rabbit is cooked with morels, in pâtés, or *à la havraise* (stuffed with truffled pigs' trotters (feet)); the blood is traditionally eaten seasoned and cooked in sanguette in Alençon (with pieces of fat pork and onions). Other meat dishes are sheep's trotters *à la rouennaise*, casseroled veal, larded calf's liver braised with carrots, and veal escalopes (scallops) in cream with mushrooms.

Normandy cheeses are mainly soft with bloomy rinds and a high fat content (many are made from double or triple cream). Besides Camembert, Livarot, and Pont l'Évêque, there are also Neufchâtel, Gournay, Trappiste de Briquebec, Lucullus, Brillat-Savarin, Bouille, Excelsior, Coeur de Bray, Bondon, etc. Particular mention must be made of *pain brié*, a white fine-textured bread that is a speciality of the Auge region.

As for desserts and pastries, the region is noted for its butter brioches (especially those from Évreux and Gisors), puff-pastry galettes with jam, puff-pastry apple turnover, *roulettes* from Rouen (small rolls of croissant dough), tarts served with fresh cream, douillons, bourdelots, craquelins, fouaces from Caen, madeleines from Illiers-Combray, sablés from Bayeux, mirlitons from Rouen, *fallues* (sweet pancakes) from Lisieux, and the traditional terrinée. Confectionery of the region includes sugar apples from Rouen, caramels from Isigny, chocolates with Calvados, mint chews from Bayeux, berlingots (boiled sweets) from Falaise, *galets* (marzipan sweets) from Le Havre, *croquettes* (small cakes) from Argentan, and duchesses (a type of macaroon) from Rouen. The meal is rounded off with Benedictine from Fécamp or perhaps with coffee spiked with Calvados.

North Africa
AFRIQUE DU NORD

The cuisine of North Africa, perhaps more than any other, tells us as much about the history of the country as its geography. The African provinces were the granary of imperial Rome. They later came under Turkish influence (in the 16th century they were occupied by the Turks, who gave the natives a taste for sweet cakes and pastry), as well as that of the Jews, whose religious ordinances often coincided with those of the Muslems, notably the exclusion from the diet of the pig and its products, fasting, and respect for ritual religious feasts. Market gardening (truck farming), fruit growing, and the introduction of the vine are due to the French and Italian colonists, who have influenced both the ancestral traditions of the 'cuisine of the desert' – based on cereals, vegetables, dried fruits, and grilled meat – and gastronomic development in the towns, particularly in Fez and Algiers, where the science of spices, the art of pastry-making, and the preparation of dishes served in sauce has reached a high degree of sophistication.

Food is always served in abundant quantities, for family life and the tradition of hospitality result in large numbers at the table. The custom of eating with the fingers is a symbol of brotherhood inspired by the Koran, which urges the appreciation of food.

Although they are neighbours, the three North African countries vary considerably in their cuisines, particularly where spices are concerned. Dishes are very highly seasoned in Algeria and Tunisia (see *harissa*), but spiced with more subtlety in Morocco, where dried lemon is widely used. In the south, the Bedouins are very fond of spit-roasted whole sheep (see *méchoui*), which may be replaced by gazelle or even camel, which supplies the Tuaregs with meat, milk, fat, and cheese.

□ **Specialities of the Maghreb** One of the distinguishing characteristics of North African cuisine is the variety of soups, always highly aromatic and often associated with religious ordinances: *chorba* in Algeria, *brudu* in Tunisia, and *harira* in Morocco. Soups combine dried vegetables or cereals (lentils, beans, chickpeas, unripe wheat) with meat (diced mutton, chicken with vermicelli) or fish.

The best-known North African culinary speciality is couscous, traditionally mixed with *smeun* fat, a sort of rancid butter. There are many kinds of couscous, with chicken, mutton, beef meatballs, or even with fish or tripe. According to local custom, hard-boiled (hardcooked) eggs, raisins, mint leaves, pumpkin, or celery may be added, as well as the usual vegetables and the sauce (*marga*). Sweet couscous may also be served for dessert, embellished with fresh fruit, pomegranate, almonds, and dates.

Another well-known speciality is tajine, a type of ragout cooked very slowly. In Tunisia it is made of mutton or rabbit with prunes, accompanied by fennel with lemon; in Algeria chicken is combined with cinnamon and onions; and Moroccan tajines are made of mutton with quinces and honey. Meat is also often served in balls (*kefta* in Tunisia) or on skewers (see *kebab*).

Vegetables are either cooked in a sauce (as ratatouille) and frequently served with scrambled eggs, as in chakchouka, or marinated and served in a salad (in the fan-shaped Tunisian *kemia*, which are served with filled pancakes, or *trids*). They may also be stuffed (artichoke hearts, cabbage leaves, peppers). Fish may be grilled or fried (sardines, red mullet), but can also be cooked in sauce (in pickle, for tuna), or marinated (as in Moroccan *charmoula*) and cooked in the oven (stuffed sea bream, shad with olives).

□ **Pastry, cakes, and drinks** Puff pastry of great delicacy is used in cooking and cake-making (particularly for baklava). In Tunisia, where it is called *malsouga*, it is the basis of egg or meat briks; while in Algeria its name is *dioul* and it is made into savoury turnovers. In Morocco it is used to make pastilla and *briouats*, which are stuffed with meat or with almonds and honey.

All the North African countries like sweetmeats (such as Turkish delight) and pastries (with walnuts, almonds, lemon, or dates), soaked with honey and syrup in Algeria and Tunisia but drier in Morocco (gazelle's horns). Cakes are eaten on special occasions and large family gatherings rather than in everyday meals.

Since the Koran forbids alcohol consumption much coffee is drunk and tea made with mint, marjoram, basil, or jasmine is served with great ceremony.

North America

AMÉRIQUE DU NORD

It would be wrong to dismiss American cuisine as being confined to fast food and the snack-bar, and to believe that its contributions to gastronomy are limited to cocktails, ice cream, corned beef, and hot dogs. The cuisine of the original European pioneers still largely survives in the American culinary heritage, which has integrated certain Indian and Mexican native dishes. It has also been enriched by traditions introduced by the Jewish, Italian, Black, and Chinese communities. In spite of the variety and abundance of products from so many different countries, American cuisine is solidly anchored to a few basic ingredients that provide a wide variety of very popular dishes. Corn (maize) is a typical example: it can be eaten as popcorn or corn on the cob, or it may be cooked as mash (hominy grits) or with red beans, as in the Indian dish succotash. Maize flour is used, according to its quality, to make the tortillas of New Mexico, as well as bread and cakes. The latter may be cooked on the grill, in ashes, or in the oven, or they may be fried like crêpes. Examples of maize dishes include hoecake, ashcake, corn bread, and johnnycake. Pumpkins are also widely used in pies, soups, cakes, and purées. Another basic ingredient is rice, which is the basis of the jambalaya of New Orleans, certain Creole dishes, 'dirty rice' (rice with giblets), and 'hopping John' (rice, bacon, and red beans).

□ **Tradition and modernity** The two main cooking utensils of the pioneer's wife were the cooking pot and the frying pan (skillet), reflected in the fact that many American dishes can be stewed or fried. Dishes that may be simmered in the cooking pot include the New England boiled dinner (boiled beef with vegetables), Boston baked beans (pickled pork and beans in tomato sauce), the Texan version of chilli con carne, Philadelphia pepperpot (a highly spiced stew), Kentucky burgoe (porridge with meat and vegetables), and the Creole dish gumbo (a thick meat and shellfish stew). Boiled dishes also include soups – particularly those made with fish (chowders) – and hot or cold fruit. Fried dishes include bacon and eggs, cod croquettes (codballs), fanny doddies (clams), and hangtown fry (oysters and beaten eggs).

The rituals of the barbecue and planked meat or fish (cooked in the oven on an oak or hickory plank, which acts as a serving dish) reflect the American taste for rustic cuisine. Fish, shellfish, and such meats as spare ribs, hamburgers, and T-bone steaks are grilled in the open air.

There are also traditional classic dishes for special occasions and Thanksgiving Day, such as turkey stuffed with corn bread and served with cranberries and orange sauce, ham cooked with cloves and whisky, fried chicken, and pecan pie.

There is one field in particular where, in spite of the widespread use of deepfrozen food and canned goods, the 'homemade' tradition remains very much alive – partly through the influence of Mormon communities. This is cake- and pastry-making, with buns, bagels and rolls, biscuits (oatmeal cookies and chocolate brownies), as well as pancakes, doughnuts, and a whole range of cakes and desserts. Typically American desserts and cakes are apple pandowdy, pound cake, strawberry shortcake, upside-down cake, lemon chiffon pie, gingerbread, brown Betty, and cheesecake. There is also a wide variety of iced desserts, including banana split, sundaes, and ice-cream sodas.

The trends of contemporary cuisine are reflected in two characteristic types of dishes – salads and dips. Most salads are based on the Caesar salad, invented by an Italian restaurateur in the 1920s and made up of romaine (cos lettuce), egg, croutons, anchovies, and Parmesan cheese. A variety of dips, i.e. thick sauces made with cream cheese, clams, tuna fish, celery, avocado, etc., are served with raw foods, toast, and sandwiches, and accompany savouries or cocktail snacks.

☐ **Regional specialities** The AngloSaxon origins of New England are reflected in its soups, pies, and roasts. The region is also noted for its seafood, especially clams, lobster, and cod. In Pennsylvania and Wisconsin the German influence is dominant, with sweetand-sour dishes and marinated meats. This region also specializes in dairy products. The Scandinavian influence is strong in Minnesota, where one finds smörgasbord, herrings, and Danish pastries. Dutch influence is noticeable in Michigan, with its stews and waffles, whilst in Oklahoma Indian cooking still survives, with such dishes as squaw

bread and jerky (smoked meat). In the Middle West, produce from the lakes and rivers is widely used. The South is particularly affected by the French presence in Louisiana, notably in its pâtisserie. In Florida turtles, crabs, and shrimps are used in cooking, while Virginia is well known for its ham and chicken dishes. The southwest is dominated by Spanish and Mexican influences – chicken with rice, filled *tamals*, *picadillo* (meat and vegetable hash), and *tacos* (savoury stuffed tortillas). On the west coast of California seafood predominates, typified by *cioppino* (thick seafood soup), and fruit is abundant. Oregon provides game for the whole country, and Washington State is renowned for its salmon and crayfish (crawfish). (See *brunch*, *Californian wines*, *whisky*.)

☐ **Canadian cuisine** The dual colonial tradition in Canandian cuisine combines both Anglo-Saxon customs and old recipes from Normandy. Fishing and hunting influence the diet, which is based on slowly cooked dishes of dried vegetables and smoked or salted meats. Particularly noteworthy are the numerous recipes for cod – even the tongue is eaten fried. Salmon is also widely used. *Chaudronnée* is a substantial soup containing several different kinds of fish. Game includes bear (a ragout can be made from its paws), reindeer, moose, hare, and river wildfowl. Savoury tarts are often the basis of meals, and pastry also figures in such desserts as rhubarb and apple pies. Pork and potatoes predominate in most dishes, notably 'pork pudding', together with *cretons* (crackling), *grillons* (cooked pork pieces), and *oreilles de crisse* (the different-shaped pork crisps and cracklings used to garnish salads). Maple syrup is used in cakes and pastries, which often contain wild berries such as rowanberries, cranberries, and wintergreen berries. It can also be added to scrambled eggs.

norvégienne (à la)

Describing several cold dishes of fish or seafood, usually glazed with aspic and garnished with such items as cucumber stuffed with smoked-salmon purée, hard-boiled (hard-cooked) eggs halved and topped with shrimp mousse, lettuce hearts, and small tomatoes. The term is also used for various hot fish dishes, such as haddock and anchovy soufflé and puff pastry filled with fish and anchovy butter and garnished with anchovy fillets.

Omelette norvégienne consists of ice cream covered with meringue and browned in the oven (see *baked Alaska*).

Nostradamus

French physician and astrologer (born Saint-Rémy-de-Provence, 1503; died Salon, 1566). Michel de Nostre-Dame, who was physician to Catherine de' Medici and Charles IX, is best known for his prophecies, set out in *Centuries astrologiques* (1555). But in the same year he published *Excellent et Moult Utile Opuscule à tous nécessaire qui désirent avoir connaissance de plusieurs exquises recettes* ('An Excellent and Most Useful Little Work, essential to all who wish to become acquainted with some exquisite recipes'). The first part is devoted to formulae for make-up, toilet waters, and scents; the second part gives recipes for various jams 'using honey as well as sugar and cooked wine' and including such fruit as cherries, ginger, limes, and oranges. There are also recipes for sugar candy, quince paste, marzipan (almond paste), and other sweets.

nougat

A sweetmeat made from sugar, honey, and nuts. Although the recipe for the Roman sweet *nucatum* (from the Latin *nux*, nut), described by Apicius, was based on honey, walnuts, and eggs, nougat in its present form appears to have been invented in Marseille in the 16th century, also based on walnuts. In about 1650, following the introduction of almond trees to the Vivarais region by Olivier de Serres, Montélimar became the manufacturing centre of nougat based on almonds.

Nougat production is now entirely mechanized and no longer exclusive to Montélimar. A paste of sugar, glucose syrup, honey, and invert sugar is beaten and usually lightened with egg white and gelatine (or egg albumen or milk), then mixed with nuts. This mixture is then spread in wooden frames lined with unleavened bread. When cold it is cut into pieces. Nougat remains a

speciality of southeastern France and is one of the traditional Provençal 'thirteen Christmas desserts'.

Several types of nougat are made in France. Nougat (or white nougat) contains at least 15% nuts; Montélimar nougat contains at least 30%, comprising toasted sweet almonds (28%) and pistachios (2%). *Pâte de nougat* contains less than 15% nuts, while in *nougat au miel* (nougat with honey) the sweetening agents contain 20% honey. The nonaerated *nougat de Provence*, made from heavily caramelized sugar syrup and honey (25%), contains almonds, hazelnuts, coriander, and aniseed (30%) and is flavoured with orange-flower water. *Noir* (black), *rouge* (red), and Parisian nougats are not aerated but contain only 15% nuts. Soft nougat contains icing (confectioners') sugar.

Vietnamese nougat, hard or soft, is made from sesame seeds, peanuts, and sugar.

RECIPE

White nougat NOUGAT BLANC Cook 250 g (9 oz, ¾ cup) honey with the same amount of sugar to the 'soft crack' stage (129 C, 264 F). Add 1 tablespoon orange-flower water and 1 stiffly whisked egg white. Melt over a very low heat, stirring constantly, and bring the temperature up to the 'soft ball' stage (109 C, 228 F). Now add 500 g (18 oz, 4½ cups) sweet almonds that have been blanched, dried, chopped, and heated through. Put the mixture into a shallow baking tin lined with sheets of rice paper and place a wooden board and weight on top. While the nougat is still slightly warm, cut into squares or rectangles.

Nougat with hazelnuts, pine kernels (nuts), or pistachios is prepared in the same way.

nougatine

A sweetmeat made from light caramel syrup and crushed almonds, sometimes also hazelnuts. Nougatine is rolled out on an oiled marble slab and cut into small pieces; alternatively it can be moulded to form cups, eggs, cornets, or other shapes for use as cake decorations.

Many sweets and chocolates have a

nougatine filling – a mixture of honey, sugar, glucose, almonds or hazelnuts, and egg white – which is cooked then mixed with pistachios, almonds, or preserved fruit. Particularly famous are the nougatines of Saint-Pourçain (small caramelized nougatine slabs) and of Poitiers (sweets made of crushed and caramelized almonds, enclosed in meringue).

Nougatine cakes usually consist of a Genoese sponge cake filled with praline or pralinized hazelnuts, brushed with apricot jam, and decorated with almonds or toasted or chopped hazelnuts. The nougatine cake of Nevers, created in 1850 by one of the town's pastrycooks, was reputedly offered to the Empress Eugénie, who was passing through the Nivernais region in 1862. It consists of a Genoese sponge filled with praline cream and iced (frosted) with chocolate fondant.

RECIPE

Nougatine Put 200 g (7 oz, scant 1 cup) caster (superfine) sugar and 20 g (¾ oz) glucose into a copper pan. Melt over a fairly high heat, stirring constantly with a wooden spoon. When the mixture turns a light reddish-brown, add 100 g (4 oz, 1 cup) ground almonds. Stir well, then pour onto an oiled baking sheet. Keep this hot by placing it at the front of an open oven. Using a lightly oiled rolling pin, roll out the nougatine to the desired thickness and cut it into shapes with a biscuit cutter (cookie cutter). If the nougatine is to form the base of a cake, pour it into an oiled cake tin the same size as the cake, or cut it to shape with an oiled knife.

nouvelle cuisine

A movement in cookery, started in 1972 by two food critics, H. Gault and C. Millau, with the aim of encouraging a simpler and more natural presentation of food. The movement combined a publicity campaign with novel recipes and a new ethic, although the idea itself was not new. Foreshadowing the apostles of nouvelle cuisine, Voltaire complained: 'I confess that my stomach does not take to this style of cooking. I cannot accept calves' sweetbreads swimming in a salty sauce, nor can I eat mince consisting of turkey, hare, and rabbit, which they try to persuade me comes from a single animal. . . . As for the cooks, I really cannot be expected to put up with this ham essence, nor the excessive quantity of morels and other mushrooms, pepper, and nutmeg with which they disguise perfectly good food.'

Advocates of nouvelle cuisine reject the over-rich, complicated, and indigestible dishes that are no longer suitable for a generation conscious of the health hazards of overeating, especially of fatty foods, known to contribute to obesity and cardiovascular disease. To counter this – and the increasing use of processed food – they espouse authenticity and simplicity in cooking. The *nouveaux cuisiniers* seek to uphold a concept – their theorists even talk of a world vision – that combines the professions of medicine and dietetics. Their guiding principles are: absolute freshness of ingredients, lightness and natural harmony in the accompaniments, and simplicity in the cooking method. This means less fat, no flour liaisons, no indigestible mixtures, and no 'disguised' dishes. Instead, they advise light sauces based on meat juices, stocks, essences, and spices; vegetables prepared so that their natural flavours are retained; and rapid cooking without fat, which allows the food to retain some of its texture. This entails dry cooking in the oven or under a grill (broiler), steaming, stewing, cooking in a bain-marie, or cooking *en papillote*. Dieticians agree that quickly cooked food retains maximum nutritional value.

Food offered by the 'new cooks' includes crisp vegetables, resplendent in their natural colours and elegantly trimmed, flanking thinly sliced meat; airy mousses accompany pink and firm fish; while vegetable purées become the stars of the culinary repertoire. Astonished gourmets scan their menus and find *gigot* applied to fish, not mutton; *darne* to meat, not salmon. They may also find gruels, rare produce, compotes not of fruit but of vegetables, and perhaps even soups as dessert.

While not discarding the wisdom of their predecessors, the new cooks are trying to widen their scope: for instance, Jacques Manière's eggs Céline, with caviar and a little vodka; Pierre Vedel's lobster soup with sweet garlic; Michel Guérard's aubergine (eggplant) purée cooked in saffron-flavoured steam; or Alain Senderens's calf's sweetbread in sea-urchin cream. All offer the diner strange, novel, exquisite, even nostalgic sensations. Sadly, it is only too easy for the exquisite to become ridiculous. In an effort to surprise, provoke, and stimulate jaded palates, nouvelle cuisine sometimes oversteps the mark: the 'pink at the backbone' rule can mean a fish oozing with blood; small vegetables become fragmented; and mousses and purées are added to every sauce. Although novel, such combinations can become pretentious, like the 'mad' salads, where lobster may find itself sharing a plate with foie gras, or herring is paired with pineapple. Where then is the much-vaunted simplicity?

Reports of a gastronomic revolution are exaggerated. Good cooking must always benefit from the old recipes and the precepts of classic cuisine. 'There are few decisive acts in cookery, each step contributes to the end result' is the dictum of Claude Peyrot, one of those craftsmen who defend both the old ways and the new. But there is no doubt that nouvelle cuisine, dedicated as it is to phasing out elaborate dishes, rigid formulae, and pompous and academic set pieces, suits the climate of the times in the same way that 'bourgeois' cookery suited the 19th century. Even the vocabulary is significant: there are no longer 'great chefs', but 'new cooks'; authority yields to craftsmanship. The satirical humorist Claude Fischler wrote an article for *Le Monde* entitled *The Socrates of the Nouvelle Cuisine*, in which he said: 'The artist in this field is no longer characterized by his overpowering authority, but rather by the opinionated modesty of an exponent of the maieutic art: in place of the cook as mercenary of the kitchen stove, we now have the Socratic cook, midwife at the birth of culinary truth.'

noyau

Any of several liqueurs, brandies, and ratafias based on an infusion of the kernels of certain fruits, particularly apricots and cherries (*noyau* is the French word for the stone that encloses the kernel). The best known of these is Noyau de Poissy, a liqueur made from cherry kernels and drunk straight or with water; it is also used to flavour ices, sorbets, fruit salads, and cocktails.

Nuits-Saint-Georges

A parish in the Côte de Nuits, in Burgundy, making mostly red wines, plus a few whites. The wines are world-famous but diverse – there are no *grands crus* but many exceptional fine wine vineyards and, as with other Burgundies, much depends on the grower and the shipper to establish character and quality.

nulle

A type of custard made with egg yolks, sugar, and cream and flavoured with musk or amber. It was in fashion at the time of Louis XIV. La Varenne gives the recipe in *Le Pâtissier français*: 'Take 4 or 5 egg yolks, some very fresh cream, a quantity of sugar, a grain of salt; beat all this well together and cook in a deep plate or a flat dish; brown the top with a salamander, sprinkle with perfumed water, and serve with musk-flavoured sugar to sweeten.'

Nicolas de Bonnefons suggests its origin: 'I think I am right in saying that a certain Italian gentleman called Nullio, groom to the kitchen of a great princess, was the inventor of this dish' (reported by Franklin).

nuoc-mâm

A condiment used in Vietnamese cookery. Meaning literally 'fish water', it is made by marinating small fish in brine then pounding them to a paste. Nuoc-mâm is very rich in protein and replaces salt in almost all culinary preparations; it is also used at table as a seasoning, served in a flask or small bowl. It has a strong taste and when heated the smell is very pronounced. Lemon juice or red pepper is sometimes added, or it can be garnished with very thinly sliced onion rings. It is a good flavouring for scrambled eggs, soups, and stews and it accompanies spring rolls.

nutcrackers

CASSE-NOIX ET
CASSE-NOISETTES

Implements used to crack walnuts and

other hard-shelled fruits. They usually take the form of a chrome-plated steel pincer with two notches to accommodate shells of different sizes. There are also wooden nutcrackers, cylindrical in shape and made of olive wood with a large screw that cracks the nuts when tightened.

nutmeg MUSCADE

The seed of the nutmeg tree, native to Indonesia but widely cultivated in tropical Asia and America. There are numerous varieties, the best known being the nutmeg tree of the Sunda Islands. The nutmeg is oval and rounded in shape, greyish-brown in colour, and wrinkled. It has a spicy flavour and aroma and is always used grated; nutmegs should be stored in an airtight container. It contains about 30% fat, and the crushed nuts are used to manufacture a 'nutmeg butter', crumbly and very fragrant, which may be used as cooking fat or as a flavouring for butters. The red web-like covering of the seed is also used as a spice (see *mace*).

Nutmeg is widely used as a spice in cooking, especially for flavouring cakes and custards and dishes with a base of potatoes, eggs (omelettes and soufflés), or cheese. It may also be included in béchamel sauces, onion soup, snail dishes, and minced (ground) meatballs. Grated nutmeg is used to spice numerous cocktails and punches and is used in the manufacture of some fortified wines and spirits.

nuts

See *fruit*. The different types of nuts are discussed under their own headings: see *almond*, *hazelnut*, *walnut*, etc.

oats AVOINE

A cereal used mainly as an animal feed (for horses and poultry), but also used for human food in the form of oatmeal, coarse, medium, or fine. Oatmeal is used for porridge, cakes, and broth.

Cultivated by the Romans, and widely consumed in gruels by the Teutons and Gauls, oats were, until the 19th century, a basic food in Scotland, Scandinavia, Germany, and Brittany. The plants are very well adapted for cultivation in cold climates. Oats contain more protein and fat than other cereals and are also rich in minerals and vitamins. They are therefore fortifying and rich in energy and are particularly suitable as food for invalids and children.

Oats are used mainly to make savoury or sweet broths and gruels. Porridge oats are eaten for breakfast with milk; they are also used for making biscuits (cookies) and pancakes, particularly in Anglo-Saxon countries. Numerous traditional Scottish, Welsh, or even Austrian recipes use oats in stews, ragouts, stuffings for meat, and for charcuterie. In the United States, they are widely used in home pastry-making by the Quakers. See also *muesli*, *porridge*.

octopus POULPE

A fairly large cephalopod mollusc (up to 80 cm, 30 in). The octopus has a head with a horny beak and eight equal-sized tentacles, each having two rows of suckers. Its flesh is fairly delicate in flavour, but it must be beaten for a long time and then blanched before use. Octopus can be prepared like lobster, cut into pieces and fried, or else simmered *à la provençale* and served with saffron rice.

RECIPE

Octopus à la provençale POULPE À LA PROVENÇALE Clean an octopus, remove the eyes and beak, and soak it under running water for a long time if it has not been prepared by the fishmonger. Drain it and beat well to tenderize the flesh. Cut the tentacles and body into chunks of the same length. Blanch the pieces in court-bouillon, drain them, and pat dry. Then brown them in oil in a saucepan, with chopped onion. Season with salt and pepper, add 4 peeled, deseeded, and chopped tomatoes, and simmer for a few minutes. Moisten with ½ bottle of dry white wine and the same quantity of cold water. Add a bouquet garni and a crushed clove of garlic. Cook, covered, for at least 1 hour. Sprinkle with chopped parsley and serve in a large bowl.

oenology OENOLOGIE

The study of the manufacture and maturing of wines (from the Greek *oinos*, wine). In France, the title oenologist was officially recognized by law on 19 March 1955, and it is possible to study for a diploma in the subject. An oenologist, therefore, is a wine technician, whereas an oenophile is a wine lover, whose knowledge may or may not be as extensive. In France a wine shop that specializes in the local wines is known as an *oenothèque*.

offal (variety meats)

ABATS DE BOUCHERIE

The edible internal parts and some extremities of an animal, which are removed before the carcass is cut up. Offal, also known as the 'fifth quarter', is divided into white and red categories.
• white offal – bone marrow, *animelles* (testicles), brain, mesentery (a membrane which holds the intestines together), feet, sweetbreads, stomach, and head. After scalding or plucking, these parts are an ivory colour. (Beef and pork cheeks are classified as meat.)
• red offal – heart, liver, tongue, lungs, spleen, and kidneys.

Offal, particularly intestines and tripe, is generally regarded as inferior meat. Only kidneys, liver, calves' sweetbreads, lambs' brains, and animelles have any real gastronomic importance. However, since it is cheap, offal is used in French home cooking, often in regional dishes (*tripous, fressure, gogues, pieds et paquets*, etc.) and also in other countries, for example in Scottish haggis, Brussels *choesels*, and Milanese *busecca* – a soup made of intestines (these are also enjoyed in Spain and Portugal).

In the past in country areas, the slaughtering of livestock was a rare event. The offal needed to be cooked and eaten quickly, and the killing of an animal (particularly a pig) was a festive occasion.

☐ **At the offal counter** The pig provides the greatest variety of offal used in cooking: brawn (a jellied mould made from the head and ears); various liver pâtés; sausages made from the chitterlings and the digestive tract; and black pudding (blood sausage). The lungs, spleen, and heart are less highly valued, but other offal provides simple and tasty dishes: pigs' trotters (breaded and grilled), kidneys (sautéed), and liver (fried).

The ox provides much edible offal, the commonest dishes being made from the tongue (boiled or pickled), stomach (intestines and tripe), and feet and tail (in pot-au-feu and ragout). The brains are less delicate than those of calves or lambs. Heifer's liver can also be cooked, but the kidneys and spleen are less popular.

Veal offal is regarded as a delicacy: mainly brains, bone marrow, kidneys, liver, and sweetbreads, but splendid dishes can also be made from the head and feet.

The brains of sheep and lamb are much prized, and the kidneys, animelles, and feet can be cooked in many ways. The liver, heart, and spleen feature in the cuisine of several regions, while sheeps' intestines and stomach are particularly valued in the south of France and in Auvergne.

oil HUILE

A fatty substance that is liquid at normal room temperatures, with a calorific value of 900 Cal per 100 g. Although there are mineral oils and animal oils (e.g. whale oil, seal oil, cod-liver oil), it is the vegetable oils that are used in cooking. These are extracted either from seeds (e.g. sunflower, groundnut (peanut), rapeseed, soya, sesame, cottonseed), from fruits (e.g. olives, cornelian cherries, walnuts), or even from roots.

Sesame oil probably has the oldest origins – it was used by the Egyptians. The ancient Greeks used olive oil: in Athens the olive was a sacred tree, symbol of the city's life. Oil was used not only for food but also as a fuel to provide light (its use as a fuel continued for many centuries in Europe).

Vegetable oils, low in cholesterol, balance animal fats in the diet. Oils extracted from a single vegetable species are known as 'pure', whereas the label 'vegetable' indicates that they are a mixture. Most oils sold in shops have been refined, with the result that their original flavour and smell have been removed leaving them quite neutral. However, it is still possible to find unrefined oils which have been obtained by cold pressing; these are termed 'virgin' or 'natural' oils and they retain the taste of their vegetable origin (olive oil, for example).

Solid oils are vegetable oils which solidify at normal room temperatures: examples are coconut oil and palm oil.

☐ Uses Oils, sometimes mixed with butter, provide the fatty element in cooking (for deep and shallow frying and browning); they are an ingredient of cold dressings (such as vinaigrette) and of sauces and condiments (mayonnaise, brandade, aïoli, etc.); and they will preserve foods (particularly fish but also goat's cheese and culinary herbs). Finally, they are used in marinades for meat, game, and fish.

In general, a distinction is made between oils used for frying and seasoning (in which the linolenic acid content must be lower than 2%) and oils used for seasoning only (particularly soyabean (soy-bean) and rapeseed oil). Linolenic acid should not be confused with linoleic acid: the former is a harmful foul-smelling substance released when oil is heated above 250 c (482 f); linoleic acid, the indispensable vitamin F, is present chiefly in sunflower, soyabean, maize (corn), grapeseed, and walnut oils.

Groundnut (peanut) and refined olive oils are the most suitable for heating to high temperatures, though the critical point must not be exceeded: this is reached when the oil begins to smoke. It is best not to heat the same batch of oil to 175 c (347 f) more than ten times.

The five most commonly used oils in the world are as follows:
• *groundnut (peanut) oil*: has many uses; remains liquid at a temperature of 5 c (41 f; withstands high temperatures best of all (up to 200 c, 390 f); if carefully filtered after each session it can be used up to 12 times.
• *rapeseed or colza oil*: light, with a neutral taste when cold because it is always refined; best at lower temperatures and used for a limited number of times.
• *cottonseed oil*: no particular flavour; widely used outside Europe.
• *soya-bean (soy-bean) oil*: light and rich, with a neutral taste; suitable for all seasonings.
• *sunflower oil*: light, with a neutral flavour when cold; remains liquid at 0 c (32 f); suitable for seasonings and low-temperature frying; its consumption is increasing owing to its dietetic properties.

Besides these major oils there are others which are more localized or less well known.
• *Olive oil* is sold under various classifications: 'virgin' (extra-fine, fine, or semi-fine) or 'pure' (i.e. mixed virgin and refined oils). Rich and easily digested, it has a fruity taste and is used a great deal in Mediterranean cooking (particularly in the south of France and Italy). It can be heated to 200 c (392 f) if it has been extracted by hot pressing or by solvents. Most aromatic oils are based on olive oil.
• *Corn (or maize)* oil is always sold refined; it has the same characteristics as sunflower oil but can be heated to 170 c (338 f).
• *Walnut oil* has a characteristic nutty taste and is used principally in dressings and seasonings. Anjou, Périgord, and various mountainous countries produce it and use it in their regional specialities, but it has the disadvantage of going rancid quickly. It is sometimes an ingredient of mixed oils.
• *Grape-seed oil* is always sold refined; it is recommended as a marinating agent as it 'feeds' the meat well.
• *Pumpkin (or marrow-seed) oil* has a delicate taste but is not suitable for all dishes because of its distinctive flavour.
• *Poppy-seed oil* has a very fine flavour when left unrefined. It is used in salads and for crudités, particularly in northern France. It is called *huile blanche* in France.

Other oils that should be mentioned are safflower and sesame oils, which are widely used in the East and in Asia; sweet almond oil, which is used in confectionery and pastry-making; and beechnut and hazelnut oil, which are not widely used.

Paraffin oil, recommended as a seasoning in some diets and also used to thinly coat dried fruit to prevent sticking, must never be heated: it is a hydrocarbon and not a vegetable oil. If taken in quantity, it can act as a laxative.

RECIPES

AROMATIC OILS

Basil oil HUILE AU BASILIC To 2 litres (3½ pints, 4½ pints) olive oil add a dozen very fresh sprigs of basil, which have been washed and dried, a small head of garlic (peeled just far enough to expose the cloves), and, if liked, a small shallot.

Put a stopper in the container and leave to marinate for 3 months before using.

Lemon oil HUILE AU CITRON Wash and dry 3 small thin-skinned lemons. Stick each one with 3 cloves. Put them in a glass jar and pour over 1 litre (1¾ pints, 4¼ cups) olive oil. Put a stopper in the jar and leave to marinate for 2 months before using.

Rosemary *or* **savory oil** HUILE AU ROMARIN OU À LA SARRIETTE Wash and dry some sprigs of rosemary or savory. Blanch them for 1 minute in boiling water, then tie the sprigs together. Put them in a glass jar and cover with 1 litre (1¾ pints, 4¼ cups) corn or olive oil. Leave to marinate for 2 months before using.

Tarragon *or* **fennel oil** HUILE À L'ES-TRAGON OU AU FENOUIL Into a glass jar put 2 fresh unpeeled garlic cloves, 1 clove, and half a dozen very fresh tarragon sprigs tied in a bunch or a small bunch of washed and dried wild fennel. Pour over 2 litres (3¼ pints, 4½ pints) corn oil (which has little smell of its own and will not mask the smell of the herbs). Leave to marinate for at least 2 months before using.

oille

Originally, a large stockpot; the word was then applied also to the contents of the pot. This sense is still preserved in Spain, with its *olla podrida*, and in certain regional dishes from southwestern France, such as *ouillade*, *ouillat*, and *oulade*.

Until the 19th century, the container (*pot-à-oille*) was a large silver pot in which a substantial soup was served. Prosper Montagné gives a recipe for an *oille à la française* which, in his opinion, made an 'excellent appetizer whose magnificence is by no means shocking or inaccessible'. Today, however, it would be considered an exceptionally rich and copious dish.

RECIPE

Oille à la française (from Prosper Montagné's recipe) Take a fine roasting chicken and 2 large pigeons. Trim and draw them and stuff with a forcemeat consisting of breadcrumbs soaked in stock mixed with 8 egg yolks, a white onion cooked over hot coals (or on a flat-topped griddle), and 3 chopped artichoke hearts, the whole being seasoned with chervil leaves and a pinch of grated nutmeg. Sew up the vents of the birds so that none of the forcemeat is lost, and truss them. In an earthenware pot put 6–8 lb beef (thinly sliced), a knuckle of veal cut into four, 3 onions, 1 parsnip, 2 carrots, 2 turnips, and 2 white leeks tied together with stalks of purslane, orache (mountain spinach), and Swiss chard. Place the stuffed birds on top and cover with stock. Heat the pot first on a very hot fire, then put on a moderate heat; skim and leave to cook gently for about 5 hours. Then lightly brown some slices of bread and put them in a *pot-à-oille* or some other large silver receptacle; stand this over a low heat, moisten the bread with some of the stock, and simmer until the bread begins to stick to the bottom. Arrange the chicken, flanked by the pigeons, on the browned bread, but do not put in the other meat. Untruss the birds and undo the vent stitches. Finally, strain the rest of the stock, skim off the fat, and pour it over the oille.

oiseau sans tête

The French name, meaning literally 'headless bird', for a slice of meat (veal, beef, or mutton) that is stuffed, rolled, tied, possibly barded, and usually cooked in a sauce or braised. In Flanders, *vogels zonder kop* (a literal translation of the French term) are slices of beef stuffed with sausagemeat (or a rasher (slice) of bacon seasoned with spiced salt), simmered in stock flavoured with aromatic herbs, served with mashed potatoes, and coated with the cooking juices thickened with kneaded butter. alternatively they may be cooked with onions and beer, as in a carbonade.

RECIPE

Oiseaux sans tête (from Raymond Oliver's recipe) Bone a shoulder of mutton and cut it into 8 slices. Beat them, trim the edges, and season with salt and pepper. Make a stuffing from breadcrumbs (soaked in milk and squeezed dry) and plenty of finely chopped parsley, chives, chervil, and tarragon and a raw egg. Put some of this stuffing in the centre of each slice of meat and roll it up. Put a small sprig of rosemary on top of each roll and wrap it in a piece of caul fat, preferably lamb's. Fry 250 g (9 oz, 2¼ cups) chopped mushrooms in a mixture of butter and oil, drain them, and spread them over the bottom of an ovenproof dish. Arrange the rolls side by side on top of the onions. Cover with buttered greaseproof (waxed) paper and cook for 25 minutes at 220 C (425 F, gas 7).

Just before serving, mix ½ teaspoon curry powder with a little fresh cream. Pour this sauce over the rolls and serve.

okra GOMBO

A tropical plant widely cultivated as a vegetable. The most widespread species, also known as ladies' fingers, gumbo, and (in France) *bamia* or *bamya*, is grown for its pods, which have longitudinal ridges and are either elongated (6–12 cm, 2½–5 in long) or short and squat (3–4 cm, 1¼–1½ in long). Another species, from New Guinea, is cultivated for its sorrel-like leaves.

Okra, which originally came from Africa or Asia and was introduced into the Americas by the black slaves, first appeared in Europe in the 17th century as a typical ingredient of Caribbean cookery. Urbain Dubois and Favre mention it in their 'American recipes'.

Rich in calcium, phosphorus, iron, and vitamin C, okra contains 40 Cal per 100 g. It is used before it is ripe, when it is green and pulpy and the seeds are not completely formed (ripe seeds were formerly used as a substitute for coffee). The New Guinea species is also rich in minerals but is a poor source of energy (23 Cal per 100 g). Okra can be obtained fresh throughout the year in exotic food stores. It is also available dried and canned. However they are prepared, okra are often best first blanched in salted water. They can be cooked in butter or cream, braised with bacon, fried, puréed, or prepared with lime, rice, etc. Okra is used as an ingredient in tajines, foutou, and Caribbean ratatouille and is eaten with mutton in Egypt and chicken in the United States.

RECIPE

Okra à la créole GOMBOS À LA CRÉOLE Wash the okra carefully. If using dried vegetables, soak them in cold water for about 12 hours. Top and tail (stem and head) and put in a saucepan. Cover them amply with cold water and cook for 10–25 minutes, skimming from time to time. Drain and dry them. Peel and finely slice 150 g (5 oz) onions and cook in 2 tablespoons (3 tablespoons) oil until soft. Add the okra and brown very gently. Scald, peel, and deseed 4 large tomatoes. Crush them and add to the okra with 2 crushed cloves of garlic, salt, pepper, and a little cayenne and powdered saffron. Cover and leave to cook very gently for at least 1 hour (more if using dried okra). Adjust the seasoning. Serve in a dish with a border of rice *à la créole*.

okrochka

A Russian soup made from *kvass* (home-made beer) and vegetables, served cold with quartered hard-boiled (hard-cooked) eggs, chopped herbs and cucumber, and soured (dairy sour) cream. The accompanying garnish may be a salpicon of left-over beef fillet, white chicken meat, pickled tongue, and ham, or of diced crayfish tails and salmon.

oleaginous plants
OLÉAGINEUX

Fruits, seeds, and plants with a high fat content (40–60%) and rich in vegetable proteins. They include walnuts, hazelnuts, almonds, pistachios, peanuts, olives, and the seeds of sesame, safflower, poppy, soya, sunflower, rape, etc. Besides their main use as a source of oil, oleaginous plants and seeds play an important role in cookery and gastronomy. They are served raw, grilled, 'roasted' (fried), or salted as snacks to eat with apéritifs and they feature in many exotic recipes, as well as in more mundane cooking. Like all fatty substances, oleaginous plants and seeds combine well with green vegetables and salads; they form an essential part of vegetarian diets.

olive

The small oval fruit of the olive tree, widely cultivated in Mediterranean regions. The fruit ripens from green to black; the fleshy pulp, enclosing an oval stone, is the source of olive oil and the whole fruit, stoned or stuffed, is used in cookery as a flavouring, ingredient, or hors d'oeuvre.

Originating in the East, the olive tree is extremely long-lived; its history is bound up with that of the Mediterranean, which since biblical times has been its native habitat. Large quantities of olives were consumed by both the Greeks and the Egyptians, who credited the goddess Isis with the discovery of oil extraction. In Greek mythology, Pallas Athene struck the Acropolis with her spear and out sprang the olive tree; she then taught men how to cultivate it and use its fruits. The Romans, too, venerated the olive tree. Throughout ancient times olives and olive oil were essential in nutrition and food preparation.

The Romans took the olive tree to all the Mediterranean countries, together with the techniques of oil extraction and the preparation of table olives. It continues to be widely grown in Italy, Spain, Greece, and Provence, where the fruity taste of olive oil dominates the cookery and even the pastries and cakes. The olive tree was introduced into Latin America in the 16th century. Nowadays, 93% of the world production of olives is used for oil extraction, the rest being prepared for the table (particularly green olives in Spain and black (ripe) olives in Greece). With a high calorific content (150–200 Cal per 100 g), olives are also rich in potassium, calcium, and vitamins.

There are two basic types of table olive, green and black (ripe).

● *Green olives* are gathered before they are ripe (October in France), treated to remove the bitter taste, then rinsed and pickled in brine. In France, varieties of green olive include the 'Picholine' from the Gard region, Corsica, and the Bouches-du-Rhône; 'Lucques' from the Hérault and Aude regions; and 'Salonenque' from the Bouches-du-Rhône.

● *Black (ripe) olives* are harvested when fully ripe (December to January in France); they are not treated with an alkali but are pickled in brine, and then sometimes in oil. Two of the best varieties grown in France are the 'Nyons' from the Drôme and the Vaucluse, and the 'Cailletier' grown around Nice.

Olives are also marketed in many other ways. 'Cracked' green olives, called *cachado*, are pickled in brine seasoned with herbs and spices and are prepared exclusively in the valley of Les Baux in France; they do not keep well and are only available in the Midi. Green olives in water (*à l'eau*) are repeatedly soaked in water to remove the bitterness; they have a strong fruity taste, but retain a slight bitterness. Green olives stuffed with anchovies, sweet peppers, pimientos, almonds, etc., are eaten as an apéritif. Black olives pickled in wine vinegar (from Calamata in Greece) are treated with brine mixed with oil and vinegar. Black olives preserved dry in salt have a good fruity slightly bitter taste, but do not keep well. The black olives from Morocco, washed and dried in the sun, are lightly salted, then packaged or barrelled in oil. Finally, black olives can simply be dried in the sun.

Table olives are an ingredient of many hors d'oeuvres and Mediterranean dishes, including pizzas, *mezze* from Greece, *tapas* from Spain, dishes *à la niçoise* and *à la provençale*, etc. They are eaten widely as cocktail snacks but are also used in cookery, either plain or stuffed, for preparing duck, daubes, paupiettes, and many other dishes.

RECIPES

Cabbage charlotte with olives CHAR LOTTE DE CHOU AUX OLIVES (from Frédérique Hébrard's recipe) Blanch a cabbage, then cook it in water and put it through a vegetable mill. To the resulting purée add ½ glass water, 1 egg yolk, and a little grated cheese. Stone (pit) and coarsely chop 30 black (ripe) olives and add them to the cabbage purée with a stiffly beaten egg white. Mix well. Butter a charlotte mould and sprinkle it with dried breadcrumbs. Pour the mixture into the mould and cook it in the oven at 220 C (425 F, gas 7) for about 30 minutes.

Cracked olives OLIVES CASSÉES Split some green olives without crushing them by giving them a light tap with a mallet on the top end. Cover with cold water and leave them for 1 week, changing the water every day. Then put them into brine (prepared using 1 kg (2¼ lb) salt per 8 litres (7 quarts, 9 quarts) water), flavoured with bay leaf, fennel, the skin of an orange, and some coriander seeds, and cover with fennel. Leave the olives for 8 days before eating them.

Duck with olives CANARD AUX OLIVES Stone 250 g (9 oz, 1½ cups) green olives, blanch them for 10 minutes in boiling water, refresh them under cold water, and drain. Rub salt and pepper on the inside and the outside of a duck weighing about 2 kg (4½ lb) and truss it. Slice 200 g (7 oz) slightly salted bacon into small strips, blanch for 5 minutes in boiling water, refresh and dry, then fry in 40 g (1½ oz, 3 tablespoons) butter. Drain.

Fry the duck until golden in the same butter, then remove it. Still using the same butter, brown 2 onions and 2 carrots, both finely chopped. Add a glass of meat stock, 1 tablespoon tomato purée, a pinch of crumbled thyme and bay leaf, and 1 tablespoon chopped parsley. Season with salt and pepper, cook gently for about 20 minutes, then strain.

Pour this sauce into a large casserole, add the duck and the fried strips of bacon, cover the pot, and bring to the boil on top of the stove. Transfer the casserole to the oven and cook at about 230 C (450 F, gas 8) for 35–40 minutes, then add the olives and continue cooking for at least another 10 minutes. Arrange the duck on a hot serving dish, cover it with the sauce, and arrange the olives all around it.

Olives à la picholine (from L. Rey-Billeton's recipe) In a large bowl mix 1 kg (2¼ lb) soda with 10 litres (2 gallons, 2¾ gallons) water. Add 5 kg (11 lb) plump green olives. Stir with a wooden spoon and leave the olives to soak for some hours, until the stones (pits) come away easily from the flesh. Take out the olives, stone (pit) them, wash them under plenty of running water, and put them into a container with enough plain water to cover them. Leave for 1 week, changing the water every day. On the ninth day, drain and rinse the olives and put them back in the container. Boil 10 litres (2 gallons, 2¾ gallons) water with 1 kg (2¼ lb) salt, 6 bay leaves, 6 sprigs of fennel, the dried skin of an orange, and 50 g (2 oz) coriander. Let this mixture get cold then pour it over the olives. Keep them for 10 days before eating.

Olives stuffed with anchovy butter OLIVES FARCIES AU BEURRE D'ANCHOIS Wash and dry some salted anchovies, remove the fillets, and pound to a purée. Mix this with butter, using 60 g (2½ oz, generous ¼ cup) butter for 5 anchovies. Season with pepper and mix everything well together. Put the anchovy butter into a piping (pastry) bag with a very narrow plain nozzle and stuff the olives. Keep them in the refrigerator until ready to serve as appetizers or with crudités.

Stuffed olives for garnish OLIVES FARCIES POUR GARNITURE Stone (pit) some green olives. Blanch them in boiling water for 5 minutes, drain them, and refresh in cold water. Stuff with quenelle forcemeat mixed with finely chopped herbs or with small slices of anchovy fillets in oil. Serve as an accompaniment to duck, chicken, sautéed rabbit, or braised beef.

Oliver (Raymond)

French chef (born Langon, 1909). His father, who had been a chef at the Savoy in London, kept a hotel in Bordeaux where Oliver started his apprenticeship. In 1948 he and Louis Vaudable, owner of Maxim's (which had been closed when France was liberated), reopened the Grand Véfour restaurant and restored it to its former glory. In 1950 Oliver became the manager of the restaurant and its success was assured:

Colette and Jean Cocteau were among the early customers, and it was soon patronized by other Parisian celebrities.

Raymond Oliver can be regarded as one of the great innovators and reformers of French cuisine, as evidenced by such dishes as red mullet with basil butter in puff pastry, ragout of pike and crayfish with aniseed, sautéed chicken in honey vinegar, stuffed guinea fowl Jean Cocteau, or the simpler lampreys *à la bordelaise* and other classic regional dishes. French cuisine has gained a great deal from his humour and his deep knowledge of the culinary arts, which he demonstrated in television programmes where he cooked his recipes himself (his son, Michel, has now taken his place). He has also lectured in other countries and is the author of various books, including *La Gastronomie à travers le mond* (1963), *La Cuisine* (new edition, 1983), *Cuisine pour mes amis* (1976), and *Les Amis du Véfour* (1983).

Olivet

A small soft French cows'-milk cheese (40% fat), made in the small town of Olivet, in the Loiret. The skin is either bluish (Olivet Bleu) or ash-covered (Olivet Cendré), having been matured in vine shoot ashes. The cheese is straw-coloured, with a fruity or spicy taste, and is made in flat discs 12–13 cm (4½–5 in) in diameter and 2–3 cm (about 1 in) thick. Balzac liked to eat it with walnuts and chilled wine.

olla podrida

A Spanish meat soup whose name, literally translated, means 'rotten soup'. A speciality of Castile, where it is served on traditional feast days, it consists of various types of meat and poultry, vegetables, and rice or lentils, cooked in a large pot. The different constituents of the soup are served separately, accompanied by spiced sauces. The broth is served first, followed by the beef or veal with chickpeas, turnips, pumpkin, and sweet potatoes; then comes the partridge or chicken with lentils or rice, followed by the mutton and offal garnished with tomatoes, and finally the smoked sausage and ham served with cabbage.

Ombiaux (Maurice des)

Belgian writer and gastronome (born Beauraing, 1868; died Paris, 1943). Nicknamed the 'Prince of Walloon story-tellers' and 'Cardinal of gastronomy', he was the rival and friend of Curnonsky, to whom he came second in a poll for 'Prince of gastronomes'. He wrote many books, including *Le Gotha des vins de France* (1925), *Les Fromages* (1926), *Le Nobiliaire des eaux-de-vie et liqueurs de France* (1927), *L'Art de manger et son histoire* (1928), and *Traité de la table* (1930). He also brought out a new edition of *Pâtissier français*, attributed to La Varenne.

ombrine

A sea fish found in the Mediterranean and the Bay of Biscay. It grows to a length of 1 m (39 in) and is silvery in colour, with golden or grey-blue stripes on the back and a marked lateral stripe. It has a short beard on the lower jaw. The flesh is as good as (if not better than) that of bass, and the same recipes can be used to cook it.

omelette

A sweet or savoury dish made from beaten whole eggs, cooked in a frying pan (skillet), and served plain or with various additions. The word comes from the French *lamelle* (small blade) because of its flat shape; in former times it was known as *alumelle*, then *alumette*, and *amelette*. (Some authorities claim that the word has a Latin origin, *ova mellita*, a classic Roman dish consisting of beaten eggs cooked on a flat clay dish with honey.)

The success of an omelette depends as much on the quality of the pan and the quantity and distribution of the butter as on the cooking. A large variety of different garnishes may be mixed with the omelette or added just before serving, with a ribbon of sauce. An omelette can be served, either flat or folded, as an entrée or a dessert, depending on whether it is savoury or sweet; it is nearly always served hot. It can also be used as a garnish for soups.

Omelettes were known during the Middle Ages, when they were also called *arboulastre d'oeufs*. In the 17th century, one of the most famous omelettes was *omelette du curé*, containing soft carp roes and tuna fish, which Brillat-Savarin much admired. Nowadays, a particularly popular French omelette is the variety known as *Mère Poulard*, which owes its fame to the high quality of the Norman butter and eggs as well as to a special knack in the making. Some chefs recommend beating the yolks and the whites separately to obtain a lighter and foamier omelette. Among the different types of savoury omelettes are:

• *omelettes cooked with the flavouring*: the flavouring is mixed with the beaten eggs before cooking.

• *filled omelettes*: the hot filling is spread on the omelette, which is then folded over and slipped onto the serving dish.

• *garnished omelettes*: filled omelettes with some garnish placed on the top; if this garnish is accompanied by a sauce or bound with butter, it is poured into a slit made in the omelette. It is usual for garnished omelette to be surrounded by a ribbon of sauce.

• *flat omelettes*: made like plain omelettes but with fewer eggs; they are cooked for a longer time and turned over in the pan halfway through cooking. The result is a sort of thick pancake which can be served cold, accompanied by the same garnishes as a plain omelette.

Sweet omelettes are usually filled with jam or poached fruit flavoured with a liqueur; they are sprinkled with sugar and glazed in the oven, or they may be flamed.

Soufflé omelettes are really a type of soufflé cooked in a long shallow dish (rather than in a deep soufflé dish). They can be flavoured with liqueur, fruit, coffee, etc.

RECIPES

Plain omelette OMELETTE NATURE Beat 8 eggs lightly and season with salt and (if liked) freshly ground pepper. (2–3 tablespoons (3–4 tablespoons) milk, or 1 tablespoon thin cream, can be added to the beaten eggs.) Heat 25–30 g (1–1½ oz, 2–3 tablespoons) butter in a scrupulously clean pan, preferably non-stick. Raise the heat and pour in the beaten eggs. Stir them with a fork,

drawing the edges to the centre as soon as they begin to set. When the omelette is cooked, slide it onto a warm serving dish and fold it in three. Rub a piece of butter over the surface to make it shiny.

FILLED OMELETTES

Chicken-liver omelette OMELETTE AUX FOIES DE VOLAILLE Slice some chicken livers, sauté them quickly in butter, and bind them with some reduced demi-glace sauce. Fill the omelette with this mixture and garnish with a ribbon of demi-glace flavoured with Madeira.

Foie gras omelette OMELETTE AU FOI GRAS (from André Daguin's recipe) Chop 200 g (7 oz) half-cooked goose foie gras into ½-cm (¼-in) cubes. Put them into a deep plate which has been rubbed with garlic, sprinkle with freshly ground pepper, and turn the pieces of foie gras so that they are covered with the pepper. Lightly beat the separated yolks and whites of 9 eggs, beating the whites until they are fairly firm. Heat some butter in a pan, pour in the eggs, and mix by shaking the handle of the pan. Season with salt. When the eggs begin to set, add the cubes of foie gras, then fold over and cook until the omelette is golden on both sides. Slide the omelette onto a lightly buttered hot dish.

Kidney omelette OMELETTE AUX ROGNONS Slice or finely dice some calves' or sheep's kidneys, sauté them in butter, and bind them with some reduced demi-glace sauce flavoured with Madeira. Fill the omelette with this mixture. Garnish with a ribbon of Madeira-flavoured demi-glace.

Omelette Argenteuil Cook an omelette and fill it with 3 tablespoons asparagus tips cooked in butter. Fold it onto a hot serving dish. Pour some cream sauce around it.

Omelette with black pudding (blood sausage) OMELETTE AU BOUDIN (from Emile Faguet's recipe) Grill (broil) some black pudding (blood sausage) and skin it while it is still hot. Mash the meat with a fork. Separate some eggs and beat the yolks and white separately, then fold them together. Cook the omelette and fill it with the black pudding before folding it.

FLAT OMELETTES

Courgette (zucchini) omelette OMELETTE AUX COURGETTES Slice some courgettes (zucchini) into thin rounds and sauté them in butter in a frying pan (skillet). Beat the eggs with chopped parsley, salt, and pepper, pour them into the pan over the courgettes, and cook the omelette on both sides like a thick pancake.

Omelette à la verdurière Cut some sorrel and lettuce into very fine strips and cook them gently in butter. Beat the eggs and add the sorrel and lettuce with some chopped parsley, chervil, and tarragon. Cook like a large pancake. Sprinkle with noisette butter.

Omelette Mistral Brown 3 tablespoons (¼ cup) diced aubergines (eggplants) in oil in a frying pan (skillet). Beat the eggs together with some diced tomato gently fried in oil, chopped parsley, and a pinch of garlic. Pour the eggs over the aubergines and cook like a large pancake.

Omelette mousseline Beat 6 egg yolks with 2 tablespoons (3 tablespoons) cream and season with salt and pepper. Whisk the egg whites to stiff peaks and fold into the mixture. Cook like a large pancake.

Omelette Parmentier Finely dice some potatoes and fry them in butter. Beat the eggs and add the potatoes and some chopped parsley. Cook like a large pancake.

Seafood omelette OMELETTE AUX FRUITS DE MER Beat the eggs with chopped parsley and chervil, salt, and pepper and make 2 flat omelettes. Put one onto a round ovenproof dish and cover it with a ragout of mussels, prawns (shrimp), small clams, or other shellfish, poached and bound with shrimp sauce. Cover with the second omelette. Coat with a cream sauce flavoured with shrimp butter and glaze in a hot oven.

Spinach omelette OMELETTE AUX ÉPINARDS Braise enough spinach leaves in butter to provide 4 tablespoons cooked spinach. Mix with 8 beaten eggs and cook like a large pancake.

GARNISHED OMELETTES

Omelette Diane Make an omelette using 8 beaten eggs and 200 g (7 oz, 2 cups) sliced mushrooms sautéed in butter and seasoned with salt and pepper. Just before folding the omelette, fill it with a salpicon of young partridge (or any other game bird) and truffles, bound with some reduced velouté sauce made from the game stock. Garnish the top of the omelette with slices of truffle tossed in butter. Surround with a ribbon of demi-glace sauce made from the game stock.

Omelette Feydeau Make a very creamy omelette and fill it with mushroom duxelles. Slide it onto an oven-proof dish, then garnish the top with poached eggs (one per guest) – choose small eggs and keep them underdone. Mask with Mornay sauce to which finely shredded truffles have been added. Sprinkle with grated Parmesan cheese and brown quickly under a hot grill (broiler).

OMELETTES COOKED WITH THEIR FLAVOURING

Anchovy omelette OMELETTE AUX ANCHOIS Soak 3 anchovy fillets until free of salt and rub them through a sieve. Add the anchovy purée to 8 eggs and beat together. Cook the omelette as usual. Garnish with a crisscross pattern of fine strips of anchovies in oil.

Artichoke omelette OMELETTE AUX ARTICHAUTS Slice 4 artichoke hearts and sauté them in butter until they are half-cooked, without letting them brown. Add the artichoke slices to 8 eggs and beat together; cook the omelette as usual. It can be garnished with a row of sliced sautéed artichoke hearts and surrounded with a ribbon of reduced veal stock.

Bacon omelette OMELETTE AU BACON Fry 3–4 tablespoons (¼–⅓ cup) diced bacon in butter and beat into 8 eggs. Cook the omelette. It can be garnished with 6 thin strips of bacon fried in butter.

Cep omelette OMELETTE AUX CÈPES Brown 200 g (7 oz, generous ¾ cup) sliced cep mushrooms in butter or oil and add them, with some chopped parsley, to 8 eggs, beating them all together. Cook the omelette. Garnish with a line of chopped ceps sautéed in butter or oil.

Any edible mushrooms can be used to flavour this omelette.

Tuna-fish omelette or **omelette du curé** OMELETTE AU THON (OU OMELETTE DU CURÉ (from Brillat-Savarin's recipe) For 6 people, wash 2 soft carp roes and blanch them for 5 minutes in lightly salted boiling water. Chop the roes together with a piece of fresh tuna about the size of a hen's egg so that they are well mixed. Put the chopped fish and roes into a pan with a small finely chopped shallot and butter and sauté until all the butter is incorporated – this is the essential characteristic of the omelette.

Blend some fresh butter with parsley and chives, and spread it onto the fishshaped dish in which the omelette will be served; sprinkle with lemon juice and put it near a hot fire.

Beat 12 eggs, add the sautéed roes and tuna, and mix well together. Cook the omelette in the usual way, keeping the shape long rather than circular, and ensure that it is thick and creamy. As soon as it is ready, arrange it on the prepared dish and serve at once.

This dish should be reserved for special luncheons for those who appreciate good food. Serve it with a good wine, and the result will be superb.

Notes on preparation: the roes and the tuna should be sautéed over a very low heat, otherwise they will harden and it will be difficult to mix them properly with the eggs. The serving dish should be fairly deep so that the sauce can be spooned up when serving. The dish should be heated enough to melt the màitre d'hôtel butter on which the omelette is placed.

SWEET OMELETTES

Omelette flambée Beat the eggs with some sugar and a pinch of salt, then cook the omelette in butter, keeping it very creamy. Dredge with sugar, sprinkle with heated rum, and set light to it immediately before serving. The rum can be replaced by Armagnac, Calvados, Cognac, whisky, or a fruit-based spirit.

Omelette with fruit compote OMELETTE À LA COMPOTE DE FRUITS Prepare a compote of peaches, plums, apples, or apricots: cook the fruit in vanilla-flavoured syrup, drain, bind with jam made from the same type of fruit, and flavour with liqueur. Beat 8 eggs with 1 tablespoon caster (superfine) sugar and a pinch of salt. Cook the omelette in butter. Just before folding, fill with 4 tablespoons (⅓ cup) fruit compote. Fold the omelette, slip it onto a round plate, and sprinkle with caster sugar. Glaze under the grill.

Soufflé omelette OMELETTE SOUF-FLÉE Mix together in a bowl 250 g (98 oz, generous cup) caster (superfine) sugar, 6 egg yolks, and 1 teaspoon vanilla sugar or 1 tablespoon grated orange or lemon rind. Beat until the mixture turns white and thick. Whisk 8 egg whites to stiff peaks and fold carefully into the yolk mixture.

Butter a long ovenproof dish and sprinkle it with caster sugar. Pour in three-quarters of the omelette mixture and smooth it into a low mound with the blade of a knife. Put the rest of the mixture into a piping (pastry) bag with a plain round nozzle and pipe an interlaced decoration on top of the omelette. Sprinkle with caster sugar. Cook at 200 C (400 F, gas 6) for about 20 minutes. Dredge with icing (confectioners') sugar and glaze under the grill (broiler).

The omelette can also be flavoured with chocolate, coffee, or a liqueur.

omelette surprise

A dessert based on the same ingredients as a baked Alaska – sponge cake coaked in syrup, ice cream, and meringue – but with the addition of fruit. The base, which may be Genoa cake, Genoese sponge, or madeleine cake mixture, is sprinkled with liqueur, covered with a bombe mixture, a fruit ice cream, or a parfait mixture, mixed with preserved fruits, pralined violets, etc. The whole is then masked with meringue and glazed in the oven. The dessert is surrounded by poached fruits, cherries in brandy, etc.

onglet

A French cut of beef consisting of two small muscles joined by an elastic membrane (the supporting muscles of the diaphragm). The butcher splits it open, trims it, and removes all the skin and membrane. Onglet must be well hung; the meat is then tender and juicy. In the past it was not a popular cut, but it is now accepted that it makes a prime steak. Whether fried or grilled (broiled), it should be eaten rare, otherwise it becomes tough.

| RECIPES

Fried onglet with shallots ONGLET POÊLÉ À L'ÉCHALOTE Make shallow criss-cross incisions on both sides of the meat. Peel and chop 3–4 shallots. Heat about 30 g (1 oz, 2 tablespoons) butter in a frying pan (skillet); when it is very hot, put in the meat and brown it quickly on both sides. Season with salt and pepper, drain it, and keep it hot. Cook the shallots in the frying pan until golden. Add 2–3 tablespoons (3–4 tablespoons) vinegar to the pan and reduce the liquid by half. Pour this gravy over the meat.

Grilled (broiled) onglet ONGLET GRILLÉ Make shallow crisscross incisions on both sides of the meat and rub it with a little oil and pepper. Cook under a very hot grill (broiler), seasoning with salt halfway through cooking, and serve rare.

onion OIGNON

A plant whose bulb is used in cooking; the bulb is formed of white fleshy leaves covered with several layers of thin papery skin, red, brown, yellow, or white in colour. It is eaten fresh or dried, raw or cooked, as a vegetable, as an ingredient in other dishes, or as a seasoning.

Originating in northern Asia and Palestine, the onion has been cultivated for more than 5000 years. It was highly esteemed by the Egyptians and the Jews, who usually ate it raw, and the Greeks attributed great therapeutic values to it. In Europe, it has been one of the mainstays of cooking since the end of the Middle Ages and is of great importance nutritionally; it features predominantly in the cookery of northern and eastern European countries (France, Belgium, Poland, Russia, the Balkans, and Hungary); in Mediterranean countries a sweet variety of onion is eaten, usually raw.

The different varieties of onion can be distinguished mainly by the colour and the production period. In France, onions are cultivated chiefly on the Côte d'Or, in the southeast, in Finistère, and in the north. They are imported from the Netherlands, Italy, Spain, and Egypt.

● *White onions*, which keep for only a short time, are available in France from April to September; those coming on the market in August, from the Midi, are fresh and crisp and have a very good flavour.

● *Spring onions (scallions)* sold in bunches with their stalks left on, are imported or available home-grown from April to July. They are either served raw with salt or in salads (the stalks can also be used for flavouring).

● *Yellow onions* are available all the year round. They include the large sweet Spanish onion, which is easy to stuff; strong-flavoured onions for storing, which are harvested in August and stored at a temperature of −3 to 0 C (27–32 F) for winter consumption; Egyptian and Polish onions, which are round and dark brown with a slight but definite flavour; and, best of all, the French variety 'Jaune Paille des Vertus', which is ideal for soups, tarts, purées, and simmered dishes.

● *Pickling onions (button onions)* are similar to white onions but they are picked when small. They can also be used whole in casseroles and stews or boiled and served in a sauce as a vegetable. They are often used as a garnish when glazed.

● *Pink and red onions*, which are less common, are sold in France from June until March and usually eaten raw. When cooked, they have much less flavour than the other varieties and taste slightly sweet.

The onion has a calorific value of only 47 Cal per 100 g and is rich in sulphur and vitamin C; it can be indigestible when eaten raw. The substance which makes the eyes water (allyl sulphide) disappears on cooking. When buying onions, look for bulbs which are quite firm: the white variety should be very shiny and the yellow or red varieties should be protected by a dry brittle skin; store them in a cool dry airy place. To peel onions in comfort, put them into the freezer for ten minutes or into the refrigerator for an hour before peeling; small pickling onions are easily peeled if they are boiled rapidly for one minute. Once peeled, onions oxidize rapidly and can eventually become toxic; peeled onions should therefore be kept covered.

The onion is a major ingredient in cooking, being used especially as a flavouring in many casseroled dishes (daube, carbonade, pot-au-feu, etc.), in which it may be chopped, sliced, or left whole and studded with cloves. They are also used for stuffings and to make sauces and braised dishes. In some French dishes they are the main ingredient, for instance in onion tart from Alsace, pissaladière, tourin, salt cod *à la bretonne*, French onion soup, beef miroton, tripe, Soubise purée and all recipes *à la Soubise*, and in many dishes cooked *à la lyonnaise*. They go particularly well with rabbit and with sausages cooked in white wine.

Stuffed onions can be served as a hot main dish or as a garnish for roast or braised meat. Fried onion rings are used as a garnish for many dishes (sautéed or fried meat or fish), and finely chopped onion is an ingredient of vinaigrette, marinades, and many cold garnishes. The onion is used with potatoes in many stews, gratins, and meat and vegetable soups and it also goes well with cabbage and with many egg dishes. Small glazed onions are an essential garnish for a whole range of meat and fish dishes (matelote, blanquette, chicken *en barbouille*, coq au vin, dishes *à la bourguignonne*, etc.). Pickled onions are used as a condiment.

RECIPES

Chopped onions OIGNONS HACHÉS Peel the onion and cut it in half down through the root. Cut each half into several slices without separating them from the root, then make 5 or 6 vertical cuts down through the halves and finally chop across these cuts. The fine dice thus produced can be chopped even more finely if required. If the onions are chopped in advance, wrap them in a cloth, sprinkle with cold water, squeeze the cloth hard to drain them, then put them aside in a dish.

Fried onions OIGNONS FRITS Peel some medium-sized onions, slice them into rings ½ cm (¼ in) thick, and separate the rings. Season with salt, dip in flour, and fry in a very hot oil. Drain them thoroughly on kitchen paper and sprinkle with fine salt. They can also be marinated in oil and lemon juice for half an hour, then dipped in batter and fried.

Onion soup SOUPE À L'OIGNON Finely chop 250 g (9 oz, 2¼ cups) onions and fry them in butter without letting them get too brown. When they are almost ready, sprinkle with 25 g (1 oz, ¼ cup) flour. Continue cooking for a minute or two, stirring the onions with a wooden spoon, then pour on 2 litres (3½ pints, 4½ pints) white stock and flavour with 2 tablespoons (3 tablespoons) port or Madeira. Continue to cook for a further 30 minutes. Put some slices of bread which have been dried in the oven into a soup tureen and pour the soup over them.

Onion tart TARTE À L'OIGNON Line a buttered 28-cm (11-in) flan tin (pie pan) with 400 g (14 oz) shortcrust or lining pastry and cook it blind. Meanwhile prepare a Soubise purée with 1 kg (2¼ lb) onions. Spread this in the flan case, sprinkle with fresh breadcrumbs, dot with butter, and brown it in a hot oven for about 15 minutes.

Stuffed onions OIGNONS FARCIS Peel some medium-sized Spanish onions, taking care not to split the outer white layer; cut them horizontally at the stalk end, leaving about three-quarters of their total height. Blanch them in salted water for 10 minutes, then refresh and drain them. Scoop out the insides, leaving a thickness all round of 2 layers.

Chop the scooped-out onion finely and mix it with some finely chopped pork, veal, beef, or mutton. Stuff the onions with this mixture, put them in a buttered sauté dish, and moisten with a few tablespoons of slightly thickened brown veal stock. Start the cooking, with the lid on, on top of the stove, then continue cooking in the oven, basting frequently to glaze the onions. A few minutes before they are cooked, sprinkle with breadcrumbs or Parmesan cheese, moisten with melted butter, and brown the surface.

Onions can also be stuffed in the following ways:

■ *à la catalane* (rice cooked in meat stock with sweet peppers fried in olive oil and chopped hard-boiled (hard-cooked) eggs).

■ *à l'italienne* (rice cooked in meat stock with finely chopped onion, cooked lean ham, and Parmesan cheese).

■ *à la parisienne* (finely chopped onion mixed with a duxelles of mushrooms and chopped cooked lean ham).

other recipes See *crêpe, gratinée, Soubise, tourin.*

Opéra

A garnish for noisettes of veal and sautéed tournedos steaks (filet mignons). It consists of small bunches of asparagus tips and tartlets or croustades filled with chicken livers sautéed in Madeira. The sauce which is poured over the meat is made by deglazing the cooking juices with Madeira and demi-glace.

This garnish is also used for eggs *sur le plat* Opéra; in this case the sauce consists of reduced veal stock enriched with butter.

The dessert *crème renversée Opéra* is cooked like a caramel custard in a mould, chilled, unmoulded, and served with the centre decorated with Chantilly cream, crushed meringue, and strawberries in Kirsch.

orache
ARROCHE BONNE-DAME

A garden plant whose green fleshy triangular leaves are used in soups and herb stocks. Orache leaves may also be cooked like spinach and used either as a vegetable or as a garnish. They may also be used to counteract the bitter taste of sorrel.

orange

The fruit of the sweet orange tree, cultivated widely in Mediterranean countries and other parts of the world. It is round with an orange or yellow skin and sweet juicy flesh, divided into segments which may or may not contain seeds. Originating in China and mentioned at the beginning of the Christian era in Indian and Chinese texts, this citrus fruit was probably known to the ancient world – the mythical golden applies from the Garden of the Hesperides were probably sweet oranges, although they would have been Seville (bitter) oranges, brought by the Arabs into Spain and by the Crusaders into France. From 1322, Nice conducted a trade in Seville oranges. Sweet oranges did not arrive in Europe until the following century or even later, coming from Arab lands via Genoese or Portuguese merchants; the latter also introduced them to America.

For centuries oranges were a rarity; they were usually made into preserves, used for a table decoration, or offered as luxury gifts. Robespierre was described as a sybarite because he had 'pyramids of oranges' served to his guests. Today in France they are the second most popular fruit, apples being the favourite. Oranges come mainly from Spain, Morocco, Israel, Italy, Algeria, and Tunisia (the best ones are available from November to May) and from South Africa and the United States in summer.

The different varieties of sweet oranges are classified into four groups:
● *Navel oranges* are characterized by a navel-like depression enclosing a small internal embryonic fruit. They are seedless and appear from the end of October. Thomsons, with a very fine smooth shiny skin, have highly-coloured fibrous pulp, not very sour and

moderately juicy but with a good flavour. Washingtons, with a firm rough skin, are juicy and slightly sour.

● *Blondes* are winter oranges, with pale flesh, coming mostly from Israel (Jaffas). Shamoutis, quite large and with a thick skin and seeds, have crisp well-flavoured juicy pulp. Salustianas, seedless and with grainy peel, are very juicy.

● *Blood oranges* have dark-red pulp and the skin may be veined with dark red. They are available from December to April. The Maltese orange, with seeds, is sour, very juicy, and has an exceptionally good flavour. Moro oranges, with a rough skin, are very juicy.

● *Late oranges* have pale flesh, few seeds, and come mainly from Spain and the southern hemisphere (Outspan). Valencia oranges, with or without seeds, have smooth firm skins and are very sharp and juicy.

Oranges contain only 44 Cal per 100 g and are very rich in vitamins, particularly vitamin C. When buying oranges, choose fruit that are shiny and heavy for their size. They are not easily damaged and will keep for some days at room temperature. If the zest or peel is to be used, the oranges should be scrubbed in warm water.

Oranges are widely used in desserts, pâtisserie, and confectionery, for fruit salads, mousses, dessert creams, frosted fruit, ices and sorbets, jams and marmalades, fritters, soufflés, filled sponges (the classic example of which is orangine), and biscuits (cookies). The candied peel is also used in numerous desserts and cakes, either as an ingredient or as a decoration. Oranges form the basis of an equally large range of drinks: syrups, sodas, juice, orangeade, punches, liqueurs, and fruit wines.

Sweet oranges are today used in recipes which, in former times, used bitter oranges: duck which nowadays is described as *à la bigarade* (with bitter oranges) is in fact cooked with sweet oranges. Some of the dishes which use oranges as an ingredient are: trout with orange butter (butter worked with orange juice, grated nutmeg, and paprika); sole *à l'orange* (surrounded with peeled orange slices, butter sauce, fresh cream, and Curaçao); young partridge roasted *à l'orange* (garnished with peeled orange segments and grapes, the cooking juices being deglazed with orange juice); fried calf's liver *à l'orange* (garnished with orange slices, the pan being deglazed with orange juice); omelette *à l'orange* (a savoury omelette flavoured with tomato sauce and grated orange peel); veal knuckle *à l'orange* (braised with a julienne of orange peel, with orange juice added to the cooking liquid); sheep's tongues *à l'orange* (cooked in water, covered with a sauce made from vinegar roux, thickened with gooseberry jelly, and garnished with orange segments); and salad of chicory (endives), beetroot (red beet), and peeled orange segments, dressed with a tarragon-flavoured vinaigrette.

See also *Seville (bitter) orange*.

RECIPES

Candied orange peel ÉCORCES D'ORANGE CONFITES Choose thick-skinned oranges. Peel them, scrape off all the white pith from the peel, and cut the peel into strips. For each orange, put ¼ litre (8 fl oz, 1 cup) water, 125 g (4½ oz, scant ⅔ cup) sugar, and 1 dl (6 tablespoons, scant ½ cup) grenadine syrup into a pan and bring to the boil. Add the peel, half-cover the pan, and let it simmer gently until the syrup is reduced by three-quarters. Leave the peel in the syrup until it is quite cold, then drain it. Sprinkle a baking sheet thickly with icing (confectioners') sugar, roll the pieces of peel in the sugar, and dry off under the grill (broiler).

Frosted oranges ORANGES GIVRÉES Choose some fine unblemished thick-skinned oranges. Cut off the top of each orange at the stalk end. Using a sharp-edged spoon scrape out all the pulp, taking care not to pierce the skin. Cut a small hole at the top of the orange caps, where the stalk was attached. Put the orange shell and the caps into the freezer. Make an orange sorbet with the pulp. When it begins to set, put it into the orange shells, smoothing the top into a dome shape. Replace the caps and insert a long lozenge-shaped piece of candied angelica into the hole, to resemble a leaf. Put back in the freezer until ready to serve.

Glacé orange segments QUARTIERS D'ORANGE GLACÉS Peel some large oranges and carefully remove all the pith, without breaking the membrane surrounding each segment. Separate the segments and set them in the front of a low oven for a few minutes to dry. Boil a sugar syrup of the 'hard crack' stage (see *sugar*). Dredge a baking sheet (or any flat cold surface) with icing (confectioners') sugar. Spike the dried orange segments on a needle, dip them into the syrup, and put them to dry on the icing sugar. When they are completely cold, arrange them in paper cases.

Orange conserve CONFITURE D'ORANGES Wash 16 juicy oranges and 3 lemons. Remove the peel without pith from 2 lemons and 4 oranges and chop it. Remove the white pith from this fruit. Cut all the fruit in half and remove the central white string. Take out the seeds, tie these in a piece of muslin (cheesecloth), and put them into a bowl with ¼ litre (8 fl oz, 1 cup) water. Slice the halved fruit finely (the peel can be left on or removed) and put them into a large bowl with the chopped peel and 4 litres (7 pints, 9 pints) water. Leave them to soak for 24 hours, turning the fruit two or three times.

Pour the contents of the bowl into a preserving pan and add the bag containing the seeds. Cover the pan and bring it to the boil. Remove the lid and simmer gently for 2 hours. Add 4 kg (9 lb) granulated or loaf sugar, bring the pan back to the boil, then reduce the heat and simmer, stirring constantly. Skim the pan and continue to cook for 30 minutes after bringing back to the boil. Pot in the usual way (see *jams, jellies, and marmalades*).

Orange marmalade MARMELADE D'ORANGES Wash and weigh 16 large oranges and 2 lemons. Peel them, including the pith, and separate them into segments. Scrape off the pith from half the peel and cut this peel into very fine strips. Put the fruit and the sliced peel into a pan and add an equal weight of water. Leave to soak for 24 hours. Pour into a preserving pan and cook until the fruit can be easily crushed; take the pan off the stove. Weigh a pan large enough to contain the cooked fruit,

pour in the fruit, and weigh again to obtain the weight of the fruit. Leave to soak for another 24 hours. Pour the fruit back into the preserving pan, add an equal weight of sugar, bring to the boil, and cook for 5–6 minutes. Pot in the usual way (see *jams, jellies, and marmalades*).

Orange salad SALADE D'ORANGES Remove all the peel and pith from some good oranges and slice them into rounds about ½ cm (¼ in) thick. Remove the seeds. Peel and finely slice some cucumber, sprinkle the slices with salt, and leave them to drain. Rinse the slices in cold water and dry them. Arrange the slices of orange and cucumber alternatively in a round glass dish. Serve with a well-seasoned vinaigrette as an entrée.

Alternatively, the oranges may be cut into small cubes and mixed with twice their volume of grated carrot. Season the salad with vinaigrette made with olive oil and raspberry vinegar and chill until ready to serve.

Orange sorbet SORBET À L'ORANGE Select 10 very large juicy oranges and remove the peel and pith. Put the pulp through a juice extractor to obtain the maximum amount of juice. Measure the juice and add 300 g (11 oz, 1⅓ cups) sugar per litre (1¾ pints) (more if the juice is very sour). Pour the juice into a sorbet maker and leave it to set (see *sorbet*).

Orange syrup SIROP D'ORANGE Select some ripe oranges and peel a few of them very thinly; put the peel to one side as it will be used to flavour the syrup. Peel the rest of the oranges. Put the pulp through a vegetable mill then strain it through a fine sieve or damp muslin (cheesecloth). Weigh the juice. Add 800 g (1¾ lb, 3½ cups) sugar to each 500 g (18 oz) juice, put into a preserving pan, and bring slowly to the boil. While the syrup is heating, line a large conical strainer with muslin and put in the reserved orange peel. Pour the syrup over the peel as soon as it comes to the boil. Let it get completely cold before bottling and sealing.

Orangine Make a Genoese sponge with 150 g (5 oz, ⅔ cup) caster (superfine) sugar, 6 eggs, 150 g (5 oz, 1¼ cup) flour, 60 g (2 oz, ¼ cup) butter, and a pinch of salt. Leave it to cool completely. Make 2.5 dl (8 fl oz, 1 cup) Curaçao-flavoured confectioners' custard (pastry cream; see *creams and custards*) and mix in 2.5 dl (8 fl oz, 1 cup) fresh cream, whisked with 1 teaspoon vanilla sugar and 30 g (1 oz, 2 tablespoons) caster sugar. Put this cream into the refrigerator. Slice the sponge into 3 equal layers. Soak each layer with 2 tablespoons (3 tablespoons) Curaçao-flavoured syrup. Spread the cream over 2 of the layers and build up the cake again. Ice (frost) the top and sides with Curaçao-flavoured fondant. Decorate the cake with pieces of candied orange peel and angelica.

orangeade

A refreshing drink made from orange juice and sugar, diluted with plain or soda water. Orangeade is best served well chilled, with ice; a little lemon juice may be added or a trace of Curaçao or rum.

orangeat

A petit four shaped like a flat disc, made from almond paste mixed with chopped candied orange peel, iced (frosted) with white fondant, and decorated with orange peel.

Orangeat perlé is a sweet (candy) consisting of candied orange peel which is dried, then covered with several layers of sugar cooked to the pearl stage. Lemon peel can be prepared in the same way (*citronnat perlé*).

orange blossom

FLEUR D'ORANGER

The fragrant flowers of the bitter (Seville) orange, which are macerated and distilled to produce orange-flower water. This is manufactured on an industrial scale and is widely used as a flavouring in pâtisserie and confectionery. Orange blossom is also used to make drinks, and orange-flower sugar is used in pâtisserie. The essential oil of orange blossom, called neroli oil, is used in perfumery and for flavouring foods.

RECIPES

Orange-flower liqueur LIQUEUR DE FLEUR D'ORANGER Add 250 g (9 oz) orange blossom, ½ teaspoons cinnamon bark, and 1 clove to 1 litre (1¾ pints, 4¼ cups) 22° (US 44°) alcohol. Leave for 1 month, then filter. Prepare a syrup with 500 g (18 oz, 2¼ cups, firmly packed) sugar and ½ litre (17 fl oz, 2 cups) water. Boil, cool, then add the flavoured alcohol. Filter once more and pour into sterilized bottles. Store in a cool dark place.

Orange-flower sugar SUCRE DE FLEUR D'ORANGER Dry some orange blossom, either in a closed container or in an oven, so as to obtain 250 g (9 oz) dry petals. Add 500 g (18 oz, 2¼ cups, firmly packed) caster (superfine) sugar to these petals and pound well in a mortar, then rub through a very fine sieve. Store in hermetically sealed jars in a dry dark place. The sugar is used mainly to flavour small cakes, creams, and custards.

oregano

See *marjoram*.

oreiller de la Belle Aurore

A large square raised pie dedicated to Brillat-Savarin's mother, Claudine-Aurore Récamier. It is one of the three pies from Belley (Bugey), Brillat-Savarin's birthplace, the recipes for which are given by Lucien Tendret in *La Table au pays de Brillat-Savarin*: the other pies are called *chapeau de Monseigneur Cortois de Quinsey* and *toque du Président Adolphe Clerc*. The *oreiller de la Belle Aurore* contains two different fillings (one of veal and pork, the other of chicken livers, young partridges, mushrooms, and truffles), to which are added marinated veal fillets, slices of breast from young red partridge and duck, a saddle of hare, white chicken meat, and blanched calves' sweetbreads.

This product of haute cuisine is said to have caused the death of Brillat-Savarin's violin teacher, who greedily ate too much of it.

oreillettes

Pastry fritters traditionally made in the Languedoc at carnival time. They are made from sweetened dough cut into long rectangles with a slit in the centre (sometimes one end is passed through this hole to form a sort of knot) and fried in oil. The oreillettes of Montpellier, flavoured with rum and orange or lemon zest, are famous.

| RECIPE

Oreillettes de Montpellier Pour 1 kg (2¼ lb, 9 cups) flour into a heap and make a well in the centre. Pour 300 g (11 oz, 1⅓ cups) melted butter into the well and work it in, gradually drawing the flour to the centre; continue to work in 5 eggs, 2 tablespoons caster (superfine) sugar, a few tablespoons rum, a small glass of milk, and the finely grated peel from 2 oranges. Knead well to obtain a smooth dough. Continue to work the dough until it becomes elastic, then form it into a ball and leave it to rest for 2 hours. Roll out the dough very thinly and cut it into rectangles 5 × 8 cm (2 × 3¼ in). Make 2 incisions in the centre of each rectangle. Fry the oreillettes in very hot fat (175 c, 340 f): they will puff up immediately and rapidly become golden. Drain them on absorbent paper, sprinkle with icing (confectioners') sugar, and arrange them in a basket lined with a white table napkin.

organic farming

AGRICULTURE BIOLOGIQUE

All farming methods which aim to maintain biological activity in the soil, particularly the action of microorganisms. The various systems that are practised have the following principal aspects in common:
● fertilization with organic matter (manure, compost, green manure) and natural minerals (phosphates, pulverized rock, wood ash);
● the exclusion of single-crop agriculture in favour of the mixing and rotation of crops, alternating demanding crops (cereals, plants which need weeding) with those that enrich the soil (leguminous);

● shallow working of the soil in order not to disturb its structure;
● using only plant-based insecticides and nonresidual fungicides.

Harder work is required, but productivity seems to be no lower than that achieved by the standard methods. Many farmers who employ these systems also practise stock-breeding (lambs, poultry, calves) and make food products: jams, preserves, cheeses, honey, wine, bread, etc.

No analysis has been able to prove the nutritional superiority of organically produced foods. For one thing, even natural fertilizers and manure are far from being harmless; whether organically or chemically produced, an excess of nitrogen will always cause the same problems. Also some cultivated varieties are not susceptible to improvement: a Golden Delicious apple, whether organically grown or not, has little flavour and no great nutritional value. On the other hand, an organically grown potato of a good variety has a higher content of vitamins and dry matter, a better flavour, and a negligible content of dangerous residues.

From a gastronomic point of view, freshly picked products sold direct to the public are unquestionably preferable, while those sold through retail shops, though much dearer, often lack freshness. Health-food shops sell bread made from organically grown cereals, and some butchers are supplied with animals raised according to 'natural' methods. There are also restaurants offering meals, mainly vegetarian, prepared with organically grown products.

organoleptic

ORGANOLEPTIQUE

Describing the qualities that determine the palatability or otherwise of a food. The organoleptic qualities of a food or drink can be defined by its flavour, smell, appearance, texture, colour, etc.

orgeat

A syrup made from sugar and milk of almonds, flavoured with orange-flower water; this is then diluted with water to make a refreshing drink. In former times it was made from barley (*orge* in French), hence its name.

orgy ORGIE

A feast at which eating and drinking is indulged in to excess and which ends in debauchery. This modern sense of the word has lost its original religious overtones. To the Greeks, and later the Romans, orgies were feasts held in honour of Dionysius, then of Bacchus, at which their followers, exalted by wine, dancing, and music, became as if possessed by the god and lost all control of themselves.

orientale (à l')

The name given to many dishes inspired by the cooking of Turkey and the Balkans and containing numerous ingredients and spices from the Mediterranean region (aubergines (eggplants), tomatoes, rice, saffron, onions, peppers, etc.). The garnish *à l'orientale* for both large and small cuts of meat consists of small tomatoes stuffed with rice pilaf (sometimes flavoured with saffron), together with okra and peppers braised in butter; the sauce is a tomato-flavoured demi-glace.

RECIPES

Oriental salad SALADE ORIENTALE
Cook some long-grain rice in salted water to which saffron has been added, keeping it fairly firm; drain thoroughly. Mix the rice with some peeled and finely chopped onion and season with vinaigrette well spiced with paprika. Pile the rice in a dome in a salad bowl. Turn some red and green peppers under a hot grill (broiler), then skin them, cut them open, take out the seeds, and cut them into strips. Peel, seed, and chop some tomatoes. Garnish the rice with the peppers, tomatoes, and some stoned black (pitted ripe) olives.

Oriental sauce SAUCE ORIENTALE
Make some tomato fondue and add saffron and a salpicon of red and green peppers. Make some very thick mayonnaise. Add the chilled tomato fondue to the mayonnaise and keep cold until ready to serve.

Orléanais

This ancient province of France can be classed among the gastronomic centres of the country. Val-de-Loire is extremely fertile. The produce of its admirable market gardens and orchards is in great demand, especially Vendôme asparagus, carrots, Chinese artichokes, garden peas, strawberries, cherries, and pears. The fertile plain of Beauce, the so-called 'granary of France', yields wheat producing one of the best-quality flours in the country; its poultry is also excellent. Perche is noted for its sheep and beef cattle, Gâtinais produces honey and poultry, and a variety of game and fish is found in the forests and lakes of Sologne. The Loire yields shad, salmon, and pike, although these are becoming rare.

The best-known Orléanais specialities are poultry and game pies and pâtés: lark pâté from Pithiviers and Blois, veal and pork pâté from Chartres, woodcock pâté from Beaugency, thrush pâté from Gien, and hare and venison pâté from Anet. Andouilles from Jargeau, rillettes and rillons from Blois and Vendôme, and pumpkin and leek soup are popular entrées. Typical of the fish dishes are carp stuffed with bacon and onions, pike with saffron (which is grown round Pithiviers) or *à la marinière*, and matelote of eel. Soup made from *corbeau* (a fish like a small bass) and vegetables, sprinkled with grated cheese, is an old favourite in the region.

Meat dishes include beef braised *à la beauceronne*, calf's mesentery *à la blésoise*, and leg of mutton (not lamb) from Sologne, cooked in water with aromatic herbs and then deglazed with vinegar. The use of game is not confined to pies and terrines: rabbit is cooked with onions and venison cutlets are prepared *à la solognote*.

Cheese production goes far beyond the Olivet beloved of Balzac. There are many other varieties, including Montoire (goats' milk), Papay (cows' milk), Pavé Blésois (goats' milk), Pithiviers, Selles-sur-Cher, Trôo (goats' milk), and Vendôme. The *tapinette* (a cheese tart) of Orléans is made with soft fresh cheese.

Orléanais pâtisserie is represented by the pithiviers, the tarte Tatin, and the financiers and croquets from Sully-sur-Loire, Montoire, and Romorantin. The delicious confectionery includes cotignac (quince paste) from Orléans, fruit pastilles, honey sweets, spiced ginger-bread, pralines from Montargis, and chocolates from Blois.

The wines of Orléanais are pleasant-tasting regional products, such as Coteaux-du-Giennois and Coteaux-du-Loir; special mention must be made of the Gris-Meunier, a rosé with a good bouquet made from the grape of the same name. Finally, both the wine vinegar and the mustard of Orléans enjoy an equally high reputation.

orléanaise (à l')

Describing large cuts of meat garnished with braised endives (chicory) and maître d'hôtel potatoes.

Orléans

The name given to tartlets of eggs (poached, soft-boiled, or *sur le plat*) which are garnished with either a salpicon of bone marrow and truffle bound with Madeira sauce, or with finely diced white chicken meat in tomato sauce. It also describes rolled sole fillets *en paupiettes*, garnished with a salpicon of shrimps and mushrooms, covered with white wine sauce, and decorated with a slice of truffle.

Orloff

The name given to a traditional recipe for cooking loin of veal: the meat is braised, sliced, stuffed with a purée of mushrooms and onions and possibly slices of truffle, then reshaped, covered with Maintenon sauce, sprinkled with Parmesan cheese, and glazed in the oven. The chef who perfected this dish was undoubtedly Urbain Dubois, who was in Prince Orloff's service for more than 20 years.

Orloff garnish for large cuts of meat consists of braised celery (or darioles lined with sticks (stalks) of braised celery and filled with a mousse made from celery purée), château potatoes, and braised lettuce.

| RECIPE

Veal Orloff VEAU ORLOFF Peel and slice thinly 500 g (18 oz, 5 cups) onions, 1 large carrot, and 750 g (1¾ lb, 7 cups) button mushrooms. Melt 50 g (2 oz, 4 tablespoons) butter in a casserole and brown 150 g (5 oz) bacon rinds, then a

boned loin of veal weighing about 1.75 kg (4 lb). Add the sliced carrot, 1 large tablespoon sliced onions, a bouquet garni, salt, and pepper. Add just enough water to cover the meat, put the lid on, and cook over a low heat for 1 hour 20 minutes.

Meanwhile, melt 30 g (1 oz, 2 tablespoons) butter in a sauté pan and quickly brown the sliced mushrooms. Chop them, replace in the pan with salt, pepper, 1 tablespoon flour, and a pinch of grated nutmeg, and cook for about 10 minutes. Put the rest of the sliced onions through a food processor or vegetable mill and cook until golden in 40 g (1½ oz, 3 tablespoons) butter. Then moisten them with water, cover the pan, and cook for 20–25 minutes until puréed. Add the mushrooms and 2 dl (7 fl oz, ¾ cup) double (heavy) cream, then boil the cream down.

Cut the veal into thin even slices, cutting transversely from one long side to the other; spread each slice with a little of the onion and mushroom purée. Put the slices together again and reshape the loin. Tie it, place in a gratin dish, and spread it with the rest of the purée. Mask it with Maintenon sauce, sprinkle with grated Parmesan cheese, dot with butter, and brown in a hot oven for 10 minutes. Skim the fat from the braising liquid and serve the latter separately.

Orly

The name given to a method of cooking fish. The fish (eel, pike, whiting, sole, smelt, salmon, etc.), which may be filleted or whole according to their size, are dipped in batter or egg and breadcrumbs, then fried, drained, and served with tomato sauce.

| RECIPE

Salmon fillets Orly with tomato sauce
FILETS DE SAUMON ORLY SAUCE TOMATE (from Plumerey's recipe) Trim 14 salmon fillets. Put them into a dish with some salt, coarsely ground pepper, a little grated nutmeg, 2 finely sliced shallots, some sprigs of parsley, the juice of 2 lemons, half a glass of olive oil, a little thyme, and a bay leaf. Be sure to turn the fillets several times in this marinade, and drain off the water which they produce. An hour before the meal

drain the fillets on kitchen paper (paper towels), sprinkle with flour, and turn them in this until they are quite dry. Pat them back into shape with the blade of a knife and dip them into 4 beaten eggs before frying them. When cooked, arrange them in a circle on a plate and serve a light tomato sauce separately.

ormer ORMEAU

A marine gastropod mollusc of the genus *Haliotis*, also called abalone, whose rimmed shell, slightly hollow and curved, resembles an ear, hence its nickname of sea-ear (*oreille de mer*). The edge of the shell is pierced with a row of holes, the interior is pearly, and the exterior reddish-brown; it measures 8–12 cm (3–5 in) across. All the muscle is edible: extracted from the shell, trimmed and beaten well to tenderize it, it is a white well-flavoured meat which can be casseroled with fresh vegetables or fried like a veal escalope (scallop).

It is eaten on the Channel coasts (braised Jersey ormers) and round the Mediterranean (*oreilles de Saint-Pierre* sautéed with garlic); the catch is now controlled.

A large exotic variety of abalone can be bought in cans.

RECIPE

Ormers with oysters ORMEAUX AUX HUÎTRES Cut off the foot of the ormers close to the shell, clean the inside, scrub it free of mucus, and beat the meat with a mallet (canned ormers could be used instead). Slice the meat and cook it in oil over a high heat for 2 or 3 minutes. Add 3 tablespoons oyster sauce (available in shops selling oriental foodstuffs), 2 tablespoons soy sauce, and pepper. Thicken with 1 tablespoon cornflour (cornstarch) moistened with a little water or ormer juices and mixed with 1 tablespoon Cognac. Sprinkle with chopped spring onions (scallions) and allow to simmer for 2 or 3 minutes.

ortolan

A small migratory bird – a species of bunting – considered since early times to be the finest and most delicate of birds to eat. Although it is now officially protected as it is becoming so rare, the law is not strictly observed in south-western France, especially in the Landes; even though it is forbidden to serve ortolans in restaurants, they continue to be captured alive and fattened up for private consumption. The bird's diet (millet, buds, berries, grapes, and small insects) gives its flesh flavour and delicacy. Weighing only 30 g (1¼ oz) when caught, it can quadruple its weight in a month.

Ortolans are usually roasted on spits or in the oven, cooked mainly in their own fat; the latter drips onto pieces of bread, which some recommend should be spread with Roquefort cheese. The bird is always eaten whole. According to James de Coquet: 'This delicate dish, costly and melting, should be cooked for no more than five or six minutes, either wrapped in greaseproof (waxed) paper or in a small casserole. A few drops of orange juice are sometimes added at the last moment. Some gourmands cover their heads with their napkins while they are eating the birds so as to lose none of the aroma. The inventor of this ritual is a priest, a friend of the Brillat-Savarin family.'

The French still regard the ortolan as one of the choicest of dishes and a symbol of luxury, which, as Grimod de La Reynière remarked, 'is prized even more by those who know only the name than by those who have tasted it'.

osmazôme

The name given by the French chemist Louis-Jacques Thenard (1777–1857), the discoverer of hydrogen peroxide, to the element in meat which gives it its flavour. The term is now obsolete, but Brillat-Savarin used it a great deal: 'It is osmazôme which gives flavour to good soups; it is the substance which, when it caramelizes, thickens the meat juices; it forms the brown crust on roasts; finally, it is the source of the aroma of venison and game . . . After the osmazôme has done its work, further elements are extracted by boiling; when these are combined with osmazôme the result is the meat juices.'

The most important application of this theory is in the pot-au-feu: if the meat is to release its goodness into the water, the later must only gradually penetrate the fibres. According to M. des Ombiaux, if the pot-au-feu boils before the meat has become swollen, 'the albumin coagulates and inhibits the extraction of the osmazôme; the result is hard meat and insipid broth. On the other hand, if the pan is allowed only to simmer, the albumin rises as scum, the broth is full of flavour, and the meat is tender.'

Ossau-Iraty

A French ewes'-milk cheese protected by an *appellation d'origine* but often sold under the name 'Fromage de Brebis des Pyrénées'. With a fat content of at least 50%, the cheese has a creamy yellow lightly pressed curd, a smooth orange-yellow to grey rind, and a pronounced flavour. It is made in the shape of a flat disc with straight or slightly convex sides, in two sizes: 24.5–25 cm (9½–11 in) in diameter, 12–14 cm (4¾–5½ in) deep, weighing 4–7 kg (9–15 lb); and 20 cm (7¾ in) in diameter, 10–12 cm (4–4¾ in) deep, weighing 2–3 kg (4½–6½ lb). It can be eaten at the end of a meal, on canapés, as a snack, or as part of a mixed salad.

osso bucco   OSSO-BUCO

An Italian dish, originally from Milan, whose name means literally 'bone with a hole'. It consists of a stew of pieces of unboned veal knuckle braised in white wine with onion and tomato. It is generally served with pasta or rice. The variation called *alla gremolata* is prepared with the addition of a mixture of chopped garlic, orange and lemon peel, and grated nutmeg.

RECIPES

Osso bucco à la milanaise   Cut 1 kg (2¼ lb) veal knuckle into 8 pieces, each about 1.5 cm (½ in) thick. Season them with salt and pepper, sprinkle with flour, then brown them in olive oil in a large casserole. Chop enough onions to give 5 level tablespoons; add these to the casserole and cook until golden. Moisten with 2 dl (7 fl oz, ¾ cup) white wine, reduce this, then add 4 large tomatoes, skinned, deseeded, and coarsely chopped. Pour in 2.5 dl (8 fl oz, 1 cup) stock. Finally add 1 large crushed garlic clove and a bouquet garni. Cover the casserole and cook in the oven at 200 C (400 F, gas 6) for 1½ hours. Arrange the

pieces of knuckle in a deep dish and cover them with the reduced cooking liquid. Squeeze on a little lemon juice and sprinkle with chopped parsley.

ostrich   AUTRUCHE

A large African bird, with tough rather flavourless meat. Its brain was considered to be a delicacy at the time of Nero. Ostrich eggs, on the other hand, are excellent. They were fashionable at the beginning of the 19th century but are not sold today. Since one ostrich egg weighs an average of 1.5 kg (3¼ lb), it would be sufficient to prepare an omelette for 8–10 people.

oublie

A small flat or cornet-shaped wafer, widely enjoyed in France in the Middle Ages, but whose origins go even further back in time. Oublies, which were perhaps the first cakes in the history of cooking, are the ancestors of waffles. They were usually made from a rather thick waffle batter and were cooked in flat round finely patterned iron moulds. Some authorities consider that the name comes from the Greek *obelios*, meaning a cake cooked between two iron plates and sold for an obol; others that it comes from the Latin *oblata* (offering), which also means an unconsecrated host.

In the Middle Ages, oublies were made by the *oubloyeurs* (or *oublieux*), whose guild was incorporated in 1270. They made and sold their wares in the open street, setting up stalls at fairs and in the open space in front of churches on feast days. It was said that the most celebrated oublies were those from Lyon, where apparently they were rolled into cornets after being cooked. The oubloyeurs would put them one inside the other and sell them in fives, called a *main d'oublies*. Often they would play dice for them with their customers or draw lots for them on a 'Wheel of Fortune', which was in fact the cover of the large pannier – or *coffin* – in which they carried their wares. By the 16th century most of the Parisian pastrycooks were established in the Rue des Oubloyers in the Cité; by night and day the apprentices would set out laden with their panniers full of *nieules* (round flat cakes), *échaudés* (a sort of brioche), oublies, and other small cakes, crying 'Voilà le plaisir, mesdames!' ('Here's pleasure, ladies!'), which led to oublies being given the popular name of *plaisirs*. The last of these pedlars disappeared after World War I.

Oublies à la parisienne Put 250 g (9 oz, 2¼ cups) sifted flour, 150 g (5 oz, ⅔ cup) sugar, 2 eggs, and a little orange-flower water or lemon juice into a bowl. Work together until everything is well mixed, then gradually add 6–7 dl (1 pint, 2½ cups) milk, 65 g (2½ oz, 5 tablespoons) melted butter, and the grated rind of a lemon. Heat the oublie iron and grease it evenly; pour in 1 tablespoon batter and cook over a high heat, turning the iron over halfway through. Peel the wafer off the iron and either roll it into a cornet round a wooden cone or leave it flat.

ouillade

In the Ariège this is a rustic soup containing garlic and eggs. In the Roussillon area it is a dish of pork boiled with vegetables. The name comes from the old French word *oille*, a large pot.

ouillat or ouliat

A soup from Béarn; the name comes from the pot in which it is cooked (the *ouille*, derived from *oille*). Based on onions, garlic, dried haricot (navy) beans or broad (fava) beans, sometimes with tomatoes or leeks, the soup (also known as *touri*) is thickened with egg and vinegar, or sprinkled with grated cheese, and poured over slices of bread.

RECIPE

ouillat (from a recipe of Simin Palay) In an earthenware casserole, heat some fat or olive oil and fry some chopped onion; when it has browned slightly, add some crushed garlic and continue cooking. Pour in the required quantity of hot water; add salt, pepper, and a bouquet of thyme and parsley. Boil for 30 minutes, then pour through a strainer over some slices of bread in a tureen.

If available, use the water in which haricot (navy) beans, dried peas, broad (fava) beans, or asparagus have been cooked. An egg and a few drops of vinegar can be added just before straining the soup into the tureen. Grated Gruyère cheese can be substituted for the egg. In season, skinned sliced tomatoes can be cooked with the onion.

oulade

A soup based on bacon, cabbage, and other vegetables, made in Rouergue, Gévaudan, and the Auvergne. The name derives from the tinned copper pot in which it is cooked (*oule*).

ourteto

A mixture of chopped spinach, sorrel, celery, and leeks boiled and flavoured with crushed garlic. It is eaten in Provence on slices of bread cut from a large round white loaf, moistened with olive oil.

ouzo

A spirit flavoured with aniseed, made in Greece and many of the Greek islands, including Cyprus. Like pastis, it turns cloudy when water is added and it should always be served together with iced water, though it should not be kept in the refrigerator for any length of time.

oven FOUR

A cooking apparatus derived from the bread oven, whose origins are lost in the mists of time. Modern domestic ovens are heated by gas jets or by a set of electric elements arranged at the bottom and top, at the sides, or at the back. The door is usually made of enamel or stainless steel, though toughened glass doors, enabling the cooking process to be seen, are gaining in popularity; there may also be an interior light. Some ovens also have additional features, such as a built-in spit, grill element, or micro waves (see *microwave oven*).

Whether the oven is a gas or electric one, it always has a thermostat which regulates the temperature (generally from 110 to 240 C, 225–475 F, gas ¼–9). Sometimes the temperature starts at 60 C (140 F), for heating plates or for very gentle cooking. There is sometimes also a warming compartment with even lower temperatures, starting at 50 C (122 F), with an independent thermostat.

In fan-assisted ovens a high-speed fan is used to distribute the heat within the oven, promoting a more uniform temperature throughout. In forced air convection ovens a circular element is fitted at the back of the oven, around a fan. These ovens heat up rapidly and the pattern in which the heat is circulated promotes speedy even cooking at temperatures that are lower than those required in an ordinary oven.

Some modern ovens are self-cleaning, either by catalysis (gas or electric) or by pyrolysis (electric ovens only).

• *Catalysis*: the sides, back, and roof of the oven are lined with a special type of porous enamel which vaporizes oven soil, e.g. splashes, etc. (the base of the oven is either enamel or nonstick). Catalytic ovens clean continuously, but work best at higher temperatures. Any surface soil should be removed from the liners carefully, using a nylon or plastic brush, then the oven is turned to maximum heat (but check with the manufacturer's handbook first). Major spills on the oven floor should be cleaned as quickly as possible.

• *Pyrolysis*: the oven is heated up to 500 c (900 f); because of the high temperature the oven is sealed so no access can be gained.The great heat carbonizes the oven soil, leaving the interior completely clean (check with the manufacturer's handbook how often to clean the oven).

overlap IMBRIQUER

To arrange food so that each piece is partially covered by the next to achieve a decorative effect. Some cold dishes are garnished in this way, using small slices of truffle set in aspic.

oxtail

A cut of meat used to make many delicious dishes, notably oxtail soup and Flemish *hochepot* (see *hotchpotch*). An ingredient of the stockpot, oxtail gives the broth body and flavour; it can also be braised and served with a flamande or nivernaise garnish, or it can be boiled, coated with breadcrumbs, and grilled (broiled) *à la Sainte-Menehould*.

Oxtail soup is a classic English soup which, according to some authorities, could have been introduced into Britain by refugees from the French Revolution. It is a clear soup made from an oxtail and traditionally it is flavoured with basil, marjoram, savory, and thyme, although these are often replaced by the classic braising vegetables: carrots, leeks, and onions. Oxtail soup can be garnished with small vegetable balls or a brunoise as well as with meat from the oxtail; it is flavoured with Madeira, brandy, or sherry.

RECIPE

Grilled (broiled) oxtail Sainte-Menehould QUEUE DE BOEUF SAINTE-MENEHOULD Cut an oxtail into sections 6–7 cm (2½–3 in) long and cook them in stock prepared as for a pot-au-feu; stop cooking before the meat begins to come away from the

	conventional oven				convection oven		
		electric				*electric*	
	gas	C	F		gas	C	F
very cool	¼	110	230			100	210
	½	120	250			110	230
cool	1	140	275		1	120	250
	2	150	300			130	265
moderate	3	160	325		2	140	275
	4		350			150	300
moderately hot	5	190	375		3	160	325
	6	200	400			165	330
hot	7	220	425			170	240
	8	230	450		4	180	350
very hot	9	240	475			190	375
						200	400

bones. Drain the pieces, bone them without breaking them up, and leave them to cool, under a weight, in the stock (from which the fat has been skimmed). Drain and dry the pieces, spread them with mustard, brown them quickly in clarified butter, then roll them in fine fresh breadcrumbs. Grill (broil) gently and serve with any of the following sauces – diable, piquante, mustard, pepper, bordelaise, or Robert – accompanied by mashed potatoes.

Oxtail soup POTAGE OXTAIL Put 1.5 kg (3½ lb) oxtail, cut into small chunks, into a casserole, on a bed of sliced carrots, leeks, and onions. Sweat in the oven for 25 minutes. Cover with 2.5 litres (4½ pints, 5½ pints) stock made by cooking 1.5 kg (3½ lb) gelatinous bones for 7–8 hours in 3.25 litres (5¾ pints, 7 pints) water. Season. Simmer gently, so that the boiling is imperceptible, for 3½–4 hours. Strain the soup and skim off surplus fat. Clarify by boiling it for an hour with 500 g (generous 1 lb) chopped lean beef and the white part of 2 leeks, finely sliced, first whisking both these ingredients with a raw white of egg. Strain the stock. Garnish with pieces of oxtail and 3 dl (½ pint, 1¼ cups) coarse brunoise of carrots, turnips, and celery sweated in butter and dropped into the stock. Add 1 tablespoon sherry.

oyonnade

A stew of young goose with Saint-Pourçain wine, thickened with the liver and blood of the bird and mixed with spirits. It used to be a traditional dish for All Saints' Day in the Bourbonnais, particularly near Montluçon, and was served with swedes (rutabaga).

| RECIPE |

Oyonnade Reserve the blood of a goose and add 2 tablespoons vinegar to prevent it from curdling. Cut the bird into pieces and brown them in a casserole, over a low heat, with 100 g (4 oz, 6 slices) fat bacon. Add 24 whole small onions and cook until they are lightly coloured. Sprinkle on 2 tablespoons flour, cook until golden, then add 2 crushed garlic cloves, a bouquet garni, ½ litre (17 fl oz, 2 cups) red wine, and ¼

litre (8 fl oz, 1 cup) hot water; season with salt and pepper. Cover the casserole, bring to the boil, then transfer to the oven at 200 C (400 F, gas 6) and cook for 2 hours.

Meanwhile, put the goose liver through a vegetable mill or blender and add the blood mixed with vinegar, 1.5 –2 dl (5–7 fl oz, ½–¾ cup) double (heavy) cream, and 1 glass liqueur brandy or Cognac. Drain the pieces of goose and keep them hot in a deep serving dish. Pour the thickening mixture into the casserole, beat it together with the cooking juices, heat through without boiling, and pour the sauce over the goose. Garnish the dish with croutons fried in the goose fat.

oyster HUÎTRE

A saltwater bivalve mollusc, of which there are many edible varieties.

The oyster has been known to man from the earliest times. The Celts, the Greeks (who reared oysters in beds), and the Romans all ate oysters in large quantities. During the Middle Ages, a distinction was made between oysters sold in their shells and those which were sold without their shells in order to facilitate rapid transport to Paris; the latter were considered to be inferior. Louis XIV's doctor maintained that oysters should always be cooked, grilled (broiled) in their shells or fried. Until the 19th century oysters were gathered in quantity from their native beds, which were thought to be inexhaustible. Ostend oysters were particularly sought-after; they were described by Maupassant in *Bel-Ami* as: 'small and rich, looking like little ears enfolded in shells, and melting between the palate and the tongue like salted sweets'.

Nowadays oysters are farmed, thus ensuring that they are not overfished and, more importantly, are free from pollution. Two species dominate the French market: the native French oyster, which is flat and round and accounts for a bare 10% of the market, and the cupped Pacific or Japanese oyster, which is almost rectangular. This variety supplies most of the market and has been farmed successfully in France since the 1970s. It was introduced as a result of a disease which almost destroyed another species, the cupped

Portuguese oyster. Portuguese oysters arrived by chance in 1868 off the coast of Aquitaine, from a wrecked ship that was carrying cargo from Portugal (hence their name). The oysters became established in the Gironde estuary and are found as far up as Marennes.

In the cultivation of oysters, seed oysters are affixed to tiles and reared in areas some way out to sea. When they have reached a certain size, they are transferred to the fattening beds, which are always situated at the mouth of a river, the mixture of fresh and sea water being essential to induce overgrowth of the liver, of which the fattening consists. The growing period lasts from three to four years and requires constant supervision. As the oyster grows, it needs more space and therefore a larger area is required for the bed. It must be protected from pollution and from its natural enemies – skate, winkles, crabs, starfish, octopus, and sea birds.

Some varieties of French flat oysters are:
- *Belon* (a name formerly reserved for the oysters from Riec-sur-Belon, near Concarneau, but nowadays applied to all flat Breton oysters): grown in deep water, most often in northern Brittany; the greyish-white flesh tastes of iodine.
- *Bouzigue*: cultivated in the Thau basin, in the Hérault region of France, from Breton seed oysters; it has a fruity salty taste; production is now low as in 1982 the beds were almost totally destroyed in a storm.
- *Gravette*: from the Arcachon region of France; entirely locally reared from spat to gathering; fleshy and greenish-yellow in colour.

Concave seed oysters can come from the Thau basin or from Arcachon, but are produced mainly in the Marennes region of France (Charente-Maritime). Marennes oysters are a characteristic green colour. This is because they are reared in *claires*: oyster beds in former salt marshes, now regularly dredged and cleaned, where the plankton includes a type of algae whose pigment causes the characteristic colour of the oysters. 'Fines de claires' are matured for two months at a concentration of 20 oysters per square metre; 'specials' are matured for six months, at five oysters per square metre.

□ **Buying and eating oysters** For generations oysters were supposed to be eaten only during the months containing the leter 'r' (i.e. from September to April). However, with modern methods of rearing and transport they can now safely be eaten at any time of the year. Demand is still heaviest from autumn to late spring, with peak consumption at Christmas and New Year. Price depends on the place of origin, the quality, and the rearing period: flat oysters, which are less common, or 'specials', with a longer fattening period, are dearer than ordinary oysters.

Oysters must always be bought live, with the shells closed or closing when tapped, and they should feel quite heavy as they should be full of water. They are not opened until the last minute. To test whether an opened oyster is alive, prick the cilia, which should instantly retract.

Oysters are sold by the dozen, by the half-dozen, or by the basket from the producer. They are also sometimes sold by weight. They should be eaten as soon as possible after purchase, but can be stored for a short time in the original basket or wrapped in seaweed or a damp cloth, round side down, in a cellar or in a refrigerator, at 0–8 c (32–44 f).

Even when described as 'fat', oysters have a low fat content (1% lipids). They are a good source of protein and are rich in minerals, trace elements, and vitamins.

Nowadays, oysters are nearly always eaten alive and raw, plainly dressed with lemon and accompanied by rye bread and fresh butter, or with a vinegar dressing containing shallot and freshly ground pepper. However, they can also be cooked and used in hot and cold dishes. Massialot, in his book *Cuisinier royal et bourgeois* (1691), gave recipes for duck with oysters and an oyster and truffle sauce which modern chefs would not scorn to use. Oysters can be poached, then chilled and served with various sauces, sometimes in barquettes; they can be browned in the oven in their shells (which are embedded in coarse salt to keep them balanced); or they are served with artichoke hearts, in croustades, etc. Browning must always be done very rapidly and the preliminary poaching is often unnecessary. Oysters can also be cooked on skewers, made into fritters, croquettes, soups, and consommés, and used as a garnish in fish recipes. English and American cookery in particular make good use of oysters – in soup, as a sauce, or as angels on horseback. Among the French regional specialities is one from Arcachon where local oysters are served with grilled chipolata sausages.

RECIPES

Angels on horseback BROCHETTES D'HUÎTRES À L'ANGLAISE Take some fine fat oysters out of their shells. Sprinkle them with a little freshly ground white pepper and wrap each one in a thin slice of bacon. Thread them on skewers and grill for 2 minutes. Arrange on pieces of hot toast.

Oyster barquettes (cold) BARQUETTES D'HUÎTRES FROIDES Poach some oysters in their own liquid, drain them, remove the beards, and let them get cold. Mask them with mayonnaise set with meat aspic. Garnish with truffles and crayfish coral and cover with jelly. Arrange them in pairs in small barquettes made from fine lining pastry, baked blind. Garnish to taste with Russian salad or a fish mousse.

Oyster barquettes (hot) BARQUETTES D'HUÎTRES CHAUDES Poach the oysters in their own liquid, drain them, and remove the beards. Make some barquettes from shortcrust pastry (basic pie dough) and bake them blind. In each barquette place a little of the chosen sauce or garnish, then the oysters, then more sauce, and finally some breadcrumbs, grated cheese, etc. Put into a hot oven for a short period.

The following are some preparations for hot oyster barquettes:

■ *à l'américaine:* garnish with américaine sauce (see *lobster (á l'américaine)*) and then sprinkle with fried breadcrumbs seasoned with cayenne.

■ *à la Nantua:* fill with a ragout of crayfish tails, cover with Nantua sauce, sprinkle with grated cheese, and brown in the oven.

■ *à la normande:* fill with a salpicon of blended prawns and mussels and then cover with a normande sauce.

Oyster bouchées à la Denis BOUCHÉES D'HUÎTRES À LA DENIS (from Chef Denis's recipe) Heat some small puff-pastry bouchées, 3–4 cm (1–1½ in) in diameter. Into each case put a small square of fresh foie gras and on this place a raw oyster. Serve at once. The oyster can be sprinkled with freshly ground white pepper.

Oyster brochettes à la Villeroi BROCHETTES D'HUÎTRES À LA VILLEROI Cook the oysters in their own liquid, drain them, and dry in a cloth. Completely cover with Villeroi sauce, thread on skewers, and fry them. Serve with Villeroi sauce.

Oyster fritters BEIGNETS D'HUÎTRES Poach the oysters in their own water and let them cool in the cooking liquid. Drain them and dry in a cloth. Leave them to soak for 30 minutes in a mixture of oil, lemon juice, pepper, and salt, then dip them in batter. Cook in very hot oil until the fritters are puffed and golden and drain them at once on absorbent paper. Sprinkle with fine salt and serve with lemon quarters.

Oysters à la Boston HUÎTRES À LA BOSTON Open a dozen flat oysters; carefully take out the flesh from the shells and drain it. In the bottom of each concave shell, place a little ground white pepper and a generous pinch of fried breadcrumbs. Replace the oysters in the shells; sprinkle them with grated Gruyère cheese and a few breadcrumbs. Dot each with a small piece of butter. Brown under the grill for 6–7 minutes. Serve with shrimp fritters or Parmesan cheese straws.

Oyster sauce SAUCE AUX HUÎTRES (English recipe) Open and poach 12 oysters. Prepare a white roux with 20 g (¾ oz, scant 2 tablespoons) butter and 20 g (¾ oz, 3 tablespoons) flour, then moisten with 1 dl (6 tablespoons, scant ½ cup) oyster cooking liquid, 1 dl (6 tablespoons, scant ½ cup) milk, and 1 dl (6 tablespoons, scant cup) single (light) cream. Adjust the seasoning. Bring to the boil and cook for 10 minutes. Pass through a sieve. Add the debearded and sliced oysters and a pinch of cayenne.

Oysters in their shells (*hot*) HUÎTRES CHAUDES EN COQUILLES Poach the oysters, replace them in their shells, and set these firmly into a layer of coarse salt in a baking tin (pan). Brown in a hot oven for a few seconds (poaching can be omitted). They can then be served in the following ways:

■ *à l'américaine*: sprinkle with a few drops of lemon juice and a pinch of cayenne.

■ *à la florentine*: replace in their shells on a layer of buttered spinach, then mask with Mornay sauce, sprinkle with grated cheese, and brown in the oven.

■ *à la polonaise*: sprinkle with chopped hard-boiled (hard-cooked) egg yolk and chopped parsley, then moisten with noisette butter mixed with fried bread-crumbs.

Oyster soup POTAGE AUX HUÎTRES Open 24 oysters, put them into a sauté pan, and pour over them their own water strained through muslin (cheesecloth). Add 2 dl (7 fl oz, ¾ cup) white wine. Bring just to the boil and take off the heat as soon as the water begins to bubble. Skim the pan; add 2 dl (7 fl oz, ¾ cup) cream, 3 tablespoons (scant ¼ cup) crushed biscuit crackers, and 100 g (4 oz, ½ cup) butter cut into small pieces. Season with salt and pepper and a pinch of cayenne. Mix well. Serve in a soup tureen.

Poached oysters HUITRES PO-CHÉES Open the oysters and put them into a sauté pan with their own water, strained through a muslin (cheesecloth) sieve. Bring almost to the boil on top of the stove, removing the pan as soon as the liquid begins to simmer.

Steak with oysters STEAK AUX HUÎTRES (from a recipe by Jean and Paul Minchelli) Open 8 oysters. Slice through a piece of beef fillet (sirloin) weighing about 300 g (11 oz), without separating the 2 halves. Flatten it slightly, season with salt and pepper, brush the inside surfaces with a mild mustard, and then sear it rapidly in a mixture of equal quantities of oil and butter. Flame it with brandy and keep hot. In another pan put the strained water from 4 oysters, a chopped garlic clove, a finely chopped shallot, a knob of butter, 3 tablespoons (scant ¼ cup) cream, and 1 teaspoon brandy. Add pepper and reduce. Slip the oysters into the steak, press it closed, and secure it with 1 or 2 cocktail sticks (toothpicks). In a small saucepan put the blood which has run from the meat, the reduced sauce, a few drops of Worcestershire sauce, pepper, and 1 tablespoon brandy; reduce again. Cover the steak with this sauce. Arrange the last 4 oysters on top of the meat. Sprinkle with chopped parsley.

oyster mushroom
PLEUROTE EN COQUILLE OU EN HUÎTRE An earlike grey or greyish-brown bracket mushroom, *Pleurotus ostreatus*, which grows in clusters on deciduous trees and stumps. It can also be cultivated and makes a pleasant substitute for the button mushroom in cooking. Abundant in autumn and winter, its flesh is firm and flavoursome, especially when young (it gets hard as it grows older). The stalk is rather tough and needs chopping and prolonged cooking. A closely related species, *Pleurotus pulmonarius* (*pleurote du panicaut*), is found in spring and autumn. It is edible, with a delicate slightly musky flavour.

Ozanne (Achille)
French chef (born La Chapelle-la-Reine, 1846; died Fontainebleau, 1896). He was chef to the king of Greece and the author of *Poésies gourmandes*. Here is his *Grive à la casserole* ('Casserole of Thrush'):

'Bien cuite dans la casserole
Avec des dés de petits lards,
Et quand on la dresse avec art,
Trônant sur sa croûte rôtie,
Puis du cresson ornant le plat,
Un vrai courant de sympathie
Se manifeste avec éclat.'

This could be roughly translated as:

'Done to a turn in the casserole
With bacon, lean and diced, I trust,
When placed with art upon the plate
Enthroned on golden savoury crust
With watercress to decorate,
The diners' goodwill is assured –
They praise the bird with one accord.'

pachade

A dessert that is a speciality of the Saint-Flour region of the Auvergne. As a rule, pachade is made from a crêpe batter mixed with fruit (particularly plums or prunes) and baked in the oven in a deep buttered dish. Sometimes, however, it is simply a thick pancake.

Pacherenc-du-Vic-Bilh

White AOC wines from the Adour Valley in southwestern France. Like the red Madiran, they are traditionally made from grapes allowed to dry on the vine, so the juice is concentrated and the wines sweet.

packaging
CONDITIONNEMENT

A wide variety of coverings and containers are used to preserve, transport, and present food products to consumers. Packaging must protect foodstuffs from anything that might affect their nutritive value or flavour, and should not itself cause any change. From the commercial point of view, it should be both attractive and practical, as well as informative (to conform with regulations on the labelling of prepacked foodstuffs).

Foodstuffs may be packed before they are put on sale, wrapped by the retailer when they are weighed, or else potted, bottled, etc., in the home. In each case, the materials used are different. The food industry uses materials which are recognized as being suitable for a particular use, sometimes being limited to a particular type of food (milk products, eggs, drinks, etc.). Formerly, specially designed containers for transporting foodstuffs included wickerwork hampers, wooden casks and barrels, stoneware pots, rush baskets, and even fresh leaves.

In the home, the use of unsuitable packaging (non-food-grade plastics, badly cleaned containers, etc.) should be avoided. When a refrigerator or freezer is used, it is essential to have some practical knowledge of packaging.

☐ **Rigid materials**

• *Glass*, which is inert as far as food is concerned, allows the passage of light (unless it is coloured), which destroys vitamins B_2 and C and causes fats to become rancid; it can be reused and is transparent, but it is heavy and cannot withstand very low or high temperatures.

• *Tin plate*, the traditional material for cans, can sometimes be reused (cake tins, sweet tins, etc.); it is waterproof and opaque and can resist high temperatures; it allows a high level of sterilization and preserving.

• *Cardboard* is used a great deal for grocery products which are solid or in powdered form; when treated with paraffin, it is waterproof and can be used as packaging for soft drinks, milk (e.g. in cartons), yogurt, and fresh cream.

• *Aluminium*, which is used for certain drinks (beer and fizzy soft drinks) is usually made into foil containers for freezing, in which food can be reheated.

• *Rigid plastics* include polystyrene (for yogurt and soft cheese), polyethylene (oil bottles), polyvinyl chloride (bottles in particular), and expanded polystyrene (which gives protection from shocks and variation in temperature). These products are light, opaque where necessary, impermeable, and have been tested for toxicity, but they are not biodegradable.

□ Flexible materials

• *Paper* (untreated) is used mostly for the retail sale of fruit and vegetables (usually in the form of paper bags) and for wrapping cakes. It allows the transmission of smells, fats, and humidity. Greaseproof (waxed) paper is used frequently in cookery.

• *Cellophane* is the product of a cellulose paste treated with acid. It is generally coated with plastic to make it waterproof. This is the traditional packaging material for pasta, rice, and dried vegetables, and also sliced bread.

• *Aluminium foil* gives the best protection against ultraviolet rays, dehydration, and odours. It insulates against very low temperatures well and withstands sharp changes in temperature (as when cooking food in foil parcels). It is also completely inert as far as food is concerned.

• *Plastic film* – the type used most is polyethylene, which is inert, waterproof, airtight, and unaffected by cold. Blister packs are packages formed from a film of plastic which adheres to a cardboard or plastic tray (industrially baked cakes, prepacked meat, etc.).

• *Complexes*, made from two or more materials (e.g. paper and polyethylene, aluminium and polyvinyl), benefit from the combined qualities of each: they are used particularly for wrapping fats and

for sealing containers which must be completely watertight.

• *Aerosols*, recently introduced, are easy to handle and hygienic, storing foodstuffs under pressure and releasing them as a foam, paste, or powder.

Finally, many products are packed industrially under a vacuum, which allows them to be kept for a very long time (vegetables for retail sale, ground and freeze-dried products, etc.).

paella

A traditional Spanish rice dish garnished with vegetables, chicken, shellfish, etc. Its name is derived from that of the vessel in which it is prepared (*paellera*).

Paella originated in the region of Valencia. Its three basic ingredients are rice, saffron, and olive oil. The garnish, which is cooked with the rice in stock, originally consisted either of chicken, snails, French (green) beans, and peas or eel, frogs, and vegetables, but it became considerably enriched and varied as it spread throughout Spain and even beyond (see *jambalaya*). The garnish may now include chicken, rabbit, duck, lobster, mussels, langoustines, prawns (shrimp), squid, chorizo, French beans, peas, red peppers, artichoke hearts, etc.; chicken, chorizo, mussels, langoustines, and peas are a minimum. Paella may be a rustic dish, cooked in the open air and eaten straight from the *paellera*, traditionally accompanied by small onions (not bread), or a very elaborate preparation, presented with great care, the different-coloured ingredients contrasting with the saffron-flavoured rice and set off by the green peas.

RECIPE

Paella Cut a chicken weighing about 1.4 kg (3 lb) into 8 pieces and season them with salt and pepper. Place the crushed backbone and the giblets in a stewpan, cover with water, season with salt and pepper, bring to the boil, and skim. Peel and chop 2 onions, cut the white part of a leek and a stick (stalk) of celery into fine strips, and chop 3 cloves of garlic. Add all the vegetables to the stewpan with a bouquet garni. Wait until the stock comes to the boil again, then simmer for 1 hour.

Wash 500 g (18 oz) squid, cut into thin strips, and put in a saucepan with some cold water. Bring to the boil, leave to boil for 5 minutes, then cool and set aside.

Heat 4 tablespoons (⅓ cup) olive oil in a deep frying pan with a metal handle (or use a paella pan) and fry the chicken pieces in it until they turn golden. Drain them. Gently reheat the same oil and add 250 g (9 oz) chorizo cut into round slices, then the squid, 2 sweet peppers seeded and cut into thin strips, and 2 chopped onions. Add a pinch of saffron and leave to soften, uncovered, for 5–6 minutes. Add 6 large tomatoes (peeled, deseeded, and crushed) and reduce for 5 minutes, still uncovered.

Measure the volume of 400 g (14 oz, 2 cups) long-grain rice, tip it into the pan, and mix everything together. Place the chicken pieces on top, then add 12 scraped and washed mussels, 12 Venus clams (if available), a handful of brushed and washed cockles, and 8–12 langoustines. Strain the giblet stock and pour into the pan a volume of it equal to two and a half times that of the rice. Cover with aluminium foil, bring to the boil over the heat, then cook in the oven at 220 C (425 F, gas 7) for 25–30 minutes. Add 250 g (8 oz, 1 cup) frozen peas, stirring them into the mixture, and leave to cook for a further 5 minutes. Switch off the oven and leave the paella there for about 10 minutes before serving, to allow the rice to finish swelling.

Paillard

A famous Parisian restaurateur of the 19th century. In 1880 he took over the establishment situated at the corner of the Rue de la Chaussée-d'Antin and the Boulevard des Italiens, kept since 1850 by the Bignon brothers. Frequented by all the élite of Europe, Paillard's restaurant became very fashionable. Favourite dishes were chicken Archduke, Georgette potatoes, calves' sweetbreads with asparagus tips, fillets of sole Chauchat, and, above all, stuffed duck, rivalling the duck *au sang* of the Tour d'Argent. Paillard opened another luxurious restaurant, the Pavillon de l'Élysée, nicknamed 'Petit Paillard'.

Referring to one of the dishes created at Paillard's, the name *paillarde* was given to a thin escalope (scallop) of veal (or a thin slice of beef), well flattened and grilled (broiled) or lightly braised. This term is obsolete in France but still used in Italy for a veal escalope.

RECIPE

Paupiettes of sole Paillard PAUPIETTES DE SOLE PAILLARD (from the recipe of A. Deland, chef of the old Paillard restaurant) Flatten some fillets of sole, season them with salt and pepper, and cover with a thin layer of fish forcemeat finished with mushroom purée. Roll them into paupiettes and place in a sauté dish lined with thinly sliced onions and mushrooms; add a bouquet garni and moisten with fish stock or dry white wine. Cook, covered, in the oven at 220 C (425 F, gas 7) for 12 minutes.

Drain the paupiettes, arrange them on artichoke hearts in a deep buttered dish, cover them, and keep them hot. Strain the cooking liquid through muslin (cheesecloth) or a fine sieve and add to it an equal volume of mushroom purée, 2 egg yolks, and 2 dl (7 fl oz, ¼ cup) fresh cream. Bring to the boil, whisking all the time, and adjust the seasoning. Coat the paupiettes with this sauce, glaze in a very hot oven, and serve immediately.

pain au chocolat

A small rectangle of croissant dough folded over one or two chocolate bars and baked in the oven. This Viennese speciality is eaten cold.

palate PALAIS

An item of red offal consisting of the fleshy membrane at the back of the roof of the mouth of animals. Regarded as a delicacy until the 19th century, ox (and sometimes sheep's) palate was soaked in cold water, blanched, cooled, cut into slices or small sticks, then prepared as fritters, in a gratin, *à la lyonnaise*, etc. It is now rarely used except as a complementary item in the preparation of ox muzzle.

Palatinate or Pfalz
PALATINAT

This wine region, a continuation of the Alsace vineyard to the north, extends along the left bank of the River Rhine in

Germany and is one of the main wine-growing areas of the Federal Republic. It produces a huge quantity of wine, mostly white, though some red is made; in the Mittelhaardt region, north of Neustadt, some truly fine wines are produced. They extend to all the quality ranges of German wines and are in general rather full and fragrant and can often be drunk even with quite robust food, unlike many of the other fine German wines from other areas. The various grapes associated with German wines are grown, including the Rheinriesling. Among famous wine villages the names of Forst, Deidesheim, Ruppertsberg, and Wachenheim are especially notable; other good wines are made around Bad Dürkheim, Kallstadt, Leistadt, and Königsbach.

Palay (Maximin, *known* as Simin)

French writer (born Casteide-Doat, 1874; died Gelos, 1965). A committee member of the Félibrige, a society of writers dedicated to preserving the Provençal language, Palay collected in his *Dictionnaire du béarnais* (1932) numerous culinary traditions of his native region. He also published *La Cuisine du pays* (1936), describing typical recipes of Armagnac, the Basque country, Béarn, Bigorre, and the Landes, including abignades, alicuit, armottes, cruchade, garbure, miques, foie gras, confits, piperade, salmis of guinea fowl, and touron. This work also includes details of the maxims, tricks of the trade, utensils, and ingredients used in these regions.

paleron

A French cut of beef including the shoulder with some of the adjoining collar. It is a fleshy meat, providing cuts for braising or boiling. Neck or chuck are the nearest British and American equivalent cuts.

RECIPE

Paleron ménagère (from Daniel Metery's recipe) Cut 1 kg (2¼ lb) chuck steak into large dice and season with salt and pepper. Brown in hot oil in a stewpan for 5 minutes. Then pour off the oil, add a large finely diced onion, and cook until brown. Sprinkle with 1 tablespoon flour, stirring well to coat the meat and the onion, then moisten with ½ litre (17 fl oz, 2 cups) dry white wine. Add 2 whole tomatoes, 2 chopped cloves of garlic, and a bouquet garni. Cover with a mixture of half water and half stock, add 1 tablespoon coarse salt, and cook gently with the lid on for 1 hour, stirring from time to time. Add 400 g (14 oz, 2⅓ cups) carrots and 200 g (7 oz) turnips cut into small sticks. Leave to simmer for 10 minutes. Finally add 20 button onions which have been cooked in salted water and adjust the seasoning. Sprinkle with coarsely chopped parsley and serve very hot.

palet

A small crisp petit four flavoured with rum, aniseed, vanilla, brown sugar, etc.; ground almonds, candied peel, or other ingredients may be added. *Palets de dames* are traditionally made with currants.

RECIPE

Palets de dames Wash 80 g (3 oz, ½ cup) currants and macerate them in a little rum. Mix 125 g (4½ oz, generous ½ cup) softened butter and 125 g (4½ oz, ½ cup) caster (superfine) sugar. Work with a whisk, then blend in 2 eggs, one after the other, and mix well. Next add 150 g (5 oz, 1¼ cups) flour, the currants with their rum, and a pinch of salt. Mix thoroughly. Butter a baking sheet, dust it lightly with flour, and arrange the mixture on it in small balls, well separated from each other. Cook in a hot oven for 25 minutes until the edges of the palets are golden.

Palette

A Provençal wine region around Mont Sainte Victoire. Red, white, and rosé wines are made, mostly very attractive, the best-known probably being that of Château Simone.

palette

A French cut of pork corresponding to the shoulder blade (butt) with the adjoining muscles. It is a tender meat that is especially suitable for stews; it is particularly good with sauerkraut, in which case it is salted and sometimes smoked. Uncured, it is good for roasting, so rich in fat that there is no need to lard it. It may also be sautéed.

RECIPE

Palette of pork with sauerkraut PALETTE DE PORC À LA CHOUCROUTE Soak a salted blade or butt of pork in cold water to remove the salt, changing the water once. Prepare some sauerkraut, place the drained shoulder in it, and cook for about 2 hours over a very low heat or in a moderate oven. The sauerkraut may be garnished with a few vegetables added 45 minutes before the end of the cooking time (potatoes, carrots, turnips, and small onions).

palette knife
See *spatula*.

palm hearts (hearts of palm)
CHOUX PALMISTES, COEURS DE PALMIER

The terminal buds of certain palm trees, in particular the West Indian cabbage palm, also called 'coconut cabbage', 'glug-glug cabbage', or 'ti-coco cabbage'. The tender parts are eaten raw, thinly sliced in salad; the firmer parts are cooked and used to prepare acras, gratins, or fillings for omelettes. The taste is similar to artichoke. Palm hearts can be sold canned.

RECIPES

Braised palm hearts CHOU PALMISTE EN DAUBE (Creole recipe) Rinse some palm hearts in water and wipe well. Melt some pork dripping (fat back) in a shallow copper frying pan (skillet). Cut some pieces of palm hearts about 5 cm (2 in) long, tie them together in bunches, and lightly brown them in the fat over a gentle heat for 30 minutes. Add 1 teaspoon flour, blending it in, then mix in 1 tablespoon tomato purée and some very concentrated chicken stock. Reduce, cook for several minutes, then put in the oven, without allowing the top to brown. Serve with a little of the sauce.

Palm hearts in salad COEURS DE PAL-MIER EN SALADE Drain a can of palm hearts, refresh them in cold water, wipe them, and cut them into round slices. Peel a cucumber, remove the seeds, and cut the pulp into dice. Peel, deseed, and dice 4 ripe firm tomatoes. Using a melon baller, scoop out some small balls from the pulp of an avocado. Mix together 2 dl (7 fl oz, ¾ cup) double (heavy) cream, some chopped chives, 2 tablespoons (3 tablespoons) vinegar, and 1 tablespoon lemon juice. Season liberally with salt and pepper. Mix the ingredients and the sauce. Garnish some individual dishes with a lettuce chiffonnade. Divide the preparation between them and chill until time to serve.

palmier
A small pastry made of a sugared and double-rolled sheet of puff pastry cut into slices, the distinctive shape of which resembles the foliage of a palm tree. First made at the beginning of the 20th century, palmiers are served with tea or as an accompaniment to ices and desserts.

RECIPE

Palmiers Prepare some 6-turn puff pastry and give it 4 more turns, dusting it generously with icing (confectioners') sugar between each rolling. Roll it out to a thickness of 5 mm (¼ in), into a rectangle 20 cm (8 in) wide (the length will depend on the quantity used). Dust again with icing sugar. Roll each of the long sides to the centre and flatten slightly, then fold the strip in half. Cut this into sections 1 cm (½ in) thick and place on a baking sheet, leaving enough space between them so that they do not stick to each other during cooking. Cook the palmiers in a hot oven for about 10 minutes, turning them over halfway through cooking to colour both sides.

palm tree PALMIER
Any of numerous tropical trees belonging to the family Palmae. Many species are commercially important as a source of food, notably the date palm, coconut palm, and sago palm. Some palms, especially the cabbage palm, have edible terminal buds (see *palm hearts*) and others yield sugar, oil, and vegetable

'butter'. The sap of some species is fermented to produce wine.

palmyra BORASSUS

A palm tree of Asia and Africa with edible buds and young shoots. The pulp of the fruit is made into a kind of flour used in numerous local dishes; in Sri Lanka, it is also used to make a popular jam. The fruit may also be eaten either raw or roasted. The sap can be used in the preparation of fermented drinks.

paloise (à la)

Describing preparations of small cuts of grilled (broiled) meat garnished with French (green) beans in cream and noisette potatoes. The paloise garnish for large grilled cuts (which is rare) comprises glazed carrots and turnips, French beans in butter, sprigs of cauliflower coated with hollandaise sauce, and croquette potatoes. True paloise sauce is a béarnaise sauce with mint (rather than tarragon), but grills *à la paloise* may be accompanied by demi-glace sauce or by classic béarnaise sauce.

RECIPE

Grilled (broiled) lamb cutlets (chops) à la paloise CÔTELETTES D'AGNEAU GRILLÉES À LA PALOISE Prepare some noisette potatoes and some French (green) beans in cream (see *bean*) and keep them hot. Season some lamb cutlets (chops) with the bone end exposed with salt and pepper, coat them very lightly with olive oil, and grill (broil) them quickly on both sides. Decorate the bone ends with white paper frills and arrange the cutlets in a crown on a large round serving dish. Place the beans in the centre and arrange the potatoes in clusters between the cutlets.

panada PANADE

A paste of variable composition used to bind and thicken forcemeats. A flour panada is used to thicken quenelle forcemeats; the flour is poured all at once into boiling salted and buttered water, and the mixture beaten well over the heat until it thickens (as for a choux paste). A frangipane panada (made with flour and egg yolks) is used for poultry and fish forcemeats; bread panada for fish forcemeats; potato panada for quenelles of white meat; and rice panada for various forcemeats.

Panada is also the name of a type of soup or gruel made from bread, stock, milk (or water), and butter. It has to simmer for a certain time and is served piping hot. The basic recipe may be enriched with eggs (whole or just yolks) or fresh cream and seasoned with nutmeg or tomato sauce.

RECIPES

Bread panada PANADE AU PAIN Soak 250 g (9 oz, 4½ cups) white breadcrumbs in 3 dl (½ pint, 1¼ cups) boiled milk until the liquid is completely absorbed. Pour this mixture into a saucepan and let it thicken over the heat, working with a wooden spoon. Pour into a buttered dish and leave to cool.

Flour panada PANADE À LA FARINE Place 3 dl (½ pint, 1¼ cups) water, 50 g (2 oz, 4 tablespoons) butter, and 2 g (⅓ teaspoon) salt in a saucepan and bring to the boil. Add 150 g (5 oz, 1¼ cups) sifted flour, beat well over the heat with a wooden spoon, then cook until the mixture comes away from the edges of the saucepan. Pour the panada into a buttered dish, smooth the surface, cover with buttered paper, and leave it to cool.

Frangipane panada PANADE À LA FRANGIPANE Place 125 g (4½ oz, generous cup) sifted flour and 4 egg yolks in a saucepan. Mix well, working with a wooden spoon, then add 90 g (3½ oz, scant ½ cup) melted butter, 2 g (½ teaspoon) salt, some pepper, and a pinch of nutmeg. Thin the mixture by blending it with 2.5 dl (8 fl oz, 1 cup) boiled milk, poured in gradually. Cook for 5–6 minutes, beating vigorously with a whisk. Pour the panada into a buttered dish, smooth the surface, cover with buttered paper, and leave to cool.

Panada soup based on meat stock SOUPE PANADE AU GRAS Remove the crusts from 250 g (9 oz) stale bread and reduce it to crumbs. Peel and deseed 500 g (18 oz) tomatoes, then crush the pulp. Peel and chop a large onion. Heat

2 tablespoons (3 tablespoons) oil in a saucepan and cook the onion until golden, then add the tomatoes and leave to cook for 5 minutes with the lid on. Moisten with 1 litre (1¾ pints, 4¼ cups) stock, add a pinch of powdered marjoram, adjust the seasoning, and leave to cook for about 30 minutes. Pour ½ litre (17 fl oz, 2 cups) stock over the breadcrumbs, leave them to soak, then add the mixture to the soup and let it cook for a further 10 minutes. Rub the soup through a sieve (or purée in a blender) and serve piping hot. 1 table-spoon oil and some coarsely chopped herbs may be added to the soup just before serving.

Panada soup with milk SOUPE PANADE AU LAIT Remove the crusts from 250 g (9 oz) stale bread and pour over it 1 litre (1¾ pints, 4¼ cups) boiling milk. Leave to soak, then cook gently for 15 minutes. Put through the blender and season with salt.

This panada may be sweetened, sprinkled with nutmeg, or enriched with an egg yolk beaten with fresh cream.

Potato panada PANADE À LA POMME DE TERRE Boil 3 dl (½ pint, 1¼ cups) milk seasoned with 2 g (½ teaspoon) salt, a pinch of pepper, and a pinch of grated nutmeg until it has reduced by one-sixth. Add 20 g (¾ oz, 2 table-spoons) butter and 250 g (9 oz, 1½ cups) thinly sliced boiled potatoes. Cook gently for 15 minutes, then mix well to obtain a smooth paste. Use this panada while still warm.

Rice panada PANADE AU RIZ Add 200 g (7 oz, 1 cup) short-grain rice to 6 dl (1 pint, 2½ cups) white unclarified consommé to which 20 g (¾ oz, 1½ tablespoons) butter has been added, and cook in the oven for about 50 minutes. Mix the cooked rice well with a wooden spoon to obtain a smooth paste. Leave to cool in a buttered dish.

pan-bagnat or bagna

A speciality of Nice consisting of a kind of sandwich sprinkled with olive oil and filled with onion, anchovy, celery, black (ripe) olives, etc.; its name means lit-erally 'bathed bread' (i.e. bathed in oil). Some people spread the bread with garlic-flavoured anchovy purée before garnishing it. Originally, this prep-aration was a salade niçoise in which stale bread was crumbled an hour be-fore serving.

| RECIPE

Pan-bagnat Split a round bread roll in two and open it out without separating the two halves. Remove two-thirds of the crumb. Rub the remaining crumb with garlic and sprinkle it with a little olive oil. Fill with slices of tomato, onion, and hard-boiled (hard-cooked) eggs, thin strips of sweet pepper, stoned black (pitted ripe) olives, and anchovy fillets in oil. Sprinkle with olive-oil vinaigrette and close up the roll.

pancake
See *crêpe*.

pandora
PAGEOT, PAGEAU
A spindle-shaped fish closely related to the sea bream, caught in the Mediter-ranean and in the Bay of Biscay. It is 30–50 cm (12–20 in) long, has a grey-green back and a white belly, and weighs up to 1 kg (2¼ lb). Pandora is prepared like sea bream but does not have as much flavour.

panetière
A small openwork cupboard, hanging on the wall or from the ceiling, which was formerly used, particularly in Brit-tany and Provence, for keeping bread. Today bread is kept in a bin, a drawer, a box with a flap, or a bag.

panetière (à la)
Describing various preparations which, after cooking, are arranged in a round hollowed-out loaf of bread which has been lightly browned in the oven. Lambs' sweetbreads, chicken livers, sal-picons, various ragouts, scrambled eggs, small birds, and fillets of fish in sauce may be presented in this way.

| RECIPE

Fillets of sole à la panetière FILETS DE SOLE À LA PANETIÈRE Cut the top off a large round loaf and remove three-quarters of the crumb. Butter the inside and lightly brown in the oven. Season some fillets of sole with salt and pepper, fold them in two, coat with flour, and cook them in butter. Prepare a ragout of mushrooms in cream. Drain the fillets of sole and arrange them in a crown in the bread. Pour into the centre the mushroom ragout and heat the preparation in the oven for 4 minutes.

panettone

A large round Italian cake that is a speciality of the city of Milan. Panettone is made from a raised dough enriched with egg yolks (which give it its colour) and containing raisins and candied orange and lemon peel. This dough is placed in a cool oven to rise and then cooked in a cylindrical mould. Traditional Christmas fare, this cake is also eaten for breakfast, with coffee, and it is sometimes served as a dessert, accompanied by a liqueur wine.

The word is derived from *pane* (bread). According to one legend, it is a contraction of *pane de Tonio*: Tonio, a poor baker from Milan, had a pretty daughter with whom a young nobleman was in love. As she could not be married without a dowry, Tonio provided all the ingredients necessary to make an excellent cake. Tonio made a fortune with his *pane* and his daughter made a good match.

panisse

In Provence, a cake made from a thick porridge of chickpeas or cornmeal which is cut into rectangles when cold. The pieces may be rolled in grated cheese and fried in olive oil, or eaten without cheese and sweetened.

In Corsica, these cakes (*panizze*) are prepared with cornmeal or chestnut flour.

pannequet

A sweet or savoury pancake filled with chopped ingredients, a purée, or a cream.

Pannequets (the name is derived from the English word 'pancake') are generally served as a small entrée, as a hot hors d'oeuvre, as a soup garnish, or as a sweet course. They are spread with the chosen filling, rolled up or folded into four, then browned or glazed under the grill (broiler) or sometimes coated with breadcrumbs and fried.

Fillings for savoury pannequets include: anchovies in béchamel or tomato sauce, spinach in Mornay sauce, melted cheese, soft roes with mushrooms, mushrooms with paprika or ham, chopped mutton with aubergines (eggplants), shrimps in Aurora sauce, game purée, puréed chicken in cream, and crayfish in Nantua sauce.

Sweet pannequets may be filled with confectioners' custard (pastry cream) flavoured with crystallized (candied) fruits, syrup, praline, or liqueur or with chestnut cream, jam, etc. They may be browned under the grill (broiler) or flamed.

RECIPES

Preparation of pannequets PRÉPARATION DES PANNEQUETS Make a batter with 250 g (9 oz, 2¼ cups) flour, a pinch of salt, 3 whole beaten eggs, 2.5 dl (8 fl oz, 1 cup) milk, 2.5 dl (8 fl oz, 1 cup) water, and 1 tablespoon melted butter. For sweet pancakes, add 1 tablespoon caster (superfine) sugar mixed with the eggs. Prepare some fairly thick pancakes. Pile them in a covered dish and keep hot over a saucepan of boiling water.

SAVOURY PANNEQUETS

Fried pannequets PANNEQUETS PANÉS ET FRITS Fill some savoury pannequets, roll them into cigar shapes, and cut into sections about 3 cm (1¼ in) long. Coat with egg and breadcrumbs and fry just before serving. Garnish with fried parsley. Fried pannequets may be filled like other savoury pannequets or in any of the following ways:

■ *à la brunoise, à la hongroise* (with a salpicon of onions and mushrooms softened in butter mixed with paprika-flavoured béchamel sauce);

■ *à la grecque* (with a salpicon of chopped braised mutton and sautéed aubergine (eggplant), bound with very thick tomato sauce);

■ *à l'italienne* (with mushroom duxelles, lean ham cut into small dice, and tomato sauce);

■ *à la Saint-Hubert* (with roebuck purée thickened with game fumet);

■ *à la strasbourgeoise* (with foie gras purée and chopped truffles).

Pannequets for soup PANNEQUETS À POTAGE Prepare some savoury pannequets (allow 6 for 8 people) and a vegetable brunoise, a cheese béchamel sauce, or a very dry mushroom duxelles. Cover half of the pannequets with the chosen garnish and cover them with the remaining pannequets. Press each pair together firmly, then cut out rounds with a fluted cutter. Place these garnishes in boiling consommé just before serving.

SWEET PANNEQUETS

Apricot pannequets PANNEQUETS AUX ABRICOTS Prepare 8 sweet pannequets. Make ¼ litre (8 fl oz, 1 cup) confectioners' custard (pastry cream) flavoured with rum (see *creams and custards*) and add to it 12 very ripe apricots (or drained canned apricots), stoned (pitted) and cut into dice, and 75 g (3 oz, ¾ cup) coarsely chopped almonds. Spread the pannequets with this preparation and roll them up. Arrange them in a buttered ovenproof dish, dust them generously with icing (confectioners') sugar, and place them for 8–10 minutes in a very hot oven.

Pannequets à la cévenole Prepare 8 sweet pannequets. Mix ¼ litre (8 fl oz, 1 cup) sweetened chestnut purée flavoured with Kirsch with 3 tablespoons (¼ cup) fresh cream and 3 tablespoons (¼ cup) fragments of marrons glacés. Spread the pannequets with this mixture and finish as for apricot pannequets.

pantler's office

PANETERIE
Under the Ancien Régime, an important office of the department of the *bouche du roi* in charge of the bread supply. At the beginning of the 15th century it comprised: one head pantler and six other pantlers; six gentlemen carvers, to prepare the trenchers; three butlers, to move the furniture, linen, and table cutlery; three *portechappes*, responsible

for looking after the bread bins, cutting the bread, and laying part of the table; an *oubloyer*, to prepare the wafers (*oublies*); a *baschonier*, to drive the horses loaded with bread; a launderer, to wash the tablecloths; and five tablecloth sevants, to look after the linen.

The pantler's office dealt not only with the bread but also with everything associated with the king's table – the linen, the plates and dishes, and sometimes the fruit and certain cakes. The senior pantler, in addition to his court duties, exercised certain legal rights over the guild of bakers; among other things, he sold masterships to apprentice bakers at prices which he determined himself. The *installation* ceremony included handing over to the senior pantler a pot of rosemary with titbits hanging from the branches. In 1650 the pot of rosemary was replaced by a 20-franc piece. The rights of the pantler, which dated from Philip Augustus, were abolished in 1711. The Duc de Brissac, last of the great pantlers, was given more than 100,000 francs in compensation for the loss of his office.

panzarotti

Rice fritters prepared in Corsica especially for religious festivals, rice being the symbol of life, abundance, and immortality. The rice cooked in milk is mixed with brandy, oil, and yeast, then egg yolks, grated lemon, and stiffly beaten egg whites. The fritters are served hot, dusted with sugar.

papaya or papaw PAPAYE

A large tropical fruit with a smooth yellowish skin; its orange-coloured flesh has a central cavity filled with black seeds. Originating in Malaysia, the papaya is now cultivated in South America, Asia, and Africa. It has a low calorific value (44 Cal per 100 g) but is rich in vitamins B and C. It can be cooked as a vegetable when green and unripe or eaten ripe, as a fruit. It is often used to make jam or pickles.

The green papaya is 'bled' (to get rid of the white acid juice) and deseeded. It may then be grated like a raw carrot, cooked like a vegetable marrow, prepared as a gratin or in gruel, or fried in slices (as is done in Vietnam).

When it is completely ripe, the

papaya is served as an hors d'oeuvre like melon, in a salad, or as a dessert with sugar and cream. Its juicy and refreshing pulp is improved by flavouring with a little rum.

paper PAPIER

A material often used in cookery for the preparation, cooking, serving, or preserving of foods and dishes. Greaseproof (waxed) paper withstands a certain amount of heat and provides insulation; it is used to wrap dishes to be cooked en papillote, to cover preparations while they are cooked in the oven so that they do not brown too quickly, and to line cake tins (pans). Cellophane paper is used to cover jams when they are put in jars.

Lace doileys, of various shapes and patterns, are used for presenting sweets and cakes. Plain doileys with a crinkled edge are used for serving fried food. Iced petits fours and bouchées are presented in little cases of pleated paper which are also used for baking small cakes. Absorbent paper is widely used in the kitchen for cleaning and wiping foodstuffs and for draining fried dishes.

papeton

A speciality of Avignon based on puréed aubergines (eggplants) and eggs, cooked in a mould which was originally shaped like a papal crown.

The creation of the papeton might have arisen after a quarrel between the cooks of Avignon and those who had come from Italy with the pontifical court, who claimed to be superior. The local cooks, wishing to prove the contrary, devised an original dish which pleased the pope.

RECIPE

Aubergine (eggplant) papeton PAPETON D'AUBERGINE Prepare ½ litre (17 fl oz, 2 cups) very reduced tomato fondue. Peel 2 kg (4½ lb) aubergines (eggplants), cut them into cubes, sprinkle with fine salt, and leave them to exude their juice for 1 hour. Wash them in cold water, wipe thoroughly, then flour them lightly and cook very gently in ½ glass of olive oil until soft. Sprinkle with salt and leave to cool, then put through a blender. Mix 7 large eggs,

beaten as for an omelette, with 1 dl (6 tablespoons, scant ½ cup) milk, 2 finely crushed cloves of garlic, some salt, pepper, and a pinch of cayenne. Add the aubergine (eggplant) purée and pour into a buttered manqué mould. Place this mould in a bain-marie, bring it to the boil on the top of the stove, then cook in the oven at 180c (350 F, gas 4), for 1 hour. Turn out onto a warmed serving dish and coat with the hot tomato fondue.

papillote

A small decorative paper frill used to garnish the bone end of a lamb or veal chop, the drumstick of a chicken, etc.

The term en papillote is used to describe a preparation cooked and served in a wrapping of greaseproof (waxed) paper or aluminium foil. Veal chops, whole stuffed fish, fish fillets, and potatoes can be prepared en papillote. The dish is generally cooked with herbs, a sauce, chopped onions or mushrooms, etc. The paper is buttered or oiled, wrapped around the food, and folded tightly so that the food is completely enclosed. The wrapping swells in the oven during cooking and the dish is served piping hot, before the wrapping collapses.

The name papillote is also given to a sweet (candy) or chocolate wrapped in brightly coloured shiny paper with fringed ends. The papillote lyonnaise contains a riddle or a motto wrapped up with the sweet: its name is attributed by some to a confectioner called Papillot, but it more probably derives from papillon (a butterfly). The cosaque is a papillote in the form of a cracker made with two papers of different colours, one of them gold. Formerly sold at fairs, these crackers have practically disappeared.

RECIPES

Fillets of fish en papillotes FILETS DE POISSON EN PAPILLOTES Cut out some rectangles of greaseproof (waxed) paper large enough to wrap up each fillet (sole, whiting, fresh cod, sea bream, etc.) folded in two. Spread 1 tablespoon double (heavy) cream in the centre of each papillote and season with salt and pepper. Place on top a fish fillet seasoned with salt and pepper, sprinkled with a little lemon juice, and folded in two. Cover with a little cream and scatter with coarsely chopped herbs. Close the papillotes, folding the edges together. Cook in a very hot oven for about 15 minutes.

A little julienne of vegetables slowly cooked in butter may be placed under and over the folded fillet.

Papillotes of lobster and scallops PAPILLOTES DE HOMARD ET DE COQUILLES SAINT-JACQUES (from André Daguin's recipe) Separate the tail from a lobster and set it aside. Open the body and take out the stomach. Crush the carcass and heat the pieces in a thick-bottomed saucepan with some chopped shallot. Add ¼ litre (8 fl oz, 1 cup) vermouth and reduce by half, then add 150 ml (¼ pint, ½ cup) cream and reduce again by half. Add the lobster tail, cook for 4 minutes, then remove the pan from the heat. Shell the tail and cut it into 8 slices. Cut a truffle into 8 thin slices. Open 8 scallops and take out the kernel and the coral. Strain the sauce.

Prepare 4 pieces of oiled greaseproof (waxed) paper. Place 2 slices of lobster on each piece of paper and top them with 2 scallops and 2 slices of truffle. Coat with the sauce and sprinkle with chopped fresh herbs. Close up the papillotes tightly, folding the edges together, and cook them in a very hot oven for a maximum of 5 minutes. Serve in a very hot stainless steel dish so that the papillotes do not collapse.

Potatoes en papillotes POMMES DE TERRE EN PAPILLOTES Wash some large potatoes but do not dry them. Wrap each potato in a piece of aluminium foil and cook for 40–45 minutes, either in a very hot oven or in the hot ashes of a fire.

Veal chops en papillotes CÔTES DE VEAU EN PAPILLOTES Sauté some veal chops in butter until they are cooked through and golden. Cut out some squares of greaseproof (waxed) paper, big enough to wrap up each chop, and oil them. Place on half of each square of paper a slice of ham cut to the dimensions of the chop, a veal chop, 1 tablespoon mushroom duxelles, and

another slice of ham the same size as the first. Fold over the paper and press the edges together. Place the papillotes in a very hot oven (240 C, 475 F, gas 9) until the paper turns golden.

Papin (Denis)

French physician and inventor (born Chitenay, near Blois, 1647; died London, 1714). Famous for his work on the properties of steam, he invented the original Papin marmite, forerunner of the pressure cooker, which he described in a treatise published in 1682 in Paris: *How to dress bones and to cook all kinds of meats in a very short time and at little cost, with a description of the machine which must be used.*

paprika

A spicy seasoning ground from a variety of sweet red pepper (*paprika* in Hungarian), used to season ragouts, stuffings, sauces, and soups, to flavour fresh cheeses, and for garnishing. Paprika is a distinctive feature of Hungarian cookery (into which it was only introduced in the 19th century, for seasoning goulash, paprikache, pörkölt and tokany, although it has been known in Europe since the time of Christopher Columbus), but it also seasons a number of French dishes (*à la zingara, à la hongroise, à l'autrichienne,* and *à l'archiduc* in particular). The shrub which supplies this pepper originated in America. Its pods, 7–13 cm (2½–5 in) long and 3 cm (1¼ in) wide, are harvested at the end of the summer, when they are red; they are then dried and crushed. Szeged, in the south of Hungary, is the main centre for producing paprika; the best variety is the 'pink' or 'sweet' pepper, which has a piquant flavour but no bitter aftertaste.

Professor Szent-Györgyi, who was awarded the Nobel prize for medicine, considered this pepper to be the plant with the highest content of vitamin C. It develops the best flavour when it is cooked with onion and lard. It should be added to the preparation away from the heat or in a moistening, otherwise the sugar which it contains may caramelize and impair the flavour and colour of the dish.

RECIPE

Sauté of lamb with paprika SAUTÉ
D'AGNEAU AU PAPRIKA Cut 1.5 kg
(3¼ lb) lamb cutlets (chops) or boned
shoulder into cubes and sauté them in
butter. When they are brown, add 150 g
(5 oz, 1¼ cups) chopped onions to the
sauté dish. Season with salt and sprinkle
with 2 tablespoons (3 tablespoons)
flour. Stir for a few minutes, then blend
in 1 teaspoon paprika away from the
heat. Moisten with 2 dl (7 fl oz, ¾ cup)
white wine, reduce by half, then add 3 dl
(½ pint, 1¼ cups) stock-pot broth and
2 tablespoons (3 tablespoons) tomato
purée. Add a bouquet garni and cook
with the lid on for 30 minutes. Drain the
pieces of lamb and put them in a sauté
dish with 250 g (9 oz, 2½ cups)
mushrooms, thinly sliced and quickly
fried in butter. Add to the sauce 2 dl (7 fl
oz, ¾ cup) fresh cream and 1 teaspoon
paprika, reduce and strain, then pour it
over the lamb. Simmer gently with the
lid on for 25 minutes.

paprikache

A Hungarian stew made with paprika,
sour cream, and either white meat or
fish (whereas goulash is made with
beef), cooked with chopped or thinly
sliced onions and garnished with
tomatoes, peppers, or potatoes.

paraffin wax   PARAFFINE

A mixture of solid neutral hydrocarbons. White, translucent, tasteless,
odourless, and melting easily, paraffin
wax is used for coating fruit and vegetables and for glazing the crust of
cheeses. It is also used for sealing jars of
jam.

parasol mushroom

LÉPIOTE

A mushroom, found in copses and clear-
ings, whose cap is usually covered in
large scales. All the large varieties are
edible, but the long woody stems surrounded by a thick ring are best discarded. Of the smaller species, one is
poisonous. The two best species for eating are the common parasol (*Lepiota
procera*) and the shaggy parasol
(*Lepiota rhacodes*). They are brown or
brownish grey with many gills, which
stand away from the stalk. The white

flesh is rather soft and insubstantial and
turns pink or reddish when exposed to
the air. They cook quickly and can be
deep-fried, shallow-fried, grilled
(broiled), or even served raw in a salad.

RECIPE

Parasol mushrooms à la suprême
LÉPIOTES À LA SUPRÊME (from Dr
Ramain's recipe) Prepare the caps of 1
kg (2¼ lb, 12 cups) young parasol
mushrooms, without washing them.
Make a white roux with 30 g (1¼ oz, 2
tablespoons) butter, 40 g (1½ oz, 6
tablespoons) flour, and ½ litre (17 fl oz,
2 cups) hot chicken stock. Let it cook
over a low heat for 15 minutes. Turn the
heat up and thicken with 1 egg yolk
mixed with 4 tablespoons (⅓ cup)
double (heavy) cream. Season with salt
and mild red paprika and keep warm in
a bain-marie. In a shallow frying pan
(skillet), cook 60 g (2½ oz, ½ cup)
chopped onions seasoned with ½ teaspoon paprika in butter. When the onions start to turn pale golden, add the
mushroom caps and sauté them briskly
for 5 minutes, then season with salt, a
little grated nutmeg, and a bouquet
garni to which extra basil and tarragon
have been added. Cover the pan and
cook for 10 more minutes over a high
heat. Drain the mushrooms and keep
them hot in the pan with a little butter.
Whisk the suprême sauce and add to the
mushrooms; check the seasoning. Serve
piled up on small slices of white bread
which have been fried golden brown in
noisette butter.

parfait

An iced dessert made with fresh cream,
which gives it smoothness, prevents it
from melting too quickly, and enables it
to be cut into slices. Originally the parfait was a coffee-flavoured ice cream;
today, the basic mixture is a flavoured
custard cream, a flavoured syrup mixed
with egg yolks, or a fruit purée, which is
blended with fresh whipped cream and
then frozen. There is a special parfait
mould in the shape of a cylinder with
one slightly rounded end. The parfait
can be served by itself or used as a base
for preparing an iced cake, an iced
soufflé, or a vacherin.

A parfait in Britain and the United

States is also the name of a whipped cream dessert.

RECIPE

Iced parfait PARFAIT GLACÉ Mix 8 cl (4 tablespoons, ⅓ cup) water with 200 g (7 oz, scant cup) caster (superfine) sugar and cook to the fine thread stage (110 C, 230 F). Place 8 egg yolks in a bowl and pour the boiling syrup over them, little by little, whisking all the time. Continue to whisk until the mixture has cooled. Then add the chosen flavouring:

■ *spirit:* 6–8 cl (3–4 tablespoons, ¼–⅓ cup) brandy or liqueur;

■ *coffee:* 7–10 cl (4–5 tablespoons, ⅓–½ cup) coffee essence (extract);

■ *chocolate:* 200 g (7 oz) plain chocolate gently melted in a bain-marie;

■ *praline:* 150 g (5 oz) powdered almond praline;

■ *vanilla:* about 10 drops of vanilla essence (extract).

Whisk 2 dl (7 fl oz, ¾ cup) double (heavy) cream with 1 dl (6 tablespoons, scant ½ cup) milk (both chilled) until very firm. Blend the whisked cream with the cooled mixture of egg yolks and syrup and pour into a parfait mould. Place in the freezer and leave to set for at least 6 hours.

parfait amour

A liqueur of Dutch origin, flavoured with lemon (or citron), cloves, cinnamon, and coriander. It originated in the 18th century and was very popular between the two World Wars. The liqueur was coloured red or violet and perfumed with violets.

Paris-Brest

A large ring-shaped cake of choux pastry, filled with praline-flavoured cream and sprinkled with shredded (slivered) almonds. It was created in 1891 by a pastrycook whose shop was situated in the suburbs of Paris on the route of the bicycle race between Paris and Brest: he had the idea of making large ring-shaped éclairs reminiscent of bicycle wheels. The Paris-Nice is a variation

without almonds, filled with Saint-Honoré cream.

RECIPE

Paris-Brest Sprinkle 100 g (4 oz, 1 cup) shredded (slivered) almonds over a baking sheet and cook them in a moderate oven (about 200 C, 400 F, gas 6) until golden. Prepare a choux pastry (see *chou*) with 100 g (4 oz, ½ cup) butter, 2 tablespoons (3 tablespoons) caster (superfine) sugar, a generous pinch of salt, 200 g (7 oz, 1¾ cups) flour, 3.5 dl (12 fl oz, 1½ cups) water, and 5 or 6 eggs, according to their size. Fill a piping bag (pastry bag) fitted with a piping tube 15 mm (¾ in) in diameter with this mixture and pipe 2 rings, 18 cm (7 in) in diameter. Glaze them with egg, sprinkle them with the shredded almonds, and cook for 35–40 minutes in the oven at 180 C (350 F, gas 4). Turn off the oven and leave the rings to cool with the door ajar, then remove from the oven and leave them to get completely cold.

Prepare a confectioners' custard (pastry cream) with 60 g (2 oz, ½ cup) flour, 175 g (6 oz, ¾ cup) sugar, 15 g (½ oz, 1 tablespoon) butter, 4 whole eggs, a generous pinch of salt, and ½ litre (17 fl oz, 2 cups) boiling milk. In another bowl make a praline-flavoured French butter cream (see *creams and custards*) with 4 dl (14 fl oz, 1¾ cups) milk, 12 eggs, 400 g (14 oz, 1¾ cups) caster sugar, 800 g (1¾ lb, 3½ cups) butter, and 160 g (5½ oz) praline. Finally, prepare 250 g (9 oz), Italian meringue.

Leave the three preparations to cool thoroughly, then mix them. Cut the choux rings in half horizontally and fill the lower halves with the cream using a piping bag with a large fluted nozzle.

Replace the top halves of the rings, dust with icing (confectioners') sugar, and put in a cool place until time to serve.

parisien

A lemon-flavoured sponge cake filled with frangipane and crystallized (candied) fruits, covered with Italian meringue, and lightly browned in a low oven.

| RECIPE

Parisien Beat 3 egg yolks with 110 g (4 oz, ½ cup) caster (superfine) sugar. When the mixture is white and thick, add 30 g (1 oz, ¼ cup) flour, 30 g (1 oz, ¼ cup) potato flour, ½ teaspoon vanilla sugar, and the grated rind of 1 lemon. Whisk 3 egg whites into stiff peaks and fold them carefully into the mixture. Pour this batter into a buttered manqué mould, 22 cm (9 in) in diameter, and cook in the oven at 180 c (350 F, gas 4), for about 35 minutes.

While the cake is cooking, prepare a frangipane: over a very low heat, warm 4 dl (14 fl oz, 1¾ cups) milk with a vanilla pod (bean) split in two. Beat 3 egg yolks in a basin with 80 g (3 oz, 6 tablespoons) caster sugar, until the mixture is white. Add 30 g (1 oz, 2 tablespoons) cornflour (cornstarch), stir well, and slowly pour in the boiling milk, mixing with a wooden spoon. Return the mixture to the saucepan and bring to the boil, whisking all the time, then pour into a bowl. When lukewarm, add 80 g (3 oz, ¾ cup) ground almonds and mix well.

Take the cake out of the oven and leave it to cool. Prepare an Italian meringue by boiling 6 cl (3 tablespoons, ¼ cup) water with 180 g (6½ oz, generous ¾ cup) caster sugar. When the syrup is at the 'ball stage', place the saucepan in a bain-marie. Whisk 3 egg whites into stiff peaks, sprinkle with the syrup, and continue to whisk for 2–3 minutes. Cut the cooled cake into layers 1 cm (½ in) thick and spread each layer with frangipane. Chop 100 g (4 oz, ¾ cup) crystallized (candied) fruits and sprinkle over the frangipane. Reassemble the cake.

Fill a piping bag (pastry bag) with a fluted nozzle with the meringue and cover the cake completely. Dust with icing (confectioners') sugar and cook in a cool oven (180 c, 350 F, gas 4) until golden. Leave to cool completely before serving.

parisienne (à la)

Describing preparations that are typical of the classic repertoire of Parisian restaurants. The term is particularly applied to meat and poultry dishes garnished with potatoes *à la parisienne* (noisettes with herbs) and accompanied by braised lettuces or artichoke hearts; the latter may be garnished with a julienne of pickled tongue and mushrooms bound with velouté, decorated with a thin slice of truffle.

Cold preparations of fish or shellfish *à la parisienne* are made with thick mayonnaise and the garnish often includes artichoke hearts garnished with macédoine in mayonnaise, stuffed hard-boiled (hard-cooked) eggs, or cubes of aspic.

The term *à la parisienne* is also applied to dishes containing chicken breasts, button mushrooms (*champignons de Paris*), pickled tongue, or vegetable macédoine. Soup *à la parisienne* is made with leeks and potatoes, finished with milk, and garnished with chervil leaves.

| RECIPES

Canapés à la parisienne Cut some slices of white bread into rectangles and remove the crusts. Spread them with chervil butter. Coat some very thin slices of chicken breast (cooked in a white stock) with a mayonnaise and decorate with a pattern of truffle and tarragon leaves.

Arrange the chicken slices on the canapés and surround them with a border of chopped aspic jelly.

Glazed salmon à la parisienne Place a whole salmon in a fish stock, bring to the boil, and simmer for 7–8 minutes. Leave it to cool in the cooking stock, then drain it and remove the skin and bones without breaking the flesh. Pat dry with absorbent paper. Coat it several times with half-set aspic jelly (prepared from the cooking stock), putting the fish in the refrigerator between applications. Cover the serving dish with a layer of aspic; when firmly set, arrange the salmon on top.

Prepare some vegetable macédoine mixed with thick mayonnaise and use it to stuff some small round tomatoes. Hard-boil (hard-cook) some eggs and cut in half; sieve the yolks and mix with some mayonnaise. Pipe the mixture into the whites. Garnish the border of the dish with the tomatoes and eggs and slices of lemon.

Omelette à la parisienne OMELETTE
GARNIE À LA PARISIENNE Beat 8
eggs with 2 tablespoons (3 tablespoons)
chopped onion softened in butter and
2–3 tablespoons (3–4 tablespoons)
chopped mushrooms quickly sautéed in
butter. Cook the omelette and roll it up
on warmed serving dish; cover it with
grilled chipolata sausages. Surround
with a thin ribbon of reduced veal stock
mixed with butter.

Parisian salad SALADE PARIS-
IENNE Prepare a vegetable macédoine
and add to it a salpicon of langouste and
truffles. Mix with mayonnaise thickened with gelatine, then pour it into a
domed mould coated with aspic and
lined with thin slices of langouste and
truffle. Put in a cold place to set, then
turn it out.

Alternatively, the ingredients may be
mixed together, turned into a salad
bowl lined with lettuce leaves, and garnished with slices of truffle and quarters
of hard-boiled (hard-cooked) eggs.

Parisian sauce SAUCE PARISIENNE
Beat 2–3 Petit-Suisse cheeses (45% butterfat) in a mixing bowl. (Alternatively,
use 2–3 oz cream cheese.) Season with
salt and sprinkle with paprika. Add 2
tablespoons (3 tablespoons) lemon
juice, then beat the sauce like a mayonnaise, adding to it, in a thin trickle, 2.5
dl (8 fl oz, 1 cup) oil. Finally add 1
tablespoon chopped chervil. This sauce
is served mainly with cold asparagus.

Parmentier (Antoine Augustin)

Military pharmacist and French agronomist (born Montdidier, 1737; died
Paris, 1813). Contrary to popular
legend, Parmentier did not 'invent' the
potato, which had been known and
cultivated in France since the 16th century, but he was an enthusiastic propa-
gator of it. While he was a prisoner-of-
war in Westphalia during the Seven
Years' War, he discovered the nutritional value of this vegetable, which was
highly prized by the local population
but considered by the French at that
time as unwholesome and indigestible,
fit only as a food for cattle or the desti-
tute. In the few provinces where it was
eaten, it was usually used in the form of
flour, mixed with wheat and rye to
make bread.

In 1772, the Academy of Besançon
offered a prize for the discovery of
plants likely to be of use to man in the
event of famine. Parmentier, who had
become an apothecary, then head
pharmacist, at Les Invalides, was one of
the seven competitors who recommended the use of the potato, which had
already been grown for a long time in
the Franche-Comté region. He won the
prize in 1773. In 1778 he published
Examen chimique de la pomme de terre,
in which he described with enthusiasm
the nutritional qualities of the tuber.
This work won him the support of Turgot, Buffon, Condorcet, Voltaire, and
even the king, Louis XVI, who personally encouraged Parmentier in his
efforts.

In 1786, after the famine of 1785, he
was granted a plot of land at Neuilly, in
the Plain of the Sablons. Later on he also
obtained permission to have potatoes
planted in the Plain of Grenelle, the
present Champ-de-Mars. Since the king
began to sport a potato flower in his
buttonhole, the aristocracy were
already won over and several noblemen
had potatoes planted on their estates. A
wily ruse gained support for the potato
from the rest of the population, who
until then were still distrustful. The
Parisian crops were guarded by the
army, a proof that the experiments performed there concerned some precious
commodity. The guard was present only
during daytime: thieves from the neighbouring district came secretly by night
to obtain supplies, and thus became the
most effective propagandists of this new
vegetable. The last prejudices vanished
during a dinner at Les Invalides given
for Benjamin Franklin; Parmentier had
a menu prepared entirely of potatoes to
ensure their gastronomic promotion.

Parmentier encouraged the spread of
the potato throughout the whole of
France by publishing booklets about its
cultivation and its uses. His works also
extended to other fields. An expert at
milling, he founded a school of baking
in Paris; he brought out numerous reports on the Jerusalem artichoke, maize
(corn), the sweet chestnut, wines,
syrups, preserves, and food hygiene. He
was appointed Inspector of Public

Health and eventually ennobled as a baron. For a time the potato itself was known as the *parmentière* in his honour, and he gave his name to various culinary preparations based on potatoes, especially *hachis Parmentier* – chopped beef covered with puréed potatoes and browned in the oven. Other dishes named after him are a cream of potato soup, various egg dishes (omelettes filled with diced fried potatoes, scrambled eggs mixed with sautéed cubes of potato, eggs cooked in nests of potato purée), and a garnish for lamb and veal.

RECIPES

Casserole of veal chops à la Parmentier CÔTES DE VEAU EN CASSEROLE À LA PARMENTIER Season 2 fairly thick veal chops with salt and pepper and brown them on both sides in 30–40 g (1–1½ oz, 2–3 tablespoons) butter in a casserole. Finish the preparation as for loin of lamb Parmentier, but cook at 200 c (400 f, gas 6) for 1 hour.

Hachis Parmentier Dice or coarsely chop 500 g (18 oz) boiled or braised beef. Melt 25 g (1 oz, 2 tablespoons) butter in a shallow frying pan (skillet) and cook 3 chopped onions in it until they are golden. Sprinkle with 1 tablespoon flour, cook until lightly brown, and then moisten with 2 dl (7 fl oz, ¾ cup) beef stock (or braising stock with water added to it). Cook for about 15 minutes, leave to cool, then add the beef, and mix well. Place the beef and onions in a buttered gratin dish, cover with a layer of potato purée, sprinkle with breadcrumbs, and moisten with melted butter. Brown in a very hot oven for about 15 minutes.

Although it is not traditional, a small cup of very reduced tomato fondue can be added to the chopped meat and a little grated cheese may be mixed with the breadcrumbs.

Loin of lamb Parmentier CARRÉ D'AGNEAU PARMENTIER Brown a trimmed loin of lamb in 30–40 g (1–1½ oz, 2–3 tablespoons) butter in a flameproof casserole. Add 400 g (14 oz) peeled diced potatoes, 40 g (1½ oz, 3 tablespoons) melted butter, and season with salt and pepper. Place the casserole in the oven at 220 c (425 f, gas 7) and cook for about 45 minutes. Drain the meat and the potatoes and keep them hot in the serving dish. Deglaze the casserole with ½ glass white wine and the same amount of stock (traditionally veal stock); reduce. Pour this sauce over the lamb and sprinkle with chopped parsley.

Parmesan

An Italian cheese made from skimmed cows' milk (32% butterfat) mixed with rennet and cooked for 30 minutes. It goes through several processes of draining and drying before being coated. Hard, yellow, and with crumbly granular consistency (hence the generic name of *grana* given in Italy to grating cheeses of the same type), Parmesan cheese has a very fruity, even piquant, flavour. It was known in Parma in the 13th century (it may have originated here or in Tuscany, in the 11th century) and by the 14th century was being used grated on pasta. It was introduced into France by a Duchess of Parma who married a grandson of Louix XV.

The true Parmesan cheese (*parmigiano reggiano*) is manufactured from 15 April to 11 November in the province of Parma and also in the provinces of Bologna and Mantua. Known and appreciated throughout the world, Parmesan cheese is formed into cylindrical millstone shapes with slightly convex sides, 33–45 cm (13–18 in) in diameter, 18–24 cm (7–9½ in) in height, and weighing about 30 kg (67½ lb). It takes at least one year to mature; the best, called *stravecchio*, takes more than three years, and some cheeses mature for up to ten years (they are then extremely hard). The cheese experts judge the cheese millstones by tapping them with a little hammer; those with a doubtful sound are sold grated. Parmesan cheese is principally used grated in cookery, for soups, pasta, soufflés, gratins, and stuffed vegetables, particularly aubergines (egg-plants). It is always preferable to grate the cheese just before using it. Parmesan is rarely included on a cheeseboard, although it is sometimes served cut into small pieces with apéritifs.

The term *à la parmesane* is used to

describe preparations which include Parmesan cheese, usually gratins.

parsley PERSIL

A herb originating in southern Europe and cultivated mainly for its aromatic leaves, which are used to flavour or garnish many dishes.

Before the reign of Charlemagne, parsley was thought to have magic powers, but since then it has become one of the most commonly used plants in cookery. There are three varieties of parsley. Common parsley, which has flat relatively smooth leaves, has the most flavour. Curly-leaved parsley, which has bright green crinkly leaves, is used mostly as a garnish. Turnip-rooted parsley is cultivated for its swollen root, which is cooked like celeriac (celery root) and used in soups. It is eaten in eastern Europe, particularly in Austria, Germany, Hungary, and the Soviet Union. In France, various other plants are known as parsley. Neapolitan or celery-leaved parsley (*persil noir*) is a type of wild celery; coriander is known as Arabian or Chinese parsley, and dill is commonly called Russian or Swedish parsley.

In cookery, fresh parsley is an ingredient of a bouquet garni and is used in marinades and stocks. When mixed with chopped garlic it is often served with sautéed or fried dishes (see *persillade*). Chopped parsley is frequently added during the final preparation of a dish or is sprinkled over food just before serving. Fried parsley is used as a garnish for fried items. Finely chopped parsley is used to flavour butter, sauces (particularly ravigote sauce, green sauce, Italian, maître d'hôtel, and poulette sauces), and vinaigrettes. Parsley can be dried and also freezes well.

In former times meat was 'larded' with parsley (i.e. parsley was inserted into it); in *Le Bourgeois Gentilhomme* (1670), Molière mentions 'a loin of mutton rich with parsley'.

RECIPES

Fried parsley PERSIL FRIT Wash, drain, and dry some curly-leaved parsley and separate it into little sprigs. Place these in a wire basket and deep-fry in very hot oil for a few seconds. Drain on kitchen paper and use immediately. Fried parsley is used as a garnish for skate with black butter sauce.

Sprigs of parsley PERSIL EN BRANCHES Pick off the leaves and small stalks from the main stalks. Wash them thoroughly in plenty of water, drain, and pat dry with kitchen paper. Fresh parsley can be used to garnish poached or grilled (broiled) fish, hot hors d'oeuvres, etc.

parsnip PANAIS

A vegetable cultivated for its white or yellowish sweet-tasting root. Widely grown by the Greeks and enjoyed in the Middle Ages and during the Renaissance, the parsnip has become a rarity in contemporary French cookery, although it is popular in other countries.

Harvested in autumn and winter, it has a fairly high calorific value (74 Cal per 100 g) and is rich in potassium and vitamin C. The parsnip is used in all the same ways as the turnip and is often preferred to it (particularly in beef broth), as it has more flavour. Parsnips may also be baked or cooked like carrots.

parson's nose

A British nickname for the fleshy part of the tail of some poultry, especially chicken and turkey; the French equivalent is *bonnet-d'evêque* (this term is also used for a table napkin folded into the shape of a mitre). See *croupion*.

partridge

PERDREAU ET PERDRIX

A highly prized game bird which is hunted throughout France and in Britain. In France, the word *perdreau* is used for partridges of either sex up to the age of one year. They have tender succulent flesh that needs very little cooking. The bird is barded or wrapped in vine leaves and roasted with juniper berries or grapes. It may also be stuffed. Young birds can be recognized by their flexible beaks and by the pointed first feather on the wing, which has a white tip. Very young partridges, found at the beginning of the season, are known as *pouillards* in France. One young partridge per serving is sufficient.

The principal species found in France are the red-legged partridge and the common or grey partridge. The former has a red back and breast, a white throat, and a red beak and feet. It is more common in south and southwestern France. The smaller and more common grey partridge has a reddish-grey back and an ash-grey breast. The male has a conspicuous brown horsehoe mark on the breast. The rock partridge is also found in France and has a high gastronomic reputation, although nowadays it is extremely rare. The American partridge, which has been introduced to France, is also highly regarded. In the United States, the word 'partridge' is also used for other game birds, especially the bobwhite and the ruffed grouse.

The mature partridge (*perdrix*) needs to be cooked longer than the young bird. The cooking time for young and tender birds is about 45 minutes, but older birds need to be braised for at least 1 hour. When really tough, they must be simmered in a covered pan for 2 hours, usually with cabbage, or they can be boiled as for a pot-au-feu. Young partridges can be prepared in a ragout, in a soufflé, as a pâté with truffles, in a casserole, in a caul, braised, in aspic, in a mousse, in a chaudfroid, etc. The classic dish for mature birds is chartreuse of partridge prepared with lentils or with cabbage, but they can also be used for forcemeats, purées, and thick soups. Charles Monselet, however, knew only one recipe worthy of the partridge:

'Gourmets! serve the bird roasted, with pink feet,

A strip of bacon to cover its modesty,

The breast sprinkled with lemon drops.'

RECIPES

Partridge croustades PERDREAUX EN CROUSTADES (from a recipe by Roger Lamazère) Completely bone 4 young partridges. Reserve the breast fillets and marinate them for 24 hours in 7.4 dl (1¼ pints, 1½ pints) red wine. Mince (grind) the meat from the thighs with the liver and season with salt and pepper. Place the bowl of forcemeat over a dish of ice and gradually work in 2 eggs, followed by 150 g (5 oz) fresh cream. Refrigerate the resulting mousse and then shape it into small quenelles.

Prepare a game stock with the partridge trimmings, the carcass, and the marinade. Boil until reduced by half, then add 3 dl (½ pint, 1¼ cups) demi-glace. Strain this stock, bring it to the boil, add the quenelles of partridge mousse, and poach them for 6 minutes.

Make 4 rectangular croustades with puff pastry. Fry 4 sliced cep mushroom caps in butter and season with salt and pepper. When the quenelles are cooked, remove from the stock and keep hot. Reduce the stock to make about 4 dl (14 fl oz, 1¾ cups) sauce, removing any scum that rises to the surface. At the last minute, thicken the sauce with 50 g (2 oz, ¼ cup) foie gras. Fry the partridge fillets in butter, season with salt and pepper, and cook for 2 minutes only on each side, so that they are still pink.

Fill the croustades with the quenelles, the fried mushrooms, and the partridge fillets. Add a little sauce and place in a very cool oven for 3 minutes. Serve the remaining sauce separately.

Partridge salad with cabbage SALADE DE PERDRIX AU CHOU (from a recipe by M. Pacaud) Select a large Savoy cabbage with a good heart. Remove about 8 of the leaves and wash them in plenty of water after removing the thick midribs. Blanch for 5 minutes in boiling salted water, cool, and drain. Pluck 6 partridges, gut them, and retain the livers. Cut the birds into quarters and use the breasts only (the thighs can be made into a terrine). Bone the breasts and season them with salt and pepper. Wipe 500 g (18 oz, 4½ cups) small firm cep mushrooms, with a damp cloth and chop them coarsely.

Brown 6 slices of belly of pork in a frying pan (skillet) and add the partridge breasts and livers. Cook for 6 minutes and then add the mushrooms. Cover the pan and braise for a further 5 minutes. Remove the contents of the pan and keep hot. Deglaze the pan with 1 dl (6 tablespoons, scant ½ cup) sherry vinegar, add some crushed peppercorns, boil down to reduce, and then thicken the sauce with 1 dl (6 tablespoons, scant ½ cup) hazelnut oil. Dip the cabbage leaves in the sauce and lay them out on the serving dish. Arrange the slices of pork, the partridge and livers, and the sliced mushrooms on the top and sprinkle with chopped chives.

Partridges with grapes PERDREAUX AUX RAISINS (from a recipe by André Daguin) Pluck, singe, and gut some young partridges. Season them with salt and pepper. Also season some large grapes with salt and pepper. Place 2 grapes and half a Petit-Suisse cheese (or ½ oz cream cheese) inside each bird. Quickly brown the birds in 50 g (2 oz, ¼ cup) butter in a heavy-based saucepan for 6 minutes. Cover the pan and cook gently for a further 10–15 minutes (the wings should be white, and the thighs pink near the bone). Drain the partridges and keep them hot.

Skim the fat from the cooking juices, add some green grapes and a small glass of Armagnac, and simmer over a low heat. Add a glass of red Banyuls wine and boil for 5 minutes to reduce. Strain the sauce and thicken with a Petit Suisse cheese (or 1 oz cream cheese). Season generously with salt and pepper. Spoon over the partridges and serve with potatoes *à la dauphinoise* and red cabbage *à la flamande.*

Partridge with lentils PERDRIX AUX LENTILLES Roast 2 partridges in 50 g (2 oz, ¼ cup) lard for 20 minutes. Then place them in a heavy saucepan with 100 g (4 oz, ½ cup) bacon pieces, 2 slices onions, 2 sliced carrots, 1 glass (¾ cup) white wine, 1 glass (¾ cup) stock, some salt, and a bouquet garni. Simmer gently for 1½ hours. In the meantime, boil in water until tender 250 g (9 oz, generous 1 cup) lentils (previously soaked for 2 hours and drained) with 200 g (7 oz) fat bacon, 4 small onions, 2 carrots (cut into quarters), 1 boiling sausage weighing 200 g (7 oz), and a pinch of salt. Arrange the lentils in a deep dish, place the partridges on top, and surround with the sliced sausage. Spoon over the cooking juices.

pascade

A pancake made in the Rouergue region of France with walnut oil, sometimes with bacon and onions added.

pascaline

A method of preparing lamb formerly traditional on Easter Day. Dumas gives a recipe which he describes as being common in France until the reign of Louis XVI: the lamb, stuffed and roasted, is served whole, like the paschal lamb sacrificed by the Jews for the feast of Passover. Monselet gives the same version and claims that he tasted it during a journey in Provence. Simon Arbellot, on the other hand, mentions a completely different pascaline of lamb, made by Montagné, who had found the recipe in the papers of Talleyrand and Carême. In this recipe lambs' heads are stuffed with liver, bacon, and herbs, lightly fried in fat, then arranged in a round dish with lambs' feet cooked in white stock, lambs' sweetbreads larded with bacon, croquettes of tongue and brain, and fried croutons; the whole is coated with a velouté sauce to which finely sliced onions have been added.

RECIPE

Pascaline (from the recipe of Alexandre Dumas) Truss a 6-month-old lamb to give a neat shape. Stuff with a forcemeat made of pounded lambs' flesh, yolks of hard-boiled (hardcooked) eggs, stale breadcrumbs, and chopped herbs, seasoned with 'four spices'. Cover the lamb with thin strips of bacon, roast it over a brisk fire, and serve it whole as a main dish following the soup, either with a green sauce or on a ragout of truffles with ham coulis.

pashka PASKHA

A traditional Russian Easter dish made of curd cheese, sugar, soured (dairy sour) cream, and butter, filled with raisins, crystallized (candied) fruits, and walnuts or almonds, and pressed in a pyramid-shaped mould. The pashka mould is usually wooden, with the sides carved with symbols representing the Passion, and with drainage holes in the base. The cake is decorated with crystallized (candied) fruits forming the letters X and B (initials, in the Cyrillic alphabet, of *Khristos Voskress*, meaning 'Christ is risen').

passion fruit

FRUIT DE LA PASSION

The edible fruit of the passionflower, a climbing plant, also known as granadilla, originating in tropical America but also grown in the West Indies, Africa, Australia, and Malaysia. The fruit is the size of a hen's egg with yellowish-green or brownish-red leathery skin, which is smooth and shiny when unripe and wrinkled when mature. The orange-yellow flesh, which is slightly acid and very fragrant, contains small edible black seeds. It contains only 46 Cal per 100 g and is rich in vitamins A and C. It can be cut in half and eaten raw, sprinkled with sugar (and sometimes with Kirsch or rum), or the pulp can be sieved and the juice made into sorbets, drinks, jellies, and creams. Passion-fruit pulp is used as a filling for the classic dessert Pavlova.

RECIPE

Passion-fruit sorbet   SORBET AUX FRUITS DE LA PASSION   Scoop out the flesh from some very ripe passion fruit and rub it through a fine sieve. Add an equal volume of cold sugar syrup and a little lemon juice (the density should then be about 1.075). Use an ice-cream maker to freeze the mixture. As a simpler alternative, granulated sugar can be added to the pulp, together with just enough water to reach a density of about 1.075; rub the pulp through a fine sieve before setting in the ice-cream maker.

pasta

PÂTES ALIMENTAIRES
A dough made from durum-wheat semolina, water, and often eggs. Pasta is shaped in various ways and sometimes flavoured. It is sold dried or fresh, ready to cook in boiling salted water (to serve with a sauce, for garnishing soups, or for gratins) or it may be sold ready stuffed and cooked, simply requiring heating up.

Durum wheat is grown in Italy, the Mediterranean, the Middle East, Russia, and North and South America. It is a hard wheat, high in gluten, which is ground into semolina. It is a popular belief that the 14th-century explorer Marco Polo introduced pasta into Italy from China, but in fact the first known reference to pasta can be traced to Sicily in the Middle Ages, when the island was under Arab domination. It had been a

basic food in Italy for many years, particularly in Naples and Rome, before Catherine de' Medici introduced it into France, although it only became really popular throughout France under the Empire.

Until the beginning of the 20th century, macaroni and vermicelli were the pastas most commonly used in France, mainly to make timbales, gratins, and sweet desserts and to garnish soups. After 1840 pasta was manufactured on an industrial scale (see *noodles*).

Pasta is made by kneading semolina with water (2–2.5 litres per 10 kg, 3–4 pints (4–5 pints) per 20 lb), adding various other ingredients if desired (eggs, flavouring, vegetable purés, etc.), and then shaping it. There are two types. Flat pastas are made industrially by rolling the dough between rollers into thin sheets that are cut into various shapes with a punch, a stamp, or some other suitable machine. The shapes include rectangles or squares with straight or wavy edges, and flat ribbons of various widths. Cylindrical forms of pasta are made by forcing the dough through a pierced plate. The hole through which the dough is forced may be straight, curved, notched, or fluted to produce solid or hollow tubes of variable size and shape. Drying is an important operation and care must be taken to ensure that the pasta will mature and keep well.

Fresh pasta, on the other hand, must be eaten quickly before it dries out. Fresh pasta (noodles, spaghetti, ravioli, cannelloni, and lasagne) is made by small businesses or in the home. It may be made with flour instead of semolina and always contains eggs.

☐ **Constituents and qualities of pasta**
● *Classic pasta* is made only with hard-wheat (durum-wheat) semolina and water; the best pastas have a translucent amber appearance. The taste of the pasta itself varies with the shape ('elbows', shells, macaroni, and tagliatelli, for example, all differ). Classic pastas are usually categorized as soup pastas, long pastas, or short pastas.
● *Egg pasta* contains 3–6 eggs per kg (2¼ lb, 6 cups) semolina. It is especially popular in Paris and Alsace.
● *Milk pasta* contains at least 6 g (¼ oz) dried milk per 450 g (1 lb, 2 cups) pasta.

• *Vegetable or flavoured pastas* contain a vegetable (usually spinach) or a flavouring (e.g. tomato), which is added during the manufacturing process. All artificial colouring is prohibited.

• *Wholewheat and buckwheat pastas* are richer in vitamins and minerals with more dietary fibre than other pastas.

Some pastas (especially lasagne, cannelloni, and ravioli) are sold fresh or frozen, ready filled.

Good-quality dried pasta is recognized by its dry smooth even appearance. The colour should be a translucent ivory, verging on yellow. It should break cleanly. Good-quality pasta quadruples in volume when cooked.

An average individual portion of pasta – about 60 g (2½ oz) – provides 230 Calories, the equivalent of 80 g (3 oz) bread, but it has almost the same protein content as beef. With a little fresh butter, fresh tomato sauce, and grated cheese (providing proteins, fats, carbohydrates, vitamins, and some dietary fibre), pasta makes a well-balanced meal.

□ Varieties of pasta Most pasta comes from Italy; it can be divided into four broad groups.

• *Pasta for soup*: very small, and made in various shapes. These include vermicelli, linguine (small grains), pennette (small quills), stelline (little stars), risoni (rice grains), conchigliette (little shells), and anellini (little rings, sometimes serrated).

• *Pasta for boiling*: the greatest variety of pasta comes into this category. Some types are flat (e.g. tagliatelle, trenette), others are cylindrical (e.g. spaghetti, spaghettini, and fideline). There are also hollow types of pasta, including macaroni, rigatoni, and penne (which are straight); pasta shells (conchiglie), nests (pappardelle), butterflies (farfalle), spirals (eliche), etc.

• *Pasta for baking*: this must first be boiled in water. It includes lasagne (smooth or wavy-edged), tortiglioni, bucatini, conchiglie, and cravattine.

• *Filled pasta*: cannelloni and ravioli are the commonest forms, but other types of filled pasta include tortellini and tortelloni (fairly large), agnolotti (small 'slippers'), cappelletti (little hats), lumache (large shells), and manicotti (large-ribbed tubes).

□ The cooking and serving of pasta Even when cooking a small quantity of pasta, a large pan must be used as plenty of boiling water is needed for the pasta to swell and move freely. Otherwise, the released starch makes it sticky. A tablespoon of oil added to the water can help prevent this. Sprinkle small pasta into briskly boiling water. Long pasta, such as spaghetti, is gradually pushed into the boiling water (without breaking the strands), until it softens and bends. It is by 'sealing' the pasta in fast-boiling water in this way that one obtains the degree of cooking known as *al dente*.

The cooking time depends on the quality of the pasta, its size, and the hardness of the water. Even if the cooking time is indicated on the packet, it is advisable to test the pasta early to avoid overcooking. As a guide, vermicelli takes 4–5 minutes, flat pasta and spaghetti take 11–12 minutes, and large macaroni takes 15 minutes; in each case timing begins when the water comes back to the boil. If the pasta is to be served in a salad, drain it, rinse in cold water, and immediately mix with a little oil, so that it will cool without sticking. When serving hot, the chosen sauce should be poured boiling hot onto the hot pasta. Stir quickly and serve immediately with grated cheese, etc., with the rest of the sauce served separately. The serving dish should also be hot.

The range of sauces for pasta is very large. The most commonly used are thick sauce based on tomatoes and often containing ham, minced (ground) meat, seafood, cheese, anchovies, chicken breasts, mushrooms, sliced vegetables, pickled ox (beef) tongue, etc. Bolognaise and milanaise sauces are the most traditional. Pasta can also be served in a timbale, a gratin, or a salad, with scrambled eggs, with mussels, in a ring, with peas, etc. Fillings include minced (ground) meat, spinach with béchamel sauce, chicken livers, cheese and herbs, sausagemeat, mushrooms, etc. In Italy, the pasta dish (*pasta asciutta*) is usually served as an entrée, whereas in France it is an accompaniment to the main dish.

RECIPE

Cooking pasta CUISSON DES PÂTES Plunge the pasta into a large quantity of boiling water (2 litres (3½ pints, 4½ pints) per 250 g (9 oz, 1½ cups) pasta) containing 1 tablespoon salt per litre (1¾ pints, 4¼ cups), unless any additional ingredients are to be very highly seasoned. Gently stir the pasta so that it does not stick together, and keep the water boiling at a constant rate. Drain the pasta completely when it is cooked, and season immediately. If the pasta is not to be used straight away, drain it and keep it hot mixed with 1 tablespoon oil. When ready to use, plunge it into boiling water, drain once more, and add the other ingredients.

Pasteur (Louis)

French chemist and biologist (born Dole, 1822; died Villeneuve-l'Étang, 1895). His work in microbiology is known by all, but less is known about his contribution to the field of nutrition. His studies on lactic, alcoholic, and butyric fermentations enabled him to perfect a method of keeping milk, beer, wine, and cider. Pasteurization is a heat treatment, intended to destroy the pathogenic bacteria which are found in a fermenting liquid and to allow food-stuffs to be kept for longer. Pasteuriza-tion is of prime importance in the dairy industry, whether the milk is intended for drinking or for manufacturing but-ter and cheese. It is also applied to beer and cider, more rarely to wine. Prepack-aged foods, such as baby foods, are also pasteurized. According to the *Dic-tionnaire de l'Académie de gastro-nomes*, on the evidence of his son-in-law, Vallery-Radot, Pasteur cared little for gastronomy: his favourite dish was a mutton cutlet with sautéed potatoes, which he ate every day except Thurs-days, when he had hot sausage gar-nished with red kidney beans.

pastillage

A paste, used in confectionery, made from a mixture of icing (confectioners') sugar and water with the addition of gelatine or gum tragacanth and pow-dered starch. It is kneaded by hand or by machine until firm enough to be rolled out and shaped easily; it may be col-oured during kneading.

The pieces shaped from the pastillage are left to dry and then fixed to the cake (or built up into shapes) with royal icing or softened pastillage.

In the hands of a skilled confectioner, pastillage can be used to create decora-tive preparations very close to sculp-ture. Artistic pastrycooks paint pictures on pastillage plaques.

pastilla or bstella

In Moroccan cookery, a kind of puff-pastry tart filled with chicken, seafood, or vegetables, which is eaten hot as an entrée. The pastilla (a Spanish word meaning 'little pie') is made with ex-tremely thin layers of pastry which are arranged in a buttered round mould, with layers of the filling inserted be-tween them. This filling, which may consist of chicken and hard-boiled (hard-cooked) eggs, quails and mushrooms, or minced (ground) beef and spinach, is always highly spiced with ginger, saffron, coriander, parsley, cinnamon, and sometimes also garlic, mint, or harissa. The pastilla is glazed with egg and traditionally cooked on glowing charcoal; halfway through cooking the tart is turned out onto a dish of the same size in order to cook the other side. It may also be cooked in the oven, moistened with melted butter, without being turned. The pastilla is served dusted with sugar and cinnamon. Dessert pastillas are also made, filled with almonds, confectioners' custard (pastry cream), or vermicelli cooked in milk with sugar and cinnamon.

pastille

A small round flat sweet (candy) manu-factured in different ways. One type of pastille is made from a cooked sugar syrup to which icing (confectioners') sugar, a flavouring, and a colouring have been added. The syrup is then dripped through a funnel to form 'drops', which are sometimes coated with chocolate. Another type of pastille is made from a mixture of icing sugar and gum tragacanth or gum arabic, which is rolled and then stamped into various shapes. These pastilles are flavoured with mint, lemon, aniseed, or with salts extracted from a mineral water (e.g. Vichy pastilles); they are rarely coloured.

The word *pastille* comes from the Spanish *pastilla*, derived from a diminutive of the Latin *panis* (bread). However, some authorities claim that these sweets were invented by and named after Jean Pastilla, a confectioner appointed by Marie de Médicis.

pastirma, pasterma, pastarma, or pastourma

Mutton, beef, or goat meat marinated with spices and garlic and then dried. Distinguished by a very strong taste, pastirma forms part of Turkish and Greek mezze and is eaten like dried ham.

pastis (drink)

In the south of France, an aniseed-flavoured rather strong drink, somewhat similar to the famous Pernod in the north. In fact the formula does not now contain any of the absinthe that originally made this type of apéritif distinctive. The name 'pastis' is a local dialect word meaning 'confused' or 'mixed' – a reference to the cloudy appearance of the drink when diluted with water (in which form it is always drunk). Sometimes the water is dripped onto the spirit through a piece of sugar held in a perforated spoon. The people of the region will spend hours sipping pastis while watching the local game of *boule* or *pétanque*. Some regional recipes include pastis, as the herby aniseed flavour is especially useful in fish dishes. There are many brands of pastis, two well-known names being Ricard and Berger.

pastis (pastry)

Any of various pastries made in south-western France (the name is derived from the word *pâté*, meaning pie). At Andernos-les-Bains (in the Gironde region), the pastis is a kind of brioche, called *landaise*. In Béarn, *pastis bourrit* is made from raised dough. The Gascon pastis is difficult to make because the dough must be spread over the whole work surface (itself covered by a large cloth), to dry for an hour. It is then saturated with goose fat and cut into rounds. Half of these are spread with thin slices of apple macerated in Armagnac brandy, covered with the other rounds, cooked in the oven, then sprinkled with Armagnac. This method of making puff pastry seems to have been brought from Spain by the Moors and is reminiscent of the Moroccan pastilla.

RECIPE

Pastis bourrit   (from a recipe by E. and J. de Rivoyre in *La Cuisine landaise*) Make some leaven with 30 g (1 oz, 2 tablespoons) flour, 10 g (¼ oz) fresh yeast (¼ cake compressed yeast), and 1 dl (3.5 fl oz, ⅓ cup) water. Leave to rise. Make a well in 1 kg (2¼ lb, 9 cups) flour in a very deep mixing bowl and add 150 g (5 oz, generous ½ cup) melted butter, a pinch of salt, 250 g (9 oz, generous cup) sugar, 6 egg yolks, 4 teaspoons vanilla-flavoured sugar, and 1 small glass of rum or anisette cordial. Stir and add 10 g (¼ oz) fresh yeast (¼ cake compressed yeast) and the leaven. Beat everything well. Whisk 6 egg whites into stiff peaks and add them to the dough. Leave to rise.

When the dough has doubled in size, butter some moulds, half-fill them with dough (this quantity of dough is enough for 2 or 3 pastis), and leave to rise to the top. Cook in a hot oven for 45 minutes until the pastis are golden. This cake is served with caramel custard or at a wedding. Cut into slices and toasted, it may be served with foie gras.

pastry
See *doughs and batters*.

pastry bag
See *piping bag*.

pastry brush   PINCEAU
A brush used for coating food with butter or oil (especially meat for grilling (broiling)), for greasing moulds and dishes, and also for brushing pastries with beaten egg or milk before they are cooked.

pastry cream
See *creams and custards*.

pastry cutter (cookie cutter)
EMPORTE-PIÈCE
A round, semicircular, oval, or triangular utensil, with a straight or fluted cutting edge, for cutting sheets of pastry

into various shapes and sizes. Pastry cutters are made of tin or stainless steel. An *emporte-pièce à colonne* (a pastry cutter column) is a cylindrical tin containing a set of pastry cutters with high edges and decreasing diameters, fitting into each other.

pastry wheel

GAUFREUSE, ROULETTE

A small fluted wheel, made of wood, steel, or plastic, mounted on a handle. It is used to cut pastry into strips or serrated narrow bands, for decorating the top of tarts, or to cut out shapes for fritters or ravioli.

pâté

This word is used in three ways in French: *pâté*, *pâté en terrine*, and *pâté en croûte*. In France the word *pâté* on its own should, strictly speaking, only be applied to a dish consisting of a pastry case (shell) filled with meat, fish, vegetables, or fruit, which is baked in the oven and served hot or cold. The best English translation of this word is 'pie', although many of these dishes are much richer and more elaborate than the sort of pie usually eaten in England and America, and are often prepared in moulds rather than pie dishes.

Pâté en terrine is a meat, game, or fish preparation put into a dish (*terrine*) lined with bacon, cooked in the oven, and always served cold. The correct French abbreviation of this is *terrine* but in common usage the French also call it *pâté*. The English have adopted both names.

Pâté en croûte is a rich meat, game, or fish mixture cooked in a pastry crust and served hot or cold.

Pâté was known to the Romans, who used to make it chiefly with pork but also used all types of marinated spiced ingredients (especially birds' tongues). In the Middle Ages, there were numerous recipes for *pâtisseries* (meats cooked in pastry) made with pork, poultry, eel, burbot, carp, sturgeon, cod, venison, capon, sheep's tongues, etc. Throughout the centuries, pâtés have been dedicated to famous people; some examples are *pâté à la mazarine* (in honour of Cardinal Mazarin), *pâté à la cardinale*, and *pâté à la reine*. In his *Grand Dictionnaire de cuisine*, Alexandre Dumas names a dozen, with numerous variants. Today there are many varieties of pâté inspired by French regional cookery, notably pâté de Chartres (made with partridge), pâté d'Amiens (duck), pâté de Pithiviers (larks), pâté de Pézenas (mutton, spices, and sugar), pâté de Ruffec (foie gras with truffles), Corsican blackbird pâté, Dieppe sole pâté, pâté lorrain, and pâté bourbonnais.

Most pâtés sold in delicatessens are actually terrines, based on pork meat or offal (in pieces or minced) bound with eggs, milk, jelly, etc. Among the best French pâtés are *pâté de campagne*, particulary that from Brittany (pure pork pâté containing offal, rind, onions, spices, and herbs); also *pâté de volaille* and *pâté de gibier* (chicken and game pâtés, containing 15% of the animal); *pâté de foie* (containing 15% pork liver and 45% fat); and *pâté de tête* (containing boned cooked pig's head mixed with cooked salted meat with the rind still on).

The pastry most often used for pâté *en croûte* is *pâte à pâté*, which is an ordinary lining pastry made with lard, but a fine pastry made with butter is also used, as well as puff pastry and unsweetened brioche dough. *Pâte à pâté* must be made well in advance, as it is easier to work after a good rest and does not brown so quickly when cooking. The pastry lid, which is sealed at the edges so that the filling cannot escape, is golden and often decorated. The centre is pierced with a 'chimney' – a small hole (often two in large pâtés) is made in the pastry and sometimes a small nozzle or cone is inserted – to enable the cooking steam to escape and prevent the pâté from splitting.

The pâté mould, which has deep sides and hinges or clips, may be round, oval, or rectangular. Dariole moulds are sometimes used for very small pâtés.

The fillings are based on pork, pork and veal, ham, chicken, fish, game, and sometimes vegetables. All the ingredients are generally minced (ground) quite finely but some of them may be cut into matchsticks, small strips, dice, etc. The ingredients may be marinated separately. They are mixed with the filling or alternated with layers of filling.

The pâté is sometimes lined with bacon barding before the filling is added.

In general, baking starts in a hot oven (200–210 C, 400–420 F, gas 6–7), which is then turned down to about 150 C (300 F, gas 2). The total cooking time is relatively long: 35–40 minutes per kg (15–18 minutes per lb). Some hot pâtés have a little sauce, gravy, or juice poured into them through the chimney before serving; for others, the sauce is served separately in a sauceboat. For pâtés that are served cold, aspic flavoured with Madeira, port, etc., can be poured through the chimney when cold to fill up the spaces made during cooking (the aspic should be ready to set). The pâté is not turned out of the mould until the aspic has set, and it is kept cool until served. Hot or cold pâtés are cut into thick slices and served as an entrée. Small individual pâtés are arranged on plates, sometimes with aspic croutons.

RECIPES

PÂTÉ EN TERRINE

Lark pâté en terrine PÂTÉ D'ALOU-ETTE EN TERRINE Pluck 8 larks, singe them, and remove the beaks and feet. Gut the birds, leaving only the liver and gizzard. Without boning them, put through a mincer (grinder), first at the medium setting and then at the fine setting. Put the purée in a bowl with 40 g (1½ oz, 3 tablespoons) foie gras and 40 g (1½ oz, 3 tablespoons) goose fat. Add 1 teaspoon salt, a generous pinch of freshly ground pepper, and 6 finely pounded juniper berries. Mix thoroughly together, then pour into a casserole. Cover the casserole and place it in a larger ovenproof dish. Fill the dish with boiling water to halfway up the casserole and cook in the oven at 180 C (350 F, gas 4), for 1½ hours.

Rub the pâté through the finest possible sieve while still hot, to obtain a very fine mousse without the slightest trace of bone. Mix this mousse with 80 g (3 oz, ¾ cup) lard and 80 g (3 oz, ¾ cup) foie gras. Pour into a small terrine, press down, and leave to cool. Melt 40 g (1½ oz, 3 tablespoons) lard over a very low heat, cool until tepid, then pour over the top. Cover the terrine and allow it to

cool completely. This lark pâté keeps for several days in a cool place.

PÂTÉS EN CROÛTE

Pâté pastry made with butter PÂTE À PÂTÉS AU BEURRE Put 500 g (18 oz, 4½ cups) sifted flour in a heap on the worktop and make a well in the centre. Add 2 teaspoons salt, 125 g (4½ oz, generous ½ cup) butter, 2 whole eggs, and about ½ dl (2½ tablespoons, 3 tablespoons) water. Mix together, then knead lightly. Roll into a ball, cover, and keep cool for 2 hours before use.

This pastry can be used for hot or cold pâtés.

Pâté pastry made with lard PÂTE À PÂTÉS AU SAINDOUX Particularly used for pork pâtés, this dough is made with 500 g (18 oz, 4½ cups) flour, 125 g (4½ oz, generous ½ cup) softened lard, 1 whole egg, 2 dl (7 fl oz, ¾ cup) water, and 3 teaspoons salt. Prepare like pâté pastry made with butter.

Ham pâté (cold) This prepared like veal and ham pâté, but lean minced (ground) ham or thin ham matchsticks are added to the forcemeat.

Pheasant pâté (cold) PÂTÉ DE FAISAN This is prepared like woodcock pâté.

Pork pâté à la hongroise (hot) PÂTÉ DE PORC À LA HONGROISE Cut 300 g (11 oz, 1½ cups) pork loin into strips and leave in a cold marinade for ingredients of pâtés and terrines for 5–6 hours. Peel and dice 150 g (5 oz, 1¼ cups) onions, wash and slice 200 g (7 oz, 2 cups) mushrooms, then sweat both vegetables in butter with salt, pepper, and paprika. Bind with 2–3 tablespoons (3–4 tablespoons) velouté sauce.

Line a pâté mould with pâté pastry. Coat the bottom with 200 g (7 oz) cream forcemeat containing chopped chives and paprika. Add the mushrooms and onions and press down gently. Drain the strips of pork, stiffen them slightly in hot butter, then put them on top of the vegetables. Cover with 200 g (7 oz) forcemeat and then with pastry (which can be shortcrust, puff, or pâté pastry). Finish the pâté in the same way as veal and ham pâté and bake in the oven at 180 c (350 f, gas 4) for 1½ hours. Pour some Hungarian sauce (see *(à la) hongroise*) into the pâté through the chimney.

Salmon pâté (hot) PÂTÉ DE SAUMON Prepare 600 g (1¼ lb) pike forcemeat and add a chopped truffle. Finely slice 600 g (1¼ lb) fresh salmon and marinate it for 1 hour in a little oil with some salt, pepper, and chopped herbs. Line a shallow oval pâté mould with pâté pastry made with butter. Cover the bottom with half the pike forcemeat, then add the salmon slices (drained) and the rest of the forcemeat. Top with a piece of pastry. Finish as for veal and ham pâté. Bake in the oven at 190 c (375 f, gas 5) for 1¼ hours.

Veal and ham pâté (cold) PÂTÉ DE VEAU ET DE JAMBON Remove the sinews from 300 g (11 oz) noix of veal and cut into matchsticks about 10 cm (4 in) long. Prepare 300 g (11 oz, 1½ cups) lean pork and 200 g (7 oz, scant cup) ham in the same way. Put all these meats into a terrine, sprinkle with 1 tablespoon spiced salt, add 1 dl (6 tablespoons, scant ½ cup) Madeira, and leave to marinate for 6–12 hours (some herbs and chopped shallots can also be added to the marinade).

Line a round or oval pâté mould with pâté pastry made with butter. Coat the bottom and sides with very thin strips of fatty bacon (200 g, 7 oz) and cover this with a layer of about 250 g (9 oz) fine forcemeat. Fill up with layers of the veal, pork, and ham matchsticks, separating them with thin layers of forcemeat. If desired, add 1 or 2 truffles cut into quarters or a few pistachio nuts. Finish with a layer of 200 g (7 oz) forcemeat. Place a sheet of pastry over the top, and pinch all round to seal. Glaze the top with egg and decorate with shapes cut out from leftover pastry (rolled out thinly). Make a hole in the centre and insert a piece of rolled-up cardboard or a small smooth nozzle. Glaze the top again.

Bake the pâté in the oven at 190 c (375 f, gas 5) for about 1¼ hours. Pour a few tablespoons of melted butter, lard, or aspic in through the 'chimney'. Turn

the pâté out of the mould when completely cool.

Woodcock pâté (cold) PÂTÉ DE BÉCASSE Prepare about 600 g (1¼ lb) game forcemeat *à gratin*. Remove the wings from 2 large woodcocks, season with salt and pepper, and roast for about 10 minutes in a very hot oven (they should still be very pink). Remove the flesh from the thighs and carcass and put through a food processor with the liver and intestines. Add this minced (ground) meat to the forcemeat and adjust the seasoning. Line an oval pâté mould with pâté pastry made with butter. Coat the bottom and sides of the mould with a layer of forcemeat, then add the 4 wings. Cover with thick slices of truffle lightly fried in butter, spread the rest of the forcemeat on top, and cover with pastry. Finish as for veal and ham pâté and bake in the oven at 190 c (375 f, gas 5) for approximately 1½ hours. Leave to cool completely, then pour in some chicken aspic through the chimney. Keep the pâté cool until it is served.

pâté pantin

A variety of pâté *en croûte*, rectangular or oblong in shape, that is not cooked in a mould. The filling (meat, chicken, game, or fish) is placed in the centre of the pastry, the edges are folded over and sealed, and the pâté is placed on a baking sheet and baked in the oven. The pâté may be baked with the sealed edges underneath or a second layer of pastry may be placed over the join and the edges sealed by pinching them together. It is served hot or cold as an entrée.

RECIPE

Chicken pâté pantin PÂTÉ PANTIN DE VOLAILLE Prepare the chicken (or use duck or young turkey) as for a ballottine. Half-cook it in a light chicken stock, drain it, and leave it to cool. Roll out about 600 g (1¼ lb) brioche dough and divide it into 2 equal portions. Coat one of the halves with very thin strips of bacon, place the filling in the centre, and turn up the edges of the dough all round the sides. Place some more thin strips of bacon on top of the filling and cover with the second piece of dough. Seal the edges, score the surface and make a small hole in the centre of the top to allow steam to escape. Glaze with egg and bake in the oven at 190 C (375 F, gas 5) for about 1 hour 10 minutes and serve hot.

pâtisserie

Sweet or savoury pastries and cakes generally baked in the oven. The term also applies to the art of the pastrycook as well as to the place where pastries are made and sold. The pastrycook (*pâtissier*), however, usually makes sweet things: hot, cold, or iced desserts, all types of cakes, pièces etc. Quiches, vols-au-vent, pâtés *en croûte* (in pastry), tarts, bouchées, rissoles, savoury crêpes, etc., are generally made by the chef or cook (*cuisinier*). Pâtisserie is closely linked with the manufacture of ice cream and confectionery (which includes working with sugar, crystallized (candied) fruits, almond paste, nougatine, decorations, etc.), and uses sweetened creams and sweet sauces.

Prehistoric man made sweet foods based on maple or birch syrup, wild honey, fruits, and seeds. It is thought that the idea of cooking a cereal paste on a stone in the sun to make pancakes began as far back in time as the Neolithic age. The Egyptians, Greeks, Romans, and then the Gauls prepared pancakes with maize (corn), wheat, or barley, mixed with poppy seeds, aniseed, fennel, or coriander. Gingerbread and puddings date back to antiquity, and the Greek *obolios* (ancestors of wafers and waffles) gave their name to the first French pastrycooks (who were known as *obloyers* or *oubloyers*) and wafers (*oublies*). In the Middle Ages in France, the work of bakers overlapped with that of pastrycooks: bakers made gingerbread and meat, cheese, and vegetable pies. Apple fritters (*beugnets*, now known in France as *beignets*) and custards were also available. However, it was the Crusaders who gave a decisive impetus to pâtisserie, by discovering sugar cane and puff pastry in the East. This led to pastrycooks, bakers, and restaurateurs all claiming the same products as their own specialities, and various disputes arose when one trade encroached upon the other. King Louis IX (1226–70) tried to create some order

by giving status to the 'master *oubloyers* and the varlets of the *oubloiries*'. In 1351, an order from King John the Good (1350–64) listed the goods coming under the description of 'pâtisserie': wafers, estrées, supplications, nieules, échaudés, fritters (made of beef bone marrow, pikes' eggs, rice, almonds, sage, etc.), tarts, gohières, popelins, marzipan, darioles, flanets, cassemuseaux, talmouses, ratons, tarts made with frangipane, pistachio, young pigeon and lark, etc. Another order, in 1440, gave the sole rights for meat, fish, and cheese pies to *pâtissiers*, this being the first time that the word appeared. Their rights and duties were also defined, and certain rules were established: prohibition of the use of spoiled meat, bad eggs, sour or skimmed milk, and the sale of reheated pies. The proprietor could not take on a worker who was not capable of an output of a thousand nieules per day. Wafers were not made on feast days.

The 1485 statutes declared the statutory feast days and that of Saint-Michel (the patron saint of the corporation) to be holidays. The final merger between *pâtissiers* and *oubloyeurs* took place in 1566; at the same time they obtained the monopoly for the organization of weddings and banquets. The corporation lasted until 1776, when Turgot abolished the trade corporations.

In the 16th century, pâtisserie products were still quite different from the ones we know today. Choux pastry is said to have been invented in 1540 by Popelini, Catherine de' Medici's chef, but the pastrycook's art only truly began to develop in the 17th century and reached its peak in the 18th and 19th centuries. Some landmarks are important: 1638 – almond tartlets were invented by Ragueneau; 1740 – the baba was introduced into France by Stanislas Leszczynski; 1760 – Avice created toasted choux and ramekins; 1805 – the horn decoration was invented by Lorsa, a Bordeaux pastrycook.

The greatest innovator at the beginning of the 19th century was indubitably Carême, to whom tradition attributes nougat, meringue, the croquembouche, vols-au-vent, and the perfecting of puff pastry. Other great 19th-century pastrycooks include Rouget, the Julien brothers, Chiboust, Coquelin, Stohrer, Quillet, Bourbonneux, Seugnoy etc., who enriched the pâtisserie repertoire with the mille-feuille, Saint-Honoré, bourdaloue, napolitain, Genoa cake, mocha cake, trois-frères, savarin, gorenflot, and many others.

There were about a hundred pastrycooks in Paris at the end of the 18th century. In 1986 the count for the whole of France was over 40,000 baker-pastrycooks and 12,500 pastrycooks.

patranque or patrenque

A speciality of Auvergne, made of stale bread soaked in milk, squeezed, and fried in butter in a frying pan (skillet). Cantal cheese (preferably fresh) is stirred into the mixture until it just melts and combines with the bread. The patranque is turned over halfway through cooking so that both sides are browned.

Pauillac

A parish (commune) in the Haut-Médoc region of Bordeaux. Many good and some very great clarets come from the estates here, as well as a number of small-scale wines. The most famous of all are the first growths – Châteaux Lafite-Rothschild, Latour, and Mouton-Rothschild. All of these are AOC Pauillac.

paulée

A feast at the end of the harvest or the grape gathering which used to be traditional in all regions of France. The word *paulée* comes from Burgundy; in other regions of France the feast is known by other names. In the Mâconnais, Dauphiné, and Lyonnais regions, for instance, it is referred to as the *revolle*, in the Bordeaux region as the *pampaillet*, in Champagne, Lorraine, and Franche-Comté as the *tue-chien*, and in central France as the *gerbaudes*.

Today, the Paulée de Vendanges (the feast after the grape harvest) only survives at Meursault and is celebrated at the end of November on the third day of the *Trois Glorieuses* (the 'Three Glorious Days') of the Côte de Beaune. The first day is devoted to the great annual chapter of the Chevaliers du Tastevin at the Clos de Vougeot, and the second to the auction of the Hospices de Beaune

wines that takes place in the fermenting room of the Hôtel-Dieu.

paupiette

A thin slice of meat spread with a layer of forcemeat and then rolled up. Paupiettes may be barded with thin rashers (slices) of fat bacon and tied up with string or secured with small wooden cocktail sticks (toothpicks). They can be braised in a little liquid or fried. Veal is most often used, but beef, lamb, and turkey escalopes, or even slices of calves' sweetbreads, are also suitable. (See *oiseau sans tête*.)

Paupiettes can also be made with cabbage (the leaves are blanched, stuffed in various ways, then rolled up, tied, and braised) or with fish (thin slices of tuna, or fillets of sole, whiting, or anchovy, are stuffed, rolled up, and cooked in stock).

RECIPES

Braised paupiettes of beef PAUPIETTES DE BOEUF BRAISÉES Flatten some thin slices of beef fillet, sirloin, or chuck steak, season with salt and pepper, and spread with a layer of well-seasoned sausagemeat. Roll them up, wrap in thin rashers of fat bacon, and tie with string. Braise the paupiettes in white wine or Madeira, drain them, untie the string, remove the bacon, and arrange them on a heated dish. Coat with the cooking juices (reduced and strained).

All the accompaniments for small cuts of braised meat are suitable for these paupiettes: noisette potatoes, braised vegetables, vegetable purée, stuffed artichoke hearts, risotto, rice pilaf, etc. Some garnishes (e.g. bourgeoise or chipolata) can be added to the casserole halfway through the braising time.

Paupiettes of beef can also be braised in red wine. In this case, the accompaniments (baby onions, bacon, and mushrooms) can also be added while the paupiettes are cooking.

Paupiettes of braised calves' sweetbreads PAUPIETTES DE RIS DE VEAU BRAISÉ (from a recipe by Georges Blanc) Blanch and clean some calves' sweetbreads and cook them gently for

15 minutes, with a little dry white wine, on a bed of carrots, celery, and leeks that have been softened in butter. Drain the sweetbreads, cut them into slices, and roll up in blanched spinach leaves. Keep hot on a serving dish. Reduce the cooking juices in the pan, thicken with kneaded butter, and add a little curry powder, a dash of mustard, and a little double (heavy) cream. Adjust the seasoning. Strain the sauce over the paupiettes on the serving dish.

Paupiettes of chicken with cabbage
PAUPIETTES DE POULE AU CHOU (from a recipe by Michel Oliver) Blanch some large leaves of green cabbage for 15 seconds. Drain and wipe them. Remove the legs, wings, and breast from an uncooked chicken and season them with salt and pepper. Wrap the chicken pieces in cabbage leaves to make 5 large paupiettes and tie them up tightly with string. Brown some chopped carrots and onions in goose fat or dripping in a pan, add the paupiettes, and cook them until they brown. Add 4 dl (14 fl oz, 1¾ cups) water, cover the pan, and cook for about 1½ hours.

The chicken pieces may be boned and skinned before use if preferred.

Paupiettes of lamb à la créole
PAUPIETTES D'AGNEAU À LA CRÉOLE Cut 6 even slices from a leg of lamb. Flatten them well and season with salt and pepper. Peel and chop 6 large onions. Deseed then chop 1 large green pepper into very small dice. Gently cook half the onions and all the pepper in 30 g (1 oz, 2 tablespoons) butter. Add 350 g (12 oz) fine pork forcemeat and season with salt and pepper. Spread the forcemeat evenly over the slices of lamb, roll them up, and tie with string. Brown the paupiettes in a casserole with 30 g (1 oz, 2 tablespoons) butter, add the rest of the onions, cook till brown, then add 3 peeled tomatoes (deseeded and chopped), some chopped parsley, 1 small crushed clove of garlic, 1 piece of lemon rind, some salt and pepper, and a little cayenne. Cover and cook in the oven at 200 c (400 f, gas 6) for 45 minutes.

Drain the paupiettes, arrange them in a circle on a serving dish, and keep warm. Reduce the pan juices until thickened, add 1 tablespoon rum, strain, and coat the paupiettes with the sauce. Fill the centre of the dish with rice *à la créole*.

Paupiettes of veal braised à brun
PAUPIETTES DE VEAU BRAISÉES À BRUN Coat some flattened veal escalopes with a pork forcemeat mixed with dry mushroom duxelles and chopped parsley and bound with egg. Roll them up, bard them with thin rashers (slices) of fat bacon, and tie with string. Arrange them in a buttered flameproof casserole lined with pieces of pork skin or bacon rinds and sliced onions and carrots browned in butter. Place a bouquet garni in the middle. Season with salt and pepper. Cover and cook over a gentle heat for 10 minutes.

Add some dry white wine or (depending on the accompaniments) Madeira (2 dl (⅓ pint, scant cup) per 10 paupiettes). Reduce almost completely, then pour in some thickened veal stock until the paupiettes are two-thirds covered. Cover and braise in the oven at 200 c (400 f, gas 6), basting frequently, for 45 minutes to 1 hour. Drain the paupiettes and remove the barding, then glaze them in the oven. Arrange them on the serving dish and coat with their braising liquor, reduced and strained. Serve with braised buttered vegetables or with vegetable purée.

pauvre homme (à la)

Describes preparations of leftover meat served with a type of clear miroton sauce made by deglazing a roux with vinegar, reducing it, and adding stock, chopped shallots, chives, or onions, and chopped parsley. In the original recipe, breadcrumbs were used instead of flour.

The term is also used for fried noisettes or cutlets of venison coated with a sauce made by deglazing the pan with vinegar and any marinade from the meat, thickening it with kneaded butter, and adding sliced gherkins. The name of the sauce (meaning poor man's sauce) derives from the fact that it was originally made with leftovers (stale bread and stock).

RECIPE

Poor man's sauce SAUCE PAUVRE HOMME Make a golden roux with 1 tablespoon butter and 1 heaped table-spoon flour. Deglaze with ½ dl (2½ tablespoons, 3 tablespoons) vinegar, boil to reduce, and add 2 dl (7 fl oz, ¾ cup) stock (or use water with a little added meat glaze or extract). Season with salt and pepper and boil for a few minutes. Just before serving, add 1 tablespoon chopped blanched shallots, 1 tablespoon chopped parsley, and 2 tablespoons (3 tablespoons) dried breadcrumbs.

Chives can be used instead of shallots or a mixture of both can be used.

pavé

This word, which literally means slab or block, is applied to several dishes, most commonly to a square-shaped cake or dessert made from Genoese sponge cake sandwiched with butter cream or squares of rice or semolina pudding.

It is also used for a cold entrée, usually a mousse, set in a square or rectangular mould, coated with aspic jelly, and garnished with slices of truffle, etc.

Pavé also describes a square block of gingerbread and a thick piece of prime grilled (broiled) beef.

RECIPE

Fried rice pavés PAVÉS DE RIZ FRITS   Make a thick rice pudding using 125 g (4½ oz, generous ½ cup) short-grain rice and 6 dl (1 pint, 2½ cups) milk, sweetened to taste (the grains must be completely soft and the mixture sticky). Butter a baking sheet and spread with a layer of rice about 1.5 cm (½ in) thick. Smooth the surface, sprinkle with a little melted butter, and leave to cool completely. Cut the rice into 5-cm (2-in) squares.

Stew 800 g (1¾ lb, 2½ cups) fruit with a little sugar until reduced to a purée (use apricots, apples, plums, oranges, or greengages). Strain the pulp into a pan, add some chopped canned pineapple, and boil to reduce by one-third. (Chestnut purée could also be used.) Spread half of the rice squares with the fruit and top with the remaining squares. Press them together, coat in breadcrumbs, and deep-fry in hot oil at 175–180 C (347–350 F) until golden brown. Drain them on absorbent kit-chen paper, and serve very hot with strawberry sauce or custard cream.

Pavé d'Auge

A Normandy cows'-milk cheese (50% fat content) with a soft straw-coloured centre and a washed crust. A firm cheese with a strong flavour, it is sold in 11-cm (4-in) squares, 5 cm (2 in) deep. Pavé d'Auge (or Pavé de Moyaux) resembles Pont-L'Évêque, but is more full-bodied and contains more fat.

paysanne

A mixture of vegetables (potatoes, car-rots, turnips, and cabbage), cut into small squares, used to make soups known as *potages taillés* or to garnish meat, fish, or omelettes. Potatoes pre-pared *en paysanne* are first cut into small sticks 8–10 mm (¼ in) thick, which are in turn cut across into thin slices. Cabbage leaves are cut into strips 8–10 mm (¼ in) wide and each strip is cut into small squares.

By extension, the term *à la paysanne* describes various braised dishes cooked with softened vegetables; the vegetables need not necessarily be cut *en paysanne*. Potatoes *à la paysanne* are cut into rounds and simmered in a herb-flavoured stock. Omelette *à la paysanne* is a potato omelette flavoured with sor-rel and herbs.

RECIPES

Casserole of veal chops à la paysanne CÔTES DE VEAU EN CASSEROLE À LA PAYSANNE   Prepare a vegetable fon-due with 4 carrots, 2 onions, 2 leeks (white part), a turnip, and 4 sticks (stalks) of celery, cut up into small squares and softened in 30 g (1 oz, 2 tablespoons) butter. Add 1 tablespoon chopped parsley and season with salt and pepper. Fry 2 firm potatoes (cut into small dice) in a mixture of 20 g (¾ oz, 1½ tablespoons) butter and 2 table-spoons (3 tablespoons) oil. Brown 200 g (7 oz) diced smoked streaky bacon in butter. Mix all these ingredients together. Fry 4 veal chops in butter, place them with the other ingredients in a casserole dish, season with salt and pepper, reheat thoroughly, and serve.

Omelette à la paysanne   For an 8-egg

omelette, prepare 3–4 tablespoons sorrel braised in butter, 200 g (7 oz) potatoes boiled in their skins, skinned, sliced, and browned in butter, and 1 tablespoon chopped parsley and chervil. Beat the eggs and add the garnish. Pour the mixture into a large frying pan (skillet) and make a flat omelette.

Potatoes à la paysanne POMMES DE TERRE À LA PAYSANNE Peel 1 kg (2¼ lb) waxy (not floury) potatoes and cut them into slices. Braise 100 g (4 oz, 3 cups) chopped sorrel in 30 g (1 oz, 2 tablespoons) butter with a crushed clove of garlic, 1 tablespoon chopped chervil, and some salt and pepper. Put a layer of potatoes in a buttered sauté pan, then a layer of the cooked sorrel, and top with the remaining potatoes. Sprinkle lightly with salt, add a generous quantity of pepper, and pour in sufficient stock to just cover the contents of the pan. Sprinkle with 30 g (1 oz, 2 tablespoons butter cut into small pieces. Cover the pan and bring to the boil. Then transfer to the oven at 200 c (400 f, gas 6) and cook for 50 minutes to 1 hour.

Soup à la paysanne POTAGE À LA PAYSANNE For 4 servings, peel and dice the following ingredients and place them in a large pan: 200 g (7 oz, 1¼ cups) carrots, 100 g (4 oz, 1 cup) turnips, 75 g (3 oz, ¾ cup) leeks (white part), 1 onion, and 2 sticks (stalks) of celery. Cover the pan and stew the vegetables in 40 g (1½ oz, 3 tablespoons) butter.

Add 1.5 litres (2¾ pints, 3½ pints) water and bring to the boil. Blanch 100 g (4 oz, 1½ cups) cabbage cut into small squares; refresh, drain, and add them to the pan. Leave to cook gently for 1 hour, then add 100 g (4 oz, ⅔ cup) diced potatoes and 100 g (4 oz, 1 cup) small fresh peas. Cook for a further 25 minutes. Crisp a long French stick in the oven. Just before serving the soup, add 30 g (1 oz, 2 tablespoons) butter and sprinkle with chopped chervil. Serve with the hot French bread.

pea PETIT POIS

The small round green seed of the plant *Pisium sativum*, up to eight of which are enclosed in a long green pod.

Peas have been cultivated as a vegetable since ancient times, but they did not become widely appreciated in France until the 17th century, when Audiger introduced a new Italian variety to the French court. However, Taillevent had already made known his recipe for *cretonnée de pois* (a type of spiced purée of peas and milk, mixed with chicken breast, and bound with eggs). Madame de Maintenon, in a letter to the Cardinal of Noailles in 1696, wrote: 'The question of peas continues. The anticipation of eating them, the pleasure of having eaten them, and the joy of eating them again are the three subjects that our princes have been discussing for four days . . . It has become a fashion – indeed, a passion.'

Nowadays, 95% of French peas come from northern and western France and the Parisian basin, where those of Saint-Germain and Clamart were once so famous that some recipes based on peas have been named after them. Peas can be canned, dried, and deep-frozen, so that they are available all the year round. Fresh garden peas, which have much more flavour, are sold in France from May to July and come mainly from southeast and southwest. In France, a distinction is made between early peas (*lisses*) and the late varieties (*ridés*).

Peas provide 92 Cal per 100 g and contain 16% carbohydrates. They are also rich in phosphorus, potassium, and vitamins and contain some protein. When buying peas, ensure that the pods are smooth and bright green. The peas should be shiny and not too large, tender, but not floury. The sooner peas are eaten after picking, the better they taste. Some cooks recommend keeping the pods for no longer than 12 hours. After this time, it is better to shell the peas, mix them with butter (125 g (4½ oz, ¾ cup) per litre (1¾ pints, 4¼ cups) shelled peas), and keep them cool until ready to cook. Peas can be easily shelled by hand and do not need to be washed. They can be boiled (*à l'anglaise*) or cooked in butter (*à la française*, with lettuce and small onions). They can also be cooked with bacon (*à la bonne femme*) or carrots (*à la fermière*) or flavoured with mint. The cooking time is quite short for freshly picked peas, but longer for those picked a few days previously. Peas are regarded as the classic accompaniment for veal, lamb, and poultry (especially duck and pigeon); they are often served with asparagus tips or artichoke hearts, as well as in a jardinière or a macédoine. Peas can also be puréed, made into soup, or used to garnish soups and broths. When cold, they can be incorporated into mixed salads and vegetable terrines. Canned or bottled peas are the most commonly eaten preserved food in France, whereas in Britain frozen peas are the most popular. Frozen peas can be used in the same way as fresh peas.

RECIPES

Boiled peas PETITS POIS À L'ANG-
LAISE Shell the peas and cook them in boiling salted water in an uncovered saucepan. They should be tender without becoming mushy or losing their colour (about 20 minutes is sufficient if they are fresh). Drain them thoroughly, and serve with fresh butter. The peas can be flavoured by cooking them with a sprig of fresh fennel or mint and serving them sprinkled with chopped fresh fennel or mint.

Peas à la bonne femme PETITS POIS À
LA BONNE FEMME Melt some butter in a frying pan (skillet) and lightly brown 12 baby onions and 125 g (4½ oz, generous ½ cup) diced scalded lean bacon. Remove the onions and bacon from the pan, add 1 tablespoon flour to the hot butter, and cook for a few minutes, stirring with a wooden spoon. Moisten with 3 dl (½ pint, 1¼ cups) white consommé, boil for 5 minutes, then add 700 g (1½ lb, 4½ cups) fresh peas. Add the onions and bacon together with a bouquet garni and cook, covered, for about 30 minutes.

Peas à la crème PETITS POIS À LA
CRÈME Boil 800 g (1¾ lb, 5¼ cups) peas, drain them, and put them back in the saucepan. Dry out a little over a brisk heat, then add 1.5 dl (¼ pint, ⅔ cup) boiling fresh cream and boil until reduced by half. Adjust the seasoning and add a large pinch of sugar. Just before serving, add 2 tablespoons (3 tablespoons) fresh cream, blend well, and serve sprinkled with chopped herbs.

Peas à la fermière PETITS POIS À LA
FERMIÈRE Clean 500 g (18 oz) baby carrots and peel 12 baby onions. Brown them in butter in a saucepan. When the carrots are brown but still firm, add 800 g (1¾ lb, 5¼ cups) fresh shelled peas, a coarsely shredded lettuce, and a bouquet garni composed of parsley and chervil. Season with salt and sugar, moisten with 2 tablespoons (3 tablespoons) water, cover the pan, and simmer gently for about 30 minutes. Remove the bouquet garni. Blend in 40 g (1½ oz, 3 tablespoons) butter just before serving.

Peas à la française PETITS POIS À LA
FRANÇAISE Place 800 g (1¾ lb, 5¼ cups) fresh shelled peas in a saucepan together with a lettuce shredded into fine strips, 12 new small onions, a bouquet garni composed of parsley and chervil, 75 g (3 oz, 6 tablespoons) butter cut into small pieces, 1 teaspoon salt, 2 teaspoons sugar, and 4½ tablespoons (generous ⅓ cup) cold water. Cover the pan, bring gently to the boil, and simmer for 30–40 minutes. When the peas are cooked, remove the bouquet garni and mix in 1 tablespoon fresh butter. Serve in a vegetable dish.

Peas with ham à la languedocienne
PETITS POIS AU JAMBON À LA LAN-
GUEDOCIENNE Cut a medium onion into quarters and brown in goose fat with 125 g (4½ oz) lean unsmoked raw ham. Add 800 g (1¾ lb, 5¼ cups) fresh peas and brown lightly. Sprinkle with 1 tablespoon flour and cook for a few minutes. Then add 3 dl (½ pint, 1¼ cups) water, season with salt and caster (superfine) sugar, add a small bouquet garni, and cook uncovered for about 45 minutes. Remove the bouquet garni and serve in a vegetable dish.

Peas with mint PETITS POIS À LA
MENTHE Proceed as described in the recipe for peas in butter, but cook the peas with a few fresh mint leaves. Arrange in a vegetable dish and sprinkle the peas with scalded chopped mint leaves.

peach PÊCHE

The fruit of the peach tree, with a velvety skin, juicy sweet flesh, which can be white or yellow in colour, and a single stone (pit). The peach tree originated in China, where it has been grown since the 5th century BC. It was introduced to Japan, and then to Persia, where it was discovered by Alexander the Great. He in turn introduced it to the Greeks. The name comes from the French *pêche*, which in turn comes from the Latin *Persicum malum* (Persian apple – an indication of its origin). Throughout the centuries, the peach has been highly regarded as a table fruit and has been used as an ingredient in many delicate desserts. In the reign of Louis XIV, splendid varieties of peach were grown in France by La Quintinie and the peach was nicknamed *téton de Venus* (Venus' breast). It was also much in favour during the Empire and the Restoration. The peach forms the basis of various refined dishes such as peach Bourdaloue, cardinal, Condé, *à l'impératrice*, and the internationally famous peach Melba.

Peaches are harvested from the end of May to September. In France, peaches come mainly from the southeast and the southwest. White peaches have a delicate fine-textured flesh which is full of flavour. They make up 30% of the total crop and are used for jams, compotes, sorbets, and soufflés, as well as being a table fruit. The majority of the crop consists of yellow peaches, which generally mature later than the white variety and are less aromatic and not as juicy. They are best suited for jams, tarts, fritters, and for decoration.

Peaches are highly digestible. They provide 62 Cal per 100 g and are rich in potassium and vitamins A, C, B_1, and B_2. They contain 12 g sugar per 100 g.

When buying peaches, ensure that they are ripe and have a fine unblemished skin. They should not be kept for more than 48 hours. Most of the vitamins are in the skin, so it is preferable not to peel them when eating them as a dessert fruit, but simply to rinse them in water. (Most dessert peaches are peeled, however.) If they are to be used to prepare other dishes, they are plunged into boiling water for 30 seconds so that the skin can be easily removed. Although peaches are used mainly for desserts and pastries, they also serve as an accompaniment for savoury dishes (calf's liver, duck, and crab in particular). They make excellent ices and sorbets and are delicious simply poached in syrup or wine. Peach liqueur and brandy are very popular after-dinner drinks and the fruit can also be crystallized (candied) as a confection.

RECIPES

Chilled peaches with raspberries PÊCHES RAFRAÎCHIES AUX FRAMBOISES Poach some peaches in a vanilla-flavoured sugar syrup and leave to cool completely; then chill. When ready to serve drain and arrange them in a glass dish. Prepare a fresh raspberry purée, add a little of the reduced sugar syrup, and flavour with a few drops of raspberry liqueur. Cover the peaches with the purée and decorate with fresh raspberries.

Peach conserve MARMELADE DE PÊCHES Plunge 1 kg (2¼ lb) peaches in boiling water for 30 seconds. Drain, peel, and remove the stones (pits). Poach in a pan with 1 dl (6 tablespoons, scant ½ cup) water and the juice of 1 lemon for about 30 minutes. Then add 900 g (2 lb, 4 cups, firmly packed) sugar. Bring back to the boil and cook until setting point is reached (about 20 minutes). Jar in the usual way (see *jams, jellies, and marmalades*).

Peaches à la bordelaise PÊCHES À LA BORDELAISE Plunge 4 peaches in boiling water for 30 seconds, peel them, cut them in half, and remove the stones (pits). Sprinkle them with sugar and leave to steep for 1 hour. Boil 3 dl (½ pint, 1¼ cups) Bordeaux wine with 8 lumps of sugar and a small piece of cinnamon. Place the peach halves in this syrup to poach for 10–12 minutes. When the fruit is cooked, drain and arrange in a glass dish. Boil the syrup to reduce it, pour over the peaches, and leave to cool. Serve with slices of brioche dusted with icing (confectioners') sugar and glazed in the oven.

Peach jam CONFITURE DE PÊCHES Put the peaches into boiling water for 30 seconds, drain, peel them, cut them in half, remove the stones (pits), and weigh them. Using 750 g (1¾ lb, 3½ cups, firmly packed) sugar and 1 dl (6 table-

variety	availability	characteristics
white peaches		
Springtime	beginning of June	colourful skin, sweet aromatic flesh
Robin	mid-June	red skin, pleasant flavour, sweet flesh
Ribet	mid-June	greenish-yellow skin, sweet juicy flesh
Charles-Roux	July	fine succulent flesh, full of flavour (excellent for jam-making)
Redwing	end of July	colourful skin, firm flesh, sweet and juicy
Michelini	mid-August	colourful skin, good quality
yellow peaches		
Earlired *and* Cardinal	June	skin almost red, firm aromatic flesh
Merril Gemfree	June	very firm flesh, medium flavour (good for poaching in wine)
Dixired	mid-June	juicy, but little flavour; plentiful on the market
Redhaven	July	good colour, firm flesh, pleasant flavour
Loring	July	pale, very large, and succulent (ideal for tarts and for decoration)
Pavie	end of July	good firm flesh; ideal for jam-making, conserves, poaching, and for fritters (named after a town in Gers where it has been produced since the 16th century)
Suncrest	beginning of August	good colour, very good quality

spoons, scant ½ cup) water per kg (2¼ lb) peaches, boil the sugar and water for 5 minutes, add the fruit, and simmer gently, stirring occasionally. The jam is ready when it coats the back of a wooden spoon (about 40 minutes). Pot in the usual way (see *jams, jellies, and marmalades*).

Peach sorbet SORBET À LA PÊCHE Prepare a sugar syrup with 350 g (12 oz, 1½ cups, firmly packed) granulated sugar and 3 dl (½ pint, 1¼ cups) of water. Bring to the boil, simmer for 3 minutes, and cool. Peel and stone 1 kg (2¼ lb) ripe peaches in the usual way, reduce to a purée in a blender, and add the juice of a lemon. Mix the cold sugar syrup and the peach purée together, pour into an ice-cream maker, and freeze (see *sorbet*).

Peach sundaes COUPES GLACÉES AUX PÊCHES Prepare ½ litre (17 fl oz, 2 cups vanilla ice cream. Plunge some peaches in boiling water for 30 seconds (allow 6 peaches for 4 sundaes), then drain, peel them, and remove the stones (pits). Reserve a few slices for decoration and chop the remainder. Sprinkle with 1 tablespoon lemon juice and 2 tablespoons (3 tablespoons) fruit liqueur (preferably strawberry liqueur). Whip 2 dl (7 fl oz, ¾ cup) double (heavy) cream. Chill 4 sundae glasses in the refrigerator, put a quarter of the peaches into each cup, cover with a layer of ice cream, and pipe the whipped cream on top, using a piping (pastry) bag fitted with a star (fluted) nozzle.

Decorate with a few thin slices of raw peach which have been soaked in liqueur.

peacock PAON

A bird of the same family as the pheasant, originating in the Middle East. Greatly prized in ancient times for its beauty, the peacock appeared on the tables of Europe under Charlemagne, essentially as a banquet dish. Throughout the Middle Ages it enjoyed great prestige, but more for the beauty of its plumage than for the succulence of its flesh. Olivier de Serre, however, considered it delectable: 'It is the king of earthly poultry, as the primacy of aquatic birds belongs to the swan. What more exquisite flesh can you eat?' For several centuries now, it has practically disappeared from cookery.

The peacock was served with great ceremony, roasted and entirely reconstituted, sometimes spitting fire (the beak covered with camphor). It was skinned, roasted (the head wrapped in a wet cloth to protect the crest), then recovered with its skin (still bearing the plumage), and its feet were gilded. The task of carving it was allotted to the most eminent guest, who carried it out to the applause of the company present and then made a vow to perform some exceptional deed, for example in a war venture or in the service of his lady or of God.

peanut ARACHIDE

The edible seed of a widely cultivated tropical plant. Originating in South America, the plant was introduced into Africa by the Portuguese slave traders and widely grown from the colonial era onwards. It is also grown in India and the United States. Each pod matures underground and contains from two to four seeds, also called groundnuts or sometimes ground pistachios.

In its country of origin and in Africa, the plant is still grown for food – the seeds may either be made into a paste, grilled (broiled), or served in a variety of dishes. In Egypt they are made into cakes. However, it is now primarily an oil crop. Groundnut oil, which has a neutral flavour, is one of the most widely used cooking oils as it is very stable. The same oil can be used for frying over and over again and it can be heated to high temperatures without losing its qualities. It is also suitable for mild-flavoured salad dressings. Furthermore, groundnut oil plays an important role in the canning industry and in the manufacture of margarine. Raw groundnuts have a high energy value (560 Cal per 100 g (4 oz)).

Grilled and salted peanuts are served as cocktail snacks. They can replace pine kernels in salads and almonds and pistachios in pâtisserie. In the United States they are made into peanut butter, which is very nutritious and is eaten in sandwiches, on canapés, etc.

pear POIRE

The fruit of the pear tree, which narrows towards the stalk and has a yellow, brown, red, or green skin, a fine white slightly granular flesh, and a central core. The tree is native to Asia Minor and grew wild in prehistoric times. It was known to the Greeks and was even more popular with the Romans, who ate it raw, cooked, or dried. They also used to prepare an alcoholic drink with the fruit.

Today there are countless varieties of pears, produced by progressive selection of cultivated varieties. Olivier de Serres sang their praises: 'The little Muscadine is the finest variety of them all. The Dorée is so called because of its golden colour on the side facing the sun; the Muscatèles smell of musk; the Brute-Bonne is named after its unappealing shape and its excellent taste. Of the summer pears, it is the Dorée that has pride of place; of the autumn pears, it is the Bergamot, and of the winter pears, it is the Williams Bon-Chrétien.'

Although certain names have changed, the varieties remain the same. A distinction is made between summer, autumn, and winter pears, which can be either dessert or cooking varieties. The fruit is used not only in a very wide range of desserts, but also in some meat dishes, confectionery (jams, crystallized (candied) fruit, etc.), and in distilling.

The first pears ripen in mid-July, but the main season is between September and January. The pear is the third most popular fruit in France. Most French varieties come from the southeast, Lot-et-Garonne, Normandy, and Maine-et-Loire. Pears are also imported from Argentina, South Africa, and Australia. In Britain many of the same varieties are grown or imported.

Pears have an energy value of 61 Cal per 100 g and are a source of vitamins C, B_1, and B_2 and potassium.

Dessert pears can be eaten raw as a table fruit or used in fruit salads, borders, etc. In the latter case they should be sprinkled with lemon juice to prevent discoloration as the flesh oxidizes quickly. Most of the cooking varieties have now disappeared and dessert pears are used instead. Nevertheless, the flavour of the Curé and Belle Angevine only becomes apparent when they have been cooked.

Pears are used in numerous desserts, including mousses, charlottes, soufflés, tarts, ice creams, sorbets, compotes, etc., and in a variety of specialities (bourdalou, cardinal, Condé, Belle-Hélène, *à l'impératrice*, etc.). Pears can also be cooked with poultry and game (e.g. duck, hare) and can be prepared as hors d'oeuvres (filled with Roquefort butter, for example). Dried pears are used especially for compotes and to accompany savoury dishes. The most common variety of pear that is canned in syrup is the Williams Bon-Chrétien, which is also used for making pear brandy and pear liqueur. The brandy (sometimes called 'Williamine') is allowed to mature for a few months in an earthenware jar or bottle; it develops a delicate bouquet very much like the natural fragrance of the fruit, which is intensified by serving it in chilled glasses. Pear liqueur, which is not as highly regarded, is made either from diluted sweetened brandy or from a mixture of steeping and distillation. Both may be drunk as digestives and used in certain desserts (ice creams, soufflés, fruit salads).

RECIPES

Pear charlotte CHARLOTTE AUX POIRES (from a recipe by Henri Boutier) Put 15 g (½ oz, 2 envelopes) gelatine to soften in 5 tablespoons (6 tablespoons cold water. Rub 350 g (12 oz) drained canned pears through a sieve and warm the pulp gently in a saucepan. Add the softened gelatine to the pear purée and stir to dissolve. Cut 350 g (12 oz) drained canned pears into 1-cm (½-in) cubes. Whip 250 g (9 oz) whipping cream with 20 g (¾ oz, scant ¼ cup) icing (confectioners') sugar.

Whisk 2 egg whites with 50 g (2 oz, 4 tablespoons, firmly packed) sugar until they form stiff peaks.

Line a charlotte mould with a ring of greaseproof (waxed) paper. Line the bottom and the sides with sponge fingers (ladyfingers) trimmed at the ends to the height of the mould. Pour the pear and gelatine mixture into a large bowl, add the diced pears and 2 cl (1½ tablespoons, 2 tablespoons) pear brandy, then incorporate the cream and the egg whites, using a spatula. Pour this mixture into the charlotte mould and chill in the refrigerator for about 10 hours until set.

Turn the charlotte out onto a serving dish and surround it with a ring of raspberry sauce. Serve the remainder of the sauce in a sauceboat.

Poirissimo (from a recipe by Christiane Massia) This dessert consists of pear compote, pear conserve, pears in wine, pear tart, and pear granita, a small portion of each being carefully arranged on individual plates. For all the recipes, the pears must be peeled quickly just before they are required, to prevent discoloration.

■ *Compote*: peel the pears, cut them into quarters, and cook them for 10 minutes over a brisk heat in a covered saucepan with sugar, lemon juice, and a little water.

■ *Conserve*: allow 750 g (1¾ lb, 3½ cups) sugar and 1 dl (6 tablespoons, scant ½ cup) water per kg (2¼ lb) fruit. Boil the sugar and water until the syrup coats the back of a spoon. Add the sliced pears to the syrup, together with vanilla essence (extract), and cook until the fruit is tender.

■ *Pears in wine*: boil a mixture of wine and honey, reducing it by half. Peel some small ripe pears without removing the stalks and cook them in the honey-and-wine mixture for 15 minutes. Cool and add some cassis (blackcurrant liqueur) to the wine syrup.

■ *Tart*: roll out some shortcrust pastry (basic pie dough) into a circle and cover with slices of pear sprinkled with lemon juice. Sprinkle with granulated sugar and cook for 20 minutes in the oven at 220 C (425 F, gas 7). Serve warm.

variety	season	characteristics
Beurré-Hardy	September to mid-November	delicate fruit, excellent quality
Comice, Doyenné-du-Comice	mid-September to January	fruit often very large; aromatic, melting, juicy, and sweet
Conference	mid-September to February	juicy, aromatic, and firm flesh; elongated shape
Passe-Crassane	November to May	fruit often very plump; flesh tender, very juicy, sometimes gritty and firm
Williams Bon-Chrétien	August, September	sweet, juicy, and fragrant; stands up very well to cooking

■ *Granita* (to be prepared the day before): make a purée with some very ripe pears and a little lemon juice and place it in the freezer. When it begins to solidify, put it through the blender, adding sugar, lemon juice, and a little pear liqueur. Return to the freezer and repeat the operation once. The resulting granita must have the colour and consistency of snow.

Wild duck with pears CANARD SAUVAGE AUX POIRES (from a recipe by Gérald Goutagny) Pluck, draw, and season a small wild duck. Roast it for approximately 30 minutes so that the flesh remains pink and leave it in its cooking dish. Make a caramel with 2 tablespoons (3 tablespoons) caster (superfine) sugar and add approximately 1.5 dl (¼ pint, ⅔ cup) red wine, a small stick of cinnamon, 6 coriander seeds, 6 black peppercorns, and the zest of an orange and a lemon. Bring it to the boil and cook 2 peeled pears in it for no longer than 15 minutes.

Remove the breast fillets of the duck, bone the legs, and put the carcass and bones to one side. Cut the pears in half, slice them, and keep them warm. Dilute the duck cooking juices with 1.5 dl (¼ pint, ⅔ cup) red wine. Add the carcass and the pear cooking syrup. Bring to the boil, reduce, and then strain. Cut the duck fillets and leg meat into thin slices. Cover with the sauce and surround with slices of pear (the finished dish may be warmed up for 30 seconds in a microwave oven just before serving).

pecan nut

NOIX DE PACANE

The fruit of a tall tree found in the north-eastern United States. It has a smooth brown fragile shell enclosing a bilobed brown kernel looking and tasting something like a walnut. Pecan pie is very popular.

Pécharmant

A red AOC wine from the Bergerac region, for which the same grape varieties as those in the Bordeaux vineyard are used.

Pecorino

An Italian ewes'-milk *grana* (grainy) cheese. Pecorino is hard-pressed with a yellow crust when mature (those made in Siena have a red crust). The name is derived from the Italian word for ewe (*pecora*). The cheese was praised by Pliny and Columella, who described its manufacture in *De re rustica*. Pecorino cheese has a white, cream, or straw-yellow centre, depending on its degree of maturity. It is produced from October to June in southern Italy. There are several varieties, the best known being Pecorino Romano, a cooked cheese from Lazion. It is matured for at least eight months and contains 36% fat. It is manufactured in cylinders 20–26 cm (8–10 in) in diameter and 14–22 cm (4–8 in) high. It has a strong flavour, and is used as a table cheese or, when sufficiently aged, as a condiment like

Parmesan cheese. Pecorino Siciliano and Pecorino Sardo, the Sicilian and Sardinian varieties, contain more fat and are uncooked cheeses. They have an equally strong flavour.

pectin PECTINE

A natural gelling agent found in plants. It is a polysaccharide and is especially abundant in certain fruits (blackberries, apples, quinces, redcurrants, oranges, lemons, etc.). Pectin can be extracted on an industrial scale from dried apple marc.

Pectin is an important ingredient in making jams and jellies. When making jellies and marmalades, a small muslin (cheesecloth) bag containing the seeds and skins of apples, quinces, and citrus fruit is boiled with the sugar and fruit juice; the pectin from the seeds and skins is released and helps set the jelly.

pediment SOCLE

An element of food presentation which was once very popular but is not often used today. Pediments of rice shaped in dariole moulds to accompany eggs or small pieces of meat remains a classic method. In catering, pediments are used for cold dishes (whole fish, poultry suprêmes, medallions of foie gras, etc.), which have been set in a mould with milk and gelatine and are cut as desired.

In former decorative cookery, pieces of meat, poultry, and fish were arranged on elaborate pediments. Turkey was served on a pediment made from 'a mixture of ordinary very white lard with a proportionate quantity of kidney and mutton fat, which must be very pure and very fresh. All filaments, fibres, and pieces of skin must be removed; it should then be cut into small pieces and soaked in water for at least four hours' (Urbain Dubois and Émile Bernard). Like *pièces montées*, pediments were influenced by architecture and by the animal and floral world; their shapes and ornamentation were very varied: 'bastions, crowns, satyrs, angels' heads, peasants, sailors, swans, wings, dolphins, claws, animals and flowers moulded in lard, butter, and wax, etc.' Carême left many designs for pediments.

peeling ÉPLUCHAGE

The action of removing the skin of fruits and vegetables. The French term is also used for the removal of stalks, ribs, wilted leaves, and roots of salad plants, spinach, and cabbage.

Peeling is generally done by hand, using a knife or peeler, although sometimes in restaurants an electric peeling machine is used; this reduces waste to 5%, whereas up to 25% can be wasted in peeling by hand. When peeling potatoes in this way, however, any 'eyes' have to be picked out afterwards. The peelings are not always thrown away: cabbage stalks are kept for soups; cucumber peel is sometimes used to decorate cocktail glasses; and truffle parings are as precious as the tuffle itself.

Peking duck
CANARD À LA PÉKINOISE

A famous dish from classical Mandarin cookery. Its preparation is intricate and involved. The duck should be drawn, washed, rapidly scalded, and dried. An air pump is used to separate the skin from the flesh, so that it swells outwards. The duck is then stuffed with a mixture of spring onions (scallions), aniseed, ginger, celery, and sesame oil, sewn up, then hung, preferably in a draught, where it is coated every half hour with a mixture of honey and flour. After three hours it is roasted in the oven and basted with its own juice and a little sesame oil.

There is a precise ritual for serving Peking duck: the skin is cut into rectangles of 3 × 4 cm (1¼ × 1½ in), which, in theory, are the only parts of the bird to be eaten, the meat being saved for other uses. In common practice, however, the meat is also cut into pieces and rolled in the pancakes. Using chopsticks, a rectangle of the skin is placed on a small hot savoury pancake; to this is added a piece of spring onion, which has been dipped in a sauce with a sour plum base; the pancake is covered with a little sugar and garlic, rolled up, still using the chopsticks, and eaten. Apart from requiring that only the skin is served, tradition also dictates that the carved re-formed duck is presented in advance to the diners.

pékinoise (à la)

A method of preparing pieces of fried fish or scampi in batter served with a sweet-and-sour sauce, inspired by Chinese cookery. The sauce is made with chopped garlic and onions mixed with slivers of ginger. These are braised in butter, then sprinkled with sugar. Soy sauce is added, followed by fresh tomato juice. The mixture is thickened with cornflour (cornstarch) and flavoured with Chinese mushrooms.

pelamid PÉLAMIDE

Another name for the bonito, one of the smallest members of the tuna family. The pelamid is no more than 70 cm (28 in) long and lives in warm seas. All recipes for tuna can be prepared with pelamid. Its flesh is considered to have a finer flavour and to be less dense than that of the albacore.

Pélardon

A small goats'-milk cheese from Cévennes (45% fat content), with a soft white centre and a very fine natural crust. Its full name depends on the region where it is produced: in Cévennes it is known as Pélardon des Cévennes; in the Ardèche as Pélardon de Ruoms; and in Gard, where it is often steeped in white wine, it is called Pélardon d'Anduze (or sometimes Péraldou). It measures 6–7 cm (2½ in) in diameter and is 2.5–3 cm (1 in) thick. This cheese is made on the farm and has a delicious nutty flavour. It is in season from May to November.

Pellaprat (Henri Paul)

French chef (born Paris, 1869; died Paris, 1950). After serving his apprenticeship with Pons, a Parisian pastrycook, Pellaprat obtained work at the Champeaux and then became assistant chef to Casimir Moisson at the Maison Dorée, where eventually he became the chef. In the army he was assigned to the officers' mess at Verdun. Pellaprat became a cookery instructor at the Cordon-Bleu schools in Paris and wrote many books on the culinary art that are still considered to be important today: *L'Art Culinaire moderne* (first edition 1935), *La Cuisine familiale et pratique*, and *Le Poisson dans la cuisine française*.

pelle

The French name for various kitchen utensils designed for lifting foods: tart or pie slice, fish slice, flour scoop, and oven shovel. Tart or pie slices can be made of porcelain, earthenware, stainless steel, or silver-plate and are often manufactured to match the cutlery or crockery. They can also be used for cakes, ice creams, etc. Fish slices are made of stainless steel or silverplate. They are sometimes slightly concave and may be slotted for lifting large fish. Flour scoops are used for scooping up flour, sugar, and other dry ingredients. Oven shovels are made of wood and have handles 2 metres (6½ ft) long. They are used in bakeries and large kitchens to remove large baking sheets of pastries from the oven.

pelmieni

A type of Russian ravioli originating from Siberia, made with noodle dough and stuffed with minced (ground) meat, potato purée with cheese, or with chicken. The pelmieni are cooked in boiling salted water and served with melted butter poured over them. Soured (dairy sour) cream, or meat juice mixed with lemon juice, can be served separately.

pelure d'oignon

A French term, meaning literally 'onion peel', that is sometimes used to describe the shade of red that certain wines acquire with age and that other rosé wines possess naturally.

pemmican

A North American Indian cake of dried and pounded meat mixed with melted fat, a food product famous since the early expeditions to North America. It is no longer in demand.

Pemmican could be kept for a long time, did not deteriorate, and took up little space. It was first made from the meat of bison (wild ox, now almost completely extinct) or from venison. The rump of the animal was cut into thin slices, dried in the sun, and pounded finely. This meat powder was then mixed with melted fat in the proportion of two parts meat to one part fat and enclosed in bags made from the animal's skin. It was eaten raw or boiled in water.

The word comes from the Algonquian *pime*, meaning fat or grease.

pepper POIVRE

A condiment derived from the pepper plant (*Piper nigrum*), a climbing vine native to India, Java, and the Sunda Islands. The plant produces berry-like fruits (peppercorns) which ripen from green, to red, and finally to brown. Peppercorns harvested at various stages of maturity provide the following types of pepper:

● *black pepper*, whole red peppercorns sold dried: very strong and pungent;
● *green pepper*, unripe peppercorns sold dried or pickled in vinegar or brine: less pungent and more fruity;
● *white pepper*, ripe peppercorns with the outer husk removed by rubbing in salt water: less spicy and particularly suitable for seasoning white sauces;
● *grey pepper*, a mixture of black and white pepper.

The name 'pepper' is also used loosely for several other seasonings and condiments, notably cayenne, paprika, and chilli powder (all derived from varieties of capsicum).

Pepper is sold either as peppercorns or ready-ground. The peppercorns must be solid, compact, of uniform colour, and they must not crumble. Ground pepper quickly loses its flavour and aroma; it is therefore best to buy whole peppercorns and grind or crush them yourself as required.

Since time immemorial, pepper has been the most popular and most widespread spice in the world. It had been in general use in India and China for centuries before Alexander the Great introduced it into Greece. The Romans used to adulterate pepper by adding juniper berries to it. Apicius even recommended its use in sweet desserts, but more importantly he suggested using it to disguise the insipid taste of boiled dishes and to hide the overpowering taste of gamey meats (as Taillevent did at a later time). Although it occupied an important place in cooking as early as the Middle Ages, it was still rare and expensive, and several times it served as exchange currency, to pay taxes or ransoms. The voyages of the great explorers were undertaken primarily to find a sure supply of spices. The struggle between the Venetians and the Dutch for the monopoly of pepper lasted until the end of the 18th century. Over the course of the centuries, pepper became so popular that mixtures of pepper and other spices were developed. Although the craze for exotic spices died down after the Renaissance, pepper remained in favour with the cooks of the western world and came into general use, as a complement to salt, for the majority of seasonings. The aptly named Pierre Poivre, governor of Fort-de-France (Martinique) in the 1770s, introduced pepper plant cultivation on the island of Bourbon (Réunion); until then it had been practised solely in Asia. Today, the annual consumption of pepper in France is 100 g (4 oz) per person.

Pepper owes its piquant flavour to essential oils, a sharp resin, and a crystalline substance, piperin. Rich in mineral salts, it stimulates the appetite and enhances digestion, but is an irritant when taken in large quantities.

□ **Pepper in cooking** Several dishes take their name and character from pepper: the French poivrade sauce, steak *au poivre*, the German *Pfefferkuchen* (gingerbread, literally pepper cake), and the Dutch 'pepper pot' (a spicy ragout of mutton with onion). Whenever a recipe states 'adjust the seasoning', salt and pepper are added at the discretion of the cook. Pepper is required in practically all savoury dishes, whether they are served hot or cold. Whole peppercorns are used in court-bouillons, marinades, and pickles; crushed pepper for grills, certain raw vegetable dishes, forcemeats, and hashes; and freshly ground pepper for salads and cooked dishes. A 'turn of the pepper mill' produces a very spicy fresh seasoning, whereas a 'pinch of pepper' gives a more discreet flavour to sauces and stews. Green peppercorns are used in specific dishes, such as *canard poêlé*, fish terrines, and avocado salad.

perch PERCHE

A freshwater fish belonging to the genus *Perca*. The common or river perch (*P. fluviatilis*) is considered in France to be one of the best freshwater fish. It is usually 25–35 cm (10–14 in) long, but can grow up to 50–60 cm (1½–2 ft) and weigh up to 3 kg (6½ lb), which is exceptional, as the fish grows slowly. It has a humped greenish-brown back marked with dark bands and bearing two dorsal fins, the first of which is spiny; the remaining fins are red. Perch must be scaled as soon as they are caught, otherwise the task becomes impossible. Small perch are fried, medium ones are prepared *à la meunière*, or in a stew, and large ones can be stuffed, like shad.

Other spiny-finned fish nicknamed 'perch' by the French include the sunfish, which is imported from the United States; the black bass; the small gudgeon, which is usually fried; and the sea bass.

percolator PERCOLATEUR

A big pot used in cafés to make large quantities of coffee and to keep it hot. It consists of two superimposed cylinders, the upper cylinder containing coffee grounds in a filter. Water is poured into the lower cylinder and heated. It is forced up a tube by the pressure of the steam into the upper cylinder, where it filters down through the ground coffee back into the lower container. The word comes from the Latin *percolare*, from *per* (through) + *colare* (to strain). The percolator is being increasingly replaced by the espresso coffee machine, which prepares and serves coffee by the cup. Certain coffee makers for domestic use work on the same principle and are also called percolators.

Pérignon (Dom Pierre)

French Benedictine monk (born Sainte-Menehould, 1638; died Épernay, 1715) whose name is associated with champagne of fine quality. While in charge of the wine cellars at the Abbey of Hautvillers, near Épernay, he evolved a method of blending the different wines from various plots to produce a harmonious whole; this making of the cuvée (a blend of champagnes) was a major development. Dom Pérignon is also credited with the rediscovery of the use of cork for sealing bottles, thereby retaining in the bottle the natural effervescence so pronounced in the wines of the Champagne region. He was also able to control its force by adding

sugar to the wine. The results were so successful that in his own lifetime customers began to ask specifically for Pérignon wines. It is sometimes erroneously claimed that he discovered champagne (until 1660 the region was noted for its red wines); nevertheless, the importance of his work in developing it cannot be overestimated. Unfortunately the records of Hautvillers were lost at the time of the French Revolution. Dom Pérignon's name is attached to the luxury cuvée made by Moët et Chandon, who now own the Abbey.

Périgord

Although certain gourmets regard the cuisine of this region as one of the best regional cuisines in France, it owes its reputation as much to the natural resources of the region as to the native talent of its cooks. The low limestone plateaux, planted with chestnut trees, walnut trees, and common oaks, is ideal terrain for finding truffles, ceps, chanterelles, and other types of mushroom and it provides good shelter for game. The wide alluvial valleys of the Dordogne and its tributaries have fields full of cereal crops, vegetables, and market garden produce, as well as orchards and vineyards, while the plains provide pasture for the sheep and cattle of Périgord. The poultry of the region is particularly famous, especially the geese and ducks. The pork of Périgord has an excellent flavour and can be prepared in many delicious ways. The rivers and pools abound with fish, and crayfish can still be found. Among the notable fish dishes are carp stuffed with foie gras, trout (grilled, (broiled), marinated, stuffed, cooked with truffles, or cooked *en papillote* in the ashes), eel in red wine, and fried gudgeon with vinegar or gudgeon *aux gardèches* in an omelette. Traditional salt cod dishes include salt cod brandade, salt cod salad, and salt cod with tomato.

The three outstanding features of the cuisine of Périgord are foie gras, confit of goose, duck, or pork (served with sorrel purée, new peas, and dried or preserved apples), and, of course, truffles. The latter in particular are used as a filling for omelettes, or are served with larks or quail, but can also be cooked in ashes, *à la serviette*, or in white wine. The cuisine of this region also makes much use of walnut oil, goose fat, and lard.

The soups of Périgord are usually seasoned with the classic fricassée périgourdine or enriched with a forcemeat. The traditional chabrot (a little red wine) is added to the last few spoonfuls of soup in the dish. The most popular soups include haricot (navy) bean or broad (fava) bean soup from Thiviers, sometimes garnished with bacon rind; blanched sorrel soup; tourin; bouillon de noces made with four kinds of meat; veal pot-au-feu; stuffed chicken in the pot; *bougras* (a cabbage, leek, and potato soup cooked in a fricassée périgourdine); *sobronade* (a country soup made with salt and fresh pork, haricot beans, leeks, celery, and root vegetables); and soups made with goose or turkey giblets, pigs' heads, miques, cabbage, oxtail, hare, rabbit, or partridge.

The range of charcuterie is impressive: besides the famous pâtés de foie gras, there are ballottines of turkey or partridge, goose or pig's rillons, stuffed goose necks, preserved pork rind, and Périgord black puddings (blood sausages) (made from blood mixed with meat from the pig's neck or head) cooked in stock with vegetables and herbs.

The poultry (turkey or goose) is excellent with truffles but may also be stuffed with ceps or chestnuts or grilled, roasted, or stewed. Turkey giblets are made into tarts. Chickens are prepared with rouilleuse sauce (made with blood), spatchcocked, fried with verjuice, or cooked *à la mode de Sorges* or in pot-au-feu. The traditional dish known as sanguette, is becoming increasingly rare. Omelettes can be flavoured with foie gras fat or garnished with various mushrooms (especially ceps, chanterelles, or morels) and also with black salsify or sorrel.

Of the game dishes, hare *à la royale* is highly regarded, although some people believe that it originated in Poitou. Hare can also be cooked *en cabessal*, made into civets, or served with cornmeal porridge. Rabbits may be stuffed, roasted, braised, or simmered in white wine (especially young rabbits). Partridges are stuffed with foie gras, and larks are grilled with chestnuts.

Beef is made into succulent dishes such as fillet steak *à la sarladaise*, grilled entrecôte *à la périgourdine*, braised loin of beef (braising steak) with cornmeal porridge or onions, beef in red wine, braised oxtail, or ox (beef) tongue with tomato sauce or gherkins. Veal is cooked in the usual ways, but there is also a speciality made with veal tripe. Pork specialities of Périgord include enchaud (with or without truffles), roast pork with chestnuts, and stuffed sucking pig. Mutton is enjoyed in the form of gigot 'with sixty cloves of garlic' or with mixed beans and as stuffed shoulder.

The vegetables of Périgord are imaginatively prepared. Cep mushrooms are cooked *à la périgourdine* (stuffed or *en cocotte*); Casesar's mushrooms are grilled; morel mushrooms are braised in verjuice; and chanterelle mushrooms are served with parsley. Potatoes are cooked *à la sarladaise*, with ceps, stuffed, or as croquettes or potato cakes. The following vegetables may also be stuffed: artichoke hearts, onions, tomatoes, cabbage, courgettes (zucchini), and cucumbers. French (green) beans *à la périgourdine*, French beans with tomatoes, purée or ragout of broad beans, and chestnut purée are some more of the succulent vegetable dishes of this region. Salads, which are seasoned with walnut oil, include dandelion salad with fresh walnuts, endives (chicory) with chapons, purslane with hard-boiled (hard-cooked) eggs, cabbage salad, and truffle salad.

The best-known Périgord cheeses are the Cujassous cheeses of Dubjac, the Thiviers cheeses (dried on hay or wrapped in chestnut leaves), and Échourgnac Abbey cheese. There are also the Cabécou cheeses, rolled in vine leaves and steeped in jars with wine vinegar.

The large range of desserts includes blanched chestnuts or chestnut gâteau, aniseed tarts, crêpes or waffles, apple pancakes (called *Jacques*), mimosa-flower fritters, merveilles, and *cornuelles*. The Périgord marzipans, Périgueux *millasses* (tarts filled with almond-flavoured egg custard), Bergerac macaroons, and walnut or aniseed biscuits are less rustic specialities. Fruits are used for flans, tarts, flaugnardes, and clafoutis. Other notable desserts are *rasimat* (a gâteau made with walnuts, grapes, lemon, and quinces), set custards, and crème caramel.

The confectionery of the region includes stuffed prunes and walnuts, marrons glacés, sugar-coated chestnuts, and chocolate truffles (a Périgord speciality).

Nearly all Périgord wines come from the vineyards of Bergerac. The whites include Monbazillac, Bergerac, Côtes-de-Bergerac, Côtes-de-Saussignac, Montravel, and Rosette, and the reds Pécharmant, Bergerac, and Côtes-de-Bergerac.

Private distillers make some good-quality brandies from plums, grapes, cherries, and pears. Finally, there are some excellent home-made liqueurs, such as walnut cordial, and quince, gin, plum, or blackcurrant ratafias.

périgourdine (à la)

Describing egg, meat, poultry, or game dishes served with périgourdine sauce or Périgueux sauce. Périgourdine sauce consists of a demi-glace sauce enriched with a little foie gras purée and truffles cut into large slices (or diced).

Many other dishes from the Périgord region are described as *à la périgourdine* despite the fact that they contain neither foie gras nor truffles.

RECIPE

Eggs en cocotte à la périgourdine OEUFS EN COCOTTE À LA PÉRIGOUR-DINE Butter some ramekins and line them with a purée of foie gras. Break 1 egg into each ramekin, place a knob of butter on top of each yolk, and cook in a bain-marie in the oven. When serving, surround the yolks with a ring of Périgueux sauce.

Périgueux

A Madeira sauce containing finely diced or chopped truffles. It is served with small cuts of meat, poultry, or game, bouchées, etc; these preparations are described as *Périgueux* or *à la périgourdine*.

RECIPES

Périgueux sauce SAUCE PÉRI-GUEUX Clean, peel, and dice some truffles and gently braise them in butter

for 10 minutes. Then add them to some Madeira sauce just before mixing in the cornflour (cornstarch) and Madeira.

Pheasant Périgueux FAISAN PÉRI-GUEUX Pluck, singe, and gut a pheasant. Season the carcass inside and out with salt and pepper, and insert some slices of truffle between the skin and flesh. Fry the truffled pheasant in butter in a heavy-based saucepan and arrange on a slice of bread fried in butter. Prepare some Périgueux sauce with the cooking juices and serve separately. The dish can be garnished with large quenelles of truffled game forcemeat.

permit CONGÉ

An official document that must accompany wines and spirits in circulation within France, attesting that the required excise tax has been paid before the wine was put on the market. Wines intended for export must be accompanied by a paper known as an *acquit*.

Pernand-Vergelesses

AOC white and red Burgundies of the Côte de Beaune. Sections of the famous vineyards of Corton and Corton-Charlemagne lie within its limits and the Pernand wines are perhaps best known for these great whites, though the red wines can also be very good.

Pernod

See *absinthe, pastis.*

perry POIRÉ

A fermented drink made like cider but with pear instead of apple juice. It has been made since ancient times in western France: Normandy, Brittany, and Maine. Sparkling perry is an inexpensive alcoholic drink in the UK.

The French word (*poiré*) should not be confused with the pear alcool blanc, referred to in full as Poire William.

persane (à la)

Describing a preparation of mutton or lamb noisettes or chops garnished with slices of fried aubergine (eggplant), fried onions, and tomato stewed with peppers. The cooking juices are flavoured with tomato and spooned over the garnishes. Pilaf *à la persane*, more obviously influenced by Iranian cuisine, consists of a mixture of rice and diced mutton fried with onions, which is simmered in stock with pepper and various condiments. The dish is finally sprinkled with melted mutton fat.

persicot

An ancient home-made liqueur made by steeping peach stones, almonds, and spices in sweetened alcohol. Persicot is used mainly for flavouring pastries.

persillade

A mixture of chopped parsley and garlic, which is added to certain dishes at the end of the cooking time.

Beef persillade is a piece of leftover boiled beef sautéed in oil and seasoned with persillade. Persillade mixed with fresh breadcrumbs provides the finishing touch to a loin of lamb *persillé* and stuffed tomatoes *à la provençale*. It is also a basic ingredient in snails *à la bourguignonne*.

The word *persillé* is also used to describe dishes finished off with persillade or with chopped fresh parsley (for example, potatoes or sautéed tomatoes) and for dishes in which a large quantity of chopped parsley is used, such as ham with parsley (*jambon persillé*).

persillé

The French term to describe certain cheeses veined with bluish-green moulds. The term is often included in the name of the cheese. For example, Persillé des Aravis, Persillé de Thônes, and Persillé du Grand-Bornand are Savoyard goats'-milk cheeses (45% fat) with pressed centres and brushed natural crusts. They have a strong flavour and are manufactured in cylinders 8–10 cm (3–4 in) in diameter and 12–15 cm (5–6 in) high. Persillé du Mont-Cenis is made with a mixture of cows' and goats' milk (45% fat) and has a lightly pressed centre and a natural crust. It also has a strong flavour and is sold in cylinders 30 cm (12 in) in diameter and 15 cm (6 in) high.

The word *persillé* is also used to describe dishes prepared with persillade and a piece of top-quality beef flecked with fat.

persimmon   KAKI

The fruit of a tree of Japanese origin that has been cultivated for centuries in China and Japan and is now cultivated commercially in Italy and other Mediterranean countries and also in the Middle East and the United States. The Japanese persimmon resembles an orange tomato, with soft sweetish orange-red flesh and up to eight seeds, depending on the variety. It contains 64 Cal per 100 g and is quite rich in potassium (200 mg) and also in vitamin C (7–22 mg). It should be eaten when very ripe, otherwise it has a bitter taste. When it ripens, the skin becomes transparent. The flesh is usually eaten fresh, but it can be made into compotes, jams, or sorbets or cooked *à l'impératrice*.

The Sharon fruit is similar to a persimmon but the flesh is sweeter, even when firm and slightly underripe. It can be used in the same recipes as the persimmon.

RECIPE

Iced persimmon à la créole   KAKIS GLACÉS À LA CRÉOLE   Cut a hole in the fruit around the stalk and scoop out the pulp with a teaspoon, taking care not to break the skin. Sprinkle a little marc brandy or liqueur into each fruit and leave to macerate for 1 hour. Mix the fruit pulp with some pineapple ice (1 tablespoon pulp to 3–4 tablespoons pineapple ice). Rub the mixture through a fine sieve and fill the fruit shells with the cream. Freeze for about 1 hour before serving.

pestle   PILON

A utensil used for crushing or pounding food in a mortar. It can be used for such items as garlic, tomatoes, butter, coarse salt, spices, nuts, parsley, or bay leaves. The rounded head may be integral with a short stem or may fit onto a separate handle. The purée pestle, nicknamed *champignon* (mushroom) in French, has a relatively long handle ending in a large solid head made of boxwood, beech, or lignum vitae, or sometimes of perforated metal. It is used for rubbing purées, forcemeats, etc., through a sieve and for pressing poultry carcasses in a strainer to extract the juices.

pétafine

A speciality from Dauphiné. Small goats'-milk and cows'-milk farmhouse cheeses, thoroughly drained (but not dry), are kneaded with yeast (dry cheeses are soaked in hot milk), then mixed with oil, a good-quality champagne, and a little anisette, and seasoned with salt and pepper. Pétafine must be steeped for a few days.

pétéram

A well-known speciality from Luchon, in the Haute-Garonne. It is a stew of sheep's feet and tripe, ham, calf's mesentery, bacon, potatoes, garlic, and herbs, cooked slowly over a period of ten hours in dry white wine.

pétillant

The term used to describe wine with a slight sparkle. This is sometimes naturally present but may also be encouraged and regulated. Although pétillant wines are made all over the world, French law requires that those produced in France must not have more than 2 atmospheres of pressure under their corks.

petit-beurre

A small square or rectangular biscuit (cookie) with fluted edges. The dough is made with flour, sugar, and fresh butter, but contains no eggs. Petits-beurres are a speciality of Nantes, where they are manufactured on an industrial scale. They are eaten for afternoon tea or served with various desserts; they are also used as an ingredient in certain desserts.

petit déjeuner

The first meal of the day in France. The French, or continental, breakfast typically consists of a cup of tea, coffee, café au lait, or hot chocolate, with buttered croissants, bread, or *biscottes* spread with jam or honey. It is very small compared with the traditional English breakfast, or even with the German or Scandinavian breakfast, which may include boiled eggs, cheeses and sausages, compotes, and fruit juices.

The petit déjeuner used to be more substantial. Known simply as *déjeuner* (meaning literally 'to break the fast'), it consisted of a bowl of soup sometimes accompanied by wine and meat (for the men). The main meal (*dîner*) was taken at midday. At the time of the Revolution, however, it became customary to eat dîner at the end of the afternoon, when the business of the day was completed, and a second 'breakfast' was needed to bridge the gap between the two meals. So the midday meal became known as déjeuner and a smaller petit déjeuner was consumed first thing in the morning.

petit-duc

A garnish for small pieces of meat, consisting of tartlets filled with chicken purée with cream, little bunches of asparagus tips, and slices of truffle. Petit-duc dishes are less prestigious versions of grand-duc dishes.

petite marmite

A type of pot-au-feu served in the receptacle in which it was cooked (originally an earthenware pot, now often small individual dishes made of flameproof procelain). The petite marmite was created in Paris in 1867, by Modeste Magny, in his famous restaurant. In theory it should contain lean beef, oxtail, chicken, marrow bone, stock-pot vegetables, and small cabbage balls. The soup is usually served with grated cheese, croutons spread with rounds of marrow and sprinkled with pepper, or slices of a long thin French loaf crisped in the oven and sprinkled with fat from the stew.

RECIPE

Petite marmite à la parisienne Pour 2.5 litres (4½ pints, 5½ pints) cold consommé into a pan. Add 500 g (18 oz) rump roast (standing rump) and 250 g (9 oz) short rib of beef. Bring to the boil and skim. Then add 100 g (4 oz) chopped carrots, 75 g (3 oz) chopped turnips, 75 g (3 oz) leeks (white part only, cut into chunks), 2 baby onions browned in a dry frying pan (skillet), 50 g (2 oz) celery hearts cut into small pieces and blanched, and 100 g (4 oz) cabbage blanched in salted water, cooled, and rolled into tight balls. Simmer these ingredients for 3 hours, occasionally adding a little consommé to compensate for the evaporation.

Lightly brown 2 sets of chicken giblets in the oven, add them to the pan, and cook for a further 50 minutes. Finally, add a large marrow bone wrapped in muslin (cheesecloth) and simmer for another 10 minutes. Skim off the surplus fat, unwrap the marrow bone, and replace it in the pan. Serve the soup hot with small slices from a long thin French loaf that have been crisped in the oven and sprinkled with a little fat from the stew. Spread some of the bread with bone marrow and season with freshly ground pepper.

petit four

A small fancy biscuit (cookie), cake, or item of confectionery. The name, according to Carême, dates back to the 18th century, when ovens were made of brick and small items had to be cooked *à petit four* (i.e. at a very low temperature), after large cakes had been taken out and the temperature had dropped.

After the bonbons, dragées, marzipans, pralines, and crystallized fruits that were in vogue during the Renaissance and in the reign of Louis XIV, other titbits were created. They required imagination and flair by the pastrycooks to reproduce the large-scale decorations in miniature. Carême himself attached great importance to the crisp petits fours known as *colifichets* – part of the pièces montées, which decorated the table and buffets. A colifichet is really a dry cake made for the birds but pastry cooks use the term to distinguish the pièces montées from the proper dishes. The elder Paul Coquelin, who became established at Passy in 1897, created 30 different types of petits fours – each one givven a female Christian name. Today, petits fours constitute an important part of pâtisserie. They are served mainly at buffets, lunches, or with cocktails, but also with tea, ice creams, and certain desserts. At a sophisticated meal in France, an assortment of petits fours (sometimes known as *mignardises*) may be served either with or after the dessert.

There are three categories of petits fours:

● *Plain petits fours*: These are dry biscuits (cookies) that keep well and are served with dessert custards, ice creams, and sorbets, and also with tea, liqueur wines, or dessert wines. They include tuiles, cigarettes, bâtonnets, palets, langues de chat, macaroons, small meringues, sponge fingers (ladyfingers), croquettes, small galettes, milanais, rochers, etc.

● *Fresh petits fours*: this category constitutes petits fours proper. It can be divided into three groups:
— Miniature reproductions of individual cakes (miniature éclairs, duchesses, choux, tartlets, barquettes, babas, etc.).
— Iced or glazed petits fours, which are the largest and most diverse group. Some consist of small geometric shapes of Genoese sponge cake filled with butter cream, ganache, confectioners' custard (pastry cream), or jam, glazed with apricot jam, iced (frosted), and decorated. Others are made with a base of almond paste, chocolate, nougatine, dacquoise, meringue, etc., topped with a square of Genoese sponge soaked in liqueur, a spoonful of cream, or diced crystallized (candied) or glacé fruit. They are then iced with fondant and decorated with piped icing (frosting), coated with chocolate, or dipped in boiled sugar and decorated with crystallized fruits, chopped almonds, or coconut.
— Sugar-coated fruits: these include prunes, dates, and cherries filled with almond paste and glazed with sugar; morello cherries and grapes coated with fondant icing; orange quarters or pineapple cubes glazed with caramel; aboukir almonds; green walnuts *en surprise*; etc.

● *Savoury petits fours*: these are served with apéritifs and cocktails and at receptions, lunches, etc. They are also referred to as *amuse-gueule* (cocktail snacks). They are made of a pastry base (matchsticks, straws, miniature turnovers, croissants, barquettes, bouchées, quiches, pizzas, etc.) and filled with a savoury filling, such as anchovy paste, flavoured butter, shellfish or foie gras mousse, cheese, smoked salmon, mayonnaise, vegetable or game purée, etc.

petit-lait

The French name for a by-product of milk, such as skimmed milk, buttermilk (liquid residue after butter has been separated from milk), or whey (the transparent pale yellow watery liquid that separates from the curd when milk is curdled).

Petit Maure

A cabaret that opened in Paris in 1618, on the corner of the Rue de Seine and the Rue Visconti. It was frequented by Voiture, Théophile de Viau, Colletet, Tallemant des Réaux, and – most notably – the poet Saint-Amant, who is said to have died there in 1661, after a violent beating occasioned by a rather biting epigram. In the following century, another Petit Maure was fashionable for a time. This was a small suburban restaurant at Vaugirard, where one could enjoy the strawberries and petits pois that grew in the surrounding district, drink the local wine, and eat the home-bred turkeys.

petit pois

Sea *pea*.

Petit-Suisse

A French cheese made with cows' milk enriched with cream, giving it a high fat content (60–75%). It is a fresh cheese, unsalted, smooth, and soft, sold in the form of 30-g (about 1-oz) wrapped cylinders. Originally, it weighed 60 g (2 oz) and was called Suisse. In spite of its name, it was first made not in Switzerland but in Normandy, in 1850, when a Swiss employee of a cheesemonger in Auvilliers had the idea of adding cream to the milk used to make the fresh Bondon cheeses. The larger cheeses are now known as double Petits-Suisses.

The cheese is served as a dessert, with sugar, honey, jam, or poached fruits, or as a savoury with salt, herbs, and pepper. It is also used to prepare cold emulsified sauces, to spread on canapés (mixed with paprika, chopped herbs, or raisins), and is added to the forcemeat for certain poultry (such as turkey and guinea fowl), to help make the flesh more tender.

pets-de-nonne

Soufflé fritters made of choux pastry, about the size of walnuts. They are fried in oil that is hot but not smoking so that the pastry swells up considerably into a light puffy ball. The name means literally 'nun's farts' and the fritters are therefore sometimes called *soupirs de nonne* (nun's sighs), thought to be less disrespectful, or *beignets venteux*. When they are cooked and golden brown, the fritters are sprinkled with sugar and served hot, sometimes with a fruit sauce. They can also be filled with cream or jam.

RECIPE

Pets-de-nonne   Make some choux pastry (see *chou*) with ¼ litre (8 fl oz, 1 cup) water, a pinch of salt, 2 tablespoons (3 tablespoons) caster (superfine) sugar, 65 g (2½ oz, 5 tablespoons) butter, 125 g (4½ oz, generous 1 cup) flour, and 3 or 4 eggs. Leave the dough to rest. Heat up some oil in a deep-fat fryer to 180 c (350 f). Drop teaspoons of the dough into the hot oil; when golden brown on one side (after about 2½ minutes), turn them over, if necessary, to cook the other side (another 2 minutes). Drain the fritters on absorbent kitchen paper and sprinkle with icing (confectioners') sugar.

Pézenas pie
PÂTÉ DE PÉZENAS

A small round pastry filled with a mixture of minced (ground) mutton, sheep's kidney fat, brown sugar, and lemon zest. It is served very hot as an entrée or even as a dessert (as recommended by Prosper Montagné). The recipe comes from Languedoc but it also claimed by Béziers, where small meat pies were being sold in the streets as early as the 17th century. According to A.-P. Alliès, a local historian, Lord Clive, viceroy and governor of India, spent the winter of 1766 at Pézenas for health reasons. During this period his Indian cook baked him some sweetened spiced mutton pies (the English were very partial to these) and the pastrycooks of Pézenas were inspired to make them themselves. They soon became popular throughout the region.

pflutters or floutes

Alsatian dumplings made with potato purée, beaten egg, and flour or semolina, sometimes moistened with milk; they are poached in boiling water and served as an entrée with melted butter. Pflutters can also be made into cakes and fried. In this case, the dough is rolled out and cut into shapes with a pastry cutter (cookie cutter) and they are served with a roast.

RECIPE

Pflutters Prepare 500 g (18 oz) very fine potato purée and mix with 2 eggs and about 75 g (3 oz, ¾ cup) flour to obtain a fairly stiff dough. Season with salt, pepper, and nutmeg. Shape the dough into balls and drop them into a saucepan of boiling salted water. Poach for 8–10 minutes, drain, and arrange in a buttered dish. Sprinkle with hot noisette butter in which fine stale breadcrumbs have been browned to give a crumbly topping.

pheasant FAISAN

A long-tailed game bird introduced into Europe from Asia in the early Middle Ages. In many countries shooting has considerably reduced the pheasant population, in spite of the periodic supply of reared birds. These are either released in January and allowed to breed in the wild, or else they are liberated just before the shoot. In the latter case, the flesh of the birds has less flavour than that of the truly wild pheasant. Hens and young cock pheasants can be roasted without being barded, but barding fat on the back and breast is necessary for old male birds. True connoisseurs prefer the hen pheasant to the cock as the hen has a finer flesh. The male bird is larger than the female. It is also more brightly coloured with iridescent blue and green feathers, bright fleshy wattles, longer tail feathers, and large leg spurs. Pheasants should be hung for a period of three days to two weeks, depending on taste and the weather, in a cool dry airy place. A bird has usually been hung for long enough when the tail feathers can be pulled out easily. Reared birds should not be hung but cooked immediately, like poultry.

The young pheasant can be distinguished from an old bird by the first wing-tip feather, which is pointed in a young bird and rounded in an old one. The upper part of the beak of a young bird is pliable to the touch. It is best roasted, or casseroled and flavoured with wine or spirits. A stock can be made from the carcass and used as a basis for sauce or consommé. A fricassee of pheasant can be made by cutting it into quarters (two suprêmes and two legs) or into six pieces (two wings, two legs, and two pieces of breast). Older birds can be prepared as a chartreuse (a mould made from game birds, cabbage, and other vegetables) or a salmis, accompanied by braised cabbage, cep mushrooms, fresh pasta, or apples with bacon and onions. Very old birds should be casseroled or made into pâtés or terrines. But the most decorative method of preparing pheasant is *à la Sainte-Alliance*, in which it is presented in all the glory of its magnificent plumage.

RECIPES

Preparation of pheasant PRÉPARATION DU FAISAN Keep the pheasant in the refrigerator for a few hours as this makes it easier to pluck. Begin by twisting the large wing feathers to remove them. Then pluck the remaining feathers in the following order: the body, legs, neck, and wings. Draw the bird in the same way as a chicken. Season the inside of the carcass with salt and pepper. Bard if necessary and truss the bird with the legs pressed as tightly as possible against the breast, especially if the bird is to be roasted.

COLD PHEASANT DISHES

Ballottine of pheasant in aspic BALLOTTINE DE FAISAN À LA GELÉE (from Carême's recipe) Take a Strasbourg foie gras. Soak in cold water and blanch. Cut each half into 4 fillets and trim. Pound 2 of these fillets in a mortar with the trimmings and the meat of a red partridge with an equal weight of pork fat. Season the mixture very well. Add 2 egg yolks and some cultivated mushrooms tossed in butter. Pound the lot thoroughly. Rub the stuffing through a quenelle sieve.

Carefully bone a well-hung fat pheasant. Lay it on a cloth and season very well. Lay on top of it half the stuffing, and then 3 fillets of foie gras, interspersing these with halved truffles. Add as much spiced salt as required. Cover the whole with half the remaining stuffing. Lay on top the rest of the foie gras and the halves of truffle. Season and cover with the rest of the stuffing.

Fold the pheasant into shape. Wrap in a cloth. Tie and cook in aspic stock flavoured with Madeira (see *aspic jelly*), to which have been added the bones and trimmings of the pheasant and partridge. Leave the ballottine to cool under a light weight. Glaze with aspic in the usual way.

Chaud-froid of pheasant CHAUD-FROID DE FAISAN Cook a prepared trussed pheasant in butter in an ovenproof casserole, taking care that the meat remains pinkish. Joint the bird into 4 or 6 pieces. Skin the pieces, trim them, and allow them to cool completely. Place in the refrigerator for about 1 hour. Prepare a brown chaud-froid sauce with some game stock, flavoured with truffle essence. Also prepare some Madeira-flavoured aspic jelly. Place the chilled pieces of pheasant on a rack, and pour the chaud-froid sauce over them twice, refrigerating in between the 2 applications. Prepare various ingredients for a garnish; for example, thinly sliced pieces of truffle cut into fancy shapes, tarragon leaves, thinly sliced carrots and leeks, pieces of hard-boiled egg white, etc. Coat each item in aspic before arranging them on the joints of pheasant. Finally, coat the pheasant with the remaining aspic and place in the refrigerator to set. To serve, arrange on a serving dish garnished with chopped aspic or slices of aspic. Alternatively, arrange in a glass bowl and coat the entire arrangement with clear seasoned aspic.

HOT PHEASANT DISHES

Casserole of pheasant FAISAN EN COCOTTE Brown a trussed pheasant in 25 g (1 oz, 2 tablespoons) butter in a flameproof casserole. Cover and continue to cook gently for 45 minutes. Add some Cognac (or other brandy) and 2 tablespoons (3 tablespoons) boiling water or stock. Season with salt and pepper. Cook for a further 5–10 minutes. Cut the pheasant into joints and serve with, for example, puréed celery.

Alternatively, halfway through the cooking time add 12 mushroom caps and some small shaped potato pieces to the casserole. Then deglaze with cream, reducing the sauce by half.

A third method is to add 2½ dl (scant ½ pint, 1 generous cup) single (light) cream to the casserole two-thirds of the way through the cooking time, basting the pheasant frequently with the cream. Just before serving, add a squeeze of lemon juice.

Grilled (broiled) pheasant à l'américaine FAISAN GRILLÉ À L'AMÉRICAINE This recipe is particularly suitable for young pheasants. Split the pheasant along the back and flatten it gently. Season with salt and pepper, and fry in butter on both sides until the flesh is firm. Coat both sides with freshly made breadcrumbs seasoned with a large pinch of cayenne. Grill (broil) the pheasant slowly. Place on a dish, and cover with grilled bacon rashers. Garnish with grilled tomatoes and mushrooms, bunches of watercress, and potato or game chips. Serve with maître d'hôtel butter.

Pheasant à la normande FAISAN À LA NORMANDE Brown the pheasant in butter in a flameproof casserole. Peel and slice 4 firm apples, and fry quickly in butter. Place them in the bottom of the casserole with the pheasant on top. Cover and cook in the oven at 240 C (475 F, gas 9) for about 45 minutes. 5 minutes before serving, pour 1 dl (6 tablespoons, scant ½ cup) cream and 1 tablespoon Calvados over the pheasant. Untruss, carve into joints, and serve very hot with the apples.

Pheasant with cabbage FAISAN AU CHOU Lard the breast and legs of an old trussed pheasant with thin strips of fat bacon and brown it in an ovenproof casserole in a very hot oven. Half-cook a large cabbage in a separate casserole with 200 g (7 oz, 10 slices) unsmoked streaky bacon, 2 diced carrots, a large bouquet garni, and some salt and pepper. Remove the pheasant from the casserole, place half the cabbage in the dish, replace the pheasant, and cover with the remaining cabbage. Replace the lid on the casserole and cook gently for 1 hour. Then add a small sausage and continue to cook gently for another hour. Untruss the pheasant and carve. Discard the bouquet garni. Slice the bacon and the sausage. Put the cabbage into a deep dish and arrange the pheasant, bacon, and sausage on top.

Pheasant with port FAISAN AU PORTO (from a recipe by P. Haeberlin) Cut 2 young pheasants, preferably hens, into 4 or 6 pieces each. Season with salt and pepper and brown in 50 g (2 oz, 4 tablespoons) butter in a frying pan (skillet). Soften 4 peeled chopped shallots in 20 g (¾ oz, 1½ tablespoons) butter in an ovenproof casserole. Add the pheasant pieces and ¼ litre (8 fl oz, 1 cup) port. Cover and simmer for 20 minutes. Fry 300 g (11 oz, 3 cups) chanterelle mushrooms in butter. Remove the pheasant pieces and deglaze the casserole with ¼ litre (8 fl oz, 1 cup) cream. Add a little juice from the pan in which the chanterelles were cooked and boil down to reduce. Bind the sauce with 60 g (2¼ oz, 4½ tablespoons) butter, cut into small pieces. Adjust the seasoning. Replace the pheasant pieces and the chanterelles in the hot sauce and allow to bubble for a few seconds. Arrange on a dish and serve with spätzle in butter.

Roast pheasant FAISAN RÔTI Truss and bard a young pheasant, brush with melted butter, and season with salt and pepper. Roast in a very hot oven at 240 C (475 F, gas 9) for 30–40 minutes, depending on the size of the bird, basting 2 or 3 times. Fry some croutons until golden brown. Untruss the pheasant and remove the barding fat. Place it on top of the croutons and keep warm. Deglaze the roasting tin (pan) with a little poultry stock and serve this gravy separately. (The pheasant can be stuffed with truffles before roasting and the croutons can be spread with a small amount of forcemeat made with the minced liver of the pheasant.)

Sautéed pheasant FAISAN SAUTÉ Cut a young tender pheasant (preferably a hen) into 4 or 6 pieces. Season with salt and pepper, brown in butter, and continue to sauté gently in an open pan. Arrange the pieces of pheasant on a warmed covered serving dish. Deglaze the sauté pan with half a glass of white wine and a little veal stock, reduce the sauce by half, and add some butter. Pour the sauce over the pheasant and serve very hot.

Slices of pheasant with orange juice FAISAN EN FILETS AU JUS D'ORANGE (from a recipe in *Ma Cuisinière Isabeau*, 1796) Remove the flesh from a pheasant. Make a sauce as follows. Crush and pound the carcass and place it in a saucepan with some veal stock and a bottle of flat champagne. Add salt and pepper, bring to the boil, and leave on a low heat to reduce. Pass through a fine sieve and return to the heat. Add the minced heart and liver; cook for another 10 minutes. Cut the pheasant flesh into long thin slices and sauté these in butter for 10 minutes, adding a handful of chopped parsley, chervil, and chives. Arrange the slices on a dish. Add the cooking juice from the pheasant to the sauce, together with the strained juice of an orange. Stir, and pour the hot sauce over the slices of pheasant.

Philippe

A Parisian restaurant established in the 19th century in the Rue Montorgueil, near Les Halles, on the site of an old post house. It began as a modest public house, but when Magny was installed as head chef in 1842, followed by Pascal, ex-chef of the Jockey Club, in 1848, the Philippe became very fashionable; it was famous for entrecôte steaks, onion soup, Normandy sole, and matelote. Its clientele was not as sophisticated as that of the neighbouring Rocher de Cancale, but people went to Philippe mainly to eat well. In the 1870s the Club des Grands Estomacs used to meet there, and it is said that their Gargantuan meals could last as long as 18 hours!

phosphorus PHOSPHORE

An element that is present in both animal and plant tissues. It is a major constituent of bone tissue, together with calcium. Phosphorus deficiency is very rare, as most foods contain considerable quantities of the element, and it only comes about as a result of certain kidney disorders.

Pic (André)

French chef (born Saint-Péray, 1893; died Valence, 1984). He began his career at the auberge Le Pin, the family inn near Valence, with his mother Sophie, who was herself a famous cook. He then became an apprentice chef at various houses in the Rhône Valley. In 1924 he returned to Le Pin, which became a famous stopping place along the road to the Midi. In 1936 he opened a restaurant in Valence itself, and in 1939 it was awarded three stars in the Michelin Guide. André Pic, Alexandre Dumaine, and Fernand Point were the three greatest French chefs in the period between the wars.

In the 1950s, however, Pic's health deteriorated and his son Jacques took over. Jacques began by reviving his father's great specialities: *poularde en vessie* (chicken in a bladder), crayfish gratin, Grignan truffle turnover, and *boudin de brochet à la Richelieu* (made with pike) – in a style similar to that of Escoffier. His own creations include bass fillets with caviar, cassolette of crayfish with morel mushrooms, calves' kidneys with sorrel or mint, and fishermen's salad with sherry.

picanchâgne

A pastry from Bourbonnais, filled with pears. The gastronome M. Dexant maintains that the name is derived from the games played by boys during the threshing season: after work they would do handstands, *piqués comme un chêne* (bristling like an oak tree), which in the local patois becomes *faisant le picanchâgne*. The pastries were decorated with small cooked pears sticking up like the legs of the boys, hence the name. Originally made with plain bread dough, the picanchâgne is now made with a richer leavened dough and covered with a layer of sliced pears (or apples or quinces) sprinkled with sugar. The dough is folded over and pressed down to incorporate the fruit, then shaped into a large ring, glazed with egg, and baked in the oven.

Picardy PICARDIE

According to some authorities this region of France is not highly regarded from a gastronomic point of view. However, it does have a very original cuisine and very ancient traditions.

The best-known dish is probably the famous *flamique à porions* (leek tart), which can also be made with onions, pumpkins, or potatoes. The market gardens around Amiens produce excellent vegetables, most of which are exported to Britain. Cattle reared in the pastures of Picardy and the famous salt-meadow sheep from the Baie de Somme yield meat of prime quality. Picardy pork is excellent, being used not only for the famous charcuterie of the region (especially andouillette sausages) but also for typical regional dishes, such as caghuse and tripe soup.

Although the area does not have a wide coastline, it has plenty of fish (especially herrings) and shellfish, including the famous *hénons* (cockles).

Picardy is famous for its wildfowl: the reputation of the legendary Amiens duck pâté has been perpetuated by the Maison Degand, which was founded in Amiens in 1643. Madame de Sévigné extolled this dish in one of her letters: 'the bird lay as if in a casket, embalmed with peppers and herbs, the secret of which doubles the pleasure.' Another well-known speciality is mallard *à la picarde* (cooked in a casserole and garnished with apples sautéed with diced duck's liver), and dishes are also prepared with teal, thrushes, and even bustard.

Excellent cheeses are made in Picardy: Maroilles, Rollot, Guerbigny, Manicamp, and Saint-Winocq; all having a strong flavour. Daussade, on the other hand, is a cream cheese steeped in vinegar and flavoured with herbs.

Beer is the standard drink in the east of the region, whereas cider and perry are traditionally drunk in the west, together with frénette, made from the fermented leaves of the ash tree.

The pâtisserie is abundant: rabottes and taliburs are similar to the douillons of Normandy, and *gâteau battu* is much appreciated, as well as the rice and

prune tarts. The region boasts a very
varied range of confectionery. Amiens
macaroons, Arras caramels and gingerbread hearts, Berck chocolate shells and
chiques, *mignonnettes sablées* from
Péronne, and chocolate slices (*tuiles*),
gaillettes, *briquettes*, and *brindinettes*
from Douai prove that – as A. de Croze
wrote in *Les Plats régionaux de France*
– 'of all French provinces, Picardy is
possibly the one that has best preserved
the old recipes of its popular dishes'.

piccalilli

An English pickle consisting of small
florets of cauliflower, sliced gherkins,
shallots, and other vegetables preserved
in a spicy mustard and vinegar sauce. It
may be strong or mild and is eaten with
cold meats, particularly ham and roast
pork.

piccata

In France, a small round veal escalope
(scallop) cut from the noix or the sous-
noix and fried in butter. Three piccatas
per person is usually sufficient. It was
originally an Italian dish, most often
served with Marsala or lemon.

RECIPE

**Veal piccata with aubergines (egg-
plants) and tomatoes** PICCATA DE
VEAU AUX AUBERGINES ET TOMATES
FRAÎCHES (from a recipe by Gilbert
Picard) Cut a fillet of veal weighing
about 1.3 kg (3 lb) into 12 round slices
(*piccatas*). Cut an aubergine (egg-plant)
into round slices and dust them with
flour. Fry the piccatas in a frying pan
(skillet) in 50 g (2 oz, ¼ cup) clarified
butter and drain them. Fry the aubergine slices in the same butter. Sauté 2
sliced white onions gently in a covered
pan. Cut a red pepper into strips and fry
them in butter for about 15 minutes.
Crush 500 g (1 lb) ripe tomatoes.

Arrange the piccatas on a serving
dish, alternating them with small strips
of cooked ham and the aubergine slices.
Garnish with the onions, the strips of
red pepper, and the crushed tomatoes.
Place in the oven for 5 minutes at 210 C
(410 F, gas 6–7). Sprinkle with noisette
butter and garnish with parsley just before serving.

pichet

An earthenware pitcher used in France
for serving water, fruit juice, cider, or
carafe wine (but not good-quality
wine). In restaurants, *vin au pichet* is an
unbottled medium-quality wine served
in large quantities.

A pichet is also an old measure for salt
and liquids. Made of tin, with or without a lid, it is one of the most handsome
regional utensils.

pickle

A condiment consisting of vegetables or
fruit (or a mixture of both) preserved in
spiced vinegar. Of Indian origin, pickles
are a milder version of the achars of
Madras and Bombay. Pickles are sold in
jars under various brand names but can
also be made at home. They are served
with cold meats, cheese, curries, etc.,
with apéritifs, and in mixed hors
d'oeuvres.

The vegetables used for pickling
(cauliflower, cucumber, cabbage,
marrow and courgettes (zucchini),
mushrooms, small onions, unripe tomatoes, etc.) are sliced if necessary and
soaked in brine or in cold water. They
are then rinsed, put into jars, and
covered with spiced vinegar. They can
also be cooked in vinegar with spices.
Fruits (plums, cherries, apples, pears,
peaches, etc.) are cut into small pieces
and usually cooked for a short time so
that they will soak up the vinegar. Eggs
and walnuts can also be pickled. The
best salt to use is coarse sea salt, as this
gives the best flavour.

Malt, wine, cider, or spirit vinegars
may be used. The spices enhance the
flavour and also act as preservatives.
The classic formula is as follows: to 1
litre (1¾ pints, 4¼ cups) vinegar, add a
stick of cinnamon (5 cm (2 in) long),
1 teaspoon cloves, 2 teaspoons fennel
seeds, 1 teaspoon black pepper, 1 teaspoon mustard seeds (or 5 teaspoons
whole pickling spice), and 2 or 3 bay
leaves. Bring the mixture to the boil and
then steep for 3 days. The vinegar is then
strained and used either cold (for vegetables, which should remain crisp) or
hot (for fruit, which should be a little
softer). Mixed pickles may combine any
number of vegetables, such as onion,
cabbage, cucumber, green beans,

carrots, and green peppers. But some vegetables and fruits are pickled on their own; for example, beetroot (red beet) with dill, red cabbage with white wine vinegar, peppers with thyme and bay leaf, lime with pepper, and peaches with spices and lemon rind.

RECIPE

Cauliflower and tomato pickle PICK-LES DE CHOU-FLEUR ET DE TO-MATE (from an American recipe by Marye Cameron Smith in *Le Grand Livre de la conserve*, Dessain et Tolra) Divide 2 medium-sized cauliflowers into florets and arrange them in layers in a terrine together with 700 g (1½ lb) firm tomatoes (quartered), 4 coarsely chopped onions, and a chopped cucumber. Sprinkle each layer with an equal quantity of salt (200 g (7 oz) altogether). Cover completely with cold water, place a sheet of kitchen foil over the top, and leave in a cool place for 24 hours.

The next day, place the vegetables in a strainer and rinse them thoroughly under the tap to wash away the excess salt. Drain and place them in a large saucepan. Sprinkle with 1 teaspoon mustard powder, 1 teaspoon ground ginger, and 1 teaspoon black pepper. Then add 250 g (9 oz, generous 1 cup, firmly packed) brown sugar. Pour in 70 cl (scant 1¼ pints, scant 1½ pints) white wine vinegar and bring to the boil over a medium heat, stirring frequently. Lower the heat and simmer for 15–20 minutes, continuing to stir, until the vegetables are just beginning to soften but are still firm when pricked with the tip of a knife.

Remove the pan from the heat, put the vegetables in clean jars, and completely cover with vinegar. The proportions given will make 3 kg (6½ lb) pickle. The jars should be stored in a cool dry place away from the light.

pickled

Describing pork or beef that has been preserved by steeping in brine to which saltpetre has been added, and then boiled.

For recipes using pickled tongue, see *écarlate (à l')*.

The word is also used to describe vegetables and fruit preserved in brine, vinegar, etc.

picnic PIQUE-NIQUE

'An informal meal in which everyone pays his share or brings his own dish', according to the Littré dictionary. That was the original meaning of the word, which is probably of French origin (the French *piquer* means to pick at food; *nique* means something small of no value). The word was accepted by the Académie française in 1740 and thereafter became a universally accepted word in many tongues.

Today, a picnic is an informal meal in the open air; the dishes are usually cold and easy to carry: for example, hard-boiled (hard-cooked) eggs, salads, pâtés, cold meats, sandwiches, cheeses, tarts, fruit, etc. These days, however, with the aid of vacuum flasks, camping stoves, and portable barbecues, picnics can take on whole new dimensions with as much hot food as cold on the menu!

Picodon

A goats'-milk cheese (45% fat content) with a soft centre and a fine natural crust that is bluish, golden, or reddish, depending on the ripeness of the cheese. Picodon – the name comes from the Languedocian word *pico* (to sting) – has a strong or nutty flavour. It is produced in several regions and is in season between May and December. Picodon de Dieulefit (in Dauphiné) is 6–7 cm (2½ in) in diameter and 2–3 cm (1 in) thick; it is steeped in white wine. Picodon de Saint-Agrève (in Languedoc) is slightly larger and has a less pronounced flavour. Picodon de Valréas is eaten when half-ripe.

picoussel or pique-aousel

A dessert from the Auvergne that is especially famous at Mur-de-Barrez. It is a type of flan made of buckwheat flour, flavoured with herbs, and filled with plums.

Picpoul

A white grape grown in the Rhône Valley and the south of France. It has been used extensively for blending and also in the making of vermouth. In fact, the name is also used for the Gros Plant vine of the Nantes region and the Folle Blanche of the Cognac area.

piddock PHOLADE

A shellfish found on the Atlantic coast of France; it is known as *dail* in Royan and *gîte* in Arcachon. It has a white shell with serrated cutting edges, which enables it to bore into soft rock. The largest piddocks are about 10 cm (4 in) long.

It is eaten raw or cooked and may be stuffed with garlic, shallots, and breadcrumbs. It is best suited for grilling (broiling).

pie

The French have adopted the English word for the classic British and American pies. A pie can be sweet or savoury and may have just a top crust of pastry or a pastry crust that encloses the filling. American pies can also have just a bottom pastry crust, and these are usually called tarts in Britain. The pastry used can be shortcrust or puff. A pie can also have a mashed potato topping, as in shepherd's pie or fish pie.

Savoury pies are usually served as a main course. The best-known are chicken pie, steak and kidney pie, game pie, and pork and apple pie. Buffalo and beer pie (made with buffalo meat, vegetables, spices, and beer), oyster pie, clam pie, and salmon pie are American specialities.

The classic dessert pies are apple pie and plum pie, but almost any stone fruit can be used as well as pears, blackcurrants, redcurrants, blackberries, gooseberries, and rhubarb. American specialities include pecan pie, pumpkin pie, and blueberry pie. These dessert pies are traditionally served with custard or fresh cream.

RECIPES

Chicken pie Joint a raw chicken weighing about 1.25 kg (2½ lb). Sprinkle the pieces with 100 g (4 oz) finely chopped onions and shallots, 150 g (5 oz, 1¼ cups) sliced mushrooms, and some chopped parsley. Season with salt and pepper. Line a buttered pie dish with 200 g (7 oz) very thin slices of veal seasoned with salt and pepper. Place the chicken in the dish, first the thighs, then the wings, and finally the breasts. Cover with 150 g (5 oz) bacon cut into very thin rashers (slices). Add 4 hard-boiled (hard-cooked) egg yolks cut in half. Pour in some chicken stock to three-quarters fill the dish.

Press a strip of puff pastry around the rim of the pie dish, brush with water, then cover the whole dish with a layer of pastry. Seal the edges, then knock up and flute with the back of a knife. Brush the whole surface with beaten egg and make a hole in the centre. Bake for 1½ hours in the oven at 190 C (375 F, gas 5). Just before serving, pour 2–3 tablespoons concentrated chicken stock into the pie.

Pear pie PIE AUX POIRES Peel and core 4 pears, cut into slices, and sprinkle with lemon juice. Arrange the pear slices in a buttered pie dish and sprinkle with 2 tablespoons (3 tablespoons) caster (superfine) sugar (a little powdered cinnamon may also be added). Dot with 30 g (1 oz, 2 tablespoons) butter.

Prepare some shortcrust pastry (see *doughs and batters*) and put a border around the rim of the dish, brush it with beaten egg, and cover the dish with a lid of pastry. Press down to seal the edges, knock up and crimp between finger and thumb, brush with beaten egg, and bake in the oven for 1 hour at 180 C (350 F, gas 4). When cooked, dust with sugar and serve very hot.

other recipes See *pâté*, *rhubarb*.

pièce montée

A large ornamental item of pâtisserie, formerly very popular, used to decorate the table at a banquet or party. It usually reflects the theme of the other decorations. Such set pieces are much rarer today than in the past, often now being replaced by arrangements of flowers, especially on sideboards. In France, the pièce montée is still popular for a wedding or baptism, and displays the artistic skills of the confectionery trade.

The pièce montée can be made of various ingredients: layers of sponge cake or Genoese sponge, nougat, shaped or blown sugar, flowers, ribbons, and leaves made out of drawn or twisted sugar, baskets of woven sugar, inedible decorative sugarwork, crests and pompoms of spun sugar, crisp petits fours, crystallized (candied) fruit, dragées, items of almond paste, chocolate shavings, etc. Classic pièces montées *à la française* are constructed on a metal framework with a central pivot that enables trays to be stacked one above the other in tiers. Pièces montées *à l'espagnole*, on the other hand, consist of separate trays of confectionery arranged in layers one on top of the other, each supported by pillars resting on the outer edges of the tray beneath. Whichever style is chosen, the confectioner may give free rein to his imagination, working on various subjects, some of which have become standard since the great era of pièces montées when Carême reigned supreme: the harp, the lyre, the globe, the Chinese pagoda, the horn of plenty, the ship, the chapel, the bandstand, the waterfall, the Louis XV carriage, the dolphin on the rock, the gleaner's basket, the temple, the cart, etc. Today a simple and popular type of pièce montée is the croquembouche made of profiteroles filled with sweetened cream, glazed with sugar, and arranged on top of one another with glazed fruit.

Pièces montée were very popular in the Middle Ages, when they were very spectacular, of gigantic proportions, and often made in the shape of an animal such as the peacock. But it was in the 18th and 19th centuries that the pièce montée reached its greatest heights, depicting allegorical subjects (for which Chiboust and Frascati were famous), and pastoral or historic subjects, such as 'The Great St Bernard Pass' or 'The Episode of the Lodi Bridge'. However, these sumptuous items were rarely edible and their function was first and foremost a decorative one. Today's pièces montées are more modest, but combine pleasure to the eye with pleasure to the taste. One 'literary' set piece has remained famous. It was conceived by Flaubert for the wedding reception of Madame Bovary: 'At the base was a piece of blue cardboard representing a temple with porticoes, colonnades, and stucco statuettes all around in tiny niches, embellished with gold stars. Above this, on the second tier, stood a castle keep of Savoy cake, surrounded by tiny fortifications made out of angelica, almonds, currants, and pieces of orange. Finally, on the top tier, was nothing less than a verdant meadow where there were rocks, pools made of jam, and boats made out of nutshells. The tiny figure of Cupid could be seen, playing on a chocolate swing, the posts of which were tipped with two real rosebuds.'

pieds et paquets

A speciality of Provence, consisting of stuffed sheep's tripe tied up to form small packets (*paquets*) and simmered in white wine and stock with bacon and sheep's trotters (feet) (*pieds*). Also sometimes called *pieds-paquets* or *pieds-en-paquets*, the dish apparently originated in the Restaurant de la Pomme, on the outskirts of Marseille.

RECIPE

Pieds et paquets de la Pomme (from a recipe of the Hôtellerie de la Fuste) Clean a sheep's tripe and cut it into 8–10-cm (3–4-in) pieces. Make a slit in one corner of each piece. In the middle of each place a spoonful of a minced (ground) mixture of 100 g (3½ oz) raw ham, 100 g (3½ oz) lamb's mesentery, a clove of garlic, and a bunch of parsley. Roll each piece of tripe around the stuffing and form a packet (*paquet*) by pushing one corner of skin into the slit; tie if necessary.

Clean, blanch, and singe some sheep's trotters (*pieds*). In an earthenware casserole place 100 g (3½ oz) diced bacon, 1 leek, and a thinly sliced onion. Brown them, then add a sliced carrot and 2 tomatoes, peeled, deseeded, and crushed. Cover with ½ litre (17 fl oz, 2 cups) white wine and 2 litres (3½ pints, 4½ pints) meat stock, then add the trotters and the 'packets'. Add a bouquet garni, 2 crushed cloves of garlic, salt, pepper, and 2 cloves. Cover and seal the lid with a flour-and-water paste. Simmer very gently for 6–7 hours.

Open the casserole, remove the packets (untie them if necessary), and remove the bones from the trotters. Skim off excess fat from the stock and reduce to the desired consistency by simmering with the lid off until ready to serve.

piémontaise (à la)

Describing various dishes that incorporate a risotto, sometimes accompanied by white Piedmont truffles. Arranged in a variety of ways – in darioles, in timbale moulds, or as croquettes – the risotto is used to garnish poultry, meat, and fish. The term *à la piémontaise* also refers to dishes of the Piedmont region of northern Italy that do not necessarily feature truffles, such as polenta, ravioli, and macaroni. Pastries *à la piémontaise* are usually based on hazelnuts, another famous product of Piedmont.

RECIPES

Attereaux à la piémontaise Prepare 400 g (14 oz) polenta; season with salt and pepper. Spread it over a lightly oiled square baking sheet and allow to cool completely. Cut into 4-cm (1½-in) squares and thread onto skewers. Coat in breadcrumbs and deep-fry in hot oil or lard (175–180 C, 350–355 F) until brown. Drain on absorbent paper and arrange on a dish garnished with fried parsley. Serve with a well-reduced tomato fondue.

Fillets of mackerel à la piémontaise FILETS DE MAQUEREAUX À LA PIÉMONTAISE Prepare a risotto *à la piémontaise* using 200 g (7 oz, 1 cup) rice. Fillet 4 mackerel; wash, pat dry with a clean cloth or absorbent paper, dip in breadcrumbs, and fry in butter on both sides. Butter a long serving dish, cover with the risotto, and arrange the fillets on top. Garnish with quarters of lemon. Serve with a slightly thickened tomato fondue.

Piémontaise sauce SAUCE À LA PIÉMONTAISE (from Carême's recipe) Finely dice 2 large onions and brown in clarified butter. Strain, then cook in a good broth, skimming off all the fat. Blend in enough béchamel sauce to accompany an entrée, together with 225 g (½ lb) diced Piedmont truffles and 2 tablespoons (3 tablespoons) pine kernels (nuts). After the sauce has boiled for a short while, add a little chicken glaze, a little garlic butter, and the juice of 1 lemon. (The quantity of truffles can be reduced without affecting the recipe.)

Spring chickens à la piémontaise POUSSINS À LA PIÉMONTAISE Prepare a risotto *à la piémontaise*, using 250 g (9 oz, 2¼ cups) rice. Chop up 75 g (3 oz) onions, soften in butter, then mix with 400 g (14 oz) finely minced (ground) sausagemeat and the minced livers of 4 spring chickens (poussins). Season the chicken with salt and pepper, stuff with the forcemeat, truss, and cook gently in a casserole containing 50 g (2 oz) butter for approximately 50 minutes in a moderate oven. Place the risotto in a ring on a heated serving dish, arrange the chickens in the centre, and keep warm. Deglaze the casserole with 2 glasses white wine and 3 tablespoons (¼ cup) tomato purée. Reduce by half, thicken with 1 tablespoon kneaded butter, add 2 tablespoons (3 tablespoons) freshly chopped parsley, and pour this sauce over the chickens.

pig COCHON

See *pork.*

pigeon

A domesticated or wild bird of which several species are eaten as poultry or game. Young pigeons (squabs; *pigeonneaux* in French) are particularly tender and are usually roasted. The rock dove, which still lives in the wild in Brittany, Provence, and in mountainous regions of southern Europe, is the ancestor of all the varieties of domestic pigeon. The most common wild pigeon in France is the wood pigeon or ring dove. Its flesh is denser and more highly flavoured than the domestic pigeon, although both are prepared in the same way. Most recipes for woodcock are applicable to pigeons. Casseroles, stews, ballottines, pâtés, and ragouts are suitable for older birds, whereas younger and more tender birds are good roasted, grilled (broiled), *à la crapaudine*, sautéed, and *en papillotes*. It is customary to leave the liver inside when dressing the bird since pigeon's liver does not contain bile. Otherwise it is drawn and prepared like other poultry. Young pigeons are only very lightly barded, if at all, whereas it is a must for adult birds.

Pigeon has been a popular dish since the Middle Ages and was much in vogue during the reign of Louis XIV, especially served with peas. The French cook La

Varenne gives a recipe for pigeon and green-pea stew in which the birds are poached in stock and then garnished with lettuce, peas, and pieces of bacon.

RECIPES

Dressing roasting pigeons HABILLAGE DES PIGEONS À RÔTIR To pluck the birds more easily, chill for a few hours in the refrigerator: the flesh will tighten and there will be less danger of tearing. Pluck each bird beginning with the large wing feathers, then the tail, and proceed upwards to finish at the head. Singe and draw. Place a thin slice of bacon on the back and breast of the bird. Truss by folding the head down between the wings.

Pigeon compote PIGEONS EN COMPOTE Season 4 pigeons with salt and pepper, inside and out, then place 3–4 juniper berries and 1 tablespoon marc brandy in each bird. Turn the birds over so that the brandy is evenly distributed inside. Put a thin strip of bacon over the breast and truss. Brown the pigeons in a flameproof casserole containing 50 g (2 oz, 4 tablespoons) butter, then remove, drain, and keep warm.

In the same butter, brown 20 small onions and 100 g (3½ oz) smoked streaky bacon, cut into small pieces. Then add 150 g (5 oz) thinly sliced mushrooms. When these have turned a good golden colour, add a bouquet garni, 2 dl (7 fl oz, ¾ cup) white wine, and the same quantity of chicken stock. Reduce by two-thirds, return the pigeons to the casserole, cover, and bring to the boil. Then cook in a hot oven (230 C, 450 F, gas 8) for approximately 30 minutes. Remove the bouquet garni, untie the pigeons, arrange them on a heated serving dish, and spoon the cooking liquid over.

Squab à la minute PIGEONNEAU À LA MINUTE Split the bird in half lengthways. Remove the small bones, gently flatten the 2 halves, and fry quickly in butter. When the squab is almost cooked, add 1 tablespoon chopped onion lightly fried in butter. Finish cooking. Arrange the squab on a dish and keep warm. Dilute the pan juices with a dash of brandy, thicken with a little dissolved meat essence, and add ½ tablespoon chopped parsley. Pour the sauce over the bird.

Squabs en papillotes PIGEONNEUX EN PAPILLOTES Take 4 squabs and split each in half lengthways. Remove as many bones as possible, especially the breastbone. Season each half with salt and pepper, and fry in a casserole containing 50 g (2 oz, 4 tablespons) butter to seal them. Prepare a duxelles from 40 g (1½ oz) mushrooms and 200 g (7 oz) raw unsmoked ham. Cut out 8 heart-shaped pieces of greaseproof (waxed) paper, oil each piece lightly on one side, and spread with the duxelles. Place a pigeon half on each and fold over the edges of the papillotes to seal. Cook in a hot oven (at least 230 C, 450 F, gas 8) until the paper cases have swollen and browned (approximately 15 minutes).

Stuffed pigeons with asparagus tips PIGEONS FARCIS AUX POINTES D'ASPERGE (from a recipe by Raymond Thuillier) Take 4 pigeons each weighing approximately 400 g (14 oz) and bone them starting at the backbone. Prepare a forcemeat with 250 g (9 oz) noix of veal, 250 g (9 oz) fat bacon, 250 g (9 oz) calves' sweetbreads, and 250 g (9 oz) foie gras. Chop all these ingredients very finely and add 30 g (1 oz) broken truffle pieces and 1 whole egg. Blend together. Stuff the pigeons and then wrap each in caul (caul fat), which will prevent the skin from drying while they are cooked.

Place the pigeons in a flameproof casserole, cover, and cook over a gentle heat for about 15 minutes. Remove the pigeons, deglaze the casserole with ½ glass vermouth, and reduce over a brisk heat before pouring the sauce over the pigeons.

Serve with a gratin of asparagus tips prepared as follows: boil 32 asparagus tips in plenty of salted water, spread on a buttered gratin dish, cover with 1 dl (6 tablespoons, scant ½ cup) fresh cream blended with 1 beaten egg yolk, and brown under the grill.

pike BROCHET

A freshwater fish with a long head and strong jaws equipped with hundreds of small sharp teeth. The body is long and thin, marbled with green or brown, and the belly is silvery. Nicknamed *grand loup d'eau* (great water wolf) in the Middle Ages because of its voracious nature, pike was much appreciated at the royal table and was reared in the Louvre fish ponds. It measures 40 cm (16 in) (the minimum size below which it is not allowed to be fished) to 70 cm (28 in); exceptional fish may reach up to 1.5 m (5 ft) and weigh up to 25 kg (56 lb) but, over 4 kg (9 lb), the flesh is only good for quenelles and mousses. In addition to the traditional preparation *au beurre blanc*, pike is prepared with white wine, *à la juive*, roasted, etc. At spawning time the roe and eggs are slightly toxic (but they are eaten in some countries, especially Romania). River pike are better than those from ponds.

RECIPES

Pike au beurre blanc   BROCHET AU BEURRE BLANC

■ *First recipe.* Gut the pike, clean it carefully, and cut off the fins and tail. Prepare a court-bouillon in a fish kettle and boil for approximately 30 minutes. Add the pike. As soon as the court-bouillon starts to boil again, reduce the temperature to keep it at a barely perceptible simmer. After 12–20 minutes remove the fish kettle from the heat.

Meanwhile, prepare the beurre blanc: boil down some vinegar containing 2–3 chopped shallots and freshly ground pepper (one turn of the pepper mill); when it has reduced by half remove from the heat. Soften a large piece of butter (about 225 g (8 oz, 1 cup) to 2 tablespoons reduced vinegar) on a plate using a spatula and incorporate it gradually into the vinegar, beating vigorously with a whisk. It will turn frothy without becoming liquid and will acquire its characteristic whiteness. Drain the pike, arrange on a long dish, and coat with the beurre blanc, adding fresh sprigs of parsley. Alternatively, serve the beurre blanc separately in a sauceboat.

■ *Second recipe.* Wash the pike in plenty of water, sprinkle with fine salt, and leave for approximately 15 minutes. Wash again and place in the fish kettle, surrounded with parsley, 2 sliced onions, 2 quartered shallots, 2 cloves of garlic, 8–20 chives or the green part of a leek, a sprig of fresh thyme, a bay leaf, and a few slices of carrot; season with salt and pepper. Cover with sprigs of parsley and add enough dry white wine to cover the whole fish. Leave to marinate for 1 hour. About 35 minutes before serving, place the fish kettle on a high heat; as soon as it begins to bubble, reduce the heat and simmer as gently as possible.

While it is cooking, prepare a beurre blanc as in the first recipe, using 250 g (9 oz, 1 cup) slightly salted butter. Keep the beurre blanc warm in a bain-marie and do not allow to boil. Trim the pike, drain for a few seconds on a cloth, and place on a long very hot dish. Using the blade of a knife, quickly slit the middle of the side, from the head to the tail, following the lateral line; detach and remove the main bone, holding the head in the left hand; reshape the fish. Quickly stir the beurre blanc with a spatula to mix the shallots in well, pour over the pike, and serve.

Pike du meunier   BROCHET DU MEUNIER   (from A. Guillot's recipe) Scale, beard, gut (clean), remove the heads from, and wash 3 young pike weighing 700–800 g (1½–1¾ lb). Cut into pieces and season; dip in milk and then flour. Cook gently in a sauté dish with 200 g (7 oz, 1 cup) butter and 1 tablespoon oil. Separately, soften 4 medium chopped onions in butter. When the pieces of pike are lightly coloured, add the onions and 5 cl (3 tablespoons, ¼ cup) very good white wine vinegar. Reduce by half. Season with salt and pepper and serve each portion with 2 croutons cooked in butter.

Terrine of pike with Nantua sauce TERRINE DE BROCHET SAUCE NANTUA   (from a recipe by J.-C. Vrinat and C. Deligne) Cut the fillets from a pike weighing approximately 1.5 kg (3 lb) and remove the skin. Cut the fillets from the belly into narrow strips, then into dice.

Prepare a frangipane by mixing 100 g (4 oz, 1 cup) flour, 40 g (1½ oz, 3 tablespoons) butter, and 3 egg yolks with 2 dl (7 fl oz, ¾ cup) hot milk; work this mixture over the heat, using a wooden spatula, until the dough collects in a ball around the spatula. Then spread the frangipane on a buttered plate and allow to cool.

Clean and finely chop 100 g (4 oz, 1 cup) button mushrooms and chop 4 or 5 good shallots.

Brown the diced pike in butter in a frying pan (skillet), then add the mushrooms and brown; finally add the shallots but do not allow them to change colour. Remove all ingredients with a skimming spoon and pour 1 dl (6 tablespoons, scant ½ cup) good dry white wine into the frying pan, stir with a spatula to deglaze, then replace the ingredients and add 20 g (1 oz, ½ cup) chopped parsley. Remove from the heat.

Pound or finely chop the remaining (approximately 500 g, 18 oz) flesh of the pike; season liberally with salt and pepper. Add the cooled frangipane in small pieces, then 3 unbeaten egg whites; mix well, then pass twice through the mincer (or chop finely in a food processor). Beat the mixture with 3.5 dl (12 fl oz, 1½ cups) double (heavy) cream and add the diced fish, mushrooms, etc.

Heat the oven to approximately 175 c (350 F, gas 4). Generously butter a pâté dish and heap the mixture into it. Cover and place in a bain-marie. Bring to the boil on top of the stove, then place in the oven and cook gently for approximately 1½ hours. The top of the terrine should turn pale gold but not brown. Serve the terrine in the container in which it was cooked, with Nantua sauce.

pike-perch SANDRE

A large fish of the perch family, living in rivers and lakes, which can reach a length of 1 m (40 in) and a weight of 15 kg (33 lb). Its back is greenish grey, striped with dark bands; the gills and dorsal fins have hard spines, which are difficult to remove, as are the scales, which are light and tend to fly around and adhere to the hands when scraped. The delicate flesh is firm and white and has few bones; it is prepared in the same way as pike or perch. The pike-perch comes from central Europe; in France it is caught in the Doubs, the Saône, and in

the small lakes into which it has been introduced.

RECIPE

Pike-perch and oyster-mushroom salad SALADE DE SANDRE AUX PLEUROTES (from Gérard Vié's recipe) Peel and wash 700 g (1½ lb) oyster mushrooms; slice thinly, sauté briskly in 1 dl (6 tablespoons, scant ½ cup) olive oil with salt and pepper, and drain. Gently heat 2 tablespoons vinaigrette with 2 tablespoons cream until warm; add the mushrooms and a vegetable julienne made from a carrot, a quarter of a root of celeriac (celery root), 100 g (4 oz) French (green) beans, and a turnip, all stewed in butter. Season 4 fillets of pike-perch, each weighing 200 g (7 oz), and cook in a moderate oven (180 c, 350 F, gas 4). Serve with the oyster-mushroom ragout, pouring a few drops of vinegar over each fillet just before serving.

pilaf or pilau

A method of preparing rice which originated in the East. The word is Turkish and is related to the Persian *pilaou* (boiled rice). In the basic recipe the rice is browned in oil or butter with onion, then cooked in stock; halfway through cooking, vegetables, meat, or fish may be added. Pilaf is always spiced, sometimes with saffron – particularly in paella.

There are many variations of pilaf, including garnishes of seafood, shrimps, prawns, lobster, foie gras, sautéed chicken livers, lambs' sweetbreads, sheep's kidneys, fish in sauce, minced (ground) meat, or thinly sliced chicken. The rice is often moulded in the shape of a crown and the garnish in its sauce is arranged in the centre. Pilaf rice can also be moulded in darioles, as a garnish for meat, fish, or poultry.

RECIPES

Chicken pilaf PILAF DE VOLAILLE Prepare some pilaf rice as in the recipe for garnished pilaf (below). Select a chicken weighing about 1.25 kg (2½ lb) and divide it into 8 pieces. Season with salt and pepper and cook in a flameproof casserole containing 50 g (2 oz, 4 tablespoons) butter. Remove with a draining spoon. Add to the casserole 1 tablespoon chopped onion, 1 glass dry white wine, 2 dl (7 fl oz, ¾ cup) chicken stock, 1 tablespoon well-reduced tomato sauce, a crushed clove of garlic, and a bouquet garni. Cook this sauce for 5 minutes, stirring, then strain and return it to the casserole with the pieces of chicken; reheat thoroughly. Shape the pilaf rice into a ring on the serving dish and pour the chicken and its sauce into the centre. Serve hot.

Garnished pilaf PILAF GARNI Thinly slice and chop 1 large onion. Heat 3 tablespoons olive oil in a flameproof casserole. Measure 250 g (9 oz, 1¼ cups) long-grain rice. Test the temperature of the oil by tossing a grain into it; when the grain begins to change colour, pour in all the rice at once and stir with a wooden spoon until the grains are transparent. Incorporate the chopped onion and stir. Add to the rice 2½ times its volume of stock or boiling water and season with salt, pepper, a small sprig of thyme, and half a bay leaf. Stir, cover, reduce the heat, and cook gently for 16–20 minutes. Turn off the heat, remove the thyme and bay leaf, then place a cloth under the lid to absorb the steam. Butter may be added just before serving.

Mould the rice to form a ring and fill the centre with any of the following garnishes: slices of foie gras and truffles, sautéed in butter and sprinkled with their cooking juices deglazed with a little Madeira; poultry liver and mushrooms, sliced, sautéed in butter, and flavoured with garlic, shallots, and parsley; halved lambs' kidneys sautéed in butter and sprinkled with their cooking juices deglazed with white wine and enriched with butter; or fish in sauce (bream in white wine or *à l'américaine*, tuna *en daube*, or monkfish *à l'américaine*.)

Shellfish pilaf PILAF DE CRUSTACÉS Dice 150 g (5 oz) cooked crab, lobster, or langouste meat. Shell 150 g (5 oz) cooked shrimps and toss in butter. Cook ½ litre (17 fl oz, 2 cups) mussels (or cockles or clams) *à la marinière*, allow them to cool in the cooking juices, then remove the shells and keep warm. Strain and measure the cooking juices, and dilute with boiling water to obtain 7 dl (23 fl oz, 2¾ cups) liquid. Wash and drain 300 g (11 oz, 1½ cups) long-grain rice. Heat 4 tablespoons (⅓ cup) olive oil in a frying pan (skillet); add the rice and stir. When it is transparent, add the diluted mussel juice, salt, and pepper; cover and cook for 15 minutes. Then add the shellfish meat (bound with lobster or langouste butter), the shrimps, and the mussels. Serve piping hot.

pilchard

A small fish related to the herring and sprat; young pilchards are called sardines. Pilchards are often sold canned in oil or tomato sauce.

pili-pili

A small hot-tasting African pepper, the name of which is a corruption of the Arabic *felfel* (strong pepper). Its use is virtually confined to Africa (especially Senegal) and Réunion Island. Crushed with gourd seeds and tomato pulp, it is a basic ingredient of rougail and numerous sauces. In Africa pili-pili is eaten with semolina, foutou, meats, and girdle cakes.

pincer

A French culinary term meaning to brown certain foods, such as bones, carcasses, or flavouring vegetables, in the oven with the addition of very little or no fat, before moistening them to make a brown stock. The word also means to caramelize meat juices slightly in their cooking fat before skimming off the fat and diluting the meat juices to make gravy.

The word also means to crimp up the edges of pies, tarts, etc., before cooking, to improve their appearance.

pinch PINCÉE

A very small quantity of a substance, usually salt, pepper, or a spice, which can be taken between the thumb and index finger. In recipes, the quantity required for a pinch is usually 3–5 g (about ¼ teaspoon), although it is not, of course, necessary to measure it! For saffron, always used in minute quantities, the expression 'measure' is used, corresponding to the small individual portions in which saffron is usually packaged.

pineapple ANANAS

A tropical plant whose fragrant fruit, weighing 1–2.5 kg (2¼–5½ lb), resembles a large pine cone and is topped with a cluster of green leaves. When the fruit is properly ripe, these leaves come away easily. Its russet skin with lozenge-shaped scales encloses the yellow juicy flesh.

Discovered in Brazil by Jean de Léry in the 16th century, the pineapple was introduced first into England and then France. The earliest pineapples ripened under glass were presented to Louis XV in about 1733. Still rare and expensive at the beginning of the 19th century, this fruit is now widely grown in the West Indies, Africa, and Asia and is common in European markets, particularly in winter. Rich in sugar and vitamins, fresh pineapple contains 51 Cal per 100 g. It is also widely consumed canned in syrup (87 Cal per 100 g) and as pineapple juice. Pineapple may be served plain or with Kirsch, in salads and in numerous sweets and desserts. It can also be used to dress fatty meats (pork and duck, as in Creole, Asian, and West Indian recipes), and even accompanies shrimps, prawns, etc., in cocktails.

Since fresh pineapple deteriorates in temperatures lower than 7 C (45 F), it is not advisable to store it in the refrigerator. When served plain, it is better to cut it along its length, as it is sweeter at the base. Round slices are always served with the centre removed.

RECIPES

Apple and pineapple jam CONFITURE DE POMMES ET D'ANANAS Dice 450 g (1 lb) peeled and cored cooking apples and 450 g (1 lb) peeled pineapple. Simmer the fruit in 4 tablespoons (⅓ cup) water until soft. Stir in 900 g (2 lb, 4 cups, firmly packed) sugar until dissolved. Boil the jam rapidly until setting point is reached.

Caribbean chicken with pineapple and rum POULET CRÉOLE À L'ANANAS ET AU RHUM Season a large chicken inside and out with salt and pepper. Brown in a flameproof casserole in chicken fat, butter, or oil and dust with a pinch of ginger and cayenne. Chop 2 large onions and 1 shallot and soften them in the fat around the chicken. Pour 5 cl (3 tablespoons) rum over the chicken and set light to it. Then add 3 tablespoons (2 fl oz, ¼ cup) pineapple syrup and 1 tablespoon lemon juice. Cover and cook in a moderate oven for 45 minutes. Dice 6 slices of pineapple and add them to the casserole. Add salt and pepper and cook for about 10 more minutes.

Duck with pineapple CANARD À L'ANANAS Prepare a young duck, season its liver with salt and pepper, and replace inside the carcass. Slowly brown the duck in butter in a flameproof casserole for 20 minutes, add salt and pepper, and then flame it in rum. Add a few tablespoons canned pineapple syrup, 1 tablespoon lemon juice, and 1 tablespoon black peppercorns. Cover the dish and finish cooking (50 minutes altogether). Brown some pineapple slices in butter and add them to the casserole 5 minutes before the end of the cooking time. Check the seasoning. Cut the duck into pieces and arrange on a warm plate. Garnish with the pineapple and pour the cooking juices over the top.

Iced pineapple à la bavaroise ANANAS GLACÉ À LA BAVAROISE Choose a large well shaped pineapple with a good cluster of fresh leaves. Cut off the top 1.5 cm (½ in) below the crown and set aside. Scoop out the flesh leaving an even 1-cm (⅓-in) thickness around the outside. Fill the inside with a mixture of pineapple Bavarian cream and a salpicon of pineapple soaked in white rum. Leave to set in a cool place or on ice. Replace the top of the pineapple before serving.

Loin of pork with pineapple CARRÉ DE PORC À L'ANANAS Brown a loin of pork in a flameproof casserole with a little butter and oil. Add salt and pepper, cover the casserole, and cook gently for about 1½ hours either on the top of the stove or in the oven heated to 200 C (400 F, gas 6). Brown some pineapple slices and apple quarters in butter and add them to the casserole 5 minutes before the end of the cooking time. Place the pork with the apples and pineapple on a warm plate and keep hot. Deglaze the casserole with a little hot water or rum, and serve this separately as a sauce.

Pineapple ice GLACE À L'ANANAS Add the crushed flesh of half a fresh pineapple to ½ litre (17 fl oz, 2 cups) sugar syrup and leave to soak for 2 hours. Reduce to a purée in a blender and flavour with rum. Measure the density with a syrup hydrometer and adjust the sugar content as necessary to achieve a density of 1.609. Freeze in an ice-cream maker.

Pineau des Charentes

A sweetish apéritif made in the Charentais, by 'stopping' grape juice from fermenting by the addition of brandy (ideally, Cognac). It varies according to the maker, in both colour and style, and is said to date from the time of King François I. It can be served with melon or even with foie gras and features in certain regional recipes.

pine kernel or nut

PIGNON

The small oblong edible seed of the stone pine, which grows in the Mediterranean region. Surrounded by a hard husk, pine kernels (or *pignoles* as they are known in the south of France) are extracted from between the scales of the pine cones.

Pine kernels have a high energy content – 670 Cal per 100 g – and are very oily (hence their tendency to go rancid); they are also rich in carbohydrates. They taste a little like almonds, but are sometimes more resinous and spicy. Although pine kernels are sometimes eaten raw, with other nuts, they are usually browned in the frying pan (skillet) and used in pâtisserie (for macaroons, biscuits (cookies), etc.) and in other recipes. They are often used to garnish rice in India and in Turkey, where they are also used in stuffed mussels, poultry forcemeats, and mutton balls. In Italy, pine kernels are used in sauces for pasta, fish forcemeats, fillings for omelettes, and to flavour sautéed chicken. In Provence they are used in charcuterie, in *tourte aux bettes niçoise*, and in raw vegetable salads dressed with olive oil.

RECIPES

Pine-kernel croissants CROISSANTS AUX PIGNONS Boil 4 tablespoons (⅓ cup) water with an equal quantity of sugar in a small saucepan, then remove the syrup from the heat. In a mixing bowl blend 50 g (2 oz, ½ cup) flour with 150 g (5 oz, 1¼ cup) ground almonds, 200 g (7 oz, scant 1 cup) caster (superfine) sugar, and 3 egg whites. When the dough is quite smooth, divide it into 30 pieces and shape into small croissants. Cover a baking sheet with lightly oiled greaseproof (waxed) paper. Dip the croissants in beaten egg, then roll them in 200 g (7 oz) pine kernels. Arrange the croissants on the baking sheet and bake in a moderately hot oven (200 C, 400 F, gas 6) for 8–10 minutes. Remove from the oven and brush the croissants with the sugar syrup. Transfer to a wire rack to cool.

Pine-kernel flan TARTE AUX PIGNONS (from J. Passedat's recipe) Spread 2 tablespoons (3 tablespoons) blackcurrant jelly over a base of sweetened enriched shortcrust pastry (see *doughs and batters*). Cover with equal quantities of confectioners' custard (pastry cream; see *creams and custards*) and ground almonds. Scatter 100 g (3½ oz) pine kernels over the top. Cook for approximately 20 minutes in a moderately hot oven (200 C, 400 F, gas 6).

Pine-kernel omelette OMELETTE AUX PIGNONS Remove the husks from 150 g (5 oz) pine kernels and grind half of them. Brown the other half in a frying pan (skillet) containing 1 tablespoon oil and 30 g (1 oz, 2 tablespoons) butter. Beat 8 eggs and add the ground pine kernels. Pour the mixture over the browned pine kernels. Cook the omelette and roll it on a warm serving dish.

Pine-kernel sauce à l'italienne SAUCE AUX PIGNOLES À L'ITALIENNE (from Carême's recipe) In a saucepan place about 60 g (2 oz, 4 tablespoons, firmly packed) brown or caster (superfine) sugar, 2 tablespoons (3 tablespoons) vinegar, 2 tablespoons veal stock, a seasoned bouquet garni, a pinch of grated nutmeg, and a pinch of coarsely ground pepper. Reduce over a moderate heat, then add 2 tablespoons (3 tablespoons) espagnole sauce and 1 glass red Bordeaux. Reduce further, then strain the sauce through coarse muslin (cheesecloth) and mix in 1 tablespoon pine kernels. Just before serving, boil the kernels rapidly in the sauce.

pinion AILERON

The wing tip, or terminal segment of a bird's wing. It can be prepared in various ways: sautéed or braised, or stuffed if it is large enough, but it is used principally for making consommé.

RECIPE

Stuffed braised turkey pinions AILERONS DE DINDONNEAU FARCIS BRAISÉS Singe and clean 6 turkey pinions and remove the bones carefully without tearing the skin. Stuff them with finely minced pork forcemeat, or a poultry or quenelle forcemeat (see *forcemeat*). Wrap each pinion in a thin slice of bacon and tie in place with kitchen thread. Line a buttered sauté pan with bacon rind, 50 g (2 oz) chopped onions, and 50 g (2 oz) thinly sliced carrots; add a bouquet garni and the pinions. Season with salt and pepper, cover, and cook gently for 15 minutes. Moisten with 2 dl (7 fl oz, ¾ cup) dry white wine or Madeira and cook uncovered until the liquid has evaporated. Add 400 ml (14 fl oz, 1¾ cups) poultry or veal stock, bring slowly to the boil, then cover and cook in a moderate oven (180 C, 350 F, gas 4) for 40 minutes. Drain the pinions, remove the bacon slices, and brown the pinions quickly in a very hot oven (250 C, 475 F, gas 9). Arrange them on a serving dish. Remove the fat from the cooking liquor, reduce and strain it, and pour over the pinions.

Serve with one of the following garnishes: Choisy, financière, forestière, Godard, jardinière, languedocienne, macédoine, milanaise, piémontaise, rice pilaf, or risotto. Braised pinions may

also be garnished with all kinds of braised or boiled vegetables, coated with butter or cream.

Pinot

One of the great grape 'families' making classic wines. Pinot grapes are grown in many countries. The Pinot Noir makes the finest red Burgundies; it and the Pinot Meunier are two of the black grapes used in Champagne. The Pinot Blanc and the Pinot Gris (often called 'Tokay' in Alsace) are two of the white varieties of Pinot.

pipe COUCHER

To force a paste, icing (frosting), cream, stuffing, or similar substance from a piping (pastry) bag. The operation must be carried out steadily, holding the nozzle of the bag at an angle. The shape of the nozzle and the way it is handled determines the final shape of the preparation – éclairs are made by piping out choux pastry into finger shapes, the mixture for langues de chat is piped out in thin tongue shapes, while the mixture for duchess potatoes is forced out into large spiral rosettes.

piperade

A Basque speciality consisting of a rich stew of tomatoes and sweet peppers (*piper* in Béarnais), sometimes seasoned with onion and garlic, cooked in olive oil or goose fat and then mixed with beaten eggs and lightly scrambled. A garnish of Bayonne ham may also be added or piperade can be eaten with slices of fried ham on the side.

RECIPE

Eggs à la piperade OEUFS À LA PIPERADE Peel and deseed 1 kg (2¼ lb) tomatoes and cut into quarters. Deseed 500 g (18 oz) red and green peppers and cut into strips. Gently fry the peppers and tomatoes, seasoned with salt and pepper, in a large frying pan (skillet) in 2 tablespoons olive oil for 30–40 minutes. Dice 140 g (5 oz) Bayonne ham and add to the fried vegetables. Beat 8 eggs in a salad bowl and pour them gently into the frying pan, stirring until they have coagulated but are still quite soft. Serve piping hot.

piping bag (pastry bag)
POCHE À DOUILLE

A cone-shaped bag fitted with nozzles of different sizes and shapes. The bag may be made of coarse linen, nylon, etc.; the nozzles, made of plastic or metal, have large or small apertures that may be plain, starred, fluted, slitlike, or serrated. Piping (or forcing) bags are used extensively in confectionery and pâtisserie for creating decorative designs of icing (frosting), cream, etc. They are also used for shaping certain pastries, notably éclairs, and for piping potato or meringues.

A rigid syringe may also be used for piping icing instead of a forcing bag but it has a restricted capacity and is not as easy to handle.

piquette

A home-made drink obtained by soaking the residue from grape-pressing in water. By extension, the word denotes a sour wine of poor quality with a low alcohol content.

piroshki or pirozhki
PIROJKI, PIROGUES

In Russian and Polish cooking, small filled pastries served with soup or as a hot entrée. They are made of choux pastry, puff pastry, or a yeast or brioche dough; the savoury filling may be based on fish, rice, game, poultry, meat, brains, cream cheese, chopped vegetables, etc. They can be baked or deep-fried.

RECIPES

Caucasian piroshki PIROJKI CAUCASIENS Spread a thin layer of cheese-flavoured choux pastry on a large baking sheet and cook in a moderate oven (180 C, 350 F, gas 4) for approximately 25 minutes. Turn the pastry out onto the work surface and cut in half. Coat one half with a layer of thick béchamel sauce to which grated cheese and cooked sliced mushrooms have been added. Cover with the other half and seal the edges well. Cut into 6 × 3-cm (2½ × 1¼-in) rectangles. Coat completely with more cheese-flavoured béchamel sauce and then with breadcrumbs. Deep-fry in very hot oil or fat,

drain on absorbent kitchen paper, and arrange on a napkin.

Cheese piroshki PIROJKI AU FROMAGE Butter 3 dariole moulds and line them with unsweetened brioche dough. Mix 220 g (8 oz) curd cheese with 75 g (3 oz) creamed butter and 3 beaten eggs; season with salt, pepper, and nutmeg. Fill the moulds with this mixture and cover with a thin layer of brioche dough. Trim this flush with the edge and press firmly onto the base. Leave to rise at room temperature away from draughts for approximately 1 hour, then cook in a hot oven (220 C, 425 F, gas 7) for 25–30 minutes. Turn out and serve very hot.

Moscow piroshki PIROJKI À LA MOSCOVITE Prepare some unsweetened brioche dough and cut out small ovals, 6–7 cm (2½ in) wide and 10 cm (4 in) long. Prepare the filling: chop and mix 125 g (4½ oz) cooked white fish fillets (whiting or pike), 75 g (3 oz) cooked *vesiga* (dried spinal marrow of the sturgeon), and 2 hard-boiled (hard-cooked) eggs. Season with salt and pepper. Put a large knob of this mixture on each oval. Moisten the edges of the ovals slightly, fold over to cover the filling, and press to seal tightly.

Leave for 30 minutes in a warm place for the dough to rise, then brush with beaten egg and cook in a hot oven (220 C, 425 F, gas 7) for approximately 25 minutes. When ready to serve, drizzle with a little melted maître d'hôtel butter.

Puff-pastry piroshki PIROJKI FEUILLETÉS Make 400 g (14 oz) puff pastry. Prepare 5 tablespoons (6 tablespoons) finely diced cooked game (wild duck, pheasant, young rabbit, or partridge) or the same amount of white fish (fillets of whiting or pike) poached in a court-bouillon. Add to the diced meat 2 chopped hard-boiled (hard-cooked) eggs and 5 tablespoons (6 tablespoons) long-grain rice cooked in meat stock. Mix this hash thoroughly and adjust the seasoning.

Roll out the pastry very thinly and cut out 12 rounds, 7 cm (3 in) in diameter. Pull slightly into oval shapes. Put a small amount of hash onto half of each piece, without going right to the edge. Brush the other half of each oval with beaten egg and fold over, pressing the edges together firmly. Score the top and brush with beaten egg. Cook in a hot oven (220 c, 425 f, gas 7) for about 20 minutes until crisp, puffy, and golden. Serve piping hot.

pirot

A speciality of Poitou consisting of pieces of sautéed kid goat seasoned with fresh garlic and sorrel.

pis

A French butchery term denoting the breast and belly meat of cattle, equivalent to brisket and flank in England, and also to plate in the United States. There is no direct translation as French cuts of meat differ from those of the English and Americans.

The word is also sometimes used for the udder of the cow, ewe, goat, or sow but this is more frequently referred to as *tétine* in French.

pissaladière

A speciality of the Nice region, consisting of a flan filled with onions and garnished with anchovy fillets and black (ripe) olives. It is traditionally coated with the condiment pissalat before being cooked, hence the name. A good pissaladière should have a layer of onions half as thick as the base if bread dough is used; if the flan is made with shortcrust pastry (basic pie dough), the layer of onions should be as thick as the flan pastry. It can be eaten hot or cold.

| RECIPE

Pissaladière Prepare 700 g (1½ lb) bread dough, and work into it 4 tablespoons (⅓ cup) olive oil. Knead it by hand, roll it into a ball, and leave to rise for 1 hour at room temperature. Soak 12 salted anchovies for a short while in cold water (or use 24 drained canned anchovy fillets).

Peel and chop 1 kg (2¼ lb) onions and fry them gently until soft in a covered frying pan (skillet) with 4–5 tablespoons (5–6 tablespoons) olive oil, a pinch of salt, a little pepper, 3 crushed cloves of garlic, thyme, and bay leaf. Fillet the anchovies. Strain 1 tablespoon pickled capers, pound them into a purée, and add to the softened onions.

Take three-quarters of the dough and flatten it to form a circle. Place on an oiled baking sheet and spread with the onion and caper mixture, leaving a rim around the edge. Roll up the anchovy fillets and press them into the onions, together with 20 or so small black (ripe) olives. Shape the rim of the dough to form a wide border that will retain the filling. Roll out the remainder of the dough and cut it into thin strips. Place these in a crisscross pattern over the filling, pressing the ends into the border. Brush the dough with oil and cook in a very hot oven (240 c, 475 f, gas 9) for approximately 20 minutes.

The strips of dough may be replaced by anchovy fillets arranged in a crisscross pattern if preferred.

pissalat or pissala

A condiment originating from the Nice region, made of anchovy purée flavoured with cloves, thyme, bay leaf, and pepper and mixed with olive oil. Originally pissalat was made from the fry of sardines and anchovies, but since this is not readily available outside the Mediterranean, anchovies in brine may be used instead. Pissalat is used for seasoning hors d'oeuvres, fish, cold meats, and the regional dish pissaladière.

| RECIPE

Escalopes of red mullet with pissalat ESCALOPES DE ROUGET AU PISSALAT (from a recipe of the Métropole Hotel, Beaulieu-sur-Mer) Fillet 3 red mullet, each weighing about 200 g (7 oz). Season with salt and pepper and cook in a frying pan (skillet) in 2–3 tablespoons (3–4 tablespoons) olive oil and 30 g (1 oz, 2 tablespoons) butter. When cooked, remove and drain on absorbent paper. Arrange the fillets in a ring on a round serving dish. Prepare some beurre blanc and mix with some pissalat to taste. Coat the fillets lightly with this sauce and garnish with small sprigs of chervil or cress.

pistache

A method of preparation from Languedoc, characterized by the presence of garlic cloves in the cooking liquid; it is used particularly for marinated and braised mutton (pistache of mutton or mutton *en pistache*) and also for partridges and pigeons.

The Saint-Gaudens pistache, a speciality of Comminges, is a somewhat richer variation comprising a mutton ragout with cloves of garlic to which are added haricot (navy) beans cooked with a shin of pork, fresh pork rind, and a bouquet garni.

RECIPE

Shoulder of mutton en pistache
ÉPAULE DE MOUTON EN PISTACHE
Roll up and tie a boned shoulder of mutton and place it in a flameproof casserole lined with a large slice of raw unsmoked (boiled) ham, 1 sliced onion, and 1 sliced carrot. Add salt, pepper, and 2 tablespoons (3 tablespoons) goose fat or lard. Cook over a very gentle heat for 20–25 minutes. Remove the mutton and ham and add 2 tablespoons (3 tablespoons) flour to the casserole. Stir and cook for a few minutes, then add 2 dl (7 fl oz, ¾ cup) white wine and the same amount of stock. Mix thoroughly, strain, and set aside.

Dice the ham and return to the casserole, together with the mutton. Add 50 cloves of garlic (blanched in boiling water and peeled), a bouquet garni, and a piece of dried orange peel. Add the strained cooking liquid, cover the casserole, and cook for approximately 1 hour in a hot oven (220 c, 425 f, gas 7). Remove and drain the shoulder, untie it, and arrange on a warm plate. Cover with the sauce (bound with breadcrumbs if necessary) and serve the cloves of garlic as a garnish.

pistachio PISTACHE

The seed of the pistachio tree, native to the Near East and reputedly introduced to Rome by Vitellius during the reign of Tiberius. The tree is now cultivated widely in Mediterranean countries and the southern United States. The pistachio nut is about the size of an olive and the pale-green kernel is surrounded by a reddish skin. It is enclosed in a smooth pale reddish-brown shell, which is easy to break and is covered by a brownish husk. Sweet and delicately flavoured, the kernel is used chiefly for decorating pastries, cakes, and confectionery. It is also used to flavour charcuterie and is eaten roasted and salted in cocktail snacks. It has a high calorific value – 630 Cal per 100 g – because it is rich in fat and carbohydrate.

In Mediterranean and oriental cooking, pistachios are used in poultry sauces and stuffings, and also in hash. In classic cuisine they garnish galantines, brawn (head cheese), and mortadella. In India, pistachio purée is used to season rice and vegetables. Pistachios go best with veal, pork, and poultry. The green colour (often accentuated artificially) makes it very popular for creams (especially for filling cakes, such as the galicien) and also for ice creams and ice-cream desserts. In confectionery it is especially associated with nougat.

RECIPE

Loin of pork with pistachios GIGUE DE PORC FRAÎCHE AUX PISTACHES
Marinate a loin of pork (or unsmoked (fresh) ham) for 24 hours in white Bordeaux wine. Soak 750 g (1¾ lb, 4½ cups) prunes in warm white Bordeaux. Stud the pork joint with garlic and pistachios. Place it in a flameproof casserole, add 3 glasses of the marinade, cover, and cook for 3 hours over a moderate heat. Then add the strained prunes, cook for a further 45 minutes, and serve very hot.

pistou

A condiment from Provence, made of fresh basil crushed with garlic and olive oil. The word (derived from the Italian *pestare*, to pound) is also used for the vegetable and vermicelli soup to which it is added. The condiment, sometimes supplemented by Parmesan cheese and tomatoes, is very similar to the Italian *pesto*, a speciality of Genoa used to season pasta and soups which consists of a thick sauce made of olive oil, Parmesan, garlic, and fresh basil.

RECIPE

Pistou soup SOUPE AU PISTOU
Soak 500 g (18 oz) mixed white and red haricot beans (navy and kidney beans) for 12 hours in cold water. Drain and place in a large saucepan or tureen

together with 2.5 litres (4½ pints, 5½ pints) cold water and a bouquet garni. Bring to the boil, boil rapidly for 10 minutes, then add a little salt, reduce the heat, and cook gently. String 250 g (9 oz) French (green) beans and cut into pieces. Dice 2 or 3 courgettes (zucchini). Scrape and dice 2 carrots and peel and dice 2 turnips. When the haricots have been cooking for 1½ hours, add the French beans, carrots, salt, and pepper. After a further 15 minutes, add the courgettes and turnips. Cook for another 15 minutes then add 200 g (7 oz) large vermicelli and cook for a further 10 minutes.

Meanwhile, pound together the pulp of 2 very ripe tomatoes, 5 peeled garlic cloves, 3–4 tablespoons (¼–⅓ cup) fresh basil leaves, and 75 g (3 oz, ¾ cup) grated Parmesan, gradually adding 4 tablespoons (⅓ cup) olive oil. Add this mixture to the soup while it is still boiling, then remove from the heat and serve piping hot.

Quartered artichoke hearts or potatoes may be added 30 minutes before the end of cooking, if wished.

pitcher CRUCHE

A pot-bellied vessel, cylindrical or truncated in shape, made of stoneware, glass, or pottery and having one or two handles and a pouring spout (or a slanting neck). Pitchers are usually used for serving cool drinks (water, fruit juices, etc.). A small pitcher (*cruchon*) is sometimes used in France for serving local wines.

Pithiviers

A cow's-milk cheese from the Orléans area, with a high fat content (40–45%), a soft texture, and a greyish-white furry crust. Ripened under a thin layer of hay, it is a supple creamy-yellow cheese when ripe, with a strong flavour. Very similar to Coulommiers, it is shaped into rounds, 12 cm (5 in) in diameter and 2.5 cm (1 in) thick.

pithiviers

A large round puff-pastry tart with scalloped edges, filled with an almond cream. A speciality of Pithiviers, in the Orléans region, it traditionally serves as a Twelfth-Night cake, when it contains a broad (fava) bean. The town of

Pithiviers is also renowned for another cake, again made of puff pastry, but filled with crystallized (candied) fruit and covered with white fondant icing (frosting). The classic pithiviers has been interpreted in various ways, the almond cream being replaced by such fillings as creamed rice, kidneys, and even chicken liver in sauce.

RECIPE

Pithiviers Cream 100 g (3½ oz, scant ½ cup butter with a spatula and mix with 100 g (3½ oz, ½ cup) caster (superfine) sugar. Then beat in 6 egg yolks, one at a time, 40 g (1½ oz) potato flour, 100 g (3½ oz, scant cup) ground almonds, and 2 tablespoons (3 tablespoons) rum. Mix this cream thoroughly. Roll out 200 g (7 oz) puff pastry and cut out a circle 20 cm (8 in) in diameter. Spread this with the almond paste, leaving a 1.5-cm (½-in) margin all round. Beat 1 egg yolk and brush it around the rim of the circle.

Roll out a further 300 g (11 oz) pastry and cut another circle the same size as the first but thicker. Place it on the first circle and seal the rim. Decorate the edge with the traditional scalloped pattern and brush with beaten egg. Score diamond or rosette patterns on the top with the point of a knife. Cook in a hot oven (220 c, 425 f, gas 7) for 30 minutes. Dust with icing (confectioners') sugar and return it to the oven for a few minutes to glaze. Serve warm or cold.

pizza

A very popular Italian dish originating from Naples. In its simplest form it consists of a thin slab of bread dough spread with thick tomato purée and Parmesan or Mozzarella cheese, seasoned with herbs and garlic, then baked in an oven. There are countless varieties of pizza, garnished with vegetables (small artichoke hearts, peas, olives, mushrooms, peppers, capers, etc.), slices of smoked sausage, ham, anchovy fillets, seafood, or mussels. It can be served as an entrée, a savoury, or a snack.

The word 'pizza' derives from a verb meaning to sting or to season. From the same origin comes *à la pizzaiola*, a piquant mixture of tomato sauce, shreds of pepper, herbs (thyme, marjoram, bay leaf), and garlic which is suitable for pasta, pork chops, or grills.

Léon Gessi in *Rome et ses environs* describes pizza as 'a blossoming flower, noble and full of fragrant odours; Mozzarella bubbles in the heat of the fire, revealing spots of oil and touches of tomato. Rust-coloured streaks soften the bright red of these touches, but it is the anchovy purée which strengthens the taste on the palate ... which is difficult to define because it subtly covers a range extending from a sweet kiss to a sharp bite ...'

Neapolitan pizza went around the world with migrating Italians, who opened pizzerias in the major cities of Europe and North America. These are typically small popular restaurants which offer Italian pasta, pizzas, and other specialities.

In classic French cuisine, pizza is prepared as a tartlet of shortcrust pastry (basic pie dough) or puff pastry garnished with a purée of tomatoes, olives, and anchovies. Miniature pizzas are used as cocktail snacks.

RECIPE

Pizza dough PÂTE À PIZZA Crumble 15 g (½ oz) fresh baker's yeast (½ cake compressed yeast) into 3 tablespoons (¼ cup) warm water containing a little sugar and leave until frothy (about 15 minutes). Alternatively, sprinkle 2 teaspoons dried yeast into the same amount of water and sugar, stir until dissolved, and leave in a warm place until frothy.

Sieve 350 g (12 oz, 3 cups) flour, make a well in the centre, and pour in 3 dl (½ pint, 1¼ cups) warm water and 4 tablespoons (⅓ cup) olive oil. Add the yeast and 1 teaspoon salt. Work the dough with the fingers then knead on a floured board until the dough becomes smooth and elastic (about 10 minutes). Roll it into a ball, dust with flour, and leave in a covered bowl in a warm place away from draughts until it has doubled in volume (about 1½ hours).

Knead for a further minute then roll out into a circle about 25 cm (10 in) in diameter. Raise the edge with the thumbs to form a rim. The pizza is ready for filling and baking in the oven.

Pizza Mario (from a recipe by Mario Vernocchi) Make some fairly short pastry with 500 g (18 oz, 4½ cups) flour, 1 glass good-quality olive oil, and a large pinch of salt. Leave overnight. Then flatten the dough by hand and line a lightly oiled tart plate with it. Open some mussels over the heat, then remove from their shells. Add them to a hash of chopped shallots, salt, pepper, 5–6 pounded anchovies, and 2–3 crushed tomatoes. Spread this mixture over the dough and decorate with 2 anchovy fillets arranged in a cross and a few black (ripe) olives. Sprinkle with grated Parmesan, and a dash of olive oil and cook for 12 minutes in a hot oven (230 C, 450 F, gas 8).

plaice PLIE

A flatfish abundant in the Atlantic, the English Channel, and the North Sea, but rare in the Mediterranean. It is 25–65 cm (10–26 in) long, with both eyes on the right-hand (i.e. uppermost) side, which is grey-brown in colour with orange spots (which are very distinct and bright in fresh fish). The blind (lower) side is pearly grey.

Plaice is available all the year round, but is best from November to April. Allow a 180–220-g (6–8-oz) whole fish per portion, because of waste. The flesh, which has a delicate taste and texture, can be prepared like sole or brill; it is particularly suitable for frying, grilling (broiling), poaching, and preparing *à la bonne femme* and even *à la Dugléré*: according to tradition, it was for plaice that the chef Dugléré of the Café Anglais originally created this dish.

RECIPE

plaice à la florentine PLIE À LA FLORENTINE Clean a large plaice, put it into a buttered dish, add equal quantities of concentrated fish stock (or court-bouillon) and white wine, and bake for approximately 35 minutes in a moderate oven (160 C, 325 F, gas 3), basting frequently. Remove from the dish and drain. Completely cover an ovenproof serving dish with spinach braised in butter. Lay the plaice on the spinach, cover with Mornay sauce, sprinkle with grated cheese and clarified *plate* **967**

butter, and glaze quickly in a very hot oven.

plaisir

A popular name, meaning literally 'pleasure', formerly given to wafers (*oublies*) rolled into a cone, which street vendors offered 'for pleasure'.

plantain

Any of various species of common herbaceous plants found growing in the wild. The young leaves may be used in salads or soups.

For plantain bananas, see *banana*.

plastics   PLASTIQUES

A wide range of synthetic materials, of polymeric structure, which can be modelled or moulded during manufacture. The first plastic – Celluloid (cellulose nitrate) – was manufactured in 1868. Modern manufacturing processes, including the use of stabilizing agents, antioxidants, and lubricants, give products with varying degrees of flexibility and transparency. Tough, light, and of various colours, plastics have replaced many traditional materials in the kitchen as well as providing some new items of equipment. For a plastic to be of 'food quality' it must contain authorized constituents that do not react with the food. Not all 'food quality' plastics are suitable for all foods. In particular, plastic bottles can only be used for a few clearly defined products.

The principal plastics used for foods are polystyrene (e.g. pots for cheese, yogurt, fresh cream, etc.); expanded polystyrene (e.g. cartons for eggs, certain cheeses, fruit and vegetable trays); polythene (corks, boxes, bottles, protective films, bags, and sachets); and polyvinyl chloride (PVC) (bottles for oil, wine, mineral water, and soft drinks; boxes for fruit, biscuits (cookies), and confectionery).

plate   ASSIETTE

A piece of crockery used to hold food, the size and shape varying according to the nature of the food it is meant to contain. In this sense, the French word *assiette* replaced the term *écuelle* (bowl) in the 16th century. The name *assiette* derives from the fact that it marked the position of the eater at the table, i.e.

where he was seated (*assis*). The word denoted the action of placing an eater or a guest at the table, then the action of putting the plates on the table, then the serving of a meal (by a tavern-keeper who *tenait assiette*, i.e. offered food to customers), and finally, it came to mean the complete range of dishes served during the course of a meal. The varied hors-d'oeuvres served on small plates were called *assiettes assorties* ('assorted plates'). Nowadays these are served on hors-d'oeuvres dishes. The name *assiettes volantes* ('flying plates') was given to different dishes served as an entrée on round plates.

In ancient times, plates, either flat or bowl-shaped, were made of terra cotta, wood, or precious or nonprecious metal. The Romans also moulded them from glass paste. By the end of the 15th century, silver plates had become a symbol of wealth in France, and up to the 17th century the tables of the rich bourgeoisie were covered with magnificent gold plate and silverware. But following the disastrous wars in the reign of Louis XIV, faïence and porcelain replaced precious metal in rich homes. Nicholas de Bonnefons commented in 1653 on the novelty of the individual soup plate, or *assiette à l'italienne*, introduced into France by Mazarin and given the name of *mazarine*: 'The plates are hollowed out so that one can be offered soup and serve oneself with the quantity one wishes to consume, without taking it spoonful by spoonful from the dish, and without the distaste that some might feel about the spoons of others being taken out of the mouth and dipped into the dish without first being wiped.' Nowadays, other materials are used: stainless or enamelled metal, treated glass, plastic, and disposable paper plates.

The centre of a hollowed-out plate is called the ombilic (navel). The edge is called marli (raised rim) or talus (slope), but some modern soup plates do not have this feature. A complete table service includes, in descending order of size: flat plates, soup plates, cheese plates, dessert plates, fruit plates, buffet plates, and bread plates. The salad plate may be half-moon-shaped. Other special plates complete the service: plates with six or twelve compartments for snails and oysters, plates for fondue bourguignonne with compartments for the sauces, suitably shaped bowls for avocados, corn-on-the-cob, and artichokes, and draining plates that are used to serve strawberries or asparagus. Presentation plates are a particular refinement: very flat and sometimes made of silver or silver-gilt, they are placed underneath a second slightly smaller flat plate. They remain on the table when each plate is changed and are only removed at the cheese course. Cake stands consist of several plates of decreasing size mounted above one another on a stand and may be used to serve crystallized (candied) fruits or petits fours.

☐ Correct use of plates Etiquette requires that two plates should never be placed on top of each other (except for presentation plates). The table is first laid with flat plates, which are replaced when the guests are seated by those for the first course. This custom is now limited to catering establishments. Changing plates, however, is necessary after the fish course and for the cheese course. Finally, it is advisable to have heated plates ready to serve hot dishes. In France, the practice of serving soup in a hot plate, just before the guests come to the table, was inaugurated by Émilie Comtat, an actress at the time of the Empire and the only woman admitted to Grimod de La Reynière's 'jury of tasters'.

Although the use of plates is widespread in most western countries, this is far from being the case in other parts of the world. In the Far East they usually use bowls. In Africa, it is often the custom to eat out of the main dish with the fingers, whilst in the Middle East flat breads are sometimes used instead of plates.

Platina (*born* Bartolomeo Sacchi)

Italian humanist (born Platina, 1421; died Rome, 1481), known as 'Il Platina'. Born near Cremona, he became the Vatican librarian after publishing in Venice in 1474 a book in Latin on the culinary art entitled *De honestia Voluptate ac Valetudine* ('Honest Pleasure and Health'). This highly successful work was published six times in 30 years and translated into French by the prior of Saint-Maurice, near Montpellier, with the help of a famous cook of the time, Nony Comeuse. Il Platina defended the then novel idea that delicacy is more important than quantity in cooking. He protested against the abuse of spices and recommended seasoning with lemon juice or wine. Furthermore, he suggested starting a meal with fresh fruit, such as melon or figs. His collection of recipes, which also contains a wealth of medical advice, is one of the first to describe regional specialities of the south of France.

plisson

A speciality of Poitou. It is a thick very sweet dessert cream obtained by heating milk and sugar very gently, several times in succession, without boiling.

plombières

An ice cream made with custard cream prepared with almond-flavoured milk and usually enriched with whipped cream and mixed with crystallized (candied) fruit steeped in Kirsch. Formerly, plombières cream was a type of custard cream, usually prepared with milk enriched with ground almonds and whipped cream, served with melted apricot jam sauce or in a pastry shell. Balzac writes in his novel *Splendeurs et Misères des courtisanes* (1847): 'After supper, ices by the name of plombières were served. Everyone knows that this type of ice is arranged in a pyramid with small very delicate crystallized fruit placed on the surface. It is served in a small glass dish and the covering of crystallized fruit in no way affects the pyramid shape.'

It has been said (incorrectly) that plombières ice cream was invented at Plombières-les-Bains, in the Vosges, at a time when Napoleon III was taking a cure there. During his visit, he entertained an Italian diplomat called Cavour, who persuaded him to intervene in the War of Liberation between Italy and Austria (1859). However, it had already been mentioned by Balzac before this, so one must assume that the etymology of plombières is connected with the lead (*plomb*) moulds in which it was originally made. The addition of crystallized fruit to the recipe, which is the distinctive feature of this dessert, dates back to the beginning of the 19th century.

RECIPE

Plombières ice cream GLACE PLOMBIÈRES Pound thoroughly in a mortar (or put through a blender or processor) 300 g (11 oz, 2 cups) blanched fresh almonds and (if desired) 10 g (½ oz, 1½ tablespoons) ground bitter almonds, gradually adding ½ glass milk. Then add 1.5 litres (2¼ pints, 2¾ pints) scalded cream and mix thoroughly. Rub through a fine sieve. Place 300 g (11 oz, 1½ cups) caster (superfine) sugar and 12 egg yolks in a large bowl and beat until the mixture becomes white and thick. Bring the almond milk to the boil and pour it onto the egg and sugar mixture, whisking continuously. Place over the heat and stir gently until the cream coats the back of the spoon. Then immerse the base of the saucepan in cold water to stop the cooking process and continue to whisk until the cream has cooled. Place in an ice-cream freezer.

When the mixture is partially frozen, mix in 200 g (7 oz, generous 1 cup) finely chopped crystallized (candied) fruit soaked in Kirsch or rum, 4 dl (14 fl oz, 1¾ cups) whipped double (heavy) cream, and 1.5 dl (¼ pint, ⅔ cup) milk, both very cold. Then place in an ice-cream mould and freeze.

plover PLUVIER

A migratory wading bird of which several species winter in western Europe. In the Middle Ages the plover was considered to be a very delicate and delicious food, served at winter feasts and in the best houses. The ringed plover frequents the marshlands and water meadows near the sea, while the golden plover, which is the most sought-after, inhabits moorlands. Plovers are considered to be excellent game and certain gastronomes insist that they should be cooked undrawn. This tradition is an old one: in the 16th century, according to Lucien Tendret, only three kinds of birds – larks, turtledoves and plovers – could be roasted without 'breaking into them'. Plover can be prepared in the same way as woodcock or lapwing, but it is usually roasted. Its

eggs are used in the same way as those of the lapwing.

pluches

The French name for the fresh leaves of certain herbs, such as chervil, tarragon, and parsley, used to flavour salads and hot dishes. Chervil pluches, for example, are used to flavour several sauces and soups, the leaves being cut with scissors rather than chopped, and added to the dish at the last minutes to give maximum flavour. It is important not to boil these herbs and thus impair their flavour, although for certain recipes the leaves may be quickly blanched in boiling water before use.

pluck FRESSURE

The heart, spleen, liver, and lungs of a slaughtered animal. The components of ox (beef) and calf's pluck are cooked separately. Lamb's or sheep's pluck is prepared as a ragout with red or white wine in several regions. Pig's pluck is a speciality of Vendée, where it is made into a ragout together with the animal's blood and skin and sometimes the head.

At one time, all these pieces of offal were made into a ragout. The French potter and writer Bernard Palissy made the following remark: 'In my time I have found that people did not want to eat sheep's feet, heads, or stomachs, yet at the moment this is what they prize most highly.'

plucking PLUMER

The process of removing the feathers from a fowl or a game bird. It is usual to start at the tail and work towards the head; care must be taken not to tear the skin. The feathers are easier to remove if the bird is put into the refrigerator to firm the flesh (especially in the case of a small bird). Poultry is usually sold ready-plucked, but small feathers often remain on the wing tips, and these should also be plucked before singeing, which burns off any residual down. Any remaining vestiges of the feathers, such as the tube-like remnants of the shafts, can be removed with the point of a knife.

plum PRUNE

A yellow, green, red, or purple stone fruit which is eaten fresh from July to

September as a dessert fruit and has numerous uses in pâtisserie and confectionery. It is also dried (see *prune*), preserved in brandy, and distilled to produce a spirit.

Originating in Asia, the plum tree was cultivated in Syria and grafted by the Romans, who preserved plums by drying (particularly damsons). It was the Crusaders who introduced the plum to western Europe. The fruit was particularly prized after the Renaissance (see *greengage*). From the 16th century plums were widely cultivated and many varieties were developed in France. Among these were the Catherine, the Impériale, the Perdrigon, the Goutte d'Or, and the Plum de Monsieur (the favourite of Louis XIII's brother).

Providing 64 Cal per 100 g, the plum is a juicy yet fairly acid fruit with quite a high sugar content and containing potassium, calcium, and vitamins. Plums selected for eating should be ripe but not soft, wrinkled, or blemished; a very slight matt white bloom on the surface proves that they have not been handled too much. The main plum-producing regions of France are in the southwest, the southeast, and the east. They are also grown in abundance in Britain with imported varieties available most of the year.

● Mid-June to mid-July: Japanese varieties are available. Fairly mediocre in quality, they are large, round, and juicy, either purplish-red with orange-coloured flesh or orange-yellow with yellow flesh.

● July: the market is dominated by the Bonne de Bry (small, blue, and rounded, with a juicy and very sweet greenish-yellow flesh) and the greengage (yellowish-green, with firm, very juicy, sweet, and fragrant flesh).

● August to September: another greengage appears (reddish-purple, as good as the green variety), followed by the Ente plum (elongated, purplish-red, with sweet but not very juicy flesh), the Alsatian quetsche (small, oblong, and purple-black, with very sweet fragrant yellow flesh), the Nancy early mirabelle, and – at the end of August – the Vosges mirabelle (small, round, and orange-red, with very fragrant, sweet, and juicy flesh).

In Britain too there are several varieties of plum, apart from the greengage and the damson.

● Czar (early August): a large dark-blue plum with golden flesh, suitable for cooking or as a dessert variety.

● Pershore (August): a conical-shaped dessert fruit with a yellow skin and rather pulpy flesh.

● Victoria (late August): a very popular fruit, large and oval with a yellowish-scarlet, skin. Sweet and juicy, it is perfect for bottling or eating as a dessert fruit.

● Kirke's Blue (late August): a large fruit with deep-purple skin with a distinct bloom and dark sweet juicy flesh; suitable for cooking or eating as a dessert fruit.

Later varieites include Warwickshire Drooper, the cherry plum, and the Monarch.

In the United States the Santa Rosa and Burbank plums are tart and juicy and are grown especially in California. They are also known as Japanese plums and are exported throughout Europe. Dark-purple beach plums grow wild in the USA, especially around Cape Cod; they are mostly used to make beach-plum jelly.

A distinction is made between the varieties of plums used for cooking, preserves, jams, and distillery, and those varieties that are enjoyed as dessert fruits. The Metz mirabelle and the quetsche, for example, are both used for distilling. The damson is used for bottling and jam-making and for making damson cheese. This traditional English preparation is a very thick damson pulp, boiled with sugar, which stores well and is served with biscuits (cookies) or used to fill tartlets.

RECIPES

Flamed plums PRUNES FLAMBÉES Stone (pit) some greengages or mirabelle plums and poach them in a vanilla-flavoured syrup until just tender. Drain them and place in a flame-proof pan. Add a little arrowroot blended with water to the cooking syrup, pour a little of this syrup over the plums, and heat. Sprinkle with quetsche or mirabelle brandy heated in a ladle, flame, and serve immediately.

Plum conserve MARMELADE DE PRUNES Stone (pit) some plums, weigh the pulp, and weigh out 750 g (generous 1½ lb, generous 3 cups) granulated sugar per kg (2¼ lb) pulp. Put the fruit in a preserving pan with 1 dl (6 tablespoons, scant ½ cup) water per kg (2¼ lb) fruit. Bring to the boil and leave to cook for about 20 minutes, stirring with a wooden spoon. Put the contents of the pan through a blender, return the purée obtained to the pan, and add the sugar. Cook until the conserve coats the wooden spoon. Pot in the usual way (see *jams, jellies, and marmalades*).

Plums in brandy PRUNES À L'EAU-DE-VIE Choose some very ripe sound plums or greengages, prick them in 3 or 4 places with a large needle, and weigh them. In a preserving pan, prepare a sugar syrup with 250 g (9 oz, generous cup) sugar and ½ dl (2½ tablespoons, 3 tablespoons) water per kg (2¼ lb) fruit, bring it to the boil, and leave to boil for 2 minutes. Add the plums, stir the pan so that the plums are evenly coated with syrup, then transfer them into jars with a skimmer. Leave to cool completely, then add some fruit spirit (1 litre (1¾ pints, 4¼ cups) per kg (2¼ lb) plums), covering the plums. Seal the jars. Leave to stand for at least 3 months before consuming.

Plum tart TARTE AUX PRUNES Prepare a lining pastry with 200 g (7 oz, 1¾ cups flour, 90 g (3½ oz, scant ½ cup) softened butter, a pinch of salt, 1 egg, and 1 tablespoon water. Roll the dough into a ball and refrigerate for 2 hours. Wash 500 g (18 oz) ripe plums and stone (pit) them without separating the halves completely. Roll out the dough to a thickness of 5 mm (¼ in) and use it to line a buttered tart tin (pan). Trim off the excess pastry and mark the edge with a crisscross pattern. Prick the bottom with a fork, sprinkle with 40 g (1½ oz 3 tablespoons) caster (superfine) sugar, and arrange the plums in the tart, opened out with curved sides downwards. Sprinkle the fruit with 40 g (1½ oz, 3 tablespoons) caster sugar. Cook in a moderately hot oven (200 C, 400 F, gas 6) for 30 minutes. Remove from the oven, leave until lukewarm, then coat the top with apricot jam.

plum cake

A traditional English cake flavoured with rum and containing currants, raisins, sultanas, and candied peel.

| RECIPE

Plum cake Soften 500 g (18 oz, 2¼ cups) butter until creamy, and beat until it turns very pale. Add 500 g (18 oz, 2¼ cups) sugar and beat again for a few minutes. Then incorporate 8 eggs, one at a time, beating well after each addition. Add 250 g (9 oz, 1½ cups) chopped candied peel (orange, citron, or lemon), 200 g (7 oz, 1¼ cups) stoned raisins, 150 g (5 oz, 1 cup) sultanas, and 150 g (5 oz, 1 cup) currants. Mix in 500 g (18 oz, 4½ cups) flour sifted with 6 g (1½ teaspoons) baking powder, the grated rind of 2 lemons, and 4 cl (3 tablespoons, 4 tablespoons) rum.

Line a 25-cm (10-in) round cake tin with greaseproof (waxed) paper so that it extends 4 cm (1½ in) above the rim. Pour the mixture into the tin, taking care not to fill it above two-thirds. Bake in a moderate oven (180 C, 350 F, gas 4) for about 2 hours or until a skewer inserted in the centre of the cake comes out clean. Cover with a piece of aluminium foil if the cake is browning too much during cooking. Leave to cool in the tin for 10 minutes, then turn out onto a wire rack to cool completely.

plum pudding

A traditional English pudding made with suet, raisins, currants, sultanas, prunes, almonds, spices, and rum. It is boiled or steamed in a pudding basin (mould) and traditionally served flamed with brandy or rum and accompanied by brandy butter or sauce.

| RECIPE

Plum pudding Place the following ingredients in a large mixing bowl: 125 g (4½ oz, scant cup) suet, 175 g (6 oz, 1½ cups) chopped blanched almonds, 250 g (9 oz, 1½ cups) each of raisins and currants, 100 g (4 oz, 1 cup) sifted flour a generous pinch of salt, 250 g (9 oz, generous cup) caster (superfine) sugar,

125 g (4½ oz, 1 cup) stale breadcrumbs, 250 g (9 oz, 1½ cups) chopped candied peel, the grated rind of half a lemon, and ½ teaspoon mixed spice, ground cinnamon, and grated nutmeg.

Beat 4 eggs with ½ glass milk and the same quantity of rum. Add to the mixing bowl.

Boil 150 g (5 oz, ⅔ cup) sugar with ½ glass cold water until golden brown, then stir in ¼ litre (8 fl oz, 1 cup) boiling water. Add this caramel to the mixing bowl.

Stir the mixture thoroughly for 15 minutes.

Butter a large pudding basin (mould) and place a circle of greaseproof (waxed) paper at the bottom. Place 125 g (4½ oz, ¾ cup) stoned (pitted) prunes (previously soaked in cold tea or water, then drained) in the basin and pour the pudding mixture on top. Cover with a circle of greaseproof paper, then with a pudding cloth or double thickness aluminium foil. Place the basin in the basket of a pressure cooker and add enough water to reach halfway up the basin. Cook for 1½ hours, beginning the timing from the moment that steam begins to escape. Alternatively, cook for 4 hours in a steamer or on an old saucer in a saucepan with enough boiling water to reach halfway up the basin. Remove the basin, wrap in aluminium foil, and store in a cool place. Steam for 1 hour more in a pressure cooker, or 2 hours in a steamer or saucepan, before serving.

Then turn the pudding out onto a serving dish and sprinkle with 3 tablespoons (4 tablespoons) sugar. Pour ½ glass warm rum over the pudding and set it alight. The pudding can also be served cold.

Plutarch PLUTARQUE

Greek biographer, essayist, and philosopher (born Chaeronea, Boeotia, c. 50 AD; died Chaeronea, c. 125 AD). His main source of inspiration was Platonism, and he wrote approximately 250 essays, of which about a third have survived in the form of his *Parallel Lives* (a series of biographies) and the *Moralia*. Among the latter are a few fragments from a *Symposium*, which deals with cooking and dietetics. The translation in 1572 by Jacques Amyot, a French bishop and classical scholar, made Plutarch the most widely read and influential ancient author in France until the 19th century. The *Symposia* were published in France under the title *Règles et Préceptes de santé de Plutarque* (Plutarch's rules and precepts about health).

poaching POCHAGE

A method of cooking food by gently simmering it in liquid. The amount of water or stock used depends on the food to be poached.

Red meat is poached in a white stock with vegetables. It is usually immersed in simmering stock, so that it is sealed and retains its juices and flavour. White meat is seldom poached.

Large poultry to be poached is put into cold white stock with vegetables; the liquid is then brought to the boil, skimmed, and seasoned. The poultry is then simmered very slowly in the stock. Poultry for poaching can be stuffed or not, and trussed. It can be larded with best lardons or studded with pieces of ham, tongue, or truffles cut into the shape of little pegs. To protect the breast while cooking, poultry should be barded. To test whether the poultry is ready, prick the thigh. When the juice which runs out is white, the bird is cooked. After cooking, drain and untruss the poultry and remove the barding. Serve on fried bread, surrounded with an appropriate garnish. The stock, strained and skimmed, is boiled down and added to the sauce to be served with the dish.

Large fish can be poached whole or in slices, and moistened with concentrated fish stock or court-bouillon. Thick slices of fish are prepared in the same way. Fillets of fish (brill, whiting, sole, turbot, etc.) to be poached are put in a buttered baking dish, seasoned, moistened with a few tablespoons of concentrated fish stock, and cooked in the oven.

Poached eggs are cooked in simmering salt water to which a few drops of vinegar have been added.

Fish or meat balls are put into a buttered pan, covered with boiling salt water, and very slowly simmered.

Fruit is poached in a sugar syrup to cook it while still retaining its shape.

A variety of foods are poached on the bain-marie principle, including mousses, mousselines, moulds, puddings, etc. They are stood in baking tins or pans half-full of hot water and cooked in a very slow oven.

pochouse or pauchouse

A Burgundy matelote (fish stew) made from a selection of pike, gudgeon, eel, perch, or carp; it should also include burbot, which is now very rare. The Bresse pochouse often includes tench, carp, and catfish. Pochouse is cooked with white wine and thickened with kneaded butter.

The name is probably derived from the French *poche*, a fisherman's game bag which in the local patois along the banks of the Doubs and the Saône is also known as a *pochouse*. The recipe comes from the Lower Doubs and is a very old one, appearing in the dispensary registers of the hospital of Saint-Louis de Chalon-sur-Saône as early as 1598. It was introduced into Burgundy by the fish merchants from Bresse. The dish is a speciality of Verdun-sur-le-Doubs where there is an association, the Confrérie des Chevaliers de la Pochouse, which is dedicated to preserving it.

| RECIPE

Pochouse   Butter a casserole generously and completely cover the bottom with 2–3 large peeled sliced onions and 2 carrots cut into rings. Clean 2 kg (4½ lb) freshwater fish and cut into uniform pieces: use 1 kg (2¼ lb) eels (skinned) and 1 kg (2¼ lb) burbot, tench, pike, carp, etc. Place the pieces of fish in the casserole with a bouquet garni in the centre. Cover with dry white wine and add 2 crushed cloves of garlic. Add salt and pepper, cover, bring to the boil, reduce the heat, and allow to simmer for approximately 20 minutes.

Meanwhile, dice 150 g (5 oz) unsmoked streaky bacon and blanch for 5 minutes in boiling water. Strain. Glaze 20 small onions. Clean and slice 250 g (9 oz, 3 cups) mushrooms and sprinkle with lemon juice. Toss the bacon and mushrooms in butter in a sauté pan. Strain the pieces of fish and add them to the sauté pan, together with the onions.

Thicken the cooking liquid from the fish with 1 tablespoon kneaded butter, strain, and pour into the sauté pan.

Simmer for a few minutes, then add 2 dl (7 fl oz, ¾ cup) fresh cream. Boil uncovered for 5 minutes to reduce. Pour the pochouse into a deep serving dish and garnish with garlic-flavoured croutons.

poêlon

A small long-handled saucepan, often with a lid. It was formerly made of earthenware (glazed or not) and was suitable for slow-cooking, simmering, or braising foods. It is still used for the same purposes, but is now made of stainless steel, black or enamelled cast iron, or enamel plate. It can also be used for browning mushrooms, making sauces, cooking paupiettes or peas with pieces of bacon, etc. The caquelon, used for preparing *fondue savoyarde* (a baked cheese fondue), is a type of poêlon, as is the pan used for making Burgundy fondue, which is deeper, fitted with a lid, and rests on a table warmer. The sugar poêlon is made of copper and is used for cooking sugar and syrups.

pogne, pognon, or pougnon

A type of brioche, sometimes filled with crystallized (candied) fruit, served either hot or cold, often with redcurrant jelly. It is a speciality of the Dauphiné. The *pogne de Romans* is famous, but pognes are also made in Crest (mainly for Easter), Die, and Valence. In certain parts of the Lyonnais and Franche-Comté regions, pognes can be brioches or tarts, made either with fruit or, in winter, with gourd or pumpkin. The word originates from *pougna* or *pugne*, a patois word for the handful of dough left over from bread-making, which housewives used to enrich with butter and eggs to make pastries.

| RECIPE

Pogne de Romans   Arrange 500 g (18 oz, 4½ cups) sifted flour in a circle on the worktop. In the middle of this circle put 8 g (¼ oz, 1¼ teaspoons) salt, 1 tablespoon orange-flower water, 25 g (1 oz) fresh yeast (1 cake compressed yeast), 250 g (9 oz, generous cup) softened butter, and 4 whole eggs. Mix together thoroughly, working the dough vigorously to give it body. Add 2 more eggs, one after the other, and finally incorporate 200 g (7 oz, scant cup) caster (superfine) sugar, little by little, kneading the dough all the while. Place this dough in a bowl sprinkled with flour, cover with a cloth, and leave it to rise for 10–12 hours at room temperature away from draughts.

Turn the dough out onto the table and knock it back with the flat of the hand. Make into 'crowns': shape two-thirds of the dough into balls, then use the remainder to shape smaller balls to place on top, like brioches. Place these crowns in buttered baking tins. Leave the dough to rise for a further 30 minutes in a warm place. Brush with beaten egg and bake in the oven at 190 C (375 F, gas 5) for approximately 40 minutes. Serve with redcurrant jelly.

point (à)

The French term describing a grilled (broiled) or sautéed steak (or other small cut of meat) that is cooked to the medium stage, i.e. between medium-rare and well-done.

By extension, a dish is referred to as *à point* when cooking has reached the desired stage and must be stopped immediately (green vegetables and pasta cooked *al dente*, fish in court-bouillon, etc.); the expression is also used to describe a dish that is ready to be served, all preparations being completed to the chef's satisfaction.

Point (Fernand)

French chef (born Louhans, 1897; died Vienne, 1955). His parents kept the station buffet at Louhans, where both his mother and grandmother were in charge of the cooking. He studied in Paris (as sauce chef at Foyot's, the Bristol, and the Majestic) then at the Hôtel Royal in Évian, where he was the fish chef. In 1922, when the P.L.M. Company refused to officially recognize the Louhans station buffet as a restaurant, Auguste Point (his father) decided to move to Vienne, where he opened a more conventional one. Two years later he left the restaurant to his son, who renamed it La Pyramide. Fernand Point concentrated on producing a cuisine that was based on good-quality food enhanced by careful cooking and meticulous preparation.

The restaurant soon became well known to gastronomes on their way to the south of France. All the famous people of the time came to sample what Curnonsky regarded as the pinnacle of culinary art. Fernand Point's personality also had a lot to do with the popularity of the restaurant: his humour, his intransigence, the warmth of his welcome, his anecdotes, his eccentricities, and his massive size, all contributed to make him one of the great French chefs. After his death, the kitchens of La Pyramide were supervised first by Paul Mercier and then by Guy Thivard, still under Madame Point's administration.

The great chef was also a first-class teacher, and his pupils, namely Thuilier, Bocuse, Chapel, the Troisgros brothers, Outhier, and Bise, bear witness of the value of his training. Point's cuisine was in the great classical mould: truffled Bresse chicken *en vessie*; stuffed almond trout braised in port wine; *délices de Saint-Antoine en feuilleté* (a dish of pigs' trotters (feet) in puff pastry which he made especially for Albert Lebrun); and the famous *marjolaine*, which took him several years to perfect (a light almond and hazelnut sponge cake filled with three different creams – chocolate, butter, and praline).

'The pharaoh of the Pyramide at Vienne' (in the words of his biographer Félix Benoît) is also remembered for his maxims, which can be found in his book *Ma gastronomie*: 'Garnishes must be matched like a tie to a suit' and 'A good meal must be as harmonious as a symphony and as well-constructed as a Norman cathedral.' He considered that the most difficult preparations were often those that appear to be the easiest: 'A béarnaise sauce is simply an egg yolk, a shallot, a little tarragon vinegar, and butter, but it takes years of practice for the result to be perfect.'

poirat

A traditional pastry of Berry that is also found in the Bourbonnais region. It is a pie filled with sweetened sliced pears soaked in brandy, served hot with fresh cream that is poured through the hole in the pastry crust.

poire

A French cut of beef that is part of the topside. It is a round lean very tender cut and is cooked as steak. It weighs approximately 500 g (18 oz).

Poitou

The variable quality of the soil has not prevented Poitou from having solid culinary traditions. The prosperity of the region is based on its cereal crops, cattle, sheep, goats, pigs, and poultry. The ground and winged game (hare, rabbit, quail, thrush, and partridge) are plentiful, and the produce of the lakes and rivers provide excellent fish dishes: tench *à la poitevine*, lamprey simmered in wine, eels sautéed in garlic, grilled (broiled), or prepared as a bouilleture. The marshland of Poitou provides frogs, and the nearby coastline of the Vendée provides sea fish (especially for chaudrée) and shellfish (especially mussels and oysters).

The cultivated marshlands are very fertile, yielding onions, artichokes, asparagus, melons, peas, white beans (*mojettes*, cooked with cream) and French beans, leeks (which are made into a succulent vegetable loaf), cauliflowers, and cabbage. Orchards are planted with apples (especially the 'Clochard' variety), cherries, peaches, and walnuts, as well as the chestnuts for which the region is famous.

Soups typical of the region include a wine soup, served either hot (known as *rôtie*) or cold (*migé*), and a pig's head potée. Charcuterie specialities include the famous *pâté de Pâques en croûte* (a pie filled with with meat, poultry, meatballs, and hard-boiled (hard-cooked) eggs), duck-liver pâtés, and the confits of Civray and Sauzé-Vaussais. Snails (*lumas*) are cooked stuffed or in wine, and frogs' legs are prepared as a blanquette or *à la luçonnaise* (sautéed in butter and garnished with fried garlic cloves). Among the most characteristic dishes of Poitou are the *sauce de pire* (pig's liver and lung simmered with onions, shallots, red wine, and spices), the gigorit of pork and poultry, the Vendée *fressure* (pigs' fry with bacon, eaten cold), the pirot prepared with goat meat, young fresh garlic, and sorrel, the Poitou *biftecks* (chopped beef bound

with bone marrow, eggs, breadcrumbs, onions, and white wine), and also the far and forcemeats.

Poitou produces some good fresh cheeses, such as caillebottes and small caillés, but is best known for its wide variety of goats'-milk cheeses, including the famous Chabichou, the Bougon, La-Mothe-Saint-Héray, Lusignan, Parthenay, Saint-Loup, Saint-Saviol, Saint-Varent, Sauzé-Vaussais, Trois-Cornes, and Xaintray.

Among the desserts should be mentioned the tourteau made with goats'-milk cheese, clafoutis, *grimolle* (a fruit pancake baked in the oven), and plum pie. Butter is used to prepare broye and *fouée* (a circle of bread dough covered with cream and butter and baked in the oven). Millas, échaudés, and craquelins are common in the west of Poitou. Some noted local products are the *berlingolettes* of Châtellerault, the macaroons of Montmorillon and Lusignan, the biscuits of Parthenay, the nougatine of Poitiers, and the candied angelica of Niort (a famous liqueur is also made from the plant).

Poitou produces pleasant vins de pays, including those of La Foye-Monjault, Loudun, Saint-Georges, Marigny-Brizay, and Maigny-Neuville.

poivrade

Any of various sauces in which pepper plays a more important role than that of a simple condiment. The best-known poivrade is a mirepoix mixed with vinegar and white wine, reduced, blended with a roux and white wine, and seasoned with crushed peppercorns. It is served with marinated meat and ground game. The other poivrade sauces are based on vinegar and shallots (hot) or vinaigrette (cold).

Poivrade is also the name of a small artichoke which is eaten *à la croque au sel* (i.e. with salt as the only accompaniment).

RECIPES

Poivrade sauce I SAUCE POIVRADE
Finely dice 150 g (5 oz) scraped or peeled carrots with cores removed, 100 g (4 oz, 1 cup) onions, and 100 g (4 oz) green streaky bacon. Cut 50 g (2 oz, ½ cup) celery into thin strips. Sweat very

gently for approximately 20 minutes with 30 g (1 oz, 2 tablespoons) butter, a sprig of thyme, and half a bay leaf. Add ½ litre (17 fl oz, 2 cups) vinegar and 1 dl (6 tablespoons, scant ½ cup) white wine, then reduce by half.

Make a brown roux with 40 g (1½ oz, 3 tablespoons) butter and 40 g (1½ oz, 5 tablespoons) flour. Add 7.5 dl (1¼ pints, 3 cups) beef or chicken stock and cook gently for 30 minutes. Skim the fat from the mirepoix and add to the roux. Deglaze the mirepoix pan with 1 dl (6 tablespoons, scant ½ cup) white wine and add to the sauce, together with 2 tablespoons (3 tablespoons) chopped mushrooms.

Cook gently for a further hour, adding a little stock if the sauce reduces too much. Crush about 10 black peppercorns, add to the sauce, and leave to simmer for 5 minutes. Then strain the sauce through coarse muslin (cheesecloth) or a very fine strainer.

If this sauce is to be served with a marinated meat, use the strained marinade to deglaze the cooking pan and dilute the roux.

If it is to be served with game, cut the trimmings from the game into small pieces and add to the mirepoix.

poivrade sauce II SAUCE POIV-RADE (from Carême's recipe) Put 2 sliced onions and 2 sliced carrots in a saucepan. Add a little lean ham, a few sprigs of parsley, a little thyme, a bay leaf, a generous pinch of mignonette, a little mace, then 2 tablespoons (3 tablespoons) good vinegar and 2 tablespoons (3 tablespoons) clear stock. Simmer over a gentle heat until the vegetables are very soft. When well reduced add 2 tablespoons (3 tablespoons) clear stock and 2 tablespoons (3 tablespoons) well-blended espagnole sauce. Boil for a few minutes, then rub the sauce through a sieve and reduce to the desired consistency.

Add a little butter to the sauce just before serving.

Pojarski

A way of serving veal chops in which the meat is detached from the bone, chopped with butter and bread soaked in milk, seasoned, re-formed on the bone, and fried in clarified butter. By extension, it has come to mean a cutlet made up of white chicken meat or salmon, covered with flour or breadcrumbs, and sautéed in clarified butter.

Kotliety pojarskie is a classic Russian dish of meatballs named after its creator, an inkeeper called Pojarski. Originally made of beef, they were a great favourite of Tsar Nicolas I. When the tsar arrived at Pojarski's unexpectedly one day, he was served with veal meatballs instead and enjoyed them just as much, so they became popular too.

RECIPE

Salmon cutlets Pojarski CÔTELETTES DE SAUMON POJARSKI Chop 300 g (11 oz) fresh salmon flesh, then add 70 g (2½ oz, generous ½ cup) stale breadcrumbs (soaked in milk and strained) and 70 g (2½ oz, 5 tablespoons) fresh butter. Season with salt and pepper and sprinkle with a pinch of grated nutmeg. Divide the mixture into 4 equal portions and shape into cutlets. Coat with breadcrumbs and brown on both sides in clarified butter. Arrange on a serving dish, sprinkle with the cooking butter, and garnish with canelled slices of lemon.

Poland POLOGNE

A country with a harsh climate and subject to numerous invasions throughout its history, Poland has a cuisine showing very diverse influences. In spite of this, it is dominated by pork, cabbage, potatoes, and spirits, not to mention an abundant and varied pâtisserie, introduced into France by Stanislas Leszczynski. A number of Slavonic dishes, notably soups, patties, and ravioli, show the Russian influence, while the religious feasts of the Catholic Church and the cookery of the Jewish community have also had their effect.

The Poles have a reputation for being solid eaters and great drinkers, as E. de Pomiane amusingly relates: 'Throughout history, the Poles have defended Europe. They would fight, and – between battles – they would eat and drink.' The morning meal often includes cold meat or charcuterie, while the evening meal traditionally consists of potatoes with curdled milk, *klouski* (a kind of savoury dumpling), patties, and large ravioli, which are traditionally served in soup. Any of the following may be served: piroshki, cyrniki, kromeskies, and other varieniki (of Russian origin), also *uszka* (small pastries stuffed with mushrooms), *kolduny* (types of ravioli stuffed with raw minced (ground) beef, prepared with bone marrow and oregano), and *paszteciki* (meat patties).

The traditional Polish meal (*obiad*) takes place at about 2 p.m. and consists of several courses. The soups are always impressive, especially *barszcz* (the Polish borsch), a clear beetroot (red beet) soup; the version eaten at Christmas is *barszcz wigilijny*, made with beetroot and mushrooms. Other soups include *zupa szczawiowa*, with sorrel and smoked bacon; *chlodnik*, with beetroot, soured (dairy sour) cream, and crayfish; *rassolnick*, with cucumber; *krupnik*, cream of barley soup with vegetables (krupnik is also a liqueur with honey and spices, which is drunk warm with the dessert); *kapusniack*, with cabbage, celery, and bacon; and *stchi*, a broth of beef, tongue, and pig's ears, flavoured with fennel.

Meat is usually braised or cooked in ragouts (see *bigos*). Stuffed dishes, which are also very popular, include braised beef stuffed with mushrooms and paupiettes stuffed with kasha. The pig provides a wide range of savoury charcuterie, including smoked and marinated ham, smoked and braised bacon, *kabanosy* (long thin sausages smoked with juniper wood), and *kielbasa tatrzanska* ('wrinkled' sausages from the Tatras).

Many of Poland's fish dishes are derived from Jewish cooking: marinated herrings, herrings in cream, jellied carp in sweet-and-sour or in horseradish sauce with sour cream, sweet-and-sour mackerel, etc. Trout *à la cracovienne* is poached and served with chopped hard-boiled (hard-cooked) eggs, lemon juice, and melted butter. Game is served with fruit; for example, roasted partridge with bilberries, apples, lemon, and cinnamon, or wild boar (smoked loin of pork) with stewed apples. Poultry is usually roasted: *ges* (goose) and *indyk* (turkey) are equally popular.

Cabbage is the most commonly used vegetable, especially in sauerkraut with apples and carrots. Boiled vegetables, such as asparagus, cauliflower, salsify, and cabbage, are prepared with chopped hard-boiled (hard-cooked) eggs and melted butter. Sweet-and-sour preparations are common, for example in salads (onions with apples in mayonnaise, cucumber with cream and sugar, peppers with walnuts) and in pickled and spiced plums.

Polish pâtisserie is sumptuous: *babka* as a kind of baba (but not soaked in rum); the *babka wielkanocna*, with raisins and richly decorated, is eaten at Easter. Other cakes include *chrust* (a very sweet sponge cake); honey and ginger cakes (Poland is a great producer of honey); *mazurek*, resembling a Linzertorte and sometimes topped with chocolate meringue; *makowiec*, a yeast cake sprinkled with poppy seeds, eaten at Christmas; *tort orzechowy*, a walnut cake with coffee icing (frosting); *paczki*, fritters filled with jam; and *nalesniki*, pancakes filled with cream cheese.

Beer is usually drunk during the meal, and tea is served at the end. Vodka is drunk at the beginning of the meal with zakuski as in Russia: *zubrowka* (vodka flavoured with 'bison herb', a very strong scented grass) is a particular favourite. Poles also appreciate iced coffee or coffee with the skin of boiled milk.

polenta

A cornmeal porridge that is the traditional basic dish of northern Italy (both Venice and Lombardy claim to have invented it). The Greeks used to eat various cereal porridges called *poltos*, but maize (corn) did not arrive from America until the beginning of the 16th century.

Polenta is traditionally made with water in a large copper pot, stirred with a big wooden spoon. The porridge is cooled in a round wooden tray and then cut into squares or lozenge (diamond) shapes. It can also be made with milk (for desserts), stock, or with a mixture of white wine and water; like rice and pasta, polenta is very versatile, and is used for a large number of dishes: fritters, croquettes, gratins, croûtes, timbales, etc. Served plain, with butter and cheese, or in a sauce, or even flavoured with vegetables, ham, or white truffle, polenta may accompany fish stews, meat ragouts, or brochettes of small birds. In Italy, the large-grained Bergamo and Verona varieties of maize, which take a long time to cook, are preferred for making polenta.

Gastronomic societies have been formed to promote polenta and its dishes: the Académie des Polentophages was founded at the beginning of the 18th century, and the P.P.P.P. Society (*Prima Patria Poi Polenta*, 'First the homeland, then polenta!') a century later.

RECIPES

Parmesan polenta POLENTA AU PARMESAN Boil 1 litre (1¾ pints, 4¼ cups) water with about 15 g (½ oz) salt, then add 250 g (9 oz, 2 cups) cornmeal and mix together thoroughly. Cook for 25–30 minutes, stirring continuously with a wooden spoon. Then add 60–70 g (2–2½ oz, 4–5 tablespoons) butter and 75 g (3 oz, ¾ cup) grated Parmesan cheese. Pour the porridge onto a damp plate, spreading it out in an even layer, and leave to cool completely. Cut into squares or lozenge shapes and fry in butter until golden. Arrange on a serving dish and sprinkle with grated Parmesan cheese and noisette butter.

Thrushes in polenta GRIVES À LA POLENTA Make some cheese polenta (as in Parmesan polenta) and pour it into a round ovenproof dish in a layer 3 cm (1 in) thick. Half-roast the thrushes for approximately 15 minutes in a hot oven (230 c, 450 c, gas 8). Using the bowl of a spoon dipped in water, make as many hollows in the layer of polenta as there are thrushes. Sprinkle the polenta with grated cheese. Place a thrush in each hollow and sprinkle with a little butter. Finish cooking in the oven for 12–15 minutes. Dilute the thrush cooking juices with white wine and pour over the polenta.

Polignac

The name of various classic French dishes dedicated to members of the Polignac family.

Suprêmes of chicken Polignac are covered with suprême sauce enriched with thinly sliced truffles and mushrooms. Flatfish are poached, dressed with a sauce made with white wine and cream, and served with a mushroom julienne. Eggs Polignac are either cooked in moulds, on thin slices of truffle, or soft-boiled and covered with Périgueux sauce.

RECIPE

Eggs in a mould Polignac OEUFS MOULÉS POLIGNAC Butter some small round moulds and line the bottom with a thin slice of truffle. Break an egg into each mould. Bake in the oven in a bain-marie. Turn each egg out onto a crouton of bread fried in butter. Heat some meat glaze and add to it an equal volume of maître d'hôtel butter. Cover the eggs with the sauce.

polka

A gâteau consisting of a ring of choux pastry on a base of shortcrust pastry (basic pie dough), filled with confectioners' custard (pastry cream) or frangipane cream, then dusted with sugar and caramelized with a red-hot skewer forming a crisscross pattern. Small polkas can also be made.

Polka bread (*pain polka*) is a traditional French bread, particularly popular in the Loire Valley. Usually round and flat, weighing 2 kg (4½ lb), it has deep crisscross grooves in the top, which enable the bread to be divided without using a knife. It is always highly baked with a thick brown crust.

In both cases, the name is derived from the dance of the same name, the crisscross pattern resembling the figures of the dance.

RECIPE

Gâteau polka Make a short pastry with 60 g (2 oz, 4 tablespoons) softened butter, 125 g (4½ oz, 1 generous cup) flour, 1 tablespoon caster (superfine) sugar, and 1 egg yolk. When smooth, roll it into a ball and chill in the refrigerator.

Make a confectioners' custard (pastry cream; see *creams and custards*) with 1 litre (1¾ pints, 4¼ cups) milks, 6 eggs, 200 g (7 oz, scant cup) caster sugar, 180 g (6½ oz, generous 1½ cups) flour, and

1 dl (6 tablespoons, ½ cup) rum. Leave to cool.

Roll out the dough thinly into a circle 20 cm (8 in) in diameter. Place it on a buttered baking tray (sheet) and prick with a fork. Make some choux pastry (see *chou*) with 1.25 dl (6 tablespoons, ½ cup) water, 30 g (1 oz, 2 tablespoons) butter, 1 tablespoon caster sugar, a pinch of salt, 65 g (2½ oz, generous ½ cup) flour, and 2 beaten eggs. Place in a piping (pastry) bag with a plain nozzle 1.5 cm (½ in) in diameter. Brush the rim of the pastry circle with beaten egg and pipe the choux pastry in a border 5 mm (¼ in) from the edge. Brush this border with beaten egg.

Bake for 20 minutes in the oven at 200 c (400 f, gas 6), covering the centre of the circle with aluminium foil if the pastry browns too quickly. Leave to cool completely, then pour the confectioners' custard (pastry cream) into the centre. Sprinkle with granulated sugar. Carefully heat a metal skewer in the flame until it is red-hot and then mark a crisscross pattern on the top of the custard.

pollack   LIEU

Either of two large sea fish (up to 70–80 cm (28–32 in) long), related to the whiting. The yellow pollack is found in the Atlantic as far south as the Bay of Biscay, while the black pollack can be found as far north as Norway and rarely further south than Brittany.

The black pollack has a grey underside and a grey-green or dark-green back; the yellow pollack is more of an olive colour, and its underside is coppery or silvery. Both varieties are very lean fish (1% fat), but the yellow variety has a finer texture. Both are sold either whole, in steaks, or filleted. Black pollack is often deep-frozen. Pollack can be prepared in the same way as cod or whiting, but the black pollack tends to disintegrate and should not be cooked for as long. In Scandinavian countries, dried pollack is called *klippfisch*; when dried and salted, it is referred to as *stockfisch*.

Polo (Marco)

Venetian voyager (born Venice, 1254; died Venice, 1324). He travelled through Armenia, Persia, and the Gobi Desert, was lavishly entertained in Peking, then returned to Europe at the end of a 16-year voyage via Sumatra and the Persian Gulf. While imprisoned by the Genoese, he wrote an account of his voyage, *The Book of the Wonders of the World.* He is given credit for the discovery and spread of rice and pastas, but more importantly he enabled Venice to trade in spices and exotic goods from the Far East. In memory of this great voyager, an annual gastronomy prize, Marco-Polo-Casanova, is awarded by a panel of journalists and restaurateurs of the best Paris restaurant specializing in foreign cooking.

polonaise (à la)

Describing a classic dish of vegetables, especially cauliflower and asparagus. The vegetables are cooked in boiling water, then sprinkled with chopped hard-boiled (hard-cooked) egg yolk and parsley (or fines herbes) and finally with breadcrumbs fried in butter. The description also refers to other recipes derived from Polish cooking.

| RECIPES

Asparagus à la polonaise   ASPERGES À LA POLONAISE   Clean some asparagus and trim to the same length. Tie into small bunches and cook for 25 minutes in plenty of boiling salted water (to which may be added 1 tablespoon flour to help the asparagus keep its colour). Drain thoroughly and arrange in a long buttered dish, in staggered rows, so that the tips show clearly. Sprinkle with sieved hard-boiled (hard-cooked) egg yolk and chopped parsley. Lightly brown some breadcrumbs in noisette butter and pour over the asparagus. Serve immediately.

Beetroot (red beet) salad à la polonaise   BETTERAVES EN SALADE À LA POLONAISE   Peel some cooked beetroot (red beet) and cut into thin slices. Season with a highly spiced vinaigrette, pile in a salad bowl, and sprinkle liberally with chopped parsley and sieved hard-boiled (hard-cooked) egg yolk. Thin apple slices sprinkled with lemon juice may be added.

Cauliflower à la polonaise   CHOU-

FLEUR À LA POLONAISE Divide a cauliflower into large florets and cook in boiling salted water until just cooked (the cauliflower should stay slightly firm). Reshape it in a round serving dish, sprinkle with 2–3 chopped hard-boiled (hard-cooked) eggs and chopped parsley, and keep in a warm place. Crumble 75 g (3 oz, 1½ cups) stale bread in 75 g (3 oz, ⅓ cup) melted butter in a frying pan (skillet). Fry until golden and sprinkle over the cauliflower; serve immediately.

polonaise or brioche polonaise

A brioche soaked in rum or Kirsch, sliced and layered with crystallized (candied) fruits mixed with confectioners' custard (pastry cream), and then covered with meringue and decorated with sliced almonds before browning in the oven. Small individual brioches can be hollowed out and filled with the custard and fruit mixture and are sometimes arranged on little pastry bases or in paper cases before being covered with meringue.

RECIPE

Brioche polonaise Make a brioche weighing about 800 g (1¾ lb). Dice about 200 g (7 oz, scant cup) crystallized (candied) fruit and steep in Kirsch. Make a syrup with 200 g (7 oz, scant cup) sugar, 2.5 dl (8 fl oz, 1 cup) water, and a liqueur glass of Kirsch. Prepare a confectioners' custard (pastry cream; see *creams and custards*) with 60 g (2 oz, ½ cup) flour, 4 egg yolks, 100 g (4 oz, ½ cup) caster (superfine) sugar, 1 teaspoon vanilla sugar, and ½ litre (17 fl oz, 2 cups) milk. Mix 40 g (1½ oz, 3 tablespoons) butter with the custard, then incorporate the drained fruit.

Cut the brioche horizontally into slices, after removing the top. Dip the slices in the syrup and spread each with a thick layer of the fruit custard. Reshape the brioche and put the top back in position. Stiffly whisk 4 egg whites, incorporating 60 g (2 oz, ¼ cup) caster sugar. Completely cover the brioche with the meringue, then sprinkle with icing (confectioners') sugar (no more than 2 tablespoons (3 tablespoons)) and scatter about 100 g (4

oz, 1 cup) shredded (slivered) almonds over the surface. Brown for 5 minutes in a very hot oven. Cool completely before serving.

pomegranate GRENADE

A shrub of Asiatic origin, cultivated for its large edible fruit. The fruit has a tough reddish-yellow or green skin enclosing many red seeds surrounded by sweet pinkish juicy pulp. The ancient Egyptians fermented pomegranates to make a heady wine. The fruit was regarded as a symbol of love and fertility because of its numerous seeds: it is mentioned in Greek mythology as well as being depicted in Christian symbolism. The dried seeds were used as a condiment by the ancients, and the fruit was used mainly as a medicine until the Renaissance. Recipes featuring the pomegranate began to appear at the time of Louis XIV, especially those for sauces and soups. It is cultivated in many tropical countries, including Central America, Lebanon, Pakistan, and India and it also grows in the south of France. In France it is usually eaten fresh or used to make refreshing drinks (see *grenadine*), but in other parts of the world it is used as an ingredient or as a condiment: pomegranate concentrate is used in certain Lebanese dishes (meatballs, stuffed fish, etc.); fresh seeds are used in salads, aubergine (egg-plant) purées, sweet couscous, and almond creams in oriental cookery; and crushed seeds are used in meat dishes in India and Pakistan.

The fruit contains only 32 Cal per 100 g and it is rich in phosphorus.

RECIPE

Lemonade with pomegranate juice LIMONADE AU SUC DE GRENADE Choose 6 very ripe pomegranates, squeeze out the juice from the seeds using a vegetable mill or blender, and then strain. Add the juice of 2 lemons and 2 oranges and the zest of 1 lemon and 1 orange. Add water (twice the volume of the fruit juice) and sugar as required. Steep for 30 minutes to 36 hours, pass through a very fine strainer, and chill before serving.

pomelo

The largest of the citrus fruits, sometimes known as shaddock. The pomelo is pear-shaped, 20–30 cm (8–12 in) long, with a thick skin and a bitter coarse flesh similar in flavour to the grapefruit. It can be eaten on its own or used in the recipes for grapefruit.

Pomerol

A Bordeaux wine region, slightly northwest of Saint-Émilion. There is some gravel in the soil, which makes the finer Pomerol wines very elegant. The most famous estate is Château Pétrus but there are many other well-known ones.

Pomaine (Édouarde Pozerski de)

French doctor and gastronome (born Paris, 1875; died Paris, 1964). Head of the food physiology laboratory at the Pasteur Institute, where he spent his entire career, Dr de Pomiane conducted research into digestion and dietetics, which led him to take an interest in cooking. He invented *gastrotechnie*, a study of the physicochemical processes to which foods are subjected during cooking. Himself a gourmet, he cooked to perfection, with an emphasis on simplicity and the harmonization of flavours. He wrote in a lively, humorous, and pleasant style, and is still one of the most popular of modern French gastronomical writers.

We are particularly indebted to him for *Bien manger pour bien vivre* (1922), *La Cuisine en six leçons* (1927), *Le Code de la bonne chère* (1924), *Radio-Cuisine* (1936; based on radio broadcasts in 1932–33 and 1934–35, on his culinary discoveries, his travels, his own creations, and his favourite recipes). In *Cuisine juive, ghettos modernes* (1929), he traces his Polish family back to its origins (his father emigrated to France in 1845). His other works include *La Cuisine pour la femme du monde* (1934), *Réflexes et Réflexions devant la nappe* (1940), and *Cuisine et Restrictions* (1940), in which Pomiane deals humorously with subjects in which cooking and contemporary life are closely associated.

Pommard

An AOC wine from a village in the Côte de Beaune in Burgundy. The red wines are both popular and widely known to drinkers all over the world who enjoy their somewhat robust style.

Pompadour (Jeanne Poisson, Marquise de)

French royal favourite (born Paris, 1721; died Versailles, 1764). The wife of Charles le Normant d'Étiolles, a farmer-general, she became Louis XV's mistress in 1745 and was made a marquise. She played an important role in the king's life and was a notable influence in the field of the arts.

Like many other courtesans of the period, she was very interested in cookery. Several dishes were named after her (dishes of apricots, lamb chops, pheasant croquettes, small iced petits fours, etc.), both during her lifetime and during the 19th century (especially by Escoffier and Urbain Dubois). Other dishes appear to be her own creations, such as fillets of sole with truffles and mushrooms, chicken breasts *en bellevue*, and tendrons of lamb *au soleil* (cooked in a white veal stock with thin escalopes and truffles).

Monselet also credits her with a sauce for asparagus containing butter and egg yolks, bound with cornmeal and seasoned with verjuice.

In classic cookery, Pompadour is the name of a dish of noisettes of lamb or tournedos fried and coated in Choron sauce, then surrounded with Périgueux sauce and artichoke hearts stuffed with lightly browned noisette potatoes.

Salpicon Pompadour (diced foie gras, pressed tongue, mushrooms, and truffles bound with a Madeira sauce) is used to fill timbales, vols-au-vent, etc.

RECIPES

Attereaux of apricots Pompadour ATTEREAUX POMPADOUR À L'ABRICOT Thread slices of stale brioche on skewers, alternating with halved apricots which have been cooked in syrup and thoroughly drained. Dip them in fried custard (see *creams and custards*) flavoured with rum or Kirsch. Coat them with breadcrumbs and deep-fry quickly in hot oil (180 C, 350 F). Drain on absorbent paper, sprinkle with caster (superfine) sugar, and serve with hot apricot sauce.

Lamb cutlets Pompadour CÔTE-
LETTES DE MOUTON POMPADOUR
Braise the cutlets, which should be
taken from the fillet end and trimmed of
fat; drain and allow to cool thoroughly.
Mask with a well-reduced Soubise
purée and leave to dry. Coat with fine
breadcrumbs and then beaten egg.
Lightly brown the cutlets in clarified
butter. Serve with lemon quarters and
small buttered turnips.

pompe

A sweet or savoury pastry, popular in
many parts of Auvergne, Lyon, and
Provence. *Pompe aux grattons*, from
the Bourbonnais area, is a type of tart or
crown-shaped brioche containing lardons or grattons, which is served as an
entrée or with an apéritif (a white Saint-
Pourçain). In the Nivernais it is called
pompe aux grignaudes; *pompe aux
poires*, a fruit tart or pie, is also found
here.

In Auvergne, *pompe* (or *pompo*) *aux
pommes* is a traditional dish for family
celebrations, Christmas, and Easter. It is
made of buttery rough puff or flaky
pastry, spiced with cinnamon and filled
with jam, plums, or even cream cheese.

In Provence, *pompe à l'huile* is a flat
Christmas cake of leavened dough made
with olive oil, flavoured with orange-
flower water, lemon zest, or saffron,
and sometimes studded with sugared
almonds (dragées). The *pompe à l'huile*
is an essential element of the 13 desserts
of the Provençal Christmas, which are
eaten with mulled wine. Its variants are
numerous (*flamado, gibassier, girodo,
resseto, toca*, etc.).

RECIPE

Christmas pompes POMPES DE
NOËL Place 1 kg (2¼ lb, 9 cups) flour
in a bowl and add 250 g (9 oz) bread-
dough leaven cut into small pieces, 250
g (9 oz, 1 cup) brown sugar, ½ teaspoon
salt, ½ glass olive oil, and 3–4 whole
eggs. Mix well. Add the grated rind of
an orange and a lemon. Knead the
dough thoroughly, and 'throw' it on the
table. When it is very soft, roll the dough
into a ball, wrap it in an oiled plastic
bag, and leave to rise in a warm
draught-free place for about 6 hours.
Knead the dough again, divide into 8

pieces, and shape into crowns. Place the
crowns on a buttered cloth and leave for
a further 2 hours. Then place in the oven
at 230 C (450 F, gas 8) and cook for 25
minutes. Remove from the oven, moisten with orange-flower water, and return to the oven for 5 minutes with the
oven door left open.

pomponnette

A small round rissole, filled with forcemeat or a finely minced salpicon, that is
fried and served as a hot hors d'oeuvre.
The name is a diminutive of *pompon*.

RECIPE

Pomponnettes Prepare 400–500 g
(14–18 oz) lining pastry (see *doughs
and batters*) and leave in a cool place for
about 2 hours. Prepare 250 g (9 oz, 1
cup) gratin or game forcemeat,
mushroom duxelles, or a ham and
mushroom salpicon bound with a very
thick béchamel sauce. Roll out the pastry to a thickness of 3–4 mm (⅛ in) and
cut into circles 8 cm (3 in) in diameter.
Place a small amount of filling on the
centre of each circle. Moisten the edges,
draw up together towards the middle
like a small pouch, and pinch firmly to
seal. Deep-fry the pomponnettes in hot
fat or oil (180 C, 350 F) until golden.
Drain on absorbent paper and serve
very hot.

Ponchon (Raoul)

French poet (born La Roche-sur-Yon,
1848; died Paris, 1937). He wrote some
150,000 verses on the themes of eating
and drinking, which were published in
daily newspapers (the best of these
appeared in the collection *La Muse au
cabaret*, 1920). He proclaimed the bottle superior to the saucepan ('One must
eat to drink, not drink to eat') and
proved to be a worthy heir of Saint-
Amant, Basselin, and Béranger. He was
elected to the Goncourt Academy in
1924.

Pont-l'Évêque

A soft cows'-milk cheese (50% fat) from
Normandy, with a washed or brushed
crust, matured for six weeks in a damp
cellar. 10 cm (4 in) square and 3 cm (1¼
in) thick, it is sold either wrapped in
waxed paper in a wooden box or un-

wrapped. It should have a smooth crust, golden yellow or orange in colour and never sticky, hard, or greyish. The interior should be soft but not runny. It has a pronounced flavour and should 'smell of the earth, not manure': if it smells too strong, it can be unpacked and wrapped in a damp cloth for half a day.

Pont-l'Évêque is served at the end of a meal with a full-bodied red wine. The name comes from the chief market town of Calvados, where it is made. Probably one of the oldest cheeses of Normandy, it was mentioned by Guillaume de Lorris in the *Roman de la Rose*, when it was known as *angelot* (from *augelot*, meaning 'cheese from Auge'). It is at its best in the autumn and winter. The cheese should be cut first in half through the centre, then progressively towards the edges, keeping the remaining portions together so that the interior does not dry out. It is still often farm-produced. The Pavé d'Auge is similar but thicker.

pont-neuf

A small Parisian pastry consisting of a tartlet of puff or shortcrust pastry, filled with frangipane or a mixture of choux pastry and confectioners' custard (pastry cream) flavoured with rum or with crushed macaroons, topped with a pastry cross, and glazed with apricot jam or redcurrant jelly after baking. This name is also given to a type of talmouse decorated with a lattice of pastry.

RECIPE

Ponts-neufs Prepare a lining pastry with 200 g (7 oz, 2 cups) flour, a pinch of salt, 25 g (1 oz, 2 tablespoons) caster (superfine) sugar, 100 g (3½ oz, ½ cup) melted butter, and 1 whole egg. Roll the dough into a ball and put it in the refrigerator. Prepare a confectioners' custard (pastry cream; see *creams and custards*) with 4 dl (14 fl oz, 1¾ cups) milk, 4 eggs, 50 g (2 oz, 4 tablespoons) sugar, half a vanilla pod (bean), and 30 g (1 oz, ¼ cup) flour; add 30 g (1 oz, ¼ cup) crushed macaroons and leave to cool. Prepare a choux pastry (see *chou*) with 1.25 dl (4 fl oz, ½ cup) water, 30 g (1 oz, 2 tablespoons) butter, a pinch of salt, 65 g (2½ oz, ½ cup) flour, 3 eggs, and ½ teaspoon sugar. Leave to cool.

Roll out the lining pastry very thinly, cut into 10 circles, and line sections of patty tins (muffin pans) of a slightly smaller diameter. Roll the remaining pastry into a ball. Mix the choux pastry with the confectioners' custard and fill the tartlets. Glaze the tops with egg yolk. Roll out the remaining pastry very thinly and cut into 20 thin strips; use to make a pastry cross on each tartlet. Cook in a moderately hot oven (190 c, 375 f, gas 5) for 15–20 minutes and cool on a wire rack.

Melt 100 g (4 oz, 5 tablespoons) redcurrant jelly over a gentle heat; coat the opposite quarters of each tartlet with the jelly and dust the remaining quarters with icing (confectioners') sugar. Keep cool until ready to serve.

pont-neuf potatoes
POMMES PONT-NEUF

A dish of fried potatoes, cut into sticks twice as thick as matches. Pont-neuf potatoes are generally used to garnish small cuts of grilled (broiled) beef, especially tournedos Henri IV (the name may come from the statue of the Vert Galant on the Pont-Neuf in Paris). In English they are popularly known as chips (French fries).

RECIPE

Pont-neuf potatoes POMMES PONT-NEUF Peel some large waxy potatoes, wash them, and cut into sticks 1 cm (½ in) thick and 7 cm (2¾ in) long. Wash well and dry in a cloth, deep-fry in fat or oil heated to 170 c (340 f) for 7–8 minutes, until they begin to colour, then drain. Just before serving, fry again in the fat or oil, reheated to 180 c (350 f), until golden. Drain and sprinkle with fine salt.

poppy

Any plant of the genus *Papaver*. The red poppy (*coquelicot* in French) has blazing red petals. These are used as colouring in confectionery, notably for *coquelicots de Nemours*, flat rectangular sweets made from cooked and flavoured sugar coloured red. Poppy leaves used to be eaten as a vegetable, much in the same way as sorrel. When in season, they are traditionally added with the flowers to the *caillettes* (flat sausages) made in Viviers.

Varieties of the opium poppy are cultivated for their blue-grey seeds, which are rich in oil (40–50%) and protein (17–23%); these seeds are not narcotic. Poppy-seed oil is extracted from varieties grown in the Balkans, Germany, Poland, the Netherlands, and (more rarely) in northern France. The oil is pale and has a pleasant taste; it is used in cooking in the same way as olive oil and in Paris and northern France is known as *huile blanche* (white oil), *olivette*, and *petite huile*.

Poppy seeds, which have a rather nutty taste, are used mainly in pâtisserie in Turkey, Egypt, and central Europe, where they are used to flavour a cream filling for certain gâteaux or are sprinkled over bread rolls (also very popular in Britain). They are also used as a condiment for cream and curd cheeses, to flavour Chinese rice-flour noodles, and as an ingredient in Indian curries.

porcelain   PORCELAINE

Fine pottery. Compact, generally white, highly vitrified, translucent, and often glazed with a colourless transparent enamel, porcelain is used for dinner, tea, and coffee services. Ovenproof porcelain or aluminite (a very hard porcelain with a low feldspar content, resistant to thermal shock) is also used for cooking utensils (moulds, gratin dishes, ramekins, etc.).

Porcelain paste basically consists of kaolin, feldspar, and water. It is fired twice and sometimes decorated with enamel fixed by a third firing.

It was during the Tang Dynasty (1st century AD) in China that porcelain was perfected. Originally a craft product, it became industrialized during the Ming period. The fineness of the paste, the purity of the shapes, the subtle glazes and floral decorations, and the fiery colours and variety of enamels created masterpieces appreciated worldwide. Large-scale production developed in Japan from the 17th century.

For a long time Europe strove to copy oriental porcelain. At the end of the 16th century a paste halfway between hard-paste and soft-paste porcelain was produced in Florence. Soft-paste porcelain was essentially a French product, which began in Rouen and Saint-Cloud at the end of the 17th century, before the discovery of kaolin in Europe. The factory at Chantilly was founded in 1725 and that of Vincennes transferred to Sèvres in 1756.

The soft-paste French porcelain had its own special beauty, derived from its velvety effect and its capacity to take rich polychrome decorations, It drew its inspiration first from China and then from the German production at Meissen in Saxony, becoming a model for the products of Tournai, Italy, and Spain, A type of phosphate porcelain was developed in England (Bow, Worcester, and Chelsea).

In 1709 the Prince Elector of Saxony's alchemist discovered a deposit of kaolin, which led to the manufacture of European porcelain closely resembling the Chinese pieces. This was the beginning of the rich production of the Meissen factory, soon copied in Vienna, Nymphenburg, Berlin, etc. Kaolin was discovered in France in 1776 at Saint-Yrieix near Limoges, which became the centre of French hard-paste porcelain manufacture. Many factories were established there at the end of the 18th century in towns that still produce soft or hard porcelain today.

porché

A Breton speciality from Dol-de-Bretagne. Based on pigs' trotters (feet), bones, and rinds, flavoured with various condiments and sorrel, it was formerly cooked overnight in the baker's oven.

pork   PORC

The flesh of the domestic pig. The male pig is called a boar, the female a sow, and the young a piglet, porker, or sucking pig, according to age. The wild boar is the ancestor of the domestic pig. It became domesticated living on refuse near human settlements, which is why pork is regarded as unclean in certain religions. From the Middle Ages the killing of a pig, an abundant source of food, was the occasion for a feast day.

Present pig-rearing (pig-raising) conditions enable selective breeding to produce a high-meat carcass, with a thin coat of fat, and fine hams. In the past, pigs had long legs and were fattened on potatoes and chestnuts and butchered at

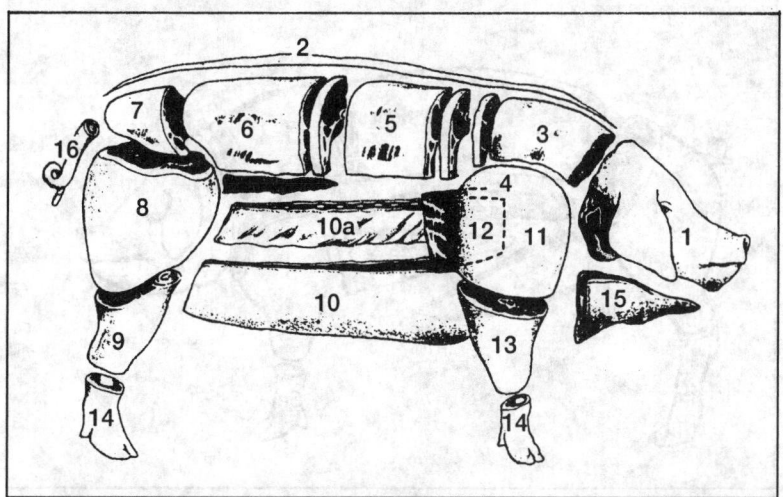

French cuts of pork. *1. tête (head); 2. lard gras (pure pork fat); 3. échine; 4. palette; 5. carré de côtes or côtes premières; 6. côtes de filet; 7. pointe; 8. jambon; 9. jambonneau arrière; 10. poitrine (belly); 10a; travers (spare ribs); 11. épaule (palette and jambonneau); 12. plat de côtes; 13. jambonneau avant; 14. pieds (feet); 15. gorge; 16. queue (tail).*

about 10 or 12 months. Today's pigs have shorter legs and provide more meat; they are fattened in six or seven months on cereal flours and weigh between 90 and 100 kg (200–225 lb). Their meat is in general less tasty and not always of the same quality. The Large White Yorkshire, Western White, Danish Landrace, and Belgian Piétrain, which is white with black patches, are four of the most common breeds. Pork is the most widely consumed meat in France, Germany, and Scandinavia, and is very popular in Britain too. Nearly 50% of French pigs are fattened in Brittany.

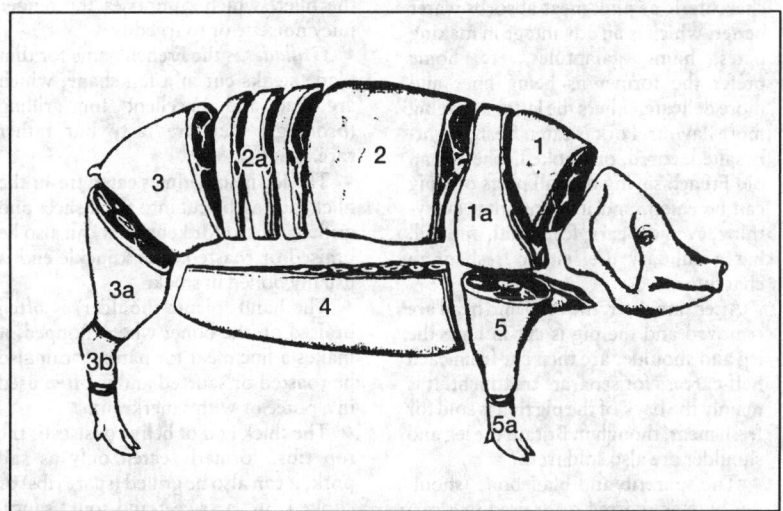

British cuts of pork. *1. spare rib; 1a. blade; 2. loin; 3. leg fillet end; 3a. leg knuckle end; 3b. hock; 4. belly; 5. hand; 5a. trotter.*

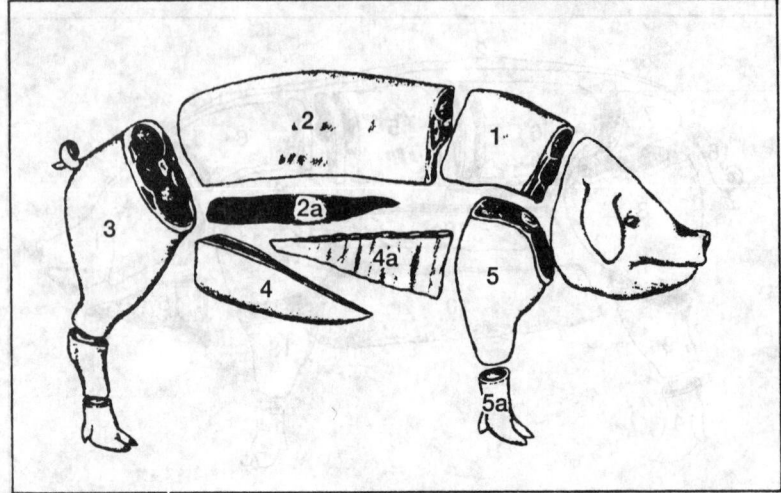

American cuts of pork. *1. blade shoulder; 2. loin; 2a. tenderloin; 3. leg; 4. side; 4a. spare rib; 5. arm shoulder; 5a. hock.*

☐ **Cuts of pork** Good-quality pork is identified by firm pink flesh, which shows no trace of moisture; whitish and damp flesh comes from a factory-farmed pig, and is therefore bland; meat that is flaccid, too red, or too fat comes from an older animal of mediocre quality. In northern and eastern France white meat is preferred; elsewhere, pink is more sought-after. In Paris, pork at the butcher's is paler than that used for charcuterie as pink meat absorbs water better, which is an advantage in making pâtés, hams, galantines, etc. Some prefer the former as being finer and more delicate, others the latter as having more flavour. Pork is eaten fresh, slightly salted, cured, or smoked. There is an old French saying that all parts of a pig can be eaten, and it is true that everything, even the ears, feet, offal, and tail, has a culinary use, either fresh or in charcuterie.

After slaughter, the offal and head are removed and the pig is cut in half; the leg and shoulder are then cut from each half-carcass for separate treatment. It is mainly the back of the pig that is sold for fresh meat, though in Britain the leg and shoulder are also sold fresh.

• The sparerib and bladebone (shoulder butt) is roasted or braised in a casserole. Moister than fillet (loin), soft, and slightly fatty, it can also be made into a stew, grilled (broiled) or fried as chops, cut into cubes for kebabs, or used for home-made sausagemeat.

• The foreloin and the unboned middle fillet give succulent roasts, but can also be prepared as chops and grilled or fried; this is lean and rather dry meat.

• The hind loin is more succulent and less fatty than the sparerib; it is usually roasted.

• The tenderloin is the middle part of the fillet, which comprises the tender juicy noisette or tournedos.

• *Grillades* is the French name for thin blade steaks cut in a fan shape, which are flat and excellent for grilling (broiling); they are tasty but rather rare.

• The leg is sometimes eaten fresh: the fillet end can be cut into thick slices and grilled or used for kebabs; it can also be braised or roasted. The knuckle end is usually boiled in stock.

• The hand (picnic shoulder) is often braised on the bone; when chopped, it makes a fine meat for pâtés. It can also be roasted or sautéed and is often used in a potée or with sauerkraut.

• The thick end of belly consists of the top ribs; formerly eaten only as salt pork, it can also be grilled (spare ribs) or cooked in a sweet-and-sour sauce, Chinese style. It is from the belly of the animal that the fat and skin are removed to make lardons and strips for barding and larding.

☐ **Pork in cookery** Pork has been enjoyed in France since the time of the Gauls. It was, however, a meat of the common people: Grimod de La Reynière saw the pig as 'an encyclopedic animal, a meal on legs' that did not provide roasts for aristocratic tables; he considered only sucking pig to be of value.

A rich and fatty meat, pork goes well with fruit (pineapple, apples, prunes) and vegetable purées. It can be enlivened with green pepper, mustard, fried onions, pepper sauce, garlic, or a Roquefort sauce. Garnished with beans, lentils, etc., it makes a substantial winter meal. Aromatic herbs (especially sage) are often used to flavour roasts and grills.

The base of all French regional potées, pork is also used in recipes inspired by Chinese, Caribbean, and Danish cookery.

RECIPE

Grilled (broiled) pork chops CÔTES DE PORC GRILLÉES Season the chops with salt and pepper, brush with melted butter or oil, and grill (broil) under a moderate heat, turning once. Arrange on a serving dish and garnish with watercress. Serve with lemon wedges.

Loin of pork bonne femme CARRÉ de porc bonne femme Salt and pepper a loin of pork. Heat in an ovenproof dish 15 g (½ oz, 1 tablespoon) butter or lard per kg (2¼ lb) meat. Brown the meat on all sides then place the dish in a moderately hot oven (200 C, 400 F, gas 6) and cook according to the weight of the meat, allowing 50 minutes per kg (22 minutes per lb). 25 minutes before the end of the cooking time, add 500 g (18 oz) peeled potatoes per kg (2¼ lb) meat and 20 small onions fried in butter. Season with salt and pepper, cover, and finish cooking. Separate the loin chops and serve very hot, sprinkled with chopped parsley.

Loin of pork with red cabbage CARRÉ DE PORC AU CHOU ROUGE Prepare a braised red cabbage while roasting a loin of pork. Arrange the pork on a hot serving dish; surround with red cabbage and boiled potatoes or braised chestnuts. Serve very hot.

Mother's cretons CRETONS DE LA MAMAN (from Juliette Lassonde's Creole recipe) In a heavy-based saucepan place 500 g (18 oz, 2¼ cups) minced (ground) shoulder of pork, 1 chopped onion, 2 crushed cloves of garlic, 1 cup breadcrumbs, 1 cup milk, 1 cup chopped parsley, salt, pepper, and cinnamon. Mix thoroughly, cover, and cook for 2 hours over a gentle heat, stirring frequently. Leave to cool, then process in a blender or food processor for 2 minutes. Pour into a buttered terrine and refrigerate until firm.

Pork chops à la bayonnaise CÔTES DE PORC À LA BAYONNAISE Stud the chops with slivers of garlic. Season with salt, pepper, powdered thyme, and bay leaf and sprinkle with oil and a dash of vinegar. Leave to marinate for 1 hour, then sauté briskly in lard. When the chops are browned on both sides, surround them with small new potatoes tossed in goose fat and cep mushrooms fried in oil. Cook for 20 minutes in a moderately hot oven (200 C, 400 F, gas 6). Arrange on a hot dish and sprinkle with chopped parsley.

Pork chops charcutière CÔTES DE PORC CHARCUTIÈRE This dish is found ready-cooked in pork butchers' shops, prepared as follows. Sauté the pork chops (they may be coated with breadcrumbs) in lard, then simmer in charcutière sauce with thinly sliced gherkins.

In restaurants, the preparation is as follows. Flatten the chops slightly, season, coat with melted butter and breadcrumbs, and gently grill (broil). Arrange them in a crown and fill the centre of the dish with mashed potato. Serve separately, in a sauceboat, a charcutière sauce to which chopped gherkins have been added at the last minute.

Roast loin of pork with various garnishes CARRÉ DE PORC RÔTI ET SES GARNITURES Salt and pepper a loin of pork 2 hours before cooking. In an ovenproof dish heat a maximum of 15 g (½ oz, 1 tablespoon) lard per kg (2¼ lb) meat. Brown the meat on all sides, place the dish in a moderately hot oven (200 c, 400 F, gas 6), and cook for about 50 minutes per kg (22 minutes per lb). Baste the loin with its cooking juices and turn it several times during cooking.

Serve with the cooking juices, skimmed of fat, and any of the following garnishes: potatoes (boulangère, dauphinoise, or puréed), a vegetable purée (celery, turnips, lentils, or chickpeas), braised vegetables (celery, endives, cabbage, Brussels sprouts, chicory, artichoke hearts, or lettuce), or fruit (apples, pears, or pineapple). The skimmed cooking juices can also be used to make various sauces, such as charcutière, piquante, Robert, or tomato.

Sautéed pork chops CÔTES DE PORC SAUTÉES Trim and flatten 4 pork chops and season with salt and pepper. Heat 25 g (1 oz, 2 tablespoons) butter or lard in a frying pan (skillet) and brown the chops on both sides. Cover the pan and cook for about 15 minutes. Remove the chops and arrange on a hot dish. Coat with the deglazed cooking juices and serve with the garnishes suggested for roast loin of pork (see recipe above).

Shoulder of pork with five spices ÉPAULE DE PORC AUX CINQ-ÉPICES (a Sino-Vietnamese recipe) In a mortar crush 2 cloves of garlic and 2 shallots with 2 teaspoons sugar and the same amount of nuoc-mâm and soy sauce, ½ teaspoon five spices, and a little black pepper. Fry the shoulder of pork, with its rind, on all sides, then add the spice mixture. Cover and cook for 30 minutes over a moderate heat, turning the meat halfway through the cooking time. Remove the lid and reduce, turn the meat in its cooking juices, then remove and slice; arrange the slices on a plate and pour over the reduced juices. Serve with plain boiled rice.

pork butchery

See *charcuterie*.

pork fat LARD

The fatty tissue lying just beneath the skin of a pig. At one time a staple item of the diet, pork fat today is used mostly as a seasoning or a cooking fat. In France a distinction is made between pure pork fat (*lard gras*) and belly fat (*lard maigre*).

Pure pork fat is usually used fresh and occurs in two layers. The layer closest to the flesh is used mostly for making lard and is called 'melting fat'. The layer next to the skin, called 'hard fat' (leaf lard), is firmer and melts less readily; it is used mostly for barding.

Belly fat consists of fat streaked with muscular tissue. It has many more culinary uses than pure pork fat and can be salted or smoked, as well as used fresh (see *lardons*, *larding*). Thinly sliced belly pork – or streaky bacon – is often served with eggs (see *bacon*).

The thick fat found especially around the fillet and the kidneys is known in France as *panne*. When melted, it yields a high-quality lard, used for preparing fine forcemeats and white sausage. In Lorraine, the residue (*chons*) obtained by gently melting this pork fat in a stewpan is used to flavour a large crusty flat cake, which is served with a dandelion salad and a rosé wine.

pörkölt

One of the four great Hungarian dishes cooked with paprika. Also flavoured with onions, pörkölt is made with meat that is too fat for goulash, cut into larger pieces. Mutton, game, pork, goose, and duck are served in this way, as are veal or even fish (carp) and sometimes shrimps (in white wine).

pork rind COUENNE

Pork rind is generally thick, hard, and very fatty. When scalded or singed and scraped, it is used to line casseroles and stewpans, adding its fat to the preparation. It is an ingredient of pork brawn (head cheese), bréjaude soup, zampone, cassoulet, and various items of charcuterie, such as coudenou. Along with calves' feet, it can be used to give the gelatinous element required in the preparation of meat aspics. After boiling in a flavoured stock, pork rind may be used to prepare ballottines (meat loaves) and roulades.

porridge

A dish of rolled oats or oatmeal cooked in boiling water or milk, which can be eaten, with or without sugar, with hot or cold milk or cream. It is a traditional breakfast dish in Anglo-Saxon countries. The name is derived from French *potage*. An ancient food of Celtic origin, it has always been very popular in Scotland's inhospitable climate, where it is eaten with salt instead of sugar, and in Ireland and Wales. It has spread throughout Britain and is especially enjoyed with golden syrup.

RECIPE

Porridge Add 15 g (½ oz) salt to 1 litre (1¾ pints, 4¼ cups) water and bring to the boil. Sprinkle 250 g (9 oz, 2½ cups) rolled oats into the water and boil gently, stirring continuously with a wooden spoon, until the mixture thickens (about 15 minutes). Each serving may be sprinkled with sugar or salt and eaten with milk or cream poured over it.

port PORTO

One of the great dessert wines of the world. It comes from a region towards the top of the Douro valley, in north Portugal, and is matured and blended downriver in the *armazens*, or wine lodges, of the shippers in Vila Nova de Gaia, opposite Oporto (the wine takes its name from this seaport). In order to qualify as true port the wine must be shipped over the bar, or the point at which the River Douro runs into the Atlantic. Port has been referred to as 'the Englishman's wine', but in fact more port is drunk in France than in Britain today, although the UK takes more of the finer wines. It is popular in other northern countries, including Belgium, West Germany, and the Scandinavian countries, and there are now a number of imitations, or port-style wines, made throughout the world, including California.

Port is a wine made from a variety of grapes blended together that has its fermentation arrested by the addition of brandy (also subject to controls); according to exactly when the spirit is added, the resulting port varies in sweetness because of the natural grape sugar retained in the wine. The majority of ports are blends of wines of various vintages and will not continue to improve after they are bottled. Vintage port, however, is made from the wine of a single year: if a shipper decides to 'declare' a vintage, the port is bottled immediately after shipping and aged in the bottle (not in wood like nonvintage ports), where it forms a heavy deposit or 'crust'. Depending on the particular vintage, it will not usually be ready to drink for eight or ten years at least and can have the lifespan of a human being.

White port, which can be dry, but in its cheaper versions may be sweetish, is made from white grapes and is drunk as an apéritif. Ruby port is a blend of young wines, full, fruity, and with the colour that gives it its name. Tawny ports are matured rubies and fine old tawnies are wines that have aged some years in wood and can achieve great quality. They may be labelled with their age. With the exception of white port, port is traditionally drunk after a meal, accompanied only by nuts and certain fruits. Vintage port should be decanted to permit the fine colour to be seen without being clouded by deposit; ruby and inexpensive tawny may be enjoyed at any time. When served as an apéritif, port is lightly chilled. In culinary use it is often associated with ham or with melon as a first course. Although it may be drunk with Stilton, it should never be mixed into the cheese.

RECIPE

Wild duck in port CANARD SAUVAGE AU PORTO Roast a duck for 20–30 minutes in a very hot oven (230 c, 450 f, gas 8). Remove the thighs and keep the rest warm. Slice the thighs, season, then brush with clarified butter and grill (broil). Reduce 1.5 dl (¼ pint, ⅔ cup) red port by half in the cooking dish. Cut the breast fillets into thin slices and arrange on a serving dish with the thigh slices. Keep warm. Crush and press the carcass, pour over the reduced port, strain, and beat 50 g (2 oz) butter in small pieces into the sauce. Pour onto the sliced duck and serve very hot.

portefeuille (en)

Describing dishes in which the food is stuffed, folded, or placed in layers one on top of the other. The term is applied to the following dishes: veal chops split, stuffed, and cooked in a caul (caul fat) or coated with breadcrumbs; a gratin of sautéed potatoes *à la lyonnaise*; and minced (ground) meat layered with sauce and topped with puréed potatoes. An omelette *en portefeuille* is folded in three, first towards the side opposite the pan handle, then towards the centre of the pan.

RECIPE

Veal chop Cussy en portefeuille CÔTE DE VEAU PANÉE CUSSY EN POR-TEFEUILLE Cut a pocket in a thick veal chop taken from the middle of the loin. Stuff with a salpicon of mushrooms, carrot, and lean ham bound with a thick seasoned béchamel sauce. Close with a wooden cocktail stick (toothpick). Coat the chop with beaten egg and breadcrumbs and cook in clarified butter until golden on both sides. Prepare a risotto and add cream, grated cheese, and a salpicon of truffles. Arrange the chop on a round dish garnished with the truffle risotto. Pour a ring of brown veal gravy, flavoured with tomato, around the dish; sprinkle the chop with noisette butter.

porte-maillot or maillot

A garnish for large pieces of braised meat, consisting of carrots, turnips, onions, and green beans. Braised lettuce or cauliflower is sometimes added to the mixture.

RECIPE

Braised ham porte-maillot JAMBON BRAISÉ PORTE-MAILLOT Braise, drain, and dress the ham. Place it in a small braising pan, pour over ½ litre (17 fl oz, 2 cups) Madeira, cover, and simmer gently for 30 minutes. Prepare a garnish of glazed carrots and onions, green beans cooked in salted water, and braised lettuce. When the ham is cooked, glaze it in the oven. Arrange on a long serving dish (platter), surrounded by the vegetables in separate piles, and keep warm. Skim the fat off the cooking juices, strain, and serve separately.

Port-Salut

A trademark granted by the monks of Port-du-Salut Abbey at Entrammes in Mayenne to a commercial enterprise making Saint-Paulin cheese. Like all Saint-Paulins, Port-Salut is made from pasteurized cows' milk (45–50% fat). The cheese is pressed but not cooked and has a washed crust. It is round, about 20 cm (8 in) in diameter and 8 cm (3 in) deep, and has a soft creamy texture. It is served at the end of a meal or on toast and is used to make croque-monsieur. The Trappist monks of Entrammes produce a similar cows'-milk cheese in the same way.

portugaise (à la)

Describing various dishes (eggs, fish, kidneys, small pieces of meat, poultry, etc.) in which tomatoes are a predominant ingredient.

RECIPES

Portuguese omelette OMELETTE FOURRÉE À LA PORTUGAISE Fill an omelette with a very thick spicy tomato fondue and surround it with a ring of the same fondue.

Portuguese sauce SAUCE PORTU-GAISE Finely chop 2 large onions and cook in 1 tablespoon olive oil until soft. Peel, deseed, and crush 4 tomatoes and add to the onions, together with 2 crushed cloves of garlic. Bring to the boil, cover, and cook slowly for 30–35 minutes, stirring from time to time, until the tomatoes are reduced to a pulp. Moisten with 1.5 dl (¼ pint, ⅔ cup) stock and season with ground pepper. Leave to cook for a further 10 minutes. Bind with 2 teaspoons kneaded butter and sprinkle with chopped parsley.

Sole à la portugaise Lightly butter a long ovenproof dish and cover with a thick tomato fondue flavoured with garlic. Trim, prepare, and season a 750-g (1½-lb) sole and lay it in the dish. Moisten with 2 tablespoons olive oil, 1 tablespoon lemon juice, and 2 tablespoons fish stock. Cook for about 10 minutes in a very hot oven (230 C, 450 F, gas 8), basting the sole from time to time with its cooking juices. Sprinkle with breadcrumbs, brown under the grill, then sprinkle with chopped parsley.

Portugal

Portuguese cookery must not be confused with that of Spain: its characteristic flavours are more varied, strong spices are less dominant, but fresh herbs and spices are more abundant. There are a number of general traits: the use of four predominant ingredients (cabbage, rice, potato, and cod), a marked taste for soups, a wide range of fish and seafood dishes, a notable selection of pork products (black pudding (blood sausage), andouille, smoked ham, and sausages flavoured with chilli peppers), and a predilection for very sweet desserts, often made with eggs.

The regions, however, preserve their own traditions. The north is famous for caldo verde, lamprey from the Minho cooked with curry, and many rice dishes accompanied by rabbit, duck, or roast partridge, with ham and lemon juice. Other classics are the *açordas* (stale-bread soups) – bread soaked in olive oil, flavoured with crushed garlic and herbs, and cooked in boiling water. These soups are garnished with vegetables, pork, chicken, fish, or snails. Seafood *açorda*, garnished with coriander and poached eggs, is particularly well known. There are several ewes'-milk cheeses (usually fresh), notably Azeitão, Serra, and Évora.

Oporto, famous for its wine (see *port*), also specializes in stewed tripe (cooked with haricot (navy) beans, chilli sausage, onions, and chicken and served with rice). Along the coast, fish and seafood dishes naturally predominate: fried skate with vegetables, grilled (broiled) sardine and red mullet, shellfish escabèche, and stewed cuttle-fish. *Caldeirada*, a type of bouillabaisse, is the best example: at Aveiro this is made with freshwater fish and sea fish with oysters, mussels, and carrots, flavoured with coriander. The convent at Aveiro is also famous for *ovos moles*, sweetmeats made of egg yolk and sugar cooked in rice water.

The cookery of Coimbra is substantial: steak *à la portugaise* originated here. Served with a purée of garlic and pepper, topped with lemon slices and grilled ham (added at the last minute), it is accompanied by sautéed potatoes. This *bife com batatas* (steak and chips) is very popular. More typical dishes are *canja* (a poultry consommé garnished with lemon and mint and sometimes also with almonds, ham, and onion

rings) and salted pigs' trotters with young turnip tops.

The national fish is salt cod (*bacalhau*), for which there are said to be a thousand recipes. The best known of these are: fried salt cod croquettes (flavoured with coriander, mint, and parsley) topped with poached eggs; salt cod poached in layers, garnished with mussels cooked in wine and tomatoes, then simmered in the oven in the cooking liquid of the mussels; and salt cod poached and cooked in the oven on a bed of potatoes and onions, garnished with black (ripe) olives and quartered hard-boiled (hard-cooked) eggs.

In Portuguese cookery there are sometimes surprising combinations of ingredients, for example: pickled pork served with shellfish stuffed with lardons; chicken and eel stew with shrimps; roast duck with ham and chorizos; and red peppers, onions, smoked ham, sausages, oysters, tomatoes, and parsley simmered together in a *cataplana* (a deep cooking pot with a handle and lid).

In Lisbon and the south seafood is always on the menu, especially lobster cooked in stock and served with tomato and pimiento sauce. In the *cervejarias* (small brasseries) the Portuguese enjoy a variety of freshly caught shellfish, including mussels, prawns, and squid (grilled with scrambled eggs). Coffee is the most widely consumed beverage in Lisbon, but lemonade and cordials are also enjoyed (through a straw) as well as aniseed drunk with candy sugar. The desserts and pastries are always highly sweetened; for example: *pudim flan*, a thick creamy dessert rich in eggs; rice with milk and cinnamon; baked caramelized figs; doughnuts with syrup; and marzipans. The most original Portuguese cake is the *lampreia de ovos*, made with egg yolks, cooked in a lamprey-shaped mould, decorated with crystallized (candied) fruits, and served on a special egg yolk custard (*ovos moles*).

The delicate cookery of the extreme south includes calf's liver marinated in red wine, *sarapatel* (a mixed lamb and kid stew), figs stuffed with almonds and chocolate, and a cake called *lardo celeste* made with almonds, lemon, and cinnamon.

Portuguese wines

VINS DU PORTUGAL

The Portuguese are great wine drinkers and export vast quantities of table wine as well as the port for which they are famous. Great improvements have been made in the past 20 years in vine-growing and wine-making, and a system of controls (*denominacão de origem*) is imposed on wines from certain regions. No comparison should be made with the wines of Spain, because the two countries are totally different.

In addition to port there are two other fortified wines: Madeira, from the island of the same name, about 850 km (530 mi) west of Lisbon; and the less well known Moscatel de Setúbal, once very famous but now not often seen outside Portugal. In the northern part of the country Minho is famous for the *vinhos verdes*; the name (literally 'green wines') refers to the youthful fresh character of the wine, which is slightly pétillant. Most people know it as a white wine, but in fact a great deal of red is also made – not always to the taste of non-Portuguese!

Also produced in the north is Mateus, the most famous rosé of all Portugal; Lancers is another popular rosé wine, particularly in the United States. Dão, also from the north but below the port region of the Douro, may be a red or white wine, robust and capable of gaining character with bottle age. Colares, from near Lisbon, is an unusual wine, as the vines, which have never been grafted against the phylloxera aphis, are planted in the sand dunes along the coast. Both red and white wines are made; they are not often seen on export lists, but are capable of providing full-bodied agreeable drinking. Bucelas, once much enjoyed by our ancestors, is a white wine also from the vicinity of Lisbon, which is light and fragrant, but the output is small. There are many other Portuguese wines now becoming more widely available outside Portugal; the Portuguese have never compromised by making use of any classic wine names and the wines can provide considerable value to the discerning.

pot

Formerly in France, a pot was a large cooking vessel. The word survives in the dishes *poule au pot* (stewed chicken) and *pot-au-feu*. It is still used in Britain too, in 'stockpot' and 'hotpot' for example.

potassium

A mineral element which plays an important role in the electric and osmotic properties of cells (together with sodium), in the autonomic functioning of the heart, and in the utilization of sugars. Widely found in food, it is especially abundant in fruit, nuts, and pulses, and in chocolate. The daily requirement is 3–4 g (but this is reduced in some diets for kidney failure). Deficiencies are rare, but even mild kidney or digestive trouble can cause a significant loss, which should be quickly restored.

potato   POMME DE TERRE

A starchy tuber, native to America, which is a major food in the form of a vegetable (always cooked); it is also processed as potato crisps (chips), etc., and used in distilling, the starch industry, and the biscuit (cracker) trade. An average-sized potato, weighing 100 g (4 oz), provides 86 Cal and is rich in carbohydrate, vitamins B and C, and fibre, with a tiny amount of protein and some mineral salts (calcium, potassium, iron, and iodine). 100 g (4 oz) potato has the same energy value as 40 g (1½ oz) bread as it contains 2½ times less carbohydrate. The food value of the potato, its taste, and its digestibility are undisputed, but the use of too much fat in cooking (chips, for example) should be avoided. Potatoes cooked in steam (not water) retain their vitamin content, vitamin C being particularly abundant in new potatoes.

□ History The potato, which was originally grown by the Incas, was discovered in Peru by Pizarro and brought to Europe in 1534. Fifty years later, Sir Walter Raleigh made the same discovery in Virginia and brought the potato to England. The English name, like the Spanish (*batata*), is derived from *patata*, the American Indian name for the sweet potato (due to early confusion between the two vegetables). The Spaniards introduced it to Italy, where it was called *tartufola* (little truffle). It was soon

Cooking and serving potatoes

cooking method	preparation	dishes
broiled or steamed	• peeled or unpeeled, whole or cut into pieces	– boiled, sprinkled with parsley – parboiled, then roast in a little lard in the oven, usually around the meat – plain mashed, *au gratin*, Mont-Doré, – mashed with butter and egg yolks (duchess potatoes, croquettes) – mashed with choux pastry (dauphine potatoes, Lorette) – mashed as a basis for gnocchi, panada, pflutters, subric, etc. – in pieces, served warm or cold in salads, etc.
deep-fried	• peeled or unpeeled, washed, dried, cut into strips, sticks, a julienne, small dice, etc.	– fried potatoes (chips (sticks), collerettes, crisps (chips), shavings, Chatouillard, potato straws, pont-neuf, nests, soufflé potatoes)
fried or sautéed in butter, oil, or fat	• grated raw • peeled, washed, blanched quickly, cut up, and sautéed • cut into slices or strips, sautéed raw or parboiled and then sautéed	– potato pancakes, potato cakes – noisette, château, cocotte, parisienne, Parmentier – à la sarladaise, with bacon, à la lyonnaise, hashed, maître d'hôtel
cooked slowly in a casserole on the hob or in the oven	• cut into slices, rings, or pieces, braised in stock, milk, cream, etc.	– Anna, Annette, fondante, à la normande, à la paysanne, à la hongroise, à la landaise, à la basquaise, à la berrichonne – dauphinois and savoyard gratins
cooked dry in a diable	• unpeeled, whole	– baked potatoes
baked in the oven or in hot embers	• unpeeled, whole • cooked, then scooped out, stuffed, and browned in the oven	– baked potatoes, stuffed potatoes

planted all over Europe: in Germany it was called *Kartoffel*, in Russia *kartoschka*, and in France *cartoufle* or *tartoufle*, being eaten there in the 16th century in the form of regional dishes, such as the *truffade* and the *truffiat*. Long regarded in France as food only fit for the poor, the potato was popularized by Parmentier and became one of the staple foods at the beginning of the 19th century. It lends itself to the most comprehensive range of recipes of all vegetables, from the popular mash and chips (French fries) to the elaborate potato straw nests, duchess potatoes, soufflé potatoes, etc.

□ **Consumption and storage** In France, the annual average consumption of potatoes is 80 kg (180 lb) per head, but the figure varies according to the region (higher in the north) and social class (up to 190 kg (420 lb) for the lower classes). On the worldwide scale, consumption reaches 200 kg (440 lb) per head in Belgium and Poland and 110 kg (240 lb) in the United Kingdom, but drops to 52 kg (120 lb) in the United States, of which half is in the form of processed products.

Potatoes should be stored in a cool dry well-ventilated place (8–10 c (46–50 F) to prevent them from sprouting or freezing). It is particularly important that the storage place is dark, to prevent the development of solanine, which causes potatoes to turn green and makes them bitter and indigestible.

There are endless varieties of potatoes but they fall into two main categories: early or new potatoes and main-crop or old ones. Early potatoes are usually dug from June to August in the United Kingdom (though imported ones are available much earlier). Main-crop potatoes are lifted from late summer onwards when they are fully mature and all their sugar has been converted into starch. They are carefully stored for distribution and use throughout the winter until the arrival of the first new potatoes the following spring or early summer. In France, the small new potatoes known as *grenailles* are available from mid-February to mid-July from the south of France or Brittany; they are firm, with a very fine skin, but do not keep. They are very similar to the Jersey new potatoes popular in the United Kingdom.

Standardization of production in France has caused the disappearance of local varieties of potatoes used for regional stews, soups, and other dishes. In Britain there are restrictions on growing certain varieties in allotments and gardens in order to bring British regulations concerning disease in line with the EEC. There is, however, still a wide range of varieties available in the shops in this country. Today two major categories of potatoes are grown: floury potatoes (labelled *consommation courante* in France), used chiefly for soups, chips, and mashes, and firm or waxy ones, for other dishes.

Numerous utensils have been designed for preparing potatoes, including the potato peeler, potato holder (for peeling a potato boiled in its skin without burning oneself), knife-guide (for producing regular slices), special knives for potato straws, waffles, and chips, the chip cutter, chopping and shredding board, scoop, masher, etc.

Potatoes can be served with most meats, poultry, fish, and even eggs. Many combinations are standard: gigot *à la boulangère*, chateaubriand with pont-neuf potatoes, hashis Parmentier, Francillon salad, poached fish and steamed potatoes, and numerous garnishes (*à la bourgeoise*, flamande, Henri IV, maraîchère, Montreuil, Parmentier, etc.). The potato also forms the basis of many traditional and regional dishes, both in France and other countries: aligot, gratin dauphinois or savoyard, goulash, Irish stew, criques, rosti, saladier lyonnais, pflutters, etc.

Its taste, which is sometimes considered to be insipid when it is not fried, can be enhanced with grated cheese, bacon, onion, cream, herbs, garlic, and spices. It is also used to give body to a number of dishes, including quenelles, gnocchi, vegetable and meat loaves, stews, soups, croquettes, panada, etc. Carême even had the idea of making a small pastry with it and the potato can be used, very successfully, mixed with wheat flour, in pastry, bread dough, and scones.

□ **Varieties of potato**

● *Early potatoes*: in France, oblong, with yellow skin and flesh, of waxy texture; limited or average storage time (except for the Resy); suitable for purées, soups, gratins, chips, and sautées. Varieties: Apollo, Bea, Jaerla, Ostara, Resy, and Sirtema. In Britain, white skin and flesh. Varieties: Ulster Sceptre, Maris Bard, Pentland Javelin, Epicure, and Arran Comet; Home Guard is usually the first early potato and is more floury than the rest.

● *Main-crop potatoes*: some are waxy with firm flesh, suitable for boiling, steaming, baking in their jackets, sautéing, and using in salads and ragouts; others are more floury and better for purées, soups, soft gratins, roasting, and chips, but are also good baked in their jackets.

French varieties include:

Belle de Fontenay: yellow skin, dark yellow flesh, firm waxy fine grain; does not keep very well (good from June to July).

B.F. 15: yellow skin and dark yellow waxy flesh; good until December.

Bintje: yellow skin and yellow floury-textured flesh, rather fine grain before complete maturity when they become coarser; suitable for sautéing or steaming; others used for purées, crisps, and powdered soups.

Kerpondy: yellow skin and flesh; floury, excellent for chips; good for soups and stews; available late in the season.

Ratte: yellow skin and firm yellow waxy flesh; particularly suitable for salads.

Roseval: red skin and yellow waxy flesh; best in autumn, but keeps quite well.

Spunta: yellow skin and flesh with floury texture; does not keep very well.

Urgenta: red skin and pale yellow flesh; does not keep very well.

Viola: pale yellow skin and firm yellow waxy flesh; average keeping qualities.

British main-crop varieties include Pentland Crown, a waxy potato similar to the American Burbank; and King Edward, with a floury texture, similar to Idaho Desiree.

RECIPES

Baked potatoes with garlic POMMES DE TERRE AU FOUR À L'AIL Peel 1.5 kg (3 lb) potatoes, cut into slices, wash, and pat dry. Heat a mixture of oil and butter in a flameproof casserole, then add the potatoes together with 4 chopped cloves of garlic and 3 thinly sliced onions. Mix together, fry gently, stirring to brown, then cover and cook in a hot oven for 30 minutes, stirring from time to time. Sprinkle with chives.

Boiled potatoes POMMES DE TERRE À L'ANGLAISE Peel some firm waxy potatoes. Leave them whole if they are small or medium-sized, otherwise cut them up. Boil them in salted water or steam them for 20–35 minutes, until tender but still whole. Serve with a little melted butter and chopped parsley as a garnish for boiled fish and some meat dishes (boiled, cooked in sauce, etc.).

Fried potatoes POMMES DE TERRE FRITES These can be cooked in oil or vegetable fat. Immerse in deep fat at a temperature of 180 C (350 F). This temperature will drop immediately to 150 C (302 F), and the fat should be reheated to 180 C (350 F). Continue cooking until the potatoes turn golden.

Pont-neuf potatoes, commonly known as chips (French fries), are removed before they have turned brown and drained in the basket; the oil or fat is reheated until smoking and then the potatoes are immersed again to crisp and brown.

When potatoes are cut very finely into potato straws, they will cause only a small drop in the temperature of the fat and will therefore need to be immersed only once.

Hashed potatoes POMMES DE TERRE HACHÉES Boil some potatoes in salted water, drain, and chop up roughly. Sauté them well in butter in a frying pan (skillet). Add salt and pepper. Press them well down into the form of a cake, leave to brown, and then turn out on a warm dish. Chopped onions fried in butter may be added to these hashed and browned potatoes, which are typical of American cooking.

Mashed potatoes PURÉE DE POMMES DE TERRE Peel some large waxy potatoes. Cut into quarters and place in a saucepan of cold salted water. Bring to the boil and leave to cook until they begin to disintegrate, then drain thoroughly. Reduce the potatoes to a pulp in a vegetable mill. Pour the mash into a saucepan and add 75 g (3 oz, 6 tablespoons) butter per 750 g (1¾ lb) potato. Stir thoroughly over a gentle heat, then add some boiling milk, beating the mash with a wooden spoon until it has a good smooth consistency. Adjust the seasoning.

The mash may be flavoured with grated cheese (75 g (3 oz, ¾ cup) per 750 g (1¾ lb) mash) or placed in a buttered dish, sprinkled with a little melted butter, and browned in the oven or under the grill.

Potato cocotte POMMES DE TERRE COCOTTE Cut some peeled potatoes into finger shapes, then trim into oblongs 4–5 cm (1½–2 in) long (keep the trimmings for a soup). Wash and drain the potatoes, place in a saucepan, cover with cold unsalted water, and bring rapidly to the boil. Drain the potatoes.

Heat a knob of butter and a little oil in a sauté pan big enough to hold the potatoes in a single layer. As soon as the fat is hot, add the potatoes, seal them over a brisk heat, then sauté them gently for approximately 15 minutes. Then cover and place in a moderately hot oven at 200 C (400 F, gas 6), and continue cooking for about 10 minutes.

Check the potatoes while cooking and remove from the oven as soon as they have browned. Drain and season them with fine salt. Serve in vegetable dish or beside the meat to be garnished, sprinkled with chopped parsley.

Potatoes à la boulangère POMMES DE TERRE À LA BOULANGÈRE Prepare 800 g (1¾ lb) peeled potatoes, cut into slices, and brown them in 40 g (1½ oz, 3 tablespoons) butter. Slice 400 g (14 oz) onions and brown in 20 g (¾ oz, 1½ tablespoons) butter. Arrange alternate layers of potatoes and onions in a buttered ovenproof dish. Season with a little salt and pepper, then cover completely with stock. Cook in a moderately hot oven at 200 C (400 F, gas 6) for approximately 25 minutes then reduce the oven temperature to 180 C (350 F, gas 4) and leave to cook for a further 20 minutes.

If required, add a little stock while they are cooking.

Potatoes à la crème POMMES DE TERRE À LA CRÈME Boil some firm unpeeled potatoes in salted water. Peel them immediately, cut into thick slices, and arrange them in a lightly buttered casserole. Cover with fresh cream, season with salt, pepper, and nutmeg, and cook them in a moderately hot oven at 200 C (400 F, gas 6) until the cream has completely reduced and the potatoes are tender. Add a little extra cream just before serving and sprinkle with chopped herbs.

Potatoes à la maître d'hôtel POMMES DE TERRE À LA MAÎTRE D'HÔTEL Place some potatoes in a saucepan of cold salted water, bring to the boil, and boil until cooked. Peel and cut into thin slices. Place in a sauté pan and cover with boiling milk or water. Add 3 tablespoons (¼ cup) butter per 800 g (1¾ lb) potatoes. Season with salt and pepper. Boil with the lid on until the liquid has reduced. Turn into a vegetable dish, and sprinkle with chopped parsley.

Potatoes au jus POMMES DE TERRE AU JUS Peel some potatoes and cut into quarters. Butter a flameproof casserole and arrange the potatoes in layers. Half-cover with meat glaze or stock. Season. Cover the pan and bring to the boil, then cook in a moderately hot oven (200 C, 400 F, gas 6) for approximately 40 minutes, adding a little stock if necessary (these potatoes must be very soft). Sprinkle with chopped parsley.

Potatoes cooked in their skins POMMES DE TERRE EN ROBE DES CHAMPS Select potatoes of similar size, wash them, and put them in a saucepan with enough salted water to cover them generously. Add 9 g (1 teaspoon) salt per litre (1¾ pints, 4¼ cups) water. Bring to the boil and cook the potatoes until the point of a knife can be easily pushed into them (20–25 minutes). Drain the potatoes and serve piping hot.

The potatoes are peeled while still hot and eaten with butter and salt, or perhaps with a herb-flavoured curd cheese. They can also be served with saveloy or herring fillets; in Alsace, the traditional accompaniment is Munster cheese.

Potatoes émiellées POMMES DE TERRE ÉMIELLÉES (from M. Verdier's recipe) Sauté some thinly sliced peeled potatoes in butter in a heavy-based frying pan (skillet), together with some small pieces of bacon and a bay leaf. Cover the pan when the potatoes are half-cooked so that they remain soft. When they are brown and well cooked, bring the pan to the table, break one egg per person into it, and stir together so that the eggs coagulate quickly. Serve with a salad.

Potatoes in oil POMMES DE TERRE À L'HUILE Place some unpeeled potatoes in a saucepan of cold salted water. Bring to the boil and boil until just cooked. Peel and cut into slices, then mix with oil, salt, pepper, and (if desired) a little crushed garlic. Finally add a hot mixture of vinegar and white wine (1 tablespoon of each per 3 tablespoons oil used). Stir and sprinkle with mixed chopped herbs. This salad can be supplemented with fillets of anchovy or herring in oil, onion rings, or thinly sliced shallots.

Potatoes with bacon POMMES DE TERRE AU LARD Heat 2 tablespoons butter or lard in a flameproof casserole and sauté in it 125 g (4½ oz) diced blanched bacon together with 10 small onions. Drain, and remove from the casserole. Cut some potatoes into oval shapes or cubes and brown them in the casserole. Season with salt and pepper, replace the bacon and onions, cover, and cook gently for approximately 15 minutes. Sprinkle with chopped parsley and, if desired, finely chopped garlic.

Potatoes with basil POMMES DE TERRE AU BASILIC Scrape some small new potatoes, wash them, and pat dry. For 1 kg (2¼ lb) potatoes, melt about 60 g (2 oz, ¼ cup) butter in a flameproof casserole. Add the potatoes, shake the pan to coat them in butter, and allow to brown slightly. Then add salt, cover, and cook in a hot oven at 220 C (425 F, gas 7) for 30 minutes, stirring from time to time. Serve in a warmed vegetable dish sprinkled with fresh chopped basil.

Potato fondantes POMMES DE TERRE FONDANTES Peel some potatoes and trim them to the shape of small eggs. Fry gently in butter for 5 minutes, then drain. Add more butter, cover, and finish cooking in a moderately hot oven. When cooked, remove from the oven, add half a glass of white stock, and leave until the potatoes have absorbed the stock. Serve in a vegetable dish, without parsley.

Alternatively, fry the potatoes in butter in a sauté pan. When cooked, remove the potatoes, wipe out the pan with absorbent paper, add fresh butter (100 g (4 oz, ½ cup) per kg (2¼ lb) potatoes), replace the potatoes, cover, and keep warm over a very gentle heat or in a very cool oven until all the butter is absorbed.

Potato mousseline POMMES DE TERRE (OU PURÉE) MOUSSELINE Bake some unpeeled potatoes in the oven, peel them, and rub the pulp through a sieve. Stir this mash over the heat, adding 200 g (7 oz, scant cup) butter per

kg (2¼ lb) mash, then 4 egg yolks. Season with salt, white pepper, and grated nutmeg. Remove from the heat and add 2 dl (7 fl oz, ¾ cup) whipped cream. Heap the mixture in a buttered ovenproof dish, sprinkle with melted butter, and brown in a very hot oven.

Potato pancakes CRÊPES DE POMMES DE TERRE Peel and wash some potatoes, pat them dry, and grate coarsely. Drain on absorbent paper, then place in a bowl. Add salt and pepper, and for every 500 g (18 oz) potatoes add 2 eggs beaten with 1 dl (6 tablespoons, scant ½ cup) milk and 5 g (¼ oz, ½ tablespoon) melted butter. Mix thoroughly. With this mixture, make some small pancakes (a little thicker than normal pancakes) in a buttered frying pan (skillet). Serve in a warm dish. A little grated cheese or grated garlic and chopped herbs can be added to this mixture. These pancakes may be served with coq au vin, roast veal, or roast venison.

Roast potatoes POMMES DE TERRE RÔTIES Peel some potatoes and cut into fairly small even-sized pieces (leave them whole if they are small). Melt some butter or lard in a casserole (approximately 100 g (4 oz, ½ cup) per kg (2¼ lb) potatoes) and put the potatoes into it (in a single layer only). Roll the potatoes in the fat, season with salt, then cook at the top of a moderately hot oven (190 C, 375 F, gas 5) for 40 minutes or more, frequently basting with the fat until they turn golden and are cooked through. Sprinkle with chopped parsley to serve.

Sautéed potatoes I POMMES DE TERRE SAUTÉES À CRU Peel and cut 750 g (1¾ lb) waxy potatoes into slices or small cubes. Wash, pat dry, and season with salt and pepper. Fry for 25 minutes in a frying pan (skillet) in butter or oil (60 g (2 oz, ¼ cup) butter or 4 tablespoons (⅓ cup) oil per 750 g (1¾ lb) potatoes) or in a mixture of equal amounts of butter and oil. Cover when brown, but toss frequently so that they cook evenly. Serve in a vegetable dish, sprinkled with chopped parsley.

Sautéed potatoes II POMMES DE TER-

RE SAUTÉES Boil 15 unpeeled potatoes in salted water until almost tender. Drain and leave to cool, then peel and cut into slices. In a sauté pan heat a mixture of equal amounts of butter and oil (or butter only: 50 g (2 oz, ¼ cup) per 750 g (1¾ lb) potatoes). Brown the potatoes evenly for 12–15 minutes, first over a brisk heat, then over a gentle heat, uncovered, turning them often. Season with salt and pepper and sprinkle with chopped parsley.

Soufflé potatoes POMMES DE TERRE SOUFFLÉES Peel some large waxy potatoes, wash, and pat dry. Cut into slices 3 mm (⅛ in) thick. Wash and dry once again. Deep-fry in oil at 150 C (300 F) for about 8 minutes. Drain on absorbent paper and leave to cool. Reheat the oil to 180 C (350 F) and replace the potatoes in it. Cook until puffy and brown, then drain on absorbent paper. Serve in a very hot dish, sprinkled with salt.

Steamed potatoes POMMES DE TERRE À LA VAPEUR Peel some potatoes and cut into quarters (leave them whole if they are small). Place them in the top of a steamer and sprinkle with salt. Pour some water into the bottom, place the top in position, cover, and cook for 30–40 minutes after the water has begun to boil.

Stuffed potatoes POMMES DE TERRE FARCIES These can be prepared in two ways:
• *Method 1.* Bake some large unpeeled potatoes in the oven. Cut a slice off the top lengthwise, and scoop out the potato without breaking the skins. Rub the pulp through a sieve and mix it with the chosen ingredients (duxelles, cheese, ham, mirepoix, fried onion, cooked hash, etc.), together with butter, salt, and pepper. Fill the empty potato skins with the stuffing, sprinkle with breadcrumbs or grated cheese (or a mixture of the two), pour melted butter over them, and brown in a very hot oven.
• *Method 2.* Peel some large potatoes, trim off the ends, and carefully scoop out the inside to leave cylinder shapes. Blanch the potato cylinders, drain, and pat dry. Season them with salt and pepper inside and out, fill them with the

chosen stuffing, then arrange them closely packed together in a buttered flameproof dish. Half-cover them with clear stock. Bring to the boil, then cover and cook in a moderately hot oven (200 C, 400 F, gas 6) for 30–35 minutes. Drain the potatoes and arrange in a buttered ovenproof dish. Sprinkle with breadcrumbs or grated cheese (or a mixture of the two), pour melted butter over them, and brown in a very hot oven. The cooking juice may be used as the base for a sauce to accompany the potatoes.

Stuffed potatoes à la cantalienne POMMES DE TERRE FARCIES À LA CANTALIENNE Prepare some stuffed potatoes using method 1. Add an equal volume of braised chopped cabbage to the pulp and adjust the seasoning. Fill the potato skins with this mixture, sprinkle with grated cheese and a little melted butter or lard, and brown in a very hot oven.

Stuffed potatoes à la charcutière POMMES DE TERRE FARCIES À LA CHARCUTIÈRE Prepare some stuffed potatoes using method 2. Fill them with sausagemeat mixed with plenty of chopped parsley and garlic and, if desired, chopped onion fried in butter. Cook in stock and then brown as in method 2.

Stuffed potatoes à la florentine POMMES DE TERRE FARCIES À LA FLORENTINE Prepare some stuffed potatoes using method 1. Mash half of the potato pulp and mix with twice its volume of spinach cooked in butter and chopped. Fill the potato skins with this mixture. Cover with Mornay sauce, sprinkle with Parmesan cheese, and brown in a very hot oven or under the grill (broiler).

Stuffed potatoes à la provençale POMMES DE TERRE FARCIES À LA PROVENÇALE Prepare some stuffed potatoes using method 2. Mix together equal amounts of canned tuna in oil and chopped hard-boiled (hard-cooked) egg yolks. Bind with well-reduced tomato fondue and adjust the seasoning; this stuffing must be highly spiced. Fill the potatoes and cook in stock. When they are done, drain, sprinkle with grated cheese and melted butter, and brown under the grill (broiler).

Stuffed potatoes à la yorkaise POM-MES DE TERRE FARCIES À LA YOR-KAISE Prepare some stuffed potatoes using method 1. Keep the pulp. Prepare equal amounts of chopped York (boiled) ham, chopped mushrooms lightly fried in butter, and chopped onions fried in butter. Mix together then bind with a little béchamel sauce. Adjust the seasoning, adding paprika if desired. Stuff the potatoes, sprinkle with breadcrumbs and melted butter, and brown in a very hot oven.

Stuffed potatoes chasseur POMMES DE TERRE FARCIES CHASSEUR Prepare some stuffed potatoes using method 1. Mix the pulp with an equal volume of thinly sliced chicken livers and mushrooms sautéed in butter. Adjust the seasoning and add a small quantity of chopped herbs. Fill the potatoes with this mixture, sprinkle with breadcrumbs and then with melted butter, and brown in a very hot oven.

Stuffed potatoes with cheese POM-MES DE TERRE FARCIES AU FROM-AGE Prepare some stuffed potatoes using method 1. Mix the pulp with 10 g (½ oz, 1 tablespoon) butter and 1 table-spoon grated cheese per potato. Fill the potatoes with this mixture, sprinkle with grated cheese and melted butter, and brown in a very hot oven.

Potatoes stuffed with chives POMMES DE TERRE FARCIES À LA CIBOULET-TE Prepare some stuffed potatoes using method 1. Mix with the pulp half its volume of double (heavy) cream, adding salt, pepper, and chopped chives. Fill the potatoes with this mixture and heat briskly in a hot oven (220 C, 425 F, gas 7).

Potatoes stuffed with duxelles POM-MES DE TERRE FARCIES À LA DUXEL-LES Prepare some stuffed potatoes using method 2. Fill them with a highly seasoned duxelles, cook them in stock, then brown in the oven.

Altrernatively, prepare the potatoes using method 1, mixing with the duxel-les half its volume of potato pulp.

Sprinkle with a mixture of breadcrumbs and grated Parmesan, then melted butter, and brown in a very hot oven.

pot-au-feu

An essentially French dish which provides at the same time soup (the broth), boiled meat (usually beef), and vegetables (root and leaf). 'The foundation of empires', according to Mirabeau, pot-au-feu is a very ancient dish with innumerable variations. Like potée and poule au pot, it is prepared in a huge pot in which all the ingredients are cooked together in water, with added flavourings. Pot-au-feu (which can also be made with poultry) is served in restaurants or at home as a warming winter dish.

For a successful pot-au-feu many flavours and textures are needed: lean cuts of meat, such as shin; fatter cuts, such as belly or flank; gelatinous cuts, such as oxtail; and thick slices of meat with marrow bone.

To improve the flavour of the broth, the meat may be put into cold water, brought to the boil, then skimmed when the first bubbles appear. The broth will be light and tasty but the meat will lack flavour. To maintain the flavour of the meat it should be put into boiling water, so the juices are sealed in and do not escape into the water. Alternatively, strongly flavoured meats may be put into boiling water while others (such as rolled boned breast) are put into cold water.

A pot-au-feu is more tasty when it is cooked the day before and the fat is skimmed from the surface before reheating. The classic vegetables are carrots, turnips, onions (often studded with cloves), leeks, celery (cut into even lengths and tied in bundles), and parsnips. A bouquet garni and aromatic herbs are also added. Potatoes are cooked separately; if a cabbage is to be used it should be blanched before it is added to the broth so that its flavour does not overpower that of the meat.

A pot-au-feu is a meal in itself. The skimmed broth is served with toasted croutons sprinkled with cheese, then the bone marrow on toast, and finally the sliced meat and vegetables, with fresh sea salt, freshly ground pepper, and accompanied by gherkins, grated horseradish, various mustards, pickles, small beetroot (red beet), pickled onions, and redcurrant jelly, as in eastern France.

The leftover meat from a pot-au-feu can be eaten hot or cold: in a salad with gherkins, potatoes, or shallots in oil; as boiled beef with sauce; or made into shepherd's pie, meatballs, croquettes, etc.

RECIPE

Broth from the pot-au-feu BOUIL-LON DU POT-AU-FEU Strain the broth from a pot-au-feu through a fine sieve. Leave to cool and refrigerate. Several hours later, skim off the fat from the surface. Thoroughly brown a chopped onion and add it to the broth to give colour. Strain again and adjust the seasoning. Bring to the boil gently and serve very hot in cups or bowls with toasted croutons. A little port or Madeira may be added to the broth.

pot-bouille

In the *Grand Dictionnaire universel* Pierre Larousse defines this word as 'everyday household cooking'. It was used in this sense by Flaubert, Richepin, Huysmans, and Vallès; Zola used the expression as the title for one of his books (1882). The term *pot-bouille* is no longer in use but the more colloquial *tambouille*, derived from *pot-en-bouille*, is still found.

potée

Any dish cooked in an earthenware pot. The term generally applies to a mixture of meat (mainly pork) and vegetables (especially cabbage and potatoes), which is cooked in stock and served as a single course. Potée is a very old dish and is found throughout rural France, often under other names (*hochepot, garbure, oille*, etc.); similar dishes exist in most other parts of the world. Each region has its own recipe, for example:

• *potée albigeoise*: leg of beef, hock of veal, raw smoked ham, preserved duck, sausage, carrots, turnips, celery, leeks, white cabbage, and haricot (navy) beans.

• *potée alsacienne*: smoked bacon fat, white cabbage, celery, carrots, and hari-cot beans. The vegetables are sweated in goose fat before the liquid is added.

• *potée artésienne*: pig's head, unsmoked (slab) bacon, breast of lamb, andouille, carrots, green cabbage, turnips, celery, white beans, and potatoes.

• *potée auvergnate*: fresh or salt pork, sausages, half a pig's head, cabbage, carrots, and turnips.

• *potée berrichonne*: knuckle of ham, sausages, and red beans cooked in red wine.

• *potée bourguignonne*: bacon, shoulder of pork, hock of pork (ham hock), cabbage head, carrots, turnips, leeks, and potatoes. Also, in the spring, green beans and peas.

• *potée bretonne*: shoulder of lamb, duck, sausages, and vegetables. An eel potée is also made in Brittany.

• *potée champenoise*: called the grape-pickers' potée: unsmoked streaky bacon, salt pork, cabbage, turnips, celeriac (celery root), roots and potatoes, sometimes sausages or smoked ham, and perhaps chicken.

• *potée franc-comtoise*: beef, bacon, Morteau sausage, mutton bones, and vegetables.

• *potée lorraine*: lean bacon, fillet or shoulder of pork, cabbage, carrots, green beans, dried or fresh white haricot beans, peas, turnips, leeks, celery, potatoes, and sometimes lentils.

• *potée morvandelle*: ham, dried sausage, smoked sausage, and various vegetables.

RECIPE

Potée lorraine Soak a pickled shoulder of pork in cold water to remove the salt. Clean and blanch a green cabbage and rinse in cold water. Line a stewpot with bacon rinds and add the pork shoulder, the cabbage, 500 g (18 oz) fat belly pork, 1 uncooked pig's tail, 6 peeled halved carrots, 6 peeled turnips, 3 leeks (cleaned, sliced, and tied in bunches), 1 or 2 sticks (stalks) of celery (strings removed), and a bouquet garni. Cover with water and bring to the boil; cook for 3 hours. 45 minutes before the end of the cooking time add a boiling sausage and some peeled potatoes. Adjust the seasoning. Serve the cut-up meat and vegetables together and the broth separately.

Potel et Chabot

A Parisian firm of caterers who work on the premises of their clients, founded in 1820 by two associates who bought Chevet's food store. Originally situated in the Rue Vivienne, they now operate from the Rue de Chaillot and are the official suppliers to the government. Their most famous engagements were the christening lunch for the Prince Imperial in 1856 and the celebrated banquet for the Mayors of France, given by President Loubet at the Tuileries in 1900.

potjevfleisch or pot-je-vleese

A Flemish speciality, well known around Dunkirk. It is a terrine of three meats (veal, bacon, and rabbit) to which calves' feet are sometimes added. The name means literally 'pot of meat'.

pot-roasting   POÊLAGE

Slow cooking by moist heat in a covered casserole after first browning in butter or other fat, then adding seasoning and a little water, stock, or wine. Pot-roasted meat, poultry, or fish should be frequently basted during cooking. It is often cooked on a bed of vegetables. When ready, the meat is removed from the casserole and the fat is skimmed from the rich full-bodied cooking liquid, which is used as a sauce. Suitable items for pot-roasting include white meat (such as rib and noix of veal and loin of pork), brisket, topside, or silverside of beef, leg or shoulder of lamb, and also poultry (particularly duck, chicken, and small turkeys).

potted char

An old English speciality consisting of a fish paste that was traditionally served at breakfast. The fish is cooked in stock with herbs and spices, then puréed, placed in shallow earthenware dishes, and covered with a layer of clarified butter. It keeps for several weeks.

Pouilly-Fuissé

An AOC white wine from the Mâconnais in southern Burgundy, made from the Chardonnay grape and produced in four parishes – Pouilly-Fuissé, Pouilly-Loché, Pouilly-Vinzelles and Pouilly-Chaintré. The wines are pleasant, even very good in some years. They have recently become popular in the United States, and therefore prices have soared.

Pouilly-sur-Loire

White wines from a vineyard near Sancerre, in the upper Loire, not to be confused with the Pouilly wines of Burgundy. Wines labelled as such are made from the Chaselas grape, but those labelled Pouilly-Fumé are superior in quality as they are made from the Sauvignon grape, called Blanc Fumé in the locality.

Poulard (Mère; *born* Annette Boutisut)

French restaurant owner (born Nevers, 1851; died Mont-Saint-Michel, 1931). Chambermaid to Édouard Corroyer, an architect in charge of restoring historic monuments, she accompanied her master when he undertook the restoration of the Abbey of Mont-Saint-Michel. There she married Victor Poulard, the local baker's son, and the couple took over the management of the hôtel-restaurant the Tête d'Or.

She made her name with Mère Poulard's omelette, the secret of which has been given a number of explanations: a long-handled pan placed on a hot wood fire, the quality of the butter and eggs, a glass of cream added to the eggs, a very short cooking time, and the proportion of whisked egg whites. Visitors crossing by boat from the mainland to Mont-Saint-Michel would work up a hearty appetite, for which Mme Poulard prescribed her omelette at any time of the day.

poule au pot

A pot-au-feu made with beef and a stuffed chicken. There are numerous variations on the stuffing ingredients and the choice of stewing vegetables. The historian Jacques Bourgeat quotes a text dating from 1664 in which Hardouin de Péréfixe, the Archbishop of Paris, recounted a conversation between Henri IV of France and the Duke of Savoy, to whom the king is reputed to have uttered his famous words: 'If God grants me a longer life, I will see to it that no peasant in my kingdom will lack the means to have a chicken in the pot (*une poule dans son pot*) every Sunday.'

RECIPE

Poule au pot à la béarnaise For a chicken weighing 2 kg (4½ lb) make a forcemeat with 350 g (12 oz, 1½ cups) fine sausagemeat, 200 g (7 oz) chopped Bayonne ham, 200 g (7 oz, 1 cup) chopped onions, 3 crushed cloves of garlic, a small bunch of parsley (chopped), and 4 chopped chicken livers. Season with salt and pepper and work these ingredients together well to make a smooth paste. Stuff the chicken and carefully sew up the openings at the neck and parson's nose (tail). Then continue as for the recipe for petite marmite, using the same vegetables. Joint the chicken, slice the forecemeat, and serve with the vegetables.

poulette (à la)

The term applied to various dishes served with poulette sauce, which is made by adding lemon juice and chopped parsley to allemande sauce. It was originally served with fricassee of chicken (*poulet*), hence its name. Nowadays the sauce is more often used with fish (eel), mussels, offal (sheep's trotters (feet), tripe, brains), snails, or mushrooms.

RECIPES

Mushrooms à la poulette CHAMPIGNONS À LA POULETTE Clean some mushrooms by rinsing them under water several times and draining well; then stew them in butter, without letting them colour. Add just enough poulette sauce to bind the mushrooms; check and adjust the seasoning if necessary. Serve the mushrooms sprinkled with chopped herbs in a warmed vegetable dish.

Poulette sauce SAUCE POULETTE Whisk 2 or 3 egg yolks with 4 dl (14 fl oz, 1¾ cups) white veal or poultry stock (or fish fumet if the sauce is to be used with fish or mussels). Heat for about 10 minutes, whisking all the time, adding lemon juice (from a half or a whole lemon) and 50 g (2 oz, 4 tablespoons)

butter. Remove from the heat when the sauce coats the spoon. Keep the sauce warm in a bainmarie until needed, stirring from time to time to stop a skin from forming.

Pouligny-Saint-Pierre

A goats'-milk cheese from Berry (45% fat content), with a smooth curd and a fine natural rind with a bluish tinge. It is firm but smooth with a pronounced flavour, and is shaped like an elongated pyramid (hence its nickname 'Eiffel Tower'). It is farmhouse-made, at its best from April to November, and protected by an AOC (which limits its production to the district of Blanc, in the department of Indre). It is sometimes matured in its mould, between plane leaves, with a little marc brandy.

poultry VOLAILLE

The generic term for farmyard birds, notably chicken, turkey, duck, goose, and guinea fowl. The meat of these birds is less fat than red meat and rich in proteins and B vitamins; it forms the basis of both simple and economical dishes and also the most elegant fare. (The French term *volaille* is used in cooking to indicate the chicken when used in basic preparations (stocks, minced (ground) or thinly sliced meat in sauces, salpicons, consommés, croquettes, salads, etc.); recipes using a particular bird will name it specifically.)

Chicken is by far the most popular poultry; next comes turkey, more widely eaten since it has been sold in joints and cuts (escalopes, legs, roasts, etc.). France is the leading world producer of guinea fowl. Geese bred in France are mainly raised nowadays for the production of foie gras, but in Britain they are fattened for the table, especially for Christmas. They remain fairly expensive and uneconomical. The breeding of ducks, on the other hand, has developed in France under the dual impetus of a fashion for duck foie gras and *magrets* (duck fillets). In Britain duck is becoming increasingly popular for special occasions, both whole and as fillets sold separately. The commercial production of poultry, particularly chickens and turkeys, has transformed what was a farmyard enterprise a couple of decades ago into a huge industry, a fact regretted by some breeders and consumers who prefer traditional methods. This has allowed prices to fall and a constant supply to be provided for the market.

In the Middle Ages, poultry (together with small game) was sold in France by *rôtisseurs-oyers* and *poulaillers* and in Britain by poulterers. They sold geese, capons, chickens, and ducks. During the time of the Renaissance poultry started to be fattened in the coop. The turkey was still rare (it was served on one of the first occasions at the marriage of Charles IX on 26 November 1570) but the guinea fowl, forgotten since Roman times, reappeared thanks to the Portuguese, who brought it back from Guinea. From the 17th century, a distinction was made between free-range farmyard chickens and those which had been specially fattened. Mme de Sévigné mentions the chicken of Caen and Rennes; in Paris, Le Mans chickens were prized above all others, while at Lyon those of Bresse were preferred. Turkey was still a luxury, and Barbary ducks and geese were both sought after. In the 18th century, goose had become a bourgeois dish but Rouen ducks were highly prized.

Until the end of the19th century, the poultry market in Paris was situated at La Vallée, around the Quai des Grands-Augustins and the neighbouring streets. La Vallée, 'whose floor is the leading and inexhaustible source of all the fur and feathers sold in Paris' (Grimod de La Reynière), was still encumbered in 1900 with 'crates full of live poultry and square hampers in which rows of dead poultry lay in deep beds. . . . On the ground, the large birds – geese, turkeys, ducks – squelched about in the dung: higher up, on three rows of shelves, flat latticed boxes contained hens and rabbits.' (Zola, *Le Ventre de Paris*).

☐ **Poultry in cooking** In former times, birds that today would be roasted were poached or boiled, and vice versa. Nowadays, the classic ways of cooking poultry are roasting (the most usual method), boiling or steaming, braising (particularly for birds which are rather old or very large, as well as for giblets), and sautéing. Forcemeat is often an essential complement to the dish.

Chicken livers, gizzards (and, more rarely, cocks' combs and kidneys) are also used in several ways in cooking.

Poultry can be served in hot or cold dishes but is never eaten raw. In home cooking, the commonest dishes are casseroles, fricassees, pilaf, hashes, blanquettes, curries, and gratin dishes; French regional dishes also include salmis, poule au pot, fritters, crépinettes, kromeskis, and gratin dishes. Among more elaborate recipes are chicken in aspic, ballottines, chauds-froids, medallions, suprêmes, turbans, soufflés, bouchées, and vols-au-vent, as well as dishes *à la reine*.

pound cake
QUATRE-QUARTS

A household cake made with equal weights of flour, sugar, butter, and eggs. The mixing method and the order in which the ingredients are added varies according to the recipe. The cake can be flavoured with vanilla, lemon, orange, etc.

RECIPE

Pound cake QUATRE-QUARTS Butter and flour a cake tin. Weigh 3 eggs, then weigh out the same amount of caster (superfine) sugar, butter, and sifted flour. Break the eggs, keeping whites and yolks separate. Beat the yolks with the sugar and a pinch of salt until the mixture becomes white and creamy. Beat in the butter, which should be melted but not hot, then the flour, and finally a small glass of rum or brandy. Whip the egg whites to stiff peaks and fold them in carefully. Pour the mixture into the cake tin and cook for about 45 minutes in the oven at 200 c (400 f, gas 6). (The temperature can be raised to 210 c (415 f, gas 6–7) when the cake has risen.) Turn the cake out of the tin as soon as it is removed from the oven and leave it to cool.

Instead of mixing in the yolks and whites separately, the whole eggs can be lightly beaten and mixed directly with the sugar: the result is not quite so light.

pountari

A speciality of Auvergne, consisting of a hash of bacon, onions, and aromatics rolled up in a cabbage leaf (or a piece of pig's intestine), tied at both ends like a sausage, and cooked in a vegetable soup. It is served in slices with the soup.

pounti

A speciality of Auvergne, consisting of a hash of bacon, onions, and Swiss chard bound with milk beaten with eggs and cooked in a cool oven in a casserole greased with lard. This rustic dish can be enriched with ham, cream, raisins, or prunes, as well as potherbs.

poupelin

An old gâteau consisting of a large flat bun made of choux pastry and filled with sweetened whipped cream, ice cream, or a fruit mousse just before serving.

poupeton

An old method of preparing meat or poultry by boning, stuffing, and rolling it into ballottines or paupiettes ready for braising. Poupeton of turkey, which Brillat-Savarin liked, was originally stuffed with ortolans (buntings) arranged on slices of foie gras.

RECIPE

Poupeton of turkey Brillat-Savarin
POUPETON DE DINDONNEAU BRIL-
LAT-SAVARIN Prepare a turkey in the same way as for a ballottine. Stuff it with a smooth mixture of fine veal forcemeat, *à gratin* forcemeat, lambs' sweetbreads braised *à blanc*, and diced foie gras and truffles. Roll the turkey into a ballottine; wrap it in a pig's caul (caul fat), then in muslin (cheesecloth), and tie it up.

Line a greased flameproof casserole with diced raw ham and slices of carrot and onion. Place the turkey in this and cook gently, covered, for 15 minutes, then add 1 glass (3 tablespoons, ¼ cup) Madeira. Reduce by half, add some gravy (or chicken stock), and continue cooking, covered, in the oven at 190 c (375 f, gas 5) for 1½ hours. Skim the fat from the cooking liquid, strain, season, and serve in a sauceboat.

The poupeton can also be served cold, as it is or in aspic.

Pourly

A goats'-milk cheese from Burgundy (45% fat content) with a soft curd and a natural rind which is fine and bluish. It is fairly smooth, with a flavour of hazelnuts and a goaty smell, and is made exclusively in Essert (Yonne). Moulded into a small cylinder with convex sides, 10 cm (4 in) in diameter, 6 cm (2½ in) high, and weighing about 300 g (11 oz), it is at its best between April and November.

pousse-café

A French slang term for a spirit, brandy, or liqueur served at the end of a meal, either in a small glass, or else in an empty coffee cup which is still warm enough to allow the flavour and aroma to develop.

In cocktail language, a *pousse-café* is a drink made by pouring one layer after another of liqueurs and spirits of differing colours and densities which do not mix into a tall glass. This kind of drink is called a *pousse-amour* when an egg yolk is used in the middle of these layers.

poutine

A dish from the south of France, consisting of a mixture of tiny young fish, particularly sardines and anchovies, which are fried like whitebait. The name comes from the dialect of Nice, from the word *poutina* (porridge). Poutine can also be made with poached fish sprinkled with lemon and oil, and can be used to garnish a soup or fill an omelette.

pouytrolle

A speciality of Languedoc, consisting of a hash of pork, Swiss chard, spinach, and herbs stuffed into pigs' intestines. Pouytrolle is poached in water, drained, baked in the oven, and served in slices.

praline   PRALIN

A preparation consisting of crushed almonds or hazelnuts (or both) that have been coated with caramelized sugar. Praline is used in pâtisserie and confectionery, for flavouring creams and ice creams and for filling sweets and chocolates. When home-made it spoils very quickly and will keep only for a day or two, stored in an airtight jar or wrapped in aluminium foil.

RECIPE

Praline PRALIN Blanch 200 g (7 oz,1½ cups) almonds and roast them in the oven or in a frying pan (skillet) without fat (they should be golden brown, but not burnt). Put 200 g (7 oz, 1 cup) granulated sugar and 1 tablespoon water into a copper pan and melt over a brisk heat. When the sugar bubbles, add a few drops of vanilla essence; as soon as it has turned brown, add the almonds and mix all together briskly for 1 minute. Pour onto a greased baking sheet, spread out, and leave to cool. Pound the praline very finely in a mortar as required.

praline (sugared almond)

A sweet consisting of an almond coated with caramelized sugar. Its granulated appearance results from the technique used in its manufacture: the almonds are heated to the hard crack stage (145 C, 285 F) in sugar syrup with a little glucose added, so that sugar crystals form around the nut. The almonds is then coated several times with sugar syrup, the last coating being coloured and flavoured, traditionally giving pink, beige, or brown pralines flavoured with chocolate or coffee.

The praline is a speciality of Montargis, since its inventor, Lassagne, who was *chef de bouche* (master of the household) to the Comte du Plessis-Praslin, chose this town to retire to. Legend has it that his creation came about in this way: seeing a kitchen boy nibbling at leftovers of caramel and almonds, Lassagne had the idea of cooking whole almonds in sugar. The sweetmeat which resulted had a great success and even, it is said, contributed to certain diplomatic triumphs, for which the Comte du Plessis-Praslin, minister to Louis XIII and Louis XIV, took all the credit (he also gave his name to the sweets). Lassagne retired to Montargis in 1630 and there founded the Maison de la Praline, which exists to this day.

Pralines have also become a tra-ditional fairground sweet, cooked in the open air in a copper 'shaker'; the almonds are sometimes replaced by peanuts, which are cheaper. The following verse was composed in honour of the 'true' praline, at about the time of its creation:

'The sweet, when created, was certainly rare;
Dented all over, its colour was brown.
Its subtle aroma delighted the nose;
You'd think it was made of a nectar divine.'

Other towns in France have also made this product a speciality, notably Aigueperse (where the almonds are coated in soft sugar) and Vabres-l'Abbaye (where they are sold in paper cones). Pralines are also used for decorating brioches and soufflés.

See also *dragée*.

RECIPE

Brioche with pralines BRIOCHE AUX PRALINES (from Claude Peyrot's recipe) Make some leavening dough with 250 g (9 oz, 2¼ cups) flour and 20 g (¾ oz) fresh yeast (¾ cake compressed yeast) or 10 g (generous ¼ oz, 2 teaspoons) dried yeast dissolved in 1.5 dl (¼ pint, ⅔ cup) warm water. Roll this dough, which will be fairly soft, into a ball and leave it to rise for at least 30 minutes; it should double in volume.

In the meantime, mix together 750 g (1¾ lb, 7 cups) flour, 15 g (½ oz, 1 tablespoon) salt, 60 g (2½ oz, 5 tabespoons) sugar, and 6 whole eggs. Knead vigorously, beating the dough against the table, and then add 900 g (2 lb, 4 cups) good-quality softened butter, a little at a time. Then mix in the leaven, and roll the dough into a ball again. Leave this to rise at room temperature for 6–7 hours. Mix some pink pralines (or candied rose petals) into the dough, then put it into a large brioche mould and cook in a moderately hot oven (200 C, 400 F, gas 6) for about 1 hour. When cooked, decorate the surface of the brioche with a few crushed pralines.

praliné

A delicate filling for sweets or chocolates, consisting of lightly roasted almonds or hazelnuts mixed with sugar, then crushed with cocoa or cocoa butter.

Praliné is also the name of a cake consisting of layers of Genoese sponge separated by a layer of praline butter cream and covered with a layer of the same cream, sprinkled with chopped almonds.

prawns

See *shrimps and prawns*.

Preservation of food

CONSERVATION

The keeping of perishable foods in a consumable form. Most of the processes of preservation, learnt by trial and error, have been handed down through the ages; the necessity of guarding against want by stocking surplus food is almost as old as human life itself. The biological discoveries of the end of the 19th century and the vast improvements in techniques have meanwhile improved and diversified methods considerably.

The principle of preservation, whether it be on an industrial or small domestic scale, is to stop or slow down the development and action of natural microorganisms and enzymes and to avoid exterior deterioration.

• *Dehydration* draws much of the water (which encourages biological reactions) from the food. Drying and smoking have been practised since antiquity and small-scale processes can still be found coexisting beside the great industrial ovens. In everyday practice, exposure to fresh air or the sun is sufficient for the dehydration of vegetables, aromatic plants, and mushrooms, and the kitchen oven will suffice for fruit. Industrial desiccation calls on three techniques (drum, plate, or vaporizer driers) according to the type of product. Freeze-drying consists of dehydrating a deep-frozen product in a vacuum.

• *Saturation* also results, albeit indirectly, in the elimination of water. This is the principle of preservation by cooking in sugar (jams, confectionery) or by salting (raw meat thrust into dry salt or into a saturated brine solution). Salting is also used to preserve butter. Preserving with oil (aromatic plants, fish) is a very old method, used by the ancients.

• *Coating* protects the food from the action of oxygen. Some traditional techniques include eggs wrapped in newspaper or dipped in lime-wash, fruit coated with wax. The gastronomical practice most common nowadays is the preserving of meat in its own fat (see *confit*), although this is of limited value if not accompanied by sterilization.

• *Preservatives* create a medium incompatible with all microbial life, hence their use among the authorized additives. Classical methods employ either vinegar, sweet-and-sour preparations (gherkins, pickles, chutneys), or alcohol (for fruit). Alcoholic fermentation (wine, beer, cider, spirits) and acidic fermentation (sauerkraut) are, in varying degree, preserving agents.

• *Heat* destroys enzymes and microorganisms as long as the temperature is sufficiently high and the period of treatment sufficiently long. Pasteurization (milk, semipreserved products) is an industrial practice allowing only short-term preservation (from a few days to several months) and foodstuffs have to be kept in the refrigerator. Sterilization (preserves, UHT milk) enables food to be kept for very long periods at room temperature (see *Appert*). These two processes, however, result in the destruction of certain vitamins sensitive to heat (C, B_1). Sterilization can be carried out in the kitchen but it must be done with care and only with a pressure cooker. Tyndallization (double sterilization with an interval of 24 hours) is no more efficient and spoils the quality of the food.

• *Refrigeration* is a very old practice but for centuries natural ice and snow had to be used. The activity of enzymes and bacteria is reduced (but germs are not destroyed) at temperatures of −8 to −10 c (18 to 14 f). Refrigeration enables vegetables, milk products, opened drinks, fresh meat, etc., to be preserved for several days. Very low temperatures, such as those used for freezing or deep-freezing, enable foods to be preserved for longer periods (up to several months or a year); the nutritive value remains the same and the taste of the food is best preserved by this method.

• *Irradiation* consists of exposing food to ionizing radiation, which destroys enzymes and microorganisms and stops germination. It is used at the industrial level for potatoes, onions, shallots, and garlic.

In everyday practice, the length of time food can be kept depends on the type of food itself and the storage methods available. A cellar enables foodstuffs to be preserved in greater quantity; a pantry, refrigerator, freezer, or deep-freeze will mean successively longer periods of preservation. Packaging also plays an important role, from the tin can for dry biscuits to plastic film and aluminium foil, which are especially suited to refrigeration.

preservative

CONSERVATEUR

An additive intended to stop deterioration (fermentation, mould, decay, etc.) in foods. Many preservatives are natural products (saltpetre, vinegar, etc.); others are synthetic.

The preservatives used most often are the antiseptics, especially sulphur dioxide (E220) and sodium and calcium sulphites (E221–226), which are used for drinks (wines, beers, fruit juices), fruit (dried and crystallized), shrimps, and potatoes. However, they can impede the metabolism of calcium and they destroy vitamin B_1 (thiamine). The nitrates and nitrites used for salting butter and in charcuterie are a modern form of saltpetre. They fix the colour of meats and salted foods and, in particular, they prevent the development of the bacillus causing botulism. Sorbic acid (E200, used in cheeses, prunes, fruit juices, wines), formic acid (E236), acetic acid (E260, vinegar), lactic acid (E270, in milk, confectionery, sodas), propionic acid (E280, in cheeses) are, with their derivatives, in current use and are quite innocuous. Many play an integral part in human metabolism. Only benzoic acid (E210) and its derivatives (E211–217) are capable of causing allergies and this is very rare.

The antifungal agents are biphenyl (diphenyl) and its derivatives (E230–232), as well as thiabendazole (E233). They are used to treat the skins of bananas, citrus fruits, the stems of pineapples, and the paper in which these are packaged. This must be printed on the label. These preservatives do not penetrate the skin but if the zest is required for use, it is preferable to choose untreated fruit.

preserves CONSERVES

Foods preserved by heating them in a container that is impervious to liquids, gas, and microorganisms. The making of preserves is practised in the home but it is more often carried out industrially.

Nowadays a large range of foods can be preserved by bottling. Vegetables are washed, sorted, graded, cleaned, cut, and very often blanched. They are then placed in cans or in glass jars, which are then filled with juice, sealed, and sterilized by heating. Fruit is sorted, tailed, seeded, washed, graded, peeled, sometimes blanched, placed in cans or jars (either in its own juice or in syrup), and then sterilized. Fish are first sorted, graded, cleaned (gutted), and the heads removed; they are then washed in brine and dried, or else cooked well in oil or tomato sauce, steamed, or cooked in brine, and finally sterilized. Meat and ready-made dishes are prepared before they are canned or placed in jars and sterilized.

Most preserved foods are put into cans, the majority of which are of tin plate, though some are of aluminium (especially small cans). The period of preservation depends on the chemical reactions between the inner wall of the can and its contents.

Canned foods will keep for the following periods, assuming optimum conditions of temperature (5–20 c, 40 –70 f) and humidity:

- berries, plums, cherries: one year
- peaches, pears, other fruits: two years
- stewed fruit and jams: one to two years
- meat, ready-made dishes: two years
- beetroot (red beet), spinach, sauerkraut, tomatoes, carrots, celery: two to three years
- peas, French beans, asparagus, cabbage, mushrooms, mixed vegetables: three to four years
- sardines, tuna, mackerel: five years and over.

The range of preserves has been greatly extended over the last 20 years. Besides the classics, such as green peas, sardines in oil, fruit salad, and tomato purée, more elaborate preparations are appearing on the market: sauerkraut, cassoulet, rice pudding, ravioli, pies, pâté, and cream desserts. More exotic foods include tropical fruits, crab, palm hearts, soya beans, and foreign foods such as goulash, vine leaves, couscous, and paella, not to mention various sauces and soups. There has also been a great improvement in high-quality foods such as foie gras, snails, truffles, ceps, morels, and ready-made classic dishes. Fruit juices and fruit in syrup and natural juices is also a thriving industry.

□ **Basic criteria** Quality largely depends on the careful selection of raw materials.

There are three operations which are fundamental to good preserving: preheating to eliminate air, efficient crimping of the covers of the containers to ensure tightness, and the use of a pressure cooker to destroy the bacteria causing food poisoning: 100 c (212 f) for acidic foods such as fruit, 115 c (240 f) for most vegetables, 120 c (248 f) for meat, 122–130 c (252–266 f) for the denser foods, which are only slowly penetrated by heat. Intense heat applied over a short period of time helps to preserve the vitamins and nutritive qualities.

Labelling should clearly mention the composition of the preserve (including additives) if it is complex, with the respective percentage of meat and garnish in the case of cooked dishes, its origin, and finally the date of canning, accompanied by a limiting date ('best before') for optimum quality.

□ **Semipreserved foods** This is food that has been preserved for a limited time, packed in glass jars, cans, aluminium sachets, or in polypropylene. The heat treatment is not as elaborate as for preserved foods – sometimes it is omitted altogether and replaced by straightforward pickling in brine. The label should display a sales deadline and the instruction 'Keep in a cold place'. The following can be found in shops in refrigerated cabinets: seafood, marinated herring (creamed or smoked), flavoured butters, anchovy, cod, mussels, fish roes, ready-to-eat dishes (quenelles, pasta, etc), cooked meats packed in plastic, pâtés, and potted meats.

preserving jar BOCAL

A wide-necked glass container, usually hermetically sealed with either a metal screw top or with a glass lid fitted with a rubber seal and a metal clasp. These jars are used for preserving fruit and vegetables in their own juice, conserves, stews, cassoulets, etc., and fruit in syrup, vinegar, or alcohol. Jars for sterilized food must not be too large, because once they are opened, their contents must be used up quickly. Also, sterilization is more difficult for large quantities. The usual size is ⅓–1½ litres (11 fl oz–2¾ pints, 1⅓ cups–3½ pints). Jars containing food should preferably be stored in the dark.

Jars for home-made jam do not need a special lid as there are various paper and plastic covers which can be used.

press PRESSE

A utensil used for producing a liquid or purée from solid ingredients. Citrus fruit squeezers made from glass, plastic, or wood enable fresh fruit juice to be squeezed from oranges and lemons. Cast-aluminium fruit squeezers, with perforated bowls, are also sometimes used for other types of fruit, but only produce small quantities of juice (for fruit cocktails). The 'half-slice' squeezer, made of metal, is used for flavouring lemon tea or for squeezing over fish or hors d'oeuvres where a wedge of lemon is needed.

Small presses made from enamelled steel are used for making jellies, jams, and wine: these crush the fruit very rapidly by the action of a screw against a face-plate. A vegetable mill (or purée press) is used to rub cooked vegetables or fruit through a sieve to reduce them to a purée. All these are now being increasingly replaced by electrically operated machines with a centrifugal action. Meat presses are used to extract the juice from raw or slightly cooked meat. The carcass (or duck) press is a piece of equipment used mainly for extracting the fatty juices from the carcass of a duck (see *Tour d'Argent*).

Some terrines, pâtés, and meats (such as tongue) need to be chilled under a press to be smoothly integrated, well moulded, or well flattened. The food is left in a cool place, covered with a small board with a heavy weight on top, or a special press with a screw-down lid can be used. In old French cookery, the term *soupresse* ('under press') was applied to a sort of fish pâté in which the crushed flesh of the fish was wrapped in a piece of muslin (cheesecloth) and pressed down hard.

pressure cooker
AUTOCUISEUR, MARMITE À PRESSION

A hermetically sealed saucepan in which food is cooked under pressure at a higher temperature and therefore much more quickly than in an ordinary pan. Temperatures range from 112–125 c (230–250 F) instead of a maximum of 100 c (212 F) – the boiling point of water at atmospheric pressure.

A type of autoclave, the pressure cooker is made of thick aluminium or stainless steel; its lid has a watertight seal that can usually be closed hermetically, either with a screw and clamp or a bayonet-type locking mechanism. A valve controls the escape of the steam once the desired pressure is reached (a safety device is included in case the valve becomes blocked). It is essential to allow the pressure to fall before opening the lid, either by letting all the steam escape through the valve, or by cooling the pressure cooker with cold water.

The pressure cooker is designed for cooking in steam or in water or stock (with a reduced quantity of liquid), but it may also be used as a sterilizer or yogurt-maker. It has the advantages of saving time and retaining the mineral salts in fruit and vegetables; it also enables the use of less fat in cooking and a better fat dispersion. However there are some disadvantages. In the opinion of gourmets, the pressure cooker cannot replace the old simmering method of cooking. Meat has a tendency to be noticeably softer, with less flavour, and the flavours of various ingredients in a dish are indiscriminately mixed.

pretzel   BRETZEL
A crisp biscuit (cookie) from Alsace, traditionally served with beer. It is usually shaped like a loose knot and is made of dough poached in boiling water, sprinkled with coarse salt and cumin seeds, and hardened in the oven. The ancient origins of this pastry are linked to the cult of the sun: it was originally made in the shape of a ring encircling a cross. Since this was too fragile, it evolved into its present shape, which is a traditional motif of bakers and pastrycooks. Pretzels of all sizes are now made as apéritif biscuits.

prickly pear
FIGUE DE BARBARIE

The edible orange-red pear-shaped fruit of a species of cactus. The fruit has a thick skin covered with large prickles and must be handled with care, preferably wearing gloves. The prickles can be removed by rubbing the skin with a thick rough cloth. The fruit is peeled and eaten raw, sprinkled with a little lemon or lime juice. It can also be cooked and puréed for use in desserts and preserves. An oil can be extracted from the seeds and the seeds can be sprouted to produce edible shoots, which are used mainly as animal feed.

primrose   PRIMEVÈRE
A meadow and woodland plant whose pale yellow flowers appear in spring. Its young tender leaves can be eaten as a salad, and its flowers are used for decorating salads and for herb teas. Primrose flowers are also used in several cookery recipes, including a dish of roast veal cooked in butter with sliced onions, carrots, and a bouquet garni, moistened with white wine, to which primrose flowers are added 30 minutes before cooking is finished; the cooking liquid is deglazed with port and thickened with cream.

Prince Albert
A method of preparing fillet of beef which was named in honour of the Prince Consort, husband of Queen Victoria. The meat is stuffed with raw foie gras with truffles, braised in a vegetable fondue, and then moistened with port; the garnish consists of whole truffles.

RECIPE

Fillet of beef Prince Albert   FILET DE BOEUF PRINCE-ALBERT   Marinate a raw goose foie gras studded with truffle in a little Cognac with salt and pepper for 24 hours in a cool place. Lard a piece of beef cut from the middle of the fillet with fine strips of bacon. Slice the meat along its length without separating the 2 halves completely. Drain the foie gras, place it in the meat, and tie together firmly to keep the liver in place. Fry the meat in butter in a braising pan over a brisk heat until it is well browned on all sides, then cover it with a layer of matignon, wrap in very thin rashers (slices) of bacon, and secure with string.

Prepare a braising stock with a calf's foot and aromatic herbs, adding the liver marinade; pour into the braising pan and add the beef. Pour on a little port, cover, bring to the boil, then transfer to a moderately hot oven (200 c, 400 f, gas 6) and cook for 1 hour. Untie the fillet, remove the bacon and the matignon, but leave the string holding the foie gras in place. Strain the braising stock, pour some over the meat, and glaze quickly in a very hot oven. Untie the meat, place it on a serving dish, and garnish with whole truffles, stewed in butter or poached in Madeira. Serve the braising stock, skimmed of fat and strained, in a sauceboat.

princesse

A rich garnish for poultry, salmon steaks, calves' sweetbreads, vols-au-vent, or egg dishes, distinguished by the inclusion of asparagus tips and slivers of truffle.

RECIPES

Chicken princesse POULARDE PRINCESSE Poach the chicken in white stock. Bake some barquette cases (shells) blind and stew some green asparagus tips in butter. Drain the chicken and place it on a serving dish and keep warm. Prepare an allemande sauce with the cooking liquid. Arrange the asparagus tips in the barquettes and use to garnish the dish. Sprinkle the barquettes with slivers of truffle heated through in butter. Pour some sauce over the chicken and serve the rest in a sauceboat.

Salmon steaks princesse DARNES DE SAUMON PRINCESSE Ask the fishmonger to cut some steaks of equal thickness from a large fresh salmon. Prepare some fish fumet, leave it to cool, and strain. Lay the steaks in a fish kettle with a small amount of fumet and poach them gently for 6 minutes from the time that the fumet starts to simmer. Drain and skin the steaks and arrange on a serving dish; keep warm. Use the cooking liquid to make a normande sauce. Garnish the steaks with slivers of truffle warmed through in butter and with green asparagus tips, also cooked in butter (these can be arranged in barquettes made of fine lining pastry). Serve the sauce separately.

Scrambled eggs princesse OEUFS BROUILLÉS PRINCESSE Prepare some scrambled eggs and pour into a bowl. Garnish with green asparagus tips stewed in butter, a julienne of white chicken meat bound with suprême sauce, and some slivers of truffle heated through in butter.

printanière (à la)

Describing various dishes (meat, poultry, eggs) which are garnished with a mixture of vegetables (in theory, spring vegetables), usually tossed in butter.

Navarin of mutton and spring vegetable soup are usually described as *printanier*.

RECIPE

Vegetable ragout à la printanière RAGOUT DE LÉGUMES À LA PRINTANIÈRE Generously grease a large flameproof casserole with butter. Prepare and wash the following new vegetables: 250 g (9 oz) baby carrots, 250 g (9 oz) baby turnips, 12 button onions, 250 g (9 oz) very small new potatoes, 2 lettuce hearts, 250 g (9 oz) finely sliced French beans, 250 g (9 oz, 1½ cups) shelled peas, and 3 trimmed artichoke hearts quartered and sprinkled with lemon juice. Separate half a very white cauliflower into tiny florets.

Put the carrots, beans, artichoke hearts, and onions into the greased casserole; just cover with chicken stock and bring to the boil. After it has boiled for 8 minutes, add the turnips, potatoes, peas, cauliflower, and lettuce hearts; adjust the seasoning and continue cooking for about 20 minutes. Drain the vegetables and arrange them in a vegetable dish. Reduce the cooking liquid, whisk in 50 g (2 oz, 4 tablespoons) butter, and pour over the vegetables.

Procope

The oldest café in Paris, which is still in existence in the Rue de l'Ancienne-Comédie. The establishment was founded in 1686 by Francesco Procopio dei Coltelli, who changed his name to Procope; he had previously worked with the Armenian Pascal, who ran a coffee stall at the Saint-Germain Fair and thus introduced the beverage to the capital. Procope opened the first permanent establishment devoted to the consumption of coffee; his café was richly decorated with chandeliers, wood panelling, and mirrors.

The Procope rapidly became the most famous centre of Parisian literary and intellectual life. From the 17th to the 19th century it was patronized by writers, actors (the Comédie-Française was situated opposite from 1687 to 1770), encyclopedists, and later by revolutionaries and Romantics. His syrup drinks, ice creams, confectionery, and cakes were also popular. Procope had the original idea of pasting up a news-sheet on the chimney of the stove which heated the room; his café thus became 'the true speaking newspaper of Paris', and a celebrated forum for the exchange of ideas.

The founder retired in 1716 and his son Alexandre succeeded him. In 1753 a certain Dubuisson bought the establishment, then later sold it to the Italian Zoppi (a friend of Marat and Danton), who managed it during the time of the Empire. The focus of literary life during the Romantic period, the Procope later began to suffer the effects of competition from the Café de la Régence. It was sold in 1872 to Baroness Thénard, and closed in 1890; it re-opened in 1893 as a literary club, then became, successively, a vegetarian restaurant and an eating house for poor students, before being used by the French administration. It reopened as a restaurant in 1952, but has never recaptured its former glory.

profiterole

A small filled sweet or savoury bun made of choux pastry. Savoury profiteroles are filled with a cheese mixture, game purée, etc., and are generally used as a garnish for soup.

Sweet profiteroles are filled with confectioners' custard (pastry cream), Chantilly cream, ice cream, jam, etc.; they are the basic ingredient of croquembouches and gâteaux Saint-Honoré. Chocolate profiteroles are filled with vanilla or coffee ice cream or Chantilly cream and are coated or served with hot chocolate sauce. Profiteroles can also be filled with Chantilly cream combined with fruit purée and can be served with zabaglione flavoured with syrup of the same fruit. The name comes from the word *profit* and originally meant a small gratuity or gift.

RECIPE

Chocolate profiteroles PROFITEROLES AU CHOCOLATE Prepare some choux pastry (see *chou*) with 2.5 dl (8 fl oz, 1 cup) water, a pinch of salt, 2 tablespoons granulated sugar, 125 g (4½ oz, generous cup) flour, and 4 eggs. Using a forcing (pastry) bag with a plain nozzle, pipe out balls of dough the size of walnuts onto a greased baking sheet and brush them with beaten egg. Cook in a moderately hot oven (200 C, 400 F, gas 6) for about 20 minutes until crisp and golden; allow to cool in the oven.

Meanwhile melt 200 g (7 oz) plain (semisweet) chocolate with 1 dl (6 tablespoons, scant ½ cup) water in a bain-marie; add 1 dl (6 tablespoons, scant ½ cup) cream and stir well. Prepare some Chantilly cream by whisking 3 dl (½ pint, 1¾ cups) double (heavy) cream with 1 dl (6 tablespoons, scant ½ cup) very cold milk, then 75 g (3 oz, 6 tablespoons) granulated sugar and 1 teaspoon vanilla sugar. Split the profiteroles on one side and fill them with the Chantilly cream, using a forcing bag. Arrange in a bowl and serve with the hot chocolate sauce.

progrès

A light and crunchy cake base made from a mixture of stiffly whisked egg whites, sugar, and ground almonds and/or hazelnuts, which is piped out in a spiral to form discs and baked in the oven. The cake is built up by placing the discs one on top of the other, sandwiched together with praline butter cream or with coffee or chocolate cream. The cake is topped with flaked (slivered) or roasted almonds, sprinkled with icing (confectioners') sugar, and iced (frosted) with fondant or decorated with butter cream, which is piped with a fluted nozzle or with a small plain nozzle to write the word 'progrès' on the top.

RECIPE

Coffee progrès PROGRÈS AU CAFÉ
Grease 3 baking sheets, dust with flour, and trace a circle, about 23 cm (9 in) in diameter, on each of them with a spoon. In a bowl mix together 150 g (5 oz, ⅔ cup) granulated sugar, 250 g (9 oz, 2 cups) ground almonds, and a pinch of salt. Whisk 8 egg whites until stiff with 100 g (4 oz, ½ cup) granulated sugar and gently fold into the first mixture with a wooden spoon. Put this mixture into a forcing (pastry) bag with an 8-mm (⅓-in) nozzle and fill the 3 circles, piping in a spiral from the centre to the edge. Bake for 45 minutes in the oven at 180 C (350 F, gas 4). Gently ease the cooked discs off the sheets and let them cool on a flat surface.

While the oven is still hot, roast 150 g (5 oz, 1 cup) flaked (slivered) almonds for 5 minutes. Put 250 g (9 oz, 1¼ cups) granulated sugar in a saucepan with 3 tablespoons water and bring to the boil. Beat 6 egg yolks in a bowl, then gradually pour over the boiling syrup, beating hard until the mixture cools. Dissolve 2 tablespoons instant coffee in 1 tablespoon boiling water. Cream 325 g (12 oz, 1½ cups) butter and gradually beat in the egg–syrup mixture; then pour in the dissolved coffee and beat well. Reserve one-quarter of this butter cream; cover each disc with one-third of the remaining cream. Then put the discs one on top of the other and cover the sides with the reserved butter cream. Decorate the top with the flaked almonds. Place in the refrigerator for about 1 hour.

Cut out some strips of thick paper 1 cm (½ in) wide and 25 cm (10 in) long. Place them on top of the cake without pressing, leaving a gap of 2 cm (¾ in) between each, and dust the cake with sifted icing (confectioners') sugar. Carefully remove the paper strips and put the progrès back in the refrigerator for at least 1 hour before serving.

prosciutto

The Italian word for ham, used in the names of raw hams coming from Italy, in particular *prosciutto di Parma* and *prosciutto di San Daniele*.

protein PROTÉINE

Any of a large group of nitrogenous compounds, present in all animals and plants, consisting of linked amino-acid units. As combustion of proteins in the body is not complete, the waste (urea and uric acid) must be eliminated. Foods of animal origin that are rich in proteins include cheese, milk, eggs, and meat; plant proteins occur in bread, pasta, and pulses. The average daily intake of proteins should be 1 gram per kg body weight, of which more than half should be of animal origin as certain essential amino acids are absent from proteins of vegetable origin.

The following are the average protein contents of some common foods (per 100 g): semi-fat meat and fish about 17 g; eggs 13 g; milk 3.5 g; cheeses 15–30 g; bread 7 g; potatoes 2 g; pulses 23 g.

provençale (à la)

Describing numerous preparations inspired by (or arising directly from) the cookery of Provence, in which olive oil, tomato, and garlic predominate. The Provençal garnish for cuts of meat or poultry includes either peeled and slowly cooked tomatoes and large mushrooms garnished with duxelles seasoned with garlic, or crushed garlic-flavoured tomatoes with stoned (pitted) olives (black (ripe) or green), or aubergines (eggplants) stuffed with a tomato fondue, French beans in butter, and château potatoes. Provençal sauce (made with tomato, onion, garlic, and white wine) is used to dress vegetables, eggs, poultry, and fish.

RECIPES

Bass (*or brill*) **à la provençale** BARS (OU BARBUES) À LA PROVENÇALE
Prepare a Provençal sauce. Scale some

bass or brill (about 400 g, 14 oz). Cut off the fins and make an incision in the top of the back, on either side of the backbone. Wash and wipe the fish. Sprinkle them with salt and pepper, dust them with flour, and brown them quickly in olive oil in a frying pan (skillet). Mask an ovenproof dish with a little provençal sauce. Arrange the fish in it and just cover with Provençal sauce. Sprinkle with fresh breadcrumbs, moisten with a little olive oil, and cook in a moderately hot oven (200 c, 400 f, gas 6) for about 20 minutes. Sprinkle with chopped parsley and serve piping hot in the cooking dish.

Fried eggs à la provençale OEUFS POÊLÉS À LA PROVENÇALE Prepare a garnish of fried tomatoes and aubergines (eggplants) by slicing, removing seeds from tomatoes and frying in olive oil, and a tomato fondue. Mask a dish with the vegetables. Lightly fry some eggs in olive oil and arrange them in the dish. Coat them with tomato fondue and sprinkle with chopped parsley and garlic.

Provençal sauce SAUCE PROVENÇALE Heat 2 tablespoons (3 tablespoons) olive oil in a heavy-based saucepan. Soften in it without browning 3 tablespoons (¼ cup) peeled and chopped onions, then add 750 g (generous 1½ lb, generous 3 cups) peeled, deseeded, and crushed tomatoes and cook gently for about 15 minutes. Add a crushed clove of garlic, a bouquet garni, 2 dl (7 fl oz, ¾ cup) dry white wine, and 2 dl (7 fl oz, ¾ cup) meat stock. Leave to cook with the lid on for 15 minutes, then adjust the seasoning, remove the lid, and reduce the sauce by half. Add some fresh chopped parsley or basil just before serving.

Sautéed veal chops à la provençale CÔTES DE VEAU SAUTÉES À LA PROVENÇALE First prepare a garlic-flavoured tomato sauce, and then some small round tomatoes stuffed with mushroom duxelles and browned in the oven. Quickly brown some veal chops in olive oil in a frying pan (skillet). Season with salt and pepper, cover, reduce the heat, and leave to complete cooking for about 15 minutes. Drain the

chops and arrange them in the serving dish surrounded by the stuffed tomatoes. Keep hot in the oven with the door ajar.

Pour the oil out of the frying pan, add the tomato sauce and ½ glass (3–4 tablespoons) white wine, stir well, and reduce by half over a brisk heat. Pour the sauce over the chops, sprinkle with chopped parsley or basil, and serve piping hot.

Provence

A vast region with a favourable climate, Provence possesses a great variety of natural resources, reflected in its colourful gastronomy, which began to be known in Paris at the time of the Revolution. The specialities were listed in *Le Cuisinier Durand*, which appeared in Nîmes in 1830, and by Maître Reboul, at the end of the 19th century. Dishes *à la provençale* are extremely varied, but all are characterized by the presence of tomato, garlic, and olive oil.

The Mediterranean coast supplies a number of fish (especially local species of rockfish) and seafood, and the inland waters provide trout, bleak, pike, tench, char, and carp.

The raising of sheep (particularly the famous Sisteron lambs) and goats produces savoury meat and local cheeses. Another speciality is the lavender honey of Vaucluse. The game of the region includes young rabbits from the Garigue, snipe, plovers (in the vicinity of Arles), and thrushes (in the Basses-Alpes).

Truffles are gathered in Tricastin (the principal market is Carpentras), but the market-garden produce and fruit dominate the market. The valleys of the Rhône and Durance are the largest fruit- and vegetable-producing areas of France; Vaucluse is the principal producer of dessert grapes. Rice is cultivated in the Camargue, figs (those of Solliès are well known) and almonds near Aix, and oranges, lemons, and even thick-skinned citrons in the Alpes-Maritimes region. Cultivation of the olive tree provides an oil which gives Provençal cookery its fruity flavour, often accentuated by aromatic herbs.

Typical Provençal soups include the following: aïgo boulido and aïgo sau d'iou (dominated by garlic); bouillabaisse with its numerous variations; and soups garnished with pistou poutine, *fielas* (conger eel), mussels, and *favouilles* (crabs). Fish and seafood predominate in the gastronomy of the coastal region, which includes the bourride of Sète, *oursinade* (dish of sea urchins), sartagnano, the *esquinade* of Toulon (crabs stuffed with mussels and browned in the oven), *favouilles* (crabs) with rice, sardines stuffed with spinach or cooked *au gratin*, fried *supions* (small cuttlefish), octopus sautéed with garlic, sea-anemone fritters or omelettes, etc. Dried salt cod is cooked *en raito* and stockfish is prepared *à la niçoise* (see *estofinado*). Small snails are eaten *à la sucarelles*, *à l'arlésienne*, or in bouillabaisse (as *limaçons*).

Among the best-known meat dishes are the excellent daube of beef *à la provençale*, with tomatoes and olives; gigot *à l'avignonnaise*; gayettes with pig's liver; the pieds et paquets of Marseille; and sou-fassum.

Vegetables are often stuffed, seasoned with many spices. Some typical Provençal vegetable dishes are stuffed gourd flowers, gratins prepared with *herbes de Provence* and garlic, tarts made with Swiss chard or courgettes (zucchini), tians, papeton of aubergines (eggplants), and panisse. Gnocchi, ravioli, macaroni, and cannelloni are very common in the Midi.

The Arles sausage has an age-old reputation, and Provence has long been known for its original sauces and condiments, such as aïoli, rouille, pissalat and the similar *melet* (typical of Martigues), tapenade, boutargue, aillade, and anchoyade.

Provençal cheeses, both goats'- and ewes'-milk cheese, are characterized by their very strong taste; they include Banon, Brousse, Bossons macérés, Cachat, and Picodon.

Pâtisserie specialities include the crisp biscuits and calissons of Aix, the bugnes of Arles, the pompe, the échaudés of Draguignan, the fouaces, the navettes of Marseille, and the soufflé cakes and croissants with pine kernels, which are included among the so-called 'thirteen desserts' of the Provençal Christmas. The confectionery of Provence includes crystallized (candied) fruits from Apt, Digne, Valréas, and Grasse; crystallized or caramelized flowers, nougat from Saint-Tropez, berlingots from Carpentras, and fig sausages.

The wines of Provence include Côtes-de-Provence and Coteaux-d'Aix, Cassis, Palette, Bellet, and Bandol, while Vaucluse prides itself on the Châteauneuf-du-Pape, accompanied by the *crus* of Gigondas, Vacqueyras, and Cairanne. Vaucluse also supplies the natural sweet wines of Beaumes-de-Venise and Rasteau.

prove (rise) POUSSER

Of dough, to increase in volume through the action of a raising (leavening) agent. To make a leavened dough rise, it should be placed away from draughts in a warm atmosphere (25–30 c, 75–85 f) to encourage fermentation; this results in the production of carbon dioxide gas, which puffs up the dough. While it is proving, the dough is covered with a cloth to prevent the formation of a crust. If brioche or bread dough has not risen sufficiently, it remains heavy and solid; when proving goes on for too long, the dough becomes acid.

Provolone

An Italian cows'-milk cheese (44% butter-fat), generally smoked, with a compressed and grained centre. It has a natural crust which is smooth, shiny, and usually golden-yellow (sometimes brown). Soft, smooth, and cream or yellow inside, Provolone cheese has a mild or piquant flavour depending on how long it has been ripened (two to six months).

Originating from Campania (where it was originally manufactured with buffaloes' milk), it is now produced throughout southern Italy. It is moulded by hand into various shapes (pear, melon, piglet, sausage, etc.), weighing 1–5 kg (2¼–11 lb). The giant Provolone is in the form of a long cylinder weighing 22–90 ₓg (50–200 lb). It generally bears the marks of the string which has been used to hang it up during ripening. Fine and soft when young, Provolone is a good table cheese which is also used for canapés, on toast, and in mixed salads; it is grated like Parmesan when mature.

prune PRUNEAU

A dried red or purple plum, which keeps

for a long time. The preparation of prunes has been known since Roman times. Traditionally the plums are dried in the sun, but most prunes today are prepared by progressive desiccation in the oven; there is also a technique of dehydration through immersion in hot syrup, producing Karlsbad plums which taste strongly of the fruit and are packed in wooden boxes for Christmas.

Several varieties of plums are processed into prunes, the finest being the Ente (or Agen) plum, the large damson of Tours, and the Catherine. The Perdrigon plum, peeled, stoned (pitted), dried in the sun, and flattened, is sold under the name of *pistole*. The same plum, unpeeled, unstoned, scalded, then dried in the shade, is called *brignole* (named after the town of Brignoles, of which it is a speciality) or *pruneau fleuri*; it was very popular during the Renaissance, being the favourite delicacy of the Duc de Guise.

With a high calorific content (290 Cal per 100 g), the prune is very rich in sugar, potassium, magnesium, and calcium. When purchased, it must be quite black, shiny, and soft but not sticky or excessively sweet. Its pulp should be amber-yellow, not caramelized. Sold loose or packaged, prunes should be stored in a place which is neither too damp nor too dry (which would cause blooming, a sugary crystallization on the surface).

Before use, prunes must be washed, then soaked (for a minimum of two hours, preferably overnight) in cold or tepid weak tea. However, they may also be cooked directly in water or red wine, particularly if they are to be made into a compote or a purée.

Stoned prunes are included in numerous pastries, either whole or boiled to a pulp with sugar (for tarts, puddings, and turnovers). They may also be used for ices, fruit salads, or fruit compotes or served soaked in liqueur or brandy, then flamed. In confectionery, they are stuffed in various ways (with almond paste, etc.) and sometimes glazed; they can also be preserved in brandy.

Prunes are also used as a condiment in cookery, particularly for rabbit and pork but also for game, goose, and turkey; they are also used to stuff paupiettes of fish. Prunes also feature in international cuisine: lamb preserved with prunes and cinnamon in Algeria; roast pork with prunes in Denmark and Poland; sweet-and-sour carp in Czechoslovakia; and bacon lightly fried with prunes in Germany.

RECIPES

Compote of prunes COMPOTE DE PRUNEAUX Soak the prunes in tepid weak tea for at least 2 hours; when swollen, drain them, stone (pit) them, and put in a saucepan. Just cover with cold water (or red or white wine) and add some granulated sugar (a maximum of 100 g (4 oz, ½ cup) per 500 g (18 oz, 3 cups) prunes), 2 tablespoons (3 tablespoons) lemon juice, and 1 teaspoon vanilla-flavoured sugar. Bring to the boil, then cook gently for about 40 minutes. Serve lukewarm or cold. When well-reduced and strained, this compote may be used to fill puff-pastry cases, turnovers, or tartlets.

The prunes may be left unstoned, and the quantity of water or wine can be increased; the prunes are then served with all their juice.

Marzipan and sugar-coated prunes PRUNEAUX DÉGUISÉS Heat in a saucepan 6 cl (3 tablespoons, ¼ cup) water, 200 g (7 oz, scant cup) caster (superfine) sugar, and 20 g (¾ oz, 1½ tablespoons) powdered glucose, until the temperature reaches 115 C (240 F). Remove from the heat and add 100 g (4 oz, 1 cup) ground almonds. Stir well with a wooden spoon until the mixture has the consistency of semolina. Cut 40 semidried Agen prunes lengthwise, without separating the halves, and take out the stones (pits).

Knead the cooled almond paste by hand; when it is soft, add 3 or 4 drops of red or green food colouring and 1 tablespoon rum. Knead the paste on a smooth worktop, gather it into a ball, roll it out into a very thin long cylinder, and cut into 40 equal sections. Roll the sections into olive shapes and insert into the prunes, making 2 or 3 slanting cuts in the visible part of the almond paste. Arrange the prunes in little cases of pleated paper.

The prunes may also be glazed with sugar syrup.

Prunes stuffed with Roquefort cheese
PRUNEAUX AU ROQUEFORT Stone
(pit) about 30 Agen prunes and flatten
them with the blade of a knife. Crumble
100 g (4 oz) Roquefort cheese with a
fork and crush 30 hazelnuts. Mix the
Roquefort cheese with the hazelnuts,
some pepper, 2 tablespoons (3 tablespoons) fresh cream, and 1 tablespoon
port. Place a small ball of this mixture in
the centre of each prune. Reshape the
prunes and put in a cool place for several hours before serving as a cocktail
snack.

Prunes with bacon   PRUNEAUX AU
BACON Take some semidried Agen
prunes and stone (pit) them by splitting
them lengthwise. Insert a shelled pistachio in place of the stone, then roll up
each prune in half a thin rasher (slice) of
bacon. Secure by means of a wooden
cocktail stick (toothpick). Arrange the
prunes in an ovenproof dish, and place
in a very hot oven (230 C, 450 F, gas 8)
until the bacon is crispy (about 8–9
minutes). Serve piping hot for a cocktail
snack.

Prunier (Alfred)

French restaurateur (died 1898). In
1872 he founded a restaurant in Paris,
in the Rue Duphot, serving oysters,
grills, and judiciously chosen wines,
which quickly became successful.
Among the customers were Sarah Bernhardt, Oscar Wilde, Clemenceau, and
the great Russian dukes.

His son Émile succeeded him and the
establishment became known for its fish
and seafood specialities, notably bass *à
l'angevine*, Boston fillet (beef with oysters), marmite dieppoise, lobster Newburg and thermidor, and, of course,
oysters and shellfish. He opened a
second restaurant, Prunier-Traktir, in
the Avenue Victor Hugo and also took
an active interest in oyster culture and
fishing, particularly sturgeon farming in
the Gironde region (for French caviar).

On his death in 1925, his daughter
Simone continued his work and opened
a third restaurant in London (Madame
Prunier), which closed in 1976.

PTFE

Polytetrafluoroethylene, a thermo-
setting plastic used for lining the inside
of cooking utensils to give a nonstick
surface.

PTFE has a very low coefficient of
friction and good insulating powers.
Heat-resistant and nonflammable, it
withstands high temperatures, does not
dissolve, and is resistant to attack by
acid. The most commonly used base is
aluminium, especially for frying pans
(skillets), baking tins, and ovenproof
dishes. Food can be cooked in PTFE-
coated utensils with a minimum of fat.
However, as the coating scratches very
easily, it is recommended that a wooden
or rubber spatula (not a fork) is used for
turning or removing foods, which
should not be cut up in the pan. PTFE is
also used to coat grills, stew-pans,
waffle moulds, etc.

pub

A public house: an establishment in
Great Britain licensed for the sale and
consumption of alcoholic drinks and
often also serving light meals. There are
usually several rooms known as bars.
The public bar is usually the most
crowded and popular room, providing
drinks at the bar and usually a buffet
service. The saloon bar, lounge bar, and
sometimes a private bar offer varying
degrees of comfort, elegance, and privacy. Most pubs offer a limited restaurant service (cold or hot dishes, especially at lunchtime). This service has
been adopted by certain restaurants in
Paris; decorated in the English fashion,
they serve beer and whisky, poached
haddock, grills, cold chicken, mixed
salads, etc.

One of the features of the English pub
lies in its very strictly regulated hours of
opening and closing. Furthermore, customers go to the bar to order and pay for
drinks, rather than being waited on at
tables.

puchero

A Spanish or Latin American stew,
highly season, made with beef, mutton,
sausage, ham, and vegetables. In Latin
American countries it is garnished with
corn on the cob.

pudding

Any of numerous dishes, sweet or
savoury, served hot or cold, which are
prepared in a variety of ways.

English suet puddings consist of a sweet or savoury filling (e.g. apples, steak and kidney) completely enclosed in a suet dough and steamed or boiled in a pudding basin (mould). Most other puddings of English origin are served as desserts, usually baked or boiled in a mould.

In the past the word 'pudding' applied to all boiled dishes; it has the same origin as the French *boudin* (black pudding, blood sausage). However, the sweet pudding that we know today did not assume its modern form until the 17th century.

Certain English puddings have now become traditional on the Continent, with their own variations. Among these are diplomat and Nesselrode puddings, bread pudding, apple or pear pudding (in a suet crust), and semolina, tapioca, and rice puddings. Soufflé pudding is made with choux pastry enriched with sugar, butter, egg yolks, and whisked egg whites and flavoured with vanilla, chocolate, orange, etc.

Iced puddings are made by lining the mould with sponge cake or finger biscuits and filling it with ice creams, sometimes combining several colours.

In France, the name 'pudding' is also given to a cake made from dry bread or stale brioche, sweetened and mixed with milk, raisins, rum, eggs, and candied orange peel, cooked in a small brioche mould, then lightly covered with fondant icing (frosting). It is similar to the English bread pudding, though much more elaborate.

RECIPES

American pudding PUDDING À L'AMÉRICAINE Put in a large bowl 75 g (3 oz, ¾ cup) stale breadcrumbs, 100 g (4 oz, 1 cup) flour, 100 g (4 oz, ½ cup) brown sugar, and 75 g (3 oz) chopped beef suet. Add 100 g (4 oz, ⅔ cup) finely diced crystallized (candied) fruit, 1 tablespoon blanched finely shredded orange peel, and the same amount of lemon peel. Bind the mixture with 1 whole egg and 3 yolks. Add a generous pinch of cinnamon, the same amount of grated nutmeg, and 1 liqueur glass of rum. Mix well and pour into a buttered and floured charlotte mould. Cook in a bain-marie in a moderately hot oven

(200 C, 400 F, gas 6) for about 50 minutes until firm. Leave to cool and turn out onto the serving dish. Serve with rum-flavoured zabaglione.

Cabinet pudding PUDDING DE CABINET Prepare 6 dl (1 pint, 2½ cups) vanilla-flavoured egg custard (see *creams and custards*). Cut 100 g (4 oz, ⅔ cup) crystallized (candied) fruit into a salpicon. Wash 100 g (4 oz, ⅔ cup) stoned raisins, then moisten them with 1 small glass of rum. Pour another small glass of rum over 150 g (5 oz, 2½ cups) sponge finger biscuits (ladyfingers) broken into pieces. Butter a charlotte mould and fill it with alternate layers of sponge fingers, raisins, and crystallized fruit. Pour the egg custard over. Place in a bain-marie and cook in a hot oven (220 C, 425 F, gas 7) for about 45 minutes. Leave the pudding until lukewarm before turning it out. Serve with a vanilla-flavoured custard cream (see *creams and custards*) or an apricot sauce.

Chocolate pudding PUDDING AU CHOCOLAT Soften 150 g (5 oz, ⅔ cup) butter at room temperature and 125 g (4½ oz) plain dessert chocolate in the oven. Work the butter with a wooden spoon in a warm mixing bowl, then beat in 75 g (3 oz, 6 tablespoons) caster (superfine) sugar and 20 g (¾ oz, 1 tablespoon) vanilla-flavoured sugar. When the mixture is white and creamy, add 8 egg yolks, one after the other. Mix the chocolate with 1 tablespoon flour and 1 tablespoon potato flour, then blend it with the mixture. Finally, add 5 stiffly beaten egg whites. Pour into a buttered and floured charlotte mould, place in a bain-marie, and cook in a moderately hot oven (200 C, 400 F, gas 6) for about 50 minutes until firm. Turn out the pudding while still lukewarm, and coat with vanilla- or coffee-flavoured custard cream (see *creams and custards*).

English almond pudding PUDDING AUX AMANDES À L'ANGLAISE Cream together 125 g (4½ oz, generous ½ cup) softened butter and 150 g (5 oz, ⅔ cup) caster (superfine) sugar in a basin. Add 250 g (9 oz, generous 2 cups) almonds, blanched and finely chopped, a pinch of salt, 1 tablespoon orange-flower water, 2 whole eggs and 2 yolks, and 4 tablespoons (⅓ cup) double (heavy) cream. Work the mixture well, then pour it into a buttered soufflé dish and cook in a moderately hot oven (200 c, 400 f, gas 6) for at least 45 minutes. Serve from the dish.

English apple pudding PUDDING AUX POMMES À L'ANGLAISE Mix together the following ingredients: 400 g (14 oz, 3½ cups) flour, 225 g (8 oz, generous 1½ cups) finely chopped beef suet, 30 g (1 oz, 2 tablespoons) caster (superfine) sugar, a little salt, and 1 dl (6 tablespoons, scant ½ cup) water. Knead thoroughly, then roll out the dough to a thickness of 8 mm (⅓ in).

Butter a 1-litre (1¾-pint) pudding basin (mould) and line it with half of the dough. Fill with finely sliced apples, sweetened with caster (superfine) sugar and flavoured with the grated rind of a lemon and some powdered cinnamon. Cover with the rest of the dough and press the edges together firmly. Wrap the basin in a cloth and tie it up firmly at the top. Place the pudding on an old saucer in a saucepan with enough boiling water to come halfway up the sides of the basin. Cover and cook for about 2 hours over a gentle heat, topping up with boiling water as necessary.

This pudding can be prepared with pears in the same way.

French bread pudding PUDDING AU PAIN À LA FRANÇAISE Crumble 14 slices of stale milk bread. Pour over the top 4 beaten eggs mixed with 100 g (4 oz, ½ cup) caster (superfine) sugar; add 4 dl (14 fl oz, 1¾ cups) tepid milk, then 4 tablespoons (⅓ cup) raisins which have been soaked in weak tea, 3 tablespoons (¼ cup) chopped crystallized (candied) fruit, the same amount of rum, a pinch of salt, and half a jar of sieved apricot jam. Mix everything together well.

Butter a pudding basin (mould) or a charlotte or manqué mould and pour half the mixture into it. Arrange 4 finely sliced canned pears over the surface, then pour in the rest of the mixture. Place the mould in a bain-marie containing boiling water. Put in the oven at 200 c (400 f, gas 6) and cook for about

1 hour until set. Dip the bottom of the mould in cold water, then turn the pudding out. Serve with blackcurrant sauce.

German bread and fruit pudding PUDDING AU PAIN ET AUX FRUITS À L'ALLEMANDE Finely dice 150 g (5 oz) white bread and fry lightly in butter. Put in a basin and pour on 2 dl (7 fl oz, ¾ cup) boiled milk. Mix, then add 2 apples cut into small cubes and cooked in butter, 50 g (2 oz, ⅓ cup) diced candied orange peel, 50 g (2 oz, ½ cup) ground almonds, and the same amount of stoned raisins, which have been soaked in water and drained. Add 75 g (3 oz, 6 tablespoons) caster (superfine) sugar, 1 tablespoon blanched and finely chopped lemon peel, and 3 egg yolks. Mix well, then blend in 3 egg whites beaten into very stiff peaks.

Pour this mixture into a buttered charlotte mould, place in a bain-marie, and cook in a moderately hot oven (200 c, 400 f, gas 6) for about 50 minutes. Turn out the pudding while still lukewarm and coat with a sauce made by mixing 2 dl (7 fl oz, ¾ cup) red wine with 2 tablespoons (3 tablespoons) sieved and warmed apricot jam.

Lemon soufflé pudding PUDDING SOUFFLÉ AU CITRON In a saucepan, work 100 g (4 oz, ½ cup) butter into a soft paste with a wooden spoon. Add 100 g (4 oz, ½ cup) caster (superfine) sugar and 100 g (4 oz, 1 cup) sifted flour, then moisten with 3 dl (½ pint, 1¼ cups) boiled milk and mix well. Bring to the boil, stirring all the time, then beat until the mixture leaves the sides of the pan clean. Remove from the heat and beat in the juice of 2 lemons and 5 egg yolks, then fold in 6 egg whites beaten into stiff peaks and 2 tablespoons (3 tablespoons) blanched and finely chopped lemon peel.

Turn the mixture into a buttered 1½-litre (2½-pint) pudding basin or soufflé mould, place in a bain-marie, and cook in a moderately hot oven (200 c, 400 f, gas 6) for 40 minutes until well risen and golden brown. Serve with a lemon-flavoured custard cream (see *creams and custards*).

Rice pudding PUDDING AU RIZ Wash 250 g (9 oz, 1¼ cups) round-grain rice and blanch it in boiling water. Drain it and place in a flameproof casserole, then add 1 litre (1¾ pints, 4¼ cups) milk boiled with 150 g (5 oz, ⅔ cup) caster (superfine) sugar, half a vanilla pod (bean), and a pinch of salt. Add 50 g (2 oz, ¼ cup) butter, stir, and bring slowly to the boil. Then cover the casserole and finish cooking in a hot oven (220 c, 425 f, gas 7), for 25–30 minutes.

Remove from the oven and beat in 8 egg yolks, mixing carefully, then 7–8 egg whites beaten into very stiff peaks. Use this mixture to fill about 10 small moulds which have been buttered and sprinkled with fine breadcrumbs. Cook in the oven in a bain-marie for 30–35 minutes. Turn out and serve with a rum-flavoured zabaglione, a custard cream, or a fruit sauce flavoured with liqueur.

The mixture may be flavoured with 50 g (2 oz, ½ cup) cocoa per 500 g (18 oz, 1¼ cups) cooked rice.

Scotch pudding Place 500 g (18 oz, 9 cups) fresh breadcrumbs in a bowl and (⅓ cup) rum. Work the mixture together thoroughly and pour it into a smooth buttered mould, filling it up to 1 cm (½ in) from the brim. Place in a bain-marie and cook in a moderately hot oven (200 c, 400 f, gas 6) for 1 hour. Serve with a rum-flavoured zabaglione or a Madeira-flavoured custard cream (see *creams and custards*).

Semolina pudding PUDDING À LA SEMOULE Sprinkle 250 g (9 oz, 1⅓ cups) semolina into 1 litre (1¾ pints, 4¼ cups) boiling milk in which has been dissolved 125 g (4½ oz, generous ½ cup) sugar, a generous pinch of salt, and 100 g (4 oz, ½ cup) butter. Mix and cook over a very gentle heat for 25 minutes. Leave to cool slightly, then add 6 egg yolks, 1 small liqueur glass of orange-flavoured liqueur, and 4 egg whites beaten into very stiff peaks. Pour this mixture into a savarin mould, buttered and dusted with semolina. Place in a bain-marie and cook in a moderately hot oven (200 c, 400 f, gas 6) until the mixture is slightly elastic to the touch. Leave the pudding to stand for 30 minutes before turning it out. Serve with custard or an orange sauce.

puffball LYCOPERDON

A globular or pear-shaped mushroom. The giant puffball is globular and its short stalk is almost unnoticeable. It is edible when young and unripe, while the flesh is still white, but the tough skin must be discarded. It can be eaten sliced, covered in breadcrumbs and fried, or as a filling for an omelette. Other varieties of puffball are pear-shaped and some are edible. *Lycoperdon echinatum*, recognizable by its brownish colour and clusters of hairs, is not edible.

puff pastry
PÂTE FEUILLETÉE, FEUILLETAGE

A rich and delicate pastry made up of very thin layers. It is said by some historians to have been invented by Claude Gellée, better known as the famous 17th-century landscape painter Claude Lorrain, who was said to have served a pastrycook's apprenticeship. Others say it was invented by a chef called Feuillet, who was chief pastrycook to the house of Condé. Carême praises Feuillet, who was undoubtedly a great pastrycook, and in his *Pâtissier royal* says: 'Richard spurred me on to work twice as hard by speaking to me often of the great Feuillet.' But Carême stops there, and nowhere in his learned treatises on pastry does he say that Feuillet was the inventor of puff pastry. But Joseph Favre is definite on this subject. In his *Dictionnaire universel de cuisine* he says that Feuillet was 'the inventor of puff pastry'.

It appears, however, from the study of documents of a much earlier date, that puff pastry was known not only in the Middle Ages but also in ancient Greece. In a charter drawn up by Robert, Bishop of Ameins (1311), puff-pastry cakes are mentioned. It therefore seems more likely that this pastry was perfected and brought back into fashion by Claude Lorrain and Feuillet in their own times.

The preparation of puff pastry is a lengthy and complicated procedure. Butter is incorporated into a rolled-out dough of flour and water. The dough is then folded, turned at right angles, rolled out, and folded again. The turning, rolling out, and folding is repeated a number of times, and the dough is left to stand and chill between each turning. The more turns there are (up to eight), the greater the number of layers in the finished pastry.

This basic preparation can be varied. Margarine, lard, oil, or goose fat may be substituted for butter, and egg yolks can be added (as in Viennese puff pastry). The so-called rough puff pastry can be made in a much shorter time by omitting the resting periods between each turning.

Puff pastry is light, golden, and crisp, but never sweetened. It is used for pies, tarts, allumettes, bouchées, vols-au-vent, mille-feuilles, and many other dishes.

The French name *demi-feuilletage* is given to any leftover pieces of dough that may then be rolled out and used, for example, to line barquettes or tartlets, or to make fleurons and other decorative items.

RECIPES

Puff pastry PÂTE FEUILLETÉE, FEUILLETAGE Put 500 g (18 oz, 4½ cups) sieved flour on a board in a circle, making a well in the middle. Since flours differ, the exact proportion of water to flour is variable. Into the centre of this circle put 1½ teaspoons salt and about 3 dl (½ pint, 1¼ cups) water. Mix and knead until the dough is smooth and elastic. Form into a ball and let it stand for 25 minutes.

Roll out the dough into a sheet about 20 cm (8 in) square and of even thickness throughout. Put 500 g (18 oz, 2¼ cups softened butter in the middle of this dough. (The butter should be softened with a wooden spatula until it can be spread easily.) Fold the ends of the dough over the butter in such a way as to enclose it completely. Leave to stand for 10 minutes in a cold place.

The turning operation (called *tourage* in French) can now begin. Roll the dough with a rolling pin on a lightly floured board in such a way as to obtain a rectangle 60 cm (24 in) long, 20 cm (8 in) wide, and 1½ cm (½ in) thick. Fold the rectangle into three, give it a quarter-turn, and, with the rolling pin at right angles to the folds, roll the dough out again into a rectangle of the same

size as the previous one. Again fold the dough into three and leave to stand for about 15 minutes and chill if too sticky. Repeat the sequence (turn, roll, fold) a further 4 times, leaving the dough to stand for about 15 minutes after each folding. After the sixth turn, roll out the dough in both directions and use according to the recipe.

Puff pastry case for flans CROÛTE FEUILLETÉE POUR TARTE Prepare some puff pastry and roll it out to a thickness of about 4 mm (¼ in). Cut it into a rectangle twice as long as it is wide. Then cut 4 small strips about 3 cm (1 in) wide, two of which are the same length as the width of the rectangle, and two the same as its length. Cut the ends of these strips at right angles so that they form corners. The remaining rectangle of the pastry forms the base of the tart. Brush some beaten egg around the edge of the base and stick the strips to it to form the sides of the pastry case. Trim the edges with a knife and mark the top edge with a decorative crisscross pattern. Prick the base to prevent the pastry from rising during cooking. Bake for about 20 minutes in the oven preheated to 230 C (450 F, gas 8). Fill the flan case with drained poached or cooked fruit covered in a fruit glaze.

Puff pastry made with oil PÂTE FEUILLETÉE À L'HUILE Make the flour and water dough as described in the traditional recipe for puff pastry, then incorporate 2 dl (7 fl oz, ¾ cup) groundnut oil (peanut oil). Roll out the dough into a 20-cm (8-in) square and brush it generously with oil. Then proceed in the usual way except that the dough is brushed with oil each time it is rolled out. Allow a total of about 3.5 dl (12 fl oz, 1½ cups) oil for 500 g (18 oz, 4½ cups) flour.

Rough puff (fast puff) pastry PÂTE FEUILLETÉE MINUTE Mix 400 g (14 oz, 3½ cups) flour, 300 g (11 oz, scant 1½ cups) butter cut into pieces, 10 g (¼ oz) salt, and 2 dl (7 fl oz, ¾ cup) very cold water in a bowl to form a soft smooth dough. Roll it out into a rectangle measuring about 60 cm (24 in) by 20 cm (8 in). Fold it into three, turn, and roll it out again into a rectangle of the same size. Repeat twice more without allowing it to stand between turns. Use immediately.

Puglia wines
VINS DE POUILLE

Puglia, on the heel of the boot of Italy, produces large amounts of wine, but the majority are usually sold for blending or for use in the manufacture of vermouth.

puits d'amour

A small pastry made of two rounds of rolled-out puff pastry placed one on top of the other, the second being hollowed out. After cooking, the centre is filled with jam or vanilla- or praline-flavoured confectioners' custard (pastry cream), which is sometimes caramelized. This pastry was probably created in 1843, after the success of a comic opera entitled *Le Puits d'amour*.

RECIPE

Puits d'amour   Roll out 500 g (18 oz) puff pastry into a rectangle 24 cm (10 in) by 18 cm (7½ in). Cut out from it 12 circles 6 cm (2½ in) in diameter. Place 6 of them on a buttered baking sheet and brush with beaten egg. Cut out the centres of the other 6 circles with a 3-cm (1¼-in) pastry (cookie) cutter; place these rings on the circles of pastry and brush with beaten egg. Cook in a hot oven (230 c, 450 f, gas 8) for 15 minutes. Allow them to cool, then dust with icing (confectioners') sugar and fill the centres with redcurrant jelly or vanilla-flavoured confectioners' custard (see *creams and custards*).

Puligny-Montrachet

A vineyard region in the Côte de Beaune in Burgundy, most famous for its white wines but also making some reds. There are several AOC wines of which the most famous is probably Le Montrachet. Some of the famous sites are actually in the adjacent parish of Chassagne-Montrachet.

pulque

A Mexican alcoholic drink obtained by fermentation of the juice of the maguey plant, a species of agave (see also *teauila, mescal*). This very popular drink is consumed in large quantities on farms, as well as in the *pulquerías*, small popular taverns.

pulses   LÉGUMINEUSES

Leguminous plants whose seeds are used as a vegetable; they include peas, beans, lentils, soya (soy) beans, and peanuts. One of the characteristics of pulses is their very high energy value (averaging 330 Cal per 100 g) and very low water content compared with fresh vegetables (which means they can be stored for long periods). Because they contain up to 23% protein, they form a vital part of a vegetarian diet. However, they do not contain all the amino acids that are essential to a balanced diet (methionine, for example) and cannot therefore be considered as a complete substitute for meat, unless combined with rice or noodles (to make up the deficit of essential amino acids). Some pulses, notably beans and lentils, contain a large proportion of iron. Pulses are rich in carbohydrates (up to 60%) and contain a high proportion of cellulose and starch, which makes them difficult to digest; for this reason, they are often ground and used as flours.

Pulses form one of the staple foods in India (see *dal*), many north African countries (particularly chickpeas and broad beans), and South America (red (kidney) beans). In France, as in all industrialized countries, the consumption of pulses has halved since 1914 as that of meat has increased.

pumpernickel

Rye bread originating from Westphalia and now manufactured throughout Germany and sometimes in Alsace. Very solid and almost black in colour, pumpernickel is made with leaven and coarsely crushed pure rye; abroad, it is often sold, packaged, in very thin slices. As it has a fairly pronounced flavour, it is eaten with smoked sausages, marinated fish, and cheese.

There are several explanations of its etymology: *pumper* could be an onomatopoeic reference to the action of the yeast, and *nickel* an abbreviation of the Christian name Nikolaus (often used in Germany to designate a halfwit); the word therefore means 'a coarse bread suitable for a half-wit'. According to another explanation, the word originated in the 1450s: as a severe famine was threatening the inhabitants of Osnabrück, the municipality baked a 'good bread' (*bonum panicum*) for the poor; its success was so great that it continued to be made and its name developed into *bumponickel*, then into *pumpernickel*.

pumpkin POTIRON

A vegetable of the marrow (squash) family, which is round, with a flattened top and base. The orange or yellow pulp is surrounded by a green, yellow, or orange ribbed rind. There are several varieties, weighing up to 100 kg (225 lb). Once the seeds and fibres have been removed, the flesh is eaten cooked, often as a soup, in a gratin, or as a purée. It is also used as a pie filling (*à la citrouille*), mixed with onion, especially in northern France, where pumpkin pie is as popular as in the United States (in the USA it is also made into a sweet pie filling). The pumpkin is cultivated in southern France, especially in the southeast, where it is harvested from October to December and keeps throughout the winter. It is low in calories (31 Cal per 100 g), rich in water, and contains potassium. When bought in slices, preferably cut from a small juicy fresh-coloured pumpkin, it does not keep long.

In French cookery pumpkin is sometimes called *citrouille*.

RECIPES

Pumpkin au jus POTIRON AU JUS Peel a pumpkin and remove the seeds and surrounding fibres. Cut the pulp into slices and blanch in boiling salted water for about 10 minutes. Drain thoroughly and put into a frying pan (skillet) with some veal stock. Cover and simmer gently for about 20 minutes. Serve sprinkled with chopped parsley.

Pumpkin gratin à la provençale GRATIN DE POTIRON À LA PROVENÇALE Peel a fine ripe pumpkin and remove the seeds and their surrounding fibres. Cut the pulp into small dice and blanch for 10 minutes in boiling salted water; refresh in cold water and drain. Peel some onions (a quarter of the weight of the pumpkin), chop, and sweat them gently for 5–6 minutes in butter. Rub the inside of a gratin dish with garlic and butter; arrange a layer of cut drained pumpkin pieces, then the onions, then the rest of the pumpkin, in the dish. Sprinkle with grated cheese and olive oil and brown in a hot oven.

Pumpkin purée PURÉE DE POTIRON Sweat the pulp of a pumpkin in butter and reduce to a purée, as for pumpkin soup. Cook some potatoes (one-third of the weight of the pumpkin) in boiling salted water and reduce to a purée. Mix the two purées, add a little boiling milk, and stir thoroughly. Then remove from the heat and beat in some fresh butter.

Pumpkin soup SOUPE DE POTIRON Peel and deseed a pumpkin to obtain 750 g (1¾ lb) pulp. Cut the pulp into small pieces and place in a saucepan with 50 g (2 oz, 4 tablespoons) butter and 8 tablespoons water. Add salt, cover the pan, and sweat for about 20 minutes. Purée the pulp, pour into the rinsed-out saucepan, and add 1 litre (1¾ pints, 4¼ cups) stock or consommé. Bring to the boil, adjust the seasoning, and whisk in 50 g (2 oz) butter cut into small pieces. Serve with small croutons fried in butter.

The purée can alternatively be diluted with 1 litre (1¾ pints, 4¼ cups) boiling milk and sweetened to taste. Thicken with 2 tablespoons ground rice blended with a little milk.

punch

An iced or hot drink, sometimes flamed, that can be made either with tea, sugar, spices, fruits, and rum or brandy, or else with rum and sugar syrup. The word originally described a British colonial drink, in which theoretically five ingredients had to be included (*pānch* means 'five' in Hindustani). In France in the 18th century, the word changed to the form *ponche* or *bouleponche* (from the English punch bowl in which the drink was served).

About 1830 the ban on the importation of rum into France from the West Indies was lifted; it had been prohibited so as not to compete with Cognac. At the same time a fashion for English things introduced the vogue for punch. A forerunner of the cocktail, it has been made according to various recipes. English punch consists of boiling tea poured over slices of lemon, with sugar, cinnamon, and rum (it was formerly flamed before being drunk). In French punch, the quantity of tea is smaller and the rum is sometimes replaced by brandy, poured in last and flamed. Marquise punch, which is hot or iced, is made with Sauternes wines, with sugar, lemon peel, and cloves; it may be flamed. Roman punch is a sorbet made with dry white wine or champagne, with orange or lemon slices, mixed with Italian meringue, over which a glass of rum is poured at the time of serving. Planter's punch is a mixture of white rum, sugar-cane syrup, and orange or lemon juice, sometimes enlivened with a dash of Angostura bitters. Brazilian batida punch, which appeared more recently in Europe, has a base of brandy, rum, and lime, guava, or mango juice.

RECIPES

Iced punch PUNCH GLACÉ Dissolve 200 g (7 oz, scant cup) sugar with the grated rind of a lemon in 1 litre (1¾ pints, 4¼ cups) sweet white wine. Heat gently then add 1 tablespoon tea leaves and leave to infuse for about 10 minutes. Strain, then add an orange and a lemon, peeled and cut into slices, and 2 dl (7 fl oz, ¾ cup) warmed flaming rum. Leave to cool. Strain and put in the freezer for 3 hours until slushy, then stir and serve in sundae dishes.

Kirsch punch PUNCH AU KIRSCH Infuse 1 tablespoon tea leaves for 8 minutes in 1 litre (1¾ pints, 4¼ cups) boiling water. Put 500 g (18 oz, 2¼ cups) sugar in a punch bowl. Pour in the strained hot tea and stir until the sugar has dissolved. Flame ¾ litre (1¼ pints, 3 cups) Kirsch and add to the punch. Serve in punch cups. The Kirsch may be replaced by rum.

Marquise punch PUNCH MAR-QUISE Put in a copper pan 1 litre (1¾ pints, 4¼ cups) Sauternes (or similar sweet white wine), 200 g (7 oz, scant cup) sugar, and the grated rind of a lemon, tied in muslin (cheesecloth) with a clove. Heat until a fine white foam has formed on the surface, then pour into a punch bowl. Add 2.5 dl (8 fl oz, 1 cup) flaming Cognac. Serve in punch cups garnished with a thin slice of lemon.

West Indian punch PUNCH AN-TILLAIS Mix in a shaker 2.5 dl (8 fl oz, 1 cup) pineapple juice, 2.5 dl (8 fl oz, 1 cup) orange juice, and 4 tablespoons (⅓ cup) orgeat or grenadine syrup. Add 5 dl (17 fl oz, 2 cups) white rum and shake thoroughly. Pour over ice cubes in frosted glasses.

purée

A creamy preparation obtained by pressing and sieving cooked foods (or by using a blender or food processor).

Vegetable purées used as a garnish or condiment are fairly thick. For making soups, they are diluted with a liquid. Certain vegetables which are too watery to give a sufficiently thick purée are thickened with a binding agent (potato purée, cornflour (cornstarch) or potato flour, thick béchamel sauce). The following vegetables may be puréed: artichoke, asparagus, aubergine (eggplant), beetroot (red beet), cardoon, carrot and other root vegetables, celery, mushrooms, endive, cauliflower, courgette (zucchini), chicory, spinach, broad beans, red or white haricot (navy) beans, green beans, lettuce, lentils, chestnuts, onions (Soubise), sorrel, split peas, green peas (Saint-Germain), potato, and pumpkin. Puréed garlic, watercress, and tarragon are usually used as condiments.

Purées of meat, game, or fish, often mixed with a brown or white sauce, are usually used as fillings for vols-au-vent, bouchées, or barquettes or as a stuffing for hard-boiled (hard-cooked) eggs, artichoke hearts, pancakes, etc.

Fruit purées, either cold or hot, are used for making ices, mousses, soufflés, and dessert sauces.

RECIPES

Anchovy purée *(for cold dishes)* PURÉE D'ANCHOIS FROIDE Desalt 75 g (3 oz) anchovies, remove the fillets, and reduce them to a purée in a mortar or in a blender with 4 hard-boiled (hard-cooked) egg yolks and 3 tablespoons, (½ cup) butter. Add 1 tablespoon chopped herbs. Mix well.

This purée is used to stuff hard-boiled (hard-cooked) eggs, artichoke hearts, fish (red mullet), etc., for serving cold.

Anchovy purée *(for hot dishes)* PURÉE D'ANCHOIS CHAUDE Desalt 75 g (3 oz) anchovies, remove the fillets, and pound them into a purée in a mortar or with a blender. Add to this purée 1.5 dl (¼ pint, ⅔ cup) thick béchamel sauce and, if desired, 2–3 sieved or pounded hard-boiled (hard-cooked) egg yolks and some coarsely chopped herbs.

This purée is used to fill bouchées, tartlets, or rissoles that are to be served hot.

Calfs *or* **chicken liver purée** PURÉE DE FOIE DE VEAU OU DE VOLAILLE Quickly fry the diced calf's liver or whole chicken livers in butter, then reduce to a purée in a blender. Season, and flavour with Madeira if desired.

This purée is used for *à gratin* forcemeats.

Chicken purée PURÉE DE VOLAILLE This is prepared like game purée; its uses are those of brain purée.

Game purée PURÉE DE GIBIER Remove the sinews from the cooked meat of pheasant, duck, young rabbit, or partridge and reduce the flesh to a purée in a blender or food processor. Incorporate the same weight of rice cooked in meat stock and purée again quickly. Adjust the seasoning.

This purée is used as an *à gratin* forcemeat.

Salmon purée PURÉE DE SAUMON Purée 250 g (9 oz) skinned and boned fresh salmon cooked in court-bouillon (or well-drained canned salmon with bones and skin removed). Add to this purée 6 tablespoons (½ cup) very thick

béchamel sauce. Heat, stirring well, then whisk in 50 g (2 oz, ¼ cup) butter. Adjust the seasoning. If desired, add a quarter of its weight of mushroom duxelles.

This purée is used for filling barquettes, pannequets, croustades, and hard-boiled (hard-cooked) eggs.

Shrimp purée PURÉE DE CREVETTES Pound in a mortar some shelled shrimp tails. Add to this purée an equal volume of béchamel sauce mixed with cream and reduced. Adjust the seasoning.

This purée is added to stuffings and sauces for fish and shellfish.

Smoked-salmon purée PURÈE DE SAUMON FUMÉE Using a blender or a food processor purée 200 g (7 oz) smoked salmon together with the juice of half a lemon and 4 egg yolks. Add 50 g (2 oz, ¼ cup) butter and work the mixture until smooth.

This purée is used for garnishing canapés, barquettes, cold pancakes, or slices of smoked salmon rolled into cornet shapes.

purslane POURPIER

A hardy plant which originated in India, was known by the Romans, and was used in the Middle Ages particularly for pickling. There are several varieties, including the golden purslane with large leaves and the *claytone de Cuba* (cultivated in the north of France and in Belgium). Rich in magnesium and with a slightly spicy flavour, this variety can be eaten as a salad, flavoured with burnet. The fleshy young leaves and the tender stalks can be cooked like spinach and cardoons (particularly with gravy, butter, or cream); the leaves can also be used as garnish for soups, omelettes, and joints of meat (instead of watercress) or to flavour sauces (béarnaise or paloise).

quadriller

A French culinary term meaning to mark the surface of grilled (broiled) food (usually meat or fish) with a crisscross pattern of lines. These scorings can be produced by contact with the very hot (but not scorching) single grill bars, which brown the surface of the food. Alternatively very hot skewers can be used to mark the surface.

Food which has been coated in egg and breadcrumbs (e.g. fish, escalopes (scallops), etc.) can be marked before cooking, using the back of a knife to trace squares or diamond shapes on the surface, to improve the appearance of the cooked dish.

In pastry- and cake-making, a crisscross pattern is achieved by placing narrow strips of pastry over an open tart. A red-hot skewer can be used to mark a dessert cream or a meringue-topped dessert. For savoury dishes, a crisscross pattern can be made with anchovy fillets on a pissaladière, a pizza, or a mixed salad.

quail CAILLE

A small migratory game bird found in Europe, in flat open country, from April to October. It is now becoming very scarce. (A breed from the Far East is at present raised like poultry in France.) In the autumn, the bird is plump and round and its flesh is full of flavour. Wild quail should never be allowed to get 'high'. Quail fattened in captivity has less flavour. The bird is drawn and usually barded with bacon. Weighing 150–200 g (5–7 oz), quails may be roasted (especially on skewers), grilled (broiled), sautéed, braised (with grapes), or stuffed and served on a canapé. They can be served chaud-froid (jellied) and can also be used in a pâté or terrine. Quails' eggs are plum-shaped and yellowish-green with brown markings: they may be served hard-boiled (hard-cooked), *en cocotte*, or in aspic. One can also buy hard-boiled quails' eggs preserved in vinegar or brine, for use as a cocktail snack.

RECIPES

Grilled (broiled) quails CAILLES GRILLÉES Pluck, draw, and singe the quails. Split them down the centre of the back from the base of the neck to the tail, and flatten them slightly. Season with salt and pepper, brush with flavoured oil or melted butter, and grill (broil) lightly for approximately 20 minutes. (Before cooking, the quails may be coated with fresh breadcrumbs.)

Grilled (broiled) quails petit-duc CAILLES GRILLÉES PETIT-DUC Coat the quails with melted butter and breadcrumbs and grill (broil). Arrange them on a bed of Anna potatoes and place a large grilled mushroom on each quail. Heat a few tablespoons game fumet with a little Madeira and butter, and sprinkle this over the quails.

Minute quails CAILLES À LA MINUTE Pluck, draw, and singe the quails. Split them down the centre of the back from the base of the neck to the tail, flatten slightly, and season with salt and pepper. Sauté them briskly in butter. After 15 minutes add a small chopped onion, some parsley, and some melted butter. Cover the pan and continue cooking for a further 5 minutes. Cut some mushrooms into thin slices, allowing 150 g (5 oz, generous 1 cup) for 4 quails. Drain the quails and arrange them on a serving dish while still hot. Brown the mushrooms in the sauté pan. Add a dash of brandy and, optionally, a few tablespoons game stock. Boil for 3–4 minutes and add a dash of lemon juice. Pour this sauce over the quails.

Quail casserole CAILLES EN CASSEROLE Pluck, draw, and singe the quails. Smear the inside of each carcass with a knob of butter kneaded with salt and pepper, then truss each bird. Heat some butter in a casserole and fry the quails until golden. Add salt and pepper, cover the dish, and place it in a very hot oven (about 240 C, 475 F, gas 9) for 12–18 minutes. When the birds are cooked, deglaze the dish with a little brandy.

Quail casserole with grapes CAILLES EN CASSEROLE AUX RAISINS Pluck, draw, and singe 8 quails. Wrap each one in a vine leaf and a very thin slice of bacon, truss, and fry in butter until golden. Add salt and pepper, cover the pan, and leave to cook for another 10 minutes. Peel and deseed about 60 large white grapes. Untruss the quails, arrange in an ovenproof dish (which can be taken to the table), and add the grapes. Sprinkle with the quails' cooking juices. Place the dish, without a lid, in a very hot oven (about 240 C, 475 F, gas 9) for 5 minutes. Just before serving, 2–3 tablespoons brandy can be added to the dish.

Quail pâté PÂTE DE CAILLES Bone the quails. Stuff each with a piece of *à gratin* forcemeat about the size of a hazelnut, and the same amount of foie gras, studded with a piece of truffle, the whole well seasoned with salt and spices and sprinkled with a dash of brandy. Wrap each quail in a very thin rasher of bacon.

Line a hinged oval or rectangular mould with fine pastry, then with thin rashers of bacon. Cover with a layer of finely pounded forcemeat made of veal and lean and fat pork in equal proportions, bound with an egg, well seasoned, sprinkled with a little brandy, and mixed with diced truffles. Over this forcemeat put a layer of *à gratin* game forcemeat, then half the stuffed quails, pressing down well. Cover with another layer of forcemeat, put in the rest of the quails, and follow with a layer of forcemeat. Cover this with a layer of truffled forcemeat, flatten it, and cover again with a layer of thin rashers of lean bacon. Seal with a pastry lid. Decorate with pieces of pastry cut in fancy shapes. Make a hole in the middle of the lid to allow steam to escape, and brush the top with beaten egg. Bake in a moderate oven (180 C, 350 F, gas 4) for about 1½ hours.

When cooked, leave the pâté to get cold, and pour liquid game aspic stock (see *aspic jelly*) through the hole in the top.

Quails' eggs in aspic with caviar ASPIC D'OEUFS DE CAILLE AU CAVIAR (from a recipe from the Restaurant Laurent) Prepare an aspic jelly with 1 litre (1¾ pints, 4¼ cups) well-reduced consommé, 20 g (generous ½ oz, 2 envelopes) gelatine, and 1 dl (6 tablespoons, scant ½ cup) port. Boil 24 quails' eggs for 1½ minutes in salted water, cool, and remove the shells.

Evenly coat the bottom and sides of 6 ramekins with aspic jelly. Garnish each ramekin with 10 g (generous ¼ oz) caviar, cover with a small amount of aspic, and leave to set. Arrange 4 boiled quails' eggs in each ramekin with the tops pointing downwards. Add 60 g (generous 2 oz) caviar to the rest of the aspic, and cover the eggs with it. When the aspic has set, remove from the moulds, and arrange on a chiffonnade of lettuce.

Make a mousse by mixing together 1 tablespoon concentrated tomato soup, ¼ litre (8 fl oz, 1 cup) crème fleurette or whipping cream, salt, pepper, and a dash of brandy. Whip the mixture and add a few grains of caviar. Serve this mousse separately.

Quails with rice CAILLES AU RIZ Pluck, draw, and singe the quails. Season with salt and pepper, truss them, and cook them in butter. Arrange them on a bed of rice pilaf. Dilute the pan juices with a dash of brandy and either game stock or game fumet. Pour the sauce over the quails.

The rice pilaf can be replaced by cheese risotto, risotto *à la piémontaise*, or polenta.

Roast quails CAILLES RÔTIES Wrap the quails in vine leaves and then in thin rashers of larding bacon. Secure with string. Roast on a spit before a lively fire, or in the oven, for 15–20 minutes. Arrange each quail on a canapé. Garnish with watercress and lemon quarters. Serve the diluted pan juices separately.

Stuffed quails à la gourmande CAILLES FARCIES À LA GOURMANDE Pluck, draw, and singe the quails. Season with salt and pepper, and stuff each bird with a mixture of butter, lean ham, and chopped truffles (or truffle peel). Truss them and brown them in butter in a sauté pan. Cover the pan and finish cooking. Drain the quails, dilute the pan juices with champagne, and reduce. Adjust the seasoning. Arrange the quails in a circle on a warm serving dish. Garnish the centre of the dish with boletus or chanterelle mushrooms sautéed in butter. Pour the pan juices over the birds.

Stuffed quails in cases CAILLES FARCIES EN CAISSES Pluck, draw, and remove the bones from 8 quails. To 175 g (6 oz, ¾ cup) *à gratin* forcemeat, add 3 or 4 chicken livers and 1 tablespoon chopped truffle peel. Stuff the quails, reshape, and then wrap each one in a piece of buttered greaseproof (waxed) paper. Arrange them in a buttered dish so that they are tightly packed together and add a little melted butter, salt, and pepper. Cook (without a lid) in a very hot oven (about 240 C, 475 F, gas 9) for 18–20 minutes. Remove the quails from the dish and unwrap them. Place each bird in an oval paper case. Deglaze the cooking juices with some Madeira, and pour over the quails. Put the cases in the oven for 5 minutes before arranging on a serving dish.

Other preparations of quails in cases use the same basic method:

■ *à l'italienne*: 1 tablespoon of Italian sauce (see (*à l'*)*italienne*) in each paper case before putting in the quails.

■ *à la Lamballe*: line the cases with a julienne of sliced mushrooms and truffles blended with cream.

■ *à la mirepoix*: add some vegetable mirepoix to the cooking liquor before it is poured over the birds.

■ *à la Mont-Bry*: replace the *à gratin* forcemeat with a poultry forcemeat mixed with truffles and deglaze the pan juices with champagne. Garnish with a ragout of cocks' combs and cocks' kidneys.

■ *à la Périgueux*: top each quail with a thick slice of truffle and pour over Périgueux sauce.

■ *à la strasbourgeoise*: stuff each bird with a salpicon of foie gras and truffles, seasoned with salt and a pinch of spices and sprinkled with a few drops of brandy.

Stuffed quails in nests CAILLES FARCIES AU NID Pluck, draw, and bone the quails. Stuff them with game forcemeat mixed with chopped truffles. Wrap each bird in a small piece of muslin and make into a roll. Poach for 18 minutes in a stock prepared from the bones and trimmings, with a jellied veal stock and Madeira. Drain the birds, unwrap, and glaze lightly in the oven. Reduce the stock. Arrange each quail in a nest of straw potatoes and pour a little reduced stock over the top.

Quart-de-Chaume

A sweetish white wine from Anjou. It

took its name from the fact that, in the past, the owner of that particular section of the Coteaux-du-Layon vineyard used to retain a quarter (*un quart*) of the vintage for his own use. The wines can be made by the action of 'noble rot' and are fragrant and capable of ageing well in the bottle.

quasi

A French cut of veal taken from the rump (corresponding to rump steak in beef). In Anjou it is called the *cul-de-veau* and is used to make many savoury dishes. It can be sliced into escalopes (more stringy and tougher than those taken from the leg) or into thicker slices for roasting, or it can be roasted whole. This cut can also be braised, sautéed, or made into a blanquette or a fricandeau. As it is lean and slightly tough, it is advisable to lard or bard it, but it is full of flavour when cooked.

The origin of the word, which is applied only to veal, is obscure; it began to appear in the culinary vocabulary at the end of the 18th century.

quassia

A shrub, found in tropical areas of America, the wood of which was traditionally used to make apéritifs and tonics.

Fizzy drinks and bitters are flavoured with quassine, the bitter extract of quassia.

Queen of Sheba

REINE DE SABA

A chocolate gâteau, usually round, made from a sponge mixture lightened by the addition of beaten egg whites. The cake is lighter still if the flour is replaced by potato flour or ground almonds (or a mixture of the two). It is served cold with a custard cream.

queen scallop   VANNEAU

A European bivalve mollusc resembling a small scallop. Measuring 4–8 cm (1½–3 in) across, the queen scallop has a creamy white shell marked with brown, with fairly wide ridges radiating from the top, and two small lugs.

quenelle

A dumpling made with a spiced meat or fish forcemeat bound with fat and eggs, sometimes with panada added: it is then moulded into a small sausage or egg shape and poached in boiling water. The most common types are veal quenelles, made from a godiveau forcemeat, and pike quenelles, a speciality of the Lyon region of France. They are served as an entrée with a sauce or *au gratin*. Small quenelles may also form part of a garnish (e.g. financière, Godard, toulousaine, etc.), particularly for poultry, or they can be added to ragouts and salpicons as a filling for vols-au-vent, croustades, etc. Quenelles are sometimes used as a garnish for soups. The name comes from the German *Knödel* (dumpling).

RECIPES

Pike quenelles   QUENELLES DE BROCHET   Fillet a pike weighing about 1.25 kg (2¾ lb). Remove the skin and take out the bones (there should be about 400 g (14 oz) flesh). Finely mince or pound the flesh, then put it in the refrigerator.

Prepare a panada: bring 3 dl (½ pint, 1¼ cups) water to the boil, adding a generous pinch of salt. Remove from the heat and shake in 150 g (5 oz, 1¼ cups) flour through a sieve; stir vigorously until smooth, then continue to stir over heat until the mixture dries out, taking care that it does not stick to the bottom of the pan. Remove from the heat and beat in 1 whole egg; leave the mixture to get cold, then refrigerate. When the panada is well chilled, put it through the blender until it is quite smooth.

Cream 200 g (7 oz, scant cup) butter. Put the pike flesh into a bowl placed in another bowl full of crushed ice; season with salt and pepper, then work it with a wooden spoon until it is smooth. Now mix in the panada, 1 whole egg and 4 yolks (one by one), and finally the butter: the mixture should be uniformly blended and smooth. (If all the ingredients are really cold, this last stage can be carried out in a blender, providing that it is powerful enough to work quickly without heating; the blender goblet itself should have been cooled in the refrigerator.) Chill the mixture for 30 minutes. Shape the quenelles, using two tablespoons dipped in hot water, and place on a lightly floured surface.

Bring 2 litres (3½ pints, 4½ pints) salted water to the boil and poach the quenelles for 15 minutes, without letting the water boil. Drain them and leave to get cold, then proceed according to the recipe.

Pike quenelles mousseline QUENELLES DE BROCHET MOUSSELINE Work 500 g (18 oz) pike flesh, 5 g (1 teaspoon) salt, a pinch of white pepper, and a pinch of grated nutmeg in a blender, then add 3 egg whites one by one. When the mixture is smooth, pour into a bowl and refrigerate. Also refrigerate 6.5 dl (generous pint, generous 2½ cups) fresh cream and the blender goblet. When the fish mixture is cold, pour it back into the blender goblet, add 2.5 dl (8 fl oz, 1 cup) chilled cream, and blend for a few seconds until the cream is thoroughly incorporated. Add a further 2 dl (7 fl oz, ¾ cup) cream, blend again, then repeat the process with the rest of the cream. Shape the mixture into quenelles and poach as for ordinary pike quenelles (see recipe above).

Salmon quenelles QUENELLES DE SAUMON These are made in the same way as pike quenelles (see recipe above), but using salmon instead of pike. Poach, arrange on a dish, then cover them completely with Nantua sauce, cream sauce, shrimp sauce, or white wine sauce.

Veal quenelles QUENELLES DE VEAU Make a godiveau with cream and chill it for at least half an hour. With floured hands, roll the mixture into balls. Press these into the shape of large olives, poach them, then proceed as in any of the recipes for pike quenelles; for example, cook them in a béchamel sauce enriched with fresh cream.

Chicken meat can be used to make quenelles in the same way.

Quercy

The French region of Quercy, and its capital Cahors, is renowned for its delectable cuisine, which is similar to that of its neighbour, Périgord.

The soups are outstanding: tourin with garlic and onion, cabbage soup accompanied by *miques* (cornmeal dumplings), and vegetable soups, of which the remains, after all the bread and vegetables have been eaten, are drunk with red or white wine (this is known as *le chabrot*).

For many, however, Quercy is best known for its truffles: these may be eaten rolled in bacon rashers (slices), enclosed in puff pastry, in salads (with hard-boiled (hard-cooked) eggs, sprinkled with verjuice, lemon juice, and walnut oil), or added to pâtés, poultry and game dishes, and omelettes.

There is a great variety of charcuterie: boudin blanc, tripe with saffron, pig's trotters (feet) *à la vinaigrette*, liver sausages, and smoked ham from the Causses make delicious introductions to a meal.

Quercy cooks have devised succulent recipes for goose, such as stuffed and preserved neck. Other poultry dishes include *alicot* (giblets stewed with cep mushrooms and chestnuts); pies made with chicken potatoes and salsify; roast guinea fowl, flambéed and arranged on a piece of bread spread with foie gras (known as *pharaonne*); chicken in a pastry case; and ballottine of turkey and chicken, in a pie or steamed. Not much fish is eaten, although it does appear in such dishes as stuffed pike and crayfish and trout in white wine (which Pierre Benoît mentions in *Le Déjeuner de Sousceyrac*) and *stoficado* (smoked cod with walnut oil and eggs).

Gigot of lamb or mutton is served crowned with garlic, not merely studded with it, garlic being an indispensable ingredient of all Quercy cooking. Other specialities of the region are veal with ceps, estouffat of pork with haricot (navy) beans, farcidures (small vegetable dumplings), *porcellous* (cabbage leaves stuffed with veal, bacon, pork, and herbs), and beef hotchpotch (cooked with chestnuts and turnips, flavoured with saffron). Mushrooms are highly esteemed, particularly ceps, a valued product of the Lot region.

The most common cheeses of the region are blue cheeses and Cabécou. For dessert, there are various types of local brioches, especially the *coques de Pâques*, flavoured with citron, and the *fouassous*, made with eggs and butter and glazed with sugar. There are also fritters (*gougnettes*) and thick pancakes, made either from wheat flour and filled with fruit (*pescajounes*) or from buckwheat flour (*bourriols* and *tour-*

tous). The plums, peaches, strawberries, melons, and grapes grown in Quercy are all of excellent quality, as are the walnuts from which oil is pressed and a liqueur and jams are made. As for wines, the most famous is the 'black' AOC wine from Cahors, where the 16th-century poet Clément Marot was born. In his *Remède contre la peste* Marot praises the cooking and the wine, recommending his readers to eat 'plenty of young pheasants' and to drink the 'delicious wines'.

queso

The Spanish word for cheese. Numerous cheeses in Spain and Latin America are called simply *queso*, followed by a qualifying adjective. For example, there is the *queso añejo* of Mexico, a dry crumbly cheese made from goats' or cows' milk, served with cornmeal pancakes, and sometimes sprinkled with red pepper (it is then known as *enchilado*); the *queso de bola* of Mexico and Spain, made from cows' milk and resembling Edam; the Chilean *queso de cabra*, a round white fresh goats'-milk cheese; the Spanish *queso de cabrales*, a type of blue goats'- or ewes'-milk cheese; the *queso de crema* of Costa Rica, a cows'-milk cheese with a pressed curd; the Spanish *queso de Mahón*, a pressed cows'-milk cheese containing a small proportion of ewes' milk; the *queso de puna* from Puerto Rico, made from skimmed cows' milk and eaten fresh; and the *queso de mano* from Venezuela, a round cows'-milk cheese wrapped in banana leaves, with a pressed and rubbery curd.

quetsche

A variety of plum with mauve skin and sweet well-flavoured yellow flesh. It is grown mostly in Alsace, from where it gets its original German name (*Zwetsche*). It is particularly suitable for tarts, compotes, and jams and is the source of a well-known brandy, which is smooth and fruity.

quiche

An open tart filled with a mixture of beaten eggs, fresh cream, and pieces of bacon, served hot as a first course or hors d'oeuvre. Originating in Lorraine (the name comes from the German *Küchen*, meaning 'cake'), it has become a classic of French cuisine and is also widely enjoyed in other countries.

Its origins go back to the 16th century; in Nancy, where it is a speciality, its local name is *féouse*. Quiches used to be made from bread dough but nowadays shortcrust or puff pastry is used. In some areas of Lorraine, any pastry tart filled with *migaine* (eggs and cream) mixed with onions, cream cheese, or pumpkin is called a quiche, and elsewhere quiches can be made with cheese, ham, bacon, onion, mushrooms, seafood, and various other ingredients.

A *quiche tourangelle* is filled with rillettes and beaten eggs, sprinkled with chopped fresh parsley, and served warm.

RECIPES

Quiche lorraine Make some lining pastry with 250 g (9 oz, 2¼ cups) flour, 125 g (4¼ oz, generous cup) butter, a generous pinch of salt, 1 egg, and 3 tablespoons (¼ cup) very cold water. Roll it into a ball and chill in the refrigerator for a few hours. Then roll it out to a thickness of 4 mm (¼ in) and line a buttered and floured tart tin or dish, 22 cm (9 in) in diameter, bringing the edges of the pastry up to extend slightly beyond the tin edge. Prick it all over and cook blind in the oven at 200 c (400 F, gas 6) for 12–14 minutes. Leave to cool.

Cut 250 g (9 oz) slightly salted pork belly into flat strips and blanch for 5 minutes in boiling water. Refresh and pat dry, then brown very lightly in butter. Spread the bacon over the pastry case. Beat 4 eggs lightly and mix in 3 dl (½ pint, 1¼ cups) double (heavy) cream; add salt, pepper, and nutmeg, then pour the mixture into the pastry case. Cook for about 30 minutes in the oven at 200 c (400 F, gas 6). Serve very hot.

Mussel quiche QUICHE AUX MOULES (from E. de Pomiane's recipe) Cook 1 litre (1¾ pints, 4¼ cups) mussels and remove them from their shells. Reserve the mussel cooking liquor.

Make a shortcrust pastry (basic pie dough) with 200 g (7 oz, 1¾ cups) flour,

100 g (4 oz, 1 cup) butter, ⅓ wineglass (4 tablespoons, ⅓ cup) water, and 3 pinches of salt. Roll out the dough to a thickness of 3 mm (⅛ in) and use to line the tart tin. Spread the mussels over the base. Mix 1 whole egg with 60 g (2 oz, ½ cup) flour, 2 egg yolks, 1.5 dl (5 fl oz, ⅔ cup) double (heavy) cream, 1 glass (8 fl oz, 1 cup) milk diluted with some of the mussel cooking liquor, and salt and pepper; pour over the mussels. Cook the quiche in a very hot oven for 30 minutes and serve with a well-chilled white wine.

Small ham and cheese quiches PE-TITES QUICHES AU JAMBON ET AU FROMAGE Prepare the lining pastry and the filling as for a quiche lorraine, but substitute 150 g (5 oz, generous ½ cup) ham cut into strips for the bacon, and add 100 g (4 oz, 1 cup) grated Gruyère cheese. Line 6 tartlet moulds, 10 cm (4 in) in diameter, with the pastry, divide the filling between them, and bake for about 18 minutes in the oven at 180 C (350 F, gas 4).

quiché

In Marseille, a slice of bread spread with anchovies, olive oil, etc., and toasted in front of the fire. Adolphe Thiers, who wrote in praise of the cookery of his native city, mentions this 'delicious croûte', which he called 'poor man's cake'.

quignon

A piece of bread, usually the end crust of a loaf. The word is a modification of *coignon*, from the Latin *cuneolus* (a small coin). In Flanders, at Christmas, they make *cougnous*, little cakes of yeast dough in the shape of a swaddled child, decorated with raisins; in Provence, these are known as *cuignots*.

quillet

A small round cake, named after the pastrycook who created it. Made from a sponge-cake mixture, it is filled and decorated with butter cream flavoured with orgeat syrup and vanilla.

| RECIPE

Quillet Into a copper or stainless steel pan put 500 g (18 oz, 2¼ cups) caster (superfine) sugar, a small pinch of salt, 15 whole eggs, and some powdered vanilla. Beat this mixture with a whisk over a gentle heat, without letting it get too hot. When white and frothy, remove from the stove and continue beating until it is nearly cold. Then add 500 g (18 oz, 4½ cups) sifted flour (added all at once) and 500 g (18 oz, 2¼ cups) melted butter. Pour the mixture into round cake tins and cook in a moderate oven. Leave the sponges to cool.

Make the butter cream: stir 450 g (1 lb, 2 cups) sugar into ½ litre (scant pint, 2¼ cups) water. Bring to the boil and boil for 1 minute. Cool, then add 1 dl (6 tablespoons, scant ½ cup) milk, 2 dl (⅓ pint, scant cup) orgeat syrup, and a split vanilla pod (bean). Bring to the boil and cook this mixture for a few minutes, then pour it over 8 egg yolks in a saucepan. Beat thoroughly with a whisk. Reheat the mixture gently without letting it boil, then leave it to get cold. Pour the cold mixture into a bowl containing 250 g (9 oz, generous cup) butter that has been rubbed through a sieve; mix well together and chill.

Cut the cakes across and spread the layers with the cream; pipe a decoration over the top with the remainder of the cream and dredge with icing (confectioners') sugar.

quince COING

The yellow fruit of a tree native to Asia but widely cultivated in temperate regions. Round or pear-shaped, it is covered with a fine down when ripe. It has a strong smell and its flesh, which is very hard and bitter when raw, is rich in tannin and pectin. Quince must always be cooked, and it is used to make some fragrant and delicate dishes. In Europe, it is used to make confectionery, liqueurs, and jam (the word marmalade comes from the Portuguese *marmelo*, meaning quince).

The quince tree is native to the Caucasus and Iran, and was known as the pear of Cydonia. It was very popular with the Greeks, who ate it hollowed out, filled with honey, and cooked in a pastry case. The Romans extracted an essential oil from the fruit that was used in perfumery. It has been known in France for centuries, and has been used not only in cookery but also in perfumery and medicine. In the 14th-century *Ménagier de Paris*, there is a recipe for quince paste (see *cotignac*), and there is an equally ancient recipe in Spain, where it is called *dulce de membrillo*. Quince is cultivated in eastern France and is marketed in the autumn. It has a low calorific value (33 Cal per 100 g) but sugar is always added. Quince is used in the preparation of compotes and jellies, as well as ratafia and fruit pastes. In the East, it may be eaten with salt, or stuffed, or used in tajines and stews. It may even be used as a garnish for roast poultry, such as quail or chicken.

RECIPES

Baked quinces COINGS AU FOUR Generously butter an ovenproof dish. Peel 4 very ripe quinces and hollow them out carefully with an apple corer. Mix 1 dl (6 tablespoons, scant ½ cup) cream with 65 g (2½ oz, 5 tablespoons, firmly packed) caster (superfine) sugar and fill the quinces with the mixture. Sprinkle the fruit with 130 g (4½ oz, 9 tablespoons, firmly packed) sugar and bake at about 220 c (425 F, gas 7) for 30–35 minutes, basting the quinces several times.

Quince liqueur or ratafia EAU OU RATAFIA DE COING Cut the quinces into quarters and remove the seeds. Shred the fruit without peeling. Place in a bowl, cover, and leave to stand in a cool place for 3 days. Squeeze them through muslin (cheesecloth) and collect the juice. Add an equal volume of spirit to the juice. For each litre of the mixture, add 300 g (11 oz, 1½ cups) caster (superfine) sugar, 1 clove, and a small piece of cinnamon. Infuse in a jar for 2 months. Then strain through muslin (cheesecloth) and bottle.

Tajine of chicken with quince POULET AUX COINGS EN TAJINE Cut a prepared chicken into 8 pieces. Peel and chop 3 onions. Brown the chicken in an ovenproof casserole in 3 tablespoons (¼ cup) olive oil. Add the chopped onions, stir, season with salt and pepper, and add a pinch of paprika, a generous pinch of powdered ginger, a few parsley and coriander leaves, and a large glass of chicken stock. Cook gently for 30 minutes with the casserole half-covered.

Meanwhile, cut 2 large quinces into 8 pieces, remove the seeds, and fry them in oil or butter over a fast heat until golden. Place the pieces of chicken and quince in a *tajine* (an earthenware dish). Pour the cooking liquid over the top and cover the dish with a piece of perforated greaseproof (waxed) paper. Cook in the oven at 225 c (437 F, gas 7–8) for about 30 minutes. Serve very hot straight from the dish.

This dish can also be made with slices of preserved quince.

Quincy

A dry white AOC wine from Berry, in the upper reaches of the River Loire. It is made from the Sauvignon grape, is of high quality, and somewhat similar to white Sancerre.

quinquina

Any of various wine-based apéritifs containing a certain proportion of crushed cinchona bark; the flavour is slightly bitter, due to the quinine in the bark. Quinquina bitters can be made at home by macerating together the zest of a Seville (bitter) orange, some cinchona bark, and some gentian root in spirits and white wine; alternatively the zest and peel of a Seville (bitter) orange, some raisins, and cinchona bark can be macerated in 90° alcohol, red wine, and cassis liqueur.

RECIPES

Home-made quinquina QUINQUINA MAISON Pour ½ litre (17 fl oz, 2 cups) 90° alcohol into a 6-litre (10-pint, 13-pint) stoneware jug. Weight out 125 g (4½ oz) cinchona bark and 30 g (1 oz) Seville (bitter) orange peel; thinly pare an orange and cut the zest into julienne strips. Put all the ingredients into the jug, cover, and leave in a cool place for 1 week. Wash a large handful of stoned raisins in warm water, drain them, and add them to the contents of the jug. Leave to macerate for a further week. Then filter the liquor and add 5 litres (9 pints, 10 pints) lively red wine and ¼ litre (8 fl oz, 1 cup) cassis liqueur. Mix well, leave to settle, filter, and bottle.

rabbit LAPIN

A small burrowing mammal, closely related to the hare, that has been regarded as a pest for many years, because of the damage it inflicts on crops and also as a result of its prolific breeding habits. An old name for the rabbit is coney or cony (in French, *connil* or *connin*), derived from the Old French *conis*, from the Latin *cuniculus*. Rabbits have been domesticated for many generations, and in 17th-century France the practice of rearing rabbits for the table was widespread. The meat was prepared as a civet, in a mustard or a poulette sauce, with onions or prunes, jellied, or made into rillettes. The tastier wild rabbit was roasted, grilled (broiled), or fried.

Rabbit was regarded as a fertility symbol, especially in Germany, and was often included in Easter menus. Domestic rabbits, which are raised not only for their meat but also for their fur, are distinguished by their size, the colour and texture of their fur, and the quality of their meat. Some notable French varieties are the Burgundy tawny, the silver field rabbit, and the Bouscat giant. A really large rabbit can weigh up to 10 kg (22 lb), but the average weight of a commercially reared specimen is 1.2–1.4 kg (2½–3 lb). The meat of the domestic rabbit is always tender and should be eaten young. The animal should be well-covered in meat, with a rounded back, pink flesh, a pale unspotted liver, and pure white fat around the kidneys (the latter should be clearly visible). The French Angevin rabbit has a superior flavour because it is fed on a special diet, but it is scarce nowadays, even on the French market, as is the wild rabbit. Myxomatosis decimated wild rabbit numbers both in France and in the UK in the 1950s.

Rabbit meat is very lean (135 Cal per 100 g), but as it is skinned before cooking, it absorbs more of the cooking fat. Steamed rabbit is perfectly digestible.

A medium rabbit should be jointed into six pieces: two front legs, two hind legs, and the two halves of the saddle. Marinating in wine seasoned with shallots, carrots, parsley, garlic, and thyme improves a commercially reared rabbit before it is made into a pie or a stew, and the addition of pig's blood brings about an even greater improvement. Rabbit can be deep-frozen either raw or cooked.

RECIPES

Boiled rabbit à l'anglaise LAPIN BOUILLI À L'ANGLAISE Prepare 500 g (1 lb) stuffing consisting of one-third breadcrumbs soaked in milk and squeezed out, one-third chopped ox (or veal) kidney, and one-third fine veal forcemeat; add 1 egg, salt, pepper, and mixed spice. Place the rabbit on its back and take out the lights (lungs) and the liver. Shape the forcemeat into a long cylinder and stuff the rabbit with it; pull down the sides and sew up the skin; place a thin strip of bacon on the seam and tie the rabbit up with string. Poach it for 1 hour in salted water to which a bouquet garni containing celery seed has been added. Serve hot with a caper sauce. The dish may also be served cold with a mayonnaise flavoured with fines herbes.

Rabbit sautéed à la minute LAPIN SAUTÉ À LA MINUTE Joint a rabbit weighing about 1.3 kg (2¾ lb). Sprinkle the pieces with salt and pepper and brown them in smoking hot butter, over a very brisk heat, stirring thoroughly so that all the pieces are evenly coloured. Arrange them in a pie dish and keep hot. Dilute the pan juices with 1.4 dl (¼ pint, ⅔ cup) white wine and add 1 chopped shallot. Boil down the sauce until it is very concentrated, then moisten with a few tablespoons of stock. Reduce again, then mix in 1 tablespoon butter and a squeeze of lemon juice. Pour the sauce over the rabbit and sprinkle with chopped parsley.

Rabbit with mustard LAPIN À LA MOUTARDE (from Michel Oliver's recipe) Joint a rabbit weighing about 1.3 kg (2¾ lb). Spread the pieces with a mixture of 2 tablespoons (3 tablespoons) strong mustard, 1 tablespoon oil, salt, and ground pepper. Place the pieces in a flameproof dish and put in a hot oven. After 5 minutes, sprinkle with 50 ml (3 tablespoons, ¼ cup) water. Continue cooking, basting with the pan juices every 5 minutes. When the pieces of rabbit are cooked, arrange them on a heated serving dish and keep hot. Skim the fat from the cooking juices and add 2 tablespoons (3 tablespoons) white wine to the pan; reduce slightly, stirring with a wooden spoon. Then add 4 tablespoons (⅓ cup) single (light) cream and some salt, stirring all the time; do not

boil. Pour this sauce over the rabbit. Serve with pasta.

Sautéed rabbit with prunes LAPIN SAUTÉ AUX PRUNEAUX Soak 350 g (12 oz, 2 cups) prunes in tea until swollen, then drain them. Sauté a rabbit of about 1.25 kg (2½ lb) as in the recipe for rabbit sautéed *à la minute*. Pound the rabbit's liver with 1 tablespoon vinegar (or put through a blender). When the rabbit is cooked, keep hot in a serving dish. Dilute the pan juices with 1.5 dl (¼ pint, ⅔ cup) white wine, add the prunes, and reduce a little. Mix in the pounded liver and adjust the seasoning. Pour the prunes and gravy over the rabbit.

Wild rabbit with Hermitage wine LAPIN DE GARENNE AU VIN DE L'HERMITAGE (from a recipe by Jacques Pic) Joint a rabbit weighing about 1.3 kg (2¾ lb) and season the pieces with salt and pepper. Cut 150 g (5 oz) fat bacon into dice. Peel 12 small white onions. Pound the rabbit's liver. Put the fat bacon in a saucepan and brown it with the onions. Place the pieces of rabbit in the saucepan and sauté them over a brisk heat; dust with flour and leave to brown slightly. Flame with 1 small glass of Hermitage marc and moisten with 2 glasses of red Crozes-Hermitage. Add a little warm water or stock. Adjust the seasoning and add a bouquet garni made of thyme, bay leaf, parsley stalks, and a clove of garlic. Cook gently for about 1 hour. When the rabbit is cooked, take it out of the saucepan and keep it hot. Remove the pan from the cooker and add the liver (pounded) and blood (to which a little vinegar has been added); blend with the pan juices away from the heat. Return the pan to the hob over a very moderate heat, so that the blood cooks without boiling. Strain the sauce and keep it hot. Arrange the rabbit in a deep earthenware dish and pour the sauce over it. Some fried croutons may be arranged around the dish.

Rabelais (François)

French humanist and writer (born Chinon, *c.* 1483; died Paris, 1553). He became successively a monk, a doctor, and a professor of anatomy before ending his days as the parish priest of

Meudon. He is best known, however, as the author of the comic satires *Pantagruel* (1532), *Gargantua* (1534), *Tiers Livre* (1546), and *Quart Livre* (1552). This powerful and original body of work, which one has to 'crack like a bone' to get to the 'real marrow', is very much occupied with eating and drinking. The terms 'pantagruelian' and 'gargantuan' are used to describe an appetite, meal, or stomach of gigantic size, worthy of a well-laden festive board.

In the *Quart Livre* (chapter XI) Rabelais gives us 'the names of the valiant and worthy cooks who, as in the Trojan horse, entered into the sow'. He mentions numerous cookery terms and dishes common in his time; for example: *Saulpicquet* (saupiquet), *Paimperdue* (pain perdu), *Carbonnade, Hoschepot* (hotchpotch), *Gualimafré* (gallimaufry), *Croque-lardon* (bacon on bread), *Salladier* (salad bowl), *Macaron* (macaroon), *Cochonnet* (suckling pig), and *Talemouse* (a pastry case with a cheese filling).

In Book IV of *Pantagruel* (chapters LIX and LX), Rabelais makes a long list of dishes and foods, giving us some idea of what was eaten in the 16th century: '. . . soups made with prime cuts of meat, bayleaf soups, soups *lionnoise* (with onion and cheese); olives pickled in brine, caviar, *boutargue* (a paste of dried salted pressed mullet or tuna roes), stockfish (salted and dried cod); roast capons with their cooking juices, cockerels, hens, and turkey-hens, ducks *à la dodiné*, pigeons, squabs, geese, swans, herons, cranes, partridges, francolins, turtledoves, rock pigeons, pheasants, quails, plovers, blackbirds, woodcocks, hazel grouse, loons, etc.; leverets, fawns, young rabbits; sausages, black puddings (blood sausage), saveloys, andouilles spread with fine mustard, potted boar's head; bleaks, eels, barbels, pike, young carp, loach, tench, trout, shad, white *apron* (small perch-like fish), whales, plaice, dolphins, sea bream, sturgeons, lobsters, oysters in their shells, fried oysters, lampreys in hippocras sauce, dabs, *laveret* (salmon-like lake fish), salted hake, Moray eels, sea anemones, sea urchins, bonito, skate, salmon, turtles, turbot, sardines, dogfish; pork cutlets with stewed onions, young goat, shoulder of mutton with capers, pigs' and calves' fry, smoked ox tongue, cold roast loin of veal sprinkled with *zinziberine* powder (mustard and ginger); cabbage with beef marrow, artichokes, spinach, rice, salads, purée of peas, salted broad beans; almond butter, raised meat pies, puff-pastry cakes; lark pâtés, chamois, capons, quinces, bacon rashers, or venison; *poupelins* (pastry cakes filled with whipped cream, etc.), tarts, wafers, curds, pancakes, *jonchées* (fresh sheeps'- or goats'-milk cheeses), *neige de beurre* (shallots and vinegar, or Muscadet, whipped up with butter), figs, pistachio nuts, Corbeil peaches, grapes, prunes, white bread, soft bread, *bourgeois* bread, wheaten bread; eggs fried, lost, suffocated, boiled, dragged over the coals, thrown into the chimney, smeared with something or other, etc.'

rabotte or rabote

An apple or pear enclosed in pastry, cooked in the oven, and served warm or cold. It is the name used in Picardy, Ardennes, and Champagne for the Norman douillon or bourdelot. In Picardy it is also called *talibur*, and in Ardennes and Champagne the name *boulaud* is sometimes used. The name *rabotte* comes from the word *rabote*, which was the old term for the ball used in real tennis.

racahout

A culinary starch used in the Middle East and the Arab countries. It is a greyish powder, consisting of salep, cocoa, sweet acorns, potato flour, rice, flour, sugar, and vanilla, which is mixed with water or milk to make a drink or soup.

Rachel

The stage name of the great tragic actress Élisabeth Félix (1821–58). She was the mistress of the famous gastronome Doctor Véron, whose dinners are still a byword, and many dishes in classic cuisine have been named after her. The Rachel garnish (for small grilled (broiled) or sautéed cuts of meat, braised calves' sweetbreads, or poached or soft-boiled eggs) consists of artichoke hearts stuffed with thin slices of beef marrow, with a bordelaise or beef marrow sauce. Artichoke hearts are also used in the Rachel mixed salad, with other ingredients. Whiting (or turbot) Rachel is poached, masked with Nantua sauce, and garnished with a julienne of truffle.

RECIPES

Poached eggs Rachel OEUFS POCHÉS RACHEL Cut some slices of white bread and fry until golden in butter or oil. Make some bone marrow sauce. Poach some slices of beef marrow in stock. Poach or soft-boil some eggs (trim the whites of poached eggs). Place an egg on each crouton, cover with sauce, and put a piece of marrow on each egg. The dish can be garnished with artichoke hearts stuffed with thin slices of beef marrow.

Rachel salad SALADE RACHEL Clean and string some celery sticks (stalks) and cut them into chunks. Cook some potatoes and some artichoke hearts in salted water and cut them into small dice. Mix equal amounts of these ingredients and dress them with a well-flavoured mayonnaise. Pile into a salad bowl and garnish with asparagus tips, cooked in salted water and well drained. If desired, the salad can be garnished with slices of truffle.

rack CLAIE

A trellis or grid of varying shape, size, material, and function.

Round or rectangular wire racks, usually with small legs, are used to cool cakes and pastries after they have been taken out of the oven and removed from their tins. This allows the steam to be released during cooling; otherwise, the cakes would retain too much moisture. A similar rack is also used in a roasting tin (pan). By roasting the meat on the rack, the joint is prevented from lying in its cooking juices.

Wooden racks serve for storing fruits or vegetables; wicker trays are used for drying crystallized fruits; and racks of stainless steel or plastic-covered wire form storage units in refrigerators and larders.

raclette

A cheese fondue from the canton of Valais in Switzerland. It is prepared by holding a half-round of the local cheese close to the fire; as it melts, the softened part is scraped off and eaten (the word *raclette* means literally a scraping). Traditionally the cheese should be grilled in front of a wood fire: it is held slantwise over a plate and the runny part is scraped off together with part of the grilled rind (after several scrapings, when the rind becomes coated with the melted cheese, it is called a *religieuse* and is a much coveted morsel). The melted cheese is shared between the guests and is eaten hot, with boiled potatoes, freshly ground pepper, gherkins, and pickled onions. Raclette should be accompanied by Fendant, a white wine from Valais, and must be made from a fatty and highly flavoured cheese: Bagnes, Conches, or Orsières. It is now possible to buy a 'raclette oven' for the table, which is fitted with a support for the cheese while it is exposed to an electric element.

radiccio TRÉVISE

A variety of chicory (endive) of Italian origin, cultivated only recently in the south of France and other countries throughout the world and available from December to March. Radiccio keeps well. Its small hearts, red with white veins, are round and crunchy and have a taste which is at once bitter, peppery, and slightly acid. It is generally used in salads, mixed with other salad vegetables, and looks particularly attractive when mixed with curly endive (chicory) and green lettuce or corn salad. It is often served with terrines, pies, and pâtés; a suitable dressing is walnut-oil vinaigrette.

radish RADIS

A plant of the cabbage family, cultivated for its edible root, which is generally eaten raw, as an hors d'oeuvre or in salads. There are many varieties of radish, differing in size, shape, and colour, the main types being 'small pink' and 'large black'. The radish has been grown in China for more than 3000 years and was esteemed by the Greeks and the Romans. In France, it was not cultivated until the 16th century and is now grown principally in the Loire region, being available throughout almost the whole year. There are three main groups:

• *Radishes available all the year round*

are small, flattish, round, or slightly elongated, and pink or scarlet, with or without a white tip. Their flavour is particularly good in March–April and September–October, when they are not too hot (in summer they may be too strong). Among the best varieties are the Flamboyant (slightly elongated, two-thirds cherry-red, one-third white), the Istar (round, two-thirds reddish-mauve, one-third white), and the National (round, bright red, with a little white collar).

• *Summer radishes*, pale pink or yellow, are round or slightly elongated. There are also some regional varieties: the Strasbourg (small, white, and top-shaped, 5 cm (2 in) across); the turnip radish (very long and narrow, with a red skin, and juicy scented flesh), which is found in eastern France and in Nice; and the golden-yellow radish (with flesh of this colour, 3–4 cm (1–1½ in) long), which is grown in Alsace.

• *Winter radishes*, which are up to 15 cm (6 in) long and 5–7 cm (2–3 in) across, have white flesh and a rough skin that is black or mauvish; among the latter is the Gournay, which is rarer and reputedly better than the black radish. (See *daikon*.)

With a calorific value of only 20 Cal per 100 g and a high water content, radishes are rich in mineral salts (especially sulphur, iron, and iodine) and in vitamins (particularly C). They must be eaten when very fresh, smooth, and firm, with an unblemished brighly coloured skin (if they are red or pink varieties); the leaves should be rather short, bright green, and stiff.

Really fresh pink radishes do not need to be peeled; the root tip and nearly all the leaves are cut off, then the radishes are washed in plenty of cold water and thoroughly dried; they are served as they are, with fresh butter and salt. Larger pink radishes are better sliced into thin rounds and added to a salad; they can also be cooked in the same way as small new turnips. Radish leaves can be added to potato soup or a sorrel or spinach purée.

The black radish, which has a more pungent flavour than the small pink variety, can also be eaten raw with salt after it has been peeled and sliced; the slices may be salted and left to stand so that some of their water is drawn out before being rinsed and dried. They can be used in the same way as celery, added to a rémoulade mayonnaise, or used in salad with a yogurt and shallot dressing.

RECIPES

Black radish as an hors d'oeuvre RADIS NOIR EN HORS D'OEUVRE Peel a black radish and slice it very thinly; soak the slices in a bowl with a small handful of table salt for an hour. Wash thoroughly, dry well, and serve in an hors d'oeuvre dish accompanied by rye bread or wholemeal bread with fresh or slightly salted butter.

Pink radishes à l'américaine RADIS ROSES À L'AMÉRICAINE Wash the radishes and cut all the leaves to the same length. Wash and then split the radishes in four from tip to leaf end without cutting through the bases; put them in a bowl of water and ice cubes. When they open out like flowers, drain and serve in an hors d'oeuvre dish, with fresh butter and table salt.

Radish-leaf soup SOUPE AUX FANES DE RADIS Cut off the leaves from a bunch of fresh radishes and cook them gently in butter in a saucepan. Pour in some chicken stock. Add 3 peeled potatoes, salt, and pepper. Cook over a low heat for 25 minutes, then pass the soup through a vegetable mill. Add 2 tablespoons (3 tablespoons) fresh cream, mix, and adjust the seasoning. Sprinkle with coarsely chopped chervil. This soup can be served with baked croutons.

ragout RAGOÛT

A stew made from meat, poultry, game, fish, or vegetables cut into pieces of regular size and shape and cooked – with or without first being browned – in a thickened liquid, generally flavoured with herbs and seasonings.

The French word *ragoût* dates from 1642; in classic French it was used to describe anything which stimulated the appetite or, in a figurative sense, awoke interest. The verb *ragoûter* meant to bring back someone's appetite. Ragouts have been enjoyed for many centuries and were even known in ancient times;

up to the Middle Ages they were probably very highly spiced.

Today there are two basic types of ragout – brown and white. For a brown ragout, of which the best known example is ragout of mutton, the meat is first browned in fat, then sprinkled with flour, cooked a little, and finally moistened with clear stock or water (or thickened meat juices, if the meat has not been floured). For a white ragout (as for a fricassee) the meat is cooked until firm but not coloured, then sprinkled with flour and diluted with stock. (A white ragout should not, however, be confused with a blanquette.) In a ragout *à l'anglaise*, in which the meat is not browned, the stew is thickened by the potatoes, which are cooked with the meat (as in Irish stew).

If fish is to be made into a ragout, its flesh must be firm enough to withstand the cooking (e.g. carp, monkfish, eel). Meat should be chosen from cuts which are suitable for braising or stewing (e.g. shoulder, chuck, or neck of beef; rib, breast, or knuckle of veal; shoulder, breast, collar, or middle neck of mutton; poultry giblets; and knuckle, chine, or blade of pork).

Vegetables for a ragout (chicory (endives), celery, mixed vegetables, mushrooms, etc.) are usually browned then cooked in their own juices, with herbs and tomatoes (peeled, seeded, and roughly chopped).

'Ragout' is also the name of a plain or mixed garnish, thickened with a white or brown liaison, with a meat or vegetable stock. It is used to fill croustades, tarts, vols-au-vent, etc., to embellish a fish or poultry dish, to garnish scrambled eggs, to fill omelettes, etc. These ragouts are made from such ingredients as crayfish tails (ragout *à la Nantua*), cocks' kidneys and combs, asparagus tips, truffles, mushrooms, calves' sweetbreads, bone marrow, and even snails or seafood; they appear in such garnishes as banquière, cancalaise, cévenole, financière, marinière, périgourdine, printanière, etc.

RECIPES

Ragout of lamb à l'anglaise RAGOÛT D'AGNEAU À L'ANGLAISE Cut 750 g (1¾ lb) shoulder of lamb, trimmed of excess fat, into cubes, and slice 500 g (18 oz) potatoes and 2 onions. Put alternate layers of lamb and vegetables into a casserole; add salt and pepper and a bouquet garni. Pour in enough hot water or stock to just cover the meat. Cover the casserole and cook in the oven at 160 C (325 F, gas 3) for 1¼ hours. Transfer to a deep dish and sprinkle with coarsely chopped parsley.

Ragout of mushrooms RAGOÛT DE CHAMPIGNONS Clean and slice 500 g (18 oz, 5 cups) large cultivated mushrooms, sauté them in butter or oil, then add a small glass of Madeira and some cream sauce. Reduce on a low heat until thick and creamy, sprinkle with coarsely chopped parsley, and serve as a garnish for roast or braised white meat or for braised fish.

Ragout of seafood RAGOÛT DE COQUILLAGES Cook the seafood in white wine (use mussels, cockles, clams, etc.), then remove from their shells and bind with a white sauce. Sprinkle with coarsely chopped parsley and arrange in the centre of a ring of rice *à la créole* or *à l'orientale*.

Ragout of shellfish RAGOÛT DE CRUSTACÉS Plunge the shellfish (use shrimps, prawns, crayfish, lobster, etc.) into boiling water for a few seconds, then cut into slices and cook in a saucepan until they become red (leave shrimps and small prawns whole). Add salt, pepper, and a chopped shallot, cover the pan, and leave to cook for 8–10 minutes. Bind with a cream or white wine sauce. Just before serving, add some savoury butter flavoured with whichever shellfish there is most of. Sprinkle with chopped herbs and serve with rice.

Ragueneau (Cyprien)

Parisian pastrycook (born Paris, 1608; died Lyon, 1654). He established himself in the Rue Saint-Honoré, displaying the sign 'Amateurs de Haulte Gresse', where he created the *tartelettes amandine* (almond tarts) mentioned by Edmond Rostand in *Cyrano de Bergerac*. He kept open house for half-starved poets and bohemians, who paid their rent in poetry. He was renowned for his tarts, marzipan confections, savoury pies flavoured with musk and amber, puff pastries, fritters, and biscuits (cookies). Charles d'Assoucy relates that he would give away these delicacies to anyone who flattered him by calling him 'Apollo reborn as a pastrycook'.

Ragueneau's shop became a sort of academy, with pastries and tartlets used as attendance tallies. He himself wrote 456 sonnets, 4 elegies, 63 odes, and 19 comic-heroic plays. He was very proud of his tragedy *Don Olibrius, occiseur d'innocents* and – hoping that Molière would produce it – he went to Béziers to join the playwright's group of actors. He was given a few bit-parts to play, but finally resigned himself to being a candle snuffer and eventually died in extreme poverty.

rail RÂLE

Any of a large family of wading birds. Two species are regarded as delicacies in France – the corncrake, found in wet meadowland, and the water rail, living in marshland. The corncrake is particularly valued; its size and the influence that it is supposed to have on quail migration has resulted in the nickname of 'the king of quails' in France. It is cooked in the same ways as quail.

raisiné

A jam made without sugar, by simmering grape juice (or even sweet wine) with various fruits cut into pieces. It is a speciality of Burgundy. Raisiné is usually spread on slices of bread; it does not keep as well as jam.

RECIPE

Burgundian raisiné RAISINÉ DE BOURGOGNE Select some very sweet grapes, either black or white, discarding any which are marked or bad. Put them into a preserving pan over a low heat and crush them with a wooden spoon. Strain the pulp through a cloth and collect the juice in a bowl. Pour half of this juice into a saucepan and boil briskly, skimming the pan carefully. When the juice rises in the pan add some of the reserved juice; do this each time the juice boils up. Stir constantly.

When the must has reduced by half, add the fruit (pears, quinces, apples, peaches, melon, etc.), peeled, deseeded or stoned (pitted), and cut into small pieces; add at least the same quantity of fruit as there were grapes. Cook until the jam becomes quite thick (a drop taken up between the thumb and index finger should form a sticky thread when the fingers are separated). The jam may be passed through a sieve (if desired) and then potted in the usual way (see *jams, jellies, and marmalades*).

raisins

See *dried vine fruits*.

Raisson (Horace-Napoléon)

French writer and gastronome (born Paris, 1798; died Paris 1854). under different pseudonyms, one of which was A. B. de Périgord, he published several cookery books, notably a *Nouvel Almanach des gourmands* (1825–30), borrowing this title from Grimond de La Reynière. His *Code gourmand* went through several editions. In 1827 he published a *Nouvelle Cuisinière bourgeoise* under the name of 'Mlle Marguerite'. This book remained popular for quite a long time, the last edition being published in 1860.

raïto, raite, or rayte

A Provençal condiment which may have originated in Greece. The sauce consists of olive oil and red wine, with tomatoes, onions, crushed walnuts, and garlic, flavoured with bay leaf, thyme, parsley, rosemary, fennel, and a clove, and sometimes garnished with capers and black (ripe) olives; the mixture is simmered for a long time until very thick, and then strained. It is served very hot with certain fried or sautéed fish dishes, often cod.

raki

A Turkish aniseed-flavoured apéritif, very similar to the Greek ouzo. The best rakis, with 45–50° alcohol, are made from selected aged brandies; some, like the Greek *mastika*, have mastic (resin of the mastic tree) added. Raki is drunk neat from a small glass in small sips, alternated with mouthfuls of iced water.

Ramadan

The ninth month of the Muslim lunar year, during which the faithful must fast from dawn until dusk. During this period, a Muslim must not drink (except to rinse the mouth out), eat, smoke, have sexual relations, or perfume himself during the daytime. At sundown he has a meal, usually consisting of soup (*harīra*), hardboiled (hard-cooked) eggs, dates, and sweet cakes. After evening prayer and before he must fast again, just before dawn, he has a second meal; this may include pancakes, honey, and sometimes also soup (*bazine*, made from semolina with butter and lemon juice added, or *halalim*, made of pulses and herbs and containing sausages, lamb, or veal and dumplings made from leavened semolina). Halfway through the month a traditional meal is served; in Morocco, for instance, this consists of pastilla, roast chicken with lemon, and a sweet pastry. The end of Ramadan is celebrated by a feast during which a sheep is ritually roasted.

Ramain (Paul)

French doctor (born Thonon, 1895; died Douvaine, 1966). He liked to describe himself as an 'independent provincial gastronome' and was a great connoisseur of wines, choosing for his motto 'Jamais en vain, toujours en vin!'

A well-known mycologist, he was the author of *Mycogastronomie* (1953), which is still regarded as an authority and gives some very good little known mushroom recipes. Writing on the best wines to accompany meals, he suggests that all good meals could well be accompanied solely by 'excellent authentic champagnes', ranging from the blanc de blancs to the blanc de rouges or the *oeil de perdrix* (pink champagne). But he also recommends locally grown wines and mentions a meal he ate in Aveyron of an 'extremely high gastronomic standard', accompanied by an old Cahors wine; apparently the wine and the food together created 'a faultless gustatory and olfactory symphony'.

Ramain offers this last admonition: 'Between each wine and each dish one should drink a mouthful of pure fresh water, preferably not (or only slightly) aerated.'

rambutan RAMBOUTAN

An exotic fruit, belonging to the same family as the lychee, originating in Malaysia and very common throughout southeast Asia. The thick red shell is covered with hooked hairs and the translucent sweet pulp has less flavour than that of the lychee. The fruit is available fresh in November and December (imported from Madagascar and Réunion) and can be bought canned in syrup all the year round. It has a calorific value of 66 Cal per 100 g and contains vitamin C. The rambutan is eaten peeled, in fruit salads, but can also accompany poultry or pork.

ramekin RAMEQUIN

A small round straight-sided soufflé dish, 8–10 cm (3–4 in) in diameter, in ovenproof china or glass; it is used to cook and serve individual portions of a variety of hot entrées: small cheese, seafood, or fish soufflés, eggs *en cocotte à la crème*, *aux fines herbes*, etc. It is equally useful for serving aspics (particularly eggs *en gelée*, served unmoulded), as well as for cold creams and custards, which may or may not be unmoulded.

In former times, a ramekin was a slice of toasted bread spread with 'meat, kidneys, cheese, onions, or garlic cloves' (according to La Varenne), moistened with cream, and, as was often done with various dishes, 'sprinkled with soot from the chimney'. Nowadays, the word is still used in the Swiss canton of Vaud for a type of toasted cheese. The word is derived from *ramken*, the diminutive of the German *Rahm* (fresh cream): thus it came to mean 'a little dish with cream'. Later on it denoted either a tartlet filled with a cream cheese or a type of gougère (choux pastry) sometimes made in a small mould.

Two French regional specialities are still called 'ramekin', used in its old sense: the *ramequin douaisien* (baked bread rolls, stuffed with a mixture of chopped kidney, breadcrumbs soaked in milk, eggs, and herbs) and the *ramequin du pays de Gex* (a blue cheese (Bleu du Haut Jura) and Gruyère cheese melted together in a saucepan with stock, red wine, butter, garlic, and mustard, served like a fondue with cubes of bread).

RECIPES

Ramekin RAMEQUIN (from Mont-Bry's recipe) Pour 1 glass (8 fl oz, 1 cup) milk into a saucepan and season with a generous pinch of salt, a small pinch of sugar, and a little white pepper. Add 25 g (1 oz, 2 tablespoons) butter and bring to the boil. As soon as the milk begins to boil, move the pan half off the heat and mix in 100 g (4 oz, 1 cup) sifted flour. Return to the heat and stir vigorously with a wooden spoon, as for choux pastry, until the mixture has dried out. When it is quite dry, take the pan off the heat and add 3 eggs, one by one, and 50 g (2 oz, ½ cup) finely diced Gruyère cheese. Put this paste into a forcing (pastry) bag with a plain nozzle and pipe small buns onto a baking sheet. Brush with beaten egg and sprinkle with tiny pieces of Gruyère. Bake in the oven at 190 C (375 F, gas 5).

Jellied eggs in ramekins OEUFS EN RAMEQUINS À LA GELÉE Arrange 2 blanched leaves of tarragon in a cross shape in the bottom of each ramekin dish. Coat the inside of each ramekin with a little tarragon-flavoured meat aspic and leave in the refrigerator to set. Then put in a small slice of very good ham, cut to the shape of the dish. Arrange a shelled soft-boiled egg on top, fill the dish with aspic, and leave to set in the refrigerator. Unmould just before serving.

Ramekin vaudois RAMEQUIN VAUDOIS Cut some thin slices from a large white loaf and slice some Gruyère cheese (300 g (11 oz) of each). Arrange alternate slices of bread and cheese in a buttered gratin dish. Beat together 2 eggs and 5 dl (17 fl oz, 2 cups) milk, season with salt, pepper, and nutmeg, and pour the mixture over the bread and cheese (the liquid should half-fill the dish). Dot with butter and cook in the oven at 190 C (375 F, gas 5) for 25 minutes.

rampion RAIPONCE

A plant of the campanula family with edible roots. These may be eaten raw in salads, for which they are cut into pieces and usually mixed with beetroot (red beet) or celery; or they can be cooked in the same way as salsify or turnips. The leaves, which have a refreshing taste, can also be eaten in salads or cooked like spinach. Rampion is rarely used in cooking today.

rancid RANCE

Describing stale fat or fatty foods which have a strong smell and an acrid taste, due to oxidation of the fat. Rancidity is accelerated by exposure to light, high temperatures, and metallic contamination.

rancio

A vin doux naturel (e.g. Banyuls or Muscat), which owes its special taste to ageing in cask over several years, in theory under the sun; the resulting oxidation produces a very smooth wine.

In Spain, the word describes the nutty taste peculiar to sherry and Málaga wines; in Portugal, it applies to the pronounced taste of some ports and Madeiras; in Italy, it applies to Marsala and other fortified wines.

range FOURNEAU

A large stove with hotplates or burners and one or more ovens, heated by solid fuel, oil, gas, or electricity. The range was originally made of masonry, and then of either thick sheet metal or cast iron. It is the main basic piece of equipment in a kitchen, especially in the restaurant trade. The range often has a polished cast-iron hotplate and pans can be moved along easily to the desired position. A hot-water boiler may also be heated by this type of stove. The most recent models are modified for use in a large kitchen: 'browning' ranges, 'live-fire' ranges, and 'simmering-plate' ranges.

The first ranges appeared in the 18th century and caused a revolution in the kitchen by replacing the large fireplace, which, until then, was the only source of heat available. The introduction of the range meant that several sources of heat at different temperatures were available, and several dishes requiring different temperatures could be cooked at the same time, i.e. items could be roasted, boiled, simmered, or simply kept warm. It is no accident that the 18th century is noted for the invention of so many new dishes. Another decisive development occurred at the end of the 18th century, when the cast-iron range, which burned coal, replaced the wood-burning stove. However, the problem of ventilation was still causing concern and led Carême to comment 'Coal is killing us.' In the 1850s in London, the chef Soyer introduced the gas cooker, and today, most modern stoves are heated by either gas or electricity.

rape COLZA

A plant related to the cabbage that is widely cultivated for the oil contained in its seeds. It was extensively cultivated in France before the introduction of groundnut (peanut) oil, and is currently regaining some of its former popularity. Although the seeds are rich in oil, they also contain toxins that have to be removed. Rapeseed oil cannot be heated to very high temperatures, but it keeps well and remains in a liquid state down to freezing point (0 C, 32 F). The flower buds of rape may be eaten in the same way as broccoli.

rās al-hānout

A mixture of powdered spices (cloves, cinnamon, and black pepper), used mainly in Morocco and in Tunisia (where it is generally less hot and perfumed with dried rosebuds). The literal meaning is 'roof of the shop'. It is used to season ragouts, the broth which accompanies the semolina in couscous, and many other North African dishes.

rascasse

See *scorpion fish*.

raspberry FRAMBOISE

The fruit of the raspberry cane, which grows wild in the woods or can be cultivated in the garden. In France, Britain, and America it is cultivated in open soil or under frames.

The raspberry has been known since prehistoric times and the Ancients attributed its origin to divine intervention: the nymph Ida pricked her finger while picking berries for the young Jupiter and thus raspberries, which had been white until then, turned red. Raspberries have been cultivated since the Middle Ages; although cultivation methods were improved in the 18th century, the fruit did not become widely cultivated until the 20th century.

Raspberries are oval or conical in shape, rather small, and have a sweet, slightly acid, flavour. They are usually fairly dark red, but yellow-coloured varieties have also been produced. Greenhouse raspberries are marketed from mid-April onwards but do not have the delicious flavour of those grown in open soil from mid-June to October. Raspberries must always be firm plump ripe fruit with a delicious flavour. The fruits are delicate and must be handled carefully: they do not keep for very long. They have a low calorific value (25 Cal per 100 g) and are rich in calcium, iron, phosphorus, fibre, and vitamins.

Regarded as a dessert fruit *par excellence*, the raspberry can be eaten with sugar or cream. Raspberries are used to make flans, desserts, jam, compotes, jellies, syrups, fermented drinks, liqueurs, and brandy, and raspberry juice can be used to flavour ice creams and sorbets. The fruit can be preserved in syrup or brandy, and can also be frozen, although the fruit becomes soft once it is defrosted. It is best to freeze raspberries by open-freezing on trays or by freezing them in sugar (dry pack), or making the bruised or slightly poor-quality ones into purée (which is made in the same way as strawberry purée (see *strawberry*).

The loganberry is a cross between a blackberry and a raspberry. It is an American hybrid named after James H. Logan, who first grew it in California in 1881. The loganberry is a large juicy dark-red fruit and is marketed in September and October. It also has a tart flavour, but is considered by some people to be less delicious than the raspberry.

RECIPES

Raspberry barquettes BARQUETTES AUX FRAMBOISES Prepare some barquettes (boat-shaped tartlets) of shortcrust pastry (basic pie dough) and leave them to cool. Spread a little confectioners' custard (see *creams and custards*) in each tartlet, and top with fresh raspberries. Coat the fruit with some warmed redcurrant or raspberry jelly.

Raspberry charlotte CHARLOTTE AUX FRAMBOISES Line a charlotte mould with sponge fingers (ladyfingers) soaked in raspberry-flavoured syrup. Whip some fresh cream with caster (superfine) sugar and vanilla sugar. Add an equal quantity of raspberry purée made with either fresh or frozen raspberries. Fill the lined mould with the mixture and cover with a layer of sponge fingers, also soaked in raspberry syrup. Press the sponge fingers down, put a plate over the mould, and refrigerate for at least 3 hours. Invert onto a plate just before serving.

Raspberry jam CONFITURE DE FRAMBOISES Select firm ripe fruit and remove the stems. Put them into a preserving pan. For each kg (2¼ lb) fruit, make a syrup with 1 kg (2¼ lb, 4½ cups, firmly packed) sugar, boiled to the 'soft ball' stage (see *sugar*). Pour the syrup over the raspberries, bring back to the boil, cook gently for 5–6 minutes, and remove from the heat. Put the jam into clean sterilized jars, cover, seal, label, and store. See *jams, jellies, and marmalades*.

Raspberry jelly GELÉE À LA FRAMBOISE This is made with equal quantities of redcurrants and raspberries. Pour the redcurrants into a pan and add 6 tablespoons (½ cup) water per kg (2¼ lb) fruit. Boil until the berries soften and the juice comes out. Leave to cool, then place the redcurrants and raspberries in a cloth over a bowl and twist the cloth to extract the juice (for a very clear jelly, pour the fruit into a jelly bag and leave to drip overnight). Pour the juice into a pan, add 1 kg (2¼ lb, 4½ cups, firmly packed) sugar per litre (1¾ pints, 4¼ cups) fruit juice, and boil quickly until the jelling stage is reached (101 C, 213.8 F). Remove from the heat and pour immediately into jars. Cover, seal, and label.

rassolnick

A Russian soup made from poultry stock flavoured with cucumber, thickened with egg yolk and cream, and garnished with cucumber cut into shapes and finely diced pieces of poultry meat (classically duck). A richer version is made by adding brisket of beef and vegetables (beetroot (red beet), leeks, cabbage) to the stock. The soup is thickened with cream and beetroot juice, seasoned with fennel and parsley, and garnished with the diced meat and possibly small grilled (broiled) sausages.

Rasteau

An AOC wine from the southern end of the River Rhône, based on the Grenache grape. The area is most famous for its vin doux naturel, but sweet white wines are also made, as well as the Côtes du Rhône Villages wines, which are red, white, and rosé. The Rasteau wines are seldom seen outside the locality.

rastegaï

A small oval Russian patty made of puff pastry and normally filled with a mixture of sturgeon spinal marrow, hard-boiled (hard-cooked) egg, and fresh salmon. It is served with melted butter as a hot entrée or as part of the *zakuski* (hors d'oeuvres).

ratafia

A home-made liqueur produced by macerating plants or fruit in sweetened spirit; some traditional ingredients are: angelica, cherries, blackcurrants, quinces, raspberries, walnuts, oranges, cherry kernels, etc.

The name is also given to a sweet apéritif made in the French provinces: this is a mixture of two-thirds fresh grape juice (must) and one-third brandy. These liqueurs are mostly intended for home consumption, but some have achieved a higher status, such as Pineau from Charentes, the Floc of Gascony, and the Ratafia Champenois from the Champagne region.

The word is of Creole French origin; it formerly referred to the alcoholic drink which clinched an agreement or a business transaction and is said to be derived from the Latin phrase *rata fiat* (let the deal be settled).

ratatouille

A vegetable ragout typical of Provençal cookery, originally from Nice, which is now found all over southeast France and is popular abroad. The word, derived from the French *touiller* (to mix or stir), at first designated an unappetizing stew.

A ratatouille from Nice (*ratatouille niçoise*) is made from onions, courgettes (zucchini), aubergines (eggplants), sweet peppers, and tomatoes simmered in olive oil with herbs. It accompanies roasts, sautéed chicken, or small cuts of meat, as well as braised fish, omelettes, and scrambled eggs. According to the purists, the different vegetables should be cooked separately, then combined and cooked together until they attain a smooth creamy consistency.

| RECIPE

Ratatouille niçoise   Trim the ends of 6 courgettes (zucchini) and cut them into rounds (do not peel them). Peel and slice 2 onions. Cut the stalks from 3 green peppers, remove the seeds, and cut them into strips. Peel 6 tomatoes, cut each into 6 pieces, and deseed them. Peel and crush 3 garlic cloves. Peel 6 aubergines (egg-plants) and cut them into rounds. Heat 6 tablespoons (½ cup) olive oil in a cast-iron pan. Brown the aubergines in this, then add the peppers, tomatoes, and onions, and finally the courgettes and the garlic. Add a large bouquet garni containing plenty of thyme, salt, and pepper. Cook over a low heat for about 30 minutes. Add 2 tablespoons (3 tablespoons) fresh olive oil and continue to cook until the desired consistency is reached. Remove the bouquet garni and serve very hot.

raton

The former name for a small tartlet filled with either sweetened cream cheese or confectioners' custard (pastry cream). A raton can also be made with a mixture of flour, sugar, crushed macaroni, pounded almonds, eggs, and milk; this is cooked in a pie dish, turned over halfway through cooking, and served hot.

Nicolas de Bonnefons, in his *Délices de la campagne* (1650), gives another recipe using puff pastry (quoted by P. Androuet in *La Cuisine au fromage*): during the last turn and rolling, a well-drained cream cheese is incorporated into the dough, which is rolled out, cut into small rectangles, brushed with beaten egg, sprinkled with grated cheese, and baked.

rave

In France, the word *rave* is used loosely for several vegetables regarded as having a low culinary status, such as kohlrabi, turnips, swedes, and black radishes. In former times, the name was applied to all root vegetables (*racines*), as opposed to *herbes* (leaf vegetables).

ravigote

A spicy sauce served hot or cold but always highly seasoned. Cold ravigote is a vinaigrette mixed with capers, chopped herbs, and chopped onion. The hot sauce is made by adding veal velouté sauce to equal quantities of white wine and wine vinegar, reduced with chopped shallots; it is finished with chopped herbs and served particularly with calf's head and brains and boiled fowl. Savoury butter and mayonnaise *à la ravigote* are flavoured with chopped herbs and shallots, and sometimes with mustard.

| RECIPE

Ravigote sauce (*cold*)   SAUCE RAVIGOTE FROIDE   (from Raymond Oliver's recipe in *La Cuisine*, Bordas, 1981) Prepare 1 dl (6 tablespoons, scant ½ cup) plain vinaigrette with mustard. Add ½ teaspoon chopped tarragon, 1 teaspoon chopped parsley, 1 teaspoon fines herbes, 2 teaspoons chervil, 1 finely chopped small onion, and 1 tablespoon dried and chopped capers.

raviole or raviolle

A dish from Nice and Corsica consisting of small square pockets of pasta stuffed with chopped spinach, Swiss chard, or cream cheese and cooked in water. The word may come from the Latin *rapum* (turnip), as a raviole was formerly a small meat and turnip pie, but it seems more likely that it has the same derivation as ravioli, which is a very similar dish.

Ravioles also exist in Savoyard cookery: these are small dumplings made of spinach, Swiss chard, flour, fresh Tomme cheese, and eggs, poached in water, then browned and served with tomato sauce.

ravioli

An Italian dish consisting of small

square envelopes of pasta dough enclosing a meat or vegetable stuffing, cooked in boiling water, and usually served with tomato sauce and grated cheese. Very small ravioli may be used as a garnish for soup. Agnolotti, a variation from Piedmont, are cut into rounds. The stuffing may be made from chopped veal or beef, chicken livers, calves' sweetbreads, or vegetables only, especially spinach.

It is said that ravioli originally came from Liguria and were invented as a means of using up leftover food, hence their original name, *rabiole* (bits and pieces, odds and ends, in Genoese dialect), which later became 'ravioli'. Whether or not leftovers are used, the ingredients of good ravioli must always be varied: one Genoese recipe includes lean bacon, basil, carrots, celery, finely sliced roast chicken, chopped loin of veal, mortadella, and Parmesan cheese. Ravioli is one of the best-known stuffed pasta dishes, famous well beyond the shores of Italy. Fresh ravioli can be bought, ready to poach and serve with a sauce, etc., and it is also available ready-prepared (canned or frozen).

RECIPES

Preparation and cooking of ravioli PRÉPARATION ET CUISSON DES RAVIOLI Make some pasta dough with eggs and roll it out thinly into 2 equal rectangles. Using a forcing (pastry) bag, pipe small quantities of the chosen stuffing onto one of the rectangles of dough, placing them in rows about 4 cm (1½ in) apart. Damp the dough between the heaps of stuffing with the fingertips. Place the second rectangle of dough over the first and gently press them together around the heaps of stuffing. Using a pastry (cookie) wheel or ravioli cutter, cut down and across the rows, producing small square envelopes of dough enclosing the stuffing. Dry in a cool place for 3–4 hours, then cook in boiling salted water for 8–10 minutes. Drain them and either treat them as a gratin or warm them through in tomato sauce.

Stuffings for ravioli FARCES À RAVIOLI

■ *Meat and vegetable*: finely chop 150 g (5 oz) beef, braised in wine or *à la mode*, or braised veal; add 100 g (4 oz, ½ cup) spinach (cooked in salted water, pressed, and chopped), 50 g (2 oz) calves' brains poached in court-bouillon, 1 shallot and 1 large onion (chopped then softened in butter), and 1 whole egg; 50 g (2 oz, ½ cup) grated Parmesan cheese can also be added if liked. Mix everything well together, adding salt, pepper, and grated nutmeg.

■ *Meat and cheese*: finely chop 200 g (7 oz) cooked veal or poultry meat, 100 g (4 oz) calves' brains cooked in court-bouillon, and 100 g (4 oz) lettuce leaves, blanched, pressed, and stewed in butter; add 50 g (2 oz, ¼ cup) well-drained curd cheese, 50 g (2 oz, ½ cup) grated Parmesan cheese, 1 lightly beaten whole egg, a pinch each of salt and pepper, and a little grated nutmeg. Mix well before using.

■ *Chicken liver*: finely chop 150 g (5 oz) chicken livers (sautéed in butter with 1 chopped shallot, a little garlic, and a pinch of salt), 100 g (4 oz, ½ cup) spinach (blanched and pressed), 1 desalted anchovy fillet, and 50 g (2 oz, ¼ cup) butter. Mix these ingredients well together, working in 1 lightly beaten whole egg and a pinch of powdered basil, salt, pepper, and nutmeg. The chicken livers can be replaced by braised veal and the spinach by Swiss chard leaves (blanched, pressed, and stewed in butter).

■ *Spinach*: blanch, press, and chop 300 g (11 oz, 1½ cups) spinach and stew it in 30 g (1 oz, 2 tablespoons) butter; add salt, pepper, and grated nutmeg. Sprinkle on 1 tablespoon flour, mix well over a high heat, then add 1 dl (6 tablespoons, scant ½ cup) milk. Bring to the boil, take off the stove, and add 50 g (2 oz, ½ cup) grated Parmesan cheese and 1 egg yolk; mix thoroughly.

Ravioli with herbs RAVIOLI AUX HERBES (from a recipe by P. and J. Gleize) Pour 1 kg (2¼ lb) flour into a circle. In the middle put 4 whole eggs, 30 g (1 oz, 1 tablespoon) salt, 1 dl (6 tablespoons, scant ½ cup) olive oil, and 2 glasses of water. Gradually mix the flour with the other ingredients: the dough should be quite soft. Leave it to rest for at least 1 hour.

Blanch 1 kg (2¼ lb) Swiss chard, 500 g (18 oz) spinach, and 100 g (4 oz) parsley for 5 minutes, refresh, then drain thoroughly. Sauté 250 g (9 oz) chanterelles in oil, add the vegetables and 3 cloves of garlic, then chop everything finely and season with salt and pepper.

Make the ravioli. Bring a large saucepan of salted water containing 1 tablespoon olive oil to the boil, drop in the ravioli, and poach gently. Drain them on a cloth and serve with melted butter and grated cheese. They can also be accompanied by a sauce made with raw tomato pulp, chopped chives, lemon juice, and olive oil.

Small ravioli for soup PETITS RAVIOLI POUR POTAGE Make some ravioli, fill with chicken-liver or calf's-brain stuffing, and cut into 2-cm (¾-in) squares. After poaching, divide them among plates of clear soup or consommé just before serving.

razor-shell (razor clam)
COUTEAU

A sand-burrowing bivalve mollusc with an elongated tubular shell. It can be made to come to the surface of its burrow by placing a little coarse salt at the opening of the hole. The two main types are the straight razor-shell (10–20 cm (4–8 in) long) and the curved razor-shell (10–15 cm (4–6 in) long). They may be eaten either raw or cooked (after cleaning), but are of little gastronomic interest.

Reblochon

A cows'-milk cheese made in Savoy (50% fat content), with a pressed uncooked curd and a washed rind, yellow, pink or orange in colour. It is very pliable, creamy, and fine-textured, with a sweet nutty taste, and was known in the 15th century. Its name comes from the French verb *reblocher*, meaning 'to milk a second time', because the cheese used to be made in the Alpine meadows from the last milk to be drawn from the cow, which is very rich in fat. Since 1958 it has been protected by an AOC, applying to the districts of Annecy, Bonne-ville, Saint-Julien-en-Genevois, and Thonon (in the department of Haute-Savoie) and Albertville and Saint-Jean-de-Maurienne (in the department of Savoie). It is shaped like a flat disc 13 cm (5 in) in diameter and 2.5 cm (1 in) thick; there is also a smaller version, 9 cm (3½ in) in diameter and 3 cm (1¼ in) thick. It is made both on farms and in dairies and can be eaten from May to October.

Reboux (Paul; *born* Henri Amillet)

French writer and journalist (born Paris, 1877; died Nice, 1963). He was the author of several recipe books, including *Plats nouveaux, 300 recettes inédites ou singulières* (1927), *Plats du jour* (1936), and *Le Nouveau Savoir-Manger* (1941), which were much criticized by chefs of the classic cuisine; he was, however, a pioneer and an enlightened lover of good food. He wrote a memorable homage to mustard: 'A touch of these mustards brings out the flavour of Gruyère cheese, seasons a salad, gives a lift to white sauces, and gives style to a ragout. The hors d'oeuvre is the first dish to feel their good effect, which only ceases with the dessert.'

Réchaud

18-century French cook. He was praised by Grimod de La Reynière in the *Manuel des amphitryons* (1808), who mentioned his spinach with goose fat and placed him in the same rank as the 'great Morillon', his father's head chef. He also gave this biographical detail: 'The late M. Réchaud, famous chef to the last Prince of Condé, founder of one of the foremost schools of the last century.'

redcurrant GROSEILLE

A shrub of the genus *Ribes* that is cultivated for its fruit – small red acid-tasting berries growing in clusters of 7–20. (The whitecurrant is a variety producing slightly sweeter white berries – it is prepared and used in the same way as the redcurrant.)

Redcurrants were introduced into France from Scandinavia in the Middle Ages. In France they are now cultivated mostly in the Rhône valley and (on a smaller scale) on the Côte d'Or and in the Loire valley.

Redcurrants are rich in citric acid (which gives them their acid taste), pectin, and vitamins. They are mostly used to make jams and jellies, used both in pâtisserie and for sauces, etc. The fruit can also be eaten raw, sprinkled with sugar, either alone or in fruit salads. It freezes well and is also used to make syrups, cold desserts, tarts, etc. A speciality in France is Bar-le-Duc jelly, made with red- and whitecurrants: the pips are removed from the fruit by hand with a quill – a technique invented in the 14th century.

RECIPES

Redcurrant jelly I GELÉE DE GROSEILLE Use either all redcurrants or two-thirds redcurrants and one-third white. 125 g (4 oz) raspberries are added to each 1 kg (2 lb) currants.

Crush the currants and raspberries together and strain them through a cloth which is wrung at both ends. Measure the juice. Allow 1 kg (2 lb, 4 cups) sugar for each litre (2 pints, 2½ pints) fruit juice. Heat the sugar in a pan with just enough water to enable it to dissolve. Add the fruit juice and cook to the jelling stage on a good heat.

Redcurrant jelly II GELÉE DE GROSEILLE Put the prepared and weighed currants in a pan, add a small glass of water for each kg (2¼ lb) currants, and heat them gently until the skins burst and the juices come out. Add raspberries (the same proportion as in the recipe above) and boil for a few seconds only. Strain the fruit and filter the juice. Continue as described above.

Redcurrant sorbet SORBET À LA GROSEILLE Slowly dissolve 175 g (6 oz, ⅔ cup) sugar in 425 ml (15 fl oz, 2 cups) water. Bring the syrup to the boil and boil steadily for 10 minutes. Cool. Mix ½ litre (17 fl oz, 2 cups) filtered redcurrant juice with ½ litre (17 fl oz, 2 cups) sugar syrup. Add a few drops of lemon juice and mix well. Then freeze the sorbet in the usual way (see *sorbet*).

redfish SÉBASTE
A fish, also called Norway haddock, related to the scorpion fish. There are two main varieties: the smaller one lives in the Mediterranean and in the Atlantic as far north as the River Loire; the larger one is found in the North Atlantic and in colder waters. The redfish has a large spiny head, like the scorpion fish, but lacks spines on its fins. It is bright pink with a silvery sheen and the inside of its mouth is black or bright red. The fish is plumper than the scorpion fish and there is less waste (40–50%) when it is prepared for cooking. It has lean firm flesh and is tastier than the scorpion fish. It yields very good fillets which taste like crab.

reduce RÉDUIRE
To concentrate or thicken a sauce, stock, etc., by boiling, which evaporates some of the water and reduces the volume. The time required will depend on the quantity of liquid and the degree of concentration desired. It takes longest to reduce a liquid to a glaze, thick and shining, so that it will coat the back of a spoon. The aim of reducing a sauce is to improve its flavour, smoothness, and consistency.

For some sauces, reduction is a preliminary operation and precedes the main preparation; it is designed to obtain a concentrated essence of white wine or vinegar (sometimes both together) or of red wine with chopped shallots, tarragon, etc.: béarnaise and bordelaise sauces and beurre blanc are prepared in this way.

When deglazing a roasting pan to prepare a sauce or gravy to accompany the meat, the fat is skimmed off and the caramelized juices are diluted with wine, fresh cream, etc.; when white wine is used, it is essential to reduce the liquid so as to remove the acidity. Clear or thickened stock is then poured into the pan and the reduction is continued until the gravy or sauce has reached the desired consistency and taste.

red wine VIN ROUGE
See *wine*.

re-emulsify REMONTER
To restore a homogeneous consistency

Categories of refrigerators

category	condenser temperature	keeping time of frozen foods
no stars	−3 to −4 c	24 hours only in the ice-making compartment
1 star	−6 c	up to 1 week
2 stars	−12 c	up to 1 month
3 stars (cabinet usually with 2 doors and freezer compartment)	−18 c	up to 3 months
4 stars (cabinet usually with 2 doors and freezer compartment, working from 1 or 2 compressors)	−18 c (−25 to −40 c during freezing)	1–12 months

to a sauce which has curdled. Mayonnaise can be re-emulsified by adding it drop by drop to any one of the following: an egg yolk, a little mustard, or a few drops of vinegar or water, while constantly beating the sauce. Hollandaise or béarnaise sauce can be reconstituted in the same way by adding a little water – hot if the sauce is cold, cold if the sauce is hot.

reform sauce RÉFORME

An English sauce based on a poivrade sauce with the addition of gherkins, hard-boiled (hard-cooked) egg whites, mushrooms, pickled tongue, and truffle. It is served with lamb cutlets or may be used to fill an omelette. The sauce can also be prepared using the same ingredients but with a base of game sauce (half poivrade and half demi-glace with redcurrant jelly added); it is served with game cutlets and small single cuts of venison.

refresh RAFRAÎCHIR

To run cold water over food which has just been blanched or cooked in water, in order to cool it down rapidly.

refrigerator

RÉFRIGÉRATEUR

A piece of equipment in the form of a cupboard designed to refrigerate and store perishable foods. It is usually made of enamelled metal with cavity walls and often contains a smaller compartment at the top that can be used as a freezer. The remaining interior space is fitted with racks and there are storage spaces in the inner door. At the bottom of the cabinet a salad drawer or vegetable crisper protects vegetables from too much cold and provides a slightly more humid atmosphere.

The low temperature is produced either by evaporation or by the expansion of a compressed refrigerant. Early refrigerators worked by evaporation. The system was absolutely noiseless but used a great deal of electricity; it is hardly ever used now except for small table-top refrigerators. Modern refrigerators work by compression and expansion and consume much less power: a gas (Freon, propane, methyl chloride), previously compressed, expands in the condenser, thus cooling itself. The drawback of this system is the noise of the motor switching on each time that the thermostat cuts in.

As the humidity in the cabinet condenses it forms ice, especially in the freezing compartment. This must be regularly removed by turning off the refrigerator to melt the ice and removing the water formed. Some refrigerators do this by a semiautomatic process (the thermostat switches off when frosting has built up, the water is emptied by

Keeping time of refrigerated foods

butter	unopened, several weeks; unwrapped, in a covered dish, a few days.
charcuterie	rillettes and pâtés in closed containers; ham and bacon in plastic wrap; sausages a few days.
cheese	cream and curd cheese in a closed container, 1–4 days; hard cheese, wrapped, up to 15 days; soft or fermented cheese (well wrapped to stop further maturing), up to 4 days (bring out 1 hour before needed).
cream	in a closed container, 2–4 days.
eggs	in closed containers or in egg boxes, preferably at the bottom of the refrigerator, away from the air which enters each time the door is opened, 2–3 weeks.
fish (cooked)	in a covered container, 1–2 days (baked or fried fish keeps longer than boiled).
fish (raw)	scaled, gutted, dried, in a covered container or a sealed bag, 1–2 days.
fruit (cooked)	in a closed container, a few days.
fruit (fresh)	redcurrants and cherries, washed and drained, in a closed container, a few days; strawberries, raspberries, plain or sugared, in a closed container, a few days.
meat (cooked)	in a covered container, 1–3 days (roast meat keeps longer than stews or casseroles).
meat (raw)	in plastic wrap or foil, not airtight, 3–4 days (may be kept in the defrosting compartment); avoid cutting the meat into small pieces; offal, 1–2 days.
milk	in a narrow-necked container or a closed bottle, standing upright, 3–4 days.
poultry and game	plucked and drawn, wrapped in foil, 2–3 days.
shellfish	large varieties wrapped in plastic wrap, small ones (shrimps) in a closed container, 1–2 days.
vegetables (cooked)	in closed containers, above the salad drawer, a few days.
vegetables (fresh)	leeks, carrots, lettuce, cabbage, fennel: cleaned, washed, but not completely drained, in the salad drawer or in plastic bags, 1 week; chicory (endives), not washed, in a plastic bag, 1 week; tomatoes, aubergines (eggplants), courgettes (zucchini), to delay ripening only, in the salad drawer, 1 week; parsley, chervil, washed and drained, in closed containers, 1 week; shelled peas, in a closed container, as short a time as possible; mushrooms, cleaned and half-cooked, in a closed container, 1–3 days; blanched spinach, in a closed container, 2 days; potatoes, turnips, and onions should not be put in the refrigerator.

REMARKS:
- Never put hot food in the refrigerator; only refrigerate preserved foods for a few hours, when they are required to be served very cold.
- Do not refrigerate fresh minced (ground) meat more than 1 day.
- Do not overcrowd the refrigerator: the air must always be able to circulate freely.
- Take prewrapped foods out of their packaging and rewrap in food bags or in foil.
- Do not keep acidic foods in metal containers once they have been opened.

hand, then the thermostat cuts in again automatically), or fully automatically.

The inner cabinet of the refrigerator may be in plastic, painted steel, enamelled steel, stainless steel, or aluminium. The interior temperatures range from −1 to 8 c (30–46 f). The coldest area is at the top, and raw meat and fish should be placed there.

régalade (à la)

Describing a method of drinking which consists of pouring the liquid into the mouth without letting the container (usually a flask or a long-necked wine bottle) touch the lips. The word originates from the Old French *gale* (making merry), from which *régaler* (to regale, entertain) also derives.

Régence

The name given to various elaborate dishes associated with the style of cooking of the Regency period in France. Régence garnish consists of quenelles (fish, poultry, or veal, according to the main dish), poached mushroom caps, and slivers of truffle. Poached oysters may be added for fish dishes, and slices of foie gras for meat, offal, or poultry dishes; fish dishes are masked with normande sauce flavoured with truffle essence, and meat dishes with a suprême or allemande sauce. Régence sauce was formerly served with calves' sweetbreads and poached or braised fowl.

RECIPES

Calves' sweetbreads Régence RIS DE VEAU RÉGENCE Prepare the sweetbreads, stud them with truffles, and braise them in white stock. Meanwhile, make some large chicken quenelles with truffles and sauté some slices of foie gras in butter. Prepare an allemande sauce using the reduced braising liquor from the sweetbreads. Arrange the sweetbreads on a hot dish and surround them with the quenelles and foie gras slices. Garnish with slivers of truffle tossed in butter and coat with the sauce.

Régence sauce Coarsely dice 100 g (4 oz) lean ham and cut 1 onion into quarters; melt 50 g (2 oz, ¼ cup) butter in a saucepan and cook the ham and onion without letting them brown. When the onion is almost cooked, add 1 sliced shallot. Deglaze the pan with 1 dl (6 tablespoons, scant ½ cup) Graves wine; reduce by two-thirds, then add 2 dl (7 fl oz, generous ¾ cup) white chicken stock. Reduce further until the sauce coats the back of a spoon, then strain.

regrater REGRATTIER

A person who used to buy food from great houses and restaurants for resale. The food might consist of cooked dishes, leftover meat, pieces of pastry or cake, etc. The word comes from the French *gratter* (to collect); it is now obsolete in English. In his book *La Vie privée d'autrefois*, Alfred Franklin describes this ancient trade, originally an honourable one, which had by the 19th century fallen to dealing in restaurant surplus and scraps. During the 14th century the regraters were almost comparable to modern grocers: 'If the housewife is in a hurry, and will put up with having less choice and paying a little more, she can get nearly all her shopping from the same place by going to the regraters, who sell everything and who are supplied by the residents and the convents of the district. There she can buy bread, salt, eggs, cheese, vegetables, sea fish, poultry, and game.' It was only with the introduction of restaurants in the 18th century that regraters began to specialize in the resale of leftover cooked dishes.

reguigneu

A speciality from the region of Avignon and Arles consisting of a slice of raw or cooked ham dipped into beaten egg and fried. Mistral defines it as: "a *riblette*, a slice of pork which is grilled (broiled) or fried' (*riblettes* were formerly thin slices of grilled or fried meat used as garnish for a large cut). He also applied the name *reguigneu* to a plain bacon omelette. This Provençal word probably comes from *reguignar*, meaning 'to wrinkle' or 'to shrivel', referring to the appearance of a piece of meat that has been quickly fried.

reheat RÉCHAUFFER

To bring a food back to the correct temperature for eating when it has already been cooked, but has been chilled or cooled. A bain-marie heated either on top of the stove or in the oven can be used for this purpose. Some cooked foods, vegetables for instance, can be reheated by putting them in a strainer and immersing them for a few minutes in salted or unsalted boiling water. Other foods (e.g. gratins or quenelles) may be reheated in a serving dish in a cool oven; stewed foods can be reheated in a saucepan over a how leat, and sautéed dishes are reheated over a high heat with added fat.

A liquid or semisolid food (soup, sauce, salpicon, etc.) can be warmed up over a moderate heat, with a wire gauze between flame and pan, and stirred constantly. It is extremely important when reheating food to watch it closely to ensure that it does not boil, dry out, or stick to the pan. Some dishes requiring long slow cooking improve when reheated and can be prepared one or two days in advance (daubes, braised dishes, etc.). Cans and jars of food are usually reheated in a bain-marie; for a frozen dish the best method of reheating is in a microwave oven.

Reims biscuit

BISCUIT DE REIMS

A small light crunchy rectangular biscuit cookie), generously dusted with sugar, 'created at the end of the 18th century by bakers wishing to make use of a hot oven after baking bread. The biscuit was originally white; it was only later that biscuit manufacturers decided to colour it pink and flavour it with vanilla. Note that the natives of Reims disdain to use the pink biscuits, preferring the white ones which retain all their natural flavour.' (Charles Sarrazin, *La France à table*). The Reims biscuit was intended to accompany champagne, which at that time was very sweet.

RECIPE

Reims biscuits BISCUITS DE REIMS Beat together in a frying pan (skillet) over a gentle heat (or in a bainmarie) 300 g (11 oz, 1½ cups) caster (superfine) sugar, 10 egg yolks, and 12 egg whites, until firm and evenly mixed. Fold in 180 g (6 oz, 1½ cups) sifted flour and 1 tablespoon vanilla sugar. Using a smooth piping nozzle, pipe the mixture onto buttered greaseproof (waxed) paper into finger shapes, well separated from each other. Bake in a preheated oven at approximately 180 C (350 F, gas 4) for about 10 minutes.

reindeer RENNE

A large deer found in Arctic regions. Reindeer milk, like whale milk, has a very high fat content; it is used to make cheese in Lapland, Norway, and Sweden. The Lapps rear reindeer, under free-range conditions, for both their milk and their meat. Venison from wild reindeer is cooked in the same way as roebuck; the meat from animals fed on grain and hay has a sweeter taste. The meat is also used to make meatballs and is cooked as steaks or in stews.

reine (à la)

A term applied to a number of elegant and delicate dishes from classic French cuisine, characterized by the presence of chicken (often with calves' sweetbreads, mushrooms, and truffles) with suprême sauce. *Reine* is the traditional name for a bird classed between a *poulet de grain* (see *chicken*) and a *poularde* (caponized hen).

The term *à la reine* is also applied to a very light milk-bread roll.

RECIPES

Chicken à la reine POULARDE À LA REINE Prepare 500 g (18 oz) panada forcemeat with butter and use it to stuff a chicken weighing about 1.8 kg (4 lb). Poach it gently in white stock. Bake some puff-pastry tartlet cases and fill them with chicken purée with cream; garnish with sliced truffles. Make a suprême sauce with the chicken stock. Arrange the chicken on a large hot serving dish and place the tartlets round it. Serve the suprême sauce separately.

Consommé à la reine Make some chicken consommé and some plain royale. Poach some chicken breasts in court-bouillon and shred the meat finely. Thicken the consommé with tapioca. Garnish the soup with the royale cut into dice or lozenges and the shredded chicken.

Croûtes à la reine Prepare some chicken purée with cream. Cut some slices from a white loaf and lightly fry in butter. Spread the croûtes with the purée, sprinkle with white breadcrumbs and clarified butter, and brown in a very hot oven.

Scrambled eggs à la reine OEUFS BROUILLÉS À LA REINE Make some very thick chicken purée and some suprême sauce. Bake a large vol-au-vent case blind and keep it hot. Make some scrambled eggs. Fill the vol-au-vent case with alternate layers of chicken purée and scrambled eggs. Serve hot, with the suprême sauce in a sauceboat.

Stuffed tomatoes à la reine TOMATES FARCIES À LA REINE Slice the tops off some large firm tomatoes; scoop out the seeds and core without breaking the skin. Make a salpicon of equal quantities of chicken breast poached in white stock and mushrooms sweated in butter; add a little diced truffle and thicken with some very thick velouté sauce. Stuff the tomatoes with this mixture and place in a buttered gratin dish. Sprinkle with fresh breadcrumbs and clarified butter and cook in a very hot oven for 10–15 minutes.

Réjane

The stage name of the great actress Gabrielle Réju (born Paris, 1856; died Paris, 1920), which has been given to various dishes. The Réjane garnish (for small pieces of sautéed meat or braised calves' sweetbreads) consists of cassolettes of duchess potatoes (which act as containers for the meat), buttered leaf spinach, quarters of steamed artichokes, and slices of poached bone marrow; the sauce consists of the braising stock or the pan juices deglazed with Madeira.

In a Réjane salad, sliced potatoes are mixed with asparagus tips and a julienne of truffles. Paupiettes of whiting Réjane, arranged on a base of duchess potatoes, are each garnished with a small metal skewer bearing an oyster, a mushroom cap, a slice of truffle, and a prawn (shrimp).

réjouissance

Traditionally, a bone or a piece of cheap meat that butchers used to include free with a purchase. According to Littré, the origin of the word (which means literally 'rejoicing') is linked to an order from Henri IV stipulating that meat should be sold boned, with the cost of the bones shared out among more expensive purchases. This order was greeted 'with rejoicing' by the common people, buyers of the cheaper cuts.

religieuse

A cake classically consisting of a large chou (filled with coffee- or chocolate-flavoured confectioners' custard (pastry cream) or Chiboust cream) surmounted by a smaller chou, similarly filled; the whole is iced (frosted) with fondant (the same flavour as the filling) and decorated with piped butter cream. The religieuse can be made either as a large cake or as small individual cakes. In one former version, the choux pastry was cooked in the form of éclairs, rings, or buns, filled with coffee or chocolate cream, and stacked on top of each other or arranged in a pyramid on a base of sweet pastry; the whole was then decorated with piped butter cream. Religieuse is a fairly recent invention, which originated in Paris. The name comes from the colour of the icing, which resembles the homespun robe worn by nuns.

Less frequently, the name is given to a puff-pastry tart filled with apple and apricot jams and raisins, and decorated with a lattice of pastry strips, recalling a convent grille.

RECIPES

Coffee religieuses RELIGIEUSES AU CAFÉ Make some choux pastry (see *chou*) with 2.5 dl (8 fl oz, 1 cup) water, a pinch of salt, 65 g (2½ oz, 5 tablespoons) butter, 1 teaspoon sugar, 125 g (4½ oz, generous 1 cup) flour, and 3 or 4 eggs. Pipe bun shapes onto a baking sheet so that half of them are twice the size of the others. Bake in a moderately hot oven (200 C, 400 F, gas 6) for 30 minutes then leave to cool in the oven with the door ajar.

Make some butter cream with 4 egg yolks, 125 g (4½ oz, generous ½ cup) caster sugar, 5 cl (3 tablespoons, scant ¼ cup) water, 125 g (4½ oz, generous

½ cup) creamed butter, and 1 teaspoon vanilla sugar.

Prepare some Chiboust cream with 6 egg yolks, 200 g (7 oz, scant 1 cup) caster (superfine) sugar, 75 g (3 oz, ¾ cup) flour or 60 g (2 oz) cornflour (cornstarch), 1 litre (1¾ pints, 4¼ cups) milk, 4 leaves of gelatine, and 4 egg whites. Flavour it with ½ teaspoon coffee essence (strong black coffee) and allow to cool completely. Fill all the choux pastries with the Chiboust cream.

Melt 400 g (14 oz) fondant icing (frosting), flavour it with ½ teaspoon coffee essence, and use it to ice all the choux pastries. Before the icing sets, stick the small buns onto the larger ones. Using a piping (pastry) bag with a fluted nozzle, decorate the top of each cake with a rosette of butter cream, then run a ribbon of butter cream around the joint of the 2 buns. Keep in a cool place until ready to serve.

Grande religieuse à l'ancienne Make some sweet pastry with 125 g (4½ oz, generous cup flour, 1 egg yolk, a pinch of salt, 35 g (1¼ oz, 2½ tablespoons) caster (superfine) sugar, and 60 g (2 oz, 4 tablespoons) butter cut into small pieces. Roll the pastry into a ball and leave it in a cool place.

Make some choux pastry (see *chou*) with 2.5 dl (8 fl oz, 1 cup) water, 65 g (2½ oz, 5 tablespoons) butter, a pinch of salt, 1 teaspoon sugar, 125 g (4½ oz, generous cup) flour, and 3 or 4 eggs. Using a piping (pastry) bag with a smooth nozzle, 1 cm (½ in) in diameter, pipe onto a baking sheet 12 strips 10 cm (4 in) long, 1 small round bun, and 4 rings decreasing in size from a diameter of 16 cm (6 in). Bake in a moderately hot oven (200 C, 400 F, gas 6) for 30 minutes, then leave to cool in the oven with the door ajar.

Meanwhile, butter a deep 19-cm (7-in) sandwich tin (layer cake pan), using 25 g (about 1 oz) butter. Roll out the sweet pastry to a thickness of 3 mm (⅛ in) and use it to line the sandwich tin; prick the bottom, cover with dried haricot (navy) beans, and bake blind for 10 minutes. Remove the beans, leave to cool, then turn it out of the tin.

Prepare some butter cream by boiling 5 cl (3 tablespoons, ¼ cup) water with 125 g (4½ oz, generous ½ cup) caster sugar; when the temperature reaches 107 C (225 F), pour slowly onto 4 egg yolks and whisk briskly until the mixture is cold; then whisk in 150 g (5 oz) creamed butter.

Prepare some Chiboust cream with 6 egg yolks, 200 g (7 oz, scant cup) caster sugar, 75 g (3 oz, ¾ cup) cornflour (cornstarch), 1 litre (1¾ pints, 4¼ cups) milk, 4 leaves of gelatine, and 4 egg whites. Mix half of this cream with 50 g (2 oz) melted chocolate and the other half with ½ teaspoon coffee essence (strong black coffee). Slit all the cooked choux pastries: into half of them pipe a filling of the chocolate cream and into the other half pipe the coffee cream.

Put 200 g (7 oz) fondant icing (frosting) into a saucepan with 1 tablespoon water and heat to 40 C (104 F), stirring constantly; add 50 g (2 oz) melted chocolate. Prepare the same quantity of fondant flavoured with ½ teaspoon coffee essence. Ice the éclairs, rings, and bun with the fondant corresponding to their filling. Boil 150 g (5 oz, ⅔ cup, firmly packed) sugar in 5 cl (3 tablespoons, scant ¼ cup) water; when the temperature reaches 145 C (293 F) brush the syrup over the bottom of the éclairs. Stick these together side by side vertically inside the pastry base, alternating the flavours, then put the 4 rings on top, beginning with the largest; place the bun at the very top. Using a fluted nozzle, pipe the butter cream along the joints of the éclairs, the rings, and the bun.

relish

A condiment, originating in India, which resembles chutney but is more highly spiced. It is a sweet-and-sour purée made from sour fruits and vegetables, with the addition of small pickled onions, gherkins, spices (mainly ginger, chilli pepper, cinnamon, white pepper, cloves, and nutmeg), which are simmered with soft brown sugar (coffee sugar) and vinegar. Relishes are served with curries and other oriental dishes and also with hamburgers, crudités, and cold meats.

Remoudou

A Belgian cows'-milk cheese with a fat content of 45%; it has a soft curd and a piquant flavour. The name is derived from the German *Rahm*, meaning 'fresh cream'. The cheese is made in the town of Battice and dates from the time of Charles V. La Confrérie du Remoudou undertakes the promotion of all dairy products from the plain of Herve. The German cheese Romadour is similar, as is Romalour from Lorraine, which Zola mentions in *Le Ventre de Paris*: 'the Romantour (*sic*) wrapped in its silver paper'.

rémoulade

A cold sauce made by adding mustard, gherkins, capers, and chopped herbs to mayonnaise; it is sometimes finished with a little anchovy essence, and chopped hard-boiled (hard-cooked) egg may be included. Its name may originate from the Picardy word *rémola*, meaning 'black radish', even though radish is not an ingredient. Rémoulade can accompany cold meat, fish, and shellfish; it sometimes appears as a simple mustard-flavoured mayonnaise spiced with garlic and pepper, and in this version is the traditional accompaniment of grated celeriac (celery root) and various mixed salads.

| RECIPE

Rémoulade sauce Make some mayonnaise with 2.5 dl (8 fl oz, 1 cup) oil, replacing, if desired, the raw egg yolk with 1 hard-boiled (hard-cooked) egg yolk rubbed through a fine sieve. Add 2 very finely diced gherkins, 2 tablespoons (3 tablespoons) chopped herbs (parsley, chives, chervil, and tarragon), 1 tablespoon drained capers, and (optional) a few drops of anchovy essence.

remove   RELEVÉ

In the days when food was served in the grand manner, this was a dish which 'came to remove' (i.e. followed) another, usually the soup. Grimod de La Reynière distinguishes between ordinary entrées and 'grosses' (large) entrées. The latter came to be called *relevés*, he says, because 'when they arrived, the soup was removed, being at each end of the table'. As examples, he gives stuffed top loin of veal with cream, calf's head *à la financière*, and a large

freshwater fish, served with sauce and garnish. This was the order of a classic menu: hors d'oeuvres; soups; relevés of the soups; fish (providing that fish was not one of the relevé dishes); relevés of fish (later eliminated); roasts, sometimes followed by relevés of roasts; and finally desserts.

Renaissance (à la)

A cookery term describing a large braised or roast cut of meat or a roast or poached chicken that is garnished with small heaps of different vegetables, such as glazed carrots and turnips (cut out with a melon baller and sometimes arranged on artichoke hearts), fondant or fried potatoes, braised lettuce, French (green) beans, asparagus tips, and cauliflower florets. The accompanying sauce is made from the meat juices or the braising stock; suprême sauce is served with chicken poached in white stock.

rennet   PRÉSURE

An extract from the stomach (abomasum) of calves and lambs which contains the enzyme rennin, which brings about the coagulation of milk. Rennet is indispensable in the manufacture of cheese and for making junket. For some French cheeses made in country regions, vegetable rennets are used: these are milk-coagulating substances obtained from certain plants, such as cardoon.

repère

A soft paste made from flour and water, used to make an airtight seal between casserole and lid prior to cooking (see *lute*).

The term also means a mixture of flour and egg white used to stick decorations onto a cake or dish (it is advisable to warm the dish before sticking on the decorations).

réserve

A word that is applied to any wine of quality in France, although it has no legal definition. Equivalents in other countries include *riserva* (Italy) and *reserva* (Spain).

reserve   RESERVER

To put aside ingredients, mixtures, or preparations, either hot or cold, for later use. Food can be kept hot in a bain-marie, over a low heat, or in a cool oven. The refrigerator is the best place to keep items cold. To ensure that food is not spoiled it may be wrapped in greaseproof (waxed) paper, kitchen foil, a cloth, etc. To prevent a skin forming on a cream or a sauce, the surface is covered with buttered paper or with fat (see *tamponner*). Pastry dough is covered with a cloth and kept cold to prevent a crust from forming. Certain cooked vegetables can be put in a dish and covered with a cloth to keep warm. Peeled potatoes can be kept immersed in cold water for a short time before cooking.

rest REPOSER

To put a dough or batter to one side in a cool place as part of its preparation. Pastry must be left to rest for at least an hour before it is used: it is rolled into a ball and wrapped in a cloth or kitchen foil, then left in the refrigerator or in a cool place away from draughts.

restaurant

An establishment where meals are served between set hours, either from a fixed menu or *à la carte*. The word appeared in the 16th century and meant at first 'a food which restores' (from *restaurer*, to restore), and was used more specifically for a rich highly flavoured soup capable of restoring lost strength. The 18th-century gastronome Brillat-Savarin referred to chocolate, red meat, and consommé as *restaurants*. From this sense, which survived until the 19th century, the word developed the meaning of 'an establishment specializing in the sale of restorative foods' (*Dictionnaire de Trévoux*, 1771).

Until the late 18th century, the only places for ordinary people to eat out were inns and taverns. (See *caterer, table d'hôte*) In about 1765, a Parisian 'bouillon-seller' named Boulanger wrote on his sign: 'Boulanger sells restoratives fit for the gods', with a motto in dog Latin: *Venite ad me omnes qui stomacho laboretis, et ego restaurabo vos* (Come unto me, all you whose stomachs are aching, and I will restore you). This was the first restaurant in the modern sense of the term. Boulanger

was followed by Roze and Pontaillé, who in 1766 opened a *maison de santé* (house of health). However, the first Parisian restaurant worthy of the name was the one founded by Beauvilliers in 1782 in the Rue de Richelieu, called the Grande Taverne de Londres. He introduced the novelty of listing the dishes available on a menu and serving them at small individual tables during fixed hours.

One beneficial effect of the Revolution was that the abolition of the guilds and their privileges made it easier to open a restaurant. The first to take advantage of the situation were the cooks and servants from the great houses, whose aristocratic owners had fled. Moreover, the arrival in Paris of numerous provincials who had no family in the capital created a pool of faithful customers, augmented by journalists and businessmen. The general feeling of wellbeing under the Directory, following such a chaotic period, coupled with the chance of enjoying the delights of the table hitherto reserved for the rich, created an atmosphere in which restaurants became an established institution.

To a certain extent, the restaurateurs guided their customers' tastes, as shown by Grimod de La Reynié's *Almanach des gourmands*, with its 'good addresses'; it was the first gastronomic guide of Paris and listed about a hundred restaurants. Fashion favoured various parts of the capital in turn: after the Palais-Royal, with such establishments as Méot, the Boeuf à la mode, the Frères Provençaux, and the Grand Véfour, came Les Halles (with the illustrious Rocher de Cancale); then it was the turn of the Grands Boulevards (Very, Hardy, Riche, etc.), the Madeleine (with Larue, Voisin, Maxim's), the Champs Élysées (Fouquet's, Laurent), the Villette, Bercy, then Montparnasse and the Left Bank (Lapérouse, the Tour d'Argent, Allard), along with Clichy and the heights of Montmartre.

Nowadays, a distinction can be made between the large restaurants, which employ a chef, and those with an owner-manager who does the cooking him- or herself.

In Paris, as in the provinces, the 20th

century has seen a tendency towards standardization and even Americanization of the restaurant trade, as evinced by snackbars, motorway pull-ins (highway rest-stops), cafeterias, takeaways, etc. In spite of this, restaurants still offer great scope for creativity. They provide both a testing ground for new ideas and a haven for more traditional recipes.

The great regional restaurants were established, in many cases, at former mail staging posts. Still near to tourist routes, and rediscovered by such gourmets as Curnonsky and M. Rouff, these establishments counterbalance the reputation of the temples of *haute cuisine*, which are the pride of Paris. In his book *Voyages gastronomiques au pays de France* (1925), J.-A. P. Cousin classifies Parisian restaurants into categories: 'perfection' (Foyot, Larue, Lapérouse, the Tour d'Argent, Voisin, and Paillard); 'the last word' (Prosper Montagné); 'very high class' (Café de Paris, Pré Catelan, Ritz, etc.); 'smart' (Laurent, Maxim's, Noël Peters, the Cascade, etc.); 'reliable' (the Boeuf à la Mode, Drouant, Lucas, Maire, Marguery, etc.); 'savoury and plentiful' (Dagorno, Jouanne, L'Escargot Montorgueil, Pharamond, etc.); and finally 'good little places' and 'good atmosphere' (the Bon Bock, the Boeuf sur le Toit, the Lapin Agile, Ramponneau, the Rotonde). He also lists wine merchants, grillrooms, inns, regional and foreign restaurants (Chinese, British, Greek, Dutch, Italian, Mexican, Russian, Swedish, and Swiss), and finally the fish bars (Prunier). In modern guides these categories are signified by means of symbols, such as crowns, stars, or crossed knives and forks. Nowadays, however, great chefs are also found in the provinces, especially since the reign of the 'three greats' (Point, Pic, and Dumaine). Tradition is giving way to new methods, such as the *service à l'assiette* (plate service) introduced in the 1960s.

There are also plenty of bistros, bars, and cafés, many of them extremely modest, where the food is simple and honest and which often specialize in one or two dishes – for example, pike *au beurre blanc de la mère Michel* or omelette *de la mère Poulard*. Other such specialities may include pieds et paquets

à la marseillaise, tripe *à la mode de Caen*, and entrecôte *marchand de vin*.

Today, restaurants are developing along two lines: on the one hand, they are attempting to fulfil their original function by feeding more and more city workers, many of whom do not go home during their lunch hour. The catering offered by works canteens and restaurants is supplemented by bars, cafés, self-service restaurants, pizzerias, etc. On the other hand, the top-ranking restaurants continue to provide their customers with luxurious surroundings, great wines, rare delicacies, and all the refinements of the culinary art.

rétès

A Hungarian pastry similar to the Austrian strudel. The dough is made from strong high-gluten flour and is stretched until very thin (the saying goes that it should be possible to read a faded love letter through the dough). It is then covered with any of various fillings, rolled up, baked, and cut into slices, which are served dusted with icing (confectioners') sugar. Suitable fillings include: cream cheese with raisins and beaten egg whites; apple jam flavoured with cinnamon; cooked cherries or plums; grated walnuts with sugar, lemon, raisins, and milk; and a cream made from poppy seeds cooked in milk and sugar, with grated apple, lemon zest, and sultanas.

retsina

A wine made in Greece and the Greek islands, either white or rosé and strongly flavoured with pine resin – hence its name. People either love it or loathe it.

Reuilly

A small region, producing AOC wines, in Berry, around the upper reaches of the River Loire, where white, red, and rosé wines are made. The whites are made from the Sauvignon grape, the others from the Pinot Noir and Pinot Gris.

réveillon

See *Christmas*.

revesset

A green bouillabaisse made in the

Toulon area, originally from Revest-les-Eaux; it contains a variety of small shore fish and tiny sardines and anchovies, with spinach, sorrel, and Swiss chard instead of potatoes.

Rhine wines
VINS DU RHIN

Rhine wines include some from the finest wine-producing regions of West Germany: the Rheingau, the Rheinhessen, and the Palatinate (or Pfalz), all in the central region of the River Rhine's course. Nearly all the wine is white, the most famous grape being the Riesling and, in some places, the Silvaner (as it is spelled on German labels); however, the renowned German wine institutes have evolved many successful crosses (such as the Müller-Thurgau, now very widely planted), which are both resistant to disease and able to withstand the cold of this northern wine-growing region.

RHEINGAU – This region has sometimes been called the German Riviera, and the vineyards, mostly in the finest sites on south-facing slopes and planted with Riesling grapes, produce many remarkable white wines. Some of these, in the higher-quality categories, have been affected by the 'noble rot' (*Botrytis cinerea*), and are outstanding and delicately luscious, the dryer wines being markedly fruity and all having a wonderful bouquet. In the Ahr Valley some red wines are made, the most famous being produced at Assmannshausen, on the Rhine itself.

RHEINHESSEN – Some very fine wines are produced here, but many are only of good average quality. This is the place of origin of much Liebfraumilch, and in addition to the Riesling grape, the Müller-Thurgau and Silvaner are also grown.

PALATINATE (PFALZ) – 'Cellar of the Holy Roman Empire' is the tag sometimes given to this region. A small amount of red wine is made, but the majority is white and some outstanding estates and growers have made their wines famous. In this region, as with the others, a wide range of different categories of wine are made, but in general many of the finer Palatinate wines have a substance, combined with delicacy, that makes it possible to drink them with food. The region itself is very picturesque and the vineyards (except those making the very finest wines) extend to the French frontier.

rhubarb RHUBARBE

A hardy perennial plant, originally from northern Asia, whose fleshy stalks are used as a pie filling or to make jams or compotes. It was the English who first introduced rhubarb to the kitchen: until the 18th century it was regarded as a medicinal and ornamental plant. The normal growing season lasts from May to July, but early forced rhubarb is delicious, bright pink, and tender; it is available from January to April. With a calorific value of only 16 Cal per 100 g, rhubarb is very sour and must always be sweetened. It contains phosphorus, potassium, magnesium, iron, and vitamins. The leaves contain a large amount of oxalic acid and should not be eaten.

There are many varieties of rhubarb, with stalks ranging from green to varying shades of mauve. The stalks should be firm, thick, and crisp and release sap when snapped. They will keep for some days in a cool place, but quickly become soft; however, rhubarb freezes well.

Rhubarb jams and compotes are often flavoured with lemon zest or ginger. The compote may also accompany fish, and rhubarb can be made into chutneys. An Italian apéritif, Rabarbaro, is made from rhubarb.

RECIPES

Rhubarb jam CONFITURE DE RHUBARBE Carefully strip the stringy fibres from some fresh rhubarb stalks, then cut up the stalks. For every kg (2¼ lb) rhubarb, put 800 g (1¾ lb) granulated sugar and ½ glass (4 fl oz, ½ cup) water into a saucepan and bring to the boil. Cook for 8 minutes, then add the rhubarb and poach it very gently until the pieces disintegrate. Then bring to a fast boil and cook until setting point is reached. Pot in the usual way (see *jams, jellies, and marmalades*).

Rhubarb pie PIE À LA RHUBARBE Make 300 g (11 oz) lining pastry (see *doughs and batters*), shape it into a ball, and leave it to rest for at least 2 hours. Roll it out to a thickness of about 3 mm (⅛ in) and cut out a piece to cover the pie dish, and also a strip to go around the edge of the dish. Remove any stringy fibres from the rhubarb and cut it into pieces 4 cm (1½ in) long. Put the rhubarb in the buttered pie dish and sprinkle with caster (superfine) sugar or soft brown sugar (coffee sugar), using 250 g (9 oz, generous cup) sugar for 750 g (1¾ lb) rhubarb; moisten with ⅓ glass (2–3 tablespoons) water.

Cover the edge of the pie dish with the strip of pastry, brush it with beaten egg, then place the pastry lid over the dish, pressing down at the edges. Decorate the lid with a diamond-shaped design, brush with egg, then sprinkle lightly with caster sugar. Insert a small pie funnel in the lid for the steam to escape, and bake the pie in a moderately hot oven (200 c, 400 f, gas 6) for 40–45 minutes.

Take the dish out of the oven, remove the funnel, and pour in some whipping cream; alternatively, this can be served separately.

rhyton

An antique drinking vessel made in the shape of the horn, head, or forepart of an animal, in use as long ago as 2000 bc. It was filled through a hole in the upper part, and the drinker could direct a stream of the drink from this hole into his mouth; more often, the contents were poured into a cup or other receptacle. It lacked a flat base, so the drinker was obliged to drain it before putting it down. Rhytons were also made of pottery, bronze, or some other metal; the finest were made of silver (in Crete) and gold (in Persia).

ribbon stage RUBAN

The stage in beating together egg yolks and caster (superfine) sugar when the mixture is sufficiently smooth and homogeneous for it to flow from the spoon or whisk in a continuous ribbon.

rice RIZ

Apart from wheat, this is the most widely cultivated cereal in the world, growing in tropical, equatorial, and temperate zones. Rice is always eaten cooked, either hot or cold, as a sweet or savoury dish. The largest consumers worldwide are China, India, Indonesia, Japan, and Bangladesh, followed by Latin America and Africa.

□ **History** Growing both on dry land and on swampy or irrigated land, rice was known and cultivated in China more than 3000 years ago. It seems, however, that the rice plant (*Oryza sativa*) may have originated in southern India, then spread to the north of the country and to China. Later it arrived in Korea, the Philippines (about 2000 bc), Japan, and Indonesia (1000 bc). The Persians imported rice to Mesopotamia and Turkestan, and Alexander the Great, who invaded India in 327 bc, brought it to Greece. Arab travellers encouraged the use of rice in Egypt, Morocco, and Spain, where it is more widely eaten than in France. Portugal and Holland introduced it into their colonies in west Africa from the 15th century onwards, and it reached America towards the end of the 17th century. Another species, *Oryza glaberrina*, was cultivated around 1500 bc in west Africa, from Senegal to the banks of the Niger, but it has been replaced by the Asian species.

It was the Crusaders who introduced rice into France, and various attempts were made to grow the cereal without much success, in spite of an edict issued by Sully in 1603. Since 1942, a relatively prosperous rice-growing area has been established in the Camargue, supplying about 20% of the national requirement. Imports to make up the balance come from the United States, Madagascar, and the Ivory Coast. Piedmont, in Italy, is also a major rice-producing area.

□ **Varieties, treatment, and products** There are two main types of rice: the subspecies *indica* (long-grain) which has long grains that remain separate when cooked, and the subspecies *japonica* (short-grain), with round grains that tend to stick together when cooked. There are also various intermediate types. Rice is classified according to the type of processing it receives after harvesting.

• *Paddy rice*: unhusked rice in its raw state, with no further treatment after threshing (contains 20–25% moisture).

• *Brown rice* (also known as *husked* or

whole rice): rice with the outer husk removed, having a characteristic beige colour; it is transported from the Far East to Europe in cargo ships; as only the outer husk is removed, the rice retains some of the B vitamins, phosphorus, and starch.

• *White rice*: brown rice from which the germ and the outer layers of the pericarp have been removed by passing the grains through machines that rasp the grain; it is also called unpolished rice.

• *Polished rice*: white rice that has been passed through machines that remove any flour still adhering to the grain.

• *Glacé rice*: polished rice covered with a fine layer of French chalk suspended in a glucose solution and specially processed to give it an attractive sheen.

• *Steamed* or *pretreated rice*: paddy rice that has been meticulously cleaned, soaked in hot water, steamed at a low pressure (leaving some of the nutritive elements), and then dehusked and blanched.

• *Precooked rice*: rice that has been husked or blanched, soaked, boiled for 1–3 minutes, then dried at 200 c (400 F). This and pretreated rice are the most popular varieties in France.

• *Camolino rice*: polished and lightly coated with oil.

• *Puffed rice*: in India it is roasted and fried on hot sand; in the United States it is subjected to heat at high pressure and then at low pressure.

• *Wild rice*: the seed of an aquatic grass, related to the rice plant, which comes from the northern United States. The seeds grow one by one up the stalk and resemble little black sticks; it is very expensive and is sometimes mixed with brown rice.

• *Basmati rice*: Indian rice with very small but long grains, with a distinctive flavour; 'old' Basmati, which is rarely available, is much prized by Indians and Pakistanis.

• *Surinam rice*: very long thin grains from Surinam; sought after by connoisseurs.

• *Perfumed rice*: long-grain rice from Vietnam and Thailand, with a distinctive taste; in Asia it is reserved for feast days.

• *Sticky rice*: long-grain rice with a very high starch content; rarely available, it is suitable for Chinese cookery (not to be confused with rice that has been badly cooked).

• *Carolina rice*: the name is no longer used to describe a particular variety; it used to be imported from the United States and was of a high quality.

• *Popped rice*: rice heated to 200 c (400 F) in oil, resembling popcorn.

• *Rice flakes*: rice that is steamed, husked, then flattened into thin flakes; it is eaten for breakfast, with milk and sugar.

• *Rice semolina, ground rice*, and *rice flour*: these are made by grinding fragments of very white rice; they are used in making cakes and pastries and to thicken sauces.

Rice is also the foundation of various alcoholic drinks: *choum* in Vietnam, *samau* in Malaysia, *sake* in Japan, *chao xing* in China (Chinese yellow or rice wine). Broken rice may sometimes be used to replace some of the malt in brewing; finally, rice bran yields an oil similar to groundnut (peanut) oil.

□ **Rice in dietetics** Rice has a very high calorific value (about 350 Cal per 100 g in whole rice, 120 Cal when blanched). It is rich in digestible starch (77%), but its proteins lack certain essential amino acids. The external layers contain vitamins B_1 and B_2 and minerals, and thus whole rice is nutritionally superior to white rice.

□ **Cooking and preparation** The amount of uncooked rice required per serving is 60–70 g (2½ oz, scant ½ cup) for a main dish, 25–30 g (1 oz, 2 tablespoons) for an hors d'oeuvre, and 40 g (1½ oz, 3 tablespoons) for a dessert. Rice is normally cooked in water, meat stock, or milk. Long-grain rice and pretreated rice are best cooked in water (the grains remain separate and retain their flavour). The former can also be sautéed in fat, but pretreated rice should not be fried, as it is too dry. Round-grain rice is best reserved for dessert dishes, as it has thickening properties and holds together.

Rice can absorb a great deal of liquid and will soak up water, milk, oil, or stock according to the recipe. The whole art of cooking rice is to ensure that the grains remain a little firm (*al dente*) but not hard, that they are separate, and that they retain their flavour (these criteria do not apply to rice cooked in milk). Unless it is precooked or pre-treated, rice should always be washed in running water and drained well before being cooked. There are four different methods of cooking rice:

• *In water* – The rice is poured into the pan with twice its volume of cold water, brought to the boil, and cooked with the pan covered until all the water is absorbed. Alternatively, it can be poured into a large quantity of boiling water (3 litres (5 pints, 6½ pints) per kg (2¼ lb, 5 cups) rice), brought back to the boil, cooked uncovered, then drained. Yet another method is to pour the rice into boiling salted water, simmer for 10 minutes, wash in cold water, drain, and put in a covered dish in a cool oven until cooking is complete. Rice cooked in water, termed *à la créole* or *à l'indienne*, is particularly suitable for mixed salads and as a garnish for meat or fish.

• *Steamed* – The rice, previously washed in cold water, is placed in a steamer over boiling water for 20–40 minutes (according to the variety); sometimes it is blanched for a few minutes before being placed in the steamer. Alternatively, the rinsed rice may be put into a saucepan with 1½ times its volume of water, brought to the boil, and cooked with the pan tightly sealed until all the water has been absorbed. Steamed rice is eaten plain or as a garnish.

• *Au gras* – This method of cooking rice is used for pilaf, risotto, paella, or rice *à la grecque*; the rice is first gently fried in fat, then twice its volume of stock or water is added, and cooking is continued until all the liquid is absorbed.

• *In milk* – This is the standard way of cooking all rice desserts. The rice is blanched in boiling water, rinsed, drained, and cooked slowly in milk, which may be flavoured in some way, until it attains the consistency of a creamy paste. It is then garnished, moulded, or flavoured in various ways.

There are numerous recipes based on rice. The most important rice dishes are risotto, pilaf, paella, and curry, but rice is also the traditional garnish for grilled

(broiled) fish, kebabs and other preparations cooked on skewers, blanquette of veal, and chicken poached in white stock (where the rice is cooked in the same stock). Rice is also an ingredient of mixed salads, garnished with fish, seafood, raw vegetables, black (ripe) olives, ham, etc., and is used as a stuffing for vegetables (tomatoes, aubergines (eggplants), peppers, and vine leaves). It may be used to garnish or thicken soups and, of course, it is the basis of the Dutch rijsttafel.

Among the desserts are rice cakes and rings garnished with fruit (Condé, *à l'impératrice*), rice tarts and moulds, and rice pudding. It may also be an ingredient in croquettes, subrics, and other desserts.

RECIPES

Savoury Rice Dishes

Boiled rice with butter RIZ AU BLANC Put 250 g (9 oz, 1¼ cups) washed and drained long-grain rice into a saucepan, cover with cold water, and add 2 teaspoons salt per litre (1¾ pints, 4¼ cups) water. Bring to the boil, cover the pan, and simmer for a maximum of 15 minutes. Drain and refresh the rice under running water, drain again, and pour it into a casserole. Add 50–75 g (2–3 oz, 4–6 tablespoons) butter cut into small pieces and mix gently with the rice. Cover the dish and place in the oven at 200 C (400 F, gas 6) for 15 minutes. Serve very hot, as a garnish.

Rice à la créole RIZ À LA CRÉOLE Thoroughly wash 500 g (18 oz, 2½ cups) long-grain rice and pour it into a sauté pan. Add salt and enough water to come 2 cm (¾ in) above the level of the rice. Bring to the boil and continue to boil rapidly with the pan uncovered. When the water has boiled down to the same level as the rice, cover the pan, and cook very gently until the rice is completely dry (about 45 minutes). The second part of the cooking process may be carried out in a cool oven.

Rice à la grecque RIZ À LA GREC-QUE Heat 3 tablespoons (4 tablespoons) olive oil in a pan until very hot, add 250 g (9 oz, 1¼ cups) unwashed long-grain rice, and stir with a wooden spoon until the grains become transparent. Then add 2½ times its volume of boiling water, a handful of raisins, salt and pepper, a small bouquet garni, a chopped onion, and a small chopped clove of garlic. Lower the heat, cover the pan, and leave to simmer for 16 minutes. Remove the bouquet garni. If wished, 2 tablespoons (3 tablespoons) finely diced red pepper (which has been cooked in butter or oil) and 1 cup peas (cooked in water and well drained) may be added to the rice.

Rice au gras RIZ AU GRAS Pour 250 g (9 oz, 1¼ cups) long-grain rice into boiling salted water, leave for 5 minutes, then drain and refresh under cold running water. Heat 30 g (1 oz, 2 tablespoons) butter in a flameproof casserole, add the rice, and mix well. Then cover with twice its volume of rather fatty stock (beef or chicken). Bring to the boil on the hob, then cover the dish and place it in the oven at 220 C (425 F, gas 7) for 20 minutes.

SWEET RICE DISHES

Rice cooked in milk RIZ AU LAIT SIMPLE Cook 200 g (7 oz, 1 cup) washed round-grain rice for 2 minutes in boiling salted water. Drain and pour it into 9 dl (1½ pints, 2 pints) boiling milk. Add 70 g (3 oz, 6 tablespoons, firmly packed) caster (superfine) sugar, a pinch of salt, and either a pinch of cinnamon or a vanilla pod (bean). Cover the pan and cook over a very low heat for 30–40 minutes. Add 50 g (2 oz, ¼ cup) butter, and, if desired, 2 or 3 egg yolks. Serve either warm or chilled.

Rice cooked in milk for ring moulds and cakes RIZ AU LAIT POUR BORDURES ET GÂTEAUX Blanch 200 g (7 oz, 1 cup) round-grain rice in boiling water for 2 minutes. Drain, refresh under cold running water, and drain again. Bring 9 dl (1½ pints, 2 pints) milk to the boil, add ½ teaspoon table salt and a vanilla pod (bean), then add the rice, together with 75 g (3 oz, 6 tablespoons, firmly packed) caster (superfine) or granulated sugar and 30 g (1 oz, 2 tablespoons) butter. Cook either over a very low heat in a covered pan for 30 minutes without

stirring, or in the oven at 200 C (400 F, gas 6) for 35 minutes. Remove the vanilla pod. Mix 4–6 egg yolks with a little of the rice, then pour it into the pan and stir well. 4 egg whites, whisked until stiff, may also be added.

Rice gâteau with caramel GÂTEAU DE RIZ AU CARAMEL Prepare some plain rice cooked in milk (see recipe above). Remove the vanilla pod (if one has been used) and add 175–200 g (6–7 oz, ⅔–¾ cup) caster (superfine) sugar and 3 egg yolks. Gently mix, then add the 3 egg whites whisked to stiff peaks. Place 100 g (4 oz, ½ cup) sugar, the juice of half a lemon, and 1 tablespoon water in a saucepan and cook until the mixture turns brown. Pour it immediately into a charlotte mould with a diameter at the top of 20 cm (8 in). Tilt the mould to line the bottom and sides with caramel. Pour the rice mixture into the mould, press it down, and place the mould in a bain-marie. Bring to the boil, then bake in the oven at 200 C (400 F, gas 6) for about 45 minutes. Leave the gâteau to cool, then turn it out onto a serving dish.

Heat a little hot water in the mould to dissolve the remaining caramel and pour it over the gâteau. Serve with custard cream or a purée of red fruits. Crystallized (candied) fruits and raisins, soaked for 2 hours in a small glass of rum, can be added to the rice before the whisked egg whites.

Rice tart TARTE AU RIZ Cut 200 g (7 oz, 1 cup) crystallized (candied) fruit into small dice and macerate in 2 tablespoons (3 tablespoons) rum. Prepare some sweet pastry with 250 g (9 oz, 2¼ cups) sifted flour, 125 g (4½ oz, ⅔ cup) caster (superfine) sugar, 1 egg, a pinch of salt, and 125 g (4½ oz, generous ½ cup) softened butter. Roll the pastry into a ball and chill it.

Boil 4 dl (14 fl oz, 1¾ cups) milk with a vanilla pod (bean). Add 100 g (4 oz, generous ½ cup) washed round-grain rice to the boiling milk, together with a pinch of salt and 75 g (3 oz, 6 tablespoons, firmly packed) caster sugar, cover the pan, and cook over a very low heat for 25 minutes. When the rice is cooked, allow it to cool slightly, then add a beaten egg, stirring it in thoroughly. Then add 2 tablespoons (3 tablespoons) fresh cream and the crystallized fruit with the rum. Mix thoroughly.

Roll out the pastry and use to line a sponge tin (cake pan). Prick the pastry base and then put in the filling. Pour 50 g (2 oz, ¼ cup) melted butter over the top and sprinkle with 5 crushed sugar cubes. Cook in a medium oven (200 c, 400 f, gas 6) for 30 minutes. Serve either warm or cold.

Riche (à la)

A term applied to two of the most famous dishes created during the 19th century at the Café Riche: roast woodcock on fried bread and sole fillets in sauce. Riche sauce exists in two versions: a velouté made from the sole fumet, flavoured with mushroom and oyster cooking liquor, bound with cream and egg yolks, then finished with the fish juices or with lobster butter; or a normande sauce made with lobster butter and truffles, seasoned with cayenne, and flavoured with Cognac – this is also called diplomat sauce and may accompany any fine fish, such as turbot, John Dory, or sole.

RECIPES

Fillets of sole à la Riche FILETS DE SOLE À LA RICHE Make a Riche sauce: prepare 2.5 dl (8 fl oz, 1 cup) normande sauce and add to it 2 tablespoons (3 tablespoons) lobster butter, 1 tablespoon chopped truffle skins, a pinch of cayenne, and 2 tablespoons (3 tablespoons) Cognac. Keep warm.

Cook a small lobster in a well-seasoned court-bouillon, drain and shell it, then cut the meat into a salpicon. Fold 8 sole fillets in two and poach them for 5 minutes in fish fumet. Drain and arrange them in a ring on a hot serving dish. Fill the centre with the lobster salpicon and mask everything with the hot Riche sauce.

Woodcock à la Riche BÉCASSE À LA RICHE Prepare 1 cup *à gratin* forcemeat. Truss a woodcock and roast it in a very hot oven for 10–12 minutes. Cut a slice of white bread large enough to hold the woodcock, fry it until golden, then spread it thickly with the forcemeat. Warm a liqueur glass of fine liqueur brandy, set it alight, and immediately pour it into the pan in which the woodcock was roasted to deglaze it. Add a purée consisting of 30 g (1 oz) foie gras pounded with the same amount of butter, and mix with the pan juices until the sauce is quite smooth. Place the woodcock on the fried bread and pour the sauce over it.

Richebourg

One of the most celebrated red wines of Burgundy, produced in the parish (commune) of Vosne-Romanée, in the Côte de Nuits area. It is classified as a *grand cru*, and the vineyard is split between a number of owners. This division into separate lots leads to variations, but the wines are usually of impressively high quality.

Richelieu

A garnish for large cuts of meat (baron, leg. etc.) comprising stuffed tomatoes and mushrooms (sometimes browned), braised lettuce, and fried new potatoes or château potatoes. The name is also applied to a method of cooking sole in which the fish is cut open, dipped in egg and breadcrumbs, and cooked in butter; the backbone is removed and the fish is garnished with maître d'hôtel butter and sliced truffle. Fillets can also be prepared in the same way.

These dishes were dedicated to the Duc de Richelieu (the Cardinal's great-nephew), whose patronage figures prominently in the culinary world. For example, *boudins à la Richelieu* are small ramekins filled with chicken forcemeat and a salpicon *à la reine*, turned out and served with Périgueux sauce and a garnish of truffles. There was also a Richelieu sauce.

RECIPE

Richelieu sauce SAUCE RICHELIEU (from Carême's recipe) Dice 4 onions and fry them in clarified butter without letting them colour; drain, then continue cooking them in 2 tablespoons (3 tablespoons) consommé with a little caster(superfine) sugar, a pinch of grated nutmeg, and some coarsely ground white pepper. When cooked, add 2 tablespoons (3 tablespoons) allemande sauce, a little chicken glaze, and a little butter. Rub the sauce through a sieve. Just before serving, add ½ table-spoon chopped and blanched chervil.

richelieu

A large cake made of several layers of almond sponge cake, usually flavoured with Maraschino, sandwiched together with apricot jam and frangipane. The richelieu is then covered with fondant icing (frosting) and decorated with crystallized (candied) fruits. It is reputed to have been invented by the chef of the Duc de Richelieu, great-nephew of the Cardinal.

Ricotta

An Italian curd cheese made from the whey produced as a by-product in the manufacture of various cows'- and ewes'-milk cheeses. Rindless, with a granular crumbly texture, Ricotta is used mainly in cooking, to spread on canapés and sandwiches, in mixed salads, for pancake fillings, in sauces for pasta, in forcemeats and stuffings, in fritter batters, or as an ingredient for gnocchi. It may also be served as a dessert with sugar or jam, or blended with Marsala, or with vinaigrette. It is an ingredient of two famous Italian specialities: Sicilian *cassata*, a cake made with chocolate, Ricotta, and crystallized (candied) fruit; and *crostata di ricotta*, a kind of tart filled with a mixture of Ricotta, grated orange and lemon peel, sugar, raisins, almonds, pine nuts, candied orange peel, and egg yolks.

Riesling

One of the great white-wine grapes of the world. Strictly, Riesling refers to the Rheinriesling or, in certain countries, Johannisberger Riesling or Weisseriesling. It is responsible for most of the greatest of German wines and for some of the finest wines of Alsace, but it is grown in many other countries. It should be stressed that a wine from outside Germany merely labelled Riesling will usually be a completely different grape variety and not usually of comparable quality.

rigodon

A sweet or savoury speciality of Burgundy. The savoury rigodon consists of a bacon or ham quiche filling thickened with potato flour and cooked without a crust in a pie dish; it is served as a hot entrée. The sweet version is a kind of pudding made from pieces of brioche moistened with milk together with chopped walnuts and hazelnuts; the pudding is flavoured with cinnamon and served warm with a fruit purée.

RECIPE

Rigodon with bacon RIGODON AU LARD Bring 4.5 dl (¾ pint, 2 cups) milk to the boil then leave to cool. Cut 250 g (9 oz) smoked streaky bacon into strips and fry them in 25 g (1 oz, 2 table-spoons) butter until transparent. Mix 3 tablespoons (¼ cup) potato flour with the milk until smooth and pour this over 3 lightly beaten whole eggs; add a large pinch of mixed spice, some pepper, and ½ teaspoon powdered thyme. Thickly butter a 22-cm (8½-in) round ovenproof pie dish and spread the bacon strips over the base. Pour in the egg mixture, dot with butter, and bake in a moderately hot oven (190 C, 375 F, gas 5) for 35–40 minutes. Serve hot from the pie dish.

Rigotte de Condrieu

A cheese from the Lyon district, made from cows' milk or mixed cows' and goats' milk; it is soft, with a naturally formed yellow or reddish rind, and contains 45–50% fat. Firm and creamy white with a mild but slightly acid flavour, it is made in the shape of squat cylinders, 4 cm (1½ in) in diameter and 3.5 cm (1¼ in) deep, usually sold in threes or more.

The very similar Rigotte des Alpes, produced in Dauphiné, is often macerated in white wine.

Rigotte de Pelussin

A cheese produced in the high regions of Forez, made from goats' milk or mixed goats' and cows' milk; it is soft with a mild and nutty taste, has a bluish naturally formed rind, and contains 40–45% fat. Made in the shape of small cylinders, 5 cm (2 in) in diameter and 3 cm (1¼ in) deep, sometimes tapering towards the top, it is best from April to October.

rijsttafel

Originally from Indonesia, this dish has become a classic of Dutch cooking. The name literally means 'rice table'; 20 or more different items are arranged around a large plate of spiced rice, including *sajur* (highly seasoned soup), *satay* (small skewers of grilled (broiled) meat), *oppordagni* (thin slices of fried beef, seasoned with coconut), fried ox liver, pork in soy sauce, curried chicken, shrimps, and scrambled eggs.

rillauds

An Angevin speciality made from very fat fresh belly or shoulder of pork with the rind on, which is cut into large cubes, each weighing 80–100 g (3–3½ oz), marinated in salt, then cooked slowly in lard. It is served either very hot or chilled, as a first course. In Anjou, the pieces were formerly arranged in a pyramid with a piece of pig's tail on the top, which was offered to the guest of honour. See also *rillons*.

rillettes

A preparation of pork, rabbit, goose, or poultry meat cooked in lard then pounded to a smooth paste, potted, and served as cold hors d'oeuvre.

Pork rillettes from Tours and Anjou are renowned for their fine texture and deep colour because they are almost caramelized by the cooking process. Balzac praised this 'brown jam' in his book *Le Lys dans la vallée*. Rillettes from Le Mans and La Sarthe, also of pork, are characterized by large pieces of meat in the fat and by their paler colour (they are cooked very slowly). Formerly, rillettes were made from the loin of old breeding sows, whose meat was rather dry; the prolonged cooking in lard tenderized the meat so that it acquired the smooth soft texture that is the hallmark of well-made rillettes.

The goose rillettes described as *pure oie* (pure goose) are prepared in the same way as the pork rillettes but they are more fatty and softer (they are only sold fresh in winter). There are also *rillettes d'oie* (made from half goose and half pork meat) and *rillettes porc et oie* (containing more pork than goose).

Rillettes of rabbit (or wild rabbit, particularly in the Orléans region) often include some veal, to make them less dry. Rillettes can also be prepared from sardines or tuna; the fish is cooked in butter and pounded to a paste with fresh butter. Outstanding among fish rillettes are those made from eels or salmon using a mixture of poached fresh fish and smoked fish.

Rillettes are always served cold, sometimes with toast; they can also be used in sandwiches and canapés.

RECIPES

Goose rillettes RILLETTES D'OIE These are made in the same way as rillettes de Tours from boned birds whose liver has been made into foie gras. Pot them as for rabbit rillettes, but use goose fat to seal the pots.

Rabbit rillettes RILLETTES DE LAPIN (from a recipe by Jean and Pierre Troisgros) Bone 4 wild rabbits, weigh the meat, and cut it into large dice. Dice 1.4 kg (3 lb) fat streaky bacon. Melt 60–80 g (2–3 oz, 4–6 tablespoons) lard in a large frying pan (skillet) and fry the bacon along with 8 peeled garlic cloves and a sprig of thyme; add the rabbit and cook until golden. Pour in 4 glasses of water and 30 g (1 oz) salt for every kg (2¼ lb) meat. Cover the pan and simmer gently for 3 hours. Adjust the seasoning. When cooked, shred the meat using 2 forks, and pour the mixture, still boiling hot, into small stoneware pots which have previously been scalded. Leave to cool. Fill the pots to the brim with melted lard, cover, and chill until ready to serve.

Rillettes de Tours Select some pieces of fat and lean pork from various cuts, such as blade, neck, belly, and leg. Separate the fat from the lean meat and remove any bones. Chop the bones, cut the lean meat into strips, and coarsely chop the fat.

Put the fat into a large saucepan, arrange the chopped bones on top, then add the strips of lean meat. Tie 4 or 5 cloves and about 12 black peppercorns in a small piece of muslin (cheesecloth) and place it in the pan, then add salt, using 20–25 g (about ¾ oz) per kg (2¼ lb) meat. Cover the saucepan, bring to the boil, and simmer gently for 4 hours.

Remove the lid, turn up the heat, and remove the bones, stripping off any adhering meat and returning it to the pan to continue cooking. Stir constantly until all the liquid has evaporated. Remove the bag of spices.

Pour the rillettes into stoneware pots, stirring well so as to mix the fat and lean; leave to cool. The fat will rise to the top so there is no need to add lard. Cover with foil and store in a cool dry place.

rillons

A speciality of Touraine, made from pieces of belly or shoulder of pork. The meat is first sprinkled with salt, then cooked in lard and browned with caramel. Balzac described them in *Le Lys dans la vallée*: 'Pork trimmings sautéed in their own fat, which look like cooked truffles.'

Rillons are also known as *rillauds*, *grillons*, or *rillots*; they are served as a first course, with various other pork products.

RECIPE

Rillons Cut some pieces of fat belly of pork into 5–6-cm (2½-in) cubes, without removing the rind. Sprinkle with salt – 25 g (1 oz) salt per kg (2¼ lb) meat – and leave for 12 hours. Put one-third as much lard as there is meat into a saucepan, heat, and then brown the pieces of pork. Lower the heat and simmer gently for 2 hours. Finally, add 2 tablespoons (3 tablespoons) caramel per kg (2¼ lb) meat, heat through quickly, and drain. The rillons may be served either very hot or thoroughly chilled.

rimotte or rimote

A cornmeal porridge from Périgord and Agenais, where it is also known in the patois as *las pous* (referring to the little whistling sounds made by bubbles breaking on the surface as it cooks over a gentle heat). The porridge may be sweetened and eaten as a dessert, but it is usually chilled, cut into squares, and eaten instead of bread. Alternatively the squares may be dipped in flour, fried in butter, lard, or goose fat, and served very hot, dredged with sugar.

rincette

A small quantity of brandy poured into a coffee cup just after it has been emptied and is therefore still warm. This residual warmth helps to release the bouquet of the brandy. The French word is an informal one, as is the practice it describes.

ring

See *border*.

Rioja

A famous Spanish wine-producing region in the northwest of the country. Both red and white wines are made in the different areas, the former often being categorized as *claretes* (light in style) or *borgognas* (heavier and fuller). Strict controls are in operation and the various *bodegas* (wine-making establishments) each make wines of individual character. Rioja has a long and proud history, and today the wines are becoming widely known and esteemed.

rioler

A French culinary term meaning to arrange straight or serrated strips of pastry on the top of a cake, tart, or flan to form a crisscross pattern, as on a linzertorte.

ripaille

An informal French name for a hearty feast, where the food is abundant and the wine flows freely. The origin of the expression *faire ripaille* (to have a good blowout) is traditionally linked to the Château de Ripaille, on the shores of Lake Geneva, where in about 1449 Amédée VIII, Duke of Savoy (the antipope Félix V) retired to indulge to excess in the delights of the table. This would be a plausible explanation if the expression had not been found in earlier texts, more than 150 years before the duke's exploits. In fact, the word comes from the Dutch word *rippen* (to scrape), undoubtedly referring to a well-laden table on which, after the meal, hardly a crumb is left!

There is also a white wine called Ripaille, which is dry and fruity and comes from Haute-Savoie.

ripopée

A French colloquial name for a mixture of liquids.

The term has now fallen into disuse, but formerly it meant either a mixture of wines (also known as *vin ripopé*) or a mixture of sauces and soups.

risotto

An Italian rice dish (the name means literally 'little rice'). The rice is fried in fat with chopped onions until golden brown, then cooked in stock. Butter and various garnishes are then added, such as vegetables, cheese, ham, mushrooms, etc. Risottos garnished *à la milanaise, à la piémontaise,* or with seafood, chicken liver, etc., can be served as a main course. When only cheese or saffron is added, it is served as an accompaniment to meat (particularly veal), eggs, or even fish. For some recipes risotto is set in moulds.

RECIPES

Risotto à la milanaise   Heat 40 g (1½ oz, 3 tablespoons) butter or 4 tablespoons (5 tablespoons) olive oil in a saucepan and cook 100 g (4 oz, 1 cup) chopped onions very gently, without browning. Then add 250 g (9 oz, 1¼ cups) rice and stir until the grains become transparent. Add twice the volume of stock and stir with a wooden spoon until the rice begins to absorb the stock. Adjust the seasoning, add a small bouquet garni, cover the pan, and continue to cook, without stirring, for 16 –18 minutes (the rice should be soft). Then add 2 dl (7 fl oz, ¾ cup) thick tomato fondue, 500 g (1 lb) pickled ox (beef) tongue, ham, and mushrooms (in equal proportions, all chopped), and a little white truffle. Keep hot without allowing the rice to cook further.

Risotto à la piémontaise   Prepare the rice as for risotto *à la milanaise* but omit the tomato fondue, tongue, ham, and mushrooms, adding insted 75 g (3 oz, ¾ cup) grated Parmesan cheese and 2 tablespoons (3 tablespoons) butter. Some safron may also be added.

Risotto with chicken livers   RISOTTO AUX FOIES DE VOLAILLE   Make a risotto *à la milanaise* but omit the final garnish. While it is cooking, prepare 1.5 dl (¼ pint, ⅔ cup) very thick tomato fondue. Sauté 200 g (7 oz, scant cup, firmly packed) diced chicken livers and 250 g (9 oz, 3 cups) sliced cultivated mushrooms in butter. Add salt and pepper and a small grated clove of garlic. Mix the tomato fondue, the chicken livers, and the mushrooms with the rice and serve very hot. 70 g (3 oz, ¾ cup) grated Parmesan cheese may be added if desired.

rissole

A small sweet or savoury pastry, usually in the form of a turnover, that contains any of various fillings and is usually deep-fried.

Puff pastry is usually used, but rissoles can also be made with lining pastry or brioche dough.

Savoury rissoles may contain chopped meat, sliced poultry, foie gras, duxelles, oysters, prawns, a salpicon bound with a sauce, a flavoured butter, a cheese cream, etc. They are served very hot, as an hors d'oeuvre or a small entrée. Very small rissoles (for example, *pomponettes,* shaped like tiny purses) may be served as appetizers, or used to garnish large joints of meat.

Sweet rissoles are filled with cooked fruit, a cream, or jam. They are eaten very hot, sprinkled with sugar and accompanied by a fruit sauce.

In former times, rissoles (or *roissoles* as they were called) were a very popular dish in France. Originally in the form of small fried pancakes, they later came to be filled with chopped meat or fish.

Rissoles de Bugey are a famous French regional speciality that were traditionally served at Christmas time. They are little oblong puff-pastry pies filled with roast turkey and ox tripe, seasoned with onion, thyme, chervil, and currants, and baked in the oven.

RECIPES

Preparation of rissoles   PRÉPARATION DES RISSOLES   Make some puff pastry or some lining pastry (see *doughs and batters*) and roll it out to a thickness of 3–4 mm (¼ in). Using a round or oval fluted pastry cutter (cookie cutter), cut out 2 pieces of pastry for every rissole required. Put a small amount of filling (about the size of a walnut) in the centre of half of the pieces of pastry, moisten the edges, cover with the second piece of pastry, and press the edges firmly together.

If the rissoles are to be made from ordinary brioche dough, cut the latter into small pieces and flatten them with the palm of the hand. Place the filling on top and leave them to rise in a warm place, away from draughts, for 30–45 minutes.

Deep-fry the rissoles, whatever dough is used, in very hot oil (175 c, 345 f) until golden brown, then drain them well on absorbent paper. Arrange the rissoles on a dish covered with a napkin; if the filling is a savoury one, garnish with fried parsley.

Rissoles à la dauphine   Make rissoles in the shape of turnovers from some brioche dough. Fill them either with a purée of foie gras (possibly mixed with chopped truffle) or with a salpicon of lobster blended with lobster butter.

Rissoles à la fermière   Cut some fluted circles, 8 cm (3 in) in diameter, from some lining pastry. Fill them with equal quantities of a salpicon of cooked ham and a mirepoix of vegetables cooked in butter, binding the mixture with a small quantity of concentrated Madeira sauce.

Ritz (César)

Swiss hotelier (born Niederwald, 1850; died Küssnach, 1918). The son of a shepherd, he rose to become the owner of some of the grandest establishments of his time. After an obscure beginning in an hotel in Brigue, he arrived in Paris in 1867, where he became a waiter at Voisin's. Ten years later, he was appointed manager of the Grand Hôtel in Monte Carlo, where he became very friendly with Escoffier. Between them, they established the reputation first of the London Savoy (1890–93) and later of the Carlton. On 15 June 1898, César Ritz opened the palatial building in Paris, in the Place Vendôme, which bears his name; at the same time he continued to manage the other great hotels – Claridge's and the Hyde Park

Hotel in London, the Grand Hôtel in Rome, the Frankfurter Hof in Frankfurt, the Villa Egeia in Palermo, and the Hôtel National in Lucerne. The splendid London Ritz was opened in 1906. There are always some of Escoffier's creations on the menu of the Paris Ritz; for example, fresh foie gras with port. One of the innovations at the Ritz was to seat diners at small tables, as in a restaurant, as opposed to the traditional table d'hôte.

Rivesaltes

One of the AOC Grand Roussillon wines, a vin doux naturel. Ordinary table wines, red, white, and rosé, are also made there.

roasting   RÔTISSAGE

Cooking meat, poultry, game, or fish by exposing it to the heat of a naked flame or grill (spit-roasting) or to the radiant heat of an oven (oven-roasting).

Spit-roasting is considered best, but it is more difficult. Some cooks consider that oven-roasted meat is spoilt because it is subjected to humidity. It is a mistake to add water to the roasting pan, because when this evaporates it tends to give a boiled taste to the meat. To ensure that the roast does not dry out or get too brown, particularly when it is to be cooked for a long time, it may be barded. The other preliminary processes are interlarding and larding. Many joints can also be stuffed before roasting.

Whichever method is used, the meat is first exposed to a high heat, which produces a surface crust and concentrates the juices inside the meat, conserving all its flavour. The meat should not be pierced while it is cooking or the juices will run out. The cooking temperature will depend on the type and the size of the joint.

□ **Spit-roasting** The intensity of the heat must always be proportionate to the type of meat to be cooked: red meat, full of juices, should first be seized and then cooked at a steady heat to make sure that it is cooked right through. For white meat and poultry, the heat must be regulated so that the inside is cooked without the outside getting too brown. The meat should be basted frequently with the fat which collects in the drip tray, but not with the meat juices underneath the fat. Cooked in this way, the meat will be tender and a good colour.

☐ **Oven-roasting** The meat should be put into a very hot oven to seal the surface. It should rest on a rack, to keep it out of its own fat and juices, and should be basted as for spit-roast meat.

If roast beef, mutton, and game are to be served rare, a few drops of deep pink blood should be emitted when the surface is lightly pricked; for a medium-rare roast, the blood should be pale pink. With veal, young lamb, and pork, the juices should run clear. Poultry should be lifted from the pan and tilted over a plate: it is done when the juice runs out clear; if there are still traces of pink, the bird is not sufficiently cooked.

As a rule, a roast should be served, with its strings and barding removed, as soon as it is taken out of the oven or off the spit; in the case of red meat, however, it is better to leave the roast to rest for a few minutes in a warm place before serving. The meat is then easier to cut.

The accompanying gravy is made by pouring into the roasting pan either a little water or a little light stock and scraping and mixing in all the juices and bits adhering to the pan. Some of the fat is poured off and the gravy is then served separately in a sauceboat with a special spout which retains the remaining fat when the gravy is poured.

Robert

A sauce based on white wine and vinegar, which is the classic accompaniment to pork chops and other grilled (broiled) meats. It is wrongly attributed to a cook named Robert Vinot active at the end of the 16th century, but its origins are older than this. Rabelais, in *Le Quart Livre* (1552), mentions 'Robert, the inventor of Robert sauce, which goes so well with roast rabbit, duck, fresh pork, poached eggs, salt cod, and a thousand other such foods'. *Le Grand Cuisinier* (1583) mentions a sauce known as *Barbe Robert*, the recipe for which had already appeared in *Le Viandier* under the name of *taille-maslée* (fried onion, verjuice, vinegar, and mustard), to be served with roast rabbit, fried fish, and fried eggs.

RECIPE

Robert sauce SAUCE ROBERT Cook 2 peeled finely chopped onions until golden brown in 25 g (1 oz, 2 tablespoons) butter or lard. Sprinkle with 1 tablespoon flour and continue to cook until it browns. Add 2 dl (7 fl oz, ¾ cup) white wine and 3 dl (½ pint, 1¼ cups) stock (or 1 dl (6 tablespoons, scant ½ cup) white wine, 2 dl (7 fl oz, ¾ cup) vinegar, and 1 dl (6 tablespoons, scant ½ cup water) and boil until reduced by one-third. Adjust the seasoning. Mix together 1 tablespoon mustard and a little of the sauce, then add it to the rest of the sauce, mixing thoroughly away from the heat.

rocambole

A variety of garlic cultivated in the French Midi, also known as 'Spanish garlic' or 'red Provençal garlic'. The large wine-red bulbs are less pungent than those of the common garlic. La Chapelle, in a recipe for sole *à la sauce aux rois* (1733), recommends using rocambole instead of shallots: the fish are fried in butter and stuffed with a forcemeat of rocambole, anchovies, and spring (green) onions, all cooked in a fish fumet over a gentle heat and sprinkled with orange juice. The name 'rocambole' comes from the German *Rockenbolle*, meaning distaff bulb, referring to its shape.

Rochambeau

A garnish for large cuts of braised or roast meat, consisting of croustades of duchess potatoes filled with Vichy carrots, alternating with stuffed lettuces, cauliflower florets *à la polonaise*, and Anna potatoes.

rocher

An item of pâtisserie or confectionery with an irregular outline and (often) a granular texture, resembling that of a rock (hence the name). Usually with a base of sugar and beaten egg whites, they can be made with almonds, coconut (*congolais*), chocolate, raisins, etc., and vary in size. For a *pièce montée* (a large structured cake), rochers are made from soufflé sugar (boiled sugar beaten with royal icing, cut into irregular pieces, and sometimes coloured), or from sponge cake (coloured pink, green, or with chocolate, etc.).

rocket (arugula)

ROQUETTE

A Mediterranean plant, with a pungent taste and smell, whose young leaves are eaten as a salad or used for flavouring salads. They should be gathered before flowering, when smooth and hairless, as later the taste becomes too mustardy. Rocket is one of the traditional ingredients of the Provençal mesclun.

rockling   MOTELLE

A Mediterranean fish, 10–40 cm (4–16 in) long, with three barbels on the head and an elongated slimy reddish-brown body speckled with black on the back. The rockling has a lean and very delicate flesh but it is only consumed locally as it does not travel well. It may be prepared in the same way as whiting.

rodent   RONGEUR

A mammal with long cutting incisor teeth. Some herbivorous rodents have quite well-flavoured meat; rabbits and hares are good examples. Other rodents have been assiduously hunted in the past and recipes for these animals, including squirrel, marmot, and beaver, are still used in some remote regions.

In some tropical countries the meat of rodents forms prime roasts: the agouti from South America and the West Indies (called *acouchi* in Guyana) is cooked in the same way as a sucking pig. There is a Guyanese proverb which says 'He who eats acouchi will always return'.

During the siege of Paris in 1870, the citizens ate rats which were sold for 10–15 sous each in the Place de l'Hôtel de Ville. In 1859, Monselet noted in *La Cuisinière poétique* that the Bordeaux coopers traditionally feasted on grilled (broiled) rat with shallots. Thomas Genin, cook and organizer of the first culinary competition (1884–89), considered rat meat to be of excellent quality.

rodgrod   ROEDGROED

A Danish dessert made from the juice of mixed red fruit (raspberries, redcurrants, blackcurrants, cherries), thickened with rice or potato flour, and

diluted with white wine. It is served very cold in a fruit dish, sprinkled with sugar and sliced almonds, and accompanied by fresh cream.

roe   OEUFS DE POISSON

The reproductive glands of male or female fish, containing the sperm and eggs respectively. This article deals with the uses of fish eggs, or hard roe; for culinary uses of the male gland, or milt, see *soft roe*. Pressed and smoked cod's roe is used as a filling for canapés, barquettes, etc., or spread on toast or crackers (see *taramasalata*). The roes of grey mullet and tuna are used for a traditional Provençal dish (see *boutargue*). Salmon and lumpfish roes are used as substitutes for caviar (the roe of the sturgeon).

RECIPES

Barquettes with roe   BARQUETTES AUX OEUFS DE POISSON   Prepare some very small barquettes, bake them blind, and leave them to cool completely. Skin a smoked cod or grey mullet roe and mix it with an equal quantity of butter. Add some finely grated lemon peel, using 1 lemon for 250 g (9 oz, generous 1 cup) roe mixture. Fill the barquettes with the mixture and ganish with fluted half-slices of lemon. Chill for 1 hour before serving.

Grilled (broiled) roes   OEUFS DE POISSON GRILLES   Season some fish roes (whiting, cod, or salmon) with salt and pepper. Brush with oil, sprinkle with a little lemon juice, and leave them for 30 minutes. Then either brush them with clarified butter and grill (broil) gently, or fry in butter over a gentle heat. Serve with rye bread, butter, and lemon.

roebuck   CHEVREUIL

A small deer common in Eurasian forests, where it is rapidly becoming popular as game (particularly in Germany), because its numbers are increasing. It is called a fawn up to 6 months, a yearling up to 18 months, and then a brocket. The flesh of young roebucks is dark red and is delicate, and does not need to be marinated (cooking should leave it pink inside). The best pieces are the cutlets and noisettes, taken from the loin, and fillets of saddle or noix of leg, which are most often sautéed; the saddle and the leg (or haunch) are on the whole eaten roasted. Stews are also made from it, accompanied by chestnut purée, poivrade sauce, cherries, redcurrant jelly, or pears in syrup.

RECIPES

3-hour leg of roebuck   GIGOT DE CHEVREUIL DE 3 HEURES   (from a recipe by Christian Dior) Trim a leg of roebuck weighing 2.5–3 kg (5½–6½ lb). Cut 300 g (¾ lb) fat bacon into thin strips and lard the leg with them. Brown on all sides in a braising pan containing 30 g (1 oz, 2 tablespoons) butter and 2 tablespoons oil. Heat a small glass of Cognac, pour it over the leg, and flame. Cover and leave to cook for 1 hour over a gentle heat. Add ¼ litre (8 fl oz, 1 cup) red wine, the juice of a lemon, 1 clove of garlic, 1 or 2 small dried chilli peppers, salt,* and pepper, and leave to cook gently for another hour, keeping the lid on. Then mix 2 teaspoons flour and 2 teaspoons strong mustard with ¼ litre (8 fl oz, 1 cup) red wine, pour over the leg, and cook for a third hour. When time to serve, strain the sauce and thicken it with 4 teaspoons raspberry jelly. Blend 1½ tablespoons thick cream with 1 litre (1¾ pints, 4 cups) thin chestnut purée and serve leg, purée, and sauce together.

Haunch of roebuck with capers   CUISSOT DE CHEVREUIL AUX CÂPRES (from a recipe by Toulouse-Lautrec) Trim the haunch and prepare a marinade with a bottle of red wine, 1½ tablespoons olive oil, pepper, 2 onions and 2 shallots (both thinly sliced), parsley, salt (in moderation), and pepper. Add the haunch and leave to marinate for at least 24 hours, basting it from time to time.

After draining, lard the meat with small strips of streaky bacon (250 g, ½ lb). Baste with melted butter, place in an oven heated to about 200 C (400 F, gas 6) and cook for at least 2 hours, basting occasionally with butter. Meanwhile simmer the marinade, also for 2 hours. When the meat has finished cooking, mix 2 teaspoons starch or arrowroot with a small cup of beef stock and add this mixture and the meat juices to the reduced marinade. To serve, add 1 tablespoon capers and about 40 g (1½ oz, 3 tablespoons) fresh butter to the sauce.

Roast haunch of roebuck   CUISSOT DE CHEVREUIL RÔTI   Heat the oven to about 220 C (425 F, gas 7). Skin and trim the haunch of young roebuck, pulling off the fine membrane which covers it. Lard with long strips of streaky bacon and place in an ovenproof dish; moisten with clarified butter, or brush with butter softened to room temperature, and sprinkle with salt and pepper. Roast the haunch in the oven, basting several times, for 12–15 minutes per kg (6–8 minutes per lb); as soon as it is browned on all sides, add 1 cup of boiling water to the dish. Serve it with a poivrade sauce and chestnut purée, together with baked apples filled with cranberry compote, or small mushroom croûtes.

Saddle of roebuck à la berrichonne   SELLE DE CHEVREUIL À LA BERRICHONNE   (from a recipe by Lucienne Dépée) Trim a saddle of roebuck, removing the sinews and keeping the trimmings. Lard it with very thin strips of fat bacon and season with salt, pepper, thyme, and a crushed bay leaf. Clean and finely dice 100 g (4 oz) carrots and 100 g (4 oz) onions. Brown the game trimmings in oil, then add the diced vegetables, 40 g (1½ oz) shallots, 30 g (1 oz) celery, 2 cloves of garlic, a bouquet garni, 8 peppercorns, and 2 cloves. Add 1.5 litres (3 pints, 7 cups) red wine (Sancerre, for example), and cook gently for 1 hour.

Drain the saddle, skim the cooking liquid and pass it through a conical strainer lined with coarse muslin, then thicken with 50 g (2 oz) brown roux. Beat the sauce with 150 g (5 oz, ½ cup) butter, salt, pepper, and finally 3 tablespoons (scant ¼ cup) pig's blood; keep hot in a bain-marie.

Cook 4 pears in ½ litre (17 fl oz, 2 cups) red wine flavoured with a generous pinch of powdered cinnamon, and braise gently in butter some quarters of celeriac (celery root) cut into half-moon shapes. Keep the pears and celeriac hot, and roast the saddle in a hot oven (about 220 c, 425 f, gas 7). Coat the bottom of the serving dish with sauce and arrange the saddle on it, garnishing it with pears and celeriac quarters alternately. Serve the rest of the sauce separately.

Roebuck filets mignons   FILETS MIG-NONS DE CHEVREUIL   In principle, filets mignons are thin tongue-shaped strips of meat situated beneath the saddle bone, but they may also be taken from the large fillets of the saddle. Trim these fillets, flatten them slightly, and lard them with fat bacon. They may then be either quickly sautéed in oil or butter, like cutlets, or oiled and grilled (broiled) under a high heat. They are served with a poivrade sauce, a chestnut purée, a fruit compote (especially of peaches), or a cherry or redcurrant sauce, according to choice. Generally speaking, all cutlet recipes may be applied to them.

Sautéed roebuck cutlets with cherries   CÔTELETTES DE CHEVREUIL SAUTÉES AUX CERISES   Place 1 glass of port with the same amount of sweetened cherry juice and redcurrant jelly in a small saucepan. Add salt and pepper, ½ teaspoon lemon juice, a pinch of powdered ginger, and, if desired, a dash of cayenne. Heat gently for about 10 minutes, then add a large glass of cherries in syrup and reheat. Sauté the cutlets and coat with the cherry sauce; serve very hot.

Sautéed roebuck cutlets with grapes   CÔTELETTES DE CHEVREUIL SAUTÉES AUX RAISINS   Fry some croutons in oil and prepare a poivrade sauce. Macerate some large skinned and seeded grapes in Cognac. Sauté the cutlets briskly, then heat the grapes in the same frying pan (skillet). Serve the cutlets with the grapes, fried croutons, and poivrade sauce.

Sautéed roebuck cutlets with juniper berries   CÔTELETTES DE CHEVREUIL SAUTÉES AU GENIÈVRE   Sauté the cutlets briskly and coat with a sauce made from the pan juice flavoured with juniper berries. Serve with an unsweetened apple purée (applesauce).

Shoulder of roebuck with olives   ÉPAULE DE CHEVREUIL AUX OLIVES (from a recipe by Danielle Spieghel) Bone a shoulder of roebuck, leaving the knuckle bone, and marinate. Cut 200 g (7 oz) fat bacon into strips, roll them in salt and pepper, and lard the shoulder with them. Roll it up and tie fairly tightly. Heat 20 g (1 oz, 2 tablespoons) butter, 2 teaspoons oil, and 30 g (1 oz) small pieces of fat bacon in a casserole. Brown the shoulder in the casserole, then cover and leave to cook gently for a good hour. Meanwhile stone (pit) some green and black (ripe) olives; blanch and drain the green ones. When the shoulder is cooked, skim the fat from the cooking liquid, add the olives, and bring to the boil. Mix 2 teaspoons arrowroot with very little water, add it to the casserole, and stir until it thickens. Pour the sauce over the shoulder and serve very hot, with a celery purée if desired.

roebuck sauce

SAUCE CHEVREUIL

An English sauce to accompany venison or meats *en chevreuil*.

| RECIPE

Roebuck sauce   SAUCE CHEVREUIL Brown in butter 1 tablespoon thinly sliced onions and 40 g (1½ oz) ham cut into small dice. Add 1 dl (6 tablespoons, scant ½ cup) vinegar and a bouquet garni, and reduce almost completely. Then add 2 dl (7 fl oz, ¾ cup) espagnole sauce and reduce for 25 minutes, skimming off the scum which forms. Remove the bouquet garni and add ½ glass of port and 2 teaspoons redcurrant jelly. Reheat, stirring well.

rognonnade

A loin of veal from which the kidney has not been removed. The loin is boned and the sinews removed, then it is beaten flat. Some of the fat is removed from the kidney, which is cut into two lengthwise; the two halves are placed end to end in the centre of the loin over the filet mignon. The loin is then rolled and tied securely and roasted, first in a hot oven to seal in the juices, then gently (30 minutes per 450 g (1 lb)).

It is advisable to baste the joint frequently during cooking and not to add salt until carved.

Rohan (à la)

The name of a garnish for braised or sautéed poultry, consisting of artichoke hearts topped with slices of foie gras and truffle, arranged alternately with tartlets filled with cocks' kidneys in suprême sauce. When the poultry has been arranged with the garnish on a large dish, cocks' combs cooked gently in butter are placed between the artichoke hearts and tartlets.

rolling pin

ROULEAU À PÂTISSERIE

A smooth cylinder, 20–50 cm (8–20 in) long and 5–6 cm (2–2½ in) in diameter, sometimes fitted with handles, used to roll out pastry (dough). Made from hardwood (beech or box), china, or glass, some rolling pins can move on an axis connecting the two handles. There are also aluminium rolling pins with a nonstick surface, and hollow plastic models, closed by a screw handle, which can be filled with hot water to soften a dough which is too hard or with iced water to firm up dough which is too soft.

Professional pastrycooks use various specialized rolling pins: fluted metal pins to pattern the surface of caramel or almond paste; fluted wooden pins to roll out puff pastry (this keeps the pieces of butter separate and ensures uniform distribution); pins covered in wickerwork to imprint a pattern on pastry; croissant-cutting rolling pins, which cut regular triangles to make into croissants; and rolling pins fitted with adjustable wheels of different sizes at either end, which automatically regulate the thickness of the dough.

rollmop

A boned herring fillet, marinated in spiced vinegar, rolled around chopped onions and a piece of gherkin *à la russe*, and secured with a cocktail stick (toothpick). The name comes from the German *rollen* (to roll) + *Mops* (a pug dog). Before being rolled up the fillets are sometimes spread with mustard and sprinkled with capers; the marinade, flavoured with juniper berries, cloves, and black peppercorns, is poured cold over the rolled fillets. The rollmops are left to marinate for five or six days in a cold place and then served as a cold hors d'oeuvre, with parsley and onion rings. They can be bought ready-prepared, imported from Denmark or Germany.

Rollot

A soft highly flavoured cows'-milk cheese from the Picardy region (45% fat content), with a washed reddish or orange-yellow rind. It was already a popular cheese in the reign of Louis XIV. Rollot is either heart-shaped or wheel-shaped (about 4 cm (1½ in) thick) and is made by small dairies, especially those in the region around Rollot, Amiens, and Beauvais. It is at its best between November and June.

romaine (à la)

The name given to various French dishes inspired by the cuisine of the Italian region of Latium; these dishes include eggs with spinach, anchovies, and Parmesan cheese; small birds casseroled with peas and ham; spinach loaf or soufflé, etc. Sauce *à la romaine* is the classic sauce to serve with roast venison; it is a sweet-and-sour sauce made with dried vine fruit, game stock, and pine kernels. Gnocchi *à la romaine* are made from semolina and grated cheese and usually served as a first course. When used to garnish large joints of meat, they are put into tartlet cases (shells) and browned in the oven; they may be accompanied by small spinach loaves with a light tomato sauce or veal stock thickened with tomato.

RECIPES

Omelette à la romaine Prepare some spinach with anchovies as for scrambled eggs *à la romaine*. Make 2 flat 5-egg omelettes garnished with chopped onions cooked in butter and chopped parsley. Spread the spinach mixture over one of the omelettes and place the second one on top. Spoon some light Mornay sauce over the omelettes, sprinkle with grated Parmesan cheese and melted butter, and brown in a hot oven or under a grill.

Quails à la romaine CAILLES À LA
ROMAINE Brown 12 chopped small
new onions and 100 g (4 oz, ½ cup)
diced cooked ham in 30 g (1 oz, 2
tablespoons) butter. Add 1 kg (2¼ lb,
6¾ cups) shelled petits pois, a pinch
each of salt and sugar, and a small
bouquet garni. Cover and braise gently
for 10 minutes. Dress, trim, and truss 8
quails and seize them in butter over a
high heat in a flameproof casserole. Tip
the vegetables onto the birds, cover, and
cook in the oven at 230 c (450 f, gas 8)
for 20 minutes. Serve directly from the
cooking dish.

Sauce à la romaine Put 1 tablespoon
each of sultanas (seedless white raisins)
and currants in warm water to soak and
swell. Cook 4 lumps of sugar to a pale
caramel in a saucepan, add 1 tablespoon
vinegar, then 2 dl (7 fl oz, ¾ cup) demi-
glace, and finally 4 tablespoons (5 tablespoons) game stock. Boil for a few minutes and strain. Brown 1 tablespoon
pine kernels either in the oven or in a
frying pan with no fat. Strain the sauce
and add the pine kernels, currants, and
sultanas.

Romanée-Conti

One of the most famous AOC red wines
of Vosne-Romanée, in the Côte de Nuits
in Burgundy. It is considered by many to
be outstanding. Only small quantities
are made and the wines are expensive,
bottled at the estate. Romanée-Saint-
Vivant, also from Vosne-Romanée, is a
slightly larger vineyard with several
owners, and also produces fine velvety
wines.

Romanov

The name given to various dishes of
classic French cooking, which were
dedicated at the beginning of the century to the Russian Imperial family. The
Romanov garnish for meat consists of
pieces of cucumber stuffed with duxelles and browned in the oven and
duchess potato cases filled with a salpicon of mushrooms and celeriac (celery
root) bound with thick velouté sauce
and seasoned with horseradish. Strawberries Romanov are macerated in
Curaçao and arranged in sundae dishes
with a decoration of Chantilly cream.

roncin

A dessert from Franche-Comté, consisting of bread soaked in milk, beaten eggs,
and fruit, particularly cherries, and
cooked in a buttered dish.

In the Vosges region, roncin is made
with semi-salted fresh soft cheese which
is melted, mixed with beaten eggs and
flour, and cooked in a cool oven. It is
served with potatoes boiled in their
skins.

rondeau

A cooking utensil used in restaurants. It
is a round shallow pan with straight
sides, a lid, and two curved handles (not
one long handle as in a sauté pan,
though it is used in a similar way). Food
can also be reheated or stewed in the
pan. In confectionery, it is used mainly
in the preparation of marrons glacés. It
may be made of aluminium, stainless
steel, tinned cast iron, or hammered
copper.

Also available are deep two-handled
pans.

Roquefort

A French ewes'-milk cheese (45% fat
content) made in the Rouergue district.
The cheese is blue-veined, smooth, and
creamy, with a naturally formed rind,
and has a strong smell and pronounced
flavour. Roquefort is one of the oldest
known cheeses: it was mentioned by
Pliny the Elder; it was Charlemagne's
favourite cheese; and in 1411 Charles
VI signed a charter giving the inhabitants of Roquefort-sur-Soulzon, a village in the Aveyron, sole rights to the
maturing of this soft cheese.

Roquefort was the first cheese to benefit from an *appellation d'origine*, conferred by a statute of 26 July 1926. The
cheese is matured in natural caves in
the mountains of Cambelou. Most of
the milk comes from the Aveyron region, then from Tarn, Lozère, Hérault,
and Gard; the Pyrenees and Corsica
make up any shortfall, but the only
place where the cheese can be matured is
the commune of Roquefort. After being
seeded with the spores of *Penicillium
roqueforti*, the cheese is matured for
three months in a damp cave, where the
fleurines (humid currents of air) encourage the development of the blue veins.

The best season is from June to December.

A Roquefort cheese is shaped like a cylinder, 19–20 cm (7½–8 in) in diameter and 8.5–10.5 cm (3¼–4¼ in) high, wrapped in foil. It can be bought in slices, portions, or even creamed, but it is always better to take a piece from the whole cheese, particularly when it is to be served at the end of a meal. It should then be accompanied by a really full-bodied red wine (such as Châteauneuf-du-Pape or Madiran) or even an old port or a Sauternes. Curnonsky recommended a Clos de Vougeot or Haut-Brion. Roquefort is also used in a number of recipes: mixed salads, sauces and flavoured butters (for spreading on canapés or to serve with a grill or roast meat), soufflés, pancakes, puff pastries, soups, etc.

RECIPES

Pears Savarin   POIRES SAVARIN Peel 12 pears, cut them in half, remove the cores, and fill the space with Roquefort cheese blended with a little butter. Arrange the pears on a plate, mask with 3 dl (½ pint, 1¼ cups) double (heavy) cream, and sprinkle with paprika. Serve chilled, as an hors d'oeuvre.

Roquefort balls   BOULETTES DE ROQUEFORT   Mix a good portion of Roquefort with an equal quantity of butter. Add pepper, a pinch of cayenne, and 1 tablespoon Cognac for every 100 g (4 oz) mixture. Shape it into little balls about the size of walnuts, roll them in golden breadcrumbs mixed with a little paprika, and chill until ready to serve, spiking each one on a cocktail stick (toothpick).

Roquefort rolls   CRUMPETS AU ROQUEFORT   In a food processor, blend 250 g (9 oz) Roquefort with the same amount of Cheddar. Add 2.5 dl (8 fl oz, 1 cup) béchamel sauce, together with salt, pepper, and 1 teaspoon mustard. Melt this mixture down in a bain-marie, then spread it on thin slices of bread cut lengthwise through the loaf, after removing the crust. Roll up each slice, bake until golden in the oven, then cut into sections 1 cm (½ in) thick.

Roquefort sauce   SAUCE AU ROQUEFORT   Mash 80 g (3 oz) Roquefort with a fork, blend in 6 Petits Suisses (or 6 oz cream cheese), and mix well. Add 3 tablespoons (¼ cup) fresh cream and 1 tablespoon Cognac, and season with pepper and salt (if necessary). Stir well and chill; serve with crudités.

Roques (Joseph)

French doctor (born Valence (now Valence d'Albigeois), 1771; died Montpellier, 1850). A friend of Grimod de La Reynière, he was a member of the latter's Jury of Tasters. He was the author of various works, the most important of which is a *Histoire des champignons comestibles et vénéneux* (1832), in which he deals with the botanical, medicinal, and culinary aspects of mushrooms. In the four volumes of his *Nouveau Traité des plantes usuelles* (1837–38), he points out the medicinal value of various fruits and vegetables.

rose

The flower of the rose bush, whose perfumed and coloured petals are used for flavouring cakes, creams, confectionery, etc. Rose-petal jam, very popular in the Middle East and the Balkans, is made from damask rose petals macerated in sugar. In France, Provins is the centre of rose-flavoured confectionery: petal jam, rose-flavoured bonbons, rose jelly, crystallized (candied) rose petals, etc.

Rose water and rose essence are used like orange-flower water to flavour creams, jellies, and ices as well as liqueurs and flower wines (very popular in the 17th century, particularly Rosolio). Rose honey is made by boiling rosebuds with honey, and rose vinegar by macerating the petals in wine vinegar in the sun. Essence of roses is found in many pastries and cakes from the East, such as *loukoum*. Dried and powdered rosebuds are used as a spice, either alone or with other ingredients (see *rās al-hānout*). In North Africa, chicken is often flavoured with rose combined with jasmine.

rose-hip   GRATTE-CUL

The red berry-like fruit of the rose, used for making jam. The hip is not a true fruit but the swollen receptacle of the plant, containing small hard seeds (the true fruits) with stiff hairs attached. When topped and tailed (stemmed and headed), the hips are placed in a dry pot to soften for a few days, then they are boiled in water and put through a food mill several times or puréed in a blender. Finally an equal volume of sugar is added, and they are cooked like jam. A white eau-de-vie can also be made from them.

roselle

OSEILLE DE GUINÉE

A species of tropical hibiscus (*Hibiscus sabdariffa*), also known as Jamaica sorrel, used as a condiment. The petals, which have a bitter taste, are used to flavour fish and meat sauces in India and Jamaica, while the red fruits are made into jam and into a refreshing sour drink called *karkade*, which is very popular in Egypt.

rosemary   ROMARIN

An aromatic shrub native to Mediterranean countries, whose evergreen leaves are used either fresh or dried as a flavouring. As they have a very pungent taste, only a few leaves are needed to flavour a marinade, a ragout, a game dish, or a grill. The name comes from the Latin *rosmarinus* (rose of the sea) and the herb combines particularly well with veal; it is also used in some tomato sauces and with oven-cooked fish. In northern Europe it is used to flavour sausagemeat, sucking pig, and roast lamb. In addition, a sprig of rosemary gives a delicate flavour to the milk used for a dessert. The flowers can be used to garnish salads and they can be crystallized (candied) in the same way as violets. Rosemary honey, a speciality of Narbonne in France, is much esteemed.

Rosette

An AOC wine from southwest France, grown on the slopes to the north of Bergerac. It is produced from Sauvignon Blanc, Sémillon, and Muscadelle grapes and is usually a semisweet wine. It is very rarely seen outside the locality.

rosette

A dry pure-pork sausage, originating in the Beaujolais region of France. Its name comes from the part of the pig's entrails into which it is stuffed – the spindle-shaped part of the intestine terminating in the rectum and commonly known as the *rosette*, because of its pink colour. The sausage is in the shape of a trussed spindle, about 30 cm (12 in) long, with a medium-coarse filling. It is cut into thin slices and eaten as an hors d'oeuvre or a snack.

rosé wine   VIN ROSÉ

A pink wine, usually best when young and drunk cool. It should never be a blend of red and white wines, except in the Champagne region, where makers can use certain of the local reds for this purpose, as well as making the wine pink by contact with the grape skins. Some rosé wines made from both black and white grapes are produced by allowing the black grapes (such as Grenache, Pinot Noir, Cabernet Franc, Gamay, Carignan, and Syrah) to ferment on their skins: the juice is then run off when a satisfactory colour has been obtained. Rosé wines are becoming more popular, and most of the wine-growing areas produce some. Some well-known rosés include Tavel, Marsannay (Burgundy), and Cabernet d'Anjou, and there are others from Alsace, Béarn, and Provence. Rosé wines are made in many other countries in Europe and in the United States.

rosquille or rousquille

A dry aniseed-flavoured cake said to have originated in Oloron-Sainte-Marie (Béarn), but also made in Arles-sur-Tech, Amélie-les-Bains, and Perpignan (Pyrenees). It is shaped like a figure of eight, like a large pretzel, and is covered with a thick layer of glacé icing (frosting). The recipe, dating apparently from the Crusades, is said to have been brought back to France by Gaston de Foix.

Rossini (Gioacchino)

Italian composer (born Pesaro, 1792; died Paris, 1868). A prolific operatic composer, he is equally well known in the field of gastronomy as a lover of good food. In his own words: 'To eat, to love, to sing, and to digest; in truth, these are the four acts in this *opéra bouffe* that we call life, and which vanishes like the bubbles in a bottle of champagne.'

Dishes named after Rossini generally include foie gras and truffles and demiglace sauce. The first and best-known dish to be named after him was tournedos Rossini (Rossini is said to have given the recipe to the chef at the Café Anglais). Other dishes that bear his name are scrambled eggs, soft-boiled or poached eggs, an omelette, roast chicken, chicken breasts, sole fillets, and a sautéed chicken dish. Truffles also feature in a salad dressing for which Rossini himself gave the recipe: 'Take some Provençal oil, some English mustard, some French vinegar, a little lemon, some pepper and salt; beat everything together; then throw in a few truffles, which should be cut up very small. The truffles lend a certain aura to this dressing which will send a gourmand into ecstasies . . . The truffle is the Mozart of mushrooms.'

The cook and historian Lacam writes that Rossini invented a way of stuffing macaroni with foie gras by means of a silver syringe.

RECIPES

Scrambled eggs Rossini OEUFS BROUILLÉS ROSSINI Make some scrambled eggs. Sauté some thin slices of foie gras in butter. Cook some sliced truffle in butter. Pour the scrambled eggs into a serving dish, garnish with the foie gras and truffle, then coat with a very reduced Madeira-flavoured demiglace sauce.

Tournedos Rossini Sauté 1 slice of foie gras and 2 slices of truffle per steak in butter. Fry some slices of bread trimmed to the shape of the steaks. Fry the fillet steaks (filets mignons) in butter and place each steak on a crouton. Arrange the foie gras and truffle slices on top. Deglaze the pan in which the steak was cooked with Madeira and pour the sauce over the meat.

rösti or roesti

A large potato cake made from layers of sliced potatoes, fried until golden. A Swiss speciality, originally from Berne, it may be flavoured with bacon strips or sliced onion.

RECIPE

Rösti Peel and grate (or finely slice) 750 g (1¾ lb) potatoes which have been cooked in their skins the night before. Add 1 teaspoon salt and, if liked, 100 g (4 oz, ½ cup) diced bacon. Melt 4 tablespoons (⅓ cup) lard in a frying pan (skillet) and add the potatoes, turning them several times so that they become impregnated with the lard. Cook over a medium heat, stirring frequently. (If the potatoes seem a little dry, cover the pan; if they start to disintegrate, leave uncovered.) When they are cooked, draw together in the pan and raise the heat until a golden crust forms underneath. Turn this cake out onto a plate, with the crust upwards. It can be served with *longeoles* (coarse Savoy sausages).

rôt

An obsolete French word for a piece of meat or fish cooked directly in front of the fire; with the pot-au-feu, it formed the basis of most meals in former times. (The equivalent today is *rôti*, roast.) The expression *être à pot et à rôt* meant to sit down to eat. By extension, the word came to mean the whole meal. However, *rôt* and *rôti* were not always synonymous: in theory, *rôti* was applied only to meat, whereas *rôt* could mean any of the dishes served in the great houses after the entrées, which might or might not contain meat.

According to Alfred Franklin in *La Vie privée d'autrefois*, Boileau, when working on his third satire, asked whether he should use *rôt* or *rôti* in the context:

'I was about to leave when the *rôt* appeared.
On a hare flanked by six scrawny chickens
Were piled three rabbits . . .'

He was told that the two words were equivalent, but that *rôt* was the nobler.

Rothomago

A dish of eggs *sur le plat* apparently invented by a cook from Rouen, the Latin name for which was *Rotomagus*. It should not be confused with dishes *à la rouennaise*.

RECIPE

Eggs sur le plat Rothomago OEUFS SUR LE PLAT ROTHOMAGO Prepare a very thick tomato sauce. Grill (broil) 2 chipolata sausages per serving. Brown some small slices of ham in butter and use them to garnish the dishes in which the eggs are to be served. Break 2 eggs into each dish and cook them *sur le plat* (see *egg*). Garnish each plate with 2 chipolatas and pour a ribbon of tomato sauce round them.

Rothschild

The name of the famous banking family has been given to a soufflé made from confectioners' custard (pastry cream) and crystallized (candied) fruit macerated in Danziger Goldwasser (a liqueur containing suspended particles of gold). Classically, this soufflé is decorated with a border of fresh strawberries.

RECIPE

Soufflé Rothschild Cut 150 g (5 oz, 1 cup) crystallized (candied) fruit into small pieces and macerate in 1 dl (6 tablespoons, scant ½ cup) Danziger Goldwasser for at least 30 minutes.

Whisk together 200 g (7 oz, scant cup) caster (superfine) sugar and 4 egg yolks until the mixture turns white and thick. Then mix in 75 g (3 oz, ¾ cup) flour and ½ litre (17 fl oz, 2 cups) boiling milk. Pour into a saucepan and bring to the boil, stirring constantly, then cook for 1–2 minutes. Pour the confectioners' custard (pastry cream) into a bowl and add 2 raw egg yolks, the pieces of fruit, and their macerating liquid. Whisk 6 egg whites to stiff peaks with a pinch of salt and fold them carefully into the cream.

Butter 2 soufflé dishes (for 4 servings each) and sprinkle the insides with 20 g (¾ oz, 1½ tablespoons) caster sugar. Divide the mixture between the 2 dishes and bake in the oven at 200 C (400 F, gas 6).

After 25 minutes, sprinkle the tops of the soufflés with icing (confectioners') sugar, taking care to leave the oven door open for the shortest possible time, then continue to cook for another 5 minutes.

Rôti-Cochon

The title of a book for children, published by Claude Michard at Dijon in about 1680. This 'very easy method of teaching children to read Latin and French' is of great interest because of the light it throws on the history of gastronomy. Many of its passages are inspired by cookery, greed, and the way of life of the period: 'After eating pears, you must drink something.' 'Sweet wafers, fritters, crackling waffles, buttered pancakes, and loaf sugar – these foods have a whiff of Lent about them.' 'Long live hot roast pork crackling.' 'Boiled capon is fine for those who have no teeth.' 'In a calf's head, the eyes and the ears are the tastiest morsels.' 'The modern way to serve salad is with the vegetables in one plate, the oil and vinegar in another.' 'Broth to take the edge off large appetites, roast meat to eat on feast days.'

rotisserie RÔTISSOIRE

An electrically powered rotating spit, designed for spit-roasting meat or poultry. It is in the form of a metal casing with a windowed front closure. An overhead infra-red element (either an ordinary guarded element or a quartz tube, more fragile but emitting more intense heat) browns the meat, which is turned automatically on the spit. The large spit is sometimes replaced by four or six automatically rotated skewers or by a container which avoids having to skewer the meat. Some models are supplied with a second heating element in the lower casing, thus simulating oven-roasting. A rack may be slid under the upper element, in place of the spit, on which food can be grilled (broiled). A removable drip tray is also supplied.

A rotisserie is also a shop or restaurant where spit-roast meat (especially chicken) is prepared and sold. In France, the term *rôtisseur* began to be used in about 1450. Before this time, the sellers of roast game and poultry were known as *oyeurs*, taking their name from the Rue des Oues (the present Rue aux Ours), in Les Halles district.

Under the Ancien Régime, the body of servants who were responsible for the king's food included an *hâteur*, a kitchen official who directed the operation of roasting. In large restaurants today the rôtisseur is in charge of all spit- or oven-roasting, as well as grilled and fried foods (meat, fish, poultry, game, and vegetables). According to custom, he also supplies the other staff with chopped parsley and fresh bread-crumbs, when required. He also slices the potatoes for frying.

In 1963, a gastronomic association, the Chaîne des Rôtisseurs, was founded to 'encourage the use of the spit and respect for the art of spit-roasting ... which in its neat and straightforward operation is the symbol and the emblem of French cookery, honest and simple.'

rouelle

A thick round slice of veal cut across the leg; it is roasted or braised. Shin of veal (veal shank) is also cut across into rounds, for example for osso bucco.

rouennaise (à la)

A description applied mainly to prepa-rations of duck or duckling, for which Rouen is famous. Some typical prepara-tions are pressed duck, invented in Rouen at the beginning of the 19th cen-tury, and stuffed duck, roasted and served with rouennaise sauce (a highly spiced bordelaise sauce to which chicken liver has been added). This sauce may also be served with poached eggs. The description *à la rouennaise* is applied to many recipes which include duck or duckling liver, as well as other specialities of Rouen, such as duck pâté, stuffed sheep's trotters (feet), fish with red wine or cider, and chicken with cream.

RECIPES

Omelette à la rouennaise For an 8-egg omelette, prepare 4 tablespoons (⅓ cup) red wine sauce and reduce until it is very thick. Whisk in 1 tablespoon but-ter. Prepare a purée of Rouen duckling livers. Cook the omelette and fill it with the purée. Place it on a serving dish and pour the sauce round it.

Rouennaise sauce SAUCE ROUEN-NAISE (from Raymond Oliver's recipe) Pound 150 g (5 oz) duck livers in a mortar. Peel and chop 75 g (3 oz, ¾ cup) shallots and cook until golden in 20 g (¾ oz, 1½ tablespoons) butter.

Pour ⅓ litre (11 fl oz, 1⅓ cups) red wine into the pan and boil until the liquid is reduced by half. Add 25 g (1 oz, ¾ cup) chopped parsley and 2 litres (3½ pints, 9 cups) demi-glace sauce. Adjust the seasoning and put aside. Just before serving, add the pounded duck livers and mix well to obtain a smooth sauce.

Stuffed duck à la rouennaise CANARD FARCI À LA ROUENNAISE (from Raymond Oliver's recipe in *La Cuisine*, new edn, Bordas, 1981) Draw, singe, and truss a duck weighing 1.5 kg (3¼ lb). Prepare a forcemeat: melt a little butter and oil in a saucepan and in this brown 25 g (1 oz, ¼ cup) chopped onion, 2 duck livers, a few sprigs of parsley, and 100 g (4 oz, 1 cup) chopped bacon fat. When all the ingredients are golden-brown, take the pan off the stove and leave it to cool.

Stuff the duck with the cold force-meat, sprinkle it with salt and pepper, and bard it. Put it in a roasting pan with a little butter and some coarsely chop-ped vegetables (1 onion, 2 carrots, 1 celery stick (stalk)). Cook for 1 hour in a very hot oven. Towards the end of the cooking time, remove the barding. When the bird is done, remove from the pan and keep hot.

Strain the cooking juices and pour off the fat. Replace the duck in the pan, sprinkle it with Madeira, bring to the boil, add the cooking juices, bring to the boil again, cover the pan, and leave it to cook for a few minutes. Place the duck on a hot serving dish and serve with either rouennaise sauce or the cooking juices, strained again and thickened with a little kneaded butter.

Rouergue

A former French province in the south-east, now part of the departments of Aveyron and Tarn-et-Garonne. The great specialities of its capital, Rodez (in Aveyron), are typical of the cooking of the whole region: veal tripe (trénels *à la ruthénoise*), game pâtés, and fricassee of pig's trotters (feet) are particularly famous.

Among the soups common to the whole Aveyron region are cabbage soup, aïgo boulido, ouillade and the very rich mourtayrol.

Specific to the Rouergue region are

sheep's tripe (called *manouls*), the dried hams from Naucelle and Najac, preserved goose, truffle omelette, stuffed pancakes from Ségala, thrushes from the Causses, and *stoficado* (dried salt cod) from the Lot valley.

Puff pastries are flavoured with Roquefort, while Laguiole, Bleu des Causses, and Cabécou cheeses can be counted among the best. Wine from Gaillac (best when it is slightly sparkling: Gaillac Perlé) goes well with the cakes and pastries of the region, of which fouace, flavoured with lemon, orange-flower water, or bergamot, and sprinkled with sugar, is most representative. In the past, fouace was sprinkled with dragées (sugared almonds) for weddings and baptisms, and at Easter it takes the form of an enormous circular cake called *coque*, which is the centrepiece of an annual procession at Najac. Other cakes surviving from a past tradition are the decorative *soleil* of Marcillac (made from yeast dough with almonds, relic of an ancient sun-worshipping cult), prune rissoles, gâteau *à la broche*, and flônes.

Rouff (Marcel)

French journalist and writer (born Geneva, 1887; died Paris, 1936). He was a colleague and friend of Curnonsky, whom he accompanied on a gastronomic tour of France, seeking out and recording her culinary resources. They published their findings in 28 little guides, written in a lively and humorous style, under the collective title of *La France gastronomique*.

Rouff portrayed Curnonsky in his novel *Guinoiseau ou le Moyen de ne pas réussir*, but he is best known for his novel *La Vie et la Passion de Dodin-Bouffant, gourmet* (1924), in which he created the archetypal perfect gastronome who sacrifices everything to the epicurean pleasures of the table. It is said that this character was based on Lucien Tendret, a distant relative of Brillat-Savarin and a well-known gastronome. In his foreword to this work, Rouff wrote: 'Light, refined, learned and noble, harmonious and orderly, clear and logical, the cooking of France is, in some strange manner, intimately linked to the genius of her greatest men.'

The famous description of Dodin-Bouffant's pot-au-feu is still often quoted: 'The lips could sense already the velvety smoothness of the thick slices of beef, nestling on a large slice of sausage, in which coarsely chopped pork was combined with the finest veal, herbs, and chopped thyme and chervil. But this delicate pork confection, cooked in the same broth as the beef, was itself resting on an ample bed of white chicken meat, including the breasts and the wings, boiled in its own liquor with a veal knuckle that had been rubbed with mint and wild thyme. And to support this magical triple edifice, there had been cleverly inserted under the white flesh of the chicken (which had been fed only on milk-soaked bread) a rich and robust foundation of a generous slice of fresh foie gras, simply poached in Chambertin.'

rougail

A highly spiced seasoning used in the cooking of the West Indies and Réunion. Made from vegetables, shellfish or fish, and pimientos, it is simmered in oil and can be eaten hot or cold, with rice-based West Indian dishes.

| RECIPE

Rougail of salt cod ROUGAIL DE MORUE Soak 300 g (11 oz) salt-cod fillets in cold water for 24 hours, changing the water 2 or 3 times. Dry the fish, cut into small pieces, and dip in flour. Heat 3 tablespoons (¼ cup) olive oil (or oil and lard) in a flameproof casserole and cook the fish until golden. Add 3 peeled and finely sliced onions, then cover and cook gently until the onions are soft. Then add 4 peeled tomatoes, deseeded and coarsely chopped. In a food processor, purée a small piece of root ginger (ginger root), 1 garlic clove, 1 small red chilli pepper, 1 teaspoon chopped parsley, and a few leaves of fresh thyme. Mix this purée into the fish, cover the casserole, and cook gently in the oven at 180 C (350 F, gas 4) for 50 minutes. Serve either hot or cold.

rouille

A Provençal sauce whose name (meaning rust) describes its colour, due to the presence of red chillies and sometimes saffron. The chillies are pounded with garlic and breadcrumbs (or potato pulp), then blended with olive oil and stock. Rouille is served with bouillabaisse, boiled fish, and octopus. Lemon juice and fish liver may be added to it.

| RECIPE

Rouille (from Raymond Oliver's recipe in *La Cuisine*, new edn, Bordas, 1981) Pound 2 small red chillies and 1 clove of garlic in a mortar (if the chillies are dried, soak them first for a few hours in cold water). Add 1 teaspoon olive oil if liked, but this is not essential and may change the taste of the sauce. Pound 2 scorpion-fish livers and 1 small potato, cooked either in the bouillabaisse or in a little fish fumet, and add the chillies. When the mixture is smooth, gradually blend it with some strained broth from the bouillabaisse (use enough to make it up to 7 times the original volume). If the sauce is to accompany a chicken bouillabaisse rather than a fish one, replace the scorpion-fish livers with chicken livers.

roulade

Any of various preparations which are stuffed and then rolled. A pork or veal roulade consists of a fairly thin slice of meat, spread with forcemeat and rolled up, then usually braised. Veal roulade can also be made using a slice from the leg or breast slit open to form a pocket, filled with a forcemeat mixed with a salpicon, then rolled into a galantine and poached in white stock. A roulade of pig's head is prepared from the boned head with the rind left on, which is salted and washed, stuffed (usually with the ears, tongue, and filets mignons), and cooked in a cloth. It is served as a cold hors d'oeuvre.

round of beef   ROND

A cut of beef taken from the top of the hind leg of the animal. Topside (top round), which forms part of the cut, gives a lean and fairly tender roasting joint with a good flavour. Silverside (bottom round) and rump are also part of the round.

Roussette

A white wine from the upper Rhône Valley, made from the Roussette (or Altesse) grape. The AOC wine Roussette-de-Savoie is pale and very dry. The Roussette grape is used for other Rhône wines, notably Seyssel.

roussette

A deep-fried pastry fritter, which is a speciality of Beauce in France. It is made from a rather thick pastry dough flavoured with orange-flower water and brandy, rolled out, and cut into rounds with a plain biscuit (cookie) cutter. Crisp, golden, and sprinkled thickly with sugar, roussettes were traditionally made at carnival time.

Roussillon

This part of Languedoc, lying to the east of the Pyrenees, with its Côte Vermeille bathed by the Mediterranean, has many resources. Game from the former county of Foix, including chamois, snow partridge, capercaillie, wild pigeon, and even bear, are prepared in ways which date from the Renaissance. The river trout are as well known as the snails, which are cooked over charcoal (see *cargolade*). Civet of langouste, monkfish, and salt cod *à la catalane* are justly famous on this coast, as are the anchovy pâtés, the mussels, and the clams. The bouillinada, a local form of bouillabaisse, is accompanied by *crémat* of garlic (puréed and diluted with stock), and the most common way of cooking fish is *à la catalane* (heavily flavoured with peppers, aubergines (eggplants), and tomatoes). Eggs are prepared in many different ways: *à la causalade* (with slices of fried local ham), scrambled with aubergines or ceps, hard-boiled (hard-cooked) with anchovies, or in an omelette with sausage or black pudding (blood sausage). The excellent early vegetables of the region are used in salads and especially in soups: escudella de nadal, ouillade, soups with mint and thyme, and braoubouffat. Broad (fava) beans are stewed *à l'étouffée* (with wine and herbs), haricot (navy) beans are prepared as an estouffat, and onions are ingredients in many spicy dishes simmered in olive oil, which make the cooking of Roussillon so typical of the Mediterranean region. Among other well-known dishes are shoulder of mutton *à la catalane* (with pistachio nuts), young partridge with morels, and pigeons simmered in a casserole with Rancio wine and flavoured with orange peel.

Several varieties of ewes'-milk cheese are made in Roussillon, but their reputation is surpassed by that of the region's fruit: peaches and apricots are of prime quality, followed by raspberries, grapes, figs, and pomegranates. The pastries and sweetmeats of the region include tartlets filled with pears, apples, dried figs, or prunes, brioche ring (or *bistorto*), pancakes with honey or bilberry or strawberry jam, turrón, honey, and nougat. The old traditions are kept alive with *biscotins* (sweet biscuits (cookies)), rosquilles, and aniseed bread.

A good ratafia is made from quinces, and some vigorous red wines are produced (Corbières-du-Roussillon and Côtes-du-Roussillon), but it is the liqueur wines and the sweet fortified wines which are considered the best (Banyuls, Muscat de Rivesaltes, and Maury).

rout RAOUT

An archaic name for a large party, social gathering, or reception. The English word is derived from the French *route*, which used to mean 'company'. The modern French word (*raout*) is derived from the English and first appeared in 1804. In the 1920s, when everything to do with the English was fashionable, the word was used to describe a cocktail party or an evening reception (Proust used it). The word has now fallen into disuse.

roux

A cooked mixture of equal amounts of flour and butter, used to thicken many sauces. The cooking period varies, depending on the colour of roux required (a white or blond roux for a white sauce; a brown roux for a brown sauce).

A white roux should, in theory, remain white. However, as it must also be cooked long enough to lose its floury taste, it is advisable to cook it until it is just beginning to take on a golden colour (blond). Blended with milk, a white or blond roux is used for a béchamel sauce; blended with white veal stock it makes a veal velouté, with

chicken stock, a chicken velouté, and with fish stock, a fish velouté.

A brown roux, cooked just long enough to obtain a light brown colour, is used to thicken espagnole and demiglace sauces.

RECIPES

White roux ROUX BLANC Melt the butter in a thick-bottomed saucepan, then clarify it. Add the same weight (or a little more) of sifted flour (up to 120 g (4½ oz, generous cup) flour for 100 g (4 oz, ½ cup) butter). To make 1 litre (1¾ pints, 4¼ cups) béchamel sauce, the roux should contain 70–80 g (about 3 oz) flour and the same weight of butter; to make 1 litre (1¾ pints, 4¼ cups) velouté sauce, use 50–60 g (2–2½ oz) flour and the same weight of butter.

Mix the butter and flour, stirring constantly with a wooden spoon and covering the whole base of the saucepan, so that the roux does not colour unevenly and become lumpy. Continue to cook in this way for 5 minutes, until the mixture begins to froth a little. Take the pan off the heat and leave it to cool until time to add the liquid (milk, white stock, fish stock). To avoid lumps forming this must be poured boiling onto the cold roux. Use a whisk to mix the roux and heat gradually while whisking constantly. (Alternatively, the cold liquid may be whisked gradually into the warm roux.)

Blond roux ROUX BLOND Make a white roux, but cook it gently for 10 minutes, stirring constantly, until it becomes a golden colour.

Brown roux ROUX BRUN Make a white roux, but cook it very gently for 15–20 minutes, stirring constantly, until it becomes a light brown colour.

rowanberry ALISE

An orange-red berry the size of a small cherry. It is the fruit of the mountain ash tree, a species of *Sorbus*. The berries are used when almost overripe to make jam or jelly (good with venison) and, on a small scale, brandy. They have a tart flavour.

royale

A moulded custard which is cut into

small dice, lozenges (diamonds), stars, etc., and used as a garnish for clear soup. Made from consommé and eggs, or a vegetable or poultry purée thickened with eggs, it is cooked in dariole moulds in a bain-marie. When it is cooked, it is unmoulded and cut into the desired shapes.

The word *royale* (royal) is also used to describe a type of icing (frosting) made from egg whites and icing (confectioners') sugar (see *icing*).

RECIPES

Plain royale ROYALE ORDINAIRE Add a generous pinch of chervil to 1.5 dl (¼ pint, ⅔ cup) boiling consommé and leave it to infuse for 10 minutes. Beat 1 whole egg with 2 yolks and add the consommé gradually, stirring constantly. Strain through a sieve lined with muslin (cheesecloth), skim, and cook in a bain-marie as for royale of asparagus.

Royale of asparagus ROYALE D'ASPERGE Cook 75 g (3 oz) asparagus tips and 5 or 6 fresh spinach leaves in boiling water for a few minutes, then drain them. Add 1½ tablespoons béchamel sauce and 2 tablespoons (3 tablespoons) consommé. Press through a sieve. Bind the mixture with 4 egg yolks, pour into dariole moulds, and cook in a bain-marie in the oven at 200 c (400 f, gas 6) for 30 minutes.

Royale of chicken purée ROYALE DE PURÉE DE VOLAILLE Poach 50 g (2 oz) white chicken meat and pound it finely. Add 2 tablespoons (3 tablespoons) béchamel sauce and the same amount of cream and press it through a sieve. Bind with 4 egg yolks and cook in a bain-marie as for royale of asparagus.

Royale of tomatoes ROYALE DE TOMATE Mix 1 dl (6 tablespoons, scant ½ cup) concentrated tomato purée with 4 tablespoons (⅓ cup) consommé. Add salt and pepper, bind with 4 egg yolks, and cook in a bain-marie as for royale of asparagus.

royale (à la)

Describing clear soups garnished with a royale; the term is also applied to various other dishes which have a light and delicate garnish.

Fish *à la royale* (salmon, turbot, trout) are poached and served hot, garnished with quenelles, mushrooms, poached oysters, and truffles, accompanied by a mousseline sauce. Poultry *à la royale* is poached, garnished with quenelles and mushrooms (sometimes with the addition of slices of foie gras), and covered with royale sauce (a thick velouté to which cream and chopped truffles are added). Hare *à la royale* is a famous dish claimed by Périgord and Orléanais. The description *à la royale* may also apply to hot or cold desserts – puddings, soufflés, stuffed pineapple, ice-cream sundaes, etc. – which are made from unusual ingredients and are presented with sophistication.

RECIPES

Consommé à la royale Make some meat or chicken consommé; prepare a plain or herb-flavoured royale. Let the royale get completely cold, unmould it onto a cloth (this will absorb any moisture), and cut it into small cubes, circles, stars, leaves, etc. Just before serving, add this garnish to the hot soup.

Hare à la royale LIÈVRE À LA ROYALE (from Claude Terrail's recipe in *Ma Tour d'Argent*, Stock) Collect the blood from a good-sized skinned hare, reserve the liver, heart, and lungs, and remove the head. Carefully grease the base and sides of a very large stewpot with goose fat. Make a bed of bacon rashers (slices) in the pot, place the hare (on its back) on top, and cover with bacon rashers. Add 1 sliced carrot, 20 garlic cloves, 40 shallots, 4 onions studded with cloves, and a bouquet garni. Pour in 25 cl (8 fl oz, 1 cup) wine vinegar and a bottle and a half of Burgundy. Season with salt and pepper. Put the pot over a low heat, cover it, and cook for 3 hours.

Finely chop 125 g (4½ oz) bacon, the hare's offal, 10 garlic cloves, and 20 shallots. Mix all these together very thoroughly. Remove the stewpot from the heat. Lift out the hare very carefully and put it on a dish, leaving the bacon and vegetables in the stewpot. Tip the contents of the pot into a strainer, pressing to extract as much liquid as possible. Add this to the chopped bacon, offal, and vegetables and pour in half a bottle of heated Burgundy. Pour this mixture into the stewpot, replace the hare, and cook over a low heat for 1½ hours. Skim off the surface fat. 15 minutes before serving, add the blood, well whisked and diluted with Cognac. When cooking is complete, arrange the hare on a serving dish and pour the sauce around it. Serve the same type of wine that was used to cook the hare.

Royale sauce SAUCE ROYALE Mix together 2 dl (7 fl oz, ¾ cup) chicken velouté sauce and 1 dl (6 tablespoons, scant ½ cup) white chicken stock. Reduce by half, adding 1 dl (6 tablespoons, scant ½ cup) cream during the reduction. Just before serving, add 2 tablespoons (3 tablespoons) finely chopped raw truffle, then whisk in 50 g (2 oz, ¼ cup) butter, and finally add 1 tablespoon sherry.

Salpicon à la royale Prepare 3 tablespoons (¼ cup) chopped mushrooms and 1 tablespoon chopped truffle. Cook the mushrooms in butter, then add the truffle and 4 tablespoons (⅓ cup) chicken purée. Mix well and use as a filling for bouchées or barquettes.

rub in SABLER

To mix the dry ingredients of a shortcrust pastry (basic pie dough) or a sablé mixture (flour, salt, fat, and sometimes sugar) to a crumbly, almost powdery, consistency. This is done first with the fingertips, fairly rapidly, then by taking small amounts of the mixture and rubbing between the palms. Water or eggs are then added and the dough is drawn into a ball and allowed to rest.

rudd ROTENGLE

A freshwater fish, known also in France as *gardon rouge* (red roach), as it is similar to the roach in appearance and habitat. It is cooked in the same ways as the roach, i.e. fried, grilled (broiled), or meunière, but it makes a very mediocre dish.

rue

A perennial herbaceous plant with small greyish-blue bitter-tasting leaves. It is an ancient herbal remedy, and during the Middle Ages was among the plants used for making liqueurs. Traditionally it was used to flavour the herb-based hippocras. Nowadays, its use is banned in France due to the mistaken idea that it can induce abortion. In Italy, however, it is used to flavour grappa (a marc brandy) – a small bunch of fresh rue sprigs is put into the bottle to macerate. In eastern Europe it is an ingredient of meat stuffings and is added to flavour cream cheeses and marinades.

ruifard

A dessert typical of the Dauphiné region of France, particularly the Valbonnais area. It is a large pie made from yeast dough, filled with sliced pears, apples, and quinces cooked in butter, sweetened, and flavoured with Chartreuse.

RECIPE

Ruifard Dissolve 15 g (½ oz) dried yeast (1 sachet active dried yeast) in 2 tablespoons warm water. Sift 250 g (9 oz, 2¼ cups) flour into a heap and pour the dissolved yeast into a well in the centre. Mix in a little of the flour to make a thick cream. Leave it to rise for 10 minutes. Then add 1 whole egg, 20 g (¾ oz, 1½ tablespoons) softened butter, 1 tablespoon oil, 100 g (4 oz, 6 tablespoons) fresh cream, 15 g (½ oz, 1 tablespoon) sugar, and ¼ teaspoon salt. Work with the hands to incorporate all the flour and knead until the dough leaves the fingers cleanly, then put it in a bowl and leave to rise for 30 minutes at 25 C (77 F).

Peel and slice 5 large apples, 5 pears, and 2 small quinces. Cook them for 10 minutes with 60 g (2 oz, ¼ cup) butter and 150 g (5 oz, ⅔ cup) sugar; flavour with 1 liqueur glass of Chartreuse. Butter a 20-cm (8-in) sandwich tin (layer cake pan) and roll out half the dough to a thickness of 0.5 cm (¼ in). Line the base and sides of the mould with this dough and pour in the cooked fruit. Roll out the rest of the dough a little more thinly and cover the fruit, sealing the edges with a little cold water.

Leave to rise for a further 10–15 minutes, then brush the surface with egg yolk. Bake for 30 minutes in a moderate oven.

Rully

The AOC of a Burgundy from the Côte Chalonnaise. The parish, adjacent to the Côte de Beaune, produces some red wine but mostly a dry and fruity white, usually drunk young. When it is made sparkling (a process to which it lends itself well) it is sold as Bourgogne Mousseux.

rum RHUM

A spirit distilled from sugar cane. The origin of the word is disputed: it may be a corruption of the Spanish *ron*; it may derive from the Latin *saccharum* (sugar); or it may be a contraction of *rumbustion* or *rumbullion*, formerly meaning 'strong liquor'. The Oxford English Dictionary prefers the latter etymology and dates use of the word 'rum' from 1654.

□ **History** According to legend, sugar cane was brought to the West Indies by Columbus from the Canaries, where it had been introduced from the Orient. Distillation from sugar cane or its by-products was taking place in Hispaniola around the start of the 17th century, but these rough spirits were only drunk by colonists in the absence of imports of anything better: a contemporary description of them is 'hot, hellish, and terrible'. Gradually rum became more refined: seafarers acquired a taste for it and introduced it into Europe, particularly western England, France, and Spain, and it eventually spread all over the known world.

Historically, rum was powerful and strong in flavour. The cane juice, or diluted molasses (the residue after cane has been pressed), would ferment violently in hot climates when in contact with natural yeasts, producing an alcoholic wash. From this rum was distilled, and often redistilled, in pot-stills (alembics). There were improvements in techniques – cultured yeasts were discovered, filtration improved, and the value of maturing appreciated – but no basic change took place in rum production until the invention in Britain of continuous (patent, or column) distillation, which was perfected in the 1830s. Patent stills were soon in operation in

the Caribbean region and they were to have a profound effect. Continuous distillation permitted increased volume with less labour and gave improved control over the final product's strength and degree of flavour.

□ **Types of rum** Some de-luxe rums are wholly from pot-stills, but most of the rums of normal commerce come from the column stills at very high strength and as almost flavourless spirit. They are either left as white rum or coloured and flavoured in various ways. Blending of rums of diverse origins is commonly practised.

Since all distillates are initially colourless, regardless of absence or presence of natural flavour, it is necessary to adjust dark rums to the required colour, ranging from pale golden, through amber, to deep brown, by the addition of caramel. Certain premium rums are matured in oak casks long enough to acquire some natural tint from the wood. Colour is, however, principally a matter of style; it has nothing to do with taste and only marginally with quality. The consumer has come to associate a dark hue with a pungent rum and white rum with virtual lack of flavour. Yet there are excellent full-flavoured rums that are almost colourless.

In speciality rums, there are two outstanding types. *Rhum agricole* is particularly relished in France and there is some demand for it in the United States. This 'agricultural rum' is made not from molasses but entirely from straight cane juice: this confers prestige in the opinion of some drinkers. The best-known (Clément) comes from Martinique and is aged for six years. British Navy Rum (Pusser's), from the British Virgin Islands, is fairly new to general commerce: formerly it was exclusively sold to be used as the Royal Navy's official daily issue of powerful highly aromatic rum. The issue was stopped in 1970.

Rum of sorts is made wherever sugar cane flourishes, often for purely local use. In world terms, by far the largest producer is Puerto Rico. All styles are made there, including some unusual *añejos* (aged) rums. However, white rum predominates, typified by Ron Bacardi, progenitor of 'Cuban' rum, whose largest distillery is in Puerto Rico. The next most important rum island is Jamaica. Jamaican rum is traditionally double-distilled in pot-stills and distinctly pungent, but Jamaica also produces light white rums by continuous distillation. Martinique is principally noted for rich fragrant rum. Other important producers are Guyana (Demerara), which distils heavy, sometimes exceptionally strong, rums, but also white varieties; Barbados, famous for Mount Gay, a smoothly medium-rich rum; and Trinidad, which produces similar types.

□ **Uses of rum** White rum is best for punches, daiquiris, and other cocktails, while the stronger and darker rums are used in grogs, flamed dishes, cooking, and pâtisserie. Old rums can be drunk as liqueurs.

There are many uses for rum in cooking, from soaking sponge cakes (for desserts and charlottes) to flavouring pancake batters, dessert creams, mousses, zabaglione, sorbets, fruit salads, etc., or sprinkling on babas and savarins, flaming pancakes and omelettes, and macerating crystallized (candied) or dried fruit.

Rum combines particularly well with sweet potatoes, pineapple, and bananas and the meat and fish dishes that these accompany (pork, sautéed chicken, turkey, scampi or monkfish kebabs, kidneys, roast duck, etc.). The aroma enhances sauces and marinades. Rum is suitable for flaming only very tender meat, such as offal and spring chicken.

Rumford
(Benjamin Thomson, Count)

American physician (born Woburn, Massachusetts, 1753; died Paris, 1814). He came to Europe to reorganize the army of the Elector of Bavaria, and during this period became interested in the problems of nutrition, in particular, how to extract the maximum benefit from food while using the minimum of fuel. As a result, he invented a brick cooker, with separate adjustable burners, which made the cook's job very much easier and also saved fuel. He also invented a pressure cooker and a kitchen stove.

Having discovered that the volatile oils in coffee were responsible for its taste, he suggested making coffee in a closed container, over a constant heat which kept the liquid just below boiling point and so avoided destroying the aroma; he could thus claim to be the inventor of the percolator. He is often credited with the invention of baked Alaska.

Rumohr
(Karl Friedrich von)

German writer and patron of the arts (born Dresden, 1785; died Dresden, 1843). Rich and independent, writer of novels and travel books, he is best known as the author of a cookery book, *Der Geist der Kochkunst*, which appeared in 1823, two years before Brillat-Savarin's *La Physiologie du goût*. Karl von Rumohr was an enlightened amateur, a fastidious connoisseur, a historian, even a dietician; his book deals with the nature of food, the origins of cookery and cooking methods, and the preparation of meat and fish, sauces, pâtés, and conserves. It then goes on to discuss vegetables, herbs, spices, sugar, and jams. The third volume is devoted to table manners, how to receive guests, etc. The book relates remarkably well to modern culinary practice.

rump steak
ROMSTECK, RUMSTECK

A cut of beef taken from between the buttock and the sirloin. Less tender than fillet but with a better flavour, the cut yields steaks for rapid grilling (broiling) or frying; when cut into pieces it can be used for kebabs or a fondue bourguignonne. It can form a roast (for which a piece at least 7 cm (2¾ in) thick is required, usually from the top rump), which is treated in the same way as a fillet or sirloin; the meat, which is dense and lean, should be lightly barded.

runner bean

A climbing bean plant widely cultivated for its edible green pods, which are cooked and prepared in the same way as French beans (see *bean*). A famous variety is the scarlet runner (*haricot d'Espagne*), named after its red flowers.

rusk   BISCOTTE
A slice of bread made from a special kind of dough (containing flour, water,

salt, yeast, fat, and sugar) and rebaked in the oven. Rusks are widely consumed in France (as *biscottes*) and also in other countries, such as Germany (as *Zwieback*) and the Netherlands. The bread is first baked in a mould, then sliced. The stale slices are rebaked in the oven, giving them a golden colour. They must have a crumbly texture with very small holes.

Rusks were originally considered as diet food. Now they are commonly eaten in France for breakfast and with meals. The composition may be modified for certain diets (salt-free, gluten-enriched, with bran, etc.). French 'toast', marketed in oblong slices, contain less fat and sugar than rusks.

Rusks are sometimes used in cookery and pastry-making, either soaked in milk for stuffings, as a garnish for gratin dishes, or powdered for use as bread-crumbs.

russe

In the restaurant trade, a round straight-sided saucepan with a long handle and a tight-fitting lid, used for cooking food in liquid.

russe (à la)

Describing preparations of shellfish coated in aspic jelly, covered with a chaudfroid sauce or a thick mayonnaise, and accompanied by a Russian salad (a macédoine of vegetables bound with mayonnaise, set in an aspic-lined mould or served in glass dishes). Russian sauce (*sauce russe*), served with crudités or cold fish, is made from mayonnaise mixed with caviar and possibly the creamy parts of lobster or crayfish.

All these dishes are inspired by the classic cuisine as practised at the time of the tsars, particularly by French chefs, and are not really representative of true Russian cookery. However, some recipes described as *à la russe* are based on Slav traditions, including those featuring cucumbers and gherkins, bitoke, herrings, stuffed peppers, fillet of beef, kacha, piroshki, etc.

RECIPES

Canapés à la russe Remove the crusts from slices of white bread and cut into small rounds, squares, or triangles. Spread with butter flavoured with herbs, cover with Russian salad, and then coat them with a thin layer of aspic. Refrigerate and serve as an hors d'oeuvre. A small slice of truffle may be placed in the centre of each canapé.

Fillets of herring à la russe FILETS DE HARENG À LA RUSSE Boil some potatoes in their skins, then peel and slice them. Take some large herring fillets in oil and slice them very thinly. Reshape them, placing a slice of potato between each slice of herring. Arrange on a long serving dish and dress with a herb vinaigrette (made with parsley, chervil, tarragon, and chives) to which some finely chopped fennel and shallots have been added.

Russian mayonnaise MAYONNAISE À LA RUSSE Melt 4 dl (14 fl oz, 1¾ cups) aspic jelly but do not let it get too warm. Mix with 3 dl (½ pint, 1¼ cups) mayonnaise and 1 tablespoon wine vinegar. Pour the mixture into a bowl placed over crushed ice and beat with a whisk until it becomes frothy (never use a wooden spoon).

This sauce can be used to bind a dry macédoine of vegetables, which is then set in aspic-lined moulds.

Russian salad SALADE RUSSE Boil and finely dice some potatoes, carrots, and turnips; boil some French beans and cut into short pieces. Mix together equal quantities of these ingredients and add some well-drained cooked petits pois. Bind with mayonnaise and pile up in a salad bowl. Garnish with a julienne of pickled tongue and truffles and add some finely diced lobster or langouste meat.

For a more elaborate dish, the ordinary mayonnaise can be replaced by thickened mayonnaise and the salad is poured into mould lined with aspic and decorated with slivers of truffle and pickled tongue. Chill in the refrigerator for 4 hours and remove from the mould just before serving.

Russian sauce (*cold*) SAUCE RUSSE FROIDE Mix equal quantities of caviar and finely sieved creamy parts (liver) of lobster. Make some mayonnaise and add the caviar mixture: use 1 part mixture to 4 parts mayonnaise.

This sauce may be seasoned with a little mild mustard.

Salmon cutlets à la russe CÔTE-LETTES DE SAUMON À LA RUSSE Cut fresh salmon steaks in two lengthwise to make the cutlets; poach them for 5 minutes in a court-bouillon. Let them cool completely in their juices, then drain, dry, and glaze them with aspic. Place a layer of shredded lettuce in vinaigrette on a large serving dish and arrange the salmon cutlets on top. Garnish with very small lettuce hearts, quartered hard-boiled (hard-cooked) eggs, black (ripe) olives, capers, and anchovy fillets in oil.

Sauce à la russe (from Carême's recipe) Chop and blanch 1 tablespoon parsley, chervil, and tarragon, drain it, and mix with a fairly thick velouté sauce. Just before serving, add 1 tablespoon fine mustard, ½ tablespoon caster (superfine) sugar, a pinch of finely ground pepper, and some lemon juice.

This sauce can be served with large joints of meat.

Russian cookery

CUISINE RUSSE

Soviet Russia, with its sea frozen over for ten months of the year in the north and its Mediterranean climate in the south, draws its resources from the granary of the Ukraine, the Armenian vineyards, the Caucasian orchards, and the Georgian tea plantations. The country has inherited diverse culinary traditions throughout its history, which reaches back over several centuries.

The Riourikides dynasty, which arrived from Scandinavia in the ninth century, brought with it smoked fish and meat, grain alcohol, and dishes containing sour cream (see *smetana*). During the tenth century, Vladimir the Great introduced oriental cooking: aubergines (eggplants), mutton, and grapes appeared on the table, although cereals and turnips were still the basic foods. Thereafter, every invasion by a neighbouring country widened the choice of foods; sauerkraut from the northern peoples and curdled milk introduced by the Tatars are notable examples. At the

feast of Ivan the Terrible and his boyars, bears' paws, haunch of reindeer, and roast fowls were served, all washed down with gallons of hydromel, kvass, and fruit liqueurs. By the end of the 17th century, Peter the Great had left his mark on Russian cookery, which was modelled on that of France: the sumptuous dinner services, embroidered cloths, and crystal glasses, the melons and caviar from the Caspian Sea, the fresh vegetables from the Ukraine, and the oysters from the Baltic all evoked the splendour of Versailles. Marriages between the tsars and German princesses introduced the custom of cooking fruit with meat and a taste for sweet-and-sour dishes.

French chefs, among them Carême and Dubois, who had been employed at the tsar's court brought back to Europe many classic Russian dishes (see *borsch, pashka, Pojarski, bitoke, piroshki, koulibiaca*). At the beginning of the 20th century, émigrés popularized other specialities from their native land – caviar, blini, vatrouchka, and zakuski – in the first Russian restaurants to be established in Paris. During the period of the Belle Époque, many dishes created by French chefs were inspired by Russian cookery – see *Demidof, Nesselrode, Orloff, Romanov, Souvarov, Vladimir, Néva (à la), tsarine (à la)*. The adoption of service *à la russe*, now standard practice, is due to the influence of a Russian ambassador to the court of Napoleon III.

☐ **Three Russian rituals** The Russian Easter is traditionally celebrated by a meal eaten on the return from Midnight Mass, between Holy Saturday and Easter Sunday. A 16th-century book, *Le Ménagier russe du XVIᵉ s.*, gives a vivid description of this meal. The table, covered with an embroidered cloth, is spread with dishes of meat, small pies, desserts, and pastries, all of which are regularly renewed throughout Sunday and Monday, to be eaten as and when desired by the family, friends, and guests. There is often a roast lamb or sucking pig on the menu, a cold jellied ham, *koulibiaca*, roast turkey or game, painted eggs, a pashka, koulitch, traditional Easter cakes (such as babas), and Polish galettes of unleavened bread.

Tea-drinking is a daily ritual. There is

always boiling water in the samovar ready to make the tea, which is very strong, sometimes flavoured or perfumed, and drunk with little or no sugar but sometimes with a spoonful of jam or with lemon (very rarely with milk).

The third major feature of Russian home entertaining is the zakuski, a selection of hors d'oeuvres served with vodka. French cuisine has adopted a number of these savouries as a small entrées. They could include any of the following: herrings (marinated, smoked, or in cream), an assortment of piroshki, pelmeni, cyrniki, kromeskies, rastegaï, tvarogi, varieniki, and sausseli, pancakes filled with cream cheese (*nalizniki*), stuffed eggs, aubergine (eggplant) caviar (and real caviar), marinated fruit and vegetables (beetroot (red beet), mushrooms, quetsche plums, pears), and cucumbers with sour cream and salt (*molossol*). With the zakuski is offered a large variety of breads: *balabouchki* (a sour-dough loaf), *boubliki* (a hard bread), *boulotchki* (milk bread sprinkled with breadcrumbs), the very white *korj*, the plaited *krouchenik* (a dense almost black rye bread), *katchapouri* with cheese, *none* with onion, *tcherek* (sprinkled with sesame seeds), and *oukrainka* (a very dark wheel-shaped bread).

□ **Regional variations** Although the entire Soviet Union seems to share a taste for cabbage, cereals, potatoes, sour soups garnished with fish or meat (often served cold), tarts, and fruit desserts, regional cookery can show many variations on these themes.

● Georgia is characterized by Mediterranean-style dishes, including *adjersandal* (aubergines cooked in the oven, with tomatoes and fried onions) and chicken *en cocotte* with tomatoes. The sauces of the region are very inventive: they are made with walnuts to accompany meat, fish, or poultry; with chopped herbs to go with kidney beans (which feature in many Georgian recipes); with prunes, served especially with chicken in aspic. Some of the great Georgian specialities are shashlyk and pastirma, yogurt and *touchouri* (a hard cheese), and *ghomi* (a cornmeal porridge).

● Armenian cookery has an oriental flavour: *matonabour* is a very popular soup made with yogurt (*matzoun*), and pastirma, dry and salty, is eaten finely sliced. The proximity of Turkey is evidenced by such dishes as *kharpout kioufta* (sliced lamb garnished with crushed wheat, pine kernels, onions, and parsley), meatballs of lamb with herbs, kebabs, baklava, and stuffed vine leaves. Desserts, all very sweet, include *ekmek*, based on toasted bread soaked in honey, and *kaimak*, a very thick rich custard.

● Central Asia produces good-quality melons, dairy produce, including *kourt* (a sun-dried ewes'-milk cheese) and *umiss* (fermented mares' milk), and some inventive delicatessen products, such as smoked lamb or horsemeat sausage. There is also *samssa* (fritters of chopped vegetables bound with egg, or of walnuts and pumpkin), ravioli filled with steamed lamb, and *patyr* (small sour-cream cakes).

● The Ukraine shows the influence of German cookery, with its *galouchki* (thick smooth egg dumplings), cabbage leaves stuffed with rice and mushrooms, *nakypliak* (a sort of steamed cabbage soufflé), and *lekchyna* (egg noodles with spinach or walnuts). The traditional Christmas dish is *koutia*, a semolina cake with poppy seeds and dried fruit. The high cereal yield of the region is reflected in such dishes as *kalatch* (a very rich white bread), *balabouchki* (small buns made from sour dough), and numerous dishes based on kasha.

● Other regions of the Soviet Union include Lithuania, with its rustic cakes and pastries (*kugelis* made from grated potato and the Christmas dish *avizine kose*, a porridge of fermented oat flakes); Estonia, with its *rossolyie* (herring and beetroot salad) and *pannkoogid* (thick pancakes served with jam); and Latvia, with its chopped meat pies, smoked sprats, and the delicious Alexander cake, filled with raspberry jam.

Common to the cookery of all these regions is a basic core of traditional dishes that typify 'Old Russia'. The repertoire of soups includes borsch, chtchi, botvinya, okrochka, rassolnick, *solianka* (cucumber, onion, and tomato, garnished with meat or fish), the famous Bagration soup, and *spass* (made with barley and yogurt, flavoured with herbs).

Fish recipes include sturgeon in aspic with horseradish sauce; fish fillets, either smoked or grilled (broiled) on skewers; smoked or fried *sigui, kilki,* and *silki* (small fish similar to sprats), accompanied by onions; carp, lamprey, or pike-perch in sweet-and-sour preparations; and eel or salmon koulibiaca. Caviar (*ikra*) is lightly salted (*molossol*) or pressed into bricks (*paiousnaia*).

Among the meat and poultry specialities are *kournik* (a croustade of chicken with rice), kholodetz, *solonina* (salted rolled beef, poached and garnished with sauerkraut and potatoes, served with horseradish sauce), and stuffed shoulder of veal, marinated with juniper berries then simmered and served with sautéed cucumbers.

Authentic Russian desserts include *halva* (a walnut custard sprinkled with toasted walnuts), *gourieva kacha* (semolina pudding containing walnuts and crystallized (candied) fruit), kissel, and *mazurek* (a walnut sponge cake covered with an icing (frosting) made with walnuts, lemon, and vinegar). *Charlotka* is of French origin, being based on the iced charlottes made by French chefs working in Russia.

There is a wide range of pastries and sweets, including *gozinakhi* (walnut and honey sweets), fritters made with cream-cheese pancakes or with yeast dough, *pampouchki* (soufflé fritters), *krendiel* (very sweet brioches shaped like pretzels), lemon waffles, *vatrouchki* (cream-cheese tartlets), *zavyvaniets* (little balls made from fruit and walnuts, covered in sweet pastry), and hazelnut nougat.

Any survey of Russian gastronomy would be incomplete if it omitted to mention vodka, which may be flavoured with aniseed, herbs (*zubrowka*), lemon zest, blackcurrant leaves, caraway seeds, peppercorns, or even with lichen. Among other traditional Russian alcoholic drinks are kvass, hydromel, Caucasian wines, and *krupnikas* (a honey-based liqueur).

One other aspect that should be mentioned is the originality of Russian Jewish cookery. Typical dishes are iced soups with hard-boiled (hard-cooked) eggs or sorrel, sweet-and-sour stuffed carp and mackerel, *petchia* (jellied calves' feet), and *klops* (minced (ground) beef pâté with veal fat and herbs, cooked on a bed of onions and herbs). Saturday is the day for *tcholent* (brisket of beef cooked in the oven with onions, kasha, and potatoes). Other favourite dishes are stuffed goose neck and *gribenes* (pieces of goose skin fried with onions, served with sorrel fritters). Sauerkraut is eaten hot with smoked beef sausages or roast goose or cold, as an hors d'oeuvre. *Tsimes*, consisting of carrot or beetroot in a sweet-and-sour sauce, is served as a first course or as a garnish for meat. There are numerous flour-based dishes, including *lokschen* (vermicelli with eggs and cream cheese) and *kendlachs* (little dumplings of flour, egg, goose fat, and ginger, which are poached or fried). The pastries resemble those typical of Austria, many being based on dried fruit, cinnamon, and poppy seeds. Jams are prepared from black radish and honey and from quetsche plums and walnuts.

russula RUSSULE

A short brightly coloured mushroom with granular crumbly flesh. There are numerous species, not all of which are edible. They can be differentiated by colour or more reliably by tasting a very small fragment of the raw mushroom: if it has a bitter or a hot taste it should not be eaten; mild-tasting species can be eaten, but experience is needed to select the edible varieties. The best species, which are cooked in the same way as cultivated mushrooms, are the green russula (*russule verdoyante* or *palomet*), with a green-patched whitish cap (excellent for grilling (broiling)), and the variety known in France as *charbonnier* or *charbonnière*, with a purple, violet, or green cap and a pleasant but rather insipid taste.

Ruster Ausbruch

An Austrian white wine, produced near Rust in the Burgenland, from late-picked grapes. It is therefore somewhat concentrated and sweet – the term *ausbruch* in the context of Austrian wines signifies that the grapes are not picked until very ripe.

rye SEIGLE

A cereal native to western Asia, which appeared in Europe before the Iron Age and is grown mainly in Nordic regions, in the mountains and on poor soil. Rye flour can be made into bread; it is usually mixed with wheat flour (which is why the two crops are sometimes mixed). This results in bread with a brown dense texture and a slightly sour taste; it keeps well. Ryebread rolls are popular served with oysters and seafood. Rye flour is also used to make gingerbread and certain cakes (*nieules* and *pain de Linz*) as well as Russian and Scandinavian pies and crispbreads. Rye flakes are also an ingredient of muesli. Rye is not as rich in protein as the other cereals but it does have a high content of phosphorus, sulphur, iron, and vitamin B. It yields 335 Cal per 100 g. Some spirits can also be made based on rye; for example, vodka and whisky.

rye whiskey

An American whiskey, produced and consumed mainly in Pennsylvania, Maryland, and Canada. It is made from nonmalted rye and barley or rye malt. It is not matured for as long as Scotch or Bourbon and it has a more pungent taste.

sabardin

A charcuterie speciality of the Loire region, made from ox intestines and pieces of pig's stomach, belly, throat, and heart. It is highly seasoned, cooked in white wine, and encased in a pig's intestine.

sabayon

See *zabaglione*.

sablage

In former times, a table decoration made with sands of different colours, which were spread on the tablecloth so as to form various patterns: flowers, landscapes, coats of arms, monograms, etc.

sablé

A crumbly biscuit (cookie) of varying size, usually round and often with a fluted edge. Sablés are made from flour, butter, egg yolks (these are sometimes omitted), and sugar, mixed rapidly until of a sandy texture. The mixture is kneaded quickly, then either rolled out to a thickness of a few millimetres and cut out with a pastry (cookie) cutter or rolled into a thick sausage shape and sliced, as for so-called Dutch sablés, which are made with two mixtures, one coloured with chocolate or cinnamon, the other flavoured with vanilla. Sablés can be flavoured with lemon, flaked (slivered) almonds, or raisins and iced (frosted) with chocolate or topped with jam (see *milanais*).

Among the French regional varieties are the sablés of Saint-Renan (with Breton butter), Lisieux (with cinnamon, brown sugar, and cream). Caen (scored with a fork and brushed with egg yolk), Noirétable, and Péronne. Shortbread and Austrian *Knusper* are also varieties of sablé. Sablé pastry is also used for making tartlets and barquettes, often filled with cream or strawberries.

RECIPE

Sablé bases FONDS DABLÉS Sift 250 g (9 oz, 2¼ cups) flour onto a work surface. Make a well in the centre and add 200 g (7 oz, scant cup) butter cut into small pieces, 2 egg yolks, 75 g (3oz, generous ⅓ cup) granulated sugar, a pinch of salt, and 1 teaspoon vanilla sugar. Mix these ingredients together, then gradually work in the flour with the fingertips. Knead the mixture quickly, gather it together into a ball, and put in a cool place.

The dough is rolled out to a thickness

of 4–5 mm (⅛–¼ in) to line pie dishes (plates) or tartlet or barquette moulds. It can also be cut up with an oval or round pastry (cookie) cutter for making biscuits (cookies), cooked on a greased baking sheet.

sabodet

A cooking sausage of the Lyon and Dauphiné areas, also known in southwestern France as *coudenas* (or *coudenat*). Made from pig's head (including the tongue), pork rind, and meat with the fat left on, it is generally eaten hot, cut into thick slices. The name (derived from *sabot*, a clog) refers to the shape this sausage originally had.

saccharometer
PÈSE-SIROP

An instrument, also called a syrup hydrometer, for measuring the density of a solution of sugar in water, in order to obtain the correct concentration. The saccharometer consists of a sealed tube with a weighted bulb at one end. A second tube is three-quarters filled with the syrup solution to be tested. The saccharometer works on the principle that any body immersed in a liquid displaces its own weight by volume, so when plunged into the syrup, the graduated tube sinks vertically and the density of the syrup is indicated by the reading at the level to which the saccharometer sinks. The saccharometer can only be used when preparing syrups at the lower temperatures – up to the light, small, or soft crack stage (129–135 C, 265–275 F).

sachertorte

A famous Viennese gâteau, created at the Congress of Vienna (1814–15) by Franz Sacher, Metternich's chief pastrycook. Sachertorte (literally, 'Sacher's cake') is a sort of chocolate Savoy cake, filled or spread with apricot jam, then covered with chocolate icing (frosting); it is traditionally served with whipped cream and a cup of coffee.

For years, Vienna was divided into two camps by the sachertorte controversy. The supporters of sachertorte as it was served at the Sacher hotel – two layers separated by jam, the top being iced – were led by the descendants of Franz Sacher, who regarded their version as the only authentic one. On the other side were the customers of the famous Demel pâtisserie, who based their claim on the rights acquired by Édouard Demel from Sacher's grandson, who authorized the so-called 'true' recipe (the cake is simply spread with jam then covered with the icing), as published in *Die Wiener Konditorei* by Hans Skrach. The Sacher Hotel finally won the day in court at the end of a case which fascinated Vienna for six years. Demel replied by claiming that his was the *Ur-Sachertorte* (the original cake).

RECIPE

Sachertorte (from Joseph Wechsberg's recipe in *Viennese Cookery*, Time-Life) Line two 20-cm (8-in) round sandwich tins (layer cake pans) with buttered greaseproof (waxed) paper. Melt 200 g (7 oz) plain cooking chocolate, broken into small pieces, in a bain-marie. Lightly beat 8 egg yolks and mix in 125 g (4½ oz, generous ½ cup) melted butter and the melted chocolate. Whisk 10 egg whites until stiff with a pinch of salt and add 140 g (5 oz, ⅔ cup caster (superfine sugar, slightly vanillaflavoured, beating all the time until the mixture stands up in stiff peaks. Fold one-third of the egg whites into the chocolate mixture, then gradually fold in the rest of the whites. Add 125 g (4½ oz, generous cup) sifted flour, sprinkling it on gradually and lightly mixing and folding together all the ingredients until all traces of white disappear. Pour equal quantities of the mixture into the 2 tins and bake in the oven at 180 C (350 F, gas 4) for about 45 minutes, until the cakes are well risen and a skewer inserted in the centres comes out clean. Turn out the cakes onto a rack and allow to cool completely.

To make the icing (frosting), put 150 g (5 oz) cooking chocolate, broken into pieces, in a saucepan together with 2.5 dl (8 fl oz, 1 cup) cream and 180 g (6 ½ oz, generous ¾ cup) vanilla sugar. Stir over a moderate heat until the chocolate has melted, then cook for 5 minutes without stirring. Beat 1 whole egg, mix in 3 tablespoons (¼ cup) of the chocolate mixture, and pour all this back into the saucepan. Cook for 1 minute, stirring, then leave to cool at room temperature.

Spread 8 tablespoons (generous ½ cup) sieved apricot jam over one of the halves of the chocolate cake, then put the other half on top. Cover the whole cake with the chocolate icing, smoothing it out with a metal spatula. Slide the cake onto a plate and chill in the refrigerator for 3 hours, until the icing hardens. Remove half an hour before serving.

sacristain

A small biscuit (cookie) made from a stick of twisted puff pastry, often sprinkled with flaked (slivered) or chopped almonds. Classically, it is one of the assortment of biscuits served with tea.

saddle RÂBLE

A cut of meat consisting of the two joined loins. The saddle of a hare or rabbit extends from the lower ribs to the tail. It is a fleshy piece of meat that can be roasted whole, often larded or barded and marinated. It can also be cooked with mustard or with cream (sautéed in a casserole), braised and served with mushroom purée, chestnuts, and poivrade sauce, or sautéed and garnished with cherries, with a sour cream sauce. When it is not cooked whole, the saddle is cut into two or three pieces and made into a civet, a stew, a sauté, etc., with the rest of the animal.

A saddle (*selle*) of venison consists of the part of the animal between the loin and the haunch (see *roebuck*).

RECIPES

Roast saddle of hare RÂBLE DE LIÈVRE RÔTI Prepare the saddle as in the recipe below, but omit the marinade. Sprinkle with salt and pepper, brush with oil, and roast it in the oven at 240 C (475 G, gas 9) for about 20 minutes (the meat should still be pink). It can also be spit-roasted.

Garnish the serving dish with fluted half-slices of lemon and watercress. Serve the saddle either with its own cooking juices (deglazing the roasting pan with white wine) or with a poivrade sauce; the pan can also be deglazed using a mixture of equal proportions of white wine and thick cream.

Saddle of hare à l'allemande RÂBLE DE LIÈVRE À L'ALLEMANDE Insert some small strips of fat bacon into the saddle and sprinkle it with table salt. Cut 1 carrot and 1 onion into slices; chop 1 shallot, 1 celery stick (stalk), and 1 garlic clove. Put some of these vegetables into a deep bowl and lay the saddle on top. Pour in 2.5 dl (8 fl oz, 1 cup) oil, sprinkle with coarsely chopped parsley, powdered thyme, a bay leaf cut into pieces, and 12 peppercorns, and add 1 small onion studded with 2 cloves. Cover the saddle with the remaining vegetables and pour in just enough white wine to cover everything. Leave to marinate for 6 hours, turning the meat once.

Oil a roasting pan and place in it the vegetables from the marinade; place the saddle on top and cook in the oven at 240 C (475 F gas 9) for 20–25 minutes (the meat should still be pink). Drain the saddle and keep it hot; pour the marinade into the roasting pan, add 2 dl (7 fl oz, ¾ cup) cream, and boil to reduce by half. Adjust the seasoning with the juice from half a lemon, strain, and pour over the saddle. Serve with unsweetened apple sauce and redcurrant jelly.

Sade (Donatien Alphonse François, Marquis de)

French writer (born Paris, 1740; died Charenton, 1814). Taking as his principle that 'nature created men only in order that they should take pleasure in everything on earth', Sade was a firm believer in the importance of good food, as well as the pleasures and pains of love. From the prisons where he spent several decades, he wrote to his wife – whom he sometimes called 'fresh pork of my thoughts' – with precise and insistent requests for food. He organized a ball in Marseille, at which he distributed among the ladies pastilles which were supposed to be chocolate but were in fact made of cantharidine, an alkaloid aphrodisiac. The marquis was also a regular at the 'chez Méot dinners' organized by Grimod de La Reynière.

safflower CARTHAME

A plant originating from Africa and Asia but cultivated in the south of France and other countries for its seeds, which yield a low-cholesterol oil used in cooking oils and margarines. The petals of its flowers are sometimes used as a saffron substitute (another name for it is 'bastard saffron'), but their taste is a little more bitter. They are mainly used to add colour and flavour to rice dishes. In Jamaica, safflower is used as a spice, mixed with chilli peppers and cloves.

saffron SAFRAN

A spice consisting of the dried stigmas of the saffron crocus, a bulbous plant originating in the East, introduced into Spain by the Arabs, and cultivated in Mediterranean regions. In France it has been grown by the *safraniers* in the Gâtinais and the Angoumois regions since the 16th century. The spice, which takes the form of dried brownish filaments or an orange-yellow powder, has a pungent smell and a bitter flavour. The best saffron comes from Valencia in Spain; it is also cultivated in Italy, Greece, Iran, and South America. As between 70,000 and 80,000 stigmas are required to make 500 g (18 oz) spice, it is very expensive and various substitutes may be used – safflower (or bastard saffron) and turmeric (or Indian saffron).

Until the Middle Ages, saffron played an important role in cooking, magic, and medicine. It was used a great deal up to the Renaissance as a perfume and colouring agent, in baking and cookery, but had lost a lot of its popularity by the 19th century (Dumas noted that this flower was used 'to colour cakes, vermicelli, and butter').

Saffron today has a privileged place in cookery, particularly in bouillabaisse, paella, the *mourtayrol* (a chicken soup) of Périgord, curry, risotto, and some recipes for mussels, white meats, and tripe. In desserts, it is used to flavour rice cooked in milk, semolina puddings, and some brioches. Saffron should be blended into hot liquid foods, never fried quickly in very hot fat.

RECIPE

Saffron rice à la néerlandaise RIZ AU SAFRAN À LA NÉERLANDAISE Wash about 175 g (6 oz, ¼ cup) shortgrain rice. Blanch it for 2 minutes, rinse in cold water, and drain. Boil 1 litre (1¾ pints, 4¼ cups) milk with ½ teaspoon

salt and 1 generous tablespoon soft light-brown sugar. Add the rice and cook for 35–40 minutes until very soft. Then add 1 tablespoon lemon juice and a generous pinch of powdered saffron and mix well. Pour the rice into individual sundae dishes and leave to cool completely. Serve as a cold dessert, sprinkled with brown sugar, accompanied by cinnamon or ginger biscuits (cookies).

Sagan

A garnish for escalopes (scallops), calves' sweetbreads, or poultry suprêmes, which consists of risotto and mushroom caps filled with a purée of calf's brain mixed with a salpicon of truffle. The accompanying sauce is made by deglazing the meat residue with Madeira and thickened veal stock. Truffles, mushrooms, and calf's brain are also ingredients of Sagan flan, and scrambled eggs Sagan are garnished with slices of brain and truffles. All these dishes are dedicated to Charles de Talleyrand-Périgord, Prince of Sagan.

RECIPE

Sagan flan FLAN SAGAN Prepare a flan base and bake it blind. Line it with a salpicon of mushrooms and truffles, bound with cream and mixed with a little curry powder. On top of this salpicon, place slices of calf's brain sautéed in butter. Place a thin slice of truffle on top of each slice of brain. Coat with Mornay sauce spiced with curry powder. Sprinkle with grated cheese, pour over some clarified butter, and brown in a hot oven.

sage SAUGE

A perennial herb that grows in temperate climates and is widely cultivated for its leaves, which have an aromatic slightly bitter flavour and are used for flavouring fatty meats (e.g. pork), forcemeats, marinades, certain cheeses (including the English Sage Derby), and various drinks. Sage is traditionally considered to have curative properties: the name comes from the Latin *salvus* (safe, in good health).

Four varieties of sage are used in France. As well as garden sage (known as *grande sauge* in France), which has thick oblong hairy leaves, greyish-green in colour, there is the small Provençal sage (*petite sauge*), the most highly prized variety, with smaller paler leaves and a more pronounced flavour; the Catalonian sage, which is even smaller; and, smallest of all, the clary sage, which has curly hairy leaves and is used to make Italian vermouth (it was formerly used to make fritters). In France, sage is used mainly in Provence, for cooking white meat and certain vegetable soups. It is used more frequently in Italian cuisine: piccata, saltimbocca, osso bucco, paupiettes, and rice minestrone are flavoured with sage. In Britain and Flanders, sage and onion are used for poultry and pork stuffings and to flavour sauces. In Germany, ham, sausages, and sometimes beer are flavoured with sage, and in the Balkans and the Middle East it is eaten with roast mutton. In China, tea is flavoured with sage.

RECIPE

Sage and onion sauce SAUCE À LA SAUGE ET À L'OIGNON Cook 2 large onions for 8 minutes in boiling salted water. Drain them and chop them. Put the chopped onion into a saucepan with 100 g (4 oz, 2 cups) fresh white breadcrumbs and 25 g (1 oz, 2 tablespoons) butter. Season with salt and pepper and add 1 tablespoon chopped sage. Cook for 5 minutes, stirring constantly. Just before serving, add 3 tablespoons (4 tablespoons) pan juices from the roast pork or goose that this sauce is served with.

sago SAGOU
A starch made from the pith of the sago palm, cultivated in the tropics. Sago comes in the form of small whitish, pinkish, or brownish grains, which are very hard and semitransparent and have a sweetish taste. Sago has been known in Europe from the time of the Renaissance. At the end of the 17th century, it was one of the most popular forms of starch in the West, used for garnishing veal or chicken broth, for thickening soup, for making soft rolls, or cooked in milk with spices. Today in Europe it is used only for thickening and to make puddings. In Indonesian cookery,

however, it is reduced to a paste with coconut pulp and milk and used for making fritters, cakes, ravioli, desserts, etc. In India it is boiled with sugar to make a dessert jelly.

sagourne
A speciality of Tours, consisting of slices of pancreas fried in butter, sprinkled with salt, pepper, and chopped parsley, and served with a squeeze of lemon juice.

Saint-Amant (Marc Antoine Girard, Sieur de)

French poet (born Quevilly, 1594; died Paris, 1661). The author of lyrical, satirical, and realist poems, he became famous for his ode *La Solitude* (1618). He divided his time between the French capital, where he frequented the taverns in the company of Cardinal de Retz, and his birthplace, Rouen, taking part in military campaigns in Catalonia and Flanders as chief administrator of the artillery. He also stayed in Poland for a time and it is thought that he visited America.

He left a large corpus of poems about eating and drinking, which figure in the best Baroque anthologies. His witty compositions were inspired by all aspects of food and drink, including cider, Brie cheese, the vine, and the melon. Although his words lose something in translation they are worth reading:

'The dear apricot which I love,
The strawberry cover'd with cream,
The manna which falls down from
heav'n,
The savour of honey's pure food,
The heavenly pear grown in Tours,
The sweetness of any green fig,
The plum with its delicate juice,
The very grape of Muscat
(A very strange title to me),
All are mere sourness and mire
Compar'd with this melon divine.'

It is said that he died in the company of a certain Montglas, tavern keeper at the Petit More where he obviously enjoyed the hospitality.

Saint-Amour

The AOC of the northernmost of the Beaujolais classified growths. It is one of the lightest, with a beautiful ruby colour.

Saint-Aubin

Red and white Burgundy wines from the Côte de Beaune. The whites, produced in vineyards next to those yielding the great Puligny-Montrachet and Chassagne-Montrachet wines, are not as good as these two and are sold under their own AOCs – Saint-Aubin or Saint-Aubin-Côte-de-Beaune. The reds may be described as Côte-de-Beaune-Villages when blended with the wines of other parishes (communes).

Sainte-Alliance (à la)

This description, evoking the festivities surrounding the signing of the Treaty of Paris (1815) by the sovereigns who had conquered Napoleon I, is given to several dishes: foie gras poached with truffles and champagne; a chicken stuffed with truffles cooked in Madeira, then fried and surrounded with slices of foie gras cooked in butter; and roast pheasant stuffed with woodcock, served on a canapé spread with woodcock purée. Brillat-Savarin supplied the recipe for the last dish in his *Physiologie du goût*, but without using this name (which was later attributed to it by Prosper Montagné).

RECIPE

Pheasant à la Sainte-Alliance FAISAN À LA SAINTE-ALLIANCE (from Brillat-Savarin's recipe) Hang a pheasant until it is very high, then pluck it and lard it with fresh firm bacon. Bone and draw 2 woodcock, separating the flesh and the offal. Make some stuffing with the flesh by chopping it together with steamed beef bone marrow, a little shredded pork fat, some pepper, salt, herbs, and truffles. Stuff the pheasant with this mixture.

Cut a slice of bread 5 cm (2 in) larger than the pheasant all round, and toast it. Pound the livers and entrails of the woodcock with 2 large truffles, 1 anchovy, a little finely chopped bacon, and a moderate-sized lump of fresh butter. Spread this paste evenly over the toast. Roast the pheasant in the oven; when it is cooked, spoon all the roasting juices over the toast on a serving dish.

Place the pheasant on top and surround it with slices of Seville (bitter) orange. This highly flavoured dish is best accompanied by wine from Upper Burgundy.

Sainte-Beuve (*Charles Augustin*)

French writer (born Boulogne-sur-Mer, 1804; died Paris, 1869). One of the greatest literary critics of his time, he was also one of the most famous gourmets. He founded, together with the Goncourts, Gavarni, Renan, and Turgenev, the 'Magny dinners'; he was also one of the regulars at Dumas's 'Wednesday suppers'. On Good Friday, 1868, he gave a dinner party for Taine, Falubert, Renan, E. About, and Prince Napoleon, at which the guests enjoyed salmon trout, fillet of beef in Madeira, buisson of prawns, and truffled pheasant.

Sainte-Croix-du-Mont

An AOC region on the right bank of the River Garonne. The wines are made with the same grapes as Sauternes and although they are slightly smaller in scale, they do resemble those of the Sauternais in their fragrance and elegant sweetness.

Sainte-Foix-Bordeaux

An AOC region east of Bordeaux, on the River Dordogne. Sweetish white and some red wines are made, all well worth trying by visitors to this beautiful region.

Sainte-Maure

A French goats'-milk cheese from Touraine (45% fat content), with a soft curd and a thin natural bluish rind, sometimes marked with pink. The best source is the Sainte-Maure plateau, where the cheese is farmhouse-made and has a particularly good flavour in summer and autumn. It is firm and creamy with a fairly pronounced goaty smell and a well-developed bouquet. It is cylindrical in shape, 15 cm (6 in) long and 4 cm (1½ in) in diameter. Sometimes a straw is inserted through the centre, running the length of the cheese. Ligueil, another cheese from the Tours area, is similar to Sainte-Maure and has the same shape.

Sainte-Menehould

Describing dishes in which the main ingredient is cooked, cooled, coated with breadcrumbs and grilled (broiled), then served with mustard or Sainte-Menehould sauce (made with mustard, onion, vinegar, and herbs). The term is typically applied to pigs' trotters (feet), a speciality of the town of Sainte-Menehould in the Marne region of France, where the recipe was developed, but it can also be used for skate, pigeon, chicken, oxtail, pigs' ears, crépinettes, and poultry wings.

The Confrérie des Compagnons du Pied'or de Sainte-Menehould, founded in 1972, points out that pigs' trotters (feet) Sainte-Menehould were served to King Charles VII in 1435 and that Louis XVI enjoyed them in 1791, at the time of the flight to Varenne.

RECIPES

Pigs' trotters (feet) Sainte-Menehould PIEDS DE COCHON SAINTE-MENEHOULD (from Yvan Desingly's recipe) Singe and clean 5 pigs' trotters (feet). Place them in a bowl with 500 g (18 oz, 1½ cups) coarse sea salt and leave to stand for 3 hours. Tie up the trotters with strips of cloth so that they do not disintegrate during cooking. Put 1 onion, 2 carrots, 2 cloves of garlic, 2 shallots, and a bouquet garni (thyme, bay leaf, basil, and parsley) in a casserole; add the pigs' trotters together with 1 wineglass white wine, 2 cloves, some salt, and plenty of water. Bring to the boil, then reduce the heat and simmer gently for 4 hours.

When the trotters are really tender, take them out of the casserole and leave to cool. When they are quite cold, untie them and cut in half lengthwise. Melt 100 g (4 oz, ½ cup) butter; break 2 eggs onto a plate and beat well. Prepare 250 g (9 oz, 4½ cups) fresh breadcrumbs. Dip the trotters in the beaten egg, then in the breadcrumbs. Place them on a grill rack and grill (broil) gently, basting with the melted butter. Arrange on a very hot dish and serve with mustard.

Sainte-Menehould sauce SAUCE SAINTE-MENEHOULD Melt 1 tablespoon butter in a saucepan. Add 1 tablespoon finely chopped onion, cover, and cook very gently for 10 minutes until soft. Season with salt, pepper, a pinch of thyme, and a pinch of powdered bay leaf and add 1 dl (6 tablespoons, scant ½ cup) white wine and 1 tablespoon vinegar. Reduce until all the liquid has evaporated, then moisten with 2 dl (7 fl oz, ¾ cup) demi-glace sauce. Boil on full heat for 1 minute, then add a pinch of cayenne. Remove from the heat and blend in 1 tablespoon each of mustard, very finely diced gherkins, chopped parsley, and chervil.

Saint-Émilion

The most robust of red Bordeaux wines, produced in Saint-Émilion and the seven neighbouring parishes (communes), making up the largest vineyard and one of the oldest in the Bordeaux region. Saint-Émilion produces generous wines that are sometimes described as the 'Burgundies of Bordeaux'. Famous names include the Château-Ausone and Château-Cheval-Blanc. The grapes are the same as in the other areas in the Gironde – Cabernet Sauvignon, Cabernet Franc, Merlot, and Malbec. There should be no confusion with the Saint-Émilion grape, also known as the Ugni Blanc, used in the Cognac region.

Saint-Estèphe

A parish (commune) in the upper Médoc, which produces more wine than any other of the AOCs in Médoc. In spite of this profusion, only five châteaux figure in the 1855 classification: Cos-d'Estournel and Montrose as second growths, Calon-Ségur as a third, Lafon-Rochet as a fourth, and Cos-Labory as fifth. Saint-Estèphe wines tend to be somewhat astringent when young, but they can develop impressively, a few even possessing some of the nobility of the Pauillacs, from the neighbouring parish.

Saint-Florentin

A French cows'-milk cheese (45% fat content), with a soft curd and a smooth reddish-brown washed rind. Saint-Florentin is a wheel-shaped cheese, 12 –13 cm (4½–5 in) in diameter and 3 cm (1¼ in) thick; it is best from November to June and has a fairly strong flavour. However, it is often sold unmatured, as a soft cheese, which tastes very sweet and milky.

The small town in the Yonne region from which it comes has also given its name to a trout dish known as *à la Saint-Florentin*, which was described by Fulbert-Dumonteil as 'flavoured with nutmeg and cloves, cooked over a clear flame in a Chablis wine which, when well heated, gives it a crown of fire'.

Saint-Florentin is also the name of a square Genoese sponge cake which is split in half, soaked with Kirsch, and filled with a cream made with Italian meringue, melted butter, Kirsch, and glacé (candied) cherries (or fresh strawberries, in season). The top of the cake is iced (frosted) with pink fondant and the sides are left uncovered, to show the fruit in the filling.

Saint Germain

The name given to various dishes containing green peas (also known as *Clamart*) or split peas; they are all named after the Comte de Saint-Germain, war minister under Louis XV. Saint-Germain purée, which is fairly thick and sometimes bound with egg yolk, is served with joints of meat and accompanied by a sauce made of clear veal stock. The purée is served separately in a vegetable dish or heaped up on top of artichoke hearts around the meat. When diluted to the required consistency with white stock or consommé, this purée becomes Saint-Germain soup, for which there are various garnishes.

The term is also applied to a method of preparing fillets of sole or brill, which are dipped in melted butter, coated with breadcrumbs, grilled (broiled), and served with a béarnaise sauce and a garnish of noisette potatoes.

RECIPES

Fillets of sole Saint-Germain FILETS DE SOLE SAINT-GERMAIN Fillet 2 soles. Flatten them out, sprinkle with salt and pepper, brush with melted butter, dip in fine fresh breadcrumbs, spoon over 50 g (2oz, ¼ cup) melted butter, and grill (broil) gently on both sides. Arrange on a long dish, surround with 600 g (generous 1¼ lb) small noisette potatoes, and serve with béarnaise sauce in a sauceboat.

Saint-Germain soup POTAGE SAINT-GERMAIN Put into a saucepan 750 g (1¾ lb, 7 cups) shelled fresh peas, a lettuce heart, 12 small new onions, a bouquet garni with chervil added, 50 g (2 oz, ¼ cup) butter, 1 teaspoon salt, and 1 tablespoon granulated sugar. Add 8 fl oz (1 cup) cold water, bring to the boil, and cook gently for 30–35 minutes. Remove the bouquet garni and rub the vegetables through an ordinary sieve, then a fine one. Add a little consommé or hot water to obtain the desired consistency and heat through. Add 25 g (1 oz, 2 tablespoons) butter, beat well, and sprinkle with chopped herbs. If desired, a few peas and croutons can be added.

Saint-Germian purée PURÉE SAINT-GERMAIN Prepare in the same way as Saint-Germain soup, but add 1–1.5 dl (¼ pint, ⅔ cup) cream to the peas after they have been sieved.

Saint-Honoré

A gâteau consisting of a layer of shortcrust pastry (basic pie dough) or puff pastry on top of which is arranged a crown of choux pastry, which is itself garnished with small choux glazed with caramel. The inside of the crown is filled with Chiboust cream (also known as 'Saint-Honoré cream') or Chantilly cream.

The Saint-Honoré is a Parisian gâteau and takes its name from the patron saint of bakers and pastrycooks. It is also said that its name comes from the fact that the pastrycook Chiboust, who created the cream which is used in it, set himself up in the Rue Saint-Honoré in Paris.

RECIPE

Saint-Honoré Prepare the dough for the base with 125 g (4½ oz, generous cup) sifted flour, 1 egg yolk, 60 g (2 oz, ¼ cup) softened butter, a pinch of salt, 15 g (½ oz, 1 tablespoon) granulated sugar, and 2 tablespoons (3 tablespoons) water. When the mixture is smooth, put it in the refrigerator.

Prepare some choux pastry (see *chou*) with 2.5 dl (8 fl oz, 1 cup) water, 60 g (2 oz, ¼ cup) butter, 15 g (½ oz, 1 tablespoon) caster (superfine) sugar, and a pinch of salt, then add 125 g (4½ oz, generous cup) sifted flour and finally 4 beaten eggs, one by one.

Roll out the dough for the base into a circle 20 cm (8 in) in diameter and 2 mm (⅛ in) thick. Place on a buttered baking sheet, prick with a fork, and brush the edge with beaten egg. Fit a piping (pastry) bag with a smooth nozzle the size of a finger and fill it with one-third of the choux pastry; pipe out a border around the edge of the base 3 mm (⅛ in) from the edge. Brush this border with beaten egg. On a second buttered baking sheet, pipe out 20 small choux about the size of walnuts. Bake the base and the choux for about 25 minutes in a moderately hot oven (200 c, 400 f, gas 6 maximum), then leave to cool completely.

Prepare a light caramel by cooking 250 g (9 oz, generous cup) granulated sugar with 1 dl (6 tablespoons, scant ½ cup) water until it reaches 145 c (293 f). Dip the choux in the caramel and stick them on top of the border so that they touch each other.

Soften 15 g (½ oz, 1 envelope) gelatine in 5 tablespoons (6 tablespoons) cold water. Boil 1 litre (1¾ pints, 4¼ cups) milk with a vanilla pod (bean). Beat 6 egg yolks with 200 g (7 oz, scant cup) caster sugar until the mixture turns white and thick and then add 75 g (3 oz, scant ¾ cup) cornflour (cornstarch). Remove the vanilla pod from the milk and pour this over the mixture, beating hard. Put back into the saucepan and bring to the boil, whisking all the time. Stir in the softened gelatine until it has completely dissolved. Stiffly whisk 4 egg whites. Bring the custard back to the boil and pour it over the egg whites, folding them in with a metal spoon. Leave until cold and on the point of setting, then fill the centre of the cake with this mixture, sprinkle with icing (confectioners') sugar, and grill (broil) rapidly until golden.

Put in a cool place until ready to serve, but do not keep for too long.

Saint-Hubert

The name of various dishes, usually based on game or including game, which take their name from the patron saint of hunters. Quails Saint-Hubert are casseroled with a piece of truffle in each bird and coated in a sauce made by deglazing the meat residue with

Madeira and game stock. The name is most often used for dishes that include game purée: for filling large mushroom caps served with saddle of hare and poivrade sauce; in tartlets with poached or soft-boiled (soft-cooked) eggs coated with poivrade sauce; in vols-au-vent, timbales, or omelettes; or for making a consommé.

<hr>

RECIPES

Consommé Saint-Hubert Make some game consommé, thicken it with tapioca, then garnish it with an ordinary royale and a julienne of mushrooms stewed in Madeira.

Saint-Hubert timbales PETITES TIMBALES SAINT-HUBERT Grease some dariole moulds, garnish them with slivers of truffle and some chopped pickled tongue, then line them with a layer of game forcemeat. Prepare a salpicon of game meat, truffles, and mushrooms, bound with demi-glace sauce made with game fumet, and divide it between the darioles. Cover with game forcemeat. Place the darioles in a bain-marie and cook in a moderately hot oven (200 c, 400 f, gas 6) for 18–20 minutes. Allow to rest for a few moments before turning out of the moulds. Serve as a hot starter, coated with poivrade sauce.

Saint-Joseph

Côtes-du-Rhône red and white wines produced in the Ardèche, on the right bank of the River Rhône, opposite the Hermitage vineyard. Saint-Joseph AOC wine may often be a robust highly coloured red, whose bouquet emerges after it has aged in the bottle for a few years. The whites are lighter in character than the white Hermitages.

Saint-Julien

A parish (commune) of the Haut-Médoc, having its own AOC. The wines are varied and some of the finest have an appealing velvety character. There are five second growths, two third growths, and four fourth growths.

Saint-Malo

A sauce for grilled (broiled) fish (brill or turbot) for which there are several recipes: Prosper Montagné recognizes at least two. The most common version is a fish velouté with the addition of reduced white wine with shallots; it can be thickened with egg yolk and may include the juice from cooked mushrooms. This sauce often has butter added, the final touch being a little mustard and/or a trickle of anchovy essence or Worcestershire sauce. Saint-Malo sauce does not in fact have anything to do with the city of Saint Malo.

RECIPE

Saint-Malo sauce SAUCE SAINT-MALO Cook 2 tablespoons (3 tablespoons) chopped onion in butter until soft but not coloured. Add 1 dl (6 tablespoons, scant ½ cup) white wine, a sprig of thyme, a piece of bay leaf, and a sprig of parsley. Reduce by two-thirds. Moisten with 2.5 dl (8 fl oz, 1 cup) velouté sauce made with fish stock, and 1 dl (6 tablespoons, scant ½ cup) fish fumet. Add 1 dl (6 tablespoons, scant ½ cup) mushroom cooking juices and reduce by one-third. Strain through muslin (cheesecloth), and mix in 1 teaspoon mustard, a trickle of Worcestershire sauce, and 1 tablespoon butter.

Saint-Mandé

A garnish for small cuts of sautéed meat, consisting of peas and French (green) beans tossed in butter, and small Macaire potatoes.

Saint-Marcellin

A French cows'-milk (formerly goats'-milk) cheese from the Dauphiné (50% fat content), with a soft curd and a thin natural rind which is bluish-grey. It has a sweet but slightly acid taste, and is marketed as small discs, 7–8 cm (2½–3 in) in diameter and 2 cm (¾ in) thick. Saint-Marcellin goes well with a light fruity Beaujolais. In Lyon it is also used for making *fromage fort* (see *cheese*), macerated in salt, herbs, and sometimes cream.

It is said to have been 'discovered' by the future Louis XI when he was governor of the Dauphiné; when he came to the throne he had it included on the royal table.

Saint-Nectaire

A French cows'-milk cheese (45% fat content) from Auvergne, with a pressed curd and a natural rind; it is matured for eight weeks on a bed of rye straw. Saint-Nectaire, which is best in summer and autumn, is soft but not flabby, with a musty smell and an earthy flavour, giving it a pronounced bouquet. It is marketed unwrapped in the form of a flat disc 20 cm (8 in) in diameter, 4 cm (1½ in) thick, weighing 1.5 kg (3¼ lb); it has a greyish rind which is sometimes marked with yellow and red. Since 1957 the cheese has been protected by an AOC (covering the Saint-Flour, Mauriac, Clermont-Ferrand, and Issoire districts).

This very old cheese was introduced to the table of Louis XIV by Henri de Sennectere, marshal of France and lord of Saint-Nectaire.

St Nicholas' Day

SAINT-NICOLAS

A traditional feast day in northern Europe, celebrated on 6 December. The legend goes that a butcher had cut three children up into pieces and put them into a salting tub; Nicholas, suspecting the crime and passing by the place, insisted on tasting the criminal's salted meat. Faced with refusal, he resuscitated the little victims. On the night between 5 and 6 December, it is traditional for children to hang stockings full of hay, oats, and bread on the fireplace, to feed the saint's donkey.

From the culinary point of view, St Nicholas' Day is celebrated with aniseed biscuits (cookies), gingerbread, chocolate, and red sugar candy in the shape of the saint, who was the bishop of Myra, in Asia Minor, in the 4th century. In Alsace, bakers used to celebrate the feast day by making a special kind of bread called *männela* (literally 'little man').

Saint-Nicolas-de-Bourgueil

The AOC of red or rosé wines from Touraine, near to Bourgueil. Like the latter, it is made exclusively from the Cabernet Franc grape. It is a fruity wine with a pronounced bouquet.

Saint-Paulin

A pasteurized cows'-milk cheese (45% fat content) with a pressed curd and a washed smooth orange rind, which shows traces of the cheesecloth in which it is wrapped when pressed. Now made all over France, it is derived from the monastery cheeses, particularly that of Port-du-Salut (the best come from Maine, Anjou, and Brittany). Saint-Paulin is soft and smooth, with a sweet taste. It looks like a small millstone, 20–22 cm (8–8½ in) in diameter and 4–6 cm (1½–2½ in) thick. It is served at the end of the meal, but can also be used for croûtes, croques-monsieur, mixed salads, etc.

Saint-Péray

A white wine from Côtes-du-Rhône vineyards opposite Valence, on the right bank of the River Rhône, with its own AOC. The still wine is not as well known as the sparkling version, which is one of the quality French sparkling wines.

Saint-Pourçain

A red, rosé, or white VDQS wine from the Bourbonnais. It is becoming known outside France and all versions can make pleasant drinking.

Saint-Romain

Red and white AOC Burgundy wines from the Côte de Beaune. Some are blended with other wines grown nearby and are sold as Côte-de-Beaune-Villages. They can be extremely agreeable and offer good value.

Saint-Saëns

The name of the famous composer has been given to a garnish for poultry suprêmes, which is typical of the rich cooking of the Second Empire. It consists of small truffle and foie gras fritters, cocks' kidneys, and asparagus tips, accompanied by a suprême sauce flavoured with truffle essence.

Saint-Véran

An AOC white Mâcon wine, made from the Chardonnay grape and now very popular in the export market for its dry robust style.

St Vincent's Day

The feast day of the patron saint of wine growers (22 January). St Vincent was a Spanish deacon and martyr whose remains are said to have been taken to Burgundy and then to Champagne. The feast day used to be celebrated with gargantuan 'pig feasts', a custom revived by the Chevaliers du Tastevin during the 1930s. The Confrérie des Vignerons de Saint-Vincent de Bourgogne et de Mâcon was founded in 1950.

sake or saké

A Japanese alcoholic drink, made from fermented rice. Sake is colourless and has a fairly sweet flavour with a bitter aftertaste.

Sake is closely linked with Japanese religious and social life and has existed for more than a thousand years. At a Shinto wedding, the couple drink several mouthfuls of cold sweetened sake from little lacquer bowls, though saké is otherwise traditionally drunk warm or even hot. There are several types, ranging from sweet to dry. In particular, a distinction is made between *mirin*, which is mostly used in cookery, *toso*, which is sweet and spicy and with which the New Year is celebrated, and *seishu*, which is often exported. Sake is drunk from tiny tumblers as an apéritif (in this case a little salt is sometimes placed on the tongue before each mouthful), or else to accompany sashimi, crudités, or grilled (broiled) or fried foods. It is also used a great deal in cookery, especially in shellfish, white fish, and prawn (shrimp) dishes. In sake bars, where men meet together, sake is drunk alternately with beer. According to a Japanese proverb, 'It is the man who drinks the first bottle of sake; then the second bottle drinks the first, and finally it is the sake that drinks the man.'

salad   SALADE

A dish of raw or cold cooked foods, usually dressed and seasoned, served as an hors d'oeuvre, side dish, etc.
● *Green salads* consist of green-leaved raw vegetables, such as lettuce, endive, chicory, watercress, dandelion leaves, spinach, mesclun, purslane, rocket (arugula), lamb's lettuce, etc. These salads (which can also be cooked as vegetables) are served as hors d'oeuvres or as an accompaniment to grills, omelettes, meat, poultry, game, etc. They are usually dressed with vinaigrette, which can be flavoured (according to the natural flavour of the vegetable) and mixed

with croutons, strips of bacon, cheese, shallots, garlic, etc.

• *Plain salads* consist of a basic ingredient, either raw or cooked, but always served cold with a cold dressing (mayonnaise, vinaigrette, mustard, gribiche, ravigote, rémoulade, Roquefort and soft cheese dressings, etc.). The basic ingredient can be a vegetable, meat, or shellfish, and the range is very varied: French (green) beans, carrots, celery, cauliflower, lentils, red or white cabbage, potatoes, rice, brawn (head cheese), crayfish, crab, cold chicken, etc.

• *Mixed salads* are more elaborate dishes combining various ingredients of contrasting (but complementary) flavours, textures, and colours. Mixed salads can include exotic ingredients, such as truffle, foie gras, or lobster medallions, or simple ones (as in salade niçoise), but should always be decorative. The accompanying dressing should blend with (rather than mask) the flavour of the ingredients. Mixed salads are served as starters, but can also accompany hot or cold roast meats. In addition to the many regional specialities, chefs often create their salads, producing an immensely wide range.

RECIPES

Dressings for Green or Plain Salads

Prepare a basic vinaigrette with 1 tablespoon wine vinegar, 3 tablespoons oil, salt, pepper, and (if desired) 1 teaspoon mustard. This vinaigrette can be embellished in different ways:

■ **with anchovies** (*for raw salads other than green ones*): thoroughly soak 4 anchovies to remove the salt and fillet them; purée them with 1 teaspoon capers; add this mixture to the vinaigrette.

■ **with bacon** (*for curly endives (chicory), red cabbage, lamb's lettuce, or dandelions*): instead of using vinaigrette, fry 100 g (4 oz) diced fairly fatty streaky bacon; put the salad in a bowl and season with salt and pepper; add 1–2 tablespoons (1–3 tablespoons) vinegar to the bacon in the pan, then pour over the salad while still hot, and toss.

■ **with cream** (*for round or cos (romaine) lettuce*): replace the oil of the vinaigrette by 4 tablespoons whipping cream.

■ **Indian** (*for cooked vegetables*): add to the vinaigrette 1 small crushed clove of garlic and 1 tablespoon finely chopped onion fried until soft in 1 tablespoon oil with 1 teaspoon curry powder.

■ **with mayonnaise**(*for all raw salads or cooked vegetables*): replace the vinaigrette by mayonnaise, plain or flavoured with herbs or garlic.

■ **with mustard and cream** (*for beetroot (red beet), macédoine, celeriac (celery root), chicory (endive), or potato*): instead of using vinaigrette, blend 1 tablespoon French mustard with 2–3 tablespoons cream; add 1 teaspoon (or more) vinegar and season with salt and pepper.

Garnishes for Plain Salads

■ **with herbs:** chop a bunch of chives, chervil, and parsley with a few tarragon and mint leaves; make some vinaigrette and mix in the chopped herbs.

■ **with nuts:** chop 50 g (2 oz, ½ cup) walnuts, peanuts, and hazelnuts; prepare a salad, season it with vinaigrette, and sprinkle with the chopped nuts; toss just before serving.

■ **with Roquefort or Fourme d'Ambert cheese:** mash 50 g (2 oz) Roquefort or Fourme d'Ambert cheese and mix in 1 Petit Suisse cheese (or 1 oz cream cheese) and 2 tablespoons (3 tablespoons) cream; add a few drops of Tabasco sauce and 1 teaspoon brandy, season with a very little salt and pepper if desired, and mix well. Pour this mixture over the salad and toss just before serving.

Mixed Salads

Alienor salad   SALADE ALIENOR
Mix 2 tablespoons grated horseradish and enough fresh cream to give a smooth sauce with a strong flavour. Trim 2 smoked trout and remove the fillets, taking out all the bones. Cover 4 plates with lettuce. Cut a large stoned

(pitted) avocado into thin slices; arrange the slices on the plates and sprinkle them with lemon juice. Arrange 2 fillets of trout, coarsely shredded, on each plate. Coat with horseradish sauce. Sprinkle with a few shredded almonds and complete with slices of gherkin.

The avocado may be replaced by pickled red cabbage.

American salad SALADE AMÉRICAINE Line some individual salad bowls with lettuce leaves. For each serving, mix together 1 tablespoon diced pineapple, 2 tablespoons (3 tablespoons) sweetcorn, either canned or cooked in boiling water, 1 tablespoon julienne of chicken breast poached in white stock, and 1 tablespoon peeled, seeded, and diced cucumber. Dress with 2 tablespoons (3 tablespoons) vinaigrette flavoured with tomato ketchup and pile up in the bowls. Garnish each bowl with quarters of hard-boiled (hard-cooked) egg and a small tomato cut to resemble a flower.

Arles salad SALADE ARLÉSIENNE Slice some boiled potatoes and quarter some boiled artichoke hearts. Mix together and dress with vinaigrette, sprinkle with chopped chervil and tarragon, and garnish with curly endive (chicory) and tomato quarters. Garnish the top with drained canned anchovy fillets arranged in a crisscross pattern, with a stoned (pitted) black (ripe) olive placed in the centre. Pour some vinaigrette (seasoned with very little salt, because of the anchovies) over the garnish just before serving.

Beef salad SALADE DE BOEUF Cut 250 g (9 oz) boiled beef into slices rather less than 5 mm (¼ in) thick. Thinly slice 6 small boiled potatoes. Sprinkle with salt and pepper while still warm and pour 1.5 dl (¼ pint, ⅔ cup) white wine and 1 tablespoon oil over them. Turn the slices over so that they get well impregnated with this dressing. Thinly slice 3 or 4 tomatoes. Slice an onion very finely. Arrange the potatoes heaped up in a salad bowl, with the slices of beef all around. Surround with the tomato slices. Garnish with the sliced onion and 1 tablespoon chopped chervil. Season with vinaigrette flavoured with mustard.

Carbonara salad SALADE CARBONARA Cook 125 g (4½ oz) macaroni in plenty of boiling water for 10 minutes, then drain it and mix immediately with 1 tablespoon olive oil. Set aside. Prepare a classic mayonnaise (using 2 egg yolks) and blend in 1 teaspoon strong mustard, a pinch of paprika, and the juice of a lemon. Mix with the cooled macaroni, then add 4 oz (1 cup) coarsely chopped hazelnuts, 100 g (4 oz) Mimolette cheese cut into matchsticks, and 8 oz (2 cups) finely chopped celery. Arrange a few lettuce leaves in a large salad bowl and pour the mixture into it. Garnish with slices of mild onion and a few whole hazelnuts.

Carrot salad with orange SALADE DE CAROTTES À L'ORANGE Put 500 g (18 oz, 4¾ cups) peeled and grated carrots in a pile in a salad bowl. Remove the peel and pith from 4 oranges and dice the flesh finely. Peel and thinly slice 2 large mild onions and break the slices up into rings. Pour some lemon vinaigrette over the carrots just before serving, and add the orange dice. Toss and garnish with the onion rings.

Cockle salad with fresh broad (fava) beans SALADE DE COQUES AUX FÈVES FRAÎCHES (from R. Courtine's recipe) Heat the cockles until they open, remove the walnut-sized pieces of flesh, and keep warm. Peel the beans, blanch them for 5 minutes in salted water, then rinse in cold water. Pour some vinaigrette mixed with chopped herbs into a salad bowl. Add the beans and the cockles, toss quickly, and serve.

German salad SALADE À L'ALLEMANDE Coarsely cut up 400 g (14 oz, 2⅓ cups) boiled potatoes and 200 g (7 oz, scant 2 cups) tart eating apples and mix with 2 tablespoons (3 tablespoons) mayonnaise. Pile up in a salad bowl; garnish with a large shredded gherkin and 2 herring fillets. Sprinkle with chopped parsley. Garnish with slices of cooked beetroot (red beet) and onion. Pour a mustard-flavoured vinaigrette over this garnish just before serving.

Maharajah salad SALADE MAHAR-
ADJAH Prepare some rice *à la créole*
and flake some crabmeat. Mix together,
dress with vinaigrette mixed with 1 teaspoon curry powder, and heap up in a
salad bowl. Around this, arrange some
shredded celeriac (celery root), alternated with blanched and diced courgettes (zucchini) and tomato quarters.
Sprinkle with sieved hard-boiled (hard-
cooked) egg yolk and chopped chives.
Pour some more of the same vinaigrette
over the garnish just before serving.

New turnip salad SALADE DE PETITS
NAVETS NOUVEAUX (from Gérard
Vié's recipe) Peel and quarter 1 kg (2¼
lb) small new turnips. Blanch them for 6
minutes in boiling water, drain, then
cook in stock, preferably chicken stock,
for about 10 minutes. Drain and leave
to cool, then sprinkle with chopped
herbs. Add some strips of smoked haddock poached in milk (1 part haddock
to 2 parts turnips) and dress with olive
oil and vinegar.

Port-Royal salad SALADE PORT-
ROYAL Mix together slices of boiled
potato, chopped cooked French (green)
beans, and slices of peeled apples lightly
sprinkled with lemon juice. Add some
mayonnaise to this mixture. Heap up in
a salad bowl, pour over some more
mayonnaise, and garnish with whole
French beans in a star shape. Surround
with small lettuce hearts and quarters of
hard-boiled (hard-cooked) eggs.

Poultry salad à la chinoise SALADE DE
VOLAILLE À LA CHINOISE Shred 200
g (7 oz) duck or chicken meat (with the
skin if it is roasted). Soak 7 or 8 black
Chinese mushrooms and 2 or 3 fragrant
Chinese mushrooms in warm water for
30 minutes. Rinse them, pat dry, and cut
into quarters. Scald 500 g (18 oz) bean
sprouts, cool under running water, and
pat dry.

Make a dressing by mixing together 1
teaspoon each of mustard and sugar, 1
tablespoon tomato ketchup, 1 tablespoon each of soy sauce and vinegar, a
pinch of black pepper, ½ teaspoon
ground ginger, a pinch each of thyme
and powdered bay leaf, a small crushed
clove of garlic, 3 tablespoons (¼ cup)

sesame oil, and, if desired, 1 tablespoon
rice spirit (or Cognac).

Mix the duck or chicken meat,
mushrooms, and bean sprouts together
and pour over the dressing. Arrange in a
salad bowl; just before serving, sprinkle
over 1 tablespoon chopped coriander
leaves.

Raphael salad SALADE RAPHAËL
Garnish a shallow salad bowl with
shredded lettuce dressed with mayonnaise and seasoned with paprika.
Arrange on top slices of peeled cucumber (previously sprinkled with salt and
left to stand, then rinsed and drained),
white asparagus tips (boiled and well
drained), small tomatoes (peeled,
seeded, and cut into quarters), small
lettuce hearts, and sliced pink radishes.
Just before serving, dress with vinaigrette made with olive oil, lemon juice,
and chopped chervil.

Raw vegetable salad SALADE DE
CRUDITÉS Clean and wash 2 toma-
toes, 3 sticks (stalks) of celery, 1 head of
fennel, and 1 lettuce. Peel and finely dice
1 beetroot (red beet). Halve 2 sweet
peppers, remove the seeds, and cut the
flesh into thin strips. Thinly slice the
fennel, celery, and tomatoes. Wash and
chop a small bunch of parsley. Line the
base of a shallow dish with the lettuce
leaves and place on top small heaps of
fennel, beetroot, celery, and peppers.
Arrange 10 green and black (ripe) olives
in the centre and surround the whole
dish with the tomato slices. Pour over
some vinaigrette and sprinkle with
chopped parsley.

Tomato salad with Mozzarella
SALADE DE TOMATES À LA MOZ-
ZARELLA Wash, peel, and slice 4
tomatoes. Thinly slice 200 g (7 oz) Mozzarella cheese. Divide the sliced tomato
between 4 plates and cover with slices of
Mozzarella. Sprinkle with salt, pepper,
and chopped fresh basil, pour over a few
drops of vinegar then a trickle of olive
oil, and serve at room temperature.

Toulouse salad SALADE
TOULOUSAINE (from Lucien Vanel's
recipe) Make some melon balls from the
flesh of a medium-sized melon. Cook 2
artichoke hearts in water and lemon

juice, cool and cut into thin strips. Thinly slice the white and green parts of a very tender leek; shred a thick slice of unsmoked ham. Mix together all these ingredients. Make a well-seasoned vinaigrette, adding chopped parsley, chives, and sage, and blend it with 1 teaspoon cream. Pour over the salad and toss gently. Place a large leaf of raw spinach, washed and patted dry, on each plate. Divide the salad between the plates; just before serving, grate a little fresh ginger over them.

Vegetable salad SALADE DE LÉGUMES This can be made with all sorts of fresh cooked vegetables: carrots and turnips (diced or cut into balls using a melon baller), chopped French (green) beans, asparagus tips, peas, sliced or diced potatoes, etc. All these vegetables are mixed together, dressed with vinaigrette, piled into a salad bowl, garnished with a floret of cauliflower, and sprinkled with chopped parsley and chervil.

salad bowl SALADIER

A deep bowl for serving salad, which traditionally comes with matching servers in wood, horn, or silver. A salad bowl should be chosen to match the salad: olive-wood salad bowls are often reserved for highly seasoned green salads, which need to be tossed easily, whereas mixed salads, with ingredients of different colours, are best displayed in a fairly shallow transparent bowl. Individual salad bowls are used for serving portions of salad at the side of the plate.

salad burnet
PIMPRENELLE
A hardy perennial herb whose serrated grey-green leaves have a cool cucumber-like flavour. It is used to season omelettes, cold sauces, marinades, and soups and its tender young leaves can be used in salads like watercress. Burnet can also be used, like borage, in cooling drinks and for flavouring vinegar.

saladier lyonnais
A speciality of the regional cookery of Lyon, traditionally served as a snack in the local bars, together with other hors d'oeuvres and charcuterie. It is a salad of sheep's trotters (feet) cooked in courtbouillon, diced sautéed chicken livers, sliced hard-boiled (hard-cooked) eggs, and pieces of pickled herring, dressed with mustard vinaigrette and chopped herbs.

salamander
SALAMANDRE
A type of oven in which the heat is directed down from the roof, used by professional cooks for glazing, browning, or caramelizing some savoury or sweet dishes. It is named after the legendary animal that was resistant to fire and lived in the bowels of the earth. Many chefs favour this method of cooking, which – according to André Guillot – 'keeps all flavours intact, in the best conditions of speed and hygiene'. The grill of a cooker (broiler of an oven) can substitute for a salamander.

A salamander is also a metal instrument, which is heated over a flame or in a fire until red-hot and then held over dishes, especially créme brûlée, to brown or caramelize the surface.

salami
A charcuterie product originating in Italy and now made in many countries. It takes the form of a fat sausage made of finely minced (ground) pork (or a mixture of meats) interspersed with pieces of fat. In Italy salami is made particularly in Lombardy (Milan) and Bologna under various official names: *salame milanese, fiorentino, di Felino, di Fabriano, di Secondigliano, calabrese*, etc. The mixture can be flavoured with red wine, smoked, or spiced with fennel or parsley. In Italy salami is also made with goose and wild boar.

Salami made in France must bear a label in French, mentioning the place of origin, to avoid confusion; a notable example is *salami de Strasbourg* (Strasbourg salami or Alsatian sausage), a smoked and fairly thin sausage usually made with beef (for the lean meat) and pork (for the fat). Salami is also made in Germany, Austria, Switzerland, Denmark, Hungary, etc. The best known are Danish salami (highly coloured, salted, and smoked) and Hungarian salami (coloured with paprika, smoked, and sometimes wrapped in horse or ox intestines). Salami is served thinly sliced as a cold hors d'oeuvre, often with an assortment of other products; it can also be used in sandwiches, canapés, etc.

salammbô

A small cake made from choux pastry, filled with confectioners' custard (pastry cream) flavoured with Kirsch, and iced (frosted) with green fondant; one end is sprinkled with chocolate vermicelli (sprinkles). Originally the salammbô was decorated with chopped pistachio nuts, pressed onto both ends, and glazed with caramel. Created at the end of the 19th century, the cake takes its name from the opera by Reyer, based on Flaubert's novel, which was very popular at the time.

salep

A type of starch extracted from the tubers of a variety of orchid and used like tapioca and sago. In the Middle East, salep is boiled in water or milk to make a jelly used for preparing desserts. Known in France since the 17th century, it was formerly served as breakfast or as a light dinner, boiled in milk flavoured with orange-flower water. In domestic cookery it has now largely been replaced by tapioca and potato flour, but it is still sold in certain delicatessens under the name of *sahlab* or *saleb*. Arrowroot is sometimes known as 'West Indian salep' and potato flour as 'poor man's salep'.

Salers

A cheese from Auvergne made from untreated whole cows' milk (45% fat), with a firm curd, pressed twice, and a greyish-brown natural brushed rind. It is protected by an *appellation d'origine*, which defines its area of production and maturing as well as its shape and conditions of manufacture. Farmhouse Salers is similar to Laguiole and Cantal; it has a strong flavour, is cylindrical (38–48 cm (15–19 in) in diameter), and weighs 30–40 kg (65–90 lb). Formerly, the milk used came exclusively from Salers cows.

salmagundi or salmagundy

SALMIGONDIS

An elaborate salad laid out on a large flat dish with each ingredient minced (ground), shredded, or sliced and arranged attractively in small rings of contrasting colour. Cold meats, fish, cooked vegetables, salads, and pickles – anything can be used. The word is also used figuratively to mean a miscellaneous collection of things.

In France, *salmigondis* is an old dish which, according to the *Dictionnaire de Trévoux*, was a 'type of ragout made from various cooked meats, reheated in a sauce'. The word would appear to come from Old French *sal* (salt) and *condir* (to season), which implies that it was a highly flavoured dish. André Guillot suggests a very appetizing recipe for game *salmigondis*: pieces of wild rabbit, partridge, pheasant, and venison, browned in butter, stewed in wine with herbs, then coated in their reduced cooking juices flavoured with garlic and cream. The term *salmigondis* was also used, during the reign of Louis XIV, to denote a supper attended by several people, or several families, each bringing his or her own dish.

salmis

A game stew. The word is an abbreviation of *salmigondis* (see *salmagundi*), and the dish is usually made with woodcock, wild duck, pheasant, or partridge, but domestic duck, pigeon, or guinea fowl can also be used. The bird is two-thirds roasted, jointed, and then cooked in a saucepan, with mushrooms, for the remainder of the time. It is served coated with salmis sauce, a kind of espagnole sauce made with the carcass and the cooking juices diluted with wine (dry white for woodcock, port for guinea fowl, Chambertin for duck).

RECIPE

Woodcock salmis SALMIS DE BÉ-CASSE Pluck and singe 2 woodcock; truss them and roast in a hot oven (220 c, 425 f, gas 7) until two-thirds cooked.

Melt 50 g (2 oz, 4 tablespoons) butter in a sauté pan and add a carrot and an onion (both diced), a pinch of dried thyme, and a pinch of powdered bay leaf; cover and cook gently for 15 minutes. Then add a generous pinch of freshly ground pepper and remove from the heat. Divide each woodcock into 4 joints, then skin them and arrange in a shallow heatproof serving dish; cover and keep warm.

Chop the skin and crush the bones of the carcasses; add to the diced vegetables, together with the roasting juices. Mix well with a wooden spoon for 4–5 minutes over a gentle heat. Then moisten with 2 dl (7 fl oz, ¾ cup) dry white wine and 4 dl (14 fl oz, 1¼ cups) thickened brown veal stock (or 8 dl (1½ pints, 3½ cups) game fumet reduced by half); bring to the boil and cook gently for 15 minutes.

Meanwhile, clean 150 g (5 oz, 1½ cups) very small button mushrooms and cook, covered, in the juice of half a lemon, 2 tablespoons water, and a pinch of salt, for 10 minutes. Drain and spoon over the joints of woodcock, then flame with 1 liqueur glass of warmed brandy. Continue to keep warm.

Strain the sauce through a fine sieve, pressing the bones hard against the sides, thicken with 1 tablespoon kneaded butter, boil, and pour over the meat. Garnish with triangles of bread fried in butter.

salmon SAUMON

A migratory fish living mainly in the sea but spawning in fresh water. Young salmon remain in fresh water for about two years; at this age, when they are 15–20 cm (6–8 in) long and are called smolt, they begin to migrate towards the sea, where they reach maturity. The duration of their stay in the sea is variable as it depends on when they become sexually mature; spawning takes place in the winter following their journey upstream. Smaller salmon, measuring 50–60 cm (20–24 in), remain in the sea for one year and migrate upstream in June or July; spring salmon, measuring 70–80 cm (28–32 in), remain for two years, migrating from March to May. The great winter salmon, which measures 90 cm to 1 m (about 3 ft), remains in the sea for three years and moves upriver from October to March. The migrating salmon at this stage is known as a grilse and its lower jaw becomes hooked as it fights against the current to return to the spawning ground. After spawning, the fish (known as kelts) either die or return to the sea. After a second migration the salmon reaches its maximum weight (up to 30 kg (65 lb) in Norway).

Salmon under three years of age are best for eating. They have pink fatty highly nourishing flesh which can be cooked fresh, smoked, or sometimes eaten raw. The salmon has a silvery-blue back with small scattered black markings that turn orange when spawning. The sides and abdomen are golden.

In France, pollution and the construction of dams have considerably reduced salmon fishing. This is despite the construction of specially designed 'lifts' to help the fish migrate upriver and counteract the effect of the dams. At one time, there were many salmon in the rivers of France and they were still fished in the 18th and 19th centuries. Today, however, only the Loire, the Allier, the mountain streams in the southwest, and certain coastal rivers of Normandy and Brittany still contain salmon. The three great centres of salmon fishing in France are Navarrenx, Châteaulin, and Brioude, the latter being famous for its hot salmon and cream tart.

Salmon were among the most popular fish in the Middle Ages: they were cooked in stock, potted, braised, served in ragouts, pâtés, or soups, or salted. When salmon became rare, it came to be regarded as one of the luxury foods. A great deal of salmon is now imported into France and England from the Pacific (Canada) and the North Sea (Scotland, Denmark, and Norway). In the Soviet Union, Germany, and Scandinavia, salmon is used in many traditional dishes, such as Russian koulibiaca or Swedish *gravadlax* (raw salmon marinated in pepper, dill, sugar, and salt). Salmon breeding in the Norwegian fjords and on the Scottish coasts has yielded excellent results, and the trials on the Breton coasts are promising. Although gourmets are not happy about the flavour of farmed salmon, most people cannot tell the difference between farmed and wild salmon and the increase in production of this 'king of fish' has made it available to many more people.

Nordic salmon, particularly the Greenland salmon (similar to French salmon), are usually eaten smoked. Fresh salmon from the Pacific (silver salmon) are also available, together with canned salmon, sold in segments with the skin still attached, which is mostly Canadian and includes the red salmon (considered to be the best), the sockeye, and the chum.

Salmon is prepared whole, or cut into segments, steaks, or slices. The middle, which is the best part, is known in France as the *mitan*. Fresh salmon, whole or cut into steaks, is usually cooked in court-bouillon and served with a hot sauce, such as anchovy, butter, caper, prawn, lobster, mousseline, Nantua, ravigote, etc. Cold salmon is accompanied by various cold sauces: mayonnaise, tartare, green, rémoulade, Vincent, etc. Salmon can also be braised whole (stuffed or otherwise), or it can be cooked on a spit (whole or in segments). Salmon steaks are cooked in court-bouillon, grilled (broiled), fried in butter, or braised, as are salmon fillets, escalopes, and 'cutlets' (trimmed steaks or shaped flesh).

□ **Smoked salmon** This is delicious served cold with lemon juice, fresh cream, or horseradish sauce, eaten with bread, toast, blinis, etc. Smoked salmon is also used in various hot and cold recipes: aspics, canapés, filled cornets, and scrambled eggs. The fish is smoked over a mixture of different types of wood (beech, birch, oak, ash, and alder) and various aromatic essences (juniper, heather, and sage).

● Wild salmon that is smoked by traditional methods and sliced from the fish as required is the most highly prized. The best is Scotch salmon, with tender orange-pink flesh. Danish smoked salmon, which is pale golden brown, is also tasty but has less flavour, whereas Norwegian smoked salmon, which is a peachy pink colour, has a more pronounced flavour. Canadian smoked salmon is less highly prized; it is a deeper red in colour and drier in texture, the best being the salmon which are frozen when caught, before being smoked.

The best smoked salmon comes from fish that have been recently smoked; it is therefore best to buy from a shop with a high turnover. The middle of the fish yields the best portions; slices near the tail are drier and saltier. If a smoked salmon is bought whole, it is better to select a side weighing 1.25–1.5 kg (2½

–3 lb) – it will have a softer finer flesh than a smaller fish.

● Industrially smoked salmon is packaged as whole sides or in slices, either vacuum-packed or frozen. It is almost always prepared from the Canadian king salmon and the flesh is sometimes stringy. It should preferably be used for mixed salads or certain recipes in which the fish is incorporated into a mixture or a forcemeat.

RECIPES

COLD SALMON DISHES

Cold poached salmon SAUMON POCHÉ FROID Poach a whole salmon (or some salmon steaks) in a court-bouillon or a fish fumet and leave to cool in the liquid. Drain the fish, wipe it, and arrange on a large dish, garnished with parsley. Alternatively, the skin can be removed and the fish garnished with lettuce hearts, hard-boiled (hard-cooked) eggs, or stuffed vegetables (cherry tomatoes, slices of cucumber, etc.).

The following garnishes are also suitable: small pieces of aspic, prawn (shrimp) or crayfish tails, lobster medallions, a macédoine of vegetables, or small barquettes or cooked artichoke hearts filled with caviar, mousse, or a seafood filling.

Cold poached salmon may be served with the following sauces: andalouse, Chantilly, gribiche, mayonnaise, ravigote, rémoulade, green, or Vincent.

Escalopes of raw salmon with pepper ESCALOPES DE SAUMON CRU AUX DEUX POIVRES (from a recipe by Jean and Paul Minchelli) Brush a cold plate lightly with olive oil and lay some thin raw escalopes of salmon on it. Brush the escalopes with olive oil. Season with two turns of the pepper mill and one turn of the salt mill, then sprinkle with crushed green peppercorns. Serve very cold.

Glazed salmon cutlets with Chambertin CÔTELETTES DE SAUMON GLACÉES AU CHAMBERTIN Cut the salmon into slices 2–3 cm (about 1 in) thick and divide each slice in half. Shape the halves into cutlets and arrange on a buttered dish. Season with salt and pepper and add some fish aspic stock made with Chambertin (use enough stock to cover the cutlets.) Poach very gently for 8–10 minutes, then drain and wipe. Allow to cool completely. Clarify the stock, then cool it but do not allow it to set. Arrange the cutlets on a grid over a dish and coat them with several layers of aspic, placing the dish in the refrigerator between each application. Put a thin layer of aspic to set on the serving dish and lay the cutlets on top.

Marinated salmon SAUMON MARINÉ (from a recipe by Georges Blanc) Fillet a fresh Scotch salmon and cut the fillets into very thin escalopes. Prepare a marinade with 1 part olive oil to 2 parts lemon juice and add some salt, freshly ground pepper, and 1 tablespoon chopped herbs (chives, chervil, and tarragon). Marinate the escalopes for a maximum of 3 minutes. Make a sauce with a little whipped fresh cream, some salt and pepper, and 1 teaspoon Meaux mustard. Drain the slices of salmon and arrange them on a serving dish. Serve the sauce separately.

Rillettes of salmon RILLETTES DE SAUMON (from Gilbert's recipe) Put a bouquet garni, some salt and pepper, a sliced carrot, and a sliced onion in a saucepan with a little water. Boil gently for 20 minutes. Add a thick piece of fresh salmon and poach very gently in the stock for 10 minutes. Leave to cool, then drain. Trim the fish and flake it with a fork. Cut 100 g (4 oz) smoked salmon into dice. Mix the 2 types of salmon thoroughly with an egg yolk, 125 g (4½ oz, generous ½ cup) butter, and 1 tablespoon olive oil. Place in an earthenware dish and leave overnight in the refrigerator before serving.

Salmon mayonnaise MAYONNAISE DE SAUMON Cut some cooked salmon into thin escalopes and season with salt, pepper, oil, and either vinegar or lemon juice. Shred some lettuce leaves and arrange in bowls. Cover the lettuce with salmon escalopes, coat with mayonnaise, and garnish with capers, anchovies, black (ripe) olives, and quarters of hard-boiled (hard-cooked) eggs. Serve well chilled.

Terrine of salmon TERRINE DE SAUMON (from a recipe by Gisèle Crouzier) Remove all the flesh from a small well-trimmed salmon and marinate it in dry white wine with salt and pepper. Prepare a forcemeat as follows: blend the flesh from 1 kg (2¼ lb) white fish and 300 g (11 oz) unpeeled shrimps in a blender or food processor. Then add 12 eggs, 12 tablespoons (¾ cup) whipped fresh cream, and some salt and pepper. Blend the ingredients thoroughly. Butter a long terrine dish; spread a layer of forcemeat on the bottom, then add a layer of salmon, and repeat the procedure, ending with a layer of forcemeat. Put the lid on the dish and cook in a bain-marie for about 1½ hours in a moderate oven (180 c, 350 f, gas 4). Allow to cool completely and serve with green sauce (see *vert*).

HOT SALMON DISHES

Escalopes of salmon ESCALOPES DE SAUMON Cut some uncooked salmon fillets into escalopes (scallops) weighing about 100 g (4 oz) each. Flatten them lightly, and trim if necessary. All the recipes for preparing salmon cutlets and steaks can be used for escalopes.

Escalopes of salmon with carrots ESCALOPES DE SAUMON AUX CAROTTES (from a recipe by Jean and Paul Minchelli) Cook 2 sliced carrots in a frying pan (skillet) with some fish fumet, a little dry vermouth, and some paprika. When cooked *al dente*, remove the carrots and set aside. Add 1 tablespoon green peppercorns and 2 dl (7 fl oz, ¾ cup) double (heavy) cream to the frying pan, season with salt and pepper, and boil to reduce. Arrange some raw escalopes of salmon with the carrots on hot buttered plates. Coat with the hot sauce and serve immediately.

Fried salmon steaks DARNES DE SAUMON FRITES Season some salmon steaks 2 cm (¾ in) thick with salt and pepper, dust well with flour, and deep-fry quickly in hot oil (180 c, 350 f) until golden brown. Serve with lemon triangles.

Grilled (broiled) salmon steaks DARNES DE SAUMON GRILLÉES Season some salmon steaks 3–5 cm (1–2 in) thick with salt and pepper. Brush them with oil and cook them gently under a moderate grill. Serve with maître d'hôtel butter, béarnaise sauce, or gooseberry sauce.

Minute steaks of salmon with aigrelette sauce MINUTES DE SAUMON À L'AIGRELETTE (from a recipe by Georges Blanc) Butter some small oven-proof plates and sprinkle with salt and pepper. Place a salmon escalope on each plate (the escalopes should be large enough to cover the plates completely). Just before serving, put the plates into a very hot oven for 2–3 minutes. Meanwhile prepare a mayonnaise with wine vinegar and lemon juice, dilute it with fish fumet, and season with salt, pepper, chopped chives, and tarragon. Serve the cooked escalopes with this sauce.

Poached salmon steaks DARNES DE SAUMON POCHÉES Place some salmon steaks 4 cm (1½ in) thick in enough court-bouillon or fish fumet to cover them. Bring to the boil, simmer for 5 minutes, then remove from the heat and drain. Serve the steaks with melted clarified butter flavoured with lemon, maître d'hôtel butter, or beurre blanc.

Salmon à l'anglaise SAUMON À L'ANGLAISE Place a cleaned trimmed salmon in a fish kettle full of salted water (9–12 g (½ oz) salt per litre (1¾ pints, 4¼ cups) water), without adding any flavourings. Bring to the boil, cover, simmer for 10 minutes, then remove from the heat and leave to poach for 30 minutes. Drain the fish, place it on a large dish, and remove the skin. Serve with melted butter and a salad of cucumber, courgettes (zucchini), or leeks dressed with vinaigrette.

Salmon brochettes with fresh duck liver BROCHETTES DE SAUMON AU FOIE DE CANARD FRAIS (from a recipe by André Daguin) Prepare the brochettes by threading cubes of raw salmon and slightly larger cubes of fresh duck liver alternately on a skewer. Arrange the brochettes (without overlapping) on a julienne of vegetables in an ovenproof dish and season with salt

and pepper. Boil some dry white wine and some shallots in a saucepan until reduced by half. Add an equal quantity of double (heavy) cream and boil for 5 minutes. Pour the sauce over the brochettes and put in a moderately hot oven to cook for 10 minutes. Drain the brochettes and put them on a hot dish. Reduce the sauce and add some truffle juice. Then whisk the sauce with 3 egg yolks, as for zabaglione, and pour it over the brochettes.

Salmon cooked in champagne SAUMON AU CHAMPAGNE Prepare a fish fumet with 1 carrot, 1 onion, 30 g (1 oz, 2 tablespoons) butter, 400 g (14 oz) fish bones (preferably without skin), a bouquet garni, 3 dl (½ pint, 1¼ cups) white wine, and 2 dl (7 fl oz, ¾ cup) water. Simmer for 30 minutes and strain. Prepare a blond roux with 50 g (2 oz, ¼ cup) butter and 40 g (1½ oz, 6 tablespoons) flour and then add the fish stock. Bring the sauce to the boil, stirring continuously, and cook for 15 minutes over a low heat.

Gut (clean) a salmon weighing about 2 kg (4½ lb). Butter a large flameproof dish and sprinkle it with salt, pepper, and 3 chopped shallots. Place the salmon in the dish and add ½ litre (17 fl oz, 2 cups) champagne. Begin cooking the fish on top of the stove and then transfer to the oven (preheated to 220 C, 425 F, gas 7) and cook for 20 minutes. Drain the salmon and place it on an ovenproof serving dish.

Boil the cooking juices to reduce by a quarter and add to the velouté sauce. Heat through, remove from the heat, and beat in 2 egg yolks mixed with 2 tablespoons (3 tablespoons) double (heavy) cream. Season with salt and pepper and strain. Coat the salmon with some of the sauce and glaze it in a very hot oven for about 5 minutes. Serve immediately with the remainder of the sauce in a sauceboat.

Salmon cutlets CÔTELETTES DE SAUMON Trim some halved salmon steaks into the shape of cutlets and fry them in butter, with or without a coating of breadcrumbs. Serve them as they are, sprinkled with the butter in which they were cooked, or serve with a sauce and garnish.

Salmon cutlets can also be made with a croquette mixture fashioned into the shape of cutlets. Coat these cutlets with beaten egg and breadcrumbs, fry in butter, and serve coated with a sauce and garnished.

Salmon cutlets can also be prepared with a salmon quenelle mixture put into cutlet-shaped moulds and poached. They are served as a hot hors d'oeuvre, coated with sauce.

Salmon cutlets à la bourguignonne CÔTELETTES DE SAUMON À LA BOUR- GUIGNONNE Poach some salmon cutlets, together with some button mushrooms, in a fish fumet made with red wine. Drain the fish and arrange it on a serving dish with the mushrooms. Garnish with glazed baby onions. Reduce the cooking liquid and thicken it with kneaded butter. Strain the sauce and pour over the fish.

Salmon cutlets à la florentine CÔTELETTES DE SAUMON À LA FLORENTINE Cook some salmon cutlets in reduced fish stock (just enough to cover them). Coarsely chop some spinach and cook gently in butter; season with salt and pepper. Drain and place on a flameproof serving dish. Drain the cutlets and arrange them on the bed of spinach. Coat with Mornay sauce, sprinkle with grated cheese and a little melted butter, and brown under a hot grill (broiler).

Salmon cutlets à l'anglaise CÔTELETTES DE SAUMON À L'ANG- LAISE Trim some halved salmon steaks into cutlet shapes, season with salt and pepper, dust with flour, dip into egg beaten with 1 tablespoon oil and some salt and pepper, and coat them with fresh white breadcrumbs. Brown the cutlets on both sides in clarified butter. Arrange them on a serving dish and coat them with slightly softened maître d'hôtel butter. Place a slice of lemon (with the peel removed) on each cutlet, and surround them with cannelled half-slices of lemon.

Salmon en croûte SAUMON EN CROÛTE Make some puff pastry with 580 g (1¼ lb, 5 cups) flour, 3 dl (½ pint,

1¼ cups) water, 3 teaspoons table salt, and 430 g (15 oz, scant 2 cups) butter.

Trim the salmon and cut off all the fins except the tail fin. Cut off the gills and scale the fish, starting from the tail and working towards the head. Gut (clean) the salmon and remove any clots of blood. Wash the inside of the fish in plenty of water, arching its back slightly. Remove the skin from one side by making an incision along the back and separating the skin from the flesh on one side of this line, beginning at the tail and working towards the head, lifting it with the thumb. Wipe the salmon.

Divide the pastry into 2 portions. Roll out one of them into a long rectangle and place it on a large buttered baking sheet. Lay the salmon on the pastry, skin side down, and season with salt and plenty of pepper. Cut the pastry around the salmon to within 4 cm (1½ in) of the fish, leaving a large piece around the tail. Fold the pastry in towards the tail, tucking in the corners, and brush the edges of the pastry with an egg yolk beaten with 1 tablespoon water. Roll out the second portion of pastry like the first and place it over the fish. Seal the edges and trim to within 2 cm (¾ in) of the fish. Fold the now projecting top edge of the pastry round the tail over the bottom piece. Using a pointed knife, lightly score the position of the head, draw a line from the head to the tail along the backbone, and trace some oblique lines from this line down the side of the fish to mark the portions. Glaze the pastry evenly, paying particular attention to the sealed edges. Bake in a hot oven (220 C, 425 F, gas 7) for 1 hour. To serve, cut the crust along the line marking the head, then cut along the median line, and finally cut along the oblique lines.

Serve only the top layer of pastry as the bottom layer will be soft and will have stuck to the skin.

Salmon fritters with apple sauce BEIGNETS DE SAUMON AU COULIS DE POMMES (from a recipe by Marie Ferrand) Beat 4 egg yolks with 2 tablespoons (3 tablespoons) double (heavy) cream and 2 tablespoons (3 tablespoons) cornflour (cornstarch). Pour the mixture into a saucepan containing ¼ litre (8 fl oz, 1 cup) boiling cider and thicken over a gentle heat. Remove from the heat and add 300 g (11 oz) diced salmon and then 2 stiffly whisked egg whites. Put to one side.

Prepare the sauce as follows. Brown 2 sliced shallots and 6 sliced apples in a pan and add ¼ litre (8 fl oz, 1 cup) cider. When cooked, purée the mixture in a blender or food processor and keep hot.

Form the salmon purée into balls using 2 teaspoons and deep-fry them in hot lard until they have puffed up and are golden brown. Serve with the apple sauce.

Salmon steaks à la meunière   DARNES DE SAUMON À LA MEUNIÈRE   Season some salmon steaks 3 cm (1 in) thick with salt and pepper and lightly dust with flour. Fry them on both sides in very hot butter. Arrange the steaks on a long dish, sprinkle with chopped parsley, and add a dash of lemon juice. Just before serving, sprinkle the steaks with the cooking butter (very hot) and surround them with cannelled half-slices of lemon.

SMOKED SALMON

See *aspic, canapé, cornet, egg* (scrambled eggs), *purée*.

salpicon

Ingredients that are diced (often very finely), then bound with sauce (in the case of vegetables, meat, poultry, game, shellfish, fish, or eggs) or with syrup or cream (for a fruit salpicon). The word comes from Spanish *sal* (salt) and *picar* (cut).

Savoury salpicons are used for filling or garnishing barquettes, vols-au-vent, canapés, croustades, croûtes, small meat pies, rissoles, tartlets, etc. They are also used for making shaped cutlets, kromeskies, and croquettes, and for stuffing or garnishing eggs, poultry, game, fish, and some cuts of meat.

Fruit salpicons are made with fresh, raw, or crystallized (candied) fruit or with fruit cooked in syrup, usually macerated in a liqueur; they are used for garnishing or filling various desserts and pastries.

RECIPES

FISH AND SHELLFISH SALPICONS

Salpicons based on fish or shellfish can be hot or cold:

■ *à l'américaine*: diced lobster or langouste flesh, bound with américaine sauce (hot);

■ *with anchovies*: diced desalted fillets, bound with tarragon vinaigrette (cold) or with béchamel sauce (hot);

■ *à la cancalaise*: poached oysters and raw mushrooms, thinly sliced, marinated in lemon juice, and bound with normande sauce or fish velouté sauce (hot);

■ *à la cardinal*: diced lobster flesh, truffles, and mushrooms, bound with cardinal sauce (hot);

■ *with crayfish*: peeled tails, bound with béchamel or Nantua sauce (hot) or with vinaigrette or mayonnaise (cold);

■ *à la dieppoise*: peeled (shelled) prawns or shrimps, *moules marinière* (see *mussel*), and sliced mushrooms, stewed and bound with normande sauce (hot);

■ *with fish*: diced poached fillets of fish, bound with béchamel, normande, or white wine sauce (hot) or with vinaigrette or mayonnaise (cold);

■ *with lobster* or *langouste*: diced flesh, bound with béchamel or Nantua sauce (hot) or with vinaigrette or mayonnaise (cold);

■ *with mussels*: cooked mussels bound with allemande, poulette, or white wine sauce (hot) or marinated and bound with vinaigrette or mayonnaise (cold);

■ *with prawns* or *shrimps*: peeled, bound with béchamel sauce (hot) or mayonnaise (cold);

■ *with skate liver*: slices of skate liver in butter, bound with velouté sauce made with fish stock (hot) or vinaigrette (cold).

MEAT, POULTRY, GAME, OFFAL, AND EGG SALPICONS

Meat or egg salpicons can be hot or cold:

■ *with brains*: diced poached brains, bound with allemande, béchamel, or velouté sauce (hot);

■ *à l'écossaise*: pickled tongue cut into small cubes and diced truffles, bound with reduced demi-glace (hot);

■ *with foie gras*: finely diced foie gras, bound with Madeira, port, or sherry sauce or game fumet (hot), or with aspic (cold); sautéed chicken livers can be added;

■ *with game*: finely diced game meat bound either with white or brown sauce made with game fumet (from the same game as the salpicon) or with aspic;

■ *with ham*: diced York, Prague, or Paris ham, bound with demi-glace (hot), or with vinaigrette or mustard-flavoured mayonnaise (cold);

■ *with hard-boiled (hard-cooked) eggs*: diced whites and yolks, bound with allemande, béchamel, cream, or velouté sauce (hot), or with vinaigrette or mayonnaise with herbs (cold);

■ *with lambs'* or *calves' sweetbreads*: sliced sweetbreads cooked in butter, bound with allemande, béchamel, demi-glace, Madeira, or suprême sauce (hot);

■ *with meat*: finely diced leftover beef, veal, mutton, or pork, bound with white or brown sauce (used particularly for croquettes and kromeskies and for filling pies);

■ *with poultry*: diced white poultry meat, bound with allemande, béchamel, cream, velouté, brown, or demi-glace sauce or with veal stock (hot, for filling vols-au-vent, barquettes, croustades, and poached eggs and for croquettes), or with vinaigrette with herbs for filling cold barquettes, hard-boiled eggs, etc.;

■ *à la reine*: diced white chicken meat, mushrooms, and truffles, bound with allemande sauce (hot);

■ *à la Saint-Hubert*: diced game meat, bound with reduced demi-glace made with game fumet (hot);

■ *with veal*: diced cooked veal, bound with allemande, béchamel, or demi-glace sauce or with veal stock (hot).

VEGETABLE SALPICONS

Vegetable salpicon with cream sauce (hot) SALPICON CHAUD DE LÉGUMES À LA CRÈME Cut partially cooked vegetables into large or small dice, according to requirements:

■ artichoke hearts half-cooked in white stock;

■ green asparagus or French beans half-cooked in boiling salted water;

■ aubergines (eggplants) half-cooked in butter or oil;

■ carrots three-quarter-cooked in water and butter;

■ celeriac (celery root) half-stewed in butter;

■ ceps or button mushrooms half-stewed in butter or oil;

■ onions half-cooked in butter;

■ tomatoes blanched for 1 minute and peeled;

■ Jerusalem artichokes or salsify half-cooked in salted water.

Finish cooking the salpicon in butter and bind with a few tablespoons of thick cream sauce or reduced velouté sauce.

Vegetable salpicon with mayonnaise (cold) SALPICON FROID DE LÉGUMES À LA MAYONNAISE Cook the chosen vegetable completely, leave to cool, cut into small dice, and bind with classic mayonnaise, which may be flavoured, coloured, or thickened. Use any of the following vegetables: artichoke hearts cooked in white stock, patted dry, and diced; asparagus tips or French (green) beans cut into short pieces, boiled in salted water, and patted dry; peeled diced celeriac (celery root) boiled in salted water and patted dry; mushrooms cooked in butter, drained, and diced; or potatoes boiled in their skins, peeled, and diced

Vegetable salpicon with vinaigrette (cold) SALPICON FROID DE LÉGUMES À LA VINAIGRETTE Cook the chosen vegetable completely, leave to cool, dice, and dress with seasoned vinaigrette flavoured with finely chopped aromatic herbs. Use any of the following vegetables: diced cooked beetroot (red beet) with chervil and parsley; raw cucumber, sprinkled with salt, left to stand, rinsed, patted dry, and diced, with fresh mint or tarragon; tomatoes, blanched for 20 seconds, peeled, seeded, and diced, with basil or tarragon.

salsify SALSIFIS

A root vegetable, also called oyster plant or vegetable oyster, of which there are two varieties: the *true salsify*, which is white and thick, with numbers of rootlets, and the *black salsify*, or *scorzonera*, which is black, longer, and tapering and has no rootlets. Black salsify is easier to peel than true salsify and is cultivated for canning. Both varieties have a fairly strong and slightly bitter flavour and tender flesh; they are prepared in the same way. The word *scorzonera* comes from Catalan *escorso* (viper), since the plant was formerly used in Spain to treat snake bites. Both vegetables are in season between October and March. They are particularly suitable for garnishing white meat.

Wild salsify, known as 'goat's beard', grows in slightly damp meadows. Its young shoots can be eaten in salad and can also be prepared like spinach; the roots are cooked like those of black salsify.

RECIPES

Preparing and cooking salsify PRÉ-PARATION ET CUISSON DES SALSI-FIS Wash the salsify well and leave to soak for 1 hour in cold water, which makes peeling easier. Scrape or peel with a potato peeler, cut into chunks 7–8 cm (3 in) long, and put them as they are prepared into water with a little lemon juice or vinegar added. Cook in boiling vegetable stock, covered, at a steady gentle simmer for 1–1½ hours, according to the quality of the vegetable, then drain and pat dry before final preparations for serving. If the salsify is not to be used immediately, it can be stored in its cooking liquid in the refrigerator for a day or two, but it will lose some of its nutritional value.

Buttered salsify SALSIFIS AU BEURRE Cook the salsify. Just before serving, make some noisette butter. Drain the salsify thoroughly while it is still very hot, quickly pat dry, then place on a heated dish and pour the noisette butter over it.

Salsify au gratin SALSIFIS AU GRATIN (from Paul and Jean-Pierre Haeberlin's recipe) Wash, scrape or peel, and roughly chop 1 kg (2¼ lb) salsify. Plunge into water with lemon juice added, then cook for 1 hour (or until tender) in salted white stock, drain, and dry. Cook 2 chopped shallots in butter until soft. Pour over 5 dl (17 fl oz, 2 cups) cream and reduce. Add the salsify and a little stock. Season with salt and pepper and pour into a gratin dish. Sprinkle with grated Gruyère and breadcrumbs and brown for 20 minutes in a very hot oven.

Salsify fritters BEIGNETS DE SALSIFIS (from Raymond Oliver's recipe) Cook 1 kg (2¼ lb) salsify, drain, and purée. Add 100 g (4 oz, ½ cup) butter and season with salt and pepper. Roll the purée into little balls, coat them in flour, and deep-fry in hot fat at 180 C (350 F) until golden all over. Remove with a slotted spoon and drain on absorbent paper. Arrange on a warmed dish and garnish with fried parsley.

Salsify in stock SALSIFIS AU JUS Wash, peel, and cook the salsify, then drain and dry. Pour over some slightly thickened white veal stock or meat gravy. Cook in a moderate oven (180 C, 350 F, gas 4) for 15–20 minutes.

Salsify Mornay SALSIFIS MORNAY Cook the salsify, drain, dry, then arrange in a gratin dish lined with a layer of Mornay sauce. Coat with boiling Mornay sauce, sprinkle with grated Parmesan, pour over some melted butter, and brown in a very hot oven.

Salsify salad with anchovies SALSIFIS EN SALADE AUX ANCHOIS Cook some salsify in white stock, drain thoroughly, and dry. Mix in some light well-seasoned mayonnaise and chopped drained canned anchovy fillets (or whole filleted anchovies that have been soaked to desalt them). Sprinkle with chopped herbs.

Salsify with mayonnaise SALSIFIS À
LA MAYONNAISE Cook the salsify
and leave to cool, then drain thoroughly
and dry. Add some well-seasoned
mayonnaise or vinaigrette. Sprinkle
with chopped herbs and serve with a
cold white meat dish – rabbit in aspic,
for example.

Sautéed salsify SALSIFIS SAUTÉS
Cook some salsify in white stock, drain,
dry and fry in butter. Sprinkle with salt,
pepper, and chopped herbs just before
serving.

salt SEL

A white crystalline odourless sharp-
tasting substance which is used as a
condiment and preserving agent. In the
pure state, salt consists of sodium chloride and is very abundant in nature.
There are two basic types: sea salt,
which is extracted from sea water by
evaporation (30 kg per cubic metre);
and rock salt, which is found in the
crystalline state in the ground. The dried
salt lakes of Asia, Africa, and America
constitute large deposits of rock salt. In
France, rock salt deposits are found in
Franche-Comté, Béarn, and especially
in Lorraine, where the salt works have
been an important industry since the
Middle Ages.

Since ancient times salt has been a
precious commodity. The Hebrews
used it in sacrifices and ceremonies.
Homer described nations as poor when
they did not mix salt with their food.
Salt is a symbol of friendship and hospitality and in some countries is still traditionally offered with bread to strangers.
The Romans used salt to preserve fish,
olives, cheese, and meat and it formed
part of the soldiers' wages (hence the
etymology of salary). In the Middle
Ages, the salt routes were used for a
solid flow of trade, both in France (especially from Saintonge) and Scandinavia,
where dried salt fish was the basic food.
There was a salt measurers' guild in
France as early as the 13th century. Its
members had the task of counting the
salt fish and quantities of butter arriving
in Paris by boat, and they also supervised the measuring of salt and grain. In
medieval Britain salt was an essential
commodity – even to peasants. It was
collected from the coastline where sea
water had evaporated leaving a crystalline deposit, and then stored in a box
near the fire.

Since salt was essential to life and to
the long-term preservation of foodstuffs, and since its production could be
easily supervised, many governments
taxed it. In France, the *gabelle* tax, created in the 14th century and abolished
in 1790, obliged private individuals to
purchase a certain amount of salt from
the king's storehouses every year at a
fixed price, even if they were not going
to use it.

Salt is an essential condiment and
remains an essential raw material in the
food industry (for canned foods, salted
meat and fish, charcuterie, cheese, etc.).
In France and Britain, the following
categories are recognized.

● *Coarse salt* (refined or unrefined) is
available in large crystals. Unrefined
salt, which is grey in colour, contains
traces of valuable minerals; it is therefore best to use it in cooking and reserve
the white salt for the table. It can be used
in its large crystal form or ground in a
salt mill.

● *Cooking salt*, which comes in the
form of small crystals, is used to season
food while cooking. It should be kept
within hand's reach in a vessel with a
lid, to keep it from becoming damp. It is
used by the handful.

● *Table salt* is always refined and is
used as a table condiment (in a salt
cellar), in pâtisserie, for seasoning, and
to finish sauces. It is used by the pinch.
To make it less hygroscopic, various
products are added to it (e.g. magnesium carbonate, sodium silicoalumin-
ate, etc.), the proportion of which must
never exceed 2%.

The essential function of salt is to
enhance the flavour of the food, to bring
out the taste, and to stimulate the appetite. It is essential for the body and
contributes to maintaining the osmotic
pressure of the body's cells. The average
requirement is about 5 g (¼ oz) salt per
day, but Western diets may provide up
to 20 g salt per day, which may cause
health problems in susceptible individuals (e.g. those with high blood
pressure). Foods rich in salt include
cheese, game, charcuterie, smoked
meats, and salt fish.

There are certain types of salt with special uses.

- *Celery salt*: a table salt mixed with dried ground celeriac (celery root). It is used to season tomato juice cocktails and other vegetable juices and also stocks and consommés.
- *Lovage salt*: a table salt flavoured with dried ground lovage root. It has more body than celery salt and is used in soups and sauces, particularly in Germany.
- *Spiced salt*: a mixture of dry table salt, white ground pepper, and mixed spices in the proportions 10:1:1. It is used to season forcemeats, pies, and terrines.
- *Tenderizing salt*: ordinary salt containing 2–3% papain. It is for tenderizing meat and is for domestic use only (prohibited in butchers' shops, delicatessens, and restaurants).
- *Iodized salt*: a mixture of table salt and sodium iodide, sold as table salt.
- *Diet salt*: a salt substitute from which the sodium chloride has been completely or partially removed.
- *Nitrite-treated salt*: a preservative used in the delicatessen and food-preserving industries (E250). Nitrite-treated salt is a salt to which a mixture of sodium or potassium nitrate (salt-petre) and sodium nitrite has been added (10% maximum).
- *Hickory salt*: an American condiment consisting of sea salt mixed with smoked finely powdered hickory wood. It has a slightly nutty taste and is used for barbecues.

In France, *sel chinois* (Chinese salt) is monosodium glutamate; and *sel de poisson* (fish salt) is nuoc-mâm.

salt box   BOÎTE À SEL

A wooden or earthenware box with a hinged lid, usually attached to the wall near a cooking surface, for easy access. Coarse and fine salt may be kept in two different boxes.

salt cellar   SALIÈRE

A small receptacle used for serving salt at the table. Made from various materials in several different shapes, such as a sprinkler or a tiny bowl and spoon, salt cellars are often incorporated in a cruet with pepper and mustard pots. Originally, salt cellars were simply hol-lowed-out lumps of bread; then silver salt cellars and rich gold-plated articles appeared, often fitted with a lock, as salt was once an extremely expensive commodity.

salt cod   MORUE

Cod that is sold ready salted and dried. For a long time France was the only country to practise two separate types of fishing – one for fresh cod, the other for cod that was salted on board. Today in France the distinction is no longer made: the fish are either frozen or salted on the same boats.

☐ **Types of salt cod**
- *Morue vert*, salted (but not dried) in casks, is hardly seen in France any more, though it is still found in some Mediterranean countries and in Portugal (*bacalao*).
- *Morue salée*, the traditional type in France, is salted on board, rinsed and brushed in port, then salted again (in barrels); it is sold in the piece (*en queue*) or cut and packed.
- *Salt-cod fillets*, skinned, boned, blanched, and slightly salted, are sold prepacked; they are often treated with sulphur dioxide (E220) to avoid mould and improve blanching.
- *Stockfish*, or Norwegian cod, is dried in the open air.

Salt cod has a greater energy value than fresh cod (350 Cal per 100 g). Its liver, rich in vitamins A and D, is used for cod-liver oil.

For centuries salt cod has formed a basic food, particularly for days of abstinence. Because it keeps so well, salt cod was a valuable food in times of siege. Cod tripe was a highly prized dish: called *noues* or *nos*, it was salted and prepared like calf's mesentery. Salt cod tongues are used in a variety of savoury recipes. Bordeaux and Marseille traditionally played an important part in the salt-cod trade, hence the spread of regional dishes (see *estofinado*, *brandade*).

Before any preparation, the fish must be carefully desalted. It can then be poached and served either cold (in vinaigrette, with mustard, in a gribiche sauce, with mayonnaise, in a salad with potatoes, etc.) or hot (in a white or Mornay sauce, *au gratin*, in scallop shells, as a soufflé or a fish loaf, in croquettes, in a cassoulet, as fritters with a tomato or onion fondue, etc.). Salt cod can also be sautéed or served in a brandade.

RECIPES

Desalting and poaching salt cod DES-SALAGE ET POCHAGE DE LA MORUE If the fish is dried, wash it thoroughly under a cold tap, then either leave it whole or cut it into sections (which speeds up the desalting process). Then place it in a colander (with the skin uppermost) in a basin of cold water, so that the fish is completely covered. Soak for 24 hours (12 hours for fillets), changing the water several times: the fish must be totally free of salt before it is cooked. Drain the cod and place it in a saucepan with plenty of cold water. Add a bouquet garni, bring the water to the boil, and keep it simmering for about 10 minutes. Drain well and prepare according to the chosen recipe.

Fillets of salt cod maître d'hôtel FILETS DE MORUE MAÎTRE D'HÔTEL Desalt the fillets whole, then drain and cut them into small tongue shapes. Flatten them slightly, coat with breadcrumbs, and cook in butter. Arrange the pieces in a serving dish and coat with half-melted maître d'hôtel butter. Serve with boiled potatoes.

Fried salt cod MORUE FRITE Desalt the cod, cut it into small tongue-shapes, and soak for 1 hour in milk which has been boiled and cooled. Drain the fish pieces, flour them, and fry in oil heated to 175 C (347 F). Place on absorbent paper and sprinkle with fine salt. Serve with lemon quarters.

Salt cod à la créole MORUE À LA CRÉOLE Desalt and poach 750 g (1¾ lb) salt cod. Prepare a fondue with 1 kg (2¼ lb) tomatoes, some olive oil, plenty of garlic and onion, and a dash of cayenne. Cut 6 medium-sized tomatoes in half and remove the seeds. Deseed 2 green peppers and cut them into small tongue-shaped pieces. Sauté the tomatoes and peppers in oil. Spread the tomato fondue in an oiled gratin dish, arrange the drained and flaked cod on top, and cover it with the tomato halves and the pieces of pepper. Sprinkle with a little oil and cook in the oven at 230 C (450 F, gas 8) for 10 minutes, moistening with a little lime juice. Serve piping hot with rice *à la créole*.

Salt cod à la florentine MORUE À LA FLORENTINE Desalt and poach 750 g (1¾ lb) cod, drain it, and flake it. Blanch 1 kg (2¼ lb) spinach for 5 minutes in salted boiling water, then drain and press it and cook slowly in 50 g (2 oz, 4 tablespoons) butter for about 10 minutes. Line a gratin dish with this spinach. Arrange the cod on top, coat with Mornay sauce, sprinkle with grated Parmesan cheese, and moisten with a little melted butter. Brown in a hot oven.

Salt cod à l'anglaise MORUE À L'AN-GLAISE Desalt the fish, poach it in water, then arrange it on a napkin in a dish, garnished with fresh parsley. Serve with boiled vegetables and melted butter, to which lemon juice, chopped hard-boiled (hard-cooked) egg, and coarsely chopped parsley have been added.

The butter may be replaced by a sauce (bâtarde, cream, hollandaise, caper, fines herbes, curry, or mustard), or the cod can be served cold with mayonnaise.

Tongues of salt cod in pistou LAN-GUES DE MORUE AU PISTOU (from a recipe of Jean and Paul Minchelli) Thoroughly desalt 800 g (1¾ lb) salt cod tongues. Poach them for 6 minutes in a mixture of equal quantities of water and milk. Drain, lightly flour, and fry quickly in olive oil. Crush 2 blanched cloves of garlic and some basil in a mortar. Mix with olive oil, add some fresh puréed tomato, and sprinkle with pepper. Place this pistou and the tongues in a nonstick frying pan (skillet), sauté, and serve piping hot.

saltimbocca

An Italian dish that is a speciality of Rome but originally came from Brescia, where the name literally means 'jump into the mouth'. It consists of fine slices of veal fried in butter, topped with small slices of ham, flavoured with sage, and gently braised in white wine.

salting SALAGE

A preserving process used mainly for pork and certain types of fish. It is sometimes combined with smoking and drying. A very ancient technique, used by the Romans for fish, olives, shrimps, and cheese, it became very much more sophisticated in the Middle Ages, for cod, herring, etc. Salting is now less widespread than before in domestic cookery, where the main methods used are bottling and freezing; it is confined to specific foods, using dry salt or brine.

• *Anchovies* – The fish are cleaned and put into salt for six to eight months.

• *Herrings, sprats, salmon, and eels* – These are salted in dry salt or brine, then smoked.

• *Cod* – The fish are split in half, flattened, and boned, then stacked between layers of salt with the addition of sulphurous anhydride (or one of its derivatives, E220), which keeps the flesh white. They are left for at least 30 days.

• *Meat* – Raw ham and bacon are rubbed with a mixture of salt and saltpetre (the operation is sometimes completed with an injection of brine into the bone joint), then the pieces are piled into salting tubs. The exuded water forms a supersaturated brine, in which the pieces are moved around every 10–15 days; salting lasts for 40–60 days. Cooked ham is placed in vats, covered with brine, and left there for 30–40 days, at a temperature of 3–5 c (37–41 f). It may also be smoked. Other traditional salted meats include beef in brine and salted tongue. Pork is also salted in brine without being cured.

• *Fruit, vegetables, and nuts* – Salting is sometimes used to preserve French (green) beans and herbs, but is particularly associated with sauerkraut, peanuts, cashews, almonds, walnuts, and hazelnuts, as well as crisps (potato chips).

• *Cheese* – Salting is an important operation in the manufacture of cheese. It accelerates drainage in soft fresh curd cheeses when sprinkled on by hand, and encourages rind formation on cooked and uncooked pressed curd cheeses immersed in brine: the more the brine is renewed, the thicker and harder the rind becomes. Some soft cheeses are salted to varying extents (slightly salted) or preserved in a light brine, as are the goats'- and ewes'-milk cheeses of Mediterranean countries.

RECIPES

Home-salted pork SALAISONS DOMESTIQUES Choose fairly even-sized pieces of belly pork, knuckles of ham, spare rib or shoulder chops, and trimmed rind. Rub them with fine salt and lay in a wooden salting tub, putting the largest pieces at the bottom: start with the pieces of belly pork, pressing them down well. Cover with cooking salt, making sure that there are as few air pockets as possible. A few cloves of garlic, peppercorns, and a bay leaf may be added, but not to excess. Then pile on the knuckles of ham, filling up the holes with the spare rib or shoulder chops. Cover each layer with salt, pressing down well, and finish with the rinds. Preservation time is 2–3 weeks for spare rib chops, 1 month for knuckles of ham, and much longer for belly pork. Knuckle, brushed and wiped, can be stored hung up in a cool airy place.

Rolled salt belly pork POITRINE ROULÉE SALÉE Choose a piece of streaky belly pork that is not too fatty. Trim it, cut into a rectangle, and slash the inside. Rub with salt mixed with chopped garlic, then sprinkle with chopped fresh thyme. Roll up the belly and tie tightly. Rub the outside – the rind side – with fine salt for some time, so that it penetrates thoroughly. Cut the belly into 2 or 3 pieces, according to the size of the salting tub.

salting tub SALOIR

A container used for salting pork. Formerly a large wooden tub, it is now a cement, earthenware, or plastic vat.

salt-meadow sheep
MOUTON PRÉ-SALÉ

A French sheep or lamb raised and fattened on the pastures close to the sea, which are impregnated with salt and iodine. In this way, the flesh acquires a unique flavour and gives high-quality meat.

saltpetre SALPÊTRE

The common name for potassium nitrate, derived from Latin *sal* (salt) and *petrae* (stone). Saltpetre takes the form of small white crystals, which were formerly obtained by scraping the walls of cellars and storerooms; it is now manufactured industrially. A powerful bactericide, saltpetre has been used since ancient times to preserve food (especially raw and cooked meats), since it strengthens the action of fermenting agents while giving a characteristic flavour to the product being treated. Its oxidizing action produces the characteristic bright pink colour of salt beef, ham, pickled tongue, etc. It is used in conjunction with salt in all types of brine, with the addition of at least twice its weight of sugar (since it has a very bitter taste). If used excessively it can be harmful so its use is controlled by very strict regulations.

salt pork   PETIT SALÉ

A piece of pork (loin, knuckle, shoulder, or hand) that has been salted in brine or dry salt and is sold raw, labelled *demisel* (slightly salted) in France. Before being cooked it is desalted by soaking in water for 1–12 hours, depending on the degree of salting. Salt pork has more flavour and cooks more quickly than unsalted meat. The classic recipe for salt pork is potée (a type of stew), but it can also be boiled and served with cabbage, pease pudding, or with lentils and carrots.

| RECIPE

Boiled salt pork with pease pudding
POITRINE DE PORC AUX POIS CASSÉS   Boil a piece of salted belly pork with some carrots, turnips, celery, leeks, onions, and parsnips. Prepare a very smooth purée of split peas (preferably yellow) using 500 g (18 oz, 2¼ cups) split peas, 100 g (4 oz, ½ cup) butter, 3 eggs, grated nutmeg, salt, and pepper. Butter a pudding basin (mould) and pour the mixture into it. Place the basin in a baking tin containing 2.5 cm (1 in) boiling water and cook in the oven at 190 C (375 F, gas 5) for 40 minutes. Drain the cooked pork, place in a serving dish, and surround with the well-drained vegetables. Turn out the pease pudding and serve separately.

samaritaine (à la)

A term applied to large braised cuts of meat garnished with rice timbales, dauphine potatoes, and braised lettuce.

sambal

An Indonesian condiment made with red chilli peppers, grated onion, lime, oil, and vinegar. The name is also used to describe the dish that it accompanies.

sambuca

A sort of colourless Italian anisette. It is very popular in Rome, where it is drunk *con la mosca* ('with the fly'): with one or two coffee beans floating in the glass, after it has been flamed. Sambuca is very strong but has a sweetish taste; the coffee beans are crunched as it is drunk.

Samos

Wine from the Greek island of Samos, which has its own AOC. Samos wines are made from a variety of the Muscat grape.

samovar

A Russian kettle that provides a permanent supply of boiling water for domestic purposes. The word comes from *samo* (itself) and *varit* (to boil). Made from brass or copper (nowadays, it may be made from aluminium or stainless steel and electrically heated), the samovar is the traditional Russian wedding gift. It consists of a potbellied container with two handles and a central chimney that rests on a grid on which embers are placed. Cold water is added at the top and heated by contact with the chimney; the boiling water is drawn off through a small tap at the bottom of the container. Since this water is used, among other things, for making tea, the name 'samovar' has been applied to a simple silver container heated by a small spirit lamp, which provided boiling water for adding to tea, during large gatherings.

samphire

CRISTE-MARINE

The common name for *Crithmum maritimum*, a perennial herb, also called rock samphire, that grows on clifftops in cracks in the rocks or on dry stony ground. In France it is also known as *perce-pierre*, *pousse-pierre*, *casse-pierre*, and *bacile*. Its fleshy leaves are rich in iodine and are used principally to flavour soups and salads. The leaves can also be pickled in vinegar like gherkins or cooked in butter or cream, like purslane.

Samphire is used in an original way in Sarah Bernhardt's recipe for wildfowl with larks: 'Pound in a mortar the flesh of two larks; add some butter, some chopped samphire, some breadcrumbs soaked in milk, some Malaga raisins, and some crushed juniper berries. Stuff a third lark with the mixture and roast it on a spit covered with samphire leaves and a strip of fat bacon. Serve on a crouton soaked in gin, and then toasted and buttered.'

See also *glasswort (marsh samphire)*.

Sampigny-lès-Maranges

AOC red and white Burgundies from the extreme south of the Côte de Beaune. Much of the wine from this area, whose production is limited, may be blended with that of neighbouring parishes (communes) and sold as Côte-de-Beaune-Villages.

Samsoë

A Danish cows'-milk cheese (45% fat), from the island of the same name, with a pressed curd and a golden yellow rind coated with paraffin wax. Mild and firm, with a few round holes, it acquires a nutty flavour after a few months' maturing. It is made in round discs 45 cm (18 in) in diameter, weighing about 15 kg (33 lb).

Sancerre

AOC wines from the upper reaches of the River Loire. The vineyards are around the picturesque little hill town of Sancerre, which stands above the river. The dry crisp fragrant white wines are especially famous and are made from the Sauvignon grape. The Pinot Noir grape is used to make fruity reds and delicious rosés, both of which are now becoming more widely known.

sanciau

A large rustic pancake or fritter which is common in several French provinces. Sweet or savoury, sanciaux are made from flour, milk, and butter and some-

times with eggs. They are cooked in a frying pan (skillet) as thick pancakes (in Berry and Nivernais, where they are also called *sauciaux*) or as batter fritters (in Bourbonnais). They are related to grapiaux, chanciaux, matefaims and other traditional flour-based dishes of rural areas of central France.

Sand (George; *born* Aurore Dupin)

French writer (born Paris, 1804; died Nohant, 1876). Together with the other great Romantic writers in Paris, she frequented the Procope, Mère Saguet's open-air café, and praised the sheep's trotters (feet) *à la poulette* served at Magny's. A cordon-bleu cook, she extolled *omelette nohentaise*, feasted on Chavignol (a soft goats'-milk cheese), and was not averse to 'fairy potatoes' (truffles). She also appreciated the wines of Berry and owned a vineyard in Mers-sur-Indre.

sand eel   ÉQUILLE

A small silvery fish, also known as a sand lance, that is very common in the Atlantic, the English Channel, and the North Sea. The sand eel grows to a length of 25 cm (10 in); it is caught in the sand at low tide and is always fried.

sand-smelt   ATHÉRINE

A small sea fish, also called silverside, living in shoals along coasts and in estuaries. The best-known species is known in France as *prêtre* or *faux éperlan* ('false smelt'). The sand-smelt is about 15 cm (6 in) long and has a conspicuous silvery stripe down each side of the body. It is sometimes passed off as smelt, but its flesh is less delicate. It is generally fried but may also be eaten smoked. The French name is derived from the Greek word *ather*, meaning 'beard of an ear of grain', as its bones resemble an ear of barley. Similar species are found in the Mediterranean.

sandwich

Two slices of bread enclosing a plain or mixed filling based on cooked meats, raw vegetables, or cheese, cut into thin slices or small pieces. Sandwiches are made with tin loaf bread (whole slices, with or without crusts, sometimes cut into triangles or rectangles after filling),

French bread (chunks of French sticks or slices of farmhouse bread), rye or brown bread in thin slices, and long or round soft rolls or brioche rolls. Various condiments complete the filling: gherkins, herbs, plain or flavoured butter, black (ripe) olives, etc. Canapé garnishes are all suitable for sandwiches.

Sandwiches are named after John Montagu, 4th Earl of Sandwich, an inveterate gambler who acquired the habit of sending for cold meat between two slices of bread so that he would not have to leave the gambling tables to eat. Although the name is relatively recent, dating from the beginning of the 19th century, the concept itself is ancient. It has long been the custom in rural France to give farm labourers working in the fields meat for their meal enclosed in two slices of brown bread. In southwestern France, it was customary to provide those setting out on a journey with slices of cooked meat (especially pork or veal), sprinkled with their juices, sandwiched between two pieces of bread. The *pan-bagnat* of Nice is also a type of sandwich, made from a copiously filled round roll impregnated with olive oil; it is found in a number of Mediterranean countries.

The greatest variety of sandwiches is found in England and the United States, where they range from very large, composed of several layers of different fillings, to small and delicate, with elaborate or exotic fillings, for serving at luncheons and cocktail parties.

RECIPES

Basil sandwich   SANDWICH AU BASILIC   Lightly toast 2 slices of bread and spread with butter mixed with chopped fresh basil. Fill with chopped hard-boiled (hard-cooked) eggs, sliced black (ripe) olives, and a few strips of sweet red pepper marinated in oil and well drained.

Club sandwich   Remove the crusts from 3 large slices of bread. Lightly toast them and spread with mayonnaise. On 2 slices place a lettuce leaf, 2 slices of tomato, some thin slices of skinned cold roast chicken breast, and sliced hard-boiled (hard-cooked) egg. Coat with more mayonnaise mixed with

a little tomato ketchup or chopped herbs and put one slice on top of the other. Cover with the third slice.

sangler

A French culinary term meaning to pack crushed ice and cooking salt around a watertight mould placed inside a container. This process is used particularly with ice-cream churns for freezing and for temporarily preserving bombe mixtures. It is being increasingly replaced by the use of the freezer.

Sangre de Toro

The registered name of one of the red wines of the Torres establishment in the Panadés area of Spain.

sangria

The Spanish version of a cup, a mixed drink based on red or white wine with added fruit and mineral water, sometimes with a spirit as well. It is served chilled. As red wine is the most usual base, the drink takes its name from *sangre*, Spanish for 'blood'.

RECIPES

Sangria with brandy   SANGRIA AU COGNAC   Mix together a lemon and an orange, both sliced, a quartered apple, 60 g (2½ oz, 5 tablespoons) sugar, 1 bottle red wine, 4 tablespoons (⅓ cup) Spanish brandy, and 750 ml (1¼ pints, 3 cups) carbonated mineral water. A pinch of cinnamon may be added.

Sangria with peaches   SANGRIA AUX PÊCHES   Cut a large can of peaches into pieces. Pour them into a large glass bowl, together with their syrup. Remove the peel and pith from 4 oranges and 2 lemons; slice them and add to the peaches. Pour over 2 litres (3½ pints, 4½ pints) Spanish or Algerian wine, 1 litre (1¾ pints, 4¼ cups) lemonade, and 2 liqueur glasses of Grand Marnier or Cointreau. Mix well and chill in the refrigerator for at least 3 hours.

Sangue di Guida

A Lombardy red wine, known also as 'Judas' blood', from the Oltrepò Pavese region of Italy.

sanguette

A rustic dish, made with the blood of a

freshly killed chicken, which used to be very popular in many regions of France, hence the diversity of its recipes and names: *sanquette, sanquet, sanguine, sanguet, sanguète*, etc.

When a hen or chicken was killed, the fresh blood was collected in an earthenware dish, sometimes lined with chopped parsley and strips of fried lean bacon. As soon as the blood had coagulated, it was cut into pieces and fried in lard or goose fat (or sometimes left whole, like a large cake). Sanguette was served with the cooking fat and the pan juices deglazed with vinegar and mixed with cream, onion, garlic, shallot, or herbs. This dish is still prepared in southwestern France.

In *La Cuisine, c'est beaucoup plus que des recettes*, Alain Chapel writes: 'Sanguette, or blood from a freshly killed chicken, should not be kept long: sprinkled with enough salt to cover the point of a knife, fried briskly, and served while still bubbling, it is a dish fit for a king.'

Santa Rosa plum

MOMBIN

A yellow or dark red fruit which is round, egg-shaped, or slightly pear-shaped, 3–5 cm (1¼–2 in) long. Also known as spondias, hog plum, and Spanish plum, it is cultivated in Mexico, the Philippines, and the West Indies. Its sweet juicy flesh tastes rather like an orange. It can be eaten plain, in a compote, as jam, or dried. Another variety of mombin – pale yellow, with firm juicy flesh and a more acid taste – is grown in India and the Pacific islands. It is served with a variety of highly seasoned dishes (notably chicken) and is used to make chutneys (especially when the fruit is green) but it can also be eaten raw when it is ripe.

santé

A thick soup derived from Parmentier soup with sorrel stewed in butter and sprigs of chervil added. Nicolas de Bonnefons, however, wrote in *Les Délices de la campagne*: 'Santé soup should be good honest soup, full of choice meats and well reduced, without chopped vegetables, mushrooms, spices, or other ingredients: it should be simple, since it bears the name *santé* (health).'

RECIPE

Santé soup POTAGE SANTÉ Prepare 1.5 litres (2¾ pints, 7 cups) fairly thin leek and potato soup. Cook 4 tablespoons (⅓ cup) shredded sorrel in butter until soft. Mix together and thicken with 3 egg yolks blended with 1 dl (6 tablespoons, scant ½ cup) cream. Beat in 50 g (2 oz) butter cut into small pieces and sprinkle with chervil. Serve with thin slices of French bread, dried out in the oven.

Santenay

AOC Burgundy from the Côte de Beaune, from the southernmost parish in the Côte-d'Or. Both red and white wines are made, the former perhaps being slightly superior in quality, but both are very good value.

sapinette

A fermented drink from the provinces of eastern France, produced on a small scale or made at home. It is made by boiling the flowering tips of the black fir tree with sugar and yeast.

sapodilla SAPOTILLE

The fruit of a Central American tree cultivated in many tropical countries. It is about the size of a lemon, covered with a rough grey or brown skin; its reddish-yellow flesh, which tastes similar to the apricot, is eaten almost overripe, peeled, and with the seeds removed.

sard

A sea fish related to the sea bream, found only off the coast of Provence. Known as *lou sar* in Provençal cookery, it may be grilled (broiled), boiled, or deep-fried.

RECIPE

Sard with chive butter SARD AU BEURRE DE CIBOULETTE (from a recipe of the Hôtel Métropole, Beaulieu) Choose a sard weighing about 800 g (1¾ lb); sprinkle with salt and pepper. Grill very rapidly until the marks of the grill begin to show, then turn the fish through 90° and repeat so that a squared pattern is formed. Carefully fillet the fish and place the fillets in a roasting tin (pan) with 2 tablespoons olive oil and a head of garlic previously cooked in its skin, split up into cloves, and peeled. Bake the fillets for 5 minutes in a very hot oven, then dry on absorbent paper. Alternatively, fillet the raw fish and prepare for the oven in the same way, but increase the cooking time slightly to compensate for not grilling beforehand. Arrange on a dish and pour over beurre blanc mixed with chopped chives. Place a walnut-sized piece of crushed tomato on top. Surround with the cloves of garlic and heart-shaped croutons spread with tapenade.

sarde (à la)

Describing cuts of meat coated with a sauce made by deglazing the pan juices with a tomato demi-glace, garnished with rice croquettes, and served either with mushrooms and beans cooked in butter or with pieces of cucumber and stuffed tomatoes.

sardine

A small fish (maximum length 25 cm, 10 in) related to the herring, with a blue-green back and silvery sides and belly. It may take its name from Sardinia, where it was once fished abundantly. The sardine is still fished intensively and is eaten fresh or canned.

Fished in spring and summer, the sardine starts growing in March and reaches its maximum size in July or August: these large sardines, which are fat and full of flavour, are known as pilchards (not to be confused with canned herrings, which are also known in French as pilchards); they are called *royans* in Charente-Maritime. A distinction is made between the small Italian sardine (12–15 cm (5–6 in) long), which should be deep-fried as it is never very oily and dries out easily; the medium-sized sardine (18–20 cm (7–8 in)), with more compact and flavoursome flesh, for grilling (broiling) or frying; and the large Brittany sardine (25 cm (10 in), which is grilled in its own fat and has a fine flavour. Fresh sardines can also be prepared as an escabèche or in a bouillabaisse, coated with breadcrumbs and fried, or stuffed and baked; they can even be eaten raw, in pâtés, or marinated.

Before cooking, the scales should be removed, the sardine gutted (cleaned) and wiped, and the head cut off, unless the fish is to be grilled (it is less likely to break up when turned if whole). Very fresh small sardines do not need to be gutted, but simply wiped; their freshness can be judged by their rigidity, the brilliance of their eyes, and the absence of bloodstains at the gills.

☐ **Preserving sardines** Sardines can be smoked or salted, but they are usually preserved in oil and canned. Breton sardines were salted and pressed as early as the Middle Ages. In the Nantes region, they were preserved in stoneware pots with vinegar and butter or oil. Around 1820 a man from Nantes, Joseph Colin, had the idea of canning sardines in oil; the first canning factory dates from 1824. Until the first half of the 20th century canning factories flourished, particularly in Brittany and the Basque country, but the Breton sardine is becoming rare, while Sète and Marseille have become important sardine ports. The Breton process consisted of canning sardines fished locally, which were therefore really fresh; the heads were removed and the fish gutted, graded, fried, packed into cans, and covered with oil. Increasing use today is being made of the Mediterranean sardines, which are considered to be less choice and are often transported before processing, winter sardines, which are leaner and less substantial, and even frozen sardines (which can be recognized by the reddish line along the spine when they are opened). All these types of sardine are braised in the oven rather than being fried; they are easier to digest but have less flavour. Sardines may be canned in olive oil, vegetable oil, oil and lemon juice, tomato sauce, or a vinegar marinade; boneless sardines are also found (but they have very little flavour). Since they improve with age, canned sardines can be stored for several years in a cool place, turned regularly, but never in the refrigerator, as the oil solidifies and can no longer penetrate the fish.

Canned sardines are eaten mainly as a cold hors d'oeuvre with various raw vegetables; they can also be served on canapés and toast and in vols-au-vent, etc., and can be used to make a flavoured butter.

RECIPES

Baked sardines SARDINES AU PLAT
Clean and gut 12 good sardines. Grease
an ovenproof dish and sprinkle the bottom with 2 or 3 chopped shallots. Lay
the sardines on the dish and pour over
a little lemon juice and 4 tablespoons
(⅓ cup) white wine; dot with 30 g
(1 oz) butter, cut into small pieces.
Bake in a hot oven (220 C, 425 F, gas 7)
for 10–12 minutes until just cooked
through. Sprinkle with chopped
parsley.

Fried sardines SARDINES FRITES
Scale, wash, and gut (clean) the sardines; open out and remove the backbone. Sprinkle the fish with lemon juice
and leave to marinate in a cool place for
30 minutes. Wipe dry, coat in breadcrumbs, and deep-fry in hot fat (180 C,
350 F) for about 3 minutes. Drain the
fish, sprinkle with a little lemon juice,
and serve very hot.

Raw sardines SARDINES CRUES
(from Christian Guillerand's recipe)
Lay the sardines on a wicker tray, without removing the scales or gutting
(cleaning) them. Put a generous pinch of
mixed salt and pepper on each head.
Refrigerate for 2 days. Remove the
heads and gut the sardines, then skin
and serve with toast and slightly salted
butter.

Raw sardine terrine TERRINE DE
SARDINES CRUES (from Jean and
Paul Minchelli's recipe) Remove the
scales from the sardines, fillet them, and
wipe dry. Pour a layer of olive oil into a
terrine, add the peel of an orange, a
clove, a small piece of bay leaf, a thinly
sliced white onion, pepper, and a few
drops of brandy; cover with a layer of
fish fillets, another layer of spices and
chopped onion, and a second layer of
fish. Leave to marinate. Serve with
farmhouse bread, toasted and buttered,
and freshly ground sea salt.

Sardine escabèche ESCABÈCHE DE
SARDINES (from Christian Guillerand's recipe) Gut (clean) the sardines,
remove the scales and heads, and wipe
thoroughly. Heat in a frying pan (skillet) enough olive oil to half-cover the

sardines. Fry, turning when golden;
drain and place in a deep dish. Add to
the cooking oil an equal quantity of
fresh oil and heat. Add to this mixture a
quarter of its volume of vinegar and an
eighth of water, some peeled garlic
cloves, thyme, rosemary, bay leaves,
parsley, Spanish chilli peppers, salt,
and pepper. Boil for 15 minutes, then
remove from the heat and leave to
cool. Marinate the sardines in this
mixture for at least 24 hours before
serving.

Sardine fritters BEIGNETS DE SARDINES (from Christian Guillerand's
recipe) Remove the scales from the sardines, fillet them, and dry thoroughly.
Dip in batter and fry for a few seconds in
grapeseed oil.

Sardines à l'anglaise Open out the
sardines, remove the backbone, and
coat with flour. Dip in beaten egg and
breadcrumbs and cook in clarified butter. Coat with half-melted maître
d'hôtel butter.

Sardines gratinées (from Pierre
Vedel's recipe) Slice 1.5 kg (3½ lb)
aubergines (eggplants); place in a colander and sprinkle with a little salt. Peel
and remove the seeds from 1 kg (2¼ lb)
tomatoes. Fillet 14 large fresh sardines
and clean thoroughly. Wash and dry the
aubergines and brown them in a frying
pan (skillet) with a little very hot olive
oil. Drain on absorbent paper. Purée the
tomatoes in a blender with 2 cloves of
garlic, 3 basil leaves, salt, pepper, and ½
teaspoon olive oil. Lay the aubergines
and the sardine fillets in an ovenproof
dish, in alternate layers, with grated
Parmesan between the layers. Cover
with the puréed tomatoes. Bake in a hot
oven (220 C, 425 F, gas 7) for about 20
minutes.

Souffléed sardines with sorrel SARDINES SOUFFLÉES À L'OSEILLE
(from Christian Guillerand's recipe)
Bone 6 good sardines through the back.
Shred a large bunch of sorrel and cook
in butter with salt and pepper until soft;
leave to cool and add a little raspberry
vinegar. Make 6 very thin savoury
crêpes. Whisk 2 egg whites until very
stiff and spread over the crêpes. Stuff the

sardines with the sorrel purée and lay a sardine on each crêpe. Roll up loosely, arrange in a wide dish, dot with a few small pieces of butter, and bake in a very hot oven.

Sardinia

See *Sicily and Sardinia*.

sargus SARGUE

A fish similar and related to the sea bream, being prepared and cooked in the same way. It has an oval squat silvery body, large eyes, a spiny dorsal fin, and a black mark on the tail fin. There are three distinct species found in the Mediterranean and in the Atlantic, south of the Bay of Biscay. The common sargus, about 20 cm (8 in) long, has a large black patch that extends along its tail as far forward as the dorsal and anal fins and a second black mark along its back behind the head. The *mouchon* or *Rondelet's sargus*, up to 40 cm (16 in) long, has, in addition to the mark on the tail, seven or eight dark vertical bands on the back and sides; the ventral fins are also black. The smallest species is the *sparaillon*, which has yellow ventral fins and four or five dark transverse bands.

sarladaise (à la)

The name given to a method of preparing potatoes in the Périgord region. The thinly sliced potatoes are sautéed (without parboiling) in goose fat. When they are cooked, they are sprinkled with chopped parsley and garlic, covered, and left to sweat. In restaurants truffles are added, but this is incorrect; truffles are an ingredient of sarladaise sauce, a cold emulsified sauce flavoured with brandy, served with grilled (broiled) or roast meat.

RECIPE

Sarladaise sauce SAUCE SARLA-DAISE Mash 4 hard-boiled (hard-cooked) egg yolks and blend with 2 tablespoons (3 tablespoons) double (heavy) cream. Add 4 tablespoons (5 tablespoons) very finely chopped fresh truffles and beat the sauce with olive oil as for mayonnaise. Add 1 tablespoon lemon juice, some salt and pepper, and 1 tablespoon brandy.

sarrasine (à la)

Describing a method of preparing large joints of meat garnished either with small buckwheat pancakes or with rice cassolettes filled with tomato and green pepper fondue, topped with fried onion rings, and served with a fairly thin demi-glace sauce.

sartagnano or sartagnado

A fish speciality of Nice, named after the pan (*sartan*) in which it is cooked. It is made with small fresh fish (such as whitebait), which are fried in olive oil and pressed together during cooking so that they can be turned over like a large pancake. It is served with a dash of hot vinegar.

sashimi

A Japanese dish of raw fish, shellfish, and molluscs. The fish (which must always be very fresh) is trimmed, boned, and cut with a long thin knife. Tuna, bonito, abalone, bass, sole, and plaice are cut into thin slices; cuttlefish and shellfish are cut into thin strips. The pieces are arranged attractively on a plate, garnished with young daikon shoots, sliced daikon, seaweed, and slices of fresh ginger, and served with slices of lemon, soy sauce, and a horseradish paste.

sasser

A French culinary term meaning to wrap thin-skinned vegetables (such as carrots, new potatoes, Japanese artichokes) in a cloth with a little coarse salt, and to shake them for a few moments. This process cleans the vegetables by friction.

sauce

A hot or cold seasoned liquid either served with, or used in the cooking of, a dish. The word comes from the Latin *salsus* (salted), since salt has always been the basic condiment. The function of a sauce is to add a flavour to a dish that is compatible with the ingredients. Talleyrand claimed that England had three sauces and 360 religions, while France had three religions and 360 sauces. In an editorial of *Cuisine et Vins de France*, Curnonsky declared: 'Sauces comprise the honour and glory of

French cookery. They have contributed to its superiority, or pre-eminence, which is disputed by none. Sauces are the orchestration and accompaniment of a fine meal, and enable a good chef or cook to demonstrate his talent.'

Medieval sauces (cameline, dodine, poivrade, Robert, etc.), which relied on such ancient condiments as garum and spikenard, were either very hot or sweet-and-sour. They consisted mainly of spicy stocks based on wine, verjuice, and cooking juices, sometimes blended with toasted breadcrumbs. It was not until the 17th and 18th centuries that more refined and aromatic preparations appeared, such as béchamel, Soubise, mirepoix, duxelles, and mayonnaise sauces.

It was Carême who began to classify sauces. The hot sauces, which are by far the more numerous, are subdivided into brown sauces and white sauces. The great, or basic, brown sauces, from which many others are derived, are espagnole, demi-glace, and tomato sauces. The basic white sauces are béchamel and velouté, and they too have innumerable derivatives. Cold sauces are usually based on mayonnaise or vinaigrette, and they too have many variations. The classical repertoire was gradually increased by sauces from other countries, often introduced by French chefs who had worked abroad (Cumberland, Albert, reform, and Cambridge sauces, sauce *à la russe*, *à l'italienne*, *à la polonaise*, etc.). The diversity of resources from the French countryside contributed to a variety of recipes based on a particular ingredient: fresh cream (normande sauce), garlic (aïoli), fresh butter (beurre blanc) mustard (dijonnaise sauce), shallots (bordelaise sauce), red or white wine (bourguignonne sauce), onions (lyonnaise sauce), etc. After the time of Escoffier, there was a tendency towards making lighter sauces. Nowadays, many chefs use mixtures based on curd cheese, yogurt, etc

A sauce may be thick or thin; it may be strained or it may contain visible ingredients. It can be used to season raw food (tomatoes with vinaigrette, celery with rémoulade), it may form part of a cooked dish (gratin *à la béchamel*, vol-au-vent financière, salmis of duck, carp

Chambord), or it may be served with a cold dish (hake with mayonnaise) or a hot dish (chateaubriand béarnaise, venison Saint-Hubert, sole normande). Some sauces are part of the dish itself (ragouts, civets, coq au vin, chicken chasseur, etc.), rather than being made separately as an accompaniment. Such sauces may, however, be served separately in a sauceboat or used to coat some other preparation (hard-boiled (hard-cooked) eggs, chaudsfroids, fish in scallop shells, etc.).

The choice of equipment is very important. Deep thick-bottomed saucepans should be used, to ensure the proper distribution of heat to prevent the sauce from burning or curdling. The bain-marie is an essential accessory, as well as a metal whisk and a spatula for scraping the residue from the base of the pan. A fine, perfectly smooth, and glossy sauce can be obtained by rubbing it through a sieve (known as 'tammying'). The preparation of sauces requires a certain amount of skill and such techniques as deglazing, reducing, thickening, preventing a skin forming, emulsifying, thinning with milk, stock, or alcohol, enriching with cream and/or egg yolks, and the judicious use of flavourings. This is why the sauce chef of the kitchen staff is considered to be such a great technician: according to Fernand Point, 'in the orchestra of a great kitchen, the sauce chef is a soloist.'

There are four basic methods for making a sauce:

● Mixing together cold ingredients. This is the simplest method, used, for example, for vinaigrette and ravigote.

● Emulsification, i.e. dispersing an insoluble solid in a liquid so that the mixture will remain stable for a certain period of time. This is used for cold sauces (mayonnaise and its derivatives, aïoli, gribiche, rouille, and tartare sauces) and hot ones (hollandaise, mousseline, béarnaise, and beurre blanc).

● Making a roux by heating together butter and flour. This method is used for béchamel sauce and its various derivatives (Mornay, Soubise, etc.).

● Cooking a stock (veal, game, chicken, or fish) and adding a white or brown roux or some other mixture (a mirepoix, marinade, mushrooms, etc.).

Sauces to accompany various dishes

food		sauces
croustades, vols-au-vent		allemande, banquière, financière, marinière, normande, périgourdine, Soubise, suprême, toulousaine, sherry
eggs	hard-boiled (hot)	allemande, aurore, béchamel, curry, white, duxelles, lyonnaise, Mornay, Soubise, tomato
	hard-boiled (cold)	aïoli, mayonnaise, ravigote, rémoulade, verte, vinaigrette, tartare
	soft-boiled or poached	américaine, andalouse, aurore, banquière, bourguignonne, bretonne, chasseur, chaudfroid, Chivry, Choron, cream, cressonnière, curry, écossaise, tarragon, hongroise, ivoire, matelote, meurette, marrow, Mornay, Nantua, périgourdine, portugaise, printanière, provençale, rouennaise, royale, Soubise, suprême, vénitienne
	omelettes	chasseur, prawn, Madeira, normande, reform, tomato, Worcestershire
fish	braised or baked	américaine, bourguignonne, bourguignotte, bretonne, cardinal, chambertin, Chambord (carp), prawn, diplomat (John Dory, sole, and turbot), crayfish, genevoise, génoise (salmon and trout), grecque, gooseberry, hongroise, italienne, Joinville, Laguipière, matelote (eel), meurette, normande, Newburg, portugaise, Riche (John Dory, sole, and turbot), rougail, tyrolienne, Véron, Victoria, white wine, red wine
	fried	nuoc-mâm, pékinoise, raïto
	smoked	cream, cold horseradish
	grilled	anchovy, Bercy, and Gascony butters; flavoured oils, pissalat; bâtarde, Beauharnais, Choron, Colbert, fennel (mackerel), italienne, bone-marrow, mustard, Saint-Malo (brill, skate, and turbot), tapenade
	marinated	escabèche, italienne, tomato
	meunière	noisette butter, Bonnefoy sauce
	poached or boiled (hot)	white butter sauce (shad and pike); melted, creamed, or noisette butter (skate); allemande (made with fish stock), anchovy (hot), aromatic, bâtarde, béchamel, Bercy, butter, white (made with fish stock), brandade (salt cod), caper, chervil, chaud-froid (white), cream, curry, prawn, écossaise, egg, française, hollandaise, oyster (fresh cod), maltaise, marinière, Mornay, mussel, mousseline, mustard, Nantua,

food		sauces
		oursinade, parsley (mackerel and salmon), poulette, rouille, sabayon, Thermidor, turtle, truffle, vénitienne, waterfish (hot)
	poached (cold)	Montpellier butter, aïoli, anchovy (cold), cinghalaise, gribiche, La Varenne, mayonnaise, orientale, sorrel, ravigote, rémoulade, Russian, tartare, tomato, verte, vinaigrette, Vincent, waterfisch (cold)
frogs		aïoli, poulette
game		aniseed, dried cherry, chaud-froid (brown), roebuck, Cumberland (cold), grand veneur, moscovite, napolitaine, onion, pauvre homme, périgourdine, pignole, apple, poivrade, reform, romaine, saupiquet (hare), smitane, Victoria
game birds		bread, chaud-froid (brown), moscovite, port, salmis
gratins		béchamel, bolognaise, duxelles, Mornay
	lamb	mint, reform
	leftovers, boiled beef	devilled, hachée, italienne, lyonnaise, bread, pauvre homme, piquante, Robert, verjuice
	large roast or braised joints	gravy (roast veal), cooking juices; Albert (hot with horseradish), anglaise, aromatic, bread, Godard, Madeira, poivrade, Régence, Richelieu, Russian, sarladaise, Talleyrand
	ham	Cumberland (cold), Madeira, saupiquet, sherry
	mutton	harissa, Cumberland (cold), curry, onion
meat	pieces of sautéed or fried meat	sweet-and-sour, béarnaise, bordelaise, bourguignonne, chasseur, Choron, duxelles, tarragon, financière, herb, hongroise, hussarde, italienne, Madeira, bone-marrow, périgourdine, portugaise, provençale, roebuck, Talleyrand, tomato, Valois, sherry, zingara
	pork	nuoc-mâm, sambal, sweet-and-sour, charcutière (grilled pork), piquante, apple, Robert, Sainte-Menehould, sage, suédoise
	white meat	aurore, bretonne, cinghalaise, cream, tarragon, hongroise, italienne, meurette, parsley, romaine (braised veal), Soubise, villageoise, truffle, zingara
	cold meat	aïoli, anchovy butter, avocado, Cambridge, chaud-froid (brown), dijonnaise, mayonnaise, mousquetaire, horseradish (cold), ravigote, rémoulade, tomato
	grilled meat	butters: anchovy, Bercy, Chivry, Colbert, snail, maître d'hôtel, marchand de vin (entrecôte steak), ravigote; sauces: barbecue, béarnaise, Beauharnais, Bonnefoy,

food		sauces
		Bontemps, bordelaise, Chateaubriand, Colbert, Foyot, harissa, oyster, morel, mustard, paloise, Robert, sarladaise, tyrolienne
	fried meat in breadcrumbs	tomato, Villeroi
	grilled meat in breadcrumbs	devilled, Saint-Menehould, mustard
mussels		marinière, poulette, ravigote
	braised, deep- or shallow-fried	sweet-and-sour, allemande (made with meat stock), banquière, noisette butter, bretonne, chaud-froid (white), écossaise, hongroise, ivoire, meurette, ravigote, Soubise, suprême, tartare, Villeroi, sherry
	ox tongue	piquante, romaine, tomato
	pig's feet	devilled, mustard, Sainte-Menehould
offal	braised calves' sweetbreads	Albufera, aurore, Chantilly, tarragon, financière, Foyot, Godard, Nantua, périgourdine, Régence
	grilled or fried kidneys	marchand de vin butter, Madeira, portugaise, tyrolienne
	calf's head	gribiche, mayonnaise, parsley, turtle
oysters		shallot, tartare, flavoured vinegars
pasta		noisette butter, bolognaise, duxelles, financière, ketchup, poulette, stufatu, vinaigrette (with salad)
	braised	Albufera, celery, duxelles, financière, Godard, onion, piémontaise, provençale, Talleyrand, villageoise, sherry
	duck	bigarade, chaud-froid (brown), dodine, apple, rouennaise
	goose	apple, sage, suédoise
poultry	poached or shallow-fried	Albufera, allemande (made with meat stock), aurore, avocado (cold), banquière, bretonne, chervil, Chantilly, chaud-froid (white), Chivry, cream, curry, écossaise, tarragon, financière, herb, ivoire, mayonnaise, Mornay, Nantua, Périgueux, parsley, printanière, ravigote (cold), Richelieu, royale, suprême, toulousaine, vénitienne
	grilled chicken	Bontemps, devilled (also for pigeon), paloise, Sainte-Menehould, tyrolienne
	roast	sweet-and-sour, cranberry (turkey), anglaise, bread, cooking juices
	sautéed	bourguignonne, chasseur, curry, duxelles, hongroise, périgourdine, portugaise, salmis, zingara
quenelles		aurore, Nantua, Soubise, tomato

food		sauces
rice	hot	chasseur, curry, duxelles, mustard, Richelieu, tomato
	cold	mayonnaise, tartare, vinaigrette
shellfish	hot	américaine, curry, prawn, lobster, Nantua, Newburg, Victoria
	cold	gribiche, kiwi, mayonnaise, rémoulade, verte
snails		snail butter, aïoli, poulette
soft roe		noisette butter
	asparagus	bâtarde, chantilly, maltaise, Pompadour, truffle, vierge
	boiled vegetables	sauces: aïoli, allemande, bâtarde, béchamel, white, Chantilly, hollandaise, mikado, Mornay, mousseline, tomato; butters: melted, Gascogne, creamed, maître d'hôtel, noisette
	cardoons	lyonnaise, marrow
	crudités and salads	anchovy, dijonnaise, curry (cold), kiwi, mayonnaise, horseradish (cold), rémoulade, Roquefort, Russian, verdurette, vinaigrette, yogurt
vegetables	haricot beans	bretonne, cream
	leeks	vierge, vinaigrette
	potatoes	cream cheese, cold horseadish (jacket potatoes) tartare (point-neuf)
	green salad	flavoured oils, Rossini and vinaigrette sauces, flavoured vinegars
	sautéed, braised	bohémienne, Colbert, cream, italienne, poulette (mushrooms), provençale, Soubise, suprême, tomato

This produces velouté and espagnole sauces and their derivatives: allemande, ivoire, poulette, normande, cardinal, and Nantua sauces (white) and bordelaise, Périgueux, chasseur, poivrade, venison sauces, etc. (brown). These sauces may be thickened with butter, cornflour (cornstarch), blood, or egg yolk or flavoured with meat, chicken, or fish glazes.

Depending on the type of dish for which the sauce is intended, the most varied ingredients, herbs, and spices can be used. Some dishes are classically accompanied by particular sauces: mutton or fish with curry sauce, salt cod with garlic sauce (aïoli), duck with bigarade (orange) sauce, game with Cumberland sauce, beef with piquante sauce, etc. Other ingredients include grated cheese, crushed tomatoes, anchovies, duxelles, chopped ham, foie gras, chopped truffles, shellfish, vinegar, fresh cream, red or white wine, alcohol, etc.

The name of a sauce often reveals its ingredients: Périgueux sauce (truffles), Hungarian sauce (paprika), Nantua sauce (crayfish), etc., but sometimes the sauce is named after its creator: Mornay, Choron, Foyot, etc.

☐ **Dessert sauces** These may be hot or cold, either served separately or poured over the dessert. Many of these sauces are based on fruit (in the form of a purée, jelly, etc.) and may be flavoured with vanilla or alcohol. Custard cream (flavoured or not) is a popular dessert sauce, usually served with puddings, fruit pies, etc. Chocolate sauce and zabaglione are also used.

RECIPES

Apple sauce SAUCE AUX POMMES Cook the apples with a small quantity of sugar until they are soft; flavour with a little ground cinnamon or cumin.

In northern Europe this sauce is served with roast pork as well as roast goose and duck.

Barbecue sauce SAUCE BARBECUE Mix ½ litre (17 fl oz, 2 cups) tomato sauce with 4 tablespoons (5 tablespoons) olive oil, 2 tablespoons (3 tablespoons) brandy, a few drops of Tabasco sauce, ½ teaspoon curry powder, 1 tablespoon chopped herbs (chives, tarragon, parsley, and chervil), and 1 tablespoon very finely chopped spring onion (scallion). Mix all the ingredients thoroughly, season with salt, and sprinkle generously with pepper.

This sauce is served with grilled (broiled) meat and sausages.

Basic white sauce SAUCE BLANCHE For 7.5 dl (1¼ pints, 1½ pints) sauce, make 100 g (4 oz, ½ cup) pale blond roux with 50 g (2 oz, ¼ cup) butter and 50 g (2 oz, ½ cup) flour. Blend in 1 litre (1¾ pints, 4¼ cups) white stock (chicken or veal). Bring to the boil and cook gently for 1½ hours, skimming from time to time.

Bâtarde sauce SAUCE BÂTARDE Mix 20 g (¾ oz, 1½ tablespoons) melted butter, 20 g (¾ oz, 3 tablespoons) flour, and 2.5 dl (8 fl oz, 1 cup) boiling salted water. Whisk the mixture vigorously, adding 1 egg yolk mixed with 1 tablespoon ice-cold water and 1 tablespoon lemon juice. Over a very low heat, gradually incorporate 100 g (4 oz, ½ cup) butter cut into small pieces, stirring constantly. Season with salt and pepper, and strain if necessary.

This sauce is served with boiled vegetables and fish.

Bread sauce SAUCE À LA CHAPELURE (from Carême's recipe) Chop 2

shallots and cut a thin slice of lean ham into small pieces. Place in a saucepan with 2–3 tablespoons white veal stock and a little coarsely ground pepper. Simmer and reduce over a low heat. Remove the ham, and add 1½ tablespoons (2 tablespoons) very fine dried breadcrumbs, a little fresh butter, 2 tablespoons (3 tablespoons) consommé, and the juice of a lemon. Boil for a few minutes and serve.

Bread sauce à l'ancienne SAUCE À LA MIE DE PAIN À L'ANCIENNE (from Carême's recipe) Chop 1 clove of garlic, 1 shallot, and some parsley. Put into a saucepan with ½ glass white wine. Reduce by half, then mix in 2 tablespoons (3 tablespoons) very fine fresh breadcrumbs, a little butter, a pinch of coarsely ground pepper, some grated nutmeg, 8 tablespoons (⅔ cup) consommé, and 4 tablespoons (⅓ cup) white veal stock. Reduce by half and add the juice of a lemon.

Brown gravy SAUCE AU JUS COLORÉ Make 2 dl (7 fl oz, 1 cup) English butter sauce and add 1 dl (6 tablespoons, scant ½ cup) juices from the roast meat, a few drops of Harvey sauce, and a few drops of ketchup.

This type of brown gravy is traditionally served with roast veal. In Britain other simple brown gravies for serving with roast meat are made with just the meat juices, flour, vegetable stock, and seasoning.

Butter sauce I SAUCE AU BEURRE Proceed as for bâtarde sauce, but use 30 g (1 oz, 2 tablespoons) butter and 30 g (1 oz, ¼ cup) flour. Do not thicken with egg yolk.

This sauce is served with fish and boiled vegetables.

Butter sauce II SAUCE AU BEURRE (from Carême's recipe) Put 1 scant tablespoon flour and a little butter into a saucepan over a gentle heat. Blend them together with a wooden spoon, remove from the heat, and add ½ glass (4½ tablespoons) water or consommé, a little salt, some grated nutmeg, and the juice of half a lemon. Stir constantly over a brisk heat, and as soon as it comes to the boil, remove the sauce. Stir in a large piece of butter. The sauce should be velvety, very smooth, with a rich but delicate flavour.

Chateaubriand sauce SAUCE CHATEAUBRIAND Mix 1 dl (6 tablespoons, scant ½ cup) white wine with 1 tablespoon chopped shallots and reduce by two-thirds. Then add 1.5 dl (¼ pint, ⅔ cup) demi-glace sauce and reduce by half. Remove from the heat and add 100 g (4 oz, ½ cup) fresh butter, 1 tablespoon chopped tarragon, a few drops of lemon juice, and a little cayenne. Mix well but do not strain.

This sauce is served with grilled (broiled) meat.

Cream sauce SAUCE CRÈME Add 1 dl (6 tablespoons, scant ½ cup) fresh double (heavy) cream to 2 dl (7 fl oz, ¾ cup) béchamel sauce and boil to reduce by one-third. Remove from the heat and add 30–50 g (1–2 oz, 2–4 tablespoons) butter and ½–1 dl (3–6 tablespoons, ¼–½ cup) double (heavy) cream. Stir well and strain.

This sauce is served with vegetables, fish, eggs, and poultry.

English bread-and-butter sauce SAUCE AU BEURRE ET AU PAIN À L'ANGLAISE (from Carême's recipe) Bring to the boil 1 tablespoon breadcrumbs in 2 large tablespoons (3 large tablespoons) consommé, adding 1 small onion cut in two and a clove. Add a little salt, grated nutmeg, and cayenne. Simmer for 10 minutes, remove the onion and the clove, and mix in 1 tablespoon butter sauce. Before serving, whisk in a little more butter. This sauce is served with roast game birds.

English butter sauce SAUCE AU BEURRE À L'ANGLAISE Make a white roux with 30 g (1 oz, 2 tablespoons) butter and 30 g (1 oz, ¼ cup) flour. Then whisk in vigorously 2.5 dl (8 fl oz, 1 cup) boiling salted water. Season with salt and pepper, and whisk in 100 g (4 oz, ½ cup) butter cut into pieces.

English cream sauce SAUCE CRÈME À L'ANGLAISE Make a white roux with 50 g (2 oz, ¼ cup) butter and 30 g (1 oz, ¼ cup) flour. Add 3.5 dl (12 fl oz, 1½ cups) white consommé, 3 tablespoons (4 tablespoons) mushroom essence, and 1 dl (6 tablespoons, scant ½ cup) double (heavy) cream. Bring to the boil, add a small bunch of parsley and a small onion, and simmer gently for 20 minutes. Remove the parsley and onion. Strain before use.

This sauce is traditionally served with roast loin of veal.

Fennel sauce SAUCE AU FENOUIL Prepare 2.5 dl (8 fl oz, 1 cup) English butter sauce and add 1 tablespoon chopped blanched fennel.

This sauce is served with boiled or grilled (broiled) fish.

French sauce SAUCE À LA FRANÇAISE (from Carême's recipe) Heat some béchamel sauce in a saucepan. When almost boiling, add a little garlic, a little grated nutmeg, and some mushroom essence. Immediately before serving, just bring to the boil, then add some crayfish butter to colour it pink. (Shelled crayfish tails and button mushrooms may also be added.) This sauce is served with fish.

Hachée sauce SAUCE HACHÉE Cook 1 tablespoon chopped onion in 1 tablespoon butter for about 15 minutes. Then add ½ tablespoon chopped shallots and cook for a further 5–10 minutes. Add 1 dl (6 tablespoons, scant ½ cup) vinegar, reduce by three-quarters, and add 1.5 dl (¼ pint, ⅔ cup) demi-glace sauce and 1 dl (6 tablespoons, scant ½ cup) tomato purée. Boil for 5 minutes. Just before serving, add 1 tablespoon lean chopped ham, 1 tablespoon dry mushroom duxelles, 1 tablespoon chopped capers and gherkins, and 1 tablespoon chopped parsley. Do not strain.

This sauce is served with slices of cooked meat or a boiled joint.

Musketeer sauce SAUCE MOUSQUETAIRE Prepare 5 dl (17 fl oz, 2 cups) mayonnaise and add 2 tablespoons chopped shallots (cooked in white wine until the liquid has completely reduced) and 1 tablespoon dissolved meat glaze. Mix together and season with a little cayenne.

This sauce is served with grilled (broiled) foods.

Mustard sauce with butter SAUCE MOUTARDE AU BEURRE Prepare 2 dl (7 fl oz, 1 cup) butter sauce or hollandaise sauce. Add 1 tablespoon mustard and strain.

This sauce is served with boiled or grilled (broiled) fish.

Mustard sauce with cream SAUCE MOUTARDE À LA CRÈME Mix 1 part Dijon mustard with 2 parts double (heavy) cream. Season with a little lemon juice and some salt and pepper. Whisk thoroughly until the sauce becomes slightly mousse-like.

This sauce is served with white meat, poultry, and fish.

Onion sauce SAUCE À L'OIGNON Cook 100 g (4 oz, 1 cup) chopped onions in 3 dl (½ pint, 1¾ cups) milk seasoned with salt, pepper, and nutmeg. As soon as the onions are cooked, strain and use the milk in which the onions were cooked to make a white sauce by stirring it into a roux made with 20 g (¾ oz, 1½ tablespoons) butter and 20 g (¾ oz, 3 tablespoons) flour. Bring to the boil, add the chopped onions, and cook gently for 8 minutes.

This typically English sauce is poured over meat: boiled mutton, chicken, braised game, or rabbit.

The onions can also be cooked in milk, then the liquid thickened with kneaded butter, using the above proportions of butter and flour.

Parsley sauce I SAUCE PERSIL Prepare a sauce with 30 g (1 oz) roux and 2.5 dl (8 fl oz, 1 cup) freshly cooked fish stock that is strongly flavoured with parsley. Cook for 8 minutes and strain. Just before serving, add 1 tablespoon chopped blanched parsley and a dash of lemon juice.

This sauce is particularly suitable to serve with salmon and mackerel.

Parsley sauce II SAUCE PERSIL Make 2.5 dl (8 fl oz, 1 cup) butter sauce add 1 tablespoon chopped blanched parsley and a little lemon juice.

This sauce is served with calf's head and feet, poached chicken, boiled rabbit. boiled ham, and braised veal.

Piquante sauce SAUCE PIQUANTE

Prepare 2.5 dl (8 fl oz, 1 cup) devilled sauce with wine vinegar. Just before serving, add 3 tablespoons (4 tablespoons) coarsely chopped gherkins and 1 generous tablespoon chopped parsley.

Serve the sauce with pork chops, boiled tongue, or slices of beef.

Port wine sauce SAUCE AU PORTO To 1 dl (6 tablespoons, scant ½ cup) port add ½ tablespoon chopped shallots, a sprig of thyme, and a piece of bay leaf. Reduce by half and then add the juice of 1 orange and half a lemon, together with a pinch of grated orange peel. Add 2 dl (7 fl oz, ¾ cup) thickened veal stock and boil for a few minutes. Strain through muslin (cheesecloth).

This English sauce is served hot with game birds, especially wild duck.

Printanière sauce SAUCE PRINTANIÈRE Add 50 g (2 oz, ½ cup) green butter sauce to 2 dl (7 fl oz, 1 cup) allemande sauce and strain.

Serve with soft-boiled (soft-cooked) or poached eggs or poached chicken.

Red wine sauce SAUCE AU VIN ROUGE Select the fish of your choice and cook it in 1.5 dl (¼ pint, ⅔ cup) mirepoix cooked in butter, 5 dl (17 fl oz, 2 cups) red wine, 1 clove of garlic, and some mushroom skins. Remove the fish, then reduce the liquid by one-third. Thicken with kneaded butter, add a few drops of anchovy essence, season with a pinch of cayenne, and strain.

This is a suitable sauce for stuffed, hard-boiled (hard-cooked), or poached eggs and fish.

Sorrel sauce SAUCE À L'OSEILLE (from a recipe by Christiane Massia) Cook 2 chopped shallots in ½ wineglass (generous ⅓ cup) dry vermouth, and reduce by half. Add 1 wineglass (¾ cup) double (heavy) cream and reduce again until the sauce is thick and smooth. Add 150 g (5 oz) finely shredded sorrel leaves, season with salt and pepper, boil again briefly, and allow to cool. Just before serving, add a few drops of lemon juice.

This sauce is especially good with fish

Verjuice sauce SAUCE AU VERJUS AIGRELETTE (from Carême's recipe) Wash 30 verjuice grapes, pound them, and press out the juice through a cloth (or use a little ready-pressed verjuice). Boil 2 generous tablespoons (3 generous tablespoons) allemande sauce with a little chicken glaze, a little butter, a pinch of nutmeg, a pinch of finely ground pepper, and enough verjuice to make the sauce sharp and appetizing.

It is particularly good served with grilled (broiled) or roasted white meat or poultry.

Vierge sauce SAUCE VIERGE Beat 125 g (4½ oz, generous ½ cup) butter until soft, then beat in 2 tablespoons (3 tablespoons) lemon juice and some salt and pepper. Continue to beat well until the mixture becomes fluffy.

This sauce is served with asparagus, leeks, and other boiled vegetables.

White wine sauce SAUCE AU VIN BLANC Boil 1.5 dl (¼ pint, ⅔ cup) fish fumet made with white wine until reduced by two-thirds. Allow to cool slightly and add 2 raw egg yolks. Whisk over a gentle heat, as for hollandaise sauce. As soon as the yolks thicken to a creamy consistency, whisk in, a little at a time, 150 g (5 oz, generous ½ cup) clarified butter. Season with salt and pepper; add ½ teaspoon lemon juice and some mushroom skins and stalks if wished. Rub through a fine sieve and reheat but do not boil.

This is a suitable sauce to serve with fish.

DESSERT SAUCES

Apricot sauce I SAUCE À L'ABRI-COT Stone (pit) 12 apricots and reduce to a pulp in a blender or food processor. Put the pulp in a thick copper saucepan and add 5 dl (scant pint, 2¼ cups) light syrup. Bring to the boil, skim, and remove the pan from the heat when the sauce coats the back of a spoon. Strain. Flavour with 1 tablespoon Kirsch or brandy.

Apricot sauce, which is served with hot or cold desserts, can be served hot or cold. If served hot, it can be made smoother by adding a little fresh butter. When stewed apricots (fresh or pre-served) are used, the syrup can be used to dilute the sauce.

An apricot sauce can also be made by mixing 3 tablespoons apricot jam, 1 tablespoon lemon juice, and a few spoonfuls of water. Heat up, strain, and flavour, as described above.

Apricot sauce II SAUCE À L'ABRI-COT (from a recipe by Paul and Jean-Pierre Haeberlin) Purée 500 g (18 oz) stoned (pitted) apricots. Put the purée in a saucepan with 5 dl (17 fl oz, 2 cups) water and 500 g (18 oz, 2¼ cups, firmly packed) sugar and boil for 5 minutes. Add 1 tablespoon cornflour (cornstarch) mixed with cold water. Bring to the boil again, stirring. Remove from the heat and add 3 tablespoons (4 tablespoons) Kirsch.

Blackcurrant sauce SAUCE AU CASSIS Put 10 lumps of sugar into a saucepan with ½ glass (scant ½ cup) water. Heat to dissolve the sugar and then boil to make a syrup. Wash 250 g (9 oz, generous 2 cups) blackcurrants in cold water, wipe them, and reduce to a purée in a blender or food processor. Rub the purée through a fine strainer. Mix the syrup with the fruit purée and add the juice of 1 lemon. Pour the sauce into a bowl and chill in the refrigerator.

Chilled blackcurrant sauce can be served with baked apples, floating islands, pineapple water ice, or fruit salad. It can also be served hot with a rice dessert, apple charlotte, or cold lemon mousse.

Blackcurrant sauce can also be made quickly by mixing 5 dl (17 fl oz, 2 cups) blackcurrant cordial with 2–3 liqueur glasses of raspberry or plum brandy. A generous handful of whole blackcurrants may be added if in season. This sauce can be used to pour over sorbets or ice-cream sundaes.

Caramel sauce SAUCE AU CARAMEL Make a pale caramel with 150 g (5 oz, generous 1 cup) icing (confectioners') sugar and 1.25 dl (4 fl oz, ½ cup) water. Boil ½ litre (17 fl oz, 2 cups) milk with a vanilla pod (bean), remove the pod, and whisk the milk into the caramel. Put 3 egg yolks into a bowl and whisk in the caramel mixture. Pour the sauce back into the saucepan and heat gently, stirring, until it thickens. When the sauce has reached a pouring consistency remove from the heat and allow to cool, stirring continuously.

This sauce is traditionally served with soufflé fritters.

Peach sauce I SAUCE AUX PÊCHES CRUES Plunge some peaches in boiling water for 30 seconds, peel them, and remove the stones (pits). Weigh the flesh and immediately sprinkle with lemon juice (the juice of 1 lemon is sufficient for 1 kg (2¼ lb) fruit). Purée the peaches, then add one-third of their weight of caster (superfine) sugar and, if desired, some fruit liqueur.

This sauce can be poured over fruit salads, charlottes, etc.

Peach sauce II SAUCE AUX PÊCHES CUITES Prepare some peach purée as in the previous recipe. Put the purée into a heavy-based saucepan together with half its weight of sugar, and cook over a brisk heat for 7–8 minutes, stirring continuously. Allow to cool, then flavour with a fruit liqueur, according to taste.

This sauce is used particularly for pouring over rice or semolina desserts.

Pineapple sauce SAUCE À L'ANA-NAS Poach some fresh pineapple in sugar syrup, or use the syrup from some canned pineapple. Thicken the syrup with arrowroot and flavour it with rum, Kirsch, brandy, or a liqueur.

This sauce can be poured over various hot or cold desserts: pies, rice or semoline puddings, etc.

sauceboat SAUCIÈRE

Part of a dinner service used for serving sauce or gravy. Sauceboats are usually oval in shape with a handle and one or two lips. A spoon or ladle is usually used to serve the sauce and there is often a matching saucer-like base. Some sauceboats, used for the gravy of roast meat, have two lips and a double bottom. The latter enables the fat to be poured off one side, leaving the gravy to be poured from the other lip afterwards. From the Middle Ages until the 18th century, sauceboats were made of tin or silver.

saucepan CASSEROLE

A cylindrical cooking utensil with a handle and usually a lid. The French word *casserole* comes from the Provençal *cassa* (oven dish). The first copper saucepans appeared in the 14th century but their tin plating was far from perfect and they were little used. However, the long handle made them more manageable than a cooking pot. With the advent of the modern cooker, the use of saucepans has become widespread. Often sold in sets of five, they are made in many materials: aluminium (with or without nonstick finishes), stainless steel, cast iron, enamelled steel nickel-plated, copper-plated, ceramic, or ovenproof porcelain. They are mainly used to heat liquids, to cook food in liquid, and to reheat prepared dishes – for which a double saucepan (bain-marie) is often used.

In the catering (food service) trade the classic saucepan is known as a *casserole russe*; other specialized saucepans are also used.

● The gravy saucepan (*casserole à jus*) has very high sides with a long handle on one side and a hand grip on the other; it is used to keep sauce and meat juices warm.

● The *casserole à pommes Anna* has low sides and a tight-fitting lid with two lugs; it is used to cook Anna potatoes, Annette potatoes, and potatoes *à la sarladaise*.

The features of a saucepan depend on the material used: the type of base must be considered, especially when cooking with electricity; the stability; the weight and ease of handling (the handle should be long enough, insulated if metal and, if desired, removable); the ease of pouring, either by a lip or better still by a pouring rim that runs around the circumference thus enabling one to pour from any point on the rim; and finally ease of cleaning.

It is not always sensible to buy saucepans in sets of five, since one or two sizes will be little used and it is often preferable to have at least two of certain sizes.

sauerkraut CHOUCROUTE

White cabbage that is finely sliced, salted, and fermented; it is generally accompanied by boiled potatoes and an assortment of meats and charcuterie. Meaning 'bitter herb', sauerkraut is a speciality of Alsace and is also made in

Lorraine and in parts of Germany, including the Black Forest and Bavaria. The most famous variety of cabbage used is the Alsace *quintal*, traditionally prepared in a small cask or a stoneware jar.

□ **Preparation** Remove the stump (core) and the green or damaged outer leaves from some white cabbages. Using a knife with a broad blade or a special shredder or food processor, cut the cabbages into very fine strips. Wash and drain thoroughly. Line the bottom of a container with large cabbage leaves or vine leaves and arrange the shredded cabbage in layers, covering each layer with coarse salt and sprinkling with juniper berries. Put a handful of coarse salt on the final layer. Cover with a cloth, then with a wooden lid that fits inside the container. Place a heavy stone on this lid. By the next day, the pressure should have forced out sufficient water to cover the lid. Ensure that it is always so. Keep in a cool place. After about three weeks, when no more foam forms above the cabbage, the sauerkraut is ready to eat. Each time some sauerkraut is taken out, remove the covering liquid, replace the cloth, the lid, and the stone, and add fresh water.

Sauerkraut should not be kept too long; eventually it turns yellow and acquires a more pronounced flavour. According to some, it should remain slightly crisp and should never be reheated. Others, on the contrary, enjoy it after repeated cooking, when it has a slightly reddish colour due to contact with the bottom of the saucepan when the water has almost evaporated.

In *La France gastronomique* of 1921, Curnonsky and M. Rouff gave a recipe for 'true sauerkraut', which included the 'three sacramental sausages' (Frankfurt, Strasbourg, and Montbéliard), mutton breast, rump of beef, legs of goose, and other salted meats.

German-style sauerkraut, cooked in Hock, is served with grilled Nuremburg sausages, Frankfurter sausages, smoked pork chops, knuckle and hand of pork (picnic shoulder), and apples.

One variation is sauerkraut with fish. Raw sauerkraut, moistened with Riesling or Sylvaner, is cooked in chicken stock or wine, then served with smoked salmon, haddock, salt cod, turbot, scallops, monkfish, or fish sausages (in various combinations as a garnish) with white butter sauce or a mousseline sauce.

□ **The symbol of Alsace** Hansi, the famous artist from Alsace, considered Colmar's sauerkraut the only true one, and gave the recipe:

'In a thick-sided metal (or earthenware) casserole, lightly brown some finely chopped onion in two good soupspoons of goose dripping or lard. Add 1 pound of sauerkraut, unwashed or very lightly washed and absolutely fresh. Add a generous glass of white wine, a dessert apple cut into pieces, then about ten juniper berries tied up in a little cloth. Pour in some stock until the sauerkraut is almost covered. Put on the lid and leave to cook for 2 to 3 hours. One hour before serving, add 1 pound of smoked belly bacon. Half-an-hour before serving, add half a small glass of Kirsch. Arrange the sauerkraut on a warmed round dish. Surround with bacon cut into little pieces, cutlets, and Colmar sausages, first heated for a good 10 minutes, either in the sauerkraut, or in almost boiling water. Serve with a few potatoes, baked in their jackets until very floury and quite dry.'

The traditional French garnish, popularized by the brasseries since the beginning of the century, generally includes smoked bacon, loin (or neck) of pork, salted pork cutlets, and poached sausages.

Sauerkraut is sometimes cooked, albeit wrongly, in champagne or, more often, in white wine – only a small amount is used so as not to accentuate the sourness of the cabbage; it can also be flavoured with a small glass of Kirsch. It is also served with juniper berries, which aid digestion. In Alsace, sauerkraut was formerly garnished with split-pea purée.

Apart from being the central ingredient in many Alsatian dishes, sauerkraut is used in preparing other dishes, often named *à l'alsacienne*, based on poultry, red meat, or even fried eggs, snails, omelettes, fish, and soup.

Julien Freund, Director of the Institute of Sociology in Strasbourg, wrote in the journal *Les Saisons d'Alsace*: 'Sauerkraut is tolerant, for it seems to be a well of contradictions. Not that it would preach a gastronomic neutrality that would endure all heresies. It rejects dogmatism and approves of individual tastes. It forms a marvellous combination with numerous spices, odours, or spirits: juniper berries, coriander seeds, peppercorns, cranberries, Reinette apples, stock, and wine; it even welcomes flakes of yeast or leftover Gruyère since it accepts being prepared *au gratin*. Its flavour sustains various potato dishes: boiled in their skins, crisps (potato chips), braised, sautéed, grilled, or simply cooked in water. It adopts many sorts of fat, including lard, butter, goose fat, or roast dripping. The variety of meats to which it consents is infinite: sausages of all kinds, such as knackwurst, white sausage, Lorraine, Montbéliard, chipolata, black pudding, hams, smoked or salted bacon, quenelles, pickled and smoked pork, goose, pheasant, etc. It makes excuses for red wine, although it has a weakness for beer and lets itself be spoilt by white wine. Each stomach may find its own happiness in it.'

RECIPES

Chicken au gratin with sauerkraut GRATIN DE VOLAILLE À LA CHOUC· ROUTE Peel and dice 1 leek (white part) and 2 carrots; stick an onion with 2 cloves; tie up in a small piece of muslin (cheesecloth) 1 tablespoon juniper berries, 1 teaspoon peppercorns, and 2 peeled cloves of garlic. Wash 1.5 kg (3¼ lb) raw sauerkraut in plenty of water, then squeeze and disentangle it by hand.

Grease a large flameproof casserole with 40 g (1½ oz, 3 tablespoons) goose fat and pile half the sauerkraut in it. On top arrange the diced vegetables and a large bouquet garni augmented with a stick (stalk) of celery and the muslin bag of spices. Cover with the remaining sauerkraut. Over the contents pour 2 dl (7 fl oz, ¾ cup) dry white wine and 3 dl (½ pint, 1¼ cups) chicken stock, season lightly with salt, cover, and bring to the boil on top of the stove. Then cook for 1 hour in a moderately hot oven (about 190 c, 375 f, gas 5).

Season a 1.5-kg (3¼-lb) chicken with salt and pepper inside and out, and place it in the midst of the sauerkraut. Return to the oven for a further 2 hours.

Then take the chicken out, cut it up, and bone it. Grease a gratin dish with goose fat. Press the sauerkraut and pile it in the dish, having removed the bag of spices and the bouquet garni. Cover with the chicken, moisten with 3 dl (½ pint, 1¼ cups) fresh cream, sprinkle 100 g (4 oz) grated Gruyère cheese on top, and brown in a very hot oven.

Sauerkraut à l'alsacienne CHOUC ROUTE À L'ALSACIENNE Thoroughly wash 2 kg (4½ lb) raw sauerkraut in cold water, then squeeze and disentangle it with the hands. Heat the oven to about 190 c (375 f, gas 5). Peel 2 or 3 carrots and cut into small cubes. Peel 2 large onions and stick a clove in each. In a small piece of muslin (cheesecloth), place 2 peeled cloves of garlic, 1 teaspoon ground pepper, and 1 tablespoon juniper berries, then tie up in a bundle.

Coat the bottom and sides of a flameproof casserole with goose fat or lard. Pile in half the sauerkraut and add the carrots, onions, muslin (cheesecloth) bundle, and a bouquet garni; then add the rest of the sauerkraut, a raw knuckle of ham, and 1 glass of dry white Alsace wine and top up with water. Season lightly with salt, cover, bring to the boil over a ring, and cook in the oven for 1 hour. Then add a medium-sized smoked shoulder of pork and 500–750 g (1¼–1¾ lb) smoked belly (salt pork); cover, bring to the boil, again over a ring, then cook in the oven for a further 1½ hours.

Meanwhile, peel 1.25 kg (2½ lb) potatoes. After 1½ hours, take out the pork belly (salt pork) and add the potatoes. Leave to cook for a further 30 minutes. During this time, poach 6–8 Strasbourg sausages in barely simmering water. When the sauerkraut is cooked, take out the muslin (cheesecloth) bundle, the bouquet garni, and the cloves and return the pork belly for 10 minutes to reheat it. Arrange the sauerkraut in a large dish and garnish with the potatoes, sausages, and meat cut into slices.

Sauerkraut au gras for garnish CHOUCROUTE AU GRAS POUR GARNI· TURE Follow the recipe for sauerkraut *à l'alsacienne* but replace the water with unskimmed stock and do not add meat.

Cook gently for 3 hours. It is served as a garnish for poultry or meat.

Sauerkraut salad à l'allemande SALADE DE CHOUCROUTE À L'ALLE-MANDE Thoroughly wash 1 kg (2¼ lb) raw sauerkraut, squeeze it, then disentangle it by hand. Place it in a saucepan along with 2–3 large onions, salt, and pepper, then cover with either stock or water to which 1 tablespoon cooking oil has been added. Cook over a gentle heat for about 2½ hours, then drain and leave to cool. Dice the onions and return them to the sauerkraut, which is then pressed, seasoned with vinaigrette, and piled into a deep dish. Garnish with quarters of hardboiled (hard-cooked) eggs and cubes of cooked beetroot (red beet).

saugrenée

'A seasoning made with butter, herbs, water, and salt. Those who say that vegetables should be cooked in salted water only have scarcely known what it is to eat.' This is the definition given for saugrenée in the *Dictionnaire de Trévoux*, and the preparation was mentioned by Rabelais in connection with broad (fava) beans. Pea and broad-bean saugrenées were common dishes in 16th-century France. The name comes from the Latin *sal* (salt) and *granum* (grain). Alain Chapel, in his recipe for young mountain hare roasted *en saugrenée*, uses the word in a different sense: the animal is coated with a sauce thickened with blood and blended with butter, which makes it 'slightly coarse, or *grenée* (granular)'.

saumonette

The name under which the lesser spotted dogfish is sold in France, usually skinned and without the head. This name reflects the salmon-pink colour of its flesh.

Saumur

Wines made around the town of Saumur, on the left bank of the River Loire. They may be AOC Coteaux de Saumur or the simpler AOC Saumur. The wines are mainly white, both still and sparkling (the latter are made mostly by the Champagne process), but there are also some reds, notably those of Saumur-Champigny. The white wines are made from the Chenin Blanc grape, the local name for which is Pineau de la Loire, and the reds from the Cabernet Franc. The former are dry to very dry, crisp, and light, and the latter are fresh with a charming bouquet typical of the grape. Although some rosé wines are also made, those of Anjou are far better known; the Saumur wines are, strictly speaking, in Anjou but the biggest pink wine region is further down the Loire, nearer to Angers.

saupiquet

In French medieval cookery, a spiced sauce made with red wine, verjuice, and onions, that was served with roast lamb or wildfowl. Just before serving, it was thickened with toasted bread. In the Languedoc and Rouergue, saupiquet is a dish of roast hare served with a highly seasoned wine sauce containing the animal's liver and blood and sliced onions. The term is used by certain cooks for variants of this dish (particularly those made with duck) which have a sauce flavoured with wine and vinegar.

Saupiquet des Amognes is a speciality of Nivernais and Morvan. Said to have been created by Jean Reynier, a culinary author of the 16th century, it consists of slices of fried ham coated with a sauce made of reduced vinegar, peppercorns, shallots, juniper berries, and tarragon, moistened with espagnole sauce and fresh cream. In another version of this ham saupiquet, the meat is coated with a very spicy velouté sauce which is finished off with cream.

The word saupiquet comes from *sau* (salt) and *piquet* (to season). It has no connection with Saupiquet, chef of the Baron de La Vieuville, who is thought to have created puff pastry.

RECIPES

Duck saupiquet SAUPIQUET DE CANARD (from Christian Schuliar's recipe) Grill (broil) or roast 300 g (11 oz) sliced duck breasts and arrange them in a hot dish. Gently cook 2 small chopped cloves of garlic in 2 tablespoons (3 tablespoons) vinegar and 2 tablespoons (3 tablespoons) white wine. Leave to cool, then put through a blender or food processor with 20 g (¾ oz, 1½ tablespoons) cream cheese, 100 g (4 oz) duck's liver, and 1 tablespoon olive oil flavoured with herbs. Cover the duck with this sauce.

Ham saupiquet JAMBON EN SAUPI-QUET Cut 8 thick slices of boned ham, which has been thoroughly desalted, and fry them in lard over a brisk heat. Make a roux with 25 g (1 oz, ¼ cup) flour and 25 g (1 oz, 2 tablespoons) butter, then add 2 dl (7 fl oz, ¾ cup) white wine and 2 dl (7 fl oz, ¾ cup) ham, chicken, or veal stock. Add the ham trimmings, 7 or 8 juniper berries, and some chopped tarragon and reduce for 15 minutes. Reduce some wine vinegar seasoned with 10 crushed peppercorns. Pour the sauce over this and simmer for another 15 minutes. Thicken with 2 dl (7 fl oz, ¾ cup) fresh cream, then rub through a very fine sieve. Drain the slices of ham, arrange them on a hot dish, and pour the sauce over them.

sausage SAUCISSE, SAUCISSON

A mixture of minced (ground) seasoned meat enclosed in a tubelike casing (the name is derived from the Latin *salsicia*, from *salsus*, meaning 'salted'). In French terminology, a *saucisse* is usually small and fresh, but some types are lightly smoked; most are cooked before eating. A *saucisson* is usually larger, smoked, dried, or otherwise preserved, and served in slices.

☐ **Saucisses** These sausages generally consist of pork meat and fat, but are sometimes made from other meats or contain added veal, beef, mutton, poultry, or offal. They are seasoned with various spices and condiments. These ingredients are minced and funnelled into a casing consisting of either pig's or sheep's intestine. Alternatively, the casing may consist of synthetic material.

● Fresh sausages for grilling (broiling), shallow-frying, or deep-frying include the British link and chipolata sausages and the Cumberland sausage; the Toulouse sausage, 3–4 cm (1½ in) in diameter, made with coarsely minced pure pork, for shallow-frying or braising; and flat sausages (see *crépinette*), with a caul (caul fat) casing. Various French regional specialities include the

small Bordeaux sausage, which is grilled with white wine and oysters; the small country sausages called *diots*, from Savoy; and white sausages, from Alsace (for deep-frying).

Some other sausages for frying and grilling include the merguez, a sausage usually made of pure beef or a mixture of beef and mutton, but sometimes of pork, coloured with sweet red peppers and seasoned with pepper; the chorizo, a mild or spicy Spanish sausage made of pure pork, or a mixture of pork and beef (it is often air-dried and eaten uncooked); the Corsican figatelli, made of pork liver; the sabodet (or coudenat), made of offal; and the Italian *luganeghe*.

● Sausages for boiling or poaching can be smoked or unsmoked. The best known is probably the German frankfurter, a smoked sausage made of finely minced (ground) pork and sold uncooked, ready for poaching. A French variety of frankfurter, called *francfort*, may contain beef and veal and is sold dried and smoked, in a beige casing, for poaching. Other sausages for poaching include the *Morteau* type, made of pure pork, which can be hung up for smoking; the *Montbéliard* sausages; and the *cervelas de Lyon*, which are made of good quality pure pork and contain pistachio nuts or truffles. *Gendarmes* are very dry heavily smoked sausages from Switzerland and Austria; they can be eaten uncooked but are often included in stews.

● Sausages made of pork which have been matured and dried, and are therefore technically known as *saucissons*, are in fact sold in France under the name of *saucisses*; examples are *saucisses de montagne* and *saucisses d'Auvergne*. The coarsely minced filling is enclosed in a section of pig's intestine 3–4 cm (1½ in) in diameter. These sausages can be semidried or dried.

☐ **German sausages** The greatest variety of sausages is found in Germany. Apart from the frankfurter, German sausages include the *Plockwurst*, made of beef and pork with a brown shiny skin, for poaching; the *Bierwurst*, for eating with beer; Holstein pork and beef sausages for cooking; the *Bratwurst* and its variations, for frying; the *Zungenwurst*, a cooked sausage containing coarsely diced lean pork, blood, and tongue, for eating cold; the smoked *Schinkenwurst*, containing beef and thick-grained lean pork, for poaching; the thin *Nuremberg sausages*, with herbs, for grilling; the Westphalian *Brägenwurst*, a long thin lightly smoked sausage made with pork fat, pig's brain, oatmeal, and onions; and the Stuttgart *Presskopf*, made of pork, veal and beef.

Sausages from other countries include Polish sausages, usually smoked, made with pork, beef, and fat with parsley, paprika, or onion, for frying or for poaching with lentils; and Madrid sausages, made of veal and fat mixed with sardines in oil.

□ **Saucisson sec** The production of dried sausage is a very ancient tradition, but since consumption is increasing, it is rare to find dried sausages made by small manufacturers. The larger manufacturers now use preservatives, additives, and various colourings. The traditional preparation of dried sausages involves a series of processes which give them their aroma, texture, and flavour: these include boning and trimming of the meat, pounding the fat and lean meat with spices to form the mixture, funnelling the mixture into the casing, predrying the sausage at 20–25 c (68 –77 f), and drying and maturing at 14 c (57.2 f) for at least four weeks. The following are examples of dried sausages:

• *saucisson de ménage*, made with fairly coarsely minced (ground) pure pork, eaten when just dry.

• *saucisson de montagne*, 5–8 cm (2–3 in) thick, made with pure pork, but more coarsely minced than the saucisson de ménage and of superior quality.

• *saucisse sèche*, made with pure pork, either collar-shaped, U-shaped, or a straight small sausage, and often labelled with the name of the region where it is produced (Auvergne, Provence, Pyrenees, Ardèche).

• *saucisson d'Arles*, made of lean beef and fatty pork, medium-minced, and traditionally containing either lean donkey meat or horse meat.

• *saucisson chasseur*, small, often quite fatty, made of pork and beef: will not keep for very long.

• *rosette*, cylindrical, tied in a string net, made with fairly coarsely minced pure pork, carefully matured when authentic.

• *jésus*, a large oval sausage, generally of finely minced pure pork.

• *saucisson de Lyon*, a straight sausage distinguished by its fine homogeneous filling, dark red colour, and the presence of small square pieces of fat (not to be confused with *cervelas de Lyon*, which is for cooking).

• *salami*, of which there are a great many varieties from several countries, including Italy, Denmark, France, and Hungary. They have a finely minced filling of pork and beef and are often smoked.

A good dry sausage is firm (even hard) to the touch and has a pronounced aroma. It should have a 'bloom', which is a sign that maturing has been carried out correctly, and it should preferably be bare, without a coating of Cellophane, flour, or ash. This type of sausage should either be kept hanging in a cool place, or stored in the salad tray in the refrigerator, especially in hot weather, and the cut surface should be protected by covering it with kitchen foil. The sausage is cut into thin slices and peeled and served as an hors d'oeuvre, as a filling for sandwiches or canapés, or as a snack with drinks. A device called a *gibet* (gibbet) is sometimes used for hanging up several sausages at the table so that the diners can help themselves; it comes with a small cutting board.

□ **Saucisson cuit** This type of sausage is used in cookery (as a filling in brioche or pastry dough) or served as a cold hors d'oeuvre.

• The *saucisson de Paris* (or *Paris ail* when flavoured with garlic) has coarsely minced meat with very little filling. It is used as a garnish for sauerkraut or served in slices. The *saucisson cuit* or *saucisson à l'ail*, either smoked or unsmoked, is similar but contains more than 25% pork. It is sometimes also referred to as *cervelas de Paris*.

• The *saucisson de Lyon* is about 5–6 cm (2½ in) in diameter and consists of finely minced meat (pork and veal); it may sometimes contain pieces of pork about the size of hazelnuts. The *saucisson princesse*, which contains diced ox (beef) tongue, is similar.

• *Saucissons de foie* (liver sausages) consist of finely minced liver, together with pork or veal. They are spread on slices of bread or canapés.

● *Saucisson de langue* (tongue sausage) is a mixture of forcemeat and tongue enclosed in a casing of pork intestine. It usually contains pistachio nuts.

● *Saucisson de Cracovie* (Cracow sausage) is smoked and based on very finely minced pork and knuckle of veal.

'Black' sausages are smoked black puddings (blood sausages). Mortadellas, which are similar to cooked sausages, are thick sausages containing large pieces of diced fat embedded in a finely minced light-coloured filling. See also *black pudding, boudin blanc, salami.*

RECIPES

Grilled (broiled) sausages SAUCISSES GRILLÉES Use chipolatas, crépinettes, or a piece of Toulouse sausage. Lay the sausages side by side in the grill pan (the Toulouse sausages should be twisted into a coil and secured with skewers). Grill (broil) gently so that they cook right through without the outside burning. Serve with mashed potato or a purée of fresh vegetables or haricot (navy) beans.

Sausage à la languedocienne SAU-CISSE À LA LANGUEDOCIENNE Twist 1 kg (2¼ lb) Toulouse sausage into a coil and secure with 2 crossed skewers. Heat 3 tablespoons (4 tablespoons) goose fat or lard in a sauté pan and place the sausage in it. Add 4 chopped cloves of garlic and a bouquet garni, cover the pan, and cook for 18 minutes, turning the sausage halfway through. Drain the sausage, remove the skewers, arrange it in a serving dish, and keep hot. Deglaze the pan with 2 tablespoons (3 tablespoons) vinegar, then add 3 dl (½ pint, 1¼ cups) stock and 1 dl (6 tablespoons, scant ½ cup) tomato purée. Boil for a few minutes, then add 3 tablespoons (4 tablespoons) pickled capers and 1 tablespoon chopped parsley. Pour this sauce over the sausage and serve with an aubergine (eggplant) gratin or tomatoes stuffed with rice.

Sausage in brioche dough à la lyonnaise SAUCISSON EN BRIOCHE À LA LYONNAISE Select a cooking sausage of pure pork weighing about 1 kg (2¼ lb) and about 30 cm (12 in) long. Boil it for 40 minutes in stock and allow to cool completely.

Dissolve 20 g (¾ oz) baker's yeast (¾ cake compressed yeast) in ½ dl (2½ tablespoons, 3 tablespoons) water. Mix 500 g (18 oz, 4½ cups) flour with 12 g (½ oz) table salt, 20 g (¾ oz, 1½ tablespoons, firmly packed) caster (superfine) sugar, 5 eggs, and the yeast in a food processor. When the dough begins to come away from the sides of the bowl, incorporate 250 g (9 oz, generous 1 cup) butter. Roll the dough into a ball, place it in a bowl, cover, and put in a warm draught-free place to rise. (Its volume should double.) When risen, knock back (punch down) the dough, flatten it, and knead it four or five times. Then replace it in the bowl, cover it, and place it in the refrigerator until ready to use.

Roll out the dough into a rectangle on a lightly floured worktop. It should be a little bit longer than the sausage. Skin the sausage, dust it lightly with flour, and roll it up in the dough. Fold the ends over, and seal the edges firmly together. Put it into a long narrow terrine dish and leave it to rise. When the brioche fills the mould, glaze with egg, and bake in the oven at 210 C (410 F, gas 6–7) for 25–30 minutes. Turn it out of the mould and serve hot (with an endive (chicory) salad, if desired).

Sausages with cabbage SAUCISSES AU CHOU Braise some green or white cabbage. At the same time, grill (broil) some Toulouse sausages. Put the cabbage into a heated serving dish and arrange the sausages on top.

Alternatively, the sausages can be braised in white wine and the cooking juices poured over the cabbage.

other recipes See *bacon, catalane (à la), crêpe.*

sausagemeat
CHAIR À SAUCISSE

A mixture of equal parts of pork (with the sinews removed) and pork fat, chopped finely and salted. Sausagemeat is used, with various seasonings, to stuff vegetables (particularly tomatoes), meat (paupiettes), or poultry, and in terrines and pâtés. In charcuterie it is used to make chipolatas and crépinettes (flat sausages). However, a range of other meats may be used in the manufacture of sausages, including lean veal, beef, mutton, poultry, or game, with different spices and seasonings, and even truffle and pistachio.

RECIPES

Sausagemeat   CHAIR À SAUCISSE Weigh out equal quantities of lean pork and fat bacon. Mince finely and add 30 g (1 oz) salt per kg (2¼ lb) mince. Chopped truffle or truffle peelings may be added, or the mince may be seasoned with finely chopped onions, garlic, salt, pepper, and herbs. Chopped mushrooms, wild or cultivated, may also be added.

Fine sausagemeat or fine pork forcemeat   CHAIR À SAUCISSE FINE OU FARCE FINE DE PORC   Using the same mixture as for the sausagemeat recipe, finely mince the ingredients twice, or chop once and sieve. The seasonings are the same.

sausage rolls

See *friand*.

sausseli

A small puff pastry in Russian cookery, related to the French dartois. Sausselis, which are served as an entrée or an hors d'oeuvre, have various fillings, but the traditional filling is a mixture of cabbage braised in lard, onions, and chopped hard-boiled (hard-cooked) eggs.

sauté

To cook meat, fish, or vegetables in fat until brown, using a frying pan (skillet), a sauté pan, or even a heavy saucepan. Small items are cooked uncovered, but slightly thicker pieces (chicken, for example) sometimes need to be covered after browning, to complete the cooking. A sauce or gravy may be made by deglazing the cooking pan. The process sometimes consists of frying food (which may be already cooked) while vigorously shaking the pan, which prevents it from sticking and ensures it is cooked on all sides.

Sautéed potatoes are made with slices of raw or cooked potato fried in butter or oil until golden. They are usually flavoured with parsley or garlic, or mixed with truffles (*à la sarladaise*) or sweated sliced onions (*à la lyonnaise*).

Sautés of meat or fish are dishes in which the meat is cut up into uniform pieces, sautéed over a brisk heat, and then moistened and covered until the cooking is completed. The cooking liquid is reduced, thickened, and sometimes strained to form the sauce. A garnish may be added during cooking.

RECIPES

Minute sauté of lamb   SAUTÉ D'AG-NEAU À LA MINUTE   Cut 800 g (1¾ lb) shoulder of lamb into small pieces and sauté in butter or oil over a brisk heat for 8 minutes. Season with salt and pepper. When the meat is well browned, add the juice of half a lemon, turn into a hot dish, and sprinkle with chopped parsley.

Minute sauté of veal   SAUTE DE VEAU À LA MINUTE   Proceed as for minute sauté of lamb but cook the veal for about 15 minutes. When serving, keep the meat hot in a serving dish and deglaze the pan with 1 small glass of white wine. Reduce, add the juice of half a lemon, and whisk in 2 tablespoons (3 tablespoons) butter. Pour the sauce over the meat and sprinkle with chopped parsley.

Sauté of lamb à l'ancienne   SAUTÉ D'AGNEAU À L'ANCIENNE   Clean 250 g (9 oz) calves' sweetbreads, blanch them for 5 minutes in salted water, drain, and then cook gently for about 5 minutes in 40 g (1½ oz, 3 tablespoons) butter in a saucepan without allowing them to brown. Clean 250 g (9 oz, 2¼ cups) small button mushrooms, add them to the sweetbreads, and braise together for another 10 minutes.

Remove all the contents of the pan, melt 30 g (1 oz, 2 tablespoons) butter in the same saucepan, and brown about 1 kg (2¼ lb) best end of neck cutlets and pieces of boned shoulder of lamb (in equal proportions) seasoned with salt and pepper.

Drain the meat, pour the butter from the pan, then replace the meat together with the sweetbreads and mushrooms.

Heat up, then sprinkle in 1 teaspoon flour. Mix together, then stir in 2 dl (7 fl oz, ¾ cup) Madeira and 2 dl (7 fl oz, ¾ cup) stock, add a bouquet garni, cover, and cook gently for about 20 minutes. Reduce by half with the lid off, then add 2 dl (7 fl oz, ¾ cup) cream mixed with 2 tablespoons (3 tablespoons) lemon juice, and reduce again until the sauce is creamy. Adjust the seasoning.

Pour into a heated dish, sprinkle with chopped parsley, and serve very hot, possibly with small croutons fried in butter.

In the traditional preparation, the quantity of sweetbreads was reduced and cocks' combs and kidneys were added.

Sauté of lamb (or veal) chasseur SAUTÉ D'AGNEAU (OU DE VEAU) CHASSEUR Cut 800 g (1¾ lb) shoulder of lamb or veal into 60-g (2-oz) pieces and brown in a mixture of 20 g (¾ oz, 1½ tablespoons) butter and 2 tablespoons (3 tablespoons) oil. Add 2 peeled chopped shallots, some stock (2 dl (7 fl oz, ¾ cup) for lamb, 3 dl (½ pint, 1¼ cups) for veal), and 2 tablespoons (3 tablespoons) tomato sauce. (1 glass of dry white wine may be added to the stock.) Season with salt and pepper, add a bouquet garni, cover, and leave to simmer for 50 minutes (lamb) or 1 hour 20 minutes (veal). When the meat is cooked, add 250 g (9 oz, 2 cups) sliced mushrooms fried in oil. Heat all the ingredients through, pour into a serving dish, and sprinkle with chopped herbs.

Sauté of lamb (or veal) with aubergines (eggplants) SAUTÉ D'AGNEAU (OU DE VEAU) AUX AUBERGINES Cut up 1.5 kg (3¼ lb) boned and trimmed best end of neck of lamb (or shoulder of veal) into pieces. Season with salt and pepper and brown in a saucepan with half butter, half oil. When the meat is cooked, arrange it in a dish and garnish with 3 aubergines (eggplants), peeled, cut into small dice, and fried in oil. Deglaze the pan juices with white wine, then mix with brown veal gravy and tomato purée flavoured with a little garlic. Reduce, strain, and pour over the meat and vegetables. Sprinkle with chopped parsley.

Sauté of lamb (or veal) with cep mushrooms SAUTÉ D'AGNEAU (OU DE VEAU) AUX CÈPES Proceed as in the previous recipe but replace the aubergines (eggplants) with 300 g (11 oz, 3 cups) cep mushrooms, which have been fried in butter or oil.

Morels may be used instead of ceps.

Sauté of lamb (or veal) with tomatoes SAUTÉ D'AGNEAU (OU DE VEAU) AUX TOMATES Proceed as for sauté of lamb with artichokes, but replace the artichokes with 8 small tomatoes, which have been peeled, deseeded, and fried in olive oil. A little finely chopped garlic may also be added.

Sauté of veal Clamart SAUTÉ DE VEAU CLAMART Cut 1 kg (2¼ lb) shoulder of veal into uniform pieces. Season with salt and pepper and brown in a heavy-based saucepan with 30 g (1 oz, 2 tablespoons) butter or 3 tablespoons (¼ cup) oil. Drain the meat, pour the fat out of the pan, deglaze the pan with 1 glass of white wine, then replace the meat and add 3 dl (½ pint, 1¼ cups) stock. Bring to the boil over a brisk heat, then reduce, cover, and leave to cook for about 1 hour. Add 1 kg (2¼ lb, 6¾ cups) shelled peas and 12 baby (pearl) onions. Bring back to the boil and continue cooking for another 30 minutes. Adjust the seasoning, pour into a hot dish, and sprinkle with chopped parsley.

Sauté of veal with red wine SAUTÉ DE VEAU AU VIN ROUGE Cut 1 kg (2¼ lb) shoulder of veal into 50-g (2-oz) pieces and brown in 30 g (1 oz) butter. Add a large sliced onion and season with salt and pepper. Then add 3 dl (½ pint, 1¼ cups) red wine, 1.5 dl (¼ pint, ⅔ cup) stock, a bouquet garni, and a crushed clove of garlic. Cover and leave to cook gently for 1¼–1½ hours. In the meantime, glaze 20 baby onions until brown and fry 150 g (5 oz, 1¼ cups) sliced mushrooms in butter. Drain the pieces of meat, strain the sauce, and thicken it with 1 tablespoon kneaded butter. Put the meat back in the sauté pan and add the onions, mushrooms, and sauce. Reheat gently for 10–15 minutes.

sauté pan SAUTEUSE

A round shallow pan with straight or slightly flared sides and a handle. It can be made of stainless steel, aluminium, or tin-plated copper. It is used to fry meat, fish, and vegetables, often cut up into pieces. The sides are slightly higher than the sides of a frying pan (skillet) and enable the ingredients to be stirred easily in order to coat them with fat, especially when cut up into small dice or chopped up and seasoned with herbs.

To make sautés in the correct sense of the word (especially those with sauce), a type of sauté pan called a *sautoir* or *plat à sauter* is preferred. It is a shallow pan with vertical sides, a handle, and a lid. Made of aluminium, cast iron, stainless steel, or tin-plated copper, it is used to make sautés of meat, poultry, or fish. The pan is covered to finish the cooking, sometimes in the oven.

Sauternes

A famous white-wine region in the Bordeaux vineyard, south of the city of Bordeaux, on the left bank of the River Garonne. On account of its situation the grapes (the usual permitted varieties for white Bordeaux wines) can be affected in some years by 'noble rot' (*Botrytis cinerea*). This acts on the ripe and eventually overripe fruit and concentrates the juice in each grape. Because of the variation in the rate of ripening and the formation of noble rot, the grapes can seldom be picked a bunch at a time, but rather in small clusters or sometimes even grape by grape, the harvesters needing to work through each vineyard several times. The resulting wine is rich, very fragrant, and luscious, and the high natural sugar content sometimes pushes the alcoholic level up to the top limits for still table wines.

The most famous Sauternes of all is undoubtedly Château d'Yquem, but there are a number of other great estates (and, these days, many small properties) making excellent Sauternes, as well as the wines sold simply as 'Sauternes'. These wines should all be drunk chilled; although they are usually served at the end of a meal with dessert fruit, etc., some enthusiasts recommend serving Sauternes with melon and also with foie gras earlier in the meal, or with Roquefort blue cheese.

Sauvignon

One of the most famous of white-wine grapes, which is grown all over the world. It is used in conjunction with other permitted varieties in the white-wine areas of the Gironde and nowadays also on its own. Other famous wines made from the Sauvignon include the fine wines of the Loire – Pouilly-Fumé, Sancerre, Menetou-Salon, Quincy, and Reuilly.

savarin

A large ring-shaped gâteau made of baba dough without raisins. After cooking, it is soaked with rum-flavoured syrup and filled with confectioners' custard (pastry cream) or Chantilly cream and fresh or crystallized (candied) fruit. The savarin was created by the Julien brothers, famous Parisian pastrycooks during the Second Empire. It was named after Brillat-Savarin, who gave Auguste Julien the secret of making the syrup for soaking the cake. Small individual savarins can also be made.

Savarin moulds can also be used for other mixtures, both sweet and savoury, such as hot or cold rice mixtures, meat, fish, or vegetable loaves or mousses, jellies, cakes, etc.

RECIPES

Savarin filled with confectioners' custard (pastry cream) SAVARIN À LA CRÈME PÀTISSIÈRE Melt 50 g (2 oz, ¼ cup) butter. In a bowl, mix 125 g (4½ oz, generous cup) flour, a good pinch of salt, 15 g (½ oz, 1 tablespoon) sugar, and 1 egg. Dissolve 5 g (¼ oz) fresh yeast (¼ cake compressed yeast) in 1 tablespoon lukewarm water and add to the dough. Add another egg and work the dough for some time until smooth and elastic. Beat in the melted butter until well blended. Pour the dough into a buttered savarin mould, 20–22 cm (8–9 in) in diameter, and leave to rest in a warm place for 30 minutes. Bake in a moderately hot oven (200 C, 400 F, gas 6) for 20–25 minutes. Turn out onto a wire rack and leave to cool. Pour some syrup over the savarin, made with ½ litre (2 cups) water, 250 g (9 oz, generous cup) sugar, and a vanilla pod (bean). Prepare some confectioners' custard (see *creams and custards*) with ¼ litre (8 fl oz, 1 cup) milk, 3 egg yolks, 50 g (2 oz, ¼ cup) sugar, 100 g (4 oz, 1 cup) flour, and 5 cl (2½ tablespoons, scant ¼ cup) rum. Spoon into the centre of the savarin and serve well chilled.

Fruit savarin SAVARIN AUX FRUITS Prepare a savarin as in the recipe above, leave it to cool, and pour some rum-flavoured syrup over it. Peel 2 white peaches, 1 pear, 1 orange, and 1 banana. Dice the fruit and sprinkle with the juice of half a lemon. Wash and deseed a small bunch of green grapes (about 75 g, 3½ cups). Clean 50 g (2 oz, scant ½ cup) raspberries and 50 g (2 oz, scant ½ cup) wild strawberries (if available). Wash and hull 50 g (2 oz, scant ½ cup) large strawberries. Put all this fruit in a bowl, pour over the rest of the syrup used to soak the savarin, and leave to steep for 1 hour. Melt 200 g (7 oz, ⅔ cup) apricot jam over a low heat and coat the savarin with it. Fill the centre of the savarin with some of the fruit and serve the rest separately.

Savarin with red fruit sauce and whipped cream SAVARIN AUX FRUITS ROUGES ET À LA CHANTILLY Make a savarin as in the recipe above and leave it to cool. Prepare a syrup by boiling ½ litre (17 fl oz, 2 cups) water with 250 g (9 oz, generous cup) sugar and a vanilla pod (bean). Put the savarin in a deep dish and pour the hot syrup over it. Leave to cool and sprinkle with 1.5 dl (¼ pint, ⅔ cup) rum. Crush and sieve 250 g (9 oz, scant 2 cups) raspberries. Mix the raspberry purée with ¼ litre (8 fl oz, 1 cup) well-reduced cherry juice and add the juice of half a lemon. Whip 2 dl (7 fl oz, ¾ cup) double (heavy) cream with ½ dl (2½ tablespoons, scant ¼ cup) very cold milk and 2 teaspoons vanilla sugar. Fill the centre of the savarin with the cream and pour over the cherry and raspberry sauce. Serve well chilled.

saveloy CERVELAS

A short thick sausage made with pork meat and a varying amount of pork fat, and seasoned with pepper or garlic. It may be smoked and is sold either cooked or raw. The saveloy formerly contained brains (*cervelles*) as well, hence its French name. Most saveloys,

also called 'cooking sausages', are intended to be simmered with vegetables.

The *cervelas de Strasbourg* takes the form of a string of segments, 6–8 cm (2½–3 in) long, in a red casing; it is eaten fried or cold, in salad, with a vinaigrette dressing containing onions. The *cervelas de Lyon*, made with pure pork, contains truffle or pistachio.

Fish saveloy, once a speciality of Reims, was prepared for Lent using pike flesh, potatoes, butter, and eggs, mixed together and then poached.

RECIPES

Saveloys in salad CERVELAS EN SALADE Cut some cold saveloys into slices. Slice a cucumber and several deseeded tomatoes into half-rounds, cut the heart of a head of celery into small rounds, and quarter some artichoke hearts that have been cooked in a court-bouillon. Arrange all the ingredients in a salad bowl, moisten with a well-seasoned vinaigrette containing white mustard, sprinkle with chopped parsley and chives, and serve chilled.

Saveloys stuffed with spinach CERVELAS FARCIS AUX ÉPINARDS Cook either 1.5 kg (3¼ lb) fresh spinach or 800 g (1¾ lb) frozen spinach in salted water. Place 4 saveloys in a saucepan of cold water and heat them gently without boiling, so that they do not burst. Drain and press the spinach and reheat it with 30 g (1 oz, 2 tablespoons) butter. Scramble 6 eggs with 20 g (¾ oz, 1½ tablespoons) butter, salt, pepper, and 1 tablespoon fresh cream. Cover the serving dish with spinach. Drain the saveloys; split them along three-quarters of their length and stuff them with the scrambled eggs. Arrange the saveloys on the spinach.

Savennières

The AOC of the Anjou-Coteaux de la Loire region around Angers. All white, these wines are made from the Chenin Blanc, have considerable elegance and charm, and can live long in bottle. Famous names are Coulée-de-Serrant and Roche-Aux-Moines.

Savigny-lès-Beaune

Red and white wines from the Côte de

Beaune, of which the former are the best known. When combined with wines of neighbouring parishes, they may be sold as Côte-de-Beaune-Villages. They can be charming wines and although they do not always have long lives, they are admirable lightweight Burgundies.

savory SARRIETTE

An aromatic herb, originating from southern Europe, with a scent resembling mint and thyme. Its name is derived from the Latin *satureia* (satyr's herb), a reference to the aphrodisiac qualities once attributed to it. There are two species. The annual summer savory, with silvery green leaves, is the species usually used in cooking. The perennial winter savory, with narrower stiffer leaves, is used mostly for flavouring soft goats'- or ewes'-milk cheeses and certain marinades; in Provence it has the nickname of *poivre d'âne* (ass's pepper). Dried or (preferably) fresh savory is the most popular herb for flavouring pulses. Fresh savory is also used to flavour Provençal salads, grilled (broiled) veal, roast lamb, and loin of pork. When dried, it is used to flavour peas, ragouts, soups, forcemeats, and pâtés.

savoury

A small savoury item, English in origin, which is served at the end of the meal, after or sometimes instead of the dessert. The range of savouries is wide: Welsh rarebit, angels on horseback, cheese straws, cheese soufflé, filled tartlets, poached eggs, various devilled items, hot or cold canapés, etc.

Savoy SAVOIE

The cuisine of Savoy, the Alpine region of southeastern France, is dominated by butter, cream, milk, and cheese. Fish from the lakes and mountain streams, game from the forests, mushrooms from the woods, meat (veal in particular), and charcuterie also play an important part. The orchards are planted with cherry, apple, pear, and walnut trees, and strawberries and raspberries are plentiful in the glades.

Soups are made with sorrel, split peas, pumpkins, nettles, or leeks, as well as with cheese. Eggs and cheese are used together in many recipes: the ancient Pont-des-Andrieux omelette, which is associated with a sun rite, goats'-milk cheese pastries, cheese pancakes, and soufflé montagnard. Other traditional dishes are vegetable or mushroom tarts with ham or bacon and little béchamel and oyster mushroom pies.

The rivers provide resources for a number of Savoyard specialities: fricassee of frogs' legs (with garlic, onions, and vinegar), Léman perch with red wine, *lavaret* (similar to trout) with white wine or capers, and *féra* (a type of salmon) meunière, quenelles, *à la thononaise*, with white wine, or with a mushroom and ham sauce. Trout are cooked *au bleu*, meunière, or stuffed and braised in the local dry white wine Apremont.

Cheese fondue, probably the best-known traditional dish, is made with dry white wine and Kirsch. Less well-known specialities include *sang de caion* (rustic black pudding (blood sausage)); diots with onion fondue and white wine; civet of fresh pork with red wine; *potée savoyarde* (made with belly of pork, knuckle of pork, and sausages, together with stockpot vegetables and chestnuts); pork ribs with Chambéry vermouth; meatballs with cheese; veal ribs *à la marmotte* (larded with anchovies and bacon and braised with onions); and leg of kid goat with mushrooms. There are some original Savoyard recipes for poultry, such as chicken blanquette, chicken with cep mushrooms or crayfish, and coq *au Crépy*. Some delicious recipes for game birds include: roast partridges stewed in white wine, then cut up and arranged in layers in a terrine with bacon, Gruyère cheese, and vermicelli browned with garlic; thrushes cooked with juniper berries; and pheasant (or grouse) cooked in Chartreuse.

In this cheese-producing region, gratins are a popular method of preparing vegetables, notably cep mushrooms, leeks, cardoons, and marrows. Other typical vegetable dishes include *salade de mouraillons* (a salad made with dandelions and bacon, seasoned with fresh cream), potato matafan (flavoured with bacon, ham, or spinach), potato and dried fruit farcement, *rambollets* (potato croquettes with prunes), gratin savoyard (without milk), crozets, and polenta.

The pâtisserie, which is rich and varied, includes some well-known traditional specialities, such as suisses, Saint-Genis brioche, and *biscuit de Savoie* (Savoy sponge cake), as well as potato bread, pear rissoles, and prune, rhubarb, or bilberry tarts.

The Savoyard cheeses include Beaufort, Reblochon, Tommes de Bonneville, Revard, Bauges, and Boudane (the latter matured in grape marc brandy), Tamié (made by Trappist monks), Toupin, and Chevrotin and Persillé des Aravis. There are also various homemade drinks, such as mulled wine, raspberry wine, cherry ratafia, and wormwood liqueur. The white brandies are also famous, as well as Chambéry vermouth.

savoyarde (à la)

The term used to describe a gratin of potatoes with milk and cheese, as well as several egg dishes: poached or soft-boiled (soft-cooked) eggs arranged on potatoes *à la savoyarde*, coated with Mornay sauce, and glazed in the oven; eggs *sur le plat* cooked with sautéed potatoes, Gruyère cheese, and fresh cream; and flat omelettes with sautéed potatoes and cheese.

RECIPE

Flat omelette à la savoyarde OMELETTE PLATE À LA SAVOYARDE Slice 250 g (9 oz) potatoes and sauté them in 40 g (1½ oz, 3 tablespoons) butter. Season with salt and pepper. Beat 8 eggs seasoned with salt and pepper and add 100 g (4 oz, 1 cup) Gruyère cheese in thin shavings. Add the potatoes to this mixture and pour it into a large frying pan (skillet). Proceed as for a flat omelette.

Savoy sponge cake

BISCUIT DE SAVOIE

A sponge cake which is extremely light due to the large proportion of stiffly beaten egg whites in the recipe. It was probably made for the first time for Amadeus VI of Savoy in about 1348. The recipe has been handed down from generation to generation, and the small town of Yenne near Lake Bourget has become famous for this speciality.

This cake is not to be confused with the Savoy gâteau, a name sometimes given to the Saint-Genis brioche, another speciality of Savoy, made from brioche dough stuffed before baking with pink pralines and cooked in the shape of a hemisphere.

RECIPE

Savoy sponge cake BISCUIT DE SAVOIE Beat 500 g (18 oz, 2¼ cups) caster (superfine) sugar, 1 tablespoon vanilla-flavoured sugar, and 14 egg yolks until the mixture is pale and thick enough to form a ribbon. Add 185 g (6½ oz, 1½ cups) potato flour or cornflour (cornstarch). Finally, fold in 14 egg whites stiffly beaten with a pinch of salt until they stand in peaks. Pour the mixture into Savoy cake tins which have been buttered and dusted with potato flour, filling them only up to two-thirds. Bake in a moderate oven (180 C, 350 F, gas 4) for about 40 minutes.

Savoy wines

VINS DE SAVOIE

The Savoy vineyards have a long history, the wines being praised by both Pliny the Elder and Columella. But they are not often seen on export lists, although they are of considerable interest and well worth the attention of visitors to this beautiful region of southeastern France. The AOCs are Crépy, Seyssel, Seyssel Mousseux, and Vins de Savoie, the latter including red as well as still white and sparkling wines. The grapes used include some of the classic varieties, as well as a number of those with purely local names, such as Altesse, Jacquère, Mondeuse Noir, and Mondeuse Blanc. The white wines are very crisp and dry and, as might be expected, the sparkling wines are also dry and somewhat distinctive in flavour. The reds are usually at their most enjoyable when drunk young and fresh. They are all definitely 'mountain wines', the altitude and the often severe winter climate affecting their character, and modern techniques of vine growing and wine making now give them far more than purely local appeal.

Sbrinz

A Swiss cows'-milk cheese (45% fat) which is produced mainly in the cantons of Lucerne, Schwyz, Uri, and Unterwald. It has a cooked pressed centre and a washed brushed smooth crust which is dark yellow or brown. Sbrinz is the oldest known Swiss cheese (it is the *caseus helveticus* mentioned by Pliny). Hard and brittle and with a strong flavour, this cheese is marketed in wheel shapes, 60 cm (24 in) in diameter and 14 cm (5½ in) deep, weighing 20 kg (44 lb). It can be eaten at the end of the meal and is also used to make canapés and toasted cheese; it can be grated like Parmesan.

scabbard fish SABRE

A very long Mediterranean fish, flattened like a ribbon, which can reach up to 2 m (6½ ft) in length. Its shiny silvery skin has no scales and its pointed snout is armed with several teeth. Nicknamed *argentin* or *jarretière* in French, it is usually sold in pieces and is particularly suitable for fish soup, since its rather soft flesh disintegrates easily.

scald

ÉBOUILLANTER, ÉCHAUDER

To dip fruit or vegetables in boiling water to remove surface impurities or eliminate tartness. Jam jars are also sterilized by scalding before they are filled.

Scald (in French *échauder*) also means to dip tripe into boiling water to remove the mucous membranes and prepare it for cooking. The head and feet of animals are also scalded to facilitate removal of the hair.

scale ÉCAILLER

To clean the scales off a fish. This task is made easier by using a scaler, which is a scraping device with vertically toothed blades, but a scallop shell can also be used.

scallop

COQUILLE SAINT-JACQUES

A bivalve mollusc found on sandy or weedy seabeds along the coast, which moves by successively opening and closing its shell. It is also known in France as the pilgrim shell. Both French names derive from the fact that it used to be found in great numbers on the coast of Galicia in Spain, where it served as an emblem for medieval pilgrims who, after a long journey, had reached Santiago de Compostella (the shrine of St James) not far inland. One side of a scallop's shell is flat and the other is curved; both are marked with deep grooves shaped like a fan. The hinge is framed by triangular lugs. When it is sold, the shell is 10–15 cm (4–6 in) long. It contains about 90 g (3¼ oz) meat including the coral, or roe (called the tongue), which is orange or pale red in colour. The flesh is firm and white and is a great delicacy.

When it is brought to market, the shell is closed. Scrub it thoroughly and place the curved side on an electric hotplate or in the oven at a low heat for a few minutes; open it with a knife. The flesh should be soaked in clear water for about 15 minutes; the beards may be used in the preparation of a fumet. Alternatively, the contents of the shell (meat and coral) may be bought already cleaned at the fishmonger's; they are also sold frozen.

Scallops are generally eaten cooked. They are served in the shell, prepared *à l'américaine*, with champagne, curried, *en gratin*, poached with various sauces, cooked on skewers, sautéed *á la provençale*, or eaten cold with a salad. After oysters and mussels they are the most popular shellfish in France, being in season from the end of September to May. They are exported in great quantities by Canada and the United States.

RECIPES

COLD SCALLOP DISHES

Raw scallops COQUILLES SAINT-JACQUES CRUES (from a recipe by Jean and Paul Minchelli) Open the scallops, remove them from their shells, wash thoroughly (after removing the beards), and dry them on a linen towel. Cut the scallops into thin slices and lay them on a cold plate which has been lightly oiled. Cover with olive oil using a brush and give one turn of the pepper mill. Garnish with thin slivers of the coral.

Scallop salad SALADE DE COQUILLES SAINT-JACQUES (from a recipe by Gerard Vie) Clean a lettuce heart, half a bunch of watercress, and the white base of 2 leeks. Slice the lettuce and the leeks and cook all these vegetables very gently in 1 tablespoon oil with salt and pepper until well reduced. Slice the flesh and corals of 12 scallops and seal them by steaming. Place the sliced scallops on the tepid vegetable mixture and sprinkle with a little olive oil and the juice of a lemon.

Scallops in mayonnaise COQUILLES SAINT-JACQUES À LA MAYONNAISE Line the deep sides of the shells with a little shredded lettuce seasoned with vinaigrette. Thinly slice the poached white flesh of the scallops, dip the slices in the vinaigrette, then roll in chopped parsley. Place the slices on the lettuce and cover with mayonnaise. Garnish each scallop with the coral, an anchovy fillet, and a few capers (or black (ripe) olives).

Scallops in salad COQUILLES SAINT-JACQUES EN SALADE Hard-boil (hard-cook) some eggs, then quarter them. Shape the flesh of a cucumber into little ovals. Poach the scallops and let them cool. Shred some lettuce and season it with vinaigrette, then line the deep part of the shells with this. Slice the scallops thinly, put them into a bowl with the cucumber, add some vinaigrette, and mix well. Place the scallop slices and the cucumber into the shells. Garnish with the egg quarters and corals, and sprinkle with mixed herbs. Fresh cream with a little ketchup may be added to the scallop slices, in addition to some lemon juice, salt, and pepper.

HOT SCALLOP DISHES

Fried scallops Colbert COQUILLES SAINT-JACQUES FRITES BEURRE COLBERT Quickly poach the white flesh of the scallops in a court-bouillon (4 minutes), then cut into slices if they are very large. Marinate them with the corals (as in the recipe for scallop brochettes), then drain, dip into batter, and fry in ample fat. Drain and serve with Colbert butter. (The meat may also be covered in breadcrumbs before frying.)

Scallop brochettes COQUILLES SAINT-JACQUES EN BROCHETTES Marinate the meat and corals of 12 good scallops in a mixture of olive oil, garlic, and chopped parsley, with a little lemon juice, salt, and pepper. Leave for 1 hour, turning the ingredients at least once during this time. Clean 12 small mushrooms. Remove the seeds from a large sweet pepper and cut into squares. Cut 200 g (7 oz) smoked brisket into small pieces. Thread all these ingredients on 4 skewers, always placing a piece of meat on either side of the scallop flesh and its coral. Dip into the marinade and grill (broil) for 15–18 minutes under a moderate heat (preferably in a vertical grill).

Scallops Mornay COQUILLES SAINT-JACQUES MORNAY Poach the white flesh of the scallops with the corals. Fill the deep side of the shell with Mornay sauce. Slice the poached flesh and place the slices, with the corals, into the shells. Cover with Mornay sauce. Sprinkle with grated cheese, baste with melted butter, and brown in a very hot oven (about 240 C, 475 F, gas 9).

Steamed scallops COQUILLES SAINT-JACQUES À LA VAPEUR Place the flesh of the scallops and their corals into the basket of a steamer. Slice the flesh if the pieces are very large. Pour a well-spiced court-bouillon into the lower part and steam for 2–3 minutes. Finely sliced vegetables (e.g. the white part of a leek, fennel, celery) may be placed in the basket and steamed for about 10 minutes, before adding the scallops. Alternatively the scallops and corals may be put into a receptacle with a cover, seasoned with salt and pepper, and cooked in the oven in their own juice.

scallop shell COQUILLE

A preparation consisting of a salpicon, purée, or ragout, thickened and covered with an appropriate garnish, and presented in a scallop shell (especially for fish and shellfish) or in a receptacle of the same shape made of metal, tempered glass, or heat-resistant porcelain. Scallop shells are normally cooked *au gratin* or with a savoury glaze and served hot as an hors d'oeuvre, or even as a light entrée. They can also be served cold. A huge number of preparations can be served in a scallop shell: armourettes *à la duxelles*, brains with an allemande or aurore sauce, brill with shrimps, crayfish tails or skate livers *au beurre blonde*, oysters *à la diable*, soft roes with spinach, viande de desserte with a tomato sauce, minced chicken, mussels, lambs' sweetbreads, fish pieces with a Mornay sauce, etc.

It once used to be *de rigueur* to garnish the border of the hot scallop shell with duchess potatoes piped from a fluted nozzle, or with thin rounds of boiled potatoes. Nowadays this border (intended to retain the various elements in the shell) tends to be left out. However, a border can still be made with chicken, veal, or fish forcemeat, depending on the dish, or with spinach purée or rice.

Cold scallop shells are normally prepared with pieces of fish in mayonnaise – cold salmon, shrimps, thin slices of lobster, oysters, or simply with shellfish in a cold sauce. They are often presented on a bed of shredded lettuce, garnished with a mayonnaise piping, with slices of lemon, black (ripe) olives, etc.

☐ **Preparation of hot scallop shells**
● Fill the bottom of the shell with the appropriate sauce.
● Add the desired filling, which should be hot and well seasoned.
● Cover with sauce.
● Sprinkle with breadcrumbs or with grated cheese, then baste with melted butter.
● Place the shells on an enamelled oven tray partly filled with water. Brown under a grill or heat in a hot oven.

| RECIPES

Scallop shells of fish à la Mornay CO-QUILLES DE POISSON À LA MORNAY Mix some cooked fish (allow about 400 g (1 lb) for 4 persons) with 3 dl (½ pint, 1¼ cups) Mornay sauce and some chopped parsley. Season to taste. Fill the scallop shells with this mixture. Sprinkle with grated Gruyère, add a few knobs of butter, and brown in a very hot oven.

Scallop shells of shrimps COQUILLES AU CREVETTES Shell some mussels, which have been cooked *à la marinière*, and strain the juice. Wash and thinly slice 250 g (9 oz, 2½ cups) mushrooms,

then sauté briskly in butter with a chopped shallot. Prepare a béchamel sauce, add the juice of the mussels, and season. Mix all these elements, adding 150 g (5 oz, 1 cup) peeled shrimps. Butter 4 scallop shells and distribute the mixture evenly. Sprinkle with fresh breadcrumbs and a little grated Parmesan cheese, baste with melted butter, and brown in a very hot oven.

Scamorze

An Italian cheese (44% fat), originally made from buffaloes' milk in the centre of the peninsula but now made from cows' milk (and sometimes goats' milk) throughout Italy. A pressed cheese with a natural crust, it is white or cream in colour with a nutty flavour. This cheese is related to Caciocavallo but it is not matured for so long. It is moulded into the shape of a narrow gourd with four little 'ears' at the top for handling. It is often eaten fresh and can be used in cookery like Mozzarella.

scampi

A type of large Italian prawn (shrimp). Scampi can be cooked in the oven, fried or sautéed with garlic, grilled (broiled) on skewers, rolled up in small slices of ham, made into a ragout with other seafoods, or boiled and served cold with lemon vinaigrette. *Scampi fritti* (fried in batter) is the best-known preparation. Recipes for langoustine can be used for scampi.

Scandinavia
SCANDINAVIE

The culinary repertoire of the Scandinavian countries relies on fish, potatoes, pork, beetroot (red beet), cucumber, fruit, dill, horseradish, cream, and butter; it preserves the distant heritage of the Vikings, who ate mutton, shellfish, wild birds, reindeer, and bear and were adept at making butter and beer.

The natural isolation of the Scandinavian countries has contributed to the survival of some very old recipes, notably raw salmon marinated with pepper, dill, sugar, and salt and served with mustard sauce. Bread is traditionally made at home, hence the variety of Scandinavian barley or rye cakes and breads. In addition, the climate is conducive to the widespread practice of drying, smoking, and marinating: cod and herring have therefore become the mainstays of the Scandinavian diet. One particularly typical dish is *surströming* – sour herrings pickled in the sun in a barrel of brine, a strong sharp dish eaten with sour black bread and potatoes.

Dairy products play an important role in Scandinavian cookery. Double (heavy) or soured (dairy sour) cream, butter, and cottage cheese or whey are much used in sweet and savoury recipes, and there are numerous cheeses, including Danish Blue and Samsoë (the best known), the Swedish Kumminost with cumin, Norwegian Gammelost, Gjetost, Nökkelost, Mysost, and Pultost, often very strong, the Finnish Kreivi, and reindeer-milk cheese.

Each of the Scandinavian countries has its own culinary characteristics. Denmark has rich fatty foods. Norway is a wilder country and consequently fish, reindeer, and mutton are important here. Finland has rustic dishes, and Sweden has the most varied cuisine.

☐ **Denmark** Solid, plentiful, and mild, Danish cookery makes much use of butter and cream. Pork and potatoes are the predominant foods. Two great classics are loin of pork stuffed with prunes and apples and roast leg of pork with crackling. Stews are also popular, especially *frikadeller* (meatballs of minced (ground) veal and pork with onion), as well as stuffed cabbage and *hakkebiff* (minced beef with onion, covered with brown sauce). Poultry dishes, which are reserved for special occasions, include chicken stuffed with parsley, and roast goose. In addition to potatoes, cabbage is widely used, especially braised red cabbage with apples, which is served with pork, goose, or duck. Boiled kale, chopped and combined with a cream sauce, is a favourite garnish for ham. The offal specialities include a famous black pudding (blood sausage), calf's head *en tortue*, and stuffed ox heart with cream sauce. Liver pâté is also very popular and is one of the main items in the cold buffet, the traditional Danish lunch which includes salads, herrings, scrambled egg with bacon and cheese on slices of buttered wholemeal or black bread, together with various foods which are easy to slice, such as *rullepoelse* (spiced rolled belly of pork).

However, the best known items of Danish cookery are the pastries and desserts, ranging from simple pancakes filled with vanilla ice cream, fruit puddings, and rodgrod, to the more elaborate apple cake (made of several layers of sweet pastry interspersed with jam and breadcrumbs mixed with melted butter and topped with whipped cream) and 'peasant maidens in veils' (with a base of crumbled rye bread, apples, chocolate, and cream). Home-made biscuits (cookies) include the *brune kage* (made with spices, almonds, and brown sugar), gingerbread, and butter shortbreads. Some Danish pastries are very popular, such as the soft flaky turnovers of various shapes, filled with cream, jam, or dried fruits. The most impressive set piece is the *kransekage*, eaten on birthdays and at weddings. As high as 80 cm (30 in), it is made of piled-up rings of pastry decorated with crystallized (candied) fruit, studded with little flags, and patterned with icing (frosting) designs.

However, a less rich culinary tradition does exist in Denmark, going back to the rural origins of the country; some examples are milk porridge topped with butter and salt-pork gravy, and *ollebrod*, a thick soup made with beer and rye bread.

☐ **Norway** The traditional Norwegian breakfast is based on salt or marinated fish, strong cheese, bacon, fried potatoes, eggs, and various types of bread, together with butter and jam. The midday meal is often only sandwiches, except in the country, where the two main foods of Norway, mutton and fish, are often eaten. The main meal of the day is dinner. Soured (dairy sour) cream is widely used: in soups and sauces, porridge, waffles, and with salt meat, pork products, and salads. The natural taste of foods is appreciated, with such dishes as salt mutton chops grilled over a birch-wood fire and served with kohlrabi purée; fried trout coated with cream and sprinkled with parsley; fish salad with horseradish, dill, and onions; and ham with *surkål*, a sort of sauerkraut with cumin. The old Norwegian national dish is *rommegrot*, a porridge made with soured cream, flour, and milk, dusted with cinnamon and sugar, and served with melted butter and redcurrant or blackberry juice; it has now given way to the more popular rice pudding.

Meat is often dried, salted, and smoked; leg of mutton prepared in this way is called *fenalår* and is cut into long thin slices, and *spekeskinke* is a dried ham eaten in the spring with new vegetables. In the winter more fortifying foods are eaten, such as *får i kål*, a mutton and cabbage stew with black pepper. There are some original recipes for game: ptarmigan casserole with cranberries, roast venison with goats'-milk cheese sauce, and smoked elk.

There are numerous ways of preparing fish. Trout is preserved by pickling as well as by the other methods, and salmon is grilled (broiled), smoked, or cooked in stock and served cold, with horseradish butter and cucumber. Sea fish are widely used. Boiled salt cod is served with melted butter and egg sauce or cooked with potatoes and young peas with mustard sauce. Another very popular dish is cods' tongues, which are often mixed with various different types of fish in aspic. As in other Scandinavian countries, herrings are prepared in many different ways, but mackerel are also highly prized: marinated and then grilled, they are served with tomato butter, aquavit, and beer. There is also a fish pudding, made with smoked haddock and cod and served with shrimp sauce, and a fish soup from Bergen, made with green vegetables, soured cream, and egg yolks.

□ **Sweden** Of all Scandinavian cookery, that of Sweden is best known abroad. The most famous culinary tradition is the smörgasbord, a sumptuous buffet which features both in domestic cookery and in all the restaurants. The Swedes are also proud of a court culinary tradition, with dishes such as *slottsstek* (braised beef *à la royale*, served with mountain cranberries and potatoes) and fillet of beef Oskar (with asparagus and béarnaise sauce).

Swedish home cooking is simpler but always full of flavour. Yellow pea soup with thyme and marjoram, served with a slice of pork, can be followed by pancakes topped with cranberry compote, fried pork sausages with pickled beetroot (red beet), beef and beer stew, and

salmon pudding (made with potatoes and onions and topped with egg custard). The potato recipes show great inventiveness: potato balls stuffed with pork, baked potatoes filled with fresh cream and topped with cods' roe, little potato pancakes with chives and pepper, as well as the famous *pytt i panna* (small potato and meat dice fried with onion, sprinkled with parsley, and served with a raw egg yolk or a fried egg).

Three other typically Swedish dishes should be mentioned: beef Lindström (minced (ground) steak with beetroot juice, capers, and onion), rolled slices of beef stuffed with anchovies and onions, and rolled slices of veal stuffed with leeks.

The pâtisserie is particularly rich and varied and saffron and cardamon are used a great deal.

Within the Arctic circle, whether in Sweden, Norway, or Finland, the meat *par excellence* is reindeer meat. Smoked to the bone and then dried, it can be kept for a long time, but it is also cooked fresh, stewed with marrow bones. The Lapps maintain some old traditions, such as salted black coffee into which they dip reindeer-milk cheese.

□ **Finland** Finnish cuisine is characterized by foods with robust flavours, such as *vorshmack* (a hash of mutton, beef, and salt herring, spiced with garlic and onion), which is accompanied by *ryyppy* (a very strong grain alcohol, which is drunk chilled). Soup made of lake fish with potatoes and onions is served with a hunk of buttered rye bread; a soup made of chopped offal cooked with carrots and potatoes is thickened with blood and garnished with barley balls. The Finns are fond of swedes (rutabaga), raw salmon (*loki*), and strong liqueurs which they make themselves, such as *lakka* (based on Arctic cranberries). They also use a lot of milk, in the form of a fairly thick buttermilk or in puddings and porridge; these include puddings made with rye, malt, treacle, and bitter-orange peel, and barley porridge served with rose-hip purée, raisins, or melted butter.

Wild mushrooms from the forests are widely used in soups, sauces, stews, pickles, and salads, and wild berries (cranberries, blackberries, and wild strawberries) are made into purées, mousses, and cream desserts. Other typical foods are burbot roe, smoked reindeer tongues, and crayfish cooked in stock with fennel. The Russian influence is significant: borsch, pashka, and blinis are common dishes, and in Karelia (formerly part of Finland) rye pastries, variants of piroshki and koulibiaca, are the typical dishes; these include *piirakka*, with a rice and fish filling, served with melted butter and hard-boiled (hard-cooked) eggs, and the famous *kalakukko*, filled with small freshwater fish and minced (ground) pork. Other Finnish dishes are liver stew with rice and mutton, pork, and veal stews.

□ **The Christmas season** Throughout Scandinavia, Christmas festivities begin on 13 December, St Lucia's Day, when the young girls dress in white and wear crowns of candles. They prepare the morning coffee and serve it with saffron biscuits (cookies). The main Christmas meal is served on Christmas Eve, with the traditional dishes: ham pie (made with rye pastry) and turnip purée in Finland; braised caramelized ham with apples, red cabbage, and mustard in Sweden; roast pork or pork ribs and sauerkraut with cumin in Norway; and roast goose stuffed with apples and prunes in Denmark. The pastries include petits fours flavoured with cloves and ginger, leavened dough fritters with brandy, Christmas loaves containing crystallized (candied) fruits, and cinnamon, butter, and almond porridges.

Meals on Christmas Day itself are served as large cold buffets. Christmas breakfast sometimes includes some special foods, such as the Swedish *julhög*, consisting of a ball of rye bread, a small wheat bun sprinkled with large sugar crystals, a heart-shaped piece of shortbread, and a red apple placed on top of each other. The Danes are particularly fond of rice pudding with whipped cream and almonds, topped with cherry sauce. The traditional punch is *glögg*, a mixture of red wine, Muscat, vermouth, and angostura bitters in which raisins, orange peel, cardamon, cloves, and cinnamon are steeped. This punch is served very hot with chopped almonds.

Schabzieger

A Swiss cheese made of skimmed cows'
milk, which is very hard and has no rind. Sharp and strong, it is flavoured with dried sweet clover, which gives it a greenish colour. The French-speaking Swiss call it Sapsago, and the German-speaking Swiss call it Kräuterkäse (herb cheese). It is shaped like a truncated cone, 7.5 cm (3 in) at the base and 10 cm (4 in) high. When completely dry, it is used like Parmesan to flavour rice, pasta, polenta, or eggs.

schenkele or schenkela

An Alsatian biscuit (cookie), traditionally eaten at Christmas (the name comes from the German *schenken*, meaning 'to offer'). Schenkeles are made from a fairly firm dough of flour, sugar, butter, eggs, and ground almonds, flavoured with brandy (or some other spirit). The dough is cut up into sticks, fried, and liberally sprinkled with sugar.

schnapps or schnaps

A spirit made in various forms in Germany (the word means literally a snatch or a gasp) and also in the Scandinavian countries and the Netherlands – aquavit is a schnapps. Often used as a chaser with beer, schnapps can accompany smoked meats and fish and cold cuts in general. It should be served ice-cold.

Schweppe (Jacob)

German industrialist (born Witzenhausen, 1740; died Geneva, 1821). He set up in Geneva as a jeweller but soon began experiments for making artificial mineral water. His research led, in 1790, to the perfecting of an industrial process. In 1792, working with two engineers and a Genevan chemist, he set up a factory in London, then continued to run it on his own, producing sodas and imitations of Seltzer, Spa, and Pyrmont waters (which were very popular at the time). The famous Schweppes Indian Tonic and Schweppes Ginger Ale were perfected in 1860 by Schweppe's successors, who made Seltzer water even more popular by adding quinine, bitter orange peel, or ginger to it. These mixtures were extremely popular in the British colonies, where malaria was rife, and it became the custom there to add gin to these drinks and drink them as 'tonics'.

Today the firm is known internationally for these and a wide range of similar drinks.

sciacce

Small Corsican pies filled with cooked mashed potato seasoned with garlic, tomato sauce, and grated cheese, bound with beaten egg. Sciacce are eaten warm, traditionally on All Saints' Day, especially in Levie.

scissors and shears

CISEAUX ET CISAILLES

Kitchen utensils having two blades, which can often be dismantled for washing, and whose handles are sometimes provided with notches or projections that can serve as bottle-openers, nutcrackers, can-openers, etc. Kitchen scissors, with solid blades ranging from 19 to 32 cm (7–12 in) long, serve for snipping herbs and trimming meat or vegetables. Strong fish scissors, with solid or serrated blades, are used for trimming and cleaning fish. Poultry shears (or secateurs), fitted with shorter very strong blades, serve to divide poultry into pieces, cut bones, etc. Grape scissors, often of silver or silver-plated, are a table accessory for dividing bunches of grapes.

scone

A small round cake made of raised dough. Originating in Scotland, it is soft and light inside and has a brown crust. Scones are eaten at breakfast or for tea, usually served hot, split in half, and buttered. They used to be traditionally cooked on a griddle (or girdle), a thick flat iron with a handle, placed on top of the stove (or, originally, on the fire). Nowadays they are more often baked in the oven.

scoop out ÉVIDER

To remove the pulp from a fresh fruit or a raw vegetable before using it in a particular recipe. The cavity is usually stuffed with a filling consisting of the pulp mixed with other ingredients.

When preparing melon balls, the seeds are removed from the melon halves and then the flesh is scooped out with a melon baller; the melon balls are then macerated in cooked wine, replaced in the hollowed-out rinds, and served chilled. In the preparation of fruit sorbets served in their skins (lemon, orange, tangerine, pineapple), the principle is the same, but the sorbet is made with the fruit pulp; when the shell has been refilled, it is served chilled.

Apples can be hollowed out with an apple corer for baking them in their skins or to slice them into rings for fritters.

scoring CERNER

Making a shallow incision, using a small knife or cutter in the skin of a fruit, vegetable, or nut. Scoring an apple around its circumference prevents it from bursting during baking. Scoring chestnuts makes them easier to peel.

For a vol-au-vent or patty, the lid is marked out by scoring the pastry with a pastry cutter (cookie cutter) or small knife before cooking.

Designs can be scored with the point of a knife or the prongs of a fork on top of a cake, pie, biscuit (cookie), etc., which has been brushed with beaten egg and is ready to cook. A puff-pastry galette is usually scored with lozenge (diamond) shapes, pithiviers with a rose pattern, and sablés, croquets, and almond biscuits (cookies) with crisscross or parallel lines.

scorpion fish RASCASSE

A fish found in warm temperate waters such as the Mediterranean, where most French supplies come from. It has a thick body and an enormous spiny head, marked with a transverse ridge and with loose skin hanging above and in front of the eyes. The dorsal fin is dotted with large spines. The small so-called brown scorpion fish (30 cm (12 in) long) is grey with a pink belly; scarce and expensive, it is much sought after and cooked like sea bream. The red scorpion fish (50 cm (20 in) long) is a pinkish-bronze colour; it is much more common and has rather tasteless and tough flesh. It is an essential ingredient of fish soups and bouilla-baisses.

RECIPE

Fillets of scorpion fish à l'antillaise
FILETS DE RASCASSE À L'ANTIL-
LAISE Cut 750 g (1¾ lb) brown scor-

pion fish fillets into strips 2 cm (¾ in) wide. Peel and deseed 1 kg (2¼ lb) very ripe tomatoes and rub the pulp through a sieve. Peel and slice 750 g (1¾ lb) potatoes and cook until golden in 4 tablespoons (⅓ cup) oil. Take the potatoes out of the pan and cook the fish until golden. Remove from the pan and put aside. Put 2 large sliced onions into the pan, then the tomato pulp, some salt and pepper, and 1 small red pepper. Bring to the boil, then add the potatoes and a bay leaf. When the potatoes are almost cooked (but still firm when pierced with a knife), add the fish and continue to cook for 7–8 minutes. Serve very hot with rice *à la créole*.

Scotch broth

A Scottish soup, also known as barley broth. The ingredients are neck or shoulder of mutton, barley, and various vegetables (carrots, turnips, onions, leeks, celery, and sometimes green peas and cabbage). It is served sprinkled with parsley. Sometimes the broth (not strained) is served first, followed by the meat with caper sauce.

scrolls COPEAUX

Light pastry confections in the shape of little scrolls. The name is also given to a chocolate decoration obtained by shaving the edge of a block of chocolate with a knife, or by pouring some melted chocolate onto marble and scraping it off when it has hardened. This type of decoration is often called *caraque* and is used on Black Forest gâteau.

Scubac or Escubac

A liqueur from Lorraine, made on a small scale. Thick and smooth, it is made by steeping spices in brandy with sugar. The usual ingredients are juniper, aniseed, coriander, cinnamon, angelica, mace, cloves, and sometimes also saffron.

sea almond

AMANDE DE MER

A small bivalve mollusc, about 5 cm (2 in) long, living on the sandy seabed. Its concentrically ribbed shell is cream, spotted with brown. Inside the shell are numerous small parallel teeth. The sea almond may be eaten raw with lemon, but is usually stuffed, like the scallop, although it is not as good.

sea bream

DAURADE, DORADE

A marine fish with gold or silvery scales. The ancient Greeks and Romans liked it cooked with seasoned sauces and accompanied with fruits. In France, it has been considered a choice dish only since the 19th century. There are three principal species.

• The gilthead (*daurade royale*) is fished in the Mediterranean and the Bay of Biscay. 30–50 cm (12–20 in) long and weighing up to 3 kg (6½ lb), it has silvery scales and a golden crescent between the eyes. The shine of the scales is a good indication of freshness; its soft white dense flesh is excellent.

• The pink sea bream (*daurade rose*) comes mainly from the Atlantic. It is gold-coloured with clear pink fins and a black mark near the gills. The flesh is less dense and has a drier texture, but is nevertheless tasty. It weighs up to 3 kg (6½ lb).

• The grey sea bream (*daurade grise*), 20–40 cm (8–16 in) long and weighing 300–500 g (11–18 oz), has flesh of a slightly coarser texture; it is much cheaper, both because of its less attractive appearance and its greater availability.

Couch's sea bream (*pagre*), known as red porgy in the United States, is found in the Mediterranean (especially on the Spanish coast) and in the Atlantic (south of the Bay of Biscay), but is now becoming rare. Up to 75 cm (30 in) long and weighing about 1.2 kg (2½ lb), it has an oval body with large scales, a grey and pink back, silvery sides, and fins marked with reddish-brown. Its flesh, though less delicate than that of the other species, is full of flavour.

Fresh sea bream is sold whole, usually gutted; the scales are numerous, wide, and sticky and should be removed by the fishmonger. The percentage of waste is very high (up to 50%); allow 300 g (11 oz) per person. Deep-frozen fillets are also available. A lean fish, containing only 80 Cal per 100 g, the sea bream is rich in magnesium. The backbone comes away easily, even when raw, and the fish is often cooked stuffed.

Sea bream can be grilled (broiled) –

slit beforehand if very large and marinated if desired – roasted, poached in a court-bouillon, or steamed with seaweed. In Mediterranean countries it is roasted on a spit and accompanied by chickpeas or haricot (navy) beans and lardons of bacon. Sliced, it can be made into soup. Finally, it is a good fish for making sashimi, provided it is absolutely fresh.

RECIPES

Braised sea bream with apples DAURADE ROYALE BRAISÉE AUX POMMES (from a recipe by Jean and Paul Minchelli) Descale a sea bream weighing about 800 g (1¾ lb), clean it through the gills, and wipe it. Retain the liver. Peel and chop 3 shallots, 1 small fennel bulb, and 1 onion. Peel and crush 2 cloves of garlic. Remove the zest from a lime and blanch, cool, and dry it. Arrange a bed of fresh fennel sprigs in a long flameproof dish; add the shallots, fennel, onion, garlic, lime zest, and some parsley stalks, moisten with ¼ litre (8 fl oz, 1 cup) fish fumet, 1 tablespoon olive oil, and 2 tablespoons white rum. Bring to the boil.

Place the bream on this bed, make three slits in the upward-facing surface, and insert lemon or orange slices and diced streaky salted bacon. Coat with olive oil and sprinkle with pepper and salt. Around it arrange the liver, cut into quarters, and 2 apples, also cut into quarters. Cover with aluminium foil and cook in a moderate oven for 20–30 minutes. Arrange on a serving dish. Strain the reduced cooking juices, adjust seasoning, and serve separately in a sauceboat.

Fillets of sea bream with vegetable julienne FILETS DE DAURADE À LA JULIENNE DE LÉGUMES Fillet a sea bream weighing about 1.75 kg (3¾ lb). Prepare a julienne of vegetables comprising the white parts of 2 leeks, 4 sliced celery sticks (stalks), half a fennel bulb, and 2 young turnips; arrange it in a buttered gratin dish. Season the fillets with salt and pepper, fold them in half, and place them in the dish. Add fresh cream and lemon juice and cook in a hot oven (about 220 c, 425 f, gas 7) for about 30 minutes, covering the dish

with a sheet of aluminium foil. (This dish is very suitable for a microwave oven.)

Sea bream stuffed with fennel DAURADE FARCIE AU FENOUIL Descale a sea bream weighing about 1.5 kg (3¼ lb). Clean it through the gills, wash, wipe, and season with salt and pepper. Cut along both sides of the backbone, then cut through the backbone at the head and tail and remove it. Take 250 g (9 oz) stale breadcrumbs and moisten with milk. Clean and thinly slice a fennel bulb. Squeeze the breadcrumbs and mix with the fennel plus 2 tablespoons (3 tablespoons) pastis, 1 tablespoon lemon juice, and a little crumbled bay leaf and thyme. Fill the bream with this stuffing and tie it up like a ballottine.

Butter a gratin dish, sprinkle with chopped shallots, and place the bream on top. One-third cover the fish with white wine (or a mixture of wine and fumet), sprinkle with olive oil, and cook for about 30 minutes in a very hot oven (about 240 c, 475 f, gas 9), basting from time to time. If necessary, protect the fish with a piece of aluminium foil towards the end of the cooking.

seafood FRUITS DE MER

A collective term for shellfish and other small edible marine animals, such as spider crabs, mussels, shrimps, winkles, clams, sea urchins, oysters, and langoustines. Seafood is often served as an hors d'oeuvre, on a bed of crushed ice and fresh clean seaweed and accompanied by butter and rye bread. It is also an ingredient of omelettes, risottos, vols-au-vent, etc.

RECIPES

Seafood bouchées BOUCHÉES AUX FRUITS DE MER Prepare and cook some savoury bouchée cases. Prepare a seafood ragout. Warm the bouchée cases in the oven (if prepared in advance), fill with the hot seafood ragout, cover with the bouchée tops, and serve immediately.

Seafood ragout RAGOÛT DE FRUITS DE MER Peel and chop 2 shallots and 1 large onion. Clean 750 g (1¾ lb) mussels and 12 langoustines. Scald and peel 5 or 6 tomatoes, remove the seeds, and crush the pulp.

Place the mussels in a pan with 2 dl (7 fl oz, ¾ cup) dry white wine, a bouquet garni, and half the chopped shallots and onion, and season with pepper. Cover the pan and cook until the shells just open, then remove and drain the mussels and strain the cooking liquid through fine muslin (cheesecloth).

Place the flesh of 15 scallops and the strained mussel liquid in a saucepan, cover, and poach very gently for 5 minutes. Remove the mussels from their shells.

Sauté the langoustines in oil in a flameproof casserole. When they have turned red, add some pepper and the rest of the chopped shallots and onion; cook until golden. Add a liqueur glass of warm brandy and flame. Add the crushed tomatoes and the cooking liquid used for the mussels and scallops, cover, cook very gently for 5–6 minutes, then remove and drain the langoustines; continue cooking the tomatoes for about 10 minutes.

Meanwhile, shell the langoustine tails, crush the shells, and add them to the casserole to flavour the mixture. Cut the langoustine tails into chunks and slice the scallop flesh. Heat 50 g (2 oz, 4 tablespoons) butter in a sauté pan until it foams, then add the langoustines, scallops, mussels, and 100 g (4 oz) shelled shrimps. Put the tomato sauce through a fine sieve, add 2 dl (7 fl oz, ¼ cup) cream, adjust the seasoning, and reduce until the mixture just starts to thicken. Pour over the seafood.

Seafood risotto RISOTTO AUX FRUITS DE MER Clean and cook 2 litres (3½ pints, 4½ pints) mussels and 1 litre (1¾ pints, 4¼ cups) cockles or clams separately in white wine seasoned with spices and herbs. Drain the shellfish and remove from their shells. Put them in a casserole with 200 g (7 oz) shelled prawn (shrimp) tails and 4 shelled scallops, previously poached in white wine and sliced. Prepare 4 dl (14 fl oz, 1¾ cups) fish velouté sauce using a white roux and the combined cooking liquids. Cook this sauce for 25 minutes until very smooth; add 6 tablespoons (scant ½ cup) cream and reduce. Then

mix in 40 g (1½ oz, 3 tablespoons) butter and put through a sieve. Pour the sauce over the shellfish and keep hot without boiling. Meanwhile, prepare a risotto *à la piémontaise* and arrange it to form a large border in a deep dish. Pour the seafood mixture into the centre.

sea kale CHOU MARIN

An English and Scottish speciality, sea kale has pale-green leaves with broad fleshy leafstalks, which are boiled and served with a seasoned sauce, sautéed with garlic, or eaten raw with a vinaigrette. The buds are eaten like asparagus, after they have been blanched. It is little known in France, although it was introduced to the royal kitchen garden at Versailles in 1820.

seal

To begin cooking of meat or poultry by sautéing it over a moderate heat until firm but not brown. The cooking is usually completed in a white sauce.

The edges of two layers of pastry, moistened with water or glaze, are sealed by pressing them gently together so that they remain stuck together during cooking. This operation is used when making tarts, pies, turnovers, rissoles, and timbales.

Bottles of wine or preserves are sealed with wax. The cork is pushed in until it is flush with the top of the bottle. Then the top of the bottle is plunged into melted wax, which hardens in about 20 minutes.

seasoning
ASSAISONNEMENT

The addition of various ingredients (salt, pepper, spices, condiments, aromatics, oil, and vinegar) in variable quantities to a culinary preparation, either to give it a particular taste or to increase its palatability without changing the nature of the foods it contains. Seasoning is a delicate art that requires a precise knowledge of basic substances to bring out the best in the different flavours by blending them. See *condiments*.

sea squirt VIOLET

A small marine invertebrate animal whose body is surrounded by a 'tunic', or saclike membrane. The edible variety resembles a large purple-brown fig, hence its French nickname, *figue de mer*. It has two orifices through which it syphons water in and out, and attaches itself to rocks or the sea bed. Found in the Mediterranean, it is split in half and the yellow part inside eaten raw, like the sea urchin.

sea urchin OURSIN

A spiny marine invertebrate, commonly known in France as the *châtaigne de mer* ('sea chestnut') or *hérisson de mer* ('sea hedgehog'). A spherical shell (test), made of chalky platelets, bears mobile spines; it encloses the digestive system, the locomotory system (the 'feet' pass through the shell), and the five yellow or orange genital glands. The latter form the edible portion (the coral). There are numerous species of sea urchin, but the one eaten in Europe is fairly flat and measures 6–8 cm (2½–3 in); it is greenish-brown or mauve. In France, where they are harvested mainly from the Mediterranean but also off Brittany, it is forbidden to collect or sell them from May to September.

When fresh, the sea urchin should have firm spines and a tightly closed mouth orifice. They are opened by cutting into the soft tissue round the mouth, using pointed scissors (and wearing gloves); by continuing right round, halfway up the shell, the top can be removed and the digestive system taken out and discarded. The coral smells strongly of iodine. The sea urchin can be eaten raw, or crushed into a paste to flavour sauces, soufflés, scrambled eggs, to fill omelettes, to accompany fish or seafood, to garnish croûtes (toast), etc. *Oursinade* is a thick sauce which, in Provence, is served as an accompaniment to poached fish; it is also the name of a fish soup of sea urchins.

RECIPES

Langoustines in sea urchin shells LANGOUSTINES AUX COQUES D'OURSIN (from Daniel Métery's recipe) Dip 4 large tomatoes into boiling water for 2 minutes, skin them, cut them in half, seed them, and dice them finely. Heat 30 g (1 oz, 2 tablespoons) butter in a saucepan and gently cook 2 small finely chopped shallots. Add the diced tomato, salt,

and pepper, cook for 15 minutes, then put the pan aside.

Open 12 sea urchins and extract the edible part; strain the liquid and put it aside. Thoroughly clean the empty shells and set aside. Cut 12 langoustines in half; cook them in a little oil over a very high heat for 2 minutes, then shell them.

Put the sea urchin liquid and 5 cl (2 tablespoons, 3 tablespoons) Cognac into a saucepan with 1 dl (6 tablespoons, scant ½ cup) dry white wine and 2 small chopped shallots; reduce by half. Add the tomatoes and reduce again for 2 minutes. Add 4 tablespoons double (heavy) cream, reduce again for 2–3 minutes, then whisk in 70 g (2¾ oz, 5 tablespoons) butter. Heat the langoustines and the corals through, without letting them boil.

To serve, heat the reserved sea urchin shells in the oven for a minute or two. Fill each with 1 tablespoon very hot sauce, a langoustine, and a coral. Arrange on hot plates. Sprinkle with chervil leaves.

Oursinade sauce SAUCE OURSINADE Melt 100 g (4 oz, ½ cup) butter in a heavy-bottomed saucepan and add 6 egg yolks. Mix together and moisten with 2 or 3 glasses of the poaching liquid from the fish which the sauce is to cover; beat until the mixture forms a smooth cream. Put into a bain-marie, add the corals from 12 sea urchins, and beat again until they are well blended.

Sea urchin purée PURÉE D'OURSINS Open the sea urchins, take out the corals, and press them through a sieve. Add an equal quantity of very reduced béchamel sauce (or hollandaise sauce); heat the mixture while stirring and then beat in 2 tablespoons butter.

This purée can be used to fill puff-pastry cases or tartlets. It can also be spread on slices of fried bread and then sprinkled with grated cheese and browned under the grill (broiler) or in the oven.

Soupe oursinade (from René Allouin's recipe) Clean 2 kg (4¼ lb) rockfish and small green crabs and cut the fish into pieces of about 5–6 cm (2 in). Make a roux with 50 g (2 oz, 4 tablespoons) butter and 70 g (3 oz, ¾ cup) flour. Pour 1.5 dl (¼ pint, ⅔ cup) olive oil into a large saucepan. Clean and finely slice 1 leek, 1 fennel bulb, and a stick (stalk) of celery; peel and crush the cloves from a small head (bulb) of garlic; peel and finely slice 2 or 3 onions. Put all the vegetables into the hot oil and cook over a low heat, adding 3 sprigs of parsley.

When the vegetables are soft, add the fish and the crabs and turn the heat up to its maximum. Add a sprig of thyme, 3 bay leaves, 5 fresh tomatoes, (peeled, seeded, and coarsely chopped), and 100 g (4 oz, ⅓ cup) tomato concentrate. Cook all these ingredients for about 10 minutes, until their juices run. Add the roux, then stir in 1 bottle white wine and finish with 4 litres (7 pints, 9 pints) water. Bring to the boil. Add salt and pepper and cook, covered, over a moderate heat (or in the oven at 180 C, 350 F, gas 4) for 30 minutes.

Then put everything through a vegetable mill or blender. Bring the soup to the boil again and add 24 sea urchins (liquid and corals), 3 dl (½ pint, 1¼ cups) double (heavy) cream, and 100 g (4 oz, ½ cup) shrimp butter. Boil for 5 minutes, then pour the soup through a fine strainer.

sedum SÉDUM

A fleshy plant which grows in dry places, two common species being the wall pepper (*Sedum acre*) and the white stonecrop (*S. album*). The plants used to be eaten as vegetables and were recommended in particular by Olivier de Serres in the 17th century. The Icelanders and Lapps still eat the roots and the Swedes use the stalks in salads.

seelac

The French name for the black pollack (and sometimes also for hake) when it has been salted, smoked, and marinated in oil. It keeps for only a short time (a month and a half in a cool place). The name appears to come from the German *See* (lake) and *Lachs* (salmon).

seize RISSOLER

To cook meat, poultry, or vegetables in hot fat or oil in a sauté pan, frying pan (skillet), or saucepan until the surface is brown. Meat is seized in the preliminary stages of cooking to seal the juices. A roast is sometimes treated in this way before being put into the oven.

Sekt

The name often used for sparkling wines in Germany. The word was first used in the 19th century by the Berlin actor Ludwig Devrient, when ordering sack in the role of Falstaff. As he was also very fond of champagne, he would use the same word to order his favourite drink in the restaurants. After this, German sparkling wines began to be referred to as 'Sekt'.

Selles-sur-Cher

A goats'-milk cheese (45% fat content) made in Sologne and protected by an *appellation d'origine*. A soft white cheese that matures slowly, it has a natural crust dusted with wood charcoal ash and is at its best from May to November. It is firm with a strong smell and a nutty flavour but it is sometimes oversalted. The cheese is shaped like a very flat truncated cone, 8 cm (3 in) at the base, 2.5 cm (1 in) thick.

Seltzer water

EAU DE SELTZ

A naturally sparkling mineral water or water which is charged with carbon dioxide gas under pressure. The name Seltzer is a corruption of Niederselters, a village in West Germany in the Taunus, whose mineral springs have been famous since the 18th century. Seltzer water is an ingredient in the preparation of many cocktails.

semolina SEMOULE

A food obtained by coarsely grinding a cereal, mainly hard (durum) wheat, into granules. White semolina is ground from rice, semolina for polenta from maize (corn), and semolina for kasha from buckwheat. Yellow semolina is made from wheat and coloured with saffron; it resembles cornmeal in appearance.

The grains are first moistened, then ground, dried, and sieved. The nutritional value of semolina (from the Latin *simila*, meaning 'flower of flour') is the same as that of flour. This food is rich in carbohydrates and is both light and nourishing; it is used to make pasta and to prepare soups, garnishes, and various dishes (couscous, tabbouleh, gnocchi, puddings, rings, cakes, custards, soufflés, etc.).

High-grade semolina is made by grinding the wheat kernel, whereas ordinary semolina contains more of the peripheral part of the grain (and therefore a higher percentage of minerals). Fine semolinas are used to make pasta, whereas medium and coarse semolinas are used in soups and desserts. Very fine semolinas are used in baby foods.

RECIPES

Baked semolina pudding SEMOULE POUR ENTREMETS Bring to the boil 1 litre (1¾ pints, 4¼ cups) milk containing 150 g (5 oz, generous cup) sugar, a pinch of salt, and a vanilla pod (bean) split in half. Mix in 250 g (9 oz, 1½ cups) semolina and 75–100 g (3–4 oz, 6–8 tablespoons) butter, then cover the pan and cook in a moderately hot oven (200 c, 400 f, gas 6) for 25–30 minutes.

Semolina subrics SUBRICS DE SEMOULE Prepare a baked semolina pudding as in the previous recipe, remove from the oven, and mix in 6 egg yolks. Leave to cool a little, then spread it in a layer 2 cm (¾ in) thick over a buttered baking sheet. Brush the surface with melted butter to prevent a crust forming and leave to cool completely. Cut out rings with a diameter of 6 cm (2½ in) with a pastry (cookie) cutter and brown them in a frying pan (skillet) in clarified butter. Arrange them in a ring in a round dish and fill the centre with redcurrant jelly or with another red jelly or jam.

Senderens (Alain)

French chef (born 1939). A native of southwestern France, he went to Paris at the age of 21, after his apprenticeship in Lourdes. He progressed from pantry-keeper to head roasting chef at the Tour d'Argent, then joined Marc Soustelle's staff at Lucas-Carton as sauce cook; after serving as head fish chef at the Berkeley, he became assistant chef at the newly opened Orly Hilton. In 1973 he opened his own restaurant in Paris, in the Rue de l'Exposition (later moved to the Rue de Varenne); he named it L'Ar-

chestrate, in honour of the ancient Greek poet and gourmet Archestratus.

Well read in gastronomy, Senderens has created imaginative new dishes using 'thousands of combinations and mixtures which have not yet been tried'. He combines ingredients, flavours, and cooking methods, creating some of the most original recipes: salads of crayfish with mango, duck, and basil or of warm calves' sweetbreads with raw cep mushrooms; veal ribs (chops) with tea and cucumber; turbot with broad (fava) beans; magrets of duck with honey and thyme blossom; hot guava charlotte with kiwi-fruit sauce; millefeuille with medlars; melon fritters with strawberry sauce; etc. However, he has also been inspired by ancient recipes to create such dishes as hare quenelles, eel broth, hot oysters with leeks, and leg of mutton.

serdeau

An officer of the king's household in France, who disposed of the leftover food cleared away by the maître d'hôtel. The term was also used for the place where the leftovers were sold. At the French court, it was the custom to keep food ready for those whose duty or business called them to the king; dishes cleared from the royal table were taken to a special room for this purpose. When the custom of serving food to the king's guests was abandoned, the king's leftovers were taken straight to the serdeau and sold by auction. This practice was still in existence during the reign of Louis XVI, and many households were provisioned in this way. The servants of the serdeau traded from the *baraques du serdeau*, next to the barracks of the French Guards at Versailles.

Serge (à la)

Describes a dish of calves' sweetbreads or veal escalopes coated with a mixture of fresh breadcrumbs, truffles, and chopped mushrooms, then fried, and garnished with small artichoke quarters stewed in butter and a coarse julienne of ham warmed in Madeira. The sauce is a demiglace flavoured with truffle essence.

serrer

A French culinary term that means to

finish whisking egg whites with a quick circular movement of the whisk, making them very stiff and homogeneous.

A sauce is described as *serrée* when its consistency is thick enough (e.g. béchamel sauce to be used for binding salpicons, etc.) or when it is reduced to make it creamier and increase its flavour.

Serres (Olivier de)

French agronomist (born Villeneuve-de-Berg, 1539; died Villeneuve-de-Berg, 1619). He studied at the university of Valence, then at Lausanne (where his Calvinist convictions had forced him to take refuge). His estate at Pradel, near Privas, became a model farm, where he was the first to grow plants and cereals on a rationalized economic basis. He introduced maize (corn), sugar beet, hops, and rice into France and also experimented with madder and silkworms. Encouraged by Sully, he also gained the support of the king, Henri IV, to whom he suggested the recipe for *poule au pot*.

In order to revive domestic gardening and animal husbandry, he published *Théâtre d'agriculture et mesnage des champs* (1600), which popularized agronomy and was highly successful (19 successive editions during the 17th century). The book offered a detailed and comprehensive study of rural farming methods and country life, covering grapes, cereals, winter stores, hunting and fishing, poultry, kitchen gardens, and even bread-making; in addition, it provided information on the culinary uses and gastronomic qualities of animal and vegetable foodstuffs, described (for the first time) the tuber that was later to be called the potato, and mentioned a process for the extraction of sweet juice from sugar beet. Serres also advocated the introduction of American poultry, such as the turkey, into France and gave a number of recipes for jam and for 'everything that can be made with wheat flour alone: biscuits, brassadeaux, cache-museaux, échaudés, fougasses, macaroons, oublies, popelins, and tourtillons'. His dictum was:

'Provision faite en saison
Et gouvernée par la raison
Fait devenir bonne la maison.'
('A thriving household depends on the

use of seasonal produce and the application of common sense.')

servery OFFICE

A room in a restaurant, etc., generally adjoining the kitchen, where all the items of table service are kept, and where certain dishes are prepared. Wines are also placed there to reach room temperature.

In classic French cuisine, the word *office* was used for the branch of the culinary art that involved, according to Carême, 'the preparation and making of all the delightful delicacies that are offered as dessert at the tables of the wealthy'. Hors d'oeuvres and salads are also prepared in the *office*.

service

Originally, the group of dishes comprising each part of a meal. There were at least three services. The term also indicated the manner in which they were presented to the guests. Service *à la française* lasted until the end of the Second Empire, when it was replaced by service *à la russe*, which is still used today.

□ Service à la française This was a continuation of the ceremony of the *grand couvert* observed during the reign of Louis XIV. As it was so costly, it was practised only by grand houses on important occasions. A meal served *à la française* was divided into three parts: the first service covered the menu from the soup to the roasts, including the hors d'oeuvre and entrées; the second from the roasts, cold second roasts, and vegetables to the sweet dishes; and the third consisted of pastries, set pieces, petit fours, sweets, ices, and fruit. The order of the menu depended on the number of entrées; the number of dishes in the first service had to be equal to that of the second service. The dishes of the first service were arranged on the table (on hotplates or under covers, if necessary) before the arrival of the guests. A dazzling display of silverware, candelabra, glasses, and flowers completed the effect.

The arrangement and order of the dishes on the table was very important. The service of a dinner for six to eight, for example, consisted of 'a main dish, two medium dishes, and four smaller dishes' (from Massialot's *Le Cuisinier royal et bourgeois*, 1691). The first service comprised: at the centre, a piece of beef garnished with small pies and sweetbreads; two soups arranged symmetrically on each side (pigeon bisque and capon soup with lettuce and asparagus tips); four other entrées arranged two by two (spit-roasted chicken and fillet steaks with lettuce on one side, hot rabbit pâté and goslings with asparagus tips on the other). During the second service three roast dishes were arranged along the centre of the table: two chickens, two hares, and eight pigeons, with two salads and two sauces in separate dishes on either side. The centrepiece of the third service was a spit-roasted ham with a cream tart and a dish of choux pastries placed at each end; a ham loaf and skewered sweetbreads on the left faced a ragout of mushrooms and asparagus on the right. Fruit was served with the dessert.

This service has often been criticized for sacrificing everything to ostentation and extravagance; the guests' appetites were not assuaged as they could not enjoy the food hot, in spite of the hotplates and covers which appeared in the 18th century. In fact, the dishes did not remain long on the table; Massialot specified that they should be left only for a quarter of an hour or a little longer. Also, as all the food was placed on the table, the guests could serve themselves immediately without having to wait for dishes to be passed. Why was it thought that so many different dishes should be offered at each service? *L'Art de bien traiter* (1674) suggests an answer: 'Many people reject and condemn good things for which they have never developed a taste . . . it is therefore necessary to provide a choice'. The former service *à la française*, which depended on a large and experienced staff (if only to avoid wasting the leftovers, some of which were often reusable), treated the guests with courtesy by offering a variety of dishes.

Horace Raisson's *Code gourmand* (1829) is a good illustration of the latter days of the service *à la française*:
'*Article one* – A grand dinner is composed of four services. The first should be the most substantial, as the appetite is sharpest; it comprises relevés and en-

trées. The roasts, escorted by salads and complementary vegetables, appear next. The third service consists of dishes hot from the oven arranged around an impressive cold dish. A dessert to delight the pretty ladies' eyes comes later.
Art. 2 – The hors d'oeuvres remain on the table until the third service, to whet the appetite.
Art. 3 – After each act of this gastronomic drama the table should be bare, but only for a moment, until the new dishes of the next service make their entrance.
Art. 4 – If it is impossible for the host to serve all the dishes himself and look after each guest individually, he should place carefully those of his friends on whose goodwill he can count.
Art. 5 – Dishes which do not require carving and which can be served with a spoon are available to all; each guest can serve himself and pass the dish on to whoever asks for it.
Art. 6 – The servants retire after the savoury courses. During the dessert each guest serves himself with whatever takes his fancy, asking his neighbour to pass him dishes that are out of reach.
Art. 7 – Jams, compotes, and ice creams are the only dishes that require a spoon (which should be gilded). Other dishes are served by hand.
Art. 8 – Ordinary wines are placed in orderly profusion along the table, but the host should pour the choice wines for his neighbours and then circulate the bottle until empty.'

☐ **Service à la russe** It was Prince Alexander Borisovitch Kourakine, the tsar's ambassador to Paris during the Second Empire, who introduced service *à la russe* into high society, from where it spread throughout the catering world. For the grand dinners he gave at the embassy he launched a new form of service, which Urbain Dubois popularized around 1880 and introduced to middle-class homes. It was characterized by less formality, less ostentation, and fewer displays of silverware; flowers and pyramids of fruit were used in their place as table decorations. The aim was to eat hot dishes as hot as possible; instead of leaving guests to choose from a variety of dishes, the order was arranged in advance and the dishes presented one after the other. Luxury and extravagance were replaced by the principle that everything should proceed as quickly as possible, so that dishes would not lose their flavour. The presentation and appearance of the food, however, remained important (especially for cold dishes, aspics, chilled chicken, etc.). It was easier to serve dishes hot, as a set time for the meal allowed the chef to calculate cooking times accordingly. In service *à la russe* the guests are divided into groups of 8, 10, or 12, each of which is served by a maître d'hôtel who is instructed in advance which guests to serve first. Dishes are served from the left of a seated person and the plates are taken away or put down from the right. The wine is served from the right in the same order as the food, but the first drops are poured into the host's glass. In a less formal meal, the master of the house carves and serves the meat himself and passes the filled plates round the table, beginning with the person on his right.

□ Catering services In catering there are four types of service which are rarely, if ever, undertaken in private households. In the 'simple' service the food is placed directly on the plates or the dishes are placed on the table (service *à l'assiette* is becoming increasingly popular, without losing the sense of occasion). In service *à la française* each guest serves himself from a dish with serving spoons. In service *à l'anglaise* the waiter places the food on the diner's plate. Finally, in service *à la russe*, also known as *à l'anglaise avec guéridon* or *au guéridon*, the dish is first offered for the guests' admiration and then the food is placed on the plates at a pedestal table (*guéridon*) beside the dining table.

Modern forms of catering permit meals to be served quickly. At snack bars the customer is served seated or, on the Continent, standing at the counter with the food he ordered already on the plate. In a self-service restaurant, he chooses from dishes on display and carries them on a tray to his place; in a semi-self-service system he helps himself to cold dishes (hors d'oeuvres, cheese, dessert, and drinks) while hot dishes are served to him on request. These methods are often used in canteens, airports, and stations and also in certain specialized establishments and the restaurants of large shops.

serviette (à la)

This describes a way of serving certain foods, particularly truffles. Truffles *à la serviette* are poached, then arranged in a timbale mould or a casserole which is placed on a napkin folded into the shape of a pocket. If they have been cooked *en papillote* in hot ashes, they are placed directly onto the napkin. Potatoes baked in their skins can also be served *à la serviette*, as can boiled asparagus, which is arranged without dressing on a white folded napkin.

Rice *à la serviette* is a dish of rice which is cooked in simmering salted water, drained, rinsed under the cold tap, and wrapped in a napkin to dry out in a cool oven.

Ham and duck liver wrapped in a cloth and tied with string are known as *à la serviette*, but should more correctly be called *au torchon*.

serving dish   PLAT

A kitchen or serving utensil that comes in a wide range of sizes and shapes – flat, oval, round, square, or rectangular – and can have raised, straight, or flared edges. Serving dishes are made of a wide variety of materials, including earthenware, china, porcelain, glass, stainless steel, aluminium, cast iron, silvered metal, and even solid silver or silver-gilt. Some are oven-to-table ware.

In the 15th century, gold serving dishes were used in the homes of the nobility, and silver in the homes of the lesser nobility, and wealthy middle class. Hammered out of a single metal sheet, the dishes were referred to as 'plate', as opposed to items assembled from several pieces. This class distinction disappeared with the coming of china and porcelain from the 18th century onwards.

Flat serving dishes, with or without raised rims, include the hors-d'oeuvre dish (often divided into compartments), radish dish, fish dish (very long and oval), roasting dish (large enough to take the garnish as well), and pie or flan dish (shaped according to function). Rounded and deeper dishes, which may have lids, include the vegetable dish, soup bowl, salad bowl, ragout dish, and compote dish. Modern oven-to-table ware includes a wide range of dishes used both for cooking and serving the food.

The word 'dish' is also used for individual preparations served during a meal. The main dish (*plat principal*, or *plat de résistance*) is the most substantial, richest, or most elaborate dish and usually consists of meat, poultry, game, or fish, served with a garnish. The rest of the menu is determined by this dish. Sometimes the meal may consist of only a single dish, possibly a regional speciality, such as sauerkraut garni, aïoli, or couscous. In the restaurant trade, the *plat du jour* (dish of the day) is suggested by the chef as the main dish, his decision depending on supplies, the season, and his personal choice; in theory, it should be different for each day of the week (see *menu*).

sesame   SÉSAME

An annual plant grown in hot countries for its seeds, from which an odourless light-coloured oil is extracted. Sesame oil is highly valued in the Middle and Far East for its sweet flavour, which resembles that of hempseed oil, and because it keeps well without turning rancid. Large amounts are used in Chinese, Japanese, and Arab cookery as a cooking oil or, more often, as a condiment or seasoning, although it loses its flavour quite quickly.

In the Middle East sesame seeds are used in halva (ground with sugar and almonds) and in *tahin* (or *tahina*). This condiment consists of a paste of ground seeds and lemon juice; pepper, garlic, and spices are often added. It is served with salads, crudités, and grilled (broiled) meats and is used to season dried beans and peas, dumplings, and poultry broths. Tahina is also used in Greece and the Lebanon to make the condiment hummus, with chickpeas.

In Africa and Asia the seeds are called *ajonjoli*; they are reddish or yellowish and are eaten roasted like peanuts. Their flour is used for pancakes. A syrupy nourishing drink is made from the seeds in China; they are also used to make biscuits (cookies) with sugar and lard. In Japan the grilled seeds are used in a number of sauces and condiments.

sétoise (à la)

Describing a dish of monkfish, a fish much used in Sète cookery (usually in bourride). The fish is cooked briskly with a julienne of vegetables stewed in olive oil and white wine; it is then drained and coated in a thick mayonnaise mixed with the reduced cooking juices.

Sévigné (Marie de Rabutin-Chantal, Marquise de)

Parisian woman of letters (born Paris, 1626; died Grignan, 1696). In letters written to her daughter, Mme de Grignan, she gave detailed accounts of meals enjoyed and culinary or gastronomic novelties, especially the first new peas of spring, chocolate, Amiens duck pâté, etc. During her travels she described regional specialities (melons, figs, and Muscat grapes from Grignan; poulardes from Rennes; fruit pâté from Apt, a town she called a 'cauldron of jams'; and calissons from Aix, sent to her by her daughter) as well as good stopping places, such as the Auberge du Dauphin at Saulieu, and M. de Chaulnes' table at Vitré: 'There is an excess of good food, whose roasts are returned to the kitchen, and the pyramids of fruit are so high that the doorways have to be raised.' In her letter of 24 April 1671 she even mentions the death of the 'great Vatel' (a famous Swiss maître d'hôtel).

A dish of soft-boiled or poached eggs on a bed of braised lettuce, covered with suprême sauce and topped with a slice of truffle, was dedicated to her.

Seville (bitter) orange

BIGARADE

A bitter orange with rough peel, mostly used for making marmalade, jams, and jellies. Seville orange trees are cultivated on a local scale in the south of France, where crystallized (candied) Seville oranges (*chinois confit*) are a speciality of Nice. The flower of the Seville orange is used in the preparation of orange-flower water. The aromatic oil extracted from the thick peel of Seville oranges is used in distilling to flavour Curaçao, Cointreau, and Grand Marnier. A traditional dish is pot-roast duck in bitter orange sauce (not to be confused with duck *à l'orange*).

RECIPES

Bitter orange sauce SAUCE BIGAR-ADE (from a recipe by Carême) Peel the zest of a Seville orange in strips running from top to bottom, ensuring that it is very thin: any pith left on it would make it bitter. Cut each strip into small pieces and place in a little boiling water. Allow to boil for a few minutes, then drain and put in a pan with some espagnole sauce, a little game extract, a pinch of coarsely ground pepper, and the juice of half a Seville orange. Boil for a few moments then add a little good-quality butter.

Brown bitter orange sauce for roast duck SAUCE BRUNE À LA BIGARADE POUR CANETON POÊLÉ OU RÔTI Cut the zest of a Seville (bitter) orange (or a sweet orange) and half a lemon into thin strips; blanch, cool, and drain. Heat 20 g (¾ oz, 2 tablespoons) granulated sugar and 1 tablespoon good wine vinegar in a saucepan until it forms a pale caramel. Add 2 dl (7 fl oz, ¾ cup) brown veal stock (or well-reduced bouillon) and boil vigorously for 5 minutes. Add the juice of the orange and a dash of lemon juice. Strain and add the blanched zest. The sauce can be flavoured with a small amount of Curaçao added just before serving.

Seville orange jelly GELÉE DE BIGAR-ADE (from a recipe by Carême) Peel the zest from 2 sound Seville oranges as thinly as possible, then squeeze the juice of 5 lemons onto the zest and strain the juice through a sieve. Mix with 420 g (14 oz, 2 cups) sugar and 45 g (1½ oz) clarified gelatine. Finish the jelly and mould in the usual manner. Set over ice.

White bitter orange sauce for roast duck SAUCE BIGARADE À BLANC POUR CANETON POÊLÉ OU RÔTI Deglaze the dish in which the duck has been cooked with a glass of dry white wine. Cut the zest of a seville orange (or an ordinary orange) and half a lemon into thin strips; blanch, cool, and drain. When the sauce has almost completely reduced, add 1.5 dl (¼ pint, ¾ cup) white consommé or stock and boil for 5 minutes. Thicken with 1 teaspoon cornflour or arrowroot mixed with 2 tablespoons (3 tablespoons) cold water. Add the juice of the orange and a dash of lemon juice. Strain, add the blanched zest, and adjust the seasoning.

Seyssel

AOC white wines of Savoy, from the two communes of Seysell, one of which is in the Ain and the other in Haute-Savoie, on either side of the River Rhône. It is made from the Altesse (or Roussette) grape, but sparkling Seyssel, locally known as Bon-Blanc, is made from the Molette and the Chasselas grapes. Dry and light, the wines are not often seen on export lists but are worth trying in the region.

shad ALOSE

A migratory fish that lives in the sea and travels up rivers in the spring to spawn. A large shad can measure up to 60 cm (2 ft). Its flesh is very fine and quite rich, but quickly deteriorates and is full of bones. At Bordeaux it is eaten grilled (broiled); in Nantes it is cooked with sorrel, but it may also be stuffed or fried as steaks. It was popular with the Romans and frequently appeared in recipes in the Middle Ages.

The *alose finte*, a smaller shad, is mainly used in soup. It does not migrate very far up the rivers and is caught mainly in estuaries and in the sea. A freshwater variety lives in the Italian lakes, and is popular locally.

RECIPES

Preparation of shad PRÉPARATION DE L'ALOSE Carefully scale and gut (clean) the shad, keeping the roe. Using plenty of cold water, wash the fish well on the outside to remove the remains of the scales, and on the inside to wash away the blood. Dry it with absorbent paper.

Fried shad ALOSE FRITE Cut the fish into slices and soak in milk. Coat them with flour and plunge into hot fat. Fry fish until golden, then drain and arrange on a napkin with fried parsley and lemon quarters.

Grilled (broiled) shad with sorrel ALOSE GRILLÉE À L'OSEILLE Gut (clean), scale, wash, and dry a medium-sized shad (about 1 kg, 2 lb). Make regular slits in the fleshy part of the back and both sides. Season with salt and pepper and marinate for an hour in oil, with a little lemon juice, chopped parsley, thyme, and a bay leaf. Drain the fish, grill (broil) under a medium heat for 30 minutes or until tender, then arrange the fish on a long dish, surrounded by lemon quarters or slices. Serve with maître d'hôtel butter and a garnish of lightly braised sorrel.

Shad au plat   ALOSE AU PLAT Choose a shad weighing 700–800 g (1½–1¾ lb). Gut (clean) the fish and fill the cavity with a mixture of 50 g (2 oz, 4 tablespoons) butter kneaded with 1 tablespoon chopped parsley, ½ tablespoon chopped shallot, salt, and pepper. Place the shad on a long buttered ovenproof dish. Season with salt and pepper, sprinkle over 1 dl (6 tablespoons, scant ½ cup) dry white wine, dot with small pieces of butter, and cook in a preheated oven (about 200 c, 400 f, gas 6) for 15–20 minutes. Baste frequently during cooking. If the liquid reduces too quickly, add a little water. Serve on the cooking dish.

Shad may also be cooked *à la provençale* and *à la bonne femme*.

shaggy cap
COPRIN CHEVELU
An edible mushroom with a cap that bends downwards and is covered with shaggy hairs. It should be picked when young and eaten soon afterwards, since the flesh is extremely delicate (it quickly becomes black and liquifies). It may be eaten raw with salt or sautéed in oil or butter with a touch of garlic.

shaker
A stainless steel or silver-plated utensil shaped like a tall goblet, slightly wider at the top, with a closely fitting lid, in which the ingredients for a cocktail are mixed by shaking them with ice. Small models contain 50 cl (17 fl oz, 1 pint), large ones 1 litre (1¾ pints, 2 pints). A shaker is especially recommended for cocktails based on cream or a syrupy liqueur or those containing egg, milk, or fruit juice.

shallot   ÉCHALOTE
A vegetable related to the onion whose name is derived from Ascalon, an ancient Palestine port, suggesting that the plant originated in the Middle East. It was already being grown in France at the time of the Carolingians (751–987 AD). The flavour of the shallot is more subtle than that of onion and less harsh than that of garlic. Varieties include grey shallots, with a small bulb and a pronounced but fine flavour; Jersey shallots, round and red and akin to the onion; pear shallots, with a large elongated bulb; and Simiane shallots, grown in the south of France, with a large bulb (these last two varieties being milder than the others).

The shallot was and still is the traditional condiment of Bordeaux cookery. Its use reached as far as Nantes, spread along the Normandy coast, and was then adopted by Parisian cuisine. Finely chopped shallot bulbs are served with salads and crudités (raw vegetable hors d'oeuvres) and with fish and grilled (broiled) or fried meats (such as red mullet and lamb's liver). Shallots are especially used to flavour sauces (Bercy, béarnaise, red wine, and white butter sauce in particular) as well as vinegar (one head of shallot is steeped for two weeks in wine vinegar) and flavoured butters. Young shallot leaves, finely chopped, can also be added to salads.

When wrapped in a cloth, put under cold water, and then pressed, the shallot loses some of its pungency. As with onion and garlic, it is unwise to keep shallots in the refrigerator, as other foods may be pervaded by the smell. As well as being in standard use in French cookery, shallots are frequently used in Vietnamese, Chinese, Indian, and Creole cookery.

RECIPES

Shallot sauce   SAUCE ÉCHALOTE Peel some shallots and chop them very finely. Add to a good wine vinegar and season with salt and pepper. This sauce is traditionally served with oysters or raw mussels.

shandy   PANACHÉ
A mixture of two drinks in almost equal quantities. The French term can mean a

mixture of coffee and alcohol, but the English term is usually used to describe a mixture of draught beer and lemonade or ginger beer.

shark REQUIN

A cartilaginous fish with an elongated body, a pointed snout, and a broad mouth. There are numerous species, ranging in size from the small dogfish (currently eaten in France) to the gigantic whale shark, which can reach a length of 18 m (60 ft). West Indians use shark meat in soups and stews, while the fins are an ingredient of a famous Chinese soup. Europeans prefer the smaller dogfish, such as the smooth hound, the tope, and the spur dogfish, sold with head and skin removed; they are prepared and cooked like rock salmon, cod, or other large fish.

RECIPE

Touffé of shark à la créole TOUFFÉ DE REQUIN À LA CRÉOLE Slice the flesh of a small shark and marinate it for several hours in the juice of 2 limes diluted with water, garlic, salt, pepper, and 1 chilli pepper. Slice 2 onions and 4–5 shallots and wash 3 tomatoes; brown all these in a saucepan along with 2 chilli peppers, 3 cloves of garlic, and a bouquet garni. Drain the fish pieces, place them on top of the vegetables, and cook with the pan covered. To serve, sprinkle with lime juice, chopped parsley, and a little grated garlic. Accompany with rice *à la créole* and red kidney beans.

shark's fins

AILERONS DE REQUIN

Fins and cartilaginous terminal segments of the tail of the dogfish (a small shark), sold dried as long yellowish-white needles. This rare and costly product, reputed to be an aphrodisiac, is made into a famous Chinese soup, traditionally served to the mandarins at their banquets. The best shark's fins come from the Philippines and China.

The fins must be soaked overnight in chicken stock, then boiled for about 3 hours. The soup is made from shrimps, sweet-smelling mushrooms, ginger, onions, and soy sauce and is garnished with the shark's fins, along with sliced ham, crabmeat, and very thin slices of bamboo.

shashlyk CHACHLIK

A Russian dish, originating from Georgia, made of skewered raw mutton taken from a well-hung leg, cut into cubes, and marinated in vinaigrette flavoured with thyme, nutmeg, bay leaf, and onions. The skewers of meat are grilled, then served with rice moistened with melted butter. Raw ham and onion rings may be inserted between the cubes of meat.

shea KARITÉ

A tree from tropical Africa with oval fruit containing oily seeds. When the seeds are dried and crushed they yield a white butter-like fat rich in calcium and vitamins, called shea butter. This is used instead of cooking fat in certain African countries. It can also be used to make soap and candles.

shelduck TADORNE

A large duck resembling a goose in shape. This and a closely related species, the ruddy shelduck, are now protected by law. Formerly, they were prepared like wild duck and usually regarded as Lenten fare. Their flesh has a pronounced fishy taste, since they eat shellfish and roe.

shellfish

Invertebrate aquatic animals with a shell or carapace that are used in cookery. There are two main classes of shellfish: crustaceans and molluscs.

□ Crustaceans These are arthropods and most of them are marine. The marine crustaceans include lobsters, langoustes (spiny lobsters), crabs, and shrimps; the only freshwater crustacean used in cookery is the crayfish. Crustaceans must be bought very fresh and are best bought live if one is to prepare them oneself. If buying ready-cooked, go to a good fishmonger. Crustaceans are also available frozen and canned. The heaviest crabs and lobsters are the best; they should still have their claws on.

Crustaceans can be prepared and cooked *à l'américaine*, as bisque soup, fried, poached in court-bouillon, or grilled (broiled), depending on the species. They are also served in cold hors d'oeuvres: the large ones are shelled (legs, claws, and trunks); the small ones are left whole or served in the form of tails by themselves, shelled.

☐ **Molluscs** These are either bivalves (clams, cockles, mussels, oysters, scallops, etc.) or gastropods (winkles, whelks, ormers, limpets, etc.). Unless they are bought where they are caught, only shellfish which come from reputable areas and are subject to some sort of quality control should be used.

Only molluscs with closed shells or which close on touching should be retained. Molluscs which are cooked in their shells and which remain closed after cooking should not be eaten. Similarly, only live gastropods, with a healthy smell of the sea, should be consumed.

See also *seafood*.

sherry XÉRÈS

The best-known fortified wine of Spain, which gets its name from the town of Jerez de la Frontera, in Andalucia. In the UK, wines of the sherry type originating from other areas or countries must have this clearly indicated on their labels: they are not strictly sherry, even though they may be perfectly good wines.

The vineyards are delimited and those producing the finest wines are usually situated on the gleaming white *albariza* soil. The main sherry grape is the Palomino, also known as the Listan, but for the great sweet sherries, the Pedro Ximenez grape is also used.

The wine is started in the same way as other wines and undergoes a vigorous fermentation, after which it goes into the *bodegas* (wine stores) of the shippers. At this stage all sherry is a completely dry wine, fully fermented so that the sugar in the original must is transformed into alcohol by the yeasts. The rather complex procedure whereby it is fortified with brandy and matured takes place in the *bodegas* and is known as the *solera* system. This varies from firm to firm, but essentially consists of a series of casks graded by age. When a consignment of sherry is required, wines are drawn off from the casks according to age and character and then blended. The arrangement and proportions in which the wines are drawn off and the

casks refreshed from other wines is both complex and individual to the particular sherry house concerned. The name *solera* is given to both the process and the casks. Very good sherries may be made by blending various wines, but a straight solera sherry will be the result of wines proceeding through a single solera and some of these are famous.

In the early stages, the various sherries are categorized according to whether or not they will develop *flor* (Spanish for 'flower'), a bacterial growth on the surface of the wine in cask that affects its character and style of maturation. Those that develop flor are the finos, those that do not are the olorosos. From this time onwards, the different sherries progress through the solera at varying rates, sometimes skipping a stage, sometimes going steadily from one cask to another. It is not always the case that, in the rows of high-piled casks in a bodega, the ones on the top row are gradually decanted off to the row beneath until they get to the bottom Nor is it necessarily true that the dates on the sherry butts or huge casks in a bodega refer to the age of the wine inside: they usually refer to the year when the solera or the particular cask was first laid down.

Sherry of all types is completely dry when first made: the sweetening takes place later to suit the various demands of the markets. Thus, although a fino will normally be dry, the fino of certain establishments may quite legally receive some sweetening to suit their customers. Similarly, oloroso is a naturally dry sherry that is slightly or definitely sweetened if required. A matured fino will turn into an amontillado; this does not necessarily mean it becomes sweeter, but merely older. Certain popular sherries may be made up from a blend of different wines (not from the wines of a single solera), which can make them more appealing to many people and slightly cheaper. Manzanilla is the sherry matured at Sanlúcar de Barrameda on the coast. Both manzanilla and fino are at their most enjoyable when young, fresh, and crisp, but the sweeter wines can sometimes gain enormous charm by ageing in the bottle. Sweet sherries described as 'cream' or 'milk' are hardly known in Spain: they were evolved for the northern markets where sweetness, in the colder climates, is still enjoyed. They can be superb wines, also capable of gaining quality with age.

Although all sherry is fortified by the addition of brandy, there are considerable variations in strength, so that in the sherry-producing region, people may be offered a *vino de pasto* or wine with a meal that is really sherry but in which the fortification is so slight that it can easily be drunk throughout a meal. For shipping abroad, a slightly higher fortification may be necessary to protect the wine from harm when it undergoes changes in temperature.

Although the production of sherry is strictly controlled, each establishment makes sherries according to its own standards and to the taste of its customers. Thus, one firm's fino may be a very dry wine, and another's may be sweetened up to the legal limits. One firm's brand of amontillado may indeed be a matured fino, whilst another's cheaper version may be made by blending in various other sherries. So the term dry sherry is very broad, depending on the establishment and certainly on how much is paid for the wine! This also applies to medium sherry, which can be a magnificent amontillado, or an agreeable but inexpensive version of this category. Very light delicate fino sherry should be lightly chilled and will cease to be at its best if the bottle is not finished within a day or two of opening. The sweeter wines should be drunk within a week or ten days. The remains of any bottle can be used up in cooking. Always serve sherry in a goblet or *copita* glass, shaped like an elongated tulip, and never fill this to the brim – sherry has a bouquet that deserves to be appreciated.

RECIPE

Chicken with sherry POULET AU XÉRÈS Cut a 1.2-kg (2¾-lb) chicken into quarters. Slightly brown 50 g (2 oz, 4 tablespoons) butter in a flameproof casserole and thoroughly brown the chicken pieces in it. Season with salt and pepper, cover, and cook for about 35 minutes, adding 1 finely chopped shallot 10 minutes before the end of cooking. Remove the chicken pieces and

keep hot on a serving dish. Blend 1 teaspoon arrowroot with 1.5 dl (¼ pint, ⅔ cup) medium sherry. Pour this mixture into the casserole and stir well while heating. Add a dash of cayenne, then pour the sauce over the chicken pieces.

shortbread

A biscuit (cookie), rich in butter, which is served with tea and is traditionally eaten at Christmas and New Year. Originating from Scotland and traditionally made with oatmeal, it is now made with wheat flour; for special occasions it is decorated with candied lemon or orange peel or flaked (slivered) almonds. In the Shetland Isles it is flavoured with cumin. Shortbread is usually baked in a large round and served cut from the centre into triangles; it is a relic of the ancient New Year cakes that were symbols of the sun.

shoulder ÉPAULE

The part of the body to which the front leg is attached. In butchery, shoulder of beef yields cuts for braising or boiling, and blade or shin (shank) is especially suitable for the stockpot. Shoulder of veal gives cuts for braising, frying, roasting, stewing (fricandeau, veal blanquette), and even for escalopes, but it can also be cooked whole, after boning and stuffing, rolled into a ballottine, and braised or roasted. Shoulder of mutton or lamb yields pieces for stewing, navarins, braising, or kebabs; it can also be cooked whole (boned or unboned) – studded with garlic, roasted, grilled (broiled), braised, or rolled up and stuffed. Shoulder of venison can be treated like haunch, but it is usually stewed.

RECIPES

LAMB

Braised shoulder of lamb with garnish ÉPAULE BRAISÉE ET SES GARNITURES Bone a shoulder of lamb, trim it, season with salt and pepper, roll it up, and tie with string. Crush the bones and brown them in butter with the trimmings. Trim the fat off some pork rind and line a braising pan with the rind. Peel and finely slice 2 carrots and 1 onion, cook in butter for 10 minutes, then add to the braising pan. Put the shoulder in the braising pan and season with salt and pepper. Add 1.5 dl (¼ pint, ⅔ cup) white wine and reduce. Add 2.5 dl (8 fl oz, 1 cup) thickened gravy (or reduced consommé – in this case add half a calf's foot to the bones and trimmings), 1 dl (5 tablespoons, scant ½ cup) tomato purée, a bouquet garni, and the bones and trimmings. Cover and cook in a hot oven (220 C, 425 F, gas 7) for about 1–1½ hours, depending on the size of the joint. Drain it, glaze in the oven, then arrange it on a serving dish.

The usual garnish consists of green or white haricot (navy) beans, vegetable purées, artichoke hearts, or haricot bean purée *à la bretonne*. It can also be served with mushrooms *à la bordelaise*, together with cooking juices deglazed with red wine and demi-glace and flavoured with shallot, thyme, and bay leaf.

Grilled (broiled) shoulder of lamb ÉPAULE D'AGNEAU DE LAIT GRIL-LÉE Trim the bone, make incisions in the flesh on both sides, brush with melted butter or oil, and grill (broil) under a medium heat for 20–25 minutes. Sprinkle with breadcrumbs and melted butter and brown under the grill (broiler). Garnish with bunches of watercress.

Roast shoulder of lamb en ballottine ÉPAULE RÔTIE EN BALLOTTINE Bone the shoulder of lamb and season with salt and pepper; insert small pieces of garlic, if desired, then roll it up as for a ballottine and tie with string. Roast, either in a dish or on a spit, in a very hot oven (240 C, 475 F, gas 9). The skin should be crisp and the centre pink. Remove the string and serve with just the cooking juices.

Stuffed shoulder of lamb à la gas-conne ÉPAULE FARCIE À LA GAS-CONNE Bone a shoulder of lamb and season it with salt and pepper. Soak 4 slices of bread in some milk. Chop up 3 or 4 slices of raw ham, 1 or 2 onions, 2 or 3 cloves of garlic, and a small bunch of parsley. Squeeze the bread and add to this mixture, along with an egg and

some salt and pepper. Mix well and spread it over the meat. Roll up the shoulder, tie with string as for a ballot-tine, and place in a roasting tin (pan). Brush with 1 tablespoon goose fat and brown quickly in a very hot oven (240 C, 475 F, gas 9).

Scald about 750 g (1¾ lb) green cabbage, cool in cold water, and squeeze dry. Peel and dice 2 carrots; peel 1 onion and stick it with cloves. Transfer the joint to a braising dish, add the cabbage, the diced carrots, the onion, and a bouquet garni, then half-cover the shoulder with stock (do not skim the fat off first). Cover and cook in a moderate oven (190 C, 375 F, gas 5) for 45 minutes. Then add 750 g (1¾ lb) peeled potatoes cut into quarters, or small whole potatoes, and cook for a further 20–25 minutes. Remove the onion and bouquet garni before serving.

MUTTON

Shoulder of mutton with various garnishes ÉPAULE DE MOUTON ET SES GARNITURES Whether whole or boned, roast or braised shoulder of mutton can be prepared and garnished in various ways:

■ *à la boulangère* (with potatoes and onions);

■ *à la bourgeoise* (boned and stuffed, with glazed carrots, baby onions, and diced blanched bacon);

■ *à la bourguignonne* (boned, stuffed, and braised in red wine with mushrooms, onions, and diced bacon);

■ *à la bretonne* (braised, with white haricot (navy) or flageolet beans);

■ *à la flamande* (braised, *en ballottine*, with red cabbage);

■ with chipolatas;

■ with turnips (braised, with hollowed-out turnips and baby onions);

■ with rice (boned, rolled up, and braised, served with boiled rice).

VEAL

Stuffed shoulder of veal ÉPAULE DE VEAU FARCIE Bone a shoulder of veal weighing about 1.5 kg (3¼ lb), flatten it out carefully, then season it with salt and pepper. Mix 450 g (1 lb) fine sausagemeat with 200 g (7 oz) mushrooms, 1 clove of garlic, and some herbs (all chopped) and season with salt and pepper. Cover the meat with this stuffing, roll it up, and tie. Braise as for shoulder of lamb. Cook until the juices are clear when the meat is pricked. Remove and drain the meat and untie. Reduce the cooking juices, strain, and pour over the joint. Glaze the joint in a very hot oven, then arrange on a serving dish and pour more juice over it. Serve the rest of the cooking juices in a sauceboat. Aubergines (eggplants) fried in oil or glazed vegetables (carrots, turnips, or onions) make an ideal garnish.

shrimp net   BALANCE

A small hanging net used for catching shrimp and crayfish.

shrimps and prawns
CREVETTES

Small shellfish that live in fresh and salt water and are commercially important as food. (The French term is the Picardy form of the word *chevrette* (a kid), an allusion to their bounding movements in the water.)

There are numerous species of edible shrimps and prawns. Those living in hot tropical waters carry their eggs inside the rather large third pair of legs. The shrimps inhabiting temperate and cold waters do not have claws on the third pair of legs and the eggs are carried outside, attached to abdominal legs.

Until the 1950s, the fishing and consumption of shrimps were mainly confined to the cold-water species, but the discovery of large deep-water shrimps with high-quality flesh in the Gulf of Mexico brought changes to the market. At the present time, 35 species of this type of shrimp are fished intensively throughout the world up to a depth of 800 m (2600 ft). The following species are most commonly found for sale in French markets:

• the sword shrimp (*crevette rose*), also called Algerian shrimp, is 15–20 cm (6–8 in) long and is fished in deep water in both the Mediterranean and the Atlantic;

• the tropical pink prawn (*crevette rose tropicale*), also known as the Senegal prawn, is 15–20 cm (6–8 in) long and paler than the sword shrimp. It is fished on the coasts and in the lagoons and estuaries of tropical Africa;

• the *caramote* or pink Mediterranean prawn (*crevette rose de Mediterranée*) is also 15–20 cm (6–8 in) long. It is generally fished on the coast of the Mediterranean.

Among the shrimps of temperate or cold waters, about 15 species have been intensively marketed over a long period, especially:

• the sword shrimp (*crevette rose 'bouquet'*), which is 7–12 cm (2½–5 in) long, greatly appreciated, and is fished on the rocky coasts of Europe and north Africa;

• the *chevrette*, which is fished in the same region but is slightly smaller and often mixed with young prawns;

• the red prawn (*crevette rouge*), which is 6–7 cm (about 3 in) long, of a high quality, and is fished in the North Atlantic;

• the common or brown shrimp (*crevette grise* or *boucaud*), 3–6 cm (1½–2½ in) long, which is translucent when raw and brownish when cooked. Considered to have the best flavour, it is fished intensively off the Channel and North Sea coasts.

Today, shrimp and prawn fishing has become industrialized, except in a few ports of Brittany, Normandy, Belgium, and Germany. Once a year, at Oostduinkerke in Flanders, the tradition of fishing on horseback (*pêche à cheval*) takes place. Large baskets are attached to the saddle of the horse, which is breast-high in water. The fishermen mount the horse and drag the baskets along parallel to the shore.

☐ **Highly prized shellfish** Prawns and shrimps are usually cooked as soon as they are caught. When fresh, the shell is very shiny, the flesh is firm, and it is easy to peel (shell) them. They are sometimes coloured artificially and may be sold whole, peeled, canned, or frozen.

Cooked in sea water or salted water, shrimps and prawns are served plain, with butter, or used in numerous hors d'oeuvres. They are consumed in great quantities in Southeast Asia, Japan, and China and are prepared in various ways.

Gambas, used in Spanish and West Indian cuisine, are often fried or grilled on skewers. Shrimps and prawns are very suitable organisms for aquaculture. In Japan, the temperature of the inland sea is ideal for the scientific rearing of the larvae.

Prawn crackers are a speciality of China and Vietnam. They are made by pounding the prawns into a paste, drying it in the sun, and cutting it into petal shapes. These are fried in very hot oil to make them swell up. They may be served either as a cocktail snack or as an accompaniment to various exotic hors d'oeuvres. Naturally an off-white colour, they are sometimes artificially coloured to pastel shades.

 | RECIPE

Fried shrimps CREVETTES FRITES Wash and drain the live shrimps and fry them in hot oil for about 1 minute. Drain, season with salt, and serve with apéritifs.

Prawn (shrimp) omelette OMELETTE FOURRÉE AUX CREVETTES Bind some peeled prawns (shelled shrimp) with prawn sauce (see below) and use them to fill an omelette. When serving, pour a thin line of sauce around the omelette.

Prawn (shrimp) salad SALADE DE CREVETTES Season some peeled (shelled) shrimps or prawns with vinaigrette or mayonnaise. Arrange them in a dish or a salad bowl garnished with quarters of hard-boiled (hard-cooked) eggs and lettuce hearts.

Prawn (shrimp) sauce SAUCE CREVETTE À L'ANGLAISE Add ½ teaspoon anchovy essence (extract) to 2.5 dl (8 fl oz, 1 cup) butter sauce *à l'anglaise* (see *sauce*). Mix 40 g (1½ oz) peeled prawns (shelled shrimp) with the sauce and season with a dash of cayenne.

Prawn (shrimp) sauce (for fish) SAUCE CREVETTE (POUR POISSONS) Blend 2 dl (7 fl oz, ¾ cup) normande sauce with 2 tablespoons (3 tablespoons) shrimp butter. Season with a dash of cayenne and put through a sieve or mix in a blender. If the sauce is to be served separately, add to it 1 tablespoon peeled prawns (shelled shrimp) just before serving.

Shrimps sautéed in whisky CREVETTES SAUTÉES AU WHISKY Wash, drain, and sauté some live shrimps in oil in a frying pan (skillet). Add some pepper, a dash of cayenne, and either whisky, Cognac, or marc (1 small glass per 500 g (18 oz) shrimps). Flame, and serve very hot.

sicilienne (à la)

Describing small pieces of meat or poultry which are fried and garnished with stuffed tomatoes, rice timbales, and crouquette potatoes.

Sicily and Sardinia

SICILE ET SARDIAIGNE

The cookery of these two Mediterranean islands is Greek (for Sicily) or Phoenician (for Sardinia) in origin, with traces of Arab and African influence and certain ancient local traditions.

● Sicily produces citrus fruit, early vegetables, olives, and almonds. Little meat is found there, but wheat abounds. Its cakes are a source of pride: they include *cannoli*, which are filled with cream cheese and crystallized (candied) fruits; and cassata. Home-made bread is common in Sicily; it is baked in huge diamond shapes or, as unleavened bread, it is dipped in oil and eaten with salted fish. There are also numerous varieties of pizza. A typical Sicilian speciality is *vasteddi*: small rolls sprinkled with cumin seeds and filled with Ricotta, pork fried in lard, and smoked ham. Pasta is also important, especially *pasta con le sarde* (with a tomato and sardine ragout). Caponata, a type of cold ratatouille, is served as an entrée or with fish or seafood, which have a special place in Sicilian cookery (notably stuffed mussels and rockfish either stuffed or *en papillote*). Speciality meat dishes include *farsu magru* (rolled stuffed beef or veal with hard-boiled (hard-cooked) eggs, herbs, and spices) and pork sausages cooked in hot ashes.

A great producer and exporter of wine, Sicily was traditionally famous for such liqueur wines as Marsala and such dessert wines as Mamertino, which was known in Julius Caesar's day. For the last 20 years the growers have turned to dry wines, white, red, or rosé, high in alcohol, a large percentage of which are exported for blending. Among the best (bottled three months after the harvest instead of maturing in the barrel as in former times) are Etna, Corvo di Casteldaccia, Alcamo, and Carasuolo di Vittoria, which are pleasant table wines, fruity and well flavoured.

• In Sardinia, livestock farming is of prime importance. It provides for such specialities as kid-goat tripe, roasted, grilled (broiled), or boiled (with peas and haricot (navy) beans), and a famous open-air dish: sucking pig, lamb, or kid cooked on a spit over a juniper or olive wood fire or on live charcoal in a ditch. Partridge and thrush are cooked whole, wrapped in myrtle leaves; Sardinian wild boar is renowned for its delicate meat. Other typical dishes are beef braised in white wine and Sardinian veal braised with tomatoes and black (ripe) olives.

Sardinian bread is often in the shape of thin pancakes, called *fogli di musica* ('sheet music'), marked with horizontal cracks. There are two pasta specialities: ravioli stuffed with Ricotta cheese, spinach, and eggs, flavoured with saffron, and served with tomato sauce and cheese; and a gratin of layers of pasta, minced (ground) meat, ham, cream cheese, and eggs, coated with tomato sauce.

Langoustes and sardines (which gave the island its name) feature prominently in Sardinian cookery, as do tuna and swordfish. Dried tuna eggs (*buttariga*) are served as an hors d'oeuvre. The best-known Sardinian cheeses are *casu marzu* (a 'rotten' cheese with a strong smell) and *fiore sardo*, a ewes'-milk cheese for grating.

Only the vine flourishes in this dry land and for the last 20 years it has given fresh dry usually white wines, the best-known of which is Vernaccia, with a slightly bitter bouquet. The island also produces quality dessert wines, full-bodied and sweet, which were its main product for many years; they are Giro, Nasco, and Moscato.

sieve TAMIS

A utensil used for sifting or straining. Sieves made of silk, horsehair, or nylon, supported on a frame, are used to sift flour or icing (confectioners') sugar. Wire sieves are used to strain forcemeat, fruit purées, cooked vegetables, doughs, flavoured butters, etc., to improve their consistency and texture, or to purée fruit and vegetables. A wooden pestle is generally used to press the food through the sieve.

silphium

A condiment, also called *laserpitium*, which was prized in Roman cookery; it is extracted from an umbelliferous plant of North African origin and looks like a rubbery resin. It was first used as a medicine and sold at the same price as gold, but was replaced by asafoetida, a similar resin from a more common plant.

silver gilt VERMEIL

Material used in the manufacture of gold and silver plate. It can take the form of a thin layer of gilding (gold applied by electrolysis to silvered metal), or gilded silver (solid silver covered with a fine layer of gold). Cutlery, plates, and serving dishes made in silver gilt are rarely suitable for practical use, with the exception of small coffee spoons or teaspoons.

silverware ARGENTERIE

Tableware made of solid silver, silver-gilt (*vermeil*), or silvered metal. Silver plate (made from a single strip of plated metal) can include not only cutlery, plates, and serving dishes but also such accessories as candelabra, table mats, hand bell, salt cellars, knife rests, etc. Silver plates and dishes were used in ancient times. In medieval France, their use spread among the nobility and rich merchants, until this mass of immobilized precious metal began to worry the monarchs. In 1310 Philip the Fair, in an attempt to solve a monetary crisis, prohibited the manufacture of gold and silver dishes. But this measure had no effect, and the custom of using silver tableware continued until the Revolution. It was nevertheless increasingly restricted to display items, after Louis

XIV had the royal tableware melted down to replenish the coffers and encouraged the development of porcelain and faïence.

It was under the Consulate that French law of 1797 fixed the legal grades for silverware, still in force at the present time. The silver used is actually an alloy of silver and copper. The two grades legally authorized in France are 925/1000 (925 parts of silver to 75 of copper) and 800/1000 (800 parts of silver to 200 of copper). The second grade is rarely used except for export, in order to compete with those of foreign manufacturers whose grades are inferior to those in France. French silverware has been hallmarked with a trade mark and guarantee since 1260. Since 1838, the hallmark for silver has been lozenge-shaped. Silvered metal (brass or nickel silver) has its brand mark (or maker's mark) inscribed in a square.

In 1840, the Englishman Elkington and the Frenchman Ruolz simultaneously invented electroplating, thus putting silverware within the reach of the less wealthy, who were able to replace their galvanized iron cutlery with silvered metal.

To prevent silver cutlery from going black, it should be stored away from contact with the air, either in cases or wrapped in special materials or tissue paper. It must be cleaned regularly with special cleaning materials applied with a very soft cloth.

simmer   M. JOTER

To cook food slowly and steadily in a sauce or other liquid over a gentle heat, just below boiling point, so that the surface of the liquid bubbles occasionally. When cooking poached dishes the liquid should be kept simmering. Meat for simmering or stewing comprises the tougher cuts, which become tender and tasty when cooked for a long time in seasoned stock, wine, or beer. The French word, *mijoter*, comes from the Old French *mijot*, meaning fruit loft, a storeroom where fruit was left to ripen slowly.

singapour

A large Genoese sponge cake, filled with jam and fruit in syrup, coated with apricot jam, and generously decorated with crystallized (candied) fruits.

RECIPE

Singapour Bring ¾ litre (1¼ pints, 3 cups) water to the boil with 600 g (1¼ lb, 2½ cups) sugar. Drain a large can of pineapple slices, add the slices to the mixture, and simmer for 1½ hours. Leave the slices to cool, then drain them.

Whip 4 eggs with 125 g (4½ oz, ⅔ cup) sugar in a bain-marie until the mixture reaches 40 C (104 F), then remove from the heat and cool completely. Mix in 125 g (4½ oz, 1 cup) plain flour, stirring with a wooden spoon, then add 50 g (2 oz, 4 tablespoons) melted butter. Pour the batter into a buttered and floured 23-cm (9-in) cake tin, place in a moderately hot oven (200 C, 400 F, gas 6), and cook for about 20 minutes or until the cake is well risen and golden and the centre springs back when lightly pressed.

Meanwhile, melt 250 g (9 oz, ¾ cup) apricot jam over a gentle heat and grill (broil) 150 g (5 oz, 1 cup) chopped almonds. Prepare a syrup with 3 dl (½ pint, 1¾ cups water and 300 g (11 oz, 1¼ cups) sugar and allow to cool, then add 5 cl (3 tablespoons, ¼ cup) Kirsch.

Cut the sponge horizontally and let it soak up the Kirsch syrup. Coat the lower half with apricot jam; cut the slices of pineapple into small dice, set a dozen aside, and sprinkle the rest over the jam. Place the upper half of the sponge in position and coat the whole cake with jam. Sprinkle with chopped almonds and decorate the top with the remaining diced pineapple, together with glacé cherries and candied angelica. Serve on the day it is made.

singeing   FLAMBAGE

The process of rotating poultry or game birds over a spirit lamp or gas flame in order to burn off any feathers or down that remain after plucking.

singer

A French culinary term meaning to sprinkle ingredients browned in fat with flour before adding liquid (wine, stock, or water) to make a sauce. The flour must cook for several minutes before the liquid is added in order to thicken the sauce.

The term previously meant to colour a sauce with caramel, which was familiarly called *jus de singe* ('monkey juice').

siphon

A bottle made of thick glass or aluminium containing water that has been made effervescent with carbonic gas under pressure. It is closed with a screwed-on plastic or metal top provided with a lever, which, when depressed, allows the liquid to flow through an interior tube. The siphon is used to jet the water directly into the glass; it is refilled with water by unscrewing the top, into which gas cartridges are placed. Until World War II siphons made of thick glass, sometimes engraved or coloured (blue or green), were often covered with wicker or metal basketwork; they were refilled with Seltzer water.

The siphon for Chantilly cream also uses gas cartridges and provides white fluffy Chantilly-like cream that lacks the richness and flavour of a classic whipped cream. It is not recommended to fill the siphon more than three-quarters full, using an equal proportion of fresh cream and sweetened milk.

sirloin   ALOYAU

A prime cut of beef from the lumbar region, which extends from the last rib to the sacrum. The sirloin includes the fillet (tenderloin), contre-filet or fauxfilet (sirloin), rump steak, and *bavette* (top of the sirloin). Cooked whole, the sirloin makes a display piece; it is, however, more usually cut into several large joints.

RECIPES

Braised sirloin   ALOYAU BRAISÉ
Ask the butcher to prepare a piece of sirloin 2–3 kg (4½–6½ lb) in weight, cut along the grain of the meat. Lard the joint with lardons of bacon which have been marinated for at least an hour with a little brandy, pepper, spices, chopped parsley, sliced carrot, and sliced onion. Tie up the sirloin, brown it on all sides in hot fat, then place it in a large braising pan on a mirepoix of vegetables. Add a

bouquet garni and pour over about 600 ml (1 pint, 2½ cups) stock. Cover the pan and braise the joint in a low oven for about 4 hours or until the meat is very tender. After braising, the meat may be sliced and served with the cooking liquor, deglazed, reduced, and strained; serve with Albufera, bourgeoise, Du Barry, or duchesse garnish.

Roast sirloin   ALOYAU RÔTI   This very large joint is not normally cooked whole except by professional chefs. They trim off the top a little to give the joint a more regular shape, then cut the ligament which runs along the chine into regular sections and remove part of the fat which surrounds the fillet. The joint is then seasoned with salt and pepper and generally roasted in the oven or on a spit (allowing 10–12 minutes per kg, 5–6 minutes per lb); it should be pink on the inside. It is served surrounded with watercress or with a bouquetière or printanière garnish.

siroper or siroter

A French culinary term meaning to put a cake of leavened dough (baba or savarin) to soak in a warm syrup or to pour syrup over it several times until it is thoroughly impregnated. The term also means to pour a trickle of syrup over a sponge cake to lightly moisten it, flavour it, and soften it before decoration.

skate   RAIE

A large flat scaleless cartilaginous fish found in cold and temperate waters. The pectoral fins are enlarged in the form of wings and the tail is long and thin. The upper side of the fish is greyish-brown and bears two eyes and a short snout; on the underside there is a large mouth with pointed slashing teeth. The cartilaginous skeleton is easily removed.

The most common, and best flavoured, skate caught off the Mediterranean coast is the thornback, 0.7–1.2 m (2–4 ft) long and marked with pale spots. It owes its name to the cartilaginous spines scattered over the back and wings (and sometimes the belly). Other edible species are the butterfly or mirror skate, 1–1.5 m (3¼–5 ft) long, with two eyespots on the wings; the spotted skate, with large black spots; and the true skate (as distinct from the ray), black or white with a pointed snout, which can exceed 2 m (6½ ft) in length and weigh more than 100 kg (220 lb).

The skin of a skate is covered with a viscous coating. As this will regenerate for ten hours or so after death, the freshness of a skate can be judged by rubbing it with a cloth and observing whether the coating reappears. It is usually just the wings of a skate that are sold, or the fish may be sold in slices; it is sometimes skinned. The pinkish-white flesh is meaty and has a fine texture. It should be washed several times to get rid of the smell of ammonia, which is most marked when the fish is quite fresh. The thick skin is always removed before cooking. Skate liver is considered to be a delicacy by some gourmets, as are the 'cheeks'.

The traditional accompaniment is black butter (or even better, noisette butter), but it may also be served with hollandaise sauce, vinaigrette with herbs, or meunière sauce, fried (especially good for small skate), as a gratin, or with béchamel sauce (particularly the Breton version of the sauce, with leeks).

RECIPES

Fried skate RAITEAUX FRITS Select some very small skinned skate (or the wings from a small or medium fish). Pour some cold milk over them and soak for 1 hour, then drain, coat with flour, and deep-fry at 180 C (350 F). When cooked, drain on absorbent paper, sprinkle with salt, and arrange on the serving dish. Garnish with fluted lemon halves.

Skate au gratin RAIE AU GRATIN Butter an ovenproof dish and sprinkle the bottom with 2 tablespoons (3 tablespoons) chopped shallots and the same amount of chopped parsley. Add 150 g (5 oz, 1¼ cups) finely sliced mushrooms. Season 2 skate wings with salt and pepper and arrange them in the dish. Moisten with ½ glass white wine, dot with 30 g (1 oz, 2 tablespoons) butter cut into small pieces, and cook in the oven at 230 C (450 F, gas 8) for 10

minutes. Remove the skate and drain it. Add 1 tablespoon fresh cream to the cooking liquor and reduce it by half. Put the skate back into the dish, pour over the cooking juices, sprinkle with breadcrumbs, dot with butter, and brown under the grill (broiler).

Skate liver with cider vinegar FOIES DE RAIE AU VINAIGRE DE CIDRE (from Jacques Le Divellec's recipe) Poach 400 g (14 oz) skate liver very gently in court-bouillon for 5 minutes. Leave it to get cold in the stock. Peel and core 4 firm apples (preferably Cox's Orange Pippins or Granny Smiths), slice them, and cook over a low heat in 15–20 g (½–¾ oz, 1–1½ tablespoons) butter. Season with salt and pepper. Slice the liver and brown in butter. Drain and arrange the slices on a hot dish. Pour the butter from the pan the livers were cooked in, then add 2 tablespoons (3 tablespoons) cider vinegar to the pan, boil for a minute or two, and pour over the liver. Surround with slices of apple and sprinkle with chopped chives.

Skate with noisette butter RAIE AU BEURRE NOISETTE Cut the skate into chunks, leaving the wings whole. Poach in court-bouillon or in water to which have been added 2 dl (7 fl oz, ¾ cup) vinegar and 1 teaspoon salt per litre (1¾ pints, 4½ cups) water. Bring to the boil, skim the pan, and simmer for 5–7 minutes, according to the thickness of the fish. Make some noisette butter. Drain the fish and arrange it on a hot dish. Sprinkle with lemon juice and chopped parsley and, just before serving, pour over the noisette butter.

skim

DÉPOUILLER, ÉCREMER, ÉCUMER

To remove the scum that rises to the surface of a stock, sauce, or ragout when it is boiled. This sense of the word is expressed in French by the words *dépouiller* or *écumer*. The skimming is carried out with a spoon, a special skimmer, or a small ladle.

To skim cream from unhomogenized milk is expressed in French by the word *écremer*. Skimming occurs spontaneously after 24 hours if whole fresh unhomogenized milk is allowed to stand; the cream rises to the surface and can be easily removed, particularly for use in home baking. In the dairy industry, skimming is done in centrifugal skimming machines. Milk is sold as full cream, semiskimmed, or skimmed in French shops.

skimmer ÉCUMOIRE

A large flat (or slightly concave) perforated spoon with a long handle, used for skimming. For skimming sauces and stocks, the skimmer is made of stainless steel, aluminium, enamelled metal, or tin. For jam, it should be made of untinned copper. A skimmer made of galvanized wire is used for removing deep-fried foods from hot oil (the French term for this is *araignée à friture*) and a concave wire skimmer is used for lifting poached items from their cooking water.

skinning DÉPOUILLER

The action of removing the skin of a game animal (e.g. a rabbit or hare) or of a fish. The French word, *dépouiller*, is also used to mean removing the outer rind of ham.

skirt HAMPE

A butchery term for the diaphragm of a beef animal or a horse: a long flat band of dark fibrous muscle. If the membranes are carefully removed and the meat is flattened out, the flank can be cut into steaks which, although rather tough, are full of flavour. It is brushed with oil, cooked under a very hot grill (broiler), and served very rare. It may also be sautéed or braised. Its flat shape makes it suitable for paupiettes.

skoal

The Scandinavian drinking toast, equivalent to 'good health' or 'à votre santé'. The word has its roots in the old Norse *skalle* (skull), commemorating an ancient warrior custom of drinking from the vanquished enemy's skull.

Today, *skoal* means to hold the glass at chest level, look directly at the person toasted, and, after slightly nodding to him, drain the glass in one gulp (if it is aquavit) or in sips (if it is wine). A further small sign of friendship is made before replacing the glass.

slang
ARGOT DE LA TABLE ET DE LA CUISINE

Strictly speaking, cooks have no slang, but they do have a professional jargon and some picturesque expressions (such as *piano* for the cooker and *gros bonnet* ('big shot') for the head chef). In catering, *chaud devant*! ('hot ahead!') is a way of clearing a passage when one has a load of dishes, and *ça marche*! ('it's going all right') signifies that the order has been recorded. There are two remaining areas where an authentic slang persists, if not in practice, at least in words. One is food as a whole, described as *becquetance, graine, jaffe*, or *tortore* (all meaning 'grub' or 'nosh'), and the verbs *becqueter* ('to stoke up'), *claper* and *grainer* (both meaning 'to eat'), and *morfaler* and *tortorer* ('to nosh'). The other relates to the items of food themselves: *brignollet* and *brigeton* (bread), *sauciflard* (large sausage), *bouillante* (soup), *barbaque* and *bidoche* (meat), *picrate, jaja, grosquitache*, and *betterave* (all meaning red wine), *roteuse* for a bottle of champagne, *frometon* (cheese), *calendo* (Camembert), and finally *caoua* (coffee).

Another picturesque area is bar slang, of which the following is not an exhaustive list: *antigel* (marc brandy), *antigrippe* (chaser), *blanc lime* (white wine and lemonade), *cercueil* (half-litre of beer), *fond-de-culotte* (suze and cassis, because it sounds like *ça ne s'use qu'assis* (it only wears out sitting down) i.e. the *fond-de-culotte* – the seat of the trousers), *marie-salope* (tomato juice and vodka, or bloody Mary), *mêlé-cass* (cassis and rum), and *rince-cochon* (white wine, lemon syrup, and soda water).

slash CISELER

To make several shallow slanting incisions on the surface of a round fish (mackerel in particular) or a chitterling. The operation allows the food to cook thoroughly when grilled (broiled) or fried.

Vegetables or herbs cut into small pieces, fine strips, or minute dice are described as *ciselés*.

slivovitz

A plum brandy from Yugoslavia; the national drink of the Bosnians and the Serbs, who also call it *prakija*. The name comes from the Serbo-Croat *slijiva* (plum). It is made from purple plums, the stones (pits) of which are usually crushed and fermented with the pulp. Slivovitz is a true *alcool blanc*, not just a brandy flavoured with plums. It is usually served as a digestive.

sloe PRUNELLE

The fruit of the blackthorn, a thorny shrub common throughout Europe. The sloe resembles a very small blue plum, with firm greenish flesh that is juicy and very sour; it is edible only after the first frosts. Sloes are used to make jam and jelly, sloe gin and sloe wine, a liqueur (in Anjou), a ratafia, and a highly prized fruit brandy (in Alsace, Franche-Comté, and Burgundy).

sloke

A foodstuff based on the seaweed laver, which was a traditional Scottish dish until recent times. Also called 'sea spinach', it was a base for soups and a sauce served with mutton.

A popular way of preparing sloke today is to cook it in milk with potatoes, purée the mixture, then add melted butter, lemon juice, and pepper.

smallage

ACHE DES MARAIS

An umbelliferous plant, also called wild celery, from which cultivated celery originated; it was used as a seasoning in Greek and Roman times. This wild plant can be included in salads and also serves as an ingredient in medicinal syrups and tisanes.

smelt ÉPERLAN

A small marine fish of the salmon family, with fine delicate flesh. It grows up to 20 cm (8 in) long, is silvery in colour, and has a second dorsal fin, which distinguishes it from similar but poorer quality fish, such as bleak and athérine, which are often used as substitutes. It spawns in estuaries but seldom runs upriver beyond the tideline.

The classic method of preparation is frying. The fish are gutted (cleaned),

washed, dried, and stored in the refrigerator (they freeze very well). They can also be marinaded, grilled (broiled), cooked in white wine, coated with flour and fried, or cooked *au gratin*. In Scandinavian countries, smelt are used in the manufacture of fish oil and fishmeal.

RECIPES

Brochettes of fried smelt ÉPERLANS FRITS EN BROCHETTES Prepare the fish as in the recipe for fried smelt. Impale on metal skewers (6–8 fish per skewer) and deep-fry.

Cold marinade of smelt ÉPERLANS MARINÉS Prepare the smelt, roll them in flour (shaking off any excess), and brown in oil in a frying pan (skillet). Drain, season with salt and pepper, and arrange in a dish. Peel and slice some onions and scald them for 1 minute in boiling water. Cool, then wipe dry and arrange over the fish. Add some peppercorns, cloves (2–3 for every 30 smelt), thyme, and bay leaves. Add vinegar and soak for at least 24 hours before serving. Arrange in an hors-d'oeuvre dish and serve accompanied by other cold hors d'oeuvres.

The vinegar in the marinade can be replaced by white wine boiled up with 2 chopped shallots, a bouquet garni, and some salt and pepper.

Fried smelt ÉPERLANS FRITS Dip the prepared smelt in salted milk, then roll them in flour and shake off the excess. Deep-fry in very hot oil (175 –180 C, 345–355 F), then drain the fish on kitchen paper (paper towels) and sprinkle with fine salt. If desired, arrange in a cluster and garnish with fried parsley. Serve with lemon quarters.

Grilled (broiled) smelt à l'anglaise ÉSPERLANS GRILLÉS À L'ANGLAISE Prepare the smelt, split them lengthways along the back, and remove the backbone. Gently open them out and season with salt, pepper, and a little cayenne. Dip them one by one in melted butter and in fresh breadcrumbs, then grill (broil) quickly. Sprinkle with fine salt and serve with maître d'hôtel butter.

Smelt velouté soup à la dieppoise
VELOUTÉ D'ÉPERLANS À LA DIEP-
POISE Prepare a velouté soup using 75
g (3 oz) white roux, 8 dl (1¼ pints, 1½
pints) fish stock, and 1 dl (6 tablespoons, scant ½ cup) mussel cooking
liquor. Cook 250 g (9 oz) cleaned smelt
and 1 tablespoon chopped onion in butter. Fillet the smelt, reduce to a purée,
add this to the velouté, then sieve. The
mixture can be thickened with 1 or 2 egg
yolks, if desired. Garnish the soup with
12 poached mussels and 12 shelled
prawns.

smetana SMITANE

A soured (dairy sour) cream, extensively
used in central and eastern Europe and
the USSR. Produced by bacterial fermentation, it does not keep well. It is
mainly used with fish, borsch, and as a
sauce for stuffed cabbage leaves, sauerkraut, and Hungarian meat stews. The
similar *sauere Sahne* of Germany has a
milder taste but is used in the same ways
and also in horseradish sauce with herrings.

smeun, smen, or smenn

Clarified butter used in Arabic and
Maghrebi cookery. Europeans loosely
describe it as rancid, but this is incorrect. Smeun is made with the butter
from ewes' milk or occasionally cows'
milk (even buffaloes' milk in Egypt),
which is liquefied, clarified, and mixed
with a little salt (or sometimes semolina). It is stored in earthenware or
stoneware pots. The traditional preparation of smeun came from the necessity of preserving fats in hot countries. As
it ages, the butter becomes refined and
develops an almond taste. It is used in
pastries and in the preparation of couscous, broths, and tajines.

smoking FUMAGE

A traditional method of preserving fresh
food, such as meat and fish, using prolonged exposure to smoke from a wood
fire. Smoking tends to dry the food, kills
bacteria and other microorganisms on
its surface, deepens its colour, and impregnates it with a smoky flavour.
Nowadays, smoking (or smoke-curing)
is rather less a means of preserving than
a process for giving flavour to meat or
fish.

Smoked meat is traditional in many
countries: *bresil*, from Franche-Comté
in eastern France, is made from lean
beef, salted and hardened, and served in
very thin slices; South American *charqui* is beef, mutton, or llama cut into
long strips and dried; *grisons* meat –
lean beef soaked in brine and dried in
the open to give a very close texture –
comes from Switzerland; and *pastirma*
from Turkey is smoked leg or shoulder
of mutton.

Smoking is mostly performed on certain cuts of pork (ham, belly, bacon),
sausages, poultry (goose, raw or cooked
chicken, cooked turkey pieces), some
game (wild boar, pheasant), and some
fish (salmon, eel, sturgeon, etc.). It is
often preceded by salting or soaking in
brine. For fish, there are two techniques.
In cold smoking (20–30 C, 70–85 F) the
fish is exposed to the smoke from a
slow-burning wood fire; in hot smoking, it is first exposed to a draught of hot
air (60–80 C, 140–175 F) emitted by a
fast-burning fire, then placed in the
thick smoke from a fire covered with
sawdust. This second type of smoking
involves a limited degree of cooking of
the fish. Meat and pork products are
hot-smoked, directly over an open fire.

The duration of smoking varies from
20 minutes to several days. The most
commonly used woods are beech, oak,
and chestnut, to which aromatic
essences (juniper, heather, laurel, sage,
and rosemary) are added. In the United
States, hickory is often used. In Savoy,
sausages are smoked over fir wood,
while in the Charente, mussels are
cooked in the smoke from pine needles.
But in general, resinous woods perform
badly and produce an acrid taste. In
Brittany, gorse is used for ham. In Andalusia, chorizo is smoked over juniper, a
plant which is also used by the Sicilians
to smoke ewes'-milk cheese. The
Chinese smoke eggs over fennel, cinamon, and poplar sawdust fires.

A smoky flavour can be produced
using a concentrate extracted from
carbonized wood. The concentrate is
sprayed over the surfaces of the foods as
they pass through a tunnel. But the food
is not thoroughly impregnated, as in
true smoking. This smoky flavour is
mostly given to foods that cannot
undergo traditional smoking, such as

biscuits (crackers), appetizers, and cheese.

smörgasbord

An abundant assortment of hot and cold dishes served in Sweden as hors d'oeuvres or a full buffet meal. The literal meaning of the word is 'table of buttered bread'; it does not simply include a few salmon canapés, cold meats, and cheese but is a vast buffet from which guests serve themselves according to their appetite. A traditional order is observed: the first course is herrings, as this is the king of Scandinavian foods. On the first plate one might mix *hareng du verrier* (marinated in sugar, vinegar, carrots, and spices) with some fried marinated herring, herring with soured (dairy sour) cream, and smoked herring with raw sliced onion or cucumber. The herring dishes are followed by other fish dishes: salmon and smoked eels, jellied trout, cod roes with fennel, hard-boiled (hard-cooked) eggs with caviar or salmon roe, lobster salad, crab with shrimps, peas, and mushrooms, or the typical smörgasbord speciality *fagelbö* (a salad of sprats, lettuce, onions, capers, sliced beetroot (red beet), and raw egg yolk). Then plates are changed for the third course, which consists of cold meats and Swedish charcuterie: veal in aspic, pressed tongue, roast beef, and liver pâté, with vegetable macédoine in mayonnaise or cold pasta salads. The fourth course includes several traditional Swedish hot dishes: 'Jason's temptation' (an anchovy gratin with potatoes, cream, and onions), stuffed onions, meatballs with peppers, etc.

Several varieties of ryebread and crisp pancakes are served with the meal; there are also several types of cheese, both strong and mild (which are often eaten first, before the herrings). The dessert is usually fruit salad. Beer and a small cask of aquavit are served for drinks.

Although smörgasbord is of Swedish origin, it is found throughout the Scandinavian countries: as *smörrebröd* in Denmark, *smorbrod* in Norway, and *voileipäpöyta* in Finland. It is also related to the Russian zakuski. The basic elements of all these meals are marinated herrings, herring salad with potatoes and beetroot (red beet), croutons of smoked goose, smoked salmon and sturgeon, and fish roe: the Norwegians add *rakorret* (fermented trout with salt and sugar); in Finland, slices of salted smoked reindeer meat with scrambled eggs; and in Denmark, meatballs with red cabbage or slices of smoked goose with sauerkraut.

Traditionally, smörgasbord is a sumptuous and carefully prepared buffet, at which the hostess can employ all her skills; at Christmas and on feast days, it is particularly lavish and artistically arranged. Historically it dates back to the ancient Norse custom of putting all the dishes for a meal on the table together. The present form dates from the 19th century, when catering helped its development considerably.

snack bar

A restaurant in which quick meals are served at all times. The limited menu offers simple dishes – hamburgers, cheese on toast, quiche, hot dogs, chicken and chips (fried potatoes) – and nonalcoholic drinks (coffee, tea, milk shakes, and soft drinks). Snack bars are found throughout the United States and were introduced to Europe in the 1950s. The formula was quickly successful in large towns and has had renewed success in the 1980s with the development of 'fast food' chains.

snail ESCARGOT

A terrestrial gastropod mollusc characterized by a spiral shell. Some species are highly prized in gastronomy. In France, two native species are most commonly eaten.

● The *Burgundy snail*, also called vineyard snail or large white, is 40–45 mm (1¾ in) long. It has a slightly mottled or veined body and a tawny-yellow shell streaked with brown; the aperture of the shell is smooth or barely rimmed. It has a slow rate of growth, taking two or three years to reach maturity. Rearing them is difficult, but wild snails are collected, especially in Burgundy, Franche-Comté, Savoy, and Champagne.

● The *petit-gris* is 26–30 mm (1 in), with an unpatterned body and a brownish shell with a spiral of fawn-grey; the aperture has a rimmed edge. It is found mostly in Provence and Languedoc, but also in Charente and Brittany. Its flesh is delicate, fruity, and slightly firm.

These snails are sold either live or freshly cooked (by pork butchers, caterers, and fishmongers), or frozen.

The French species are becoming increasingly rare and, although the petit-gris has been reared with limited success, imports have increased to meet the demand. These include large snails from Algeria and Turkey, which have a striped shell, and snails from central Turkey, which are imported either live or frozen. 'Achatines' snails, less delicate and sold preserved, come from China, Indonesia, and Africa.

The types of live snail available depend on the season: spring and autumn for the *coureurs* ('runners'); summer and winter when they are *operculés* (i.e. the shell's aperture is sealed off for hibernation) or *voilés* ('veiled' – these are the best and, because they have fasted, the leanest). In France, the collection of Burgundy and petit-gris snails is governed by regulations.

☐ **History** Snails were among the first animals to be eaten by man, on the evidence of the heaps of shells found in prehistoric sites. It was the Romans who first prepared them for cooking. They had 'snaileries' where the snails were fattened on wine and bran, and Pliny speaks of grilled snails, eaten with wine as a snack before or after meals. The Gauls, it seems, enjoyed them as a dessert. In the Middle Ages, the Church permitted consumption of snails on days of abstinence. They were fried with oil or onion, cooked on skewers, or boiled. But Nicolas de Bonnefons was 'astonished that the odd tastes of man have led him as far as this depraved dish in order to satisfy the extravagance of gluttony.'

In the 17th century, the consumption of snails was appreciably reduced. But Talleyrand brought them back into fashion by asking Carême to prepare some for the dinner which he gave for the Czar of Russia.

☐ **Gastronomy** All the regions of France have their own name for the snail: it is called *cagouille* in Saintonge, *lumas* in Poitou, *caracol* in Flanders, *carnar* in Lorraine, *carago* or *cacalau* in Provence, *carcaulada* in Roussillon, and *cantaleu* in Nice. In the south, it is usual-

ly prepared in wine, with bacon or ham, spices, garlic, and olive oil; it is also included in tarts, pastries, and turnovers, cooked in broths, fricassees, or on skewers, or grilled (broiled) on a wood fire (see *cargolade*). But for the classic entrée, snails are stuffed with butter *à la bourguignonne* (snail butter) and served piping hot in their shells (or in tiny individual pots), six to twelve at a time, on a special grooved dish, the *escargotière*; they are eaten using a pair of tongs and a small two-pronged fork. For Joseph Delteil, the *quanta de consommation* (i.e. the quantity normally consumed per gourmet) is about a hundred: 'No fewer may be swallowed.'

Suçarelle is a typical regional dish from southeastern France: small snails (preferably) are cooked in courtbouillon with fennel and rosemary, then browned in olive oil with onion, tomatoes, bay leaf, garlic, and pepper; they are then floured, sprinkled with stock and lemon juice, and simmered for a long time; the bottom of the shell is pierced and the flesh sucked through the hole.

Grimod de La Reynière gives recipes which use only the shells: 'In the season when snails are unobtainable we sometimes divert ourselves by deceiving the senses through a semblance which is not unamusing. We make an excellent fine forcemeat, either of game or of fish, with anchovy fillets, nutmeg, delicate spices, herbs, and a binding of egg yolks. Well-washed and very hot snail shells are used. Each one is filled with the forcemeat and they are served burning hot.' The recipe for *escargots simulés Comtesse Riguidi* is as follows: 'In large well-washed snail shells (from which, naturally, you will have expelled any undesirable inhabitant) place rounds of lambs' sweetbreads sautéed in butter. Fill the cavity of the shells with a fine forcemeat of creamed chicken, to which some chopped white truffle has been added. Place the snails disguised in this way in an ovenproof dish or a snail dish; sprinkle with breadcrumbs and cook for a few minutes in the oven.'

Snails served with butter in their shells may be prepared *à l'alsacienne* (using flavoured aspic, garlic butter, and aniseed), *à la dijonnaise* (maître d'hôtel butter), *à l'italienne* (maître d'hôtel butter and Parmesan cheese), or *à la valaisane* (chilli-flavoured gravy, garlic butter, and chives). Snails served with sauce may be prepared *à la poulette*; other sauces include garlic-flavoured mayonnaise and béarnaise sauce. They can also be cooked in red wine or white wine, flamed in Armagnac, or lightly fried.

☐ **Preparation** Ideally use vineyard or petit-gris snails that are hibernating; otherwise, make them fast for about ten days (in Provence, instead of fasting, they are put on a diet of thyme, which helps the molluscs to eliminate poisonous material and flavours their flesh). Some authorities recommend that snails should not be purged with salt, because that risks spoiling their gastronomic quality. If they are purged, a small handful of coarse salt is required for four dozen large snails, together with half a glass of vinegar and a pinch of flour. Cover the vessel containing the snails and place a weight on top: leave to soak for three hours, stirring from time to time. Next wash the snails in several lots of water to remove all the mucus, then blanch them for 5 minutes in boiling water. Drain and rinse in fresh water. Shell them and take out the black part (cloaca) at the end of the 'tail', but do not remove the mantle, comprising the liver and other organs, which represents a quarter of the total weight of the animal and is the most delicious and nutritious part.

RECIPES

Butter for snails BEURRE D'ESCAR-GOT, BEURRE À LA BOURGUIG-NONNE Finely chop 35 g (1¼ oz) shallots and enough parsley to fill 1 tablespoon. Crush 2 cloves of garlic. Add all these ingredients to 350 g (12 oz, 1½ cups) softened butter, 15 g (½ oz) salt, and a good pinch of pepper. Mix well. (This quantity is sufficient to fill about 50 snail shells).

Snail broth BOUILLON D'ESCAR-GOTS (from an ancient recipe) Prepare 36 snails. Shell them and put them in a saucepan containing 3 litres (5¼ pints, 6½ pints) water. Add 400 g (14 oz) calf's head, a lettuce, cleaned and quartered, a handful of purslane leaves, and

a little salt. Heat, then skim. Bring to the boil, then reduce the heat and simmer for about 2 hours. Adjust the seasoning and strain.

Snails à la bourguignonne ESCAR-GOTS À LA BOURGUIGNONNE Put the shelled snails in a saucepan and cover them with a mixture of equal parts of white wine and stock. Add 1 tablespoon chopped shallot, 10 g (½ oz) onion, and 75 g (3 oz) carrot per litre (1¾ pints, 4¼ cups) liquid, and a large bouquet garni. Add salt, allowing 8 g (¼ oz) per litre.

Simmer for about 2 hours, then leave to cool in the cooking liquor. Meanwhile, boil the empty shells in water containing 1 tablespoon soda crystals per litre. Drain them, wash in plenty of water, and dry in the oven, without letting them colour. Prepare some butter for snails (see recipe above); at least 50 g (2 oz) is required for a dozen snails. Remove the snails from the liquor. Place a little butter in the bottom of each shell, insert a snail, and fill up the shell with more butter. Arrange in snail dishes and heat without letting the butter brown. Serve piping hot.

Snails à la poulette ESCARGOTS À LA POULETTE Cook 48 shelled snails as for snails *à la bourguignonne* (see above), then drain. Prepare a white roux using 25 g (1 oz, 2 tablespoons) butter and 25 g (1 oz, ¼ cup) flour. Add 250 ml (8 fl oz, 1 cup) chicken stock, 250 ml (8 fl oz, 1 cup) white wine, and a bouquet garni. Cook briskly for 15 minutes or until the sauce is reduced by one-third. Soften a large chopped onion in 20 g (¾ oz, 1½ tablespoons) butter in a saucepan. Add the snails and the sauce and cook for 5 minutes.

Meanwhile, mix 2 egg yolks and the juice of a lemon; chop a small bunch of parsley. Remove the bouquet garni from the saucepan. Blend a little of the hot sauce with the egg yolks and lemon juice, then add to the saucepan. Stir briskly and remove from the heat. Sprinkle with chopped parsley and serve piping hot.

Snails grilled à la mode du Languedoc ESCARGOTS GRILLÉS À LA MODE DU LANGUEDOC Arrange some shelled snails on a grid (grill). Prepare a fire of vine shoots; as soon as the embers form a light ash, place the grid on top, sprinkle the snails with salt, pepper, thyme, and crushed fennel, and grill. Meanwhile, cook some diced fatty bacon in a frying pan (skillet) until soft. Tip the cooked snails into a dish and baste with the sizzling bacon fat. Serve immediately with farmhouse bread and red wine.

snake SERPENT

Practically all snakes, poisonous or not, are edible: the boas of South America, the pythons of Africa, the cobras of Asia, the rattlesnakes of Mexico, and the grass snakes and adders of Europe. Until the 18th century, adder-based diets were very fashionable in France for their beneficial effects on health and beauty. Mme de Sévigné, who obtained her adders from Poitou, advised her daughter to go on a month's adder diet once a year. Recipes of the period are full of suggestions: the adders should be skinned and gutted, cooked with herbs, used to stuff a capon, cooked in stock, jellied, made into oils, etc. Louis XIV controlled the adder trade by restricting their sale to doctors and apothecaries. Grass snakes, which were served for a long time in various dishes in suburban taverns, are now protected species in France, as is the smooth snake in Britain.

In China, an ancient recipe mentions the three cobras necessary to make a very complex dish called 'the meeting of the tiger, the phoenix, and the dragon'. In Cameroon, a ragout of adder and spices is prepared. Paul Corcellet, a specialist in exotic cookery, suggests a recipe for python stew: the snake is skinned, cut into pieces, dusted with flour, and sealed in the frying pan (skillet) with palm oil, then flamed with Armagnac and stewed for five hours in a rich tomato and onion sauce (fondue) flavoured with shallots, thyme, bay leaf, and peppers. This dish is considered to taste like sautéed chicken.

snipe BÉCASSINE

A migratory game bird, similar in appearance to the woodcock but smaller (wingspan 50 cm, 20 in); it is found in marshes, ponds, and water

meadows. Snipe are hunted from August to April (but are best in the autumn) and are more easily caught than woodcock. The plumage is brownish-black on the head and back and white underneath. It is prepared in the same way as woodcock. See also *Lucullus*.

snowball

BOULE-DE-NEIGE

An ice-cream dessert made using a spherical (bombe) mould. The mould is lined with chocolate ice cream, filled with a mousse mixture, and, when turned out, covered with Chantilly cream.

soak TREMPER

To immerse a foodstuff in cold water for a variable length of time. Soaking is carried out to reconstitute dried vegetables or fruits, to facilitate the cooking of dried vegetables (lentils, beans), to desalt salt fish (especially salt cod), or to clean and wash vegetables or preserve them in the short term.

Tremper la soupe means to place pieces of stale or lightly toasted bread in the soup tureen or dishes so that they become saturated with soup.

sobressada

SOUBRESSADE

A speciality of Spanish charcuterie: an unsmoked spreading sausage that consists of small pieces of lean meat in a fatty stuffing, highly seasoned and coloured with sweet pepper. The name *sobressada de Mallorca* is protected so no imitations can be made.

sobronade

A rustic soup from Périgord made from haricot (navy) beans, potatoes, root vegetables, celery, and flavourings, garnished with both fresh and salt pork or sometimes with ham.

RECIPE

Sobronade Soak 750 g (1¾ lb, 4 cups) dried haricot (navy) beans in cold water for 12 hours. Peel 2 medium-sized turnips and cut into thick slices. Brown a third of these in a pan with 100 g (4 oz) chopped fat bacon. Drain the beans and put them into a large saucepan, cover completely with cold water, and add 250 g (9 oz) diced ham and a piece of fresh pork (fat and lean) weighing about 750 g (1¾ lb). Bring to the boil and skim; add all the turnip, a bouquet garni, an onion studded with 2 cloves, 4 carrots, 2 sliced celery sticks (stalks), a bunch of parsley, and 2 chopped cloves of garlic. Boil for about 20 minutes, then add 250 g (9 oz) potatoes cut into thick slices and leave to cook for about another 40 minutes. Garnish a soup tureen with slices of dried bread and pour the soup on top.

socca

A flour made from chickpeas in the Nice region. A thick porridge is made from it, which can be cooked *au gratin*, used to fill a tart, or sliced (when cold), fried in olive oil, and served with sugar. The latter is a popular delicacy, which is sold in the streets.

soda water   SODA

Effervescent mineral water formerly sold in a siphon but now usually bottled. Soda water is used to dilute spirits, syrups, fruit juices, etc.

sodium

A mineral which, with potassium, plays a vital role in the hydration of cells and also helps to maintain the acid-base balance. The daily requirement of 1–1.5 g is generally met by normal nutrition, which yields 4–6 g sodium (many nutritionists consider this too much: excessive intake of sodium may cause high blood pressure). The main dietary source of sodium is salt (sodium chloride), although some foodstuffs are naturally rich in sodium (milk, seafood, egg white, dried fruits, and truffles).

soft roe   LAITANCE

The sperm or milt of a male fish. It is a soft white smooth substance, which is rich in phosphorus. Roes can be eaten fresh, smoked, or preserved in oil. Herring roes are the most widely available variety, followed by carp (one of Brillat-Savarin's favourite dishes when used as an omelette filling) and mackerel. Whether poached in a court-bouillon or cooked *à la meunière*, they can be served as hot hors d'oeuvres (barquettes, bouchées, canapés, fritters, etc.) or used as a garnish in fish dishes.

RECIPES

Cooking soft roes in court-bouillon CUISSON DES LAITANCES AU COURT-BOUILLON   Soak the roes in cold water for 2 hours, then remove the small blood vessels that run down the sides. Prepare a simple court-bouillon with cold water, a little lemon juice, salt, and oil (2 tablespoons (3 tablespoons) for every ½ litre (17 fl oz, 2 cups) water). Put the roes in this liquid, bring slowly to a very gentle simmer, and poach for about 4 minutes. Drain and cool.

Soft roes à la meunière LAITANCES À LA MEUNIERE   Soak the roes and blot them dry. Coat them with flour, shake off any excess, and fry in butter seasoned with salt and pepper. Sprinkle with lemon juice.

Soft roes à l'anglaise LAITANCES À L'ANGLAISE   Poach the roes in a court-bouillon and allow to cool. Coat them in flour, then dip them in egg and breadcrumbs. Fry in butter, browning on both sides. Arrange on a serving dish and sprinkle with a mixture of melted butter and lemon juice. Garnish with a circle of half slices of lemon.

Soft roes in noisette butter LAITANCES AU BEURRE NOISETTE   Poach the roes in court-bouillon, dry on absorbent kitchen paper, and arrange on a long dish. Sprinkle with capers and chopped parsley, together with a little lemon juice. Top with a few tablespoons of noisette butter.

The lemon juice may be replaced with a few drops of vinegar, and the chopped parsley with 2 tablespoons (3 tablespoons) chervil added to the noisette butter.

Soft roes in scallop shells à la normande LAITANCES EN COQUILLES À LA NORMANDE   Poach the roes in court-bouillon and drain them. Put them in scallop shells edged with a border of duchess potatoes, previously browned in the oven. Top the roes in each shell with a poached drained oyster, a cooked mushroom, and a scant tablespoon shrimps and mussels. Coat with normande, Mornay, or butter sauce, and garnish each shell with a generous strip of truffle.

sole

A flat sea fish, almost a perfect oval in shape, with eyes on the right side (which is grey or brown, the blind side being creamy white). The minimum size for marketing is 21 cm (8 in), but some sole measure up to 60 cm (2 ft). The weight ranges from 180–200 g (7 oz) to 800 g (1¾ lb).

The sole was the favourite fish in the cookery of ancient Rome, where it was called *solea Jovi* (Jupiter's sandal). In former times it was preserved (marinated in salt), sweated, fried, made into pâté or soup, stewed, or roasted. During the reign of Louis XIV it became a 'royal dish', since when the fillets have been used in a number of elaborate dishes, one of which was created by the Marquise de Pompadour. The great chefs of the 19th century, especially Dugléré and Marguery, exercised all their skill in preparing sole dishes.

• **Dover sole** is the best known. Well shaped and brown or grey in colour, it is fished in the English Channel and the Atlantic and also in the Baltic and North Seas. It is exported from Holland, Belgium, Denmark, and England (Dover and Ostend have the greatest reputation). French sole fished on the line is called *sole de ligne*: it is firm and delicate with an exquisite taste.

• **Partridge sole** (or **sand sole**) has dark stripes and is smaller and less tasty than Dover sole. It is fished in the English Channel and the Atlantic, as far as Nantes.

• **Séteau** is a very small elongated variety of sole, 7.5–10 cm (3–4 in) long, brown in colour, which is fished on the Vendée and Charentes coasts. It is called *langue d'avocat* ('lawyer's tongue') in Bordeaux.

• **Dakar sole** (or **Moroccan sole**) is elongated with large scales and is fished in large numbers. It is of inferior quality, with firm but bland flesh.

The witch or Torbay sole is not a true sole but a variety of plaice with a reasonable flavour. It is an inexpensive substitute for Dover sole, as is the lemon sole (see *dab*).

As a general rule the finest sole are fished in deep (rather than coastal) waters; cold-water varieties are better than those of warmer seas. Since 50% of the weight is lost in trimmings, sole is usually bought gutted (cleaned) and skinned or filleted. Its freshness is indicated by a very white blind side, coloured gills, and, above all, by a very sticky skin. There are very few bones in the flesh, but there is a long fin armed with straight sharp spines all around the fish, which should be carefully removed with a fish knife. The large bones linked to the backbone are easily removed. The fishmonger will often skin and fillet the fish (see *filleting fish*). Sole is a lean fish (containing only 1% fat) with firm white flesh that has a delicate flavour and is easily digested.

Usual cooking methods are deep-frying for the smallest fish, pan-frying or grilling (broiling) for medium sole or sole fillets (220–250 g, 7–9 oz), and poaching in stock for larger fish. Stuffed sole are braised or cooked in the oven. Fillets, rolled into paupiettes or left flat, are poached and served with a sauce or coated with breadcrumbs and fried.

There are more recipes for sole than for any other fish: *à l'amiral*, *à la bonne femme*, *au gratin*, *à la dieppoise*, Colbert, Dugléré, Mornay, Joinville, Nantua, *à la normande*, etc.

Fillets lend themselves to even more recipes: *à la batelière*, *à la bordelaise*, *en goujonnettes*, *à la hongroise*, Riche, Walewska, etc., not forgetting aspics, kebabs, croquettes, fritters, pâtés, timbales, vol-au-vent fillings, etc. In 1733 Chapelle offered sole *à la sauce aux rois* (stuffed with chopped herbs, capers, and anchovy fillets, poached in white wine, and served with the juice of a freshly squeezed orange); in 1739 Marin presented blanquette of fillets of sole. During the Belle Époque the chef of the Ritz created quenelles of sole coated with a Rhine wine sauce and garnished with shrimp tails, but undoubtedly the most popular dish is a succulent sole meunière, as described by Proust in *À l'ombre des jeunes filles en fleurs*: '. . . from the leathery skin of a lemon we squeezed a few golden drops on two sole, which soon left their bones on our plates, light as a feather and sonorous as a zither.'

RECIPES

Preparation of sole and fillets of sole
PREPARATION DES SOLES ET DES
FILETS To skin a sole, take hold of the
tail fin with a cloth and cut the black
skin at a slight angle just above the fin.
Gently detach the skin with your
thumb, then take hold of it with the
cloth and remove it with one sharp pull
towards the head. Remove the head
and, for the white side, pull the skin
from the head towards the tail. Cut the
side fins close to the flesh with scissors.
The head can also be cut in half at an
angle. To remove the fillets, cut the flesh
down to the bones on each side of the
backbone with a filleting knife. Detach
the flesh with the knife, from the backbone to the sides, to make four fillets.
Remove any debris attached to the flesh
and flatten slightly. Wash under running water.

Fillets of sole à la cantonnaise FILETS
DE SOLE À LA CANTONNAISE (from
Lysiane Luong Lap's recipe) Trim 2
good fillets for each guest. Sprinkle each
one with a very small pinch of coriander, cinnamon, mixed spice, nutmeg,
and chopped onion. Add 2 slices of fresh
ginger and fold the fillets in half.
Sprinkle with oil and a little more
seasoning, then steam for 10–12 minutes. Arrange on a warm plate and
season with salt and pepper.
  Prepare the sauce separately. Heat 4
tablespoons oil in a pan and add 2 large
chopped green peppers, 50 g (2 oz)
sliced mushrooms, 8 thin strips of
smoked pork, a slice of ham cut in
strips, 100 g (4 oz) chopped shrimps,
and a drained 250-g (8-oz) can of crabmeat. Cook for 5 minutes stirring continuously. Beat 2 eggs with 1 tablespoon
soy sauce; stir into the pan and dilute
with a little stock blended with 2 tablespoons tomato purée. Reheat and pour
over the fillets of sole.

Fillets of sole à l'anglaise FILETS DE
SOLE À L'ANGLAISE Coat 8 fillets of
sole with egg and breadcrumbs and
cook them in clarified butter. Arrange
on a long plate and cover with maître
d'hôtel butter. Serve with potatoes or a
boiled or steamed green vegetable
(leeks, spinach, etc.).

Fillets of sole poached in salted water
and milk are also known by this name.
They are served with boiled potatoes
and melted butter. Whole sole can be
cooked in the same way.

Fillets of sole au gratin FILETS DE
SOLE AU GRATIN Butter a gratin dish
and coat the base with 4 tablespoons
dry mushroom duxelles. Arrange 8 seasoned fillets of sole on top. Garnish with
sliced mushrooms around the dish and
place 2 mushroom caps cooked in butter on each fillet. Coat with a little duxelles sauce to which some concentrated
fish fumet has been added, sprinkle with
breadcrumbs and clarified butter, and
cook in a preheated very hot oven until
brown. Sprinkle with the juice of half a
lemon and serve in the cooking dish.

Fillets of sole Cubat FILETS DE SOLE
CUBAT Poach fillets of sole in mushroom stock and butter. Place on a long
ovenproof dish and cover with a thick
mushroom duxelles. Place 2 slices of
truffle on each fillet. Coat with Mornay
sauce and brown in the oven.
  This dish is named after Pierre Cubat,
chef at the court of Russia in 1903.

Fillets of sole Marco Polo FILETS DE
SOLE MARCO POLO (from
Marinette's recipe) Roughly chop some
tarragon, fennel, and a celery stick
(stalk). Crush some lobster or langouste
shells and put them in a frying pan
(skillet). Flame with brandy and add the
trimmings from 4 sole. Moisten with 3
dl (½ pint, 1¼ cups) white wine and
simmer, allowing the liquid to reduce
slightly.
  Place 50 g (2 oz, 4 tablespoons) butter, half a chopped shallot, and half a
peeled, deseeded, and crushed tomato in
a saucepan and moisten with 2 dl (7 fl
oz, ¾ cup) Champagne. Season with
salt and pepper. Poach the fillets in this
mixture for 5–6 minutes.
  Sieve the cooking juices of the shells,
crushing the latter firmly, then strain
through muslin. Add 100 g (4 oz, ½
cup) butter and whisk in 2 egg yolks and
1 dl (6 tablespoons, scant ½ cup) fresh
cream.
  Serve the fillets in their cooking juices,
well reduced, separately from the lobster sauce.

Fillets of sole Robert Courtine FILETS DE SOLE ROBERT COURTINE (from Jacques Manière's recipe) Fillet two 600–700-g (1½-lb) sole. Sprinkle with lemon juice and keep cool. Sweat 2 chopped shallots in a knob of butter over a gentle heat, moisten with 1 dl (6 tablespoons, scant ½ cup) white wine, and add a pinch of salt and pepper. Reduce slightly and add ¼ litre (8 fl oz, 1 cup) soured (dairy sour) cream. Reduce to two-thirds, remove from heat, and whisk in 150 g (5 oz) butter cut into small pieces. Strain into a sauceboat and keep warm in a bain-marie. Reserve the shallots for the forcemeat.

Flake 200 g (7 oz) white fish in a bowl, mix with the reserved shallots, and season with salt and pepper. Place bowl over crushed ice and work in 150 ml (¼ pint, ⅔ cup) double (heavy) cream. Lay the fillets of sole skin side up and season lightly. Spread the forcemeat along the fish and fold into three. Steam (on seaweed, if possible) for 7–8 minutes. Arrange on a dish and sprinkle with a little sevruga caviar. Add the remaining caviar (about 80 g (3 oz) altogether) to the sauce, mix gently, and pour over the fillets.

Garnish with chunks of peeled blanched steamed cucumber bound with soured cream, or, better still, make a garnish of small potato pancakes: rub 250 g (8¾ oz) boiled potatoes through a fine sieve into a basin. Add 3 tablespoons flour and 2 tablespoons double (heavy) cream, mix with a fork, and beat in 5 whole eggs, one at a time. Heat a heavy pan on a gentle heat, lightly cover the base with oil, and pour in the mixture to make small pancakes, which require about 3 minutes cooking on each side. The potato pancakes can be made in advance and kept warm.

Fillets of sole with apples FILETS DE SOLE AUX POMMES (from Jean and Paul Minchelli's recipe) Boil 2 teaspoons green peppercorns with 2 tablespoons fish fumet in a pan. Add 3 tablespoons fresh cream, freshly ground pepper, and a pinch of salt. Reduce, add 2 sliced tart apples, and cook for a few seconds. Gently poach 4 fillets of sole in a little fish fumet for 2 minutes. Drain, arrange on a plate, and surround with the apples. Add the cooking juices of the

fish to the peppercorn mixture and bring to the boil. Pour over the fish and serve.

Fillets of sole with basil FILETS DE SOLE AU BASILIC (from Claude Delign's recipe) Cover the bottom of an ovenproof dish with a mixture of 4 finely chopped shallots, 1 tablespoon basil, and 1 tablespoon olive oil. Arrange the seasoned fillets of two 750-g (1¾-lb) sole on top. Moisten with 5 tablespoons (6 tablespoons) fish stock and an equal amount of white wine. Cover with aluminium foil and bring to the boil on a brisk heat, then place in a very hot oven for 5 minutes. Drain the fish and keep warm between 2 plates. Reduce the cooking juices to a third. Whisk in 120 g (4½ oz) butter in small pieces, adjust the seasoning, and add the juice of half a lemon. Plunge a tomato into boiling water for 30 seconds, peel, deseed, and dice, then place the tomato on the fillets and coat with the sauce. Sprinkle with chopped basil.

Fillets of sole with mushrooms FILETS DE SOLE AUX CHAMPIGNONS Fold each fillet over 2 large mushroom caps and cook over a gentle heat in a fish fumet prepared with white wine. Carefully invert the drained fish onto a long dish so that the mushrooms face upwards. Add an equal quantity of fresh cream to the cooking juices and reduce by half. Whisk in 30 g (1 oz, 2 tablespoons) butter, strain, and pour over the fish.

Fillets of sole with vermouth FILETS DE SOLE AU VERMOUTH (from Louis Outhier's recipe) Place the fillets in a buttered pan. Moisten with 1 dl (6 tablespoons, scant ½ cup) fish fumet and 1 dl (6 tablespoons, scant ½ cup) dry vermouth. Poach gently for 10 minutes. Remove the fish and keep warm. Cook 125 g (4 oz) sliced mushroom caps in butter over a brisk heat, for 4 minutes, with salt, pepper, and lemon juice. Strain both cooking juices into a pan and reduce to 4 tablespoons; add 4 dl (14 fl oz, 1¾ cups) double (heavy) cream, and boil. Remove from the heat and bind with 3 egg yolks. Reheat, stirring, without allowing the mixture to boil. Garnish the fillets with the mushrooms and coat with the sauce.

Fried fillets of sole en goujons FILETS DE SOLE FRITS EN GOUJONS Cut 2 large fillets of sole diagonally across in slices about 2 cm (¾ in) wide. Dip in salted milk, drain, coat with flour, and fry in hot fat or oil (180 C, 350 F). Drain on absorbent paper, sprinkle with fine salt, and arrange in a heap on a napkin. Garnish with fried parsley and lemon wedges. The fillets, also known as *goujonnettes*, can be used as a garnish for large braised fish and for sole *à la normande.*

Grilled (broiled) fillets of sole FILETS DE SOLE GRILLÉS Season the fillets, baste with oil or clarified butter, and grill (broil) each side for 4 minutes. Arrange on a long dish surrounded with lemon slices and fried parsley. Serve with melted butter flavoured with lemon juice.

Fried sole SOLES FRITES Skin, gut (clean), and trim the sole, which should weigh no more than 250 g (9 oz) each. Soak in milk, drain, and deep fry in oil heated to 180 C (350 F) at least. As soon as they are golden, drain on absorbent paper. Sprinkle with fine salt and serve with lemon quarters.

Golden sole SOLE DORÉE Season and flour the sole. Brown lightly in clarified butter. Garnish with peeled lemon slices and sprinkle with noisette butter.

Grilled (broiled) sole SOLE GRIL-LÉE Skin a sole of at least 400 g (14 oz). Lightly season, soak in oil, and drain well. Grill (broil) on both sides. Serve with half slices of canelled lemon, fried parsley, and any sauce suitable for grilled fish.

Paupiettes of sole PAUPIETTES DE SOLE Prepare a forcemeat from 500 g (18 oz) puréed whiting, salt, pepper, and 2 dl (7 fl oz, ¾ cup) fresh cream, working in a bowl over crushed ice.

Remove and prepare the fillets from 2 large (750-g, 1¾-lb) sole. Lightly flatten them on a damp worktop and season both sides. Spread the forcemeat on the 8 fillets, roll them up, and tie loosely, so that the forcemeat does not escape. Butter a flameproof dish large enough to hold the fillets upright, side by side, then sprinkle it with 2 or 3 chopped shallots and arrange the fillets in it. Season. Moisten with 175 ml (6 fl oz, ¾ cup) each of white wine and fish fumet. Cover with aluminium foil, bring to the boil, then place in a hot oven (230 C, 450 F, gas 8) and cook for 10–15 minutes. Drain the paupiettes and arrange on a serving dish. Keep warm.

Strain the cooking juices into a small saucepan and whisk in 1 tablespoon butter. Pour this onto 2 egg yolks beaten with the juice of half a lemon, then return it to the saucepan and whisk until thick, without allowing it to boil. Pour over the paupiettes and serve very hot.

Sole à la meunière Skin, gut (clean), wash, and trim 4 sole, each weighing 250–300 g (9–11 oz); lightly flour and season with pepper. Heat 75–100 g (3 –4 oz, 6–8 tablespoons) clarified butter and 1 tablespoon oil in a frying pan (skillet). Brown the sole for 6–7 minutes on each side. Drain and arrange on a heated serving dish. Pour over 75 g (3 oz, 6 tablespoons) butter melted in a saucepan with the juice of a lemon. Sprinkle with chopped parsley. Serve with fried mushrooms, aubergines (eggplants), or courgettes (zucchini), buttered boiled potatoes, spinach, etc.

Sole and mushroom brochettes BROCHETTES DE SOLE AUX CHAMPIGNONS Cut the fish into square pieces of equal size. Sandwich them together two by two with a stuffing made from hard-boiled (hard-cooked) egg yolks, fresh soft breadcrumbs, and chopped parsley. Thread them on skewers, alternating with mushrooms tossed in melted butter. Season with salt and pepper and baste with clarified butter. Cover with white dried breadcrumbs and grill (broil).

Sole with orange SOLE À L'ORANGE Brown a trimmed floured sole in a knob of butter until cooked through on both sides. Place on a hot serving dish and season with pepper. Garnish with thin slices of peeled orange with the seeds removed. Melt a little butter in a bain-marie, season with salt, and add a little fresh cream and Curaçao. Pour over the sole.

Sole with pan-fried vegetables SOLE AUX LÉGUMES POÊLES Cook a sole *à la meunière*. Surround it with sliced vegetables fried in oil or butter; sprinkle with chopped parsley, a little lemon juice, and a little hot oil or hot melted butter.

Suitable vegetables include: aubergines (eggplants) and courgettes (zucchini) fried in oil, chunks of cucumber sweated in butter, sliced artichoke hearts fried in butter, mushrooms (especially ceps) fried in butter or oil, and red or green peppers cut into thick julienne strips and sweated in oil.

Stuffed sole Auberge de l'Ill SOLES FARCIES AUBERGE DE L'ILL (from Paul and Jean-Pierre Haeberlin's recipe) Remove the black skin from two 750-g (1¾-lb) sole and cut off the heads at an angle. Cut along the backbone and open out. Remove the bone, taking care that the fillets remain attached.

Put 100 g (4 oz) whiting fillets, 1 egg white, salt, pepper, and a pinch of grated nutmeg in a blender or processor. Run the machine and add ¼ litre (8 fl oz, 1 cup) very cold double (heavy) cream, a little at a time. Mix the forcemeat with 150 g (5 oz) diced salmon fillets and 50 g (2 oz) chopped pistachios in a terrine. Stuff the sole with the mixture, season, and arrange on a buttered ovenproof dish. Sprinkle with chopped shallots and moisten with ¼ litre (8 fl oz, 1 cup) Riesling and ¼ litre (8 fl oz, 1 cup) fish fumet. Cover with aluminium foil and cook in a hot oven (220 C, 425 F, gas 7) for 25 minutes. Arrange on a plate and keep warm.

Pour the cooking juices into a pan, add ¼ litre (8 fl oz, 1 cup) double (heavy) cream, and reduce by half. Whisk in 100 g (4 oz, ½ cup) butter, a little at a time. Add the juice of a lemon. Adjust the seasoning and pour over the sole. Garnish with slices of truffle glazed in butter and puff-pastry flowers.

solilemme or solilem

A type of brioche, rich in eggs, butter, and cream, which is cut in half after cooking, while still warm, and sprinkled with melted salted butter. Solilemme is usually served with tea, but it can also be served in slices with smoked fish. It originated in Alsace; Carême gave a recipe for it. It is similar to, though richer than, the English tea bread Sally Lunn, made by a Bath pastrycook of the same name in the 1780s. She sold her cakes to the fashionable people who came to take the local waters. The Sally Lunn is also sliced while still warm and spread generously with butter.

| RECIPE

Solilemme Mix together 125 g (4 oz, 1 cup) sifted flour and 15 g (½ oz) fresh yeast (½ cake compressed yeast), creamed with 2–3 tablespoons warm water. Leave to rise for about 2 hours at room temperature, away from draughts. Break up the dough, mix in 2 eggs and 50 ml (3 tablespoons, ¼ cup) fresh cream, then add 375 g (13 oz, 3½ cups) sifted flour. Knead the dough. Mix 125 g (4 oz) butter cut into small pieces, 50 ml (3 tablespoons, ¼ cup) double (heavy) cream, and 2 eggs into the dough. Knead thoroughly, adding a little more cream if necessary (the dough should be fairly soft). Place in a buttered charlotte mould and leave to double in volume, away from draughts. Cook in a hot oven (220 C, 425 F, gas 7) for 40 minutes. Turn out the solilemme and cut into two layers. Sprinkle each with 40 g (1½ oz, 3 tablespoons) melted slightly salted butter and sandwich together again.

solognote (à la)

Describing a preparation for duck. The bird is stuffed, preferably the day before, with its liver, which has been marinated in Armagnac and herbs then finely minced with fresh soft breadcrumbs. The duck is then pot-roasted.

Gigot *à la solognote* is a leg of lamb marinated in white wine and wine vinegar with flavourings, then roasted. The marinade, well reduced, is used as a sauce.

sommelier

Originally, the monk who had charge of the crockery, linen, bread, and wine in a monastery, i.e. the cellarer. During the Ancien Régime, the king's household had several sommeliers, whose primary function was to receive the wine brought by the *sommiers* (from French *bêtes de somme*, 'beasts of burden'). The name sommelier was also applied to the officials who took care of royal furniture; later, it was used for any bearer of burdens. During the reign of Louis XIV, the sommelier was the official in charge of the transport of baggage when the court moved. In the household of a great lord he was the official who chose the wines, table settings, and desserts.

Nowadays, the sommelier of a large restaurant is the wine waiter, a job which requires extensive knowledge of the subject and the ability to choose the appropriate wine for a dish. The *caviste* (cellarman) is responsible for supervising the wines in the cellar.

sorb apple CORME

The fruit of the service tree. Sorb apples resemble small greenish or reddish pears; they are gathered after the first frosts and become pulpy and sweet when they are overripe. They can then be eaten without further preparation, like medlars, but they have a more delicate flavour.

In the west of France, they are also used to make a fermented drink known as *cormé*, which is a little like cider.

sorbet

A type of water ice that is softer and more granular than ice cream as it does not contain any fat or egg yolk. The basic ingredient of a sorbet is fruit juice or purée, wine, spirit, or liqueur, or an infusion (tea or mint). A sugar syrup, sometimes with additional glucose or one or two invert sugars, is added. The mixture should not be beaten during freezing. When the sorbet has set, some Italian meringue can be added to give it volume.

Historically, sorbets were the first iced desserts (ice creams did not appear until the 18th century). The Chinese introduced them to the Persians and Arabs, who introduced them to the Italians. The word *sorbet* is a gallicization of the Italian *sorbetto*, derived from Turkish *chorbet* and Arab *charab*, which simply meant 'drink'. Sorbets were originally made of fruit, honey, aromatic substances, and snow. Today, the sorbet is served as a dessert or as a refreshment (in a cornet) between meals; at large formal dinners in France, sorbets with an alcoholic base are served between the main courses, taking the place of the liqueurs (*trou normand*) that were formerly served in the middle of the meal. Sorbets are served in sundae dishes or tall glasses; they are sometimes sprinkled with a liqueur or alcohol to match their flavour (vodka on lime, clear spirits on the appropriate fruit). Other ingredients, such as raisins, pine nuts, etc., can be incorporated into the mixture before freezing.

RECIPES

Fruit sorbet SORBET AUX FRUITS
For soft fruit, prepare a syrup using 200 g (7 oz, scant cup) sugar and 150 ml (¼ pint, ⅔ cup) water per 500 g (18 oz) fruit. Poach the fruit in the syrup then purée in a blender or processor: the density of the mixture should be 1.1513. For citrus fruit use 100 g (4 oz, ½ cup) sugar and 150 ml (¼ pint, ⅔ cup) water for every 3–4 fruit. Finely grate the zest then squeeze the juice from the fruit and mix with the syrup: the density of the mixture should be 1.1697. Correct the density by adding more sugar (if it is too weak) or more water (if it is too strong). Pour into an ice-cream maker and allow to freeze. Halfway through the cycle some Italian meringue (one-third of the volume of the sorbet) can be added.

Peach sorbet SORBET À LA PÊCHE
Prepare a syrup by boiling 1 dl (6 tablespoons, scant ½ cup) water with 300 g (11 oz, scant 1½ cups) sugar and allow to cool. Peel 1 kg (2¼ lb) white peaches, cut into quarters, and purée in a blender or processor. Add the juice of a large lemon and mix the purée with the cold syrup. Pour into an ice-cream maker and set in operation for an hour. When the sorbet has frozen, switch off the machine and put the container in the freezer, together with 4 sorbet glasses, for about an hour. To serve: place 2 balls of sorbet in each glass and pour over some well-chilled champagne (½ bottle for the 4 glasses).

Pear sorbet SORBET À LA POIRE
Peel 4 juicy pears and cut into quarters.
Remove the pips and dice the flesh.
Sprinkle with the juice of a lemon. Reduce to a fine purée, with 300 g (11 oz,
scant 1½ cups) sugar, in a blender or
processor. Pour the purée into an ice-
cream maker and operate for 1½ hours,
until the sorbet freezes. Put the container into the freezer until required or
serve immediately.

Raspberry sorbet SORBET À LA
FRAMBOISE Prepare a syrup by boiling 250 g (9 oz, generous cup) sugar and
4 dl (14 fl oz, 1¾ cups) water. Allow to
cool. Pour in 400 g (14 oz, 3 cups)
raspberries and the juice of half a lemon.
Purée in a blender or food processor and
then pass through a sieve if wished. Pour
the mixture into an ice-cream maker,
and set in operation for about an hour.
When the sorbet begins to freeze, pour
into a mould and place in the freezer
until required.

Sorbet of exotic fruits SORBET AUX
FRUITS EXOTIQUES Peel a very ripe
pineapple, cut into 4, remove the centre,
and dice the pulp, retaining the juice.
Cut 2 mangoes in half, remove the
stones (pits), and scoop out the flesh
with a spoon. Peel and slice a banana.
Put the fruit into a blender or processor
with juice of a lemon and purée it.
Measure the juice obtained. Add 75 g (3
oz, 6 tablespoons) caster (superfine)
sugar per ¼ litre (8 fl oz, 1 cup) juice.
Mix with a fork and add 1 teaspoon
vanilla sugar and a pinch of cinnamon.
Pour into an ice-cream maker and set in
operation for 1½ hours. When the sorbet begins to freeze, put into the freezer.
Serve in chilled sundae dishes.

Sorbet with Calvados SORBET AU
CALVADOS Dissolve 200 g (7 oz,
scant cup) caster (superfine) sugar in ⅓
litre (11 fl oz, 1⅓ cups) water. Add a
vanilla pod (bean) cut in half. Bring to
the boil to obtain a light syrup. Remove
from heat; discard the vanilla pod. Add
the juice of a lemon and a pinch of
cinnamon. Mix well. Whisk (beat) 3 egg
whites to stiff peaks and mix them
gently into the syrup. Pour into the ice-
cream maker. When the sorbet begins to
freeze add 4–5 liqueur glasses old Cal-

vados. Beat for a few moments, turn
into a mould and freeze until required.

Sorbet with cocoa and raisins SORBET
AU CACAO ET AUX RAISINS Thoroughly mix 1 litre (1¾ pints, 4¼ cups)
water, 600 g (1¼ lb, 2½ cups) sugar,
250 g (8¾ oz, 2 cups) cocoa, 50 g (2 oz)
vanilla essence, and 3 cl (1½ tablespoons, 2 tablespoons) dark rum. After
processing in the ice-cream maker, add
100–150 g (4–5 oz, scant cup) raisins
soaked in whisky and pour into a
mould. Freeze until required.

Sorbet with honey and pine nuts SOR-
BET AU MIEL ET AUX PIGNONS DE
PIN Mix 900 g (2 lb, 2⅔ cups) orange-
blossom honey, the juice of a lemon, a
few drops orange-flower water, and 1
litre (1¾ pints, 4¼ cups) water. After
processing in the ice-cream maker, add
some lightly toasted pine nuts, then
pour into a mould and place in the
freezer.

Strawberry sorbet SORBET À LA
FRAISE Wash and hull 1 kg (2¼ lb, 7
cups) strawberries and purée in a
blender or food processor. Add 300 g
(11 oz, scant 1½ cups) caster (superfine)
sugar. Mix well to dissolve, then add the
juice of half a lemon and an orange.
Pour into the ice-cream maker. Set in
operation for about an hour. Pour the
sorbet into a mould and put into the
freezer for a further 1½–2 hours to
allow the sorbet to freeze completely.

sorghum SORGHO

A cereal that is grown in hot countries
and has the highest world consumption
after rice. Also known as Indian millet,
guinea-corn, or durra, sorghum provides flour, which is not suitable for
bread but is used for porridges and flat
cakes. Fermented drinks are also made
from its seeds.

Records of sorghum cultivation in
India date back to 1900 BC. It was
grown in Italy in the days of Pliny and
was possibly named *surgo* (I rise) at this
time; the name could also be derived
from Latin *syricus* (from Syria). Its cultivation was abandoned in Europe at
the end of the 15th century, but it remains a staple food crop in Africa and
China. Cakes made from sorghum are
served with spicy sauces or milk and

butter. A type of couscous is made from sorghum in Mali, while in Tunisia the traditional *sohleb*, a sorghum porridge with ginger, is sold in the streets. In China such porridges are a staple food: sorghum appeared 3000 years before rice. *Pombé*, a beer made with sorghum and okra, is traditionally brewed by women in the Sudan. An alcohol flavoured with rose petals, called *caoliang*, is made from sorghum in China; it is also used in cookery for marinades and sauces.

soringue

An eel dish typical of 15th-century cookery. Skinned steamed pieces of eel were simmered in a thick sauce of toasted breadcrumbs mixed with verjuice and flavoured with ginger, cinnamon, cloves, and saffron, with added fried onion rings and chopped parsley. Finally, the dish was enhanced with wine, verjuice, and vinegar.

sorrel OSEILLE

A culinary plant originating in northern Asia and Europe; its edible green leaves have a slightly bitter taste (from the oxalic acid they contain). It has only 25 Cal per 100 g and is rich in potassium, magnesium, and vitamin C. In France several varieties with large or small crinkled leaves, either dark or pale green, are available from March to August; the most common variety is the 'Large de Belleville'. When sorrel is for sale it should be shiny and firm; it will keep for some days in the bottom of the refrigerator. It is prepared and cooked in the same way as spinach; when made into a purée or shredded, it can be given extra smoothness by adding a white roux or some cream. Sorrel is a traditional accompaniment for fish (shad, pike) and veal (topside (rump), breast). It can also be used as a filling for omelettes, as an accompaniment to eggs *en cocotte*, and to prepare soup and velouté sauce. When the leaves are very young and tender they can be eaten in a salad.

RECIPES

Chiffonade of sorrel CHIFFONADE D'OSEILLE Pick over the sorrel leaves and remove the hard stalks. Wash and dry the leaves and shred them finely. Melt some butter in a saucepan without letting it colour (allow 30 g, 1 oz, 2 tablespoons butter for 200 g, 7 oz, 1 cup leaves); add the sorrel, three-quarters cover the pan with a lid, and let it cook gently until all the vegetable liquid has disappeared. The chiffonade can be used as it is as a garnish; it can also be mixed with thick cream and reduced. A 'mixed' chiffonade is a combination of sorrel and lettuce.

Preserved sorrel CONSERVE D'OSEILLE Clean some sorrel, shred it finely, and cook it in butter until it is completely dry. Pack it into a widemouthed jar. When it is quite cold, seal the jar and sterilize it. The sorrel can also be packed into containers and frozen. It is advisable to prepare only small quantities at a time.

Sorrel purée PURÉE D'OSEILLE Pick over and clean some sorrel, taking out the hard stalks. Put the leaves into a large saucepan and pour in boiling water, allowing 1 litre (1¾ pints, 4¼ cups) water per kg (2¼ lb) sorrel. Bring to the boil, cook for 4–5 minutes, then remove from the heat; drain in a sieve. In a casserole, make a white roux using 60 g (2½ oz, 5 tablespoons) butter and 40 g (1½ oz, 6 tablespoons) flour. Add the sorrel and mix well together. Pour in 5 dl (17 fl oz, 2 cups) white stock and add salt and a pinch of sugar.

Cover the casserole, bring to the boil on top of the stove, then transfer it to the oven and cook at 180 C (350 F, gas 4) for 1½ hours. Purée the sorrel in a blender and return it to the hob to reheat. Bind it with 3 whole eggs beaten with 1 dl (6 tablespoons, scant ½ cup) cream. Finally add 100 g (4 oz, ½ cup) butter, cut into small pieces.

sot-l'y-laisse

The small piece of chicken meat in the hollow of each of the iliac bones, just above the tail. The French name of this delicacy, which literally means 'the fool leaves it there', confirms its choiceness. Its English name is the oyster. The carver usually keeps it for himself or offers it to a guest.

Soubise

The name given to dishes containing an

onion sauce (a béchamel to which onion purée has been added) or an onion purée (usually thickened with rice). These preparations were named in honour of Charles de Rohan, Prince of Soubise and marshal of France, who, like other 18th-century French aristocrats, did not despise the culinary art. It is particularly applied to dishes of eggs, served on the purée or sometimes covered with the sauce. The purée may also be used to garnish cuts of meat or as a stuffing for vegetables.

RECIPES

Hard-boiled eggs à la Soubise OEUFS DURS À LA SOUBISE Hard-boil (hard-cook) some eggs; cool and shell them. Prepare 2 tablespoons Soubise purée per egg and pour into a buttered dish. Place the eggs in the purée at regular intervals and coat with cream sauce.

Soubise purée PURÉE SOUBISE Peel and thinly slice 1 kg (2¼ lb) white onions and place in a saucepan with plenty of salted water. Bring to the boil, then drain the onions and place in a saucepan with 100 g (4 oz, ½ cup) butter, salt, pepper, and a pinch of sugar. Cover and cook over a gentle heat for 30–40 minutes (the onions should not change colour). Then add to the onions one-quarter of their volume of boiled rice or thick béchamel sauce. Mix thoroughly and cook for a further 20 minutes. Adjust the seasoning, pass through a very fine sieve, and mix in 75 g (3 oz, 6 tablespoons) butter.

Soubise sauce SAUCE SOUBISE Prepare a Soubise purée with béchamel sauce. When it is well thickened, add 1 dl (6 tablespoons, scant ½ cup) whipping cream. Blend thoroughly.

Stuffed potatoes Soubise POMMES DE TERRE FARCIES SOUBISE Bake some firm medium-sized unpeeled potatoes in the oven, then scoop them out into a bowl. Prepare a well-reduced Soubise purée. Add a quarter of its volume of cream and reduce still further until the mixture is extremely thick. Beat into the scooped-out potato until well blended. Stuff the potato skins with this mixture, arrange them in an ovenproof dish, and sprinkle with breadcrumbs and small knobs of butter. Brown in a very hot oven.

sou du franc

A former practice whereby the housekeeper or cook, responsible for buying food, was given a cash discount of 5%. It was officially accepted by the employers that this profit, which could be quite considerable, should be kept by the housekeeper or cook over and above their basic wages. On the other hand, any servant caught trying to make an illicit profit by falsifying the accounts was immediately dismissed.

sou-fassum

In the cookery of Nice, a whole cabbage stuffed with a forcemeat of Swiss chard, bacon, onions, rice, and sausagemeat. Traditionally wrapped in a net known as a *fassumier*, it is cooked in the stock of a mutton pot-au-feu. In Grasse, there is a variation of this dish in which the cabbage leaves are arranged alternately with the forcemeat in a terrine lined with slices of streaky bacon. The sou-fassum, which is said to be of Greek origin, apparently dates back to the founding of Antibes.

RECIPE

Sou-fassum Trim a large green cabbage, blanch for 8 minutes in boiling salted water, then cool and drain. Detach the large leaves, remove their ribs, and spread them out flat on a net or muslin (cheesecloth), soaked and wrung out. Chop the remainder of the cabbage and arrange it on the leaves, then add in layers: 250 g (8¾ oz) blanched chopped Swiss chard leaves; 200 g (7 oz) lean bacon, diced and browned; 100 g (4 oz, 1 cup) chopped onions, fried in butter; 2 large tomatoes, peeled, deseeded, and crushed; 100 g (4 oz, ⅔ cup) blanched rice; and 750 g (1¾ lb, 3½ cups) sausagemeat with a crushed garlic clove added. Shape this mixture into a large ball, then fold round the leaves to enclose the stuffing. Tie up the net, plunge the cabbage into a mutton pot-au-feu stock, and boil very gently for approximately 3½ hours. Drain the cabbage, unwrap, and arrange on a round dish. Pour over a few tablespoons of stock and serve hot.

soufflé

A hot preparation which is served straight from the oven, so that it is well risen above the height of the mould in which it is cooked. There are two basic types: savoury soufflés, which are served as hors d'oeuvres or hot entrées; and sweet soufflés, which are served as desserts.

• *Savoury soufflés* are made from a thick béchamel sauce or a purée, bound with egg yolks, to which are then added stiffly beaten egg whites. Ingredients added to the basic mixture (in the form of a salpicon or purée), which determine the name of the soufflé, include vegetables, ham, cheese, white poultry meat or poultry livers, fish or shellfish, or a game or offal salpicon. During cooking, the air trapped in the egg whites expands and increases the volume of the preparation, which must be served immediately, before it collapses. A soufflé must never be left to stand but the basic mixture can be prepared in advance and kept in a bain-marie or in a cool place until the stiffly beaten egg whites are added, just before cooking. The egg whites are whisked with a pinch of salt until stiff and folded in very gently. First a little of the egg white is beaten with the mixture to slacken it, then the remainder is folded in quickly, a little at a time, until the mixture is smooth.

The cooking mould is cylindrical, so that the preparation can rise evenly; it is buttered and often covered with flour, and only filled three-quarters full. For individual soufflés, ramekins are used. Special care must be taken not to open the oven door while the soufflé is cooking. As the soufflé is served straight from the mould, the latter is made of an attractive material that withstands high temperatures, such as fireproof porcelain (the material most frequently recommended), enamelled cast iron (which guarantees good distribution of heat), or fireproof glass (which takes longer to heat).

• *Dessert soufflés* are based either on a milk mixture or a fruit purée and cooked sugar mixture. For the former, a confectioner's custard (pastry cream) is used, which is bound with egg yolks and flavoured (with vanilla, liqueur, spirit,

etc.) before folding in the stiffly beaten egg whites. Alternatively a blond roux can be used: it is mixed with boiling sweetened vanilla-flavoured milk and bound with yolks (or yolks and whole eggs) before adding the stiffly beaten egg whites and the flavouring. These soufflés are cooked in buttered sugar-coated moulds. Dessert soufflés may be filled with pieces of sponge finger biscuits (ladyfingers) or Genoese cake (soaked in liqueur or spirit), which are either sandwiched in three layers in the soufflé mixture or placed all together in the centre of the soufflé. The top is smoothed or sometimes grooved.

Soufflés made from a fruit mixture have a base of sugar cooked to the 'hard crack' stage, to which a fruit purée is added. The mixture is then reheated just to the 'soft ball' stage (110 c, 230 f). The egg whites are whisked into the hot mixture, which is poured over them. The fruit flavour is enhanced by a little alcohol or liqueur. Fresh fruit soufflés are usually prepared using this recipe, but you can also make them with confectioner's custard (pastry cream): very dense fruit purée is then added to the custard before the whites are incorporated.

The appearance of a dessert soufflé can be enhanced by sprinkling it with icing (confectioners') sugar a few minutes before the end of cooking: the icing sugar caramelizes to give the soufflé a glossy surface.

Before cooking a savoury or sweet soufflé, it is advisable to stand it for a few minutes in a bain-marie of very hot water; alternatively put the soufflé in a hot oven (220 c, 425 f, gas 7), then immediately reduce the heat to 190 c (375 f, gas 5) and cook for 25–30 minutes (for a large soufflé) or 12 minutes (for small individual soufflés). The soufflé is served by placing it, still in its mould, on a plate, which in classic cuisine is covered with a dish paper (for a savoury soufflé) or a paper doily (for a sweet dessert soufflé).

☐ **Iced soufflés** These are iced desserts that superficially resemble genuine soufflés: the mixture is placed in a soufflé mould or a timbale whose height is increased by a band of paper; after freezing, the paper is removed so that the soufflé rises above the level of the mould, like a baked soufflé.

An iced soufflé is made either of a simple ice cream or, more frequently, of alternate layers of mousse and either ice cream, parfait, or bombe mixture, variously flavoured and coloured. These layers may be separated by layers of sponge cake soaked in liqueur, thick sweetened fruit purée, fruit in syrup, crystallized (candied) fruits, etc. The top is often decorated with Chantilly cream, coffee beans in liqueur, or any other sugar decoration. These soufflés are also made in ramekins. Iced soufflés are usually served with champagne or a dessert wine.

Chilled soufflés can also be made in this way but dissolved gelatine is incorporated in the mixture. The soufflé is then placed in the refrigerator to set rather than frozen.

RECIPES

Dessert Soufflés

Banana soufflé SOUFFLÉ AUX BANANES Mix together in a saucepan 1 tablespoon sifted flour and a pinch of salt with 1 dl (5 tablespoons, scant ½ cup) milk, which has been boiled with 30 g (1 oz, 2 tablespoons) caster sugar and half a vanilla pod (bean) and then cooled. Boil the mixture for 2 minutes, whisking all the time, then remove from the heat and add the pulp of 4 finely sieved bananas, 2 egg yolks, and 20 g (¾ oz, 1½ tablespoons) butter. Flavour if required with Kirsch or rum. Fold in 3 stiffly whisked egg whites. Pour the mixture into a 20-cm (8-in) buttered soufflé mould (or small ramekins) coated with caster (superfine) sugar. Cook in the oven at 200 C (400 F, gas 6) for 30 minutes (for a large soufflé) or about 12 minutes for ramekins.

Chestnut soufflé SOUFFLÉ AUX CHÂ-TAIGNES (from a recipe by Jean and Pierre Troisgros) Place 300 g (11 oz) peeled chestnuts in a saucepan with 2 dl (7 fl oz, ¾ cup) milk, 20 g (¾ oz, 1½ tablespoons) sugar, and a pinch of salt; boil for 10 minutes with the lid on, then remove the lid and continue to boil for a further 5 minutes to allow the milk to evaporate. Set 4 whole chestnuts aside and rub the remainder through a sieve or put in a blender or processor. Blend the purée with 4 dl (14 fl oz, 1¾ cups) double (heavy) cream and place in a bain-marie of very hot water.

Butter a 20-cm (8-in) soufflé mould and coat with flour. Whisk 5 egg whites until stiff together with a pinch of salt. Return the chestnut purée to the heat and, when it is just boiling, remove from the heat and mix in 3 egg yolks. Stir thoroughly. Add a quarter of the stiffly whisked egg whites and mix thoroughly. Crumble 2 of the reserved chestnuts and add them. Carefully fold in the remaining egg whites using a metal spoon. Pour this mixture into the mould and smooth the surface; sprinkle with the 2 remaining chestnuts cut into 12 pieces. Place in a preheated moderate oven (180 C, 350 F, gas 4), switch off the oven, and leave to cook for 15–20 minutes without opening the door. Serve immediately with a tangerine sorbet.

Chocolate soufflé SOUFFLÉ AU CHOCOLAT Follow the recipe for coffee soufflé, but dissolve 75 g (3 oz) plain chocolate in the milk instead of instant coffee and sweeten with 75 g (3 oz, scant ½ cup) caster (superfine) sugar.

Coffee soufflé SOUFFLÉ AU CAFÉ Over a low heat, dissolve 2 tablespoons (3 tablespoons) instant coffe in 1 tablespoon milk taken from a ¼ litre (8 fl oz, 1 cup). Then add the remainder of the milk and bring to the boil. Beat 2 egg yolks with 30 g (1 oz, 2 tablespoons) caster (superfine) sugar until the mixture turns thick and white, then incorporate 30 g (1 oz, ¼ cup) flour in a trickle. Gradually pour the boiling coffee-flavoured milk into the mixture, beating briskly. Pour the mixture into a saucepan and bring to the boil, stirring all the time. Once it has boiled, transfer it to a large bowl and allow to cool. Butter a 20-cm (8-in) soufflé mould and sprinkle it with 25 g (1 oz), caster (superfine) sugar. Beat 6 egg whites until they are stiff. Incorporate a further 2 egg yolks into the coffee preparation, then carefully fold in the whites using a metal spoon. Pour the mixture into the mould and cook in the oven at 190 C (375 F, gas 5) for 20 minutes. Then sprinkle the soufflé with icing (confectioners') sugar and return to the oven for 5 minutes to glaze the surface. Serve immediately.

Curaçao soufflé SOUFFLÉ AU CURAÇAO Whisk 250 g (9 oz, generous cup) sugar with 8 egg yolks until the mixture turns pale and thick. Incorporate 1 dl (6 tablespoons, scant ½ cup) Curaçao, then fold in the whites of 12 eggs very stiffly whisked with a pinch of salt. Pour the mixture into a large buttered soufflé mould coated with sugar, place in the oven at 200 C (400 F, gas 6), and bake for 15 minutes. Sprinkle icing (confectioners') sugar over the top and return to the oven for 5–6 minutes. Serve immediately.

Another liqueur may be used instead of Curaçao.

Fruit soufflé made with sugar syrup SOUFFLÉ AUX FRUITS AU SIROP DE SUCRE Mix 1 kg (2¼ lb, 4½ cups) sugar with 1 dl (6 tablespoons, scant ½ cup) water and boil until the temperature reaches 140 C (284 F). Then add 1.2 kg (2½ lb) finely sieved fruit purée. Fold in 12 stiffly whisked egg whites and cook in a large soufflé mould in a moderately hot oven (190 C, 375 F, gas 5) for about 35–40 minutes.

Strawberries and raspberries are used raw.

Apricots, cherries, pears, and apples are cooked in sugar beforehand; apples should be reduced until very dry before being sieved.

Lime soufflé SOUFFLÉ AU CITRON VERT (from Daniel Valluet's recipe) Boil 1.25 dl (7 tablespoons, scant ⅔ cup) milk together with the zest of a lime. Whisk 50 g, ¼ cup) sugar, 2 egg yolks, 25 g (1 oz, 2 tablespoons) cornflour (cornstarch), and 1.25 dl (7 tablespoons, scant ⅔ cup) lime juice. Pour the boiling milk onto this mixture, then return to the heat and bring to the boil, whisking all the time. Leave to cool.

Butter 4 ramekins liberally and coat with sugar. Add 2 egg yolks to the confectioner's custard (pastry cream). Stiffly whisk the whites of 6–8 eggs (depending on their size), blend in 75 g (3 oz, scant ½ cup) caster (superfine) sugar, and fold the mixture into the confectioner's custard (pastry cream). Pour the mixture into the moulds and

place in the oven at 200 C (400 F, gas 6). After 12 minutes, place a thin slice of lime on each soufflé, cover with a sheet of greaseproof (waxed) paper, and cook a further 3 minutes. Serve immediately with a warm custard cream (see *creams and custards*) flavoured with blanched lime zest.

soufflé ambassadrice Prepare a confectioner's custard (pastry cream; see *creams and custards*) using 1 litre (1¾ pints, 4¼ cups) milk, 8 egg yolks, a generous pinch of salt, 120 g (4 oz, 1 cup) flour (or 4 tablespoons (⅓ cup) cornflour or potato flour), and 300 g (11 oz, scant 1½ cups) sugar. Add 1 teaspoon vanilla essence, 8 crushed macaroons, and 6 tablespoons (½ cup) shredded (slivered) almonds soaked in rum. Fold in 12 stiffly whisked egg whites, turn into a large prepared soufflé dish, and cook in a moderately hot oven (200 C, 400 F, gas 6) for about 30–35 minutes.

ICED SOUFFLÉS

Iced fruit soufflé SOUFFLÉ GLACÉ AUX FRUITS Cook 300 g (11 oz, scant 1½ cups) caster (superfine) sugar in 1 dl (6 tablespoons, scant ½ cup) water to the soufflé stage (see *sugar*). Pour this syrup over 5 very stiffly whisked egg whites, whisking until completely cold. Purée 350 g (12 oz) fresh strawberries or raspberries, or apricots, peaches, or pears cooked in sguar. Fold the purée into the egg white and sugar mixture together with ½ litre (17 fl oz, 2 cups) stiffly whipped cream.

Cut out a strip of greaseproof (waxed) paper or aluminium foil 24 cm (9 in) wide and longer than the circumference of the soufflé mould. Fold in half to reduce its width to 12 cm (4½ in). Surround the mould with this double strip so that it comes well above the edge and keep it in place with an elastic band or adhesive tape. Pour the soufflé mixture into the mould until it reaches the top of the paper, smooth over the surface, and freeze until firm (approximately 4 hours). Remove the paper to serve.

Iced raspberry soufflé SOUFFLÉ GLACÉ AUX FRAMBOISES (from

Charles Bérot recipe) Sort and clean 400 g (14 oz, scant 3 cups) raspberries. Put the best 20 to one side; crush the others and press through a sieve. Mix this purée with an equal amount of caster (superfine) sugar and add ½ litre (17 fl oz, 2 cups) Chantilly cream. Whisk the whites of 2 eggs very stiffly, whisking in 50 g (2 oz) caster (superfine) sugar. Fold lightly into the purée and cream mixture, then pour it into a 15-cm (6-in) soufflé mould around which has been wrapped a band of oiled greaseproof (waxed) paper 6 cm (2½ in) higher than the mould. Place in a freezer for at least 8 hours. When the soufflé is firm, remove the paper. Decorate with the reserved raspberries and serve immediately, with a light sweetened purée of fresh raspberries and almond tuiles. Serve with a dry Champagne.

SAVOURY SOUFFLÉS

Basic recipe METHODE DE BASE Make a béchamel sauce using 40 g (1½ oz, 3 tablespoons) butter, 40 g (1½ oz, scant ½ cup) flour, and 2 dl (⅓ pint, scant cup) cold milk. Season with salt, pepper, and nutmeg and incorporate the chosen garnish. Then add 4–5 egg yolks (use fairly large eggs) and fold in 4–5 egg whites whisked to stiff peaks. Preheat the oven for 15 minutes to 220 C (425 F, gas 7). Butter a soufflé mould 20 cm (8 in) in diameter and coat with flour. Pour in the mixture and bake in the oven at 200 C (400 F, gas 6) for 30 minutes, without opening the door during cooking, until well-risen and a deep golden-brown on top.

Cheese and poached egg soufflé SOUFFLÉ AU FROMAGE ET AUX OEUFS POCHÉS (from Paul and Jean-Pierre Haeberlin's recipe) Mix ¼ litre (8 fl oz, 1 cup) milk with 50 g (2 oz, ½ cup) flour and an equal amount of softened butter. Bring to the boil, stirring continuously, then beat in 5 egg yolks, and 100 g grated Gruyère cheese. Gently fold in 6 stiffly whisked egg whites. Pour half the mixture into a 20-cm (8-in) buttered soufflé mould and cook in the oven at 200 C (400 F, gas 6) for 10 minutes. Meanwhile, poach 4 eggs in vinegar water for 4 minutes, then drain, plunge into fresh water, drain again, and trim.

Take the soufflé out of the oven and place the eggs in it. Add the remainder of the soufflé mixture, put back into the oven, and continue cooking at the same temperature for 10–15 minutes.

Cheese soufflé SOUFFLÉ AU FROMAGE Add to the béchamel sauce 75 –90 g (3–3½ oz, scant cup) grated Gruyère (or 60 g (2 oz, ½ cup) grated Parmesan) cheese and a pinch of grated nutmeg. Proceed as in the basic recipe.

Crab soufflé SOUFFLÉ AU CRABE Prepare a béchamel sauce from 40 g (1½ oz, 3 tablespoons) butter, 40 g (1½ oz, scant ½ cup) flour, 1.5 dl (¼ pint, scant cup) milk, and 1 dl (5 tablespoons, scant ½ cup) reduced crab cooking liquid. Incorporate 200 g (7 oz) crab purée and adjust the seasoning. Add 4–5 eggs (the yolks, then the stiffly whisked whites) and cook as in the basic recipe.

Shrimp or lobster soufflés are prepared in the same way.

Ham soufflé SOUFFLÉ AU JAMBON Put into a processor 150 g (5 oz, generous ½ cup) chopped lean ham, or finely mince (grind) twice. Prepare a cheese soufflé mixture, add the ham, and proceed as in the basic recipe.

Potato soufflé SOUFFLÉ À LA POMME DE TERRE Bind 400 g (14 oz, 1¾ cups) mashed potato with 4 tablespoons (⅓ cup) cream, add 3 egg yolks, and then fold in 4 stiffly whisked egg whites. Cook by the basic method.

Chestnut, sweet potato, or Jerusalem artichoke soufflés may also be made in this way; they can be flavoured with 75 g (3 oz, ¾ cup) grated Gruyère or 50 g (2 oz, ½ cup grated Parmesan cheese.

Poultry soufflé SOUFFLÉ À LA VOLAILLE Reduce to a purée in a blender or processor 250 g (9 oz, 1¼ cups) cooked game or poultry meat (pigeon, chicken, turkey, or guinea fowl) and 30 g (1 oz, 2 tablespoons) butter. Season well. Mix this purée with béchamel sauce and finish according to the basic recipe.

Add 2 tablespoons (3 tablespoons) chopped truffle to the purée mixture to produce a soufflé *à la reine*. The truffles can be replaced by a few spoonfuls of mirepoix. This soufflé is usually cooked in ramekins.

Salmon soufflé SOUFFLÉ AU SAUMON (from Raymond Thuillier's recipe) Skin a salmon and remove all the bones with a small pair of tweezers (you must have 400 g (14 oz) flesh). Pass this flesh through a blender or processor very quickly so as not to heat it. Add 4 whole eggs and ¼ litre (8 fl oz, 1 cup) fresh cream. Stir this mixture with a spatula for 15 minutes, keeping it on ice. Rub through a sieve and adjust the seasoning. Stiffly whisk 4 slightly salted egg whites and fold gently into the salmon mixture. Pour into a buttered soufflé mould and bake in a moderately hot oven (200 C, 400 F, gas 6) for approximately 25 minutes.

This recipe can also be made using salmon trout or brown trout.

Soumaintrain

A French cows'-milk cheese (45% fat) that is soft-textured and has a washed reddish damp rind. A speciality of the Yonne region, it has a penetrating odour and a spicy flavour. It is sold without a wrapping in a round slab 12–13 cm (4½–5) in in diameter and 2.5–3 cm (1–1¼ in) deep. It is farm made and is at its best from the end of spring to autumn, accompanied by a full-bodied Burgundy.

soup POTAGE, SOUPE

A liquid food served at the beginning of a meal or for lunch, a snack, etc.

Originally in France, the *soupe* was the slice of bread on which was poured the contents of the cooking pot (*potage*). *Soupe* and *potage* are now often synonymous, although the former is also used to designate unstrained vegetable, meat, or fish soups garnished with bread, pasta, or rice; it is also used for regional or classical soups with bread added to them, such as French onion soup (*soupe à l'oignon gratinée*).

Soups can be classified into two broad groups: clear soups and thick soups.

Clear soups are discussed in the articles on *bouillon* and *consommé*.

Thick soups can be further subdivided according to the type of thickening used:
• purée soups (vegetable soups thick-ened with the starch contained in the puréed vegetables);
• bisques (made with puréed shellfish and fresh cream);
• cream soups (thickened with béchamel sauce);
• velouté soups (thickened with egg yolks, butter, and cream).

In addition to these, there are soups and broths thickened with arrowroot, rice, and tapioca.

RECIPES

Artichoke velouté soup VELOUTÉ D'ARTICHAUT Prepare a white roux with 40 g (1½ oz, 3 tablespoons) butter and 40 g (1½ oz, 6 tablespoons) flour. Moisten with 8 dl (1⅓ pints, 1¾ pints) chicken consommé. Blanch 8 small artichoke hearts, cut into slices, and simmer in 40 g (1½ oz, 3 tablespoons) butter for about 20 minutes. Add them to the consommé, bring to the boil, and cook until the vegetables break up. Reduce the mixture to a purée in a blender or food processor. Dilute with a little consommé to obtain the desired consistency, and heat. Remove from the heat and thicken the soup with a mixture of 3 egg yolks beaten with 1 dl (6 tablespoons, scant ½ cup) cream. Finally, whisk in 60 g (3 oz, generous ¼ cup) butter. Reheat but do not boil.

Asparagus velouté soup VELOUTÉ D'ASPERGE Prepare a thickened chicken consommé as described in the recipe for artichoke velouté soup. Cut 400 g (14 oz) washed asparagus into pieces, blanch for 5 minutes in boiling water, drain, and then simmer with 40 g (1½ oz, 3 tablespoons) butter for about 10 minutes. Reduce to purée in a blender or food processor and add it to the consommé. Finish as for artichoke velouté soup.

Celeriac (celery root) velouté soup VELOUTÉ DE CÉLERI Proceed as for artichoke velouté soup but use 300 g (11 oz) celeriac (celery root), blanched, sliced, and simmered in 40 g (1½ oz, 3 tablespoons) butter, instead of artichokes.

Chicken velouté soup VELOUTÉ DE VOLAILLE Thicken 8 dl (1⅓ pints,

1¾ pints) chicken consommé with a white roux made with 40 g (1½ oz, 3 tablespoons) butter and 40 g (1½ oz, 6 tablespoons) flour. Add a small young chicken and simmer gently until it breaks up with a fork. Drain and bone the chicken, reserve some breast meat for a garnish, and reduce the remainder to a purée in a blender or food processor, adding a little of the cooking liquid. Mix with the rest of the cooking liquid and complete as for artichoke velouté soup. Cut the reserved meat into very fine strips and add to the soup just before serving.

Game or any other meat can be used instead of chicken to make a game or meat velouté soup.

English chicken soup   SOUPE DE POULET À L'ANGLAISE   Put a medium-sized chicken into a stewing pot and pour in 1.75 litres (3 pints, 7½ cups) plain stock. Boil, skim, season with salt, and then add an onion studded with a clove, a bouquet garni, a stick (stalk) of celery, and 100 g (4 oz, ½ cup) rice. Leave to simmer until the chicken meat comes away from the bones. Drain the chicken and cut the flesh into small pieces, discarding the skin. Remove the bouquet garni and the onion. Put the chicken meat back into the pot, add 1.5 dl (¼ pint, ⅔ cup) chopped vegetables cooked in butter, and bring to the boil. Serve piping hot.

Fish soup with mussels   SOUPE DE POISSON AUX MOULES   (from Roland de Reu's recipe) Shred the cleaned white part of 3 leeks, 2 carrots, and 1 stick (stalk) of celery and fry in 1 dl (6 tablespoons, scant ½ cup) olive oil. Add a pinch of saffron, a sprig of thyme, a bay leaf, a crushed clove of garlic, and 250 g (9 oz, generous cup) fresh crushed tomatoes. Add 150 g (5 oz) each of fillets of brill, monkfish, red mullet, and weever (sand lance), together with 1.5 litres (2¾ pints, 7 cups) fish fumet. Simmer for 15 minutes. Season with salt and pepper and add 500 g (18 oz) shelled mussels. Serve piping hot.

Hungarian soup with liver dumplings SOUPE AUX BOULETTES DE FOIE À LA HONGROISE   Cut 150 g (5 oz) veal or chicken liver into dice and sauté briskly in 15 g (½ oz, 1 tablespoon) lard. Season with salt and pepper. Braise 50 g (2 oz, ½ cup) thinly sliced onions in butter. Put all these ingredients through a blender or food processor, together with 1 tablespoon chopped parsley, 1 large egg, 50 g (2 oz, ¼ cup) butter, salt, pepper, 1 teaspoon paprika, and a generous pinch of grated nutmeg. Shape the mixture into small dumplings and simmer them in stock for 15 minutes. Prepare 1.5 litres (2¾ pints, 7 cups) chicken consommé and serve garnished with the dumplings.

Iced avocado velouté soup   VELOUTÉ GLACÉ À L'AVOCAT   (from Lionel Jounault's recipe) Using a melon baller, scoop out some balls of pulp from a small peeled and deseeded cucumber. Blanch them rapidly in boiling water. Skin a firm ripe tomato after dipping it in boiling water, and cut the flesh into very small dice. Halve 3 avocados, remove the stones, and scoop out all the pulp with a spoon. Put the pulp through a blender or food processor, adding the juice of a lemon, 4 tablespoons (5 tablespoons) fresh cream, and 1 dl (6 tablespoons, scant ½ cup) milk. Season with salt and dust with cayenne. Place in the refrigerator to chill. Pour the soup into 4 bowls and garnish with the cucumber balls, the diced tomato, and finely chopped mint leaves (6 in all). Serve ice-cold.

Mushroom velouté soup   VELOUTÉ DE CHAMPIGNON   Proceed as for artichoke velouté soup but use 400 g (14 oz, 3½ cups) cultivated mushrooms, sliced and simmered in 40 g (1½ oz, 3 tablespoons) butter, instead of artichokes.

Potato and leek soup   SOUPE AUX POIREAUX ET AUX POMMES DE TERRE   Cut off the green part of 12 leeks and remove the withered leaves. Peel and quarter 4 large potatoes. Thinly slice the cleaned green parts of the leeks and fry in 30 g (1 oz, 2 tablespoons) butter. Add 1.5 litres (2¾ pints, 7 cups boiling water, bring to the boil, and then add the potatoes. Season with salt and pepper and leave to cook gently with the lid on for approximately 1 hour. Put through a blender or food processor, pour into a soup tureen, sprinkle with chopped parsley, and serve piping hot with small slices of bread dried in the oven.

Purée of Brussels sprout soup POT-AGE-PURÉE AUX CHOUX DE BRUXELLES Trim 500 g (18 oz) Brussels sprouts and blanch them for 2 minutes in boiling water. Rinse in cold water and drain thoroughly, then sweat gently in 50 g (2 oz, 4 tablespoons) butter. Finish as for purée of celery soup.

Purée of celery soup POTAGE-PURÉE DE CÉLERI Scrub 500 g (18 oz) celery sticks (stalks), chop, and sweat in 50 g (2 oz, 4 tablespoons) butter. (The celery may be replaced by the same weight of blanched peeled celeriac (celery root).) Purée the cooked celery in the blender or food processor. Pour the purée into a saucepan and add 1.75 litres (3 pints, 7½ cups) chicken stock and 250 g (9 oz) floury potatoes, cut into quarters. Bring to the boil and cook for about 30 minutes. Rub through a sieve and add sufficient stock to obtain the desired consistency. Adjust the seasoning. Just before serving, beat in 50 g (2 oz) butter in small pieces.

Purée of chestnut soup POTAGE-PURÉE DE MARRONS Peel 600 g (1¼ lb) chestnuts and cook in a saucepan with 1.5 litres (2¾ pints, 7 cups) stock or consommé until they begin to fall apart. Peel 200 g (7 oz) celeriac (celery root), cut it into slices, and blanch for 2 minutes in boiling water. Wipe. Sweat in 30 g (1 oz, 2 tablespoons) butter with 1 tablespoon finely chopped onion. Add the celeriac to the cooked chestnuts and cook together for a further 10 minutes. Put through a blender or food processor. Dilute with a little stock or boiled milk, and whisk in 50 g (2 oz) butter cut into small pieces. Serve with small croutons fried in butter.

Purée of tomato soup POTAGE-PURÉE DE TOMATES Peel and chop 50 g (2 oz, ½ cup) onions. Sweat them in 30 g (1 oz, 2 tablespoons) butter, then add 750 g (1¾ lb) peeled tomatoes, a crushed garlic clove, a small bouquet garni, salt, and pepper. Cook gently for

20 minutes, add 100 g (4 oz, ½ cup) long-grain rice, and stir. Add 1.5 litres (2¾ pints, 7 cups) boiling stock, stir, cover, and leave to cook for 20 minutes. Remove the bouquet garni. Reduce to a purée in a blender, then return to the saucepan and whisk in 50 g (2 oz) butter cut into small pieces. Sprinkle with chopped parsley or basil. Serve with croutons flavoured with garlic and fried in olive oil.

Soissonais soup POTAGE-PURÉE SOISSONNAIS Soak 350 g (12 oz, 1¾ cups) dried white haricot (navy) beans in cold water for 12 hours. Put them in a saucepan with 1.5 litres (2¾ pints, 7 cups) cold water and bring to the boil. Add an onion studded with 2 cloves, a peeled diced carrot, a bouquet garni, and 75 g (3 oz) slightly salted belly of pork or unsmoked streaky bacon, blanched, diced, and fried in butter. Cover, bring to the boil, and cook until the beans break up. Remove the onion and the bouquet garni. Put the beans and some of the liquid through a blender or food processor. Return the purée to the saucepan, dilute with stock or consommé, adjust the seasoning, bring to the boil, and whisk in 50 g (2 oz, 4 tablespoons) butter. Serve with croutons fried in butter.

Soupe à la bonne femme Heat 40 g (1½ oz, 3 tablespoons) butter in a saucepan but do not let it brown. Add the cleaned white part of 4 medium-sized finely sliced leeks and cook gently until quite soft. Then add 3 litres (5¼ pints, 6½ pints) ordinary consommé and bring to the boil. Add 350 g (12 oz, 2 cups) thinly sliced potatoes, bring to the boil again, season with salt and pepper, then lower the heat and leave to cook for 1 hour. Just before serving, remove the saucepan from the heat and whisk in 60 g (2 oz, ¼ cup) butter and 1 tablespoon chervil leaves.

Soupe hollandaise (from Hubert's recipe) Peel an onion, wash a small stick (stalk) of celery, and chop together. Lightly brown this hash for 10 minutes in 15 g (½ oz, 1 tablespoon) butter over a gentle heat. Add 3 tomatoes, peeled, deseeded, and cut into quarters. Continue cooking for 10 minutes. Purée the vegetables in a blender or food processor and return to the saucepan. Add a pinch of pili-pili and bring to the boil. Dilute with 1.5 litres (2¾ pints, 7 cups) water and cook for 15 minutes.

Cut 200 g (7 oz) stale bread into very small pieces and place in a soup tureen with 150 g (5 oz) grated Gouda. Remove the saucepan from the heat, add 1 dl (6 tablespoons, scant ½ cup) fresh cream, and pour into the tureen. Cover and leave to stand for 5 minutes before serving.

Stracciatella soup SOUPE STRACCIATELLA Pour into a bowl 100 g (4 oz, 2 cups) fine fresh breadcrumbs and add 2 eggs beaten as for an omelette. Mix, then add 50 g (2 oz, ½ cup) grated Parmesan cheese, salt, pepper, and nutmeg. Pour this mixture into 1.5 litres (2¾ pints, 7 cups) boiling chicken consommé, whisking vigorously. Cook very gently for 8 minutes. Give a final whisk just before serving.

Viennese sour cream soup SOUPE VIENNOISE À LA CRÈME AIGRE Prepare 1.5 litres (2¾ pints, 7 cups thin velouté sauce and add a medium-sized onion studded with a clove, a bouquet garni, a pinch of cumin powder, and grated nutmeg. Cook gently for 20 minutes, then rub through a fine sieve. Add 1 dl (6 tablespoons, scant ½ cup) soured (dairy sour) cream (or double (heavy) cream mixed with 2 tablespoons (3 tablespoons) lemon juice) and serve with small fried croutons.

soup tureen SOUPIÈRE

A wide deep bowl, fitted with two handles, used for serving soup. A lid, sometimes with a notch to accommodate the ladle, keeps the soup warm. For a formal dinner, most soups are served directly into soup dishes or cups, and the soup tureen does not appear on the table. However, it is used for serving bisques and velouté and cream soups, for which it can be made of gold- or silver-plate or fine porcelain (the first such tureens appeared in the 18th century). Thick substantial soups with solid ingredients tend to be served in tureens made of earthenware, glazed clay, fireproof porcelain, etc. Gratinées are often served in small individual soup tureens made of fireproof porcelain.

souris

The small sweet rounded piece of meat at the knuckle end of a leg of lamb or mutton. Stronger-tasting than the noix, it is regarded as a delicacy in France. It can be eaten on its own, with a thin strip of grilled (broiled) skin, or it can be accompanied by a slice of rare meat from the rest of the joint, the contrasting flavours being delicious. Although not so highly prized in Britain, the carver often keeps it for himself as it is so good!

South Africa
AFRIQUE DU SUD

A dual tradition inherited from the English and Dutch colonists has left its mark on South African cuisine. Local produce is also used: *biden*, for example, is boiled and chopped like spinach or mixed with peanut flour. A principal characteristic is the widespread use of meat and rice, while fish is usually eaten smoked (shellfish are not very popular). The most typical speciality is biltong (charqui), which is beef, mutton, or antelope meat, dried, salted, and sometimes sweetened. Also noteworthy are *beoerewors* (beef sausages), *sosati* (mutton which is marinated, dried, then barded and grilled on skewers), and *boboti* (chopped and spiced beef mixed with onions and almonds, then cooked in the oven with beaten eggs). Chutney and piquant sauces are very widely used. Much maize is eaten (as flour made into *kakou* bread or as sweet semolina) and an enormous quantity of fruit, but few vegetables. Meals end with tarts, porridge, waffles, or preserves. There is a thriving wine industry, but beer and fruit juices are also commonly drunk.

South African wines
VINS D'AFRIQUE DU SUD

Vines were first planted at the Cape in 1655 and wine traditions here are of historic importance. Today, although some other regions and countries in southern Africa are planting vine and making wine, the most important area is still that of the Cape. Whereas in the past the stress was on the production of sweet dessert wines and brandy – both still produced in quantity – there has been an enormous increase in the making of apéritif wines according to the procedures followed in the sherry region of Spain; there are also port-type wines and a huge range of table wines of all types, including sparkling wines. These days legislation decrees how the wines are labelled: different coloured bands on the seal attached to the capsule of many wines in bottle indicate the wine's status.

The regions in alphabetical order are: Boburg, Breede River Valley, Caledon, Constantia, Durbanville, Klein Karoo (the Little Karoo), Olifantsrivier, Paarl, Piquetberg, Robertson, Stellenbosch, Swartland, Swellendam, Tulbagh, and Worcester. A fairly wide range of vines – here referred to as 'cultivars' – are grown. For white wines these include Chenin Blanc (also known here as Steen), Palomino, Clairette Blanche, Cape Riesling, Rheinriesling, Colombar (or Colombard), Sémillon (or 'Green Grape'), Gewurstraminer, Bukettraube, Kerner, Sauvignon Blanc, Chardonnay, and Muscat d'Alexandrie (or Hanepoot). Some of the black grapes grown are: Cabernet Sauvignon, Cinsaut, Pinotage, Pinot Noir, Shiraz (Syrah), and some Zinfandel. Recently it has become very fashionable to make 'Blanc de Noir', a white or pale pink wine from black grapes vinified as white.

There are a number of wine estates, some of which have their wines made for them by one of the huge firms, of which the co-op, known by its initials as K.W.V., is the most important and influential – it is the largest winery in the world. Other important concerns are Stellenbosch Farmers' Winery, Die Bergkelder, Union Wine, and Douglas Green. Considerable educational programmes and promotions are undertaken by several of these, operating throughout the Republic of South Africa. In addition to brandy and other basic spirits, liqueurs are also made, notably one called Van der Hum, which is based on brandy and flavoured with the maartjie (a type of bitter orange).

South America

AMÉRIQUE DU SUD

The highly spiced cuisine of the South American countries betrays its Spanish or Portuguese origin, in stews, fish, and seafood dishes, with an emphasis on fried food. By another route, the Black slaves introduced their own dietary habits, as did the European colonists: the Italians to Argentina, where pasta is very popular; the Germans to Bolivia, where more beer is drunk than in other Latin-American countries; and the French to Guyana and Venezuela, where the cuisine is more delicate. A lot of meat is eaten in livestock-breeding regions, sometimes dried (*charqui*) but more often grilled as open-air cooking is popular everywhere. Local recipes remain colourful, however; armadillo is still eaten as well as iguana eggs and large grilled ants. All South American countries use red beans, potatoes, rice, and, above all, maize (corn) – its flour, leaves, and ears (see *empanada, tamal*). Tropical fruits, which are extremely varied, are eaten either with vegetables, in salads, as juice, or as jellies. Desserts are primarily sweet dishes such as mashes and milk jellies. (For drinks, see *aguardiente, coffee, chicha, maté, pulque, tequila.*)

● **Argentina** – The Argentinian eats a lot of meat, particularly beef, which he likes in large portions, either roast (*asado*) or grilled (*churrasco*). But this does not exclude more elaborate dishes, such as beef broth garnished with pumpkin and ears of maize (corn). *Matambre* ('hunger-killer') is typically Argentinian, made from marinated beef stuffed with vegetables and hard-boiled (hard-cooked) eggs, roasted and boiled, and served cold at the beginning of a meal. Another Argentinian meat dish is *carbonada criolla*, a stew simmered in a gourd skin. This great livestock-breeding country also produces such cheeses as *tafi*, which is like Cantal, and *dulce de leche*, a sweet spread made from aromatized condensed milk and eaten throughout South America. See also *Argentinian wines*.

● **Bolivia** – With Peru, Bolivia is the country of origin of the potato, and prides itself on producing more than 300 varieties. Particularly popular are *chuños*, frozen and dried potatoes, which are very light and are soaked before using. Apart from highly spiced soups and small fried dishes cooked in the open air, Bolivian cuisine has one speciality – *conejo estirado*, a dish made from rabbit which has been stretched out to make its flesh very delicate.

● **Brazil** – Influenced by the Portuguese, Brazilian cuisine is, with that of Peru, the most varied and refined in South America. The Indians have contributed cassava flour, cocoa, sweet potatoes, and peanuts; the Blacks have imported yams, bananas, coconuts, and above all palm oil (*dende*), which gives its flavour to all fried dishes. The national dish is *feijoada*, traditionally preceded by a *batida*, a cocktail shake of eau-de-vie mixed with lime. There are many local variants of the national dish, for the personality of each region of Brazil is reflected in its cuisine. Fish and seafood are widely consumed in the northeast. *Fritada de mariscos* is a dish of mussels, oysters, and pieces of crab coated in fritter batter and fried, and large shrimps are prepared in many ways – in sauces, with coconut for *vatapa*, in balls, fried with red beans, and even in *xinxin de galinha*, a chicken fricassee with peanuts and cassava. The cakes and pastries of this region are highly prized and include flavoured custards, cakes made with coconut or prunes, and egg yolks beaten with sugar and given picturesque names such as angel's cheeks, young girl's saliva, and mother-in-law's eye. The typical dish of central Brazil is *churrasco* (grilled meat) and everywhere cream cheese is eaten with guava jelly. The south has a copious and abundant cuisine with such dishes as offal in ragouts and fruit-stuffed poultry. The basic dish is a purée of black beans, cassava flour, and bacon pieces. Amazonian fauna provides some culinary curiosities – pickled peccary and sea cow cooked in coconut milk – and there is also an impressive range of fruits.

● **Chile** – The quality of the meat is excellent, particularly the grilled mutton, and there is a great variety of *empanadas* (meat pies). The abundance of seafood is reflected in the cuisine, which is invariably seasoned with pimiento and onion. Conger-eel soup is a famous speciality. Hotch-potches (*chupes*) are made from offal, vegetables, or dried meat.

● **Colombia** – Colombians are great

eaters. Scrambled eggs with tomatoes and onions are served from breakfast onwards and *tamales* and *empanadas* are nibbled all day. Stews are very substantial – *ajiaco* is made from meat or poultry, maize (corn), potatoes, and avocado, and seasoned with pimiento, and *sancocho* is made from meat or fish, with cassava and unripe bananas. Maize biscuits (*arepa*) are used as bread. Coconut, which is very popular, may be found as often in sauces as in desserts. Strawberries and oranges are as plentiful as papaw and passion fruit.

● **Ecuador** – Varieties of banana are particularly numerous, and bananas occur in all the recipes. As well as *tamales*, soups, and filled pies, a lot of marinated raw fish is eaten. At All Saints, the major holiday of the year, hundreds of little decorated sugar cakes are made and families come to eat them on the graves of their loved ones.

● **Guyana, French Guiana, and Surinam** – Some authentic Indian dishes are still eaten in this region, such as armadillo ragout, alligator kebabs, and roast peccary, but the day-to-day diet is based on Creole cooking.

● **Paraguay and Uruguay** – Here the food is the same as in Argentina, with the addition of freshwater fish and abundant game. Palm hearts (terminal buds) are mainly produced in this region. The national dish is again a stew, *bori bori*, made of meat balls, vegetables, pieces of cream cheese, and maize (corn).

● **Peru** – Peruvian cooking, as highly spiced as that of Mexico, has kept up the tradition of the *pachamanca* – an oven dug out of the earth in which is cooked a pig, goat, or chickens with corn on the cob, potatoes, and aromatic herbs. Peru is the country of *ceviche*, marinated raw fish served with sweet limes, onions, tomatoes, and maize (corn). Their *chupes* (thick stews), more liquid than the Chilean variety, have milk added to them and are garnished with vegetables or poached eggs. Potatoes are prepared in various ways: with cream cheese, onions, and orange juice; mashed with shrimps, olives, and hard-boiled (hard-cooked) eggs; as an accompaniment to dried meat; and of course in all the stews. Another Peruvian speciality is *anticucho*, kebabs of highly spiced ox or calf hearts. Among sweetmeats, Lima nougat is renowned.

• Venezuela – This country has the mildest cuisine in South America, again featuring beef, red beans mixed with rice, and maize. The *arepa*, or maize biscuit, accompanies every dish. *Hayaca*, the typical dish prepared traditionally at Christmas, consists of maize pancakes filled with meat or fish, eggs, olives, raisins, almonds, and condiments, and is cooked in banana leaves. *Sancocho* is the classic stew of meat, offal, or fish. Papaw jelly is the favourite dessert but, like bananas, it is also served with savoury dishes.

Southeast Asia
ASIE DU SUD-EST

The cuisine of China's neighbouring countries resembles Chinese cooking in many ways. China's influence is particularly noticeable in Korea, Vietnam, Laos, and Cambodia. In Burma and Thailand, the cuisine is influenced by the proximity of India.

As in China, the dishes of a meal, often a great number of them, are served all together. The concepts of hors d'oeuvres and dessert are unknown, and between meals the Indochinese eat sweetmeats and cocktail snacks such as *nems* (stuffed and fried rice pancakes), imperial pâtés, and spring rolls.

Garnished stocks and soups are prominent everywhere; for example, the Vietnamese *pho* (spiced beef stock garnished with noodles, vegetables, and very thin slices of meat), the acid-flavoured Thai *tom yam*, or the Burmese *hincho*, with vegetables. They take the place of breakfast, and they are served with or at the end of the main meals.

The most common meats are pork and chicken. Beef is sometimes eaten, but never mutton. A great deal of fish is eaten, and crabs and shrimps are even more popular. Vegetables – turnips, cabbage, cucumbers, and many varieties of mushrooms – are cooked in small pieces. They are also served raw in salad, which never happens in China.

Spices and aromatics used in Southeast Asia are those which are found all over the East (pimiento, ginger, saffron, and cinnamon), but many fresh plants are also used, such as shallots, lemon balm, and coriander. Turmeric, from which curry is made, is widely used in Burma, but it is *nuoc-mâm* in particular (unknown in China) that gives Indochinese cooking its characteristic flavour. Rice is a traditional accompaniment, together with very fine vermicelli used in soups and ragouts. Whether food is simmered, marinated, fried, or braised, the dishes are generally less elaborate and lighter than those of China.

The most widely grown fruits are pineapple, lychees, mandarins (tangerines), papaw, rambutan, ginkgo, jujube, kumquat, and mango. They may be eaten fresh or preserved, but are also used to garnish savoury dishes and may be mixed with raw vegetables in certain recipes. Durian, with its very distinctive 'rotten' smell, is much appreciated in Vietnam. Popular sweetmeats include little cakes made of almonds, lotus cream, or sesame, and other specialities include preserved ginger, mandarins (tangerines), and gourds.

Typical Vietnamese dishes are *bi-thanh* (scooped-out gourd, steamed and filled with sliced chicken, lotus seeds, dried mushrooms, ham, crab, and ginger), pork ribs with lemon balm (marinated, then grilled), and *vit-tim* (steamed duck stuffed with prunes, mushrooms, and shallots). There is also a vast range of filled omelettes. *Lap* (crushed and spiced raw meat), fried crab's claws, and chicken with spices are specialities in Laos and Thailand, while *bahmi* (a mixture of meat, fish, and noodles) and *bahuri* (ragout of pork and salted fish mixed with pineapple and mango) are special Thai dishes. Cabbage with ginger and turnips and *bulgogi* (marinated beef) are popular Korean dishes.

Souvarov

A method of preparing pheasant, partridge, woodcock, or quail, which is also suitable for chicken. The bird is stuffed with foie gras and truffle, fried until three-quarters cooked, then finished off in a casserole together with the frying pan juices deglazed with demi-glace sauce, truffle fumet, and Madeira. Foie gras Souvarov is seized in butter, then cooked in a sealed terrine with truffles and a truffle-flavoured demi-glace sauce.

These dishes were named in honour of a certain Prince Souvorov, who used to frequent Paris restaurants and was a descendant of the governor of the Crimea. His name, corrupted to Souvarov, Souvaroff, or Souwaroff, has also been given to a petit four made of two small sablés sandwiched together with jam.

RECIPE

Foie gras Souvarov Season a goose foie gras weighing 500 g (18 oz) with salt and pepper and leave to steep for 24 hours in Cognac. Drain off the excess liquid, then seize the foie gras in 30 g (1 oz, 2 tablespoons) butter. Place it in a terrine just big enough to contain it, surrounded by quartered truffles. Half-cover it with reduced demi-glace sauce flavoured with truffle. Cover the terrine and seal the lid with a strip of dough. Cook for 40 minutes in a moderately hot oven (200 c, 400 f, gas 6). Serve in the terrine.

Partridge à la Souvarov PERDREAU À LA SOUVAROV Stuff a partridge with fois gras and truffles cut into large dice, seasoned with salt and pepper, and sprinkled with a dash of brandy. Truss the bird and seize it in butter, then place it in a small oval terrine, surrounded by diced or whole truffles, peeled and seasoned with salt and pepper. Moisten with 1 dl (6 tablespoons, scant ½ cup) Madeira-flavoured game fumet to which the pan juices, diluted with Madeira, have been added. Sprinkle with a dash of brandy. Cover the terrine, seal the lid with a strip of dough, and cook in a moderately hot oven (190 c, 375 f, gas 5) for 45 minutes. Serve in the terrine.

Woodcock, pheasant, and chicken can be prepared in the same way, but fry the latter in butter until it is three-quarters done, then finish cooking in the oven for 30 minutes.

Petits four Souvarov Make a sablé mixture using 600 g (generous 1½ lb, 6½ cups) flour, 400 g (14 oz, 1¾ cups) butter, 200 g (7 oz, scant cup) caster (superfine) sugar, and 1 tablespoon cream. Leave to stand for 1 hour in a cool place. Roll it out to a thickness of 4 mm (¼ in) and cut out shapes with a round or fluted oval pastry (cookie) cutter. Place on a baking sheet and cook in a moderately hot oven (200 c, 400 f, gas 6) for 15 minutes. Leave to cool, then spread the sablés with thick sieved apricot jam, sandwich together in pairs, and sprinkle with icing (confectioners') sugar.

Sovietski

A Russian pasteurized pressed cows'-milk cheese (50% fat). It is elastic in consistency and has rather a piquant taste. After it has been ripening for a few months, small holes appear in it. It comes in a rectangular slab, 50 cm (20 in) by 20 cm (8 in), weighing 12–16 kg (26–36 lb). It is usually eaten for breakfast and is also used in cooking.

Soviet wines
VINS D'URSS

Wine has been made in Russian for many centuries, notably in the Caucasus, but the area under vines has increased enormously in recent years and continues to do so. Not much reaches export markets as yet – the labels present problems to many potential customers – and in fact the USSR imports significant quantities of a variety of wines, both from the Iron Curtain countries near its borders and from certain Mediterranean vineyards. By far the largest amount of wine made is sparkling and much of this is sweet or very sweet, but various table wines and fortified wines are also produced, the latter being extremely popular – as such sweetish wines usually are in northern countries where the climate is severe.

A wide range of grapes is used, including such classic varieties as the Cabernets, Muscats, Riesling, and Sylvaner as well as local varieties. A number of hybrids are also cultivated. As might be expected, wine making is carried out in large-scale cooperatives, but the different wine regions are demarcated and it is possible that, in the future, controls may be applied to establish a certain conformity of quality. The use of certain classic wine names – port, sherry, and so on – is at present misleading, but terms such as 'claret', 'Chablis', and 'Sauternes' were often used until quite recently for wines quite separate (and indeed different) from those of France.

The Crimea is one of the quality wine-producing regions, where a variety of wines are now made. The River Don, Moldavia, the Ukraine, Stavropol, Krasnodar, Azerbaijan, and Armenia are other wine-producing regions; Georgia is well-known for many old-established vineyards and produces many sparkling wines and also an amount of brandy. The USSR makes and consumes a considerable amount of spirits, notably vodka; flavoured vodkas are extensively made.

sow thistle (milkweed)

LAITERON

A plant which has something of the flavour of both endive (chicory) and lettuce. It exudes a copious white sap when cut. The young leaves of the culti-vated sow thistle are used in salads, while the tougher more leathery ones are cooked in boiling salted water like spinach. In winter the roots can be eaten and are cooked in the same way as salsify.

soya (soy) bean   SOJA

A pulse that probably originated in Manchuria, which the Chinese call *dadou* (big bean) and the Japanese *daizu*. The stem bears leaves in groups of three and brown or greenish pods, each containing three small pea-sized seeds.

The plant is used all over the world for forage, to produce oil and flour, and as a foodstuff in various forms. There are garden varieties grown for their seeds, which are eaten like beans or peas, or for their sprouts. A basic food-stuff in the Far East, the soya bean was known in China well before our era. It was introduced to Japan in the 6th cen-tury, where it was called the 'meat vegetable'. European travellers dis-covered it in the 17th century and made known certain soya-based oriental dishes: soups, cakes, and porridges. A century later the first seeds arrived in Paris at the Jardin des Plantes. In 1874 a variety of soya with yellow seeds was produced at Etampes, but it was only after World War I that the United States and Europe became interested in its commercial production for forage and oil. As a vegetable it remained 'exotic'. Today, in the West, it is usually the bean sprouts that are used, in salads, or as a garnish for pork or chicken, but the use of dried soya beans as a source of veg-etable protein, particularly for vegeta-rian diets, is increasing.

A number of different products are obtained from the plant.

● *Fresh soya beans* are sold (in special-ist shops) in their pods or shelled (they may also be frozen or canned). They contain 12% protein, which is directly assimilated, and are boiled. The Chinese serve them with beef as well as seafood.

● *Dried soya beans*, yellow, green, black or bicoloured, have a high calor-ific value (422 Cal per 100 g) and are twice as rich in protein as beef. Soaked and boiled, they are eaten in soups or salads. In Japan the black beans are cooked for a long time with cloves and sugar, flavoured with soy sauce, and served with rice.

● *Soya bean sprouts* are the seeds and their shoots, which are a few inches long. Mung and alfalfa seeds and sprouts are milder and more tender than the true soya and more common in Europe. In Vietnamese cookery the sprouts are usually eaten in spring rolls, as a sweet-and-sour vegetable, or in salads.

● *Soya flour* (twice as rich in protein as wheat flour) is used in cakes and to bind sauces. In Japan it is used to coat sticky rice pâtés.

Japanese cookery has always made extensive use of soya-based products: *natto* (fermented black beans), used as a garnish for rice dishes and dishes for special occasions; *tofu*, or soya cheese, with many uses; and *miso*, made of rice, barley, or soya, which is fermented and used in broths, soups, or as a garnish for fish with vegetables. Vietnamese pan-cakes of soya flour and soya milk, served plain or with honey, should also be mentioned.

RECIPES

Soya bean salad   SALADE DE SOJA
Prepare 500 g (18 oz, 9 cups) soya (soy)

bean sprouts as for soya bean sprout hors d'oeuvre and lightly fry with 3 tablespoons hot oil; drain and allow to cool completely. Hard-boil (hard-cook) and peel 4 eggs. Turn the bean sprouts into a salad bowl and dress with a spicy vinaigrette seasoned with a touch of cayenne. Add a few slices white chicken meat or cold roast duck. Mix, and garnish with the quartered hard-boiled (hard-cooked) eggs.

Soya bean sprout hors d'oeuvre HORS-D'OEUVRE AU SOJA Cook a large crab in stock and 200 g (7 oz) prawns (shrimp) in salted water. Shell the crab and the prawns. Place 500 g (18 oz, 9 cups) soya (soy) bean sprouts in cold water, remove the debris that comes to the surface, drain, and blanch for no more than a minute in boiling salted water. Drain and refresh in very cold water, then wipe them. Place the flaked crab, prawns, and bean sprouts in a salad bowl. Finely slice 2 spring onions (scallions) and add ½ teaspoon soy sauce, ½ teaspoon mustard, a pinch of sugar, 1 tablespoon brandy or sherry, 1 tablespoon vinegar, 2–3 tablespoons oil, pepper, a little salt, and a few drops of Tabasco (or a small pinch of cayenne). Pour the sauce onto the salad, mix well, and sprinkle with chopped coriander.

Soyer (Alexis)

French cook (born Meaux, 1810; died London, 1858). He started out at the age of 16 at Grignon's in Paris and became the deputy chef in the kitchens of the Ministry of Foreign Affairs. After the July Revolution he emigrated to England, where he was chef at the Reform Club, whose kitchens he installed. After the sudden death of his wife, an English actress, Emma Jones, he devoted himself to charity, opening canteens for the underprivileged in London and Dublin. He worked for the British government during the Crimean War and designed an 'economical bivouac and camp kitchen' for the army. He also invented a 'magic oven', the ancestor of the table hotplate, which was heated by a spirit lamp. Soyer, who had a sense of publicity, launched Soyer sauce (for meat dishes) and Soyer nectar (based on fruit juice and aerated water).

He wrote several books, both for wealthy gourmets and for the less fortunate, including *The Gastronomic Regenerator* (1846), *The Poor Man's Regenerator* (1848), and *A Shilling Cookery* (1854).

soy sauce SAUCE SOJA

A basic condiment from Southeast Asia and Japan (it is called *shoyu* in Japan and *jiang yong* in China). The sauce is made from soya beans, wheat, water, and salt. Other ingredients can be used: chopped pork in Canton, ginger and mushrooms in Peking. Sometimes nuoc-mâm or anchovy paste is added. In Japan there is a dark spicy soy sauce for cooking and a light soy sauce for seasoning. Soy sauce has the same nutritional value as meat extract and improves with age. In Japanese cooking it is used mainly to season grilled kebabs, tofu, cold vegetable and fish salads, fritters, and sashimi. It can be enriched with grated daikon, taro, ginger, horseradish sauce, or finely sliced vegetables. In China soy sauce is mainly used in marinades and stewed dishes, while in Indonesia it is mainly a table condiment.

RECIPE

Soy sauce SAUCE SOJA (from a collection of traditional Chinese recipes mentioned by Jean Suyeux in *Le Grand Livre des produits et de la cuisine exotiques*, Le Sycomore, 1980) Boil 2.5 kg (5½ lb, 13 cups) soya (soy) beans in water until they are reduced to a purée. Add 1 kg (2¼ lb, 9 cups) flour and knead well to produce a thick dough. Leave in a cool dark place for 2 days, then hang the container in a draught for a week. When a yellow mould appears on the dough, place a jar containing 5 litres (9 pints, 11 pints) water and 1.5 kg (3¼ lb, 4¼ cups) salt in a sunny place. When the water is warm to the touch put the dough into the jar. Leave uncovered for a month, pounding vigorously every day with a stick. The mixture will turn black as it ages. Do not touch for 4–5 months unless the weather is bad, in which case the jar should be covered. Decant and store the sauce in hermetically sealed bottles.

spaghetti

One of the most popular of Italian pasta products. Originating in Naples, it spread to other parts of Italy (especially to the kitchens of Rome and Liguria) and then abroad. Spaghetti consists of long solid threads (*spago* means string). Originally made in the home, it began to be marketed in the Renaissance period, at the same time as macaroni. Abroad, it is usually prepared *alla napoletana* (with a tomato sauce base), *alla bolognese* (with a sauce based on minced (ground) meat and tomato), and *alla carbonara* (with bacon, Parmesan cheese, and eggs).

Cooked *al dente*, spaghetti is traditionally served with tomato sauce and Parmesan cheese, as an accompaniment for poultry or veal. There is a large number of other original recipes, especially in Latium (west central Italy): *a cacio e pepe* (with cheese and pepper), *alla carrettiera* (with mushrooms and tuna), *con le vongole* (with clams and chopped parsley), and *all'amatriciana* (with tomatoes, onion, bacon and Pecorino cheese). In Naples it is eaten with mushrooms, peas, and Mozzarella cheese, or *alla zappatora* (with sweet and chilli peppers). In Capri it is cooked with squid, and in Umbria it is served with chopped white truffles marinated in olive oil with garlic and anchovies.

RECIPES

Spaghetti à la ligurienne   Peel and crush 2 cloves of garlic. Strip and chop 2 sprigs of basil. Place these ingredients in a mortar together with 40 g (1½ oz, scant ½ cup) dry crumbled Pecorino Romano cheese and 25 g (1 oz, ¼ cup) pine nuts. Cover with 4 tablespoons (⅓ cup) olive oil and leave to soak for 2 hours. Then pound all these ingredients with a pestle to obtain a fluid paste. Cook the spaghetti *al dente*, drain, pour into a heated serving dish, and cover with the condiment. Stir and serve immediately.

Spaghetti alla carbonara   Cook 250 g (9 oz) spaghetti *al dente*. While it is cooking, cut 100 g (4 oz) rindless streaky bacon into small pieces and fry over a gentle heat until crisp. Beat 2 eggs in a bowl, adding 50 g (2 oz, ½ cup) grated Parmesan cheese and salt and pepper to taste. When the spaghetti is cooked, drain, return it to the pan, and stir in the beaten egg and hot bacon. (The heat of the pasta is sufficient to cook the eggs). Serve immediately, with 50 g (2 oz, ½ cup) grated Parmesan cheese.

Spaghetti with basil   SPAGHETTI AU BASILIC   Cook 250 g (9 oz) spaghetti for 10–12 minutes in plenty of boiling salted water, stirring frequently. When the spaghetti is *al dente*, drain it. While it is cooking, peel and crush 3 cloves of garlic, then strip and chop 3 sprigs of basil. Pound these ingredients in a mortar and form a fine paste by gradually adding 3 tablespoons (¼ cup) olive oil. Pour the drained spaghetti into a heated serving dish, add 50 g (2 oz, ¼ cup) butter cut into small pieces, the pounded condiment, then 100 g (4 oz, ⅔ cup) stoned black (pitted ripe) olives cut into small dice. Mix thoroughly and serve piping hot, with grated Parmesan cheese in a separate dish.

Spain   ESPAGNE

There is an old Spanish saying, 'All you find to eat in a Spanish inn is what you bring with you.' Fortunately, the advent of tourism has changed all this.

Dishes vary from the south (rice and pork) to the north (beef and potatoes) while the poor central provinces generally eat lean mutton and chickpeas. Fish and shellfish are caught all along the coast, and are usually fried in oil.

There is one dish better known than any of the others: olla podrida, a soup that combines the flavours of meats and vegetables. Other good Spanish soups are puchero, which is often a substitute for olla podrida, cocido, and gazpacho, the model for all cold soups.

Paella is a hearty dish that includes pork, chicken, duck, chorizos, fish, shellfish, frogs, snails, and a large number of vegetables, pulses, and cereals. Simpler paellas are made in the home.

Other special Spanish dishes are empanadas, roast sucking pig, and various egg dishes, including eggs *à la flamenca* (cooked in the oven on a spiced mixture of chopped meat and vegetables and garnished with peas, asparagus, and chilli peppers). Rice was introduced into Spain by the Moors, but it was the Spaniards who discovered how the chilli peppers could be used in cooking and introduced them to the rest of Europe, together with various dishes based on tomatoes.

Fish and shellfish have always been popular and feature in various dishes: *bacalao à la biscaïenne* (cod served with tomatoes, onions, green peppers, and hardboiled (hard-cooked) eggs); escabèches; and shellfish ragouts (e.g. calderata from Asturias, zarzuela from the Basque region).

□ **Refinements and subtleties** The Spanish, like the French, have developed the art of cooking with wine. Sherry is often used in various recipes for cooking veal escalopes (scallops), crab, and kidneys. Cooking with chocolate is a memento of the days when Mexico was a colony; it is used to prepare rabbit, pigeon, and crayfish.

Game is highly prized and is used in certain high-class dishes such as partridge, boar, and chamois. On the other hand, the regional cuisine is more basic with such foods as *serrano* (very dry ham) and pimiento-flavoured sausages such as the chorizo, longaniza and boutifar. Spanish cheeses have a piquant taste and are made from goats' milk (*cabrales*), ewes' milk (*villalón* and *manchego*), and sometimes cows' milk (*roncal*).

The streets of the bustling Spanish towns are filled with the smell of *churros* (hot fritters) and of sweet *turrón* (a kind of nougat). In the cafés, *tapas* (well-seasoned cocktail snacks) are nibbled with a glass of wine. Orange trees grow in the heart of the cities, and juicy water melons are sold in the public squares, while there is usually an aroma of cinnamon-flavoured chocolate or aniseed liqueur. Beer and cider are manufactured in addition to wine, and other specialities include *horchata*, a very thirst-quenching drink made from orgeat, and sangria, a very popular punch based on red wine. This deep red colour is also typical of the pâtisserie, which always contains large quantities of sugar and almonds and includes flaky pastries, jam swiss rolls, biscuits flavoured with cinnamon and aniseed, quince paste, orange flans, and the curious speciality of Avila, *yemas de*

Santa Teresa (soft creamy balls made with a base of egg yolk and sugar).

spalla

A speciality of Italian charcuterie, made in the same way as coppa but with shoulder of pork (*spalla* in Italian), boned, trimmed, salted, then wrapped and tied in a casing, steamed, and only partially dried.

Spanish wines
VINS D'ESPAGNE

Spain is world-famous as the homeland of sherry, one of the great fortified wines. But sherry is only one of the many wines of Spain. The country has the largest area under vines in Europe, although it is not the top producer – Italy and France make more wine. The first vines were probably planted by the Phoenicians in Andalucia around 1100 BC and the Romans subsequently improved and consolidated the methods of cultivation and wine making.

Until fairly recently, Spanish table wines were not well known outside the Iberian peninsula, where *vino corriente* tended to be drunk, often straight from the cask, by the inhabitants of the different regions. But in fact some of the table wines, notably those of the Rioja area in the northwest, had been reputed for quality almost since medieval times and were, in addition, subject to controls. The rather full robust wines of several Spanish regions became popular as blending wines in various export markets. When these wines (especially those of Rioja) began to attract attention as wines in their own right, certain French terms, such as *clarete* and *borgogna*, were used to describe the characteristics of some of the reds.

Today, many Spanish regions are making a name in export markets, including the areas of Valdepeñas, Navarra, La Mancha, and Léon; modern technology has enabled the white wines to achieve a crisp, clean, and dry style and the reds to attain a fullish agreeable warm character. The Penedés region, in the hinterland of Barcelona, is particularly successful, thanks to the dedication of some wine makers who – like certain old-established firms in Rioja – have become world-famous for their red, white, and rosé wines.

An enormous quantity of sparkling wines is made in the northeast, again mainly in the Penedés region. Some of these are made according to the champagne process and others are produced in *cuves closes* (sealed vats). Since 1973, these sparkling wines cannot legally be referred to as 'Xampaña', but many Spaniards will continue to do so! The gigantic installations of the sparkling-wine makers, who export huge amounts of wine to America, are impressive even to the makers of champagne in France!

In addition to the huge range of sherries, both dry and sweet, there are the wines of Montilla, similar in style to sherry but not fortified, and also the wines of Málaga and Tarragona, which can be dry but are best known as sweetish or definitely sweet.

Sparassis crispa
SPARASSIS CRÉPU

A mushroom with a thick stalk, divided into a large number of flattened branches. It looks like a large yellowish curly endive (chicory) and grows near the trunks of conifer trees. It has a hazelnut taste and is best eaten young.

spare ribs TRAVERS

The upper part of the pork belly, cut in long narrow strips, the flesh and fat surrounding the pieces of bone and ribs. The appearance of this cut justifies its French nickname of *cartouchière* (cartridge belt). The best spare ribs are the fleshiest and the leanest. They are either boiled (in potées, as a sauerkraut garnish, or processed as salt pork), or grilled (broiled). Spare ribs of pork, marinated in spices and soy sauce then grilled, make a popular Chinese dish. In the United States, spare ribs are marinated in a mixture of soy sauce, ketchup, sugar, ginger, and often garlic, then grilled (broiled) or barbecued.

| RECIPE

Spare ribs Prepare a marinade with 1 tablespoon sugar, 1 teaspoon salt, a pinch of ground ginger, 4 tablespoons (⅔ cup) soy sauce and the same quantity of ketchup, a chopped clove of garlic, and some black pepper. Marinate the spare ribs for at least 30 minutes, then drain and grill (or broil) briskly on one side, baste with a little marinade, and grill the other side. Baste once more and grill the ribs until they are stickily glazed on both sides. The ribs may also be baked in a moderate oven, basting occasionally, or cooked in a microwave.

sparerib (shoulder butt)
ÉCHINE

A cut of pork taken from the back of the animal, near the head. This part yields a soft slightly fatty meat. Chops are cut from here, as well as pieces for grilling (broiling) on skewers and roasting on a spit (they do not need to be barded). It is also used for stews. The usual word in French for this cut is *échine*, but it is also known as *épinée* (spined) because of the spiny knobs of the vertebrae. The sparerib (shoulder butt) kept whole, either boned or not, is a roasting joint, which Zola describes in *L'Assommoir*: 'And there was no time to draw breath—the *échine* was arriving in a dish, surrounded by big round potatoes, as if in a cloud. What a wonderful joint! Soft yet solid, and you could feel it slipping down the whole length of your innards right to your feet.'

sparkling wines
MOUSSEUX

A fully sparkling wine may be produced by several methods. The finest are made according to the procedure followed for making champagne. Very good sparkling wines are made according to a process known as *Charmat* or *cuve close*; others, which may be pleasant inexpensive wines, can be made by carbonating a still wine. Most sparkling wines are white, varying from dry to sweetish, but a number of rosés are also made and there are some red sparkling wines, notably in Touraine and Burgundy.

spatula
PALETTE, SPATULE

Any of several types of kitchen utensil with a flat blunt blade. The *palette knife* has a long flexible stainless-steel blade with a rounded end, mounted on a short handle. It is used to ice (frost) cakes, to loosen pastries from the baking sheet, to smooth the surface of a preparation, etc. This and other types of spatula are used for loosening or turning over fried or braised foods in the pan and for transferring them to the serving dish. The *fish slice*, which has a wide flat blade, sometimes perforated, and is fitted with a flat handle, is especially designed for turning over and serving whole fish and large fillets. The *wooden spatula* is designed for mixing and stirring various mixtures, liquids, or sauces while they are cooking, to prevent them from sticking and to avoid scratching receptacles with a nonstick surface. It has the advantage over the wooden spoon of doubling up as a turning and lifting instrument. There are also rubber or plastic spatulas for scraping out batter, sauces, or other mixtures from the sides of the mixing bowl (these should not be used over heat).

spätzle

A speciality common to Alsace and southern Germany, consisting of small dumplings made of flour, eggs, and cream poached in boiling water. They are used to garnish sauced meat dishes (especially game) or are eaten as an entrée, *au gratin*, with cream or noisette butter, or with small fried croutons. In Württemberg, spätzle are similar to small quenelles and are made with liver purée or cheese. The word literally means 'little sparrow'; in Alsace, it is also spelt *spatzele* or *spetzli*.

RECIPE

Spätzle with noisette butter SPÄTZLE AU BEURE NOISETTE Blend together 500 g (18 oz, 4½ cups) sifted flour, 4 whole eggs, 2 tablespoons (3 tablespoons) double (heavy) cream, and 1 tablespoon fine salt. Season with pepper and nutmeg. Boil plenty of salted water in a large pan. Drop small spoonfuls of the dough into the boiling water, using a second spoon to shape them into little dumplings. Leave the spätzle to poach until they rise to the surface. Drain on absorbent paper and serve piping hot, liberally coated with noisette butter. (They may be fried in butter before being coated with noisette butter.)

spéculos or speculoos

A Belgian speciality consisting of small flat gingerbread cakes cut into the shapes of legendary and traditional characters. Speculos are traditionally sold at Flemish fairs; they are also found in southern Germany (as *Spekulatius*). The name comes from the Latin *speculator* ('he who sees'), the nickname for St Nicholas, the original model for these cakes.

RECIPE

Spéculos Put 500 g (18 oz, 4½ cups) sifted flour in a pile on the worktop, make a well in the centre, and add a pinch of salt, 1 teaspoon bicarbonate of soda, ½ tablespoon ground cinnamon, 3 eggs, 4 finely crushed (or ½ teaspoon ground) cloves, 300 g (11 oz, 1½ cups) brown sugar, and 200 g (7 oz, scant cup) softened butter. Mix these ingredients thoroughly, gradually incorporating the flour. Roll the dough into a ball and leave in a cool place overnight. Divide into several pieces and roll them out. Mould them in spéculos moulds coated with flour. Turn out on to a lightly buttered baking sheet and bake in a moderately hot oven (190 C, 375 F, gas 5) until the cakes have browned (about 20 minutes).

spelt ÉPEAUTRE

An ancient variety of wheat with small brown grains that adhere strongly to the chaff; it is quite unlike modern varieties. Widely grown until the beginning of the 20th century, especially in upland regions of Germany, Switzerland, and France, spelt is now rare. Its nutritional value is comparable with soft wheat and it does not need rich soil. A famous German bread is made with spelt and rye. After threshing, spelt is cooked like rice; it is still an ingredient in certain country soups, especially in Provence.

RECIPE

Spelt broth SOUPE D'ÉPEAUTRE Place either 1 kg (2¼ lb) shoulder or leg of mutton (on the bone) or 1 large saucisson de ménage (see *sausage*) in a saucepan, and add 3 litres (5 pints, 6½ pints) water. Bring to the boil, then skim. Add an onion studded with 2 cloves, 2 carrots, 1 turnip, 1 leek, a stick (stalk) of celery, a clove of garlic, and a bouquet garni. Season with salt, add 4 small handfuls of spelt, then simmer gently for 3 hours. When ready, remove the meat and vegetables and serve together. The remaining swollen spelt makes a smooth and creamy broth.

spice ÉPICE

One of many aromatic substances derived from plants, that have a fragrant or sharp flavour and are used to season food. The French distinguish between *épices* (spices) and *aromates* (aromatic substances), although there is still much confusion between the two. In France, a *condiment* is a prepared or cooked product seasoned with herbs or spices.

□ **The spice route** Most spices come from the East, and the first spice to be introduced to Europe was pepper, from India, which long remained a rare and expensive commodity. Roman food was always liberally spiced, ginger being a particular favourite, and the practice of adding spices continued through the Middle Ages and remained common until the 18th century.

The use of spices in cooking was originally introduced by the Byzantines. Food-stuffs were preserved in spiced sauces, sometimes to hide the fact that the meat was high, sometimes to replace the flavour lost after lengthy boiling.

Supplies increased as a result of the Crusades, and control of the 'spice route' aroused much rivalry. Venice managed to obtain a near-monopoly over the distribution of spices in Europe, and the quest for alternative sources of supply was one of the reasons for the great voyages of discovery to America and the West Indies. Spices became more plentiful and less expensive, with British and Dutch companies in particular trading in them. Meanwhile, belief in the miraculous properties of spices waned, and spices were used in cookery with much greater discretion. Nowadays only saffron can be considered a genuinely precious spice.

Because of their rarity and value, spices were highly esteemed as gifts. It is reported that in the 16th century, a German banker called Fugger, wishing to honour Charles V, had a faggot of cinnamon burnt in his honour. Taxes, ransoms, or customs dues were sometimes paid in spices. Thus, the word *épices* had a special meaning under the Ancien Régime: it was the gift that litigants, especially successful ones, would make to the judge; it consisted at first of confectionery, and later of coin of the realm. Subsequently, *épices* became a compulsory tax, paid to the judge as remuneration. The poor were exempted from this tax, but on certain documents one could read: 'Justice will not be rendered to those who do not pay *épices*'. The practice was abolished by the Revolution.

□ **Spices in cookery** Etymologically derived from *espèce* (species), and thus with connotations of the more general *marchandise* (goods), the word *épice* was originally applied to sugary items as well as spices. There was a distinction between *épices de chambre* (fennel or aniseed dragées, nougat, marzipan, jams, and crystallized (candied) fruits) and *épices de cuisine*. The latter term covered products which are no longer considered to be spices, such as milk, sugar, and honey, as well as others which have totally disappeared (galingale, amber, and musk).

Taillevent gave a list of the spices he thought were necessary in a well-stocked kitchen: 'ginger, cinnamon, cloves, cardamom, chillies and peppercorns, spikenard, cinnamon flower, saffron, nutmeg, bay leaves, galingale, mastic, orris, cumin, sugar, almonds, garlic, onions, chives, and shallots', to which should be added 'green-colouring spices' (parsley, *salmonde*, sorrel, vine leaves, redcurrant leaves, and green wheat) and 'steeping spices' (white wine, verjuice, vinegar, water, fatty stock, cows' milk, and almond milk). Thus, 'spice' covered both liquids and solids used in cookery. Taillevent also referred to *poudres* (powders – what we would call spices) without indicating their composition. In the Middle Ages and up to the 17th century, *poudre* meant 'powder made of ground spices'. *Poudres forts* (strong powders) were distinguished from *poudres douces* (mild powders), according to whether the spices were sharp or not. *Le Trésor de santé* (1607) gives the composition of the 'powder' used for sauces and soups: ginger, 4 ounces; cinnamon, 3½ ounces; peppercorns, 1½ ounces; chilli, 1 ounce; nutmeg, 2 ounces; cardamom and galingale, 1 ounce each; cloves, 1 ounce. The author added: 'All the powders will keep for one month, or even 40 days, without spoiling. They must be kept in leather bags, to avoid exposure to the air, since they have already been overexposed on the long journey from their place of origin. From Spain to Calcutta (India), where pepper and ginger come from, is 4000 leagues by sea, and from there to the Spice Islands and nearby islands, where cloves and nutmeg come from, is 2000 leagues.'

In France, professional chefs now use ready-prepared mixed spice, especially for forcemeats, terrines, pâtés, and ragouts. The classic formula is as follows: 10 g thyme; 10 g bay leaf; 5 g marjoram, 5 g rosemary; 20 g nutmeg; 20 g cloves; 6 g cayenne; 12 g white pepper; and 10 g coriander.

Another formula, devised by Escoffier, is especially suited to Provençal cooking: 25 g thyme; 25 g bay leaf; 25 g rosemary; 25 g basil; 25 g nutmeg; 20 g cloves; 20 g white pepper; 10 g coriander; 20 g savory; and 3 g lavender.

Carême regarded the abuse of spices as one of the enemies of good cookery, and in his memoirs he recalls that before his arrival at the court of King George IV of England, the cooking was 'so strong and over-flavoured that the prince often had pains lasting all day and night'.

Spices were widely reputed to have aphrodisiac qualities as well as being the mark of refined and high-class cuisine. Baudelaire's response to Flaubert's Pécuchet, who was afraid of spices because they might 'set his body on fire', was that spices ennoble food. He scorned 'simple meats and insipid fish' and summoned 'the whole of nature's pharmacy to the aid of the kitchen'. 'Peppers, English powders, saffron-like substances, and exotic dusts' seemed essential to him to make a dish elegant and attractive.

□ The present day In Europe, spices are now used much more judiciously in accordance with the dish: cloves and peppercorns for marinades; nutmeg and cinnamon for wine sauces; saffron for bouillabaisse and paella; cumin and aniseed in biscuit-making; juniper berries and coriander for game, etc. Very strong spices are rarely used, except

chilli (chili pepper) in Spanish and Latin American cooking and paprika in Hungarian dishes. Spices are usually sold either as seeds or in powder form. It is always preferable to buy small quantities, because they spoil on exposure to air and quickly lose their properties. It is also advisable to store them in fairly large jars to maintain a certain amount of ventilation. (See *five spices, four spices*.)

In non-European counties, spices are used to a much greater extent. In India, for example, the preparation of spices, either in powder or paste form, is as complex as that of sauces in French cuisine. Chinese cookery also uses many spices, selected according to elaborate harmonies of flavour. Of particular importance are aniseed, coriander, ginger, dried chilli, dried mushrooms, and sesame. African and West Indian cookery use spices unknown in Europe, obtained from a variety of flowers, seeds, and roots and also from dried insects and fish. Arab cuisine combines salty, piquant, and sweet flavours, such as dried fruits, saffron, rose water, pepper, and chilli.

spice box BOÎTE À ÉPICES

A small cylindrical or rectangular box with a lid, usually forming part of a set. The containers may vary in size and are designed to store, within easy reach, the ingredients that are frequently used in cooking. They were very common in kitchens until the 19th century and were usually arranged in a line on the mantel shelf. Spice boxes, which were as decorative as they were functional, are now reappearing in contemporary kitchens, being made of wood, enamelled or painted metal, porcelain, or pottery (spices keep better, however, in airtight opaque bottles).

Restaurant chefs keep a metal spice box within easy reach. This is a rectangular box with compartments containing pepper, nutmeg, etc.

spider crab
ARAIGNÉE DE MER

The name given to several species of crab having a spiny shell, slender hairy legs, and long claws. In France the most common spider crab is the *maïa*, usually found on the Atlantic coast. Its shell is about 20 cm (8 in) across, compared with the giant spider crab, which lives on the coasts of Japan and has a body 40 cm (16 in) wide and a claw span of nearly 3 m (10 ft). Considered by some to be the finest of all shellfish, the spider crab is prepared in a court-bouillon and is traditionally served cold on a dish of seafood, accompanied by mayonnaise.

spikenard NARD

A bitter and highly scented aromatic extract obtained from certain valerianaceous plants. It was highly esteemed in ancient and medieval cookery, being used in sauces, meat dishes, and wines. Indian spikenard, which tastes of ginger and verbena, is still used in Malaysian and Sri Lankan cooking, but Celtic spikenard, formerly used as a substitute for the Indian variety, fell into disuse when oriental spices were introduced into Europe.

spinach ÉPINARD

A vegetable with dark-green curled or smooth leaves, generally cooked, but also eaten raw in salads when young and tender.

Spinach originated in Persia. In the Middle Ages it was sold either fresh or cooked, chopped, and pressed into balls, under the name of *espinoche*. It was very fashionable in the 17th century, when it was cooked with sugar, and at least ten varieties were grown, including 'Monstrueux de Viroflay' and 'Merveille de Versailles'.

Nowadays, spinach is available all the year round, but especially from March to May. The winter varieties have much larger and lighter-coloured leaves than the summer ones. Spinach has a high water content, contains only 20–32 Cal per 100 g, and is very digestible. It is rich in minerals, especially iron, and vitamins. Scalded, drained, and served with fresh butter, spinach is a classic accompaniment to veal and poultry, as well as eggs, but it is also used in regional dishes, such as tarts and pâtés. It is used for stuffings (mixed with other vegetables, particularly sorrel), soufflés, purées, and gratins. It is an essential ingredient for Florentine dishes. Spinach is also available preserved in jars (whole, chopped, or as purée) and deep-frozen.

Because of its pronounced flavour, people either love or hate spinach. Le Prudhomme in Flaubert's *Dictionnaire des idées reçues* declared: 'I dislike it, and am happy to dislike it because if I liked it I would eat it, and I cannot stand it.' Maupassant hated spinach too, and it is said that his valet managed to make him eat it by calling it 'Tetragonian spinach' (in fact a variety of spinach from Australia and New Zealand).

A Mexican shrub known in France as *épinard géant du Mexique* (giant Mexican spinach) has large leaves that are cooked and eaten like spinach.

RECIPE

Preparation and cooking of spinach PRÉPARATION ET CUISSON DES ÉPINARDS (from a method by Paul Bocuse) Cut off the stalks, wash the spinach in plenty of water, and remove any yellowing or wilting leaves. The flavour and nutritional qualities are best preserved if it is cooked very quickly and served immediately. Boil a large quantity of water in an untinned copper pan and add the prepared and drained spinach. Boil briskly for 8 minutes. Check if the spinach is cooked by pinching a piece between your fingers. More mature leaves take longer than younger ones. Drain in a large colander or sieve, refill the pan with cold water, and replace the spinach. Repeat this several times to cool the spinach quickly. Then, taking handfuls at a time, squeeze hard to extract all the water. If the spinach is not to be served immediately, keep it in an earthenware dish in the refrigerator or in a cool place.

Scallop broth with spinach BROUET DE SAINT-JACQUES AUX ÉPINARDS CRUS (from a recipe by Guy Delmotte) Cut up 12 prepared scallops into slices, 5 mm (¼ in) thick, and place in a buttered frying pan (skillet). Add salt and a glass of fish stock, poach for 2 minutes, then remove and drain. Add 20 cl (7 fl oz, ¾ cup) fresh cream to the stock and reduce until it is the consistency of a light soup. Add 500 g (18 oz) chopped fresh spinach and heat for 2 minutes. Then bind with a mixture consisting of 1 dl (6 tablespoons) cream, 2 egg yolks, and the juice of a lemon. Then add the scallop slices and adjust the seasoning. Serve in hot dishes garnished with hot roughly chopped tomatoes.

Spinach à l'anglaise ÉPINARDS À L'ANGLAISE Clean and parboil some spinach rapidly in boiling salted water. Drain and dry in a cloth. Arrange the leaves (whole) in a heated vegetable dish. Serve with fresh butter.

Spinach au gratin ÉPINARDS AU GRATIN Clean, parboil, and dry the spinach. Lightly butter a gratin dish, and spread out the spinach leaves in it. Cover with a light béchamel sauce flavoured with nutmeg and grated cheese. Sprinkle with more grated cheese and then with melted butter, and brown in a very hot oven. Hard-boiled (hard-cooked) egg halves may be arranged on top of the sauce before sprinkling with cheese, if desired.

Spinach bouillabaisse BOUILLA-BAISSE D'ÉPINARDS (from a recipe by J. B. Reboul) Wash and trim 1 kg (2¼ lb) spinach, cook for 5 minutes in boiling water, cool, and drain. Squeeze with your hands to extract all the water, then chop. Place 1.5 dl (¼ pint, ⅔ cup) olive oil in a flameproof casserole, add a chopped onion and brown lightly, then add the spinach and stir over a low heat for 5 minutes. When the spinach is dry, add 5 potatoes cut into slices. Season with salt and pepper and a little saffron. Add 1 litre (1¾ pints, 4¼ cups) boiling water, 2 chopped cloves of garlic, and a stick of fennel and cook with the lid off over a low heat. When the potatoes are cooked, break 4 eggs, one by one, onto the surface, and allow to cook very gently. This dish can be served straight from the casserole.

Spinach croquettes CROQUETTES D'ÉPINARDS Mix 2 parts chopped spinach cooked in butter with 1 part duchess potato mixture. Shape this mixture into balls the size of tangerines, and gently flatten. Coat with egg and breadcrumbs, deep-fry in very hot oil (175 –180 c, about 350 f) until golden, then drain on absorbent paper. Serve with grilled (broiled) or roast meat or poultry.

Spinach in butter ÉPINARDS AU BEURRE Clean and parboil some spinach, then drain and dry in a cloth. Heat a little butter in a frying pan (skillet) and add the spinach. Season with salt, pepper, and a little nutmeg. When all the moisture has evaporated, add more butter, allowing 50 g (2 oz, 4 tablespoons) butter to 500 g (generous lb, 2 cups) spinach. Arrange in a vegetable dish and garnish with fried croutons. The spinach may also be sprinkled with noisette butter, if desired.

Spinach in cream ÉPINARDS À LA CRÈME Clean, parboil, and dry the spinach. Arrange it in a warm vegetable dish and pour heated fresh cream (or cream sauce) over the top; stir before serving. The spinach may be slightly sweetened, and served with fried croutons cut into the shape of sponge fingers (ladyfingers).

Spinach purée PURÉE D'ÉPINARDS Clean, parboil, and dry the spinach, then rub it through a sieve or use a blender to form a purée. Add 50 g (2 oz, 4 tablespoons) butter for every 500 g (generous lb, 2 cups) cooked spinach. If desired, add one-third of its volume of potato purée, or bind with a quarter of its volume of béchamel sauce.

Spinach salad SALADE D'ÉPI-NARDS Plunge the prepared spinach into boiling water for a few seconds. Cool under running water, drain, and dry in a cloth. Arrange in a salad bowl, sprinkle with chopped hard-boiled (hard-cooked) eggs, and dress with oil, vinegar, salt, and pepper.

Raw spinach may be finely sliced and mixed with flakes of smoked haddock, sliced scallops, or new potatoes.

spiny lobster

See *langouste.*

spit BROCHE

A pointed iron rod with which a piece of meat or a whole animal is speared for roasting, either horizontally or vertically, traditionally over or in front of a fire (see *barbecue, brochette, kebab, rotisserie.*

When all cooking was carried out at

the hearth, the roasting spit was a most important piece of equipment. It is used much less nowadays, although this method of cooking provides the best roasts: according to Escoffier, 'cooking a roast on a spit is performed in the open air, in a dry atmosphere, which leaves the joint with all its unique flavour.'

Spit-roasting owes its perfect cooking to the regular and constant rotation of the spit. From the technical point of view, this method of cooking, which is closer to grilling (broiling) than oven-roasting, comprises two phases: in the first, the meat is cooked quickly at a high temperature to seal the outside (particularly for red meat and juicy game, which require rapid sealing before actual cooking); the second phase, which requires a lower temperature and skill on the part of the roaster, is intended to cook the inside of the joint to the required degree. White meat and poultry, on the other hand, require simultaneous cooking of the inside and the outside, at a lower temperature than for red meat. While it is cooking, the meat is basted with the drippings.

split peas POIS CASSÉS
Small pale green dried peas that are split in two. They are obtained from mature peas, picked in summer, which are mechanically stripped of their cellulose skins and then split in two, dried, and often polished by friction. Certain varieties of pea, such as Rondo, are specially grown for producing split peas.

Split peas have a very high energy content (351 Cal per 100 g) and are rich in carbohydrates, proteins, phosphorus, and potassium. They can be stored in a dry place for several months and are always soaked before being cooked. They can be used for preparing soups, stews, and purées, especially as a garnish for preparations cooked *à la Sainte-Menehould*, and also with roast pork or veal. They can also be served as a vegetable with boiled ham.

| RECIPE

Cooking split peas CUISSON DES POIS CASSÉS Soak some split peas for 1½ hours in cold water, drain, then place them in a saucepan with 2 litres (3½ pints, 4½ pints) fresh cold water per 500 g (18 oz, 2¼ cups) peas. Add a carrot, a stick (stalk) of celery, the white part of a leek, and an onion, all chopped as for a mirepoix. Then add a bouquet garni including the green part of the leek and, if possible, a knuckle of ham and some lettuce leaves. Bring slowly to the boil, skim, and season with salt and pepper. Simmer gently with the lid on for approximately 2½ hours. Then remove the bouquet garni and the ham. Strip the meat off the bone and discard the skin. Dice and serve with the peas if wished.

Split-pea purée PURÉE DE POIS CASSÉS Rub some cooked split peas through a fine sieve or reduce to a purée in a blender or processor. Pour the purée into a heavy-based saucepan and heat, stirring continuously with a wooden spoon and slowly pouring in a little of the strained cooking liquid. Blend in some cream, remove from the heat, add a knob of butter, and serve piping hot.

Split-pea soup POTAGE DE POIS CASSÉS Rub some cooked split peas through a fine sieve (or use a blender or processor), together with the vegetables they were cooked with. Add equal amounts of the cooking liquid and milk (or use one-third of this volume of cream instead of milk and replace the cooking liquor with consommé). Stir well and adjust the seasoning. Sprinkle with chervil. Fry some croutons in butter or oil and serve separately. The ham used for cooking the split peas may also be added after being cut into very small dice.

sponge cake BISCUIT
A cake that is usually lightened with baking powder or whisked egg whites. There are many varieties, the best known in France being Savoy sponge cake, sponge roll (*biscuit roulé*), manqué, and pound cake. They are often enriched with almonds and flavoured with lemon zest, vanilla, liqueurs, etc., and can be filled with jam or butter cream.

| RECIPE

Basic sponge cake recipe PÂTE À BISCUIT Using a large bowl and a spatula, beat 500 g (18 oz, 2¼ cups) caster (superfine) sugar with 25 g (1 oz, 2 tablespoons) vanilla sugar and 10 egg yolks until the mixture is very pale and thick enough to form a ribbon trail. Then carefully fold in 125 g (4½ oz, 1 cup) sifted flour and an equal quantity of cornflour (cornstarch), 10 stiffly beaten egg whites, and a pinch of salt. (A slightly heavier mixture can be made using 250 g (9 oz, 1 cup) sugar, 8 eggs (separated), 125 g (4½ oz, 1 cup) sifted flour, and a pinch of salt.)

LARGE SPONGE CAKES

Almond sandwich cake BISCUIT AUX AMANDES Prepare a sponge cake mixture using 500 g (18 oz, 2¼ cups) caster (superfine) sugar, 1 tablespoon vanilla sugar, 14 egg yolks, 185 g (6½ oz, 1½ cups) sifted flour and an equal quantity of cornflour (cornstarch). When the egg and sugar mixture is very pale and thick enough to form a ribbon, add the flour and cornflour (cornstarch), then 200 g (7 oz, 1½ cups) blanched almonds (with 4 or 5 bitter almonds if desired), which have been pounded to a paste with 2 egg whites and a few drops of orange-flower water. Butter a very large round cake tin and dust the inside with caster sugar. Pour in the mixture, which should only two-thirds fill the tin. Bake at 180 C (350 F, gas 4) until risen and springy to the touch – about 1–1¼ hours depending on the size of the tin. Turn the cake out on to a cooling tray, and when cool, slice into three equal rounds. Spread the bottom round with apricot jam and the middle round with raspberry jelly. Reassemble the cake and coat the top and sides with apricot glaze. It may be iced with vanilla fondant icing (frosting) and decorated with chopped almonds on the top and sides.

Italian sponge cake BISCUIT À L'ITALIENNE Using a large bowl and a spatula, beat 500 g (18 oz, 2¼ cups) caster (superfine) sugar with 10 g (¼ oz) vanilla sugar and 10 egg yolks. Beat the egg whites with a pinch of salt until stiff and fold into the mixture. Quickly fold in 125 g (4½ oz, 1 cup) flour and 125 g (4½ oz, 1 cup) cornflour (cornstarch) sifted together. Butter a charlotte mould and dust the inside with caster sugar and

cornflour. Pour the mixture into the mould, no more than two-thirds full. Bake in a preheated oven at approximately 180 C (350 F, gas 4) until risen, golden, and firm to the touch.

Orange sandwich cake BISCUIT MOUSSELINE À L'ORANGE Prepare the same mixture as for Italian sponge cake. Grease a charlotte mould with hot clarified butter and dust generously with icing (confectioners') sugar. Pour the mixture into the mould, no more than two-thirds full. Bake in a preheated oven at approximately 160 C (325 F, gas 3) until risen, golden, and firm to the touch. Turn the cake out onto a cooling tray and leave until just warm. Cut into two rounds of equal thickness. Pour a little Curaçao onto the bottom half and spread with a thick layer of orange jam or marmalade. Place the other half on top. Coat the top and sides with orange jam or warmed sieved marmalade. Coat with fondant icing (frosting) flavoured with Curaçao. Decorate with candied orange peel.

Sponge roll BISCUIT ROULÉ Prepare a sponge cake mixture using half the quantities for almond sponge cake. Line a rectangular baking sheet with greaseproof (waxed) paper and brush with clarified butter. Spread the mixture evenly using a metal spatula until it covers the whole buttered area to a thickness of about 1 cm (½ in). Cook in a preheated oven (about 180 C, 350 F, gas 4) for 10 minutes. The top of the cake should be just golden. Meanwhile, prepare a syrup using 75 g (3 oz, ¾ cup) sugar, 7 cl (4 tablespoons, ⅓ cup) water, and 5 cl (3 tablespoons, ¼ cup) rum. Lightly toast 125 g (4 oz, 1 cup) flaked (slivered) almonds. When the cake is cooked, turn it over onto a cloth and sprinkle with the syrup. Spread it with apricot jam or raspberry jelly. Using a cloth, roll up the cake. Cut the ends off crosswise. Cover the whole cake with apricot glaze and, if required, decorate with toasted almonds.

SPONGE DROPS AND SMALL SPONGE CAKES

Chocolate soufflé biscuits (cookies) BISCUITS SOUFFLÉS AU CHOCOLAT

Melt 300 g (11 oz) dessert (semi-sweet) chocolate and stir in 2 egg yolks. Beat 500 g (18 oz, 2¼ cups) caster (super-fine) sugar with 10 egg whites in a small saucepan over a very low heat (or in a bain-marie). When the meringue is fairly firm, add the chocolate mixture. Butter and flour a baking sheet and pipe the mixture onto it, in the shape of macaroons or sponge fingers. Bake at approximately 180 c (350 f, gas 4) for about 10 minutes.

Geneva sponge fingers BISCUITS GENEVOIS Beat 125 g (4½ oz, ⅔ cup) caster (superfine) sugar with a little grated lemon zest, a pinch of salt, 1 whole egg, and 3 egg yolks until the mixture is thick enough to form a rib-bon. Add 45 g (2 oz, 4 tablespoons) clarified butter, 35 g (1½ oz, ⅓ cup) ground almonds, 125 g (4½ oz, 1 cup) sifted flour, and 3 stiffly beaten egg whites. Pour into finger-shaped moulds that have been buttered and dusted with caster sugar and cornflour (cornstarch) and bake at about 180 c (350 f, gas 4). Turn the sponge fingers out of the moulds and leave to dry at the front of the oven with the oven door open. Leave to cool and store in an airtight con-tainer.

Italian sponge drops BISCUITS ITALIENS Put 250 g (9 oz, 1 cup) sugar into a small saucepan with ½ litre (17 fl oz, 2 cups) water and boil until the syrup reaches the hard ball stage. Par-tially cool, then add 4 egg yolks and 125 g (4½ oz, 1 cup) sifted flour. Beat 4 egg whites stiffly with a pinch of salt and add to the mixture. Pipe into small flat rounds and finish as for lemon sponge drops.

Lemon sponge drops BISCUITS AU CITRON Using a large bowl and a spatula, beat 250 g (9 oz, 1 cup) caster (superfine) sugar with 8 egg yolks until the mixture is thick enough to form a ribbon. Add the grated zest of a lemon, 125 g (4 oz, 1 cup) sifted flour, 80 g (3 oz, ¾ cup) cornflour (cornstarch), 1 good tablespoon ground almonds, and 3 egg whites stiffly beaten with a pinch of salt. Using a forcing (pastry) bag with a smooth nozzle, pipe small flat rounds, 3 cm (1 in) in diameter, and dust with caster sugar. Bake at approximately 180 c (350 f, gas 4) for about 10 minutes or until lightly browned and set. Cool completely before storing in an airtight container.

Punch cakes BISCUITS PUNCH Us-ing a large bowl and a spatula, beat together 375 g (13 oz, 1⅔ cups) caster (superfine) sugar, ½ tablespoon orange-flavoured sugar, ½ tablespoon lemon-flavoured sugar, 3 whole eggs, and 12 egg yolks until light and fluffy. Continue beating and add 3 tablespoons rum and 375 g (13 oz, 3 cups) sifted flour, then 8 stiffly beaten egg whites and 300 g (11 oz, 1½ cups) clarified butter. Butter some small paper cases and fill them with the mixture. Bake at 180 c (350 f, gas 4) for about 15 minutes, until risen and golden.

Sponge biscuits (cookies) BISCUITS FINS Make a sponge cake mixture. Flavour with Curaçao and add chopped candied orange peel. Using a forcing (pastry) bag with a smooth nozzle, pipe the mixture onto a sheet of greaseproof (waxed) paper in figures of eight. Dust with icing (confectioners') sugar. Bake at 180 c (350 f, gas 4) for about 10 minutes. Remove the biscuits from the paper while still warm and allow to cool completely before storing them in an airtight container.

sponge finger
BISCUIT À LA CUILLER

A small elongated sponge cake made of a mixture similar to that used for Savoy sponge cake, but lighter. Sponge fingers are served with fruit creams and purées and are often used as a border for cold charlottes or with ice creams. They can be kept for two to three weeks in an airtight container.

RECIPE

Sponge fingers BISCUITS À LA CUILLER Beat 250 g (9 oz, 1 cup) caster (superfine) sugar with 8 egg yolks until the mixture is thick enough to form a ribbon. Flavour with 1 table-spoon orange-flower water. Add 190 g (7 oz, 1¾ cups) sifted flour and fold in 8 egg whites stiffly beaten with a pinch of salt. Using a forcing (pastry) bag with a smooth nozzle, pipe the mixture onto sheets of greaseproof (waxed) paper. Dust with icing (confectioners') sugar and gently lift and tap the sheets of paper to remove any excess sugar. Bake in a cool oven (about 160 C (325 F, gas 3)) for about 10 minutes or until pale golden.

The mixture can be flavoured with orange or lemon zest.

spoom

A sort of frothy sorbet, which used to be a great favourite in England, made with a lighter syrup than that required for a true sorbet. As it is beginning to set, it is mixed with half its volume of Italian meringue. Like sorbet, it is made from fruit juice, wine, sherry, port, etc.; it is served in a tall glass. The name comes from the Italian *spuma* (foam). In Italy, *spumone* is a light frothy ice cream made with egg whites, a flavouring, and whipped cream.

spoon
CUILLER, CUILLÈRE

A utensil consisting of a hollow part (the bowl) and a handle of varying length. The French word for spoon derives from the Latin *cochlea* (snail), as a *cuiller* was originally a spatula used for eating snails, as well as eggs and shellfish.

The spoon is as old as the knife and was used both to prepare and eat the meal. The first spoons were cut in a simple fashion out of wood, sometimes sweet-smelling (juniper, box). During the Middle Ages and the Renaissance, however, the spoon became a luxurious table utensil, made of crystal, serpentine, or cornelian, but always with a fairly short handle studded with precious stones or enamels. In the 17th century chased silver was used for the first time and the handle became longer. Ever since then, the sizes and shapes of spoons have varied according to their uses.

□ **Table spoons** These are usually made of metal (silver, silver plate, or stainless steel), or at least the bowl is. A distinction is made between the individual spoon and the serving spoons. A table setting includes three sizes of spoons: the serving spoon (tablespoon), the soupspoon, and the dessertspoon. In addition to these basic spoons there are many others with specific uses, according to the dish to be consumed: for grapefruit (serrated edge), oysters (which some people prefer to eat with a fork), boiled eggs, sauces, ice cream, coffee, etc. Other spoons of various shapes complete this individual set: spoons for breakfast, cocktails or syrups (with a very long handle, called a *diablotin*), and for tea.

Table settings may also include specific spoons for serving salad, often made of wood, horn, or plastic. The spoon for serving sauce has a bowl with two compartments (with fat and without). Other serving spoons of special shape include those used for salt, mustard, sugar, jam, honey (often of ivory, bone, wood, or stainless metal, matching the serving container), fruit salads (with a pouring spout), olives (made of wood pierced with holes), strawberries, and ice cream (made of perforated metal, in the shape of a spatula or a paddle).

□ **Cooking spoons** The shape and material used for cooking spoons are suited to their uses: for example, basting spoons are small ladles with a lateral pouring spout for basting roasts; ragout spoons have a straight lip; and spoons for tasting are made of porcelain so that one does not burn oneself. Spoons for stirring and mixing are usually made of wood, which is strong and a poor conductor of heat. Some have a corner on the bowl which gets into the crevice in the base of a pan. There are also sets of spoons for measuring. The ice-cream spoon is used for filling bombe moulds and the ice-cream scoop for shaping balls for sundaes and cornets. Finally, the melon baller, which has a small oval, fluted, or round bowl, is used to make ball shapes out of potatoes, carrots, and fruits (apples or melons).

sprat

A small fish (12–15 cm (4½–6 in) long) similar to a sardine, with a bluish-green back and silvery sides. It is most common in the Baltic, the North Sea, and the English Channel, but is also found in the Atlantic. When fresh, sprats are usually fried; the fish is held in the fingers and the flesh is eaten off either side, leaving the head and tail intact. They are often sold smoked, preserved, or marinated. Norway (where smoked sprats are called anchovies) is a major producer. Sprats are used a great deal in Scandinavian cooking (for gratins, open sandwiches, salads, etc.).

RECIPE

Sprats à la vinaigrette Remove the heads and skin from some fresh sprats. Arrange them in a small bowl and sprinkle liberally with chopped shallots and parsley. Coat with oil and shallot-flavoured (or white distilled) vinegar. Leave to marinate in a cool place for 10 hours. Serve with parsley, rye bread, and shallot butter.

spring onion (scallion)
CIBOULE
A variety of onion that produces small white mild-flavoured bulbs with a long neck of stiff leaves. Spring onions (scallions) are usually eaten raw and thinly sliced in salads.

spring roll
PÂTÉ IMPÉRIAL, ROULEAU DE PRINTEMPS
An oriental preparation, so called because it is often served during the New Year celebrations, known in China and Vietnam as the Spring Festival. The Chinese spring roll differs slightly from the Vietnamese version; it consists of a square of dough made with eggs and wheat flour that is rolled around a filling of pork, onions, prawns (shrimp), bamboo shoots or bean sprouts, flavoured mushrooms, chives, and sometimes water chestnuts. The filling is bound with egg and a seasoning based on soy sauce, ginger, pepper, and rice wine. The rolls are deep-fried, served with soy sauce flavoured with garlic and lemon, and garnished with lettuce leaves, raw bean sprouts, mint leaves, parsley, or coriander leaves.

The Vietnamese spring roll is called a *nem*. Chicken can be used in the filling instead of pork and crab instead of prawns, but the distinctive feature is that the filling is seasoned with *nuoc-mâm* and wrapped in a very thin rice pancake. These spring rolls are either deep-fried or shallow-fried and served with lightly peppered *nuoc-mâm*, mint leaves, and lettuce leaves. Very tiny spring rolls are known as *cha gio*.

spunchade
An iced dessert made, like a sorbet, from a sugar syrup with a fruit base, sometimes flavoured with Kirsch. It is then mixed with Italian meringue or egg whites and chilled thoroughly until iced. Spunchade is served in sorbet glasses.

RECIPE

Lemon spunchade SPUNCHADE AU CITRON (from a recipe by Darenne and Duval in *Traité de pâtisserie moderne*, Flammarion) Prepare ¼ litre (8 fl oz, 1 cup) sugar syrup with a density of 1.2624 (use 100 g (4 oz, ½ cup) sugar to ¼ litre (8 fl oz, 1 cup) water). Add the juice of 4 lemons, then dilute the mixture to a density of 1.1609 with soda water (about 2 tablespoons, 3 tablespoons) and add half a plain egg white or some Italian meringue made from 1 egg white. Place immediately in an ice-cream maker and work the mixture thoroughly until icy. Serve straight away.

squash
An edible gourd that is cooked and served as a vegetable. The best-known varieties are the American winter squashes, varying in size and shape and also in colour from white, yellow, and orange to green squashes. A green variety called a *pâtisson* is available in the south of France from August to September. It can measure up to 25 cm (10 in) in diameter and is edged with rounded serrations, like a pie crust (hence its name). The flesh is firm, floury, and milky white, with a slightly sweet taste resembling that of an artichoke.

Squashes are blanched and then usually sautéed as part of a highly seasoned dish or they can be peeled, cut up, boiled, and mashed with butter and a little orange juice. They are also good stuffed or baked in the oven with butter and brown sugar or maple syrup. Very small squashes can be pickled in vinegar. Most recipes for marrow (see *gourd*) and pumpkin are suitable for squashes.

squeeze out EXPRIMER

To use pressure to extract the juice of a fruit, etc., or to remove excessive liquid from a food. The liquid and seeds may be removed from tomatoes by halving them and pressing them in a colander with a spoon before crushing the flesh. Excess liquid in blanched drained spinach is squeezed out by hand. A special lemon squeezer is used to squeeze the juice from citrus fruits.

squid CALMAR

A marine mollusc, also called calamary or calamari, related to the cuttlefish. In France its other names are *calamar*, *encornet*, or *chipiron* (on the Basque coast) and *supion* (in the south of France). Its spindle-shaped body (about 50 cm (20 in) long) is covered with blackish membranes. It has two triangular fins at the tail end and its head bears ten arms, or tentacles, two of which are very long. Like cuttlefish, squid have an ink bag situated near the heart. Squid are sold whole or cleaned, and sometimes dried. They are enjoyed in Mediterranean countries, where they may be stuffed with tomato, cooked in sauce *à l'américaine* or in a white wine sauce, served cold with aïoli, or fried. The classic Spanish speciality is to cook them *en su tinta*, in a black sauce made from their ink (this preparation is also found in Venice, served with polenta). Squid are best to eat when they are quite tender and well-seasoned.

RECIPES

Fried or sautéed squid CALMARS FRITS OU SAUTÉS Wash and dry 1 kg (2¼ lb) very small cleaned squid. Put them in a frying pan (skillet) with half a glass of cold olive oil. Heat and cook over a brisk heat for 10 minutes, turning continually. Season with salt and pepper, cover the pan, reduce the heat, and cook for 15 minutes more. Add 2 or 3 chopped large cloves of garlic and 1 tablespoon chopped parsley. Increase the heat and stir. Serve very hot.

Squid à l'andalouse CALMARS À L'ANDALOUSE Wash and dry 1 kg (2¼ lb) white squid flesh and cut it into thin strips. Fry the strips in very hot olive oil. Place 3 or 4 peppers in a very hot oven for a few minutes so that the skin swells. Peel, remove the seeds, and cut the flesh into thin strips. Peel 3 onions and slice them into rounds. Peel 4 or 5 tomatoes, remove the seeds, and crush the pulp. Dice 100 g (4 oz) farmhouse bread and brown in very hot olive oil. Add the strips of pepper to the squid, then the onions, and finally the tomatoes. Brown the mixture, add 1 glass very dry white wine, and cook for 35–45 minutes over a low heat. Chop and mix together the diced fried bread, a small bunch of parsley, and 3 or 4 large cloves of garlic. Add a pinch of saffron, 75 g (3 oz, ¾ cup) ground almonds, and 2 tablespoons oil. Pour this mixture over the cooked squid, mix well, and adjust the seasoning. Serve piping hot with well drained rice.

Stuffed squid à la marseillaise CALMARS FARCIS À LA MARSEILLAISE Buy some small cleaned squid complete with their tentacles. Chop the tentacles finely together with 2 large onions. Soak 100 g (4 oz) stale bread in milk, then squeeze it out. Chop and mix together some garlic and parsley. Brown the chopped tentacles and onions in olive oil, then add 2 peeled and crushed tomatoes. Mix all the ingredients together. Add 2 or 3 egg yolks, salt, pepper, and a pinch of cayenne, and blend well. Fill the squid with this stuffing, sew them up, and pack tightly together in an oiled baking dish. Sprinkle with chopped garlic and parsley, add a roughly crushed onion, salt, pepper, 1 glass white wine, and an equal amount of hot water. Cover the dish with oiled greaseproof (waxed) paper. Start the cooking on the top of the cooker and then transfer the dish to a moderate oven (180 C, 350 F, gas 4) for about 30 minutes. Uncover the dish to reduce the liquid, then sprinkle the squid with olive oil and dried white breadcrumbs and brown under the grill.

Additional recipe See *basquaise (à la)*.

squilla SQUILLE

A large shrimp-like crustacean living on the muddy bed of the Mediterranean; it has a pair of large grasping appendages like those of a praying mantis (hence its common name of mantis shrimp). Up to 25 cm (10 in) long, it is prepared in the same way as scampi, but is less of a delicacy.

squill-fish
CIGALE DE MER

A crustacean of the rocky seabed, closely related to the lobster, with a brown or greenish body and a powerful tail. Its flesh is very delicate. Two species exist: the large squill, found only in the Mediterranean, can reach 45 cm (18 in) in length and weigh up to 2 kg (4½ lb), while the small squill measures 7–10 cm (3–4 in). Squills have no claws but possess two pairs of antennae, one of which is blade-shaped.

RECIPE

Squill-fish on skewers with saffron BROCHETTES DE CIGALES DE MER AU SAFRAN Wash and wipe some small squill-fish. Marinate them for at least 30 minutes in a mixture of saffron (1 pinch per 500 g (18 oz) squill-fish), olive oil, lemon juice, chopped garlic (1 clove per 500 g (18 oz) squill-fish), chopped parsley, crumbled thyme, salt, and pepper. Thread the squill-fish onto skewers and grill (broil) them quickly.

stabilizing agent
STABLILISANT

A food additive used to ensure that a product keeps its texture and consistency. Stabilizing agents are indicated by the numbers E322–E339 and E400–E495. Rarely used on their own, these additives are usually associated with an emulsifying agent, a thickener, or a gelling agent. Among the most commonly used stabilizing agents are lecithin (egg yolk), tartaric acid, alginates, pectin, carob, tamarind, agar-agar, and guar (vegetable gums).

stale RASSIS

Describing food, particularly bread, which is no longer fresh, being rather dry and hard. For some dishes (croûtes, pain perdu, etc.) the bread or brioche should be slightly stale. The large white French loaf known as *pain de campagne*

is better if eaten two or three days after cooking. Bread can be kept fresh if it is stored in the freezer.

Stanley

The name of various onion dishes seasoned with curry powder, named after the British explorer Sir Henry Morton Stanley. Eggs Stanley, soft-boiled or poached, are arranged on tartlets filled with Soubise purée and coated with curried sauce. Chicken Stanley is sautéed with onions, then coated with a Soubise sauce spiced with curry powder. This sauce also accompanies poached chicken.

RECIPE

Sautéed chicken Stanley POULET SAUTÉ STANLEY Cut a chicken into 6 pieces and sauté them in butter in a casserole without allowing them to brown. After 30 minutes, add 2 large finely sliced onions, cover, and finish cooking over a low heat (about 20 minutes). Cook some mushrooms in butter. Arrange the chicken and mushrooms in the serving dish and keep warm. Deglaze the casserole juices with 2 dl (7 fl oz, ¾ cup) cream, reduce by a quarter, and pass through a sieve. Add ½ teaspoon curry powder and a pinch of cayenne, then whisk in 40 g (1½ oz, 3 tablespoons) butter. Cover the chicken with this sauce and (if desired) garnish with a few strips of truffle.

star anise BADIANE

The fruit of a shrub native to the Far East. It is shaped like an eight-pointed star and contains seeds with a slightly hot aniseed flavour. It was first imported into Europe by the English during the Renaissance, and is used most commonly in infusions and in the preparation of liqueurs (anisette). In Scandinavian countries it is also used in pastry- and biscuit-making. Star anise is a spice commonly used in oriental cuisine. In China it is used as a seasoning for fatty meats (pork and duck) and sometimes as an ingredient of scented tea. In India it is used in all ground spice mixtures and is chewed as a breath freshener.

starch   AMIDON, FÉCULE

A type of carbohydrate stored in the seeds, stalks, roots, and tubers of numerous plants. Fruits and vegetables that are rich in starch include potatoes, chestnuts, sweet potatoes, bananas, cassava, and yams. They are also rich in vitamin C (which is lacking in cereals, the other large category of starchy foods) and in sugars, but are lacking in proteins and minerals. Starchy foods are used principally as a source of energy.

Starch for culinary uses is extracted from the roots or tubers of certain plants (such as cassava, yam, or potato) or from the grain of wheat, rice, or maize (corn). It is in the form of a fine white powder that swells and forms a gelatinous paste in a hot liquid. Potato starch is used in large quantities in the food industry. In the kitchen, starch is used to thicken purées, broths, and sauces. The main types used are cornflour (cornstarch), potato flour, arrowroot, and tapioca.

steak   BIFTECK

A slice of beef (or sometimes horsemeat in France), weighing 100–200 g (4–8 oz), that can be grilled (broiled) or fried. Introduced to France after the Battle of Waterloo by the occupying English forces, steak was originally cut from the fillet, rump, or sirloin. It then became customary to cut steaks from all roasting joints and subsequently from braising joints as well. Fillet is usually prepared as tournedos, and sirloin and rump provide first-class steaks that are both tender and full of flavour. Steaks cut from topside are almost as tender. Top of sirloin, thin flank, blade, top rump, and skirt are very tasty cuts; silverside and flank are darker in colour.

Steak tartare is a preparation of raw chopped meat, with an egg and condiments. The origins of steak *au poivre* are controversial, as discussed by R. Lallemand in his book *Vraie Cuisine de l'Île-de-France*. Chefs who claim to have created this dish include E. Lerch in 1930, when he was chef at the Restaurant Albert on the Champs-Élysées; and M. Deveaux in about 1920, at Maxim's. However, M. G. Comte certifies that steak *au poivre* was already established as a speciality of the Hôtel de Paris at Monte Carlo in 1910, and O. Becker states that he prepared it in 1905 at Paillard's!

RECIPES

Steak au poivre   (from R. Lallemand's recipe) Generously sprinkle a thick steak (preferably rump steak) with coarsely ground black pepper. Seal the steak in hot clarified butter or oil in a sauté pan; when half-cooked, season with salt. When it has finished cooking, remove from the pan and keep hot. Skim the fat from the sauté pan and dilute the cooking juices with white wine and brandy. Boil down a little, then add 2 tablespoons (3 tablespoons) demi-glace sauce or thick veal stock. Reduce further until the sauce becomes thick and glossy. Finish off with fresh butter and adjust the seasoning with salt.

Serve the steak coated with the sauce. Some cooks flame it with Cognac, Armagnac, whisky, or liqueur brandy, and it is standard practice to finish the sauce with cream. It has recently become common practice to prepare this dish using whole green peppercorns.

Steak Dumas   BIFTECKS DUMAS (from a recipe of the Lasserre restaurant) Poach 12 rounds of beef marrow in court-bouillon. Sauté 4 sirloin steaks in butter, season with salt and pepper, and garnish with the marrow slices; remove from the frying pan (skillet) and keep warm. Add 1 dl (6 tablespoons, scant ½ cup) dry white wine and 2 tablespoons (3 tablespoons) chopped shallots to the frying pan (skillet) and reduce by three-quarters. Add 1 dl (6 tablespoons, scant ½ cup) stock, bring to the boil, stir in 100 g (4 oz, ½ cup) butter, and adjust the seasoning. Coat the steaks with the sauce and sprinkle with chopped parsley.

steak and kidney pie

A British speciality consisting of a hot pie with a filling of lean beef and kidney to which are added onions and mushrooms, or sometimes potatoes, hard-boiled (hard-cooked) eggs, or oysters (for steak, kidney, and oyster pie).

Steak and kidney pudding uses the same filling, which is packed raw in a pudding basin lined with suet dough and cooked by boiling or steaming for several hours.

RECIPE

Steak and kidney pie Make some puff pastry, using 225 g (8 oz, 2 cups) plain flour and the same quantity of butter. (Traditionally, steak and kidney pie can also be made with flaky or shortcrust pastry.)

Cut 675 g (1½ lb) stewing steak into cubes. Clean an ox (beef) kidney and cut it into small pieces. Season 25 g (1 oz, ¼ cup) flour with salt and pepper to taste and coat the steak and kidney with the mixture. Peel and finely chop an onion. Heat 50 g (2 oz, ¼ cup) butter in a saucepan, add the meats and onion, and fry until golden. Stir in 600 ml (1 pint, 2½ cups) beef stock. Continue to stir until the mixture boils and thickens, then cover the pan, reduce the heat, and simmer for about 1½ hours, until the meat is almost tender.

Spoon the mixture into a 1.2-litre (2 pint, 5-cup) pie dish, reserving excess liquid for gravy. Wet the rim of the pie dish and put a strip of pastry around it; brush with water, then cover the dish with pastry. Trim, knock up, and flute the edges with the back of a knife and brush with beaten egg. Make a small hole in the centre of the pie crust to allow steam to escape, and bake in a moderately hot oven (190 C, 375 F, gas 5) for about 45 minutes. Cover the pastry with foil if overbrowning. Serve piping hot in the pie dish.

steak batt

BATTE À CÔTELETTE

A square flat stainless steel instrument with handle, with one side plain and the other with two sloping sides. Relatively heavy in proportion to its size (about 900 g, 2 lb), the steak batt is used for flattening cutlets, escalopes (scallops), rib steaks, and fillets of fish.

steaming

CUISSON À LA VAPEUR

A method of cooking whose origins, according to Raymond Oliver, go back to the time before the discovery of fire, using the stones of hot springs. Jacques Manière, a poioneer of steaming, claims for it an enormous range of gastronomic possibilities: fish, vegetables, and poultry in particular may be prepared in this way with aromatic and subtle results. The essential factor in steaming is the perfect quality of the ingredients used, since the slightest doubtful smell is accentuated. In Britain, suet and sponge puddings are also steamed.

The classic process for steaming consists of quarter-filling a saucepan or casserole with water or stock flavoured as desired, then placing the item to be cooked in a perforated container or basket, the base of which is just above the level of the boiling liquid; the saucepan or steamer is covered and the item is cooked gently in the steam from the water or stock. Foods may also be cooked in their own steam without any liquid, either in a casserole over a low heat or in aluminium foil over glowing embers. The main advantage of steaming is that food cooked in steam retains more of the vitamins and minerals which would otherwise be lost in the cooking water. On the other hand, the cooking time is relatively long unless the food is cut into small pieces. When cooking meat in this way the steam causes the fat to melt and fall into the stock, thus reducing its fat content.

In his *Physiologie du goût* Brillat-Savarin recalls how he solved the problem of how to cook a very large turbot; placing the fish on a grid covered with aromatic herbs, which was then suspended over a pot of boiling water, he found that 'the fish prepared in this way was incomparably better than if it had been cooked in a turbot kettle . . . it had lost nothing of its essential characteristics and had, moreover, drawn out all the aroma of the seasonings'. The famous gourmet concluded from this that the advantages of steaming in domestic cookery had not been fully exploited.

RECIPES

Steamed fillets of sole in tomato sauce FILETS DE SOLE À LA VAPEUR AU COULIS DE TOMATE (from Jacques Manière's recipe) Arrange 6–7 sprigs of basil in the basket of a steamer and place on top 4 sole fillets folded in two; season with salt and pepper. Pour a little water into the lower pan, bring to the boil, and cook with the lid on for about 8 minutes. Keep the sole fillets hot.

Poach 1 egg for 3 minutes in water with vinegar added; mash well. Cook a chopped shallot gently in olive oil in a saucepan. Away from the heat, add the mashed poached egg, a dash of French mustard, the juice of a lemon, salt, and pepper, as well as the basil leaves, finely chopped. Place on a low heat and whisk the mixture. While whisking, gradually add 100 ml (4 fl oz, ½ cup) olive oil to thicken the sauce to the consistency of a hollandaise. Then add 3 tomatoes, peeled, seeded, and cut into dice, and 1 tablespoon chopped chervil.

Serve the sole fillets coated with the sauce.

Veal steamed with vegetables ÉTOUF-FÉ DE VEAU À LA VAPEUR DE LÉGUMES (from André Daguin's recipe) Cut a shoulder of veal into 24 pieces and place in a heavy-based casserole together with 18 small trimmed carrots, 18 olive-sized turnip pieces, the white part of 18 leeks cut into 2-cm (¾-in) pieces, and 18 small young onions. Cover and cook over a very low heat without fat or liquid, shaking the pan occasionally to prevent sticking. At the end of 20 minutes remove the turnips, season them with salt, and keep hot; 10 minutes later remove and season the leeks; after a further 10 minutes do the same with the carrots and onions. Continue to cook the veal over a very low heat, so that it does not burn, for a further 20 minutes. Moisten with 1 glass of white wine and reduce until almost dry. Then add ½ litre (17 fl oz, 2 cups) whipping cream and leave to cook for 10 minutes. Replace the vegetables in the casserole and bring to a final boil. Serve the veal with its vegetables piled into a dish.

steel ACIER

A very resistant alloy of iron and carbon in varying proportions. Other minerals are added to obtain special types of steel.

In household equipment, ordinary steel is used for certain knife blades and various utensils (larding needles, corkscrews, apple corers), but since it will rust it is being increasingly replaced in all kitchen equipment by stainless steel. This is an alloy of steel and chromium, and sometimes nickel for superior quality. Knife blades contain 13% chromium, lids 16%, pans, bowls, and cooking utensils 18%. Stainless steel does not rust, nor is it attacked by acids or alkalis. Chalky water leaves no deposit on it, and it does not retain smells. When sufficiently thick (0.8–2 mm (0.03–0.08 in) for pans), stainless steel is resistant to shocks and to overheating, but as it is a poor conductor of heat it takes time to heat up and the heat is distributed unevenly, so that food tends to stick. To remedy this defect, manufacturers have perfected the 'sandwich' base (copper or aluminium between two layers of stainless steel), which much improves the heat conduction. However ordinary steel is a good conductor and absorbs heat, so it is given a black mat finish and used for frying pans (skillets) and baking trays (baking sheets). Better quality enamelled steel saucepans make excellent heavy-duty pans.

steels and sharpeners
FUSILS

A steel is a cylindrical grooved rod made from a high-carbon steel, used for honing knife blades. The handle usually has a ring on the end for hanging it up. A steel only gives a temporary edge, and sharp knives, especially butcher's and kitchen knives, should be ground periodically on a grindstone to sharpen them.

Electric sharpeners have slots for knives and kitchen scissors. When the electricity is switched on, a wheel spins fast, putting a sharp edge to the knife.

Oilstones are made of a very hard silicon carbide. The very fine grain gives a good edge to the knife, making it extremely sharp.

steep IMBIBER

To saturate certain cakes with syrup, alcohol, or liqueur to make them moist and to add flavour. Babas, savarins, plum pudding, sponge fingers (ladyfingers), and Genoese sponge may be treated in this way.

sterilizer STÉRILISATEUR

A container designed for sterilizing

household preserves (autoclaves are used in the food industry). A simple sterilizer, which is made of galvanized metal sheeting, is equipped with two handles and is closed by means of a hard plastic lid, which incorporates a thermometer. It can contain 12 1-litre (1¾-pint) jars. An electric sterilizer of smaller capacity (five or six jars only) is made of heat-resistant plastic. A thermostat controls the temperature. The disadvantage of the sterilizer is that it does not raise the temperature of the water surrounding the jars above boiling point; it is therefore necessary to surround it with a salt solution (250 g (9 oz) salt per litre (1¾ pints) water) to obtain a boiling point of 108 c (226 f). (The correct sterilization temperature is between 110 and 115 c (230–239 f).)

sterlet

A small sturgeon, less than 1 m (about 3 ft) long, very common in eastern Europe and western Asia. It is prized for its delicate flesh and used as a source of high-quality caviar. Eaten fresh, dry, or marinated, it may be prepared in the same way as salmon, salmon trout, and sturgeon but is most frequently braised in white wine.

Stilton

An English cheese made from cows' milk (55% fat); it is firm and cream-coloured, uniformly mottled with bluish veins, and has a natural brushed rind. Considered as one of the best cheeses in the world, some say it was originally made in the village of Stilton in Cambridgeshire, where its production dates back to 1730. Others say it was first served at the Bell Inn, Stilton, in the 18th century but it was – and still is – made in parts of Leicestershire, Derbyshire, and Nottinghamshire, and its production is protected, even today. Stilton is moulded in a cylinder, 15 cm (6 in) in diameter by 25 cm (10 in) high, and weighs 4–4.5 kg (9–10 lb). It is still farm-made and is at its best from autumn to spring.

Stilton is traditionally accompanied by a glass of old port or Burgundy, together with fresh walnuts or grapes. Some people soak it in port, Madeira, or sherry, by pouring the wine into a hollow cut out of the centre of the cheese, which is eaten after a week or two with a small spoon. This is not considered advisable by cheese enthusiasts, who, to revive a slightly drying cheese, would simply wrap it in a moistened cloth and leave it until the dampness restored the proper consistency.

stir   REMUER

To agitate ingredients gently with a spatula, wooden spoon, or whisk, either before or during cooking, to ensure that the mixture is smooth and free from lumps and that it does not stick to the pan while cooking. To prevent a liquid, sauce, purée, or cream from sticking, a special spatula is used.

Rice and pasta need to be stirred when immersed in boiling water.

stock   FOND

A flavoured liquid base for making a sauce, stew, or braised dish. A white stock (*fond blanc*) is prepared by placing the ingredients directly into the cooking liquid; in a brown stock (*fond brun*) the ingredients are first browned in fat. Sauces made from white stock are always called white sauces, whether they are basic or variation sauces (e.g. allemande, poulette, aurore, suprême, etc.); all sauces made from brown stock are called brown sauces (e.g. espagnole, bordelaise, Bercy, piquante, etc.).

Stocks can be used in thickened or unthickened form. They are based on veal, beef, poultry, game, vegetables, aromatic ingredients, or fish. Other basic cooking stocks include velouté, consommé, essence, aspic, marinade, matignon, court-bouillon, and brine.

White and brown stocks, which used to be essential bases for almost all the great classic sauces, take a long time to make and are often expensive. In practice, they belong to the realm of the restaurant and their use has been considerably reduced in domestic cookery. The advent of stock cubes – solid extracts which need only be dissolved in boiling water – has reduced the use of traditional stocks.

There are three main stocks:
• white stock is made with white meat or poultry, veal bones, chicken carcasses, and aromatic vegetables. It is used to make white sauces, blanquettes, fricassees, and poached chicken dishes.

- brown stock (formerly called *jus brun* in French) is made with beef, veal, poultry meat and bones, and vegetables which have been browned in fat and then had the liquid added to them. It is used to make brown sauces and gravies, braised dishes, and brown stews, for deglazing fried meats, and for making glazes by reduction.
- vegetable stock is made by boiling vegetables and aromatic herbs which have first been gently fried in butter.

In general, stocks are aromatic but not salty, since they have to remain unseasoned until the sauce is perfected. Nevertheless, an optional pinch of salt enhances the blending of the ingredients and the liquid. The meats used to make the stocks can be used afterwards to make minced (ground) dishes, purées, salpicons, stuffings, etc.

RECIPES

Brown veal stock FOND BRUN DE VEAU Bone 1.25 kg (2¼ lb) shoulder of veal and the same amount of knuckle of veal. Tie them together with string and brush with melted dripping. Crush 500 g (18 oz) veal bones as finely as possible. Brown all these ingredients in a large flameproof casserole or saucepan. Peel and slice 150 g (5 oz, (1½ cups) carrots and 100 g (4 oz, 1 cup) onions, then add them to the pan. Cover and leave to sweat for 15 minutes. Add ¼ litre (8 fl oz, 1 cup) water and reduce to a jelly (consistency). Repeat the process. Add 2 litres (5 pints) water or white stock and bring to the boil. Skim and season. Leave to simmer very gently for 6 hours. Skim off the fat and strain through a fine sieve or (better still) through muslin (cheesecloth).

Game stock FOND DE GIBIER Tie together 1.5 kg (3¼ lb) shoulder, breast, and other pieces of venison. Draw and truss 1 old partridge and 1 old pheasant. Brush all the meat with butter and brown in the oven in a roasting tin. Slice 150 g (5 oz, 1½ cups) carrots and 150 g (5 oz, 1¼ cups) onions. Line a large flameproof casserole with fresh pork rind, then add the carrots and onions, 1 kg (2¼ lb) hare or wild rabbit trimmings, and the rest of the game. Deglaze the roasting tin with

½ litre (17 fl oz, 2 cups) red wine and ½ litre (17 fl oz, 2 cups) water, and reduce to a jelly (consistency). Pour into the casserole, add 2.5 litres (4½ pints, 9 cups) water, bring to the boil, then skim and season lightly. Add a large bouquet garni, a sprig of sage, 10 juniper berries, and 1 clove. Simmer for 3 hours. Skim off the fat, then strain through a fine sieve or (better still) through muslin (cheesecloth).

Light brown stock FOND BRUN CLAIR Scald 150 g (5 oz) fresh pork rind and 125 g (4½ oz) knuckle of ham for 4–5 minutes. Bone 1.25 kg (2¾ lb) lean stewing beef (leg or blade) and cut into cubes, together with the same amount of knuckle of veal. Peel 150 g (5 oz, 1½ cups) carrots and 150 g (5 oz, 1¼ cups) onions, cut into slices, then brown on top of the stove in a large flameproof casserole with all the meat, 500 g (18 oz) crushed veal or beef bones, and the pork rind. Add a bouquet garni, 1 clove of garlic, ½ litre (17 fl oz, 2 cups) water, and reduce to a jelly consistency. Add another ½ litre (17 fl oz, 2 cups) water and reduce to a jelly again. Add 2.5–3 litres (4½–5 pints) water and 15 g (½ oz, 2 teaspoons) coarse salt, bring to the boil, and simmer very gently for 8 hours. Skim off the fat and strain through a fine sieve or (better still) through muslin (cheesecloth).

Thick veal stock FOND DE VEAU LIÉ Reduce 2 litres (3½ pints, 7 cups) brown veal stock to three-quarters of its volume. Thicken with 15 g (½ oz, 2 tablespoons) arrowroot blended with 3 tablespoons clear cold veal stock. Strain through muslin (cheesecloth) or a fine sieve and keep hot in a bain-marie.

Tomato veal stock FOND DE VEAU TOMATÉ Add 2 dl (7 fl oz, ¾ cup) tomato purée to 2 litres (3½ pints, 7 cups) brown veal stock. Reduce to three-quarters of its volume. Strain through a fine sieve or (better still) through muslin (cheesecloth).

White stock FOND BLANC ORDINAIRE Bone a 750-g (1¾-lb) shoulder of veal and a 1-kg (2¼-lb) knuckle of veal, then tie them together with string. Crush the bones. Place the bones, meat, and 1 kg (2¼ lb) chicken giblets or carcasses in a saucepan, add 3.5 litres (3 quarts, 3¾ quarts) water, bring to the boil, and skim. Add 125 g (4½ oz, 1½ cups) sliced carrots, 100 g (4 oz, 1 cup) onions, 75 g (3 oz, ¾ cup) leeks (white part only), 75 g (3 oz, ¾ cup) celery, and a bouquet garni. Season. Simmer gently for 3½ hours. Skim off the fat and put through a very fine strainer or (better still) through muslin (cheesecloth).

White chicken stock FOND BLANC DE VOLAILLE Prepare in the same way as for ordinary white stock, but add a small chicken (which can be used afterwards for making croquettes) or double the quantity of giblets.

stockfish STOCKFISCH

Dried and salted cod, used in traditional dishes both in Scandinavia and in southern and central France (see *estofinado*). Its name comes from the German *Stock* (stick) and *Fisch* (fish), as it was formerly dried on sticks. It was referred to by Rabelais, in his novel *Pantagruel*, under the name of *stocficz*, and *Le Ménagier de Paris* states: 'If you wish to keep cod for 10 to 12 years, gut it, remove its head, and dry it in the open air or in the sun, never by the fire or with smoke. And having done this, it is called stofix.'

RECIPE

Stockfish à la niçoise Soak 1 kg (2¼ lb) stockfish in water for 48 hours, then chop it into pieces. Prepare ¾ litre (1¼ pints, 1½ pints) rich tomato fondue flavoured with garlic. Put the cod and the tomato sauce in a saucepan, cover, and let it poach gently for 50 minutes. Then add 400 g (14 oz) thickly sliced potatoes and 250 g (8 oz, 1½ cups) stoned black (pitted ripe) olives. Cook for a further 25 minutes. 5 minutes before it is ready, add 1 tablespoon of chopped fresh basil.

stockpot FAIT-TOUT

A fairly deep cylindrical two-handled pan with a heavy close-fitting lid. Such pans are usually made of hardened aluminium but some are stainless steel, enamel, or cast iron. The translation of the French name (literally 'do-all') is a good description of this type of pan, which is used for cooking food with or without liquid. Two handles are needed as the pan is very heavy when full.

Stohrer

A Parisian confectioner who set up shop at the beginning of the 19th century at 51 Rue Montorgueil, in Les Halles. The shop still bears the decorative panels of the *Renommées*, painted by P. Baudry in 1864. Stohrer achieved fame by introducing the baba to Paris, bringing the recipe with him from his native Lorraine; the cake was created at the court of the king of Poland at Luneville. Noisettines, chocolatines, and puits d'amour are still specialities of the house.

stollen

A sort of brioche made with dried fruits: a German speciality traditionally eaten at Christmas. There are several recipes, the best known being that from Dresden.

RECIPE

Dresden stollen Make a well in the centre of 750 g (1¾ lb, 6½ cups) sifted flour. Add 20 g (¾ oz) fresh yeast (¾ cake compressed yeast), 1 tablespoon of caster (superfine) sugar, and 2.5 dl (8 fl oz, 1 cup) warm milk. When bubbles form in the mixture knead it thoroughly, incorporating the flour to make a smooth dough. Cover with a cloth and leave to rise in a warm place free from draughts.

Soak 200 g (7 oz, 1¼ cups) currants in ½ dl (3 tablespoons, 4 tablespoons) rum. Soften 500 g (18 oz, 2¼ cups) butter at room temperature, then beat it with 150 g (5 oz, ⅔ cup, firmly packed) sugar and 3 eggs until light and creamy; add the currants and the rum, 200 g (7 oz, 1¼ cups) candied orange and lemon peel (finely chopped), a pinch of powdered vanilla (or a few drops of essence) and 1 teaspoon grated lemon rind.

Add this mixture to the dough with just enough milk to keep it soft but not sticky. Knead it well, knocking it on the table several times, as for a brioche dough, and set it to rise again under a cloth. When it has doubled in size turn it onto a floured work surface, stretch it into a thick sausage shape, and fold it in two. Put this on a buttered baking sheet and leave it to rise again for 15 minutes in a warm place. Brush with clarified butter and cook in a moderate oven (180 C, 350 F, gas 4) for 50 minutes.

When cooked, brush again with clarified butter, dust with icing (confectioners') sugar, and leave to cool before serving.

stoneware GRÈS

Dense hard pottery which is fired at a very high temperature. It may be brown, red, yellow, or grey, depending on the colour of the clay. Fine stoneware consists of a mixture of clay and feldspar and is usually enamelled; for example, Alsace stoneware. It is generally used for making serving dishes and preserving jars.

stopper BOUCHON

A piece of cork, glass, or rubber, usually in the shape of a cylinder or truncated cone, which is inserted into the neck of a bottle, carafe, or flask to form a more or less airtight seal. The French word *bouchon*, which comes from the Old French *bousche*, meaning a bunch of hay, corn, or leaves to be used as a stopper, can also apply to modern metal or plastic screw tops.

☐ For wine Originally, wine was protected by a layer of oil poured onto the surface; then wooden pegs covered with hemp soaked in oil were used. Its elasticity, flexibility, and durability make cork ideal for stopping wine bottles; wines that are to be drunk young are given a softer cork than wines that are laid down for several years, allowing the young wine to 'breathe' more readily. Corks must be 4–4.5 cm (about 1¼ in) long; for cider and champagne they are held in place with wire. Sometimes the cork is sealed with wax or covered with a sheet of tinfoil.

☐ Special stoppers There are several different kinds of stopper that allow an opened bottle to be resealed or to facilitate pouring from a bottle:

• glass pourer for serving apéritifs;
• chrome-plated metal pourer to measure out syrups or liqueurs;
• dropper to measure out a dash of spirit or bitters into a cocktail;

• pressure cork to close an opened bottle of champagne;
• spring stopper to close a bottle of sparkling mineral water or an opened bottle of beer.

storzapreti

A Corsican speciality, particularly associated with Bastia, consisting of dumplings made of chopped green vegetables (spinach, Swiss chard, or both), mixed with fresh Broccio cheese and bound with eggs, grated cheese, salt, and pepper. They are poached in boiling salt water, drained, and browned in the oven.

stout

A strong English and Irish dark beer with a high proportion of hops. Some roasted barley is added to the malts which give the beer its distinctive taste.

Stracchino

An Italian cows'-milk cheese (48% fat), with a washed rind and a soft centre. Traditionally made on the return of the cows from the Alpine pastures (when they are 'tired', *stracche* in Italian), Stracchino is a speciality of the Lombardy region.

strainer PASSOIRE

A utensil used to filter drinks, liquids, and sauces or to drain raw or cooked foods. Strainers are of various sizes and shapes according to their uses. Small strainers generally have a handle to enable them to be held under a pouring spout; examples are the tea or infusion strainer, made of stainless steel or aluminium and perforated with small holes, and the milk strainer, made of fine metal netting, to retain the milk 'skin'. The finest strainer, used for pressing sauces, straining broths, creams, etc., is the conical chinois. The vegetable strainer, which is much larger, is made of metal or plastic netting. Colanders are strainers with a base for standing in the sink.

Cloth strainers of horsehair, wool, silk, or yarn were formerly used for sieving, sifting, or filtering. Today, they are usually made of linen, cotton, or nylon and are used particularly in confectionery for the preparation of fruit jellies and syrups. See also *muslin*.

strasbourgeoise (à la)

Describing a dish consisting of large cuts of meat or poultry which are braised or lightly fried and garnished with braised sauerkraut, thin strips of streaky bacon cooked with the sauerkraut, and thin slices of foie gras sautéed in butter; the pan juices are used to make the sauce.

The term *à la strasbourgeoise* is also used to describe sautéed tournedos (filet mignons) served on thin slices of foie gras and coated with a sauce made by deglazing the pan juices with Madeira-flavoured demi-glace. Consommé *à la strasbourgeoise* is seasoned with juniper berries, thickened with starch, and garnished with a julienne of red cabbage and slices of Strasbourg sausage; grated horseradish is served separately.

straw CHALUMEAU

A hollow tube of straw, glass, plastic, or waxed paper, used for sipping cold drinks, such as milk shakes, soda, and cocktails, from tall glasses. Curved straws are used to drink cocktails served in small glasses. Straws may accompany coffee and chocolate liégeois and other iced desserts served in tall glasses.

strawberry FRAISE

The red, roughly conical, fruit of the strawberry plant, cultivated in numerous varieties throughout Europe and America. The strawberry was valued in Roman times for its therapeutic properties. The alchemists of the Middle Ages considered it to be a panacea, and as late as the 18th century Fontenelle (who died aged 100) attributed his longevity to his fondness for strawberries: he ate them daily when they were in season.

Strawberries began to be cultivated in the 13th century. From the five or six species then known, a number of varieties with larger fruit and a longer fruiting season have been cultivated. La Quintinie, gardener to Louis XIV, managed to grow strawberries in the greenhouses of Versailles from May onwards, and the king was very fond of them. At the beginning of the 18th century, the scarlet Virginia strawberry (*Fragaria virginiana*) was introduced into France from the United States and Canada, and the explorer Antoine Amédée Frézier imported some new plants from Chile (*Fragaria chiloensis*). These strawberries were larger than the European hautbois strawberry (*Fragaria moschata*) and were grown in the region of Plougastel, where they are still cultivated to the present day. The growing of strawberries became very popular in the 19th century and more than 600 varieties were developed. These are constantly being added to by crossbreeding.

In France strawberries are marketed from the beginning of April to September, with a high season in June. French strawberries are grown mainly in the southwest, the southeast, the Rhône Valley, and the Loir-et-Cher Valley. In Britain strawberries are imported from Spain, Israel, America, and Holland but the majority are home-grown. Some of the favourite varieties are Cambridge Favourite, Gorella, and Ostara. The strawberry is both refreshing and full of flavour and contains only 26 Cal per 100 g. It is low in sugar, a good source of vitamin C, and relatively rich in potassium and other minerals. Strawberries are delicate fruit and must be eaten when freshly gathered as they do not keep for long (a maximum of 48 hours in the refrigerator, loosely covered, if not too ripe). Strawberries should be red, shiny, unbruised, firm, and fragrant. They need not necessarily be large as the larger ones are often full of water and have less flavour.

Strawberries should be rinsed quickly if dirty before hulling them. They should never be soaked, handled too much, or exposed to heat and should be eaten within one hour after preparation. They are often served as a dessert with sugar or cream. They may also be steeped in wine, champagne, or Kirsch, or used in fruit salads, sundaes, flans, soufflés, Bavarian creams, mousses, ice creams, jams, and liqueurs.

☐ **Wild strawberries** (*fraises des bois*) These can be picked in the woods from June to July in flat country, and in August and September in mountainous regions. The berries are small (up to 12 mm (½ in) long), very dark red, and matt and do not have to be hulled. The European varieties of cultivated strawberry are derived from the wild strawberry, but the flavour and scent of really ripe wild strawberries surpasses them. All the recipes given for cultivated strawberries can be prepared using wild strawberries.

RECIPES

Iced strawberry mousse MOUSSE GLACÉE À LA FRAISE Dissolve 90 g (2 lb, 4 cups, firmly packed) sugar in ½ litre (17 fl oz, 2 cups) water, and boil until a thick syrup is obtained (104.5 c, 220 F). Add 900 g (2 lb, 4 cups) sieved freshly prepared strawberry purée and then fold in 1 litre (1¾ pints, 4¼ cups) very stiffly whipped cream. Freeze in the usual way. (Raspberry mousse can be prepared in the same way.)

Strawberries à la maltaise FRAISES À LA MALTAISE Cut some oranges in half and scoop out the flesh. Trim the bases of the orange halves so that they can stand upright. Place them in the refrigerator. Squeeze the pulp and sieve to obtain the juice. Wash, wipe, and hull some small strawberries. Add some sugar and a little Curaçao or Cointreau to the orange juice, and pour the mixture over the strawberries. Store in the refrigerator. When serving, fill the orange halves with the strawberries and arrange them in a dish on a bed of crushed ice.

Strawberry jam CONFITURE DE FRAISES Select perfect unblemished fruit. Wash the strawberries carefully

variety	appearance	characteristics	season
Gorella (Périgord and Ardèche)	large, elongated, and conical; firm red flesh	soft and juicy; easy to hull; good flavour	early April to late June
Surprise des Halles (grown in the open ground in Périgord; preferred to the bright red greenhouse berries, available March–April but lacking flavour)	medium-sized, round or conical, and dark red; quite firm	acid and full of flavour	May to late July
Cambridge Favourite (Loire Valley in France; most widely grown variety in UK – 70%)	large, orange-red; firm and shiny	melting, sweet, and easy to hull; good for freezing	late May to late June
Belrubi	very large, elongated, and bright red; firm	sweet but rather lacking in flavour; easy to hull	early May to late June
Red Gauntlet (climbing variety)	medium-sized to large; light red, firm, and shiny	acid and full of flavour (for 2nd crop)	August–September
Unigento (Loire Valley)	large and elongated; firm	juicy and sweet; difficult to hull	late June to October
Sans Rivale (throughout France)	small, bright red, and shiny; round with pointed end	sweet and full of flavour; excellent	May–July
Senga Sengana (north and east France)	medium-sized, dark red, round, and shiny	musky flavour; delicious	May–July
Vicomtesse Héricart de Thury (very rare)	small and very pale pink	excellent and full of flavour	August–September

only if necessary; otherwise wipe them, remove the hulls, and weigh them. Use 750 g (1½ lb, 3 cups, firmly packed) preserving or granulated sugar and 1 dl (6 tablespoons, scant ½ cup) water per kg (2¼ lb) fruit. Dissolve the sugar and water in a preserving or large pan over gentle heat, then cook to the 'ball stage' (116 c, 240 f); see *sugar*. Skim the syrup, add the prepared strawberries, and cook for a few minutes so that the juice is released. Drain the strawberries and boil the syrup again until it is at the ball stage once more. Replace the strawberries in the pan and cook for another 5 or 6 minutes, until the jam reaches the jelling stage (101 c, 213.8 f). To enable the jam to keep longer, boil until the temperature reaches 104 c (220 f), the 'thread stage'. Put into sterilized jars, seal, label, and store (see *jams, jellies, and marmalades*).

Strawberry purée preserved by bottling CONSERVE DE PURÉE DE FRAISES STERILISÉE Prepare the purée as for freezing, place in jars, and seal. Put the jars in a large preserving pan, separating them with either paper or cloths. Cover the jars with cold water and bring to the boil for 10 minutes. Leave in the pan to cool, then wipe, label, and store in a cool dry place.

Strawberry purée preserved by freezing CONSERVE DE PURÉE DE FRAISES CONGELÉE Wash or wipe the strawberries carefully, hull them, reduce to a purée, and strain the purée through a fine sieve. Add 300 g (11 oz, scant 1½ cups, firmly packed) granulated sugar per kg (2¼ lb) fruit. Place in special freezer containers, leaving a 2-cm (¾-in) space between the top of the purée and the lid. Close the container, label, and freeze. The purée must be defrosted at room temperature or in the refrigerator, before opening the container.

Strawberry syrup SIROP DE FRAISE Wash, wipe, and hull some very ripe strawberries. Crush them and squeeze through a cloth. Pour the strained strawberry juice into a bowl and check the density, which depends on the sugar content of the fruit and determines the amount of sugar to be added. This will range from 1.75 kg (3¾ lb, 7½ cups, firmly packed) sugar per kg (2¼ lb) fruit if the density at boiling point is 1.007, to 1.25 kg (2½ lb, 5 cups) if the density at boiling point is 1.075. Boil the sugar and the juice from the strawberries for 2–3 minutes. The density of the syrup should then be 1.3319. Pour the strawberry syrup into sterilized jars, cover, seal, and store in a cool dry dark place.

straw potatoes PAILLE

Potatoes cut into long very thin strips and deep-fried. Cooked, they resemble straw and are served mainly with grills.

RECIPE

Straw potatoes POMMES PAILLE Peel some large firm potatoes, cut them into very thin strips, and leave them to soak in plenty of cold water for 15 minutes. Drain and wipe thoroughly, then cook them in very hot deep-frying oil (180–190 c, 356–374 f) until they are golden (about 5 minutes). Drain them on absorbent paper, dust them with fine salt, and serve them piping hot.

street cries of Paris
CRIS DE PARIS

The right of Parisian street hawkers to cry their wares was established in 1220. Wine, oil, onions, water, vegetables, meat, fish, pastries, and cooked dishes could all be advertised in this way. It was also possible to announce the times of meetings, a death, or the loss of a child, or an animal, or a possession in the same way. The Paris of former years resounded with such cries.

In the course of time the cries gradually changed and evolved into their modern forms. The first simple cries included 'Je vends de l'eau' ('I sell water!'), 'Crapois y'a!' ('Here's crapois!') for salted whale meat, 'Voilà le plaisir!' ('What a delight!') for wafers, and 'Marchand d'ail!' ('Garlic merchant!'), which rapidly became shortened to 'chand d'ail' and eventually to 'chandail' (the jersey that vegetable hawkers traditionally wore became known as a *chandail*).

The following are some examples of Parisian street cries.

The herring crier, or fishwife, called out:

'Harens seretz appétissants,
Ce sont petits morceaux friands
Pour desjeuner au matinet,
Avec vin blanc, clair, pur et net!'
('Herrings will be tempting,
They are tasty little morsels
To eat for breakfast,
With white wine, clear, pure and
clean!')

The selling of vegetables inspired veritable poetry to describe their quality:

'Choux gelés, les bons chou gelés!
Ils sont plus tendres que rosée,
Ils ont crû parmi les poirées
Et n'ont jamais été grêlés!'
('Frozen cabbages, good frozen
cabbages!
They are more tender than the dawn,
They have grown amongst the white
beet
And never been struck by hail!')

The merchant selling wafers was the only street hawker to have continued with this custom until the end of the 19th century. In the Middle Ages, the cry was:

'Chaudes oublies renforcées,
Galettes chaudes, eschaudés,
Rissoles, flans chauds, gâteaux rassis,
Je les apporte tôt faits!'
('Hot strong wafers,
Hot cakes, canary bread,
Rissoles, hot flans, stale cakes,
I bring them without delay!')

Until 1415, innkeepers had to hire a public crier first to taste and then to announce the quality and price of their wines. It was also customary for the king's wine to be cried before any other (the proclamation was known as *droit de banvin*):

'Aucune fois, ce m'est avis,
Crie-t-on le ban du roi Loys,
Si crie-l'en en plusieurs lieux
Le bon vin fort à trente-deux sous,
À seize, à douze, à huit!'
('Sometimes, or so I think,
They do cry the proclamation of King
Louis,
In several places is cried
The good strong wine at thirty-two
sous,
At sixteen, at twelve, at eight!')

The street cries of Paris are now scarcely heard except occasionally in open-air markets.

strengthen CORSER

To reinforce the flavour and aroma of a preparation by adding concentrated substances (meat glaze to a sauce, for example) or strong and piquant ones (spices or condiments). The flavour of a liquid preparation can also be strengthened by reducing it (by boiling).

string FICELLE

Fine cord made of hemp or flax used to tie joints of meat or poultry before roasting or braising. It is also used to truss poultry. Fine thread is also used to sew up meat and poultry after they have been stuffed, and to secure paupiettes, stuffed cabbage, etc. *Gigot à la ficelle* is leg of lamb roasted in front of a hot fire suspended by a piece of string that allows it to be rotated as it is roasting. This method of preparation (more picturesque than gastronomic) is attributed to Alexandre Dumas.

Stroganov

A preparation of thinly sliced beef coated with a cream-based sauce and garnished with onions and mushrooms.

This traditional dish of classic Russian cookery has been known in Europe, in various forms, since the 18th century. The Stroganovs were a family of wealthy merchants, financiers, and patrons of the arts, originally from Novgorod. They set up trading posts as far as the Netherlands; one of them, raised to the nobility by Peter the Great, employed a French cook, who might have given his master's name to one of his creations. (Some authorities give an etymology derived from the Russian verb *strogat*, 'to cut into pieces').

Thin strips of beef (fillet, sirloin, or rump steak), seasoned with salt, pepper, and paprika, are sautéed over a brisk heat, then coated with a sauce made by deglazing the pan juices with white wine, cream, and thickened veal stock, to which onions sautéed in butter have been added. The dish is served with pilaf rice and sautéed mushrooms. In one version, regarded as more 'Russian', the onions and mushrooms are sautéed together and then added to the thin strips of sautéed meat; the whole mixture is then coated with a sauce made by blending a roux with soured (dairy sour) cream and seasoning it with mustard and lemon juice. The meat alternatively may be marinated then sautéed, flamed, and coated with a sauce made from the reduced marinade blended with cream.

RECIPE

Beef Stroganov BOEUF STROGANOV Cut 750 g (1¾ lb) fillet of beef into fine strips 2.5 cm (1 in) long. Sprinkle them with salt and pepper and put them in a small ovenproof dish with 4 sliced onions, 3 chopped shallots, 1 large carrot cut into slices, a crushed bay leaf, and a small sprig of crumbled fresh thyme. Add just enough white wine to cover the meat and leave to marinate in a cool place, with the lid on, for 12 hours. Drain and dry the meat; reduce the marinade by half and set it aside.

Sauté 2 thinly sliced onions in a shallow frying pan in 30 g (1 oz, 2 tablespoons) butter until soft and lightly brown; set aside. Lightly brown 200 g (7 oz, 2 cups) thinly sliced mushrooms in the same pan with 30 g (1 oz, 2 tablespoons) butter, then add them to the onions. Wipe the pan and melt 50 g (2 oz, 4 tablespoons) butter in it; when hot, add the meat and sauté over a brisk heat, turning it frequently. When the meat is well-browned (about 5 minutes), sprinkle it with 1 small glass of warmed brandy and flame it. Keep warm in a serving dish.

Tip the onions and mushrooms into the frying pan together with the reduced and strained marinade and 1.5 dl (¼ pint, ⅔ cup) double (heavy) cream; stir over a brisk heat until thickened. Adjust the seasoning and coat the meat with the sauce. Sprinkle with chopped parsley and serve piping hot.

strudel

Wafer-thin pastry rolled around a sweet or savoury filling (the name literally means 'whirlwind').

One of the most famous Viennese pastries, inspired by the Turkish baklava, the recipe was apparently created by a Hungarian. The dough, which must be made with strong (high-gluten) flour, is difficult to prepare and to handle. It is sprinkled with breadcrumbs and ground almonds, then with the chosen filling, and rolled up. The usual filling is apples and raisins flavoured with cinnamon and grated lemon zest. Other classic fillings include stoned (pitted) morello cherries, sugar, lemon zest, and ground almonds; and cream cheese mixed with egg yolks, lemon zest, raisins, cream, and stiffly whisked egg whites. In Austria, savoury strudels can be filled with chopped boiled beef with bacon, onions, paprika, and parsley; another version uses chopped cabbage, baked with fat and sugar.

RECIPE

Apple strudel STRUDEL AUX POMMES Mix 150 ml (¼ pint, ⅔ cup) tepid water in a bowl with a pinch of salt, 1 teaspoon vinegar, and 1 egg yolk; add 1 tablespoon oil. Make a well in 250 g (9 oz, 2¼ cups) strong flour in a mixing bowl; pour the egg mixture into the centre, mix with the blade of a knife, then knead until the dough is elastic. Gather it into a ball, place it on a floured board, cover it with a scalded basin, and leave it to stand for 1 hour.

Peel and finely dice 1 kg (2¼ lb) cooking apples; sprinkle them with 3 tablespoons (¼ cup) caster (superfine) sugar. Wash and wipe 200 g (7 oz, generous cup) raisins.

Spread a large floured cloth over the worktop and place the dough on it. Stretch the dough carefully with the knuckles, working from underneath it, brush with melted butter, then keep on stretching it until it is very thin, taking care not to tear it. Trim the edges to the shape of a large even rectangle.

Lightly brown a handful of breadcrumbs and 100 g (4 oz, 1 cup) chopped fresh walnuts in 75 g (3 oz, scant ½ cup) melted butter; spread this mixture evenly over the dough. Sprinkle with the apples and raisins, then dust with 1 teaspoon cinnamon and 8 tablespoons (⅔ cup) caster (superfine) sugar. Roll up the dough carefully to enclose all the ingredients, then slide the strudel onto a buttered baking sheet. Brush with 2 tablespoons (3 tablespoons) milk. Cook for 40–45 minutes in a moderately hot oven (200 C, 400 F, gas 6). When golden, take it out of the oven, dust it with icing (confectioners') sugar, and serve it lukewarm.

stud CLOUTER

To insert one or several cloves into a large raw onion, which is then added to a preparation to flavour it during cooking.

A piece of meat, poultry, or game can be studded with small thin sticks cut from truffle, cooked ham, anchovy fillets, or gherkins; the meat thus flavoured is usually braised. Large joints of firm meat are most often treated in this way.

stufatu or stufato

A Corsican ragout of meat with tomatoes and onions, which is generally served with pasta. It is prepared with braising beef, loin of pork, and diced ham, browned in oil with tomato, onion, garlic, and parsley. The mixture is sprinkled with white wine and flavoured with bay leaves and herbs from the Maquis (rosemary and thyme). Stufatu (the word literally means 'slowly cooked in a closed container') can also be prepared with mutton, pigeons or partridges, rabbit, or chicken giblets. It is commonly served in a soup tureen, in alternating layers with pasta cooked *al dente* and sprinkled with cheese.

stuff FARCIR

To fill the interior of poultry, game birds, prepared joints of meat, fish, shellfish, hollowed-out vegetables, eggs, fruit, or other preparations (pancakes, croquettes, etc.) with a forcemeat, a salpicon, a purée, or any other appropriate mixture. This is usually carried out before cooking except in the case of certain cold dishes.

Practically all poultry and game birds can be stuffed, unless they are very small. Cuts of meat that are suitable for stuffing include boned shoulder, leg, and breast, paupiettes (rolled-up fillets), and chops; whole milk-fed lamb and sucking pig can also be stuffed. Most types of river and sea fish can be stuffed: round fish are stuffed whole, while fillets of flat fish are wrapped around the stuffing. Scallops, mussels, clams, and snails are also suitable for stuffing. The most suitable vegetables are tomatoes,

large mushrooms, cabbage (whole or leaves), aubergines (eggplants), courgettes (zucchini), peppers, potatoes, onions, chicory, vine leaves, lettuce hearts, etc. The best fruits for stuffing are avocados, citrus fruits, melon, pears, and apples.

stuffings

See *forcemeat or stuffing*.

sturgeon ESTURGEON

A large migratory fish that lives in the sea and migrates up rivers to spawn. It was once plentiful in certain French rivers, but is now rarely found except in the Garonne. It is mainly fished in the Black Sea and the Caspian Sea, essentially for its roe (see *caviar*) rather than its flesh, which, although quite tasty, can be rather indigestible.

Up to 9 m (29 ft) long and weighing up to 1400 kg (3150 lb), the sturgeon's tapering body is covered with large scales; its flesh is firm and fairly fatty. In Russia, a breed of sturgeon known as the sterlet is caught in the Volga. It is eaten fresh, salted, or smoked and the dried spinal marrow (*vesiga*) is used in the preparation of a hot fish pie (see *koulibiaca*).

Two breeds are found in European waters; the great sturgeon (called in England the royal sturgeon) and the common sturgeon.

In France, sturgeon is cut into steaks or thick slices and braised like veal (fricandeau of sturgeon), grilled (broiled), sautéed, or roasted. The traditional Russian method of preparing sturgeon is called *en attente* (waiting): the fish is cooked in court-bouillon for several hours with aromatic vegetables. It is served cold with cooked parsley, olives, mushrooms, crayfish tails, horseradish, lemon, and Molossol gherkins, or hot with a tomato sauce finished with crayfish butter. It is also served smoked.

RECIPE

Fricandeau of sturgeon à la hongroise FRICANDEAU D'ESTURGEON À LA HONGROISE Brown a thick slice of sturgeon in butter with finely diced onions. Season with salt, paprika, and a bouquet garni. Moisten with 2 dl (⅓ pint, scant cup) white wine. Boil down.

Add 3 dl (½ pint, 1¼ cups) velouté sauce based on fish stock. Finish cooking in a slow oven. Add butter to the sauce and pour it over the fish. Serve with boiled potatoes, cucumber balls, or a purée of sweet peppers.

subric

A small croquette sautéed in clarified butter and served as an hors d'oeuvre, a hot entrée, or a garnish. It is usually garnished with fried parsley and accompanied by a fairly highly seasoned sauce. Subrics are made from ready-cooked ingredients (leftover meat, diced chicken livers, fish, vegetable purée, cooked rice, etc.) bound with allemande or béchamel sauce, beaten eggs and flour, cream and grated cheese, etc. They are never coated in egg and breadcrumbs and deep-fried like most croquettes. Sweet subrics, made with rice or semolina, are served with jam or poached fruit as a dessert.

In ancient times, subrics were cooked *sur les briques* (i.e. on hot bricks from the kitchen fire), hence their name.

RECIPES

Potato subrics SUBRICS DE POMMES DE TERRE Finely dice 500 g (18 oz) potatoes, blanch for 2 minutes in salted water, drain and wipe, then cook slowly in butter. Remove from the heat and bind them with 2.5 dl (8 fl oz, 1 cup) thick béchamel sauce. Add 3 egg yolks and 1 whole egg and season with salt, pepper, and nutmeg. Proceed with moulding and cooking as for spinach subrics.

Spinach subrics SUBRICS D'ÉPINARDS Cook some well-washed spinach gently in a covered saucepan without water. Drain and cool it. For 500 g (18 oz, 2⅓ cups) pressed chopped spinach, add 1.5 dl (¼ pint, ⅔ cup) very thick béchamel sauce, 1 whole egg and 3 yolks, lightly beaten as for an omelette, then 2 tablespoons double (heavy) cream. Season with salt, pepper, and nutmeg, then leave to cool completely. Mould this mixture into small balls and cook in 40 g (1½ oz, 3 tablespoons) clarified butter in a frying pan until golden (about 3 minutes). Serve piping hot, with a cream sauce well-seasoned with nutmeg.

Sweet rice subrics SUBRICS D'ENTREMETS AU RIZ Prepare 750 g (scant 1¾ lb) rice in milk. Blend with it 100 g (4 oz, ⅔ cup) chopped crystallized (candied) fruits soaked in liqueur and spread the mixture over a buttered baking sheet, in a layer 2 cm (¾ in) thick. Brush the whole surface with 40 g (1½ oz, 3 tablespoons) melted butter and leave to cool. Cut this rice into rounds, rings, or squares and cook in clarified butter in a frying pan until golden on both sides. Arrange in a serving dish and decorate each subric with 1 teaspoon redcurrant or raspberry jelly, apricot purée, or an apricot-half poached in syrup.

succés

A round cake made from two layers of meringue mixture containing almonds, separated by a layer of praline-flavoured butter cream, and topped with a smooth layer of the butter cream. It is decorated with shredded (slivered) almonds, sugar hazelnuts, marzipan leaves, and, traditionally, by a rectangle of almond paste with the word 'succès' piped in royal icing (frosting).

The succès mixture is also used for making petits fours, usually filled with butter cream, as well as various pastries.

RECIPE

Succès base FOND À SUCCÈS Crush 250 g (9 oz, scant 2 cups) blanched dried almonds with 250 g (9 oz, generous cup) sugar until reduced to a powder. Fold in 350 g (12 oz) egg whites (about 8) whisked into very stiff peaks with a pinch of salt. Pour this mixture into two 18–20-cm (7–8-in) flan-rings set on buttered and floured baking sheets; it should form a layer about 5 mm (¼ in) thick. Cook for 12–15 minutes in a moderate oven (180 C, 350 F, gas 4). Cool on a wire rack after removing the rings.

sucking pig or suckling pig
COCHON DE LAIT,
PORCELET

A young piglet, usually slaughtered at two months old, when it generally weighs less than 15 kg (33 lb). Often roasted whole, it forms a sumptuous dish; it is also cooked in a blanquette and in a ragout. Its succulent flesh has been appreciated throughout Europe since the Middle Ages. The grilled skin and ears were once a choice dish; in Spain, the skin is still eaten, lightly fried, cut into fine strips, and accompanied by Rioja, a heady red wine.

Sucking pig roasted *à l'anglaise* (stuffed with onions and sage, moistened with its own juice and Madeira, and served with a purée of apples and raisins) was well-known in the 1890s in restaurants of the Boulevard. Another speciality, sucking pig in aspic, was particularly famous in the East. In *Madame Bovary*, sucking pig is the main attraction of the wedding breakfast: 'The table was set up inside the cartshed. On it there were four sirloins of beef, six fricassees of chicken, casseroled veal, three legs of mutton and, in the centre, a beautiful roasted sucking pig, flanked by four chitterlings with sorrel.'

RECIPES

Roast sucking pig PORCELET RÔTI Clean out the animal as for the stuffed sucking pig *à l'occitane*, without boning or stuffing it. Sew it up and tie up the trotters. Marinate as in following recipe. Cook the sucking pig on a spit over a high heat for about 1 hour 45 minutes: the skin should be golden and crisp. Baste the pig with a little of the marinade during cooking. Serve on a dish garnished with watercress.

Stuffed sucking pig à l'occitane POR-CELET ÉTOFFÉ À L'OCCITANE (traditional recipe) Clean out the sucking pig through an incision in the belly. Bone it, leaving only the leg bones. Season the interior with salt and four spices, sprinkle with brandy, and leave for several hours.

Prepare a forcemeat: slice the pig's liver and an equal amount of calves' or lambs' liver, season, and brown briskly in very hot butter. Drain and set aside. In the same butter, still on a high heat, lightly brown the pig's heart and kidneys and 150 g (5 oz) calves' sweetbreads (trimmed, blanched, rinsed in cold water, and sliced). Drain these ingredients and add to the liver. Put 3

tablespoons butter into the same pan and brown 200 g (7 oz, scant 2 cups) finely chopped onions, then add 2 tablespoons chopped shallots and 75 g (3 oz, ¾ cup) shredded mushrooms and cook for a few moments. Add a pinch of powdered garlic, cover with dry white wine, and reduce, then add 4 dl (14 fl oz, 1¾ cups) stock and boil. Add 150 g (5 oz) fresh bacon rinds, cooked and cut into small pieces, and 100 g (4 oz, ¾ cup) blanched stoned (pitted) green olives. Cook for a few minutes, then add the above ingredients and heat without boiling. Mix well and leave to cool. Then add an equal amount of fine sausage meat and bind with 4 whole eggs. Add chopped parsley and ½ glass brandy, mix well, and adjust seasoning.

The day before the sucking pig is to be cooked, stuff it with this mixture, sew it up, truss, and marinate in a mixture of oil, brandy, sliced carrots and onions, crushed garlic cloves, chopped parsley, thyme, bay leaf, and pepper.

On the day of cooking, lay the pig out in a large braising pan lined with bacon rinds and sliced carrots and onions (those from the marinade, with others if necessary). Do not hesitate to add plenty of vegetables, as they will be used as a garnish; small carrots and onions may be used whole. Brush the sucking pig with melted lard, cover, and cook on the top of the stove until the vegetables begin to fry. Moisten with 3 dl (½ pint, 1¼ cups) dry white wine, reduce, then add a few tablespoons stock and a bouquet garni. Finish cooking in a moderately hot oven (200 C, 400 F, gas 6). The total cooking time should be about 2½ hours, when the skin will be slightly crisp.

Drain and untruss the sucking pig and lay out on a serving dish. Garnish with pork crépinettes with mixed herbs and small black puddings (blood sausages) cooked in butter. Add the sliced onions and carrots from the braising pan and pour over the strained cooking juices. Serve with a celery purée or mashed potatoes.

suédoise

A cold dessert, made of fruits cooked in syrup, arranged in layers in a mould or an earthenware dish, then covered with a jelly flavoured with fruit, wine, or liqueur. When set, the suédoise is turned out and served with fresh whipped cream or a fruit sauce.

suédoise (à la)

A term describing various dishes reminiscent of Scandinavian cookery. Mixed salads *à la suédoise* combine vegetables, fruit, mushrooms, cheese, and shellfish or fish, dressed with a herb-flavoured vinaigrette. Mayonnaise *à la suédoise* is mixed with grated horseradish and apple sauce, made with white wine but no sugar. Roast pork *à la suédoise* is stuffed with stoned (pitted) prunes and served with apples stuffed with prunes.

| RECIPE

Anchovy salad à la suédoise SALADE AUX ANCHOIS À LA SUÉDOISE Peel and dice 500 g (18 oz) cooking apples and sprinkle with lemon juice. Dice the same weight of cooked beetroot (red beet). Mix these ingredients with a vinaigrette seasoned with mild mustard. Heap in a salad bowl and garnish with desalted anchovy fillets, the whites and yolks of hard-boiled (hard-cooked) eggs chopped separately, and thin slices of blanched mushrooms.

sugar SUCRE

Any of a class of sweet-tasting carbohydrates, formed naturally in the leaves of numerous plants but concentrated mainly in their roots, stems, or fruits. The plants' energy reserve may be in the form of simple sugars or high-molecular-weight polymers of simple sugars (known as starch). Although sugar is extracted from the maple tree in Canada, the date palm in Africa, and from sorghum, grapes, etc., the two main commercial sources of sugar are sugar cane in tropical regions and sugar beet in temperate regions.

The term 'sugar', in the singular, usually denotes cane sugar or beet sugar, the scientific name of which is sucrose (or saccharose); it consists of a molecule of glucose combined with a molecule of fructose; its sweetening power is by definition equal to 1. In the plural, 'sugars' denotes the class of soluble simple carbohydrates to which

sucrose belongs. Other sugars include glucose (or dextrose); glucose syrup (partially hydrolysed starch, sweetening power typically 0.7); fructose (or levulose), which is the sugar of fruit and honey (sweetening power 1.1 to 1.3); galactose; and lactose (milk sugar).

☐ **History** A few thousand years ago sugar was already being used in Asia, in the form of cane syrup, whereas in Europe at that time honey and fruit were the only source of sweetening. According to legend, the Chinese and Indians have always known how to manufacture granulated sugar. In about 510 BC, at the time of the expedition of Darius to the valley of the Indus, the Persians discovered a 'reed which yields honey without the assistance of bees'. They brought it back with them and jealously guarded the secret of how this sugary substance could be obtained and traded as a rarity. In the 4th century Alexander the Great also brought back the 'sweet reed', from which was extracted *çarkara* (a Sanskrit word meaning 'grain'), a crystal obtained from the juice of the plant. Cultivation of this reed extended to the Mediterranean basin and to Africa. A new food had just been created: *saccharose* for the Greeks, *saccharum* for the Romans, *sukkar* for the Arabs, then *zucchero* in Venice, *çucre* (then *sucre*) in France, *sugar* in England, *azúcar* in Spain, *Zucker* in Germany.

During the Crusades the French discovered this 'spice', sold at a very high price by apothecaries. Stone or rock sugar and brown, muscarrat, and candied sugar (sugar candy) were types of sugar which had been refined to various degrees. Loaf sugar, crystalline sugar, and powdered sugar were often flavoured with rose, violet, lemon, or redcurrant. Sugar was instrumental in the development of confectionery and pâtisserie, but it was at that time also commonly used for seasoning meats and savoury dishes.

In the 15th century the Spanish and Portuguese introduced cultivation of the cane into their African possessions (the Canary Islands, Madeira, Cape Verde islands), so as to free themselves from the monopoly of the Mediterranean producers. Lisbon soon superseded Venice as the principal city of refining. The discovery of the New World and colonial conquests generally favoured the extension of sugar-cane cultivation, firstly in Cuba, Brazil, and Mexico, then in the islands of the Indian Ocean, then in Indonesia, and finally as far as the Philippines and Oceania. The West Indies, which had become the 'Sugar Islands', provided sugar for the refineries of the European ports. In the 17th century the fashion for coffee, tea, and chocolate appreciably increased the consumption of sugar, which nevertheless remained an expensive and precious commodity. The first French sugar refinery was built at Bordeaux in 1633; after that, through the impetus of Colbert, others were created at Rouen, Nantes, La Rochelle, and Marseille.

Sugar beet remained unexploited, although Olivier de Serres had drawn attention to its high sugar content as early as 1575. It was not until 1747 that the German Marggraf succeeded in extracting sugar from beet and solidifying it. In 1786 his follower Achard, a Frenchman, tried to produce it on an industrial basis, but the output was still small, with a very high cost. It was necessary to wait for Chaptal, who published some conclusive findings in 1800. Blockades during the Napoleonic Wars gave an additional impetus, and in 1811 Delessert perfected the industrial extraction of beet sugar in his Passy refinery; on 2 January 1812 he offered Napoleon I the first sugar loaf. In 1875, France, the first sugar producer in Europe, could boast 525 sugar refineries, which processed 450,000 tons of sugar. Today France remains the biggest producer in the EEC and lies second in the world for beet sugar production, after the USSR.

□ **Manufacture of raw sugar** Once harvested, the beets and cane must be converted quickly to crystalline raw sugar. This is to ensure there is no microbiological degradation and no loss of their rich sugar content. For this reason raw sugar factories are established close to the growing areas and work without a break during the whole harvesting campaign, which usually lasts 80–100 days.

The principle of raw sugar production from beet or cane consists of extracting the sucrose by successively eliminating the other constituent parts of the plant.

The root of the beet is sliced and the sweet juice is extracted by diffusion in hot water. The juice, which contains 13–15% sugar, is then treated with milk of lime and carbon dioxide. This results in the production of chalk, which traps much of the insoluble non-sugar material which is filtered off to give a clear juice.

In the case of cane sugar, the cut cane is shredded, crushed, and sprayed with hot water. The juice is heated, treated with lime, and then filtered.

Both clarified cane and beet juices are then concentrated by evaporation under reduced pressure until crystallization is induced. The concentrated crystallized mass is transferred to mixers (crystallizers) where crystal growth continues. The crystalline raw sugar is then separated from the remaining syrup by centrifugation. Not all of the sugar may have been extracted from the juice at this stage, so the remaining liquor may be recycled. When it is no longer economically practical to extract more sugar the remaining liquor is called molasses, either cane (blackstrap) or beet (which is inedible).

Some raw cane sugars are prepared with extra care and to recognized standards; these sugars are marketed for consumption as unrefined brown sugars and include such sugars as raw cane demerara and muscovado sugars. In the main, however, raw sugars are not in a fit condition for human consumption and require further refining. Raw sugar is a stable product, which may be handled, stored, and transported to wherever it is to be refined.

Unlike the production of raw sugar, refining may continue all year and need not be in the country of origin. Cane refineries tend to be in the importing country, while raw beet is often refined adjacent to the raw beet sugar factory.

□ **Refining of raw cane sugar** Refining raw cane sugar removes all impurities, leaving an end-product of pure natural sucrose. This product contains no artificial colourings, preservatives, or flavourings of any kind. White refined sugar contains 99.95% pure sucrose; brown sugars contain a small proportion of molasses, which imparts colour and flavour.

The raw sugar consists of brown sugar crystals containing many impurities and covered with a coating of molasses. The outer layers are first softened with warm syrup (called magma) which is passed into centrifugal machines to separate the syrup from the crystals. The crystals are rewashed to remove remaining impurities and treated again with lime and carbon dioxide. The emerging liquor, which is a clear amber colour, is passed over bone charcoal or another decolorizing agent (such as resin) to remove nearly all the soluble impurities and any nonsweetening colouring matter. The liquor is now colourless and clear and ready for recrystallization.

The liquor is boiled under a vacuum to avoid colouring or destroying the sugar by heat. When the liquor reaches the correct thickness crystallization is started by adding a controlled quantity of very small crystals to the liquor. These tiny crystals are known as 'seeds' and are the size of grains of icing (confectioners') sugar. When the tiny crystals have grown to the required size, they are separated from the mother liquor in centrifugal machines and dried in granulators. The boiling and crystallization process is repeated three times before the sugar starts to discolour. This liquor is then used to make other sugar products, such as golden syrup, or is boiled and crystallized again together with syrup separated from the raw sugar magma in the 'recovery house'. The final syrup is called 'refinery molasses'.

Different sizes of crystals are normally produced by variations in boiling technique and duration. The crystals are graded by screening before being packed as either granulated or caster (superfine) sugar. Icing sugar is made by pulverizing the crystals in a mill.

A little less than half the sugar produced is used in direct form; the remainder is sold to food industries or to specialists producing items containing sugar: confectionery, chocolates, biscuits (cookies), manufactured desserts, cakes, dietetic foods, yogurts, jellied milks, dessert creams and ice cream, evaporated and powdered milks, jams, tinned fruits and vegetables, fizzy drinks, fruit juices, squashes, syrups, cordials, champagnes, sparkling wines, liqueurs and creams, fortified wines, and aniseed apéritifs.

□ **The different varieties of sugar**

• *Refined sugar* or *refined extra white sugar*: beet or cane sugar containing at least 99.7% sucrose (typically more than 99.9%), less than 0.06% moisture (by being oven-dried at 105 c), and less than 0.04% invert sugar. It has the highest purity and may be sold as granulated, caster (superfine), grain, or lump sugars.

• *White sugar*: containing at least 99.7% sucrose (typically 99.8–99.9%). It is sold in the same forms as refined sugar (above).

• *Brown sugar*: unrefined (or raw) cane sugar containing 85–99.5% sucrose and certain impurities (which give it its varying shades of brown). Marketed in granulated, lump, or cube form, it possesses a distinctive flavour. There are various types – the very dark moist soft molasses sugar and muscovado, through a pale muscovado to the large crystallized demerara. Some essential minerals and vitamins may be present, but probably in insufficient quantities to substantiate claims that it is nutritionally superior to white sugar. Some commercial brown sugars, however, are refined white sugar with caramel or molasses added to colour and flavour them. This is indicated on the label under 'Ingredients'. The natural product will have no such list.

□ **Various types of commercial white sugars**

• *Granulated sugar*: produced directly from crystallization of the syrup; it forms fairly coarse crystals. It is the most common variety for general use and is generally sold in 500-g (1.1-lb) and 1-kg (2.2-lb) packets.

• *Caster (superfine) sugar* or *fine sugar*: this can be made from crushed and sieved granulated sugar, but in Britain it is mostly boiled to a small crystal size. Sold in paper, cardboard, or polythene packets of 500 g (1.1 lb), 1 kg (2.2 lb), or 2 kg (4½ lb), it is used for making desserts, pastries, cakes, ices, and sweet dishes as well as for sweetening dairy products drinks, pancakes etc.

• *Lump sugar*: this is obtained by moulding moistened granulated sugar while hot, then drying it in order to fuse the crystals together (agglomerated sugar). Invented in 1854 by Eugène François, a Paris grocer, lump sugar takes the form of cubes, tablets, or irregular chunks (in France). Quick-dissolving cubes are compressed only, to give an open texture and quicker dissolution. They are arranged in cartons to prevent them from rubbing against each other and so preserve their shape.

In cafés and restaurants lump sugar is served in wrappers containing one, two, or three cubes. Lump sugar is suitable for sweetening all hot drinks and also for preparing sugar syrup and caramel. For some recipes sugar cubes can be used to rub the zest from citrus fruit.

• *Sugar loaf*: sugar moulded into a cone shape, with the base wrapped in blue-paper; it is today mainly manufactured for export to Arab countries.

• *Icing (confectioners') sugar*: granulated sugar milled very finely into a powder, mixed with 3% starch in France (calcium phosphate in Britain, cornflour (cornstarch) in the United States) to prevent it caking. It is used for dusting, decorating, or icing cakes and buns and is included in many kinds of confectionery.

• *Sucre adant* (or *'de luxe' sugar*): sugar obtained by slow crystallization of very pure syrups, cast into small slabs with shining crystals, which are then sawn or broken into pieces. This is mainly sold in France.

• *Sugar nibs*: rounded grains, obtained by crushing pieces or blocks of white sugar, sorted for size in a sieve: used for the manufacture of sweetened products and for decorating pastries, e.g. Bath buns.

• *Preserving sugar*: large crystals designed for jam-making because they dissolve quickly without forming a lot of scum.

• *Special jam sugar*: gelling sugar, consisting of caster or granulated sugar, natural pectin (0.4–1%), and citric acid (0.6–0.7%, sometimes partially or completely replaced by tartaric acid): helps produce a good-quality set in jams and jellies. Boiling time is often reduced, which gives better colour and retention of aromatic fruit flavours.

• *Vanilla sugar*: caster sugar to which has been added at least 10% powdered extract or essence of natural vanilla, sold in 7-g (¼-oz) sachets for flavouring sweet dishes and pastries; it is available in France and in specialist shops in the United States and Britain. Vanilla-flavoured sugar, blended with synthetic vanilla or with a mixture of ethylvanilline and natural extract of vanilla, has the same uses.

• *Liquid sugar* (*sugar syrup*): literally, a sugar solution, normally prepared by dissolving white sugar in water. In industry, however, it is more closely defined. It is a colourless or golden solution of cane sugar containing at least 62% dissolved solids (usually 66% for better microstability), of which not more than 3% consists of invert sugar. The cane industry has a wide range of liquid sugars, most of which are prepared from intermediate liquors from the refinery process. Cane molasses has a pleasant flavour (unlike beet), hence there is no equivalent to these products in the beet industry. Liquid sugars are used in the food and brewing industries and also for preparing punches or desserts (1 coffeespoon is equivalent to 3 g (⅛ oz) sugar).

• *Invert sugar*: sugar obtained by the action of acids and an enzyme (invertase) on sucrose, consisting of a mixture of glucose and fructose with a little noninverted sucrose; it is used mainly by professional pastrycooks and industries (brewing, confectionery), in the form of 'invert sugar solution' (62% dissolved solids, of which 3–5% is invert sugar) or 'invert sugar syrup' (62% dissolved solids, of which over 50% is invert sugar and syrups).

• *Candy sugar*: very large crystals of white or brown sugar (the latter being white sugar sprayed with caramel colour), obtained by means of slow crystallization on wire-mesh frames.

• *Vergeoise*: solid residue from refining beet or cane sugar, giving a product of soft consistency, golden or brown, with a pronounced flavour: used mostly in Flemish pâtisserie and found mainly in France.

• *Fondant*: sugar syrup worked when cool into a thick white paste with a quantity of glucose syrup or cream of tartar, used for flavouring and decorating in pâtisserie and confectionery. Fondant can also be made with icing sugar, egg white, and glucose syrup worked together. A ready-mixed dry fondant can also be bought (just add water) and ready-to-roll fondant in blocks is also marketed.

• *Liquid caramel*: liquid sugar ready for use without cooking, sold in small bottles or sachets for flavouring yogurts, puddings, and ices.

• *Pastillage*: icing sugar mixed with gelatine, starch, potato starch, or gum, intended for professional pastrycooks. It is available mainly in France.

• *Syrups, molasses, and black treacle*: some syrups, such as maple syrup and palm syrup, occur naturally, but golden syrup (slightly sweeter than sugar) is a by-product of sugar refining which undergoes its own refining process. It is used a great deal in biscuit (cookie) manufacture and in the brewing industry as well as having a useful role in home baking for melted mixtures (such as brandy snaps and flapjacks) and in cakes and desserts. Corn syrup, produced from sweetcorn, can be light or dark (the darker one being more strongly flavoured). It is used in the same way as golden syrup. Molasses and black treacle are dark and viscous, with a strong distinctive flavour, and they are are less sweet than honey. Molasses is the natural syrup drained from sugar cane. Black treacle is a refined molasses-like sugar syrup. They are interchangeable in cooking for such recipes as gingerbread, rich fruit cakes, treacle toffee, and the American speciality Boston baked beans. Treacle is also used in the pharmaceutical industry for lozenges and linctuses.

□ **Sugar in nutrition** All cells in the human body need energy derived from nutrients in the food we eat. Sugar forms the fuel necessary for providing energy for metabolism in the body's tissues, particularly the muscles and the brain. The human digestive system contains enzymes which break down foods into their basic units, small enough to be absorbed into the bloodstream and carried to the cells in the body. Sugar is present naturally in many foods. Refined sugar is a pure carbohydrate which contains 375 Cal per 100 g, or 16 Cal per 5-ml teaspoon. Digestion of sugar breaks it down and results in the release of glucose, which is used in the body. The proportion of glucose in the blood must remain constant (about 1 g per litre); a lower level than this causes faintness.

□ **Sugar in the food industry and cooking** Sugar is widely used in the industrial preparation of foods, including ice creams, yogurts and pre-sweetened desserts, biscuits, chocolates, and confectionery (bonbons, nougats, caramels, barley sugars, etc.).

In cookery, it is also an important ingredient for enhancing flavour, preserving, etc., as well as for sweetening. It is used as a condiment in a number of savoury dishes (glazed onions, carrots and turnips, caramelized brown sauces, glazed ham, carbonades and ragouts, sweet-and-sour dishes, etc.). The versatility and high solubility of sugar mean that it plays an important part as a preservative: for jams, jellies, and marmalades, fruit jellies, preserved or glacé fruits, and crystallized (candied) flowers. It is added to numerous hot or cold drinks, the flavour of which it completes, strengthens, improves, or just sweetens (coffee, tea, chocolate, infusions, fruit juices, sodas); it performs the same function with numerous dairy products, fruit salads, and compotes. Finally, it is one of the essential ingredients of pâtisserie and sweet dessert dishes.

□ **The properties and cooking of sugar** White, shining, odourless, and with a particularly sweet flavour, granulated sugar in its pure state is in rhomboidal prisms; its true density is 1.6 by volume but its practical density is about 1.2 by volume. Its degree of solubility in water depends on the temperature: 1 litre (1¾ pints, 4¼ cups) water can dissolve 2 kg (4½ lb, 9 cups) sugar at 19 c (66 f) and nearly 5 kg (11 lb) at 100 c (212 f). It is not easily dissolved in alcohol. Heated when dry, it begins to dissolve at about 160 c (325 f); rapid cooling at this stage produces barley sugar. Sugar caramelizes above 170 c (337 f) and burns at about 190 c (375 f). Beaten with egg yolks, it forms a creamy foam used in numerous recipes for desserts; when added to stiffly whisked egg whites it provides the basis for meringues.

The cooking of sugar should be carried out progressively, in a heavy-based pan made of untinned copper or stainless steel, which must be absolutely clean and without traces of grease; a simple heavy-based saucepan can be substituted. (The copper pan kept for this use is called a *casson*). Use refined white sugar (granulated, caster (superfine), or, better still, lump), which is barely moistened (a maximum of 300 g (11 oz) water per kg (2¼ lb) sugar). As refined sugar is the purest, there is less risk of crystallization (massing) under the action of an impurity, which would render it unusable; for greater precautions, 50–100 g (2–4 oz) glucose (powder or liquid) is added per kg (2¼ lb) sugar. The sugar must never be stirred during cooking, but the container can be shaken. Cooking begins over a low heat until the sugar is dissolved; the heat is then increased and the sugar should be constantly watched, as the different stages of cooking, which correspond to specialized uses, follow very closely on each other. When a cooking stage is reached, the pan must be removed quickly from the heat; a few drops of cold water can be added in order to lower the temperature of the syrup naturally, but when the syrup begins to turn golden it is then irreversible. The physical characteristics of the sugar indicate the point reached and the degree of cooking is measured manually, either with a saccharometer (also called a syrup hydrometer), which measures the density, or with a sugar (candy) thermometer, graduated up to 200 c (400 f).

☐ **The different stages of cooking sugar**

● *Coated* (100 c, 212 f): absolutely translucent syrup brought to come to the boil; when a skimmer is dipped in it and withdrawn immediately the syrup coats its surface. It is used for fruits in syrup.

● *Small thread* or *small gloss* (101 c, 214 f): professional chefs test the consistency of this sugar by plunging the fingers first in cold water, then quickly in the sugar syrup, which has become thicker; on parting the fingers carefully, short threads will form, about 2–3 mm

(⅛ in) wide, which break easily. It is used for almond paste.

● *Large thread* or *large gloss* (102–103 c, 215–217 f): the thread obtained between the fingers is now stronger and about 0.5 cm (¼ in) wide. This syrup is used in recipes requiring 'sugar syrup' (without any further qualification) – for butter creams, icings, frostings, etc.

● *Small pearl* (103–105 c, 217–221 f): a few minutes after the large thread stage, round bubbles form on the surface of the syrup; when a little is collected on a spoon and taken between the fingers, it forms a wide solid thread. It is used in jams and *torrone* (a type of nougat).

● *Large pearl* or *soufflé* (107–109 c, 224–228 f): the thread of sugar between the fingers may reach a width of 2 cm (¾ in); if it drops back forming a twisted thread (at 1 degree higher) it is described as 'in a pigtail'; when one blows on the skimmer after plunging it into the syrup, bubbles are formed on the other side. It is used in jams, sugar-coated fruits, marrons glacés, and icings (frostings).

● *Small* or *soft ball* (116–118 c, 241–244 f): when a little syrup, which has obviously thickened, is removed with a spoon and plunged into a bowl of cold water, it will roll into a soft ball; if one blows on the skimmer dipped into the syrup, bubbles break loose and blow away. It is used in jams and jellies, soft caramels, nougats, and Italian meringue.

● *Large* or *hard ball* (121–124 c, 250 –255 f): after several boilings, the previous operation is repeated and a harder ball is obtained; if one blows through the skimmer, snowy flakes are formed. It is used in jams, sugar decorations, Italian meringue, fondant, and caramels.

● *Light, small,* or *soft crack* (129–135 c, 265–275 f): a drop of syrup in cold water hardens immediately and will crack and stick to the teeth when chewed. (A saccharometer cannot be used at these higher temperatures.) It is used mainly for toffee.

● *Hard crack* (149–150 c, 295–300 f): the drops of syrup in cold water become hard and brittle (like glass), but not sticky; the sugar acquires a pale straw-yellow colour at the edges of the saucepan; it must be watched carefully to avoid it turning into caramel, which would spoil it at this stage. It is for boiled sweets and candies, spun sugar decorations, icings, sugar flowers, candy floss.

- *Light caramel* (151–160 c, 302–325 F): the syrup, which now contains hardly any water, begins to change into barley sugar, then into caramel; yellow at first, it becomes golden and then brown. It is used in the caramelization of crème caramel, sweets, and nougatine and for flavouring sweet dishes, puddings, cakes, biscuits (cookies), and icings.

- *Brown* or *dark caramel* (blackjack) (161–170 c, 326–338 F): when it has turned brown, sugar loses its sweetening power; extra sugar is added to preparations with a basis of dark caramel. As the last stage of cooked sugar before carbonization (sugar burns and smokes at about 190 c, 375 F) brown caramel is used mainly for colouring sauces, cakes, and stocks.

In addition, there are several methods for fashioning sugar, for making confectionery and decorating pastries and cakes.

- *Spun sugar* (*sucre filé* or *angels' hair*): cooked to nearly 155 c (312 F). The pan is taken off the heat and left to cool for 1–2 minutes, then placed in a saucepan of hot water to keep the syrup hot. Two forks are dipped into the syrup and flicked quickly backwards and forwards above a lightly greased rolling pin; the threads obtained are then spread over a marble slab and flattened lightly with the blade of a knife in order to obtain ribbons, or collected and used to decorate cakes or make a veil. The strands should be used within an hour, otherwise they will melt.

- *Poured sugar* (*sucre coulé*): cooked to cracking point, possibly coloured, then moulded into cups, pompoms, little bells, and other decorative shapes.

- *Fashioned*, *drawn*, or *pulled sugar*: cooked so that it loses its transparency. Colourings are added at 140 c (284 F), and the syrup is heated to 155 c (312 F). It is then cooled, poured onto a greased marble slab or other cold surface, and then pulled, kneaded, or moulded into flowers, candies, etc., with a satinized finish. (These should be stored in an airtight container.)

The stages of cooking sugar

name	degrees Celsius	degrees Fahrenheit	density	manual assessment
coated	100	212	1.240	translucent coating
small thread or small gloss	101	214	1.251	2–3-mm thread
large thread or large gloss	102–103	215–217	1.262	0.5-cm thread
small pearl	103–105	217–221	1.296	rounded bubbles
large pearl or soufflé	107–109	224–228	1.319	bubbles with skimmer, 2-cm thread
small or soft ball	116–118	241–244	1.344	soft ball
large or hard ball	121–124	250–255	1.357	harder ball
light (small or soft) crack	129–135	265–275		hard but sticky ball
hard crack	149–150	295–300		brittle but not sticky ball
light caramel	151–160	302–325		
brown or dark caramel (blackjack)	161–170	326–338		

• *Rock sugar* (*sucre rocher*): cooked to nearly 125 C (260 F), emulsified with royal icing (coloured or not), then used especially to give a rocky effect. It keeps well when exposed to the air.
• *Brown sugar*: cooked to nearly 145 –150 C (285–300 F), which may be coloured and is blown like glass.

These types of sugar are used in pâtisserie chiefly for constructing *pièces montées*: flowers and leaves, ribbons, knots, and shells of drawn and coloured sugar; flowers of fashioned or pulled sugar (rolled out into thin sheets); moiré ribbons (in strips shaped over a spirit lamp and flattened by hand on a board); various types of baskets of plaited sugar (sugar spun into the shape of small cords, plaited, and cooled); objects made of cut, compacted, or pressed sugar (moistened and moulded, then dried out in a closed container); plumes of spun sugar, etc. Coloured sugars are made from granulated or coarse caster (super-fine) sugar, which is heated, then sprinkled with colourings soluble in alcohol.

For making biscuits, pastries, and petits fours sugar may be flavoured with the zest of citrus fruits, cinnamon, aniseed, clove, ginger, or dried and pounded flower petals (orange blossom, thyme, lime, violet, rose, etc.).

RECIPES

Aniseed sugar SUCRE D'ANIS Dry out 50 g (2 oz) aniseed wrapped in paper in a cool oven. Pound it finely in a mortar with 500 g (18 oz, 2½ cups) caster (superfine) sugar. Sift through a sieve. Store in a tightly corked jar, in a dry place. Use as required.

Cinnamon sugar SUCRE DE CANNELLE Chop 1 thin stick of cinnamon, mix with 1 tablespoon caster (superfine) sugar, then pound with another tablespoon of sugar. Sift through a fine sieve. Pound the cinnamon remaining in the sieve with another tablespoon of sugar and sift. Store as for aniseed sugar.

Clove sugar SUCRE DE GIROFLE Proceed and store as for aniseed sugar, using 20 g (¾ oz) whole cloves and 500 g (18 oz, 2½ cups) sugar.

Ginger sugar SUCRE DE GINGEMBRE Proceed and store as for aniseed sugar, using 30 g (1 oz) fresh root ginger and 500 g (18 oz, 2½ cups) sugar.

Orange sugar SUCRE D'ORANGE (from Carême's recipe) Take some sweet Maltese oranges with fine skins. Grate the zest on sugar lumps, but take care not to reach the white pith which is immediately under the zest, since this is extremely bitter and would spoil the orange flavour. As the surface of the sugar becomes coloured, scrape off the layer of zest which becomes attached to it through repeated rubbing. Continue until all the zest is removed. Then dry the sugar in a sealed container or in a cool oven. Crush the sugar lumps and sift through a fine sieve.

The procedure is the same for Seville (bitter) orange, lemon, citron, or tangerine sugars.

Sugar icing (frosting) GLACE DE SUCRE Mix some icing (confectioners') sugar with a little water; flavour it with coffee, melted chocolate, liqueur, vanilla, or finely grated orange, tangerine, or lemon zest. The quantity of water should be increased if a softer icing is desired. Use it to coat small and large cakes and biscuits.

Vanilla sugar SUCRE VANILLE Split 60 g (2 oz) vanilla pods (beans) and chop them up finely. Pound them finely in a mortar with 500 g (18 oz, 4 cups) lump sugar and sift through a fine sieve.

sugar bowl SUCRIER

A container for serving sugar at table. It may be of porcelain, earthenware, glass or crystal, stainless steel, silver, or silver plate and sometimes forms part of a tea or coffee service. Bowls for lump sugar are accompanied by a pair of sugar tongs and often fitted with a lid. Prototypes of sugar bowls, called 'sugar pots', appeared in the 18th century. Caster (superfine) sugar can be served in a sugar bowl with a small ladle, but a sugar sprinkler (dredger) is more practical.

sugar cane
CANNE À SUCRE

A plant, originating in Indonesia, that is cultivated widely in tropical and subtropical regions for its sugar-rich stems, which contain 14% sucrose. References to 'an Indian reed with juice sweeter than honey' occur in Roman literature; however, the cultivation of sugar cane did not develop until after the discovery of America, where it was planted on a large scale.

A cane known as 'eating cane' is grown by the locals, who remove the husk and chew it to extract the sweet juice.

Industrial cane juice, obtained by crushing the stems, is used to make sugar. It also ferments spontaneously and can be distilled to produce various spirits, particularly rums.

sugar dredger
GLACIÈRE À SUCRE

A small cylindrical container with a screw top pierced with small holes, used for sprinkling icing or caster sugar (confectioners' or superfine sugar) over the top of cakes, waffles, and desserts, or dishes to be caramelized.

sugared almonds
See *dragée*, *praline*.

sugar pea (snow pea)
POIS GOURMAND

A type of pea, also known in France as *princesse* and nicknamed *mange-tout* as the whole pod is eaten. The pods have no parchment lining, but as they can be stringy it is best to eat only the young pods. They are marketed in winter and in early spring. There are two varieties, Carouby de Maussane and Corne-de-Bélier. They have a lower calorific value than peas but are quite rich in sugar, potassium, and vitamins. Sugar peas are very tender and brilliant green in colour and can be stored for a few days in the refrigerator. They can be used, either whole or sliced, for the same recipes as fresh peas.

suisse
A traditional pastry of Valence (Drôme) in the shape of a little man, made of sweetened brioche dough flavoured with orange. The original suisse was said to have been modelled on the Emperor Napoleon, whose legendary hat was, over the years, confused with the cocked hats of the Swiss Guard at the Vatican. A diffferent explanation exists: 'As a prisoner of the republican army, Pope Pius VI . . . came to end his days at Valence. It was the picturesque costume of the soldiers of his Swiss Guard (designed, it is said, by Michelangelo), soon a familiar sight to the inhabitants of Valence, which inspired an astute pastrycook to make little men from crisp pastry flavoured with orange, to which he gave the name of *suisses*, which they have kept to this day.' (Ned Rival, *Traditions pâtissières de nos provinces*.)

Suisses were formerly baked as a speciality for Palm Sunday, but nowadays they are sold all the year round.

sukiyaki
A typically Japanese dish, of the type described as *nabemono* (cooked directly on the table). Its origin goes back to the era when religion banned the consumption of meat. In country districts, however, the peasants used to cut birds and game into fine strips and grill them secretly out in the fields (*sukiyaki* means literally 'grilled on a ploughshare'). Nowadays sukiyaki usually consists of thin slices of beef, chopped vegetables, vermicelli, or small noodles, and bean curd, sautéed in a copper pan over a table hotplate, then dipped in raw egg just before being eaten. Pork, chicken, and fish are also prepared in this way. In Japan each guest serves himself directly from the pan, as the cooking proceeds.

RECIPE

Sukiyaki Before proceeding with the cooking, which is done in the course of the meal, prepare the ingedients: 450 g (1 lb, 2 cups) lean beef (fillet or sirloin), cut into very fine strips; 240 g (8½ oz, generous cup) *shirataki* (vermicelli made with starch), dipped in boiling water and drained (this may be replaced by fresh small noodles); 100 g (4 oz, 1 cup) thinly sliced mushrooms; 150 g (5 oz, 1 cup) canned bamboo shoots, drained and finely sliced; 4 large leeks, thinly sliced; 150 g (5 oz, ¾ cup) bean curd cut into small dice; 100 g (4 oz, 1½ cups) blanched shredded Chinese cabbage; and (optional) a few coarsely shredded spinach leaves.

Heat a large heavy-based pan on a table hotplate, over a brisk flame, and grease it lightly with a piece of beef fat, which should be removed before cooking begins. Place one-third of the strips of meat in the pan, heat through, then add 4 tablespoons (⅓ cup) soy sauce and 2 tablespoons (3 tablespoons) sugar; turn over the meat, cook for 1–2 minutes, then push towards the edge of the pan. Next add one-third of the vegetables, together with some *shirataki* and bean curd, and sprinkle with 4 tablespoons (⅓ cup) saké; leave to cook for 4–5 minutes. Distribute the vegetables and meat between the plates (the proportions given are for 4 guests), and repeat the operation until the ingredients are used up.

Sukiyaki is eaten with chopsticks: each mouthful is dipped in raw beaten egg before being eaten; each guest breaks an egg into a small bowl for this purpose. Sukiyaki is served with plain boiled rice.

sultanas

See *dried vine fruits*.

sultane (à la)

A term describing various preparations characterized by pistachio nuts, either in the form of a flavoured butter to finish a chicken velouté or to accompany fish, or chopped, or used as a flavouring for ice cream or for fruit-based desserts (apricots, pears, peaches, etc.). The sultane garnish, for suprêmes of chicken served on a chicken forcemeat, consists of small tartlets filled with truffle purée and studded with peeled pistachio halves. There is, however, another sultane garnish, for large cuts of meat, which does not contain pistachio nuts: it consists of duchess potatoes cut into the shape of Islamic crescents (to which it owes its name) with a julienne of stewed red cabbage.

sumac, sumach, or shoomak

A shrub originating in Turkey, certain varieties of which are cultivated in southern Italy and in Sicily. Its fleshy petals and small berries are dried and reduced to purple powder, which has an acid taste and is very popular in Middle Eastern cookery. Mixed with water, it can be used in the same way as lemon juice, particularly in preparations of tomatoes and onions, chicken forcemeats, marinades of fish, and dishes with a lentil base.

Varieties of sumac cultivated in Britain are ornamental and not used in cookery. The dried and ground leaves are also used in tanning and dyeing.

sumptuary laws

LOIS SOMPTUAIRES

Government regulations issued to keep down expenses in banquets and also designed to control personal extravagance. In ancient Rome the sumptuary laws forbade the consumption of very young animals and the slaughter of certain species. They also put a stop to ostentatious displays of luxury, and once even decreed that everyone should eat with their doors wide open so that the laws could be enforced. This type of controlling legislation was also introduced during the Ancien Régime in France (pre-1789), when it was extended to customs and traditions, notably to wedding feasts: 'To put an end to ruinous extravagance . . . members of the upper classes shall no longer be allowed to serve more than eight courses at table; these will include the entrée, entremets, and set pieces; as for wedding feasts, the number of dishes will henceforth be restricted to a maximum of six.'

sundae

A dessert from the United States, consisting of ice cream and fruit coated with jam or syrup. Originally it was reserved for the family meal on Sundays: at the end of the 19th century, North America was fairly puritanical, and the consumption of sweets and delicacies was still frowned upon. But the fashion for ice creams, encouraged by the first manually operated ice-cream freezers, was increasing and gradually the nickname 'sundae' was given to the traditional ice which could be served on Sundays 'without offending God'. Today there is a wide variety of sundaes.

Henri Troyat, in *La Case de l'oncle Sam*, describes it thus: '. . . I shall remember that sundae all my life. In a sumptuous confectioner's shop, light, airy, full of fragrance, we were served with a mountain of coffee ice cream, sprinkled with cream and scattered with walnuts, honey, peanuts, and various fruits. When I carried the first spoonful to my mouth . . . my taste buds experienced a violent ecstasy. A whole opera of sensation rolled off my tongue . . .'

Recipes for sundaes can be found under the article for *coupe*.

sunflower TOURNESOL

An annual plant, originally from Mexico and Peru, also known as helianthus. Nowadays it is widely cultivated both for ornament and for its seeds, from which an oil is extracted. Sunflower-seed oil contains a high proportion of essential fatty acids and is recommended by dietitians as a cooking oil. Its good emulsifying quality makes it very suitable for mayonnaise. It is also useful for dressings, sautéing, and roasting, but does not withstand heating beyond 170 c (340 f). As it is sensitive to light, it should be kept in an opaque container. Sunflower-seed oil from the first cold press, which is fruity, light, and digestible, is the best. In Russia and Poland, sunflower seeds are nibbled, like almonds, as a snack: they are an excellent source of energy.

superstitions of the table

SUPERSTITIONS DE TABLE

There have always been superstitions associated with eating. Some have a rational explanation; others remain a mystery.

Spilt salt is supposed to bring bad luck. The origins of this superstition go back to the times when it was very expensive (and therefore not to be wasted). In addition, salt has been a symbol of friendship and welcome from the earliest times: to offer salt and bread remains a traditional gesture of greeting in a number of countries. On the other hand, the act of throwing a pinch of salt over one's shoulder to ward off bad luck arises purely from superstition; as Léon de Fos wrote: 'Upon my faith, the essential thing is for no salt to be dropped into the stewed fruit or custard!'

Crossed knives, another bringer of bad luck, evoke both the cross on which St Andrew was crucified and the murderous gesture of crossing swords with an enemy.

Ought one to break the shell of an egg after eating the contents? This custom has its roots in the past; it is referred to by ancient and modern writers. The Romans attached great importance to it. The egg was regarded as an emblem of nature, a substance that was both mysterious and sacred. People were convinced that magicians used eggs in their incantations, emptying them and drawing magic characters from inside the shell. These had the power to cause much harm. One crushed the shell to destroy the evil spell. Occasionally it was enough to pierce it with a knife, or to rap it three times.

Why will you marry within the year (or, if you are already married, why will you have a daughter) if the last drop of a bottle of wine is poured into your glass? This has been seen as an allusion to the poverty which befalls the married man, or the one who has too many daughters to marry off and provide with dowries. On the other hand, wine spilt over the table is an omen of good luck, in memory of the ancient libations.

The presence of 13 people at table is regarded as unlucky because of its association with the Last Supper, where the 13 participants included Judas Iscariot, who betrayed his master and hanged himself. This superstition was shrugged off by Grimod de La Reynière who said that it is only dangerous to be 13 at table if the dinner is prepared for only 12.

There are various popular superstitions attached to the food itself. Cabbage is not supposed to be eaten on St Stephen's Day, because the saint, according to the legend, hid in a cabbage field to try and escape from his persecutors. Melon was said to cause fever in autumn, and jams were supposed to ferment when the fruit trees begin to blossom. The custom of throwing handfuls of rice over newly married couples as they come out of the church is supposed to symbolize abundance and prosperity.

supper SOUPER

A light meal taken in the evening, often after a night out.

Originally the only evening meal (now called dinner), supper usually consisted of soup (hence the name) and was eaten relatively early. (In Provence, the midnight feast at Christmas is still called the *souparoun*.) The fashion for supper as an intimate late dinner became established in French high society in the 18th century. Saint-Simon recalls the famous suppers of the Regent hotel: 'For small suppers, dishes were prepared in kitchens specially set up on the same floor, using utensils made of silver. The roués often gave the cooks a hand.' Rich and extravagant dishes were prepared, including marinated wild boar kidneys, oysters with cream, followed by cakes, tarts, salads, and entremets (pigs' trotters (feet) Sainte-Menehould, peas with poached eggs, apples *à la chinoise*). The supper vogue continued under Louis XV. Marquises and duchesses often prepared the dishes themselves, as the servants were kept away from these intimate evening parties; these aristocratic creations included Soubise cutlets, gigot *à la duchesse*, and bouchée *à la reine*.

Until the middle of the 19th century, supper was the essential conclusion of any successful evening. At a ball, the orchestra gave the signal for supper by means of a fanfare. Gradually, however, the supper was abandoned, because it was becoming too expensive and was causing too many difficulties. It was sometimes replaced by buffets or refreshments brought on trays, and sometimes, very late in the evening, by a punch and pastries. At dawn, the guests were revived with tea, broth, chocolate, coffee, sandwiches, and wines. However, private households continued to hold quiet suppers: 'When only a chosen few are left in the drawing room, the master of the house gathers them together quietly around a table concealed in some cosy nook, and there they see in the day, chatting about the events of the past night. Wit and appetite normally find their best openings in these private suppers, which have a certain smack of the forbidden fruit' (E. Briffault, *Paris à table*). The supper vogue also became established with the restaurateurs, especially those who had private rooms.

suprême

The breast and wing of chicken or game; the term is also used for a fine fillet of fish (sole or brill, for example). Suprêmes of chicken or game (which are often garnished with truffles, a delicate and stylish preparation, hence their name) are usually cooked rapidly, either brushed with butter, sprinkled with lemon juice, and baked quickly in the oven in a covered casserole or wrapped in foil, or poached in a very little liquid (without boiling), or browned quickly in butter, or coated with breadcrumbs and fried or grilled (broiled).

Suprêmes are usually served with fresh vegetables (asparagus tips, French (green) beans, or green peas) bound with butter or cream, but the classic garnishes for fried or poached chicken can also be used. The accompanying sauce is white or brown, depending on the method of cooking and the garnish. Fillets of turkey and duck are now readily available and can be cooked in the same way.

Suprêmes of fish are generally poached and served with a garnish and a white-wine, shrimp, Nantua, américaine, or normande sauce.

The term is also applied to preparations of luxury foods (suprêmes of foie gras, for example). Suprême sauce, which accompanies poached and fried poultry, is a reduced velouté mixed with chicken stock and fresh cream, sometimes finished with mushroom essence and lemon juice.

RECIPES

Suprêmes (*preparation*) Pull the leg of the bird away from the body; slice down to where the thigh joins the carcass. Cut through the joint and remove the whole leg. Repeat with the other leg and set both legs aside for another dish. Separate the flesh on either side of the breastbone, cutting down towards the wing joints. Then sever the joints of the wings from the body, without separating them from the breast meat. Finally cut through each wing at the second joint to remove the pinion (wing tip). Carefully ease off the skin.

Garnishes for suprêmes of chicken
SUPRÊMES DE VOLAILLE ET LEUR
GARNITURE Prepare the suprêmes *à
blanc* or *à brun*. The following garnishes can be used: diced aubergines (eggplants) sautéed in butter, braised lettuce or chicory, pieces of cucumber slowly cooked in butter, spinach in butter or gravy, artichoke hearts slowly cooked or sautéed in butter, French (green) beans or macédoine of vegetables in butter, peas *à la française*, asparagus tips in butter or cream, or a vegetable purée.

Suprême sauce SAUCE SUPRÊME
Prepare a velouté with a white roux (40 g (1½ oz, 3 tablespoons) butter and 40 g (1½ oz, 6 tablespoons) flour) and 8 dl (1¼ pints, 3 cups) well-seasoned and well-reduced chicken consommé. Add 5 dl (17 fl oz, 2 cups) white chicken stock and reduce it by at least half. Add 3–4 dl (½ pint, 1½ cups) fresh cream and reduce the sauce to about 6 dl (1 pint, 2½ cups), at which point it should coat the spoon. Remove from the heat and stir in 50 g (2 oz, 4 tablespoons) butter. Strain through a very fine sieve and keep in a bain-marie until ready to use.

Suprêmes of chicken à blanc SUP-
RÊMES DE VOLAILLE À BLANC Season the suprêmes with salt and pepper, brush with clarified butter, arrange in a buttered casserole, and sprinkle with a little lemon juice. Cover the casserole and cook in the oven at 220 C (425 F, gas 7) for about 15 minutes. Drain the suprêmes and arrange them on a serving dish with the chosen garnish.

Suprêmes of chicken à brun SUP-
RÊMES DE VOLAILLE À BRUN Season the suprêmes with salt and pepper, coat them in flour, and cook them in clarified butter in a sauté pan until golden on both sides. Arrange on a serving dish with the chosen garnish.

Suprêmes of chicken à l'anglaise SUP-
RÊMES DE VOLAILLE À L'ANGLAISE Season the suprêmes with salt and pepper, then coat them with beaten egg and breadcrumbs. Cook in clarified butter in a sauté pan until golden and cooked through. Arranged on a bed of Anna potatoes, surround with grilled (broiled) tomatoes, and garnish each

suprême with a grilled rasher (slice) of bacon.

Surati

An Indian cheese made from buffaloes' milk, sometimes also from cows' milk, with a soft whitish centre and a slightly sour yet salty flavour. It is matured and sold in its whey in large terracotta containers. It takes its name from the city of Surat, where it is manufactured.

surprise (en)

A term describing certain dishes that are presented in such a way as to give a false impression of their flavour, consistency, etc., which are revealed, when they are eaten, as a delightful surprise. The most obvious example of such a dish is baked Alaska, in which ice cream is hidden inside a meringue which has been placed for a short time in a hot oven.

The term *en surprise* is generally given to fruits which are scooped out and filled with ice cream or sorbet and frozen, or filled with a soufflé, mousse, or other preparation and chilled. Good examples are oranges, tangerines, melons, and pineapples, which can all have their 'lids' replaced to hide what is inside. Sugar-coated fruits are also described as *en surprise*.

In one of his *Lettres gourmandes* to the playwright Émile de Najac, Charles Monselet mentions eggs *en surprise*, for which he gives an ancient recipe from the royal château of Marly: 'Take 12 fine eggs; in each one make two small holes at the ends. Pass a straw through one of these holes to burst the yolk, then empty the eggs by blowing through one of the ends. Rinse the shells in water, drain them, and dry in the open air. Fill up one of the holes in each egg with a mixture of flour and egg yolk and leave to dry, then fill the eggs through the remaining hole with chocolate custard cream mixture, coffee custard cream mixture, or orange-blossom custard cream mixture made with the blown-out egg); for this purpose use a very small funnel. Stop up the holes of the eggshells with the flour and egg yolk mixture and cook them in plenty of hot water (which should not be allowed to boil) to set the custard cream. Remove the 'plugs' from the two ends of the eggs, wipe the eggs, and serve them under a folded napkin as a dessert. Two years ago eggs *en surprise* came back into fashion and our leading confectioners began to make them, especially at Easter time.'

Pineapple en surprise ANANAS EN SURPRISE Cut the top off a choice pineapple close to the leaves and hollow it out carefully, without splitting the skin. Cut the pulp into dice and macerate these with 100 g (4 oz, ½ cup, firmly packed) caster (superfine) sugar and 5 cl (2 tablespoons, 3 tablespoons) rum for 2 hours.

Boil 6.5 dl (1 pint, 2½ cups) milk with a vanilla pod (bean) split in two. In a mixing bowl beat 1 whole egg with 3 yolks and 100 g (4 oz, ½ cup, firmly packed) caster sugar; when the mixture is white and thick, blend in 60 g (2¼ oz, generous ½ cup) flour to obtain a very smooth paste. Pour the boiling milk over the paste fairly slowly to avoid cooking the yolks, whisking rapidly all the time. Replace the mixture over a gentle heat and stir until the cream has thickened. Then remove from the heat and add the juice in which the pineapple has been macerated.

Cool this cream in the refrigerator, then mix it gently with the diced pineapple, 3 egg whites whisked to very stiff peaks, and 1 dl (6 tablespoons, scant ½ cup) fresh cream. Fill the pineapple with this preparation, replace its top, and refrigerate until time to serve.

other recipes See *chartreuse, melon, tangerine, walnut.*

Suzette

A type of sweet pancake flavoured with tangerine and coated with a tangerine flavoured sauce. In the recipe given by Escoffier, tangerine juice and Curaçao are used to flavour the pancake batter and the melted butter and sugar (to which tangerine zest has been added) used to mask the pancakes.

Henri Charpentier, who was Rockefeller's cook in the United States, falsely claimed to have invented crêpes Suzette in 1896, at the Café de Paris in Monte Carlo, as a compliment to the Prince of Wales and his companion whose first name was Suzette; in actual fact, at that date Charpentier was not old enough to be the head waiter serving the prince. Back in the United States he introduced the fashion for flamed crêpes Suzette. Elsewhere, Léon Daudet, in *Paris vécu* (1929), speaks of pancakes called Suzette which in about 1898 were one of the specialities of Marie's Restaurant (famous for its oeufs Toupinel and its entrecôte bordelaise): they were made with jam and flavoured with brandy 'which improved them greatly'.

Crêpes Suzette Prepare a crêpe batter with 250 g (9 oz, 2¼ cups) flour, 3 whole eggs, 2 glasses of milk, and a pinch of salt. Add the juice of a tangerine, 1 tablespoon Curaçao, and 2 tablespoons olive oil. Leave to stand for 2 hours at room temperature. Work 50 g (2 oz, 4 tablespoons) butter with the juice of a tangerine, its grated rind, 1 tablespoon Curaçao, and 50 g (2 oz, 4 tablespoons) caster (superfine) sugar.

Make some thin crêpes in a heavybased frying pan (skillet) (never washed, but wiped each time with clean paper). Mask them with a little of the tangerine butter, fold them in four, return them one by one to the frying pan, and heat them. Arrange them in a warm dish, slightly overlapping.

swan CYGNE

A large aquatic web-footed bird with oily leathery flesh, regarded today purely as an ornamental bird. From the Middle Ages to the Renaissance, however, it ranked with the peacock in pro viding a sumptuous roast at banquets The bird was carefully plucked and roasted on a spit. It was dressed in its feathers and brought ceremoniously to the table with a piece of blazing cam phor or wick in its beak

sweat SUER

To cook vegetables (generally cut up small) in fat over a gentle heat, so that they become soft (but not brown) and their juices are concentrated in the cooking fat. When the pan is covered during cooking, the ingredients retain a certain amount of their natural mois ture, as in a vegetable fondue; when the pan is not covered, the preparation is relatively dry, as in a mushroom duxelles.

swede (rutabaga)

RUTABAGA

A root vegetable with orange-yellow flesh. Originally from Scandinavia (where it is called *rotabagge*), it has a low calorific value and is fairly rich in minerals. It can be cooked in the same way as the turnip and is often included in stews, to which it gives a distinctive flavour.

sweet-and-sour

AIGRE-DOUX

The association of two contrasting flavours, acid and sweet, in the same dish is a very old culinary practice still common today in many countries. Honey with vinegar and verjuice were among the basic ingredients of the seasonings of dishes in Roman times and in medieval cooking, with its sauces and ragouts. Many meat, game, or fish (particularly river fish) dishes, marinated or boiled in wine or beer, have dried fruit in the sauce, or the jelly of red berries as an accompaniment: this is one of the distinguishing features of Russian, Scandinavian, German, Alsatian, Jewish, and Flemish cooking. Fruits preserved in vinegar – plums, cherries, cranberries – are a typical example of the sweet-and-sour combination, and there is a large range of cooked condiments – chutneys, sweet mustards, achars – some of which are of exotic origin (from India and the West Indies) and were adopted in Europe under British influence. But it is undoubtedly in China that sweet-and-sour cooking is at its finest, particularly for pork and duck.

RECIPE

Sweet-and-sour sauce SAUCE AIGRE-DOUX Soak 1 tablespoon raisins in water. Using a small thick-bottomed saucepan, cook 3 lumps of sugar moistened with 2 tablespoons vinegar until they caramelize slightly. Add 1.5 dl (¼ pint, ⅔ cup) dry white wine and 2 teaspoons chopped shallots; cook briskly until the liquid has evaporated. Add 225

ml (8 fl oz, 1 cup) demi-glace sauce and boil for a few moments. Press the sauce through a fine sieve, then return to the pan and slowly bring to the boil. Drain the raisins and add them to the sauce with 2 teaspoons capers. This sauce can be served with poultry or roast pork.

sweetbread RIS

The culinary term for the thymus gland (in the throat) and the pancreas (near the stomach) in calves, lambs, and pigs, although the latter are not much used. Thymus sweetbreads are elongated and irregular in shape; pancreas sweetbreads are larger and rounded. Lambs' and calves' sweetbreads are cooked in the same way, but the latter are considered to be superior; they can be used in fillings and ragouts for moulds and vols-au-vent. Sweetbreads are blanched, refreshed, and cooled; they can then be fried, braised, roasted, grilled (broiled), poached, cooked *au gratin*, on skewers, etc.

RECIPES

Preparation of lambs' *or* calves' sweetbreads PRÉPARATION DE RIS D'AGNEAU OU DE VEAU Soak the sweetbreads in cold water until they become white, changing the water from time to time until it remains clear (at least 5 hours). Put them into a saucepan with cold salted water to cover and bring them slowly to the boil. At the first sign of boiling, remove and drain the sweetbreads and refresh them under cold running water. Then drain and wipe dry, remove the skin and fibres, and press them between 2 cloths under a board with a weight on top. Leave for 1 hour.

Depending on the recipe chosen, they can be studded with thin pieces of bacon, truffle, tongue, or ham.

CALVES' SWEETBREADS

Calves' sweetbreads braised in brown stock RIS DE VEAU BRAISÉS À BRUN Prepare the sweetbreads as in the following recipe. Put bacon rinds and finely sliced carrots and onions into a buttered sauté dish, add salt, pepper, and a bouquet garni, cover, and cook gently for 10 minutes. Then moisten with a few tablespoons of brown veal stock (or stock with 1 tablespoon tomato purée mixed in) and a few tablespoons of white wine. Boil down rapidly to reduce the liquid to a glaze. Finish as for sweetbreads braised in white stock, but glaze for a little longer. Serve with a Clamart or périgourdine garnish.

The dish may also be served with vegetables that have been braised or browned in butter, and cooked in the reduced cooking liquid, or accompanied by a vegetable purée served separately.

Calves' sweetbreads braised in white stock RIS DE VEAU BRAISÉS À BLANC Blanch and refresh some calves' sweetbreads. Cool and press in the usual way (they may be larded, studded, or left plain, depending on the recipe). Put some bacon rinds and some finely sliced onions and carrots into a buttered sauté pan and lay the sweetbreads on top. Add salt and pepper and a bouquet garni. Cover the pan and begin the cooking slowly over a gentle heat. Then moisten with a few tablespoons of white stock. Transfer the covered dish to the oven at 200 C (425 F, gas 7) and continue the cooking for 25–30 minutes, basting frequently with the stock. When the sweetbreads are cooked, they can be glazed very lightly by removing the lid and leaving the dish in the oven for a further 5–6 minutes, basting with the fat in the stock. Serve with one of the following garnishes: anversoise, Nantua, princesse, or Régence.

Escalopes of calves' sweetbreads à l'ancienne RIS DE VEAU ESCALOPÉS À L'ANCIENNE Make a puff-pastry shell and bake it blind. Cut some calves' sweetbreads into thick round slices and braise them in white stock. Arrange the slices in a circle in the pastry case. Reduce the braising stock and pour it over the sweetbreads. Fill the centre of the circle with mushrooms cooked in butter and blended with a thick Madeira-flavoured velouté sauce. Garnish each slice of sweetbread with a sliver of truffle.

In the original recipe, cocks' combs and kidneys were added to the mushrooms.

Escalopes of calves' sweetbreads au gratin RIS DE VEAU EN ESCALOPES AU GRATIN Cut some braised sweetbreads into slices and arrange them in a circle in a buttered ovenproof dish. Surround with sliced mushrooms, cover with a duxelles sauce, and sprinkle with breadcrumbs. Brown in the oven. To serve, sprinkle with a little lemon juice and chopped parsley.

Fried calves' sweetbreads RIS DE VEAU POÊLÉS Blanch, cool, and press the sweetbreads. Cut each one into 3 or 4 slices, season with salt and pepper, dip each slice in flour, and fry in butter until brown.

Alternatively, clean the sweetbreads well, dry them thoroughly, put them into a sauté pan with some melted butter, add salt and pepper, cover the pan, and let them cook gently for 30–35 minutes.

Fried sweetbreads are sprinkled with chopped parsley and can be served on Anna potatoes, for example, with a thick béarnaise sauce served separately.

Fritters of calves' sweetbreads BEIGNETS DE RIS DE VEAU Blanch and trim some calves' sweetbreads and cool under a board with a weight on top. Cut into slices and dip them first in flour, then in a light fritter batter, and deep-fry at 180 C (350 F) until golden brown on both sides. Drain the fritters on kitchen paper. Serve with quarters of lemon and either a well-reduced tomato fondue or a herb mayonnaise.

Grilled (broiled) calves sweetbreads RIS DE VEAU GRILLÉS Rinse, blanch, cool, and press the sweetbreads. Brush them with oil or clarified butter, season with pepper, and grill (broil) slowly, either whole or sliced, under a moderate flame. Serve either with a green salad or with a seasonal vegetable, steamed and tossed in fresh butter. Alternatively, the grilled sweetbreads may be served with a purée of carrots, peas, or turnips.

Poached calves' sweetbreads RIS DE VEAU POCHÉS Blanch, skin, cool, and press the sweetbreads, put them into a sauté pan, barely cover them with white stock, and let them simmer very gently for 35–40 minutes, according to their thickness. Drain them and keep hot. Reduce the cooking liquor and pour this over the sweetbreads. Serve with buttered green beans, young broad beans (fava beans), or a macédoine of spring vegetables.

Roast calves' sweetbreads RIS DE VEAU RÔTIS Prepare some good-sized blanched pressed calves' sweetbreads, larded if wished. Season with salt and pepper and wrap each one in a small piece of pig's caul (caul fat). Thread them onto a skewer and roast them in a hot oven for about 30 minutes.

Terrine of calves' sweetbreads TERRINE DE RIS DE VEAU (from a recipe of the Hôtel de la Poste, at Avallon) Prepare 4 calves' sweetbreads in the usual way, blanch them, take out any gristle, stud them with slices of truffle, and press them under a light weight for 24 hours. Brown a finely chopped mirepoix of onions, carrots, shallots, and a clove of garlic in some butter. Season the sweetbreads, then sauté them with the mirepoix, without allowing them to brown. Pour in 1 glass white wine, 1 glass Madeira, and ½ glass port. Add a bouquet garni and braise gently for 40 minutes. Take out the sweetbreads and reduce the cooking liquor by a quarter. Strain and set aside.

Make a fine forcemeat with 250 g (9 oz, generous cup, firmly packed) minced (ground) fat pork, an equal quantity of minced noix of veal, 75 g (3 oz, ⅓ cup) minced ham, 1 dl (6 tablespoons, scant ½ cup) fresh cream, 1 egg, 1 tablespoon foie gras, salt, and pepper. Line a terrine with thin strips of bacon. Fill the dish with alternate layers of sweetbreads and forcemeat, covering each layer of forcemeat with very thin bacon rashers (slices). Pour a little of the reduced cooking liquor onto each layer. Finish with a layer of forcemeat topped with bacon rashers.

Cover the terrine and cook gently in a bain-marie in the oven at 180 C (350 F, gas 4) for 1½ hours. Before it gets completely cold, cover with port-flavoured aspic jelly. Chill for 1 or 2 days.

LAMBS' SWEETBREADS

All the recipes given for cooking calves' sweetbreads are suitable for lambs' sweetbreads and the garnishes are the same. However, here are two original recipes.

Lambs' sweetbreads with mushroom purée RIS D'AGNEAU AU COULIS DE CHAMPIGNONS (from a recipe by Gérard Vié) Blanch some lambs' sweetbreads in boiling salted water for 5 minutes, then refresh, drain, and skin them. Wipe some horn-of-plenty mushrooms thoroughly, sauté them in oil, drain them, and purée them in a food processor or blender with some hot Banyuls wine, salt, pepper, and a little butter. Sauté the sweetbreads for 5 minutes and serve them surrounded by the mushroom purée.

Morels stuffed with lambs' sweetbreads MORILLES FARCIES AU RIS D'AGNEAU (from a recipe by M. E. Tabourdiau) For 6 people, use 500 g (18 oz) medium-sized morels. Wash and drain them thoroughly. Cut half the stalk from each morel, chop them, and use to prepare a duxelles; set aside. Blanch 400 g (14 oz) lambs' sweetbreads and braise them in port as for veal sweetbreads, adding some herbs. Chop them and add the duxelles, a pinch of chopped chervil, and 1 tablespoon braising stock. Bind the stuffing with an egg yolk, put into a forcing (pastry) bag, and fill the morels. Season the morels and sauté them in butter. Arrange them in a casserole and add the reduced juices in which they were cooked, together with a little port and the braising stock from the sweetbreads. Cover the casserole, seal it with a flour-and-water paste, and cook in a bain-marie in the oven for about 20 minutes.

sweeten ADOUCIR

To reduce the sharpness, tartness, bitterness, sourness, acidity, or excessive seasoning in a dish by adding to it a little water, milk, fresh cream, sugar, etc., or by prolonging the cooking time considerably. A pinch of sugar will sweeten crushed tomatoes, and the acidity of a sauce may be lessened by boiling up the wine that is added to the meat juices in the pan.

sweetener ÉDULCORANT

A chemical substance with a high sweetening power but no nutritional value and containing no calories. The best-known is saccharine. Sweeteners are used in the food industry and in sugar-free diets.

sweet lime LIME

A small citrus fruit that is often confused with other varieties, but which constitutes a separate species. It is spherical, 2.5–4 cm (1–1½ in) in diameter, greenish-yellow, strongly scented, and produces a large quantity of acid juice. It is used for making sharp-tasting sauces in exotic cookery, notably Brazilian duck with rice, Peruvian ceviche, Indian saffron rice, Tunisian dried vegetable soup, and also certain oriental salads, stews, and grilled (broiled) fish dishes. Its grated rind is an ingredient in certain chutneys, and lime syrup is sprinkled on some pastries.

sweet pepper

See *capsicum*.

sweet potato

PATATE DOUCE

An edible tuber originating in South America and brought to Africa by the Portuguese. It has a reddish, violet, or grey skin and a sweet and floury flesh, orange-yellow, pink, or violet in colour, which is always eaten cooked, as a vegetable, a garnish, or as the basis for a dessert. With a fairly high calorific value (110 Cal per 100 g), the sweet potato is rich in chlorine, potassium, and vitamins B and C.

When bought it should be really firm, without bruises and without smell. It is prepared like the potato but is much sweeter. Sweet potatoes may be baked, puréed, cooked in their skins, in cream, as croquettes, in gratins, and in souffleés. Caribbean cookery offers the most original recipes for them. There are several varieties of sweet potato: the 'Virginia', with yellow flesh, and the pink Malaga variety are the most delicious; the latter can be used to make a delicate jam. The young leaves of the plants are prepared like spinach.

| RECIPES

Sweet-potato cake GÂTEAU DE PA-TATES DOUCES Soak 150 g (5 oz, 1 cup) seeded raisins in some rum. Boil 5 unpeeled sweet potatoes in unsalted water. When they are cooked, peel them and purée finely in a blender. Blend 1 teaspoon vanilla-flavoured sugar and 1 tablespoon flour with the potato purée and beat the mixture hard. Soften with a little milk, then add 3 whole eggs, one by one, and finally 1 egg yolk. Whisk 1 egg white into stiff peaks and blend it with the purée to produce a smooth light mixture. Add the raisins and pour the mixture into a buttered charlotte mould. Place the mould in a bain-marie, bring it to the boil, then cook in the oven at 200 C (400 F, gas 6) for about 40 minutes. Turn out onto a wire rack, leave to cool, and serve with a custard cream.

Sweet potatoes à l'impériale PATATES À L'IMPÉRIALE Place equal quantities of sliced sweet potatoes, sliced dessert apples, and thinly sliced bananas in a well-buttered gratin dish. Mix everything together well, add salt, and sprinkle with paprika. Scatter the surface with tiny fragments of butter and cook in a cool oven until tender.

This gratin is served as an accompaniment for meat, roast poultry, or game; it may be coated with redcurrant jelly.

sweets (candies)

BONBONS

Items of confectionery based on sugar. The French word *bonbon* dates from 1604, but sweets were made before the introduction of sugar into Europe, using fruit, honey, or grain, flavoured with cinnamon. The true sweet appeared from the 12th and 13th century onwards when sugar cane was brought back from the Orient by the crusaders. Catalogues of recipes from this period quote *gingembraz*, *pomidilon*, and *diadragam*. Almond and fruit pastes, apple sugar, jams, marzipan, and pignolat were specialities in the 14th century. *Épices de chambre* ('chamber spices'), coated in sugar and sucked at the end of a meal to aid digestion, were also widely consumed. Although the sweet was still considered to be basically an apothecary's product, it was also regarded as a luxury food, packaged in decorative boxes and offered as a gift to kings and queens. Sugared almonds and pralines date from the Renaissance, when the fashion for sweets was upheld by François I and Henri IV. The confectioners' shops of Paris in the 17th and 18th centuries became the meeting places of the bourgeois rich. Marrons glacés, pastilles, twists, crystallized (candied) fruits, and lollipops were sold in abundance. Liqueur-filled sweets also appeared at this time. A professional monogram published in 1887 notes: 'Sweets include honey pastilles, surprise boxes, whistling snakes, sugar pipes, chocolate swans, and liquorice sticks, in other words, all those sweet things designed to ensure the peace and tranquillity of nannies and parents.'

The first sweet factories were opened towards the end of the 19th century, and today the manufacture of sweets is a large branch of the confectionery industry. The Americans are the largest producers of sweets, but average consumption is highest in Great Britain. The most important manufacturing centres in France are the north, the Paris area, the Lyon area, the Drôme, and the Clermont-Ferrand area. Traditional sweets continue to be made, with crystallized fruits from Vaucluse, nougat from Montélimar, sugared almonds from eastern France, fruit pastes from Dauphiné, etc. The principal raw materials used in the manufacture of sweets are sucrose, glucose syrup, milk (full cream or skimmed), gum arabic, almonds and hazelnuts, vegetable fat, fruit, honey, and butter. Artificial flavouring, acidulation, and colouring are also permitted. Boiled sweets are the most popular of the confectionery products that are currently manufactured. These are followed by chewing gum, chews, caramels, toffees, crystallized fruits, fruit jellies, sugared almonds, pastilles, gums, and liquorice.

☐ **Boiled-sugar sweets** The standard method of manufacture consists of heating a mixture of sucrose and glucose that is then flavoured and coloured. This is then cooled, and either shaped to make solid sweets or moulded for filled sweets.

Solid sweets, such as acid drops, caramels, barley sugars, lollipops, humbugs, etc., are shaped between two cylinders, set in pill-shaped moulds (round sweets), or in a press. Rocks are sweets with relief patterns of flowers, fruits, etc.

Filled sweets consist of an outside mould with a creamy or liquid centre. The filling may consist of fruit pulp, praline, coffee cream, liqueurs, honey, etc.

Other boiled sweets include layered sweets (alternating layers of boiled sugar and praline), sugar twists, and *miel des Vosges* (honey-flavoured diamond-shaped sweets), etc.

The flavour is a very important aspect of the quality of a sweet and accuracy is essential in this respect: a sweet with a 'pure fruit' centre contains only the pulp of the fruit indicated. If it is simply a fruit centre, it contains the pulp of several fruits and natural flavouring. If it has a 'fruit flavoured' filling, then this is a syrup containing natural or concentrated flavouring.

The mean annual consumption of sweets is approximately 3 kg (6½ lb) per head in France.

swimming crab ÉTRILLE

A small brown crab with paddle-shaped back legs that is particularly common on the shores of the Atlantic and the English Channel. It is covered with short stiff hairs and measures about 10 cm (4 in) across. When cooked in court-bouillon, the flesh is full of flavour, though difficult to remove from the shell. It is also used to enhance the flavour of a bisque or a coulis.

Swiss chard BETTE

A variety of beet whose leaves are eaten as a vegetable. Swiss chard is also known as spinach beet. The leaves, which have broad tender midribs, have a slightly less pronounced flavour than spinach and are prepared in the same way. Except for curled Swiss chard with red stalks, which has a rather mediocre taste, the different varieties of Swiss chard are all of good quality. The most common summer variety in France is *bette blonde à carde blanche* (cultivated particularly in the Lyon region), with light green leaves; *bette verte frisée à carde blanche* (also much appreciated in Switzerland) is also sold in autumn. Green Swiss chard, with dark green leaves, is available all year round except in summer.

Although Swiss chard contains less iron than spinach, it has tonic qualities. It often appears in local and regional French dishes (especially in the Lyon region and Corsica): tarts, stuffings, and soups using the green leaves, and gratin dishes and garnishes using the stalks. Swiss chard tart is a speciality of Nice and is served as a dessert.

RECIPES

Preparation of Swiss chard PRÉPARA-TION DES BETTES Remove the green parts of the leaves, then break the veins and leafstalks (it is important not to cut them with a knife) and remove the stringy parts. Divide into sections 6–8 cm (2–3 in) long. Cook in salted water or, better still, in a white vegetable stock. Once drained, these sections are ready for use in all kinds of dishes. Wash the green parts, blanch for 5 minutes in boiling water, salted or unsalted, rinse in cold water, drain, and pat dry.

Swiss chard au gratin BETTES AU GRATIN Prepare Swiss chard in béchamel sauce and pour into an ovenproof dish. Smooth the surface, sprinkle with grated cheese and melted butter, and brown at the hottest possible temperature in the oven or under the grill (broiler).

Swiss chard in gravy BETTES AU JUS Cook 750 g (2 lb) Swiss chard in a court-bouillon and drain. Place in a deep frying pan (skillet) with 3 dl (½ pint, 1¼ cups) brown veal stock, cover, and simmer for at least 10 minutes. Transfer the chard to a vegetable dish. Add 80 g (3 oz, ⅓ cup) butter to the gravy and pour it over the chard.

Swiss chard tourte TOURTE AUX FEUILLES DE BETTE Marinate 100 g (4 oz, ¾ cup) raisins in brandy. Make the pastry using 500 g (18 oz, 14½ cups) flour, a pinch of salt, 60 g (2 oz, 4 tablespoons) sugar, 1 sachet easy-blend dried yeast (1 envelope dry yeast), 1 egg yolk, and 2 dl (7 fl oz, ¾ cup) oil. Mix the dough, adding a few teaspoons very cold water, and leave to stand.

Blanch 500 g (18 oz) Swiss chard leaves in salted water, dry very thoroughly, and chop roughly. Peel 2 cook-ing apples, slice thinly, and sprinkle with lemon juice; cut 2 dried figs into quarters; crumble 1 macaroon. Mix these ingredients (including the chopped leaves) with the raisins, 2 whole eggs, a little grated lemon zest, and approximately 40 g (1½ oz) pine kernels (nuts).

Grease an ovenproof flan dish, 27 cm (8 in) in diameter. Line with half the pastry, spread the filling over, and coat with 3 tablespoons (4 tablespoons redcurrant jelly. Cover with the remaining pastry and pinch the edges to join the two halves. Place a small pastry funnel in the lid. Bake at 200–210 C (400 F, gas 6) for 30–40 minutes. Dust with icing (confectioners') sugar and serve hot or cold.

Swiss wines

VINS DE SUISSE

According to recent figures, the area under vines in Switzerland is about 14,000 hectares, which yield approximately 1 million hectolitres. Of these two-thirds are white wines and one-third red. Vineyards are very much divided, the average size of a holding being between one and three hectares.

Rather oddly, it is the Chasselas that is the chief variety cultivated – one usually regarded as a table grape, but no grapes are grown for the table in Switzerland. The altitude (500 m and above) and latitude (46–47° N) mean that Swiss vineyards are at the very edge of the region where the wine vine may be grown, and therefore the procedures of deacidification and chaptalization are legally undertaken in many areas.

On 1 January 1980 a new law came into force, relating to the declassification of wines; it is opposite to the AOC in France, which restricts the amount from a specified area, declassifying any excess produced. The Swiss law declassifies wines which, subsequent to the vintage, have not attained the requisite degrees Oechsle that have been determined for both the year and the particular region.

The most important wine regions are in the Suisse Romande: Valais, Vaud, Geneva, and Neuchâtel; there is a plantation in the Tessin and the remainder of the vines are cultivated mainly along the upper Rhine Valley.

☐ **White wines** The Chasselas makes wines distinguished by their flowery light bouquet, displaying marked regional characteristics. This grape makes the Fendant of the Valais, the Dorin of the Vaud, the Perland of Geneva, and the white Neuchâtel; it is also known as Gutedel in German Switzerland. Other grape varieties include Sylvaner, which makes the Johannisberg and the Riesling-Sylvaner (also known as the Müller-Thurgau). In addition, there is the white Marsanne (which makes the Ermitage of the Valais), the Pinot Gris (called Malvoisie in the Valais), the Chardonnay, Traminer, Riesling, Muscat, Pinot Blanc, and the Aligoté. The few indigenous Valais grapes, which now produce very little (which is no great loss), include the Amigne, Arvine, Petite Arvine, and Humagne (black as well as white). The 'Glacier wine' of the Anniviers Valley, in former times made from the native Rèze grape, is more often made from the Fendant. In the highest vineyard in Europe, in the Haut Valais at Visperterminen, a wine is made from the Pagan (Païen) grape, called Heida in German, which in fact is a type of Traminer.

☐ **Red wines** These are made from the Pinot Noir (Blauburgunder or Clevner in German regions), the Gamay, and (in the Tessin) the Merlot. The Pinot Noir is sometimes made as a rosé wine, called Oeil de Perdrix (Partridge Eye). The Pinot Noir and Gamay are often combined and sold in the Vaud as 'Pinot-Gamay'. A specific quality label is 'Salvagnin'. In the Valais, Dôle is made either from the same mix, with the Pinot predominating, or from straight Pinot. Goron wine, on the contrary, is lighter in alcohol than Dôle and contains more Gamay than Pinot, possibly even being wholly Gamay.

The Grisons region is principally under Pinot Noir, of which some are of fine quality – notably Maienfeld. The Tessin, where 98% black grapes are cultivated, is increasingly planting Merlot, which gives a popular wine, capable of improving in bottle. The label 'VITI' is bestowed on about 40% of the wines, made from Merlot.

In general, the Swiss white wines are of superior quality to the reds, which often make only a small amount. The best-known whites come from the cantons of the Valais and Vaud, the best Fendants of the Valais being those of Sion, Uvrier, Montibeux, Molignon, and others. Vaud makes the various types of Dorin (from the Chasselas) which, after official approval, may be labelled as 'Terravin', from the vineyards along the slopes of Lake Geneva. From Coppet to Lausanne, the viticultural area is known as La Côte and accounts for 50% of the vineyards of the canton, with six delimited regions: Féchy, Mont-sur-Rolle, Tartegnin, Vinzel, Luins, and Coteaux de Vincy. Lavaux is the wine region from Lausanne to Montreux, the most famous wine being Dézaley, especially that coming from the Lausanne area; Lavaux is made up of six parishes: Lutry, Villette, Épesses, Saint-Saphorin, Chardonne, and Vevey. From Montreux up to the frontier of the Valais Chablais wine is produced from the parishes of Bex, Ollon, Aigle, Yvorne, and Villeneuve. There are also vineyards in the north of the Vaud: Côtes de l'Orbe and Rives Vadoises, from both Lake Neuchâtel and from Vully.

Switzerland SUISSE

Swiss cookery reflects the multinational origins of the country. The French-speaking cantons are familiar with the dishes of the Jura and Savoy; the German-speaking cantons share the German and Austrian traditions; while the cookery of Tessin is related to that of northern Italy. The Grisons have a relatively original cuisine, and central Switzerland boasts a number of ancient sweet-and-sour recipes. The common feature of all these regions is the charcuterie: an assortment of sausages of all types (especially smoked), salted or cured meats, and bacon, which are used to garnish sauerkraut or Swiss potée – national dishes on a par with cheese fondue and raclette.

Switzerland produces some 150 cheeses, some of which are solely for local consumption. Among the best-known hard cheeses are Gruyère, Emmental, Sbrinz, and cheeses *à rebibes* (for scraping into fine shavings); semi-hard ones include Tilsit, Vacherin de Fribourg, Appenzell, and raclette cheeses; while the Mont d'Or Vacherin is outstanding among the soft varieties. Just as famous as Swiss cheese is Swiss chocolate, and the chocolate industry deserves its reputation for producing a vast range of fine bars, particularly of milk chocolate.

There is no typically Swiss cuisine, but each of the cantons has its own culinary traditions.

The pâtisserie of Basle is distinguished by the spicy leckerli and the *brünsli* (little Christmas biscuits (cookies) made with almonds, hazelnuts, and chocolate). Bern is famous for its *Bernerplatte*, an assortment of meats and charcuterie (served with sauerkraut in winter and French beans in summer), and also for its rösti; among Bernese pastries and confectionery are leckerli made with hazelnuts, honey, and cinnamon, meringues (said to have been invented by a pastrycook from Meiringen), and a plaited loaf eaten throughout the country. Specialities of Fribourg include Vacherin fondue served warm with potatoes, chalet soup (made of vegetables, wild herbs, pasta, cheese, milk, cream, and butter), and *cuchaule* (a brioche spiced with saffron).

Geneva is the home of longeole (fresh sausage made from pork meat and rinds), *attriaux* (small sausages of pig's liver with herbs), cardoons with bone marrow or *au gratin*, and fillets of perch, fried or meunière. Veal boudin blanc (served with creamed potatoes, prunes, and an onion sauce) and pear bread are specialities of Glarus. The Grisons are well known for their cured meat (salt beef dried in the open air, then pressed), *capuns* (stuffed Swiss chard), ragout of mutton with potatoes (very like Irish stew), and the famous walnut tart of the Engadine.

In the Swiss Jura the feast of St Martin of Ajoie in November is the occasion for a meal that includes *grelatte* (aspic of pig's trotters (feet), tail, head, and ears, with knuckle of ham) and a meat and leek pie. The area can also boast wild trout, mushroom stews, an unusual ragout of mutton with milk, *floutes* made of potatoes moistened with noisette butter, and all kinds of tarts.

In Lucerne people enjoy *chügelipastete* (a timbale of rice and veal) and a dish of fried potatoes, dried pears, and bacon. At Neuchâtel boiled tripe (served with vinaigrette, mayonnaise, and pickles), duck in red wine, and a soup of lake fish are cooked. At Schaffhouse a famous onion tart and a delicious sausage roll are produced; the traditional dish at Schwyz is a cheese soup, simmered with stale bread and stock; and at Soleure the inhabitants feast on roast beef which has been marinated in red wine and vinegar. Saint-Gall produces its famous veal sausages (roasted and served with onions) and smoked pork sausages.

The Tessin has the atmosphere of northern Italy, with its tripe soup, *minestrone ticinese* (with vegetables and white haricot (navy) beans), osso bucco, ravioli, and *torta di pane* (a cake with a base of stale bread). Specialities of the Valais are raclette and a tart containing potatoes, leeks, bacon, and cheese; this region also preserves the traditions of the *sil* (a dessert, formerly served at weddings, consisting of crumbled rye bread sprinkled with red wine, then heated with elder syrup, raisins, and fresh cream until thick) and Cardinal Schiner's stew (made with roast beef, knuckle, oxtail, quails, partridges, and vegetables, served with a sauce thickened with breadcrumbs).

The canton of Vaud possesses a multitude of specialities, including *papet* (leek stew thickened with mashed potatoes), sausages with cabbage or liver, Payerne smoked sausage, the *pote de la Broye* (pig's snout stuffed with a tenderloin and then braised), as well as *malakoffs* (cheese puffs) and cakes containing white or red wine. Zoug is noted for its small salmon trout, prepared *au bleu* or meunière, and its Kirsch-flavoured tarts. Zurich is famous for its *Geschnetzeltes* (thinly sliced veal served with a sauce made by deglazing the par with white wine and cream) and its kebabs of calf's liver and bacon flavoured with sage. Finally, mention should be made of the apple tart of Thurgau, in which the fruit is cut in half and pressed into the surface of a raised dough, and the *stunggis* of Unterwald, a traditional stew made with pork, garden vegetables, and potatoes.

The high reputation of hotels and restaurants in Switzerland has been firmly established for well over a century, but recently there has been a marked increase in those specializing in regional and French dishes. The latter are exemplified by Freddy Girardet of Crissier-Lausanne, creator of a range of simple and elaborate dishes, which include ramekins of Belon oysters poached in sherry and served with celery fritters, lobster ragout with creamed Brussels sprouts, and bitter-chocolate meringues.

swordfish ESPADON

A very large food and game fish, 2–5 m (6–16 ft) long and weighing 100–500 kg (225–1250 lb), that is abundant in all warm seas. It has an elongated upper jaw resembling a sword. Its flesh is considered to be excellent and is similar to that of tuna. It may be eaten fresh, frozen, or canned.

sybarite

A person devoted to luxurious and voluptuous living, after the fashion of the inhabitants of Sybaris, a city in the ancient Greek colony in Italy famous for its wealth and luxury, situated in a region which corresponds to present-day Calabria. Founded in about 720 BC and made rich by trade, Sybaris experienced a prosperity which became proverbial until it was destroyed in the 6th century BC. Smindrydes, the richest of the Sybarites, owned 1000 slaves, fishermen, bird-catchers, and cooks.

syllabub

A dessert made of whipped cream, white wine to which sherry or brandy may be added, lemon, and sugar. The dish is of English origin and goes back to the time of Elizabeth I.

Sylvaner

A white-wine grape cultivated in many countries, including Germany, Austria, Chile, California, and the north of Italy. In Alsace it makes a light pleasant wine that, depending on the producer and the vineyard, can attain considerable quality.

symposium

In ancient Greece, a symposium was a continuation of dinner, during which it was customary to serve wine accompanied by fresh and dried fruit, cheeses, salted cakes, or even preserved cicadas, which provoked a thirst and therefore maintained the desire to drink – the word is derived from the Greek *sumposion* (banquet), from *sun* (with) and *potein* (to drink). Women, with the exception of slaves, dancing girls, and courtesans, were excluded from the symposium, which could provide the opportunity for philosophical discussion, as in Plato's *Symposium*. More often, however, it was an occasion for musical pageants and dancing, acrobatic, and similar displays: the symposiasts, who arrived at the end of the dinner, joined the diners in drinking goblets of wine.

The symposium traditionally began with a libation from the master of the house, who opened the session by striking up a 'symposiacal paean', a hymn in the honour of Dionysius. A 'symposiarch' was appointed to decide the number of goblets to be drunk, the quantity of wine they would contain, and the proportion of water to wine (Greek wine, at the time, was very thick and highly alcoholic). The servants drew the wine from the bowl, prepared the mixtures, and served them to the guests in goblets (*cyathae*). It was customary to dilute the wine more as the night progressed. In Xenophon's *Symposium*, Socrates expresses a wise precept regarding this: 'If the servants cause a fine and frequent rain to fall into our small goblets of wine . . . we shall not reach a state of drunkenness under the influence of alcohol, but its sweet persuasion will lead to more gaiety.' The tradition of the symposium continued into Roman times, but often degenerated into a drinking bout.

syringe SERINGUE

A small hollow metal or plastic cylinder with a plunger, a handle, and a threaded tip to which various nozzles can be attached. The rigidity of the syringe makes it more manageable than a piping (pastry) bag, but its capacity is limited. It is used for decorating cakes and pastries.

The basting syringe, which is made of plastic and has a bulb at one end, is for sucking up cooking fat to baste a roasting joint. Unfortunately, it sucks up all the juices, not just the fat, and this is not conducive to a good roast, which should be basted with the fat only, leaving the juices moist in the tin for making a good gravy.

Other syringes are used in charcuterie to inject brine into salted meat.

syrup   SIROP

A concentrated solution of sugar in water, which can be used hot or cold in the preparation of jams and ices with syrup and for many operations in pâtisserie and confectionery (soaking babas and savarins, dipping biscuits, working fondant, etc.).

Syrups flavoured with fruit or other flavourings can be diluted with water to make a refreshing drink. Fruit syrups are usually based on red fruit (strawberry, raspberry, blackcurrant), to the juice of which sugar is added (1.8 kg (4 lb) cube sugar to the juice of 1 kg (2¼ lb) fruit in 1.5 litres (2¾ pints, 3½ pints) water); they are cooked on full heat until they reach 32 c (90 f) on a sugar thermometer, then cooled and bottled. Some syrups are a mixture of a sugar syrup and an essence or concentrate (mint, grenadine, aniseed, orange, or lemon). These are diluted in a proportion of five to eight with a flat or effervescent water, lemonade (diabolo), or milk. They are also used in many cocktails.

Syrups were formerly more popular as refreshments than they are today: violets and roses were used, in addition to fruits. The word has the same origin as *sorbet*, from Arabic *charab* (drink).

Tabasco

An American sauce, popular in cookery the world over, that consists of chilli peppers marinated in spirit vinegar with salt. Sold in small bottles, this condiment is used to season (among other foods) meat, egg and red kidney bean dishes, sauces, and a number of cocktails.

tabbouleh   TABBOULÉ

A Lebanese speciality made of bulgur (crushed wheat) mixed with aromatic herbs, tomatoes, onion, mint, and sometimes sweet pepper and lemon. Served as a cold entrée, it is traditionally wrapped in cos (romaine) lettuce leaves and eaten with the hands.

RECIPE

Tabbouleh   TABBOULÉ   Pour into a salad bowl 250 g (9 oz) bulgur wheat (or use wheat semolina instead). Moisten with ½ litre (17 fl oz, 2 cups) boiling water, adding it gradually so as to moisten but not soak the grains. Leave to stand for a few minutes. Add 500 g (18 oz) finely diced juicy tomatoes with their juice, 250 g (9 oz, 2¼ cups) finely chopped onions, 2 tablespoons (3 tablespoons) chopped fresh mint, and the same amount of parsley. Season with salt and pepper. Moisten with 6 tablespoons (4 fl oz, ½ cup) olive oil (or sesame oil) and the juice of 3 lemons, thoroughly mixing all the ingredients. Leave in a cool place for 2–3 hours, stirring occasionally to aerate the ingredients and complete the mixing process. Just before serving, garnish with 8 peeled spring onions (scallions) and leaves of fresh mint.

tabil

A mixture of spices in Arab cookery, consisting of three parts fresh (or dried) coriander to one part caraway (fresh or dried), crushed with garlic and red pepper. Tabil is dried in the sun, finely ground, and stored in a dry place. In particular, it is used to spice semolina dishes, mutton ragout, and purée of broad beans (fava beans) in oil. It is also used to season vinaigrette for crayfish cooked in court-bouillon and as a sauce to accompany snails – two dishes enjoyed by Arabs.

table

A piece of furniture on which food is served. In a wider sense, the word also refers to the meal itself, while the French *tablée* means a group of people having a meal around a table.

table **1263**

□ **Tableware over three centuries** At the beginning of the 17th century, the usefulness of items still took precedence over their decorativeness. The conventional plate had a wide raised rim and in France was called a 'cardinal's hat'; the fork, which was still rare, had only two prongs. The drinking glass was beginning to replace the metal goblet, although pewter ewers were very common. Also to be found was the metal cup for tisane, a very popular drink, with a lid to keep the drink hot. The flat candlesticks were also made of pewter.

The beginning of the 18th century saw the introduction of more elaborate silverware. Forks and spoons were adorned with architectural motifs; forks had four prongs, but the knives still did not match the forks and spoons. The plate evolved into its modern shape and the drinking glass came into general use. The flat candlestick became a sconce. New items appeared, such as the sugar sprinkler, the egg cup, and the salt cellar.

The Regency and the reign of Louis XV were the heyday of silverware. Decoration became more complex, with mouldings and borders. Fork, spoon, and knife formed a matching set. The sconce became a candelabrum with several branches. The broth bowl on its stand appeared, soon followed by the soup plate. Glasses became more and more delicate. The fashion for coffee and drinking chocolate gave rise to the coffee pot and sets of coffee cups. The '*oille* pot' was used to serve soups and ragouts of game.

From the time of Louis XVI to the First Empire, neoclassical decoration replaced the rococo style. The heavy silver or pewter plate gave way to porcelain and the newly invented silver- or gold-plated metal (*pomponne*). Industrial processes influenced shapes: for example, glasses were moulded rather than blown. More new objects appeared, including oil and vinegar cruets, sauceboats, and pepper pots. Sideboards had more shelves to accommodate all the silverware, glasses, and other items.

It was under Napoleon III that the decorative craze reached its peak. Styles were at their most ornate and heaviest; the electroplating process provided an infinite number of pieces at widely varying prices. On the same table Empire plates, rococo cutlery, a Renaissance pitcher, and Venetian glassware could be found clustered around enormous and elaborate centrepieces.

At the end of the 19th century, a reaction began: craftsmanship reasserted itself and many older styles disappeared. The revolution in the arts at the beginning of the 20th century inspired such designers as the Art Nouveau exponent Van de Velde (1900) and Puiforcat (1920s) and led to the appearance of the Tiffany and Scandinavian styles.

□ **Table decoration** More than 20 years ago, *New Larousse Gastronomique* offered the following advice: 'Table decorations should not in any way impede the service or make it difficult to speak to or see one another. The fashion for complicated "pâtisserie" decorations, candelabra, or monumental flower arrangements went out long ago; nowadays, one or two low baskets or glass bowls of flowers make an elegant and practical decoration. Centrepieces, such as mirrors with Japanese gardens arranged on them or statuettes made of Sèvres porcelain, are suitable for formal occasions. *Chemins de fleurs* in little crystal jardinières, arranged end to end, make a charming border of roses, violets, or nasturtiums. Also attractive are sprays of autumn leaves on the tablecloth. Bowls or baskets of fruit can replace floral decorations. Low fruit dishes, plates, or baskets with handles that are easy to hold are preferable to symmetrical pyramidal arrangements on high dishes. Fruit should be arranged without too much fuss, interspersed, if necessary, with clusters of leaves, and should please the eye as well as the appetite. . . . Dishes, silver, and glass must be spotlessly clean. A thick felt padding should be placed under the tablecloth. The fork should be placed on the left-hand side of the plate, the spoon and knife on the right; the cutting edge of the latter should be turned inwards towards the plate. Glasses for water, wine, Madeira, and champagne are arranged either in a group or in a line, in order of size. Carafes of water and *vin ordinaire* are grouped along the table alternately with the salt cellars and pepper pots.'

Nowadays, the tendency is towards simplification. Whereas formerly the fork had to be placed prongs down on the tablecloth, so that the figure engraved on the back of the handle was visible, the tendency in restaurants nowadays is to spare the tablecloth, placing the fork prongs uppermost, as is the custom in Britain and the United States. Also, it is better to make do with two glasses, one for water and one for wine, the latter being changed when a different wine is poured.

table d'hôte

Formerly, a large communal table at an inn at which people sat as and when they arrived and where everyone could be served meals that were prepared throughout the day. A communal table d'hôte was also the rule in boarding houses, where meals were served at a set time. They still exist in provincial areas, in certain hotels for commercial travellers. In Paris, in a few restaurants with regular customers, they are again becoming fashionable. When the inn was superseded by the restaurant, customers were served at separate tables.

At the end of the 18th century, Sébastien Mercier gave this description: 'Tables d'hôte are intolerable for outsiders, but they have no choice. They have to take a knife and fork and go and eat in the midst of a dozen strangers. Those who are polite and shy do not manage to get enough to eat for their money. The centre of the table, near what are called the *pièces de résistance*, is occupied by the regular customers, who seize these important seats. . . . Equipped with tireless jaws, they devour the food without ceremony. Unhappy are those who are slow eaters.'

Originally, when restaurateurs were permitted to invite customers into their dining room, table d'hôte meant that the owner allowed the customer to sit 'at his own table' to eat the cooked dishes he had purchased on the premises, instead of taking them home.

table etiquette and manners

SAVOIR-VIVRE ET ETIQUETTE DE LA TABLE

A set of rules which govern the serving and eating of a meal; the strictness with which they are adhered to depends on the degree of formality of the meal, lunch generally being rather less formal than dinner. Brillat-Savarin said: 'To invite someone to one's table is to assume responsibility for his happiness during the time he is under your roof.' The guest's enjoyment will be increased if a tasteful arrangement of the table and a flawless service are added to the good quality of the food.

□ **Etiquette through the centuries** With the Greeks, etiquette required that shoes were exchanged for light sandals before entering the dining room. The best place was given to the stranger and it was customary to offer him, before the meal, a bath or a foot wash. Roman diners, who used to eat reclining and crowned with flowers, changed not only their shoes but also their clothes, putting on a woollen tunic provided for this purpose. It was essential to make the first step into the *triclinium* with the right foot. The dishes were presented first to the master of the house, accompanied by music, by a servant executing a dance step.

Under the Merovingian kings an elaborate ceremony, inspired by the Byzantine court, was introduced and honorific duties were created, such as that of the *mapparius*, who presented a tablecloth to the monarch. With Charlemagne the ceremonial became even more complicated: the emperor was seated on the highest chair, while dukes, chiefs, and kings of other nations passed him the dishes to the sound of fifes and oboes. These lesser ranks did not eat themselves until the imperial meal was finished; they were served in their turn by counts, prefects, and dignitaries, who did not themselves dine until after this second service, and so on (the people of the lowest ranks usually had to make do with leftovers, towards the middle of the night). From feudal times, the king usually dined alone and it was a rare honour to be admitted to his table.

The table of François I was magnificent but the preoccupation with eating well, strengthened by the arrival of the Florentine cooks, took precedence over formal presentation. Henri III, on the other hand, reintroduced a strict etiquette and his enemies accused him of multiplying the 'idolatrous bows' not only to himself but also to his personal belongings.

When Louis XIV dined *au grand couvert* he ate alone but in public, and the courtiers were allowed to watch him eat while each victualling officer carried out his duties according to a complicated ceremonial. At the *petit couvert*, in intimate surroundings, the etiquette was relaxed and the Duc de Luynes relates that the king threw little balls of bread to the ladies and allowed them to throw them at him. The *grand couvert* was maintained under Louis XV (who aroused admiration through the skill with which he cut the top off a boiled egg with a single stroke of the fork) and under Louis XVI. Marie-Antoinette, anxious to withdraw from the obligation of eating in public, appeared only once a week at this meal, which, according to Arthur Young, 'had more peculiarity than magnificence'. Before the 17th century it was the custom to keep a hat on one's head while eating. Under the Empire and until the end of the monarchy, etiquette imposed strict rules.

□ **Rules when eating** Table manners have developed through the ages and vary in every country. The Gauls used to eat sitting down, and the Romans lying down, while the Japanese traditionally squat on their heels at the table. The French are taught to keep their hands over the table throughout the meal, whereas English etiquette requires that they should be placed in the lap when not actually eating. Belching, regarded as the grossest indelicacy in western countries, was a sign of politeness in ancient Rome and still is in the Middle East.

One of the first collections of the rules of etiquette was compiled by Robert de Blois, since the rules of chivalry extended to good table manners. His advice was always to have clean hands and fingernails, not to eat bread before the first course, not to take the largest pieces of food, not to pick one's teeth or scratch oneself with one's knife, not to talk with one's mouth full, and not to laugh too loudly. Washing one's hands before and after the meal was a compulsory ritual, for which servants would bring a copper basin full of perfumed water and a towel. When we realize that there were no forks at that time, that a bowl and goblet were shared by several guests, and that meals could last for hours, these precautions were not negligible.

Erasmus wrote a *Treatise on Manners* in 1526, in which he advised his readers to wash their hands and clean their fingernails before going to the table. We also read: 'Starting a meal by drinking is for drunkards: one begins to drink only with the second course, after the soup, and first one must wipe one's lips with one's handkerchief. It is coarse to put your fingers in your soup, and it is unseemly to put chewed items back on your plate. It is absolutely not done to throw your bones under the table or to lick your plate.'

An important turning point came at the beginning of the 17th century, when the Italian influence on French society as a whole was reflected in the refinement of both table manners and the vocabulary of the menu. *Soupe* became *potage* and the *plat de chair* became a *plat de viande*. This concern for refinement became affectation in the next century, with the *petits soupers*, *médianoche*, and *ambigu* (new French names for snacks taken at various times of the day). Nevertheless, advice on good manners was still plentiful: in 1765 Antoine Le Courtin wrote a *Traité de civilité*, in which he prohibits 'lapping like an animal', while La Bruyère, in his *Caractères*, describes what one does not do at table by depicting Gnathon the guzzler, 'for whom the table is a hay rack'. After the French Revolution, treatises multiplied, although manners were still sometimes slow to develop. It was not until the middle of the 19th century that people stopped eating chicken with their fingers and stopped mixing the salad with their hands, and that table cutlery in a well-to-do house began to include leg-of-mutton and cutlet holders.

□ **The placing of guests** Today, table arrangement and the places allotted to guests are still subject to a number of rules. Guests sitting at the same table face each other, whereas formerly they used to sit at tables arranged in a U-shape so that everyone looked towards the centre.

Except at very formal meals, where the guests enter the dining room in couples, women enter the dining room first. When there are up to eight guests, the mistress of the house shows each one where to sit. Above that number, it is a good idea to provide small cards. For a party meal, a table plan must be prepared. (The number 13 should be avoided, out of consideration for the superstitious.) The subtleties of French etiquette sometimes present problems of precedence (whereas in England, Burke's *Peerage* makes provision for all cases).

In France, apart from the official protocol of the Ministry of Foreign Affairs, there are only general rules, which are sometimes contradictory when, for example, there are diplomats, clergy, and members of the aristocracy at the same table. It is customary to honour the guest who is invited for the first time by placing him on the right hand of the mistress of the house (if it is a lady who is invited, on the right hand of the master of the house), but this rule is modified according to the age or the merits of the other guests. The traditional order is as follows: members of the clergy, foreign diplomats, French diplomats, politicians, representatives of the army. But a foreign prince comes before a cardinal. Here is an example of precedence: bishop, canon, prefect or subprefect, deputy, mayor, president of the tribunal, public prosecutor, chairman of the chamber of commerce, etc. Title generally takes precedence over age, but among guests of equal rank age comes first.

It is sometimes a good idea to set two or more tables, naming for each a table chairman. The right hand of the table chairman becomes a place of honour, although that of the mistress of the house remains the most honoured. In the United States and in Britain, it is customary for the master of the house to place himself at the end of the table, in order to leave the best places for the guests, a custom sometimes practised in France. The mistress of the house may preside with her chosen guest opposite her or, in the case of a royal guest, let the guest preside in her place.

In ancient times the place of honour was on the left of the master of the house, on the side of the heart. In the Middle Ages the table hierarchy was much less precise, but the master of the house honoured his guest by having a choice morsel brought to him, inviting him to cut off a piece of meat, or drinking to his health (see *toast*). In China, the place of honour is situated opposite the door of the dining room, and if possible, facing south. Precedence is determined by age, degree of relationship, and social rank, rarely by sex.

☐ **Rules for guests** All meals to which guests are invited are social occasions which require mutual deference and courtesy. Guests must not arrive before the indicated time, but custom dictates that a guest should not keep his host waiting for more than a quarter of an hour.

When the guests are taken into the dining room, they should remain standing until the lady of the house is seated; it is she who, when each course is served, gives the signal to take the first mouthful. It is also she who rises first from the table when the meal is over.

At lunch, ladies wearing hats may keep them on (a custom which crossed from England to France at the beginning of the century).

Nothing is touched with the fingers except bread, which is broken up into pieces and never cut with a knife, and a few occasional foods (artichokes and certain seafoods), which are usually reserved for intimate gatherings.

The cutlery should be handled without any noise, and the knife should never be put in the mouth. When a dish is offered to him, the guest should serve himself with moderation, taking the portion closest to him without ostensible selection. At intimate gatherings, the dish is placed in the middle of the table.

It is the custom to wait a little before beginning to drink. The master of the house will pour (or order the pouring of) the first few drops of each bottle of wine into his own glass, in case it is corked. Wine glasses are filled only two-thirds full, to bring out the flavour of the wine.

When a course is over, the guest should leave his cutlery on his plate, side by side (never crossed). The person who clears the table should remove the plates one by one, without stacking them up. Clean cutlery must be used after shellfish and fish.

In certain countries it is polite for the guest to leave a little food on his plate to indicate that he has had enough to eat. In France, however, it is good manners to clear one's plate as a compliment to the quality of the food, but one should not mop up sauce with bread (in 1950 a sauce spoon was introduced at the Restaurant Lapérouse, for diners to spoon up their sauce).

The fingerbowl usually appears on the table with the fruit course, but sometimes also after a platter of seafood or artichokes. The guests should dip their fingers into it discreetly.

To smoke during the meal is extremely bad manners and ashtrays should never be placed on the table. Smoking is, however, customary in English-speaking countries, but only if the lady of the house gives her express permission and preferably not before the cheese.

☐ **The rules of etiquette**

● *Soup* – The soup should be sipped from the side of the spoon. Any sucking noises should be avoided. In France, the bowl is never tilted to spoon up the last mouthfuls though it is acceptable to tilt it away from the eater in England and many other countries.

● *Boiled eggs* – In France the top should be removed with the spoon and the egg should never be taken out of the egg cup. Once empty, the shell should be crushed. In England the top may be cut off (never peeled) and the shell left intact.

● *Asparagus* – The tips are cut off with a fork and the rest is left, unless the lady of the house invites the guests to use their fingers. It is however acceptable these days to eat the whole thing in the fingers, leaving any woody stalk on the side of the plate afterwards.

● *Artichokes* – These are eaten leaf by leaf, the leaves being detached with the fingers. However, at formal meals only the hearts are served, garnished or stuffed.

● *Salad* – This is sometimes served in a small individual dish to the left of the diner. Salad is never cut with a knife as, in theory, it is prepared so that the leaves can be eaten in small mouthfuls.

● *Melon* – This is generally eaten with a spoon but certain gourmets recommend using a fork, or a knife and fork.

● *Cheese* – It is preferable to serve cheese already cut, in order not to embarrass the guests, who would hesitate to start a new cheese. Rectangular cheeses are cut lengthwise in even strips, round cheeses (like Camembert) are cut along the radius into small wedges, Brie-shaped cheeses are usually served in a wedge and are cut 'on the cross', i.e. diagonally, ensuring that not only crust is left for the next diner. In France, cheese is eaten in small pieces, placed with the knife on a fragment of bread (never use your fork or eat the cheese from the tip of your knife). Lastly, the cheeseboard is never offered a second time (to take a second helping would indicate that you had not had enough to eat). This custom is, of course, deplored by certain cheese-lovers.

● *Fruit* – This is peeled with a small knife with a silver blade, while being held with a fork (not the fingers). If you only require half a large fruit (at an intimate gathering) you should leave the part with the stalk attached (and the stone, if any) in the bowl.

● *Coffee and liqueurs* – These are served in the drawing room, not at the dining-room table. The lady of the house should never be complimented on the success of the meal, as this could possibly imply that one is surprised that it was good. But at informal meals with close friends compliments are acceptable.

Whatever blunders he may commit, the guest is always treated with respect: the ultimate courtesy, on the part of the host or hostess, consists of voluntarily committing the same mistake as the guest, to show that it is quite all right.

table napkin SERVIETTE

An individual piece of linen which is used to protect the clothing or wipe the mouth during a meal. On a set table the napkins are folded, sometimes with a bread roll inside, and placed on the plate. The guests spread the unfolded napkins on their laps and place the roll at the right of their plate. Decorative folding is sometimes used in restaurants. It is good manners to wipe the mouth before drinking and whenever a trace of sauce or other food remains on the lips. Tying the napkin around the neck is regarded as inelegant, unless the dish consists of shrimps or seafood which require peeling.

The Romans used a *sudarium* (cloth) to mop the forehead and face while slaves brought round basins of water for washing. The use of napkins was not widespread at the beginning of the Middle Ages, although tablecloths did exist. Guests wiped their hands and mouths on the cloth or on the *longuière*, a band of linen running along the edge of the table for this purpose. Around the 13th century *touailles* came into use: these were cloths hung on the wall for guests to use as required; they were also used to cover the remains of the food. This led to individual napkins of cotton or linen, sometimes embroidered, which were worn on the shoulder or over the left arm. With the fashion for ruffs during the reign of Henri III it became acceptable to tie the napkin around the neck.

In catering the maître d'hôtel traditionally carries a folded napkin on his left arm as a mark of office, as do waiters. The Serviette au cou, a gastronomic society, was founded in Paris in 1934 by Paul Colombier; it had a monthly dinner, served at a precise time, at which there was no place of honour and tying the napkin round the neck was compulsory!

It is customary to arrange certain dishes on white napkins instead of dish papers or doilies: a 'gondola' for a whole fish served on a long dish, for example, or a folded napkin for hot toast or a bombe.

table setting
SERVICE DE TABLE

The linen, crockery, and cutlery laid out for a meal. Everything should coordinate – matching tablecloth and napkins, all the crockery of same design, or at least toning, and matching sets of wine glasses. A few flowers, not strongly scented, may be arranged in small clusters or in a single flower bowl. The tablecloth, white or of an unobtrusive pattern, is placed on a table felt, to deaden the sound; table mats placed directly on the table are suitable for less formal meals. Each guest must have sufficient room (about 60 cm, 2 ft). The places are laid symmetrically: fork on the left of the plate, soupspoon and main knife on the right, together with the fish knife or oyster fork (if required); the knife rest, which is tending to disappear, should not be used for a formal dinner. According to the number of wines, several glasses (not more than three), of decreasing size, are placed in front of the plate. The napkin, folded in the simplest possible manner, is put on the plate and may contain a bread roll in a fold. Salt cellars and carafes are placed at either end of the table, or possibly in the centre if the table is round. The wine, uncorked in advance, remains in its original bottle, but clarets may be decanted into a carafe; fresh water is also provided in a carafe.

The setting can also include several pieces designed to be used together for a particular dish. An asparagus set comprises a cradle or draining dish, in which the boiled asparagus is placed, and tongs or a scoop for serving. A fondue set has a heater, a pan, long-handled forks, and sometimes dishes with compartments for various sauces. A cake set has a serving plate (round or long), a cake slice, matching plates, and cake forks. A fish set has a long plate, sometimes a sauceboat, and fish knives and forks. A cheese set has a cheeseboard, small plates, and a cheese knife. The strawberry set, with its drainer, small plates, and scoop, and the snail set, with its dimpled plates and pincers, should also be mentioned. Finally, there is the carving set, a large knife and fork (sometimes with a holder) used to cut joints of meat, poultry, or game at the table. As for drinks: a liqueur or port set consists of small glasses and a decanter. A tea or coffee service comprises cups and saucers of the appropriate size, small spoons, a teapot or coffeepot, a sugar basin, and a milk jug, sometimes on a tray. The *tête-à-tête* is a tea, coffee, or breakfast service for two people.

table song
CHANSON DE TABLE

The custom of singing at table at the end of a meal arose from the natural tendency of the guests to express their satisfaction. According to Ecclesiastes: 'There is nothing under the sun better for man than to eat, drink, and be merry. Go, therefore, eat your bread with joy and drink your wine with cheer.' Greek and Roman banquets usually ended with great spectacles, and in the Middle Ages all feasts were punctuated by interludes of song or mime, but the table song, or rather, the drinking song, began in the 15th century with Olivier Basselin, creator of the *vau de vire*, from which the term vaudeville is derived.

The custom was at its peak at the time of the Empire and the Restoration. E. Briffault notes in *Paris à table* (1846): 'Under the Empire, part of the old freedom of the past returned: people used to sing at table during dessert, sometimes drinking songs, most often fashionable ballads; there were also verses to celebrate festivals and weddings. It was then that singing dinners were formed, dinners for bachelors, dinners for friends, dinners for corporations, etc.' As early as 1804, Grimod de La Reynière complained of patriotic songs ('true signs of carnage') sung during the Revolution and rejoiced in the return of drinking songs and love songs, symbols of ('healthy French gaiety') composed by Désaugiers, Pannard, Collé, Favart, and others. Practising what he preached, he published drinking and eating songs in the successive editions of his *Almanach des gourmands*.

The tradition of singing during dessert has been upheld to the present day, but is now regarded as a rather vulgar habit. As early as 1830, Henri Monnier ridicules it through the character of Monsieur Prudhomme, singing at table being a sign of the lower middle classes. Songs are hardly ever sung now except at weddings, or banquets for old comrades, or at meals to celebrate a first communion.

tablier de sapeur

A speciality of Lyon, made of pieces of tripe cut from the so-called 'honeycomb', dipped in beaten egg, and covered with breadcrumbs. They are then fried or grilled (broiled), and served piping hot with snail butter, gribiche sauce, or tartare sauce. The name means literally 'sapper's apron', and according to Christian Guy, the dish was named by the maréchal de Castellane, the military governor of Lyon under Napoleon III and a former sapper (engineer), whose uniform included a leather apron. Another explanation is that in the traditional Lyon puppet theatre, the cobbler character, Gnafron, the regular companion of Guignol, always used to wear a wide leather apron (which explains the apron, but not the sapper).

RECIPE

Tablier de sapeur (from a recipe by Léa Bidaut) For 4 servings, rinse a scalded ox stomach (tripe) in cold water, place it in a large saucepan or cooking pot, cover with water, bring to the boil, and add 2 onions, 2 carrots, 2 leeks, 3 sticks (stalks) of celery, 2 turnips, salt, and pepper. Simmer for 4 hours and allow to cool in the court-bouillon. Drain, then marinate for 3 hours in a little white wine (Pouilly-Fuissé) seasoned with lemon juice, a few drops of oil, strong mustard, salt, and pepper.

Spread out the ox stomach on a board and cut it up into large triangles with sides about 12 cm (5 in) long. Dry them and dip them in a mixture of 2 beaten eggs, salt, pepper, 1 tablespoon oil, and a little cold water. Drain the triangles and coat them with finely crushed dried breadcrumbs; press hard to make the breadcrumbs stick and shake to remove the excess. Without delay, gently heat 2 tablespoons (3 tablespoons) oil in a frying pan (skillet) and put in the triangles. They must be cooked gently, without browning, otherwise they will become hard.

Finely chop some shallots and reduce in white wine until soft. Blend with butter and chopped tarragon. While still hot, mix this shallot cream with mayonnaise and serve with the tripe.

The tripe trimmings obtained when cutting out the triangles can be cut into strips, sautéed with finely sliced onions (already lightly browned in oil), seasoned with salt and pepper, and moistened with a dash of vinegar when the cooking process is over. The result is tripe lyonnais.

taco

In Mexican cookery, a cornmeal pancake (tortilla) filled with a thick sauce, or minced (ground) meat seasoned with chilli pepper, or black beans, or avocado purée with onion. When filled, the pancake is rolled and eaten straight away or fried gently. Tacos are a popular snack or hot entrée.

tafia

Originally, the name given to rum by the natives of the French West Indies. The word is now used to mean a second-rate form of the spirit.

tagliatelle

Italian egg pasta in the form of flat ribbons, 6 mm (¼ in) wide and golden or green in colour (green tagliatelle contains spinach). They are a speciality of Emilia-Romagna, where, according to legend, their invention was inspired by a nobleman's love for the hair of Lucrezia Borgia. They are usually served with a meat sauce (beef, pork, and smoked ham minced (ground) with carrots, celery, onion, herbs, nutmeg, and fresh cream). Tagliatelle literally means 'small cut-up things'. In Italy, there are variant forms: *taglierini*, which are narrower (3 mm, ⅛ in); and *tagliolini*, which are shorter. *Fettucine* is a wider ribbon pasta.

Tahiti

An island in the Windward group of the Society Islands in the South Pacific. Natural and simple, Polynesian cookery makes use of abundant fish and fruit, particularly breadfruit, which is roasted, boiled, grilled (broiled), ground, or reduced to a paste (notably in *popoï*, a basic foodstuff to which meat or fish is added). The great speciality of Tahiti is raw fish: diced, steeped in lime juice, sprinkled with chopped onion and crushed garlic, and seasoned with salt and pepper, it is served sprinkled with coconut milk. The latter, extracted from the pulp of grated coconut, constitutes a very popular drink, either fresh or fermented. As in the West Indies, shark is used in cooking, as are shrimps and land crabs.

Taro, yam, spinach, and salad crops all grow in abundance. So do pineapple and banana. Tahitians also enjoy roast wild birds, duck, and a type of small wild boar, which is roasted on hot stones to provide the feast dish, *ahi moha*. Pork chops are cooked in the oven between layers of young spinach shoots and banana leaves, sprinkled with chopped garlic and finely sliced onion. Again, this dish is sprinkled with coconut milk.

Coconut pulp is also used to make various desserts (creams, jams, meringues). Papaw purée mixed with arrowroot, cooked like a cream and flavoured with vanilla, is a popular dessert, as in *poe meia*, a banana dessert served sprinkled with sugar and topped with fresh cream.

tahitienne (à la)

A term for raw fillets of fish (gilt-head bream, monkfish, grouper, or turbot) cut into thin strips or small dice, marinated for several hours in lemon juice and oil with salt and pepper, then served with deseeded tomato quarters or tomato pulp and sprinkled with grated coconut. Fish *à la tahitienne* can also be included in a mixed salad along with avocado, grapefruit quarters, and a chiffonnade of lettuce and tomatoes, all seasoned with lemon mayonnaise.

tail   QUEUE

The caudal appendix of an animal, classed as a cheap cut of meat.

The most widely used is oxtail, which makes many delicious dishes, notably oxtail soup (see *oxtail*).

Lamb's or sheep's tail is not often used, although it can be boiled and then grilled (broiled), or braised with curry.

Pig's tail can be cooked in the same way as pig's trotters (boned and stuffed, braised, or boiled, coated with breadcrumbs, and grilled; it can also be pickled in brine).

The tail of prawns, scampi, crayfish, and similar crustaceans is often the only edible portion after shelling.

Taillevent (*born* Guillaume Tirel)

French cook (born Pont-Audemer, c. 1310; died Pont-Audemer, c. 1395), author of *Le Viandier*, one of the oldest cookery books written in French. Four manuscripts were discovered by Baron Jérôme Pichon, who, assisted by Gabriel Vicaire, published the book in 1892 and included some information about the author's life and career.

The name Guillaume Tirel is found in a manuscript dated 1326 describing the coronation of Jeanne d'Évreux – the young Tirel was in the service of the latter as a kitchen boy. In 1346 he entered the service of Philippe de Valois (who later gave him a house in Saint-Germain-en-Laye), then he joined the household of the Dauphin, as squire, becoming cook in 1355. He subsequently held the same position in the households of the Duke of Normandy (1359–61) and of Charles V (1368–73). Finally, in 1381, he entered the service of Charles VI, who ennobled him and under whom, in 1392, he was elevated to master of the king's kitchen provisions, the crowning title of his career. Guillaume Tirel, known as Taillevent (or Taillevant), a nickname apparently inspired by the length of his nose, was buried in the priory of Notre-Dame, in Hennebont.

It is thought that *Le Viandier*, the first professional cookery treatise written in France, predates 1380. It was commissioned by Charles V, who was anxious to have the specialists of his time write about various 'learned' subjects. For expertise concerning cookery, Taillevent was an obvious choice – at the pinnacle of his career and in charge of the royal kitchens. The full title of the work (translated into English) is: 'Hereafter follows the Viandier describing the preparation of all manner of foods, as cooked by Taillevent, the cook of our noble king, and also the dressing and preparation of boiled meat, roasts, sea and freshwater fish, sauces, spices, and other suitable and necessary things as described hereafter.' The word *viande* in the original French means all foodstuffs, not simply meat, and one of the most interesting features of the work is that it details the foodstuffs eaten in the 14th century: some of the more unusual meats include *connins* (rabbits), wild boars, plovers, swans, peacocks, storks, herons, bustards, cormorants, and turtledoves. Lamprey, loach, eel, pike, carp, and other freshwater fish were common, whereas sea fish were less numerous (conger-eel, dogfish, mackerel, sole, herring, cod, turbot, sturgeon, mussels, and oysters, not forgetting whales). Green vegetables were uncommon, but spices, eggs, milk, and cheeses were all important.

Numerous copies of the *Le Viandier* circulated among noblemen and chefs before the printing press popularized this 'dispensatory'. The author of *Le Ménagier de Paris* (1393) quoted extensively from it, and Villon mentions it in his *Testament*: 'See Taillevent – the chapter on fricassees.' First printed around 1490 and enlarged with notes, new recipes and banquet menus. *Le Viandier* was published several times up to the beginning of the 18th century. Its predecessors included *Traité où l'on enseigne à appareiller et à assaisonner toutes viandes* (1306) and *Le Grand Cuisinier de toute cuisine*, which appeared anonymously in 1350, but *Le Viandier* provides a complete synthesis of all aspects of cookery in the 14th century. Its influence was felt until the advent of the Florentine chefs under Catherine de' Medici, and the publication of the *Le Cuisinier français* by La Varenne in 1651, which introduced a new conception of culinary art. The main contribution of *Le Viandier* lies in its emphasis on spicy sauces (predominantly saffron, ginger, pepper, and cinnamon), soups, and ragouts, which included the preparation not only of meat, poultry, and game, but also fish. Also noteworthy is the common use of verjuice and also of liaisons with toasted breadcrumbs. Another aspect of 'gothic' cookery was the popularity of sweet-and-sour dishes throughout Europe: German gruel with almonds, onion, and larding bacon; rice with milk and fatty bouillon; pies of meat with raisins and sugar; eels with prunes; goose with apples and cinnamon; and not forgetting hippocras and wines flavoured with honey or herbs. The principal cooking methods were roasting and boiling. Stuffed dishes and pies and flans based on minced (ground) meat were numerous. Furthermore, cookery often had to conform to the strictures of the Church, and considerable attention was given to the cookery of the days of abstinence (in Lent, for example).

The cookery of Taillevent is often depicted as a series of heavy complex, and overspiced dishes. Nevertheless, the recipes in the *Le Viandier* also include simpler preparations, for example aigo boulido from Provence, tourin from Périgord, bouilleture of eels, saupiquet, hotchpotch, Pézenas pâtés, Pithiviers gâteau with frangipane, and pears in wine. Some of the recipes can be prepared quite easily today, almost without changing anything: cretonnée of new peas, almond blancmange, watercress soup, and Bourbonnais tart, for instance.

Moreover, today's nouvelle cuisine has drawn on Taillevent, updating such old dishes as salmon pâté with sorrel, civet of hot oysters, and fresh ham with leek.

tajine

A deep glazed-earthenware dish with a conical lid that fits flush with the rim. It is used throughout North Africa for preparing and serving a range of dishes that are cooked slowly in a flavoured basting liquid; these preparations themselves are also called tajines and are made with vegetables (potatoes, courgettes (zucchini), etc.), fish, chicken (with quinces or dates), meat (mutton with prunes, veal with tomatoes and aubergines (eggplants), etc.), and even fruit.

RECIPES

Tajine of carrots TAJINE DE CAR-OTTES Put 1 kg (2¼ lb) sliced carrots into a tajine or saucepan. Add 5 tablespoons (6 tablespoons) olive oil then add 450 g (1 lb) finely sliced onions, a bouquet of coriander, the same amount of parsley, 2 chopped cloves of garlic, 1 teaspoon ginger, a pinch each of cumin, paprika, and saffron powder, 2 turns of the pepper mill, and a large pinch of salt. Mix together, put on the lid, and cook over a very low heat for 1½ hours (using a heat diffuser). Just before serving, add 150 g (5 oz, 1 cup) black (ripe) olives and sprinkle with lemon juice.

Tajine of mutton with prunes and honey TAJINE DE MOUTON AUX PRUNEAUX ET AU MIEL (from *Les*

Meilleures Recettes de cuisine dans les ustensiles en terre by Aglae Gaussen; Robert Morel, 1980) In a tajine (or saucepan) put 1 kg (2¼ lb) mutton cut into pieces, 5 tablespoons (6 tablespoons) olive oil, a pinch of salt, 1 finely sliced onion, a pinch of ginger, a bouquet of coriander, a pinch of saffron powder, and 1 cinnamon stick. Cover with water, put the lid on, and simmer over a very low heat for 2 hours (using a heat diffuser). When the meat is cooked, take off the lid and allow the sauce to reduce and thicken. Remove the coriander, meat, and cinnamon. Add 450 g (1 lb, 2½ cups) prunes to the sauce and cook for 20 minutes. Then pour in 5 tablespoons (6 tablespoons) honey and simmer for a further 10 minutes. In a frying pan (skillet) brown 1 tablespoon sesame seeds. Return the meat to the tajine along with 1 teaspoon orange-flower water. Replace the lid, reheat, and serve very hot. Just before serving, sprinkle with the fried sesame seeds.

Taleggio

An Italian cows'-milk cheese (48% fat); pressed, uncooked, and white or creamy yellow, it has a soft texture and a washed thin pale-pink rind. The fruity taste is accompanied by a pronounced smell. Originally from Taleggio (a province of Bergamo), it is now made throughout Lombardy and is sold as slabs, 20 cm (8 in) square by 5 cm (2 in) thick, in silver paper. Benefiting from an AOC, it is best between June and November.

talibur

A pastry from Picardy, consisting of an apple, peeled, hollowed out, and filled with sugar, which is cooked in a square of puff pastry or shortcrust pastry (basic pie dough) with the edges sealed with beaten eggs. Also called *rabotte* or *pomme en cage*, talibur is the equivalent of the Norman bourdelot, the galopin of the Orléans region, and the bourdaine of the Perche.

Talleyrand-Périgord (Charles Maurice de)

French statesman (born Paris, 1754; died Paris, 1838), who not only managed to retain high office and good fortune throughout the Revolution until the Restoration, but was also a celebrated host and connoisseur of good food, whose table was considered one of the finest in Europe. He employed the famous pastrycook Avice and the great chef Antonin Carême, whose fortune he made. He also stole from Cambacérès, his rival in gastronomy, a cook who invented for him snails *à la bourguignonne*, which Talleyrand made fashionable.

With his head cook Bouchée, who came from the Condé household, Talleyrand (for whom lunch was of little importance) devised some epoch-making dinners. His menu regularly consisted of two soup courses, two removes (including one of fish), four entrées, two roasts, four sweets, and dessert – a menu which became the rule for all the best tables. Talleyrand himself would carve the meat and poultry and he used to serve his guests according to their status. In his eyes, however, the culinary art was not simply a question of gastronomic pleasure; it was above all an invaluable aid in government and diplomacy. 'Sire, I have more need of saucepans than instructions,' he said to Louis XVIII as he left for the negotiations at the Congress of Vienna, and it was at the meal table that he secured great advantages for France.

In classic cuisine, Talleyrand's name is associated with numerous preparations: veal chops, calves' sweetbreads, tournedos, large pieces of beef or veal, and poultry – garnished with buttered macaroni flavoured with cheese and served with a julienne of truffles, diced foie gras, and Périgueux sauce. His name is also given to various other dishes, such as stuffed anchovy fillets rolled into paupiettes, a curried omelette filled with calves' sweetbreads, and semolina croquettes stuffed with a salpicon of poultry, pickled tongue, truffles, and mushrooms and covered with demi-glace sauce. Talleyrand sauce (chicken velouté sauce with Madeira, mirepoix, truffles, and pickled tongue) is used in the same way as Périgueux sauce (see *Sagan*.) Finally, a talleyrand is a savarin cake made with chopped pineapple, soaked in syrup, covered with apricot glaze, and decorated with pineapple pieces.

RECIPE

Anchovy fillets Talleyrand FILETS D'ANCHOIS TALLEYRAND Thoroughly desalt some anchovy fillets and trim them. Mask them with a purée of pickled tuna mixed with finely chopped truffles and bound with a little mayonnaise. Roll the fillets into paupiettes. Arrange each one on a thick slice of hard-boiled (hard-cooked) egg. Serve them on an hors-d'oeuvre dish, garnished with a chiffonnade of lettuce and slices of lemon and cooked beetroot (red beet). Sprinkle with vinaigrette.

Omelette Talleyrand Lightly fry in butter some onions, finely diced and seasoned with curry powder. Drain them. Beat some eggs, add the onions, and use to make a flat omelette; put to one side and keep warm. Dip some slices of calves' sweetbreads in egg and breadcrumbs and sauté in butter. Garnish the omelette with the sweetbreads and serve with cream sauce.

Talleyrand sauce SAUCE TALLEYRAND Prepare 2 dl (7 fl oz, ¾ cup) chicken velouté sauce and add 2 dl (7 fl oz, ¾ cup) white stock. Mix and reduce by half. Add 4 tablespoons (⅓ cup) fresh cream and ½ dl (3 tablespoons, scant ¼ cup) Madeira. Boil for a few moments. Remove from the heat and blend in 50 g (2 oz, 4 tablespoons) butter. Strain the sauce and add 1 tablespoon vegetable mirepoix, then the same amount of finely chopped truffles and pickled tongue.

talmouse

A small savoury pastry made with soft fresh cheese and dating back to the Middle Ages. The Saint-Denis talmouses, which used to be made for the Archbishop of Paris, are mentioned by François Villon and referred to by Balzac in *Un début dans la vie*: 'On entering Saint-Denis, Pierrotin stopped in front of the door of the innkeeper who sells the famous talmouses and where all travellers alight. . . . Georges bought them some talmouses and a glass of Alicante wine.' *Le Viandier* and *Le Ménagier de Paris* both give a recipe for them (at that time, the spelling was *talmous, talmose,* or *talemouse*): 'Made with fine cheeses, cut into squares as small as beans. A generous amount of eggs are added and it is all mixed together. The pastry case is coated with eggs and butter.'

In 1742, Menon recommended that the moulds used for making talmouses should be lined with puff-pastry in such a way that it hangs over the edge; the pastry cases should then be filled with cheese béchamel sauce, after which the corners of the pastry should be folded over to form a tricorn shape. *Le Cuisinier gascon* (18th century) advocates rolled-out puff-pastry bases, which are filled with soft cheese blended with eggs, then 'trussed, brushed, and cooked in the oven'. *Le Cuisinier des cuisiniers* (1882) gives the following variant: soufflé-fritter batter mixed with well-drained soft cheese, divided into small shapes, brushed, and puffed up in the oven. The name 'Saint-Denis talmouses' is also given to tartlets made of shortcrust pastry (basic pie dough) filled with a mixture of soft cheese, rindless Brie, whole eggs, and whisked egg whites.

As can be seen, recipes for talmouses have varied through the ages. Several kinds of talmouse are made today. The type known as a *pont-neuf* is a tartlet made of puff or lining pastry, filled with choux pastry mixed with thick cheese-flavoured béchamel sauce, with two thin strips of pastry forming a cross on top; it is brushed with egg and cooked in a hot oven. In the Bagration talmouse, the tartlet is filled with cheese-flavoured choux pastry; after cooking it is covered with cheese-flavoured béchamel sauce piped through a forcing (pastry) bag. For the talmouse marquise, the tartlet is masked with cheese-flavoured béchamel sauce, filled with choux pastry, then brushed and cooked. These talmouses are served piping hot with sprigs of parsley, as hors d'oeuvres.

Another variety, known as *talmouses en tricorne*, are based on an older recipe: they take the form of circles or squares of puff pastry, which are brushed with egg, filled with a thick béchamel sauce bound with egg yolks and flavoured with cheese, then shaped into tricorns or crowns by folding the corners inwards; they are cooked in a hot oven. Various ingredients may be added, including spinach purée and diced ham. These talmouses are again served as hot hors d'oeuvres.

There are also sweet talmouses made with frangipane: tartlets or barquettes of puff pastry are filled with a mixture of confectioners' custard (pastry cream) and frangipane cream, covered with granulated sugar or shredded (slivered) almonds, then cooked in a moderate oven and sprinkled with icing (confectioners') sugar.

The word *talmouse* may derive from the old French word for bakers, *talemeliers*, although it has been suggested that it is a combination of *taler* (to beat) and *mouse* (muzzle).

RECIPES

Bagration talmouses TALMOUSES BAGRATION Line some fluted tartlet tins with very fine lining pastry (see *doughs and batters*). Fill with cheese-flavoured choux pastry (see *chou*) and sprinkle with a little diced Gruyère cheese. Brush with egg. Cook in a moderately hot oven (190 C, 375 F, gas 5) for about 15 minutes. Serve piping hot. After cooking, the talmouses may be topped with a little cheese-flavoured béchamel sauce.

Talmouses à la Florentine These are prepared in the same way as talmouses *à l'ancienne*, but the cheese soufflé mixture is replaced by spinach soufflé mixture mixed with grated cheese.

Talmouses à l'ancienne Roll out some puff pastry to a thickness of 5 mm (¼ in) and cut it into 10-cm (4-in) squares. Brush with egg yolk and in the centre of each square place 1 large tablespoon cheese soufflé mixture, then on top sprinkle a little diced Gruyère cheese. Fold the corners of each square to the centre, keeping the filling in the middle. Put the talmouses on a buttered baking sheet and cook in a moderately hot oven (200 C, 400 F, gas 6) for 12 minutes. Serve piping hot.

tamal

An ancient Mexican dish in which highly spiced chopped meat (pork, turkey, or chicken) on a bed of ground corn mixed with lard is cooked in the husk of a corn cob, generally by steaming.

Tamals are served hot as an entrée. The forcemeat may also contain chopped olives or small fish.

tamarind TAMARIN

The fruit of a leguminous evergreen tree, which originated in west Africa but is now grown in the West Indies, India, tropical Africa, and southeast Asia. The brown pods, 10–15 cm (4–6 in) long and 2 cm (¾ in) wide, contain a bitter-sweet pulp dotted with a few hard seeds. Tamarinds are mostly used for preparing jams, sorbets, chutneys, drinks, and condiments. In India, the pulp of dried tamarind – a major ingredient in spice mixtures – is also used in salads, broths, and purées of dried vegetables. The juice of fresh tamarind is used to season crudités. In China, crystallized (candied) tamarind is used to garnish certain sweet-and-sour soups.

Tamié

A cows'-milk cheese from Savoy (40–45% fat), made by the Trappist monks of the monastery of Tamié. Pressed and uncooked, with a soft and elastic texture, Tamié has a washed smooth clear rind, a fairly pronounced lactic taste, and is made in the form of rounds, 18 cm (7 in) in diameter and 4–5 cm (1½–2 in) thick. Also called Trappiste de Tamié, it is served at the end of the meal or grilled (broiled) on croûtes.

tamponner

A French culinary term meaning to carefully place flecks of butter on the surface of a hot preparation, such as a sauce (especially béchamel) or a soup; as the butter melts it forms a thin film of grease over the sauce, which prevents a skin forming while it is kept hot.

tandoori TANDOURI

In Indian cookery, particularly in the Punjab and Pakistan, a method of cooking chicken or other meat. The pieces of chicken are skinned, then coated in yogurt mixed with chilli powder, turmeric, ginger, spices, onion, and chopped garlic. After marinating overnight, the chicken is sprinkled with saffron or chilli powder and cooked on a bed of embers in a special cylindrical clay oven called a *tandoor*, until the flesh is tender,

but the outside crispy. Tandoori chicken is served with salads: onions and tomatoes with tamarind juice and coriander; cucumber with yogurt and cumin; or grated cabbage with pepper and lemon juice. Fish and galettes can also be cooked in the *tandoor*.

tangelo

A citrus fruit produced by crossing a tangerine and a grapefruit. It can be peeled as easily as a tangerine. Irregular in shape, the tangelo (an American hybrid) is bigger and more acid than an orange, but it is used in the same way – as fresh fruit, for fruit salad, and for fruit juice.

tangerine MANDARINE

A citrus fruit resembling a small slightly flattened orange; it originated in China and is also called a mandarin. In France tangerines are available from January to April; the Moroccan variety Wilking, which appears rather late in the season, is particularly popular. Tangerines are very easy to peel and the pulp is sweet and fragrant, but contains many pips. Clementines (a variety developed in the 19th century), with thinner skins and no pips, are gradually replacing tangerines. Yielding 40 Cal per 100 g, the tangerine is rich in vitamin C and calcium. Usually eaten fresh for dessert, it can also be preserved and used in cooking and pâtisserie in the same way as orange; in sweet preparations its flavour can be enhanced with Kirsch or liqueur brandy. The peel is used to flavour liqueurs.

In France, the word *tangerine* is used for the hybrid produced by crossing an orange with a tangerine.

RECIPES

Frosted tangerines MANDARINES GIVRÉES Choose fine even-sized tangerines with thick skins. Cut off the tops and remove the segments without breaking the peel. Place the empty shells and tops in the freezer. Squeeze the pulp, strain the juice, and add 300 g (11 oz, 1⅓ cups) caster (superfine) sugar for every 500 ml (17 fl oz, 2 cups) juice. Dissolve the sugar completely in the juice. Add a little more juice if too thick or a little more sugar if too thin. Place in an ice-cream maker but stop the process before the ice sets. Fill the frosted shells with the iced pulp and cover each with its top. Return to the freezer to allow the ice to set.

Tangerine gâteau GÂTEAU À LA MANDARINE Crush 125 g (4½ oz, 1 cup) almonds in a mortar or grind in a food processor, and then add 4 eggs, one by one, 4 pieces finely chopped candied tangerine peel, 125 g (4½ oz, ⅔ cup) sugar, 3 drops of vanilla essence (or 1 teaspoon vanilla sugar), 2 drops of almond essence, and 2 tablespoons (3 tablespoons) sieved apricot jam. Mix well together.

Roll out 300 g (11 oz) flan pastry and line a flan tin (pie pan). Spread a layer of tangerine marmalade on the bottom and fill with the almond mixture. Carefully smooth the top. Cook in the oven at 200 C (400 F, gas 6) for about 25 minutes. Take the cake out of the oven and allow to cool. Sieve 3 tablespoons (scant ¼ cup) apricot jam and spread over the top of the cake. Decorate with flaked (slivered) almonds and place under the grill to colour the almonds. Store in a cool place until serving.

Tangerine syrup SOUPE DE MAN-DARINES (from René Lasserre's recipe) Remove the peel from 4 tangerines, cut it into julienne strips, and steep in a syrup made with 1 dl (6 tablespoons, scant ½ cup) water and 300 g (11 oz, 1⅓ cups) sugar. Add a sprig of fresh mint and allow to cool completely: leave the mint to infuse in the syrup for 2 hours. Carefully remove the white pith from the tangerine segments and cut them into small pieces. Remove the mint from the syrup and pour this onto the fruits. Put in a cool place until time to serve.

tannin TANIN

A substance contained in vegetable matter, such as tea, and oak or walnut bark, and also in the skin, pips, and stalks of grapes. In wine-making it dissolves in the alcohol and is one of the main constituents of red wine, responsible for its character and longevity. Tannin is particularly abundant in Bordeaux wines, which explains why they take so long to mature. Excess tannin makes wine astringent and leads to the formation of a deposit in the bottle.

tansy TANAISIE

A common European plant with tall stems and golden-yellow aromatic flowers. Its leaves have a bitter flavour and were included in the pharmacopoeias compiled by monks in the Middle Ages. They are still occasionally used for seasoning, particularly in northern Europe and Britain, in forcemeats, pies, marinades, courts-bouillons, and sometimes also pastries. In former times, a highly flavoured household liqueur was made with tansy. When Stanislas Leszczyński 'invented' the baba, he sprinkled it with tansy water.

tant-pour-tant

A mixture comprising equal proportions of caster (superfine) sugar and powdered almonds, used by professional pastrycooks and confectioners to make biscuit (cookie) batters, almond cream, petit-four bases, etc.

tapas

In Spain, an assortment of hors d'oeuvres or cocktail snacks, served to accompany Málaga, sherry, or Manzanilla. The custom of nibbling tapas while drinking apéritifs, particularly in the evening, is widespread in bars and restaurants. The word comes from *tapa* (lid), since it originally meant a slice of bread which was used to cover a glass of wine to protect it from flies.

Tapas can sometimes take the place of dinner because they are so varied and abundant; they may include cubes of ham garnished with sweet red pepper; white haricot (navy) beans with vinaigrette; squares of thick filled omelettes; seafood in sauce; sautéed kidneys; fried shrimps; black (ripe) olives in brine; tuna rissoles; cauliflower in vinaigrette; small eels fried with red pepper; squid *en su tinta* (in their ink); stuffed peppers; and even snails in a piquant sauce, pigs' trotters (feet) with tomato, or chicken fricassee with mushrooms. These tapas are served in small earthenware dishes, into which people dip using their fingers or cocktail sticks.

tapenade

A condiment from Provence, made with capers (from Toulon), desalted anchovies, and stoned black (pitted ripe) olives, pounded in a mortar and seasoned with olive oil, lemon juice, aromatics, and possibly a drop of marc brandy. Tapenade is sometimes augmented by small pieces of tuna, mustard, garlic, thyme, or bay leaf. It accompanies crudités (in particular, celery, fennel, and tomato), meat, or grilled (broiled) fish, is spread on slices of toast, and can garnish hard-boiled (hard-cooked) eggs (mixed with yolk).

The word is derived from the Provençal *tapeno* (caper).

RECIPE

Tapenade Desalt 100 g (4 oz) canned anchovies, peel 4 cloves of garlic, and stone (pit) 350 g (12 oz, 2 cups) black (ripe) olives. Blend, using a food processor, 100 g (4 oz) tuna in oil (drained), the anchovy fillets, 100 g (4 oz) capers, the juice of 1 lemon, the olives, and the garlic. Press the ingredients through a very fine strainer, then pound the purée in a mortar (or use a food processor), gradually adding ¼ litre (8 fl oz, 1 cup) olive oil and the juice of 1 large lemon. The finished tapenade should be thick and smooth.

tapinette

A speciality of the Orléanais, also known as *tarte au caillé* (curdled milk tart), consisting of a shortcrust pastry (basic pie dough) case filled with a precooked mixture of well-drained curd cheese, milk, and flour to which beaten eggs are added; it is then cooked in a hot oven.

tapioca

A starchy food extracted from the roots of the manioc plant, which is hydrated, cooked, then ground. Used mainly for thickening soups and broths and making milk puddings and other desserts, tapioca contains 360 Cal per 100 g. Highly digestible, it is low in mineral salt and vitamins. True tapioca (the word is derived from the Tupi-Guarani *typioca*) comes from Guyana, Brazil, and the West Indies.

RECIPES

Tapioca consommé CONSOMMÉ AU TAPIOCA Sprinkle 80–100 g (3–4 oz, about ½ cup) tapioca in 1.5 litres (2¾ pints, 7 cups) boiling consommé and cook for 10 minutes. Serve piping hot.

Tapioca dessert ENTREMETS AU TAPIOCA Boil ½ litre (17 fl oz, 2 cups) milk with a pinch of salt, 30 g (1 oz, 2 tablespoons) sugar, and 1 teaspoon vanilla sugar. Sprinkle in 80 g (3 oz, ½ cup) tapioca, stir, then add 2 beaten egg yolks. Continue mixing, then blend in 3 egg whites whisked to stiff peaks with 80 g (3 oz, ¾ cup) icing (confectioners') sugar. Serve thoroughly chilled.

Tapioca with milk TAPIOCA AU LAIT Boil 1 litre (1¾ pints, 4¼ cups) milk with a pinch of salt, 2 tablespoons (3 tablespoons) sugar, and, as desired, either a vanilla pod (bean) or ½ teaspoon orange-flower water. Sprinkle in 80–100 g (3–4 oz, about ½ cup) tapioca, mix, and cook for 10 minutes, stirring regularly. Remove the vanilla pod.

taramasalata TARAMA

A Greek speciality, traditionally served as one of the mezze dishes or as an hors d'oeuvre. It consists of a smooth creamy pink paste of fish roe (botargo) crushed with breadcrumbs soaked in milk, egg yolk, lemon juice, a little vinegar, salt, and pepper, then emulsified with olive oil.

taro

A perennial plant grown in tropical regions for its large starchy tuberous rhizomes, which have twice the calorific value of the potato. Taro originally came from India (where it is called *katchu*). It is known as *chou-chine* or *chou caraïbe* in Martinique, *malanga* in Cuba and Haiti, *songe* in Réunion, and *madère* in Guadeloupe. Up to 40 cm (16 in) long, the roots have a smooth skin and are variously coloured – white, purplish-blue, red, or yellowish, according to the variety. They are scrubbed and peeled, then used in the same way as the potato: boiled, fried, or cooked *au gratin*, etc. In China, balls of steamed taro are stuffed with meat then fried. In

Japan it is used in vegetable stews. In Haiti, the grated raw pulp is used to prepare acras. Taro is also used in sweet desserts.

tarragon ESTRAGON

An aromatic perennial plant originating in central Asia. Its name is derived, via the Arabic *tarkhūn*, from the Greek *drakontion* (a serpent-eating bird) – the herb was formerly reputed to cure snakebite.

The toothed green leaves have a fine delicate flavour, and are used to season salads, sauces, pickles, etc. They may be fresh or they may be preserved by drying or freezing. Russian tarragon is lighter in colour and more piquant, but does not have such a delicate taste.

RECIPES

Bottled tarragon CONSERVE D'ESTRAGON PAR ÉBULLITION Wash and dry young sprigs of fresh tarragon and press them down well in small bottles, which have been cleaned and dried. Cork the bottles, secure the corks with string, and place them either in a saucepan or a pressure cooker lined with paper. Separate the individual bottles with paper or cloth. Cover them with cold water and boil (for 40 minutes in a saucepan, 20 minutes in a pressure cooker). Cool, then drain and dry the bottles, and store in a cool dark place. Treated in this way, tarragon can be kept for a very long time without losing any of its aroma. It is used in the same way as fresh tarragon.

Dried tarragon CONSERVE D'ESTRAGON PAR SÉCHAGE Wash some very fresh sprigs of tarragon and wipe them thoroughly. Tie them into a bunch with some string and hang them up in a cool dry place. Wait until the tarragon has completely dried before storing it either in airtight tins or plastic food bags.

The microwave oven ensures ultra-rapid drying, which retains both the colour and the flavour of the herb. Place the washed tarragon sprigs on a sheet of absorbent paper and place in the microwave oven. Cook on full power for 1–5 minutes, depending on the quantity. Turn the leaves over, and repeat the operation if necessary. Remove the tarragon from the oven and wait for about 10 minutes before storing it either in airtight tins or small plastic bags.

The flavour of dried tarragon is more pronounced than that of fresh or bottled tarragon, so slightly less should be used.

Tarragon cream CRÈME D'ESTRAGON Boil 100 g (4 oz, 1 cup) fresh crushed tarragon leaves with 1.5 dl (¼ pint, ⅔ cup) dry white wine. When almost completely dry, add 3.5 dl (generous ½ pint, 1½ cups) thick béchamel sauce, season with salt and pepper, bring to the boil for a few seconds, and rub through a sieve. Reheat and add a little butter.

This purée is used as a filling for small vols-au-vent, barquettes, or canapés and also for stuffing certain vegetables such as artichoke hearts, mushrooms, etc.

Tarragon preserved by freezing CONSERVE D'ESTRAGON PAR CONGÉLATION Wash and wipe the freshest leaves and freeze in small freezer bags. The leaves may also be chopped and placed in ice trays with water. The ice cubes containing the herb can then be stored in the freezer. Frozen tarragon may be added directly to hot dishes without defrosting; alternatively it may be defrosted at room temperature.

Tarragon purée (*cold*) PURÉE D'ESTRAGON À FROID Blanch 100 g (4 oz, 1 cup) tarragon leaves and cool under running water. Wipe them and pound in a mortar (or use a blender) with the yolks of 6 hard-boiled (hard-cooked) eggs, 2 tablespoons (3 tablespoons) fresh butter, salt, and pepper.

Tarragon purée (*hot*) PURÉE D'ESTRAGON À CHAUD This is prepared in the same way as tarragon cream, but with a very reduced béchamel sauce. It can also be made by adding a purée of tarragon leaves (blanched, cooled under running water, drained, pounded in a mortar, and sieved) to twice its volume of mashed potatoes.

Tarragon sauce for poached fowl SAUCE À L'ESTRAGON POUR VOLAILLES POCHÉES Add a large handful of tarragon to the white stock in which the chicken was poached. Skim the fat from the stock, strain, reduce, and thicken with arrowroot (cornstarch). Add some freshly chopped tarragon just before serving.

Tarragon sauce for small cuts of meat SAUCE À L'ESTRAGON Sauté the meat in butter, then remove from the pan. Make a sauce from the pan juices by adding 1 dl (6 tablespoons, scant ½ cup) white wine, 1 tablespoon chopped tarragon leaves, and 2 dl (⅓ pint, scant cup) stock. Boil down by half, adjust the seasoning, and thicken with kneaded butter.

Tarragon sauce for soft-boiled *or* **poached eggs** SAUCE À L'ESTRAGON POUR OEUFS MOLLETS OU POCHÉS Coarsely chop 100 g (4 oz, 1 cup) washed and wiped tarragon leaves, add 1 dl (6 tablespoons, scant ½ cup) white wine, and boil down. Add 2 dl (7 fl oz, ¾ cup) demi-glace or thickened brown veal stock and boil for a few moments. Strain through a very fine sieve. Add 1 tablespoon fresh coarsely shredded tarragon just before serving.

Tarragona

Wine from one of the specific wine regions of Spain (DOC), which comes from Catalonia and vineyards south of Barcelona. Today it is not often seen outside Spain but in former times it was popular; the rather rich dessert Tarragonas were sometimes known as the 'poor man's port'. It is not always a fortified wine and dry versions are also made.

tart TARTE

A pastry case filled, before or after baking, with savoury or sweet ingredients. The words 'tart' (*tarte*) and 'flan' are often used interchangeably in Britain and France to designate a pastry filled with fruit, jam, custard, or some other filling. The American term most often used is open or single-crusted pie. Almost all such dishes are cooked and served in the United States in a pie dish, whereas in Britain and France a metal flan or pastry ring, placed on a metal baking sheet, is used.

Savoury tarts are served as hot en-

trées, and include flans, quiches, onion, tomato, or cheese tarts, pissaladière, flamiche, and goyère. Sweet tarts are usually filled with fruit or a flavoured cream; they are one of the commonest and most varied pastries.

To prepare a tart, a baking ring, pie dish, or tin is lined with suitable pastry – shortcrust (basic pie dough), puff, or sablé – and the filling is placed in it. If the fruit (particularly strawberries and raspberries) is to remain uncooked, the case is baked blind and filled after baking. When the case is to receive a liquid filling, it is half-baked, then filled. Tarts of the galette type (which can be rectangular or square) are baked directly on a baking sheet without a tin: these are filled with narrow strips of fruit and sprinkled with sugar.

Tarts baked with their filling are usually of shortcrust pastry or puff pastry. Those baked blind and filled afterwards are made with sablé or shortcrust pastry. Some puff-pastry tarts are baked blind as rectangles edged with puff-pastry strips; they are then usually filled with confectioners' custard (pastry cream) and poached fruit, then glazed. Other varieties include: upside-down tarts, modelled on the Tatin tart; tarts decorated with crisscrossed pastry strips, known in France as *alsaciennes* and including the Austrian Linzertorte; and *tartes à l'anglaise*, which are actually fruit pies cooked in a pie dish and covered with a pastry lid. Tart pastry may be enriched with ground almonds, cinnamon, etc., and the filling may be glazed with apricot or covered with meringue.

Since the Middle Ages there have been innumerable tart recipes from all parts of France. The *tarte bourbonnaise* cited in Taillevent's *Viandier* ('fine cheese mixed with cream and preserved plums' in a case 'moulded with eggs') is still a speciality of the Bourbonnais, now called *gouéron*. The tarts of Alsace are well-known for the variety of their fillings: strawberries, cherries, bilberries (blueberries), redcurrants, mirabelle plums, quetsches, rhubarb, etc. Everyday tarts are often made with ordinary pastry, whereas those for feast days are made of fine pastry. In northern and eastern France, fresh-cheese tarts are a traditional speciality; this tart is found in Corsica under the name of *imbrucciata*. A simple mixture of beaten eggs, sugar, milk, and cream is used as a filling for the *tarte au goumeau* of Franche-Comté and the *tarte en quemeu* of Chaumont. Confectioners' custard is used as a bed for fruit in some tarts (pears for the *tarte Bourdaloue*, cherries or plums in Alsace). In northern France and Switzerland rice or sugar tarts are made, similar to the Canadian maple syrup tarts. In western France, apples and pears are the most popular filling.

In Germany and Austria, tarts are called *Torte* (e.g. *Linzertorte*) or *Kuchen* (e.g. *Kirschenkuchen*, or cherry tart); they are frequently made with apples, cherries, plums, or mixed fruits and are often decorated with whipped cream. Also worth mentioning are the Russian *vatrouchka*, the American pecan pie, and the Swiss wine tart.

RECIPES

SAVOURY TARTS

Curd cheese tart TARTE AU FROMAGE BLANC Mix 500 g (18 oz) well-drained curd cheese with 5 tablespoons (6 tablespoons) flour, the same amount of fresh cream, 2 eggs, salt, and a very little pepper. Pour this mixture into an unbaked tart case (pie shell) made of shortcrust pastry (basic pie dough), sprinkle with knobs of butter, and bake in a moderately hot oven (200 C, 400 F, gas 6) for about 45 minutes. Serve cold.

Spinach tart TARTE AUX ÉPINARDS (from a recipe by Raymond Thuillier) Quickly blanch 1.5 kg (3¼ lb) young fresh spinach. Chop coarsely and blend with 40–50 g (1½–2 oz, 3–4 tablespoons) butter. Season with salt and pepper. Line a 20-cm (8-in) tart tin (preferably made of cast iron for more rapid and more even baking) with puff pastry rolled out to a thickness of 4–5 mm (¼ in). Fill it with the spinach. Take 4 anchovy fillets in oil, drain them, and lay them on top of the tart in a crisscross pattern. Sprinkle the tart with a few knobs of butter and bake in a hot oven for 20 minutes. The anchovy fillets may be replaced by fresh sardines cooked very rapidly in a frying pan (skillet) with a little olive oil.

Tomato tart TARTE À LA TOMATE (from a recipe by Renée Delaporte) Make some puff pastry, roll it out, and use it to line a greased flan tin; gently prick the bottom. Mix together 6 whole eggs, 1 dl (6 tablespoons, scant ½ cup) fresh cream, 30 g (1 oz, 2 tablespoons) butter, and 50 g (2 oz) grated Gruyère cheese. Add 1 kg (2¼ lb) tomatoes, peeled, deseeded, and crushed. Mix well and season with salt and pepper. Fill the tart with this mixture and bake in a moderate oven (180 C, 350 F, gas 4) for about 45 minutes.

SWEET TARTS

Alsace tart TARTE ALSACIENNE Beat 1 whole egg with 250 g (9 oz, generous 1 cup) caster (superfine) sugar, then add 125 g (4½ oz, generous ½ cup) melted butter. Work the mixture together. Gradually blend in 250 g (9 oz, 2 cups) sifted flour, then 250 g (9 oz, generous 2 cups) ground almonds. Knead thoroughly, adding 1–2 tablespoons water if the dough is difficult to work. Roll out three-quarters of the dough to form a circle 1 cm (½ in) thick; place this on a buttered baking sheet. Roll out the remaining dough very thinly and cut it into narrow strips. Surround the pastry circle with one of the strips and arrange the others crisscross fashion on the disc. Fill each compartment with a different sort of jam (strawberry, plum, or apricot, for example) and bake in a moderately hot oven (200 C, 400 F, gas 6) for 20 minutes. Serve lukewarm or cold.

Apple tart TARTE AUX POMMES RONDE In a food processor blend 250 g (9 oz, 2¼ cups) flour, 125 g (4½ oz, generous ½ cup) butter cut into pieces, and a large pinch of salt until the dough sticks to the sides of the bowl. Add ½ dl (3 tablespoons, scant ¼ cup) water (or a little more), and operate the food processor again until the dough begins to bind together. Quickly shape the dough into a ball, wrap it in aluminium foil, and refrigerate for 2 hours.

Peel and finely slice 750 g (1¾ lb) apples and sprinkle with lemon juice. Roll out the dough to a thickness of 3 mm (⅛ in) and use it to line a buttered and floured 26-cm (10-in) tart tin.

Arrange the slices of apple over the pastry base in concentric circles; sprinkle generously with granulated sugar and 60 g (2 oz, 4 tablespoons) melted butter. Bake in a hot oven (220 C, 425 F, gas 7) for about 30 minutes, until the apples caramelize slightly. Serve lukewarm, accompanied by fresh cream.

Cherry tart TARTE AUX CERISES Line a flan tin with shortcrust pastry (basic pie dough) and fill with ripe stoned (pitted) cherries. Whisk together 100 g (4 oz, ½ cup) caster (superfine) sugar and 2 whole eggs, then blend in 2 dl (7 fl oz, ¾ cup) milk and 50 g (2 oz, ½ cup) flour. Pour this cream over the cherries and bake the tart for about 30 minutes in a moderately hot oven (200 C, 400 F, gas 6).

Chocolate tart TARTE AU CHOCOLAT (from a recipe by Georges Blanc) Gently melt in a bain-marie 100 g (4 oz) plain chocolate and the same amount of butter. In a mixing bowl, blend 50 g (2 oz, ½ cup) flour, 100 g (4 oz, ½ cup) caster (superfine) sugar, and 3 eggs. Blend in the melted chocolate and work the mixture with a wooden spatula for 10 minutes. When the mixture is smooth and forms ribbons, pour it into a buttered tart tin and bake in a moderately hot oven (200 C, 400 F, gas 6) for 20 minutes. Turn out onto a rack and allow to cool. Melt 80 g (3 oz) bitter chocolate with 10 g (½ oz, 1 tablespoon) butter in a bain-marie. Add 80 g (3 oz) boiling whipping cream to obtain a smooth paste. Spread this cream over the top of the tart. Allow to harden slightly, then trace a chequered pattern with a knife and sprinkle with cocoa powder.

German goosebery tart (or Stachelbeer-kuchen) TARTE AUX GROSEILLES À MAQUEREAU À L'ALLEMANDE Clean some large ripe gooseberries. Prepare a puff-pastry tart base and bake blind. Mix the gooseberries in a saucepan with an equal weight of sugar cooked to the crack stage (see *sugar*): when the sugar has melted, drain the fruit and boil down the juice until it sets into a jelly. Put the gooseberries back into the syrup, boil together for a moment, then pour into a basin. When

cool, use it to fill the tart; mask with whipped cream.

Lemon tart TARTE AU CITRON (from a recipe by Dominique Nahmias) Make a tart case (shell) of shortcrust pastry (basic pie dough) and bake blind until the pastry is crisp but not completely cooked. Mix together 3 eggs, 100 g (4 oz, ½ cup) sugar, 80 g (3 oz) melted butter, the juice of 5 lemons, and their grated zest. Whisk and pour into the tart case. Bake in a very hot oven for 10–15 minutes.

This recipe can be made using 3 oranges or 7 tangerines instead of the lemons.

Pineapple tart TARTE À L'ANANAS Prepare some pastry with 150 g (5 oz, 1¼ cups) flour, 75 g (3 oz, 6 tablespoons) softened butter, a pinch of salt, and a little cold water. When it is pliable and well-mixed, roll it out and use it to line a 22-cm (8½-in) buttered flan tin; prick the base with a fork. Leave in a cool place for 2 hours, then bake blind in a moderately hot oven (200 C, 400 F, gas 6) for 20 minutes.

Meanwhile, mix together 2 egg yolks, 80 g (3 oz, 6 tablespoons) caster (superfine) sugar, 1 teaspoon flour, and 1 glass of milk. Stir this mixture over a low heat until it thickens, then add the juice of half a lemon and 4 tablespoons (⅓ cup) reduced pineapple syrup. Take the tart case out of the oven, allow it to cool, then pour in the cream and arrange on top 6 slices of canned pineapple, well-drained. Whisk 2 egg whites to stiff peaks, pour over the fruit, and sprinkle with 30 g (1 oz, 2 tablespoons, firmly packed) caster (superfine) sugar. Return to the oven at the same temperature and bake for 10 minutes to brown the meringue mixture. Leave in a cool place until just before serving.

Puff-pastry apple tart TARTE FEUIL-LETÉE AUX POMMES Prepare an apple compote with 750 g (1¾ lb) apples, the juice of half a lemon, 150 g (5 oz, ⅔ cup, firmly packed) caster (superfine) sugar, and 1 teaspoon vanilla sugar. Sieve, and heat gently to dry off the excess liquid. Prepare 400 g (14 oz) puff pastry. Roll it out to form a rectangle 30 cm (12 in) by 13 cm (5 in). Make a border with a small strip of pastry about 1.5 cm (½ in) wide. Bake blind. Thinly slice 500 g (18 oz) crisp apples and sauté them in 50 g (2 oz, 4 tablespoons) butter until they are brown but still intact. Spread the apple compote over the cooked base, garnish with the slices of apple, sprinkle with 2 tablespoons (3 tablespoons) icing (confectioners') sugar, and glaze in the oven or under the grill.

Strawberry tart TARTE AUX FRAISES Sort, wash, and hull 1 kg (2¼ lb, 7¼ cups) strawberries. Put them in an earthenware bowl and sprinkle with the juice of 1 lemon and 50 g (2 oz, 4 tablespoons) caster and (superfine) sugar. Prepare some pastry using 300 g (11 oz, 2¾ cups) flour, 150 g (5 oz, generous ½ cup) softened butter, a pinch of salt, and 2 tablespoons (3 tablespoons) water. Roll it into a ball and leave it in a cool place for 2 hours. Then roll out the pastry and use it to line a buttered and floured 28-cm (11-in) tart tin. Prick the base with a fork and bake blind. When the tart is cool, fill it with the strawberries. Mix 4 tablespoons (⅓ cup) redcurrant jelly with the juice drained from the strawberries and pour this syrup over the tart. The top can be decorated with whipped cream.

Swiss wine tart TARTE SUISSE AU VIN Mix 350 g (12 oz, 3 cups) flour, a pinch of salt, and 1 tablespoon caster (superfine) sugar. Add 80 g (3 oz, 6 tablespoons) softened butter and 15 g (½ oz) fresh yeast (½ cake compressed yeast) mixed with 3 tablespoons (¼ cup) milk. Alternatively, sprinkle 1½ teaspoons dried (active dry) yeast over the milk, whisk with a balloon whisk until dissolved, and leave in a warm place until frothy before adding it to the other ingredients. Rapidly work the ingredients, then roll the dough into a ball and set aside for 2 hours. Roll it out and use it to line a buttered tart tin. Beat 3 eggs with 100 g (4 oz, ½ cup) sugar until the mixture becomes thick and creamy, then add 1 dl (6 tablespoons, scant ½ cup) dry white wine. Pour the mixture into the tart case (shell). Bake in a hot oven for 20 minutes. Take out the tart, sprinkle with caster (superfine) sugar and knobs of butter, then return it to the

oven for a further 15 minutes. Serve lukewarm.

tartar TARTRE

A brownish-red crystalline deposit left inside wine casks after racking. This by-product of wine consists mainly of crude potassium hydrogen tartrate, which, when purified, gives cream of tartar, used in baking.

Tartaric acid is the principal acid found in grapes and is responsible for half the total acidity of wine. It is the most important of the fixed acids of wine (with malic and citric acids). If the must lacks acidity, some tartaric acid may be added to it. However, too much tartaric acid gives an astringent, or even harsh, wine. Acidity also helps to preserve wine and affects its stability and colour.

tartare (à la)

A term originally describing dishes covered with breadcrumbs, grilled (broiled), and served with a highly seasoned sauce, but now usually used for a sauce or a raw meat dish. Tartare sauce is a mayonnaise made with hard-boiled (hard-cooked) egg yolks, onion, and chives and is served with fish, calves' feet, oysters, and pontneuf potatoes. Steak tartare is made with minced (ground) beef (or horse meat, according to the purists) served raw with egg yolk and seasoning. In Belgium, this dish is called *filet américain*. The expression *à la tartare* is also applied to various highly seasoned cold or hot dishes: paupiettes of anchovies with horseradish butter or fried eggs on a bed of minced beef with paprika, for example.

RECIPES

Steak tartare Mince (grind) 150–200 g (5–7 oz) lean beef (rump steak, sirloin, or top rump). Season with salt and pepper, a little cayenne, and a few drops of Worcestershire sauce or Tabasco. Shape the meat into a ball, place it on a plate, hollow out the centre, and put a raw egg yolk in the hollow. Around the meat arrange 1 tablespoon each of chopped onion, chopped parsley, and chopped shallots and 1 teaspoon drained capers. Serve with tomato ketchup, olive oil, and Worcestershire sauce.

Tartare sauce SAUCE TARTARE Prepare some mayonnaise, replacing the raw egg yolk with hard-boiled (hardcooked) egg yolk. Add some finely chopped chives and chopped spring onion (scallion).

Alternatively, a mixture of raw egg yolk and hard-boiled egg yolk can be used, and chopped herbs can replace the chives and onion.

other recipes See *egg (eggs en cocotte)*, *feet and trotters*.

tartine

The French word for a slice of bread spread with butter, jam, or any other suitable substance of spreading consistency.

M. des Ombiaux describes the very elaborate *tartine de Meursault* in his *Traité de la table*: 'Bone a woodcock that is two or three days old and finely chop the meat together with the liver and the heart. Grate some larding bacon and mix it with the meat to make a paste. Season with salt and spread the paste on a piece of French bread cut lengthways and hollowed out. Put some largish knobs of butter on the tartine and cook in the oven for about 20 minutes. Just before serving, moisten with a little chicken stock. The result will be a woodcock tartine, greatly superior to plain woodcock, which is often very dry. Drink with it a Santenot de Volany or a Meursault.

Le Dictionnaire de l'Académie des gastronomes refers to *fripe*, which, in the west of France, is any substance that can be spread on bread (butter, cheese, jam, etc.); in *Le Lys dans la vallée*, Balzac writes: 'rillettes from Tours are the best of *fripes*'.

RECIPE

Tartines marquise Cut some crustless bread into squares or rounds 6 cm (2 in) thick and spread them with thick béchamel sauce bound with egg yolks and mixed with grated Gruyère cheese. Deep-fry the tartines in boiling oil, keeping the side spread with sauce uppermost, until they are crisp. Serve as a hot entrée.

tartiner

The French term meaning to spread butter, paste, etc., on a slice of bread; a special knife with a rounded edge (a *tartineur*) is used for this purpose. The word is also used to describe spreading forcemeats or fillings on escalopes, crêpes, cakes, etc., and lining or coating dariole or charlotte moulds.

tartlet TARTELETTE

A small individual tart made in the same way as a large tart and with the same fillings. Tartlets filled with fruit, creams, or other sweet mixtures are served as a dessert; savoury tartlets are served as hors d'oeuvres or small entrées.

RECIPES

Coffee or chocolate tartlets TARTELETTES AU CAFÉ OU AU CHOCOLAT (from Raymond Oliver's recipe) Line some greased tartlet tins with sablé pastry (see *doughs and batters*). Prick the bottom with a fork and bake blind for about 10 minutes. Allow to cool. Then, using a forcing (pastry) bag, fill some of the cases with French coffee butter cream (see *creams and custards*) and the remainder with Chantilly cream flavoured with chocolate and rum.

Walnut and honey tartlets TARTELETTES AUX NOIX ET AU MIEL (from Raymond Oliver's recipe) Line some greased tartlet tins with shortcrust pastry (basic pie dough). Sprinkle them with crushed walnuts and arrange some narrow strips of pastry in a crisscross pattern on the top. Brush with beaten egg and bake in a hot oven for about 15 minutes. When they are cooked, coat them with acacia honey.

tart or flan ring
CERCLE À TARTE

A ring of tinplate of varying diameter (6–34 cm, 2¼–13¼ in). Many pastrycooks prefer it to a mould for preparing tarts and flans. When placed directly on the baking sheet, it ensures a better diffusion of heat through the pastry and enables the cooked tart or flan to be easily removed.

tartouillat

A dessert of Nivernais and Morvan. Thick pancake batter mixed with peeled and chopped apples is poured onto cabbage leaves which have been thoroughly washed and dried; they are then carefully folded and baked in the oven. In Burgundy, tartouillats are made with cherries instead of apples.

tassau

A meat dish that is typical of West Indian and Central American cookery. It is made by steeping some pieces of meat (beef, veal, or poultry) for several hours in a chilled very spicy court-bouillon containing pepper, cloves, thyme, chilli, onion, limes, and chives. The meat is then poached rapidly in the court-bouillon, drained, and then either grilled (broiled) or fried. Tassau is served either with boiled bananas or with fried sweet potatoes.

taste GOÛT

The sense by which the flavours of food are perceived, the organ used being the tongue, which is equipped with taste buds. It is possible to distinguish four basic tastes: salt, acid, sweet, and bitter, which, combined in different ways, determine the taste of everything we eat. From a gastronomic point of view, the sense of taste is closely associated with the sense of smell. The aroma of a dish provides a good deal of information about its taste, and the sense of smell contributes greatly to the sense of taste while actually eating – this is why food seems tasteless when one has a cold.

taster GOÛTEUR

A specialist who judges the quality of a drink or a food by its taste (see *tasting*). No instrument has been devised to rival a properly trained human palate, particularly in the area of wine tasting, where the test consists of savouring the wine by rolling it in one's mouth so that all its qualities are brought out. In Paris there is still a Compagnie de Courtiers-Gourmets-Piqueurs de Vins, which dates back to the time of Philip the Fair (reigned 1285–1314); the duties of these officials include the tasting of wines at the request of the courts or authorities. The word *piqueur* derives from a tool called a *coup de poing*, a sort of gimlet used to puncture (*piquer*) the barrel to take a sample. The food industry often makes use of professional tasters. Tea, coffee, butter, foie gras, oil, etc., are tested by panels, which consist of groups of tasters whose opinions are cross-checked.

tasting DÉGUSTATION

The critical appraisal of a food or drink via its impression on the senses. Although many foods are tasted, from basic items such as butter, oil, and tea to the luxury foods, such as foie gras and fine chocolates, the word is usually applied to the tasting of wines and spirits.

The professional taster adopts the same procedure for both wines and spirits, but a spirit, whether on its own or 'broken down' with water, is seldom actually put in the mouth: it is mainly sniffed. In 'blind tasting' the identity of the liquid is not known. There are three main stages in tasting: looking, sniffing, and appraising the liquid in the mouth. The taster will look at the colour and limpidity of the liquid (in wine the colour is known as the 'robe'), and will then sniff at it. Then a small quantity is taken into the mouth, usually with a certain amount of air, which is drawn through the liquid; the sample is pulled around to make contact with the top and sides of the mouth and the tongue.

The registering of impressions conveyed by the smell is of great importance and much may be learned from this stage of tasting, although only experience can enable one to interpret the messages received by the nose from a wine or spirit. When the wine gets into the mouth, another set of impressions are registered – flavours associated with particular grapes, regions, and even makers – and, with both the smells and the tastes, certain faults in the wine can be picked out. Each part of the mouth can often contribute to the overall impression, although it should be remembered that tasting young wines, before they are ready to drink, is an experience that the beginner can find unpleasant: time is needed before the development of a wine can be judged, except by the very experienced. In general, though, wine should be a unified harmonious beverage, each element being in balance with the others – fruit, acidity, alcohol.

A professional taster will usually spit out a wine – to taste and drink a number of assorted ones, even those that have reached the stage of being agreeable drinks, can be highly confusing when several dozen or more samples have to be tasted. With the fortified wines, the number that can be judged at one session is fairly small, even for the professionals. When the wine has either been swallowed or spat out, the taster breathes sharply out through the mouth; this process circulates the aromas within the facial cavities and registers the aftertaste, which can be very revealing. A wine that leaves the palate clean, refreshed, and with a definite impression of interest and quality is said to have good finish.

tâte-vin or taste-vin

A small receptacle made of pewter, silver, or silver plate with a handle surmounted by a support for the thumb; it is used for examining and tasting wine. Known also as a *coupole* or simply (as in Burgundy) a *tasse*, its shape varies from region to region: the tâte-vin from Burgundy has rounded sides that are ornamented with bosses to reflect the colour of the wine, while those of Bordeaux have smooth funnel-shaped rims.

Tatin

The name given to an apple tart that is cooked under a lid of pastry, but served with the pastry underneath and the fruit on top. This delicious pastry, in which the taste of caramel is combined with the flavour of apples cooked in butter under a golden crispy pastry crust, established the reputation of the Tatin sisters, who ran a hotel-restaurant in Lamotte-Beuvron at the beginning of the century. However, the 'upsidedown' tart, made with apples or pears, is an ancient speciality of Sologne and is found throughout Orléanais. Having been made famous by the Tatin sisters, it was first served in Paris at Maxim's, where it remains a speciality to the present day.

RECIPE

Tarte Tatin Make about 350 g (12 oz) shortcrust pastry (basic pie dough), roll it into a ball, and leave it in a cool place for 2 hours. Then roll it out into a circle 3 mm (⅛ in) thick. Peel and core 750 g (1¾ lb) apples and cut them into quar-

ters. Butter a fairly deep flan dish 24 cm (10 in) in diameter, sprinkle with 60 g (2½ oz, ⅓ cup), firmly packed) caster (superfine) sugar, and arrange the quartered apples in concentric circles. Sprinkle with another 60 g (2½ oz, ⅓ cup, firmly packed) caster sugar and then dot some small knobs of butter over the apples (about 80 g, 3 oz, scant ½ cup). Cover with the pastry, tucking it under inside the edge of the dish so that the fruit is contained within the lid. Bake in the oven at 230 c (450 f, gas 8) for 30–35 minutes. Place a serving dish on top of the flan dish and turn the tart upside down. Remove the flan dish. The top of the apples should be caramelized. Serve warm, with fresh cream.

Tavel

Possibly the best-known rosé wine in the world, which has its own AOC and comes from the bottom of the Rhône Valley, in the vicinity of Avignon. It is composed from several different grapes, according to the maker, and there are estate Tavels as well as the more ordinary ones. Robust and with a pronounced bouquet (unusual for a rosé wine), Tavel is one of the world's few pink wines that can benefit by some bottle age if it comes from a reputable maker; the more usual examples, however, are at their pleasantest when drunk young and fresh.

tavern TAVERNE

Originally, a tavern in France was simply a wine shop, as distinct from the cabaret, which also provided meals. In 1698 tavern-keepers were given permission to serve meat, provided that it was prepared elsewhere, at the rôtisserie or the charcuterie. Ten years later, they were allowed to cook meat on the premises but they were still forbidden to cook ragouts, which were the prerogative of the traiteurs. Nowadays, a tavern is a brasserie or a restaurant with traditional decor that is often in keeping with regional kitchens, especially those of the Alsace.

Jean Favier describes Paris taverns in the 1450s in his book *François Villon* (Fayard, 1982): 'Taverns are everywhere, particularly during the new wine season, when the burghers of Paris obtain authorization from the provost of the merchants to sell off their excess production to the community. To sell at a tavern is to be a Parisian with vineyards. To be a tavern-keeper is something else. Throughout the year, the established tavern-keepers (through paying the duty) offer Parisians wine to take away or to drink on the premises. Their benches and trestles serve as a social link for an entire population who cannot afford to entertain at home. The tavern is the place where people chat, confide in one another, and make merry. They go there to conspire against the government and the provost. . . .

'The cellar count of 1457 officially records 200 professional tavern-keepers and a hundred or so amateur tavern-keepers. At that time, they were situated along the Rue Saint-Jacques and the Rue de la Harpe on the Left Bank, along the Rues Saint-Martin and Saint-Denis on the Right Bank, and also in the district of Les Halles and the Place de Grève. The most famous tavern at that time was the Pomme de Pin, opposite the Palais. Others include the Grand Godet in the Place de Grève, and the Quatre Fils Aymon in the Rue de la Juiverie. François Villon, in his *Testament*, mentions the tavern-keeper Arnoul Turgis, a wine merchant, at La Chasse.

'The ordinary wines that were sold in those days were from Conflans, Vitry, Fleury-lès-Clamart, Fontenay-sous-Bagneux, and Montreuil-sous-Bois: these wines were of a fairly mediocre quality, either white acidic light wines treated with chalk, or else dark red wines called *morillons*, which were rough and harsh. There were also wines from the vineyards of Vanves, Issy, Clamart, and Meudon, which were of better quality. When the wine was excessively bad, it was blended, diluted, sweetened with honey, or strengthened. However, taverns also sold the wines of Argenteuil, Chaillot, and Suresnes, which were the greatest wines of that period, together with the wine of Auxerrois and wines from Burgundy, Auvergne, and the Loire Valley, which arrived in the capital by boat. But these wines were reserved for the rich. The circles in which Villon mixed were content to drink hippocras or *morillon* at the taverns, eating pickled herrings to give themselves a thirst and chancing their luck at gambling.'

Taverne anglaise

The name given to several Parisian restaurants that specialized in English food. The first Taverne anglaise, which was also known as the Grande Taverne de Londres, was opened by Beauvilliers at the Palais-Royal in 1782. Later, he founded another establishment in his own name. There was also a Taverne anglaise in the Rue Taranne, in Saint-Germain-des-Prés.

The Englishman Richard Lucas opened a Taverne anglaise in 1832 and the menu included roast beef and Yorkshire pudding. This establishment became the Restaurant Lucas and subsequently the Lucas-Carton. A fourth Taverne anglaise opened in 1870 in the Rue de Richelieu; it served rare meat, rib of beef, and rhubarb tart.

Anglomania persists to this day with the setting up of various English pubs, some more authentic than others, where English beer and typical British lunches are served.

tchorba

A thick soup from Arab cookery made with pieces of sheep tail and mutton cutlets. The meat is browned in oil with onions and tomatoes, mixed with courgettes (zucchini), garlic, thyme, and bay leaves, then cooked in plenty of water with white haricot (navy) beans or chickpeas, and seasoned with red pepper, black pepper, and saffron. Before serving, some macaroni or vermicelli or dried fruit are added to the soup.

Similar dishes are found in Balkan cookery: Yugoslav *corba* (beef soup with sweet pepper and onion, thickened with rice) and Romanian or Bulgarian *ciorba* (a sharp-tasting soup made with beef and vegetables (or sometimes fish), which may be seasoned with lemon).

tea THÉ

The most universally consumed beverage, made by infusing the dried leaves of an Asiatic evergreen shrub, *Camellia sinensis*. There are two main varieties of tea plant, that of China and that of India, with numerous local varieties and hybrids. Climate, soil, altitude, and orientation all affect the growth and quality of the plants, and therefore the colour, fragrance, and taste of the tea. The best teas are cultivated at an altitude of about 2000 m (6500 ft) and are picked in the spring. Growing areas are situated at latitudes between 42N and 31S, in regions with a hot humid climate and winters that are neither too cold nor too dry.

It is thought that tea cultivation originated in China around 3000 BC and spread to Japan in about 780 AD. It was not grown in India until the 1840s, and in Ceylon (now Sri Lanka) the first tea estate was planted in 1867. The beverage was brought to Europe in the 17th century by the Dutch, and reached England in 1644. It arrived in America in the early 18th century. At first regarded primarily as a medicinal beverage, tea drinking soon became fashionable with the aristocracy and then popular at all levels of society.

Today the principal tea producers are, in order of output, India, Sri Lanka, China, Japan, Indonesia, East Africa, Latin America, and the Soviet Union. In France and in Britain, where tea has become the national beverage, the most popular varieties are Ceylon teas. The drinking of tea is important in China and in Japan, where the tea ceremony (*kaiseki*) has influenced social life, art, religion, and philosophy.

In the wild, the plant can reach a height of 10 m (32½ ft), but in cultivated plantations the shrubs are limited to a height of 1.2 m (4 ft), so that the leaves can more easily be picked by hand. The downy terminal bud (the 'pekoe', from the Chinese *pa ko*, meaning down) and the top two leaves are plucked from each stem. The smaller and younger the leaves, the better the tea. The different grades of tea are *orange pekoe* (the tip of the bud is yellowish-orange), *pekoe* (shorter leaves without buds), *pekoe souchong* (even shorter, coarser, and older leaves), and *souchong* (leaves older still and rolled into balls). The broken leaves are sold under the same names but preceded by the word 'broken'.

There are three types of tea, depending on the treatment of the leaves: *green tea*, which is unfermented and roasted immediately after harvesting and gives a strong, bitter, although quite clear infusion; *black tea*, by far the most common, which is fermented and dried; and *oolong tea*, which is semifermented and intermediate between green and black tea.

☐ Green tea A speciality of China and Japan prepared by subjecting the leaves to fierce heat. It is highly favoured by the Chinese and also the Muslims, who are forbidden to drink fermented tea. The varieties are: Gunpowder (known as Chao Chen in China), the rolled leaves of which are similar to small shot about 3 mm long; Tychen (also known as Coarse Gunpowder or Imperial Tea), having larger pellet-sized rolled leaves; Moroccan mint tea, which is very refreshing; and Japanese tea (Shincha), which gives a highly coloured infusion.

☐ Black tea Whether from China or elsewhere, there are five stages in its preparation: withering (the leaf is dried and softened), rolling (the cells of the leaves are broken down to release and mix the constituents), moist fermentation (2–3 hours at 27 C, 81 F), desiccation (20 minutes at 90 C, 194 F), and sorting or grading. The three main types of black tea come from Sri Lanka (Ceylon), India, and China.

● *Ceylon teas* – These are quite strong infusions, with a natural simple taste, and can be drunk at any time. Among the best varieties are: Superior Orange Pekoe (large very fragrant leaves, with a delicate taste, giving an amber-coloured infusion, served preferably without milk); Flowery O Pekoe (rolled leaves which open out fully during infusion, giving a fragrant tea, blending well with lemon); Uva Highland (a great growth, obtained from large leaves, drunk without milk); Medium Grown Broken Orange Pekoe (a full-bodied tea, usually drunk with milk); and High Grown (a coloured very fragrant tea, excellent in the morning).

● *Indian teas* – These are particularly fragrant teas, the most prestigious of which are Darjeeling (fruity, delicious with pastries, the taste varying depending on the soil, altitude, and weather conditions of the estates where they are grown – Selimbong, Sington, Jungpana, etc.) and Assam (small broken leaves with golden tips, producing a full-bodied tea often drunk with a little milk). Bengal tea has large leaves, giving a delicate tea with an almond taste, suitable for breakfast.

• *China teas* – There are two types: ordinary teas (which does not mean ordinary quality) and steamed teas. Among the former are: Yunnan, known as the 'mocha' of teas, stimulating and with a full-bodied taste (well-formed leaves with golden tips); Caravan, fragrant, low in caffeine, recommended for drinking in the evening; Keemun, with digestive properties; and Great Mandarin, flavoured with jasmine and a perfect accompaniment to oriental cookery. Steamed teas include Imperial Souchong (young tender leaves blended with jasmine flowers), suitable for the afternoon; Lapsang Souchong (a well-formed broad-leaved tea with a smoky taste and aroma), steamed more than Imperial Souchong; and Tarry Souchong (broad leaves), with a very pronounced smoky flavour.

☐ **Oolong** This tea from Taiwan is made from semifermented leaves. Its quality varies from season to season (it is at its best in the summer). It is very popular in the United States, where it is divided into eight grades ranging from 'choicest' to 'common'. The best is Fancy Grade Oolong, characterized by well-formed whole leaves and giving a unique mellow infusion best drunk without milk. Other varieties taste of honey.

☐ **Scented teas** Apart from the classic teas, there is a large variety of teas perfumed with flowers or fruits, the most famous of which is Earl Grey. A black unsteamed China tea to which oil of bergamot is added, it is named after the 2nd Earl Grey, for whom it was created. There is also Georgia tea, flavoured with citrus fruits and flowers. Vanilla, mulberrry, raspberry, coconut, grapefruit, apple, apricot, ginger, cinnamon, passion fruit, etc., give various scented teas that may be drunk either hot or iced. However, apart from the traditional flavourings of jasmine, rosehip, bergamot, orange flower, and lotus, other fragrances produce infusions which, for tea-lovers, have little to do with tea.

In addition, a number of classic blended unscented teas are sold. Companies have also marketed instant tea, freeze-dried tea, decaffeinated tea, and scented tea in powdered form.

☐ **Tea and health** The many beneficial qualities of tea have been recognized since ancient times: it stimulates the nervous system because of its caffeine (or theine) content, it aids digestion, stimulates the circulation and heartbeat (by means of theophylline), and it is a diuretic; it is rich in manganese, iodine, and copper.

The properties and flavour of tea can be preserved by storing it in a dry airtight tin away from the light. Tea stored in this way will keep for up to about 18 months.

☐ **To make tea** Tea is made according to a few simple rules.

• Use water that is as lime-free as possible (purists avoid tap water, which makes the tea cloudy). The water should be free from iron, which would precipitate tannins in the cup, and should not be chlorinated. In the absence of spring water, connoisseurs choose a light mineral water, such as Évian or Volvic. Do not use water that has already been boiled once in order to save time.

• Rinse out the teapot with boiling water just before putting in the tea. The general rule is one teaspoon of tea per person and one 'for the pot'. The better the tea, the smaller the quantity required, but you can never compensate for an insufficient quantity of tea by letting it infuse over a longer period.

• Pour the water onto the tea just as it reaches boiling point, taking the pot to the kettle.

• The infusion time is three to five minutes, depending on whether the tea leaves are whole or broken. After this time, the flavour does not improve, and the tannins spread and make the infusion more bitter and darker. (Because of this, tea balls or tea infusers are recommended.)

• Just before serving, stir the tea in the teapot with a spoon; if the tea leaves are left in the pot, use a strainer when pouring.

A good-quality tea is generally drunk on its own, or sometimes with a dash of milk always cold). Tea-lovers avoid lemon, which denatures the flavour of tea, and they often do without sugar. Some, however, like tea sweetened with honey.

There are various traditions associated with the preparation and tasting of tea in different countries. Russian tea is quite dark and strong and is served in glasses. Sometimes a lump of sugar is placed in the mouth and the tea is sipped and allowed to filter through it. The reserve of boiling water in the samovar enables tea to be prepared continuously, and it is traditionally offered to all visitors. China tea is served in small fine porcelain cups without handles. It is sometimes flavoured with bergamot or jasmine, and can be drunk at any time of the day, except during meals. According to Vietnamese tradition, tea is drunk in cups with a closely fitted lid, which retains the flavour and heat. In Arab countries, tea is infused with mint and drunk very sweet, out of small glasses. The Japanese drink tea in accordance with an elaborate ceremony, governed down to the minutest detail and requiring years of experience.

In exotic cookery, tea is used as an aromatic in cooking.

RECIPES

China tea THÉ CHINOIS Boil 1 litre (1¾ pints, 4¼ cups) water in an enamel kettle. When the water starts to boil vigorously, pour a little into a teapot (made of earthenware or porcelain). shake the teapot for 30 seconds so that it is heated evenly. Throw the water away. Put 2 teaspoons black tea into the teapot, fill with boiling water, put on the lid, and leave for 2 minutes. Pour the tea into a large cup, then immediately pour it back into the teapot (this operation brings out the fragrance of the tea). Allow to infuse for a further 2 minutes, then serve.

Duck with tea leaves (*Chinese cookery*) CANARD AUX FEUILLES DE THÉ Draw a duck weighing about 1.3 kg (3 lb). Rub the inside and outside of the carcass with salt, then with sugar. Place the duck in a deep ovenproof dish sprinkled with 20 g (¾ oz) fresh ginger cut into thin strips, 5 g (¼ oz) crushed cinnamon, and 5 g (¼ oz) star anise. Sprinkle with 1 glass (¾ cup) saké (or use sherry). Add 1 dl (6 tablespoons, scant ½ cup) water, cover, and cook in a bain-marie for 2 hours. Drain the duck

and leave to cool on a plate. Heat a deep cast-iron pan and pour in 80 g (3 oz) green tea. Place over a moderate heat until a light white smoke is given off. Then put the duck in the hot pan, cover, leave it to absorb the smoke for 4 minutes, then remove from the heat. Heat a little groundnut (peanut) oil in a large deep frying pan (skillet) and brown the duck on all sides over a brisk heat for 5 minutes. Carve and serve piping hot, garnished with braised broccoli.

Eggs with tea leaves(*Chinese cookery*) OEUFS AUX FEUILLES DE THÉ Put 6 eggs into a saucepan with ½ litre (17 fl oz, 2 cups) cold water. Leave the pan uncovered and simmer for 20 minutes. Allow to cool. Remove the eggs and crack the shells by tapping with the back of a spoon over the entire surface. Put the eggs back into the saucepan with ½ litre (17 fl oz, 2 cups) cold water, 1 tablespoon salt, 2 tablespoons (3 tablespoons) soy sauce, 1 bulb of star anise, and 2 coffee spoons black China tea. Bring to the boil, then reduce the heat as much as possible and cook gently for 2 hours. The eggs must always be covered with liquid (add boiling water as necessary). Remove the saucepan from the heat and allow the eggs to steep in the cooking liquid for 8 hours. Just before serving, shell the eggs. Cut them in half lengthways and serve them with thin strips of cold roast pork and a salad of soya-bean sprouts with mushrooms, seasoned with soy sauce vinaigrette.

Iced tea THÉ GLACÉ Prepare an infusion of green tea and add a sprig of fresh mint. Strain the tea, pour it into a carafe, sweeten it slightly, allow it to cool, then chill it in the refrigerator for at least an hour.

Just before serving, add 4 tablespoons (5 tablespoons) rum per litre (1¾ pints, 4¼ cups) tea.

Indian tea with milk and spices THÉ INDIEN AU LAIT AUX ÉPICES Pour ½ litre (17 fl oz, 2 cups) milk into a saucepan and add 1 cinnamon stick, 2 crushed cloves, 2 crushed cardamon seeds, and, if possible, 1 piece of fresh ginger (peeled and chopped). Bring to the boil, then add 1½ tablespoons (2 tablespoons) tea and some caster (superfine) sugar (according to taste). Boil for 1–2 minutes, cover, remove from the heat, and allow to infuse for at least 7–8 minutes. Strain the infusion and serve very hot.

Lamb with prunes, tea, and almonds (*Algerian cookery*) AGNEAU AUX PRUNEAUX, AU THÉ ET AUX AMANDES Bone 1 kg (2¼ lb) shoulder of lamb, remove the fat, and cut the meat into large dice. Sprinkle with finely ground salt and cook it in a casserole with butter until golden brown. Drain. Add to the butter in the casserole ¼ litre (8 fl oz, 1 cup) water, 1 cinnamon stick chopped into pieces, ½ cup blanched almonds, 200 g (7 oz, 1 cup) caster (superfine) sugar, and 2 tablespoons (3 tablespoons) orange-flower water. Bring this mixture rapidly to the boil, stirring continuously. Replace the meat, cover the pan, and allow to simmer over a low heat for 45 minutes. Meanwhile, soak 350 g (12 oz, 2 cups) stoned (pitted) prunes in very strong green tea. Add the prunes and tea to the casserole and cook for a further 10 minutes.

Tea sorbet SORBET DE THÉ Prepare quite a strong infusion of a tea according to taste. Add sugar in the proportion of 300 g (11 oz, scant 1½ cups) per litre (1¾ pints, 4¼ cups) and allow to set in a churn freezer. Prunes cut up into tiny pieces may be added to the sorbet. Green tea flavoured with jasmine gives excellent results.

Tuna fish in tea (*Vietnamese cookery*) THON AU THÉ Brown a bluefin tuna steak, weighing about 800 g (1¾ lb), in oil in a frying pan (skillet). Meanwhile, prepare an infusion of fairly strong tea (black China tea or lotus tea). Put the tuna into a saucepan together with 100 g (4 oz, ½ cup) diced fresh unsalted belly of pork. Add a piece of fresh ginger cut into thin strips, pepper, 1–2 teaspoons *nuoc-mâm*, a lump of sugar, and the tea (ensure that the liquid just covers the fish). Simmer over a gentle heat for 1 hour.

tea (the meal) THÉ

A light meal in the afternoon, at which sandwiches, pastries, cakes, etc., are served with tea. A rather more substantial meal is high tea (or meat tea), which is taken particularly in the north of England, where the evening meal is replaced by tea served with cold meat, fish, salads, etc., as well as buttered rolls, toast, cakes, etc. Afternoon tea taken at five o'clock was launched by the Duchess of Bedford in about 1830 (at that time lunch was served quite early and dinner was served late). It provided an opportunity to display tea services made of porcelain or silver plate, to create recipes of cakes, biscuits (cookies), etc., and to lay down rules of etiquette associated with the occasion (the correct way in which to hold the cup, put down the spoon, etc.). An English tea sometimes includes savoury canapés but the most common items are bread-and-butter, scones, muffins, crumpets, buns, cakes, biscuits, gingerbread, and shortbread, with jams and jellies, lemon curd, etc.

On the Continent, tea was adopted during the period of Anglomania at the end of the 19th century, especially in towns. It was also served as a kind of buffet during balls and soirées. 'A prefect was reproached for bribing the electors of his *département* by inviting them to dine at his sumptuous table. He announced that henceforth he would confine himself to offering them tea. . . . The precious infusion with a dash of cream was served on magnificent trays with small dry crispy pastries. The country electors . . . could not understand people liking this insipid beverage, which, to them, was like hot water. The prefect's secretary discreetly led them to the back of the room. There, sideboards had been arranged, suitably decked with cold items, capable of satisfying the heartiest of appetites. They found pâtés, fish, galantines, and venison, with wines to match. And so these worthy folk then understood what tea was. In France, tea is the supper of the salons.' (Eugène Briffault, *Paris à table*)

teal SARCELLE

A small wild duck, several species of which are hunted in France, including the common teal, which rarely migrates and is found in France and Britain all year round, the summer teal, which comes from Africa, as well as the Baikal teal, the marbled teal, and the sickled teal. In the United States there are various species, the most common being the green-winged teal. The teal is more difficult to hunt than the mallard because of its jerky flight, but is cooked in the same way. Its brownish and rather bitter meat is much sought-after by connoisseurs; in the Middle Ages it was considered to be a lean meat, i.e. one that could be eaten on fast days. Teal, like all wild ducks, is roasted blood-rare and seldom braised.

teapot THÉIÈRE

A receptacle with a lid, a spout, and a handle, used to prepare and serve tea. Teapots come in various sizes and can be made of various materials: porcelain, faïence, earthenware, metal, etc.

An innovation appeared in the 19th century: a trellis, or a screen pierced with small holes, is placed inside, at the base of the spout, thereby preventing the leaves from pouring into the cup with the infusion. However, this does not mean that a strainer need not be used. Some models also have an internal strainer, which is fitted to the opening of the teapot. The tea leaves are placed in it before the water is poured in. The first metal teapots appeared in France at the end of the 17th century. Those made of porcelain and faïence came initially from China and Japan, then later from Meissen and Sèvres.

tea room SALON DE THÉ

An establishment in which tea, hot chocolate, coffee, soft drinks, and cakes (and sometimes savoury pastries or egg dishes, salads, sandwiches, croque-monsieur, etc.) are served in the afternoon or at lunch time. Nowadays tea rooms are usually part of a bakers' shop or a large store. The luxurious Parisian tea rooms of the first half of the 20th century, where society ladies met for 'five o'clock tea', are now disappearing.

telfairia

A plant of the gourd family, resembling a water melon, grown in Réunion. The telfairia, or oyster nut, contains numerous flat seeds which enclose the kernels. A light yellow oil, of good quality for cooking, is extracted from them and they are also pleasant to eat.

Tellier (Charles)

French engineer (born Amiens, 1828; died Paris, 1913), nicknamed 'the father of refrigeration' in 1908 by d'Arsonval. In 1856 he developed the first industrial refrigerator, and in 1876 the first plant to produce ice consistently for preserving foodstuffs. In the same year an attempt was made to transport meat preserved by refrigeration from Rouen to Buenos Aires on board the steamship *Frigorifique*, which had been specially fitted out for that purpose. The experiment was successful and marked the first victory for the refrigeration industry.

tench TANCHE

A European freshwater fish found in ponds and quiet waterways. 15–30 cm (6–12 in) long, with a barbel on each side of the mouth, it has tiny olive-green to reddish-brown scales covered with thick mucus. Fish caught in clear water are delicious, especially since tench do not have too many bones. But ones caught in muddy waters may be tainted and should be soaked in water. This is why fishermen pour a spoonful of vinegar into its mouth as soon as the fish is taken out of the water. Tench is generally used in matelotes and can also be fried or prepared *à la meunière*. In the past it was more popular, being cooked in court-bouillon, or *à la bonne femme* and used in soups, ragouts, and pies.

tende-de-tranche

A French cut of beef taken from the top of the thigh. Classified as second-category beef, it nevertheless provides cuts for steaks: *dessous-de-tranche* (rather firm), *merlan* (long and flat), *poire* (round and fleshy), and *morceaux du boucher* (delicious tender cuts of meat). Tende-de-tranche can also be roasted.

tenderizing ATTENDRIR

Even good-quality meat may be tough for several hours after slaughtering. It may be made more tender by several methods. The storage of meat at low temperatures (0–2 c, 32–36 f) enables it to mature and tenderize. Small meat joints may be flattened with a mallet, which has the effect of making them more tender. Meat may also be tenderized by immersing it for varying periods in a marinade or in brine. The introduction of small strips of fat bacon into a piece of meat makes it more tender and also gives it a better flavour (see *larding*). Generally speaking, the effect of prolonged cooking is to make food more tender.

Tendret (Lucien)

French lawyer and gastronome (born Belley, 1825; died Belley, 1896). He was a compatriot and distant relative of Brillat-Savarin and a scholar who was passionately interested in food. In 1892 he published *La Table au pays de Brillat-Savarin*, in which he recorded, among others, the recipe for the famous chicken Celestine, a Lyonnais speciality, as well as recipes for the three famous *pâtés en croûte* of Belley: the *oreiller de la Belle Aurore*, the *toque du président Adolphe Clerc*, and the *chapeau de monseigneur Gabriel Cortois de Quincey*, rich in game, poultry, truffles, and foie gras.

The following aphorism is attributed to him: 'Gourmandism seeks out all the courtesies and all the refinements. It is the only passion that does not leave behind any remorse, sorrow, or suffering.' Rouff undoubtedly modelled his character Dodin-Bouffant upon Lucien Tendret.

In her *Livre de cuisine* (published by Minuit, 1981), Alice Toklas maintained that she actually had the recipe book of Lucien Tendret in her possession, from which she extracted a magnificent composite salad. 'Put into a salad bowl some olive oil of the best quality, some white wine vinegar, 4 tablespoons roast turkey juice, ½ teaspoon tarragon mustard, the inside of a lobster, salt, and pepper. Stir until the mixture is perfectly smooth. Then add slices of lobster flesh, slices from the breast of a braised chicken and the breast of a roast turkey without the skin, the breast of three young partridges (keep the best slices for decoration), some thinly sliced truffles cooked in an excellent dry white wine, some mushrooms prepared in the same way, and a number of shelled crayfish. Cover with a layer of blanched endive (chicory) leaves. Add a second layer of the mixture, then a further layer of en-

dive. Then on top, tastefully arrange the reserved slices of meat, a few strips of ham from which the fat has been removed, a few large slices of truffle and mushroom, a border of shelled crayfish, a tablespoon of capers washed in white wine, and a cupful of stoned (pitted) green olives. Put a mound of thick mayonnaise in the centre with the largest truffle on top. Serve with the finest dry champagne, very cold but not iced.'

tendron

A piece of beef or veal cut from the extremities of the ribs, from the point at which the chops are generally cut, to the sternum. Tendrons of veal, which contain a few small cartilages, are streaked with fat and are very smooth. They are used for blanquette, braised or sautéed veal, or veal Marengo. If they include sufficient lean meat, they can be cut into slices, pot-roasted or braised as *côtes parisiennes*, and then garnished with fresh pasta, risotto, braised spinach in butter, or braised carrots. Tendrons of beef are streaky pieces of meat used for braising and for pot-au-feu.

RECIPE

Braised tendrons of veal à la bourgeoise TENDRONS DE VEAU BRAISÉS À LA BOURGEOISE Braise 4 tendrons of veal; when half-cooked, add 12 small glazed onions, 12 shaped and glazed carrots, and 50 g (2 oz, ¼ cup) diced streaky bacon (blanched and fried). Finish the cooking, drain the tendrons, and arrange them on an ovenproof serving dish. Sprinkle them with a little of the cooking juices and glaze in the oven. Serve piping hot, garnished with the vegetables and the diced bacon.

tequila

A spirit made in several Mexican states from the plant *Agave tequilana*. The pulp of this plant is chopped up and baked to extract the sap. Then it is shredded and pressed, so that the juice runs out and begins to ferment. Subsequently it undergoes a double distillation. Some tequila is aged in wood, gaining colour; the best is usually five years old and golden in tone. Unless tequila is part of a cocktail, it is traditionally drunk from a small glass; the drinker puts some salt in the join of his thumb and forefinger, licks a slice of lime or lemon, and knocks the reflex of the wrist so that the salt jumps up to the mouth. (One can, alternatively, just lick the salt.) The tequila is then drunk in a single gulp.

terrine

A fairly deep dish with straight sides, grips or handles, and a tightly fitting lid that rests on an inner lip. Terrines are manufactured in a wide range of sizes; they can be made of glazed earthenware (with the lid sometimes shaped like an animal) or of porcelain, ovenproof glass, or even enamelled cast iron. The food cooked or served in such a container is also known as a terrine.

The word terrine in France is also the name of a stoneware utensil shaped like a truncated cone with a wide rim and, sometimes, a pouring spout; it is used to hold milk or cream, to work a forcemeat or a paste, to steep a foodstuff, etc. A terrine may also be a simple serving utensil used to present pickled herring fillets, mushrooms *à la grecque*, etc.

The preparations known as terrines are numerous and varied. They are usually made with mixed meats, but can also be made with fish, seafood, and even vegetables. They are served cold in the container in which they are cooked (or in slices taken from the latter), accompanied by gherkins, pickled onions, and cherries or grapes as a sweet-and-sour garnish. Fish or vegetable terrines are sometimes served with a sauce and may be eaten warm. They are generally prepared with cooked ingredients set in aspic jelly, or ingredients reduced to a mousse and cooked in a bainmarie.

The majority of meat terrines contain a certain amount of pork (fat and lean), or sometimes veal, mixed with the meat that gives the dish its name: chicken, chicken liver, game, foie gras, etc. The ingredients are used in varying proportions and are cut up in different ways, depending on the recipe (reduced to a forcemeat, cut into strips, dice, or fillets, coarsely chopped, etc.). Seasoning always plays an important part in the preparation, as does marinating the ing-

redients in alcohol. The containers are usually lined with bacon fat and the preparation covered with jelly or lard. They are often autumn dishes, as this is the game season, and may be decorated with mushrooms, nuts (walnuts, almonds), aromatic herbs (thyme, bay leaf, juniper berries), etc.

This is how René Boylesve describes the terrine in *L'Enfant à la balustrade*: 'She took us to the dining room and ran to the sideboard. She took out a brown glazed earthenware terrine, which had a recumbent animal roughly moulded on the lid. . . . The contents formed an egg-shaped dome which was reddish-bronze in colour, decorated with strips of bacon fat, glazed and half-melted, which still seemed to sizzle, and small bay leaves, also cooked, like greenish copper ornaments. A snow-white grease enshrined it all like a crackled wall, milky-blue in colour. It was a pâté made with game from the *bourriche* (game bag).'

Terrines, which are cooked covered in the oven, in a bain-marie, are often rustic dishes, suitable for slicing; others, however, are sophisticated preparations, such as terrine de Nérac (red-legged partridge, chicken livers, ham, and truffles), terrines of goose liver (very much in vogue in the 18th century, before goose liver pâté was invented), and terrines of venison, wild rabbit, or thrushes with juniper berries. Contemporary chefs have a preference for terrines of fish and shellfish: crayfish with small vegetables, scorpion fish, red mullet, burbot, pike, etc.

Terrines are also prepared as desserts made with fruit set in jelly, which are served with fresh cream or a fruit sauce.

RECIPES

Terrine de Body (from Gérard Magman's recipe) Cut 600 g (1¼ lb) veal escalopes and 400 g (14 oz) smoked belly of pork into fine strips. Finely chop 16 shallots and a bunch of parsley and season with 2 teaspoons ground black pepper. Arrange the ingredients in a terrine as follows: first a layer of pork belly, then a layer of veal, then a layer of shallots and parsley, continuing this way until the ingredients are used up, finishing with a layer of pork. Moisten each layer with a little dry white wine and press down hard.

Cover the terrine and place it in a bainmarie. Bring to the boil on top of the stove, then cook in the oven at 180 C (350 F, gas 4) for 1 hour. Place a small board with a weight on the terrine before allowing it to cool. Refrigerate for at least 24 hours before serving.

Terrine de l'océan (from Yves Cullerre's recipe) Scale, gut, and clean a 1-kg (2¼-lb) turbot, a 1-kg (2¼-lb) pike, 500 g (18 oz) fresh salmon, and 2 large red mullet. Lift out the fillets and ensure that no bones remain. Reserve the trimmings.

Cut an 800-g (1¾-lb) lobster in half, seal it in 40 g (1½ oz, 3 tablespoons) slightly salted butter, then remove the shell and put it to one side. Clean 1 kg (2¼ lb) mussels and cook in a covered pan until they open. Remove the flesh and retain the cooking juices.

Prepare the forcemeat as follows: wash 500 g (18 oz) leeks and finely slice the white parts; chop 2 cloves of garlic and 4 shallots. Soften all these vegetables in 40 g (1½ oz, 3 tablespoons) slightly salted butter. Add 200 g (7 oz) coarsely chopped sorrel, then the leaves of a sprig of tarragon. Use a coarse grater to shred the fillets of pike and then the lobster flesh. Blend in the leek and sorrel mixture. Season with salt and pepper; add a pinch of 'four spices', 2 tablespoons (3 tablespoons) mustard, and 3 whole eggs. Mix thoroughly, then add the mussels.

Now prepare the terrine: line a white porcelain ballottine mould with bards, leaving the ends hanging over the side of the dish, and brush with egg white, then spread in it the first layer of forcemeat and cover with the fillets of turbot and salmon. Add a second layer of forcemeat, then the flesh and corals of 1 kg (2¼ lb) scallops, pointing the corals towards the centre of the mould. Chop 1 large truffle and sprinkle over the scallops, then add another layer of forcemeat, then the red mullet fillets, and finally the rest of the forcemeat. Put a bay leaf in the centre. Dissolve ¼ oz (1 envelope) powdered gelatine in 4 tablespoons water; pour over the terrine. Fold down the bards to seal the terrine, cover, and cook in a bain-marie in a hot oven (190–200 C, 375–400 F, gas 5–6) for 1¼ hours.

Prepare an aspic with the fish trimmings, the shell of the lobster, the juice of the mussels, the green parts of the leeks, and some gelatine. Pour this over the terrine when it has cooled. Keep cool until just before serving. To serve, stand the mould in a little hot water then turn it out onto a serving dish. Garnish with lettuce leaves and parsley. Serve some herb-flavoured mayonnaise separately.

Terrine of duckling TERRINE DE CANETON Bone a duckling weighing about 1.25 kg (2¾ lb) without damaging the breast meat. Cut the latter into even strips, together with 300 g (11 oz) bacon fat. Put the meat into a bowl with salt, pepper, ½ teaspoon 'four spices', 4 tablespoons (5 tablespoons) brandy, a chopped bay leaf, and a small sprig of fresh thyme with the leaves removed. Thoroughly soak the meat in this mixture and marinate for 24 hours in a cool place. Put the rest of the duck in the refrigerator. Soak an intact pig's caul (caul fat) in cold water, then squeeze and wipe it dry.

Prepare a duxelles with 250 g (9 oz, 3 cups) button mushrooms, 2 or 3 shallots, salt, and pepper.

Finely chop 350 g (12 oz) fresh belly of pork, 1 onion, the remaining duck meat, and the blanched zest of an orange. Mix the duxelles and the chopped meat in a bowl with 2 eggs, pepper, and salt. Work the mixture well to make it homogeneous, adding the marinade in which the strips of bacon fat and duck were steeped.

Line the terrine with the caul. Arrange half of the forcemeat in an even layer. Cover with alternating strips of the marinated duck and bacon fat. Cover with the rest of the forcemeat. Press down the caul on the contents of the terrine and trim. Place a bay leaf and 2 small sprigs of fresh thyme on top and then put on the lid.

Place the terrine in a bain-marie, bring to the boil on top of the stove, then cook in the oven at 180 C (350 F, gas 4) for 1½ hours. Remove from the oven and allow to cool. When lukewarm, take off the lid and replace with a weighted board. Allow the terrine to cool completely.

An aspic flavoured with port can be poured into the terrine and allowed to set. In order to preserve the terrine, cover with a fine layer of melted goose fat.

Terrine of fruit with honey jelly TER-RINE DE FRUITS À LA GELÉE DE MIEL (from M. Lachize's recipe) 2 rectangular terrines are required for this recipe. Add 2 tablespoons (3 tablespoons) honey, 500 g (18 oz, 2¼ cups, firmly packed) caster (superfine) sugar, some orange and lemon peel, and a few leaves of lemon-balm to 1.5 litres (2¾ pints, 3½ pints) water in a pan. Boil for 30 minutes then strain through coarse muslin (cheesecloth). Soak 3 oz (12 envelopes) powdered gelatine in a little cold water, add to the strained liquid, then chill. Meanwhile, clean some strawberries, raspberries, and alpine strawberries, cut some peeled pears into quarters, deseed some grapes, and dice some candied orange and lemon peel. Pour the half-set jelly onto the fruit and gently mix together. Put into the terrine and leave to set in a cool place for at least 2 hours. Serve with raspberry purée decorated with a band of honey.

Terrine of pheasant, partridge, *or* quail TERRINE DE FAISAN, DE PER-DREAU, OU DE CAILLE Proceed as for terrine of duckling, but arrange the forcemeat in 3 layers, one separated by strips of meat, and the next by a thin layer of foie gras and diced truffle.

Terrine of vegetables Fontanieu TER-RINE DE LÉGUMES FONTANIEU (from a recipe of the Hôtel Métropole, Beaulieu-sur-Mer) Cook separately, in very lightly salted water, 7 fluted carrots, 300 g (11 oz) French (string) beans, and 150 g (5 oz, scant cup) petits pois. Cut the following vegetables into sticks and cook separately: 500 g (18 oz) turnips, 500 g (18 oz) courgettes (zucchini), and 1 small root of celeriac (celery root). Peel, halve, and deseed 3 tomatoes. Cool the vegetables and dry them thoroughly.

Bring 1 litre (1¾ pints, 4¼ cups) double (heavy) cream just to the boil, then blend in 500 g (18 oz, 6 cups) shredded button mushrooms. Season with salt and pepper. Remove the mushrooms after 5 minutes and chop them. Do not boil down the cream, but blend in, while it is still hot, 35 g (1 oz, 4 envelopes) powdered gelatine, ½ glass (4½ tablespoons) dry vermouth, and the chopped mushrooms. Keep the mixture warm, ready for building up the terrine.

Pour a thin layer of this mixture into the bottom of a china mould. Arrange the French beans lengthways, covering the whole of the bottom of the terrine, then mask them with a little of the mushroom cream. In this way, build up the terrine, alternating the layers of vegetables according to colour. (The purpose of the cream mixture is simply to bind the ingredients – it should not take precedence over the vegetables.) Place the tomato halves in the middle. When the terrine is full, settle the ingredients by lightly tapping the bottom and refrigerate for at least half a day. When serving, turn out of the mould and serve with small diced tomatoes sprinkled with chopped basil. Sprinkle the terrine with a dash of raspberry vinegar and olive oil. Season with salt and pepper

terrinée

A cold dessert that is a speciality of Normandy. It was formerly an indispensable item of food at village fêtes and on special occasions and still remains a traditional family dish. It consists of rice cooked in milk in a glazed earthenware terrine, with sugar and a little salt, traditionally flavoured with cinnamon and sometimes with nutmeg. The cooking process lasts at least 5 hours (formerly it was cooked in the baker's oven) and the finished dish has a.thick tasty golden crust. It is particularly nourishing, especially as it was often eaten with a slice of *fallue* (brioche). Terrinée is also commonly called *teurt-goule, teurgoule, tor-goule,* or *bourre-gueule.*

Tête-de-Moine

A Swiss cows'-milk cheese (40% fat) from the canton of Berne. Pressed and uncooked, it is a firm yet pliable cheese with a washed brownish-yellow rather sticky rind. It has a spicy flavour and a pronounced aroma. The cheese is creamy yellow and becomes reddish as it matures. It is sold unwrapped in cylinders that are as high as they are wide

(9–12 cm, 3½–4¾ in). The best Tête-de-Moine comes from Bellelay, where, long ago, it was customary for the prior of the abbey to receive one cheese *par tête-de-moine* (per monk) each year as a fee. Nowadays it is produced on a small scale, as a cottage industry, and is in season between September and March.

This cheese is served at the end of the meal. Traditionally the upper layer is sliced off and kept as a cover and the inside is scooped out in small quantities. It is also used for sandwiches and canapés. (It should not be confused with Tête-de-Mort or Tête-de-Maure, the name given in France to Dutch Edam cheese.)

tête de nègre

A ball-shaped confection, consisting of two meringues sandwiched together with chocolate-flavoured butter cream. The ball is then coated with more cream and covered with grated chocolate or, more rarely, with grated coconut (or coconut on one half and cocoa powder on the other).

The name is also given to a dome-shaped rice cake entirely coated with chocolate sauce and surrounded with a ring of whipped cream, and to a small patty made of very light sweet pastry arranged on a wafer and coated with chocolate (this confection is also called *baiser de nègre*).

texturing agent

AGENT DE TEXTURE
An additive designed to give a specific structure and consistency to certain foods. Texturing agents affect the physical properties of the product – density, fluidity, viscosity – and hence its smoothness, oiliness, creaminess, etc. They may be emulsifiers (poly-phosphates in pork products, lecithin in chocolates), thickeners (agar-agar in soups and broths, carrageenin in ice creams, pectin in jams, gum arabic in confectionery), gelling agents (alginates in custards and desserts), or stabilizers (softening salts in cream cheeses, algin-ates in wine).

tfina

A slowly cooked ragout of Arab cuisine, made with brisket of beef, calf's foot, chickpeas (or white haricot (navy) beans), peeled potatoes, and whole eggs in their shells, arranged in layers with olive oil, garlic, paprika, and honey. Meatballs and spices may also be added. Tfina must simmer for several hours. Traditionally the meat is served in one dish and the vegetables and eggs in another. In wheat tfina, the potatoes are replaced by wheat or pearl barley and the eggs are omitted: this is the typical Sabbath dish of Algerian-Jewish cookery. Tfinas are also made with spinach or vermicelli.

thermidor

The name of a lobster dish, created in January 1894 at Maire's, a famous restaurant in the Boulevard Saint-Denis in Paris, on the evening of the premiere of *Thermidor*, a play by Victorien Sardou (according to the *Dictionnaire de l'Académie des gastronomes*). Other authors attribute it to Léopold Mourier of the Café de Paris, where the chef Tony Girod, his assistant and successor, created the recipe used today: cubes or escalopes of lobster mixed with Bercy sauce (or cream) seasoned with mustard and served in the two halves of the shell, either sprinkled with grated cheese and cooked *au gratin*, or covered with Mornay sauce and glazed in the oven or under the grill. Sometimes small mushrooms or truffles are added.

The name 'thermidor' is also given to a dish consisting of sole poached in white wine and fish fumet, with shallots and parsley, and covered with a sauce made from the reduced cooking liquid thickened with butter and seasoned with mustard.

RECIPE

Lobster thermidor HOMARD THER-MIDOR (from Tony Girod's recipe) Split a live lobster in two, lengthwise. Crack the shell of the claws and remove the gills from the carcass. Season both halves of the lobster with salt, sprinkle with oil, and roast in the oven for 15–20 minutes. Remove and dice the flesh from the tail and claws.

Prepare a stock using equal proportions of meat juices, fish fumet, and white wine, flavoured with chervil, tarragon, and chopped shallots. Boil it down to a concentrated consistency, then add a little very thick béchamel sauce and some English mustard. Boil the sauce for a few moments, then whisk in some fresh butter (one-third of the volume of the sauce). Pour a little of this sauce into the two halves of the shell. Fill the shells with the flesh of the lobster, cover with the remainder of the sauce, sprinkle with a little grated Parmesan cheese and melted butter, and brown rapidly in a very hot oven.

More simply, the lobster can be split into two and grilled (broiled). The two halves of the shell are then emptied out, lined with a little cream sauce seasoned with mustard, and the sliced lobster flesh is put back, covered with the same sauce, and glazed in the oven. Arrange the lobster on a long dish and serve piping hot.

thermometer
THERMOMÈTRE
An instrument used to measure temperature. The graduation is in degrees Celsius (centigrade) or Fahrenheit on a scale varying according to the use intended: monitoring the temperature of a freezer, cooking sugar syrup, deep-frying, etc. Most thermometers used in the kitchen consist of a glass tube containing a liquid which expands as the temperature increases. For roast meat, there are bimetallic thermometers, consisting of metals with different expansion coefficients. The meat thermometer has a pointed end and is graduated from +30 c (86 f) to 120 c (248 f) and has markings for well-done, medium, and rare meat. It is implanted in the centre of a joint of meat to measure the internal temperature. The frozen meat thermometer is graduated from −30 to +30 c (−22 to +86 f).

thickening LIAISON
A process used to give body to a sauce, soup, gravy, etc.

There are several different methods, depending on the thickening agent used.
● *Thickening with starch* (such as cornflour (cornstarch), arrowroot, or ground rice) is effected by making a stable paste through the action of heat. The thickening agent is blended with water to make a thin paste and then added to the boiling liquid that needs to be thickened. The mixture is stirred constantly over the heat until it thickens.
● *Thickening with egg yolk, blood, cream, or liver* results in the formation of an emulsion. Soups and sauces for meat or poultry dishes are thickened in this way, but as the thickening agents are proteins the liquids should never be allowed to boil as proteins curdle at a high temperature. It is best to keep the temperature below 80 c (175 f).
● *Thickening with a roux* (flour cooked with butter) is achieved by adding the liquid to be thickened, while boiling, to the cold roux and then whisking the mixture over the heat until it comes to the boil. It is then simmered for a few minutes. This method is used for thickening béchamel and velouté sauces. The same principle is involved when flour is sprinkled onto ingredients that have been sautéed in fat, before the stock is added (see *braising, ragout*).
● *Thickening with a mixture of eggs and flour*, possibly adding other ingredients to a boiling liquid, is used when making confectioners' custard (pastry cream), etc.
● Some rapid methods of thickening are used just before serving. These include incorporating whipped cream (for Chantilly sauce, for example) and whisking butter into sauces: in neither case should the thickened liquid be allowed to boil, otherwise the sauce will curdle. Kneaded butter (*beurre manié*) can also be dropped into the liquid in small lumps and then whisked to thicken.

RECIPES

Thickening with arrowroot LIAISON À L'ARROW-ROOT Mix 1 teaspoon arrowroot with 2–3 tablespoons cold stock. Pour this mixture into ½ litre (scant pint, 2¼ cups) boiling stock or juice and whisk until it thickens. Strain.

Thickening with blood LIAISON AU SANG Add 1 tablespoon vinegar to a small bowl of liquid blood (rabbit, hare, pork, or duck) to prevent it curdling. To thicken the sauce, remove it from the heat and add this mixture, whisking continuously. Do not let it boil again. Sometimes the puréed liver of the animal can be added as well.

Thickening with butter LIAISON AU BEURRE Heat the strained sauce or stock. Cut the butter into small pieces and add it all at once to the hot liquid. Whisk well. 1 tablespoon liquid can absorb up to 50 g (2 oz, ¼ cup) butter.

Thickening with cream LIAISON À LA CRÈME Mix the cream with a little of the sauce, stock, or soup to be thickened and then pour it back into the preparation. Whisk until it begins to boil, then lower the heat and let it reduce until it has reached the desired consistency.

Thickening with kneaded butter LIAISON AU BEURRE MANIÉ To thicken ½ litre (17 fl oz, 2 cups) stock or sauce, work together 30 g (1¼ oz, 2 tablespoons) butter and 30 g (1¼ oz, 5 tablespoons) flour. Add this paste to the boiling liquid and whisk over the heat for 2 minutes.

Thickening with liver LIAISON AU FOIE Clean the liver of the appropriate animal and purée it finely. Add one-quarter of its weight of double (heavy) cream and mix well. Remove the boiling liquid from the heat and whisk in the cream and liver mixture at once.

thigh CUISSE

The upper fleshy part of the leg of animals.

The thigh of beef provides choice pieces of meat for roasting, such as topside (beef round), rump, silverside (bottom round), and also steak.

A thigh of veal provides the fillet (round) and the rump, which may be roasted whole or cut into paupiettes or escalopes. (For thigh of mutton or lamb, see *gigot*; for pork thigh, see *ham*.)

In poultry, the thigh ends in the drumstick. Both thigh and drumstick are used for ragouts and fricassees. The thigh may be boned and stuffed. In France, a thigh of turkey, together with the drumstick, is sold under the name of *gigolette* of turkey.

The thigh of a frog's leg is the only edible part of the animal.

thin RELÂCHER

To add a liquid (broth, stock, milk, consommé, water, etc.) to a sauce, purée, stuffing, etc., to render it less thick. For example, mayonnaise is thinned by adding a mixture of boiling water and vinegar.

Thouarsais wines
VINS DU THOUARSAIS

White, red, and rosé wines of the Loire Valley, produced around Thouars, in the Deux-Sèvres. The whites are slightly reminiscent of Saumur wines, which, like them, are made from the Chenin Blanc. The reds and rosés come from the Cabernet Franc. They have a pleasant fragrance.

thread-fin CAPITAINE

A sea fish related to the mullet, sometimes called *grand pourceau* ('great swine') in France. About 50 cm (20 in) long, it inhabits coastal regions of west Africa and can be found in the estuaries and rivers. Caught in large numbers, it has tasty flesh and is an important local food, particularly in Senegal, where it is used in *tié bou diéné*.

thrush GRIVE

A small bird belonging to the same family as the blackbird. There are a dozen species in France, which are hunted in autumn and winter for their delicate flesh, the flavour of which depends on their diet (grapes, juniper berries, peas, etc.). The song thrush makes excellent eating. The larger mistle thrush feeds on mistletoe berries, which make its flesh taste rather bitter. The smaller redwing is also highly prized; the fieldfare, imported from northern Europe, has a rather insipid flavour but firmer flesh.

All thrushes are prepared in the same way as quails and there are in addition certain regional specialities, particularly pies and terrines. They are often cooked with juniper berries. Although common in England and the United States, thrushes are rarely, if ever, eaten there. In England they are protected birds and may not be killed.

thyme THYM

A perennial plant with small grey-green aromatic leaves and small purplish flowers, much used as a culinary herb and also to prepare infusions. Thyme contains an essential oil, Thymol, which has a very aromatic odour and antiseptic properties. Thyme is one of the basic herbs used in cooking. Alone or in a bouquet garni, fresh or dried, it is used in stuffings, casseroles, stews, soups, baked fish, etc. Fresh thyme is particularly good for flavouring scrambled eggs, salads, tomato dishes, and lentils. It is also used in the preparation of certain home-made liqueurs.

Wild thyme (called *serpolet* in France) has clusters of rose-pink flowers and a less pronounced flavour than garden thyme. It is used mostly with chicken or white meats, and in Provençal cookery (where it is called *farigoule* or *farigoulette*) it is traditionally used to flavour trout, mutton, and rabbit. It is also used in the production of a liqueur.

tian

An earthenware ovenproof dish from Provence. Square or rectangular, with slightly raised edges, it is used to prepare all kinds of gratin dishes, which are also called tians. Potato tian (a speciality of Apt) consists of alternate layers of sliced potatoes and chopped onion with sliced tomato, sprinkled with thyme, salt and pepper, covered with grated cheese, and sprinkled with olive oil. Prepared in the same way are tians of artichoke hearts with anchovies, aubergines (eggplants) with tomatoes, salt cod (especially in Carpentras), white haricot (navy) beans, spinach, etc. In Corsica, the *tianu* is a type of small earthenware saucepan used for preparing ragouts (red kidney beans in wine, garnished with slices of preserved sausage and leeks). Rice is also cooked in it.

tié bou diéné

A Senegalese dish consisting of chunks or steaks of lean fish (conger eel, gilthead bream, cod, or hake), sometimes stuffed with chopped onion, parsley, and red pepper. Browned in groundnut (peanut) oil, the fish is simmered on a bed of vegetables (onions, tomatoes, sweet potatoes, aubergines (eggplants), turnips, shredded cabbage) that have been sautéed in oil, then seasoned with chilli powder and pepper, and mixed with pieces of dried fish. Also called *tiep dien* or *tiébédienne*, the dish is served with steamed rice and the sauce it is cooked in.

Tilsit

A Swiss cows'-milk cheese (45% fat) from the cantons of Saint-Gall and Thurgovie. It is pressed, uncooked, pliable, and golden yellow, with small regular holes and a polished yellow-brown rind. It has a very fruity flavour and a strong odour and takes the form of a small round slab about 35 cm (14 in) in diameter and 7–8 cm (2¾–3¼ in) high.

Originally from Holland, the cheese was imported several centuries ago into Tilsit, east Prussia (now Sovietsk, in the Soviet Union). It was not until the end of the 19th century that it was introduced into Switzerland. It is also made in northern Germany and central Europe, but has a stronger taste and is sometimes flavoured with aniseed. Used for canapés and toasted croutes, it is also served at the end of a meal and may replace Emmental in gratin dishes and soufflés, which it flavours more strongly. When it has matured for more than four months, it is used like Parmesan cheese.

timbale

This word is used in various senses. Originally a timbale was a small metal drinking goblet; such timbales are now usually made of silver or silver plate and are purely decorative, being given to babies at birth or as christening presents.

The word also refers to a serving dish similar to a vegetable dish, made of silverplated metal, stainless steel, or heatproof porcelain, in which vegetables, scrambled eggs, ragouts, etc., are served.

Today, however, the word is applied chiefly to a plain round high-sided mould and the preparation cooked in it – a pie crust baked blind and then filled with meat of various kinds, forcemeat, pasta, etc., blended with a sauce. The crust is often decorated with patterns cut out with a pastry (cookie) cutter. The filling may be breast of chicken, calves' or lambs' sweetbreads, fish or seafood (fillets of sole, crayfish, scampi, etc.), truffles, quenelles, or any of the fillings for vols-au-vent or bouchées. Sometimes layers of meat or forcemeat are alternated with layers of pasta (as in timbale *à la milanaise*).

The name timbale is also given to small preparations moulded into darioles, consisting of various salpicons, vegetables, risotto, etc., served as an entrée or a garnish.

Finally, a timbale can also be a dessert: a pastry case (shell) baked blind then filled with various fruits, creams, or ice cream.

RECIPES

Large timbale case (shell) CROÛTE À TIMBALE GARNIE Butter a large timbale or charlotte mould. Decorate the inside with little shapes of very firm noodle paste (slightly moistening them so that they will adhere to the pastry used to line the mould).

Prepare 400 g (14 oz) lining pastry (see *doughs and batters*) and roll it out into a round 20 cm (8 in) in diameter and 6 mm (¼ in) thick. Sprinkle lightly with flour and fold in half, then bring the ends into the centre until they meet. Roll out again to smooth away the folds. Place this round of pastry in the mould and press it firmly against the base and sides without disturbing the noodle-paste decorations. Cut off any excess pastry.

Line the pastry case with buttered paper (buttered side inwards), then fill it up with dried beans. Place a circle of paper on top of the dried beans (which should be heaped into a dome) then, on top of this, a thin round sheet of pastry 1.5 cm (½ in) thick. Join the edges of the pastry together by pressing them between the fingers, then make the rim of the pie by pinching this border with pastry pincers.

Moisten the lid with water and decorate with little shapes (leaves, rosettes, fluted rings) cut from a thin sheet of pastry. Make a chimney in the centre of the lid. Brush with egg and bake in a moderate oven (190 c, 375 f, gas 5) for 35–40 minutes.

Take the timbale out of the oven, cut round the lid with a sharp-pointed knife, and remove it. Take out the paper and dried beans and brush the inside of the pastry case with egg. Put the timbale back in the oven with the door open, to dry for a few minutes, then remove it, turn it out of the mould onto a wire rack, and keep it hot together with the lid. Fill as desired and replace the lid. Serve immediately.

Small timbales as an entrée PETITES TIMBALES D'ENTRÉE Butter some dariole moulds and sprinkle with truffle, pickled tongue, or lean ham (chopped or cut into decorative shapes). Line evenly with a layer ½ cm (¼ in) thick of fine poultry or fish forcemeat, rice *au gras* (cooked in a meat stock), vegetable brunoise, etc. Fill the middle with a cooled salpicon or a barquette filling. Cover with a layer of the forcemeat, etc., used to line the moulds and cook in the oven, in a bain-marie, for 15–18 minutes. Leave for a few moments, then turn the timbales out of the moulds onto a dish or onto rounds of fried bread or artichoke hearts. Serve with a sauce in keeping with the main ingredient.

small timbales à l'épicurienne TIMBALES À L'ÉPICURIENNE Sprinkle some buttered dariole moulds with dried breadcrumbs and line them with an even layer, 5 mm (¼ in) thick, of rice *au gras* (cooked in meat stock) mixed with chopped truffle. Fill with a salpicon of lambs' sweetbreads, truffle, and pickled tongue, blended with mushroom purée. Cover with a layer of rice *au gras*. Cook in the oven for 10–15 minutes (without a bain-marie), then leave to stand for 5 minutes before turning out of the mould. Serve with tomato sauce.

Timbales Élysée (from a recipe of the Restaurant Lasserre) Prepare 8 pastry cups (shells) from a short biscuit-type (cookie-type) pastry made by thoroughly blending 100 g (4 oz, 1 cup) flour, 100 g (4 oz, 1 cup) sugar, 1 egg, and 50 g (2 oz, ¼ cup) rather soft butter. Flavour with vanilla. Divide dough into 8 then roll into very thin rounds and arrange on a buttered and floured baking sheet. Bake in the oven at 200 c (400 f, gas 6) for 6–8 minutes.

While the pastry rounds are still hot, mould each of them into a cup shape. Place a small slice of sponge cake soaked in a Kirsch-flavoured syrup at the bottom of each pastry cup. Add a spoonful of vanilla ice cream and cover with fresh fruit (strawberries, raspberries, etc.). Coat this with a spoonful of Kirsch-

flavoured redcurrant jelly, then pipe
rosettes of Chantilly cream round the
inside edge of the cup.

Cover each of the filled cups with a
cage of spun sugar: cook 200 g (7 oz,
1¼ cups) sugar and 40 g (1½ oz) glucose to the 'hard crack' stage (see *sugar*),
then thread this sugar in as delicate a
lattice as possible over the bowl of a
suitably-sized ladle. Top with a rosette
of Chantilly cream.

tin   ÉTAIN

A very malleable white metal often used
in the form of 'silver paper' or tinfoil for
wrapping food products (tea, chocolate,
confectionery, cheeses, etc.). It is also
used for tinning sheet metal (tin plate)
and the copper used for manufacturing
kitchen utensils. Tin was formerly used
for manufacturing the majority of pots
and pans in common use. Today it is
included in a number of alloys, including pewter. As tin does not alter the taste
of wine, beer, or tea, it is used especially
for manufacturing pitchers, tankards,
and teapots.

tin plate   FER-BLANC

Thin steel sheet, coated on both sides
with a layer of tin. It is resistant to
corrosion by acids, does not rust, and is
a very good conductor of heat. Tin plate
is the most suitable material for the
manufacture of cans for preserving
foods. It is also used to manufacture
certain kitchen utensils, such as baking
tins, ladles, etc., but nowadays, aluminium or stainless steel utensils are preferred as there is a risk of the tin plate
melting when subjected to very high
temperatures; for example, during
frying or jam-making.

tire-larigot (à)

To drink *à tire-larigot* is a colloquial
expression meaning to drink a lot. This
old phrase, which is used in the writings
of Ronsard and Rabelais, comes,
according to the historian Jacques
Bourgeat, from the name of the Bishop
of Rouen, Rigault, who donated to the
cathedral a bell, which was nicknamed
la Rigaude by the people. The bell-
ringers, thirsty from the effort of ringing
the large bell, used it as an excuse to
drink large amounts of cider *à tire la
Rigaude.*

tisane

An infusion of herbs and dried plants
that is drunk hot, on its own or slightly
sweetened. The word derives from the
Greek *ptisanê* (barley water) and originally designated a decoction of this
cereal.

Today most tisanes are made from
medicinal plants. Digestive infusions,
which are said by some to be beneficial
at the end of a meal, can include the
following: aniseed, a stimulant and
sedative; camomile, effective against
neuralgia, migraines, and fever pains;
corn poppy, a sedative and supposed to
be effective against asthma; ground ivy,
antitussive (good for coughs); marjoram, for spasms and insomnia; lemon
balm, for giddiness, palpitations, migraines, and sleep disorders; mint, a tonic
and stimulant; meadowsweet, a sudorific and diuretic, effective against in-
fluenza and rheumatism; rosemary,
beneficial to the liver; sage, a tonic,
stomachic, and digestive; wild thyme,
an antiseptic, good for the respiratory
tract and the stomach; lime blossom, an
antispasmodic and sudorific; verbena, a
digestive; and violet, an antitussive, ex-
pectorant, sudorific, and diuretic.
Tisanes can combine two plants
blended together: for example, lime
blossom and mint, or lime blossom and
star anise.

Formerly, the expression *tisane de
champagne* referred to a lighter sweeter
champagne than classic champagne.
Nowadays, in colloquial usage, tisane is
simply a bad champagne.

Formerly, *tisane de Richelieu* was a
colloquial name for Bordeaux wine.

tisanière

A tall cup used for making an infusion.
Made of porcelain, faïence, or stoneware, it is fitted with an internal strainer
(in which the leaves are placed before
the boiling water is poured in) and a lid.
The infusion is prepared directly in the
cup, with the lid closed, so that it can be
drunk from a hot vessel. The forerunner
of the tisanière, the *timbale à tisane*, was
already in existence in the 17th century.
It had a lid to keep the tisane – at that
time a very popular beverage – hot.

Tivoli

The name given, in the 18th and 19th

centuries, to several Parisian establishments providing illuminations, fireworks and other attractions, together with refreshments (including ice cream), and evoking the famous Villa d'Este with its water gardens, built in Tivoli, not far from Rome, in the 16th century. In Paris, in the Saint-Lazare district, the old Folie-Boutin was renamed Tivoli and enlivened by the firework-maker Ruggieri after the Reign of Terror (1793–94). Other establishments renamed Tivoli were the Folie-Richelieu, also modernized by Ruggieri, which operated between 1811 and 1826, and the Tivoli-Vauxhall, at St Martin's gate, very popular up to 1848 and where pigeon shooting was introduced from England.

In classic cookery, the name Tivoli has been given to a garnish for small cuts of meat, consisting of bunches of asparagus tips and grilled mushroom caps, filled with a salpicon of cocks' combs and kidneys blended with suprême sauce.

toad in the hole

A popular British dish. It originally consisted of pieces of cooked meat mixed with smoked bacon, covered with batter, and baked in the oven. Now it is made with small fresh pork sausages arranged in a dish and covered with thick pancake batter. It is cooked in a very hot oven and served hot.

toast RÔTIE

A slice of bread grilled (broiled) on both sides in a toaster or under the grill (broiler) and served hot. Pieces of toast can be served in a toast rack, which will keep them crisp; they can also be served in a basket, loosely wrapped in a napkin to keep them warm.

Buttered toast is traditionally eaten for breakfast or tea, often spread with marmalade, honey, or jam. It is also an accompaniment to caviar, foie gras, smoked fish, etc., and is used as a base for various other savoury preparations: cheese, flavoured butters, scrambled eggs, grilled kidneys, mushrooms, asparagus tips with béchamel sauce, grilled bacon, etc. Slices of toast spread with forcemeat are served with roast game birds, especially woodcock and snipe.

A toast is also a proposal to drink someone's health. This sense of the word derives from the old habit of placing a slice of toast in a glass of hot spiced wine: the glass of wine was passed round among the guests and the slice of toast was offered to the guest of honour.

RECIPE

Garlic toast RÔTIES À L'AIL Cut some slices about ½ cm (¼ in) thick from a loaf of brown or white bread and grill them lightly. Spread them with garlic purée and sprinkle with a thin layer of breadcrumbs and a little olive oil. Brown quickly in a hot oven and serve very hot with a salad of endive (chicory), cherry tomatoes, or mesclun (mixed green salad).

toaster GRILLE-PAIN

A device used for toasting bread. Electric toasters are either semiautomatic (the bread has to be removed when toasted) or automatic (the slices are ejected once they have been toasted the correct amount). Some models have vertical slots, others have horizontal slots, of variable length and width. (The latest models even toast thick slices of bread, such as French bread.) Those which heat from above, the horizontal models, can be used to toast brioches, croissants, and rolls.

tofu

A basic foodstuff of Far Eastern cookery, especially Japanese, prepared from soya (soy) beans, which are soaked, reduced to a purée, then boiled and sieved. The liquid obtained is jellified by the addition of a coagulant. In French, tofu is called *fromage de soja* since its appearance and colour are reminiscent of fresh cheese.

Originally from China, where it is said to have been prepared as early as the 2nd century BC, Mongolian *doufu* was introduced into Japan during the 8th century by Buddhist priests. It traditionally constituted the basis of vegetarian dishes. Western travellers referred to tofu as early as the 17th century but it is only since the 20th century that we have been familiar with its method of manufacture and its uses.

Relatively neutral in taste and very rich in vegetable proteins, tofu is used in a wide variety of Japanese recipes: combined with sweet and sour sauces in vegetable and seaweed salads; diced with noodle dishes; crumbled and cooked like scambled eggs, with mushrooms and aromatics, etc. It is used in sukiyaki, in fish and shellfish dishes, and in soups; garnished with spring onions (scallions) or onions, it is shaped into small patties or fried in balls; it is coated with *miso* and grilled on skewers. It can also be cut into cubes, fried, and eaten with grated ginger and soy sauce. In summer it is served chilled, in a salad with spring onions (scallions), dried bonito, grated daikon, and sesame seeds. In winter, it is scalded and accompanied by *konbu* (a type of seaweed).

Chinese doufu is firmer than Japanese tofu. It is usually used in steamed dishes, soups, and broths. Cut into dice or strips, it also accompanies fish. Doufu can also be pressed, plain or flavoured in various ways (with curcuma, green tea, or red pepper), and fried with vegetables or added to marinated dishes. Fermented doufou, which has quite a strong flavour, is often seasoned with pepper and used to garnish *riz gluant* (sticky rice) and potées.

In Vietnam, the Philippines, Indonesia, and Korea, tofu is prepared with various condiments: dried shrimps, mint, rice spirit, etc.

tokány

A Hungarian beef stew in which paprika is not the principal seasoning (unlike goulash or paprikache). The meat is cut into thin strips, which are lightly cooked with onions in lard. The basting liquid is white wine and the seasoning is based in particular on pepper and marjoram. Sometimes, halfway through cooking, some pieces of fried smoked larding bacon are added; the stew is finished off with soured (dairy sour) cream.

Tokay

A world-famous pale amber-coloured white wine made near the little town of the same name in northeastern Hungary. Known for many centuries, it is made mainly from the Furmint grape. It is important to realize that the Tokay

d'Alsace and the Tocai of Italy are not versions of Hungarian Tokay.

There are several different types of Hungarian Tokay, the most usual being the sweet or very sweet wines that are categorized as being from three to five (sometimes even six) *puttonyos* – the higher the number, the sweeter the wine. The *puttony* is a wooden basket or cask, holding six gallons, in which overripe grapes, affected with the 'noble rot' (*Botrytis cinerea*), are piled; such grapes are referred to as *aszú*. The legendary 'Tokay Eszencia', a precious and mysteriously sweet wine that has been credited with semimagical properties (including that of being an elixir of life), is made from the juice that flows from the *aszú* grapes through the pressure of their own weight. This juice is combined with the juice of Furmint grapes, and the wine label indicates how many *puttonyos* of *aszú* were added to the Furmint must. Szamarodni can be either sweet or dry.

The production of Tokay is complex and lengthy and any visitor to the strange cellars underground in the region will be astounded by the thick blanket of mould that covers the walls and must obviously have a marked effect on the wines that mature many years in the small casks known as *gönci*. The bottles for the sweet wines are 50 cl, slightly dumpy in shape with elongated necks. Although the dry wines can be enjoyed on many occasions, the sweet ones are possibly best served at the end of a meal, lightly chilled.

tomate

An apéritif made in Corsica with the local and excellent pastis (aniseed-flavoured) and grenadine, which results in a drink looking exactly like tomato juice.

tomato TOMATE

An annual plant cultivated for its red fruits, which are widely used, cooked or raw, as vegetables, in salads, to make a sauce or juice, etc. Originally from Peru (the name comes from the Aztec *tomatl*), the tomato was imported into Spain in the 16th century. Until the 18th century it was thought to be poisonous and remained an ornamental plant (called 'Peruvian apple' or 'acacia apple').

In the south of France, it was nicknamed 'love apple' or 'golden apple', a name also used in Italy (*pomodoro*). When its properties as a vegetable-cum-fruit were discovered, the tomato became established in Spain, then in the Spanish kingdom of Naples, then in the north of Italy, the south of France, and Corsica. It was not until 1790 that it reached the Paris area and the north of France. The story goes that the people of Marseille, who had come to Paris for the Federation festival, urged the restaurateurs to have this fruit sent from the south of France and to advise the Parisian market gardeners to cultivate it.

Nowadays, the southeast and southwest of France account for 68% of French production, mainly between June and September. Imports from Morocco, Spain, Italy, Holland, and Belgium cover the needs of the French market all year round. The numerous varieties of tomato are distinguished according to shape and size: round, ribbed and flattened, elongated, or oval. Some are used while still green.

With a high water content but low in calories (23 Cal per 100 g), the tomato is rich in vitamins A, B, and C. Diuretic, laxative, and refreshing, it is slightly acidic (this problem is often rectified by adding sugar to the cooking liquid). As its skin is sometimes difficult to digest, it is scalded and skinned for some preparations.

Tomatoes are also available in preserved form: canned peeled whole tomatoes, concentrated tomato purée in cans or tubes, condiments and sauces, tomato juice, etc.

Fresh tomatoes must be firm, fleshy, and shiny, without wrinkles or cracks, and preferably of uniform colour. Tomatoes that are rather green ripen quickly in a warm place. They can be kept for ten days or so in the salad drawer of a refrigerator.

Iberian, Italian, Provençal, Basque, and Languedocian cookery are unimaginable without the tomato, and it is also used in the cookery of most other European countries, including Hungary and Britain. The tomato is also indispensable in classic French cookery (chicken Marengo, stuffed tomatoes, Aurora, américaine, and Choron sauces, etc.). Crushed or diced tomato pulp is used to season a number of stocks and garnishes, and raw tomato is used in various salads and garnishes for cold dishes. Tomato blends perfectly with many seasonings (garlic, shallot, basil, tarragon, even cumin), and its association with olives, sweet peppers, and aubergines (eggplants) is by now classical. It is also a good accompaniment to tuna fish, salt cod, sardines, and red mullet, as well as beef, veal, chicken, and eggs. Green tomatoes are used in pickles and chutneys, and the fruit can also be made into jam (red or green) and even sorbets.

Typical dishes based on the tomato clearly reflect its southern origins: *à l'algérienne, à l'andalouse, à l'arlésienne, à la bolognaise, à l'espagnole, à la grecque, à la languedocienne, à la marseillaise, à la mexicaine, à la napolitaine, à la niçoise, à l'orientale, à la portugaise, à la provençale, à la tyrolienne,* and zingara.

RECIPES

Cold tomato mousse MOUSSE FROIDE DE TOMATE Lightly fry in butter 500 g (18 oz, 2 cups) coarsely chopped tomato pulp (net weight after skinning and deseeding). When it is well dried out, add 1 dl (6 tablespoons, scant ½ cup) velouté sauce to which 4 leaves (1½ tablespoons, 2 tablespoons) gelatine softened in cold water have been added. Strain this mixture through coarse muslin (cheesecloth), then put in a bowl and whisk until smooth. When cool, add half its volume of fresh whipped cream. Season with salt, pepper, and a little cayenne and add a few drops of lemon juice. Mix well, then pour into a glass dish.

The mousse can also be used as a garnish for cold dishes (particularly fish). In this case, pour into dariole moulds lined with aspic jelly, set in the refrigerator, then turn out of the mould.

Concentrated tomato glaze GLACE DE TOMATE, SUC DE TOMATE CONCENTRÉ Immerse some ripe tomatoes in boiling water for 30 seconds, then skin them. Pound in a mortar and cook over a brisk heat until they are boiled down by half, then strain through a fine strainer. Cook once more very gently until the pulp thickens and becomes syrupy. (It can be made even smoother by straining it twice in the course of cooking.) This tomato glaze keeps for a long time in the refrigerator. It is used in the same way as tomato purée.

Fresh tomato pulp PULPE DE TOMATE FRAÎCHE Wash some very ripe perfectly sound tomatoes. Pound and rub them, still raw, through a sieve. Put this pulp into a saucepan and boil for about 5 minutes. Strain through a cloth and collect the thick pulp remaining in the cloth. Tomato pulp is used to flavour salads, hot or cold sauces, etc.

Green tomato jam CONFITURE DE TOMATES VERTES Select some green tomatoes and prepare them in the same way as for red tomato jam, but steep for 24 hours in the sugar and use special sugar for jams. The cooking time is 4 minutes after the syrup has come to the boil.

Grilled (broiled) tomatoes TOMATES GRILLÉES Cut a circle around the stalk of some round firm sound tomatoes. Remove the seeds with a teaspoon. Lightly season the tomatoes with salt and pepper, brush with olive oil, and grill (broil) them rapidly so that they do not collapse.

Red tomato jam CONFITURE DE TOMATES ROUGES Choose some very ripe firm tomatoes that are free of blemishes. Remove the stalks and plunge them in boiling water for 1 minute. Peel, cut into small pieces, then steep for 2 hours with their weight of granulated sugar and the juice of 2 lemons per kg (2¼ lb) tomatoes. Put the mixture in a pan and bring to the boil. Cook very gently until the syrup reaches the jelling stage: this takes 1–1¼ hours. Pot in the usual way (see *jams, jellies, and marmalades*).

To help the jam to set, either add 3 dl (½ pint, 1¼ cups) apple juice per kg (2¼ lb) tomatoes or replace the granulated sugar with special sugar for jams. The cooking time, after boiling, is then reduced to 4 minutes.

Sautéed tomatoes à la provençale TOMATES SAUTÉES À LA PROVENÇALE Remove the stalks from 6 firm round tomatoes. Cut them in two, remove the

seeds, and season with salt and pepper. Heat 3 tablespoons (¼ cup) olive oil in a frying pan (skillet) and put in the tomato halves cut side downwards. Brown them, then turn them over. Sprinkle the browned sides with a mixture of chopped parsley and garlic (3 generous tablespoons, generous ¼ cup). When the other side is browned, arrange the tomatoes on a hot serving dish. Add some breadcrumbs to the frying pan and brown lightly in the oil, then pour the contents of the pan over the tomatoes.

Alternatively, the breadcrumbs can also be added to the chopped parsley and garlic mixture; the stuffed tomatoes are then arranged in a gratin dish and the cooking finished in a hot oven.

Soufflé tomatoes TOMATES SOUFFLÉES Remove the seeds from some firm regular-shaped tomatoes. Sprinkle with oil or clarified butter and cook for 5 minutes in the oven at 240 c (475 F, gas 9). Allow to cool and fill with tomato soufflé mixture. Smooth the surface, sprinkle with grated Parmesan cheese, and put back in the oven at 200 c (400 F, gas 6) for 15 minutes.

Stuffed tomatoes (preparation) TOMATES FARCIES (PRÉPARATION) Choose some ripe but firm tomatoes, of medium size and regular shape. Cut a circle round the stalk end and, with a teaspoon, remove the seeds and juice. Still using the spoon, enlarge the hole slightly until it is large enough to receive the stuffing. Lightly season the inside with salt and turn the tomatoes upside down on a cloth to drain (if preferred, lightly season the inside with salt and pepper without draining). Arrange the tomatoes on an oiled baking sheet and warm them for 5 minutes in a hot oven. Drain again, then stuff them, heaping up the stuffing to form a dome. Complete according to the recipe.

Hot stuffed tomatoes are usually sprinkled with breadcrumbs and oil or clarified butter before being cooked.

Stuffed tomatoes à la bonne femme (hot) TOMATES FARCIES CHAUDES À LA BONNE FEMME For 8 medium tomatoes, mix together 250 g (9 oz, generous cup) sausagemeat, 75 g (3 oz, ¾ cup) onion lightly fried in butter, 2 tablespoons fresh breadcrumbs, 1 tablespoon chopped parsley, 1 crushed clove of garlic, and salt and pepper. Stuff the tomatoes with this mixture. Sprinkle with breadcrumbs and oil or clarified butter and cook for 30–40 minutes in the oven at 220 c (425 f, gas 7).

The stuffing can be precooked very gently in a frying pan for 15 minutes. The tomatoes are then stuffed and cooked *au gratin*. If this method is used the tomatoes will not collapse.

Stuffed tomatoes à la languedocienne (hot) TOMATES FARCIES CHAUDES À LA LANGUEDOCIENNE These are prepared in the same way as tomatoes *à la bonne femme*, but a chopped hard-boiled (hard-cooked) egg is added to the stuffing. Use olive oil.

Stuffed tomatoes à la niçoise (hot) TOMATES FARCIES CHAUDES À LA NIÇOISE Make a stuffing consisting of equal proportions of rice cooked in meat stock and aubergine (eggplant) diced very small and tossed in olive oil. Add chopped parsley, garlic, and breadcrumbs fried in olive oil. Stuff the tomatoes, put them in an ovenproof dish, sprinkle them with breadcrumbs and olive oil, and cook for 30–40 minutes in the oven at 220 c (425 f, gas 7).

Stuffed tomato nests (hot) TOMATES FARCIES CHAUDES EN NID Prepare some tomatoes for stuffing and cook them in the oven. Break an egg in each tomato. Lightly season with salt and pepper, place a small knob of butter on top, and cook for 6 minutes in the oven at 230 c (450 f, gas 8).

Tomatoes stuffed with tuna (cold) TOMATES FARCIES FROIDES AU THON Mix together equal amounts of rice pilaf and fragments of canned tuna. Add 1 tablespoon mayonnaise for every 4 tablespoons (⅓ cup) rice/fish mixture and mix in some chopped herbs and finely diced lemon pulp. Stuff the tomatoes, garnish each with a black (ripe) olive, and put in the refrigerator until just before serving; serve with sprigs of parsley.

Tomato loaf PAIN DE TOMATE Boil down some tomato pulp over a low heat until it becomes very thick. Blend in some beaten eggs (6 eggs per 500 g (18 oz, 2 cups) purée). Season with salt, pepper, and a pinch of mixed spice. Fill a round well-buttered tin (or dariole moulds) with this mixture and cook in a bain-marie in the oven at 180 c (350 f, gas 4) for 40 minutes. Allow the loaf to stand for a few moments before unmoulding. Serve coated with tomato sauce mixed with butter.

Tomato salad SALADE DE TOMATES Immerse some ripe firm sound tomatoes in boiling water for 30 seconds. Skin them, cut into slices, and place in a colander to drain off the liquid. Arrange the slices in a salad bowl. Add some finely chopped mild onion (100 g (4 oz, 1 cup) onion per kg (2¼ lb) tomatoes) and dress with a tarragon-flavoured vinaigrette. Leave in a cool place. Just before serving, sprinkle with chervil, parsley, basil, or chopped tarragon.

Tomato sauce SAUCE TOMATE Cut 100 g (4 oz, 6 slices) fresh streaky bacon into small dice. Blanch, drain, and lightly cook in 3–4 tablespoons (¼–⅓ cup) oil. Add 100 g (4 oz, 1 cup) each of diced carrots and diced onion. Cover and lightly fry for 25–30 minutes. Sprinkle in 60 g (2 oz, ½ cup) sifted flour and lightly brown. Add 3 kg (6½ lb) fresh tomatoes, skinned, deseeded, and pounded, 2 crushed cloves of garlic, a bouquet garni, and 150 g (5 oz, generous ½ cup) blanched lean ham. Add 1 litre (1¾ pints, 4¼ cups) white stock. Season with salt and pepper, add 20 g (¾ oz, 1½ tablespoons) sugar, and bring to the boil while stirring. Cover and leave to cook very gently for 2 hours. Strain the sauce into a basin. Carefully pour some tepid melted butter on the surface to prevent a skin forming.

Tomato sorbet SORBET À LA TOMATE Peel 1 kg (2¼ lb) very ripe tomatoes, press them, and filter the juice. Measure the volume (250 ml (8 fl oz, 1 cup) is needed). Make a cold syrup with 150 ml (5 fl oz, generous ½ cup) water and 300 g (11 oz, scant 1½ cups) special sugar for jams. Mix the syrup with the tomato juice and add 1 liqueur glass of vodka, then pour into an ice-cream mould and freeze for at least 1 hour. Beat 1 egg white with 50 g (2 oz) icing (confectioners') sugar over a pan of water (the water must be at about 60 c, 140 F). When the sorbet begins to set, whisk it, gently fold in the beaten egg white, and put back in the freezer until it sets (about 2 hours).

tomber

A French term meaning to cook watery vegetables, either whole (e.g. spinach) or cut up (e.g. chiffonade of sorrel, finely sliced onions), over a low heat with or without fat. Under the action of the heat, they cook in their own juices without browning.

In the terminology of old French cookery, *tomber* referred to a method of cooking meat in a saucepan, without any liquid other than that produced by the meat itself. The reduced syrupy meat juices were used for the sauce. The expression *tomber à glace* still means to boil down a cooking liquid (stock, juice, etc.) until it is syrupy.

Tomme or Tome

The generic name of two large families of cheeses: one made from goats' or ewes' milk, especially in southeastern France and the Dauphiné and sometimes in Savoy; the other from cows' milk, pressed and uncooked, typical of Savoy and Switzerland. Tomme is also the name given to Cantal and Laguiole at the first stage of their preparation, when they are still fresh.

☐ **Goats'- or ewes'-milk Tommes** The goats'-milk *Tomme des Allues* (from the Haute Tarentaise), pressed and uncooked (45% fat), is shaped like a flat disc, pliable, soft, and pale yellow with a thin smooth grey or light yellow rind; it has a mild lightly seasoned flavour and a strong smell. The *Tomme de Belley* (from Franche-Comté) is soft (40–45% fat), shaped like a small flat disc or briquette, and smooth and homogeneous with a thin bluish rind; it has a nutty flavour and a pronounced bouquet and is sometimes made of cows' and goats' milk mixed together. Ewes'-milk *Tomme de Brach* (from Limousin) is soft (45% fat), in the shape of a tall cylinder, with a pronounced flavour; it is firm and rich, sometimes blue-veined, and has a natural rind. Ewes'-milk *Tomme de Camargue* (45%

fat) is a fresh cheese flavoured with thyme and bay leaf, with a mild creamy taste. *Tomme de Combovin* (from the Dauphiné) is produced from goats' milk (45% fat) and is soft with a thin bluish natural rind, similar to Pélardon, and has a *bouqueté* flavour. Goats'-milk *Tomme de Corps* (from the Dauphiné) is soft (45% fat), with a thin smooth natural rind, which is bluish to pinky-grey, and has a pronounced goatlike smell. Goats'-milk *Tomme de Courchevel* is similar to Tomme des Allues but has slightly more bouquet. *Tomme de Crest* (from Valence) is shaped like a small round disc, firm (45% fat), with a thin bluish rind and a pronounced flavour, similar to Picodon. It is also used to make strong cheeses (*fromages forts*). *Tomme de Sospel* (from the Alpes-Maritimes), made from ewes' or goats' milk (45% fat), is pressed, uncooked, and has a natural rind; shaped like a wide flat cylinder, it is eaten either young (with a mild slightly acid creamy flavour) or old (with a piquant flavour and strong smell) and is sometimes used grated as a condiment. Goats'-milk *Tomme de Vercors* (45% fat) is shaped like a small disc; soft, with a thin bluish natural rind and a spicy flavour, it is used in the preparation of pétafine.

☐ **Cows'-milk Tommes** These are usually pressed, uncooked, and have a natural polished rind. *Tomme de Belleville* (from Tarentaise), *Tomme de Boudane* (from Savoy), and *Tomme de Revard* are variants of *Tomme de Savoie* (20–40% fat), pliable and homogeneous, with a uniform yellow or red rind, a pronounced smell of mould, and a nutty flavour; it is best from June to November and eaten at the end of the meal and in sandwiches. It is sometimes flavoured with fennel. *Tomme au marc* has a strong smell of alcoholic fermentation and a fairly piquant taste: the cheeses are dried slightly, then arranged in layers with marc brandy, in a cask sealed with clay, and left to ferment (it should not be confused with *Tome au raisin*, a kind of processed cheese, coated with roasted grape seeds). *Tomme de Romans* (from the Dauphiné), shaped like a flat disc, is thoroughly pliable, with a mild to nutty flavour and a lactic smell. *Tomme vaudoise* (or *de Payerne*) is a soft almost rindless Swiss cheese, white and springy, with a creamy taste; it is sometimes flavoured with cumin. Finally there is *Tomme de Sixt*, which is eaten very dry, and *Tomme de Vivarais*, which Charles Forot recommends kneading with rapeseed oil, a little vinegar, salt, and pepper, and serving with potatoes cooked in their skins.

tom-pouce

A small pastry consisting of two squares of shortcrust pastry (basic pie dough) sandwiched together with a cream made of butter, crushed nuts, sugar, and coffee essence; it is iced (frosted) with coffee fondant and decorated with a grilled hazelnut.

tongs PINCE

A utensil comprising two arms made of metal, wood, or plastic. They are either pivoted or connected by a spring and are used for grasping a variety of foods, including asparagus, gherkins, snails, salads, ice cream, sugar, and ice (sugar and ice tongs sometimes have claws to help grasp the cubes). Lobster tongs are used for crushing the claws to extract the flesh. Working on the same principle, the pastry crimper is used for pinching the edges of pastries.

tongue LANGUE

Fleshy organs from the heads of slaughtered livestock, which are classed as offal for culinary purposes. Ox (beef) tongue (weighing up to 2 kg, 4½ lb), calf's tongue (considered to be superior in quality and quicker to cook, pig's tongue, and lamb's tongue are all used and can be prepared in many different ways: in ragouts, stewed, boiled and served with highly seasoned sauces (charcutière, piquante, Italian), in fritters, *au gratin*, and often cold, with a vinaigrette. In earlier days, tongue was cooked with verjuice or chestnuts, made into small sausages, or grilled on skewers. Pickled ox (beef) tongue (*à l'écarlate*) is preserved in brine and can be used in many ways, sometimes as a garnish for other meats. It can also be smoked.

Pink flamingo tongues were considered to be a delicacy in ancient Rome, and blackbird tongues were popular in the Middle Ages. Deep-fried salt-cod

tongues served with tartare sauce are a Canadian speciality.

RECIPES

Preparation of tongue PRÉPARATION DE LA LANGUE Soak the tongue in cold water for 12 hours, renewing the water 2 or 3 times (use plenty of water). Then trim it, removing the fat parts, and dip it in boiling water. Skin it by making an incision in the skin at the base and on the top and pull the skin towards the tip. Wash and wipe the skinned tongue, then sprinkle it with fine salt and leave it in a cool place for 24 hours. Wash it again, then wipe it.

CALF'S TONGUE

Boiled calf's tongue LANGUE DE VEAU BOUILLIE Calf's tongue prepared in this way is always served with calf's head. Prepare and skin the tongue. Prepare a cooking stock separately: blend flour with cold water, using 1 tablespoon flour per litre (1¾ pints, generous quart) water, until smooth. Strain the mixture and pour into a large saucepan. Season with 1 teaspoon salt and add 1 tablespoon vinegar per litre water. Bring to the boil, then add 1 large onion stuck with 2 cloves and a bouquet garni. Put in this stock the tongue and the calf's head (weighing about 1 kg, 2¼ lb), well tied up with string. Add about 200 g (8 oz, 2 cups) chopped veal fat, bring back to the boil, and cook for 2½ hours.

The tongue may be served with a simple vinaigrette or with various other sauces: caper, fines herbes, hongroise, piquante, ravigote, Robert, etc.

Braised calf's tongue LANGUE DE VEAU BRAISÉE Prepare the tongue and brown it in 40–50 g (2 oz, ¼ cup) butter; drain. Brown 1 kg (2¼ lb) crushed veal knuckle bones in the oven. Blanch 1 boned calf's foot. Peel and dice 2 large onions and 3 carrots, cook them in butter in a pan until golden, then take them out. Line this pan with a large piece of pork rind with the fat removed, add the diced onion and carrot, the veal bones, the boned calf's foot, the tongue, a bouquet garni, and a crushed clove of garlic.

Blend 2 tablespoons tomato purée with 3 dl (½ pint, 1¼ cups) white wine and the same quantity of stock (the wine may be replaced by Madeira, cider, or beer); pour over the tongue. Add 2 tablespoons brandy, season with salt and pepper, cover, and bring to the boil. Place the pan in a moderately hot oven (200 c, (400 f, gas 6) and leave for about 2½ hours to finish cooking.

Drain the tongue and cut it into slices. Cut the flesh of the calf's foot into dice. Take out the bouquet garni, the remainder of the rind, and the bones. Blend the stock and vegetables in a blender and coat the tongue with the mixture.

Calf's tongue à l'italienne LANGUE DE VEAU À L'ITALIENNE Braise the tongue as in the previous recipe, adding some crushed tomatoes to the pan at the same time as the bouquet garni. Blanch 200 g (7 oz, 1¼ cups) green olives in boiling water, add them to the blended braising stock, and spoon them over the tongue.

LAMB'S OR SHEEP'S TONGUE

Devilled lambs' (*or* sheep's) tongues LANGUES DE MOUTON À LA DIABLE Braise the tongues and leave to cool in their stock. Cut them in half and spread each half with mustard seasoned with a touch of cayenne. Baste with butter. Dip in breadcrumbs, pour butter over them, and grill (broil) slowly. Serve with devilled sauce.

Lamb's (*or* sheep's) tongue brochettes LANGUES DE MOUTON EN BROCHET-TES Prepare some lambs' or sheep's tongues and braise them as for calf's tongue, taking care that they remain slightly firm. Allow them to cool completely, then cut them lengthwise into thin tongue-shaped slices. Marinate them for 30 minutes with some mushroom caps in a mixture of olive oil and lemon juice, with a crushed garlic clove. Cut some smoked belly bacon into strips. Roll up the tongue slices and thread them on skewers, alternating with the strips of bacon and the mushroom caps. Soak once again in the marinade and grill (broil) slowly.

The marinade may be omitted: in this case, lightly brown the mushrooms and the strips of bacon in butter before skewering them, then baste the skewers with melted butter and coat with breadcrumbs. Sprinkle again with a little melted butter and grill gently. Serve with a tomato sauce.

Lambs' (*or* sheep's) tongues à la vinaigrette LANGUES DE MOUTON À LA VINAIGRETTE Prepare the tongues and cook them in a white stock, as for calf's head. Drain and skin them. Serve cold with a vinaigrette.

OX (BEEF) TONGUE

Ox tongue à la bourgeoise LANGUE DE BOEUF À LA BOURGEOISE Prepare the tongue and braise it as for a calf's tongue. Prepare a bourgeoise garnish with 500 g (1 lb) carrots cut to uniform size and half-cooked, about 20 small onions glazed and half-cooked, and 20 or so strips of larding bacon (slightly salted belly bacon) blanched and lightly fried in butter. 15 minutes before the end of cooking, drain the tongue and strain the braising stock. Return the tongue to the braising pan, add the bourgeoise garnish, and pour the strained braising stock over everything. Finish cooking in a moderate – moderately hot oven (180–200 c, 350–400 f, gas 4–6).

Valenciennes stuffed ox tongue LANGUE DE BOEUF FOURRÉE DE VALEN-CIENNES (from a recipe by François Benoist) Trim a smoked tongue and cut it into thin slices. Prepare a mixture consisting of two-thirds foie gras and one-third fine-quality butter; work it with a glass of port, some finely chopped fresh truffles, salt, and pepper. Coat the slices of tongue with this preparation and reshape the tongue; wrap it in muslin (cheesecloth) and keep it in a cool place. To serve, unwrap the tongue, glaze it with clear aspic, and arrange it on a bed of aspic.

tonic

An aerated drink, containing carbon dioxide and sugar, flavoured with natural fruit and plant extracts, usually including quinine. Tonic, usually mixed with gin, was made fashionable by British colonists as a refreshing alcoholic antipyretic drink. It can also be drunk straight, with ice and a slice of lemon, or in a cocktail.

tonkinois

An almond manqué cake sliced into two and filled with praline butter cream. The sides are masked with this cream and decorated with grilled shredded (slivered) almonds; the top is iced (frosted) with orange fondant and sprinkled with grated coconut.

The name is also given to a square-shaped petit four made of nougatine and filled with frangipane flavoured with praline. The top is iced (frosted) with chocolate and decorated with chopped pistachios.

topknot CARDINE

A marine flatfish, 20–50 cm (8–20 in) long, which has two eyes side by side, a large mouth, and fins with long filaments. Its dorsal side is greyish, marked with brown or pink, and it has a very clear lateral line. The thick firm white flesh is lean and comes away easily from the bones. Sometimes also known as megrim, the topknot can be used for many dishes, particularly when filleted.

top rump
TRANCHE GRASSE

Part of the leg of beef consisting of the group of three muscles situated in the front, in the femoral region. The *rond* (round), *plat* (flat), and *mouvant* (moving) muscles provide very good roasts and tender tasty steaks, which are fairly lean. The *rond* is less homogeneous than the other two muscles. The top rump also provides meat for spit-roasting or minced (ground) beef (for hamburgers or steak tartare).

toque du président Adolphe Clerc

One of the three pies from Belley, described by L. Tendret in *La Table au pays de Brillat-Savarin*. Served cold, it is made of hare, woodcock, red-legged partridge, thrush, black truffles, and goose liver. The original recipe was found by Brillat-Savarin's mother among the papers of the judge Adolphe Clerc, president of the local law court. The shape of this pie is reminiscent of the magistrates' cap (*toque* in French). See also *oreiller de la Belle Aurore*.

torteil or tourteau

A typically Catalan pastry, the authentic name being *tortell*. This crown-shaped brioche is a speciality of Ville-franche-de-Conflent and Arles-sur-Tech, where it is flavoured with aniseed. In Limoux, where it is traditionally eaten on Twelfth Night, it is decorated with crystallized (candied) citron, raisins, and pine kernels, then flavoured with orange, lemon, and rum.

tortellini

Italian pasta made with small pieces of thinly rolled dough, filled with a stuffing, folded, and shaped into rings. They exist in different sizes and shapes (rolled-up narrow strips or small rounded turnovers) and are called *tortelli*, *tortelletti* (mentioned in a 13th-century recipe book), *tortellini*, *tortelloni*, and *tortiglioni*. All these words derive from *torta* (tart), with various diminutives and augmentatives.

The pasta used may be made simply with eggs or coloured with tomato or spinach. The stuffing is usually made from chicken or ham, chopped with lemon zest, nutmeg, egg yolks, or Parmesan cheese. Tortellini is a speciality of the Bolognese Christmas dinner (filled with turkey, ham, and sausage forcemeat). Poached in a consommé or cooked in water, tortellini and tortelloni are served with melted butter or in a sauce – tomato or cream (sometimes with mushrooms) – and with Parmesan cheese. This stuffed pasta is of ancient origin: legend has it that a young apprentice pastrycook made them in the shape of a navel out of love for his mistress.

tortilla

A thin pancake made of cornmeal – an important item of the diet in Latin American countries. It was named by the Spanish conquistadors: in Spanish cookery, a tortilla is a flat omelette, usually filled with salt cod or potatoes, which is cut into quarters like a cake (the word has the same origin as *torta*, a tart).

Cornmeal has been used since time immemorial for preparing pancakes, which are traditionally grilled on earthenware utensils. They are used as bread or as tart bases and are stuffed for turnovers and sandwiches. The old Indian method of preparation consists of kneading the cornmeal dough, or *masa*, on a stone called a *metate*, then shaping it into circles about 20 cm (8 in) in diameter and 3 mm (⅛ in) thick, which is quite a delicate operation. Nowadays, *tortillerias* provide ready-made tortillas, which can be bought cooked or uncooked. Grilled tortillas, lightly browned, have a thin but tough crust on each side. They can also be puffed up like soufflé potatoes, then stuffed. Tortillas are always eaten hot, either on their own (as bread) or filled with various ingredients, usually with a piquant sauce.

The range of condiments and stuffings used include *guacamole* (avocado purée with red pepper), chopped raw onion, red pepper, green tomato coulis, grated *queso* (cheese), thin strips of chicken breast, etc. The main dishes prepared with tortillas are *tacos* (a very popular type of sandwich), *enchiladas* (tortillas rolled around their filling – fried sausages or pieces of roast chicken – then coated with a sauce and cooked in the oven), *tostadas* (small very crisp tortillas, covered with sautéed or fried red kidney beans and sometimes embellished with chopped meat, served as a hot hors d'oeuvre), *chilaquiles* (thin strips of fried tortilla covered with a highly spiced sauce and cooked in the oven), and *quesadillas* (tortillas filled with meat in sauce or vegetables with cheese, folded into turnovers, then fried in lard).

The tortilla even forms part of the Mexican breakfast, which basically consists of *huevos rancheros*: fried eggs arranged on fried tortillas and garnished with tomatoes crushed with red pepper and slices of avocado. At lunch, the soup is sometimes thickened with small pieces of tortilla. *Sopa seca* is a dish consisting of pieces of tortilla generously coated with sauce and served piping hot. Equally popular are *sopes* – tortillas filled with meat, beans, and highly spiced sauce. Among the specialities of Yucatán, mention should

be made of the *papatzul* (literally, food of lords): tortillas stuffed with pieces of pork or hard-boiled (hard-cooked) eggs, served with a sauce made from ground pumpking seeds, tomato purée, and pumpkin-seed oil. In Venezuela, cornmeal pancakes are found in the form of *arepas*. These are thicker than tortillas and are often raw in the middle, even after cooking. Butter, eggs, spices, or fried maize (corn) grains are sometimes added to the dough.

tortillon

A dry petit four, usually made of twisted puff pastry (like a sacristain) with crystallized (candied) or dried fruits or shredded almonds; alternatively it is made of choux pastry moulded into a zigzag shape.

Tortillon is also another name for the brassadeau.

RECIPE

Tortillons (from Jean Chaumontel's recipe) Fill a medium-sized forcing (pastry) bag with choux pastry. Holding the bag at 45° and making a zigzag pattern, pipe onto a baking sheet some sawtooth shapes 15 cm (6 in) long. Sprinkle each tortillon with a dozen currants steeped in rum. Dust very lightly with icing (confectioners') sugar and bake in a moderate oven (175 c, 350 f, gas 4) for 25 minutes.

Tortoni

A café, restaurant, and ice-cream parlour opened in Paris in 1798, at the corner of Rue Taitbout and Boulevard des Italiens, by a Neapolitan called Velloni. Shortly afterwards, it was purchased by his head clerk, Tortoni, who gave the place its name. It closed in 1893. Every celebrity in Paris climbed the steps of the famous ice-cream parlour, which was also a highly regarded restaurant, well known for its cold buffets. Its meats in aspic, papillotes of young hare, and salmon escalopes attracted as many customers as the ice-cream cakes, sorbets, and granitas, Italian specialities that Tortoni made fashionable in Paris. A *Tableau de Paris*, dated 1834, quoted by R. Héron de Villefosse in *Histoire géographique et gourmande de Paris*, describes the activity of the establishment: 'In the morning, its excellent cold lunches brought in the stockbrokers, bankers, and the fashionable set from the Chaussée d'Antin. At four o'clock, the speculators from the Stock Exchange met in front of its facade. . . . Finally, in the evening, the regular customers from the Boulevard came to savour the imperial tea and the flavour of the iced pyramids in the shape of fruits and plants.'

tortue (en)

A method of preparing calf's head. It is cooked in white court-bouillon, simmered with the tongue and sweetbreads in a white wine sauce with olives, mushrooms, and gherkins added, then heaped on a platter in a mound usually garnished with small quenelles of veal forcemeat and fried croutons. This French dish, which dates back to the Middle Ages, is also highly esteemed in Belgium.

Calf's head *en tortue* was once a large and spectacular entrée: the head was surrounded by small quenelles of veal forcemeat, cocks' combs and kidneys, cooked mushrooms, stuffed poached olives, slivers of truffle, and escalopes of calf's tongue. Small fried eggs, small slices of calf's brain cooked in court-bouillon, gherkins shaped like olives, dressed crayfish, and fried heart-shaped croutons completed the garnish.

Nowadays, calf's head *en tortue* is usually prepared using pieces of head, simmered in tortue sauce and arranged on fried croutons, surrounded by a more modest garnish. When served whole, it is stuffed and cooked in a braising stock seasoned with 'turtle herbs', a mixture of basil, thyme, bay leaf, sage, rosemary, and marjoram, with coriander seeds and peppercorns, inside a muslin (cheesecloth) bag.

Tortue sauce, made with white wine, mirepoix, a roux, and stock and flavoured with tomato, traditionally accompanies calf's head *en tortue*; it was originally intended for turtle, hence its name, and is also used for fish and offal.

RECIPES

Calf's head en tortue TÊTE DE VEAU EN TORTUE Prepare a white court-bouillon (see *head*) and cook the calf's head and, separately, the tongue and sweetbreads. Cut all this offal into pieces and keep warm in their stock. Make some tortue sauce. Cook in butter, without browning, 250 g (9 oz) diced mushrooms. Stone 150 g (5 oz) green olives, blanch for 3–4 minutes in boiling water, and dice them. Also dice 7–8 gherkins. Strain the sauce and add the gherkins, olives, and mushrooms. Heat thoroughly and adjust the seasoning by adding a pinch of cayenne. Take out the pieces of offal and cover them with the sauce. Garnish the dish with small quenelles of veal forcemeat and croutons fried in butter.

Tortue sauce SAUCE TORTUE Infuse a bouquet garni and a few sprigs of basil in ½ litre (17 fl oz, 2 cups) dry white wine. Lightly cook in butter 150 g (5 oz) smoked ham, 3 onions, and 3 carrots (both cut into dice). Sprinkle with 3 tablespoons flour and brown. Add the strained white wine and 3 dl (½ pint, 1¼ cups) beef stock. Add 2–3 tablespoons concentrated tomato purée, cover, and cook very gently for at least 30 minutes.

toscane (à la)

A term used in France to describe various dishes prepared with Parmesan cheese and ham, specialities of Emilia-Romagna; true Tuscan cookery, however, is characterized by grilled beefsteak, bean dishes, and Chianti. Macaroni *à la toscane* is bound with a purée of foie gras and sprinkled with diced truffles sautéed in butter.

RECIPE

Allumettes à la toscane Cut some puff pastry into strips 8 cm (3 in) wide and 5 mm (¼ in) thick. Mix equal amounts of cooked ham cut into small dice and poultry forcemeat, season, and add a little chopped truffle. Completely coat the strips of puff pastry with this mixture. Cover with a very little béchamel sauce, sprinkle with grated Parmesan cheese, and cook for 12–15 minutes in a very hot oven (240 c, 475 f, gas 9).

toss REMUER

To turn over the leaves of a salad to ensure they are evenly coated with seasoning or dressing. This is always done immediately before serving.

totelots

A dish of Lorraine cookery, consisting of small squares of noodle pasta cooked in boiling water and served cold in a salad, with sliced hard-boiled (hard-cooked) eggs and a vinaigrette flavoured with onion, garlic, and shallot. It was once the traditional dish for Good Friday. *Vitelots*, which are quite similar, are bands of pasta, either cooked in milk and served as a hot dessert or cooked in water and served cold or hot, as an entrée, with a piquant sauce.

tôt-fait

A type of pound cake usually flavoured with lemon. This typical family cake is served at tea on its own or as a dessert, with jam, compote, or fruit poached in syrup. It can also be cut in two and filled with plum or apricot compote lightly flavoured with a fruit spirit or rum.

Another type of tôt-fait is made from sugar and flour mixed with milk and eggs, then melted butter, and flavoured with vanilla. Cooked in a shallow buttered dish, it is eaten hot, straight from the oven, before it collapses (the dough becomes very puffy).

RECIPE

Tôt-fait Mix in a basin 4 beaten whole eggs with the same weight of sifted flour and of caster (superfine) sugar. Add the same weight of melted butter, a pinch of salt, and the grated zest of a lemon. Butter and flour a manqué mould, pour in the mixture, and bake in a moderately hot oven (200 c, 400 f, gas 6) for about 45 minutes. Turn out of the mould onto a rack and allow to cool.

touiller

A French word meaning to mix or stir a preparation, or various ingredients, without special care, using a wooden spatula. The word is colloquial and comes from Latin *tudiculare* (to pound). *Touiller la salade* formerly meant 'to toss the salad'.

toulousaine (à la)

Describing a garnish for poached or pot-roasted poultry or a filling for croustades, tarts, or vols-au-vent. It consists of a ragout of small quenelles of poultry, lambs' sweetbreads or cocks' combs and kidneys, mushrooms, and truffles, bound with allemande sauce (or toulousaine sauce, i.e. a suprême sauce thickened with egg yolks and cream). Nowadays, the expression is more frequently applied to various dishes from southwestern France.

RECIPE

Aubergines (eggplants) au gratin à la toulousaine Peel 4 aubergines (eggplants) and cut them into slices lengthways. Sprinkle with salt and leave to steep for an hour. Rinse, dry thoroughly, and lightly cook on both sides in a pan of olive oil. Take an equal weight of tomatoes, remove the stalks, cut into slices, deseed, and cook in olive oil. Arrange the aubergines (eggplants) and tomatoes in alternate layers in an oiled gratin dish. Sprinkle generously with finely grated fresh breadcrumbs mixed with 2 tablespoons chopped parsley. A little finely chopped garlic may be added. Sprinkle with oil. Brown in a very hot oven.

Toulouse-Lautrec (Henri de)

French painter (born Albi, 1864; died Château de Malromé, 1901). This great artist, noted for his drawings, paintings, lithographs, and posters, was also an excellent amateur cook, the creator of recipes in which originality vied with soundness of taste (chickpeas with spinach, perch with anchovies, plums in rum) and also with humour (grilled grasshoppers, seasoned with salt and pepper). Thanks to his friend Maurice Joyant, the traditional and regional recipes that he cooked were collected in *La Cuisine de Monsieur Momo*, of which 100 copies were printed in 1930; the work was republished in 1966 under the title *L'Art de la cuisine*, with illustrations of menus by Lautrec.

Paul Leclercq, in *Autour de Toulouse-Lautrec* (1921), describes him as a discriminating gourmet: 'The precise degree of cooking, the quality of the butter and spices, and great care were, according to him, the secrets of good food. . . . He was a connoisseur of vintage wines and spirits. And when, clicking his tongue against his palate, he announced that such-and-such a Burgundy "fanned out like a peacock's tail in the mouth", this magnificent image drew attention to the full-flavoured rich bouquet of the wine. . . . The cooking of a leg of mutton *de sept heures* or the preparation of a lobster *à l'américaine* held no secrets for him.'

Leclercq also describes him in an impromptu role as a barman, during a Parisian soiree: 'Lautrec's imagination was inexhaustible. After a series of drinks that had to be swallowed in a single draught, he presented a range of pink cocktails with an affected taste that had to be sipped slowly with a straw. . . . Lautrec also invented that evening some "solid" cocktails, in the form of sardines in gin and port. He flamed them in a long silver dish and they, in turn, did not fail to light fires in imprudent throats.'

toupin

An earthenware pan or small stewpot, used in Savoy to prepare soups, fondues, ragouts, etc. Its name has been given to a pressed cows'-milk cheese (45% fat), in the shape of a tall cylinder, made in the Vallée d'Abondance. It is firm and honogeneous, with a fruity flavour, and has a thin, rather rough, rind.

Toupinel

A poached egg dish, said to have been created in the restaurant Maire at the end of the 19th century. It apparently owes its name to a vaudeville by A. Bisson, *Feu Toupinel*, which was playing at that time on the boulevards. Eggs Toupinel are arranged in scooped-out baked potatoes. The pulp is crushed with butter and cream, seasoned with salt and nutmeg, then put back into the potatoes, which are coated with Mornay sauce. Finally, a poached egg is placed on top of each potato, also covered with Mornay sauce, and the dish is glazed in the oven or under the grill (broiler). Celery purée or shredded lean ham is sometimes added to the mashed pulp. Eggs Toupinel are traditionally served with fried parsley.

Touraine

Homeland of Gargantua and known as the 'garden of France', Touraine produces an abundance of delicious vegetables and fruits. As well as fish from the Loire, the Cher, and the Indre, there are breeding stocks in the ponds and abundant wild fowl. Its poultry has been famous since the Middle Ages, and cattle from nearby Maine provide quality animals. Rich in resources, this province has a simple and delicate cuisine, with many ancient recipes (green walnuts in verjuice, *bijane*, megrim with cream, noisettes of pork with prunes, braised veal in red wine, and the fouaces enjoyed by Rabelais). In addition, the long periods spent by the court in the Loire Valley established a tradition for sumptuous dishes, such as carp *à la Chambord* and game pâtés.

The meal may start with rillons, rillettes, andouillettes, and black puddings (blood sausages) from Tours, Vouvray, or Chinon (quiche tourangelle with rillettes should also be mentioned); alternatively, one might prefer leek and turnip soup garnished with bacon and peas, or pâtés and jambons of game and poultry from Richelieu. Marinated shad (grilled or roasted), matelotes of eels in Chinon wine with lardons, pike with shallot butter, perch stuffed with mushrooms or sorrel, and lamprey sautéed in walnut oil and simmered in red wine all bear witness to the wealth of fish recipes. Meat is prepared in a number of delicate dishes, particularly *cul de veau* (chump end of loin of veal) with spring onions (scallions), fricassee of chicken, and hare *à la chinonaise*. Sanguette with onions and the rustic sagourne should also be mentioned.

The famous prunes of Tours, introduced into the Loire Valley from Damascus by the Crusaders, are widely used in cooking to garnish wild hare, roast pork, matelote of eel, or lamprey.

Touraine is famous for its asparagus, celery, chicory (endives), lettuce, leeks, and beans, particularly broad (fava) beans *à la tourangelle* (with ham and onions, bound with egg yolks, and sprinkled with chervil), French (green) beans with béchamel sauce, and peas with savory.

There are numerous goats'-milk

cheeses: Sainte-Maure, Saint-Loup, Ligueil, Loches, and Chouzé (which sometimes contains cows' milk). Chasselas grapes from the slopes above the Loire, Williams and Passe-Crassane pears, Reinette and Golden Delicious apples, and greengages and plums from Rochecorbon are all well known. Apart from the traditional pastries – fouaces, cassemuseaux, and *gâteaux cordés* and *russeroles* (similar to pets-de-nonne), there are stuffed prunes, biscuits (cookies) and barley sugar from Tours, dried pears from Rivarennes, croquets from Sully-sur-Loire, and crystallized (candied) walnuts and macaroons from Cormery.

Touraine wines

VINS DE TOURAINE

Many writers (including Rabelais) and poets (such as Ronsard) have praised the wines of Touraine: a combination of soil and climate, together with very old-established traditions of wine making, have resulted in the region's wines being among the most charming of the Loire Valley. Although, until fairly recently, some of them were not supposed to travel well, these days they appeal to drinkers all over the world and the variety is considerable. Among the best known, each with an AOC, are Vouvray and Montlouis (white) and Chinon, Bourgueil, and St Nicolas de Bourgueil (red), but there are many others and also some rosé. The grape varieties for the white wines are dominated by the Chenin Blanc (known locally as the Pineau de la Loire) and those for the reds by the Cabernet Franc (its regional nickname being Breton), but other varieties are grown, including Gamay, Groslot, and Cot (Malbec). A great deal of sparkling wine is also made, mainly white, according to the Champagne method.

tourangelle (à la)

Describing large pieces of roast lamb or mutton served with their thickened juices and a garnish of French (green) beans and flageolet beans bound with butter. The expression is also applied to poached or soft-boiled eggs arranged on tartlets filled with flageolet bean purée and coated with cream sauce.

Tour d'Argent

The oldest Parisian restaurant. It originated in 1582, as an inn on the Quai de la Tournelle, standing on the remains of a castle, built by Charles V, of which a white stone tower still remained. A certain Rourteau (or Rourtaud) used to prepare heron and wild duck pies, which Henri III himself ate there. Later, Richelieu enjoyed goose with prunes at the inn, his great-nephew, the Duke of Richelieu, had his 'all beef' menu prepared there. Madame de Sévigné praised its chocolate and Madame de Pompadour its champagne. The Tour d'Argent vies with the Procope as to which serves the freshest coffee. Under Napoleon I, Lecoq, head of the imperial kitchens, took over the restaurant, which had suffered during the Revolution. Roast duck and leg of lamb were at that time the best-known dishes. Paillard succeeded Lecoq, and George Sand and Musset were among the restaurant's regular customers.

It was after 1890 that the Tour d'Argent acquired the prestige that it retains to this day, with the famous Frédéric, first maître d'hôtel then manager, who invented the recipe for *canard au sang* and had the idea of attributing a serial number to each bird served. The tradition has continued, and the *canardiers* in white aprons who now officiate on the small stage of the *théâtre du canard*, where two magnificent presses occupy the place of honour, had registered, by 1982, the number 613,000. The great Frédéric, who made the Tour d'Argent the 'Bayreuth of cookery' (according to Jean Cocteau), was succeeded by André Terrail, then by his son, Claude Terrail, who now presides over the famous restaurant, with its top-floor dining room overlooking the Seine and Notre-Dame. Its specialities, apart from pressed duck, are lobster Lagardère, lamb chops Tour d'Argent, fillets of sole Frédéric, lemon, chocolate, or violet soufflés, and all the great classics of French and foreign cookery.

tourer

A French term meaning to give the necessary turns to puff-pastry dough to make it puff up during baking. This entails successive operations of folding, rolling out, turning the dough through 90°, then refolding, etc. Professional pastrycooks do this on a *tour de pâtisserie*, which is a refrigerated marble or metal slab.

tourifas

A speciality of the Auvergne, consisting of thin strips of toasted bread on which are arranged thin strips of raw cured ham and bacon (smoked or unsmoked), with mushrooms and fines herbes. The tourifas are then coated with breadcrumbs and fried.

tourin

Onion soup, sometimes with garlic or tomato, prepared with lard or goose fat; it is common to the Périgord and Bordeaux areas. The food historian Jean-Jacques Dubern writes: 'Tourin is onion soup made with good fat and a little garlic, bound with egg yolk in a trickle of vinegar and poured over slices of stale home-made bread. When there is no more bread left in the soup bowl, a good glass of strong red wine of the year is poured in. The colour is certainly not attractive, I admit, but we are on our own, and this warm beverage, flowing and generous, is an exceptional tonic.'

Tourin, which is also spelled *tourain*, *thourin*, *tourrin*, *touril* (in Rouergue) or *touri* (in Béarn), was traditionally taken to newly-weds on the morning after their wedding and bore the name *tourin des mariés* or *tourin des noces* (with vermicelli added). In Quercy, some variants are *tourin à l'aoucou* (cooked with a preserved goose leg), *tourin à la poulette* (onion and flour browned in goose fat before adding the liquid), and *tourin aux raves* (shredded kohlrabi, browned in lard). In Périgord, a crushed clove of garlic and a little tomato purée or fresh tomatoes are usually added.

RECIPE

Périgord tourin TOURIN PÉRIGOUDIN Lightly brown in goose fat, in a frying pan (skillet), 150 g (5 oz, 1¼ cups) finely chopped onion. Sprinkle with 1 tablespoon flour and add 2 crushed cloves of garlic and a few tablespoons boiling water. Stir to avoid lumps. Cook 2 large deseeded tomatoes in 2 litres (3½ pints, 4½ pints) stock.

Drain, crush, and return to the stock. Add the contents of the frying pan and boil for 45 minutes. Just before serving, blend in 2 egg yolks mixed with a few tablespoons of stock. Pour into a soup tureen over some thin slices of farmhouse bread.

tournebride

An obsolete name for an inn situated near a château or country residence, where visitors' servants and horses were lodged. Already old-fashioned at the beginning of the 20th century, the word *tournebride*, which originally meant 'turnabout', is still used to describe a quiet welcoming country inn.

tournedos (filet mignon)

A small round slice, 2 cm (¾ in) thick, taken from the heart of a fillet of beef and sautéed or grilled. In French butchery, the classic presentation of the tournedos, barded and tied up, enables other roasting cuts to be used in the same way as fillet; these cuts are called *façon tournedos* (tournedos style).

The *Dictionnaire de l'Académie des gastronomes* explains the etymology of the word, which appeared around 1864, as follows: 'In the last century, the stalls backing onto (*tournant le dos*) the central alleys of the fresh fish pavilion, in the Paris Halles, were assigned fish of doubtful freshness. By analogy, the name *tournedos* was given to pieces of fillet of beef that were kept for a few days in storage. An indiscretion is said to have led to the word's appearing on a restaurant menu one day; the public, not knowing its origin, adopted it.' Another explanation is connected with the dish ordered by Rossini (with foie gras and truffles), which surprised the head waiter so much that he had the dish served behind the backs (*dans le dos*) of the other customers. This cut of meat has one of the largest varieties of garnishes and sauces.

RECIPES

Sautéed or grilled (broiled) tournedos TOURNEDOS SAUTÉS OU GRILLÉS Sauté the tournedos very rapidly in butter, oil, or a mixture of both, so that the interior remains pink. They can also be grilled. Depending on the choice of garnish, or to prevent the garnish from masking the tournedos, the steaks are sometimes arranged on fried or grilled croutons, potato cakes, artichoke hearts, rice, etc. Here are a few suggestions for garnishes and sauces:

■ *à la d'Abrantès*: season with paprika, sauté in oil, and arrange on a grilled slice of aubergine (eggplant); add to the cooking juices some lightly fried onion, a salpicon of sweet pepper, and tomato sauce.

■ *archiduc*: sauté in butter and arrange on a potato cake; garnish with croquettes of calves' brains and slivers of truffle; cover with the pan juices diluted with sherry, fresh cream, and veal stock and flavoured with paprika.

■ *with anchovies*: sauté in butter and arrange on a slice of fried bread; pour over a sauce made from the pan juices mixed with thickened veal stock, white wine, and a little anchovy butter; garnish with half fillets of anchovies in oil, placed in a crisscross pattern on the tournedos.

■ *à la béarnaise*: grill and garnish with château potatoes; serve béarnaise sauce separately.

■ *with mushrooms*: sauté in butter; pour over a sauce made from the pan juices mixed with thickened veal stock and Madeira; garnish with mushrooms sautéed in butter.

■ *Clamart*: sauté in butter and garnish with artichoke hearts filled with peas or fresh pea purée; pour over a sauce made from the pan juices mixed with white wine and veal stock.

■ *à la périgourdine*: sauté in butter; place on a fried crouton; garnish with slices of truffle tossed in butter; pour over a sauce made from the pan juices mixed with Madeira.

■ *Saint-Germain*: sauté in butter, place on a fried crouton, and garnish with thick pea purée.

Tournedos Brillat-Savarin (from Georges Blanc's recipe) Wash 250 g (9 oz) fresh morels, cut off the stems, and make small cuts in the caps. Simmer them in a little water for 15 minutes, then drain. Brown a chopped shallot in butter in a frying pan (skillet). Add the morels with a little mustard and a few tablespoons thick cream. Finish cooking over a low heat. Adjust the seasoning and keep warm.

Gently fry the tournedos in butter. Remove and keep warm. Stir into the pan a wine glass of port and a small cup of gravy and heat. Remove from the heat and thicken the sauce with butter. Adjust the seasoning. Arrange the morels around the tournedos and pour over the strained sauce.

tourner

See *turn*.

tourte

A round pie or tart, which can be savoury or sweet. The name originally designated a round loaf (from the Latin *tortus*). A tourte consists of a shortcrust or puff pastry case (shell), filled either with a mixture of meat, poultry, game, fish, or vegetables (with aromatics and additional ingredients) or with fruit and cream. It is covered with a lid of the same pastry. Some sweet tourtes do not have lids: these are high-sided tarts. Large rustic brioches are also called tourtes.

Similar to English pies, tourtes nowadays derive from rustic or regional cookery. They once played a major role as classic entrées or desserts: tourtes with truffles, oysters, pigeons, foie gras, béatilles, godiveaux, etc., very fashionable until the 17th century, gave way to the lighter vols-au-vent, croûtes, and timbales, as Carême pointed out in his *Traité des entrées chaudes*: 'The tourte is no longer elegant enough to appear on our opulent tables, because its shape is too common; even the middle classes scorn it and eat only hot pâtés and vols-au-vent, whereas rich merchants and their families used to regale themselves with the humble tourtes.'

In medieval cookery and during the Renaissance, it was one of the commonest dishes and was sometimes highly decorative: mention should be made of the frangipane tourte, similar to the Pithiviers gâteau, and the *tourtes parmeriennes* of Taillevent (large round tall pies filled with mutton, veal, or pork, with spices and raisins, coloured with saffron, and with castellated edges in which small flags bearing the guests' coats of arms were placed).

Tourte specialities of the French provinces include the tourte of Poitou (chicken, rabbit, and pork belly meatballs); the salmon tourte of Brioude; the tourte of Nice, with Swiss chard, sugar, and raisins; the *tourte bitteroise* (mutton fat, cassonade, lemon zest, and crystallized (candied) melon rind), and the Rouergue tourte, made with Roquefort and Laguiole cheeses. Among the fruit tourtes, the *poirat* of Berry, the *picanchagne bourbonnais*, the *ruifard valbonnais*, and the *croustade* of Languedoc are worthy of mention.

RECIPES

Apricot tourte TOURTE AUX ABRICOTS (from Mont-Bry's recipe) Place some thinly rolled-out shortcrust pastry (basic pie dough) in a tourtière (or deep flan dish) lightly moistened in the middle. Trim it to size, prick the base, and moisten the edge, fixing around it a band of puff pastry 3 cm (1¼ in) wide and 1 cm (½ in) thick to form the rim. Fill the tourte with stoned (pitted) fresh apricots, without letting the fruit touch the pastry rim, (which would prevent it from rising evenly during cooking). Brush the upper surface of the rim with egg and score it lightly with the point of a knife. Bake for about 45 minutes in a moderate oven. 5 minutes before it is cooked, sprinkle lightly with icing (confectioners') sugar to provide a glaze.

Many other fruits can be used, cooked or uncooked, whole or cut up: pineapple, cherries, nectarines, pears, apples, plums, etc.

Tourte of veal with Parmesan cheese TOURTE DE VEAU AU PARMESAN (from Hubert's recipe) Make 400 g (14 oz) shortcrust pastry (basic pie dough). Soak a pig's (caul fat) in cold water. Cut into strips 250 g (9 oz) noix of veal, a large slice of smoked ham, and 200 g (7 oz) bacon fat; marinate in a bowl with 1 dl (6 tablespoons, scant ½ cup) white wine, 1 liqueur glass Cognac, thyme, salt, and pepper.

Meanwhile, chop up 200 g (7 oz) breast of veal, a large slice of smoked ham, 200 g (7 oz) bacon fat, 300 g (11 oz) calf's liver, and 3–4 shallots. Add 100 g (4 oz, 1 cup) grated Parmesan cheese and mix with 2 beaten whole eggs, salt, and pepper.

Roll out two-thirds of the pastry and line a buttered tourtière (or deep flan dish) with it. Lay the caul inside, letting the edges overhang. Spread half of the forcemeat on top; add the strips of meat, then the rest of the forcemeat. Fold over the edges of the caul. Roll out the rest of the pastry and place it on top of the flan dish, sealing the edges by moistening and pinching them. Make a small hole in the middle and slide a kitchen-foil funnel inside to let the steam escape. Brush the top of the tourte with beaten egg and bake in a hot oven (220 C, 425 F, gas 7) for 1½ hours. Serve with corn salad.

Tourtes à la mode béarnaise Melt 500 g (18 oz, 2¼ cups) butter and pour it over 100 g (4 oz) fresh yeast (4 cakes compressed yeast) in a bowl. Mix together. Add 500 g (18 oz, 2¼ cups) caster (superfine) sugar, 12 eggs, 1 small glass rum, the grated zest of 2 lemons, a pinch of salt, and enough flour to obtain a firm mixture. Leave to rise for 24 hours. Divide into balls and put into buttered moulds. Bake for about 45 minutes in a hot oven (220 C, 425 F, gas 7).

tourteau

A French name for the common edible crab, the biggest European crab, fished both in the Atlantic and in the Mediterranean, where it lives on rocks and stones at depths of up to 100 m (330 ft). Its oval yellowish-brown carapace is wider than it is long and is lightly scalloped around the edge. The first pair of legs, which are highly developed and have large black-tipped pincers, contain a delicate flesh.

tourteau fromagé

In Poitou and Vendée, a gâteau made with goats'-milk cheese; it is shaped like a slightly flattened ball with a smooth, almost black, surface. It is prepared by filling a deep pastry case (pie shell) with a mixture of fresh goats'-milk cheese, eggs, fresh cream, sugar, and flour, flavoured with Cognac. There are numerous variants, which sometimes incorporate candied angelica. This gâteau, originally from Lusignan, is also found in Niort, Poitiers, and as far away as Ruffec. The prune torteau of the same region is a puff-pastry tart filled with prune purée and covered with a pastry lattice.

RECIPE

Tourteau fromagé Make some short pastry with 250 g (9 oz, 2¼ cups) flour, 125 g (4½ oz, 9 tablespoons) butter, 1 egg yolk, 1–2 tablespoons water, and a pinch of salt. Leave in a cool place for 2 hours, roll out to a thickness of 3 mm (⅛ in), and line a buttered tourtière (or deep flan dish) 20 cm (8 in) in diameter. Bake blind for about 10 minutes. Mix 250 g (9 oz) well-drained fresh goats'-milk cheese with 125 g (4½ oz, ⅔ cup) caster (superfine) sugar, a pinch of salt, 5 egg yolks, and 30 g (1 oz, ¼ cup) potato starch. Mix well, then add 1 teaspoon brandy or 1 tablespoon orange-flower water. Whisk 5 egg whites to very stiff peaks and gently fold them into the mixture. Pour into the pastry case (shell) and bake in a moderately hot oven (200 c, 400 f, gas 6) for about 50 minutes. Serve warm or cold.

tourtière

A round mould of variable diameter, slightly wider at the top, with high fluted or smooth sides. Made of ovenproof white porcelain, earthenware, or ovenproof glass, it is used for cooking and serving tourtes, tarts, or pies, sometimes with a removable base.

The word is also used in France for any kind of pie dish, tart mould, or flan ring.

tourtou or tourton

A small buckwheat pancake, the Limousin equivalent of the Breton galette, traditionally cooked in a frying pan (skillet) greased with pork fat. Tourtous are a speciality of the Tulle region, where they are still made at home by housewives and taken to the local village shops to be sold.

In Périgord, Quercy, and Rouergue, *tourteaux* are small cornmeal pancakes (not to be confused with the tourteau fromagé).

trace element

OLIGO-ÉLÉMENT

An element that is essential for healthy growth and development but is present only in minute quantities in the body. The most important trace elements are manganese, copper, zinc, cobalt, iron, iodine, fluorine, aluminium, lithium, and bismuth.

trait

A small quantity of a spirit or liqueur used for making a cocktail. It is generally measured by means of a measuring cap.

Trappiste

A generic name for various cheeses made by monks, particularly in the Trappist monasteries of Cîteaux, Belval, Briquebec, Mont-des-Cats, and Tamié, as well as in certain Belgian monasteries (e.g. Orval). They bear the name of the abbey where they are made, sometimes preceded by the words 'Trappiste de...'. Made from cows' milk (40–45% fat), they take the form of discs of varying sizes. *Trappiste de Belval*, originating in Picardy, is a pressed uncooked cheese with a smooth washed rind, straw yellow to greyish in colour. Pliable and delicate, the ivory yellow cheese has a mild flavour. *Trappiste de Cîteaux* (Burgundy), with the same characteristics, has a more fruity flavour. *Trappiste de Briquebec* (Manche), another pressed cheese with a washed rind, is characterized by a slight smell of the cellar and a bland flavour. *Trappiste d'Échourgnac* (Périgord), an ivory yellow cheese pierced with very small holes, which has a mild flavour, and *Trappiste d'Entrammes* (Maine), which has a fruity flavour, should also be mentioned.

Trappisten is an Austrian cheese made from cows' milk (sometimes mixed with ewes' or goats' milk), matured to a varying degree; pale yellow, with a mild flavour, it is also made in Bosnia and Hungary.

Trappistine

A yellowish-green liqueur, made from Armagnac and macerated herbs; it is manufactured by Trappistine nuns, notably at the abbey of Grâce-de-Dieu, in Doubs.

travailler

A French term meaning to beat or mix together the elements of a dough, batter, or any liquid preparation, in order to blend in various ingredients, to make it homogeneous or smooth, or to give it body. Depending on the type of preparation (forcemeat, purée, dough, cream, sauce, etc.), the operation is carried out either on the stove or away from the heat, sometimes on ice, with a wooden spatula, a manual or electric whisk, a blender, a mixer, or even with the hand.

The intransitive form of the verb *travailler* is applied to rising dough or fermenting alcohol.

tray PLATEAU

A large flat low-rimmed container, sometimes with handles, used for presenting and carrying to table various foods. It may be made of wood, wicker, glass, or metal. A *plateau de fruits de mer* ('seafood platter') is an assortment of shellfish served on a tray decorated with crushed ice or seaweed.

Tremellodon gelatinosum

TRÉMELLODON
GÉLATINEUX

A whitish or brownish mushroom, commonly known as the jelly-spore fungus; it has soft translucent prickles and grows on the decaying stumps of conifers. Its flesh, of a gelatinous consistency, has a resinous taste and is eaten raw in salads.

trencher TRANCHOIR

Formerly, a wooden board used for carving meat. In the Middle Ages, the trencher was a thick slice of bread which was used as a plate. These were changed when they became too impregnated with sauce or broth; at the end of the meal, they were given to the poor. Parisian trencher bread, according to the *Ménagier de Paris*, was a fairly coarse loaf made in Corbeil and sold in the Place Maubert.

trénels

A mutton tripe dish typical of the Millau region in Aveyron. The rumen is cut into large pieces, in each of which is placed a clove of garlic studded with cloves, a few thin strips of ham, and some small pieces of mutton tripe. The trénels are then tied or sewn up and simmered in a stewpan containing bacon rinds, carrots, thyme, bay leaves, water, and white wine.

trescat

A mutton tripe dish that is cooked with egg yolks (a characteristic of the cookery of southwestern France). A special feature of the dish is that the tripe is plaited (*tressé*), hence its name. It is also called *galutres*.

Tricholoma

TRICHOLOME

A genus of fleshy robust mushrooms with white or pink gills, indented near the stalk, and without a ring (or volva). They are available from spring to the end of autumn and most species are edible; the tastiest are *Tricholoma gambosum* (St George's mushroom, also called *mousseron* in French), which is white or buff (and sometimes a little indigestible), and the wood blewit (*pied-bleu*), which is a brownish-violet colour (the fibrous base of its stalk must be cut off and the rather sticky skin of its cap must be removed). Both of these are excellent when prepared like chanterelles and can even be eaten raw. The wood blewit also grows in winter and can be cultivated. Other species worthy of note are *Tricholoma argyraceum*, which is brownish-grey with a very delicate flavour after cooking; *Tricholoma equestre* (firewood agaric or *jaunet*), which tastes like a carnation; the pinkish-white *Tricholoma columbetta*; and *Tricholoma terreum* (or *petit-gris*).

triclinium

In ancient Rome, a dining room containing three couches arranged parallel to three sides of a table, the fourth side remaining free for the service. Each couch accommodated three guests. Rich patricians had three tricliniums: one for summer, one for winter, and one for spring and autumn.

Triggerfish BALISTE

A flat lozenge-shaped fish from warm seas. Its French name, *baliste*, comes from the name of a Roman war machine (*balista*) and derives from the dorsal trigger which it displays in times of danger. The best-known species is the Mediterranean triggerfish, which is prepared in the same way as tuna and has a similar flavour.

trim PARER

To remove all the parts of a piece of meat, chicken, fish, vegetable, or any other item of food that are not required for its preparation. Vegetables, particularly potatoes, carrots, and turnips, are peeled before being cut into the desired shape. The trimming of a roasting joint includes not only removing the sinews and the excess fat but also tying it up with string.

Some dishes are trimmed, either before or after cooking, to improve their appearance. For example, tarts are trimmed of excess pastry before baking, and poached eggs are trimmed after cooking to remove the rough edges.

Trimalcion

A character created by Petronius, a Roman writer of the 1st century AD, in the *Satyricon*, an account of the wanderings of a young dissolute Roman. Trimalcion is a typical parvenu who exhibits vulgar ostentation in his private life, particularly at table. Trimalcion offers his friends and courtesans a gargantuan feast with a multiplicity of courses: fish, plump chickens, wild boars, sows' udders, pigs stuffed with sausages and black puddings (blood sausages), oysters, snails, etc. In Trimalcion, Petronius caricatures the nouveaux riches: the habits described are not representative of the usual Roman practice of the time (see *ancient Rome*).

The expression *festin de Trimalcion* (Trimalcion's feast) is often used to describe a magnificent meal, but in view of its true meaning it is hardly a compliment.

trimmings PARURES

The parts of meat, poultry, fish, etc., that are trimmed off before cooking. The trimmings, which can include pieces of skin, fat, sinews, fish heads, etc., can be used for making stock, sauces, soups, and purées.

tripe

GRAS-DOUBLE, TRIPES

The stomach of ruminants (especially ox, calf, or sheep) used as food. It is usually sold specially prepared or cleaned for cooking but is also available ready-cooked or pickled.

Tripe can be prepared in a variety of ways. The best-known French dish is *tripes à la mode de Caen*, the authenticity of which has been defended by the Norman Confrérie de la Tripière d'Or since 1952; each year they award a prize to the best manufacturer. Tripe can also be marinated and then fried or grilled (broiled); sautéed with onions; slowly stewed with tomatoes; cooked *au gratin*; cooked in a sauce with vegetable flavourings; or cooked in broth, wine, or cider. Particular mention should be made of tripe *en meurette* (cooked with vinegar, shallots, and fresh cream), Bugey tripe (sautéed, flamed with marc brandy, and slowly stewed in white wine with tomatoes and spices), and tripe *à la dauphinoise* (slowly stewed with bacon rinds and pork skin, tomatoes, garlic, and spicy stock).

Tripe is used in a large number of regional French dishes, usually highly seasoned. In the provinces of western France, ox tripe is preferred. Apart from the famous tripe dish of Caen, which Alex Pharamond brought to Paris before 1870 and which is still cooked in its small earthenware pan, mention should be made of those of Coutances (with cream, rolled into small packets), Authon-du-Perche (arranged in layers with bacon and simmered in cider with carrots and onions), Vannes (also cooked in cider, with calves' feet, onions, carrots, and leeks), Saint-Malo or Pont-l'Abbé (ox feet, calves' feet, and sheep and ox stomach with pieces of pickled pork, shallots, and onions), Angoulême (calf's rumen, psalterium, and feet, cooked in white wine with tomato and garlic, with studded onions and shallots), and La Ferté-Macé (threaded in little bundles on skewers).

In northern France, a tripe dish (ox stomach and feet) is prepared in Cambrai with garlic and thyme, simmered in cider or white wine, and served with fried potatoes (ox tripe is traditionally garnished with steamed potatoes). In eastern France, in Marmesse, tripe is cooked with tomatoes and cream.

In southern France, mutton tripe is preferred. In Rouergue and Auvergne, specialities include trénels, tripous, manouls, pétéram, and cabassol. In Quercy and Albigeois, tripe is seasoned with saffron (according to a typically medieval recipe, *tripes au jaunet*). *Tripes de jeune bouc châtré*, an old Olargues speciality, is also worthy of note. Mutton tripe is equally popular in Provence, where it is cooked in white wine and garlic or sometimes sautéed. Mention should also be made of the pieds et paquets of Marseilles. In Gascony, calf's tripe is cooked with goose fat; in Roussillon a blanquette of tripe is prepared; whereas in Corsica, *tripettes* are sautéed with tomatoes.

Cooked tripe preparations sold by French butchers do not necessarily correspond to the authentic regional dishes. These cooked preparations include *tripes de Caen* (ox rumen, reticulum, abomasum, and feet, cooked with slices of carrot in a seasoned stock), *tripes à l'auvergnate* (ox tripe and pig's trotters), *tripous du Cantal* (calf's mesentery, feet, and forcemeat made with bacon, onion, garlic, and parsley), and *tripes à la provençale* (ox tripe, pig's trotters, and pieces of pig's head in tomato sauce).

Notable tripe dishes of other countries include *busecca* from Lombardy (a soup made with calf's-tripe and green vegetables); Spanish *tripes à la madrilène* (highly spiced and garnished with chorizo, chilli peppers, garlic, and thin strips of sweet red pepper); Bulgarian tchorba (tripe soup); Arab *annrisse* (tripe and pluck boiled with cumin, pepper, and orange and lemon rind), *barbouche*, or tripe couscous (tripe simmered with oil, garlic, cumin, caraway, white haricot (navy) beans, and beef sausage); and the British tripe and onions, simmered in milk with bay leaves.

Tripe à la bourgeoise GRAS-DOUBLE DE BOEUF À LA BOURGEOISE Cut 750 g (1¾ lb) blanched tripe into squares. Peel and blanch 24 small new carrots. Peel 36 small onions, Half-cook 24 of them in stock and brown the remainder in 50 g (2 oz, ¼ cup) butter. Sprinkle the browned onions with 1 tablespoon flour, brown lightly, and add 6 dl (1 pint, 2½ cups) stock; stir and boil for 6 minutes. Add the tripe, salt, pepper, a pinch of cayenne, and a bouquet garni, and boil very rapidly. Add the blanched carrots and the half-cooked onions, cover, and cook for about 1½ hours. Serve in a deep dish, sprinkled with chopped parsley.

Tripe à la lyonnaise GRAS-DOUBLE DE BOEUF À LA LYONNAISE Cook and drain 750 g (1¾ lb) tripe and cut into thin strips. Sauté in sizzling butter or lard. Season with salt and pepper and add 4 tablespoons (⅓ cup) finely chopped onions fried in butter or lard. Mix and cook together until the tripe is browned. Arrange in a deep dish, add a dash of vinegar heated in the frying pan (skillet), and sprinkle with chopped parsley.

Tripe à la mode de Caen TRIPES À LA MODE DE CAEN Line the bottom of a marmite or casserole with 500 g (18 oz) finely sliced onions and 500 g (18 oz) sliced carrots. On top of these put 2 calves' feet, boned and cut into pieces, together with their long bones split in half lengthways. Add a mixture of 2 kg (4½ lb) ox tripe, consisting of the psalterium (or manyplies), rennet (or reed), reticulum, and rumen, cut into 5-cm (2-in) pieces. Insert among the tripe 4 cloves garlic, a large bouquet garni (mostly thyme and bay leaf), and 300 g (11 oz) leeks, tied in a bunch. Season with 15 g (½ oz, 3 teaspoons) coarse salt, 4 g (1 teaspoon) freshly ground pepper, and a pinch of 'four spices'. Cover with a few slices of beef fat, then pour in enough cider, mixed with a few tablespoons Calvados, to cover.

Begin cooking on the stove without a lid, then cover and seal with a flour-and-water luting paste. Cook in a cool oven (140 C, 275 F, gas 1) for about 10 hours. Before serving, remove the layer of fat, drain the tripe, and take out the bouquet garni, all the bones, and the leeks. Put the tripe into a serving dish and pour over the cooking stock, strained and skimmed of fat. Keep as hot as possible until serving. Serve on heated plates or in small earthenware bowls, with steamed potatoes.

Tripe à la poulette   GRAS-DOUBLE À LA POULETTE   (from Carême's recipe) Cut the tripe into pieces 2.5 cm (1 in) square. Keep hot in a double boiler or bain-marie with a little butter and meat glaze. Make some light allemande sauce, adding some lightly fried blanched chopped parsley. Mix half of it with the tripe and add the juice of a lemon. Heat in a dish, and cover with the rest of the allemande sauce, adding 250 g (9 oz, 2¼ cups) peeled mushrooms.

Tripe soup à la milanaise   SOUPE AU GRAS-DOUBLE À LA MILANAISE   Cut into julienne strips 500 g (18 oz) calf's tripe, which has been blanched, cooled, and drained. In a casserole heat 100 g (4 oz, ½ cup) bacon cut into small cubes, a medium-sized onion, and the shredded white part of a leek. Add the julienne strips of tripe and brown for a few minutes on the stove. Sprinkle with 1 tablespoon flour. Add 2 litres (3½ pints, 4½ pints) stock or water and bring to the boil. Cut the heart of a medium-sized cabbage into small pieces, blanch for 6 minutes in boiling water, then drain. Peel and deseed 2 tomatoes and crush the pulp. Add to the boiling soup the cabbage, the tomatoes, 5 tablespoons (6 tablespoons) peas, and a few small sprigs of broccoli. Season with salt and pepper and cook rapidly for at least 1½ hours.

tripe (à la)

Describes a dish of hard-boiled (hard-cooked) eggs, cut into slices and covered with thick béchamel sauce mixed with onion lightly fried in butter. It is also known as hard-boiled eggs *en tripes*. In Berry, however, eggs *à la tripe* are eggs poached in a white-wine sauce with onions and aromatic herbs. There is no apparent connection with tripe, apart from the presence of onions.

RECIPE

Eggs à la tripe   OEUFS À LA TRIPE Hard-boil (hard-cook) 8 eggs for 9 minutes, then cool and shell them. Cut into fairly thick slices, put in a shallow dish, and keep warm. Lightly fry, without browning, 100 g, (4 oz, 1 cup) sliced onion with 50 g (2 oz, 4 tablespoons) butter. Sprinkle with 40 g (1½ oz, 6 tablespoons) sifted flour and stir well, over the heat. Pour in ½ litre (17 fl oz, 2 cups) cold milk and cook for 10 minutes, stirring regularly. Season with nutmeg, salt, and pepper. Cover the eggs with this sauce while it is still hot and serve immedaitely.

Alternatively, use a béchamel sauce mixed with an equal volume of onion purée.

triperie

In France, all the offal of slaughtered animals, which is sold mainly by the tripe butcher. However, kidneys and liver may be sold at an ordinary butcher's and pig's offal is sold and processed by the pork butcher. In the Middle Ages, the tripe butchers' corporation was founded in Paris by six families, who purchased white or red offal from butchers on a wholesale basis. They prepared the offal and resold it to merchants, who peddled it about the streets, in copper containers, especially ox tripe with saffron.

tripotcha or tripotch

A Basque speciality, which Curnonsky defined as a mutton *boudin* (black pudding, blood sausage) but which is usually made from the intestines, lungs, and blood of a calf, all highly spiced. In Biriatou, near Hendaye, tripotcha is eaten with apple purée.

tripous or tripoux

In Rouergue, small bundles of sheep's tripe tied up and braised over a low heat. They are prepared with pieces of sheep's stomach (or calf's sweetbread) and sheep's feet, herbs, and vegetable flavourings. Tripous are found almost everywhere in central France. In Espalion, where they are also called *petites*, they are made with sheep's stomach cut into long thin strips, which are wrapped around a forcemeat made from ham, garlic, parsley, and flavourings. The small bundles, held together with knotted intestines, are cooked in a broth or veal stock with white wine. There are many variants, including the trénels of Millau, the trescats of southwestern France, or the manouls of Aveyron. They are sometimes seasoned with saffron.

Trois-Cornes

A triangular cheese from Poitou, formerly made from ewes' milk. Now rare, it is usually made from cows' milk today. Because of its characteristic triangular shape, it is also known as *trébèche*, from the Celtic *tri* (three) and *bézeck* (point).

trois-frères

A pastry created in the 19th century by the three Julien brothers, celebrated Parisian pastrycooks, for which a special mould, in the shape of a large twisted crown, was invented. A mixture of rice flour and melted butter is poured onto eggs whisked (beaten) with sugar, flavoured with vanilla or maraschino, cooked, then set on a base of sweet pastry. Trois-frères is traditionally glazed with apricot and decorated with candied angelica. A variant of this pastry is made with ground almonds, sugar, eggs, and whipped cream, flavoured with orange, iced, then decorated with fruit. The special trois-frères mould is sometimes replaced by a savarin mould.

RECIPE

Trois-frères Make 250 g (9 oz) pâte sablée (see *doughs and batters*). Preheat the oven to 200 c (400 F, gas 6). Put 7 whole eggs into a heatproof basin and whisk (beat), on the top of the stove, over hot water, with 250 g (9 oz, 1 cup) caster (superfine) sugar. When the mixture is thick and creamy, pour in 225 g (8 oz, 2 cups) rice flour, 200 g (7 oz, scant cup) melted butter, and 1 liqueur glass Maraschino or rum. Mix thoroughly, then pour into a well buttered trois-frères mould. Roll out the dough to a round shape 4 mm (¼ in) thick and a little larger than the mould. Place on a buttered and floured baking sheet. Bake both preparations in the oven at the same time, the first for 45 minutes and the second for 20 minutes. Remove from the oven, turn out of the mould, and allow to cool. Set the crown-shaped cake on the pastry base, cover generously with apricot syrup, sprinkle with chopped shredded (slivered) almonds, and decorate with diamond shapes of candied angelica.

Troisgros (Jean *and* Pierre)

French cooks and restaurateurs in Roanne (Loire). Jean (1926–83) and Pierre (born 1928) were born in Chalon-sur-Saône, the sons of Jean-Baptiste Troisgros, a café-owner who later became proprietor of the small station hotel at Roanne, where his sister and his wife were in charge of the kitchens. The two brothers were sent to Lucas-Carton in Paris for their apprenticeship, then to Fernand Point in Vienna. In 1954 they began to practise their trade in the family hotel, then took over the management; from that point on their progress was continuous (one star in the Michelin guide in 1955, two in 1965, three in 1968).

Their cookery was inspired by recipes handed down from past generations, sometimes almost peasant in character: for example, pigeons *à la gouse d'ail en chemise*, snails *en poêlon* with green butter, and foie gras fried with spinach. But they also brought family dishes to a peak of perfection, notably their famous escalope of salmon with sorrel and their *mosaïque* of vegetables stuffed with truffles. Pierre proved to be the meat specialist, whereas Jean was a wine connoisseur. Together they created rib of beef *au fleurie* and *à la moelle*, accompanied by a gratin of potatoes *à la forézienne* (without cheese), aiguillettes of mallard with St George's mushroom, or, in a more modern vein, scallops *en croûte* with Nantes butter, and *salade riche* (foie gras, lobster, and truffle).

troquet

A popular term in France for a drinking establishment (synonymous with *bistrot*). It is a shortened form of *mastroquet* (wine retailer), which appears to come from the Dutch *meesterke* (small employer), allied to the slang word *stroc* (a measure of wine).

trotters

See *feet and trotters*.

trou normand

The former custom, also called *coup de milieu*, of drinking a small glass of spirits in the middle of a large meal to aid digestion and stimulate the appetite for the remaining courses. The spirit was Calvados (hence the name – Calvados being distilled in Normandy), but Cognac, Kirsch, or a fruit brandy could also be drunk, usually after the entrées and before the roasts. Nowadays, in place of the *trou normand*, a fruit sorbet is sometimes served, sprinkled with an appropriate spirit: orange and Cognac, pineapple and Kirsch, pear and pear brandy, lemon and vodka, etc.

trousser

A French term meaning to arrange fowl or winged game in the appropriate form before trussing, with the legs straight out for roasting and folded in for braising or poaching. The term *troussé* is particularly applied to a bird with a small incision made in its sides for inserting the leg and thigh joint. For some small fowl, *troussage* may make trussing unnecessary.

Crayfish (and sometimes langoustines) are often *troussé* for a particular garnish: the operation consists of sticking the ends of the pincers into the base of the 'tail' (that is, the abdomen).

trout TRUITE

A fish of mountain streams, lakes, and rivers, highly sought-after by fishermen. This carnivorous fish, with tasty flesh (its name comes from Greek *troktes*, meaning 'voracious'), is also bred on a large scale in trout farms. Since 1961, when the Guillon law was passed, only specially bred rainbow trout have been sold in fish shops or served in restaurants in France, whereas the majority of regional trout dishes are, in principle, intended for trout caught locally.

The common brown trout constitutes 5% of bred trout, but young fish are rapidly reintroduced into their natural environment to restock well-oxygenated rivers. Adult trout are a golden colour, with spots on the top half of the body, but the degree of colouring depends on habitat, sex, and age; they can grow as long as 60 cm (2 ft). Highly esteemed in the Middle Ages, trout was then cooked in a court-bouillon or a pie. A variety called the lake trout, living in lakes and fast-flowing streams, can grow as long as 1 metre (39 in). Its diet, rich in shellfish, turns its flesh pink; it is then called salmon trout. The same is true of the sea trout, which lives in coastal rivers near the English Channel and swims down to the sea, returning to the rivers in autumn. Fishing for the brown trout, lake trout, and sea trout requires a permit. They are reserved for private consumption.

The rainbow trout is a species imported from the United States (where it lives in open water); it is bred in fish farms on a large scale. It is a silvery fish, sometimes with a purplish-blue band down its side. It has spots over its entire body, including the fins. There are now 700 trout-breeding farms in France, with production rising from 10,000 tons to 20,000 tons over 10 years. The brown trout was the first fish to be bred successfully by artificial insemination, as early as the 15th century. At the Réomé monastery (Côte-d'Or), Dom Pinchon took and fertilized some trout eggs, put them in boxes on a bed of sand, and replaced the fish in the river. Known to a number of fishermen and kept secret, this method was rediscovered in 1842 by two Vosgians. But the expansion of trout farming did not occur until the beginning of the 20th century, when the rainbow trout was imported. The milt of stud males is poured onto the eggs of selected females; the eggs are left to incubate in water at a constant temperature, rich in oxygen. The alevins are then placed in tanks; while they are growing, they are sorted into batches of uniform size. At about five months, the alevin measures 6 cm (2½ in) and already has the general shape of a trout. Between 6 and 16 cm (2½–6¼ in), or 40–80 g (1½–3 oz), it is called a troutlet (*truitelle*), which becomes a *truite-portion* between 18 months and 2 years, when it measures 28 cm (11 inches) and weighs 150–300 g (5–11 oz). It can live for a further ten years and reach 6–8 kg (13–18 lb), but this only happens to those specimens selected for reproduction.

The diet of the bred trout (fish meal and soya (soy) flour) is carefully measured; the trout cannot be force-fed in order to make it grow. Furthermore, it needs space, otherwise it will die. The defects attributed to trout from breeding farms (tasteless or flaccid flesh) are usually caused by the treatment they receive at the fishmonger's or at the restaurant, where the water in which they are kept may be too warm or insufficiently oxygenated.

Smoked trout are also sold whole or in skinned fillets (rainbow or sea trout, sometimes salmon trout). In Norway, in particular, salmon trout bred in fjords are smoked, frozen, or bottled.

☐ **Trout cookery** Trout *à la meunière* and *au bleu* are well-known preparations, which are succulent when made with freshly caught brown trout. There are, in addition, a variety of tasty ancient recipes from the French provinces. In Auvergne, trout is fried with chopped bacon and garlic; stuffed *à la montdorienne* (with breadcrumbs, cream, herbs, and mushrooms); cooked in a fumet and coated with cream sauce; or poached in fillets and served on a julienne of cabbage simmered in cream. Trout *à la d'Ussel* is poached, then, the next day, rolled in breadcrumbs and cooked *au gratin*. In southwestern France, trout (known as *trouéte* or *truchet*) is fried or braised in white wine with cep mushrooms or stuffed with whiting flesh ground with duck foie gras and cooked *en papillote*. In Savoy, trout is cooked *au bleu*, *à la meunière* (a speciality of Lake Annecy), in a court-bouillon (served with a mousseline sauce), or stuffed and braised *à l'apremont*. In Corsica (where Corte is a major river-fishing centre), it is traditionally cooked with aromatics and red wine in a *poêlon* (a long-handled metal pan). In Normandy, trout is pot-roasted with bacon *à la mode de Vire*; cooked in a matelote with cider (in the Andelys); cooked en papillote, with apple, herbs, cream, and Calvados; or made into a hot pie (a traditional dish of the bishops of Rouen). Mention should also be made of trout *à la beauvaisienne* (roasted with peppercorns); trout *à la montbardoise* (stuffed with spinach and shallot and cooked in a court-bouillon), also called *caprice de Buffon* (in honour of the naturalist Buffon, who was born in Montbard); trout pâté *à la lorraine* (fillets ground with nutmeg and herbs, mixed with chopped morels, and garnished with whole fillets); trout flambé from Périgord, served with melted butter; and plain grilled trout, as described by Austin de Croze: 'The trout were gutted, scraped, and washed, while some broad flat pebbles were being heated in a hole with burning twigs. The hot pebbles were removed with forked branches; on each was placed a few drops of oil or a tiny piece of butter, followed immediately by the seasoned trout, in which some diamond-shaped incisions had been made: hot pebbles were used to seal the other side of the trout . . . , which were eaten *au naturel* on large hunks of bread.' Jean Giono, a great connoisseur, denounces trout with almonds, a classic restaurant dish that is despised by many gourmets: 'Never with butter, never with almonds. That's not cookery, it's cardboard-making. . . . Apart from trout *au bleu*, people don't know how to cook trout.'

Despite the prejudice against them, bred trout are widely used in restaurants in various dishes, hot or cold, some more elaborate than others. Chefs have prepared them in a variety of imaginative ways. Laguipière served the Emperor Napoleon grilled (broiled) trout, which had been marinated in olive oil and lemon, with a maître d'hôtel sauce seasoned with nutmeg. Fernand Point devised a recipe for trout stuffed with mushrooms, truffle, carrots, and celery, sealed in a court-bouillon, sprinkled with port, and finished off in the oven *en papillote*, coated with the cooking juices thickened with kneaded butter. Classic preparations include trout poached in a court-bouillon and served with a hollandaise sauce; cooked in red wine *à la bourguignonne*; fried *à la Colbert*; or cold, in jelly, with various garnishes. In addition, any salmon recipe can be used for trout.

RECIPES

Blue trout TRUITES AU BLEU 10 minutes before serving, take the fish out of the water and kill them with a hard blow on the head; gut and clean rapidly, without wiping. Sprinkle with vinegar, then plunge into a boiling court-bouillon containing a high proportion of vinegar. Simmer, allowing 6–7 minutes for fish weighing about 150 g (5 oz). Drain and arrange on a napkin. Garnish with fresh parsley and serve with melted butter or hollandaise sauce.

Fried trout TRUITES FRITES Clean,

gut, and dry some very small trout. Season with salt and pepper and dust with flour. Deep-fry in sizzling oil, then drain and arrange on a napkin. Serve with a green salad and slices of lemon.

Salmon trout Beauharnais TRUITE SAUMONÉE BEAUHARNAIS Stuff a salmon trout weighing about 900 g (2 lb) with 250 g (9 oz) forcemeat of whiting and cream mixed with 4 tablespoons (⅓ cup) vegetable mirepoix lightly cooked in butter. Place on the buttered grid of a fish kettle, half-cover with fish fumet made with white wine and cook in a hot oven (230 c, 450 f, gas 8), or place the fish kettle across two burners of the stove, for about 20 minutes. Drain the trout, place in a serving dish, and garnish with noisette potatoes cooked in butter and small artichoke hearts cooked in butter and filled with béarnaise sauce.

Strain the cooking liquid; reduce, thicken with butter, and serve with the trout.

Salmon trout with salad TRUITES SAUMONÉES EN SALADE (from Daniel Jourdan's recipe) Clean and fillet 4 salmon trout. Slice the fillets into thin strips, lay on a porcelain dish, season with salt and pepper, and sprinkle with olive oil. Turn them over and repeat the operation. Leave to marinate overnight in a cool place.

On the day of the meal, cook some small artichokes, keeping them crisp, peel 2 very ripe avocados, poach 3 quails' eggs per guest, and prepare a very fine julienne or orange zest and ginger. Cook 3 crayfish per person in a highly flavoured court-bouillon.

Arrange the raw trout fillets in a fan shape on the plates. Place the crayfish, with their tails shelled, at the base of the fan, then complete the fan with avocado slices, artichoke quarters, and quails' eggs. Sprinkle with the julienne of orange and ginger, then season with a dash of lemon juice and olive oil.

In autumn, make the garnish with thin strips of Caesar's mushrooms, a boletus cap marinated with the trout fillets, small shaped pieces of beetroot (red beet), crisp French (green) beans, artichoke hearts, poached quails' eggs, and a julienne of orange zest and fresh ginger.

Trout à la bourguignonne TRUITES À LA BOURGUIGNONNE Clean and dry 4 trout and season with salt and pepper inside and out. Finely slice 250 g (9 oz) cleaned mushrooms, a carrot, and an onion, lightly cook in butter, and use to line a buttered ovenproof dish. Place the trout in the dish and add a bouquet garni and just enough red Burgundy to cover the fish. Bring to the boil on top of the stove, then cover and cook in a hot oven (220 c, 425 f, gas 7) for about 10 minutes. Glaze 12 small (pearl) onions. Drain the trout and place in a heated serving dish, with the onions as a garnish. Keep hot. Strain the cooking liquid, thicken with 1 tablespoon kneaded butter, and put back on the heat for 2–3 minutes. Add 2 tablespoons (3 tablespoons) fresh butter, whisk, and pour over the trout.

Trout with almonds TRUITES AUX AMANDES Clean and dry 4 (9-oz) trout, each weighing 250 g (9 oz). Season with salt and pepper and dust with flour. Heat 50 g (2 oz, 4 tablespoons) butter in a large oval frying pan (skillet) and brown the trout on both sides, then lower the heat and cook for 10–12 minutes, turning once. Brown 75 g (3 oz, ¾ cup) shredded (slivered) almonds in a dry frying pan or in the oven and add to the trout. Drain the cooked trout and arrange on a serving dish. Sprinkle with 2 tablespoons lemon juice and some chopped parsley. Keep warm. Add 20 g (¾ oz, 1½ tablespoons) butter and 1 tablespoon vinegar to the frying pan, heat, and pour over the trout with the almonds.

Trout with leeks TRUITE AUX POIREAUX (from the Restaurant Pharamond's recipe) Remove the backbone from an uncooked trout, season with salt and pepper, and stuff with a fine forcemeat of whiting and cream. Roll up in blanched whole leaves of young leeks. Cook in a buttered dish with a little white wine and shallots. Drain the fish. Reduce the cooking liquid, if necessary, and thicken with cream; adjust the seasoning and pour over the trout.

trucha

A flat rustic omelette from Nice, made with spinach and Swiss chard. It is served as an entrée, sometimes cold, with tomato coulis.

truffade or truffado

A speciality from Auvergne, made of cooked potatoes, peeled, coarsely shredded, then fried in lard over a brisk heat, with thin strips of Tomme (fresh Cantal cheese) added. It is stirred until the cheese melts and combines with the potato to form a thick pancake, which is turned over, covered, cooked for a few more minutes over a low heat, and then served as a hot entrée. Connoisseurs of this dish consider that the best Tomme for truffade is that of la Planèze, which is particularly high in fat. Fried lardons or chopped garlic are sometimes added. The name comes from *truffe*, or *troufle*, a former name for 'potato' in country areas.

truffer

A French culinary term meaning to impart the aroma of truffles to a dish by incorporating pieces of truffle. It is mainly foie gras, forcemeats (for pâtés, poultry, quenelles, black puddings (blood sausages), etc.), salpicons, and ragouts that have diced or chopped truffle added to them. A chicken can be 'truffled' by sliding strips of truffle between the flesh and skin. As Grimod de La Reynière stated: 'Maraschino can be "truffled" as well as turkey.' But overuse is not recommended, as the *Dictionnaire de l'Académie des gastronomes* makes clear: 'Let us be truffophiles, even truffivores at times, but let us refrain from truffomania!'

truffiat or truffat

A speciality of Berry, made by cooking grated raw potatoes with curd cheese in a casserole. Truffiat may also be made from a mixture of grated raw potatoes, butter, and beaten eggs, seasoned with salt and pepper, poured into a flan dish, cooked in the oven, and served hot. Formerly, the potatoes (which were called *truffes*, hence the name of the dish), butter, and eggs were mixed with shortcrust pastry (basic pie dough), giving rise to the nickname *bourre-chrétien* (from *bourer*, 'to stuff').

truffle   TRUFFE

A subterranean fungus which lives in symbiosis with certain trees, mainly the oak but also the chestnut, hazel, and beech. A highly esteemed foodstuff, the truffle (from the Latin *tuber*, meaning 'outgrowth' or 'excrescence') is rounded, of variable size and irregular shape, and black, dark brown, or sometimes grey or white in colour; it is found especially in chalky soil or clay, quite near the surface (less than 30 cm (12 in) deep). French truffle production (particularly in the southwest and southeast) has greatly declined since the beginning of the 20th century, because of deforestation, the deterioration of suitable land, the use of pesticides, etc. Before 1914, some 1800 tons of truffles were harvested each year in Périgord alone. Nowadays 200 tons are harvested in the whole of France. These figures explain why the liberal use of truffles in certain classic recipes is now impracticable. Methodical truffle cultivation has not yet given conclusive results.

☐ **Mysterious origins and small-scale harvesting** The truffle has been known and appreciated since ancient times. The Egyptians ate truffles coated in goose fat and cooked *en papillote*. The ancient Greeks and Romans attributed therapeutic and aphrodisiac powers to them: the latter quality was still recognized in the 19th century, when Alexandre Dumas wrote, 'They can, on certain occasions, make women more tender and men more lovable.' Up to the beginning of the 18th century, their origin was shrouded in mystery: 'Since, during storms, flames leap from the humid vapours and dark clouds emit deafening noises, is it surprising that lightning, when it strikes the ground, gives rise to truffles, which do not resemble plants?' asked Plutarch. In the Middle Ages, when they were looked upon as a manifestation of the devil, they fell into oblivion. Having returned to popularity during the Renaissance, they subsequently suffered a further eclipse, but came back into favour under Louis XIV and have reigned supreme since then. La Varenne recommended ragout of dried or fresh truffles as an entrée: washed, cooked in wine, seasoned with salt and pepper, and served on a napkin or in a dish garnished with flowers. In 1711, Claude Joseph Geoffroy, a French botanist, published a paper entitled *Végétation de la truffe*, which definitely classified the truffle among the mushrooms.

The practice of using muzzled pigs to seek out truffles was common in the 17th century; in 1705 Lémery wrote: 'There are dogs which can detect them as well as pigs. Some peasants, in areas where truffles are found, have taught themselves through long experience to recognize the places where they are hidden.' Nowadays, the many varieties of truffles are always gathered with the assistance of an animal (pig or dog) that can detect their presence. In some cases, the movement of a fly may reveal that truffles are nearby. With the animal on a leash, the 'digger' closely follows its footsteps and unearths the truffles as soon as the animal begins to root in the ground. He then carefully replaces the clods of earth so that no traces remain – the other truffles must be left to mature and the curiosity of potential poachers must not be aroused. Truffle cultivation remains essentially empirical and small-scale: truffles are neither sown nor planted. They spring up spontaneously when the fungal spores or mycelia encounter the rootlets of an oak tree (or another symbiotic species) and form a mycorrhiza, which takes its nutrients from the tree; the truffle itself is the fruiting body of the fungus and does not appear to be connected by any filaments to the mycorrhiza.

□ **Varieties of truffles** There are 70 varieties of truffles, 32 of which are found in Europe. The most highly esteemed is the black truffle of Périgord, which matures after the first frosts: it has black flesh streaked with whitish veins and gives off a strong aroma. In fact, it mainly comes from Tricastin, Vaucluse, Lot, Quercy, and Gard, but it retains the prestigious appellation which established its reputation (it is also found in Piedmont, Tuscany, and Aragon). The *truffe d'été*, or *truffe de Saint-Jean*, dark brown and white-veined, the grey truffle of Champagne and Burgundy, and the truffles of Alsace and Vaucluse, brown with black veins, have less of an aroma, like the *terfez* (the snow-white truffle, which

grows in North African, in the Atlas mountains).

The white truffle of Piedmont enjoys a measure of popularity. It has a delicate aroma, especially marked in the truffle of the Alba region, and is in season from October to December. In cookery, it is served with capon, veal, and sometimes langouste. It is also eaten cooked in Asti, sprinkled with Parmesan, and seasoned with lemon vinaigrette. A sauce made with Piedmont truffles, butter, cream, garlic, and anchovy is poured over spaghetti or vegetables served cold. The truffle is also used raw, grated or cut into thin strips (with a *coupe-truffe*, a special utensil), as a garnish for grilled meat, chicken, agnolotti, or risotto.

□ **The truffle in cookery** A good black truffle must be well rounded and in a single piece. It is not at its best until ripe, which prompted Grimod de La Reynière to say: 'Truffles are only really good after Christmas. . . . So let us allow ignorant fops, beardless gourmands, and inexperienced palates the petty triumph of eating the first truffles.'

Although its use in cookery is more restrained than in the past, because of its rarity and high price, the prestige of the truffle remains intact and the superlatives attributed to it bear witness to its almost mythical quality: 'diamond of cookery' (Brillat-Savarin), 'fairy apple' (George Sand), 'black queen' (Émile Goudeau), 'gem of poor lands' (Colette), 'fragrant nugget' (J. de Coquet), 'black pearl' (Fulbert Dumonteil), and 'holy of holies for the gourmet' (Alexandre Dumas). Regarding their cost, J.-L. Vaudoyer is said to have observed: 'There are two types of people who eat truffles: those who think truffles are good because they are dear and those who know they are dear because they are good.'

Truffles are eaten raw or cooked, cut into strips or slices, diced or shredded, in the form of juice, fumet, or essence, or simply for their fragrance: 'When you feel like eating boiled eggs, if you have some truffles in the house, put them in a basket with the eggs and the next day you will have the best boiled eggs you have ever tasted in your gastronomic life' (M. des Ombiaux). Truffles occur, frequently associated with foie gras, in all recipes called *Périgueux* or *à la péri-gourdine*; these can include game, meat, poultry, pâte, forcemeat, black puddings (blood sausages), egg dishes, and salads. They also feature in various sauces (diplomat, financière, Joinville, régence, and riche) and garnishes (banquière, Belle-Hélène, Berny, cardinal, Chambord, Demidof, favorite, Frascati, Godard, Lorette, Lucullus, réforme, and Rohan). Other prestigious dishes including truffles are: fillet of beef Prince Albert; timbale Talleyrand; chicken *à la d'Albufera*, demi-deuil, and Edward VII; fillets of sole *à l'impériale* and Renaissance; lobster with Victoria sauce; tournedos Rossini; etc.

However, as Colette says, 'You pay its weight in gold for it, then in most cases you put it to some paltry use. You smear it with foie gras, you bury it in poultry overloaded with fat, you chop it up and drown it in brown sauce, you mix it with vegetables covered in mayonnaise. . . . To hell with thin slices, strips, trimmings, and peelings of truffles! Is it not possible to like them for themselves?' Indeed, the true connoisseur enjoys truffles whole and fresh, either raw, with butter or salad, or cooked (in embers, braised with white wine or champagne, or in a puff pastry case).

Colette also gives us a delicious recipe: 'Steep in good very dry white wine (keep your champagne for banquets; the truffle does very well without it), lightly seasoned with salt and pepper. Cook in a covered black cocotte. For 25 minutes it dances in the boiling liquid with 20 or so lardons – like Tritons playing around a black Amphitrite – which give substance to the cooking juices. No other spices whatsoever! And to hell with the pressed napkin, tasting and smelling of chlorine, the final bed of the cooked truffle! Your truffles should come to the table in their court-bouillon. Take a generous helping: the truffle whets the appetite and assists the digestion.'

□ **Canning** Truffles are now sold in cans, peeled or scrubbed, ripe and whole. They are graded: *surchoix* (with firm flesh, black, and of a uniform size and colour), *extra* (with firm flesh, more or less black, and slightly irregular in size), *premier choix* (with more or less firm flesh, sometimes light in colour, of irregular size, and possibly with abrasions). They are also canned in pieces (at least 5 mm (¼ in) thick, dark in colour, with up to 2% impurities), peelings (of variable colour, with 20% cracks at most and up to 3% impurities), and fragments (with up to 5% impurities).

RECIPES

Frozen truffles CONSERVE DE TRUFFES CONGÉLÉES Clean but do not peel the truffles; leave them to dry at the entrance of an open oven for about a minute (or, better, use an electric dryer). Put them into very small freezer containers, seal, and place inside a polythene (plastic) freezer bag. Seal, label, and freeze.

Ragout of truffles RAGOÛT DE TRUFFES (from Georges Garin's recipe) Peel 8 fresh 40-g (1½-oz) truffles, cut into quarters, and season with salt and pepper. Add 1 dl (6 tablespoons, scant ½ cup) dry Banyuls and marinate for 20 minutes at room temperature.

Reduce by half 2 dl (7 fl oz, ¾ cup) good full-bodied red wine in an ovenproof casserole, lightly rubbed with garlic. Blend in 1 teaspoon flour mixed with 2 teaspoons butter, bring to the boil, then add the truffles and the marinade.

Cover with aluminium foil and put on the lid, bringing the edges of the foil over the top; cook in a moderate oven for 10 minutes.

Cut some stale bread into 3–4-cm (1½-in) croutons, dry them slightly in the oven, then rub with garlic and spread the soft side with goose or duck fat. Serve the ragout in its casserole, with the croutons in a separate dish.

Sauté of Piedmont truffles SAUTÉ DE TRUFFES DU PIÉMONT (from Plumerey's recipe) White or black truffles may be used for this recipe, which can be prepared at table as follows: Finely slice the truffles. Put in a silver dish a few tablespoons olive oil or butter and some good meat glaze, the size of an egg, cut into small pieces. Place the truffles on top with a little salt, white pepper, and grated nutmeg. Sprinkle with a few tablespoons oil or a few pieces of fine butter. The silver dish, covered with its lid, is placed on a spirit heater in front of the host, who frequently stirs the truffles with a spoon, replacing the lid of the dish each time. 7–8 minutes' cooking should be sufficient. The host then adds the juice of a lemon and serves his guests.

Sterilized preserved truffles CONSERVE DE TRUFFES STÉRILISÉES Soak the truffles in lukewarm water, then clean them by scrubbing under cold water. Peel and reserve the peelings. With the point of a knife, remove all the earth lodged in the holes and folds. Sprinkle with fine salt mixed with 'four spices' and pepper and leave for 2 hours. Boil some Madeira and add the truffle peelings with a pinch of salt; cover with an airtight lid and leave to cool, then strain. Put the truffles in small jars and cover generously with the stock. Seal, sterilize, and allow to cool completely before storing in a dry place.

Truffle ice cream GLACE AUX TRUFFES (from André Daguin's recipe) Boil 3 large well-scrubbed truffles in 1 litre (1¾ pints, 4¼ cups) milk for about 1 hour. In the meantime, whisk (beat) 8 egg yolks with 250 g (9 oz, 1 cup) sugar. Drain, dry, and trim the truffles. Pour the milk over the sugar and egg mixture to make a custard; cook until it forms ribbons when the spoon is lifted, then add the chopped truffle trimmings. Allow to cool, then leave to set in an ice-cream maker. Cut the truffles into julienne strips. Fill tulip glasses with alternate layers of ice cream and truffle, finishing with a decoration of julienne strips. This ice cream is served as a dessert.

Truffles à la croque au sel TRUFFES À LA CROQUE AU SEL Cut fresh truffles, well-scrubbed and peeled, into slices and serve with good butter. Only truffles gathered between December and March, after the first frosts and before the spring, are suitable for this dish.

Truffle salad SALADE DE TRUFFES Clean some raw truffles and slice finely or cut into julienne strips. Make a vinaigrette with oil, vinegar, salt, pepper, and lemon juice, but without aromatic herbs. (When fresh truffles are not available, preserved truffles can be used.)

The truffles may be mixed with sliced boiled potatoes (demi-deuil salad) or sliced artichoke hearts (impératrice salad).

Truffle sauce SAUCE À LA TRUFFE (from Chef Denis's recipe) Cook a very black fresh truffle in a mixture of half Madeira, half meat stock, with a little tomato purée, for 10 minutes. Drain and cut into julienne strips. Cover the pan tightly and reduce the liquid to a few teaspoons, then add 2 egg yolks and the julienne. Thicken with 200 g (7 oz, ¾ cup) clarified butter, as for a béarnaise sauce. Season with salt and pepper.

This sauce is served with poached fish, white meats, and Lauris asparagus.

Truffles for garnishes TRUFFES POUR GARNITURES Depending on the dish to be garnished, fresh raw truffles are peeled then cut into strips or dice of varying size, or into quarters, or shaped like olives. Cook gently in butter for a few minutes only, so as not to impair their flavour or texture. Add a few tablespoons dessert wine and keep hot, but do not boil.

Sterilized truffles or truffles in goose fat, which have already been cooked, need only be heated with the dish that they are to accompany.

Truffles preserved in goose fat CONSERVE DE TRUFFES À LA GRAISSE D'OIE Prepare and cook the truffles as for sterilized preserved truffles, replacing the Madeira infusion with melted goose fat, as in a confit. Seal hermetically and store in a very cool place. Reserve the peelings for flavouring.

Truffle tourte à la périgourdine TOURTE DE TRUFFES À LA PÉRIGOURDINE Line a pie dish, 4–5 cm (1½–2 in)deep, with lining pastry (see *doughs and batters*) and place on a baking sheet. Arrange on the bottom a layer of uncooked foie gras cut into large dice, seasoned with salt and pepper, and sprinkled with 'four spices' and Cognac, covering the pastry to within 1.5 cm (⅝ in) of the edge. Top with scrubbed and peeled whole truffles, seasoned with salt and pepper, and sprinkled with 'four spices' and Cognac. Place small slices of foie gras, seasoned with salt and pepper, on the truffles. Cover with a thin layer of pastry and seal the edges. Decorate the top with cut-out shapes of pastry and place a funnel in the centre. Brush with egg and cook in a moderately hot oven (200 c, 400 f, gas 6) for 40–45 minutes. Pour through the funnel a few tablespoons reduced demi-glace sauce, flavoured with Madeira and truffle essence. The tourte is served hot or cold.

Truffle turnovers TRUFFES EN CHAUSSONS Peel medium-sized truffles and sprinkle with spiced salt. Wrap each in a thin rasher of fat bacon and place on a small round of puff pastry. Moisten the edges of the pastry with water, fold over, and pinch together. Place the turnovers on a baking sheet, brush with egg, make a little opening in the centre and bake in a very hot oven (240 c, 475 f, gas 9) for 18–20 minutes.

truffle (confectionery)
See chocolate truffle.

trumpet of death
TROMPETTE-DES-MORTS
See horn of plenty.

truss BRIDER
To thread one or two pieces of trussing twine through the body of a poultry or game bird with a trussing needle to hold the legs and wings in place during cooking. This operation is performed after dressing the bird (i.e. when it has been plucked, cleaned, trimmed, and singed); if the bird is to be braised, poached, or fried whole (rather than roasted), the legs are tucked under the skin before trussing.

A well-trussed bird sits better on its roasting or cooking dish. It is easier to baste and turn and easier to cook and prepare, especially if it is to be served whole. It is always untied after cooking so that the parts which are protected by the legs can be checked to see that they are properly cooked.
● **Trussing poultry** (1) The bird is placed on its back, with the neck to-wards the left. Using a trussing needle threaded with 50 cm (20 in) twine, pierce between the bone and the fleshy part of the thigh. Pass the thread through from one side of the bird to the other. (2) Turn the bird onto its breast, neck still to the left. Hold the wing tips together and wrap the loose neck skin neatly round over the back to cover the neck cavity. Now insert the needle into the first joint of the wing then over the wing tip, through the neck skin and body, over the next wing tip, through the wing joint, and out on the other side. Tie the two pieces of twine securely together and cut off the ends (not too short). (3) Replace the bird on its back. Fold the legs tightly along the body and insert the needle into the tail end of the body (close to the join with the fleshy part of the thigh), pushing it through to the other side. (4) Return the needle over the thigh, through the belly, and out over the leg. (5) Pull the ends of the twine firmly to hold the legs against the body and tie tightly in place. Trim the twine.

trussing needle
AIGUILLE À BRIDER
A rod of stainless steel, 15–30 cm (6–12 in) long and 1–3 mm (about ⅛ in) in diameter, pointed at one end and having an eye at the other. It is used to pass one or two strings of thread through the body in order to keep the legs and wings of a chicken or game bird in place. Trussing needles often come in a case containing an assortment of needles of different sizes.

tsarine (à la)
A term that describes poached poultry garnished with olive-shaped pieces of cucumber in cream, or poached fish (sole or brill) garnished with cucumber cooked in butter and coated with Mornay sauce seasoned with paprika. The expression also refers to various dishes directly inspired by classic Russian cookery: cream of hazel grouse and celery garnished with a julienne of celery; poached eggs arranged on tartlets filled with hazel grouse purée, coated with cream and mushroom sauce; soft roes poached in white wine and garnished with chopped vesiga and caviar.

ttoro or tioro

A soup or fricassee of fish from Basque cookery, of which there are numerous variants. Ttoro classically consists of a highly seasoned fish fumet made with white wine, mixed with crushed tomatoes and chopped sweet pepper, and spiced with chilli pepper; it is poured boiling hot over chunks of fish (monkfish, conger eel, gurnard, hake) that have been dusted with flour and browned in hot olive oil. Ttoro is usually garnished with mussels and langoustines and served with chopped parsley and croutons fried in oil. In Biarritz, it is made with lean fish; sorrel is added to the broth, which is thickened with egg yolk. The fish can be served separately from the broth.

tuile

A crisp thin petit four, in the shape of a curved tile. The basic dough (sugar, shredded (slivered) or ground almonds, eggs, and flour), sometimes with added butter and flavoured with vanilla and orange, is spread onto a baking sheet. The tuile acquires its characteristic shape by being bent over a rolling pin while still hot, then left to harden. Flat round tuiles (called *mignons*) are stuck together in pairs with meringue, then dried in the oven.

RECIPE

Tuiles Whisk (beat) together 125 g (4 oz, ½ cup) caster (superfine) sugar, 1 teaspoon vanilla sugar, 75 g (3 oz, ¾ cup) sifted flour, 2 eggs, and a small pinch of salt. Blend in 30 g (1 oz, 2 tablespoons) melted butter and 75 g (3 oz, ¾ cup) shredded (slivered) almonds (optional). Using a teaspoon, place small quantities of the mixture, well apart from one another, on a buttered baking sheet. Spread them out slightly with the back of a fork dipped in cold water. Bake for about 4 minutes in a very hot oven; the edges of the tuiles should be golden brown, the centres remaining white. Take out of the oven, remove from the tray, and bend them, while still hot, over a rolling pin or a very clean bottle; leave to cool.

tuna THON

Any of several large sea fish, which are similar in appearance and shape.

Tuna was highly appreciated in ancient times. The Phoenicians used to salt and smoke it. Archestratus recommended the great tuna of Samos and that of Sicily but, he said, 'If one day you go to Hippone, a town in illustrious Italy (in North Africa), the tuna there are better than all the rest.' When using the female tuna, he recommended cutting the tail into pieces, roasting it, sprinkling it with salt and oil, and pickling it in a strong brine. In the Middle Ages, pickled tuna was appreciated, particularly *tonnine* (cut up, roasted or fried in olive oil, then salted and strongly spiced). In the time of Louis XIV, the grocers still traded in pickled tuna. From the 19th century, tuna fishing gradually extended to the Atlantic. Since 1947, Breton fishermen have been fishing off the coast of Africa. Five species of tuna are now fished: the albacore, yellowfin tuna bluefin tuna, blackfin tuna, and skipjack.

• The *albacore* or *white tuna* (called *germon* or *thon blanc* in France) is widely used for canning. Formerly much more abundant than it is today, it weighs 10–30 kg (22–66 lb) and is fished from the Azores to Ireland. Its white flesh, slightly rose-tinted and very tasty, resembles veal and is cooked in a similar way. Formerly, it was nicknamed 'veal of the Carthusians', as it could be eaten on days of abstinence. Breton *germon* is sold fresh from the end of May to the beginning of October. It is sliced and braised (after marinating) or grilled (broiled).

• The *yellowfin tuna* (called *albacore* in France) is bigger and heavier than the albacore (up to 2½ m (8 ft) long and 250 kg (5 cwt) in weight); it has a steel blue back, greyish sides, and a silvery belly (like the albacore) but its fins are yellow and its flesh pale pink. It is fished practically throughout the year in tropical and equatorial waters. Rarely sold fresh, it is widely used by the canning industry.

• The *bluefin tuna* is fished in the Mediterranean, the Bay of Biscay, and a few tropical seas. When it is young, its belly has green stripes and its flesh is white. The flesh of adult fish is dark red. The average weight of a bluefin tuna is 100–125 kg (220–275 lb) but some very old fish are more than 3½ m (11½ ft) long and weigh 700 kg (13¾ cwt). The bluefin tuna is almost always sold fresh. In France it is prepared by Basque, Sicilian, or Provençal cooking methods: cut into slices, marinated, then braised or cooked *en daube*, rather than grilled. The flesh of the bluefin tuna is best when it has been kept for about eight days: by that time it is shiny and bright red, with a more pronounced taste than that of the albacore. When its colour is verging on light brown, the fish has gone bad.

• The *blackfin tuna* (called bigeye in the United States) is caught in the same areas as the yellowfin. It does not exceed 100 kg (220 lb) and is usually eaten fresh, but it does not have the flavour of albacore.

• The *skipjack* is a bonito. Its flesh is as good as that of the bluefin tuna but less firm. It is used mostly in canning for tuna-based preparations.

Several other fish resemble tuna and are prepared in similar ways: the *pelamide* (pelamid or bonito), which is cooked in steaks like albacore but does not have its quality and taste; *melva* (frigate mackerel), a small fish found in warm seas, with a dark blue back and often smoked; *thonine* (little tunny), a bonito with a speckled belly and brown flesh, used in canning.

Tuna are migratory fish which travel in dense shoals. As early as the 2nd century BC, the Greeks knew of their migratory habits and ancient fishing methods have been practised for a long time in Sicily and Yugoslavia. In Provence, at the end of the 19th century, the approach of shoals of tuna was still heralded by lookouts blowing their horns. At the outbreak of World War I, fishing for bluefin tuna was still on a small scale and restricted to the Mediterranean, whereas fishing for albacore, which had been modernized around 1850, was thriving in the Bay of Biscay. The first boat designed for fishing tuna for the canning industry was built in 1906. Around 1930, a few shipowners in Saint-Jean-de-Luz fitted their boats with refrigerated holds. Today tuna fishing is industrialized and

scientific: locating the migrating shoals by helicopter or even satellite.

Tuna is a fatty fish (13% lipids), and fresh tuna provides 225 Cal per 100 g. It is a good source of protein, phosphorus, iodine, iron, and vitamins A, B, and D.

☐ **Preserved tuna** Tuna is usually consumed in a wide range of preserved forms, which are used to make mixed salads, stuffed vegetables (avocados, peppers, tomatoes) and various hors d'oeuvres, and even filled or garnished omelettes.

Canned tuna is presented either whole (the slab is in fact composed of pieces tightly packed together), in small fragments, or in fillets (long strips taken from the belly of the fish).

Cans labelled 'tunny' or 'tuna fish' almost always contain tropical tuna (yellowfin, skipjack, or blackfin). Those labelled 'albacore', 'white tuna', or 'germon' must contain that variety, which is more expensive and of better quality. In France they are marketed in various forms.

• *Tuna in brine*: cut into slices and then pieces, which are boned, trimmed, washed, dipped in brine, cooked by heat sterilization, then covered with lightly salted water; always comprises whole tuna.

• *Tuna in oil*: head and tail removed, cooked in a court-bouillon or braised, dried, then cut up, boned, and skinned; slabs, fragments, or fillets are canned in oil (in the case of olive or groundnut oil, this is specified).

• *Tuna in tomato sauce*: cooked, dried, and canned whole, in fillets, or in fragments with a sauce containing at least 8% tomato extract and 10% oil.

• *Marinated tuna* (sometimes with aromatics): prepared like tuna in oil, covered with sauce seasoned with vinegar and aromatized, whole, in fillets, or in fragments.

• *Tuna à la ravigote* or *aux achards*: usually fillets in olive oil, aromatized, or with seasoning added.

• *Tuna hors d'oeuvre*: prepared with a very variable quality of tuna, a spicy sauce, shredded vegetables, etc.

Tuna in oil keeps very well and improves with age. Plain tuna, on the other hand, gains nothing from the ageing process.

RECIPES

Chopped white tuna steak with seaweed STEAK DE THON BLANC HACHÉ AUX ALGUES (from Robert Courtine's recipe) Trim a steak of fresh white tuna (albacore). Remove the skin and bones. Cut into dice, then chop coarsely. Prepare a tartare sauce and season the fish with it. Arrange in small bowls, surrounded by seaweed blanched in salted water for 30 seconds. Season with pepper, lemon juice, and olive oil.

Grilled (broiled) tuna THON GRILLÉ Take some steaks of white tuna (albacore) 4–5 cm (1½–2 in) thick. Mix some olive oil with lemon juice, salt, pepper, a little cayenne, some finely chopped parsley, and, if desired, a crushed clove of garlic. Marinate the fish in this mixture for at least 30 minutes. Grill (broil) the drained steaks under a low heat for 10 minutes on each side. Serve with a flavoured butter (sweet pepper or anchovy).

Tuna en daube THON EN DAUBE Prepare like tuna *à la provençale*, but replace the white wine by red wine (for example, Côtes-du-Rhône).

Tuna en daube à la provençale THON EN DAUBE À LA PROVENÇALE Stud a round slice of bluefin tuna with anchovy fillets. Marinate in olive oil, lemon juice, salt and pepper for 1 hour. Brown the fish in olive oil in a stew pan. Add 1 chopped onion lightly cooked in oil, 2 large tomatoes (peeled, deseeded, and crushed), a small crushed clove of garlic, and a bouquet garni. Cover and cook for 15 minutes. Pour in 1.5 dl (¼ pint, ⅔ cup) white wine and finish cooking in the oven, basting often, for 40 minutes. Drain the fish and place on a serving dish. Cover with the concentrated cooking liquor and sprinkle with chopped parsley.

Tuna salads SALADES DE THON

■ Drain some tuna in olive oil. Mix with cooled cooked rice (possibly flavoured with saffron), raisins, strips of green pepper rapidly fried in oil and well drained, and some almonds. Season with vinaigrette and herbs.

■ Drain some plain white tuna (albacore). Mix with some blanched and drained bean sprouts, shredded palm hearts, and shredded raw mushrooms, sprinkled with lemon. Season with vinaigrette mixed with soy sauce.

■ Drain some tuna fillets in oil. Prepare some grated carrots, diced beetroot (red beet), diced apples sprinkled with lemon, hard-boiled (hard-cooked) eggs and tomatoes (both quartered). Arrange all these in clusters, seasoned with vinaigrette and sprinkled with chopped herbs, on a bed of finely shredded lettuce.

turban

A word used to describe certain foods arranged in a circle on the dish: fillets of fish, crown of lamb, etc. The term also refers to a preparation of forcemeat, salpicon, etc., cooked in a ring mould: *turban* of fish, shellfish, poultry, rice, or game; these are generally served as a hot or cold entrée, coated with sauce. Mousses and ice creams are also moulded in a turban.

RECIPES

Iced turban TURBAN GLACÉ Pour into a ring mould some vanilla ice cream mixed with a salpicon of crystallized (candied) fruits steeped in rum. Leave to set in the freezer. Turn out of the mould onto a layer of nougatine and fill the centre with vanilla-flavoured Chantilly cream.

Turban of poultry TURBAN DE VOLAILLE Line a buttered ring mould with thin slices of raw poultry, cut from the breast, so that the slices slightly overhang both edges. Mask with a thin layer of poultry forcemeat, then fill the mould with a salpicon of cooked poultry, mixed with truffle and mushrooms, and bound with allemande sauce. Cover with a thin layer of forcemeat and fold the overhanging slices over the top. Cook in a bain-marie in the oven for about 40 minutes then leave to stand for 10 minutes before turning out of the mould onto a round dish. Fill the centre of the turban with braised slices of calves' sweetbreads and sautéed morels. Coat with suprême sauce.

Turbigo

A dish consisting of lambs' kidneys cut in half, sautéed, garnished with grilled chipolatas and sautéed mushrooms, and covered with a sauce made from the cooking juices mixed with white wine and tomato-flavoured demi-glace sauce. This recipe, named after the Lombardy town where the French won two victories over the Austrians under the First and Second Empire, dates back to an era when restaurateurs and cooks named their creations after military victories or generals.

RECIPE

Lambs' kidneys Turbigo ROGNONS D'AGNEAU TURBIGO Cut the kidneys in half; remove the thin skin that surrounds them and the white central part. Season with salt and pepper and fry briskly in butter. Arrange them in a circle on a round dish, possibly on a bed of croutons browned in butter, and keep hot.

Cook some small button mushrooms in the butter used to cook the kidneys and grill (broil) as many small chipolatas as there are kidney halves. Arrange the chipolatas between the kidney halves and place the mushrooms in the centre. Mix the cooking juices with white wine and tomato-flavoured demi-glace sauce; reduce and pour over the kidneys.

turbiner

A French term meaning to freeze an ice-cream or sorbet mixture until it solidifies, the preparation being automatically mixed during the operation. *Turbinage* is carried out in a freezer or a machine.

turbot

A flatfish living on the sandy pebbly beds of the Atlantic (called *berdonneau* or *triboulet* in French) and the Mediterranean (nicknamed *rombu* or *clavelat*). It is one of the best sea fish. Both eyes are on one side of its body, which is brownish, dotted with black and white marks. The blind side is sometimes pigmented as well, which is

unusual with flatfish. Its lozenge-shaped body, which is broader than it is long and made round by its fins, has led to the invention of a special turbot kettle (*turbotière*). Its tough skin lacks visible scales but is covered with small bony tubercles (hence its name, which derives from the Scandinavian word for a thorn).

Highly esteemed since ancient times and nicknamed *roi du carême* (king of Lent) for centuries, turbot has been prepared in the most sumptuous ways. For Napoleon, Laguipière created turbot *à l'impériale* (cut into slices, poached in milk, arranged with crayfish tails, and coated with a truffle sauce). The way in which it was cut up at table, with a silver fish slice, was formerly governed by precise rules.

Turbot is sold whole and gutted (cleaned) or in chunks, depending on its size. Most fish measure 40–50 cm (16–20 in) and weigh between 2 and 4 kg (4½–9 lb), although some, which are not necessarily less delicate, reach 90 cm (3 ft) and 20 kg (44 lb). Chicken turbot (*turbotin*) is the name given to small turbot weighing 1–1½ kg (2¼–3¼ lb), which are often cheaper than large turbot, although they have the same qualities. There is always a large amount of waste: about 50% of the weight (slightly less for the biggest fish).

Its white firm flaky flesh, which is particularly delicate and tasty, makes turbot an expensive fish. Whether it is poached (in milk, to ensure that its flesh remains white), braised, grilled (broiled), or pot-roasted, its cooking must be carefully controlled. If it is cooked for too long, the flesh loses its flavour and texture. All recipes for brill and John Dory are suitable for whole turbot, and all recipes for fillets of sole are suitable for fillets of turbot.

As in the past, the great chefs give turbot pride of place in their creations. Some classic preparations for turbot are Dugléré, *à l'amiral*, Bercy, *à la cancalaise*, Saint-Malo, and Victoria, and (cold dishes) in scallop shells or with mayonnaise, green sauce, tartare, remoulade, or gribiche sauce. In turbot *à la pèlerine*, created by Prosper Montagné, the fish is sprinkled with melted butter and cooked on a baking tray lined with onion lightly cooked in butter, coated with the cooking juices mixed with white wine, cream, and butter, then glazed in the oven and garnished with fried scallops arranged *en buisson*). Such a large fish is rarely deep-fried, but Brillat-Savarin recommended this method to his cook La Planche: 'You tried my hellish idea and you were the first to have the glory of offering the startled world a huge fried turbot. That day, there was great jubilation among the lucky guests.' Notable creations of contemporary chefs include turbot braised in vermouth (Fernand Point), *suprême de turbot de ligne* (studded with anchovies, roasted with parsley, and steeped in a champagne sauce; A. Chapel), *blanc de turbotin* with sorrel fondue (R. Vergé), blanquette of turbot (André Guillot), chicken turbot with grapes and tea (Alain Senderens), and chicken turbot studded with anchovies and steamed with saffron (M. Guérard). But many gastronomes consider that turbot should simply be grilled or poached on its own.

RECIPES

Escalopes of turbot with buttered leeks ESCALOPES DE TURBOT À L'EMBEURRÉE DE POIREAUX (from Simone Lemaire's recipe) Slice some fillets of turbot into escalopes and make a fumet with the trimmings. Seal the escalopes in butter, on both sides, then cover with the fumet. Simmer for 5 minutes. Drain the fish. Mix the cooking juices with an equal amount of double (heavy) cream. Arrange the escalopes on a hot dish and pour over the sauce. Serve with an *embeurrée* of leeks: cook 1 kg (2¼ lb) shredded white parts of leeks in the oven with 200 g (7 oz, scant 1 cup) butter and 1 glass water, covered, for 20 minutes; season with salt and pepper.

Turbot with morels TURBOT AUX MORILLES (from Jacques Pic's recipe) For 5 or 6 servings, soak 300 g (11 oz) dried morels in plenty of water (or use fresh morels when in season). Remove the stalks and wash thoroughly. Cook in salted water, strain, squeeze gently, and brown in a saucepan, adding 2 finely chopped shallots at the last moment. Add 2 dl (7 fl oz, ¾ cup) double

(heavy) cream and bring to the boil. Adjust the seasoning and simmer for about 10 minutes.

Fillet, skin, and trim a 3–4-kg (6½–9-lb) turbot and cut into 100-g (4-oz) escalopes. Season with salt and pepper on both sides. Garnish half the escalopes with small piles of morels and cover with the remaining escalopes. Cook in a frying pan with a little butter, then in the oven for about 10 minutes. Arrange in a dish and coat with américaine sauce. Put a medallion of lobster on each escalope.

turbot kettle TURBOTIÈRE

A square- or diamond-shaped fish kettle, provided with a grid with handles and a lid. Made of smooth or hammered aluminium, copper, tin-plated iron, or stainless steel, the turbot kettle is designed for cooking large whole flatfish: turbot, brill, and skate.

turinois

A cake that does not require cooking, made from chestnut purée, sugar, butter, and grated chocolate and flavoured with Kirsch. The purée is poured into a buttered square mould lined with paper at the bottom, pressed down firmly, and left to cool for several hours. The cake is then turned out of the mould, cut into slices, and served.

The name *turinois* (or *turin*) is also given to a square petit four made of sweet pastry, garnished with chestnut purée flavoured with Kirsch, then spread with apricot syrup and decorated with chopped pistachios.

Turkey TURQUIE

Midway between Europe and the East, Turkish cookery draws equally on Muslim, Jewish, Orthodox, and Christian traditions. In turn, it has left its mark in numerous countries: Russia, Greece, North Africa, the Middle East.

In France, a number of dishes of Turkish origin were adopted centuries ago, such as pilaf, lamb kebabs, stuffed aubergines (eggplants), and dried figs, not to mention coffee and patisserie. The Turks also invented mezze, böreks, halva, baklava, *kadaïf* (a shredded wheat dough used for pastries), Turkish delight, and all kinds of confectionery with picturesque names (beloved's lips, vizier's fingers, lady's navel, etc.).

Proper Turkish cookery gives pride of place to hors d'oeuvres and small entrées. Apart from soup (meat or vegetable *chorba*), they eat *cacik* (cucumber in yogurt), mussels stuffed with rice, pine kernels, chopped onion, raisins, and spices, sheep's trotters (feet) in aspic, pastirma (dried and spiced beef), and the whole range of dolmas (stuffed vine or cabbage leaves).

The most sought-after fish are gilthead bream, mackerel, sardine, tuna, turbot, and eel (often cooked in a courtbouillon and served with an aubergine (eggplant) and honey sauce). The Turks also enjoy fillets of salt cod (soaked in milk to remove the salt), coated with unsweetened almond milk, bound with cream, and sprinkled with shredded (slivered) almonds.

Among Turkish meat dishes mutton reigns supreme, being used in a great variety of preparations. The *döner kebab* consists of layers of meat and fat placed on top of one another on a vertical spit, forming a large distaff which revolves in front of the flame, and from which long thin strips are carved when they are cooked to the right degree. There is also *adjem pilaf* (diced roast shoulder of mutton with finely sliced onion, rice, and broth), *unkar beyendi* (pieces of leg of mutton, sheep's tails, and fat, threaded onto skewers, grilled, and served on aubergine purée), meatballs (mixed with courgette (zucchini) pulp, onion, and grated cheese, then fried and eaten hot or cold), not forgetting shish kebab (frequently served with shredded almonds and sour cream). The Turks also enjoy young goat, chicken (*à la circassienne*, with a red pepper and walnut sauce), and beef (particularly in meatballs).

The main vegetable is the aubergine, indispensable for the famous imam bayildi and moussaka, but Turkish recipes also include courgettes and stuffed peppers (generally eaten half-cooled in their cooking juices), gombos, cabbage, spinach, and mange-tout (snap) beans (often cooked in water or butter and served with spicy sauces, such as a sauce made from crushed anchovies in lemon juice, mixed with stock and oil). Bulgur wheat and rice are also basic ingredients, the former being used in stuffings and soups, the latter in the famous pilaf (mixed with raisins, pine kernels, or almonds). Curd cheese is used to garnish crudités and make sauces (particularly for ravioli) and puff-pastry cakes, as is yogurt (in soups or for pouring over fried aubergines and grilled meat).

Apart from very sweet pastries, the Turks sometimes serve puddings, such as *azure* (made from chickpeas, rice, flour, milk, sugar, and dried fruit, flavoured with rose-water or orangeflower water), at the end of the meal. Roses are also used in the preparation of jams and to flavour loukoum.

The national drink is coffee – a Turk drinks on average ten cups per day – but *raki*, a kind of anisette drunk alternately with mouthfuls of cold water while nibbling mezze, should also be mentioned.

At the end of the last century, Istanbul was described as a city where people ate day and night and where itinerant merchants sold cooked rice, chickpeas, lamb or chicken tripe kebabs, curd cheese and grilled fish, tea, coffee, salep and ice cream, pancakes, melons, water melons, etc. This atmosphere continues today in small popular restaurants with their *djindjères* – large round pans made of tin-plated copper – in which stews and soups simmer all day long, and their spits, on which lambs and döner kebabs, dripping with fat, are continuously cooking.

turkey
DINDE, DINDON, ET DINDONNEAU

A farmyard bird raised for its delicate flesh. The size of the bird will vary according to its variety and breeding. Although the traditional large birds are still available, particularly at festive seasons, medium-sized and small birds have been developed which are suitable for smaller gatherings all the year. Large turkeys are still produced for cutting up into joints and for charcuterie. In French, the word *dinde* is used for both male and female birds, although strictly speaking it applies only to turkey hens. The flesh of turkey cocks is drier and it is advisable to lard it with bacon strips.

The word *dindonneau* (young turkey) is often used on menus.

The turkey was called 'Indian chicken' by the Spanish conquerors, who thought they were still in the Indies when they discovered it in Mexico (hence the French name – a contraction of *poule d'Indes*). It first appeared on a French table in 1570, at the marriage feast of Charles IX, but it was not commonly used in cooking until about 1630. In England it eventually replaced the Christmas goose. The turkey still lives in the wild in the United States and Mexico but it was already domesticated in Mexico at the time of the Aztecs; prepared with a sauce containing chocolate, it constitutes the national dish (*mole poblano de guajolote*). In the United States turkey is the traditional dish on Thanksgiving Day, since the arrival of the first colonists who were saved from famine by the wild turkey. It is stuffed with corn bread, roasted, and served with chestnuts and orange and cranberry sauce.

Brillat-Savarin, who proclaimed himself a 'dindonophile' (turkey-lover), dedicated a long paragraph in *The Sixth Meditation* to the 'Indian chicken': 'The turkey appeared in Europe towards the end of the 17th century; it was imported by the Jesuits, who raised a large number of them, particularly in a farm they owned near Bourges; it was from there that they gradually spread over the whole of France. This is why the colloquial name for a turkey is still *jésuite* in many places.'

☐ **How to buy and prepare a turkey** A good turkey should be young, plump, and short-necked, with a supple windpipe. If the bird is old, its feet are reddish and scaly. The sinews must be drawn from the legs (it is best to ask the butcher to do this). The bird may be easier to carve if the wishbone is removed. Usually, the entire breast is barded so that the flesh is protected from drying out during cooking.

Apart from dishes using turkey joints or giblets, turkey is usually stuffed and roasted. However, it is sometimes braised or cooked in a ragout (like goose) and garnished *à la bourgeoise* or *à la chipolata*. Turkey meat may also be grilled, cooked in a fricassee like chicken, or casseroled and garnished with such vegetables as aubergines (eggplants), artichokes, mushrooms, small onions, or browned potatoes.

RECIPES

Braised turkey legs CUISSES DE DINDONNEAU BRAISÉES This recipe uses the legs of young turkeys; the wings or suprêmes can be used for another dish. Bone the legs, fill with a suitable poultry stuffing, and roll them into small ballottines. Braise in white or brown stock, then drain and glaze in the oven. Arrange on a serving dish and coat with the cooking stock. Serve with a vegetable purée, braised vegetables (such as carrots or celery), rice, or creamed potatoes.

Daube of turkey à la bourgeoise DINDONNEAU EN DAUBE À LA BOURGEOISE This dish is made with a very tender turkey hen, rather than a young turkey cock. Braise the bird in a suitable brown stock; when three parts cooked, drain. Strain the braising stock. Replace the bird in the braising pan and surround with a bourgeoise garnish. Add the strained braising stock, cover the pan, and finish cooking over a gentle heat.

Poached turkey vinaigrette DINDONNEAU POCHÉ VINAIGRETTE (from a recipe by Jean and Pierre Troisgros) Prepare a 2.75-kg (6-lb) turkey and place it in a large casserole dish, add the neck, feet, and some poultry giblets. Cover with water. Season with coarse salt, bring to the boil, and skim. Add a bouquet garni and simmer very slowly for 1 hour 10 minutes. Then add 2 or 3 carrots, 1 or 2 turnips, the white part of 2 leeks, and 1 large celeriac (all sliced) and cook for a further 20 minutes or until tender. Cook half a cauliflower separately for 10 minutes in some stock from the turkey casserole. Untruss the turkey and serve on a heated dish surrounded by the vegetable garnish. Serve chervil-flavoured vinaigrette separately.

Roast turkey DINDONNEAU RÔTI Season and truss a small turkey and bard the breast and back with bacon. Roast either on a spit, allowing 20 minutes per 500 g (lb), or in the oven, allowing 25 minutes per 500 g (lb) at 160 c (325 f, gas 3). Remove the bacon before the bird is completely cooked so that it browns. Serve with the skimmed strained cooking juices and garnish with watercress.

Roast turkey à l'anglais DINDON-NEAU RÔTI À L'ANGLAISE Stuff the turkey with a sage and onion stuffing prepared as follows: bake the onions in their skins in the oven, peel and chop them, then toss in butter. Season with a pinch of chopped sage. Mix with an equal quantity of breadcrumbs, dipped in milk and squeezed, and half their quantity of chopped suet. Roast the turkey in the usual way. Put it on a serving dish surrounded with slices of bacon or grilled sausages. Serve with the cooking gravy and bread sauce.

Roast turkey stuffed with chestnuts DINDONNEAU RÔTI FARCI AUX MAR-RONS Scald and peel 1 kg (2¼ lb) chestnuts. Half-cook them in stock, drain, and wrap in a large piece of soaked pig's caul. Enclose in the boned turkey, tie up neatly, and roast in the usual way.

Roast turkey stuffed with dessert apples DINDONNEAU FARCI AUX POMMES REINETTES Season the turkey and, if desired, insert some slices of truffle between the skin and the flesh. Remove the gall bladder from the liver and pound the liver with a small can of goose foie gras mousse, 40 g (1½ oz, 3 tablespoons) butter, and 2 tablespoons (3 tablespoons) port. Peel and remove the seeds from 750 g (1¾ lb) dessert apples, cut them into thick slices, and brown them in a frying pan in 75 g (3 oz, 6 tablespoons) butter. Mix half the apples with the liver mixture and use to stuff the turkey. Keep the remaining apples hot. Place a very thin strip of bacon on the breast and on the back of the bird, and tie up firmly.

Cook the turkey in a hot oven (about 200 c, 400 f, gas 6) for about 2 hours for a 3-kg (6½-lb) bird. The bird is cooked if the juices released when the skin is pricked are clear. Remove the bacon slices and quickly brown the turkey breast, if necessary, in a very hot oven. Carve in the usual way. Put the

remaining hot apples into a small vegetable dish, sprinkle them with the cooking juices from the turkey, and serve with the slices of turkey.

Turkish delight
LOUKOUM
A Middle Eastern confectionery made of sugar, honey, glucose, syrup, and flour – usually cornflour (cornstarch). It is flavoured and coloured, usually either pink or green, and often decorated with almonds, pistachio nuts, pine kernels, or hazelnuts. Turkish delight (*loukoum*, or *rahat loukoum*, meaning literally 'rest for the throat') has a rubbery consistency and is presented as large cubes covered in icing (confectioners') sugar.

turmeric CURCUMA
A tropical herbaceous plant with an aromatic underground stem. The powdered stem is used as a spice and as a colorant. The extract is known as curcumine (E100) and is used to colour certain dairy products, confectionery, drinks, and mustards. Turmeric has a more bitter taste than saffron and is an ingredient in curry powder. It is used mainly in the cuisine of India and of Southeast Asia.

turn TOURNER
To shape vegetables, using an appropriate knife, into a specific regular form: vegetables 'turned' in a similar way cook uniformly. Potatoes are 'turned' into the shape of balls, olives, or pods of different sizes, depending on the dish. Carrots and turnips are also 'turned' for a bouquetière garnish, as are cucumber (into olive shapes), mushroom caps, and olives (in a spiral around the stone (pit), the latter having been removed and the olive reformed).

In French, the word has several other meanings. It can mean to turn a piece of meat, without pricking it, while it is roasting in the oven, so that it roasts evenly on all sides. Applied to a mixture, the term means to stir during preparation or cooking, either with a whisk (e.g. for confectioners' custard (pastry cream)), or with a spatula (e.g. for custard). *Tourner la salade* means to toss the salad, i.e. to mix the lettuce, etc., in the dressing in the salad bowl, using salad servers.

In baking, *tourner* describes the action of folding and shaping the dough for croissants. The *tourne* is also the weighing and moulding of bread dough before it is put into breadbaskets.

In its intransitive form, the verb *tourner* refers to the transformation of certain foodstuffs: ripe fruit that has begun to deteriorate; milk that is going sour.

Tourne is also a defect of wine, which turns it frothy and gives it an unpleasant odour and taste.

turnip NAVET

A fleshy root vegetable, yellow or white in colour and often tinged with purple near the leaf bases. European in origin, the vegetable has been cultivated in India for centuries. It was a popular pot vegetable in France, especially in soups and stews, principally in northern and coastal regions. The turnips of Nantes, Meaux, Belle-Île-en-Mer, and Orléans have been famous for centuries, like those from Teltow in Berlin, which were even praised by Goethe.

Today the turnip is less popular and suffers from prejudice. Nevertheless, its distinctive flavour makes it suitable for a garnish, purée, and soup (Freneuse). It can even be eaten raw, grated and flavoured with lemon juice. Some chefs are now rediscovering its virtues and are preparing stuffed turnips, braised turnips in cider, turnip mousse with sorrel and chives, and sautéed turnips.

Among the varieties of garden turnip are Purple Top Milan (Milan), which is round and white with a purple collar and is available as a spring vegetable, and Golden Ball (Boule d'Or), a round yellow winter variety with a very good flavour. The French varieties Nantais and Croissy are elongated and white and are sold in spring and summer. There is also a black variety, which may be elongated or round.

The turnip has a low calorific value (36 Cal per 100 g), a high water content, and is rich in sulphur, potassium, and sugar. Turnips should be firm and heavy with an unblemished smooth shiny skin. Spring turnips are often sold complete with their leaves, which can also be cooked (like spinach). Spring turnips must be used within a short time of purchase; winter turnips, on the other hand, will keep for 2 months in a cool place.

Turnips should be peeled and washed just before they are cooked, otherwise they will darken; small new turnips need only be scrubbed. Winter turnips are improved by blanching for 10 minutes before further preparation to reduce their very strong flavour. An essential ingredient of pot-au-feu and hearty meat soups, turnips can also be prepared in the same way as carrots (glazed *à l'anglaise*, sautéed in butter, or cooked with cream), or puréed, used in a vegetable loaf, or in a soufflé. They have the property of absorbing large quantities of fat, and for this reason they are traditionally served with fatty meat (mutton, duck, etc.).

RECIPES

Stuffed turnips braised in cider NAVETS FARCIS BRAISÉS AU CIDRE (from a recipe by Alain Senderens) Peel and blanch 600 g (1¼ lb) small round young turnips. Slice off and reserve the tops, then scoop out a shallow hollow in each and cook the scooped-out flesh in boiling salted water. When soft, reduce to a purée in a blender. Sauté the hollowed-out turnips and tops in equal quantities of olive oil and butter and cook until browned. Sprinkle with salt and pepper.

Meanwhile, boil half a bottle of dry cider and reduce to half its original volume. Drain the turnips and tops well and add them to the cider. Pour in a little stock and braise in the oven for 15 minutes. Drain them, reserving the cooking juices. Add the purée to the liquid to thicken it, and adjust the seasoning. Add 50 g (2 oz, 4 tablespoons) butter, beat the mixture, and keep hot.

Mix together 100 g (4 oz, ½ cup) sausagemeat, 30 g (1 oz, 2 tablespoons) *à gratin* forcemeat, some basil, rosemary, and thyme flowers. Shape the mixture into small balls and cook them in butter over a low heat. Place one ball into each hollow turnip, adding the tops to form lids. Pour the sauce over and serve very hot.

Turnip mousse MOUSSE DE NAVETS (from a recipe by Georges Paineau) Peel and cook 1 kg (2¼ lb) round turnips. Reduce to a very smooth purée in a blender and add 4 egg yolks, 8 tablespoons (⅔ cup) fresh cream, and 50 g (2 oz, ½ cup) potato flour. Season with salt and white pepper. Butter 8 dariole moulds and place a sorrel leaf in the bottom of each. Divide the mousse between the moulds and cook in a bain-marie for 20 minutes in a moderate oven (180 c, 350 f, gas 4). Prepare some cream sauce and reduce it to 2 dl (7 fl oz, ¾ cup); just before serving, blend in 100 g (4 oz, 1 cup) chopped chives. Turn out the mousses onto a hot serving dish, pour a thin ribbon of sauce around them, and serve the remainder of the sauce separately.

Turnip sauerkraut CHOUCROUTE DE NAVETS Peel some large turnips and cut out any woody bits. Grate the remainder into long strips. Put a layer about 10 cm (4 in) deep into a large earthenware pot and sprinkle with salt. Add some peppercorns and juniper berries. Repeat this procedure until 5 or 6 layers have been packed into the pot. Place a weight on the top, cover with a cloth, and leave for 12 days or so in the refrigerator. Pour off the juices that will have accumulated in the pot and rinse the turnips thoroughly. Then put them into boiling water for a few minutes. This turnip 'sauerkraut' can be braised and served with the same accompaniments as traditional sauerkraut.

Turnips au gratin NAVETS AU GRA-TIN Peel some turnips and slice them into rounds. Blanch them in boiling salted water, drain and refresh under cold running water, and braise in butter. Place the turnip rounds in a buttered gratin dish, smooth the top, and coat with Mornay sauce. Sprinkle with grated cheese and brown in a very hot oven (240 c, 475 f, gas 9).

turnover CHAUSSON

A pastry in the shape of a semicircle made from a thinly rolled round of puff pastry folded over a filling of stewed fruit, traditionally (but not necessarily) apples. Most are individual, but large turnovers, using a simple shortcrust pastry (basic pie dough), may be prepared for several people. All these pastries are eaten warm or cold.

Turnovers can also be savoury. They are usually small and served very hot, as an hors d'oeuvre or entrée, filled with various salpicons (fish, poultry, game, ham, mushrooms, etc.). See *empanada, rissole.*

RECIPES

Preparation of turnovers PRÉPARA-TION DES CHAUSSONS Whether savoury or sweet, the method is the same. Roll out some puff pastry to a thickness of about 3 mm (1/10 in). Cut out circles 5–15 cm (2–6 in) in diameter. Place a fairly dry filling on half of each circle, without going right up to the edge, fold the free half back over the filled half and join the two edges firmly, pinching them to prevent the filling from leaking during cooking. Decorate with lines made with the tip of a knife and glaze with egg yolk.

SAVOURY TURNOVERS

Turnovers for light entrées CHAUS-SONS POUR PETITS ENTRÉES Following the method of preparation above, use any of these savoury fillings:

■ *à la lyonnaise* (creamed pike with butter and crayfish tails, truffle, and Cognac);

■ *à la Nantua* (ragout of crayfish tails *à la Nantua*);

■ *à la périgourdine* (salpicon of foie gras and truffle sprinkled with Cognac);

■ *à la reine* (purée of chicken mixed with diced truffles and mushrooms).

SWEET TURNOVERS

Apple and prune turnovers CHAUS-SONS AUX POMMES ET AUX PRUNEAUX Soak 250 g (9 oz, 1½ cups) stoned (pitted) prunes in tepid water and 50 g (2 oz, ⅓ cup) washed currants in a small glass of rum. Peel and thinly slice 4 good apples, then place in a stewpan with ½ glass of water and 50 g (2 oz, 4 tablespoons) caster (superfine) sugar. Leave to cook for 20 minutes, then blend and return to the pan with the drained currants and 30 g (1 oz, 2 tablespoons) butter; stir over a gentle heat to dry out. Put the drained prunes in another stewpan with 1 dl (6 tablespoons, scant ½ cup) weak tea, 50 g (2 oz, 4 tablespoons) sugar, and the grated rind of a lemon; boil gently for 10 minutes, then blend and return to the pan to dry uncovered over a gentle heat.

Heat the oven to about 225 c (425 f, gas 7). Roll out 500 g (18 oz) puff pastry thinly on a floured board. Cut it out into 8 rounds, using a cutter 15 cm (6 in) in diameter, and elongate them slightly. Brush over the edges of the rolled-out pastry with beaten egg and fill half of each round with stewed apples and stewed prunes, without mixing them. Fold over the pastry and join the edges together, tucking them over each other and pressing down well. Arrange the turnovers on a moistened baking sheet and brush with beaten egg. Trace light diamond-shaped cuts in the pastry. Bake in the oven for about 25 minutes, then take out the turnovers and serve them either warm, or cold and dusted with icing (confectioners') sugar.

turnspit (roasting jack)
TOURNEBROCHE

A mechanism for rotating a roasting spit in front of a heat source. The modern turnspit is an oven or barbecue accessory, usually operating by electricity.

In the Middle Ages, turnspits were operated by *galopins* (urchins), young apprentice rôtisseurs, who turned the handles of heavy spits in front of glowing fires. Subsequently, dogs were used to turn the spit by running inside a wheel. Self-turning spits appeared at the end of the 16th century; Montaigne, in his *Voyage en Italie*, describes these appliances 'operating by a spring or a system of weights and counterweights'. In the 18th century, when clockwork mechanisms were perfected, turnspits could function automatically for one or two hours. A bell sounded when they needed to be reset. There were also spits operated by the heat of the fireplace, which turned a bladed wheel. In some restaurants there were giant spit roasters for cooking several dozen chickens at the same time.

turque (à la)
A term that describes various dishes inspired by oriental cookery, particularly rice pilaf, either arranged in a ring with a garnish in the centre, or moulded in darioles as an accompaniment to shirred eggs, omelette, or lamb noisettes, served with sautéed aubergines (eggplants).

The term refers specifically to a dish of chicken livers (sautéed with chopped onion and tomato-flavoured demi-glace sauce added), or aubergines (or sweet peppers) stuffed with minced (ground) mutton, rice, and duxelles, baked with tomato-flavoured onion fondue. Vegetables stuffed *à la turque* can be used to garnish pot-roasted loin or saddle of lamb.

RECIPE

Lamb noisettes à la turque NOISETTES D'AGNEAU À LA TURQUE Prepare some rice pilaf and sauté some diced aubergine (eggplant) flesh in oil. Fry the lamb noisettes in butter and arrange in a serving dish; garnish with the aubergine and the rice pilaf moulded in darioles. Keep hot. Dilute the pan juices with tomato-flavoured veal stock and pour over the noisettes.

turrón or touron
Confectionery of Spanish origin, made from ground almonds, egg whites, and sugar. Of various colours and flavours, it can also contain pistachios, whole almonds, walnuts, or dried fruit. There are numerous varieties, which are all southern specialities.

● The Spanish turrón, also called *jijona* (from the name of the town where it is a speciality), is made from honey and sugar, with walnuts, hazelnuts, pine kernels, and sometimes coriander and cinnamon. The Alicante turrón, a traditional Christmas sweetmeat, is more crunchy. Both are made in the form of slabs, which are cut into slices.

● The Catalan turrón, which resembles the black nougat of Provence, contains hazelnuts but no almonds.

● The Basque turrón, made simply from almond paste, coloured red, takes the form of small balls similar to arbutus berries.

● The Bayonne touron is similar to almond paste. It looks like a chequerboard, with squares of different colours and flavours, with or without almonds.

• The honey touron of Gap, made from sugar and honey, contains almonds and hazelnuts.

The name *touron* is also given to a round petit four, made from almond paste, royal icing (frosting), chopped pistachios, and orange zest.

RECIPE

Tourons (petits fours) Pound 250 g (9 oz, scant 2 cups) blanched almonds with 2 egg whites; add 200 g (7 oz, scant cup) caster (superfine) sugar and knead the mixture on a marble worktop. Sprinkle with 2 tablespoons icing (confectioners') sugar and roll out to a thickness of 1.5 cm (⅝ inch). Mix 100 g (4 oz, 1 cup) chopped pistachios with 200 g (7 oz, scant cup) caster (superfine) sugar and the zest of half an orange, very finely chopped. Add 100 g (4 oz) royal icing (frosting) and 2 whole eggs. Mix well with a spatula. Spread this mixture evenly over the almond paste. Cut into circles or rings and arrange on a buttered and floured baking sheet. Dry in a very cool oven.

Tursan

VDQS wine from southwestern France. It has been known since Gallo-Roman times and was exported even in the Middle Ages. The vineyards are between Béarn and the Basque country, in the Landes. Tursan is best known as a dry sinewy white wine, made from a local vine called the Baroque. There are red and rosé versions, the former being fairly full-bodied. They are mostly made from the Tannat grape.

turtle TORTUE

A short-legged reptile, amphibious or terrestrial, whose body is enclosed in a scaly carapace. There are several edible varieties, but they are increasingly rare and protected, so their preparation for the table is chiefly a matter of gastronomic curiosity. The hawksbill turtle, which is quite small, used to be common on the east coast and islands of tropical America. Sought-after for its shell, it also provides highly esteemed meat and eggs. The loggerhead, the largest turtle, is considered to be leathery, with a taste of the sea. The diamondback turtle or terrapin, which lives in fresh water, is bred in the United States. Boiled in salted water and boned, it is prepared according to local recipes in Maryland.

At the beginning of the 19th century in New York, a popular entertainment was barbecuing turtles imported live from the West Indies. West Indian cookery has the greatest variety of dishes prepared from turtle, particularly the green turtle, which provides excellent flesh; the head, legs, tail, intestines, and eggs are also edible. In addition, its fat provides very good oil. It is traditionally made into soup, daubes, fricassee, stew, and colombo. Turtle steaks, marinated in vinegar, oil, and garlic, are cooked like beef and served highly seasoned with pepper. In Egypt, turtle meat is prepared in a stew, with onions and pomegranate juice. The flippers make a highly esteemed braised dish, served with a spicy sauce. In Europe, turtle soup is made: this was a British contribution to classic French cookery (mock turtle soup, made from calf's head, was also invented in Britain). It was being made in France as early as the 16th century, since, as stated by Delamare (quoted by Franklin), 'the blood of turtles, even live turtles, is cold. Therefore, the turtle is a true fish, and can be eaten without qualm on days of abstinence.'

RECIPES

Mock turtle soup FAUSSE SOUPE À LA TORTUE Boil a boned calf's head in a white court-bouillon (see *head*) for 1½ hours, with carrots, an onion studded with cloves, celery, a bouquet garni, salt, and pepper. Drain the head and cut off the ears (which are not used for this soup); trim the rest of the meat and put it under a press between 2 plates. When it is quite cold, cut it into small round or square pieces and reheat in a little of the stock.

While the calf's head is cooking, make a clear brown gravy in a stewpan, by adding some stock to slices of salt leg of pork, veal knuckle, and a half-roasted chicken. When these meats are almost cooked and the gravy reduced, add the calf's head cooking juices and vegetables and simmer gently for about 2 hours.

Strain, thicken with a little arrowroot

diluted with cold stock, then add an aromatic infusion of basil, spring onion (scallion), marjoram, thyme, and bay leaf in Madeira or port.

Strain the soup and pour it into a soup tureen; garnish with pieces of calf's head and, if desired, small quenelles made from sausagemeat mixed with mashed hard-boiled (hard-cooked) egg yolks.

Thick turtle soup POTAGE À LA TOR-TUELIÉ Proceed as for turtle soup. After straining the soup, thicken with 30 g (1 oz) blond roux or 50 g (2 oz) arrowroot per litre (1¾ pints, 4¼ cups) of soup.

turtle herbs
HERBE À TORTUE

A mixture of aromatic herbs (basil, marjoram, chervil, savory, and fennel), used to flavour turtle soup and also turtle sauce, which is served with calf's head and boiled ox (beef) tongue.

tutti-frutti

An expression of Italian origin, meaning 'all the fruits'. It is used to describe various desserts that combine the flavours of several fruits or contain mixed fruits, crystallized (candied), poached, or fresh, generally cut into small pieces.

Tutti-frutti ice cream contains diced crystallized fruits steeped in Kirsch. A tutti-frutti bombe may be coated with strawberry ice cream, with a lemon ice cream mixed with diced crystallized fruit inside.

Tutti-frutti is also a pastry made of a thin layer of sweet pastry covered with a layer of crystallized or poached fruit, finely diced, then a second layer of pastry. The top is covered with apricot syrup, iced, and generously sprinkled with shredded (slivered) almonds or pieces of candied orange peel.

| RECIPE

Tutti-frutti bombe BOMBE TUTTI FRUTTI Line a bombe mould with 1 litre (1¾ pints, 4¼ cups) pineapple ice and harden in the freezer. Then make a sugar syrup using 250 g (9 oz) sugar and 6 tablespoons (4 fl oz, ½ cup) water,

pour into a saucepan in a bain-marie, and blend in 8 egg yolks. Whisk (beat) on the top of the stove until thick and frothy. Strain, then whisk again in a basin. Blend in 400 g (14 oz) Chantilly cream. Flavour with 1 tablespoon Kirsch and add a salpicon of 400 g (14 oz) crystallized (candied) fruits steeped in Kirsch, together with 100 g (4 oz, ⅔ cup) raisins soaked in rum and well drained. Pour the mixture into the mould and freeze for 4 hours. Turn out of the mould and decorate with glacé (candied) cherries, candied angelica, and shredded (slivered) almonds.

tvarog

In Russian cookery, a mixture of drained and sieved curd cheese, softened butter (or soured (dairy sour) cream), and beaten eggs, usually seasoned with salt and pepper. It is used to stuff small patties, which are served cold as an hors d'oeuvre. Tvarog can also be used to fill tartlets, pastry cases (shells), or rolled pancakes.

Twelfth-Night cake
GÂTEAU DES ROIS

A traditional cake eaten on the day of Epiphany. A bean is inserted in the cake before cooking, and the person whose portion contains the bean is appointed 'king' or 'queen' for the occasion. This ceremony probably dates back to Roman times. During the Saturnalia the 'king of the day' was chosen by lot, using a bean concealed in a galette. It was only in the Middle Ages that this cake ceremony began to be associated with the festival of Epiphany. From this time the Church attached a different significance to it – the sharing of the holy bread – but the tradition of the 'elected king' survived. Formerly, in many provinces, the cake was cut according to a particular ritual, with songs, processions of children collecting alms, etc. During the Revolution an unsuccessful attempt was made to replace the Twelfth-Night cake with a cake of Equality or Liberty, shared out during a 'good neighbour' festival.

Nowadays, France has two major traditional Twelfth-Night cakes: in the north, in Lyon and in the Paris area, the cake is a puff-pastry galette, sometimes filled with frangipane; in the south, the cake is like a brioche, often decorated with crystallized (candied) fruit or flavoured with brandy or orange-flower water. In Provence and Auvergne the Twelfth-Night cake is like a crown-shaped brioche and in Bordeaux and Limoux the cake is flavoured with citron. The bean is replaced by a china figurine of a baby, animal, etc.

RECIPE

Bordeaux   Twelfth-Night   cake
GÂTEAU DES ROIS DE BORDEAUX,
GÂTEAU TORTILLON   Make a well in
500 g (18 oz, 4½ cups) sifted flour and crumble in 20 g (¾ oz) fresh yeast (¾ cake compressed yeast) and 10 g (2 teaspoons) salt. Work in 8 whole eggs, one by one, the zest of a grated lemon, 200 g (7 oz, ⅞ cup) caster (superfine) sugar in small quantities, and 200 g (7 oz, scant cup) butter softened until creamy. Knead the dough well until evenly blended, then leave it to rise in a warm place for 10 hours. Knock back (punch down) the dough as for brioche dough and divide it into 4 equal parts. Shape each one into a crown and place these crowns, after inserting the bean on the underside of one of them, on a piece of buttered paper. Allow to rise in a very cool oven, then leave to cool. Brush the crowns with beaten egg. Decorate with thin slices of citron and crystallized sugar. Bake in a moderately hot oven (200 c, 400 f, gas 6).

Traditionally, the 4 crowns are placed on top of each other.

tyndallization
TYNDALLISATION
A method of sterilization invented in 1876 by the Irish physicist John Tyndall; it occurs in several stages to obtain better preservation. In normal sterilization, the majority of bacteria are killed, but a few resistant spores may remain and revive during cooling. A second sterilization kills them off. Tyndallization has the additional advantage of reducing the alteration of products due to the 'cooking' effect of normal sterilization, since a series of heating processes are less damaging than a single heating process.

tyrolienne (à la)
A term given to preparations of meat, chicken, grilled kidneys, soft-boiled or poached eggs, or baked brill, garnished with fried slices of onion and a tomato fondue (or crushed tomato). Tyrolienne sauce is a tomato-flavoured béarnaise sauce, thickened with oil instead of butter.

RECIPE

Grilled (*broiled*) **chicken à la tyrolienne**   POULET GRILLÉ À LA TYROLIENNE   Prepare a 1-kg (2¼-lb) chicken *en crapaudine*. Season with salt and pepper, brush with flavoured oil, and grill (broil) for 25–30 minutes. Meanwhile, peel and slice 2 large onions and separate into rings. Dust the rings with flour and fry in oil at 180 c (350 f). Cut 4 medium-sized tomatoes into quarters, remove the seeds, and lightly fry in 30 g (1 oz, 2 tablespoons) butter. Arrange the grilled chicken on a hot dish, surrounded by the onions and tomato fondue, seasoned with salt and pepper, and possibly garnished with parsley.

udder TÉTINE

The mammary gland of an animal, especially that of a cow. Cow's udder should first be sliced, soaked in cold water, blanched, and cooled. It can then be braised (possibly studded with small pieces of bacon fat) in the same way as noix of veal and served with mushrooms or rice. It can also be used in pâtés and terrines, but its gastronomic role is now fairly limited, in contrast to former times. Apicius gives a recipe for a puff-pastry pie of sow's udders, fish, and chicken spiced with pepper and pine kernels. In the Middle Ages, people enjoyed cow's udder with verjuice, while heifer's udder was quite a common constituent of forcemeat.

Ude (Louis-Eustache)

French cook, a contemporary of Carême, who was one of the first to introduce the French culinary art into Britain.

Having been Louis XVI's head cook, then Princess Letizia Bonaparte's maître d'hôtel, he became chef to Lord Sefton, then to the Duke of York, and finally director of St James's Club in London. An annuity bequeathed by Lord Sefton, a gourmet and epicurean, enabled Ude to retire and write The French Cook or the Art of Cookery developed in all its various branches (1813, republished several times up to 1833). This is a 'practical good cookery course' for organizing 'elegant and inexpensive dinners', with anecdotes, advice on choosing menus, and a list of 'several new French recipes'.

ugli ÆGLE

A tropical plant, originally from eastern India, similar to the lemon tree and having fragrant fruit resembling medium-sized oranges. The Indians (who call them bilva or mahura) cook ugli fruit in ashes because of their leatheriness, then eat them with sugar. They can also be made into jam.

UHT milk

See milk, uperization.

ulluco or ullucus

A plant from western South America, cultivated in Bolivia and Peru for its small pinkish edible tubers. Attempts to introduce the ulluco into Europe as a substitute for the potato have not been very successful.

unleavened bread

AZYME

Describing a dough that is without leaven, or yeast. Unleavened bread plays an important role in Jewish ritual, as Orthodox Jews consider fermented bread to be profane. According to tradition, unleavened bread symbolizes absolutely pure food, the fermentation brought about by the leavening agent marking the beginning of the process of decay. Each year, biblical Jews made *matzo* (from a verb meaning 'to extract'), round ritual bread resembling the offertory cakes of the Mediterranean peoples. Later, *matzo* was eaten in place of bread during the seven days of Passover, to commemorate the deliverance of the children of Israel (see Exodus XII, 33).

In earlier times the rabbis ordained that three women should work simultaneously in making *matzo*: one to knead the dough, another to shape the biscuits (cookies), and the third to put them into the oven. The custom of making patterns and interlaced designs on the *matzo* was abandoned, however, and the biscuits are now crisp, round, or square, and of varying thickness and size. They may sometimes be shaped in moulds with geometric patterns. In England, in 1875, *matzo* was first made industrially under rabbinical control.

The composition of unleavened bread for religious purposes must be scrupulously respected: water and wheat flour (harvested in a prescribed way), without salt, sugar, or fats. Barley, spelt, oats, or rye may also be used. Sometimes the dough is flavoured with wine or fruit, but only 'pure' *matzo* is eaten on the first night of Passover. A whole cuisine has built up around the use of unleavened flour (*matzo* meal), including traditional soups containing *matzo* balls, fritters, and cakes. Some of these recipes may account for the name 'celestial bread' in the Cabbala.

unmould DÉMOULER

To turn out a cake, jelly, ice cream, etc., from a tin or mould. This is often a delicate operation and should be carried out with care.

● *Aspics and jellies* – Plunge the base of the mould in hot (but not boiling) water for a few seconds. Remove and shake lightly from side to side. Loosen the jelly around the edge with the blade of a knife, place a serving plate on top of the mould, turn over quickly, and lift off the mould steadily, keeping it vertical. The same procedure can be used for cream desserts and flans.

● *Sponge cakes* – Unmoulding is made easier if the mould or tin has a nonstick surface. Otherwise, it needs to be greased and lightly dusted with flour before adding the mixture. Another alternative is to line the tin or mould with greaseproof (waxed) paper. Turn out onto a wire cooling tray immediately after removing from the oven.

● *Cakes that seem to have stuck to the tin* – Either turn the tin over onto a plate and cover the base with a damp cloth, or place it immediately on a cold surface such as a marble slab. Either method should facilitate the unmoulding. A loose-bottomed tin also makes unmoulding easier.

● *Unmoulding ices* – Dip the mould briefly into cold water and then into lukewarm water. Loosen the ice with the blade of a knife, taking care not to cut into the ice cream. Place a napkin or a paper doily and then the serving dish on top of the mould. Turn over quickly and lift off the mould, keeping it vertical.

uperization UPÉRISATION

A milk sterilization process, in which the milk is heated to a temperature of 140–150 c (285–300 f) for a very short period (one to three seconds) and immediately cooled under vacuum.

The word is a contraction of *ultra* and *pasteurization*. Uperized milk (also called UHT (ultra-heat-treated) milk) retains its flavour and nutritive qualities.

Vacherin

The name given to several cows'-milk cheeses (45% fat content) from Switzerland or France (Savoy or Franche-Comté), having a soft texture and a washed rind.

Vacherin d'Abondance, a Savoyard farm cheese, is in the shape of a thick pancake 25 cm (10 in) in diameter and 4 cm (1½ in) deep, encircled by a thin strip of spruce bark and set into a box, adhering to the base. A soft runny sweet-tasting cheese with a smooth red or pink rind, it should be served with a white fruity wine from Savoy or Burgundy and the rind should not be discarded (the flavour is exceptional). *Vacherin des Bauges* (or *des Aillons*) is similar but sometimes creamier. These traditional cheeses were made as long ago as the 12th century, when they were called *vachelins*, though the cooked cheese process of present-day Vacherin was not known until the appearance of cooperative cheese dairies much later. *Vacherin Fribourgeois*, from the Swiss canton of Fribourg, is shaped like a small millstone, 40 cm (16 in) in diameter and about 8 cm (3 in) deep (it is similar to Tomme d'Abondance); it is a soft cheese with a smooth yellowish-grey or pink rind, smelling a little of resin and with a slightly acid taste. It is used particularly to make fondue fribourgeoise. Finally, *Vacherin Mont-d'Or*, made on the farms in the Joux district of Franche-Comté and in Switzerland in the canton of Vaud (where it is also called *Mont-d'Or de Joux*), comes in the form of a flat cylinder, 15–30 cm (6–12 in) in diameter and 3–5 cm (1¼–2 in) deep, also in a box and encircled by a strip of resinous sapwood. Excellent at the end of autumn and in winter, this creamy cheese has a sweet slightly aromatic flavour; the rind is smooth and pink, slightly damp, and the cheese is soft, almost liquid in the case of Swiss Vacherin (which is not cut into portions but served with a spoon after the rind has been removed).

A good Vacherin may be recognized by the colour and appearance of its rind. Before being broached it should be stored in a cool damp place. Once started, a block of wood should be placed against the cut surface to prevent it running too much, but it is a cheese which should be eaten quickly, as it rapidly loses its fragrance and flavour.

vacherin

A cold dessert, made of a ring of

meringue or almond paste filled with ice cream or whipped cream (or both). It owes its name to its shape and colour, which resemble the cheese of the same name. The classic vacherin is made of rings of meringue placed on top of each other, filled with ice cream of one or more flavours, to which may be added fresh or crystallized (candied) fruit, sponge biscuits soaked in liqueur, marrons glacés, etc., on a base of sweetened pastry. Whipped cream is piped over the top and the dessert is decorated with crystallized flowers, sugar-coated 'pearls', fruit, etc.

Sometimes the name vacherin is given to rounds of meringue layered with cream or ice cream.

RECIPE

Iced vacherin VACHERIN GLACÉ (from François Châtel's recipe) Prepare 3 layers of meringue: draw 3 circles on sheets of greaseproof (waxed) paper, marking their centres. Grease the paper on the side on which the circles have been drawn, then place the ungreased side on baking sheets. Whisk 8 egg whites to very stiff peaks with a pinch of salt; towards the end of this operation scatter in 500 g (18 oz, 2¼ cups) caster (superfine) sugar (the mixture will be pearly). Fill a large piping (pastry) bag fitted with a large smooth nozzle with this meringue mixture, then, starting from the centre of the circles, cover these with meringue, forming a flat spiral. Place the baking sheets in the oven preheated to 100 C (212 F), close the door, switch off the oven, and cook for 1½–2 hours as it cools. Allow the meringues to become completely cold.

Now prepare some vanilla ice cream: make a light custard cream (see *creams and custards*) with 5 egg yolks, 150 g (5 oz, ⅔ cup) sugar, 1 dl (6 tablespoons, scant ½ cup) milk, a vanilla pod (bean), and 4 dl (14 fl oz, 1¾ cups) double (heavy) cream. Freeze this cream in an ice-cream maker, making sure that it remains soft. Prepare ½ litre (17 fl oz, 2 cups) soft strawberry ice cream in the same way.

To assemble the vacherin, remove the greaseproof paper from the meringue layers with the point of a knife. Place a ball of vanilla ice cream in the centre of one layer, then, place the second layer on top, pressing sufficiently to allow the ice cream to come to the edges of the layer. Replace in the freezer to harden the ice cream, then remove and repeat the process with the strawberry ice cream between the second and third layers. Replace the vacherin in the freezer and prepare the decoration.

Heat 100 g (4 oz, 1 cup) sugar with 4 dl (14 fl oz, 1¾ cups) water and boil for 1 minute. Whisk 2 eggs whites to very stiff peaks, pour the boiling syrup over them, and whisk until the mixture is cold. Add ½ litre (17 fl oz, 2 cups) double (heavy) cream and whisk until the mixture has set. Chill in the refrigerator, then put into a piping bag with a fluted nozzle and pipe decoratively on the top of the cake; alternatively, simply apply a smooth covering over the top and sides of the vacherin, giving it the appearance of a cheese. The vacherin may also be decorated with crystallized (candied) fruits or violets.

Valençay (cheese)

A goats'-milk cheese from Berry (45% fat content), also made in Touraine and the Charentes. It has a soft texture and a natural rind that is dusted with charcoal if it comes from a farm (in which case it is in season from April to November); otherwise the rind may have bloomed surface (it is sometimes also dusted with charcoal if the cheese is industrially produced). Made in the shape of a truncated pyramid (8 cm (3 in) across by 6–7 cm (2½ in) high), it is firm to the touch, with a musty smell and a nutty flavour.

Valençay (wine)

A smallish vineyard of the upper Loire, making white, red, and rosé VDQS wines which are seldom found outside the locality.

valencienne (à la)

The term applied to a rice dish inspired by Spanish cooking and prepared in the Valencian style, cooked in meat stock and garnished with a salpicon of peppers and smoked ham, sometimes with peeled and seeded tomatoes; peas and green beans may also be added to the rice. It may accompany noisettes of lamb, sautéed tournedos steak (filet mignon), or fried chicken, which are coated with a demiglace sauce.

These dishes *à la valencienne* should not be confused with those described as *à la Valenciennes*, which are typical of northern France, notably rabbit *à la Valenciennes* (with prunes and raisins) and tongue *à la Valenciennes* (slices of smoked tongue covered with foie gras purée).

In France, the name *valence* is often used to designate Spanish oranges and, by extension, all oranges.

valesniki

In Russian or Polish cookery, small savoury pancakes, coated with a mixture of cream cheese, beaten eggs, and butter, then folded, rolled, and fried in very hot oil. They are served as a hot hors d'oeuvre.

vallée d'Auge

The name of a chicken dish typical of Normandy cooking: chicken pieces are browned in butter, flamed in Calvados, and cooked in cider; cream is added to the reduced cooking juices to provide a sauce. Apples cut into small dice are added to the chicken at the start of cooking, or else the chicken is served garnished with apple halves cooked in butter.

The name *vallée d'Auge* is also given to a dish of roast duck, accompanied by a sweet-and-sour sauce made with apple jelly and slices of apple fried in butter.

Valois

The name of a garnish for fried or sautéed poultry or small cuts of meat. It consists of Anna potatoes and sliced artichoke hearts sautéed in butter, sometimes with the addition of stuffed olives. The sauce is made by deglazing the pan with white wine and butter-enriched veal stock.

The name Valois is also given to béarnaise sauce mixed with meat glaze.

Valpolicella

The best-known red wine from the Veneto region of Italy. At its best, it has a charming colour, a certain distinctive fragrance, and a full appealing taste. Recioto della Valpolicella, which has a DOC, is a rather more important type of wine, made to be a dry, half-dry, or sweet and sparkling wine (*frizzante*). The word *recioto* means 'ears', and it is the outer bunches of the grapes that become ripe first; these are picked separately and, in some instances, slightly dried before being pressed. Valpolicella is traditionally supposed to have been the wine of the lovers of Verona – Romeo and Juliet.

vandyke HISTORIER

To embellish a decorative feature of a dish: usually applied to tomato, lemon, or orange halves with their edges cut into zigzags. These are often used to garnish poached, grilled (broiled), or fried fish, platters of oysters or seafood, etc.

The French term, *historier*, also means to cut lemons into basket shapes, with a strip of peel forming the handle, and to flute or otherwise shape mushroom caps, which are then poached and used chiefly to decorate dishes served in a sauce. In a more general sense, *historier* can mean to embellish a dish with small items of garnish; for example, dishes in aspic or covered with a chaud-froid sauce are garnished with small pieces of truffle or pieces of pickled ox (beef) tongue fixed in place with egg white. Finally, the word can be used to describe metal moulds with an inlaid decorative pattern.

vanilla VANILLE

A climbing plant native to Mexico (where it was discovered by Cortés) and now also cultivated in some islands of the Indian Ocean and the West Indies for its pods (beans). The word derives from the Spanish *vainilla* (little sheath), referring to the long thin shape of the pod. Harvested when barely ripe, it is plunged into boiling water and dried, or exposed to the sun (under covers), until it is dark brown; the pod becomes frosted with vanillin crystals, which give it its characteristic smell and flavour. According to its appearance, it is graded into *fine vanilla*, with a black, frosted, and very fragrant pod 20–30 cm (8–12 in) long; *woody vanilla*, 13–20 cm (5–8 in) long, reddish-brown with a dry dull surface and not very frosted; and *vanillon*, with thicker flatter pods, 10–12 cm (4–5 in) long, which are brown and soft, partly opened, and rarely frosted, having a stronger slightly bitter smell. Finally, there is a variety of yellowish almost odourless vanilla from the West Indies.

Mexican vanilla (*ley* or *leg*) is the most highly prized; next comes that from the Indian Ocean (Bourbon vanilla), followed by that from Guyana, Guadeloupe, Réunion, Tahiti, etc. Vanilla is sold in various ways: in pods; in powdered form (the pods are dried and ground, giving a fine dry dark brown powder, sold pure or sugared); as an essence (a liquid obtained by maceration in alcohol then percolation, or infusion in sugar syrup of varying concentrations, and sold in small bottles); or in the form of vanilla sugar (with at least 10% vanilla, obtained by mixing dried vanilla extract with sucrose).

Vanilla is used particularly in pâtisserie and confectionery, to flavour creams, cake mixtures, ices, compotes, poached fruit, desserts, sweets (candy), chocolate, etc. It is also used in distillery and flavours punch, hot chocolate, mulled wine, and sangria. In cookery a trace of vanilla is sometimes used to season fish soup, the cooking juices of mussels, certain white meats, and even creamed vegetables.

| RECIPES

Vanilla ice cream GLACE À LA VANILLE Prepare a custard cream (see *creams and custards*) with 1 dl (6 tablespoons, scant ½ cup) milk and a vanilla pod (bean) cut in two, 5 or 6 egg yolks, 150 g (5 oz, ⅔ cup) caster (superfine) sugar, and 4 dl (14 fl oz, 1¾ cups) double (heavy) cream. Pour the custard cream into an ice-cream maker and allow to set in the freezer for 4 hours. Pile up the mixture in a mould and replace in the freezer to complete the setting of the ice cream.

It may be unmoulded onto a serving dish and decorated with crystallized (candied) fruit or fruit poached in syrup or coated with cold fruit purée (strawberry, peach, or mango, for example), or else used in balls in sundaes or to fill profiteroles.

Vanilla soufflé SOUFFLÉ À LA VAN-ILLE Add 1 whole vanilla pod (bean) to the milk used in the preparation of the soufflé mixture. Boil this milk and leave to infuse for about 10 minutes. Complete according to the basic recipe (see *soufflé*).

vanillin VANILLINE

A chemical substance responsible for the aroma of vanilla pods (beans). It may also be produced synthetically by using eugenol, an essence extracted from the clove tree. This consists of colourless crystals with a strong smell and a pronounced vanilla flavour. Synthetic vanillin competes widely with natural vanilla, being used in pâtisserie, confectionery, and chocolate-making, but should be avoided by discriminating cooks and gourmets.

vanner

A French culinary term meaning to stir a hot cream, sauce, or mixture until it is cold, with a wooden spatula or a whisk, to keep it smooth and particularly to prevent a skin forming on its surface. This process also shortens the cooling time.

variegate PANACHER

To mix two or more ingredients of different colours, flavours, or shapes. Variegated beans (*haricots panachés*) consist of equal proportions of French (green) and flageolet beans. Many ices and ice-cream desserts are variegated, as the alternation of colours and flavours plays an important part.

varieniki

In Russian cooking, a large form of ravioli filled with a mixture of drained curd cheese, butter, and beaten eggs, seasoned with pepper and nutmeg, poached in boiling water, and served as an entrée with soured (dairy sour) cream or melted butter. Lithuanian varieniki are stuffed with chopped cooked beef, onion, and suet, bound with a parsley sauce; they are served in the same way as the Russian variety.

variety meats
See *offal*.

Vatel (*born* Fritz Karl Watel)
Maître d'hôtel of Swiss origin (born

Paris, 1635; died Chantilly, 1671). Employed as a steward by the financier Fouquet, he later became attached to the noble house of Chantilly. Although traditionally described as a cook, in reality he was in charge of everything concerning the catering and administrative services of the château.

In April 1671 the prince of Condé entrusted him with the task of organizing a fête in honour of Louis XIV, with 3000 guests. The celebrations began on a Thursday evening; in the course of the supper following a hunting party, several tables lacked roast meat because a number of unexpected guests turned up. Later, the planned firework display was spoiled by the cloudy sky. These incidents, which were later recounted by Mme de Sévigné in a letter of 26 April, persuaded Vatel that his honour was lost. Learning at dawn on the following day that only two loads of the fresh fish ordered for the meals of the day had arrived, he gave way to despair: declaring 'I shall not survive this disgrace,' he shut himself in his room and ran his sword through his body, at the very moment when the fish carts were entering the castle gates.

Philéas Gilbert, chef and associate of Prosper Montagné, severely criticized this loss of equanimity: 'If we *chefs de cuisine*, whose coat sleeve may be decorated with four or five stripes each indicating ten years of service, recalled our experiences, we could all remember disasters which suddenly strike the catering services and which, according to Vatel's example, would call for *harakiri*. But recourse to the cook's knife (in the absence of a sword) would solve nothing, and it is in such difficult circumstances that firmness of character emerges in the one who commands; he should find within himself unerring judgment, an iron will, a high sense of responsibility, and the experience which dictates prompt and energetic decisions. Such a one will never lose his head and would not dream of committing suicide. An authoritative appeal to the goodwill of his team temporarily at a loss, some brief and clear orders called out over the tumult of the upset pots and pans, and the problem is resolved: the service continues . . .'

vatrouchka

A Russian cheesecake consisting of a sablé base, covered with a mixture of eggs, sugar, crystallized (candied) or sometimes dried fruits, and curd cheese, usually topped with a lattice of pastry and dusted with sugar after cooking. Another Russian culinary speciality are *vatrouchki*, small turnovers made of ordinary brioche dough, filled with a savoury curd cheese filling.

RECIPE

Vatrouchka (from the restaurant Dominique's recipe) Macerate 200 g (7 oz, 1 generous cup) diced crystallized (candied) fruits in 5 cl (2 tablespoons, 3 tablespoons) Cognac, Armagnac, or rum.

To prepare the pastry, beat together in a bowl 3 egg yolks and 1 white with 200 g (7 oz, 1 cup) caster (superfine) sugar until the mixture is thick and creamy. Whisk in 125 g (4½ oz, ½ cup) softened butter, then sprinkle with 350 g (12 oz, 3 cups) sifted flour. Form the pastry into a ball and place in the refrigerator for about 1 hour. Roll it out on a floured surface into a circle 3 mm (⅛ in) thick. Cover a baking sheet with a circle of buttered greaseproof (waxed) paper, 28 cm (11 in) across, and place the pastry on it; roll the leftover pastry into a ball and reserve. Prick the pastry with a fork and bake blind in the oven at 200 c (400 f, gas 6), for 12–15 minutes, then leave to cool.

Meanwhile prepare the filling: combine 4 whole eggs and 5 yolks with 400 g (14 oz, 2 cups) caster sugar in a bowl until the mixture is thick and creamy; add the crystallized fruits with the alcohol in which they have been macerating, and 1 kg (2¼ lb, 4½ cups) curd cheese; mix well together.

Pour the filling onto the cooled pastry base and smooth the surface. Roll out the reserved pastry into a rectangle 3 mm (⅛ in) thick and cut into narrow strips. Arrange these in a lattice pattern on top, sealing down the ends at the sides of the cake. Glaze the filling and the pastry strips with egg and bake in the oven at 150 c (350 f, gas 4) for 40–50 minutes. Take out the vatrouchka, dust with icing (confectioners') sugar, and leave until completely cold before serving.

VDQS

See *appellation d'origine.*

veal VEAU

The meat of a calf up to one year old, specially reared for slaughter when weaned. Veal is a white, tender, and delicate meat, highly prized in cooking, but its quality varies considerably according to the methods of rearing.

☐ **High-quality veal** When the calf has been fed exclusively on its mother's milk (the most ancient and natural method), it gives a very pale pink meat smelling of milk, with satiny white fat having no tinge of red (which would indicate that the animal had eaten cereals or grass). In certain regions, including Normandy, the calf used to be 'finished' for the market by giving it up to 10 eggs daily, the yolks of which coloured its mouth: it was then said to have a *palais royal* (royal palate). According to *L'Art culinaire*, published at the beginning of the 20th century: 'The calf of the Seine valley, or river calf, so esteemed for the whiteness of its meat, is the product of special breeding. Its diet ... consists only of milk and raw eggs, sometimes

barley flour mixed with milk, and échaudés.' The Pontoise calf, also fed on biscuits soaked in milk, had an equally high reputation. Today the best localities for veal include Corrèze and Lot-et-Garonne, where the calves are raised *au pis* (on the udder) and their delicately grained flesh is slightly pink.

When the meat is reddish, or greyish-white, and rather soft and damp with thick shiny tendons, the animal has been fed not with its mother's milk but with reconstituted milk; at the worst, it may have received hormone treatment (totally prohibited since 1976); its meat, of mediocre quality, cooks badly, gives off water, and reduces in volume, whereas 'white' or 'pink' veal remains moist and does not dry out. Among the best products of French breeding is the Saint-Étienne calf (not weaned, but fed supplements of protein-rich flours), whose pink meat is very tender, as well as the Lyon calf (weaned and intensively fattened indoors), which provides roasting and grilling (broiling) joints of excellent flavour. The Limousin milk calf, raised exclusively at the udder, is the only one to have been awarded that seal of approval, the *label rouge*.

☐ **Cuts and methods of cooking** The cutting up of the calf in the so-called

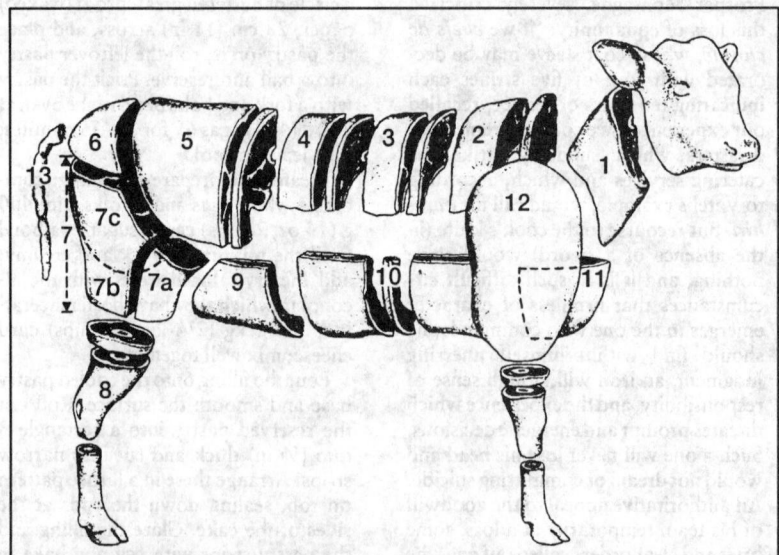

French cuts of veal.
1. *collier*; 2. *bas de carré*; 3. *côtes secondes*; 4. *côtes premières*; 5. *longe*; 6. *quasi*; 7. *cuisseau*: 7a. *noix-pâtissière*, 7b. *sous-noix*, 7c. *noix*; 8. *jarret*; 9. *flanchet*; 10. *tendron*; 11. *poitrine*; 12. *épaule*; 13. *queue (tail)*.

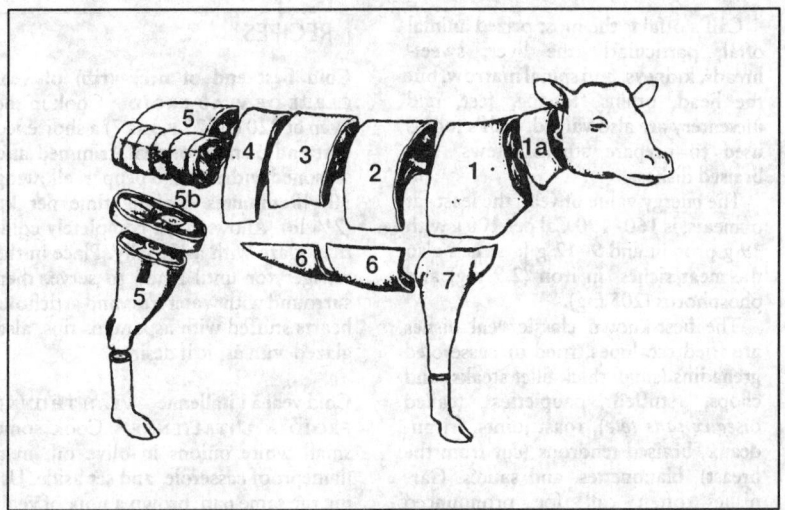

American cuts of veal.
1. shoulder; 1a. blade; 2. rib; 3. loin; 4. sirloin; 5. leg (round); 5a. boneless rump roast; 5 b. round steak; 6. breast; 7. fore shank.

'Parisian' manner, which is the most widespread, provides for the following: first-category cuts, comprising the chump (rump) end of loin, the leg (giving the parts known in French as the *noix, sousnoix,* and *noix pâtissière* and escalopes (scallops) cut from the noix or the noix pâtissière), the loin, and the fillet, as well as the best end of neck (ribs and shortened best end of neck); second-category cuts, comprising the shoulder, breast, tendron (not usually sold separately from the breast in Britain and the USA), flank, and upper ribs; and finally third-category cuts, the scrag end (neck) and the knuckles.

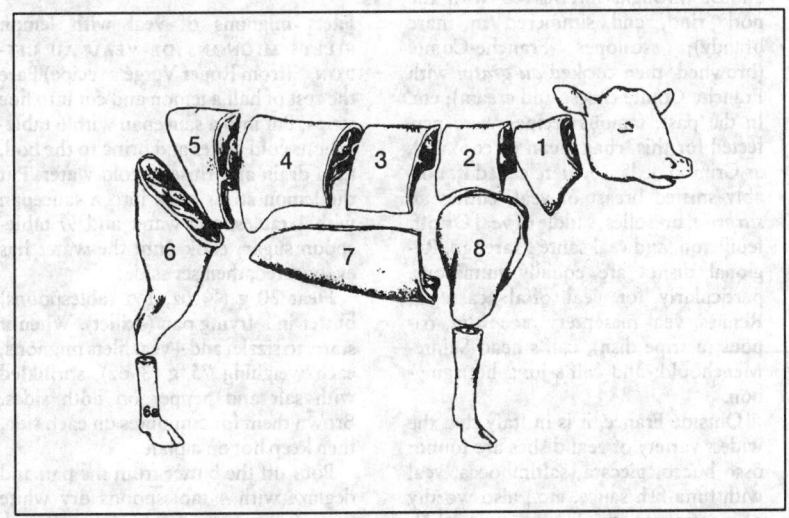

British cuts of veal.
1. scrag end; 2. middle neck; 3. best end; 4. loin; 5. fillet; 6. leg; 6a. knuckle; 7. breast; 8. shoulder.

Calf's offal is the most prized animal offal, particularly the liver, sweet-breads, kidneys, and spinal marrow, but the head, brains, tongue, feet, and mesentery are also valued. Calf's foot is used to prepare stocks, stews, and braised dishes.

The energy value of veal, the least fat of meats, is 160–190 Cal per 100 g with 19 g protein and 9–12 g fats; it is also the meat richest in iron (2.9 mg) and phosphorus (205 mg).

The best-known classic veal dishes are fried escalopes, fried or casseroled grenadins (small thick fillet steaks) and chops, stuffed paupiettes (called *oiseaux sans tête*), roast joints, fricandeaux, braised tendrons (cut from the breast), blanquettes, and sautés. Garnishes often call for pronounced flavours: fricandeau with sorrel, Foyot veal chops with onion, rump of veal *à l'angevein* accompanied by Soubise purée, and loin of veal stuffed with mushrooms. Aubergines (eggplants), tomatoes, or spinach go equally well with this meat, which is often prepared with cream, wine and spirits, or cheese: veal chop vallée d'Auge (with cream and Calvados) or *à la Dreux* (larded with ox tongue, fat bacon, and truffle, simmered in Madeira); veal steamed in red wine; Lorraine veal with pork rind (sliced almost through, interleaved with the pork rind, and simmered in marc brandy); escalopes Franche-Comté (browned, then cooked *au gratin* with Franche-Comté cheese and cream); etc. In the past, famous recipes were perfected for this 'chameleon of cooking', as Grimod de la Reynière called it, notably stuffed breast of veal, cutlets *en surprise*, brésolles, saddle of veal Orloff, feuilleton, and veal sauté Marengo. Regional dishes are equally numerous, particularly for veal offal: casse of Rennes, veal mesentery *au gratin*, tripous (a tripe dish), calf's head Sainte-Menehould, and calf's lung bourguignon.

Outside France, it is in Italy that the widest variety of veal dishes are found: osso bucco, piccata, saltimbocca, veal with tuna-fish sauce, etc.; also worthy of mention are the Hungarian pörkölt with paprika, the Austrian Wiener schnitzel (breaded escalopes), and the British veal and ham pie.

RECIPES

Cold best end of neck (rib) of veal CARRÉ DE VEAU FROID Cook in the oven at 220 C (425 F, gas 7) a shortened best end of neck of veal, trimmed and seasoned with salt and pepper, allowing 30–40 minutes cooking time per kg (2¼ lb). Allow to get completely cold, then glaze with aspic jelly. Place in the refrigerator until ready to serve, then surround with watercress and artichoke hearts stuffed with asparagus tips, also glazed with aspic if desired.

Cold veal à l'italienne VEAU THONNÉ FROID À L'ITALIENNE Cook some small white onions in olive oil, in a flameproof casserole, and set aside. Using the same pan, brown a noix of veal; then add to the casserole 300 g (11 oz) canned tuna in oil, 100 g (4 oz) desalted anchovy fillets, 2 peeled and diced lemons, salt, pepper, and a bouquet garni. Replace the onions in the casserole. Moisten with an equal mixture of white wine and veal stock, cook for 1½ hours, then allow to cool in the casserole. Remove the veal and pass the rest of the contents of the casserole through a blender or processor. Prepare a mayonnaise, add the strained sauce to it, and serve with the veal.

Filets mignons of veal with lemon FILETS MIGNONS DE VEAU AU CITRON (from Roger Vergé's recipe) Pare the zest of half a lemon and cut into fine strips. Put into a saucepan with 6 tablespoons cold water and bring to the boil, then drain and rinse in cold water. Put the lemon strips back into a saucepan with 1 tablespoon water and ½ tablespoon sugar; cook until the water has evaporated, then set aside.

Heat 20 g (¾ oz, 1½ tablespoons) butter in a frying pan (skillet). When it starts to sizzle, add 4 veal filets mignons, each weighing 75 g (3 oz), sprinkled with salt and pepper on both sides. Brown them for 5 minutes on each side, then keep hot on a plate.

Pour off the butter from the pan and deglaze with 4 tablespoons dry white wine, reducing to 1 tablespoon liquid. Mix in 40 g (1½ oz, 3 tablespoons) butter, then 1 tablespoon chopped parsley.

Transfer the filets mignons to hot serving plates, pouring any meat juices into the sauce, and coat the fillets with the sauce. Garnish each fillet with a peeled slice of lemon and a little of the shredded zest cooked in sugar.

Braised veal chops à la Custine CÔTES DE VEAU BRAISÉES À LA CUSTINE (from Carême's recipe) Braise some veal chops; coat them first with 1 generous tablespoon duxelles, then with bread-crumbs, then dip in beaten egg, and finish with another coating of bread-crumbs. Fry in well-browned butter and serve with a light tomato sauce.

Breaded veal chops à la milanaise CÔTES DE VEAU PANÉES À LA MILA-NAISE Flatten the chops and season with salt and pepper. Dip in beaten egg and coat in a mixture of half bread-crumbs and half grated Parmesan cheese. Cook gently in clarified butter in a sauté pan, then arrange on a serving dish garnished with cannelled lemon slices and sprinkled with noisette butter. Serve macaroni *à la milanaise* separately.

Carême recommended replacing the cheese in the breadcrumb coating with finely chopped truffle, and serving the chops (which would then be called *à la Morland*) with a mushroom purée.

Casseroled veal chops CÔTES DE VEAU EN CASSEROLE Season some veal chops with salt and pepper and cook gently in 20 g (¾ oz, 1½ table-spoons) butter or 2 tablespoons oil per chop, at first uncovered, then covered, until they are browned. Deglaze the sauté pan with 2 tablespoons each of veal stock and white wine per chop, reduce by half, and pour over the chops.

Alternatively, half-cook the chops, remove them from the pan, put in the chosen accompanying vegetable (also half-cooked), replace the chops in the pan, and complete the cooking. These accompanying vegetables could include: diced aubergine (eggplant) sautéed in butter or oil; glazed carrots, turnips, or small onions, Vichy carrots; mushrooms sautéed in butter; celeriac (celery root), cucumber, or artichoke hearts cut into quarters and cooked in butter; or green beans cooked in water.

Alternatively, the chops may be completely cooked and garnished with vegetables cooked separately, either by braising, sautéeing, or steaming.

Other vegetables which may be used are chicory, Brussels sprouts, cauliflower, endive, spinach, hop shoots, flageolets, beans, lettuce, chestnuts, sorrel, peas, or tomatoes. Buttered noodles or rice can also be served.

Casseroled veal chops à la bonne femme CÔTES DE VEAU EN CASSEROLE À LA BONNE FEMME Sauté the chops in a flameproof dish until they are half-cooked. Add the bonne femme garnish comprising, for each chop, 4 small pieces of bacon, 5 small onions, and 6 small new potatoes, all well browned. Cover and complete in the oven, at 220 c (425 f, gas 7).

Grilled (broiled) veal chops CÔTES DE VEAU GRILLÉES Flatten the chops and season with salt and pepper; coat with tarragon-flavoured oil and leave to marinate for 30 minutes. Grill (broil) gently until the meat is cooked through (about 15 minutes), turning over once. Serve the chops with a green salad, a mixed salad, or green beans, steamed and served with green butter (see *butter*).

Grilled (broiled) veal chops vertpré CÔTES DE VEAU GRILLÉES VERT-PRÉ Grill (broil) the veal chops and garnish with rounds of maître d'hôtel butter. Serve surrounded with bunches of watercress and straw potatoes.

Sautéed veal chops à la crème CÔTES DE VEAU SAUTÉES À LA CRÈME Brown some veal chops, seasoned with salt and pepper, in a frying pan (skillet) using 1 tablespoon oil per chop; cover and finish cooking over a low heat (about 15 minutes). Strain off the oil from the pan and add 1 chopped shallot per chop; cook, uncovered, until browned. Remove the chops and shallots and keep hot. Add to the pan 2–3 tablespoons cider or white wine and 1 tablespoon double (heavy) cream per chop; boil over a brisk heat until the sauce is reduced and smooth. Adjust the seasoning and coat the chops with the sauce.

All garnishes suggested for escalopes of veal may accompany sautéed veal chops.

Veal chops in aspic   CÔTES DE VEAU À LA GELÉE   Trim the chops and lard them a little with fat bacon and pickled tongue. Braise them, then drain thoroughly and leave to cool under a press. Strain the braising liquid and leave to cool; coat the chops with the cold liquid before it sets, arrange them on a serving dish, and refrigerate. Just before serving, garnish them with squares of aspic flavoured with port or sherry.

veganism   VÉGÉTALISME

A strict form of vegetarianism in which the diet is based on cereals, fruit, fresh and dried vegetables, and vegetable oils. It excludes all animal products – even eggs, milk, and honey.

With the ready availability today of a wide variety of fresh fruit and vegetables and modern production of items like soya (soy) milk, vegetable protein products, and pure vegetable margarines, it is now possible to have a reasonably varied and nutritious vegan diet. It is, however, still difficult to maintain a good balance of essential nutrients and vegans must take great care to avoid dietary deficiencies in protein, calcium, iron, and vitamin B_{12}.

vegetable dish
LÉGUMIER

A rectangular, oval, or round dish with a lid in which vegetables are served when they are not arranged as a garnish around meat, poultry, or fish. In France, the covered vegetable dish appeared during the Regency period, when it was made of silver, porcelain, or earthenware. Vegetable dishes are now also made in stainless steel, which enables them to keep hot for longer, and in enamelled iron, which makes it possible to cook the vegetables and serve them in the same dish. This is particularly useful for braised vegetables.

vegetables   LÉGUMES

Herbaceous plants cultivated for food.

According to the species, different parts of the vegetable are eaten: the fruit (courgettes (zucchini), aubergines (eggplants), sweet peppers, tomatoes, etc.); the seed (peas, lentils, beans, etc.); the leaves (spinach, lettuce, cabbage, etc.); the bulb (onions, shallots, fennel, etc.); the tuber (potatoes, yams); the germ (soya); or the root (carrots, turnips, parsnips, radishes, etc.). Mushrooms and other fungi are also usually regarded as vegetables. For culinary purposes, a distinction is made between fresh vegetables (including greens), dried vegetables (see *pulses*), and salads.

Vegetables form an essential part of our diet. They contain glucose, proteins, mineral salts, and vitamins in varying proportions in a form that can be easily absorbed by the body. They also help to maintain a healthy digestive system. They are extremely valuable in cookery as they can be prepared in so many different ways (hors d'oeuvres, soups, garnishes, pickles, etc.).

Fresh vegetables play a particularly vital role in a balanced diet as their alkaline content neutralizes the acids in high-protein food. They are rich in iron, sodium, sulphur, magnesium, copper, and iodine, as well as vitamins (A, B_1, B_2, and C), all of which contribute to maintaining a healthy nervous system. Fresh vegetables can be eaten raw or cooked. Whether or not the mineral and vitamin content of the vegetables is destroyed in cooking depends on the method used. The best method is to steam them unpeeled, though certain vegetables can be grilled (broiled). Boiling in large quantities of water and blanching result in the loss of up to half the content of mineral salts, although these can be reclaimed by using the cooking liquid to make soup.

Vegetables are usually served as a garnish with meat or fish, but they can also constitute a complete dish by themselves (in the form of soups or gratins, or stuffed). Seasoning and sauces can transform bland vegetables, such as courgettes, cooked lettuce, endive (chicory), etc. The simplest way of preparing fresh vegetables is *à l'anglaise* (i.e. cooking them in water).

Vegetables can be stored for several days at the bottom of the refrigerator without losing their nutritive value.

Modern storage methods (such as freezing) and the great increase in imported vegetables mean that fresh vegetables can be eaten at any time of the year, but many people still prefer the flavour of a fresh vegetable in season. With foreign cookery becoming increasingly popular, many exotic vegetables now appear in the shops (plantains, sweet potatoes, etc.).

vegetarianism
VÉGÉTARISME

A type of diet that totally excludes meat, poultry, and sometimes fish, but permits eggs, milk, cheese, and sometimes butter. Vegetarians also prefer foods that are mainly unrefined (whole-grain cereals and wholemeal bread, for example). Vegetarian meals can be of a good gastronomic standard (there are some excellent vegetarian restaurants) and vegetarianism is compatible with a balanced diet, as the animal by-products provide the necessary proteins and enough calcium is present in milk and cheese. Moreover, the advantage of such a diet is that it is rich in unsaturated fats: it is universally recognized that an excess of saturated fatty acids, present in animal fats, may be harmful.

veine

A French cut of beef from the neck, subdivided into fat veine (or *saignée*) and lean veine (or second clod), both rich in connective tissue. Thus meat is used for braising and stewing (daube, carbonade, etc.).

velours

The name given to a carrot soup to which consommé, substantially thickened with tapioca, is added. This gives the soup a thick velvety consistency.

velouté sauce

One of the basic white sauces, made with a white veal or chicken stock or a fish fumet, thickened with a white or golden roux. Numerous other sauces are derived from it: allemande, caper, poulette, and mushroom sauces (from veal velouté); ivoire, suprême, and aurore sauces (from chicken velouté); and bretonne, cardinal, and Nantua sauces (from fish velouté).

RECIPES

Basic velouté sauce VELOUTÉ, SAUCE BLANCHE GRASSE For 2.5 litres (4½ pints, 5½ pints) stir 2.75 litres (scant 5 pints, 6 pints) white stock made with veal or chicken into a pale blond roux made with 150 g (5 oz, generous ½ cup) butter and 150 g (5 oz, 1¼ cups) flour. Blend well together. Bring to the boil, stirring with a wooden spoon until the first bubbles appear. Cook the velouté very slowly for 30 minutes, skimming frequently. Strain through a cloth. Stir until it is completely cold.

Velouté may be prepared either in advance or just before it is required. As the white stock used for making it is seasoned and flavoured, it is not necessary to add other flavourings. An exception is made for skins and trimmings of mushrooms, which may be added when available, this addition making the sauce yet more delicate.

Velouté sauce based on fish stock VELOUTÉ DE POISSON, VELOUTÉ MAIGRE Make like basic velouté sauce, replacing the veal or chicken stock with fish stock.

velouté soup
See *soup*.

Venaco

A Corsican cheese made from goats' or ewes' milk (45% fat content), with a soft texture and a greyish scraped natural rind. It comes from Venaco and Corte and is made only on a small scale as a cottage industry, in season from June to September. It is made in the form of a 13-cm (5-in) square slab, 6 cm (2½ in) high. Venaco is a whitish fatty cheese, firm to the touch, with a strong smell and sometimes a piquant flavour. It is served with a full-bodied red wine. Sometimes the cheese is crumbled and soaked in wine and marc brandy.

Vendée

The coastal strip of Poitou is known as the Vendée, and the cuisine of this region combines the resources of the sea with the culinary traditions of the hinterland.

The pastureland of the Vendée is

stock-breeding country and many cattle are raised, providing excellent meat. Cereals and vegetables are also grown, including the famous Vendée green cabbages and *mogettes* (white haricot (navy) beans, which are cooked in the usual way and dressed with butter and cream). Other popular dishes are broadbean purée in stock, *chouée* (green cabbage boiled in salted water, drained and pressed, and mixed with plenty of butter), and also buttered cabbage. The channels of the marshland which extend from Challans to Beauvoir-sur-Mer are famous for ducks, which are bred for the markets of Nantes and Paris.

Rivers and ponds provide eels for fish stews; frogs' legs are prepared *à la luçonnaise* (cooked in water flavoured with vinegar, then sautéed in butter and garnished with fried cloves of garlic) and snails are grilled (broiled) or prepared *à la mode d'Oléron* (cooked in boiling water with fennel, then simmered in a white sauce with potatoes).

Rabbit and hare are cooked in particularly interesting ways; for example, rabbit pâté (a terrine with alternate layers of fillets of wild rabbit and a forcemeat of the remaining flesh mixed with onion and shallot) and hare *à la vendéenne*, a speciality of La Roche-sur-Yon, birthplace of the poet Raoul Ponchon. Pork from this region also has an excellent flavour and specialities include boar's-head stew and *fressure vendéenne* (chopped pork offal and bacon mixed with congealed pig's blood and cooked slowly for a long time).

The recipes for fish and seafood are many and varied and include cotriade, chaudrée, mouclade, salt cod soup, and oyster soup. The langoustes of the island of Yeu, the sardines of Les Sables-d'Olonne, and mussels from L'Aiguillon-sur-Mer are justly famous.

The cheeses, pâtisserie, and sweets of Poitou are also found in the Vendée, but there are some additional specialities, such as brioche vendéenne, alize pâquaude, bottereaux, fouaces, caillebottes, and *flan maraîchin* (eggs in milk under a caramelized crust).

Vendôme

A cows'-milk cheese (50% fat) made in Orléans. It is in season from June to December and has a soft texture and a natural bluish or ash-grey rind. It is a small round cheese, 11 cm (4¼ in) in diameter and 3.5 cm (1¼ in) high. Vendôme is firm to the touch; the cheese with a grey rind has a more fruity flavour and a more pronounced smell than that with the blue rind. It is made only on farms and is becoming increasingly rare.

venison VENAISON

The meat of any kind of deer. In French, however, the term is used not only for deer meat but also for the meat of any large game animal (including wild boar). Hare and wild rabbit are known in French as *base venaison*. The word venison comes from the Latin *venatio* (hunt).

Haunch or quarter of venison is generally a leg and loin of deer, which is roasted after being marinated or hung.

There are also various venison sauces to accompany game meat, of which the classic is a poivrade (pepper) sauce mixed with fresh cream and redcurrant jelly.

RECIPE

Venison sauce SAUCE VENAISON (from Carême's recipe) Pour into a saucepan a glass of old Burgundy wine, 2 tablespoons (3 tablespoons) ordinary vinegar, 2 tablespoons (3 tablespoons) sugar, the flesh of half a deseeded lemon, and half a pot of redcurrant jelly. Boil to reduce and add 2 tablespoons (3 tablespoons) espagnole sauce. Reduce again, gradually mixing in the contents of a second glass of Burgundy. When the sauce has reached the correct consistency, rub it through a sieve.

vénitienne (à la)

The name given to poached fillets of sole, slices of conger eel sautéed in butter, poached chicken, or soft-boiled (soft-cooked) or poached eggs when accompanied by vénitienne sauce. This sauce is made with a mixture of vinegar, tarragon, and allemande sauce, reduced, mixed with green butter, strained, and garnished with herbs. Fish served with a normande sauce mixed with herbs and chopped capers may also be called *à la vénitienne*.

RECIPES

Fillets of sole à la vénitienne FILETS DE SOLE À LA VÉNITIENNE Fold the fillets of sole in half and poach them in a fish fumet made with white wine. Drain and wipe them and arrange them in a ring on a serving dish, alternating with heart-shaped croutons fried in butter. Coat them with vénitienne sauce mixed with the reduced cooking liquid from the sole.

Vénitienne sauce SAUCE VÉNITIENNE (from Carême's recipe) Boil together in a saucepan 2 tablespoons (3 tablespoons) allemande sauce, a generous pinch of chopped tarragon blanched and drained on a fine silk strainer, 1 tablespoon chicken glaze, a little Isigny butter, a pinch of grated nutmeg, and a few drops of good tarragon vinegar.

Ventadour

The name given to a dish of tournedos steaks or noisettes of lamb, garnished with slices of bone marrow and truffle and served with artichoke purée and potato cocotte.

venue

The French culinary term for the process of assembling the necessary ingredients in the correct proportions to make an item of pâtisserie or confectionery.

verbena VERVEINE

Any of several ornamental flowering plants. An infusion of the leaves and flowers of lemon verbena, sweetened with honey, is recommended for liver and kidney ailments and for soothing the nerves. Some chefs also use fresh verbena leaves with their lemony fragrance to flavour stocks. Alain Chapel, for example, suggests steaming pieces of langouste wrapped in endive (chicory) leaves over stock with verbena leaves added; the langoustes are served coated with a champagne fumet chickened with butter and surrounded with a ragout of chanterelle mushrooms.

Dried powdered verbena leaves can be added to meat and fish stuffings to give a delicate flavour.

Verdier

The name given to a dish of hard-boiled (hard-cooked) eggs stuffed with foie gras, placed on a bed of cooked sliced onions, coated with a béchamel sauce containing truffles, sprinkled with Parmesan cheese, and browned in the oven. The dish is attributed to the proprietor of the Maison Dorée.

RECIPE

Hard-boiled (hard-cooked) eggs Verdier OEUFS DURS VERDIER Hard-boil (hard-cook) the eggs, shell them, and halve them. Remove the yolks, rub them through a sieve, and mix them with one-third of their volume of foie gras cut into very small dice. Fill the halves of egg white with the mixture. Slice some onions, gently soften them in butter, blend them with a very little béchamel sauce seasoned with curry powder, and spread in a layer in a gratin dish. Place the stuffed eggs on top, and coat with béchamel sauce mixed with a julienne of truffles. Sprinkle with Parmesan cheese and brown in a very hot oven.

The foie gras may be replaced by diced chicken livers sautéed in butter and the truffles with a julienne of sweet peppers, but in this case the dish should not be called by the classic name.

verdure

A term used in French cuisine to describe a green salad or a mixture of green pot herbs. Chopped verdure is used especially to make forcemeats or purées. The name *verdurette* is given to a vinaigrette sauce mixed with chopped chives, hard-boiled (hard-cooked) eggs, chervil, tarragon, and parsley. Kitchen staff in the times of the Ancien Régime included a *verdurier*, whose job was to provide the herbs and vinegar. (See *vert*.)

vergeoise

A type of French soft brown sugar (beet or cane) crystallized from a syrup remaining at the end of the refining process, the colour and smell of which is determined by the components of the raw material used. Its name is taken from the old sugar moulds, the *vergeoises*, in which large sugar loaves were made.

There are two kinds of vergeoise, light and dark brown: the former is obtained by recooking the syrup removed at the first stage of the sugar-refining process; dark brown vergeoise, with a more unusual smell, results from recooking the syrup removed at the second stage of sugar refinement.

In northern France and Belgium, vergeoise is commonly used to make pastries, especially *tarte au sucre* (sugar tart), and also to sprinkle on or fill crêpes and waffles.

verjuice VERJUS

The acid juice extracted from large un-ripened grapes, which was formerly widely used as a sauce ingredient, a condiment, and in deglazing. In the Middle Ages, *vertjus* (literally 'green juice') was an acid-tasting stock pre-pared with the juice of unripe grapes, sometimes mixed with lemon or sorrel juice, herbs, and spices. It was used in most sauces and liaisons.

RECIPE

Soft roes of herring with verjuice LAI-TANCES DE HARENG AU VERJUS (from Joël Robuchon's recipe) Soak 800 g (1¾ lb) soft roes of herring for 1 hour in cold water with 1 dl (6 tablespoons, scant ½ cup) white wine vinegar. Drain and wipe. Season with salt and pepper, coat with flour, shaking off any excess, then prick with a needle to prevent them from bursting during cooking. Heat 40 g (1½ oz, 3 tablespoons) butter and 5 cl (3 tablespoons, ¼ cup) oil in a frying pan (skillet). Carefully place the roes in the hot fat and cook for 3–4 minutes on each side.

Heat 80 g (3 oz, 6 tablespoons) butter in a separate frying pan and brown 80 g (3 oz, 1 cup) diced mushrooms and an equal quantity of diced sour apples for 4 minutes. Then add 80 g (3 oz) diced tomatoes, cook for 1 minute, and add 50 g (2 oz) capers, salt, and pepper. Arrange the roes on warmed plates, sprinkle with 50 g (2 oz, 1½ cups) small sprigs of parsley, and garnish with the browned vegetables.

Remove the fat from the pan in which the roes were cooked and add, over a brisk heat, 5 cl (3 tablespoons, ¼ cup) cider vinegar and an equal quantity of verjuice. Bring to the boil and pour over the roes.

vermicelli VERMICELLE

A pasta made in the form of fine strands (the name means 'small worms'), often used in soups but also served like spaghetti. 'Angel's hair' is a very fine variety of vermicelli, used only in con-sommés and clear soups. Vermicelli is also used to make certain puddings and soufflés.

Chinese vermicelli, prepared with soya flour, comes in long lustrous skeins. Boiled or fried, it is used in soups, vegetable mixtures, forcemeats, etc. In the Far East, there is a type of vermicelli made with rice flour. It con-sists of long flat whitish strands and is cooked in the same way as noodles.

vermouth

An aromatized wine whose name is de-rived from the German W*ermut* (worm-wood or absinthe) this being an in-gredient of many recipes of vermouth.

Vermouth is now made in many re-gions where wine is made, although commercial production began in Turin in the 18th century. Prior to this, va-rious versions of wine incorporating herbs, spices, barks, and peels were made, often for semimedicinal pur-poses; records of these drinks exist from about the 5th century BC. By the end of the 18th century establishments for making vermouth were in production in Marseille and Chambéry in France and these places, with Turin, remain the world centres for vermouth.

There are several main methods of production: the ingredients may be in-fused, macerated, or even distilled in the base wine, or a combination of all these processes can be followed. Any good vermouth is subject to a certain matu-ration period.

Each of the great vermouth establish-ments makes a range of vermouths, the main types being dry and white, sweet-ish and red, and rosé. An Italian special-ity is Bianco, or white vermouth, which is slightly sweet (although many drinkers suppose it to be dry on account of the pale colour). It is a common error to categorize Italian vermouth as sweet and French as dry – as may be noted from the fact that the world's most famous cocktail, the dry martini, is thought to have been originally made with Italian vermouth of the world-famous firm, Martini Rossi. However, because of the obviously different methods of production and the secret formulae of the great establishments, French vermouth is, overall, different from Italian. Chambéry vermouth, from Savoy, is very delicate and aromatic and traditionally always served straight. There is a 'strawberry vermouth' also made in Chambéry. There are hundreds of vermouth producers, as well as Noilly Prat, Cinzano, and Gancia, and many chains of wine retailers have their 'own label' brands of vermouth in the main types.

In the kitchen vermouth is extremely useful, because the herby ingredients make it suitable for stuffings, seasonings, sauces, and poaching stock, notably for fish and shellfish. Although vermouth, like wine, will decline in quality after the bottle has been opened and the contents exposed to the air (in a few weeks for the dry versions), it will remain perfectly usable for culinary purposes almost indefinitely.

vernis

A bivalve mollusc that inhabits the sandy ocean bed and belongs to the same family as clams – it is cooked in the same way. Its shells, 6–10 cm (2½–4 in) long, are smooth, shiny, and brown, marked with dark radiating stripes.

RECIPE

Vernis à la mode de Klébert Haedens (from R. Dumay's recipe in *Du silex au barbecue*, Julliard) Place the molluscs in a pan, cover, and heat until they open, shaking the pan occasionally; remove the flesh and dice it, and reserve the shells. Cook a mixture of chopped shallots and breadcrumbs in butter in a flameproof dish for 5 minutes. Add the diced vernis, salt and pepper, and 2–3 tablespoons fresh cream; continue cooking but do not allow to boil. Remove from the heat and mix thoroughly with chopped garlic and parsley. Fill the shells with the mixture, return to the

dish, and brown in a very hot oven. Serve very hot.

Vernon

The name of a dish of sautéed small cuts of meat, which are garnished with artichoke hearts topped with asparagus tips, turnips stuffed with mashed potato, and hollowed-out apples filled with peas in butter.

Veronica VÉRONIQUE

A genus of plants of which there are numerous species found throughout temperate regions. *Veronica officinalis*, the common speedwell, nicknamed the 'tea of Europe' in France, was used as long ago as the early 18th century as a substitute for tea. *Veronica beccabunga*, the brooklime, often confused with watercress, can be eaten raw in salads or cooked like spinach.

Véron (Louis Désiré)

French doctor and journalist (born Paris, 1798; died Paris, 1867). After practising medicine in fashionable circles, he became a critic and the editor of various literary reviews, then administrator of the Opéra, and finally a political journalist at the head of *Constitutionnel*, which supported the cause of Louis-Napoléon and the Empire. He owes his place in the history of gastronomy to his role as a lavish host, at first in his apartment in the Rue de Rivoli, then at Auteuil. Among his guests, Sainte-Beuve, Nestor Roqueplan, and Arsène Houssaye rubbed shoulders with Halévy, Auber, Trousseau, Velpeau, and various famous actresses, including Rachel, his mistress. On Fridays, dinner was more formal and guests included certain political personalities, sometimes even the Prince-President himself.

The reputation of Véron's table depended heavily on the talents of his cook-housekeeper, Sophie, who is said to have surpassed herself with such dishes as duck with olives and braised leg of lamb with beans. During his lifetime Véron gained a reputation with some for ostentatious luxury and gourmandism, but in fact the doctor was a sober and moderate man: 'He eats only two courses, and his normal drink is very old Bordeaux, greatly diluted with water', a journalist wrote of him. Véron thanked the writer of the article, and even added: 'At the Café de Paris, they would charge to me everything that was being eaten and drunk around me.' However, in a novel entitled *Cinq Cent Mille Livres de rente*, Véron contributed a menu consisting of a fabulous collection of dishes, including chicken suprêmes reine scattered with pickled tongue and truffles, Lake Geneva trout *au bleu* with green sauce, Alpine rock partridges *sur piédestal*, ortolans *en litière*, Swiss mousse, and Italian cascade.

In classic cuisine, Véron's name has been given to a normande sauce with herbs mixed with veal fumet or stock, served with breaded or grilled (broiled) fish.

RECIPES

Fillets of brill Véron FILETS DE BARBUE VÉRON Cut the fillets in half lengthways, season with salt and pepper, dip in melted butter and breadcrumbs, sprinkle with more melted butter, and cook gently under the grill (broiler). Arrange the fillets on a hot serving dish and coat with Véron sauce.

Véron sauce SAUCE VÉRON Prepare a reduced herb mixture as for a béarnaise sauce. Then add 2 dl (7 fl oz, ¾ cup) normande sauce and 2 tablespoons (3 tablespoons) very concentrated brown veal stock or fish glaze. Season with a pinch of cayenne, rub through a sieve, and add 1 tablespoon snipped chervil or tarragon.

vert

In Flemish cooking, the name *au vert* (literally, green) is given to a dish of eels cooked with numerous herbs (up to 15), which vary according to the season and may include sorrel, spinach, salad cress, white deadnettle, parsley, chervil, tarragon, fresh mint, sage, burnet, lemon balm, etc.

Sauce verte (green sauce) is a mayonnaise containing a purée of herbs. In former times, the sauce was more of a vinaigrette, which the Parisian *sauciers* in the reign of Louis XII used to sell in the streets:

'Vous faut-il point de sauce verte?
C'est pour manger carpes et limandes,
Ça qui en veut, qui en demande,
Tant que mon pot est ouvert.'
('Do you need any green sauce?
It's for eating with carp or dabs,
For those who want it, let them ask for it,
While my pot is open.')

The modern recipe was perfected by Balvay, formerly chef to Napoleon III, then chef at the restaurant Le Doyen, where it became a speciality, particularly when served with sea trout. *Beurre vert* (green butter) is a flavoured butter made with chopped herbs.

RECIPE

Green sauce SAUCE VERTE For 4 dl (14 fl oz, 1¾ cups) sauce, prepare 3 dl (10 fl oz, 1¼ cups) mayonnaise and 1 dl (6 tablespoons, scant ½ cup) purée of green herbs (spinach, watercress, parsley, chervil, and tarragon), blanched for 1 minute in boiling water, cooled under the tap, thoroughly dried, and then pounded in a mortar. Mix the 2 preparations together and rub through a sieve.

Use the sauce like classic mayonnaise, especially to accompany cold poached fish.

vert-cuit

A French culinary term used when food is cooked very lightly and served almost raw (by analogy with fruit, which is described as *vert* (green) before it has ripened). Duck *au sang* and woodcock, in particular, are served *vert-cuits*.

vert-pré

The term describing preparations of grilled (broiled) meat (kidneys, steaks, chops, noisettes, etc.) garnished with straw potatoes and watercress and served with maître d'hôtel butter, which is either placed on the meat in rounds, or melted and served in a sauceboat. The name is also given to preparations of white meat, duckling, vols-au-vent, etc., garnished with a mixture of peas, asparagus tips, and green beans, tossed in butter. Chicken or fish coated with green sauce are also called *vert-pré*.

RECIPES

Croustades vert-pré Prepare croustades with duchess potatoes and fill them with a mixture of equal quantities of peas, asparagus tips, and French beans (cut into small pieces), all bound together with butter. Serve hot.

Entrecôte vert-pré Prepare some maître d'hôtel butter, shape it into a roll, and wrap in aluminium foil. Put it in the refrigerator to harden. Grill (broil) an entrecôte steak on both sides and place it on a hot serving dish. Slice rounds of maître d'hôtel butter and place on top of the steak. Garnish with bunches of watercress and straw potatoes.

Viard

A 19th-century French chef, author of a collection of recipes entitled *Le Cuisinier impérial, ou l'Art de faire la cuisine et la pâtisserie pour toutes les fortunes, avec la manière de servir une table depuis vingt jusqu'à soixante couverts* (1806). This 'dispensatory' was published in at least 32 successive editions, with titles that varied according to the prevailing political circumstances; in 1817, at the time of the Restoration, it became *Le Cuisinier royal* (with a supplementary chapter on wines, by Pierhugue), and in 1852, in its 22nd edition, *Le Cuisinier national de la ville et de la campagne*, whose authors were given as Viart (*sic*), Fouret, and Délan. In 1853, published as *Le Cuisinier impérial de la ville et de la campagne*, it included 200 new articles by Bernardi. This culinary encyclopedia continued to be the basic reference book for professional chefs throughout the 19th century.

Vicaire (Gabriel)

French poet (born Belfort, 1848; died Paris, 1900). In a collection appearing in 1884, entitled *les Émaux bressans*, he sang the praises of his native Bresse, the cuisine of which is among the most famous. He also published gastronomic articles. His writing was deliberately anti-Symbolist, as is shown by this verse extracted from *Victime du réveillon* (he is writing of the pig):

'Et braves gens, que de joie
Lorsqu'en forme de boudin
Ressuscitera soudain
Le bon habillé de soie.'
('And good people, what joy
When the good pig
Suddenly comes back again
In the shape of a black pudding (blood
sausage).')

Vicaire (Georges)

French scholar (born Paris, 1853; died Chantilly, 1921). A cousin of the poet Gabriel Vicaire, he wrote a *Manuel de l'amateur de livres au XIXᵉ siècle* (in eight volumes) and also a study on Balzac as a publisher and printer. However, he is best known to collectors of books on cuisine for his valuable *Bibliographie gastronomique* (1890), which records and describes some 2500 works on gastronomy and cuisine, from the time when printing first began up to 1890. The work is dedicated to Baron Jérôme Pichon, with whom he published Taillevent's *Viandier* in 1892.

Vichy

The name given to a dish of sliced carrots cooked over a low heat (traditionally with sugar and bicarbonate of soda, or 'Vichy salt') until all the moisture is absorbed. To justify the name, the water used for cooking should be Vichy Saint-Yorre mineral water. Vichy carrots, or carrots à la Vichy, with fresh butter and parsley, are often served with veal cutlets and sautéed chicken, coated with a sauce made by deglazing the cooking pan with veal stock.

RECIPE

Vichy carrots CAROTTES VICHY Peel 800 g (1¾ lb) young carrots and cut into thin rounds. Place in a sauté pan and just cover with water, adding 1 teaspoon salt and a generous pinch of sugar per ½ litre (17 fl oz, 2 cups) water. Cook gently until all the liquid is absorbed. Serve the carrots in a vegetable dish, sprinkled with small pieces of butter and chopped parsley.

vichyssoise

A leek and potato soup thickened with fresh cream and served cold, garnished with chopped chives. Vichyssoise was created in the United States by a French chef from the Bourbonnais. The name vichyssoise is also given to any cold soup based on potatoes and another vegetable, such as courgettes (zucchini).

RECIPE

Vichyssoise Slice 250 g (9 oz) leeks (white part only) and cut 250 g (9 oz) peeled potatoes into quarters. Soften the leeks in 50 g (2 oz, ¼ cup) butter in a covered pan without allowing them to brown. Then add the potatoes, stir, and pour in 1.75 litres (3 pints, 3¾ pints) water. Add salt, pepper, and a small bouquet garni. Bring to the boil and cook for 30–40 minutes. Purée the potatoes and leeks in a blender or processor and return to the pan. Blend in at least 2 dl (7 fl oz, ¾ cup) fresh cream and return just to the boil, stirring frequently. Allow the soup to cool and place in the refrigerator for 1 hour. Serve in consommé cups sprinkled with chopped chives.

Victoria

There are a number of dishes and sauces dedicated to Queen Victoria, all characterized by rich ingredients or an elegant presentation. Barquettes and bouchées, fillets of sole, poached and soft-boiled (soft-cooked) eggs, and filled omelette Victoria all contain a salpicon of lobster and truffle, bound in various ways. Scallop shells of fish Victoria, with mushrooms and truffles, are coated with Nantua sauce and garnished with slices of truffle.

Salad Victoria is a mixed salad of diced cucumber, a salpicon of langouste, sliced celeriac (celery root), sliced artichoke hearts, sliced potatoes, and thin strips of truffle, dressed with pink mayonnaise.

Victoria garnish consists of small tomatoes stuffed with mushroom purée and browned under the grill (broiler), and quartered artichoke hearts cooked in butter. It is served with small sautéed pieces of meat coated with a sauce made by deglazing the pan juices with either Madeira or port and thickened veal stock. Victoria sauces are served with poached fish (white wine sauce with lobster butter and a salpicon of lobster and truffles) or with venison (espagnole

sauce flavoured with port, redcurrant jelly, orange juice, and spices).

Bombe Victoria has a plombières ice cream centre coated with strawberry ice cream, and Victoria cake is a kind of rich fruit cake with spices and glacé cherries (instead of dried fruit).

Victoria sandwich cake was also named after the queen. After the death of her husband, Prince Albert, in 1861, Queen Victoria used to spend time every year in retreat at Osborne House, on the Isle of Wight. She was encouraged to give tea parties, during which the Victoria sandwich, made of sponge cake filled with various preserved fruits, was served. Its popularity soon spread throughout England.

RECIPES

Scallop shells of salmon Victoria CO-QUILLES DE SAUMON VICTORIA Fill the scallop shells with a mixture of salmon poached in fumet, sliced mushrooms cooked in butter, and small diced truffles. Coat with Nantua sauce, dust with grated Parmesan cheese, sprinkle with clarified butter, and brown in a very hot oven. Garnish each scallop shell with a slice of truffle heated in butter.

Victoria sauce for fish SAUCE VIC-TORIA POUR POISSON Prepare 2.5 dl (8 fl oz, 1 cup) white wine sauce. Add 2 tablespoons (3 tablespoons) lobster butter, a dash of cayenne, and 2 tablespoons (3 tablespoons) diced lobster flesh and truffles.

Victoria sauce for venison SAUCE VICTORIA POUR VENAISON Prepare 2.5 dl (8 fl oz, 1 cup) espagnole sauce; add 1.5 dl (¼ pint, ⅔ cup) port and 3 tablespoons (4 tablespoons) redcurrant jelly. Then add 8 peppercorns, 2 cloves, a small stick of cinnamon, and the blanched zest of an orange. Boil until reduced by one-third, add the juice of the orange and a little cayenne, and rub through a sieve.

videler

A French culinary term meaning to make a border around the edge of a piece of pastry by gently easing it with the fingers a little at a time, upwards then towards the centre, to form a rolled edge. The rim of a tart case (shell) is treated in this way before being cooked in a flan ring, to give a neat even edge.

viennoise (à la)

The description *à la viennoise* is given to veal escalopes or to fillets of poultry or fish coated with egg and breadcrumbs, sautéed, and served with chopped hard-boiled (hard-cooked) egg (white and yolk separated), fried parsley, and capers; the meat or fish is usually topped with a slice of lemon with skin and pith removed and with a stoned (pitted) green olive surrounded by an anchovy fillet. The serving dish is coated with thickened veal stock and noisette butter is served separately.

This dish is a French interpretation of the classic Austrian dish *Wiener schnitzel* (made with veal), which is coated with egg and breadcrumbs, cooked in lard, and served with a slice of lemon and a potato salad or with a green salad and browned or mashed potatoes.

Spring chickens or chicken joints coated with breadcrumbs and sautéed or fried are also described as *à la viennoise*.

RECIPE

Escalopes à la viennoise Flatten 4 escalopes well and sprinkle with salt on both sides. Put 4 tablespoons (⅓ cup) flour with a little salt on one plate, 175 g (6 oz, 2 cups) dried breadcrumbs on another, and 2 beaten eggs on the third. Melt 100 g (4 oz, ½ cup) lard in a large frying pan (skillet). Dip the escalopes into the flour so that they are completely covered with a very fine coating, then in the beaten egg, and finally in the breadcrumbs, coating them evenly on both sides. Place in the lard when it is on the point of smoking and cook gently for 8 minutes on each side. Serve well browned.

viennoiserie

A French term used to describe bakery products other than bread, traditionally comprising croissants, milk-bread rolls, fruit buns, brioches, etc.; i.e., items made from raised dough or puff or rough-puff pastry, and excluding biscuits (cookies), sablés, etc., which come into the category of pâtisserie. Fancy breads, such as Viennese, granary, large brioche, etc., grouped under the term *panasserie*, are sometimes also included in viennoiserie.

vigneronne (à la)

The description given to dishes prepared with grapes or autumn produce or in 'wine-growers' style'. Salad *à la vigneronne* consists of dandelion leaves (sometimes also lamb's lettuce) and browned chopped bacon, dressed with walnut oil. The bacon pan is deglazed with vinegar, and this is used to season the salad. Small birds *à la vigneronne* are usually cooked in a casserole with grapes. Snails *à la vigneronne* are shelled, sautéed with garlic and shallots, coated in batter containing chives, then fried.

RECIPE

Partridge à la vigneronne PERDREAU À LA VIGNERONNE Pluck, clean, and truss a partridge. Cook it in butter in a saucepan for about 30 minutes, then drain and untruss it. Put into the saucepan 24 skinned and deseeded grapes, 3 tablespoons game fumet, and 1 tablespoon flamed brandy. Cover the pan and cook gently for 5 minutes, then replace the partridge on top, heat through, and serve.

villageoise (à la)

The description given to poached white meat or poultry accompanied by villageoise sauce. This is either a béchamel sauce mixed with onions softened in butter, veal or poultry stock, and mushroom essence, which is strained, thickened with egg yolk, and finished with butter, or a light velouté sauce mixed with onion purée, thickened with egg yolk and cream, and finished with butter.

Leek consommé, usually garnished with pasta, is also called *villageois*.

RECIPE

Villageoise sauce SAUCE VILLAGEOISE Slice 400 g (14 oz, 3½ cups) onions and cook gently for 20 minutes with a piece of butter (about 50 g, 2 oz). Add 3 dl (½ pint, 1¼ cups) very thick béchamel sauce, then 2 dl (7 fl oz, ¾ cup) veal or poultry stock and a little mushroom essence. Continue to cook over a low heat, stirring constantly. Strain the sauce and thicken it with an egg yolk. Away from the heat, beat in 40 g (1½ oz, 3 tablespoons) butter cut in small pieces.

Villeroi

The name of a sauce used to coat various foods which are then covered with egg and breadcrumbs and deep-fried. These preparations are described as *à la Villeroi* and include attereaux of offal, brochettes of seafood, fish steaks, sweetbreads, chicken pieces, or mutton cutlets; they are served with a tomato, devilled, chasseur, or mushroom sauce.

Villeroi sauce (dedicated to Marshal de Villeroi, mentor of Louis XV) is an allemande sauce, made either with meat stock (for coating meat) or fish stock (to coat fish), mixed with white stock and mushroom essence and then reduced; the sauce may be finished with truffle essence or purée of tomatoes or onions, or mixed with chopped truffles or mushrooms or a mirepoix.

When the sauce has reached the right consistency, it should be left to cool before being used to coat the food.

RECIPES

Scallop and oyster brochettes à la Villeroi BROCHETTES DE COQUILLES SAINT-JACQUES ET D'HUÎTRES À LA VILLEROI Poach the white flesh and the coral of the scallops in water, then the shelled oysters in their own water; allow to get cold. Drain and thread alternately onto skewers; coat with Villeroi sauce then breadcrumbs, fry, and serve as for attereaux of lambs' brains *à la Villeroi*.

Villeroi sauce SAUCE VILLEROI Prepare 2 dl (7 fl oz, ¾ cup) allemande sauce, dilute with 4 tablespoons (⅓ cup) white stock flavoured with a little mushroom essence, then reduce until it coats the spoon. Put through a strainer and stir until the sauce is barely tepid.

vinaigrette

A cold sauce made from a mixture of vinegar, oil, pepper, and salt, to which various flavourings may be added: shallot, onion, herbs, capers, garlic, gherkins, anchovies, hard-boiled (hard-cooked) egg, mustard, etc.

Vinaigrette is used especially for dressing green salads. The choice of oil (olive, sunflower, walnut, etc.) and vinegar is made according to the nature of the salad; the vinegar may be replaced by lemon juice or is sometimes flavoured with it. Vinaigrette is also used to dress various other cold dishes: vegetables (tomatoes, asparagus, cauliflower, leeks, artichoke hearts, etc.), meat (sheep's trotters (feet), brawn (head cheese), boiled beef, calf's head), and fish in court-bouillon. It is considered to be a typically French sauce and is often called 'French dressing' in Britain. It was a French émigré, Chevalier d'Albignac, who started the fashion in London high society for salads dressed in this way.

RECIPE

Vinaigrette (from Raymond Oliver's recipe) Put a little salt into a bowl and dissolve it in 1 tablespoon vinegar (salt does not dissolve in oil); add 3 tablespoons oil and some pepper. Mix well. The vinegar may be replaced by another acid substance, such as lemon, orange, or grapefruit juice, in which case the mixture is half juice, half oil. The oil may also be replaced by fresh cream.

Other flavourings, such as herbs, mustard, or garlic, may be added to taste. The mixture may also be placed in a screw-top jar and shaken vigorously to form an emulsion.

vinaigrier

The French name for the small glass bottle, usually with a glass stopper, used for serving vinegar at the table; it forms a pair together with the oil bottle as part of a cruet.

In France the name is also given to a large earthenware or stoneware cask traditionally used to make home-made vinegar. Shaped like a bottle or jug, usually with a capacity of 5 litres (9 pints), it has a tap at its base allowing the vinegar to be drawn off as required.

Vincent

The name of a mayonnaise that contains

chopped herbs or herb purée as well as chopped hard-boiled (hard-cooked) egg. It is served with crudités, cold meat, and fish.

RECIPE

Vincent sauce SAUCE VINCENT Prepare a mayonnaise with 1 egg yolk, 1 teaspoon white mustard, 1 tablespoon white-wine vinegar, 2.5 dl (8 fl oz, 1 cup) oil, salt, and pepper. Blanch the following herbs for 1 minute in boiling water: chervil, chives, watercress, sorrel, and parsley (a little mint, sage, or burnet may also be added). Rub the mixed herbs through a sieve and add 1 generous tablespoon of the resulting purée to the mayonnaise. Mix in a finely chopped hard-boiled (hard-cooked) egg and adjust the seasoning.

vin de liqueur

The French term for a fortified wine, such as port, in which fermentation has been arrested by the addition of spirit.

The term *vin de liqueur* or *vin liquoreux* also signifies a sweet wine, but not one of more than table-wine strength.

vin de paille

Straw wine: dessert wine coming mainly from the vineyards of the Jura, made from grapes that are slightly dried after picking, either by being laid on straw mats (hence the name) or hung on racks. This drying before pressing concentrates the juice, but straw wines are not necessarily all sweet, rather more rich in style. Very little vin de paille is now made although in the past it was produced in other areas, including the Rhône Valley.

vin d'honneur

A wine offered at receptions, as on certain civic occasions. Historic examples quoted by MM Renouil and Traversay in their *Dictionnaire du vin* include the following: the medieval *vin de bourgeoisie*, offered to the mayor and municipal magistrates by anyone who became a burgher of the town; the *vin de coucher*, offered by newly-weds to the wedding guests; the *vin de curé*, offered to the priest by a family whose child had been baptized; and the *vin du*

clerc, offered to the clerk of the court by a litigant, if the judgment had gone in his favour.

vin doux naturel

In France, a wine that has been fortified with brandy, which increases its strength to more than that of table wines and arrests the working of the yeasts, so that some of the natural sweetness in the grapes remains in the finished wine. Both red and white examples are made and the majority come from the Grand Roussillon region in the south, on the Franco-Spanish border; others come from the mouth of the Rhône. The grapes are predominantly Muscat, as in the well-known Muscat de Frontignan, Muscat de Beaumes de Venise, and many others. But other grapes used include the Malvoisie and the Grenache.

Our ancestors loved these soft fragrant wines (the name literally means 'naturally sweet wine') and drank them on many occasions – as apéritifs, between meals, and after meals or with dessert. They are less well-known than they deserve in the UK because their strength makes them liable to higher duty than table wines. However, they are enjoyed in the holiday regions of Banyuls (which makes a reputable vin doux naturel) and the French-Spanish hinterland from Collioure.

vinegar VINAIGRE

A sour liquid, widely used as a condiment, consisting of a dilute solution of acetic acid obtained by natural fermentation of wine or any other alcoholic solution. Vinegar (the French name literally means 'sour wine') has been produced and used since the Gallo-Roman era; vinegar diluted with water was a common drink of the Roman legionaries. Orléans, an important centre for wine transport on the Loire, soon became the vinegar capital, and half the French wine vinegar is still produced there. The vinegar merchants' corporation was created in this city in 1394, and in 1580 Henri IV ordered that the profession of vinegar and mustard merchant should be a 'recognized occupation in the town and its suburbs', which resulted in the perfection of carefully developed production methods.

In 1862 Pasteur discovered that acetification was caused by a bacterium. Acetification takes place on contact with air; it gives a good vinegar if the wine – red or white – is light, acid, and thoroughly strained to get rid of any residue. The operation takes place at a temperature of 20–30 c (68–86 f). The fermentation is caused by bacteria present in an even velvety grey film, which forms on the surface and slowly sinks into the liquid in a folded sticky mass; this is the vinegar mother (*mère de vinaigre*). The quality of vinegar always depends on the quality of the wine or other alcohol used to make it; it must contain at least 6% acetic acid and be clear, transparent, and colourless if it comes from white wine or differing shades of pink if it comes from red wine. Spirit or wine vinegars are mostly used in France, but in Britain and the USA malt and cider vinegars are also widely used and vinegar may also be made from champagne or even honey. There are also differently flavoured or coloured vinegars (e.g. using beetroot (red beet) or caramel).

☐ **Varieties of vinegar** Some French vinegars traditionally produced by craftsmen are still made, including *vinaigre vieux à l'ancienne* and *vinaigre d'Orléans*; these are obtained by pouring red or white wine into oak casks already containing the *souche*, a small quantity of vinegar always kept in the cask. The vinegar drawn off is filtered and bottled, sometimes after ageing in a cask; it is fresh and perfumed, acid but without bitterness. Sherry vinegar, also made by craftsmen, is a little more full-bodied. It is these traditional vinegars which are often aromatized, using tarragon, basil, garlic, shallot, lemon, raspberry, or even rose and elderflowers (making *rosat* and *surard* vinegars). In Britain flavoured vinegars, especially those flavoured with herbs or garlic, are also popular.

Malt vinegar (particularly popular in Britain) is obtained from malted barley and is very mild; cider vinegar is also mild and golden in colour. Other vinegars are made from maple, rice, and even milk (in Switzerland).

Industrially produced wine vinegar is made in 24 hours with red or white wine, which is brewed with beech-wood shavings soaked in vinegar, a quick method (called the 'German method') which gives a pungent unperfumed product. Spirit vinegar is obtained by forcing air into a mixture of vinegar and beetroot alcohol; it is colourless or tinted with caramel.

☐ **Uses of vinegar** Essential in the preparation of mustards, cold sauces, and vinaigrettes (in which it is sometimes replaced by, or mixed with, lemon juice), vinegar also plays a major role in cooked reduced sauces and in deglazing. It is indispensable for sweet-and-sour preparations and for marinades and conserves (pickles, fruit and vegetable chutneys, etc.).

Different types of vinegar have different uses. Spirit vinegar is used to clean fish and mushrooms; it is also used to prepare cocktail onions and gherkins. White-wine vinegar is suitable for seasoning endive, cos (romaine) lettuce, and chicory, for meat, game, and fish marinades, to prepare *beurre blanc* (white butter sauce) and hollandaise and béarnaise sauces, and to finish noisette butter, as well as for deglazing. The traditional French white-wine vinegar is preferred for making aromatized vinegar at home.

Red-wine vinegar is preferable for seasoning delicate or rather flavourless salads (e.g. lettuce), as it has a more pronounced taste. It is used to cook red cabbage, and a trickle of this pink vinegar also improves fried calf's liver, sanguette, red meat dishes, pepper sauce, or even eggs *sur le plat*.

Cider vinegar, like white-wine vinegar, is used in fish and shellfish court-bouillons; it is also used for chicken in vinegar, dressings, and even in stewed apples. Malt vinegars are often preferred for marinated mackerel or herring, chutneys, and salads in which fruits and vegetables are mixed (sweetcorn, grapefruit, apples, walnuts, etc.).

☐ **Home-made vinegar** The method consists of pouring some good-quality white or red wine into a cask and placing delicately on the surface a piece of vinegar mother; the vessel is then sealed with a paper stopper (to allow air to pass) and left at room temperature for a minimum of one month and a maximum of two. The vinegar may then be drawn off as required and replaced by an equal quantity of wine. If a vinegar mother is unobtainable, wine vinegar should be mixed with red wine in equal proportions (or cider vinegar with non-pasteurized cider) and then left, as before, for acetification to take place; in this case, however, it will take at least three or four months for the vinegar to be produced. The vinegar mother should always stay on the surface, without mixing with the alcohol. The cask should never be placed in a wine cellar.

RECIPES

Herb vinegar VINAIGRE AUX HERBES Peel and slice 2 small onions and 2 shallots and blanch for 30 seconds in boiling water with 5 chives. Cool and wipe them and place in a 1-litre (1¾-pint) bottle of traditional French wine vinegar. Leave to macerate for a month before use.

Raspberry vinegar VINAIGRE FRAMBOISÉ Pour into a stoneware jug 2 litres (3½ pints, 4½ pints) red-wine vinegar and as many cleaned raspberries as it will hold. Leave to macerate for 8 days, then strain through a very fine sieve or jelly bag, without pressing the fruit, and decant into bottles.

Rose vinegar VINAIGRE ROSAT Put 100 g (4 oz) red rose petals in 1 litre (1¾ pints, 4¼ cups) red-wine vinegar and leave to macerate for 10 days. Strain and bottle.

Tarragon vinegar VINAIGRE À L'ESTRAGON Blanch 2 sprigs of tarragon for 10 seconds in boiling water; cool, wipe dry, and place in a 1-litre (1¾-pint) bottle of white-wine vinegar. Leave to macerate for a month before use.

vin gris

Very pale rosé wine made only in small quantities. The term is sometimes used for other pale-toned rosé wines.

vin jaune

Yellow AOC wine from the Jura, coming from Château-Chalon, Arbois, L'Étoile, and several other regions. The grapes, all Savagnin, are picked late and the wine is put into oak casks which are then sealed. The wine stays in the casks for a minimum of six years, during which time a yeast film forms on the surface of the wine, similar to *flor* on sherry. This method results in an unusual dry wine, yellow in colour, of slightly more than table-wine strength, and with an odd flavour, described as 'nutty' by some. Good vintages will 'fill out' in the mouth. Vin jaune keeps admirably, even for many years. It is one of the few white wines drunk at room temperature. In cooking, it may be best known for *coq au vin jaune*, a speciality of Franche-Comté.

violet VIOLETTE

A small perennial plant whose purple flowers, when newly opened, may be used to decorate salads or in stuffings for poultry or fish. The sweet violet, a common European species, was formerly used in a cough medicine; nowadays, it is used mainly in confectionery and preserves. Crystallized (candied) violets are a speciality of Toulouse and are popular in Britain: the complete flowers are immersed in sugar syrup, sometimes coloured, which is allowed to come up to the boil. After crystallization they are drained and dried, then used as decoration or to aromatize desserts, sometimes with crystallized mimosa flowers. Sweets (candies) can be made with cooked sugar perfumed with essence of violets and coloured and moulded in the shape of violets.

RECIPE

Violet soufflé SOUFFLÉ AUX VIOLETTES Prepare a dessert soufflé mixture and flavour it with 5–6 drops of essence of violets before folding in the stiffly whisked egg whites. Add a dozen chopped crystallized (candied) violets and complete the soufflé.

Viroflay

The name of a spinach dish consisting of subrics (a kind of croquette) made with spinach purée, wrapped in blanched spinach leaves, then coated with Mornay sauce and browned in the oven. Spinach subrics also feature in the Viroflay garnish to accompany large joints of roast meat served with thickened gravy, quartered sautéed artichoke hearts, and château potatoes.

visitandine

A small round or boat-shaped cake, made of a rich mixture of egg whites, ground almonds, butter, and sugar. After cooking, it is sometimes glazed with apricot jam and iced (frosted) with fondant flavoured with Kirsch. Visitandines, which were first made in monasteries, were invented as a means of using up surplus egg whites.

␣ RECIPE

Visitandines Mix 500 g (18 oz, 2¼ cups) caster (superfine) sugar and 500 g (18 oz, 4½ cups) ground almonds. Add 150 g (5 oz, 1¼ cups) sieved flour, then mix in 12 very lightly beaten egg whites little by little, stirring in well, and finally 750 g (scant 1¾ lb, scant 3½ cups) melted butter (barely tepid). To finish, add 4 stiffly whisked egg whites. Fill buttered barquette moulds with small quantities of the mixture, using a piping (pastry) bag with a large smooth nozzle. Place in the oven at 220 c (425 F, gas 7) and cook for about 10 minutes or just long enough for the cakes to be browned and the insides soft.

vitamin VITAMINE

An organic substance contained in foods and indispensable for healthy growth and development. The quantities of vitamins required are very small (see table) but it is vital that they be provided in the diet, daily if possible (since few vitamins are stored by the body), or disorders will result. Vitamin deficiencies can be serious but are rare providing food is balanced and varied.

The concept of the vitamin dates only from the end of the 19th century. In a Java penitentiary, a Dutch doctor, Christiaan Eijckmann, observed that the incidence of beriberi increased with a diet consisting entirely of white rice, from which he deduced that whole rice contained a preventive factor. This factor, isolated in 1911, was given the name *vitamin* ('amine necessary to life') but it was later discovered that not all vitamins are amines. Many illnesses are now known to be caused by vitamin

deficiency, including scurvy, beriberi, pellagra, etc.

Vitamins are classified as water-soluble (C, and the B vitamins) or fat-soluble A, D, E, and K). The latter are found mainly in meat, milk, milk products, and fats, while the former are in fruits, vegetables, and meat; as the water-soluble vitamins pass into the water when the food is soaked or cooked in water, it is desirable, when possible, to use the cooking liquid.

viveur

Now a synonym for 'reveller' or 'gay dog', this term was used, mainly in the 19th century, to describe various fairly rich or spiced culinary preparations: viveurs or des viveurs soup is a chicken consommé seasoned with cayenne, garnished with fine strips of celery, and served with paprika diablotins. It may also be coloured with beetroot (red beet) juice and garnished with small poultry quenelles. Viveur omelette is made with celeriac (celery root), artichoke hearts, and beef cut into small dice.

␣ RECIPE

Viveur omelette OMELETTE VIVEUR Cook 2 artichoke hearts in white stock, drain them, and cut into dice. Boil 2 tablespoons (3 tablespoons) diced celeriac (celery root) in salted water and drain. Cut 100 g (4 oz) beef fillet into small cubes, salt them, and dust with cayenne. Sauté all these ingredients in butter in a large frying pan (skillet) and pour over them 8 beaten eggs, seasoned with salt and pepper. Make into a flat omelette and serve very hot.

Vladimir WLADIMIR

A name given to various dishes dating from the Edwardian era, probably dedicated to a grand duke of this name. Turbot or sole Vladimir are poached, coated with white-wine sauce containing crushed tomatoes and poached clams, then glazed in the oven. Small cuts of meat Vladimir are sautéed, garnished with small pieces of braised cucumber and diced sautéed courgettes (zucchini), and covered with a sauce

The principal vitamins

vitamin	role	daily requirement	principal sources
fat-soluble			
A (retinol)	Required for healthy skin; essential for good vision, particularly at night; resistance to infection	750 μg	Liver, butter, egg yolk, milk, carrots, tomatoes, spinach, fruits
D (calciferol)	Enhances intestinal absorption of calcium; regulates metabolism of calcium in the body; essential for healthy bone formation	Very variable according to age; 10 μg for children and pregnant women	Mainly formed in the skin through the action of sunlight; fish liver oil
E (tocopherol)	Prevents oxidation of polyunsaturated fatty acids in cell membranes	10–12 mg	Wheatgerm, vegetable oils, margarine, eggs, butter
K	Required for blood coagulation	Normally synthesized by intestinal bacteria	Green vegetables, liver, eggs
water-soluble			
B₁ (thiamine)	Required for metabolism of carbohydrates	1.3–1.5 mg	Yeast, dried vegetables, liver, pork, whole cereals, milk, eggs, cheese
B₂ (riboflavin)	Involved in many metabolic processes	1.5–1.8 mg	Offal, meat, fish, milk, cheese
B₆ (pyridoxine)	Vital for healthy tissues	Deficiency rare	Green vegetables, meat, whole grains
B₁₂ (cyanocobalamin)	Required for formation of red blood cells (prevents pernicious anaemia)	3–4 mg	Liver, meat
C (ascorbic acid)	Required for healthy connective tissues (prevents scurvy); aids resistance to infection	30 mg	Citrus fruits, herbs, fresh vegetables

made of the cooking liquid deglazed with soured (dairy sour) cream and seasoned with paprika and grated horseradish; this preparation is reminiscent of Russian cookery. Eggs *sur le plat* Vladimir are fried, then sprinkled with Parmesan and garnished with diced truffles and asparagus tips.

voandzeia

A variety of bean, also called groundnut or (in French) *pois arachide*, with yellow pods containing round edible seeds, very rich in starch and protein. It has considerable economic importance in tropical Africa, where it is widely used as food, being one of the most nutritive vegetable products (367 Cal per 100 g). It has also been introduced into Central America.

vodka

An alcoholic drink made from grain, molasses, potatoes, or various other vegetables that are available for distillation. It probably originated in Poland (although the Soviet Union often disputes this) and is now made in many countries, including the UK. Vodka (a Russian word derived from *voda*, 'water') goes through the distillation and rectification in a continuous process. It is a neutral spirit and basically has neither taste nor smell. It is mainly appreciated for the stimulus given by the alcohol.

Various vodkas may be flavoured with spices (such as pepper), plants, leaves, or fruits (such as lemons). From Poland, for example, comes *zubrowka*, made of a maceration of grasses called 'bison grass', mentioned by Somerset Maugham in his novel *The Razor's Edge* as a drink which 'smells of freshly mown hay and spring flowers'.

Vodka is now an international drink, often served with caviar and smoked fish (especially herring). It is also used to flame various fish preparations and a special sweet omelette, and to deglaze certain dishes, particularly poultry.

The West was slow to take to vodka, but in recent years it has become enormously popular in the United States. It is used in a variety of mixes, including Bloody Mary (vodka and tomato juice).

Vodka fizz Mix 1 tablespoon sugar and 1 measure of vodka in a tumbler, add pineapple juice, and finish off with carbonated mineral water. Mix well. Serve with ice cubes and a swizzle stick.

voiler

A French cookery term meaning to coat certain pastries or iced desserts with a veil of sugar, consisting of fine threads of sugar cooked to the 'hard crack' stage.

Voisin

A restaurant in the Rue Saint-Honoré in Paris, considered to be one of the foremost in the capital between 1850 and 1930.

Its first manager was Bellanger, who set up a cellar of reputable Burgundies. The menu of the Christmas Eve midnight feast in 1870, consisting of the choicest meat of animals from the Paris Zoo, has remained famous: elephant consommé, civet of kangaroo, haunch of wolf with roebuck sauce, antelope terrine with truffles, etc. Taken over by Braquessac, who came from Bordeaux, the restaurant kept up its reputation with its chef, Choron, who created, among other things, a béarnaise sauce with tomatoes. Daudet, the Goncourts, and Zola were regular customers, as was the Prince of Wales.

In *Un gastronome se penche sur son passé*, S. Arbellot mentions the Voisin as the most exclusive restaurant in Paris: 'Rumours were put about well calculated to discourage undesirables: only whole animals are served, Château-Lafite is drunk only in magnums.' In his *Guide des restaurants de Paris* (1925), Cousin classifies it in his 'perfection' class, with the note: 'No specialities, everything is recommended', but several enthusiasts selected its partridge salmis with sherry and its saddle of lamb as being particularly worthy of mention. Its name is still used for a timbale of duckling fillets with truffles in aspic.

Duck Voisin CANARD VOISIN Roast a duckling so that the meat remains slightly pink (about 30 minutes at

230 c, 450 f, gas 8). Let it get completely cold, then remove the fillets. Break up the carcass and trimmings and use these to prepare a salmis. Strain the salmis, remove the fat, and add to it an equal quantity of meat aspic. Reduce and strain. Place a layer of this sauce in a timbale mould; when it has set, place on top a layer of finely sliced duckling fillets. Coat them with more of the sauce, then cover with a layer of sliced truffle. Continue to fill the timbale with alternating layers of duck and truffle, coating each layer with a little half-set aspic. Finish with a layer of aspic. Place in the refrigerator until set. Turn out and serve very cold.

vol-au-vent

A round case of puff pastry, 15–20 cm (6–8 in) in diameter, having a pastry lid. The vol-au-vent is filled after baking and served as a hot entrée or hors d'oeuvre. Its invention is attributed to Carême, who had the idea of replacing a shortcrust pastry case with puff pastry of such delicacy that 'it flew away in the wind (*s'envola au vent*) on coming out of the oven'. The celebrated chef also said: 'This entrée is attractive and undoubtedly very good; it is almost always eaten with pleasure on account of its extreme delicacy and lightness.'

The filling for a vol-au-vent is bound with sauce; there are many different kinds: *à la financière*, *à la reine*, *à la bénédictine*, *à la toulousaine*, *à la Nantua*, seafood, mushrooms in béchamel sauce, sole fillets, poultry or veal quenelles, veal sweetbreads, or escalopes, sliced chicken fillets, lobster escalopes, salmon, etc. Purées of shellfish, chicken, or game finished with a salpicon of the basic ingredient can also be used, and even spaghetti in tomato sauce with diced ham. The classic presentations, however, are vols-au-vent *financière* and *marinière*.

Both the filling and the pastry case must be very hot, and the filling takes place at the last moment, so as not to soak the pastry. The vol-au-vent is served immediately, though it may be placed briefly in the oven to reheat after filling.

The classic vol-au-vent has been adapted to modern tastes. Individual ones are now popular and bite-sized cocktail ones are often made to serve with drinks (see *bouchée*).

RECIPE

Vol-au-vent case   CROÛTE À VOL-AU-VENT   Prepare 500 g (18 oz) fine puff pastry. Divide it into 2 equal parts and roll out each one to a thickness of 4 mm (¼ in). From each part cut a disc 15 cm (6 in) in diameter, using a flan ring (pie pan) as a guide. Place one of the discs on a slightly dampened baking sheet. Using a 12–13-cm (4¾–5-in) pastry (cookie) cutter, remove the centre of the second disc, leaving a border of even width all around. Dampen the top of the first disc and place the border of the second one on top, turning it over.

Roll the cut-out circle of pastry to the same size as the vol-au-vent, again cutting round the 15-cm (6-in) flan ring. Dampen the border of the vol-au-vent and place this third layer on top. Glaze the surface with beaten egg then, with a small knife, trace the circumference of the lid (around the inner 12–13-cm (4¾–5-in) circle), following the shape of the central 'well'. Perforate the circular border (to aid removal after cooking) and score the top of the lid.

Bake in a hot oven (220 c, 425 f, gas 7) for about 15 minutes until well-risen and golden-brown. After taking it out of the oven, place the vol-au-vent on a wire tray; carefully cut out the lid without breaking it, place it on the wire tray, and remove the soft pastry from the inside of the vol-au-vent. Keep hot. Reheat the filling, fill the case with it, place the lid on top, and serve very hot.

volière (en)

Describing a very decorative method of presenting game birds, particularly pheasant and woodcock. This method was in common use up to the 19th century but is now obsolete. On the cooked bird, the head, tail, and outspread wings were placed in position and fixed on with small wooden pegs. In the Middle Ages, peacocks, swans, and herons were presented *en volière* and a piece of burning tow was placed in their beaks. Under the Ancien Régime various game birds, complete with their feathers, were served on a large silver dish and presented as *chasse royale* (royal hunt).

Volnay

An AOC red Burgundy wine from the Côte de Beaune. The white wines produced here are sold as Meursault. The favourite wine of Louis XI, Volnay is famous for its elegance, quality, and charming bouquet.

Vosne-Romanée

AOC red Burgundy wines of the Côte de Nuits; the best, counted among the greatest red wines in the world, are sold under their own AOCs: Romanée-Conti, Richebourg, Romanée, La Tâche, Romanée-Saint-Vivant, Echez-eaux, and Grands-Échezaux. The small size of the vineyard unfortunately makes these wines rare and very expensive, but when successful, they can be superb memorable Burgundies, with great style and elegance.

Vouvray

AOC white wines from the Loire Valley near Tours. Made from the Chenin Blanc and Arbois grapes (mostly the former), Vouvray may be still, *pétillant* (slightly sparkling), or *mousseux* (fully sparkling), and often ages in cellars dug into the limestone. It can vary from dry to very sweet, depending on both the year and the maker and on how long it is allowed to mature. The great sweet Vouvrays are outstanding wines, and the wines made by certain individual growers have charm and distinction, in all the categories. Much Vouvray, however, is bought by large wine-making establishments who may achieve a consistent pleasant style but rarely anything outstanding.

Vuillemot (Denis-Joseph)

French chef (born Crépy-en-Valois, 1811; died Saint-Cloud, 1876). Son and grandson of maîtres d'hôtel, he started his apprenticeship under Véry, became the pupil of Carême, then set up on his own account at Crépy, and later at Compiègne. He then assumed the management of the Restaurant de France at the Place de la Madeleine in Paris, and finished his career at the Hôtel de la Tête-Noire, at Saint-Cloud.

A long-standing friend of Alexandre Dumas, he was his technical associate for the recipes in the *Grand Dictionnaire de la cuisine* (1873). He also organized a banquet in the novelist's honour on his return from Russia, which has remained famous for its culinary creations, all bearing names evoking the titles of Dumas' works: soups *à la Buckingham* and *aux Mohicans*, trout *à la Henri III*, lobster *à la Porthos*, fillet of beef *à la Monte-Cristo*, bouchées *à la reine Margot*, bombe *à la dame de Monsoreau*, salad *à la Dumas*, gâteau *à la Gorenflot*, crème *à la reine Christine*, etc.

wafer GAUFRETTE

A small very crisp light biscuit made of a dough similar to that for waffles but less runny. Wafers are mainly produced industrially. They can be plain, shaped like a fan, rolled up like cigarettes, or filled with jam or praline cream. Wafer dough is also used to make ice-cream cornets. See also *oublie*.

RECIPE

Dutch wafers GAUFRETTES HOLLANDAISES Make a well in 250 g (9 oz, 2¼ cups) sifted flour and add 125 g (4¼ oz, generous cup) sugar, a pinch of salt, and the chosen flavouring (vanilla, cinnamon, or orange or lemon zest). Add an egg white, then 125 g (4½ oz, generous ½ cup) softened butter, and mix all the ingredients. Shape the dough into a ball and cook as for waffles.

waffle GAUFRE

A thin light batter cooked on the stove between the two buttered and heated plates of a waffle iron. The waffle is made of flour, butter, sugar, eggs, and water or milk, with a flavouring (usually vanilla or orange-flower water, but sometimes cinnamon, aniseed, brandy, or citrus fruit zest).

The ancient Greeks used to cook very flat cakes, which they called *obelios*, between two hot metal plates. This method of cooking continued to be used in the Middle Ages by the *obloyeurs* who made all sorts of *oublies*, which were flat or rolled into cornets. The *oublie* became the waffle in the 13th century, when a craftsman had the idea of forging some cooking plates reproducing the characteristic pattern of honeycombs, which at that time were called *gaufres* (from the Old French *wāfla*).

Waffles, like fritters and pancakes, were one of the most common foods in country cooking. Sometimes they were simply made of flour and water or milk. The richer country people added eggs, *cassonade* (semirefined sugar) or honey, sugar, and aromatized wine. Nowadays each area has its own recipe for waffles. They can even be savoury, made with ham, cheese, or pumpkin. The dough can be enriched with fresh cream or butter, or made lighter with whisked egg whites.

Waffles from the central regions of France are delicate and crunchy and can be kept in a tin. In Champagne and Franche-Comté the waffles are very crisp and sprinkled with sugar. The waffles of northern France, called *étrennes*, are thick and greasy and eaten hot. The batter contains a lot of butter and fresh cream, and the flour is mixed with milk rather than water.

Waffles, like pancakes, continue to be sold in the street and at fairs, particularly in the northern provinces of France and Flanders.

Waffles are usually eaten hot, sprinkled with sugar, and accompanied by whipped cream or jam. They can also be filled.

RECIPES

Waffles GAUFRES In a large earthenware bowl sift 500 g (18 oz, 4½ cups) plain flour with 2 teaspoons bicarbonate of soda (baking soda), 4 teaspoons baking powder, and 10 g (2 teaspoons) salt. Add 30–40 g (1–1½ oz, 2–3 tablespoons) caster (superfine) sugar, 150 g (5 oz, ⅔ cup) melted butter, 5 beaten eggs, and 8 dl (1⅓ pints, 3¼ cups) milk (or more, if very light waffles are preferred). Mix well until batter is runny and completely smooth. Leave to stand for 1–2 hours, as for pancake batter. Heat and, if necessary, grease the waffle mould. Pour a small ladle of batter in one half of the open waffle iron. Close the mould and turn it over so that the batter is distributed equally in both halves. Leave to cook. Open the waffle iron, take out the waffle, sprinkle with icing (confectioners') sugar, and serve.

Filled waffles GAUFRES FOURRÉES Mix 15 g (½ oz, ½ cake) fresh (compressed) yeast or 1½ teaspoons dried yeast with 3 dl (½ pint, 1¼ cups) tepid water. Blend in 500 g (18 oz, 4½ cups) flour, then add 125 g (4½ oz, generous ½ cup) butter, 40 g (1½ oz, 3 tablespoons) caster (superfine) sugar, and 10 g (2 teaspoons) salt and knead to obtain a smooth dough. Leave to prove (rise) under a cloth overnight. Then shape it into little balls and again leave to rise on a floured board for 1–2 hours.

When the balls have doubled in size, heat the waffle iron, grease it if necessary, place a ball of dough in it, close it, and leave to cook. As soon as the waffle has turned brown, take it out, slice it in two horizontally, and leave to cool completely. Do the same with the other balls. In a warm basin, whip together 250 g (9 oz, generous cup) butter, 200 g (7 oz, 1½ cups) icing (confectioners') sugar, and 200 g (7 oz) praline. Use to fill the waffles.

Liège waffles GAUFRES LIÉGEOISES Take 500 g (18 oz, 4½ cups) sifted flour. Mix 15 g (½ oz, ½ cake) fresh (compressed) yeast or 1½ teaspoons dried yeast with 125 ml (4 fl oz, ½ cup) tepid water and blend with a quarter of the flour. Leave to rise until it has doubled in size. Then add the rest of the flour, a generous pinch of salt, 125 g (4½ oz, generous ½ cup) caster (superfine) sugar, 4 beaten eggs, and 200 g (7 oz, scant cup) softened butter. Mix well. Work the dough with the palm of the hand. Divide it into balls (the size of an egg). Roll into the shape of sausages. Leave to stand on a floured board for 30 minutes. Heat the waffle iron and, if necessary, grease it. Put one of the sausage shapes between the plates, close the waffle iron, and leave to cook. Serve the waffle lukewarm or cold, sprinkled with icing (confectioners') sugar.

waffle iron GAUFRIER

A hinged cast-iron mould, consisting of two honeycomb-patterned plates between which waffle batter is cooked.

Hand-operated waffle irons, of which the oldest date back to the 15th century, are sometimes veritable masterpieces, richly adorned with designs and engraved with coats of arms, crosses, religious or magic symbols, etc. They are placed over a heat source (glowing embers, electric hotplate, or burner) and are turned over halfway through cooking. They are equipped with long handles.

Nowadays, waffle irons are often electric. They are fitted with a thermostat and sometimes have a nonstick coating so that the plates do not need to be greased and the waffles can be taken out of the mould more easily. Some models have a set of interchangeable plates so that toasted sandwiches, grills, and even pancakes can also be made in them.

Waldorf

A mixed salad consisting of diced apple and celeriac (celery root) or celery and shelled green (fresh) walnuts, dressed with a thin mayonnaise. Banana slices are sometimes added. It is named after the prestigious New York hotel, the Waldorf Astoria.

This name has also been given to a dish of marinated conger eel fillets, floured, grilled (broiled), and sprinkled with melted butter. It is served with small baked potatoes and a mayonnaise américaine (with mustard and the coral of a lobster or langouste added).

Walewska (à la)

The name given to fish poached in a fumet, garnished with slices of lobster (or other crustacean) and thinly sliced truffle, coated with Mornay sauce finished with lobster butter, and glazed in the oven. This dish, typical of the rich cuisine of the Second Empire, appears to have been dedicated to Count Walewski, natural son of Napoleon I and Marie Walewska, who was ambassador in London and Minister for Foreign Affairs under Napoleon II.

RECIPE

Fillets of sole à la Walewska FILETS DE SOLE À LA WALEWSKA Poach some sole fillets in a fish fumet for 5 minutes, using very little liquid. Arrange on a long ovenproof dish and on each fillet place a slice of lobster or langouste flesh (cooked in court-bouillon) and a slice of raw truffle. Coat with Mornay sauce containing 1 tablespoon lobster or langouste butter to every 1.5 dl (¼ pint, ⅔ cup) sauce. Glaze quickly in a very hot oven.

walnut NOIX

The fruit of the walnut tree, consisting of a hard-shelled nut surrounded by an outer green fleshy husk, called a shuck. The delicious kernel is shaped like the two halves of a brain (the reason why the ancient Greeks and Romans believed that walnuts cured headaches). The kernel comprises 35–50% of the total weight, depending on the quality of the nut. It is covered with a fine skin, light- to dark-yellow in colour, and the

kernel is white, turning greyish with age. Some thin-shelled varieties can be crushed in the hand, but normally a nutcracker is required.

Grown originally on the shores of the Caspian Sea and in northern India, walnuts were valued by the Greeks for their oil. The Romans extended cultivation of the walnut tree to other parts of Europe and from the 4th century it was cultivated in the Grésivaudan region of France. Nowadays, French walnuts are grown mainly in Périgord and Dauphiné. The name 'noix de Grenoble', an *appellation d'origine*, can be applied to any of the three best-known varieties – Franquette, Mayette, or Parisienne (delicate and fruity, the most sought-after dessert walnut) – and guarantees their place of origin, quality, and flavour. The main variety grown in Périgord is Corne; others are Marbot and Grandjean. They are usually sold shelled.

From mid-September to around All Saints' Day (1 November), dehusked fresh walnuts are sold in France: they should be eaten within a fortnight of harvesting and kept in a wicker basket in a cool place, never in the refrigerator, where the oil they contain would harden and destroy their flavour. Later in the season, as they mature, the husk falls off and the nuts are sold dried. If the kernels are soaked in milk overnight they will regain their fresh flavour. Walnuts have a very high calorific content (650 Cal per 100 g); they are also rich in fats and protein and are a good source of phosphorus and vitamins B and D. They are therefore an important item in vegetarian diets.

Walnuts are used chiefly in cakes and pastries, either as an ingredient (ground or chopped) or as a decoration (half kernels). But they are also used in salads; with meat, poultry, or fish dishes (especially with chicken, salt cod, and snails); and for flavouring sauces (for pasta), forcemeats (for pâtés or rissoles), and savoury butter. They can also be prepared with verjuice or preserved in vinegar (pickled walnuts). Walnut oil, with its fruity taste, is reserved for flavouring salads. Ratafias and liqueurs (especially *brou de noix*) are made from the shucks, and there are also walnut-flavoured wines.

RECIPES

Cream soup with walnuts POTAGE CRÈME AUX NOIX Blend 1 egg yolk into 1 litre (1¾ pints, 4¼ cups) chicken stock. Peel some fresh walnuts, pound them in a mortar, and add them to the soup. Finish with a little double (heavy) cream.

Green walnuts in verjuice CERNEAUX DE NOIX AU VERJUS Clean some fresh green (i.e. unripe) walnuts without breaking them, place them in cold water, drain and dry them, sprinkle with coarse salt, then pour over some verjuice (the acid juice of unripe grapes). Scatter some chopped herbs over the walnuts and serve with cold meat, such as roast veal or pork.

Pheasant with walnuts FAISAN AUX NOIX Pound together 60 peeled fresh walnut kernels, 3 Petit-Suisse cheeses (or 3 oz cream cheese), ½ wine glass grape juice, the juice of 1 lemon, a few drops of port, ½ cup very strong tea, salt, and pepper. Stuff a pheasant with this mixture. Brown the pheasant in butter, then season with salt and pepper, cover the pan, and cook until tender (about 40 minutes).

Pickled walnuts NOIX AU VINAIGRE Choose fairly large green walnuts with husks that can easily be pierced with a pin. Wipe them and prick deeply all over. Marinate the nuts for 3 days in brine, made with 100 g (4 oz, 1 cup) salt per litre (1¾ pints, generous quart) water, then bring them to the boil. Repeat this operation 3 times, marinating the nuts for 3 days between each boiling. Then drain the walnuts and put them into jars. Boil 5 litres (4½ quarts, 5½ quarts) vinegar for 15 minutes with 80 g (3 oz, ¾ cup) black peppercorns, 35 g (1½ oz, ⅓ cup) fennel flower, 35 g (1½ oz, ⅓ cup) cloves, 35 g (1½ oz, ⅓ cup) mace, and 40 g (1½ oz, ¾ cup) crushed root ginger. Fill the jars to the top with boiling spiced vinegar, ensuring that the walnuts are completely covered. Seal the jars and store them in a cool place. Serve with cold meat, ham, etc.

Scampi with walnuts LANGOUS-TINES AUX NOIX Soak the walnut kernels in cold water overnight. Dry, peel, and fry quickly in hot oil, then drain them and keep hot. Season some shelled scampi with white wine, fresh ginger juice, salt, and pepper. Roll them in flour and fry in very hot oil. In another pan, quickly fry some green onion stalks. Turn all these ingredients out on a hot dish, mix together, and sprinkle with stock to which white wine, soy sauce, and ground ginger have been added.

Walnut cake GÂTEAU AUX NOIX Cream 125 g (4½ oz, generous ½ cup) butter, then whisk in 300 g (11 oz, 1½ cups) caster (superfine) sugar, 5 eggs (one by one), 125 g (4½ oz, generous 1 cup) ground almonds, and 125 g (4½ oz) ground green walnut kernels. Then fold in 2 tablespoons (3 tablespoons) rum and 80 g (3 oz, ¾ cup) sifted flour and mix well until smooth. Butter a 20-cm (8-in) sandwich tin (layer cake pan), line the base with a circle of buttered greaseproof (waxed) paper, and transfer the mixture to the tin. Bake for 35–40 minutes in a moderately hot oven (200 C, 400 F, gas 6). Allow the cake to cool in the tin before turning it out. Decorate the top with walnut halves.

Walnut surprises NOIX EN SUR-PRISE In a heavy-based saucepan heat 250 g (9 oz, generous cup) granulated sugar, 7.5 dl (1¼ pints, 3 cups) water, and 25 g (1 oz) glucose. When the temperature reaches 115 C (240 F), take the pan off the heat and add, all at once, 125 g (4½ oz, generous cup) ground almonds. Stir until the mixture acquires a sandy texture, then knead it by hand, blending in 5 drops of coffee essence (strong black coffee). Roll the paste out into a long thin sausage and cut it into 50 equal slices; roll each slice into a ball and flatten it slightly; moisten each side and press in a walnut half. Store in a cool place. To serve, put each petit four into a pleated paper case.

warbler BECFIGUE

A small songbird of which there are many species, including the garden warbler and blackcap. During the autumn migration, they cross the south of France when the figs and grapes are ripe and eat the seeds. Brillat-Savarin was particularly enthusiastic about them, although they were already appreciated in Roman times. Once hunted to excess, they are now a protected species.

washing LAVER

Any impurities in food (sand, soil, insects, etc.) are removed by immersion in cold water. Vegetables – especially root vegetables – need to be washed several times to remove all traces of soil, especially if they are to be eaten raw. A little vinegar may be added to the water. Lettuce is among the vegetables that need several washes, but this should be done with care to avoid damaging the leaves. Some very delicate items (such as cultivated mushrooms and raspberries) are simply wiped.

Washington

A garnish for poached or braised chicken consisting of boiled sweetcorn bound with very thick cream. The name is somewhat paradoxical, since although maize (corn) is considered the national cereal of the United States, George Washington is renowned for having encouraged the growing of wheat!

water EAU

Water accounts for about two-thirds of an adult's weight and is essential for almost every physiological process: man can survive for several weeks without food but only for a few ways without water. The average adult must consume about 40 ml water per kg of the body's weight (2½ tablespoons per lb).

Drinking water must be clear, odourless, and above all free of dangerous bacteria (rainwater often contains impurities suspended in the atmosphere). It must also have the correct proportions of calcium salts, magnesium, phosphates, carbonates, etc., and it must be aerated, i.e. it must contain dissolved oxygen. Insufficiently aerated water is said to be 'heavy'. If water is too hard (i.e. contains too much calcium), it is less suitable for cooking vegetables. If water contains a large proportion of mineral salts, it may have a salty, alkaline, earthy, bitter, or brackish taste.

Water piped to our homes is chemically treated nowadays, and often has a slight taste of chlorine. Water from a natural spring, when pure and balanced, is considered to be the best.

Mineral waters contain variable proportions of minerals. They are subject to health control, and some of them are excellent table waters. Sold in glass or plastic bottles, they are becoming very popular in many parts of the world. These should not be confused with sparkling waters, which have had pure gases added to them and are used widely with apéritifs. True mineral waters have therapeutic properties, come from authorized springs, and generally contain carbon dioxide and mineral salts.

Water is not only the ideal dietary drink, it is also an essential raw material for the beer and fruit-juice industries in particular. Moreover, it plays an essential part in cookery (for boiling, and in soups, stocks, and stews). It is also used for making beverages, notably tea and coffee.

water carrier
PORTEUR D'EAU

Large houses and princely residences were the first to have private water sources, at least their own wells, but the rest of the population had to make do with public fountains which were few and unevenly distributed. It was not until 1860, under the auspices of Baron Haussmann, that these fountains began to be systematically sited in Paris, heralding the gradual installation of running water to buildings. Before this, people relied on the services of the water carriers.

A team of 58 water carriers was mentioned in a fiscal document of 1292. They bore a yoke on their shoulders, at the ends of which hung two buckets. When a customer replied to their cry of 'Who wants water? It's everyone's right, it's one of the four elements', they carried the water upstairs to him. They used the water of the Seine but were not allowed to draw water between the Place Maubert and the Pont-Neuf 'because of the infection and impurity of the stagnant water'.

In the 18th century the yoke was replaced by a diagonal strap, with a lattice to hold the bucket in place away from the body; a round piece of wood floated on the surface of the water to reduce its movement while the carrier walked. The corporation had about 20,000 members. Two buckets of water cost two sous for the first two floors and three sous for higher floors. The office of water carrier was worth about 1200 livres at the time.

water chestnut

MACRE, MADI

The tuber of an aquatic plant originating in Southeast Asia, having a prickly coat enclosing crunchy white flesh with a delicate flavour. Water chestnuts are sold either fresh or canned and are used in Chinese and Vietnamese cooking to accompany hot fried dishes and to give texture to stuffings. They are often served as a garnish mixed with green vegetables and bamboo shoots. A popular dish is lotus leaves stuffed with water chestnuts and rice. The tuber can also be used fresh as a dessert or preserved in sugar.

watercress

See *cress, cressonière (à la)*.

waterfisch

A hot or cold sauce for freshwater fish, of Dutch origin. Hot waterfisch sauce (mainly for pike and perch) is made by cooking a julienne of vegetables in white wine until reduced, then moistening with court-bouillon, reducing once more, then adding hollandaise sauce and parsley.

Cold waterfisch sauce is an aspic jelly prepared with the court-bouillon of the fish it is accompanying, with the addition of a julienne of vegetables, sweet red pepper, gherkins, and capers; the fish is coated with the aspic, then decorated with thin strips of anchovy and served with rémoulade sauce.

RECIPES

Cold waterfisch sauce   SAUCE WATERFISCH FROIDE   Prepare a julienne of vegetables as for hot waterfisch sauce; moisten with 2 dl (7 fl oz, ¾ cup) of the court-bouillon used to cook the fish that the sauce is to accompany, and simmer until evaporated. Dissolve 2 leaves (¼ oz, 1 envelope)

gelatine in 2 dl (7 fl oz, ¾ cup) fish court-bouillon, add the vegetable julienne while still hot, then allow to cool. Add 1 tablespoon each of chopped gherkins, chopped sweet red pepper, and capers; mix together.

Hot waterfisch sauce   SAUCE WATERFISCH CHAUDE   Cut into very fine strips 50 g (2 oz) carrots, 25 g (1 oz) white part of leeks, 25 g (1 oz) celery, 30 g (1 oz) Hamburg parsley roots, and 2 teaspoons grated orange zest. Place the julienne in a saucepan, moisten with 2 dl (7 fl oz, ¾ cup) dry white wine, and boil until all the liquid has evaporated. Add 2 dl (7 fl oz, ¾ cup) fish court-bouillon made with white wine, and reduce completely once again. Prepare 5 dl (17 fl oz, 2 cups) hollandaise sauce and mix the vegetables into it, together with 1 tablespoon blanched chopped parsley sprigs. Keep hot in a bain-marie until ready to serve.

watermelon   PASTÈQUE

A large spherical or oval fruit, weighing 3–5 kg (6½–11 lb), with a dark green rind and pink flesh that is sweet and very refreshing but slightly insipid; the pulp is studded with large flat black seeds.

Of tropical origin, known since antiquity, the watermelon is grown in many countries, particularly Spain and parts of the United States. It has a high water content (92%), a low calorific value (30 Cal per 100 g), and contains vitamins B and C. When it is bought, it should be heavy and not sound hollow. It is generally cut into slices and eaten just as it is, to quench the thirst (it is sold in the streets in Mediterranean countries). When the seeds have been removed, watermelon pulp may be included in fruit salads (possibly served in the empty rind). In certain countries, it is picked when green and unripe and prepared like a vegetable marrow.

RECIPE

Watermelon à la provençale   PASTÈQUE À LA PROVENÇALE   Make a circular incision around the stalk of a ripe watermelon. Cut off the end and scoop out some flesh. Shake the fruit so that some of the seeds fall out. Fill the watermelon with Tavel wine, stop it up with the cut-off end, and seal it with wax. Place in the refrigerator for at least 2 hours. Just before serving, take off the end, strain the wine, cut the watermelon into slices, and serve it with the wine.

water parsnip   BERLE

A perennial herb with tuberous roots, which are prepared like salsify, and leaves which can be eaten in salads. Cultivated in Japan and China, water parsnips were introduced into Europe in the 16th century and were once highly esteemed as a vegetable; they have now practically disappeared.

waterzooï or waterzootje

WATERZOÏ

A Flemish speciality comprising freshwater fish and eel cooked in a court-bouillon with herbs, Hamburg parsley roots, and vegetables. The preparation is finished with a generous amount of butter and fresh cream and is sometimes thickened with breadcrumbs. Waterzooï (the word is formed from 'water' plus *ziedem*, to simmer) is also made in Ghent, using chicken.

RECIPES

Chicken waterzooï   WATERZOÏ DE POULET   Poach a chicken until three-quarters cooked (about 40 minutes) in a white stock containing an onion stuck with 2 cloves, a bouquet garni, and 1 stick (stalk) of celery and 1 leek, both sliced. Prepare a julienne of leek and celery and cook it in a flameproof casserole with some of the chicken stock, as for fish waterzooï. Cut the chicken into 8 pieces and arrange them on the julienne. Add sufficient stock to cover the chicken and cook for a further 30 minutes. Remove the chicken pieces and the vegetables with a slotted spoon; add to the casserole 2 dl (7 fl oz, ¾ cup) double (heavy) cream and reduce to a smooth sauce; adjust the seasoning. Replace the chicken and vegetables and serve from the casserole, accompanied with bread and butter or buttered toast.

Fish waterzooï   WATERZOÏ DE POISSONS   Cut 200 g (7 oz) white part of leeks and the same quantity of celery into fine strips; butter a large flameproof casserole and cover the base with the vegetables; add salt, pepper, and a bouquet garni containing 4 sage leaves. Add sufficient fish fumet (or court-bouillon) to cover 2 kg (4½ lb) fresh-water fish (about 1.25 litres, 2¼ pints, 5¼ cups) and add 100 g (4 oz, ½ cup) butter in small pieces. Cover and cook gently for about 30 minutes, then allow to cool. Meanwhile, clean the fish and cut into sections. Place them in the cold cooking liquid, adding a little more court-bouillon if necessary, partly cover the pan, bring to the boil, and poach for at least 20 minutes. Remove the fish with a slotted fish slice, discard the bouquet garni, and mix 2 dl (7 fl oz, ¾ cup) double (heavy) cream into the cooking liquid. Reduce this sauce, then replace the fish and reheat. Serve from the casserole, accompanied with bread and butter or slices of buttered toast.

Weber

A café-restaurant that opened in the Rue Royale in Paris in 1865; an 'American bar' was added in 1898. Léon Daudet paints a lively picture of it in *Paris vécu*: Caran d'Ache sported pink or butter-coloured suits there, in company with Forain; Welsh rarebit, a speciality of the house, was praised by Paul Mariéton, who wrote in the Provençal language, and the author Paul-Jean Toulet would sit at a table in front of a whisky and soda. 'On the stroke of midnight, a young gentleman with a fawnlike expression . . . entered proudly and asked for a bunch of grapes, or two pears, or two apples; it was Marcel Proust.' York ham and cold *boeuf mode* (stewed beef) were also served at Weber's, as well as *assiette anglaise* (a plate of cold meats), which was said to have originated there. Alphonse Daudet, F. Coppée, P. Déroulède, and General de Gallifet were regular customers, together with Curnonsky and A. Scholl. Considered a 'chic' restaurant until about 1935, the premises had a terrace frequented by fashionable society and the regular patrons of Maxim's. The restaurant closed in 1961.

wedding   MARIAGE

A social and religious event in which the ceremonial meal has a very important role. According to the New Testament, it was at a wedding feast (in Cana) that Jesus performed one of his miracles – turning the water into wine; this illustrates the importance of the wedding feast as a social gathering from the earliest times.

In former times, the festivities of the wedding feasts of the nobility and royalty lasted for several days. On these occasions, roast meat, cakes, and public fountains of wine were offered to the people. Marriages with princes or princesses from foreign lands were also occasions when new kinds of food were introduced into France (fruit and vegetables from Italy, chocolate from Spain, etc.).

More recently, in rural areas where ordinary fare was, until World War I, rather poor and monotonous, the wedding feast often lasted for several days and included a great variety of meat dishes.

In *Fêtes, Coutumes et Gâteaux* (N. Vielfaure and A. C. Beauviala; published by Christine Bonneton), the authors mention the wedding of a particularly affluent bridegroom in Lorraine: 'The first meal was for 150 guests, the festivities lasted for three days, and included 3 calves, 3 sheep, 75 kilos of beef, 12 sucking pigs, 20 geese, 3 batches of bread, 9 batches of oven-baked pies, and 24 *hottes* (i.e. nearly 1000 litres of wine).'

The most outstanding feature of wedding feasts is the cake or cakes, which are remarkable either for their size or their quantity. Nowadays in France, an ornamental tiered cake (*pièce montée*), topped by figurines representing the bridal couple, is very fashionable, but the wedding cakes of bygone days were more varied. In some parts of France the emphasis is on the variety and number of cakes: fruit, jam, or cheese tarts; small cakes and fritters (particularly in the south of France and in Corsica); brioches, crystallized (candied) fruit, and filled pastries; piles of wafers and waffles; etc.

In other regions it is the spectacular size or nature of the cake that is important. In southeastern France and Burgundy, a *pièce montée* of considerable size might be constructed using marzipan (almond paste) and Savoy sponge cakes. In the Pyrenees and in Rouergue, the traditional wedding cake is a *gâteau à la broche*, constructed with great difficulty on a wooden cone turned in front of the fire. The wedding cake of the Vendée is the *gâtais*, a huge brioche presented by the godfathers and godmothers of the bridal couple. Weighing up to 35 kg (77 lb) and either round (up to 1.3 m (4 ft) in diameter) or rectangular (2.5 m × 80 cm (8 × 3 ft)) in shape, this monumental cake is carried in by bearers who execute a kind of dance step to demonstrate that the cake is not too heavy. After the cake has been 'danced', the bride cuts it up and distributes a piece to each guest, setting aside portions for relatives who have not attended the wedding. Sharing and distribution rituals are found in all regions. Often the cake is eaten several days later when the guests are at home, so that they are reminded of the ceremony. This custom is similar to the British tradition of sending pieces of the wedding cake in small decorative boxes specifically designed for the purpose, to relatives and friends who, for various reasons, could not attend the ceremony.

wedge-shell
OLIVE DE MER

A small marine bivalve mollusc with a pastel-coloured wedge-shaped shell, 3–4 cm (1¼–1½ in) long, which lives in the sand at the water's edge. In France it is also known as *haricot-de-mer*, *flion*, *vanneau*, etc. It is eaten in the same way as cockles, either raw or cooked, after having been soaked to clean it; it has a very good flavour.

weever VIVE

A sea fish which often lies buried in the sand on the sea bed. It is appreciated for the quality of its flesh but feared for its poisonous spines; the spines and the fins should therefore be cut off before any other preparation, handling the fish with gloves on. The greater weever, which is usually 25 cm (10 in) long but may reach 40 cm (16 in), has a long body (brown back striped with blue, yellow sides, and white belly) and a short head, with a wide mouth and large eyes close together. Its flesh is firm and fragrant and fillets are cooked in the same way as sole fillets. Whole and cleaned, it may be grilled (broiled) or prepared like red mullet. Weever steaks can be used in a matelote made with white wine. The lesser weever (the size of a sardine) has hardly any flavour.

A related fish, the star-gazer (called *uranoscope*, *rat*, or *rascasse blanche* in French), is found only in the Mediterranean and is used in bouillabaisse.

RECIPE

Grilled (*broiled*) **weever** VIVES GRIL-LÉES Gut and clean the weevers. Make shallow slits on the back of each fish and on each side of the central fin. Marinate them for an hour in a mixture of oil, lemon juice, salt, pepper, and chopped parsley, with a little chopped garlic. Then gently grill (broil) them for about 15 minutes, turning once.

Serve with melted butter strongly flavoured with lemon and mixed with chopped herbs, or with a mixture of olive oil and raw crushed tomato pulp.

weights and measures

POIDS ET MESURES

Since the metric system became compulsory in France (1 January 1840), most recipes give measures of ingredients in kilograms, grams, litres, centilitres, etc. However, in addition to these, standard recipes still give measures corresponding to the contents of standard utensils: tablespoon, teaspoon, bowl, glass, cup, etc. The measure shown is sometimes even more approximate: a handful, a pinch, a little, etc. In cooking in the old days the weights and measures of ingredients were rarely specified: the number of eggs was given, but the quantity of liquids, spices, etc., was left vague. Indications such as 'plenty' and 'very little' were in common usage.

Before the 19th century, a wide variety of weights and measures was used in France, with notable regional variations. The most frequent old measures are as follows:

— *boisseau* (bushel; for grain and salt) = 12.5 litres
— *chopine* (for liquids) = ½ litre (approx.)
— *grain* = one-twentieth of a gram
— *gros* (one-eighth of an *once*) = 3.824 g
— *litron* (one-sixteenth of a bushel) = 0.813 litre

Approximate measures and their equivalents

1 ordinary glass	2–2.5 dl (7–8 fl oz, 1 cup)
5 tablespoons	1 dl (4 fl oz, scant ½ cup)
1 wine glass	1–1.5 dl (4–5 fl oz, ½–⅔ cup)
1 Madeira glass	5–6 cl (1½–2 fl oz, 3–4 tablespoons)
1 liqueur glass	2.5–3 cl (1–1½ tablespoons, 1–2 tablespoons)
1 large bowl	
liquid	½ litre (17 fl oz, 2 cups)
caster (superfine) sugar	425 g (15 oz, 1 cup)
flour	300 g (11 oz, 2¾ cups)
rice	470 g (1 lb, 2¼ cups)
pulses	440 g (1 lb, 1 cup)
1 soup plate	¼ litre (8 fl oz, 1 cup) liquid or 250 g (8 oz)
1 tea cup	1.2–1.5 dl (4–5 fl oz, ½–⅔ cup)
1 coffee cup	1 dl (4 fl oz, scant ½ cup)

— *livre* (pound; equivalent to 16 *onces* in Paris (0.489 kg), 12 *onces* in Lyon) = 500 g
— *minot* (for dry substances; varied according to the region) = 51 litres (Paris), 52 litres (Lyon)

— *muid* (for liquids and grains; still used for casks of wine) = (in Paris) 274 litres (wine); 1873 litres (corn)

— *once* (in Paris, one-sixteenth of a *livre* (30.594 g), or, as used by Carême, an old weight equivalent to 24–33 g)

— *picotin* (mainly for oats) = 3 litres

— *pinte* (pint; for liquids) = (in Paris) 0.93 litre

— *quarteron* (¼ *livre* or one-quarter of 100 items (i.e. 25) but actually 26 in Paris, as Furetière states: 'A quarteron of apricots consists of 26, namely 25 which is a quarter of 100, plus one for good measure')

— *scrupule* (either one-twentieth of an *once* or 24 *grains*) = 1.137 g

— *setier* (in Paris, either 12 bushels of wheat (150 litres), or 24 bushels of oats (300 litres).

It was the task of measurers, who were public officials, to ensure that the quantities measured were adhered to during commercial transactions concerning grain, coal, garlic, onions, walnuts, apples, medlars, chestnuts, oil, salt, and firewood.

Grain measurers used minas and minots personally authorized by the king. There were 63 such officials in Paris in 1633. Gaugers determined the capacity of barrels of wine, vinegar, oil, honey, grease, beer, and cider. In 1719 there were 24 of them. Salt measurers, whose existence went back to 1200, were known as 'salt counters' when they counted the salted fish and the butter, which arrived in Paris by boat, and 'stampers' when they stamped the minots, boisseaux, picotins, etc., after examining these weights. Garlic and onion measurers operated according to a precise ritual: they filled the minot on their knees so that the 'excess onions which fall on the floor will belong to the vendor and those which remain in the minot will belong to the purchaser'.

☐ **British and American measures** In the UK, the Imperial system of measures is still widely used in cooking (pounds and ounces, pints and fluid ounces), although most recipe books give metric equivalents. The United States uses a system based on the cup measure. In 1965 the British government agreed to adopt the metric system as the primary system of weights and measures by 1975. The date was later amended to

Metric measures with imperial and American equivalents

metric	imperial	American
liquid measures		
150 ml	¼ pint	⅔ cup
300 ml	½ pint	1¼ cups
450 ml	¾ pint	2 cups
600 ml	1 pint	2½ cups
1 litre	1¾ pints	4¼ cups
weights		
25 g	1 oz	
50 g	2 oz	
100 g	4 oz	
225 g	8 oz	
350 g	12 oz	
450 g	1 lb	
1 kg	2¼ lb	

1980, with a provision 'for the continued use of Imperial units of measurement for explanatory purposes'. The United States has also begun to adopt the metric system but, like the UK, is reluctant to give up its own system for culinary use.

Weisslacker

A German cows'-milk cheese produced in foil-wrapped blocks weighing about 1.5 kg (3¼ lb). Golden-yellow right through, with a dense texture and a washed rind, it has a pronounced flavour and smell. It originated in Bavaria and is also called *Bierkäse* (beer cheese). It is traditionally served with rye bread and *Doppelbock* beer.

well   PUITS

The hollow made in a heap of flour on a work surface (ideally a marble top) or in a bowl, to receive the various ingredients which will be used to make the dough. They are gradually incorporated into the flour by working the edges of the flour towards the centre. When liquid is added to the dough, the well must be large enough to take all the liquid without any spilling out.

Welsh rarebit

A British speciality consisting of a slice of toasted bread covered with a mixture of Cheshire or Cheddar cheese melted in pale ale with English mustard, pepper, and sometimes a dash of Worcestershire sauce and an egg yolk. It is then grilled (broiled) and served very hot. In Great Britain Welsh rarebit is served as a quick and delicious snack, often accompanied by beer. On the Continent, where this dish was popular in 'English taverns' in the 19th century, it is more usually served as a hot entrée.

RECIPE

Welsh rarebit Cut 250 g (9 oz) Cheshire cheese into thin slices and place in a saucepan. Add 20 cl (7 fl oz, ¼ cup) pale ale, 1 large teaspoon English mustard, and a pinch of pepper. Heat gently, stirring constantly, until the mixture is smooth and runny. Toast 4 slices of sandwich bread and butter them. Put each slice on an individual flameproof plate, also buttered, and coat with the cheese mixture without spilling any over the edges of the bread. Brown under the grill for 3–4 minutes. Serve very hot.

West Indies ANTILLES

The cuisine of the West Indies owes much to African and Indian influences, with contributions from France (Guadeloupe and Martinique) and also from Spain and America (Haiti, Cuba, Jamaica, and Puerto Rico). It is characterized by sweet-and-savoury mixtures, fried dishes, and highly spiced ragouts but does not feature grilled (broiled) dishes. Seafood, meats, and tropical vegetables are prepared by traditional family methods, using recipes that require slow cooking and the expert use of spices. The Caribbeans are proud of their culinary secrets; they make it a point of honour, for example, to use the *lélé*, a three-branched stick that replaces the wooden spoon and the blender, without which they would be unable to prepare broths such as *calalou* (a thick spiced purée of herbs with bacon and sweet potato leaves, sorrel,

okra, cucumber, Caribbean cabbage, *mousambe*, *siguine*, etc.) or *soupe des habitants*, made with beef, sweet potatoes, pumpkin, celery, purslane, and green beans. There are also numerous soups made with *cribiches* or *ouassous* (large crayfish also made into kebabs), *tourlourous* (land crabs), *pisquettes* or *tiritis* (small fish and alevins, also used in omelettes and ragouts), or tripe; these are always mixed with vegetables and a variety of herbs and spices, including pimiento, garlic, onion, cloves, thyme, and bay.

Another starter to a Caribbean meal is crudités (raw vegetables, such as bamboo shoots, palm cabbage, palm-hearts, breadfruit, and papaw) in vinaigrette, served with the famous acras and accompanied by *féroce* (spiced avocado purée, with salt cod). Other starters include stuffed avocados, the highly seasoned Creole pudding, and omelettes made with shellfish, *pisquettes*, or pineapple.

☐ **Fish and seafood** Fish and seafood are a speciality, usually simmered in a marinade of lime and pimiento seasoned with spices. Such dishes include *blaff*, made with devilfish, bonito, *coulirous* (mackerel), or *chadrons* (sea urchins' eggs); *touffé*, made from shark that is first marinated, then braised and served coated with tomato sauce; *broulai* (fish sautéed with cassava, tomatoes, and onions); and turtle colombo. Salt cod is widely used, cooked in such dishes as *macadam* (browned in a roux, then simmered in sauce) or *chiquetaille* (flaked over rice and tomatoes). Fish (fried, marinated, or stuffed), spiny lobsters, crabs (stuffed or cooked in a stew), and molluscs (lambis) are traditionally served, as are meats, with rice and red beans. Among the most exotic recipes are smoked fish with mangoes, bass with ginger, and *sopito*, a kind of bouillabaisse made with coconut milk.

☐ **Meat and vegetables** Meat dishes are prepared using the same variety and richness of spices. In the French Antilles, curry and calumba are used with beef, chicken, and mutton. Specialities are *pâté en pot* (sheep's belly, head, feet, breast, and liver cooked with vegetables) and pork *vindaye* (cooked coated with a thick paste of ginger, garlic, onion, saffron, and pimiento). Ham with rum and pineapple, pork braised with maize, and chicken with coconut milk and bananas complete the range. Vegetables are prepared in traditional ways – *giraumonade* (pumpkin purée), *mange-mêle* (vegetables with bacon), and calabash stew with peanut bread and shrimps. In Jamaica, curried young goat is served with unripe bananas and saffron rice. In Puerto Rico, the South American influence can be seen in *pasteles* (stuffed and steamed plantain leaves), *piononos* (stuffed fried banana slices), and *asapao*, a chicken ragout that is served as a soup. In Curaçao, a noteworthy dish is *stoba*, a goat ragout seasoned with cumin, capers, and olives, cooked with cucumbers and lemon.

□ **Desserts** Besides the classic tropical fruits, the sapodilla plum should be mentioned, as well as the custard apple and cinnamon apple. Fruit salads, compotes, jellies and jams, flans and blancmanges (flavoured with coconut, vanilla, and cinnamon), soufflés, and very sweet fritters – all flavoured with rum – are the most popular desserts.

whale BALEINE

A large aquatic mammal hunted for its fat in some parts of the world (the Canadian Far North and Japan), in spite of increasingly strict measures enforced to protect it from complete extinction.

Throughout the Middle Ages, when whales were still to be found off the coasts of Europe, in particular the Bay of Biscay, they were also hunted for their oil (which was used for lighting) and for their flesh which, since it came from a 'fish', was considered a suitable food during Lent. According to Ambroise Paré, 'the flesh has no value, but the tongue, which is soft and delicious, is preserved in salt. The same applies to the blubber, which is eaten with peas during Lent.' This blubber, known as *craspols* or *lard de carème* ('Lenten fat'), was the main diet of the poor during the Easter period. However, the tail, and particularly the tongue, were considered to be delicacies.

19th-century cookery books suggested recipes for grilled flipper escalopes, poached brains, or slices of liver grilled in anchovy butter. Whale meat is very red and contains more protein than beef. Eskimos eat it dried and the Norwegians eat grilled whale meat. A traditional Icelandic dish is cooked whale blubber preserved in vinegar. The Japanese are the largest consumers of whale meat and eat it raw, cooked with ginger, or marinated. Meat from the tail or throat is particularly prized. The blubber is cut into thin strips and served with *sake*. It is also used in the manufacture of many preserved foods (soups, tinned meat, edible fat, etc.).

wheat BLÉ

A cereal used to produce flour and semolina that can also be eaten cooked, crushed, etc.

Wheat was cultivated in Neolithic times and was used in girdle cakes and broth. The Egyptians, followed by the Greeks and Romans, used it to make bread, and it is in this form that wheat has mostly been used in southern and western Europe. It has virtually replaced other cereals in this part of the world, whereas other civilizations have grown up on rice or maize.

Each grain of wheat consists of a husk (bran) and a kernel. The latter is made of starch and a mixture of proteins called gluten. Inside the kernel is the seed or embryo (known as wheat germ), which is rich in nitrogenous material and fatty substances. The external portion of the grain contains phosphorus, calcium, and other mineral salts as well as numerous vitamins.

There are several varieties of wheat with different uses within the food industry. Gluten-rich hard wheat is used for making semolina, especially for pasta and couscous. Soft wheat is ground for flour of varying degrees of whiteness, depending on how much of the husk is removed.

Growing interest in vegetarian cookery has led to the rediscovery of the use of wheat as a natural food. Ground whole wheat is used to make gruel, croquettes, biscuits, etc. Germinated wheat is particularly rich in amino acids, mineral salts, and vitamins (especially vitamin C). See also *bulgur*.

RECIPE

Germinated wheat BLÉ GERMÉ
Place wheat grains in a flat container
and cover them with water. Leave for 24
hours. Wash the grains in running
water, then replace in the container,
without water, for another 24 hours.
The grains must, however, remain
moist. Wash again the next day. The
grains now have a little white point (this
is the germ) and are ready for use. They
do not keep and must be used the same
day. They are eaten either in their natural state or dried and ground and then
added to soups, salads, or purées.

whelk BUCCIN

A marine snail with a whitish conical
pointed shell, very common on the
Channel and Atlantic coasts. Cooked
for 10 minutes in salted water, whelks
are eaten cold with bread and butter; if
they are cooked any longer they become
fairly tough. Whelks can also be cooked
in a white wine sauce.

whisk FOUET

A kitchen utensil made of tinned or
stainless steel wire bent into loops and
held together in a handle.
• An egg whisk, which is short and
rounded, with flexible wires attached by
a ring to a wooden or metal handle, is
used for whisking egg whites. It is also
used to make potato purée, to beat egg
yolks with sugar (especially for zabaglione), and to whisk fresh cream.
• A sauce whisk, which is longer and
has stiffer wires and a metal handle, is
used to beat and emulsify sauces and
also to beat custards and various mixtures so that they will not be lumpy.
Nowadays electric beaters, fitted with
steel or plastic attachments, are often
used instead of hand whisks. Whisking
is made much easier, especially for egg
whites and mayonnaise, but the results
are inferior for delicate mixtures, such
as hollandaise and béarnaise sauces and
Chantilly cream.

whisky

A spirit originating from Scotland and
made from malted grain. It is spelled
'whiskey' in Ireland and the United
States, but Irish whiskey is different
from American whiskey, which is made
from rye or maize (corn).
• *Scotch whisky*, the Scottish national
drink, is made from malted barley and
has changed little over the centuries.
After germination, the malted barley is
dried over the heat of peat fires: it is the
aroma of the peat which will give the
whisky its particular flavour. The barley
is then ground and mixed with water to
form the wort; the wort is fermented
and goes through two distilling operations, according to the methods of the
craft. Malt whisky is obtained in this
way, called single malt when it comes
from one distillery only and pure malt
when it is a blend of different malt
whiskies.
Grain whisky is made from a mixture
of any malted and unmalted cereals. A
long maturation period is the key to the
mellow flavour of Scotch whisky. Law
requires that it be matured in oak casks
in Scotland for a minimum of three
years before becoming Scotch whisky.
This is true of malt and grain whiskies.
In fact most Scotch whisky is matured
for five or six years, or longer. The label
frequently states the age of a brand. In
the case of a blended Scotch whisky, law
demands that the age of the youngest
individual whisky in the blend is
stated.
Constantly increasing demand since
World War I led producers to develop
the market for blended whiskies, resulting from blends of malt and grain
whisky. The latter, produced in a much
more industrial way, has a less distinctive flavour. The blend takes its
aroma mainly from the malt whisky, of
which the proportion in the composition of the blend may vary from 15 to
40%. Extremely widely drunk, blended
Scotch whiskies are now recognized
throughout the world; there are about
ten great brands, each corresponding to
a particular blend of different whiskies,
with its own fine and full-bodied aroma.
Though connoisseurs may remain
attached to malt whisky, it is blended
whisky which has given rise to most
imitations abroad.
• *Irish whiskey* was for a long time
produced and consumed on a small-
scale family basis. Made from barley,
but also from wheat, rye, and oats, it is
not dried over peat. Distilled three

times, it undergoes, like Scotch whisky, various blends before being sold.

• *Canadian whisky*, made from cereals, is marketed under numerous names and has a fairly light taste. Maize (corn) is found in large proportions in the mixtures, which are fermented under the action of malted barley as for other whiskies.

• *Corn whiskey* is an American grain spirit, produced from a mixture of cereals containing at least 80% maize (corn).

• *Bourbon whiskey*, the most widely drunk of the American whiskies, originated from Kentucky and is made from a mixture of maize (at least 51%), rye, and malted barley; it is aged for at least two years in oak casks charred inside.

• *Rye whiskey* is an American grain spirit produced from rye.

Many countries produce different spirits under the name of 'whisky' or 'whiskey', which covers all sorts of products. But, whatever the results of the various attempts and researches, none, have been able to equal the particular delicate flavour of the original Scotch whisky.

Whisky is generally drunk as an apéritif, on ice, either neat or with plain or soda water; the Scots drink it with a glass of plain water beside it. This spirit is also used to make numerous cocktails, such as 'whisky Collins', 'whisky sour', and 'Bourbon sour' (see *Irish coffee*). It is also an ingredient in various cookery recipes (for chicken and shellfish, particularly), and some enthusiasts prefer it to Cognac or Armagnac for flamed dishes.

In Geneva there is a Confrérie du Bon Vieux Whisky, and in France, Great Britain, and the United States, an Academy of Pure Malt Whisky. In France, this Academy bestows the Glenfiddich Award each year.

whitebait BLANCHAILLE

The young of herrings, sprats, etc., which are very common along coasts and in river estuaries. These small fish are usually fried and eaten whole.

The French word *blanchaille* is also used to describe various small freshwater fish.

white pudding (sausage)

See *boudin blanc*.

white wine VIN BLANC

See *wine*.

whiting MERLAN

A sea fish similar to haddock and cod but without barbs. The whiting is 25–40 cm (10–16 in) long, with a greenish-grey back, golden-coloured sides, and a silvery belly with a line of small brownish-yellow streaks above the pectoral fin. It lives near the coast and is fished mainly in the Atlantic, from the north of Norway to Spain. Available most of the year, it is sold either whole or in fillets.

Whiting flesh is fine-textured and friable and contains less than 1% fat, making it easy to digest. It must be cooked carefully because the flesh tends to fall apart fairly easily. Whiting is an essential ingredient in certain regional soups along the French coast. It literally dissolves in the soup, giving it a velvety texture. It can be prepared in many ways: fried, grilled (broiled), fried in breadcrumbs, or poached in wine. It can also be stuffed, rolled into paupiettes, or used in forcemeats, fish loaves, or mousses. However, it needs to be fairly well-seasoned (with flavoured butter, lemon, herbs, etc.), as the flesh is rather tasteless.

RECIPES

Fried whiting en colère MERLAN FRIT EN COLÈRE Soak the whiting for 10 minutes in milk or pale (light) ale. Drain, pat it dry, season with salt and pepper, and roll it in flour. Shape the fish into a circle by putting the tail into the mouth and clenching the jaws so that it remains in this position during cooking. Deep-fry in hot (but not smoking) fat, ensuring that it is evenly browned on both sides. Drain it on absorbent paper and serve with fried parsley, slices of lemon, and tartare sauce. Whiting can also be fried flat, but in this case a shallow incision should be made along its back.

Fried whiting en lorgnette MERLANS FRITS EN LORGNETTE Make a deep incision in the fish along each side of the backbone. Do not separate the fillets from the head. Remove the backbone, starting at the tail and breaking it off at the base of the head. Season with salt and pepper and dip in egg and breadcrumbs. Roll up the fillets on either side of the head and secure each of them with a small wooden skewer so that they stay in position (see illustration). Deep-fry in very hot (but not smoking) fat. Arrange on a napkin and garnish with fried parsley and slices of lemon.

Paupiettes of whiting   MERLANS EN PAUPIETTES   Fillet 3 whiting and remove the skin. Put the bones and heads into a saucepan together with 2 grated carrots, 1 shredded onion, 2 chopped shallots, 2 glasses (12 fl oz, 1½ cups) dry white wine, a large glass of water, a bouquet garni, salt, and pepper. Boil gently for 30 minutes, then strain the fumet and boil it down by half. Leave it to cool.

Prepare a fish mousse in the following way. Reduce 2 whiting fillets to a purée in a blender and put it into a basin. Place the basin in a second bowl containing crushed ice. Gradually add 2 dl (7 fl oz, ¾ cup) fresh cream, working the mixture briskly until it becomes mousse-like. Flatten the 4 remaining fillets, season with salt and pepper, and coat evenly with the fish mousse. Roll the fillets up tightly and tie them with string. Arrange the paupiettes in a buttered flameproof dish, pour the reduced stock over the top, and cover. Bring to the boil on top of the stove, then cook in the oven at 220 c (425 f, gas 7) for 20–25 minutes.

Make some kneaded butter by mixing 1 tablespoon butter with an equal quantity of flour. Drain the paupiettes and keep them hot on a serving dish. Thicken the sauce with the kneaded butter. Untie the paupiettes, coat them with the sauce, and serve piping hot.

Poached whiting with melted butter   MERLAN POCHÉ AU BEURRE FONDU   Put a large whiting into a cold court-bouillon in a pan. Bring to the boil, cover, and poach gently for 10 minutes. Drain the fish and arrange it on a serving dish. Pour a little melted butter over the top and sprinkle with chopped parsley.

Serve the remaining butter in a sauce-boat. Garnish with steamed potatoes, rice, cucumber slices, spinach, or leeks cooked in butter, or sautéed courgettes (zucchini) or aubergines (eggplants).

Stuffed whiting with cider   MERLANS FARCIS AU CIDRE   (from a recipe by J. Granville) Remove the backbone from 4 whiting, each weighing about 300 g (11 oz). Gut (clean) them through the back and season with salt and pepper. Cut 2 carrots, 2 sticks (stalks) of celery, and the white parts of 2 leeks into very fine slices. Cook them very gently for 5 minutes in a covered pan with 30 g (1 oz, 2 tablespoons) butter, salt, and pepper. Stuff the fish with the vegetables and place them in a dish with 1 tablespoon olive oil. Pour 2 glasses (1½ cups) cider and 1 glass (¾ cup) fish fumet over the fish. Cook in a hot oven for 10–20 minutes, or until cooked. Remove the fish, boil down the stock until it is almost dry, then add 250 g (9 oz, generous 1 cup) curd cheese (*fromage blanc*) and cook for 5 minutes. Pour this sauce over the whiting, sprinkle with chopped chives, and serve very hot.

Whiting à l'anglaise   MERLAN PANÉ À L'ANGLAISE   Open the fish from the back and remove the backbone. Season with salt and pepper, roll in flour, dip in egg and breadcrumbs, and brown in butter on both sides. Arrange it on a dish and coat with slightly softened maître d'hôtel butter. Serve with plain boiled potatoes.

Whiting à l'espagnole   MERLAN À L'ESPAGNOLE   Dip the whiting in egg and breadcrumbs, brown it in oil, and serve on a bed of tomato fondue seasoned with a little crushed garlic. Garnish with fried onion rings.

Whiting hermitage   MERLAN HERMITAGE   (from Raymond Oliver's recipe) Remove the bone from a large whiting and gut (clean) it through the back. Stuff it with a mixture of breadcrumbs, creamed butter, chopped shallot, egg, chopped herbs, salt, and a pinch of cayenne. Put it into a buttered gratin dish with a little cream and some fish stock. Cover with buttered greaseproof (waxed) paper and bake in the oven for 15 minutes. Drain the whiting and keep it hot. Boil down the cooking liquid to reduce and add some butter, cream, salt, and pepper. Bring to the boil again, and pour the sauce over the fish.

Whiting in white wine MERLANS AU VIN BLANC Gut (clean) 2 large whiting and season with salt and pepper. Butter a gratin dish, line it with a layer of chopped onions and shallots, and place the fish on top. Add equal quantities of white wine and fish stock so that the fish are half-covered. Cover the dish, begin the cooking on the top of the stove, then place in the oven at 220 C (425 F, gas 7) for about 20 minutes. Drain the fish and keep them hot in a serving dish. Boil the cooking liquid to reduce by half and add 2 dl (7 fl oz, ¾ cup cream. Boil down further and pour the sauce over the fish. Glaze for 5 minutes in a very hot oven.

Wiener schnitzel

See *viennoise (à la)*.

wild boar SANGLIER

The ancestor of the domestic pig, which has been hunted since ancient times and is now increasingly rare. It is known in French hunting terms as *bête noire*. The young animals have delicate flesh, but the flavour of the meat becomes more pronounced with age and is very strong in the adults.

Horace was one of the first to acclaim wild boar as a noble highly flavoured dish: 'If you shun insipid meat, let a wild boar from Umbria, fed on ilex acorns, make your table bend under its weight ...', and Martial was equally enthusiastic: 'May your joyful aroma fill my home, may the wood burn in my kitchen as on a feast day. But my cook must use plenty of pepper and must be generous with the Falernian wine and the mysterious garum.' During and after the Middle Ages wild boar continued to be popular, particularly 'wild boar tails in hot sauce' (*Ménagier de Paris*), boar's head, stewed shoulder, roast loin, and pâtés.

Up to the age of six months, the wild boar is known in France as a marcassin; its light-coloured fur is striped with dark bands from head to tail (it is said to be 'in livery'). It is forbidden to hunt an animal younger than three months. From six months to a year it is called *bête rousse* (red beast), because of its colour, and from one to two years, *bête de compagnie*. At that age, its flesh is excellent for cooking. Then its black coat appears. At the age of two years, the wild boar is called *ragot*; at three, it is a *tiers-an*; at four, a *quartenier*; older, a *porc entier*. An animal of advanced years (it can reach the age of 30) is called a *solitaire* or *ermite*. In an eight-year-old male the flesh, although tough and very strongly flavoured, is still edible. The delicate flesh of the marcassin does not need to be marinated. The *bête rousse* and *bête de compagnie* should be marinated in red wine for two to three hours, older animals for five to eight hours; at this stage long slow cooking is essential.

Most recipes for pork are suitable for wild boar, apart from roasting (marcassins excepted). The cutlets, whether marinated or not, can be fried; slices cut from the tenderest parts can be cooked like escalopes. The leg, or ham, should be braised in sweet-and-sour sauce with its marinade, with the possible addition of raisins, prunes, or orange peel. Marcassin fillet can be barded and roasted in a moderate oven (20–25 minutes per lb, basting frequently). Wild boar fillet can be cooked in a daube: it is first browned, then simmered on a layer of pork rind with the marinade (30–45 minutes per lb, according to age). The best cuts are usually cooked in a civet: there is a variation in which curry powder is sprinkled over the pieces after they have been browned. They are then cooked in a covered pan with onions, carrots, garlic, and white wine; the sauce can be thickened with cream. Wild boar meat can also be minced (ground) and cooked in a pie with prunes.

RECIPE

Boar's-head brawn (head cheese) HURE DE SANGLIER Cook in courtbouillon 4 pigs' tongues which have been blanched, peeled, and soaked in brine for 4–5 days. Singe a boar's head weighing about 5 kg (11 lb), scrape it out carefully, and bone it completely, without tearing the skin. Cut off the ears and set aside; remove the tongue and the fleshy parts attached to the skin. Cut the pieces of lean meat into large even-sized cubes; leave them, with the tongue and the skin of the head, to marinate for 10 hours with 5 carrots, 4 chopped onions, thyme, bay leaf, salt, pepper, and 1 teaspoon mixed spice.

Cut into dice 2 cm (¾ in) square the boar's tongue, the cooked pigs' tongues, 500 g (18 oz) pickled tongue, 750 g (1¾ lb) ham, 1 kg (2¼ lb) boned and trimmed chicken meat, and 500 g (18 oz) fat bacon. Add 400 g (14 oz) truffles (peeled and coarsely diced), 150 g (5 oz, 1 cup) shelled pistachio nuts, and the pieces of lean meat from the head. Marinate for 2 hours in brandy, salt, pepper, and ½ teaspoon mixed spice. Add 4.5 kg (10 lb) fine pork forcemeat and 4 whole eggs; mix all together well.

Spread out the skin of the head, with the outside underneath, on a cloth that has been soaked in cold water and wrung out; lay the stuffing in the middle and fold the skin over the mixture. Wrap the head in the cloth, reshaping it in its original form, and tie firmly.

Cook in aspic-jelly stock to which the bones and trimmings from the boar's head and the carcass and trimmings from the chicken have been added; simmer very gently for about 4½ hours. One hour before it is ready, put the ears into the stock to cook. Drain, leave to stand for 30 minutes, then unwrap the head, wash the cloth, and wring it out well. Roll the head in the cloth again and bind with wide tape, taking care to keep the shape (start binding at the snout end). Leave to cool for at least 12 hours, then unwrap and wipe dry.

Using thin wooden cocktail sticks (toothpicks) fix the ears, coated with a layer of brown chaud-froid sauce or dissolved meat glaze, in their correct positions. Place the head on a rack and coat with the same sauce; put the tusks back in their sockets and make eyes with hard-boiled (hard-cooked) egg white and truffles. Lay the head on a large dish, garnish with truffles and shelled pistachio nuts, and glaze with the aspic (which should have the consistency of unbeaten egg white). Chill in the refrigerator. In domestic cookery, where the truffles are omitted, the cooled head is simply covered with golden bread-crumbs. The ears are diced and added to the rest of the stuffing.

wine VIN

A drink made from the juice of the grape, the sugar in the fruit being converted into alcohol by the action of yeasts in the process of fermentation.

According to the definition of the Wine & Spirit Association of Great Britain, wine is: 'The alcoholic beverage obtained from the juice of freshly gathered grapes, the fermentation of which has been carried through in the district of its origin and according to local tradition and practice.' This means that drinks made from fruits other than grapes are not, strictly speaking, 'wines': in the UK these are categorized as country wines. Nor can alcoholic drinks made from dried grapes and grape and fruit extracts be described as 'wine' in the UK – they are categorized as 'British wines' or 'British ... style wine'. Alcoholic drinks made from wine kits and fermented with various types of yeast are known in the UK as 'made wines'. All of these can be acceptable and agreeable beverages, and anyone who makes some form of alcoholic drink, and thereby understands something of what is involved, may go on to learn and enjoy true wines. But it is important to recognize the distinction between 'British wine' (as defined above) and 'English wine', which is made from grapes grown in England. Although various countries have definitions that differ in detail from the above, the latter is generally widely accepted.

Red, rosé, or white, still or sparkling, wine is enjoyed by millions of people and plays an important role in all kinds of celebrations. Its history is as old as that of civilization. The vine grew wild in Europe and the East, and the idea of obtaining a drink from it goes back probably to the very remote past.

At Ur, in Mesopotamia, a panel has been discovered representing a drink-offering scene. The Egyptians were including wine in their funeral ceremonies some 3000 years before Christ. The Bible makes numerous allusions to the Hebrews as being great lovers of wine.

The art of cultivating the vine and making wine was, according to mythology, taught to the Greeks by Dionysus. In fact, it was undoubtedly the Egyptians who spread this art throughout the Mediterranean, particularly in Sicily and southern Italy. The Romans inherited it and their immense empire derived the benefits. The Gauls were familiar with the vine well before the Roman conquest (1st century BC), but the quality of Roman wines and new methods introduced by the conquerors gave considerable impetus to viticulture. The Gauls became excellent vine growers and may have invented the cask, which took the place of the amphorae which had been used until that time for the storing and transport of wine. The high quality of Gallic production gave such pride of place to their wines that in the year 92 AD the Roman Emperor Domitian, on the pretext of encouraging wheat growing, but in reality to protect Roman vine growers from formidable competition, ordered that half the Gallic vines should be pulled up.

In the Middle Ages, viticulture was linked to the propagation of Christianity, each monastery producing its own wine for the Mass and therapeutic use and working hard at improving the quality. Many famous wines of France, notably in Burgundy, are still grown around what were formerly monasteries.

French wines were exported to England and Scotland, the Scandinavian countries, and as far away as the Near East (in spite of the Islamic ban, which at one time obliged certain Bordeaux exporters to label as 'mineral water' the casks of wine sent to Turkey). In this way they acquired a reputation which continued to grow until the 18th century. The use of bottles for maturing wines became general in the 18th century. The French Revolution resulted in the parcelling out among innumerable small landowners of the vineyards which had belonged to the nobility and the religious communities. In 1867 phylloxera, a plant bug which spread to Europe from North America, destroyed the vines in the majority of European vineyards. Built up again later with vines grafted onto American rootstocks, resistant to phylloxera, French vineyards now extend over an enormous and increasing area and wine is of major importance in the French economy.

The Institut National des Appellations d'Origine des Vins et Eaux-de-Vie (INAO) has classified French wines as follows:

● *Vins de table*: wines for daily consumption. Their labels must indicate the alcoholic strength and the capacity of the bottle. *Vin de Table Français* is a blend of French wines, *Vin de Différents Pays de la Communauté Européenne* is a blend from several EEC countries. *Vin de la CEE* is one made in a different country from that producing the grapes.

● *Vins de pays*: wines made from specified vines produced in a particular region, having satisfied a tasting panel.

● *Vins Délimités de Qualité Supérieure (VDQS)*: wines which comply with conditions relating to the exact area of production, varieties of vines, and cultivation and production methods; these are also subject to tasting panels. (This category is soon to be phased out.)

● *Appellations d'Origine Contrôlées (AOC)*: wines representing the finest of France, whose production is strictly controlled at each stage. However, it should be borne in mind that a wine made wholly in compliance with all the strictest regulations may somehow, through natural chance or human error, fail to attain the highest standards of quality. The local syndicates within each region determine the conditions governing the area's AOCs, but it is important to understand that the regulations can change, and therefore some laid down in works of reference may be out of date; also, in many areas, the overall AOC (such as 'Bordeaux') has less detailed significance than a more specific AOC (for example, 'Bordeaux Supérieur' or 'Pauillac'). Essentially, the AOC determines: the exact area within which the vines are grown; the varieties of vines; the way they are grown and pruned; the permitted yield per hectare; and the alcoholic strength in the finished wine. There are some complications and anomalies, and anyone seriously interested should consult a detailed work of reference. The only great French wine that does not have to state its AOC on its label is champagne.

□ **Wine production** Normally harvested when they are fully ripe, the grapes are then treated differently according to whether they are to make red, white, or rosé wine. In making red wine, the first stage is the crushing, the aim of this being to make the grapes discharge their juice without squashing the seeds or splitting the stalks and stems. This crushing was formerly done with bare feet, but is now carried out mechanically in various ways. Stalks are sometimes removed prior to crushing, by a destalking machine. The crushed grapes are then usually placed in a vat, formerly of wood, today sometimes of cement but increasingly of stainless steel; here the must (grape juice) undergoes fermentation by the action of yeast bacteria, which transforms it into wine. The colour of red wine is produced by leaving the skins of black grapes in the must so that the pigments tint it. The yeasts convert the natural sugar in the juice into ethyl alcohol and carbonic gas. The length of the fermentation varies; on average it is about eight to ten days although it can go on for much longer. The fermented must (now wine) is then drawn off and goes either into another vat or tank or into casks. The marc (the solid residue of the grapes) is then pressed, and this *vin de presse* may either be mixed with the main wine or, in certain instances, be kept for domestic consumption by the personnel.

White wine is made in two main ways. Either it comes solely from white grapes (and is called *blanc de blancs*) or it is made from a mixture of black and white grapes, the skins of the black grapes being removed before the pigments in them can impart colour to the must. As nearly all grape juice is pale yellowish-green anyway, it is possible to make a white wine solely from black grapes (*blanc de noirs*) if the skins are removed early in the vinification process.

For rosé wine, the skins of black grapes remain in contact with the must for long enough to impart colour. There are some grapes that have pinkish juice, but none of these are involved with the finer wines.

When the first stage of fermentation has been completed, the wine – either in cask or vat – may be subjected to certain forms of treatment. One of these is a type of clarification known as 'fining', in which one of various substances (egg white is a well-known fining agent) is introduced into the cask, attracts particles in suspension in the wine, and causes them to cling to it and gradually sink to the bottom of the vessel. In addition, wine in cask is 'racked off' – that is, it is pumped off any deposit that may have been formed in the cask and that may cause it to continue 'working' (fermenting) because of the yeasts in it. Finally, before bottling, wine will usually be filtered to ensure that it is 'star bright' as customers prefer.

☐ **The cellar** The best storage place for wine is the cellar, but this is sadly becoming a rarity in modern houses. The first requirement for a wine cellar is a constant temperature, preferably fairly cool: the ideal temperature is about 12 c (54 f). The ageing of the wine may be slowed down below this temperature and accelerated slightly above it; sudden changes of temperature are particularly harmful. The cellar must also be aerated and have a reasonable degree of humidity so that the corks do not dry out; but a very damp atmosphere, although good for the long-lasting wines, can damage labels. A strong light can cause white wines to turn brownish, particularly if it comes from fluorescent tubes. More difficult to eliminate in towns is the shaking, due to the passage of underground trains or motor traffic; this can cause wine to age prematurely. Finally, products giving off a strong smell, such as paraffin or paint, should not be stored in the cellar, neither should fruit, which could ferment: delicate wines easily take on flavours through their corks, even when these are covered with a metal or plastic capsule.

There are now on sale portable cellars (*caves d'appartement*) having constant temperature and atmospheric humidity, mounted on shock absorbers which absorb vibrations. These are obviously of a limited capacity, but can be placed anywhere.

Ideally, even modest wines should be rested, lying in their bins or on their sides, before being broached. Any classic wine that may have thrown some kind of deposit must have a period of rest after being brought home, even if this is merely a day or two standing upright, to allow the deposit to settle. In general, white wines do not last as long as reds, but this depends on the quality of the wine, the maker, and the vintage; some great white Burgundies, for example, can last a surprisingly long time. Champagne and sparkling wines are sold when they are ready to drink, but even a few months', 'landing age' to a non-vintage champagne can endow it with additional quality. Many dry white wines bearing a vintage date are probably most enjoyable when consumed within five years of their vintage; the very finest, including certain great white Burgundies and the finest Alsace wines, may have much longer lives. The luscious sweet wines, such as the Sauternes and Barsacs, will certainly not decline in quality for many years. The longevity of white wines from other countries depends on their type, maker, and vintage. Rosé wines do not usually have long lives, with the possible exception of certain estate Tavels. Red wines, however, vary enormously – the lighter ones may well be at their most enjoyable when young and fresh, whereas the great clarets and red Burgundies can have very long lives in certain vintages. Some, indeed, may last as long as a human lifespan. But generalizations are risky and personal tastes vary a great deal. Many French drinkers prefer to drink their wines young, but the British tend to like aged wines, sometimes absurdly so, as age in itself is not necessarily a virtue and a wine can lose its freshness when allowed to get too old.

☐ **Serving and tasting** Whether it is coming out of a home cellar or the dealer's, wine should ideally rest for several hours, standing up, before being drunk, so that any deposit sinks to the bottom of the bottle. The wine cradle, which allows the bottle to be served lying down, as drawn from the bin, is justified only for very old red wines, which have a lot of sediment; the bottle must not be set upright at any time after coming out of the rack. Decanting is the careful transferring of the wine into a carafe, allowing the sediment to be eliminated and aerating the wine, which usually improves it. Bordeaux wines are decanted when they are considered to be a little 'closed' or have thrown a heavy deposit, so that they may open out on contact with the air. If you have to uncork bottles of red wine several hours before serving to make sure they are as

they should be, they can be closed again if the wine is *à point* (as you think it should be) or left with the stoppers out if the wine seems too 'hard' and 'closed up'. For white wines, about ten minutes of aeration suffices to remove any bottle stink.

White wines, both dry and fuller-bodied, should be drunk between 5 and 8 c (41–46 F), rosé wines between 8 and 10 c (46–50 F), and light red wines between 10 and 12 c (50–54 F); full-bodied red wines are served chambré, that is between 15 and 18 c (59–64 F). A fine red Burgundy is usually served between 15 and 17 c (59–63 F), a great Bordeaux around 18 c (64 F). The bringing of a wine to the correct temperature must always be gradual; white wine must not be cooled by putting it in the freezer, nor should a red wine be warmed by placing it near the fire or over the stove.

When opening a bottle, first wipe the capsule, then, after removing this, wipe the cork. Once this is drawn the inside of the neck of the bottle is also wiped with a clean cloth. The wine is poured as steadily as possible, avoiding any shaking, preferably into a thin colourless glass, with a sufficiently long stem to enable it to be held without the hand heating its contents. A tulip glass, large enough to bring out the bouquet, but narrow at the opening so that this does not escape too quickly, is suitable for all wines.

Champagne and rosé wine can accompany all dishes, but this is often a too easy option. When a meal includes several wines, they are served in a certain order. According to Brillat-Savarin, 'The order of the drinks goes from the most moderate to the headiest and the most fragrant.' As a general rule, dry whites are served before sweet whites, white wines before reds, young wines before old ones. The wine should also go with the dish it accompanies. For example, serving a great sweet white wine with game or red meat should be avoided, as should serving a great red wine with fish or shellfish. But all this is often a matter of personal taste and opportunity. Here are some suggestions by Dr Paul Ramain, a French expert in oenology, about possible food and wine combinations:

- Local white wines: charcuterie, fish, crayfish, roast or grilled (broiled) meat, cheese.
- Dry white wines: eggs, hors d'oeuvres, white fish, shellfish soups, shellfish, charcuterie, veal, fresh (i.e. nonfermented) cheeses.
- Fuller-bodied white wines: melon, oily fish, spiced shellfish, foie gras, chicken *à la crème*.
- Sweet white wines: foie gras without truffles, desserts, and sweet dishes.
- Dry champagne: may be drunk throughout the meal.
- Sweet champagne: desserts.
- Vins gris and light rosés: charcuterie, hors d'oeuvres, cold meats, veal, quail.
- Full-bodied rosés: crayfish, caviar, fish soup, *brandade* (salt cod), roast meats, poultry, cooked cheeses.
- Local red wines: family meals, snacks, and in cooking.
- Light red wines: poultry, white meats, lamb, thrush, quail, cold meats, charcuterie, meat pies, cheese.
- Full-bodied red wines: red meats, game, cheese.

□ **Wine vocabulary** Professional tasters and well-informed wine enthusiasts sometimes use technical jargon when discussing wine, of which the following are among the most commonly used terms.

acerbe (bitter): rough and acid.

ambré (amber-coloured): describing an old white wine which has acquired a golden colour like that of amber, due to the oxidation of its colouring matter; this colour is a defect in a young wine.

arôme (aroma): the specific smell imparted by each variety of grape to the wine which is made from it; particularly evident in young wines, but tends to blur with age.

astringent: having excessive tannin; this characteristic can disappear with age.

bouchonné (corked): having a smell or taste of the cork; this defect, which is harmless but makes the wine unpleasant, is due to various factors and should not be put down as a fault on the part of the grower or bottler.

bouquet: the sum of the olfactory qualities acquired by the wine in the course of its fermentation and ageing.

brillant (brilliant): perfectly clear.

brut (extra-dry): very dry (describing champagne).

caractère (character): describing a wine whose qualities are very marked and easily recognizable.

charnu (fleshy): having body; giving the impression of filling the mouth.

charpenté (constructed): full-bodied and *charnu*.

corsé (full-bodied): seemingly rich, well-coloured, and of marked character.

coulant (flowing): fresh, pleasant to drink.

court (short): not leaving a durable impression on the palate.

croûté (crusty): said of an old red wine whose sediment has stuck to the inside of the bottle and which needs to be decanted.

délicat (delicate): rather light, fine, and elegant.

distingué (distinguished): a high class.

doux (sweet): some wines are naturally sweet because of the sugar in the grape juice: they are quite different from wines that are sweetened. Sugar not converted into alcohol is referred to as 'residual sugar'.

dur (hard): lacking charm, through excessive tannin or acidity: this defect sometimes disappears as the wine matures.

élégant (elegant): fine and high-class.

enveloppé (wrapped): mellow and velvety because it contains glycerine (a by-product of the alcoholic fermentation).

épanoui (opening out): describing a bouquet which fills the mouth.

équilibré (balanced): describing a wine whose characteristics are neither too weak nor too marked.

éventé (flat): oxidized, generally because of either aeration during bottling or being too old.

faible (weak): low, usually in both alcohol and bouquet.

fin (fine): distinguished: most AOC wines should be *fin*.

frais (fresh): describing a young wine which is fruity and not excessively acid. (However, the instruction *servir frais* means 'serve cool'.)

franc (clean): healthy; straightforward.

fruité (fruity): having a flavour of fruit; few wines either smell or taste of grapes, but the fruity character should be evident.

généreux (generous): full-bodied; rich in alcohol.

gouleyant (mouth-filling): easily drunk; 'moreish': sometimes describes a light wine that is served chilled.

gras (fat): *charnu*, mellow, and supple.

jeune (young): describing a wine which has not reached maturity, when describing a wine which has to age.

léger (light): low in alcohol.

liquoreux (liqueur-like): sweet, usually in relation to white wine.

louche (dubious): cloudy.

lourd (heavy): dull; undistinguished.

madérisé (browning): oxidized. When used of a white wine, the colour and smell are said to be reminiscent of Madeira.

maigre (lean): insufficiently fruity; lacking agreeable character.

moelleux (mellow): sweetish: usually describing white wines.

nerveux: vigorous, sinewy: describing a wine of definite character and style.

nouveau (new): young: the term is often used nowadays for wines made to be drinkable without ageing.

onctueux (smooth): full-bodied; fat.

perlant (forming minute bubbles): giving off a very slight amount of carbonic acid gas, which creates a sensation of tingling in the mouth.

pétillant (slightly sparkling): less than fully sparkling but more so than *perlant*.

piqué (tart): having a 'pricked' taste, an indication that is may shortly turn to vinegar.

plat (flat): (when describing a sparkling wine) no longer sparkling; (when describing a still wine) uninteresting.

plein (full): rounded; ample.

racé (distinguished): implies breeding.

robe (appearance): indicates the colour.

robuste (robust): full-bodied and assertive.

rond (rounded): well-balanced; harmonious.

sain (healthy): clean-tasting; in good condition.

sec (dry): used mainly to describe dry still white wines. A champagne described as *sec* is actually slightly sweet.

séché (dried): describing a wine which has lost its freshness and fruit.

souple (supple): on the smooth side.

suave (pleasant): agreeable, possibly sweetish.

taché (stained): describing a white wine that has become slightly pink, either because it has been in a cask which has contained red wine, or because it has been allowed to take on colour from the skins of black grapes.

tendre (tender): young, fresh, agreeable, and easy to drink.

terne (dull): lacking character.

tranquille (still): not sparkling.

tuilé (tile-coloured): describing a red wine which has taken on a tawny tone because it is getting old.

usé (worn out): describing a wine which has lost its qualities.

velouté (velvety): mellow, smooth.

vert (green): coming from insufficiently ripe grapes; high in acidity.

vif (lively): young, fresh, and attractive.

vineux (vinous): somewhat alcoholic and without lingering fragrance.

☐ **Cooking with wine** The custom of using wine in the preparation of food goes back to ancient times. White, red, and rosé wines, as well as champagne, figure in numerous recipes; in regional dishes, the local wines are used.

There are certain general rules on the use of wine in cooking. Whatever its colour, the wine must be clean and without a harsh aggressive taste. Very cheap table wine sometimes does not react well in cooking, and it is better to use something slightly superior in quality, although this does not have to be a great wine. Red wine, which should be fairly full-bodied, is indispensable for coq au vin, daubes, game ragouts, beef bourguignon, fish stews, and marinades. Accompanied by garlic, onion, and often mushrooms, it is also used in numerous thickened sauces. Red wine may be used to cook certain vegetables, such as red kidney beans, and it also features in some desserts, being used to macerate strawberries or cook pears. White wines suitable for cooking are usually dry and rather acid, such as Muscadet and Aligoté. Their natural acidity is even increased by the addition of lemon juice when deglazing the pan used for frying meats; for long slow cooking, on the other hand, it is sometimes necessary to reduce this acidity by boiling the wine, uncovered, for about ten minutes. White wine is included as an ingredient of a court-bouillon used for cooking fish or shellfish. It goes well with chicken and white meats cooked in fricassees.

wine cellar CAVE À VIN

A cellar is the ideal place to store wines, being (ideally) dark, airy, and quiet, with a constant temperature and protected from unpleasant smells. It should not be subject to seasonal temperature changes, and should also be slightly damp and draught-free. If conditions are too damp, moulds may grow on the outside of the corks and the labels may deteriorate, although this does not affect the wine. Bottles of wine are stored horizontally in wooden or metal racks and arranged by region and year, preferably with their labels visible. A cellar book, which lists all the wines by name with their vintage, price, supplier, date of receipt, date of consumption, and any tasting notes, is an invaluable asset. Once or twice a year it is a good idea to examine every bottle to ensure that each is well corked and filled; the cork must remain in contact with the liquid if it is to function properly as an air filter. Wine must be stored lying down, so that the cork remains wet and swollen. Spirits, however, must stand up, as the cork or stopper may rot if in contact with the spirit.

If no true cellar is available, a dark quiet place, of constant temperature, can be fitted with wine bins and, if necessary, with a humidifier.

wing AILE

Either of the front limbs of a bird, including the muscles which operate it. The latter form the delicate white meat of the breast. When cooked whole, both the wing and breast of young and tender birds (especially chicken or young turkey) is called a suprême; on older birds it is called – incorrectly – a 'poultry cutlet'.

winkle BIGORNEAU

A small marine snail harvested from coastal waters. It is recognized by its brown or black shell with its pointed spine: the hard operculum must be removed before eating.

Winkles are eaten cold with bread and butter, after poaching for five minutes in salted water (it should be possible to remove them whole from their shells with a pin; if they are cooked for too long, they become brittle). They are also eaten in salads.

Winterthur

A dish of langouste prepared like lobster cardinal but filled with shrimps and a salpicon of langouste. It named after a Swiss town in the canton of Zurich.

wok

A large open cast-iron pan with a rounded base and two handles. It is widely used in Chinese cooking, mainly to prepare stir-fried dishes, but also for roasts, sautés, steamed dishes, and even soups. The wok's main advantage is that it allows food to be tossed and stirred constantly while cooking: in this way it can be cooked rapidly over a high heat without absorbing too much fat. Stir-frying is the most common method in China for cooking small pieces of food.

woodcock BÉCASSE

A migratory bird with a wingspan of 60 cm (24 in), a long bill, and short legs. In France woodcock are hunted in March –April and October–November (they are fatter and more tender in the autumn); in Great Britain they are classified as game birds and can only be shot between September and January. The bird is fairly rare and difficult to find because it is well-camouflaged – its plumage is the colour of dead leaves; it has long been regarded as a delicacy. In classic cuisine, it is hung for 4–8 days (until the skin on the belly is shiny, the feathers and tail come away easily, and the beak can be broken with the fingers) and then used to make salmis, pâtés, and mousses. Modern recipes however, prefer it not to be hung and it is usually roasted undrawn, except for the gizzard, and often served on a toast base.

The parts of the bird most esteemed by such French authors on gastronomy as Godard d'Aucour are the entrails. These should be collected from cooked birds, seasoned with spices and lemon juice, then mixed with chopped fatty bacon or foie gras, laced with brandy and eaten spread on fried bread or toast.

RECIPES

Preparation of woodcock PRÉPARA-
TION DE LA BÉCASSE Unlike poultry
and other game, woodcock is not
trussed with string; it trusses itself. The
long pointed beak goes through the
thighs and the legs are raised and held
together. It is customary to remove the
eyes of the woodcock, but not the intestines (except for the gizzard). After
cooking, the intestines are spread on
toast.

Casserole of woodcock BÉCASSE EN
CASSEROLE OU EN COCOTTE Truss
the woodcock and bard with thin
bacon. Brown in some butter, season,
then place in an ovenproof dish and
roast in a hot oven (240 C, 475 F, gas 9)
for 15–18 minutes until bird is cooked,
basting frequently. Drain the bird, remove the bacon, and keep warm. Pour a
dash of brandy into the casserole dish
and, if possible, a few tablespoons of
game stock. Remove the intestines and
chop with an equal quantity of fresh
bacon. Add salt and pepper, a pinch of
grated nutmeg, and a dash of Cognac,
Armagnac, or Calvados. Fry a slice of
bread (white or brown), spread it with
the intestines, and then put it in a very
hot oven for a few minutes to cook the
bacon. Serve the woodcock on the toast
canapé and moisten with the cooking
juices.

casserole of woodcock à la crême
BÉCASSE EN COCOTTE À LA CRÈME
Prepare and cook a woodcock as in the
recipe for casserole of woodcock. Add
to the casserole a dash of Cognac,
Armagnac, or Calvados and a few tablespoons of fresh cream. Return to the
oven to warm through.

Cold timbale of woodcock TIMBALE
DE BÉCASSE FROIDE Line a raised pie
dish with lining pastry (see *doughs and
batters*) and then with thin slices of
bacon. Cover the bottom and sides of
the lined dish with a game forcemeat
flavoured with diced truffle. Bone 2
woodcocks, stuff with foie gras studded
with truffle, roll into ballottines, and
seal by frying in butter. Place the woodcock in the dish and fill in the gaps
between with the birds' fine forcemeat

mixed with foie gras and the chopped
intestines, well seasoned, and flavoured
with a dash of Cognac. Spread a layer of
game forcemeat over the whole, shaping
it into a dome, then top with thin
rashers of fat bacon. Cover with hot-
water crust shaped to fit the top of the
pie. Seal the edges to form a crimped
ridge and decorate the top of the pie
with pastry shapes. Make a small hole in
the pastry lid to allow steam to escape.
Bake for 1¼ hours at 180 C (350 F, gas
4). Allow to cool thoroughly before
turning out of the mould. Serve on a
dish covered with a napkin.

Cold woodcock à la Diane BÉCASSE
FROIDE À LA DIANE (from a recipe by
Leopold Mourier) Roast the woodcock
until rare and slice the meat. Pound the
intestines with a knob of foie gras, a
knob of butter, nutmeg, and brandy.
Sieve and season well. Reshape the
sliced flesh round the intestine mixture,
arranging it on large slices of raw truffle
marinated in brandy to resemble a
woodcock, and coat with a firm game
aspic (see *aspic jelly*). Chill well in the
refrigerator before serving.

Hot woodcock pâté à la perigourdine
PÂTÉ CHAUD DE BÉCASSE À LA PÉRI-
GOURDINE Bone 2 woodcocks,
spread out the birds on a table, and fill
with stuffing as in the recipe for woodcock casserole *à la perigourdine*. Roll
the woodcocks into ballottines and
wrap each one separately in muslin
(cheesecloth). Poach for 12 minutes in a
Madeira braising stock prepared with
the carcass and trimmings. Drain and
allow to cool. Unwrap when cold.
Meanwhile, prepare a fine forcemeat
composed of two-thirds game forcemeat and one-third veal forcemeat (see
forcemeat). Line the bottom and sides
of an oval pâté mould with a thin layer
of shortcrust pastry (basic pie dough)
and spread the forcemeat over this.
Place the ballottines side by side in the
mould. Cover with 10 slices of foie gras
fried in butter and 20 slices of truffle.
Cover with the remaining forcemeat.
Cover the pâté with a layer of pastry and
seal and trim the edges. Make a hole in
the pastry lid for the steam to escape.
Garnish with shaped pastry trimmings
and brush with egg. Place the pâté on a

baking sheet and bake for 1¼ hours at 180 c (350 f, gas 4). Just before serving, pour a few tablespoons of Perigueux sauce into the pâté through the hole in the lid.

Roast woodcock on toast BÉCASSE RÔTIE SUR CANAPÉ Truss the woodcock, bard, tie up with string, and roast on a spit or in a very hot oven (approximately 240 c, 475 f, gas 9) for 18–20 minutes. Prepare a canapé as for woodcock casserole and serve the woodcock on top of the canapé. The dish may be garnished with large peeled grapes.

Sautéed woodcock in Armagnac BÉCASSE SAUTÉE À L'ARMAGNAC Cut the woodcock into pieces. Use the carcass and the trimmings to prepare a fumet and add rich demi-glace. Put the pieces of woodcock in a sauté pan just big enough to hold them and brown briskly in butter. Cover the pan and simmer for 8 minutes. Drain the pieces, arrange in a timbale or in a shallow dish, and keep hot. Dilute the pan juices with 2 tablespoons Armagnac, add the strained concentrated woodcock fumet, and boil for a few moments. Thicken this sauce with the chopped intestines, season with a small pinch of cayenne, and add 1 teaspoon butter and a dash of lemon juice. Strain the sauce and pour it over the woodcock, piping hot.

wood pigeon

PALOMBE, RAMIER

A species of pigeon that is prepared in the same way as ordinary pigeon, although its flesh is more delicate and flavoursome. In the Bordeaux region it is enjoyed in a salmis or roasted; in the Basque country it is eaten lightly grilled (broiled) or as a confit.

In southwestern France, where it is known as *palombe*, the wood pigeon is traditionally hunted with nets (*palombières*) during its annual migration over the Pyrenees.

Worcestershire sauce

An English condiment whose recipe was apparently discovered in the East Indies by Sir Marcus Sandys, a native of Worcestershire. On returning home, he asked the English grocers Lea & Perrins to make up a sauce that resembled his favourite condiment. It was launched commercially in 1838. The present-day 'Original and Genuine Worcestershire sauce', which still bears the names of its inventors, is made of malt vinegar, molasses, sugar, shallot, garlic, tamarind, clove, anchovy essence, and meat extract. It is used to season ragouts, soups, stuffings, vinaigrette, devilled or tomato sauces, steak tartare, and exotic dishes; it also flavours various cocktails and tomato juice. A similar condiment, based on soy sauce, is Harvey's, which was introduced in the late 18th century.

wrasse VIEILLE

A medium-sized fish (less than 30 cm, 12 in) with a thick mouth armed with many teeth. The superb colours of its body, with green or red predominating, are flecked with gold lights, but its soft and rather insipid flesh is riddled with bones. The pearly or ballan wrasse, the best and most common variety, found in the English Channel and the Atlantic, is usually baked. The green wrasse, which is elongated in shape, and the more thickset *merle* are smaller Mediterranean fish, used in making bouillabaisse; the *coquette*, found on rocky sea beds, is also used in fish soups.

| RECIPE |

Wrasse with potatoes VIEILLES AUX POMMES DE TERRE (from Jacques Le Divellec's recipe) Blanch 250 g (9 oz) thick streaky lightly salted bacon in water and cut into small strips. Peel and slice 150 g (5 oz, generous cup) shallots. Peel 1 kg (2¼ lb) potatoes, cut into thin slices, wash, and wipe dry. Grease an ovenproof dish with lard and arrange the strips of bacon and potatoes in it in alternate layers, sprinkled with shallots. Season with salt and pepper. Moisten with 5 dl (17 fl oz, 2 cups) white wine. Place in a medium oven (200 c, 400 f, gas 6) for 30 minutes.

Meanwhile, scale, clean, and wash 4 wrasse, each weighing about 400 g (14 oz), and rub them outside and inside with salt and pepper. Place them on the potatoes, sprinkle with small pieces of lard, and return to the oven for 10 minutes. Turn the fish over and continue cooking for a further 5 minutes. Serve very hot in the baking dish.

Wuchteln

An Austrian dessert consisting of squares of yeast dough folded over a plum jam filling, put in a warm place to rise, then baked and served hot, dusted with icing sugar (confectioners' sugar) and accompanied with a compote of prunes.

Xavier

A cream soup or consommé thickened with arrowroot or rice flour and garnished with diced plain or chicken royale. It may also be flavoured with Madeira, garnished with small savoury pancakes, or served with *oeufs filés* (threads of egg white cooked in the soup).

RECIPE

Xavier soup POTAGE XAVIER Pre-pare 1.5 litres (2¾ pints, 7 cups) chicken consommé. Thicken it with 3 tablespoons (¼ cup) *crème de riz* (rice flour slaked with milk or water). Away from the heat, add 3 egg yolks mixed with 1 dl (6 tablespoons, scant ½ cup) double (heavy) cream. Stir in 60 g (2 oz, 4 tablespoons) butter. Garnish with diced chicken royale and serve in cups.

ximenia XIMÉNIA

A small tropical shrub with edible, though rather sour, fruit.

yak YACK

A long-haired domesticated ruminant that lives on mountainous pastures of central Asia. It is used as a pack animal and also provides meat and milk. Yak meat (*gyak* in Tibetan) is cooked mainly as thin slices fried quickly in butter or grilled (broiled) on bamboo sticks; larger joints are boiled, after marinating if the animal is old. Dried complete with bones, the meat is sometimes reduced to a coarse powder used as a basis for soups and porridges made with yak's milk. The Tibetans use yak's milk also to make small very hard cube-shaped cheeses and butter, which is eaten when rancid.

yakitori

A Japanese dish of chicken kebabs cooked over charcoal embers. They usually include pieces of chicken meat and liver, balls of minced (ground) chicken mixed with spring onions (scallions), mushrooms, and sometimes quail's eggs, peppers, or ginkgo nuts. These items are threaded onto thin bamboo skewers, soaked in a sauce called *teriyaki* (rice beer, soy sauce, sugar, and ginger), then grilled for 4–5 minutes. In Japan, restaurants specialize in yakitori, offering a whole range of these kebabs. They are also sold in the streets.

yam IGNAME

The round or elongated edible tuber of a tropical climbing plant, cultivated in Africa, Asia, and America. The flesh is white, yellow, or pink and the skin may be rough or smooth and white, pink, yellow, or blackish-brown in colour, depending on the variety. Yielding 102 Cal per 100 g and with a very high starch content, the yam is a basic food in many tropical countries. Very small yams can be cooked in their skins. Larger ones, weighing up to 20 kg (45 lb), are peeled, washed in cold water, and blanched for 10–20 minutes in boiling salted water. They can then be used in the same way as potatoes or sweet potatoes (in soups, ragouts, purées, soufflés, croquettes, fritters, gratins, chips, etc., as well as various sweet dishes). A starch extract from yams, called 'Guiana arrowroot', is widely used in cookery and confectionery.

yassa

A Senegalese dish consisting of pieces of grilled (broiled) mutton, chicken, or fish (originally monkey) which have been marinated in lime juice and highly seasoned condiments. It is served with rice or millet and the marinade, used as a sauce.

yeast LEVURE

A microscopic fungus that multiplies rapidly in suitable conditions and is used as a raising (leavening) agent in various kinds of dough. When yeast is added to the dough, it causes alcoholic fermentation and converts the sugar and starch into ethanol (ethyl alcohol) and carbon dioxide. This gas causes the dough to rise. The use of brewer's yeast in baking goes back to 1665, when a baker had the idea of adding some to his leaven: Archduchess Maria Theresa of Austria was so delighted with the bread produced in this way that the loaf was called a 'queen loaf'.

There are three main types of yeast – fresh, dried, and brewer's. Fresh and dried yeast are used in making bread and some cakes and should always be stored in the refrigerator. Dried yeast can be substituted for fresh yeast in recipes, but only half the amount should be used as it is more concentrated. Brewer's yeast (which is slightly liquid) is used mainly in the brewing of beer and ale. Yeast is a good source of vitamin B and is often prescribed, medicinally, in the form of yeast tablets or concentrated extract.

yogurt or yoghurt

YAOURT

A fermented milk product, of custard-like consistency and slightly sour taste, obtained by the combined action of two species of bacteria, *Streptococcus thermophilus* and *Thermobacterium bulgaricum*; these were discovered by the Russian biologist Metchnikoff, assistant to Pasteur.

Made for centuries in the Balkans, Turkey, and Asia, yogurt appeared briefly in France during the reign of François I: a Jewish doctor from Constantinople treated the king's intestinal trouble with yogurt, but later returned to the East with the secret of its preparation. The product only really caught on after World War I, when Greek and Georgian immigrants started serving it in their restaurants or producing it on a small scale for local dairymen. Marcel Aymé, in *Maison basse* (1935), still considered it necessary to explain the term: 'One morning, he was putting away some pots of yogurt, a kind of curdled milk which was rather popular, but whose spelling was uncertain.'

Yogurt (both the product and the word) is of Turkish origin, although many French dictionaries give the French *yaourt* as derived from the Bulgarian *jaurt*. However, the product is also traditional in India, Arabic countries, central Asia, and countries of the former Ottoman Empire, whose peoples attribute to it their health and longevity. Authentic Turkish yogurt is quite different from the yogurt with which we are familiar: the milk of the cow, ewe, or buffalo (the latter, according to connoisseurs, gives a denser and better-tasting product) is boiled until reduced by about one-third, then poured into a leather bottle or terracotta jar and left to ferment naturally.

Today, a multitude of brands and flavours are produced industrially. Yogurt may also be made at home with an electric yogurt-maker or simply using an insulated vessel and a thermometer. It is slightly laxative, easily digested, and replenishes the intestinal flora. Natural unflavoured low-fat yogurt contains only 37–46 Cal per 100 g, 0.2–1.5% fat (according to the milk used), 3.5% protein, mineral salts (especially calcium and phosphorus), and vitamins. A great variety of coloured and flavoured yogurts, often containing fruit, are also available. In France, a 'Bulgarian flavour' yogurt, of a creamy consistency, is also produced.

In Europe, yogurts are usually eaten as a dessert or for breakfast; plain yogurt is often sweetened with sugar, honey, jam, or fresh or dried fruit. In the kitchen, yogurt is used to prepare refreshing drinks, cold or iced dessserts, and sauces, instead of fresh cream (in this case, it may be stabilized with a little potato flour if it is to be cooked, as in soups, ragouts, gratins, stuffings, etc.).

In Asia and the East there is a host of traditional uses for yogurt. Apart from an iced drink, prepared by beating it with a little water, it is used to cook meat and vegetables, to dress raw vegetable salads (such as Indian *raitas* or Turkish *cacik* made of cucumbers, seasoned with herbs), to prepare soups, or in sauces for kebabs.

RECIPES

Cucumber salad with yogurt SALADE DE CONCOMBRE AU YAOURT Peel a large cucumber, split lengthways, and remove the seeds. Cut the flesh into very thin half-slices, dust with 1 teaspoon fine salt, and leave for 30 minutes in a colander for the cucumber to lose some of its water. Rinse under the cold tap, wipe well, and mix with 3 tablespoons (¼ cup) yogurt sauce.

Iced yogurt bombe BOMBE GLACÉE AU YAOURT (from a recipe gy André Daguin) The day before the meal, cook 90 g (3½ oz) dried haricot beans in twice their volume of water sweetened with 100 g (4 oz, ½ cup, firmly packed) sugar per litre (1¾ pints, 4¼ cups), and 2 vanilla pods (beans). When completely cooked, put through a blender or processor and mix with 4 pots of natural yogurt, 3 yogurt pots of caster (superfine) sugar, and 1 yogurt pot of honey; work well with a spatula. Put the mixture in a churn freezer, then set it in a decorative mould.

On the day of serving, scald 300 g (11 oz) strawberries for 1 minute then reduce to a purée without sugar. Poach 2 pears in enough wine syrup to cover them (make the syrup by heating 100 g (4 oz, ½ cup) caster (superfine) sugar in 1 litre (1¾ pints, 4¼ cups) wine). Reduce the pears to a purée, thin with a little of the syrup, and reheat. Unmould the bombe and serve accompanied with the hot fruit purée in a sauceboat.

Yogurt cocktail COCKTAIL AU YAOURT Reduce to a purée 1 small peeled banana and 2 slices canned pineapple, using a blender or processor. Blend in 2 pots of natural yogurt and 1 tablespoon pineapple syrup. Add sugar to taste.

This cocktail may also be made with banana and strawberries, pear and peach, or mango and lemon.

Yogurt sauce SAUCE AU YAOURT Mix 1 small pot of natural yogurt with 1 teaspoon paprika; season with salt and pepper, then add 1 teaspoon lemon juice

and the same quantity of chopped chervil and chopped chives.

Use to dress a salad of cucumber, tomatoes, courgettes (zucchini), sweet peppers, cauliflower, green beans, or potatoes.

yorkaise (à la)

A term used for egg dishes containing York ham. Cold eggs *à la yorkaise* are poached, arranged on small round thick slices of ham, garnished with chervil and tarragon, then coated with Madeira jelly. Fried eggs *à la yorkaise* are made with hard-boiled (hard-cooked) eggs: these are cut in half and the yolks sieved and mixed with a salpicon of ham bound with béchamel sauce; the eggs are then reassembled, breaded, fried, and served with tomato sauce.

Yorkshire pudding

A British speciality made of a batter of eggs, flour, and milk, which is traditionally baked in the fat of roast beef, for which it is the classic accompaniment. Fat from the cooked roast is poured into a shallow ovenproof dish and the pudding batter then added; it is cooked in the oven until well-risen, crisp, and brown, and served with the roast, together with gravy, roast potatoes, a green vegetable, mustard. and horseradish sauce

RECIPE

Yorkshire pudding Whisk 2 eggs until frothy with ½ teaspoon salt; mix in 150 g (5 oz, 1¼ cups) flour, whisking constantly. Add ¼ litre (8 fl oz, 1 cup) milk in a thin stream and beat until the mixture is smooth. Put in a cool place for 1 hour. In an ovenproof dish heat 2 tablespoons (3 tablespoons) roast beef fat (or, failing this, lard) until it sizzles; beat the batter once more, adding 3–4 tablespoons cold water, and pour into the dish. Bake in the top of a hot oven (220 c, 425 F, gas 7) for 15 minutes, then lower the temperature to 200 c (400 F, gas 6) and bake for about a further 15 minutes; the pudding should be well-risen, crisp, and brown. Serve very hot.

zabaglione

SABAYON, SAMBAYON

A light foamy dessert of Italian origin, made by whisking egg yolks, wine, and sugar together over a gentle heat. Zabaglione is served barely warm in cups or glasses (like those of the Café Greco, in Rome, of which it is a speciality); it can also be poured over a dessert, poached fruit, a pastry, or ice cream. The word is derived from the Neapolitan dialect word *zapillare*, meaning 'to foam'.

Zabaglione can be made with dry white wine (Asti or champagne), sweet white wine (Sauternes), Marsala, fortified wine (Frontignan, Málaga, Banyuls), port, or else a mixture of white wine and a liqueur (Chartreuse, Kümmel), or white wine and a spirit (brandy, whisky, rum, Kirsch). It can also be flavoured with lemon or vanilla. Its preparation requires some skill, as the yolks must thicken without coagulating and the end result must be very frothy. Sometimes whisked egg whites are added to zabaglione after it has been beaten up, just before serving.

The term 'sabayon' is also applied to a sort of mousseline sauce, usually made with champagne, which is served with fish or shellfish.

RECIPES

Zabaglione SABAYON Put 5 egg yolks into a basin and add the grated zest of half a lemon, a pinch of powdered vanilla or a few drops of vanilla essence (extract), and 180 g (6½ oz, generous ¾ cup) granulated sugar. Whisk until the mixture is thick and pale, then place the basin in a bain-marie and continue whisking, adding 2 dl (7 fl oz, ¾ cup) white wine and 1 dl (6 tablespoons, scant ½ cup) Marsala, a little at a time. When the zabaglione is thick and frothy, take the basin out of the bain-marie. Frost the rim of 6–8 sundae dishes with lemon juice and granulated sugar. Divide the zabaglione between these dishes and serve with plain petits fours.

Rum zabaglione with marrons glacés SABAYON AU RHUM ET AUX MARRONS GLACÉS (from Christian Con-stant's recipe) Beat 10 egg yolks and 200 g (7 oz, scant cup) granulated sugar with a whisk in a bain-marie, until the mixture becomes pale and thick. Mix in 3 wineglasses white wine and 3 tablespoons (¼ cup) white rum, beating all the time, until the mixture becomes thick and frothy. Flavour lightly with a few drops of vanilla essence (extract). Arrange some marrons glacés in sundae dishes, cover with zabaglione, and chill in the refrigerator until required.

zakuski ZAKOUSKI

In Russian cooking, an assortment of small hot or cold savouries served before a meal, with vodka, as hors d'oeuvres. In former times the zakuski constituted part of the meal, although they were served in a room adjacent to the dining room. The extent and variety of the zakuski reflected the prosperity of the host and the status accorded to the guest. A full zakuski table, which is similar to the Scandinavian smörgasbord, may consist of: caviar and smoked fish eggs on buttered black bread canapés; rye bread croutons, hollowed out and filled with sauerkraut and slices of smoked goose; piroshki with different fillings; soused or smoked fish (salmon, eel, sturgeon); meatballs; herring pâté; stuffed eggs; fish or chicken salads; beetroot (red beet) and potatoes dressed with herbs; sweet-and-sour gherkins; and pickled beetroot, quetsche plums, and mushrooms. These are accompanied by different sorts of bread, mainly rye bread flavoured with cumin, onion, or poppy-seed. Zakuski are arranged on a sideboard or on trays for guests to help themselves. If intended simply as cocktail snacks with the vodka, zakuski are often restricted to filled canapés and piroshki.

zampone

An Italian speciality from Modena, consisting of a boned and stuffed pig's trotter (foot), sold ready to cook or precooked and served hot or cold. It is stuffed with a forcemeat of pork, green (unsmoked) bacon, truffles, and seasoning, and then cured, smoked, boiled, and often served with lentils.

The word comes from *zampa* (paw): a large trotter is called a *zampone*; a small one a *zampino*.

Zampone Soak a ready-to-cook zampone in cold water for 3 hours; scrape the skin well and prick it all over with a barding needle. Wrap it in a thin cloth, tie at each end and in the centre, then put it into a casserole and cover with cold water. Bring to the boil and poach for 3 hours. Serve either hot, with mashed potatoes or lentil purée and braised spinach or cabbage; or cold, sliced like a sausage, with parsley.

zarzuela

A Catalan speciality consisting of a fish and seafood ragout. Zarzuela (the name literally means 'operetta') combines many kinds of seafood (*mariscos*), such as clams, mussels, squills, squid, shrimps and scampi, as well as various rock fish, cut into sections; lobster, langouste (crawfish), or scallops may also be added. The ingredients are cooked with onions and peppers browned in olive oil and garlic, together with sliced smoked ham, chopped tomatoes, ground almonds, bay leaf, saffron, parsley, and pepper, all moistened with white wine and lemon juice.

Zarzuela is served in the casserole in which it is cooked, with small croutons fried in oil; it is sometimes seasoned with a few drops of absinthe.

zephyr ZÉPHYR

The name (meaning literally 'a light wind') given to various savoury or sweet dishes, served hot or cold, characterized by a light and frothy consistency.

A zephyr is often a soufflé. The name is also given to quenelles, mousses, or small savoury puddings made in dariole moulds and consisting of pounded lean veal, chicken meat, or fish mixed with butter, egg yolks, and either fresh cream or stiffly whisked egg whites.

In the West Indies zephyrs are balls of vanilla-and-rum ice cream surrounded by meringue shells and accompanied by a chocolate zabaglione, served as a dessert. Zephyrs may also be small light cakes made of layers of sweet pastry or meringue covered with praline- or coffee-flavoured butter cream, sandwiched together, then iced (frosted) with fondant.

Seafood zephyr ZÉPHYR AUX FRUITS DE MER (from Marie-Louise Cordillot's recipe, published by Flammarion) Wash 2 litres (3½ pints, 4½ pints) mussels and open them; shell 300 g (11 oz) shrimps. Reserve 6 mussels and 12 shrimps and finely chop the remainder together.

Now prepare a soufflé: mix together over a low heat 60 g (2 oz, 4 tablespoons) butter and 75 g (2½ oz, scant ¾ cup) flour, then mix in ½ litre (17 fl oz, 2 cups) cold milk and bring to the boil. Add 5 egg yolks then the chopped seafood. Whisk the 5 egg whites to stiff peaks and fold them lightly into the mixture. Butter a 20-cm (8-in) soufflé dish and empty the mixture into it, three-quarters filling it. Level the surface by shaking the dish. Cook in a moderately hot oven (190 C, 375 F, gas 5).

Meanwhile, dip the reserved mussels and shrimps in a mixture of half an egg yolk and 30 g (1 oz) grated Gruyère cheese. When the soufflé is almost cooked (after about 20 minutes) scatter these mussels and shrimps over the top, together with a little grated cheese (this must be done extremely rapidly so that the soufflé does not collapse). Brown in a very hot oven for about 5 minutes and serve immediately.

zest ZESTE

The coloured and perfumed outer rind of an orange, lemon, or other citrus fruit. The zest is separated from the whitish part of the skin by using a special knife (called a zester) or a potato peeler. Cut into fine strips or small pieces, the zest is used to flavour creams, cake mixtures, and desserts. It may also be candied, pickled in vinegar, grated, or rubbed onto lump sugar. Candied orange zest, sometimes chocolate coated, is called *écorces d'orange* or *orangettes*.

Lemon zest preserved in vinegar ZESTES DE CITRON CONFITS AU VINAIGRE Remove the zest from 3 lemons and cut into fine strips, making a julienne. Put this into a small saucepan of boiling water and boil gently for 10–15 minutes. Remove and drain the julienne, clean the saucepan, then replace the julienne along with 1 tablespoon sugar and 1 wineglass vinegar. Cook very gently until all the liquid has evaporated, then thoroughly mix the julienne with the caramel which has formed.

Zests prepared in this way are used particularly to flavour chicken terrines and can also be used as a condiment, like chutney.

zingara

A sauce or garnish containing paprika and tomato (*zingara* means 'gypsy' in Italian). Zingara sauce is a mixture of demi-glace and tomato sauce mixed with ham, pickled tongue, and mushrooms (truffle is an optional extra) and seasoned with paprika. It is served with small cuts of meat, poultry, and soft-boiled or poached eggs. The garnish consists of the same ingredients and goes with veal escalopes or sautéed chicken, dusted with paprika and served with a sauce made by deglazing the pan juices with tomato sauce and Madeira.

| RECIPES

Sautéed chicken a la zingara POULET SAUTÉ À LA ZINGARA Season a 1.25-kg (2½-lb) chicken with salt and pepper, cut it into 4 pieces, and dust with paprika. Brown the pieces in oil in a flameproof casserole, reduce the heat, cover, and continue cooking. After 30 minutes add 4 tablespoons (⅓ cup) strips of ham and the same quantity of pickled tongue and mushrooms; add a little truffle and a small sprig of tarragon. When the chicken is cooked, arrange it on a serving dish, together with its garnish (without the tarragon), and keep hot.

Deglaze the casserole with ½ dl (3 tablespoons, scant ¼ cup) Madeira and 2 tablespoons (3 tablespoons) tomato fondue. Reduce until almost dry, then add 1.5 dl (¼ pint, ⅔ cup) demi-glace sauce and heat through. Toast 4 slices of sandwich bread; quickly fry in butter 4 small round slices of ham; place the ham on the pieces of toast and arrange alongside the chicken. Coat the chicken with the sauce and sprinkle with chopped parsley. Serve very hot.

Zingara sauce SAUCE ZINGARA Prepare 2.5 dl (8 fl oz, 1 cup) demi-glace sauce, 2 tablespoons (3 tablespoons) sieved tomato sauce, and a julienne comprising 1 tablespoon each of cooked ham, pickled tongue, and mushrooms cooked gently in butter, plus a little truffle. Add the julienne to the demi-glace sauce and mix in the tomato sauce. Add a dash of paprika and keep hot in a bain-marie until ready to serve.

zucchini

See *courgette*.

zuppa inglese

A dessert invented by Neapolitan pastrycooks and ice-cream makers who settled in the big cities of Europe during the 19th century. Inspired by the English puddings that were fashionable at the time, zuppa inglese (literally 'English soup') usually consists of a sponge soaked with Kirsch, filled with confectioners' custard (pastry cream) and crystallized (candied) fruits macerated in Kirsch or Maraschino, then covered with Italian meringue and browned in the oven. In another version, alternate layers of slices of brioche loaf browned in the oven and crystallized fruits macerated in rum are placed in a gratin dish and soaked in boiling milk mixed with beaten eggs and sugar; after cooking, the dessert is covered with Italian meringue and browned in the oven.

Index

à gratin forcemeat 537
abattis babylas 590
abattis de dinde aux navets 590
abattis en fricassée 590
abattis en ragoût 590
abattis à l'anglaise 590
abricots au sirop 39
abricots Bordaloue 149
abricots Condé 39
abricots sterilisés au naturel 39
achard de légumes au citron 3
agneau aux pruneaux, au thé et aux amandes 1290
agneau de lait farci 715
Agnès Sorel tartlets 6
aigo boulido 7
aiguillettes de boeuf en gelée 7–8
aiguillettes de canard au vinaigre de miel 652
aiguillettes of duckling with honey vinegar 652
ailerons de dindonneau farcis braisés 961
aillade sauce 8
Albufera sauce 9
alcazar gateau 10
alexandra 318
Ali-Bab salad 12
Alienor salad 1102
aligot 13
allemande sauce 13
allumettes au cumin 406
allumettes à la toscane 14, 1312
allumettes salées 14
almond batonnets 83
almond butter 188
almond choux fritters 300
almond cream 380
almond croquets 394
almond darioles 417
almond financiers 512
almond milk jelly 15
almond paste 16
almond sandwich cake 1217
alose: preparation 1165
alose au plat 1166
alose frite 1165
alose grillée à l'oseille 1165
aloyau braisé 1175
aloyau rôti 1175
Alsace tart 1280
amandes salées 15
American mincemeat 810
American pudding 1017
American salad 1103
americano 318
Amiens duck pâté 459
amourettes: preparation 21
amourettes au gratin 22
ananas en surprise 1251
ananas glacé à la bavaroise 959
ananas glacé à la creole 385
anchovy butter 188
anchovy dartois 418
anchovy fillets à la silesienne 23
anchovy fillets Talleyrand 1273
anchovy fritters 561
anchovy mayonnaise 785
anchovy omelette 880
anchovy purée (for cold dishes) 1023

anchovy purée (for hot dishes) 1024
anchovy salad à la suedoise 1238
anchoyade corse aux figues 509
andalouse sauce 26
andouillettes à la tourangelle 27
angelique confit 27–8
angels on horseback 897
Angevin bouilleture 144
anguille: préparation 471
anguille à la bonne femme 472
anguille à la diable 471
anguille à la provençale 472
anguille à l'anglaise en brochettes 472
animelles: preparation 29
animelles frites 29
aniseed biscuits (cookies) 29
aniseed sugar 1245
Anna potatoes 30–1
appareil à Condes 337
appareil à Maintenon 761
appareil à matignon 782
apple charlotte 255
apple compote 333
apple conserve 36
apple delicieux 430
apple flamusse 518
apple fritters 560
apple jelly 681
apple and mango chutney 306
apple paste 567
apple and pineapple jam 959
apple and prune turnovers 1342
apple puffs a la normande 862
apple sauce 1131
apple soufflé 36
apple strudel 1234
apple tart 1280
apples bonne femme 36
apples with cream and Kirsch 697
apricot barquettes 79
apricot bouchées 141
apricot cocktail 319
apricot compote 334
apricot fritters 560
apricot Genoese sponge 584
apricot jam 681
apricot jam dartois 418
apricot liqueur 738
apricot marmalade 38
apricot pannequets 907
apricot paste 567
apricot sauce 1134
apricot tourte 1318
apricots Bourdaloue 149
apricots Condé 39
apricots preserved au naturel 39
apricots preserved in syrup 39
Arabic coffee 327
arbolade 41
Ardèche caillettes 201
Argenteuil salad 42
Arles salad 1103
aromatic sauce 45
arrowroot liaison 46
artichauts bouillis 47
artichauts Clamart 312
artichauts à la barigoule 77
artichauts à la lyonnaise 47
artichoke hearts: preparation 47

artichoke hearts cooked in butter or à la creme 47
artichoke hearts à la cevenole 47
artichoke hearts à la nicoise 47
artichoke omelette 880
artichoke velouté soup 1198
artichokes Clamart 312
artichokes à la barigoule 77
artichokes à la lyonnaise 47
asparagus: preparation 50
asparagus au gratin 50
asparagus à la flamande 517
asparagus à la polonaise 979
asparagus served hot 50
asparagus served warm 50
asparagus tart 50
asparagus tips: cooking 50–1
asparagus tips for cold garnishes 51
asparagus velouté soup 1198
asperges: préparation 50
asperges au gratin 50
asperges à la flamande 517
asperges à la polonaise 979
asperges servies chaudes 50
asperges servies tiedes 50
aspic croutons 400
aspic de foie gras 51–2
aspic de jambon et de veau (ou de volaille) 51
aspic de saumon fumé 52
aspic d'oeufs de caille au caviar 1026
aspic of ham and veal (or chicken 51
aspic mayonnaise 785
aspic moulds and dishes: preparation 51
attereaux of apricots Pompadour 981
attereaux d'ananas 54
attereaux de foies de volaille à la mire-poix 54
attereaux d'huitres 54
attereaux à la piemontaise 954
attereaux of oysters 54
attereaux of pineapple 54
attereaux Pompadour à l'abricot 981
aubergine (eggplant) caviar 55
aubergine (eggplant) fritters 561
aubergine (eggplant) papeton 908
aubergine au cumin 406
aubergines (eggplants): preparation 55
aubergines (eggplants) au gratin, à la toulousaine (or à la languedocienne) 55, 1313
aubergines (eggplants) with cumin 406
aubergines (eggplants) imam bayildi 666
aubergines farcies 55
aubergines farcies à la catalane 235
aubergines sautées 55
avocado à la coque 353
avocado salad Archestrate 59
avocados stuffed with crab 59
avocat à la coque 353
avocats farcis au crabe 59

babas au rhum 61
Bacardi 318
backenofe 63
bacon bread 158
bacon omelette 881
Bagration meat soup 63
Bagration talmouses 1274
baked Alaska 65
baked eggs à la cressonière 391
baked foie gras 528
baked gurnard 630
baked potatoes with garlic 995
baked potatoes with raw goose foie
  gras 528
baked quinces 1032
baked red mullet with fennel 835
baked red mullet à la livournaise
  835
baked sardines 1124
baked semolina pudding 1160
ballottine of chicken in aspic 68
ballottine d'agneau à la gelee 69
ballottine de faisan à la gelee 946
ballottine de porc 69
ballottine de poularde à la gelee 68
ballottine de veau 69
*ballottine d'oie au
  Savigny-les-Beaune* 603
ballottine of goose with
  Savigny-les-Beaune 603
ballottine of lamb in aspic 69
ballottine of pheasant in aspic 946
ballottine of pork 69
ballottine of veal 69
banana cocktail 319
banana croutes à la maltaise 764
banana fritters 560
banana souffle 1195
banas flambé 72
bananas à la creole au gratin 72
banquière sauce 74
bar: préparation 80
bar braisé 81
bar grillé 82
bar à la portugaise 81
bar poché chaud 82
barbecue sauce 1131
barbue: préparation 166
barbue au chambertin 166
barbue au champagne 166
barbue braisée 166
barbue cardinal 221
barbue à la Berry 105
barbue à la dieppoise 437
barbue saumonée 166
baron d'agneau à la périgourdine
  79
baron of lamb à la périgourdine 79
barons de lapereau à la menthe 812
barquettes au fromage 79
barquettes aux abricots 79
barquettes aux champignons 79
barquettes aux framboises 1042
barquettes aux oeufs de poisson
  1069
barquettes d'huitres chaudes 897
barquettes d'huitres froides 897
barquettes à la bouquetière 148
barquettes with roe 1069
bars (ou barbues) à la provençale
  1012
basic sponge cake recipe 1216
basic velouté sauce 1359
basic white sauce 1131
basil oil 874

basil sandwich 1121
basket of crudites 401
bass: preparation 81
bass braised in red Graves 81
bass a la portugaise 81
bass (or brill) à la provençale 1012
bastion d'anguilles 82
bastion of eels 82
bâtarde sauce 1131
batonnets aux amandes 83
Bavarian cream 84
Bavarian cream à la cevenole 244
Bavarian fruit cream 84
bavarois aux fruits 84
Bavarois à la cevenole 244
bavarois à la crème 84
bavaroise 84
bavette grillée 520
bavette à l'échalote 520
bearnaise sauce 89
Beauharnais bananas 91
Beauharnais sauce 91
Beauvilliers timbales (small) 93
bécasse: préparation 1400
bécasse en casserole ou en cocotte
  1400
becasse en cocotte à la crème 1400
becasse froide à la Diane 1400
bécasse rôtie sur canapes 1400
bécasse sauté à l'Armagnac 1401
bécasses à la fine champagne 513
bechamel sauce 93
beef bourguignon 95
beef croquettes 395
beef émincés with mushrooms 484
beef hash à l'italienne 640
beef à la mode 95
beef à la mode de Beaucaire 90
beef miroton 815
beef salad 1103
beef Stroganov 1234
beetroot à la lyonnaise 101
beetroot (red beet) salad à la
  polonaise 979
beetroot soup (cold) 101
beignets d'ananas 561
beignets d'anchois 561
beignets d'aubergines 561
beignets de bananes 560
beignets de champignons 561
beignets de dattes 419
beignets de figures 561
beignets de fleurs d'acacia 810
beignets de foie gras à l'ancienne
  527
beignets de foies de volaille 561
beignets de fromage 561
beignets de gourilos 486
beignets de laitances 561
beignets de langoustines 561, 719
beignets de pommes 560
beignets de ris de veau 1253
beignets de riz 561
beignets de salsifis
  1114
beignets de sardines 1124
*beignets de saumon au coulis de
  pommes* 1111
beignets d'huitres 897
beignets à la creole 385
beignets à la florentine 522
beignets à l'imbrucciata 667
beignets Mont-Bry 821
beignets soufflés 561
beignets soufflés 561

beignets soufflés fourrés aux cerises
  275
Belgian cassonade tart 232
Bercy butter or shallot butter 104
Bercy sauce or shallot sauce 105
Besançon matafaim 781
best end of neck of lamb à la
  languedociènne 721
best end of neck (rib) of veal (cold)
  1356
betteraves étuvées à la crème 101
betteraves à la lyonnaise 101
bettes: préparation 1257
bettes au gratin 1257
bettes au ius 1257
bettraves en salade à la polonaise
  979
beurre Bercy ou beurre d'échalote
  104
beurre blanc 107
beurre clarifié 189
beurre Colbert 330
beurre composé: préparation 187
beurre d'ail 188
beurre d'amandes 188
beurre d'anchois 188
beurre de citron 188
beurre de crabe ou de crevettes 188
beurre de cresson 189
beurre de homard 188
beurre de laitances 189
beurre de Montpellier 188
beurre de moutarde 188
beurre de noisettes 188
beurre de piment 188
beurre de raifort 188
beurre de roquefort 189
beurre de sardines 189
beurre d'échalote 189
*beurre d'escargots, beurre à la
  bourguignonne* 1182
beurre d'estragon 189
beurre fondu 190
beurre hotelier 188
beurre à la broche 189
beurre landais 190
beurre maître d'hotel 762
beurre manié 189
beurre marchand de vin 769
beurre mousseux 189
beurre noir 189
beurre noisette 190
beurre vert 188
bichof au vin du rhin 112
bière de ménage 101
bifteck à cheval 278
bigos 108
bilberry flan 109
bilberry jam 109
bird's-nest consommé 110
bireweck 110
biscuit aux amandes 1217
biscuit de Savoie 1147
biscuit glacé au cassis 661
biscuit à l'italienne 1217
biscuit mousseline à l'orange 1217
biscuit roulé 1217
biscuits au citron 1218
biscuits de Reims 1051
biscuits fins 1218
biscuits genevois 1218
biscuits italiens 1218
biscuits à la cuiller 1218
biscuits punch 1218
biscuits soufflés au chocolat 1217

bisque de homard 113
bisque d'écrevisses 113
bitoke 113–14
bitter orange sauce 1165
black butter 189
Black Forest gateau 203
black pudding 117
black pudding à la normande 117
black radish as an hors d'oeuvre 1037
black velvet 319
blackberry jam 115
blackberry tartlets 115–16
blackcurrant ice cream cake 661
blackcurrant jelly 116
blackcurrant sauce 1134
blackcurrant sorbet 117
blackcurrant wine 364
blanc de champignons 839
blanc for offal and meat 119
blanc pour abats et viandes 119
blanc pour légumes 119
blanc for vegetables 119
blancs de pintade aux pommes de terre Alex Humbert 628
blancs de Saint-Pierre au velouté de whisky et sa julienne de légumes 688
blanquette: préparation 120
blanquette d'agneau à l'ancienne 121
blanquette de veau 121
blanquette of lamb a l'ancienne 121
blanquette of veal 121
blé germé 1389
blinis à la francaise 122
blond roux 1081
Bloody Mary 319
blue trout 1326
boar's head brawn (head cheese) 1392
boeuf bourguignon 95–6
boeuf gros sel ou boeuf bouilli 96
boeuf à la mode 95
boeuf à la mode de Beaucaire 90
boeuf miroton 815
boeuf pressé 97
boeuf salé 97
boeuf Stroganov 1234
boiled artichokes 47
boiled beef 96
boiled beef hash 640
boiled beef à la hongroise 145
boiled beef à la provençale 145
boiled calf's tongue 1308
boiled carrots 228
boiled chestnuts 277
boiled leeks 726
boiled (or poached) eggs à l'americaine 21
biled peas 930
boiled pigs' ears 465
boiled potatoes 995
boiled rabbit à l'anglaise 1033
boiled rice with butter 1060
boiled salt pork with pease pudding 1119
boisson frénette 49
boisson marquise 777
bolognaise sauce 126
bombe Aida 127
bombe Alhambra 127
bombe archiduc 127
bombe cardinal 221
bombe Chateaubriand 127

bombe diplomate 127
bombe Doria 127, 444
bombe duchesse 127
bombe glacée au yaourt 1405
bombe glacée Montmorency 823
bombe Grimaldi 127
bombe mixture 127
bombe Monselet 127
bombe tutti-frutti 1345
bone-marrow canapes 128
bone-marrow sauce 128
Bontemps sauce 129
Bordeaux Twelfth-Night cake 1346
bordelaise sauce 131
bordure de riz garnie 132
bordure de riz à la creole 133
bordure de semoule aux fruits 133
bordure de soles à la normande 132
bordure d'oeufs Brillat-Savarin 132
bordure d'oeufs princesse 132
borsch 133
bottereaux 134
bottled tarragon 1278
botvinya 137
bouchées: preparation 140
bouchées aux fruits de mer 1156
bouchées de lotte au chou nouveau 819
bouchées à la benedictine 104
bouchées à la financière 140
bouchées à la julienne 690
bouchées à la perigourdine 140
bouchées à lareine 140
bouchées with mushrooms 140
bouchées with prawns (shrimps) 140
boudin antillais 142
boudin blanc 142
boudin de volaille à la richelieu 142
boudin a la Richelieu 142
boudin noir 117
boudin noir à la normande 117
bougras 143
bouillabaisse 144
bouillabaisse d'épinards 1215
bouilleture angevine 144
bouilli de boeuf à la hongroise 145
bouilli de boeuf à la provençale 145
bouillon aux herbes 145
bouillon d'abattis 145
bouillon de légumes 146
bouillon de légumes dietiques 145
bouillon d'escargots 1182
bouillon du pot-au-feu 1000
bouillon ménagers modernes 146
boulettes de harengs à la suedoise 649
boulettes de Roquefort 1074
bourguignonne sauce for fish 150
bourguignonne sauce for meat and poultry 150
bourride 151
brain souffle à la chanoinesse 250
brains: preparation 152
brains in noisette butter 152
braised bass 81
braised beetroot with cream 101
braised brill 166
braised cabbage 192
braised calf's tongue 1308
braised celery 240
braised chestnuts 277
braised chicory 286
braised cod à la flamande 323
braised duck 459

braised endive 486
braised ham 636
braised ham with Madeira 758
braised ham with pineapple 636
braised ham porte-maillot 990
braised joint of beef 97
braised leeks 726
braised leg of lamb with baby onions 591
braised lettuce au gratin 733
braised lettuce in meat stock 733
braised mutton cutlets 845
braised ox cheek 265
braised palm hearts 903
braised paupiettes of beef 926
braised pigs' ears 466
braised rib of beef 98
braised sea bream with apples 1156
braised shoulder of lamb with garnish 1169
braised sirloin 1175
braised tendrons of veal à la bourgeoise 1292
braised turkey legs 1339
braised veal chops à la Custine 1357
braised veal grenadins 621
brandade de morue nimoise 155
brandade sauce à la provencale 154
brayaude omelette 156
Brazilian cocktail 320
bread croustades 398
bread panada 904
bread sauce 160, 1131
bread sauce à l'ancienne 1131
breaded lamb cutlets 713
breaded veal chops à la milaniase 1357
bream à la vendangeuse 161
breast of guinea fowl with potatoes Alex Humbert 628
breast of lamb fritots 162
brèdes de cresson 162
brème à la vendangeuse 161
Bressane salad 163
Bresse chicken-liver terrine 741
Breton sauce 164
brik with egg 165
brik a l'oeuf 165
brill: preparation 166
brill cardinal 221
brill in Chambertin 166
brill in champagne 166
brillà la Bercy 105
brill à la dieppoise 437
brill stuffed with salmon 166
Brimont mixed salad 169
brioche antillaises 171
brioche aux framboises 171
brioche aux fruits 171
brioche aux pralines 1005
brioche Parisienne 170
brioche polonaise 980
brioche with pralines 1005
brioche with raspberries 171
brioches with anchovies 171
brioches aux anchois 171
brioches aux champignons 171
brioches aux fromage 171
brioches with cheese 171
brioches with mushrooms 171
brioches Parisiennes individuelles 170
broccoli with cream 173
broccoli à la vendéenne 173

brochet au beurre blanc 956
brochet du meunier 956
brochettes d'agneau 174
brochettes de cigales de mer au
   safran 1222
brochettes de coquilles
   Saint-Jacques et d'huitres à la
   Villeroi 1368
brochettes de filet de boeuf mariné
   174
brochettes de foies de volaille è
   l'italienne 741
brochettes de fruits de mer 174
brochettes de fruits en papillotes
   565
brochettes de lotte 174
brochettes de moules 842
brochettes de porc aux pruneaux
   174
brochettes de queues de langoustine
   719
brochettes de rognons 175
brochettes de saumnon au foie de
   canard frais 1110
brochettes de sole aux
   champignons 1188
brochettes d'huitres à la Villeroi
   897
brochettes d'huitres à l'anglaise 897
brochettes of fried smelt 1178
brochettes of frogs' legs 562
brochettes of langoustine tails 719
brochettes of marinated fillet of
   beef 174
bronx 174
broth from the pot-au-feu 1000
brouet de Saint-Jacques aux
   épinards crus 1214
broufado 176
brouillade de truffes 479
brown bitter orange sauce for roast
   duck 1165
brown chaud-froid sauce for fish
   and game 263
brown chaud-froid sauce for
   various meats 263
brown gravy 1131
brown roux 1081
brown veal stock 1227
broyé béarnaise 177
broyé poitevin 177
brunoise pannequets 178
Brussels sprout purée 178
Brussels sprouts au gratin 178
Brussels sprouts à l'anglaise 178
bûche aux marrons 304
bûche de Noël 304
bûche de Noël au chocolat 305
buckwheat crepes (galettes) 387
bugnes 180
buisson of asparagus in pastry 181
buisson of crayfish 181
buisson d'asperges en croustade
   181
buisson d'écrevisses 181
buns 181
Burgundian raisine 1039
butter sauce 1131
butter for snails 1182
buttered cardoons 222
buttered cucumber 404
buttered noodles à l'alsacienne 860
buttered salsify 1114

cabbage charlotte with olives 876

cabbage à l'anglaise 192
cabillaud braisé à la flamande 323
cabillaud frit 324
cabillaud grillée 324
cabillaud à la boulangère 147
cabillaud à l'anglaise 324
cabillaud à l'indienne 669
cabillaud pochà chaud 324
cabillaud rôti 324
cabinet pudding 1017
café arabe 327
cafe glacé 327
caillebottes poitevines 201
cailles au riz 1027
cailles en casserole 1025
cailles en casserole aux raisins 1016
cailles en chemise 272
cailles farcies au nid 1027
cailles farçies en caisses 1027
cailles farçies en caisses à la
   Lamballe 716
cailles farçies à la gourmande 1027
cailles grillées 1025
cailles grillées petit-duc 1026
cailles à la minute 1026
cailles à la romaine 1072
cailles rôties 1027
caillettes ardéchoises 201
cake 203
cake au gingembre 594
cake au miel et aux cerises confites
   204
calf's or chicken liver purée 1024
calf's head: preparation 643
calf's head bonne femme 644
calf's head en tortue 1312
calf's head (hot) with cold sauce
   644
calf's head (hot) with hot sauce 644
calf's head à l'anglaise 644
calf's heart à l'anglaise 645
calf's kidney à la bonne femme 695
calf's liver with bacon 62
calf's liver à la bourgeoise 149
calf's liver à la bourguignonne 740
calf's liver à l'anglaise 740
calf's liver à l'espagnole 492
calf's mesentery calf's l'indienne
   800
calf's tongue à l'italienne 1309
calf's-brain fritots 153
calmars farçis à la marseillaise
   1221
calmars frits ou sautés 1221
calmars à l'andalouse 1221
calves' brains en matelote 153
calves' brains à l'allemande 14
calves' feet with tartare sauce 504
calves' kidneys with chicken livers
   695
calves' liver à la creole 385
calves' sweetbreads braised in
   brown stock 1252
calves' sweetbreads braised in white
   stock 1253
calves' sweetbreads Regence 1050
Cambridge sauce 207
Camerani soup 208
canapés: preparation 209
canapés with anchovies 209
canapés arlequins 210
canapés with asparagus 209
canapés au crabe 210
canapés au cresson 210
canapés au fromage 210

canapés au saumon fumé 210
canapés aux anchois 209
canapés aux asperges 209
canapés aux champignons 210
canapés aux crevettes (au homard,
   à la langouste) 209
canapés with cheese 210
canapés with crab 210
canapés à la bayonnaise 209
canapés à la danoise 210
canapés à la moelle 128
canapés à la moelle 128
canapés à la parisienne 912
canapés à la russe 1086
canapés à l'ecarlate 468
canapés with mushrooms 210
canapés with shrimps, lobster, or
   langouste 209
canapés with smoked salmon 210
canapés with watercress 210
canard aux feuilles de thé 1289
canard aux olives 877
canard braisé 459
canard farçi à la rouennaise 1078
canard à l'agenaise 460
canard à l'ananas 959
canard à l'orange Lasserre 460
canard rôti 460
canard rôti aux peches 461
canard sauvage au chambertin 461
canard sauvage au porto 989
canard sauvage aux pires 935
canard sauvage à la tyrolienne 461
canard sauvage à la Walter Scott
   461
canard Voisin 1374
canasta 319
candied angelica 27–8
candied orange peel 885
caneton au miel de lavande et au
   citron 729
cannelloni aux fruits de mer 212
cannelloni à la bechamel 212
cannelloni à la florentine 212
cannelloni à la viande 212
cannelloni pasta 212
cape gooseberry compote 214
caper sauce 214
caponata 215
capucins 218
caramel cream for garnishing
   desserts 380
caramel cream with honey 652
caramel ice cream 663
caramel à napper 219
caramel sauce 219, 1134
caramel-flavoured custard 381
caramels durs au café 220
caramels mous à la crème 220
carbonara salad 1103
carbonnade à la flamande 221
cardinal sauce 222
cardons au beurre 222
cardons frits 222
cardoon purée 222
cardoon salad 222
cari d'agneau 410
cari de lotte à la creole 410
cari de poulet 409
Caribbean brioche 171
Caribbean chicken with pineapple
   and rum 959
Caribbean cocktail 319
carolines Joinville 225
carolines à la hollandaise 225

carottes aux raisins 228
carottes glacées 228
carottes à la creme 228
carottes à la forestière 539
carottes à l'anglaise 228
carottes râpées aux anchois 229
carottes Vichy 1365
carp Chambord 247
carp à la chinoise 226
carp à la juive 689
carpe farcie à l'ancienne 226
carpe frite 226
carpe grillé à la mâitre d'hotel 226
carpe à la chinoise 226
carpe à la juive 689
carré d'agneau grillé 715
carré d'agneau à la bonne femme 715
carré d'agneau à la bordelaise 715
carré d'agneau à la languedocienne 721
carré d'agneau à la nicoise 857
carré d'agneau La Varenne 724
carré d'agneau Parmentier 914
carré d'agneau rôti 715
carré de porc au chou rouge 987
carré de porc bonne femme 987
carré de porc a l'ananas 959
carré de porc rôti et ses garnitures 987
carré de veau froid 1356
carrot flan 228
carrot loaves 742
carrot purée 228
carrot salad with orange 1103
carrots with cream 228
carrots à la forestière 539
carrots with raisins 228
casbah 320
casserole au riz à l'ancienne 231
casserole of calf's heart 645
casserole of pheasant 947
casserole veal chops 1357
casserole veal chops à la bonne femme 1357
casserole of veal chops à la Parmentier 914
casserole of veal chops à la paysanne 928
casserole of woodcock 1400
casserole of woodcock à la crème 1400
cassis 232
cassolettes de Saint-Jacques aux endives 287
cassoulet 234
Caucasian piroshki 962
cauliflower au gratin 238
cauliflower à la polonaise 979
cauliflower à l'anglaise 238
cauliflower salad 238
cauliflower and tomato pickle 951
caviar d'aubergine 55
caviar mayonnaise 785
céléri branche: preparation 240
céléri en remoulade 240
céléri-branche à la milanaise 806
céléri-ravé: préparation 239
celeriac: preparation 239
celeriac (celery root) velouté soup 1198
celeriac croquettes 239
celeriac en remoulade 240
celeriac julienne 240
celeris au beurre 240

celeris braisés (au gras ou au maigre) 240
celery: preparation 240
celery in butter 240
celery à la milanaise 806
celery sauce 240
cep omelette 881
cepes grillés 243
cepes marinés a chaud 243
ceps au gratin 242
ceps en terrine 242
ceps à la brodelaise 242
ceps à la mode bearnaise 242
cerises Condé 337
cerises confites fourrées à la pâte d'amande 565
cerises deguisées dites 'marquises' 565
cerises flambées à la bourguignonne 274
cerises jubilé 275
cerises à l'eau-de-vie 275
cerneaux de noix au verjus 1380
cervelas en salade 1145
cervelas farcis aux epinards 1145
cervelle au beurre noisette 152
cervelle de veau en fritots 153
cervelle de veau frite à l'anglaise 153
cervelle de veau à l'allemande 13
cervelles: préparation 152
chair à saucisse 1142
chair à saucisse fine ou farce fine de porc 1142
Chambertin sauce 246
Chambord sauce 247
champagne cocktail 319
champignons en garniture 840
champignons farcis 840
champignons à la crème 840
champignons à la poulette 1002
champignons à l'anglaise 839
champigny gateau 249
Chantilly cream 251
Chantilly cream puffs 301
Chantilly sauce 251
charcutiere sauce 253
charlotte au chocolat 255
charlotte aux framboises 255, 1043
charlotte aux poires 255, 934
charlotte aux pommes 255
charlotte aux pommes à la cassonade brune 35–6
charlotte aux rougets 256
charlotte de chou aux olives 876
charlotte de légumes 256
charlotte glacée aux marons 256
charlotte glacée a la vanille 256
Chartreuse crêpes 388
chartreuse de perdreau 258
chartreuse of eggs in a mould 257
chartreuse of partridge 258
chasseur sauce 253
chateau potatoes 262
chateaubriand grillé 259
chateaubriand sauce 1132
chateaubriand sauté 259
Chatouillard potatoes 262
chaud-froid of chicken with tarragon 263
chaud-froid de faisan 947
chaud-froid de poulet à l'estragon 263
chaud-froid de saumon 264
chaud-froid of pheasant 947

chaud-froid of salmon 264
chaussons: préparation 1342
chaussons aux pommes et aux pruneaux 1342
chaussons pour petits entrées 1342
chayotes braisés au jus 411
chayotes à la martiniquaise 411
cheese barquettes 79
cheese croissants 393
cheese croquettes 396
cheese darioles 417
cheese diablotins 437
cheese flan 519
cheese fondue 532
cheese fritters 561
cheese piroshki 962
cheese and poached egg souffle 1197
cheese puffs 300
cheese souffle 1197
cherries in brandy 275
cherries Condé 337
cherries flambéed à la bourguignonne 274
cherries preserved au naturel 275
cherry blossom 319
cherry cocktail 320
cherry compote 334
cherry crêpes 388
cherry flan 519
cherry jam 275
cherry liqueur 738
cherry paste 567
cherry soup 273
cherry tart 1280
cherry-filled souffle fritters 275
chervil essence 494
chervil soup 275
chestnut compote 334
chestnut cream 277
chestnut croquembouche 394
chestnut croquettes 396
chestnut custards 604
chestnut log 304
chestnut preserve 277
chestnut purée 277
chestnut souffle 1195
chestnut souffle Mont-Bry 277
Chiboust cream 279
chiche-kebab 693
chicken ambassadrice 20
chicken au blanc 118
chicken au gratin sauerkraut 1137
chicken with bamboo shoots 170
chicken bonne femme 129
chicken casserole 282
chicken with celery 241
chicken with cider 307
chicken Clamart 312
chicken cooked in beer 100–1
chicken crepinettes 389
chicken curry 409
chicken demi-deuil 431
chicken Demidof 431
chicken Doria 444
chicken en capilotade 215
chicken en vessie Marius Vettard 118
chicken hash 641
chicken with hazelnuts 642
chicken jambalaya 678
chicken jambonneaux 678
chicken à la bourguignonne 150
chicken à la Chantilly 251
chicken à la creole 385

chicken à la matignon 782
chicken à la Nantua 849
chicken à la Neva 855
chicken à la polonaise 281
chicken à la reine 1051
chicken with lemon 728
chicken à l'ivoire 676
chicken Maryland 282
chicken medallions Beauharnais 790
chicken medallions à l'egyptienne 481
chicken mousse 831
chicken oysters with morels 825
chicken pâté pantin 924
chicken pie 952
chicken pilaf 957
chicken princesse 1010
chicken purée 1024
chicken with rice and supreme sauce 282
chicken in a salt crust 282
chicken with sherry 1169
chicken with tarragon 282
chicken with tarragon in aspic 282
chicken velouté soup 1198
chicken waterzooi 1383
chicken yassa 1404
chicken-liver brochettes 175
chicken-liver brochettes à l'italienne 741
chicken-liver croustades 741
chicken-liver flan chavette 519
chicken-liver fritters 561
chicken-liver omelette 879
chicken-liver timbale 741
chicorée au gratin 486
chicorée braisée 486
chicory au gratin 286
chicory fritots 286
chicory with ham 287
chicory salad à la flamande 286
chiffonade d'oseille 1192
chiffonade of sorrel 1192
chiffonnade de laitue crue 287
chiffonnade of raw lettuce 287
chilled melon ices 793
chilled peaches with raspberries 931
chilli purée 217
chilli-pepper oil 217
China tea 1289
Chinese artichokes: preparation 290
chipolatas au risotto 291
chipolatas with risotto 291
Chivry butter 292
Chivry sauce for eggs and poultry 292
chocolat frappé 296
chocolat mousseux 296
chocolat viennois 296
chocolate cake 294
chocolate charlotte 255
chocolate cream 380
chocolate cream puffs 301
chocolate eclairs 468
chocolate egg custard 381
chocolate ice cream 294
chocolate icing 295
chocolate log 305
chocolate marquise 777
chocolate mousse 832
chocolate profiteroles 1011
chocolate pudding 1017

chocolate sauce 295
chocolate souffle 1195
chocolate souffle biscuits 1217
chocolate and strawberry mousse 831
chocolate tart 1280
chocolate truffles with butter 297
chocolate truffles with cream 297
chocolate-flavoured confectioners' custard (pastry cream) 381
choesels a la bruxelloise 297
chop suey 299
chopped onions 883
chopped white tuna steak with seaweed 1335
Choron sauce 299
chou braisé 192
chou chinois à la sseutch'ouannaise 290
chou farçi 193
chou à l'anglaise 192
chou palmiste en daube 903
chou rouge à la flamande 193
chou rouge mariné 193
chou-fleur au gratin 238
chou-fleur à la polonaise 979
chou-fleur à l'anglaise 238
chou-fleur sauté 238
choucroute au gras pour garniture 1137
choucroute de navets 1342
choucroute à l'alsacienne 1137
choux au café 301
choux au chocolat 301
choux au fromage 300
choux de Bruxelles en purée 178
choux de Bruxelles gratinnés 178
choux de Bruxelles à l'anglaise 178
choux de Bruxelles sautés 178
choux with foie gras mousse 300
choux à la creme Chantilly 301
choux à la mousse de foie gras 300
choux à la Nantua 300
choux à la normande 301
choux pastry 300
Christmas pompes 982
Christmas pudding 304
Christmas yule log 304
chump end of lamb Callas 305
chutney aux oignons d'Espagne 306
chutney aux pommes et aux mangues 305
cider cup 406
cider fruit cup 307
cigarettes russes 308
cinghalaise sauce 308
cinnamon sugar 1245
citrons confits 729
citrons farcis 729
citrons givrés 729
civet de homard 310
civet de lièvre 310
civet of hare 310
civet of lobster 310
clafoutis 311
clam soup 312
clarification du bouillon 313
clarification of stock 313
clarified butter 189
clarified fish colle for desserts 331
clarified white consommé 344
classic fine brioche dough 170
classic macaroons 754
classic madeleines 759

classic mayonnaise 785
clove sugar 1245
club sandwich 1121
coating caramel 219
Cocabana 319
Cocabricot 319
cock-a-leekie 317
cockle salad with fresh broad (fava) beans 1103
cocks' combs: preparation 318
cocks' combs en attereaux à la Villeroi 318
cocks' kidneys for garnishing 695
cocktail au yaourt 1405
Cocktomate 319
coconut cake 322
coconut preserve 322
coconut preserve 322
cod à la boulangere 147
cod à l'anglaise 324
cod à l'indienne 669
coeur de veau en casserole 645
coeur de veau farci 645
coeur de veau grillé en brochettes 645
coeur de veau à l'anglaise 645
coeur de veau rôti 645
coeur de veau sauté 645
coeurs d'agneau à l'anglaise 645
coeurs d'agneau sautés 645
coeurs d'artichaut 47
coeurs de palmier en salade 903
coffee and brandy ice cream 663
coffee or chocolate tartlets 1283
coffee cream puffs 301
coffee dacquoise 413
coffee éclairs 469
coffee essence 494
coffee ice cream 327
coffee progrès 1012
coffee religieuses 1052
coffee souffle 1195
coffee-flavoured confectioners' custard (pastry cream) 381
coings au four 1032
Colbert butter 330
Colbert sauce 330
colin à la boulangère 633
colle de poisson clarifiée pour entremets 331
colvert au poivre vert 460
cominée degelines 333
Commercy madeleines 759
complete cocktail 319
compote d'abricots 334
compote d'alkekenges 214
compote d'ananas 334
compote de cerises 334
compote de figures fraîches 334
compote de figures sèches 334
compote de fraises 335
compote de fruit en conserve 335
compote de marrons 334
compote de pêches 334
compote de poires 334
compote de pommes 333
compote de pruneaux 1015
compote de prunes 335
compote quatre fruits 334, 541
compote de rhubarbe 335
compote poires-pommes caramelisée 334
compote of prunes 1015
concentrated tomato glaze 1304
concombres: préparation 403

concombres étuvés au beurre 404
concombres farcis 404
concombres farcis au crabe 404
concombres à la crème 404
Condé icing 337
Condé soup 336
confectioners' custard (pastry cream) 380
confit d'oie 339
confit d'oie à la béarnaise 339
confit d'oie à la landaise 339
confit of goose 339
confit of goose à la béarnaise 339
confit of goose à la landaise 339
confiture d'abricots 681
confiture d'airelles 374
confiture de cerises 275
confiture de citron 730
confiture de figues 509
confiture de fraises 1231
confiture de framboises 1043
confiture de marrons 277
confiture de melons 794
confiture de mirabelles 814
confiture de mures 115
confiture de myrtilles 109
confiture de noix de coco 322
confiture de peches 931
confiture de pommes de d'ananas 959
confiture de raisin 614
confiture de reines-claudes 681
confiture de rhubarbe 1057
confiture de tomates vertes 1305
confiture d'oranges 886
conserve de champignons au naturel 840
conserve de foie gras de canard (ou d'oie) au naturel en terrine 528
conserve de purée de fraises congelée 1232
conserve de purée de fraises sterilisée 1232
conserve de truffes congelées 1330
conserve de truffes à la graisse d'oie 1331
conserve de truffes sterilisées 1331
conserve d'estragon par congelation 1278
conserve d'estragon par ebullition 1278
conserve d'estragon par séchage 1278
conserve d'oseille 1192
conserve de cerises au naturel 275
consommé au fumet de gibier 345
consommé au riz ou a la semoule 345
consommé au tapioca 1277
consommé au vin 345
consommé aux nids d'hirondelle 110
consommé aux profiteroles 346
consommé blanc clarifié 344
consommé blanc simple 344
consommé Brillat-Savarin 345
consommé chasseur 345
consommé Colbert 345
consommé croute au pot 345
consommé Dalayrac 345
consommé flavoured with game fumet 345
consommé Florette 345
consommé julienne 690
consommé à la brunoise 178

consommé à la madrilene 759
consommé à la parisienne 345
consommé à la reine 1051
consommé à la royale 1082
consommé à l'amiral 21
consommé Leopold 345
consommé à l'essence de truffe 345
consommé à l'essence d'estragon 345
consommé à l'orge perle 77
consommé Monte-Carlo 345
consommé Nesselrode 853
consommé with pearl barley 77
consommé Princess Alice 346
consommé with profiteroles 346
consommé with rice or semolina 346
consommé Saint-Hubert 1099
consommé simple de gibier 344
consommé simple de poisson 344
consommé simple de volaille 344
consommé with wine 345
conversations 347
cooked' meringues 798
cooking pasta 919
cooking soft-roes in court-bouillon 1184
coq au cidre 307
coq au vin 352
coq à la biere 100
coqilles Saint-Jacques crues 1148
coqilles Saint-Jacques en brochettes 1149
coqilles Saint-Jacques en salade 1149
coqilles Saint-Jacques frites beurre Colbert 1149
coqilles Saint-Jacques à la mayonnaise 1149
coqilles Saint-Jacques à la vapeur 1149
coqilles Saint-Jacques Mornay 1149
coquelets en crapaudine à l'americaine 353
coquilles au crevettes 1150
coquilles de poisson à la Mornay 1150
coquilles de saumon Victoria 1366
coquilles Saint-Jacques crues au caviar 239
coquilles Saint-Jacques gratinées à la dieppoise 438
coquilles Saint-Jacques à la nage 847
corn en soso with chicken giblets 763
cornbread 763
cornets de jambon à la mousse foie gras 356
cornets de saumon fumé aux oeufs de poisson 356
cornichons au vinaigre, à chaud 589
cornichons au vinaigre, à froid 589
cornichons à la russe 588
cornmeal pancakes with avocados 59
Corsican anchoyade with figs 509
coté de boeuf braisée 98
coté de boeuf (garnitures) 98
coté de boeuf rotie au four 98
côté de boeuf rôtie à la bouqetiàre 148
côté de veau Foyot 542

côté de veau panée Cussy en portefeuille 990
côtelettes composées 411
côtelettes d'agneau aux figures et au miel 510
côtelettes d'agneau grillées 713
côtelettes d'agneau grillées à la paloise 904
côtelettes d'agneau à la maréchale 769
côtelettes d'agneau à l'anversoise 32
côtelettes d'agneau panées 713
côtelettes de chevreuil sautées au enièvre 1071
côtelettes de chevreuil sautées aux cerises 1071
côtelettes de chevreuil sautées aux raisins 1071
côtelettes de lièvre aux champignons 639
côtelettes de marcassin aux coings 768
côtelettes de mouton braisées 845
côtelettes de mouton chasseur 845
côtelettes de mouton à la cevenole 244
côtelettes de mouton à la fermière 845
côtelettes de mouton Maintenon 760
côtelettes de mouton Pompadour 982
côtelettes de saumon 1110
côtelettes de saumon glacées au Chambertin 1108
côtelettes de saumon à la bourguignonne 1111
côtelettes de saumon à la florentine 1111
côtelettes de saumon à la russe 1087
côtelettes de saumon à l'anglaise 1111
côtelettes de saumon Pojarski 976
côtelettes de volaille Helder 646
côtelettes de mouton Champvallon 250
côtes de porc aux kiwis 701
côtes de porc charcuterie 987
côtes de porc grillées 987
côtes de porc à la bayonnaise 987
côtes de porc sautées 988
côtes de veau aux fines herbes 513
côtes de veau braisées a la Custine 1357
côtes de veau en casserole 1357
côtes de veau en casserole à la bonne femme 1357
côtes de veau en casserole à la Parmentier 914
côtes de veau en casserole à la paysanne 928
côtes de veau en papillotes 909
côtes de veau grillées 1357
côtes de veau grillées vert-pré 1357
côtes de veau à la gelée 1358
côtes de veau panées à la milanaise 1357
côtes de veau sautées à la crème 1357
côtes de veau sautées à la duxelles 463
côtes de veau sautées à la provencale 1013

cotignac 362
cotriade 362
coulis de framboises 363
coulis de fruits frais 363
coupe de fruits du cidre 307
coupes aux poires à la crème au
*   caramel* 365
coupes de crème Hawaï 365
coupes glacées aux peches 932
coupes à la cevenole 365
coupes à la cevenole Malmaison
*   365*
courge au gratin 608
courgette (zucchini) omelette 880
courgette (zucchini) purée 366
courgette (zucchini) salad 367
courgettes farcies 367
courgettes glacées 367
courgettes sautées 367
courgettes (zucchini): preparation
    366
courgettes (zucchini) à la
    mentonnaise 795
courgettes (zucchini) à la nicoise
    367
courgettes (zucchini) à la
    provencale 367
courgettes (zucchini) à l'indienne
    367
court-bouillon au citron ou au
    vinaigre 368
court-bouillon au lait 368
court-bouillon au vin 368
court-bouillon eau de sel 368
court-bouillon with milk 368
court-bouillon with wine 368
couscous 369
couscous au poisson 370
couscous aux legumes 370
couscous with fish 370
couscous à la viande 370
couscous with meat 370
couscous with vegetables 370
cousinette 371
crab cocktail 320
crab feuilletes 507
crab à la bretonne 373
crab (or prawn) butter 188
crab salad 373
crab souffle 1197
crabe à la bretonne 373
crabes farcis au gratin 373
crabes farcis à la martiniquaise 373
cracked olives 877
cramique 373
cranberry jam 374
cranberry jelly 374
cranberry sauce 374
crapiaux with apples 375
crapiaux aux pommes 375
craquelins en forme de petits fours
*   375*
craquelins as petits fours 375
crayfish bisque 113
crayfish à la bordelaise 376
crayfish sauce 376
crayfish tails au gratin 377
crayfish tails au gratin à la façon de
    Maitre La Planche 377
cream of asparagus soup 383
cream of chicken soup 383
cream forcemeat 536
ream of mushroom soup 383

cream sauce 1132
cream soup with walnuts 1380
cream soups: preparation 383
creamed butter 189
Crécy soup 384
creme anglaise 381
creme anglaise collée 381
creme anglaise à la liqueur 381
creme au beurre au cafe 382
creme au beurre au chocolat 382
creme au beurre au sirop 382
crème au beurre nature au sucre
*   382*
crème au beurre nature à l'anglaise
*   382*
crème au beurre pralinée 382
crème au café ou au thé 381
crème au caramel 381
crème au caramel pour garnir des
*   entremets* 380
crème au chocolat 380
crème au citron 381, 382
crème caramel au miel 652
crème Chantilly 251
crème Chiboust 279
crème d'amandes 380
crème d'asperges 383
crème de champignons 383
crème de marrons 277
crème de volaille 383
crème d'estragon 1278
crème en ramequins 380
crème fouette 383
crème frangipane 542
crème frite en beignets 382
crème ganache 575
creme pâtissière 380
creme pâtissière au café 381
creme pâtissière au chocolat 381
creme renversée 381
creme renversée au chocolat 381
crème-potage: methode de base 383
crêpes au citron 389
crêpes au jambon 387
crêpes au Roquefort 387
crêpes aux cerises 388
crêpes aux champignon 387
crêpes aux mais aux avocats 59
crêpes de pommes de terre 99
crêpes des chartreux 388
crêpes gratinees aux épinards 38.
crêpes à la cevenole 244, 388
crêpes à la confiture 389
crêpes à la frangipane 542
crêpes à l'oeuf et au fromage 387
crêpes normandes 388
crêpes (ou galettes) de sarrasin 387
crêpes Suzette 1251
crépinettes de porc 389
crépinettes de volaille 389
cresson étuvé 390
crêtes de coq: préparation 318
crêtes de coq en attereaux à la
*   Villeroi* 318
cretons de la maman 987
crevettes frites 1172
crevettes sautées au whisky 1172
croissants au fromage 393
croissants aux crevettes 393
croissants aux pignons 960
croissants parisiens 392
croissants viennois 392
croissants viennois à la confiture
*   393*
cromesquis: preparation 706

croque-Emmental 484
croque-monsieur a la brandade 394
croquembouche de marrons 394
croquets aux amandes 394
croquette mixture: preparation 395
croquettes aux champignons 839
croquettes de boeuf 395
croquettes de celeri 239
croquettes de fromage 396
croquettes de macaroni 396
croquettes de marrons 396
croquettes de morue 396
croquettes de pommes de terre
*   396*
croquettes de riz 396
*   sweet* 397
croquettes de riz à l'indienne 396
croquettes d'epinards 1215
croquettes Montrouge 824
croquignoles parisiennes 397
crosnés: préparation 290
croustades de foies de volaille 741
croustades de pain de mie 398
croustades de pâté feuilletée 398
croustades de pommes de terre
*   duchesse* 398
croustades de riz ou de semoule
*   398*
croustades à la grecque 398
croustades à la langouste 718
croustades à la marinière 398
croustades vert-pré 1365
croûte feuilletée pour tarte 1020
croûte à flan cuite à blanc 518
croûte à timbale garnie 1300
croûte à vol-au-vent 1375
croûte à vol-au-vent 1375
croûtes: preparation 399
croûtes au pot 400
croûtes aux bananes à la maltaise
*   764*
croûtes aux champignons 399
croûtes aux fruits 399
croûtes aux fruits de mer 399
croûtes Brillat-Savarin 168
croûtes for consomme 400
croûtes en couronne à la
*   Montmorency* 399
croûtes à la diable 399
croûtes à la reine 1052
crouton omelette 400
croutons de gelée 400
croutons 400
crown of croutes à la
    Montmorency 399
crumpets 402
crumpets with Roquefort 1074
cucumber cocktail 321
cucumber salad 404
cucumber salad with yoghurt 1405
cucumber soup (cold) 404
cucumber stuffed with crab 404
cucumbers: preparation 403
cucumbers with cream 404
cuisses de dindonneau braisées
*   1339*
cuisses de grenouille aux fines
*   herbes* 562
cuisses de grenouille en brochettes
*   562*
cuisses de lièvre rôties 640
cuisson: macaroni 753
cuisson à blanc d'un fond de tarte
*   64*
cuisson des haricots 87
cuisson des haricots verts 86

*cuisson des laitances au
   court-bouillon* 1184
cuisson des pâtés 919
cuisson des ravioli 1045
cuisson à l'eau 50
cuissot de chevreuil aux capres
   1070
cuissot de chevreuil rôti 1070
*culotte de boeuf au poireaux à la
   bière* 727
*culotte de boeuf aux poireaux à la
   bière* 727
Cumberland sauce 405
cumin allumettes 406
Curacao 407
Curacao souffle 1196
curd cheese tart 1280
Curnonsky 319
curried beef hash 641
curried haddock 632
curry or Indian sauce 669
custard cream 381
custard cream with gelatine 381
custard cream with liqueur 381
custard flavoured with coffee or tea
   381
custard marrows braised in gravy
   411
custard marrows à la martiniquaise
   411
cutlets of marcassin with quinces
   768

dacquoise au café 413
daiquiri 319, 414
damier 415
dampfnudeln 415
dandelion and bacon salad 416
danicheff gateau 416
Danish canapes 210
Danish cherry flan 275
darioles au fromage 417
darioles aux amandes 417
darnes de saumon frites 1109
darnes de saumon grillées 1110
darnes de saumon à la meunière
   1112
darnes de saumon pochées 1110
darnes de saumon princesse 1010
Darphin potatoes 417
dartois aux anchois 418
dartois aux fruits de mer 418
dartois à la confiture d'abricots 418
dartois à la frangipane 418
dartois Laguipere 713
d'Artois soup 48
date fritters 419
daube of beef à la provencale 420
daube de boeuf à la provencale 420
daube de pieds de porc 504
daube of pigs' trotters 504
daube of turkey à la bourgeoise
   1339
dauphine potatoes 422
daurade de citron confit 729
daurade farcie au fenouil 1156
daurade (ou bar) à la meunière 801
daurade royale braisée aux pommes
   1156
delices aux noix 430
delicieux aux pommes 430
delicieux surprise 430
demi-glace 432
desalting and poaching salt cod
   1117

dessalage et pochage de la morue
   1117
*dessert de mangues et de fruits de la
   passion au rhum* 765
devilled eeel 471
devilled herrings 436
devilled lambs' (or sheep's) tongues
   1309
devilled meat dishes 436
devilled oyster 436
devilled sauce 436
devilled spring chicken 285
diablotins au fromage 437
diablotins aux noix et au Roquefort
   437
diablotins with walnuts and
   Roquefort cheese 437
dietetic vegetable bouillon 145
dijonnaise sauce 439
dinde etoffée grand-duc 610
*dindonneau en daube à la
   bourgeoise* 1339
dindonneau poché vinaigrette 1339
dindonneau rôti 1339
dindonneau rôti farci aux marrons
   1340
*dindonneau rôti farci aux pommes
   reinettes* 1340
dindonneau rôti à l'anglaise 1340
diplomat pudding 440
diplomat sauce 440
diplomate au bavarois 440
dodine de canard 442
dodine of duck 442
Doria salad 444
dorines 444
doughnuts 444
douillons 449
Dresden stollen 1228
dressing roasting pigeons 955
dried tarragon 1278
drying apples and pears 455
drying herbs 455
drying vegetables 455
Du Barry salad 456
Dubonnet fizz 319
duchess potato croustades 398
duchess potato mixture 457
duchess potatoes for garnish 457
duchesses (petits fours) 456
duck foie gras with banana purée
   and truffles 527
duck foie gras with grapes 614
duck foie gras with oysters and
   crayfish 527
duck foie gras with white pepper
   and green leeks 527
duck à l'agenaise 460
duck à l'orange Lasserre 460
duck with olives 877
duck (or goose) foie gras escalopes
   with grapes (hot) 528
duck (or goose) foie gras escalopes
   with grapes and truffles 526
duck (or goose) foie gras mousse
   527
duck pâté (cold) 460
duck with pineapple 959
duck saupiquet 1138
duck with tea leaves 1289
duck Voisin 1374
duckling with lavender-honey and
   lemon 729
Dumaine, Alexandre 462
Dumas, Alexandre 462

dumpling 462
Dutch wafers 1377
duxelles de champignons 463
duxelles sauce 463

eau de ratafia de coing 1032
eau de reglisse à l'orange 739
éclairs au cafe 469
éclairs au chocolat 469
écorcé de melon au vinaigre 794
écorcés de citron confites 730
écorcés d'orange confites 885
ecossaise sauce 469
écrevisses grillees au beurre d'ail
   377
écrevisses à la bordelaise 376
eel: preparation 471
eel brochettes à l'anglaise 472
eel à la bonne femme 472
eel à la provencale 472
eel matelote 782
eel pie 472
eel pie aux fines herbes 472
egg or caramel custard 381
egg and cheese crépes 387
egg custard 479
egg ring Brillat-Savarin 132
egg ring à la princesse 132
egg sauce 480
egg yolk stuffing (cold) 536
egg yolk stuffing (hot) 536
eggnog with beer 479
eggplants *see under* aubergines
eggs au miroir 475
eggs in cups à la hollandaise 651
eggs en cocotte: preparation 475
eggs en cocotte Brillat-Savarin 168
eggs en cocotte with cream 475
eggs en cocotte à la périgourdine
   941
eggs en cocotte à la tartare 475
eggs en cocotte with tarragon 475
eggs à la bruxelloise 179
eggs à la chevalière 278
eggs à la coque: preparation 475
eggs à la piperade 961
eggs à la tripe 1323
eggs in a mould: preparation 475
eggs in a mould Bizet 475
eggs in a mould Carème 223
eggs in a mould Polignac 978
eggs sur le plat: preparation 475
eggs sur le plat au bacon 476
eggs sur le plat Carmen 224
eggs sur le plat à la Chaveille 476
eggs sur le plat à la maraichère 768
eggs sur le plat à l'agenaise 476
eggs sur le plat à l'antiboise 476
eggs sur le plat à l'orientale 476
eggs sur le plat Meyerbeer 803
eggs sur le plat Montrouge 476
eggs sur le plat Rothomago 1077
eggs with tea leaves 1289
eierkuckas 481
elder-flower wine with lime
   blossom 481
émincés d'agneau 715
émincés de boeuf aux champignons
   484
*émincés de veau ou de volaille à
   blanc* 484
émincés a l'italienne 674
enchaud 485
endive salad with bacon 486
endives au gratin 286, 486

endives au jambon 287
endives en fritots 286
endives a l'étuvée 286
English almond pudding 1017
English apple pudding 1018
English bread-and-butter sauce
1132
English butter sauce 1132
English chicken soup 1199
English cream sauce 1132
English mincemeat 810
English muffins 833
entrecôte grand-mere 611
entrecôte grillée 487
entrecôte à la menagere 794
entrecôte marchand de vin 769
entrecôte poelée 486
entrecôte poelée aux champignons
487
entrecôte poelée à la
bourguignonne 487
entrecôte vert-pré 1365
entrecôtes Mirabeau 813
entremets au tapioca 1277
épaule braisée et ses garnitures
1169
épaule d'agneau de lait grillée 1170
épaule d'agneau à l'albigeoise 9
épaule de chevreuil aux olives 1071
épaule de mouton en pistache 964
épaule de mouton et ses garnitures
1170
épaule de porc aux cinq-épices 988
épaule de veau farcie 1170
épaule farcie à la gasconne 1170
épaule rotie en ballottine 1170
éperlans frits 1178
éperlans frits en brochettes 1178
éperlans grillés à l'anglaise 1178
éperlans marinés 1178
epigrammes 489
épinards: preparation et cuisson
1214
épinards au beurre 1215
épinards au gratin 1215
épinards à la creme 1215
épinards à l'anglaise 1215
escabèche de sardines 1124
escalopes of bass with pepper and
cream of ginger 81
escalopes of calves' sweetbreads au
gratin 1253
escalopes of calves' sweetbreads à
l'ancienne 1253
escalopes chaudes de foie gras de
canard (ou d'oie) au raisin 528
escalopes de homard à la parisienne
744
escalopes de lotte à la crème de
poiyron 818
escalopes de loup au poivre et à la
crème de gingembre 81
escalopes de rouget au pissalat 963
escalopes de saumon 1109
escalopes de saumon aux carottes
1109
escalopes de saumon cru aux deux
poivres 1108
escalopes de turbot a l'embeurrée
de poireaux 1337
escalopes froides de foie gras de
canard (ou d'oie) au raisin et aux
truffes 526
escalopes à la Brancas 154
escalopes à la Madelieu 490

escalopes à la viennoise 1367
escalopes à l'anversoise 491
escalopes of monkfish with
creamed peppers 818
escalopes of raw salmon with
pepper 1108
escalopes of red mullet with
pissalat 963
escalopes of salmon 1109
escalopes of salmon with carrots
1109
escalopes of turbot with buttered
leeks 1337
escargots grillés à la mode du
Languedoc 1182
escargots à la bourguignonne 1182
escargots à la poulette 1182
escargots à l'arlesienne 43
espagnole sauce 492, 493
essence d'ail 494
essence de café 494
essence de cerfeuil 494
essence de champignons 494
essence de tomate 494
essence de truffe 494
essence d'estragon 494
estouffade of beef 495
estouffade de boeuf 495
estouffat de haricots à l'occitane
495
estouffat of haricot (navy) beans à
l'occitane 495
etouffe de veau à la vapeur de
légumes 1225
Evening delight 319
exotic fruit salad with lime 567

faisan: préparation 946
faisan au chou 947
faisan au porto 948
faisan aux noix 1380
faisan en cocotte 947
faisan en filets au jus d'orange 948
faisan grillé a l'americaine 947
faisan à la languedocienne 721
faisan à la normande 947
faisan à la Sainte-Alliance 1096
faisan à l'alsacienne 18
faisan Periguex 941
faisan rôti 948
faisan sauté 948
falettes 498
far breton 499
farce au foie gras 537
farce aux champignons 538
farce d'ail 578
farce de champignons 840
farce de crevettes 536
farce de crustace 536
farce de foie 537
farce de gibier 537
farce de harengs saurs ou de
sardines 536
farce de jaunes d'oeuf à chaud 536
farce de jaunes d'oeuf à froid 536
farce de veau 538
farce de volaille 538
farce à gratin 537
farce à la crème 536
farce à la panade et au beurre 538
farce à la panade et à la crème 538
farce mousseline 537
farce mousseline pour mousses et
mousselines de poisson 536
farce pour poissons 538

farce pour volailles 537
farce: préparation 536
farce à ravioli 1045
farci 500
fausse soupe à la tortue 1344
faux-filet rôti 502
fennel braised in meat stock 505
fennel sauce 1132
fenouil braisé au gras 505
fenouil cru en salade 505
fermented cherry juice 566
feuilletage 1020
feuillete aux pommes à la
normande 862
feuilletes au crabe 507
feuilletes au Roquefort 508
feuilleton de veau l'Echelle 508
feuilleton of veal l'Echelle 508
feves frâiches à la francaise 173
feves frâiches à l'anglaise 173
fig (dried) compote 334
fig (fresh) compote 334
fig fritters 561
fig jam 509
fig tart 509
figs with raspberry mousse 509
figues fraîches au jambon cru 510
figues à la mousse de framboise 509
filet de boeuf froid en gelée 511
filet de boeuf froid à la nicoise 511
filet de boeuf à la Frascati 545
filet de boeuf à la perigourdine 511
filet de boeuf rôti au four 511
filet de boeuf rôti à la brioche 511
filets d'anchois à la silesienne 23
filets d'anchois Talleyrand 1273
filets de barbue Veron 1364
filets de daurade à la juliene de
légumes 1156
filets de hareng à la russe 1086
filets de harengs frits à l'anglaise
649
filets de harengs à la livonienne 650
filets de harengs marinés à l'huile
650
filets de lièvre: préparation 639
filets de lièvre rôtis 639
filets de lotte braisés au vin blanc
818
filets de lotte à la crème et aux
poireaux 819
filets de lotte à l'anglaise 818
filets de maquereaux à la dijonnaise
756
filets de maquereaux à la
piemontaise 954
filets de morue maître d'hotel 1117
filets de poisson au cidre 307
filets de poisson en papillotes 908
filets de rascasse à l'antillaise 1154
filets de Saint-Pierre au citron 687
filets de Saint-Pierre au melon 687
filets de Saint-Pierre au poivron
rouge 687
filets de Saint-Pierre soufflés 687
filets de sole au basilic 1187
filets de sole au Chambertin 246
filets de sole au gratin 1186
filets de sole au vermouth 1187
filets de sole aux champignons
1187
filets de sole aux pommes 1187
filets de sole Crécy 384
filets de sole Cubat 1186
filets de sole frits en goujons 1189

filets de sole grilles 1188
filets de sole Joinville 688
filets de sole à la bordelaise 131
filets de sole à la cancalaise 210
filets de sole à la cantonnaise 1186
filets de sole à la panetiere 905
filets de sole à la Riche 1062
filets de sole à la vapeur au coulis de tomate 1224
filets de sole à la venitienne 1361
filets de sole à la Walewska 1379
filets de sole à l'anglaise 1186
filets de sole Marco Polo 1186
filets de sole Marquery 771
filets de sole Mornay 826
filets de sole Nantua 849
filets de sole Robert Courtine 1187
filets de sole Saint-Germain 1098
filets de sole au vin rouge 845
filets mignons of beef en *chevreuil* 278
filets mignons de boeuf en chevreuil 278
filets mignons de chevreuil 1071
filets mignons de veau au citron 1356
filets mignons grillés 511
filets mignons poelés 511
filets mignons of veal with lemon 1356
filled omelette à la japonaise 683
filled waffles 1378
fillet of beef in aspic (cold) 511
fillet of beef à la Frascati 545
fillet of beef à la nicoise (cold) 511
fillet of beef à la périgourdine 511
fillet of beef Prince Albert 1009
fillets of brill Veron 1364
fillets of fish in cider 307
fillets of fish en papillotes 908
fillets of hare: preparation 639
fillets of herring à la russe 1086
fillets of mackerel à la dijonnaise 756
fillets of mackerel à la piemontaise 954
fillets of monkfish braised in white wine 818
fillets of monkfish à l'anglaise 818
fillets of monkfish with leeks and cream 819
fillets of salt cod maître d'hotel 1117
fillets of scorpion fish à l'antillaise 1154
fillets of sea bream with vegetable julienne 1156
fillets of sole with apples 1187
fillets of sole au gratin 1186
fillets of sole with basil 1187
fillets of sole with Chambertin 246
fillets of sole Crecy 384
fillets of sole Cubat 1186
fillets of sole Joinville 688
fillets of sole à la bordelaise 131
fillets of sole à la cancalaise 210
fillets of sole à la cantonnaise 1186
fillets of sole à la panetiere 905
fillets of sole à la Riche 1062
fillets of sole à la venitienne 1361
fillets of sole à la Walewska 1379
fillets of sole à l'anglaise 1186
fillets of sole Marco Polo 1186
fillets of sole Marguery 771
fillets of sole Mornay 826

fillets of sole with mushrooms 1187
fillets of sole Nantua 849
fillets of sole Robert Courtine 1187
fillets of sole Saint-Germain 1098
fillets of sole with vermouth 1187
financière garnish 512
financière sauce 512
financiers aux amandes 512
fine sausagemeat or fine pork forcemeat 1142
fish aspic 51
fish in escabèche 490
fish fumet 570
fish hamburgers 637
fish loaf 742
fish mousse 831
fish and shellfish salpicons 1112
fish soup with mussels 1199
fish waterzooi de poissons 1383
five-fruit cocktail 320
flamed plums 970
flamiche aux poireaux 517
flamri 518
flamusse aux pommes 518
flan au fromage 519
flan au lait 519
flan aux carottes 228
flan aux cerises 519
flan aux fruits de mer 519
flan aux mirabelles 814
flan Brillat-Savarin 168
flan case (pie shell) baked blind 64, 518
flan de cerises à la danoise 275
flan de poireaux au fromage 726
flan de volaille chavette 519
flan à la florentine 519
flan Sagan 1094
flank with shallots 520
flat omelette à la jardiniere 684
flat omelette à la lorraine 748
flat omelette à la savoyarde 1147
flaugnarde 521
flavoured butter: preparation 187
Flemish salad 517
fleurs de courge en beignets 608
floating islands 522
flour panada 904
foamy chocolate 296
foie d'agneau à l'ail 741
foie de porc à la moutarde 741
foie de veau au bacon 62
foie de veau à la bourgeoise 149
foie de veau à la bourguignonne 740
foie de veau à la creole 385
foie de veau à l'anglaise 740
foie de veau à l'espagnole 492
foie de veau rôti 740
foie de veau sauté à la florentine 740
foie gras au four 528
foie gras cru: préparation 526
foie gras de canard au poivre blanc et au vert de poireau 527
foie gras de canard au raisin 614
foie gras de canard aux huitres et aux écrevisses 527
foie gras de canard glacé 527
foie gras de canard à la purée de bananes truffée 527
foie gras de canard à la vapeur au fumet de Sauternes 528
foie gras d'oie aux raisins 529
foie gras en brioche 528

foie gras forcemeat 537
foie gras fritters à l'ancienne 527
foie gras omelette 879
foie gras Souvarov 1205
foies de raie au vinaigre de cidre 1176
fond blanc de volaille 1228
fond blanc ordinaire 1227
fond brun clair 1227
fond de gibier 1227
fond de veau lié 1227
fond de veau tomate 1227
fond noix ou noisettes 530
fond perle 530
fond à succes 1236
fondant icing 530
fondant-coated or marquise cherries 565
fonds d'artichaut: préparation 47
fonds d'artichaut étuvés au beurre ou à la crème 47
fonds d'artichaut garnis pour plats chauds 47
fonds d'artichaut garnis pour plats froids 47
fonds d'artichaut à la nicoise 47
fonds d'artichaut à la revenole 47
fonds sablés 1091
fondue 532
fondue de tomate 532
fondue du Valais 532
forcemeat for fish 538
forcemeat for poultry 537
forcemeats: preparation 536
fouace or fougasse 540
four-fruit compote 334
four-fruits compote 541
Foyot sauce 542
fraise de veau frite 800
fraise de veau à l'indienne 800
fraises Condé 337
fraises à la maltaise 1231
frangipane cream 544
frangipane dartois 418
frangipane panada 904
freezing mushrooms 839
French bean salad 86–7
French beans: cooking 86
French beans sautéed à la provencale 87
French bread pudding 1018
French butter cream à l'anglaise 382
French butter cream made with sugar 382
French butter cream made with syrup 382
French chocolate butter cream 382
French coffee butter cream 382
French sauce 1132
French toast 555
frenette cordial 49
fresh broad beans à la francaise 173
fresh broad beans à l'anglaise 173
fresh corn au naturel 763
fresh corn with bechamel sauce 763
fresh figs with Parma ham 510
fresh fruit coulis 363
fresh grape tart 614
fresh tomato pulp 1305
friands à la viande 556
fricandeau de veau à l'oseille 557
fricandeau d'esturgeon à la hongroise 1235

fricandeau of sturgeon à la
hongroise 1235
fricassée of chicken à la
berrichonne 557
fricassée d'agneau 558
*fricassée de mer au sabayon de
Bellet* 557
fricassée de poulet à la berrichonne
557
fricassée de poulet à la minute 558
fricassée of giblets 590
fricassée of sea fish with Bellet
zabaglione 557
fried animelles 29
fried bread sauce 160
fried calf's brain à l'anglaise 153
fried calf's liver à la florentine 740
fried calf's mesentery 800
fried calves' sweetbreads 1253
fried cardoons 222
fried carp 226
fried cod 324
fried custard fritters 382
fried eggs: preparation 476
fried eggs à la bayonnaise 476
fried eggs à la catalane 235
fried eggs à la charcutiere 253
fried eggs à la provencale 1013
fried eggs à l'italienne 674
fried entrecôte 486
fried entrecôte à la bourguignonne
486
fried entrecôte with mushrooms
487
fried fillet steaks 511
fried fillets of sole en goujons 1188
fried frogs' legs 562
fried herring 649
fried herring fillets à l'anglaise 649
fried mussels 841
fried onglet with shallots 882
fried onion 883
fried parsley 915
fried potatoes 995
fried red mullet 835
fried rice paves 928
fried salmon steaks 1109
fried salt cod 1117
fried sardines 1124
fried or sauteed squid 1221
fried scallops Colbert 1149
fried shad 1165
fried shrimps 1172
fried skate 1176
fried smelt 1178
fried sole 1188
fried supremes 604
fried trout 1326
fried whiting en colere 1390
fried whiting en lorgnette 1390
fritots d'abattis de volaille 559
fritots de Grenouilles 559
fritots de moules 559
fritots de saumon 559
fritots de sole 559
fritots de viande ou de volaille 559
fritots d'huitres 559
fritots of meat or poultry 559
fritter batter 560
fritters of calves' sweetbreads 1253
fritters à la creole 385
fritters à la florentine 522
fritters à l'imbrucciata 667
fritters Mont-Bry 821
frogs' legs: preparation 562

fromage blanc aux herbes 271
frosted lemons 729
frosted oranges 885
frosted tangerines 1275
frozen truffles 1330
fruit brioche 170
fruit brochettes en papillotes 565
fruit cake 203
fruit croutes 399
fruit salad with gin 568
fruit salad with Kirsch and
Maraschino 568
fruit salad with kiwi fruit 701
fruit salad à la maltaise 568
fruit salad à la normande 568
fruit salad à l'occitanienne 568
fruit savarin 1145
fruit sorbet 1190
fruit souffle 1196
*fruits rafraîchis au Kirsch et au
Marasquin* 568
fruits rafraîchis à la maltaise 568
fruits rafraîchis à la normande 568
fruits rafraîchis à l'occitanienne
568
frying batter 448
fumet de champignon 570
fumet de poisson 570

galantine of chicken 572
galantine de volaille 572
galette de plomb 573
galette de pomme de terre 573
galette des rois 573
galicien 573
game forcemeat 537
game purée 1024
game stock 1227
ganache cream 575
garbure 576
gargantuan hard-boiled egg 476
garlic butter 188
garlic essence 494
garlic oil 578
garlic purée 578
garlic stuffing 578
garlic toast 1302
garnished pilaf 958
garnishes for plain salads 1102
garnishes for rib of beef 98
garnishes for supremes of chicken
1250
garniture financière 512
gaspacho de Seville 582
gâteau alcazar 10
gâteau au chocolat 294
gâteau aux noisettes 643
gâteau aux noix 1380
gâteau bréton 203
gâteau champigny 249
gâteau de crêpes 388
gâteau de foies blonds de volaille
741
gâteau de haddock 632
gâteau de la Forêt-Noire 203
gâteau de patates douces 1255
gâteau de riz au caramel 1061
gâteau des rois de Bordeaux 1346
gâteau à la mandarine 1276
gâteau à la noix de coco 322
gâteau le Parisien 204
gâteau manqué 767
gâteau marbre 204
gâteau moka 816
gâteau Montmorency 823

gâteau Montpensier 823
gâteau nantais 848
gâteau polka 978
gâteau Tortillion 1346
gâteaux de morilles 825
gaufres 1378
gaufres fourrées 1378
gaufres liégeoises 1378
gaufrettes hollandaises 1377
gelée d'airelle 374
gelee de bigarade 1165
gelée de cassis à chaud 116
gelée de cassis à froid 116
gelée de groseille 1047
gelée de groseilles à maquereau 605
gelée de poisson 52
gelée de pomme 681
gelée de viande 52
gelée à la framboise 1043
Geneva sponge fingers 1218
genevoise sauce 583
Genoa cake 583
Genoese sponge 584
genoise à l'abricot 584
genoise sauce 583
German bread and fruit pudding
1018
German gooseberry tart
(Stachelbeerkuchen) 1281
German salad 1104
germinated wheat 1389
Germiny soup 587
gherkins à la russe 588
gherkins pickled in vinegar
(prepared cold) 589
gherkins pickled in vinegar
(prepared hot) 589
giblet bouillon 145
giblet ragoût 590
giblets babylas 590
giblets à l'anglaise 590
gigot bouilli à l'anglaise 592
*gigot braisé aux petits oignons
nouveaux* 591
gigot de chevreuil de 3 heures 1070
gigot à la boulangère 147
gigot à la brioche persille 593
gigot rôti 592
gigot rôti aux ananas 593
*gigot rôti aux quarante gousses
d'ail* 592
gigot rôti de Lea 592
gigot rôti en chevreuil 592
gigue de porc fraiche aux pistaches
964
gimblettes a l'orange 593
gin fizz 319
ginger cake 594
ginger sugar 1245
gingerbread 595
glacage au chocolat 295
glace au café 327
glace au café et à la fine champagne
663
glace au caramel 663
glace au chocolat 294
glace au fondant 530
glace au Grand Marnier 663
glace aux truffes 1331
glacé (candied) cherries filled with
almond paste 565
glace de sucre 1245
*glace de tomate, suc de tomate
concentré* 1304
glace de viande 599

glace à la liqueur 663
glace à la mangue 664
glace à la vanille 1352
glace à la vanille pour coupes glacées 365
glace à l'ananas 960
glacé orange segments 886
glace plombières 969
glace royale 664
glazed carrots 228
glazed courgettes 367
glazed duck foie gras 527
glazed ham with caramel 637
glazed salmon cutlets with Chambertin 1108
glazed salmon en bellevue 103
glazed salmon à la parisienne 912
gnocchi à la parisienne 601
gnocchi à la romaine 601
gnocchi à l'alsacienne 601
Godard sauce 602
godiveau with cream 602
godiveau à la creme 602
godiveau lyonnais ou farce de brochet à la lyonnaise 602
godiveau lyonnais or pike forcemeat à la lyonnais 602
gogues 603
golden sole 1188
gombos à la creole 875
goose foie gras with sultanas 529
goose à la bourguignonne 604
goose à l'anglaise 604
goose in the pot 604
goose rillettes 1064
gooseberry jelly 605
gooseberry sauce 605
gougères 607
goulache 607
gourilos fritters 486
goyère 609
Grand Mariner ice 663
grand veneur sauce 611
grande religieuse à l'ancienne 1053
granita 612
granite 612
grape jam 614
grapefruit ices 615
grapefruit with prawns 615
grapefruit salad 615
gras-double de boeuf à la bourgeoise 1322
gras-double de boeuf à la lyonnaise 1322
gras-double à la poulette 1323
grated carrots with anchovies 229
gratin dauphinois 616
gratin de pommes de terre à la hongroise 654
gratin de potiron à la provencale 1022
gratin de queues d'écrevisse 377
gratin de queues d'écrevisse à la facon de Maître La Planche 377
gratin de volaille à la choucroute 1137
gratin d'oeufs bruillés à l'antiboise 478
gratin of potatoes à la hongroise 654
gratin of scrambled eggs à l'antiboise 478
gratinée 616
green butter 188
green sauce 1364

green tomato jam 1305
green walnuts in verjuice 1380
green-cabbage salad 193
greengage jam 681
grenadins de veau braisés 621
grenouilles: preparation 562
gribiche sauce 622
grilled bass 82
grilled beef fillet steaks 511
grilled (broiled) calves' sweetbreads 1253
grilled (broiled) chicken à la tyrolienne 1346
grilled (broiled) and devilled breast of mutton 161
grilled (broiled) fillets of sole 1188
grilled (broiled) fresh corn on the cob 763
grilled (broiled) lamb cutlets (chops) à la paloise 904
grilled (broiled) onglet 882
grilled (broiled) oxtail Sainte-Menehould 894
grilled (broiled) pheasant 947
grilled (broiled) pheasant à l'americaine 947
grilled (broiled) pork chops 987
grilled (broiled) quails 1025
grilled (broiled) quails petit-duc 1026
grilled (broiled) red mullet 835
grilled (broiled) red mullet à la nicoise 857
grilled (broiled) roes 1069
grilled (broiled) salmon steaks 1109
grilled (broiled) sausages 1141
grilled (broiled) shad with sorrel 1165
grilled (broiled) shoulder of lamb 1170
grilled (broiled) smelt 1178
grilled (broiled) sole 1188
grilled (broiled) tomatoes 1305
grilled (broiled) tuna 1335
grilled (broiled) veal chops 1357
grilled (broiled) veal chops vertpre 1357
grilled (broiled) weaver 1385
grilled butter 189
grilled calf's heart on skewers 645
grilled calf's kidney 695
grilled carp à la maitre d'hotel 226
grilled ceps 243
grilled chateaubriand 259
grilled cod 324
grilled crayfish with garlic butter 377
grilled and devilled calves' ears 465
grilled entrecôte 487
grilled filets mignons 511
grilled flank 520
grilled haddock 632
grilled herring 649
grilled lamb cutlets 713
grilled langouste with basil butter 718
grilled lobster 743
grilled loin of lamb 715
grilled pepper salad 217
grilled pigeon (or chicken) en crapaudine 375
grilled pigs' trotters 504
grilled saffron milk caps à la Lucifer 711
grives en croute à l'ardennaise 42

grives à la liégoise 734
grives à la polenta 978
groudins au four 630
grouper with Corcellet sauce 626
guinea fowl with chestnuts 629
guinea fowl salad with fruit 629

habillage des pigeons à rôtir 955
hachée sauce 1132
hachis de boeuf bouilli 640
hachis de boeuf à l'indienne 641
hachis de boeuf à l'italienne 640
hachis de veau Mornay 641
hachis de volaille 641
hachis Parmentier 914
haddock gateau 632
haddock grillé 632
haddock à l'indienne 632
haddock poché 632
haddock rillettes 632
hake à la boulangère 633
half and half 319
halicot de mouton 634
halicot of mutton 634
ham cornets with foie gras mousse 356
ham crépes 387
ham mousse (cold) 637
ham pâté (cold) 923
ham saupiquet 1138
ham souffle 1197
hamburgers 637
hamburgers de poisson 637
hard coffee caramels 220
hard-boiled egg cutlets 477
hard-boiled egg with sorrel 477
hard-boiled eggs: preparation 476
hard-boiled eggs in breadcrumbs 477
hard-boiled eggs à la Chimay 288
hard-boiled eggs à la Soubise 1193
hard-boiled eggs Verdier 1361
hare with cherries 274
hare with chocolate 639
hare cutlets with mushrooms 639
hare en cabessal 195
hare à la royale 1082
hare pâté 639
harengs frits 649
harengs grillés 649
harengs à la diable 436
harengs marinés 649
harengs sautés à la lyonnaise 649
haricot bean salad 87
haricot beans: cooking 87
haricot beans in cream 87
haricot beans à la lyonnaise 87
haricots à la crème 87
haricots rouges à la bourguignonne 87
haricots verts sautés à la provencale 87
harlequin canapes 210
hashed potatoes 995
haunch of rabbit with mint 812
haunch of roebuck with capers 1070
Hawaiian cream coupes 365
hazelnut butter 188
hazelnut and Caesar's mushroom soup 196
hazelnut cake 643
hazelnut macaroons 755
herb broth 145
herb vinegar 1371

herring fillets à la livonienne 650
herring fillets marinated in oil 650
hippocras with angelica 650
hippocras with juniper berries 650
hollandaise sauce 651
hollandaise sauce au supreme 651
homard au court-bouillon 744
homard en chemise 744
homard à l'americaine 743
homard sauté a l'orange 745
homard surprise 745
homard thermidor 1296
homard grillés 743
homards à la Newburg 855
home-brewed beer 101
home-made quinquina 1032
home-alted pork 1118
honey and cherry cake 204
honey pastry for tarts 652
hop shoots in cream 655
hors d'oeuvre au soja 1207
hors d'oeuvre de moules à la ravigote 841
hors d'oeuvre of mussels à la ravigote 841
horseradish butter 188
horseradish sauce (cold) 656
horseradish sauce (hot) (or Albert sauce) 657
hotelier butter 188
huile au basilic 874
huile au citron 874
huile au romarin ou à la sarriette 874
huile d'ail 578
huile à l'estragon ou au fenouil 874
huile pimentée 217
huitres chaudes en coquilles 898
huitres à la Boston 897
huitres à la diable 436
huitres pochées 898
Hungarian goulash 607
Hungarian omelette 654
Hungarian sauce 654
Hungarian soup with liver dumplings 1199
hure de sanglier 1392
hypocras au geniévre 650
hypocras à l'angelique 650

iced avocado velouté soup 1199
iced charlotte with chestnuts 256
iced chocolate 296
iced coffee 327
iced cream mousse 831
iced fruit mousse 831
iced fruit souffle 1196
iced mussel soup 842
iced parfait 911
iced persimmon à la creole 942
iced pineapple à la bavaroise 959
iced pineapple à la creole 385
iced punch 1023
iced raspberry souffle 1196
iced strawberry mousse 1231
iced tea 1289
iced turban 1335
iced vacherin 1350
iced yoghurt bombe 1405
ile flottante au caramel 666
ile flottante with caramel 666
Indian salad dressing 1102
Indian tea with milk and spices 1289
individual chocolate creams 380

individual diplomats with crystallized fruit 441
individual Parisian brioches 170
Italian meringue 798
Italian sauce 674
Italian sponge cake 1217
Italian sponge drops 1218
ivoire sauce 676

jalousies with apricot jam 677
jalousies à l'abricot 677
jam crépes 389
jambalaya de poulet 678
jambon braisé 636
jambon braisé au Madere 758
jambon braisé au Madere 758
jambon braisé a l'ananas 636
jambon braisé porte-maillot 990
jambon en saupiquet 1138
jambon glacé au caramel 637
jambon landais au miel 654
jambon poché en pate à l'ancienne 637
jambonneaux de volaille 678
jarret de veau à la provencale 704
jellied eggs in ramekins 1041
jellied beef aiguillettes 7–8
Jerusalem artichokes à l'anglaise 685
jesus à la vigneronne 686
jets de houblon à la crème 655
John Dory fillets with lemon 687
John Dory fillets with melon 687
John Dory fillets with red peppers 687
John Dory fillets in a souffle 687
John Dory with rhubarb 688
John Dory steaks in whisky velouté sauce with vegetable julienne 688
joues de boeuf en daube 265
Jubilee cherries 275
julienne de celeri 240

kacha polonaise à l'orge 692
kacha russe 693
kacha russe au Parmesan 693
kakis glaces à la creole 942
kaltschale 692
keshy yena 470
kidney brochettes 175
kidney omelette 879
Kirsch punch 1023
kissel aux airelles 697
kissel with cranberries 697
kiwi fruit sauce 701
klosse à la viennoise 701
kneaded butter 189
knuckle of beef à la provencale 704
kouing-aman 705
koulibiac de saumon 705
kromeskies: preparation 706
kromeskies à la bonne femme 706
kromeskies à la florentine 707
kugelhopf 707

La Varenne sauce 724
lactaires grillés à la Lucifer 711
Laguipère sauce 713
Laguipère sauce for fish 713
lait d'amande pour coupes glacées 15
lait de poule à la bière 479
laitances au beurre noisette 1184
laitances de hareng au verjus 1362

laitances en coquilles à la normande 1184
laitances à la meunière 1184
laitances à l'anglaise 1184
laitues braisées au gras 733
laitues braisées au gratin 733
laitues braisées au maigre 733
laitues farcies 733
laitues à la crème 733
laitues à l'italienne 674
lamb brochettes 174
lamb curry 410
lamb cutlets (chops) è la marechale 769
lamb cutlets with figs and honey 510
lamb cutlets à l'anversoise 32
lamb cutlets Pompadour 982
lamb fricassée 558
lamb noisettes à la turque 1343
lamb noisettes Melba 792
lamb (or mutton) chops Maintenon 760
lamb with prunes, tea, and almonds 1290
Lamballe soup 716
lambs' or calves' sweetbreads: preparation 1252
lambs' hearts à l'anglaise 645
lambs' kidneys à l'anglaise 696
lambs' kidneys sauteed with mushrooms 696
lambs' kidneys Turbigo 1336
lamb's lettuce mixed salad 716
lamb's lettuce salad with bacon 716
lamb's liver iwth garlic 741
lambs' (or sheep's) tongue brochettes 1309
lambs' (or sheep's) tongues à la vinaigrette 1309
lambs' sweetbreads with mushroom puree 1254
lamprey à la bordelaise 717
lamproie à la bordelaise 717
landais butter 190
Landes ham with honey 654
langouste croustades 718
langouste des chroniqueurs 718
langouste du grincheux 718
langouste grillé au beurre de basilic 718
langouste salad 718
langoustine fritters 719
langoustines aux coque d'oursin 1158
langoustines aux noix 1380
langoustines pochées 719
langoustines in sea urchin shells 1158
langue: préparation 1308
langue de boeuf fourrée de Valenciennes 1309
langue de boeuf à la bourgeoise 1309
langue de boeuf à l'écarlate 467
langue de veau bouillie 1308
langue de veau braisée 1308
langue de veau à l'italienne 1308
langue de morue au pistou 1117
langue-de-chat 720
lapereau de campagne au cidre fermier 307
lapin bouilli à l'anglaise 1033
lapin de Garenne au vin de l'Hermitage 1034

lapin à la moutarde 1034
lapin sauté aux pruneaux 1034
lapin sauté à la minute 1034
lapwings' eggs princesse 722
lark pate en terrine 923
lark pie (cold) 723
le jeu de pommes 36
Lea's roast leg of lamb 592
leckerli 725
leek flamiche 517
leek flan with cheese 726
leeks au gratin 727
leeks à la creme 727
leeks à la vinaigrette 727
leg of lamb boiled à l'anglaise 592
légumes chop suey 299
légumes à la grecque 620
lemon butter 188
lemon cream 382
lemon crepes 389
lemon curd 731
lemon custard 381
lemon delice 430
lemon jam 730
lemon manque 767
lemon meringue pie 730
lemon mousse 832
lemon oil 874
lemon sorbet 730
lemon souffle pudding 1018
lemon sponge drops 1218
lemon spunchade 1220
lemon tart 730, 1281
lemon or vinegar court-bouillon 368
lemon zest preserved in vinegar 1409
lemonade with pomegranate juice 980
lentil purée 732
lentil salad (hot) 732
lepiotes à la supreme 910
lettuce à la creme 733
lettuce à l'italienne 674
lettuce purée 733
lettuce salad 733
liaison au beurre 1298
liaison au beurre manié 1298
liaison au beurre mani– 1298
liaison au foie 1298
liaison au sang 1297
liaison à la crème 1298
liaison à l'arrow-root 46, 1297
Liège waffles 1378
lièvre aux cerises 274
lièvre en cabessal 195
lièvre en chocolat 640
lièvre à la royale 1082
lièvre rôti en saugrenée 640
light brown stock 1227
lime souffle 1196
limonade au suc de grenade 980
lining pastry 448
linzertorte 737
liqueur d'abricot 738
liqueur de cerise 738
liqueur de fleur d'oranger 887
liqueur de fraise 728
liqueur d'orange 738
liqueur ice 663
liver forcemeat 537
lobster bisque 113
lobster butter 188
lobster in court-bouillon 744
lobster en chemise 744

lobster escalopes à la parisienne 744
lobster à l'americaine 743
lobster mayonnaise 785
lobster Newburg 855
lobster sauce 745
lobster sautéed a l'orange 745
lobster surprise 745
lobster thermidor 1296
loin of lamb à la bonne femme 715
loin of à la bordelause 715
loin of La Carenne 724
loin of lamb Parmentier 914
loin of pork bonne femme 987
loin of pork with pistachios 964
loin of pork with red cabbage 987
loin of veal 745
Longchamp soup 746
longe de veau 745
Lorette potatoes 747
lotte pochée 819
lotte rôtie 820
loup braisé au graves rouge 81
lyonnaise potatoes 751
lyonnaise sauce 751

Macaire potatoes 753
macaroni: cooking 753
macaroni croquettes 396, 754
macaroni à l'anglaise 754
macaroni à l'italienne 754
macaroni Lucullus 749
macaroni with mustard 843
macaroni with seafood 754
macaroni in stock 754
macaronis au jus 754
macaronis aux fruits de mer 754
macaronis en croquettes 754
macaronis à la moutarde 843
macaronis à l'anglaise 754
macaronis à l'italienne 754
macarons aux noisettes 755
macarons classiques 754
macarons moelleux 755
macedoine de légumes au beurre ou à la crème 755
mackerel in cider Pierre Traiteur 757
mackerel with noisette butter 757
mackerel with sorrel 757
mackerel with two-mustard sauce 757
Madeira sauce 758
madeleines classiques 759
madeleines de Commercy 759
magrets de canard 759
maharajah salad 1104
Maintenon mixture 761
mais en soso aux abattis de poulet 763
mais frais au naturel 763
mais frais grillé 763
mais frais à la béchamel 763
maitre d'hotel butter 762
mallard with green peppercorns 460
maltais 764
maltaise sauce 764
mandarines givrées 1275
mango dessert with passion fruit and rum 765
mango ice 664
mango sorbet 766
Manhattan 319
Manhattan dry 319

manque au citron 767
maple-syrup tart 767
maquereaux au beurre noisette 757
maquereaux au cidre Pierre Traiteur 757
maquereaux aux deux moutardes 757
maquereaux à l'oseille 757
marble cake 204
marchand de vin butter 769
marignan 772
Marigny soup 772
marinade for ingredients of pates and terrines 773
marinade for large cuts of meat and game 774
marinade for meat and venison 773
marinade for meats en chevreuil 279
marinade pour elements de pâtés et de terrines 773
marinade pour grosses viandes de boucherie et gibier 774
marinade pour petites viandes de boucherie, volailles et poissons 774
marinade pour viandes de boucherie et venaison 773
marinade pour viandes en chevreuil 278
marinade for small cuts of meat and poultry 774
marinade of smelt (cold) 1178
marinated fish à la grecque 619
marinated herring 649
marinated salmon 1109
marinière sauce 775
marmelade d'abricots 38–9
marmelade de peches 931
marmelade de pommes 36
marmelade de prunes 971
marmelade d'oranges 886
marquise au chocolat 777
marquise (drink) 777
marrons bouillis 277
marrons braisés 277
marrons grillés 277
marrow au gratin 608
marrow flower fritters 608
marzipan and sugar-coated prunes 1015
marzipan sweets 778, 779
mascotte 779
mashed potatoes 995
massepains communs 779
massillons 781
matafaim savoyard 781
matafans biontons 781
matelote d'anguille 778
matelote à la canotière 213
matignon mixture 782
mayonnaise 784
mayonnaise au cresson 785
mayonnaise aux anchois 785
mayonnaise aux crevettes 785
mayonnaise classique 785
mayonnaise collée 785
mayonnaise de caviar 785
mayonnaise de homard 785
mayonnaise de saumon 1109
mayonnaise de volaille 785
mayonnaise à la russe 785, 1086
meat aspic 52
meat cannelloni 212
meat, game, or poultry loaf 742

meat glaze 599
meat, poultry, game, offal, and egg
  salpicons 1112
mechoui 789
*medaillons de lotte au beurre de
  poivron rouge* 819
medallions de volaille Beauharnais
  790
*medallions de volaille à
  l'egyptienne* 481
medallions of monkfish with a
  red-pepper sauce 819
melon en surprise à la parisienne
  793
melon frappé 793
melon jam 794
melted butter 190
meringue à l'italienne 798
meringue-topped fruit and rice
  798
meringues cuites 798
meringues suisses 798
meringues vanillées à la Chantilly
  799
merlan frit en colère 1390
merlan hermitage 1391
merlan à l'espagnole 1391
merlan pané à l'anglaise 1391
merlan poché au beuree fondu
  1391
merlans au vin blanc 1392
merlans en paupiettes 1391
merlans farcis au cidre 1391
merlans frits en lorgnette 1390
merou sauce Corcellet 626
merveilles 799
mets endiables 436
meurette de poisson 802
meurette of fish 802
mignonettes d'agneau de lait 804
nignonettes of milk lamb 804
mikado salad 805
milanais sables 805
milk flan 519
milk rolls 158
millas aux fruits 808
millas en bouillie 808
miñas with fruit 808
*mille-feuille de Saint-Jacques aux
  poivrons* 217
*mille-feuille de saumon frais au
  beurre rose* 808
mille-feuille of fresh salmon au
  beurre rose 808
îmille-feuille gâteau 808
mille-feuille rond 808
mille-feuille of scallops with sweet
  peppers 217
millet tartlets 809
mimosa flower fritters 810
mimosa ratafia 810
mimosa salad 810
mince pies 811
mincemeat americain 810
mincemeat anglais 810
minestrone 811
mint cocktail 320
mint sauce 813
mint tea 813
minute de saumon a l'aigrelette
  1110
minute fricassée of chicken 558
minute quails 1026
minute sauté of lamb 1142
minute sauté of veal 1142

minute steaks of salmon with
  aigrelette 1110
miques 813
mirabelle custard pudding 814
mirabelle jam 814
mirepoix au gras 814
mirepoix au maigre 814
mirepoix with meat 814
mirlitons de Rouen 814
mixed salad with banana .71–2
Mme Maigret's coq au vin 352
mocha cake 816
mock turtle soup 1344
moelle de sureau 481
monkfish brochettes 174
monkfish curry à la creole 410
monkfish pieces in cabbage leaves
  819
mont-blanc 821
Montpellier butter 188
morel creams 825
morels in herb sauce 826
morels à la creme 825
morels stuffed with lambs'
  sweetbreads 1254
morilles farcies au ris d'agneau
  1254
morilles à la creme 825
Mornay sauce 826
morue en bamboche 70
morue frite 1117
morue à la creole 1117
morue à florentine 1117
morue à la languedocienne 721
morue à la lyonnaise 752
morue à l'anglaise 1117
Moscow piroshki 962
mother's cretons 987
mouclade des boucholeurs 828
moules frites 841
moules à la crème 842
moules marinière 775
moules (ou palourdes) farcies 842
moussaka 830
mousse au chocolat 832
*mousse au chocolat et aux fraises
  confites* 831
mousse de citron 832
mousse de crevette ou de homard
  831
*mousse de foie gras de canard (ou
  d'oie)* 527
mousse de navets 1341
mousse de poisson 831
mousse de volaille 831
mousse froide de jambon 637
mousse froide de tomate 1304
mousse glacée aux fruits 831
mousse glacée à la crème 831
mousse glacée à la fraise 1231
mousseline of apples with walnuts
  832
*mousseline de fumet de moules aux
  huitres de Zelandre* 833
mousseline de reinettes aux noix
  832
mousseline forcemeat 537
mousseline forcemeat for fish
  mousses and mousselines 536
mousseline sauce 833
mulled wine with cinnamon and
  cloves 309
Muscat grape tartlets 614
museau de boeuf 837
mushroom barquettes 79

mushroom crépes 387
mushroom croutes 399
mushroom duxelles 463
mushroom essence 494
mushroom forcemeat 538
mushroom fritters 561
mushroom fumet 570
mushroom salad 839
mushroom souffles 840
mushroom stuffing 840
mushroom veloute soup 1199
mushrooms blanc 839
mushrooms cooked in cream 840
mushrooms croquettes 839
mushrooms (cultivated):
  preparation 839
mushrooms for garnishing 840
mushrooms à la poulette 1002
mushrooms à l'anglaise 839
musketeer sauce 1132
mussel brochettes 842
mussel fritots 559
mussel quiche 1030
mussel salad 842
mussel sauce 842
mussel-farmers' mouclade 828
mussels in cream 842
mustard butter 188
mustard sauce 844
mustard sauce with cream 1133
mustard sauce (for cold fish) 844
mustard sauce (for grills) 844
mutton broth 845
mutton cutlets Champvallon 250
mutton cutlets chasseur 845
mutton cutlets à la cevenole 244
mutton cutlets à la fermière 845
mutton fillets in red wine 845

Nantes cakes 848
Nantua sauce 849
napolitain 850
napolitain biscuits (cookies) 850
napolitaine sauce 850
navarin de mouton printanier 851
navarin of mutton with spring
  vegetables 851
navets au gratin 1342
navets farcis braisés au cidre 1341
nègre en chemise 852
Negrillonne 320
Negroni 319
Nesselrode pudding 853
new turnip salad 1104
nids de pommes paille ou gaufrettes
  854
nimes brandade 155
noisette butter 190
noisettes chasseur 859
noisettes d'agneau à la turque 1343
noisettes d'agneau Melba 792
noisettes d'agneau Montpensier
  823
noisettes des Tournelles 859
noisettes of lamb Montpensier 823
noix au vinaigre 1380
noix de veau Brillat-Savarin 860
noix de veau rôti 860
noix en surprise 1380
noix of veal Brillat-Savarin 860
noodles au gratin 861
noodles (fresh) 861
noodles à la lyonnaise 861
noques à la viennoise 861
noques à l'alacienne 861

normande sauce 862
nougat blanc 867
nougatine 868
nouilles au beurre à l'alsacienne 860
nouilles au gratin 861
nouilles fraîches 861
nouilles à la lyonnaise 861
nut delices 430

octopus à la provencale 871
oeuf dur gargantua 476
oeuf pochés Rachel 1036
oeufs au lait 479
oeufs au miroir 475
oeufs aux feilles de thé 1289
oeufs Bernis mollets ou pochés 21, 23, 106, 125
oeufs brouillés au saumon fumé 478
oeufs brouillés aux ceps 478
oeufs brouillés aux crevettes 478
oeufs brouillés aux foies de volaille 478
oeufs brouillés à la reine 1052
oeufs brouillés princesse 1010
oeufs brouillés Rossini 1076
oeufs de poisson grillés 1069
oeufs de vanneau princesse 722
oeufs durs en cotelettes 477
oeufs durs à la Chimay 288
oeufs durs à la Soubise 1193
oeufs durs à l'oseille 477
oeufs durs panés 477
oeufs durs Verdier 1361
oeufs en cocotte Brillat-Savarin 168
oeufs en cocotte à la crème 475
oeufs en cocotte à là périgourdine 941
oeufs en cocotte à la tartare 475
oeufs en cocotte à l'estragon 475
oeufs en ramequins à la gelée 1041
oeufs en tasses à la hollandaise 651
oeufs frits à la bayonnaise 476
oeufs frits à la charcutiere 253
oeufs frits à l'italienne 674
oeufs à la bruxelloise 179
oeufs à la chevalière 278
oeufs à la neige 522
oeufs à la piperade 961
oeufs à la tripe 1323
oeufs mollets Aladin 479
oeufs mollets Beranger 479
oeufs mollets Chenier 479
oeufs mollets (ou poches) Careme 223
oeufs mollets (ou poches) à la chatelaine 262
oeufs mollets (ou poches) à la florentine 522
oeufs mollets (ou poches) à la forestière 539
oeufs mollets (ou poches) a l'écossaise 469
oeufs mollets (ou pochés) Mornay 826
oeufs moulés Bizet 475
oeufs moulés Careme 223
oeufs moulés en chartreuse 257
oeufs moulés Polignac 978
oeufs pochés: préparation 477
oeufs pochés au caviar 477
oeufs pochés en gelée 477
oeufs pochés à la cressoniere 391
oeufs pochés à la Daumont 421

oeufs pochés à la duchesse 457
oeufs pochés à la duxelles 463
oeufs pochés masques Almaviva 477
oeufs poelés a la catalane 235
oeufs poelés à la provencale 1013
oeufs sur le plat: préparction 475
oeufs sur le plat au bacon 476
oeufs sur le plat Carmen 224
oeufs sur le plat Condé 336
oeufs sur le plat à la Chaveille 476
oeufs sur le plat à la cressonière 391
oeufs sur le plat a la maraichère 768
oeufs sur le plat à l'agenaise 476
oeufs sur le plat à l'antiboise 476
oeufs sur le plat à l'orientale 476
oeufs sur le plat Meyerbeer 803
oeufs sur le plat Montrouge 476
oeufs sur le plat Rothomago 1077
oie au pot 604
oie à la bourguignonne 604
oie à l'anglaise 604
oie rôtie aux fruits 605
oignons farcis 883
oignons frits 883
oignons hâches 883
oille à la française 874
oiseau sans tête 875
okra à la creole 875
old-fashioned barley sugar 78
olives cassées 877
olives farcies au beurre d'anchois 877
olives farcies pour garniture 877
olives à la picholine 877
olives stuffed with anchovy butter 877
omelette Argenteuil 879
omelette au bacon 881
omelette au boudin 879
omelette au foie gras 879
omelette au thon (ou omelette du curé) 881
omelette aux anchois 880
omelette aux artichauts 880
omelette aux cepes 881
omelette aux clitocybes verts 314
omelette aux courgettes 880
omelette aux croutons 400
omelette aux épinards 880
omelette aux foies de volaille 879
omelette aux fruits de mer 880
omelette aux pignons 960
omelette aux rognons 879
omelette with black pudding (blood sausage) 879
omelette brayaude 156
omelette chasseur 258
omelette Diane 880
omelette farcie a l'espagnole 492
omelette Feydeau 880
omelette flambée 881
omelette fourrée aux crevettes 1172
omelette fourrée à la duxelles 463
omelette fourrée à la japonaise 683
omelette fourrée à la portugaise 990
omelette with fruit compote 881
omelette garnie aux fines herbes 513
omelette garnie à la parisienne 913
omelette garnished with fines herbes 513

omelette with green clitocybes 314
omelette à la Bercy 105
omelette à la Celestine 241
omelette à la compote de fruits 881
omelette à la duxelles 463
omelette à la hongroise 654
omelette à la lyonnaise 752
omelette à la menagere 794
omelette a la morvandelle 827
omelette à la parisienne 913
omelette à la paysanne 928
omelette a la romaine 1072
omelette a la rouennaise 1078
omelette à la verdurie 880
omelette Mistral 880
omelette mousseline 880
omelette nature 879
omelette norvégienne 65
omelette Parmentier 880
omelette plate à la jardinière 684
omelette plate a la lorraine 748
omelette plate à la savoyarde 1147
omelette soufflée 881
omelette sucrée à la dijonnaise 439
omelette sucrée à la normande 863
omelette Talleyrand 1273
omelette viveur 1372
onglet grillé 882
onglet poelé à l'échalote 882
onion and honey tart 664
onion sauce 1133
onion soup 883
onion tart 883
onions stuffed with garlic puree 604
orange conserve 886
orange gimblettes 593
orange liqueur 738
orange marmalade 886
orange salad 886
orange sandwich cake 1217
orange sorbet 886
orange sugar 1245
orange syrup 886
orange wine 364
orange-flavoured liquorice water 739
orange-flower liqueur 887
orange-flower sugar 887
oranges givrées 885
orangine 886
oreilles de porc bouillies 465
oreilles de porc braisées 466
oreilles de porc farcies et frites 466
oreilles de veau farcies du Bugey 465
oreilles de veau grillés à la diable 465
oreillettes de Montpellier 888
Oriental salad 889
Oriental sauce 889
Orly de filets de saumon sauce tomate 890
ormeaux aux huitres 891
ormers with oysters 891
osso buco à la milanaise 892
oubliés à la parisienne 893
ouillat 893
oursinade sauce 1158
oven-roast rib of beef 98
ox kidney with lardons 696
ox muzzle 837
ox tongue à la bourgeoise 1309
oxtail hotchpotch 657
oxtail soup 895

oyonnade 895
oyster barquettes (cold) 897
oyster barquettes (hot) 897
oyster bouchées à la Denis 897
oyster bnrochettes à la Vilelroi 897
oyster fritots 559
oyster fritters 897
oyster sauce 897
oyster soup 898
oysters à la Boston 897
oysters in their shells 898

paella 900
pain aux lardons 158
pain blanc 159
pain complèt 159
pain de genes 583
pain de mais 763
pain de tomate 1306
pain d'épice 596
pain perdu 555
pains au lait 158
pains aux raisins 159
pains de carotte 742
pains de crustace 743
pains de Nantes 848
*pains de viande, de gibier, ou de
    volaille* 742
pains à l'anis 29
paleron menagère 902
palets de dames 902
palette de porc à la chou-croute
    903
palette of pork with sauerkraut 903
palm hearts in salad 903
palmiers 903
pamplemousse aux crevettes 615
pamplemousse glacés 615
pan-bagnat 905
panache of chicken and mushrooms
    with Mimolette 809
*panache de volaille et de
    champignons à la Mimolette* 809
panada forcemeat with butter 538
panada forcemeat with cream 538
panada soup based on meat stock
    904
panada soup with milk 905
panade au pain 904
panade au riz 905
panade à la farine 904
panade à la frangipane 904
panade à la pomme de terre 905
panier de crudités 401
pannequets: préparation 906
pannequets aux abricots 907
pannequets à la brunoise 178
pannequets à la cevenole 907
pannequets à potage 907
pannequets for soup 907
papeton d'aubergine 908
*papillotes de homard et de coquilles
    Saint—jacques* 909
papillotes of lobster and scallops
    909
parasol mushrooms à la supreme
    910
parfait glace 911
Paris-Brest 911
Parisian brioche 170
Parisian croissants 392
Parisian croquignoles 397
Parisian salad 913
Parisian sauce 913
parisien 912

Parmesan polenta 978
parsley sauce 1133
parsley, sprigs of 915
partridge croustades 916
partridge à la Souvarov 1205
partridge à la vigneronne 1367
partridge with lentils 917
partridge Monselet 820
partridge salad with cabbage 916
partridges with grapes 917
pascaline 917
passion-fruit sorbet 918
pasta: à la provencale 1382
pasteque à la provencale 1382
pastis bourrit 921
patates à l'imperiale 1255
pâté à beignets (ou pâté à frire)
    560
pâté à biscuit 1216
pâté à brioche classique fine 170
pâté à brioche commune 170
pâté brisée 449
pâté à cannelloni 212
*pâté chaud de bécasse à la
    périgourdine* 1400
pâté à choux 300
pâté à crépes salée 387
pâté à crépes sucrée 388
pâté d'abricots 567
pâté d'alouette en terrine 923
pâté d'alouette en terrine 923
pâté d'amandes 16
pâté d'anguille 472
pâté d'anguille aux fines herbes 472
pâté de bécasse 924
pâté de cailles 1026
pâté de canard d'Amiens 459
pâté de canard froid 460
pâté de cerises 567
pâté de faisan 923
pâté de foie gras truffé 529
pâté de fraises 567
pâté de lièvres 640
pâté de pommes 567
pâté de porc à la hongroise 923
pâté de prunes 567
pâté de saumon 924
pâté de veau et de jambon 924
pâté feuilletée 1020
pâté feuilletée à l'huile 1021
pâté feuilletée minute 1020
pâté à foncer 448
pâté à frire 448
pâté froid d'alouettes 723
pâté à genoise 584
pâté levée pour tartes 449
pâté pantin de volaille 924
pâté pastry made with butter 923
pâté pastry made with lard 923
pâté à pates au beurre 923
pâté à pates au sandoux 923
pâté sablee 448
pâté à tarte au miel 652
paupiettes of braised calves'
    sweetbreads 926
paupiettes of cabbage 193
paupiettes of chicken with cabbage
    927
paupiettes d'agneau à la creole 927
paupiettes de boeuf braisées 926
paupiettes de chou 193
paupiettes de poule au chou 927
paupiettes de ris de veau braisé 926
paupiettes de sole 1188
paupiettes de sole Paillard 901

paupiettes de veau braisées à brun
    927
paupiettes of lamb à la creole 927
paupiettes of sole 1188
paupiettes of sole Paillard 901
paupiettes of veal braised à brun
    927
paupiettes of whiting 1391
pavés de riz frits 928
peach compote 334
peach conserve 931
peach jam 931
peach melba 792
peach sauce 1135
peach peach sorbet 932, 1190
peach peach sundaes 932
peaches dame blanche 414
peaches à la bordelaise 931
peaches à la duchesse 456
pear and apple caramel compote
    334
pear and caramel-cream coupes
    365
pear charlotte 255, 934
pear compote 334
pear pie 952
pear sorbet 1191
pearl fond 530
pears Savarin 1074
peas with ham à la languedocienne
    930
peas à la bonne femme 930
peas à la crème 930
peas à la fermière 930
peas à la francaise 930
peas with mint 930
peches dame blanche 414
pêche à la bordelaise 931
pêches à la duchesse 456
pêches melba 792
pêches rafraîchies aux framboises
    931
pepper butter 188
peppers à la piemontaise 217
peppers à l'orientale 217
perdreau à la Souvarov 1205
perdreau à la vigneronne 1367
perdreau Monselet 820
perdreaux aux raisins 917
perdreaux en courstades 916
perdrix aux lentilles 917
Perigord tourin 1316
Perigueux sauce 941
persil en branches 915
persil frit 915
petite marmite à la parisienne 943
petites galettes orangines 573
*petites quiches au jambon et au
    fromage* 1031
petites tartes au muscat 614
petites timbales d'entrée 1300
petites timbales à la fermière 1300
petites timbales Saint-Hubert 1099
petits choux amandines en beignets
    300
petits croissants aux amandes 393
petits diplomates aux fruits confits
    441
petits fours Souvarov 1205
*petits pois au jambon à la
    languedocienne* 930
petits pois à la bonne femme 930
petits pois à la crème 930
petits pois à la fermière 930
petits pois à la francaise 930

petits pois à la menthe 930
petits pois à l'anglaise 930
petits ravioli pour potage 1045
pets-de-nonne 945
pflutters 946
pheasant: preparation 946
pheasant with cabbage 947
pheasant à la languedocienne 721
pheasant à la normande 947
pheasant à la Sainte-Alliance 1096
pheasant à l'alsacienne 18
pheasant pâté (cold) 923
pheasant Périgueux 941
pheasant with port 948
pheasant with walnuts 1380
*piccata de veau aux aubergines et
    tomates fraîches* 950
pickled melon rind 794
pickled ox tongue 467
pickled red cabbage 193
pickled walnuts 1380
pickles de chou-fleur et de tomate
    951
pie aux poires 952
pie à la rhubarbe 1057
pièce de boeuf braisée 97–8
pieds de cochon Sainte-Menehould
    1097
pieds de mouton à la poulette 504
pieds de mouton à la vinaigrette
    504
pieds de porc grillés 504
pieds de veau à la tartare 504
pieds de et paquets de la Pomme
    953
piemontaise sauce 954
pigeon compote 955
pigeon (or chicken) en crapaudine:
    preparation 375
pigeonneau à la minute 955
pigeonneaux en papillotes 955
pigeons en compote 955
pigeons farcis aux pointes d'asperge
    955
pigs' kidneys: preparation 696
pig's liver with mustard 741
pigs' trotters (feet)
    Sainte-Menehould 1097
pike au beurre blanc 956
pike du meunier 956
pike quenelles 1028
pike quenelles mousseline 1029
pike-perch and oyster-mushroom
    salad 1391
pilaf de crustaces 958
pilaf de volaille 957
pilaf garni 958
pine-kernel croissants 960
pine-kernel flan 960
pine-kernel omelette 960
pine-kernel sauce à l'italienne 960
pineapple comote 334
pineapple en surprise 1251
pineapple sauce 1135
pineapple tart 1281
pink radishes à l'americaine 1037
pintadeaux aux marrons 629
piquante sauce 1133
pirojki au fromage 962
pirojki caucasiens 962
pirojki feuilletés 962
pirojki à la moscovite 962
pissaladiere 963
pistou soup 964
pithiviers 965

pizza dough 966
pizza Mario 966
plaice à la florentine 966
plain marzipan sweets (candies)
    779
plain omelette 879
plain royale 1082
Planter's 319
plie à la florentine 966
plombières ice cream 969
plum cake 971
plum compote 335
plum conserve 971
plum paste 567
plum pudding 971
plum tart 971
plums in brandy 971
poached bass (hot) 82
poached calves' sweetbreads 1253
poached chicken à l'anglaise 283
poached cod (cold) 324
poached cod (hot) 324
poached eggs: preparation 477
poached eggs Almaviva 477
poached eggs in aspic 477
poached eggs with caviar 477
poached eggs à la Daumont 421
poached eggs à la duchesse 457
poached eggs à la duxelles 463
poached eggs à la cressonière 391
poached eggs Rachel 1036
poached haddock 632
poached ham in pastry à l'ancienne
    637
poached langoustines 719
poached monkfish 819
poached oysters 898
poached salmon (cold) 1108
poached salmon steaks 1110
poached turkey vinaigrette 1339
poached whiting with melted butter
    1391
pochouse 973
pogne de Romans 973
pointes d'asperge: cuisson 50–51
*pointes d'asperge pour garnitures
    froides* 51
poireaux au gratin 727
poireaux braisés 726
poireaux à la crème 727
poireaux à la vinaigrette 727
poireaux à l'anglaise 726
poires Savarin 1074
poirissimo 934
pois casses: cuisson 1216
poissons en escabèche 490
poissons marinés à la grecque 619
Poitou caillebottes 201
poitrine d'agneau en fritots 162
poitrine d'agneau farcie 162
*poitrine de mouton farcie à
    l'ariegeoise* 42
poitrine de porc aux pois cassés
    1119
*poitrine de veau braisé à
    l'alsacienne* 161
poitrine roulée salée 1118
poivrade sauces 975, 976
poivrons en ragoût à l'éspagnole
    492
poivrons farcis 218
poivrons grillés en salade 217
poivrons à la piemontaise 217
poivrons à l'orientale 217
polenta au Parmesan 978

Polish kasha with barley 692
pommes Anna 30
pommes bonne femme 36
pommes Chatouillard 262
pommes chips 391
pommes dauphine 422
pommes de terre au basilic 997
*pommes de terre au four au foie
    d'oie cru* 528
pommes de terre au four a l'ail 995
pommes de terre au jus 996
pommes de terre au lard 997
pommes de terre au chateau 262
pommes de terre cocotte 995
pommes de terre Cussy 410
pommes de terre Darbin 417
pommes de terre emiellées 996
pommes de terre en papillottes 909
*pommes de terre en robe des
    champs* 996
*pommes de terre farcies:
    préparation* 998
pommes de terre farcies au fromage
    999
pommes de terre farcies chasseur
    999
*pommes de terre farcies à la
    basquaise* 80
*pommes de terre farcies à la
    cantalienne* 998
*pommes de terre farcies à la
    charcutrie* 998
*pommes de terre farcies à la
    ciboulette* 999
*pommes de terre farcies à la
    duxelles* 999
*pommes de terre farcies à la
    florentine* 998
*pommes de terre farcies à la
    provençale* 998
*pommes de terre farcies à la
    yorkaise* 999
pommes de terre farcies Soubise
    1193
pommes de terre fondantes 997
pommes de terre frites 995
pommes de terre hachées 995
pommes de terre à la berrichonne
    106
pommes de terre à la boulangère
    996
pommes de terre à la crème 996
pommes de terre à la landaise 717
pommes de terre à la lyonnaise 751
pommes de terre à la maître d'hotel
    996
pommes de terre à la normande
    863
pommes de terre à la paysanne 929
pommes de terre à la vapeur 998
pommes de terre à l'anglaise 995
pommes de terre à l'huile 996
pommes de terre Lorette 747
pommes de terre Macaire 753
*pommes de terre (ou purée)
    mousseline* 997
pommes de terre rôties 997
pommes de terre sautées 997
pommes de terre soufflées 998
pommes duchesse: appareil 457
pommes duchesse pour garniture
    457
pommes à la crème au Kirsch 697
pommes paille 1232
pommes pont-neuf 983

pommes soufflées 36
pommes de terre arcies à la Maintenon 761
pompes de Noel 982
pomponnettes 982
pont-neuf potatoes 983
ponts-neufs 983
poor man's sauce 927
porcelet étoffé à l'occitane 1237
porcelet rôti 1237
pork brochettes with prunes 174
pork chops charcuterie 987
pork chops with kiwi fruit 701
pork chops à la bayonaise 987
pork crepinettes 389
pork pate à la hongroise (hot) 923
porridge 989
port wine sauce 1133
Port-Royal salad 1104
Portuguese omelette 990
Portuguese sauce 990
potage au cerfeuil 275
potage au mouton 845
potage aux huitres 898
potage aux oronges et aux noisettes 196
potage Bagration au gras 63
potage bonne femme 129
potage camberani 208–9
potage Condé 336
potage Crécy 384
potage crème aux noix 1380
potage cultivateur 405
potage d'Artois 48
potage de pois cassés 1216
potage fermière 506
potage froid au concombre 404
potage froid de betteraves 101–2
potage Germiny 587
potage julienne Darblay 417
potage à la Du Barry 456
potage à la paysanne 929
potage à la tortuelie 1345
potage Lamballe 716
potage Longchamp 746
potage Marigny 772
potage oxtail 895
potage Saint-Germain 1098
potage santé 1122
potage Xavier 1403
potage-purée aux choux de Bruxelles 1200
potage-purée de celeri 1200
potage-purée de marrons 1200
potage-purée de marrons 1200
potage-purée de tomates 1200
potage-purée soissonnais 1200
potato cocotte 995
potato crisps 391
potato croquettes 396
potato fondantes 997
potato galette 573
potato and leek soup 1199
potato mousseline 997
potato nests 854
potato panada 905
potato pancakes 997
potato souffle 1197
potato subrics 1236
potatoes au jus 996
potatoes with bacon 997
potatoes with basil 997
potatoes cooked in their skins 996
potatoes emiellées 996
potatoes en papillottes 909

potatoes à la berrichonne 106
potatoes à la boulangere 996
potatoes à la créme 996
potatoes à la Cussy 410
potatoes à la landaise 717
potatoes à la maître d'hotel 996
potatoes à la normande 863
potatoes à la paysanne 929
potatoes in oil 996
potatoes stuffed with chives 999
potatoes stuffed with duxelles 999
potée lorraine 1000
potiron au jus 1022
potted foie gras with truffles 529
poularde au blanc 118
poularde au celeri 241
poularde au riz sauce supreme 282
poularde Clamart 312
poularde demi-deuil 431
poularde Demidof 431
poularde Doria 444
poularde en casserole ou en cocotte 282
poularde en vessie Marius Vettard 118
poularde à la bonne femme 129
poularde à la bourguignonne 150
poularde à la Chantilly 251
poularde à la Chivry 292
poularde à la matignon 782
poularde à la Nantua 849
poularde à la Neva 855
poularde à la reine 1051
poularde à l'estragon 282
poularde à l'estragon dans sa gelée 282
poularde à l'ivoire 676
poularde pochée à l'anglaise 283
poularde princesse 1010
poule au pot à la béarnaise 1002
poulet au citron 728
poulet au xeres 1169
poulet aux coings en tajine 1032
poulet aux noisettes 642
poulet aux poussés de bambou 70
poulet creole à l'ananas et au rhum 959
poulet en barbouille 76
poulet en capilotade 215
poulet en croute de sel 282
poulet farci à la mode de Sorges 284
poulet frit Maryland 282
poulet à la creole 385
poulet à la polonaise 281
poulet rôti 283
poulet sauté Alexandra 11
poulet sauté Annette 283
poulet sauté archiduc 41
poulet sauté au basilic 284
poulet sauté au vinaigre 284
poulet sauté aux cepes 284
poulet sauté aux huitres 284
poulet sauté aux mangues 766
poulet sauté à blanc 283
poulet sauté à brun 283
poulet sauté chasseur 259
poulet sauté Demidof 431
poulet sauté à la biarrotte 108
poulet sauté à la bohemienne 125
poulet sauté à la bordelaise 132
poulet sauté à la crème 284
poulet sauté à la minute 283
poulet sauté à la nicoise 283
poulet sauté à la zingara 1410

poulet sauté à l'estragon 284
poulet sauté Stanley 1222
poulette sauce 1002
poulpe à la provencale 871
poultry forcemeat 538
poultry mayonnaise 785
poultry salad à la chinoise 1104
poultry souffle 1197
pound cake 1003
poupeton de dindonneau Brillat-Savarin 1004
poupeton of turkey Brillat-Savarin 1004
poussin grillé à la diable 285
poussins à la piemontaise 954
poussins à la sicilienne 285
pralin 1005
praline 1005
Praline butter cream 382
prawn cocktail 320
prawn (shrimp) forcemeat 536
prawn (shrimp) omelette 1172
prawn (shrimp) salad 1172
prawn (shrimp) sauce 1172
prawn (shrimp) sauce (for fish) 1172
preserved fruit compote 335
preserved lemon peel 730
preserved lemons 729
preserved mushrooms (au naturel) 840
preserved potted duck (or goose) foie gras in goose fat 528
preserved sorrel 1192
pressed beef 97
printanière sauce 1133
profiteroles au chocolat 1011
progres au cafe 1012
provençal sauce 1013
pruneaux au bacon 1016
pruneaux au Roquefort 1016
pruneaux deguisés 1015
prunes with bacon 1016
prunes flambées 970
prunes à l'eau-de-vie 971
prunes stuffed with Roquefort cheese 1016
pudding au chocolat 1017
pudding au pain et aux fruits à l'allemand 1018
pudding au pain à la francaise 1018
pudding au riz 1018
pudding aux amandes à l'anglaise 1017
pudding aux pommes à l'anglaise 1018
pudding de cabinet 1017
pudding à la chipolata 291
pudding à la semoule 1019
pudding à l'americaine 1017
pudding Nesselrode 853
pudding souffle au citron 1018
puff pastry 1020
puff pastry case for flans 1020
puff pastry croustades 398
puff pastry made with oil 1020
puff-pastry apple tart 1281
puff-pastry piroshki 962
puits d'amour 1021
pulpe de tomate fraîche 1305
pumpkin au jus 1022
pumpkin gratin à la provencale 1022
pumpkin purée 1022
pumpkin soup 1022

punch antillais 1023
punch au kirsch 1023
punch cakes 1218
punch glace 1023
punch marquise 1023
purée of Brussels sprout soup 1200
purée of celery soup 1200
purée of chestnut soup 1200
purée d'ail 578
purée d'anchois chaude 1024
purée d'anchois froide 1023
purée de cardons 222
purée de carottes 228
purée de courgettes 366
purée de cresson 390
purée de crevettes 1024
purée de foie de veau ou de volaille
    1024
purée de gibier 1024
purée de laitues 733
purée de lentilles 732
purée de marrons 277
purée de piment 217
purée de pois cassés 1216
purée de pommes de terre 995
purée de potiron 1022
purée de saumon 1024
purée de saumon fumée 1024
purée de volaille 1024
purée d'épinards 1215
purée d'estragon à chaud 1278
purée d'estragon à froid 1278
purée d'oseille 1192
purée d'oursins 1158
purée Saint-Germain 1098
purée Soubise 1193
purée of tomato soup 1200

quail casserole 1026
quail casserole with grapes 1026
quail pâté 1026
quails' eggs in aspic with caviar
    1026
quails en chemise 272
quails à la romaine 1072
quails with rice 1027
quartiers d'orange glacés 886
quatre-quarts 1003
quenelles de brochet 1028
quenelles de brochet mousseline
    1029
quenelles de saumon 1029
quenelles de veau 1029
queue de boeuf en hochepot 657
queue de boeuf Sainte-Menehould
    894
quiche aux moules 1030
quiche lorraine 1030
quillet 1031
quine liqueur or ratafia 1032
quinquina maison 1032

rabbit with mustard 1034
rabbit rillettes 1064
rable de lièvre à la minute 1034
rable de lièvre rôti 1093
Rachel salad 1036
rack of lamb à la nicoise 857
radis noir en hos d'oeuvre 1037
radis roses à l'americaine 1037
radish-leaf soup 1037
ragout of beatilles 89
ragout of calf's head 644
ragout of crayfish tails à la Nantua
    849

ragout d'agneau à l'anglaise 1038
ragout de champignons 1038
ragout de coquillages 1038
ragout de crustaces 1038
ragout de fruits de mer 1156
ragout de légumes à la printanière
    1010
ragout de mouton aux pois chiches
    285
ragout de mouton à la bonne
    femme 845
ragout de patés aux gesiers et aux
    cous de canards confits 597
ragout de queues d'écrevisse à la
    Nantua 849
ragout de truffes 1330
ragout of lamb à l'anglaise 1038
ragout of mushrooms 1038
ragout of mutton with chickpeas
    295
ragout of mutton à la bonne femme
    845
ragout of pasta with preserved
    ducks' gizzards and necks 597
ragout of seafood 1038
ragout of shellfish 1038
ragout of sweet peppers à
    l'espagnole 492
ragout of truffles 1330
raie au beurre noisette 1176
raie au gratin 1176
raising tart 453
raisine de Bourgogne 1039
raiteaux frits 1176
ramekin 1041
ramekin vaudois 1041
ramequin 1041
ramequin vaudois 1041
raphael salad 1104
raspberry barquettes 1042
raspberry charlotte 255, 1043
raspberry coulis 363
raspberry jam 1043
raspberry jelly 1043
raspberry sorbet 1191
raspberry vinegar 1371
ratafia 1032
ratafia d'acacia 810
ratatouille nicoise 1044
ravigote sauce (cold) 1044
ravioli: preparation 1045
ravioli aux herbes 1045
ravioli with herbs 1045
raw fennel salad 505
raw foie gras: preparation 526
raw sardine terrine 1124
raw sardines 1124
raw scallops 1148
raw scallops with caviar 239
raw vegetable salad 1104
recasse à la Riche 1062
red cabbage à la flamande 193
red cabbage salad 195
red (kidney) beans à la
    bourguignonne 87
red mullet charlotte 256
red mullet grilled (broiled) in cases
    835
red mullet with jasmine 684
red mullet à la nantaise 848
red mullet poached à la nage with
    basil 836
red tomato jam 1305
red wine sauce 1133
redcurrant jelly 1047

redcurrant sorbet 1047
Regence sauce 1050
reheated sliced lamb in sauce 715
Reims biscuits 1051
religieuses au café 1052
remoulade sauce 1054
Rhine wine Bishop 112
rhubarb compote 335
rhubarb jam 1057
rhubarb pie 1057
rice au gras 1061
rice casserole à l'ancienne 231
rice cooked in milk 1061
rice cooked in milk for ring moulds
    and cakes 1061
rice croquettes 396
    sweet 397
rice croquettes à l'indienne 396
rice fritters 561
rice gateau with caramel 1061
rice à la creole 1060
rice à la grecque 1060
rice à l'imperatrice 667
rice à l'indienne or a l'orientale 669
rice panada 905
rice pudding 1018
rice ring à la creole 133
rice ring with various garnishes 132
rice or semolina croustades 398
rice tart 1061
rice sweetened shortcrust pastry
    448
Richelieu sauce 1062
rigodon au lard 1063
rigodon with bacon 1063
rilletes of salmon 1109
rillettes de haddock 632
rillettes de lapin 1064
rillettes de lapin 1064
rillettes de saumon 1109
rillettes de Tours 1064
rillettes d'oie 1064
rillons 1065
ring of sole à la normande 132
ris d'agneau au coulis de
    champignons 1254
ris d'agneau ou de veau:
    preparation 1252
ris de veau braisés à blanc 1253
ris de veau braisés à brun 1252
ris de veau en escalopes au gratin
    1253
ris de veau en escalopes à
    l'ancienne 1253
ris de veau grillés 1253
ris de veau pochés 1253
ris de veau poelés 1253
ris de veau Regence 1050
ris de veau rôtis 1254
risotto aux foies de volaille 1066
risotto aux fruits de mer 1156
risotto with chicken livers 1066
risotto à la milanaise 1066
risotto à la piemntaise 1066
rissoles: preparation 1066
rissoles à la dauphine 1067
rissoles à la fermière 1067
riz au blanc 1060
riz au gras 1061
riz au lait pour bordures et gâteaux
    1061
riz au lait simple 1061
riz au safran à la neerlandaise 1094
riz à la creole 1060
riz à la grecque 1060

riz à l'imperatrice 667
riz à l'indienne ou à l'orientale 669
roast calf's heart 645
roast calf's liver 740
roast calves' sweetbreads 1254
roast chestnuts 277
roast chicken 283
roast cod 324
roast duck 460
roast duck with peaches 461
roast faux-filet 502
roast fillet of beef 511
roast fillets of hare 639
roast goose with fruit 605
roast grouse 626
roast hare en saugrenee 640
roast haunch of roebuck 1070
roast leg of lamb en chevreuil 592
roast leg of lamb with forty cloves
of garlic 592
roast leg of lamb à la boulangère
147
roast leg of lamb with pineapple
593
roast legs of hare 640
roast loin of lamb 715
roast loin of pork with various
garnishes 987
roast monkfish 820
roast noix of veal 860
roast pheasant 948
roast pork with lime sorbet and
mint 735
roast potatoes 997
roast quails 1027
roast rib of beef à la bouquetière
148
roast saddle of hare 1093
roast shoulder of lamb en ballottine
1170
roast sirloin 1175
roast sucking pig 1237
roast turkey 1339
roast turkey à l'anglaise 1340
roast turkey stuffed with chestnuts
1340
roast turkey stuffed with dessert
apples 1340
roast wood cock on toast 1401
Robert sauce 1068
roebuck filets mignons 1071
roebuck sauce 1071
rognon de boeuf aux lardons 696
rognon de veau grillé 695
rognon de veau à la bonne femme
695
*rognon de veau sauté aux trois
moutardes* 695
*rognon de veau sauté à la
bordelaise* 132
rognons d'agneau à l'anglaise 696
*rognons d'agneau sautés aux
champignons* 696
rognons d'agneau Turbigo 1336
rognons de coq pour garnitures 695
rognons de porc: preparation 696
*rognons de veau aux foies de
volaille* 695
rolled salt belly pork 1118
Roquefort balls 1074
Roquefort butter 188
Roquefort feuilletes 508
Roquefort rolls 1074
Roquefort sauce 1074
Roquefort-cheese crépes 387

rose vinegar 1371
rosemary or savory oil 874
rosti 1076
*rôti de porc au sorbet de citron vert
et à la menthe* 735
rôties à l'ail 1302
rouennaise sauce 1078
rougail de morue 1079
rougail of salt cod 1079
rougets au four au fenouil 835
rougets au four à la livournaise 835
rougets au jasmin 684
rougets frits 835
rougets grillés 835
rougets grillés en caisse 835
rougets grillés à la nicoise 857
rougets à la nantaise 848
rougets pochés à la nage au basilic
836
rough puff (fast puff) patry 1020
rouille 1080
roux blanc 1081
roux blond 1081
roux brun 1081
royal icing 664
royale of asparagus 1082
royale of chicken purée 1082
royale d'asperge 1082
royale de purée de volaille 1082
royale de tomates 1082
royale d'ordinaire 1082
royale sauce 1083
royale of tomatoes 1082
ruifard 1083
rum babas 61–2
rum zabaglione with marr5ons
glacés 1407
rump of beef with leeks and beer
727
Russian kasha 693
Russian kasha with Parmesan
cheese 693
Russian mayonnaise 785, 1086
Russian salad 1086
Russian sauce (cold) 1086

sabayon 1407
*sabayon au rhum et aux marrons
glacés* 1407
sablé bases 1091
sablés milanais 805
sachertorte 1092
saddle of hare à l'allemande 1093
saddle of roebuck grand veneur
611
saddle of roebuck à la berrichone
1070
saffron rice à la neerlandaise 1094
Sagan flan 1094
sage and onion sauce 1095
Saint James's cup 406
Saint-Germain purée 1098
Saint-Germain soup 1098
Saint-Honoré 1098
Saint-Hubert timbales 1099
Saint-Malo sauce 1100
Saint-Pierre à la rhubarbe 688
Sainte-Menehould sauce 1097
salad dressing with anchovies 1102
salad dressing with bacon 1102
salad dressing with cream 1102
salad dressing with mayonnaise
1102
salad dressing with mustard and
cream 1102

salad of girolles with endive
(chicory) 597
salad of Jerusalem artichokes 685
salad à la favorite 503
salade Ali-Bab 12
salade alienor 1102
salade americaine 1103
salade Argenteuil 42
salade arlesienne 1103
salade aux anchois à la suedoise
1238
salade Bressane 163
salade carbonara 1103
salade composee à la bananae 71
salade d'avocat Archestrate 59
salade de betteraves à la scandinave
102
salade de boeuf 1103
salade de cardons 222
salade de carottes a l'orange 1103
salade de champignons 839
salade de chicoree aux lardons 486
salade de chou rouge 195
salade de chou vert 193
salade de chou-fleur 238
salade de choucroute à l'allemande
1138
salade de concombre 404
salade de concombre au yaourt
1405
salade de coqilles Saint-Jacques
1148
salade de crabe 373
salade de cresson 390
salade de crevettes 1172
salade de croques aux feves fraiches
1103*salade de crudités* 1104
salade de fruits au gin 568
salade de fruits aux kiwi 701
salade de girolles à la chicorée 597
salade de haricots 87
salade de haricots verts 86
salade de laitue 733
salade de langouste 718
salade de l»gumes 1105
salade de lentilles chaude 732
salade de mache aux petits lardons
716
salade de mache panachée 716
salade de moules 842
salade de pamplemousse 615
salade de perdrix au chou 916
salade de petits navets nouveaux
1104
salade de pintadeau aux fruits 629
salade de pissenlit au lard 416
salade de sandre aux pleurotes 957
salade de soja 1206
salade de tomates 1306
salade de tomates à la Mozzarella
1104
salade de topinambours 685
salade de truffes 1331
salade de volaille à la chinoise 1104
salade d'endives à la flamande 286
salade d'épinards 1215
salade d'oranges 886
salade Doria 444
salade Du Barry 456
salade exotique au citron vert 567
salade à la favorite 503
salade à l'allemande 1103
salade maharadjah 1104
salade mikado 805
salade mimosa 810

salade panachée Brimont 169
salade parisienne 913
salade Port-Royal 1104
salade Rachel 1036
salade raphael 1104
salade russe 1086
salade toulousaine 1104
salade de thon 1335
salade flamande 517
salade domestiques 1118
salade de bécasse 1106
salmon brochettes with fresh duck
   liver 1110
salmon with champagne 248
salmon cooked in champagne 1110
salmon cutlets 1110
salmon cutlets à la borguignonne
   1111
salmon cutlets à la florentine 1111
salmon cutlets à la russe 1087
salmon salmong cutlets à l'anglaise
   1111
salmon cutlets Pojarski 976
salmon en croute 1111
salmon fillets Orly with tomato
   sauce 890
salmon fritots 559
salmon fritters with apple sauce
   1111
salmon koulibiaca 705
salmon à l'anglaise 1110
salmon mayonnaise 1109
salmon pté (hot) 924
salmon purée 1024
salmon quenelles 1029
salmon souffle 1198
salmon steaks à la meuniàre 1112
salmon steaks princesse 1010
salmon trout Beauharnais 1327
salmon trout Berchoux 104
salmon trout with salad 1327
salpicon chaud de légumes à la
   crème 1113
salpicon froid de légumes à la
   mayonnaise 1113
salpicon froid de légumes à la
   vinaigrette 1113
salpicon à la bohemienne 125
salpicon à la royale 1083
salsifis au beurre 1114
salsifis au gratin 1114
salsifis au jus 1114
salsifis en salade aux anchois 1114
salsifis à la mayonnaise 1115
salsifis Mornay 1114
salsifis sautés 1115
salsify: preparation 1114
salsify au gratin 1114
salsify fritters 1114
salsify with mayonnaise 1115
salsify Mornay 1114
salsify sandwich with anchovies
   1114
salsify in stock 1114
salt beef 97
salt cod à la creole 1117
salt cod à la florentine 1117
salt cod à la languedocienne 721
salt cod à la lyonnaise 752
salt cod à l'anglaise 1117
salt-cod acras 4
salt-cod croquettes 396
salt-cod en bamboche 70
salted almonds 15
sandwich au basilic 1121

sangria au cognac 1121
sangria aux pêches 1121
sangria with brandy 1121
sangria with peaches 1121
santé soup 1122
sard au beurre de ciboulette 1122
sard with chive butter 1122
sardine butter 188
sardine escabèche 1124
sardine fritters 1124
sardines au plat 1124
sardines crües 1124
sardines frites 1124
sardines gratinées 1124
sardines à l'anglaise 1124
sardines soufflées à l'oseille 1124
sarladaise sauce 1124
sauce aigre-doux 1252
sauce aillade 8
sauce Albufera 9
sauce allemande 13
sauce andalouse 26
sauce aromatique aux morilles 826
sauce au beurre 1131
sauce au beurre et au pain à
   l'anglaise 1132
sauce au beurre à l'anglaise 1132
sauce au caramel 1134
sauce au cassis 1134
sauce au celeri 240
sauce au chocolat 295
sauce au fromage blanc 270
sauce au porto 1133
sauce au raifort chaude, Albert
   sauce 657
sauce au raifort froide 656
sauce au verjus 1134
sauce au vin 1134
sauce au vin rouge 1133
sauce au yaourt 1405
sauce aurore 56
sauce aux airelles 374
sauce aux aromates 45
sauce aux écrevisses 376
sauce aux fines herbes 513
sauce aux groseilles à maquereau
   605
sauce aux huitres 897
sauce aux kiwis 701
sauce aux moules 842
sauce aux pêches crues 1135
sauce aux pêches cuites 1135
sauce aux pignons à l'italienne 960
sauce aux pommes 1131
sauce banquière 74
sauce barbecue 1131
sauce bâtarde 83, 1131
sauce béarnaise 89
sauce Beauharnais 91
sauce béchamel 93
sauce Bercy ou sauce à l'échalote
   105
sauce bigarade 1165
sauce bigarade à blanc pour
   caneton poelé ou rôti 1165
sauce blanche 1131
sauce bolognaise 126
sauce Bontemps 129
sauce bordelaise 131
sauce bourguignonne pour poissons
   150
sauce bourguignonne pour viandes
   et volailles 150
sauce brandade à la provençale 154

sauce Bretonne 164
sauce brune à la bigarade pour
   caneton poelé ou rôti 1165
sauce Cambridge 207
sauce cardinal 222
sauce Chambertin 246
sauce Chantilly 251
sauce charcutière 253
sauce chasseur 258
sauce Chateaubriand 1132
sauce chaud-froid blanche pour
   abats blancs, oeufs, et volailles
   264
sauce chaud-froid brune pour
   poissons et gibiers 263
sauce chaud-froid brune pour
   viandes diverses 263
sauce chaud-froid à la tomate 264
sauce chevreuil 1071
sauce Chivry pour oeufs et volailles
   292
sauce Choron 299
sauce cinghalaise 308
sauce Colbert 330
sauce for couscous 370
sauce crème 1132
sauce crème à l'anglaise 1132
sauce cressonière 391
sauce crevette à l'anglaise 1172
sauce crevette (pour poissons)
   1172
sauce diplomate 440
sauce echalote 1166
sauce ecossaise 469
sauce espagnole 492, 493
sauce financière 512
sauce with fines herbes 513
sauce forte 370
sauce Foyot 542
sauce genevoise 583
sauce genoise 583
sauce Godard 602
sauce grand veneur 611
sauce gribiche 622
sauce hâchée 1132
sauce hollandaise 651
sauce homard 745
sauce hongroise 654
sauce italienne 674
sauce à la chapelure 1131
sauce à la diable 436
sauce à la duxelles 463
sauce à la francaise 1132
sauce à la grecque for fish 619
sauce à la grecque pour poissons
   619
sauce à la menthe 813
sauce à la mie de pain à l'ancienne
   1131
sauce à la moelle 128
sauce à la piemontaise 954
sauce à la rmaine 1072
sauce à la russe 1087
sauce à la sauge et à l'oignon 1095
sauce à la truffe 1331
sauce La Varenne 724
sauce à l'abricot 1134
sauce Laguipere 713
sauce Laguipere pour poissons 713
sauce à l'ananas 1135
sauce à l'anglaise 28
sauce à l'avocat 59
sauce à l'estragon 1279
sauce à l'estragon pour oeufs
   mollets ou pochés 1279

sauce à l'estragon pour volailles pochées 1278
sauce à l'indienne 669
sauce à l'oignon 1133
sauce à l'oseille 1133
sauce lyonnaise 751
sauce Madère 758
sauce maltaise 764
sauce marinière 775
sauce Mornay 826
sauce mousquetaire 1132
sauce mousseline 833
sauce moutarde 844
sauce moutarde au beurre 1133
sauce moutarde à la crème 1133
sauce Nantua 849
sauce napolitaine 850
sauce normande 862
sauce oursinade 1158
sauce parisienne 913
sauce pauvre homme 927
sauce Perigueux 941
sauce persil 1133
sauce piquante 1133
sauce poivrade 975, 976
sauce portugaise 980
sauce poulette 1002
sauce printanière 1133
sauce provençale 1013
sauce ravigote froide 1044
sauce Regence 1050
sauce Richelieu 1062
sauce Robert 1068
sauce with Roquefort 1074
sauce rouennaise 1078
sauce royale 1083
sauce russe froide 1086
sauce Saint-Malo 1100
sauce Sainte-Menehould 1097
sauce sarladaise 1124
sauce soja 1207
sauce Soubise 1193
sauce supreme 1250
sauce Talleyrand 1273
sauce tartare 1283
sauce tomate 1306
sauce tortue 1312
sauce venaison 1360
sauce venitienne 1361
sauce Veron 1364
sauce verte 1364
sauce Victoria pour poisson 1366
sauce Victoria pour venaison 1366
sauce vierge 1134
sauce villageoise 1367
sauce Villeroi 1368
sauce Vincent 1369
sauce waterfish chaude 1382
sauce waterfish froide 1382
sauce zingara 1410
sauce aux capres 214
saucisse à la languedocienne 1141
saucisses au bacon en brochettes 62
saucisses au chou 1141
saucisses grillées 1141
saucisson en brioche à la lyonnaise 1141
sauerkraut au gras for garnish 1137
sauerkraut à l'alsacienne 1137
sauerkraut salad à l'allemande 1138
saumon au champagne 248, 1110
saumon en croute 1111
saumon glacé en bellevue 103
saumon à l'anglaise 1110

saumon mariné 1109
saumon poché froid 1108
saupiquet de canard 1138
sausage nd bacon brochettes 62
sausage in brioche dough à la lyonnaise 1141
sausage à la languedocienne 1141
sausage rolls 556
sausagemeat 1142
sausages with cabbage 1141
sauté of chicken archiduc 41
sauté d'agneau au paprika 910
sauté d'agneau à la minute 1142
sauté d'agneau à l'ancienne 1142
sauté d'agneau (ou de veau) aux aubergnes 1143
sauté d'agneau (ou de veau) aux cepes 1143
sauté d'agneau (ou de veau) aux tomates 1143
sauté d'agneau (ou de veau) chasseur 1143
sauté de truffes du Piemont 1330
sauté de veau à la minute 1142
sauté de veau Marengo 770
sauté of lamb à l'ancienne 1142
sauté of lamb (or veal) with aubergines (eggplant) 1143
sauté of lamb (or veal) chasseur 1143
sauté of lamb (or veal) with tomatoes 1143
sauté of lamb with paprika 910
sauté of Piedmont truffles 1330
sauté chicken à la zingara 1410
sautéed aubergines 55
sautéed Brussels sprout 178
sautéed calf's heart 645
sautéed calf's kidney à la bordelaise 132
sautéed calf's kidney with three mushrooms 695
sautéed cauliflower 238
sautéed chateaubriand 259
sautéed chicken Alexandra 11
sautéed chicken Annette 283
sautéed chicken à blanc 283
sautéed chicken à brun 283
sautéed chicken with cep mushrooms 284
sautéed chicken chasseur 259
sautéed chicken with cream 284
sautéed chicken Demidof 431
sautéed chicken à la biarrote 108
sautéed chicken à la bohemienne 125
sautéed chicken à la bordelaise 132
chicken à la minute 283
sautéed chicken à la nicoise 283
sautéed chicken with mangoes 766
sautéed chicken with oysters 284
sautéed chicken Stanley 1222
sautéed chicken with tarragon 284
sautéed chicken with vinegar 284
sautéed courgettes 367
sautéed or grilled (broiled) tournedos 1316
sautéed herrings à la lyonnaise 649
sautéed lamb cutlets 714
sautéed lambs' hearts 645
sautéed pheasant 948
sautéed pork chops 988
sautéed potatoes 997
sautéed rabbit with prunes 1034

sautéed roebuck cutlets with cherries 1071
sautéed roebuck cutlets with grapes 1071
sautéed roebuck cutlets with juniper berries 1071
sautéed salsify 1115
sautéed tomatoes provencale 1305
sautéed veal chops à la creme 1357
sautéed veal chops à la duxelles 463
sautéed veal chops à la provencale 1013
sautéed veal Marengo 770
sautéed woodcock in Armagnac 1401
Sauternes cup 407
savarin aux fruits 1145
savarin aux fruits rouges et à la Chantilly 1145
savarin filled with confectioners' custard (pastry cream) 1144
savarn à la crème patîsserie 1144
savarin with red fruit sauce and whipped cream 1145
saveloys in salad 1145
saveloys stuffed with spinach 1145
savoury allumettes 14
savoury crêpe batter 387
savoury souffle: preparation 1197
Savoy matafan 781
Savoy sponge cake 1147
scallop brochettes 1149
scallop broth with spinach 1214
scallop and chicory cassolettes 287
scallop and oyster brochettes à la Villeroi 1368
scallop salad 1148
scallop shells of fish à la Mornay 1150
scallop shells of salmon Victoria 1366
scallop shells of shrimps 1150
scallops au gratin à la dieppoise 438
scallops à la nage 847
scallops in mayonnaise 1149
scallops Mornay 1149
scallops in salad 1149
scampi fritters 561
scampi with walnuts 1380
Scandinavian beetroot salad 102
Scotch pudding 1019
scrambled eggs: preparation 478
scrambled eggs with cep mushrooms 478
scrambled eggs with chicken livers 478
scrambled eggs à la reine 1052
scrambled eggs Massenet 780
scrambled eggs princesse 1010
scrambled eggs Rossini 1076
scrambled eggs with shrimps 478
scrambled eggs with smoked salmon 478
scrambled eggs with truffles 479
sea bream (or bass) à la meuniere 801
sea bream with preserved lemons 729
sea bream stuffed with fennel 1156
sea urchin purée 1158
seafood bouchées 1156
seafood brochettes 174
seafood cannelloni 212

seafood croutes 399
seafood dartois 418
seafood flan 519
seafood omelette 880
seafood ragoût 1156
seafood risotto 1156
seafood zephyr 1408
selle d'agneau Callas 305
selle de chevreuil grand veneur 611
selle de chevreuil à la berrichone 1070
semolina pudding 1019
semolina ring with fruit 133
semolina subrics 1160
semoule pour entremets 1160
Seville gazpacho 582
Seville orange jelly 1165
shad: preparation 1165
shad au plat 1166
shallot butter 188
shallot sauce 1166
shaped chicken cutlets Helder 646
shaped cutlets 411
sheep's trotters à la poulette 504
shellfish forcemeat 536
shellfish loaf 743
shellfish pilaf 958
sherry cobbler 319
shirred eggs Condé 336
shish kebab 693
shortcrust pastry 449
shoulder of lamb à l'albigeoise 9
shoulder of mutton en pistache 964
shoulder of mutton with various garnishes 1170
shoulder of pork with five spices 988
shoulder of roebuck with olives 1071
shrimp croissants 393
shrimp or lobster mousse 831
shrimp or prawn mayonnaise 785
shrimp purée 1024
shrimps sautéed in whisky 1172
Sidecar 319
simple chicken consommé 344
simple fish consommé 344
simple game consommé 344
simple white consommé 344
singapour 1174
sirop au café 327
sirop de fraise 1232
sirop d'oranges 886
six-vegetable cocktail 321
skate au gratin 1176
skate liver with cider vinegar 1176
skate with noisette butter 1176
sliced meat à l'italienne 674
slices of pheasant with orange juice 948
small almond croissants 393
small ham and cheese quiches 1031
small orange galettes 573
small ravioli for soup 1045
small timbales à l'épicurienne 1300
small timbales as an entree 1300
smelt velouté soup à la dieppoise 1179
smoked herring or sardine forcemeat 536
smoked salmon aspic 52
smoked salmon cornets iwth fish roe 356
smoked-salmon purée 1024
snail broth 1182

snails grilled à la mode du Languedoc 1182
snails à la bourguignonne 1182
snails à la poulette 1182
snails à l'arlesienne 43
sobronade 1183
soft boiled (or poached) eggs à l'écossaise 469
soft butter caramels 220
soft fresh cheese with herbs 271
soft macaroons 755
soft roe fritters 561
soft roes of herring with verjuice 1362
soft roes à la meuniere 1184
soft roes à l'anglaise 1184
soft roes in noisette butter 1184
soft roes in scallop shells à la normande 184
soft-boiled (or porached) eggs: preparation 479
soft-boiled (or poached) eggs Aladdin 479
soft-boiled (or poached) eggs Beranger 479
soft-boiled (or poached) eggs Bernis 106
soft-boiled (or poached) eggs Carème 223
soft-boiled (or poached) eggs Chenier 479
soft-boiled (or poached) eggs à la bohemienne 125
soft-boiled (or poached) eggs à la chatelaine 262
soft-boiled (or poached) eggs à la florentine 522
soft-boiled (or poached) eggs à la forestière 539
soft-boiled (or poached) eggs à l'ancienne 23
soft-boiled (or poached) eggs Mornay 826
soft-cheese sauce 270
soft-roe butter 188
soissonnais soup 1200
sole: preparation 1186
sole Armenonville 44
sole aux légumes poeles 1189
sole Colbert 330
sole diplomate 440
sole dorée 1188
sole fritots 559
sole grillée 1188
sole à la meunière 1188
sole à la normande 863
sole à la portugaise 990
sole à l'orange 1188
sole and mushroom brochettes 1188
sole with orange 1188
sole with pan-fried vegetables 1189
soles de ligne à la fondue de poireau 727
soles farcies Auberge de l'Ill 1189
soles frites 1188
soles with leek fondue 727
soles meunière Mont-Bry 821
solilemme 1189
sorbet au cacao et aux raisins 1191
sorbet au Calvados 1191
sorbet au cassis 117
sorbet au citron 730
sorbet au miel et aux pignons 1191

sorbet aux fruits 1190
sorbet aux fruits de la passion 918
sorbet aux fruits exotiques 1191
sorbet with Calvados 1191
sorbet with cocoa and raisins 1191
sorbet de thé 1290
sorbet d'oranges 886
sorbet of exotic fruits 1191
sorbet with honey and pine nuts 1191
sorbet à la fraise 1191
sorbet à la framboise 1191
sorbet à la groseille 1047
sorbet à la mangue 766
sorbet à la pêche 932, 1190
sorbet à la poire 1191
sorbet à la tomate 1306
sorrel purée 1192
sorrel sauce 1133
sot-l'y-laisse aux morilles 825
sou-fassum 1193
Soubise purée 1193
Soubise sauce 1193
soufflé ambassadrice 1196
soufflé au café 1195
soufflé au chocolat 1195
soufflé au citron vert 1196
soufflé au crabe 1197
soufflé au Curacao 1196
soufflé au fromage 1197
soufflé au fromage et aux oeufs pochés 1197
soufflé au jambon 1197
soufflé au saumon 1198
soufflé aux bananes 1195
soufflé aux champignons 840
soufflé aux chataignes 1195
soufflé aux fraises ou aux framboises 1196
soufflé aux fruits au sirop de sucre 1196
soufflé aux violettes 1371
soufflé de cervelle à la chanoinesse 250
soufflé fritters 561
soufflé glace aux framboises 1196
soufflé glace aux fruits 1196
soufflé à la pomme de terre 1197
soufflé à la vanille 1352
soufflé à la volaille 1197
soufflé omelette 881
soufflé potatoes 998
soufflé Rothschild 1077
soufflé tomatoes 1305
souffléd sardines with sorrel 1124
soup au pistou 964
soup à la paysanne 929
soupe au gras-double à la milanaise 1323
soupe aux boulettes de foie à la hongroise 1199
soupe aux cerises 273
soupe aux clams 312
soupe aux fanes de radis 1037
soupe aux poireaux et aux pommes de terre 1199
soupe de mandarines 1276
soupe de poisson aux moules 1199
soupe de potiron 1022
soupe de poulet à l'anglaise 1199
soupe d'epeautre 1211
soupe glacée aux moules 842
soupe hollandaise 1200
soupe à la bonne femme 1200
soupe à l'oignon 883

soupe orsinade 1158
soupe panade au gras 904
soupe panade au lait 905
soupe stracciatella 1201
soupe viennoise à la crème aigre 1201
soy sauce 1207
soya bean salad 1206
soya bean sprout hors d'oeuvre 1207
spaghetti alla carbonara 1208
spaghetti au basilic 1208
spaghetti with basil 1208
spaghetti à la ligurienne 1208
Spanish omelette 492
Spanish-onion chutney 306
spare ribs 1210
spatzle au beurre noisette 1211
spatzle with noisette butter 1211
speculos 1211
spelt broth 1211
spiced tomato juice 319
spinach: preparation and cooking 1214
spinach au gratin 1215
spinach bouillabaisse 1215
spinach in butter 1215
spinach in cream 1215
spinach crêpes au gratin 387
spinach croquettes 1215
spinach à l'anglaise 1215
spinach omelette 880
spinach purée 1215
spinach salad 1215
spinach subrics 1236
spinach tart 1280
spit-roast leg of lamb with parsley 593
spit-roasted fillet of beef 511
split peas: cooking 1216
split-pea purée 1216
split-pea soup 1216
sponge biscuits (cookies) 1218
sponge fingers 1218
sponge roll 1217
sprats à la vinaigrette 1220
spring chickens à la piemontaise 954
spring chickens à la sicilienne 283
spunchade au citron 1200
squab à la minute 955
squabs en papillotes 955
squid à l'andalouse 1221
squill-fish on skewers with saffron 1222
standard brioche dough 170
steak au poivre 1223
steak aux huitres 898
steak à cheval 278
steak de thon blanc hâche aux algues 1335
steak Dumas 1223
steak and kidney pie 1224
steak with oysters 898
steak tartare 1282
steaks of hake à la duxelles 633
steamed duck foie gras with Sauternes 528
steamed fillets of sole in tomato sauce 1224
steamed potatoes 998
steamed scallops 1149
sterilized preserved truffles 1331
stockfish à la nicoise 1228
stocks (quick) 146

stracciatella soup 1201
straw potatoes 1232
strawberries Condé 337
strawberries à la maltaise 1231
strawberry compote 335
strawberry delices 431
strawberry jam 1231
strawberry liqueur 738
strawberry purée preserved by bottling 1232
strawberry purée preserved by freezing 1232
strawberry sorbet 1191
strawberry syrup 1232
strawberry tart 1282
strudel aux pommes 1234
stuffed artichoke hearts as garnish for cold dishes 47
stuffed artichoke hearts as garnish for hot dishes 47
stuffed aubergines 55
stuffed aubergines à la catalane 235
stuffed braised turkey pinions 961
stuffed breast of mutton à l'arigeoise 42
stuffed breasts of lamb 162
stuffed cabbage 193
stuffed calf's heart 645
stuffed calves' ears du Bugey 465
stuffed carp à l'ancienne 226
stuffed chicken à la mode de Sorges 284
stuffed courgettes 367
stuffed crabs au gratin 373
stuffed crabs à la martiniquaise 373
stuffed cucumber 404
stuffed dates 419
stuffed duck à la rouennaise 1078
stuffed and fried pigs' ears 466
stuffed goose legs en ballottines 604
stuffed lemons 729
stuffed lettuce 733
stuffed milk lamb 715
stuffed mushrooms 840
stuffed mussels (or clams) 842
stuffed olives for garnish 877
stuffed onions 883
stuffed peppers 218
stuffed pigeons with asparagus tips 955
stuffed potatoes 998
stuffed potatoes chasseur 999
stuffed potatoes with cheese 999
stuffed potatoes à la basquaise 80
stuffed potatoes à la cantailienne 998
stuffed potatoes à la charcuterie 998
stuffed potatoes à la florentine 998
stuffed potatoes à la Maintenon 761
stuffed potatoes à la provenale 998
stuffed potatoes à la yorkaise 999
stuffed potatoes Soubise 1193
stuffed quails in cases 1027
stuffed quails in cases à la Lamballe 716
stuffed quails à la gourmande 1027
stuffed quails Lucullus 749
stuffed quails in nests 1027
stuffed shoulder of lamb à la gasconne 11770
stuffed shoulder of veal 1170

stuffed sole Auberge de l'Ill 1189
stuffed squid à la marseillaise 1221
stuffed sucking pig à l'occitane 1237
stuffed tomato nests (hot) 1306
stuffed tomatoes 1305
stuffed tomatoes à la bonne femme 1305
stuffed tomatoes à la languedocienne (hot) 1306
stuffed tomatoes à la nicoise (hot) 1306
stuffed tomatoes à la reine 1052
stuffed turkey grand-duc 610
stuffed turnips braised in cider 1341
stuffed whiting with cider 1391
stuffings for ravioli 1045
subrics de pommes de terre 1236
subrics de semoule 1160
subrics d'entremets au riz 1236
subrics d'épinards 1236
suc de cerise 566
succes base 1236
sucre d'anis 1245
sucre de cannelle 1245
sucre de fleur d'oranger 887
sucre de gingembre 1245
sucre de girofle 1245
sucre d'orange 1245
sucre d'orge à l'ancienne 78
sucre vanille 1245
sugar icing (frosting) 1245
sukiyaki 1246
supreme sauce 1250
supremes: preparation 1249
supremes of chicken à blanc 1250
supremes of chicken à brun 1250
supremes of chicken à la financière 513
supremes of chicken à la florentine 522
supremes of chicken à l'anglaise 1250
supremes de volaille à blanc 1250
supremes de volaille à brun 1250
supremes de volaille et leur garniture 1250
supremes de volaille a la financière 513
supremes de volaille à la florentine 522
supremes de volaille è l'anglaise 1250
Swedish herring balls 649
sweet crépe batter 388
sweet omelette à la dijonnaise 439
sweet omelette à la normande 863
sweet potatoes à l'imperiale 1255
sweet rice subrics 1236
sweet-and-sour sauce 1252
sweet-potato cake 1255
Swiss chard: preparation 1257
Swiss chard au gratin 1257
Swiss chard tourte 1257
Swiss meringues 798
Swiss wine tart 1282
Szechwan-style Chinese cabbage 290

tabbouleh 1262
tablier de sapeur 1269
tajine of carrots 1272
tajine of chicken with quine 1032
tajine de carottes 1272

tajine de mouton aux pruneaux et au miel 1272
tajine of mutton with prunes and honey 1272
Talleyrand sauce 1273
Italmouses Bagration 1274
talmouses à la Florentine 1274
talmouses à l'ancienne 1274
tangerine gâteau 1278
tangerine syrup 1276
tapenade 1277
tapioca au lait 1277
tapioca consommé 1277
tapioca dessert 1277
tapioca with milk 1277
tarragon butter 188
tarragon cream 1278
tarragon essence 494
tarragon or fennel oil 874
tarragon preserved by freezing 1278
tarragon purée (cold) 1278
tarragon purée (hot) 1278
tarragon sauce for poached fowl 1278
tarragon sauce for small cuts of meat 1279
tarragon sauce for soft-boiled or poached eggs 1279
tarragon vinegar 1371
tarragon -flavoured consomme 345
tart cauchoise 236
tartare sauce 1283
tarte alsacienne 1280
tarte au chocolat 1281
tarte au citron 730, 1281
tarte au raisin frais 614
tarte au riz 1061
tarte aux asperges 50
tarte aux cerises 1281
tarte aux figues 509
tarte aux fraises 1282
tarte aux groseilles à maquereau à l'allemande 1281
tarte aux myrtilles 109
tarte aux oignons et au miel 654
tarte aux pignons 960
tarte aux pommes ronde 1280
tarte aux prunes 971
tarte aux raisins 453
tarte feuilletée aux pommes 1281
tarte à la cassonade 232
tarte à l'ananas 1281
tarte à l'oignon 883
tarte meringuée au citron 730
tarte suisse au vin 1282
tarte Tatin 1285
tartelettes Agnès Sorel 6
tartelettes au café ou au chocolat 1283
tartelettes au millet 809
tartelettes aux murés 115–16
tartelettes aux noix et au miel 1283
tartines marquise 1283
tea punch 320
tea sorbet 1290
tendrons de veau braisés à la bourgeoise 1292
terrine of calves' sweetbreads 1254
terrine de Body 1293
terrine de brochet sauce Nantua 956
terrine de caneton 1294
terrine de faisan, de perdreau ou de caille 1295

terrine de foie gras aux truffes 529
terrine de fruits à la gelée de miel 1295
terrine de légumes Fontanieu 1295
terrine de l'ocean 1294
terrine de ris de veau 1254
terrine de sardines crues 1124
terrine de saumon 1109
terrine of duckling 1294
terrine of fruits with honey jelly 1295
terrine of pheasant, partridge or quail 1295
terrine of pike with Nantua sauce 956
terrine of salmon 1109
terrine of vegetables Fontanieu 1295
tête de veau: préparation 643
tête de veau bonne femme 644
tête de veau chaude en sauce chaude 644
tête de veau chaude en sauce froide 644
tête de veau en ragoût 644
tête de veau en tortue 1312
tête de veau à l'anglaise 644
tetras rôti 626
thé chinois 1289
thé glace 1289
thé indien au lait aux epices 1289
thé à la mente 813
thick turtle soup 1345
thick veal stock 1227
thickening with arrowroot 1297
thickening with blood 1297
thickening with butter 1298
thickening with cream 1298
thickening with kneaded butter 1298
thickening with liver 1298
thon au thé 1290
thon en daube 1335
thon en daube à la provencale 1335
thon grillé 1335
three-hour leg of roebuck 1070
thrushes en croute à l'ardennaise 42
thrushes à la liegoise 734
thrushes in polenta 978
timbale Brillat-Savarin 168
timbale case (shell), large 1300
timbale de bécasse froide 1400
timbale de foies de volaille 741
timbale of woodcock (cold) 1400
timbales beauvilliers (petites) 93
timbales Elysée 1399
Tom Collins 319
tomates farcies: preparation 1305
tomates farcies chaudes en nid 1306
tomates farcies chaudes à la bonne femme 1305
tomates farcies chaudes à la languedocienne 1306
tomates farcies chaudes à la nicoise 1306
tomates farcies froides au thon 1306
*tomates farcies à la reine*1052
tomates sautees à la provencale 1305
tomates soufflés 1305
tomato chaud-froid sauce 264
tomato coulis (condiment) 363
tomato coulis (sauce) 363

tomato essence 494
tomato fondue 532
tomato loaf 1306
tomato mousse (cold) 1304
tomato salad 1306
tomato salad with Mozzarella 1104
tomato sauce 1306
tomato sorbet 1306
tomato tart 1280
tomatoes veal stock 1227
tomatoes stuffed with tuna (cold) 1306
tongue: preparation 1308
tongues of salt cod in pistou 1117
topinambours à l'anglaise 685
tortillons 1311
tortue sauce 1312
tot-fait 1313
touffe de requin à la creole 1167
touffe of shark à la creole 1167
Toulouse salad 1104
tourin perigoudin 1316
tournedos Helder 647
tournedos Brillat-Savarin 1317
tournedos Marguery 772
tournedos Marigny 772
tournedos Massena 780
tournedos Rossini 1076
tournedos sautés ou grillés 1316
tourons (petits fours) 1344
tourte au sirop d'erable 767
tourte aux abricots 1318
tourte aux feuilles de better 1257
tourte de truffes à la perigourdine 1331
tourte de veau au Parmesan 1318
tourte of veal with Parmesan cheese 1318
tourteau fromage 1319
tourtes à la mode béarnaise 1318
traditional almond blancmange 120
tranches de colin à la duxelles 633
tranches de filet de boeuf grillees 511
tranches de flet de boeuf à la poele 511
tripe à la bourgeose 1322
tripe à la lyonnaise 1322
tripe à la mode de Caen 1322
tripe à la poulette 1323
tripe soup à la milanaise 1323
trois-frères 1324
trout with almonds 1327
trout à la bourguignonne 1327
trout with leeks 1327
truffes au champagne 248
truffes au paprika 297
truffes en chaussons 1332
truffes en chocolat au beurre 297
truffes en chocolat à la creme 297
truffes à la croque au sel 1331
truffes pour garnitures 1331
truffle essence 494
truffle ice cream 1331
truffle salad 1331
truffle sauce 1331
truffle truffle tourte à la perigourdine 1331
truffle turnovers 1332
truffle-flavoured consomme 345
truffled pâté de foie gras 529
truffles with champagne 248
truffles for garnishes 1331
truffles à la croque au sel 1331
truffles in paprika 297

truffles preserved in goose fat 1331
truite aux poireaux 1327
truite saumonee Berchoux 104
truites au bleu 1326
truites aux almonds 1327
truites frites 1326
truites à la bourguignonne 1327
truites saumonée Beauharnais 1327
truites saumonées en salade 1327
tuiles 1333
tuna en daube 1335
tuna en daube à la provencale 1335
tuna fish in tea 1290
tuna salads 1335
tuna-fish omelette or omelette du
cure 881
turban de volaille 1335
turban glacé 1335
turban of poultry 1335
turbot aux morilles 1337
turbot with morels 1337
turkey giblets with turnips 590
turnip mousse 1341
turnips au gratin 1342
turnips sauerkraut 1342
turnovers: preparation 1342
turnovers for light entrées 1342
tutti-frutti bombe 1345
Twelfth-Night cake 573

vacherin glace 1350
Valenciennes stuffed ox tongue
1309
vanilla ice cream 1352
vanilla ice cream charlotte 256
vanilla ice cream for coupes glacees
365
vanilla meringues with Chantillt
cream 799
vanilla souffle 1352
vanilla sugar 1245
vatrouchka 1353
veal or chicken emincés a blanc 484
veal chop Cussy en portefeuille 990
veal chop Foyot 542
veal chops in aspic 1358
veal chops aux fines herbes 513
veal chops en papillotes 909
veal forcemeat 538
veal fricandeau with sorrel 557
veal and ham pâté (cold) 924
veal hash à la Mornay 641
veal à l'italienne (cold) 1356
veal Orloff 890
veal piccata with aubergines
(eggplants) and tomatoes 950
veal quenelles 1029
veal steamed with vegetables 1225
veau Orloff 890
veau thonne froid à l'italienne 1356
vegetable achar with lemon 3
vegetable bouillon 145
vegetable charlotte 256
vegetable macedoine with butter or
cream 755

vegetable mirepoix 814
vegetable ragôut à la printanière
1010
vegetable salad 1105
vegetable salpicon with cream
sauce 1113
vegetable salpicon with mayonnaise
1113
vegetable salpicon with vinaigrette
1113
vegetable soup bonne femme 129
vegetables à la grecque 620
vegetarian braised lettuce 733
veloute d'artichaut 1198
veloute d'asperge 1198
veloute de celeri 1198
veloute de champignons 1199
veloute de poisson, veloute maigre
1359
velouté de volaille 1198
velouté d'éperlans à la dieppoise
1179
velouté glacé à l'avocat 1199
velouté sauce blanche graisse 1359
venison sauce 1360
venitienne sauce 1361
verjuice sauce 1134
vernis à la mode de Klebert
Haedens 1363
Veron sauce 1364
Vichy carrots 1365
vichysoisse 1366
Victoria sauce for fish 1366
Victoria sauce for venison 1366
vieilles aux pommes de terre 1401
Viennese chocolate 296
Viennese croissants 392
Viennese currants buns 159
Viennese jam croissants 393
Viennese sour cream soup 1201
vierge sauce 1134
villageoise sauce 1367
Villeroi sauce 1368
vin chaud à la cannelle et au girofle
309
vin de cassis 364
vin d'oranges 364
vinaigre aux herbes 1371
vinaigre framboise 1371
vinaigre à l'estragon 1371
vinaigre roast 1371
vinaigrette 1368
Vincent sauce 1369
violet souffle 1371
visitandines 1372
vives grillées 1385
viveur omelette 1372
vodka fizz 1374
vol-au-vent case 1375

waffles 1378
walnut cake 1380
walnut or hazelnut fond 530
walnut and honey tartlets 1283
walnut surprises 1380

watercress brèdes 162
watercress butter 188
watercress (cooked) 390
watercress mayonnaise 785
watercress purée 390
watercress sauce 391
waterfisch sauce (cold) 1382
waterfisch sauce (hot) 1382
watermelon à la provencale 1382
waterzoi de poissons 1383
waterzoi de poulet 1383
Welsh rarebit 1387
West Indian punch 1023
whipped cream 383
white bread 159
white butter orange sauce for roast
duck 1165
white chaud-froid sauce for white
offal, eggs, and poultry 264
white chicken stock 1228
white nougat 867
white roux 1081
white stock 1227
white wine sauce 1134
whiting hermitage 1391
whiting à l'anglaise 1391
whiting à l'espagnole 1391
whiting in white wine 1392
wholewheat bread 159
wild duck au chambertin 461
wild duck à la tyrolienne 461
wild duck à la Walter Scott 461
wild duck with pears 935
wild duck in port 989
wild rabbit with farm cider 307
wild rabbit with Hermitage wine
1034
woodcock: preparation 1400
woodcock à la Diane (cold) 1400
woodcock à la fine champagne 513
woodcock à la Riche 1062
woodcock pât (cold) 924
woodcock pâté à la périgourdine
(hot) 1400
woodcock salmis 1106
wrasse with potatoes 1401

Xavier soup 1403

Yalanci dolmas 443
yeast dough for tarts 449
yoghurt cocktail 1405
yoghurt sauce 1405
Yorkshire pudding 1406
young artichoke hearts 47

zabaglione 1407
zampone 1408
Zeeland oysters with mussel
mousseline 833
zephyr aux fruits de mer 1408
zestes de citron confits au vinaigre
1409
zucchini *see under* courgette